Leslie Halliwell was born in Bolton. He buys most of the feature films and series screened by the ITV network and goes twice a year to Hollywood in search of them; he has been an enthusiast for the medium since childhood. He has managed several Rank Organisation and specialist cinemas and is a member of two National Film Archive committees.

Mr Halliwell spent several years as a film reviewer for *Picturegoer* and *Sight and Sound* and has contributed to other national publications. His published works include *The Filmgoer's Book of Quotes, The Clapperboard Book of the Cinema* (co-author), *Halliwell's Filmgoer's Companion* (also available in Paladin), *Mountain of Dreams* and *Halliwell's Teleguide.*

HALLIWELL'S FILM GUIDE

To Over 10,000 Films

Second Edition

Leslie Halliwell

A PALADIN BOOK

GRANADA

London Toronto Sydney New York

Published in paperback by Granada Publishing Limited in 1979
Reprinted 1980 (twice)
Second edition 1982, 1983

ISBN 0 586 08389 8

First published in Great Britain by
Granada Publishing 1977
Copyright © Leslie Halliwell 1977, 1979

Granada Publishing Limited
Frogmore, St Albans, Herts AL2 2NF
and
36 Golden Square, London W1R 4AH
515 Madison Avenue, New York, NY 10022, USA
117 York Street, Sydney, NSW 2000, Australia
60 International Blvd, Rexdale, Ontario, R9W 6J2, Canada
61 Beach Road, Auckland, New Zealand

Made and printed in Great Britain by
Richard Clay (The Chaucer Press) Ltd,
Bungay, Suffolk

Granada ®
Granada Publishing ®

Contents

Introduction to the First Edition (1977)

During the twelve years which have elapsed since *The Filmgoer's Companion* first appeared, I have often been asked why I do not produce a complete compendium of all the films ever made, giving a minimum of useful information for each title. Some people even complain because the *Companion* does not provide all this. Plainly, with more than 25,000 English-speaking titles alone to contend with – and I am speaking here of feature-length films only – no one volume could hope to be comprehensive, and even if it were possible the attempt would be fairly pointless, for the book would be cluttered up with endless lists of routine second features of long ago, which no one in his right mind would even wish to remember, let alone see again.

In the *Companion* I do treat separately some seven or eight hundred titles which I consider significant either historically or as pure entertainment, and some readers have been annoyed when looking up films they consider memorable to discover that their titles have not accorded with my prejudices. Ever anxious to please, I have rearranged and amplified the information given in these entries, and multiplied the number of entries tenfold: hence the volume you hold in your hand, which I hope will provide an instant reference when what you want to look up is a movie rather than a person, a theme or a technical expression.

The key to the volume must still be selection, even with a goal of eight thousand entries. To some extent the selection must be personal, but readers of the *Companion* will be helped by having sensed the extent of my memory and the balance of my inclinations. (I think I may claim to have as reasonable a set of hang-ups as anyone now writing about films, except that I tend to hark back towards the old rather than the new, which is not a bad qualification for the job in hand.) I did feel it necessary, however, to restrict myself, at least in the first edition, to films wholly or partly financed in America or Britain. Obviously there are many foreign-language films which demanded inclusion, but it would have been impossible to select them on the same level: I could have given only a smattering of the better-known ones, which seemed unfair. The same is true of silent films, so I firmly put both problems aside for another day and limited myself to English-speaking talking films, which gave me fifty years of product to play with.

I have tried to include every film which seemed likely or worthy of remembrance by the keen filmgoer or student, whether with affection for its own sake as good entertainment, for showcasing memorable work by a particular talent, for sheer curiosity value or for box office success. This brings in virtually everything which played as a main feature in Britain or America. Co-features, 'programmers' and second features are included if they are known to have special merit or to show promise in some department; I have tried to omit the absolutely routine, and specifically excluded a few hundred westerns on the Audie Murphy and Randolph Scott level or below. Another way of looking at my choice is to say that the main studios to suffer are Republic, Monogram, PRC, Nettlefold and Mancunian. Other deliberate exclusions are porno films (hard or soft); underground films; documentaries and shorts; features below fifty-five minutes; exploitation and horror films from independent sources; from-the-stalls versions of ballet, opera and Shakespeare; and pop concerts on film.

I shall be disappointed if the regular reader of the *Companion* cannot find in this volume any film he is likely to require, unless he is a specialist in the early work of Edgar G. Ulmer, Maurice Elvey, or Harry d'Abbabie d'Arrast. Complaints of omissions will nevertheless be welcome: if only one reader sees merit in an excluded film, it has to be worthy of reconsideration next time. Be assured, however, that I already have another three thousand titles half researched . . .

Here is a note of the information given for each film:

Title, with alternatives if used

Italicizing, as in the *Companion*, of any talent involved who makes a particularly outstanding or typical contribution

A rating system

Country of origin

Date of completion/release

Production company, with producer bracketed if named. (Distributor precedes production company if different)

Colour, including name of process, or black and white, and wide-screen or 3-D systems if applicable

Brief synopsis

Brief appraisal (intended as an amalgam of the general view)

Writer, including original source

Director

Photographer

Composer of music score

Other credits as available and applicable

Principal cast with comments

Brief quotes from well-known critics (for about a fifth of the titles)

The compilation of such a tome is an enterprise both daunting and challenging. I could not have accomplished it without the help of many predecessors on whose research I have leaned. I salute especially the work of Leonard Maltin, James Robert Parish, Denis Gifford, Douglas Eames and the unsung anonymous heroes who compiled the reviews of the BFI's *Monthly Film Bulletin* during the fifties and sixties.

The least the reader will derive from this book, I hope, is a notion of the enormous variety of talent which has been poured into the film business during the last half-century. It is often said with justice that far too many film books are published: I hope this may be one of the most useful and comprehensive. I have certainly tried to pour a quart of information into a pint pot of paper, and any corrections or additions will certainly be welcomed. They should be sent to me, please, care of Granada TV, 36 Golden Square, London W.1.

August 1976   L.H.

Preface to the Second Edition

Apart from bringing in films released up to the autumn of 1978, this second edition has the following significant additions:

A selection of the most outstanding silent films which are still shown and discussed, or which are important to the history of the industry;

A selection of foreign-language films of significance, mainly those which have been shown and appreciated in Britain and America;

A further gleaning of English-speaking films omitted from the first edition, bringing the total of new entries to about 1,500.

To make room for the above, the TV movie entries have been transferred to my new *Teleguide*, which will be published at about the same time as this edition.

More than two thousand additions and corrections have been made to existing entries. Many of these clarify music credits, a matter of some complication; there are also many more critical quotes. I have also thought it worthwhile to list principal Academy Awards (AA) and also nominations (AAN). The final choice of these awards is sometimes a matter of fashion, but any nominated work is surely worth recording as being thought outstanding of its kind, even though it will be seen that these choices do not always accord with my own italics, and with some I would be in violent disagreement!

Further corrections, and suggestions for films to be included, will continue to be most welcome.

November 1978   L.H.

Acknowledgements

I am most grateful to all who have written with suggestions, and it has been my aim to reply to all letters. I have found especially useful the careful notes of Jack Docherty, T. G. Wheatley and Derrick Mighall.

Explanatory Notes

Title   The complete title is given, though the definite and indefinite articles are not of course counted in the alphabetical arrangement. The spelling of the country of origin is used, e.g. *My Favorite Blonde* rather than *My Favourite Blonde*.

Alphabetical order   Hyphenated or apostrophized words are counted as one word, and as usual in reference books the order is taken not by the complete title but a word at a time, e.g. *No Room at the Inn* comes before *Nob Hill*. Mac and Mc are regarded as interchangeable under Mac.

Ratings   It would be absurd to classify films selected from a period of forty-five years as to which are the best or the worst. Techniques improve, standards change, and personal preferences have to be accounted for. I have tried, however, to give credit for what seemed excellent or innovative at the time, even though it may have been overtaken by imitators; I have tried to judge each film by its own standards (how could one sensibly compare *Frankenstein Meets the Wolf Man* with *Gone with the Wind*?), and I have rescrutinized it now to see what historical or artistic interest it retains. Mere entertainment value has not been derided, nor have films which may seem naïve but give an accurate picture of the standards of their own time. To sum up in one word, the ratings indicate how much *interest* a film is thought to have for the modern viewer, whether he be a student or a reasonably alert seeker of entertainment.

Four stars, then, indicate a film outstanding in many ways, a milestone in cinema history, remarkable for acting, direction, writing, photography or some other aspect of technique. Three stars indicates a very high standard of professional excellence or high historical interest: or if you like three strong reasons for admiring it. Two stars indicate a good level of competence and a generally entertaining film. One star draws attention to minor points of merit, usually in a film not very satisfactory as a whole; it could be a failed giant or a second feature with a few interesting ideas among the dross. No stars at all indicates a totally routine production or worse; such films may be watchable but are at least equally missable.

It will be seen that my judgements are fairly harsh, but I hope they are consistent. For further elucidation of my personal prejudices see the essay, 'The Decline and Fall of the Movie', on p. 1216.

Country of origin   First item on second line.

Year of release   Comes after country of origin, and is intended to be the year in which the film was first shown. If it was made earlier and held back, I have tried to indicate the fact. Dating is sometimes an onerous task, and the result debateable, please be sympathetic.

Running time   In minutes, signified by 'm'. As far as possible this is the original release time. Very many films are cut when they cross the water, sometimes by twenty minutes or more, but I have not tried to indicate this, as when the film appears on television the new print is usually taken from the original negative (but may be cut again). Remember, however, that an engineering function of British television results in an imperceptible speeding-up of projection and a consequent loss of one minute in every twenty-five. A hundred-minute film, therefore, will run only ninety-six minutes on the box, so check your facts before complaining.

Black and white or colour   I have given the colour process where known (it is not always stated these days) and have coined the single word Eastmancolor to equate with Technicolor.

Other notable points   are given at the end of the second line: Whether the film is in some special process (3-D, Vistavision, etc).

Production credit   The central credit on the third line is the production company. To the left, however, comes the distributor if different from the production company, in brackets if his rights subsequently lapsed. To the right is the actual producer, except for early thirties films in which he was seldom credited. He is also in brackets unless he has a stake in the production.

Alternative title   This is given on a separate line, usually with a note of the country in which it was used. If no such fine line exists, I have used the formula *aka* (also known as). Indexes of alternative titles will be found at the end of the book, and should be consulted if any film for which the reader is looking cannot at first be found.

Synopsis   Self-explanatory, with brevity and accuracy the keynote.

Assessment   Again very brief, so flippancy will inevitably be suspected. Not so, but for more considered judgements look for books which have more space.

Writer credit   It seems to me that this is, at least sometimes, more important than the director credit, and as script in any case precedes direction, it comes first in this book. The author of the screenplay is always given; if this derives from a novel, play or story, this is given next, together with the original author.

Director credit *d*.

Photography credit *ph*.

Music Credit *(m)*   This means the composer of the background music score. Sometimes there is only a music director *(md)* who orchestrates library or classical music.

Other credits   Production designer *(pd)*, music and lyrics *(m/ly)*, art director *(ad)*, special effects *(sp)*, montage, etc, are given when they seem important and can be found. In some cases it has not been possible to track down all the credits one would wish.

Cast   The principal actors are given where possible, roughly in order of importance. I have stopped before the bit parts, and given fewer names in the case of foreign films, where the actors tend to be less well known.

Additional notes   Any other significant remarks about the film are given after the symbol †.

Comments from critics   To a quarter or so of the items I have appended brief quotes from well-known professional critics, sometimes because they wittily confirm my own findings, and sometimes because they disagree with me entirely. I hope these will be enjoyable and illuminating; the absence of a quote casts no reflection whatever on the film, only on my own ability as a researcher.

Italics   These denote a contribution of a particularly high standard. Arguments are expected and additions welcomed.

Academy Awards   Awards (AA) and also nominations (AAN) are listed for all principal categories, including acting, direction, photography, music score, songs and best picture.

A

À Bout de Souffle **
France 1959   90m   bw
SNC (Georges de Beauregard)
aka: *Breathless*

Casual, influential, New Wave reminiscence of
both *Quai des Brumes* and innumerable
American gangster thrillers. (The film is
dedicated to Monogram.)

*w François Truffaut d Jean-Luc Godard
ph Raoul Coutard m Martial Solal*

Jean-Paul Belmondo, Jean Seberg, Daniel
Boulanger, Jean-Pierre Melville

  'A film all dressed up for rebellion but with no
real tangible territory on which to stand and
fight.'—*Peter John Dyer*

À Double Tour
France/Italy 1959   110m   Eastmancolor
Paris/Panitalia (Robert and Raymond Hakim)
aka: *Web of Passion*

A wealthy wine grower has trouble with his wife,
his children, his best friend, and his mistress
across the way, who is murdered.
Talented but irritating mixture of Hitchcock and
Les Parents Terribles; rather an
undergraduatish romp.

*w Paul Gégauff, novel La Clé de la Rue Saint-
Nicolas d Claude Chabrol ph Henri Decaë
m Paul Misraki*

Jacques Dacqmine, Madeleine Robinson, Jean-
Paul Belmondo, Bernadette Lafont, Antonella
Lualdi, André Jocelyn

A-Haunting We Will Go *
US 1942   68m   bw
TCF (Sol M. Wertzel)

Gangsters dupe Laurel and Hardy into escorting
a coffin, which is accidentally switched with one
used in a magic act.
Nothing whatever to do with haunting: a poor
comedy with no typical material for the stars, but
interesting as a record of the touring show of
Dante the Magician.

*w Lou Breslow d Alfred Werker ph Glen
MacWilliams m Glen MacWilliams*

Stan Laurel, Oliver Hardy, *Dante*, Sheila Ryan,
John Shelton, Elisha Cook Jnr

À Nous la Liberté ****
France 1931   95m   bw
Tobis

A factory owner is blackmailed about his past,
and helped by an old prison friend, with whom he
finally takes to the road.
Operetta-style satirical comedy with leftish
attitudes and several famous sequences later
borrowed by Chaplin for *Modern Times*. In
terms of sheer film flair, a revelation, though the
plot has its tedious turns.

*wd René Clair ph Georges Périnal m Georges
Auric pd Lazare Meerson*

Raymond Cordy, Henri Marchand, Rolla
France, Paul Olivier

À Propos de Nice **
France 1930   30m   bw

A satirical documentary on the millionaire's
paradise of the French Riviera.
Cheaply made and rather naive-looking after
fifty years, this amusingly belligerent lampoon
still has its striking moments.

wd Jean Vigo ph Boris Kaufman

Aan *
India 1952   190m approx (English version
    130m)   Technicolor
All India Film Corporation/Mehboob
    Productions
aka: *Savage Princess*

A usurping young prince and his sister are tamed
by an athletic peasant and his girl friend.
One of the few examples to reach the west of
Indian costume melodrama with music,
spectacle and swashbuckling. Distinctly
intriguing, if overpowering.

*w Chaudary, Ali Raza d Mehboob
ph Faredoon A. Irani m Naushad Dilip Kumar,
Nimmi, Premnath, Nadira*

  'Disarmingly enthusiastic . . . exotic and yet
charmingly naive.'—*MFB*

Aaron Slick from Punkin Crick *
US 1952   95m   Technicolor
Paramount (William Perlberg, George
    Seaton)
GB title: *Marshmallow Moon*

A small-town girl is tricked into selling her farm
and moving to the city, but eventually marries
the simple farmer who rescues her.
Homespun entertainment based on a staple
success of the American provincial theatre, with
pleasant songs added.

wd Claude Binyon, *play* Walter Benjamin
Hare *ph* Charles B. Lang Jnr *m/ly* Jay
Livingston, Ray Evans *ch* Charles O'Curran

Alan Young, Dinah Shore, Robert Merrill, Adele
Jergens, Minerva Urecal

Abbott and Costello Go to Mars
US 1953 76m bw
U-I (Howard Christie)

Two incompetents accidentally launch a space
ship and land first in Louisiana, then on Venus.
Dismal knockabout, badly made.

w John Grant, D. D. Beauchamp *d* Charles
Lamont
ph Clifford Stine *m* Joseph Gershenson

Bud Abbott, Lou Costello, Mari Blanchard,
Robert Paige, Martha Hyer

Abbott and Costello in Hollywood*
US 1945 85m bw
MGM (Martin Gosch)

Two agents have hectic adventures in a film
studio.
Tolerable star romp on one of their biggest
budgets, climaxing in a roller coaster ride.

w Nat Perrin, Lou Breslow *d* S. Sylvan
Simon *ph* Charles Schoenbaum

Bud Abbott, Lou Costello, Francis Rafferty,
Warner Anderson, Robert Z. Leonard

Abbott and Costello in the Foreign Legion
US 1950 80m bw
U-I (Robert Arthur)

Incompetent legionaires become heroes to the
fury of their sergeant.
Dull star vehicle on ramshackle sets, with no
memorable routines.

w John Grant, Leonard Stern, Martin
Ragaway *d* Charles Lamont *ph* George
Robinson *m* Joseph Gershenson

Bud Abbott, Lou Costello, Patricia Medina,
Walter Slezak, Douglass Dumbrille

Abbott and Costello Lost in Alaska
US 1952 76m bw
U-I (Howard Christie)

Two San Francisco firemen take a melancholy
prospector back to Alaska to find a gold mine.
Sub-standard comedy vehicle with poor
production.

w Martin Ragaway, Leonard Stern *d* Jean
Yarbrough
ph George Robinson *m* Joseph Gershenson

Bud Abbott, Lou Costello, *Tom Ewell*, Mitzi
Green, Bruce Cabot

Abbott and Costello Meet Captain Kidd*
US 1952 70m Supercinecolor
Warner / Woodley (Alex Gottlieb)

Two servants have a treasure map, and a
fearsome pirate wants it.
Crude knockabout: the stars are way below their
best, and a famous actor is embarrassed.

w Howard Dimsdale, John Grant *d* Charles
Lamont
ph Stanley Cortez *m* Raoul Kraushaar

Bud Abbott, Lou Costello, Charles Laughton,
Hillary Brooke, Leif Erickson

Abbott and Costello Meet Dr Jekyll and Mr Hyde*
US 1953 77m bw
U-I (Howard Christie)

In Victorian London, two rookie policemen
catch a monster.
Quite a lively spoof with some well-paced
comedy sequences.

w John Grant, Lee Loeb *d* Charles
Lamont *ph* George Robinson *m* Joseph
Gershenson

Bud Abbott, Lou Costello, Boris Karloff,
Reginald Denny, Craig Stevens, Helen Westcott,
John Dierkes

'Gracious Boris Karloff is superior to his
surroundings.'—*MFB*. (Though it is doubtful
whether he ever got behind the Hyde make-up.)
† In Britain, the film was given an 'X' certificate,
though it later played on children's television.

Abbott and Costello Meet Frankenstein**
US 1948 83m bw
U-I (Robert Arthur)
GB title: *Abbott and Costello Meet the Ghosts*

Two railway porters deliver crates containing the
Frankenstein monster, Dracula, and the Wolf
Man.
Fairly lively spoof which put an end to
Universal's monsters for a while. Good typical
sequences for the stars, a few thrills, and some
good lines. (Dracula to Costello, lovingly: 'What
we need is young blood . . . and brains . . .')

*w Robert Lees, Frederic I. Rinaldo, John
Grant d Charles Barton ph Charles van
Enger m Frank Skinner*

Bud Abbott, Lou Costello, Bela Lugosi, Lon

Chaney Jnr, Glenn Strange, Lenore Aubert, Jane Randolph

† Probably the Abbott and Costello film which survives best.

Abbott and Costello Meet the Invisible Man*

US 1951 82m bw
U-I (Howard Christie)

A boxer accused of murder makes himself invisible while two detectives clear him.
Quite a bright comedy with good trick effects.

w Robert Lees, Frederic I. Rinaldo, John Grant *d* Charles Lamont *ph* George Robinson *m* Joseph Gershenson

Bud Abbott, Lou Costello, Arthur Franz, Nancy Guild, Adele Jergens, Sheldon Leonard

Abbott and Costello Meet the Keystone Kops*

US 1954 79m bw
U-I (Howard Christie)

In pioneer film days, two incompetents are sold a dud studio by a con man, but succeed as stunt men.
Flabby comedy which never seems to get going until the chase finale; notable chiefly for a guest appearance by Mack Sennett.

w John Grant *d* Charles Lamont *ph* Reggie Lanning *m* Joseph Gershenson

Bud Abbott, Lou Costello, Lynn Bari, Fred Clark, Frank Wilcox, Maxie Rosenbloom

Abbott and Costello Meet the Killer, Boris Karloff*

US 1948 84m bw
U-I (Robert Arthur)

Two bellboys help to solve mysterious murders in a remote hotel.
This clumsily titled comedy really does not work until the last sequence in a cavern. Boris Karloff is not the killer and appears very little.

w Hugh Wedlock Jnr, Howard Snyder, John Grant
d Charles Barton *ph* Charles van Enger *md* Milton Schwarzwald

Bud Abbott, Lou Costello, Boris Karloff, Gar Moore, Lenore Aubert, Alan Mowbray

Abbott and Costello Meet the Mummy*

US 1955 77m bw
U-I (Howard Christie)

A missing medallion leads to a lost tomb and a living mummy.
The comedians show their age in this one, but there is some typical if predictable humour and a thrill or two.

w John Grant *d* Charles Lamont *ph* George Robinson
m Joseph Gershenson

Bud Abbott, Lou Costello, Kurt Katch, Marie Windsor, Michael Ansara, Dan Seymour

The Abdication

GB 1974 102m Technicolor
Warner (Robert Fryer, James Cresson)

17th-century Queen Christina of Sweden journeys to Rome to embrace the Catholic church and falls in love with a cardinal.
Sombre historical fantasia, more irritating than interesting.

w Ruth Wolff, from her play *d* Anthony Harvey *ph* Geoffrey Unsworth *m* Nino Rota

Liv Ullmann, Peter Finch, Cyril Cusack, Paul Rogers, Graham Crowden, Michael Dunn, Lewis Fiander, Harold Goldblatt

'Dainty debauchery and titillating tease straight from twenties women's pulp magazines.'—*Variety*

The Abductors*

US 1957 80m bw Regalscope
TCF / Regal (Ray Wander)

Around 1870, criminals steal Lincoln's body as ransom to effect a convict's release.
Interesting minor melodrama, but not sufficiently well made.

w Ray Wander *d* Andrew V. McLaglen *ph* Joseph La Shelle

Victor McLaglen, Gavin Muir, George Macready

Abdul the Damned**

GB 1935 111m bw
BIP / Capitol (Max Schach)

In 1900 Turkey, an opera star gives herself to a villainous sultan to protect her fiancé.
Thoroughgoing hokum, well produced, which pleased a lot of people at the time.

w Ashley Dukes, Warren Chetham Strode, Roger Burford
d Karl Grune

Fritz Kortner, Adrienne Ames, Nils Asther, John Stuart, Esme Percy, Walter Rilla, Patric Knowles, Eric Portman

Abdulla the Great

GB / Egypt 1954 103m Technicolor
(Gregory Ratoff)
aka: *Abdulla's Harem*

A pleasure-loving European potentate sets his sights on an English girl.

Feeble satire on King Farouk, inept and relentlessly boring.

w George St George, Boris Ingster d Gregory Ratoff ph Lee Garmes

Gregory Ratoff, Kay Kendall, Sydney Chaplin

Abe Lincoln in Illinois**
US 1940 110m bw
RKO (Max Gordon)
GB title: *Spirit of the People*

Episodes in the political and domestic life of Abraham Lincoln.

Pleasant, muted, careful film based on a Broadway success: generally informative and interesting.

w Grover Jones, *play* Robert E. Sherwood d John Cromwell ph *James Wong Howe* m Roy Webb

Raymond Massey, Ruth Gordon, Gene Lockhart, Mary Howard, Dorothy Tree, Minor Watson, Howard da Silva

'If you want attitudes, a five gallon hat, famous incidents, and One Nation Indivisible, they're all here. As a picture and as a whole, it just doesn't stick.'—*Otis Ferguson*

AAN: Raymond Massey, James Wong Howe

Abie's Irish Rose
US 1946 96m bw
(UA) Bing Crosby Productions

Flat filming of the twenties Broadway play about Irish girl marrying Jewish boy, leading to a clash of families.

w Anne Nichols, from her play d Edward A. Sutherland
ph William Mellor m John Scott Trotter

Joanne Dru, Richard Norris, Michael Chekhov, Eric Blore, Art Baker

† There had been a silent version in 1928, and the plot was borrowed, to say the least, for the 1972 TV series *Bridget Loves Bernie*.

The Abominable Dr Phibes**
GB 1971 94m Movielab
AIP (Louis M. Heyward, Ron Dunas)

A disfigured musical genius devises a series of horrible murders, based on the ten curses of Pharaoh, for the surgeons who failed to save his wife.

Brisk but uninspired treatment of a promising theme, with more unintended nastiness than intended laughs. Some good moments and interesting low-budget thirties sets.

w James Whiton, William Goldstein d Robert

Fuest ph Norman Warwick m Basil Kirchen, Jack Nathan pd Brian Eatwell

Vincent Price, Joseph Cotten, Hugh Griffith, Terry-Thomas, Peter Jeffrey, Virginia North, Aubrey Woods

† Sequel: *Dr Phibes Rises Again* (1973).

The Abominable Snowman*
GB 1957 91m bw Hammerscope
Hammer / Clarion (Aubrey Baring)

Himalayan explorers are attacked one by one by the Yeti and their own fear.

A thin horror film with intelligent scripting: more philosophizing and characterization than suspense. The briefly glimpsed Yeti are disappointing creations.

w *Nigel Kneale*, from his TV play d Val Guest ph Arthur Grant m Humphrey Searle

Peter Cushing, Forrest Tucker, Maureen Connell, Richard Wattis, Robert Brown, *Arnold Marle*

About Face
US 1952 96m Technicolor
Warner (William Jacobs)

Moronic remake of *Brother Rat* (qv), shorn of all wit, pace and style.

w Peter Milne d Roy del Ruth ph Bert Glennon songs Charles Tobias, Peter de Rose

Eddie Bracken, Gordon Macrae, Dick Wesson, Virginia Gibson, Phyllis Kirk, Joel Grey

About Mrs Leslie*
US 1954 104m bw
Paramount (Hal B. Wallis)

An ageing nightclub singer has a platonic affair with a mysterious wealthy man, who leaves her enough money to buy a boarding house.

Odd, likeable romantic drama tailored for an unusual star; but its plot is too thin and its direction too drab for real success.

w Ketti Frings, Hal Kanter d Daniel Mann ph Ernest Laszlo m Victor Young

Shirley Booth, Robert Ryan, Alex Nicol, Marjie Miller, Eilene Janssen

'This quiet and curious film has an unexpectedly gentle, civilized flavour.'—*Gavin Lambert*

'It's all sunny disposition and sweet sadness for Miss Booth.'—*Judith Crist*

'One is reminded alternately of Chekhov and of *Back Street*.'—*Sight and Sound*

Above and Beyond*
US 1952 122m bw
MGM (Melvin Frank, Norman Panama)

The training of Colonel Paul Tibbetts, who
dropped the first atomic bomb on Japan.
Overstretched flagwaver with laborious
domestic interludes. Of little real interest then or
now.

w Melvin Frank, Norman Panama, *story* Beirne
Lay Jnr d Melvin Frank, Norman
Panama ph Ray June m Hugo Friedhofer

Robert Taylor, Eleanor Parker, James
Whitmore, Larry Keating, Larry Gates

AAN: Beirne Lay Jnr, Hugo Friedhofer

Above Suspicion*
US 1943 91m bw
MGM (Victor Saville)

Just before World War II, an Oxford professor
on a continental honeymoon is asked to track
down a missing agent.
Patchy, studio-bound spy comedy-drama with a
couple of good sequences. Notable also for Mr
MacMurray's impersonation of a professor who
hails a Nazi as 'Hiya, dope!'

w Keith Winter, Melville Baker, Patricia
Coleman, *novel* Helen MacInnes d Richard
Thorpe ph Robert Planck m Bronislau Kaper

Fred MacMurray, Joan Crawford, Conrad
Veidt, *Basil Rathbone*, Reginald Owen, Felix
Bressart, Richard Ainley

Above Us the Waves*
GB 1955 99m bw
(Rank) London Independent Producers
(William Macquitty)

In World War II, midget submarines attack a
German battleship in a Norwegian fjord.
Archetypal stiff-upper-lip war drama with good
action sequences.

w Robin Estridge d Ralph Thomas ph Ernest
Steward m Arthur Benjamin

John Mills, John Gregson, Donald Sinden,
James Robertson Justice, Michael Medwin, Lee
Patterson, Lyndon Brook

Abraham Lincoln**
US 1930 97m bw
UA / D. W. Griffith

An account of Lincoln's entry into politics and
his years of power.
Rather boring even at the time, this
straightforward biopic has the virtues of
sincerity and comparative fidelity to the facts.

w Stephen Vincent Benet, Gerrit Lord d *D. W.
Griffith* ph Karl Struss m Hugo
Riesenfeld pd William Cameron Menzies

Walter Huston, Una Merkel, Edgar Dearing,
Russell Simpson, Henry B. Walthall

'A treasure trove of magnificent moments.'—
MFB, 1973

Abroad with Two Yanks*
US 1944 80m bw
Edward Small

Adventures around the Pacific with two woman-
chasing sailors.
This simple-minded farce with its punny title was
a great success in its day, and still generates a
laugh or two.

w Charles Rogers, Wilkie Maholey, Fred
Redsills d Allan Dwan ph Charles
Lawton m Lud Gluskin

Dennis O'Keefe, William Bendix, Helen Walker,
John Abbott, John Loder

Abschied von Gestern*
West Germany 1966 90m bw
Kairos Film/Alexander Kluge/Independent
aka: *Yesterday Girl*

A Jewish girl escapes from East to West
Germany but is disillusioned and gives herself
up.
Witty and remarkably light-hearted satirical
comedy which can be fully understood only by
those living in Germany in the sixties.

wd *Alexander Kluge* ph Edgar Reitz, Thomas
Mauch Alexandra Kluge, Gunther Mack, Hans
Korte, Eva Marie Meinecke

The Absent-Minded Professor*
US 1960 97m bw
Walt Disney (Bill Walsh)

A lighter-than-air substance called flubber
enables its inventor to drive his Model-T through
the sky and catch some spies.
Foolishly engaging fantasy comedy with
goodish trick effects.

w Bill Walsh d Robert Stevenson ph Edward
Colman m George Bruns sp Robert A. Mattey,
Peter Ellenshaw, Eustace Lycett

Fred MacMurray, Tommy Kirk, Keenan Wynn,
Nancy Olson, Leon Ames, Ed Wynn, Edward
Andrews
† Sequel: *Son of Flubber* (1964).

AAN: Edward Colman

Accattone*
Italy 1961 120m bw
Cino del Duca/Arco (Alfredo Bini)

A Roman pimp and thief is beset by troubles,
and is finally killed escaping from the police.
Sordid and rough-edged but vividly realistic
melodrama.

wd Pier Paolo Pasolini ph Tonino delli Colli
md Carlo Rustichelli

Franco Citti, Franca Pasut, Roberto
Scaringella, Adele Cambria

Accent on Youth*
US 1935 77m bw
Paramount (Douglas Maclean)

A secretary falls in love with her middle-aged
playwright employer.
Reasonably sparkling comedy from a popular
play, later remade as *Mr Music* and *But Not for
Me.*

w Herbert Fields, Claude Binyon, *play* Samson
Raphaelson *d* Wesley Ruggles *ph* Leon
Shamroy

Herbert Marshall, Sylvia Sidney, Philip Reed,
Astrid Allwyn, Holmes Herbert

Accident**
GB 1967 105m Eastmancolor
London Independent Producers
    (Joseph Losey, Norman Priggen)

An Oxford undergraduate is killed in a car crash;
his tutor looks back over the tangle of personal
relationships that contributed to his death.
Ascetic drama in which the audience is too often
left to observe at length and draw its own
conclusions; good characterizations
nevertheless.

w Harold Pinter, *novel* Nicholas Mosley
d Joseph Losey *ph* Gerry Fisher *m* Johnny
Dankworth

Dirk Bogarde, Stanley Baker, Jacqueline
Sassard, Vivien Merchant, Michael York

'The whole thing is such a teapot tempest, and
it is so assiduously underplayed that it is neither
strong drama nor stinging satire. It is just a sad
little story of a wistful don.'—*Bosley Crowther*

'Everything is calm, unruffled, lacquered in a
veneer of civilization, yet underneath it all, one
gradually begins to realize, the characters are
tearing each other emotionally to shreds.'—
MFB

'Uneven, unsatisfying, but with virtuoso
passages of calculated meanness.'—*New
Yorker, 1977*

The Accused*
US 1948 101m bw
Paramount (Hal B. Wallis)

In self-defence a lady professor kills a student
who has sexually attacked her.
Dullish suspenser with the outcome never in
doubt, though the production values are beyond
reproach.

w Ketti Frings *d* William Dieterle *ph* Milton
Krasner *m* Victor Young

Loretta Young, Robert Cummings, Wendell
Corey, Sam Jaffe, Douglas Dick

Ace Eli and Rodger of the Skies
US 1973 92m De Luxe Panavision
TCF (Robert Fryer, James Cresson)

Adventures of a father-and-son aerial
barnstorming act after World War I.
Poorly written melodrama, very tame apart from
the flying shots.

w Claudia Salter, *story* Steven Spielberg *d* John
Erman *ph* David M. Walsh, Bill Birch, Don
Morgan *m* Jerry Goldsmith

Cliff Robertson, Pamela Franklin, Eric Shea,
Rosemary Murphy, Bernadette Peters, Alice
Ghostley

'A tediously inane flop. Nostalgia isn't what it
used to be.'—*Variety*

Ace in the Hole****
US 1951 1.11m bw
Paramount (Billy Wilder)
aka: *The Big Carnival*

In order to prolong the sensation and boost
newspaper sales, a self-seeking journalist delays
the rescue of a man trapped in a cave.
An incisive, compelling melodrama taking a sour
look at the American scene; one of its director's
masterworks.

w Billy Wilder, Lesser Samuels, Walter
Newman *d Billy Wilder ph* Charles B. Lang
Jnr *m* Hugo Friedhofer

Kirk Douglas, Jan Sterling, Porter Hall, Bob
Arthur, Frank Cady, Ray Teal

'Few of the opportunities for irony, cruelty
and horror are missed.'—*Gavin Lambert*

'Style and purpose achieve for the most part a
fusion even more remarkable than in *Sunset
Boulevard.*'—*Penelope Houston*

'As stimulating as black coffee.'—*Richard
Mallett, Punch*

AAN: Billy Wilder

Aces High*
GB 1976 114m Technicolor
EMI / S. Benjamin Fisz / Jacques Roitfeld

In the air force during World War I, young pilots
are needlessly sacrificed.
Spirited if rather unnecessary remake of
Journey's End transposed to the air war, which
makes it almost identical to *The Dawn Patrol.*

w Howard Barker *d* Jack Gold *ph* Gerry
Fisher, Peter Allwork *m* Richard Hartley

Malcolm McDowell, Christopher Plummer,

Simon Ward, Peter Firth, John Gielgud, Trevor Howard, Richard Johnson, Ray Milland

Across 110th Street*
US 1972   102m   De Luxe
UA / Film Guarantors (Fouad Said, Ralph Serpe)

A tough New York cop loses his own life tracking down three Harlem criminals who have robbed the Mafia.
Brutish, noisy, incoherent police melodrama, with fashionable sadism and predictable performances. Good location work, though.

w Luther Davis, *novel* Wally Ferris d Barry Shear ph Jack Priestley m J. J. Johnson

Anthony Quinn, Anthony Franciosa, Yaphet Kotto, Paul Benjamin, Ed Bernard
'Not for the squeamish . . . a virtual blood bath, leaving no relief from depression and oppression.'—*Variety*

Across the Bridge*
GB 1957   103m   bw
Rank / IPF (John Stafford)

A fugitive financier kills his pursuer, finds he was a murderer, and tries to hide out across the Mexican border.
This star *tour de force* is unconvincing in detail and rather unattractive to watch (British films never could cope with American settings), but the early sequences have suspense.

w Guy Elmes, Denis Freeman, *novel* Graham Greene d Ken Annakin ph Reg Wyer m James Bernard

Rod Steiger, David Knight, Marla Landi, Noel Willman, Bernard Lee

Across the Pacific***
US 1942   99m   bw
Warner (Hal B. Wallis)

Just before Pearl Harbor, an army officer is cashiered by arrangement in order to contact pro-Japanese sympathizers.
Hasty, easy-going and very enjoyable hokum, partly ship-set and successfully reteaming three stars of *The Maltese Falcon*.

w Richard Macauley, *serial* Aloha Means Goodbye by Robert Carson d John Huston ph Arthur Edeson m Adolph Deutsch

Humphrey Bogart, Mary Astor, Sydney Greenstreet, Sen Yung, Richard Loo, Monte Blue
'A spy picture which tingles with fearful uncertainties and glints with the sheen of blue steel.'—*Bosley Crowther*

Across the Wide Missouri*
US 1951   77m   Technicolor
MGM (Robert Sisk)

In the 1820s, a trapper marries an Indian girl and lives with her people.
Promising credits produce an unsatisfactory western: despite honest efforts, the elements do not jell into a convincing whole.

w Talbot Jennings d William Wellman ph William C. Mellor m David Raksin

Clark Gable, Ricardo Montalban, John Hodiak, Adolphe Menjou, Maria Elena Marques, J. Carrol Naish, Jack Holt, Alan Napier

Act of Love*
US 1954   104m   bw
UA / Benagoss (Anatole Litvak)

In Paris in 1944, an American with the liberation army falls in love with a French girl, who commits suicide when he is posted and cannot make their rendezvous.
Cheerless romantic drama, rather thin and unmemorable despite the efforts of all concerned.

w Irwin Shaw, *novel* The Girl on the Via Flaminia by Alfred Hayes d Anatole Litvak ph Armand Thirard m Michael Emer, Joe Hajos pd Alexander Trauner

Kirk Douglas, Dany Robin, Barbara Laage, Robert Strauss, Gabrielle Dorziat, Gregoire Aslan, Fernand Ledoux, Serge Reggiani, Brigitte Bardot
† Made in France, an early Hollywood foreign location film.

An Act of Murder**
US 1948   90m   bw
U-I (Jerry Bresler)
aka: *Live Today for Tomorrow*

A judge insists on being tried for the mercy killing of his incurably ill wife.
Earnest social drama which despite excellent acting can only reach an inconclusive ending.

w Michael Blankfort, Ernest Thoeren, *novel* The Mills of God by Ernst Lothar d Michael Gordon ph Hal Mohr m Daniele Amfitheatrof
Fredric March, Florence Eldridge, Edmond O'Brien, Geraldine Brooks

Act of Murder**
GB 1964   62m   bw
Merton Park (Jack Greenwood)

A couple arrange a holiday by swapping houses with strangers, and a complex plot ensues.
Slick, superior example of the Edgar Wallace second feature series.

w Lewis Davidson *d Alan Bridges ph* James Wilson *m* Bernard Ebbinghouse

John Carson, Anthony Bate, Justine Lord, Duncan Lewis, Dandy Nichols

'This uncommonly intelligent little thriller is just the sort of film which is likely to arouse critical sneers for reaching too high on a low budget.'—*Tom Milne*

Act of Violence**
US 1948   82m   bw
MGM (William Wright)

After the war, an ex-GI tracks down a prison camp informer.

Moody, glossy melodrama with tension well sustained, though the sentimental ending is a cop-out.

w Robert I. Richards, *story* Collier Young *d Fred Zinnemann ph Robert Surtees m* Bronislau Kaper

Van Heflin, Robert Ryan, Janet Leigh, Mary Astor

'Strong characterization, fine direction and good photography combine to put this film high among its kind.'—*MFB*

'An effortless narrative control and a real power to maintain tension.'—*Richard Winnington*

Act One*
US 1963   110m   bw
Warner (Dore Schary)

Poor Brooklyn boy Moss Hart rises to Broadway eminence via his writing partnership with George S. Kaufman.

Incredibly stilted film version of an excellent autobiography, notable only for fragments of acting and the fact that a film so totally uncommercial was made at all.

wd Dore Schary *ph* Arthur J. Ornitz *m* Skitch Henderson

George Hamilton (Hart), Jason Robards Jnr (Kaufman), Jack Klugman, Sam Levene, George Segal, Ruth Ford, Eli Wallach

'From the moment young Hart takes pencil in hand, we have nowhere to go except to that happy ending; and despite all the painstaking detail, we don't believe a word of it.'—*Judith Crist*

Action for Slander*
GB 1937   83m   bw
London Films / Saville (Victor Saville)

A bankrupt officer, accused of cheating at cards, defends his honour with a writ.

Lively melodrama of the old school.

w Ian Dalrymple, Miles Malleson, *novel* Mary Borden *d* Tim Whelan

Clive Brook, Ann Todd, Margaretta Scott, Arthur Margetson, Ronald Squire, Athole Stewart, Percy Marmont, Frank Cellier, Morton Selten

Action in the North Atlantic*
US 1943   127m   bw
Warner (Jerry Wald)

An American convoy bound for Russia comes under U-boat attack.

Efficient propaganda potboiler; studio bound, but still works as a war actioner.

w John Howard Lawson, *story* Guy Gilpatric *d* Lloyd Bacon *ph* Ted McCord *m* Adolph Deutsch

Humphrey Bogart, Raymond Massey, Alan Hale, Julie Bishop, Ruth Gordon, Sam Levene, Dane Clark

'The production has interludes of tremendous power. What is lacking is dramatic cohesion.'—*Howard Barnes*

'Directly in line of descent from *The Perils of Pauline*.'—*Time*

AAN: Guy Gilpatric

Action of the Tiger
GB 1957   93m   Technicolor
   Cinemascope
MGM / Claridge (Kenneth Harper)

An adventurer helps a French girl to rescue her brother from political imprisonment in Albania. Dull and poorly constructed action melodrama.

w Robert Carson *d* Terence Young *ph* Desmond Dickinson *m* Humphrey Searle

Van Johnson, Martine Carol, Herbert Lom, Gustavo Rocco, Anthony Dawson, Helen Haye, Sean Connery

Actors and Sin*
US 1952   91m   bw
(UA) Sid Kuller (Ben Hecht)

Two short stories. When an unsuccessful actress commits suicide, her father makes it look like murder so that for once she shall get attention. The authoress of a romantic script bought by Hollywood is discovered to be a horrid little 9-year-old.

Interesting but incompetent compendium which descends almost to the home movie level and leaves the actors struggling.

wd Ben Hecht *ph* Lee Garmes *m* George Antheil

Edward G. Robinson, Marsha Hunt, Dan

O'Herlihy, Rudolph Anders, Eddie Albert, Alan
Reed, Jenny Hecht

'A depressing double bill.'—*Lindsay
Anderson*

An Actor's Revenge*

Japan 1963   113m   Daieicolor
Daieiscope
Daiei (Masaichi Nagata)
original title: *Yukinojo Henge*

In the early 19th century, a touring actor comes
upon the rich merchant who had ruined his
parents, and his revenge involves several deaths.
Complex, fascinating period melodrama, both
rich and strange, with strong echoes of Jacobean
melodrama.

w Daisuke Ito, Teinosuke Kinugasa, Natto
Wada, *novel* Otokichi Mikami *d Kon
Ichikawa ph* Setsuo Kobayashi *m* Yasushi
Akutagawa

Kazuo Hasegawa, Fujiko Yamamoto, Ayako
Wakao, Ganjiro Nakamura

The Actress*

US 1928   90m approx (24 fps)   bw   silent
MGM
GB title: *Trelawney of the Wells*

A young Victorian actress marries a rich
admirer.
Pleasing, well-cast version of a celebrated play.

w Albert Lewin, Richard Schayer, *play* Sir
Arthur Wing Pinero *d* Sidney Franklin

Norma Shearer, Ralph Forbes, O. P. Heggie,
Owen Moore, Roy D'Arcy
† Opening attraction at London's Empire
Theatre, Leicester Square.

The Actress

US 1953   91m   bw
MGM (Lawrence Weingarten)

Ruth Jones becomes an actress against the
wishes of her stubborn seafaring father.
Episodes from Ruth Gordon's early life, based
on her Broadway play *Years Ago*, make a
pleasant though scarcely engrossing film: it is all
a shade too discreet and wanly winning, and the
few key events take place offscreen.

w Ruth Gordon *d* George Cukor *ph* Harold
Rosson *m* Bronislau Kaper *ad* Cedric Gibbons,
Arthur Lonergan

Jean Simmons, Spencer Tracy, Teresa Wright,
Anthony Perkins, Ian Wolfe, Mary Wickes

Ada*

US 1961   109m   Metrocolor
Cinemascope
MGM / Avon / Chalmar (Lawrence
Weingarten)

A political candidate marries a call girl who
becomes his strong right arm and weathers a
threat to reveal her past.
Indecisive romantic drama which pulls too many
punches but has interesting background detail.

w Arthur Sheekman, William Driskill, *novel* Ada
Dallas by Wirt Williams *d* Daniel
Mann *ph* Joseph Ruttenberg *m* Bronislau
Kaper

Susan Hayward, Dean Martin, Wilfrid Hyde
White, Ralph Meeker, Martin Balsam
'A bonanza for connoisseurs of perfectly
awful movies.'—*Judith Crist*

Adalen 31**

Sweden 1969   115m   Technicolor
Techniscope
Svensk Filmindustri

A prolonged strike at a small-town paper mill
ends in tragedy when the troops move in.
Effective period piece which emphasizes the
idyllic qualities of the backgrounds rather than
the foreground terrors.

wd Bo Widerberg *ph* Jorgen Persson

Peter Schildt, Kerstin Tidelius, Roland Hedlund,
Stefan Feierbach, Anita Bjork

Adam and Evelyne

GB 1949   92m   bw
Rank / Two Cities (Harold French)

A society playboy adopts his dead friend's
daughter, and falls in love with her.
Undernourished romantic drama, a mild
variation on *Daddy Longlegs*.

w Noel Langley, Lesley Storm, George Barraud,
Nicholas Phipps *d* Harold French *ph* Guy
Green *m* Mischa Spoliansky

Stewart Granger, Jean Simmons, Helen Cherry,
Edwin Styles, Beatrice Varley, Wilfrid Hyde
White

Adam Had Four Sons*

US 1941   81m   bw
Columbia (Robert Sherwood)

A widower's family is cared for by a governess.
Modest magazine fiction which established
Ingrid Bergman as an American star.

w Michael Blankfort, William Hurlbut, *novel*
Legacy by Charles Bonner *d* Gregory
Ratoff *ph* Peverell Marley
m W. Franke Harling

Warner Baxter, *Ingrid Bergman*, Susan
Hayward, Richard Denning, Fay Wray

Adam's Rib***

US 1949   101m   bw
MGM (Lawrence Weingarten)

Husband and wife lawyers are on opposite sides of an attempted murder case.

A superior star vehicle which also managed to introduce four promising personalities; slangily written and smartly directed, but perhaps a shade less funny than it once seemed.

w Ruth Gordon, Garson Kanin d George Cukor ph George J. Folsey m Miklos Rozsa

Spencer Tracy, Katharine Hepburn, David Wayne, Tom Ewell, Judy Holliday, Jean Hagen, Hope Emerson, Clarence Kolb
† A 1972 TV series of the same title provided a boring imitation, with Ken Howard and Blythe Danner.

The Adding Machine*
GB 1968   99m   Technicolor
Universal / Associated London (Jerome Epstein)

Downtrodden clerk Mr Zero rebels against society by murdering his boss. Tried and executed, he spends thirty years in heaven before being 'laundered' and sent back to start again as another nonentity.

Elmer Rice's satirical fantasy of the twenties is here robbed of its expressionist staging and presented naturalistically, a fatal error from which the film never for one moment recovers.

wd Jerome Epstein ph Walter Lassally m Mike Leander, Lambert Williamson

Phyllis Diller, Milo O'Shea, Billie Whitelaw, Sydney Chaplin, Julian Glover, Raymond Huntley, Phil Brown, Libby Morris

Address Unknown*
US 1944   72m   bw
Columbia (William Cameron Menzies)

A German-American becomes a Nazi and is incriminated by false letters from his one-time friend.

Reasonably engrossing, cheaply-made adaptation of a slim little thriller which was widely read during World War II.

w Kressman Taylor, Herbert Dalmass, novel Kressman Taylor d William Cameron Menzies ph Rudolf Maté m Ernst Toch

Paul Lukas, Peter Van Eyck, Mady Christians, Emory Parnel

AAN: Ernst Toch

Adieu Philippine*
France/Italy 1962   106m   bw
Unitec/Alpha/Rome-Paris (Georges de Beauregard)

A young TV cameraman is torn between two girls.

Flimsy but attractive romantic comedy, slightly marred by New Wave improvisation with consequent rough edges.

w Michèle O'Glor, Jacques Rozier d Jacques Rozier ph René Mathelin m various

Jean-Claude Aimini, Yveline Céry, Stefania Sabatini, Vittorio Caprioli

The Admirable Crichton*
GB 1957   93m   Technicolor   Vistavision
Columbia / Modern Screenplays (Ian Dalrymple)
US title: *Paradise Lagoon*

Lord Loam and his family are shipwrecked on a desert island, where his manservant proves the undisputed leader.

Few laughs are to be had from this blunt, sentimental version of a famous play, but the photography and decor are excellent.

w Vernon Harris, play J. M. Barrie d Lewis Gilbert ph Wilkie Cooper m Douglas Gamley ad William Kellner costumes Bernard Nevill devices Emmett

Kenneth More, Cecil Parker, Sally Ann Howes, Diane Cilento, Martita Hunt, Jack Watling, Peter Graves, Gerald Harper

'Barrie's play now seems more remote than Gammer Gurton.'—*David Robinson*

Adolf Hitler—My Part in His Downfall*
GB 1972   102m   Technicolor
UA / Norcon (Gregory Smith, Norman Cohen)

Episodes in the life of a conscript at the beginning of World War II.

Lumbering anarchic comedy based on Spike Milligan's own sidesplitting memoirs; an enfeebled British $M^*A^*S^*H$.

w Johnny Byrne d Norman Cohen ph Terry Maher m Wilfred Burns

Jim Dale, Spike Milligan (as his own father), Arthur Lowe, Bill Maynard, Windsor Davies, Pat Coombs, Tony Selby, Geoffrey Hughes

'A convincing period shabbiness and sleaziness which are endearing when they're not being overstated.'—*MFB*

Adorable*
US 1933   85m   bw
Fox

A Ruritanian princess falls in love with a naval officer.

Charming, lightweight romance of the old school.

w George Marion Jr, Jane Storm, story Paul Frank, Billy Wilder d William Dieterle ph John Seitz

Janet Gaynor, Henri Garat, C. Aubrey Smith, Herbert Mundin, Blanche Friderici, Hans von Twardowski

Adorable Creatures

France 1952   105m   bw
Jacques Roitfeld/Sirius

A Paris fashion executive recalls his love affairs.
A collection of four short sex comedies which did well on the heels of *La Ronde*.

w Charles Spaak, Jacques Companeez
d Christian-Jaque *ph* Christian Matras
m Georges Van Parys

Daniel Gélin, *Danielle Darrieux*, Edwige Feuillère, Antonella Lualdi, Martine Carol, Marilyn Buferd

Advance to the Rear*

US 1964   97m   bw   Panavision
MGM / Ted Richmond
GB title: *Company of Cowards?*

After the Civil War, a troop of misfits is sent west out of harm's way, but manages to capture a rebel spy and save a gold shipment.
Semi-satirical western action comedy with a farcical climax; quite sharply made.

w Samuel A. Peeples, William Bowers *d* George Marshall *ph* Milton Krasner *m* Randy Sparks

Glenn Ford, *Melvyn Douglas*, Stella Stevens, Jim Backus, Joan Blondell, Andrew Prine, Alan Hale, James Griffith, Preston Foster

Adventure*

US 1945   126m   bw
MGM (Sam Zimbalist)

A roughneck sailor marries a librarian, but only settles down to love her when their child is born.
Uniquely embarrassing (and fascinating) mishmash of pretentious dialogue and cardboard characters. 'Gable's back and Garson's got him!' squealed the posters, but the stars would have done better not to meet.

w Frederick Hazlitt Brennan, Vincent Lawrence, *novel* Clyde Brion Davis *d* Victor Fleming *ph* Joseph Ruttenberg *m* Herbert Stothart

Clark Gable, Greer Garson, Thomas Mitchell, Joan Blondell, John Qualen, Richard Haydn

'MGM proudly announce *Adventure* as the meeting of a red-blooded man with a blue-blooded woman. Its impact on the bloodstream of your critic was a chilling one. Fifty years of the cinema, he thought, and this is where we've landed.'—*Richard Winnington*

Adventure in Baltimore

US 1949   89m   bw
RKO (Richard H. Berger)
GB title: *Bachelor Bait*

In 1905, a young society girl becomes a suffragette.
Inconsequential period comedy which did nothing for its young star's fading career.

w Lionel Houser, *story* Christopher Isherwood, Lesser Samuels *d* Richard Wallace *ph* Robert de Grasse *m* Frederick Hollander

Shirley Temple, Robert Young, John Agar, Albert Sharpe, Josephine Hutchinson, Johnny Sands, John Miljan, Norma Varden

Adventure in Diamonds

US 1940   76m   bw
Paramount (George Fitzmaurice)

A British adventurer in South Africa falls in love with a lady diamond thief.
Acceptable romantic comedy-drama.

w Leonard Lee, Franz Schultz *d* George Fitzmaurice *ph* Charles Lang

George Brent, Isa Miranda, John Loder, Nigel Bruce, Elizabeth Patterson, Matthew Boulton, Cecil Kellaway, Ernest Truex, E. E. Clive

Adventure in Manhattan

US 1936   73m   bw
Columbia
GB title: *Manhattan Madness*

An actress helps an ace reporter to foil a bank robbery by a master criminal.
Flat romantic mystery comedy which wastes a good cast.

w Sidney Buchman, Harry Sauber, Jack Kirkland *d* Edward Ludwig

Jean Arthur, Joel McCrea, Thomas Mitchell, Reginald Owen, Herman Bing

The Adventure of Sherlock Holmes' Smarter Brother

GB 1975   91m   De Luxe
TCF / Jouer (Richard A. Roth)

More by good luck than good management, Sherlock's younger brother solves one of his cases.
Infuriating parody with little sense of the original and a hit-or-miss style all of its own. Amusing moments fail to atone for the general waste of opportunity.

wd Gene Wilder *ph* Gerry Fisher *m* John Morris *pd* Terry Marsh

Gene Wilder, Marty Feldman, Madeleine Kahn, Leo McKern, Dom De Luise, Roy Kinnear,

John Le Mesurier, Douglas Wilmer, Thorley Walters

'Like a compilation of the kind of numbers actors like to do at parties.'—*Howard Kissel*

'He has bitten off more than he can chew or I can swallow.'—*John Simon*

'A few stray chuckles but nothing more.'—*Sight and Sound*

The Adventurer***
US 1917   21m approx (24 fps)   bw   silent
Mutual

An escaped convict rescues two wealthy women from drowning and is invited to their home. Hilarious early Chaplin knockabout, with his physical gags at their most streamlined.

wd Charles Chaplin *ph* William C. Foster, Rollie Totheroh

Charles Chaplin, Edna Purviance, Eric Campbell, Henry Bergman

The Adventurers
GB 1950   86m   bw
Rank / Mayflower (Maxwell Setton, Aubrey Baring)
US title: *The Great Adventure*

In 1902, two Boers and a cashiered English officer set out to recover stolen diamonds. Lethargic South African western in the wake of *Treasure of the Sierra Madre*; clumsy and unconvincing, with cardboard characters.

w Robert Westerby *d* David MacDonald *ph* Oswald Morris *m* Cedric Thorpe Davie

Dennis Price, Jack Hawkins, Siobhan McKenna, Peter Hammond, Bernard Lee, Grégoire Aslan

The Adventurers*
US 1970   170m   Technicolor   Panavision
Paramount / Avco Embassy / Adventurers Film
(Lewis Gilbert)

A sensualist brought up amid Europe's luxuries returns to his Central American homeland to take vengeance on the brutal security chief who raped and murdered his mother.
Sprawling, sexy, bloodstained extravaganza from a Harold Robbins novel. Expensive to look at and riddled with sensation, but that's about all.

w Michael Hastings, Lewis Gilbert *d* Lewis Gilbert *ph* Claude Renoir *m* Antonio Carlos Jobim *pd* Tony Masters

Bekim Fehmiu, Alan Badel, Candice Bergen, Ernest Borgnine, Olivia de Havilland, Rossano Brazzi, Charles Aznavour, Sidney Tafler,

Fernando Rey, Leigh Taylor-Young, Thommy Berggren, John Ireland

'A three-hour slog through every imaginable cliché of writing and direction . . . in addition to an abundance of flaccid sex and violence, it offers drugs, sadism, orchids, fireworks, orgies, lesbianism, a miscarriage, a private torture chamber, and the hell of several fashion shows with loud pop music accompaniment. This might well be described as the film with everything; trouble is, it is difficult to imagine anybody wanting any of it.'—*MFB*

'Lovers of rotten movies and close-up violence can revel in it.'—*Judith Crist*

The Adventures of Arsène Lupin*
France/Italy 1956   103m   Eastmancolor
Chavane-SNE-Gaumont/Lambor-Costellazione (Robert Sussfeld)

In 1912, the famous jewel thief conducts several successful robberies and outwits the Kaiser. The most stylish Lupin film, though not based on the original stories.

w Jacques Becker, Albert Simonin, based on the character created by Maurice Leblanc *d* Jacques Becker *ph* Edmond Séchan *ad* Rino Mondellini

Robert Lamoureux, Lisolotte Pulver, Otto Hasse, Henri Rolland

The Adventures of Barry Mackenzie*
Australia 1972   114m   Eastmancolor
Columbia / Longford (Philip Adams)

A sex-hungry Australian gets into all kinds of trouble on a visit to the Old Country. Occasionally funny, defiantly crude and tasteless, but poorly produced comedy-misadventure from the *Private Eye* comic strip. Australian slang combines with bad sound recording to make much of the film unintelligible.

w Barry Humphries, Bruce Beresford *d* Bruce Beresford *ph* Don McAlpine *m* Peter Best

Barry Crocker, Barry Humphries (as Aunt Edna Everage), Peter Cook, Spike Milligan, Dennis Price, Avice Landon, Dick Bentley, Joan Bakewell, William Rushton

'A wildly uneven concoction of antipodean bad taste, probably only fully appreciated by Earls Court exiles.'—*Sight and Sound*
† Sequel 1974: *Barry Mackenzie Holds His Own.*

The Adventures of Bullwhip Griffin**
US 1965   110m   Technicolor
Walt Disney (Bill Anderson)

In the 1849 California Gold Rush, two

aristocrats and their butler head west.
Rather splendid spoof western with careful
attention to detail and comedy pointing, well
above the average Disney standard.

w Lowell S. Hawley, novel By the Great Horn
Spoon by Sid Fleischman *d* James Neilson
ph Edward Colman *m* George
Bruns *titles Ward Kimball*

Roddy McDowall, Suzanne Pleshette, Bryan
Russell, Karl Malden, Harry Guardino, Richard
Haydn, Mike Mazurki, Hermione Baddeley,
Cecil Kellaway

The Adventures of Captain Fabian
US 1951   100m   bw
Republic / Silver (William Marshall)

A sea captain returns to New Orleans to revenge
himself on the family which had defrauded his
father.
Stilted, old-fashioned *Monte Cristo*ish
melodrama with some curiosity value but little
verve in the playing or production. An awful
warning to independent producers.

w Errol Flynn, novel Fabulous Ann Medlock by
Robert Shannon *d* William
Marshall *ph* Marcel Grignon *m* René Cloerec

Errol Flynn, Micheline Presle, Agnes
Moorehead, Vincent Price, Victor Francen, Jim
Gerald
† Made in France.

The Adventures of Don Juan**
US 1949   110m   Technicolor
Warner (Jerry Wald)
GB title: *The New Adventures of Don Juan*

A reformed 17th-century rake saves his queen
from the machinations of her first minister.
Expensive, slightly uneasy, but generally very
entertaining swashbuckler with elements of self-
spoofery. Flynn's last big-budget extravaganza.

w George Oppenheimer, Harry Kurnitz
d Vincent Sherman *ph* Elwood Bredell *m* Max
Steiner

Errol Flynn, Viveca Lindfors, Romney Brent,
Robert Douglas, Alan Hale, Ann Rutherford,
Robert Warwick, Jerry Austin, Douglas
Kennedy, Una O'Connor, Aubrey Mather,
Raymond Burr

The Adventures of Gerard**
GB 1970   91m   De Luxe   Panavision
UA / Sir Nigel Films (Peter Beale)

A hussar of Napoleon becomes involved in a
double spy game but comes out trumps and wins
a fair lady.
A lighthearted historical spoof of military pomp,
with plenty of attractive elements which

unfortunately fail to jell into a satisfying film.

w H. A. L. Craig and others, from stories by
Arthur Conan Doyle *d* Jerzy
Skolimowski *ph* Witold Sobocinski *m* Riz
Ortolani

Peter McEnery, Claudia Cardinale, Eli Wallach,
Jack Hawkins, Mark Burns, Norman
Rossington, John Neville

'Enormously graceful and witty . . . picks its
way with amazing delicacy through the reefs of
facetiousness.'—*Tom Milne*

The Adventures of Hajji Baba*
US 1954   93m   De Luxe   Cinemascope
Allied Artists / Walter Wanger

In ancient Arabia, a barber helps and falls in love
with an escaping princess.
A reasonably dashing sword and sandal romp
which no one takes very seriously.

w Richard Collins *d* Don Weis *ph* Harold
Lipstein *m* Dmitri Tiomkin *pd* Gene Allen

John Derek, Elaine Stewart, Thomas Gomez,
Amanda Blake, Paul Picerni, Rosemarie Bowe

The Adventures of Huckleberry Finn: see
Huckleberry Finn

The Adventures of Marco Polo*
US 1938   100m   bw
Samuel Goldwyn

The medieval Italian explorer discovers China,
fireworks, and a beautiful maiden.
One gets the impression that this began as a
standard adventure and that during production it
switched to comedy; whatever the cause, lively
and amusing scenes fail to add up to more than a
thinly scripted pantomime.

w Robert E. Sherwood *d* Archie Mayo
ph Rudolph Maté *m* Hugo Friedhofer
md Alfred Newman *ad* Richard Day

Gary Cooper, Sigrid Gurie, Basil Rathbone,
Ernest Truex, Binnie Barnes, Alan Hale, George
Barbier

The Adventures of Mark Twain**
US 1944   130m   bw
Warner (Jesse L. Lasky)

The life of America's foremost humorous writer,
from a Mississippi riverboat to his becoming an
honorary fellow of Oxford University.
Conventional biopic, quite watchable and with
unusual side turnings, but eventually lacking the
zest of the subject.

w Harold M. Sherman, Alan le May, Harry
Chandler *d* Irving Rapper *ph* Sol Polito
m Max Steiner

Fredric March, Alexis Smith, Donald Crisp,
Alan Hale,
C. Aubrey Smith, John Carradine, William
Henry, Robert Barrat, Walter Hampden

AAN: Max Steiner

The Adventures of Robin Hood****
US 1938   102m   Technicolor
Warner (Hal B. Wallis)

Rebel outlaw Robin Hood outwits Guy of
Gisbourne and the Sheriff of Nottingham, and
saves the throne for the absent King Richard.
A splendid adventure story, rousingly operatic in
treatment, with dashing action highlights, fine
comedy balance, and incisive acting all round.
Historically notable for its use of early three-
colour Technicolor; also for convincingly
recreating Britain in California.

w Seton I. Miller, Norman Reilly
Raine *d William Keighley, Michael
Curtiz ph Tony Gaudio, Sol Polito, Howard
Green m Erich Wolfgang Korngold ad Carl
Jules Weyl*

Errol Flynn, Olivia de Havilland, *Basil
Rathbone, Claude Rains,* Eugene Pallette, Alan
Hale, Patric Knowles, Melville Cooper, Una
O'Connor, Ian Hunter, Herbert Mundin,
Montagu Love
  'Magnificent, unsurpassable . . . the film is
lavish, brilliantly photographed, and has a great
Korngold score.'—*NFT, 1974*
  'Has the supreme virtue of a movie . . . it keeps
moving.'–*James Shelley Hamilton*

AA: Erich Wolfgang Korngold
AAN: best picture

The Adventures of Robinson Crusoe***
Mexico 1953   89m   Pathecolor
Tepeyac (Oscar Dancigers, Henry F. Ehrlich)

A 17th-century mariner is shipwrecked on an
uninhabited tropical island.
Fascinating version of a famous story, with only
one character on screen until the belated arrival
of Friday and the escape to civilization. Subtle
and compelling, with only the colour
unsatisfactory.

w Luis Bunuel, Phillip Roll, *novel* Daniel Defoe
d Luis Bunuel *ph* Alex Phillips *m* Anthony
Collins

Dan O'Herlihy, James Fernandez
  'A film of which the purity, the tense poetic
style, evokes a kind of wonder.'—*Gavin
Lambert*
  'Free of that deadly solicitude which usually
kills off classics.'—*New Yorker, 1977*

AAN: Dan O'Herlihy

The Adventures of Sherlock Holmes***
US 1939   83m   bw
TCF (Gene Markey)
GB title: *Sherlock Holmes*

Moriarty sends Holmes on a false trail while he
plots to steal the Crown jewels.
Highly engaging piece of Hollywood Victoriana,
with all elements perfect except for an
unconvincing plot.

w Edwin Blum, William Drake *d* Alfred
Werker *ph* Leon Shamroy *m* Cyril Mockridge
Basil Rathbone, Nigel Bruce, George Zucco, Ida
Lupino, Alan Marshal, E. E. Clive, Mary
Gordon
  'Told with more movie art per foot than seven
reels of anything the intellectual men have been
finding good this whole year or more.'—*Otis
Ferguson*
† This was the second and last of Rathbone's
costume outings as Holmes, and the one in which
he sang a comic song in disguise.

The Adventures of Tartu*
GB 1943   103m   bw
MGM (Irving Asher)
US title: *Tartu*

During World War II, a British spy goes to
Czechoslovakia to dismantle a poison gas
factory.
Halting and artificial comedy-thriller, saved only
by a graceful star performance.

w Howard Emmett Rogers, John Lee Mahin,
Miles Malleson *d* Harold S. Bucquet *ph* John J.
Cox *m* Hubert Bath *md* Louis Levy

Robert Donat, Valerie Hobson, Walter Rilla,
Glynis Johns, Martin Miller

The Adventures of Tom Sawyer***
US 1938   91m   Technicolor
David O. Selznick (William H. Wright)

Small-town Mississippi boy tracks down a
murderer, Injun Joe.
Set-bound but excellent version of the children's
classic by Mark Twain.

w John Weaver *d* Norman Taurog *ph* James
Wong Howe, Wilfrid Cline *m* Max Steiner
ad William Cameron Menzies

Tommy Kelly, Ann Gillis, *May Robson,* Victor
Jory, Jackie Moran, Walter Brennan, Spring
Byington, Margaret Hamilton, Victor Kilian
  'Should make Mark Twain circulate in his
grave like a trout in a creel.'—*Otis Ferguson*

Advise and Consent**
US 1962   139m   bw   Panavision
Columbia / Otto Preminger

The President's choice of an unpopular secretary of state leads to divisions in the Senate and the blackmail and suicide of a senator.

Absorbing political melodrama from a novel which aimed to lift the lid off Washington. Many character actors make their mark, but the harsh-contrast photography seems misjudged.

w Wendell Mayes, *novel* Allen Drury d Otto Preminger *ph* Sam Leavitt *m* Jerry Fielding *titles* Saul Bass

Don Murray, *Charles Laughton,* Henry Fonda, Walter Pidgeon, Lew Ayres, Edward Andrews, Burgess Meredith, Gene Tierney, Franchot Tone, George Grizzard, Paul Ford, Peter Lawford, Inga Swenson, Will Geer

'The result is supremely ambivalent, a battle between fascinatingly real props and procedures and melodramatically unreal characters and situations.'—*Peter John Dyer*

Aelita*
USSR 1924   70m approx   bw   silent
Mezhrabpom

Two Russian rocket pioneers land on Mars and start a revolution against the planet's queen. Notable early space fiction, with footage of twenties Moscow as well as interesting set designs.

w Fedor Ozep, Alexei Faiko, *novel* Alexei Tolstoy d Yakov Protazanov *ph* Yuri Zhelabuzhsky *pd* Sergei Kozlovsky

Yulia Solntseva, Nikolai Batalov, Igor Ilinsky

Aerograd**
USSR 1935   81m   bw
Mosfilm-Ukrainfilm
aka: *Frontier*

Guards keep Japanese spies out of Siberia, where an airport is being built.

An action film with style and pretensions.

wd *Alexander Dovzhenko* ph Edouard Tissé, Mikhail Gindin

Semyon Shagaida, Stepan Shkurat, Sergei Stolyarov

Affair in Trinidad*
US 1952   98m   bw
Columbia / Beckworth (Vincent Sherman)

A nightclub singer whose husband is killed by gangsters works undercover for the police and routs the gang with the help of her husband's brother.

A tired tropical melodrama intended to follow up the success of *Gilda*, but without the verve. Some routine pleasures, though.

w Oscar Saul, James Gunn d Vincent

Sherman *ph* Joseph Walker *m* Morris Stoloff, George Dunning

Rita Hayworth, Glenn Ford, Alexander Scourby, Torin Thatcher, Valerie Bettis, Steve Geray, Karel Stepanek, George Voskovec

'Improbable, foolish, but glossy.'—*Penelope Houston*

An Affair to Remember**
US 1957   114m   Eastmancolor
    Cinemascope
TCF (Leo McCarey)

An ex-nightclub singer falls in love with a wealthy bachelor on a transatlantic liner, but an accident prevents her from attending their subsequent rendezvous.

Remake of *Love Affair*, a surprisingly successful mixture of smart lines, sentiment and tears, all applied with style and assurance.

w Delmer Daves, Leo McCarey d Leo McCarey *ph* Milton Krasner *m* Hugo Friedhofer

Cary Grant, Deborah Kerr, Cathleen Nesbitt, Richard Denning, Neva Patterson

'A lush slice of Hollywood romanticism.'—*MFB*

'90 masterly minutes of entrancing light comedy and 25 beastly minutes of beastly, melodramatic, pseudo-tragic guff.'—*Paul Dehn*

AAN: Milton Krasner; Hugo Friedhofer; title song (*m* Harry Warren, *ly* Harold Adamson, Leo McCarey)

Affair with a Stranger*
US 1953   87m   bw
RKO (Robert Sparks)

Five friends reminisce about a marriage which seems about to break up.

This would-be-smart comedy has a good idea unsatisfactorily worked out, and could have used a more sparkling cast.

w Richard Flournoy d Roy Rowland *ph* Harry J. Wild *m* Roy Webb

Jean Simmons, Victor Mature, Mary Jo Tarola, Monica Lewis, Jane Darwell, Nicholas Joy, Wally Vernon, Dabbs Greer

L'Affaire est dans le Sac*
France 1932   47m   bw
Pathé/Nathan
aka: *It's in the Bag*

Two would-be kidnappers end up (a) married to and (b) employed by their intended victims. Semi-professional nonsense comedy with political jokes.

w Jacques Prévert d Pierre Prévert *ph* A.

Giboury, Eli Lotar m Maurice Jaubert
J.-P. Le Chanois, Jacques Brunius, Etienne
Decroux, Lucien Raimbourg, Julien Carette,
Lora Hays

The Affairs of Annabel*
US 1938 69m bw
RKO (Lee Marcus, Lou Lusty)

A crackpot Hollywood press agent sends his star
to jail as a publicity stunt.
An amusing frenetic comedy of its time,
successful enough to warrant a sequel, *Annabel
Takes a Tour*, in the same year.

w Bert Granet, Paul Yawitz *d* Lew
Landers *ph* Russell Metty *m* Roy Webb

Lucille Ball, Jack Oakie, Ruth Donnelly, Bradley
Page, Fritz Feld, Thurston Hall, Elizabeth
Risdon, Granville Bates, James Burke

The Affairs of Cellini*
US 1934 90m bw
Twentieth Century (Darryl F. Zanuck)

The complex amours of a 16th-century
Florentine rake.
Lively period bedroom farce somewhat
hampered by censorship.

w Bess Meredyth, *play* The Firebrand by Edwin
Justus Mayer *d* Gregory La Cava *ph* Charles
Rosher

Fredric March, Constance Bennett, *Frank
Morgan*, Fay Wray, Vince Barnett, Louis
Calhern, Jessie Ralph

'Gay and entertaining though whipped up
synthetically like circus ice cream.'—*Variety*

AAN: Charles Rosher; Fredric March

The Affairs of Dobie Gillis
US 1953 74m bw
MGM (Arthur M. Loew Jnr)

Adventures of an indolent and accident-prone
university student.
Scatty comedy with good talent and musical
numbers encased in a tatty production.

w Max Shulman *d* Don Weis *ph* William
Mellor *md* Jeff Alexander

Bobby Van, Debbie Reynolds, Hans Conried,
Barbara Ruick, Bob Fosse

The Affairs of Susan**
US 1945 110m bw
Paramount (Hal B. Wallis)

Four men in Susan's life see her differently.
Occasionally witty comedy designed as a
champagne vehicle for its star. It seemed quite
good at the time.

w Richard Flournoy, *original story* Laszlo
Gorog, T. Monroe
d William A. Seiter *ph* David Abel *m* Frederick
Hollander

Joan Fontaine, George Brent, Walter Abel, Don
Defore, Dennis O'Keefe
'The cast enters into the irresponsibilities with
gusto.'—*MFB*
'A bright thing, a bit too long.'—*Richard
Mallett, Punch*

AAN: Laszlo Gorog, T. Monroe

Affectionately Yours
US 1941 88m bw
Warner (Mark Hellinger)

A foreign correspondent hurries home when he
hears that his wife plans to divorce him.
Thin lightweight comedy, unsuitably cast.

w Edward Kaufman *d* Lloyd Bacon *ph* Tony
Gaudio *m* Heinz Roemheld

Merle Oberon, Dennis Morgan, *Rita Hayworth*,
George Tobias, Ralph Bellamy, James Gleason,
Hattie McDaniel

Africa Texas Style*
GB 1967 109m Eastmancolor
Paramount / Vantors (Andrew Marton)

A Kenyan settler hires two Texas cowboys to
help in his scheme of wild game ranching.
Excellent location sequences are dragged down
by a very boring script, but it's a good family film
nevertheless.

w Andy White *d* Andrew Marton *ph* Paul
Beeson *m* Malcolm Arnold

John Mills, Hugh O'Brian, Nigel Green, Tom
Nardini, Adrienne Corri, Ronald Howard
† Forerunner of TV series, *Cowboy in Africa*.

The African Queen****
GB 1951 103m Technicolor
IFD / Romulus–Horizon (Sam Spiegel)

In 1915, a gin-drinking river trader and a prim
missionary make odd companions for a boat trip
down a dangerous river, culminating in an attack
on a German gunboat.
Despite some unfortunate studio sets mixed in
with real African footage achieved through great
hardship by all concerned, this is one of those
surprising films that really work, a splendidly
successful mixture of comedy, character and
adventure.

w James Agee, novel C. S. Forester *d John
Huston ph* Jack Cardiff *m Allan Gray*

Humphrey Bogart, Katharine Hepburn, Robert
Morley, Peter Bull

'Entertaining but not entirely plausible or original.'—*Robert Hatch*

AA: Humphrey Bogart
AAN: James Agee; John Huston; Katharine Hepburn

After Office Hours*
US 1935   75m   bw
MGM (Bernard H. Hyman)

A newspaperman and his socialite reporter solve a murder mystery.
Crisply-written, fast-moving comedy melodrama; good stuff of its time and type.

w Herman J. Mankiewicz *d* Robert Z. Leonard *ph* Charles Rosher

Clark Gable, Constance Bennett, Stuart Erwin, Billie Burke, Harvey Stephens, Katherine Alexander, Henry Travers, Henry Armetta
  'One of the best balanced pix of the season; it has practically everything.'—*Film Daily*

After the Ball*
GB 1957   89m   Eastmancolor
IFD / Beaconsfield (Peter Rogers)

The life and loves of music-hall singer Vesta Tilley, who married into the nobility.
Adequate if uninspired biopic with entertaining detail and songs.

w Hubert Gregg *d* Compton Bennett

Pat Kirkwood, Laurence Harvey, Clive Morton, Jerry Verno, June Clyde

After the Fox*
US / Italy 1966   103m   Technicolor
Panavision
UA / Nancy / CCM (John Bryan)

The Fox escapes from jail to execute a gold bullion caper and save his young sister from the streets.
Unlikeable and unfunny farce which sets its star among excitable Italians and hopes for the best, adding a few wild stabs at satire on movie-making styles.

w Neil Simon, Cesare Zavattini *d* Vittorio de Sica *ph* Leonida Barboni *m* Burt Bacharach

Peter Sellers, *Victor Mature* (agreeably sending up his old image), Britt Ekland, Lilia Brazzi, Paola Stoppa, Akim Tamiroff, Martin Balsam
  'Never even begins to get off the ground.'—*MFB*

After the Thin Man**
US 1936   113m   bw
MGM (Hunt Stromberg)

Nick and Nora Charles, not forgetting Asta, solve another murder.

Overlong but well-carpentered sequel to *The Thin Man*, developing the thesis that a married couple, even if they are detectives and drink too much, can be interesting and lovable.

w Frances Goodrich, Albert Hackett *d* W. S. Van Dyke II
ph Oliver T. Marsh *m* Herbert Stothart, Edward Ward

William Powell, Myrna Loy, James Stewart, Elissa Landi, Joseph Calleia, Jessie Ralph, Alan Marshal, Sam Levene

AAN: Frances Goodrich; Albert Hackett

Against All Flags*
US 1952   83m   Technicolor
U-I (Howard Christie)

A daring British seaman routs Spanish ships at the request of the king.
Standard pirate yarn, almost Flynn's last swashbuckler; production below par.

w Aeneas Mackenzie, Joseph Hoffman *d* George Sherman *ph* Russell Metty *m* Hans Salter

Errol Flynn, Maureen O'Hara, Anthony Quinn, Mildred Natwick
† Remade as *The King's Pirate* (qv).

Against the Wind**
GB 1947   96m   bw
Ealing (Sidney Cole)

In London during World War II, men and women are trained as saboteurs, and one of them is a traitor.
Thoughtful, well-made spy thriller with good performances.

w T. E. B. Clarke, Michael Pertwee *d* Charles Crichton *ph* Lionel Banes *m* Leslie Bridgewater

Simone Signoret, Robert Beatty, Jack Warner, Gordon Jackson, Paul Dupuis, Gisele Preville, John Slater, Peter Illing, James Robertson Justice

L'Âge d'Or**
France 1930   63m   bw
Vicomte de Noailles

A collection of strange events satirizing religion and the social order.
Deliberately shocking and possibly quite meaningless, this truly surrealist film is chiefly interesting now for its flashforwards to Bunuel's later work.

w Luis Bunuel, Salvador Dali *d* Luis Bunuel *ph* Albert Dubergen

Gaston Modot, Lya Lys, Max Ernst, Pierre Prévert, Jacques Brunius

Age of Consent*

Australia 1969   103m   colour
Columbia / Nautilus (James Mason, Michael Powell)

An artist seduces the granddaughter of a drunken harridan with whom he shares a Barrier Reef island.
Mildly likeable but self-conscious and overlong South Pacific idyll.

w Peter Yeldham, *novel* Norman Lindsay
d Michael Powell ph Hannes Staudinger
m Stanley Myers

James Mason, Helen Mirren, Jack McGowran, Neva Carr-Glyn, Frank Thring

Age of Innocence

Canada/GB 1977   101m   Eastmancolor
Judson/Willoughby (Henning Jacobsen)

After World War I, an English teacher in Canada develops pacifist views which stir up local resentment and lead to violence.
Rather uninteresting melodrama which never really comes to the boil despite care all round.

w Ratch Wallace d Alan Bridges ph Brian West m Lucio Agostini

David Warner, Honor Blackman, Trudy Young, Cec Linder, Tim Henry, Lois Maxwell, Robert Hawkins

The Agitator*

GB 1944   98m   bw
British National (Louis H. Jackson)

An embittered mechanic becomes a loud-mouthed union spokesman, but fate eventually takes him into management.
Fairly absorbing, modest narrative of the flaws of socialism.

w Edward Dryhurst, *novel* Peter Pettinger by William Riley d John Harlow

William Hartnell (then being built into a star), Mary Morris, John Laurie, Moore Marriott, George Carney, Edward Rigby, Elliot Mason, Frederick Leister, Cathleen Nesbitt, Moira Lister

The Agony and the Ecstasy*

US 1965   140m   De Luxe   Todd-AO
TCF / International Classics Inc (Carol Reed)

Pope Julius II persuades Michelangelo to leave his sculptures and paint the ceiling of the Sistine Chapel.
Dully reverent comic strip approach to art and history; generally heavy going, but good looking.

w Philip Dunne, *novel* Irving Stone d Carol Reed ph Leon Shamroy m Alex North pd John de Cuir

Charlton Heston, Rex Harrison, Diane Cilento, Harry Andrews, Alberto Lupo, Adolfo Celi
'The vulgarity of the whole concept has none of the joyfully enthusiastic philistinism of a de Mille; rather its tone is a dry, almost cynical, condescension.'—*Brenda Davies*
'All agony, no ecstasy.'—*Judith Crist*
AAN: Leon Shamroy; Alex North

Ah, Wilderness**

US 1935   101m   bw
MGM (Hunt Stromberg)

Problems of a small-town family at the turn of the century.
Well-acted, affectionately remembered version of a play later musicalized as *Summer Holiday*. The commercial success of this film led to the Hardy family series.

w Albert Hackett, Frances Goodrich, *play* Eugene O'Neill d Clarence Brown ph Clyde de Vinna m Herbert Stothart

Wallace Beery, Lionel Barrymore, Eric Linden, Spring Byington, Mickey Rooney, Aline MacMahon, Charley Grapewin, Cecilia Parker, Frank Albertson, Bonita Granville

Aida

Italy 1953   95m   Ferraniacolor
Oscar Film (Ferrucio de Martino, Federico Teti)

A young Egyptian army officer loves the captive princess of the Ethiopians.
Stuffy, over-dressed, pantomimish version of the opera, with some pretension to cinematic vitality.

w various, from Verdi's opera d Clemente Fracassi ph Piero Portalupi ad Flavio Mogherini

Sophia Loren (sung by Renata Tebaldi), Lois Maxwell, Luciano della Marra

Ain't Misbehavin'*

US 1955   81m   Technicolor
U-I (Samuel Marx)

A young millionaire marries a cabaret girl, who determines to improve her mind and manners.
Lively American version of *Pygmalion*, with musical numbers and some bright lines.

w Edward Buzzell, Philip Rapp, Devery Freeman d Edward Buzzell ph Wilfrid Cline m Joseph Gershenson ch Kenny Williams, Lee Scott

Rory Calhoun, *Piper Laurie, Reginald Gardiner*, Jack Carson, Barbara Britton, Mamie Van Doren

Air Force*

US 1943   124m   bw
Warner (Hal B. Wallis)

A Flying Fortress and its crew see action in
Manila, Pearl Harbor and the Coral Sea.
Propaganda piece concentrating on the
characters of the crew members, with action set
pieces largely provided by newsreel; but skilled
direction still conveys plenty of punch.

w Dudley Nichols d Howard Hawks ph James
Wong Howe, Elmer Dyer, Charles Marshall
m Franz Waxman

John Garfield, Gig Young, Arthur Kennedy,
Charles Drake, John Ridgley, Harry Carey,
George Tobias, Stanley Ridges, Moroni Olsen,
Edward Brophy

AAN: Dudley Nichols; James Wong Howe,
Elmer Dyer, Charles Marshall

Air Raid Wardens*

US 1943   67m   bw
MGM (B. F. Zeidman)

Rejected by the armed services, two incompetent
air raid wardens accidentally round up Nazi
spies.
Well below par star comedy: their incomparable
dignity has disappeared.

w Jack Jevne, Martin Rackin, Charles Rogers,
Harry Crane d Edward Sedgwick ph Charles
Rogers, Harry Crane m Nathaniel Shilkret

Stan Laurel, Oliver Hardy, Edgar Kennedy,
Jacqueline White, Stephen McNally, Nella
Walker, Donald Meek

Airport***

US 1969   136m   Technicolor   Todd-AO
Universal / Ross Hunter (Jaque Mapes)

Events of one snowy night at a midwestern
international airport, culminating in airborne
melodrama when a mad bomber is killed and the
damaged plane has to be talked down.
Glossy, undeniably entertaining, all-star version
of a popular novel, with cardboard characters
skilfully deployed in Hollywood's very best style.

w George Seaton, novel Arthur Hailey d George
Seaton ph Ernest Laszlo m Alfred Newman

Burt Lancaster, Dean Martin, Jean Seberg,
Helen Hayes, Van Heflin, Jacqueline Bisset,
George Kennedy, Maureen Stapleton, Barry
Nelson, Dana Wynter, Lloyd Nolan, Barbara
Hale, Gary Collins, Jessie Royce Landis
   'The best film of 1944.'—Judith Crist
   'For sheer contentment there is nothing to beat
the sight of constant catastrophe happening to
others.'—Alexander Walker

AA: Helen Hayes

AAN: best picture; George Seaton; Ernest
Laszlo; Alfred Newman; Maureen Stapleton

Airport 1975

US 1974   105m   Technicolor   Panavision
Universal (Jennings Lang, William Frye)

A private aircraft collides with a jet plane and
kills or immobilizes its crew, so a stewardess has
to manoeuvre the jumbo to safety.
Inept airborne suspenser loaded with stars who
do nothing and marred by continuity lapses and
boring dialogue.

w Don Ingalls d Jack Smight ph Philip
Lathrop m John Cacavas

Charlton Heston, Karen Black, George
Kennedy, Helen Reddy, Efrem Zimbalist Jnr,
Susan Clark, Myrna Loy, Gloria Swanson,
Linda Blair, Dana Andrews, Roy Thinnes, Sid
Caesar, Ed Nelson, Nancy Olson, Martha Scott
   'Aimed squarely for the yahoo trade.'—
Variety

Airport '77

US 1977   114m   Technicolor   Panavision
Universal (William Frye)

A private airliner loaded with guests and art
treasures hits an oil rig and settles underwater on
a sandbank.
Hysteria, rescue, and guest stars with nothing to
do; the mixture as before.

w Michael Scheff, David Spector d Jerry
Jameson ph Philip Lathrop m John Cacavas
pd George C. Webb

Jack Lemmon, James Stewart, Brenda Vaccaro,
Joseph Cotten, Olivia de Havilland, Lee Grant,
Darren McGavin, Christopher Lee, Robert
Foxworth, Robert Hooks, Monte Markham,
Kathleen Quinlan, James Booth
   'Neither as riveting as it should be, nor as
much fun as its absurd plotline would
suggest.'—Verina Glaessner, MFB

Al Capone**

US 1959   105m   bw
Allied Artists (John H. Burrows, Leonard J.
Ackerman)

An account of Chicago's most famous gangster,
up to his arrest for income tax evasion.
Only slightly overplayed, semi-documentary
retelling of a larger-than-life true story.

w Marvin Wald, Henry Greenberg d Richard
Wilson ph Lucien Ballard m David Raksin

Rod Steiger (a clever impersonation on the
border of caricature), Fay Spain, Murvyn Vye,
Nehemiah Persoff, Martin Balsam, James
Gregory, Joe de Santis

Alakazam the Great*

Japan 1960   88m   Eastmancolor
Toei (Hiroshi Okawa)
original title: *Saiyu-ki*

The arrogant monkey king of the animals is sent
by his human master on a pilgrimage; he defeats
evil King Gruesome and returns a hero.
Smartly animated, Disney-inspired cartoon
based on the same legend as *Monkey,* translated
by Arthur Waley.

w Osamu Tezuka, Keinosuke Uekusa *d* Taiji
Yabushita

The Alamo*

US 1960   193m   Technicolor   Todd-AO
UA / John Wayne

In 1836 a small southern fort becomes the centre
of Texas' fight for independence, but it is
suddenly annihilated by a Mexican raid, and all
its defenders killed.
Sprawling historical epic with many irrelevant
episodes and distracting changes of mood.

w James Edward Grant   *d* John
Wayne   *ph* William H. Clothier   *m* Dmitri
Tiomkin

John Wayne (as Crockett), Richard Widmark
(Bowie), Laurence Harvey (Travis), Richard
Boone (Houston), Frankie Avalon, Patrick
Wayne, Linda Cristal, Chill Wills, Joseph
Calleia

'Its sole redeeming feature lies in one of those
crushing climaxes of total massacre which
Hollywood can still pull off thunderingly well.'—
Peter John Dyer

AAN: best picture; William H. Clothier; Dmitri
Tiomkin; Chill Wills; song 'The Green Leaves of
Summer' (*m* Dmitri Tiomkin, *ly* Paul Francis
Webster)

Alaska Seas

US 1953   78m   bw
Paramount (Mel Epstein)

Alaska fishermen oppose the crooked owner of
the local cannery.
Insipid remake of *Spawn of the North (qv).*

w Geoffrey Homes, Walter Doniger   *d* Jerry
Hopper   *ph* William C. Mellor   *md* Irvin Talbot

Robert Ryan, Gene Barry, Jan Sterling, Brian
Keith, Richard Shannon

Albert RN**

GB 1953   88m   bw
Dial (Daniel M. Angel)
US title: *Break to Freedom*

Prisoners of war construct a lifelike dummy to
cover the absence of escaping prisoners.

Competent, entertaining version of a successful
play: an archetypal POW comedy drama.

w Guy Morgan, Vernon Harris, *play* Guy
Morgan, Edward Sammis   *d* Lewis
Gilbert   *ph* Jack Asher   *m* Malcolm Arnold

Jack Warner, Anthony Steel, Robert Beatty,
William Sylvester, Anton Diffring, Eddie Byrne,
Guy Middleton, Paul Carpenter, Frederick Valk

Alex and the Gypsy

US 1976   99m   De Luxe
TCF/Richard Shepherd

A cynical California bailbondsman involved in
illicit activities chooses romantic freedom with a
gypsy girl.
Incoherent hardbitten romance with an
unconvincing set of characters.

w Lawrence B. Marcus, *novel* The
Bailbondsman by Stanley Elkin   *d* John Korty
ph Bill Butler   *m* Henry Mancini

Jack Lemmon, Genevieve Bujold, James
Woods, Gino Ardito, Robert Emhardt

   'Even if it were well done (which it is not) it
would be banal, predictable and cloying.'—
Frank Rich

Alex in Wonderland

US 1970   109m   colour
MGM (Larry Tucker)

A Hollywood director finds life tedious.
So did the small paying audiences who saw this
pale imitation of Fellini. (Some wags called it
One and a Half.)

w Paul Mazursky, Larry Tucker   *d* Paul
Mazursky

Donald Sutherland, Jeanne Moreau, Ellen
Burstyn, Federico Fellini

Alexander Hamilton*

US 1931   73m   bw
Warner

The life of America's 18th-century financier.
Star biopic, highly satisfying in its day.

w Julian Josephson, Maude Howell, George
Arliss   *d* John G. Adolfi   *ph* James Van Trees

George Arliss, Doris Kenyon, Montagu Love,
Dudley Digges, Lionel Belmore, Ralf Harolde,
Alan Mowbray

Alexander Nevsky****

USSR 1938   112m   bw
Mosfilm

In 1242, Prince Alexander Nevsky defeats the
invading Teutonic Knights in a battle on the ice
of Lake Peipus.
A splendid historical pageant which shows the

director at his most inventively pictorial and climaxes in a superb battle sequence using music instead of natural sound.

w Pyotr Pavlenko, Sergei Eisenstein d Sergei Eisenstein ph Edouard Tissé m Prokofiev ad I. Shpinel, N. Soloviov, K. Yeliseyev

Nikolai Cherkassov, Nikolai Okhlopkov, Andrei Abrikosov, Dmitri Orlov

'Superb sequences of cinematic opera that pass from pastoral to lamentation and end in a triumphal cantata.'—Georges Sadoul

Alexander the Great*
US 1956 135m Technicolor
 Cinemascope
UA / Robert Rossen

The life and early death at thirty-three of the Macedonian warrior who conquered the entire known world.
Dour impassive epic which despite good intelligent stretches makes one long for Hollywood's usual more ruthless view of history.

wd Robert Rossen m Mario Nascimbene
ph Robert Krasker ad Andrei Andreiev

Richard Burton, Fredric March, Danielle Darrieux, Claire Bloom, Barry Jones, Harry Andrews, Peter Cushing, Stanley Baker, Michael Hordern, Niall MacGinnis

'Not a scene is held for a second longer than it is worth; greatness is pictured in constant dissolve.'—Alexander Walker

Alexander's Ragtime Band***
US 1938 106m bw
TCF (Darryl F. Zanuck, Harry Joe Brown)

Between 1911 and 1939, two songwriters vie for the affections of a rising musical comedy star.
Archetypal chronicle musical with 26 songs: well-paced, smartly made, and bursting with talent.

w Kathryn Scola, Lamar Trotti, Richard Sherman d Henry King ph Peverell Marley m/ly Irving Berlin md Alfred Newman

Tyrone Power, Alice Faye, Don Ameche, Ethel Merman, Jack Haley, Jean Hersholt, Helen Westley, John Carradine, Paul Hurst, Wally Vernon, Ruth Terry, Eddie Collins, Douglas Fowley, Chick Chandler

AA: Alfred Newman
AAN: best picture; Irving Berlin (for original story); Irving Berlin (for song, 'Now It Can Be Told')

The Alf Garnett Saga
GB 1972 90m colour
Columbia / Associated London Films (Ned Sherrin, Terry Glinwood)

Bigoted Alf is exasperated by his council flat, his son-in-law, and the possibility that his daughter is pregnant by a black man.
Second inflation of the TV series, Till Death Us Do Part, even cruder and less funny than the first; listlessly written and developed.

w Johnny Speight d Bob Kellett ph Nic Knowland m Georgie Fame

Warren Mitchell, Dandy Nichols, Adrienne Posta, Mike Angelis, John Le Mesurier, Joan Sims, John Bird, Roy Kinnear

'One long, repetitive and unfunny diatribe.'—MFB

Alfie**
GB 1966 114m Techniscope
Paramount / Sheldrake (Lewis Gilbert)

A Cockney Lothario is proud of his amorous conquests, but near-tragedy finally makes him more mature.
Garish sex comedy, an immense box office success because of its frankness and an immaculate performance from its star.

w Bill Naughton, from his play d Lewis Gilbert ph Otto Heller m Sonny Rollins

Michael Caine, Vivien Merchant, Shirley Anne Field, Millicent Martin, Jane Asher, Julia Foster, Shelley Winters, Eleanor Bron, Denholm Elliott

'Paramount thought it was a good bet because it was going to be made for 500,000 dollars, normally the sort of money spent on executives' cigar bills.'—Lewis Gilbert

AAN: best picture; Bill Naughton; Michael Caine; Vivien Merchant; title song

Alfred the Great*
GB 1969 122m Metrocolor Panavision
MGM / Bernard Smith

In AD 871 Alfred takes over kingship from his weak elder brother.
A 'realistic' youth-oriented view of history: blood and four-letter words alternate with cliché to make a dispiriting, disunified whole, though the background detail is interesting and the battle scenes vivid.

w Ken Taylor, James R. Webb d Clive Donner ph Alex Thomson m Ray Leppard pd Michael Stringer

David Hemmings, Michael York, Prunella Ransome, Colin Blakely, Julian Glover, Ian McKellen, Alan Dobie

Alf's Button Afloat*
GB 1938 89m bw
Gainsborough (Edward Black)

Six itinerants encounter a genie, whose granting

of their wishes brings riches and embarrassment. Archetypal music hall farce descending at moments into surrealism (the lovers are eaten by a bear). All concerned are on top form.

w Marriott Edgar, Val Guest, Ralph Smart, novel Alf's Button by W. A. Darlington *d Marcel Varnel ph* Arthur Crabtree *md* Louis Levy

Bud Flanagan, Chesney Allen, Jimmy Nervo, Teddy Knox, Charles Naughton, Jimmy Gold (the six original members of the Crazy Gang), *Alastair Sim,* Wally Patch, Peter Gawthorne

Algiers**
US 1938 95m bw
Walter Wanger

A romantic Casbah thief makes the mistake of falling in love.
Seminal Hollywood romantic drama based closely on a French original, *Pepe le Moko*; laughed at for years because of the alleged line 'Come with me to the Casbah' (which is never actually said), it holds up remarkably well in its fashion.

w John Howard Lawson, James M. Cain *d John Cromwell ph James Wong Howe m* Vincent Scott, Mohammed Igorbouchen

Charles Boyer, Hedy Lamarr, Sigrid Gurie, Gene Lockhart, Joseph Calleia, Alan Hale, Johnny Downs

'Few films this season, or any other, have sustained their mood more brilliantly.'—*New York Times*

'The general tone is that of the decent artistry we must demand and enjoy in pictures, which should someday be as respectable as books, only more near and vivid.'—*Otis Ferguson*

'This version is pure Hollywood, sacrificing everything to glamour, and the heavy make-up and studio lighting make it seem so artificial one can get giggly.'—*New Yorker, 1977*
† Remake: *Casbah* (qv).

AAN: James Wong Howe; Charles Boyer; Gene Lockhart

Ali Baba and the Forty Thieves*
US 1944 87m Technicolor
U-I (Paul Malvern)

A deposed prince pretending to be a bandit regains his rightful throne.
Absurd but likeable wartime pantomime without much humour: a typical big-budget production of its studio and period.

w Edmund L. Hartmann *d* Arthur Lubin *ph* George Robinson *m* Edward Ward

Jon Hall, Maria Montez, Scotty Beckett, Turhan Bey, Frank Puglia, Andy Devine, Kurt Katch

† Remake: *Sword of Ali Baba,* which over twenty years later used much of the same footage.

Ali Baba and the Forty Thieves*
France 1954 90m Eastmancolor
Films du Cyclope

Ali Baba is sent to buy a new wife for his master, and accidentally finds a thieves' treasure cave . . . Sporadically amusing but finally disappointing version of the Arabian Nights story; it looks hasty.

w Jacques Becker, Marc Maurette, Maurice Griffe *d* Jacques Becker *ph* Robert Le Fèbvre *m* Paul Misraki

Fernandel, Samia Gamal, Dieter Borsche, Henri Vilbert

Ali Baba Goes to Town*
US 1937 81m bw
TCF (Lawrence Schwab)

A hobo falls off a train into a film set and thinks he is back in the Arabian Nights.
Rather flat star vehicle with a few compensations.

w Harry Tugend, Jack Yelten *d* David Butler *ph* Ernest Palmer

Eddie Cantor, Tony Martin, Roland Young, John Carradine, June Lang

Alias Jesse James*
US 1958 92m Technicolor
Hope Enterprises (Jack Hope)

An incompetent insurance salesman sells a policy to Jesse James and has to protect his client until he can get it back.
Ho-hum star comedy saved by a climax in which Hope is protected by every cowboy star in Hollywood.

w William Bowers, D. D. Beauchamp *d* Norman Z. McLeod *ph* Lionel Lindon *m* Joseph J. Lilley

Bob Hope, Rhonda Fleming, Wendell Corey, Jim Davis, Will Wright

Alias Nick Beal***
US 1949 93m bw
Paramount (Endre Boehm)
GB title: *The Contact Man*

A politician is nearly corrupted by a mysterious stranger offering wealth and power.
Highly satisfactory modern version of *Faust*, done in gangster terms but not eschewing a supernatural explanation. Acting, photography and direction all in the right key.

w Jonathan Latimer, story Mindret Lord

d John Farrow ph Lionel Lindon m Franz Waxman

Ray Milland, Thomas Mitchell, Audrey Totter, George Macready, Fred Clark

Alibi*

US 1929 90m bw
Roland West

An ex-convict marries a policeman's daughter and uses her in his plan for the perfect murder. Early talkie drama, mostly risible now but with interesting fragments of technique and imagination.

wd Roland West ph Ray June

Chester Morris, Eleanor Griffith, Regis Toomey, Mae Busch, Harry Stubbs

Alibi*

GB 1942 82m bw
Corona (Josef Somlo)

A nightclub mindreader forces the lady owner to give him a murder alibi.
Interesting but disappointing minor suspenser copied from a sharper French original.

w uncredited, *novel* Marcel Achard *d* Brian Desmond Hurst *ph* Otto Heller *m* Jack Beaver

Margaret Lockwood, Hugh Sinclair, James Mason, *Raymond Lovell,* Enid Stamp-Taylor, Hartley Power, Jane Carr, Rodney Ackland, Edana Romney, Elizabeth Welch, Olga Lindo, Muriel George

Alibi Ike**

US 1935 73m bw
Warner

A baseball pitcher gets involved in all kinds of trouble.
Above average star comedy vehicle.

w William Wister Haines, *story* Ring Lardner *d* Ray Enright *ph* Arthur Todd *md* Leo F. Forbstein

Joe E. Brown, Olivia de Havilland, Ruth Donnelly, Roscoe Karns, William Frawley

Alice Adams**

US 1935 99m bw
RKO (Pandro S. Berman)

A social-climbing small-town girl falls in love. Dated but interesting star vehicle with good production values.

w Dorothy Yost, Mortimer Offner, *novel* Booth Tarkington *d George Stevens ph* Robert de Grasse *m* Max Steiner, Roy Webb

Katharine Hepburn, Fred MacMurray, Evelyn Venable, Frank Albertson, Fred Stone, Ann

Shoemaker, Charles Grapewin, Grady Sutton, Hedda Hopper

'A nice middle-class film, as trivial as a schoolgirl's diary, and just about as pathetically true.'—*C. A. Lejeune*

AAN: best picture; Katharine Hepburn

Alice Doesn't Live Here Any More**

US 1975 112m Technicolor
Warner (David Susskind, Audrey Maas)

A widow sets off with her young son for Monterey and a singing career.
Realistically squalid and foul-mouthed but endearing look at a slice of America today, with firm handling and excellent performances in a surprisingly old-fashioned theme.

w Robert Getchell d Martin Scorsese ph Kent L. Wakeford *m* various *pd* Toby Carr Rafelson

Ellen Burstyn, Alfred Lutter, Kris Kristofferson, Billy Green Bush, *Diane Ladd,* Lelia Goldoni, Jodie Foster

'What Scorsese has done is to rescue an American cliché from the bland, flat but much more portentous naturalism of such as *Harry and Tonto* and restore it to an emotional and intellectual complexity through his particular brand of baroque realism.'—*Richard Combs*

'Full of funny malice and breakneck vitality.'—*New Yorker*

'A tough weepie, redeemed by its picturesque locations and its eye for social detail.'—*Michael Billington, Illustrated London News*

AA: Ellen Burstyn
AAN: Robert Getchell; Diane Ladd

Alice in Wonderland**

US 1933 90m bw
Paramount

Intriguing but disappointing version of the nonsense classic, keeping to the Tenniel drawings by dressing an all-star cast in masks, thereby rendering them ineffective.

w Joseph L. Mankiewicz, William Cameron Menzies, *novel* Lewis Carroll *d* Norman Z. McLeod *ph* Henry Sharp, Bert Glennon *m* Dmitri Tiomkin

Charlotte Henry, W. C. Fields (Humpty Dumpty), Cary Grant (Mock Turtle), Gary Cooper (White Knight), Edward Everett Horton (Mad Hatter), Edna May Oliver (Red Queen), Jack Oakie (Tweedledum), Leon Errol (Uncle), Charles Ruggles (March Hare), May Robson (Queen of Hearts), Louise Fazenda (White Queen), Ned Sparks (Caterpillar), Alison Skipworth (Duchess)

'Lavishly produced, with great care given to

costumes and settings and make-up, but the spirit is missing.'—*New Yorker, 1977*

Alice in Wonderland*
US 1951   75m   Technicolor
Walt Disney

Fully animated cartoon version which has good moments but modernizes and Americanizes the familiar characters.

w various   *d* Clyde Geronomi, Hamilton Luske, Wilfred Jackson   *supervisor* Ben Sharpsteen   *m* Oliver Wallace

AAN: Oliver Wallace

Alice's Adventures in Wonderland*
GB 1972   101m   Eastmancolor   Todd-AO
TCF / Josef Shaftel (Derek Horne)

Live-action version which starts amiably enough but soon becomes flat and uninventive, with a star cast all at sea and tedium replacing the wit of the original.

wd William Sterling   *ph* Geoffrey Unsworth   *m* John Barry   *pd* Michael Stringer

Fiona Fullerton, Michael Crawford (White Rabbit), Robert Helpmann (Mad Hatter), Dudley Moore (Dormouse), Spike Milligan (Gryphon), Peter Sellers (March Hare), Dennis Price (King of Hearts), Flora Robson (Queen of Hearts), Rodney Bewes (Knave of Hearts), Peter Bull (Duchess), Michael Hordern (Mock Turtle), Ralph Richardson (Caterpillar), etc

Alice's Restaurant*
US 1969   110m   De Luxe
UA / Florin (Harold Levanthal)

Folk singer Arlo Guthrie, on the verge of being drafted, gets some varied experience of life among the drop-outs of Montana, Massachusetts and New York.
Typical of the freakish, anti-Vietnam, do-as-you-please movies which splurged from Hollywood in the wake of *Easy Rider*, this has the minor benefits of good production values and a few jokes.

w Venable Herndon, Arthur Penn   *d* Arthur Penn   *ph* Michael Nebbia   *m/songs* Arlo Guthrie

Arlo Guthrie, Pat Quinn, James Broderick, Michael McClanathan, Geoff Outlaw

AAN: Arthur Penn

Alive and Kicking*
GB 1958   94m   bw
ABP (Victor Skuzetsky)

Three old ladies escape from a home to an Irish island.

Agreeable minor comedy, a showcase for its elderly but vigorous stars.

w Denis Cannan   *d* Cyril Frankel   *ph* Gilbert Taylor
m Philip Green

Sybil Thorndike, Kathleen Harrison, Estelle Winwood, Stanley Holloway, Joyce Carey, Eric Pohlmann, Colin Gordon

All About Eve****
US 1950   138m   bw
TCF (Darryl F. Zanuck)

An ageing Broadway star suffers from the hidden menace of a self-effacing but secretly ruthless and ambitious young actress.
A basically unconvincing story with thin characters is transformed by a screenplay scintillating with savage wit and a couple of waspish performances into a movie experience to treasure.

wd Joseph L. Mankiewicz   *ph* Milton Krasner   *m* Alfred Newman

Bette Davis (a supremely bitchy performance), *George Sanders* (caricaturing his usual image), Anne Baxter, Celeste Holm, Gary Merrill, Hugh Marlowe, Gregory Ratoff, Thelma Ritter, Marilyn Monroe, Barbara Bates
  'The wittiest, the most devastating, the most adult and literate motion picture ever made that had anything to do with the New York Stage.'—*Leo Mishkin*
  'The dialogue and atmosphere are so peculiarly remote from life that they have sometimes been mistaken for art.'—*Pauline Kael, 1968*
  'Plenty of surface cynicism, but no detachment, no edge and no satire. Boiled down it is a plush backstage drama.'—*Richard Winnington*
  'Long, but continuously, wonderfully entertaining in a way I had almost forgotten was possible for films.'—*Richard Mallett, Punch*
AA: best picture; Joseph L. Mankiewicz (as writer); Joseph L. Mankiewicz (as director); George Sanders
AAN: Milton Krasner; Alfred Newman; Bette Davis; Anne Baxter; Celeste Holm; Thelma Ritter

The All-American
US 1952   83m   bw
U-I (Aaron Rosenberg)
GB title: *The Winning Way*

When his parents are killed on the way to a match, a college football hero rejects sport for the *groves of academe*.
Very modest formula drama.

w D. D. Beauchamp *d* Jesse Hibbs *ph* Maury
Gertsman
m Joseph Gershenson

Tony Curtis, Mamie Van Doren, Lori Nelson,
Gregg Palmer, Richard Long, Paul Cavanagh

All Ashore

US 1952   80m   Technicolor
Columbia (Jonie Taps)

Three sailors on shore leave work their passage
to Catalina.
Very lightweight musical, no rival for *On the
Town.*

w Blake Edwards, Richard Quine *d* Richard
Quine *ph* Charles Lawton Jnr *m* Morris Stoloff,
George Duning *ly* Robert Wells

Mickey Rooney, Dick Haymes, Ray McDonald,
Peggy Ryan, Barbara Bates, Jody Lawrance

All Creatures Great and Small*

GB1974   92m   Eastmancolor
EMI / Venedon (David Susskind, Duane
Bogie)

The pre-war Yorkshire life of a country vet.
Simple-minded popular entertainment of a long-
forgotten kind, oddly sponsored by American
TV in the shape of Readers' Digest and the
Hallmark Hall of Fame.

w Hugh Whitemore, *novel* James
Herriot *d* Claude Whatham *ph* Peter
Suschitzky *m* Wilfred Josephs

Anthony Hopkins, Simon Ward, Lisa Harrow,
Freddie Jones, Brian Stirner, T. P. McKenna,
Brenda Bruce, John Collin
    †1976 sequel: *It Shouldn't Happen to a Vet.*

All Fall Down*

US 1962   111m   bw
MGM (John Houseman)

A young man reveres his ne'er-do-well elder
brother but determines to shoot him when he
causes a girl's death.
Another gallery of middle American failures,
competently portrayed by a writer and actors
very practised at this sort of thing.

w William Inge, *novel* James Leo
Herlihy *d* John Frankenheimer *ph* Lionel
Lindon *m* Alex North

Warren Beatty, Brandon de Wilde, Angela
Lansbury, Karl Malden, Eva Marie Saint

All for Mary*

GB 1956   82m   Eastmancolor
Rank / Paul Soskin

Two rivals for the hand of the pretty daughter of
a Swiss hotelier are struck down by chicken pox

and cared for by the old nanny of one of them.
Simple-minded farce in which two grown men
quail like children before a forceful old lady; on
the strength of the latter characterization and a
few funny lines the original play was a
considerable West End success.

w Peter Blackmore, Paul Soskin, *play* Harold
Brooke, Kay Bannerman *d* Wendy
Toye *ph* Reg Wyer *m* Robert Farnon
Kathleen Harrison, Nigel Patrick, David
Tomlinson, Jill Day, David Hurst, Leo McKern

All Hands on Deck

US 1961   98m   De Luxe   Cinemascope
TCF (Oscar Brodney)

Romantic and farcical adventures of sailors on
leave.
Tired musical comedy romp with a second team
cast.

w Jay Sommars, *novel* Donald R.
Morris *d* Norman Taurog *ph* Leo
Tover *m* Cyril Mockridge *songs* Jay
Livingston, Ray Evans

Pat Boone, Buddy Hackett, Dennis O'Keefe,
Barbara Eden, Warren Berlinger, Gale Gordon,
Joe E. Ross

All I Desire

US 1953   79m   bw
U-I (Ross Hunter)

A woman who had deserted her husband and
family for a life on the stage returns for her
daughter's graduation and is reconciled.
Resilient star melodrama with all stops out.

w James Gunn, Robert Blees *d* Douglas
Sirk *ph* Carl Guthrie *m* Joseph Gershenson
Barbara Stanwyck, Richard Carlson, Lyle
Bettger, Maureen O'Sullivan, Richard Long,
Lori Nelson

All in a Night's Work

US 1961   94m   Technicolor
Paramount / Hal B. Wallis—Joseph Hazen

A publishing heir falls for a girl he suspects of
having been his uncle's mistress.
Unpolished and not very amusing comedy which
falters after an intriguing start.

w Edmund Beloin, Maurice Richlin, Sidney
Sheldon *d* Joseph Anthony *ph* Joseph La
Shelle *m* André Previn

Shirley Maclaine, Dean Martin, Charles
Ruggles, Cliff Robertson, Norma Crane, Gale
Gordon, Jerome Cowan, Jack Weston
    'Tame and aimless sex-and-big-business
comedy.'—*MFB*

All Mine To Give*

US 1956   102m   Technicolor   RKOscope
RKO (Sam Wiesenthal)
GB title: *The Day They Gave Babies Away*

In 1856, a pioneer couple in Wisconsin train
their children to carry on the family after their
own deaths.

Weird sentimental sob story, even odder under
its English title. Surprisingly, some of it works
quite well.

w Dale and Katherine Eunson (apparently about
their own ancestors) *d* Allen
Reisner *ph* William Skall *m* Max Steiner

Glynis Johns, Cameron Mitchell, Patty
McCormack, Rex Thompson, Ernest Truex,
Hope Emerson, Alan Hale

'A strong mood folksy western
reminiscence.'—*MFB*

All My Sons*

US 1948   94m   bw
U-I (Chester Erskine)

A young man establishes that his father sold
defective airplanes during the war.
Heady family melodrama from a taut and
topical stage play. The film is well-meaning but
artificial and unconvincing.

w Chester Erskine, *play* Arthur Miller *d* Irving
Reis *ph* Russell Metty *m* Leith Stevens

Edward G. Robinson, Burt Lancaster, Mady
Christians, Howard Duff

All Neat in Black Stockings

GB 1969   99m   Eastmancolor
Anglo Amalgamated / Miton (Leon Clore)

Sex adventures of an amorous window cleaner.
Modish comedy drama with surface
entertainment of a sort, but no depth.

w Jane Gaskell, Hugh Whitemore
d Christopher Morahan *ph* Larry Pizer
m Robert Cornford

Victor Henry, Susan George, Jack Shepherd,
Anna Cropper, Clare Kelly, Terence de Marney

All Night Long*

GB 1961   95m   bw
Rank / Bob Roberts (Michael Relph, Basil
Dearden)

Because of rumour set about by a jealous rival, a
jazz trumpeter at an all-night party tries to
strangle his wife.
Cheeky updating of *Othello* with jazz
accompaniment, played a shade too grimly by
an excellent cast. An interesting misfire.

w Nel King, Peter Achilles *d* Basil Dearden
ph Ted Scaife *m* Philip Green

Patrick McGoohan, Richard Attenborough,
Keith Michell, Betsy Blair, Marti Stevens, Paul
Harris, Bernard Braden; and on the sound track
Dave Brubeck, Tubby Hayes, Johnny
Dankworth etc

All of Me

US 1934   70m   bw
Paramount (Louis Lighton)

An engineering professor on his way to Boulder
Dam finds his life affected by the problems of a
criminal.
Confused and uninteresting romantic
melodrama with a good cast all at sea.

w Sidney Buchman, Thomas Mitchell, *play*
Chrysalis by Rose Porter *d* James Flood
ph Victor Milner *m/ly* Ralph Rainger, Leo
Robin

Fredric March, Miriam Hopkins, George Raft,
Helen Mack, Nella Walker, William Collier Jnr,
Gilbert Emery, Blanche Friderici, Edgar
Kennedy

'The most startling glorification of criminals
that even the movies have ever dared.'—*New
York Sun*

All Over the Town*

GB 1949   88m   bw
Rank / Wessex (Ian Dalrymple)

Two reporters revivify a West of England local
newspaper, and expose local corruption.
Fresh, agreeable romantic comedy on sub-
Ealing lines.

w Derek Twist and others *d* Derek Twist *ph* C.
Pennington-Richards *m* Temple Abady

Norman Wooland, Sarah Churchill, *Fabia
Drake* (as a local gorgon), Cyril Cusack, James
Hayter

All Quiet on the Western Front****

US 1930   130m approx.   bw
Universal (Carl Laemmle Jnr)

In 1914, a group of German teenagers volunteer
for action on the Western Front, but they
become disillusioned, and none of them survives.
A landmark of American cinema and
Universal's biggest and most serious
undertaking until the sixties, this highly emotive
war film with its occasional outbursts of bravura
direction fixed in millions of minds the popular
image of what it was like in the trenches, even
more so than *Journey's End* which had shown
the allied viewpoint. Despite dated moments, it
retains its overall power and remains a great
pacifist work.

w Lewis Milestone, Maxwell Anderson, Del
Andrews, George Abbott, *novel* Erich Maria

Remarque d Lewis Milestone (in a manner reminiscent of Eisenstein and Lang) ph Arthur Edeson m David Broekman

Lew Ayres, Louis Wolheim, Slim Summerville, John Wray, Russell Gleason, Richard Griffith, Beryl Mercer, Ben Alexander

'A trenchant and imaginative audible picture . . . most of the time the audience was held to silence by its realistic scenes.'—New York Times

'The sound and image mediums blend as one, as a form of artistic expression that only the motion screen can give.'—National Board of Review

AA: best picture; Lewis Milestone (as director)
AAN: Lewis Milestone, Maxwell Anderson, Del Andrews, George Abbott; Arthur Edeson

All That Heaven Allows
US 1955   89m   Technicolor
U-I (Ross Hunter)

A sad widow falls in love with the gardener at her winter home, and marries him despite local prejudice.
Standard tearjerker in the tradition of Magnificent Obsession, reuniting the same stars, producer and director in the same rich musical and photographic sauce.

w Peg Fenwick d Douglas Sirk ph Russell Metty m Frank Skinner

Jane Wyman, Rock Hudson, Agnes Moorehead, Conrad Nagel, Virginia Grey, Charles Drake
'As laboriously predictable as it is fatuously unreal.'—MFB

All That Money Can Buy****
US 1941   106m   bw
RKO / William Dieterle (Charles L. Glett)
aka:The Devil and Daniel Webster; Daniel and the Devil; Here Is a Man

A hard-pressed farmer gives in to the Devil's tempting, but is saved from the pit by a famous lawyer's pleading at his 'trial'.
A brilliant Germanic Faust set in 19th-century New Hampshire and using historical figures, alienation effects, comedy asides and the whole cinematic box of tricks which Hollywood had just learned again through Citizen Kane. A magic act in more ways than one.

w Dan Totheroh, based on The Devil and Daniel Webster by Stephen Vincent Benet d William Dieterle ph Joseph August m Bernard Herrmann ad Van Nest Polglase sp Vernon L. Walker

Walter Huston ('Mr Scratch', a great performance), James Craig, Anne Shirley, Simone Simon, Edward Arnold (Daniel

Webster), Jane Darwell, Gene Lockhart, John Qualen, H. B. Warner
AA: Bernard Herrmann
AAN: Walter Huston

All the Brothers Were Valiant*
US 1953   94m   Technicolor
MGM (Pandro S. Berman)

Rivalry between brothers on a whaling schooner. Remake of a silent melodrama with predictable vengefulness and formula heroism, capably but unmemorably portrayed.

w Harry Brown, novel Ben Ames Williams
d Richard Thorpe ph George Folsey m Miklos Rozsa

Stewart Granger, Robert Taylor, Ann Blyth, Betta St John, Keenan Wynn, James Whitmore, Kurt Kasznar, Lewis Stone

All the Fine Young Cannibals
US 1960   122m   Metrocolor
Cinemascope
MGM / Avon (Pandro S. Berman)

The son of a country clergyman loves the daughter of another clergyman; they both find the realities of life in New York a horrid shock. The glum joys of sex and dope in the big city are revealed in this boring rather than daring farrago which is not even unintentionally funny.

w Robert Thom, novel The Bixby Girls by Rosamond Marshall d Michael Anderson ph William H. Daniels m Jeff Alexander

Robert Wagner, Natalie Wood, Pearl Bailey, Susan Kohner, George Hamilton, Jack Mullaney, Onslow Stevens, Anne Seymour

All the King's Men***
US 1949   109m   bw
Columbia (Robert Rossen)

An honest man from a small town is elected mayor and then governor, but power corrupts him absolutely and he ruins his own life and those of his friends before being assassinated. Archetypal American political melodrama based on the life of southern senator Huey Long. The background is well sketched in and there are excellent performances, but the overall narrative is rather flabby.

w Robert Rossen, novel Robert Penn Warren d Robert Rossen ph Burnett Guffey m Louis Gruenberg ad Sturges Carne

Broderick Crawford, John Ireland, Mercedes McCambridge, Joanne Dru, John Derek, Anne Seymour, Shepperd Strudwick
'More conspicuous for scope and worthiness of intention than for inspiration.'—Gavin Lambert

'A superb pictorialism which perpetually crackles and explodes.'—*Bosley Crowther*

AA: Broderick Crawford

AAN: best picture; Robert Rossen (as writer);, Robert Rossen (as director); John Ireland; Mercedes McCambridge

All the President's Men***
US 1976   138m   Technicolor
Warner / Wildwood (Robert Redford, Walter Coblenz)

A reconstruction of the discovery of the White House link with the Watergate affair by two young reporters from the *Washington Post*. An absorbing drama from the headlines which despite its many excellences would have been better with a more audible dialogue track, less murky photography and a clearer introduction of the characters concerned. The acting however is a treat.

w William Goldman, *book* Carl Bernstein, Bob Woodward *d* Alan J. Pakula *ph* Gordon Willis *m* David Shire *pd* George Jenkins

Robert Redford, Dustin Hoffman, Jason Robards Jnr, Martin Balsam, Hal Holbrook, Jack Warden, Jane Alexander, Meredith Baxter

AA: William Goldman; Jason Robards Jnr
AAN: best picture; Alan J. Pakula; Jane Alexander

All the Right Noises*
GB 1969   91m   Eastmancolor
(TCF) Trigon (Anthony Hope)

The electrician of a touring company has an affair with a 15-year-old actress, but finally returns to his wife.
Sharp, sensible treatment of a cliché situation, as watchable as a superior television play.

wd Gerry O'Hara ph Gerry Fisher *m* John Cameron

Tom Bell, Judy Carne, Olivia Hussey, John Standing

'Built on a solid framework of disciplined direction and animated performances.'—*MFB*

All the Way Home**
US 1963   107m   bw
Paramount / Talent Associates (David Susskind)

In 1916 Tennessee, the beloved father of a family is killed in a car crash, and after the trauma wears off, mother helps the children to rebuild their lives.
Tactful, charming though finally depressing slice of small town period Americana, with generally eloquent performances.

w Philip Reisman Jnr, *play* Tad Mosel, *novel* A Death in the Family by James Agee *d* Alex Segal *ph Boris Kaufman m* Bernard Green

Robert Preston, Jean Simmons, Aline MacMahon, Pat Hingle, Michael Kearney
'A heart-wrenching blend of nostalgia and sorrow.'—*Judith Crist*

All the Way Up*
GB 1970   97m   Technicolor
Granada / EMI (Philip Mackie)

Social-climbing Dad makes his way by treachery and blackmail, but gets his come-uppance when his son takes after him.
Crudely farcical adaptation of a thoughtful comedy of its time; the treatment works in fits and starts but leaves one in no mood for the talkative finale.

w Philip Mackie, *play* Semi Detached by David Turner *d* James MacTaggart *ph* Dick Bush *m* Howard Blake

Warren Mitchell, Pat Heywood, Elaine Taylor, Kenneth Cranham, Vanessa Howard, Richard Briers, Adrienne Posta, Bill Fraser

All the Young Men
US 1960   87m   bw
Columbia (Hall Bartlett / Jaguar)

A marine patrol in Korea is commanded by a black man, and racial tensions take precedence over fighting the enemy.
Simple-minded, parsimoniously-budgeted war melodrama.

wd Hall Bartlett *ph* Daniel Fapp *m* George Duning

Alan Ladd, Sidney Poitier, Ingemar Johansson, Glenn Corbett, James Darren, Mort Sahl
'Strenuously engaged in exploiting the entertainment values of nostalgia, fear, suspense, hatred and sex.'—*MFB*

All This and Heaven Too**
US 1940   143m   bw
Warner (Jack L. Warner, Hal B. Wallis)

A 19th-century French nobleman falls in love with his governess and murders his wife.
Romantic, melodramatic soap opera from a mammoth best seller; well made for those who can stomach it, with excellent acting and production values.

w Casey Robinson, *novel* Rachel Field *d* Anatole Litvak *ph* Ernest Haller *m* Max Steiner

Charles Boyer, Bette Davis, Barbara O'Neil, Virginia Weidler, Jeffrey Lynn, Helen Westley, Henry Daniell, Harry Davenport, Walter

Hampden, George Coulouris, Janet Beecher, Montagu Love

AAN: best picture; Ernest Haller; Barbara O'Neil

All Through the Night **
US 1942 107m bw
Warner (Jerry Wald)

Gangsters help to track down fifth columnists in World War II New York.
Highly entertaining muddle of several styles which somehow works well and allows several favourites to do their thing.

w Leonard Spiegelgass, Edwin Gilbert
d Vincent Sherman ph Sid Hickox m Adolph Deutsch

Humphrey Bogart, Conrad Veidt, Peter Lorre, Karen Verne, Judith Anderson, Jane Darwell, Frank McHugh, Jackie Gleason, William Demarest, Phil Silvers

Allegheny Uprising
US 1939 81m bw
RKO (P. J. Wolfson)
GB title: The First Rebel

A young frontiersman smashes liquor traffic with the Indians.
Modestly efficient western with an impressive cast.

w P. J. Wolfson, story Neil Swanson d William A. Seiter ph Nicholas Musuraca

John Wayne, Claire Trevor, Brian Donlevy, George Sanders, Wilfrid Lawson, Robert Barrat, Moroni Olsen, Eddie Quillan, Chill Wills

An Alligator Named Daisy
GB 1955 88m Technicolor Vistavision
Rank (Raymond Stross)

A young songwriter finds himself saddled with a pet alligator.
The ultimate in silly animal comedies, this does score a few laughs.

w Jack Davies, novel Charles Terrot d J. Lee-Thompson ph Reg Wyer m Stanley Black

Donald Sinden, Diana Dors, Jean Carson, James Robertson Justice, Stanley Holloway, Roland Culver, Margaret Rutherford, Avice Landone, Richard Wattis, Frankie Howerd, Jimmy Edwards, Gilbert Harding

'Apart from a fairly Kafkaesque scene in which Daisy is discovered in an upright piano, the situation is treated with little wit or comic invention.'—MFB

Aloma of the South Seas
US 1941 77m Technicolor
Paramount (Monte Bell)

A young Polynesian chieftain returns to quell trouble on his island after being educated in the US.
Hoary goings-on in gory colour, a remake of a silent epic devised to display the star's sarong and the backlot's expensive volcano.

w Frank Butler, Seena Owen, Lillie Hayward d Alfred Santell ph Karl Struss, Wilfrid M. Cline, William Snyder m Victor Young sp Gordon Jennings

Dorothy Lamour, Jon Hall, Lynne Overman, Philip Reed, Katherine de Mille, Fritz Leiber, Dona Drake, Esther Dale

'The mountain has the privilege of belching when it is dissatisfied, which is something no well-bred critic should do.'—C. A. Lejeune
† A silent version in 1926 had starred Gilda Gray. Directed by Maurice Tourneur, it adhered more closely to the original play (by John B. Hymer and Leroy Clemens).

AAN: Karl Struss, Wilfrid M. Cline, William Snyder

Alone on the Pacific **
Japan 1963 104m Eastmancolor Cinemascope
Ishihara-Nikkatsu (Akira Nakai)
original title: Taiheiyo Hitoribochi

A young man crosses from Osaka to San Francisco in a small yacht.
Fascinating Robinson-Crusoe-like exercise, with flashbacks to life on dry land.

w Natto Wada, based on the experiences of Kenichi Horie d Kon Ichikawa ph Yoshihiro Yamazaki m Yasushi Akatagawa, Tohru Takemitsu

Yujiro Ishihara, Masayuki Mori, Kinuyo Tanaka, Ruriko Asaoko

'Wonderfully comic moments emerge, but they never overshadow the film's sheer pictorial value.'—Brenda Davies, MFB

Along Came Jones *
US 1945 90m bw
(UA) Cinema Artists Corporation (Gary Cooper)

Two cowboys are mistaken for killers.
Very mild western comedy melodrama, with the star at his most self-effacing and production only mediocre.

w Nunnally Johnson, novel Alan le May d Stuart Heisler ph Milton Krasner m Charles Maxwell, Arthur Lange, Hugo Friedhofer

Gary Cooper, Loretta Young, William Demarest, Dan Duryea, Russell Simpson

Along the Great Divide
US 1950   88m   bw
Warner (Anthony Veiller)

A marshal prevents an old man from being hanged for murder, and eventually discovers the real culprit.

Adequate, modest western with an unusual detective element.

w Walter Doniger, Lewis Meltzer d Raoul Walsh ph Sid Hickox m David Buttolph

Kirk Douglas, Virginia Mayo, Walter Brennan, John Agar, Ray Teal

The Alphabet Murders
GB 1965   90m   bw
MGM (Ben Arbeid)

Hercule Poirot solves a series of murders by an apparent lunatic choosing his victims in alphabetical order.

Ruination of a classic whodunnit novel, misguided both in its attempt to mix slapstick with detection and in its terrible central performance.

w David Pursall, Jack Seddon, novel The ABC Murders by Agatha Christie d Frank Tashlin ph Desmond Dickinson m Ron Goodwin

Tony Randall, Robert Morley, Anita Ekberg, Maurice Denham, Guy Rolfe, James Villiers, Clive Morton

Alphaville*
France/Italy 1965   98m   bw
Chaumiane/Filmstudio (André Michelin)

A special agent travels across space to find out what happened to his predecessor, and finds himself in a loveless society.

A rather chill futuristic fantasy on the lines of 1984 but with an outer space background and a hero borrowed from Peter Cheyney. Interesting but not endearing.

wd Jean-Luc Godard ph Raoul Coutard m Paul Misraki

Eddie Constantine, Anna Karina, Akim Tamiroff, Howard Vernon, Laszlo Szabo

Alvarez Kelly*
US 1966   116m   Technicolor   Panavision
Columbia / Ray David (Sol C. Siegel)

The owner of a herd of 2500 cattle finds himself between two sides in the American Civil War.

Unusual if rather tepid western which balances historical interest against social conscience and throws in a variety of other elements.

w Franklin Coen d Edward Dmytryk ph Joseph MacDonald m John Green

William Holden, Richard Widmark, Janice Rule, Patrick O'Neal, Victoria Shaw, Roger C. Carmel, Richard Rust

Always Goodbye
US 1938   75m   bw
TCF (Raymond Griffith)

An unwed mother gives up her baby and later wants it back.

Tired sentimental warhorse, a remake of Gallant Lady (qv).

w Kathryn Scola, Edith Skouras d Sidney Lanfield ph Robert Planck md Louis Silvers

Barbara Stanwyck, Herbert Marshall, Ian Hunter, Cesar Romero, Lynn Bari, Binnie Barnes

Always in My Heart*
US 1942   92m   bw
Warner (Walter McEwen, William Jacobs)

A convict returns home to find his daughter a stranger and his wife about to marry again.

Well acted sentimental drama.

w Adele Commandini, play Fly Away Home by Dorothy Bennett, Irving White d Joe Graham ph Sid Hickox m Heinz Roemheld

Walter Huston, Kay Francis, Gloria Warren, Frankie Thomas, Sidney Blackmer, Una O'Connor

AAN: title song (m Ernest Lucuona, ly Kim Gannon)

Always Leave Them Laughing*
US 1949   116m   bw
Warner (Jerry Wald)

A vaudeville comedian craves the spotlight at the expense of his private life.

Raucous backstage vehicle, crammed with sentimental and melodramatic cliché but affording tantalizing glimpses of the stage acts of its two stars.

w Jack Rose, Mel Shavelson d Roy del Ruth ph Ernest Haller ly Sammy Cahn md Ray Heindorf

Milton Berle, Bert Lahr, Virginia Mayo, Ruth Roman, Alan Hale, Jerome Cowan

Les Amants*
France 1958   88m   bw   Dyaliscope
Nouvelles Editions
aka: The Lovers

A rich provincial wife has a secret life in Paris, but finds real satisfaction in an affair with a young man.

A passionate romance which had some censorship difficulties at the time, this rather gloomy film never quite whirls one away as it should, and it doesn't have the eye for detail of *Brief Encounter*.

wd Louis Malle, *novel* Point de Lendemain by Dominique Vivant, Baron de Denon *ph* Henri Decaë *m* Brahms

Jeanne Moreau, Alain Cluny, Jean-Marc Bory, Judith Magre

Les Amants de Vérone*

France 1948 110m bw
CICC (Raymond Borderie)
aka: *The Lovers of Verona*

In modern Venice a film is being made of *Romeo and Juliet*, and the stand-ins for the stars feel they are re-enacting the old story.
A superbly stylish if rather empty piece, the dazzling detail being much more interesting than the main story.

w André Cayatte, Jacques Prévert *d* André Cayatte *ph* Henri Alekan *m* Joseph Kosma *ad* Moulaert

Pierre Brasseur, Serge Reggiani, Anouk Aimée, Louis Salou, Marcel Dalio
'Visually exciting, immaculately made.'— *Penelope Houston*

Amarcord**

Italy/France 1973 123m Technicolor
FC Produzione/PECF (Franco Cristaldi)

Memories of a small Italian town during the fascist period.
A bizarre, intriguing mixture of fact, fantasy and obscurity, generally pleasing to watch though hardly satisfying. The title means 'I remember'.

w Federico Fellini, Tonino Guerra *d* Federico Fellini *ph* Giuseppe Rotunno *m* Nino Rota *ad* Danilo Donati

Puppela Maggio, Magali Noel, Armando Brancia, Ciccio Ingrassia
'A rich surface texture and a sense of exuberant melancholia.'—*Michael Billington, Illustrated London News*
'Peaks of invention separated by raucous valleys of low comedy.'—*Sight and Sound*

The Amateur Gentleman*

GB 1936 102m bw
Criterion (Marcel Hellman, Douglas Fairbanks Jnr)

A Regency innkeeper's son poses as a travelling pugilist in order to clear his father's name of theft.
Dated but rather fascinating period adventure, quite a lively production of its time.

w Clemence Dane, Edward Knoblock, Sergei Nolbandov *d* Thornton Freeland

Douglas Fairbanks Jnr, Elissa Landi, Gordon Harker, Basil Sydney, Hugh Williams, Irene Browne, Margaret Lockwood, Coral Browne, Frank Pettingell, Athole Stewart, Esmé Percy

The Amazing Colossal Man*

US 1957 80m bw
AIP / Malibu (Bert I. Gordon)

A plutonium explosion causes an army colonel to grow at the rate of ten feet a day.
Modest, quite well written sci-fi let down by shaky trick work.

w Bert I. Gordon, Mark Hanna *d* Bert I. Gordon *ph* Joe Biroc *m* Albert Glasser

Glenn Langan, Cathy Downs, William Hudson, James Seay
† Sequel: *Revenge of the Colossal Man* (GB: *The Terror Strikes*).

The Amazing Dr Clitterhouse**

US 1938 87m bw
Warner (Robert Lord)

A criminologist researcher joins a gangster's mob and becomes addicted to crime.
Amusing, suspenseful, well acted comedy-melodrama.

w John Huston, John Wexley, *play* Barre Lyndon *d* Anatole Litvak *ph* Tony Gaudio *m* Max Steiner

Edward G. Robinson, Humphrey Bogart, Claire Trevor, Allen Jenkins, Gale Page, Donald Crisp, Maxie Rosebloom

The Amazing Mr Blunden**

GB 1972 99m Eastmancolor
Hemdale / Hemisphere (Barry Levinson)

In 1918, a widow and her two children meet a kindly gentleman who offers them work in his old mansion. Here they meet two ghost children, discover that he is a ghost too, and travel a hundred years back in time to right a wicked wrong.
Involved ghost story for intellectual children, made generally palatable by oodles of period charm and good acting.

wd Lionel Jeffries, *story* The Ghosts by Antonio Barker *ph* Gerry Fisher *m* Elmer Bernstein *pd* Wilfrid Shingleton

Laurence Naismith, Diana Dors, James Villiers, David Lodge, Lynne Frederick, Dorothy Alison, Rosalyn Lander, Marc Granger
'Easy period charm . . . fills every crevice.'— *Clyde Jeavons*

The Amazing Mr Williams*

US 1939 86m bw
Columbia (Everett Riskin)

About-to-be-marrieds investigate a murder.
Brisk comedy-thriller on *Thin Man* lines.

w Dwight Taylor, Sy Bartlett, Richard
Maibaum *d* Alexander Hall *ph* Arthur Todd
md Morris Stoloff

Melvyn Douglas, Joan Blondell, Ruth Donnelly,
Clarence Kolb, Ed Brophy, Donald MacBride,
Don Beddoe

The Amazing Mrs Holliday
US 1943   98m   bw
Universal (Bruce Manning, Frank Shaw)

Torpedoed in mid-Pacific, a missionary's
daughter arrives in San Francisco with eight
Chinese orphans.
Unusual sentimental vehicle for its star; of no
particular interest or merit in itself, but with the
usual interludes for song.

w Frank Ryan, John Jacoby *d* Bruce Manning
ph Elwood Bredell *m* Hans Salter, Frank
Skinner *md* Charles Previn

Deanna Durbin, Edmond O'Brien, Frieda
Inescort, Barry Fitzgerald

AAN: Hans Salter, Frank Skinner

The Amazing Quest of Ernest Bliss
GB 1936   80m   bw
Garrett–Klement (Robert Garrett, Otto
Klement)
US title: *Romance and Riches*

A millionaire accepts a wager that he can live
independently of his riches for one year.
Formulary comedy drama of its era on the theme
that money isn't everything. Very dated.

w John L. Balderston *d* Alfred Zeisler *ph* Otto
Heller

Cary Grant (on home leave after his first
Hollywood success), Mary Brian, Henry
Kendall, Leon M. Lion, Garry Marsh, Moore
Marriott, Peter Gawthorne, Ralph Richardson

The Ambassador's Daughter*
US 1956   102m   Technicolor
Cinemascope
UA / Norman Krasna

An American senator in Paris decides that the
presence of US forces in Paris constitutes a
moral danger. The ambassador's daughter
decides to investigate.
Thin comedy of the old-fashioned type: smart
lines and intimate playing not helped by the vast
screen.

wd Norman Krasna *ph* Michael Kelber
n Jacques Metehen

Olivia de Havilland, John Forsythe, Edward
Arnold, Adolphe Menjou, Myrna Loy, Francis

Lederer, Tommy Noonan, Minor Watson
   'An experienced cast approach the story's
frivolities with poise and style.'—*MFB*

Ambush*
US 1949   89m   bw
MGM (Armand Deutsch)

An army scout leads a posse to capture an
Indian chief who is holding a white woman
hostage.
Good, clean, robust western, well produced and
acted.

w Marguerite Roberts *d* Sam Wood *ph* Harold
Lipstein *m* Rudolph Kopp

Robert Taylor, John Hodiak, Arlene Dahl, Don
Taylor, Jean Hagen, Leon Ames

Ambush at Tomahawk Gap
US 1953   73m   Technicolor
Columbia (Wallace MacDonald)

Four ex-convicts seek hidden loot in a ghost
town.
Standard co-feature western with rather more
violence than usual for its date.

w David Lang *d* Fred F. Sears *ph* Henry
Freulich *m* Ross Di Maggio

John Hodiak, John Derek, David Brian, Maria
Elena Marques, Ray Teal, John Qualen

Ambush Bay
US 1966   109m   De Luxe
UA / Aubrey Schenck

In 1944, nine Marines try to escape from a
Japanese-held island.
Routine, lengthy, sub-standard heroics for
action addicts.

w Marve Feinberg, Ib Melchior *d* Ron Winston
ph Emanuel Rojas *m* Richard La Salle

Hugh O'Brian, Mickey Rooney, James
Mitchum, Tisa Chang, Harry Lauter

The Ambushers
US 1967   102m   Technicolor
Columbia / Meadway / Claude (Irving Allen)

An experimental flying disc disappears on a test
run, and the trail leads Matt Helm to the
Mexican jungle.
The third Matt Helm adventure had such a
stupid script that all concerned decided to send it
up, unfortunately with too obvious a tendency to
smirk at their own bravado.

w Herbert Baker *d* Henry Levin *ph* Burnett
Guffey, Edward Colman *m* Hugo Montenegro

Dean Martin, Senta Berger, Janice Rule, Kurt
Kasznar, James Gregory, Albert Salmi
   'Plot, jokes and gadgets all well below par.'—
MFB

America**

US 1924 · 136m (16 fps) bw silent
(UA)

Various characters experience the
Revolutionary War.
The Birth of a Nation, one war back. Much of
interest, but nothing new; Griffith was basically
repeating himself.

w John Pell d D. W. Griffith ph Billy Bitzer,
Hendrick Sartow, Marcel le Picard, Hal
Sintzenich

Neil Hamilton, Carol Dempster, Lionel
Barrymore, Erville Alderson
† As the English were the villains, the film was
banned in Britain, but later released under the
title *Love and Sacrifice*.

America, America*

US 1963   177m bw
Warner (Elia Kazan)
GB title:*The Anatolian Smile*

In 1896 Turkey, a young Greek dreams of
emigrating to America, and finally does so.
A massive piece of self-indulgence by a one-man
band, fascinating for his family circle but so
poorly constructed as to be of very limited
interest elsewhere.

wd Elia Kazan ph Haskell Wexler m Manos
Hadjidakis

Stathis Giallelis, Frank Wolff, Harry Davis,
Elena Karam, Estelle Hemsley, Lou Antonio
 'Kazan has failed to film the adventure implicit
in his material, and a potentially exciting story
has gone to waste.'–*MFB*
 'If he sinks his teeth in a scene or a sequence
that he enjoys, the audience can just sit around
and be damned.'—*Stanley Kauffmann*

AAN: Elia Kazan (as writer); Elia Kazan (as
director); Haskell Wexler

An American Dream

US 1966   103m   Technicolor
Warner (William Conrad)
GB title: *See You in Hell, Darling*

A TV commentator is goaded into murdering his
wife, becomes involved with gangsters and,
tortured by guilt, allows them to kill him for
shielding the girl friend of one of them.
Ludicrously heavy-handed version of a semi-
surrealist book which presumably had
something to say about modern America, at
least in its author's mind. Nothing comes
through but relentless boredom at watching
sordid and unlikely events, and sympathy for
those involved.

w Mann Rubin, *novel* Norman Mailer d Robert
Gist

ph Sam Leavitt m Johnny Mandel

Stuart Whitman, Janet Leigh, Eleanor Parker (in
a one-scene role of screaming bitchery that has
to be seen to be believed), J. D. Cannon, Lloyd
Nolan, Barry Sullivan, Murray Hamilton

AAN: title song (m Johnny Mandel, *ly* Paul
Francis Webster)

American Graffiti***

US 1973   110m   Techniscope
Universal / Lucasfilm / Coppola Company
(Francis Ford
  Coppola, Gary Kurtz)

In 1962 California, four young men about to
leave for college gather for a night's girl-chasing
and police-baiting.
Nostalgic comedy recalling many sights and
sounds of the previous generation and carefully
crystallizing a particular time and place.
Successful in itself, it led to many imitations.

wd George Lucas ph Ron Eveslage, Jan
D'Alquen m popular songs

Richard Dreyfuss, Ronny Howard, Paul le Mat,
Charlie Martin Smith, Cindy Williams, Candy
Clark, Mackenzie Philips

AAN: best picture; George Lucas (as writer);
George Lucas (as director); Candy Clark

An American Guerrilla in the Philippines*

US 1950   105m   Technicolor
TCF (Lamar Trotti)
GB title: *I Shall Return*

World War II, Pacific Zone: two American
sailors try to make their way to Australia after
MacArthur's surrender at Bataan.
Rather dull adventure story shot in the actual
locations.

w Lamar Trotti, *novel* Ira Wolfert d Fritz Lang
ph Harry Jackson m Cyril Mockridge

Tyrone Power, Micheline Presle, Tom Ewell,
Bob Pattern, Tommy Cook, Robert Barrat (as
MacArthur), Jack Elam
 'Cannot be regarded as a serious war film.'—
Penelope Houston

American Hot Wax

US 1978   91m   Metrocolor
Paramount (Art Limson)

The early days of rock and roll as seen by a
prominent disc jockey of the time.
Mildly entertaining ragbag of semi-historical
facts and authentic music, strictly for the youth
market.

w John Kaye d Floyd Mutrux ph William A.
Fraker *md* Kenny Vance

Tim McIntire (as Alan Freed), Fran Drescher,

Jay Lena, Laraine Newman, Chuck Berry, Jerry Lee Lewis, Screamin' Jay Hawkins

An American in Paris****
US 1951   113m   Technicolor
MGM (*Arthur Freed*)

A carefree young artist scorns a rich woman's patronage and wins the love of a gamine.
Altogether delightful musical holiday, one of the highspots of the Hollywood genre, with infectious enthusiasm and an unexpected sense of the Paris that was.

w Alan Jay Lerner d Vincente Minnelli ph Al Gilks, John Alton m George Gershwin ly Ira Gershwin ch Gene Kelly ad Cedric Gibbons, Preston Ames

Gene Kelly, Oscar Levant, Nina Foch, Leslie Caron, Georges Guetary

'Too fancy and overblown, but the principal performers are in fine form and the Gershwin music keeps everything good-spirited.'—*New Yorker, 1977*

AA: best picture; Alan Jay Lerner; Al Gilks, John Alton; musical arrangements (Saul Chaplin, Johnny Green)
AAN: Vincente Minnelli

American Madness**
US 1932   80m   bw
Columbia

When a bank failure threatens, hundreds of small savers increase their deposits to save the situation.
Vivid, overstressed topical melodrama with crowd scenes typical of its director's later output.

w Robert Riskin d Frank Capra ph Joseph Walker

Walter Huston, Pat O'Brien, Kay Johnson, Constance Cummings, Gavin Gordon, Berton Churchill

'The sequence of the mounting panic and the storming of the bank are effectively staged, but the resolution is the usual Capra/Riskin populist hokum.'—*New Yorker, 1977*

An American Romance*
US 1944   151m   Technicolor
MGM (King Vidor)

The life of a European immigrant who becomes a master of industry.
Mind-boggling pageant of the American dream, coldly presented and totally humourless. Its saving grace is its smooth physical presentation.

w Herbert Dalmas, William Ludwig d King Vidor ph Harold Rosson m Louis Gruenberg

Brian Donlevy, Ann Richards, John Qualen, Walter Abel, Stephen McNally

'A thousand chances to inform, excite or even interest have been flung away.'—*Richard Winnington*
'The whole aim of it is to boost The American Way.'—*Richard Mallett, Punch*

An American Tragedy**
US 1931   95m   bw
Paramount

An ambitious young man murders his pregnant fiancée when he has a chance to marry a rich girl.
Dated but solidly satisfying adaptation of a weighty novel, more compelling than the 1951 remake *A Place in the Sun.*

wd Josef Von Sternberg, novel Theodore Dreiser *ph* Lee Garmes *ad* Hans Dreier

Phillips Holmes, *Sylvia Sidney,* Frances Dee, Irving Pichel, Frederick Burton, Claire McDowell

'It is the first time, I believe, that the subjects of sex, birth control and murder have been put into a picture with sense, taste and reality.'—*Pare Lorentz*
'An ordinary program effort with an unhappy ending. Slow, heavy and not always interesting drama.'–*Variety*

The Americanization of Emily*
US 1964   115m   bw
MGM / Filmways (John Calley)

World War II: just before the Normandy landings, a war widow driver falls for an American commander who is a self-confessed coward.
Bizarre comedy full of eccentric characters, an uneasy choice for its female star but otherwise successful in patches in its random distillation of black comedy, sex and the tumbling of old-fashioned virtues.

w Paddy Chayevsky, novel William Bradford Huie *d* Arthur Hiller *ph Philip Lathrop, Chris Challis m* Johnny Mandel

Julie Andrews, James Garner, *Melvyn Douglas,* James Coburn, Liz Fraser, Joyce Grenfell, Edward Binns, Keenan Wynn, William Windom

'Out of it all there comes the definite feeling that Hitler's war is incidental to Paddy Chayevsky's war of ideas . . . no plot synopsis could begin to suggest how much the characters talk.'—*MFB*

AAN: Philip Lathrop

The Americano
US 1916   60m approx (24 fps)   bw   silent
Triangle (D. W. Griffith)

A young American engineer becomes involved in a revolution in Patagonia.

Early star adventure vehicle, an immense popular success; the last film Fairbanks made for Griffith.

w Anita Loos, John Emerson, *novel* Blaze Derringer by Eugene P. Lyle Jnr d John Emerson ph Victor Fleming

Douglas Fairbanks, Alma Rubens, Spottiswoode Aitken, Lillian Langdon

The Americano
US 1955 85m Technicolor
(RKO) Robert Stillman

A westerner takes three prize bulls to Brazil, but finds the buyer has been murdered.
A western with a twist, but otherwise extremely dull, with poor pace, colour and use of settings.

w Guy Trosper d William Castle ph William Snyder m Roy Webb

Glenn Ford, Frank Lovejoy, Abbe Lane, Cesar Romero, Ursula Thiess

Un Ami Viendra ce Soir
France 1946 111m bw
CGC (R. Artus)

During World War II a French patriot uses a lunatic asylum as a resistance headquarters.
Rather glum wartime melodrama, lacking in tension.

w Jacques Companeez, Raymond Bernard d Raymond Bernard ph Robert Le Fèbvre m Arthur Honegger

Michel Simon, Louis Salou, Saturnin Fabre, Paul Bernard, Madeleine Sologne, Marcel André

Le Amiche*
Italy 1955 90m bw
Trionfalcine
aka: *The Girl Friends*

The interaction of five girls living together in Turin.
Highbrow lending library stuff, quite watchable but equally forgettable.

w Suso Cecchi d'Amico, Alba de Cespedes, *story* Tra Donne Sole by Cesare Pavese d Michelangelo Antonioni ph Gianni di Venanzo m Giovanni Fusco

Eleanora Rossi Drago, Valentina Cortese, Yvonne Furneaux, Gabriele Ferzetti, Franco Fabrizi, Madeleine Fischer

Among the Living*
US 1941 68m bw
Paramount (Sol C. Siegel)

In a small town live twin brothers, one of whom is a murderer.
Offbeat suspenser with effective performances.

w Lester Cole, Garrett Fort d Stuart Heisler ph Theodor Sparkuhl

Albert Dekker, Susan Hayward, Frances Farmer, Harry Carey, Gordon Jones

The Amorous Adventures of Moll Flanders
GB 1965 125m Technicolor Panavision
Paramount / Winchester (Marcel Hellman)

An ambitious servant girl loses her virtue to a succession of rich gentlemen but finally settles for a highwayman.
The aim was to make a female *Tom Jones*, but this bawdy romp never achieves the freewheeling fluency of that surprise success, and a vacuous central performance makes the constant couplings more boring than exciting.

w Dennis Cannan, Roland Kibbee, *novel* Daniel Defoe d Terence Young ph Ted Moore m John Addison pd Syd Cain

Kim Novak, Richard Johnson, George Sanders, Lilli Palmer, Angela Lansbury, Leo McKern, Vittorio de Sica, Cecil Parker, Daniel Massey

'Further from Defoe than *Tom Jones* was from Fielding, but with much the same combination of crude table manners and clean sets to stand in for period flavour.'—*MFB*

The Amorous Prawn*
GB 1962 89m bw
BL / Covent Garden (Leslie Gilliat)
US title: *The Playgirl and the War Minister* (an attempt to
     cash in on the Profumo case)

A hard-up general's wife invites American paying guests to their official highland home.
This film version of a stage success seems very mild, but the cast is eager to please: the result is a frantic high class farce.

w Anthony Kimmins, Nicholas Phipps, *play* Anthony Kimmins d Anthony Kimmins ph Wilkie Cooper m John Barry

Joan Greenwood, Ian Carmichael, Cecil Parker, Dennis Price, Robert Beatty, Finlay Currie, Liz Fraser, Derek Nimmo

Amsterdam Affair
GB 1968 91m Eastmancolor
LIP / Trio / Group W (Gerry Willoughby)

Inspector Van der Valk investigates when a writer is accused of murdering his mistress.
Tolerable *roman policier.*

w Edmund Ward, *novel* Love in Amsterdam by Nicholas Freeling d Gerry O'Hara ph Gerry Fisher m Patrick John Scott

Wolfgang Kieling, William Marlowe, Caterina Von Schell

The Amsterdam Kill

Hong Kong 1977   93m   Technicolor
Panavision

Golden Harvest / Fantastic Films / Raymond Chow

An American ex-Drug Enforcement Agency officer tries to protect an old friend caught in the Hong Kong drug wars.

Roughlyu made and uninventive thriller in which the Hong Kong film makers fail to consolidate the international ground they gained with kung fu films.

w Robert Clouse, Gregory Teifer *d* Robert Clouse *ph* Alan Hume *m* Hal Schaffer

Robert Mitchum, Bradford Dillman, Richard Egan, Leslie Nielsen, Keye Luke

Anastasia **

US 1956   105m   Eastmancolor
Cinemascope

TCF (Buddy Adler)

In 1928 Paris, a group of exiled White Russians claim to have found the living daughter of the Tsar, presumed executed in 1918; but the claimant is a fake schooled by a general, with whom she falls in love.

Slick, highly theatrical entertainment for the upper classes; it dazzles and satisfies without throwing any light on history.

w Arthur Laurents, *play* Marcelle Maurette, Guy Bolton *d* Anatole Litvak *ph* Jack Hildyard *m* Alfred Newman *ad* Andrei Andreiev, Bill Andrews

Ingrid Bergman (her Hollywood comeback after some years in Europe under a cloud for her 'immoral' behaviour), Yul Brynner, *Helen Hayes,* Martita Hunt, Akim Tamiroff, Felix Aylmer, Ivan Desny

'Little weight but considerable and urbane charm.'—*John Cutts*

AA: Ingrid Bergman
AAN: Alfred Newman

Anatahan

Japan 1953   92m   bw
Daiwa (K. Takimura)
aka: *The Saga of Anatahan*

During World War II, Japanese seamen are shipwrecked on the same deserted island as a man and a woman; the latter causes jealousy and murder.

Downright peculiar studio-set melodrama, based on true events and directed by its creator through interpreters, with results far from happy.

wd, ph Josef Von Sternberg   *m* A. Ifukube

Akemi Negishi, T. Sugunuma, K. Onoe, T. Bandoh

'The main impression is of tedium relieved by moments of far from intentional humour.'—
Penelope Houston

Anatomy of a Murder **

US 1959   161m   bw   Cinemascope
Columbia / Otto Preminger

A small-town lawyer successfully defends an army officer accused of murdering a bartender who had assaulted his wife.

Overlong and over-faithful version of a highly detailed courtroom bestseller. The plot is necessarily equivocal, the characterizations overblown, but the trial commands some interest, and the use of 'daring' words in evidence caused controversy at the time.

w Wendell Mayes, *novel* Robert Traver *d* Otto Preminger *ph* Sam Leavitt *m* Duke Ellington *pd* Boris Leven

James Stewart, Ben Gazzara, Lee Remick, *Eve Arden,* Arthur O'Connell, *George C. Scott* (his first notable role, as the prosecutor), Kathryn Grant, Orson Bean, Murray Hamilton
† The trial judge was played by Joseph N. Welch, a real-life judge who had gained fame by his supervision of the McCarthy hearings.

AAN: best picture; Wendell Mayes; Sam Leavitt; James Stewart; Arthur O'Connell; George C. Scott

Anchors Aweigh **

US 1945   139m   Technicolor
MGM (Joe Pasternak)

Two sailors on leave in Los Angeles get involved with a small boy who wants to join the navy. Rather droopy musical most notable as a forerunner of *On the Town,* though on much more conventional lines. Amiable performances, and a brilliant dance with a cartoon mouse, save the day.

w Isobel Lennart *d* George Sidney *ph* Robert Planck, Charles Boyle *principal songs* Jule Styne *ly* Sammy Cahn *m* George Stoll *pd* Cedric Gibbons

Frank Sinatra, Gene Kelly, Kathryn Grayson, Jose Iturbi, Sharon McManus, Carlos Ramirez, Dean Stockwell, Pamela Britton

AA: George Stoll
AAN: best picture; Robert Planck; Gene Kelly; song 'I Fall in Love Too Easily' (*m* Jule Styne, *ly* Sammy Cahn)

And Baby Makes Three

US 1950   83m   bw
Columbia (Robert Lord)

A wife divorces her compromised husband before discovering that she is pregnant.

Thin marital comedy with minor compensations.

w Lou Breslow, Joseph Hoffman *d* Henry
Levin *ph* Burnett Guffey *m* George Duning

Robert Young, Barbara Hale, Billie Burke,
Robert Hutton, Janis Carter, Nicholas Joy,
Lloyd Corrigan

'It has everything but a story that hangs
together.'—*New York Herald Tribune*

And God Created Woman
France 1956   92m   Eastmancolor
  Cinemascope
Iena/UCIL/Cocinor (Raoul Lévy)
original title: *Et Dieu Créa la Femme;* aka: *And
Woman...*
  Was Created

An 18-year-old finds herself fatally attracted
towards men.
Rather a feeble excuse for its star to strip on the
St Tropez beach.

w Roger Vadim, Raoul Lévy *d* Roger Vadim
ph Armand Thirard *m* Paul Misraki

Brigitte Bardot, Curt Jurgens, Jean-Louis
Trintignant, Christian Marquand, Georges
Poujouly, Jane Marken, Paul Faivre

And Now For Something Completely
Different**
GB 1971   88m   colour
(Columbia) Kettledrum / Python (Victor
Lowndes / GSF)
  (Patricia Casey)

Useful round-up of the more famous sketches
from BBC TV's zany comedy series *Monty
Python.*
Side-splitting for those who want Groucho Marx
updated; baffling for reactionaries; movie
presentation perfunctory.

written by and starring *John Cleese, Graham
Chapman, Terry Gilliam, Eric Idle, Michael
Palin, Terry Jones*

d Ian Macnaughton *ph* David Muir

And Now Miguel*
US 1965   95m   Technicolor
Universal / Robert B. Radnitz

A 10-year-old Mexican boy proves himself
worthy to work on the mountain with the sheep.
A children's film typical of its producer: good to
look at, documentarily convincing, but too slight
and too slow.

w Ted Sherdeman, Jane Clove, *novel* Joseph
Krumgold *d* James B. Clark *ph* Clifford Stine
m Phillip Lambro

Pat Cardi, Guy Stockwell, Clu Gulager, Michael
Ansara, Joe de Santis

And Now Tomorrow*
US 1944   86m   bw
Paramount (Fred Kohlmar)

A rich girl goes deaf, loses her fiancé, but wins
the poor doctor who cares for her.
Bestselling slush turned into a routine star
romance.

w Frank Partos, Raymond Chandler (!), *novel*
Rachel Field *d* Irving Pichel *ph* Daniel L. Fapp
m Victor Young

Loretta Young, Alan Ladd (his first film in
confirmed top-star status after a meteoric rise
interrupted by war service), Susan Hayward,
Beulah Bondi, Cecil Kellaway, Barry Sullivan.

'A vernal sign of the boys getting back to one
of their favourite legends after the wintry days of
war.'—*Richard Winnington*

And So They Were Married
US 1935   74m   bw
Columbia (B. P. Schulberg)

A widow and a widower try to get married
despite the ill-feeling of their children.
Predictable romantic farce.

w Doris Anderson, Joseph Anthony *d* Elliott
Nugent *ph* Henry Freulich *m* Howard Jackson

Melvyn Douglas, Mary Astor, Edith Fellows,
Jackie Moran, Donald Meek, Dorothy Stickney

And Soon the Darkness*
GB 1970   99m   Technicolor
Associated British (Albert Fennell, Brian
Clemens)

Of two young nurses on a cycling holiday in
France, one is murdered by a local sex maniac
and the other almost shares her fate.
Slow, overstretched, often risible suspenser on
vanishing lady lines; long on red herrings and
short on humour, but with some pretension to
style. The action all takes place along a mile or
two of sunlit country road.

w Brian Clemens, Terry Nation *d* Robert
Fuest *ph* Ian Wilson *m* Laurie Johnson

Pamela Franklin, Michele Dotrice, Sandor Eles,
John Nettleton

And the Angels Sing*
US 1944   95m   bw
Paramount (E. D. Leshin)

Four singing sisters have hectic adventures with
a bandleader.
Mildly disarming romantic comedy with music,
more firmly set in a recognizable social milieu
than the usual fan product from this studio.

w Melvin Frank, Norman Panama *d* Claude
Binyon *ph* Karl Struss *m* Victor Young
songs Johnny Burke, Jimmy Van Heusen

Dorothy Lamour, Diana Lynn, Betty Hutton, Mimi Chandler, Fred MacMurray, Raymond Walburn, Eddie Foy Jnr, Frank Albertson, Mikhail Rasumny

'Slapstick sophistication in a sub-Sturges manner.'—*MFB*

And Then There Were None ****
US 1945   97m   bw
Harry M. Popkin
GB title: *Ten Little Niggers*

Ten people are invited to a house party on a lonely island, and murdered one by one.
A classic mystery novel is here adapted and directed with the utmost care to provide playful black comedy, stylish puzzlement, and some splendid acting cameos.

*w*Dudley Nichols, *novel* Agatha Christie (aka Ten Little Niggers) *d* René Clair *ph* Lucien Andriot *m* Mario Castelnuovo-Tedesco

Walter Huston, Barry Fitzgerald, Louis Hayward, June Duprez, *Roland Young, Richard Haydn,* C. Aubrey Smith, Judith Anderson, Queenie Leonard, Mischa Auer

And Then There Were None
GB 1974   98m   Technicolor
EMI / Filibuster (Harry Alan Towers)

Ten people are lured to an isolated Persian hotel and murdered one by one.
Listless remake, often so inept you could scream.

w Peter Welbeck (Harry Alan Towers) *d* Peter Collinson *ph* Fernando Arribas *m* Bruno Nicolai

Oliver Reed, Richard Attenborough, Elke Sommer, Herbert Lom, Gert Froebe, Stéphane Audran, Charles Aznavour, Adolfo Celi, Alberto de Mendoza, Maria Rohm

The Anderson Tapes *
US 1971   98m   Technicolor   Panavision
Columbia / Robert M. Weitman

An ex-con forms a gang to rob a building, not knowing that police and others, for various purposes, are making tape recordings of his conversations.
Superficially slick and fashionable crime thriller, marred by unnecessarily flashy direction, a failure to explain enough about the tapes, and a climax which oddly mixes bloodshed and farce.

w Frank R. Pierson, *novel* Lawrence Sanders *d* Sidney Lumet *ph* Arthur J. Ornitz *m* Quincy Jones

Sean Connery, *Martin Balsam*, Dyan Cannon, Alan King, Ralph Meeker

Andrei Rublev **
USSR 1966   181m   colour (part)
Cinemascope Mosfilm

Imaginary episodes from the life of a 15th-century icon painter.
A superb recreation of medieval life dramatizes the eternal problem of the artist, whether to take part in the life around him or merely comment on it.

w Andrei Mikhalkov-Konchalovsky, Andrei Tarkovsky *d* Andrei Tarkovsky *ph* Vadim Yusov *m* Vyacheslav Tcherniaiev

'The one indisputable Russian masterpiece of the last decade.'–*Nigel Andrews, MFB, 1973*
'With the exception of the great Eisenstein, I can't think of any film which has conveyed a feeling of the remote past with such utter conviction . . . a durable and unmistakable masterpiece.'—*Michael Billington, Illustrated London News*

Androcles and the Lion **
US 1952   96m   bw
RKO (Gabriel Pascal)

A slave takes a thorn from the paw of a lion which later, in the arena, refuses to eat him.
Shavian drollery, with interpolated discussions on faith, is scarcely ideal cinema material, but gusto in the performances keeps it going despite stolid direction.

w Chester Erskine, *play* Bernard Shaw *d* Chester Erskine *ph* Harry Stradling *m* Frederick Hollander *ad* Harry Horner

Alan Young, Jean Simmons, Robert Newton, Victor Mature, Maurice Evans (as Caesar), Reginald Gardiner, Elsa Lanchester, Alan Mowbray, Gene Lockhart

The Andromeda Strain **
US 1970   131m   Technicolor   Panavision
Universal / Robert Wise

Scientists work frantically to neutralize an infected village, knowing that the least infection will cause their laboratory to self-destruct.
Solemn and over-detailed but generally suspenseful thriller, with a sense of allegory about man's inhumanity to man.

w Nelson Gidding, *novel* Michael Crichton *d* Robert Wise *ph* Richard H. Kline *m* Gil Melle *ad* Boris Leven

Arthur Hill, David Wayne, James Olson, Kate Reid, Paula Kelly

Andy Hardy Comes Home *
US 1958   81m   bw
MGM (Red Doff)

Fortyish Andy returns to Carvel, his home town, to negotiate a land deal.
Rather dismal sequel to the celebrated series of *Hardy* (qv) family comedies which were enormously popular in the early forties: a thirteen-year gap is too long, and although most of the family is reunited the old Judge is sadly missed.

w Edward Everett Hutshing, Robert Morris Donley *d* Howard W. Koch *ph* William W. Spencer, Harold E. Wellman *m* Van Alexander

Mickey Rooney, Fay Holden, Cecilia Parker, Patricia Breslin, Sara Haden, Jerry Colonna

Angel**
US 1937   98m   bw
Paramount (Ernst Lubitsch)

The wife of an English diplomat finds herself neglected and almost has an affair with his old friend.
A curious romantic comedy in many ways typical of its time, yet with very few laughs, showing none of its director's usual cinematic sense, and compromised by the censor's refusal to let a spade be called a spade. Underplaying, and a sense that we watch a way of life about to be swept away, just about save it.

w Samson Raphaelson, *play* Melchior Lengyel *d* Ernst Lubitsch *ph* Charles Lang *m* Frederick Hollander

Marlene Dietrich, Herbert Marshall, Melvyn Douglas, Edward Everett Horton, Laura Hope Crews, Ernest Cossart

Angel and the Badman*
US 1947   100m   bw
Republic (John Wayne)

The love of a Quaker girl converts a wounded gunslinger to an honourable life.
Thoughtful western with good background detail and a fair measure of action.

wd James Edward Grant *ph* Archie Stout *m* Richard Hageman *pd* Ernest Fegte

John Wayne, Gail Russell, Harry Carey, Bruce Cabot, Irene Rich, Tom Powers

Angel Baby*
US 1960   97m   bw
Madera (Thomas F. Woods)

A mute girl is cured by an evangelist, and renounces her sins.
Strident, vigorous low-budget melodrama.

w Oris Borstem, Samuel Roeca, Paul Mason, *novel* Jenny Angel by Elsie Oaks Barbour *d Paul Wendkos ph* Haskell Wexler, Jack Marta *m* Wayne Shanklin

Salome Jens, George Hamilton, Joan Blondell, Mercedes McCambridge, Henry Jones, Burt Reynolds

Angel Face*
US 1952   91m   bw
RKO (Otto Preminger)

A demented girl murders her father and stepmother, involving her chauffeur, whom she finally kills, and commits suicide.
Outrageous melodrama, so absurd as to be almost endearing.

w Frank Nugent, Oscar Millard *d* Otto Preminger *ph* Harry Stradling *m* Dmitri Tiomkin

Jean Simmons, Robert Mitchum, Herbert Marshall, Barbara O'Neil, Leon Ames, Mona Freeman, Kenneth Tobey, Raymond Greenleaf
'The one lyrical nightmare in the cinema.'—
Ian Cameron

An Angel from Texas*
US 1940   69m   bw
Warner

Misadventures of a country boy in New York.
Modest revamping of a much filmed farce, also made as *The Tenderfoot* (1928) and *Dance Charlie Dance* (1937).

w Fred Niblo Jnr, Bertram Millhauser, *play* The Butter and Egg Man by George F. Kaufman *d* Ray Enright *ph* Arthur L. Todd

Eddie Albert, Rosemary Lane, Wayne Morris, Ronald Reagan, Milburn Stone

Angel in Exile
US 1948   90m   bw
Republic

An ex-con heads for an abandoned Arizona mine to recover stolen gold.
Modest, effective western about a baddie who reforms.

w Charles Larson *d* Allan Dwan, Philip Ford *ph* Reggie Lanning *m* Nathan Scott

John Carroll, Adele Mara, Thomas Gomez

The Angel Levine*
US 1970   105m   De Luxe
UA / Belafonte Enterprises (Chiz Schultz)

An elderly Jewish tailor complains to God of his bad luck; a black angel appears and seems to help him for a while.
Muddled and seemingly pointless parable with occasional felicities.

w Bill Gunn, Ronald Ribman, *story* Bernard Malamud *d* Jan Kadar *ph* Richard Kratina *pd* George Jenkins *m* Zdenek Linka

Zero Mostel, Harry Belafonte, Ida Kaminska, Milo O'Shea, Eli Wallach, Anne Jackson, *Gloria Foster*

'A prolonged variation on the theme that faith can produce miracles, but only if there is enough of it.'—*John Gillett*

Angel on My Shoulder**
US 1946   101m   bw
UA / Charles R. Rogers

The devil promises leniency to a dead gangster if he will return to earth and take over the body of a judge who is stamping out evil.
Crude but lively fantasy on the tail-end of the *Here Comes Mr Jordan* cycle, and by the same author.

w Harry Segall, Roland Kibbee d Archie Mayo ph James Van Trees m Dmitri Tiomkin

Paul Muni, Claude Rains, Anne Baxter, Erskine Sanford, Hardie Albright

'The story is so imitative that it's hard to feel any more towards it than a mildly nostalgic regard.'—*Bosley Crowther*

Angel on the Amazon
US 1948   86m   bw
Republic (John H. Auer)
GB title: *Drums Along the Amazon*

An elderly white lady resident of the Amazon jungle looks only 25 after being scared by a panther . . .
Ludicrous melodrama which the actors take seriously.

w Lawrence Kimble d John H. Auer ph Reggie Lanning m Nathan Scott

George Brent, Constance Bennett, Vera Hruba Ralston, Brian Aherne, Fortunio Bonanova, Alfonso Bedoya, Gus Schilling

The Angel Who Pawned Her Harp*
GB 1954   76m   bw
Group Three (Sidney Cole)

A real angel arrives on a goodwill visit to seamy Islington, and manages to right a few wrongs.
Simple-minded whimsy, spottily effective, with good performances.

w Charles Terrot, Sidney Cole d Alan Bromly ph Arthur Grant m Antony Hopkins

Diane Cilento, Felix Aylmer, Robert Eddison, Jerry Desmonde, Sheila Sweet, Alfie Bass

The Angel with the Trumpet
GB 1949   98m   bw
British Lion / London Films (Karl Hartl)

An Austrian lady has an affair with a crown prince but marries for security and dies in defiance of the Nazis.

Curious European cavalcade, dully directed to keep the budget down and accommodate long stretches of an Austrian original. An eccentricity.

w Karl Hartl, Franz Tassie, *novel* Ernst Lothar d Anthony Bushell ph Robert Krasker m Willy Schmidt-Gentner

Eileen Herlie, Basil Sydney, Norman Wooland, Anthony Bushell, Maria Schell, John Justin, Oskar Werner, Andrew Cruickshank

The Angel Wore Red
US 1960   105m   bw
MGM / Titanus / Spectator (Gottfredo Lombardo)

The love story of a priest and a prostitute in the Spanish Civil War.
Turgid farrago, unsatisfactory both romantically and politically.

wd Nunnally Johnson ph Giuseppe Rotunno m Bronislau Kaper

Ava Gardner, Dirk Bogarde, Joseph Cotten, Vittorio de Sica, Aldo Fabrizi, Finlay Currie

'The stars show no apparent surprise that a film so empty of reward should take itself so seriously.'—*Peter John Dyer*

Angelina*
Italy 1947   98m   bw
Lux

An impoverished housewife becomes the spokeswoman for her community on flooding, housing and other slum problems.
Reasonably rewarding star vehicle in the neo-realist tradition, this time angled for comedy.

w Suso Cecchi d'Amico, Piero Tellini, Luigi Zampa d Luigi Zampa ph Mario Craveri m Enzio Masetti

Anna Magnani, Nando Bruno, Gianni Glori, Franco Zeffirelli

Angélique
France / West Germany / Italy 1964   116m
   Eastmancolor   Dyaliscope
Francos / CICC / Gloria / Fona Roma (Francis Cosne)

Adventures of a nobleman's daughter at the court of Louis XIV.
Watchable swashbuckling nonsense, a kind of French *Forever Amber*. Several sequels were made.

w Claude Brûlé, Bernard Borderie, Francis Cosne, *novel* Serge and Anne Golon d Bernard Borderie ph Henri Persin m Michel Magne

Michèle Mercier, Robert Hossein, Giuliano Gemma, Jean Rochefort, François Maistre, Jacques Toja

Angels in the Outfield
US 1952   99m   bw
MGM (Clarence Brown)
GB title: *Angels and the Pirates*

The profane and bad-tempered manager of an unsuccessful baseball team gets help from an angel.

Unamusing, saccharine whimsy which does not deserve its excellent production values.

w Dorothy Kingsley, George Wells *d* Clarence Brown *ph* Paul C. Vogel *m* Daniele Amfitheatrof

Paul Douglas, Janet Leigh, Keenan Wynn, Lewis Stone, Donna Corcoran, Spring Byington, Bruce Bennett

Angels One Five *
GB 1952   98m   bw
Associated British (John W. Gossage, Derek Twist)

A slice of life in an RAF fighter station during the Battle of Britain.

Underplayed semi-documentary drama with stiff upper lips all round and the emphasis on characterization rather than action. A huge commercial success in Britain.

w Derek Twist *d* George More O'Ferrall *ph* Christopher Challis *m* John Wooldridge

Jack Hawkins, John Gregson, Michael Denison, Andrew Osborn, Cyril Raymond, Humphrey Lestocq, Dulcie Gray, Veronica Hurst

Angels Over Broadway *
US 1940   80m   bw
Columbia (Ben Hecht, Douglas Fairbanks Jnr)

During one rainy New York night, three of life's failures have one last stab at success.

Would-be poetic, moralizing melodrama very typical of its author; interesting but not a success.

w Ben Hecht *d* Ben Hecht, Lee Garmes *ph* Lee Garmes

Douglas Fairbanks Jnr, Rita Hayworth, Thomas Mitchell, John Qualen, George Watts, Ralph Theodore

'There's a genial, original spirit to it.'—*New Yorker, 1978*

'It has excitement, fast talk, some knowable people, cynicism and sentiment.'—*Otis Ferguson*

AAN: Ben Hecht (as writer)

Angels Wash Their Faces *
US 1939   86m   bw
Warner (Max Siegel)

A bad boy joins the Dead End Kids, but they all reform in the end.

Routine programmer, hastily concocted after the success of *Angels with Dirty Faces*.

w Michael Fessier, Niven Busch, Robert Buckner *d* Ray Enright *ph* Arthur Todd *m* Adolph Deutsch

Ann Sheridan, Ronald Reagan, the Dead End Kids, Bonita Granville, Frankie Thomas, Henry O'Neill, Berton Churchill, Eduardo Ciannelli

Angels with Dirty Faces ****
US 1938   97m   bw
Warner (Sam Bischoff)

A Brooklyn gangster is admired by slum boys, but for their sake pretends to be a coward when he goes to the electric chair.

A shrewd, slick entertainment package and a seminal movie for all kinds of reasons. It combined gangster action with fashionable social conscience; it confirmed the Dead End Kids as stars; it provided archetypal roles for its three leading players and catapulted the female lead into stardom. It also showed the Warner style of film-making, all cheap sets and shadows, at its most effective.

w John Wexley, Warren Duff, *original story* Rowland Brown *d* Michael Curtiz *ph* Sol Polito *m* Max Steiner

James Cagney (gangster with redeeming features), *Pat O'Brien* (priest), *Humphrey Bogart* (gangster with no redeeming features), *The Dead End Kids, Ann Sheridan,* George Bancroft, Edward Pawley

'A rousing, bloody, brutal melodrama.'—*New York Mirror*

AAN: Rowland Brown; Michael Curtiz; James Cagney

Les Anges du Péché *
France 1943   73m   bw
Synops / Robert Paul

A novice nun has trouble with the mother superior because of her obsessive interest in a rebellious delinquent girl, and dies before taking her vows.

Interesting study of an enclosed society, notable as its director's first film.

w R. P. Bruckberger, Jean Giraudoux, Robert Bresson *d Robert Bresson ph* Philippe Agostini *m* Jean-Jacques Grunenwald

Renée Faure, Jany Holt, Sylvie, Mila Parély, Marie-Hélène Dasté

The Angry Hills
GB 1959 105m bw
MGM / Raymond Stross

In 1940, an American war correspondent is
helped by Greek freedom fighters.
Laboured war melodrama with pretentious
dialogue but little characterization.

w A. I. Bezzerides, *novel* Leon Uris d Robert
Aldrich ph Stephen Dade m Richard Rodney
Bennett ad Ken Adam

Robert Mitchum, Gia Scala, Elisabeth Mueller,
Stanley Baker, Donald Wolfit, Kieron Moore,
Theodore Bikel, Sebastian Cabot, Peter Illing,
Marius Goring, Leslie Phillips

The Angry Silence*
GB 1960 94m bw
British Lion / Beaver (Richard Attenborough,
Bryan
    Forbes)

A worker who refuses to join an unofficial strike
is 'sent to Coventry' by his mates; the matter hits
national headlines, and the communists use it to
their own advantage.
Irresistibly reminding one of a po-faced *I'm All
Right Jack*, this remains a fresh and urgent film
which unfortunately lost excitement in its
domestic scenes.

w Bryan Forbes, *story* Michael Craig, Richard
Gregson d Guy Green ph Arthur Ibbetson
m Malcolm Arnold

Richard Attenborough, Michael Craig, Pier
Angeli, Bernard Lee, Alfred Burke, Laurence
Naismith, Geoffrey Keen

AAN: Bryan Forbes

Animal Crackers*
US 1930 98m bw
Paramount

Thieves covet a valuable oil painting unveiled at
a swank party.
An excuse for the Marx Brothers, and a lively
one in patches, though sedate and stage bound in
treatment. The boys are all in top form, and
many of the dialogue exchanges are classics.

w *Morrie Ryskind*, from musical play by himself
and *George F. Kaufman* d Victor Heerman
ph George Folsey m/ly Bert Kalmar, Harry
Ruby

Groucho, Chico, Harpo, Zeppo, *Margaret
Dumont*, Lillian Roth, Louis Sorin, Robert
Greig, Hal Thompson

Animal Farm*
GB 1955 75m Technicolor
Louis de Rochemont / Halas and Batchelor

Oppressed by the cruelty and inefficiency of their
master, the animals take over a farm but find
fresh tyrants among themselves.
George Orwell's political fable—'all animals are
equal but some animals are more equal than
others'—is faithfully followed in this ambitious
but rather disappointingly flat cartoon version.

w/pd John Halas and Joy Batchelor
voices Maurice Denham

The Animal Kingdom*
US 1932 95m bw
RKO (Darryl F. Zanuck)
GB title: *The Woman in His House*

An intellectual publisher tries to justify keeping
both a wife and a mistress.
Smart comedy-drama from a Broadway success,
later bowdlerized as *One More Tomorrow* (qv).

w Horace Jackson, *play* Philip Barry d Edward
H. Griffith ph Lucien Andriot

Leslie Howard, Ann Harding, Myrna Loy, Neil
Hamilton, William Gargan, Henry Stephenson,
Ilka Chase

The Animal World*
US 1956 80m Technicolor
Warner / Windsor (Irwin Allen)

The evolution of animals from their primitive
beginnings.
Ambitious documentary with a popular science
approach; very variable, with poorish model
work.

wd Irwin Allen ph Harold Wellman m Paul
Sawtell sp Willis O'Brien, Ray Harryhausen

Ann Vickers*
US 1933 72m bw
RKO (Pandro S. Berman)

A feminist social worker is taught a thing or two
by life and settles down with a corrupt judge.
Reasonably effective version of a popular though
heavy-going novel of the time.

w Jane Murfin, *novel* Sinclair Lewis d John
Cromwell ph David Abel, Edward Cronjager
m Max Steiner

Irene Dunne, Walter Huston, Conrad Nagel,
Bruce Cabot, Edna May Oliver, Mitchell Lewis,
Murray Kinnell

Anna
Italy 1952 100m bw
Lux (Ponti / de Laurentiis)

A novice nun recalls her former life and almost
gives up her vocation.
Soupy woman's picture of no particular merit.

w various d Alberto Lattuada ph Otello
Martelli m Nino Rota

Silvana Mangano, Raf Vallone, Vittorio
Gassman, Gaby Morlay, Jacques Dumesnil

Anna and the King of Siam**
US 1946   128m   bw
TCF (Louis D. Lighton)

In 1862 an English governess arrives in Bangkok
to teach the 67 children of the king.
Unusual and lavish drama, tastefully handled
and generally absorbing despite miscasting and
several slow passages.

w Talbot Jennings, Sally Benson, *book* Margaret
Landon d John Cromwell ph *Arthur Miller*
m Bernard Herrmann *ad Lyle Wheeler,*
William Darling

Irene Dunne, Rex Harrison, Linda Darnell, Gale
Sondergaard, Lee J. Cobb, Mikhail Rasumny
'A film that never touches the imagination, a
film that leaves the mind uninformed and the
memory unburdened.'—*Richard Winnington*

AA: Arthur Miller
AAN: Talbot Jennings, Sally Benson; Bernard
Hermann; Gale Sondergaard

Anna Christie**
US 1930   74m   bw
MGM

A waterfront prostitute falls in love with a young
seaman.
Primitive sound version of an earthy theatrical
warhorse: it has a niche in history as the film in
which Garbo first talked.

w Frances Marion, *play* Eugene O'Neill
d Clarence Brown ph William Daniels

Greta Garbo, Charles Bickford, *Marie Dressler,*
James T. Mack, Lee Phelps
'A very talkie, uncinematic affair, more old-
fashioned than the silent movies. If it were not so
well acted it would be pretty tiresome.'—
National Board of Review

AAN: Clarence Brown; Greta Garbo

Anna Karenina**
US 1935 95m bw
MGM (David O. Selznick)

The wife of a Russian aristocrat falls for a
dashing cavalry officer.
Well-staged but finally exasperating romantic
tragedy, sparked by good performances and
production.

w Clemence Dane, Salka Viertel, *novel* Leo
Tolstoy *d Clarence Brown ph William Daniels*
m Herbert Stothart

Greta Garbo, Fredric March, *Basil Rathbone,*

Freddie Bartholemew, Maureen O'Sullivan,
May Robson, Reginald Owen, Reginald Denny
† Previously filmed as a 1928 silent called *Love,*
with Garbo and John Gilbert.

AAN: William Daniels

Anna Karenina*
GB 1947   139m   bw
London Films (Alexander Korda)

Tiresomely overlong but very handsomely
staged remake marred by central miscasting.

w Jean Anouilh, Guy Morgan, Julien Duvivier
d Julien Duvivier ph *Henri Alekan m* Constant
Lambert

Vivien Leigh, Kieron Moore, *Ralph Richardson,*
Marie Lohr, Sally Ann Howes, Niall MacGinnis,
Michael Gough, Helen Haye, Mary Kerridge

Anna Lucasta*
US 1949   86m   bw
Columbia / Security (Philip Yordan)

The bad girl of a farming family comes home to
marry, but her past catches up with her.
Polish immigrant melodrama, a touring
company staple, adequately transferred to the
screen.

w Philip Yordan, Arthur Laurents, *play* Philip
Yordan *d* Irving Rapper *ph* Sol Polito *m* David
Diamond

Paulette Goddard, Oscar Homolka, Broderick
Crawford, William Bishop, Gale Page, Mary
Wickes

Anna Lucasta*
US 1958   97m   bw
(UA) Longridge Enterprises (Sidney Harmon)

Black version of the long-running play;
performances standard.

w Philip Yordan d Arnold Laven ph Lucien
Ballard m Elmer Bernstein

Eartha Kitt, Frederick O'Neal, Sammy Davis
Jnr, Henry Scott, Rex Ingram, James Edwards

Anna of Brooklyn
Italy/France/US 1958   106m   Technirama
Circeo Cinematografica / France
Cinema / RKO (Milko
   Skofic)

An attractive widow returns from New York to
her native Italian village in search of a husband.
Footling romantic drama which wastes its cast
and budget.

w Ettore Margadonna, Dino Risi d Reginald
Denham, Carlo Lasticati ph Giuseppe
Rotunno m Alessandro Cicognini, Vittorio de
Sica

Gina Lollobrigida, Dale Robertson, Vittorio de Sica, Amedeo Nazzari, Peppino de Felippo, Gabriella Palotta

Anne of Green Gables*
US 1934 79m bw
RKO (Kenneth MacGowan)

An orphan girl goes to the country to live with her aunt.
Standard version of the classic for young girls.

w Sam Mintz, *novel* L. M. Montgomery
d George Nicholls Jnr *ph* Lucien Andriot

Anne Shirley (who had been known as Dawn O'Day and legally adopted the name of her character in this, her first starring role), Tom Brown, O. P. Heggie, Helen Westley, Sara Haden, Charley Grapewin

'Made up and monotonous—tragedy having its breakfast in bed.'—*Otis Ferguson*

Anne of the Indies*
US 1951 87m Technicolor
TCF (George Jessel)

Lady pirate Anne Bonney, the terror of the Caribbean, is at odds with her former master Blackbeard.
Routine swashbuckler, generally well handled.

w Philip Dunne, Arthur Caesar d Jacques Tourneur *ph* Harry Jackson *m* Franz Waxman

Jean Peters, Louis Jourdan, Debra Paget, Herbert Marshall, Thomas Gomez, James Robertson Justice, Sean McClory, Francis Pierlot

Anne of the Thousand Days*
GB 1969 146m Technicolor Panavision
Universal / Hal B. Wallis

Henry VIII divorces his wife to marry Anne Boleyn, but soon finds evidence of adultery.
A somewhat unlikely view of history, rather boringly presented on a woman's magazine level, but with occasional good moments from a cast of British notables.

w John Hale, Bridget Boland, *play* Maxwell Anderson d Charles Jarrott *ph* Arthur Ibbetson *pd* Maurice Carter *m* Georges Delerue

Richard Burton, Geneviève Bujold, John Colicos (as Cromwell), Irene Papas, Anthony Quayle, Michael Hordern, Katharine Blake, Peter Jeffrey, William Squire, Esmond Knight, Nora Swinburne

'The costumes, beautiful in themselves, have that unconvincing air of having come straight off the rack at Nathan's.'—*Brenda Davies*

'A decent dullness is, alas, the keynote.'—*Michael Billington, Illustrated London News*

AAN: best picture; John Hale, Bridget Boland; Arthur Ibbetson; Georges Delerue; Richard Burton; Geneviève Bujold; Anthony Quayle

Annie Get Your Gun*
US 1950 107m Technicolor
MGM (Arthur Freed)

A young female hillbilly joins Frank Butler's sharpshooting act, and is sophisticated by her love for him.
Gaudy, stagey, generally uninspired screen version of the famous musical show based remotely on a historical character of post-wild-west days. There is a lack of dancing, the direction is stodgy, and in general flair the production falls disappointingly below MGM's usual standard.

w Sidney Sheldon, *musical play* Herbert and Dorothy Fields d George Sidney *ph* Charles Rosher *m/ly* Irving Berlin *md* Adolph Deutsch, Roger Edens *ch* Robert Alton *ad* Cedric Gibbons, Paul Grosse

Betty Hutton (who took over when temperament ousted Judy Garland), *Howard Keel*, Edward Arnold, J. Carrol Naish, Louis Calhern

AAN: Charles Rosher; Adolph Deutsch, Roger Edens

Annie Hall***
US 1977 93m De Luxe
UA/Jack Rollins-Charles H. Joffe (Fred T. Gallo)

Against the neuroses of New York and Los Angeles, a Jewish comedian has an affair with a midwestern girl.
Semi-serious collage of jokes and bits of technique, some of the former very funny and some of the latter very successful. For no very good reason it hit the box office spot and turned its creator, of whom it is very typical, from a minority performer to a superstar.

w Woody Allen, Marshall Brickman d Woody Allen *ph* Gordon Willis *m* various

Woody Allen, Diane Keaton, Tony Roberts, Carol Kane, Paul Simon, Shelly Duvall
†The narrative supposedly mirrors the real-life affair of the stars, who separated before the film came out.

Annie Oakley*
US 1935 90m bw
RKO (Cliff Reid)

The historical story, more or less, of the lady later immortalized in *Annie Get Your Gun*.
Lively semi-western with good dialogue but gluey plot development.

w Joel Sayre, John Twist d George Stevens

ph J. Roy Hunt *m* Alberto Columbo *ad* Van Nest Polglase

Barbara Stanwyck, Preston Foster, Melvyn Douglas, Moroni Olsen, Pert Kelton, Andy Clyde, Chief Thunderbird

The Anniversary*
GB 1968   95m   Technicolor
Hammer (Jimmy Sangster)

A malevolent one-eyed widow will stop at nothing to prevent her grown sons from leaving the family orbit, and they meet each year to mourn the death of the husband she really hated. Agreeable but over-talkative black comedy with a splendid role for its star and some good scattered moments, marred by a general lack of style.

w Jimmy Sangster, *play Bill MacIlwraith d* Roy Ward Baker *ph* Harry Waxman *m* Philip Martell

Bette Davis, Jack Hedley, *James Cossins,* Sheila Hancock, Elaine Taylor, Christian Roberts, Timothy Bateson

'Magisterially grotesque in elegantly tailored eye-patch and exotic gown, she snaps out her bitchy insults with all 57 varieties of relish.'— *MFB*

Another Dawn
US 1937   73m   bw
Warner (Harry Joe Brown)

In a British army post in Africa, a wife is torn between duty and romance.
Absurdly sudsy melodrama, a potboiler for stars between more important assignments.

w Laird Doyle *d* William Dieterle *ph* Tony Gaudio *m* Erich Wolfgang Korngold

Errol Flynn, Kay Francis, Ian Hunter, Frieda Inescort, Herbert Mundin
† In every Warner film where a cinema canopy was shown, the title advertised was *Another Dawn*, so its use here as an actual title is presumably a piece of cynicism.

Another Language
US 1933   75m   bw
MGM (Walter Wanger)

A young wife does not fit in with her husband's snobby family and falls in love with his nephew. Flat treatment of a dated play.

w Herman J. Mankiewicz, Gertrude Purcell, Donald Ogden Stewart, *play* Rose Franken *d* Edward H. Griffith *ph* Ray June

Helen Hayes, Robert Montgomery, John Beal, Louise Closser Hale, Henry Travers, Margaret Hamilton

Another Man, Another Chance
France / US 1977   132m   Eastmancolor
UA / Films 13 / Ariane (Alexandre Mnouchkine, George Dancigers)
French title: *Un Autre Homme, Une Autre Chance*

A Yank vet and a French widow meet and fall in love in the old west.
Pretty, overlong, rather enervating romance with an unusual and not entirely convincing setting.

wd Claude Lelouch *ph* Jacques Lefrançois *m* Francis Lai

James Caan, Geneviève Bujold, Francis Huster, Susan Tyrrell

Another Man's Poison*
GB 1951   89m   bw
Douglas Fairbanks Jnr / Daniel M. Angel

A lady novelist poisons her husband and lover, then unwittingly takes a fatal dose herself. Hysterical vehicle for a fading Hollywood star reduced to repeating her tantrums in an English studio on a low budget; she should have stayed home, as should her director.

w Val Guest, *play* Deadlock by Leslie Sands *d* Irving Rapper *ph* Robert Krasker *m* John Greenwood

Bette Davis, Anthony Steel, Gary Merrill, Emlyn Williams, Barbara Murray, Reginald Beckwith, Edna Morris

'Barnstormers as rich and improbable as this are rare . . . the general atmosphere takes one back to 1935.'—*Gavin Lambert*
'Like reading Ethel M. Dell by flashes of lightning.'
—*Frank Hauser*

Another Part of the Forest*
US 1948   108m   bw
U-I (Jerry Bresler)

In the post-Civil War years, Marcus Hubbard leads his family to worldly success by cheating and the misuse of power: he lives to regret it, as the children learn their lessons all too well. This backwards sequel to *The Little Foxes*, showing how the characters of that play got to be their nasty selves, is quite absorbingly acted but stagily presented, with plenty of care but no style.

w Vladimir Pozner, *play Lillian Hellman d* Michael Gordon *ph* Hal Mohr *m* Daniele Amfitheatrof

Fredric March, Florence Eldridge, Ann Blyth, Dan Duryea, Edmond O'Brien, John Dall

Another Shore*
GB 1948 77m bw
Ealing (Hal Mason)

A young Irishman dreams of life in the South
Seas but gives up his fancies for love.
Curiously whimsical, artificial and unconvincing
comedy drama from a famous studio, but not
without its moments of interest.

w Walter Meade, novel Kenneth Reddin
d Charles Crichton ph Douglas Slocombe
m Georges Auric

Robert Beatty, Stanley Holloway, Moira Lister

Another Time, Another Place
GB 1958 98m bw Vistavision
Paramount / Kaydor (Lewis Allen, Smedley
Aston)

During World War II an American
newspaperwoman has an affair with a British
war correspondent; when he is killed in action,
she consoles his widow.
Drippy romance, unsympathetically played and
artificially set in a Cornish village.

w Stanley Mann, novel Lenore Coffee d Lewis
Allen ph Jack Hildyard m Douglas Gamley

Lana Turner, Barry Sullivan, Glynis Johns, Sean
Connery, Sidney James

Anthony Adverse*
US 1936 141m bw
Warner (Henry Blanke)

Adventures of an ambitious young man in early
19th-century America.
A rousing spectacle of its day, from a bestselling
novel, this award-winning movie quickly dated
and now seems very thin and shadowy despite
the interesting talents involved.

w Sheridan Gibney, novel Hervey Allen
d Mervyn Le Roy ph Tony Gaudio ad Anton
Grot m Erich Wolfgang Korngold

Fredric March, Olivia de Havilland, Gale
Sondergaard, Edmund Gwenn, Claude Rains,
Anita Louise, Louis Hayward, Steffi Duna,
Donald Woods, Akim Tamiroff, Ralph Morgan,
Henry O'Neill
    'A bulky, rambling and indecisive photoplay
which has not merely taken liberties with the
letter of the original but with its spirit.'—Frank
S. Nugent, New York Times
    'In the dramatizing there is shown no relish or
conviction, only a retentive memory for all the
old clothes of show business.'—Otis Ferguson

AA: Tony Gaudio; Erich Wolfgang Korngold;
Gale Sondergaard
AAN: best picture

Antoine et Antoinette*
France 1947 87m bw
SNEG

A young married couple find they have won a
lottery but lost the ticket.
A bubbly soufflé, most expertly served but leaving one still a little hungry; not quite in the Clair
class.

w Françoise Giroud, M. Griffe, Jacques Becker
d Jacques Becker ph Pierre Montazel m Jean-
Jacques Grunenwald

Roger Pigaut, Clair Maffei

Antony and Cleopatra*
GB 1972 170m Technicolor Todd-AO
35
Transac (Zurich) / Izaro (Madrid) / Folio Films
(London)
    (Peter Snell)

Well-meaning, well-mounted, but quite uninspired rendering.

wd Charlton Heston, play William Shakespeare
ph Rafael Pacheco m John Scott pd Maurice
Pelling

Charlton Heston, Hildegarde Neil, Eric Porter,
John Castle (as Octavius), Fernando Rey, Freddie Jones, Peter Arne, Roger Delgado

Any Number Can Play*
US 1949 103m bw
MGM (Arthur Freed)

A gambling casino owner has health problems, is
reconciled with his son and retires from the
game.
Rather boring drama redeemed by slightly
offbeat dialogue and excellent star acting, albeit
in routine roles.

w Richard Brooks, novel E. H. Heth d Mervyn
Le Roy ph Harold Rosson m Lennie Hayton

Clark Gable, Alexis Smith, Mary Astor, Wendell
Corey, Audrey Totter, Lewis Stone, Frank
Morgan, Marjorie Rambeau, Barry Sullivan

Any Wednesday*
US 1966 109m Technicolor
Warner (Julius J. Epstein)
GB title: Bachelor Girl Apartment

A millionaire businessman spends every
Wednesday with his mistress, but complications
arise when his young associate is accidentally
sent to use the company flat.
Overlong screen version of a thinly scripted
Broadway success in which yawns gradually
overtake laughs.

w Julius J. Epstein, play Muriel Resnik d Robert
Ellis Miller ph Harold Lipstein m George
Duning

Jane Fonda, Dean Jones, Jason Robards Jnr, *Rosemary Murphy* (a breath of air as the deceived wife who doesn't mind), Ann Prentiss, King Moody

Anything Can Happen*
US 1952   93m   bw
Paramount / William Perlberg, George Seaton

Adventures of a Russian immigrant family in New York.
A standard Hollywood product based on a sentimental best-seller.

w George Seaton, George Oppenheimer, *book* George and Helen Papashvily d George Seaton *ph* Daniel L. Fapp *m* Victor Young

Jose Ferrer, Kim Hunter, Kurt Kasznar, Alex Danaroff, Oscar Beregi
'Exploits to the hilt the somewhat limited possibilities of quaintness and whimsicality with a broken accent.'—*Penelope Houston*

Anything Goes**
US 1936   92m   bw
Paramount (Benjamin Glazer)
TV title: *Tops is the Limit*

Romantic adventures on board a transatlantic liner.
Amiably batty musical comedy, zestfully directed and blithely performed.

w Guy Bolton, P. G. Wodehouse, Howard Lindsay, Russell Crouse, from their Broadway show d Lewis Milestone *ph* Karl Struss *songs* Cole Porter *md* Victor Young *ad* Hans Dreier

Bing Crosby, Ethel Merman, Charles Ruggles, Grace Bradley, Ida Lupino, Chill Wills, the Avalon Boys, Arthur Treacher

Anything Goes*
US 1956   106m   Technicolor   Vistavision
Paramount (Robert Emmett Dolan)

The male stars of a musical comedy each sign a girl to play the female lead; resulting complications are ironed out during a transatlantic voyage.
Below-par reworking of the 1936 film in which technical gloss and dull sets virtually reduce the characters to puppets. A few good moments transcend the general lack of imagination.

w Sidney Sheldon, from show as credited in 1936 version d Robert Lewis *ph* John F. Warren *songs* Cole Porter *md* Joseph J. Lilley *ch* Nick Castle, Roland Petit *ad* Hal Pereira, Joseph M. Johnson

Bing Crosby, Donald O'Connor, Zizi Jeanmaire, Mitzi Gaynor, Phil Harris, Kurt Kasznar

Anzio
Italy 1968   117m   Technicolor   Panavision
(Columbia) Dino de Laurentiis (Marcel Bebert)
GB title: *The Battle for Anzio*

A war correspondent joins American and British troops preparing for the 1944 landing in Italy.
Threadbare war film which wastes an all-star American cast.

w H. A. L. Craig, *book* Anzio by Wynford Vaughan Thomas d Edward Dmytryk *ph* Giuseppe Rotunno *m* Riz Ortolani

Robert Mitchum, Peter Falk, Arthur Kennedy, Robert Ryan, Earl Holliman, Mark Damon, Reni Santoni, Anthony Steel, Patrick Magee
'It must be a long time since a script managed to pack in so many crassly portentous statements about why men fight wars.'—*MFB*

Apache*
US 1954   91m   Technicolor
UA / Hecht–Lancaster (Harold Hecht)

After the surrender of Geronimo, one Apache leader is unconquered; after creating much havoc, he settles for domesticity, and the white men let him go unharmed.
Sober western in the wake of *Broken Arrow*, with a predictably sympathetic star performance and a surprising happy ending. More decency than excitement along the way.

w James R. Webb, *novel* Bronco Apache by Paul I. Wellman d Robert Aldrich *ph* Ernest Laszlo *m* David Raksin

Burt Lancaster, Jean Peters, John McIntire, Charles Bronson, John Dehner, Paul Guilfoyle, Walter Sande, Monte Blue

Apache Drums
US 1951   75m   Technicolor
U-I (Val Lewton)

A gambler helps a town under Indian attack.
Standard co-feature western, perfectly adequate but showing no sign of its producer's former tastes and skills.

w David Chandler d Hugo Fregonese *ph* Charles Boyle *m* Hans Salter

Stephen McNally, Willard Parker, Coleen Gray, Arthur Shields, James Griffith

Aparajito***
India 1956   113m   bw
Epic Films Private Ltd (Satyajit Ray)
aka: *The Unvanquished*

After his father's death, a poor country boy is helped by his mother to study for the university. A detailed and moving study of two characters who are universally familiar despite an unusual background.

wd Satyajit Ray *ph* Subrata Mitra *m* Ravi Shankar

Pinaki Sen Gupta, Karuna Banerjee, Kanu Banerjee

The Apartment***
US 1960 125m bw Panavision
UA / Mirisch (Billy Wilder)

A lonely, ambitious clerk rents out his apartment to philandering executives and finds that one of them is after his own girl.
Overlong and patchy but agreeably mordant and cynical comedy with a sparkling view of city office life and some deftly handled individual sequences.

w Billy Wilder, I. A. L. Diamond *d* Billy Wilder *ph* Joseph La Shelle *m* Adolph Deutsch *ad* Alexander Trauner

Jack Lemmon, Shirley Maclaine, Fred MacMurray, Ray Walston, Jack Kruschen, Edie Adams, David Lewis

'Without either style or taste, shifting gears between pathos and slapstick without any transition.'—*Dwight MacDonald*

AA: best picture; Billy Wilder, I. A. L. Diamond (as writers); Billy Wilder (as director)
AAN: Joseph La Shelle; Jack Lemmon; Shirley Maclaine; Jack Kruschen

Apartment for Peggy*
US 1948 98m Technicolor
TCF (William Perlberg)

A retired professor finds a new lease of life through caring for the homeless family of an ex-GI.
Sentimental comedy with serious undertones (the professor twice attempts suicide). Signs of enterprise are smothered by regulation charm.

wd George Seaton, *story* Faith Baldwin *ph* Harry Jackson *m* David Raksin

Edmund Gwenn, Jeanne Crain, William Holden, Gene Lockhart, Henri Letondal, Charles Lane, Houseley Stevenson

The Ape
US 1940 61m bw
Monogram

Dr Adrian seeks to cure polio by means of a serum which can only be obtained from the spinal fluid of a human being. He kills an escaped ape and dresses in its skin to seek victims.

Silly and rather boring addition to the mad doctor cycle.

w Curt Siodmak, Richard Carroll, *play* Adam Shirk *d* William Nigh *ph* Harry Neumann

Boris Karloff, Maris Wrixon, Gertrude Hoffman, Henry Hall

The Ape Man
US 1943 64m bw
Monogram
GB title: *Lock Your Doors*

A scientist injects himself with spinal fluid which turns him into an ape creature.
Cheap rubbish shot in a couple of corners and offering no thrill whatever.

w Barney A. Sarecky, *story* They Creep in the Dark by Karl Brown *d* William Beaudine *ph* Mack Stengler

Bela Lugosi, Wallace Ford, Louise Currie, Minerva Urecal

† A supposed sequel the following year, *Return of the Ape Man,* had in fact no plot connection. In this Lugosi thawed out a neanderthal man, inserted John Carradine's brain, and the composite turned into George Zucco!

The Appaloosa*
US 1966 99m Techniscope
Universal (Alan Miller)
GB title: *Southwest to Sonora*

A cowboy's plan to start a stud farm with his magnificent horse is interrupted by badmen who think he has molested their girl.
Mannered, slow western set on the Mexican border, with star and director apparently striving to upstage each other.

w James Bridges, Roland Kibbee, *novel* Robert MacLeod *d* Sidney J. Furie *ph* Russell Metty *m* Frank Skinner

Marlon Brando, Anjanette Comer, John Saxon, Rafael Campos, Frank Silvera

'Seems intent less on telling a story than in carving out the incidental details.'—*MFB*

'The camerawork concentrates on beady eyes, sweaty foreheads, spurred boots and anonymous midriffs being studied through a variety of frames, ranging from tequila bottles to cook fires to grillwork to fingers to feet.'—*Judith Crist*

Applause***
US 1929 78m bw
Paramount (Jesse L. Lasky, Walter Wanger)

A vaudeville star gradually loses the love of her daughter.
Absorbing treatment of a hasbeen tearjerking

theme, full of cinematic touches and with unusual use of New York locations.

w Garrett Fort, *novel* Beth Brown *d* Rouben Mamoulian *ph* George Folsey

Helen Morgan, Joan Peers, Henry Wadsworth, Fuller Mellish Jnr

'An oasis of filmic sophistication in a desert of stage-bound early talkies.'—*William Everson, 1966*

The Appointment*
US 1969   100m   colour
MGM (Martin Poll)

A businessman suspects his wife of spare time prostitution.

Unusual sophisticated fable, dressed to kill but rather stretched out for its substance. Shades of *El* and *The Chinese Room*.

w James Salter *d* Sidney Lumet *m* John Barry, Don Walker

Omar Sharif, Anouk Aimée, Lotte Lenya

Appointment for Love*
US 1941   89m   bw
Universal

A doctor and a playwright agree to marry 'without love'.

A familiar theme quite amusingly explored by a practised cast.

w Bruce Manning, Felix Jackson *d* William A. Seiter

Charles Boyer, Margaret Sullavan, Eugene Pallette, Rita Johnson, Gus Schilling, Reginald Denny, Ruth Terry

Appointment in Berlin
US 1943   77m   bw
Columbia (Sam Bischoff)

An RAF wing commander expresses unpopular views and is recruited by the Nazis as a 'voice of truth' broadcaster.

World War II potboiler.

w Horace McCoy, Michael Hogan *d* Alfred E. Green *ph* Franz Planer *m* Werner Heymann

George Sanders, Marguerite Chapman, Gale Sondergaard, Onslow Stevens, Alan Napier, H. P. Sanders (the star's father)

Appointment in London*
GB 1952   96m   bw
Mayflower (Aubrey Baring, Maxwell Setton)

The exploits of a squadron of Bomber Command during one month in 1943.

Dullish war film with standard credits.

w John Wooldridge, Robert Westerby *d* Philip Leacock *ph* Stephen Dade *m* John Wooldridge

Dirk Bogarde, Ian Hunter, Dinah Sheridan, Bill Kerr, Bryan Forbes, William Sylvester, Charles Victor

Appointment with Danger*
US 1949   89m   bw
Paramount (Robert Fellows)

A nun becomes the government's chief witness in identifying the murderers of a US postal inspector.

Routine but entertaining star thick-ear.

w Richard Breen, Warren Duff *d* Lewis Allen *ph* John Seitz *m* Victor Young

Alan Ladd, Phyllis Calvert, Paul Stewart, Jan Sterling, Jack Webb, Henry Morgan

Appointment with Venus**
GB 1951   89m   bw
GFD / British Film Makers (Betty E. Box)
US title: *Island Rescue*

During World War II, a pedigree cow is rescued from the German-occupied Channel Islands.

Curious but generally agreeable mixture of comedy and war adventure, pleasantly shot on Sark.

w Nicholas Phipps, *novel* Jerrard Tickell *d* Ralph Thomas *ph* Ernest Steward *m* Benjamin Frankel

David Niven, Glynis Johns, George Coulouris, Barry Jones, Kenneth More, Noel Purcell, Bernard Lee, Jeremy Spenser

The Apprenticeship of Duddy Kravitz*
Canada 1974   121m   Bellevue–Pathe Panavision
Duddy Kravitz Syndicate (Gerald Schneider)

An ambitious young Jew finds that it is best to be liked.

Amusing adventures of an anti-hero; good scenes but rather patchy technique.

w Mordecai Richler, from his novel *d* Ted Kotcheff *ph* Miklos Lente *m* Stanley Myers

Richard Dreyfuss, Micheline Lanctot, Jack Warden, Randy Quaid, Denholm Elliott, Joseph Wiseman

The April Fools*
US 1969   95m   Technicolor   Panavision
Cinema Center / Jalem (Gordon Carroll)

An unhappy New York husband elopes to Paris with an unhappy wife.

Whimsical romantic comedy which rather strains its resources without giving full value for money in romance, humour or simple charm.

Good moments, though.

w Hal Dresner *d* Stuart Rosenberg *ph* Michel

Hugo *m* Marvin Hamlisch *pd* Richard Sylbert

Jack Lemmon, Catherine Deneuve, Myrna Loy, Charles Boyer, Peter Lawford, Jack Weston, Harvey Korman, Sally Kellerman

'Painfully modish, from the opening party in an apartment filled with fashionable objets d'art to the final mad dash to the airport in an expensive sports car.'—*MFB*

April in Paris*
US 1952 100m Technicolor
Warner (William Jacobs)

A chorus girl is mistakenly invited to a US Arts Festival in Paris, and bewitches the bureaucrat in charge.

Poorly produced star musical with a thin plot and a few redeeming wisps of wit.

w Jack Rose, Melville Shavelson *d* David Butler *ph* Wilfrid Cline *md* Ray Heindorf *ch* Le Roy Prinz *songs* Sammy Cahn, Vernon Duke, E. Y. Harburg

Doris Day, *Ray Bolger*, Claude Dauphin, Eve Miller, George Givot

April Love
US 1957 99m Eastmancolor
Cinemascope
TCF (David Weisbart)

For stealing a car, a teenager is sent on probation to his uncle's stud farm, where circumstances seem once again to put him in trouble with the law.

Easygoing star vehicle with little to recommend it to adults.

w Winston Miller, *novel* George Agnew Chamberlain *d* Henry Levin *ph* Wilfrid Cline *songs* Sammy Fain, Paul Francis Webster

Pat Boone, Shirley Jones, Dolores Michaels, Arthur O'Connell, Jeanette Nolan

† A remake of *Home in Indiana*.

AAN: title song (*m* Sammy Fain, *ly* Paul Francis Webster)

April Showers*
US 1948 94m bw
Warner (William Jacobs)

In a family vaudeville act, Dad takes to drink. Hoary musical melodrama enlivened by occasional acts.

w Peter Milne *d* James V. Kern *ph* Carl Guthrie *md* Ray Heindorf *m adaptation* Max Steiner *songs* various

Jack Carson, Robert Alda, Ann Sothern, Robert Ellis, S. Z. Sakall

The Arab see The Barbarian

Arabesque**
US 1966 118m Technicolor Panavision
Universal (Stanley Donen)

An Oxford professor is asked by Middle Eastern oil magnates to decipher a hieroglyphic, and finds afterwards that he is marked for assassination.

The ultimate in sixties spy kaleidoscopes, in which the working out of the plot matters much less than the stars, the jokes and the lavish backgrounds. Fast moving, amusing and utterly forgettable.

w Julian Mitchell, Stanley Price, Pierre Marton *d* Stanley Donen *ph Christopher Challis ad* Reece Pemberton *m* Henry Mancini

Gregory Peck, Sophia Loren, *Alan Badel*, Kieron Moore, Carl Duering

'Nothing could look more "with it", or somehow matter less.'—*MFB*

'A strikingly visual chase and intrigue yarn.'—*Robert Windeler*

'All rather too flashy for comfort.'—*Sight and Sound*

Arabian Nights*
US 1942 86m Technicolor
Universal (Walter Wanger)

The Caliph of Baghdad is deposed by his half-brother but wins back his throne with the help of a dancer and an acrobat.

Well presented oriental adventure which has nothing to do with its source material but entertained multitudes in search of relief from total war and was followed by several vaguely similar slices of hokum with the same stars.

w Michael Hogan *d John Rawlins ph* Milton Krasner, William V. Skall, W. Howard Greene *m* Frank Skinner

Jon Hall, Maria Montez, Sabu, Leif Erickson, Thomas Gomez, Turhan Bey, John Qualen, Billy Gilbert, Shemp Howard

AAN: Milton Krasner, William V. Skall, W. Howard Greene; Frank Skinner

Arch of Triumph*
US 1948 120m bw
Enterprise (Lewis Milestone)

In postwar Paris, an embittered refugee seeks his former Nazi tormentor and has a tragic romance with a would-be suicide.

Doleful, set-bound melodrama knee-deep in misery and artificial melodramatics. An expensive, ambitious failure, both commercially and artistically, but an interesting one.

w Lewis Milestone, Harry Brown, *novel* Erich Maria Remarque *d* Lewis Milestone *ph* Russell Metty

Ingrid Bergman, Charles Boyer, Charles
Laughton, Louis Calhern

Are Husbands Necessary?
US 1942 79m bw
Paramount

A bickering couple decide to adopt a baby.
Mild marital comedy in a familiar mould.

w Tess Slesinger, Frank Davis, *novel* Mr and
Mrs Cugat by Isabel Scott Rorick d Norman
Taurog ph Charles Lang

Ray Milland, Betty Field, Patricia Morison,
Eugene Pallette, Charles Dingle, Cecil Kellaway,
Leif Erickson, Richard Haydn, Elizabeth Risdon

'A chaos of farcical situations, conceived
without gusto and played without conviction.'—
Richard Mallett, Punch

Are You Being Served
GB 1977 95m Technicolor
EMI (Andrew Mitchell)

The staff of the clothing section of a department
store go on holiday to the Costa Plonka.
Feeble enlargement of an old-fashioned but very
popular TV series relying heavily on sexual
badinage and ancient jokes.

w Jeremy Lloyd, David Croft d Bob Kellett
ph Jack Atcheler m various

John Inman, Frank Thornton, Mollie Sugden,
Trevor Bannister, Wendy Richard, Arthur
Brough, Nicholas Smith, Arthur English, Harold
Bennett, Glyn Houston

'A withering selection of patent British
puns.'—*John Pym, MFB*

Are You With It?*
US 1948 90m bw
U-I

An insurance executive with doubts joins a fun
fair and has a whale of a time.
Pleasantly lively low-budget musical.

w Oscar Brodney, *musical comedy* Sam Perrin,
George Balzer d Jack Hively ph Maury
Gertsman md Walter Scharf

Donald O'Connor, Olga San Juan, Martha
Stewart, Lew Parker

Arena
US 1953 83m Anscocolor 3-D
MGM (Arthur M. Loew Jnr)

A rodeo rider regains his wife and his sense when
his best friend is killed.
Routine actioner, distinguished by 3-D
camerawork.

w Harold Jack Bloom d Richard Fleischer
ph Paul C. Vogel m Rudolph G. Kopp

Gig Young, Jean Hagen, Polly Bergen, Henry
Morgan, Barbara Lawrence, Robert Horton,
Lee Van Cleef

Aren't Men Beasts!*
GB 1937 66m bw
BIP (Walter Mycroft)

A dentist poses as his aunt to stop a plot to
prevent his son's marriage.
Archetypal British star farce.

w Marjorie Deans, William Freshman, *play*
Vernon Sylvaine d Graham Cutts

Robertson Hare, Alfred Drayton, June Clyde,
Billy Milton, Judy Kelly

Arise My Love***
US 1940 113m bw
Paramount (Arthur Hornblow Jnr)

American reporters in Europe and in love
survive the Spanish Civil War, a wrathful editor
in Paris and the sinking of the *Athenia*.
Unique sophisticated entertainment gleaned
from the century's grimmest headlines, ending
with a plea against American isolationism. A
significant and stylish comedy melodrama.

w *Charles Brackett, Billy Wilder d Mitchell
Leisen ph* Charles Lang m Victor Young

Claudette Colbert, Ray Milland, Walter Abel
(who as the harassed editor inaugurated his
celebrated line 'I'm not happy. I'm not happy at
all . . .'), Dennis O'Keefe, George Zucco, Dick
Purcell

AA: original story (Benjamin Glazer, John S.
Toldy)
AAN: Charles Lang; Victor Young

The Aristocats**
US 1970 78m Technicolor
Walt Disney

Two cats are deliberately lost by a butler who
fears they will inherit his mistress's wealth; but a
variety of animal friends restore them to their
rightful place.
Cartoon feature, a moderate example of the
studio's work after Disney's death, with rather
too few felicitous moments.

d Wolfgang Reitherman

Arizona
US 1941 125m bw
Columbia (Wesley Ruggles)

A Tucson wildcat meets her match in a travelling
Missourian who helps her outwit villains who are
sabotaging her wagon trains.
Loosely built, deliberately paced western which
for all its pretensions makes very little impact.

w Claude Binyon d Wesley Ruggles ph Joseph
Walker, Harry Hollenberger, Fayte Brown
m Victor Young

Jean Arthur, William Holden, Warren William,
Porter Hall, Paul Harvey, George Chandler,
Byron Foulger, Regis Toomey, Edgar Buchanan
   'Lacks the sweep and dramatic impulse that
would have made it a great picture.'—*Variety*

AAN: Victor Young

Arizona Bushwhackers
US 1968 86m Techniscope
Paramount (A. C. Lyles)

A Confederate prisoner is given a chance as a
western sheriff.
Stolid western, notable only, as is usual with this
producer, for its gallery of ageing but still reliable
familiar faces.

w Steve Fisher d Lesley Selander ph Lester
Shorr m Jimmie Haskell

Howard Keel, Yvonne de Carlo, Brian Donlevy,
John Ireland, Marilyn Maxwell, Scott Brady,
Barton Maclane, James Craig

Armored Car Robbery*
US 1950 67m bw
RKO (Herman Schlom)

A police lieutenant leads the recovery of half a
million dollars stolen by gangsters.
Good competent second feature with Los
Angeles locations and detailed observation of
police methods.

w Earl Felton, Gerald Drayson Adams
d Richard Fleischer ph Guy Roe m Constantin
Bakaleinikoff

Charles McGraw, Adele Jergens, William
Talman, Douglas Fowley, Steve Brodie

Armored Command
US 1961 105m bw
Allied Artists (Ron W. Alcorn)

During the Battle of the Bulge, a ravishing Nazi
spy is infiltrated into an American army outpost.
Incredible Mata Hari melodrama posing as a
war film, nicely shot in bleak snowscapes. Not
exactly rewarding, but unusual.

w Ron W. Alcorn d Byron Haskin ph Ernest
Haller m Bert Grund

Howard Keel, Tina Louise, Burt Reynolds, Earl
Holliman, Warner Anderson, Carleton Young,
Marty Ingels

Arnold
US 1973 95m De Luxe
Avco/Fenady (Charles A. Pratt, Andrew
Fenady)

Via cassette recordings, a dead man toys with his
would-be heirs, and several are murdered.
Unpleasant and very laboured black comedy on
the lines of *And Then There Were None* and a
hundred others, all better than this.

w Jameson Brewer, John Fenton Murray
d Georg Fenady ph William Jurgenson
m George Duning

Stella Stevens, Roddy McDowell, Elsa
Lanchester, Shani Wallis, Farley Granger,
Victor Buono, John McGiver, Bernard Fox,
Patric Knowles
† Apparently made back to back with *Terror in
the Wax Museum*, which has very similar
credits.

Around the World
US 1943 81m bw
RKO (Allan Dwan)

Kay Kyser's band goes on a world tour to
entertain troops overseas.
Typical wartime patriotic musical, now of
sociological interest.

w Ralph Spence d Allan Dwan ph Russell
Metty md Constantin Bakaleinikoff m George
Duning

Kay Kyser, Ish Kabibble, Ginny Simms, Joan
Davis, Mischa Auer

Around the World in Eighty Days*
US 1956 178m Technicolor Todd-AO
UA / Michael Todd

A Victorian gentleman and his valet win a bet
that they can go round the world in eighty days.
Amiable large-scale pageant resolving itself into
a number of sketches, which could have been
much sharper, separated by wide screen
spectacle. What was breathtaking at the time
seems generally slow and blunted in retrospect,
but the fascination of recognizing 44 cameo stars
remains. The film is less an exercise in traditional
skills than a tribute to its producer's energy.

w James Poe, John Farrow, S. J. Perelman, *novel*
Jules Verne d Michael Anderson, Kevin
McClory ph Lionel Lindon m Victor Young
titles Saul Bass

David Niven, Cantinflas, Robert Newton, Shirley
Maclaine, Charles Boyer, Joe E. Brown, Martine
Carol, John Carradine, Charles Coburn, *Ronald
Colman*, Melville Cooper, *Noel Coward*, Finlay
Currie, Reginald Denny, Andy Devine, Marlene
Dietrich, Luis Dominguin, Fernandel, *John
Gielgud*, Hermione Gingold, Jose Greco, Cedric
Hardwicke, Trevor Howard, Glynis Johns,
Buster Keaton, Evelyn Keyes, Beatrice Lillie,
Peter Lorre, Edmund Lowe, A. E. Matthews,
Mike Mazurki, Tim McCoy, Victor McLaglen,

John Mills, Alan Mowbray, Robert Morley, Jack Oakie, George Raft, Gilbert Roland, Cesar Romero, Frank Sinatra, *Red Skelton*, Ronald Squire, Basil Sidney, *Harcourt Williams*, Ed Murrow

'Michael Todd's "show", shorn of the ballyhoo and to critics not mollified by parties and sweetmeats, is a film like any other, only twice as long as most . . . the shots of trains and boats seem endless.'—*David Robinson*

AA: best picture; James Poe, John Farrow, S. J. Perelman; Lionel Lindon; Victor Young

Around the World under the Sea
US 1966   110m   Metrocolor   Panavision
MGM / Ivan Tors (Andrew Marton)

An ultra-modern underwater craft travels around the seabed fixing sensors to give early warning of volcanoes.
Earnest, dullish, elementary sci-fi with cardboard characters providing routine five men-one woman skirmishes.

w Arthur Weiss, Art Arthur *d* Andrew Marton, Ricou Browning *ph* Clifford Poland, Lamar Boren *m* Harry Sukman

Lloyd Bridges, Shirley Eaton, Brian Kelly, David McCallum, Keenan Wynn, Marshall Thompson, Gary Merrill

The Arrangement**
US 1969   127m   Technicolor   Panavision
Warner / Athena (Elia Kazan)

A wealthy advertising man fails in a suicide attempt and spends his convalescence reflecting on his unsatisfactory emotional life.
A lush, all-American melodrama, rich in technique but peopled by characters who have nothing to say; the film makes no discernible point except as a well-acted tirade against the compromises of modern urban living.

wd Elia Kazan, from his own novel *ph* Robert Surtees *m* David Amram *pd* Malcolm C. Bert

Kirk Douglas, Faye Dunaway, Deborah Kerr, Richard Boone, Hume Cronyn

'The sort of collage that won't fit together, no matter where you stand.'—*PS*

Arrowhead
US 1953   105m   Technicolor   3D
Paramount (Nat Holt)

Enmity between an army scout and an Indian chief is resolved by single combat.
Standard western, good-looking but rather lifeless.

w Charles Marquis Warren, *novel* W. R. Burnett *d* Charles Marquis Warren *ph* Ray Rennahan *m* Paul Sawtell

Charlton Heston, Jack Palance, Katy Jurado, Brian Keith, Milburn Stone

Arrowsmith*
US 1932   108m   bw
Samuel Goldwyn

The self-sacrificing career of a doctor.
Emotionally satisfactory, dramatically slow and unsurprising variation on a theme which has since been treated far too often.

w Sidney Howard, *novel* Sinclair Lewis *d* John Ford *ph* Ray June *m* Alfred Newman

Ronald Colman, Helen Hayes, Richard Bennett, Myrna Loy, Charlotte Henry, Beulah Bondi, A. E. Anson

AAN: best picture; Sidney Howard; Ray June

Arsenal**
USSR 1929   99m (16 fps)   bw   silent
VUFKU

The 1914 war is made worse by strikes at home. Patchy propagandist drama with brilliant sequences.

wd Alexander Dovzhenko *ph* Danylo Demutsky

S. Svashenko, A. Buchma, M. Nademsky
'A romantic and lyrical masterpiece.'—*Georges Sadoul*

Arsene Lupin**
US 1932   75m   bw
MGM

The Parisian gentleman thief accomplishes some daring robberies and is almost caught stealing the Mona Lisa.
Amusing crook comedy with a few flat passages but much sparkle in between, and a lively finale.

w Carey Wilson, Lenore Coffee, Bayard Veiller *d* Jack Conway *ph* Oliver Marsh

John Barrymore, Lionel Barrymore, Karen Morley, Tully Marshall, John Miljan

Arsenic and Old Lace***
US 1942 (released 1944)   118m   bw
Warner (Frank Capra)

Two dear, well-meaning old ladies invite lonely old men to their Brooklyn home, poison them with elderberry wine, and have their mad brother, who believes the corpses are yellow fever victims, bury them in the cellar. A homicidal nephew then turns up with bodies of his own.
A model for stage play adaptations, this famous black farce provided a frenzy of hilarious activity, and its flippant attitude to death was better received in wartime than would have been

the case earlier or later. The director coaxes some perfect if overstated performances from his star cast, and added his own flair for perpetuating a hubbub.

w Julius J. and Philip G. Epstein, from the play by Joseph Kesselring with help from Howard Lindsay and Russell Crouse *d* Frank Capra *ph* Sol Polito *m* Max Steiner

Cary Grant (registering nineteen double takes to the minute), *Josephine Hull, Jean Adair, Raymond Massey, Peter Lorre, Priscilla Lane, Edward Everett Horton, James Gleason, John Alexander, Jack Carson, Grant Mitchell*

The Art of Love
US 1965   99m   Technicolor
Universal / Ross Hunter

To stimulate interest in his work, a penniless artist fakes suicide, subsequently becoming so famous that he finds it difficult to reappear.
A pleasant black comedy idea is buried under lush production, dull direction and a host of unattractive Parisian sets.

w Carl Reiner *d* Norman Jewison *ph* Russell Metty *m* Cy Coleman

James Garner, Dick Van Dyke, Angie Dickinson, Elke Sommer, Ethel Merman, Pierre Olaf

Artistes at the Top of the Big Top: Disorientated**
West Germany 1968   103m   bw/colour
Kairos Film

The daughter of a dead trapezist dreams of creating the ideal circus with a moral for mankind but step by step gives up her ambition. A melancholy satire, told in fragmented fashion with some brilliant tricks and memorable sequences.

wd *Alexander Kluge ph* Gunther Hörmann, Thomas Mauch

Hannelore Hoger, Siegfried Graue, Alfred Edel, Bernd Höltz

'Those who interpret it simply as an allegory of German politics or of the present crisis in film-making narrow it unnecessarily.'—*Jan Dawson, MFB*

Artists and Models*
US 1937   97m   bw
Paramount (Lewis E. Gensler)

An advertising man has to find the right girl as symbol for a silverware company.
Fairly stylish comedy musical with many elements typical of its studio.

w Walter de Leon, Francis Martin *d* Raoul

Walsh *ph* Victor Milner *m* Victor Young *songs* various

Jack Benny, Ida Lupino, Richard Arlen, Gail Patrick, Ben Blue, Judy Canova, Martha Raye, Donald Meek, Hedda Hopper, André Kostelanetz and his Orchestra, Louis Armstrong and his Orchestra

AAN: song 'Whispers in the Dark' (*m* Frederick Hollander, *ly* Leo Robin)

Artists and Models*
US 1955   109m   Technicolor   Vistavision
Paramount / Hal B. Wallis

A goonish young man receives telepathic top secret information in his nightmares, which are used by his artist friend in comic strips; foreign agents and the CIA get interested.
A good zany idea is worked into an overlong dyspeptic comedy which neither the stars nor frantic treatment can hope to save.

w Frank Tashlin, Don McGuire *d* Frank Tashlin *ph* Daniel Fapp *m* Walter Scharf

Dean Martin, Jerry Lewis, Shirley Maclaine, Dorothy Malone, Eddie Mayehoff, Eva Gabor, Anita Ekberg, George 'Foghorn' Winslow, Jack Elam

Artists and Models Abroad*
US 1938   90m   bw
Paramount (Arthur Hornblow Jnr)
GB title: *Stranded in Paris*

Stranded in Paris, a troupe of girls and their manager are helped by a Texas oil millionaire.
Generally agreeable comedy musical with emphasis on fashion.

w Howard Lindsay, Russell Crouse, Ken Englund *d* Mitchell Leisen *ph* Ted Tetzlaff *md* Borris Morros *songs* various *ad* Hans Dreier, Ernest Fegte

Jack Benny, Joan Bennett, Mary Boland, Charley Grapewin, Joyce Compton, the Yacht Club Boys, Fritz Feld, G. P. Huntley, Monty Woolley

The Aryan*
US 1916   75m (16 fps)   bw   silent
Triangle (Thomas Ince)

A gold prospector is cheated by a woman and becomes an outlaw.
Striking early star western.

w C. Gardner Sullivan *d* William S. Hart, Clifford Smith *ph* Joseph August, Clyde de Vinna

William S. Hart, Bessie Love, Louise Glaum, Hershall Mayall

As Long as They're Happy*
GB 1955   91m   Eastmancolor
Rank / Group (Raymond Stross)

The suburban home of a London stockbroker is
invaded by an American sob singer.
Frantic farce expanded from a stage satire of the
Johnnie Ray cult; a patchy but sometimes funny
star vehicle.

w Alan Melville, *play* Vernon Sylvaine d J. Lee-
Thompson

Jack Buchanan, Brenda de Banzie, Diana Dors,
Jean Carson, Janette Scott, Susan Stephen, Jerry
Wayne, Hugh McDermott

As You Desire Me*
US 1931   71m   bw
MGM (George Fitzmaurice)

The amnesiac mistress of a novelist rediscovers
her real husband and falls in love with him again.
Interesting star vehicle with good cast and
production.

w Gene Markey, *play* Luigi Pirandello d George
Fitzmaurice ph William Daniels

Greta Garbo, Melvyn Douglas, Erich Von
Stroheim, Owen Moore, Hedda Hopper, Rafaela
Ottiano

As You Like It*
GB 1936   96m   bw
TCF / Inter-Allied (Joseph M. Schenck, Paul
Czinner)

The fortunes of an exiled king take a turn in the
Forest of Arden.
Stylized, rather effete but often amusing version
of Shakespeare's pastoral comedy.

w J. M. Barrie, Robert Cullen, *play* William
Shakespeare d Paul Czinner m William Walton

Elisabeth Bergner, Laurence Olivier, Sophie
Stewart, Leon Quartermaine, Henry Ainley,
Richard Ainley, Felix Aylmer, Mackenzie
Ward, Aubrey Mather, John Laurie, Peter Bull
   'Rather too respectably lighthearted, but by
no means a contemptible production.'—*New
Yorker, 1978*

As Young as You Feel*
US 1951   77m   bw
TCF (Lamar Trotti)

An elderly employee, forced to retire,
impersonates the company president, saves the
firm from bankruptcy, and proves his continued
worth.
Good-natured comedy, ably presented.

w Lamar Trotti, *story* Paddy Chayevsky
d Harmon Jones ph Joe MacDonald m Cyril
Mockridge

Monty Woolley, Constance Bennett, Thelma
Ritter, David Wayne, Jean Peters, Marilyn
Monroe, Allyn Joslyn, Albert Dekker

Ash Wednesday*
US 1973   99m   Technicolor
Sagittarius (Dominick Dunne)

An ageing American beauty rejuvenates herself
via plastic surgery, leads a vivid sex life, and
leaves her stolid husband.
The bloodthirsty operation scenes are revolting,
yet this joyless saga seems meant as a
celebration of the wonders of cosmetic surgery
and Sex for the Aged. Hypnotic but hardly
rewarding.

w Jean Claude Tramont d Larry Peerce
ph Ennio Guarnieri m Maurice Jarre

Elizabeth Taylor, Henry Fonda, Helmut Berger,
Keith Baxter, Maurice Teynac
   'Endless shots of Elizabeth Taylor expensively
attired against the plush background of
Cortina.'—*Michael Billington, Illustrated
London News*

Ashes and Diamonds**
Poland 1958   104m   bw
Film Polski
original title: *Popiol y Diament*

A Polish partisan is confused by the apparent
need to continue killing after the war is over.
A chilling account of the intellectual
contradictions to which war leads, and a moving
and sensitive film in its own right.

wd *Andrzej Wajda, novel* Jerzy Andrzejewski
ph Jerzy Wojcik

Zbigniew Cybulski, Ewa Krzyzanowska, Adam
Pawlikowski

Ask a Policeman**
GB 1938   82m   bw
Gainsborough (Edward Black)

In a small coastal village, incompetent policemen
accidentally expose smugglers who are scaring
the locals with a headless horseman legend.
One of the best comedies of an incomparable
team, with smart dialogue, good situations and a
measure of suspense.

w *Marriott Edgar, Val Guest, J. O. C. Orton*
d Marcel Varnel ph Derek Williams

Will Hay, Moore Marriott, Graham Moffatt,
Glennis Lorimer, *Peter Gawthorne, Herbert
Lomas,* Charles Oliver

Ask Any Girl*
US 1959   98m   Metrocolor
   Cinemascope
MGM / Euterpe (Joe Pasternak)

A husband-hunting receptionist in New York catches the eye of a wealthy playboy but finally settles for his elder brother.
Predictable Cinderella story with a lively but forgettable script and actors going through familiar paces.

w George Wells, *novel* Winifred Wolfe d Charles Walters *ph* Robert Bronner *m* Jeff Alexander

David Niven, Shirley Maclaine, Gig Young, Rod Taylor, Jim Backus, Claire Kelly
  'Like a comic strip transposed to the glossy pages of *Vogue*'.—*MFB*

Asphalt*
Germany 1929   101m   bw
UFA

A young policeman accidentally kills his rival for a worthless girl.
Heavily expressionist melodrama, overlong but good to watch.

w Rolf Vanloo, Fred Majo, Hans Szekely *d Joe May ph* Günther Rittau

Gustav Fröhlich, Betty Amann, Else Heller, Louise Brooks

The Asphalt Jungle***
US 1950   112m   bw
MGM (Arthur Hornblow Jnr)

An elderly crook comes out of prison and assembles a gang for one last robbery.
Probably the very first film to show a 'caper' from the criminals' viewpoint (a genre which has since been done to death several times over), this is a clever character study rather than a thriller, extremely well executed and indeed generally irreproachable yet somehow not a film likely to appear on many top ten lists; perhaps the writer-director stands too far back from everybody, or perhaps he just needed Humphrey Bogart.

w Ben Maddow, John Huston, *novel* W. R. Burnett *d John Huston ph* Harold Rosson *m* Miklos Rozsa

Sterling Hayden, *Sam Jaffe, Louis Calhern*, Jean Hagen, Marilyn Monroe, James Whitmore, John McIntire, Marc Lawrence, Barry Kelley
  'Where this film excels is in the fluency of its narration, the sharpness of its observation of character and the excitement of its human groupings.'—*Dilys Powell*
  'I wouldn't walk across the room to see a thing like that.'—*Louis B. Mayer*
† Apart from imitations, the film has been directly remade as *The Badlanders, Cairo* and *A Cool Breeze*.

AAN: Ben Maddow, John Huston (writers); John Huston (as director); Harold Rosson; Sam Jaffe

The Assassin**
Italy/France 1961   105m   bw
Titanus-Vides-SGC (Franco Cristaldi)

A prosperous antique dealer is accused of murder and his unsavoury past is revealed; but when he is freed, he prides himself on his new personality.
A careful, detailed and wholly enjoyable character study, somewhere between comedy and drama.

w Elio Petri and others *d Elio Petri ph* Carlo di Palma *m* Piero Piccioni

Marcello Mastroianni, Salvo Randone, Micheline Presle, Andrea Checci

Assassin
GB 1973   83m   Technicolor
Pemini (David M. Jackson)

MI5 arranges the liquidation of an Air Ministry spy.
Old hat espionage melodrama, topheavy with artiness which makes it look like an endless TV commercial.

w Michael Sloan *d* Peter Crane *ph* Brian Jonson *m* Zack Lawrence

Ian Hendry, Edward Judd, Frank Windsor, Ray Brooks, John Hart Dyke

The Assassination Bureau*
GB 1968   110m   Technicolor
Paramount / Heathfield (Michael Relph)

In 1906 a lady journalist breaks up an international gang of professional killers by falling in love with their leader.
Black comedy period pastiche which resolves itself into a series of sketches leading up to a spectacular zeppelin climax. Plenty going on, but the level of wit is not high.

w Michael Relph, with Wolf Mankowitz *d* Basil Dearden *ph Geoffrey Unsworth m* Ron Grainer

Oliver Reed, Diana Rigg, Telly Savalas, Curt Jurgens, Philippe Noiret, Warren Mitchell, Clive Revill, Beryl Reid, Kenneth Griffith

The Assassination of the Duc de Guise*
France 1908   15m (16 fps)   bw   silent
Film d'Art

Henry III arranges the killing of the Duc de Guise when he comes to court.
Influential early story film.

w Henri Lavedan *d* Charles le Bargy *m* Saint-Saëns

Charles le Bargy, Albert Lambert, Gabrielle Lavinne

The Assassination of Trotsky*
Italy / GB / France 1972   103m
  Technicolor
Dino de Laurentiis / Josef Shaftel / Cinetel
  (Norman Priggen, Joseph Losey)

In 1940, Trotsky is hiding out in Mexico; a
Stalinist infiltrates his presence and kills him with
an ice pick.
Glum historical reconstruction with much
fictitious padding; basically undramatic.

w Nicholas Mosley, Masolino d'Amico
d Joseph Losey ph Pasquale de Santis m Egisto
Macchi

Richard Burton, Alain Delon, Romy Schneider,
Valentina Cortese, Jean Desailly
   'Not for anyone who knows, or cares,
anything about Leon Trotsky.'—*New Yorker,
1977*

Les Assassins du Dimanche
France 1956   94m   bw   Cinepanoramic
EDIC
aka: *Every Second Counts*

Dozens of people help to track down a holiday
car which has been driven away from a garage in
a dangerous condition.
Watchable but artificial suspenser.

w Alex Joffe, Gabriel Arout d Alex Joffe
ph Jean Bourgoin

Barbara Laage, Jean-Marc Thibault, Dominique
Wilms, Paul Frankeur

Assault
GB 1970   91m   Eastmancolor
Rank / Peter Rogers (George H. Brown)

An art mistress helps police to solve a case of
multiple rape in an English village.
Old-fashioned police mystery with new-fangled
shock treatment. Routine excitements.

w John Kruse, *novel* Kendal Young d Sidney
Hayers ph Ken Hodges m Eric Rogers

Frank Finlay, Suzy Kendall, James Laurenson,
Lesley-Anne Down, Freddie Jones, Tony
Beckley, Anthony Ainley, Dilys Hamlett
   'All right for that wet afternoon.—*Michael
Billington, Illustrated London News*

Assault on a Queen
US 1966   106m   Technicolor   Panavision
Paramount / Seven Arts / Sinatra Enterprises
  (William Goetz)

Crooks dredge up a submarine and use it to hi-
jack the *Queen Mary*.
Strained caper film which remains uncertain
whether to play for drama or thrills, and achieves
neither. Special effects unconvincing.

w Rod Serling, *novel* Jack Finney d Jack
Donohue ph William Daniels m Duke Ellington

Frank Sinatra, Virna Lisi, Tony Franciosa, Alf
Kjellin, Errol John, Richard Conte, Murray
Matheson, Reginald Denny
   'Just about as enthralling as plastic boats in
the bath.'—
MFB

Assault on Precinct 13*
US 1976   91m   Metrocolor   Panavision
CKK (Joseph Kaufman)

Gang members on a vendetta attack a police
station.
Violent but basically efficient and old-fashioned
programmer which shows that not all the
expertise of the forties in this then-familiar field
has been lost.

wd/m John Carpenter ph Douglas Knapp

Austin Stoker, Darwin Joston, Laurie Zimmer,
Martin West

Assignment in Brittany
US 1943   96m   bw
MGM (J. Walter Ruben)

A Free French soldier stays in occupied France
to fight the Nazis.
Routine propagandist actioner, totally
unbelievable.

w Anthony Veiller, William Wright, Howard
Emmett Rogers, *novel* Helen MacInnes d Jack
Conway

Jean Pierre Aumont, Signe Hasso, Susan Peters,
Reginald Owen, Richard Whorf, Margaret
Wycherly, John Emery, Miles Mander, George
Coulouris

Assignment K
GB 1968   97m   Techniscope
Columbia / Mazurka (Ben Arbeid, Maurice
Foster)

The European head of a toy firm is also head of a
special spy unit.
Dreary espionage thriller, instantly forgettable,
and only watchable at odd moments while it's
on.

w Val Guest, Bill Strutton, Maurice Foster, *novel*
Hartley Howard d Val Guest ph Ken Hodges
m Basil Kirchen

Stephen Boyd, Michael Redgrave, Camilla
Sparv, Leo McKern, Jeremy Kemp

Assignment Paris
US 1952   85m   bw
Columbia (Sam Marx, Jerry Bresler)

A reporter on the Paris staff of the *New York*

Herald-Tribune goes to Yugoslavia, is arrested as a spy, and has to be exchanged.

Dim cold war melodrama with occasional entertaining moments.

w William Bowers, *novel* Trial by Terror by Paul Gallico *d* Robert Parrish *ph* Burnett Guffey, Ray Cory *m* George Duning

George Sanders, Dana Andrews, Sandra Giglio, Marta Toren, Audrey Totter, Herbert Berghof

Assignment to Kill

US 1967 99m Technicolor Panavision
Warner Seven Arts (William Conrad)

A New York insurance company hires a private eye to investigate a dubious European financier. Routine international intrigue with muddled plot and unusual cast. A nice production wasted.

wd Sheldon Reynolds *ph* Harold Lipstein
m William Lava

Patrick O'Neal, John Gielgud, Peter Van Eyck, Joan Hackett, Herbert Lom, Eric Portman, Oscar Homolka, Leon Greene

The Astonished Heart*

GB 1949 89m bw
Gainsborough / Sydney Box (Antony Darnborough)

A psychiatrist is permitted by his wife to fall in love with another woman but finds the situation intolerable and kills himself.

The star, looking like a Chinese mandarin, reached his nadir in this unwise screen adaptation, inelegantly directed, of one of his slightest short plays about boring and effete people. It sank without trace.

w Noel Coward, from his play *d* Terence Fisher, Antony Darnborough *ph* Jack Asher *m* Noel Coward

Noel Coward, Margaret Leighton, Celia Johnson, Graham Payn, Joyce Carey, Ralph Michael, Michael Hordern

Asylum*

GB 1972 88m Eastmancolor
Amicus (Max J. Rosenberg, Milton Subotsky)

A doctor applies for a job at an asylum, hears weird stories from four patients, and finds himself in the middle of a weirder one.

Lively horror compilation with echoes of *Caligari* and *Dead of Night*. Gruesomeness sometimes overdone.

w Robert Bloch *d* Roy Ward Baker *ph* Denys Coop *m* Douglas Gamley

Patrick Magee, Robert Powell, Geoffrey Bayldon, Barbara Parkins, Sylvia Syms, Richard Todd, Peter Cushing, Barry Morse,

Britt Ekland, Charlotte Rampling, James Villiers, Megs Jenkins, Herbert Lom

At Long Last Love

US 1975 114m Technicolor
TCF / Copa de Oro

The 1935 romance of a New York millionaire and a musical star.

An attempt to recapture the simple pleasures of an Astaire-Rogers musical; unfortunately true professionalism is lacking and the wrong kind of talent is used. The result is awful to contemplate.

wd Peter Bogdanovich *ph* Laszlo Kovacs
m Cole Porter *pd* Gene Allen

Burt Reynolds, Cybill Shepherd, Eileen Brennan, Madeleine Kahn, Duilio del Prete, John Hillerman, Mildred Natwick

'He works hard at reducing all his sets and costumes to variations of black against silver or white on white, and uncovers in his most oft-repeated visual motif—the elegant mirrors before which his cast seem at all times to be posed—the perfect metaphor for this endlessly narcissistic, thoroughly calcified enterprise.'— *Richard Combs*

'It just lies there, and it dies there.'—*Variety*

'Studios bury more films than the public or the critics. Fox gave up on *At Long Last Love* instantly. A six million dollar film was written off while it was doing well because their lawyers told them they could make more money that way.'— *Peter Bogdanovich*

At Sword's Point*

US 1951 81m Technicolor
RKO (Jerrold T. Brandt)
GB title: *Sons of the Musketeers*

The sons of the three musketeers rally round their ageing queen to prevent her daughter's marriage to a villain.

Adequate swashbuckler with plenty of pace and a sound cast.

w Walter Ferris, Joseph Hoffman *d* Lewis Allen *ph* Ray Rennahan *m* Roy Webb

Cornel Wilde, Maureen O'Hara, Gladys Cooper, Robert Douglas, Dan O'Herlihy, Alan Hale Jnr, Blanche Yurka, Nancy Gates

At the Circus**

US 1939 87m bw
MGM (Mervyn Le Roy)

A shyster lawyer and two incompetents save a circus from bankruptcy.

This film began the decline of the Marx Brothers; in it nothing is ill done but nothing is very fresh either apart from the rousing finale which shows just what professionalism meant in the old

Hollywood. Highlights include Groucho singing about Lydia the tattooed lady, his seduction of Mrs Dukesbury, and the big society party.

w Irving Brecher d Edward Buzzell ph Leonard M. Smith songs Harold Arlen m Franz Waxman

Groucho, Chico, Harpo, Margaret Dumont, Florence Rice, Kenny Baker, Eve Arden, Nat Pendleton, Fritz Feld

At the Earth's Core
GB 1976 90m Technicolor
Amicus (John Dark)

Scientists testing a geological excavator are carried by it to the centre of the earth, and find a prehistoric land inhabited by feuding tribes.
Mainly feeble science fiction for kids, with occasional amusing moments.

w Milton Subotsky, novel Edgar Rice Burroughs d Kevin Connor ph Alan Hume m Mike Vickers sp Ian Wingrove pd Maurice Carter

Doug McClure, Peter Cushing, Caroline Munro, Cy Grant, Godfrey James, Keith Barron
  'Papier mâché people-eaters, idiotic situations, and a frequent sense of confusion as to what is going on.'—David Stewart, Christian Science Monitor

At War with the Army
US 1951 93m bw
Paramount / Fred K. Finklehoffe

A couple of song and dance men have trouble as army recruits.
American service farce, based on a play and confined largely to one set; rather untypical of Martin and Lewis, yet oddly enough the film which sealed their success.

w Fred K. Finklehoffe, play James Allardice d Hal Walker ph Stuart Thompson m Joseph Lilley

Dean Martin, Jerry Lewis, Mike Kellin, Polly Bergen, Jimmie Dundee

L'Atalante*
France 1934 89m bw
J. L. Nounez-Gaumont

A barge captain takes his new wife down river.
One of those classics which no longer provides the authentic thrill; its lack of incident and plot leads quickly to boredom.

w Jean Guinée, Jean Vigo, Albert Riera d Jean Vigo ph Boris Kaufman, Louis Berger m Maurice Jaubert

Jean Dasté, Dita Parlo, Michel Simon, Giles Margarites

Athena
US 1954 96m Eastmancolor
MGM (Joe Pasternak)

A young lawyer falls in love with the eldest of seven sisters brought up to high standards of moral conduct and physical fitness.
Promising but unfulfilling light musical which smothers a good idea in routine treatment.

w William Ludwig, Leonard Spiegelgass d Richard Thorpe ph Robert Planck songs Hugh Martin, Ralph Blane

Edmund Purdom, Jane Powell, Debbie Reynolds, Louis Calhern, Evelyn Varden, Vic Damone, Linda Christian, Ray Collins

Atlantic City*
US 1944 87m bw
Republic

Before World War I, a young showman aims to make Atlantic City the entertainment centre of the world.
Simple-minded romantic musical, quite pacy and effectively staged for a Republic product.

w Doris Gilbert, Frank Gill Jnr, George Carlton Brown d Ray McCarey ph John Alton m/ly various

Constance Moore, Brad Taylor, Jerry Colonna, Charley Grapewin

Atlantic Ferry*
GB 1941 108m bw
Warner (Max Milder)
US title: Sons of the Sea

In 1837 Liverpool, two brothers build the first steamship to cross the Atlantic.
Ponderous historical romance with points of interest.

w Gordon Wellesley, Edward Dryhurst, Emeric Pressburger d Walter Forde ph Basil Emmott m Jack Beaver

Michael Redgrave, Valerie Hobson, Griffith Jones, Margaretta Scott, Hartley Power, Bessie Love, Milton Rosmer
  'Probably the finest collection of model shots in captivity.'—C. A. Lejeune

L'Atlantide*
France 1921 125m approx (16 fps) bw silent
Thalman

Two explorers find the lost continent of Atlantis and fall in love with its queen.
Highly commercial adventure fantasy of its day; it cost two million francs and ran in Paris for a year. Some scenes still sustain, and the desert scenes are impressive.

wd Jacques Feyder, *novel* Pierre Benoît
ph Georges Specht, Victor Morin

Jean Angelo, Stacia Napierkowska, Georges Melchior

† Other versions include *Queen of Atlantis* (Germany 1932, *d* G. W. Pabst, with Brigitte Helm); *Siren of Atlantis* (US 1948, *d* Gregg Tallas, with Maria Montez); *L'Atlantide* (France/Italy 1961, *d* Edgar G. Ulmer).

Atlantis, the Lost Continent
US 1961   91m   Metrocolor
MGM / Galaxy / George Pal

A Greek fisherman is imprisoned when he returns a maiden he has rescued to her island home of Atlantis, but escapes just before volcanic eruption overtakes the decadent nation.
Penny-pinching fantasy spectacle with very little entertainment value.

w Daniel Mainwaring, *play* Sir Gerald Hargreaves *d* George Pal *ph* Harold E. Wellman *m* Russell Garcia

Anthony Hall, Joyce Taylor, John Dall, Edward Platt, Frank de Kova, Jay Novello

The Atomic City *
US 1952   85m   bw
Paramount (Joseph Sistrom)

The young son of a leading atomic scientist is kidnapped but his father and the FBI rescue him.
Routine but well-paced thriller with a documentary background of research at Los Alamos.

w Sidney Boehm *d* Jerry Hopper *ph* Charles B. Lang Jnr *m* Leith Stevens

Gene Barry, Lydia Clarke, Lee Aaker, Nancy Gates, Milburn Stone

AAN: Sidney Boehm

The Atomic Kid
US 1954   86m   bw
Republic

After an atomic blast, a prospector accidentally left in the area proves immune to uranium, and after various adventures rounds up some communist spies.
Inane romp which raises a few laughs.

w Benedict Freeman, John Fenton Murray, *story* Blake Edwards *d* Leslie H. Martinson *ph* John L. Russell Jnr *m* Van Alexander

Mickey Rooney, Robert Strauss, Elaine Davis, Bill Goodwin, Whit Bissell

The Atonement of Gosta Berling **
Sweden 1924   200m approx (16 fps)   bw
  silent
Svensk Filmindustri
original title: *Gosta Berlings Saga*

A pastor is defrocked for drinking, becomes a tutor, and has various love affairs.
Lumpy but often engrossing picturization of a famous novel, veering mostly into melodrama but finding its way to a happy ending.

w Mauritz Stiller, Ragnar Hylten-Cavallius, *novel* Selma Lagerlof *d* Mauritz Stiller *ph* Julius Jaenzon

Lars Hanson, Gerda Lundeqvist, Ellen Cederstrom, Mona Martensson, Jenny Hasselqvist, Otto Elg-Lundberg, Greta Garbo.
† It was her small role in this film which led directly to Greta Garbo's American stardom.

Attack **
US 1956   104m   bw
UA / Associates and Aldrich

In 1944 Belgium, an American infantry command is led by a coward.
High-pitched, slick, violent and very effective war melodrama, even though by the end we seem to be in the company of raving lunatics rather than soldiers.

w James Poe, play Fragile Fox by Norman Brooks *d Robert Aldrich ph Joseph Biroc m* Frank de Vol

Jack Palance, Eddie Albert, Lee Marvin, Buddy Ebsen, Robert Strauss, Richard Jaeckel, William Smithers, Peter Van Eyck

'The film does not so much tackle a subject as hammer it down.'—*Penelope Houston*

Attack on the Iron Coast
GB 1967   90m   De Luxe
US / Mirisch (John Champion)

In World War II, a Canadian commando unit destroys a German installation on the French coast.
Stagey low-budgeter with modest action sequences.

w Herman Hoffman *d* Paul Wendkos *ph* Paul Beeson *m* Gerard Schurmann

Lloyd Bridges, Andrew Keir, Mark Eden, Sue Lloyd

Attila the Hun
Italy/France 1944   79m   Technicolor
Lux Ponti de Laurentiis/LCCF (Georgio Andriani)
original title: *Attilo Flagello di Dio*

The barbarian chief attacks the forces of the

Emperor Valentinian and marches on Rome. Predictably violent adventures after de Mille; a bit slow to start.

w Ennio de Concini, Primo Zeglio *d* Pietro Francisci *ph* Aldo Tonti *m* Enzo Masetti

Anthony Quinn, Sophia Loren, Henri Vidal, Irene Papas, Ettore Manni, Claude Laydu

Au dela des Grilles
Italy/France 1949   90m   bw
Italia Produzione/Francinex (Alfredo Guarini)
aka: *Beyond the Gates*; Italian title: *La mura de Malapaga*

A murderer on the run in Genoa falls in love with a waitress and loses his chance of escape. *Quai des Brumes* reworked against an Italian neo-realist setting; dramatic values less interesting now than historical ones.

w Jean Aurenche, Pierre Bost, Cesare Zavattini, Suso Cecchi d'Amico *d* René Clément *ph* Louis Page *m* Roman Vlad

Jean Gabin, *Isa Miranda*, Vera Talchi, Andrea Checci

Au Royaume des Cieux
France 1949   108m   bw
Regina (Julien Duvivier)
aka: *Woman Hunt*

An 18-year-old girl suffers at a reform school. Shoddy melodrama, more sensational than Hollywood ever dared to be.

wd Julien Duvivier *ph* Victor Armenise

Suzanne Cloutier, Serge Reggiani, Monique Mélinand, Suzy Prim, Jean Davy, Juliette Greco
'A depressing exhibit from a director who once had a serious reputation.'—*Gavin Lambert*

Aunt Clara
GB 1954   84m   bw
London Films (Colin Lesslie, Anthony Kimmins)

A pious old person inherits from a reprobate uncle five greyhounds, a pub and a brothel. Extremely mild star vehicle with a gallery of comedy character cameos.

w Kenneth Horne, *novel* Noel Streatfeild *d* Anthony Kimmins *ph* C. Pennington-Richards *m* Benjamin Frankel

Margaret Rutherford, Ronald Shiner, A. E. Matthews, Fay Compton, Nigel Stock, Jill Bennett, Reginald Beckwith, Raymond Huntley

Auntie Mame*
US 1958   144m   Technirama
Warner (Morton da Costa)

An orphan boy is adopted by his volatile extravagant aunt, whose giddy escapades fill his memory of the twenties and thirties.
A rather unsatisfactory star revue from a book and play later turned into a musical, *Mame*. A few splendid moments, otherwise rather dull and irritating.

w Betty Comden, Adolph Green, *novel* Patrick Dennis, *play* Jerome Lawrence, Robert E. Lee *d* Morton da Costa *ph* Harry Stradling *m* Bronislau Kaper *ad* Malcolm Bert

Rosalind Russell, Forrest Tucker, *Coral Browne*, Fred Clark, Roger Smith, Patric Knowles, Peggy Cass, Lee Patrick, Joanna Barnes

AAN: best picture; Harry Stradling; Rosalind Russell; Peggy Cass

Une Aussi Longue Absence*
France/Italy 1961   96m   bw
Procinex/Lyre/Galatea (Jacques Nahum)
aka: *The Long Absence*

A widow who owns a Paris café meets an amnesiac tramp who may be her long-lost husband.
Romantic character study which just about comes off thanks to good acting.

w Marguerite Duras, Gérald Jarlot *d* Henri Colpi *ph* Marcel Weiss *m* Georges Delerue

Alida Valli, Georges Wilson, Jacques Harden

Austerlitz
France/Italy/Lichtenstein/Yugoslavia 1959   166m   Eastmancolor   Dyaliscope
CFPI/SCLF/Galatea/Michael Arthur/Dubrava (Alexander and Michael Salkind)
aka: *The Battle of Austerlitz*

Napoleon defeats the Austro-Russian army. Elaborate pageant with a hopelessly cluttered narrative line arranged to take in a roster of guest stars who merely distract from the central theme.

wd Abel Gance *ph* Henri Alekan, Robert Juillard *m* Jean Ledrut

Pierre Mondy, Jean Mercure, Jack Palance, Orson Welles, Michel Simon, Jean-Louis Trintignant, Martine Carol, Leslie Caron, Claudia Cardinale, Rossano Brazzi, Ettore Manni, Jean Marais, Vittorio de Sica
'Strictly for connoisseurs of Gance's brand of hyperbolic history.'—*Peter John Dyer, MFB*

Autumn Leaves*
US 1956   108m   bw
Columbia / William Goetz

A middle-aged spinster marries a young man who turns out to be a pathological liar and tries to murder her.

Skilfully tailored star vehicle for female audiences.

w Jack Jeyne, Lewis Meltzer, Robert Blees *d* Robert Aldrich *ph* Charles Lang *m* Hans Salter

Joan Crawford, Cliff Robertson, Lorne Greene, Vera Miles, Ruth Donnelly, Shepperd Strudwick

Autumn Sonata*
Sweden / West Germany / GB 19 97m colour
Martin Starger / GMBH / ITC Personafilm (Ingmar Bergman)

When her lover dies, a concert pianist visits the daughter she has not seen for many years.
Typically Bergmanesque, understated conversation piece with no obvious happy ending for anybody.

wd Ingmar Bergman *ph* Sven Nykvist

Ingrid Bergman, Liv Ullmann, Halvar Bjork

Avalanche
US 1978 91m Metrocolor
New World (Roger Corman)

Snow threatens holidaymakers at a ski lodge.
A disaster movie which, while quite competent in most ways, is no better than TV movies of this kind, esp-ecially as it resorts for its climaxes to scratched old stock film.

w Claude Pola, Corey Allen *d* Corey Allen *ph* Pierre-William Glenn *m* William Kraft

Rock Hudson, Mia Farrow, Robert Forster, Jeanette Nolan, Rick Moses, Steve Franken, Barry Primus

Avanti!**
US 1972 144m De Luxe
UA / Mirisch / Phalanx / Jalem (Billy Wilder)

A young American goes to Ischia to collect the body of his father who has died on holiday. He finds that the fatal accident had also killed his father's mistress, and amid overwhelming bureaucratic problems proceeds to fall in love with her daughter.
Absurdly overlong black comedy, with compensations in the shape of a generally witty script and some fine breakneck sequences of culminating confusion.

w Billy Wilder, I. A. L. Diamond, play Samuel Taylor *d Billy Wilder ph* Luigi Kuveiller *m* Carlo Rustichelli

Jack Lemmon, Juliet Mills, Clive Revill, Edward Andrews, Gianfranco Barra

L'Avventura**
Italy/France 1960 145m bw
Cino del Duca/PCE/Lyre (Amato Pennasilico)

Young people on a yachting holiday go ashore on a volcanic island. One of them disappears; this affects the life of the others, but she is never found.
Aimless, overlong parable with lots of vague significance; rather less entertaining than the later *Picnic at Hanging Rock* (qv), it made its director a hero of the highbrows.

w Michelangelo Antonioni, Elio Bartolini, Tonino Guerra *d Michelangelo Antonioni ph* Aldo Scavarda *m* Giovanni Fusco

Monica Vitti, Lea Massari, Gabriele Ferzetti, Dominique Blanchar, James Addams, Lelio Luttazi

'A film of complete maturity, sincerity and creative intuition.'—*Peter John Dyer, MFB*

Away All Boats!
US 1956 114m Technicolor Vistavision
U-I (Howard Christie)

Adventures of a small transport boat during the Pacific War.
Competent drum-beating war heroics with expensive action sequences.

w Ted Sherdeman *d* Joseph Pevney *ph* William Daniels, Clifford Stine *m* Frank Skinner

Jeff Chandler, George Nader, Julie Adams, Lex Barker, Keith Andes, Richard Boone, Frank Faylen

The Awful Truth***
US 1937 90m bw
Columbia (Leo McCarey)

A divorcing couple endure various adventures which lead to reconciliation.
Classic crazy comedy of the thirties, marked by a mixture of sophistication and farce and an irreverent approach to plot.

wd Leo McCarey, play Arthur Richman *ph* Joseph Walker *md* Morris Stoloff

Irene Dunne, Cary Grant, Ralph Bellamy, Alexander D'Arcy, Cecil Cunningham, Molly Lamont, Esther Dale, Joyce Compton

'The funniest picture of the season.'—*Otis Ferguson*

† Remade 1953 as *Let's Do It Again* (qv).

AA: Leo McCarey (as director)
AAN: best picture; Irene Dunne; Ralph Bellamy

B

B.F.'s Daughter*
US 1948   106m   bw
MGM (Edwin A. Knopf)
GB title: *Polly Fulton*

The wife of a penniless lecturer secures her
husband's rise to fame without his knowing that
she is the daughter of a millionaire.
Solid upper class romantic drama with a touch of
Peg's Paper.

w Luther Davis, *novel* John P. Marquand
d Robert Z. Leonard ph Joseph Ruttenberg
m Bronislau Kaper

Barbara Stanwyck, Van Heflin, Charles Coburn,
Richard Hart, Keenan Wynn, Margaret
Lindsay, Spring Byington, Marshall Thompson

Babbitt*
US 1934   74m   bw
Warner (Sam Bischoff)

Problems of a middle-aged man in a small
American town.
A minor attempt to film a major novel: quite
tolerable but lacking density.

w Mary McCall Jnr, *novel* Sinclair Lewis
d William Keighley ph Arthur Todd

Guy Kibbee, Aline MacMahon, Claire Dodd,
Maxine Doyle, Minor Watson, Minna Gombell,
Alan Hale, Berton Churchill, Russell Hicks, Nan
Grey
† Previously filmed in 1924 with Willard Louis.

The Babe Ruth Story
US 1948   107m   bw
Allied Artists

The biography of a baseball player who was
thought of as something of a saint.
Dim, sentimental and faintly mystical biopic,
throughout which the star presents his familiar
image.

w Bob Considine, George Callahan d Roy del
Ruth ph Philip Tunnura, James Van Trees
m Edward Ward

William Bendix, Claire Trevor, Charles Bickford

Babes in Arms**
US 1939   96m   bw
MGM (Arthur Freed)

The teenage sons and daughters of retired
vaudevillians put on a big show.
Simple-minded backstage musical which marked
the first enormously successful teaming of its two
young stars.

w Jack McGowan, Kay Van Riper, from the
Broadway show by Rodgers and Hart
d/ch Busby Berkeley ph Ray June
songs Rodgers and Hart m Roger Edens,
George Stoll

Judy Garland, Mickey Rooney, Charles
Winninger, Douglas Macphail, Leni Lynn, June
Preisser

AAN: Roger Edens, George Stoll; Mickey
Rooney

Babes in Toyland**
US 1934   77m   bw
Hal Roach
aka: *Wooden Soldiers; Laurel and Hardy in
Toyland*

Santa Claus's incompetent assistants
accidentally make some giant wooden soldiers,
which come in useful when a villain tries to take
over Toyland.
Comedy operetta in which the stars have
pleasant but not outstanding material; the style
and decor are however sufficient to preserve the
film as an eccentric minor classic.

w Nick Grinde, Frank Butler, *original
book/ly* Glen MacDonough d Gus Meins,
Charles Rogers ph Art Lloyd, Francis Corby
m Victor Herbert

Stan Laurel, Oliver Hardy, Charlotte Henry,
Henry Brandon, Felix Knight, Florence Roberts,
Johnny Downs, Marie Wilson

Babes in Toyland
US 1961   105m   Technicolor
Walt Disney

A misfiring remake, all charm and no talent
apart from some excellent special effects at the
climax.

w Ward Kimball, Joe Rinaldi, Lowell S. Hawley
d Jack Donohue ph Edward Colman
md George Bruns sp Eustace Lycett, Robert A.

Mattey, Bill Justice, Xavier Atencio, Yale Gracey

Ray Bolger (miscast as the villain), Annette Funicello, Tommy Kirk, Gene Sheldon (imitating Stan Laurel), Henry Calvin (imitating Oliver Hardy), Ed Wynn, Kevin Corcoran

AAN: George Bruns

Babes on Broadway **
US 1941   118m   bw
MGM (Arthur Freed)

A sequel to *Babes in Arms*, in which the kids get to Broadway and share some disillusion.
Inflated and less effective than the original, but with good numbers.

w Fred Finkelhoffe, Elaine Ryan *d/ch* Busby Berkeley *ph* Lester White *songs* Burton Lane and Ralph Freed

Judy Garland, Mickey Rooney, Virginia Weidler, Ray Macdonald, Richard Quine, Fay Bainter

AAN: song 'How About You' (*m* Burton Lane, *ly* Ralph Freed)

Babette Goes to War
France 1959   103m   Eastmancolor
  Cinemascope
Iéna (Raoul Lévy)
original title: *Babette S'en Va-t-en Guerre*

In 1940 a French refugee girl is sent by British intelligence from London to Paris as bait in a plot to kidnap a German general and delay the Nazi invasion of England.
Witless war farce which goes on for ever.

w Raoul Lévy, Gérard Oury *d* Christian-Jaque *ph* Armand Thirard *m* Gilbert Bécaud

Brigitte Bardot, Jacques Charrier, Hannes Messemer, Yves Vincent, Ronald Howard, *Francis Blanche*

  'A kind of *Private's Progress* without comedians.'—*MFB*

The Baby and the Battleship
GB 1956   96m   Eastmancolor
Jay Lewis / British Lion (Antony Darnborough)

Two sailors hide an Italian baby on their battleship.
Simple-minded lower decks farce, with lots of confusion and cooing over the baby, but not much to laugh at.

w Jay Lewis, Gilbert Hackforth-Jones, Bryan Forbes *d* Jay Lewis *ph* Harry Waxman

John Mills, Richard Attenborough, André Morell, Bryan Forbes, Michael Howard, Lisa Gastoni, Ernest Clark, Lionel Jeffries, Thorley Walters

Baby Blue Marine *
US 1976   90m   Metrocolor
Columbia / Spelling—Goldberg (Robert LaVigne)

In 1943, a failed marine returns home and pretends to be a war hero.
Careful small-town drama with good period feel but not much dramatic punch: *Hail the Conquering Hero* did it better.

w Stanford Whitmore *d* John Hancock *ph* Laszlo Kovacs *m* Fred Karlin

Jan-Michael Vincent, Glynnis O'Connor, Katherine Helmond, Dana Elcar, Bert Remsen, Richard Gere

Baby Doll **
US 1956   116m   bw
Warner / Elia Kazan

In the deep South, the child wife of a broken-down cotton miller is seduced by her husband's revenge-seeking rival.
An incisive, cleverly-worked-out study of moral and physical decay; whether it was worth doing is another question, for it's a film difficult to remember with affection.

wd Elia Kazan, *play* Tennessee Williams *ph* Boris Kaufman *m* Kenyon Hopkins *ad* Richard Sylbert

Karl Malden, Eli Wallach, Carroll Baker, Mildred Dunnock, Lonny Chapman

  'Just possibly the dirtiest American-made motion picture that has ever been legally exhibited, with Priapean detail that might well have embarrassed Boccaccio.'—*Time*

  'He views southern pretensions with sardonic humor, and builds an essentially minor story into a magnificently humorous study of the grotesque and the decadent.'—*Hollis Alpert*

  'A droll and engrossing carnal comedy.'—*Pauline Kael, 1968*

AAN: Elia Kazan; Boris Kaufman; Carroll Baker; Mildred Dunnock

Baby Face **
US 1933   70m   bw
Warner (Ray Griffith)

Amorous adventures of an ambitious working girl.
Sharp melodrama very typical of its time, with fast pace and good performances.

w Gene Markey, Kathryn Scola, Mark Canfield (Darryl F. Zanuck) *d* Alfred E. Green *ph* James Van Trees

Barbara Stanwyck, George Brent, Donald Cook, Margaret Lindsay, Arthur Hohl, John Wayne, Henry Kolker, Douglass Dumbrille

Baby Face Nelson*
US 1957   85m   bw
UA / Fryman–ZS (Al Zimbalist)
Fragmentary account of the life of a thirties
public enemy, with the star over the top and the
technicians doing what they can on an obviously
low budget.

w Irving Shulman, Daniel Mainwaring d Don
Siegel ph Hal Mohr m Van Alexander

Mickey Rooney, Cedric Hardwicke, Carolyn
Jones, Chris Dark, Ted de Corsia, Leo Gordon,
John Hoyt, Anthony Caruso, Jack Elam

Baby Love
GB 1968   93m   Eastmancolor
(Avco) Avton / Michael Klinger (Guido Coen)
An orphaned nymphet causes trouble among the
men in her foster home.
Ludicrous sexploiter which embarrasses a good
cast and descends into bathos.

w Alastair Reid, Guido Coen, Michael Klinger,
novel Tina Chad Christian d Alastair Reid
ph Desmond Dickinson m Max Harris

Linda Hayden, Ann Lynn, Keith Barron, Derek
Lamden, Diana Dors, Patience Collier, Dick
Emery

Baby, the Rain Must Fall
US 1964   100m   bw
Columbia / Pakula–Mulligan (Alan Pakula)
A parolee rejoins his wife and daughter in a
Southern town, but his outbursts of violence
separate them again.
Hard work by all concerned scarcely produces
absorbing interest in this filmed play of the
Tennessee Williams school.

w Horton Foote, from his play The Travelling
Lady d Robert Mulligan ph Ernest Laszlo
m Elmer Bernstein

Steve McQueen, Lee Remick, Don Murray, Paul
Fix, Josephine Hutchinson, Ruth White, Charles
Watts

The Bachelor and the Bobbysoxer*
US 1947   95m   bw
RKO (Dore Schary)
GB title: Bachelor Knight
A lady judge allows her impressionable young
sister to get over her crush on an errant playboy
by forcing them together.
Simple but unexpectedly delightful vehicle for
top comedy talents, entirely pleasant and with
several memorable moments.

w Sidney Sheldon d Irving Reis ph Robert de
Grasse, Nicholas Musuraca m Leigh Harline
Cary Grant, Myrna Loy, Shirley Temple, Ray

Collins, Rudy Vallee, Harry Davenport, Johnny
Sands, Don Beddoe
AA: Sidney Sheldon

Bachelor Apartment
US 1931   77m   bw
RKO (William Le Baron)
A virtuous working girl in New York falls for a
rich woman-chasing bachelor.
Mildly agreeable early talking romantic comedy.

w J. Walter Ruben, John Howard Lawson
d Lowell Sherman ph Leo Tover

Irene Dunne, Lowell Sherman, Mae Murray,
Norman Kerry, Claudia Dell, Ivan Lebedeff

Bachelor Father
US 1931   90m   bw
MGM
A much-married elderly man visits his grown
children.
Unremarkable star comedy of its day.

w Laurence E. Johnson, play Edward Childs
Carpenter d Robert Z. Leonard ph Oliver T.
Marsh

Marion Davies, C. Aubrey Smith, Ray Milland,
Ralph Forbes, Halliwell Hobbes, Guinn
Williams, David Torrence

Bachelor in Paradise
US 1961   109m   Metrocolor
    Cinemascope
MGM / Ted Richmond
A famous writer of advice to the lovelorn settles
incognito in a well-heeled Californian
community to observe its social habits.
Mildly amusing satire is too frequently
interrupted by unsuitable romantic interludes in
this rather ill-considered star comedy.

w Valentine Davies, Hal Kanter d Jack Arnold
ph Joseph Ruttenberg m Henry Mancini

Bob Hope, Lana Turner, Janis Paige, Don
Porter, Paula Prentiss, Jim Hutton, Virginia
Grey, Reta Shaw, John McGiver, Agnes
Moorehead

AAN: title song (m Henry Mancini, ly Mack
David)

Bachelor Mother*
US 1939   82m   bw
RKO (B. G. De Sylva)
A shopgirl finds an abandoned baby and is
thought to be its mother; the department store
owner's son is then thought to be the father.
Blithely-scripted comedy which stands the test of
time and provided several excellent roles.

w Norman Krasna d Garson Kanin ph Robert de Grasse

Ginger Rogers, David Niven, Charles Coburn, Frank Albertson, E. E. Clive, Ernest Truex

'An excellent comedy, beautifully done.'— *Richard Mallett, Punch*

† Remade as *Bundle of Joy* (qv).

AAN: Felix Jackson (for original story)

Bachelor of Hearts

GB 1958   94m   Technicolor

Rank / Independent Artists (Vivian A. Cox)

Adventures of a German student at Cambridge University.

Sometimes agreeable, sometimes annoying, especially when romance gets in the way of the possibilities for fun.

w Leslie Bricusse, Frederic Raphael *d* Wolf Rilla *ph* Geoffrey Unsworth

Hardy Kruger, Sylvia Syms, Ronald Lewis, Eric Barker, Newton Blick

The Bachelor Party***

US 1957   93m   bw

UA / Norma (Harold Hecht)

New York book-keepers throw a wedding eve party for one of their fellows, but drink only brings to the fore their own private despairs. Though the last half-hour lets it down, most of this is a brilliantly observed social study of New York life at its less attractive, and the acting matches the incisiveness of the script.

w Paddy Chayevsky, from his TV play *d* Delbert Mann *ph* Joseph La Shelle *m* Alex North

Don Murray, E. G. Marshall, Jack Warden, Philip Abbott, Larry Blyden, Patricia Smith, Carolyn Jones

AAN: Carolyn Jones

The Bachelor's Daughters*

US 1946   90m   bw

UA / Andrew Stone

GB title: *Bachelor Girls*

Four shopgirls and a floorwalker rent a Long Island house and pass themselves off as a wealthy family in order to lure suitable husbands for the girls.

Mildly amusing comedy with good performances.

wd Andrew Stone *ph* Theodor Sparkuhl

Adolphe Menjou, Gail Russell, Claire Trevor, Billie Burke

Back from Eternity

US 1956   97m   bw

RKO (John Farrow)

An airliner is forced to crashland in headhunter country, and when repairs are made only five of the eight survivors can be carried.

Remake by the same producer-director of his own 1939 'B', *Five Came Back,* this time to considerably less effect despite superior production.

w Jonathan Latimer *d* John Farrow *ph* William Mellor *m* Franz Waxman

Robert Ryan, Anita Ekberg, Rod Steiger, Phyllis Kirk, Gene Barry, Keith Andes, Beulah Bondi, Fred Clark, Cameron Prud'homme, Jesse White

Back Street*

US 1932   93m   bw

Universal (Carl Laemmle Jnr)

A married man has a sweet-tempered mistress who effaces herself for twenty years.

Popular version of a sudsy bestselling novel.

w Gladys Lehman, Lynn Starling, *novel* Fannie Hurst *d* John M. Stahl *ph* Karl Freund

Irene Dunne, John Boles, June Clyde, George Meeker, Zasu Pitts, Doris Lloyd

Back Street*

US 1941   89m   bw

Universal (Bruce Manning)

Competent remake.

w Bruce Manning, Felix Jackson *d* Robert Stevenson *ph* William Daniels *m* Frank Skinner

Margaret Sullavan, Charles Boyer, Richard Carlson, Frank McHugh, Tim Holt, Frank Jenks, Esther Dale, Samuel S. Hinds

AAN: Frank Skinner

Back Street*

US 1961   107m   Technicolor

U-I / Ross Hunter / Carrollton

Glossy remake typical of its producer: unfortunately it fails to work because the heroine suffers too luxuriously.

w Eleanore Griffin, William Ludwig *d* David Miller *ph* Stanley Cortez *m* Frank Skinner

Susan Hayward, John Gavin, Vera Miles, Virginia Grey, Charles Drake, Reginald Gardiner

'Though there is a lot to be said for this new version's thesis that one can be just as lonely in a series of apartments and lovers' nests apparently never less than a hundred yards wide, the illusion is quickly shattered the moment one gets the impression that the lovers prefer to keep much the same distance during their moments of passion.'—*Peter John Dyer*

Back to Bataan
US 1945   97m   bw
RKO (Robert Fellows)

When Bataan is cut off, a Marine colonel
organizes guerrilla resistance.
Modestly made and rather dislikeable flagwaver.

w Ben Barzman, Richard Landau d Edward
Dmytryk ph Nicholas Musuraca m Roy Webb

John Wayne, Anthony Quinn, Beulah Bondi,
Fely Franquelli, Leonard Strong, Richard Loo,
Philip Ahn, Lawrence Tierney, Paul Fix

Back to God's Country
US 1953   78m   Technicolor
U-I (Howard Christie)

A sea captain battles the Canadian winter and a
villain who wants his wife and his cargo of furs.
Old-fashioned adventure story, moderately well
presented.

w Tom Reed, novel James Oliver Curwood
d Joseph Pevney ph Maury Gertsman m Frank
Skinner

Rock Hudson, Steve Cochran, Marcia
Henderson, Hugh O'Brian

Backfire
US 1949   90m   bw
Warner (Anthony Veiller)

A war veteran solves the murder of which his
best friend is accused.
Confusing murder mystery of a very familiar
kind, adequately made but with no particular
style. Flashbacks don't help.

w Larry Marcus, Ivan Goff, Ben Roberts
d Vincent Sherman ph Carl Guthrie ad Anton
Grot m Ray Heindorf

Gordon Macrae, Virginia Mayo, Edmond
O'Brien, Dane Clark, Viveca Lindfors, Ed
Begley

Background*
GB 1953   82m   bw
Group Three (Herbert Mason)
US title: Edge of Divorce

Two people decide on divorce, but thoughts of
their children bring them together again.
Low budget, stiff-upper-lip marriage guidance
tract, well acted but more well-intentioned than
memorable.

w Warren Chetham Strode, from his play, with
Don Sharp d Daniel Birt ph Arthur Grant

Valerie Hobson, Philip Friend, Norman
Wooland, Janette Scott, Mandy Miller, Jeremy
Spenser, Richard Wattis

Background to Danger**
US 1943   80m   bw
Warner (Jerry Wald)

An adventurer thwarts Nazi intrigue in Turkey.
Good routine war action yarn, well presented
and performed.

w W. R. Burnett, novel Uncommon Danger by
Eric Ambler d Raoul Walsh ph Tony Gaudio

George Raft, Brenda Marshall, Sydney
Greenstreet, Peter Lorre, Osa Massen, Turhan
Bey, Kurt Katch
    'You could use this film for one kind of
measurement of the unconquerable difference
between a good job by Hitchcock and a good job
of the Hitchcock type.'—James Agee

Backlash*
US 1956   84m   Technicolor
U-I (Aaron Rosenberg)

A gunman seeks the father he has never met,
who turns out to be a villain who sold his
partners for gold to attacking Indians.
Rather unusual suspense western, very
watchable for its mystery elements.

w Borden Chase d John Sturges ph Irving
Glassberg m Herman Stein

Richard Widmark, Donna Reed, John McIntire,
William Campbell, Barton Maclane

The Bad and the Beautiful**
US 1952   118m   bw
MGM (John Houseman)

A director, a star, a screenwriter and an
executive recall their experiences at the hands of
a go-getting Hollywood producer.
Very much a Hollywood 'in' picture, this rather
obvious flashback melodrama offers good acting
chances and a couple of intriguing situations;
never quite finding the style it seeks, it offers
good bitchy entertainment along the way, and
there are references back to it in Two Weeks in
Another Town, made ten years later.

w Charles Schnee d Vincente Minnelli
ph Robert Surtees m David Raksin

Kirk Douglas, Walter Pidgeon, Lana Turner,
Dick Powell, Barry Sullivan, Gloria Grahame,
Gilbert Roland, Leo G. Carroll, Vanessa Brown,
Paul Stewart
    'For all the cleverness of the apparatus, it lacks
a central point of focus.'—Penelope Houston

AA: Robert Surtees; Gloria Grahame
AAN: Charles Schnee; Kirk Douglas

Bad Bascomb*
US 1946   110m   bw
MGM (Orville Dull)

A sentimental bank robber becomes the hero of a group of travelling Mormons.

Pleasing though overlong star western, with good production values.

w William Lipman, Grant Garrett d S. Sylvan Simon ph Charles Schoenbaum m David Snell

Wallace Beery, Margaret O'Brien, Marjorie Main, J. Carrol Naish, Russell Simpson, Sara Haden

Bad Company**

US 1972 92m Technicolor
Paramount (Stanley R. Jaffe)

During the Civil War, two youths on the run team up and become outlaws.

A successful attempt to recreate the feeling of past time, by the writers of another criminal myth, *Bonnie and Clyde*.

w *David Newman, Robert Benton* d Robert Benton ph Gordon Willis m Harvey Schmidt

Jeff Bridges, Barry Brown, Jim Davis, David Huddleston, John Savage

Bad Day at Black Rock****

US 1954 81m Eastmancolor
Cinemascope
MGM (Dore Schary)

A one-armed stranger gets off the train at a sleepy desert hamlet and is greeted with hostility by the townsfolk, who have something to hide.

Seminal suspense thriller—the guilty town motif became a cliché—with a terse script and professional presentation. The moments of violence, long awaited, are electrifying.

w *Millard Kaufman, story* Bad Time at Hondo by Howard Briskin d *John Sturges* ph William C. Mellor m André Previn

Spencer Tracy, Robert Ryan, Dean Jagger, Walter Brennan, Ernest Borgnine, Lee Marvin, Anne Francis, John Ericson, Russell Collins

'A very superior example of motion picture craftsman- ship.'—*Pauline Kael*

AAN: Millard Kaufman; John Sturges; Spencer Tracy

Bad for Each Other

US 1954 83m bw
Columbia (William Fadiman)

A doctor back from the army scorns his home town for high society, but a mine disaster reverses his decision.

Misleadingly titled cliché drama, patterned after *The Citadel*. Actors ill at ease, handling competent but routine.

w Irving Wallace, Horace McCoy, from the latter's novel d Irving Rapper ph Franz Planer md Mischa Bakaleinikoff

Charlton Heston, Lizabeth Scott, Dianne Foster, Mildred Dunnock, Arthur Franz, Ray Collins, Marjorie Rambeau

The Bad Lord Byron*

GB 1948 85m bw
Rank / Sydney Box (Aubrey Baring)

Byron lies dying, and imagines his life and loves under review in a heavenly court.

Thought risible at the time, this historical romance in flashback now seems no worse and even a little more stylish than most, though the script suffers from too many cooks.

w Terence Young, Anthony Thorne, Peter Quennell, Laurence Kitchin, Paul Holt d David MacDonald ph Stephen Dade m Cedric Thorpe Davie

Dennis Price, Mai Zetterling, Linden Travers, *Joan Greenwood*, Sonia Holm, Raymond Lovell, Leslie Dwyer

† The end of the British costume cycle which began with *The Man in Grey*.

The Bad Man

US 1940 70m bw
MGM (J. Walter Ruben)
GB title: *Two Gun Cupid*

A Mexican outlaw helps a former friend and unites two lovers.

Forgettable western comedy drama with a sterling cast.

w Wells Root, *play* Porter Emerson Brown d Richard Thorpe

Wallace Beery, Lionel Barrymore, Laraine Day, Ronald Reagan, Henry Travers

† Previously produced by First National in 1923, and in 1930 with Walter Huston and O. P. Heggie.

Bad Man's River

Spain / Italy / France 1972 90m
Eastmancolor Franscope
Zurbano / Apollo / Roitfeld (Bernard Gordon)

Four outlaws accept the job of blowing up a government arsenal in Mexico.

Lurid western with comedy leanings and a somewhat eccentric cast.

w Philip Yordan, Eugenio Martin d Eugenio Martin ph Alexander Ulloa m Waldo de Los Rios

Lee Van Cleef, James Mason, Gina Lollobrigida, Simon Andreu, Diana Lorys

'When shooting a western in Spain one should

not say to oneself, "Never mind, no one is going to see it," because that will be just the film which the Rank Organization will choose to release in England.'—*James Mason*

The Bad News Bears
US 1976   103m   Movielab
Paramount (Stanley Jaffe)

An ex-baseball professional coaches a team of tough kids.
Rough-tongued, sentimental star comedy.

w Bill Lancaster *d* Michael Ritchie *ph* John A. Alonzo *m* Jerry Fielding (after Bizet)

Walter Matthau, Tautm O'Neal, Vic Morrow, Joyce Van Patten

†Two inferior sequels were made. *The Bad News Bears in Breaking Training* (1977; 100m; *d* Michael Pressman: with William Devane); *The Bad News Bears Go to Japan* (1978; 91m; *d* John Berry; with Tony Curtis).

The Bad Seed*
US 1956   129m   bw
Warner (Mervyn Le Roy)

A sweet-looking 8-year-old girl is a liar and a murderess; her mother finds out and attempts to kill her and commit suicide.
A real curiosity from an unexpected stage hit: absurd melodrama treated with astonishing high literary style and some censor-induced levity: at the end, after the little villainess has been struck by lightning, a curtain call shows her being soundly spanked.

w John Lee Mahin, *play* Maxwell Anderson, *novel* William March *d* Mervyn Le Roy *ph* Harold Rosson *m* Alex North

Nancy Kelly (rather uneasily recreating her stage role as the mother), *Patty McCormack*, Henry Jones, Eileen Heckart, Evelyn Varden, William Hopper, Paul Fix, Jesse White

AAN: Harold Rosson; Nancy Kelly; Patty McCormack; Eileen Heckart

Bad Sister
US 1931   71m   bw
Universal (Carl Laemmle Jnr)

A small-town coquette falls for a city slicker, and her quiet sister gets her steady boy friend.
A teenage potboiler of its day, remarkable only for its cast.

w Raymond L. Schrock, Tom Reed, *story* The Flirt by Booth Tarkington *d* Hobart Henley *ph* Karl Freund

Conrad Nagel, Sidney Fox, Bette Davis, Humphrey Bogart, Zasu Pitts, Slim Summerville, Emma Dunn, Bert Roach

Badge 373
US 1973   116m   Technicolor
Paramount (Howard W. Koch)

A police detective is enraged by the murder of his partner and his own suspension after the death of a suspect.
'Realistic' (i.e. violent and foul-mouthed) cop thriller in the wake of *The French Connection*, tolerable only for action highlights.

w Pete Hamill, from the exploits of Eddie Egan *d* Howard W. Koch *ph* Arthur J. Ornitz *m* J. J. Jackson

Robert Duvall, Verna Bloom, Henry Darrow, Eddie Egan, Felipe Luciano, Tina Christiana, Marina Durell

'A deeply divided and scarcely reassuring addition to the movies' composite portrait of the American police force.'—*John Gillett*

'Nasty, violent and humourless.'—*Sight and Sound*

'A movie well worth protesting about.'—*Michael Billington, Illustrated London News*

The Badlanders*
US 1958   83m   Metrocolor
Cinemascope
MGM / Arcola (Aaron Rosenberg)

Crooked westerners plan to rob a goldmine.
Rather sloppy western remake of *The Asphalt Jungle*.

w Richard Collins *d* Delmer Daves *ph* John Seitz

Alan Ladd, Ernest Borgnine, Katy Jurado, Claire Kelly, Kent Smith, *Nehemiah Persoff*, Robert Emhardt

Badlands***
US 1973   94m   Consolidated Color
(Columbia) Pressman / Williams / Badlands
(Terrence Malick)

A teenage girl and a young garbage collector wander across America leaving a trail of murder behind them.
A violent folk tale for moderns; very well put together if somewhat lacking in point, it quickly became a cult film.

wd Terrence Malick *ph* Brian Probyn, Tak Fujimoto, Stevan Larner *m* George Tipton

Martin Sheen, Sissy Spacek, Warren Oates, Ramon Bieri

'One of the finest literate examples of narrated cinema since the early days of Welles and Polonsky.'—*Jonathan Rosenbaum*

'So preconceived that there's nothing left to respond to.'—*New Yorker*

Bagdad
US 1949   81m   Technicolor
U-I (Robert Arthur)

A chieftain's daughter seeks revenge for her
father's death.
Thinly-conceived Arabian Nights
modernization, unsure whether to take itself
seriously.

w Robert Hardy Andrews d Charles Lamont
ph Russel Metty m Frank Skinner, Jack Brooks

Maureen O'Hara, Vincent Price, Paul Christian,
John Sutton, Jeff Corey, Frank Puglia

Bahama Passage
US 1941   82m   Technicolor
Paramount (Edward H. Griffith)

A sophisticated girl is determined to live on a
salt-mining island in the West Indies.
Forgettable tropical romance in very pleasing
early colour.

w Nelson Hayes d Edward H. Griffith ph Leo
Tover

Madeleine Carroll, Sterling Hayden, Flora
Robson, Leo G. Carroll, Cecil Kellaway,
Dorothy Dandridge

La Baie des Anges**
France 1962   85m   bw
Sud-Pacifique (Paul-Edmond Decharme)
GB title: *Bay of Angels*

A bank clerk who has had unexpected winnings
at the Nice Casino falls in love with a compulsive
gambler.
Good-looking romantic drama utilizing many of
the cinema's most dazzling resources.

wd Jacques Demy ph Jean Rabier m Michel
Legrand

Jeanne Moreau, Claude Mann, Paul Guers,
Henri Nassiet

'Immense lightness, speed and gaiety . . .
stunning visual texture.'—*Tom Milne, MFB*

Bait
US 1954   79m   bw
Columbia (Hugo Haas)

Gold prospectors fall out over a mine and a
woman.
Antediluvian melodrama typical of this director,
made more risible than usual by Cedric
Hardwicke's introduction in the shape of Satan.

w Samuel W. Taylor d Hugo Haas ph Edward
P. Fitzgerald m Vaclav Divina

Hugo Haas, Cleo Moore, John Agar, Emmett
Lynn

Balalaika*
US 1939   102m   bw
MGM (Lawrence Weingarten)

Russian exiles gather in Paris.
Mildly pleasing star musical.

w Jacques Deval, Leon Gordon, *play* Eric
Maschwitz d Reinhold Schunzel ph Joseph
Ruttenberg, Karl Freund m Herbert Stothart
songs various

Nelson Eddy, Ilona Massey, Charles Ruggles,
Frank Morgan, C. Aubrey Smith, Lionel Atwill,
Walter Woolf King, Joyce Compton

The Balcony*
US 1963   86m   bw
Walter Reade / Sterling / Allen Hodgdon /
   City Film   (Joseph Strick, Ben Maddow)

In a war-torn world, a brothel continues to
attract customers of every variety.
Low-budget adaptation of a rather confused
allegorical play: vivid moments hardly atone for
reels of surrealist groping.

w Ben Maddow, *play* Jean Genet d Joseph
Strick ph George Folsey m Igor Stravinsky

Shelley Winters, Peter Falk, Lee Grant, Peter
Brocco, Kent Smith, Ruby Dee, Jeff Corey,
Leonard Nimoy

Ball of Fire*
US 1942   111m   bw
Samuel Goldwyn

Seven professors compiling a dictionary give
shelter to a stripteaser on the run from gangsters.
Rather overstretched but fitfully amusing romp
inspired by *Snow White and the Seven Dwarfs*.

w *Charles Brackett, Billy Wilder* d Howard
Hawks ph Gregg Toland m Alfred Newman

Barbara Stanwyck, Gary Cooper, Oscar
Homolka, Henry Travers, S. Z. Sakall, Tully
Marshall, Leonid Kinskey, Richard Haydn,
Aubrey Mather, Allen Jenkins, Dana Andrews,
Dan Duryea

AAN: original story (Theodore Monroe, Billy
Wilder); Alfred Newman; Barbara Stanwyck

Ballad in Blue
GB 1964   88m   bw
(Warner) Alexander and Miguel Salkind
   (Herman Blaser)
US title: *Blues for Lovers*

A famous pianist becomes friendly with a blind
boy and helps reconcile his parents.
Curious sentimental drama with the star playing
himself; competent but hardly rousing.

w Burton Wohl d Paul Henreid ph Ron Taylor
m Ray Charles, Stanley Black

Ray Charles, Mary Peach, Dawn Addams, Tom Bell, Piers Bishop, Betty McDowell

Ballad of a Soldier**
USSR 1959 89m bw
Mosfilm
original title: *Ballada o Soldate*

A soldier is granted four days' home leave before returning to be killed at the front.
Lyrical tear-jerker most notable for its impeccably photographed detail of Russian domestic and everyday life.

w Valentin Yoshov, Grigori Chukrai *d Grigori Chukrai ph Vladimir Nikolayev, Era Saveleva m* Mikhail Ziv

Vladimir Ivashev, Sharma Prokhorenko, Antonina Maximova

'In an epoch when the entertainment in most entertainment films is little more than offensive, its persuasive charm is particularly welcome.'— *MFB*

AAN: Valentin Yoshov, Grigori Chukrai

The Ballad of Cable Hogue*
US 1970 121m Technicolor
Warner (Sam Peckinpah)

A gold prospector takes a lengthy and ineffectual revenge on men who robbed him, and dies trying to be a hero.
Curious peripatetic western with the director in uncharacteristically experimental and comparatively non-violent mood. All concerned seem to be enjoying themselves, but the fun is not always communicated.

w John Crawford, Edward Penney *d Sam Peckinpah ph Lucien Ballard m* Jerry Goldsmith

Jason Robards, David Warner, Strother Martin, Slim Pickens, L. Q. Jones, Peter Whitney, R. G. Armstrong, Gene Evans

The Ballad of Josie
US 1967 102m Techniscope
Universal (Marty Melcher)

Cleared of the manslaughter of her husband, a western widow renovates a derelict ranch and sets up as a sheep farmer.
Tediously whimsical, unsuitably cast women's lib comedy with so few laughs that it may require to be taken seriously.

w Harold Swanton *d* Andrew V. McLaglen *ph* Milton Krasner *m* Frank de Vol

Doris Day, Peter Graves, George Kennedy, William Talman, Andy Devine, Audrey Christie

Balthazar*
France / Sweden 1966 95m bw
Parc / Ardos / Athos / Svenska Filminstitutet (Mag Bodard)
original title: *Au Hasard, Balthazar*

The life of a talented donkey, born in the Swiss alps and eventually killed during a smuggling escapade.
Something between *Black Beauty* and a Christian parable, this quiet, episodic film is counted by some as its director's best work.

wd Robert Bresson *ph* Ghislain Cloquet *m* Jean Wiener (and Schubert)

Anne Wiazemsky, François Lafarge, Walter Green (amateur cast)

Baltic Deputy*
USSR 1937 100m bw
Lenfilm

An old professor is finally reconciled to the 1917 revolution.
Propagandist biography (of scientist K. A. Timiriazev) with interesting scenes and a strong central performance.

w the directors and others *d* Alexander Zharki, Josef Heifits *ph* M. Kaplan *m* M. Timofeyev

Nikolai Cherkassov, M. Damasheva, A. Melnikov

Bambi****
US 1942 72m Technicolor
Walt Disney

The story of a forest deer, from the book by Felix Salten.
Anthropomorphic cartoon feature, one of Disney's most memorable and brilliant achievements, with a great comic character in Thumper the rabbit and a climactic forest fire sequence which is genuinely thrilling. A triumph of the animator's art.

supervisor David Hand *m* Frank Churchill, Edward Plumb

AA: song 'Love Is a Song' (*m* Frank Churchill, *ly* Larry Morey)
AAN: Frank Churchill, Edward Plumb

Bananas*
US 1971 81m De Luxe
UA / Rollins and Joffe (Jack Grossberg)

A meek and mild product tester for a New York corporation accidentally becomes a South American rebel hero.
Disjointed anarchic comedy with a few good jokes typical of their author.

w Woody Allen with Mickey Rose *d* Woody

Allen *ph* Andrew M. Costikyan *m* Marvin
Hamlisch

Woody Allen, Louise Lasser, Carlos Montalban,
Jacobo Morales

'Full of hilarious comic ideas and lines,
supplied by Allen and his collaborator; then
Allen, the director and actor, murders them.'—
Stanley Kauffmann

† Asked why his film was called *Bananas*, Allen
replied: 'Because there are no bananas in it.'

Band of Angels
US 1957   127m   Warnercolor
Warner (no producer credited)

In 1865, a Kentucky girl learns that her mother
was black and is sold as a slave, but quickly
becomes her owner's mistress.

Long-winded romantic adventure, rather lamely
scripted and developed. The star's presence
reinforces the impression of sitting through the
ghost of *Gone with the Wind.*

w John Twist, Ivan Goff, Ben Roberts, *novel*
Robert Penn Warren *d* Raoul Walsh *ph* Lucien
Ballard *m* Max Steiner

Clark Gable, Yvonne de Carlo, Sidney Poitier,
Efrem Zimbalist Jnr, Patric Knowles, Rex
Reason, Torin Thatcher, Andrea King

'Too absurd to be dislikeable.'—*MFB*

Band Waggon*
GB 1939   85m   bw
Gainsborough (Edward Black)

Comedians running a pirate TV station in a
ghostly castle round up a gang of spies.

Film version of a long-running radio comedy
series; quite a serviceable record of a
phenomenon.

w Marriott Edgar, Val Guest *d* Marcel Varnel

Arthur Askey, Richard Murdoch, Jack Hylton
and his band, Pat Kirkwood, Moore Marriott,
Peter Gawthorne, Wally Patch, Donald
Calthrop

The Band Wagon***
US 1953   112m   Technicolor
MGM (Arthur Freed)

A has-been Hollywood dancer joins forces with
a temperamental stage producer to put on a
Broadway musical.

Simple but sophisticated musical with the bare
minimum of plot, told mostly in jokes, and the
maximum of music and song. Numbers include
'Shine on My Shoes', 'Triplets', 'Dancing in the
Dark', 'I Guess I'll Have to Change My Plan',
'Louisiana Hayride' and 'That's Entertainment',
and there is a spoof Mickey Spillane ballet finale.
Level of technical accomplishment very high.

w Adolph Green, Betty Comden *d* Vincente
Minnelli *ph* Harry Jackson *songs* Howard
Dietz, Arthur Schwarz *m* Adolph Deutsch
ad Cedric Gibbons, Preston Ames

Fred Astaire, Jack Buchanan, Oscar Levant,
Cyd Charisse, Nanette Fabray

AAN: Adolph Green, Betty Comden; Adolph
Deutsch

Bande à Part
France 1964   95m   bw
Anouchka / Orsay (Philippe Dussart)
aka: *The Outsiders*

Aimless young people plan a robbery which ends
in murder.

Despite the plot, the emphasis is on fragments of
lyricism, and the film is not among its director's
greatest successes.

wd Jean-Luc Godard, *novel* Fool's Gold by
Dolores and B. Hitchens *ph* Raoul Coutard
m Michel Legrand

Anna Karina, Claude Brasseur, Sami Frey,
Louisa Colpeyn

'In a sense, the whole film is a metaphor
illustrating this glancing collision, when fantasy
and reality merge but one may still remain
unsure which is which.'–*Tom Milne, MFB*

Bandido
US 1956   92m   De Luxe   Cinemascope
UA / Robert L. Jacks

Mexico 1916: an American adventurer helps a
rebel leader to defeat a gun runner.

Standard action fare, rather slackly handled.

w Earl Felton *d* Richard Fleischer *ph* Ernest
Laszlo *m* Max Steiner

Robert Mitchum, Gilbert Roland, Zachary
Scott, Ursula Thiess

The Bandit*
Brazil 1953   119m   bw
Companhia Cinematographica (Cid Leite da
Silva)
original title: *O'Cangaceiro*

The leader of a gang of outlaws comes to grief
after falling out with his second in command
over a woman.

One of the few Brazilian films to achieve
international popularity, mainly because of its
memorable theme tune. The film itself looks
attractive but becomes a bit of a bore.

wd Lima Barreto *ph* Chick Fowle *m Gabriel
Migliori*

Alberto Ruschel, Milton Ribeiro, Marisa Prado

The Bandit of Sherwood Forest**

US 1946   87m   Technicolor
Columbia (Leonard S. Picker, Clifford
Sanforth)

Robin Hood frustrates the Regent who plans to
usurp the throne from the boy king.
A lively romp through Sherwood Forest with a
capable cast.

w Wilfrid H. Pettit, Melvin Levy, *novel* Son of
Robin Hood by Paul A. Castleton *d* George
Sherman, Henry Levin *ph* Tony Gaudio,
William Snyder, George Meehan *m* Hugo
Friedhofer

Cornel Wilde, Anita Louise, Edgar Buchanan,
Jill Esmond, Henry Daniell, George Macready,
Russell Hicks, John Abbott, Lloyd Corrigan

Bandits of Orgosolo

Italy 1961   98m   bw
Titanus

A Sardinian shepherd shelters some bandits and
becomes one of them.
Rather slow character adventure which achieved
some international reputation in its first release.

wd Vittorio de Seta *m* Valentino Bucchi

Michele Cossu, Peppeddu Cuccu, and amateur
cast

Bandolero!*

US 1968   108m   De Luxe   Panavision
TCF (Robert L. Jacks)

In Texas, fugitive outlaw brothers run into
trouble with their Mexican counterparts.
Dour and downbeat but well-staged western with
emphasis on hanging and rape; an unusual
mixture but smoothly assembled.

w James Lee Barrett *d* Andrew V. McLaglen
ph William H. Clothier *m* Jerry Goldsmith

James Stewart, Dean Martin, Raquel Welch,
George Kennedy, Will Geer, Andrew Prine

Bang the Drum Slowly

US 1973   96m   Movielab
Paramount (Maurice and Lois Rosenfield)

A baseball star finds that he is dying of leukemia.
Cliché-ridden tearjerker in the modern style.

w Mark Harris, from his novel *d* John Hancock
ph Richard Shore *m* Stephen Lawrence

Michael Moriarty, Robert de Niro, Vincent
Gardenia, Phil Foster

AAN: Vincent Gardenia

Bang, You're Dead

GB 1954   88m   bw
British Lion / Wellington (Lance Comfort)

A small boy accidentally shoots a local villain,
and another man is arrested.
Singularly pointless and unattractive
melodrama, a long way behind *The Window* and
The Yellow Balloon.

w Guy Elmes, Ernest Borneman *d* Lance
Comfort *ph* Brendan J. Stafford *m* Eric Spear

Jack Warner, Derek Farr, Veronica Hurst,
Gordon Harker, Michael Medwin, Anthony
Richmond, Philip Saville

Banjo on my Knee**

US 1936   95m   bw
TCF (Nunnally Johnson)

In a Mississippi riverboat shanty town, a
wedding night is interrupted when the groom is
arrested during a brawl.
Unusual, easy-going comedy in which the stars
sing and dance as well as fool around.

w Nunnally Johnson, novel Harry Hamilton
d John Cromwell *ph* Ernest Palmer *m* Arthur
Lange

Barbara Stanwyck, Joel McCrea, Buddy Ebsen,
Walter Brennan, Helen Westley, Walter Catlett,
Tony Martin, Katherine de Mille

The Bank Dick**

US 1940   73m   bw
Universal
GB title: *The Bank Detective*

In Lompoc, California, a ne'er-do-well
accidentally stops a hold-up, is made a bank
detective, acquires deeds to a worthless mine and
interferes in the production of a film.
Imperfect, but probably the best Fields vehicle
there is: the jokes sometimes end in mid-air, but
there are delicious moments and very little
padding. The character names are sometimes
funnier than the script: they include Egbert
Sousè (accent grave over the 'e'), J. Pinkerton
Snoopington, Ogg Oggilbie and Filthy
McNasty.

w Mahatma Kane Jeeves (W. C. Fields) *d* Eddie
Cline *ph* Milton Krasner *md* Charles Previn

W. C. Fields, Franklin Pangborn, Shemp
Howard, Jack Norton, Grady Sutton, Cora
Witherspoon

'One of the great classics of American
comedy.'—*Robert Lewis Taylor*

'When the man is funny he is terrific . . . but the
story is makeshift, the other characters are stock
types, the only pace discernible is the distance
between drinks or the rhythm of the fleeting
seconds it takes Fields to size up trouble coming
and duck the hell out.'—*Otis Ferguson*

Bank Holiday*
GB 1938 _86m bw
Gainsborough (Edward Black)
US title: *Three on a Weekend*

The lives of various people intertwine during a
day out in Brighton.
Simple but effective slice-of-life comedy-drama,
establishing several actors and a director. Still
quite refreshing.

w Hans Wilhelm, Rodney Ackland, Roger
Burford *d* Carol Reed

*Margaret Lockwood, Hugh Williams, Kathleen
Harrison*, Wally Patch, Rene Ray, Linden
Travers, Garry Marsh, Wilfrid Lawson

The Bank Shot*
US 1974 83m De Luxe
UA / Hal Landers, Bobby Roberts

Using house-moving equipment, an escaped
convict steals a whole bank.
Extended chase comedy with scenes of gleeful
destruction. Acceptable for those in the mood,
but a shade overdone.

w Wendell Mayes, *novel* Donald E. Westlake
d Gower Champion *ph* Harry Stradling Jnr
m John Morris

George C. Scott, Joanna Cassidy, Sorrell
Brooke, G. Wood, Clifton James

Bannerline*
US 1951 87m bw
MGM (Henry Berman)

To comfort a dying old man, a young reporter
prints a fake newspaper showing the indictment
of the old man's gangster enemy. By an odd
chain of events, the story becomes true.
Worthy but rather dull MGM 'B', typical of the
regime of Dore Schary, boasting a pleasing
small-town atmosphere and a remarkable cast of
old actors.

w Charles Schnee, *story* Samson Raphaelson
d Don Weis *ph* Harold Lipstein *m* Rudolph
Kopp

Lionel Barrymore, Keefe Brasselle, Sally
Forrest, Lewis Stone, Elizabeth Risdon, J.
Carrol Naish, Spring Byington, Larry Keating

Banning
US 1967 102m Techniscope
Universal (Dick Berg)

A tennis pro has sporting and amorous
adventures at a country club.
Tedious, complexly plotted melodrama of life
among the idle rich; handling generally laboured.
A showcase for the studio's young contract
talent.

w James Lee *d* Ron Winston *ph* Loyal Griggs
m Quincy Jones

Robert Wagner, Anjanette Comer, Jill St John,
Guy Stockwell, James Farentino, Susan Clark,
Howard St John, Mike Kellin, Sean Garrison,
Gene Hackman

AAN: song 'The Eyes of Love' (*m* Quincy
Jones, *ly* Bob Russell

Barabbas*
Italy / US 1962 144m Technirama
Columbia / Dino de Laurentiis

Pardoned instead of Christ, Barabbas is
sentenced to the silver mines, turns Christian,
and becomes a gladiator.
Overblown epic which starts with a genuine
eclipse of the sun and has nowhere to go but
down. The cast sparks a few moments, but it is
generally a gaudy display of carnage.

w Christopher Fry, Nigel Balchin, Diego Fabbri,
Ivo Perilli, *novel* Pär Lagerkvist *d* Richard
Fleischer *ph* Aldo Tonti *m* Mario Nascimbene
ad Mario Chiari

Anthony Quinn, Silvana Mangano, Vittorio
Gassman, Ernest Borgnine, Jack Palance,
Arthur Kennedy, Norman Wooland, Valentina
Cortese, Harry Andrews, Katy Jurado, Michael
Gwynn

'Unacceptable in its pain-preoccupation and
its religiosity.'—*Peter John Dyer*

Barbarella*
France / Italy 1967 98m Technicolor
Panavision
Marianne / Dino de Laurentiis

A beautiful young 40th-century astronaut
prevents the positronic ray from getting into the
wrong hands.
Campy and slightly sick adventures with angels
and other space people, from a highly censorable
comic strip; some ingenious gadgetry and
design, but not much of interest in the
foreground.

w Terry Southern, *book* Jean-Claude Forest
d Roger Vadim *ph* Claude Renoir *pd* Mario
Garbuglia *m* Bob Crewe, Charles Fox

Jane Fonda, John Phillip Law, Anita Pallenberg,
Milo O'Shea, David Hemmings, Marcel
Marceau, Ugo Tognazzi, Claude Dauphin

'A leading science fiction authority has
claimed that if Lewis Carroll were alive today he
would inevitably have written not *Alice's
Adventures in Wonderland* but *Lolita*. He might
perhaps equally well have written *Barbarella*.'—
Jack Ibberson

The Barbarian
US 1933   90m approx   bw
MGM
GB title: *A Night in Cairo*

An American lady travelling in the Middle East
falls for a local potentate.
Shades of *The Sheik*. Actually this version was
first made in 1924 as *The Arab*, with the same
leading man. Either version would seem fairly
hysterical now.

w Anita Loos, Elmer Harris, *play* Edgar
Selwyn *d* Sam Wood

Ramon Novarro, Myrna Loy, Reginald Denny,
C. Aubrey Smith, Louise Closser Hale, Edward
Arnold

The Barbarian and the Geisha *
US 1958   105m   Eastmancolor
  Cinemascope
TCF (Eugene Frenke)

In 1856 the first US diplomat to visit Japan
meets local opposition but is helped by a geisha.
Episodic semi-historical romance which scarcely
suits the talents of those involved.

w Charles Grayson *d* John Huston *ph* Charles
G. Clarke *m* Hugo Friedhofer

John Wayne, Eiko Ando, Sam Jaffe, So
Yamamura

Barbary Coast **
US 1935   91m   bw
Samuel Goldwyn

During San Francisco's gold rush days a
ruthless club owner builds a lonely girl into a star
attraction but cannot win her love.
Juicy melodrama tailored for its stars, but with
excellent background detail, sets and lighting.

w Ben Hecht, Charles MacArthur *d* Howard
Hawks *ph* Ray June *m* Alfred Newman

Edward G. Robinson, Miriam Hopkins, Joel
McCrea, Walter Brennan, Frank Craven, Brian
Donlevy, Donald Meek
† David Niven made his first screen appearance
as an extra.

AAN: Ray June

Barbary Coast Gent
US 1944   87m   bw
MGM (Orville Dull)

A bandit from the Californian goldfields tries to
go straight in San Francisco.
Star comedy drama, somewhat below par
despite attractive settings and good production.

w William Lipman, Grant Garrett, Harry
Ruskin *d* Roy del Ruth

Wallace Beery, Binnie Barnes, Frances Rafferty,
Chill Wills, Ray Collins, John Carradine, Noah
Beery, Morris Ankrum, Henry O'Neill, Donald
Meek, Paul Hurst, Louise Beavers

Barefoot Battalion
Greece 1954   89m   bw
Peter Boudoures

War orphans inhabit a derelict barge and band
together to harass the Germans.
Unlikely true story, roughly dramatized and
poorly produced.

w Nico Katsiotes *d* Gregg Tallas *ph* Mixalis
Gaziadis *m* Mikis Theodorakis

Maria Costi, Nico Fermas, Stavros Krozos

The Barefoot Contessa **
US 1954   128m   Technicolor
UA / Figaro (Forrest E. Johnston)

A glamorous barefoot dancer in a Spanish
cabaret is turned into a Hollywood star, but her
sexual frustrations lead to a tragic end.
A fascinating farrago of addled philosophy and
lame wisecracks, very typical of a writer-director
here not at his best, decorated by a splendid
gallery of actors and some attractive settings.

wd Joseph L. Mankiewicz ph Jack Cardiff
m Mario Nascimbene

Humphrey Bogart, Ava Gardner, Edmond
O'Brien, Marius Goring, Valentina Cortese,
Rossano Brazzi, Elizabeth Sellars, Warren
Stevens
  'This example of the Higher Lunacy must vie
with *Johnny Guitar* for the silliest film of the
year.'—*Gavin Lambert*
  'A trash masterpiece: a Cinderella story in
which the prince turns out to be impotent.'—
Pauline Kael, 1968

AA: Edmond O'Brien
AAN: Joseph L. Mankiewicz (as writer)

The Barefoot Executive *
US 1970   96m   Technicolor
Walt Disney (Bill Anderson)

A TV network discovers that its most infallible
average viewer is a chimpanzee.
Quite a beguiling little farcical comedy with mild
doses of satire.

w Joseph L. McEveety *d* Robert Butler
ph Charles F. Wheeler *m* Robert F. Brunner

Kurt Russell, Harry Morgan, Joe Flynn, Wally
Cox, Heather North, Alan Hewitt, Hayden
Rorke

Barefoot in the Park **
US 1967   109m   Technicolor
Paramount / Hal B. Wallis

A pair of New York newlyweds rent a cold water flat at the top of a liftless building, and manage to marry the bride's mother to an eccentric neighbour.

Breezy but overlong adaptation of a stage play which succeeded through audience response to its one-liners, which on the screen sometimes fall flat. The people are nice, though.

w Neil Simon, from his play *d* Gene Saks *ph* Joseph La Shelle *m* Neal Hefti

Robert Redford, Jane Fonda, *Mildred Natwick*, Charles Boyer, Herb Edelmann, Mabel Albertson

AAN: Mildred Natwick

The Barefoot Mailman
US 1951 82m Supercinecolor
Columbia (Robert Cohn)

In 19th-century Florida, the mailman is joined by a confidence trickster who later has a change of heart.

Inept comedy adventure which never really gets started.

w James Gunn, Francis Swann, *novel* Theodore Pratt *d* Earl McEvoy *ph* Ellis W. Carter *m* George Duning

Robert Cummings, Jerome Courtland, Terry Moore, John Russell, Will Geer, Arthur Shields, Trevor Bardette

† This is the title parodied by the Magoo cartoon *Barefaced Flatfoot.*

The Bargee*
GB 1964 106m Techniscope
AB / Galton–Simpson (W. A. Whitaker)

A canal barge Casanova is trapped into marriage.

The long-awaited comedy which was supposed to make a film star out of TV's Young Steptoe turned out to be rough and vulgar but not very funny.

w Ray Galton, Alan Simpson *d* Duncan Wood *ph* Harry Waxman *m* Frank Cordell

Harry H. Corbett, Ronnie Barker, Hugh Griffith, Eric Sykes, Julia Foster. Miriam Karlin, Eric Barker, Derek Nimmo, Norman Bird, Richard Briers

The Barkleys of Broadway*
US 1949 109m Technicolor
MGM (Arthur Freed)

A quarrelling couple of musical comedy stars split up, and she becomes a serious actress.
A rather flat and unattractive reunion for a famous pair, with a witless script, poorish numbers and very little style. The compensations are minor.

w Adolph Green, Betty Comden *d* Charles Walters *ph* Harry Stradling *songs* Harry Warren, Ira Gershwin

Fred Astaire, Ginger Rogers, Oscar Levant, Jacques François, Billie Burke

AAN: Harry Stradling

Barnacle Bill
US 1941 90m bw
MGM (Milton Bren)

A fishing boat skipper gets romantic in the hope of financing his enterprises.
Adequate waterfront comedy on *Min and Bill* lines, consolidating a popular star teaming.

w Jack Jevne, Hugo Butler *d* Richard Thorpe *ph* Clyde de Vinna

Wallace Beery, Marjorie Main, Leo Carrillo, Virginia Weidler, Donald Meek, Barton Maclaine, Connie Gilchrist, Sara Haden

Barnacle Bill*
GB 1957 87m bw
Ealing (Michael Balcon)
US title: *All at Sea*

The last of a long line of sailors suffers from seasickness, and takes command of a decaying Victorian pier at an English seaside resort.
Quite an amusing comedy which had the misfortune to come at the tag-end of the Ealing classics and so seemed too mild and predictable. Perhaps it was a little staid.

w T. E. B. Clarke *d* Charles Frend *ph* Douglas Slocombe *m* John Addison

Alec Guinness, Irene Browne, Percy Herbert, Harold Goodwin, Maurice Denham, George Rose, Lionel Jeffries, Victor Maddern

Le Baron Fantôme*
France 1943 100m bw
Consortium de Productions de Films (Robert Florat)
GB title: *The Phantom Baron*

In the early 19th-century, the disappearance of a nobleman causes problems for his heirs.
Macabre fairy tale with effective scenes which seem to relate to Cocteau's later fantasies; the film as a whole is less effective.

wd Serge de Poligny *dialogue* Jean Cocteau *ph* Roger Hubert *m* Louis Beydts

Jany Holt, Odette Joyeux, Alain Cuny, Gabrielle Dorziat

Baron Munchausen*
Czechoslovakia 1962 81m Agfacolor
Ceskoslovensky Film
original title: *Baron Prasil*

An astronaut finds on the moon the famous liar
Baron Munchausen, who takes him back to
earth and a variety of exaggerated adventures.
Amusing variation on the old stories, using live
action against deliberately artificial
backgrounds.

wd Karel Zeman, from the novel by Gottfried
Burger and the illustrations by Gustave Doré
ph Jiri Tarantik *m* Zdenek Liska

Milos Kopecky, Rudolf Jelinek, Jana Becjchova

The Baron of Arizona

US 1950   85m   bw
Lippert (Carl Hittleman)

In the 19th century a clerk tries to claim the
whole of Arizona by false land grants.
Initially appealing but basically rather feeble tall
tale, ineffectively worked out and decidedly
undernourished as a production.

wd Samuel Fuller *ph* James Wong Howe
m Paul Dunlap

Vincent Price, Ellen Drew, Beulah Bondi,
Vladimir Sokoloff, Reed Hadley, Robert Barrat

The Baroness and the Butler

US 1938   75m   bw
TCF (Raymond Griffith)

The Hungarian prime minister's butler is loved
by a princess.
Thin mittel-European romantic star whimsy.

w Sam Hellman, Lamar Trotti, Kathryn Scola,
play The Lady Has a Heart by Ladislaus Bus-
Fekete *d* Walter Lang *ph* Arthur Miller
md Louis Silvers

William Powell, Annabella, Henry Stephenson,
Nigel Bruce, Helen Westley, Joseph Schildkraut,
J. Edward Bromberg, Lynn Bari

Barquero!

US 1970   114m   De Luxe
Aubrey Schenck (Hal Klein)

A western ferryman is taken prisoner by bandits
but turns the tables.
Long, violent, rather uninteresting western in the
Spanish manner.

w George Schenck, William Marks *d* Gordon
Douglas *ph* Jerry Finnermann *m* Dominic
Frontiere

Lee Van Cleef, Forrest Tucker, Warren Oates,
Kerwin Mathews, Mariette Hartley, Brad
Weston, John Davis Chandler

The Barretts of Wimpole Street **

US 1934   109m   bw
MGM (Irving Thalberg)
TV title: *Forbidden Alliance*

Invalid Elizabeth Barrett plans to marry poet
Robert Browning, against her tyrannical father's
wishes.
Claustrophobic but well-acted adaptation of a
stage play which has become more forceful than
history. Stilted now, but still better than the
remake.

w Ernst Vajda, Claudine West, Donald Ogden
Stewart, *play* Rudolf Besier *d* Sidney Franklin
ph William Daniels *m* Herbert Stothart

Norma Shearer, Fredric March, *Charles
Laughton,* Maureen O'Sullivan, Katherine
Alexander, Ralph Forbes, Una O'Connor, Ian
Wolfe

AAN: best picture; Norma Shearer

The Barretts of Wimpole Street

GB 1956   105m   Metrocolor
     Cinemascope
MGM (Sam Zimbalist)

Dreadful, miscast remake of the above, with
emphasis on the Freudian father-daughter
relationship. An unattractive and boring film.

w John Dighton *d* Sidney Franklin
ph Frederick A. Young *m* Bronislau Kaper

Jennifer Jones, Bill Travers, John Gielgud,
Virginia McKenna

Barricade

US 1939   71m   bw
TCF (Edward Kaufman)

A newsman and a girl with a past fight
Mongolian bandits in North China.
A bagful of clichés which does not quite add up
to entertainment.

w Granville Walker *d* Gregory Ratoff *ph* Karl
Freund

Warner Baxter, Alice Faye, Charles Winninger,
Arthur Treacher, Keye Luke, Willie Fung, Doris
Lloyd

Barricade

US 1949   75m   Technicolor
Warner (Saul Elkins)

A tough mine-owner who runs a camp miles
from civilization meets his come-uppance when
three strangers are forced to accept his
hospitality.
Rough western only notable as an (almost)
scene-for-scene steal from *The Sea Wolf:* a textbook adaptation.

w William Sackheim *d* Peter Godfrey *ph* Carl
Guthrie *m* William Lava

Raymond Massey, Dane Clark, Ruth Roman,
Robert Douglas, Morgan Farley

Barry Lyndon **
GB 1975 187m Eastmancolor
Warner / Hawk / Peregrine (Stanley Kubrick)

Adventures of an 18th-century Irish gentleman of fortune.

A curiously cold-hearted enterprise, like an art gallery in which the backgrounds are sketched in loving detail and the human figures totally neglected; there is much to enjoy, but script and acting are variable to say the least, and the point of it all is obscure, as it certainly does not tell a rattling good story.

wd Stanley Kubrick, novel W. M. Thackeray
ph John Alcott md Leonard Rosenman *pd Ken Adam*

Ryan O'Neal, Marisa Berenson, Patrick Magee, Hardy Kruger, Steven Berkoff, Gay Hamilton, Marie Kean, Murray Melvin, André Morell, Leonard Rossiter, Philip Stone *narrator* Michael Hordern

'The motion picture equivalent of one of these very large, very expensive, very elegant and very dull books that exist solely to be seen on coffee tables.'—*Charles Champlin*

'Watching the movie is like looking at illustrations for a work that has not been supplied.'—*John Simon*

'All art and no matter: a series of still pictures which will please the retina while denying our hunger for drama. And far from re-creating another century, it more accurately embalms it.'—*Michael Billington, Illustrated London News*

AA: John Alcott; Leonard Rosenman
AAN: best picture; Stanley Kubrick (as writer); Stanley Kubrick (as director)

Bartleby *
GB 1970 79m Eastmancolor
Pantheon (Rodney Carr-Smith)

A young clerk gradually refuses to take part in life.

A non-action film from an independent source, praiseworthy but overlong and fairly lacking in any kind of appeal except to literary connoisseurs.

w Anthony Friedmann, Rodney Carr-Smith, *story* Herman Melville *d* Anthony Friedmann *ph* Ian Wilson *m* Roger Webb

Paul Scofield, John McEnery, Thorley Walters, Colin Jeavons

Les Bas-fonds *
France 1936 92m bw
Albatros
aka: *The Lower Depths*

A clash of temperaments flares up between derelicts in a dosshouse.

Uneven transposition of a famous work, with patches of good acting.

w Jean Renoir, Charles Spaak and others, *play* Maxim Gorky *d* Jean Renoir *ph* Jean Bachelet

Jean Gabin, Louis Jouvet, Vladimir Sokoloff, Robert Le Vigan, Suzy Prim

The Bat
US 1959 78m bw
AA / Liberty (C. J. Tevlin)

A lady mystery writer rents a spooky old house and finds herself and her guests at the mercy of a maniac in search of hidden loot.

Poor remake of a standard twenties stage thriller; everyone chews the scenery.

wd Crane Wilbur, *play* Mary Roberts Rinehart *ph* Joseph Biroc *m* Louis Forbes

Vincent Price, Agnes Moorehead, Gavin Gordon, John Sutton, Lenita Lane, Darla Hood

The Bat Whispers **
US 1930 70m bw
UA / Roland West

Classic early sound version of *The Bat* (qv) by the director of the 1926 silent version. Excellent use of camera, sets, and unusual models.

wd Roland West ph Ray June, Robert Planck

Chester Morris, Una Merkel, Chancer Ward, Grayce Hampton, Maude Eburne, Spencer Charters, Gustav Von Seyffertitz

Bataan *
US 1943 114m bw
MGM (Irving Starr)

Thirteen soldiers holding a bridge against the Japanese die one by one.

Uncredited remake of *The Lost Patrol* (qv) transposed to the Pacific war, with stereotyped characters and much flagwaving. Very dated, but a big box office film of its time, despite its studio jungles.

w Robert D. Andrews *d* Tay Garnett *ph* Sidney Wagner *m* Bronislau Kaper

Robert Taylor, George Murphy, Thomas Mitchell, Lloyd Nolan, Lee Bowman, Robert Walker, Desi Arnaz, Barry Nelson, Philip Terry

La Bataille du Rail **
France 1945 87m bw
CGCF

Reconstructions of heroic resistance work by the French railwaymen during World War II.

Reasonably compulsive documentary fiction

which was plainly more inspiring at the time than it seems now.

wd René Clément *ph* Henri Alekan *m* Yves Baudrier

Salina, Daurand, Lozach, Tony Laurent

Bathing Beauty
US 1944   101m   Technicolor
MGM (Jack Cummings)

A songwriter plans to retire and settle down, but his publisher schemes to set his fiancée against him.
Witless, artificial aqua-musical, with plenty of unpersuasive high jinks but no real style despite a capable cast.

w Dorothy Kingsley, Allen Boretz, Frank Waldman *d* George Sidney *ch* John Murray Anderson

Esther Williams, Red Skelton, Basil Rathbone, Keenan Wynn, Ethel Smith, Xavier Cugat, Bill Goodwin

Batman*
US 1966   105m   De Luxe
TCF / Greenlawn / National Periodical
    Publications (William Dozier)

The cloaked avenger saves an important executive from the clutches of four of the world's most notorious criminals.
Glossy feature version of the old and new serials about the comic strip hero who scurries around in his Batmobile making sure that justice is done. The scriptwriter's invention unfortunately flags halfway, so that despite a fairly sharp production the result is more childish than camp.

w Lorenzo Semple Jnr *d* Leslie Martinson *ph* Howard Schwarz *m* Nelson Riddle

Adam West, Burt Ward, Cesar Romero, Frank Gorshin, Burgess Meredith, Lee Meriwether, Alan N:)ier, Neil Hamilton

The Battle*
France 1934   85m   bw
Gaumont (Leon Garganoff)
English language version aka: *Thunder in the East, Hara Kiri*

A Japanese aristocrat urges his wife to befriend an English naval attaché and steal secrets from him; she does, and falls in love.
Stagey but discreet melodrama of the old school, quite well made and acted.

w Nicolas Farkas, Bernard Zimmer, Robert Stevenson, *novel* Claude Farrère *d* Nicolas Farkas

Charles Boyer, Merle Oberon, John Loder, Betty Stockfield, Miles Mander

Battle beneath the Earth*
GB 1967   92m   Technicolor
MGM / Reynolds / Vetter (Charles Reynolds)

Enemy agents burrow under the US by means of a giant laser.
Agreeable schoolboy science fiction with fair special effects.

w L. Z. Hargeaves *d* Montgomery Tully *ph* Kenneth Talbot *m* Ken Jones *sp* Tom Howard

Kerwin Mathews, Vivienne Ventura, Robert Ayres, Peter Arne, Martin Benson

Battle Circus
US 1952   90m   bw
MGM (Pandro S. Berman)

A patriotic nurse and a disillusioned major fall in love at a mobile army hospital in Korea.
A flat, studio-bound potboiler with miscast stars, bound to provoke hilarity now as a serious version of *M*A*S*H*.

wd Richard Brooks *ph* John Alton *m* Lennie Hayton

Humphrey Bogart, June Allyson, Keenan Wynn, Robert Keith, William Campbell

Battle Cry
US 1954   148m   Warnercolor
    Cinemascope
Warner (producer not credited)

During World War II, marines endure tough training before combat in Saipan; their sex lives come a close second to the war.
Interminable cheapie epic with both eyes on the box office: the cast salvages an odd moment or two, but violence of all kinds is the key to the entertainment.

w Leon Uris, from his novel *d* Raoul Walsh *ph* Sid Hickox *m* Max Steiner

Van Heflin, Aldo Ray, Mona Freeman, Dorothy Malone, Raymond Massey, Nancy Olson, James Whitmore, Tab Hunter, Anne Francis, William Campbell

AAN: Max Steiner

Battle for Music*
GB 1943   87m   bw
Strand Films (Donald Taylor)

The story of the wartime ups and downs of the London Philharmonic Orchestra.
Not many films feature a classical orchestra, and this simple tribute, a mediocre production at best, has considerable historical interest.

w St John L. Clowes *d* Donald Taylor

Hay Petrie, Joss Ambler, Charles Carson, Jack Hylton,

J. B. Priestley, Eileen Joyce, Moiseiwitch, Sir Adrian
Boult, Sir Malcolm Sargent

Battle Hymn
US 1957   108m   Technicolor
   Cinemascope
U-I (Ross Hunter)

An American preacher with a guilt complex
volunteers to help the South Koreans and after
many adventures founds an orphanage.
Earnest, somnolent biopic of one Dean Hess; its
mixture of drama, comedy, religion and war
heroics is indigestible despite professional
handling.

w Charles Grayson, Vincent B. Evans
d Douglas Sirk ph Russell Metty m Frank
Skinner

Rock Hudson, Anna Kashfi, Dan Duryea, Don
Defore, Martha Hyer, Jock Mahoney, James
Edwards, Carl Benton Reid
   'The film seems to infer that heroic self-
sacrifice, a little homely Eastern philosophy and
a capacity for combining battle experience with
an awareness of spiritual values are enough to
overcome all emergencies.'—*John Gillett*

The Battle of Algiers*
Algeria / Italy 1965   135m   bw
Casbah / Igor (Antonio Musi, Yacef Saadi)
original title: *La Battaglia di Algeri*

In 1954 Algiers, an ex-convict joins the terrorists
in rebellion against the French government.
Politically oriented reconstruction of a bitter
period of French colonial history, made better
propaganda by its wealth of effective detail.

w Franco Solinas d Gillo Pontecorvo
ph Marcello Gatti m Ennio Morricone, Gillo
Pontecorvo

Brahim Haggiag, Jean Martin, Yacef Saadi,
Tommaso Neri

AAN: Franco Solinas; Gillo Pontecorvo (as
director)

Battle of Britain*
GB 1969   131m   Technicolor   Panavision
UA / Spitfire (Harry Saltzman, Ben Fisz)

Summer 1940: England defends itself against
aerial onslaught.
Plodding attempt to cover an historic event from
too many angles and with too many guest stars,
all indistinguishable from each other when
masked in the cockpit during the repetitive and
interminable dogfight sequences. On the ground,
things are even duller.

w James Kennaway, Wilfrid Greatorex d Guy
Hamilton ph Frederick A. Young m William
Walton, Ron Goodwin

Laurence Olivier (as Dowding), Robert Shaw,
Michael Caine, Christopher Plummer, Kenneth
More, Susannah York, Trevor Howard, Ralph
Richardson, Patrick Wymark, Curt Jurgens,
Michael Redgrave, Nigel Patrick, Robert
Flemyng, Edward Fox

The Battle of Paris
US 1929   71m   bw
Paramount

A lady music seller teams up with a pickpocket
and falls for an American artist.
Primitive sound musical notable chiefly for its
cast.

w Gene Markey d Robert Florey ph Bill
Steiner songs Cole Porter

Gertrude Lawrence, Charles Ruggles, Walter
Petrie, Arthur Treacher, Gladys du Bois

Battle of the Bulge**
US 1965   167m   Technicolor   Ultra
Panavision
Warner / United States Pictures (Sidney
   Harmon, Milton Sperling, Philip Yordan)

In December 1944, the Allies take longer than
expected to win a land battle in the Ardennes
because of a crack Nazi Panzer commander.
Bloody and unbowed war spectacle, quite
literate and handsome but deafeningly noisy and
with emphasis on strategy rather than character.

w Philip Yordan, Milton Sperling, John Melson
d Ken Annakin ph Jack Hildyard m Benjamin
Frankel

Henry Fonda, Robert Shaw, Robert Ryan, Telly
Savalas, Dana Andrews, George Montgomery,
Ty Hardin, Pier Angeli, Barbara Werle, Charles
Bronson, James MacArthur, Werner Peters

The Battle of the River Plate*
GB 1956   119m   Technicolor   Vistavision
Rank / Powell and Pressburger
US title: *Pursuit of the Graf Spee*

Semi-documentary account of the 1939 trapping
of the German pocket battleship *Graf Spee* in
Montevideo Harbour, and of her subsequent
scuttling.
A sympathetic view of a German hero,
Commander Langsdorff (not unexpected from
these producers) is the most notable feature of
this disappointingly patchy and studio-bound
war epic, with too many actors in ill-defined bit
parts, too undisciplined a storyline, and too
confusing scenes of battle.

wd Michael Powell, Emeric Pressburger
ph Christopher Challis m Brian Easdale

John Gregson, Anthony Quayle, Peter Finch, Bernard Lee, Ian Hunter, Jack Gwillim, Lionel Murton, Anthony Bushell, Peter Illing

'It is difficult to understand how English film-makers can have done thus badly with material so apt to their gifts.'—*Stanley Kauffmann*

The Battle of the Sexes*
GB 1960   83m   bw
Prometheus (Monja Danischewsky)

A lady efficiency expert upsets the even tenor of life at an Edinburgh tweed manufactory, and the chief accountant plans to eliminate her.
Sub-Ealing black comedy which tends to misfire despite effort all round.

w Monja Danischewsky, from James Thurber's story The Catbird Seat *d* Charles Crichton *ph* Freddie Francis *m* Stanley Black

Peter Sellers, Constance Cummings, Robert Morley, Jameson Clark, Moultrie Kelsall, Alex Mackenzie, Roddy McMillan, Donald Pleasance, Ernest Thesiger

The Battle of the V1
GB 1958   109m   bw
Maynard–Sewell (George Maynard)
US titles: *Unseen Heroes; Missiles from Hell*

Polish patriots sabotage the German rocket installation at Peenemunde.
Effective though schoolboyish war adventure shot on a low budget: story development reasonably brisk though predictable.

w Jack Hanley, Eryk Wlodek, *book* Bernard Newman *d* Vernon Sewell *ph* Basil Emmott *m* Robert Sharples

Michael Rennie, Patricia Medina, Milly Vitale, David Knight, Esmond Knight, Christopher Lee

The Battle of the Villa Fiorita
GB 1964   111m   Technicolor   Panavision
Warner (Delmer Daves)
US title: *Affair at the Villa Fiorita*

Two children aim to break up their mother's romance with an Italian concert pianist.
Quite lively, old-fashioned romantic comedy-drama largely set in a splendid Mediterranean villa; happy ending never in doubt.

wd Delmer Daves, *novel* Rumer Godden *ph* Oswald Morris *m* Mischa Spoliansky

Maureen O'Hara, Rossano Brazzi, Richard Todd, Phyllis Calvert, Olivia Hussey, Martin Stephens, Elizabeth Dear

Battleground*
US 1949   118m   bw
MGM (Dore Schary)

How a group of American soldiers in 1944 endured the Battle of the Bulge.
Enormously successful at the box office, this studio-bound production now seems stilted and unpersuasive, despite some good writing and direction.

w Robert Pirosh *d* William Wellman *ph* Paul C. Vogel *m* Lennie Hayton

Van Johnson, John Hodiak, Ricardo Montalban, George Murphy, Marshall Thompson, Jerome Courtland, Don Taylor, Bruce Cowling, James Whitmore, Douglas Fowley, Leon Ames

'Engrossingly well done.'—*Richard Mallett, Punch*

AA: Robert Pirosh; Paul C. Vogel
AAN: best picture; William Wellman; James Whitmore

The Battleship Potemkin****
USSR 1925   75m approx (16 fps)   silent;
            sound version 65m
Goskino
original title: *Bronenosets Potemkin*

An account of the mutiny at Odessa, an episode in the 1905 revolution. (The film was made as part of the 20th anniversary celebrations.)
A textbook cinema classic, and masterpiece of creative editing, especially in the famous Odessa Steps sequence in which innocent civilians are mown down in the bloodshed; the happenings of a minute are drawn into five by frenzied cross-cutting. The film contains 1,300 separate shots, and was judged the best film ever made in 1948 and 1958 by a panel of international judges.

wd Sergei Eisenstein *ph* Edouard Tissé, V. Popov

A. Antonov, Grigori Alexandrov, Vladimir Barsky, Levshin

Battling Butler*
US 1926   68m approx (24 fps)   bw   silent
MGM

A young millionaire pretends to be a boxer in order to win a sweetheart.
Middling star comedy.

w Al Boasberg, Charles Smith, Paul Gerard Smith, Lex Neal *d* Buster Keaton

Buster Keaton, Sally O'Neil

The Bawdy Adventures of Tom Jones
GB 1976   94m   Technicolor
Universal / Robert Sadoff

See *Tom Jones*, of which this is a musical version.

Not quite as bad as one would expect, but not up to the original.

w Jeremy Lloyd, *play* Don McPherson *songs* Paul Holden *d* Cliff Owen *ph* Douglas Slocombe *m* Ron Grainer

Nicky Henson, Trevor Howard, Terry-Thomas, Arthur Lowe, Georgia Brown, Joan Collins, William Mervyn, Murray Melvin, Geraldine McEwan, Michael Bates, James Hayter, Isabel Dean, Gladys Henson

Baxter*

GB 1972   100m   Technicolor
(EMI) Performing Arts (Arthur Lewis)

An American son of divorced parents comes to London with his mother, meets tragedy in the shape of a friend's death, and responds to treatment for a speech defect.
Slight, appealing case history of a maladjusted 12-year-old; a rather unnecessarily uncommercial slice of life with no easy solution offered.

w Reginald Rose *d* Lionel Jeffries *ph* Geoffrey Unsworth *m* Michael J. Lewis

Patricia Neal (as the therapist), Scott Jacoby, Britt Ekland, Jean-Pierre Cassel, Lynn Carlin, Paul Eddington

Beach Party*

US 1963   104m   Pathecolor   Panavision
AIP / Alta Vista (James H. Nicholson)

An anthropologist sets up house on a California beach to study the mating habits of young people but becomes personally involved when one of them falls for him.
Vaguely satirical pop musical with relaxed performances; quite tolerable in itself, it started an excruciating trend.

w Lou Rusoff *d* William Asher *ph* Kay Norton *m* Les Baxter

Robert Cummings, Dorothy Malone, Annette Funicello, Frankie Avalon, Vincent Price, Harvey Lembeck, Morey Amsterdam, Jody McCrea

Beach Red*

US 1967   105m   Technicolor
UA / Theodora (Cornel Wilde)

In 1943, American assault craft take a Jap-held Pacific island.
Brutal, pacifist war film, simply and clearly portrayed but not exactly entertaining.

w Clint Johnston, Donald A. Peters, Jefferson Pascal *d* Cornel Wilde *ph* Cecil R. Cooney *m* Antonio Buenaventura

Cornel Wilde, Rip Torn, Burr de Benning, Jean Wallace

The Beachcomber*

GB 1954   90m   Technicolor
GFD / London Independent (William MacQuitty)

An alcoholic ne'er-do-well in the Dutch East Indies reforms after an unexpected adventure with a lady missionary.
Styleless remake of *Vessel of Wrath* (qv); the acting just about holds the interest, but all other contributions are flat.

w Sydney Box, from Somerset Maugham's story *d* Muriel Box *ph* Reg Wyer *m* Francis Chagrin

Robert Newton, Glynis Johns, Donald Sinden, Paul Rogers, Donald Pleasance, Walter Crisham, Michael Hordern, Ronald Lewis

Bear Country see The Living Desert

The Bears and I

US 1974   89m   Technicolor
Walt Disney (Winston Hibler)

An army veteran goes to live near an Indian settlement and adopts three bear cubs, later becoming a Park Ranger.
Simple, pleasing outdoor family film.

w John Whedon, *novel* Robert Franklin Leslie *d* Bernard McEveety *ph* Ted D. Landon *m* Buddy Baker

Patrick Wayne, Chief Dan George, Andrew Duggan, Michael Ansara

The Beast from Twenty Thousand Fathoms

US 1953   80m   bw
Warner (Hal Chester, Jack Dietz)

Heat generated by an atomic bomb test in the Arctic thaws out a prehistoric rhedosaurus which travels down the American coast to cause havoc in New York until cornered and destroyed on Coney Island.
Flat-footed addition to the monster cycle, with an interminable wait for the beast's appearance and inferior trick work when he goes on the rampage.

w Lou Morheim, Fred Freiburger *d* Eugène Lourié *ph* Jack Russell *m* David Buttolph *sp* Ray Harryhausen

Paul Christian, Paula Raymond, Cecil Kellaway (as a professor gobbled up in a bathysphere), Kenneth Tobey, Donald Woods, Lee Van Cleef

The Beast in the Cellar

GB 1970   87m   Eastmancolor
Tigon-Leander (Tony Tenser, Graham Harris)

A rampaging killer in the Lancashire woods

turns out to be the deranged ex-soldier brother of two elderly spinsters who have kept him locked up for thirty years.
Idiotically boring farrago, totally lacking in suspense and wasting good talent.

wd James Kelly *ph* Harry Waxman, Desmond Dickinson *m* Tony Macaulay

Flora Robson, Beryl Reid, Tessa Wyatt, John Hamill, T. P. McKenna

The Beast Must Die*
GB 1974 93m Technicolor
BL / Amicus (Milton Subotsky)

A millionaire big game hunter holds a weekend party to track down a werewolf, but his guest list rapidly gets smaller . . .
A savage variation on *Ten Little Niggers*, not badly done, with such gimmicks as a 'guess who' break near the end.

w Michael Winder, *story* James Blish *d* Paul Annett *ph* Jack Hildyard *m* Douglas Gamley

Calvin Lockhart, Peter Cushing, Charles Gray, Anton Diffring, Marlene Clark, Ciaran Madden, Michael Gambon

Beast of the City
US 1932 80m bw
MGM

A police captain is determined to get a ruthless racketeer by fair means or foul.
Curiously dour little crime melodrama with a high death rate; the cast does not quite save it.

w John Lee Mahin, *story* W. R. Burnett *d* Charles Brabin *ph* Barney McGill

Walter Huston, Jean Harlow, Wallace Ford, Jean Hersholt, Dorothy Petersen, Tully Marshall, John Miljan
  'Endowed with vitality and realism.'—*New York Times*

The Beast with Five Fingers*
US 1946 88m bw
Warner (William Jacobs)

A famous pianist dies and his severed hand returns to commit murder.
Slow-moving, Italian-set horror thriller which wastes an excellent original; a superb central performance and clever trick effects can hardly redeem the stodgy script or the ending which reveals the hauntings as an hallucination.

w Curt Siodmak, *story* W. F. Harvey *d* Robert Florey *ph* Wesley Anderson *m* Max Steiner

Peter Lorre, Andrea King, Robert Alda, J. Carrol Naish, Victor Francen, Charles Dingle

The Beat Generation
US 1959 95m bw Cinemascope
Albert Zugsmith
aka: *This Rebel Age*

A vicious rapist joins the beatniks.
Bankrupt exploitation melodrama, not easy to sit through.

w Richard Matheson, Lewis Meltzer *d* Charles Haas *ph* Walter H. Castle *m* Albert Glasser

Ray Danton, Steve Cochran, Fay Spain, Mamie Van Doren, Jackie Coogan, Louis Armstrong, Maggie Hayes, Jim Mitchum, Irish McCalla, Maxie Rosenbloom
  'An enervating mixture of slapstick, religiosity, psychological hokum and grubby sensationalism.'—*MFB*

Beat the Devil*
GB 1953 100m bw
Romulus / Santana (Jack Clayton)

In a small Mediterranean port, and subsequently on a boat bound for the African coast, oddly assorted travellers plan to acquire land known to contain uranium deposits.
Unsatisfactory, over-talkative and inconsequential burlesque of the director's own *The Maltese Falcon* and *Across the Pacific*. Good fun was obviously had by the cast, but audiences were mostly baffled by the in-jokes, the extra-strange characters, and the lack of attention to pace, suspense and plot development.

w Truman Capote, John Huston, *novel* James Helvick *d* John Huston *ph* Oswald Morris *m* Franco Mannino

Humphrey Bogart, Gina Lollobrigida, Jennifer Jones, *Edward Underdown*, Peter Lorre, Robert Morley, *Ivor Barnard*, Bernard Lee
  'A potential treat emerged as a wet firecracker . . . the incidents remain on a naggingly arch and lagging verbal keel.'—*New York Times*
  'Each of its cinematic clichés appears to be placed in the very faintest of mocking quotation marks.'—*Time*

Beau Brummell*
GB 1954 111m Eastmancolor
MGM (Sam Zimbalist)

A Regency dandy enjoys a close relationship with the Prince of Wales, and when this is eventually withdrawn he dies in penury.
Stodgy historical romance with entertaining patches; the main story is too graceful and conventional to be believed.

w Karl Tunberg, *play* Clyde Fitch *d* Curtis Bernhardt *ph* Oswald Morris *m* Richard Addinsell *ad* Alfred Junge

Stewart Granger, Elizabeth Taylor, *Peter Ustinov* (as the Prince), *Robert Morley* (as George III), James Donald, James Hayter, Rosemary Harris, Paul Rogers, Noel Willman, Peter Bull, Peter Dyneley

Beau Geste **

US 1926   120m approx (24 fps)   bw
  (colour sequences)   silent
Paramount (Herbert Brenon)

Three English brothers join the Foreign Legion, suffer under a brutal sergeant, and die fighting the Arabs.

Although outmoded even when first filmed, this tale of derring-do and self sacrifice usually works, and in this case it gave its star a fresh image. One of the best remembered silents of the twenties.

w Paul Schofield, *novel* P. C. Wren *d* Herbert Brenon *ph* Roy Hunt *ad* Julian Boone Fleming

Ronald Colman, Neil Hamilton, Ralph Forbes, Alice Joyce, Mary Brian, *Noah Beery*, William Powell, Victor McLaglen

† Remade 1939 and 1966; sequel, *Beau Ideal,* 1931.

Beau Geste **

US 1939   120m   bw
Paramount (William Wellman)

Spirited remake, with the famous flashback opening of the desert fort defended by corpses. Style and acting generally satisfactory.

w Robert Carson *d* William Wellman
ph Theodor Sparkuhl, Archie Stout *m* Alfred Newman

Gary Cooper, Ray Milland, Robert Preston, *Brian Donlevy, J. Carrol Naish*

AAN: Brian Donlevy

Beau Geste

US 1966   105m   Techniscope
Universal (Walter Seltzer)

The central desert section of the story is here augmented, with violence stressed, and Beau allowed to survive at the end.

A cheap leery melodrama is what results from the jettisoning of all the romantic portions of the original.

wd Douglas Heyes *ph* Bud Thackery *m* Hans Salter

Telly Savalas (rampant as the sadistic sergeant), Guy Stockwell, Doug McClure, Leslie Nielsen, Leon Gordon, Michael Constantine

Beau Ideal

US 1931   75m   bw
RKO (William Le Baron)

John Geste and a new legionnaire friend become involved in a religious war started by a rascally emir.

Lame sequel to *Beau Geste*, fettered by primitive dialogue.

w Paul Schofield, *novel* P. C. Wren *d* Herbert Brenon
ph J. Roy Hunt

Lester Vail, Ralph Forbes, Don Alvarado, Loretta Young, Irene Rich

Beau James *

US 1957   107m   Technicolor   Vistavision
Paramount / Hope Enterprises (Jack Rose)

The vaguely crooked career of Jimmy Walker, mayor of New York in the twenties.

Romanticized biopic with few funny moments: Hope cannot cope with the drama, and the result is a creaking vehicle apart from a well-recreated twenties atmosphere and excellent production values.

w Jack Rose, Melville Shavelson, *book* Gene Fowler *d* Melville Shavelson *ph* John F. Warren

Bob Hope, Paul Douglas, Vera Miles, Alexis Smith, Darren McGavin, Joe Mantell, Walter Catlett *guest stars* Jack Benny, George Jessel, Jimmy Durante *narrator* Alistair Cooke

Le Beau Serge *

France 1958   97m   bw
AYJM (Jean Cotet)

A student returns to his home town and tries to redeem his old friend who has become a drunkard.

Enjoyable character drama with well observed village backgrounds. Credited with being the spearhead of the 'new wave'.

wd Claude Chabrol ph Henri Decaë m Emile Delpierre

Gérard Blain, Jean-Claude Brialy, Michèle Meritz, Bernadette Lafont

La Beauté du Diable ***

Italy / France 1949   96m   bw
AYJM

The Faust story with the protagonists agreeing to change places.

Dazzling plot twists and cinematic virtuosity make this a richly enjoyable fantasy, though perhaps not among Clair's greatest works.

w René Clair, Armand Salacrou *d René Clair*

ph Michel Kelber *m* Roman Vlad *ad* Léon Barsacq

Michel Simon, Gérard Philipe, Raymond Cordy, Nicole Besnard, Gaston Modot, Paolo Stoppa

The Beautiful Blonde from Bashful Bend*
US 1949 77m Technicolor
TCF (Preston Sturges)

A temperamental saloon entertainer accidentally shoots the sheriff and takes refuge as a schoolmistress.
A dishevelled western farce unworthy of its creator, but with the advantage of appearances by many of his usual repertory of players.

wd Preston Sturges *ph* Harry Jackson *m* Cyril Mockridge

Betty Grable, Cesar Romero, El Brendel, Hugh Herbert, Rudy Vallee, Olga San Juan, Sterling Holloway, Porter Hall, Esther Howard, Margaret Hamilton
   'She's got the biggest six-shooters in the west!'—*publicity*
   'It erects a fabric of roaring slapstick on a conventional western foundation, and from time to time it succeeds in being very funny.'—*Richard Mallett, Punch*
   'Somehow the ramshackle air of Bashful Bend itself seems to have permeated the whole film.'—*MFB*

Beautiful Stranger
GB 1954 89m bw
Maxwell Setton, John R. Sloan
US title: *Twist of Fate*

On the Riviera, an actress discovers that her fiancé is a criminal.
Tawdry star melodrama of virtually no interest.

w Robert Westerby, Carl Nystrom *d* David Miller *ph* Robert Day, Ted Scaife *m* Malcolm Arnold

Ginger Rogers, Jacques Bergerac, Herbert Lom, Stanley Baker, Margaret Rawlings, Eddie Byrne, Coral Browne

The Beauty Jungle*
GB 1964 114m Eastmancolor
   Cinemascope
Rank / Val Guest
US title: *Contest Girl*

A typist enters a beauty contest and step by step becomes Miss Globe; but her descent is equally rapid.
Wicked show biz and the road to ruin in one glossy package, predictable, but not badly done; always something going on, and performed with gusto.

w Robert Muller, Val Guest *d* Val Guest *ph* Arthur Grant *m* Laurie Johnson

Janette Scott, Ian Hendry, Ronald Fraser, Edmund Purdom, Kay Walsh, Norman Bird, Janina Faye, Tommy Trinder, Francis Matthews

Because of Him*
US 1946 88m bw
U-I

A waitress pesters a Broadway author and actor for a leading role in their new show.
Moderately sprightly star vehicle with bonuses in the leading men; handling disappointingly routine.

w Edmund Beloin *d* Richard Wallace *ph* Hal Mohr

Deanna Durbin, Charles Laughton, Franchot Tone
† A remake of *The Good Fairy*.

Because of You
US 1952 95m bw
U-I (Albert J. Cohen)

A female ex-convict marries on parole but does not tell her husband of her past. Her old associates involve her innocently in another crime, and her husband divorces her; but years later she gets him and their child back.
Soap opera of the stickiest kind, made quite tolerable by good production.

w Ketti Frings *d* Joseph Pevney *ph* Russell Metty *m* Frank Skinner

Loretta Young, Jeff Chandler, Alex Nicol, Frances Dee, Lynne Roberts, Alexander Scourby, Mae Clarke
   'Shows the most whole-hearted devotion to woman's magazine conventions.'—*MFB*

Because They're Young
US 1960 98m bw
Columbia / Drexel (Jerry Bresler)

A high school teacher helps one of his tougher pupils not to slip into crime.
Routine sentimental melodrama, slightly redeemed by directorial expertise.

w James Gunn, *novel* Harrison High by John Farris *d* Paul Wendkos *ph* Wilfrid Cline *m* Johnny Williams

Dick Clark, Michael Callan, Tuesday Weld, Victoria Shaw, Warren Berlinger, Doug McClure

Because You're Mine
US 1952 103m Technicolor
MGM (Joe Pasternak)

An opera singer becomes a GI and wins the sergeant's sister.

Lumberingly inept star vehicle, giving the impression of nothing at all happening between the songs.

w Leonard Spiegelgass, Karl Tunberg *d* Alexander Hall *ph* Joseph Ruttenberg *md* Johnny Green

Mario Lanza, Doretta Morrow, James Whitmore, Dean Miller, Paula Corday, Jeff Donnell, Spring Byington

AAN: title song (*m* Nicholas Brodszky, *ly* Sammy Cahn)

Becket****
GB 1964 149m Technicolor Panavision
Paramount / Hal B. Wallis

Henry II leans on his boisterous Saxon friend Thomas à Becket, but when the latter is made first chancellor and then archbishop a rift between them widens and ends in Becket's assassination by Henry's over-eager knights. Jean Anouilh's bitter stage comedy is filmed literally and soberly as a rather anaemic epic, so that the point is lost and the edge blunted. The paucity of physical action causes good scenes to alternate with long stretches of tedium.

w Edward Anhalt *d* Peter Glenville *ph Geoffrey Unsworth m* Laurence Rosenthal

Richard Burton, Peter O'Toole, Donald Wolfit, *John Gielgud*, Martita Hunt, Pamela Brown, Sian Phillips, Paolo Stoppa
   'Handsome, respectable and boring.'—*John Simon*

AA: Edward Anhalt
AAN: best picture; Peter Glenville; Geoffrey Unsworth; Laurence Rosenthal; Richard Burton; Peter O'Toole; John Gielgud

Becky Sharp****
US 1935 83m Technicolor
(RKO) Kenneth MacGowan

An ambitious girl makes her way into Regency society.

Chiefly notable as the first feature in three-colour Technicolor, this rather theatrical piece has its civilized enjoyments and the director made a few predictable cinematic experiments; the overall effect, however, is patchy.

w Francis Edward Faragoh, *play* Landon Mitchell, *novel* Vanity Fair by W. M. Thackeray *d Rouben Mamoulian ph Ray Rennahan m* Roy Webb *pd Robert Edmond Jones*

Miriam Hopkins, *Cedric Hardwicke*, Frances Dee, Billie Burke, Alison Skipworth, Nigel

Bruce, Alan Mowbray, Colin Tapley, G. P. Huntley Jnr
   'As pleasing to the eye as a fresh fruit sundae, but not much more.'—*Otis Ferguson*
AAN: Miriam Hopkins

The Bed Sitting Room*
GB 1969 91m De Luxe
UA / Oscar Lewenstein (Richard Lester)

Surrealist romance; after a nuclear war, motley survivors in the waste lands turn into bed sitting rooms, cupboards and parakeets.

Arrogantly obscure fantasy, a commercial flop which kept its director in the wilderness for four years. Fans of Monty Python may salvage a joke or two.

w John Antrobus, from the play by himself and Spike Milligan *d* Richard Lester *ph* David Watkin *m* Ken Thorne *pd* Assheton Gorton

Ralph Richardson, Rita Tushingham, Michael Hordern, Arthur Lowe, Mona Washbourne, Peter Cook, Dudley Moore, Spike Milligan, Harry Secombe, Marty Feldman, Jimmy Edwards

Bedazzled*
GB 1968 96m De Luxe Panavision
TCF / Stanley Donen

A short order cook is saved from suicide by Mr Spiggott, who offers him seven wishes in exchange for his soul.

A camped-up version of Faust which resolves itself into a series of threadbare sketches for the stars. All rather desperate apart from the leaping nuns.

w Peter Cook *d* Stanley Donen *ph* Austin Dempster *m* Dudley Moore

Peter Cook, Dudley Moore, Michael Bates, Raquel Welch, Eleanor Bron

Bedelia
GB 1946 90m bw
John Corfield (Isadore Goldsmith)

A psychotic woman is discovered to have poisoned three husbands.

Dreary upper-class British murder drama, totally devoid of style or suspense but a big star hit of the time.

w Vera Caspary, Moie Charles, Herbert Victor, Roy Ridley, Isadore Goldsmith, *novel* Vera Caspary *d* Lance Comfort

Margaret Lockwood, Ian Hunter, Barry K. Barnes, Anne Crawford, Jill Esmond, Ellen Pollock

Bedevilled
US 1955   86m   Eastmancolor
Cinemascope
MGM (Henry Berman)

In Paris, a novice priest befriends a girl on the run from gangsters. She turns out to be a murderess and is shot by her victim's brother.
Absurd high-flown bosh, unsuitably cinemascoped in ugly colour, and surprisingly badly handled by old professionals.

w Jo Eisinger d Mitchell Leisen ph Frederick A. Young m William Alwyn

Anne Baxter, Steve Forrest, Simone Renant, Victor Francen, Maurice Teynac, Joseph Tomelty
   'This mixture of melodrama and religion provides a most unedifying entertainment.'—
MFB

The Bedford Incident***
GB 1965   102m   bw
Columbia / Bedford Productions (James B. Harris)

A ruthlessly efficient US destroyer captain in the Arctic chases a Russian submarine and accidentally fires an atomic weapon.
Gripping mixture of themes from *Dr Strangelove* and *The Caine Mutiny*, very tense and forceful, with excellent acting.

w James Poe, novel Mark Rascovitch d James B. Harris ph Gilbert Taylor m Gerald Schurrmann

Richard Widmark, Sidney Poitier (his first role with no reference to his colour), James MacArthur, Eric Portman, Wally Cox, Martin Balsam, Phil Brown, Michael Kane, Garry Cockrell, Donald Sutherland
   'Strong on virtues of a rather negative kind.'—
Penelope Houston

Bedknobs and Broomsticks
US 1971   117m   Technicolor
Walt Disney (Bill Walsh)

In 1940 three evacuee children and a kindly witch ride on a magic bedstead and defeat the invasion of England.
Extraordinarily dishevelled and incompetent Disney follow-up to *Mary Poppins*, a very muddled narrative with few high points and evidence of much cutting. Redeemed occasionally by camera trickery.

w Bill Walsh, Don DaGradi d Robert Stevenson ph Frank Philips m/ly Richard M. Sherman, Robert B. Sherman sp Eustace Lycett, Alan Maley, Danny Lee

Angela Lansbury, David Tomlinson, Roy Smart, Cindy O'Callaghan, Sam Jaffe, Roddy McDowall, Bruce Forsyth, Tessie O'Shea, Reginald Owen

AAN: Richard M. Sherman, Robert B. Sherman; song 'The Age of Not Believing' by the Shermans

Bedlam**
US 1946   80m · bw
RKO (*Val Lewton*)

In 18th-century London, a sane girl is confined by the malevolent asylum master.
Interesting but rather flatly handled addition to the Val Lewton gallery of horrors, perhaps too carefully and discreetly done for pace or suspense.

w Mark Robson, Carlos Keith d Mark Robson ph Nicholas Musuraca m Roy Webb

Boris Karloff, Anna Lee, Billy House, Richard Fraser, Glenn Vernon

Bedtime for Bonzo
US 1951   83m   bw
U-I (Michael Kraike)

To prove that environment determines character, a chimpanzee is brought up as a human baby.
Very moderate fun and games which proved successful enough for a sequel, *Bonzo Goes to College.*

w Val Burton, Lou Breslow d Frederick de Cordova ph Carl Guthrie m Frank Skinner

Ronald Reagan, Diana Lynn, Walter Slezak, Lucille Berkely, Herbert Heyes

A Bedtime Story*
US 1933   89m   bw
Paramount (Emmanuel Cohen)

A breezy Frenchman has to interrupt his romances to look after an abandoned baby.
Mild star vehicle in which the agreeable comedy is largely supplanted by sentimental cooing.

w Benjamin Glazer, *novel* Bellamy the Magnificent by Roy Horniman d Norman Taurog ph Charles Lang songs Ralph Rainger, Leo Robin

Maurice Chevalier, Helen Twelvetrees, Baby LeRoy, Edward Everett Horton, Adrienne Ames

Bedtime Story*
US 1941   85m   bw
Columbia (B. P. Schulberg)

A playwright's wife wants to retire instead of acting in his next play.
Pleasantly sparkling comedy with good performances.

w Horace Jackson, Grant Garrett, Richard

Flournoy *d* Alexander Hall *ph* Joseph Walker

Fredric March, Loretta Young, Robert
Benchley, Allyn Joslyn, Eve Arden, Helen
Westley, Joyce Compton, Tim Ryan

Bedtime Story*
US 1964   99m   Eastmancolor
U-I / Lankershim / Pennebaker (Stanley
Shapiro)

Two Riviera confidence tricksters outwit each
other.
A fairly lively script is defeated by dull handling,
but performances and backgrounds are
attractive.

w Stanley Shapiro, Paul Henning *d* Ralph Levy
ph Clifford Stine *m* Hans Salter

David Niven, Marlon Brando, Shirley Jones,
Dody Goodman, Aram Stephan, Marie Windsor

Before Hindsight**
GB 1977   78m   Eastmancolor
Elizabeth Taylor-Mead

Interviews and clips show how inadequately
cinema newsreels covered world events in the
1930s.
Hard tack for entertainment seekers, but a clear
exposition of a proven case of importance to
film-makers and politicians.

w Elizabeth Taylor-Mead *d* Jonathan Lewis
'Certainly not the kind of picture people will
pay money to see.'—*Variety*

Before I Hang*
US 1940   71m   bw
Columbia

A research scientist experiments with a new
serum which turns him into a murderer.
Archetypal Karloff mad doctor flick, Jekyll and
Hyde model: still quite tolerable.

w Robert D. Andrews *d* Nick Grinde
ph Benjamin Kline

Boris Karloff, Evelyn Keyes, Bruce Bennett,
Pedro de Cordoba, Edward Van Sloan, Don
Beddoe

Before Winter Comes*
GB 1968   107m   Technicolor
Columbia / Windward (Robert Emmett
Ginna)

Austria 1945: a British major in charge of
displaced persons is helped and hindered by a
cheerful Yugoslav refugee who turns out to be a
Russian deserter.
Likeable, well-produced drama hampered by a
plot which becomes unnecessarily schematic.

coincidental and downbeat in its attempts to tug
at the heartstrings.

w Andrew Sinclair, *novel* The Interpreter by
Frederick L. Keefe *d* J. Lee-Thompson
ph Gilbert Taylor *m* Ron Grainer

David Niven, Topol, Ori Levi, Anna Karina,
John Hurt, Anthony Quayle
'One of those films with a message on every
page of its script.'—*MFB*

The Beggar's Opera**
GB 1952   94m   Technicolor
British Lion / Imperadio (Herbert Wilcox,
Laurence Olivier)

A highwayman in Newgate jail devises an opera
based on his own exploits.
Exuberant potted version of the 1728 low opera,
generally likeable but lacking a strong coherent
approach and marred by violent colour and
raggedly theatrical presentation. It nearly but
not quite comes off.

w Dennis Cannan, Christopher Fry, *opera* John
Gay *d* Peter Brook *ph* Guy Green *ad* George
Wakhevitch, William C. Andrews *musical
arrangement and additions* Arthur Bliss

Laurence Olivier, Stanley Holloway, Dorothy
Tutin, Daphne Anderson, Mary Clare, George
Devine, Athene Seyler, Hugh Griffith, Margot
Grahame, Sandra Dorne, Laurence Naismith
'The failure is equalled only by the
ambition.'—*Gavin Lambert*

The Beginning or the End
US 1947   112m   bw
MGM (Samuel Marx)

During World War II American scientists
continue to perfect the atom bomb despite their
own misgivings, and one dies in an explosion.
Semi-documentary marred by sentimental
personal asides and of very little continuing
interest.

w Robert Considine *d* Norman Taurog *ph* Ray
June

Brian Donlevy, Robert Walker, Tom Drake,
Beverly Tyler, Hume Cronyn, Audrey Totter,
Godfrey Tearle (as Roosevelt)

The Beguiled*
US 1971   109m   Technicolor
Universal / Malpaso (Don Siegel)

A wounded Unionist soldier hides out in a
Confederate ladies' school; the teachers fend for
him until he causes trouble among the sexually
frustrated women, who eventually kill him.
Eccentric melodrama which does not really
work despite its credentials and patient work all
round.

w John B. Sherry, Grimes Grice, *novel* Thomas Cullinan *d* Don Siegel *ph* Bruce Surtees *m* Lalo Schifrin *pd* Ted Haworth

Clint Eastwood, Geraldine Page, Elizabeth Hartman, Jo Ann Harris, Darleen Carr, Mae Mercer

'A must for sadists and woman-haters.'— *Judith Crist*

Behave Yourself*
US 1951   81m   bw
RKO (Jerry Wald, Norman Krasna)

A young married couple and their dog get mixed up in a chain of murders.
Zany black comedy in the wake of *A Slight Case of Murder* and *The Thin Man*. The humour is spread too thin for success.

wd George Beck *ph* James Wong Howe *m* Leigh Harline

Farley Granger, Shelley Winters, William Demarest, Francis L. Sullivan, Margalo Gillmore, Lon Chaney, Hans Conried, Elisha Cook Jnr

Behind the High Wall
US 1956   85m   bw
U-I (Stanley Rubin)

A prison warder, taken as hostage by escaping convicts, steals some of the money they have taken.
Glum melodrama, capably presented.

w Harold Jack Bloom *d* Abner Biberman *ph* Maury Gertsman *m* Joseph Gershenson

Tom Tully, Sylvia Sidney, John Gavin, Betty Lynn, John Larch, Barney Phillips, Don Beddoe

Behind the Mask*
GB 1958   99m   Eastmancolor
BL / GW Films (Sergei Nolbandov, Josef Somlo)

Political infighting causes tension on the board of a local hospital.
Oddly titled social drama with interesting detail but not much tension or conclusion.

w John Hunter, *novel* The Pack by John Rowan Wilson *d* Brian Desmond Hurst *ph* Robert Krasker *m* Geoffrey Wright

Michael Redgrave, Tony Britton, Carl Mohner, Niall MacGinnis, Vanessa Redgrave, Ian Bannen, Brenda Bruce, Lionel Jeffries, Miles Malleson, John Welsh, Ann Firbank

Behind the Rising Sun*
US 1943   88m   bw
RKO

An American-educated Japanese goes home in the thirties, comes under the influence of warmongers, and causes his father to commit hara-kiri.
Outrageous wartime flagwaver designed to vilify 'Uncle Tojo's dogs', from the writer and director of the similar *Hitler's Children* (qv).

w Emmet Lavery *d* Edward Dmytryk *ph* Russell Metty *m* Roy Webb

J. Carrol Naish, Tom Neal, Margo, Robert Ryan, Gloria Holden, Don Douglas, Adeline de Walt Reynolds

Behold a Pale Horse*
US 1964   121m   bw
Columbia / Highland / Brentwood (Fred Zinnemann, Alexander Trauner)

A Spanish guerrilla goes into exile at the end of the Civil War. Twenty years later he is persuaded to return and kill a brutal police chief.
An action film which unfortunately insists on saying something significant about morality, destiny and death. Impeccably made, but somehow not very interesting apart from the action sequences.

w J. P. Miller, *novel* Killing a Mouse on Sunday by Emeric Pressburger *d* Fred Zinnemann *ph* Jean Badal *m* Maurice Jarre *ad* Alexander Trauner

Gregory Peck, Omar Sharif, Anthony Quinn, Raymond Pellegrin, Paolo Stoppa, Mildred Dunnock, Daniela Rocca, Christian Marquand
'A fine example of a high class failure.'— *Judith Crist*

Behold My Wife
US 1934   79m   bw
Paramount (B. P. Schulberg)

A wealthy young man brings back and marries a New Mexico Indian girl to show up his snobbish family.
Dated melodrama, of interest solely for its racial theme.

w William R. Lippman, Oliver LaFarge, *novel* The Translation of a Savage by Sir Gilbert Parker *d* Mitchell Leisen *ph* Leon Shamroy

Sylvia Sidney, Gene Raymond, Juliette Compton, Laura Hope Crews, H. B. Warner, Monroe Owsley, Ann Sheridan

Believe in Me
US 1971   90m   colour
MGM (Irwin Winkler, Robert Chartoff)

Two young marrieds take to drugs.
Tedious and unenlightening modern drama which seems to think it's saying something new.

w Israel Horowitz *d* Stuart Hagmann

Michael Sarrazin, Jacqueline Bisset, Jon Cypher, Allen Garfield

Bell, Book and Candle*
US 1958 103m Technicolor
Columbia / Phoenix (Julian Blaustein)

A publisher slowly becomes aware that his new girl friend is a witch.
A gossamer stage comedy has been fatally flattened in translation; most of the actors are miscast, and sentiment soaks the script. But it remains a civilized entertainment.

w Daniel Taradash, play John Van Druten d Richard Quine ph James Wong Howe m George Duning

James Stewart, Kim Novak, Jack Lemmon, Ernie Kovacs, Hermione Gingold, Elsa Lanchester, Janice Rule

A Bell for Adano*
US 1945 104m bw
TCF (Louis D. Lighton, Lamar Trotti)

An American major takes over an Italian town and wins affection by replacing the local bell.
Slight end-of-war mood piece, still quite pleasant but without the undercurrents of feeling it had at the time.

w Lamar Trotti, Norman Reilly Raine, novel John Hersey d Henry King ph Joseph La Shelle m Alfred Newman

John Hodiak, Gene Tierney, William Bendix, Glenn Langan, Richard Conte, Stanley Prager, Henry Morgan

The Bellboy*
US 1960 72m bw
Paramount / Jerry Lewis Productions (Jerry Lewis)

An incompetent bellboy causes havoc in a Miami hotel.
Plotless essence of a comedian who divides opinion and will never be better than variable.
This ragbag of old gags at least prevents his usual sentimental excesses, and is mercifully short.

wd Jerry Lewis ph Haskell Boggs m Walter Scharf

Jerry Lewis, Alex Gerry, Bob Clayton, Herkie Styles, Milton Berle

Belle de Jour***
France / Italy 1967 100m Eastmancolor
Paris Film / Five Film (Robert and Raymond Hakim)

A surgeon's wife finds herself drawn to afternoon work in a brothel.

Fascinating Bunuel mixture of fact and fantasy, impeccably woven into a rich fabric.

w Luis Bunuel, Jean-Claude Carrière d Luis Bunuel ph Sacha Vierny m none

Catherine Deneuve, Jean Sorel, Michel Piccoli, Genevieve Page, Pierre Clémenti

La Belle Equipe*
France 1936 74m bw
Ciné Arts

Five unemployed Parisians win the lottery and open a restaurant, but things do not go smoothly.
Interesting but rather lumpy star drama which finally descends into melodrama; alternative tragic and happy endings were originally offered.

w Charles Spaak, Julien Duvivier d Julien Duvivier ph Jules Kruger, Marc Fessard m Maurice Yvain

Jean Gabin, Charles Vanel, Viviane Romance, Raymond Aimes, Robert Lynen, Raymond Cordy, Raphael Medina

La Belle et la Bête**
France 1946 95m bw
André Paulvé

Beauty gives herself to the Beast who has kidnapped her father; through love the monster turns into a handsome prince.
Slightly heavy-handed though usually stunning-looking adaptation of the fairy tale.

wd Jean Cocteau ph Henri Alekan m Georges Auric ad Christian Bérard

Jean Marais, Josette Day, Mila Parély, Marcel André, Michel Auclair

Belle le Grand
US 1951 89m bw
Republic

The proprietress of a Barbary Coast gambling house is plagued by an ex-husband on whose account she served a prison term.
Confused and incompetent period melodrama.

w D. D. Beauchamp d Allan Dwan ph Reggie Lanning m Victor Young

Vera Ralston, John Carroll, William Ching, Hope Emerson, Stephen Chase, Grant Withers, John Qualen

The Belle of New York*
US 1952 82m Technicolor
MGM (Arthur Freed)

A nineties playboy falls for a Salvation Army girl.
A rather dreary version of the old musical, with undistinguished additions.

w Robert O'Brien, Irving Elinson *d* Charles Walters *ph* Robert Planck *m/ly* Johnny Mercer, Harry Warren *ad Jack Martin Smith*

Fred Astaire, Vera-Ellen, Marjorie Main, Keenan Wynn, Alice Pearce, Clinton Sundberg, Gale Robbins

Belle of the Nineties*
US 1934   75m   bw
Paramount (William Le Baron)

A saloon entertainer loves two men, one of whom is a crook.
Much-laundered star vehicle which despite superior production seems a pale shadow of the star's better pieces.

w Mae West *d* Leo McCarey *ph* Karl Struss

Mae West, Roger Pryor, John Miljan, John Mack Brown, Katherine de Mille, Duke Ellington and his Orchestra

Belle of the Yukon*
US 1945   84m   Technicolor
International

A troupe of saloon entertainers in the Yukon become involved with a bank robbery.
Threads of plot support comedy, dancing and songs in this thin but reasonably fresh musical imitation of *The Spoilers*.

w James Edward Grant *d* William A. Seiter *ph* Ray Rennahan *md* Arthur Lange

Gypsy Rose Lee, Randolph Scott, Dinah Shore, Charles Winninger, Bob Burns

AAN: Arthur Lange; song 'Sleigh Ride in July' (*m* Jimmy Van Heusen, *ly* Johnny Burke)

Belle Starr
US 1941   87m   Technicolor
TCF (Kenneth MacGowan)

Absurdly laundered version of the life of the west's most notorious female outlaw, with the star laughably miscast.

w Lamar Trotti *d* Irving Cummings *ph* Ernest Palmer, Ray Rennahan *m* Alfred Newman

Gene Tierney, Randolph Scott, Dana Andrews, Shepperd Strudwick, Elizabeth Patterson, Chill Wills, Louise Beavers

Les Belles de Nuit**
France / Italy 1952   89m   bw
Franco London / Rizzoli

A discontented music teacher dreams of beautiful women through the ages.
Charming but very slight dream fantasy with many of the master's touches. (He claims to have intended a comic *Intolerance*.)

wd René Clair ph Armand Thirard, Robert Juilliard, Louis Née *m Georges Van Parys ad* Léon Barsacq

Gérard Philipe, Gina Lollobrigida, Martine Carol, Magali Vendeuil, Paolo Stoppa, Raymond Bussières, Raymond Cordy

The Belles of St Trinian's*
GB 1954   91m   bw
BL / London Films / Launder and Gilliat

At an unruly and bankrupt school for girls, more time is spent backing horses than studying subjects, and the headmistress's bookmaker brother has a scheme or two of his own.
Fairly successful film version of Ronald Searle's awful schoolgirl cartoons, the emphasis shifted to a grotesque older generation with the star in drag. An enormous commercial success, but the three sequels *Blue Murder at St Trinian's, The Pure Hell of St Trinian's, The Great St Trinian's Train Robbery* went from bad to awful.

w Frank Launder, Sidney Gilliat, Val Valentine *d* Frank Launder *ph* Stan Pavey *m* Malcolm Arnold

Alastair Sim, George Cole, Joyce Grenfell, Hermione Baddeley, Betty Ann Davies, Renée Houston, Beryl Reid, Irene Handl, Mary Merrall
  'Not so much a film as an entertainment on celluloid, a huge charade, a rich pile of idiot and splendidly senseless images.'—*David Robinson*

Belles on Their Toes
US 1952   89m   Technicolor
TCF (Samuel G. Engel)

Further adventures in the growing up of the twelve Gilbreth children.
Flat sequel to *Cheaper by the Dozen* (qv) with sentimentality instead of Clifton Webb. Period atmosphere attractive.

w Phoebe and Henry Ephron, *book* Frank B. Gilbreth Jnr and Ernestine Gilbreth Carey *d* Henry Levin *ph* Arthur E. Arling *m* Cyril Mockridge

Myrna Loy, Jeanne Crain, Debra Paget, Jeffrey Hunter, Edward Arnold, Hoagy Carmichael, Barbara Bates, Robert Arthur

Bellissimà*
Italy 1951   100m   bw
Bellissimà Films (Salvo d'Angelo)

A mother struggles to get a part in a film for her 7-year-old daughter.
Highly detailed, very noisy star vehicle with neo-realist working-class backgrounds. Exhausting.

w Suso Cecchi d'Amico, Francesco Rosi, Luchino Visconti, Cesare Zavattini *d* Luchino

Visconti *ph* Piero Portalupi *m* Franco Mannino

Anna Magnani, Walter Chiari, Tina Apicella, Gastone Renzelli, Alessandro Blasetti

Bells are Ringing*
US 1960 126m Metrocolor
  Cinemascope
MGM (Arthur Freed)

A telephone answering service operator becomes passionately involved in the lives of her clients.
Dull, rather ugly and boring transcription of a Broadway musical, with all talents below par, not enough dancing and too much plot.

w/ly Betty Comden, Adolph Green, from their play *d* Vincente Minnelli *ph* Milton Krasner *m* Jule Styne *md* André Previn *ad* George W. Davis, Preston Ames *ch* Charles O'Curran

Judy Holliday, Dean Martin, Fred Clark, Eddie Foy Jnr, Jean Stapleton, Ruth Storey, Frank Gorshin

AAN: André Previn

The Bells Go Down**
GB 1943 89m bw
Ealing (Michael Balcon)

The exploits of a London firefighting unit during World War II.
Tragi-comedy with lively scenes, a good record of the historical background of the blitz.

w Roger Macdougall, Stephen Black *d* Basil Dearden *ph* Ernest Palmer *m* Roy Douglas

Tommy Trinder, James Mason, Mervyn Johns, Philippa Hyatt, Finlay Currie, Philip Friend, Meriel Forbes, Beatrice Varley, Billy Hartnell

The Bells of St Mary's**
US 1945 126m bw
RKO (Leo McCarey)

At a big city Catholic school, Father O'Malley and Sister Benedict indulge in friendly rivalry, and succeed in extending the school through the gift of a building.
Sentimental and very commercial sequel to *Going My Way*, with the stars at their peak and the handling as cosy and well-paced as might be expected.

w Dudley Nichols *d* Leo McCarey *ph* George Barnes *m* Robert Emmett Dolan

Bing Crosby, Ingrid Bergman, Henry Travers, William Gargan, Ruth Donnelly, Rhys Williams, Una O'Connor, Eva Novak

AAN: Leo McCarey; George Barnes; Robert Emmett Dolan; Bing Crosby; Ingrid Bergman; song 'Aren't You Glad You're You' (*m* Jimmy Van Heusen, *ly* Johnny Burke)

Beloved Enemy*
US 1936 90m bw
Samuel Goldwyn (George Haight)

During the 1921 Irish rebellion, the fiancée of a British army officer falls in love with the leading revolutionary.
Dreamy-eyed romance with little relevance to the real situation; not badly done of its kind.

w John Balderston, Rose Franken, William Brown Meloney, David Hart *d* H. C. Potter *ph* Gregg Toland

Brian Aherne, Merle Oberon, David Niven, Karen Morley, Jerome Cowan, Henry Stephenson, Donald Crisp

Beloved Infidel*
US 1959 123m De Luxe Cinemascope
TCF / Company of Artists (Jerry Wald)

Sheilah Graham, a British chorus girl turned Hollywood columnist, marries Scott Fitzgerald but fails to cure him of alcoholism.
A bitter and even sordid true story becomes a slice of Hollywood romance, with stars unsuitably cast. On all levels it falls between two stools, satisfying nobody.

w Sy Bartlett, *book* Sheilah Graham and Gerald Frank *d* Henry King *ph* Leon Shamroy *m* Franz Waxman

Gregory Peck, Deborah Kerr, Eddie Albert, Philip Ober, Herbert Rudley, Karin Booth, Ken Scott
  'Catastrophically misguided.'—*Penelope Houston*

The Beloved Vagabond*
GB 1936 78m bw
Ludovico Toeplitz

At the turn of the century, a jilted French artist becomes a vagabond and falls in love with an orphan girl.
Mildly amusing bi-lingual production from a bestselling picaresque novel; production quite lively.

w Wells Root, Arthur Wimperis, Hugh Mills, Walter Creighton, *novel* W. J. Locke *d* Curtis Bernhardt

Maurice Chevalier, Margaret Lockwood, Betty Stockfield, Desmond Tester, Austin Trevor, Peter Haddon, Cathleen Nesbitt

The Belstone Fox*
GB 1973 103m Eastmancolor Todd-AO 35
Rank / Independent Artists (Sally Shuter)

A fox and a hound grow up together but the fox leads to tragedy for its masters.

Good animal and countryside photography barely compensate for a fragmentary story with unpleasant moments or for a muddled attitude towards humans and animals; one is not clear what audience the result is supposed to appeal to.

wd James Hill, *novel* David Rook *ph* John Wilcox, James Allen *m* Laurie Johnson

Eric Porter, Rachel Roberts, Jeremy Kemp, Bill Travers, Dennis Waterman

Ben

US 1972   92m   De Luxe
Cinerama / Bing Crosby (Mort Briskin)

A sickly boy inherits an army of trained rats. Boring reprise of *Willard* in which the audience knows only too well what to expect. Production and development quite routine.

w Gilbert A. Ralston *d* Phil Karlson *ph* Russell Metty *m* Walter Scharf

Lee Harcourt Montgomery, Arthur O'Connell, Rosemary Murphy, Meredith Baxter, Kaz Garas, Paul Carr, Kenneth Tobey

AAN: title song (*m* Walter Scharf, *ly* Don Black)

Ben Hur***

US 1925   170m approx (16 fps)   bw
silent
MGM

In the time of Christ, a Jew suffers mightily under the Romans.
The American silent screen's biggest epic; the sea battle and the chariot race are its most famous sequences.

w Bess Meredyth, Carey Wilson, *novel* Lew Wallace *d Fred Niblo* *ph* Karl Struss, Clyde de Vinna, and others   *ad* Horace Jackson, Ferdinand Pinney Earle

Ramon Novarro, Francis X. Bushman, Carmel Myers, May McAvoy, Betty Bronson
   'A masterpiece of study and patience, a photodrama filled with artistry.'—*New York Times*
† Previously filmed in 1907.

Ben Hur**

US 1959   217m   Technicolor   Camera 65
MGM (Sam Zimbalist)

Solid, expensive, surprisingly unimaginative remake; generally less sprightly than the silent version.

w Karl Tunberg *d* William Wyler, *Andrew Marton* *ph* Robert L. Surtees *m* Miklos Rozsa *ad* William A. Horning, Edward Carfagno

Charlton Heston, Haya Harareet, Jack

Hawkins, Stephen Boyd, Hugh Griffith, Martha Scott, Sam Jaffe, Cathy O'Donnell, Finlay Currie, Frank Thring, Terence Longdon, André Morell, George Relph

AA: best picture; William Wyler; Robert L. Surtees; Miklos Rozsa; Charlton Heston; Hugh Griffith
AAN: Karl Tunberg

Bend of the River**

US 1952   91m   Technicolor
U-I (Aaron Rosenberg)
GB title: *Where the River Bends*

1880 wagon trains arrive in Oregon, and the pioneers have trouble with the local bad man. Good standard western with pace and period feeling.

w Borden Chase, *novel* Bend of the Snake by William Gulick *d* Anthony Mann *ph* Irving Glassberg *m* Hans Salter

James Stewart, Arthur Kennedy, Rock Hudson, Julia Adams, Lori Nelson, Jay C. Flippen, Henry Morgan, Royal Dano, Stepin Fetchit

Beneath the Twelve Mile Reef

US 1953   102m   Technicolor
   Cinemascope
TCF (Robert Bassler)

Jealousy, tragedy and romance among the Florida sponge fishers.
Fox's second Cinemascope production involved much underwater shooting, a trick octopus, and predictable plot devices.

w A. I. Bezzerides *d* Robert D. Webb *ph* Edward Cronjager *m* Bernard Herrmann

Robert Wagner, Terry Moore, Gilbert Roland, Peter Graves, J. Carrol Naish, Richard Boone, Angela Clarke, Jay Novello
   'The dead weight of a melodramatic script overtaxes the gallant attempts at conviction.'—*MFB*

AAN: Edward Cronjager

Bengal Brigade

US 1954   87m   Technicolor
U-I (Ted Richmond)
GB title: *Bengal Rifles*

In 19th-century India, an officer is cashiered through false evidence, and becomes an undercover man with the wicked local rajah. Routine Hollywood heroics with a few unintended laughs.

w Richard Alan Simmons, *novel* Bengal Tiger by Hall Hunter *d* Laslo Benedek *ph* Maury Gertsman *m* Joseph Gershenson

Rock Hudson, Dan O'Herlihy, Ursula Thiess, Torin Thatcher, Michael Ansara, Arnold Moss

Bengazi
US 1955   79m   bw   Superscope
RKO / Panamint (Sam Wiesenthal, Eugene
Tevlin)

Various unsavoury characters set out into the
African desert to look for gold hidden by the
Nazis.
Poor potboiler on predictable lines.

w Endre Boehm, Louis Vittes d John Brahm
ph Joseph Biroc m Roy Webb

Richard Conte, Victor McLaglen, Richard
Carlson, Mala Powers, Richard Erdman,
Gonzales Gonzales, Hillary Brooke

**Benjamin, or The Diary of an Innocent
Young Man**
France 1966   104m   Eastmancolor
Paramount / Parc / Marianne (Mag Bodard)

In the 18th century, a 17-year-old orphan is
taken in hand by his wealthy aunt and initiated
into the mysteries of sex.
Imitation *Tom Jones*, quite good to look at but
rather boring.

w Nina Companeez d Michel Déville
ph Ghislain Cloquet

Pierre Clémenti, Michèle Morgan, Catherine
Deneuve, Michel Piccoli, Francine Bergé, Anna
Gaël, Odile Versois

'Heavy with Gallic naughtiness rather than
airy charm . . . a plethora of colourful costumes,
foliage and fireworks.'
—*MFB*

Benji*
US 1974   86m   CFI color
Mulberry Square (Joe Camp)

A stray mongrel dog saves two kidnapped
children.
Family film par excellence which rang the box
office bell in a big way in the US. Its modest
merits are rather beside the point.

wd Joe Camp ph Don Reddy m Euel Box

Peter Breck, Edgar Buchanan, Terry Carter,
Christopher Connelly
† A sequel, *For the Love of Benji*, followed in
1977.

AAN: song 'I Feel Love' (m Euel Box, ly Betty
Box)

The Benny Goodman Story*
US 1955   117m   Technicolor
U-I (Aaron Rosenberg)

A clarinettist from the Jewish section of Chicago
becomes internationally famous.
Sentimental biopic of a familiar figure which

comes to life when the sound track is given its
head (and the real Goodman's clarinet).

wd Valentine Davies ph William Daniels
md Joseph Gershenson

Steve Allen, Donna Reed, *Berta Gersten*,
Herbert Anderson, Robert F. Simon, Sammy
Davis Snr, Harry James, Martha Tilton, Gene
Krupa
'The customary fictional liberties appear to
have been taken.'—*MFB*

Bequest to the Nation*
GB 1973   116m   Technicolor
Universal / Hal B. Wallis
US title: *The Nelson Affair*

The story of Nelson's long affair with the
tempestuous Lady Hamilton.
Undistinguished historical drama from a thin
play which despite hard work all round makes
very ordinary screen entertainment.

w Terence Rattigan, from his play d James
Cellan Jones ph Gerry Fisher pd Carmen
Dillon m Michel Legrand

Peter Finch, Glenda Jackson (way over the top),
Michael Jayston, Anthony Quayle, Margaret
Leighton, Dominic Guard, Nigel Stock, Roland
Culver
'As empty as an out-of-town matinee.'—*MFB*

Berkeley Square**
US 1933   87m   bw
Fox (Jesse L. Lasky)

A London house reincarnates its owner as his
18th-century ancestor.
Romantic fantasy on a time lapse theme, the first
of many and perhaps the most stylish and self-
assured. Remade as *I'll Never Forget You* (qv).

w Sonya Levien, John Balderston, from
Balderston's play d Frank Lloyd ph Ernest
Palmer m Louis de Francesco ad William
Carling

Leslie Howard, Heather Angel, Valerie Taylor,
Irene Browne, Beryl Mercer, Colin Keith-
Johnson, Alan Mowbray

AAN: Leslie Howard

Berlin Correspondent
US 1942   70m   bw
TCF (Bryan Foy)

In pre-war Germany an American reporter is
kidnapped by the Nazis and replaced by a
double . . .
Preposterous melodrama, so silly as to be often
quite funny.

w Steve Fisher, Jack Andrews d Eugene Forde
ph Virgil Miller md Emil Newman

Dana Andrews, Virginia Gilmore, Mona Maris, Martin Kosleck, Sig Rumann, Kurt Katch, Torben Meyer

Berlin Express*
US 1948 87m bw
RKO (Bert Granet)

Police of four nations guard a German VIP on a crack train to Berlin.
Rather muddled suspenser with attempts at political moralizing; the cast provides some good moments.

w Harold Medford d Jacques Tourneur
ph Lucien Ballard m Frederick Hollander

Merle Oberon, Robert Ryan, Charles Korvin, Paul Lukas, Robert Coote

Berlin, Symphony of a Great City***
Germany 1927 78m bw silent
Fox-Europa
original title: Berlin die Symphonie einer Grosstadt

An impression of the life of a city from dawn to midnight, expressed by cinematic montages, angles, sequences, etc, and set to music. A most influential documentary.

w Walter Ruttman, Karl Freund, Carl Mayer d Walter Ruttman ph Reimar Kuntze, Robert Baberske, Laszlo Schäffer m Edmund Meisel

Berliner Ballade*
Germany 1948 77m bw
Comedia Film (Alf Teichs)
aka: The Ballad of Berlin

Otto Nobody, an unwilling soldier, returns home to find himself at the mercy of bureaucrats and black marketeers.
Melancholy satire presented as a series of sketches, almost a forerunner of That Was the Week That Was.

w Gunter Neumann d Robert Stemmle ph Georg Krause m/ly Gunter Neumann, Werner Eisbrenner

Gert Fröbe, Anton Zeithammer, Tatjana Sais, O. E. Hasse
'Very much the film of a defeated people.'— Penelope Houston

Bernardine*
US 1957 95m Eastmancolor
Cinemascope
TCF (Samuel G. Engel)

A college student forced to swot for exams asks a friend's elder brother to look after his girl.
Henry Aldrich-style high school comedy, showing the lighter side of Rebel without a

Cause. Notable for the clean-living hero played by a clean-living singing star, and the reappearance of Janet Gaynor for the only time since 1939, in a routine mother role.

w Theodore Reeves, play Mary Chase d Henry Levin ph Paul Vogel m Lionel Newman

Pat Boone, Richard Sargent, Terry Moore, Janet Gaynor, Walter Abel, Dean Jagger, Natalie Schaefer, James Drury

Berserk!
GB 1968 96m Technicolor
Columbia (Herman Cohen)

A lady circus owner revels in the publicity brought about by a series of murders.
Grisly and unattractive thriller with an ageing star in a series of unsuitably abbreviated costumes; the script is beyond redemption.

w Herman Cohen, Aben Kandel d Jim O'Connolly ph Desmond Dickinson m Patrick John Scott

Joan Crawford, Diana Dors, Ty Hardin, Judy Geeson, Michael Gough, Robert Hardy, Geoffrey Keen, Sidney Tafler, Philip Madoc

Best Foot Forward
US 1943 94m Technicolor
MGM (Arthur Freed)

A glamorous publicity-seeking film star accepts an invitation to a military college ball.
Old-fashioned formula musical based on a lightweight Broadway success.

w Irving Brecher, Fred Finklehoffe, play John Cecil Holmes d Edward Buzzell ph Leonard Smith md Lennie Hayton songs Hugh Martin, Ralph Blane ch Charles Walters

Lucille Ball, William Gaxton, Virginia Weidler, Harry James and his Orchestra, June Allyson, Gloria de Haven

The Best House in London*
GB 1968 96m Eastmancolor
MGM / Bridge / Carlo Ponti (Philip Breen, Kurt Unger)

A Victorian publicity agent tries to organize a government-sponsored brothel.
Cheerful slam-bang historical send-up with as many dull thuds of banality as pleasant witticisms.

w Denis Norden d Philip Savile ph Alex Thompson m Mischa Spoliansky pd Wilfrid Shingleton

David Hemmings, George Sanders, Joanna Pettet, Warren Mitchell, Dany Robin, William Rushton

The Best Man***
US 1964   104m   bw
UA / Stuart Millar, Lawrence Turman

Two contenders for a presidential nomination
seek the support of the dying ex-president.
Brilliant political melodrama, ingeniously
adapted on a low budget from an incisive play,
with splendid dramatic scenes, memorable
performances and good convention detail.

w Gore Vidal from his play *d Franklin
Schaffner ph* Haskell Wexler *m* Mort Lindsey

Henry Fonda, Cliff Robertson, Lee Tracy,
Margaret Leighton, Edie Adams, Kevin
McCarthy, *Shelley Berman,* Ann Sothern, Gene
Raymond, Mahalia Jackson

'A fine opportunity to watch pros at work in a
hard-hitting and cogent drama that seems to
become more topical and have more relevance
with each showing.'—*Judith Crist*

'Some of the wittiest lines since *Strangelove*
. . . the acting fairly crackled with
authenticity.'—*Isabel Quigly*

AAN: Lee Tracy

The Best of Enemies
US / Italy 1961   104m   Technirama
Columbia / Dino de Laurentiis

During the Abyssinian campaign of 1941, an
Italian and a British officer learn mutual respect.
Mild satirical comedy drama with a few points to
make about war; the elements blend rather
obviously and dispiritingly.

w Jack Pulman *d* Guy Hamilton *ph Giuseppe
Rotunno m* Nino Rota

David Niven, Alberto Sordi, Michael Wilding,
Amedeo Nazzari, Harry Andrews, David
Opatoshu, Kenneth Fortescue, Duncan Macrae

The Best of Everything*
US 1959   121m   De Luxe   Cinemascope
TCF (Jerry Wald)

Personal problems of a New York publisher's
female staff.
Slick novelette on the lines of a naughty Peg's
Paper: pure Hollywood gossamer.

w Edith Sommer, Mann Rubin, *novel* Rona
Jaffe *d* Jean Negulesco *ph* William C. Mellor
m Alfred Newman

Hope Lange, Stephen Boyd, Joan Crawford,
Louis Jourdan, Suzy Parker, Martha Hyer,
Diane Baker, Brian Aherne, Robert Evans, Brett
Halsey, Donald Harron

'A cautionary tale sensationally told.'—
Alexander Walker

AAN: title song (*m* Alfred Newman, *ly* Sammy
Cahn)

Best of the Badmen*
US 1951   84m   Technicolor
RKO (Herman Schlom)

At the end of the Civil War Jeff Clanton
organizes the break-up of Quantrell's Raiders,
but is himself arrested on a trumped-up charge
and needs the Raiders' help.
Standard western notable for a good cast and for
bringing in a remarkable number of historical
outlaws, doing rather unhistorical things.

w Robert Hardy Andrews, John Twist
d William D. Russell *ph* Edward Cronjager

Robert Ryan, Claire Trevor, Jack Buetel, Robert
Preston, Walter Brennan, Bruce Cabot, John
Archer, Lawrence Tierney

The Best Things in Life Are Free*
US 1956   103m   Eastmancolor
    Cinemascope
TCF (Henry Ephron)

From Broadway to Hollywood in the twenties,
the story of songwriting team De Sylva, Brown
and Henderson.
Gangsters, movie studios and the writing of
'Sonny Boy' for Al Jolson all figure in this
amiable musical which spends more time on
jokes than romance; the numbers are
disappointing despite good tunes.

w William Bowers, Phoebe Ephron *d* Michael
Curtiz *ph* Leon Shamroy *md* Lionel Newman

Ernest Borgnine, Gordon Macrae, Dan Dailey,
Sheree North, Jacques d'Amboise, Norman
Brooks, Murvyn Vye

AAN: Lionel Newman

The Best Years of Our Lives****
US 1946   182m   bw
Samuel Goldwyn

Three men come home from war to a small
middle-American community, and find it
variously difficult to pick up where they left off.
The situations and even some of the characters
now seem a little obvious, but this was a superb
example of high-quality film-making in the
forties, with smiles and tears cunningly spaced,
and a film which said what was needed on a vital
subject.

w Robert Sherwood, novel Glory for Me by
Mackinlay Kantor *d William Wyler ph* Gregg
Toland m Hugo Friedhofer

Fredric March, Myrna Loy, Teresa Wright,
Dana Andrews, Virginia Mayo, Cathy
O'Donnell, *Hoagy Carmichael, Harold Russell*
(a handless veteran whose only film this was),
Gladys George, Roman Bohnen, Ray Collins

'The result is a work of provocative and

moving insistence and beauty.'—*Howard Barnes*

AA: best picture; Robert Sherwood; William Wyler; Hugo Friedhofer; Fredric March; Harold Russell

Le Béte Humaine*
France 1938   99m   bw
Paris Films
aka: *The Human Beast; Judas Was a Woman*

A psychopathic train driver falls for a married woman, plans with her to kill her husband, but finally strangles her instead.
Curious melodrama with strong visual sequences, flawed by its ambivalent attitude to its hero-villain.

wd Jean Renoir, *novel* Emile Zola *ph* Curt Courant *m* Joseph Kosma

Jean Gabin, Simone Simon, Julien Carette, Fernand Ledoux, Jean Renoir

'Marvellous atmosphere and a fine cast, but the material turns oppressive.'—*New Yorker, 1978*

† Remade in Hollywood as *Human Desire*.

Betrayal from the East
US 1945   83m   bw
RKO (Herman Schlom)

Japanese out to sabotage the Panama Canal are thwarted by a carnival showman.
Extravagant but penny-pinching flagwaver.

w Kenneth Gamet, Aubrey Wisberg, *novel* Alan Hynd *d* William Berke *ph* Russell Metty *m* Roy Webb

Lee Tracy; Nancy Kelly, Richard Loo, Abner Biberman, Regis Toomey, Philip Ahn, Addison Richards, Sen Yung, Drew Pearson

Betrayed
US 1954   108m   Eastmancolor
MGM (Gottfried Reinhardt)

In 1943 a Dutch intelligence officer works with a resistance leader who turns out to be a traitor.
Slow-moving, studio-set romantic melodrama of the old school; not very lively.

w Ronald Millar, George Froeschel *d* Gottfried Reinhardt *ph* Frederick A. Young *m* Walter Goehr

Clark Gable, Victor Mature, Lana Turner, Louis Calhern,
O. E. Hasse, Wilfrid Hyde White, Ian Carmichael, Niall MacGinnis, Nora Swinburne

The Betsy
US 1977   125m   Technicolor
Allied Artists / Harold Robbins International (Robert R. Weston)

Jockeying for power in the boardroom and the family life of an aged car manufacturer.
Rather tame and obvious melodrama enlivened by its star performance.

w William Bast, Walter Bernstein, *novel* Harold Robbins *Daniel Petrie ph* Mario Tosi *m* John Barry

Laurence Olivier, Robert Duvall, Tommy Lee Jones, Katharine Ross, Jane Alexander, Lesley-Anne Down, Joseph Wiseman, Edward Herrmann

Between Heaven and Hell
US 1956   94m   Eastmancolor
   Cinemascope
TCF (David Weisbart)

After Pearl Harbor a young southern landowner is called up and finds himself on active service with mixed racial types.
Vaguely anti-war, pro-understanding action thriller which ends up going through predictable heroics in a professional but not too sympathetic manner.

w Harry Brown, *novel* The Day the Century Ended by Francis Gwaltney *d* Richard Fleischer *ph* Leo Tover *m* Hugo Friedhofer

Robert Wagner, Buddy Ebsen, Broderick Crawford, Brad Dexter, Mark Damon, Robert Keith, Ken Clark, Skip Homeier, Harvey Lembeck

AAN: Hugo Friedhofer

Between Midnight and Dawn
US 1950   89m   bw
Columbia (Hunt Stromberg)

Radio policemen track down a racketeer.
Competent, undistinguished programmer.

w Eugene Ling *d* Gordon Douglas *ph* George E. Diskant *m* George Duning

Mark Stevens, Edmond O'Brien, Gale Storm, Donald Buka, Gale Robbins, Roland Winters

Between Two Worlds*
US 1944   112m   bw
Warner (Mark Hellinger)

A number of air-raid victims, and two lovers who have committed suicide, find themselves on a luxury ship en route to the next world.
Nice-looking but slow and turgid remake of *Outward Bound* (qv), largely sunk in its own misery but redeemed by two performances.

w Daniel Fuchs, *play* Sutton Vane *d* Edward A.

Blatt *ph* Carl Guthrie *m* Erich Wolfgang
Korngold

John Garfield, *Edmund Gwenn*, Eleanor Parker,
Paul Henreid, *Sydney Greenstreet*, Sara
Allgood, George Tobias, Faye Emerson, George
Coulouris, Dennis King, Isobel Elsom

Between Us Girls
US 1942 89m bw
Universal

A mother and daughter are both involved in
romances which tend to cross.
Mild comedy, a disappointing debut for a
disappointing young star.

w Myles Connolly, True Boardman, *play* Le
Fruit Vert by Regis Gignoux, Jacques Thery
d Henry Koster *ph* Joseph Valentine *m* Frank
Skinner

Diana Barrymore, Kay Francis, Robert
Cummings, John Boles, Scotty Beckett, Ethel
Griffies

Beware My Lovely
US 1952 77m bw
RKO / Filmmakers (Collier Young)

A handyman employed by a widow turns out to
be a mental defective who imprisons and
threatens to rape and murder her.
Dismal suspenser with a lot of screaming and
running around but very little flair.

w Mel Dinelli, from his play The Man *d* Harry
Horner *ph* George E. Diskant *m* Leith Stevens

Ida Lupino, Robert Ryan, Taylor Holmes,
Barbara Whiting

'Inept characterization and ludicrously
repetitive situations will surely rank this among
the silliest films of the year.'—*MFB*

Beware of Pity*
GB 1946 106m bw
Two Cities (W. P. Lipscomb)

An officer courts a crippled girl out of pity. She
finds out and kills herself.
Ambitious but rather artificial and dreary
drama, a shade too pleased with its own
literariness; performances straitjacketed by
production.

w W. P. Lipscomb, Elizabeth Baron, Margaret
Steen, *novel* Stefan Zweig *d* Maurice Elvey
ph Derick Williams

Lilli Palmer, Albert Lieven, Cedric Hardwicke,
Gladys Cooper, Linden Travers, Ernest
Thesiger, Emrys Jones

Bewitched
US 1945 65m bw
MGM (Arch Oboler)

A girl with twin personalities has her murderous
element exorcized by a spiritualist.
Hilarious nonsense, ancestor of the Eve/Lizzie
schizos of the fifties.

wd Arch Oboler, from his story Alter Ego
ph Charles Salerno Jnr

Phyllis Thaxter, Edmund Gwenn, Addison
Richards, Kathleen Lockhart

Beyond a Reasonable Doubt*
US 1956 80m bw
RKO (Bert Friedlob)

A novelist is persuaded by a crusading
newspaper proprietor to fake circumstantial
evidence incriminating himself in a murder, thus
proving the uselessness of such evidence. He
does it so well that he is convicted . . . but that
doesn't matter as he was guilty all the time.
Ingenious but rather cheerless and mechanical
thriller. The actors extract what they can from a
script intent on sleight of hand, but the
distinguished director is at his most flatulent.

w Douglas Morrow *d* Fritz Lang *ph* William
Snyder *m* Herschel Burke Gilbert

Dana Andrews, Joan Fontaine, Sidney
Blackmer, Philip Bourneuf, Shepperd Strudwick,
Arthur Franz, Edward Binns

Beyond Glory
US 1948 82m bw
Paramount

The honour of a West Point cadet is vindicated.
Proficient but dramatically turgid vehicle for an
absurdly over-age star.

w Jonathan Latimer, Charles Marquis Warren,
William Wister Haines *d* John Farrow *ph* John
F. Seitz

Alan Ladd, Donna Reed, George Coulouris,
George Macready, Audie Murphy

Beyond Mombasa
GB 1955 90m Technicolor
Columbia / Hemisphere (Adrian Worker)

In East Africa, an American avenges his
brother's death at the hands of the Mau Mau
(here called the Leopard Men and revealed to be
run by a mad English missionary).
Tasteless and rather humdrum jungle adventure
using real-life problems purely as a backdrop.

w Richard English, Gene Levitt, *novel* Mark of
the Leopard by James Eastwood *d* George
Marshall *ph* Frederick A. Young *m* Humphrey
Searle

Cornel Wilde, Donna Reed, Leo Genn, Ron
Randell, Christopher Lee

Beyond the Blue Horizon*
US 1942   76m   Technicolor
Paramount (Monta Bell)

An orphan white girl grows up on a tropical
island with a chimpanzee and a swimming tiger;
when rescued and her story doubted, she leads
an expedition back to prove it.
The most tongue-in-cheek of the Lamour jungle
extravaganzas, with plenty of simple fun.

w Frank Butler d Alfred Santell ph Charles
Boyle m Victor Young

Dorothy Lamour, Richard Denning, Jack
Haley, Patricia Morison, Walter Abel, Helen
Gilbert, Elizabeth Patterson

Beyond the Curtain
GB 1960   88m   bw
Rank / Martin (John Martin)

A flying officer rescues a stewardess whose plane
has been forced down in East Germany.
Inept, penny-pinching cold war melodrama in
which very little happens.

w John Cresswell, Compton Bennett,
novel Thunder Above by Charles F. Blair
d Compton Bennett ph Eric Cross m Eric
Pakeman

Richard Greene, Eva Bartok, Marius Goring,
Lucie Mannheim, Andree Melly, George Mikell,
John Welsh

Beyond the Forest*
US 1949   96m   bw
Warner (Henry Blanke)

The discontented wife of a small-town doctor has
an affair with a wealthy Chicagoan, murders a
witness, attempts suicide, and dies of fever.
The star caricatures herself in this overblown
melodrama which marked the unhappy end of
her association with the studio. The rest of the
cast suffer more dumbly from the script's
unintentional hilarities.

w Lenore Coffee, novel Stuart Engstrandt
d King Vidor ph Robert Burks m Max Steiner

Bette Davis, Joseph Cotten, David Brian, Ruth
Roman, Minor Watson, Dona Drake, Regis
Toomey
   'Nobody's as good as Bette when she's
bad!'—publicity
   'This peerless piece of camp.'—New Yorker,
1978
   'Miss Davis makes a regrettably
melodramatic mess of what is undoubtedly one

of the most unfortunate stories she has ever
tackled.'—Newsweek
AAN: Max Steiner

Beyond the Time Barrier
US 1959   75m   bw
AIP / Pacific International / Miller-
   Consolidated (Robert Clarke)

A test pilot crosses the fifth dimension and finds
himself in 2024 when civilization has gone
underground to avoid nuclear contamination.
Crude science fiction, roughly on the level of
Flash Gordon but less entertaining.

w Arthur G. Pierce d Edgar G. Ulmer
ph Meredith Nicholson m Darrell Calker

Robert Clarke, Darlene Tompkins, Adrienne
Arden, Vladimir Sokoloff, Stephen Bekassy

Beyond the Valley of the Dolls
US 1970   109m   De Luxe   Panavision
TCF (Russ Meyer)

Three girls in Hollywood enjoy the wilder
reaches of show biz high life.
The skinflick director's first film for a major
studio, with positively no connection with Valley
of the Dolls, is not explicitly pornographic but
pussyfoots around with as many general
excesses as can be crammed into two hours. If
taken as high camp it provides a laugh or two,
but is chiefly notable as marking a major studio's
deepest dip into muddy waters.

w Roger Ebert d Russ Meyer ph Fred J.
Koenekamp
m Stu Phillips, William Loose

Dolly Read, Cynthia Myers, Marcia McBroom,
John La Zar, Michael Blodgett, Edy Williams
   'If one can resist walking out, the last half hour
is quite manic.'—MFB
   'A film whose total, idiotic, monstrous
badness raises it to the pitch of near-irresistible
entertainment.'—Alexander Walker

Beyond This Place*
GB 1959   90m   bw
Renown / Georgefield (Maxwell Setton, John
   R. Sloan)
US title: Web of Evidence

An American visiting London finds his
supposedly dead father in prison serving a life
sentence for murder; he delves into history and
finds the real culprit.
Spiritless murder mystery with less serious intent
than the original novel; tolerable entertainment.

w Kenneth Taylor, novel A. J. Cronin d Jack
Cardiff ph Wilkie Cooper m Douglas Gamley
ad Ken Adam

Van Johnson, Vera Miles, Bernard Lee, Emlyn Williams, Jean Kent, Moultrie Kelsall, Leo McKern, Ralph Truman

Bezhin Meadow**
USSR 1937   31m   bw
Mosfilm
original title: *Bezhin Lug*

Fragments from an incomplete Eisenstein film are held together by freeze frames.
Even this collection of bits and pieces shows the power of the monster.

w Alexander Rozhdestvenski, *story* Ivan Turgenev *d Sergei Eisenstein ph* Edouard Tissé

Vitya Kartashov, Boris Zakhava, Igor Pavlenko

Bhowani Junction*
GB 1955   110m   Eastmancolor
  Cinemascope
MGM (Pandro S. Berman)

Adventures of an Anglo-Indian girl during the last years of British India.
Disappointingly anaemic semi-epic from a gutsy novel, variably handled by all concerned.

w Sonya Levien, Ivan Moffat, *novel* John Masters *d* George Cukor *ph* Frederick A. Young *m* Miklos Rozsa

Ava Gardner, Stewart Granger, *Francis Matthews*, Bill Travers, Abraham Sofaer, Marne Maitland, Peter Illing, Freda Jackson, Edward Chapman
  'An unwieldy, flatly-conceived charade.'—*MFB*

The Bible*
US / Italy 1966   174m   De Luxe
  Dimension 150 (70mm)
TCF / Dino de Laurentiis (Luigi Luraschi)

Through the Old Testament from Adam to Isaac.
A portentous creation with whispered commentary gives way to a dull misty Eden with decorous nudes, a sprightly Noah's Ark, a spectacular Babel, a brooding Sodom and a turgid Abraham. The pace is killingly slow and the script has little religious sense, but the pictures are often pretty.

w Christopher Fry and others *d* John Huston *ph Giuseppe Rotunno m* Toshiro Mayuzumi *ad* Mario Chiari

Michael Parks (Adam), Ulla Bergryd (Eve), Richard Harris (Cain), *John Huston* (Noah), Stephen Boyd (Nimrod), George C. Scott (Abraham), Ava Gardner (Sarah), Peter O'Toole (the three angels)

  'An Old Testament spectacular like any other.'—*David Robinson*
  'At a time when religion needs all the help it can get, John Huston may have set its cause back a couple of thousand years.'—*Rex Reed*

AAN: Toshiro Mayuzumi

Les Biches**
France / Italy 1968   99m   Eastmancolor
La Boétie / Alexandra (André Génovès)
aka: *The Does*

Two lesbians form an uneasy *ménage à trois* with a young architect, who loves both of them.
Fascinating and well-detailed character study with more depth than at first appears.

w Paul Gégauff, Claude Chabrol d Claude Chabrol ph Jean Rabier m Pierre Jansen

Stéphane Audran, Jacqueline Sassard, Jean-Louis Trintignant

Bicycle Thieves****
Italy 1948   90m   bw
PDS-ENIC (Umberto Scarparelli)
original title: *Ladri di Biciclette*

An Italian workman, long unemployed, is robbed of the bicycle he needs for his new job, and he and his small son search Rome for it.
The epitome of Italian neo-realism, the slight human drama is developed so that it has all the force of *King Lear*, and both the acting and the backgrounds are vividly compelling.

w Cesare Zavattini d Vittorio de Sica ph Carlo Montuori *m* Alessandro Cicognini

Lamberto Maggiorani, Enzo Staiola
  'A film of rare humanity and sensibility.'—*Gavin Lambert*
  'A memorable work of art with the true flavour of reality. To see it is an experience worth having.'—*Richard Mallett, Punch*
  'My idea is to de-romanticize the cinema.'—*Vittorio de Sica*

AA: best foreign film; Cesare Zavattini

Il Bidone**
Italy / France 1955   109m   bw
Titanus / SGC
aka: *The Swindlers*

A group of petty swindlers fails to move into the higher criminal bracket.
Sharply observed but rather sentimental melodrama with tragic pretensions.

w Federico Fellini, Ennio Flaiano, Tullio Pinelli *d Federico Fellini ph* Otello Martelli *m* Nino Rota

Broderick Crawford, Richard Basehart, Franco Fabrizi, Giulietta Masina

Big Bad Mama

US 1974　85m　Metrocolor
Santa Cruz (Roger Corman)

In 1932 Texas, a desirable widow becomes a
bank robber.
Fast moving, violent nonsense, like a caricature
of *Bonnie and Clyde*, which was itself a
caricature.

w William Norton, Frances Doel　*d* Steve
Carver　*ph* Bruce Logan　*m* David Grisman

Angie Dickinson, William Shatner, Tom
Skerritt, Susan Sennett, Robbie Lee

The Big Blockade *

GB 1941　73m　bw
Ealing (Alberto Cavalcanti)

A semi-documentary showing the importance of
blockading Germany in winning the war.
A curious all-star propaganda revue with some
sketches more effective than others.

w Charles Frend, Angus Macphail　*d* Charles
Frend

Leslie Banks, Michael Redgrave, John Mills,
Will Hay (his only serious role), Frank Cellier,
Robert Morley, Alfred Drayton, Michael
Rennie, Marius Goring, Bernard Miles

The Big Boodle

US 1957　83m　bw
UA / Monteflor (Lewis F. Blumberg)
GB title: *Night in Havana*

A croupier in an Havana gambling casino is
suspected of knowing where counterfeit plates
are hidden . . .
An undistinguished chase film with the star very
tired and a long way from home.

w Jo Eisinger, *novel* Robert Sylvester　*d* Richard
Wilson　*ph* Lee Garmes　*m* Raoul Lavista

Errol Flynn, Pedro Armendariz, Gia Scala,
Rossana Rory

The Big Bounce

US 1969　102m　Technicolor　Panavision
Warner / Greenway (William Dozier)

An ex-GI with a criminal record gets into sexual
and criminal trouble while working at a
California motel.
Unattractive melodrama with no discernible
point, certainly not to entertain.

w William Dozier, *novel* Elmore Leonard　*d* Alex
March　*ph* Howard R. Schwartz　*m* Michael
Curb

Ryan O'Neal, Leigh Taylor-Young, Van Heflin,
James Daly, Robert Webber, Lee Grant

The Big Broadcast **

US 1932　78m　bw
Paramount

A failing radio station is saved by an all-star
show.
Revue-style show with a minimum of plot,
valuable as archive material covering many stars
of the time.

w George Marion Jnr, *novel* Wild Horses by
William Ford Manley　*d* Frank Tuttle
ph George Folsey

Bing Crosby, Kate Smith, George Burns, Gracie
Allen, Stuart Erwin, Leila Hyams, Cab
Calloway, the Mills Brothers, the Boswell Sisters

The Big Broadcast of 1936 **

US 1935　97m　bw
Paramount (Ben Glazer)

The 'radio lover' of a small radio station is
kidnapped by a man-hungry countess.
Zany comedy with interpolated variety acts and
a totally Marxian climax.

w Walter de Leon, Francis Martin, Ralph
Spence　*d* Norman Taurog　*ph* Leo Tover
songs various　*ch* LeRoy Prinz

Jack Oakie, George Burns, Gracie Allen, Henry
Wadsworth, Wendy Barrie, Lyda Roberti, C.
Henry Gordon, Benny Baker, Bing Crosby,
Ethel Merman, Richard Tauber, Amos 'n Andy,
Mary Boland, Charles Ruggles, Virginia
Weidler, Guy Standing, Gail Patrick, Bill
Robinson, the Nicholas Brothers, the Vienna
Boys Choir, Akim Tamiroff

The Big Broadcast of 1937 **

US 1936　100m　bw
Paramount (Lewis Gensler)

A radio station manager has trouble with his
sponsors.
More recorded acts separated by a measure of
plot.

w Edwin Gelsey, Arthur Kober, Barry Travers,
Walter de Leon, Francis Martin　*d* Mitchell
Leisen　*ph* Theodor Sparkuhl　*songs* various

Jack Benny, George Burns, Gracie Allen, Bob
Burns, Martha Raye, Shirley Ross, Ray Milland,
Benny Fields, Benny Goodman and his
Orchestra, Leopold Stokowski and the
Philadelphia Orchestra, Eleanore Whitney,
Larry Adler, Louis da Pron

'It isn't a comedy and it isn't a musical, but it
has a lot of laughs, the best in several types of
music, and I don't know where in the world you
will see anything like it.'—*Otis Ferguson*

The Big Broadcast of 1938**
US 1937   90m   bw
Paramount (Harlan Thompson)

A steamship owner engaged in a transatlantic race is hampered by his practical joking twin brother.
Glamorous, empty-headed all-star nonsense with the expected bevy of interpolated acts.

w Walter de Leon, Francis Martin, Ken Englund, Frederick Hazlitt Brennan *d* Mitchell Leisen *ph* Harry Fischbeck *songs* various

W. C. Fields, Bob Hope (debut), Martha Raye, Dorothy Lamour, Shirley Ross, Lynne Overman, Ben Blue, Leif Erickson, Kirsten Flagstad, Tito Guizar, Shep Fields and his Rippling Rhythm Orchestra

AAN: song 'Thanks for the Memory' (*m* Ralph Rainger, *ly* Leo Robin)

Big Brown Eyes
US 1936   76m   bw
Paramount (Walter Wanger)

A private detective and his wisecracking girl friend catch a jewel thief.
Minor league Thin Man stuff, quite acceptably done.

w Raoul Walsh, Bert Hanlon *d* Raoul Walsh *ph* George Clemens *m* Gerald Carbonara *md* Morris Stoloff

Cary Grant, Joan Bennett, Walter Pidgeon, Lloyd Nolan, Alan Baxter, Marjorie Gateson, Isabel Jewell, Douglas Fowley

The Big Bus
US 1976   88m   Movielab   Panavision
Paramount (Fred Freeman, Lawrence J. Cohen)

Misadventures of a giant atomic-powered bus on its first cross-country trip.
Rather feeble spoof on disaster pictures, with some good moments.

w Fred Freeman, Lawrence J. Cohen *d* James Frawley *ph* Harry Stradling Jnr *m* David Shire *pd* Joel Schiller

Joseph Bologna, Stockard Channing, John Beck, René Auberjonois, Ned Beatty, Bob Dishy, Jose Ferrer, Ruth Gordon, Harold Gould, Larry Hagman, Sally Kellerman, Richard Mulligan, Lynn Redgrave

The Big Circus*
US 1959   109m   Technicolor
  Cinemascope
AA (Irwin Allen)

A bankrupt circus owner tries to get his show

back on the road despite the murderous schemes of his ex-partners.
Fast-paced melodrama which makes little sense but generally provides the expected thrills.

w Irwin Allen, Charles Bennett, Irving Wallace *d* Joseph Newman *ph* Winton C. Hoch *m* Paul Sawtell, Bert Shefter

Victor Mature, Red Buttons, Rhonda Fleming, Kathryn Grant, Vincent Price, Peter Lorre, *Gilbert Roland*, David Nelson, Adele Mara, Steve Allen

The Big City
US 1927   80m approx (24 fps)   bw   silent
MGM

A cabaret owner has a jewel robbery gang as a sideline.
Minor star melodrama.

w Waldemar Young, Tod Browning *d* Tod Browning

Lon Chaney, Betty Compson, James Murray, Marceline Day

The Big City*
US 1937   80m   bw
MGM (Norman Krasna)

An honest cab driver and his wife hold out against corruption.
Sentimental realism of the type expected of its director. Smooth and syrupy.

w Dore Schary, Hugo Butler *d* Frank Borzage *ph* Joseph Ruttenberg *m* William Axt

Spencer Tracy, Luise Rainer, Charley Grapewin, Janet Beecher, Irving Bacon, William Demarest, Eddie Quillan

Big City
US 1948   103m   bw
MGM (Joe Pasternak)

In New York's East Side, a little girl is the adopted daughter of three bachelors, but trouble looms when they all get ideas of romance.
Later-day star vehicle for which the young star is really too old and all else is excessively sentimental and sprawling.

w Whitfield Cook, Ann Morrison *d* Norman Taurog
ph Robert Surtees

Margaret O'Brien, Robert Preston, Danny Thomas, George Murphy, Karin Booth, Jackie Butch Jenkins, Betty Garrett

The Big City**
India 1963   131m   bw
R. D. Bansal
original title: *Mahanagar*

A poverty-stricken Calcutta bank accountant sends his wife out to work; then the bank crashes, and she becomes the sole breadwinner. Immensely detailed, overlong, but mainly fascinating account of modern urban India and its attitudes.

wd, m Satyajit Ray, *novel* Narendra Nath Mitra *ph* Subrata Mitra

Madhabi Mukherjee, Anil Chatterjee, Haren Chatterjee, Haradhan Banerjee

The Big Clock*
US 1947   95m   bw
Paramount (John Farrow)

A publishing magnate murders his mistress and assigns one of his editors to solve the crime.
Slick but rather empty thriller with judicious use of adequate talent.

w Jonathan Latimer, from his novel *d* John Farrow *ph* John Seitz *m* Victor Young

Charles Laughton, Ray Milland, Maureen O'Sullivan, Rita Johnson, Elsa Lanchester

The Big Combo*
US 1955   80m   bw
Allied Artists / Security-Theodora (Sidney Harmon)

The police crush a crime syndicate.
An otherwise uninspired thriller memorable for starting the new violence, with some ugly scenes of torture which suffered at the time from the censor.

w Philip Yordan *d* Joseph H. Lewis *ph* John Alton *m* David Raksin

Cornel Wilde, Richard Conte, Jean Wallace, Brian Donlevy, Robert Middleton, Lee Van Cleef, Ted de Corsia, Helen Walker, John Hoyt

The Big Country***
US 1958   165m   Technirama
UA / Anthony / Worldwide (William Wyler, Gregory Peck)

The Ter
ills and the Hannesseys feud over water rights, and peace is brought about only with the deaths of the family heads.
Big-scale western with a few pretensions to say something about the Cold War. All very fluent, star-laden and easy to watch.

w James R. Webb, Sy Bartlett, Robert Wilder, *novel* Donald Hamilton *d William Wyler ph Franz Planer m Jerome Moross*

Gregory Peck, Jean Simmons, Charlton Heston, Carroll Baker, *Burl Ives, Charles Bickford,* Alfonso Bedoya, Chuck Connors

AA: Burl Ives
AAN: Jerome Moross

Big Fella*
GB 1937   73m   bw
Fortune (J. Elder Wills)

In Marseilles, a black man returns a lost child to his English parents.
Pleasant light vehicle with the star in typical easy form.

w Fenn Sherie, Ingram d'Abbes, *novel* Banjo by Claude McKay *d* J. Elder Wills

Paul Robeson, Elizabeth Welch, Roy Emerton, Marcelle Rogez

The Big Fisherman
US 1959   166m   Technicolor   Panavision
Centurion (Rowland V. Lee)

An Arab princess meets disciple Simon Peter, who dissuades her from her plan to assassinate her stepfather Herod.
Well-meaning but leaden adaptation of a bestselling novel which followed on from *The Robe*. Too reverent by half, and in many respects surprisingly incompetent.

w Howard Estabrook, Rowland V. Lee, *novel* Lloyd C. Douglas *d* Frank Borzage *ph* Lee Garmes *m* Albert Hay Malotte *pd* John de Cuir

Howard Keel, Alexander Scourby, Susan Kohner, John Saxon, Martha Hyer, Herbert Lom, Ray Stricklyn, Beulah Bondi

'Its overall flatness of conception and execution is a stiff price to pay for the lack of spectacular sensationalism characterizing its fellow-epics.'—*MFB*

AAN: Lee Garmes

The Big Gamble*
US 1960   100m   De Luxe   Cinemascope
TCF / Darryl F. Zanuck

Three people drive an ailing truck to a remote African township where they hope to start a haulage business.
Curious comedy-drama-adventure which starts off with family matters in Dublin and gradually develops into a lighter-hearted *Wages of Fear*. It has its moments.

w Irwin Shaw *d* Richard Fleischer, Elmo Williams *ph* William Mellor, Henri Persin *m* Maurice Jarre

Stephen Boyd, Juliette Greco, David Wayne, *Gregory Ratoff*, Sybil Thorndike, Fernand Ledoux

A Big Hand for the Little Lady **

US 1966 96m Technicolor
Warner / Eden (Fielder Cook)
GB title: *Big Deal at Dodge City* (though the
action clearly takes place in Laredo)

Five rich poker players are outwitted by a family
of confidence tricksters.

Diverting but thinly stretched acting-piece from
a much shorter TV original; still, suspense builds
nicely until the disappointingly handled
revelation.

w Sidney Carroll, from his own TV play
d Fielder Cook ph Lee Garmes *m* David
Raksin

Henry Fonda, *Joanne Woodward*, Jason
Robards, Paul Ford, Kevin McCarthy, *Charles
Bickford*, Robert Middleton, *Burgess Meredith*,
John Qualen

The Big Hangover

US 1950 82m bw
MGM (Norman Krasna)

A lawyer struggling to mingle with the mighty
finds he is allergic to strong drink.
Woefully unfunny comedy with virtually no plot.

wd Norman Krasna *ph* George Folsey
m Adolph Deutsch

Van Johnson, Elizabeth Taylor, Percy Waram,
Fay Holden, Leon Ames, Edgar Buchanan,
Rosemary de Camp, Gene Lockhart, Selena
Royle

The Big Heat **

US 1953 90m bw
Columbia (Robert Arthur)

A police detective's wife is killed by a bomb
meant for himself; he goes undercover to track
down the gangsters responsible.
Considered at the time to reach a new low in
violence (boiling coffee in the face), this dour
little thriller also struck a new note of realism in
crime films and produced one of Glenn Ford's
most typical performances.

w Sydney Boehm, *novel* William P. McGivern
d Fritz Lang *ph* Charles Lang *m* Arthur
Morton *md* Mischa Bakaleinikoff

Glenn Ford, Gloria Grahame, Alexander
Scourby, Jocelyn Brando, Lee Marvin, Jeanette
Nolan, Peter Whitney
   'The main impression is of violence employed
arbitrarily, mechanically and in the long run
pointlessly.'—*Penelope Houston*

The Big House **

US 1930 88m bw
MGM

Tensions in prison lead to an attempted break-
out and a massacre.
Archetypal prison melodrama and a significant
advance in form for early talkies. Its sets were re-
used by Laurel and Hardy in *Pardon Us*.

w Frances Marion d George Hill ph Harold
Wenstrom

Chester Morris, Wallace Beery, Robert
Montgomery, Lewis Stone, Leila Hyams,
George F. Marion, J. C. Nugent, Karl Dane

AA: Frances Marion
AAN: best picture; Wallace Beery

Big House USA

US 1954 82m bw
UA / Bel Air (Aubrey Schenck)

Convicts stage a break-out to get at hidden loot.
Though less explicit in its violence than many
later films, this is a singularly unpleasant
melodrama with not one attractive character.

w John C. Higgins *d* Howard W. Koch
ph Gordon Avil *m* Paul Dunlap

Broderick Crawford, Ralph Meeker, Lon
Chaney, Charles Bronson, William Talman,
Reed Hadley

Big Jack

US 1949 85m bw
MGM (Gottfried Reinhardt)

Adventures of a couple of amiable scoundrels in
1890 Virginia.
The elements don't jell in this outdoor comedy-
drama, which was its star's last film.

w Gene Fowler, Marvin Borowsky, Otto Van
Eyss *d* Richard Thorpe *ph* Robert Surtees
m Herbert Stothart

Wallace Beery, Marjorie Main, Richard Conte,
Edward Arnold, Vanessa Brown, Clinton
Sundberg, Charles Dingle, Clem Bevans

Big Jake *

US 1971 110m Technicolor Panavision
Batjac / Cinema Center (Michael A. Wayne)

An elderly Texas cattleman swings into action
when his grandson is kidnapped.
Satisfactory example of the star's later vehicles,
with efficient production and familiar cast and
brawling.

w Harry Julian Fink, R. M. Fink *d* George
Sherman *ph* William Clothier *m* Elmer
Bernstein

John Wayne, Richard Boone, Maureen O'Hara,
Patrick Wayne, Chris Mitchum, Bobby Vinton,
Bruce Cabot, Glenn Corbett, Harry Carey Jnr,
John Agar
   'Another genial celebration of Big John's

ability to carry a film practically single-handed.'—*MFB*

Big Jim McLain
US 1952   90m   bw
Wayne / Fellows (Robert Fellows)

A special agent for the House of UnAmerican Activities Committee routs communists in Hawaii.

Curious and rather offensive star vehicle in which the right-wing political shading interferes seriously with the entertainment value.

w James Edward Grant *d* Edward Ludwig
ph Archie Stout *m* Emil Newman

John Wayne, Nancy Olson, James Arness, Alan Napier, Veda Ann Borg, Hans Conried, Gayne Whitman

'Brings to the screen all the unattractively hysterical mentality of the witch hunt.'—*Penelope Houston*

The Big Knife*
US 1955   111m   bw
UA / Aldrich and Associates

A depressed Hollywood star who wants better things for himself is blackmailed into signing a new contract.

Overheated argument between Art and Mammon, with rather disagreeable people shouting at each other, for too long a time. Limited interest is provided by the acting.

w James Poe, *play* Clifford Odets *d* Robert Aldrich *ph* Ernest Laszlo *m* Frank de Vol

Jack Palance, Ida Lupino, *Rod Steiger*, Everett Sloane, Jean Hagen, Shelley Winters, Wendell Corey, Ilka Chase, Wesley Addy

'Everything in it is garish and overdone: it's paced too fast and pitched too high, immorality is attacked with almost obscene relish, the knife turns into a buzz saw.'—*Pauline Kael, 1968*

The Big Land
US 1957   92m   Warnercolor
(Warner) Jaguar
GB title: *Stampeded*

Cattlemen encourage the building of a rail link for Texas.

Undistinguished star western.

w David Dortort, Martin Rackin, *novel* Buffalo Grass by Frank Gruber *d* Gordon Douglas

Alan Ladd, Virginia Mayo, Edmond O'Brien, Anthony Caruso, Julie Bishop, John Qualen

'Hackneyed, humdrum western.'—*Howard Thompson*

The Big Lift*
US 1949   119m   bw
TCF (William Perlberg)

When the Russians blockade Berlin, British and American airmen get supplies there via a massive airlift; two men on one plane hold opposite views of the matter, and both have chastening experiences.

Rather heavy-going fiction based on fact, with earnest performances and good production.

wd George Seaton *ph* Charles G. Clarke
m Alfred Newman

Montgomery Clift, Paul Douglas, Cornell Borchers,
O. E. Hasse, Bruni Lobel

'There are some acute touches . . . just enough to make the slick evasions of the rest all the more regrettable.'—*Gavin Lambert*

The Big Money
GB 1956   86m   Technicolor   Vistavision
Rank

A family of petty crooks is ashamed of its eldest son, who is an incompetent thief.

A would-be high-spirited lark in which none of the jokes comes off, and a note of forced artificiality hangs over the whole production.

w John Baines *d* John Paddy Carstairs *ph* Jack Cox *m* Van Phillips

Ian Carmichael, Belinda Lee, Kathleen Harrison, Robert Helpmann, James Hayter, George Coulouris, Jill Ireland, Renee Houston, Leslie Phillips

The Big Mouth
US 1967   107m   Pathecolor
Columbia (Jerry Lewis)

A meek bank auditor finds he is the double of a dying gangster and is put on the trail of stolen diamonds.

The comedian at his worst, most repetitive and long drawn out.

w Jerry Lewis, Bill Richmond *d* Jerry Lewis
ph W. Wallace Kelley, Ernest Laszlo *m* Harry Betts

Jerry Lewis, Harold J. Stone, Susan Day, Buddy Lester, Del Moore

The Big Night
US 1951   75m   bw
(UA) Philip A. Waxman

A 17-year-old youth goes on the rampage in the underworld to avenge the beating up of his father by gangsters.

Hysterical melodrama presenting a rather false

and dismal view of the world. Amazingly typical of its director's later output.

w Stanley Ellin, Joseph Losey, *novel* Dreadful Summit by Stanley Ellin d Joseph Losey ph Hal Mohr m Lyn Murray

John Barrymore Jnr, Preston Foster, Howard St John, Philip Bourneuf, Howland Chamberlin, Emile Meyer, Dorothy Comingore, Joan Lorring

'We are in that familiar underworld of the American cinema: dark streets gleaming with rain, sleazy apartments, garish night clubs, with Negro singers, drunks who spout philosophy, discontented blondes and fierce pock-marked thugs.'—*Gavin Lambert*

The Big Noise
US 1944   74m   bw
TCF (Sol M. Wurtzel)

Two incompetent detectives accidentally round up a spy gang.
Very thin star vehicle consisting largely of poorly staged and warmed up versions of a few old routines.

w Scott Darling d Mal St Clair ph Joe MacDonald

Stan Laurel, Oliver Hardy, Doris Merrick, Arthur Space, Jack Norton

The Big Operator
US 1959   91m   bw   Cinemascope
MGM / Albert Zugsmith-Fryman (Red Doff)
The racketeer head of a labour union goes berserk when the government has him investigated.
Unpleasant gangster exploitation melodrama from the bottom of the barrel.

w Robert Smith, Allen Rivkin d Charles Haas ph Walter H. Castle m Van Alexander

Mickey Rooney, Steve Cochran, Mamie Van Doren, Mel Tormé, Ray Danton, Jim Backus, Jackie Coogan, Ray Anthony, Charles Chaplin Jnr

The Big Parade***
US 1925   115m approx (24 fps)   bw
silent
MGM

A young American enlists in 1917, learns the realities of war, is wounded but survives.
Enormously successful commercially, this 'anti-war' film survives best as a thrilling spectacle and a well-considered piece of film-making.

w Lawrence Stallings, Harry Behn d King Vidor ph John Arnold m William Axt, David Mendoza

John Gilbert, Renee Adoree, Hobart Bosworth, Karl Dane, George K. Arthur

'The human comedy emerges from a terrifying tragedy.'—*King Vidor*

The Big Parade of Comedy**
US 1964   90m approx   bw
MGM (Robert Youngson)
aka: *MGM's Big Parade of Comedy*

A compilation by Robert Youngson, including material as diverse as *Ninotchka*, Laurel and Hardy and the Marx Brothers.
One is grateful for the excerpts but the assembly of them is somewhat graceless.

The Big Pond*
US 1930   79m   bw
Paramount (Monta Bell)

The son of an important French family acts as a tourist guide in Venice.
Reasonably lively, semi-satirical early musical with Americans the butt of the jokes.

w Robert Presnell, Garrett Fort, Preston Sturges, *play* George Middleton, A. E. Thomas d Hobart Henley ph George Folsey
songs various

Maurice Chevalier, Claudette Colbert, George Barbier, Nat Pendleton, Marion Ballou

AAN: Maurice Chevalier

Big Red
US 1962   89m   Technicolor
Walt Disney (Winston Hibler)

An orphan boy protects a dog which later saves him from a mountain lion.
Simple boy-and-dog yarn with impressive Canadian settings.

w Louis Pelletier d Norman Tokar ph Edward Colman

Walter Pidgeon, Gilles Payant, Emile Genest

The Big Shakedown
US 1934   64m   bw
Warner (Sam Bischoff)

A racketeer finds a new gimmick: cut-price medicine.
Action programmer with emphasis on the young couple forced into helping the racket.

w Niven Busch, Rian James d John Francis Dillon ph Sid Hickox

Bette Davis, Ricardo Cortez, Charles Farrell, Glenda Farrell, Allen Jenkins, Henry O'Neill, Samuel S. Hinds

'A routine assortment of gang-film impedimenta.'—*New York Times*

The Big Shot*
US 1942   82m   bw
Warner (Walter MacEwen)

An ill-fated criminal has trouble with women and
his former companions.
Dullish star vehicle.

w Bertram Millhauser, Aben Finkel, Daniel
Fuchs d Lewis Seiler ph Sid Hickox

Humphrey Bogart, Irene Manning, Richard
Travis, Donald Crisp, Stanley Ridges, Henry
Hull, Arthur Kennedy, Susan Peters, Howard da
Silva

The Big Show
US 1961   113m   De Luxe   Cinemascope
TCF / API (Ted Sherdeman)

A circus proprietor dominates his sons; after his
death they fight for supremacy.
Another remake of *House of Strangers*, which
was also remodelled as *Broken Lance*. Not too
bad as circus melodramas go.

w Ted Sherdeman d James B. Clark ph Otto
Heller m Paul Sawtell, Bert Shefter

Esther Williams, Cliff Robertson, *Nehemiah
Persoff*, Robert Vaughn, Carol Christensen,
Margia Dean, David Nelson

The Big Sky*
US 1952   122m   bw
RKO (Howard Hawks)

In 1830 two Kentucky mountain men join an
exploration up the Missouri and become
preoccupied with Indian trouble.
A large-scale adventure, loaded with talent,
which becomes oddly tedious.

w Dudley Nichols, *novel* A. B. Guthrie Jnr
d Howard Hawks ph Russell Harlan m Dmitri
Tiomkin

Kirk Douglas, Arthur Hunnicutt, Elizabeth
Threatt, Dewey Martin, Buddy Baer, Steve
Geray, Jim Davis
   'It has the timeless, relentless quality of the
long American historical novel.'—*Penelope
Houston*

AAN: Russell Harlan; Arthur Hunnicutt

The Big Sleep***
US 1946   114m   bw
Warner (Howard Hawks)

Private eye Philip Marlowe is hired to protect
General Sternwood's wild young daughter from
her own indiscretions, and finds several murders
later that he has fallen in love with her elder
sister.
Inextricably complicated, moody thriller from a
novel whose author claimed that even he did not

know 'who done it'. The film is nevertheless
vastly enjoyable along the way for its slangy
script, star performances and outbursts of
violence, suspense and sheer fun.

w *William Faulkner, Leigh Brackett, Jules
Furthman, novel Raymond Chandler d Howard
Hawks ph Sid Hickox m Max Steiner*

Humphrey Bogart, Lauren Bacall, Martha
Vickers, John Ridgely, Dorothy Malone, Regis
Toomey, Charles Waldron, Elisha Cook Jnr
   'A sullen atmosphere of sex saturates the film,
which is so fast and complicated you can hardly
catch it.'—*Richard Winnington*
   'A violent, smoky cocktail shaken together
from most of the printable misdemeanours and
some that aren't.'—*James Agee*
   'Harder, faster, tougher, funnier and more
laconic than any thriller since.'—*NFT, 1974*
   'Wit, excitement and glamour in generous
doses.'—*Francis Wyndham*

The Big Sleep
GB 1977   99m   De Luxe
ITC / Elliott Kastner, Michael Winner

Straight remake of the 1946 film, curiously and
ineffectively set in London.

wd Michael Winner ph Robert Paynter m Jerry
Fielding

Robert Mitchum, Sarah Miles, Richard Boone,
Candy Clark, Edward Fox, Joan Collins, John
Mills, James Stewart, Oliver Reed, Harry
Andrews, Richard Todd, James Donald, Colin
Blakely
   'The 1946 film takes on even more stature in
light of this. For a Winner film, however, it's
quite good.'—*Variety*

The Big Steal**
US 1949   72m   bw
RKO (Jack J. Gross)

An army officer is framed for the theft of a
payroll, and sets off across Mexico in hectic
pursuit of the real culprit.
Unexpectedly enjoyable comedy melodrama
with a plethora of twists and a pace that never
lets up. Routine Hollywood at a level seldom
achieved, and short enough to leave one asking
for more.

w *Gerald Drayson Adams, Geoffrey Homes,
story* The Road to Carmichael's by Richard
Wormser d Don Siegel ph Harry J. Wild
m Leigh Harline

Robert Mitchum, Jane Greer, William Bendix,
Ramon Novarro, Patric Knowles, Don
Alvarado, John Qualen
   'Vigour and excellent craftsmanship.'—*Gavin
Lambert*

The Big Store*
US 1941   83m   bw
MGM (Louis K. Sidney)

An eccentric private eye saves a department store from the hands of crooks.
Reckoned to be the Marx Brothers' weakest MGM vehicle, but it has its moments, especially the first reel and the bedding department scene, also Groucho's rendering of 'Sing While You Sell'.

w Sid Kuller, Hal Fimberg, Ray Golden d Charles Reisner ph Charles Lawton m George Stoll

Groucho, Chico, Harpo, Margaret Dumont, Douglass Dumbrille, Tony Martin, Virginia Grey, Virginia O'Brien, Henry Armetta

The Big Street*
US 1942   88m   bw
RKO (Damon Runyon)

A Broadway nightclub waiter falls in love with a crippled singer who selfishly accepts his help without loving him in return.
Unusual but mawkish material from an author who never really suited the screen; a mixture of laughs, tears and sentimentality, with a comic gangster background.

w Leonard Spiegelgass, *story* Little Pinks by Damon Runyon d Irving Reis ph Russell Metty m Roy Webb

Henry Fonda, Lucille Ball, Eugene Pallette, Virginia Weidler, Agnes Moorehead, Barton MacLane, Ozzie Nelson and his Orchestra, Sam Levene, Ray Collins, Marion Martin

The Big Trail*
US 1930   125m   bw
Fox

A wagon train struggles along the Oregon trail.
Simple-minded early talkie western spectacular with a new young star who took another nine years to make it big. Originally shown on a giant 70mm gauge and intended for big screens.

w Jack Peabody, Marie Boyle, Florence Postal d Raoul Walsh ph Lucien Andriot, Arthur Edeson

John Wayne, Marguerite Churchill, El Brendel, Tully Marshall, Tyrone Power Snr, David Rollins, Ward Bond, Helen Parrish

The Big Trees**
US 1952   89m   Technicolor
Warner (Louis F. Edelmann)

An unscrupulous lumberman tries to exploit California's giant redwood forests but is won over by the local Quakers who hold the trees in awe.

Pleasing, old-fashioned outdoor drama with a plot which allows the star much opportunity for derring-do.

w John Twist, James R. Webb d Felix Feist ph Bert Glennon m Heinz Roemheld

Kirk Douglas, Eve Miller, Patrice Wymore, Edgar Buchanan, John Archer, Alan Hale Jnr

The Big Wheel
US 1949   92m   bw
(UA) Popkin / Stiefel / Dempsey (Samuel H. Stiefel)

The son of a racing driver is determined to follow in father's footsteps.
Grubby star actioner.

w Robert Smith d Edward Ludwig ph Ernest Laszlo m Nat W. Finston

Mickey Rooney, Spring Byington, Thomas Mitchell, Mary Hatcher, Allen Jenkins

The Bigamist*
US 1953   80m   bw
Filmmakers (Collier Young)

A travelling salesman has two wives.
Minor melodrama which took its subject seriously but failed to make absorbing drama of it. Very much a family affair, starring the producer's present and past wives, the latter also directing.

w Collier Young d Ida Lupino ph George Diskant m Leith Stevens

Edmond O'Brien, Joan Fontaine, Ida Lupino, Edmund Gwenn, Jane Darwell
   'The film seems to have summoned all its energy to shout defiantly that bigamous marriages exist and, finding no one to defy, retires deflated.'—*MFB*

The Bigamist*
Italy / France 1956   97m   bw
Royal / Filmel / Alba

An innocent young salesman is accused of bigamy and dragged into court.
Noisy comedy of mistaken identity; some laughs, but the talents are not at their best.

w Sergio Amidei, Age Scarpelli, Franco Rosi, Elio Talarico d Luciano Emmer ph Mario Montuori m Alessandro Cicognini

Marcello Mastroianni, Vittorio de Sica, Franca Valeri, Giovanna Ralli

Bigger than Life*
US 1956   95m   Eastmancolor Cinemascope
TCF / James Mason

A small-town schoolteacher is prescribed

cortisone for arthritis; it gradually turns him into a bullying megalomaniac full of grandiose schemes.
Exaggerated and sensationalized but still not very dramatic expansion of a genuine case history. A curious choice for all concerned.

w Cyril Hume, Richard Maibaum d Nicholas Ray ph Joe MacDonald m David Raksin

James Mason, Barbara Rush, Walter Matthau, Robert Simon, Roland Winters

The Biggest Bundle of Them All
US 1967 110m Metrocolor Panavision
MGM / Shaftel–Stewart

A retired gangster is kidnapped by other gangsters and shows them how to steal five million dollars worth of platinum.
Very moderately amusing international comedy caper.

w Josef Shaftel, Sy Salkowitz d Ken Annakin ph Piero Portalupi m Riz Ortolani

Raquel Welch, Robert Wagner, Vittorio de Sica, Edward G. Robinson, Godfrey Cambridge, Davy Kaye
'It begins like one of these really bad movies that are unintentionally funny. Then it becomes clear that it intends to be funny, and it isn't.'— Renata Adler

A Bill of Divorcement **
US 1932 76m bw
David O. Selznick

A middle-aged man, released from a mental institution, comes home and meets his strong-willed daughter.
Pattern play which became a celebrated star vehicle; now very dated but the performances survive.

w Howard Estabrook, Harry Wagstaff Gribble, play Clemence Dane d George Cukor ph Sid Hickox

John Barrymore, Katharine Hepburn (her debut), Billie Burke, David Manners, Paul Cavanagh, Henry Stephenson, Elizabeth Patterson

A Bill of Divorcement *
US 1940 69m bw
David O. Selznick
GB title: Never To Love

Virtually a scene-for-scene remake of the above. Again the acting holds the material together.

w Dalton Trumbo d John Farrow ph Nicholas Musuraca

Adolphe Menjou, Maureen O'Hara, Patric

Knowles, Herbert Marshall, C. Aubrey Smith, Dame May Whitty

Billie
US 1965 87m Techniscope
UA / Peter Lawford (Don Weis)

A teenage tomboy runs into trouble because she is better at sport than her boy friends.
Routine American college/domestic comedy with a young star and good comedy support.

w Ronald Alexander, from his play Time Out for Ginger d Don Weis ph John Russell m Dominic Frontière

Patty Duke, Jim Backus, Jane Greer, Warren Berlinger, Billy de Wolfe, Charles Lane, Dick Sargent, Richard Deacon

Billion Dollar Brain
GB 1967 111m Technicolor Panavision
UA / Lowndes (Harry Saltzman)

Ex-secret agent Harry Palmer agrees to take a mysterious canister to Finland and becomes involved in an American megalomaniac's bid to take over the world.
Incomprehensible spy story smothered in the kind of top dressing now expected from this director, but which almost killed his career at the time. Occasional pictorial pleasures, but the total kaleidoscopic effect is enough to drive most audiences to the exit.

w John McGrath, novel Len Deighton d Ken Russell ph Billy Williams m Richard Rodney Bennett pd Syd Cain

Michael Caine, Oscar Homolka, Françoise Dorléac, Karl Malden, Ed Begley

Billy Budd *
GB 1962 125m bw Cinemascope
Anglo-Allied (A. Ronald Lubin, Peter Ustinov)

In 1797 the sadistic master at arms of a British warship terrorizes the crew and is killed by young Billy Budd, who must hang for his unpremeditated crime.
Handsomely photographed but obtusely scripted and variously acted attempt at the impossible, an allegory of good and evil more suited to opera or the printed page than film: in any case, a hopelessly and defiantly uncommercial enterprise. Some actors bore, others chew the scenery.

w Peter Ustinov, Robert Rossen, novel Herman Melville d Peter Ustinov ph Robert Krasker m Anthony Hopkins

Peter Ustinov, Robert Ryan, Terence Stamp, Melvyn Douglas, Paul Rogers, John Neville, Ronald Lewis, David McCallum, Lee

Montague, John Meillon, Thomas Heathcote,
Niall MacGinnis, Cyril Luckham

AAN: Terence Stamp

Billy Jack*
US 1971   113m   Technicolor
Warner / National Student Film Corporation
(Mary Rose Solti)

A half-breed Vietnam veteran roams the
Arizona desert protecting wild mustangs and a
runaway teenager.

A trendy radical drama, virtually a one-man
show which had an enormous success in the US
and led to a sequel, *The Trial of Billy Jack* (qv).

w Tom Laughlin, Delores Taylor *d* Tom
Laughlin (T. C. Frank) *ph* Fred Koenekamp,
John Stephens *m* Mundell Lowe

Tom Laughlin, Delores Taylor, Bert Freed,
Clark Howat, Julie Webb, Ken Tobey, Victor
Izay

'A plea for the alternative society with a
format of the crudest melodrama.'—*MFB*

Billy Liar*
GB 1963   98m   bw   Cinemascope
Vic Films (Joe Janni)

In a drab North Country town, an undertaker's
clerk lives in a world of fantasy.

Flawed only by its unsuitable Cinemascope
ratio, this is a brilliant urban comedy of its time,
seminal in acting, theme, direction and
permissiveness. From a novel and play no doubt
inspired by Thurber's Walter Mitty, it was later
turned into a TV series and a successful stage
musical, making Billy a universal figure of the
period.

w *Keith Waterhouse, Willis Hall*, from KW's
novel and their play *d* *John Schlesinger*
ph Denys Coop *m* Richard Rodney Bennett

Tom Courtenay, Julie Christie, Wilfred Pickles,
Mona Washbourne, *Ethel Griffies*, Finlay
Currie, Rodney Bewes, Leonard Rossiter

Billy the Kid*
US 1930   90m   bw
MGM

A young western outlaw is relentlessly pursued
by Sheriff Pat Garrett.

Mildly interesting early talkie western with the
usual romanticized view of Billy. Originally
made and shown in 70mm.

w Wanda Tuchock, Laurence Stallings, Charles
MacArthur *d* King Vidor

Johnny Mack Brown, Wallace Beery, Kay
Johnson, Karl Dane, Roscoe Ates

Billy the Kid*
US 1941   95m   Technicolor
MGM

Remake of the above, equally false and rather
less well acted, but a striking outdoor colour film
of its period.

w Gene Fowler *d* David Miller *ph* Leonard
Smith, William V. Skall *m* David Snell

Robert Taylor, Brian Donlevy, Ian Hunter,
Mary Howard, Gene Lockhart, Henry O'Neill,
Frank Puglia, Cy Kendall, Ethel Griffies

AAN: Leonard Smith, William V. Skall

Billy Two Hats
US 1973   99m   Technicolor
UA / Algonquin (Norman Jewison, Patrick
Palmer, Mitchell Lifton)

The friendship of an old Scottish outlaw and a
young half-breed is broken only by the old man's
death.

Curiously miscast western shot in Israel; it
makes no discernible point and is not very
entertaining.

w Alan Sharp *d* Ted Kotcheff *ph* Brian West
m John Scott

Gregory Peck, Desi Arnez Jnr, Jack Warden,
Sian Barbara Allen, David Huddleston

**The Bingo Long Traveling All-Stars and
Motor Kings**
US 1976   111m   Technicolor
Universal (Rob Cohen)

Adventures of a black baseball team in the
1940s.

High-spirited japes and exhibitions of athleticism
which dramatically do not add up to very much.

w Hal Barwood, Matthew Robbins, *novel*
William Brashler *d* John Badham *ph* Bill
Butler *m* William Goldstein

Billy Dee Williams, James Earl Jones, Richard
Pryor, Rico Dawson

Biography (of a Bachelor Girl)*
US 1935   84m   bw
MGM

The biography of a sophisticated lady portrait
painter reveals surprising details of her love life.
Leaden, bowdlerized screen version of a
sparkling Broadway play, fragments of which do
however survive.

w Anita Loos, *play* S. N. Behrman *d* Edward H.
Griffith *ph* James Wong Howe

Ann Harding (miscast), Robert Montgomery,
Edward Everett Horton, Edward Arnold, Una
Merkel, Charles Richman, Donald Meek

Bird of Paradise
US 1932   80m   bw
RKO

An adventurer on a South Sea island marries a native girl and causes trouble.
Never-never romance which remains stilted despite care obviously taken.

w Wells Root d King Vidor ph Clyde de Vinna m Max Steiner

Joel McCrea, John Halliday, Dolores del Rio, Skeets Gallagher

Bird of Paradise
US 1951   100m   Technicolor
TCF (Harmon Jones)

Opulent remake of the above; the trappings make it even more absurd, and the ritual sacrifice of the heroine seems misplaced in what is otherwise a pantomime.

wd Delmer Daves ph Winton Hoch m Daniele Amfitheatrof

Louis Jourdan, Jeff Chandler, Debra Paget, Maurice Schwartz, Everett Sloane, Jack Elam
'The Kahuna is a naively grotesque figure, with a Central European accent and carrying what appears to be an outsize radish: he personifies the film's dubious approach to Polynesian myth and culture.'—Gavin Lambert

Birdman of Alcatraz *
US 1961   148m   bw
UA / Hecht–Lancaster (Stuart Millar, Guy Trosper)

An imprisoned murderer makes a name for himself as an ornithologist.
Overlong and rather weary biopic of Robert Stroud, who spent nearly sixty years in prison and became a cause célèbre. One cannot deny many effective moments, notably of direction, but it's a long haul.

w Guy Trosper, book Thomas E. Gaddis d John Frankenheimer ph Burnett Guffey m Elmer Bernstein

Burt Lancaster, Karl Malden, Thelma Ritter, Edmond O'Brien, Betty Field, Neville Brand, Hugh Marlowe, Telly Savalas, James Westerfield

AAN: Burnett Guffey; Burt Lancaster; Thelma Ritter; Telly Savalas

The Birds ***
US 1963   119m   Technicolor
Universal / Alfred Hitchcock

In a Californian coastal area, flocks of birds unaccountably make deadly attacks on human beings.

A curiously absorbing work which begins as light comedy and ends as apocalyptic allegory, this piece of Hitchcockery has no visible point except to tease the audience and provide plenty of opportunity for shock, offbeat humour and special effects (which despite the drumbeating are not quite as good as might be expected). The actors are pawns in the master's hand.

w Evan Hunter, story Daphne du Maurier d Alfred Hitchcock ph Robert Burks sound consultant Bernard Herrmann sp Lawrence A. Hampton

Rod Taylor, Tippi Hedren, Jessica Tandy, Suzanne Pleshette, Ethel Griffies
'Enough to make you kick the next pigeon you come across.'—Judith Crist
'The dialogue is stupid, the characters insufficiently developed to rank as clichés, the story incohesive.'—Stanley Kauffmann

The Birds and the Bees
US 1956   94m   Technicolor   Vistavision
Paramount (Paul Jones)

On a transatlantic voyage a wealthy simpleton is fleeced by a card sharp and his daughter; but the latter falls in love with her victim.
Competent but uninspired reworking of The Lady Eve as a vehicle for a rather charmless comic. Lacking Preston Sturges at the helm, the mixture of slapstick and sentiment fails to jell.

w Sidney Sheldon after Preston Sturges d Norman Taurog ph Daniel Fapp m Walter Scharf

George Gobel, David Niven, Mitzi Gaynor, Fred Clark, Reginald Gardiner, Harry Bellaver, Hans Conried

Birds Come to Die in Peru
France 1968   98m   Technicolor   Franscope
Universal (Jacques Natteau)

On a Peruvian beach a tormented nymphomaniac makes love to several men and attempts suicide, but is rescued by her true love. Elaborate high-flown bosh, quite fun to watch.

wd Romain Gary ph Christian Matras m Kenton Coe

Jean Seberg, Maurice Ronet, Danielle Darrieux, Pierre Brasseur

Birds Do It
US 1966   88m   colour
Columbia (Ivan Tors, Stanley Colbert)

A janitor at an atomic plant is accidentally ionized and finds he can fly, which enables him to catch a spy or two.
Childish stunt comedy.

w Arnie Kogen *d* Andrew Marton *ph* Howard Winner *m* Samuel Maltovsky

Soupy Sales, Tab Hunter, Arthur O'Connell, Edward Andrews, Doris Dowling, Beverly Adams, Louis Quinn

The Birds, the Bees and the Italians
Italy / France 1965 98m colour
Dear Film / Films du Siècle (Robert Haggiag, Pietro Germi)
original title: *Signore e Signori*

Stories of adultery in an Italian provincial town. Mainly tedious sex comedy full of gesticulating actors.

w Furio Scarpelli, Luciano Vincenzoni, Pietro Germi *d* Pietro Germi *ph* Aiace Parolin *m* Carlo Rustichelli

Gastone Moschin, Virna Lisi, Alberto Lionello, Gigi Ballista, Beba Loncar, Franco Fabrizi

The Birth of a Nation****
US 1915 approx 185m (16 fps) bw silent
Epoch (D. W. Griffith, Harry E. Aitken)

Northern and southern families are caught up in the Civil War.

The cinema's first and still most famous epic, many sequences of which retain their mastery despite negro villains, Ku Klux Klan heroes, and white actors in blackface. Originally shown as *The Clansman*; a shorter version with orchestral track was released in 1931.

w D. W. Griffith, Frank E. Woods, *novel* The Klansman by Thomas Dixon Jnr *d D. W. Griffith ph G. W. Bitzer*

Henry B. Walthall, Mae Marsh, Miriam Cooper, Lillian Gish, Robert Harron, Wallace Reid, Donald Crisp, Joseph Henaberry, Raoul Walsh, Eugene Pallette, Walter Long

The Birth of the Blues*
US 1941 85m bw
Paramount (B. G. De Sylva, Monta Bell)

Trials and tribulations of a jazz band in New Orleans.

Thin fiction on which is strung a multitude of dark brown musical entertainment. Not bad, even now.

w Harry Tugend, Walter de Leon *d* Victor Schertzinger *ph* William C. Mellor *md* Robert Emmett Dolan

Bing Crosby, Mary Martin, Brian Donlevy, Jack Teagarden, Eddie Rochester Anderson, Carolyn Lee

AAN: Robert Emmett Dolan

The Birthday Party*
GB 1968 126m Technicolor
Palomar (Max Rosenberg, Milton Subotsky)

The down-at-heel lodger in a seaside boarding house is menaced by two mysterious strangers, who eventually take him away.

Overlong but otherwise satisfactory film record of an entertaining if infuriating play, first of the black absurdities which proliferated in the sixties to general disadvantage, presenting structure without plot and intelligence without meaning.

w Harold Pinter, from his play *d* William Friedkin *ph* Denys Coop *m* none *pd* Edward Marshall

Sidney Tafler, Patrick Magee, Robert Shaw, *Dandy Nichols*, Moultrie Kelsall

The Birthday Present*
GB 1957 100m bw
BL / Jack Whittingham

A toy salesman's life is changed when he is charged with smuggling a watch through the customs.

Downcast, prolonged and rather uninteresting domestic drama; attention is held by generally good acting.

w Jack Whittingham *d* Pat Jackson *ph* Ted Scaife *m* Clifton Parker

Tony Britton, Sylvia Syms, Jack Watling, Walter Fitzgerald, Geoffrey Keen, Howard Marion Crawford, John Welsh

The Bishop's Wife**
US 1947 108m bw
Samuel Goldwyn

An angel is sent down to mend the ways of a bishop whose absorption with cathedral buildings has put him out of touch with his wife and parishioners.

Whimsical, stolid and protracted light comedy saved by its actors and its old-fashioned Hollywood style.

w Robert E. Sherwood, Leonardo Bercovici, *novel* Robert Nathan *d* Henry Koster *ph* Gregg Toland *m* Hugo Friedhofer

Cary Grant, Loretta Young, David Niven,–Monty Woolley, James Gleason, Gladys Cooper, Elsa Lanchester, Sara Haden, Regis Toomey

AAN: best picture; Henry Koster; Hugo Friedhofer

Bite the Bullet*
US 1975 131m Metrocolor Panavision
Columbia / Persky–Bright / Vista (Richard Brooks)

Several cowboys compete in a 700-mile
endurance horse race.
Episodic adventure story with too much
muddled chat and a very thin connecting story
line; good to look at, though.

wd Richard Brooks *ph* Harry Stradling *m* Alex
North

Gene Hackman, Candice Bergen, James
Coburn, Ben Johnson, Ian Bannen, Jan-Michael
Vincent, Paul Stewart

AAN: Alex North

Bitter Harvest
GB 1963   96m   Eastmancolor
Rank / Independent Artists (Albert Fennell)

An innocent Welsh girl comes to London, is
deflowered, and sets off in search of wealth and
luxury at any price.
Naive sixties version of the road to ruin, quite
well done if you like that kind of thing.

w Ted Willis *d* Peter Graham Scott *ph* Ernest
Steward *m* Laurie Johnson

Janet Munro, John Stride, Anne Cunningham,
Alan Badel, Thora Hird, Vanda Godsell,
Terence Alexander

Bitter Rice*
Italy 1949   108m   bw
Lux Films
original title: *Riso Amaro*

In the rice fields of the Po valley, a thief on the
run meets a girl who tries to steal his loot.
Well-made exploitation melodrama which made
a star of the well-endowed Mangano but is not
otherwise more memorable than its innumerable
American counterparts.

w Carlo Lizzani, Carlo Musso, Gianni Puccini,
Corrado Alvaro, Ivo Perillo, Giuseppe de Santis
d Giuseppe de Santis *ph* Otello Martelli
m Goffredo Petrassi

Silvana Mangano, Raf Vallone, Doris Dowling,
Vittorio Gassman

Bitter Springs*
GB 1950   89m   bw
Ealing (Leslie Norman)

A pioneer family in Australia buys a patch of
ground but has trouble with aborigines.
Thinnest of the Ealing attempts to make movies
down under, suffering from a lack of pace and
sharpness as well as obvious studio settings.

w Monja Danischewsky, W. P. Lipscomb
d Ralph Smart *ph* George Heath *m* Vaughan
Williams

Chips Rafferty, Tommy Trinder, Gordon
Jackson, Jean Blue, Charles Tingwell

Bitter Sweet
GB 1933   93m   bw
British and Dominion (Herbert Wilcox)

In 1875 Vienna, a violinist marries a girl dancer
and is later killed by a gambler.
Rather feeble filming of Noel Coward's operetta:
it pleased a lot of people at the time.

w Lydia Hayward, Herbert Wilcox, Monckton
Hoffe *d* Herbert Wilcox

Anna Neagle, Fernand Gravet, Ivy St Helier,
Miles Mander, Esmé Percy, Hugh Williams, Pat
Peterson, Kay Hammond

Bitter Sweet
US 1940   94m   Technicolor
MGM (Victor Saville)

Remake of the above, retailored for unsuitable
leads and with the story and music unattractively
rearranged.

w Lesser Samuels, *operetta* Noel Coward *d* W.
S. Van
Dyke II *ph* Oliver T. Marsh, Allen Davey

Jeanette Macdonald, Nelson Eddy, George
Sanders, Felix Bressart, Ian Hunter, Fay
Holden, Sig Rumann, Herman Bing, Curt Bois

AAN: Oliver T. Marsh, Allen Davey

The Bitter Tea of General Yen**
US 1933   89m   bw
Columbia (Walter Wanger)

An American lady missionary in Shanghai is
captured by a Chinese warlord and falls in love
with him.
Arty miscegenation story which bids fair to
become a cult film and certainly has a number of
interesting sequences.

w Edward Paramore, *story* Grace Zaring Stone
d Frank Capra *ph* Joseph Walker *m* W. Frank
Harling

Barbara Stanwyck, Nils Asther, Toshia Mori,
Walter Connolly, Gavin Gordon, Lucien
Littlefield
† The film chosen to open Radio City Music
Hall.

Bitter Victory
US / France 1957   100m   bw
  Cinemascope
Columbia / Transcontinental / Robert Laffont

Two officers sent on a document raid in Libya
during World War II become poor soldiers
because one suspects the other of an affair with
his wife.
Glum desert melodrama, turgidly scripted and
boringly made.

w René Hardy, Nicholas Ray, Gavin Lambert,

novel Bitter Victory by René Hardy *d* Nicholas
Ray *ph* Michel Kelber *m* Maurice Le Roux

Richard Burton, Curt Jurgens, Ruth Roman,
Raymond Pellegrin, Anthony Bushell, Andrew
Crawford, Nigel Green, Christopher Lee

Black Angel*
US 1946 80m bw
U-I (Roy William Neill, Tom McKnight)

A drunk sets out to find the murderer of his wife,
and finds it was himself.
Stylish but empty version of a tired theme,
interesting for performances and atmosphere.

w Roy Chanslor, *novel* William Irish *d* Roy
William Neill *ph* Paul Ivano *m* Frank Skinner

Dan Duryea, Peter Lorre, Broderick Crawford,
June Vincent, Wallace Ford, Hobart
Cavanaugh, Constance Dowling

The Black Arrow
US 1948 76m bw
Columbia
GB title: *The Black Arrow Strikes*

During the Wars of the Roses, an English knight
seeks the murderer of his father.
Pennypinching swashbuckler which contrives to
entertain despite total disregard of probability.

w Richard Schayer, David P. Sheppard, Thomas
Seller, *novel* R. L. Stevenson *d* Gordon
Douglas *ph* Charles Lawton Jnr

Louis Hayward, Janet Blair, George Macready,
Edgar Buchanan, Paul Cavanaugh

Black Bart
US 1948 80m Technicolor
U-I (Leonard Goldstein)
GB title: *Black Bart, Highwayman*

Lola Montez, on an American tour, falls for an
American bandit.
Acceptable western programmer with historical
trimmings and some evidence of tongue-in-cheek
attitudes.

w Luci Ward, Jack Natteford, William Bowers
d George Sherman *ph* Irving Glassberg
m Frank Skinner

Yvonne de Carlo, Dan Duryea, Jeffrey Lynn,
Percy Kilbride, Lloyd Gough, Frank Lovejoy,
John McIntire, Don Beddoe

Black Beauty
US 1946 74m bw
(TCF) Edward L. Alperson

In Victorian England, a girl searches for her lost
colt.
Stilted children's film with little relation to the
book.

w Lillie Hayward, Agnes Christie Johnson, *novel*
Anna Sewell *d* Max Nosseck *m* Dmitri
Tiomkin

Mona Freeman, Richard Denning, Evelyn
Ankers,
J. M. Kerrigan, Terry Kilburn

Black Beauty*
GB 1971 106m colour
Tigon / Chilton (Tony Tenser)

A luckless horse passes from hand to hand but is
finally restored to its original young master and
has a happy retirement.
Pleasant, episodic animal story which stays
pretty close to the book. A shade yawn-inducing
for adults, but fine for children.

w Wolf Mankowitz, *novel* Anna Sewell *d* James
Hill *ph* Chris Menges *m* Lionel Bart, John
Cameron

Mark Lester, Walter Slezak, Peter Lee
Lawrence, Patrick Mower, John Nettleton,
Maria Rohm

The Black Bird
US 1975 98m colour
Columbia / Rastar (Michael Levee, Lou
Lombardo)

Sam Spade's son finds himself beset by crooks
still after the Maltese falcon.
Dismal, witless, boring parody of a classic crime
film, with none of the humour of the original.

wd David Giler *ph* Philip Lathrop *m* Jerry
Fielding

George Segal, Stéphane Audran, *Lee Patrick*,
Elisha Cook Jnr, Lionel Stander, John Abbott,
Signe Hasso, Felix Silla

'It doesn't work because it has nothing to
say.'—*Michael Billington, Illustrated London
News*

The Black Book*
US 1949 88m bw
Eagle–Lion
GB title: *Reign of Terror*

A member of a secret organization which plans
to replace Robespierre with a moderate goes
undercover with the French Revolutionaries.
Moderate period melodrama with an attractive
though artificial look.

w Philip Yordan, Aeneas Mackenzie *d* Anthony
Mann *ph* John Alton *m* Sol Kaplan

Robert Cummings, Arlene Dahl, Richard
Basehart, Richard Hart, Arnold Moss

The Black Cat*
US 1934   65m   bw
Universal
GB title: *House of Doom*

A revengeful doctor seeks out the Austrian architect and devil-worshipper who betrayed his country in World War I.

Absurd and dense farrago set in a modernistic but crumbling castle which is eventually blown to bits just as its owner is skinned alive. Mostly rather dull despite the extraordinary plot, but the thing has moments of style, a delightful cod devil worship sequence (especially for audiences with a rudimentary knowledge of Latin) and nothing at all to do with the title or Edgar Allan Poe.

w Peter Ruric *d* Edgar G. Ulmer *ph John Mescall m* Heinz Roemheld *ad* Charles D. Hall

Boris Karloff, *Bela Lugosi*, David Manners, Jacqueline Wells, Egon Brecher

The Black Cat*
US 1941   70m   bw
Universal

Murder follows the summoning of the family to the spooky house of a cat-loving recluse.

Disappointing mystery which squanders a splendid cast on a script full of non-sequiturs and makes heavy weather of its light relief.

w Robert Lees, Fred Rinaldo, Eric Taylor, Robert Neville *d* Albert S. Rogell *ph* Stanley Cortez

Basil Rathbone, Gladys Cooper, Broderick Crawford, Hugh Herbert, Gale Sondergaard, Anne Gwynne, Alan Ladd, Cecilia Loftus, Bela Lugosi

Black Friday*
US 1940   70m   bw
Universal

After an accident, a college professor is given a gangster's brain, and the surgeon encourages him to believe that he is the gangster so as to find hidden loot.

Plot-packed melodrama which fails to provide the chills suggested by the cast, but passes the time agreeably enough.

w Curt Siodmak, Eric Taylor *d* Arthur Lubin *ph* Woody Bredell *m* Hans Salter

Boris Karloff, Bela Lugosi, *Stanley Ridges*, Anne Nagel, Anne Gwynne, Virginia Brissac, Paul Fix

† Lugosi was originally cast as the professor, but proved wrong for the part; Stanley Ridges replaced him and walked off with the movie.

Black Fury*
US 1935   95m   bw
Warner (Robert Lord)

A coal miner comes up against union problems, unsafe conditions and corruption.

Typical Warner social drama, good for its time but now very obvious.

w Abem Finkel, Carl Erickson, *play* Bohunk by Harry R. Irving *d* Michael Curtiz *ph* Byron Haskin

Paul Muni, Karen Morley, William Gargan, Barton MacLane, John Qualen, J. Carrol Naish, Vince Barnett, Tully Marshall, Henry O'Neill

Black Hand*
US 1949   92m   bw
MGM (William H. Wright)

In New York at the turn of the century, an Italian boy avenges his father's death at the hands of the Mafia.

Neatly produced, studio-set melodrama, unusual in subject but very stereotyped and artificial in treatment.

w Luther Davis *d* Richard Thorpe *ph* Paul C. Vogel *m* Alberto Colombo

Gene Kelly, J. Carrol Naish, Teresa Celli, Marc Lawrence, Frank Puglia, Barry Kelley

The Black Knight
GB 1954   85m   Technicolor
Warwick (Irving Allen, Albert R. Broccoli)

A humble swordmaker reveals a traitor to King Arthur.

Hilarious travesty of English historical legend, meant seriously for Anglo-American consumption. Shades of *Zorro, Babes in the Wood* and *1066 and All That*.

w Alec Coppel *d* Tay Garnett *ph* John Wilcox *m* John Addison

Alan Ladd, Peter Cushing, Patricia Medina, Harry Andrews, André Morell, Anthony Bushell, Patrick Troughton, Laurence Naismith, John Laurie

  'Alan Ladd galahads with wild west *gentillesse* in this Technicolored rampage through British history.'—*MFB*

Black Legion**
US 1936   83m   bw
Warner (Robert Lord)

A factory worker becomes involved with the Ku Klux Klan.

Social melodrama typical of its studio, and good of its kind.

w Robert Lord, Abem Finkel, William Wister Haines *d* Archie Mayo *ph* George Barnes

Humphrey Bogart, Erin O'Brien Moore, Dick Foran, Ann Sheridan, Robert Barrat, John Litel, Charles Halton

'An honest job of film work, and one of the most direct social pieces released from Hollywood.'—*Otis Ferguson*

AAN: Robert Lord (original story)

Black Limelight*
GB 1938 70m bw
ABPC (Walter C. Mycroft)

The wife of a man convicted of killing his mistress proves that a 'moon murderer' did it. Naive but effective little chiller.

w Dudley Leslie, Walter Summers, *play* Gordon Sherry d Paul Stein

Raymond Massey, Joan Marion, Walter Hudd, Henry Oscar, Coral Browne

Black Magic*
US 1949 105m bw
Edward Small (Gregory Ratoff)

Cagliostro the magician becomes involved in a plot to supply a double for Marie Antoinette. Deliriously complicated historical romp which unfortunately suffers from a stolid script and production which kill all the flights of fancy.

w Charles Bennett d Gregory Ratoff ph Ubaldo Arata, Anchise Brizzi m Paul Sawtell

Orson Welles, Nancy Guild, Akim Tamiroff, Valentina Cortese, Margot Grahame, Charles Goldner, Frank Latimore, Stephen Bekassy

Black Narcissus***
GB 1946 100m Technicolor
GFD / The Archers (Michael Powell, Emeric Pressburger)

Anglo-Catholic nuns in the Himalayas have trouble with climate, morale, and one of their number who goes mad of sex frustration. An unlikely theme produces one of the cinema's most beautiful films, a visual and emotional stunner despite some narrative uncertainty.

wd Michael Powell, Emeric Pressburger, *novel* Rumer Godden *ph Jack Cardiff*

Deborah Kerr, David Farrar, Sabu, Jean Simmons, Kathleen Byron, Flora Robson, Esmond Knight, Jenny Laird, May Hallatt, Judith Furse

AA: Jack Cardiff

Black on White*
Finland 1967 95m Eastmancolor
Jorn Donner / FJ Film

A successful young executive falls in love with a

girl hitch-hiker, but when his wife leaves him the girl is no longer interested.
Showy romantic melodrama which tries to make rather too much of a slender theme.

wd Jorn Donner ph Esko Nevaleinen m George Riedel

Jorn Donner, Kristina Halkola, Liisamaija Laaksonen

The Black Orchid*
US 1958 95m bw Vistavision
Paramount (Carlo Ponti, Marcello Girosi)

A widower incurs hostility from his daughter when he plans to marry a gangster's widow. Rather solemn New York/Italian romantic melodrama, with much gesticulation all round.

w Joseph Stefano d Martin Ritt ph Robert Burks m Alessandro Cicognini

Sophia Loren, Anthony Quinn, Ina Balin, Jimmy Baird, Mark Richman

Black Orpheus*
France / Italy / Brazil 1958   106m
  Eastmancolor Cinemascope
Dispatfilm / Gemma / Tupan (Sacha Gordine)
original title: *Orfeu Negro*

Against a background of the Rio carnival, a black tram driver accidentally kills his girl friend, and after seeking her in the nether regions kills himself to be with her.
Rather irritating and noisy attempt to update a legend, without showing very much reason for doing so.

w Vinitius de Moraes d Marcel Camus ph Jean Bourgoin m Luis Bonfa, Antonio Carlos Jobim

Breno Mello, Marpessa Dawn, Ademar da Silva, Lourdes de Oliviera

The Black Pirate***
US 1926 76m approx (24 fps)
  Technicolor silent
Douglas Fairbanks

A shipwrecked mariner swears revenge on the pirates who blew up his father's ship.
Cheerful swashbuckler with the star in top form.

w Douglas Fairbanks, Jack Cunningham d Albert Parker ph Henry Sharp ad Oscar Borg, Dwight Franklin

Douglas Fairbanks, Billie Dove, Donald Crisp, Sam de Grasse

The Black Room*
US 1935 70m bw
Columbia

A nobleman's power is claimed by his evil twin brother.

Rather splendid old barnstormer with touches of horror, a neatly produced star vehicle.

w Henry Myers, from the writings of Arthur Strawn d *Roy William Neill* ph Al Siegler

Boris Karloff, Marian Marsh, Katherine de Mille, Thurston Hall

The Black Rose*
US 1950   120m   Technicolor
TCF (Louis D. Lighton)

A 13th-century English scholar journeys to the land of the Mongols, and after many adventures returns to a knighthood for his scientific discoveries.
Portentous and slow-moving adventure with good things along the way.

w Talbot Jennings, *novel* Thomas B. Costain d Henry Hathaway ph *Jack Cardiff* m Richard Addinsell ad Paul Sheriff

Tyrone Power, Orson Welles, Cecile Aubry, Jack Hawkins, Finlay Currie, Henry Oscar, Michael Rennie

The Black Scorpion
US 1957   88m   bw
Warner (Frank Melford, Jack Dietz)

Volcanic explosions uncover a nest of prehistoric giant scorpions near a Mexican village.
Apart from a genuinely terrifying sequence in the scorpion's lair, this is a poor monster movie in which excessively dark photography seems intended to cover up very variable trick work.

w David Duncan, Robert Bless d Edward Ludwig ph Lionel Lindon m Paul Sawtell sp Willis O'Brien

Richard Denning, Mara Corday, Carlos Rivas, Mario Navarro

The Black Sheep of Whitehall*
GB 1941   80m   bw
Ealing (S. C. Balcon)

An incompetent teacher is mistaken for an economics expert and saves the real expert from spies who run a nursing home.
Pretty good wartime star comedy, with a succession of briskly timed gags.

w Angus Macphail, John Dighton d Basil Dearden, Will Hay

Will Hay, John Mills, Basil Sydney, Frank Cellier, Felix Aylmer

The Black Shield of Falworth*
US 1954   99m   Technicolor
     Cinemascope
U-I (Robert Arthur, Melville Tucker)

The film in which Tony Curtis says 'Yonda lies the castle of my fodda' (or something like it) is an amiable romp which alternates between comic strip dialogue and a surprisingly convincing sense of medieval custom. The training scenes are as sharp as the romantic asides are pallid.

w Oscar Brodney, *novel* Men of Iron by Howard Pyle d Rudolph Maté ph Irving Glassberg m Joseph Gershenson

Tony Curtis, Janet Leigh, David Farrar, Barbara Rush, Herbert Marshall, Rhys Williams, Dan O'Herlihy, Torin Thatcher
   'A straightforward piece of hokum with no pretensions, and spoken in a variety of accents that only Hollywood could muster.'—*John Gillett*

The Black Sleep
US 1956   81m   bw
UA / Bel Air (Howard W. Koch)

A Victorian brain surgeon experiments on human beings and produces freaks who eventually turn on him.
Gruesome and humourless horror film notable only for its gallery of wasted talent.

w John C. Higgins d Reginald Le Borg ph Gordon Avil m Les Baxter

Basil Rathbone, Bela Lugosi, Lon Chaney Jnr, John Carradine, Akim Tamiroff, Tor Johnson, Herbert Rudley, Patricia Blake

Black Sunday*
US 1977   143m   Movielab   Panavision
Paramount (Robert Evans)

The Black September movement threatens a football game to be held in Miami's Superbowl.
Spectacular, heavily detailed, but somehow unexciting disaster melodrama.

w Ernest Lehman, Kenneth Ross, Ivan Moffat, *novel* Thomas Harris d John Frankenheimer ph John A. Alonzo m John Williams

Robert Shaw, Marthe Keller, Bruce Dern, Fritz Weaver, Steven Keats, Bekim Fehmiu, Michael V. Gazzo, William Daniels, Walter Gotell

The Black Swan***
US 1942   85m   Technicolor
TCF (Robert Bassler)

Morgan the pirate is made governor of Jamaica and enlists the help of his old friends to rid the Caribbean of buccaneers.
Rousing adventure story with comic asides: just what action hokum always aimed to be, with a spirited gallery of heroes and villains and an entertaining narrative taken at a spanking pace.

w *Ben Hecht, Seton I. Miller, novel* Rafael Sabatini d *Henry King* ph Leon Shamroy m Alfred Newman

Tyrone Power, Maureen O'Hara, *Laird Cregar, Thomas Mitchell, George Sanders*, Anthony Quinn, George Zucco, Edward Ashley

AA: Leon Shamroy
AAN: Alfred Newman

The Black Tent

GB 1956 93m Technicolor Vistavision
Rank / William MacQuitty

During a Libyan battle a wounded army captain is cared for by Arabs and marries the sheik's daughter. Ten years later, after his death, his son elects to live with the tribe.
Pleasantly shot but otherwise dull, formless and interminable romantic drama, all very stiff upper lip.

w Robin Maugham, Bryan Forbes *d* Brian Desmond Hurst *ph Desmond Dickinson m* William Alwyn

Anthony Steel, Donald Sinden, *André Morell*, Anna Maria Sandri, Ralph Truman, Donald Pleasance, Anthony Bushell, Michael Craig

The Black Torment*

GB 1964 85m Eastmancolor
Compton-Tekli (Robert Hartford-Davis)

The second wife of an 18th-century baronet investigates the hauntings which have followed the apparent suicide of his first.
Agreeably unpretentious period ghost story (with a rational explanation). Not exactly good, but better than one might expect.

w Donald and Derek Ford *d* Robert Hartford-Davis *ph* Peter Newbrook *m* Robert Richards

John Turner, Heather Sears, Ann Lynn, Joseph Tomelty, Peter Arne, Raymond Huntley

Black Tuesday*

US 1954 80m bw
UA / Leonard Goldstein (Robert Goldstein)

A killer escapes from Death Row and hides out with hostages in a disused warehouse.
Starkly melodramatic gangster vehicle with the star up to his oldest tricks. Good tension, but generally rather unpleasant.

w Sydney Boehm *d* Hugo Fregonese *ph* Stanley Cortez *m* Paul Dunlap

Edward G. Robinson, Jean Parker, Peter Graves, Milburn Stone, Warren Stevens, Jack Kelly, James Bell

Black Widow*

US 1954 95m De Luxe Cinemascope
TCF (Nunnally Johnson)

A Broadway producer is suspected of the murder of an ambitious young girl.

Reasonably classy whodunnit with glamorous settings and an able cast, but a little lacking in wit and pace.

wd Nunnally Johnson, *novel* Fatal Woman by Patrick Quentin *ph* Charles G. Clarke *m* Leigh Harline

Ginger Rogers, Van Heflin, George Raft, Gene Tierney, Peggy Ann Garner, Reginald Gardiner, Virginia Leith, Otto Kruger, Hilda Simms, Cathleen Nesbitt

The Black Windmill*

GB 1974 106m Technicolor Panavision
Universal / Zanuck–Brown (Don Siegel)

A secret service agent has to fight a lone battle when his young son is kidnapped by spies.
Unconvincing variant on *The Man Who Knew Too Much*, with an unwieldy and incoherent plot and more borrowings from Hitchcock than you can count. It ends up as fair predictable fun despite its jaded air.

w Leigh Vance, *novel* Seven Days to a Killing by Clive Egleton *d* Don Siegel *ph* Ousama Rawi *m* Roy Budd

Michael Caine, Janet Suzman, Joseph O'Conor, Donald Pleasance, Delphine Seyrig, John Vernon, Joss Ackland

'A flaccid spy thriller, vaguely reminiscent of Hitchcock and *Foreign Correspondent*, with direction as blank as the expression on Michael Caine's face throughout.'—*Sight and Sound*

Black Zoo

US 1962 88m Eastmancolor
Panavision
Allied Artists / Herman Cohen

The owner of a private Los Angeles zoo trains his animals to kill his enemies.
Stultifyingly inept and uninteresting horror film.

w Herman Cohen *d* Robert Gordon *ph* Floyd Crosby *m* Paul Dunlap

Michael Gough, Jeanne Cooper, Rod Lauren, Virginia Grey, Jerome Cowan, Elisha Cook Jnr, Marianna Hill

Blackbeard the Pirate*

US 1952 99m Technicolor
RKO (Edmund Grainger)

In the 17th century, reformed pirate Sir Henry Morgan is commissioned to rid the Caribbean of the rascally Blackbeard.
A farrago of action clichés with the star giving his eye-rolling all. The romantic element is dreary and the whole a shade bloodthirsty for family fare.

w Alan le May *d* Raoul Walsh *ph* William E.
Snyder *m* Victor Young

Robert Newton, Linda Darnell, Keith Andes,
William Bendix, Torin Thatcher, Irene Ryan,
Alan Mowbray, Richard Egan

Blackbeard's Ghost
US 1967 107m Technicolor
Walt Disney (Bill Walsh)

The famous pirate returns as a ghost to help the
old ladies who own a hotel he loved.
Ponderous and lengthy comedy, partially
salvaged by performances.

w Bill Walsh, Ben Da Gradi *d* Robert
Stevenson *ph* Edward Colman *m* Robert F.
Brunner

Peter Ustinov, Dean Jones, Suzanne Pleshette,
Elsa Lanchester, Richard Deacon

The Blackboard Jungle*
US 1955 101m bw
MGM (Pandro S. Berman)

In a slum school, a teacher finally gains the
respect of his class of young hooligans.
Seminal fifties melodrama more notable for its
introduction of 'Rock Around the Clock' behind
the credits than for any intrinsic interest.

wd Richard Brooks, *novel* Evan Hunter
ph Russell Harlan *m* Bill Haley and the Comets

Glenn Ford, Anne Francis, Louis Calhern,
Margaret Hayes, John Hoyt, Richard Kiley,
Emile Meyer, Warner Anderson, Basil
Ruysdael, *Sidney Poitier, Vic Morrow*, Rafael
Campos

·AAN: Richard Brooks (as writer); Russell
Harlan

Blackmail***
GB 1929 78m bw
BIP (John Maxwell)

A Scotland Yard inspector finds that his girl is
involved in a murder; he conceals the fact and is
blackmailed.
Hitchcock's first talkie is now a very hesitant
entertainment but fully bears the director's
stamp and will reward patient audiences in
several excitingly staged sequences.

w Alfred Hitchcock, Benn W. Levy, Charles
Bennett, *play* Charles Bennett *d Alfred
Hitchcock ph* Jack Cox *m* Campbell and
Connelly

Anny Ondra, Sara Allgood, John Longden,
Charles Paton, Donald Calthrop, Cyril Ritchard

Blackmail
US 1939 81m bw
MGM (John Considine Jnr)

A man is released from prison after serving a
sentence
for a crime he did not commit. Immediately a
blackmailer
pounces...
Co-feature drama for a star marking time; not
bad in its way.

w David Hertz, William Ludwig *d* H. C. Potter
ph Clyde de Vinna

Edward G. Robinson, Ruth Hussey, Gene
Lockhart, Guinn Williams, Esther Dale

Blackmailed
GB 1950 85m bw
GFD / Harold Huth

Several victims of a blackmailer are involved in
his murder.
Interestingly plotted and well cast melodrama
which suffers from a flat script and production.

w Hugh Mills, Roger Vadim, *novel* Mrs
Christopher by Elizabeth Myers *d* Marc
Allégret *ph* George Stretton *m* John
Wooldridge

Dirk Bogarde, Mai Zetterling, Fay Compton,
Robert Flemyng, Michael Gough, James
Robertson Justice, Joan Rice, Wilfrid Hyde
White, Harold Huth

Blackwell's Island
US 1939 71m bw
Warner (Bryan Foy)

A reporter goes to jail to get the goods on a smart
gangster.
Forgettable exposé of the lighter kind.

w Crane Wilbur *d* William McGann

John Garfield, Rosemary Lane, Dick Purcell,
Victor Jory, Stanley Fields

Blacula
US 1972 93m Movielab
AIP (Joseph T. Naar)

In 1815 in Transylvania, an African prince falls
victim to Dracula. A hundred and fifty years
later, his body is shipped to Los Angeles and
accidentally revivified.
Jaded semi-spoof notable chiefly as the first
black horror film. The star's performance is as
stately as could be wished in the circumstances.

w Joan Torres, Raymond Koenig *d* William
Crain *ph* John Stevens *m* Gene Page

William Marshall, Vonetta McGee, Denise
Nicholas, Gordon Pinsent, Charles Macaulay

Blanche Fury
GB 1948 95m Technicolor
GFD / Cineguild (Anthony Havelock-Allan)

A governess marries a wealthy heir, then with a steward connives at his murder.
Chilly Victorian melodrama without much interest outside the decor: the actors have unplayable roles and the handling is very flat.

w Audrey Erskine Lindop, Hugh Mills, Cecil McGivern, *novel* Joseph Shearing *d* Marc Allégret *ph* Guy Green, Geoffrey Unsworth *m* Clifton Parker

Valerie Hobson, Stewart Granger, Walter Fitzgerald, Michael Gough, Maurice Denham, Sybilla Binder

Blaze of Noon
US 1947 91m bw
Paramount (John Farrow)

Three stunt flier brothers in the twenties leave their circus to start a commercial air-line.
Predictable romantic drama with little flying: tragic pretensions, routine performances.

w Frank Wead, Arthur Sheekman *d* John Farrow

William Holden, Anne Baxter, Sonny Tufts, Sterling Hayden, William Bendix, Howard da Silva

The Blazing Forest
US 1952 90m Technicolor
Paramount / Pine–Thomas (William H. Pine, William C. Thomas)

A lady landowner has trouble with her rival timber bosses.
Fair period programmer.

w Lewis R. Foster, Winston Miller *d* Edward Ludwig *ph* Lionel Lindon *m* Lucien Caillet

John Payne, Agnes Moorehead, William Demarest, Richard Arlen, Susan Morrow, Roscoe Ates, Lynne Roberts

Blazing Saddles*
US 1974 93m Technicolor Panavision
Warner / Crossbow (Michael Herzberg)

A black railroad worker and an alcoholic ex-gunfighter foil a crooked attorney and his henchmen.
Wild western parody in which the action eventually shifts to the Warner backlot, after which the actors repair to Grauman's Chinese Theatre to find out what happened at the end of the story. At least as many misses as hits, and all aimed squarely at film buffs.

w Norman Steinberg, Mel Brooks, Andrew Bergman, Richard Pryor, Alan Unger *d* Mel Brooks *ph* Joseph Biroc *m* John Morris

Cleavon Little, Gene Wilder, Slim Pickens, Harvey Korman, Madeleine Kahn, Mel Brooks, Burton Gilliam, Alex Karras

'One suspects that the film's gradual disintegration derives not from the makers' inability to end it, so much as from their inability to stop laughing at their own jokes.'—*Jan Dawson*

'A surfeit of chaos and a scarcity of comedy.'—*Judith Crist*

AAN: Madeleine Kahn; title song (*m* John Morris, *ly* Mel Brooks)

Bless the Beasts and Children*
US 1973 110m colour
Columbia / Stanley Kramer

Six boys on an adventure holiday try to free a herd of buffalo earmarked for destruction.
Rather obviously pointed melodrama, well enough done but not very interesting.

w Mac Benoff, *novel* Glendon Swarthout *d* Stanley Kramer

Bill Mumy, Barry Robins, Miles Chapin, Jesse White, Ken Swofford

AAN: title song (*m/ly* Barry de Vorzon, Perry Botkin Jnr)

Blessed Event**
US 1932 84m bw
Warner (Ray Griffith)

A gossip columnist gets himself into hot water.
Amusing vehicle for a fast-talking star, and quite an interesting historical document.

w Howard Green, *play* Manuel Seff, Forest Wilson *d* Roy del Ruth *ph* Sol Polito

Lee Tracy, Ned Sparks, Mary Brian, Dick Powell, Ruth Donnelly, Frank McHugh, Allen Jenkins

Blind Alley**
US 1939 61m bw
Columbia

An escaped killer takes refuge in the home of a psychiatrist, who explores his subconscious and tames him.
Unusual lowercase thriller with effective dream sequences; it was much imitated.

w Philip MacDonald, Albert Blankfort, Michael Duffy, *play* James Warwick *d* Charles Vidor *ph* Lucien Ballard *m* Morris Stoloff

Chester Morris, Ralph Bellamy, Ann Dvorak, Melville Cooper, Rose Stradner, Marc Lawrence

'As un-Hollywood as anything that has come from France this year.'—*New York Daily News*
† Remake: *The Dark Past* (qv).

Blind Date*
GB 1959 95m bw
Rank / Sydney Box / Independent Artists
(David Deutsch)

A young Dutch painter in London discovers his
mistress's body and finds himself in a web of
deceit.
Tolerable, comparatively sophisticated murder
puzzle; rather glum looking, but the plot holds
the interest.

w Ben Barzman, Millard Lampell, *novel* Leigh
Howard d Joseph Losey ph Christopher
Challis m Richard Rodney Bennett

Hardy Kruger, Stanley Baker, Micheline Presle,
Robert Flemyng, Gordon Jackson, John Van
Eyssen

The Blind Goddess
GB 1947 88m bw
Gainsborough (Betty Box)

The private secretary to a public figure finds that
his idol has feet of clay, and suffers in court for
his discovery.
Courtroom drama from an old-fashioned stage
play: surefire for addicts, but routine as a film.

w Muriel and Sydney Box, *play Patrick
Hastings* d Harold French

Eric Portman, Anne Crawford, Hugh Williams,
Michael Denison, Nora Swinburne, Claire
Bloom, Raymond Lovell, Frank Cellier

Blind Husbands*
US 1918 90m approx (24 fps) bw silent
Universal

An Austrian officer, on holiday in the Alps,
seduces the wife of a rich American.
Stroheim's first comedy of sexual manners, now
of mainly archival interest.

wd, ad Erich Von Stroheim ph Ben Reynolds

Erich Von Stroheim, Sam de Grasse, Gibson
Gowland, Francella Billington

Blind Terror
GB 1971 89m colour
Columbia / Filmways / Genesis (Basil
Appleby)
US title: *See No Evil*

A blind girl is the sole, hunted survivor of a
maniac's rampage on a lonely estate.
Shocks, screams and starts fill a cliché-ridden
but still effective script which is faithfully turned
into a competent but routine heart-stopper.

w Brian Clemens d Richard Fleischer ph Gerry
Fisher m Elmer Bernstein

Mia Farrow, Robin Bailey, Dorothy Alison,

Diane Grayson, Norman Eshley, Brian
Rawlinson

  'For those who like to watch folks pull the
wings off flies.'—*Judith Crist*

Blindfold**
US 1965 102m Technicolor Panavision
Universal (Marvin Schwarz)

A society psychiatrist is enlisted by the CIA to
make regular blindfold journeys to a secret
destination where he treats a neurotic physicist.
Discovering that his contacts are really enemy
agents, he tracks down the destination by sound
and guesswork, and routs the villains.
Lively spy spoof with rather too much
knockabout between the Hitchcockian suspense
sequences; it has indeed the air of a script which
Hitchcock rejected, but provides reliable
entertainment.

w Philip Dunne, W. H. Menger, *novel* Lucile
Fletcher d Philip Dunne ph Joseph
MacDonald m Lalo Schifrin

Rock Hudson, Claudia Cardinale, Jack Warden,
Guy Stockwell, Brad Dexter

The Bliss of Mrs Blossom
GB 1968 93m Technicolor
Paramount (Josef Shaftel)

The wife of a bra manufacturer keeps her lover in
the attic.
Silly, wild-eyed sex comedy decorated with the
flashy tinsel of swinging London's dying fall.

w Alec Coppel, Denis Norden d Joe McGrath
ph Geoffrey Unsworth m Riz Ortolani
pd Assheton Gorton

Richard Attenborough, Shirley Maclaine, James
Booth, Freddie Jones, William Rushton, Bob
Monkhouse, Patricia Routledge

Blithe Spirit**
GB 1945 96m Technicolor
Two Cities / Cineguild (Anthony Havelock-
Allan)

A cynical novelist's second marriage is disturbed
when the playful ghost of his first wife
materializes during a séance.
Direction and acting carefully preserve a
comedy which on its first West End appearance
in 1941 achieved instant classic status. The
repartee scarcely dates, and altogether this is a
most polished job of film-making.

w Noel Coward, from his play *scenario* David
Lean, Anthony Havelock-Allan, Ronald
Neame d David Lean ph Ronald Neame
m Richard Addinsell

*Rex Harrison, Kay Hammond, Constance
Cummings, Margaret Rutherford,* Hugh
Wakefield, Joyce Carey, Jacqueline Clark

The Blob

US 1958   83m   De Luxe
Tonylyn / Jack H. Harris

A small town combats a slimy space invader.
Padded hokum for drive-ins, with a few effective
moments.

w Theodore Simonson, Kate Phillips d Irwin S.
Yeaworth Jnr ph Thomas Spalding m Ralph
Carmichael

Steve McQueen, Aneta Corseaut, Olin Howlin,
Earl Rowe

† Sequel 1971: *Beware! The Blob* (GB: *Son of
Blob*).

Blockade*

US 1938   84m   bw
Walter Wanger

During the Spanish Civil War, a peace-loving
young farmer has to take up arms to defend his
land.
Much touted as Hollywood's first serious
contribution to international affairs, this dogged
drama was in fact so bland that audiences had
difficulty ascertaining which side it was on,
especially as neither Franco nor the Fascists
were mentioned. As a romantic action drama,
however, it passed muster.

w John Howard Lawson d William Dieterle
m Werner Janssen

Henry Fonda, Madeleine Carroll, Leo Carrillo,
John Halliday, Vladimir Sokoloff, Robert
Warwick, Reginald Denny

'The film has a curious unreality considering
the grim reality behind it.'—*Frank S. Nugent*

AAN: John Howard Lawson; Werner Janssen

Blockheads***

US 1938   60m   bw
Hal Roach / Stan Laurel

Twenty years after World War I, Stan is still
guarding a trench because nobody told him to
stop. Olly takes him home to meet the wife, with
disastrous consequences.
The last first-class Laurel and Hardy comedy is
shapeless but hilarious, a fragmented reworking
of earlier ideas, all of which work beautifully.
Gags include encounters with a tip-up truck and
an automatic garage, and a brilliantly worked
out sequence up and down several flights of
stairs.

w James Parrott, Harry Langdon, Felix Adler,
Charles Rogers, Arnold Belgard d John G.
Blystone ph Art Lloyd m Marvin Hatley

Stan Laurel, Oliver Hardy, Billy Gilbert,
Patricia Ellis, Minna Gombell, James Finlayson

AAN: Marvin Hatley

Blonde Crazy*

US 1931   74m   bw
Warner
GB title: *Larceny Lane*

A bellhop and a chambermaid set out to fleece
all-comers.
Smart con man comedy with the star in excellent
form.

w Kubec Glasmon, John Bright d Roy del Ruth
ph Sid Hickox

James Cagney, Joan Blondell, Ray Milland,
Louis Calhern, Guy Kibbee, Polly Walters,
Charles Lane, Maude Eburne

'A chipper, hard-boiled, amusing essay in
petty thieving.'—*Time*

A Blonde in Love: see *Loves of a Blonde*

Blonde Venus*

US 1932   97m   bw
Paramount

A German café singer marries an American
research chemist, but their marriage doesn't run
smoothly.
Rather dreary, fragmented star vehicle with
good moments, notably the star's opening
appearance as a gorilla.

w Jules Furthman, S. K. Lauren d Josef Von
Sternberg ph Bert Glennon m Oscar Poteker

Marlene Dietrich, Herbert Marshall, Cary
Grant, Dickie Moore

'The story has all the dramatic integrity of a
sashweight murderer's tabloid
autobiography.'—*Pare Lorentz*

Blondie*

US 1938   68m   bw
Columbia

Misadventures of a harassed suburban family
man.
Dagwood Bumstead and his wife Blondie were
Mr and Mrs Small Town America throughout
the thirties and forties, and received their perfect
screen incarnations in this unambitious but quite
watchable series, which provided familiar and
often quite observant fun.

w Richard Flournoy, from the comic strip by
Chic Young d Frank R. Strayer

*Arthur Lake, Penny Singleton, Larry Simms,
Daisy* the Dog, *Jonathan Hale* (as the boss, Mr
Dithers), Gene Lockhart, Ann Doran, Irving
Bacon (as the mailman)

Other episodes were as follows:
1939: BLONDIE MEETS THE BOSS,
BLONDIE TAKES A VACATION,
BLONDIE BRINGS UP BABY

1940: BLONDIE ON A BUDGET, BLONDIE
HAS SERVANT TROUBLE, BLONDIE
PLAYS CUPID
1941: BLONDIE GOES LATIN, BLONDIE
IN SOCIETY
1942: BLONDIE GOES TO COLLEGE,
BLONDIE'S BLESSED EVENT, BLONDIE
FOR VICTORY
1943: IT'S A GREAT LIFE, FOOTLIGHT
GLAMOUR
1945: LEAVE IT TO BLONDIE
1946: BLONDIE KNOWS BEST, LIFE WITH
BLONDIE, BLONDIE'S LUCKY DAY
1947: BLONDIE'S BIG MOMENT,
BLONDIE'S HOLIDAY, BLONDIE IN THE
DOUGH, BLONDIE'S ANNIVERSARY
1948: BLONDIE'S REWARD
1949: BLONDIE'S SECRET, BLONDIE'S
BIG DEAL, BLONDIE HITS THE JACKPOT
1950: BLONDIE'S HERO, BEWARE OF
BLONDIE
† TV series were started in the fifties and sixties,
but both failed.

Blondie of the Follies*
US 1932   97m   bw
MGM (Marion Davies)

Two New York showgirls graduate from
tenements to luxury.
Adequate comedy-melodrama with an
interesting cast and good dialogue.

w Frances Marion, Anita Loos d Edmund
Goulding ph George Barnes m William Axt

Marion Davies, Jimmy Durante, Robert
Montgomery, Billie Dove, James Gleason, Zasu
Pitts, Sidney Toler, Douglass Dumbrille

Blood Alley
US 1955   115m   Warnercolor
  Cinemascope
Warner / Batjac (no producer credited)

An American sailor is helped by local people to
escape from a Chinese jail; he then escorts them
to Hong Kong.
Rudimentary anti-Red heroics with expensive
spectacle punctuating a tacky script.

w A. S. Fleischmann, from his novel d William
Wellman ph William H. Clothier m Roy Webb
pd Alfred Ybarra

John Wayne, Lauren Bacall, Paul Fix, Joy Kim,
Berry Kroger, Mike Mazurki, Anita Ekberg

Blood and Roses
France / Italy 1960   87m   Technirama
Eger / Documento (Raymond Eger)
original title: *Et Mourir de Plaisir*

Carmilla takes on the vampiric personality of her
ancestress Millarca, whom she closely
resembles.
A rather half-hearted attempt to make an elegant
horror story; boring rather than charming or
frightening.

w Claude Brûlé, Claude Martin, Roger Vadim
d Roger Vadim ph Claude Renoir m Jean
Prodromidès

Mel Ferrer, Elsa Martinelli, Annette Vadim,
Marc Allégret

Blood and Sand*
US 1922   80m (24 fps)   bw   silent
Paramount

A matador falls under the spell of an aristocratic
woman.
Elegant star vehicle which established his image.

w June Mathis, *novel* Vicente Blasco Ibanez
d Fred Niblo

Rudolph Valentino, Nita Naldi, Lila Lee, Walter
Long

Blood and Sand*
US 1941   123m   Technicolor
TCF (Darryl F. Zanuck, Robert T. Kane)

Rather boring remake, fine to look at but
dramatically deadly.

w Jo Swerling, *novel* Vicente Blasco Ibanez
d Rouben Mamoulian ph Ernest Palmer, Ray
Rennahan m Alfred Newman ad Richard Day,
Joseph C. Wright

Tyrone Power, Rita Hayworth, Linda Darnell,
Nazimova, Anthony Quinn, J. Carrol Naish,
John Carradine, Lynn Bari, Laird Cregar,
Monty Banks

AA: Ernest Palmer, Ray Rennahan

The Blood Beast Terror
GB 1967   88m   Eastmancolor
Tigon (Arnold L. Miller, Tony Tenser)

A Victorian entomologist creates human beings
who can change themselves into monster
death's-head moths.
Unpersuasive and totally idiotic cheapjack
horror fare.

w Peter Bryan d Vernon Sewell ph Stanley A.
Long m Paul Ferris

Robert Flemyng, Peter Cushing, Wanda
Ventham, Vanessa Howard, David Griffin, John
Paul, Kevin Stoney, Roy Hudd

Blood from the Mummy's Tomb*
GB 1971   94m   Technicolor
Hammer (Howard Brandy)

Twenty years after a female mummy is brought
back to England, members of the expedition are

killed one by one, and their leader's daughter is possessed by the spirit of the dead princess. Interesting but over-complicated and hard-to-enjoy attempt to maintain the mummy saga without an actual marauding mummy. Intelligently handled but sadly lacking in a sense of humour.

w Christopher Wicking, *novel* Jewel of the Seven Stars by Bram Stoker *d* Seth Holt *ph* Arthur Grant *m* Tristam Cary

Andrew Keir, Valerie Leon, James Villiers, Hugh Burden, George Coulouris, Mark Edwards, Rosalie Crutchley, Aubrey Morris, David Markham

'Makes the genre seem like new.'—*Tony Rayns*

The Blood of a Poet**

France 1930   58m   bw
Vicomte de Noailles
original title: *Le Sang d'un Poète*

Aspects of a poet's vision, taking place while a chimney is falling down.

An indescribable film full of striking imagery which may, or may not, be meaningful. Its author claims that it is not surrealist, but that label for most people will do as well as any other.

wd Jean Cocteau *ph* Georges Périnal *m* Georges Auric *ad* Jean Gabriel d'Aubonne

Lee Miller, Pauline Carton, Odette Talazac

Blood on Satan's Claw

GB 1970   93m   Eastmancolor
Tigon-Chilton (Tony Tenser, Malcolm B. Heyworth, Peter L.
    Andrews)
aka: *Satan's Skin*

A devil's claw wreaks havoc among children in a 17th-century English village.
Moderately frightening, rather silly but at least original period horror comic.

w Robert Wynne-Simmons *d* Piers Haggard *ph* Dick Bush *m* Marc Wilkinson

Patrick Wymark, Linda Hayden, Barry Andrews, Avice Landon, Simon Williams, Tamara Ustinov, Anthony Ainley

Blood on the Moon*

US 1948   88m   bw
RKO

A homesteader finds that his best friend is the villainous leader of a group of cattlemen.
Good-looking but rather pedestrian western, generally well handled.

w Lillie Hayward *d* Robert Wise *ph* Nicholas Musuraca *m* Roy Webb

Robert Mitchum, Barbara Bel Geddes, Robert Preston, Walter Brennan

Blood on the Sun*

US 1945   94m   bw
William Cagney

In the twenties, the American editor of a Tokyo newspaper reveals a Japanese militarist plan for world conquest.
Satisfactory star actioner with good production and exciting highlights.

w Lester Cole *d* Frank Lloyd *ph* Theodor Sparkuhl *m* Miklos Rozsa

James Cagney, Sylvia Sidney, Wallace Ford, Rosemary de Camp, Robert Armstrong, John Emery, Leonard Strong, Frank Puglia

'It ought to be fine for those who enjoy a good ninety-minute massacre.'—*New Yorker*

Bloodbrothers

US 1978   116m   Technicolor
Warner / Stephen Friedman / Kings Road

The disintegration through fialure and inadequacy of a noisy Italian-American family. The kind of self-indulgence that has one seeking the exit before it's half over.

w Walter Newman, *novel* Richard Price *d* Robert Mulligan *ph* Robert Surtees *m* Elmer Bernstein *pd* Gene Callahan

Paul Sorvino, Tony Lo Bianco, Richard Gere, Lelia Goldoni

'Why should filmgoers pay to see what they can already hear in the next apartment?'—*Variety*

Bloodhounds of Broadway*

US 1952   90m   Technicolor
TCF (George Jessel)

With the help of a gangster, an orphan girl and her pet bloodhounds make a big hit in cabaret. Absurd but sporadically amusing gangster burlesque, typical of its author. Lively production values.

w Sy Gomberg, *story* Damon Runyon *d* Harmon Jones *ph* Edward Cronjager *md* Lionel Newman

Mitzi Gaynor, Scott Brady, Mitzi Green, Marguerite Chapman, Michael O'Shea, Wally Vernon, George E. Stone

Bloody Mama*

US 1971   90m   Movielab
AIP (Roger Corman)

In the thirties, outlaw Kate Barker and her four sons conduct a reign of terror until what's left of the gang is riddled with machine gun bullets.

Violent gangster story with a star on the rampage; the attempt to philosophize is more than the facts will bear, but the production moves smartly enough.

w Robert Thom *d* Roger Corman *ph* John Alonzo *m* Don Randi

Shelley Winters, Pat Hingle, Don Stroud, Diane Varsi, Bruce Dern, Clint Kimbrough, Robert de Niro, Robert Walden, Alex Nicol

Bloomfield
GB 1969 95m Technicolor
World Film Services / Limbridge (John Heyman, Wolf Mankowitz)

A 10-year-old Israeli boy hitchhikes to Jaffa to see his football idol play his last game.
Sentimental whimsy, unattractively interpreted.

w Wolf Mankowitz *d* Richard Harris *ph* Otto Heller *m* Johnny Harris

Richard Harris, Romy Schneider, Kim Burfield, Maurice Kaufmann, Yossi Yadin

Blossoms in the Dust **
US 1941 99m Technicolor
MGM (Irving Asher)

A woman who loses her husband and child founds a state orphanage.
Archetypal tearjerker of the forties, a glossy 'woman's picture' which distorts the facts into a star vehicle. Excellent colour helped to make it an enormous success.

w Anita Loos, based on the life of Edna Gladney *d* Mervyn Le Roy *ph* Karl Freund, W. Howard Greene *m* Herbert Stothart

Greer Garson, Walter Pidgeon, Felix Bressart, Marsha Hunt, Fay Holden, Samuel S. Hinds

AAN: best picture; Karl Freund, W. Howard Greene; Greer Garson

Blow Up **
GB 1966 110m Eastmancolor
MGM / Carlo Ponti

A London fashion photographer thinks he sees a murder, but the evidence disappears.
Not a mystery but a fashionable think-in on the difference (if any) between fantasy and reality.
Agreeable to look at for those who can stifle their irritation at the non-plot and non-characters; a huge audience was lured by flashes of nudity and the trendy 'swinging London' setting.

wd Michelangelo Antonioni *ph* Carlo di Palma *m* Herbert Hancock *ad* Assheton Gorton

David Hemmings, Sarah Miles, Vanessa Redgrave

AAN: Michelangelo Antonioni (as writer and director)

Blowing Wild *
US 1953 88m bw
(Warner) United States (Milton Sperling)

A Mexican oil driller becomes involved with the psychotic wife of an old friend; the triangle leads to murder and retribution.
Pot-boiling star vehicle with adequate melodramatic interest, full of reminiscences of other movies, with a wicked lady to end them all.

w Philip Yordan *d* Hugo Fregonese *ph* Sid Hickox *m* Dmitri Tiomkin

Gary Cooper, Barbara Stanwyck, Anthony Quinn, Ruth Roman, Ward Bond

Blue
US 1968 113m Technicolor Panavision
Paramount / Kettledrum (Judd Bernard, Irwin Winkler)

The white adopted son of a Mexican bandit prevents his cohorts from raping a white girl, and falls in love with her.
Pretentious, self-conscious, literary western without much zest.

w Meade Roberts, Ronald M. Cohen *d* Silvio Narizzano *ph* *Stanley Cortez* *m* Manos Hadjidakis

Terence Stamp, Joanna Pettet, Karl Malden, Ricardo Montalban

'I don't know which is worse—bad cowboy movies or bad *arty* cowboy movies. *Blue* is both.'—*Rex Reed*

The Blue Angel ****
Germany 1930 98m bw
UFA (Erich Pommer)

A fuddy-duddy professor is infatuated with a tawdry night-club singer. She marries him but is soon bored and contemptuous; humiliated, he leaves her and dies in his old classroom.
A masterwork of late twenties German grotesquerie, and after a slowish beginning an emotional powerhouse, set in a dark nightmare world which could be created only in the studio.
Shot also in English, it was highly popular and influential in Britain and America.

w Robert Liebmann, Karl Zuckmayer, Karl Vollmoeller, *novel* Professor Unrath by Heinrich Mann *d* Josef Von Sternberg *ph* Gunther Rittau, Hans Schneeberger *m* Frederick Hollander (inc 'Falling in Love Again', 'They Call Me Wicked Lola') *ad* Otto Hunte, Emil Hasler

Emil Jannings, Marlene Dietrich (who was instantly catapulted to international stardom), Kurt Gerron, Hans Albers

The Blue Angel
US 1959   107m   De Luxe   Cinemascope
TCF (Jack Cummings)

Ill-advised attempt at a 'realistic', updated remake of the above; the result is a total travesty, with the actors aware that stylized melodrama is turning before their eyes into unintentional farce.

w Nigel Balchin d Edward Dmytryk ph Leon Shamroy m Hugo Friedhofer

Curt Jurgens, May Britt, Theodore Bikel, John Banner

'It totally lacks the stifling atmosphere of sordid and oppressive sexuality which is essential to give conviction to the German sadism of the story.'—Brenda Davies

Blue Blood
GB 1973   86m   Technicolor
Mallard-Impact Quadrant

A German governess arrives at an English stately home and finds the malevolent butler plotting to show his supremacy over his effete master.
An extremely unattractive, would-be satirical melodrama which plays like a Grand Guignol version of The Servant.

wd Andrew Sinclair, novel The Carry-Cot by Alexander Thynne ph Harry Waxman m Brian Gascoigne

Oliver Reed, Derek Jacobi, Fiona Lewis, Anna Gael, Meg Wynn Owen

Blue Collar*
US 1978   114m   Technicolor
Universal / TAT (Don Guest)

Three car factory workers try to improve their lot by unionization and robbery.
Salty, rough, downbeat but impressively realistic modern drama, a belated American equivalent of Saturday Night and Sunday Morning.

w Paul Schraeder, Leonard Schraeder d Paul Schraeder ph Bobby Byrne m Jack Nitzche

Richard Pryor, Harvey Keitel, Yaphet Kotto, Ed Begley Jnr, Harry Bellaver

The Blue Dahlia**
US 1946   99m   bw
Paramount (John Houseman)

A returning war veteran finds his faithless wife murdered and himself suspected.
Hailed on its first release as sharper than average, this mystery suspenser is now only moderately compelling despite the screenplay credit; direction and editing lack urgency and the acting lacks bounce.

w Raymond Chandler d George Marshall

ph Lionel Lindon m Victor Young

Alan Ladd, Veronica Lake, William Bendix, Howard da Silva, Doris Dowling, Tom Powers, Hugh Beaumont, Howard Freeman, Will Wright

'It threatens to turn into something, but it never does.'—New Yorker, 1978

AAN: Raymond Chandler

Blue Denim*
US 1959   89m   bw   Cinemascope
TCF (Charles Brackett)
GB title: Blue Jeans

Teenagers confronted with the prospect of illegitimate parenthood consult an abortionist, but all ends with wedding bells.
First of its rather dreary kind but better than most, this only slightly mawkish domestic drama has its heart in the right place and steers surprisingly towards a nick-of-time chase climax.

w Edith Sommer, Philip Dunne, play James Leo Herlihy, William Noble d Philip Dunne ph Leo Tover m Bernard Herrmann

Carol Lynley, Brandon de Wilde, Macdonald Carey, Marsha Hunt, Nina Shipman, Warren Berlinger

The Blue Gardenia
US 1953   90m   bw
Warner (Alex Gottlieb)

A girl gets drunk and wakes up in a strange apartment with a dead man by her side.
Totally undistinguished mystery which leaves egg on the actors' faces.

w Charles Hoffman d Fritz Lang ph Nicholas Musuraca m Raoul Krashaar

Anne Baxter, Richard Conte, Ann Sothern, Raymond Burr, Jeff Donnell, Richard Erdman, Nat King Cole

Blue Hawaii
US 1961   101m   Technicolor   Panavision
Hal B. Wallis

A GI comes home to Honolulu and becomes a beachcomber.
Lifeless star vehicle shot on glamorous locations.

w Hal Kanter d Norman Taurog ph Charles Lang Jnr m Joseph J. Lilley

Elvis Presley, Joan Blackman, Nancy Walters, Roland Winters, Angela Lansbury, John Archer, Howard McNear

The Blue Lagoon*
GB 1949   103m   Technicolor
GFD / Individual (Frank Launder, Sidney Gilliat)

A shipwrecked boy and girl grow up on a desert island, ward off smugglers, have a baby, and eventually sail away in search of civilization. Rather lifeless, though pretty, treatment of a famous novel: the story never becomes vivid despite splendid Fijian locations.

w Frank Launder, John Baines, Michael Hogan, *novel* H. de Vere Stacpoole *d* Frank Launder *ph Geoffrey Unsworth m* Clifton Parker

Jean Simmons, Donald Houston, Noel Purcell, Cyril Cusack, James Hayter

The Blue Lamp***
GB 1949   84m   bw
Ealing (Michael Relph)

A young man joins London's police force. The elderly copper who trains him is killed in a shootout, but the killer is apprehended.
Seminal British police film which spawned not only a long line of semi-documentary imitations but also the twenty-year TV series *Dixon of Dock Green* for which the shot PC was happily revived. As an entertainment, pacy but dated; more important, it burnished the image of the British copper for a generation or more.

w *T. E. B. Clarke d* Basil Dearden *ph* Gordon Dines *md* Ernest Irving

Jack Warner, Jimmy Hanley, Dirk Bogarde, Meredith Edwards, Robert Flemyng, Bernard Lee, Patric Doonan, Peggy Evans, Gladys Henson, Dora Bryan

'The mixture of coyness, patronage and naive theatricality which has vitiated British films for the last ten years.'—*Gavin Lambert*

'A soundly made crime thriller which would not be creating much of a stir if it were American.'—*Richard Mallett, Punch*

The Blue Max**
US 1966   156m   De Luxe   Cinemascope
TCF (Christian Ferry)

In Germany after World War I an ambitious and skilful pilot causes the death of his comrades and steals the wife of his High Command superior, who eventually finds a means of revenge.
For once, an action spectacular not too badly let down by its connecting threads of plot, apart from some hilarious and unnecessary bedroom scenes in which the female star's bath towel seems to become conveniently adhesive.

w David Pursall, Jack Seddon, Gerald Hanley, *novel* Jack Hunter *d* John Guillermin *ph* Douglas Slocombe *m* Jerry Goldsmith

George Peppard, *James Mason*, Ursula Andress, Jeremy Kemp, Karl Michael Vogler, Anton Diffring, Derren Nesbitt

The Blue Peter
GB 1955   93m   Eastmancolor
British Lion/Beaconsfield (Herbert Mason)

A confused war hero becomes a trainer at an Outward Bound school for boys.
Pleasant but uninspired open air adventure for young people.

w Don Sharp, John Pudney *d* Wolf Rilla *ph* Arthur Grant *m* Anthony Hopkins

Kieron Moore, Greta Gynt, Sarah Lawson, Mervyn Johns, Ram Gopal, Edwin Richfield, Harry Fowler, John Charlesworth

Blue Skies*
US 1946   104m   Technicolor
Paramount (Sol C. Siegel)

A dancing star and a nightclub owner fight for years over the same girl.
Thin musical with splendid Irving Berlin tunes and lively individual numbers.

w Arthur Sheekman *d* Stuart Heisler *ph* Lionel Lindon *md* Robert Emmett Dolan

Fred Astaire (dancing 'Putting On the Ritz'), Bing Crosby, Joan Caulfield, Billy de Wolfe, Olga San Juan, Robert Benchley, Frank Faylen, Victoria Horne, Jack Norton

AAN: Robert Emmett Dolan; song 'You Keep Coming Back Like a Song' (*m*/*ly* Irving Berlin)

The Blue Veil*
US 1951   114m   bw
(RKO) Wald–Krasna (Raymond Hakim)

The vocational career of a children's nurse who descends into poverty but is rescued by one of her own charges, now grown up.
Sober American remake of a French tearjerker (*Le Voile bleu*) with the star suffering nobly but being upstaged by the cameo players.

w Norman Corwin, from the original by François Campaux *d* Curtis Bernhardt *ph* Franz Planer *m* Franz Waxman

Jane Wyman, Charles Laughton, Richard Carlson, Joan Blondell, Agnes Moorehead, Don Taylor, Audrey Totter, Everett Sloane, Cyril Cusack, Natalie Wood, Warner Anderson

AAN: Jane Wyman; Joan Blondell

Bluebeard*
US 1944   73m   bw
PRC

A strangler of young girls is at large in Paris. Poverty Row chiller with effective moments; possibly the most interesting film ever to come from PRC (which isn't saying *very* much).

w Pierre Gendron *d Edgar G. Ulmer ph* Jockey Feindel

John Carradine, Jean Parker, Ludwig Stossel, Nils Asther, Iris Adrian

Bluebeard

France / Italy / Germany 1972   124m
Technicolor
Barnabé / Gloria / Geiselgasteig (Alexander Salkind)

The lady killer in this case is an Austrian aristocrat who has been driven to desperation and murder by a long line of mistresses whose bodies he keeps frozen in his cellar.
Would-be macabre comedy which becomes totally off-putting by its emphasis on close-up death agonies.

w Ennio di Concini, Edward Dmytryk, Maria Pia Fusco d Edward Dmytryk ph Gabor Pogany m Ennio Morricone

Richard Burton, Raquel Welch, Joey Heatherton, Virna Lisi, Nathalie Delon, Marilu Tolo

'Somewhere between (and a long way behind) *Kind Hearts and Coronets* and *The Abominable Dr Phibes*.'—*Clyde Jeavons, MFB*

Bluebeard's Eighth Wife*

US 1938   80m   bw
Paramount (Ernst Lubitsch)

The daughter of an impoverished French aristocrat marries for money a millionaire who has had seven previous wives, and determines to teach him a lesson.
Very thin sophisticated comedy with unsympathetic characters and little wit after the first scene; a disappointment from the talent involved.

w Charles Brackett, Billy Wilder, *story* Alfred Savoir d Ernst Lubitsch ph Leo Tover

Claudette Colbert, Gary Cooper, David Niven, Edward Everett Horton, Elizabeth Patterson, Herman Bing, Warren Hymer, Franklin Pangborn

Bluebeard's Ten Honeymoons

GB 1960   93m   bw
Anglo-Allied (Roy Parkinson)

Another version of the story of Landru, alternating wildly between fantasy, farce and melodrama. Not a success in any of its moods.

w Myles Wilder d W. Lee Wilder ph Stephen Dade m Albert Elms

George Sanders, Corinne Calvet, Patricia Roc, Ingrid Hafner, Jean Kent, Greta Gynt, Maxine Audley, Selma Vaz Diaz, George Coulouris

'The unedifying narrative is developed along the most obvious lines imaginable.'—*MFB*

The Bluebird***

US 1940   98m   Technicolor (bw prologue)
TCF (Gene Markey)

In a Grimm's Fairy Tale setting, the two children of a poor woodcutter seek the bluebird of happiness in the past, the future and the Land of Luxury, but eventually discover it in their own back yard.
An imaginative and often chilling script clarifies Maurice Maeterlinck's fairy play, and the art direction is outstanding, but the children are necessarily unsympathetic and the expensive production paled beside the success of the more upbeat *Wizard of Oz*, which was released almost simultaneously. Slashed for re-release, the only existing prints now open with confusing abruptness and no scene-setting before the adventures begin.

w Ernest Pascal d Walter Lang ph Arthur Miller, Ray Rennahan m Alfred Newman

Shirley Temple, Johnny Russell, *Gale Sondergaard* (as the cat), *Eddie Collins* (as the dog), Nigel Bruce, Jessie Ralph, Spring Byington, Sybil Jason, Helen Ericson, Russell Hicks, Al Shean, Cecilia Loftus

AAN: Arthur Miller, Ray Rennahan

A Blueprint for Murder*

US 1953   77m   bw
TCF (Michael Abel)

After the death of his brother and nephew, a man proves that his sister-in-law is a murderess.
Unpleasant but efficient murder story with enough twists to keep one watching.

wd Andrew Stone ph Leo Tover m Lionel Newman

Jean Peters, Joseph Cotten, Gary Merrill, Catherine McLeod, Jack Kruschen

Blueprint for Robbery*

US 1960   87m   bw
Paramount (Bryan Foy)

Crooks plan and execute a robbery, agreeing not to touch the proceeds for two and a half years. But some get tired of waiting. . .
Minor but effective crime melodrama in semi-documentary vein.

w Irwin Winehouse, A. Sanford Wolf d Jerry Hopper ph Loyal Griggs m Van Cleave

J. Pat O'Malley, Robert Gist, Romo Vincent, Marion Ross, Tom Duggan

'A not uninteresting entry in the screen log-book on crime.'—*MFB*

Blues in the Night *
US 1941   88m   bw
Warner (Henry Blanke)

Career and romantic problems for the members
of a travelling jazz band.
Atmospheric little melodrama with good score
and smart dialogue.

w Robert Rossen, *play* Hot Nocturne by Edwin
Gilbert *d* Anatole Litvak *ph* Ernest Haller

Priscilla Lane, Richard Whorf, Lloyd Nolan,
Betty Field, Jack Carson, Elia Kazan, Wallace
Ford, Billy Halop, Peter Whitney

AAN: title song (*m* Harold Arlen, *ly* Johnny
Mercer)

Blume in Love **
US 1973   116m   Technicolor
Warner (Paul Mazursky)

A divorced American lawyer in Venice
reminisces about his love life.
Shapeless but enjoyable 'serious comedy' with
star and director in good form.

wd Paul Mazursky *ph* Bruce Surtees *m* various

George Segal, Susan Anspach, Kris
Kristofferson, Marsha Mason, Shelley Winters

The Boatniks *
US 1970   100m   Technicolor
Walt Disney (Ron Miller)

An accident-prone coastguard officer creates
havoc at a yachting marina but is acclaimed a
hero after catching three jewel thieves.
Simple fresh-air farce for the family, pleasantly
set but flatly directed.

w Arthur Julian *d* Norman Tokar *ph* William
Snyder *m* Robert F. Brunner

Phil Silvers, Robert Morse, Stefanie Powers,
Norman Fell, Mickey Shaughnessey, Wally
Cox, Don Ameche, Joey Forman

Bob and Carol and Ted and Alice **
US 1969   105m   Technicolor
Columbia (Larry Tucker)

Two California couples, influenced by a group
therapy session advocating natural spontaneous
behaviour, decide to admit their extra-marital
affairs and narrowly avoid a wife-swapping
party.
Fashionable comedy without the courage of its
convictions: it starts and finishes very bashfully,
but there are bright scenes in the middle. An
attempt to extend it into a TV series was a failure.

w Paul Mazursky, Larry Tucker *d* Paul
Mazursky *ph* Charles E. Lang *m* Quincy Jones

Natalie Wood, Robert Culp, Elliott Gould,
Dyan Cannon, Horst Ebersberg

'An old-fashioned romantic comedy disguised
as a blue picture.'—*Arthur Schlesinger Jnr*

AAN: Paul Mazursky, Larry Tucker; Charles
E. Lang; Elliott Gould; Dyan Cannon

Bobbikins
GB 1959   90m   bw   Cinemascope
TCF (Oscar Brodney, Bob McNaught)

A downtrodden variety artist finds that his baby
can not only talk but also give him tips on the
stock exchange.
Not at all a good idea, and feebly executed.

w Oscar Brodney *d* Robert Day *ph* Geoffrey
Faithfull *m* Philip Green

Max Bygraves, Shirley Jones, Billie Whitelaw,
Barbara Shelley, Colin Gordon, Charles
Tingwell, Lionel Jeffries, Rupert Davies

The Bobo
US 1967   105m   Technicolor
Warner / Gina (Elliott Kastner, Jerry
   Gershwin) (David R. Schwarz)

An unsuccessful and timid bullfighter is offered a
contract if within three days he can seduce the
local belle.
Stylized, silly and boring comedy from an
obviously dated play; hopefully the star's last
attempt to provide Chaplinesque pathos.

w David R. Schwarz, from his play and the novel
Olimpia by Burt Cole *d* Robert Parrish
ph Gerry Turpin *m* Francis Lai

Peter Sellers, Britt Ekland, Rossano Brazzi,
Adolfo Celi, Hattie Jacques, Ferdy Mayne,
Kenneth Griffith, John Wells

Boccaccio '70 *
Italy / France 1962   210m   Eastmancolor
TCF / CCC / Cineriz / Francinex / Gray Films
   (Antonio Cervi, Carlo Ponti)

Four modern stories which Boccaccio might
have written (on an off day).
Overlong portmanteau with inevitable bright
moments but many more longueurs.

'THE TEMPTATION OF DR ANTONIO':
w Federico Fellini, Tullio Pinelli, Ennio Flaiano
d Federico Fellini *ph* Otello Martelli; with Anita
Ekberg
'THE JOB': *w* Suso Cecchi d'Amico, Luchino
Visconti *d* Luchino Visconti *ph* Giuseppe
Rotunno; with Romy Schneider, Tomas Milian
'THE RAFFLE': *w* Cesare Zavattini *d* Vittorio
de Sica *ph* Otello Martelli; with Sophia Loren
'RENZO AND LUCIANA': *d* Mario
Monichelli

Body and Soul*
US 1947   104m   bw
Enterprise (Bob Roberts)

A young boxer fights his way unscrupulously to
the top.
Melodramatic but absorbing study of
prizefighting's seamy side. (Is there any other?)
Inventively studio-bound and almost
impressionist in treatment.

*w Abraham Polonsky d Robert Rossen
ph James Wong Howe md* Rudolph Polk
m Hugo Friedhofer

John Garfield, Lilli Palmer, Hazel Brooks, Anne
Revere, William Conrad, Joseph Pevney,
Canada Lee

AAN: Abraham Polonsky; John Garfield

The Body Disappears
US 1941   72m   bw
Warner (Ben Stoloff)

A professor invents an invisibility formula.
Uninspired comedy switch on a familiar theme.

w Scott Darling, Erna Lazarus *d* D. Ross
Lederman *ph* Allen G. Seigler

Edward Everett Horton, Jeffrey Dell, Jane
Wyman, Herbert Anderson, Marguerite
Chapman, Craig Stevens, David Bruce, Willie
Best

The Body Snatcher*
US 1945   77m   bw
RKO (Val Lewton)

In 19th-century Edinburgh a doctor obtains
'specimens' from grave-robbers, and murder
results when supplies run short.
A familiar theme very imaginatively handled,
and well acted, though the beginning is slow. The
best of the Lewton thrillers.

w Philip MacDonald, Carlos Keith (Val
Lewton), *story* R. L. Stevenson *d Robert Wise
ph Robert de Grasse m* Roy Webb

Henry Daniell, Boris Karloff, Bela Lugosi, Edith
Atwater, Russell Wade

'A humane sincerity and a devotion to good
cinema . . . However, most of the picture is more
literary than lively.'—*Time*

Boeing-Boeing
US 1965   102m   Technicolor
(Paramount) Hal B. Wallis

By successfully juggling with plane schedules, a
Paris journalist manages to live with three air
hostesses at the same time.
Frenetic, paper-thin sex comedy from a one-joke
play; film style generally undistinguished.

w Edward Anhalt, *play* Marc Camoletti *d* John
Rich *ph* Lucien Ballard *m* Neal Hefti

Tony Curtis, Jerry Lewis (his only 'straight'
part), Dany Saval, Christiane Schmidtner,
Suzanna Leigh, *Thelma Ritter*

'A sort of jet-age French farce.'—*Judith Crist*

The Bofors Gun**
GB 1968   105m   Technicolor
Rank / Everglades (Robert A. Goldson, Otto
    Plaschkes)

In 1954 Germany a British army unit runs into
trouble when a violent and unstable Irish
sergeant picks on a weakly National Service
corporal.
Keen, fascinating, but often crude and eventually
rather silly expansion of a TV play chiefly
notable for the excellent acting opportunities
provided by its unattractive but recognizable
characters.

w John McGrath *d* Jack Gold *ph* Alan Hume
m Carl Davis

Nicol Williamson, John Thaw, *David Warner*,
Ian Holm

The Bohemian Girl*
US 1936   74m   bw
Hal Roach

Gypsies kidnap a nobleman's daughter and
bring her up as their own.
One of several operettas reworked for Laurel
and Hardy, this is an inoffensive entertainment
which devotes too little care to their need for
slowly built-up gag structure; their sequences
tend to fizzle out and the singing is a bore.

w Alfred Bunn, *operetta* William Balfe *d* James
Horne, Charles Rogers *ph* Art Lloyd, Francis
Corby

Stan Laurel, Oliver Hardy, Mae Busch, Antonio
Moreno, Jacqueline Wells, Darla Hood, Zeffie
Tilbury, James Finlayson, Thelma Todd (for one
song, apparently dubbed: presumably before her
sudden death she had been cast as the heroine)

The Bold and the Brave
US 1956   87m   bw   Superscope
RKO / Hal E. Chester

An assortment of American types come together
in the Italian campaign of 1944.
Routine war heroics chiefly remembered (if at
all) for a crap game sequence.

w Robert Lewin *d* Lewis Foster *ph* Sam
Leavitt *m* Herschel Burke Gilbert

Wendell Corey, *Mickey Rooney*, Nicole Maurey,
Don Taylor

AAN: Robert Lewin; Mickey Rooney

Bolero*
US 1934   85m   bw
Paramount

A New York dancer neglects his personal life to
become king of the European night club circuit.
Lively romantic drama which performed
remarkably at the box office and led to a kind of
sequel, *Rumba*.

w Carey Wilson, Kubec Glasmon, Ruth
Ridenour, Horace Jackson d *Wesley Ruggles*
ph Leo Tover

George Raft, Carole Lombard, Sally Rand
(doing her fan dance), Frances Drake, William
Frawley, Ray Milland, Gertrude Michael

Bomba the Jungle Boy
US 1949   65m   bw or sepia
Monogram (Walter Mirisch)

Photographers in Africa meet a junior Tarzan
who rescues their girl friend.
Cut-rate hokum starring the lad who had played
Johnny Weissmuller's 'son' in earlier Tarzan
movies; it led to several tedious sequels.

w Jack de Witt, from the comic strip by Roy
Rockwell d Ford Beebe ph William Sickner
m Edward Kay

Johnny Sheffield, Peggy Ann Garner, Onslow
Stevens, Charles Irwin

Bombardier
US 1943   99m   bw
RKO (Robert Fellows)

Cadet bombardiers learn the realities of war on
raids over Japan.
Totally routine recruiting poster heroics.

w John Twist d Richard Wallace ph Nicholas
Musuraca m Roy Webb

Pat O'Brien, Randolph Scott, Anne Shirley,
Eddie Albert, Walter Reed, Robert Ryan,
Barton Maclane

Bombay Talkie*
India 1970   105m   Eastmancolor
Merchant-Ivory (Ismail Merchant)

A sophisticated American woman comes to
Bombay and falls for two men involved in film-
making.
Interesting but unsatisfactory romantic drama,
rather pointlessly set against film studio
backgrounds.

w Ruth Prawer Jhabvala, James Ivory d James
Ivory ph Subrata Mitra m Shankar Jaikishan

Jennifer Kendal, Shashi Kapoor, Zia
Mohyeddin

Bombers B-52
US 1957   106m   Warnercolor
   Cinemascope
Warner (Richard Whorf)
GB title: *No Sleep till Dawn*

A USAF sergeant considers applying for a
discharge so that he can earn more money in
civilian life.
Glossy domestic melodrama punctuated by
aircraft shots.

w Irving Wallace d Gordon Douglas
ph William Clothier m Leonard Rosenman

Karl Malden, Marsha Hunt, Natalie Wood,
Efrem Zimbalist Jnr, Don Kelly

   'No one questions the basic assumption—that
the good life consists of servicing bigger and
better bombers.'—*MFB*

Bombshell***
US 1933   91m   bw
MGM (Hunt Stromberg)
GB title and aka title: *Blonde Bombshell*

A glamorous film star yearns for a new image.
Crackpot farce which even by today's standards
moves at a fair clip and enabled the star to give
her best comedy performance.

w Jules Furthman, John Lee Mahin,
play Caroline Francke, Mack Crane d *Victor
Fleming ph* Chester Lyons, Hal Rosson

Jean Harlow, Lee Tracy, Frank Morgan,
Franchot Tone, Pat O'Brien, Ivan Lebedeff, Una
Merkel, Ted Healy, Isabel Jewell, C. Aubrey
Smith, Louise Beavers, Leonard Carey, Mary
Forbes

Bon Voyage*
US 1962   133m   Technicolor
Walt Disney (Bill Walsh, Ron Miller)

An American family spends a holiday in Paris.
Simple-minded, overlong comedy of mishaps,
with daddy finally trapped in the sewer.
Smoothly done of its kind.

w Bill Walsh, *novel* Marrijane and Joseph
Hayes d James Neilson ph William Snyder
m Paul Smith

Fred MacMurray, Jane Wyman, Michael
Callan, Deborah Walley, Jessie Royce Landis,
Tommy Kirk, Ivan Desny

Bond Street
GB 1948   107m   bw
ABP / World Screenplays (Anatole de
   Grunwald)

Four stories, each concerning an item of an
expensive wedding trousseau.
Mild and laboured short story compendium.

w Anatole de Grunwald *d* Gordon Parry
ph Otto Heller *m* Benjamin Frankel

Roland Young, Jean Kent, Paula Valenska,
Kathleen Harrison, Derek Farr, *Kenneth
Griffith*, Hazel Court, Ronald Howard
'Even a glimpse of actual Bond Street makes
little contact with reality.'—*MFB*

Le Bonheur*

France 1965   79m   Eastmancolor
Parc / Mag Bodard

A young carpenter is happy with his wife and
family, happier still when he finds a mistress,
whom he marries when his wife is found
drowned.
Slight, good looking, ambivalent little fable
which finally expires in a surfeit of style.

wd Agnès Varda *ph* Jean Rabier, Claude
Beausoleil *m* Mozart

Jean-Claude Drouot, Claire Drouot, Marie-
France Boyer

Bonjour Tristesse*

GB 1957   93m   Technicolor
   Cinemascope
(Columbia) Wheel Films (Otto Preminger)

A teenage girl becomes involved with her
sophisticated father's amours and causes the
death of his would-be mistress.
The novel's rather repellent characters are here
played like royal personages against a
background of Riviera opulence. The result is
very odd but often entertaining, especially when
it slips into self-parody.

w Arthur Laurents, *novel* Françoise Sagan
d Otto Preminger *ph* Georges Périnal
m Georges Auric *pd* Roger Furse

David Niven, Deborah Kerr, Jean Seberg,
Mylene Demongeot, Geoffrey Horne, Juliette
Greco, Martita Hunt, Walter Chiari, Jean Kent,
Roland Culver
'An elegant, ice-cold charade of emotions.'—
Judith Crist
'Sagan not so much translated as traduced—
opened out, smartened up, the sickness overlaid
with Riviera suntan.'—*Alexander Walker*
† Shot in monochrome for Paris, colour for the
Riviera.

La Bonne Soupe

France / Italy 1963   97m   bw
Belstar / Du Siècle / Dear Film (André Hakim)

A high-class prostitute tells her life story.
A saucy frolic complete with three-in-a-bed and
rapidly closing doors; quite enjoyable of its kind.

wd Robert Thomas, *play* Félicien Marceau
ph Roger Hubert *m* Raymond le Sénéchal

Annie Girardot, Marie Bell, Gérard Blain,
Bernard Blier, Jean-Claude Brialy, Claude
Dauphin, Sacha Distel, Daniel Gélin, Blanchette
Brunoy, Jane Marken, Raymond Péllégrin.
Franchot Tone

Bonnie and Clyde****

US 1967   111m   Technicolor
Warner / Seven Arts / Tatira / Hiller (*Warren
   Beatty*)

In the early thirties, a car thief and the daughter
of his intended victim team up to become
America's most feared and ruthless bank
robbers.
Technically brilliant evocation of sleepy mid-
America at the time of the public enemies, using
every kind of cinematic trick including fake
snapshots, farcical interludes, dreamy soft-focus
and a jazzy score. For all kinds of reasons a very
influential film which even made extreme
violence quite fashionable (and very bloody it is).

*w David Newman, Robert Benton d Arthur
Penn ph Burnett Guffey m Charles Strouse*,
using 'Foggy Mountain Breakdown' by Flatt
and Scruggs

Warren Beatty, Faye Dunaway, Gene
Hackman, Estelle Parsons, *Michael J. Pollard*,
Dub Taylor, Denver Pyle, Gene Wilder
'They're young . . . they're in love . . . and they
kill people!'—*publicity*
'It is a long time since we have seen an
American film so perfectly judged.'—*MFB*
'. . . all to the rickety twang of a banjo and a
saturation in time and place.'—*Judith Crist*
'The formula is hayseed comedy bursting
sporadically into pyrotechnical bloodshed and
laced with sentimental pop-Freudianism.'—
John Simon
'A film from which we shall date reputations
and innovations in the American cinema.'—
Alexander Walker

AA: Burnett Guffey; Estelle Parsons
AAN: best picture; David Newman, Robert
Benton; Arthur Penn; Warren Beatty; Faye
Dunaway; Gene Hackman; Michael J. Pollard

Bonnie Prince Charlie

GB 1948   140m approx (later cut to 118m)
   Technicolor
British Lion / London Films (Edward Black)

The hope of the Stuarts returns from exile but is
eventually forced to flee again.
Good highland photography combines with
appalling studio sets, an initially confused
narrative, a draggy script and uneasy
performances to produce an ill-fated attempt at a
British historical epic. Alexander Korda, who
masterminded it, sulked in public at the critical

roasting, but on this occasion the critics were
right.

w Clemence Dane d Anthony Kimmins
ph Robert Krasker m Ian Whyte

David Niven, Margaret Leighton, Jack
Hawkins, Judy Campbell, Morland Graham,
Finlay Currie, John Laurie

'I have a sense of wonder about this film,
beside which *The Swordsman* seems like a
dazzling work of veracity and art. It is that
London Films, having surveyed the finished
thing, should not have quietly scrapped it.'—
Richard Winnington.

Bonnie Scotland**
US 1935   80m   bw
MGM / Hal Roach

Two Americans journey to Scotland to collect a
non-existent inheritance, then follow their friend
in the army and wind up in India.
Generally disappointing star comedy which still
contains excellent sequences when it is not vainly
trying to preserve interest in a boring plot. An
obvious parody on *Lives of a Bengal Lancer*,
released earlier that year; Scotland has almost
nothing to do with it.

w Frank Butler, Jeff Moffitt d James Horne
ph Art Lloyd, Walter Lundin

Stan Laurel, Oliver Hardy, James Finlayson,
Daphne Pollard, William Janney, June Lang

The Boogie Man Will Get You
US 1944   66m   bw
Columbia

Bodies accumulate when mad doctors get to
work creating supermen in a small village.
Desperately unfunny spoof notable only for the
fact that it was attempted with these players and
at that time.

w Edwin Blum d Lew Landers ph Henry
Freulich

Boris Karloff, Peter Lorre, Maxie Rosenbloom,
Jeff Donnell, Larry Parks, Maude Eburne, Don
Beddoe

Boom!
GB 1968   113m   Technicolor   Panavision
Universal / World Film Services / Moon Lake
    Productions (John Heyman, Norman
    Priggen)

On the volcanic Mediterranean island which she
owns, a dying millionairess plans to take as her
last lover a wandering poet who is the angel of
death.
Pretentious, boring nonsense, showing that when
talent goes awry it certainly goes boom.

w Tennessee Williams, from his play *The Milk
Train Doesn't Stop Here Any More* d Joseph
Losey ph Douglas Slocombe m John Barry

Elizabeth Taylor, Richard Burton, *Noel
Coward*, Michael Dunn, Joanna Shimkus

Boom Town**
US 1940   120m   bw
MGM (Sam Zimbalist)

Two friendly oil drillers strike it rich.
Enjoyable four-star, big-studio product of its
time: world-wide entertainment of assured
success, with a proven mix of romance, action,
drama and comedy.

w John Lee Mahin, *story* James Edward Grant
d Jack Conway ph Harold Rosson m Franz
Waxman ad Cedric Gibbons

Clark Gable, Spencer Tracy, Claudette Colbert,
Hedy Lamarr, *Frank Morgan,* Lionel Atwill,
Chill Wills

AAN: Harold Rosson

Boomerang***
US 1947   88m   bw
TCF (Louis de Rochemont)

In a New England town, a clergyman is shot
dead on the street. The DA prevents an innocent
man from being convicted, but cannot track
down the guilty party.
Incisive real life thriller: based on a true case, it
was shot in an innovative documentary style
which was much copied, and justice is not seen to
be done, though the murderer is known to the
audience. A milestone movie of its kind.

w *Richard Murphy* d Elia Kazan ph Norbert
Brodine m David Buttolph

Dana Andrews, Jane Wyatt, Lee J. Cobb, Cara
Williams, Arthur Kennedy, Sam Levene, Taylor
Holmes, Robert Keith, Ed Begley

'A study of integrity, beautifully developed by
Dana Andrews against a background of political
corruption and chicanery that is doubly
shocking because of its documentary
understatement.'—*Richard Winnington*

AAN: Richard Murphy

Boots Malone
US 1952   103m   bw
Columbia (Milton Holmes)

A would-be jockey tags along with a down-at-
heel agent who gets him work and finally
persuades him not to throw a crooked race.
Dullish racetrack melodrama bogged down by
repetitive and unsympathetic plot twists.

w Milton Holmes d William Dieterle
ph Charles Lawton m Elmer Bernstein

William Holden, Johnny Stewart, Stanley
Clements, Basil Ruysdael, Carl Benton Reid, Ed
Begley, Henry Morgan

Border Incident
US 1949   93m   bw
MGM (Nicholas Nayfack)

Police stop the illegal immigration of labourers
from Mexico.
Routine semi-documentary cops and robbers,
well enough made.

w John C. Higgins d Anthony Mann ph John
Alton m André Previn

Ricardo Montalban, George Murphy, Howard
da Silva, James Mitchell, Alfonso Bedoya

Bordertown*
US 1935   90m   bw
Warner (Robert Lord)

In a North Mexican town, a shabby lawyer
becomes infatuated with the neurotic wife of a
businessman.
Satisfying melodrama whose plot climax was
later borrowed for *They Drive by Night.*

w Laird Doyle, Wallace Smith, *novel* Carroll
Graham d Archie Mayo ph Tony Gaudio

Paul Muni, Bette Davis, Margaret Lindsay,
Eugene Pallette, Robert Barrat, Henry O'Neill,
Hobart Cavanaugh
† *Blowing Wild* (qv) was also a partial
uncredited remake.

Born Again
US 1978   110m   Technicolor
Robert L. Munger / Frank Capra Jnr

Charles Colson, sent to prison after Watergate,
becomes a devout Christian.
Part evangelism, part reconstruction through
rose-tinted spectacles; not particularly
entertaining or instructive as either.

w Walter Block d Irving Rapper ph Harry
Stradling Jnr m Les Baxter

Dean Jones, Anne Francis, Jay Robinson, Dana
Andrews, Raymond St Jacques, George Brent,
Harry Spillman (as Nixon)

Born Free**
GB 1965   95m   Technicolor   Panavision
Columbia / Open Road (Carl Foreman)

A Kenyan game warden and his wife rear three
lion cubs, one of which eventually presents them
with a family.
Irresistible animal shots salvage this rather
flabbily put together version of a bestselling
book. An enormous commercial success, it was
followed by the even thinner *Living Free*, by a

TV series, and by several semi-professional
documentaries.

w Gerald L. C. Copley, *book* Joy Adamson
d James Hill ph Kenneth Talbot m *John Barry*

Virginia McKenna, Bill Travers, Geoffrey Keen

AA: John Barry; title song (*m* John Barry,
ly Don Black)

Born Losers
US 1967   112m   colour
AIP (Delores Taylor)

California teeny-boppers claim to have been
gang-raped by wandering motorcyclists.
Teenage shocker, only notable for its credits, and
for being the first Billy Jack film.

wd Tom Laughlin ph Gregory Sandor

Tom Laughlin, Jane Russell, Elizabeth James,
Jeremy Slate, William Wellman Jnr

Born to be Bad
US 1934   61m   bw
Twentieth Century (William Goetz, Raymond
    Griffith)

A girl schemes to seduce the man who has
adopted her illegitimate son.
Batty mother-love melodrama.

w Ralph Graves d Lowell Sherman ph Barney
McGill

Loretta Young, Cary Grant, Jackie Kelk, Henry
Travers, Russell Hopton, Andrew Tombes,
Harry Green

Born to be Bad
US 1950   94m   bw
RKO (Robert Sparks)

An ambitious girl marries a millionaire but
continues her affair with a novelist; finally both
men discover her true character.
Tentative bad girl novelette, just about passable.

w Edith Sommer, *novel* All Kneeling by Anne
Parrish d Nicholas Ray ph Nicholas
Musuraca m Frederick Hollander

Joan Fontaine, Robert Ryan, Zachary Scott,
Joan Leslie,
Mel Ferrer

Born to Dance*
US 1936   108m   bw
MGM (Jack Cummings)

A sailor meets a girl in New York.
Well remembered musical with good numbers
but a rather lame look.

w Jack McGowan, Sid Silvers, B. G. De Sylva
d Roy del Ruth ph Ray June songs Cole Porter

Eleanor Powell, James Stewart, Virginia Bruce,

Una Merkel, Sid Silvers, Frances Langford, Raymond Walburn, *Reginald Gardiner*, Buddy Ebsen

AAN: song 'I've Got You Under My Skin'

Born to Kill*
US 1947   92m   bw
RKO
GB title: *Lady of Deceit*

A psychotic involves his new wife in his criminal pursuits.

Unusual, heavy-going, well acted melodrama.

w Eve Greene, Richard Macauley *d* Robert Wise *ph* Robert de Grasse

Lawrence Tierney, Claire Trevor, Walter Slezak, Philip Terry, Elisha Cook Jnr

Born to Love
US 1931   84m   bw
RKO

During World War I a nurse bears the child of an army pilot who is reported missing; but he turns up after she has married an English milord.

A useful compendium of thirties romantic clichés, quite attractively packaged.

w Ernest Pascal *d* Paul Stein *ph* John Mescall

Constance Bennett, Joel McCrea, Paul Cavanagh, Frederick Kerr, Anthony Bushell, Louise Closser Hale, Edmond Breon, Mary Forbes

Born Yesterday**
US 1950   103m   bw
Columbia (S. Sylvan Simon)

The ignorant ex-chorus girl mistress of a scrap iron tycoon takes English lessons, falls for her tutor, and politically outmanoeuvres her bewildered lover.

Pleasant film version of a cast-iron box office play, subtle and intelligent in all departments yet with a regrettable tendency to wave the flag.

w Albert Mannheimer, *play Garson Kanin* *d* George Cukor *ph* Joseph Walker *m* Frederick Hollander

Judy Holliday, Broderick Crawford, William Holden, Howard St John

AA: Judy Holliday
AAN: best picture; Albert Mannheimer; Garson Kanin

Borsalino*
France / Italy 1970   126m   Eastmancolor
Adel-Marianne-Mars (Alain Delon)

In the thirties two Marseilles gangsters become firm friends and join forces.

Semi-spoof, but with 'real' blood, and period

atmosphere laid on thick. The stars just about keep it ticking over.

w Jean-Claude Carrière, Claude Sautet, Jacques Deray, Jean Cau *d* Jacques Deray *ph* Jean-Jacques Tarbès *m* Claude Bolling

Jean-Paul Belmondo, Alain Delon, Michel Bouquet, Catherine Rouvel, Corinne Marchand

'Rather like a Hollywood musical where someone has forgotten to insert the production numbers.'—*MFB*

The Boss*
US 1956   89m   bw
UA / Frank N. Seltzer

After World War I, a ne'er-do-well becomes a corrupt small town political boss.

Low budgeted, complexly plotted, occasionally quite powerful and efficient crime melodrama.

w Ben L. Parry *d* Byron Haskin *ph* Hal Mohr

John Payne, William Bishop, Gloria McGhee, Doe Avedon, Joe Flynn

Boston Blackie
An American second feature series made by Columbia between 1941 and 1949. There had been silent films about the character, a reformed crook and con man who has to solve crimes because he is suspected by the law. Cheap but sometimes vigorous productions, they had a loyal following, and starred Chester Morris with George E. Stone as his assistant the Runt.

The titles were:

1941: MEET BOSTON BLACKIE, CONFESSIONS OF BOSTON BLACKIE
1942: ALIAS BOSTON BLACKIE, BOSTON BLACKIE GOES TO HOLLYWOOD
1943: AFTER MIDNIGHT WITH BOSTON BLACKIE
1944: ONE MYSTERIOUS NIGHT
1945: BOSTON BLACKIE BOOKED ON SUSPICION, BOSTON BLACKIE'S RENDEZVOUS
1946: A CLOSE CALL FOR BOSTON BLACKIE, THE PHANTOM THIEF
1947: BOSTON BLACKIE AND THE LAW
1948: TRAPPED BY BOSTON BLACKIE
1949: BOSTON BLACKIE'S CHINESE VENTURE

† A television series starring Kent Taylor followed in 1951.

The Boston Strangler**
US 1968   118m   De Luxe   Panavision
TCF (Robert Fryer)

A semi-factual account of the sex maniac who terrified Boston in the mid-sixties.

Ambitious *policier* rendered less effective by

pretentious writing and flashy treatment,
including multi-image sequences; the
investigation is more interesting than the
psychoanalysis.

w Edward Anhalt, *book* Gerold Frank
d Richard Fleischer *ph* Richard Kline *m* Lionel
Newman

Henry Fonda, *Tony Curtis* (as the murderer),
George Kennedy, Mike Kellin, Hurd Hatfield,
Murray Hamilton, Sally Kellerman, Jeff Corey,
George Voskovec

Botany Bay
US 1952   94m   Technicolor
Paramount (Joseph Sistrom)

On a convict ship in 1787 an American student
unjustly accused of robbery clashes with the
brutal captain for the favours of the only woman
aboard.
Cramped and brutal action melodrama, a let-
down considering the talent involved.

w Jonathan Latimer, *novel* Charles Nordhof and
James Hall   *d* John Farrow   *ph* John Seitz
m Franz Waxman

James Mason, Alan Ladd, Patricia Medina,
Cedric Hardwicke, Murray Matheson, Jonathan
Harris

The Bottom of the Bottle
US 1956   86m   Eastmancolor
   Cinemascope
TCF (Buddy Adler)
GB title: *Beyond the River*

A wealthy attorney is visited by his drunken
brother, on the run from the police and needing
help to escape into Mexico.
Dreary drama in muddy colour, a clearly
misguided enterprise.

w Sydney Boehm, *novel* Georges Simenon
d Henry Hathaway   *ph* Lee Garmes

Joseph Cotten, Van Johnson, Ruth Roman, Jack
Carson

Bottoms Up
US 1934   85m   bw
Fox (B. G. De Sylva)

A slick promoter in Hollywood disguises his pals
as British nobility and gets them lucrative jobs.
Mild musical with a rather interesting cast.

w B. G. De Sylva, David Butler, Sid Silvers
d David Butler   *ph* Arthur Miller   *md* Constantin
Bakaleinikoff

Spencer Tracy, Pat Patterson, John Boles,
Harry Green, Herbert Mundin, Sid Silvers,
Thelma Todd, Robert Emmett O'Connor

Le Boucher**
France / Italy 1969   94m   Eastmancolor
La Boétie / Euro International (André
Génovès)
aka: *The Butcher*

Murders in a small French town are traced to the
inoffensive-seeming young butcher who is
courting the local schoolmistress.
Curious, mainly charming film which can't make
up its mind whether to be an eccentric character
study or a Hitchcock thriller, but has its
moments as each.

wd Claude Chabrol   *ph* Jean Rabier   *m* Pierre
Jansen

Stéphane Audran, Jean Yanne, Antonio
Passalia, Mario Beccaria

Boudu Sauvé des Eaux***
France 1932   87m   bw
Michel Simon / Jean Gehret
aka: *Boudu Saved from Drowning*

A scruffy tramp is not grateful for being rescued
from suicide, and plagues the family who invite
him to stay.
A minor classic of black comedy, interesting
equally for its characterizations, its acting, and
its film technique.

wd Jean Renoir, *play* René Fauchois   *ph* Marcel
Lucien   *m* from Raphael and Johann Strauss

Michel Simon, Charles Grandval, Marcelle
Hainia, Séverine Lerczinska, Jean Dasté,
Jacques Becker

'A beautifully rhythmed film that makes one
nostalgic for the period when it was made.'—
New Yorker, 1977

Bought
US 1931   70m   bw
Warner

An ambitious working girl rebels against her
slum existence and seeks a rich man.
Typical star vehicle of its time, with a predictable
and unlikely change of heart for a finale.

w Charles Kenyon, Raymond Griffith, *novel*
Jackdaw's Strut by Harriet Henry   *d* Archie
Mayo   *ph* Ray June

Constance Bennett, Ben Lyon, Richard Bennett,
Dorothy Peterson, Ray Milland, Doris Lloyd,
Maude Eburne

Bound for Glory*
US 1976   148m   De Luxe   Panavision
UA (Charles Mulvehill)

In 1936 Woody Guthrie leaves the Texas dust
bowl for California, and after various hardships
his musical talent is recognized.

Care and occasional beauty in the photography do not obscure memories of *The Grapes of Wrath*, which told much the same story more dramatically and succinctly, and with less earnestness and self-pity.

w Robert Getchell, from Guthrie's autobiography *d* Hal Ashby *ph Haskell Wexler m* Leonard Rosenman *songs* Woody Guthrie *pd* Michael Haller

David Carradine, Ronny Cox, Melinda Dillon, Gail Strickland, John Lehne

AAN: best picture; Robert Getchell; Haskell Wexler

The Bowery***
US 1933   92m   bw
Twentieth Century (Darryl F. Zanuck) (Raymond Griffith,
    William Goetz)

In nineties New York, two boisterous rivals settle their differences after one has jumped off the Brooklyn Bridge for a bet.
Roistering saga of cross and double cross on the seamy side, splendidly vigorous in acting and treatment.

w Howard Estabrook, James Gleason d Raoul Walsh ph Barney McGill *m* Alfred Newman *ad* Richard Day

Wallace Beery, George Raft, Pert Kelton, Jackie Cooper, Fay Wray, Herman Bing

The Bowery Boys
A cheap and cheerful series of American second features, immensely popular between 1946 and 1958, these adventures of a group of ageing Brooklyn layabouts had their origin in the 1937 film *Dead End*, from which the Dead End Kids graduated to other features at Warner: *Crime School, They Made Me a Criminal, Angels with Dirty Faces, Angels Wash their Faces*, etc. A couple of the 'boys' then defected to Universal and made *Little Tough Guy* and a series of half a dozen subsequent pictures; while in 1940 Monogram took a couple more and built up another group called the East Side Kids. In 1946 a formal merger of talent at Monogram consolidated the remaining members into the Bowery Boys. The members were Leo Gorcey, Huntz Hall, Bobby Jordan, Gabriel Dell (all from the Dead End Kids), Bernard Gorcey, David Gorcey, Billy Benedict, and Bennie Bartlett.

The films are:

1946: IN FAST COMPANY, BOWERY BOMBSHELL, LIVE WIRES, SPOOK BUSTERS, MR HEX
1947: BOWERY BUCKAROOS, HARD BOILED MAHONEY, NEWS HOUNDS, ANGELS' ALLEY
1948: JINX MONEY, SMUGGLER'S COVE, TROUBLE MAKERS
1949: ANGELS IN DISGUISE, FIGHTING FOOLS, HOLD THAT BABY, MASTER MINDS
1950: BLONDE DYNAMITE, BLUES BUSTERS, LUCKY LOSERS, TRIPLE TROUBLE
1951: BOWERY BATALLION, CRAZY OVER HORSES, GHOST CHASERS, LET'S GO NAVY
1952: FEUDIN' FOOLS, HERE COME THE MARINES, HOLD THAT LINE, NO HOLDS BARRED
1953: CLIPPED WINGS, JALOPY, LOOSE IN LONDON, PRIVATE EYES
1954: THE BOWERY BOYS MEET THE MONSTERS, JUNGLE GENTS, PARIS PLAYBOYS
1955: BOWERY TO BAGDAD, HIGH SOCIETY, JAIL BUSTERS, SPY CHASERS
1956: DIG THAT URANIUM, CRASHING LAS VEGAS, FIGHTING TROUBLE, HOT SHOTS
1957: SPOOK CHASERS, HOLD THAT HYPNOTIST, LOOKING FOR DANGER
1958: UP IN SMOKE, IN THE MONEY.

Bowery to Broadway
US 1944   94m   bw
Universal (John Grant)

In the nineties, a Bowery songstress makes it to the big time.
Simple-minded musical in which the drama has no drive and the guest stars are given inferior material.

w Joseph Lytton, Arthur T. Horman *d* Charles Lamont *ph* Charles Van Enger *md* Edward Ward

Maria Montez, Turhan Bey, Susanna Foster, Jack Oakie, Donald Cook, Louise Allbritton, Andy Devine, Rosemary de Camp, Ann Blyth, Donald O'Connor, Peggy Ryan, Frank McHugh, Leo Carrillo, Evelyn Ankers, Mantan Moreland

Boxcar Bertha*
US 1972   88m   De Luxe
AIP (Roger Corman)

In early thirties Arkansas, an unhappy girl falls in with gangsters and train robbers.
Competent imitation of *Bonnie and Clyde*.

w Joyce H. and John W. Corrington *d Martin Scorsese ph* John Stephens *m* Gilb Guilbeau, Thad Maxwell

Barbara Hershey, David Carradine, Barry Primus, Bernie Casey, John Carradine

A Boy a Girl and a Bike
GB 1947 92m bw
Gainsborough (Ralph Keene)

Romantic jealousies arise between members of a Yorkshire cycling club.

Mild comedy drama with the advantage of fresh air locations.

w Ted Willis d Ralph Smart

John McCallum, Honor Blackman, Patrick Holt, Diana Dors, Leslie Dwyer, Thora Hird, Anthony Newley, Megs Jenkins, Maurice Denham

The Boy and the Bridge
GB 1959 91m bw
Xanadu (Kevin McClory)

A boy who believes he has committed a murder hides in the ramparts of Tower Bridge.
This tiny fable adds up to very weak entertainment, despite inventive photography, because it has virtually no plot development.

w Geoffrey Orme, Kevin McClory, Desmond O'Donovan d Kevin McClory ph Ted Scaife m Malcolm Arnold

Ian MacLaine, Liam Redmond, James Hayter, Norman Macowan, Geoffrey Keen, Jack MacGowran, Royal Dano, Rita Webb

Boy, Did I Get a Wrong Number
US 1966 99m De Luxe
UA / Edward Small (George Beck)

Trying to phone his wife, an estate agent gets involved with a runaway actress.
Lifeless and generally resistible star comedy, the first of several hard and unfunny vehicles for an ageing Bob Hope seeming to hark back to the least attractive aspects of burlesque rather than the sympathetic wisecracking which suits him best.

w Burt Styler, Albert E. Lewin, George Kennett d George Marshall ph Lionel Lindon m Richard Lasalle ly By Dunham

Bob Hope, Elke Sommer, Phyllis Diller, Marjorie Lord, Cesare Danova, Benny Baker

The Boy Friend*
GB 1971 125m Metrocolor Panavision
MGM / Russflix (Ken Russell)

On a wet Wednesday afternoon in Portsmouth in the late twenties, a tatty company with backstage problems puts on an empty-headed musical.

Russell the mastermind effectively destroys

Sandy Wilson's charming period pastiche, sending up all the numbers (via badly staged dream sequences on the wrong shape screen) in a Busby Berkeley manner which had not yet been invented. Moments do work, but a non-star doesn't help, and the whole thing is an artistic disaster of some significance both to Russell's career and to the cinema of the early seventies.

w Ken Russell, from Sandy Wilson's musical play d Ken Russell ph David Watkin md Ian Whittaker, Peter Greenwell, Peter Maxwell Davies pd Tony Walton

Twiggy, Christopher Gable, *Max Adrian*, Tommy Tune, Barbara Windsor, Moyra Fraser, Bryan Pringle, Vladek Sheybal, *Antonia Ellis*, *Glenda Jackson*

'The glittering, joyless numbers keep coming at you: you never get any relief from Russell's supposed virtuosity.'—*New Yorker, 1977*

AAN: Ian Whittaker, Peter Greenwell, Peter Maxwell Davies

The Boy from Oklahoma*
US 1953 88m Warnercolor
Warner (David Weisbart)

A genial plainsman studying law becomes sheriff of a small town and uncovers its mayor as a killer.
Modest, pleasing western with the star imitating his father.

w Frank David, Winston Miller d Michael Curtiz ph Robert Burks m Max Steiner

Will Rogers Jnr, Nancy Olson, Lon Chaney Jnr, Anthony Caruso, Wallace Ford, Clem Bevans, Merv Griffin

Boy Meets Girl**
US 1938 86m bw
Warner (George Abbott)

Two crazy Hollywood scenario writers make a star of an infant yet unborn.
Freewheeling film version of a hilarious play: fine crazy comedy and excellent Hollywood satire.

w Bella and Sam Spewack, from their play d Lloyd Bacon ph Sol Polito m Leo Forbstein

James Cagney, Pat O'Brien, Marie Wilson, Ralph Bellamy, Frank McHugh, Dick Foran, Bruce Lester, Ronald Reagan, James Stephenson

Boy on a Dolphin*
US 1957 111m Eastmancolor
Cinemascope
TCF (Samuel G. Engel)

A Greek girl diver discovers a sunken artifact of great value and the news spreads to an American

archaeologist and an unscrupulous collector.
Likeable, sunswept Mediterranean adventure
romance marred by the miscasting of the male
lead.

w Ivan Moffatt, Dwight Taylor, *novel* David
Divine *d* Jean Negulesco *ph Milton Krasner*
m Hugo Firedhofer *md* Lionel Newman

Alan Ladd, Sophia Loren, *Clifton Webb*,
Laurence Naismith, Alexis Minotis, Jorge
Mistral

AAN: Hugo Friedhofer

The Boy with Green Hair
US 1948   82m   Technicolor
RKO (Dore Schary)

When he hears that his parents were killed in an
air raid, a boy's hair turns green; other war
orphans encourage him to parade himself
publicly as an image of the horror and futility of
war.
Muddled, pretentious and unpersuasive fantasy,
typical of this producer's do-goodery. One of
those oddities which make Hollywood
endearing, but not very entertaining apart from
Pat O'Brien's garrulous grandpa.

w Ben Barzman, Alfred Lewis Levitt, *story* Betsy
Beaton *d* Joseph Losey *ph* George Barnes
m Leigh Harline

Dean Stockwell, Pat O'Brien, Robert Ryan,
Barbara Hale

The Boys
GB 1962   123m   Cinemascope
Gala / Columbia (Sidney J. Furie)

Four boys are on trial for killing a garage
attendant.
Elaborate courtroom drama with flashbacks,
stars for counsel, a tricksy director, and about
forty minutes too much footage.

w Stuart Douglass *d* Sidney J. Furie *ph* Gerald
Gibbs *m* The Shadows

Richard Todd, Robert Morley, Felix Aylmer,
Dudley Sutton, Ronald Lacey, Tony Garnett,
Jess Conrad, Wilfrid Brambell, Allan
Cuthbertson, Colin Gordon

The Boys From Brazil **
US / GB 1978   124m   De Luxe
ITC / Producer Circle (Martin Richards,
Stanley O'Toole)

A renegade Nazi in hiding has a sinister plot to
reconquer the world.
Suspense fantasy firmly based on a gripping
book; excellent performances, but a shade too
long.

w Heywood Gould, *novel* Ira Levin *d* Franklin

Schaffner *ph* Henri Decaë *m* Jerry Goldsmith
pd Gil Parrando

Gregory Peck, Laurence Olivier, James Mason,
Lilli Palmer, Uta Hagen, Steven Buttenberg,
Denholm Elliott, Rosemary Harris, John
Dehner, John Rubenstein, Anne Meara, David
Hurst, Michael Gough

The Boys from Syracuse *
US 1940   74m   bw
Universal (Jules Levey)

The Comedy of Errors with modern wisecracks,
and a few songs.
Predictable well-drilled confusion arises from
master and slave having identical twins, but the
general tone is a bit flat for an adaptation from a
hilarious Broadway success. Still, the songs are
lively and the chariot race finale shows spirit.

w Leonard Spiegelgass, Charles Grayson, Paul
Gerard Smith, from the play by George Abbott
and William Shakespeare *d* Edward A.
Sutherland *ph* Joseph Valentine *m* Frank
Skinner *md* Charles Previn *songs* Rodgers and
Hart

Allan Jones, Joe Penner, Charles Butterworth,
Rosemary Lane, Irene Hervey, Martha Raye,
Alan Mowbray
† The writing credit on screen ends: 'After a play
by William Shakespeare . . . long, long after!'

Boys in Brown
GB 1949   84m   bw
Gainsborough (Antony Darnborough)

Life in a Borstal institution.
The stars make elderly boys, but Jack Warner is
a cuddly governor. Boring and unpersuasive
non-documentary fiction in Britain's most
tiresome style.

wd Montgomery Tully, *play* Reginald Beckwith
ph Gordon Lang, Cyril Bristow *m* Doreen
Carwithen

Jack Warner, Dirk Bogarde, Michael Medwin,
Jimmy Hanley, Richard Attenborough, Alfie
Bass, Barbara Murray, Thora Hird
† Made by the Independent Frame method,
which blended real backgrounds with studio sets.

The Boys in Company C
Hong Kong 1977   125m   Technicolor
Panavision
Golden Harvest (Andre Morgan)

Five marines find their lives changed by the
Vietnam war.
Crude action melodrama.

w Rick Natkin, Sidney J. Furie *d* Sidney J.

Furie *ph* Godfrey Godar *m* Jaime Mendoza-Nava

Stan Shaw, Andrew Stevens, James Canning, Michael Lembeck, Craig Wasson, James Whitmore Jnr

'Laden with barrack room dialogue and played at the enlisted man's level.'—*Variety*

The Boys in the Band*
US 1970 120m Technicolor
Cinema Center / Leo (Mart Crowley, Kenneth Utt)

Tempers fray and true selves are revealed when a heterosexual is accidentally invited to a homosexual party.
Careful but claustrophobic filming of a Broadway play, which at the screen's closer quarters becomes overpowering well before the end.

w Mart Crowley, from his play *d* William Friedkin *ph* Arthur J. Ornitz *m* none

Leonard Frey, Kenneth Nelson, Cliff Gorman, Frederick Combs, Reuben Greene, Robert La Tourneaux, Laurence Luckinbill, Keith Prentice, Peter White

'They crack jokes while their hearts are breaking.'—*New Yorker*

Boys' Night Out
US 1962 115m Metrocolor
Cinemascope
MGM / Filmways (Martin Ransohoff)

Three married men and their bachelor friend share a flat and a 'mistress'.
Would-be saucy comedy in which nothing sexy ever happens and the helpless players are as witless as the script.

w Ira Wallach *d* Michael Gordon *ph* Arthur E. Arling *m* Frank de Vol

James Garner, Kim Novak, Tony Randall, Howard Duff, Howard Morris, Oscar Homolka, Janet Blair, Patti Page, Jessie Royce Landis

Boys' Town**
US 1938 93m bw
MGM (John W. Considine Jnr)

The story of Father Flanagan and his school for juvenile delinquents.
Well-made, highly successful, but sentimental crowd pleaser.

w John Meehan, Dore Schary, *original story* Eleanor Griffin, Dore Schary *d* Norman Taurog *ph* Sidney Wagner

Spencer Tracy, Mickey Rooney, Henry Hull, Gene Reynolds, Sidney Miller, Frankie Thomas, Bobs Watson, Tommy Noonan

AA: Eleanor Griffin, Dore Schary; Spencer Tracy
AAN: best picture; John Meehan, Dore Schary; Norman Taurog

The Brain
France / US 1969 115m colour
Paramount (Alain Poiré)

A British colonel leads an international crew in an attempt to rob NATO.
Exhausting and generally misfiring international crook comedy.

w Gerard Oury, Marcel Julian, Daniele Thompson *d* Gerard Oury *ph* Vladimir Ivanov, Armand Thirard *m* Georges Delerue

David Niven, Jean-Paul Belmondo, Bourvil, Eli Wallach, Silvia Monti

Brainstorm
US 1965 110m bw Panavision
Warner / Kodima (William Conrad)

A passer-by saves a married woman from suicide, has an affair with her, and conspires to murder her husband. This accomplished, she leaves him and he goes insane.
Overlong thriller which starts off agreeably in the *Double Indemnity* vein; but goes slow and solemn around the half way mark.

w Mann Rubin *d* William Conrad *ph* Sam Leavitt *m* George Duning

Jeffrey Hunter, Anne Francis, Dana Andrews, Viveca Lindfors, Stacy Harris

'A sub-B potboiler for those who find comic books too intellectual.'—*Judith Crist*

The Bramble Bush
US 1960 105m Technicolor
Warner / United States (Milton Sperling)

A doctor returns to his home town and finds himself involved in old tragedies including the mercy killing of his friend.
Sordid small-town melodrama in the *Peyton Place* vein, with adequate production values but dispiriting treatment.

w Milton Sperling, Philip Yordan, *novel* Charles Mergendahl *d* Daniel Petrie *ph* Lucien Ballard *m* Leonard Rosenman

Richard Burton, Barbara Rush, Jack Carson, Angie Dickinson, James Dunn, Tom Drake, Henry Jones, Frank Conroy, Carl Benton Reid, William Hansen

Branded
US 1950 104m Technicolor
Paramount (Mel Epstein)

A gunman poses as a rancher's lost heir, but redeems himself by finding the real one.
Competent, brisk western.

w Sydney Boehm, Cyril Hume *d* Rudolph Maté *ph* Charles Lang Jnr *m* Roy Webb

Alan Ladd, Charles Bickford, Mona Freeman, Robert Keith, Joseph Calleia, Peter Hansen, Selena Royle, Tom Tully

Brandy for the Parson*
GB 1951   79m   bw
Group Three (Alfred O'Shaughnessy)

A couple on a yachting holiday find themselves unwittingly smuggling brandy into Britain.
Pleasant little sub-Ealing comedy with agreeable locations but not much drive.

w John Dighton, Walter Meade, *story* Geoffrey Household *d* John Eldridge *ph* Martin Curtis *m* John Addison

James Donald, Kenneth More, Jean Lodge, Frederick Piper, Charles Hawtrey, Michael Trubshawe, Alfie Bass, Reginald Beckwith

Brannigan*
GB 1975   111m   De Luxe   Panavision
UA / Wellborn (Jules Levy, Arthur Gardner)

A Chicago policeman is sent to London to pick up a gangster.
Cheerful crime pastiche and tour of London, quite an agreeable entertainment despite its obviously over-age star.

w Christopher Trumbo, Michael Butler, William P. McGivern, William Norton *d* Douglas Hickox *ph* Gerry Fisher *m* Dominic Frontière

John Wayne, Richard Attenborough, Judy Geeson, Mel Ferrer, John Vernon, Daniel Pilon, John Stride, James Booth, Barry Dennen

The Brasher Doubloon*
US 1946   72m   bw
TCF
GB title: *The High Window*

Philip Marlowe investigates the theft of a rare coin and finds himself involved in a series of murders.
The poorest of the Chandler adaptations, previously filmed as *Time to Kill*, still contains good moments, though the star is lightweight and the production low-budget.

w Dorothy Bennett, *novel* The High Window by Raymond Chandler *d* John Brahm *ph* Lloyd Ahern

George Montgomery, Nancy Guild, Florence Bates, Conrad Janis, Fritz Kortner

The Brass Bottle
US 1964   89m   Eastmancolor
U-I / Scarus (Robert Arthur)

A young architect finds an old brass bottle which contains a troublesome genie.
Simple-minded farce with little invention and poor trickwork.

w Oscar Brodney, *novel* F. Anstey *d* Harry Keller *ph* Clifford Stine *m* Bernard Green *sp* Roswell Hoffman

Tony Randall, Burl Ives, Barbara Eden, Edward Andrews, Ann Doran

The Bravados*
US 1958   98m   Eastmancolor
      Cinemascope
TCF (Herbert B. Swope)

A widower chases four killers who, he believes, raped and murdered his wife.
Dour western with a downbeat ending; production good, but entertainment uneasy.

w Philip Yordan, *novel* Frank O'Rourke *d* Henry King *ph* Leon Shamroy *m* Lionel Newman

Gregory Peck, Stephen Boyd, Joan Collins, Albert Salmi, Henry Silva, George Voskovec, Barry Coe, Lee Van Cleef

The Brave Bulls
US 1951   108m   bw
Columbia (Robert Rossen)

A Mexican matador regains his courage but loses his girl in a car crash.
Muddled narrative with dollops of bull-fighting mystique; a rather miserable movie despite effort all round.

w John Bright, *novel* Tom Lea *d* Robert Rossen *ph* James Wong Howe, Floyd Crosby

Mel Ferrer, Miroslava, Anthony Quinn, Eugene Iglesias

The Brave Don't Cry*
GB 1952   90m   bw
Group Three (John Baxter)

Over a hundred men are rescued in a Scottish mine disaster.
Semi-documentary based on a real incident: well done on a small budget, but hardly memorable.

w Montagu Slater *d* Philip Leacock *ph* Arthur Grant *m* none

John Gregson, Meg Buchanan, John Rae, Fulton Mackay, Andrew Keir, Russell Waters, Jameson Clark, Jean Anderson, Eric Woodburn

The Brave One*
US 1956   100m   Technicolor
Cinemascope
King Brothers

A small boy saves the life of his pet bull when it is sent into the ring.
Mildly beguiling minor drama for those who adore small boys and bulls.

w Harry Franklin, Merrill G. White, *original story* Robert Rich d Irving Rapper ph Jack Cardiff m Victor Young

Michel Ray, Rodolfo Hoyos, Elsa Cardenas, Joi Lansing, Carlos Navarro

AA: Robert Rich: there was much confusion when the mysterious Rich turned out to be Dalton Trumbo, who was blacklisted at the time.

Brazil
US 1944   91m   bw
Republic

A lady novelist goes to Brazil for material; a local composer poses as her guide in order to pay her back for her previous remarks about his country.
Acceptable lower case musical with pleasant tunes and humour.

w Frank Gill Jnr, Laura Kerr d Joseph Dantley ph Jack Marta *songs* Bob Russell and others m Walter Scharf

Virginia Bruce, Tito Guizar, Edward Everett Horton, Roy Rogers

AAN: song 'Rio de Janeiro' (m Ary Barrosa, *ly* Ned Washington); Walter Scharf

Bread, Love and Dreams*
Italy 1953   90m   bw
Titanus (Marcello Girosi)

The new sergeant of police in a small rural village comes looking for a wife.
Pleasant rather than exciting rural comedy which spun off a number of vaguely related sequels (*Bread, Love and Jealousy*, etc).

w Luigi Comencini, *original story* Ettore Margadonna d Luigi Comencini ph Arturo Gallea m Alessandro Cicognini

Vittorio de Sica, Gina Lollobrigida, Marisa Merlini, Roberto Risso

AAN: Ettore Margadonna

Break of Hearts
US 1935   80m   bw
RKO (Pandro S. Berman)

A girl composer falls in love with a distinguished conductor who becomes a dipsomaniac.

Well acted soap opera, not really worthy of its stars.

w Sarah Y. Mason, Victor Heerman, Anthony Veiller d Philip Moeller ph Robert de Grasse m Max Steiner

Katharine Hepburn, Charles Boyer, Jean Hersholt, John Beal, Sam Hardy

Break the News*
GB 1938   78m   bw
GFD / Jack Buchanan

A dancer arranges his partner's 'death' for publicity reasons but is sent to jail when the partner disappears.
Thin but lively comedy with a remarkable couple of song and dance men. Negative apparently lost.

w Geoffrey Kerr, *novel* La Mort en Fuite by Loid de Gouriadec d René Clair

Jack Buchanan, Maurice Chevalier, June Knight, Marta Labarr, Garry Marsh, Felix Aylmer, Robb Wilton
† Various remakes include *The Art of Love* (qv).

Breakfast at Tiffany's*
US 1961   115m   Technicolor
Paramount (Martin Jurow, Richard Shepherd)

A young New York writer has as neighbour the volatile Holly Golightly, a slightly crazy call girl with an exotic social and emotional life.
Impossibly cleaned up and a sexual version of a light novel which tried to be the American *I Am a Camera*. Wild parties, amusing scenes and good cameos, but the pace is slow, the atmosphere is unconvincingly clean and luxurious, and the sentimentality kills it.

w George Axelrod, *novel* Truman Capote d Blake Edwards ph Franz Planer m Henry Mancini

Audrey Hepburn, George Peppard, Patricia Neal, Buddy Ebsen, Martin Balsam, *John McGiver* (as the Tiffany salesman), Mickey Rooney

AA: Henry Mancini; *song* 'Moon River' (m Henry Mancini, *ly* Johnny Mercer)
AAN: Audrey Hepburn

Breakfast for Two*
US 1937   65m   bw
RKO (Edward Kaufman)

A Texas heiress turns a playboy into a businessman.
Star crazy comedy with some wildly funny scenes.

w Charles Kaufman, Paul Yawitz, Viola Brothers Shore d Alfred Santell ph J. Roy Hunt

Barbara Stanwyck, Herbert Marshall, Donald Meek, Glenda Farrell, Eric Blore, Etienne Girardot

Breakheart Pass*
US 1975   94m   De Luxe
UA / Elliott Kastner (Jerry Gershwin)

Various mysterious passengers on an 1873 train across the frozen west to Fort Humboldt turn out to have smuggling and murder in mind.
Botched murder mystery on wheels: there are some exciting scenes, but the plot makes little sense and the 'action finale' is muddled.

w Alistair MacLean, from his book d Tom Gries ph Lucien Ballard m Jerry Goldsmith

Charles Bronson, Ben Johnson, Richard Crenna, Jill Ireland, Charles Durning, Archie Moore, Ed Lauter

The Breaking Point*
US 1950   97m   bw
Warner (Jerry Wald)

A charterboat owner becomes involved with crooks but turns them in when they have killed his friend.
Adequate if slightly humdrum attempt by Warners to atone for what they had done to a Hemingway novel, the infidelity of *To Have and Have Not* and the unauthorized variation of *Key Largo*. (See also: *The Gun Runners*.)

w Ranald MacDougall, *novel* To Have and Have Not by Ernest Hemingway d Michael Curtiz ph Ted McCord m (uncredited) William Lava, Max Steiner

John Garfield, Patricia Neal, Phyllis Thaxter, Juano Hernandez, Wallace Ford, Edmon Ryan, William Campbell

Breaking Point
Canada 1976   92m   colour   Panavision
TCF / Astral Belle Vue (Harold Greenberg, Harold Pariser)

An innocent witness against the Mafia takes off against them vigilante style when his partner is murdered and his own life is threatened.
Comic strip thuggery with performances to match; plenty of excitement for toughies.

w Roger E. Swaybill, Stanley Mann d Bob Clark ph Marc Champion m David McLey

Bo Svenson, Robert Culp, John Colicos, Belinda J. Montgomery, Stephen Young

Breakthrough
US 1950   91m   bw
Warner (Bryan Foy)

Adventures of a US army unit in Normandy after D-Day.
Routine low-budgeter which improves after a slow start.

w Bernard Girard, Ted Sherdeman, Joseph I. Breen Jnr d Lewis Seiler ph Edwin DuPar m William Lava

David Brian, John Agar, Frank Lovejoy, William Campbell, Paul Picerni, Greg McClure, Edward Norris, Matt Willis, Dick Wesson

A Breath of Scandal
US 1960   98m   Technicolor
Paramount / Titanus / Ponti–Girosi (Carlo Ponti, Marcello Girosi)

A spirited Ruritanian princess falls for an American industrialist.
Exceedingly flat-footed and boring international co-production of an old Molnar play; if anyone concerned had bright ideas, they don't show.

w Sidney Howard (presumably in the thirties, for he died in 1939), *play* Olimpia by Ferenc Molnar d Michael Curtiz, Mario Russo ph Mario Montuori m Alessandro Cicognini

Sophia Loren, Maurice Chevalier, John Gavin, Isabel Jeans, Angela Lansbury, Roberto Risso, Frederick Ledebur, Tullio Carminati, Milly Vitale

Breezy
US 1973   107m   Technicolor
Universal / Malpaso (Robert Daley)

A divorced 50-year-old real estate agent is rejuvenated by an affair with a young girl hippy.
An abrasive veneer covers the most stereotyped of January–May love stories. Technically an attractive piece of work.

w Jo Heims d Clint Eastwood ph Frank Stanley m Michel Legrand

William Holden, Kay Lenz, Roger C. Carmel, Marj Dusay, Joan Hotchkis

Brewster's Millions*
GB 1935   84m   bw
British and Dominion (Herbert Wilcox)

If he can spend a million pounds within two months, a playboy will inherit many millions more.
Artless but lively version of a famous comedy which provided a good role for its star.

w Arthur Wimperis, Paul Gangelin, Douglas Furber, Clifford Grey, Donovan Pedelty, Wolfgang Wilhelm, *play* George Barr McCutcheon and Winchell Smith, *original novel* George Barr McCutcheon d Thornton Freeland

Jack Buchanan, Lili Damita, Nancy O'Neil, Amy Veness, Sydney Fairbrother, Fred Emney, Sebastian Shaw

Brewster's Millions*
US 1945 79m bw
Edward Small

Competent American remake of the above.

w Winchell Smith, Cryon Ongley *d* Allan Dwan *ph* Charles Lawton Jnr

Dennis O'Keefe, Eddie 'Rochester' Anderson, Helen Walker

† Remade as *Three on a Spree* (GB 1961).

Brewster McCloud
US 1970 105m Metrocolor Panavision
MGM / Adler–Phillips / Lion's Gate (Lou Adler)

A man hides out under the roof of the Houston Astrodrome, prepares to learn to fly with man-made wings, and refuses all offers of help; when he launches himself, he falls to his death.
Anarchic, allegorical fantasy, a delight no doubt for connoisseurs of way-out humour. Everyone else, forget it.

w Doran William Cannon *d* Robert Altman *ph* Lamar Boren, Jordan Cronenweth *m* Gene Page

Bud Cort, Sally Kellerman, Michael Murphy, William Windom, Shelley Duvall, René Auberjonois, Stacy Keach, John Shuck, Margaret Hamilton

'Amorphous and rather silly . . . the idea seems to be left over from a Victorian fable, but the style is like a Road Runner cartoon.'—*New Yorker, 1974*

The Bribe*
US 1949 98m bw
MGM (Robert Z. Leonard)

A US agent tracks down a group of criminals in Central America.
Steamy melodrama with pretensions but only moderate entertainment value despite high gloss. The rogues' gallery, however, is impressive.

w Marguerite Roberts *d* Robert Z. Leonard *ph* Joseph Ruttenberg *m* Miklos Rozsa

Robert Taylor, Ava Gardner, Charles Laughton, Vincent Price, John Hodiak

The Bridal Path*
GB 1959 95m Technicolor
British Lion / Sidney Gilliat, Frank Launder

A stalwart Hebridean islander journeys to the mainland in search of a wife.

Mild, episodic, very pleasant open-air comedy set amid splendid locations.

w Frank Launder, Geoffrey Willans, *novel* Nigel Tranter *d* Frank Launder *ph* Arthur Ibbetson *m* Cedric Thorpe Davie

Bill Travers, Fiona Clyne, George Cole, Duncan Macrae, Gordon Jackson, Dilys Laye, Bernadette O'Farrell

The Bride Came C.O.D.*
US 1941 92m bw
Warner (Hal B. Wallis)

A charter pilot agrees to kidnap a temperamental heiress, but is stuck with her when they crashland in the desert.
Feeble comedy with a script totally unworthy of its stars. The mass of talent does however provide a smile or two towards the end.

w Julius J. and Philip G. Epstein *d* William Keighley *ph* Ernest Haller

Bette Davis, James Cagney, Harry Davenport, Stuart Erwin, Eugene Pallette, Jack Carson, George Tobias, William Frawley, Edward Brophy, Chick Chandler

'Neither the funniest comedy ever made, nor the shortest distance between two points, but for the most part a serviceable romp.'—*Theodore Strauss*

'Both of them mug good-naturedly, and it's pleasantly fast.'—*New Yorker, 1977*

The Bride Comes Home*
US 1935 82m bw
Paramount (Wesley Ruggles)

A penniless socialite helps a wealthy man and his roughneck bodyguard in a magazine venture.
Slight but freshly handled romantic comedy, still worth a look.

w Elizabeth Sanxay Holding, Claude Binyon *d* Wesley Ruggles *ph* Leo Tover

Claudette Colbert, Robert Young, Fred MacMurray, William Collier Snr, Donald Meek, Edgar Kennedy, Richard Carle, Jimmy Conlin

Bride for Sale
US 1949 87m bw
RKO (Jack H. Skirball)

A practical-minded businesswoman has two admirers.
Skittish romantic comedy for ageing stars.

w Bruce Manning, Islin Auster *d* William D. Russell *ph* Joseph Valentine *m* Frederick Hollander

Claudette Colbert, George Brent, Robert Young,

Max Baer, Gus Schilling, Charles Arnt, Thurston Hall

The Bride Goes Wild
US 1948 98m bw
MGM (William H. Wright)

As his lady illustrator finds out, a writer of children's books is not quite the sober uncle she expected, especially when he has to pretend to adopt an unruly orphan.
Scatty comedy with farcical interludes, quite pleasantly played but lacking style.

w Albert Beich d Norman Taurog ph Ray June m Rudolf Kopp

June Allyson, Van Johnson, Jackie 'Butch' Jenkins, Hume Cronyn, Richard Derr

The Bride of Frankenstein****
US 1935 85–90m bw
Universal (Carl Laemmle Jnr)

Baron Frankenstein is blackmailed by Dr Praetorious into reviving his monster and building a mate for it.
Frankenstein was startlingly good in a primitive way; this sequel is the screen's sophisticated masterpiece of black comedy, with all the talents working deftly to one end. Every scene has its own delights, and they are woven together into a superb if wilful cinematic narrative which, of its gentle mocking kind, has never been surpassed.

w *John L. Balderston, William Hurlbut* d *James Whale* ph *John Mescall* m *Franz Waxman*

Boris Karloff, Colin Clive, *Ernest Thesiger*, Valerie Hobson, *E. E. Clive*, Dwight Frye, O. P. Heggie, Una O'Connor, *Elsa Lanchester* (as Mary Shelley and the monster's mate), Gavin Gordon (as Byron), Douglas Walton (as Shelley)

'It is perhaps because Whale was by now master of the horror film that this production is the best of them all.'—*John Baxter, 1968*

'An extraordinary film, with sharp humour, macabre extravagance, and a narrative that proceeds at a fast, efficient pace.'—*Gavin Lambert, 1948*

'A great deal of art has gone into it, but it is the kind of art that gives the healthy feeling of men with their sleeves rolled up and working, worrying only about how to put the thing over in the best manner of the medium—no time for nonsense and attitudes and long hair.'—*Otis Ferguson*

†The regular release version runs 75m, having dropped part of the Mary Shelley prologue and a sequence in which the monster becomes unsympathetic by murdering the burgomaster.

††The title was originally to have been *The Return of Frankenstein.*

Bride of Vengeance*
US 1948 91m bw
Paramount (Richard Maibaum)

The story of the Borgias (whitewashing Lucretia) and the Duke of Ferrara.
Superb looking but appallingly acted and rather stodgily directed piece of historical melodrama. Totally studio-bound, but one of these days it could find a sympathetic audience.

w Cyril Hume, Michael Hogan d Mitchell Leisen ph Daniel L. Fapp m Hugo Friedhofer ad Hans Dreier, Roland Anderson, Albert Nozaki

Paulette Goddard, John Lund, Macdonald Carey, Albert Dekker, Raymond Burr

The Bride Walks Out
US 1936 81m bw
RKO (Edward Small)

A successful mannequin tries to manage on her engineer husband's lowly salary.
Thin, pleasant marital comedy with no surprises.

w P. J. Wolfson, Philip G. Epstein d Leigh Jason ph J. Roy Hunt m Roy Webb

Barbara Stanwyck, Gene Raymond, Robert Young, Ned Sparks, Helen Broderick, Willie Best, Robert Warwick, Billy Gilbert, Hattie McDaniel, Irving Bacon

The Bride Wore Black*
France / Italy 1967 107m Eastmancolor
Films du Carrosse / Artistes Associés / Dino de Laurentiis (Marcel Bébert)
original title: *La Mariée Était en Noir*

A melancholy lady traces and kills the five men responsible for her fiancé's death.
Uncertain and not very entertaining attempt to turn a Hitchcock situation into a character study.

w François Truffaut, Jean-Louis Richard, *novel* William Irish d François Truffaut ph Raoul Coutard m Bernard Herrmann

Jeanne Moreau, Jean-Claude Brialy, Michel Bouquet, Charles Denner, Claude Rich, Michel Lonsdale

The Bride Wore Boots
US 1946 86m bw
Paramount (Seton I. Miller)

A woman who loves horses is married to a man who does not.
Flimsy, silly, but mainly quite tolerable light comedy sustained by its stars.

w Dwight Mitchell Wiley *d* Irving Pichel
ph Stuart Thompson *m* Frederick Hollander

Barbara Stanwyck, Robert Cummings, Diana
Lynn, Patric Knowles, Peggy Wood, Robert
Benchley, Willie Best, Natalie Wood

The Bride Wore Red*
US 1937 103m bw
MGM (Joseph L. Mankiewicz)

A whimsical count arranges for a chorus girl to
spend two weeks at an aristocratic Tyrol resort,
where she is pursued by two rich men.
Cinderella retold in fancy dress; a typically
unreal but quite entertaining star confection of
its day.

w Tess Slesinger, Bradbury Foote, *play* The Girl
from Trieste by Ferenc Molnar *d* Dorothy
Arzner *ph* George Folsey *m* Franz Waxman

Joan Crawford, Robert Young, Franchot Tone,
Billie Burke, Reginald Owen, George Zucco,
Lynne Carver, Mary Phillips, Paul Porcasi

Brides of Dracula**
GB 1960 85m Technicolor
U-I / Hammer / Hotspur (Anthony Hinds)

Baron Meinster, a disciple of Dracula, is locked
up by his mother; but a servant lets him out and
he goes on the rampage in a girls' school.
The best of the Hammer *Draculas*, with plenty of
inventive action, some classy acting and a good
sense of place and period.

w Jimmy Sangster, Peter Bryan, Edward Percy
d Terence Fisher ph Jack Asher *m* Malcolm
Williamson

David Peel (as Meinster), *Peter Cushing*, Freda
Jackson, *Martita Hunt*, Yvonne Monlaur,
Andrée Melly, Mona Washbourne, Henry
Oscar, Miles Malleson

The Bridge*
West Germany 1959 106m bw
Fono / Jochen Severin (Hermann Schwerin)

In 1945, only a handful of 16-year-old
schoolboys is left to defend the bridge of a small
German town.
Painful but memorable war vignette, almost an
updating of *All Quiet on the Western Front*.

w Michael Mansfield, Karl-Wilhelm Vivier,
novel Manfred Gregor *d Bernhard Wicki*
ph Gerd Von Bonen *m* Hans-Martin Majewski

Volker Bohnet, Fritz Wepper, Michael Hinz,
Frank Glaubrecht, Karl Michael Balzer,
Gunther Hoffman

The Bridge at Remagen*
US 1968 116m De Luxe Panavision
UA / Wolper (David L. Wolper)

February 1945: Germans and Americans fight
over a Rhine bridge.
Disenchanted, violent war film in which
incessant bang-bang, adroitly staged, is all that
matters.

w Richard Yates, William Roberts *d* John
Guillermin *ph* Stanley Cortez *m* Elmer
Bernstein

George Segal, Robert Vaughn, Ben Gazzara,
Bradford Dillman, E. G. Marshall, Peter Van
Eyck

'Viable viewing if explosions and clichés are
your shtick and exciting if you're not sure who
won that war.'—*Judith Crist*

The Bridge of San Luis Rey*
US 1944 85m bw
(UA) Benedict Bogeaus

Five people die when a Peruvian rope bridge
collapses; the film investigates why they were
each on the bridge at the time.
An intriguing novel is turned into tedious film
drama, with actors, director, scenarist and
production designer all making heavy weather.

From the novel by Thornton Wilder *d* Rowland
V. Lee *ph* John Boyle *m* Dmitri Tiomkin

Lynn Bari, Francis Lederer, Nazimova, Louis
Calhern, Akim Tamiroff, Blanche Yurka,
Donald Woods

AAN: Dmitri Tiomkin

The Bridge on the River Kwai***
GB 1957 161m Technicolor
  Cinemascope
Columbia / Sam Spiegel

British POWs in Burma are employed by the
Japs to build a bridge; meanwhile British agents
seek to destroy it.
Ironic adventure epic with many fine moments
but too many centres of interest and an
unforgivably confusing climax. It is
distinguished by Guinness' portrait of the
English CO who is heroic in his initial stand
against the Japs but finally cannot bear to see his
bridge blown up: and the physical detail of the
production is beyond criticism.

w Carl Foreman, *novel* Pierre Boulle *d* David
Lean *ph* Jack Hildyard *m* Malcolm Arnold

Alec Guinness, Jack Hawkins, William Holden,
Sessue Hayakawa, Percy Herbert, *James
Donald*, Geoffrey Horne, André Morell

AA: best picture; Carl Foreman (credited as

Michael Wilson); David Lean; Jack Hildyard;
Malcolm Arnold; Alec Guinness

AAN: Sessue Hayakawa

Bridge to the Sun*
France / US 1961   112m   bw
MGM / Cité Films (Jacques Bar)

Just before Pearl Harbor, an American girl
marries a Japanese diplomat and goes to live in
Tokyo.
Romantic drama which oddly sides with the
Japanese and shows America in a poor light.
Interesting if not very compelling, with some
unfamiliar views of Japan.

w Charles Kaufman, *autobiography* Gwendolen
Terasaki d Etienne Périer ph Marcel Weiss,
Seiichi Kizuka, Bill Kelly m Georges Auric

Carroll Baker, James Shigeta, James Yagi,
Tetsuro Tamba

'In yet another burst of national flagellation,
Hollywood turns on itself and unthinking
Americans for being so beastly about the
wartime Japanese.'—*MFB*

A Bridge Too Far**
US / GB 1977   175m   Technicolor
   Panavision
UA / Joseph E. Levine (John Palmer)

The story of the Allied defeat at Arnhem in 1944.
Like all large-scale military films, this one fails to
make its tactics clear, and its sober intent
conflicts with its roster of guest stars. For all
that, there are impressive moments of acting and
production.

w William Goldman, *book* Cornelius Ryan
d Richard Attenborough (and Sidney Hayers)
ph *Geoffrey Unsworth, Harry Waxman, Robin
Browne* pd Terence Marsh

Dirk Bogarde, James Caan, Michael Caine,
Sean Connery, Edward Fox, Elliott Gould, Gene
Hackman, Anthony Hopkins, Hardy Kruger,
Laurence Olivier, Ryan O'Neal, Robert
Redford, Maximilian Schell, Liv Ullmann,
Arthur Hill, Wolfgang Preiss

'A film too long.'—*Anon.*

'So wearily, expensively predictable that by
the end the viewer will in all likelihood be too
enervated to notice Attenborough's prosaic
moral epilogue.'—*John Pym, MFB*

The Bridges at Toko-Ri*
US 1954   104m   Technicolor
Paramount / Perlberg–Seaton

The comradeship and death of two jet pilots
during the Korean War.
Ambitiously staged action thriller with points to

make about war, death and politics: a well-worn
American formula pitched very hard.

w Valentine Davies, *novel* James E. Michener
d Mark Robson ph Loyal Griggs m Lyn
Murray

William Holden, Mickey Rooney, Grace Kelly,
Fredric March, Robert Strauss, Charles
McGraw, Earl Holliman, Willis Bouchey

Brief Encounter****
GB 1945   86m   bw
Cineguild (Anthony Havelock-Allan, Ronald
Neame)

A suburban housewife on her weekly shopping
visits develops a love affair with a local doctor;
but he gets a job abroad and they agree not to see
each other again.
An outstanding example of good middle-class
cinema turned by sheer professional craft into a
masterpiece; even those bored by the theme must
be riveted by the treatment, especially the use of
a dismal railway station and its trains.

w Noel Coward, from his one-act play Still Life
d David Lean ph Robert Krasker
m Rachmaninov

Celia Johnson, Trevor Howard, Stanley
Holloway, Joyce Carey, Cyril Raymond

'Both a pleasure to watch as a well-controlled
piece of work, and deeply touching.'—*James
Agee*

'Polished as is this film, its strength does not lie
in movie technique, of which there is plenty, so
much as in the tight realism of its detail.'—
Richard Winnington

AAN: David Lean; Celia Johnson

Brigadoon*
US 1954   108m   Anscocolor
   Cinemascope
MGM (Arthur Freed)

Two Americans in Scotland find a ghost village
which awakens only once every hundred years.
Likeable but disappointing adaptation of a Lost
Horizonish Broadway musical, marred by
artificial sets and jaded direction.

w Alan Jay Lerner, from his play d Vincente
Minnelli ph Joseph Ruttenberg md Johnny
Green songs Frederick Loewe, Alan Jay Lerner

Gene Kelly, Cyd Charisse, Van Johnson, Jimmy
Thompson, Elaine Stewart, Barry Jones, Eddie
Quillan

'The whimsical dream world it creates holds
no compelling attractions.'—*Penelope Houston*

The Brigand*
US 1952   93m   Technicolor
Columbia

A Moroccan adventurer looks like the king and is reprieved from execution if he will impersonate the latter and root out his enemies.
Cheeky revamp of *The Prisoner of Zenda*, quite acceptably done.

w Jesse Lasky Jnr *d* Phil Karlson *ph* W. Howard Greene *m* Mario Castelnuovo-Tedesco

Anthony Dexter, Jody Lawrance, Gale Robbins, Anthony Quinn, Carl Benton Reid, Ron Randell

The Brigand of Kandahar
GB 1965   81m   Technicolor   'Scope
EMI / Hammer (Anthony Nelson Keys)

A cashiered Bengal Lancer officer throws in his lot with a troublesome bandit.
Feeble frontier adventure with nothing ringing true.

wd John Gilling *ph* Reg Wyer *m* Don Banks *pd* Bernard Robinson

Oliver Reed, Ronald Lewis, Duncan Lamont, Yvonne Romain, Catherine Woodville, Glyn Houston

Brigham Young**
US 1940   112m   bw
TCF (Kenneth MacGowan)

The story of the Mormon trek to Utah.
Ambitious but rather dull interpretation of history, seen as a western with romantic fictional trimmings.

w Lamar Trotti, *story* Louis Bromfield *d* Henry Hathaway *ph* Arthur Miller *m* Alfred Newman

Dean Jagger, Tyrone Power, Linda Darnell, Brian Donlevy, Jane Darwell, John Carradine, Mary Astor, Vincent Price, Moroni Olsen

Bright Eyes*
US 1934   84m   bw
TCF

An orphan finds herself torn between foster-parents.
The first of Shirley Temple's genuine star vehicles has a liveliness and cheerfulness hard to find today. As a production, however, it is decidedly economical.

w William Conselman *d* David Butler *ph* Arthur Miller *m* Samuel Kaylin

Shirley Temple, James Dunn, Lois Wilson, *Jane Withers*, Judith Allen

Bright Leaf
US 1950   110m   bw
Warner (Henry Blanke)

A 19th-century tobacco farmer builds a cigarette empire.
Quite agreeable but disjointed fictional biopic, more about love than tobacco.

w Ranald MacDougall *d* Michael Curtiz *ph* Karl Freund *m* Max Steiner

Gary Cooper, Lauren Bacall, Patricia Neal, Jack Carson, Donald Crisp, Gladys George, Elizabeth Patterson, Jeff Corey, Taylor Holmes

Bright Road*
US 1953   69m   bw
MGM (Sol Baer Fielding)

In an all-black school, a problem child finds himself when he helps to rid the school of a swarm of bees.
Slight but attractive second feature, unostentatiously set in a black community.

w Emmet Lavery *d* Gerald Mayer *ph* Alfred Gilks *m* David Rose

Dorothy Dandridge, Harry Belafonte, Robert Horton, Philip Hepburn, Barbara Ann Sanders

Bright Victory*
US 1951   97m   bw
Universal (Robert Buckner)
GB title: *Lights Out*

A blinded soldier adjusts to civilian life.
Well-meaning if rather slow and sticky, this drama is more sentimental than realistic but has good performances.

w Robert Buckner, *novel* Bayard Kendrick *d* Mark Robson *ph* William Daniels *m* Frank Skinner

Arthur Kennedy, Peggy Dow, Julia Adams, James Edwards, Will Geer, Minor Watson, Jim Backus

AAN: Arthur Kennedy

Brighton Rock***
GB 1947   92m   bw
Associated British / The Boultings
US title: *Young Scarface*

The teenage leader of a racetrack gang uses a waitress as alibi to cover a murder, and marries her. He later decides to be rid of her, but fate takes a hand in his murder plot.
A properly 'seedy' version of Graham Greene's 'entertainment', very flashily done for the most part but with a trick ending which allows the heroine to keep her illusions.

w Graham Greene, Terence Rattigan *d John Boulting ph* Harry Waxman *m* Hans May

Richard Attenborough, Hermione Baddeley, *Harcourt Williams*, William Hartnell, Alan Wheatley, Carol Marsh

'The film is slower, much less compelling, and, if you get me, less cinematic than the book, as a child's guide to which I hereby offer it.'—*Richard Winnington*

Bring Me the Head of Alfredo Garcia

US 1974   112m   De Luxe
UA / Optimus / Churubusco (Martin Baum)

A wealthy Mexican offers a million dollars for the head of a man who seduced his daughter, and claimants find that grave robbing is involved.
Gruesome, sickly action melodrama with revolting detail; the nadir of a director obsessed by violence.

w Gordon Dawson, Sam Peckinpah *d* Sam Peckinpah *ph* Alex Phillips Jnr *m* Jerry Fielding

Warren Oates, Gig Young, Isela Vega, Robert Webber, Helmut Dantine, Emilio Fernandez, Kris Kristofferson

Bring On the Girls

US 1945   92m   Technicolor
Paramount (Fred Kohlmar)

A millionaire joins the navy in the hope that a girl will love him for himself.
A good example of the gaily-coloured but witless drivel which occasionally came out of the big studios towards the end of the war.

w Karl Tunberg, Darrell Ware *d* Sidney Lanfield *ph* Karl Struss *md* Robert Emmett Dolan

Veronica Lake, Eddie Bracken, Sonny Tufts, Marjorie Reynolds, Grant Mitchell, Alan Mowbray, Porter Hall

Bringing Up Baby***

US 1938   102m   bw
RKO (Howard Hawks)

A zany girl causes a zoology professor to lose a dinosaur bone and a pet leopard in the same evening.
Outstanding crazy comedy which barely pauses for romance and ends up with the whole splendid cast in jail.

w Dudley Nichols, Hagar Wilde *d* Howard Hawks *ph* Russell Metty *m* Roy Webb

Katharine Hepburn, Cary Grant, May Robson, Charles Ruggles, Walter Catlett, Fritz Feld, Jonathan Hale, Barry Fitzgerald

'I am happy to report that it is funny from the word go, that it has no other meaning to recommend it . . . and that I wouldn't swap it for practically any three things of the current season.'—*Otis Ferguson*

'It may be the American movies' closest equivalent to Restoration comedy.'—*Pauline Kael*

'Crazy comedies continue to become crazier, and there will soon be few actors and actresses left who have no straw in their hair.'—*Basil Wright*

Britannia Mews

GB 1948   91m   bw
TCF (William Perlberg)
US title: *The Forbidden Street*

In Victorian times, the widow of a puppetmaster eventually marries his lookalike who rebuilds their puppet theatre.
Curious and uncertain comedy drama set among yesterday's high society, with poorly played leads but an interesting supporting cast and technical assurance.

w Ring Lardner Jnr, *novel* Margery Sharp *d* Jean Negulesco *ph* Georges Périnal *ad* Andrei Andreiev *m* Malcolm Arnold

Dana Andrews, Maureen O'Hara, Sybil Thorndike, Wilfrid Hyde White, Fay Compton, A. E. Matthews

British Agent*

US 1934   81m   bw
Warner (Henry Blanke)

In 1910 Russia, a Britisher falls in love with a lady spy.
Sluggish and dated romantic melodrama, notable only for Howard's performance and some directional felicities.

w Laird Doyle, *novel* H. Bruce Lockhart *d* Michael Curtiz *ph* Ernest Haller *ad* Anton Grot

Leslie Howard, Kay Francis, William Gargan, *Irving Pichel*, Philip Reed, Walter Byron, J. Carrol Naish, Halliwell Hobbes

British Intelligence

US 1940   63m   bw
Warner
GB title: *Enemy Agent*

During World War I a German lady spy becomes a guest in the house of a British war official, the butler of which is the leader of a German spy ring.
Second feature remake of *Three Faces East* (qv); still quite an entertaining melodrama.

w Lee Katz, *play* Anthony Paul Kelly *d* Terry Morse *ph* Sid Hickox

Boris Karloff, Margaret Lindsay, Maris Wrixon, Bruce Lester, Leonard Mudie, Holmes Herbert

Broadway
US 1942 90m bw
Universal (Bruce Manning)

George Raft recalls his days as a hoofer in a New York speakeasy, and in particular a murder involving gangsters and chorus girls.
Minor crime melodrama which after interminable scene-setting paints an effective picture of the twenties but has too slack a grip on narrative.

w Felix Jackson, John Bright, *play* Philip Dunning, George Abbott *d* William A. Seiter *ph* George Barnes *md* Charles Previn

George Raft, Pat O'Brien, S. Z. Sakall, Janet Blair, Broderick Crawford, Marjorie Rambeau

Broadway Bill**
US 1934 104m bw
Columbia (Frank Capra)
GB title: *Strictly Confidential*

A cheerful horse trainer finds he has a winner.
Easygoing romantic comedy with the energetic Capra style in fairly full bloom.

w Robert Riskin, *story* Mark Hellinger *d Frank Capra ph* Joseph Walker

Warner Baxter, Myrna Loy, Walter Connolly, Helen Vinson, Douglass Dumbrille, Raymond Walburn, Lynne Overman, Clarence Muse, Margaret Hamilton, Paul Harvey, Claude Gillingwater, Charles Lane, Ward Bond

'It will be a long day before we see so little made into so much: it is gay and charming and will make you happy, and I am sorry to say I do not know recommendations much higher.'— *Otis Ferguson*
† Remade as *Riding High* (qv).

Broadway Limited*
US 1941 75m bw
Hal Roach
GB title: *The Baby Vanishes*

On an express train, a Hollywood publicity stunt backfires.
Wild farce which is not very funny as a whole but has entertaining comic performances.

w Rian James *d* Gordon Douglas *ph* Henry Sharp *m* Charles Previn

Victor McLaglen, Patsy Kelly, *Leonid Kinskey*, Marjorie Woodworth, Dennis O'Keefe, Zasu Pitts, George E. Stone

Broadway Melody*
US 1929 110m bw (Technicolor scenes)
MGM

Chorus girls try to make it big on Broadway.
The screen's very first musical, exceedingly primitive by the standards of even a year later, but rather endearing and with a splendid score.

w James Gleason, Norman Houston, Edmund Goulding *d* Harry Beaumont *ph* John Arnold *songs* Nacio Herb Brown, Arthur Freed

Charles King, Anita Page, Bessie Love, Jed Prouty, Kenneth Thomson, Mary Doran, Eddie Kane

AAN: Bessie Love

Broadway Melody of 1936*
US 1935 103m bw
MGM (John W. Considine Jnr)

A Broadway producer is at loggerheads with a columnist.
Fairly lively musical with lavish numbers.

w Jack McGowan, Sid Silvers, *original story* Moss Hart *d* Roy del Ruth *ph* Charles Rosher *songs* Nacio Herb Brown, Arthur Freed

Jack Benny, Robert Taylor, Una Merkel, *Eleanor Powell*, June Knight, Vilma and Buddy Ebsen, Nick Long Jnr

AAN: best picture; Moss Hart

Broadway Melody of 1938*
US 1937 110m bw
MGM (Jack Cummings)

Backstage problems threaten the opening of a musical show.
Lavish but fairly forgettable musical with top talent.

w Jack McGowan, Sid Silvers *d* Roy del Ruth *ph* William Daniels *songs* Nacio Herb Brown, Arthur Freed

Eleanor Powell, George Murphy, *Sophie Tucker*, Judy Garland, Robert Taylor, Buddy Ebsen, Sid Silvers, Billy Gilbert, Raymond Walburn

Broadway Melody of 1940*
US 1939 102m bw
MGM (Jack Cummings)

A dance team gets to the top.
Splendidly produced but thinly plotted extravaganza with good numbers.

w Leon Gordon, George Oppenheimer *d* Norman Taurog *ph* Oliver T. Marsh, Joseph Ruttenberg *songs* Cole Porter

Fred Astaire, Eleanor Powell, George Murphy, Douglas Macphail, Florence Rice, Frank Morgan, Ian Hunter

Broadway Rhythm*
US 1943 113m Technicolor
MGM (Jack Cummings)

Originally intended as *Broadway Melody of 1944*, this putting-on-a-show extravaganza had only the numbers to commend it.

w Dorothy Kingsley, Harry Clark, from the Kern/Hammerstein operetta Very Warm for May *d* Roy del Ruth *ph* Leonard Smith *songs* various

George Murphy, Ginny Simms, Charles Winninger, Gloria de Haven, Lena Horne, Nancy Walker, Hazel Scott, Eddie Anderson, Ben Blue, Tommy Dorsey and his Orchestra

Broadway Serenade
US 1939   114m   bw
MGM (Robert Z. Leonard)
GB title: *Serenade*

Career problems split the marriage of a songwriter and his singing wife.
Lavish but rather dull romantic drama with music.

w Lew Lipton, John T. Foote, Hans Kraly *d* Robert Z. Leonard *md* Herbert Stothart

Jeanette MacDonald, Lew Ayres, Frank Morgan, Ian Hunter, Rita Johnson, Virginia Grey, William Gargan, Katherine Alexander

Broadway thru a Keyhole *
US 1933   90m   bw
UA / William Goetz, Raymond Griffith

A tough New York gangster falls for a singer in his nightclub.
Reputed acid observation of the New York scene distinguishes this low-budget gangster drama.

w Gene Town, *story* Walter Winchell *d* Lowell Sherman *ph* Barney McGill *songs* Mack Gordon, Harry Revel

Constance Cummings, Russ Columbo, Paul Kelly, *Blossom Seeley*, Gregory Ratoff, *Texas Guinan*, Hobart Cavanaugh, C. Henry Gordon

Broken Arrow *
US 1950   92m   Technicolor
TCF (Julian Blaustein)

A US army scout brings about peace between white man and Apache.
Solemn western which at the time was acclaimed for giving the Indian's point of view (something which had scarcely happened since silent days). As entertainment it was not exciting, but it set Jeff Chandler off on a career playing Cochise with variations, and a TV series of the same name surfaced in 1956.

w Michael Blankfort, *novel* Blood Brother by Elliott Arnold *d* Delmer Daves *ph* Ernest Palmer *m* Hugo Friedhofer *md* Alfred Newman

James Stewart, Jeff Chandler, Debra Paget, Basil Ruysdael, Will Geer, Arthur Hunnicutt, Jay Silverheels
'It has probably done more to soften racial hostilities than most movies designed to instruct, indict and inspire.'—
Pauline Kael

AAN: Michael Blankfort; Ernest Palmer; Jeff Chandler

Broken Blossoms **
US 1919   105m (16 fps)   bw
UA / D. W. Griffith

In slummy Limehouse, a young Chinaman loves the daughter of a brute, who kills her; the Chinaman then kills him and commits suicide.
Victorian-style melodrama presented by Griffith with all the stops out; sometimes striking, but very dated even on its first appearance.

wd D. W. Griffith, story The Chink and the Child in Thomas Burke's Limehouse Nights *ph* G. W. Bitzer

Lillian Gish, Donald Crisp, Richard Barthelmess
† Leslie Henson appeared in a parody, Broken Bottles, in 1920.

Broken Blossoms *
GB 1936   84m   bw
Twickenham (Julius Hagen)

A remake originally intended to be directed by Griffith. Quite stylish, and in some ways more interesting than its predecessor.

w Emlyn Williams *d John Brahm*

Dolly Haas, Arthur Margetson, Emlyn Williams, Donald Calthrop, Ernest Sefton, Kathleen Harrison, Basil Radford

Broken Journey
GB 1948   89m   bw
Gainsborough (Sydney Box)

A plane crashes in the Alps, and the survivors take different attitudes to their situation.
Unpersuasive and stagey melodrama which wastes some good talent.

w Robert Westerby *d* Ken Annakin *ph* Jack Cox *m* John Greenwood

Phyllis Calvert, James Donald, Margot Grahame, Francis L. Sullivan, Raymond Huntley, Derek Bond, Guy Rolfe, David Tomlinson

Broken Lance *
US 1954   96m   De Luxe   Cinemascope
TCF (Sol C. Siegel)

An autocratic cattle baron causes dissension among his sons.

Western remake of *House of Strangers*, quite well done.

w Richard Murphy, *original story* Philip Yordan *d* Edward Dmytryk *ph* Joe MacDonald *m* Leigh Harline

Spencer Tracy, Robert Widmark, Robert Wagner, Jean Peters, Katy Jurado, Earl Holliman, Hugh O'Brian, Eduard Franz, E. G. Marshall

AA: Philip Yordan
AAN: Katy Jurado

Broken Lullaby*
US 1932 77m bw
Paramount
GB and original title: *The Man I Killed*

A young Frenchman goes to Germany to seek out the family of the man he killed in the war, and is accepted by them as a friend.

This most untypical Lubitsch film now seems very dated but was deeply felt at the time and has plenty of cinematic grip.

w Ernest Vajda, Samson Raphaelson, *play* L'Homme que J'ai Tué by Maurice Rostand *d* Ernst Lubitsch *ph* Victor Milner *ad* Hans Dreier

Lionel Barrymore, Phillips Holmes, Nancy Carroll, Tom Douglas, Zasu Pitts, Lucien Littlefield, Lois Carver, Emma Dunn

'The best talking picture that has yet been seen and heard.'—*Robert E. Sherwood*

The Broken Wing
US 1932 71m bw
Paramount

A Mexican girl jilts a bandit for an American pilot.

Hokey romantic melodrama.

w Gordon Jones, William Slavens McNutt, *play* Paul Dickey, Charles Goddard *d* Lloyd Corrigan *ph* Henry Sharp

Lupe Velez, Leo Carrillo, Melvyn Douglas, George Barbier, Willard Robertson

Broth of a Boy
Eire 1958 77m bw
Emmet Dalton (Alec Snowden)

TV covers the village festivities celebrating an old poacher's 110th birthday.

Mildly amusing regional comedy.

w Patrick Kirwan, Blanaid Irvine, *play* The Big Birthday by Hugh Leonard *d* George Pollock *ph* Walter J. Harvey *m* Stanley Black

Barry Fitzgerald, June Thorburn, Tony Wright,

Harry Brogan, Eddie Golden, Maire Kean, Godfrey Quigley, Dermot Kelly

Brother John*
US 1970 94m Eastmancolor
Columbia / E and R (Joel Glickman)

A mysterious black man comes to town for a family funeral and is suspected by the townsfolk of various sinister motives, but when they imprison him he is freed by a sympathizer. The humans are all mean-minded, the saintly visitor is either Christ or an emissary from another planet. Either way, we have been here before, but although this little fantasy has nothing clear to say it is quite enjoyable on the surface.

w Ernest Kinoy *d* James Goldstone *ph* Gerald Perry Finnerman *m* Quincy Jones

Sidney Poitier, Bradford Dillman, Will Geer, Beverly Todd, Ramon Pieri, Warren J. Kemmerling, Paul Winfield, Lincoln Kilpatrick

'It starts out as an engaging mystery with sociological overtones but ends up as a muddle-headed doomsday parable.'—*Judith Crist, 1977*

Brother Orchid*
US 1940 91m bw
Warner (Hal B. Wallis)

A gangster, 'taken for a ride' by his former friends, escapes and becomes a monk. Rather uneasy blend of comedy, drama and religion, with some good scenes.

w Earl Baldwin, *story* Richard Connell *d* Lloyd Bacon *ph* Tony Gaudio

Edward G. Robinson, Humphrey Bogart, Donald Crisp, Ann Sothern, Ralph Bellamy, Allen Jenkins, Cecil Kellaway

Brother Rat*
US 1938 89m bw
Warner (Robert Lord)

Fun and games with the cadets at a military academy.

Brisk but dated farce from a highly successful Broadway original; remade as *About Face*.

w Richard Macaulay, Jerry Wald, *play* Fred Finklehoffe, John Monks *d* William Keighley *ph* Ernest Haller

Wayne Morris, Eddie Albert, Ronald Reagan, Priscilla Lane, Jane Bryan, Jane Wyman, Johnnie Davis, Henry O'Neill

Brother Rat and a Baby
US 1939 87m bw
Warner (Robert Lord)
GB title: *Baby Be Good*

Scatty follow-up to the above, with the cadets graduating.

w Jerry Wald, Richard Macauley *d* Ray Enright *ph* Charles Rosher

Wayne Morris, Eddie Albert, Ronald Reagan, Priscilla Lane, Jane Wyman, Jane Bryan, Arthur Treacher, Moroni Olsen

Brother Sun, Sister Moon

GB / Italy 1972   122m   Technicolor
Panavision
Paramount / Vic Films / Euro International
(Luciano Perugia)

The life of Francis of Assisi.
Good-looking but relentlessly boring view of a medieval saint as a kind of early flower person.

w Suso Cecchi d'Amico, Kenneth Ross, Lina Wertmuller, Franco Zeffirelli *d* Franco Zeffirelli *ph* Ennio Guarnieri *m* Donovan

Graham Faulkner, Judi Bowker, Alec Guinness (as Pope Innocent III), Leigh Lawson, Kenneth Cranham, Lee Montague, Valentina Cortese
'If I were Pope, I would burn it.'—*Stanley Kauffmann*

The Brotherhood*

US 1968   96m   Technicolor
Paramount / Brotherhood Company

A Mafia executive welcomes his younger brother into the syndicate, but is finally executed by him.
Dour melodrama with tragic pretensions: well made but rather tedious and violent.

w Lewis John Carlino *d* Martin Ritt *ph* Boris Kaufman *m* Lalo Schifrin

Kirk Douglas, Alex Cord, *Luther Adler*, Irene Papas, Susan Strasberg, Murray Hamilton, Eduardo Ciannelli

The Brotherhood of Satan*

US 1970   93m   Techniscope
Columbia / LQJAF / Four Star Excelsior (L. Q. Jones, Alvy Moore)

A village is isolated by an outbreak of diabolism.
Fresh and intriguing minor horror film with imaginative touches.

w William Welch *d* Bernard McEveety *ph* John Arthur Morrill *m* Jaime Mendoza-Nava

Strother Martin, L. Q. Jones, Charles Bateman, Anna Capri, Charles Robinson, Alvy Moore, Geri Reischl

The Brothers**

GB 1947   98m   bw
GFD / Sydney Box

An orphan girl comes to a Skye fishing family at the turn of the century, and causes superstition, sexual jealousy and tragedy.
Wildly melodramatic but good-looking open-air melodrama, a surprising and striking British film of its time.

w Muriel and Sydney Box, *novel* L. A. G. Strong *d* David Macdonald *ph* Stephen Dade

Patricia Roc, Maxwell Reed, *Duncan Macrae* (a splendidly malevolent performance), Will Fyffe, Andrew Crawford, Finlay Currie

Brothers in Law*

GB 1957   97m   bw
British Lion / the Boultings

A young barrister has comic misdemeanours in and out of court.
The lighter side of the law, from a bestseller by a judge; mechanically amusing and not in the same street as its predecessor *Private's Progress*, though it seemed hilarious at the time.

w Roy Boulting, Frank Harvey, Jeffrey Dell, *novel Henry Cecil* *d* John Boulting *ph* Max Greene *m* Benjamin Frankel

Ian Carmichael, Terry-Thomas, Richard Attenborough, *Miles Malleson, Eric Barker*, Irene Handl, John Le Mesurier, Olive Sloane, Kynaston Reeves

The Brothers Karamazov*

US 1958   146m   Metrocolor
MGM (Pandro S. Berman)

In 19th-century Russia, the father of three sons is murdered and the wrong brother is found guilty.
Decent but decidedly unenthralling Hollywood compression of a classic, faithful to the letter but not the spirit of the book, and with few memorable moments or performances.

w Richard Brooks, *novel* Fedor Dostoievsky *d* Richard Brooks *ph* John Alton *m* Bronislau Kaper *ad* William A. Horning, Paul Groesse

Yul Brynner, Maria Schell, Richard Basehart, Claire Bloom, Lee J. Cobb, Albert Salmi, William Shatner, Judith Evelyn

AAN: Lee J. Cobb

The Brothers Rico

US 1957   91m   bw
Columbia / William Goetz (Lewis J. Rachmil)

An accountant fails to retrieve his brothers from a life of crime.
Moderate gangster fare with good credentials but more talk than action.

w Lewis Meltzer, Ben Perry, *novel* Georges Simenon *d* Phil Karlson *ph* Burnett Guffey *m* George Duning

Richard Conte, James Darren, Dianne Foster, Kathryn Grant, Larry Gates, Lamont Johnson, Harry Bellaver

Brown on Resolution*
GB 1935   80m   bw
Gaumont (Michael Balcon)
Later retitled: *Forever England*; US title: *Born for Glory*

In the 1914 war in the Mediterranean, a seaman holds a German warship at bay with a rifle.
Uneasy amalgam of adventure heroics and character study, interesting for its effort.
Remade as *Singlehanded* (qv).

w Michael Hogan, Gerard Fairlie, J. O. C. Orton, *novel* C. S. Forester d Walter Forde

John Mills, Betty Balfour, Barry Mackay, Jimmy Hanley, Howard Marion Crawford, H. G. Stoker

The Browning Version*
GB 1951   90m   bw
GFD / Javelin (Teddy Baird)

Retiring through ill health, a classics master finds that he is hated by his unfaithful wife, his headmaster and his pupils. An unexpected act of kindness gives him courage to face the future.
A rather thin extension of a one-act play, capped by a thank-you speech which is wildly out of character. Dialogue and settings are smooth, but the actors are not really happy with their roles.

w Terence Rattigan, from his play d Anthony Asquith ph Desmond Dickinson

Michael Redgrave, Jean Kent, Nigel Patrick, Wilfrid Hyde White, Bill Travers, Ronald Howard

The Brute*
Mexico 1952   83m   bw
International Cinematografica
original title: *El Bruto*

Victimized slum tenants call for help to a slow-witted giant, who kills the landlord and falls in love with his daughter.
Eccentric melodrama which doesn't quite seem to make its point.

wd Luis Bunuel ph Augustin Jiminez m Rafael Larista

Pedro Armendariz, *Katy Jurado*, Rosita Arenas, Andres Soler

Brute Force**
US 1947   96m   bw
U-I

Six violent convicts revolt against a sadistic warden and try to escape.

Vivid and rather repellent prison melodrama leading up to an explosive climax; its savagery seemed at the time to break fresh ground.

w *Richard Brooks d Jules Dassin ph* William Daniels m Miklos Rozsa

Burt Lancaster, Charles Bickford, Hume Cronyn, Ella Raines, Yvonne de Carlo

The Buccaneer*
US 1938   90m   bw
Paramount (Cecil B. de Mille)

During the 1812 war, pirate Jean Lafitte helps president Andrew Jackson to repel the British.
Sprightly adventure romance with generally good production and acting.

w Jeanie Macpherson, Edwin Justus Mayer, Harold Lamb, C. Gardner Sullivan d Cecil B. de Mille ph Victor Milner md Boris Morros m Georges Antheil

Fredric March, Franciska Gaal, *Akim Tamiroff*, Margot Grahame, Walter Brennan, Ian Keith, Spring Byington, Douglass Dumbrille, Robert Barrat, Hugh Sothern, Beulah Bondi, Anthony Quinn, Montagu Love

AAN: Victor Milner

The Buccaneer
US 1958   121m   Technicolor   Vistavision
Paramount / Cecil B. de Mille (Henry Wilcoxon)

Slow, slack and stolid remake of the 1938 film, with practically no excitement or interest and very obvious studio sets.

w Jesse L. Lasky Jnr, Berenice Mosk, from the earlier screenplay d Anthony Quinn ph Loyal Griggs m Elmer Bernstein

Yul Brynner, Claire Bloom, Charles Boyer, Inger Stevens, Henry Hull, Charlton Heston, E. G. Marshall, Douglass Dumbrille, Lorne Greene, Ted de Corsia, Robert F. Simon

Buck and the Preacher
US 1971   103m   colour
Columbia / E and R / Belafonte (Joel Glickman)

Nightriders chasing escaped slaves are outwitted by a wagon train guide and a con man.
Lively, easygoing western with a largely black cast, and a message of militancy sugar-coated by Hollywood hokum.

w Ernest Kinoy d Sidney Poitier ph Alex Phillips m Benny Carter

Sidney Poitier, Harry Belafonte, Ruby Dee, Cameron Mitchell, Denny Miller, Nita Talbot, John Kelly

Buck Privates*
US 1941   84m   bw
Universal (Alex Gottlieb)
GB title: *Rookies*

Two incompetents in the army accidentally
become heroes.

Abbott and Costello's first starring vehicle is a
tired bundle of army jokes and old routines
separated by plot and romance, but it sent the
comedians right to the top, where they stayed for
ten years.

w Arthur T. Horman   *d* Arthur Lubin   *ph* Milton
Krasner   *md* Charles Previn

Bud Abbott, Lou Costello, Lee Bowman, Alan
Curtis, Jane Frazee, *The Andrews Sisters, Nat
Pendleton*, Samuel S. Hinds, Shemp Howard

AAN: Charles Previn; song 'The Boogie Woogie
Bugle Boy of Company B' (*m* Hugh Prince,
ly Don Raye)

Buck Privates Come Home
US 1946   77m   bw
U-I
GB title: *Rookies Come Home*

Incompetent war veterans are demobilized and
find civilian life tough.

Thin star comedy with a good final chase.

w John Grant, Frederic I. Rinaldo, Robert Lees
d Charles T. Barton   *ph* Charles Van Enger

Bud Abbott, Lou Costello, Beverly
Simmons,Tom Brown, Nat Pendleton

Buckskin
US 1968   97m   Pathecolor
Paramount / A. C. Lyles

In the frontier town of Gloryhole a gambler is
routed by the new marshal.

Routine old-fashioned western with this
producer's predictable gallery of weatherbeaten
familiar faces.

w Michael Fisher   *d* Michael Moore   *ph* W.
Wallace Kelley   *m* Jimmie Haskell

Barry Sullivan, Joan Caulfield, Lon Chaney Jnr,
John Russell, Richard Arlen, Barbara Hale, Bill
Williams, Barton Maclane

The Buddy Holly Story
US 1978   113m   colour
Columbia / Innavisions / ECA (Fred Bauer)

The life of a fifties rock-and-roller who died
young in an accident.

Solidly carpentered showbiz biopic for the youth
market.

w Robert Gitler   *d* Steve Rash   *ph* Stevan
Larner   *md* Joe Renzetti

Gerry Busey, Dan Stroud, Charles Martin
Smith, Bill Jordan, Maria Rochwine

Buffalo Bill*
US 1944   89m   Technicolor
TCF (Harry Sherman)

A moderately fictitious account of the life of
William Cody, from buffalo hunter to wild west
showman.

Easygoing entertainment which turns from
western excitements to domestic drama.
Generally watchable.

w Aeneas Mackenzie, Clements Ripley, Cecile
Kramer   *d* William Wellman   *ph* Leon Shamroy
m David Buttolph

Joel McCrea, Maureen O'Hara, Linda Darnell,
Thomas Mitchell, Edgar Buchanan, Anthony
Quinn, Moroni Olsen

**Buffalo Bill and the Indians, or Sitting
Bull's History Lesson**
US 1976   118m   colour   Panavision
UA / Robert Altman

During winter camp for his wild west show,
Buffalo Bill Cody and his friends discuss life and
his own myth.

Anti-action, alienation-effect talk piece which
has some points of interest for sophisticates but
is likely to set western addicts asking for their
money back.

w Alan Rudolph, Robert Altman, *play* Indians
by Arthur Kopit   *d* Robert Altman   *ph* Paul
Lohmann   *m* Richard Baskin

Paul Newman, Burt Lancaster, Joel Grey, Kevin
McCarthy, Geraldine Chaplin, Harvey Keitel,
John Considine, Denver Pyle

'The western is an enormously resilient form,
but never has that resilience been tested quite so
much as in this movie . . . it isn't really a movie,
it's a happening.'—*Arthur Knight*

'Whereas Kopit's play offered a hallucinatory
mosaic, Altman's script has the one-dimensional
clarity of a cartoon.'—*Michael Billington,
Illustrated London News*

Bug
US 1975   101m   Movielab
Paramount / William Castle

Large rocklike insects appear after an
earthquake and set fire to themselves and their
victims.

Absurd, overlong and rather nasty horror film
with no visible redeeming features.

w William Castle, Thomas Page, *novel* The
Hephaestus Plague by Thomas Page   *d* Jeannot
Szwarc   *ph* Michel Hugo, Ken Middleham
m Charles Fox

Bradford Dillman, Joanna Miles, Richard
Gilliland, Jamie Smith Jackson, Alan Fudge,
Patty McCormack

'The finer scientific points are to say the least
elusive.'—
David Robinson

The Bugle Sounds
US 1941   101m   bw
MGM (J. Walter Ruben)

An old cavalry sergeant, discharged for
insubordination, rounds up fifth columnists and
is reinstated.

Ho-hum star vehicle on familiar lines but at
undue length.

w Cyril Hume *d* S. Sylvan Simon *ph* Clyde de
Vinna *m* Lennie Hayton

Wallace Beery, Marjorie Main, Lewis Stone,
George Bancroft, William Lundigan, Henry
O'Neill, Donna Reed, Chill Wills, Roman
Bohnen, Jerome Cowan, Tom Dugan, Guinn
Williams, Jonathan Hale.

Bugles in the Afternoon
US 1952   85m   Technicolor
William Cagney

In the US army at the time of Custer's last stand,
a young officer is victimized by a jealous rival.
Modest, adequate western with nice scenery but
no surprises.

w Geoffrey Homes, Harry Brown, *novel* Ernest
Haycox *d* Roy Rowland *ph* Wilfrid Cline
m Dmitri Tiomkin

Ray Milland, Hugh Marlowe, Helena Carter,
Forrest Tucker, Barton Maclane, George
Reeves, James Millican, Gertrude Michael

Bugsy Malone * *
GB 1976   93m   Eastmancolor
Rank / Bugsy Malone Productions (David
   Puttnam, Allan Marshall)

New York 1929: gangster Fat Sam fights it out
with Dandy Dan, and the best man wins the girl.
Extremely curious musical gangster spoof with
all the parts played by children and the guns
shooting ice cream. Very professionally done,
but one wonders to whom it is supposed to
appeal.

wd Alan Parker *ph* Michael Seresin, Peter
Biziou *m*/*songs* Paul Williams *pd* Geoffrey
Kirkland

Scott Baio, Jodie Foster, Florrie Digger, John
Cassisi

'If for nothing else, you would have to admire
it for the sheer doggedness of its eccentricity.'—
David Robinson, Times

'All the pizazz in the world couldn't lift it

above the level of empty camp.'—*Frank Rich,
New York Post*

'I only wish the British could make adult
movies as intelligent as this one.'—*Michael
Billington, Illustrated London News*

Bulldog Drummond *
US 1929   90m   bw
Samuel Goldwyn

After advertising for adventure, ex-war hero
Drummond is approached by an American girl
whose uncle is being held prisoner in a fake
nursing home by villainous Carl Petersen.
This is the closest the screen ever came to the
original Drummond character, debonair yet
taking personal and unnecessary vengeance on
the chief villain. A fairly primitive talkie with
little movement, yet consistently interesting.

w Sidney Howard, *play* 'Sapper' (H. C.
McNeile)
d F. Richard Jones *ph* George Barnes, Gregg
Toland *ad* William Cameron Menzies

Ronald Colman, Joan Bennett, *Claud Allister*
(as Algy), Lilyan Tashman, Montagu Love,
Lawrence Grant

AAN: Ronald Colman

Bulldog Drummond Strikes Back *
US 1934   83m   bw
Samuel Goldwyn

Drummond gets married, but delays his
honeymoon to investigate a mysterious London
house with a disappearing body.
Slow-starting, then intriguing light mystery
which becomes repetitive and silly.
Performances and production enjoyable.

w Nunnally Johnson *d* Roy del Ruth
ph Peverell Marley

Ronald Colman, Loretta Young, C. Aubrey
Smith, *Charles Butterworth* (Algy), Warner
Oland, Mischa Auer, Una Merkel
† Later Drummond films included a few from
Paramount in the late thirties with John Howard,
three in the late forties with Tom Conway, and
two totally unrecognizable sixties
personifications by Richard Johnson, *Deadlier
than the Male* and *Some Girls Do*.

Bulldog Jack *
GB 1935   72m   bw
Gaumont (Michael Balcon)
US title: *Alias Bulldog Drummond*

A playboy poses as Bulldog Drummond when
the real man is injured, and manages to foil the
thieves and save the girl.
After a slowish start, this comedy thriller works
up into a fine frenzy with exciting scenes on the

London Underground and in the British
Museum.

w H. C. McNeile, Gerard Fairlie, J. O. C. Orton,
Sidney Gilliat *d Walter Forde*

*Jack Hulbert, Ralph Richardson, Claude
Hulbert,* Fay Wray, Athole Fleming, Paul
Graetz

'There is . . . a mad train ride towards the
terminus and destruction, as good as anything in
screen melodrama.'—*Peter John Dyer, 1965*

'A sense of showmanship that is rewarded in a
full quota of thrills and laughs.'—*Kine Weekly*

A Bullet for Joey
US 1955 85m bw
UA / Sam Bischoff, David Diamond

A Canadian policeman prevents the murder of
an atomic scientist.
Listless low-budgeter with familiar stars below
par.

w Geoffrey Homes, A. I. Bezzerides *d* Lewis
Allen *ph* Harry Neumann *m* Harry Sukman

Edward G. Robinson, George Raft, Audrey
Totter, George Dolenz, Peter Hanson, Peter Van
Eyck

A Bullet is Waiting
US 1954 82m Technicolor
Columbia / Welsch (Howard Welsch)

A plane accident brings a policeman and his
prisoner to a lonely farm, where a girl and her
father bring a fresh twist to the situation.
Disappointing melodrama full of pretentious
moralizing and fey characterization.

w Thames Williamson, Casey Robinson *d* John
Farrow *ph* Franz Planer *m* Dmitri Tiomkin

Jean Simmons, Rory Calhoun, Stephen
McNally, Brian Aherne

Bullets or Ballots*
US 1936 81m bw
Warner (Lou Edelman)

A city cop goes undercover to break the mob.
Vivid routine gangster thriller, not quite of the
top flight, but nearly.

w Seton I. Miller *d* William Keighley *ph* Hal
Mohr *m* Heinz Roemheld

Edward G. Robinson, Joan Blondell, Humphrey
Bogart, Barton Maclane, Frank McHugh, Dick
Purcell, George E. Stone

The Bullfighter and the Lady
US 1950 87m bw
Republic / John Wayne (Budd Boetticher)

A young American in Mexico is fascinated by
bullfighting but during training accidentally

causes the death of a great matador.
Predictable, rather boring plot given routine
treatment: for aficionados only.

w James Edward Grant *d* Budd Boetticher
ph Jack Draper *m* Victor Young

Robert Stack, Gilbert Roland, Joy Page, Katy
Jurado, Virginia Grey, John Hubbard

AAN: original story (Budd Boetticher, Ray
Nazarro)

The Bullfighters*
US 1945 60m bw
TCF (William Girard)

Two detectives in Mexico find that one of them
resembles a famous matador.
Laurel and Hardy's last American feature is
poor enough as a whole, but at least has a few
sequences in their earlier style.

w Scott Darling *d* Mal St Clair *ph* Norbert
Brodine

Stan Laurel, Oliver Hardy, Richard Lane, Carol
Woode

Bullitt**
US 1968 113m Technicolor
Warner / Solar (Philip D'Antoni)

A San Francisco police detective conceals the
death of an underground witness in his charge,
and goes after the killers himself.
Routine cop thriller with undoubted charisma,
distinguished by a splendid car chase which
takes one's mind off the tedious plot. Technical
credits first class.

w Harry Kleiner, Alan R. Trustman, *novel* Mute
Witness by Robert L. Pike *d Peter Yates*
ph William A. Fraker m Lalo Schifrin

Steve McQueen, Jacqueline Bisset, Robert
Vaughn, Don Gordon, Robert Duvall, Simon
Oakland

'It has energy, drive, impact, and above all,
style.'—
Hollis Alpert

Bundle of Joy
US 1956 98m Technicolor RKOscope
RKO / Edmund Grainger

A shopgirl finds an abandoned baby and
everyone thinks it is hers.
Tame musical remake of *Bachelor Mother*;
some laughs, but poor numbers.

w Norman Krasna, Arthur Sheekman, Robert
Carson *d* Norman Taurog *ph* William Snyder
m Josef Myrow

Debbie Reynolds, Eddie Fisher, Adolphe
Menjou, Melville Cooper, Tommy Noonan, Nita
Talbot, Una Merkel, Robert H. Harris

Bunny Lake is Missing**

GB 1965   107m   bw   Panavision
Columbia / Wheel (Otto Preminger)

The 4-year-old illegitimate daughter of an
American girl in London disappears, and no one
can be found to admit that she ever existed.
A nightmarish gimmick story, with more
gimmicks superimposed along the way to say
nothing of a *Psycho*ish ending; some of the
decoration works and makes even the
unconvincing story compelling, while the cast is
alone worth the price of admission.

w John and Penelope Mortimer, *novel* Evelyn
Piper d Otto Preminger ph Denys Coop
m Paul Glass pd Don Ashton *titles* Saul Bass

Laurence Olivier, Carol Lynley, Keir Dullea,
Noel Coward, Martita Hunt, Finlay Currie,
Clive Revill, Anna Massey, Lucie Mannheim

  'It has the enjoyable hallmarks of really high
calibre professionalism.'—*Penelope Houston*

Bunny O'Hare

US 1971   92m   Movielab
AIP (Gerd Oswald, Norman T. Herman)

A middle-aged widow and an ex-con plumber
become bank robbers, dressed as hippies and
escaping on a motor cycle.
Unappealing, ill-thought-out comedy with
pretensions to satire, an unhappy venture for
both stars.

w Stanley Z. Cherry, Coslough Johnson d Gerd
Oswald ph Loyal Griggs, John Stephens
m Billy Strange

Bette Davis, Ernest Borgnine, Jack Cassidy,
Joan Delaney, Jay Robinson, John Astin

Buona Sera Mrs Campbell*

US 1968   113m   Technicolor
UA / Connaught (Melvin Frank)

Wartime USAF comrades reassemble twenty
years later in an Italian village, and three find
that they have been paying paternity money to
the same local glamour girl.
Agreeably cast, pleasantly set and
photographed, quite funny in parts, this comedy
of middle age unfortunately outstays its welcome
and lets its invention peter out.

w Melvin Frank, Denis Norden, Sheldon Keller
d Melvin Frank ph Gabor Pogany m Riz
Ortolani

Gina Lollobrigida, Telly Savalas, Phil Silvers,
Peter Lawford, Lee Grant, Marian Moses,
Shelley Winters

The Burglar*

US 1957   80m   bw
Columbia (Louis W. Kellerman)

A burglar is shadowed by a policeman who is
also after the loot.
Slightly pretentious but watchable low-budgeter.

w David Goodis from his novel d/ed Paul
Wendkos ph Don Malkames m Sol Kaplan

Dan Duryea, Jayne Mansfield, Martha Vickers,
Peter Capell

The Burglars

France / Italy 1971   120m   Eastmancolor
  Panavision
Columbia / Vides (Henri Verneuil)
original title: *La Casse*

A determined policeman chases three burglars
and their girl accomplice.
Expensive, camped-up version of *The Burglar*,
with plenty going on, most of it borrowed from
other films.

w Vahe Katcha, Henri Verneuil, *novel* The
Burglar by David Goodis d Henri Verneuil
ph Claude Renoir m Ennio Morricone

Omar Sharif, Jean-Paul Belmondo, Dyan
Cannon, Robert Hossein, Nicole Calfan, Renato
Salvatori

  'Electronic equipment, wild action, exotic
locales and bland villainy.'—*Tom Milne, MFB*

Burke and Hare

GB 1971   91m   De Luxe
UA / Kenneth Shipman / Armitage (Guido
  Coen)

The story of anatomist Dr Knox and his body
snatchers, retold with emphasis on the local
brothel. Depressing in its childish attempts to be
gruesome and perverted.

w Ernie Bradford d Vernon Sewell
ph Desmond Dickinson m Roger Webb

Harry Andrews, Derren Nesbitt, Glynn
Edwards, Yootha Joyce, Dee Sjendery, Alan
Tucker

The Burmese Harp***

Japan 1956   116m   bw
Nikkatsu (Masayuki Takagi)
original title: *Biruma no tategoto*

A shell-shocked Japanese soldier stays in the
Burmese jungle to bury the unknown dead.
Deeply impressive and horrifying war film with
an epic, folk-tale quality, emphasized by
superbly controlled direction.

w Natto Wada, *novel* Michio Takeyama d Kon
Ichikawa ph Minoru Yokoyama m Akira
Ifukube

Shoji Yasui, Rentaro Mikuni, Tatsuya Mihashi

Burnt Offerings
US 1976   115m   De Luxe
UA/PEA-Dan Curtis (Robert Singer)

An evil house restores itself by feeding on its
tenants.

An agreeably macabre idea for a five-page story
is dragged out to interminable length, and seizes
the attention only by a few shock moments. The
title is mysteriously irrelevant.

w William F. Nolan, Dan Curtis, *novel* Robert
Marasco d Dan Curtis *ph* Jacques Marquette
m Robert Colbert *pd* Eugene Lourie

Oliver Reed, Karen Black, Bette Davis, Lee
Montgomery, Burgess Meredith, Eileen
Heckart, Dub Taylor

Bus Riley's Back in Town*
US 1965   93m   Eastmancolor
U-I (Elliott Kastner)

An ex-sailor wants to settle back into small-town
life but finds that his girl friend has married.
Watchable, middling, routine small-town drama
in the style of *Picnic*.

w Walter Gage (William Inge) d *Harvey Hart*
ph Russell Metty m Richard Markowitz

Michael Parks, Ann-Margret, Jocelyn Brando,
Janet Margolin, Kim Darby, Brad Dexter, Larry
Storch, Crahan Denton, Mimsy Farmer, David
Carradine

Bus Stop*
US 1956   96m   Eastmancolor
Cinemascope
TCF (Buddy Adler)
TV title: *The Wrong Kind of Girl*

In a rodeo town, a simple-thinking cowboy
meets a café singer and asks her to marry him.
Sex comedy-drama, a modest entertainment in
familiar American vein, very well done but
rather over-inflated by its star.

w George Axelrod, *play* William Inge d Joshua
Logan *ph* Milton Krasner m Alfred Newman,
Cyril Mockridge

Marilyn Monroe, Don Murray, Betty Field,
Arthur O'Connell, Eileen Heckart, Robert Bray,
Hope Lange, Hans Conried, Casey Adams
  'The film demands of its principal performers a
purely physical display of their bodies viewed as
sexual machinery.'—*David Robinson*

AAN: Don Murray

Busman's Honeymoon*
GB 1940   99m   bw
MGM (Harold Huth)
US title: *Haunted Honeymoon*

Lord Peter Wimsey finds a murder to be solved
in his honeymoon cottage.
Pleasant, slightly flat film version of a favourite
old-fashioned detective novel.

w Monckton Hoffe, Angus Macphail, Harold
Goldman, *novel* Dorothy L. Sayers d Arthur
Woods

Robert Montgomery, Constance Cummings,
Leslie Banks, *Seymour Hicks*, Robert Newton,
Googie Withers, Frank Pettingell, Joan Kemp-
Welch

The Buster Keaton Story*
US 1957   91m   bw   Vistavision
Paramount (Sidney Sheldon, Robert Smith)

A biopic of the great silent comedian, with the
emphasis on his years of downfall through drink.
An interesting recreation of Hollywood in the
twenties and thirties is the main asset of this
otherwise dismal tribute to a man whose
greatness the star is unable to suggest apart from
a few acrobatic moments.

w Robert Smith, Sidney Sheldon d Sidney
Sheldon *ph* Loyal Griggs m Victor Young

Donald O'Connor, Rhonda Fleming, Ann Blyth,
Peter Lorre, Larry Keating, Richard Anderson,
Dave Willock

Busting
US 1973   92m   De Luxe
UA/Chartoff-Winkler (Henry Gellis)

Two Los Angeles vice squad officers fight
corruption inside and outside the force.
Violent, exhausting, but totally routine police
caper of the seventies.

wd Peter Hyams *ph* Earl Rath m Billy
Goldenberg

Elliott Gould, Robert Blake, Allen Garfield,
Antonio Fargas
  'The farcical version of *Serpico*."—*Michael
Billington, Illustrated London News*

The Busy Body
US 1966   102m   Techniscope
Paramount / William Castle

A gangster is buried in a suit with a million dollar
lining which various people are out to get.
Unfunny black comedy; laboured handling
makes it a joke in poor taste.

w Ben Starr, *novel* Donald E. Westlake
d William Castle *ph* Hal Stine m Vic Mizzy

Robert Ryan, Sid Caesar, Arlene Golonka,
Anne Baxter, Kay Medford, Charles McGraw

But Not for Me

US 1959   105m   bw
Paramount (William Perlberg, George
Seaton)

An ageing, washed-up Broadway producer is
loved by his young drama student secretary.
Rather heavy-going remake of *Accent on Youth*,
efficiently performed but lacking the original
gaiety.

w John Michael Hayes *d* Walter Lang
ph Robert Burks *m* Leith Stevens

Clark Gable, Carroll Baker, Lilli Palmer, Lee J.
Cobb, Barry Coe, Thomas Gomez

Butch Cassidy and the Sundance Kid***

US 1969   110m   De Luxe   Panavision
TCF / Campanile (John Foreman)

A hundred years ago, two western train robbers
keep one step ahead of the law until finally
tracked down to Bolivia.
Humorous, cheerful, poetic, cinematic account
of two semi-legendary outlaws, winningly acted
and directed. One of the decade's great
commercial successes, not least because of the
song 'Raindrops Keep Fallin' on My Head'.

w William Goldman d George Roy Hill
ph Conrad Hall m Burt Bacharach

Paul Newman, Robert Redford, Katharine Ross,
Strother Martin, Henry Jones, Jeff Corey, Cloris
Leachman, Ted Cassidy, Kenneth Mars

AA: William Goldman; Conrad Hall; Burt
Bacharach; song 'Raindrops Keep Fallin' on My
Head' (*m* Burt Bacharach, *ly* Hal David)
AAN: best picture; George Roy Hill

Butley*

US / GB 1973   130m   Eastmancolor
American Express / Ely Landau / Cinevision

Personal problems assail an English lecturer at a
university college.
Adequate but not outstanding transcription (for
the American Film Theatre) of a successful and
percipient play.

w Simon Gray, from his play *d* Harold Pinter
ph Gerry Fisher *m* none

Alan Bates, Jessica Tandy, Richard Callaghan,
Susan Engel, Michael Byrne

The Buttercup Chain*

GB 1970   95m   Technicolor   Panavision
Columbia (Leslie Gilliat, John Whitney, Philip
Waddilove)

A hothouse sex quartet changes partners with
bewildering rapidity against a background of
European splendour.
Chi-chi romance with a fashionably disillusioned
and tragic ending. As watchable as the best TV
commercials, but totally empty.

w Peter Draper, *novel* Janice Elliott *d* Robert
Ellis Miller *ph* Douglas Slocombe *m* Richard
Rodney Bennett

Hywel Bennett, Leigh Taylor-Young, Jane
Asher, Sven-Bertil Taube, Clive Revill, Roy
Dotrice

Butterfield Eight

US 1960   108m   Metrocolor
Cinemascope
MGM / Afton / Linebrook (Pandro S. Berman)

A society call girl has a complex love life.
This coy sex drama seemed mildly daring in
1960, but has since been well outclassed in that
field and certainly has nothing else going for it
except good production values.

w Charles Schnee, John Michael Hayes, *novel*
John O'Hara *d* Daniel Mann *ph* Joseph
Ruttenberg, Charles Harten *m* Bronislau Kaper

Elizabeth Taylor, Laurence Harvey, Eddie
Fisher, Dina Merrill, Mildred Dunnock, Betty
Field, Jeffrey Lynn, Kay Medford, Susan Oliver
   'The mixture resolutely refuses to come to the
boil.'—*John Gillett*

AA: Elizabeth Taylor
AAN: Joseph Ruttenberg, Charles Harten

Butterflies are Free

US 1972   109m   Eastmancolor
Columbia / M. J. Frankovich

An aspiring actress falls for a blind neighbour
but is handicapped by his possessive mother.
Three-character comedy-drama from a slight,
sentimental but successful Broadway play.

w Leonard Gershe, from his play *d* Milton
Katselas *ph* Charles B. Lang *m* Bob Alcivar

Goldie Hawn, Edward Albert, Eileen Heckart

AA: Eileen Heckart
AAN: Charles B. Lang

Buy Me That Town*

US 1941   70m   bw
Paramount (Sol C. Siegel)

Gangsters take over a small town and pull the
community out of bankruptcy.
Unusual comedy-drama, quite well done for a
second feature.

w Gordon Kahn *d* Eugene Forde *ph* Theodor
Sparkuhl

Lloyd Nolan, Albert Dekker, Constance Moore,
Sheldon Leonard, Vera Vague, Edward Brophy,
Horace MacMahon, Warren Hymer

Bwana Devil

US 1952 79m Anscocolor 3D
(UA) Arch Oboler

At the turn of the century, two man-eating lions
threaten an African railroad.

Inept actioner notable only as the first film in 3-D
('Natural Vision'), advertised with the famous
slogan 'A lion in your lap'.

wd Arch Oboler *ph* Joseph Biroc *m* Gordon
Jenkins

Robert Stack, Barbara Britton, Nigel Bruce,
Ramsay Hill

By Love Possessed*

US 1961 116m De Luxe Panavision
UA / Mirisl (Walter Mirisch)

A Massachusetts lawyer reflects on the
outlandish sexual mores of himself, his family
and friends.

Peyton Place moved up in the social scale; a
reasonably absorbing melodrama but hardly
memorable.

w John Dennis, *novel* James Gould Cozzens
d John Sturges *ph* Russell Metty *m* Elmer
Bernstein

Lana Turner, Efrem Zimbalist Jnr, Jason
Robards Jnr, Barbara Bel Geddes, George
Hamilton, Susan Kohner, Thomas Mitchell,
Yvonne Craig, Everett Sloane

'A talky succession of soap opera
situations.'—*Robert Windeler*

By the Light of the Silvery Moon*

US 1953 101m Technicolor
Warner (William Jacobs)

In a small American town in 1918, the Winfield
family has several problems arising from the
return of daughter Marjorie's soldier boyfriend.

A sequel to *On Moonlight Bay* (qv), presenting
further situations from the Penrod stories
retailored for Doris Day. Inoffensive, well-made,
old-fashioned entertainment with nostalgic
songs and an archetypal family.

w Robert O'Brien, Irving Elinson, from stories
by Booth Tarkington *d* David Butler *ph* Wilfrid
M. Cline *m* Max Steiner

Doris Day, Gordon Macrae, *Leon Amis,
Rosemary de Camp, Mary Wickes*

Bye Bye Birdie

US 1963 112m Eastmancolor
  Panavision
Columbia / Fred Kohlmar / George Sidney

Havoc suffuses the last TV show of a pop star
before he goes into the army.

Noisy, frenetic musical, hard to follow and even
harder to like, with all the satire of the stage
original subtracted. For young audiences who
enjoy incoherence.

w Irving Brecher, from musical by Michael
Stewart *d* George Sidney *ph* Joseph Biroc
md Johnny Green *songs* Charles Strouse, Lee
Adams

Janet Leigh, Dick Van Dyke, Maureen
Stapleton, Ann-Margret, Bobby Rydell, Jesse
Pearson, Ed Sullivan, Paul Lynde, Robert Paige

AAN: Johnny Green

Bye Bye Braverman*

US 1968 92m Technicolor
Warner / Sidney Lumet

New Yorkers get drunk and disillusioned on their
way home from the funeral of a friend.

Witty, downbeat Jewish comedy which does not
quite come off and would in any case be caviare
to the general.

w Herbert Sargent, *novel* To an Early Grave by
Wallace Markfield *d* Sidney Lumet *ph* Boris
Kaufman *m* Peter Matz

George Segal, Jack Warden, Joseph Wiseman,
Sorrell Booke, Jessica Walter, Phyllis Newman,
Zohra Lampert, Alan King, Godfrey Cambridge

C

Cabaret***
US 1972   123m   Technicolor
ABC Pictures / Allied Artists (Cy Feuer)

In the early thirties, Berlin is a hotbed of vice and anti-semitism. In the Kit Kat Klub, singer Sally Bowles shares her English lover with a homosexual German baron, and her Jewish friend Natasha has troubles of her own.
This version of Isherwood's Berlin stories regrettably follows the plot line of the play *I Am a Camera* rather than the Broadway musical on which it is allegedly based, and it lacks the incisive remarks of the MC, but the very smart direction creates a near-masterpiece of its own, and most of the songs are intact.

w Jay Presson Allen, from Goodbye to Berlin by Christopher Isherwood *d/ch* Bob Fosse *m* John Kander *ly* Fred Ebb *ph* Geoffrey Unsworth *md* Ralph Burns *pd* Rolf Zehetbauer

Liza Minnelli, Joel Grey, Michael York, Helmut Griem, Fritz Wepper, Marisa Berenson

‘A stylish, sophisticated entertainment for grown-up people.’—*John Russell Taylor*

‘Film journals will feast for years on shots from this picture; as it rolled along, I saw page after illustrated page from a not-too-distant book called *The Cinema of Bob Fosse*.’—*Stanley Kauffmann*

AA: Bob Fosse (as director); Geoffrey Unsworth; Ralph Burns; Liza Minnelli; Joel Grey
AAN: best picture; Jay Presson Allen

Cabin in the Cotton*
US 1932   79m   bw
Warner (Hal B. Wallis)

A sharecropper is almost ruined by a southern belle.
Dated melodrama with interesting style and performances.

w Paul Green, *novel* Harry Harrison Knoll *d* Michael Curtiz *ph* Barney McGill

Richard Barthelmess, Dorothy Jordan, Bette Davis, David Landau, Tully Marshall, Henry B. Walthall, Hardie Albright

Cabin in the Sky**
US 1943   99m   bw
MGM (Arthur Freed)

An idle, gambling husband is reformed by a dream of his own death, with God and Satan battling for his soul.
Consistently interesting, often lively, but generally rather stilted all-black musical which must have seemed a whole lot fresher on the stage. Still, a good try.

w Joseph Schrank, *musical play* Lynn Root *d* Vincente Minnelli *ph* Sidney Wagner *md* George Stoll *new songs: m* Harold Arlen, *ly* E. Y. Harburg *show songs: m* Vernon Duke, *ly* John Latouche, Ted Fetter

Eddie 'Rochester' Anderson, Ethel Waters, Lena Horne, Cab Calloway, Louis Armstrong, John W. Bublett

AAN: song 'Happiness Is Just a Thing Called Joe' (*m* Harold Arlen, *ly* E. Y. Harburg)

The Cabinet of Caligari
US 1962   105m   bw   Cinemascope
TCF / Lippert (Roger Kay)

A young woman whose car breaks down near a country house is held prisoner by the sinister Caligari. Eventually it transpires that the mystery is all in her imagination: he is a psychiatrist and she an old lady whose sexual fantasies he has been curing.
Interminably talkative and frequently (unintentionally) funny trick film with the odd moment of effective suspense. The original ending, which cast some doubt on who was mad and who sane, is no longer available. The actors do not entirely escape absurdity.

w Robert Bloch *d* Roger Kay *ph* John Russell *m* Gerald Fried

Glynis Johns, Dan O'Herlihy, Constance Ford, Dick Davalos, Lawrence Dobkin

‘It is impossible to be grateful for the film on any of its levels.’—*MFB*
† The fact that the story is told through the eyes of a mad person is the only link with the 1919 classic.

The Cabinet of Dr Caligari****
Germany 1919   90m approx (16 fps)   bw
  silent
Decla-Bioscop (Erich Pommer)

A fairground showman uses a somnambulist for
purposes of murder and is finally revealed to be
the director of a lunatic asylum; but the whole
story is only the dream of a madman.
Faded now, but a film of immense influence on
the dramatic art of cinema, with its odd angles,
stylized sets and hypnotic acting, not to mention
the sting in the tail of its story (added by the
producer).

w Carl Mayer, Hans Janowitz d Robert Wiene
ph Willy Hameister ad Hermann Warm,
Walter Röhrig, Walter Reiman

Werner Krauss, Conrad Veidt, Lil Dagover,
Friedrich Feher, Hans von Twardowski

Cabiria**
Italy / France 1957   110m   bw
Dino de Laurentiis / Les Films Marceau
original title: Le Notti di Cabiria; aka: Nights of
  Cabiria

A Roman prostitute has dreams of romance and
respectability.
A bitter Cinderella story which was later turned
into the Broadway musical Sweet Charity. Much
of interest, but the leading lady is too
Chaplinesque.

w Federico Fellini, Ennio Flaiano, Tullio Pinelli
d Federico Fellini ph Aldo Tonti m Nino Rota

Giulietta Masina, François Périer, Amedeo
Nazzari, Franca Marzi, Dorian Gray
  'Any nobility in the original conception slowly
suffocates in an atmosphere of subjective
indulgence bordering dangerously on self-
pity.'—Peter John Dyer

Caccia Tragica*
Italy 1947   89m   bw
Lux / ANPI
aka: The Tragic Pursuit

A bandit is hunted through the Po valley but
finally allowed to escape.
Minor peripatetic melodrama, well-handled and
exciting but uncertain in mood.

w Giuseppe de Santis, Michelangelo Antonioni,
Cesare Zavattini, Carlo Lizzani, Unberto
Barbaro d Giuseppe de Santis ph Otello
Martelli m Giuseppe Rosati

Massimo Girotti, Andrea Checci, Vivi Gioi

Cactus Flower*
US 1969   103m   Technicolor
Columbia / M. J. Frankovich

To deceive his mistress, a dentist employs his
starchy secretary to pose as his wife, and falls for
her when she loosens up.
Amusing sophisticated comedy, generally well
handled.

w I. A. L. Diamond, play Abe Burrows, French
original by Pierre Barillet, Jean Pierre Gredy
d Gene Saks ph Charles E. Lang m Quincy
Jones pd Robert Clatworthy

Ingrid Bergman, Walter Matthau, Goldie Hawn,
Jack Weston, Rick Lenz, Vito Scotti, Irene
Hervey

AA: Goldie Hawn

The Caddy
US 1953   95m   bw
Paramount (Paul Jones)

A music hall comedy act recall how they got
together.
Less a feature than a series of short sketches, this
ragbag has its choice moments, but they are few.

w Edmund Hartmann, Danny Arnold
d Norman Taurog ph Daniel L. Fapp m Joseph
L. Lilley

Dean Martin, Jerry Lewis, Donna Reed,
Barbara Bates, Joseph Calleia, Fred Clark,
Clinton Sundberg, Marshall Thompson

AAN: song 'That's Amore' (m Harry Warren,
ly Jack Brooks)

Caesar and Cleopatra**
GB 1945   135m   Technicolor
Rank / Gabriel Pascal

An elaborate screen treatment of Bernard
Shaw's comedy about Caesar's years in
Alexandria.
Britain's most expensive film is an absurd
extravaganza for which the producer actually
took sand to Egypt to get the right colour. It has
compensations however in the sets, the colour,
the performances and the witty lines, though all
its virtues are theatrical rather than cinematic
and the play is certainly not a major work.

w Bernard Shaw d Gabriel Pascal ph F. A.
Young, Robert Krasker, Jack Hildyard, Jack
Cardiff m Georges Auric decor,
costumes Oliver Messel sets John Bryan

Claude Rains, Vivien Leigh, Cecil Parker,
Stewart Granger, Flora Robson, Francis L.
Sullivan, Raymond Lovell, Anthony Harvey,
Anthony Eustrel, Basil Sydney, Ernest Thesiger,
Stanley Holloway, Leo Genn, Jean Simmons,
Esmé Percy, Michael Rennie
  'It cost over a million and a quarter pounds,
took two and a half years to make, and well and
truly bored one spectator for two and a quarter
hours.'—Richard Winnington

Café Metropole
US 1937 83m bw
TCF (Nunnally Johnson)

An heiress in Paris romances a Russian
nobleman who is actually a penniless American.
Lighter-than-air romance which passed the time
at the time.

w Jacques Duval *d* Edward H. Griffith
ph Lucien Andriot *md* Louis Silvers

Loretta Young, Adolphe Menjou, Tyrone
Power, Charles Winninger, Gregory Ratoff,
Christian Rub, Helen Westley

Café Society
US 1939 84m bw
Paramount

A publicity-seeking socialite impulsively marries
a reporter who has annoyed her, but instead of
making a fool of him she falls in love.
Faded light comedy which was never
outstanding.

w Virginia Van Upp *d* Edward H. Griffith

Madeleine Carroll, Fred MacMurray, Shirley
Ross, Claude Gillingwater

Cage of Gold*
GB 1950 83m bw
Ealing (Michael Relph)

A girl's philandering ex-husband comes back
into her life and is murdered.
Mild mystery melodrama in which the puzzle
comes too late.

w Jack Whittingham *d* Basil Dearden
ph Douglas Slocombe *m* Georges Auric

Jean Simmons, David Farrar, James Donald,
Madeleine Lebeau, Maria Mauban, Herbert
Lom, Bernard Lee, Gladys Henson, Harcourt
Williams, Grégoire Aslan

Caged*
US 1950 96m bw
Warner (Jerry Wald)

After being involved in a robbery a 19-year-old
girl is sent to prison, and finds the staff more
terrifying than the inmates.
Slick, superficial, hysterically harrowing women-
in-prison melodrama; predictably overblown but
also effective and powerful.

w Virginia Kellogg, Bernard Schoenfeld *d* John
Cromwell *ph* Carl Guthrie *m* Max Steiner

Eleanor Parker, Agnes Moorehead, Ellen
Corby, *Hope Emerson*, Betty Garde, Jan
Sterling, Lee Patrick, Olive Deering, Jane
Darwell, Gertrude Michael, Joan Miller
† Remade in 1961 as *House of Women*, directed
by Walter Doniger, with Shirley Knight.

AAN: Virginia Kellogg, Bernard Schoenfeld;
Eleanor Parker; Hope Emerson

Cahill, US Marshal
US 1973 103m Technicolor Panavision
Warner / Batjac (Michael A. Wayne)

A stalwart western marshal finds that his own
young sons are involved in a robbery he is
investigating.
Satisfactory but sentimental John Wayne vehicle
with the star too often yielding place to the rather
boring young folk.

w Harry Julian Fink, Rita M. Fink *d* Andrew V.
McLaglen *ph* Joseph Biroc *m* Elmer Bernstein

John Wayne, George Kennedy, Gary Grimes,
Neville Brand, Clay O'Brien, Marie Windsor,
Royal Dano, Denver Pyle, Jackie Coogan

Cain and Mabel*
US 1936 90m bw
Warner (Sam Bischoff)

Tribulations of a prizefighter in love with a
showgirl.
Generously produced but weakly written
comedy drama with rather unexpected musical
numbers; not a successful whole, but interesting.

w Laird Doyle, H. C. Witwer *d* Lloyd Bacon
ph George Barnes

Clark Gable, Marion Davies, Allen Jenkins,
Roscoe Karns, Walter Catlett, Hobart
Cavanaugh, Pert Kelton, Ruth Donnelly, E. E.
Clive

The Caine Mutiny**
US 1954 125m Technicolor
Columbia / Stanley Kramer

Jealousies and frustrations among the officers of
a peacetime destroyer come to a head when the
neurotic captain panics during a typhoon and is
relieved of his post. At the resulting trial the
officers learn about themselves.
Decent if lamely paced version of a bestseller
which also made a successful play; the film
skates too lightly over the characterizations and
even skimps the courtroom scene, but there are
effective scenes and performances.

w Stanley Roberts, *novel* Herman Wouk
d Edward Dmytryk *ph* Franz Planer *m* Max
Steiner

Humphrey Bogart, Jose Ferrer, Van Johnson,
Fred MacMurray, Robert Francis, May Wynn,
Tom Tully, E. G. Marshall, Lee Marvin, Arthur
Franz

AAN: best picture; Stanley Roberts; Max
Steiner; Humphrey Bogart; Jose Ferrer

Cairo*
US 1941   100m   bw
MGM

An American war reporter in Egypt meets a
screen star and thinks she is a spy.
Mildly pleasing light comedy-drama with self-
spoofing elements.

w John McClain d W. S. Van Dyke II ph Ray
June md Herbert Stothart

Jeanette MacDonald, Robert Young, Ethel
Waters, Reginald Owen, Lionel Atwill, Mona
Barrie, Eduardo Ciannelli, Dennis Hoey, Dooley
Wilson

Cairo
GB 1963   91m   bw
MGM (Ronald Kinnoch)

Crooks plan to steal Tutankhamun's jewels from
the Cairo Museum.
Spiritless remake of *The Asphalt Jungle* (qv).

w Joanne Court d Wolf Rilla ph Desmond
Dickinson m Kenneth V. Jones

George Sanders, Richard Johnson, Faten
Hamama, John Meillon, Eric Pohlmann, Walter
Rilla

Cairo Road
GB 1950   95m   bw
ABP (Aubrey Baring)

An Egyptian police chief lays traps for drug
smugglers.
Oddly cast, reasonably lively but routine police
adventure in an unfamiliar setting.

w Robert Westerby d David MacDonald
ph Oswald Morris m Robert Gill

Eric Portman, Laurence Harvey, Maria
Mauban, Karel Stepanek, Harold Lang,
Camelia, Grégoire Aslan, Oscar Quitak

Calabuch*
Spain / Italy 1956   93m   bw
Aguila / Constellaxione (Jose Luis Jerez)

An atomic scientist settles delightedly in a
peaceful Spanish village, but sacrifices his own
privacy when he invents a sky rocket.
Semi-satirical Ealing-type comedy which starts
engagingly but runs out of steam.

w Leonardo Martin, Ennio Flaiano, Florentino
Soria, Luis Berlanga d Luis Berlanga
ph Francisco Sempere m Francesco Lavagnino

Edmund Gwenn, Valentina Cortese, Franco
Fabrizi

Calamity Jane**
US 1953   101m   Technicolor
Warner (William Jacobs)

Calamity helps a saloon owner friend find a star
attraction, and wins the heart of Wild Bill
Hickok.
Agreeable, cleaned-up, studio-set western
musical patterned after *Annie Get Your Gun*, but
a much friendlier film, helped by an excellent
score.

w James O'Hanlon d David Butler ph Wilfrid
Cline songs *Sammy Fain, Paul Francis
Webster* md Ray Heindorf ch Jack Donohue

Doris Day, Howard Keel, Allyn McLerie, Phil
Carey, Dick Wesson, Paul Harvey

AA: song 'Secret Love' (*m* Sammy Fain, *ly* Paul
Francis Webster)
AAN: Ray Heindorf

Calcutta
US 1948   83m   bw
Paramount (Seton I. Miller)

Two fliers seek the murderer of their friend in the
hotels and bazaars of Calcutta.
Studio-bound action potboiler, simple-minded
but quite good fun.

w Seton I. Miller d John Farrow ph John F.
Seitz m Victor Young

Alan Ladd, Gail Russell, William Bendix, June
Duprez, Lowell Gilmore

California
US 1946   97m   Technicolor
Paramount (Seton I. Miller)

An army deserter joins the 1848 California gold
rush.
Standard glamorized star western; not bad if you
accept the conventions.

w Frank Butler, Theodore Strauss d John
Farrow ph Ray Rennahan m Victor Young

Ray Milland, Barbara Stanwyck, Barry
Fitzgerald, Albert Dekker, George Coulouris,
Anthony Quinn

California Split*
US 1974   109m   Metrocolor   Panavision
Columbia / Won World (Robert Altman,
Joseph Walsh)

Two cheerful gamblers get drunk, laid, cheated
and happy.
Sporadically entertaining character comedy
sunk in a sea of chatter.

w Joseph Walsh d Robert Altman ph Paul
Lohmann

Elliott Gould, George Segal, Gwen Welles, Ann
Prentiss, Joseph Walsh

'The film seems to be being improvised . . . we
catch at events and personalities by the ends of
threads.'—*New Yorker*

California Straight Ahead*
US 1937 67m bw
Universal (Trem Carr)

A nationwide race is held between a special train
and a convoy of high-powered trucks.
Unusual and quite lively second feature shot on
location.

w Herman Boxer d Arthur Lubin ph Harry
Neumann

John Wayne, Louise Latimer, Robert McWade,
Tully Marshall

Call Her Savage
US 1932 88m bw
Paramount (Sam E. Rork)

Trials and tribulations of a half-breed Indian girl
who marries a cad and later takes to the streets.
Rough and ready melodrama for female
audiences; the penultimate appearance of a star
who did not take to talkies.

w Edwin Burke, *novel* Tiffany Thayer d John
Francis Dillon ph Lee Garmes

Clara Bow, Gilbert Roland, Monroe Owsley,
Thelma Todd, Estelle Taylor

Call It a Day*
US 1937 89m bw
Warner (Henry Blanke)

An upper-class British family has problems
during a single day.
Surprising, and not very effective, Hollywood
treatment of a very British comedy.

w Casey Robinson, *play* Dodie Smith d Archie
Mayo ph Ernest Haller

Olivia de Havilland, Ian Hunter, Anita Louise,
Alice Brady, Roland Young, Frieda Inescort,
Bonita Granville, Peggy Wood, Walter Woolf
King, Una O'Connor, Beryl Mercer

Call Me Bwana*
GB 1962 93m Eastmancolor
Rank / Eon (Harry Saltzman, Albert R.
  Broccoli)

A fake African explorer is sent to the jungle to
recover a space capsule.
Moderate star farce with occasional bright
moments.

w Nate Monaster, Johanna Harwood d Gordon
Douglas ph Ted Moore m Monty Norman

Bob Hope, Anita Ekberg, Edie Adams, Lionel
Jeffries, Percy Herbert, Paul Carpenter, Orlando
Martins

Call Me Madam*
US 1953 114m Technicolor
TCF (Sol C. Siegel)

A Washington hostess is appointed Ambassador
to Lichtenberg and marries the foreign minister.
Studio-bound but thoroughly lively transcription
of Irving Berlin's last big success, with most of
the performers at their peak and some topical
gags which may now be mystifying.

w Arthur Sheekman, *play* Howard Lindsay,
Russel Crouse m/ly *Irving Berlin* md Alfred
Newman ph Leon Shamroy d Walter Lang
ch Robert Alton

*Ethel Merman, Donald O'Connor, George
Sanders, Vera-Ellen,* Billy de Wolfe, Helmut
Dantine, Walter Slezak, Steve Geray, Ludwig
Stossel

AA: Alfred Newman

Call Me Mister
US 1951 95m Technicolor
TCF (Fred Kohlmar)

A husband-and-wife dance team entertain the
troops in Japan and after the war.
Passable musical of a very predictable kind.

w Albert E. Lewin, Burt Styler d Lloyd Bacon
ph Arthur E. Arling m Leigh Harline ch Busby
Berkeley songs various original show credits:
m Harold Rome, book Arnold Auerbach,
Arnold B. Horwitt

Betty Grable, Dan Dailey, Danny Thomas, Dale
Robertson, Richard Boone

Call Northside 777**
US 1948 111m bw
TCF (Otto Lang)

A Chicago reporter helps a washerwoman prove
her son not guilty of murdering a policeman.
Overlong semi-documentary crime thriller based
on a real case. Acting and detail excellent, but the
sharp edge of *Boomerang* is missing.

w Jerome Cady, Jay Dratler d Henry
Hathaway ph Joe MacDonald

James Stewart, Lee J. Cobb, Helen Walker,
Kazia Orzazewski, Betty Garde

Call of the Wild*
TCF (Darryl F. Zanuck)
US 1935 81m bw

A young widow falls in love with a wild Yukon
prospector.
Inaccurate but pleasing adaptation of an
adventure novel with dog interest.

w Gene Fowler, Leonard Praskins, *novel* Jack
London d William Wellman ph Charles Rosher

Clark Gable, Loretta Young, Jack Oakie,
Reginald Owen, Frank Conroy

Call of the Wild
GB / Ger / Sp / It / Fr 1972   105m
Eastmancolor
Massfilms / CCC / Izaro / Oceania / UPF
    (Harry Alan Towers)

During the Klondike gold rush, a stolen dog
becomes a miner's best friend before joining the
wolf-pack.
Closer to the book than the previous version, but
curiously scrappy and unsatisfactory.

w Harry Alan Towers, Wyn Wells, Peter
Yeldman d Ken Annakin ph John Vabrera,
Dudley Lovell m Carlo Rustichelli

Charlton Heston, Michèle Mercier, Raimund
Harmstorf, George Eastman

Callan*
GB 1974   106m   Eastmancolor
EMI / Magnum (Derek Horne)

A former secret agent is seconded to a
government section devoted to the elimination of
undesirables.
Expanded rewrite of the first episode of a long-
running TV series, quite fresh and vivid in the
circumstances, especially as it comes at the tail
end of ten years of similar bouts of blood and
thunder.

w James Mitchell, from A Magnum for
Schneider d Don Sharp ph Ernest Steward
m Wilfred Josephs

Edward Woodward, Eric Porter, Carl Mohner,
Catherine Schell, Peter Egan, Russell Hunter,
Kenneth Griffith

Callaway Went Thataway*
US 1951   81m   bw
MGM (Melvin Frank, Norman Panama)
GB title: The Star Said No

The old movies of a Hollywood cowboy become
popular on TV, but the star has become a
hopeless drunk and an actor is hired to pose as
him for public appearances.
Reasonably engaging comedy using charm
rather than acid.

wd Melvin Frank, Norman Panama ph Ray
June m Marlin Skiles

Dorothy McGuire, Fred MacMurray, Howard
Keel, Jesse White, Natalie Schaefer

Calle Mayor*
Spain / France 1956   95m   bw
Play Art Iberia / Cesareo Gonzales
aka: Grand Rue

In a small Spanish town, a young stud pretends
for a bet to be in love with a plain spinster.
Interesting but rather unattractive and certainly

unconvincing little comedy-drama, rather too
obviously styled for its American star after her
success in Marty.

wd Juan Antonio Bardem ph Michel Kelber
m Joseph Kosma

Betsy Blair, Yves Massard, René Blancard, Lila
Kedrova

Calling Bulldog Drummond
GB 1951   80m   bw
MGM (Hayes Goetz)

Drummond goes undercover to catch a gang of
thieves.
Minor-league quota quickie addition to the
exploits of a long-running character (see Bulldog
Drummond).

w Howard Emmett Rogers, Gerard Fairlie,
Arthur Wimperis d Victor Saville ph Graham
Kelly m Rudolph Kopp

Walter Pidgeon, Margaret Leighton, Robert
Beatty, David Tomlinson, Peggy Evans, Charles
Victor, Bernard Lee, James Hayter

Camelot**
US 1967   181m   Technicolor   Panavision
70
Warner (Jack L. Warner)

King Arthur marries Guinevere, loses her to
Lancelot, and is forced into war.
A film version of a long-running Broadway show
with many excellent moments. Unfortunately the
director cannot make up his mind whether to go
for style or realism, and has chosen actors who
cannot sing. The result is cluttered and overlong,
with no real sense of period or sustained
imagination, but the photography and the music
linger in the mind.

w Alan Jay Lerner m Frederick Loewe
d Joshua Logan ph Richard H. Kline
pd/costumes John Truscott ad Edward Carere
md Ken Darby, Alfred Newman

Richard Harris, Vanessa Redgrave, David
Hemmings, Lionel Jeffries, Laurence Naismith,
Franco Nero

'One wonders whether the fashion for
musicals in which only the chorus can actually
sing may be reaching its final stage.'—MFB
    'Three hours of unrelieved glossiness,
meticulous inanity, desperate and charmless
striving for charm.'—John Simon
    'The sets and costumes and people seem to be
sitting there on the screen, waiting for the
unifying magic that never happens.'—New
Yorker, 1977

AAN: Richard H. Kline; Ken Darby, Alfred
Newman

The Cameraman***

US 1928   78m approx (24 fps)   bw   silent
MGM / Buster Keaton Productions

In order to woo a film star, a street photographer
becomes a newsreel cameraman.
Highly regarded chapter of farcical errors,
among the star's top features.

w Clyde Bruckman, Lex Lipton, Richard
Schayer d Edward Sedgwick ph Elgin Lessley,
Reggie Manning

Buster Keaton, Marceline Day, Harry Gribbon,
Harold Goodwin

† The film was remade in 1948 for Red Skelton
as *Watch the Birdie*, with Keaton sadly
supervising the gags but getting no credit.

Camille**

US 1936   108m   bw
MGM

A dying courtesan falls for an innocent young
man who loves her, and dies in his arms.
This old warhorse is an unsuitable vehicle for
Garbo but magically she carries it off, and the
production is elegant and pleasing.

w Frances Marion, James Hilton, Zoe Akins,
novel Alexandre Dumas *d George Cukor*
ph William Daniels m Herbert Stothart

Greta Garbo, Robert Taylor, Lionel Barrymore,
Henry Daniell, Elizabeth Allan, Lenore Ulric,
Laura Hope Crews, Rex O'Malley, Jessie Ralph,
E. E. Clive

'The slow, solemn production is luxuriant in its
vulgarity: it achieves that glamor which MGM
traditionally mistook for style.'—*Pauline Kael,
1968*

'The surprise is to find a story that should by
rights be old hat coming to such insistent life on
the screen.'—*Otis Ferguson*

AAN: Greta Garbo

Il Cammino della Speranza*

Italy 1950   105m   bw
Lux (Luigi Rovere)
aka: *The Road to Hope*

Unemployed Sicilian miners travel to France in
search of work.
Episodic location melodrama with a social
conscience, a kind of Italian *Grapes of Wrath*.
Very watchable, but not moving. .

w Federico Fellini, Tullio Pinelli d *Pietro Germi*
ph Leonido Barboni m Carlo Rustichelli

Raf Vallone, Elena Varzi, Saro Urzi, Franco
Navarra

The Camp on Blood Island

GB 1958   81m   bw   Megascope
Columbia / Hammer (Anthony Hinds)

The sadistic commandant of a Japanese POW
camp swears to kill all the inmates. Japan
surrenders, and a great effort is made to prevent
the news from reaching him.
Dubious melodrama parading sadism and
brutality as entertainment.

w Jon Manchip White, Val Guest d Val Guest
ph Jack Asher m Gerard Schurmann

André Morell, Carl Mohner, Edward
Underdown, Michael Goodliffe, Ronald Radd,
Walter Fitzgerald, Phil Brown, Barbara Shelley,
Michael Gwynn, Richard Wordsworth, Marne
Maitland, Mary Merrall

Campbell's Kingdom*

GB 1957   102m   Eastmancolor
Rank (Betty E. Box)

A young man who thinks he is dying arrives in
the Canadian Rockies to take over his father's oil
valley, but a scheming contractor opposes him.
Competent and entertaining romantic thick-ear.

w Robin Estridge, *novel* Hammond Innes
d Ralph Thomas ph Ernest Steward

Dirk Bogarde, Stanley Baker, Barbara Murray,
Athene Seyler, Mary Merrall, James Robertson
Justice

Can Can

US 1960   131m   De Luxe   Todd-AO
TCF (Jack Cummings)

A Parisian nightclub dancer in the nineties is
sued for performing the Can Can.
Flat film of a dull musical, with just a few plums
in the pudding.

w Dorothy Kingsley, Charles Lederer, *play* Abe
Burrows *songs* Cole Porter d Walter Lang
ph William Daniels ch Hermes Pan md Nelson
Riddle

Frank Sinatra, Shirley Maclaine, Maurice
Chevalier, Louis Jourdan, Juliet Prowse, Marcel
Dalio, Leon Belasco

AAN: Nelson Riddle

Can Heironymus Merkin Ever Forgive Mercy Humppe and Find True Happiness?

GB 1969   117m   Technicolor
Universal / Taralex (Anthony Newley)

A performer on a beach assembles a huge pile of
personal bric-à-brac and reminisces about his life
in the style of a variety show.
Obscure and pointless personal fantasy,
financed at great expense by a major film
company as a rather seedy monument to
Anthony Newley's totally uninteresting sex life,
and to the talent which he obviously thinks he

possesses. The few mildly amusing moments are not provided by him.

w Herman Raucher, Anthony Newley
d Anthony Newley *ph* Otto Heller *m* Anthony Newley

Anthony Newley, Joan Collins, George Jessel, Milton Berle, Bruce Forsyth, Stubby Kaye, Patricia Hayes, Victor Spinetti

'If I'd been Anthony Newley I would have opened it in Siberia during Christmas week and called it a day.'—*Rex Reed*

'The kindest thing for all concerned would be that every available copy should be quietly and decently buried.'—*Michael Billington, Illustrated London News*

The Candidate **
US 1972   110m   Technicolor
Warner / Redford–Ritchie (Walter Coblenz)

A young Californian lawyer is persuaded to run for senator; in succeeding, he alienates his wife and obscures his real opinions.
Put together in a slightly scrappy but finally persuasive style, this joins a select band of rousing, doubting American political films.

w Jeremy Larner. *d* Michael Ritchie *ph* Victor J. Kemper *m* John Rubinstein

Robert Redford, Peter Boyle, *Don Porter*, Allen Garfield, Karen Carlson, Quinn Redeker, Morgan Upton, *Melvyn Douglas*

'Decent entertainment . . . it is never boring, but it is never enlarging, informationally or emotionally or thematically.'—*Stanley Kauffmann*

AAN: Jeremy Larner

Candide
France 1960   90m   bw
CLM / SN Pathé (Clément Duhour)

Ever optimistic, a 20th-century Candide tours Nazi prison camps, communist countries and various South American revolutions.
Scrappily-made satire which soon overstays its welcome.

wd Norbert Carbonneaux, from Voltaire
ph Robert Le Fèbvre *m* Hubert Rostaing

Jean-Pierre Cassel, Daliah Lavi, Pierre Brasseur, Nadia Gray, Michel Simon, Louis de Funès

Candleshoe
GB 1977   101m   Technicolor
Walt Disney Productions (Hugh Attwooll)

An attempt to pass off a fake heiress to an English stately home is prevented by the resourceful butler.
Slackly handled comedy adventure full of easy targets and predictable incidents.

w David Swift, Rosemary Anne Sisson, *novel* Christmas at Candleshoe by Michael Innes
d Norman Tokar *ph* Paul Beeson *m Ron Goodwin*

David Niven, Helen Hayes, Jodie Foster, Leo McKern, Veronica Quilligan, Ian Sharrock, Vivian Pickles

Candy
US 1968   124m   Technicolor
Selmur / Dear / Corona (Robert Haggiag)

An innocent girl defends herself from a fate worse than death in a variety of international situations.
Witless and charmless perversion of a sex satire in which the point (if any) was that the nymphet gladly surrendered herself to all the gentlemen for their own good. A star cast flounders helplessly in a morass of bad taste, bad film-making, and boredom.

w Buck Henry, *novel* Terry Southern
d Christian Marquand *ph* Giuseppe Rotunno *m* Dave Grusin

Ewa Aulin, Richard Burton, Marlon Brando, James Coburn, Walter Matthau, Charles Aznavour, John Huston, Elsa Martinelli, Ringo Starr, John Astin

'Hippy psychedelics are laid on with the self-destroying effect of an overdose of garlic.'—*MFB*

'As an emetic, liquor is dandy, but *Candy* is quicker.'—*John Simon*

Cannon for Cordoba
US 1970   104m   De Luxe   Panavision
UA / Mirisch (Stephen Kandel, Vincent Fenelly)

In 1912, the Mexican bandit Cordoba is outgunned and outwitted by a US army captain. Fast-moving but rather uninteresting action adventure.

w Stephen Kandel *d* Paul Wendkos *ph* Antonio Macasoli *m* Elmer Bernstein

George Peppard, Raf Vallone, Giovanna Ralli, Pete Duel, Don Gordon, Nico Minardos, John Russell

Cannonball
US / Hong Kong 1976   93m   Metrocolor
Harbor / Shaw Brothers (Samuel W. Gelfman)
GB title: *Carquake*

Aggressive drivers compete in the Trans-American Grand Prix.
The plot is a thin excuse for multiple pile-ups and

other road disasters. Moments amuse, but the violence quickly palls.

w Paul Bartel, Donald C. Simpson *d* Paul Bartel *ph* Tak Fujimoto *m* David A. Axelrod

David Carradine, Bill McKinney, Veronica Hamel, Gerrit Graham, Judy Canova

'A free-wheeling, stunt-studded, dented and demented story of a road racer without rules.'— *publicity*

Canon City*
US 1948 82m bw
Eagle Lion

Convicts break out of the Colorado State Prison. Minor semi-documentary melodrama, quite effectively presented.

wd Crane Wilbur *ph* John Alton

Scott Brady, Jeff Corey, Whit Bissell, Stanley Clements, De Forrest Kelley

Can't Help Singing*
US 1944 90m Technicolor
Universal (Frank Ross)

A Washington heiress chases her army lieutenant lover across the wild west to California.
Lively star musical which could have used a little more wit in its lighthearted script.

w Lewis Foster, Frank Ryan *d* Frank Ryan *ph* Woody Bredell, W. Howard Greene *m* Jerome Kern

ly E. Y. Harburg *md* Jerome Kern, Hans Salter

Deanna Durbin, David Bruce, Robert Paige, *Akim Tamiroff, Leonid Kinskey*, Ray Collins, Thomas Gomez

'This could have been a beautiful and gay picture, but it is made without much feeling for beauty or gaiety.'—*James Agee*

AAN: Jerome Kern, Hans Salter; song 'More and More' (*m* Jerome Kern, *ly* E. Y. Harburg)

A Canterbury Tale*
GB 1944 124m bw
Rank / Archers (Michael Powell, Emeric Pressburger)

A batty magistrate is unmasked by a land girl, an army sergeant and a GI.
Curious would-be propaganda piece with Old England bathed in a roseate wartime glow, but the plot seems to have little to do with Chaucer. Indeed, quite what Powell and Pressburger thought they were up to is hard to fathom, but the detail is interesting.

wd Michael Powell and Emeric Pressburger

Eric Portman, Sheila Sim, John Sweet, Dennis Price, Esmond Knight, Charles Hawtrey, Hay Petrie, George Merritt, Edward Rigby

The Canterville Ghost*
US 1943 95m bw
MGM (Arthur Field)

The young girl heiress of an English castle introduces GIs to the resident ghost.
Leaden comedy a long way after Oscar Wilde, sunk by slow script and direction, but partly salvaged by the respective roguishness and infant charm of its stars.

w Edwin Blum *d* Jules Dassin *m* George Bassman

Charles Laughton, Margaret O'Brien, Robert Young, William Gargan, Rags Ragland, Peter Lawford, Una O'Connor, Mike Mazurki

Canyon Passage*
US 1946 99m Technicolor
Universal (Walter Wanger)

In the 1850s along the pioneering tracks the west's first towns were being built . . .
Simple, scrappy but generally pleasing film which gives a vivid picture of pioneering life while minimizing its hardships.

w Ernest Pascal, William Fosche *d* Jacques Tourneur *ph* Edward Cronjager *m* Frank Skinner

Dana Andrews, Patricia Roc, Hoagy Carmichael, Brian Donlevy, Susan Hayward, Ward Bond, Andy Devine, Lloyd Bridges

AAN: song 'Ole Buttermilk Sky' (*m* Hoagy Carmichael, *ly* Jack Brooks)

Cape Fear
US 1962 106m bw
U-I / Melville–Talbot (Sy Bartlett)

An ex-convict blames a lawyer for his sentence and threatens to rape the lawyer's wife.
Unpleasant and drawn out suspenser with characters of cardboard and situations from stock.

w James R. Webb, *novel* The Executioners by John D. MacDonald *d* J. Lee-Thompson *ph* Sam Leavitt *m* Bernard Herrmann

Gregory Peck, Robert Mitchum, Polly Bergen, Martin Balsam, Lori Martin, Jack Kruschen, Telly Savalas

The Caper of the Golden Bulls
US 1966 104m Pathecolor
Embassy (Clarence Greene)
GB title: *Carnival of Thieves*

Ex-air-aces rob banks in order to pay for the restoration of a French cathedral they had to bomb; to avoid incrimination they are blackmailed into doing one last job in Pamplona. Ingeniously plotted, flatly executed suspenser set in Pamplona during the bull run.

w Ed Waters, William Moessinger, *novel* William P. McGivern *d* Russel Rouse *ph* Hal Stine *m* Vic Mizzy

Stephen Boyd, Giovanna Ralli, Yvette Mimieux, Walter Slezak, Vito Scotti

Capetown Affair

US / SA 1967   100m   De Luxe
TCF / Killarney (Robert D. Webb)

A pickpocket on a South African bus steals a purse containing secret microfilm.
Flatulent remake of *Pickup on South Street* with nothing but the unfamiliar locale to recommend it.

w Harold Medford, Samuel Fuller *d* Robert D. Webb *ph* David Millin *m* Bob Adams

James Brolin, Jacqueline Bisset, Claire Trevor, Bob Courtney, Jon Whiteley

Capone

US 1975   101m   De Luxe
TCF / Santa Fe (Roger Corman)

Exploitation version of the Capone story, with the emphasis on unpleasant violence.

w Howard Browne *d* Steve Carver *ph* Vilis Lapenieks *m* David Grisman

Ben Gazzara, Sylvester Stallone, Susan Blakely, Harry Guardino, John Cassavetes, John Davis Chandler, Peter Maloney, Royal Dano

Caprice*

US 1967   98m   De Luxe   Cinemascope
TCF / Aaron Rosenberg, Marty Melcher

A career girl investigating the death of her boss discovers that a cosmetics empire is the front for international drug smuggling.
Incoherent kaleidoscope which switches from farce to suspense and Bond-style action, scattering in-jokes along the way. Bits of it however are funny, and it looks good.

w Jay Jayson, Frank Tashlin *d* Frank Tashlin *ph* Leon Shamroy (who also appears) *m* Frank de Vol

Doris Day, Richard Harris, Edward Mulhare, Ray Walston, Jack Kruschen, Lilia Skala, Irene Tsu, Michael Romanoff, Michael J. Pollard

Capricious Summer*

Czechoslovakia 1968   75m   Eastmancolor
Ceskoslovensky Film (Jan Libora)

The beautiful assistant of a wandering tightrope walker sets up sexual tensions when they stop at a sleepy riverside town.
Amusing little period comedy in a period setting.

wd Jiri Menzel ph Jaromir Sofr *m* Jiri Sust

Rudolf Hrusinksy, Vlastimil Brodsky, Frantisek Rehak, Jana Drchalova, Jiri Menzel

Capricorn One

US 1978   128m   CFI colour
Associated General / Lew Grade (Paul N. Lazarus III)

A reporter discovers that the first manned space flight to Mars was a hoax.
Smartly packaged topical adventure thriller rather marred by its all star cast.

wd Peter Hyams ph Bill Butler *m* Jerry Goldsmith *pd* Albert Brenner

Elliott Gould, James Brolin, Brenda Vaccaro, Sam Waterston, O. J. Simpson, Hal Holbrook, Telly Savalas, Karen Black, David Huddleston

Captain Apache

US / Spain 1971   94m   Technicolor
'Scope
Benmar (Milton Sperling, Philip Yordan, Irving Lerner)

An Indian serving with US army intelligence tracks down a gun runner.
An old formula tarted up with the new violence.
Very ho-hum.

w Philip Yordan, Milton Sperling, *novel* S. E. Whitman *d* Alexander Singer *ph* John Cabrera *m* Dolores Claman

Lee Van Cleef, Carroll Baker, Stuart Whitman, Percy Herbert, Tony Vogel

Captain Blood**

US 1935   119m   bw
Warner (Harry Joe Brown)

A young British surgeon, wrongly condemned by Judge Jeffreys for helping rebels, escapes and becomes a Caribbean pirate.
Modestly produced but quite exhilarating pirate adventure notable for making a star of Errol Flynn. Direction makes the most of very limited production values.

w Casey Robinson, *novel* Rafael Sabatini *d Michael Curtiz ph* Hal Mohr *ad Anton Grot*

Errol Flynn, Olivia de Havilland, *Basil Rathbone*, Lionel Atwill, Guy Kibbee, Ross Alexander, Henry Stephenson, Forrester Harvey, Hobart Cavanaugh, Donald Meek

AAN: best picture

Captain Boycott*
GB 1947 93m bw
GFD / Individual (Frank Launder, Sidney
    Gilliat)

In 1880, poor Irish farmers rebel against their
tyrannical English landlords.
Modest historical drama in which a splendid cast
is rather subdued.

w Wolfgang Wilhelm, Frank Launder, Paul
Vincent Carroll, Patrick Campbell, novel Philip
Rooney· d Frank Launder ph Wilkie Cooper
m William Alwyn

Stewart Granger, Kathleen Ryan, Alastair Sim,
Robert Donat (a cameo as Parnell), Cecil
Parker, Mervyn Johns, Noel Purcell, Niall
MacGinnis

Captain Carey USA
US 1951 83m bw
Paramount (Richard Maibaum)
GB title: After Midnight

After the war, a military officer returns to an
Italian village to expose the informer who
betrayed his comrades.
Muddled and rather boring melodrama with a
labyrinthine plot which seems to have stultified
all concerned. It did produce a hit song, 'Mona
Lisa'.

w Robert Thoeren, novel Dishonoured by
Martha Albrand d Mitchell Leisen ph John F.
Seitz m Hugo Friedhofer

Alan Ladd, Francis Lederer, Wanda Hendrix,
Joseph Calleia, Celia Lovsky, Angela Clarke,
Jane Nigh, Frank Puglia, Luis Alberni

AA: song 'Mona Lisa' (m/ly Ray Evans, Jay
Livingstone)

Captain Caution
US 1940 84m bw
Hal Roach

In 1812, a girl takes over her dead father's ship
and fights the British.
Lively though unconvincing adventure with
emphasis on comedy.

w Grover Jones d Richard Wallace ph Norbert
Brodine m Phil Ohman

Victor Mature, Louise Platt, Bruce Cabot, Leo
Carrillo, Robert Barrat, Vivienne Osborne, Alan
Ladd

Captain China
US 1949 97m bw
Paramount / Pine-Thomas (William H. Pine,
    William C. Thomas)

A wandering seafarer seeks the mate who
betrayed him.

Action melodrama with a second team look; all
rather listless.

w Lewis R. Foster, Gwen Bagni d Lewis R.
Foster ph John Alton m Lucien Caillet

John Payne, Gail Russell, Jeffrey Lynn, Lon
Chaney Jnr, Michael O'Shea, Ellen Corby

Captain Clegg*
GB 1962 82m Technicolor
Universal / Hammer (John Temple-Smith)
US title: Night Creatures

The vicar of an 18th-century village in Romney
Marsh is really a retired pirate, now doing a little
smuggling on the side.
Mild remake of Dr Syn with a few moments of
violence added; watchable for those who like
totally predictable plot development.

w John Elder d Peter Graham Scott ph Arthur
Grant m Don Banks

Peter Cushing, Patrick Allen, Michael Ripper,
Oliver Reed, Derek Francis, Milton Reid, Martin
Benson, David Lodge

Captain Eddie
US 1945 107m bw
TCF / Eureka

Eddie Rickenbacker, adrift on a life raft after a
plane crash in the Pacific, thinks back on his
adventurous life in aviation.
Flat and surprisingly poorly made biopic with
little to hold the attention.

w John Tucker Battle d Lloyd Bacon ph Joe
MacDonald

Fred MacMurray, Lynn Bari, Thomas Mitchell,
Lloyd Nolan, Charles Bickford

Captain from Castile
US 1947 140m Technicolor
TCF (Lamar Trotti)

A young 15th-century Spaniard hopes for fame
and fortune in the New World.
Rather empty and boring adventure epic from a
bestseller; high production values produce
moments of interest.

w Lamar Trotti, novel Samuel Shellabarger
d Henry King ph Charles Clarke, Arthur E.
Arling m Alfred Newman ad Richard Day,
James Basevi

Tyrone Power, Jean Peters, Lee J. Cobb, Cesar
Romero, John Sutton, Antonio Moreno,
Thomas Gomez, Alan Mowbray, Barbara
Lawrence, George Zucco, Roy Roberts, Marc
Lawrence

AAN: Alfred Newman

Captain Fury*
US 1939   91m   bw
Hal Roach

In 19th-century Australia, an adventurer fights
the evil head of a penal colony.
Shades of Zorro and Robin Hood in a brawling,
comic actioner typical of this producer.

w Grover Jones, Jack Jevne, William de Mille
d Hal Roach ph Norbert Brodine m Marvin
Hatley

Brian Aherne, Victor McLaglen, Paul Lukas,
June Lang, John Carradine

The Captain Hates the Sea*
US 1934   92m   bw
Columbia

Crime and comedy on an ocean voyage.
Zany, rather endearing comedy which gave the
star his last role.

w Wallace Smith d Lewis Milestone ph Joseph
August

John Gilbert, Victor McLaglen, Walter   .
Connolly, Alison Skipworth, Wynne Gibson,
Helen Vinson, Leon Errol, Walter Catlett,
Donald Meek, Arthur Treacher, Akim Tamiroff

'The best neglected picture in two years.'—
Otis Ferguson, 1936

Captain Horatio Hornblower RN
GB 1951   117m   Technicolor
Warner (Raoul Walsh)

Events from the adventure novels about a 19th-
century sailor who outwits the Spaniards and the
French and marries his admiral's widow.
Sprawling, plotless sea saga with the cast ill at
ease in highly unconvincing sets: no air seems to
blow across the decks of the *Lydia.*

w Ivan Goff, Ben Roberts, Aeneas Mackenzie,
novels C. S. Forester d Raoul Walsh ph Guy
Green m Robert Farnon ad Tom Morahan

Gregory Peck, Virginia Mayo, Robert Beatty,
James Robertson Justice, Terence Morgan,
Moultrie Kelsall, Richard Hearne, Denis O'Dea

'No point makes a strong enough impression
to suggest a main line of criticism.'—*Richard
Mallett, Punch*

Captain January*
US 1936   74m   bw
TCF (Darryl F. Zanuck)

A little girl is rescued from a shipwreck by a
lighthouse keeper.
Standard Shirley Temple vehicle with pleasing
dialogue and numbers.

w Sam Hellman, Gladys Lehman, Harry

Tugend, *novel* Laura E. Richards d David
Butler ph John F. Seitz

Shirley Temple, Guy Kibbee, Buddy Ebsen, Slim
Summerville, June Lang, Sara Haden, Jane
Darwell

Captain Kidd
US 1945   90m   bw
Benedict Bogeaus

A pirate tricks King William III into giving him
royal orders, but enemies he believes dead return
to see him hanged.
Rather poorly produced vehicle for a star who
however rants and raves to some effect.

w Norman Reilly Raine d Rowland V. Lee
ph Archie Stout m Werner Janssen

Charles Laughton, Randolph Scott, Barbara
Britton, Reginald Owen, John Carradine,
Gilbert Roland, Sheldon Leonard

AAN: Werner Janssen

Captain Lightfoot
US 1955   92m   Technicolor print
          Cinemascope
U-I (Ross Hunter)

Adventures of a 19th-century Irish rebel.
Dullish adventure story with the star ill at ease.

w W. R. Burnett, Oscar Brodney d Douglas
Sirk ph Irving Glassberg m Joseph Gershenson

Rock Hudson, Barbara Rush, Jeff Morrow,
Kathleen Ryan, Finlay Currie, Denis O'Dea,
Geoffrey Toone

Captain Nemo and the Underwater City
GB 1969   106m   Metrocolor   Panavision
MGM / Omnia (Steven Pallos, Bertram
          Ostrer)

Six survivors from an Atlantic shipwreck are
picked up by a mysterious submarine and have
adventures in a spectacular underwater city.
Further adventures of Jules Verne's engaging
Victorian character from *Twenty Thousand
Leagues under the Sea.* Here however the
general production values are stolid rather than
solid, and the script makes heavy weather.

w Pip Baker, Jane Baker, R. Wright Campbell
d James Hill ph Alan Hume, Egil Woxholt
m Walter Stott ad Bill Andrews

Robert Ryan, Chuck Connors, Bill Fraser,
Kenneth Connor, Nanette Newman, John
Turner, Luciana Paluzzi, Allan Cuthbertson

Captain Newman MD*
US 1963   126m   Eastmancolor
Universal–Brentwood–Reynard (Robert
          Arthur)

At an army air base during World War II, a psychiatrist has varied success with his patients. A decidedly curious comedy drama on the fringe of bad taste; it should have turned out better than it does, but will entertain those who like hospital heroics drenched in bitter-sweet sentimentality.

w Richard L. Breen, Phoebe and Henry Ephron, *novel* Leo Rosten *d* David Miller *ph* Russell Metty *m* Joseph Gershenson

Gregory Peck, Tony Curtis, Angie Dickinson, Eddie Albert, Bobby Darin, James Gregory, Jane Withers, Bethel Leslie, Robert Duvall, Larry Storch, Robert F. Simon, Dick Sargent

AAN: Bobby Darin

Captain Sinbad*

US / Germany 1963   88m   Eastmancolor
Wonderscope
King Brothers

Sinbad returns to Baristan and by means of magic deposes a sultan.
Rather splendid adventure fantasy with a European flavour, good trick effects and full-blooded performances.

w Samuel B. West, Harry Relis *d* Byron Haskin *ph* Gunther Senftleben, Eugen Shuftan *m* Michel Michelet *sp* Tom Howard *ad* Werner and Isabell Schlicting

Guy Williams, Pedro Armendariz, Heidi Bruhl, Abraham Sofaer

Captains Courageous**

US 1937   116m   bw
MGM (Louis D. Lighton)

A spoiled rich boy falls off a cruise liner and lives for a while among fisherfolk who teach him how to live.
Semi-classic Hollywood family film which is not all that enjoyable while it's on but is certainly a good example of the prestige picture of the thirties. (It also happened to be good box office.)

w John Lee Mahin, Marc Connelly, Dale Van Every, *novel* Rudyard Kipling *d* Victor Fleming *ph* Harold Rosson *m* Franz Waxman

Spencer Tracy, Lionel Barrymore, Freddie Bartholemew, Mickey Rooney, Melvyn Douglas, Charley Grapewin, Christian Rub, John Carradine, Walter Kingsford, Leo G. Carroll, Charles Trowbridge

'Another of those grand jobs of movie-making we have come to expect from Hollywood's most profligate studio.'—*Frank S. Nugent, New York Times*

† 1977 brought a TV movie remake.

AA: Spencer Tracy
AAN: best picture

Captains of the Clouds

US 1942   113m   Technicolor
Warner (Hal. B. Wallis, William Cagney)

A flippant Canadian Air Force pilot proves his worth under fire.
Recruiting poster heroics, reasonably well done but lacking the vital spark.

w Arthur T. Horman, Richard Macaulay, Norman Reilly Raine *d* Michael Curtiz *ph* Sol Polito, Wilfrid M. Cline *m* Max Steiner

James Cagney, Dennis Morgan, Brenda Marshall, George Tobias, Alan Hale, Reginald Gardiner, Reginald Denny, Paul Cavanagh, Clem Bevans, J. M. Kerrigan

'Pure tribute to the unchanging forcefulness of James Cagney.'—*New York Post*

AAN: Sol Polito, Wilfrid M. Cline

The Captain's Paradise*

GB 1953   89m   bw
BL / London (Anthony Kimmins)

The captain of a steamer plying between Gibraltar and Tangier has a wife in each port, one to suit each of his personalities.
Over-dry comedy in which the idea is much funnier than the script. One is left with the memory of a pleasant star performance.

w Alec Coppel, Nicholas Phipps *d* Anthony Kimmins *ph* Ted Scaife *m* Malcolm Arnold

Alec Guinness, Celia Johnson, Yvonne de Carlo, Charles Goldner, Miles Malleson, Bill Fraser, Nicholas Phipps, Ferdy Mayne, George Benson

AAN: original story (Alec Coppel)

The Captain's Table*

GB 1958   89m   Eastmancolor
Rank (Joseph Janni)

A cargo skipper is given command of a luxury liner and has to watch his manners.
Lively adaptation of a frivolous book of obvious jokes, most of which come up quite funny amid the luxurious surroundings.

w John Whiting, Bryan Forbes, Nicholas Phipps, *novel* Richard Gordon *d* Jack Lee *ph* Christopher Challis *m* Frank Cordell

John Gregson, Peggy Cummins, *Donald Sinden, Reginald Beckwith*, Nadia Gray, Richard Wattis, Maurice Denham, Nicholas Phipps, Joan Sims, Miles Malleson

The Captive City**

US 1951   91m   bw
UA / Aspen (Theron Warth)

Small-town corruption imposed by the Mafia is revealed by a crusading editor who defies threats to his wife and family and tells all to the Kefauver Commission.

Excellent documentary melodrama made in a style then original, also notable for use of the Hoge deep focus lens.

w Karl Lamb, Alvin Josephy Jnr d Robert Wise ph Lee Garmes m Jerome Moross

John Forsythe, Joan Camden, Harold J. Kennedy, Marjorie Crossland, Victor Sutherland, Ray Teal, Martin Milner, Hal K. Dawson

The Captive Heart**
GB 1946   108m   bw
Ealing (Michael Relph)

Stories of life among British officers in a German POW camp, especially of a Czech who has stolen the papers of a dead Britisher.
Archetypal POW drama lacing an almost poetic treatment with humour and melodrama.

w Angus Macphail, Guy Morgan d Basil Dearden ph Lionel Banes, Douglas Slocombe m Alan Rawsthorne

Michael Redgrave, Jack Warner, Basil Radford, Mervyn Johns, Jimmy Hanley, Gordon Jackson, Ralph Michael, Derek Bond, Karel Stepanek, Guy Middleton, Jack Lambert, Gladys Henson, Rachel Kempson, Meriel Forbes

The Car
US 1977   98m   Technicolor   Panavision
Universal (Peter Saphier)

A small southwestern town is terrorized by a driverless car which may be a creation of the devil.
Silly suspenser with a draggy midsection.

w Dennis Shyrack, Michael Butler, Lane Slate d Elliot Silverstein ph Gerald Hirschfeld m Leonard Rosenman

James Brolin, Kathleen Lloyd, John Marley, R. G. Armstrong, John Rubenstein

Caravan
US 1934   101m   bw
Fox

A countess marries a gypsy.
Odd romantic drama with music: too whimsical to succeed.

w Samson Raphaelson d Erik Charell ph Ernest Palmer, Theodor Sparkuhl songs Werner B. Heymann, Gus Kahn

Loretta Young, Charles Boyer, Jean Parker, Phillips Holmes, Louise Fazenda, Eugene Pallette, C. Aubrey Smith, Charley Grapewin, Noah Beery, Dudley Digges

Caravan
GB 1946   122m   bw
Gainsborough (Harold Huth)

A young man on a mission in Spain is left for dead by emissaries of his rival in love; he is nursed back to health by a gypsy girl who falls in love with him.
Artificial, romantic, high-flown period tosh without the courage of its lack of convictions. At the time, an exhibitor's dream.

w Roland Pertwee, novel Lady Eleanor Smith d Arthur Crabtree ph Stephen Dade

Stewart Granger, Jean Kent, Anne Crawford, Robert Helpmann, Dennis Price, Gerard Heinz, Enid Stamp-Taylor, David Horne, John Salew

Caravan to Vaccares
GB / France 1974   98m   Eastmancolor
    Panavision
Crowndale (Geoffrey Reeve)

An American drifter on the Riviera is employed to escort a mysterious Hungarian to New York.
Lumpy Alistair MacLean action thriller, all a bit déjà vu.

w Paul Wheeler d Geoffrey Reeve ph Frederic Tammes m Stanley Myers

David Birney, Charlotte Rampling, Michel Lonsdale, Marcel Bozzuffi, Michael Bryant
  'An undernourished plot advanced only by a series of venerable clichés.'—MFB
  'The biggest load of schoolboy hokum since Boy's Own Paper ceased circulation.'—Michael Billington, Illustrated London News

Carbine Williams
US 1952   93m   bw
MGM (Armand Deutsch)

An imprisoned bootlegger perfects a new gun and is pardoned.
Flat fictionalization of a true story, with the star miscast.

w Art Cohn d Richard Thorpe ph William Mellor m Conrad Salinger

James Stewart, Jean Hagen, Wendell Corey, Carl Benton Reid, Paul Stewart, Otto Hulett, James Arness

The Card**
GB 1952   91m   bw
Rank / British Film Makers (John Bryan)
US title: The Promoter

A bright young clerk from the potteries finds many ingenious ways of improving his bank account and his place in society.
Pleasing period comedy with the star in a made-to-measure role and excellent production values.

w Eric Ambler, *novel* Arnold Bennett *d* Ronald
Neame *ph* Oswald Morris *ad* T. Hopwell Ash
m William Alwyn

Alec Guinness, Glynis Johns, Petula Clark,
Valerie Hobson, Edward Chapman, Veronica
Turleigh, Gibb McLaughlin, Frank Pettingell

Card of Fate see Le Grand Jeu

Cardboard Cavalier*
GB 1949 96m bw
Rank / Two Cities

In Cromwellian England, royalists commission a
barrow boy to carry a secret letter. Helped by
Nell Gwynn, he succeeds after encounters with a
castle ghost and custard pies.
A pantomime crossed with an Aldwych farce in
a period setting. It failed at the time but now
seems a brave try, with nice judgment all round.

w Noel Langley *d* Walter Forde *ph* Jack
Hildyard *m* Lambert Williamson

Sid Field, Margaret Lockwood, Mary Clare,
Jerry Desmonde, Claude Hulbert, Irene Handl,
Brian Worth, Edmund Willard (as Cromwell)

The Cardinal*
US 1963 175m Technicolor Panavision
70
Gamma / Otto Preminger

A 1917 ordinand becomes a Boston curate, a
fighter of the Ku Klux Klan, a Rome diplomat,
and finally gets a cardinal's hat.
Heavy-going documentary melodrama with
many interesting sequences marred by lack of
cohesion, too much grabbing at world problems,
and over-sensational personal asides.

w Robert Dozier, *novel* Henry Morton
Robinson *d* Otto Preminger *ph* Leon Shamroy
m Jerome Moross *pd* Lyle Wheeler *titles* Saul
Bass

Tom Tryon, *Carol Lynley*, Dorothy Gish,
Maggie Macnamara, Cecil Kellaway, John
Saxon, *John Huston*, Robert Morse, Burgess
Meredith, Jill Haworth, Raf Vallone, Tullio
Carminati, Ossie Davis, Chill Wills, Arthur
Hunnicutt, Murray Hamilton, Patrick O'Neal,
Romy Schneider

'Very probably the last word in glossy
dishonesty posturing as serious art.'—*John
Simon*

'Mere and sheer wide screen Technicolor
movie.'—*Stanley Kauffmann*

AAN: Otto Preminger; Leon Shamroy; John
Huston

Cardinal Richelieu*
US 1935 83m bw
Twentieth Century (Darryl F. Zanuck)

Fictionalized biography of the unscrupulous
cardinal who was the grey eminence behind
Louis XIII.
One of George Arliss' better star vehicles, with
not much conviction but excellent production
values.

w Maude Howell, Cameron Rogers, W. P.
Lipscomb *d* Rowland V. Lee *ph* Peverell
Marley *m* Alfred Newman

George Arliss, Maureen O'Sullivan, Edward
Arnold, Cesar Romero

Career
US 1939 80m bw
RKO (Robert Sisk)

A respected small-town storekeeper has old
scores to settle against the local banker.
Modest, pleasing, rather faded 'B' picture.

w Dalton Trumbo, Bert Granet, *novel* Phil
Stong *d* Leigh Jason *ph* Frank Redman

Edward Ellis, Samuel S. Hinds, Anne Shirley,
Janet Beecher, Leon Errol, Raymond Hatton,
Hobart Cavanaugh

Career*
US 1959 105m bw
Paramount / Hal B. Wallis (Paul Nathan)

An actor from the midwest finally gets his
chance in New York.
A location melodrama with the feel of a
documentary, well played but slow and rather
indeterminate.

w James Lee, from his play *d* Joseph Anthony
ph Joseph La Shelle *m* Franz Waxman

Anthony Franciosa, Dean Martin, Shirley
Maclaine, Carolyn Jones, Joan Blackman,
Robert Middleton, Frank McHugh, Donna
Douglas

AAN: Joseph La Shelle

Carefree*
US 1938 85m bw
RKO (Pandro S. Berman)

A humourless lawyer sends his undecided girl
friend to an alienist, with whom she falls in love.
Slight, frothy comedy musical; quite palatable,
but it signalled the end of the Astaire–Rogers
series.

w Allan Scott, Ernest Pagano *d* Mark Sandrich
ph Robert de Grasse *m/ly* Irving Berlin
ch Hermes Pan *md* Victor Baravelle

Fred Astaire, Ginger Rogers, Ralph Bellamy,
Luella Gear, Clarence Kolb, Jack Carson,

Franklin Pangborne, Walter Kingsford, Hattie
McDaniel

AAN: Victor Baravelle; song 'Change Partners'
(*m/ly* Irving Berlin)

Careful, Soft Shoulder*
US 1942   69m   bw
TCF (Walter Morosco)

A Washington socialite becomes a spy for both
sides.

Modest, slightly unusual second feature which
over the years has gathered for itself more
reputation than it really deserves.

wd Oliver H. P. Garrett   *ph* Charles Clarke

Virginia Bruce, James Ellison, Aubrey Mather,
Sheila Ryan, Ralph Byrd

The Caretaker*
GB 1964   105m   bw
Caretaker Films (Michael Birkett)
US title: *The Guest*

Two brothers invite a revolting tramp to share
their attic.

Rather doleful filming of the fashionable play
with its non-plot, irregular conceits and
interesting interplay of character. It remains a
theatrical experience.

w Harold Pinter   *d* Clive Donner   *ph* Nicolas
Roeg   *m* Ron Grainer

Alan Bates, Robert Shaw, Donald Pleasance

The Caretakers*
US 1963   97m   bw
UA / Hall Bartlett
GB title: *Borderlines*

The interrelationship of several cases in a state
mental hospital.

Rather hysterical melodrama, lacking in the
stature required for its subject, but sometimes
perversely entertaining.

w Henry F. Greenberg, *novel* Daniel Telfer
d Hall Bartlett   *ph* Lucien Ballard   *m* Elmer
Bernstein

Polly Bergen, Robert Stack, Joan Crawford,
Diane McBain, Janis Paige, Van Williams,
Robert Vaughn, Herbert Marshall, Constance
Ford

AAN: Lucien Ballard

The Carey Treatment*
US 1972   101m   Metrocolor   Panavision
MGM (William Belasco)

A Boston pathologist investigating the death of
an abortion victim becomes the potential murder
victim of a father turned killer.

Pretentious thriller with a tendency to make

moral points among the bloodshed; vigorously
but variably made.

w James P. Bonner, *novel* A Case of Need by
Jeffrey Hudson   *d* Blake Edwards   *ph* Frank
Stanley   *m* Roy Budd

James Coburn, Jennifer O'Neill, Skye Aubrey,
Pat Hingle, Dan O'Herlihy, Elizabeth Allen,
Alex Dreier, Regis Toomey

Caribbean
US 1952   94m   Technicolor
(Paramount) Pine–Thomas (William H. Pine,
   William C. Thomas)
GB title: *Caribbean Gold*

An 18th-century pirate captures the nephew of
his old enemy.

Adequate but not very exciting swashbuckler
with fair production values.

w Frank L. Moss, Edward Ludwig   *d* Edward
Ludwig   *ph* Lionel Lindon   *m* Lucien Cailliet

John Payne, Arlene Dahl, Cedric Hardwicke
(incredibly cast as the pirate), Francis L.
Sullivan, Dennis Hoey

Carlton-Browne of the FO
GB 1958   88m   bw
British Lion / Charter Films (John Boulting)
US title: *Man in a Cocked Hat*

When valuable mineral deposits are found in a
small British colony, the diplomat sent to cement
good relations does quite the reverse.

Hit-or-miss farcical comedy several rungs below
the Ealing style, with all concerned in poor form.

wd Jeffrey Dell, Roy Boulting   *ph* Max Greene
m John Addison

Terry-Thomas, Peter Sellers, Ian Bannen,
Thorley Walters, Raymond Huntley, John Le
Mesurier, Luciana Paluzzi, Miles Malleson,
Kynaston Reeves, Marie Lohr

Carmen Jones*
US 1954   105m   De Luxe   Cinemascope
TCF (Otto Preminger)

A factory girl marries a pilot, and is strangled by
him for infidelity.

Black American updating of Bizet's opera, not
really satisfactory but given full marks for trying,
though the main singing is dubbed and the effect
remains doggedly theatrical.

w Harry Kleiner   *d* Otto Preminger   *ph* Sam
Leavitt   *ly* Oscar Hammerstein II   *titles* Saul
Bass   *md* Herschel Burke Gilbert

Dorothy Dandridge, Harry Belafonte, *Pearl
Bailey*, Olga James, Joe Adams, Roy Glenn,
Nick Stewart, Diahann Carroll, Brock Peters

'All one regrets is that the director has been

unable to impose a unifying style on this promising material.'—*Gavin Lambert*

AAN: Herschel Burke Gilbert; Dorothy Dandridge

Carnal Knowledge*
US 1971 97m Technicolor Panavision
Avco Embassy / Icarus (Mike Nichols)

A college student embarks on an enthusiastic and varied sex life but by middle age is bored and empty.

Hampered by an unsuitable wide screen, this pretentious but fragmented comedy drama is embarrassingly conscious of its own daring in subject and language, and good performances are weighed down by an unsubtle script and tricksy direction.

w Jules Feiffer *d* Mike Nichols *ph* Giuseppe Rotunno *m* various songs *pd* Richard Sylbert

Jack Nicholson, *Arthur Garfunkel*, Candice Bergen, *Ann-Margret*, Rita Moreno

AAN: Ann-Margret

Carnegie Hall
US 1947 134m bw
Federal Films

The story of New York's music centre, based on a fiction about a cleaner who finally becomes a concert organizer when her son is a famous pianist.

Slim and risible excuse for a classical concert, featuring among others Bruno Walter, Leopold Stokowski, Artur Rubenstein, Jascha Heifitz, Lily Pons, Rise Stevens, Ezio Pinza, Jan Peerce, Harry James, Vaughn Monroe and the New York Philharmonic Symphony Orchestra.

w Karl Lamb *d* Edgar G. Ulmer *ph* William Miller

'The thickest and sourest mess of musical mulligatawny I have yet had to sit down to.'— *James Agee*

Un Carnet de Bal**
France 1936 120m bw
Lévy / Strauss / Sigma
aka: *Christine*

A rich widow seeks her partners at a ball she remembers from her youth, finding that they are all failures and the ball a village hop.
Considering its fame, this is a lumpy porridge of a picture, good in parts but often slow, pretentious and banal. Its gallery of actors is, however, unique.

w Jean Sarment, Pierre Wolff, Bernard Zimmer, Henri Jeanson, Julien Duvivier *d* Julien Duvivier *ph* Michel Kelber, Philippe Agostini *m* Maurice Jaubert

Marie Bell, Françoise Rosay, *Louis Jouvet, Raimu, Harry Baur, Fernandel, Pierre Blanchar*

† The film's international success took Duvivier to Hollywood, where he half-remade it as *Lydia* and went on to other multi-story films such as *Tales of Manhattan* and *Flesh and Fantasy*.

Carnival
GB 1946 93m bw
Rank / Two Cities

In the nineties, a ballet dancer marries a dour Cornish farmer, who shoots her when her erstwhile lover comes after her.
Flimsy screen version of a solidly old-fashioned romantic drama.

w Eric Maschwitz, *novel* Compton Mackenzie *d* Stanley Haynes *ph* Guy Green

Sally Gray, Michael Wilding, Bernard Miles, Cathleen Nesbitt

Carnival in Costa Rica
US 1947 97m Technicolor
TCF

A young Costa Rican, engaged to an American singer, returns home to find that his parents expect him to marry his childhood sweetheart.
Decidedly rundown musical in which incessant carnival largely supplants the wispy plot.

w John Larkin, Samuel Hoffenstein, Elizabeth Reinhardt *d* Gregory Ratoff *ph* Harry Jackson *ch* Leonide Massine *m/ly* Harry Ruby, Ernesto Lecuona

Dick Haymes, Vera-Ellen, Celeste Holm, J. Carrol Naish, Cesar Romero

Carnival Story
US / Germany 1954 95m Technicolor
The King Brothers

A starving girl becomes a trapezist at a German circus and stirs up jealousy among her partners.
Bleak reworking of *The Three Maxims* (qv), reworked again with more expertise in *Trapeze* (qv); this version is a cheap and unattractive co-production.

w Kurt Neumann, Hans Jacoby *d* Kurt Neumann *ph* Ernest Haller *m* Willi Schmidt-Genter

Anne Baxter, Steve Cochran, Lyle Bettger, George Nader, Jay C. Flippen

Carolina
US 1934 85m bw
Fox (Darryl F. Zanuck)

A Yankee farmer's daughter falls in love with a Southern plantation owner.
Mildly pleasing period piece.

w Reginald Berkeley, *play* The House of Connelly by Paul Green *d* Henry King *ph* Hal Mohr

Janet Gaynor, Lionel Barrymore, Robert Young, Henrietta Crosman, Mona Barrie, Richard Cromwell

Caroline Chérie

France 1951   115m approx   bw
SNEG / Cinéphonie

Adventures of an attractive and willing young French girl in the days of the revolution.
A cheerful French imitation of *Forever Amber*; witless and not very entertaining despite good period sense and a certain amount of self-mockery.

w Jean Anouilh, *novel* Cécil Saint-Laurent *d* Richard Poitier *ph* Maurice Barry *m* Georges Auric

Martine Carol, Jacques Dacqmine, Marie Déa, Paul Bernard, Pierre Cressoy

† After several sequels, a colour remake appeared in 1967.

Carousel*

US 1956   128m   Eastmancolor
   Cinemascope 55
TCF (Henry Ephron)

A ne'er-do-well dies while committing a hold-up. Fifteen years later he returns from heaven to set his family's affairs in order.
Based on a fantasy play with an honourable history, this super-wide-screen version of an effective stage musical is hollow and boring, a humourless whimsy in which even the songs seem an intrusion.

w Phoebe and Henry Ephron, from the musical based on Ferenc Molnar's play Liliom *d* Henry King *ph* Charles G. Clarke *m/ly* Rodgers and Hammerstein *ch* Rod Alexander, Agnes de Mille

Gordon Macrae, Shirley Jones, Cameron Mitchell,Gene Lockhart, Barbara Ruick, Robert Rounseville

The Carpetbaggers**

US 1964   150m   Technicolor   Panavision
Paramount / Embassy (Joseph E. Levine)

A young playboy inherits an aircraft business, becomes a megalomaniac tycoon, and moves to Hollywood in his search for power.
Enjoyable pulp fiction clearly suggested by the career of Howard Hughes. Lashings of old-fashioned melodrama, quite well pointed by all concerned.

w John Michael Hayes, *novel* Harold Robbins *d* Edward Dmytryk *ph* Joseph MacDonald

m Elmer Bernstein *ad* Hal Pereira, Walter Tyler

George Peppard, Carroll Baker, *Alan Ladd* (his last film), *Martin Balsam*, Bob Cummings, Martha Hyer, Elizabeth Ashley, Lew Ayres, Ralph Taeger, Archie Moore, Leif Erickson, Audrey Totter

'One of those elaborate conjuring tricks in which yards and yards of coloured ribbon are spread all over the stage merely to prove that the conjuror has nothing up his sleeve.'—*Tom Milne*

Carrie**

US 1952   122m   bw
Paramount (William Wyler)

In the early 1900s a country girl comes to Chicago, loses her innocence and goes on the stage, meanwhile reducing a wealthy restaurant manager to penury through love for her.
A famous satirical novel is softened into an unwieldy narrative with scarcely enough dramatic power to sustain interest despite splendid production values. Heavy pre-release cuts remain obvious, and the general effect is depressing; but it is very good to look at.

w Ruth and Augustus Goetz, *novel* Sister Carrie by Theodore Dreiser *d* William Wyler *ph* Victor Milner *m* David Raksin *ad* Hal Pereira, Roland Anderson

Laurence Olivier, Jennifer Jones, Miriam Hopkins, Eddie Albert, Basil Ruysdael, Ray Teal, Barry Kelley, Mary Murphy

Carrie*

US 1976   98m   MGM-De Luxe
UA / Red Bank (Paul Monash)

A repressed teenager with remarkable mental powers takes a macabre revenge on classmates who taunt and persecute her.
Stylish but unattractive shocker which works its way up to a fine climax of gore and frenzy, and takes care to provide a final frisson just when the audience thinks it can safely go home.

w Laurence D. Cohen, *novel* Stephen King *d* Brian de Palma *ph* Mario Tosi *m* Pino Donaggio

Sissy Spacek, *Piper Laurie*, Amy Irving, William Katt, John Travolta

AAN: Sissy Spacek; Piper Laurie

Carrington VC*

GB 1954   106m   bw
British Lion / Romulus (Teddy Baird)
US title: *Court Martial*

An army major is courtmartialled for embezzling mess funds.
Good courtroom drama with a few plot

surprises, convincing characters, and very serviceable acting and direction.

w John Hunter, play Dorothy and Campbell Christie d Anthony Asquith ph Desmond Dickinson

David Niven, Margaret Leighton, Noelle Middleton, Laurence Naismith, Clive Morton, Mark Dignam, Allan Cuthbertson, Victor Maddern, John Glyn-Jones, Raymond Francis, Newton Blick, John Chandos

Carry on Sergeant

GB 1958 83m bw
Anglo Amalgamated / Insignia (Peter Rogers)

An army training sergeant accepts a bet that his last platoon of raw recruits will win the Star Squad award.
Shabby farce with humdrum script and slack direction, saved by energetic performances.

w Norman Hudis, play The Bull Boys by R. F. Delderfield d Gerald Thomas ph Peter Hennessy m Bruce Montgomery

Bob Monkhouse, William Hartnell, Kenneth Williams, Charles Hawtrey, Shirley Eaton, Eric Barker, Dora Bryan, Bill Owen, Kenneth Connor
† From this unlikely beginning sprang almost twenty years of *Carry Ons*, their plots gradually disappearing under an accumulation of old jokes which grew steadily bluer. Colour did little to disguise their makeshift construction, and they never raised their sights as high as satire, but they became a British institution like fish and chips, and many of the regulars became stars. Apart from Williams, Hawtrey and Connor, those most regularly featured in the sequels were Sid James, Bernard Bresslaw, Jim Dale, Joan Sims, Hattie Jacques, Peter Butterworth, and Jack Douglas, with occasional guests such as Harry H. Corbett, Juliet Mills and even Phil Silvers. All were produced by Peter Rogers and directed by Gerald Thomas; most were written (or recollected) by Talbot Rothwell. Delivered at the rate of roughly two a year, the sequence of titles was CARRY ON NURSE (a surprising hit in the US), CARRY ON TEACHER, CARRY ON CONSTABLE, CARRY ON REGARDLESS, CARRY ON CRUISING, CARRY ON CABBY, CARRY ON JACK, CARRY ON SPYING, CARRY ON CLEO, CARRY ON COWBOY, CARRY ON SCREAMING, FOLLOW THAT CAMEL (Beau Geste), DON'T LOSE YOUR HEAD (the Scarlet Pimpernel), CARRY ON DOCTOR, CARRY ON UP THE KHYBER, CARRY ON CAMPING, CARRY ON AGAIN DOCTOR, CARRY ON LOVING, CARRY ON UP THE JUNGLE, CARRY ON

HENRY (Henry VIII), CARRY ON AT YOUR CONVENIENCE, CARRY ON MATRON, CARRY ON ABROAD, CARRY ON GIRLS, CARRY ON DICK, CARRY ON BEHIND, CARRY ON ENGLAND.
† CARRY ON ADMIRAL and WHAT A CARRY ON are not part of the series.

Carson City*

US 1952 87m Warnercolor
Warner (David Weisbart)

A stagecoach service suffers from bandit raids, so a local banker finances a railroad.
Agreeably conventional western with plenty of reliable plot and a satisfactory outcome for the goodies.

w Sloan Nibley, Winston Miller d André de Toth ph John Boyle m David Buttolph

Randolph Scott, Raymond Massey, Lucille Norman, Richard Webb, James Millican, Larry Keating, George Cleveland

Cartouche

Italy / US 1954 85m approx bw
Venturini / RKO (John Nasht)

A French prince clears himself of a murder charge and brings the villain to book.
Flat costume drama.

w Louis Stevens, Tullio Pinelli d Steve Sekely, Gianni Vernuccio ph Massimo Dallamano m Bruce Montgomery

Richard Basehart, Patricia Roc, Massimo Serato, Akim Tamiroff

Cartouche**

France / Italy 1961 114m Eastmancolor Dyaliscope
Ariane / Filmsonor / Vides (Georges Danciger)
aka: *Swords of Blood*

An 18th-century cooper's son becomes a quick-witted and gallant thief.
Slightly bitter fairy tale based on a French legend, vigorously encompassing tragedy, farce, violence and high-flown adventure.

w Daniel Boulanger, Philippe de Broca d Philippe de Broca ph Christian Matras m Georges Delerue

Jean-Paul Belmondo, Claudia Cardinale, Odile Versois, Marcel Dalio, Philippe Lemaire, Jean Rochefort
'A tour de force of virtuosity.'—*Peter John Dyer, MFB*

Carve Her Name with Pride*

GB 1958 119m bw
Rank / Keyboard (Daniel M. Angel)

In 1940, the young British widow of a French officer is enlisted as a spy, and after various adventures dies before a German firing squad.
Slightly muddled if ultimately moving biopic in which initial light comedy gives way to romance, documentary, character study, blazing war action and finally tragedy. Generally well made.

w Vernon Harris, Lewis Gilbert, *book* R. J. Minney *d Lewis Gilbert ph* John Wilcox *m* William Alwyn

Virginia McKenna (as Violette Szabo), *Paul Scofield*, Jack Warner, Sidney Tafler, Denise Grey, Alain Saury, Maurice Ronet, Nicole Stèphane, Noel Willman, Bill Owen, William Mervyn, Anne Leon

'What is missing is the deeply charged passion which would have gone beyond the quietly decent statement intermittently achieved.'— *John Gillett*

Casablanca****
US 1942   102m   bw
Warner *(Hal B. Wallis)*

Rick's Café in Casablanca is a centre for war refugees awaiting visas for America. Rick abandons his cynicism to help an old love escape the Nazis with her underground leader husband.
Cinema par excellence: a studio-bound Hollywood melodrama which after various chances just fell together impeccably into one of the outstanding entertainment experiences of cinema history, with romance, intrigue, excitement, suspense and humour cunningly deployed by master technicians and a perfect cast.

w *Julius J. Epstein, Philip G. Epstein, Howard Koch*, from an unproduced play, Everybody Comes to Rick's, by Murray Burnett and Joan Alison *d Michael Curtiz ph Arthur Edeson m Max Steiner*

Humphrey Bogart, Ingrid Bergman, Claude Rains, Paul Henreid, Conrad Veidt, S. Z. Sakall, Sidney Greenstreet, Peter Lorre, Dooley Wilson (singing 'As Time Goes By'), *Marcel Dalio, Leonid Kinskey*

'A picture which makes the spine tingle and the heart take a leap . . . they have so combined sentiment, humour and pathos with taut melodrama and bristling intrigue that the result is a highly entertaining and even inspiring film.'—*New York Times*

'Its humour is what really saves it, being a mixture of Central European irony of attack and racy Broadway–
Hollywood Boulevard cynicism.'—*Herman G. Weinberg*

'The happiest of happy accidents, and the most decisive exception to the *auteur* theory.'— *Andrew Sarris, 1968*

'A film which seems to have been frozen in time . . . the sum of its many marvellous parts far exceeds the whole.'—*NFT, 1974*

'You can tell by the cast it's important! gripping! big!'—*publicity*

AA: best picture; Julius J. and Philip G. Epstein, Howard Koch; Michael Curtiz
AAN: Arthur Edeson; Max Steiner; Humphrey Bogart; Claude Rains

Casanova Brown
US 1944   99m   bw
International / Christie (Nunnally Johnson)

Just as his divorce comes through, a man discovers that his wife is pregnant.
Very mild star comedy which tiptoes round its subject.

w Nunnally Johnson, *play* Bachelor Father by Floyd Dell, Thomas Mitchell *d* Sam Wood *ph* John F. Seitz *m* Arthur Lange

Gary Cooper, Teresa Wright, Frank Morgan, Anita Louise, Patricia Collinge, Edmond Breon, Jill Esmond, Isobel Elsom, Mary Treen, Halliwell Hobbes

AAN: Arthur Lange

Casanova's Big Night
US 1954   86m   Technicolor
Paramount (Paul Jones)

In old Italy, the great lover is fleeing from his creditors and changes places with a tailor's apprentice.
The last of Bob Hope's big-budget, big-studio burlesques is a lumbering vehicle which wastes its star cast and mistimes its laughs.

w Hal Kanter, Edmund Hartmann *d* Norman Z. McLeod *ph* Lionel Lindon

Bob Hope, Joan Fontaine (an unhappy comedy foil), Basil Rathbone, Vincent Price, Audrey Dalton, Hugh Marlowe, John Carradine, Primo Carnera, Arnold Moss, Lon Chaney Jnr

Casbah
US 1948   94m   bw
Universal (Erik Charell)

Remake of *Algiers* (qv) with songs added.
Not too bad in the circumstances, but a wholly artificial exercise, and another version was really not needed. The sets seem overlit and claustrophobic.

w (not credited) *d* John Berry *ph* Irving Glassberg *m* Harold Arlen

Tony Martin, Yvonne de Carlo, Marta Toren, *Peter Lorre,* Hugo Haas

AAN: song 'For Every Man There's a Woman'
(*m* Harold Arlen, *ly* Leo Robin)

The Case against Mrs Ames
US 1936 85m bw
Paramount (Walter Wanger)

The prosecutor in a murder case is convinced of
the defendant's innocence.
Tired rehash of a familiar theme.

w Gene Towne, Graham Baker *d* William A.
Seiter *ph* Lucien Andriot

Madeleine Carroll, George Brent, Arthur
Treacher, Alan Baxter, Beulah Bondi, Alan
Mowbray, Esther Dale, Ed Brophy

Casey's Shadow
US 1978 116m Metrocolor Panavision
Columbia / Ray Stark (Michael Levee)

A Cajun family in New Mexico breeds a
champion horse which wins the annual race.
Shades of *Maryland*: an old-fashioned movie of
the kind which absolutely nobody should want to
revive, at least not so ineptly or at such length.

w Carol Sobieski, *story* Ruidoso by John
McPhee *d* Martin Ritt *ph* John A. Alonzo
m Patrick Williams

Walter Matthau, Alexis Smith, Robert Webber,
Murray Hamilton, Andrew A. Rubin, Stephan
Burns, Michael Hershewe

Cash McCall
US 1960 102m Technicolor
Warner (Henry Blanke)

A Napoleon of the stock market gets into trouble
for the first time when love interferes with
business.
Slightly unusual comedy drama, quite sharply
made and played, but not adding up to much.

w Lenore Coffee, Marion Hargrove, *novel*
Cameron Hawley *d* Joseph Pevney *ph* George
Folsey *m* Max Steiner

James Garner, Natalie Wood, Nina Foch, Dean
Jagger, E. G. Marshall, Henry Jones, Otto
Kruger, Roland Winters

Cash on Demand*
GB 1963 86m bw
Columbia / Woodpecker / Hammer (Michael
Carreras)

A fussy bank manager outwits a classy robber.
Quietly effective suspenser with an admirable
middle-aged cast and no love interest.

w Lewis Greifer, David T. Chantler, from
Jacques Gillies' TV play *d* Quentin Lawrence
ph Arthur Grant *m* Wilfred Josephs

Peter Cushing, André Morell, Richard Vernon,
Norman Bird, Edith Sharpe

Casino Royale
GB 1967 130m Technicolor Panavision
Columbia / Famous Artists (Charles K.
Feldman, Jerry Bresler)

The heads of the allied spy forces call Sir James
Bond out of retirement to fight the power of
SMERSH.
Woeful all-star kaleidoscope, a way-out spoof
which generates far fewer laughs than the
original. One of the most shameless wastes of
time and talent in screen history.

w Wolf Mankowitz, John Law, Michael Sayers,
novel Ian Fleming *d* John Huston, Ken Hughes,
Val Guest, Robert Parrish, Joe McGrath,
Richard Talmadge *ph* Jack Hildyard *m* Burt
Bacharach *pd* Michael Stringer

David Niven, Deborah Kerr, Orson Welles,
Peter Sellers, Ursula Andress, Woody Allen,
William Holden, Charles Boyer, John Huston,
Joanna Pettet, Daliah Lavi, Kurt Kasznar,
Jacqueline Bisset, Derek Nimmo, George Raft,
Ronnie Corbett, Peter O'Toole, Jean-Paul
Belmondo, Geoffrey Bayldon, Duncan Macrae

'One of those wild wacky extravaganzas in
which the audience is expected to have a great
time because everybody making the film did. It
seldom works out that way, and certainly doesn't
here.'—*John Russell Taylor*

AAN: song 'The Look of Love' (*m* Burt
Bacharach, *ly* Hal David)

Casque d'Or***
France 1952 96m bw
Speva / Paris
aka: *Golden Marie*

1898. In the Paris slums, an apache finds
passionate love but is executed for murder.
A tragic romance which on its first release
seemed bathed in a golden glow and is certainly
an impeccable piece of film-making.

w Jacques Becker, Jacques Companeez
d Jacques Becker ph Robert Le Fèbvre
m Georges Van Parys

Simone Signoret, Serge Reggiani, Claude
Dauphin, Raymond Bussières, Gaston Modot

'Takes its place alongside *Le Jour Se Lève*
among the masterpieces of the French
cinema.'—*Karel Reisz*

Cass Timberlane*
US 1947 119m bw
MGM (Arthur Hornblow Jnr)

A judge marries a working class girl, who is

unsettled at first but finally comes to realize her
good fortune.
Solid drama with an understanding star
performance and good production values.

w Donald Ogden Stewart, *novel* Sinclair Lewis
d George Sidney ph Robert Planck m Roy
Webb

Spencer Tracy, Lana Turner, Zachary Scott,
Tom Drake, Mary Astor, Albert Dekker, Selena
Royle, Josephine Hutchinson, Margaret Lindsay

The Cassandra Crossing

GB / Italy / West Germany 1976   129m
  Technicolor   Panavision
AGF / CCC / International Cine (Lew Grade,
  Carlo Ponti)

A terrorist carrying a deadly plague virus boards
a transcontinental train.
Disaster spectacular with a number of
fashionable interests but no observable film-
making technique.

w Tom Mankiewicz, Robert Katz, George Pan
Cosmatos d George Pan Cosmatos ph Ennio
Guarnieri m Jerry Goldsmith pd Aurelio
Crugnola

Sophia Loren, Richard Harris, Ava Gardner,
Burt Lancaster, Martin Sheen, Ingrid Thulin,
Lee Strasberg, John Phillip Law, Lionel Stander,
Ann Turkel, O. J. Simpson, Alida Valli

Cast a Dark Shadow*

GB 1955   82m   bw
Frobisher / Daniel M. Angel (Herbert Mason)

A wife-murderer marries an ex-barmaid and tries
again.
Unambitious but enjoyable melodrama, well
acted though with directorial opportunities
missed.

w John Cresswell, *play* Murder Mistaken by
Janet Green d Lewis Gilbert ph Jack Asher
m Antony Hopkins

Dirk Bogarde, *Margaret Lockwood*, Kay
Walsh, Kathleen Harrison, Robert Flemyng,
Mona Washbourne, Walter Hudd

Cast a Giant Shadow*

US 1966   141m   De Luxe   Panavision
UA / Mirisch / Llenroc / Batjac (Melville
  Shavelson)

An American military lawyer and ex-colonel
goes to Israel in 1947 to help in the fight against
the Arabs.
Spectacular war biopic with all concerned in
good form but lacking the clarity and narrative
control of a real smash.

w Melville Shavelson, from Ted Berkman's
biography of Col. David Marcus d Melville

Shavelson *ph Aldo Tonti m* Elmer Bernstein
pd Michael Stringer

Kirk Douglas, Angie Dickinson, Senta Berger,
Luther Adler, Stathis Giallelis, Chaim Topol,
John Wayne, Frank Sinatra, Yul Brynner, James
Donald, Gordon Jackson, Michael Hordern,
Gary Merrill, Allan Cuthbertson, Jeremy Kemp

The Castaway Cowboy*

US 1974   91m   Technicolor
Walt Disney (Ron Miller, Winston Hibler)

In 1850, a Shanghaied sailor on Hawaii helps a
lady potato farmer to turn her land into a cattle
ranch.
Unexciting and unexceptional family fare.

w Don Tait d Vincent McEveety ph Andrew
Jackson m Robert F. Brunner

James Garner, Vera Miles, Robert Culp, Eric
Shea, Elizabeth Smith

Castle Keep*

US 1969   107m   Technicolor   Panavision
Columbia / Filmways (Martin Ransohoff,
  John Calley)

During World War II seven battle-weary
American soldiers occupy a 10th-century castle
filled with art treasures, then die defending it.
Or are they dead all the time? The film version of
this fantastic novel never seems quite sure, and
the uncertainty finally deadens it despite careful
work all round.

w Daniel Taradash, David Rayfiel, *novel*
William Eastlake d Sydney Pollack ph Henri
Decaë m Michel Legrand

Burt Lancaster, Peter Falk, Jean Pierre Aumont,
Patrick O'Neal, Al Freeman Jnr, Scott Wilson,
Tony Bill, Bruce Dern, Astrid Heeren

Castle on the Hudson*

US 1940   77m   bw
Warner (Sam Bischoff)
GB title: *Years without Days*

A hardened criminal is not helped by his years in
prison.
Adequate, gloomy remake of *Twenty Thousand
Years in Sing Sing*.

w Seton I. Miller, Brown Holmes, Courtney
Terrett d Anatole Litvak ph Arthur Edeson

John Garfield, Pat O'Brien, Ann Sheridan,
Burgess Meredith, Jerome Cowan, Henry
O'Neill, Guinn Williams, John Litel

Cat and Mouse*

GB 1958   79m   bw
(Eros) Anvil (Paul Rotha)

The daughter of a man executed for murder is

threatened by criminals seeking hidden loot.
Interesting rather than exciting second feature
thriller directed by a documentary maker.

wd Paul Rotha, *novel* Michael Halliday
ph Wolfgang Suschitsky

Lee Patterson, Ann Sears, Hilton Edwards,
Victor Maddern, George Rose, Roddy
McMillan

The Cat and the Canary***
US 1927 84m (24 fps) bw silent
Universal

Greedy relatives assemble in an old house to
hear an eccentric's will, and a young girl's sanity
is threatened.
Archetypal spooky house comedy horror, here
given an immensely stylish production which
influenced Hollywood through the thirties and
was spoofed in *The Old Dark House*.

*w Alfred Cohn, Robert F. Hill, play John
Willard d Paul Leni ph Gilbert Warrenton
ad Charles D. Hall*

Creighton Hale, Laura La Plante, Forrest
Stanley, Tully Marshall, Flora Finch, Gertrude
Astor, Arthur Carewe
† Remade for sound by Rupert Julian in 1931 as
The Cat Creeps, with Raymond Hackett, Helen
Twelvetrees and Jean Hersholt. This title was
also used for a grade Z 1946 second feature with
a different plot.

The Cat and the Canary***
US 1939 72m bw
Paramount (Arthur Hornblow Jnr)

A superbly staged remake, briskly paced,
perfectly cast and lusciously photographed. The
comedy-thriller par excellence, with Bob Hope
fresh and sympathetic in his first big star part.

*w Walter de Leon, Lynn Starling d Elliott
Nugent ph Charles Lang m Dr Ernst Toch
ad Hans Dreier, Robert Usher*

*Bob Hope, Paulette Goddard, Gale
Sondergaard, John Beal, Douglass
Montgomery, Nydia Westman, Elizabeth
Patterson, John Wray, George Zucco*
  'Beautifully shot, intelligently constructed.'—
Peter John Dyer, 1966

Cat Ballou**
US 1965 96m Technicolor
Columbia (Harold Hecht)

Young Catherine Ballou hires a drunken
gunfighter to protect her father from a vicious
gunman, but despite his efforts he is shot, so she
turns outlaw.
Sometimes lively, sometimes somnolent western
spoof which considering the talent involved

should have been funnier than it is. The linking
ballad helps.

*w Walter Newman, Frank R. Pierson, novel Roy
Chanslor d Eliot Silverstein ph Jack Marta
m Frank de Vol*

Jane Fonda, *Lee Marvin*, Michael Callan,
Dwayne Hickman, Nat King Cole, Stubby
Kaye, Tom Nardini, John Marley, Reginald
Denny
  'Uneven, lumpy, coy and obvious.'—*Pauline
Kael*

AA: Lee Marvin
AAN: Walter Newman, Frank R. Pierson;
Frank de Vol; song 'The Ballad of Cat Ballou'
(*m* Jerry Livingston, *ly* Mack David)

The Cat Creeps see The Cat and the Canary
(1927)

The Cat from Outer Space
US 1978 103m Technicolor
Walt Disney Productions (Ron Miller)

A superintelligent extraterrestrial cat is forced to
land on earth for running repairs.
Fairly modest studio offering which pleased its
intended market but could have been sharper.

*w Ted Key d Norman Tokar ph Charles F.
Wheeler m Lalo Schifrin sp Eustace Lycett, Art
Cruickshank, Danny Dee*

Ken Berry, Roddy McDowall, Sandy Duncan,
Harry Morgan, McLean Stevenson, Jesse White,
Alan Young, Hans Conried

Cat on a Hot Tin Roof**
US 1958 108m Metrocolor
MGM (Lawrence Weingarten)

A rich plantation owner, dying of cancer, finds
his two sons unsatisfactory: one is a conniver,
the other a neurotic who refuses to sleep with his
wife.
Slightly bowdlerized version of Tennessee
Williams' most straightforward melodrama,
watchable for the acting but still basically a
theatrical experience.

*w Richard Brooks, James Poe d Richard
Brooks ph William Daniels m uncredited*

Paul Newman, Burl Ives, Elizabeth Taylor, Jack
Carson, Judith Anderson, Madeleine Sherwood,
Larry Gates

AAN: best picture; Richard Brooks, James Poe;
Richard Brooks (as director); William Daniels;
Paul Newman; Elizabeth Taylor

Cat People**
US 1942 73m bw
RKO (*Val Lewton*)

A beautiful Yugoslavian girl believes she can turn into a panther; before she is found mysteriously dead, several of her acquaintances are attacked by such a beast.

The first of Lewton's famous horror series for RKO is a slow starter but has some notable suspense sequences. It was also the first monster film to refrain from showing its monster.

w De Witt Bodeen d Jacques Tourneur
ph Nicholas Musuraca m Roy Webb

Simone Simon, Kent Smith, Tom Conway, Jane Randolph, Jack Holt

'(Lewton) revolutionized scare movies with suggestion, imaginative sound effects and camera angles, leaving everything to the fear-filled imagination.'—Pauline Kael, 1968
† Curse of the Cat People (qv) was a very unrelated sequel.

Catch Me a Spy

GB 1971 94m Technicolor
Rank / Ludgate / Capitol / Films de la Pleiade (Steven
Pallos)

A British agent smuggling Russian manuscripts into England falls for the wife of a Russian spy and finally gets his money as well.
Complex, patchy comedy thriller with dispirited action scenes in Bucharest and Scotland. Technical credits rather dim.

w Dick Clement, Ian La Frenais, novel George Marton, Tibor Meray d Dick Clement
ph Christopher Challis m Claude Bolling

Kirk Douglas, Trevor Howard, Tom Courtenay, Marlene Jobert, Patrick Mower, Bernadette Lafont, Bernard Blier

Catch 22 *

US 1970 122m Technicolor Panavision
Paramount (John Calley, Martin Ransohoff)

At a US Air Force base in the Mediterranean during World War II, one by one the officers are distressingly killed; a survivor paddles towards neutral Sweden.
Intensely black comedy, more so than M*A*S*H and less funny, effectively mordant in places but too grisly and missing several tricks.

w Buck Henry, novel Joseph Heller d Mike Nichols ph David Watkin m none pd Richard Sylbert

Alan Arkin, Martin Balsam, Richard Benjamin, Art Garfunkel, Jack Gilford, Buck Henry, Bob Newhart, Anthony Perkins, Paula Prentiss, Jon Voight, Martin Sheen, Orson Welles

'There are startling effects and good revue touches here and there, but the picture keeps going on and on, as if it were determined to impress us.'—New Yorker, 1977

Catch Us if You Can

GB 1965 91m bw
Anglo Amalgamated / Bruton (David Deutsch)
US title: Having a Wild Weekend

Freelance stuntmen have various adventures in the west of England.
The first film of a pretentious director is a bright but wearisomely high-spirited imitation of A Hard Day's Night.

w Peter Nichols d John Boorman ph Manny Wynn m Dave Clark

The Dave Clark Five, Barbara Ferris, David Lodge, Robin Bailey, Yootha Joyce

The Catered Affair *

US 1956 93m bw
MGM (Sam Zimbalist)
GB title: Wedding Breakfast

When the daughter of a New York taxi driver gets married, her mother insists on a bigger function than they can afford.
Rather heavy-going comedy with amusing dialogue, from the period when Hollywood was seizing on TV plays like Marty and Twelve Angry Men.

w Gore Vidal, TV play Paddy Chayevsky
d Richard Brooks ph John Alton m André Previn

Bette Davis, Ernest Borgnine, Debbie Reynolds, Barry Fitzgerald, Rod Taylor, Robert Simon, Madge Kennedy, Dorothy Stickney

Catherine the Great *

GB 1934 93m bw
Alexander Korda

How Catherine married the mad prince and slowly conquered the Russian court.
Dated but well acted and written account, sober by comparison with The Scarlet Empress which came out at the same time.

w Lajos Biro, Arthur Wimperis, Marjorie Deans, play The Czarina by Melchior Lengyel, Lajos Biro d Paul Czinner

Elisabeth Bergner, Douglas Fairbanks Jnr, Flora Robson, Gerald du Maurier, Irene Vanbrugh, Griffiths Jones, Joan Gardner, Diana Napier

Catlow *

GB 1971 101m Metrocolor
MGM / Euan Lloyd

A maverick cattleman tricks his enemies and winds up as sheriff.

Light-hearted, cheerfully cast, fast-moving, Spanish-located western.

w Scot Finch, J. J. Griffith, *novel* Louis L'Amour *d* Sam Wanamaker *ph* Ted Scaife *m* Roy Budd

Yul Brynner, Leonard Nimoy, Richard Crenna, Daliah Lavi, Jo Ann Pflug, Jeff Corey, Bessie Love, David Ladd

Cattle King
US 1963 90m Metrocolor
MGM (Nat Holt)
GB title: *Guns of Wyoming*

A big rancher opposes a cattle trail and starts a range war.
Moderately expert but very familiar star western.

w Thomas Thompson *d* Tay Garnett *ph* William E. Snyder

Robert Taylor, Joan Caulfield, Robert Middleton, Robert Loggia, Larry Gates, Malcolm Atterbury

Caught*
US 1948 88m bw
Enterprise (Wolfgang Reinhardt)

The ill-treated wife of a vicious millionaire leaves him for a doctor, but finds she is to have the millionaire's baby.
Pretentious *film noir*, rather typical of its time, with much talent squandered on a very boring plot.

w Arthur Laurents, *novel* Wild Calendar by Libbie Block *d* Max Ophuls *ph* Lee Garmes *m* Frederick Hollander

James Mason (the doctor), Robert Ryan (the millionaire), Barbara Bel Geddes, Natalie Schaefer, Curt Bois

Caught in the Draft**
US 1941 82m bw
Paramount (B. G. De Sylva)

A nervous film star cannot avoid being drafted into the army.
Sprightly comedy from the star's best period, with gags and supporting cast well up to form.

w Harry Tugend *d* David Butler *ph* Karl Struss *m* Victor Young

Bob Hope, Lynne Overman, Dorothy Lamour, Clarence Kolb, Eddie Bracken, Paul Hurst, Irving Bacon

Cause for Alarm*
US 1951 74m bw
MGM (Tom Lewis)

A housewife tries frantically to retrieve a posted letter containing manufactured evidence which may put her on a murder charge.
Minor-league suspenser, watchable but disappointingly handled.

w Mel Dinelli, Tom Lewis *d* Tay Garnett *ph* Joe Ruttenberg *m* André Previn

Loretta Young, Barry Sullivan, Bruce Cowling, Margalo Gillmore, Irving Bacon

Cavalcade**
US 1933 109m bw
Fox (Winfield Sheehan)

The story of an upper-class English family between the Boer War and World War I.
Rather static version of the famous stage spectacular, very similar in setting and style to TV's later *Upstairs Downstairs*. Good performances, flat handling.

w Reginald Berkeley, *play* Noel Coward *d* Frank Lloyd *ph* Ernest Palmer *war scenes* William Cameron Menzies *ad* William Darling

Clive Brook, Diana Wynyard, Ursula Jeans, Herbert Mundin, Una O'Connor, Irene Browne, Merle Tottenham, Beryl Mercer, Frank Lawton, Billy Bevan

'If there is anything that moves the ordinary American to uncontrollable tears, it is the plight—the constant plight—of dear old England . . . a superlative newsreel, forcibly strengthened by factual scenes, good music, and wonderful photography.'—*Pare Lorentz*

AA: best picture; Frank Lloyd
AAN: Diana Wynyard

Ceiling Zero*
US 1935 95m bw
Warner / Cosmopolitan (Harry Joe Brown)

Amorous and airborne adventures of an irresponsible but brilliant civil airlines pilot.
Splendid star vehicle which turns maudlin in the last reel but until then provides crackling entertainment.

w Frank 'Spig' Wead, from his play *d* Howard Hawks *ph* Arthur Edeson

James Cagney, Pat O'Brien, June Travis, Stuart Erwin, Henry Wadsworth, Isabel Jewell, Barton Maclane

'The best of all airplane pictures.'—*Otis Ferguson, 1939*
'Directed at a breakneck pace which emphasizes its lean fibre and its concentration on the essentials of its theme.'—*Andrew Sarris, 1963*

† Remade in 1939 as *International Squadron*.

Cela s'appelle l'Aurore*

France / Italy 1955   108m   bw
Marceau / Laetitia

A Corsican company doctor falls for a young widow while his wife is on holiday, and events lead to tragedy.

Efficient melodrama, given an extra dimension by its *auteur*.

w Luis Bunuel, Jean Ferry, *novel* Emmanuel Robles d Luis Bunuel ph Robert Le Fèbvre m Joseph Kosma

Georges Marchal, Lucia Bose, Gianni Esposito, Julien Bertheau, *Henri Nassiet*

Cell 2455 Death Row

US 1955   77m   bw
Columbia (Wallace MacDonald)

A convicted murderer staves off execution with appeal after appeal.

Cheap run-off of the case of Caryl Chessman, who was executed ten years after his trial for rape and murder. Retold in a 1977 TV movie, *Kill Me If You Can*.

w Jack de Witt, *book* Caryl Chessman d Fred F. Sears ph Fred Jackman Jnr md Mischa Bakaleinikoff

William Campbell, Kathryn Grant, Harvey Stephens, Marian Carr, Vince Edwards

Centennial Summer**

US 1946   102m   Technicolor
TCF (Otto Preminger)

A Philadelphia family responds to the Great Exposition of 1876.

Pleasing family comedy with music, the kind of harmless competence Hollywood used to throw off with ease but can no longer manage.

w Michael Kanin, *novel* Albert E. Idell d Otto Preminger ph Ernest Palmer m Alfred Newman *songs* Jerome Kern, Oscar Hammerstein II, E. Y. Harburg, Leo Robin

Jeanne Crain, Cornel Wilde, Linda Darnell, William Eythe, Walter Brennan, *Constance Bennett*, Dorothy Gish

AAN: Alfred Newman; song 'All Through the Day' (*m* Jerome Kern, *ly* Oscar Hammerstein II)

The Ceremony

US / Spain 1963   107m   bw
UA / Magla (Laurence Harvey)

In a Tangier jail, a bank robber awaits the firing squad, but he and his brother have an escape plan.

Murky and pretentious melodrama with aspirations to high style and symbolism. A bore.

w Ben Barzman, *novel* Frederic Grendel

d Laurence Harvey ph Oswald Morris m Gerard Schurmann

Laurence Harvey, Sarah Miles, Robert Walker, John Ireland, Ross Martin, Lee Patterson, Jack McGowran, Murray Melvin, Fernando Rey

A Certain Smile*

US 1958   105m   Eastmancolor
Cinemascope
TCF (Henry Ephron)

A girl student falls in love with her philandering uncle.

Another sordid novella by Françoise Sagan (see *Bonjour Tristesse*), transformed by Hollywood into a glowing romantic saga of life among the Riviera rich. On this level, very competent.

w Frances Goodrich, Albert Hackett d Jean Negulesco ph Milton Krasner m Alfred Newman

Christine Carere, Rossano Brazzi, Joan Fontaine, Bradford Dillman, Eduard Franz, Kathryn Givney, Steve Geray

AAN: title song (*m* Sammy Fain, *ly* Paul Francis Webster)

Cervantes

Spain / Italy / France 1968   119m
Eastmancolor   Supertotalvision
Prisma / Protor / Procinex (Alexander Salkind)

Cervantes, an assistant papal envoy, helps persuade Philip of Spain to join the Holy League, then turns soldier and has various adventures.

Rather boring spectacular with conventional set pieces.

w Enrique Llovet, Enrico Bomba, *novel* Bruno Frank d Vincent Sherman ph Edmond Richard m Jean Ledrut

Horst Buchholz, Gina Lollobrigida, Louis Jourdan, Jose Ferrer, Fernando Rey, Francisco Rabal

César see Marius

César and Rosalie*

France / Italy / West Germany 1972   105m
Eastmancolor
Fildebroc / UPS / Mega Paramount / Orion
(Michèle de Broca)

A divorcee living with a rich merchant becomes attracted to a young artist. Unexpectedly, the two men become friends . . .

Wryly amusing comedy for adults.

w Jean-Loup Dabadie, Claude Sautet d Claude Sautet ph Jean Boffety m Philippe Sarde
Yves Montand, Romy Schneider, Sami Frey, Umberto Orsini

Chad Hanna*
US 1940   86m   Technicolor
TCF (Darryl F. Zanuck, Nunnally Johnson)

Life in a New York state circus in the 1840s.
Mild romantic drama from a bestseller; local
colour excellent, dramatic interest thin.

w Nunnally Johnson, *novel* Red Wheels Rolling
by Walter D. Edmonds d Henry King
ph Ernest Palmer m David Buttolph

Henry Fonda, Dorothy Lamour, Linda Darnell,
Guy Kibbee, Jane Darwell, John Carradine, Ted
North, Roscoe Ates

Chain Lightning
US 1950   94m   bw
Warner (Anthony Veiller)

After World War II a bomber pilot learns how to
control the new jets.
Absolutely routine romance and heroics.

w Liam O'Brien, Vincent Evans d Stuart
Heisler ph Ernest Haller m David Buttolph

Humphrey Bogart, Eleanor Parker, Raymond
Massey, Richard Whorf, James Brown, Roy
Roberts, Morris Ankrum

Chained*
US 1934   77m   bw
MGM (Hunt Stromberg)

A devoted wife has a shipboard romance with
another man.
Moderate star romantic drama.

w John Lee Mahin d Clarence Brown
ph George Folsey m Herbert Stothart

Joan Crawford, Clark Gable, Otto Kruger,
Stuart Erwin, Una O'Connor, Akim Tamiroff

The Chalk Garden*
GB 1964   106m   Technicolor
U-I / Quota Rentals (Ross Hunter)

The governess in a melancholy household has an
effect on the lives of her aged employer and the
young granddaughter.
Sub-Chekhovian drama in a house by the sea,
flattened by routine handling into something
much less interesting than it was on the stage.

w John Michael Hayes, *novel* Enid Bagnold
d Ronald Neame ph Arthur Ibbetson
m Malcolm Arnold

Edith Evans, Deborah Kerr, Hayley Mills, John
Mills, Felix Aylmer, Elizabeth Sellars, Lally
Bowers, Toke Townley

'Crashing symbolism, cracker-motto
sententiousness.'—
MFB

AAN: Edith Evans

A Challenge for Robin Hood*
GB 1967   96m   Technicolor
Hammer (Clifford Parkes)

A retelling of the original Robin Hood legend.
Unassuming, lively, predictable adventure
hokum.

w Peter Bryan d C. Pennington-Richards
ph Arthur Grant m Gary Hughes

Barrie Ingham, James Hayter, Leon Greene,
John Arnatt

Chamber of Horrors
US 1966   99m   Warnercolor
Warner (Hy Averback)

A maniacal murderer is finally trapped by two
amateur criminologists who run a wax museum
in Baltimore.
Zany horror thriller originally meant for TV; it
turned out a shade too harrowing. Advertised as
'the picture with the Fear Flasher and the Horror
Horn', shock gimmicks which proved much
more startling than the crude events they
heralded.

w Stephen Kandel d Hy Averback ph Richard
Kline m William Lava

Patrick O'Neal, Cesare Danova, Wilfrid Hyde
White, Laura Devon, Patrice Wymore, Suzy
Parker, Jeanette Nolan, Tony Curtis (guest)

The Champ*
US 1931   87m   bw
MGM

A young boy has faith in a washed-up
prizefighter.
Maudlin drama, highly commercial in its day
and a box office tonic for its two stars. Remade
as *The Clown* (qv).

w Leonard Praskins, Frances Marion d King
Vidor ph Gordon Avil

Wallace Beery, Jackie Cooper, Irene Rich,
Roscoe Ates, Edward Brophy

AA: Leonard Praskins, Frances Marion;
Wallace Beery
AAN: best picture; King Vidor

Champagne Charlie*
GB 1944   107m   bw
Ealing (John Croydon)

The life of Victorian music hall singer George
Leybourne and his rivalry with the Great Vance.
Careful period reconstruction and good songs
and acting are somehow nullified by
unsympathetic handling and photography.

w Austin Melford, Angus Macphail, John
Dighton d Alberto Cavalcanti

Tommy Trinder, Stanley Holloway, Betty

Warren, Austin Trevor, Jean Kent, Guy
Middleton, Frederick Piper, Harry Fowler

Champagne for Caesar*
US 1950   99m   bw
Cardinal (George Moskov)

A self-confessed genius with a grudge against a
soap company determines to win astronomical
sums on its weekly radio quiz.
Agreeable, mildly satirical star comedy which
tends to peter out halfway.

w Hans Jacoby, Fred Brady d Richard Whorf
ph Paul Ivano m Dmitri Tiomkin

Ronald Colman, Vincent Price, Celeste Holm,
Barbara Britton, Art Linkletter

The Champagne Murders
France 1967   107m   Techniscope
Universal (France) (Jacques Natteau)
original title: *Le Scandale*

A disturbed champagne millionaire thinks he
may be a murderer.
Complex but uninvolving mystery story in which
the director's eye seems to be more on satire than
on narrative.

w Claude Brûlé, Derek Prouse, Paul Gégauff
d Claude Chabrol ph Jean Rabier m Pierre
Jansen

Anthony Perkins, Maurice Ronet, Stéphane
Audran, Yvonne Furneaux, Suzanne Lloyd

Champion**
US 1949   99m   bw
Stanley Kramer

An ambitious prizefighter alienates his friends
and family, and dies of injuries received in the
ring.
Interesting exposé of the fight racket, presented
in good cinematic style and acted with great
bravura.

w Carl Foreman, story Ring Lardner d Mark
Robson ph Franz Planer m Dmitri Tiomkin

Kirk Douglas, Arthur Kennedy, Marilyn
Maxwell, Paul Stewart, Ruth Roman, Lola
Albright, Luis Van Rooten

AAN: Carl Foreman; Franz Planer; Dmitri
Tiomkin; Kirk Douglas; Arthur Kennedy

Chance of a Lifetime*
GB 1950   93m   bw
Pilgrim Pictures (Bernard Miles)

The owner of a small engineering works,
impatient with the unionism of his men, gives
them a chance to run the factory themselves.
Quiet comedy-drama on sub-Ealing lines;

always interesting, it never quite catches fire
despite a reliable cast.

w Walter Greenwood, Bernard Miles d Bernard
Miles ph Eric Cross

Bernard Miles, Basil Radford, Niall MacGinnis,
Geoffrey Keen, Julien Mitchell, Josephine
Wilson, Kenneth More, Hattie Jacques

Chandu the Magician*
US 1932   74m   bw
Fox

A spiritualist battles against a madman with a
death ray which could destroy the world.
Rather dim serial-like thriller, with interesting
talent not at its best.

w Philip Klein, Barry Conners d Marcel Varnel,
William Cameron Menzies ph James Wong
Howe

Edmund Lowe, Bela Lugosi, Irene Ware,
Herbert Mundin, Henry B. Walthall

Chang**
US 1927   71m (24 fps)   bw   silent
Paramount

The life of a rice-grower in Thailand.
Influential but now rather boring documentary
with animal interest.

wd, ph, ed Merian C. Cooper, Ernest B.
Schoedsack

Change of Heart
US 1934   74m   bw
Fox

Four young California students make good in
New York.
Minor fairy tale which marked the last of twelve
teamings for Gaynor and Farrell.

w Sonya Levien, James Gleason, Samuel
Hoffenstein, novel Kathleen Norris d John G.
Blystone ph Joseph Aiken

Janet Gaynor, Charles Farrell, Ginger Rogers,
James Dunn, Beryl Mercer, Gustav Von
Seyffertitz, Shirley Temple

Change of Mind
US 1969   98m   Eastmancolor
Sagittarius (Seeleg Lester, Richard Wesson)

The life of a liberal white DA can only be 'saved'
by transplanting his brain into the body of a dead
black man.
Fantasy melodrama with a social conscience,
about a half-and-half which is acceptable to
neither whites nor blacks. Very obvious and
rather boring.

w Seeleg Lester, Richard Wesson d Robert
Stevens ph Arthur J. Ornitz m Duke Ellington

Raymond St Jacques, Susan Oliver, Janet
McLachlan, Leslie Nielsen

Chapayev*
USSR 1934   94m   bw
Lenfilm

Exploits of a Red Army commander during the
1919 battles.
Moderately striking propaganda piece.

wd Sergei and Georgy Vasiliev *ph* Alexander
Sigayev *m* Gavril Popov

Boris Babochkin, B. Blinov, Leonid Kmit

The Chapman Report
US 1962   125m   Technicolor
(Warner) Darryl F. Zanuck (Richard D. Zanuck)

Dr Chapman conducts a study of female sex
behaviour in an American suburb.
Influenced by the Kinsey report, this
melodramatic compendium takes itself far too
seriously, and the director's smooth style is
barely in evidence.

w Wyatt Cooper, Don M. Mankiewicz, *novel*
Irving Wallace *d* George Cukor *ph* Harold
Lipstein *m* Leonard Rosenman

Shelley Winters, Claire Bloom, *Glynis Johns*,
Efrem Zimbalist Jnr, Jane Fonda, Ray Danton,
Ty Hardin, Andrew Duggan, John Dehner,
Henry Daniell, Corey Allen, Harold J. Stone
  'We had a preview which went very well, and
then it was sent over to Mr Zanuck, who did
what I thought was a most horrendous job of
cutting it up.'—*George Cukor*

Charade**
US 1964   113m   Technicolor
Universal / Stanley Donen

A Parisienne finds her husband murdered. Four
strange men are after her, and she is helped by a
handsome stranger . . . but is he hero, spy or
murderer?
Smoothly satisfying sub-Hitchcock nonsense,
effective both as black romantic comedy and
macabre farce.

w Peter Stone *d* Stanley Donen *ph* Charles
Lang Jnr *m* Henry Mancini

Cary Grant (sixty but concealing the fact by
taking a shower fully clothed), *Audrey Hepburn,
Walter Matthau*, James Coburn, George
Kennedy, Ned Glass, Jacques Marin

AAN: song 'Charade' (*m* Henry Mancini,
ly Johnny Mercer)

The Charge at Feather River*
US 1953   96m   Warnercolor
Warner (David Weisbart)

An army platoon composed of men from the
guardhouse tries to rescue two women
kidnapped by Indians.
Formula western distinguished by 3-D
photography, probably the best to be achieved in
the brief life of the medium. Warnerphonic sound
was less successfully added; the sum total would
be trying for nervous people.

w James **R**. Webb *d* Gordon Douglas
ph Peverell Marley m Max Steiner

Guy Madison, Frank Lovejoy, Vera Miles,
Helen Westcott, Dick Wesson, Onslow Stevens,
Steve Brodie
  'From the start we are involved in a whirl of
frenzied activity: a cavalry charge, knife
throwing, sabre practice, flaming arrows—not a
trick missed.'—*MFB*

The Charge of the Light Brigade***
US 1936   115m   bw
Warner (Hal B. Wallis, Sam Bischoff)

An army officer deliberately starts the Balaclava
charge to even an old score with Surat Khan,
who's on the other side.
Though allegedly 'based on the poem by Alfred
Lord Tennyson', this is no more than a travesty
of history, most of it taking place in India. As
pure entertainment however it is a most superior
slice of Hollywood hokum and the film which set
the seal on Errol Flynn's superstardom.

w Michael Jacoby, Rowland Leigh *d Michael
Curtiz ph* Sol Polito, Fred Jackman *m* Max
Steiner

Errol Flynn, Olivia de Havilland, Patric
Knowles, Donald Crisp, C. Aubrey Smith,
David Niven, Henry Stephenson, Nigel Bruce,
C. Henry Gordon, Spring Byington, E. E. Clive,
Lumsden Hare, Robert Barrat, J. Carrol Naish

The Charge of the Light Brigade
GB 1968   141m   De Luxe   Panavision
US / Woodfall (Neil Hartley)

An historical fantasia with comic, sociological
and cartoon embellishments.
This version for the swinging sixties has a few
splendid moments but apes *Tom Jones* all too
obviously and leaves audiences with an even
dimmer view of history than they started with.

w Charles Wood *d* Tony Richardson *ph* David
Watkin, Peter Suschitsky *m* John Addison
animation Richard Williams ad Edward
Marshall

Trevor Howard, John Gielgud, David
Hemmings, Vanessa Redgrave, Jill Bennett,
Harry Andrews, Peter Bowles, Mark Burns
  'Considering the lucid book on which it is
largely based, it is almost as inexcusably

muddled as the British commanders at
Balaclava.'—*John Simon*
    'The point of the film is to recreate mid-
Victorian England in spirit and detail.'—*Stanley
Kauffmann*
    'Notions for at least three interesting films are
on view . . . what seems signally lacking is a
guiding hand, an overriding purpose.'—*John
Coleman*

Charley and the Angel*
US 1974   93m   Technicolor
Walt Disney (Bill Anderson)

A small-town sporting goods storekeeper in the
thirties escapes death three times and finds an
impatient angel waiting for him.
Mild sentimental whimsy on the lines of *On
Borrowed Time*, but with a happy ending and
attractive period trappings.

w Roswell Rogers, *novel* The Golden Evenings
of Summer by Will Stanton *d* Vincent
McEveety *ph* Charles F. Wheeler *m* Buddy
Baker

Fred MacMurray, Cloris Leachmann, Harry
Morgan, Kurt Russell, Kathleen Cody, Edward
Andrews, Barbara Nichols

Charley Moon*
GB 1956   92m   Eastmancolor
Colin Lesslie, Aubrey Baring

A music hall comic becomes swollen-headed but
returns to his home village and marries his
childhood sweetheart.
Faltering musical lacking the gusto of its
background, but providing a generally believable
impression of life on the halls.

w/songs Leslie Bricusse, *novel* Reginald Arkell
d Guy Hamilton *ph* Jack Hildyard

Max Bygraves, Dennis Price, Michael Medwin,
Florence Desmond, Shirley Eaton, Patricia
Driscoll, Reginald Beckwith

Charley Varrick**
US 1973   111m   Technicolor
Universal (Don Siegel)

A bank robber discovers he has stolen Mafia
money, and devises a clever scheme to get
himself off the hook.
Sharp, smart, well-observed but implausible
thriller, astringently handled and agreeably set in
Californian backlands. Accomplished,
forgettable entertainment.

w Howard Rodman, Dean Reisner, *novel* The
Looters by John Reese *d* Don Siegel
ph Michael Butler *m* Lalo Schifrin

Walter Matthau, Joe Don Baker, Felicia Farr,

Andy Robinson, John Vernon, Sheree North,
Norman Fell
    'It proves there is nothing wrong with an
auteur director that a good script can't cure.'—
Stanley Kauffmann
    'The narrative line is clean and direct, the
characterizations economical and functional,
and the triumph of intelligence gloriously
satisfying.'—*Andrew Sarris*

Charley's Aunt**
US 1941   81m   bw
TCF (William Perlberg)
GB title: *Charley's American Aunt*

For complicated reasons, an Oxford
undergraduate has to impersonate his own rich
aunt from Brazil (where the nuts come from).
Very adequate version of the Victorian farce,
with all concerned in excellent form.

w George Seaton, *play* Brandon Thomas
d Archie Mayo *ph* Peverell Marley *m* Alfred
Newman *ad* Richard Day, Nathan Juran

Jack Benny, Kay Francis, James Ellison, Anne
Baxter, *Laird Cregar*, Edmund Gwenn,
Reginald Owen, Richard Haydn, Arleen
Whelan, Ernest Cossart
† See also: *Where's Charley?*

Charley's Big-Hearted Aunt
GB 1940   76m   bw
Gainsborough (Edward Black)

Rather disappointing British version of the
famous farce, dully assembled and rather
unsuitably cast.

w Marriott Edgar, Val Guest *d* Walter Forde

Arthur Askey, Phyllis Calvert, Moore Marriott,
Graham Moffatt, Richard Murdoch, Jeanne de
Casalis, J. H. Roberts, Felix Aylmer, Wally
Patch

Charlie Bubbles***
GB 1968   91m   Technicolor
Universal / Memorial (Michael Medwin,
    George Pitcher)

A successful novelist loathes the pointlessness of
the good life and tries unsuccessfully to return to
his northern working class background.
A little arid and slow in its early stages, and with
a rather lame end (our hero escapes by air
balloon), this is nevertheless a fascinating,
fragmentary character study with a host of wry
comedy touches and nimbly sketched
characters; in its unassuming way it indicts
many of the symbols people lived by in the
sixties.

*w Shelagh Delaney d Albert Finney ph Peter
Suschitsky m* Mischa Donat

Albert Finney, Billie Whitelaw, Liza Minnelli, Colin Blakely, Timothy Garland, Diana Coupland, Alan Lake, Yootha Joyce, Joe Gladwin

'A modest thing, but like all good work in minor keys it has a way of haunting the memory.'—*Richard Schickel*

Charlie Chan

The Oriental detective created by Earl Derr Biggers began his film career as a minor character (played by George Kuwa) in a 1926 serial called HOUSE WITHOUT A KEY. In 1928 Kamiyama Sojin had a bigger role in THE CHINESE PARROT, but in 1929 E. L. Park did almost nothing in BEHIND THAT CURTAIN. In 1931 however began the fully-fledged Chan movies, which entertained a generation. Chan, based on a real-life Chinese detective named Chang Apana, became a citizen of Honolulu and was developed as a polite family man, aided by his impulsive number one or number two son (out of a family of fourteen), in solving murder puzzles. He had a treasury of aphorisms (a whole book of which has been published), and his technique was to gather all the suspects into one room before unmasking one as the murderer. The films built to a peak around 1936–9, but tailed off disastrously in the mid-forties. They were never noted for production values, but many retain interest for their scripts, their puzzles, and their casts of budding stars, as well as the central character. This is a complete list:

For Fox (later Twentieth Century Fox), with *Warner Oland* as Chan:
1931: CHARLIE CHAN CARRIES ON*, THE BLACK CAMEL
1932: CHARLIE CHAN'S CHANCE
1933: CHARLIE CHAN'S GREATEST CASE
1934: CHARLIE CHAN'S COURAGE, CHARLIE CHAN IN LONDON
1935: CHARLIE CHAN IN PARIS*, CHARLIE CHAN IN EGYPT, CHARLIE CHAN IN SHANGHAI
1936: CHARLIE CHAN'S SECRET*, CHARLIE CHAN AT THE CIRCUS*, CHARLIE CHAN AT THE RACE TRACK, CHARLIE CHAN AT THE OPERA**
1937: CHARLIE CHAN AT THE OLYMPICS, CHARLIE CHAN ON BROADWAY*, CHARLIE CHAN AT MONTE CARLO

For Twentieth Century Fox, with *Sidney Toler*:
1938: CHARLIE CHAN IN HONOLULU
1939: CHARLIE CHAN IN RENO, CHARLIE CHAN ON TREASURE ISLAND**, CITY OF DARKNESS

1940: CHARLIE CHAN IN PANAMA, CHARLIE CHAN'S MURDER CRUISE, CHARLIE CHAN AT THE WAX MUSEUM*, MURDER OVER NEW YORK
1941: DEAD MEN TELL, CHARLIE CHAN IN RIO, CASTLE IN THE DESERT*

For Monogram, with Sidney Toler:
1944: CHARLIE CHAN IN THE SECRET SERVICE, THE CHINESE CAT, BLACK MAGIC
1945: THE SCARLET CLUE, THE JADE MASK, SHANGHAI COBRA, RED DRAGON
1946: SHADOWS OVER CHINATOWN, DANGEROUS MONEY
1947: THE TRAP

For Monogram, with Roland Winters:
1947: THE CHINESE RING
1948: DOCKS OF NEW ORLEANS, SHANGHAI CHEST, THE GOLDEN EYE, THE FEATHERED SERPENT
1949: SKY DRAGON

In the late fifties J. Carrol Naish appeared in a half-hour TV series as Chan, but the episodes were dull. In 1971 Universal tried to revive the character in a 96-minute pilot film *Happiness is a Warm Clue*, but Ross Martin was woefully miscast.

Charlotte's Web

US 1972   96m   Technicolor
Hanna-Barbera for Sagittarius

Farmyard animals who sense their fate are stimulated and encouraged by a resourceful spider.
Interesting but overlong and rather plodding version of a stylish book for children; the animation has no style at all.

w Earl Hanmer Jnr, *novel* E. B. White *d* Charles A. Nichols, Iwao Takamoto

Charly*

US 1968   106m   Techniscope
Selmur / Robertson Associates (Ralph Nelson)

New methods of surgery cure a mentally retarded young man, who becomes a genius, but the effects wear off.
Smooth, unconvincing, rather pointless fantasy which ultimately leaves a bad taste in the mouth.

w Sterling Silliphant, *novel* Flowers for Algernon by Daniel Keyes *d* Ralph Nelson *ph* Arthur J. Ornitz *m* Ravi Shankar

Cliff Robertson, Claire Bloom, Leon Janney, Lilia Skala

'The most distressing thing about *Charly* is not its ticklish subject, nor yet its clumsily

modish surface, but its insistent, persistent
sentimentality.'—*Tom Milne*

AA: Cliff Robertson

Charro

US 1969 98m Technicolor Panavision
National General (Charles Marquis Warren)

A reformed outlaw is framed for the theft of a
cannon.
Dismal western with a singing star playing
straight. A bad experience.

wd Charles Marquis Warren *ph* Ellsworth
Fredericks *m* Hugo Montenegro

Elvis Presley, Ina Balin, Barbara Werle, Lynn
Kellogg, Victor French, Solomon Sturges

The Chase*

US 1947 84m bw
Nero Pictures (Seymour Nebenzal)

A shell-shocked ex-serviceman foils a criminal
and falls for his wife.
Weird Cuban-set *film noir* with a strange cast
and stranger atmosphere. A genuine bomb, but
worth a look for its pretensions, its cast, and its
trick ending.

w Philip Yordan, *novel* The Black Path of Fear
by Cornell Woolrich *d* Arthur Ripley *ph* Franz
Planer *m* Michel Michelet

Robert Cummings, Michèle Morgan, Peter
Lorre, Steve Cochran, Lloyd Corrigan, Jack
Holt

The Chase*

US 1966 135m Technicolor Panavision
Columbia / Sam Spiegel

When a convict escapes and heads for his small
Texas home town, almost all the inhabitants are
affected in one way or another.
Expensive but shoddy essay in sex and violence,
with Brando as a masochistic sheriff lording it
over Peyton-Place-in-all-but-name. Literate
moments do not atone for the general
pretentiousness, and we have all been here once
too often.

w Lillian Hellman, *novel* Horton Foote *d* Arthur
Penn *ph* Joseph La Shelle *pd* Richard Day
m John Barry

Marlon Brando, Jane Fonda, Robert Redford,
Angie Dickinson, Janice Rule, James Fox,
Robert Duvall, E. G. Marshall, Miriam Hopkins
Henry Hull

'The worst thing that has happened to movies
since Lassie played a war veteran with
amnesia.'—*Rex Reed*

'Considering all the talent connected with it, it
is hard to imagine how *The Chase* went so
haywire.'—*Philip T. Hartung*

Chase a Crooked Shadow**

GB 1957 87m bw
ABP / Associated Dragon Films (Douglas
Fairbanks Jnr)

An heiress finds her home invaded by a stranger
posing as her dead brother.
Tricksy, lightly controlled suspense melodrama
with a perfectly fair surprise ending. Handling
equivocal but competent.

w David D. Osborn, Charles Sinclair *d* Michael
Anderson *ph* Erwin Hillier *m* Matyas Seiber

Richard Todd, Anne Baxter, Faith Brook,
Herbert Lom, Alexander Knox, Alan Tilvern

† The plot was borrowed from an episode in *The
Whistler* TV series, and later reversed for a 1975
TV film, *One of my Wives is Missing*.

The Chastity Belt

Italy 1967 110m Eastmancolor
Warner / Julia (Francesco Mazzei)
aka: *On My Way to the Crusades I Met a Girl
Who . . .*

A 12th-century knight is called to the Crusades
just as he is consummating his marriage, and
when he locks his wife in a chastity belt she
follows him.
Abysmal international romp which looks nice
but is killed stone dead by writing, dubbing and
direction.

w Luigi Magni, Larry Gelbart *d* Pasquale Festa
Campanile *ph* Carlo di Palma *m* Riz Ortolani

Tony Curtis, Virna Lisi, Hugh Griffith, John
Richardson, Nino Castelnuovo

Chato's Land

GB 1971 100m Technicolor
UA / Scimitar (Michael Winner)

An Apache half-breed kills a man in self-defence,
subsequently eluding and destroying the sheriff's
posse.
Exhaustingly violent western in which the
audience is spared no gory detail; efficiently put
together for those who like this kind of fracas.

w Gerald Wilson *d* Michael Winner *ph* Robert
Paynter *m* Jerry Fielding

Charles Bronson, Jack Palance, Richard
Basehart, James Whitmore, Simon Oakland,
Richard Jordan, Ralph Waite, Victor French,
Lee Patterson

Chatterbox

US 1943 77m bw
Republic (Albert J. Cohen)

A radio cowboy gets a film contract but can't
stand horses.
Flat star comedy which borrows some well-worn
situations but handles them badly.

w George Carleton Brown, Frank Gill Jnr
d Joseph Santley *ph* Ernest Miller *md* Walter
Scharf

Joe E. Brown, Judy Canova, Rosemary Lane,
John Hubbard, Chester Clute

Che!
US 1969   94m   De Luxe   Panavision
TCF (Sy Bartlett)

Fidel Castro is helped in his subversion of
Batista's Cuban regime by an Argentinian
doctor named Che Guevara.
Fictionalized biography, and a dull one, of a man
who became a myth.

w Michael Wilson, Sy Bartlett *d* Richard
Fleischer *ph* Charles Wheeler *m* Lalo Schifrin

Omar Sharif, Jack Palance (as Castro), Cesare
Danova, Robert Loggia, Woody Strode,
Barbara Luna

The Cheap Detective
US 1978   92m   Metrocolor   Panavision
Columbia / Ray Stark

Forties private eye Lou Peckinpaugh is involved
in a complex case with echoes of *Casablanca*,
The Big Sleep, *The Maltese Falcon* and *Farewell
My Lovely*.
Lame spoof which might have seemed funnier on
a small screen in black and white; as it is, the
strain is evident and desperate.

w Neil Simon *d* Robert Moore *ph* John A.
Alonzo *m* Patrick Williams

Peter Falk (Bogart), John Houseman
(Greenstreet), Nicol Williamson (Veidt), *Louise
Fletcher* (Bergman), Fernando Lamas
(Henreid), Madeleine Kahn (Astor), Dom de
Luise (Lorre), Paul Williams (Cook), Marsha
Mason (Gladys George), Ann-Margret (Claire
Trevor), Eileen Brennan (Bacall), Stockard
Channing (Lee Patrick), Sid Caesar (Miles
Mander), Scatman Crothers (Dooley Wilson);
and James Coco, Phil Silvers, Abe Vigoda, Vic
Tayback
†The film was a follow-up to the not much more
effective but at least more controlled *Murder by
Death*.

Cheaper by the Dozen**
US 1950   86m   Technicolor
TCF (Lamar Trotti)

Efficiency expert Frank Gilbreth and his wife
Lillian have twelve children, a fact which
requires mathematical conduct of all their lives.
Amusing family comedy set in the twenties,
unconvincing in detail though based on a book
by two of the children. A great commercial

success and a Hollywood myth-maker. Sequel:
Belles on their Toes (qv).

w Lamar Trotti, *book* Frank B. Gilbreth Jnr,
Ernestine Gilbreth Carey *d* Walter Lang
ph Leon Shamroy *m* Cyril Mockridge
md Lionel Newman *ad* Lyle Wheeler, Leland
Fuller

Clifton Webb, Myrna Loy, Jeanne Crain, Edgar
Buchanan, Barbara Bates, Betty Lynn, Mildred
Natwick, Sara Allgood

The Cheat*
US 1915   95m (16 fps)   bw   silent
Famous Players Lasky / Paramount

A society lady borrows from a rich Japanese,
and he brands her when she refuses to become
his mistress.
Hoary melodrama which caused a sensation in
its day.

w Hector Turnbull *d* Cecil B. de Mille *ph* Alvin
Wyckoff

Fanny Ward, Jack Dean, Sessue Hayakawa,
James Neill
† Remade in 1923 by George Fitzmaurice, in
1931 by George Abbott, and in 1937 (in France,
as *Forfaiture*) by Marcel L'Herbier.

The Cheaters*
US 1945   86m   bw
Republic

A selfish and ostentatious family is reformed by
the ministrations of a down-and-out actor.
Fairly engaging variation on *The Passing of the
Third Floor Back*, with sweetness and light
brought into people's lives by a fireside recital of
A Christmas Carol.

w Francis Hyland *d* Joseph Kane

Joseph Schildkraut, Billie Burke, Eugene
Pallette, Ona Munson, Raymond Walburn

Check and Double Check
US 1932   71m   bw
RKO

Comic adventures of a couple of black
handymen.
Feeble comedy notable only for the film
appearance of radio's immensely popular Amos
'n Andy, played by white actors in blackface.

w Bert Kalmar, Harry Ruby, J. Walter Ruben
d Melville Brown *ph* William Marshall

Freeman F. Gosden, Charles V. Correll, Sue
Carol, Charles Morton, Irene Rich, Ralf
Harolde, Duke Ellington and his Orchestra

Checkpoint*
GB 1956   84m   Eastmancolor
Rank (Betty Box)

A tycoon sends an industrial spy to Italy in
search of new motor racing car designs.
Acceptable hokum, cleanly assembled, with
motor race highlights.

w Robin Estridge d Ralph Thomas ph Ernest
Steward m Bruce Montgomery

Anthony Steel, Stanley Baker, James Robertson
Justice, Odile Versois, Maurice Denham,
Michael Medwin, Lee Patterson

Cheers for Miss Bishop*
US 1941   94m   bw
Paramount (Richard A. Rowland)

The life of a schoolmistress in a small
midwestern town.
Acceptable sentimental hokum, quite pleasantly
done.

w Adelaide Heinbron, novel Bess Streeter
Aldrich d Tay Garnett ph Hal Mohr
m Edward Ward

Martha Scott, William Gargan, Edmund
Gwenn, Sterling Holloway, Sidney Blackmer,
Mary Anderson, Dorothy Petersen

AAN: Edward Ward

Cheyenne Autumn*
US 1964   170m   Technicolor   Panavision
70
Warner / Ford-Smith (Bernard Smith)

In the 1860s, Cheyenne Indians are moved to a
new reservation 1500 miles away; wanting aid,
they begin a trek back home, and various battles
follow.
Dispirited, shapeless John Ford western with
little of the master's touch; good to look at,
however, with effective cameos, notably an
irrelevant and out-of-key comic one featuring
James Stewart as Wyatt Earp.

w James R. Webb, novel Mari Sandoz d John
Ford ph William H. Clothier m Alex North

Richard Widmark, Carroll Baker, Karl Malden,
Dolores del Rio, Sal Mineo, Edward G.
Robinson, James Stewart, Ricardo Montalban,
Gilbert Roland, Arthur Kennedy, Patrick
Wayne, Elizabeth Allen, Victor Jory, John
Carradine, Mike Mazurki, John Qualen, George
O'Brien
   'Although one would like to praise the film for
its high-minded aims, it is hard to forget how
ponderous and disjointed it is.'—Moira Walsh
   'The acting is bad, the dialogue trite and
predictable, the pace funereal, the structure

fragmented and the climaxes puny.'—Stanley
Kauffmann

AAN: William H. Clothier

The Cheyenne Social Club*
US 1970   102m   Technicolor   Panavision
National General (James Lee Barrett, Gene
   Kelly)

Two itinerant cowboys inherit a high-class
brothel.
Disappointing star comedy western with
pleasing moments and a lively climactic shoot-
out. Perhaps the girls are just a shade too
winsome.

w James Lee Barrett d Gene Kelly ph William
H. Clothier m Walter Scharf

James Stewart, Henry Fonda, Shirley Jones, Sue
Anne Langdon, Robert Middleton, Arch
Johnson
   'Co-starring Shirley Jones and Rigor Mortis,
who enters early and stays through the very last
scene.'—Rex Reed

Chicago Calling*
US 1951   75m   bw
UA / Arrowhead / Joseph Justman (Peter
   Berneis)

A drunk cannot pay his phone bill and is waiting
for a vital call about his daughter's involvement
in a car crash.
Moderate, location-shot minor melodrama with
a few good ideas.

w John Reinhardt, Peter Berneis d John
Reinhardt ph Robert de Grasse

Dan Duryea, Mary Anderson, Gordon Gebert,
Ross Elliot

Chicago Deadline
US 1949   87m   bw
Paramount (Robert Fellows)

A reporter researches the life of a lonely girl who
died of tuberculosis.
Flat star vehicle consisting mainly of overplayed
cameos.

w Warren Duff, Tiffany Thayer d Lewis Allen
ph John F. Seitz m Victor Young

Alan Ladd, Donna Reed, June Havoc, Berry
Kroeger, Arthur Kennedy, Gavin Muir,
Shepperd Strudwick
   † Remade for TV as the TV movie Fame Is the
Name of the Game.

Chicken Every Sunday*
US 1949   94m   bw
TCF

The Hefferans have run a boarding house for

twenty years, but dad's wild schemes run away with any possible profit.

Archetypal, folksy, American small-town chronicle, reasonably well made, for an audience that now watches *The Waltons*.

w George Seaton, Valentine Davies *d* George Seaton *ph* Harry Jackson *m* Alfred Newman

Dan Dailey, Celeste Holm, Colleen Townsend, Alan Young, Natalie Wood

Chief Crazy Horse
US 1954 86m Technicolor
Cinemascope
U-I (William Alland)
GB title: *Valley of Fury*

The tribal problems of the Indian chief who defeated Custer at Little Big Horn.
Competent pro-Indian western.

w Franklin Coen, Gerald Drayson Adams *d* George Sherman *ph* Harold Lipstein *m* Frank Skinner

Victor Mature, Suzan Ball, John Lund, Ray Danton, Keith Larsen, Paul Guilfoyle, David Janssen

Un Chien Andalou*
France 1928 17m bw silent
Luis Bunuel

Famous surrealist short which includes dead donkeys on pianos and starts with a woman's eyeball being cut by a razor blade.
It had meaning for its makers, but very few other people saw anything in it but sensationalism.

w Luis Bunuel, Salvador Dali d, ed Luis Bunuel ph Albert Dubergen

Simone Mareuil, Pierre Batcheff, Jaime Miravilles, Salvador Dali, Luis Bunuel

La Chienne*
France 1931 85m bw
Braunberger-Richebé

A bank clerk falls for a prostitute and later kills her; her pimp is executed for the crime and the bank clerk becomes a tramp.
Heavy-going, old-fashioned melodrama with some interesting detail.

wd Jean Renoir, novel Georges de la Fouchardière *ph* Theodor Sparkuhl, Roger Hubert

Michel Simon, Janie Marèze, Georges Flament, Jean Gehret
† Remade as Scarlet Street (qv).

Child in the House
GB 1956 88m bw
Eros / Golden Era (Ben Fisz)

When her mother is ill and her father in hiding from the police, a 12-year-old girl goes to stay with her fussy uncle and aunt.
Modest family drama of the novelette type in which adult problems are put right by the wisdom of a child.

wd C. Raker Endfield, *novel* Janet McNeill *ph* Otto Heller *m* Mario Nascimbene *ad* Ken Adam

Eric Portman, Phyllis Calvert, Stanley Baker, Mandy Miller, Dora Bryan, Joan Hickson, Victor Maddern, Percy Herbert

A Child is Born
US 1939 79m bw
Warner (Sam Bischoff)

A slice of life in the maternity ward.
Adequately dramatic sequence of cameos, with mothers-to-be including a gangster's moll: a remake of *Life Begins*.

w Robert Rossen, *play* Mary M. Axelson *d* Lloyd Bacon *ph* Charles Rosher

Geraldine Fitzgerald, Jeffrey Lynn, Gladys George, Gale Page, Spring Byington, Henry O'Neill, John Litel, Gloria Holden, Eve Arden, Nanette Fabares, Hobart Cavanaugh, Johnny Downs, Johnnie Davis

A Child is Waiting**
US 1963 104m bw
UA / Stanley Kramer

A mixed-up spinster joins the staff of a school for mentally handicapped children.
Worthy semi-documentary marred by having a normal boy play the central character (albeit very well). A little over-dramatized but cogent and unsentimental.

w Abby Mann *d* John Cassavetes *ph* Joseph La Shelle *m* Ernest Gold

Burt Lancaster, *Judy Garland, Bruce Ritchey*, Steven Hill, Gena Rowlands, *Paul Stewart*, Lawrence Tierney

The Childhood of Maxim Gorky***
USSR 1938–40 bw
Soyuzdetfilm

Orphan Gorky is raised by his grandparents, and becomes a ship's cook and a painter before going on to university.
This simple and direct story is told in three beautifully detailed if rather overlong films:
'The Childhood of Maxim Gorky': 101m
'Out in the World': 98m
'My Universities': 104m

w Mark Donskoi, I. Grudzev *d Mark Donskoi*

ph Pyotr Yermolov *m* Lev Schwartz *ad* I. Stepanov

Alexei Lyarsky, Y. Valbert, M. Troyanovski, Valeria Massalitinova

Children of Hiroshima**
Japan 1952 97m bw
Kendai Eiga Lyokai / Gekidan Mingei

A young teacher returns to Hiroshima seven years after the bomb.
Restrained yet harrowing social documentary in fiction form, with the most effective use of flashbacks to show the horror of the bomb and its aftermath.

wd Kaneto Shindo, novel Arata Osada
ph Takeo Itoh m Akira Ifukube

Nobuko Otowa, Chikako Hoshawa, Niwa Saito

The Children of Sanchez
US / Mexico 1978 126m colour
Hall Bartlett

A macho Mexican and one of his daughters have ideas above the semi-slum in which they live. The star is still looking for another *Zorba the Greek*, but this isn't it. Glum, glum, glum.

w Cesare Zavattini, Hall Bartlett, *novel* Oscar Lewis *d* Hall Bartlett *ph* Gabriel Figueroa *m* Chuck Mangione

Anthony Quinn, Dolores del Rio, Lupita Ferrer, Katy Jurado, Stathis Giallelis

Children of the Damned*
GB 1964 90m bw
MGM (Ben Arbeid)

Six super-intelligent children of various nations are brought to London by UNESCO, and turn out to be invaders from another planet.
Moderate sequel to *Village of the Damned*, well made but with no new twists.

w John Briley *d* Anton M. Leader *ph* David Boulton *m* Ron Goodwin

Ian Hendry, Alan Badel, Barbara Ferris, Alfred Burke, Sheila Allen, Ralph Michael, Martin Miller, Harold Goldblatt

The Children's Hour*
US 1961 108m bw
UA / Mirisch (William Wyler)
GB title: *The Loudest Whisper*

A spoilt schoolgirl spreads a rumour that her schoolmistresses are lesbians.
Frank sixties version of a play originally filmed in a much bowdlerized version as *These Three*. Unfortunately frankness in this case leads to dullness, as nothing is done with the theme once it is stated, and the treatment is heavy-handed.

w Lillian Hellman, from her play *d* William Wyler *ph* Franz Planer *m* Alex North

Audrey Hepburn, Shirley Maclaine, James Garner, Miriam Hopkins, Fay Bainter, Karen Balkin

'All very exquisite, and dead as mutton.'— *Tom Milne*

AAN: Franz Planer; Fay Bainter

Child's Play*
US 1972 100m Movielab
Paramount (David Merrick)

In a Catholic boarding school for boys, an unpopular master is hounded and discredited by another whose motives may be diabolic.
Enjoyable overblown melodrama with hints of many nasty goings on, rather spoiled by too much talk and too little local colour.

w Leon Prochnik, *play* Robert Marasco *d* Sidney Lumet *ph* Gerald Hirschfeld *m* Michael Small

James Mason, Robert Preston, Beau Bridges, Ronald Weyand

The Chiltern Hundreds*
GB 1949 84m bw
Rank / Two Cities (George H. Brown)

An aged earl is bewildered when his son fails to be elected to parliament as a socialist but his butler gets in as a tory.
Satisfactory filming of an amusing stage comedy, with the aged A. E. Matthews repeating his delightful if irrelevant act as the dotty earl.

w William Douglas Home, Patrick Kirwan, *play William Douglas Home d* John Paddy Carstairs *ph* Jack Hildyard *m* Benjamin Frankel

A. E. Matthews, Cecil Parker, David Tomlinson, Marjorie Fielding, Joyce Carey

Chimes at Midnight*
Spain / Switz 1966 119m bw
Internacional Films Espanola / Alpine (Alessandro Tasca)
aka: *Falstaff*

Prince Hal becomes King Henry V and rejects his old friend Falstaff.
Clumsy adaptation of Shakespeare with brilliant flashes and the usual Welles vices of hasty production, poor synchronization and recording, etc. One wonders why, if he wanted to make a telescoped version of the plays, he did not spare the time and patience to make it better.

w Orson Welles *d* Orson Welles *ph* Edmond Richard *m* Angelo Francesco Lavagnino

Orson Welles, Keith Baxter, John Gielgud

(Henry IV), Margaret Rutherford (Mistress
Quickly), Jeanne Moreau (Doll Tearsheet),
Norman Rodway, Alan Webb, Marina Vlady,
Tony Beckley, Fernando Rey

China
US 1943   79m   bw
Paramount (Richard Blumenthal)

An oil salesman joins a Chinese guerrilla force
and sacrifices himself.
Solemnly hilarious propaganda piece tailored to
its star, showing the immense superiority of one
lone American to the entire Japanese army.

w Frank Butler, *novel* The Fourth Brother by
Reginald Forbes *d* John Farrow *ph* Leo Tover

Alan Ladd, Loretta Young, William Bendix,
Philip Ahn, Iris Wong, Sen Yung, Richard Loo,
Tala Birell

China Clipper*
US 1936   89m   bw
Warner (Sam Bischoff)

An aviator neglects his wife while building up a
trans-Pacific civil aviation link.
Solid entertainment feature of its day, with
adequate production and performance.

w Frank 'Spig' Wead *d* Ray Enright *ph* Arthur
Edeson

Pat O'Brien, Beverly Roberts, Ross Alexander,
Humphrey Bogart, Marie Wilson, Henry B.
Walthall, Joseph Crehan, Addison Richards

China Doll
US 1958   99m   bw
Romina / Batjac (Frank Borzage)

In 1943 an American air force officer
accidentally buys the services of a young
Chinese housekeeper. He marries her but they
are both killed in action; years later their
daughter is welcomed to America by members of
his old air crew.
Incurably sentimental and icky romantic drama
in the style of the director's silent films;
something of a curiosity for historians.

w Kitty Buhler *d* Frank Borzage *ph* William H.
Clothier *m* Henry Vars

Victor Mature, Li Li Hua, Bob Mathias, Ward
Bond, Stuart Whitman

China Gate
US 1957   90m   bw   Cinemascope
TCF (Samuel Fuller)

A Eurasian girl guides her American husband to
a communist arms dump.
Anti-Red thick ear, slick but undistinguished.

wd Samuel Fuller *ph* Joseph Biroc *m* Victor
Young, Max Steiner

Gene Barry, Angie Dickinson, Nat King Cole,
Paul Dubov, Lee Van Cleef, George Givot

China Girl
US 1943   95m   bw
TCF (Ben Hecht)

A newsreel cameraman in China falls in love
with a Eurasian schoolteacher.
Routine adventure romance with splodges of
love and self-sacrifice.

w Ben Hecht *d* Henry Hathaway *ph* Lee
Garmes *m* Hugo Friedhofer

Gene Tierney, George Montgomery, *Lynn Bari*,
Victor McLaglen, Alan Baxter, Sig Rumann,
Myron McCormick, Philip Ahn

China Seas**
US 1935   89m   bw
MGM (Albert Lewin)

Luxury cruise passengers find themselves
involved with piracy.
Omnibus shipboard melodrama, tersely scripted
and featuring a splendid cast all somewhere near
their best; slightly dated but very entertaining.

w Jules Furthman, James Kevin McGuinness,
novel Crosbie Garstin *d Tay Garnett ph* Ray
June

Clark Gable, Jean Harlow, Wallace Beery,
Rosalind Russell, Lewis Stone, C. Aubrey
Smith, Dudley Digges, Robert Benchley

China Sky
US 1945   78m   bw
RKO (Maurice Geraghty)

Two American doctors live with Chinese
guerrillas; the jealousy of the wife of one of them
causes problems.
Routine adventure romance with generally
unconvincing production and performance.

w Brenda Weisberg, Joseph Hoffman, *novel*
Pearl Buck *d* Ray Enright *ph* Nicholas
Musuraca *m* Roy Webb

Randolph Scott, Ellen Drew, Ruth Warrick,
Anthony Quinn, Carol Thurston, Richard Loo,
Philip Ahn

Chinatown***
US 1974   131m   Technicolor   Panavision
Paramount / Long Road (Robert Evans)

In 1937, a Los Angeles private eye takes on a
simple case and burrows into it until it leads to
murder and a public scandal.
Pretentious melodrama which is basically no
more serious than the Raymond Chandler

mysteries from which it derives; the tragic ending is merely an irritation, and the title only allusive. Superficially, however, it is eminently watchable, with effective individual scenes and performances and photography which is lovingly composed though tending to suggest period by use of an orange filter.

w Robert Towne d Roman Polanski ph John A. Alonso m Jerry Goldsmith pd Richard Sylbert

Jack Nicholson, Faye Dunaway, John Huston, Perry Lopez, John Hillerman, Roman Polanski, Darrell Zwerling, Diane Ladd

AA: Robert Towne

AAN: best picture; Roman Polanski; John A. Alonso; Jerry Goldsmith; Jack Nicholson

The Chinese Bungalow
GB 1939   72m   bw
George King

A Chinese merchant plots to kill the lover of his English wife.

Stolid version of an old melodrama which can hardly fail; previously filmed in 1926 with Matheson Lang and Genevieve Townsend (directed by Sinclair Hill) and in 1930 with Matheson Lang and Anna Neagle (directed by J. B. Williams).

w A. R. Rawlinson, George Wellesley, play Matheson Lang, Marian Osmond *d George King*

Paul Lukas, Jane Baxter, Robert Douglas, Kay Walsh, Jerry Verno

Chisum*
US 1970   110m   Technicolor   Panavision
Warner / Batjac (Michael Wayne, Andrew J. Fenady)

A corrupt businessman plots against the head of a vast cattle empire, who is saved by the intervention of numerous friends including Pat Garrett and Billy the Kid.

Desultory, overlong, friendly western in the Ford manner. Easy to watch and easier to forget.

w Andrew J. Fenady d Andrew V. McLaglen ph William H. Clothier m Dominic Frontière

John Wayne, Forrest Tucker, Christopher George, Ben Johnson, Glenn Corbett, Bruce Cabot, Andrew Prine, Patric Knowles, Richard Jaeckel, Linda Day George, John Agar, Ray Teal, Glenn Langan, Alan Baxter, Abraham Sofaer

'A curious mixture of styles and myths.'— *John Gillett*

Chitty Chitty Bang Bang
GB 1968   145m   Technicolor   Super Panavision 70
UA / Warfield / DFI (Albert R. Broccoli)

An unsuccessful inventor rescues a derelict car and gives it magical properties, then helps the children who own it to overthrow the government of a country which hates children.

A bumpy ride. Sentiment, slapstick, whimsy and mild scares do not combine but are given equal shares of the limelight, while poor trickwork prevents the audience from being transported.

w Roald Dahl, Ken Hughes d Ken Hughes ph Christopher Challis m Irwin Kostal songs the Sherman Brothers ad Ken Adam decor Rowland Emmett

Dick Van Dyke, Sally Ann Howes (as Truly Scrumptious), Lionel Jeffries, Robert Helpmann, Gert Frobe, Benny Hill, James Robertson Justice

AAN: title song

The Chocolate Soldier*
US 1941   102m   bw
MGM (Victor Saville)

Married opera singers fall out backstage.

Talky musical remake of *The Guardsman*: nearly comes off but not quite.

w Keith Winter, Leonard Lee d Roy del Ruth ph Karl Freund songs Oscar Straus m Herbert Stothart, Bronislau Kaper

Nelson Eddy, Rise Stevens, Nigel Bruce, Florence Bates, Nydia Westman

AAN: Karl Fruend; Herbert Stothart, Bronislau Kaper

The Choirboys
US 1978   119m   Technicolor
Lorimar / Airone (Lee Rich, Merv Adelson)

Members of a police department are if anything more delinquent, vicious and mentally retarded than their quarries.

A vulgar and repellent anti-establishment display, apparently intended as black comedy. Just the thing to put an end to the art of the movie once and for all.

w Christopher Knopf, novel Joseph Wambaugh d Robert Aldrich ph Joseph Biroc m Frank de Vol

Charles Durning, Lou Gossett Jnr, Perry King, Stephen Macht, Tim McIntyre, Clyde Kusatu, Randy Quaid, Don Stroud, Robert Webber, Blair Brown

Chosen Survivors

US 1974 98m colour
Alpine / Metromedia (Charles Fries)

Ten people with special skills are chosen to test
human reaction to thermo-nuclear war, but find
themselves at the mercy of vampire bats.
Another misfit group united by disaster; more
shocks than suspense, and not much
characterization, but for adventure/horror
addicts it will pass the time.

w H. B. Cross, Joe Red Moffly d Sutton Roley
ph Gabriel Torres m Fred Karlin

Jackie Cooper, Alex Cord, Richard Jaeckel,
Diana Muldaur, Lincoln Kilpatrick, Bradford
Dillman, Pedro Armendariz Jnr, Gwen Mitchell,
Barbara Babcock, Christina Moreno

A Christmas Carol*

US 1938 69m bw
MGM (Joseph L. Mankiewicz)

Scrooge the miser is reformed when four ghosts
visit him on Christmas Eve.
Standard Dickensian frolic, quite well mounted.

w Hugo Butler d Edwin L. Marin ph Sidney
Wagner m Franz Waxman

Reginald Owen, Gene Lockhart, Kathleen
Lockhart, Terry Kilburn, Leo G. Carroll, Lynne
Carver
† See also *Scrooge*.

Christmas Eve*

US 1947 92m bw
Benedict Bogeaus
aka: *Sinners' Holiday*

An old lady needs the help of her three adopted
sons to prevent herself from being swindled.
Basically three short stories sealed by a
Christmas Eve reunion, this is old-fashioned
sentimental stuff, but it works on its level and the
cast is interesting.

w Lawrence Stallings d Edwin L. Marin
ph Gordon Avil m Heinz Roemheld

Ann Harding, George Raft, Randolph Scott,
George Brent, Joan Blondell, Virginia Field,
Reginald Denny

Christmas Holiday

US 1944 93m bw
Universal (Felix Jackson)

A young girl marries a murderer, and later, as a
shady songstress in a nightclub, is forced to help
him escape.
A weird change of pace for Deanna Durbin,
whose forte had been sweetness and light, this
relentlessly grim and boring melodrama was also
a travesty of the novel on which it was based.

w Herman J. Mankiewicz, *novel* Somerset
Maugham d Robert Siodmak ph Elwood
Bredell m Hans Salter

Deanna Durbin, Gene Kelly, Dean Harens,
Gladys George, Richard Whorf, Gale
Sondergaard

AAN: Hans Salter

Christmas in Connecticut*

US 1945 101m bw
Warner (William Jacobs)
GB title: *Indiscretion*

The spinster writer of a successful column about
love and marriage has to conjure up a family for
herself in the cause of publicity.
Predictable but fairly brisk comedy with
excellent talent well deployed.

w Lionel Houser, Adele Commandini d Peter
Godfrey ph Carl Guthrie m Frederick
Hollander

Barbara Stanwyck, Dennis Morgan, Sydney
Greenstreet, Reginald Gardiner, S. Z. Sakall,
Robert Shayne, Una O'Connor, Frank Jenks

Christmas in July**

US 1940 67m bw
Paramount

A young clerk and his girl win first prize in a big
competition.
Slightly unsatisfactory as a whole, this Preston
Sturges comedy has echoes of Clair and a dully
predictable plot line, but is kept alive by inventive
touches and a gallery of splendid character
comedians.

wd Preston Sturges ph Victor Milner
m Sigmund Krumgold

Dick Powell, Ellen Drew, Ernest Truex, *Al
Bridge*, Raymond Walburn, William Demarest
'The perfect restorative for battered humors
and jangled nerves.'—*Bosley Crowther*
'Agreeable enough, but it lacks the full-fledged
Sturges lunacy.'—*New Yorker, 1977*

The Christmas Tree

France / Italy 1969 110m Eastmancolor
Corona / Jupiter (Robert Dorfmann)

The small son of a millionaire widower is fatally
infected by radioactivity.
Painfully sentimental and overdrawn weepie, the
most lachrymose film of the sixties.

wd Terence Young, *novel* Michel Bataille
ph Henri Alekan m Georges Auric

William Holden, Virna Lisi, Brook Fuller,
Bourvil
'Depending on your taste threshold, there may

not be a dry eye—nor a full stomach—in the house.'—*Judith Crist*

Christopher Columbus
GB 1948   104m   Technicolor
Rank (Betty Box)

Columbus seeks and receives the patronage of the Spanish court for his voyage to the west.
An extraordinarily tediously paced historical account of basically undramatic events; interesting without being stimulating.

w Muriel and Sydney Box, Cyril Roberts
d David MacDonald *ph* Stephen Dade
m Arthur Bliss

Fredric March, Florence Eldridge, Francis L. Sullivan, Linden Travers

Christopher Strong*
US 1933   72m   bw
RKO (Pandro S. Berman)

A daring lady aviator has an affair with a married businessman and commits suicide when she finds herself pregnant.
A curious and unsatisfactory yarn for Hepburn's second film; well enough made, it died at the box office.

w Zoe Akins, *novel* Gilbert Frankau *d* Dorothy Arzner *ph* Bert Glennon *m* Max Steiner

Katharine Hepburn, Colin Clive, Billie Burke, Helen Chandler, Ralph Forbes, Irene Browne, Jack La Rue

'The personal story of a million daughters.'—*publicity*

Chronique d'un Eté*
France 1961   90m   bw
Argos

Parisians talk about their lives.
Curious but rather stimulating acted documentary, with two interviewers pontificating; saved by shrewd editing to keep interest at its maximum.

wd Jean Rouch, Edgar Morin *ph* various

Chu Chin Chow*
GB 1934   102m   bw
Gaumont British / Gainsborough (Michael Balcon)

In old Arabia, a slave girl foils a robber posing as a dead mandarin.
Second screen version (the first was silent) of the old Arabian Nights stage musical. A curiosity.

w Edward Knoblock, L. DuGarde Peach, Sidney Gilliat, *play* Oscar Asche and Frederick Norton *d* Walter Forde *songs* Frederick

Norton *md* Louis Levy *ph* Max Greene
ch Anton Dolin

George Robey, Fritz Kortner, Anna May Wong, John Garrick, Pearl Argyle, Malcolm MacEachern, Dennis Hoey, Francis L. Sullivan, Sydney Fairbrother

'Gaumont British have broken away for the first time from their careful refinement, and produced something that has guts as well as grace.'—*C. A. Lejeune*

Chubasco
US 1967   100m   Technicolor   Panavision
Warner Seven Arts (William Conrad)

A wild beach boy takes a job on a tuna fishing boat.
Old-fashioned boy-makes-good melodrama à la Captains Courageous. Excellent action sequences at sea.

wd Allen H. Miner *ph* Louis Jennings, Paul Ivano *m* William Lava

Chris Jones, Richard Egan, Susan Strasberg, Ann Sothern, Simon Oakland, Preston Foster, Audrey Totter, Peter Whitney

Chuka
US 1967   105m   Technicolor
Paramount / Rod Taylor

A wandering gunfighter defends the inhabitants of a fort against Indian attack.
Ill-assorted characters under stress is the theme of this rather pedestrian and slightly pretentious western.

w Richard Jessup *d* Gordon Douglas
ph Harold Stine *m* Leith Stevens

Rod Taylor, Ernest Borgnine, John Mills, Luciana Paluzzi, James Whitmore, Louis Hayward, Angela Dorian

A Chump at Oxford**
US 1939   63m   bw
Hal Roach

Two street cleaners foil a bank hold-up and are presented with an Oxford education.
Patchy but endearing Laurel and Hardy romp, starting with an irrelevant two reels about their playing butler and maid, but later including Stan's burlesque impersonation of Lord Paddington.

w Charles Rogers, Harry Langdon, Felix Adler
d Alfred Goulding *ph* Art Lloyd

Stan Laurel, Oliver Hardy, James Finlayson, Forrester Harvey, Wilfrid Lucas, Peter Cushing

'Ranks with their best pictures—which, to one heretic, are more agreeable than Chaplin's. Their clowning is purer; they aren't out to better an unbetterable world; they've never wanted to play Hamlet.'—*Graham Greene*

Cimarron*

US 1931 130m bw
RKO (Louis Sarecky)

The life of an Oklahoma homesteader from 1890 to 1915.
Sprawling western family saga; a big early talkie, it dates badly.

w Howard Estabrook, *novel* Edna Ferber
d Wesley Ruggles *ph* Edward Cronjager

Richard Dix, Irene Dunne, Estelle Taylor, Nance O'Neill, William Collier Jnr, Roscoe Ates, George E. Stone, Stanley Fields, Edna May Oliver

AA: best picture; Howard Estabrook
AAN: Wesley Ruggles; Edward Cronjager; Richard Dix; Irene Dunne

Cimarron

US 1961 147m Metrocolor
Cinemascope
MGM (Edmund Grainger)

Flabby, relentlessly boring remake of the above.

w Arnold Schulman *d* Anthony Mann
ph Robert L. Surtees *m* Franz Waxman

Glenn Ford, Maria Schell, Anne Baxter, Lili Darvas, Russ Tamblyn, Henry Morgan, David Opatoshu, Charles McGraw, Aline MacMahon, Edgar Buchanan, Arthur O'Connell, Mercedes McCambridge, Vic Morrow, Robert Keith, Mary Wickes, Royal Dano, Vladimir Sokoloff

The Cincinnati Kid**

US 1965 113m Metrocolor
MGM / Filmways (Martin Ransohoff, John Calley)

In New Orleans in the late thirties, stud poker experts compete for supremacy.
This is to poker what *The Hustler* was to pool, a fascinating suspense study of experts at work; as before, the romantic asides let down the effectiveness of the others.

w Ring Lardner Jnr, Terry Southern, *novel* Richard Jessup *d* Norman Jewison *ph* Philip Lathrop *m* Lalo Schifrin

Steve McQueen, *Edward G. Robinson*, Karl Malden, Ann-Margret, Tuesday Weld, Joan Blondell, Rip Torn, Jack Weston, Cab Calloway, Jeff Corey

Cinderella**

US 1950 75m Technicolor
Walt Disney

The Perrault fairy tale embroidered with animal characters.
A feature cartoon rather short on inspiration, though with all Disney's solid virtues. The mice are lively and the villainous cat the best character.

supervisor Ben Sharpsteen *d* Wilfred Jackson, Hamilton Luske, Clyde Geronomi *m* Oliver Wallace, Paul J. Smith

AAN: Oliver Wallace, Paul J. Smith; song 'Bibbidy Bobbidy Boo' (*m/ly* Mack David, Al Hoffman, Jerry Livingston)

Cinderella Jones

US 1946 89m bw
Warner (Alex Gottlieb)

To collect an inheritance, a girl must marry a brainy man.
Witless comedy for the easily pleased.

w Charles Hoffman, *story* Philip Wylie *d* Busby Berkeley *ph* Sol Polito *m* Frederick Hollander

Joan Leslie, Robert Alda, S. Z. Sakall, Edward Everett Horton, Julie Bishop, William Prince, Charles Dingle, Ruth Donnelly, Elisha Cook Jnr, Hobart Cavanaugh, Chester Clute

Cinderella Liberty

US 1974 117m De Luxe Panavision
TCF / Sanford (Mark Rydell)

A sailor on shore leave picks up a prostitute and falls in love with her.
Assertively 'modern' yet glutinously sentimental love story in squalid settings. It presumably has an audience.

w Darryl Ponicsan, from his novel *d* Mark Rydell *ph* Vilmos Zsigmond *m* John Williams

James Caan, Marsha Mason, Eli Wallach, Kirk Calloway, Allyn Ann McLerie

'A sordid, messy affair which wants to jerk tears but just doesn't have the knack.'—*New Yorker*

AA: song 'Nice To Be Around' (*m* John Williams, *ly* Paul Williams)
AAN: John Williams; Marsha Mason

Cinderfella

US 1960 91m Technicolor
Paramount / Jerry Lewis

Luxury pantomime featuring a male Cinderella.
Annoyingly lavish and empty star vehicle with precious little to laugh at: Lewis' own jokes are strung out to snapping point and no one else gets a look in.

wd Frank Tashlin *ph* Haskell Boggs *m* Walter Scharf

Jerry Lewis, Ed Wynn, Judith Anderson, Anna

Maria Alberghetti, Henry Silva, Robert Hutton,
Count Basie

'A drought of comic inspiration, followed by a
flood of mawkish whimsy, gradually increases
one's early misgivings to a degree which finally
verges on revulsion.'—*Peter John Dyer*

Circle of Danger*
GB 1951   89m   bw
Coronado / David Rose (Joan Harrison)

An American in England investigates the strange
death some years earlier of his brother during a
commando raid.
Individual scenes are well milked for suspense
and dramatic emphasis, but the plot line has
virtually no mystery and absolutely no danger. It
all seems mildly reminiscent of several
Hitchcock films.

w Philip MacDonald *d Jacques Tourneur*
ph Oswald Morris *m* Robert Farnon

Ray Milland, Patricia Roc, Marius Goring,
Hugh Sinclair, Naunton Wayne, Marjorie
Fielding, Edward Rigby, Colin Gordon, Dora
Bryan

Circle of Deception
GB 1960   100m   bw   Cinemascope
TCF (T. H. Morahan)

An officer is parachuted into Germany with the
intention that he should crack under
interrogation and reveal false information.
Depressing World War II tall tale, with suspense
sacrificed by flashback structure.

w Nigel Balchin, Robert Musel, *novel* Alec
Waugh *d* Jack Lee *ph* Gordon Dines *m* Clifton
Parker

Bradford Dillman, Harry Andrews, Suzy
Parker, Robert Stephens, John Welsh, Paul
Rogers, Duncan Lamont, Michael Ripper

The Circus*
US 1928   72m (24 fps)   bw   silent
(UA) Charles Chaplin

A tramp on the run from the police takes refuge
in a circus and falls for an equestrienne.
Pathos often descends to bathos in this self-
constructed star vehicle which has far too few
laughs.

wd Charles Chaplin ph Rollie Totheroh, Jack
Wilson, Mark Marlott

Charles Chaplin, Merna Kennedy, Allan Garcia,
Harry Crocker

AAN: Charles Chaplin (as actor and director)

Circus of Horrors
GB 1960   91m   Eastmancolor
Anglo Amalgamated / Lynx / Independent
   Artists (Norman Priggen)

A plastic surgeon staffs a semi-derelict circus
with criminals whose faces he has altered, and
murders any who try to flee.
Stark horror comic; quite professionally made,
but content-wise a crude concoction of sex and
sadism.

w George Baxt *d* Sidney Hayers *ph* Douglas
Slocombe *m* Franz Reizenstein, Muir
Mathieson

Anton Diffring, Erika Remberg, Yvonne
Monlaur, Donald Pleasance, Jane Hylton,
Kenneth Griffith, Conrad Phillips, Jack Gwyllim

Circus World
US 1964   138m   Super Technirama
Bronston / Midway (Samuel Bronston)
GB title: *The Magnificent Showman*

An American circus owner tours Europe in
search of his alcoholic ex-wife who left him when
her lover fell to death from the trapeze.
Lethargic big-screen epic which exhausts its
spectacle in the first hour and then settles down
to a dreary will-daughter-guess-who-the-
strange-lady-is plot, without even the plus of an
exciting finale.

w Ben Hecht, Julian Halevy, James Edward
Grant *d* Henry Hathaway *ph* Jack Hildyard
pd John de Cuir *m* Dmitri Tiomkin

John Wayne, *Rita Hayworth*, Claudia
Cardinale, John Smith, Lloyd Nolan, Richard
Conte, Wanda Rotha, Kay Walsh

The Cisco Kid
The Cisco Kid, a ruthless Mexican bandit
originally created by O. Henry in a short story,
was turned by Hollywood into a dashing wild
western Robin Hood in twenty-three sound
features (following a few silent ones) and a long-
running TV series. In most of them he was
accompanied by his fat side-kick Pancho.

For Fox:
1929: IN OLD ARIZONA (Warner Baxter)
1931: THE CISCO KID (Baxter)

For Twentieth Century Fox:
1939: THE RETURN OF THE CISCO KID
(Baxter), THE CISCO KID AND THE LADY
(Cesar Romero: who played the role in all the
remaining TCF movies).
1940: VIVA CISCO KID, LUCKY CISCO
KID, THE GAY CABALLERO
1941: ROMANCE OF THE RIO GRANDE,
RIDE ON, VAQUERO

For Monogram:
1945: THE CISCO KID RETURNS (Duncan Renaldo), THE CISCO KID IN OLD NEW MEXICO (Renaldo), SOUTH OF THE RIO GRANDE (Renaldo)
1946: THE GAY CAVALIER (Gilbert Roland), SOUTH OF MONTEREY (Roland), BEAUTY AND THE BANDIT (Roland)
1947: RIDING THE CALIFORNIA TRAIL (Roland), ROBIN HOOD OF MONTEREY (Roland), KING OF THE BANDITS (Roland)

For United Artists (all with Renaldo):
1949: THE VALIANT HOMBRE, THE GAY AMIGO, THE DARING CABALLERO, SATAN'S CRADLE
1950: THE GIRL FROM SAN LORENZO

† The fifties TV series starred Renaldo with Leo Carrillo.

Cisco Pike

US 1971　94m　Eastmancolor
Columbia / Acrobat (Gerald Ayres)

A former pop group leader and drug pusher is blackmailed by a cop into selling heroin.
Low-key, would-be realistic study of a section of life in seventies LA. Flashy, boring and almost plotless.

wd Bill L. Norton　*ph* Vilis Lapenieks　*m* various

Kris Kristofferson, Gene Hackman, Karen Black, Harry Dean Stanton

'A moody, melancholy little film whose strength lies in its evocation of the rootless, aimless, irresponsible life-style of the pop/drug culture.'—*Brenda Davies*

The Citadel**

GB 1938　113m　bw
MGM (Victor Saville)

A young doctor has a hard time in the mining villages but is later swayed by the easy rewards of a Mayfair practice.
Solidly produced adaptation of a bestseller; the more recent deluge of doctors on television make it appear rather elementary, but many scenes work in a classical way. One of the first fruits of MGM's British studios which were closed by World War II.

w Elizabeth Hill, Ian Dalrymple, Emlyn Williams, Frank Wead, *novel* A. J. Cronin
d King Vidor　*m* Louis Levy

Robert Donat, Rosalind Russell, Ralph Richardson, Emlyn Williams, Penelope Dudley Ward, Francis L. Sullivan

'I think any doctor will agree that here is a medical picture with no *Men in White* hokum, no hysterical, incredible melodrama, but with an honest story, honestly told. And that's a rare picture.'—*Pare Lorentz*

AAN: best picture; script; King Vidor; Robert Donat

Citizen Kane****

US 1941　119m　bw
RKO (Orson Welles)

A newspaper tycoon dies, and a magazine reporter interviews his friends in an effort to discover the meaning of his last words.
A brilliant piece of Hollywood cinema using all the resources of the studio; despite lapses of characterization and gaps in the narrative, almost every shot and every line is utterly absorbing both as entertainment and as craft.
See *The Citizen Kane Book* by Pauline Kael, and innumerable other writings.

w Herman J. Mankiewicz, Orson Welles
d Orson Welles　*ph* Gregg Toland　*m* Bernard Herrmann　*ad* Van Nest Polglase　*sp* Vernon L. Walker

Orson Welles, Joseph Cotten, Dorothy Comingore, Everett Sloane, Paul Stewart, Ray Collins, Ruth Warrick, *Erskine Sanford, Agnes Moorehead, George Coulouris*, William Alland, Fortunio Bonanova

'On seeing it for the first time, one got a conviction that if the cinema could do that, it could do anything.'—*Penelope Houston*

'What may distinguish *Citizen Kane* most of all is its extracting the mythic from under the humdrum surface of the American experience.'—*John Simon, 1968*

'Probably the most exciting film that has come out of Hollywood for twenty-five years. I am not sure it isn't the most exciting film that has ever come out of anywhere.'—
C. A. Lejeune

'At any rate Orson Welles has landed in the movies, with a splash and a loud yell.'—*James Shelley Hamilton*

'More fun than any great movie I can think of.'—*Pauline Kael, 1968*

AA: Herman J. Mankiewicz, Orson Welles (script)
AAN: best picture; Orson Welles (as director); Gregg Toland; Bernard Herrmann; Orson Welles (as actor)

La Città Si Difende

Italy 1951　90m　bw
Cines (Carlo Civallero)

A gang is recruited to rob a football stadium.
Moderate forerunner of *The Good Die Young, The Killing*, and a hundred other caper films.

w Federico Fellini, Tullio Pinelli, Luigi Comencini　*d* Pietro Germi　*ph* Carlo Montuori
m Carlo Rustichelli

Fausto Tozzi, Gina Lollobrigida, Patrizia
Manca, Enzo Maggio
'As anonymous as the average B picture.'—
Gavin Lambert

City across the River

US 1949   91m   bw
U-I (Howard Christie)

Brooklyn delinquents get involved in murder.
Semi-documentary throwback to the Dead End
Kids, with location shooting influenced by *The
Naked City*. Dull.

w Maxwell Shane, Dennis Cooper, *novel* The
Amboy Dukes by Irving Shulman *d* Maxwell
Shane *ph* Maury Gertsman *m* Walter Scharf

Stephen McNally, Barbara Whiting, Peter
Fernandez, Al Ramsen, Joshua Shelley,
Anthony Curtis (Tony Curtis in his first film
role)

City beneath the Sea

US 1953   87m   Technicolor
U-I (Albert J. Cohen)

Deep sea divers fall out over a sunken treasure.
Adequate double-biller with little to stir the
interest.

w Jack Harvey, Ramon Romero *d* Budd
Boetticher *ph* Charles P. Boyle

Robert Ryan, Anthony Quinn, Mala Powers,
Suzan Ball, George Mathews, Karel Stepanek,
Lalo Rios

City beneath the Sea

US 1970   98m   De Luxe   TVM
Warner / Kent / Motion Pictures International
(Irwin Allen)
GB theatrical release title: *One Hour to
Doomsday*

An undersea city is threatened by an errant
planetoid.
Futuristic adventure from a familiar stable; it
will satisfy followers of *Voyage to the Bottom of
the Sea*.

w John Meredyth Lucas *d* Irwin Allen
ph Kenneth Peach *m* Richard La Salle
ad Roger E. Maus, Stan Jolley

Stuart Whitman, Robert Wagner, Rosemary
Forsyth, Robert Colbert, Burr de Benning,
Richard Basehart, Joseph Cotten, James
Darren, Sugar Ray Robinson, Paul Stewart

City for Conquest**

US 1940   106m   bw
Warner (Anatole Litvak)

An East Side truck driver becomes a boxer but is
blinded in a fight; meanwhile his composer

brother gives up pop music for symphonies.
Phony but oddly persuasive melodrama set in a
studio in New York and heavily influenced by
the pretensions of the Group theatre.

w John Wexley, *novel* Aben Kandel *d* Anatole
Litvak *ph* Sol Polito, James Wong Howe
m Max Steiner

James Cagney, Ann Sheridan, Frank Craven,
Donald Crisp, *Arthur Kennedy*, Frank McHugh,
George Tobias, Anthony Quinn, Jerome Cowan,
Lee Patrick, Blanche Yurka, Thurston Hall
  'Sometimes we wonder whether it wasn't
really the Warner brothers who got New York
from the Indians, so diligent and devoted have
they been in feeling the great city's pulse,
picturing its myriad facets and recording with
deep compassion the passing life of its seething
population.'—*Bosley Crowther*

City Girl*

US 1930   77m   bw
Fox

A city girl finds rural life has its own drama.
Rural drama distinguished by directorial
touches.

w Berthold Viertel, Marion Orth, *play* The Mud
Turtle by Elliot Lester *d* F. W. Murnau
ph Ernest Palmer *m* Arthur Kay

Charles Farrell, Mary Duncan, David Torrence,
Edith Yorke, Dawn O'Day

City Lights***

US 1931   87m   bw   silent (with music
and effects)
(UA) Charles Chaplin

A tramp befriends a millionaire and falls in love
with a blind girl.
Sentimental comedy with several delightful
sequences in Chaplin's best manner.

wd, m Charles Chaplin ph Rollie Totheroh,
Mark Marlott, Gordon Pollock

Charles Chaplin, Virginia Cherrill, Harry Myers

City of Bad Men*

US 1953   82m   Technicolor
TCF (Leonard Goldstein)

In Carson City during the Corbett–Fitzsimmons
boxing match, outlaws plan to rob the arena of
its receipts.
Slightly unusual western suspenser with
generally accomplished handling.

w George W. George, George Slavin *d* Harmon
Jones *ph* Charles G. Clarke *md* Lionel
Newman

Dale Robertson, Jeanne Crain, Richard Boone,

Lloyd Bridges, Carl Betz, Carole Mathews,
Whitfield Connor

City of Fear*
US 1958 81m bw
Columbia / Orbit (Leon Chooluck)

A convict escapes with a canister of radioactive
cobalt, which he believes to be heroin. After
terrifying the city, he finally dies of exposure to it.
Rough-edged but occasionally gripping minor
thriller from an independent company.

w Steven Ritch, Robert Dillon d Irving Lerner
ph Lucien Ballard m Jerry Goldsmith

Vince Edwards, John Archer, Patricia Blair,
Steven Ritch, Lyle Talbot

City of the Dead*
GB 1960 78m bw
Vulcan (Donald Taylor)
US title: Horror Hotel

In Massachusetts, a woman burned as a witch
250 years ago is still 'alive', running a local hotel
and luring unwary strangers into becoming
sacrificial victims.
A deadly first half gives way to splendid
cinematic terror when the scene shifts to the
village by night, all dry ice and limpid fog, and
the heroine becomes a human sacrifice. A
superior horror comic.

w George Baxt d John Moxey ph Desmond
Dickinson m Douglas Gamley, Ken Jones

Patricia Jessel, Betta St John, Christopher Lee,
Dennis Lotis, Valentine Dyall, Venetia
Stevenson, Norman Macowan, Fred Johnson

City Streets**
US 1931 86m bw
Paramount

A gangster's daughter is sent to jail for a murder
she did not commit, and on release narrowly
escapes being 'taken for a ride'.
Tense, dated gangland melodrama of primary
interest because of its director's very cinematic
treatment.

w Max Marcin, Oliver H. P. Garrett, Dashiell
Hammett d Rouben Mamoulian ph Lee
Garmes

Sylvia Sidney, Gary Cooper, Paul Lukas, Guy
Kibbee, William (Stage) Boyd, Stanley Fields,
Wynne Gibson

City That Never Sleeps
US 1953 90m bw
Republic (John H. Auer)

The work of the Chicago police force during one
night.

Adequate minor semi-documentary police yarn.

w Steve Fisher d John H. Auer ph John I.
Russell
m R. Dale Butts

Gig Young, Mala Powers, William Talman,
Edward Arnold, Chill Wills, Paula Raymond,
Marie Windsor

City under the Sea
GB 1965 84m Eastmancolor
   Colorscope
Bruton / AIP (Daniel Haller)
US title: War Gods of the Deep

An American heiress in Cornwall meets
Victorian smugglers who have lived a hundred
years under the sea in Lyonesse.
Childlike, unpersuasive nonsense which wastes
some good talent.

w Charles Bennett, Louis M. Heyward
d Jacques Tourneur ph Stephen Dade
m Stanley Black

Vincent Price, David Tomlinson, Susan Hart,
Tab Hunter, Henry Oscar, John Le Mesurier

Civilization***
US 1916 68m (1931 'sound' version) bw
   silent
Triangle

A mythical country starts war, but one of the
principals has a vision of Christ on the
battlefields and the king is persuaded to sign a
peace treaty.
Surprisingly impressive parable showing this
early director at his best; intended as a pacifist
tract in the middle of World War I.

w C. Gardner Sullivan d Thomas Ince ph Irwin
Willat

Enid Markey, Howard Hickman, J. Barney
Sherry

The Clairvoyant*
GB 1934 80m bw
Gainsborough (Michael Balcon)

A fraudulent mindreader predicts a disaster
which comes true.
Effective minor suspenser on predictable but
enjoyable lines.

w Charles Bennett, Bryan Edgar Wallace,
Robert Edmunds d Maurice Elvey

Claude Rains, Fay Wray, Jane Baxter, Mary
Clare, Athole Stewart, Ben Field, Felix Aylmer,
Donald Calthrop

Clambake
US 1967 98m Techniscope
UA / Rhodes (Laven–Gardner–Levy)

The son of an oil millionaire sets out to see life. Painless, forgettable star vehicle.

w Arthur Browne Jnr *d* Arthur H. Nadel *ph* William Margulies *m* Jeff Alexander

Elvis Presley, Shelley Fabares, Bill Bixby, James Gregory, Will Hutchins, Gary Merrill

Clarence the Cross-Eyed Lion
US 1965   98m · Technicolor
MGM (Leonard Kaufman)

Adventures of animal farmers in Africa. Amiable theatrical 'pilot' for the *Daktari* TV series.

w Alan Caillou, Marshall Thompson, Art Arthur *d* Andrew Marton

Marshall Thompson, Betsy Drake, Richard Haydn, Cheryl Miller

Clash by Night*
US 1952   105m   bw
RKO (Harriet Parsons) (A Wald–Krasna Production)

In a northern fishing village, jealousy and near-tragedy are occasioned by the return home of a hardened girl from the big city.
Absurdly overblown melodrama of the *Anna Christie* school, burdened with significance and doggedly acted by a remarkable cast.

w Alfred Hayes, *play* Clifford Odets *d* Fritz Lang *ph* Nicholas Musuraca *m* Roy Webb

Barbara Stanwyck, Paul Douglas, Robert Ryan, Marilyn Monroe, J. Carrol Naish, Keith Andes

Class of '44
US 1973   95m   Technicolor   Panavision
Warner (Paul Bogart)

Sex problems of college students during World War II.
Thin sequel to *Summer of '42*, nostalgic to Americans over forty but not much of a trip for anyone else.

w Herman Raucher *d* Paul Bogart *ph* Andrew Laszlo *m* David Shire

Gary Grimes, Jerry Houser, Oliver Conant, William Atherton, Sam Bottoms, Deborah Winters

The Class of Miss McMichael
GB 1978   90m   colour
Brut / Kettledrum (Judd Bernard)

A dedicated schoolmistress has no chance against her slum surroundings.
The Blackboard Jungle lives on, very boringly.

W Judd Bernard, *novel* Sandy Hutson *d* Silvio Narizzano *ph* Alex Thomson *m* Stanley Myers

Glenda Jackson, Oliver Reed, John Standing, Michael Murphy, Rosalind Cash
   'Poorly mannered, simple minded, badly disciplined . . . gives social science a bad name.'—*Variety*

Claudelle Inglish
US 1961   99m   bw
Warner (Leonard Freeman)
GB title: *Young and Eager*

A poor farmer's daughter scorns a wealthy man for a succession of young studs.
Would-be sensational novelette from the author of *Tobacco Road*; it does not begin to be interesting.

w Leonard Freeman, *novel* Erskine Caldwell *d* Gordon Douglas *ph* Ralph Woolsey *m* Howard Jackson

Diane McBain, Arthur Kennedy, Constance Ford, Chad Everett, Claude Akins, Will Hutchins, Robert Colbert, Ford Rainey, James Bell

Claudia***
US 1943   92m   bw
TCF (William Perlberg)

A middle-class husband helps his child-wife to mature.
Typical of the best of Hollywood's 'woman's pictures' of the period, this is a pleasant domestic comedy-drama featuring recognizably human characters in an agreeable setting.

w Morrie Ryskind, *novel* and *play* Rose Franken *d* Edmund Goulding *ph* Leon Shamroy *m* Alfred Newman

Dorothy McGuire (her film debut), *Robert Young, Ina Claire*, Reginald Gardiner, Olga Baclanova, Jean Howard, Elsa Janssen

Claudia and David*
US 1946   78m   bw
TCF

Claudia and her husband survive assorted crises including their son's illness and David's involvement in a car crash.
Patchwork sequel to *Claudia*, quite pleasant but obviously contrived quickly from scraps.

w Rose Franken, William Brown Meloney *d* Walter Lang *ph* Joseph La Shelle

Dorothy McGuire, Robert Young, Mary Astor, John Sutton, Gail Patrick, Florence Bates

The Clay Pigeon**
US 1949   63m   bw
RKO (Herman Schlom)

An amnesiac sailor finds himself courtmartialled

for treason, but discovers the real culprit.
Tidily efficient second feature thriller; good
enjoyable stuff of its kind.

*w Carl Foreman d Richard Fleischer
ph* Robert de Grasse *m* Paul Sawtell

Bill Williams, Barbara Hale, Richard Quine,
Richard Loo, Frank Fenton

Cleo from Five to Seven*
France / Italy 1961   90m   part colour
Rome / Paris (Bruno Drigo)

A girl waiting for the result of a medical
examination wanders around Paris thinking she
has cancer.
Impressively handled character sketch with
gratifying attention to detail.

wd Agnès Varda ph Jean Rabier m Michel
Legrand

Corinne Marchand, Antoine Bourseiller,
Dorothée Blanck, Michel Legrand

Cleopatra**
US 1934   101m   bw
Paramount / Cecil B. de Mille

After Julius Caesar's death, Cleopatra turns her
attention to Mark Antony.
More of the vices than the virtues of its producer
are notable in this fustian epic, which is almost
but not quite unwatchable because of its stolid
pace and miscasting. Some of the action
montages and the barge scene, however, are
superb cinema.

*w Waldemar Young, Vincent Lawrence d Cecil
B. de Mille ph Victor Milner m* Rudolph Kopp
md Alex North

Claudette Colbert, Henry Wilcoxon (Antony),
Warren William (Caesar), Gertrude Michael,
Joseph Schildkraut, Ian Keith, C. Aubrey Smith,
Leonard Mudie, Irving Pichel, Arthur Hohl

'It is remarkable how Cecil B. de Mille can
photograph so much on such a vast scale and
still say nothing . . . it reeks of so much pseudo-
artistry, vulgarity, philistinism, sadism, that it
can only be compared with the lowest form of
contemporary culture: Hitlerism. This is the type
of 'culture' that will be fed to the audience of
Fascist America.'—*Irving Lerner, 1968*

'He has certainly made the most sumptuous of
Roman circuses out of Roman history . . . a
constant succession of banquets, dancers,
triumphs, and a fleet set on fire.'—*The Times*

AA: Victor Milner
AAN: Alex North

Cleopatra
US 1963   243m   De Luxe   Todd-AO
TCF (Walter Wanger)

The unsurprising story is told at inordinate
length and dullness in this ill-starred epic, one of
the most heralded, and mismanaged, in film
history. (Its story is best told in the producer's
My Life with Cleopatra.) The most expensive
film ever made, for various reasons which do not
appear on the screen.

w Joseph L. Mankiewicz, Ranald MacDougall,
Sidney Buchman, and others *d* Joseph L.
Mankiewicz (and others) *ph* Leon Shamroy
m Alex North *ad* John de Cuir, Jack Martin
Smith, and others

Elizabeth Taylor, Richard Burton, Rex
Harrison, Pamela Brown, George Cole, Hume
Cronyn, Cesare Danova, Kenneth Haigh,
Andrew Keir, Martin Landau, Roddy
McDowall, Robert Stephens, Francesca Annis,
Martin Benson, Herbert Berghof, Grégoire
Aslan, Richard O'Sullivan

'Whatever was interesting about it clearly
ended up somewhere else: on the cutting room
floor, in various hotel rooms, in the newspaper
columns . . . it lacks not only
the intelligent spectacle of *Lawrence of Arabia*
but
the spectacular unintelligence of a Cecil B. de
Mille
product . . .'—*John Simon*

'The small screen does more than justice to
this monumental mouse.'—*Judith Crist*

'I only came to see the asp.'—*Charles
Addams*

AA: Leon Shamroy
AAN: best picture; Rex Harrison

The Climax*
US 1944   86m   Technicolor
Universal (George Waggner)

A young opera singer is hypnotized by a mad
doctor, who has kept his murdered mistress
embalmed for ten years.
Gothic romantic melodrama invented to
capitalize on the success—and the sets—of
Phantom of the Opera. Curiously endearing,
with a good eye-rolling part for Karloff.

w Curt Siodmak, Lynn Starling, *play* Edward
Cochran *d* George Waggner *ph* Hal Mohr, W.
Howard Greene *m* Edward Ward

Boris Karloff, Susanna Foster, Gale
Sondergaard, Turhan Bey, Thomas Gomez,
Scotty Beckett

'All quite unalarming, which is a bit of a
handicap.'—*New Yorker, 1978*

The Clinging Vine*
US 1926   71m (24 fps)   bw   silent
Cecil B. de Mille

The president's secretary is the real driving force of a paint company, but finds that love is more important than business.

Interesting silent predecessor of many career girl comedies of the thirties and forties.

w Jeannie McPherson d Paul Sloane

Leatrice Joy, Tom Moore, Toby Claude, Robert Edeson

Clive of India*

US 1935   90m   bw
TCF (Darryl F. Zanuck, William Goetz, Raymond Griffith)

The life of the 18th-century empire builder, with special emphasis on his marriage.

A very tame and now faded epic, with more romance than adventure. The production relies more on stars than technique, but it works.

w W. P. Lipscomb, R. J. Minney, from their play d Richard Boleslawski ph Peverell Marley m Alfred Newman

Ronald Colman, Loretta Young, Colin Clive, Francis Lister, Montagu Love, Robert Greig, Leo G. Carroll, C. Aubrey Smith, Mischa Auer

'Patriotic pageantry, undistorted by facts.'— *J. R. Parish*

Cloak and Dagger*

US 1946   106m   bw
United States Pictures (Milton Sperling)

A physics professor joins the secret service and is parachuted into Germany to interview a kidnapped scientist.

Supposedly authoritative espionage adventure which turned out dull and humourless; plot routine, direction absent-minded.

w Albert Maltz, Ring Lardner Jnr d Fritz Lang ph Sol Polito m Max Steiner

Gary Cooper, Lilli Palmer, Robert Alda, Vladimir Sokoloff, J. Edward Bromberg, Ludwig Stossel, Helene Thimig, Marc Lawrence

Clochemerle

France 1948   93m   bw
Cinéma Productions (Ralph Baum)

The progressive mayor of a French village erects a gentlemen's convenience in the main street and shocks the local reactionaries.

Most of the book's political satire was ironed out in this cheap and opportunist production which got a few easy laughs but failed to sustain itself.

w Gabriel Chevalier, from his novel d Pierre Chénal ph Robert Le Fèbvre m Henri Sauguet

Brochard, Maximilienne, Simone Michels, Jane Marken, Paul Demange, Felix Oudart, Saturnin Fabre

The Clock**

US 1945   90m   bw
MGM (Arthur Freed)
GB title: *Under the Clock*

A girl meets a soldier at New York's Grand Central Station and marries him during his 24-hour leave.

Everyone now seems far too nice in this winsome romance full of comedy cameos and real New York locations, but if you can relive the wartime mood it still works as a corrective to the Betty Grable glamour pieces.

w Robert Nathan, Joseph Schrank, *story* Paul and Pauline Gallico d *Vincente Minnelli* ph George Folsey m George Bassman

Judy Garland, Robert Walker, James Gleason, Lucile Gleason, Keenan Wynn, Marshall Thompson, Chester Clute

'Sweetly charming, if maybe too irresistible . . . fortunately the director fills the edges with comic characters.'—*New Yorker, 1978*

A Clockwork Orange*

GB 1971   136m   colour
Warner / Polaris (Bernard Williams)

In a future Britain of desolation and violence, a young gangster guilty of rape and murder obtains a release from prison after being experimentally brainwashed: he finds society more violent than it was in his time.

A repulsive film in which intellectuals have found acres of social and political meaning; the average judgement is likely to remain that it is pretentious and nasty rubbish for sick minds who do not mind jazzed-up images and incoherent sound.

wd Stanley Kubrick, *novel* Anthony Burgess ph John Alcott m Walter Carlos pd John Barry

Malcolm McDowell, Michael Bates, Adrienne Corri, Patrick Magee, Warren Clarke

'Very early there are hints of triteness and insecurity, and before half an hour is over it begins to slip into tedium . . . Inexplicably the script leaves out Burgess' reference to the title.'—*Stanley Kauffmann*

AAN: best picture; Stanley Kubrick (as writer and director)

Close Encounters of the Third Kind

US 1977   135m   Metrocolor   Panavision
Columbia / EMI (Julia and Michael Phillips)

A series of UFOs takes Indiana by surprise, and a workman is led by intuition and detection to the landing site which as been concealed from the public.

There's a lot of padding in this slender fantasy, which has less plot and much less suspense than *It Came from Outer Space* which was made on a tiny budget in 1955; but the technical effects are masterly though their exposure is over-prolonged, and the benevolent mysticism filled a current requirement of popular taste, accounting for the enormous box-office success of a basically flawed film. Much of the dialogue is inaudible.

wd Steven Spielberg *ph* Vilmos Zsigmond *m* John Williams *sp* Douglas Trumbull *pd* Joe Alves

Richard Dreyfuss, Françoise Truffaut, Teri Garr, Melinda Dillon, Cary Guffey
†The cost of this film was estimated at 20,000,000 dollars.

Close to My Heart
US 1951 90m bw
Warner (William Jacobs)

An adopted baby is discovered to have a murderer for a father; but environment is proved to be more important than heredity.
Routine sentimental drama.

wd William Keighley, *story* A Baby for Midge by James R. Webb *ph* Robert Burks *m* Max Steiner

Ray Milland, Gene Tierney, Fay Bainter, Howard St John, Mary Beth Hughes

Closely Observed Trains**
Czechoslovakia 1966 92m bw
Ceskoslovensky Film (Zdenek Oves)

During World War II, an apprentice railway guard at a country station falls in love and becomes a saboteur.
Warm, amusingly detailed comedy with a disconcerting downbeat ending.

wd Jiri Menzel, *novel* Bohumil Hrabal *ph* Jaromir Sofr *m* Jiri Pavlik

Vaclav Neckar, Jitka Bendova, Vladimir Valenta, Josef Somr
'Like Forman, Menzel seems incapable of being unkind to anybody.'—*Tom Milne*

The Clouded Yellow*
GB 1950 96m bw
Sydney Box (Betty Box)

A sacked secret service agent gets work tending a butterfly collection and finds that this involves him in a murder plot.
Implausible but quite engaging thriller in the Hitchcock style, involving a chase across the Lake District.

w Janet Green, Eric Ambler *d* Ralph Thomas

Trevor Howard, Jean Simmons, Barry Jones, Sonia Dresdel, Maxwell Reed, Kenneth More, André Morell

The Clown
US 1952 91m bw
MGM (William H. Wright)

A drunken clown, once a great star, is idolized by his son who believes in a comeback.
Maudlin reworking of *The Champ* (qv), with not a surprise in the plot and a star way over the top.

w Martin Rackin *d* Robert Z. Leonard *ph* Paul C. Vogel *m* David Rose

Red Skelton, Jane Greer, Tim Considine, Loring Smith, Philip Ober

Cluny Brown**
US 1946 100m bw
TCF (Ernst Lubitsch)

A plumber's niece goes into service and falls for a Czech refugee guest.
Romantic comedy in a never-never pre-war England; it does no more than poke casual fun at upper-class conventions, but the smooth direction and some excellent character comedy keep it well afloat.

w Samuel Hoffenstein, Elizabeth Reinhardt, *novel* Margery Sharp *d* Ernst Lubitsch *ph* Joseph La Shelle *m* Cyril Mockridge, Emil Newman

Jennifer Jones, Charles Boyer, *Richard Haydn*, Una O'Connor, Peter Lawford, Helen Walker, Reginald Gardiner, Reginald Owen, C. Aubrey Smith, Sara Allgood, Ernest Cossart, Florence Bates, Billy Bevan

Cobra Woman
US 1944 71m Technicolor
U-I (George Waggner)

A South Seas girl is abducted by snake worshippers ruled by her evil twin.
A monument of undiluted hokum with some amusing sets and performances but not enough self-mockery in the script.

w Richard Brooks, Gene Lewis *d* Robert Siodmak *ph* George Robinson, W. Howard Greene *m* Edward Ward

Maria Montez, Jon Hall, Sabu, Lon Chaney Jnr, Mary Nash, Edgar Barrier, Lois Collier, Samuel S. Hinds, Moroni Olsen

The Cobweb
US 1955 124m Eastmancolor
Cinemascope
MGM (John Houseman)

Tensions among the staff of a private mental clinic reach a new high over the purchase of curtains.
The patients seem saner than the doctors in this strained and verbose character drama which

despite its cast and big studio look never begins
to engage the interest.

w John Paxton, *novel* William Gibson
d Vincente Minnelli *ph* George Folsey
m Leonard Rosenman

Richard Widmark, Lauren Bacall, Charles
Boyer, *Lillian Gish*, Gloria Grahame, John
Kerr, Susan Strasberg, *Oscar Levant*, Tommy
Rettig, Paul Stewart, Adèle Jergens

'An overwrought and elaborately artificial
exercise, made scarcely more plausible by
reliance on the basic jargon of psychiatry.'—
Penelope Houston

The Cockeyed World*
US 1929   115m   bw
Fox

Further adventures of Sergeants Flagg and
Quirt, the boisterous heroes of *What Price
Glory*.
Lively early talkie; the adventure comedy
remains interesting, though the technique is
badly faded.

w William K. Wells, Laurence Stallings, Michael
Anderson, Wilson Mizner, Tom Barry *d* Raoul
Walsh *ph* Arthur Edeson

Victor McLaglen, Edmund Lowe, Lili Damita,
Lelia Karnelly, El Brendel, Bobby Burns, Stuart
Erwin

Cockfighter
US 1974   83m   Metrocolor
Rio Pinto / New World / Artists
   Entertainment Complex (Roger Corman)
aka: *Born to Kill*

A professional cockfighter ends a run of bad luck
but loses his girl.
Not badly made but rather seedy film about
appalling people.

w Charles Willeford, from his novel *d* Monte
Hellman *ph* Nestor Almendros *m* Michael
Franks

Warren Oates, Richard B. Shull, Harry Dean
Stanton, Ed Begley Jnr, Laurie Bird, Troy
Donahue

Cockleshell Heroes
GB 1955   97m   Technicolor
   Cinemascope
Columbia / Warwick (Phil C. Samuel)

During World War II, ten marines are trained to
travel by canoe into Bordeaux harbour and
attach limpet mines to German ships.
Absolutely predictable semi-documentary war
heroics, with barrack-room humour turning
eventually into tragedy. The familiar elements,

including a display of stiff upper lips, ensured
box office success.

w Bryan Forbes, Richard Maibaum *d* Jose
Ferrer *ph* John Wilcox, Ted Moore *m* John
Addison

Jose Ferrer, *Trevor Howard*, Dora Bryan, Victor
Maddern, Anthony Newley, Peter Arne, David
Lodge, Walter Fitzgerald, Beatrice Campbell

The Cocoanuts**
US 1929   96m   bw
Paramount (Walter Wanger, James R. Cown)

A chiselling hotel manager tries to get in on the
Florida land boom.
Considering its age and the dismal prints which
remain, this is a remarkably lively if primitive
first film by the Marxes, with some good routines
among the excess footage.

w George S. Kaufman, Morrie Ryskind
d Robert Florey *ph* George Folsey *m/ly* Irving
Berlin

The Four Marx Brothers, Margaret Dumont,
Oscar Shaw, Mary Eaton, Kay Francis, Basil
Ruysdael

'The camerawork showed all the mobility of a
concrete fire hydrant caught in a winter
freeze.'—*Paul D. Zimmermann*

Coconut Grove
US 1938   85m   bw
Paramount (George Arthur)

A band is fired from an excursion boat but
makes it big in a Los Angeles night club.
Vacuous comedy musical with a watchable
number or two.

w Sy Bartlett, Olive Cooper *d* Alfred Santell
ph Leo Tover *songs* various

Fred MacMurray, Harriet Hilliard, The Yacht
Club Boys, Ben Blue, Eve Arden, Billy Lee, Rufe
Davis

Coiffeur pour Dames
France 1952   87m approx   bw
Hoche (Jean Boyer)
GB title: *An Artist with Ladies*

A Provençal sheep shearer becomes a
fashionable ladies' hairdresser with a Champs-
Élysées salon, and finds that his clients are all
susceptible to his charms.
Obvious star comedy with a fair measure of
laughs; more in fact than the much later
Shampoo.

w Serge Véber, Jean Boyer, *play* P. Armont, M.
Gerbidon *d* Jean Boyer *ph* Charles Suin
m Paul Misraki

Fernandel, Blanchette Crunoy, Renée Devillers,
Arlette Poirier

Cold Turkey*
US 1970   102m   De Luxe
UA / Tandem / DFI (Bud Yorkin, Norman
Lear)

A tobacco company offers 25 million dollars to
any town which can give up smoking for thirty
days.
Rather wild and strained but sporadically
amusing satirical comedy, aggressively littered
with unpleasant detail.

w Norman Lear, *novel* I'm Giving Them Up for
Good by Margaret and Neil Rau *d* Norman
Lear *ph* Charles F. Wheeler *m* Randy Newman

Dick Van Dyke, Pippa Scott, Tom Poston,
Edward Everett Horton, Bob Newhart, Vincent
Gardenia, Jean Stapleton
  'An eager desire to debunk and shock at the
same time.'—*David McGillivray*

A Cold Wind in August*
US 1960   77m   bw
UA / Troy Films (Robert L. Ross, Philip
Hazleton)

An ageing stripper seduces a 17-year-old janitor
but the affair ends when he sees her do her act.
Roughly-made, well-acted sex drama which at
the time seemed mildly shocking but can only
survive for its central acting performance.

w Burton Wohl, from his novel *d* Alexander
Singer *ph* Floyd Crosby *m* Gerald Fried

Lola Albright, Scott Marlowe, Joe de Santis,
Herschel Bernardi

The Colditz Story**
GB 1954   97m   bw
British Lion / Ivan Foxwell

Adventures of British POWs in the German
maximum security prison in Saxony's Colditz
Castle during World
War II.
Probably the most convincing of the British
accounts of POW life, with a careful balance of
tragedy and comedy against a background of
humdrum, boring daily existence. A TV series
followed in 1972.

w Guy Hamilton, Ivan Foxwell, *book* P. R. Reid
d Guy Hamilton *ph* Gordon Dines *m* Francis
Chagrin

John Mills, Eric Portman, Christopher Rhodes,
Lionel Jeffries, Bryan Forbes, Ian Carmichael,
Richard Wattis, Frederick Valk, Anton Diffring,
Eugene Deckers, Theodore Bikel

The Collector*
US 1965   119m   Technicolor
Columbia (Jud Kinberg, John Kohn)

An inhibited young butterfly specialist kidnaps a
girl to add to his collection.
Talkative and unrewarding suspenser with
pretensions, sluggishly handled and not very
interestingly acted.

w Stanley Mann, John Kohn, *novel* John Fowles
d William Wyler *ph* Robert L. Surtees, Robert
Krasker *m* Maurice Jarre

Terence Stamp, Samantha Eggar, Mona
Washbourne

AAN: Stanley Mann, John Kohn; William
Wyler; Samantha Eggar

Colleen*
US 1936   89m   bw
Warner (Robert Lord)

Boy meets Irish girl in New York.
Typical light musical of the period with standard
studio talent.

w Peter Milne, F. Hugh Herbert, Sig Herzig
d Alfred E. Green *ph* Byron Haskin, Sol Polito
m/ly Harry Warren, Al Dubin *ch* Bobby
Connolly *gowns* Orry-Kelly

Dick Powell, Ruby Keeler, Jack Oakie, Joan
Blondell, Hugh Herbert, Louise Fazenda, Paul
Draper, Marie Wilson, Luis Alberni, Hobart
Cavanaugh, Berton Churchill

College Holiday
US 1936   87m   bw
Paramount (Harlan Thompson)

Bright young specimens are invited to spend a
summer with a lady hotelier interested in
eugenics.
Boisterous fun and games which may have
seemed funny at the time.

w J. P. McEvoy, Harlan Ware, Jay Gorney,
Henry Myers *d* Frank Tuttle *ph* Theodor
Sparkuhl *songs* various

Jack Benny, George Burns, Gracie Allen, Mary
Boland, Martha Raye, Etienne Girardot,
Marsha Hunt, Leif Erickson, Eleanore Whitney,
Johnny Downs, Olympe Bradna, Ben Blue, Jed
Prouty

College Humor
US 1933   84m   bw
Paramount

A freshman discovers that football and necking
are at least as important as studies.
Easy-going comedy-musical which helped to
establish its star.

w Dean Fales *d* Wesley Ruggles

Bing Crosby, Jack Oakie, George Burns, Gracie
Allen, Richard Arlen, Mary Carlisle

College Swing
US 1938   86m   bw
Paramount (Lewis Gensler)
GB title: *Swing, Teacher, Swing*

A dumb girl must graduate if a college is to
inherit a fortune.
Mild comedy more notable for its cast than its
script.

w Walter de Leon, Francis Martin *d* Raoul
Walsh *ph* Victor Milner *songs* various

George Burns, Gracie Allen, Martha Raye, Bob
Hope, Edward Everett Horton, Florence
George, Ben Blue, Betty Grable, Jackie Coogan,
John Payne, Cecil Cunningham, Robert
Cummings

Colonel Effingham's Raid
US 1946   70m   bw
TCF (Lamar Trotti)

A retired southern colonel tries to straighten out
a corrupt Georgia town.
Competent, unsurprising programmer.

w Kathryn Scola, *novel* Berry Fleming *d* Irving
Pichel *ph* Edward Cronjager *m* Cyril
Mockridge

Charles Coburn, Joan Bennett, William Eythe,
Allyn Joslyn, Elizabeth Patterson, Donald
Meek, Frank Craven, Thurston Hall, Cora
Witherspoon, Emory Parnell, Henry Armetta,
Roy Roberts, Charles Trowbridge

Colorado Territory*
US 1949   93m   bw
Warner (Anthony Veiller)

An outlaw escapes from prison planning one last
robbery but is shot in the attempt.
Moderate western remake of *High Sierra*.

w John Twist, Edmund H. North *d* Raoul
Walsh *ph* Sid Hickox *m* David Buttolph

Joel McCrea, Virginia Mayo, Dorothy Malone,
Henry Hull, John Archer, James Mitchell,
Morris Ankrum, Basil Ruysdael, Frank Puglia

Coma
US 1978   113m   Metrocolor
MGM (Martin Erlichman)

A lady doctor suspects that patients are being
put deliberately into coma so that their organs
can be sold, and finds herself in deadly peril.
Hitchcockian suspense thriller with nobody but
the audience believing the heroine; the fact that
there are more dead than living characters makes
it slightly too ghoulish at times.

wd Micheal Crichton, *novel* Robin Cook
ph Victor J. Kemper, Gerald Hirschfeld *m* Jerry
Goldsmith *pd* Albert Brenner

Geneviève Bujold, Michael Douglas, Richard
Widmark, Elizabeth Ashley, Rip Torn, Lois
Chiles, Harry Rhodes

The Comancheros**
US 1961   107m   De Luxe   Cinemascope
TCF (George Sherman)

A Texas Ranger and his gambler prisoner join
forces to clean up renegade gunmen operating
from a remote armed compound.
Easy-going, cheerfully violent western with lively
roughhouse sequences.

w James Edward Grant, Clair Huffaker
d Michael Curtiz *ph* William H. Clothier
m Elmer Bernstein

John Wayne, Stuart Whitman, Nehemiah
Persoff, Lee Marvin, Ina Balin, Bruce Cabot

Come and Get It*
US 1936   99m   bw
Samuel Goldwyn (Merritt Hulburd)

The life and loves of a lumber tycoon in 19th-
century Wisconsin.
Disappointingly conventional, mainly studio-
bound action drama using top talent of the
period.

w Jules Furthman, Jane Murfin, *novel* Edna
Ferber *d* Howard Hawks, William Wyler
ph Gregg Toland, Rudolph Maté

Edward Arnold, Joel McCrea, Frances Farmer,
Walter Brennan, Andrea Leeds

AA: Walter Brennan

Come Back Little Sheba*
US 1952   99m   bw
Paramount (Hal B. Wallis)

An ex-alcoholic is let down not only by his
slovenly wife but by the young girl he idolizes.
Stagey but theatrically effective transcription of
a popular domestic drama, with one outstanding
performance.

w Ketti Frings, *play William Inge d* Daniel
Mann *ph* James Wong Howe *m* Franz
Waxman

Shirley Booth, Burt Lancaster, Terry Moore,
Richard Jaeckel

AA: Shirley Booth
AAN: Terry Moore

Come Blow Your Horn*
US 1962   112m   Technicolor   Panavision
Paramount / Lear and Yorkin

A country boy in New York is envious of his
older brother's sophisticated life.
Amusing characters and funny lines permeate
this stolid transcription of an early Neil Simon

success; the big screen is not the place for them.

w Norman Lear, *play Neil Simon d* Bud Yorkin
ph William Daniels *m* Nelson Riddle

Frank Sinatra, Tony Bill, Lee J. Cobb, Molly
Picon, Jill St John, Barbara Rush, Dan Blocker

Come Fill the Cup*
US 1951 113m bw
Warner (Henry Blanke)

An alcoholic newspaperman cures himself, then
his boss's alcoholic son who is involved with
gangsters.
Unlikely but solidly entertaining melodrama,
powerfully cast.

w Ivan Goff, Ben Roberts, *novel* Harlan Ware
d Gordon Douglas *ph* Robert Burks *m* Ray
Heindorf

James Cagney, Gig Young, Raymond Massey,
Phyllis Thaxter, James Gleason, Selena Royle,
Larry Keating

AAN: Gig Young

Come Fly with Me
US 1962 109m Metrocolor Panavision
MGM / Anatole de Grunwald

The romantic adventures of three air hostesses.
Good-looking girls and airplanes but little else
make thin entertainment.

w William Roberts *d* Henry Levin *ph* Oswald
Morris

Hugh O'Brian, Dolores Hart, Karl Malden,
Pamela Tiffin, Lois Nettleton, Karl Boehm

Come Live with Me*
US 1941 86m bw
MGM (Clarence Brown)

In order to stay in America, a girl refugee from
Vienna arranges a strictly platonic marriage with
a struggling author.
Hypnotically predictable comedy, quite well
presented and performed.

w Patterson McNutt, Virginia Van Upp
d Clarence Brown *ph* George Folsey *m* Herbert
Stothart

James Stewart, Hedy Lamarr, Ian Hunter,
Verree Teasdale, Donald Meek, Barton
MacLane, *Adeline de Walt Reynolds*

Come Next Spring*
US 1955 92m Trucolor
Republic

A drunkard returns to his Arkansas farm family
and wins the respect of them and the community.
D. W. Griffith-type pastoral melodrama which
surprisingly works pretty well and leaves one
with the intended warm glow.

w Montgomery Pittman *d* R. G. Springsteen
ph Jack Marta *m* Max Steiner

Ann Sheridan, Steve Cochran, Walter Brennan,
Sherry Jackson, Richard Eyer, Edgar
Buchanan, Sonny Tufts, Mae Clarke
'An unpretentious film with a good deal of
charm.'—*MFB*

The Come On
US 1956 83m bw Superscope
AA (Lindley Parsons)

Husband and wife confidence tricksters get
homicidal when she falls in love.
In trade parlance, strictly a lower berth item; but
with points of mild interest.

w Warren Douglas, *novel* Whitman Chambers
d Russell Birdwell *ph* Ernest Haller *m* Paul
Dunlap

Anne Baxter, Sterling Hayden, John Hoyt, Jesse
White, Paul Picerni

Come on George*
GB 1939 88m bw
ATP (Jack Kitchin)

A stableboy calms a nervous racehorse and rides
him to victory.
Standard comedy vehicle, well mounted, with the
star at his box office peak.

w Anthony Kimmins, Leslie Arliss, Val
Valentine *d* Anthony Kimmins

George Formby, Pat Kirkwood, Joss Ambler,
Meriel Forbes, Cyril Raymond, George Carney,
Ronald Shiner

Come September
US 1961 112m Technicolor
Cinemascope
Universal (Robert Arthur)

A wealthy American discovers that his Italian
villa is being used as a hotel by his once-a-year
mistress, who is about to marry.
Clumsy sex farce with lush trimmings and
generation gap asides; effort more noticeable
than achievement.

w Stanley Shapiro, Maurice Richlin *d* Robert
Mulligan *ph* William Daniels *m* Hans J. Salter

Rock Hudson, Gina Lollobrigida, Sandra Dee,
Bobby Darin, Walter Slezak, Brenda de Banzie,
Joel Grey, Rosanna Rory, Ronald Howard

Come to the Stable*
US 1949 94m bw
TCF (Samuel G. Engel)

Two French nuns arrive in New England to build
a local hospital, and melt the hearts of the local
grumps.

This old-time charmer simply brims with sweetness and light and is produced with high-class studio efficiency.

w Oscar Millard, Sally Benson, *story* Clare Boothe Luce *d* Henry Koster *ph* Joseph La Shelle *md* Lionel Newman *m* Cyril Mockridge

Loretta Young, Celeste Holm, Hugh Marlowe, Elsa Lanchester, Thomas Gomez, Dorothy Patrick, Basil Ruysdael, Dooley Wilson, Regis Toomey, Henri Letondal

AAN: Clare Boothe Luce; Joseph La Shelle; Loretta Young; Celeste Holm; Elsa Lanchester; song 'Through a Long and Sleepless Night' (*m* Alfred Newman, *ly* Mack Gordon)

The Comedians*
US / Bermuda / France 1967   160m Metrocolor
  Panavision
MGM / Maximilian / Trianon (Peter Glenville)

A variety of English-speaking eccentrics are caught up in the violent events of Haiti under Papa Doc Duvalier.
Clumsy and heavy-going compression of a too-topical novel, with most of the plot left in at the expense of character. Neither entertaining nor instructive, but bits of acting please.

w Graham Greene, from his novel *d* Peter Glenville *ph* Henri Decaë *m* Laurence Rosenthal

Richard Burton, Elizabeth Taylor, *Alec Guinness*, Peter Ustinov, Lillian Gish, Paul Ford, Roscoe Lee Browne, James Earl Jones, Raymond St Jacques, Cicely Tyson

'So thick and fast do the clichés come that one feels the script can only have been salvaged from some *New Statesman* competition.'—*Tom Milne*

'It's pleasant to spend two hours again in Greeneland, still well-stocked with bilious minor crucifixions, furtive fornication, cynical politics, and reluctant hope.'—*Stanley Kauffmann*

The Comedy Man*
GB 1964   92m   bw
British Lion—Gray-Consort (Jon Pennington)

A middle-aged actor on the skids desperately rounds up his contacts and becomes the star of a TV commercial.
Determinedly depressing satirical melodrama with engaging moments; comedy emphasis would have better suited the talents.

w Peter Yeldham, *novel* Douglas Hayes *d* Alvin Rakoff *ph* Ken Hodges *m* Bill McGuffie

Kenneth More, Cecil Parker, Dennis Price, Billie Whitelaw, Norman Rossington, Angela

Douglas, Edmund Purdom, Frank Finlay, Alan Dobie

The Comedy of Terrors*
US 1963   88m   Pathecolor   Panavision
Alta Vista / AIP (Anthony Carras, Richard Matheson)

Two impecunious funeral directors decide to speed up the demise of their prospective clients.
Disappointingly slackly-handled and rather tiresome macabre frolic, notable for a few splendid moments and an imperishable cast.

w Richard Matheson *d* Jacques Tourneur *ph* Floyd Crosby *m* Les Baxter

Vincent Price, Peter Lorre, Boris Karloff, Basil Rathbone, Joe E. Brown, Joyce Jameson

The Comic**
US 1969   95m   Technicolor
Columbia (Carl Reiner)

The success, downfall and old age of a silent film comedian in Hollywood.
Remarkably bright and cinematic tragi-comedy obviously based on Buster Keaton, with a *Citizen Kane*-type framework. Not a commercial success, but a must for professionals.

w Carl Reiner, Aaron Rubin *d* Carl Reiner *ph* W. Wallace Kelley *m* Jack Elliott

Dick Van Dyke, Mickey Rooney (more or less playing Ben Turpin), Cornel Wilde, Carl Reiner, Michele Lee, Pert Kelton
'Offers a variety of delights.'—*Judith Crist*

Coming Home
US 1978   128m   De Luxe
UA / Jerome Hellman

An embittered Vietnam veteran falls for the wife of a serving soldier.
Self-pitying romantic wallow which must mean more to American audiences than to others. Goodish acting.

w Waldo Salt, Robert C. Jones, *story* Nancy Dowd *d* Hal Ashby *ph* Haskell Wexler *pd* Mike Haller *m* various

Jane Fonda, Jon Voight, Bruce Dern, Robert Carradine, Penelope Milford

The Command
US 1954   94m   Warnercolor
  Cinemascope
Warner (David Weisbart)

A cavalry troop escorts a wagon train through Indian country.
Competent but unsurprising 'second team' western.

w Russell Hughes, *novel* James Warner Bellah *d* David Butler *ph* Wilfrid M. Cline *m* Dmitri Tiomkin

Guy Madison, Joan Weldon, James Whitmore, Carl Benton Reid, Harvey Lembeck, Ray Teal, Bob Nichols

Command Decision*
US 1949 111m bw
MGM (Sidney Franklin)

War among the back-room boys; a general, his staff and his peers debate the aerial bombardment of Germany.
Plainly reproduced version of a determinedly serious play, with a remarkable cast partly at sea.

w William R. Laidlaw, George Froeschel, *play* William Wister Haines *d* Sam Wood *ph* Harold Rosson *m* Miklos Rozsa

Clark Gable, Walter Pidgeon, Van Johnson, Brian Donlevy, John Hodiak, Charles Bickford, Edward Arnold, Marshall Thompson, Richard Quine, Cameron Mitchell, Clinton Sundberg, Ray Collins, Warner Anderson, John McIntire, Moroni Olsen

The Commandos Strike at Dawn*
US 1942 98m bw
Columbia (Lester Cowan)

Norwegian commandos outwit the Nazis with the help of the British navy.
Standard war adventure shot in Newfoundland.

w Irwin Shaw, *story* C. S. Forester *d* John Farrow *ph* William C. Mellor *m* Louis Gruenberg

Paul Muni, Anna Lee, Lillian Gish, Cedric Hardwicke, Robert Coote, Ray Collins, Rosemary de Camp, Richard Derr, Alexander Knox, Rod Cameron

AAN: Louis Gruenberg

Common Clay
US 1930 68m bw
Fox

A speakeasy hostess becomes maid in a wealthy household and falls in love with her betters.
Archetypal soap opera which caused a mild sensation and sent its star into half a dozen imitations.

w Jules Furthman, *novel* Cleves Kincaid *d* Victor Fleming *ph* Glen MacWilliams

Constance Bennett, Lew Ayres, Tully Marshall, Matty Kemp, Purnell Pratt, Beryl Mercer

The Common Touch*
GB 1941 104m bw
British National (John Baxter)

A rich young man poses as a tramp to save a dosshouse from destruction.
Naive drama with a social conscience, remade from the 1932 talkie *Dosshouse.* A brave try.

w Barbara K. Emery, Geoffrey Orme, *novel* Herbert Ayres *d* John Baxter

Geoffrey Hibbert, Greta Gynt, Joyce Howard, Harry Welchman, Edward Rigby, George Carney, Bransby Williams, Wally Patch, Eliot Makeham, Bernard Miles, Bill Fraser, John Longden; *guests* Sandy Macpherson, Scott Sanders, Mark Hambourg, Carrol Gibbons

Company Limited*
India 1971 112m bw
Bharat Shumshere Rana

The young export sales manager of a firm of Delhi electrical appliance manufacturers is saved from boredom by his wife's younger sister.
Quietly pleasing but overlong comedy-drama of modern urban India, very typical of its director.

wd Satyajit Ray, novel Shankar *ph* Soumendu Roy

Barun Chanda, Sharmilla Tagore, Parumita Chowdhary

'Subtle, witty, intelligent, and beautifully acted.'—*Michael Billington, Illustrated London News*

The Company She Keeps
US 1950 83m bw
RKO (John Houseman)

A self-sacrificing parole officer allows a parolee to steal her fiancé.
Considering the credits, a dismally novelettish drama of almost no interest.

w Ketti Frings *d* John Cromwell *ph* Nicholas Musuraca *m* Leigh Harline

Lizabeth Scott, *Jane Greer,* Dennis O'Keefe, Fay Baker, John Hoyt, James Bell, Don Beddoe, Bert Freed

Compulsion**
US 1959 103m bw Cinemascope
TCF (Richard D. Zanuck)

In the twenties, two Chicago students kidnap and murder a young boy for kicks.
Rather dogged but earnest fictionalization of the Leopold-Loeb case with solid performances and production.

w Richard Murphy, *play* Meyer Levin *d* Richard Fleischer *ph* William C. Mellor *m* Lionel Newman

Dean Stockwell, Bradford Dillman, Orson
Welles (in a cameo court appearance as
Clarence Darrow), Diane Varsi, E. G. Marshall,
Martin Milner, Richard Anderson, Robert
Simon

Comrade X*
US 1940   89m   bw
MGM (Gottfried Reinhardt)

An American correspondent in Russia is
blackmailed into smuggling a girl out of the
country.
Lame satirical comedy in the wake of
Ninotchka; a few good moments, but generally
heavy-handed.

w Ben Hecht, Charles Lederer, *original story*
Walter Reisch d King Vidor m Bronislau
Kaper

Clark Gable, Hedy Lamarr, Felix Bressart,
Oscar Homolka, Eve Arden, Sig Rumann

AAN: Walter Reisch

Condemned*
US 1930   86m   bw
Samuel Goldwyn

A bank robber is sent to Devil's Island and falls
in love with the wife of the brutal warden.
Slow-moving but pictorially attractive
melodrama with old-style performances.

w Sidney Howard, *novel* Condemned to Devil's
Island by Blair Niles d Wesley Ruggles
ph George Barnes, Gregg Toland sets William
Cameron Menzies

Ronald Colman, Ann Harding, Louis Wolheim,
Dudley Digges, William Elmer

AAN: Ronald Colman

The Condemned of Altona*
Italy / France 1962   113m   bw
(TCF) Titanus / SGC (Carlo Ponti)

The head of a German shipping empire discovers
he has only a few months to live and tries to bring
his family to order.
Strident intellectual melodrama whose credits
tell all. Watchable for the acting, but very glum.

w Abby Mann, Cesare Zavattini, *play* Jean-Paul
Sartre d Vittorio de Sica ph Roberto Gerardi
m Dmitri Shostakovich

Fredric March, Sophia Loren, Robert Wagner,
Maximilian Schell, Françoise Prévost, Alfredo
Franchi
  'This film is such a hopeless mess that it is
difficult to know where to begin criticizing it.'—
Tom Milne

Condemned to Death*
GB 1932   75m   bw
Twickenham (Julius Hagen)

A condemned killer hypnotizes a judge into
murdering those who turned him in.
Irresistible nonsense of the old school, with
spirited direction and a good cast.

w Bernard Merivale, Harry Fowler Mear, Brock
Williams, *play* Jack O'Lantern by George
Goodchild and James Dawson d Walter Forde
ph Sidney Blythe, William Luff

Arthur Wontner, Gillian Lind, Edmund Gwenn,
Gordon Harker, Jane Welsh, Cyril Raymond
  'It would be difficult to find a dull moment.'—
The Bioscope

Conduct Unbecoming*
GB 1975   107m   Technicolor
British Lion / Crown (Michael Deeley, Barry
    Spikings)

In an officers' mess in India in the nineties, a
cadet is accused of assault on a lady but the real
culprit is a paranoic who has taken to pigsticking
in quite the wrong way.
Disappointingly flatly-handled and quite
unatmospheric picturization of an absorbing
West End melodrama. The cast is largely
wasted, but stretches of dialogue maintain their
interest.

w Robert Enders, *play* Barry England
d Michael Anderson ph Bob Huke m Stanley
Myers

Michael York, Stacy Keach, Trevor Howard,
Christopher Plummer, Richard Attenborough,
Susannah York, James Faulkner, James Donald

Cone of Silence*
GB 1960   92m   bw
British Lion / Bryanston (Aubrey Baring)
US title: *Trouble in the Sky*

A seasoned pilot is condemned for an error
which caused a crash and later dies in similar
circumstances. A flying examiner discovers
scientific reasons for exonerating him.
Tolerable suspense drama let down by thin
dialogue and confused characterization.

w Robert Westerby, *novel* David Beaty
d Charles Frend ph Arthur Grant m Gerhard
Schurmann

Michael Craig, Bernard Lee, Peter Cushing,
George Sanders, Elizabeth Seal, André Morell,
Gordon Jackson, Delphi Lawrence, Noel
Willman, Charles Tingwell

Coney Island**
US 1943   96m   Technicolor
TCF (William Perlberg)

Two fairground showmen vie for the affections of a songstress.
Brassy, simple-minded, entertaining musical. Very typical of its time; later remade as *Wabash Avenue* (qv).

w George Seaton *d Walter Lang ph* Ernest Palmer *songs* Leo Robin, Ralph Rainger *m* Alfred Newman *ch* Hermes Pan *ad* Richard Day, Joseph C. Wright

Betty Grable, George Montgomery, Cesar Romero, Charles Winninger, Phil Silvers, Matt Briggs, Paul Hurst, Frank Orth, Andrew Tombes, Alec Craig, Hal K. Dawson

AAN: Alfred Newman

Confession

US 1937 90m bw
Warner (Henry Blanke)

An errant mother shoots her former lover to protect her daughter.
Stilted romantic melodrama copied scene for scene from a 1936 German film *Mazurka*.

w Julius J. Epstein, Margaret Le Vino, *original screenplay* Hans Rameau *d* Joe May *ph* Sid Hickox *m* Peter Kreuder *md* Leo F. Forbstein *ad* Anton Grot

Kay Francis, Ian Hunter, Basil Rathbone, Jane Bryan, Donald Crisp, Dorothy Peterson, Laura Hope Crews, Robert Barrat

The Confession*

France / Italy 1970 160m Eastmancolor
Films Corona / Films Pomereu / Selena Cinematografica (Robert Dorfmann)
original title: *L'Aveu*

In Prague in 1951, a minister is secretly imprisoned and interrogated, and finally confesses under duress to anti-communist activities.
Brutally long but frequently impressive anti-Soviet tract, extremely well acted but less exciting than *Z*. Based on a true account.

w Jorge Semprun, *book* Lise and Artur London *d Costa-Gavras ph* Raoul Coutard *m* not credited

Yves Montand, Simone Signoret, Gabriele Ferzetti, Michel Vitold

Confessions of a Nazi Spy***

US 1939 102m bw
Warner (Robert Lord)

How G-men ferreted out Nazis in the United States.
Topical exposé with all concerned in top form; a semi-documentary very typical of Warner product throughout the thirties and forties, from

G-Men to *Mission to Moscow* and *I Was a Communist for the FBI*: well made, punchy, and smartly edited, with a loud moral at the end.

w Milton Krims, John Wexley, from materials gathered by former FBI agent Leon G. Turrou *d Anatole Litvak ph* Sol Polito *m* Max Steiner

Edward G. Robinson, Paul Lukas, George Sanders, Francis Lederer, Henry O'Neill, Lya Lys, James Stephenson, Sig Rumann, Dorothy Tree, Joe Sawyer

'The Warner brothers have declared war on Germany with this one . . . with this precedent there is no way any producer could argue against dramatizing any social or political theme on the grounds that he's afraid of domestic or foreign censorship. Everybody duck.'—*Pare Lorentz*

'Has a remarkable resemblance to a full-length *Crime Does Not Pay.*'—*David Wolff*

'One of the most sensational movie jobs on record, workmanlike in every respect and spang across the headlines.'—*Otis Ferguson*

Confessions of an Opium Eater

US 1962 85m bw
Albert Zugsmith
GB title: *Evils of Chinatown*

In San Francisco in the nineties, a seaman falls into the clutches of a tong.
The hero is called De Quincey, but that is the only association with the famous book of the same title. This absurd melodrama is just about bad enough to be funny, but not very.

w Robert Hill *d* Albert Zugsmith *ph* Joseph Biroc *m* Albert Glasser *ad Eugene Lourié*

Vincent Price, Linda Ho, Richard Loo, Philip Ahn, June Kim

'Has to be seen to be believed . . . starved girls captive in cages, secret panels, sliding doors, sewer escape routes, opium dens and nightmares . . .'—*MFB*

Confidential Agent**

US 1945 122m bw
Warner (Robert Buckner)

An emissary of Franco's Spain comes to England in the late thirties to make a munitions deal, and falls in love with the tycoon's daughter.
Heavy-going simplification of Graham Greene's lowering novel, with cast and (especially) set designers all at sea but nevertheless providing striking moments.

w Robert Buckner *d* Herman Shumlin *ph James Wong Howe m* Franz Waxman

Charles Boyer, Lauren Bacall, Katina Paxinou, Peter Lorre, Victor Francen, George Coulouris, Wanda Hendrix, George Zucco, Miles Mander

Confidential Report*
Spain 1955   99m   bw
Sevilla Studios (Louis Dolivet, Orson Welles)
aka: *Mr Arkadin*

A wealthy and powerful financier employs a
young American to seek out figures from his own
past, who are soon found dead . . .
Silly melodrama which might have been
suspenseful if done by Hitchcock, or even by
Welles at his peak; as it is, weak writing and
sloppy production remove most of the interest
and reveal it as a very obvious bag of tricks.

wd Orson Welles *ph* Jean Bourgoin *m* Paul
Misraki

Orson Welles, Michael Redgrave, Katina
Paxinou, Akim Tamiroff, Mischa Auer, Patricia
Medina, Jack Watling, Peter Van Eyck, Paola
Mori, Robert Arden, Grégoire Aslan, Suzanne
Flon

   'Tilted camera angles, heavy atmospheric
shots, overlapping dialogue—all the trademarks
are here, sometimes over-used to an almost
hysterical degree, but they have little significance
. . . (the film) springs not from life but from the
earlier cinematic world of Welles himself and
from the kind of thriller written about thirty
years ago by E. Philips Oppenheim.'—*Gavin
Lambert*

Confirm or Deny*
US 1941   78m   bw
TCF (Len Hammond)

An American reporter falls for a wireless
operator in wartime London.
Artificial but watchable minor romantic
melodrama.

w Jo Swerling, Henry Wales, Samuel Fuller
d Archie Mayo *ph* Leon Shamroy

Don Ameche, Joan Bennett, Roddy McDowall,
Arthur Shields, Raymond Walburn, John Loder

Conflict*
US 1945   86m   bw
Warner (William Jacobs)

A man murders his wife and is apparently
haunted by her; but the odd happenings have
been arranged by a suspicious psychiatrist.
Leaden and artificial melodrama with both stars
miscast; a few effective moments.

w Arthur T. Horman, Dwight Taylor *d* Curtis
Bernhardt *ph* Merritt Gerstad *m* Frederick
Hollander

Humphrey Bogart, Sydney Greenstreet, Alexis
Smith, Rose Hobart, Charles Drake, Grant
Mitchell

Conflict of Wings*
GB 1953   84m   Eastmancolor
Group Three (Herbert Mason)
US title: *Fuss over Feathers*

East Anglian villagers fight to save a bird
sanctuary from being taken over by the RAF as
a rocket range.
Sub-Ealing comedy-drama with a highly
predictable outcome; generally pleasant but
without much bite.

w Don Sharp, John Pudney *d* John Eldridge
ph Arthur Grant *m* Philip Green

John Gregson, Muriel Pavlow, Kieron Moore,
Niall MacGinnis, Sheila Sweet, Harry Fowler,
Barbara Hicks, Charles Lloyd Pack

Congo Crossing
US 1956   85m   Technicolor
U-I (Howard Christie)

Assorted fugitives from justice gather at
Congotanga, which has no extradition laws.
The poor man's *Casablanca*, quite good looking
but dully written and presented.

w Richard Alan Simmons *d* Joseph Pevney
ph Russell Metty *m* Joseph Gershenson

George Nader, Virginia Mayo, *Peter Lorre*,
Michael Pate, Rex Ingram

Congress Dances*
Germany 1931   92m   bw
UFA (Erich Pommer)
original title: *Der Kongress Tanzt*

At the Congress of Vienna, Metternich attempts
to decoy the Tsar with a countess; but the Tsar
has a double.
Lubitsch-like treatment of sexual dalliance in
high places; no doubt a stunner in its time, but
rather faded now.

w Norbert Falk, Robert Liebmann *d Erik
Charrell ph* Carl Hoffmann *m Werner
Heymann*

Conrad Veidt, Henri Garat/Willy Fritsch, Lilian
Harvey

A Connecticut Yankee*
US 1931   96m   bw
Fox

A man dreams himself back to the court of King
Arthur, and teaches the Middle Ages a thing or
two about modern living.
First sound version of Mark Twain's classic
fantasy, also filmed in 1921 and 1949. Creaky
now, but amiable.

w William Conselman *d* David Butler
ph Ernest Palmer

Will Rogers, Maureen O'Sullivan, Myrna Loy, Frank Albertson, William Farnum

A Connecticut Yankee in King Arthur's Court*
US 1949   106m   Technicolor
Paramount
GB title: *A Yankee in King Arthur's Court*

Gossamer musical version of the above with the emphasis on song and knockabout. Palatable, with the 'Busy Doin' Nothin' ' sequence the most memorable.

w Edmund Beloin *d* Tay Garnett *ph* Ray Rennahan *md* Victor Young

Bing Crosby, Rhonda Fleming, William Bendix, *Cedric Hardwicke*, Murvyn Vye

Connecting Rooms
GB 1969   103m   Technicolor
Telstar / Franklin Gollings (Harry Field)

In a seedy Bayswater boarding house, a dismissed schoolmaster befriends a failed cellist whose protégé is a sponging songwriter. Aggressively dismal melodrama which would be hilarious if it were not so sadly slow and naive.

wd Franklin Gollings, *play* The Cellist by Marion Hart *ph* John Wilcox *m* Joan Shakespeare

Bette Davis, Michael Redgrave, Alexis Kanner, Kay Walsh, Gabrielle Drake, Leo Genn, Olga Georges-Picot, Richard Wyler, Brian Wilde

The Connection
US 1961   110m   bw
Shirley Clarke / Lewis Allen

Junkies hang around waiting for a fix and are filmed by a documentary unit.
Unattractive low-budgeter with occasional impressive moments.

w Jack Gelber *d* Shirley Clarke *ph* Arthur J. Ornitz *m* Freddie Redd *ad* Richard Sylbert

Warren Finnerty, Jerome Raphael, Jim Anderson, Carl Lee, Roscoe Browne

The Conqueror
US 1955   112m   Technicolor
   Cinemascope
Howard Hughes (Dick Powell)

A romance of the early life of Genghis Khan, who captures and is enamoured by the daughter of an enemy.
Solemn pantomime with a measure of bloodthirsty action and dancing girls, but featuring too many dull spots between, especially as the star is the most unlikely of eastern

warriors and the production values careful but not too steady.

w Oscar Millard *d* Dick Powell *ph* Joseph La Shelle, Leo Tover, Harry J. Wild *m* Victor Young

John Wayne, Susan Hayward, Pedro Armendariz, Agnes Moorehead, Thomas Gomez, John Hoyt, William Conrad, Ted de Corsia, Lee Van Cleef

The Conquerors
US 1932   88m   bw
RKO
TV title: *Pioneer Builders*

Nebraska settlers in the 1870s set the seeds of a banking empire.
Routine family epic with the star playing himself and his own grandson.

w Robert Lord, *story* Howard Estabrook *d* William Wellman *ph* Edward Cronjager *m* Max Steiner

Richard Dix, Ann Harding, Edna May Oliver, Guy Kibbee, Donald Cook, Julie Haydon, Jed Prouty

Conquest**
US 1937   115m   bw
MGM (Bernard Hollyman)
GB title: *Marie Walewska*

The life of Napoleon's most enduring mistress. Measured, dignified, and often rather dull historical fiction, lightened by excellent performances and production.

w Samuel Hoffenstein, Salka Viertel, S. N. Behrman, from a Polish play dramatized by Helen Jerome *d* Clarence Brown *ph* Karl Freund

Greta Garbo, *Charles Boyer*, Reginald Owen, Alan Marshal, Henry Stephenson, Dame May Whitty, Leif Erickson

AAN: Charles Boyer

Conquest of Space
US 1955   80m   Technicolor
Paramount (George Pal)

In 1980, the Americans have built a space station in the atmosphere, and plan a voyage to the moon but are sent to Mars instead.
So history catches up with science fiction. This sober prophecy looks good but very little happens and the result is as dull as it is bright and shiny.

w James O'Hanlon *d* Byron Haskin *ph* Lionel Lindon *m* Van Cleeve *ad* Hal Pereira, James McMillan Johnson *sp* John P. Fulton, Irmin Roberts, Paul Lerpae, Ivyl Burks, Jan Domella

Eric Fleming, Walter Brooke, Mickey
Shaughnessy, William Hopper, Ross Martin

Conrack*
US 1974   106m   De Luxe   Panavision
TCF (Martin Ritt, Irving Ravetch)

A young white teacher is assigned to an all-black
school in South Carolina, and after some
difficulty makes friends with children and
parents.
Nostalgically mellow happy-film, lit by bright
smiles all round.

w Irving Ravetch, Harriet Frank Jnr, *novel* The
Water Is Wide by Pat Conroy d Martin Ritt
ph John Alonzo m John Williams

Jon Voight, Paul Winfield, Hume Cronyn,
Madge Sinclair, Tina Andrews
    'For all its craftsman-like virtues, it seems a
conscious turning aside from the complexities of
modern cinema to the simpler alternatives of
yesteryear. Indeed, with underprivileged white
children instead of black and Greer Garson
substituting for Jon Voight, the film might have
been made all of thirty years ago.'—*John
Raisbeck*

Conspiracy of Hearts*
GB 1960   113m   bw
Rank (Betty E. Box)

During World War II, Italian nuns smuggle
Jewish children across the border from a nearby
prison camp.
Highly commercial combination of exploitable
sentimental elements: Germans, Jews, nuns,
children, war, suspense. Remarkably, it gets by
without causing nausea.

w Robert Presnell Jnr d Ralph Thomas
ph Ernest Steward m Angelo Lavagnino

Lilli Palmer, Sylvia Syms, Yvonne Mitchell,
Albert Lieven, Ronald Lewis, Peter Arne, Nora
Swinburne, Michael Goodliffe, Megs Jenkins,
David Kossoff, Jenny Laird, George Coulouris,
Phyllis Neilson-Terry

Conspirator
GB 1949   87m   bw
MGM (Arthur Hornblow Jnr)

A guards officer, unknown to his young wife, is a
communist spy.
Singularly awful romantic melodrama which
never convinces or entertains for a moment.

w Sally Benson, Gerard Fairlie, *novel* Humphrey
Slater d Victor Saville ph E. A. Young m John
Wooldridge

Robert Taylor, Elizabeth Taylor, Harold
Warrender, Robert Flemyng, Marie Ney

The Conspirators*
US 1944   101m   bw
Warner (Jack Chertok)

A Dutch underground leader escapes to Lisbon
and clears up international intrigue.
Interestingly cast but often listless wartime
melodrama, a doomed attempt to reprise
Casablanca without Humphrey Bogart.

w Vladimir Pozner, Leo Rosten, *novel* City of
Shadows by Frederick Prokosch d Jean
Negulesco ph Arthur Edeson m Max Steiner

Hedy Lamarr, Paul Henreid, Sydney
Greenstreet, Peter Lorre, *Victor Francen*, Carol
Thurston, Vladimir Sokoloff, Joseph Calleia,
Edward Ciannelli, Steve Geray, Kurt Katch,
George Macready

The Constant Husband*
GB 1954   88m   Technicolor print
British Lion / London Films (Frank Launder,
    Sidney Gilliat)

An amnesiac discovers that he is a multiple
bigamist, still wanted by each of his five wives.
Flimsy comedy which never really gets going
despite an attractive cast.

w Sidney Gilliat, Val Valentine d Sidney Gilliat
ph Ted Scaife m Malcolm Arnold

Rex Harrison, Kay Kendall, Margaret Leighton,
Cecil Parker, Nicole Maurey, George Cole,
Raymond Huntley, Michael Hordern, Eric
Pohlmann, Robert Coote

The Constant Nymph*
GB 1933   98m   bw
Gaumont (Michael Balcon)

In the Tyrol, a composer leaves his rich wife for a
schoolgirl suffering from a heart condition.
Archetypal romantic drama from Margaret
Kennedy's book, first filmed in 1928 by the same
producer (directed by Adrian Brunel, with Ivor
Novello and Mabel Poulton). A standard
production of its time, which seems to have
vanished with the literary copyright.

w Margaret Kennedy, Basil Dean, from their
play based on her novel d Basil Dean

Brian Aherne, Victoria Hopper, Leonora
Corbett, Lyn Harding, Mary Clare, Jane Baxter
    'One can say that it has a beginning, a middle
and an end, but it lacks something vital.'—*E. V.
Lucas, Punch*

The Constant Nymph*
US 1943   112m   bw
Warner (Henry Blanke)

Artificially well-produced, overlong Hollywood
version of the above.

w Kathryn Scola *d* Edmund Goulding *ph* Tony Gaudio *m* Erich Wolfgang Korngold

Charles Boyer, *Joan Fontaine*, Alexis Smith, Brenda Marshall, Charles Coburn, Dame May Whitty, Peter Lorre, Joyce Reynolds, Jean Muir, Edward Ciannelli, Montagu Love, André Charlot

AAN: Joan Fontaine

Contraband**
GB 1940 92m bw
British National (John Corfield)
US title: *Blackout*

A Danish merchant captain and a girl in wartime London expose a gang of spies using a cinema as headquarters.
Enjoyable lightweight comedy melodrama on Hitchcock lines, reuniting the unlikely star team from *The Spy in Black*.

w Emeric Pressburger, Michael Powell, Brock Williams *d* Michael Powell

Conrad Veidt, Valerie Hobson, Esmond Knight, Hay Petrie, Raymond Lovell, Harold Warrender, Charles Victor, Manning Whiley

Convention City*
US 1933 78m bw
Warner (Henry Blanke)

Extra-marital fun and games at a Chicago convention.
Amusing and rather risqué comedy which helped to bring down on Hollywood the wrath of the Legion of Decency.

w Robert Lord *d* Archie Mayo *ph* William Rees

Joan Blondell, Guy Kibbee, Adolphe Menjou, Dick Powell, Mary Astor, Frank McHugh, Ruth Donnelly, Hugh Herbert, Hobart Cavanaugh

The Conversation**
US 1974 113m Technicolor
Paramount / Francis Ford Coppola

A bugging device expert lives only for his work, but finally develops a conscience.
Absorbing but extremely difficult to follow in detail, this personal, timely (in view of Watergate), Kafkaesque suspense story centres almost entirely on director and leading actor, who have a field day.

wd Francis Ford Coppola ph Bill Butler *m* David Shire

Gene Hackman, John Cazale, Allen Garfield, Frederick Forrest
'A private, hallucinatory study in technical expertise and lonely guilt.'—*Sight and Sound*

'A terrifying depiction of a ransacked spirit.'—*New Yorker, 1977*
'Alert, truthful, unarty and absolutely essential viewing.'—*Michael Billington, Illustrated London News*
AAN: best picture; Francis Ford Coppola (as writer)

Conversation Piece
Italy / France 1974 121m Technicolor
Todd AO 35
Rusconi / Gaumont (Giovanni Bertolucci)
original title: *Gruppo di Famiglia in un Interno*

When a reclusive professor is persuaded to let his top floor to a young couple he is brought face to face with his latent homosexuality and his approaching death.
Death in Venice revisited, but with much less style and even more obscurity.

w Luchino Visconti, Suso Cecchi d'Amico, Enrico Medioli *d* Luchino Visconti
ph Pasqualino de Santis *m* Franco Mannino

Burt Lancaster, Helmut Berger, Claudia Marsani, Silvana Mangano

Convict 99**
GB 1938 91m bw
Gainsborough (Edward Black)

A seedy schoolmaster accidentally becomes a prison governor and lets the convicts run the place.
Patchily funny if overlong and in some ways rather serious Will Hay comedy, not quite typical of him.

w Marriott Edgar, Val Guest, Ralph Smart, Jack Davies *d* Marcel Varnel *ph* Arthur Crabtree *md* Louis Levy

Will Hay, Graham Moffatt, Moore Marriott, Googie Withers, Garry Marsh, Peter Gawthorne, Basil Radford, Kathleen Harrison

Convicted*
US 1950 91m bw
Columbia (Jerry Bresler)

When a prison informer is killed, one convict knows who did it.
Routine, over-plotted, strongly cast prison melodrama.

w William Bowers, Fred Niblo Jnr, Seton I. Miller, *play* Martin Flavin *d* Henry Levin *ph* Burnett Guffey *m* George Duning

Glenn Ford, Broderick Crawford, Millard Mitchell, Dorothy Malone, Frank Faylen, Carl Benton Reid, Will Geer

Convicts Four*

US 1962   106m   bw
Allied Artists–Lubin–Kaufman (A. Ronald
Lubin)
original and GB title: *Reprieve*

A convict reprieved from the electric chair
spends eighteen years in prison, becomes a
painter, and is rehabilitated.

Odd and unsatisfactory mixture of
documentary, melodrama, sentimentality and
character study, with stars unexpectedly
popping in for cameo appearances. Something
worthier was obviously intended.

wd Millard Kaufman, from the autobiography of
John Resko *ph* Joseph Biroc *m* Leonard
Rosenman

Ben Gazzara, Vincent Price, Rod Steiger,
Broderick Crawford, Stuart Whitman, Ray
Walston, Jack Kruschen, Sammy Davis Jnr

Convoy*

GB 1941   90m   bw
Ealing (Sergei Nolbandov)

A German pocket battleship menaces a British
convoy, and a merchant ship sacrifices itself to
prevent disaster.

Fluent British war film of the early days, the only
substantial work of a much vaunted director who
was subsequently killed.

w Pen Tennyson, Patrick Kirwan *d Pen
Tennyson*

Clive Brook, John Clements, Edward Chapman,
Judy Campbell, Penelope Dudley Ward,
Edward Rigby, Allan Jeayes, Albert Lieven

Convoy

US 1978   110m   De Luxe   Panavision
UA / EMI (Robert M. Sherman)

A folk hero truck driver survives several crashes
and his policeman nemesis.

A virtually plotless anthology of wanton
destruction. Too noisy to sleep through.

w B. W. L. Norton, based on the song by C. W.
McCall *d* Sam Peckinpah *ph* Harry Stradling
Jnr

Kris Kristofferson, Ali MacGraw, Ernest
Borgnine, Burt Young, Madge Sinclair

'There's a whole lot of nothing going on here
... strictly a summer popcorn picture for the
nondiscriminating.'—*Variety*

Coogan's Bluff**

US 1968   94m   Technicolor
Universal (Don Siegel)

An Arizona sheriff takes an escaped killer back
to New York, and when the man escapes uses
western methods to recapture him.

Violent, well-done police story which inspired
the TV series *McCloud.*

w Herman Miller, Dean Riesner, Howard
Rodman *d Don Siegel ph* Bud Thackery
m Lalo Schifrin

Clint Eastwood, Lee J. Cobb, Susan Clark, Don
Stroud, Tisha Sterling, Betty Field, Tom Tully

Cool Breeze

US 1972   102m   Metrocolor
MGM / Penelope (Gene Corman)

A miscellaneous gang of crooks is rounded up to
commit a robbery, which ultimately fails.

Third, all-black remake of *The Asphalt Jungle*
(the others being *The Badlanders* and *Cairo*).
Fashionable violence against a Los Angeles
backdrop, but not at all memorable.

wd Barry Pollack *ph* Andy Davis *m* Solomon
Burke

Thalmus Rasulala, Judy Pace, Jim Watkins,
Raymond St Jacques, Lincoln Kilpatrick

Cool Hand Luke**

US 1967   126m   Technicolor   Panavision
Jalem / Warner (Gordon Carroll)

Sentenced to two years' hard labour with the
chain gang, a convict becomes a legend of
invulnerability but is eventually shot during an
escape.

Allegedly a Christ-allegory, this well-made and
good-looking film is only partially successful as
an entertainment; slow stretches of soul-
searching alternate with brutality, and not much
acting is possible.

w Donn Pearce, Frank R. Pierson, *novel* Donn
Pearce *d* Stuart Rosenberg *ph* Conrad Hall
m Lalo Schifrin

Paul Newman, George Kennedy, Jo Van Fleet,
J. D. Cannon, Lou Antonio, Robert Drivas,
Strother Martin, Clifton James

AA: George Kennedy
AAN: Donn Pearce, Frank R. Pierson; Lalo
Schifrin; Paul Newman

The Cool Ones

US 1967   96m   Technicolor   Panavision
Warner (William Conrad)

Former pop singer makes a comeback.
Zazzy showbiz saga with ear-splitting track,
quite professionally assembled.

w Joyce Geller *d* Gene Nelson *ph* Floyd
Crosby *m* Ernie Freeman

Roddy McDowall, Debbie Watson, Robert
Coote, Phil Harris, Nita Talbot

The Co-Optimists*
GB 1929 83m bw
New Era (Gordon Craig)

A revue by a popular pierrot troupe of the time.
Famous as Britain's first musical, this is a dated
but valuable record of a stage performance of the
kind long vanished.

d Edwin Greenwood, Laddie Cliff

Davy Burnaby, Stanley Holloway, Laddie Cliff,
Phyllis Monkman, Melville Gideon, Gilbert
Childs, Betty Chester, Elsa MacFarlane, Peggy
Petronella, Harry S. Pepper

Copacabana
US 1947 91m bw
(UA) Sam Coslow

A quick-thinking agent forms two acts out of one
client, which makes things awkward when both
are needed at once.
Thinly produced comedy with both stars doing
what is expected of them in surroundings less
glamorous than those to which they were
previously accustomed.

w Laslo Vadnay, Allen Boretz, Howard Harris
d Alfred E. Green

Groucho Marx, Carmen Miranda, Steve
Cochran, Gloria Jean, Andy Russell

Cops***
US 1922 20m (24 fps) bw silent
Associated First National

An innocent disrupts a parade and is pursued by
a horde of policemen.
The perfect Keaton short, a careful assembly of
perfectly timed gags.

wd Buster Keaton

Buster Keaton, Virginia Fox

Cops and Robbers*
US 1973 89m De Luxe
UA / EK Corp (Elliott Kastner)

Two New York cops turn crook and pull off a job
for the Mafia.
Trendily anti-establishment comedy, quite
snappy and smart when you can follow it.

w Donald E. Westlake d Aram Avakian
ph David L. Quaid m Michel Legrand

Cliff Gorman, Joe Bologna, Dick Ward,
Shepperd Strudwick, Ellen Holly, John P. Ryan

Le Corbeau**
France 1943 92m bw
L'Atelier Français

Poison pen letters disturb a small provincial
town.
Impressively characterized whodunnit with the
usual French qualities of detail and discretion.
Remade in Hollywood to less effect as *The
Thirteenth Letter* (qv).

w Louis Chavance d Henri-Georges Clouzot
ph Nicholas Hayer m none

Pierre Fresnay, Pierre Larquey, Ginette Leclerc,
Hélène Manson

The Corn is Green*
US 1945 118m bw
Warner (Jack Chertok)

In 1895 Miss Moffat starts a village school for
Welsh miners, and after some tribulations sees
one of them off to Oxford.
A very theatrical production with unconvincing
sets and mannered acting, but the original play
has its felicities.

w Casey Robinson, Frank Cavett, *play Emlyn
Williams* d Irving Rapper ph Sol Polito m Max
Reiner ad Carl Jules Weyl

Bette Davis, John Dall, Nigel Bruce, Joan
Lorring, Rhys Williams, Rosalind Ivan, Mildred
Dunnock, Arthur Shields

'It's very apparent that Hollywood isn't Wales
. . . but the film lingers in the memory
anyway.'—*New Yorker, 1978*
† Remade as a TV movie in 1978, with
Katharine Hepburn.

AAN: John Dall; Joan Lorring

Cornered*
US 1945 102m bw
RKO

After demobilization, a French-Canadian pilot
tracks down the collaborationist responsible for
the death of his wife.
Well-made but humourless revenge thriller.

w John Paxton, *story* John Wexley d Edward
Dmytryk ph Harry J. Wild

Dick Powell, Micheline Cheirel, Walter Slezak,
Morris Carnovsky

The Corpse Came COD
US 1947 87m bw
Columbia (Sam Bischoff)

Rival reporters try to solve the mystery of a
wandering body.
Routine crime comedy with too few smart lines.

w George Bricker, Dwight Babcock, *novel*
Jimmy Starr d Henry Levin ph Lucien Andriot
m George Duning

George Brent, Joan Blondell, Adele Jergens, Jim
Bannon, Leslie Brooks, Grant Mitchell, Una
O'Connor

Corridor of Mirrors
GB 1948   105m   bw
Cartier–Romney–Apollo (Rudolph Cartier)

An eccentric art collector believes that he and his
mistress are reincarnations of 400-year-old
lovers in a painting; but they are separated by
murder.
Pretentious melodrama of no urgent narrative
interest, with all concerned sadly at sea.

w Rudolph Cartier, Edana Romney d Terence
Young ph André Thomas m Georges Auric

Eric Portman, Edana Romney, Barbara Mullen,
Hugh Sinclair

'It has aimed at Art. It is, in fact, Effect. Some
members of the cast wander in and out of the
scenes as if they are not quite sure what has
happened to them. Their confusion is not beyond
comprehension.'—MFB

Corridors of Blood*
GB 1958   86m   bw
Producers' Associates (John Croydon)

Seeking to discover anaesthetics, a Victorian
doctor falls a prey to resurrection men.
Unpleasant but well-mounted semi-horror
backed by strong cast and art direction.

w Jean Scott Rogers d Robert Day ph Geoffrey
Faithfull m Buxton Orr ad Anthony Masters

Boris Karloff, Christopher Lee, Finlay Currie,
Frank Pettingell, Betta St John, Francis
Matthews, Adrienne Corri, Marian Spencer

Corruption
GB 1967   91m   Technicolor
Columbia / Titan (Peter Newbrook)

A surgeon kills for pituitary gland fluid to restore
his fiancée's beauty.
Highly derivative shocker with no inspiration of
its own except an accumulation of gory detail.

w Donald and Derek Ford d Robert Hartford
Davis ph Peter Newbrook m Bill McGuffie

Peter Cushing, Sue Lloyd, Noel Trevarthen,
Kate O'Mara, David Lodge

The Corsican Brothers*
US 1942   111m   bw
Edward Small

Siamese twins are separated but remain
spiritually tied through various adventures.
Adequately exciting picturization of the Dumas
swashbuckler.

w George Bruce, Howard Estabrook d Gregory
Ratoff ph Harry Stradling m Dmitri Tiomkin

Douglas Fairbanks Jnr, Akim Tamiroff, Ruth

Warrick,
J. Carrol Naish, H. B. Warner, Henry Wilcoxon
AAN: Dmitri Tiomkin

Corvette K 225*
US 1943   97m   bw
Universal (Howard Hawks)
GB title: The Nelson Touch

A Canadian corvette commander encounters
submarines and bombers in mid-Atlantic.
Good war film of its period, marred by romantic
interest.

w Lt John Sturdy d Richard Rosson ph Tony
Gaudio m David Buttolph

Randolph Scott, James Brown, Ella Raines,
Barry Fitzgerald, Andy Devine, Richard Lane
AAN: Tony Gaudio

Cottage on Dartmoor
GB 1929   75m   bw
BIP (Bruce Woolfe)

A farmer's wife shelters her ex-lover when he
breaks jail.
Crude early talkie notable only as an immature
work of its director.

wd Anthony Asquith

Norah Baring, Uno Hemming, Hans Schlettow,
Judd Green

Cottage to Let*
GB 1941   90m   bw
Gainsborough (Edward Black)
US title: Bombsight Stolen

Evacuated to Scotland, a Cockney helps prevent
spies from kidnapping his inventor foster-father.
Stagey but often amusing comedy-thriller which
after a shaky start becomes agreeably
Hitchcockian.

w Anatole de Grunwald, J. O. C. Orton, play
Geoffrey Kerr d Anthony Asquith

Leslie Banks, Alastair Sim, John Mills, Jeanne
de Casalis, George Cole, Carla Lehmann,
Michael Wilding, Frank Cellier, Wally Patch,
Muriel Aked, Muriel George, Catherine Lacey,
Hay Petrie

Council of the Gods*
Germany 1950   106m   bw
DEFA (Adolf Fischer)

A research chemist working for a big chemical
company denounces them after the war when he
finds they have been producing poison gas for
the concentration camps.
Self-flagellatory expiation of war crimes encased
in an absorbing drama.

w Friedrich Wolff, Philipp Gebb *d* Kurt
Maetzig *ph* Friedl Behn-Grund *m* Hanns
Eisler, Erwin Lehn

Paul Bildt, Agnes Windeck, Yvonne Merin, Fritz
Tillman

Counsellor at Law*
US 1933   78m   bw
Universal

Life in the New York office of a successful
Jewish lawyer.
Practised film-making from a Broadway hit.

w Elmer Rice, from his play *d William Wyler*
ph Norbert Brodine

John Barrymore, Bebe Daniels, Melvyn
Douglas, Doris Kenyon, Onslow Stevens, Isabel
Jewell, Thelma Todd, Mayo Methot

Count Five and Die*
GB 1957   92m   bw   Cinemascope
TCF / Zonic (Ernest Gartside)

British intelligence seeks to give the Nazis false
information about the 1944 invasion, but
conviction grows that a double agent is among
them.
Terse, downbeat war suspenser, gripping in parts
but quite forgettable.

w Jack Seddon, David Pursall *d* Victor Vicas
ph Arthur Grant *m* John Wooldridge

Nigel Patrick, Jeffrey Hunter, Anne-Marie
Duringer, David Kossoff

The Count of Monte Cristo***
US 1934   114m   bw
Edward Small / Reliance

After spending years in prison, Edmond Dantes
escapes and avenges himself on those who
framed him.
Classic swashbuckler, extremely well done with
due attention to dialogue as well as action; a
model of its kind and period.

w Philip Dunne, Dan Totheroh, Rowland V.
Lee, *novel* Alexandre Dumas *d Rowland V. Lee*
ph Peverell Marley *m* Alfred Newman

Robert Donat, Elissa Landi, Louis Calhern,
Sidney Blackmer, Raymond Walburn, O. P.
Heggie, William Farnum

Count Three and Pray
US 1955   92m   Technicolor
    Cinemascope
Columbia (Ted Richmond)

After the Civil War a roistering Southerner
comes home to rebuild his town and become its
parson.

Moderate semi-western, fresh and pleasing but
not memorable.

w Herb Meadow *d* George Sherman *ph* Burnett
Guffey *m* George Duning

Van Heflin, Joanne Woodward (debut), Phil
Carey, Raymond Burr, Allison Hayes, Myron
Healey, Nancy Kulp, James Griffiths

Count Yorga Vampire
US 1970   90m   Movielab
Erica / AIP (Michael Macready)

Inquisitive Los Angeles teenagers are
vampirized by a suave foreign visitor.
A semi-professional film that looks it but amid
the longueurs provides one or two nasty frissons.

wd Bob Kelljan *ph* Arch Archambault
m William Marx

Robert Quarry, Roger Perry, Michael Murphy,
Michael Macready, Donna Anders, Judith Lang
† *The Return of Count Yorga* followed a year
later.

Count Your Blessings
US 1959   102m   Metrocolor
    Cinemascope
MGM (Karl Tunberg)

An English girl marries an aristocratic
Frenchman, but the war and other
considerations make them virtual strangers until
their son is nine years old, when it becomes clear
that daddy is a philanderer.
Slight upper-crust comedy, basically rather
tedious but kept buoyant by Chevalier as
commentator.

w Karl Tunberg, *novel* The Blessing by Nancy
Mitford *d* Jean Negulesco *ph* Milton Krasner,
George Folsey *m* Franz Waxman

Deborah Kerr, *Maurice Chevalier*, Rossano
Brazzi, Martin Stephens, Tom Helmore, Ronald
Squire, Patricia Medina, Mona Washbourne
    'Negulesco's aspirations to elegance are now
familiar . . . this is far too absurd an example of
Hollywood's infatuation with Old Europe to
arouse much interest.'—*MFB*

Countdown*
US 1967   101m   Technicolor   Panavision
Warner (William Conrad)

Russian and American spaceships race for the
moon.
Earnest, simply-plotted science-fiction in which
technology is the centre of interest.

w Loring Mandel *d* Robert Altman *ph* William
W. Spencer *m* Leonard Rosenman *ad* Jack
Poplin

James Caan, Robert Duvall, Barbara Baxley,
Joanna Moore, Charles Aidman, Steve Ihnat

Counterattack
US 1945   89m   bw
Columbia
GB title: One against Seven
Resistance fighters go behind enemy lines for
purposes of sabotage.
Standard World War II actioner, the star
appearing above his surroundings.

w John Howard Lawson, play Janet and Philip
Stevenson d Zoltan Korda m Louis Gruenberg

Paul Muni, Marguerite Chapman, Larry Parks,
George Macready, Roman Bohnen

The Counterfeit Traitor*
US 1962   140m   Technicolor
Paramount / Perlberg–Seaton
An oil importer, a naturalized Swede born in
America, is blackmailed by the Allies into
becoming a spy.
Heavy-going espionage drama which divides its
time between action and moralizing. Excellent
production does not quite make it exciting.

wd George Seaton, book Alexander Klein
ph Jean Bourgoin m Alfred Newman

William Holden, Lilli Palmer, Hugh Griffith,
Werner Peters, Eva Dahlbeck

Counterpoint*
US 1967   107m   Techniscope
Universal (Dick Berg)
In 1944, an American symphony orchestra is
captured by the Germans and threatened with
execution.
Bizarre war suspenser, quite unconvincing but
with effectively suspenseful moments and an old-
fashioned portrayal of the Nazis as sadistic
music-loving Huns.

w James Lee, Joel Oliansky, novel The General
by Alan Sillitoe d Ralph Nelson ph Russell
Metty m Bronislau Kaper

Charlton Heston, Maximilian Schell, Anton
Diffring, Kathryn Hays, Leslie Nielsen

A Countess from Hong Kong
GB 1967   120m   Technicolor
Universal (Jerome Epstein)
An American millionaire diplomat is followed
from Hong Kong by his Russian émigrée girl
friend, and complications mount when his wife
boards the ship at Hawaii.
Flatulent comedy with neither the sparkle of
champagne nor even the fizz of lemonade:
Chaplin's writing, direction and music are alike
soporific, and commiserations are due to the
cast.

wd/m Charles Chaplin ph Arthur Ibbetson
pd Don Ashton

Marlon Brando, Sophia Loren, Patrick Cargill,
Margaret Rutherford, Charles Chaplin, Sydney
Chaplin, Oliver Johnston, John Paul
'An unfunny, mindless mess.'—Robert
Windeler

Country Dance
GB 1969   112m   Metrocolor
MGM / Keep–Windward (Robert Emmett
Ginna)
aka: Brotherly Love
An eccentric baronet's incestuous love for his
sister finally breaks up her marriage.
Rambling melodrama with O'Toole going mad
in squire's tweeds; tediously fashionable but too
pallid for general success, it was barely released.

w James Kennaway, from his novel Household
Ghosts
d J. Lee-Thompson ph Ted Moore m John
Addison

Peter O'Toole, Susannah York, Michael Craig,
Harry Andrews, Cyril Cusack, Judy Cornwell,
Brian Blessed

The Country Doctor*
US 1936   94m   bw
TCF (Darryl F. Zanuck)
A rural physician becomes famous when
quintuplets are born to one of his patients.
Fictionalization of the birth of the Dionne
Quintuplets; pleasantly nostalgic even forty
years after its raison d'être.

w Sonya Levien d Henry King ph John F. Seitz,
Daniel B. Clark

Jean Hersholt, the Dionne Quins, Dorothy
Petersen, June Lang, Slim Summerville, Michael
Whalen, Robert Barrat
† Sequels: Reunion (1936), Five of a Kind
(1938).

The Country Girl*
US 1954   104m   bw
Paramount (William Perlberg)
The wife of an alcoholic singer blossoms when he
is stimulated into a comeback.
Theatrically effective but highly unconvincing,
this rather glum stage success made a cold film,
miscast with an eye on the box office.

w George Seaton, play Clifford Odets d George
Seaton ph John F. Warren m Victor Young
songs Ira Gershwin, Harold Arlen

Bing Crosby, Grace Kelly, William Holden,
Anthony Ross, Gene Reynolds

'How far should a woman go . . . to redeem the man she loves?'—*publicity*

'The dramatic development is not really interesting enough to sustain a film of the intensity for which it strives.'—*Karel Reisz*

AA: George Seaton (as writer); Grace Kelly
AAN: best picture; John F. Warren; Bing Crosby

The Court Jester***
US 1955 101m Technicolor Vistavision
Paramount / Dena (Melvin Frank, Norman Panama)

Opposition to a tyrannical king is provided by the Fox, but it is one of the rebel's meekest men who, posing as a jester, defeats the usurper.
One of the star's most delightful vehicles, this medieval romp has good tunes and lively action, not to mention an exceptional cast and the memorable 'chalice from the palace' routine.

wd Norman Panama, Melvin Frank ph Ray June *songs* Sylvia Fine, Sammy Cahn *ad* Hal Pereira, Roland Anderson

Danny Kaye, Glynis Johns, *Basil Rathbone*, Cecil Parker, *Mildred Natwick*, Angela Lansbury, Edward Ashley, Robert Middleton, Michael Pate, Alan Napier

The Court Martial of Billy Mitchell*
US 1955 100m Warnercolor
Cinemascope
United States Pictures (Milton Sperling)
GB title: *One Man Mutiny*

In the early twenties, an American general of the Army Air Service is court-martialled for accusing the war department of criminal negligence.
Adequate recreation of a historical incident, with a cast of excellent actors converging for a courtroom scene of some effectiveness.

w Milton Sperling, Emmet Lavery *d* Otto Preminger *ph* Sam Leavitt *m* Dmitri Tiomkin

Gary Cooper, *Rod Steiger*, Ralph Bellamy, Charles Bickford, Elizabeth Montgomery, Fred Clark, Darren McGavin, James Daly

AAN: Milton Sperling, Emmet Lavery

The Courtneys of Curzon Street*
GB 1947 120m bw
British Lion / Herbert Wilcox
US title: *The Courtney Affair*

In Victorian times, a baronet's son marries a lady's maid . . . and many years later, their grandson marries a factory worker.
Unbelievable upstairs-downstairs romantic drama spanning three generations; all to be taken with a gigantic pinch of salt, but a huge success when released.

w Nicholas Phipps, *novel* Florence Tranter *d* Herbert Wilcox *ph* Max Greene

Anna Neagle, Michael Wilding, Gladys Young, Coral Browne, Michael Medwin, Daphne Slater, Jack Watling, Helen Cherry, Bernard Lee

'The dignity of Curzon Street is Hollywoodized, and it is rare in 1945 that people in their sixties look as though they have one foot in the grave.'—*MFB*

The Courtship of Eddie's Father*
US 1962 117m Metrocolor Panavision
MGM / Joe Pasternak

The small son of a widower tries to interest Dad in another woman.
Fairly icky American-style sentimental comedy with most of the stops pulled out; way over-length and too self-indulgently solemn in the last part, but with professional touches.

w John Gay, *novel* Muriel Toby *d* Vincente Minnelli *ph* Milton Krasner *m* George Stoll

Glenn Ford, Ronnie Howard, Shirley Jones, Stella Stevens, Dina Merrill
† A TV series starring Bill Bixby followed in 1971.

Les Cousins*
France 1958 110m bw
AJYM (Claude Chabrol)

A law student stays with his sophisticated cousin in Paris, and his life is altered.
The country cousin fable filled with undramatic detail and given a rather perverse ending without any apparent point.

wd Claude Chabrol ph Henri Decaë *m* Paul Misraki

Jean-Claude Brialy, Gérard Blain, Juliette Mayniel, Claude Cerval

A Covenant with Death
US 1966 97m Technicolor
Warner (William Conrad)

A half-Mexican judge in a border town convicts a man who accidentally kills the hangman just as the real murderer confesses.
Dreary moral melodrama with accents, nicely photographed but cold, remote and drawn out.

w Larry Marcus, Saul Levitt, *novel* Stephen Becker *d* Lamont Johnson *ph* Robert Burks *m* Leonard Rosenman

George Maharis, Katy Jurado, Earl Holliman, Sidney Blackmer, Laura Devon, Gene Hackman

Cover Girl **
US 1944   107m   Technicolor
Columbia (Arthur Schwartz)

The road to success for magazine cover models.
Wartime glamour musical with a stronger
reputation than it really deserves apart from
Kelly's solos; it does however manage a certain
joie de vivre which should not be despised.

w Virginia Van Upp *d* Charles Vidor
ph Rudolph Maté *md* Morris Stoloff, Carmen
Dragon *songs* Jerome Kern, Ira Gershwin

Rita Hayworth, Gene Kelly, Phil Silvers, Lee
Bowman, Jinx Falkenberg, Otto Kruger, Eve
Arden, Ed Brophy

　'Kelly and Silvers are better than Kelly and
Hayworth, though she does look sumptuous,
and her big smile could be the emblem of the
period.'—*New Yorker, 1977*

AA: Morris Stoloff, Carmen Dragon; song
'Long Ago and Far Away'
AAN: Rudolph Maté

The Covered Wagon *
US 1923   103m (24 fps)   bw   silent
Paramount / Famous Players-Lasky

Pioneer settlers travel west by wagon train.
A classic western which now seems painfully
undernourished in terms of plot and character
but still retains moments of epic sweep.

w Jack Cunningham, *novel* Emerson Hough
d James Cruze *ph* Karl Brown

Ernest Torrence, Tully Marshall, J. Warren
Kerrigan, Lois Wilson, Alan Hale

　'There wasn't a false whisker in the film.'—
James Cruze

　'Forthright, impressive and vigorous, it
brought a breath of fresh air into the jazz-ridden
film world.'—*Lewis Jacobs*

The Cow and I
France 1959   119m   bw
Cyclope / Omnia (Walter Rupp)
original title: *La Vache et le Prisonnier*

A French soldier escapes from a prison camp
and takes a farm cow as cover.
Curiously overlong war adventure which hovers
uncertainly between comedy and suspense.

w Henri Verneuil, Henri Jeanson, Jean Manse
d Henri Verneuil *ph* Roger Hubert *m* Paul
Durand

Fernandel, René Havard, Albert Remy, Bernard
Musson

Cowboy *
US 1957   92m   Technicolor
Columbia (Julian Blaustein)

Frank Harris becomes a cattle herder for love of
a lady but is quickly disillusioned with the
outdoor life.
Fashioned from a lively autobiography, this has
interesting moments but is never as fascinating
as one would expect.

w Edmund H. North, *book* On the Trail by
Frank Harris *d* Delmer Daves *ph* Charles
Lawton Jnr *m* George Duning

Jack Lemmon, Glenn Ford, Brian Donlevy,
Anna Kashfi, Dick York, Richard Jaeckel, King
Donovan

The Cowboy and the Lady
US 1938   91m   bw
Samuel Goldwyn

The daughter of a presidential candidate
becomes infatuated with a rodeo cowboy.
Insubstantial and witless romantic comedy
which suffered many sea changes from script to
screen.

w Leo McCarey, S. N. Behrman, Sonya Levien
d H. C. Potter *ph* Gregg Toland *m* Alfred
Newman

Gary Cooper, Merle Oberon, Patsy Kelly,
Walter Brennan, Fuzzy Knight, Henry Kolker,
Harry Davenport

　'Just a lot of chestnuts pulled out of other
people's dead fires.'—*Otis Ferguson*

AAN: Alfred Newman; title song (*m* Alfred
Newman, *ly* Arthur Quenzer)

The Cowboys *
US 1972   128m   Technicolor   Panavision
70
Sanford / Warner (Mark Rydell)

Deserted by his ranch hands, a cattle drover on a
long trail enlists the help of eleven schoolboys,
who later avenge his death.
Ambling, climactically violent, extremely
unlikely western with good scenes along the way.

w Irving Ravetch, Harriet Frank Jnr, *novel*
William Dale Jennings *d* Mark Rydell
ph Robert Surtees *m* John Williams

John Wayne, Roscoe Lee Browne, Bruce Dern,
Colleen Dewhurst, Slim Pickens, Sarah
Cunningham

† A TV series followed in 1974 but was
shortlived.

Crack in the Mirror
US 1960   97m   bw   Cinemascope
TCF / Darryl F. Zanuck

A young lawyer and his ageing mentor are at
opposite sides of a murder case.
Pointless Paris-set melodrama in which for no

obvious reason each of the three stars plays two roles. Relentlessly boring.

w Mark Canfield (Darryl F. Zanuck) *d* Richard Fleischer *ph* William C. Mellor *m Maurice Jarre*

Orson Welles, Bradford Dillman, Juliette Greco, William Lucas, Alexander Knox, Catherine Lacey

Crack in the World
US 1965   96m   Technicolor
Paramount / Security (Philip Yordan, Bernard Glasser, Lester A. Sansom)

A dying scientist fires a missile into the earth's centre, and nearly blows the planet apart.
Jaded science-fiction melodrama, overburdened with initial chat but waking up when the special effects take over.

w Jon Manchip White, Julian Halevy *d* Andrew Marton *ph* Manuel Berenguer *m* John Douglas *ad Eugene Lourié sp John Douglas*

Dana Andrews, Janette Scott, Kieron Moore, Alexander Knox, Peter Damon, Gary Lasdun

Crack Up*
US 1946   93m   bw
RKO

A museum curator with an eye for forgery is discredited by crooks who make him appear drunk or half-crazed when he recounts a set of strange events which have happened to him . . .
The intriguing mystery of the opening reels, when solved, is replaced by rather dull detection, but this remains a thriller with a difference, generally well presented.

w John Paxton *d* Irving Reis *ph* Robert de Grasse

Pat O'Brien, Claire Trevor, Herbert Marshall, Ray Collins

Craig's Wife*
US 1936   77m   bw
Columbia

A middle-class wife lets her house take precedence over her husband.
Capable picturization of a Broadway success, later remade as *Harriet Craig* (qv).

w Mary McCally Jnr, George Kelly, *play* George Kelly *d* Dorothy Arzner *ph* Lucien Ballard *md* Morris Stoloff

Rosalind Russell, John Boles, Billie Burke, Jane Darwell, Dorothy Wilson, Alma Kruger, Thomas Mitchell, Elizabeth Risdon, Raymond Walburn

Crainquebille*
France 1922   70m approx (16 fps)   bw silent
Trarieux Films

A street trader is unjustly accused and imprisoned, afterwards finding happiness as a tramp.
Somewhere between Chaplin and Kafka, this fable was long admired for its style.

wd Jacques Feyder, story Anatole France *ph* Léonce Burel

Maurice de Féraudy, Françoise Rosay, Felix Oudart

† Remade 1933 by Jacques de Baroncelli with Maurice Tramel; 1954 by Ralph Habib with Yves Deniaud.

The Cranes Are Flying**
USSR 1957   94m   bw
Mosfilm
original title: *Letyat Zhuravli*

When her lover goes to war, a girl refuses to believe later reports of his death even though she has suffered much, including marriage to a bully, in the interim.
Sleek, moving love story with most of the Hollywood production virtues plus an attention to detail and a realism which are wholly Russian.

w Victor Rosov d Mikhail Kalatozov ph Sergei Urusevski

Tatiana Samoilova, Alexei Batalov, Vasili Merkuriev

Crash
US 1976   96m   Technicolor   Panavision
Warner (Fred Weintraub, Paul Heller)

The problems of competitors in a 1000-mile motor race across the Philippines.
Cheapjack cash-in on the *Cannonball* school; only violence catches the eye.

w Michael Allin *d* Alan Gibson *ph* Alan Hume *m* Art Freeman

Joe Don Baker, Susan Sarandon, Larry Hagman, Alan Vint, Michael Pitton

Crash Dive*
US 1943   105m   Technicolor
TCF (Milton Sperling)

A submarine lieutenant and his commander love the same girl.
Well-staged war thrills in the final reels are prefaced by a long romantic comedy build-up, which probably seemed good propaganda at the time.

w Jo Swerling, *story* W. R. Burnett *d* Archie

Mayo *ph* Leon Shamroy *m* David Buttolph
md Emil Newman *sp Fred Sersen*

Tyrone Power, Anne Baxter, Dana Andrews,
James Gleason, Dame May Whitty, Henry
Morgan, Frank Conroy, Minor Watson
   'One of those films which have no more sense
of reality about this war than a popular song.'—
Bosley Crowther

Craze
GB 1973   95m   Technicolor
(EMI) Harbour (Herman Cohen)

An African idol accidentally causes a death
which brings money to its owner, who kills again
and again in the hope of more loot.
Crude shocker from the bottom of even this
producer's barrel, notable for the star cast which
was surprisingly roped in.

w Aben Kandel, Herman Cohen, *novel* Infernal
Idol by Henry Seymour *d* Freddie Francis
ph John Wilcox *m* John Scott

Jack Palance, Diana Dors, Julie Ege, Edith
Evans, Hugh Griffith, Trevor Howard, Michael
Jayston, Suzy Kendall, Martin Potter, Percy
Herbert, Kathleen Byron

Crazy House
US 1943   80m   bw
Universal (Erle C. Kenton)

Olsen and Johnson go to Hollywood to make a
film.
Lame sequel to *Hellzapoppin;* after an
explosively well edited first reel of panic in the
studio, it degenerates into a slew of below-par
variety turns.

w Robert Lees, Frederic I. Rinaldo *d* Edward
Cline *ph* Charles Van Enger *md* George Hale,
Milt Rosen

Ole Olsen, Chic Johnson, Martha O'Driscoll,
Patric Knowles, Percy Kilbride, Cass Daley,
Thomas Gomez, Edgar Kennedy
† Sherlock Holmes fans may or may not wish to
record a two-line comic bit by Basil Rathbone
and Nigel Bruce in character.

The Crazy World of Laurel and Hardy**
US 1964   83m   bw
Hal Roach / Jay Ward

A compilation of Laurel and Hardy extracts
from their classic period.
Although the material is in itself excellent and
some of the build-up sequences well done, the
clips are all too short to achieve maximum
impact, and virtually none is identified.

w Bill Scott *m* Jerry Fielding *narrator* Garry
Moore

The Creature from the Black Lagoon
US 1954   79m   bw   3-D
U-I (William Alland)

Up the Amazon, scientists encounter a fearful
fanged creature who is half man, half fish.
Unpersuasive and unsuspenseful horror hokum
from the bottom drawer of imagination: it did,
however, coin enough pennies to generate two
even worse sequels, *Revenge of the Creature*
(1955) and *The Creature Walks Among Us*
(1956). And the underwater photography is
super.

w Harry Essex, Arthur Ross *d* Jack Arnold
ph William E. Snyder

Richard Carlson, Julie Adams, Richard
Denning, Antonio Moreno, Nestor Paiva, Ricou
Browning (in the rubber suit)

Creatures the World Forgot
GB 1970   95m   Technicolor
Columbia / Hammer (Michael Carreras)

Quarrels break out between rival tribes of Stone
Age men.
Feeble follow-up to *One Million Years BC* and
When Dinosaurs Ruled the Earth: someone
forgot to order any monsters.

w Michael Carreras *d* Don Chaffey *ph* Vincent
Cox *m* Mario Nascimbene

Julie Ege, Brian O'Shaughnessy, Robert John,
Marcia Fox, Rosalie Crutchley

The Creeping Flesh*
GB 1972   91m   Eastmancolor
Tigon / World Film Services (Michael
Redbourn)

A Victorian scientist discovers that water causes
the recomposing of tissue on the skeleton of a
Neanderthal man.
Absurd but persuasive horror film, quite well
done in all departments.

w Peter Spenceley, Jonathan Rumbold
d Freddie Francis *ph* Norman Warwick *m* Paul
Ferris

Peter Cushing, Christopher Lee, Lorna
Heilbron, George Benson, Kenneth J. Warren,
Duncan Lamont, Michael Ripper

Crescendo*
GB 1969   95m   Technicolor
Warner / Hammer (Michael Carreras)

A girl researcher goes to stay with the widow of a
famous composer, and finds herself in mortal
danger . . .
Lunatic Hammer horror with the courage of its
shameless borrowings from *Taste of Fear,
Fanatic, Nightmare, Maniac* and all the films

about mad twin brothers, to which this chaotic brew adds dollops of sex and heroin addiction.

w Jimmy Sangster, Alfred Shaughnessy *d Alan Gibson ph* Paul Beeson *m* Malcolm Williamson

Stefanie Powers, James Olson, Margaretta Scott, Jane Lapotaire, Joss Ackland

Cries and Whispers***

Sweden 1972   91m   Eastmancolor
Cinematograph (Ingmar Bergman)
original title: *Viskingar och Rop*

A young woman dying of cancer in her family home is tended by her two sisters.
Quiet, chilling, classical chapter of doom which variously reminds one of Chekhov, Tolstoy and Dostoievsky but is also essential Bergman. Tough but important viewing, it lingers afterwards in the mind like a picture vividly painted in shades of red.

*wd Ingmar Bergman ph Sven Nykvist
m* Chopin and Bach

Harriet Andersson, Kari Sylwan, Ingrid Thulin, Liv Ullmann

'Harrowing, spare and perceptive, but lacking the humour that helps to put life and death into perspective.'—*Michael Billington, Illustrated London News*

AA: Sven Nykvist
AAN: best picture; Ingmar Bergman (as writer)

Crime and Punishment*

US 1935   88m   bw
Columbia

A student kills a pawnbroker and is tortured by remorse.
Heavy-going rendering of Dostoievsky with some pictorial interest.

w S. K. Lauren, Joseph Anthony *d Josef Von Sternberg ph* Lucien Ballard *m* Arthur Honegger *md* Louis Silvers

Peter Lorre, Edward Arnold, Tala Birell, Marian Marsh, Elizabeth Risdon, Mrs Patrick Campbell

Crime and Punishment USA

US 1958   96m   bw
Allied Artists / Sanders Associates (Terry Sanders)

A student murders an old pawnbroker and is driven mad by guilt.
Pointless updating of Dostoievsky by two young film-makers who seemed for years to be on the brink of a masterpiece but never actually produced it. Some points of interest, but the low budget is cramping.

w Walter Newman *d* Denis Sanders *ph* Floyd Crosby *m* Herschel Burke Gilbert

George Hamilton, Frank Silvera, Mary Murphy, John Harding, Marian Seldes

'There is about it a strange quality of aimlessness which nullifies much of its effect.'—*MFB*

Crime by Night*

US 1944   72m   bw
Warner (William Jacobs)

A private detective reluctantly solves a small-town murder, and finds a spy.
Second feature which was thought at the time to have established a new pair of married detectives in the tradition of *The Thin Man*. However, one poor sequel, *Find the Blackmailer*, put paid to the idea.

w Richard Weil, Joel Malone, *novel* Forty Whacks by Geoffrey Homes *d* William Clemens *ph* Henry Sharpe

Jerome Cowan, Jane Wyman, Faye Emerson, Charles Lang, Eleanor Parker, Cy Kendall, Creighton Hale

Crime Doctor*

US 1943   66m   bw
Columbia

An amnesiac becomes a successful psychiatrist, then discovers that he was once a wanted gangster.
Time-passing second feature from a popular radio series. Ten *Crime Doctor* films were made between 1943 and 1949, all starring Warner Baxter, all except the first being locked room mysteries which seldom played fair with the audience.

w Graham Baker, Louise Lantz *d* Michael Gordon

Warner Baxter, Margaret Lindsay, John Litel, Ray Collins, Harold Huber, Leon Ames, Don Costello

The sequels:
1943: CRIME DOCTOR'S STRANGEST CASE
1944: SHADOWS IN THE NIGHT, CRIME DOCTOR'S COURAGE
1945: CRIME DOCTOR'S WARNING
1946: CRIME DOCTOR'S MANHUNT, JUST BEFORE DAWN
1947: THE MILLERSON CASE
1948: CRIME DOCTOR'S GAMBLE
1949: CRIME DOCTOR'S DIARY

Crime in the Streets*

US 1956   91m   bw
Allied Artists (Vincent M. Fenelly)

Rival knife gangs bring havoc to tenement dwellers.

Lively semi-documentary low-life melodrama; routine subject, excellent credits.

w *Reginald Rose*, from his TV play d *Don Siegel* ph Sam Leavitt

John Cassavetes, James Whitmore, Sal Mineo, Mark Rydell

The Crime of Monsieur Lange**
France 1935   85m   bw
Obéron (André Halley des Fontaines)

When the hated boss of a publishing house is believed killed, the workers turn it into a successful co-operative. When he reappears, they kill him.

The political elements of this fable now seem unimportant, but it still shows its original charm and cinematic skill.

w *Jacques Prévert* d Jean Renoir ph Jean Bachelet m Jean Wiener

René Lefèbvre, Jules Berry, Florelle, Sylvie Bataille, Henri Guisol

Crime of Passion
US 1956   86m   bw
UA / Bob Goldstein (Herman Cohen)

An executive's wife sleeps his way to the top, but when the boss does not come through with promotion she shoots him.

Old-fashioned star melodrama on a low budget.

w Jo Eisinger d Gerd Oswald ph Joseph La Shelle m Paul Dunlap

Barbara Stanwyck, Sterling Hayden, Raymond Burr, Fay Wray, Royal Dano, Virginia Grey

Crime School*
US 1938   86m   bw
Warner (Bryan Foy)

Problems of the warden of a reform school. Predictable vehicle for the Dead End Kids; watchable at the time.

w Crane Wilbur, Vincent Sherman d Lewis Seiler ph Arthur Todd

Humphrey Bogart, Gale Page, Billy Halop, Huntz Hall, Leo Gorcey, Bobby Jordan, Gabriel Dell, Bernard Punsley, Paul Porcasi, Al Bridge

Crime without Passion**
US 1934   82m   bw
Paramount (Ben Hecht, Charles MacArthur)

A lawyer is driven to commit murder.

Effective melodrama notable for then-new techniques which were blended into the mainstream of movie-making, and for the first appearance in Hollywood of a smart new writer-producer-director team.

wd *Ben Hecht, Charles MacArthur*, from their story Caballero of the Law ph Lee Garmes sp Slavko Vorkapitch

Claude Rains, Margo, Whitney Bourne, Stanley Ridges

'The whole venture seems to take a long stride forward for the movies.'—*Otis Ferguson*

'A flamboyant, undisciplined, but compulsively fascinating film classic.'—*Peter John Dyer, 1966*

Crimes at the Dark House
GB 1939   69m   bw
Pennant (George King)

A Victorian landowner kills his wife and conceals the fact by using a lunatic as her double. Cheeky adaptation of a classic to make one of the star's most lip-smacking barnstormers.

w Edward Dryhurst, Frederick Hayward, H. F. Maltby from The Woman in White by Wilkie Collins d George King

Tod Slaughter, Hilary Eaves, Sylvia Marriott, Hay Petrie, David Horne

The Criminal*
GB 1960   97m   bw
Merton Park (Jack Greenwood)
US title: *The Concrete Jungle*

Sent to jail for a racecourse snatch, a gangster comes out fifteen years later to regain the loot and is followed by other criminals who kill him. Relentlessly grim saga of prison life, with a few sensational trimmings.

w Alun Owen, Jimmy Sangster d Joseph Losey ph *Robert Krasker* m Johnny Dankworth

Stanley Baker, Sam Wanamaker, Margit Saad, *Patrick Magee*, Noel Willman, Grégoire Aslan, Jill Bennett, Kenneth J. Warren, Nigel Green, Patrick Wymark, Murray Melvin

'A savage, almost expressionistic picture of English underworld life.'—*NFT, 1973*

The Criminal Code*
US 1931   97m   bw
Columbia (Harry Cohn)

A young man kills in self-defence, is railroaded into jail and becomes involved in another murder.

Impressive melodrama with good performances and sharp handling.

w Seton I. Miller, Fred Niblo Jnr, *play* Martin Flavin d *Howard Hawks* ph James Wong Howe, William O'Connell

Walter Huston, Phillips Holmes, Constance Cummings, Mary Doran, De Witt Jennings, John Sheehan, Boris Karloff

† Remade as *Penitentiary* (1938) with Walter Connolly and *Convicted* (1950) with Broderick Crawford.

AAN: Seton I. Miller, Fred Niblo Jnr

The Criminal Life of Archibaldo de la Cruz*
Mexico 1955   91m   bw
Alianza Cinematografica (Roberto Figueroa)
original title: *Ensayo de un Crimen*

A fantasist determines to kill all women who cross his path, but fate intervenes.
Cheaply made macabre joke, one of its director's throwaway oddities: not too smooth, but often amusing.

w Luis Bunuel, E. Ugarte *d* Luis Bunuel *ph* Augusto Jimenez *md* Jorge Perez

Ernesto Alonso, Ariadna Welter, Miroslava Stern, Rita Macedo

The Crimson Curtain*
France 1952   43m   bw
Argos
original title: *Le Rideau Cramoisi*

An officer billeted with a bourgeois family is visited at night by the beautiful daughter, who finally dies in his arms.
A curious polished fragment with narration replacing spoken dialogue. For those in the mood, it works.

wd Alexandre Astruc, from a story by Barbey d'Aurevilly *ph* Eugene Schufftan *m* Jean-Jacques Grunenwald

Jean-Claude Pascal, Anouk Aimée, Madeleine Garcia, Jim Gerald

'In its limited time, with the greatest economy of means, it evokes an authentic sense of the past, as well as telling a story movingly and dramatically.'–*Richard Roud*

The Crimson Kimono
US 1959   82m   bw
Columbia / Globe (Samuel Fuller)

Detectives seeking the murderer of a stripper in Los Angeles' Little Tokyo both fall in love with a witness.
Self-conscious local colour, though quite freshly observed and well photographed, finally overwhelms an ordinary little murder mystery.

wd Samuel Fuller *ph* Sam Leavitt *m* Harry Sukman

Glenn Corbett, James Shigeta, Victoria Shaw, Anna Lee, Paul Dubov

The Crimson Pirate*
GB 1952   104m   Technicolor
Warner / Harold Hecht

An 18th-century pirate and an eccentric inventor lead an island's people in rebellion against a tyrant.
One suspects that this started off as a straight adventure and was turned halfway through production into a spoof; at any rate, the effect is patchy but with spirited highlights, and the star's acrobatic training is put to good use.

w Roland Kibbee *d* Robert Siodmak *ph* Otto Heller *m* William Alwyn

Burt Lancaster, Nick Cravat, Eva Bartok, Torin Thatcher, James Hayter, Margot Grahame, Noel Purcell, Frank Pettingell

Crin Blanc**
France 1953   47m   bw
Albert Lamorisse
aka: *Wild Stallion*

A small boy befriends and rides a wild horse in the Camargue.
A favourite short film of great beauty, but a shade overlong for its content.

wd Albert Lamorisse ph Edmond Séchan *m* Maurice Le Roux

Alain Emery, Pascal Lamorisse

Crisis*
US 1950   96m   bw
MGM (Arthur Freed)

A brain surgeon is forced to operate secretly on a South American dictator, and his wife is kidnapped by revolutionaries.
Dour intellectual suspense piece, in key with the genteel enlightenment of the Dore Schary regime at MGM. Well made but cold.

wd Richard Brooks, *story* George Tabori *ph* Ray June *m* Miklos Rozsa

Cary Grant, Jose Ferrer, Signe Hasso, Paula Raymond, Ramon Navarro, Antonio Moreno, Leon Ames, Gilbert Roland

Criss Cross*
US 1948   87m   bw
U-I (Michael Draike)

An armoured car guard and his double-crossing ex-wife get mixed up with vicious gangsters.
Sordid *film noir* with a poor plot but suspenseful sequences.

w Daniel Fuchs *d* Robert Siodmak *ph* Franz Planer *m* Miklos Rozsa

Burt Lancaster, Yvonne de Carlo, Dan Duryea, Stephen McNally, Richard Long, Tom Pedi, Alan Napier

'Siodmak's talent for brooding violence and the sombre urban setting gives the film a relentlessly mounting tension.'—*Peter John Dyer*

Critic's Choice
US 1963   100m   Technicolor   Panavision
Warner / Frank P. Rosenberg

A ruthless Broadway critic is forced by his scruples to write a bad review of his wife's play. Unsuitable vehicle for stars who have shorn a good comedy of wit and strive vainly for sentiment, wisecracks and pratfalls.

w Jack Sher, *play* Ira Levin *d* Don Weis *ph* Charles Lang *m* George Duning

Bob Hope, Lucille Ball, Marilyn Maxwell, Rip Torn, Jessie Royce Landis, John Dehner, Jim Backus, Marie Windsor
    'For instant stultification.'—*Judith Crist*

Cromwell*
GB 1970   141m   Technicolor   Panavision
Columbia / Irving Allen (Andrew Donally)

An account of the rise of Cromwell to power, the execution of Charles I, and the Civil War. Disappointingly dull schoolbook history, with good production values but glum handling.

wd Ken Hughes *ph* Geoffrey Unsworth *m* Frank Cordell *pd* John Stoll

Richard Harris, Alec Guinness, Robert Morley, Dorothy Tutin, Frank Finlay, Timothy Dalton, Patrick Wymark, Patrick Magee, Nigel Stock, Charles Gray, Michael Jayston, Anna Cropper, Michael Goodliffe
    'It tries to combine serious intentions with the widest kind of popular appeal and falls unhappily between the two. It will offend the purists and bore the kiddies.'—*Brenda Davies*

AAN: Frank Cordell

Crooks and Coronets
GB 1969   106m   Technicolor
Warner Seven Arts / Herman Cohen

American gangsters plan to rob a stately home but are taken over by the dowager in charge. Overlong and mainly flatulent comedy, with a good climax involving a vintage plane.

wd Jim O'Connelly *ph* Desmond Dickinson *m* Patrick John Scott

Telly Savalas, Edith Evans, Warren Oates, Nicky Henson, Cesar Romero, Harry H. Corbett

Crooks Anonymous*
GB 1962   87m   bw
Anglo Amalgamated (Nat Cohen)

A petty thief joins an organization for reforming criminals, but is tempted again . . . and so are they.
Amusingly devised and plotted minor comedy with an exceptional cast.

w Jack Davies, Henry Blyth *d* Ken Annakin

Leslie Phillips, Stanley Baxter, Wilfrid Hyde White, Julie Christie, James Robertson Justice, Robertson Hare, Charles Lloyd Pack

Crooks' Tour*
GB 1940   84m   bw
British National (John Corfield)

English tourists are mistaken for spies by Nazis in Baghdad.
Amusing vehicle for two comic actors who excelled at portraying the English abroad.

w John Watt, Max Kester, from the radio serial by Sidney Gilliat and Frank Launder *d* John Baxter *ph* James Wilson *m* Kennedy Russell

Basil Radford, Naunton Wayne, Greta Gynt, Abraham Sofaer, Gordon McLeod

Cross My Heart*
US 1945   83m   bw
Paramount (Harry Tugend)

A romantic girl confesses to murder, is acquitted, and finds the real murderer.
Modest remake of *True Confession* (qv), with frenetic pace but not much style.

w Claude Binyon, Harry Tugend, Charles Schnee *d* John Berry *ph* Charles Lang Jnr *m* Robert Emmett Dolan

Betty Hutton, Sonny Tufts, Michael Chekhov, Rhys Williams, Ruth Donnelly, Al Bridge, Howard Freeman, Iris Adrian

Cross of Iron*
GB / West Germany 1976   133m
    Technicolor
EMI—Rapid Film / Terra Filmkunst (Wolf C. Hartwig)

Militarily and emotionally at the end of its tether, a German battalion is decimated while fighting the Russians in 1943.
Painful to follow, occasionally beautiful to watch, this quite horrid film offers too much opportunity for its director to wallow in unpleasant physical details, and its main plot of bitter rivalry offers no relief.

w Julius J. Epstein, Herbert Asmodi *d* Sam Peckinpah *ph* John Coquillon *m* Ernest Gold

James Coburn, James Mason, Maximilian Schell, David Warner, Klaus Löwitch
    'Morally dubious but technically brilliant.'—*Michael Billington, Illustrated London News*

The Cross of Lorraine*

US 1944 91m bw

MGM (Edwin Knopf)

In a German camp for French prisoners, an escape leads to a rising by local villagers. Standard war propaganda piece, made with enthusiasm on unconvincing sets.

w Michael Kanin, Ring Lardner Jnr, Alexander Esway, Robert Andrews *d* Tay Garnett *ph* Sidney Wagner *m* Bronislau Kaper

Gene Kelly, Jean-Pierre Aumont, Cedric Hardwicke, Peter Lorre, Joseph Calleia, Richard Whorf, Hume Cronyn

Crossed Swords

Italy / USA 1954 83m Pathecolor

Viva Films (J. Barrett Mahon, Vittorio Vassarotti)

original title: *Il Maestro di Don Giovanni*

The son of an Italian duke prevents an uprising. A thin swashbuckler showing the perils of early co-production.

wd Milton Krims *ph* Jack Cardiff

Errol Flynn, Gina Lollobrigida, Cesare Danova, Nadia Gray, Paola Mori

Crossfire****

US 1947 86m bw

RKO (Adrian Scott)

A Jew is murdered in a New York hotel, and three soldiers are suspected.

Tense, talky thriller shot entirely at night with pretty full expressionist use of camera technique; notable for style, acting, experimentation, and for being the first Hollywood film to hit out at racial bigotry.

w John Paxton, *novel* The Brick Foxhole by Richard Brooks *ph* J. Roy Hunt *d* Edward Dmytryk *m* Roy Webb

Robert Young, Robert Mitchum, *Robert Ryan*, Gloria Grahame, *Paul Kelly*, Sam Levene, Jacqueline White, Steve Brodie

AAN: best picture; John Paxton; Edward Dmytryk; Robert Ryan; Gloria Grahame

The Crossing of the Rhine*

France / Italy / West Germany 1960 125m

bw

Franco-London-Gibe-Jonia-UFA (Ralph Baum)

original title: *Le Passage du Rhin*

Two French soldiers escape from the Germans in 1940 and after various adventures meet up again in Paris in 1945.

Two crowded plots and not a great deal of point emerge from this watchable war film full of conventional set pieces.

w André Cayatte, Armand Jammot *d* André Cayatte *ph* Roger Fellous *m* Louiguy

Charles Aznavour, Nicole Courcel, Georges Rivière, Cordula Trantow

Crossplot

GB 1969 97m Eastmancolor

UA / Tribune (Robert S. Baker)

An advertising executive gets involved in a spy ring.

Old-fashioned, London-set amalgam of secret codes, disappearing bodies, helicopter attacks, and a finale frustrating the assassination of a statesman in Hyde Park.

w Leigh Vance *d* Alvin Rakoff *ph* Brendan J. Stafford *m* Stanley Black

Roger Moore, Martha Hyer, Alexis Kanner, Francis Matthews, Bernard Lee

Crossroads**

Japan 1928 80m approx bw silent

Shochiku

original title: *Jujiro*

A woman kills her seducer. Her brother thinks he has killed a man and takes refuge with her, only to die of shock when he sees the man alive.

The only widely distributed Japanese silent film, this curious piece is fragmentarily told and will remind many of *Rashomon* with its mixture of flashbacks and dreams.

wd Teinosuke Kinugasa *ph* Kohei Sugiyama

J. Bandoha, A. Tschihaya, Yujiko Ogawa, I. Sohma

Crossroads*

US 1942 84m bw

MGM (Edwin Knopf)

A French diplomat who once lost his memory is blackmailed by crooks who claim he was once a criminal.

Smooth mystery melodrama adapted from the French film *Carrefour*.

w Howard Emmett Rogers, John Kafka *d* Jack Conway *ph* Joseph Ruttenberg *m* Bronislau Kaper

William Powell, Hedy Lamarr, Basil Rathbone, Claire Trevor, Margaret Wycherly, Felix Bressart, Sig Rumann

The Crowd***

US 1928 98m bw silent

MGM (King Vidor)

Episodes in the life of a city clerk.

A deliberately humdrum story, chosen to show

that drama can exist in the lowliest surroundings, retains much of its original power, though some of the director's innovations have become clichés.

w King Vidor, John V. A. Weaver, Harry Behn d King Vidor ph Henry Sharp ad Cedric Gibbons, Arnold Gillespie ed Hugh Wynn

James Murray, Eleanor Boardman, Bert Roach, Estelle Clark

AAN: King Vidor

The Crowd Roars*
US 1932   85m   bw
Warner

A star motor-racing driver tries to prevent his young brother from following in his footsteps. Typical early Cagney vehicle, still spectacularly pacy but dated in its dialogue scenes.

w Kubec Glasmon, John Bright, Niven Busch d Howard Hawks ph Sid Hickox, John Stumar md Leo Forbstein

James Cagney, Joan Blondell, Ann Dvorak, Eric Linden, Guy Kibbee, Frank McHugh, Regis Toomey

'As so often Hawks seems bitter at the world men have created but respects those who have to attempt to live it to the full.'—NFT, 1963
† Remade in 1939 as Indianapolis Speedway.

The Crowd Roars*
US 1938   90m   bw
MGM (Sam Zimbalist)

A young boxer becomes involved with the underworld.
Standard star vehicle with efficient trimmings.

w Thomas Lennon, George Bruce, George Oppenheimer d Richard Thorpe ph John Seitz m Edward Ward

Robert Taylor, Frank Morgan, Edward Arnold, Maureen O'Sullivan, William Gargan, Frank Craven, Jane Wyman, Lionel Stander, Nat Pendleton
† Remade as Killer McCoy.

The Crowded Sky
US 1960   104m   Technicolor
Warner (Michael Garrison)

As two planes fly unwittingly towards each other, the passengers muse on their personal problems. An emergency landing averts total disaster.
The format goes back as far as Friday the Thirteenth, and forward to Airport 75, but this was in fact a cut-rate rehash of The High and the Mighty, with dull characters and insufficiently

tense handling, not to mention a second team cast.

w Charles Schnee d Joseph Pevney ph Harry Stradling m Leonard Rosenman

Dana Andrews, Rhonda Fleming, Efrem Zimbalist Jnr, John Kerr, Anne Francis, Keenan Wynn, Troy Donahue, Joe Mantell, Patsy Kelly

The Cruel Sea**
GB 1952   126m   bw
Ealing (Leslie Norman)

Life and death on an Atlantic corvette during World War II.
Competent transcription of a bestselling book, cleanly produced and acted; a huge box office success.

w Eric Ambler, novel Nicholas Monsarrat d Charles Frend ph Gordon Dines, Jo Jago, Paul Beeson m Alan Rawsthorne

Jack Hawkins, Donald Sinden, Stanley Baker, John Stratton, Denholm Elliott, John Warner, Bruce Seton, Virginia McKenna, Moira Lister, June Thorburn

'One is grateful nowadays for a film which does not depict war as anything but a tragic and bloody experience, and it is this quality which gives the production its final power to move.'—John Gillett

AAN: Eric Ambler

The Crusades**
US 1935   127m   bw
Paramount / Cecil B. de Mille

Spurred by his wife Berengaria, Richard the Lionheart sets off on his holy wars.
Heavily tapestried medieval epic, spectacular sequences being punctuated by wodges of uninspired dialogue. A true de Mille pageant.

w Harold Lamb, Waldemar Young, Dudley Nichols d Cecil B. de Mille ph Victor Milner sp Gordon Jennings

Henry Wilcoxon, Loretta Young, C. Aubrey Smith, Ian Keith, Katherine de Mille, Joseph Schildkraut, Alan Hale,
C. Henry Gordon, George Barbier, Montagu Love, Lumsden Hare, William Farnum, Hobart Bosworth, Pedro de Cordoba, Mischa Auer

'Mr de Mille's evangelical films are the nearest equivalent today to the glossy German colour prints which decorated mid-Victorian bibles. There is the same lack of a period sense, the same stuffy horsehair atmosphere of beards and whiskers, and, their best quality, a childlike eye for detail.'—Otis Ferguson

AAN: Victor Milner

Cry for Happy
US 1961   110m   Eastmancolor
  Cinemascope
Columbia (William Goetz)

Four navy cameramen in Japan help geishas to found an orphanage.

As bad as it sounds, a repellent mixture of sentiment and knockabout.

w Irving Brecher *d* George Marshall *ph* Burnett Guffey *m* George Duning

Glenn Ford, Donald O'Connor, Miiko Taka, James Shigeta, Mikoshi Umeki, Joe Flynn, Howard St John

'Any film which expends most of its energies on a protracted joke about how far you can go with a geisha could hardly fail to be as charmless and witless as this.'—*MFB*

A Cry from the Streets
GB 1958   100m   bw
Film Traders (Ian Dalrymple)

Episodes from the work of child welfare officers. Mildly pleasing but unconvincing semi-documentary, with children competing with the star at scene-stealing.

w Vernon Harris, *novel* The Friend in Need by Elizabeth Coxhead *d* Lewis Gilbert *ph* Harry Gillan *m* Larry Adler

Max Bygraves, Barbara Murray, Colin Petersen, Dana Wilson, Elizabeth Harrison, Eleanor Summerfield, Mona Washbourne

Cry Havoc
US 1943   97m   bw
MGM (Edwin Knopf)

War nurses are caught up in the Bataan retreat. An all-woman cast adequately handles a stagey melodrama about a tragic situation.

w Paul Osborn, *play* Proof thro' the Night by Allen R. Kenward *d* Richard Thorpe

Margaret Sullavan, Joan Blondell, Ann Sothern, Fay Bainter, Marsha Hunt, Ella Raines, Frances Gifford, Diana Lewis, Heather Angel, Connie Gilchrist

'A sincere fourth-rate film made from a sincere fifth-rate play.'—*James Agee*

A Cry in the Night
US 1956   75m   bw
Warner / Jaguar (George C. Bertholon)

A peeping Tom, caught by a teenage couple, abducts the girl and threatens rape.
Odd little domestic thriller, with parents and police working together. Watchable, but a bit over the top.

w David Dortort *d* Frank Tuttle *ph* John Seitz *m* David Buttolph

Edmond O'Brien, Brian Donlevy, Natalie Wood, Raymond Burr, Richard Anderson, Irene Hervey, Anthony Caruso

Cry of the Banshee
GB 1970   87m   Movielab
AIP (Gordon Hessler)

A 16th-century magistrate is cursed by a witch, who sends a devil in the form of a young man to destroy him.
Modest horror film which fails to do justice to its interesting plot.

w Tim Kelly, Christopher Wicking *d* Gordon Hessler *ph* John Coquillon *m* Les Baxter

Vincent Price, Elisabeth Bergner, Patrick Mower, Essy Persson, Hugh Griffith, Hilary Dwyer, Sally Geeson

Cry of the City**
US 1948   96m   bw
TCF

A ruthless gangster on the run is pursued by a policeman who was once his boyhood friend.
Very well produced but relentlessly miserable New York thriller on the lines of *Manhattan Melodrama* and *Angels with Dirty Faces*.

w Richard Murphy *d* Robert Siodmak *ph* Lloyd Aherne *m* Alfred Newman

Victor Mature, Richard Conte, Mimi Agulia, Shelley Winters, Tommy Cook, Fred Clark, Debra Paget

Cry Terror**
US 1958   96m   bw
MGM / Andrew Stone

As security against ransom money being delivered, an airline bomber kidnaps a family. Unabashed suspenser which screws panic situations as far as they will go and farther.

wd Andrew Stone *ph* Walter Strenge *m* Howard Jackson

James Mason, Rod Steiger, Inger Stevens, Neville Brand, Angie Dickinson, Kenneth Tobey, Jack Klugman, Jack Kruschen

Cry the Beloved Country*
GB 1951   96m   bw
London Films (Alan Paton)
US title: *African Fury*

In South Africa, a white farmer and a black preacher find friendship through linked family tragedies.
Well-intentioned, earnest, rather high-flown racial drama.

w Alan Paton, from his novel *d* Zoltan Korda *ph* Robert Krasker *m* Raymond Gallois-Montbrun

Canada Lee, Sidney Poitier, Charles Carson, Charles McRae, Joyce Carey, Geoffrey Keen, Michael Goodliffe, Edric Connor

Cry Wolf
US 1947 83m bw
Warner (Henry Blanke)

A widow claims her husband's estate and finds his mysterious uncle very difficult to deal with . . .
Rather obvious old dark house mystery with a not very interesting solution, all relying too heavily on star performances.

w Catherine Turney, *novel* Marjorie Carleton *d* Peter Godfrey *ph* Carl Guthrie *m* Franz Waxman

Barbara Stanwyck, Errol Flynn (as the apparent heavy), Geraldine Brooks, Richard Basehart, Helene Thimig

The Crystal Ball*
US 1943 82m bw
(Richard Blumenthal)

A failed beauty contestant becomes a fortune teller and is involved in a land swindle.
Pleasant comedy with fanciful moments, ending with a pie-throwing contest.

w Virginia Van Upp *d* Elliott Nugent *ph* Leo Tover *m* Victor Young

Paulette Goddard, Ray Milland, Gladys George, Virginia Field, Cecil Kellaway, William Bendix, Ernest Truex

Cuba Si!*
France 1961 58m bw
Films de la Pléiade

A documentary on the Cuban revolution and Castro's rise to power.
Remarkable and influential at the time for its use of techniques which are now the commonplaces of television, this documentary still has its flashes of interest.

wd, ph Chris Marker *m* E. G. Mantici, J. Calzada *ed* Eva Zora
  'An eloquent, personal record of history in the making.'—*Georges Sadoul*

Cuban Love Song
US 1931 86m bw
MGM

A marine on leave in Cuba falls in love; years later he returns to retrieve his illegitimate child, whose mother has died.

Pathetic musical melodrama which did not advance its singing star's film career.

w John Lynch *d* W. S. Van Dyke *ph* Harold Rosson *songs* various

Lawrence Tibbett, Lupe Velez, Jimmy Durante, Ernest Torrence, Karen Morley, Louise Fazenda

A Cuckoo in the Nest*
GB 1933 85m bw
Gaumont (Ian Dalrymple, Angus MacPhail)

A newlywed husband is forced to spend a night at an inn with an old flame pretending to be his wife.
Classic Aldwych farce with the stage company in excellent form; directorial style on the stagey side.

w Ben Travers, A. R. Rawlinson, *play Ben Travers d* Tom Walls

Ralph Lynn, Tom Walls, Yvonne Arnaud, Mary Brough, Veronica Rose, Gordon James, Cecil Parker, Roger Livesey
† Remade 1955 as *Fast and Loose*.

Cul de Sac
GB 1966 111m bw
Compton–Tekli (Gene Gutowski)

Two gangsters on the run take refuge in an old castle on a desolate Northumbrian island, but find their nemesis in the effeminate owner and his voluptuous wife.
Overlong, eccentric black comedy, more perplexing than entertaining.

w Roman Polanski, Gerard Brach *d* Roman Polanski *ph* Gilbert Taylor *m* Komeda

Lionel Stander, Donald Pleasence, Jack MacGowran, Françoise Dorléac, William Franklyn, Robert Dorning, Renée Houston

The Culpeper Cattle Company*
US 1972 92m De Luxe
TCF (Paul A. Helmick)

A 16-year-old would-be cowboy joins a cattle trail but is shocked at the harsh realities of western life.
Excellent moody photography helps to convince us that the old west was really like this, but the story is more brutal than interesting.

w Eric Bercovici, Gregory Prentiss *d* Dick Richards *ph* Lawrence Edward Williams, Ralph Woolsey *m* Tom Scott, Jerry Goldsmith

Gary Grimes, Billy 'Green' Bush, Luke Askew, Bo Hopkins, Geoffrey Lewis, Wayne Sutherlin

The Cure****
US 1917 20m approx bw silent
Mutual

A dipsomaniac sent to a spa gets his booze
mixed up with the spa water.
One of the funniest of the Chaplin shorts, with no
pathos intervening (nor come to that much plot);
it is simply a succession of balletic slapstick
scenes of the highest order.

wd Charles Chaplin ph William C. Foster,
Rollie Totheroh

Charles Chaplin, Edna Purviance, Eric
Campbell, Henry Bergman

The Cure for Love
GB 1949 98m bw
London Films (Robert Donat)

An ex-soldier goes home and tries to get married.
Thin Lancashire comedy which seemed an
astonishing choice for Robert Donat, whose
acting and direction were equally ill at ease.

w Robert Donat, Alexander Shaw, Albert
Fennell, *play* Walter Greenwood *d* Robert
Donat *ph* Jack Cox *m* William Alwyn

Robert Donat, Renée Asherson, Dora Bryan,
Marjorie Rhodes, Charles Victor, Thora Hird,
Gladys Henson
'Antediluvian regional farce.'—*MFB*

Curly Top*
US 1935 78m bw
TCF (Darryl F. Zanuck, Winfield Sheehan)

An orphan waif is adopted by a playboy, and not
only sets his business right but fixes his romantic
interest in her sister.
Archetypal Temple vehicle, a loose remake of
Daddy Longlegs.

w Patterson McNutt, Arthur Beckhard *d* Irving
Cummings *ph* John Seitz

Shirley Temple, John Boles, Rochelle Hudson,
Jane Darwell, Rafaela Ottiano, Esther Dale,
Arthur Treacher, Etienne Girardot

The Curse of Frankenstein**
GB 1957 83m Eastmancolor
Warner / Hammer

A lurid revamping of the 1931 *Frankenstein*, this
time with severed eyeballs and a peculiarly
unpleasant and uncharacterized creature, all in
gory colour. It set the trend in nasty horrors from
which we have all suffered since, and launched
Hammer Studios on a long and profitable career
of charnelry. But it did have a gruesome sense of
style.

w Jimmy Sangster d Terence Fisher ph Jack
Asher *m James Bernard ad* Ted Marshall

Peter Cushing, Christopher Lee, Hazel Court,
Robert Urquhart, Valerie Gaunt, Noel Hood

The Curse of the Cat People*
US 1944 70m bw
RKO (*Val Lewton*)

A child is haunted by the spirit of the cat people.
A gentle film ordered by the studio as a sequel to
Cat People but turned by Lewton into a fantasy
of childhood. Slow to start but finally
compelling, it's a pleasing and unusual film in a
minor key.

w De Witt Bodeen *d* Robert Wise, Gunther
Fritsch *ph* Nicholas Musuraca *m* Roy Webb

Kent Smith, Simone Simon, Jane Randolph,
Julia Dean, Ann Carter, Elizabeth Russell
'Full of the poetry and danger of
childhood.'—*James Agee*

Curse of the Crimson Altar
GB 1968 89m Eastmancolor
Tigon / AIP (Tony Tenser)

Witchcraft, diabolism and mystery in an English
country house.
A derivative, muddled scribble of a horror film,
making no sense and wasting much talent.

w Mervyn Haisman, Henry Lincoln *d* Vernon
Sewell *ph* John Coquillon *m* Peter Knight

Boris Karloff (his last appearance), Christopher
Lee, Rupert Davies, Mark Eden, Barbara Steele,
Michael Gough

Curse of the Werewolf
GB 1961 92m Technicolor
U-I / Hammer (Anthony Hinds)

A beggar rapes a servant girl and their offspring
grows up to be a werewolf.
Doleful Hammer horror in a Spanish setting,
with an absurd but predictable plot and a lack of
sympathy for its fancy, hairy hero.

w John Elder (Anthony Hinds) *d* Terence
Fisher *ph* Arthur Grant *m* Benjamin Frankel

Oliver Reed, Clifford Evans, Catherine Feller,
Yvonne Romain, Anthony Dawson, Richard
Wordsworth, Warren Mitchell

Curtain Call*
US 1940 63m bw
RKO

Two Broadway producers buy an awful play in
order to get even with a temperamental star, but
she likes it.
Amusing second feature, a kind of flashforward
to *The Producers*. A reprise the following year,
Footlight Fever, did not work.

w Dalton Trumbo *d* Frank Woodruff

ph Russell Metty *m* Roy Webb

Alan Mowbray, Donald MacBride, Helen Vinson, Barbara Read, John Archer

Curtain Call at Cactus Creek*
US 1949   83m   Technicolor
U-I (Robert Arthur)
GB title: *Take the Stage*

A travelling repertory company in the old west exposes a gang of bank robbers.
Cheerful minor comedy with good pace and amusing burlesques of old melodramas.

w Oscar Brodney *d* Charles Lamont *ph* Russell Metty

Donald O'Connor, Gale Storm, Eve Arden, Vincent Price, Walter Brennan, Chick Chandler

Curtain Up*
GB 1952   85m   bw
Rank / Constellation (Robert Garrett)

A seaside repertory company runs into trouble when the producer is at loggerheads with the author of next weeks's play.
Fairly amusing farce which has now acquired historical value for the light it throws on the old weekly reps.

w Michael Pertwee, Jack Davies, *play* On Monday Next by Philip King *d* Ralph Smart *ph* Stanley Pavey *m* Malcolm Arnold

Margaret Rutherford, Robert Morley, Olive Sloane, Joan Rice, Charlotte Mitchell, Kay Kendall, Liam Gaffney, Michael Medwin

Custer of the West
US 1968   146m   Super Technirama 70
Cinerama / Security (Louis Dolivet, Philip Yordan, Irving Lerner)

After the Civil War, Custer is offered a cavalry command, becomes disillusioned, and is massacred with his troops at Little Big Horn.
Gloomily inaccurate spectacular with pauses for Cinerama carnival thrills and dour bits of melodrama.

w Bernard Gordon, Julian Halevy *d* Robert Siodmak *ph* Cecilio Paniagua *m* Bernardo Segall

Robert Shaw, Mary Ure, Robert Ryan, Jeffrey Hunter,
Ty Hardin, Lawrence Tierney, Kieron Moore

The Cyclops
US 1956   65m   bw
B and H (Bert I. Gordon)

Explorers in Mexico find animals turned by radiation into monsters, plus a one-eyed 25-foot-tall human.

Modest monster movie, quite palatable of its kind.

wd Bert I. Gordon *ph* Ira Morgan *m* Albert Glasser

James Craig, Lon Chaney Jnr, Gloria Talbot, Tom Drake

Cynara**
US 1933   78m   bw
Samuel Goldwyn

A London barrister has an affair with a young girl who commits suicide when he goes back to his wife.
Solidly carpentered, effective star vehicle of the old school, now dated but preserving its dignity.

w Frances Marion, Lynn Starling, *novel* An Imperfect Lover by Robert Gore Brown *d* King Vidor *ph* Ray June

Ronald Colman, Kay Francis, Phyllis Barry, *Henry Stephenson*, Paul Porcasi

Cynthia
US 1947   98m   bw
MGM
GB title: *The Rich Full Life*

An over-protected girl finds an outlet in music and her parents finally allow her to lead her own life.
An overlong domestic drama in which thin writing and acting are backed by unsound psychology.

w Harold Buchman, Charles Kaufman, *play* Vina Delmar *d* Robert Z. Leonard *ph* Charles Schoenbaum

Elizabeth Taylor, George Murphy, Mary Astor, S. Z. Sakall, James Lydon, Gene Lockhart, Spring Byington

Cyrano de Bergerac*
US 1950   112m   bw
Stanley Kramer

In the 17th century a long-nosed poet, philosopher and buffoon writes letters enabling a friend to win the lady he loves himself.
The classic romantic verse play does not take kindly to a hole-in-corner black-and-white production, but at the time it was lapped up as a daring cultural breakthrough.

w Brian Hooker, *play* Edmond Rostand *d* Michael Gordon *ph* Franz Planer *m* Dmitri Tiomkin

Jose Ferrer, Mala Powers, William Prince, Morris Carnovsky, Ralph Clanton, Virginia Farmer, Edgar Barrier, Elena Verdugo

AA: Jose Ferrer

D

Daddy Longlegs*
US 1931   73m   bw
Fox

An orphan girl grows up to fall in love with her
mysterious benefactor.
Cinderella-like romance, adequately adapted
from a novel which became the classic American
version of the January–May romance.

w Sonya Levien, *novel* Jean Webster d Alfred
Santell ph Lucien Andriot

Janet Gaynor, Warner Baxter, Una Merkel,
John Arledge, Claude Gillingwater, Louise
Closser Hale
† Other versions were made in 1919 with Mary
Pickford and Mahlon Hamilton, directed by
Marshal Neilan; in 1935
disguised as *Curly Top* (qv) and in 1955 (see
below).

Daddy Longlegs*
US 1955   126m   Technicolor
   Cinemascope
TCF (Samuel G. Engel)

Overlong and unsuitably wide-screened musical
version of a popular story (see above). Generally
clumsy and dispirited, but Astaire is always
worth watching and a couple of the dances are
well staged.

w Phoebe and Henry Ephron d Jean Negulesco
ph Leon Shamroy m Alfred Newman *songs*
Johnny Mercer

Fred Astaire, Leslie Caron, *Fred Clark*, Thelma
Ritter, Terry Moore, Charlotte Austin, Larry
Keating

AAN: Alfred Newman; song 'Something's
Gotta Give' (*m/ly* Johnny Mercer)

Daddy's Gone A-Hunting
US 1969   108m   Technicolor
Warner / Red Lion (Mark Robson)

A child and its mother are threatened by her
deranged ex-husband.
Unpleasant and protracted suspenser with the
emphasis on sex rather than thrills.

w Larry Cohen, Lorenzo Semple Jnr d Mark
Robson ph Ernest Laszlo m John Williams

Carol White, Paul Burke, Scott Hylands, Mala
Powers, Andrea King

Dad's Army**
GB 1971   95m   Technicolor
Columbia / Norcon (John R. Sloan)

Misadventures of a number of elderly gents in
Britain's wartime Home Guard.
Expanded big-screen version of the long-running
TV series, a pleasant souvenir but rather less
effective than was expected because everything is
shown—the town, the Nazis, the wives—and
thus the air of gentle fantasy disappears,
especially in the face of much coarsened
humour.

w Jimmy Perry, David Croft d Norman Cohen
ph Terry Maher m Wilfred Burns

*Arthur Lowe, John Le Mesurier, John Laurie,
James Beck*, Ian Lavender, *Arnold Ridley*, Liz
Fraser, *Clive Dunn*, Bill Pertwee, Frank
Williams, Edward Sinclair

Daisy Kenyon
US 1947   99m   bw
TCF (Otto Preminger)

A fashion designer has two men in her life.
Adequate woman's picture which hardly justifies
its cast.

w David Hertz, *novel* Elizabeth Janeway d Otto
Preminger ph Leon Shamroy m David Raksin

Joan Crawford, Henry Fonda, Dana Andrews,
Ruth Warrick, Martha Stewart, Peggy Ann
Garner

Daisy Miller*
US 1974   92m   Technicolor
Paramount / Copa de Oro (Peter
   Bogdanovich)

In the 19th century, an American girl tourist in
Europe falls in love but dies of the Roman fever.
Curious attempt to film a very mild and
uneventful Henry James story, with careful
production but inadequate leads. The first sign
that Bogdanovich was getting too big for his
boots.

w Frederic Raphael d Peter Bogdanovich
ph Alberto Spagnoli m classical themes
ad Ferdinando Scarfiotti

Cybill Shepherd, Barry Brown, Cloris
Leachman, Mildred Natwick, Eileen Brennan,
James MacMurtry

'A historical film bereft of any feeling for
history, and a literary adaptation which reveals a
fine contempt for literary subtlety.'—*Jan
Dawson*

'Appallingly crass . . . directed with all the
subtlety of a sledgehammer.'—*Michael
Billington, Illustrated London News*

'Trying to make that little thing he's with into
Daisy Miller was hilarious. God almighty
couldn't do that. She's so coy.'—*Henry
Hathaway*

Dakota
US 1945 82m bw
Republic (Joseph Kane)

The daughter of a railroad tycoon elopes with a
cowboy and becomes involved in a land war.
Adequate star western.

w Lawrence Hazard, *story* Carl Foreman
d Joseph Kane *ph* Jack Marta *m* Walter Scharf.

John Wayne, Vera Hruba Ralston, Walter
Brennan, Ward Bond, Ona Munson, Hugo
Haas, Mike Mazurki, Paul Fix, Grant Withers,
Jack La Rue

Daleks: Invasion Earth 2150 AD see Dr
Who and the Daleks

Dallas*
US 1950 94m Technicolor
Warner (Anthony Veiller)

A renegade ex-Confederate colonel is pardoned
for bringing law and order to Dallas.
Routinely competent top-of-the-bill western.

w John Twist *d* Stuart Heisler *ph* Ernest Haller
m Max Steiner

Gary Cooper, Ruth Roman, Raymond Massey,
Steve Cochran, Barbara Payton, Leif Erickson,
Antonio Moreno, Jerome Cowan

The Dam Busters**
GB 1954 125m bw
ABPC (Robert Clark)

In 1943 the Ruhr dams are destroyed by Dr
Barnes Wallis' bouncing bombs.
Understated British war epic with additional
scientific interest and good acting and model
work, not to mention a welcome lack of love
interest.

w R. C. Sheriff, *books* by Guy Gibson and Paul
Brickhill *d* Michael Anderson *ph* Erwin Hillier
m Leighton Lucas, *Eric Coates* *sp* George
Blackwell

Michael Redgrave, Richard Todd, Basil Sydney,
Derek Farr, Patrick Barr, Ernest Clark,
Raymond Huntley, Ursula Jeans

Dames**
US 1935 90m bw
Warner (Robert Lord)

A millionaire purity fanatic tries to stop the
opening of a Broadway show.
Typical Warner musical of the period: its real
raison d'être is to be found in the splendidly
imaginative numbers at the finale, but it also
gives very full rein to the roster of comic actors
under contract at the time.

w Delmer Daves *d* Ray Enright *ch* Busby
Berkeley *ph* Sid Hickox, George Barnes
m various

*Joan Blondell, Hugh Herbert, Guy Kibbee, Zasu
Pitts*, Dick Powell, Ruby Keeler

Les Dames du Bois de Boulogne*
France 1946 90m bw
Films Raoul Ploquin

Hélène revenges herself on her bored lover by
arranging for him to marry a prostitute.
Spare, symbolic melodrama which has
occasioned as much irritation as applause.

w Robert Bresson, Jean Cocteau, from Diderot's
Jacques Le Fataliste *d Robert Bresson*
ph Philippe Agostini *m* Jean-Jacques
Grunenwald

Maria Casarès, Elina Labourdette, Lucienne
Bogaert, Paul Bernard

'Through abstraction, Bresson has been able
to make a film in which the tragedy is implicit not
only in the plot but also in the form.'—*Richard
Roud, MFB, 1966*

Damien: Omen Two
US 1978 109m De Luxe Panavision
TCF (Harvey Bernhard)

The antichrist who got rid of the entire cast of
The Omen now, as a teenager, starts in on his
foster parents.
Once was enough.

w Stanley Mann, Michael Hodges *d* Don
Taylor *ph* Bill Butler *m* Jerry Goldsmith

William Holden, Lee Grant, Jonathan Scott-
Taylor, Robert Foxworth, Lucas Donat, Lew
Ayres, Sylvia Sidney, Elizabeth Shepherd

Damn Yankees**
US 1958 110m Technicolor
Warner (George Abbott, Stanley Donen)
GB title: *What Lola Wants*

The devil interferes in the fortunes of a failing baseball team.

Smartly-styled but very American musical based on *Faust*; brilliant moments but some tedium.

w George Abbott, *novel* Douglas Wallop *d* George Abbott, Stanley Donen *ph* Harold Lipstein *m/ly* Richard Adler, Jerry Ross *md* Ray Heindorf

Gwen Verdon, Tab Hunter, Ray Walston, Russ Brown, Shannon Bolin

AAN: Ray Heindorf

Damnation Alley

US 1977   95m   De Luxe
TCF / Hal Landers, Bobby Roberts, Jerome M. Zeitman

Four survivors from World War Three try to reach a colony of fellow-survivors in New York. Feeble attempt at a low-budget blockbuster.

w Alan Sharp, Lukas Heller, *novel* Roger Zelazny *d* Jack Smight *ph* Harry Stradling Jnr *m* Jerry Goldsmith *pd* Preston Ames

Jan-Michael Vincent, George Peppard, Dominique Sanda, Paul Winfield

The Damned*

France 1947   105m   bw
Speva Film
original title: *Les Maudits*

In 1945 fanatical Nazis escape in a submarine but make the mistake of stopping to sink a freighter.
Unusual melodrama with a brilliant sense of claustrophobia, good characterization and much suspense.

w Jacques Remy, René Clément, Henri Jeanson *d* René Clément *ph* Henri Alekan *m* Yves Baudrier

Paul Bernard, Henri Vidal, Marcel Dalio, Michel Auclair, Florence Marly

The Damned*

GB 1961   87m   bw   Hammerscope
Columbia / Hammer–Swallow (Anthony Hinds)
US title: *These Are the Damned*

A scientist keeps radioactive children in a cliff cave, sealed off from the world's corruption. Absurdly pompous, downcast and confused sci-fi melodrama set in Weymouth, with a secondary plot about motor-cycling thugs.

w Evan Jones, *novel* The Children of Light by H. L. Lawrence *d* Joseph Losey *ph* Arthur Grant *m* James Bernard

Macdonald Carey, Shirley Ann Field, Alexander

Knox, Viveca Lindfors, Oliver Reed, Walter Gotell, James Villiers

'A *folie de grandeur.*'—*Tom Milne*

'Out of this wild mishmash some really magnificent images loom.'—*John Coleman*

The Damned**

West Germany / Italy 1969   164m
Eastmancolor
Praesidens / Pegaso
original title: *Götterdammerung*

A family of German industrialists divides and destroys itself under Nazi influence.
A film which has been called baroque, Wagnerian, and just plain unpleasant; it is also rather a strain to watch, with exaggerated colour and make-up to match the rotting theme.

w Nicola Badalucco, Enrico Medioli, Luchino Visconti *d* Luchino Visconti *ph* Armando Nannuzzi, Pasquale de Santis *m* Maurice Jarre *ad* Enzo del Prato, Pasquale Romano

Dirk Bogarde, Ingrid Thulin, Helmut Berger, Renaud Verley, Helmut Griem, René Kolldehof, Albrecht Schönhals, Umberto Orsini

'One is left lamenting that such a quondam master of realism as Visconti is making his films look like operas from which the score has been inexplicably removed.'—*MFB*

AAN: script

The Damned Don't Cry

US 1950   103m   bw
Warner (Jerry Wald)

A middle-class housewife leaves her husband for a gambler, and becomes involved with gangsters, but eventually reforms.
Rather dreary stimulation for female audiences who like safe dreams of danger.

w Harold Medford, Jerome Weidman, *novel* Case History by Gertrude Walker *d* Vincent Sherman *ph* Ted McCord *m* Daniele Amfitheatrof

Joan Crawford, Kent Smith, David Brian, Steve Cochran, Hugh Sanders, Selena Royle, Morris Ankrum, Richard Egan

A Damsel in Distress*

US 1937   101m   bw
RKO (Pandro S. Berman)

An American dancing star falls for an aristocratic young Englishwoman.
Astaire without Rogers, but the style is the same and there are some very good numbers.

w P. G. Wodehouse, S. K. Lauren, Ernest Pagano *d* George Stevens *ph* Joseph H. August *m/ly* George and Ira Gershwin *ch* Hermes Pan

Fred Astaire, George Burns, Gracie Allen, Joan Fontaine, Reginald Gardiner, Constance Collier, Ray Noble, Montagu Love
† Rogers had demanded a break from musicals, so she was replaced by the demure Miss Fontaine, who was generally thought disappointing.

Dance Fools Dance
US 1931 82m bw
MGM

A lady reporter in Chicago proves her worth.
Bizarrely-titled gangster thriller based on the Jake Lingle killing. Very moderate of its kind.

w Richard Schayer, Aurania Rouverol *d* Harry Beaumont *ph* Charles Rosher

Joan Crawford, Lester Vail, Cliff Edwards, William Bakewell, William Holden (the other one), Clark Gable, Earle Foxe, Joan Marsh

Dance Girl Dance *
US 1940 88m bw
RKO (Erich Pommer)

Private problems of the members of a nightclub dance troupe.
Competent and sometimes interesting formula drama with a harder edge than usual.

w Tess Slesinger, Frank Davis, *story* Vicki Baum *d* Dorothy Arzner *ph* Russell Metty

Maureen O'Hara, Louis Hayward, Lucille Ball, Maria Ouspenskaya, Ralph Bellamy, Virginia Field, Mary Carlisle, Walter Abel, Edward Brophy, Harold Huber

Dance Hall *
GB 1950 80m bw
Ealing (E. V. H. Emmett)

Four factory girls seek relaxation and various kinds of romance at the local palais.
Untypically flat Ealing slice of life, now watchable only with a smile as musical nostalgia.

w E. V. H. Emmett, Diana Morgan, Alexander Mackendrick *d* Charles Crichton *ph* Douglas Slocombe *md* Ernest Irving

Natasha Parry, Donald Houston, Diana Dors, Bonar Colleano, Jane Hylton, Petula Clark, Gladys Henson, Sydney Tafler; the bands of Geraldo and Ted Heath

The Dance of Death *
GB †1968 149m Technicolor
BHE / National Theatre (John Brabourne)

Edgar and Alice live alone on an island, their marriage having become a constant war.
Too-literal film transcription of an applauded

theatrical production, with the camera anchored firmly in the middle of the stalls.

w August Strindberg (*translation* by C. D. Locock) *d* David Giles *ph* Geoffrey Unsworth

Laurence Olivier, Geraldine McEwan, Robert Lang, Carolyn Jones

Dancing Co-ed
US 1939 90m bw
MGM (Edgar Selwyn)
GB title: *Every Other Inch a Lady*

A college girl makes it in show business as well as the groves of academe.
Mindless vehicle for a 19-year-old star.

w Albert Mannheimer, *story* Albert Treynor *d* S. Sylvan Simon

Lana Turner, Richard Carlson, Artie Shaw, Leon Errol, Ann Rutherford, Lee Bowman, Monty Woolley, Roscoe Karns, June Preisser, Walter Kingsford

Dancing in the Dark *
US 1949 92m Technicolor
TCF (George Jessel)

A silent movie idol makes a comeback as a talent scout, and spots his own daughter.
Thin but unusual Hollywood drama with music; in the long run too sentimental.

w Mary C. McCall Jnr, *play* The Band Wagon by George F. Kaufman, Howard Dietz, Arthur Schwarz *d* Irving Reis *ph* Harry Jackson *m* Alfred Newman

William Powell, Adolphe Menjou, Mark Stevens, Betsy Drake, Hope Emerson, Lloyd Corrigan, Walter Catlett, Jean Hersholt

Dancing Lady *
US 1933 94m bw
MGM (David O. Selznick)

A successful dancer chooses between a playboy and her stage manager.
Routine backstage semi-musical with interesting talent applied.

w Allen Rivkin, P. J. Wolfson, *novel* James Warner Bellah *d* Robert Z. Leonard *ph* Oliver T. Marsh *m* various

Joan Crawford, Clark Gable, *Fred Astaire*, Franchot Tone, May Robson, Ted Healy and his Stooges (the Three Stooges), Winnie Lightner, Robert Benchley, Nelson Eddy

The Dancing Masters
US 1943 63m bw
TCF (Lee Marcus)

Laurel and Hardy run a ballet school, and get involved with gangsters and inventors.

Insubstantial star comedy featuring reworkings of old routines, and a back-projected runaway bus climax.

w Scott Darling, George Bricker *d* Mal St Clair *ph* Norbert Brodine

Stan Laurel, Oliver Hardy, Trudy Marshall, Bob Bailey, Margaret Dumont, Matt Briggs, Robert Mitchum

The Dancing Years
GB 1949   97m   Technicolor
ABPC (Warwick Ward)

A composer loves a singer who leaves him after a misunderstanding but later bears his son . . . all in the Alps pre-1914.
Lamentable transcription of an operetta; precisely the ingredients which worked so well on stage seem embarrassing on film, and the performances and direction do not help.

w Warwick Ward, Jack Whittingham, from Ivor Novello's operetta *d* Harold French *ph* Stephen Dade *m* Ivor Novello

Dennis Price, Gisèle Préville, Patricia Dainton, Anthony Nicholls, Grey Blake, Muriel George, Olive Gilbert

A Dandy in Aspic
GB 1968   107m   Technicolor   Panavision
Columbia (Anthony Mann)

A double agent in Berlin is given orders to kill himself.
Muddled, pretentious spy thriller; flat, nebulous and boring.

w Derek Marlowe, from his novel *d* Anthony Mann *ph* Christopher Challis *m* Quincy Jones

Laurence Harvey, Tom Courtenay, Lionel Stander, Mia Farrow, Harry Andrews, Peter Cook, Per Oscarsson
† Anthony Mann died during shooting, and Laurence Harvey completed the direction.

Danger: Diabolik
Italy / France 1967   105m   Technicolor
Dino de Laurentiis / Marianne (Bruno Todini)

International police bait a golden trap for a master criminal.
Superior Batman-type adventures with a comic strip hero-villain.

w Dino Maiuri, Adriano Baracco, Mario Bava *d* Mario Bava *ph* Antonio Rinaldi *m* Ennio Morricone

John Phillip Law, Marisa Mell, Michel Piccoli, Adolfo Celi, Terry-Thomas

Danger Route
GB 1967   92m   De Luxe
UA / Amicus (Max J. Rosenberg, Milton Subotsky)

An 'eliminator' for the British secret service finds after a series of adventures that he must dispose of his own girl friend.
Dour sub-Bondian thriller with little to commend it.

w Meade Roberts, *novel* The Eliminator by Andrew York *d* Seth Holt *ph* Harry Waxman *m* John Mayer

Richard Johnson, Diana Dors, Sylvia Syms, Carol Lynley, Barbara Bouchet, Gordon Jackson, Sam Wanamaker, Maurice Denham, Harry Andrews

Danger Within**
GB 1958   101m   bw
British Lion / Colin Lesslie
US title: *Breakout*

Escape plans of officers in a prisoner-of-war camp are threatened by an informer.
Familiar comedy and melodrama with an added whodunnit element, smartly handled and very entertaining.

w Bryan Forbes, Frank Harvey, *novel* Michael Gilbert *d* Don Chaffey *ph* Arthur Grant *m* Francis Chagrin

Richard Todd, Bernard Lee, Michael Wilding, Richard Attenborough, Dennis Price, Donald Houston, William Franklyn, Vincent Ball, Peter Arne

Dangerous*
US 1935   78m   bw
Warner (Harry Joe Brown)

An alcoholic actress is rehabilitated.
Unconvincing and only adequately handled melodrama which won the star her first Oscar, presumably from sympathy at her losing it the previous year for *Of Human Bondage*.

w Laird Doyle *d* Alfred E. Green *ph* Ernest Haller

Bette Davis, Franchot Tone, Margaret Lindsay, Alison Skipworth, John Eldridge, Dick Foran
† Remade 1941 as *Singapore Woman*.

AA: Bette Davis

Dangerous Corner*
US 1934   67m   bw
RKO

After dinner conversation reveals what might have been if friends had spoken the truth about a long-ago suicide.

A fascinating trick play makes interesting but scarcely sparkling cinema.

w Anne Morrison Chapin, Madeleine Ruthven, *play* J. B. Priestley d Phil Rosen *ph* J. Roy Hunt

Melvyn Douglas, Conrad Nagel, Virginia Bruce, Erin O'Brien Moore, Ian Keith, Betty Furness, Henry Wadsworth

Dangerous Crossing*
US 1953   75m   bw
TCF (Robert Bassler)

At the start of an Atlantic sea voyage a woman's husband disappears, and she is assured that he never existed. He does, and is trying to murder her.

Adequately handled twist on the vanishing lady story: grade A production covers lapses of grade B imagination.

w Leo Townsend, *story* John Dickson Carr d Joseph M. Newman *ph* Joseph La Shelle *md* Lionel Newman

Jeanne Crain, Michael Rennie, Carl Betz, Casey Adams, Mary Anderson, Willis Bouchey

Dangerous Curves
US 1929   75m   bw
Paramount

A bareback rider loves a high wire artist. Obvious circus melodrama, a modest star vehicle.

w Donald David, Florence Ryerson d Lothar Mendes *ph* Harry Fischbeck

Clara Bow, Richard Arlen, Kay Francis, David Newell, Anders Randolf

Dangerous Exile
GB 1957   90m   Eastmancolor
   Vistavision
Rank (George H. Brown)

After the French Revolution, the young would-be Louis XVII is brought across the Channel and hidden in Pembrokeshire, where enemies attack him.

Historical romance, ineptly plotted but quite well produced.

w Robin Estridge, *novel* Vaughan Wilkins d Brian Desmond Hurst *ph* Geoffrey Unsworth *m* Georges Auric

Louis Jourdan, Belinda Lee, Keith Michell, Richard O'Sullivan, Martita Hunt, Finlay Currie, Anne Heywood, Jacques Brunius

Dangerous Moonlight*
GB 1941   98m   bw
RKO (William Sistrom)
US title: *Suicide Squadron*

A Polish pianist escapes from the Nazis and loses his memory after flying in the Battle of Britain.

Immensely popular wartime romance which introduced Richard Addinsell's Warsaw Concerto. Production values and script somewhat below par.

w Shaun Terence Young, Brian Desmond Hurst, Rodney Ackland d Brian Desmond Hurst

Anton Walbrook, Sally Gray, Derrick de Marney, Cecil Parker, Percy Parsons, Kenneth Kent, Guy Middleton, John Laurie, Frederick Valk

Dangerous to Know*
US 1938   70m   bw
Paramount

A ruthless Chicago gangster comes a cropper when his Chinese mistress discovers he has fallen for a socialite.

Flatly handled but mildly interesting adaptation of a highly successful play, the potential of which seems to have been thrown away.

w William R. Lippmann, Horace McCoy, *play* On the Spot by Edgar Wallace d Robert Florey *ph* Theodor Sparkuhl

Akim Tamiroff, Anna May Wong, Gail Patrick, Lloyd Nolan, Harvey Stephens, Anthony Quinn, Porter Hall

Dangerous When Wet**
US 1953   95m   Technicolor
MGM (George Wells)

An entire Arkansas family is sponsored to swim the English Channel.

A bright and lively vehicle for an aquatic star, who in one sequence swims with Tom and Jerry. Amusing sequences give opportunities to a strong cast.

w *Dorothy Kingsley* d Charles Walters *ph* Harold Rosson *songs* Johnny Mercer, Arthur Schwarz

Esther Williams, Charlotte Greenwood, William Demarest, Fernando Lamas, Jack Carson, Denise Darcel, Barbara Whiting

Dangerously They Live
US 1941   77m   bw
Warner (Ben Stoloff)

American Nazi agents try to get a secret memorized by a British girl agent injured in a car crash.

Watchable, routine spy propaganda fare.

w Marion Parsonnet d Robert Florey *ph* William O'Connell

John Garfield, Raymond Massey, Nancy

Coleman, Moroni Olsen, Lee Patrick, Christian Rub, Frank Reicher

Dante's Inferno**
US 1935 89m bw
TCF (Sol M. Wurtzel)

A ruthless carnival owner gets too big for his boots, and has a vision of hell induced by one of his own attractions.

Curiously unpersuasive melodrama with a moral, but the inferno sequence is one of the most unexpected, imaginative and striking pieces of cinema in Hollywood's history.

w Philip Klein, Robert Yost d Harry Lachman ph Rudolph Maté

Spencer Tracy, Claire Trevor, Henry B. Walthall, Alan Dinehart, Scotty Beckett, Rita Hayworth (her first appearance, as a dancer)

'We depart gratefully, having seen papier maché photographed in more ways than we had thought possible.'—Robert Herring

'One of the most unusual and effectively presented films of the thirties.'—John Baxter, 1968

Darby O'Gill and the Little People*
US 1959 90m Technicolor
Walt Disney

An Irish caretaker falls down a well and is captured by leprechauns, who allow him three wishes to rearrange his life.

Pleasantly barmy Irish fantasy with brilliant trick work but some tedium in between.

w Lawrence Edward Watkin, stories H. T. Kavanagh d Robert Stevenson ph Winton C. Hoch m Oliver Wallace sp Peter Ellenshaw, Eustace Lycett, Joshua Meador

Albert Sharpe, Jimmy O'Dea, Sean Connery, Janet Munro, Kieron Moore, Estelle Winwood, Walter Fitzgerald, Denis O'Dea, J. G. Devlin, Jack MacGowran

'One of the best fantasies ever put on film.'—Leonard Maltin

Darby's Rangers
US 1957 121m bw
Warner (Martin Rackin)
GB title: The Young Invaders

A tough American commando unit is trained in Britain before seeing action in Africa and Sicily.

Standard World War II actioner, adequately executed.

w Guy Trosper, book Major James Altieri d William Wellman ph William H. Clothier m Max Steiner

James Garner, Etchika Choureau, Jack Warden, Edward Byrnes, Venetia Stevenson, Torin

Thatcher, Stuart Whitman, Andrea King, Frieda Inescort, Reginald Owen, Adam Williams

The Daring Game
US 1967 101m Eastmancolor
Paramount / Tors (Gene Levitt)

A commercial group experiments with airborne and underwater inventions, and rescues a scientist from a police state.

Well photographed but haphazardly assembled adventures, aimed at TV.

w Andy White d Laslo Benedek ph Edmund Gibson m George Bruns

Lloyd Bridges, Nico Minardos, Joan Blackman, Michael Ansara

The Dark Angel*
US 1935 105m bw
Samuel Goldwyn

During World War I, a blinded officer tries to dismiss his fiancée without her learning of his infirmity.

Tearstained melodrama from another age, neatly packaged for the romantic 1935 public.

w Lillian Hellman, Mordaunt Sharp, play Guy Bolton d Sidney Franklin ph Gregg Toland m Alfred Newman

Merle Oberon, Fredric March, Herbert Marshall, Janet Beecher, John Halliday, Henrietta Crosman, Frieda Inescort, George Breakston, Claud Allister

† A 1925 silent version had starred Ronald Colman and Vilma Banky.

AAN: Merle Oberon

The Dark at the Top of the Stairs**
US 1960 124m Technicolor
Warner (Michael Garrison)

Twenties small town drama about a young boy's awakening to the sexual tensions around him.

Archetypal family drama set in that highly familiar American street. The perfect essence of this playwright's work, with high and low spots, several irrelevancies, but a real feeling for the people and the place.

w Harriet Frank Jnr, Irving Ravetch, play William Inge d Delbert Mann ph Harry Stradling m Max Steiner

Robert Preston, Dorothy McGuire, Angela Lansbury, Eve Arden, Shirley Knight, Frank Overton, Lee Kinsolving, Robert Eyer

† The curious title turns out to be a synonym for life, which one should never be afraid of.

AAN: Shirley Knight

The Dark Avenger*

GB 1955 85m Eastmancolor
Cinemascope
Allied Artists
US title: *The Warriors*

The Black Prince quells some French rebels.
Good-humoured historical romp with the ageing
star in his last swashbuckling role, helped by a
good cast and brisk pace.

w Daniel B. Ullman *d* Henry Levin *ph* Guy
Green *m* Cedric Thorpe Davie

Errol Flynn, Peter Finch, Joanne Dru, Yvonne
Furneaux, Patrick Holt, Michael Hordern,
Moultrie Kelsall, Robert Urquhart, Noel
Willman

Dark City

US 1950 97m bw
Paramount / Hal B. Wallis

A bookmaker finds himself on the run from a
revenge-seeking psychopath.
Unattractive and heavily-handled underworld
melodrama, a disappointment from the talents
involved.

w John Meredyth Lucas, Larry Marcus
d William Dieterle *ph* Victor Milner *m* Franz
Waxman

Charlton Heston (his first Hollywood
appearance), Lizabeth Scott, Viveca Lindfors,
Dean Jagger, Don Defore, Jack Webb, Ed
Begley, Henry Morgan, Mike Mazurki
  'A jaded addition to a type of thriller which
has become increasingly tedious and unreal.'—
MFB

Dark Command*

US 1940 92m bw
Republic (Sol C. Siegel)

In pre-Civil War Kansas, an ambitious ex-
schoolteacher named Cantrill organizes guerrilla
bands to pillage the countryside.
Semi-historical hokum, quite well done with a
good cast.

w Grover Jones, Lionel Houser, F. Hugh
Herbert,
novel W. R. Burnett *d* Raoul Walsh *ph* Jack
Marta
m Victor Young

John Wayne, Claire Trevor, Walter Pidgeon,
Roy Rogers, George 'Gabby' Hayes, Porter
Hall, Marjorie Main

AAN: Victor Young

The Dark Corner*

US 1946 98m bw
TCF (Fred Kohlmar)

A private eye with a criminal record thinks he is
being menaced by an old adversary, but the
latter is found murdered.
Moody, brutish, well-made thriller with a plot
put together from bits and pieces of older, better
movies, notably Clifton Webb's reprise of his
Laura performance and William Bendix ditto
The Glass Key.

w Jay Dratler, Bernard Schoenfeld, *story* Leo
Rosten *d* Henry Hathaway *ph* Joe MacDonald
m Cyril Mockridge

Mark Stevens, Clifton Webb, Lucille Ball,
William Bendix, Kurt Kreuger, Cathy Downs,
Reed Hadley, Constance Collier
  'Not so much a whodunnit as a whodunnwhat
. . . all seem bent on "getting" each other and
their internecine plottings add up to an alpha
thriller.'—*Daily Mail*

Dark Eyes of London*

GB 1939 75m bw
Pathe / Argyle (John Argyle)
US title: *The Human Monster*

The proprietor of a home for the blind uses a
mute giant to drown insured victims.
Reasonably effective British horror, a rarity at
the time.

w John Argyle, Walter Summers, Patrick
Kirwan, *novel* Edgar Wallace *d* Walter
Summers

Bela Lugosi, Hugh Williams, Greta Gynt,
Wilfrid Walter, Edmon Ryan

Dark Journey*

GB 1937 82m bw
London Films / Victor Saville

In 1915 Stockholm, a French woman spy
masquerading as a traitor falls in love with her
German spy contact.
Unconvincing but entertaining romantic
adventure with good star performances.

w Lajos Biro, Arthur Wimperis, *play* Lajos Biro
d Victor Saville *ph* Georges Périnal, Harry
Stradling

Conrad Veidt, Vivien Leigh, Joan Gardner,
Anthony Bushell, Ursula Jeans, Eliot Makeham,
Austin Trevor, Edmund Willard

The Dark Man

GB 1950 91m bw
Rank / Independent Artists (Julian Wintle)

A mysterious murderer haunts a seaside resort.
Limp, disappointing location police thriller, with
too much chat and generally mishandled
moments of suspense

wd Jeffrey Dell *ph* Eric Cross *m* Hubert Clifford

Maxwell Reed, Edward Underdown, Natasha Parry, Barbara Murray, William Hartnell, Cyril Smith, Geoffrey Sumner

'The contrivances of the script are not helped by stilted dialogue.'—*MFB*

The Dark Mirror**
US 1946   85m   bw
International

A police detective works out which of identical twin girls is a murderer.

Unconvincing but highly absorbing thriller with all credits plus; the best brand of Hollywood moonshine.

w Nunnally Johnson, *original story* Vladimir Posner *d* Robert Siodmak *ph* Milton Krasner

Olivia de Havilland, Lew Ayres, Thomas Mitchell, Garry Owen

AAN: Vladimir Posner

Dark Passage**
US 1947   106m   bw
Warner (Jerry Wald)

A convicted murderer escapes from jail and proves his innocence.

Loosely assembled, totally unconvincing star thriller which succeeds because of its professionalism, some good cameos, and a number of narrative tricks including subjective camera for the first half hour.

w Delmer Daves, *novel* David Goodis *d* Delmer Daves *ph* Sid Hickox *m* Franz Waxman

Humphrey Bogart, Lauren Bacall, Agnes Moorehead, Bruce Bennett, *Tom D'Andrea, Houseley Stevenson*

'An almost total drag.'—*New Yorker, 1977*

The Dark Past**
US 1948   75m   bw
Columbia

A psychiatrist turns the tables on convicts who break into his home.

Tense, economical remake of *Blind Alley* (qv); a fresh look at a familiar situation (*The Small Voice, The Desperate Hours*, etc) helped by excellent performances.

w Philip Macdonald, Malvin Wald, Oscar Saul *d* Rudolph Maté *ph* Joseph Walker *m* George Duning

William Holden, Lee J. Cobb, Nina Foch, Adele Jergens, Stephen Dunne

'A picture so packed with skill and imagination that every minute is absorbing.'—*Richard Mallett, Punch*

Dark Star
US 1974   83m   Metrocolor
Jack H. Harris

In the 22nd century, the bored crew of a starship on an intergalactic mission become prey to their own phobias and to the alien mascot they are taking back to earth.

A semi-professional film which turned out to be one of the screen's neatest low-budget entries in the pulp science fiction genre. That doesn't make it wholly entertaining, but its credentials are impeccable.

w John Carpenter, Dan O'Bannon *d* John Carpenter *pd, ed* Dan O'Bannon *ph* Douglas Knapp *m* John Carpenter

Brian Narelle, Dre Pahich, Cal Kuniholm, Dan O'Bannon

The Dark Tower
GB 1943   93m   bw
Warner

A circus hypnotist possessively controls a girl trapezist.

Heavy-handed but quite effective melodrama.

w Brock Williams, Reginald Purdell, *play* Alexander Woolcott, George S. Kaufman *d* John Harlow

Ben Lyon, Anne Crawford, David Farrar, Herbert Lom, William Hartnell, Frederick Burtwell, Josephine Wilson

Dark Victory**
US 1939   106m   bw
Warner (David Lewis)

A good-time society girl discovers she is dying of a brain tumour.

A highly commercial tearjerker of its day, this glutinous star vehicle now works only fitfully.

w Casey Robinson, *play* George Brewer Jnr, Bertram Bloch *d* Edmund Goulding *ph* Ernest Haller *m* Max Steiner

Bette Davis, George Brent, Humphrey Bogart, Ronald Reagan, Geraldine Fitzgerald, Henry Travers, Cora Witherspoon, Dorothy Peterson

'A completely cynical appraisal would dismiss it all as emotional flim-flam . . . but it is impossible to be that cynical about it.'—*Frank S. Nugent*

'A gooey collection of clichés, but Davis slams through them in her nerviest style.'—*New Yorker, 1976*

† Remade 1963 as *Stolen Hours*, with Susan Hayward; 1975 as *Dark Victory* (TV movie) with Elizabeth Montgomery.

AAN: best picture; Bette Davis; Max Steiner

Dark Waters**
US 1944   90m   bw
Benedict Bogeaus

Recovering from being torpedoed, an orphan girl
visits her aunt and uncle in Louisiana and has
some terrifying experiences.
Competent frightened-lady melodrama helped
by its bayou surroundings. Possibly discarded by
Hitchcock, but with sequences well in his
manner.

w Joan Harrison, Marian Cockrell d André de
Toth ph John Mescall

Merle Oberon, Franchot Tone, *Thomas
Mitchell, Fay Bainter, John Qualen*, Elisha
Cook Jnr, Rex Ingram

Darker than Amber
US 1970   96m   Technicolor
Cinema Center / Major Films

A Florida private eye rescues a girl who is
subsequently murdered and turns out to be part
of a confidence racket.
Routine suspenser from the Travis McGee
books; not very stimulating.

w Ed Waters, *novel* John D. MacDonald
d Robert Clouse ph Frank Phillips m John
Parker

Rod Taylor, Suzy Kendall, Theodore Bikel,
James Booth, Jane Russell, Janet McLachlan,
William Smith

Darling**
GB 1965   127m   bw
Anglo-Amalgamated / Vic / Appia (Joseph
Janni,
    Victor Lyndon)

An ambitious young woman deserts her
journalist mentor for a company director, an
effeminate photographer and an Italian prince.
Fashionable mid-sixties concoction of smart
swinging people and their amoral doings.
Influential, put over with high style, and totally
tiresome in retrospect.

w Frederic Raphael d John Schlesinger ph Ken
Higgins m John Dankworth

Julie Christie, Dirk Bogarde, Laurence Harvey,
Roland Curram, Alex Scott, Basil Henson,
Pauline Yates
    'As empty of meaning and mind as the empty
life it's exposing.'—*Pauline Kael*

AA: Frederic Raphael; Julie Christie
AAN: best picture; John Schlesinger

Darling How Could You
US 1951   96m   bw
Paramount (Harry Tugend)
GB title: *Rendezvous*

Children long separated from their parents have
fantasies about them.
Faded-looking Edwardian comedy which does
not quite have the style or the cast for success.
(Or the title, come to that.)

w Dodie Smith, Lesser Samuels, *play* Alice Sit
by the Fire by J. M. Barrie d Mitchell Leisen
ph Daniel L. Fapp m Frederick Hollander

Joan Fontaine, John Lund, Mona Freeman,
Peter Hanson, David Stollery, Lowell Gilmore,
Robert Barrat, Gertrude Michael

Darling Lili*
US 1970   136m   Technicolor   Panavision
Paramount / Geoffrey (Owen Crump)

During World War I, an American air ace falls
for a German lady spy, and waits till the war is
over to marry her.
Farce and romance mix oddly with aerial
acrobatics in this expensive and dull
extravaganza which bore the sub-title *Where
Were You the Night I Shot Down Baron Von
Richthofen?* (which probably sums up its aims
and its failure). A coffee table film, good to look
at and with occasional striking moments.

wd Blake Edwards ph Russell Harlan, Harold
E. Wellman m Henry Mancini pd Fernando
Carrere

Julie Andrews, Rock Hudson, Jeremy Kemp,
Lance Percival, Michael Witney, Jacques Marin,
André Maranne

AAN: Henry Mancini; song 'Whistling Away
the Dark' (*m* Henry Mancini, *ly* Johnny Mercer)

The Darwin Adventure*
GB 1971   91m   Eastmancolor
(TCF) Palomar (Joseph Strick, Irving Lerner)

In 1831, Charles Darwin becomes ship's
naturalist on the *Beagle* and studies wild life in
South America.
Rather naive biopic of Darwin which tries to
cover too much with too slender resources but
makes a pleasant introduction to the subject.

w William Fairchild d Jack Couffer ph Denys
Coop, Jack Couffer m Marc Wilkinson

Nicholas Clay, Susan Macready, Ian
Richardson, Christopher Martin, Robert
Flemyng, Aubrey Woods, Hugh Morton
    'The biopic plague, which has ravaged the
screen lives of Pasteur, Juarez, Cole Porter and
countless others, has now struck down the
memory of famed naturalist Charles Darwin.

The filmgoing public's own version of Darwin's natural selection theory will immediately weed out this inferior species.'—*Variety*

A Date with Judy
US 1948 113m Technicolor
MGM (Joe Pasternak)

A teenager wrongly suspects her friend of an illicit affair.
Ambitious but flat comedy musical which neatly wraps up all kinds of forties people and institutions: teenagers, small towns, families, Carmen Miranda and Miss Taylor, not to mention the producer.

w Dorothy Cooper, Dorothy Kingsley
d Richard Thorpe ph Robert Surtees
m/ly various

Wallace Beery, Elizabeth Taylor, Jane Powell, Carmen Miranda, Xavier Cugat, Robert Stack, Selena Royle, Scotty Beckett, Leon Ames

Daughter of Darkness
GB 1947 91m bw
Kenilworth–Alliance (Victor Hanbury)

A murderous Irish servant girl has a fatal flair for men.
Absurd melodrama, almost Grand Guignol, louringly set on the Yorkshire moors but lethargically handled all round.

w Max Catto, from his play They Walk Alone
d Lance Comfort

Siobhan McKenna, Anne Crawford, Maxwell Reed, George Thorpe, Barry Morse, Honor Blackman, Liam Redmond, David Greene

The Daughter of Rosie O'Grady*
US 1950 104m Technicolor
Warner (William Jacobs)

A girl determines to follow in her dead mother's musical comedy footsteps against the wishes of her still-grieving father.
Absolutely standard period musical, quite pleasantly handled but with below-par musical numbers.

w Jack Rose, Mel Shavelson, Peter Milne
d David Butler ph Wilfred M. Cline md David Buttolph

June Haver, Gordon Macrae, *James Barton*, S. Z. Sakall, Gene Nelson, Debbie Reynolds, Sean McClory, Jane Darwell

Daughters Courageous*
US 1939 107m bw
Warner (Hal B. Wallis)

A prodigal father returns to his family and sorts out their problems.

Following the success of *Four Daughters* (qv) the cast was reassembled to make this amiable rehash about a different family.

w Julius and Philip Epstein, *play* Fly Away Home by Dorothy Bennett, Irving White
d Michael Curtiz ph James Wong Howe

Claude Rains, John Garfield, Jeffrey Lynn, Fay Bainter, Priscilla Lane, Rosemary Lane, Lola Lane, Gale Page, Donald Crisp, May Robson, Frank McHugh, Dick Foran, Berton Churchill

'For its intelligent use of small town locations, its skilled acting, fine camerawork and evenly paced, sympathetic direction, it surpasses everything of its type.'—*John Baxter, 1968*

'Attractive people, good dialogue and camerawork, and skilful direction can work wonders.'—*Richard Mallett, Punch*

David and Bathsheba*
US 1952 116m Technicolor
TCF (Darryl F. Zanuck)

King David loves the wife of one of his captains, and ensures that the latter is killed in battle.
Deliberately sober bible-in-pictures, probably intended as a riposte to Cecil B. de Mille. Somewhat lacking in excitement, but you can't call it gaudy.

w Philip Dunne d Henry King ph Leon Shamroy m Alfred Newman

Gregory Peck, Susan Hayward, James Robertson Justice, Raymond Massey, Kieron Moore, Jayne Meadows, John Sutton, Dennis Hoey, Francis X. Bushman, George Zucco

'Hardly a single unintentional laugh.'—*Richard Mallett, Punch*

AAN: Phillip Dunne; Leon Shamroy; Alfred Newman

David and Lisa*
US 1963 94m bw
Continental (Paul M. Heller)

Two disturbed adolescents at a special school fall in love.
Case history drama, earnest and well meaning rather than exciting.

w *Eleanor Perry, book* Theodore Isaac Rubin
d Frank Perry ph Leonard Hirschfield m Mark Lawrence

Keir Dullea, Janet Margolin, Howard da Silva, Neva Patterson, Clifton James, Richard McMurray

AAN: Eleanor Perry; Frank Perry

David Copperfield****
US 1935 132m bw
MGM (David O. Selznick)

Disliked by his cruel stepfather and helped by his eccentric aunt, orphan David grows up to become an author and eventually to marry his childhood sweetheart.

Only slightly faded after forty years, this small miracle of compression not only conveys the spirit of Dickens better than the screen has normally managed but is a particularly pleasing example of Hollywood's handling of literature and of the deployment of a great studio's resources. It also overflows with memorable character cameos, and it was a box office giant.

w Hugh Walpole, Howard Estabrook, *novel* Charles Dickens *d George Cukor ph* Oliver T. Marsh *m* Herbert Stothart *montages* Slavko Vorkapitch *ad Cedric Gibbons*

Freddie Bartholemew (young David), *Frank Lawton* (David as a man), *W. C. Fields* (Micawber), *Roland Young* (Uriah Heep), *Edna May Oliver* (Aunt Betsy), *Lennox Pawle* (Mr Dick), *Basil Rathbone* (Mr Murdstone), Violet Kemble Cooper (Miss Murdstone), Maureen O'Sullivan (Dora), Madge Evans (Agnes), Elizabeth Allan (Mrs Copperfield), *Jessie Ralph* (Peggotty), Lionel Barrymore (Dan Peggotty), Hugh Williams (Steerforth), Lewis Stone (Mr Wickfield), *Herbert Mundin* (Barkis), Elsa Lanchester (Clickett), Jean Cadell (Mrs Micawber), Una O'Connor (Mrs Gummidge), John Buckler (Ham), Hugh Walpole (the Vicar), Arthur Treacher (donkey man)

'Though half the characters are absent, the whole spectacle of the book, Micawber always excepted, is conveyed.'—*James Agee*

'The most profoundly satisfying screen manipulation of a great novel that the camera has ever given us.'—*André Sennwald*

AAN: best picture

David Harum*
US 1934   83m   bw
TCF

A wily old rancher plays matchmaker. Simple, pleasing small-town comedy-drama, ably fashioned for its star.

d James Cruzé

Will Rogers, Evelyn Venable, Kent Taylor, Louise Dresser, Stepin Fetchit, Charles Middleton, Noah Beery

Davy*
GB 1957   84m   Technirama
Ealing (Basil Dearden)

A member of a family music hall act auditions at Covent Garden.

Curiously unsuccessful vehicle for a popular

singing comic; the script and continuity are simply poor, and swamped by the wide screen.

w William Rose d Michael Relph ph Douglas Slocombe m various classics

Harry Secombe, Ron Randell, George Relph, Alexander Knox, Susan Shaw, Bill Owen

Davy Crockett*
US 1955   93m   Technicolor
Walt Disney

Episodes in the career of the famous Tennessee hunter and Indian scout who died at the Alamo. Disjointed and naive but somehow very fresh and appealing adventures; made for American television (as 3 × 50m episodes) but elsewhere an enormous hit in cinemas.

w Tom Blackburn d Norman Foster ph Charles Boyle m George Bruns

Fess Parker, Buddy Ebsen, Basil Ruysdael, William Bakewell, Hans Conried, Kenneth Tobey, Nick Cravat

† 1956 sequel on similar lines: *Davy Crockett and the River Pirates.*

The Dawn Patrol**
US 1930   82m   bw
Warner

In France during World War I, flying officers wait their turn to leave on missions which may mean death.

The second version (see below) is more watchable today, but this early talkie was highly effective in its time, and much of its aerial footage was re-used.

w John Monk Saunders, Dan Totheroh, Seton I. Miller d Howard Hawks ph Ernest Haller

Richard Barthelmess, Douglas Fairbanks Jnr, Neil Hamilton, William Hanney, *James Finlayson*, Clyde Cook, Edmund Breon, Frank McHugh

'Bare, cleancut, uncluttered technique, a stark story line, terse dialogue . . . and a pervasive atmosphere of hopelessness captured with economy and incisiveness.'—*Andrew Sarris, 1963*

AAN: John Monk Saunders

The Dawn Patrol**
US 1938   103m   bw
Warner (Hal B. Wallis)

A remarkably early but trim and competent remake of the above, using much of the same aerial footage.

w Seton I. Miller, Dan Totheroh d Edmund Goulding ph Tony Gaudio

Errol Flynn, Basil Rathbone, David Niven,

Melville Cooper, Donald Crisp, Barry
Fitzgerald, Carl Esmond

A Day at the Races****
US 1937 109m bw (blue-tinted ballet
sequence)
MGM (Max Siegel)

The Marxes help a girl who owns a sanatorium
and a racehorse.
Fashions in Marxism change, but this top quality
production, though lacking their zaniest
inspirations, does contain several of their
funniest routines and a spectacularly well
integrated racecourse climax. The musical and
romantic asides are a matter of taste but
delightfully typical of their time.

w *Robert Pirosh, George Seaton, George
Oppenheimer d Sam Wood ph Joseph
Ruttenberg m Franz Waxman*

Groucho, Chico, Harpo, Margaret Dumont,
Maureen O'Sullivan, Allan Jones, *Douglass
Dumbrille, Esther Muir, Sig Rumann*

Day for Night***
France / Italy 1973 116m Eastmancolor
Films du Carrosse / PECF / PIC (Marcel
Bébert)
original title: *La Nuit Américaine*

Frictions and personality clashes beset the
making of a romantic film in Nice.
Immensely enjoyable, richly detailed, insider's-
eye-view of the goings-on in a film studio. A fun
film with melodramatic asides.

w François Truffaut, Jean-Louis Richard,
Suzanne Schiffman *d François Truffaut
ph* Pierre-William Glenn *m* Georges Delerue

Jacqueline Bisset, Valentina Cortese, Jean-Pierre
Aumont, Jean-Pierre Léaud, Dani, Alexandra
Stewart, Jean Champion, François Truffaut,
David Markham
    'I thought I'd had my last dram of enjoyment
out of the Pagliacci theme and studio magic, and
Truffaut shows there's life in the old whirl yet.'—
Stanley Kaufmann
    'Made with such dazzling craftsmanship and
confidence that you can never quite believe
Truffaut's point that directing a movie is a
danger-fraught experience.'—*Michael
Billington, Illustrated London News*
† Graham Greene, as Henry Graham, played an
insurance representative.

AAN: script; François Truffaut (as director);
Valentina Cortese

A Day in the Death of Joe Egg**
GB 1971 106m Eastmancolor
Columbia / Domino (David Deutsch)

A teacher and his wife are frustrated by their
own inability to cope with the problem of their
spastic daughter.
A well-filmed version of a sincerely human play,
with humour and fantasy sequences leavening
the gloom.

w *Peter Nichols*, from his play *d Peter Medak
ph* Ken Hodges *m* Elgar

Alan Bates, Janet Suzman, Peter Bowles, Sheila
Gish, *Joan Hickson*
    'It's unsatisfying, and it's not to be missed.'—
Stanley Kauffmann

The Day of the Animals
US 1976 98m De Luxe Todd AO 35
Film Ventures International

In the Californian High Sierras, animals of all
kinds suddenly turn on human beings, but a day
later are all found dead.
Irritatingly pointless horror fable borrowing
heavily from *The Birds*; basically an exploitation
shocker, most efficient when most unpleasant.

w William and Eleanor Norton *d* William
Girdler *ph* Tom McHugh *m* Lalo Schifrin

Christopher George, Lynda Day George, Leslie
Nielsen, Robert Sorrentino, Richard Jaeckel,
Michael Ansara, Ruth Roman, Paul Mantee, Gil
Lamb

The Day of the Dolphin*
US 1973 104m Technicolor Panavision
Avco–Embassy / Icarus (Robert E. Relyea)

A marine biologist researching dolphins off the
Florida coast discovers they are being used in a
plot to blow up the President's yacht.
A strangely unexpected and unsuccessful
offering from the talent involved: thin and
repetitive as scientific instruction (the dolphins'
language in any case topples it into fantasy), and
oddly childlike as spy adventure.

w Buck Henry, *novel* Robert Merle *d* Mike
Nichols *ph William A. Fraker m* Georges
Delerue *pd* Richard Sylbert

George C. Scott, Trish Van Devere, Paul
Sorvino, Fritz Weaver
    'The whole thing seems to have been shoved
through the cameras as glibly as possible, so that
everyone concerned could grab the money and
run.'—*Stanley Kauffmann*
    'An eight and a half million dollar Saturday
afternoon special for sheltered nine-year-
olds.'—*Judith Crist*

AAN: Georges Delerue

The Day of the Evil Gun*
US 1968 93m Metrocolor Panavision
MGM (Jerry Thorpe)

Returning home after three years, a rancher finds that his wife and child have been carried off by Indians.

Competent standard western which resolves itself into a duel of wits between the hero and his rival.

w Charles Marquis Warren, Eric Bercovici *d* Jerry Thorpe *ph* W. Wallace Kelley *m* Jeff Alexander

Glenn Ford, Arthur Kennedy, Dean Jagger, Paul Fix, John Anderson, Nico Minardos

The Day of the Jackal**
GB / France 1973   142m   Technicolor
Universal / Warwick / Universal France
   (John Woolf, David Deutsch)

British and French police combine to prevent an OAS assassination attempt on de Gaulle by use of a professional killer.

An incisive, observant and professional piece of work based on a rather clinical bestseller. Lack of a channel for sympathy, plus language confusions, are its main drawbacks.

w Kenneth Ross, *novel* Frederick Forsyth *d* Fred Zinnemann *ph* Jean Tournier *m* Georges Delerue

Edward Fox, Michel Lonsdale, Alan Badel, Eric Porter, Cyril Cusack, Delphine Seyrig, Donald Sinden, Tony Britton, Timothy West, Olga Georges-Picot, Barrie Ingham, Maurice Denham, Anton Rodgers

'Before *Jackal* is five minutes old, you know it's just going to be told professionally, with no flavour and no zest.'—*Stanley Kauffmann*

'All plot, with scarcely a character in sight.'—*Michael Billington, Illustrated London News*

The Day of the Locust**
US 1975   143m   Technicolor
Paramount / Long Road (Jerome Hellman, Sheldon
   Shrager)

In Hollywood in the 1930s, a novice art director is bewildered by the eccentricities of life and an innocent man is martyred by the crowd.
A curious and interesting work from a savagely satirical novel; full of stimulating scenes and characters, it barely succeeds as a whole and was a disaster at the box office.

w Waldo Salt, *novel* Nathanael West *d* John Schlesinger *ph* Conrad Hall *m* John Barry *pd* Richard MacDonald

Donald Sutherland, William Atherton, Karen Black, Burgess Meredith, Geraldine Page, Richard A. Dysart, Bo Hopkins, Lelia Goldoni

AAN: Conrad Hall; Burgess Meredith

The Day of the Outlaw**
US 1958   96m   bw
US / Security Pictures (Sidney Harmon)

Two rival cattlemen forget their differences to fight six outlaws who ride into town.
Bleak and wintry western, well done and sufficiently unusual to stick in the mind.

w Philip Yordan, *novel* Lee Wells *d* André de Toth *ph* Russell Harlan *m* Alexander Courage

Robert Ryan, Burl Ives, Tina Louise, Nehemiah Persoff, David Nelson, Venetia Stevenson, Jack Lambert, Lance Fuller
   'In the best William S. Hart tradition.'—*MFB*

The Day of the Triffids*
GB 1962   95m   Eastmancolor
   Cinemascope
Philip Yordan

Almost everyone in the world is blinded by meteorites prior to being taken over by intelligent plants.
Rough and ready adaptation of a famous sci-fi novel, sometimes blunderingly effective and with moments of good trick work.

w Philip Yordan, *novel* John Wyndham *d* Steve Sekely *ph* Ted Moore *m* Ron Goodwin

Howard Keel, Nicole Maurey, Kieron Moore, Janette Scott, Alexander Knox

Day of Wrath***
Denmark 1943   105m   bw
Palladium
original title: *Vredens Dag*

In a 17th-century village an old woman is burned as a witch and curses the pastor who judged her. He dies and his mother accuses her daughter-in-law, in love with another man, of using witchcraft to kill him.
Harrowing, spellbinding melodrama with a message, moving in a series of Rembrandtesque compositions from one horrifying sequence to another. Depressing, but marvellous.

w Carl Dreyer, Poul Knudsen, Mogens Skot-Hansen, *play* Anne Pedersdotter by Hans Wiers Jenssen *d* Carl Dreyer *ph* Carl Andersson *m* Poul Schierbeck *ad* Erik Ases, Lis Fribert

Thorkild Roose, Lisbeth Movin, Sigrid Neiiendam, Preben Lerdoff Rye, Anna Svierkier

The Day the Earth Caught Fire**
GB 1961   99m   bw with filters
   Dyaliscope
British Lion / Pax (Val Guest)

Nuclear tests knock the world off its axis and send it careering towards the sun.
A smart piece of science fiction told through the

eyes of Fleet Street journalists and showing a
sharp eye for the London scene. Rather
exhaustingly talkative, but genuinely frightening
at the time.

*w Wolf Mankowitz, Val Guest d Val Guest
ph Harry Waxman m Monty Norman*

Edward Judd, Janet Munro, Leo McKern,
Arthur Christiansen (ex-editor of the Daily
Express), Michael Goodliffe, Bernard Braden,
Reginald Beckwith, Austin Trevor, Renée
Asherson, Edward Underdown

The Day the Earth Stood Still**
US 1951   92m   bw
TCF (Julian Blaustein)

A flying saucer arrives in Washington and its
alien occupant, aided by a robot, demonstrates
his intellectual and physical power, warns the
world what will happen if wars continue, and
departs.
Cold-war wish-fulfilment fantasy, impressive
rather than exciting but very capably put over
with the minimum of trick work and the
maximum of sober conviction.

*w Edmund H. North d Robert Wise ph Leo
Tover m Bernard Herrmann*

Michael Rennie, Patricia Neal, Hugh Marlowe,
Sam Jaffe, Billy Gray
'Quite wry and alarmingly smooth.'—*New
Yorker, 1977*

The Day the Fish Came Out
GB / Greece 1967   109m   De Luxe
TCF / Michael Cacoyannis

Atomic material contaminates a Mediterranean
island.
Addle-pated, would-be satirical mod fantasy
with establishment figures cast as world villains.

*wd Michael Cacoyannis ph Walter Lassally
m Mikis Theodorakis*

Tom Courtenay, Colin Blakely, Sam
Wanamaker, Candice Bergen, Ian Ogilvy,
Patricia Burke

The Day They Robbed the Bank of England*
GB 1960   85m   bw
MGM / Summit (Jules Buck)

In 1901 Irish patriots plan a coup against the
British government . . .
Small-scale, well-detailed period caper story,
marred by a slow-starting script and
unsympathetic acting.

*w Howard Clewes, Richard Maibaum, novel
John Brophy d John Guillermin ph Georges
Périnal m Edwin Astley*

Peter O'Toole, Aldo Ray, Elizabeth Sellars,
Kieron Moore, Albert Sharpe, Hugh Griffith,
John Le Mesurier, Joseph Tomelty, Miles
Malleson, Colin Gordon

The Day Will Dawn*
GB 1942   98m   bw
Paul Soskin
US title: *The Avengers*

Norwegian freedom fighters destroy a U-boat
base and are saved by commandos.
Dated propaganda piece with an interesting cast.

*w Terence Rattigan, Anatole de Grunwald,
Patrick Kirwan d Harold French*

Ralph Richardson, Deborah Kerr, Hugh
Williams, Griffith Jones, Francis L. Sullivan,
Roland Culver, Niall MacGinnis, Finlay Currie,
Bernard Miles, Patricia Medina

Daybreak*
US 1931   85m approx   bw
MGM

An Austrian guardsman falls in love out of his
class.
Elegant romantic fable comparable with *Letter
From an Unknown Woman*; equally unpopular
and quite forgotten.

*w Ruth Cummings, Zelda Sears, Cyril Hume,
play Arthur Schnitzler d Jacques Feyder*

Ramon Novarro, Helen Chandler, C. Aubrey
Smith, Karen Morley, Kent Douglass, Jean
Hersholt, Glenn Tryon

Daybreak
GB 1946   81m   bw
GFD / Triton (Sydney Box)

A barber and part-time hangman marries a
destitute girl, loses her to a Swedish seaman, and
kills himself in such a way as to implicate the
other man.
Dockside melodrama of extraordinary
pretentious gloominess; laughable in most
respects. A curious follow-up from the *Seventh
Veil* team.

*w Muriel and Sydney Box, play Monckton
Hoffe d Compton Bennett*

Ann Todd, Eric Portman, Maxwell Reed,
Edward Rigby, Bill Owen, Jane Hylton, Maurice
Denham

Days of Glory
US 1944   86m   bw
RKO (Casey Robinson)

Russian peasants fight the invading Nazis.
Lower-berth wartime propaganda piece chiefly

notable for introducing Gregory Peck to the screen.

w Casey Robinson, *story* Melchior Lengyel *d* Jacques Tourneur *ph* Tony Gaudio *m* Daniele Amfitheatrof

Tamara Toumanova, Gregory Peck, Alan Reed, Maria Palmer, Lowell Gilmore, Hugo Haas

Days of Heaven**
US 1978 95m Metrocolor
Paramount/OP (Bert and Harold Schneider)

In the early 20th century, three young immigrants leave Chicago for the wheatfields. Superb period slice of life, with fine visuals and emotional pull; worthy to be compared with *The Grapes of Wrath*.

wd Terrence Malick *ph* Nestor Almendros *m* Ennio Morricone

Richard Gere, Brooke Adams, Sam Shepard, Linda Manz

Days of Thrills and Laughter***
US 1961 93m bw
(TCF) *Robert Youngson*

Appealing if rather miscellaneous silent film compilation with the accent on action and thrills as well as comedy. Like the other Youngson histories, a boon to film archivists despite a facetious commentary.

m Jack Shaindlin *narrator* Jay Jackson

Stan Laurel, Oliver Hardy, Snub Pollard, Douglas Fairbanks, Charles Chaplin, Pearl White, Houdini, Harry Langdon, Ben Turpin, Charlie Chase, Boris Karloff, Warner Oland, Fatty Arbuckle, Keystone Kops

Days of Wine and Roses**
US 1962 117m bw
Warner (Martin Manulis)

A PR man becomes an alcoholic; his wife gradually reaches the same state, but he recovers and she does not.
Smart satirical comedy confusingly gives way to melodrama, then sentimentality; quality is evident throughout, but all concerned are happiest with the first hour.

w J. P. Miller *d* Blake Edwards *ph* Philip Lathrop *m* Henry Mancini

Jack Lemmon, Lee Remick, Charles Bickford, Jack Klugman, Alan Hewitt, Debbie Megowan, Jack Albertson

AA: title song (*m* Henry Mancini, *ly* Johnny Mercer)
AAN: Jack Lemmon; Lee Remick

A Day's Pleasure*
US 1919 20m bw silent
First National

Mishaps of a family picnic.
Very mild Chaplin, reaching for but not achieving a kind of lyric quality. Amusing bits rather than scenes.

wd Charles Chaplin *ph* Rollie Totheroh

Charles Chaplin, Edna Purviance, Henry Bergman, Babe Lincoln

Dayton's Devils
US 1968 103m Eastmancolor
Madison / Harold Goldman (Robert W. Stabler)

A former USAF colonel assembles a group of misfits and adventurers to steal an army payroll. Overlong, routine caper film with a surprisingly crisp climax (when it comes).

w Fred de Gorter *d* Jack Shea *ph* Brick Marquard *m* Martin Skiles

Leslie Nielsen, Rory Calhoun, Lainie Kazan, Hans Gudegast

D-Day the Sixth of June
US 1956 106m Eastmancolor
Cinemascope
TCF (Charles Brackett)

On the way to invade France in 1944, a British colonel and an American captain reminisce about their love for the same woman.
Turgid war romance with some good action scenes and the usual hilarious Hollywood view of London. General effect very wooden.

w Ivan Moffat, Harry Brown, *novel* Lionel Shapiro *d* Henry Koster *ph* Lee Garmes *m* Lyn Murray

Robert Taylor, Richard Todd, Dana Wynter, Edmond O'Brien, John Williams, Jerry Paris, Richard Stapley

'Reminiscent of *Mrs Miniver* in style and feeling.'—*MFB*

De Sade*
US / Germany 1969 113m Movielab
AIP / CCC / Transcontinental (Louis M. Heyward, Artur Brauner)

The unbalanced Marquis de Sade is tormented by his wicked uncle with thoughts of his past. Mildly interesting attempt by AIP at European debauchery, with a good theatrical framework for the fantasies but too much flailing about by all concerned, especially in the slow motion orgy sequences, which are relentlessly boring, as is the film.

w Richard Matheson *d* Cy Endfield *ph Heinz
Pehlke ad Jurgen Kiebach m* Billy Strange

Keir Dullea, *John Huston*, Lilli Palmer, Senta
Berger, Anna Massey, Uta Levka

Dead End***
US 1937   92m   bw
Samuel Goldwyn

A slice of life in New York's east side, where
slum kids and gangsters live in a river street next
to a luxury apartment block.
Highly theatrical film of a highly theatrical play,
more or less preserving the single set and
overcoming the limitations of the script and
setting by sheer cinematic expertise. It is chiefly
remembered, however, for introducing the Dead
End Kids to a delighted world.

w Lillian Hellman, *play Sidney Kingsley
d William Wyler ph Gregg Toland ad Richard
Day m* Alfred Newman

Joel McCrea, Sylvia Sidney, *Humphrey Bogart*,
Wendy Barrie, Claire Trevor, Allen Jenkins,
Marjorie Main, James Burke, Ward Bond, *The
Dead End Kids* (Billy Halop, Leo Gorcey,
Bernard Punsley, Huntz Hall, Bobby Jordan,
Gabriel Dell)

AAN: best picture; Gregg Toland; Claire Trevor

The Dead End Kids
The films in which the original gang of young
'hooligans' (see above) appeared were as follows:

1937: DEAD END
1938: CRIME SCHOOL, ANGELS WITH
DIRTY FACES
1939: THEY MADE ME A CRIMINAL,
HELL'S KITCHEN, ANGELS WASH
THEIR FACES
1940: THE DEAD END KIDS ON DRESS
PARADE
Subsequently they broke up into the LITTLE
TOUGH GUYS, the EAST SIDE KIDS, and
the BOWERY BOYS (all qv)

Dead Heat on a Merry Go Round
US 1968   108m   Technicolor
Columbia (Carter de Haven)

An ex-con breaks parole and plans to rob Los
Angeles Airport.
Boringly arty caper comedy-melodrama,
concentrating less on the robbery than on its
hero's sexual prowess. All very superficially
flashy, and what the title means is anybody's
guess.

wd Bernard Girard *ph* Lionel Lindon *m* Stu
Phillips

James Coburn, Camilla Sparv, Aldo Ray, Nina

Wayne, Robert Webber, Rose Marie, Todd
Armstrong, Marian Moses, Severn Darden
'Just fills the space between a frisky title and a
tricky TV-comedy ending, but doesn't fill it with
any revels that require a viewer's complete
attention.'—*Time*

Dead of Night****
GB 1945   104m   bw
Ealing (Michael Balcon)

An architect is caught up in an endless series of
recurring dreams, during which he is told other
people's supernatural experiences and finally
murders the psychiatrist who is trying to help
him.
Chillingly successful and influential
compendium of the macabre, especially effective
in its low-key handling of the linking sequence
with its circular ending.

w John Baines, Angus Macphail, based on
stories by themselves, H. G. Wells, E. F. Benson
*d Cavalcanti, Charles Crichton, Robert Hamer,
Basil Dearden ph* Douglas Slocombe, Stan
Pavey *m Georges Auric ad Michael Relph*

Mervyn Johns, Roland Culver, Mary Merrall,
Judy Kelly, Anthony Baird, *Sally Ann Howes*,
Frederick Valk, Googie Withers, Ralph
Michael, Esmé Percy, Basil Radford, Naunton
Wayne, Miles Malleson, *Michael Redgrave*,
Hartley Power, Elizabeth Welch
'In a nightmare within a nightmare are
contained five separate ghost stories . . . they
have atmosphere and polish, they are eerie, they
are well acted.'—*Richard Winnington*
'One of the most successful blends of laughter,
terror and outrage that I can remember.'—
James Agee
'The five ghost stories accumulate in intensity
until the trap closes in the surrealist climax.'—
Pauline Kael, 1968

Dead or Alive
Italy / US 1967   89m   Eastmancolor
Documento / Selmur (Albert Band)

A gunman with a paralysed right arm helps a
state governor rid a town of bandits.
Semi-spaghetti western with a strong cast and
violent action scenes.

w Ugo Liberatore, Louis Garfinkle *d* Franco
Giraldi *ph* Aiace Parolin *m* Carlo Rustichelli

Robert Ryan, Arthur Kennedy, Alex Cord,
Nicoletta Machiavelli

Dead Reckoning*
US 1947   100m   bw
Columbia (Sidney Biddell)

Two war veterans are on their way to be

decorated in Washington when one disappears. Dour, complexly plotted thriller, a typical Hollywood *film noir* of the post-war years but a long way behind *Gilda* in likeability. The hero confesses the plot to a priest, and all the way it is more glum than fun.

w Oliver H. P. Garrett, Steve Fisher *d* John Cromwell *ph* Leo Tover *m* Marlin Skiles *md* Morris Stoloff

Humphrey Bogart, Lizabeth Scott, *Morris Carnovsky*, Charles Cane, William Prince, Marvin Miller, Wallace Ford, James Bell

Dead Ringer*
US 1964   116m   bw
Warner (William H. Wright)
GB title: *Dead Image*

A woman shoots her rich twin sister and assumes her identity.
High camp star vehicle, full of memories of long ago but rather drearily assembled and far too long, though Miss Davis as ever is in fighting form.

w Albert Beich, Oscar Millard *d* Paul Henreid *ph* Ernest Haller *m* André Previn

Bette Davis, Karl Malden, Peter Lawford, Philip Carey, Jean Hagen, Estelle Winwood, George Chandler, Cyril Delevanti

Deadfall
GB 1968   120m   De Luxe
TCF / Salamanda (Paul Monash, Jack Rix)

Robbery turns sour when a cat burglar falls in love with the wife of his homosexual partner. Drearily fashionable romantic melodrama with far too few high spots and generally dull performances.

w Bryan Forbes, *novel* Desmond Cory *d* Bryan Forbes *ph* Gerry Turpin *m* John Barry

Michael Caine, Eric Portman, Giovanna Ralli, Nanette Newman, David Buck
'Exhausted no doubt by their past passions and childhood traumas, the principal protagonists move like so many somnambulists through the turgid labyrinth . . . whatever the intention, *Deadfall* merely falls flat on its somewhat ludicrous face.'—*MFB*

Deadlier Than the Male
GB 1967   101m   Techniscope
Rank / Sydney Box (Betty E. Box)

Bulldog Drummond traces the death of oil company executives to a master criminal using glamorous female assassins.
Just about tolerable recreation of Drummond in the modern world, with too little style, too much

violence and sex, and an almost total lack of self-mockery. A sequel *Some Girls Do* (qv), was an unmitigated disaster.

w Jimmy Sangster, David Osborn, Liz Charles-Williams *d* Ralph Thomas *ph* Ernest Steward *m* Malcolm Lockyer *ad* Alex Vetchinsky

Richard Johnson, Nigel Green, Elke Sommer, Sylva Koscina, Suzanna Leigh, Zia Mohyeddin, Steve Carlson
'The original Drummond would have found the whole thing rather distasteful.'—*MFB*

Deadline at Dawn
US 1946   82m   bw
RKO

A sailor on leave passes out, finds the girl he was with has been murdered, and is helped by a philosophical taxi driver and a girl.
This could have been another *Crossfire*, but is smothered by pretentious writing and uncertain direction. The credits are interesting, though.

w Clifford Odets *d* Harold Clurman *ph* Nicholas Musuraca

Paul Lukas, Bill Williams, Susan Hayward, Osa Massen, Lola Lane

Deadline USA*
US 1952   87m   bw
TCF (Sol C. Siegel)
GB title: *Deadline*

Despite threats and the killing of a witness, a crusading newspaper editor goes ahead with a story about the crimes of a powerful gangster. Watchable newspaper melodrama with nothing much to say except that America must wake up to the enemy within. Smooth production, but too much semi-pretentious talk.

wd Richard Brooks *ph* Milton Krasner *m* Cyril Mockridge

Humphrey Bogart, Kim Hunter, Ethel Barrymore, Ed Begley, Paul Stewart, Warren Stevens, Martin Gabel, Joe de Santis, Audrey Christie, Jim Backus

The Deadly Affair**
GB 1966   106m   Technicolor
Columbia / Sidney Lumet

A Foreign Office man apparently commits suicide; his colleague is unconvinced and finally uncovers a spy ring.
Compulsive if heavy-going thriller from the sour-about-spies era, deliberately glum, photographed against the shabbiest possible London backgrounds in muddy colour. Solidly entertaining for sophisticated grown-ups.

w Paul Dehn, novel Call for the Dead by John Le Carré *d Sidney Lumet ph* Frederick A. Young *m* Quincy Jones

James Mason, Simone Signoret, Harry Andrews, Maximilian Schell, Harriet Andersson, Kenneth Haigh, *Max Adrian*, Robert Flemyng, Roy Kinnear, Lynn Redgrave

The Deadly Companions*
US 1961 90m Pathecolor Panavision
Warner / Pathe America (Charles B. Fitzsimmons)

An army sergeant, a deserter, a trigger-happy gunman and a saloon hostess join forces to rob a bank.
Disjointed but rather attractive little western let down by corny moments in the script.

w A. S. Fleishman *d Sam Peckinpah ph* William H. Clothier

Brian Keith, Maureen O'Hara, Chill Wills, Steve Cochran

Deadly Strangers
GB 1974 93m Eastmancolor
Rank / Silhouette (Peter Miller)

A girl accepts a lift from a motorist at a time when a mad strangler is on the loose.
Sub-Hitchcock melo-thriller with enough red herrings to sink a ship. Smartly enough done, but the grisliness needed balancing by humour.

w Philip Levene *d* Sidney Hayers *ph* Graham Edgar *m* Ron Goodwin

Hayley Mills, Simon Ward, Sterling Hayden, Ken Hutchison, Peter Jeffrey

The Deadly Trackers
US 1973 104m Technicolor
Warner / Cine Film (Ed Rosen, Fouad Said)
A sheriff stalks the bandits who killed his wife and son.
Lurid and ludicrous western started, and abandoned, by Samuel Fuller; the challenge need not have been taken up.

w Lukas Heller *d* Barry Shear *ph* Gabriel Torres *m* various

Rod Taylor, Richard Harris, Al Lettieri, Neville Brand, William Smith

'It is no more than the outline of a shadow.'— *Tony Rayns*

'An incoherent, blood-soaked chase story.'— *New Yorker, 1977*

Dear Brigitte
US 1965 100m De Luxe Cinemascope
TCF / Fred Kohlmar

The small son of an American professor writes a love letter to Brigitte Bardot, and when they finally go to Paris she is charming to them.
Mild family comedy quaintly set around a decaying Mississippi riverboat home; despite assured performances, it all gets a bit icky at times.

w Hal Kanter, *novel* Erasmus with Freckles by John Haase *d* Henry Koster *ph* Lucien Ballard *m* George Duning

James Stewart, Glynis Johns, Fabian, Cindy Carol, Billy Mumy, John Williams, Jack Kruschen, Brigitte Bardot, Ed Wynn, Alice Pearce

Dear Heart*
US 1964 114m bw
Warner (Martin Manulis)

At a postmasters' convention in New York, two middle-aged delegates fall in love.
Charming, understated, overlong romantic drama in the *Marty* tradition; all quite professional and satisfying.

w Tad Mosel d Delbert Mann *ph* Russell Harlan *m* Henry Mancini

Glenn Ford, Geraldine Page, Angela Lansbury, Michael Anderson Jnr, Barbara Nichols, Patricia Barry, Charles Drake, Ruth McDevitt, Neva Patterson, Alice Pearce, Richard Deacon
AAN: title song (*m* Henry Mancini, *ly* Jay Livingston, Ray Evans)

Dear John*
Sweden 1964 111m bw
Sandrew (Bo Jonsson)
original title: *Käre John*

An unmarried mother in a seaside village falls for a seaman.
A slight story effectively tricked out with all manner of cinematic devices including a multitude of flashbacks. Very watchable if a little self-conscious.

wd Lars Magnus Lindgren, novel Olle Lansburg *ph* Rune Ericson *m* Bengt-Arne Wallin

Jarl Kulle, Christina Schollin, Helena Nilsson, Morgan Anderson
'It shines with the cool clear light of the Swedish summer, and despite its glossy surface manages also to convey strong sensual pleasure.'—*Brenda Davies*

Dear Mr Prohack
GB 1949 91m bw
GFD / Wessex (Ian Dalrymple, Dennis Van Thal)

A treasury official copes admirably with public

money but is helpless when he comes into a private fortune.
Flat little comedy in which the minor amusements are incidental to the story.

w Ian Dalrymple, Donald Bull, *novel* Arnold Bennett *d* Thornton Freeland *ph* H. E. Fowle *m* Temple Abady

Cecil Parker, Hermione Baddeley, Dirk Bogarde, Sheila Sim, Glynis Johns, Heather Thatcher, Henry Edwards, Judith Furse

Dear Murderer

GB 1947   94m   bw
GFD / Gainsborough (Betty E. Box)

Plot and counterplot among an adulterous triangle.
Thoroughly artificial pattern play set among the unreal rich, from one of those unaccountable West End successes, here boringly filmed.

w Muriel and Sydney Box, Peter Rogers, *play* St John L. Clowes *d* Arthur Crabtree *ph* Stephen Dade

Eric Portman, Greta Gynt, Dennis Price, Maxwell Reed, Jack Warner, Hazel Court, Andrew Crawford, Jane Hylton

Dear Octopus**

GB 1943   86m   bw
GFD / Gainsborough (Edward Black)
US title: *The Randolph Family*

Members of a well-to-do British family reunite for Golden Wedding celebrations.
Traditional upper-class British comedy drama, and very well done too, with opportunities for excellent character acting.

w R. J. Minney, Patrick Kirwan, *play* Dodie Smith *d* Harold French

Margaret Lockwood, Michael Wilding, *Helen Haye, Frederick Leister, Celia Johnson, Roland Culver, Athene Seyler,* Basil Radford, Nora Swinburne, Jean Cadell, Kathleen Harrison, Ann Stephens, Muriel George, Antoinette Cellier, Graham Moffatt

Dear Ruth*

US 1947   95m   bw
Paramount (Paul Jones)

A schoolgirl causes confusion when she writes love letters to a soldier using her elder sister's photograph.
Smoothly amusing family comedy from a Broadway success.

w Arthur Sheekman, *play* Norman Krasna *d* William D. Russell *ph* Ernest Laszlo *m* Robert Emmett Dolan

Joan Caulfield, William Holden, Mona

Freeman, Billy de Wolfe, Edward Arnold, Mary Philips, Virginia Welles
† Two less amusing sequels were made using virtually the same cast: *Dear Wife* (1949, 88m, *d* Richard Haydn); *Dear Brat* (1951, 82m, *d* William A. Seiter).

Death at Broadcasting House*

GB 1934   71m   bw
ABFD / Phoenix (Hugh Perceval)

A radio actor is murdered during a broadcast. Intriguing little murder mystery with an unusual background.

w Basil Mason, *novel* Val Gielgud *d* Reginald Denham

Ian Hunter, Austin Trevor, Mary Newland, Henry Kendall, Val Gielgud, Peter Haddon, Betty Ann Davies, Jack Hawkins, Donald Wolfit

Death in Venice**

Italy 1971   128m   Technicolor Panavision
Warner / Alfa (Mario Gallo)
original title: *Morte a Venezia*

In a lush Venetian hotel one summer in the early years of the century, a middle-aged German composer on holiday falls for the charms of a silent young boy, and stays in the city too long to escape the approaching plague.
Incredibly extended and rather pointless fable enriched by moments of great beauty and directorial style; these do not quite atone for the slow pace or the muddled storyline.

w Luchino Visconti, Nicola Bandalucco, *novel* Thomas Mann *d* Luchino Visconti *ph* Pasquale de Santis *m* Gustav Mahler *md* Franco Mannino *ad* Ferdinando Scarfiotti

Dirk Bogarde, Bjorn Andresen, Silvana Mangano, Marisa Berenson, Mark Burns
'Maybe a story as elusive as *Death in Venice* simply can't be filmed. Visconti has made a brave attempt, always sensitive to the original; but it's finally not quite the same thing.'—*David Wilson, MFB*

Death of a Cyclist*

Spain / Italy 1955   85m   bw
Guion-Suevia / Trionfalcine
original title: *Muerte de un Ciclista*

An accident – a cyclist is knocked down and killed by an adulterous couple – tragically affects the lives of many people.
Rather like a politically conscious version of *An Inspector Calls*, this mannered and unemotional film was most interesting because of its almost Hollywoodian self-assurance.

wd Juan Antonio Bardem story Luis de Igoa
ph Alfredo Fraile *m* Isrido Maiztegui

Lucia Bose, Alberto Closas, Otello Toso, Carlos
Casaravilla

Death of a Gunfighter*
US 1969   100m   Technicolor
Universal (Richard E. Lyons)

An unpopular marshal refuses to resign, and the
situation leads to gunplay.
Downcast character western set in the early
years of the century.

w Joseph Calvelli *d* Robert Totten, Don Siegel
ph Andrew Jackson *m* Oliver Nelson

Richard Widmark, Lena Horne, John Saxon,
Carroll O'Connor, Larry Gates, Kent Smith

Death of a Salesman***
US 1952   112m   bw
Columbia (Stanley Kramer)

An ageing travelling salesman recognizes the
emptiness of his life and commits suicide.
A very acceptable screen version of a milestone
play which has become an American classic;
stage conventions and tricks are cleverly
adapted to cinematic use, especially when the
hero walks from the present into the past and
back again.

w Stanley Roberts, *play Arthur Miller d* Laslo
Benedek *ph* Franz Planer *m* Alex North
md Morris Stoloff

Fredric March, Kevin McCarthy, Cameron
Mitchell, Mildred Dunnock, Howard Smith,
Royal Beal, Jesse White

'Its time shifts with light, which were poetic in
the theatre, seemed shabby in a medium that can
dissolve time and space so easily.'—*Stanley
Kauffmann*

AAN: Franz Planer; Alex North; Fredric
March; Kevin McCarthy; Mildred Dunnock

Death of a Scoundrel*
US 1956   119m   bw
RKO / Charles Martin

A Czech in New York becomes rich by fraud.
Unconvincing but intermittently entertaining
melodrama, a vehicle for a male Bette Davis.

wd Charles Martin *ph* James Wong Howe
m Max Steiner

George Sanders, Yvonne de Carlo, Coleen Gray,
Victor Jory, Zsa Zsa Gabor, Nancy Gates, John
Hoyt, Tom Conway

'Vague moralizing and some attempts at social
comment scarcely enliven this protracted study
in megalomania.'—*MFB*

Death on the Nile*
GB 1978   140m   Technicolor
EMI (John Brabourne, Richard Goodwin)

Hercule Poirot solves the mystery of who killed
the spoilt heiress on a steamer cruising down the
Nile.
A pleasant thirties atmosphere and the travel
poster backgrounds are the chief assets of this
rather hesitant who-dunnit which plays fair
enough with the audience but gives its popular
cast too little to do, while its constant repetitions
of the crime become rather ghoulish. On the
whole, though, a very passable representation of
an old-fashioned genre, and a few points up on
Murder on the Orient Express.

w Anthony Shaffer, *novel* Agatha Christie
d John Guillermin *ph* Jack Cardiff *pd* Peter
Murton *m* Nino Rota

Peter Ustinov, Bette Davis, Mia Farrow, Angela
Lansbury, Jane Birkin, David Niven, George
Kennedy, Jack Warden, Simon MacCorkindale,
Lois Chiles, Jon Finch, Maggie Smith, Olivia
Hussey, Harry Andrews, *I. S. Johar*

Death Race 2000*
US 1975   79m   colour
New World (Roger Corman)

In the year 2000, the world's most popular sport
involves motor racers who compete for the
highest total of human casualties.
Cheaply made macabre satire, quite well enough
made to please addicts of the blackest of black
comedy.

w Robert Thom, Charles Griffith, Ib Melchior
d Paul Bartel *ph* Tak Fujimoto *m* Paul Chihara

David Carradine, Simone Griffeth, Sylvester
Stallone, Mary Woronov

'The script is hardly Swiftian and therefore
treads a thin delicate line between mockery and
exploitation.'—*Michael Billington, Illustrated
London News*

Death Takes a Holiday**
US 1934   78m   bw
Paramount (E. Lloyd Sheldon)

In the form of a mysterious prince, Death visits
an Italian noble family to see why men fear him
so.
A somewhat pretentious classic from a popular
play of the twenties; interesting handling and
performances, but a slow pace by modern
standards.

w Maxwell Anderson, Gladys Lehman, Walter
Ferris based on plays by Maxwell Anderson and
Alberto Casella *d* Mitchell Leisen *ph* Charles
Lang *ad* Ernst Fegte

Fredric March, Evelyn Venable, Sir Guy

Standing, Katherine Alexander, Gail Patrick,
Helen Westley, Kathleen Howard, Henry
Travers, Kent Taylor

Death Wish*
US 1974   94m   Technicolor
Paramount / Dino de Laurentiis (Hal Landers,
Bobby Roberts, Michael Winner)

When his wife dies and his daughter becomes a
vegetable after an assault by muggers, a New
York businessman takes the law into his own
hands.

After a highly unpleasant and sensational
opening, this curious and controversial film
settles down into what amounts to black
comedy, with the audience well on the vigilante's
side. It's not very good, but it keeps one
watching.

w Wendell Mayes, *novel* Brian Garfield
d Michael Winner *ph* Arthur J. Ornitz
m Herbie Hancock

Charles Bronson, Hope Lange, Vincent
Gardenia, Stuart Margolin, Stephen Keats,
William Redfield

Deathsport
US 1978   83m   Metrocolor
New World (Roger Corman)

A popular game of the future involves gladiators
willing to lose their lives against lethal
motorcyclists.

Low-budget shocker for teenagers, by *Rollerball*
out of *Death Race*. Of no possible interest except
as exploitation.

W Henry Suso, Donald Stewart *d* Henry Suso,
Allan Arkush *ph* GaRY Graver *m* Andrew
Stein

David Carradine, Claudia Jennings, Richard
Lynch, William Smithers

Decameron Nights
GB 1952   94m   Technicolor
Film Locations (M. J. Frankovich)

Young Boccaccio entertains a glamorous widow
and her three guests with stories.
Feeble costume charade with all the cuckolding
off-screen: insipid and artificial.

w George Oppenheimer *d* Hugo Fregonese
ph Guy Green *m* Antony Hopkins

Louis Jourdan, Joan Fontaine, Binnie Barnes,
Joan Collins, Godfrey Tearle, Eliot Makeham,
Noel Purcell
   'The sort of hybrid international production of
which experience has made one mistrustful.'—
Gavin Lambert

Deception**
US 1946   112m   bw
Warner (Henry Blanke)

A European cellist returning to America after the
war finds that his former girl friend has a rich and
jealous lover.

Downcast melodrama made when its star was
beginning to slide; today it seems irresistible
bosh with a background of classical music, done
with intermittent style especially by Claude
Rains as the egomaniac lover.

w John Collier, *play* Monsieur Lamberthier by
Louis Verneuil *d* Irving Rapper *ph* Ernest
Haller *m* Erich Wolfgang Korngold

Bette Davis, *Claude Rains*, Paul Henreid, John
Abbott, Benson Fong
   'It's like grand opera, only the people are
thinner . . . I wouldn't have missed it for the
world.'—*Cecelia Ager*
   'Exquisitely foolish: a camp classic.'—*New
Yorker, 1977*
† Previously filmed in 1929 as *Jealousy*, with
Fredric March and Jeanne Eagels.

Decision before Dawn*
US 1951   119m   bw
TCF (Anatole Litvak, Frank McCarthy)

In 1944, anti-Nazi German POWs are
parachuted into Germany to obtain information.
Meticulous, well made but unexciting spy story
which seldom comes vividly to life.

w Peter Viertel, *novel* Call It Treason by George
Howe *d* Anatole Litvak *ph* Franz Planer
m Franz Waxman

Oskar Werner, Richard Basehart, Gary Merrill,
Hildegarde Neff, Dominique Blanchar, Helene
Thimig, O. E. Hasse, Hans Christian Blech

AAN: best picture

The Decision of Christopher Blake
US 1948   75m   bw
Warner (Ranald MacDougall)

A 12-year-old boy reunites his divorcing parents.
Sentimental slop, surprisingly ill done, but with a
few good lines.

w Ranald MacDougall, *play* Moss Hart *d* Peter
Godfrey *ph* Karl Freund *m* Max Steiner

Alexis Smith, Robert Douglas, *Cecil Kellaway*,
Ted Donaldson, *Harry Davenport*, John Hoyt,
Mary Wickes, Art Baker, Lois Maxwell

The Decks Ran Red
US 1958   84m   bw
MGM / Andrew and Virginia Stone

Unscrupulous sailors plan to murder the entire
crew of a freighter and claim the salvage money.

Solidly crafted but basically uninteresting melodrama.

w Andrew and Virginia Stone *d* Andrew Stone *ph* Meredith M. Nicholson

James Mason, Broderick Crawford, Dorothy Dandridge, Stuart Whitman

Decline and Fall
GB 1968   113m   De Luxe
TCF / Ivan Foxwell

An innocent, accident-prone Oxford undergraduate is expelled and after various adventures in high and low society is convicted as a white slaver.
Flabby, doomed attempt to film a satirical classic which lives only on the printed page. Odd moments amuse.

w Ivan Foxwell, *novel* Evelyn Waugh *d* John Krish *ph* Desmond Dickinson *m* Ron Goodwin

Robin Phillips, Donald Wolfit, Genevieve Page, Robert Harris, Leo McKern, Colin Blakely, Felix Aylmer, Donald Sinden, Griffith Jones

Dédée d'Anvers*
France 1948   95m   bw
Sacha Gordine (André Paulvé)
aka: *Woman of Antwerp; Dédée*

A dockside prostitute falls for a sailor and arouses the jealousy of her protector.
Seamy low life melodrama, presented *con brio*, but rather like a tenth copy of *Quai des Brumes*.

w Yves Allégret, Jacques Sigurd *d* Yves Allégret *ph* Jean Bourgoin *m* Jacques Besse

Simone Signoret, Marcel Pagliero, Bernard Blier, Marcel Dalio, Jane Marken

The Deep
US 1977   124m   Metrocolor   Panavision
Columbia / EMI (Peter Guber)

Underwater treasure seekers off Bermuda clash with black villains seeking a lost consignment of morphine.
An expensive action picture which is singularly lacking in action and even in plot, but oozes with brutality and overdoes the splendours of submarine life, forty per cent of it taking place under water.

w Peter Benchley, Tracy Keenan Wynn, *novel* Peter Benchley *d* Peter Yates *ph* Christopher Challis, Al Giddings, Stan Waterman *m* John Barry *pd* Tony Masters

Jacqueline Bisset, Robert Shaw, Nick Nolte, Lou Gossett, Eli Wallach

'The ultimate disco experience . . . it dances on the spot for two hours, taking voodoo, buried treasure, morphine, violence and sea monsters in its stride.'—*Time Out*

'Peter Yates has knocked himself out doing masterly underwater action sequences in the service of a woefully crummy book.'—*Russell Davies, Observer*

The Deep Blue Sea*
GB 1955   99m   Eastmancolor
   Cinemascope
TCF / London Films (Anatole Litvak)

A judge's wife attempts suicide when jilted by her ex-RAF lover.
Undistinguished adaptation of a very good play, hampered by wide screen and muddy colour, helped by thoughtful performances.

w Terence Rattigan, from his play *d* Anatole Litvak *ph* Jack Hildyard *m* Malcolm Arnold

Vivien Leigh, Kenneth More, Eric Portman, *Emlyn Williams*, Moira Lister, Arthur Hill, Dandy Nichols, Jimmy Hanley, Miriam Karlin

Deep End*
West Germany / USA 1970   88m
   Eastmancolor
Maran / Kettledrum / Bavaria Atelier (Judd Bernard)

Sexual problems of two young people on the staff of a London municipal bathhouse.
Interestingly made but rather dreary and vaguely symbolic modern fable.

w Jerzy Skolimowski, Jerzy Gruza, Boleslaw Sulik *d* Jerzy Skolimowski *ph* Charly Steinberger *m* Cat Stevens

Jane Asher, John Moulder-Brown, Diana Dors, Karl Michael Vogler, Christopher Sandford

'A study in the growth of obsession that is both funny and frighteningly exact.'—*Nigel Andrews, MFB*

Deep in My Heart*
US 1954   132m   Eastmancolor
MGM (Roger Edens)

Sigmund Romberg, a composer-waiter in New York, is helped by writer Dorothy Donnelly and showman Florenz Ziegfeld to become a famous writer of musicals.
Standard fictionalized biopic with plenty of good turns and a sharper script than usual.

w Leonard Spiegelgass *d* Stanley Donen *ph* George Folsey *m* Sigmund Romberg *ad* Cedric Gibbons, Edward Carfagno *ch* Eugene Loring

Jose Ferrer, Merle Oberon, Paul Henreid (as Ziegfeld), Walter Pidgeon, Helen Traubel, Doe Avedon, Tamara Toumanova, Paul Stewart, Isobel Elsom, David Burns, Jim Backus . . . and

Gene Kelly, Fred Kelly, Rosemary Clooney,
Jane Powell, Ann Miller, Cyd Charisse, James
Mitchell, Howard Keel, Tony Martin, Joan
Weldon

The Deep Six
US 1958   110m   Warnercolor
Jaguar (Martin Rackin)

A Quaker is unhappy at being drafted into the
submarine service, but after initial unpopularity
becomes a hero.

An ageing star contends with many hazards:
slipshod production, poor colour, a dull script,
and an unplayable part.

w John Twist, Martin Rackin, Harry Brown
d Rudolph Maté ph John Seitz m David
Buttolph

Alan Ladd, William Bendix, Efrem Zimbalist
Jnr, Dianne Foster, Keenan Wynn, James
Whitmore, Joey Bishop, Jeanette Nolan

Deep Valley
US 1947   104m   bw
Warner (Henry Blanke)

The daughter of a poor California farmer falls
for a convict on a work gang.

Downright peculiar melodrama, a cross between
Tobacco Road and *Cold Comfort Farm*, with
touches of *High Sierra*. For collectors.

w Salka Viertel, Stephen Morehouse Avery,
novel Dan Totheroh d Jean Negulesco ph Ted
McCord m Max Steiner

Ida Lupino, Dane Clark, Wayne Morris, Henry
Hull, Fay Bainter, Willard Robertson

Deep Waters
US 1948   85m   bw
TCF

A problem orphan boy is content when adopted
by a lobster fisherman.

Forgettable family film, smoothly directed and
photographed.

w Richard Murphy d Henry King ph Joseph La
Shelle m Cyril Mockridge

Jean Peters, Dana Andrews, Dean Stockwell,
Cesar Romero, Anne Revere

The Deer Hunter*
US 1978   182m   Technicolor
Universal / EMI (Barry Spikings, Michael
   Deeley, Michael Cimino, John Pevera)

Three friends from a small Pennsylvania town go
to fight in Vietnam.

The three-hour running time is taken up with
crosscutting of a wedding, a deer hunt and a game
of Russian roulette. Presumably the audience

has to guess the point, if any; meanwhile it may
be repelled by this lonag and savage if frequently
engrossing film.

w Deric Washburn, story Michael Cimino,
Louis Garfinkle, Quinn K. Redeker and
Washburn d Michael Cimino ph Vilmos
Zsigmond m Stanley Myers

Robert De Niro, John Cazale, John Savage,
Christopher Walken, Meryl Streep

The Defector
France / West Germany 1966   101m
   Eastmancolor
PECF / Rhein Main (Raoul Lévy)
original title: L'Espion

An American physicist in East Germany gets
involved in the spy game.

Disenchanted espionage 'realism', not very well
styled and hampered by a star at the end of his
tether.

w Robert Guenette, Raoul Lévy, novel The Spy
by Paul Thomas d Raoul Lévy ph Raoul
Coutard m Serge Gainsbourg

Montgomery Clift, Hardy Kruger, Macha Meril,
Roddy McDowall, David Opatoshu, Christine
Delaroche, Jean-Luc Godard

The Defiant Ones**
US 1958   96m   bw
US / Stanley Kramer

A black and a white convict escape from a chain
gang, still linked together but hating each other.

Schematic melodrama with a moral, impeccably
done and with good performances.

w Nathan E. Douglas, Harold Jacob Smith
d Stanley Kramer ph Sam Leavitt m Ernest
Gold

Tony Curtis, Sidney Poitier, Theodore Bikel,
Charles McGraw, Lon Chaney Jnr, King
Donovan, Claude Akins, Lawrence Dobkin,
Whit Bissell, Carl 'Alfalfa' Switzer, Cara
Williams

   'Probably Kramer's best picture. The subject
matter is relatively simple, though "powerful";
the action is exciting; the acting is good. But the
singleness of purpose behind it all is a little
offensive.'—Pauline Kael

AA: Nathan E. Douglas, Harold Jacob Smith;
Sam Leavitt

AAN: best picture; Stanley Kramer; Tony
Curtis; Sidney Poitier; Theodore Bikel; Cara
Williams

Le Defroqué*
France 1953   111m   bw
SFC / SNEG

A defrocked priest performs a gallant action which persuades an acquaintance to become a priest himself and try to draw his friend back into the fold.

Curious but holding moral melodrama embellished by good acting.

w Leo Joannon, Denys de la Patellière *d Leo Joannon ph* Nicolas Toporkoff *m* Jean-Jacques Grunenwald

Pierre Fresnay, Pierre Trabaud, Nicole Stéphane, Marcelle Geniat, Guy Decomble, Leo Joannon, René Blancard

A Delicate Balance*
US 1975 134m colour
American Express / Ely Landau / Cinevision

A quarrelsome Connecticut family is dominated by an ageing matriarch, and tensions mount to a climax of fear and threats.

Honourable but slightly boring film version of an essentially theatrical play: the acting is the thing.

w Edward Albee, from his play *d* Tony Richardson *ph* David Watkin *m* none

Katharine Hepburn, Paul Scofield, Joseph Cotten, Lee Remick, Kate Reid, Betsy Blair

The Delicate Delinquent
US 1956 101m bw Vistavision
Paramount / Jerry Lewis

A New York policeman tries to make friends with an eccentric youth who mixes with thugs; the boy decides to train as a policeman.

Jerry Lewis' first film without Dean Martin: a sobering experience combining zany comedy, sentiment, pathos and social comment. The mixture fails to rise.

wd Don McGuire *ph* Haskell Boggs *m* Buddy Bregman

Jerry Lewis, Darren McGavin, Martha Hyer, Robert Ivers, Horace McMahon

Delicious
US 1931 106m bw
Fox

An Irish girl in New York falls for a rich man. Early musical, very thin, but an agreeable museum piece for collectors.

w Guy Bolton, Sonya Levien *d* David Butler *ph* Ernest Palmer *songs* George and Ira Gershwin

Janet Gaynor, Charles Farrell, El Brendel, Lawrence O'Sullivan, Virginia Cherrill, Mischa Auer

Deliverance**
US 1972 109m Technicolor Panavision
Warner / Elmer Enterprises (John Boorman)

Four men spend a holiday weekend canoeing down a dangerous river, but find that the real danger to their lives comes from themselves and other humans.

Vigorous, meaningful, almost apocalyptic vision of man's inhumanity, disguised as a thrilling adult adventure.

w James Dickey, from his novel *d* John Boorman *ph* Vilmos Zsigmond *m* Eric Weissberg

Burt Reynolds, Jon Voight, Ned Beatty, Ronny Cox, James Dickey

'There is fundamentally no view of the material, just a lot of painful grasping and groping.'—*Stanley Kauffmann*

AAN: best picture; John Boorman

Dementia 13*
US / Eire 1963 81m bw
Filmgroup / AIP (Roger Corman)
GB title: *The Haunted and the Hunted*

An axe murderer attacks members of a noble Irish family at their lonely castle.

Nastily effective macabre piece with interesting credits.

wd Francis Ford Coppola *ph* Charles Hannawalt *m* Ronald Stein

Luana Anders, William Campbell, Bart Patton, Mary Mitchell, Patrick Magee, Eithne Dunn

Demetrius and the Gladiators**
US 1954 101m Technicolor
Cinemascope
TCF (Frank Ross)

A Greek slave who keeps Christ's robe after the crucifixion is sentenced to be one of Caligula's gladiators and becomes involved in Messalina's wiles.

Lively, efficient sequel to *The Robe*, with emphasis less on religiosity than on the brutality of the arena and our hero's sexual temptations and near-escapes. Good Hollywood hokum.

w Philip Dunne *d* Delmer Daves *ph* Milton Krasner *m* Franz Waxman

Victor Mature, Susan Hayward, Michael Rennie (as Peter), Debra Paget, Anne Bancroft, Jay Robinson, Barry Jones, William Marshall, Richard Egan, Ernest Borgnine

The Demi-Paradise*
GB 1943 114m bw
Two Cities (Anatole de Grunwald)
US title: *Adventure for Two*

In 1939, a Russian inventor is sent to observe the British way of life.

Pleasant, aimless little satirical comedy in which this blessed plot seems to be peopled entirely by eccentrics.

w Anatole de Grunwald *d* Anthony Asquith

Laurence Olivier, Penelope Dudley Ward, *Margaret Rutherford*, Leslie Henson, Marjorie Fielding, Felix Aylmer, Guy Middleton, Michael Shepley, George Thorpe, Edie Martin, Muriel Aked, Joyce Grenfell

'A backhanded way of showing us poor juvenile-minded cinemagoers that the England of Mr Punch and Mrs Malaprop lives forever.'—*Richard Winnington*

Demon Seed
US 1977　95m　Metrocolor　Panavision
MGM (Herb Jaffe)

A scientist invents too perfect a computer: it locks up his wife, rapes her, and incubates a child . . .

Science fiction at the end of its tether, all very smart and self-conscious, but at this length very tasteless. Hitchcock would have got it into a television half-hour.

w Robert Jaffe, Roger O. Hirson, *novel* Dean R. Koontz *d* Donald Cammell *ph* Bill Butler *m* Jerry Fielding *pd* Edward Carfagno

Julie Christie, Fritz Weaver, Gerrit Graham, Berry Kroeger, Lisa Lu

Derby Day
GB 1952　84m　bw
British Lion / Wilcox-Neagle (Maurice Cowan)
US title: *Four Against Fate*

Intercut comic and melodramatic stories of four people who go to the Derby.

Quietly efficient, class-conscious entertainment on the lines of *Friday the 13th* and *The Bridge of San Luis Rey*. No surprises, but plenty of familiar faces.

w John Baines, Monckton Hoffe, Alan Melville *d* Herbert Wilcox *ph* Max Greene *m* Anthony Collins

Anna Neagle, Michael Wilding, Googie Withers, Gordon Harker, John McCallum, Peter Graves, Suzanne Cloutier, Gladys Henson, Ralph Reader, Alfie Bass, Edwin Styles, Nigel Stock

'Excessive loyalty to a formula has produced far from happy results.'—*Penelope Houston, MFB*

Le Dernier Milliardaire*
France 1934　90m　bw
Pathé-Natan

The queen of a small principality invites a financial wizard to pay court to her daughter. The girl elopes with a bandleader, the financier is engaged to the queen, and is then revealed as a sham.

Rather too determined to be satirical, this comedy sadly lacks the pace and flair of the director's best work but there are several sequences of interest.

wd René Clair *ph* Rudolph Maté, Louis Née *m* Maurice Jaubert

Max Dearly, Renée Saint-Cyr, Marthe Mellot, Raymond Cordy

Les Dernières Vacances*
France 1947　95m　bw
Pathé

During a country house holiday in the twenties, the last before the house is sold, old friends conduct amorous intrigues and so do their teenage progeny.

A moderately charming little fable making a rather obscure social point.

w R. Breuil, Roger Leenhardt *d* Roger Leenhardt *ph* Philippe Agostini

Berthe Bovy, Renée Devillers, Pierre Dux, Jean d'Yd, Odile Versois, Michel François

The Desert Fox**
US 1951　88m　bw
TCF (Nunnally Johnson)
GB title: *Rommel, Desert Fox*

Rommel returns, disillusioned, to Hitler's Germany after his North African defeat, and is involved in the July plot.

Vivid but scrappy account of the last years of a contemporary hero. At the time it seemed to show a new immediacy in film-making, and was probably the first film to use an action sequence to arrest attention before the credit titles.

w Nunnally Johnson, *book* Rommel by Desmond Young *d* Henry Hathaway *ph* Norbert Brodine

James Mason, Jessica Tandy, Cedric Hardwicke, Luther Adler (as Hitler), Everett Sloane, *Leo G. Carroll, George Macready*, Richard Boone, Eduard Franz, Desmond Young

Desert Fury
US 1947　96m　Technicolor
Paramount (Hal B. Wallis)

Against advice, a girl is attracted to a neurotic gambler who may have murdered his first wife. Muddled melodrama slightly helped by Arizona colour settings; unconvincing characters mouth unspeakable lines in an airless tedium.

w Robert Rossen *d* Lewis Allen *ph* Charles Lang, Edward Cronjager *m* Miklos Rozsa

Lizabeth Scott, Wendell Corey, Burt Lancaster, John Hodiak, Mary Astor, Kristine Miller

'The only fury I could sense was in my corner of the balcony.'—*C. A. Lejeune*

Desert Legion

US 1953 86m Technicolor
Universal (Ted Richmond)

A Foreign Legion captain rids a lost city of menacing bandits.
Schoolboy stuff, impudent in its silly story and its unconvincing Shangri-La, but quite entertaining for those prepared to let their hair down.

w Irving Wallace, Lewis Meltzer *d* Joseph Pevney *ph* John Seitz *m* Frank Skinner

Alan Ladd, Richard Conte, Arlene Dahl, Akim Tamiroff, Leon Askin

The Desert Rats *

US 1953 88m bw
TCF (Robert L. Jacks)

An English captain commands an Australian detachment in the siege of Tobruk, and survives an encounter with Rommel.
Actioner made to cash in on the success of *The Desert Fox* (qv). Stars and battle scenes survive a studio look.

w Richard Murphy *d* Robert Wise *ph* Lucien Ballard *m* Leigh Harline *md* Nathaniel Finston

James Mason (as Rommel), Richard Burton, Robert Newton, Robert Douglas, Torin Thatcher, Chips Rafferty

The Desert Song

US 1929 106m bw
Warner

A romantic and mysterious figure leads North African natives against evil Arabs.
Primitive sound version of the highly successful 1926 operetta.

w Harvey Gates, *play* Otto Harbach, Lawrence Schwab, Frank Mandel *d* Roy del Ruth *ph* Barney McGill *m* Sigmund Romberg *ly* Oscar Hammerstein II

John Boles, Carlotta King, Louise Fazenda, Johnny Arthur, Edward Martindel, Jack Pratt

The Desert Song

US 1943 96m Technicolor
Warner (Robert Florey)

Updated version with Nazis as the real villains.

adaptation Robert Buckner *d* Robert Florey *ph* Bert Glennon

Dennis Morgan, Irene Manning, Bruce Cabot, Lynne Overman, Gene Lockhart, Victor Francen, Faye Emerson, Curt Bois, Jack La Rue, Marcel Dalio, Nestor Paiva, Gerald Mohr

The Desert Song

US 1953 110m Technicolor
Warner (Rudi Fehr)

Well staged straight version of the musical, with full score.

adaptation Roland Kibbee *d* Bruce Humberstone *ph* Robert Burks *m adaptation* Max Steiner

Gordon Macrae, Kathryn Grayson, Steve Cochran, Raymond Massey, Dick Wesson, Allyn McLerie, Ray Collins, Paul Picerni, William Conrad

The Deserter

Italy / Yugoslavia / USA 1970 99m
  Technicolor Panavision
Dino de Laurentiis / Jadran / Heritage
  (Norman Baer, Ralph Serpe)
original title: *La Spina Dorsale del Diavolo*

In the southwest in 1886, a cavalry captain tracks down the Apaches who tortured his wife to death.
Brutal revenge western, as muddled as its international credits would suggest.

w Clair Huffaker *d* Burt Kennedy *ph* Aldo Tonti *m* Piero Piccione *pd* Mario Chiari

Bekim Fehmiu, John Huston, Richard Crenna, Chuck Connors, Ricardo Montalban, Ian Bannen, Brandon de Wilde, Slim Pickens, Albert Salmi, Woody Strode, Patrick Wayne, Fausto Tozzi

Design for Living **

US 1933 88m bw
Paramount (Ernst Lubitsch)

Two friends love and are loved by the same worldly woman, and they set up house together. Elegant but miscast version of a scintillating play, with all the sex and the sting removed (at the insistence of the Legion of Decency, then coming into power). Ben Hecht claimed to have removed all but one line of Coward's dialogue.

w Ben Hecht, *play* Noel Coward *d* Ernst Lubitsch *ph* Victor Milner *m* Nathaniel Finston *ad* Hans Dreier

Gary Cooper, Fredric March, Miriam Hopkins, Edward Everett Horton, Franklin Pangborn, Isabel Jewell

Designing Woman *
US 1957   118m   Metrocolor
  Cinemascope
MGM (Dore Schary)

A sports reporter marries a dress designer and
finds that their common interests are few.
Lumbering comedy which aims for
sophistication but settles for farce: tolerable for
star watchers who have dined well.

w George Wells *d* Vincente Minnelli *ph* John
Alton *m* André Previn

Gregory Peck, Lauren Bacall, Dolores Gray,
Sam Levene, Tom Helmore, Mickey
Shaughnessey, Jesse White, Chuck Connors,
Jack Cole

AAN: George Wells

Desire **
US 1936   89m   bw
Paramount (Ernst Lubitsch)

In Spain, an American car designer falls for a
glamorous jewel thief.
Romantic comedy which the producer should
have worked on longer: it begins brilliantly and
keeps its style, but the pace and wit ebb away.

w Edwin Justus Mayer, Waldemar Young,
Samuel Hoffenstein, from a German film Die
schönen Tage von Aranjuez and a play by Hans
Szekely and R. A. Stemmle *d Frank Borzage*
ph Charles Lang, Victor Milner *m* Frederick
Hollander *ad* Hans Dreier, Robert Usher

Marlene Dietrich, Gary Cooper, *John Halliday*,
William Frawley, Ernest Cossart, Akim
Tamiroff, Alan Mowbray, Zeffie Tilbury
  'It sparkles and twinkles . . . one of the most
engaging pictures of the season.'—*Frank S.*
Nugent, New York Times

Desire in the Dust
US 1960   102m   bw   Cinemascope
TCF / Associated Producers (William F.
Claxton)

A wealthy southern aristocrat is involved in a
fatal car crash and persuades a young farmhand
to take the blame.
Derivative hothouse drama, a little better than its
title, with a cast breathing heavily in imitation of
refugees from Tennessee Williams or William
Faulkner.

w Charles Lang, *novel* Harry Whittington
d William F. Claxton *ph* Lucien Ballard *m* Paul
Dunlap

Raymond Burr, Martha Hyer, Joan Bennett,
Ken Scott, Brett Halsey, Anne Helm, Jack Ging,
Edward Binns

Desire Me
US 1947   91m   bw
MGM (Arthur Hornblow Jnr)

The wife of a Normandy villager hears that he
has died in a concentration camp. She marries
the bearer of the news, who turns out to be a
psychotic who has left her husband for dead . . .
but he is not.
Dreary drama, troubled during production and
offering little for the actors to chew on.

w Marguerite Roberts, Zoe Akins, Casey
Robinson, *novel* Leonhard Frank *d* not credited,
but mostly by George Cukor, Melvyn Le Roy,
Jack Conway *ph* Joseph Ruttenberg *m* Herbert
Stothart

Greer Garson, Robert Mitchum, Richard Hart,
George Zucco, Morris Ankrum
  'The supporting cast includes a number of
characters who give the appearance of having
come out of a dusty cupboard marked "French
Types—Assorted".'—*MFB*

Desire under the Elms
US 1958   111m   bw   Vistavision
Paramount (Don Hartman)

A New England farmer brings home a young
bride and causes friction with his son.
This bid for culture turns out like a hoary and
very slow melodrama, not exactly risible but
annoying because it teeters between several
styles.

w Irwin Shaw, *play* Eugene O'Neill *d* Delbert
Mann *ph* Daniel L. Fapp *m* Elmer Bernstein

Sophia Loren, Burl Ives, Anthony Perkins,
Frank Overton, Pernell Roberts, Anne Seymour
  'The film is consistently and unhappily out of
its depth.'—*Penelope Houston*

AAN: Daniel L. Fapp

Desirée
US 1954   110m   De Luxe   Cinemascope
TCF (Julian Blaustein)

Fictionalized biopic of one of Napoleon's
mistresses.
Heavy-going costume piece, with all
contributors distinctly uncomfortable.

w Daniel Taradash, *novel* Annemarie Selinko
d Henry Koster *ph* Milton Krasner *m* Alex
North

Jean Simmons, Marlon Brando, Merle Oberon,
Michael Rennie, Cameron Mitchell, Elizabeth
Sellars, Cathleen Nesbitt, Isobel Elsom

The Desk Set**
US 1957 103m Eastmancolor
Cinemascope
TCF (Henry Ephron)
GB title: *His Other Woman*

Ladies in a broadcasting company's reference
section are appalled when an electronics expert is
sent to improve their performance.
Thin comedy, altered from a Broadway success;
patchy as a whole, but with several splendid
dialogue scenes for the principals.

w Phoebe and Henry Ephron, *play* William
Marchant *d* Walter Lang *ph* Leon Shamroy
m Cyril Mockridge

Spencer Tracy, Katharine Hepburn, Joan
Blondell, Gig Young, Dina Merrill, Neva
Patterson

The Desperados
US 1968 90m Technicolor
Columbia / Meadway (Irving Allen)

After the Civil War, a fanatic 'parson' leads a
tribe of violent outlaws including his three sons.
Rough-and-tumble western in the modern
savage manner; made in Spain.

w Walter Brough *d* Henry Levin *ph* Sam
Leavitt *m* David Whitaker

Vince Edwards, Jack Palance, George Maharis,
Neville Brand, Sylvia Syms, Christian Roberts,
Kate O'Mara, Kenneth Cope, John Paul

Desperate Characters*
US 1971 106m colour
ITC (Frank D. Gilroy)

Residents of New York's east side find the
rigours of life hard to take.
Curious but interesting suburban drama, a kind
of deglamorized and updated *City for Conquest*.

wd Frank D. Gilroy, *novel* Paula Fox *ph* Urs
Furrer

Shirley Maclaine, Gerald S. O'Loughlin,
Kenneth Mars, Sada Thompson, Jack Somack
'The most blistering indictment of New York
City since *Midnight Cowboy*.'—*Rex Reed*
'A film of authenticity, of delicately realized
intangibles.'—*Stanley Kauffmann*

The Desperate Hours*
US 1955 112m bw Vistavision
Paramount (William Wyler)

Three escaped convicts take over a suburban
house but are finally outwitted by the family.
Ponderous treatment of an over-familiar
situation with only the acting and an 'A' picture
look to save it.

w Joseph Hayes, from his novel and play
d William Wyler *ph* Lee Garmes *m* Gail Kubik

Fredric March, Humphrey Bogart, Martha
Scott, Arthur Kennedy, Gig Young, Dewey
Martin, Mary Murphy, Robert Middleton,
Richard Eyer
'A solid, deliberate and long-drawn-out
exercise in the mechanics of suspense.'—
Penelope Houston

Desperate Journey**
US 1942 109m bw
Warner (Hal B. Wallis)

Three POWs in Nazi Germany fight their way
back to freedom.
When you pit Errol Flynn against the Nazis,
there's no doubt who wins; and the last line is
'Now for Australia and a crack at those Japs!'
Exhilarating adventure for the totally uncritical;
professional standards high.

w Arthur Horman *d* Raoul Walsh *ph* Bert
Glennon

Errol Flynn, Alan Hale, Ronald Reagan, Nancy
Coleman, Raymond Massey, Arthur Kennedy,
Ronald Sinclair, Albert Basserman, Sig
Rumann, Ilka Gruning, Pat O'Moore

Desperate Moment
GB 1953 88m bw
Rank / George H. Brown

In Poland, a man imprisoned for murder finds he
didn't do it, escapes, and tracks down the real
criminal, his best friend.
Cliché-ridden melodrama climaxing in a car
chase; poor in all departments.

w Patrick Kirwan, George H. Brown,
novel Martha Albrand *d* Compton Bennett
ph C. Pennington-Richards *m* Ronald Binge

Dirk Bogarde, Mai Zetterling, Philip Friend,
Albert Lieven, Carl Jaffe, Gerald Heinz

Destination Gobi*
US 1953 90m Technicolor
TCF (Stanley Rubin)

American soldiers get Mongol help against the
Japanese in the Gobi desert.
A curious war adventure, a kind of camel opera,
apparently based on fact; mildly enjoyable,
though the outlandish is gradually replaced by
the predictable.

w Everett Freeman *d* Robert Wise *ph* Charles
G. Clarke *m* Sol Kaplan

Richard Widmark, Don Taylor, Casey Adams,
Murvyn Vye, Darryl Hickman, Martin Milner,
Ross Badgasarian, Rodolfo Acosta

Destination Moon*
US 1950 91m Technicolor
Universal / George Pal

An American inventor gets private backing to
build a rocket so that the US can reach the moon
before the Russians.

Semi-documentary prophecy with impressive
gadgetry encased in a tedious and totally
unsurprising script.

w Rip Van Ronkel, Robert Heinlan, James
O'Hanlon d Irving Pichel ph Lionel Lindon
m Leith Stevens

Warner Anderson, John Archer, Tom Powers,
Dick Wesson

'Heavy-handed, unimaginative and very badly
acted.'—MFB

Destination Tokyo*
US 1943 135m bw
Warner (Jerry Wald)

A US submarine is sent into Tokyo harbour.
Solid, well acted war suspenser, but overlong.

w Delmer Daves, Albert Maltz, original
story Steve Fisher d Delmer Daves ph Bert
Glennon m Franz Waxman

Cary Grant, John Garfield, Alan Hale, John
Ridgely, Dane Clark, Warner Anderson,
William Prince, Robert Hutton, Tom Tully,
Peter Whitney, Faye Emerson, John Forsythe

'We don't say it is credible; we don't even
suggest that it makes sense. But it does make a
pippin of a picture from a purely melodramatic
point of view.'—Bosley Crowther

AAN: Steve Fisher

Destiny*
Germany 1921 100m approx bw silent
Decla-Bioscop
original title: Der Mude Tod

In the 19th-century a young woman tries to save
her lover from the presence of Death, who shows
her that whatever she does it is inevitable.

A solemn fantasy on the lines of Appointment in
Samarra, the framing story being more effective
than the 'illustrations'.

w Thea Von Harbou, Fritz Lang d Fritz Lang
ph Fritz Arno Wagner, Erich Nitschmann,
Hermann Saalfrank

Lil Dagover, Rudolph Klein-Rogge, Bernhard
Götzke, Walter Janssen

Destiny*
US 1944 65m bw
Universal (Roy William Neill)

An escaped convict on the run finds refuge with a
blind girl on a lonely farm.

Curious second feature, interesting because it
began as a story eliminated from Flesh and
Fantasy (qv); extra footage was added to bring it
up to the required length. The original footage is
mainly the nightmare suffered by the girl.

w Roy Chanslor (F and F Ernest Pascal)
d Reginald Le Borg (F and F Julien Duvivier)
ph George Robinson (F and F Paul Ivano)

Gloria Jean, Alan Curtis (who died in the
original but here survives), Frank Craven, Grace
McDonald

Destiny of a Man**
USSR 1959 98m bw
Sovexportfilm / Mosfilm (G. Kuznetsov)
original title: Sudba Cheloveka

During World War II a Russian is captured by
Nazis but escapes and returns home only to find
his family dead.

Strikingly styled sob story whose very glumness
prevented it from being hailed as a masterpiece;
in technique however it is in the best Russian
tradition.

w Y. Lukin, F. Shakhmagonov, story Mikhail
Sholokhov d Sergei Bondarchuk ph Vladimir
Monakhov m V. Basnov

Sergei Bondarchuk, Zinaida Kirienko, Pavlik
Boriskin

'Of all Soviet post-war films, this will be looked
on as the greatest and most original work of the
period.'—MFB

Destroyer
US 1943 99m bw
Columbia (Louis F. Edelmann)

An old sea dog talks himself into a job on a
World War II destroyer but works his men too
hard.

Flat propaganda piece, not too well made.

w Frank Wead, Lewis Meltzer, Borden Chase
d William A. Seiter ph Franz Planer
m Anthony Collins

Edward G. Robinson, Glenn Ford, Marguerite
Chapman, Edgar Buchanan, Leo Gorcey, Regis
Toomey, Ed Brophy

Destry*
US 1954 95m Technicolor
U-I (Stanley Rubin)

Almost scene-for-scene remake of Destry Rides
Again (qv). Well enough made and tolerably
acted, but it doesn't have the sparkle, despite
employing the same director.

w Edmund H. North, D. D. Beauchamp
d George Marshall ph George Robinson
m Joseph Gershenson

Audie Murphy, Mari Blanchard, Lyle Bettger, Thomas Mitchell, Edgar Buchanan, Wallace Ford, Lori Nelson, Alan Hale Jnr, Mary Wickes
'The impression is of a school revival of the original production.'—*MFB*

Destry Rides Again****
US 1939   94m   bw
Universal (Joe Pasternak)

A mild-mannered sheriff finally gets mad at local corruption and straps on his guns.
Classic western which manages to encompass suspense, comedy, romance, tenderness, vivid characterization, horseplay, songs and standard western excitements, without moving for more than a moment from a studio main street set. It starts with a sign reading 'Welcome to Bottleneck' and an outburst of gunfire; it ends with tragedy followed by a running joke. Hollywood expertise at its very best.

w Felix Jackson, Gertrude Purcell, Henry Myers, novel Max Brand *d George Marshall ph Hal Mohr songs Frederick Hollander, Frank Loesser m Frank Skinner*

James Stewart, Marlene Dietrich, Brian Donlevy, Charles Winninger, Samuel S. Hinds, Mischa Auer, Irene Hervey, Jack Carson, *Una Merkel,* Allen Jenkins, Warren Hymer, *Billy Gilbert*

† An early sound version in 1932 starred Tom Mix; *Frenchie* (1950) was a slight variation. See also *Destry.*

The Detective**
US 1968   114m   De Luxe   Panavision
TCF / Arcola / Millfield (Aaron Rosenberg)

A New York police detective fights crime and corruption.
Determinedly sleazy and 'frank' cop stuff, quite arrestingly narrated and with something to say about police methods. Good violent entertainment, with just a shade too many homosexuals and nymphomaniacs for balance.

w Abby Mann, novel Roderick Thorp *d Gordon Douglas ph Joseph Biroc m Jerry Goldsmith*

Frank Sinatra, Lee Remick, Jacqueline Bisset, Ralph Meeker, Jack Klugman, Horace MacMahon, Lloyd Bochner, William Windom, Tony Musante, Al Freeman Jnr, Robert Duvall
'It vacillates uncertainly between murder mystery, political allegory, and a psychological study of the hero.'—*Jan Dawson*

Detective Story***
US 1951   103m   bw
Paramount (William Wyler)

A day in a New York precinct police station,

during which a detective of almost pathological righteousness discovers a stain on his family and himself becomes a victim of violence.
Clever, fluent transcription of a Broadway play with some of the pretensions of Greek tragedy; it could have been the negation of cinema, but professional handling makes it the essence of it.

w Philip Yordan, Robert Wyler, play Sidney Kingsley d William Wyler ph Lee Garmes

Kirk Douglas, Eleanor Parker, William Bendix, Cathy O'Donnell, George Macready, Horace MacMahon, Gladys George, *Joseph Wiseman, Lee Grant,* Gerald Mohr, Frank Faylen, Luis Van Rooten
'The admirably directed interaction of movement and talk all over the big room is what gives the thing its satisfying texture.'—*Richard Mallett, Punch*

AAN: Philip Yordan, Robert Wyler; William Wyler; Eleanor Parker; Lee Grant

Devi*
India 1960   93m   bw
Satyajit Ray Productions
aka: *The Goddess*

While his son is away at university, a farmer persuades his daughter-in-law that she is a goddess, and the events which follow, including the death of her son, are too much for her reason.
A curious, 'foreign' story which does not have the usual Ray tempo or feeling for character, but wins one's attention by its very strangeness.

wd Satyajit Ray, *story* Prabhat Kumar Mukherjee *ph* Subrata Mitra *m* Ali Akbar Khan

Chhabi Biswas, Sharmila Tagore, Soumitra Chatterjee, Karuna Bannerjee

The Devil and Miss Jones**
US 1941   97m   bw
RKO / Frank Ross, Norman Krasna

A millionaire masquerades as a clerk in his own department store to investigate worker complaints.
Attractive comedy with elements of the crazy thirties and the more socially conscious forties.

w Norman Krasna d Sam Wood *ph* Harry Stradling

Jean Arthur, *Charles Coburn,* Robert Cummings, Spring Byington, S. Z. Sakall, William Demarest

AAN: Norman Krasna; Charles Coburn

Devil and the Deep*
US 1932   73m   bw
Paramount

A submarine commander goes mad with jealousy of his faithless wife.
A turgid melodrama notable for its stars.

w Benn Levy d Marion Gering ph Charles Lang

Tallulah Bankhead, Charles Laughton, Gary Cooper, Cary Grant, Paul Porcasi

The Devil and the Nun*
Poland 1960   108m   bw
Kadr
original title: *Matka Joanna od Aniolow;* aka: *Mother Joan of the Angels*

In a 17th-century convent nuns are possessed by devils. A priest who tries to help is burned at the stake; another becomes possessed himself. Reasonably dispassionate and fairly stylized version of the same facts that were treated so hysterically by Ken Russell in *The Devils*.

w Tadeusz Konwicki, Jerzy Kawalerowicz, *novel* Jaroslav Iwaszkiewicz d Jerzy Kawalerowicz ph Jerzy Wojcik m Adam Walacinski

Lucyna Winnicka, Mieczyslaw Voit, Anna Ciepielewska

The Devil at Four o'Clock
US 1961   126m   Eastmancolor
Columbia / Leroy / Kohlmar (Fred Kohlmar)

A drunken missionary and three convicts save a colony of leper children from a South Seas volcano.
Muddled adventure melodrama with a downbeat ending long delayed.

w Liam O'Brien, *novel* Max Catto d Mervyn Le Roy ph Joseph Biroc m George Duning

Spencer Tracy, Frank Sinatra, Kerwin Mathews, Jean-Pierre Aumont, Grégoire Aslan, Alexander Scourby, Barbara Luna

The Devil Commands*
US 1941   65m   bw
Columbia

An electrical scientist tries to communicate with his dead wife through a medium.
Modestly effective horror thriller, though rather too deliberately paced.

w Robert D. Andrews, Milton Gunzberg, *story* The Edge of Running Water by William Sloane d Edward Dmytryk ph Allan G. Siegler

Boris Karloff, Richard Fiske, Amanda Duff, Anne Revere, Ralph Penney

Devil Dogs of the Air**
US 1935   86m   bw
Warner (Lou Edelman)

Rivalry and romance in the Marine Flying Corps.
Standard, lively vehicle for Cagney and O'Brien, with excellent stunt flying sequences.

w Malcolm Stuart Boylan, Earl Baldwin, *novel* John Monk Saunders d Lloyd Bacon ph Arthur Edeson md Leo F. Forbstein

James Cagney, Pat O'Brien, Margaret Lindsay, Frank McHugh, Helen Lowell, John Arledge, Robert Barrat, Russell Hicks, Ward Bond
'A loud and roughneck screen comedy, both amusing and exciting.'—*André Sennwald*

The Devil Doll**
US 1936   79m   bw
MGM

A refugee from Devil's Island disguises himself as an old lady who sells human dolls which murder those responsible for his imprisonment. Interesting rather than exciting tall tale with a Paris backdrop; despite impressive moments it does not quite have the right *frisson*.

w Tod Browning, Garrett Fort, Erich Von Stroheim, Guy Endore, *novel* Burn Witch Burn by A. A. Merritt d Tod Browning ph Leonard Smith m Franz Waxman ad Cedric Gibbons

Lionel Barrymore, Maureen O'Sullivan, Frank Lawton, Henry B. Walthall, Rafaela Ottiano, Grace Ford, Arthur Hohl

The Devil Is a Sissy
US 1936   92m   bw
MGM (Frank Davis)
aka: *The Devil Takes the Count*

The young son of divorcing parents gets into bad company.
Adequate juvenile melodrama

w John Lee Mahin, Richard Schayer, Roland Brown
d W. S. Van Dyke ph Harold Rosson, George Schneidermann m Herbert Stothart

Freddie Bartholemew, Jackie Cooper, Mickey Rooney, Ian Hunter, Peggy Conklin, Katherine Alexander, Gene Lockhart, Dorothy Peterson

The Devil Is a Woman*
US 1935   82m   bw
Paramount

In Seville in th 1890s a *femme fatale* has several admirers.
The last Dietrich vehicle to be directed by Von Sternberg, and rather splendid in its highly decorative and uncommercial way; a treat for addicts.

w John Dos Passos, S. K. Winston, *novel* La Femme et le Pantin by Pierre Louÿs d Josef Von

Sternberg *ph* Josef Von Sternberg, Lucien Ballard *ad* Hans Dreier

Marlene Dietrich, Lionel Atwill, Cesar Romero, Edward Everett Horton, Alison Skipworth, Don Alvarado, Morgan Wallace, Tempe Pigott

'One of the most sophisticated films ever produced in America.'—*André Sennwald, New York Times*

'Light and shadow are splashed liberally around over the white-painted sets; cafés, tobacco factories, stairs and balconies are decorated with every conceivable device and camera-level.'—*Peter John Dyer, 1964*

'A clever, perversely dehumanized picture said to be one of Von Sternberg's favourites.'—*New Yorker, 1977*

The Devil Makes Three
US 1952 90m bw
MGM (Richard Goldstone)

An American intelligence officer in post-war Germany becomes involved with neo-Nazis.
A curious break from dancing for Gene Kelly, this obscurely titled thriller has little to commend it but authentic locations.

w Jerry Davis, *story* Lawrence Bachmann *d* Andrew Marton *ph* Vaclav Vich *m* Rudolph G. Kopp

Gene Kelly, Pier Angeli, Richard Rober, Richard Egan, Claus Clausen

The Devil Rides Out *
GB 1967 95m Technicolor
Hammer (Anthony Nelson Keys)
US title: *The Devil's Bride*

The Duc de Richleau rescues a friend from a group of Satanists.
Rather stodgy adaptation of a frightening novel; moments of suspense.

w Richard Matheson, *novel* Dennis Wheatley *d* Terence Fisher *ph* Arthur Grant *m* James Bernard

Christopher Lee, *Charles Gray*, Leon Greene, Patrick Mower, Gwen Ffrangcon Davies

The Devil to Pay *
US 1931 65m bw
Samuel Goldwyn

The prodigal son of a snooty English family returns to cheer them all up.
Agreeably lighthearted star comedy in the drawing-room tradition.

w Frederick Lonsdale *d* George Fitzmaurice

Ronald Colman, Loretta Young, Myrna Loy, Frederick Kerr

'Six reels of Mr Colman being charming . . . a

polished, tasteful and entirely likeable screen comedy.'—*New York Herald Tribune*

A Devil with Women
US 1930 76m bw
Fox (George Middleton)

Soldiers of fortune in a banana republic end the regime of a notorious bandit and compete for a fair señorita.
Primitive Flagg-and-Quirt knockabout.

w Dudley Nichols, Henry M. Johnson, *novel* Dust and Sun by Clements Ripley *d* Irving Cummings *ph* Arthur Todd *m* Peter Brunelli

Victor McLaglen, Humphrey Bogart, Mona Maris, Michael Vavitch

The Devils *
GB 1970 111m Technicolor Panavision
Warner / Russo (Robert H. Solo, Ken Russell)

An account of the apparent demoniacal possession of the 17th-century nuns of Loudun, climaxing in the burning of their priest as a sorcerer.
Despite undeniable technical proficiency this is its writer-director's most outrageously sick film to date, campy, idiosyncratic and in howling bad taste from beginning to end, full of worm-eaten skulls, masturbating nuns, gibbering courtiers, plague sores, rats and a burning to death before our very eyes . . . plus a sacrilegious dream of Jesus. A pointless pantomime for misogynists.

wd Ken Russell, *play* John Whiting, *book* The Devils of Loudun by Aldous Huxley *ph* David Watkin *m* Peter Maxwell Davies *ad* Robert Cartwright

Vanessa Redgrave, Oliver Reed, Dudley Sutton, Max Adrian, Gemma Jones, Murray Melvin, Michael Gothard, Graham Armitage

'Ken Russell doesn't report hysteria, he markets it.'—*New Yorker, 1976*

'Russell's swirling multi-colored puddle . . . made me glad that both Huxley and Whiting are dead, so that they are spared this farrago of witless exhibitionism.'—*Stanley Kauffmann*

'A garish glossary of sado-masochism . . . a taste for visual sensation that makes scene after scene look like the masturbatory fantasies of a Roman Catholic boyhood.'—*Alexander Walker*

The Devil's Advocate
West Germany 1977 109m colour
Geria (Lutz Hengst)

A dying priest is summoned to Rome to investigate the cult of a dead partisan nominated for sainthood.
Well-meaning but rather tepid and inconclusive

adaptation of a bestseller which presumably made its points more firmly.

w Morris West, from his novel d Guy Green
ph Billy Williams m Bert Grund

John Mills, Stéphane Audran, Jason Miller, Timothy West, Patrick Mower, Paola Pitagora, Daniel Massey, Leigh Lawson, Raf Vallone, Jack Hedley

The Devil's Brigade
US 1968 132m De Luxe Panavision
UA / David L. Wolper

For combat in Norway and Italy during World War II a US officer assembles a platoon of thugs and misfits to work with crack Canadian commandos.
Flagrant but routine imitation of *The Dirty Dozen*, quite undistinguished.

w William Roberts d Andrew V. McLaglen
ph William Clothier m Alex North

William Holden, Cliff Robertson, Vince Edwards,
Andrew Prine, Claude Akins, Carroll O'Connor, Richard Jaeckel

Devil's Canyon
US 1953 92m Technicolor 3-D
RKO / Edmund Grainger

Life in a notorious Arizona prison in the eighties; a marshal is unjustly convicted but wins his pardon.
Fairly brutal western, quite unmemorable.

w Frederick Hazlitt Brennan d Alfred Werker
ph Nicholas Musuraca m Daniele Amfitheatrof

Dale Robertson, Virginia Mayo, Stephen McNally, Arthur Hunnicutt, Robert Keith, Jay C. Flippen, Whit Bissell

The Devil's Disciple*
GB 1959 82m bw
UA / Hecht–Hill–Lancaster / Brynaprod (Harold Hecht)

In 1777 an American ne'er-do-well almost allows himself to be hanged by the British in mistake for a rebel pastor.
Star-studded but indifferently staged adaptation of a minor Shavian frolic. Patchy, with good moments.

w John Dighton, Roland Kibbee, *play* Bernard Shaw d Guy Hamilton ph Jack Hildyard
m Richard Rodney Bennett ad Terence Verity, Edward Carere

Burt Lancaster, Kirk Douglas, *Laurence Olivier* (as General Burgoyne), Eva Le Gallienne, Janette Scott, Harry Andrews, Basil Sidney,

George Rose, Neil McCallum, David Horne, Mervyn Johns

Devil's Doorway
US 1950 84m bw
MGM (Nicholas Nayfack)

A Shoshone Indian fights valiantly in the Civil War but on his return to Wyoming finds himself hated and threatened by his former colleagues.
Dull pro-Indian western with a most unsuitable star.

w Guy Trosper d Anthony Mann ph John Alton m Daniele Amfitheatrof

Robert Taylor, Louis Calhern, Paula Raymond, Marshall Thompson, James Mitchell, Edgar Buchanan, Rhys Williams, Spring Byington

The Devil's Eye*
Sweden 1960 90m bw
Svensk Filmindustri

An old proverb says that a woman's chastity is a stye in the devil's eye. So when Satan has a sore eye he comes down to earth to put things right. Surprisingly shoddily-made comedy with just a few of the sharpnesses of technique and mystifications of plot which one had come to expect from this maestro.

wd Ingmar Bergman ph Gunnar Fischer
m Domenico Scarlatti

Jarl Kulle, Bibi Andersson, Nils Poppe, Stig Järrel, Gunnar Björnstrand

The Devil's General
West Germany 1955 121m bw
Ryal (Gyula Trebitsch)

In 1941 a German air ace becomes estranged from the high command and is tortured by the Gestapo. On release he helps a Jewish couple . . .
Heavy-going melodrama which nevertheless paints a convincing picture of Berlin during the war.

w George Hurdalek, Helmut Kautner, *play* Carl Zuckmayer d Helmut Kautner ph Albert Benitz

Curt Jurgens, Victor de Kowa, Karl John, Eva-Ingeborg Scholz

The Devil's Hairpin
US 1957 83m Technicolor Vistavision
Paramount / Cornel Wilde

A former motor racing champion makes a comeback, and redeems his past boorish behaviour.
Efficient routine melodramatics with good action sequences.

w James Edmiston, Cornel Wilde *d* Cornel Wilde *ph* Daniel Fapp *m* Van Cleave

Cornel Wilde, Jean Wallace, Arthur Franz, *Mary Astor*, Paul Fix

The Devil's Playground*

Australia 1976   107m   Eastmancolor
The Feature Film House (Fred Schepsi)

Tensions between masters and boys in a Catholic seminary in the fifties.
Well made but rather dislikeable intrusion into *Mr Perrin and Mr Traill* country with the addition of modern frankness.

wd Fred Schepsi *ph* Ian Baker *m* Bruce Smeaton

Arthur Dignam, Nick Tate, Simon Burke, Charles McCallum, John Frawley

The Devil's Rain

US 1975   86m   colour   Todd-AO 35
Sandy Howard

Witchcraft in the modern west causes victims to melt; the son of one of them takes arms against the leading Satanist.
Interestingly cast example of the low-budget seventies exploitation picture, with more nastiness than logic.

w Gabe Essoe, James Ashton, Gerald Hopman *d* Robert Fuest *ph* Alex Phillips Jnr *m* Al de Lory

Ernest Borgnine, Ida Lupino, Eddie Albert, William Shatner, Keenan Wynn, Tom Skerritt

The Devil's Wanton*

Sweden 1949   80m   bw
Terrafilm
original title: *Fängelse*

Film-makers discuss some rather unpleasant projects but put them aside as unsatisfactory.
A bit of a Scandinavian wallow, with heavy expressionism and low-life themes.

wd Ingmar Bergman *ph* Göran Strindberg *m* Erland von Koch

Doris Svedlund, Birger Malmsten, Eva Henning, Hasse Ekman

'It employs all the paraphernalia associated with Scandinavian angst.'—*John Gillett, MFB*

Devotion**

US 1944   107m   bw
Warner (Robert Buckner)

A highly romanticized account of the lives of the Brontë sisters and their brother Branwell.
An enjoyably bad example of a big-budget Hollywood production which tampers with things it cannot understand, in this case life in a

Yorkshire parsonage in Victorian times. An excuse is found to give the curate an Austrian accent to fit the available actor, but this and other *faux pas* are atoned for by the vividness of Emily's recurrent dream of death as a silhouetted man on horseback. In general, an interesting period piece in more senses than one.

w Keith Winter *d* Curtis Bernhardt *ph* Ernest Haller *m* Erich Wolfgang Korngold

Ida Lupino (Emily), Olivia de Havilland (Charlotte), Nancy Coleman (Anne), Arthur Kennedy (Branwell), Montagu Love (Revd Brontë), Paul Henreid (Revd Nicholls), Ethel Griffies (Aunt Branwell), Sidney Greenstreet (Thackeray), Eily Malyon, Forrester Harvey, Victor Francen

'I found it painless. It never got nearer to the subject than names and consequently didn't hurt. But I would like to know who was devoted to whom and why.'—*Richard Winnington*

The DI

US 1957   106m   bw
Warner / Mark VII (Jack Webb)

A tough marine drill instructor takes a special interest in a backward member of his platoon.
Noisy recruiting poster heroics in which the producer gives himself a loud but boring part.
The drill sequences are well done, but the film is overlong and repetitive.

w James Lee Barrett *d* Jack Webb *ph* Edward Colman *m* David Buttolph

Jack Webb, Don Dubbins, Jackie Loughery, Lin McCarthy, Monica Lewis

Le Diable au Corps*

France 1947   110m   bw
Transcontinental
US title: *Devil in the Flesh*

When her husband is away at war, a young married woman falls for a college student and dies bearing his child.
A love story of World War I; a great commercial success, but tending to be slow and dreary.

w Jean Aurenche, Pierre Bost, *novel* Raymond Radiguet *d* Claude Autant-Lara *ph* Michel Kelber *m* René Cloërc

Micheline Presle, Gérard Philipe, Jean Debucourt, Denise Grey, Jacques Tati

Les Diaboliques***

France 1954   114m   bw
Filmsonor (Henri-Georges Clouzot)
aka: *Diabolique; The Fiends*

A sadistic headmaster's wife and mistress conspire to murder him; but his body disappears and evidence of his presence haunts them.

Highly influential, suspenseful and scary thriller with a much-copied twist typical of its authors.
Slow to start and shabby-looking as befits its grubby school setting, it gathers momentum with the murder and turns the screw with fine professionalism.

w Henri-Georges Clouzot, G. Geronimi, *novel* The Woman Who Was by Pierre Boileau and Thomas Narcejac *d* Henri-Georges Clouzot *ph* Armand Thirard *m* Georges Van Parys

Simone Signoret, Vera Clouzot, Charles Vanel, Paul Meurisse
    'Scary, but so calculatedly sensational that it's rather revolting.'—*New Yorker, 1978*
† Remade in 1976 as a TV movie, *Reflections of Murder.*

Diagnosis: Murder
GB 1974   90m   Eastmancolor
Silhouette (Patrick Dromgoole, Peter Miller)
A psychiatrist's wife disappears, and the police suspect her husband.
Well-upholstered but sadly old-fashioned domestic crime thriller; one is vaguely surprised to see it in colour, having seen it so often in black-and-white.

w Philip Levene *d* Sidney Hayers *ph* Bob Edwards *m* Laurie Johnson

Jon Finch, Judy Geeson, Christopher Lee, Tony Beckley, Dilys Hamlett, Jane Merrow, Colin Jeavons

Dial M For Murder**
US 1954   105m   Warnercolor   3-D
Warner (Alfred Hitchcock)
An ageing tennis champion tries to arrange the death of his wife so that he will inherit, but his complex plan goes wrong.
Hitchcock did not try very hard to adapt this highly commercial play for the cinema, nor did he exploit the possibilities of 3-D. But for a one-room film with a not very exciting cast the film holds its grip pretty well.

w Frederick Knott, from his play *d* Alfred Hitchcock *ph* Robert Burks *m* Dmitri Tiomkin

Ray Milland, John Williams, Grace Kelly, Robert Cummings, Anthony Dawson
    'All this is related with Hitchcock's ghoulish chic but everyone in it seems to be walking around with tired blood.'—*Pauline Kael, 1968*

Dial 1119*
US 1950   75m   bw
MGM (Richard Goldstone)
GB title: *The Violent Hour*

An assortment of people are held up in a bar by a maniac.
Suspenseful thriller when it sticks to its central theme; dullish when it tries characterization. A good second feature.

w John Monks Jnr *d Gerald Mayer ph* Paul Vogel *m* André Previn

Marshall Thompson, Virginia Field, Andrea King, Leon Ames, Keefe Brasselle, Richard Rober, James Bell, William Conrad

Diamond City
GB 1949   90m   bw
GFD / Gainsborough (A. Frank Bundy)
Law and order is maintained during the working of a South African diamond field.
British imitation of a Wyatt Earp western; very milk-and-water.

w Roger Bray, Roland Pertwee *d* David MacDonald *ph* Reginald Wyer *m* Clifton Parker

David Farrar, Honor Blackman, Diana Dors, Niall MacGinnis, Andrew Crawford, Mervyn Johns, Bill Owen, Phyllis Monkman

Diamond Head
US 1962   107m   Eastmancolor
  Panavision
Columbia (Jerry Bresler)
A domineering Hawaiian landowner almost ruins the lives of his family.
Predictable, heavy-going transcription of a bestseller.

w Marguerite Roberts, *novel* Peter Gilman *d* Guy Green *ph* Sam Leavitt *m* Johnny Williams

Charlton Heston, Yvette Mimieux, George Chakiris, France Nuyen, James Darren, Aline MacMahon, Elizabeth Allen, Richard Loo

Diamond Horseshoe
US 1945   104m   Technicolor
TCF (William Perlberg)
aka: *Billy Rose's Diamond Horseshoe*
A nightclub singer gives up her career for a medical student.
Lavish but humourless star vehicle with standard numbers.

wd George Seaton, *play* The Barker by Kenyon Nicholson *ph* Ernest Palmer *songs* Mack Gordon, Harry Warren

Betty Grable, Dick Haymes, *William Gaxton*, Phil Silvers, Beatrice Kay, Carmen Cavallero, Margaret Dumont

Diamond Jim*
US 1935 93m bw
Universal (Edmund Grainger)

A fantasia on the life of the nineties millionaire
who sailed pretty close to the wind in business,
adored Lillian Russell, and developed a
gargantuan appetite.
Cheerful period comedy drama with plenty of
gusto.

w Preston Sturges d A. Edward Sutherland
ph George Robinson m Ferde Grofe, Franz
Waxman

Edward Arnold, Jean Arthur, Binnie Barnes,
Cesar Romero, Eric Blore

Diamonds
US 1975 108m Eastmancolor
Avco Embassy / AmeriEuro (Menahem
Golan)

A London diamond merchant sets himself up to
be robbed so that he can blackmail the culprits
into a raid on the Tel Aviv diamond repository.
Cheerful but unremarkable caper movie with an
upbeat ending.

w David Paulsen, Menahem Golan d Menahem
Golan ph Adam Greenberg m Roy Budd

Robert Shaw, Richard Roundtree, Barbara
Seagull, Shelley Winters

Diamonds Are Forever*
GB 1971 120m Technicolor Panavision
UA / Eon / Danjaq (Harry Saltzman, Albert R.
Broccoli)

Seeking a diamond smuggler, James Bond has
adventures in Amsterdam, a Los Angeles
crematorium, various Las Vegas gambling
parlours, and a secret installation in the desert.
Campy, rather vicious addition to a well-worn
cycle, with an element of nastiness which big-
budget stunts cannot conceal. Panavision does
not help, and Connery's return to the role for a
final throw is disappointing.

w Richard Maibaum, Tom Mankiewicz, novel
Ian Fleming d Guy Hamilton ph Ted Moore
m John Barry pd Ken Adam

Sean Connery, Jill St John, Charles Gray, Lana
Wood, Jimmy Dean, Bruce Cabot, Bernard Lee,
Lois Maxwell

Diamonds for Breakfast
GB 1968 102m Eastmancolor
Paramount / Bridge Films (Carlo Ponti, Pierre
Rouve)

An impoverished Russian aristocrat decides to
retrieve from a museum the crown jewels of his
ancestors, and seduces seven female
accomplices.
Yawning caper yarn embellished with sex and
slapstick.

w N. F. Simpson, Pierre Rouve, Ronald
Harwood d Christopher Morahan ph Gerry
Turpin m Norman Kay

Marcello Mastroianni, Rita Tushingham, Elaine
Taylor, Warren Mitchell, Nora Nicholson, Bill
Fraser, Leonard Rossiter

Diane
US 1956 110m Eastmancolor
 Cinemascope
MGM (Edwin H. Knopf)

Diane de Poitier becomes a consultant to the
king and falls in love with his son.
Solidly boring slice of Hollywood history, with
all concerned out of their depth.

w Christopher Isherwood d David Miller
ph Robert Planck

Lana Turner, Roger Moore, Cedric Hardwicke,
Pedro Armendariz, Marisa Pavan

The Diary of a Chambermaid*
US 1946 86m bw
Benedict Bogeaus (Burgess Meredith,
Paulette Goddard)

A 19th-century serving girl causes sexual
frustration and other troubles in two households.
Hollywood notables were all at sea in this wholly
artificial and unpersuasive adaptation of a minor
classic.

w Burgess Meredith, novel Octave Mirbeau
d Jean Renoir ph Lucien Andriot pd Eugene
Lourié

Paulette Goddard, Burgess Meredith, Hurd
Hatfield, Francis Lederer, Judith Anderson,
Florence Bates, Irene Ryan, Reginald Owen,
Almira Sessions

The Diary of a Chambermaid*
France / Italy 1964 98m bw Franscope
Speva / Ciné Alliance / Filmsonor / Dear
 (Serge Silberman, Michel Sabra)
original title: Le Journal d'une Femme de
 Chambre

Interesting but not especially successful Bunuel
version: the subject is certainly up his street, but
the novel seems to restrict him and the visual
quality is unattractive.

w Luis Bunuel, Jean-Claude Carrière d Luis
Bunuel ph Roger Fellous m none

Jeanne Moreau, Georges Géret, Michel Piccoli,
Françoise Lugagne

The Diary of a Country Priest**

France 1950 120m bw
Union Générale Cinématographique (Léon Carré)
original title: *Journal d'un Curé de Campagne*

A lonely young priest fails to make much impression in his first parish; and, falling ill, he dies alone.
Striking, depressing, slow and austere, with little dialogue but considerable visual beauty; a very typical work of its director.

wd Robert Bresson, *novel* Georges Bernanos *ph* L. Burel *m* Jean-Jacques Grunenwald

Claude Laydu, Jean Riveyre, Armand Guibert, Nicole Ladmiral

Diary of a Lost Girl**

Germany 1929 110m approx bw silent
G. W. Pabst Film
original title: *Tagebuch einer Verlorenen*

A rich man's daughter is seduced, has an illegitimate child, is placed in a house of correction and finds herself later in a brothel.
Heavily Germanic Road to Ruin, superbly mounted in best cinematic style, with several memorable sequences. Heavily mutilated by censors; according to the screenwriter the film ends just after the middle of his script.

w Rudolf Leonhardt, *novel* Margaret Böhme *d G. W. Pabst ph* Sepp Allgeier

Louise Brooks, Fritz Rasp, Josef Ravensky
† A previous version had been made in 1918, written and directed by Richard Oswald.

Diary of a Mad Housewife**

US 1970 95m Technicolor
Universal / Frank Perry

The bored and repressed wife of a lawyer tries an affair, walks out on her husband, and opts for group therapy.
An agreeably mordant view of the contemporary American scene, with good dialogue and performances, but the little bits of satire do not really add up to a satisfactory film.

w Eleanor Perry, novel Sue Kaufman *d Frank Perry ph* Gerald Hirschfeld

Carrie Snodgress, Richard Benjamin, Frank Langella, Lorraine Cullen, Frannie Michel
'A prototypical contemporary American artifact . . . all its assorted talents and technological smartness are turned to the varnishing of mediocrity.'—*Stanley Kauffmann*

AAN: Carrie Snodgress

The Diary of a Madman

US 1962 96m Technicolor
UA / Admiral (Robert E. Kent)

A murderer explains to a magistrate that he was possessed by an evil spirit.
Ponderous transcription of a Maupassant story with a few moments of horror.

w Robert E. Kent *d* Reginald Le Borg *ph* Ellis W. Carter *m* Richard La Salle

Vincent Price, Nancy Kovack, Chris Warfield, Stephen Roberts

The Diary of a Married Woman

Germany 1953 83m bw
Magna
original title: *Tagebuch einer Verliebten*

A wife divorces her adulterous husband, but their small son brings them together again.
One long Hollywood cliché, assembled with some spirit; notable only as one of the rare post-war German films to get distribution in English-speaking countries.

w Emil Burri, Johann Mario Simmel *d* Josef Von Baky *ph* Oskar Snirch *m* Alois Melichar

Maria Schell, O. W. Fischer, Franco Andrei

The Diary of Anne Frank**

US 1959 170m bw Cinemascope
TCF / George Stevens

In 1942, a family of Dutch Jews hides in an attic from the Nazis; just before the war ends they are found and sent to concentration camps.
Based on the famous diaries of a girl who died at Auschwitz, this solemn adaptation is elephantine in its length, its ponderousness and its use of Cinemascope when the atmosphere is supposed to be claustrophobic.

w Frances Goodrich, Albert Hackett, from their play based on Anne Frank's diaries *d* George Stevens *ph William C. Mellor m* Alfred Newman

Millie Perkins, *Joseph Schildkraut, Shelley Winters, Ed Wynn*, Richard Beymer, Gusti Huber, Lou Jacobi, Diane Baker

AA: William C. Mellor; Shelley Winters
AAN: best picture; George Stevens; Alfred Newman; Ed Wynn

The Diary of Major Thompson

France 1955 83m bw
SNE Gaumont / Paul Wagner
original title: *Les Carnets de Major Thompson;* US title: *The French They Are a Funny Race*

An Englishman married to a Frenchwoman keeps notes on the French way of life.

Tatty filming of a mildly amusing book; it falls away into a number of badly-timed and presented gags, and one can't believe that its creator was once the top comedy genius of Hollywood.

wd Preston Sturges *ph* Maurice Barry, Christian Matras *m* Georges Van Parys

Jack Buchanan, Martine Carol, Noel-Noel, Genevieve Brunet

'Even allowing for the appalling editing and the frequently incomprehensible dubbed soundtrack, there is little evidence to suggest that this film could ever have been anything but a shambles.'—*Peter John Dyer, MFB*

Dick Tracy
US 1945 61m bw
RKO (Herman Schlom)

The jut-jawed detective routs a disfigured criminal named Splitface.
Vigorous second feature from the comic strip.

w Eric Taylor, *strip* Chester Gould *d* William Berke *ph* Frank Redman *m* Roy Webb

Morgan Conway, Jane Greer, Mike Mazurki, Anne Jeffreys, Lyle Latell, Joseph Crehan, Trevor Bardette
† Sequels: *Dick Tracy vs Cueball* (1946) with Morgan Conway, *d* John Rawlins; *Dick Tracy Meets Gruesome* (1947) with Ralph Byrd, Boris Karloff, *d* John Rawlins; *Dick Tracy's Dilemma* (1947), with Ralph Byrd, *d* John Rawlins. There had been several Republic serials featuring Tracy, and in the fifties a cartoon series appeared.

Dick Turpin
GB 1933 79m bw
Stoll-Stafford (Clyde Cook)

In this version the highwayman's ride to York is to prevent an enforced marriage.
Mild British costume piece which sent its star to Hollywood.

w Victor Kendall, *novel* Rookwood by Harrison Ainsworth *d* Victor Hanbury, John Stafford

Victor McLaglen, Jane Carr, Frank Vosper, James Finlayson, Gillian Lind

The Dictator*
GB 1936 86m bw
Toeplitz
aka: *For Love of a Queen; The Loves of a Dictator*

In 18th-century Denmark, a country doctor falls in love with his queen and overthrows the mad king.
Stiff-backed middle-class romance, an

interesting example of English-German co-production at the time.

w Benn Levy, Hans Wilhelm, H. G. Lustig, Michael Hogan *d* Victor Saville, Alfred Santell

Clive Brook, Madeleine Carroll, Helen Haye, Emlyn Williams, Isabel Jeans, Alfred Drayton, Frank Cellier

Did You Hear the One about the Travelling Saleslady?
US 1967 96m Techniscope
Universal (Si Rose)

In a Kansas town in 1910 an eccentric saleslady offers pianolas which tend to go berserk.
Cornbelt comedy vehicle for an unappealing star.

w John Fenton Murray *d* Don Weis *ph* Bud Thackery *m* Vic Mizzy

Phyllis Diller, Bob Denver, Joe Flynn, Jeanette Nolan

Dieu A Besoin des Hommes*
France 1950 100m bw
Transcontinental (Paul Graetz)
aka: *Isle of Sinners; God Needs Men*

The priest of a Breton island leaves in horror at the sinfulness of his flock, and the fisherfolk appoint one of their number as priest.
Cold, gloomy, rather pointless fable, often a pleasure to look at.

w Jean Aurenche, Pierre Bost, *novel* Un Recteur de l'Ile de Sein by H. Quefflec *d* Jean Delannoy *ph* Robert Le Fèbvre *m* René Cloërc

Pierre Fresnay, Madeleine Robinson, Daniel Gélin, Andrée Clément, Sylvie, Jean Brochard

A Different Story
US 1978 106m CFI color
Avco / Alan Belkin

A homosexual falls in love with a lesbian.
One supposes it had to come, but one doesn't really have to watch it.

w Henry Olek *d* Paul Aaron *ph* Philip Lathrop *m* David Frank

Perry King, Meg Foster, Valarie Curtin, Peter Donat

Dillinger*
US 1945 70m bw
Monogram

The life of American public enemy number one who was shot by the police in 1934.
Slick, speedy gangster thriller, possibly the most tolerable movie to come from this low-budget studio.

w Philip Yordan d *Max Nosseck* ph Jackson
Rose

Lawrence Tierney, Edmund Lowe, Anne
Jeffreys

AAN: Philip Yordan

Dillinger*
US 1973   107m   Movielab
AIP (Buzz Feitshans)

Violence-soaked version, with black comedy
touches, of the last year of Dillinger's life. Not
badly done, with a style reminiscent of *Bonnie
and Clyde.*

wd *John Milius* ph Jules Brenner m Barry
Devorzon

Warren Oates, Ben Johnson (as Melvin Purvis),
Michelle Philips, Cloris Leachman, Harry Dean
Stanton, Richard Dreyfuss

Dimples**
US 1936   82m   bw
TCF (Darryl F. Zanuck, Nunnally Johnson)

In the New York Bowery in pre-Civil War days,
a child and her reprobate grandfather win the
hearts of high society.
Excellent Temple vehicle with good period
flavour.

w Arthur Sheekman, Nat Perrin d William A.
Seiter ph Bert Glennon m Louis Silvers

Shirley Temple, Frank Morgan, Helen Westley,
Berton Churchill, Robert Kent, Delma Byron,
Astrid Allwyn

Dinner at Eight***
US 1933   113m   bw
MGM

Guests at a society dinner party all find
themselves in dramatic circumstances.
Artificial but compelling pattern play from a
Broadway success.

w Frances Marion, Herman J. Mankiewicz, *play*
George S. Kaufman, Edna Ferber d George
Cukor ph William Daniels

Marie Dressler, John Barrymore, Lionel
Barrymore, Billie Burke, Wallace Beery, *Jean
Harlow,* Lee Tracy, Edmund Lowe, Madge
Evans, Jean Hersholt, Karen Morley, Louise
Closser Hale, Phillips Holmes, May Robson,
Grant Mitchell, Elizabeth Patterson

Dinner at the Ritz
GB 1937   77m   bw
New World (Robert T. Kane)

A French girl exposes swindlers who faked her
father's suicide.

Once-diverting comedy melodrama with an
international cast.

w Roland Pertwee, Romney Brent d Harold
Schuster

Annabella, Paul Lukas, David Niven, Romney
Brent, Stewart Rome, Francis L. Sullivan, Nora
Swinburne, Frederick Leister

The Dion Brothers
US 1974   96m   colour   TVM
Tomorrow (Roger Gimbel)
GB theatrical title: *The Gravy Train*

Two coal miners seek a quick fortune in the city
as armed robbers.
Adequate modern gangster stuff.

w Bill Kerby, David Whitney (Terrence Malick)
d Jack Starrett m Fred Karlin

Stacy Keach, Frederic Forrest, Margot Kidder,
Barry Primus

Diplomatic Courier*
US 1952   98m   bw
TCF (Casey Robinson)

American and Russian agents clash on a train
between Salzburg and Trieste; an unexpected
master spy is revealed after several chases.
Lively cold war intrigue, well produced and
played with relish.

w Casey Robinson, Liam O'Brien, *novel* Sinister
Errand by Peter Cheyney d Henry Hathaway
ph Lucien Ballard md Lionel Newman m Sol
Kaplan

Tyrone Power, Patricia Neal, Stephen McNally,
Hildegarde Neff, Karl Malden, James Millican,
Herbert Berghof
    'A reversion to the oldest tradition of spy
fiction.'—*Penelope Houston*

Dirigible*
US 1931   102m   bw
Columbia

The story of an airship disaster.
Economical epic with a few Capra touches.

w Jo Swerling, Dorothy Howell, *story* 'Spig'
Wead d Frank Capra ph Joe Wilbur, Elmer
Dyer

Jack Holt, Fay Wray, Ralph Graves, Hobart
Bosworth, Roscoe Karns

Dirty Dingus Magee
US 1970   91m   Metrocolor   Panavision
MGM (Burt Kennedy)

A likeable western outlaw crosses swords with
an old enemy.

Fair burlesque western often stooping to
vulgarity.

w Tom Waldman, Frank Waldman, Joseph
Heller, *novel* David Markson *d* Burt Kennedy
ph Harry Stradling *m* Jeff Alexander

Frank Sinatra, George Kennedy, Anne Jackson,
Lois Nettleton, Jack Elam, John Dehner, Henry
Jones, Harry Carey Jnr, Paul Fix

'Skittish burlesque, scripted in the brash and
undisciplined style of a TV show . . . heavily
reliant on the *Carry On* brand of humour.'—
David McGillivray

The Dirty Dozen**
US / Spain 1967   150m   Metrocolor
    70mm
MGM / Kenneth Hyman (Raymond Anzarut)

In 1944, twelve convicts serving life sentences
are recruited for a commando suicide mission.
Professional, commercial but unlikeable slice of
wartime thick ear; pretensions about capital
punishment are jettisoned early on in favour of
frequent and violent bloodshed. Much imitated,
e.g. by *The Devil's Brigade, A Reason to Live, a
Reason to Die,* etc.

w Nunnally Johnson, Lukas Heller *d Robert
Aldrich ph* Edward Scaife *m* Frank de Vol

Lee Marvin, Ernest Borgnine, Robert Ryan,
Charles Bronson, Jim Brown, John Cassavetes,
George Kennedy, Richard Jaeckel, Trini Lopez,
Telly Savalas, Ralph Meeker, Clint Walker,
Robert Webber, Donald Sutherland

AAN: John Cassavetes

Dirty Harry**
US 1971   103m   Technicolor   Panavision
Warner / Malpaso (Don Siegel)

A violently inclined San Francisco police
inspector is the only cop who can bring to book a
mad sniper. When the man is released through
lack of evidence, he takes private revenge.
A savage cop show which became a cult and led
to a spate of dirty cop movies, including two
sequels. *Magnum Force* (qv) and *The Enforcer.*
Well done for those who can take it.

w Harry Julian Fink, Rita M. Fink, Dean
Riesner *d Don Siegel ph* Bruce Surtees *m* Lalo
Schifrin

Clint Eastwood, Harry Guardino, Reni Santoni,
John Vernon, Andy Robinson, John Larch, John
Mitchum

Dirty Little Billy
US 1972   92m   Eastmancolor
Columbia / WRG / Dragoti (Jack L. Warner)
The violent young life of Billy the Kid.

Squalid little western with few attractive aspects
except that it presents its hero as the mentally
retarded delinquent which history says he was.

w Charles Moss, Stan Dragoti *d* Stan Dragoti
ph Ralph Woolsey *m* Sascha Burland

Michael J. Pollard, Lee Purcell, Richard Evans,
Charles Aidman

'The gap between its ostensible aims and its
manner of realizing them continually leaves the
film bogged down in its own scrupulously
realistic mud.'—*Tony Rayns*

Dirty Mary, Crazy Larry
US 1974   92m   De Luxe
Academy Pictures Corporation (Norman T.
Herman)

Two racing drivers and a kooky groupie rob a
supermarket and almost elude their police
pursuers.
Elaborately stunted chase film, agreeable enough
to watch if the characters were not so
disagreeable.

w Leigh Chapman, Antonio Santean, *novel* The
Chase by Richard Unekis *d* John Hough
ph Mike Margulies *m* Jimmie Haskell

Peter Fonda, Susan George, Adam Roarke, Vic
Morrow, Kenneth Tobey, Roddy McDowall,
Eugene Daniels

'The film's general delight in destruction and
despoilation makes one wonder if it is the cinema
that reflects the ugliness of modern society or the
ugliness of modern society that reflects trends in
the cinema.'—*Michael Billington, Illustrated
London News*

Dirty Work
GB 1934   78m   bw
Gaumont (Michael Balcon)

Shop assistants pose as crooks in order to catch
thieves.
Rather thin Ben Travers farce with some
authentic moments.

w Ben Travers, from his play *d* Tom Walls

Ralph Lynn, Gordon Harker, Robertson Hare,
Lillian Bond, Basil Sydney, Cecil Parker,
Margaretta Scott, Gordon James, Peter
Gawthorne

**The Discreet Charm of the
    Bourgeoisie*****
France / Spain / Italy 1972   105m
    Eastmancolor
Greenwich (Serge Silberman)
original title: *Le Charme Discret de la
    Bourgeoisie*

The efforts of a group of friends to dine together are continually frustrated.
A frequently hilarious, sometimes savage surrealist fable which makes all its points beautifully and then goes on twenty minutes too long. The performances are a joy.

w Luis Bunuel, Jean-Claude Carrière *d* Luis Bunuel *ph* Edmond Richard

Fernando Rey, Delphine Seyrig, Stéphane Audran, Bulle Ogier, Jean-Pierre Cassel, Paul Frankeur, Julien Bertheau

'A perfect synthesis of surreal wit and blistering social assault.'—*Jan Dawson, MFB*

AAN: Luis Bunuel, Jean-Claude Carrière (script)

Dishonored**
US 1931   91m   bw
Paramount

An officer's widow turned streetwalker is hired by the German government as a spy.
Rather gloomy melodrama which helped to establish its star as a top American attraction; but the heavy hand of her Svengali, Von Sternberg, was already evident.

w Daniel H. Rubin   *d* Josef Von Sternberg *ph* Lee Garmes   *m* Karl Hajos

Marlene Dietrich, Victor McLaglen, Lew Cody, Gustav Von Seyffertitz, Warner Oland, Barry Norton, Wilfred Lucas

'The most exciting movie I have seen in several months . . . yet I hope I may die young if I ever again have to listen to a manuscript so full of recusant, stilted, outmoded theatrical mouthings.'—*Pare Lorentz*
'The whole film has a kind of magnificent grandeur embellished, of course, by its shining central performance.'—*John Gillett, 1964*

Dishonored Lady
US 1947   85m   bw
Mars Film (Hedy Lamarr)

A girl with a past is cleared of a murder charge by her psychiatrist.
Melodramatic showpiece designed for herself by a glamorous star; OK for the silly season.

w Edmund H. North, *play* Edward Sheldon, Margaret Ayer Barnes   *d* Robert Stevenson *ph* Lucien Andriot

Hedy Lamarr, John Loder, Dennis O'Keefe, Paul Cavanagh, William Lundigan, Natalie Schaefer, Morris Carnovsky

Dishonour Bright*
GB 1936   82m   bw
GFD / Cecil (Herman Fellner, Max Schach)

An ageing playboy is blackmailed about a past affair.
Interesting semi-smart comedy of the period, tailored for its star.

w Ben Travers   *d* Tom Walls

Tom Walls, Eugene Pallette, Betty Stockfield, Diana Churchill, Arthur Wontner, Cecil Parker, George Sanders, Henry Oscar, Basil Radford

A Dispatch from Reuters**
US 1940   90m   bw
Warner (Hal B. Wallis)
GB title: *This Man Reuter*

The story of the man who provided Europe's first news service.
Acceptable if slightly dull addition to Warner's prestige biopics; well made and acted.

w Milton Krims   *d* William Dieterle *ph* James Wong Howe

Edward G. Robinson, Edna Best, Eddie Albert, Albert Basserman, Gene Lockhart, Otto Kruger, Montagu Love, Nigel Bruce, James Stephenson

Disputed Passage*
US 1939   90m   bw
Paramount (Harlan Thompson)

A young scientist who wants to marry meets resistance from his mentor.
Adequate screen version of a bestseller.

w Anthony Veiller, Sheridan Gibney, *novel* Lloyd C. Douglas   *d* Frank Borzage   *ph* William C. Mellor   *m* Frederick Hollander, James Leopold

Dorothy Lamour, John Howard, Akim Tamiroff, Judith Barrett, William Collier Snr, Victor Varconi, Keye Luke, Elizabeth Risdon

Disraeli*
US 1929   89m   bw
Warner

Fictionalized episodes in the life of the Victorian statesman, including his activities as a matchmaker.
Very early star talkie, of primarily archival interest; Arliss had appeared in a silent version in 1921.

w Julian Josephson, *play* Louis N. Parker *d* Alfred E. Green   *ph* Lee Garmes

George Arliss, Joan Bennett, Florence Arliss, Anthony Bushell, David Torrence, Ivan Simpson, Doris Lloyd

AA: George Arliss
AAN: best picture; Julian Josephson

Distant Drums
US 1951   101m   Technicolor
United States Pictures (Milton Sperling)

In 1840 Florida, an army officer rescues
prisoners from an Indian fort and decimates the
Seminoles who threaten their return journey.
Overlong action saga, with dull stretches
compensated by a dominating star and some
lively incident.

w Niven Busch, Martin Rackin d Raoul Walsh
ph Sid Hickox m Max Steiner

Gary Cooper, Mari Aldon, Richard Webb, Ray
Teal, Arthur Hunnicutt, Robert Barrat

A Distant Trumpet
US 1964   116m   Technicolor   Panavision
Warner (William H. Wright)

The new commander of a cavalry outpost
tightens up discipline, which serves him well
when Indian trouble erupts.
Moderate western, quite well staged but with a
second team cast.

w John Twist, novel Paul Horgan d Raoul
Walsh ph William Clothier m Max Steiner

Troy Donahue, Suzanne Pleshette, James
Gregory, Diane McBain, William Reynolds,
Claude Akins, Kent Smith, Judson Pratt

Ditte, Child of Man*
Denmark 1946   106m   bw
Nordisk
original title: Ditte Menneskebarn

An unmarried mother abandons her daughter,
who grows up to be a servant and to be seduced
in her turn.
Impressive, doom-laden Scandinavian saga,
highly thought of on its release.

wd Astrid and Bjarne Henning-Jensen,
novel Martin Andersen ph Werner Jenssen
m Herman Koppel

Tove Maes, Rasmus Ottesen, Karen Poulsen

Dive Bomber*
US 1941   133m   Technicolor
Warner (Hal B. Wallis)

Aviation scientists work to eliminate pilot
blackout.
Somewhat rarefied propaganda piece with too
many reels of romantic banter but tense
climactic scenes and good star performances.

w Frank 'Spig' Wead, Robert Buckner
d Michael Curtiz ph Bert Glennon, Winton C.
Hoch m Leo Steiner md Leo F. Forbstein

Errol Flynn, Fred MacMurray, Ralph Bellamy,
Alexis Smith, Regis Toomey, Robert

Armstrong, Allen Jenkins, Craig Stevens,
Moroni Olsen, Gig Young, William Hopper,
Charles Drake, Russell Hicks, Addison
Richards, Ann Doran, Herbert Anderson

AAN: Bert Glennon, Winton C. Hoch

The Divided Heart*
GB 1954   89m   bw
Ealing (Michael Truman)

A boy believed to be a war orphan is lovingly
brought up by foster parents; then his real
mother turns up and wants him back.
Effective 'woman's picture' set in Europe and
giving a genuine sense of post-war feelings and
problems.

w Jack Whittingham d Charles Crichton
ph Otto Heller m Georges Auric

Cornell Borchers, Yvonne Mitchell, Armin
Dahlen, Alexander Knox, Geoffrey Keen,
Michel Ray, Liam Redmond, Eddie Byrne

The Divine Lady*
US 1929   100m   bw
Warner

The adventures of Emma, Lady Hamilton.
Historical charade which titillated at the time.

w Agnes Christine Johnson, Forrest Halsey
d Frank Lloyd ph John Seitz

Corinne Griffith, Victor Varconi, H. B. Warner,
Montagu Love, Marie Dressler

AAN: Frank Lloyd; John Seitz

The Divine Woman*
US 1927   95m approx (24 fps)   bw   silent
MGM

The loves of Sarah Bernhardt.
Garbo's first star role; a typical Hollywood
melodramatization of facts.

w Dorothy Farnum, play Starlight by Gladys
Unger d Victor Sjostrom

Greta Garbo, Lars Hanson, Lowell Sherman,
John Mack Brown, Polly Moran

Divorce American Style*
US 1967   109m   Technicolor
Columbia / Tandem (Norman Lear)

Well-heeled Los Angeles suburbanites toy with
divorce but eventually resume their domestic
bickering.
Rather arid and patchy but often sharply
sardonic comedy about a society in which people
can't afford to divorce.

w Norman Lear d Bud Yorkin ph Conrad Hall
m David Grusin pd Edward Stephenson

Dick Van Dyke, Debbie Reynolds, Jean

Simmons, Jason Robards Jnr, Van Johnson, Joe Flynn, Shelley Berman, Martin Gabel, Lee Grant, Tom Bosley, Dick Gautier

AAN: Norman Lear

Divorce Italian Style**
Italy 1961   108m   bw
Lux / Vides / Galatea (Franco Cristaldi)
original title: *Divorzio all'Italiana*

A Sicilian nobleman explains how, wishing to be rid of his wife, he arranged for her to be seduced and later shot by a jealous lover.
Sardonic, stylized comedy which, rather in the manner of *Kind Hearts and Coronets*, manages while retailing a black comedy plot to satirize Italian manners and institutions.

w Ennio de Concini, Pietro Germi, Alfredo Gianetti d Piero Germi ph Leonida Barboni *m* Carlo Rustichelli

Marcello Mastroianni, Daniela Rocca, Stefania Sandrelli, Leopoldo Trieste

AAN: script; Pietro Germi; Marcello Mastroianni

The Divorce of Lady X**
GB 1937   92m   Technicolor
London Films (Alexander Korda)

A nobleman's daughter wins a barrister by posing as a divorce client.
Pleasing comedy with high production standards of its time, deftly performed by a distinguished cast.

w Lajos Biro, Arthur Wimperis, Ian Dalrymple, *play* Counsel's Opinion by Gilbert Wakefield *d Tim Whelan*

Laurence Olivier, Merle Oberon, Binnie Barnes, Ralph Richardson, Morton Selten, J. H. Roberts

The Divorcee*
US 1930   83m   bw
MGM

Would-be liberal young marrieds divorce when she puts up with his affairs but he can't tolerate hers. She falls in love with another married man but sends him back to his wife.
Rather wan illustration of the double standard which was being much discussed in society at the time.

w John Meehan, Nick Grinde, Zelda Sears, *novel* Ex-Wife by Ursula Parrott *d* Robert Z. Leonard *ph* Norbert Brodine *ad* Cedric Gibbons

Norma Shearer, Chester Morris, Conrad Nagel, Robert Montgomery, Florence Eldridge

AA: Norma Shearer

AAN: best picture; Robert Z. Leonard; John Meehan, Nick Grinde, Zelda Sears

Dixie*
US 1943   90m   Technicolor
Paramount (Paul Jones)

The life of old-time minstrel man Dan Emmett. Lighter-than-air fictionalized biography with pleasing mid-19th-century settings.

w Karl Tunberg, Darrell Ware *d* A. Edward Sutherland *ph* William C. Mellor *songs* Johnny Burke, Jimmy Van Heusen

Bing Crosby, Dorothy Lamour, Marjorie Reynolds, *Lynne Overman, Eddie Foy Jnr, Billy de Wolfe, Raymond Walburn*, Grant Mitchell

DOA**
US 1949   81m   bw
Cardinal Pictures (Leo C. Popkin)

A businessman discovers that he has effectively been murdered by a slow-acting poison. In the few hours left to him he tracks down and kills his murderer, and confesses to the police.
Unusual and effective thriller, well photographed on location in San Francisco and Los Angeles.

w Russell Rouse, Clarence Greene d Rudolph Maté *ph Ernest Laszlo m* Dmitri Tiomkin

Edmond O'Brien, Luther Adler, Pamela Britton, William Ching
† Remade 1970 as *Colour Me Dead*, with Tom Tryon.

Do Not Disturb
US 1965   102m   De Luxe   Cinemascope
TCF / Melcher / Arcola (Aaron Rosenberg, Martin Melcher)

An American wool executive is posted to London; his dizzy wife makes him jealous by flirting with a French antique dealer.
Silly farce which paints a lunatic picture of English and French life but occasionally raises a wild laugh or two. Thin script and production.

w Milt Rosen, Richard Breen, *play* William Fairchild *d* Ralph Levy *ph* Leon Shamroy *m* Lionel Newman

Doris Day, Rod Taylor, *Sergio Fantoni*, Reginald Gardiner, Hermione Baddeley, Leon Askin

Do You Like Women?
France / Italy 1964   100m   bw
Francoriz / Number One / Federiz (Pierre Kalfon)
original title: *Aimez-Vous Les Femmes?*

Secret rival sects of woman-eaters cause an outbreak of murders in Paris.

Bizarre black comedy that doesn't quite work but provides ghoulish fun along the way.

w Roman Polanski, Gérard Brach, *novel* Georges Bardawil *d* Jean Léon *ph* Sacha Vierny *m* Ward Swingle

Sophie Daumier, Guy Bédos, Edwige Feuillère, Grégoire Aslan, Roger Blin

'It has the provoking quality of a carefully-prepared firework display which, due to faulty timing or bad connections, is never actually ignited.'—*MFB*

Do You Love Me?

US 1946 91m Technicolor
TCF (George Jessel)

The lady dean of a music school gets herself glamorized.
Thin, mildly agreeable but forgettable musical.

w Robert Ellis, Helen Logan *d* Gregory Ratoff *ph* Edward Cronjager *songs* various

Maureen O'Hara, Dick Haymes, Harry James and his Orchestra, Reginald Gardiner, Richard Gaines, Stanley Prager

Doc**

US 1971 96m De Luxe
UA / Frank Perry

Doc Holliday goes to Tombstone to die of TB, but is drawn into the feud between the Clantons and his friend Wyatt Earp, whose motives are not of the highest.
A somewhat glum debunking of the west's most heroic myth, backing dour character study with grubby pictures. The result lacks excitement but maintains interest.

w Pete Hamill *d* Frank Perry *ph* Gerald Hirschfeld *m* Jimmy Webb

Stacy Keach (Doc), Harris Yulin (Earp), Faye Dunaway (Kate Elder), Mike Witney, Denver John Collins, Dan Greenberg

'The physical realism that *Doc* is at pains to establish becomes simply a convention of its own.'—*Richard Combs*

Doc Savage, Man of Bronze

US 1975 100m Technicolor
Warner (George Pal)

A thirties superman and his assistants the Amazing Five fly to South America to avenge the death of Doc's father.
Stolid, humourless adaptation from a comic strip, totally lacking in the necessary panache.

w George Pal, Joe Morhaim, *stories* Kenneth Robeson *d* Michael Anderson *ph* Fred Koenekamp *m* John Philip Sousa

Ron Ely, Paul Gleason, Bill Lucking, Michael Miller, Eldon Quick

'A slick, ultra-self-conscious camp that denies the material its self-respect.'—*Colin Pahlow*

'Nothing in this unfortunate enterprise is likely to please anyone: former Savage fans will be enraged, newcomers bored, and children will probably feel superior to the whole mess . . .'—*New Yorker*

The Dock Brief

GB 1962 88m bw
(MGM) Dimitri de Grunwald
US title: *Trial and Error*

An incompetent barrister defends his client on a murder charge. The client is found guilty but the sentence is quashed on the grounds of inadequate defence.
Flat filming of a TV play which was a minor milestone; the film is twice the length and half as funny, and both stars quickly become tiresome.

w John Mortimer, Pierre Rouve, *play* John Mortimer *d* James Hill *ph* Ted Scaife *m* Ron Grainer

Peter Sellers, Richard Attenborough

Docks of New York**

US 1928 80m (24 fps) bw silent
Paramount

A stoker marries a girl he has saved from suicide. Further unfortunate incidents result in his going to prison, but she waits for him.
Glum melodrama chiefly remarkable for its sets and lighting, reminiscent of the later *Quai des Brumes*.

w Jules Furthman, *story* The Dock Walloper by John Monk Saunders *d* Josef Von Sternberg *ph* Harold Rosson *ad* Hans Dreier

George Bancroft, Betty Compson, Olga Baclanova, Clyde Cooke, Gustav Von Seyffertitz

Dr Christian

Following the success of THE COUNTRY DOCTOR (qv), a rival studio (RKO) made a series of second features about a fictional country doctor, the rights to Dr Dafoe's life story being unavailable. Jean Hersholt again played the leading role and the films were immensely popular in small towns. A TV series followed in the fifties, starring Macdonald Carey.

1939: MEET DR CHRISTIAN
1940: THE COURAGEOUS DR CHRISTIAN, DR CHRISTIAN MEETS THE WOMEN, REMEDY FOR RICHES

1941: MELODY FOR THREE, THEY MEET
AGAIN

Dr Crippen*
GB 1962   98m   bw
ABP / John Clein

A quiet doctor murders his wife and elopes with
a typist.
Straightforward account of a famous and rather
unsurprising Edwardian murder case; well
enough made but with no special *raison d'être*.

w Leigh Vance d Robert Lynn ph Nicolas Roeg

Donald Pleasence, Coral Browne, Samantha
Eggar, Donald Wolfit

Dr Cyclops*
US 1940   76m   Technicolor
Paramount (Merian C. Cooper)

Jungle travellers are captured and miniaturized
by a mad scientist.
Splendid special effects and an appropriately
sombre atmosphere are hampered by a slow-
paced narrative in this minor horror classic.

w Tom Kilpatrick d Ernest Schoedsack
ph Henry Sharp, Winton Hoch m Ernst Toch,
Gerard Carbonera, Albert Hay Malotte

Albert Dekker, Janice Logan, Victor Kilian,
Thomas Coley, Charles Halton

Dr Dolittle
US 1967   152m   De Luxe   Todd-AO
TCF / APJAC (Arthur P. Jacobs)

In a Victorian English village, Dr Dolittle is a
veterinary surgeon who talks to his patients;
escaping from a lunatic asylum, he travels with
friends to the South Seas in search of the Great
Pink Sea Snail.
Lumpish family spectacular with no imagination
whatever, further handicapped by charmless
performances and unsingable songs.

w/songs Leslie Bricusse, novels Hugh Lofting
d Richard Fleischer ph Robert Surtees
pd Mario Chiari md Lionel Newman, Alex
Courage

Rex Harrison, Anthony Newley, Samantha
Eggar, *Richard Attenborough*, William Dix,
Peter Bull

AA: song 'Talk to the Animals'
AAN: best picture; Robert Surtees; Lionel
Newman, Alex Courage; Leslie Bricusse (m)

Dr Ehrlich's Magic Bullet***
US 1940   103m   bw
Warner (Wolfgang Reinhardt)
aka: *The Story of Dr Ehrlich's Magic Bullet*

A German scientist develops a cure for venereal
disease.
Excellent period biopic: absorbing, convincing
and extremely well put together.

w John Huston, Heinz Herald, Norman
Burnside d William Dieterle ph James Wong
Howe m Max Steiner

Edward G. Robinson, Ruth Gordon, Otto
Kruger, Donald Crisp, Maria Ouspenskaya,
Montagu Love, Sig Rumann, Donald Meek,
Henry O'Neill, Albert Basserman, Edward
Norris, Harry Davenport, Louis Calhern, Louis
Jean Heydt
    'A superb motion picture.'—*Pare Lorentz*

AAN: John Huston, Heinz Herald, Norman
Burnside

Dr Faustus
GB 1967   93m   Technicolor
Columbia / Oxford University Screen
    Productions / Nassau Films / Venfilms
    (Richard Burton, Richard McWhorter)

A medieval scholar conjures up Mephistopheles
and offers his soul in exchange for a life of
voluptuousness.
Marlowe's play has been adapted and
'improved', and there is some good handling of
the poetry, but the production is flat, dingy and
uninspired, as well as ludicrous when Miss
Taylor makes her silent appearances.

w Nevill Coghill, *play* Christopher Marlowe
d Richard Burton, Nevill Coghill ph Gabor
Pogany m Mario Nascimbene pd John de Cuir

Richard Burton, Andreas Teuber, Ian Marter,
Elizabeth Donovan, Elizabeth Taylor (as Helen
of Troy)
    'It is of an awfulness that bends the mind. The
whole enterprise has the immense vulgarity of a
collaboration in which academe would sell its
soul for a taste of the glamour of Hollywood, and
the stars are only too happy to appear a while in
academe.'—*John Simon*
    'It turns out to be the story of a man who sold
his soul for Elizabeth Taylor.'—*Judith Crist*

Dr Goldfoot and the Bikini Machine
US 1965   90m   Pathecolor   Panavision
AIP (Anthony Carras)

Dr G. makes girl robots programmed to lure
wealthy men into their clutches.
Way-out farce for the jaded end of the teenage
market; a few lively touches and a climactic
chase partly atone for the general tastelessness.

w Elwood Ullman, Robert Kaufman d Norman
Taurog ph Sam Leavitt m Les Baxter
ad Daniel Halier

Vincent Price, Fred Clark, Frankie Avalon, Dwayne Hickman, Susan Hart, Jack Mullaney

Doctor in the House **
GB 1954   91m   Eastmancolor
Rank (Betty Box)

Amorous and other misadventures of medical students at St Swithin's Hospital.
A comedy with much to answer for: several sequels and an apparently endless TV series. The original is not bad, as the students, though plainly over age, constitute a formidable mass of British talent at its peak.

w Nicholas Phipps, book Richard Gordon d Ralph Thomas *ph* Ernest Steward *m* Bruce Montgomery

Dirk Bogarde, Kenneth More, Donald Sinden, Donald Houston, Kay Kendall, Muriel Pavlow, *James Robertson Justice*, Geoffrey Keen
'Works its way with determined high spirits through the repertoire of medical student jokes.'—*MFB*
† Sequels: *Doctor at Sea* (1955) with Dirk Bogarde, *Doctor at Large* (1957) with Dirk Bogarde, *Doctor in Love* (1960) with Michael Craig, *Doctor in Distress* (1963) with Dirk Bogarde, *Doctor in Clover* (1966) with Leslie Phillips, *Doctor in Trouble* (1970) with Leslie Phillips.

Doctor in the Village *
Holland 1958   92m   bw
Nationale Filmproductie Maatschappij
  (Bobby Roosenboom)
original title: *Dorp aan de Rivier*

Stories are recalled of an eccentric but respected country doctor at the turn of the century.
Tragi-comic incidents in the vein of Pagnol, a little too rich in farce and melodrama to be convincingly human.

w Hugo Claus, *novel* Antoon Coolen *d* Fons Rademakers *ph* Eduard J. R. van der Enden *m* Jurriaan Andriessen

Max Croiset, Mary Dresselhuys, Bernhard Droog, Jan Teulings
'Scenes which should have had disturbing power crowd one upon another with an almost repellent relish which falls over into parody.'—*Peter John Dyer, MFB*

Doctor Jack *
US 1922   72m approx (24 fps)   bw   silent
Pathé / Rolin

A quack country doctor does more good than the licensed medicos.
Pleasing but not hilariously funny star vehicle.

w Sam Taylor, Jean Havez *d* Fred Newmeyer
Harold Lloyd, Mildred Davis, John Prince, Eric Mayne

Doctor Jekyll and Mr Hyde ****
US 1932   90m   bw
Paramount (Rouben Mamoulian)

A Victorian research chemist finds a formula which separates the good and evil in his soul; when the latter predominates, he becomes a rampaging monster.
The most exciting and cinematic version by far of the famous horror story; the make-up is slightly over the top, but the gas-lit London settings, the pace, the performances and clever camera and sound tricks make it a film to enjoy over and over again. Subjective camera is used at the beginning, and for the first transformation the actor wore various layers of make up which were sensitive to different colour filters and thus produced instant change.

w Samuel Hoffenstein, Percy Heath, novel Robert Louis Stevenson d Rouben Mamoulian ph Karl Struss ad Hans Dreier

Fredric March, Miriam Hopkins, Rose Hobart, Holmes Herbert, Halliwell Hobbes, Edgar Norton
'As a work of cinematic imagination this film is difficult to fault.'—*John Baxter, 1968*
† The screenplay with 1,400 frame blow-ups was published in 1976 in the Film Classics Library (editor Richard J. Anobile).
AA: Fredric March
AAN: Samuel Hoffenstein, Percy Heath; Karl Struss

Dr Jekyll and Mr Hyde **
US 1941   122m   bw
MGM (Victor Saville, Victor Fleming)

Curiously misconceived, stately, badly cast version with elaborate production including Freudian dream sequences. Always worth watching, but not a success.

w John Lee Mahin *d* Victor Fleming *ph* Joseph Ruttenberg *m* Franz Waxman

Spencer Tracy, Ingrid Bergman, Lana Turner, Ian Hunter,
C. Aubrey Smith, Donald Crisp, Sara Allgood
'Not so much evil incarnate as ham rampant . . . more ludicrous than dreadful.'—*New York Times*
† Other versions: *The Two Faces of Dr Jekyll* (1960),
I Monster (1970). Variations: *Daughter of Dr Jekyll* (1957), *Abbott and Costello Meet Dr Jekyll and Mr Hyde* (1954), *Son of Dr Jekyll* (1951), *The Ugly Duckling* (1960), *House of*

Dracula (1945), *The Nutty Professor* (1963), *Dr Jekyll and Sister Hyde* (1970).

AAN: Joseph Ruttenberg; Franz Waxman

Dr Jekyll and Sister Hyde *
GB 1971   97m   Technicolor
Hammer

A twist: Jekyll now turns into a young and beautiful woman, and kills prostitutes so that he can continue his research.
Half-successful attempt to link the legend with Jack the Ripper, killed by gore and overlength.

w Brian Clemens *d* Roy Ward Baker
ph Norman Warwick *m* David Whitaker

Ralph Bates, Martine Beswick, Gerald Sim, Lewis Fiander, Dorothy Alison

Dr Kildare
This long-running screen hero was a young intern at Blair Hospital, under the cranky tutelage of old Dr Gillespie. Created by Max Brand in a series of novels, he first appeared on the screen in a 1937 Paramount double-biller called INTERNS CAN'T TAKE MONEY, played by Joel McCrea with Barbara Stanwyck, no less, providing the love interest. Kildare came up against gangsters; Gillespie did not appear. MGM then took over the property and went to town with it, making fifteen films in nine years. They were as follows:

1938: YOUNG DR KILDARE
1939: CALLING DR KILDARE, THE SECRET OF DR KILDARE
1940: DR KILDARE'S STRANGEST CASE, DR KILDARE GOES HOME, DR KILDARE'S CRISIS
1941: DR KILDARE'S WEDDING DAY
1942: DR KILDARE'S VICTORY, CALLING DR GILLESPIE
1943: DR GILLESPIE'S NEW ASSISTANT, DR GILLESPIE'S CRIMINAL CASE
1944: THREE MEN IN WHITE, BETWEEN TWO WOMEN
1947: DARK DELUSION

Lew Ayres played Kildare, but in 1942 declared himself a conscientious objector and was dropped. The emphasis shifted to Gillespie, played by Lionel Barrymore from a wheelchair, and he proceeded to deal with a whole series of interns. The films were well enough made on medium budgets; nine were directed by Harold S. Buquet and the last five by Willis Goldbeck, one by W. S. Van Dyke. In 1961 a TV series began with Richard Chamberlain and Raymond Massey, and ran for seven years.

Doctor Mabuse ***
Germany 1922   101m (24 fps)   bw   silent
UFA
original title: *Doktor Mabuse, der Spieler*

A criminal mastermind uses hypnotism and blackmail in his efforts to obtain world domination, but when finally cornered is discovered to be a raving maniac.
A real wallow in German post-war depression and melodrama, in the form of a Fu Manchu/Moriarty type thriller. Fascinating scene by scene, but by now a slightly tiresome whole.

w Thea Von Harbou, Fritz Lang, *novel* Norbert Jacques *d Fritz Lang ph* Carl Hoffman *ad* Otto Hunte, Stahl-Urach, Erich Kettelhut, Karl Vollbrecht

Rudolph Klein-Rogge, Alfred Abel, Gertrude Welcker, Lil Dagover, Paul Richter
† Originally issued in Germany in two parts, *Der Grosse Spieler* and *Inferno*, adding up to a much longer running time.
†† See sequels, *The Testament of Dr Mabuse* and *The Thousand Eyes of Dr Mabuse*.

Doctor No ***
GB 1962   111m   Technicolor
UA / Eon (Harry Saltzman, Albert R. Broccoli)

A British secret service agent foils a master criminal operating in the West Indies.
First of the phenomenally successful James Bond movies, mixing sex, violence and campy humour against expensive sets and exotic locales. Toned down from the original novels, they expressed a number of sixties attitudes, and proved unstoppable box office attractions for nearly fifteen years. The first was, if not quite the best, reasonably representative of the series.

w Richard Maibaum, Johanna Harwood, Berkely Mather, *novel* Ian Fleming *d* Terence Young *ph* Ted Moore *m Monty Norman*

Sean Connery, Ursula Andress, Jack Lord, Joseph Wiseman, John Kitzmiller, Bernard Lee, Lois Maxwell, Zena Marshall, Eunice Gayson, Anthony Dawson
† The subsequent titles, all qv, were *From Russia with Love* (1963), *Goldfinger* (1964), *Thunderball* (1965), *You Only Live Twice* (1967), *On Her Majesty's Secret Service* (1969), *Diamonds Are Forever* (1971), *Live and Let Die* (1973), *The Man with the Golden Gun* (1974). *Casino Royale* (1967) was a Bond spoof made by other hands.

Dr Phibes Rises Again *
GB 1972   89m   De Luxe
AIP (Richard Dalton)

The immortal Phibes and his wife rise from the dead to seek an Egyptian elixir of life, and cross swords with a satanic Egyptologist.
Uncertainly paced but generally zippy comic strip for adults, with all concerned entering gleefully into the evil spirit of the thing. See prequel, *The Abominable Dr Phibes*.

w Robert Fuest, Robert Blees d Robert Fuest
ph Alex Thomson m John Gale ad Brian Eatwell

Vincent Price, Robert Quarry, Valli Kemp, Fiona Lewis, Peter Cushing, Beryl Reid, Terry-Thomas, Hugh Griffith, *Peter Jeffrey*, Gerald Sim, John Thaw, John Cater, Lewis Fiander

'It's refreshing to find a sequel which is better than its prototype.'—*Philip Strick, MFB*

Dr Socrates**
US 1935   70m   bw
Warner (Robert Lord)

A small-town doctor is forced to help wounded gangsters, and becomes involved.
Good star melodrama.

w Robert Lord, *novel* W. R. Burnett d William Dieterle ph Tony Gaudio md Leo F. Forbstein

Paul Muni, Ann Dvorak, Barton Maclane, Robert Barrat, John Eldridge, Hobart Cavanaugh, Mayo Methot, Samuel S. Hinds, Henry O'Neill
† Remade as *King of the Underworld* and *Bullet Scars*.

Dr Strangelove; or, How I Learned to Stop Worrying and Love the Bomb***
GB 1963   93m   bw
Columbia / Stanley Kubrick (Victor Lyndon)

A mad USAF general launches a nuclear attack on Russia, and when recall attempts fail, and retaliation is inevitable, all concerned sit back to await the destruction of the world.
Black comedy resolving itself into a series of sketches, with the star playing three parts (for no good reason): the US president, an RAF captain, and a mad German-American scientist. Historically an important film in its timing, its nightmares being those of the early sixties, artistically it clogs its imperishable moments by untidy narrative and unattractively contrasty photography.

w Stanley Kubrick, Terry Southern, Peter George, *novel* Red Alert by Peter George
d Stanley Kubrick ph Gilbert Taylor m Laurie Johnson ad Ken Adam

Peter Sellers, George C. Scott, Peter Bull, Sterling Hayden, Keenan Wynn, Slim Pickens, James Earl Jones, Tracy Reed
† *Fail Safe* (qv), which took the same theme

more seriously, was released almost simultaneously.

AAN: best picture; script; Stanley Kubrick (as director); Peter Sellers

Dr Syn*
GB 1937   80m   bw
Gaumont

The vicar of Dymchurch in 1780 is really a pirate believed dead.
This now obscure, lively pirate yarn was its star's last film.

w Michael Hogan, Roger Burford, *novel* Russell Thorndike d Roy William Neill ph Jack Cox md Louis Levy

George Arliss, Margaret Lockwood, John Loder, Roy Emerton, Graham Moffatt, Frederick Burtwell, Meinhart Maur, George Merritt

Dr Syn Alias the Scarecrow
GB 1962   98m   Technicolor
Walt Disney (Bill Anderson)

The vicar of Dymchurch is really a smuggler who manages to outwit a rascally general and save a prisoner from Dover Castle.
Oddly released the same year as another version of the story, *Captain Clegg*, this rather set-bound adventure yarn turns its hero into a Robin Hood figure. It was originally made to be shown in three parts on American TV.

w Robert Westerby, *novel* Christopher Syn by Russell Thorndike, William Buchanan d James Neilson ph Paul Beeson m Gerard Schurmann

Patrick McGoohan, George Cole, Tony Britton, Geoffrey Keen, Kay Walsh, Patrick Wymark, Alan Dobie, Eric Pohlmann

The Doctor Takes a Wife*
US 1940   89m   bw
Columbia (William Perlberg)

A young doctor has to pretend to be the husband of a socialite.
Typical high life comedy of its period, quite brisk and diverting.

w George Seaton, Ken Englund d Alexander Hall ph Sid Hickox m Frederick Hollander md Morris Stoloff

Loretta Young, Ray Milland, Edmund Gwenn, Reginald Gardiner, Gail Patrick, Frank Sully, George Metaxa, Charles Halton, Chester Clute

Dr Terror's House of Horrors
GB 1965   98m   Techniscope
Amicus (Milton Subotsky)

An eccentric, who turns out to be Death himself, tells the fortunes of five men in a railway carriage.

One of the first Amicus horror compendiums and a weak one, not helped by wide screen, a couple of naïve scripts and ho-hum acting. The book-ends are quite pleasant, though.

w Milton Subotsky *d* Freddie Francis *ph* Alan Hume *m* Elisabeth Lutyens

Peter Cushing, Ursula Howells, Max Adrian, Roy Castle, Alan Freeman, Bernard Lee, Jeremy Kemp, Kenny Lynch, Christopher Lee, Michael Gough, Donald Sutherland
† Later collections from the same stable include *Torture Garden, Tales from the Crypt, Vault of Horror* and *Asylum.*

Dr Who and the Daleks

GB 1965   83m   Techniscope
British Lion / Regal / Aaru (Milton Subotsky,
   Max J. Rosenberg)

Three children and their grandfather accidentally start his time machine and are whisked away to a planet where villainous robots rule.

Junior science fiction from the BBC series. Limply put together, and only for indulgent children.

w Milton Subotsky *d* Gordon Flemyng *ph* John Wilcox *m* Malcolm Lockyer

Peter Cushing, Roy Castle, Jennie Linden, Roberta Tovey, Barrie Ingham
† A sequel, no better, emerged in 1966: *Daleks: Invasion Earth 2150 AD,* with similar credits except that Bernard Cribbins instead of Roy Castle provided comic relief.

Dr X **

US 1932   82m   Technicolor
Warner

A reporter investigates a series of moon murders and narrows his search to one of several doctors at a medical college.

Fascinating, German-inspired, overblown and generally enjoyable horror mystery whose armless villain commits murders by growing limbs from 'synthetic flesh'.

w Earl Baldwin, Robert Tasker, *play* Howard W. Comstock, Allen C. Miller *d* Michael Curtiz *ph* Richard Tower, Ray Rennahan

Lee Tracy, Lionel Atwill, Preston Foster, Fay Wray, George Rosener, Mae Busch, Arthur Edmund Carewe, John Wray
'The settings, lighting and final battle with the man-monster are quite stunning.'—*NFT, 1974*

Doctor You've Got to be Kidding

US 1967   93m   Metrocolor   Panavision
MGM / Trident (Douglas Laurence)

A girl arrives at a maternity hospital chased by three prospective husbands.

Wild and wacky farce which leaves little impression.

w Phillip Shuken, *novel* Patte Wheat Mahan *d* Peter Tewkesbury *ph* Fred Koenekamp *m* Kenyon Hopkins

Sandra Dee, George Hamilton, Celeste Holm, Bill Bixby, *Dwayne Hickman,* Dick Kallman, Mort Sahl, Allen Jenkins

Doctor Zhivago ***

US 1965   192m   Technicolor   Panavision
70
MGM / Carlo Ponti

A Moscow doctor is caught up in World War I, exiled for writing poetry, forced into partisan service and separated from his only love.

Beautifully photographed and meticulously directed, this complex epic has been so reduced from the original novel that many parts of the script simply do not make any kind of sense. What remains is a collection of expensive set pieces, great for looking at if not listening.

w Robert Bolt, *novel* Boris Pasternak *d* David Lean *ph* Frederick A. Young *m* Maurice Jarre

Omar Sharif, Julie Christie, Rod Steiger, Alec Guinness, Rita Tushingham, Ralph Richardson, Tom Courtenay, Geraldine Chaplin, Siobhan McKenna, Noel Willman, Geoffrey Keen, Adrienne Corri
'A long haul along the road of synthetic lyricism.'—*MFB*
'David Lean's *Doctor Zhivago* does for snow what his *Lawrence of Arabia* did for sand.'—*John Simon*
'It isn't shoddy (except for the music); it isn't soap opera; it's stately, respectable, and dead.'—*Pauline Kael*

AA: Robert Bolt; Frederick A. Young; Maurice Jarre
AAN: best picture; David Lean; Tom Courtenay

The Doctor's Dilemma *

GB 1958   99m   Metrocolor
MGM / Anatole de Grunwald

Eminent Harley Street surgeons debate the case of a devoted wife and her tubercular artist husband.

Well acted but curiously muffled filming of Shaw's Edwardian play about ethics and human values.

w Anatole de Grunwald, *play* Bernard Shaw
d Anthony Asquith *ph* Robert Krasker
m Joseph Kosma *ad* Paul Sheriff

Leslie Caron, Dirk Bogarde, *John Robinson*,
Alastair Sim, Felix Aylmer, Robert Morley,
Michael Gwynn, Maureen Delany, Alec
McCowen

Doctors' Wives

US 1970   102m   Eastmancolor
Columbia / M. J. Frankovich

When Dr Dellman shoots his unfaithful wife, his
colleagues reconsider their sex lives.
Adult soap opera from talents who at other times
have found better things to do. In the sensational
circumstances, two sanguinary operation
sequences are tastelessly irrelevant.

w Daniel Taradash, *novel* Frank G. Slaughter
d George Schaefer *ph* Charles B. Lang
m Elmer Bernstein

Richard Crenna, Janice Rule, Gene Hackman,
John Colicos, Dyan Cannon, Diana Sands,
Rachel Roberts, Carroll O'Connor, Cara
Williams, Ralph Bellamy, Richard Anderson
  'Crisis follows hard on crisis to breathlessly
ludicrous effect.'—*Tom Milne*

Dodge City***

US 1939   104m   Technicolor
Warner (Robert Lord)

An ex-soldier and trail boss helps clean up the
west's great railroad terminus.
Standard, satisfying big-scale western with all
clichés intact and very enjoyable, as is the soft,
rich early colour. The story is plainly inspired by
the exploits of Wyatt Earp.

w Robert Buckner *d Michael Curtiz ph Sol
Polito, Ray Rennahan m* Max Steiner

Errol Flynn, Olivia de Havilland, Ann Sheridan,
Bruce Cabot, Alan Hale, Frank McHugh, John
Litel, Victor Jory, William Lundigan, Henry
Travers, Henry O'Neill, Guinn Williams, Gloria
Holden

Dodsworth***

US 1936   101m   bw
Samuel Goldwyn

An American businessman takes his wife on a
tour of Europe, and their lives are changed.
Satisfying, well-acted drama from a bestselling
novel; production values high.

*w Sidney Howard, novel Sinclair Lewis
d William Wyler ph* Rudolph Maté *m* Alfred
Newman

Walter Huston, Mary Astor, Ruth Chatterton,
David Niven, Paul Lukas, Gregory Gaye, *Maria*

Ouspenskaya, Odette Myrtil, Spring Byington,
John Payne

AAN: best picture; Sidney Howard; William
Wyler; Walter Huston; Maria Ouspenskaya

Dog Day Afternoon**

US 1975   130m   Technicolor
Warner / AEC (Martin Bregman, Martin
  Elfland)

Two incompetent robbers are cornered in a
Brooklyn bank.
Recreation of a tragi-comic episode from the
newspaper headlines; for half its length a
fascinating and acutely observed film which then
bogs itself down in a surplus of talk and excessive
sentiment about homosexuality.

w Frank Pierson, *book* Patrick Mann *d Sidney
Lumet ph* Victor J. Kemper *m* none
Al Pacino, John Cazale, *Charles Durning*, Sully
Boyar, James Broderick, *Chris Sarandon*
  'There is plenty of Lumet's vital best here in a
film that at least glancingly captures the
increasingly garish pathology of our urban
life.'—*Jack Kroll*
  'Scattered moments of wry humour, sudden
pathos and correct observation.'—*John Simon*
  'The mask of frenetic cliché doesn't spoil
moments of pure reporting on people in
extremity.'—*New Yorker*
  'A long and wearying case history of the
beaten, sobbing, despairing and ultimately
powerless anti-hero.'—*Karyn Kay, Jump Cut*
  'Full of galvanic mirth rooted in human
desperation.'
—*Michael Billington, Illustrated London News*

AA: Frank Pierson
AAN: best picture; Sidney Lumet; Al Pacino;
Chris Sarandon

A Dog of Flanders

US 1959   97m   De Luxe   Cinemascope
TCF / Associated Producers (Robert B.
  Radnitz)

A small boy wants to be an artist; when he runs
away in frustration, his shaggy dog, formerly a
stray, leads his family to him.
Old-fashioned tear-jerker for well-brought-up
children, previously filmed as a silent; quite
accomplished in presentation.

w Ted Sherdeman, *novel* Ouida *d* James B.
Clark *ph* Otto Heller *m* Paul Sawtell, Bert
Shefter

David Ladd, Donald Crisp, Theodore Bikel,
Max Croiset, Monique Ahrens

A Dog's Life*
US 1918   30m approx   bw   silent
First National

A tramp and a stray mongrel help each other
towards a happy ending.
Threatening sentiment is kept at bay by amusing
sight gags in this pleasing star featurette.

wd Charles Chaplin ph Rollie Totheroh

Charles Chaplin, Edna Purviance, Chuck
Riesner, Henry Bergman, Albert Austin, Scraps

La Dolce Vita**
Italy / France 1960   173m   bw
   Totalscope
Riama / Pathé Consortium (Giuseppe Amato)
aka: *The Sweet Life*

A journalist mixes in modern Roman high
society and is alternately bewitched and sickened
by what he sees.
Episodic satirical melodrama, a marathon self-
indulgent wallow with a wagging finger never far
away. Not a successful whole, but full of choice
moments such as a statue of Christ being flown
by helicopter over the city.

w Federico Fellini, Tullio Pinelli, Ennio Flaiano,
Brunello Rondi *d Federico Fellini ph* Otello
Martelli *m* Nino Rota *ad* Piero Gherardi

Marcello Mastroianni, Anita Ekberg, Anouk
Aimée, Alain Cuny, Yvonne Furneaux, Magali
Noel, Nadia Gray, Lex Barker

   'Its personification of various familiar
symbols—love, death, purity, sin, reason and so
on—never succeeds in reflecting human values
or creating intellectual excitement . . . Its actual
significance rests in the way its (albeit specious)
social attack has stirred the imagination of other
Italian film-makers, as well as public interest in
their work.'—*Robert Vas, MFB*

AAN: best film; script

Doll Face
US 1945   80m   bw
TCF (Bryan Foy)

A burlesque queen goes to Broadway.
Lower case musical of minimal interest.

w Leonard Praskins *d* Lewis Seiler *ph* Joseph
La Shelle *songs* Harold Adamson, Jimmy
McHugh

Vivian Blaine, Dennis O'Keefe, Carmen
Miranda, Perry Como, Martha Stewart, Michael
Dunne, Reed Hadley, George E. Stone, Donald
McBride, Edgar Norton

Dollars*
US 1971   120m   Technicolor
Columbia / M. J. Frankovich
GB title: *The Heist*

An American security expert installs an
electronic system in a Hamburg bank which he
plans to rob himself.
Overlong caper comedy-drama which is quite
good to watch when it starts moving, though the
quick cutting, short takes and deliberately
obscure narrative leave one breathless.

wd Richard Brooks *ph* Petrus Schloemp
m Quincy Jones

Warren Beatty, Goldie Hawn, Gert Frobe,
Robert Webber, Scott Brady, Arthur Brauss

   'An essay in virtuoso film construction . . .
rather as if one were watching a perfect machine
in full throttle but with nowhere to go.'—*John
Gillet*

A Doll's House*
GB 1973   95m   Eastmancolor
Elkins / Freeward (Hillard Elkins)

A wife begins to resist her husband's will.
Ibsen's feminist play was always good value; set
in Norway in the nineties, it was taken up eighty
years later as a precursor of women's lib, which
accounts for two film versions in one year. This
one is simply staged and well performed, but
suffers from a bad translation.

w Christopher Hampton, *play* Henrik Ibsen
d Patrick Garland *ph* Arthur Ibbetson *m* John
Barry

Claire Bloom, Anthony Hopkins,
Ralphchardson, Denholm Elliott, Anna Massey,
Edith Evans

A Doll's House
GB / France 1973   106m   Eastmancolor
World Film Services / Les Films de la Boétie
   (Joseph Losey)

Opened out but less effective version of the
above, with too much solemnity and the central
part miscast.

w David Mercer, *play* Henrik Ibsen *d* Joseph
Losey *ph* Gerry Fisher *m* Michel Legrand

Jane Fonda, David Warner, Trevor Howard,
Edward Fox, Delphine Seyrig, Anna Wing

The Dolly Sisters**
US 1945   114m   Technicolor
TCF (George Jessel)

The lives of a Hungarian sister act in American
vaudeville.
Fictionalized biographical musical, only fair in
the script department but glittering to look at in

superb colour, and enriched by splendid production values. Undoubtedly among the best of its kind.

w John Larkin, Marian Spitzer *d* Irving Cummings *ph Ernest Palmer* md Alfred Newman, Charles Henderson *songs* various *ch* Seymour Felix *ad Lyle Wheeler, Leland Fuller*

Betty Grable, June Haver, John Payne, S. Z. Sakall, Reginald Gardiner, Frank Latimore, Gene Sheldon, Sig Rumann, Trudy Marshall

AAN: song 'I Can't Begin to Tell You' (*m* Johnny Monaco, *ly* Mack Gordon)

The Domino Principle
US 1977 100m CFI color
Associated General Films (Lew Grade, Martin Starger) / Stanley Kramer
GB title: *The Domino Killings*

A murderer is offered his freedom if he will assassinate a national figure.
Fashionable, complex and rather boring political thriller.

w Adam Kennedy, from his novel *d* Stanley Kramer *ph* Fred Koenekamp, Ernest Laszlo *m* Billy Goldenberg

Gene Hackman, Richard Widmark, Candice Bergen, Mickey Rooney, Edward Albert, Eli Wallach, Ken Swofford, Neva Patterson

Don Camillo's Last Round*
Italy 1955 98m bw
Rizzoli
original title: *Don Camillo e l'Onorevole Peppone*

The village Catholic priest tries to stop the re-election of the communist mayor.
Pleasant third collection of encounters with familiar characters.

w Giovanni Guareschi and others, from his books *d* Carmine Gallone *ph* Anchise Brizzi *m* Alessandro Cicognini

Fernandel, Gino Cervi, Claude Silvain, Leda Gloria

'The episodic narrative is full of mildly amusing incident.'—*MFB*

The Don is Dead
US 1973 117m Technicolor
Universal / Hal B. Wallis (Paul Nathan)

Cross and double cross among Mafia families.
A failed attempt to cash in on *The Godfather*, this endless melodrama is boringly violent and totally predictable.

w Marvin H. Albert, from his novel *d* Richard

Fleischer *ph* Richard H. Kline *m* Jerry Goldsmith

Anthony Quinn, Frederic Forrest, Robert Forster, Al Lettieri, Angel Tompkins, Charles Cioffi

Don Q Son of Zorro*
US 1925 170m (16 fps) bw silent
United Artists

Further adventures in the manner of the star's 1920 hit (see *The Mark of Zorro*).

w K. and H. Pritchard *d* Donald Crisp

Douglas Fairbanks, Mary Astor, Donald Crisp, Jack McDonald, Jean Hersholt

Don Quixote*
France 1933 82m bw
Vandor / Nelson / Wester

An adequate potted version starring Fedor Chaliapin and in the English version George Robey (French version: Dorville).

w Paul Morand, Alexandre Arnoux, from Cervantes *d* G. W. Pabst *ph* Nikolas Farkas, Paul Portier *ad* André Andreiev *m* Jacques Ibert

Don Quixote**
USSR 1957 105m Agfacolor Sovscope
Lenfilm

An extremely handsome version with a commanding star performance.

w E. Schwarz *d* Grigori Kozintsev *ph* Andrei Moskvin, Apollinari Dudko *ad* Yevgeny Yenei *m* Kara-Karayev

Nikolai Cherkassov, Yuri Tolubeyev
† Other versions came from France in 1902 and 1908, Italy in 1910, France in 1911, USA in 1915, Britain in 1923, Denmark in 1926, Spain in 1927, Britain in 1972, and Britain (ballet version with Nureyev) in 1975.

Donovan's Brain*
US 1953 81m bw
UA / Dowling (Tom Gries)

An unscrupulous tycoon is fatally injured, but his brain is kept alive by a surgeon who finds himself dominated by it.
Modest competence marks this version of a much filmed novel, with quiet suspense and a firm central performance.

w Felix Feist, *novel* Curt Siodmak *d* Felix Feist *ph* Joseph Biroc *m* Eddie Dunstedter

Lew Ayres, Gene Evans, Nancy Davis, Steve Brodie, Lisa K. Howard

Donovan's Reef
US 1963   108m   Technicolor
Paramount (John Ford)

War veterans settle down on a South Sea island;
when the daughter of one of them comes to visit,
his reputation must be protected.
Good-humoured but finally enervating mixture
of rough-house and slapstick, with the
appearance of an old friends' benefit and the
director in familiar sub-standard form.

w Frank Nugent, James Edward Grant d John
Ford ph William H. Clothier m Cyril
Mockridge

John Wayne, Lee Marvin, Jack Warden,
Elizabeth Allen, Dorothy Lamour, Cesar
Romero, Mike Mazurki

Don't Bother to Knock*
US 1952   76m   bw
TCF (Julian Blaustein)

A deranged girl gets a baby-sitting job in a hotel
and terrifies all concerned by threatening to kill
her charge.
Curious vehicle for the emergent Monroe, who is
not up to it, as who would be? Technical credits
par, but entertainment value small.

w Daniel Taradash, novel Charlotte Armstrong
d Roy Baker ph Lucien Ballard m Lionel
Newman

Marilyn Monroe, Richard Widmark, Anne
Bancroft, Donna Corcoran, Jeanne Cagney,
Lurene Tuttle, Jim Backus, Elisha Cook Jnr

Don't Bother to Knock
GB 1961   89m   Technicolor
Cinemascope
ABP / Haileywood (Frank Godwin)
US title: Why Bother to Knock

A Casanova travel agent gives each of his girl
friends a key to his Edinburgh flat.
Poorly developed and self-conscious sex farce.

w Dennis Cannan, Frederick Gotfurt, Frederic
Raphael, novel Clifford Hanley d Cyril Frankel
ph Geoffrey Unsworth m Elisabeth Lutyens

Richard Todd, Judith Anderson, Elke Sommer,
June Thorburn, Nicole Maurey, Rik Battaglia,
Eleanor Summerfield, John Le Mesurier

Don't Go Near the Water*
US 1957   107m   Metrocolor
Cinemascope
MGM (Lawrence Weingarten)

The US Navy sets up a public relations unit on a
South Pacific island.
Loosely cemented service farce full of fumbling
lieutenants and bumbling commanders, a more

light-hearted M*A*S*H. Boring romantic
interludes separate some very funny farcical
sequences.

w Dorothy Kingsley, George Wells, novel
William Brinkley d Charles Walters ph Robert
Bronner m Bronislau Kaper

Glenn Ford, Fred Clark, Gia Scala, Romney
Brent, Mickey Shaughnessey, Earl Holliman,
Anne Francis, Keenan Wynn, Eva Gabor, Russ
Tamblyn, Jeff Richards, Mary Wickes

Don't Just Stand There
US 1967   99m   Techniscope
Universal (Stan Margulies)

A mild-mannered watch smuggler gets himself
involved with kidnapping, murder, and finishing
a sex novel.
Frantic but ineffective farce which keeps on the
move but does not arrive anywhere.

w Charles Williams, from his novel The Wrong
Venus d Ron Winston ph Milton Krasner
m Nick Perito

Mary Tyler Moore, Robert Wagner, Barbara
Rhoades, Glynis Johns, Harvey Korman
  'Paris locations might have helped, but we're
stuck with the San Fernando Valley.'—Robert
Windeler

Don't Look Now***
GB 1973   110m   Technicolor
BL / Casey / Eldorado (Peter Katz)

After the death of their small daughter, the
Baxters meet in Venice two old sisters who claim
mediumistic connection with the dead girl. The
husband scorns the idea, but repeatedly sees a
little red-coated figure in shadowy passages by
the canals. When he confronts it, it proves to be a
maniac dwarf who stabs him to death.
A macabre short story has become a pretentious
and puzzling piece of high cinema art full of
vague suggestions and unexplored avenues.
Whatever its overall deficiencies, it is too brilliant
in surface detail to be dismissed. Depressingly
but fascinatingly set in wintry Venice, it has to be
seen to be appreciated.

w Allan Scott, Chris Bryant, story Daphne du
Maurier d Nicolas Roeg ph Anthony
Richmond m Pino D'Onnagio ad Giovanni
Soccol

Donald Sutherland, Julie Christie, Hilary
Mason, Clelia Matania, Massimo Serrato
  'The fanciest, most carefully assembled
enigma yet seen on the screen.'—New Yorker
  'A powerful and dazzling visual texture.'—
Penelope Houston

Don't Look Now . . . We're Being Shot At!*

France 1966   130m   Eastmancolor
Panavision
Les Films Corona (Robert Dorfmann)
original title: *La Grande Vadrouille*

During World War II three members of a British bomber crew bale out over Paris and make a frantic escape to the free zone by means of various wild disguises.

Freewheeling star farce, a shade lacking in control, but with some funny sequences.

wd Gérard Oury *ph* Claude Renoir *m* Georges Auric

Terry-Thomas, Bourvil, Louis de Funès, Claudio Brook, Mike Marshall

'Both the sight gags and the characters evoke pale echoes of Laurel and Hardy, but it is not familiarity that breeds contempt here so much as the debasement of the familiar.'—*MFB*

Don't Make Waves

US 1967   97m   Metrocolor   Panavision
MGM / Filmways (Julian Bercovici)

A swimming-pool salesman attempts to get his own back on an impulsive young woman who has wrecked his car.

Malibu beach farce for immature adults, made by professionals helpless in the face of a weak script, but boasting a funny climax with a house teetering on the edge of a cliff.

w Ira Wallach, George Kirgo, *novel* Muscle Beach by Ira Wallach *d* Alexander Mackendrick *ph* Philip Lathrop *m* Vic Mizzy

Tony Curtis, Claudia Cardinale, Robert Webber, Joanna Barnes, Sharon Tate, Jim Backus, Mort Sahl

Don't Raise the Bridge, Lower the River

GB 1967   100m   Technicolor
Columbia / Walter Shenson

An American turns his English wife's home into a discotheque.

Dreary comedy apparently intent on proving that its star can be just as unfunny abroad as at home.

w Max Wilk *d* Jerry Paris *ph* Otto Heller *m* David Whitaker

Jerry Lewis, Terry-Thomas, Jacqueline Pearce, Bernard Cribbins, Patricia Routledge, Nicholas Parsons, Michael Bates

Don't Take it to Heart*

GB 1944   90m   bw
GFD / Two Cities (Sydney Box)

A genial castle ghost is unleashed by a bomb and affects the love affair of a researcher with the daughter of the house.

Amiably lunatic British-upper-class extravaganza with eccentric characters and some felicitous moments.

wd Jeffrey Dell

Richard Greene, *Edward Rigby*, Patricia Medina, Alfred Drayton, Richard Bird, Wylie Watson, Moore Marriott, Brefni O'Rourke, Amy Veness, Claude Dampier, Joan Hickson, Joyce Barbour, Ronald Squire, Ernest Thesiger

'A cheerful and rewarding entertainment.'— *Richard Mallett, Punch*

Doomwatch

GB 1972   92m   colour
Tigon (Tony Tenser)

An investigator of coastal pollution discovers a village in which dumped chemicals have given all the inhabitants a distorting disease called acromegaly.

An unsatisfactory horror film is drawn from a moderately serious TV series about ecology.

w Clive Exton *d* Peter Sasdy *ph* Kenneth Talbot *m* John Scott

Ian Bannen, Judy Geeson, John Paul, Simon Oates, George Sanders, Percy Herbert, Geoffrey Keen, Joseph O'Conor

The Door in the Wall*

GB 1956   29m   Technicolor   Vistavision
AB Pathé / BFI / Lawrie (Howard Thomas)

A man is obsessed by a childhood dream of a green door which leads into a beautiful garden. The story is chosen to experiment with Dynamic Frame, a system in which the picture changes shape and size according to the subject matter. In this case the results are entertaining enough.

wd Glenn H. Alvey Jnr ph Jo Jago *m* James Bernard

Stephen Murray, Ian Hunter

The Door with Seven Locks

GB 1940   89m   bw
Rialto (John Argyle)
US title: *Chamber of Horrors*

A mad doctor abducts an heiress in the hope of gaining her wealth.

Old-fashioned barnstormer, ineptly made.

w Norman Lee, John Argyle, Gilbert Gunn, *novel* Edgar Wallace *d* Norman Lee

Leslie Banks, Lilli Palmer, Romilly Lunge, Gina Malo, Richard Bird, David Horne, Cathleen Nesbitt

Dosshouse*

GB 1933   53m   bw
Sound City

An escaped convict is captured by a reporter and detective posing as tramps.

Low-budget featurette which deserves a footnote in film history for its social consciousness, rare at the time, especially in the dosshouse scenes.

w Herbert Ayres   d John Baxter

Frank Cellier, Arnold Bell, Herbert Franklyn, J. Hubert Leslie

Double Confession

GB 1950   85m   bw
ABP / Harry Reynolds

At a seaside resort, a man finds his wife dead and tries to frame her lover, but becomes confused with two real murderers with a different purpose.

Confused and unlikely melodrama which signally lacks the ancient mariner's eye.

w William Templeton, novel All on a Summer's Day by John Garden   d Ken Annakin
ph Geoffrey Unsworth   m Benjamin Franklin

Derek Farr, Peter Lorre, William Hartnell, Joan Hopkins, Naunton Wayne, Ronald Howard, Kathleen Harrison, Leslie Dwyer, Edward Rigby

Double Dynamite

US 1951 (produced 1948)   80m   bw
RKO (Irving Cummings)
aka: It's Only Money

A bank teller wins a fortune at the race track but is afraid his winnings will be thought the proceeds of a bank robbery.

Insultingly mild comedy, nearly saved by a few quips from Groucho.

w Melville Shavelson, Harry Crane, Leo Rosten
d Irving Cummings   ph Robert de Grasse
m Leigh Harline

Frank Sinatra, Jane Russell, Groucho Marx, Don McGuire, Howard Freeman

Double Indemnity****

US 1944   107m   bw
Paramount (Joseph Sistrom)

An insurance agent connives with the glamorous wife of a client to kill her husband and collect.

Archetypal film noir of the forties, brilliantly filmed and incisively written, perfectly capturing the decayed Los Angeles atmosphere of a Chandler novel but using a simpler story and more substantial characters. The hero/villain was almost a new concept.

w Billy Wilder, Raymond Chandler, novel

James M. Cain   d Billy Wilder   ph John Seitz
m Miklos Rozsa

Fred MacMurray, Barbara Stanwyck, Edward G. Robinson, Tom Powers, Porter Hall, Jean Heather, Byron Barr, Richard Gaines

'The sort of film which revives a critic from the depressive effects of bright epics about the big soul of America or the suffering soul of Europe and gives him a new lease of faith.'—Richard Winnington

'Masturbation fantasy triple distilled.'—James Agee

'The most pared-down and purposeful film ever made by Billy Wilder.'—John Coleman, 1966

'Profoundly, intensely entertaining,'—Richard Mallett, Punch

AAN: best picture; Billy Wilder, Raymond Chandler; John Seitz; Miklos Rozsa; Barbara Stanwyck

A Double Life**

US 1947   103m   bw
Kanin Productions

An actor playing Othello is obsessed by the role and murders a woman he imagines to be Desdemona.

An old theatrical chestnut (cf Men Are Not Gods) is decked out with smartish backstage dialogue but despite a pleasant star performance remains unrewarding if taxing, and the entertainment value of the piece is on the thin side considering the mighty talents involved

w Ruth Gordon, Garson Kanin   d George Cukor   ph Milton Krasner   m Miklos Rozsa

Ronald Colman, Shelley Winters, Signe Hasso, Edmond O'Brien, Millard Mitchell

AA: Miklos Rozsa; Ronald Colman
AAN: Ruth Gordon, Garson Kanin; George Cukor

The Double Man*

GB 1968   105m   Technicolor
Warner / Hal E. Chester

A CIA agent investigates the death of his son on a Swiss skiing holiday and finds the murder was a lure to get him there so that an enemy lookalike can substitute for him.

Rather ruthless but good-looking and generally watchable spy melodrama.

w Frank Tarloff, Alfred Hayes, novel Henry S. Maxfield   d Franklin Schaffner   ph Denys Coop

Yul Brynner, Clive Revill, Anton Diffring, Britt Ekland, Moira Lister

Double Wedding
US 1937   87m   bw
MGM (Joseph L. Mankiewicz)

A bohemian artist makes a play for the lady of
his choice by romancing her sister.
Zany star comedy which doesn't quite come off.

w Jo Swerling, *play* Great Love by Ferenc
Molnar d Richard Thorpe ph William Daniels
m Edward Ward

William Powell, Myrna Loy, John Beal,
Florence Rice, Jessie Ralph, Edgar Kennedy,
Sidney Toler, Barnett Parker, Katherine
Alexander, Donald Meek

Douce*
France 1943   106m   bw
Société Parisienne de l'Industrie
   Cinématographique

In 1887 Paris a sheltered young rich girl falls for
a steward and encounters family opposition.
A charming old-fashioned story which provides
a well-taken opportunity for a portrait of the old
bourgeoisie.

w Jean Aurenche, Pierre Bost d Claude Autant-
Lara ph Gaston Thonnart m René Cloërc

Odette Joyeux, Jean Debucourt, Marguerite
Moreno, Roger Pigaut, Madeleine Robinson
   'Direction and camerawork constantly reveal
touches of felicity.'—*MFB*

Doughboys*
US 1930   80m approx   bw
MGM

A young eccentric joins the army.
Simple-minded farce with a few good routines
for the star.

w Richard Schayer d Edward Sedgwick

Buster Keaton, Sally Eilers, Cliff Edwards,
Edward Brophy

The Doughgirls*
US 1944   102m   bw
Warner (Mark Hellinger)

In a crowded wartime Washington hotel, a
honeymoon is frustrated by constant
interruption, not to mention the discovery that
the wedding was not legal.
Frantic farce, generally well adapted, and
certainly played with gusto.

w James V. Kern, Sam Hellman, *play* Joseph
Fields d James V. Kern ph Ernest Haller
m Adolph Deutsch

Alexis Smith, Jane Wyman, Jack Carson, Ann
Sheridan, Irene Manning, *Eve Arden*, Charlie
Ruggles, John Alexander, John Ridgely, Craig
Stevens, Alan Mowbray, Donald MacBride

'There's nothing so good in it that you must
attend, just as there is nothing bad enough to
keep you away.'—*Archer Winsten*

The Dove*
US 1974   104m   Technicolor   Panavision
St George Productions (Gregory Peck)

Yachtsman Robin Lee Graham makes a five-
year voyage around the world.
Bland, rather stolid adventure story for boatniks,
based on real incidents; good to look at.

w Peter Beagle, Adam Kennedy d Charles
Jarrott ph Sven Nykvist m John Barry

Joseph Bottoms, Deborah Raffin, John McLiam,
Dabney Coleman
   'Postcard views flick by to the strains of a
saccharine score.'—*David McGillivray*

Down Argentine Way*
US 1940   94m   Technicolor
TCF (Harry Joe Brown)

A wealthy American girl falls in love with an
Argentinian horse-breeder.
A very moderate musical which happened to
bring both Grable and Miranda to star stature
and set Fox off on their successful run of forties
extravaganzas, reasonably pleasant to look at but
but empty-headed.

w Karl Tunberg, Darrell Ware d Irving
Cummings ph Ray Rennahan, Leon Shamroy
songs Harry Warren, Mack Gordon

Betty Grable, Carmen Miranda, Don Ameche,
Charlotte Greenwood, J. Carrol Naish, Henry
Stephenson, Leonid Kinskey, The Nicholas
Brothers
   'I dislike Technicolor in which all pinks
resemble raspberry sauce, reds turn to sealing
wax, blues shriek of the washtub, and yellows
become suet pudding.'—*James Agate*
   'So outrageous—that it's hard to believe it
isn't at least partly intentional—but why would
anybody make this picture on purpose.'—*New
Yorker, 1976*

AAN: Ray Rennahan, Leon Shamroy; title song
(*m* Harry Warren, *ly* Mack Gordon)

Down Three Dark Streets*
US 1954   85m   bw
UA / Edward Small (Arthur Gardner, Jules V.
Levy)

An FBI agent is shot on duty, and his friend
avenges him in the course of clearing up three
cases in which he was involved.
Competent, enjoyable police film with three
cases for the price of one.

w The Gordons, Bernard C. Schoenfeld, *book*

Case File FBI by the Gordons *d Arnold Laven*
ph Joseph Biroc *m* Paul Sawtell

Broderick Crawford, Ruth Roman, Martha
Hyer, Marisa Pavan, Casey Adams, Kenneth
Tobey

† One of the first collaborations of the prolific
production company Laven-Gardner-Levy.

Down to Earth*
US 1947   101m   Technicolor
Columbia

The muse Terpsichore comes down to help a
Broadway producer fix a new show in which she
is featured.
Pleasant but undistinguished musical fantasy, a
sequel to *Here Comes Mr Jordan*. The heavenly
sequences promise more amusement than they
produce.

w Edwin Blum, Don Hartman *d* Alexander
Hall *ph* Rudolph Maté *m* Heinz Roemheld

Rita Hayworth, Larry Parks, Roland Culver (as
Mr Jordan), *Edward Everett Horton* (repeating
as Messenger 7013), Marc Platt, James Gleason
'Just the film to make the spectator forget the
troubles of life.'—*MFB*
'Celestial whimsy musical, with arch acting
and a dull score.'—*New Yorker, 1977*

Down to the Sea in Ships*
US 1948   120m   bw
TCF

An old whaling skipper wants his grandson to
follow in his footsteps.
Seagoing spectacle with strong characters; all
concerned show Hollywood in its most
professional form, but the film somehow fails to
catch the imagination or live in the memory.

w John Lee Mahin, Sy Bartlett *d* Henry
Hathaway *ph* Joe MacDonald *m* Alfred
Newman

Lionel Barrymore, Dean Stockwell, Richard
Widmark, *Cecil Kellaway*, Gene Lockhart

Downhill
GB 1927   80m approx (24 fps)   bw   silent
Gainsborough (Michael Balcon)
US title: *When Boys Leave Home*

A sixth-form schoolboy, accused of theft, is
expelled and goes to the bad in Marseilles before
being found innocent.
Absurd novelette with only marginal glimpses of
the director's emerging talent.

w Eliot Stannard, *play* Ivor Novello and
Constance Collier *d* Alfred Hitchcock
ph Claude McDonnell *ed* Ivor Montagu

Ivor Novello, Ben Webster, Robin Irvine, Sybil
Rhoda, Lillian Braithwaite, Isabel Jeans, Ian
Hunter

Downhill Racer*
US 1969   101m   Technicolor
Paramount / Wildwood (Richard Gregson)

An ambitious American skier gains a place on
the team competing in Europe.
Virtually plotless, casually assembled study of a
man and a sport, good to look at, often exciting,
but just as frequently irritating in its throwaway
style.

w James Salter, *novel* Oakley Hall *d* Michael
Ritchie *ph* Brian Probyn *m* Kenyon Hopkins

Robert Redford, Gene Hackman, Camilla
Sparv, Joe Jay Jalbert, Timothy Kirk, Dabney
Coleman

Dracula***
US 1930   84m   bw
Universal (Carl Laemmle Jnr)

A Transylvanian vampire count gets his come-
uppance in Yorkshire.
A film which has much to answer for. It started
its star and its studio off on horror careers, and it
launched innumerable sequels (see below). In
itself, after two eerie reels, it becomes a pedantic
and slow transcription of a stage adaptation, and
its climax takes place offscreen; but for all kinds
of reasons it remains full of interest.

w Garrett Fort, *play* Hamilton Deane, John
Balderston, *novel* Bram Stoker *d* Tod
Browning *ph* Karl Freund *m* none

Bela Lugosi, Helen Chandler, David Manners,
Dwight Frye, Edward Van Sloan
'A too literal adaptation of the play (*not* the
book) results in a plodding, talkative
development, with much of the vital action
taking place off-screen.'—*William K. Everson*
'The mistiest parts are the best; when the lights
go up the interest goes down.'—*Ivan Butler*
† Sequels include *Dracula's Daughter* (qv), *Son
of Dracula* (qv); the later Hammer sequence
consists of *Dracula* (see below), *Brides of
Dracula* (qv), *Dracula Prince of Darkness* (qv),
Dracula Has Risen From the Grave (qv), *Taste
the Blood of Dracula* (qv), *Scars of Dracula*
(qv), *Dracula AD 1972* (qv), *The Satanic Rites
of Dracula* (qv). Other associated films in which
the Count or a disciple appears include (all qv)
Return of the Vampire (1944), *House of
Frankenstein* (1945), *House of Dracula* (1945),
Abbott and Costello Meet Frankenstein (1948),
The Return of Dracula (1958), *Kiss of the
Vampire* (1963), *The Fearless Vampire Killers*
(1967), *Count Yorga Vampire* (1969), *Countess
Dracula* (1970), *Vampire Circus* (1970), *The*

House of Dark Shadows (1970), *Vampire Lovers* (1971), *Blacula* (1972). Minor potboilers are legion.

Dracula***
GB 1958 82m Technicolor
Hammer (Anthony Hinds)
US title: *Horror of Dracula*

A remake of the 1930 film.
Commendably brief in comparison with the later Hammer films, this was perhaps the best horror piece they turned out as well as the most faithful to its original. Decor and colour were well used, and the leading performances are striking.

w Jimmy Sangster d Terence Fisher ph Jack Asher m James Bernard ad Bernard Robinson

Peter Cushing (as Van Helsing), *Christopher Lee* (as Dracula), Melissa Stribling, Carol Marsh, Michael Gough, John Van Eyssen, Valerie Gaunt, Miles Malleson

Dracula AD 1972
GB 1972 95m Eastmancolor
Warner / Hammer (Josephine Douglas)

Dracula reappears among Chelsea teenagers practising black magic.
Depressed attempt to update a myth; the link with modern sin makes it seem not only tarnished but tasteless, and the film itself is lamentably short on excitement.

w Don Houghton d Alan Gibson ph Richard Bush m Michael Vickers

Peter Cushing, Christopher Lee, Stephanie Beacham, Michael Coles, Christopher Neame, William Ellis

Dracula's Daughter**
US 1936 70m bw
Universal

The daughter of the old count follows his remains to London.
Lively sequel which develops in the manner of a Sherlock Holmes story.

w Garrett Fort d Lambert Hillyer ph George Robinson

Otto Kruger, Marguerite Churchill, Edward Van Sloan, Gloria Holden, Irving Pichel, Nan Grey, Hedda Hopper, Gilbert Emery, Claud Allister, E. E. Clive, Halliwell Hobbes, Billy Bevan

Dracula Has Risen from the Grave
GB 1968 92m Technicolor
Hammer (Aida Young)

Dracula again terrorizes the village in the shadow of his castle, and is routed by a bishop.
Tedious, confined and repetitive shocker with

little conventional action and an unusual emphasis on sex.

w John Elder (Anthony Hinds) d Freddie Francis ph Arthur Grant m James Bernard

Christopher Lee, Rupert Davies, Veronica Carlson, Barbara Ewing, Barry Andrews, Ewan Hooper

'A bloody bore.'—*Judith Crist*

Dracula Prince of Darkness
GB 1965 90m Techniscope
Warner / Hammer (Anthony Nelson Keys)

Stranded travellers are made welcome at the late count's castle by his sinister butler, who proceeds to use the blood of one of them to revivify his master.
Ingenious rehash of incidents from the original story, largely dissipated by poor colour and unsuitable wide screen.

w John Sansom d Terence Fisher ph Michael Reed m James Bernard

Christopher Lee, *Philip Latham*, Barbara Shelley, Thorley Walters, Andrew Keir, Francis Matthews, Suzan Farmer, Charles Tingwell

'Run-of-the-coffin stuff... only for ardent fang-and-cross fans.'—*Judith Crist*

Dragnet*
US 1954 93m Warnercolor
Mark VII (Jack Webb)

Sgt Joe Friday solves the murder of an ex-convict.
Moderately interesting but overlong attempt to transfer television techniques to the big screen; laconic dialogue, question and answer, cheap sets, close-ups and convenient Los Angeles locations.

w Richard Breen d Jack Webb ph Edward Colman

Jack Webb, Ben Alexander, Richard Boone, Stacy Harris, Ann Robinson, Virginia Gregg

Dragon Seed*
US 1944 144m bw
MGM (Pandro S. Berman)

Chinese peasants fight the Japs.
Ill-advised attempt to follow the success of *The Good Earth*; badly cast actors mouth propaganda lines in a mechanical script which provokes more boredom and unintentional laughter than sympathy.

w Marguerite Roberts, Jane Murfin, novel Pearl S. Buck d Jack Conway, Harold S. Bucquet ph Sidney Wagner m Herbert Stothart

Katharine Hepburn, Walter Huston, Turhan Bey, Aline MacMahon, Akim Tamiroff, Hurd

Hatfield, Frances Rafferty, Agnes Moorehead, Henry Travers, J. Carrol Naish

AAN: Sidney Wagner; Aline MacMahon

Dragonwyck*
US 1946 103m bw
TCF (Darryl F. Zanuck)

In the 1840s a farmer's daughter marries her rich cousin, not knowing that he has poisoned his first wife.
Good-looking but rather tedious romance of the Jane Eyre/Rebecca school: tyrannical recluse, mystery upstairs, spooky house, etc. Heavy going.

w Joseph L. Mankiewicz, *novel* Anya Seton
d Joseph L. Mankiewicz ph *Arthur Miller*
m Alfred Newman

Gene Tierney, Vincent Price, Glenn Langan, Walter Huston, Anne Revere, Spring Byington, Henry Morgan, Jessica Tandy

Drake of England
GB 1935 104m bw
Wardour (Walter C. Mycroft)
US titles: *Drake the Pirate; Elizabeth of England*

Sir Francis Drake is knighted by Queen Elizabeth for his seafaring exploits, and defeats the Spanish Armada.
Stiffly moving historical pageant; you can smell the mothballs.

w Clifford Grey, Akos Tolney, Marjorie Deans, Norman Watson d Arthur Woods

Matheson Lang, Athene Seyler, Jane Baxter, Donald Wolfit, Henry Mollison, George Merritt, Amy Veness, Sam Livesey, Ben Webster

Dramatic School*
US 1938 80m bw
MGM

Young actresses compete for success.
Another, less lively, *Stage Door*; tolerable but not exciting.

w Ernst Vajda, Mary McCall Jnr, *play* School of Drama by Hans Szekely, Zoltan Egyed
d Robert B. Sinclair Jnr ph William Daniels

Luise Rainer, Paulette Goddard, Alan Marshal, Lana Turner, Anthony Allan (later John Hubbard), Henry Stephenson, Genevieve Tobin, Gale Sondergaard, Melville Cooper, Erik Rhodes, Ann Rutherford, Margaret Dumont, Virginia Grey, Hans Conried

Drango
US 1957 92m bw
UA / Hall Bartlett

After the Civil War, a Union Army officer is assigned to bring law and order to a Georgia community.
Eccentric, downbeat semi-western with aspirations to be some kind of *film noir*; does not come off.

wd Hall Bartlett ph *James Wong Howe*
m Elmer Bernstein

Jeff Chandler, Ronald Howard, Joanne Dru, Julie London, Donald Crisp, John Lupton, Morris Ankrum

Dream Girl
US 1947 86m bw
Paramount (P. J. Wolfson)

A girl revels in her own romantic dreams, one of which nearly comes true.
Potentially pleasant comedy about a female Walter Mitty does not work because the director has run out of ideas, the star is miscast and Hollywood has insisted on making the girl rich to begin with, which robs the dreams of any point.

w Arthur Sheekman, *play* Elmer Rice d Mitchell Leisen ph Daniel L. Fapp m Victor Young

Betty Hutton, Macdonald Carey, Walter Abel, Patric Knowles, Virginia Field, Peggy Wood, Lowell Gilmore

A Dream of Kings
US 1969 110m Technicolor
National General (Jules Schermer)

Episodes in the life of an improvident, lusty, poetical Chicago Greek with a dying son.
The part screamed for Anthony Quinn and got him, with the result that it has all been seen before, too frequently. Well made, with strong appeal to Chicago Greeks.

w Harry Mark Patrakis, Ian Hunter, *novel* Harry Mark Patrakis d Daniel Mann
ph Richard H. Kline m Alex North

Anthony Quinn, Irene Papas, Inger Stevens, Sam Levene, Val Avery, Tamara Daykarhanova

A Dream of Passion
Greece 1978 110m Eastmancolor
Branfilm / Melinafilm (Jules Dassin)

A Woman who, Medea-like, has killed her children is drawn into an eccentric relationship with an actress playing Medea on the stage.
Weird and ineffective character drama which badly needs discipline.

wd Jules Dassin ph George Arvanitis m Ionnis Markopoulos

Melina Mercouri, Ellen Burstyn, Andreas Voutsinas, Despo Diamantidou

Dream Wife

US 1953   99m   bw
MGM (Dore Schary)

An executive leaves his ambitious wife for a
sheik's daughter schooled in the art of pleasing
men, but naturally finds drawbacks.
Very moderate comedy with strained situations
and few laughs. The stars work hard.

w Sidney Sheldon, Herbert Baker, Alfred L.
Levitt d Sidney Sheldon ph Milton Krasner
m Conrad Salinger

Cary Grant, Deborah Kerr, Walter Pidgeon,
Betta St John, Eduard Franz, Buddy Baer, Les
Temayne

Dreamboat*

US 1952   83m   bw
TCF (Sol C. Siegel)

A romantic star of the silent film era is
embarrassed when his old movies turn up on
television.
Hollywood rather blunderingly makes fun of its
arch enemy in this sometimes sprightly but often
disappointing comedy which should have been a
bulls-eye.

wd Claude Binyon ph Milton Krasner m Cyril
Mockridge

Clifton Webb, Ginger Rogers, Anne Francis,
Jeffrey Hunter, Elsa Lanchester, Fred Clark,
Ray Collins, Paul Harvey

Dreaming Lips*

GB 1937   94m   bw
Trafalgar (Paul Czinner)

The wife of an invalid musician has an affair with
another man and commits suicide.
Standard star fare, possibly Miss Bergner's most
notable film, also available in a German version.

w Margaret Kennedy, Lady Cynthia Asquith,
Carl Mayer, play Henry Bernstein d Paul
Czinner, Lee Garmes ph Lee Garmes
m William Walton

Elisabeth Bergner, Romney Brent, Raymond
Massey, Joyce Bland, Sydney Fairbrother, Felix
Aylmer, Donald Calthrop

Dreams That Money Can Buy*

US 1946   81m   Technicolor
Art of the Century (Hans Richter, Peggy
    Guggenheim, Kenneth MacPherson)

A young itinerant sells dreams to people who
need them.
Semi-underground surrealist film, momentarily
of interest, but disjointed and with no real
apparent purpose.

wd Hans Richter ph Arnold Eagle md Louis
Applebaum

† The individual dreams are directed by Max
Ernst, Man Ray, Fernand Leger, Marcel
Duchamp and Alexander Calder as well as
Richter.

'Arch, snobbish and sycophantic, about as
genuinely experimental as a Chemcraft set.'—
James Agee

Drei von der Tankstelle*

Germany 1930   80m   bw
UFA

Three penniless young men find happiness as
petrol station attendants.
Light-hearted operetta of the Depression era,
well received at the time.

w Franz Schultz, Paul Frank d William Thiele
ph Franz Planer m Werner Heymann

Willy Fritsch, Lilian Harvey, Oskar Karlweis,
Heinz Ruhmann, Olga Tchekhova
† Remade 1955 by Hans Wolff, with a cast still
led by Willy Fritsch.

Die Dreigroschenoper**

Germany 1931   114m   bw
Warner / Tobis / Nero
US title: The Threepenny Opera

In turn-of-the-century London, Mack the Knife
marries the daughter of the beggar king and runs
into trouble.
Heavy-footed but interesting updating of The
Beggar's Opera, with splendid sets.

w Bela Balazs, Leo Lania, Ladislas Vajda, from
Bertolt Brecht's version d G. W. Pabst ph Fritz
Arno Wagner m Kurt Weill ad Andrei
Andreiev

Lotte Lenya, Rudolf Forster, Fritz Rasp,
Caroline Neher, Reinhold Schunzel, Valeska
Gert, Vladimir Sokoloff
† Brecht disliked the film and sued the makers,
but lost.
†† A French version was also released under the
title L'Opéra de Quat'sous, with Albert Préjean.

Dreyfus*

GB 1931   90m   bw
Wardour (F. W. Kraemer)

In 1894 France, a Jewish officer is accused of
spying.
Primitive version of a much-filmed story (cf The
Life of Emile Zola, I Accuse).

w Rehfisch Herzog, Reginald Berkeley, Walter
C. Mycroft d F. W. Kraemer, Milton Rosmer

Cedric Hardwicke, George Merritt (as Zola),

Charles Carson, Sam Livesey, Garry Marsh (as Esterhazy), Randle Ayrton, George Zucco

Drifters*
GB 1929   40m approx   bw
Empire Marketing Board

A documentary of the North Sea fishing fleet. A highly influential documentary, made at a time when British films were totally unrealistic and studio-bound. Unfortunately it now seems extremely dull.

wd, ed John Grierson *ph* Basil Emmott

Drive a Crooked Road
US 1954   82m   bw
Columbia (Jonie Taps)

A garage mechanic falls in with bank robbers. Terse crime melodrama, quite watchable.

w Blake Edwards *d* Richard Quine *ph* Charles Lawton Jnr *md* Ross di Maggio

Mickey Rooney, Kevin McCarthy, Dianne Foster

Drive He Said
US 1970   90m   colour
Columbia / Drive Productions / BBS (Steve Blauner)

An easygoing college basketball star is helped by an eccentric rebel to ensure his own unfitness for military service. Both run into trouble.
Flabby celebration of against-the-government attitudes, expressed partly through sex and bad language. Defiantly hard to like.

w Jeremy Larner, Jack Nicholson *d* Jack Nicholson *ph* Bill Butler *m* David Shire

Michael Margotta, William Tepper, Bruce Dern, Karen Black, Robert Towne, Henry Jaglom

The Driver*
US 1978   91m   De Luxe
TCF / EMI / Lawrence Gordon

A detective determines to catch an old enemy, a getaway driver. Noisy melodrama, very proficient in the screeching tyre department but extremely empty as to character.

wd Walter Hill *ph* Philip Lathrop *m* Michael Small

Ryan O'Neal, Bruce Dern, Isabelle Adjani, Ronee Blakeley

Drôle de Drame*
France 1936   100m approx   bw

A complicated chain of bizarre events is set in motion when a botanist pretends not to be a detective story writer, a bishop tries to be a detective, and a murderer seeks revenge for libel.

A curious satirical comedy which is never quite as funny as it seems about to be, but should be seen for its downright peculiar London sets and its array of actors in top form.

w Jacques Prévert, *novel* The Lunatic at Large by J. Storer Clouston *d* Marcel Carné

Françoise Rosay, Michel Simon, Louis Jouvet, Jean-Louis Barrault, Jean-Pierre Aumont

   'No one with any taste for nonsense should miss it.'—*Richard Mallett, Punch*

Drop Dead Darling
GB 1966   100m   Technicolor   Panavision
Seven Arts (Ken Hughes)
US title: *Arriverderci Baby*

A con man who marries and murders rich women meets a con lady with similar intentions. Loud, restless black comedy which squanders its moments of genuine inventiveness among scenes of shouting, confusion and action for action's sake.

wd Ken Hughes, *story* The Careful Man by Richard Deeming *ph* Denys Coop *m* Dennis Farnon

Tony Curtis, Rosanna Schiaffino, Lionel Jeffries, Zsa Zsa Gabor, Nancy Kwan, Fenella Fielding, Anna Quayle, Warren Mitchell, Mischa Auer

The Drowning Pool
US 1975   108m   Technicolor   Panavision
Warner / Coleytown (Lawrence Turman, David Foster)

Private eye Lew Harper goes to New Orleans to investigate an anonymous letter which ends in murder.
Dreary sequel to *Harper* (qv), full of boring characters uninventively deployed.

w Tracy Keenan Wynn, Lorenzo Semple Jnr, Walter Hill, *novel* John Ross MacDonald *d* Stuart Rosenberg *ph* Gordon Willis *m* Michael Small

Paul Newman, Joanne Woodward, Coral Browne, Tony Franciosa, Murray Hamilton, Gail Strickland, Linda Hayes, Richard Jaeckel

   'The impenetrable mystery is not particularly gripping; and the general air of pointlessness is only intensified by the sudden rush of clarifications at the end.'—*Tom Milne*

   'It recycles every private eye cliché known to civilized man as it crawls through Louisiana talking all the way.'—*Paul D. Zimmermann*

The Drum*
GB 1938   96m   Technicolor
London Films (Alexander Korda)
US title: *Drums*

The British army helps an Indian prince to resist his usurping uncle.

Reasonably entertaining story of the Raj, with adequate excitement after a meandering start.

w Lajos Biro, Arthur Wimperis, Patrick Kirwan, Hugh Gray *d* Zoltan Korda *ph* Georges Périnal *m* John Greenwood, Miklos Rozsa

Sabu, Roger Livesey, Raymond Massey, Valerie Hobson, Desmond Tester, David Tree, Francis L. Sullivan, Roy Emerton, Edward Lexy

Drumbeat
US 1954   111m   Warnercolor
Jaguar (no producer credited)

An Indian fighter sets out to make peace with a renegade.

Long, dull western, stolid all round.

wd Delmer Daves *ph* J. Peverell Marley *m* Victor Young

Alan Ladd, Audrey Dalton, Marisa Pavan, Robert Keith, Rodolpho Acosta, Charles Bronson, Warner Anderson, Elisha Cook Jnr, Anthony Caruso

Drums along the Mohawk***
US 1939   103m   Technicolor
TCF (Raymond Griffith)

Colonists survive Indian attacks in upstate New York during the Revolutionary War.

Patchy, likeable period adventure story with domestic and farming interludes; in its way a key film in the director's canon.

w Lamar Trotti, Sonya Levien, *novel* Walter Edmonds *d John Ford ph Bert Glennon, Ray Rennahan m* Alfred Newman

Claudette Colbert, Henry Fonda, *Edna May Oliver*, Eddie Collins, John Carradine, Dorris Bowdon, Jessie Ralph, Arthur Shields, Robert Lowery, Roger Imhof, Ward Bond

AAN: Edna May Oliver

Dry Rot
GB 1956   87m   bw
Romulus (Jack Clayton)

Three bookmakers plot to make a fortune by substituting a doped horse for the favourite.

Flat filming of a long-running theatrical farce.

w John Chapman, from his play *d* Maurice Elvey *ph* Arthur Grant *m* Peter Akister

Ronald Shiner, Brian Rix, Sid James, Michael Shepley, Joan Haythorne, Joan Sims, Heather Sears, Lee Patterson, Peggy Mount.

Dual Alibi
GB 1947   81m   bw
British National (Louis H. Jackson)

Twin trapezists fall out over a lottery ticket and a worthless woman, but later extract a unique revenge.

Sprightly circus melodrama, shot on a shoestring.

w Alfred Travers, Stephen Clarkson *d* Alfred Travers *ph* James Wilson

Herbert Lom, Phyllis Dixey, Ronald Frankau, Terence de Marney, Abraham Sofaer, Eugene Deckers

Dubarry Was a Lady
US 1943   101m   Technicolor
MGM (Arthur Freed)

A New Yorker imagines himself back at the court of Louis XIV.

Dull, stiff adaptation of a Broadway musical comedy, with changed songs.

w Irving Brecher, *book* B. G. De Sylva, Herbert Fields *d* Roy del Ruth *ph* Karl Freund *songs* Cole Porter

Gene Kelly, Lucille Ball, Red Skelton, Virginia O'Brien, Zero Mostel, Rags Ragland, Tommy Dorsey and his Orchestra

The Duchess and the Dirtwater Fox
US 1976   104m   De Luxe   Panavision
TCF (Melvin Frank)

A Barbary Coast con man and a saloon singer have various hectic adventures.

Wild and woolly spoof western which fires off aimlessly in a variety of styles and becomes merely tiresome despite good scenes.

w Melvin Frank, Barry Sandler *d* Melvin Frank *ph* Joseph Biroc *m* Charles Fox

George Segal, Goldie Hawn, Conrad Janis, Thayer David, Roy Jenson, Bob Hoy, Bennie Dobbins

'The classic western has now been shot to death by Sam Peckinpah, laughed to death by Mel Brooks and pondered to death by Arthur Penn, and Frank is like a scavenger picking up stray relics from its body.'—*Newsweek*

The Duchess of Idaho
US 1950   98m   Technicolor
MGM (Joe Pasternak)

Romantic misunderstandings among candidates for Miss Idaho Potato.

Lightweight musical, quite pleasant if routine, with guest spots.

w Dorothy Cooper, Jerry Davis *d* Robert Z. Leonard *ph* Charles Schoenbaum *md* Georgie Stoll

Esther Williams, Van Johnson, John Lund,

Paula Raymond, Clinton Sundberg; guests Red Skelton, Eleanor Powell, Lena Horne

Duck Soup****
US 1933   68m   bw
Paramount

An incompetent becomes President of Fredonia and wages war on its scheming neighbour.
The satirical aspects of this film are fascinating but appear to have been unintentional. Never mind, it's also the most satisfying and undiluted Marx Brothers romp, albeit the one without instrumental interludes. It does include the lemonade stall, the mirror sequence, and an endless array of one-liners and comedy choruses.

w Bert Kalmar, Harry Ruby, Arthur Sheekman, Nat Perrin d Leo McCarey ph Henry Sharp m/ly Bert Kalmar, Harry Ruby ad Hans Dreier, Wiard Ihnen

The Four Marx Brothers, Margaret Dumont, Louis Calhern, Edgar Kennedy, Raquel Torres
  'So much preliminary dialogue is necessary that it seems years before Groucho comes on at all; and waiting for Groucho is agony.'—*E. V. Lucas, Punch*

Due Soldi di Speranza*
Italy 1952   98m   bw
Universalcine (Sandro Ghenzi)
GB title: *Two Pennyworth of Hope*

Demobilized after World War II, Antonio finds life in his native village hard to take.
Neo-realist comedy-melodrama full of gesticulating rustics; good for those who like this sort of thing.

w Renato Castellani, Titina de Filippo d Renato Castellani ph Arturo Gallea m Alessandro Cicognini

Vincenzo Musolino, Maria Fiore, Filumena Russo, Luigi Astarita

Duel at Diablo*
US 1965   103m   De Luxe
UA / Nelson / Engel / Cherokee / Rainbow / Brien

White and black man fight together as apaches attack.
Well-paced, old-fashioned, shoot-em-up star western.

w Marvin H. Albert, Michel M. Grilikhes d Ralph Nelson ph Charles F. Wheeler m Neal Hefti

Sidney Poitier, James Garner, Bibi Andersson, Bill Travers, William Redfield, John Hoyt, John Hubbard

Duel at Silver Creek
US 1952   77m   Technicolor
U-I (Leonard Goldstein)

An honest man is murdered by claim jumpers, and the Silver Kid is suspected.
Modest, efficient western.

w Gerald Drayson Adams, Joseph Hoffman d Don Siegel ph Irving Glassberg m Hans Salter

Audie Murphy, Stephen McNally, Faith Domergue, Susan Cabot, Gerald Mohr, Eugene Iglesias, Lee Marvin, Walter Sande

Duel in the Jungle
GB 1954   101m   Technicolor
ABP / Marcel Hellman

An African explorer intends to defraud an insurance company and sets traps for the investigator who pursues him.
Lackadaisical romp in the studio jungle, none of it with much style or film sense.

w Sam Marx, T. J. Morrison d George Marshall ph Erwin Hillier m Mischa Spoliansky

Dana Andrews, Jeanne Crain, David Farrar, Patrick Barr

Duel in the Sun***
US 1946   135 or 138m   Technicolor
David O. Selznick

A half-breed girl causes trouble between two brothers.
Massive western, dominated and fragmented by its producer, who bought the best talent and proceeded to interfere with it, so that while individual scenes are marvellous, the narrative has little flow. The final gory shoot-up between two lovers was much discussed at the time.

w David O. Selznick, Oliver H. P. Garrett, novel Niven Busch d King Vidor (and others) second unit B. Reeves Eason, Otto Brower ph Lee Garmes, Harold Rosson, Ray Rennahan m Dmitri Tiomkin ad James Basevi pd J. McMillan Johnson

Jennifer Jones, Joseph Cotten, Gregory Peck, Lionel Barrymore, Lillian Gish, Walter Huston, Herbert Marshall, Charles Bickford, Tilly Losch, Joan Tetzel, Harry Carey, Otto Kruger, Sidney Blackmer

AAN: Jennifer Jones; Lillian Gish

The Duellists*
GB 1977   101m   colour
Scott Free / NFFC / David Puttnam

In the early 1800s, two Hussar Officers challenge each other to a series of duels; after sixteen years an ironic truce is called. A singularly pointless anecdote; its main virtue is that it is coldly attractive to look at.

w Gerald Vaughan-Hughes, *story* The Point of Honour by Joseph Conrad *d* Ridley Scott *ph* Frank Tidy *m* Howard Blake *pd* Peter J. Hampton

Keith Carradine, Harvey Keitel, Albert Finney, Edward Fox, Cristina Raines, Tom Conti, Robert Stephens, John McEnery

Duffy
GB 1968 101m Technicolor
Columbia / Martin Manulis

Two half-brothers plan to rob their millionaire father.
Would-be with-it caper film, all flashy fragments and pop art, like sitting through a feature-length commercial. Exasperating.

w Donald Cammell, Harry Joe Brown Jnr *d* Robert Parrish *ph* Otto Heller *m* Ernie Freeman

James Coburn, James Mason, James Fox, Susannah York, John Alderton, Guy Deghy, Tutte Lemkow, Carl Duering, Marne Maitland

Duffy's Tavern
US 1945 97m bw
Paramount (Danny Dare)

The owner of a bar is helped by Hollywood stars.
Flat comedy based on a radio show and not helped by dismal guest star appearances.

w Melvin Frank, Norman Panama *d* Hal Walker *ph* Lionel Lindon

Ed Gardner, Victor Moore, Marjorie Reynolds, Barry Sullivan and guests including Bing Crosby, Bob Hope, Betty Hutton, Alan Ladd, Dorothy Lamour, Veronica Lake, William Bendix, Joan Caulfield

The Duke of West Point *
US 1938 112m bw
Edward Small

An extrovert army cadet finds the going tough.
Dated romantic flagwaver which pleased at the time.

w George Bruce *d* Alfred E. Green *ph* Robert Planck

Louis Hayward, Joan Fontaine, Tom Brown, Richard Carlson, Alan Curtis, Donald Barry, Gaylord Pendleton, Jed Prouty, Marjorie Gateson

Dulcima
GB 1971 98m Technicolor
EMI (Basil Rayburn)

A farmer's daughter reluctantly moves in with a persistent, lecherous old miser.
Weird sex melodrama from *Cold Comfort Farm* country, more risible than interesting.

wd Frank Nesbitt, *story* H. E. Bates *ph* Tony Imi *m* Johnny Douglas

John Mills, Carol White, Stuart Wilson, Bernard Lee, Dudley Foster

Dumbo ***
US 1941 64m Technicolor
Walt Disney

A baby circus elephant finds that his big ears have a use after all.
Delightful cartoon feature notable for set pieces such as the drunken nightmare and the crows' song.

w various *d* Ben Sharpsteen *m* Frank Churchill, Oliver Wallace

AAN: Frank Churchill, Oliver Wallace; song 'Baby Mine' (*m* Frank Churchill, *ly* Ned Washington)

Dunkirk **
GB 1958 135m bw
MGM / Ealing (Michael Balcon)

In 1940 on the Normandy beaches, a small group gets detached from the main force.
Sober, small-scale approach to an epic subject; interesting but not inspiring, with performances to match.

w W. P. Lipscomb, David Divine *d* Leslie Norman *ph* Paul Beeson *m* Malcolm Arnold

John Mills, Richard Attenborough, Bernard Lee, Robert Urquhart, Ray Jackson

The Dunwich Horror *
US 1970 90m Movielab
AIP (Roger Corman, Jack Bohrer)

A young warlock plans to use his girl friend in a fertility rite.
Bookish horror story, quite well done against a village background.

w Curtis Lee Hanson, Henry Rosenbaum, Ronald Silkosky, *story* H. P. Lovecraft *d* Daniel Haller *ph* Richard C. Glouner *m* Les Baxter

Dean Stockwell, Sandra Dee, Ed Begley, Sam Jaffe, Lloyd Bochner

Duped Till Doomsday *
East Germany 1957 97m bw
DEFA (Adolf Fischer)
original title: *Betrogen bis zum Jungsten Tag*

Three Nazi NCOs go to the bad.
Propagandist anti-Nazi war melodrama, very well made in parts.

w Kurt Bortfeldt, *novel* Kameraden by Franz
Fuhmann d Kurt Jung-Alsen ph Walter
Fehdmer

Wolfgang Kieling, Rudolph Ulrich, Hans-
Joachim Martens

Dust Be My Destiny*
US 1939 88m bw
Warner (Lou Edelman)

A young misfit tries to find himself in the
country.
Dated but well made social melodrama.

w Robert Rossen, *story* Jerome Odlum d Lewis
Seiler ph James Wong Howe m Max Steiner

John Garfield, Priscilla Lane, Alan Hale, Frank
McHugh, John Litel, Charles Grapewin, Billy
Halop, Bobby Jordan, Stanley Ridges

  'You can tell from the title that John Garfield
has his usual part—the angry, bitter, tough, poor
young man with slight persecution mania.'—
Richard Mallett, Punch
† Remade 1942 as *I Was Framed*, with Michael
Ames.

Dutchman*
GB 1966 56m bw
Gene Persson

On a New York subway train a woman
humiliates a black man and finally knifes him.
An allegory for addicts who can ferret out the
meaning; on the surface, vaguely Pinterish and
mainly boring.

w LeRoi Jones, from his play d Anthony
Harvey ph Gerry Turpin m John Barry

Shirley Knight, Al Freeman Jnr

Dynamite**
US 1929 129m bw
Paramount (Cecil B. de Mille)

In order to gain an inheritance, a socialite
marries a man about to be executed . . . but he is
reprieved.
Dated but still dynamic social melodrama of the
early talkie period.

w Jeanie Macpherson d Cecil B. de Mille
ph Peverell Marley m Herbert Stothart

Kay Johnson, Charles Bickford, Conrad Nagel,
Julia Faye, Joel McCrea

  'Exuberant, wonderfully vigorous, the film
skilfully evokes the look and character of the
Jazz Age.'—*Charles Higham*

E

Each Dawn I Die*
US 1939 84m bw
Warner (David Lewis)

A crusading reporter is framed for manslaughter and becomes a hardened prisoner.
Efficient, vigorous yet slightly disappointing star vehicle; the talents are in the right background, but the script is wobbly.

w Norman Reilly Raine, Warren Duff, Charles Perry, *novel* Jerome Odlum d William Keighley *ph* Arthur Edeson *m* Max Steiner

James Cagney, George Raft, Jane Bryan, George Bancroft, Maxie Rosenbloom, Stanley Ridges, Alan Baxter, Victor Jory

The Eagle and the Hawk**
US 1933 72m bw
Paramount

In 1918 France, two American army fliers dislike each other but come together before the death of one of them.
Dawn Patrol melodrama, well done with unusually vivid dialogue and acting.

w Bogart Rogers, Seton I. Miller, *story* John Monk Saunders d Stuart Walker *ph* Harry Fischbeck

Fredric March, Cary Grant, Carole Lombard, Sir Guy Standing, Jack Oakie, Forrester Harvey

The Eagle and the Hawk
US 1949 86m bw
(Paramount) Pine-Thomas

During the Mexican wars, a US government agent tracks down a traitor who is supplying arms to the rebel Juarez.
Stolid adventure yarn, energetically played.

w Geoffrey Homes, Lewis R. Foster d Lewis R. Foster *ph* James Wong Howe *m* David Chudnow

John Payne, Dennis O'Keefe, Rhonda Fleming, Thomas Gomez, Fred Clark, Frank Faylen, Eduardo Noriega

The Eagle Has Landed*
GB 1976 135m Eastmancolor Panavision
ITC / Associated General (Jack Wiener, David Niven Jnr)

During World War II, enemy aliens infiltrate an English village in the hope of killing Churchill.
Elaborately plotted but uninvolving spy melodrama, lethargically directed, muddily coloured and too concerned to create some good Germans.

w Tom Mankiewicz, *novel* Jack Higgins d John Sturges *ph* Anthony Richmond *m* Lalo Schifrin

Michael Caine, Donald Sutherland, Robert Duvall, Jenny Agutter, Donald Pleasence, Anthony Quayle, Jean Marsh, Sven-Bertil Taube, John Standing, Judy Geeson, Larry Hagman, Maurice Roeves

Eagle in a Cage*
GB 1970 103m Eastmancolor
Group W / Ramona (Millard Lampell, Albert Schwarz)

In 1815, a professional soldier becomes governor of St Helena and jailer to Napoleon.
Talkative, anecdotal, heavily serious historical reconstruction with good acting but little control.

w Millard Lampell d Fielder Cook *ph* Frano Vodopivec *m* Marc Wilkinson

John Gielgud, Ralph Richardson, Kenneth Haigh, Billie Whitelaw, Moses Gunn, Ferdy Mayne, Lee Montague

Eagle Squadron
US 1942 102m bw
Universal (Walter Wanger)

During World War II, American fliers join the RAF.
Studio-bound air epic, leavened with conventional romance but little humour or sympathy.

w Norman Reilly Raine, *story* C. S. Forester d Arthur Lubin *ph* Stanley Cortez .m Frank Skinner

Robert Stack, Diana Barrymore, John Loder, Eddie Albert, Nigel Bruce, Leif Erickson, Edgar Barrier, Jon Hall, Evelyn Ankers, Isobel Elsom,

Alan Hale Jnr, Don Porter, Fredericorlock,
Gladys Cooper

Earl Carroll Vanities
US 1945   91m   bw
Republic (Albert J. Cohen)

A Ruritanian princess in need of a loan becomes
the singing star of a New York night club.
Nit-witted musical with no style but an engaging
cast.

w Frank Gill Jnr *d* Joseph Santley *ph* Jack
Marta *md* Walter Scharf *songs* Walter Kent,
Kim Gannon

Constance Moore, Dennis O'Keefe, Alan
Mowbray, Eve Arden, Otto Kruger (as Earl
Carroll), Pinky Lee, Mary Forbes, Stephanie
Bachelor, Parkyakarkus, Leon Belasco, Robert
Greig

AAN: song 'Endlessly' (*ly* Kim Gannon,
m Walter Kent)

The Earl of Chicago*
US 1940   87m   bw
MGM (Victor Saville)

An American gangster accedes to an English
earldom but is tried for murder.
Unusual but unsatisfactory comedy-drama
which rambles to a dismal conclusion but has
entertaining passages.

w Lesser Samuels, *novel* Brock Williams
d Richard Thorpe *m* Werner Heymann

Robert Montgomery, Edward Arnold, Reginald
Owen, Edmund Gwenn

The Early Bird
GB 1965   98m   Eastmancolor
Rank / Hugh Stewart

A milkman gets involved in an inter-company
war.
Star farcical comedy; not the worst of Wisdom,
but overlong and mainly uninventive.

w Jack Davies, Norman Wisdom, Eddie Leslie,
Henry Blyth *d* Robert Asher *ph* Jack Asher
m Ron Goodwin

Norman Wisdom, Edward Chapman, Jerry
Desmonde, Paddie O'Neil, Bryan Pringle,
Richard Vernon, John Le Mesurier, Peter Jeffrey

Earth*
USSR 1930   63m approx (24 fps)   bw
   silent
VUFKU
original title: *Zemlya*

Trouble results in a Ukrainian village when a
landowner refuses to hand over his land for a
collective farm.

The melodramatic little plot takes second place
to lyrical sequences of rustic beauty, illustrating
life, love and death in the countryside.

wd, ed Alexander Dovzhenko *ph* Danylo
Demutsky

Semyon Svashenko, Stephan Shkurat, Mikola
Nademsky, Yelena Maximova
   'Stories in themselves do not interest me. I
choose them in order to get the greatest
expression of essential social forms.'—
Dovzhenko

Earthquake*
US 1974   123m   Technicolor   Panavision
Universal / Jennings Lang / Mark Robson

Various personal stories intertwine in a Los
Angeles earthquake.
Dreary drama with very variable special effects,
gimmicked up by Sensurround. A box office
bonanza.

w George Fox, Mario Puzo *d* Mark Robson
ph Philip Lathrop *m* John Williams
pd Alexander Golitzen *sp* Albert Whitlock

Charlton Heston, Ava Gardner, Lorne Greene,
Marjoe Gortner, Barry Sullivan, George
Kennedy, Richard Roundtree, Geneviève
Bujold, Walter Matthau (under the alias of his
real name)

East Lynne
US 1931   102m   bw
Fox

A Victorian lady is unjustly divorced by her
husband, and later loses both her lover and her
sight.
Much caricatured melodrama, here presented in
stolidly acceptable form.

w Bradley King, Tom Barry, *novel* Mrs Henry
Wood *d* Frank Lloyd *ph* John Seitz *m* Richard
Fall

Ann Harding, Clive Brook, O. P. Heggie,
Conrad Nagel, Cecilia Loftus, Beryl Mercer,
Flora Sheffield
† Previous versions had been made by Fox, in
1916 with Theda Bara and in 1925 with Alma
Rubens.

AAN: best picture

East of Eden**
US 1954   115m   Warnercolor
   Cinemascope
Warner (Elia Kazan)

In a California farming valley in 1913 a wild
adolescent rebels against his stern father and
discovers that his mother, believed dead, runs a
nearby brothel.

Turgid elaboration of Genesis with strong
character but nowhere to go. Heavily overdirected and rousingly acted.

w Paul Osborn, *novel* John Steinbeck *d* Elia
Kazan ph Ted McCord *m* Leonard Rosenman
ad James Basevi, Malcolm Bert

Raymond Massey, James Dean (his first star
role), Julie Harris, Dick Davalos, *Jo Van Fleet*,
Burl Ives, Albert Dekker

'Of what a boy did . . . of what a girl did . . . of
ecstasy and revenge!'—*publicity*

'The first distinguished production in
Cinemascope.'—
Eugene Archer

AA: Jo Van Fleet
AAN: Paul Osborn; Elia Kazan; James Dean

East of Elephant Rock
GB 1976 92m colour
Boy's Company / Kendon

In 1948 Malaya a womanizing civil servant is
shot by his jealous mistress.
Style-less and quite uncredited re-hash of *The
Letter*, striving vainly to recreate the spirit of
Somerset Maugham.

wd Don Boyd *ph* Keith Goddard *m* Peter
Skellern

Judi Bowker, Jeremy Kemp, John Hurt,
Christopher Cazenove, Anton Rodgers, Vajira,
Tariq Yunus

'Punishingly inept in every department.'—
David Badder, MFB

East of Piccadilly
GB 1940 79m bw
ABPC (Walter C. Mycroft)
US title: *The Strangler*

A novelist and a girl reporter catch a silk
stocking murderer.
Adequate lower case mystery with good
atmosphere.

w Lesley Storm, J. Lee-Thomson, *novel* Gordon
Beckles *d* Harold Huth

Sebastian Shaw, Judy Campbell, Henry
Edwards, Niall MacGinnis, George Pughe,
Martita Hunt, George Hayes, Cameron Hall,
Edana Romney

East of Sudan
GB 1964 94m Techniscope
Columbia / Ameran (Charles H. Schneer)

A trooper, a governess and others escape
downriver from one of General Gordon's
outposts.
Shameless borrowing of plot from *The African
Queen* and footage from *The Four Feathers*. The
purest hokum.

w Jud Kinberg *d* Nathan Juran *ph* Wilkie
Cooper *m* Laurie Johnson

Anthony Quayle, Sylvia Syms, Jenny Agutter.
'Nathan Juran could direct this kind of thing
blindfold, and for once would appear to have
done so.'—*MFB*

East of Sumatra*
US 1953 82m Technicolor
U-I (Albert J. Cohen)

A mining engineer has trouble with the ruthless
chief of a Pacific island.
A good example of routine Hollywood hokum,
efficiently staged and acted.

w Frank Gill Jnr *d* Budd Boetticher *ph* Clifford
Stine

Jeff Chandler, Anthony Quinn, Marilyn
Maxwell, John Sutton

East Side West Side*
US 1949 108m bw
MGM (Voldemar Veltuguin)

A New York businessman is torn between his
wife and another woman.
High class soap opera with all the production
stops pulled out; generally well acted and
reasonably entertaining.

w Isobel Lennart, *novel* Marcia Davenport
d Mervyn Le Roy *ph* Charles Rosher *m* Miklos
Rozsa

James Mason, Barbara Stanwyck, Van Heflin,
Ava Gardner, *Gale Sondergaard,* Cyd Charisse,
Nancy Davis, William Conrad

'No company is quite so adept as MGM at
presenting basically uninteresting material with
such style, and such a strong cast, that it cannot
fail to entertain.'—*Penelope Houston*

Easter Parade**
US 1948 109m Technicolor
MGM (Arthur Freed)

A song and dance man quarrels with one partner
but finds another.
A musical which exists only in its numbers,
which are many but variable. All in all, an
agreeable lightweight entertainment without the
style to put it in the top class.

w Sidney Sheldon, Frances Goodrich, Albert
Hackett *d* Charles Walters *ph* Harry Stradling
m/ly Irving Berlin *md* Roger Edens, Johnny
Green

Fred Astaire, Judy Garland, Ann Miller, Peter
Lawford, Clinton Sundberg, Jules Munshin

AA: Roger Edens, Johnny Green

Easy Living* **
US 1937 91m bw
Paramount (Arthur Hornblow Jnr)

A fur coat is thrown out of a window and lands
on a typist . . .
Amusing romantic comedy with farcical
trimmings; it now stands among the classic
crazy comedies of the thirties.

w Preston Sturges d Mitchell Leisen ph Ted
Tetzlaff *md* Boris Morros

Jean Arthur, Ray Milland, *Edward Arnold*, Luis
Alberni, Mary Nash, Franklin Pangborn,
William Demarest, Andrew Tombes

'Secretaries, millionaires, jokes, sight gags,
furies, attacks of cool sense—there are always
three things going on at once.'—*New Yorker,
1977*

Easy Living
US 1949 77m bw
RKO (Robert Sparks)

An ageing football star wants to retire but has to
satisfy the living standards of his ambitious wife.
Dim drama.

w Charles Schnee, *story* Irwin Shaw *d* Jacques
Tourneur *ph* Harry J. Wild *m* Roy Webb

Victor Mature, Lucille Ball, Lizabeth Scott,
Sonny Tufts, Lloyd Nolan, Paul Stewart, Jack
Paar, Jeff Donnell

Easy Money
GB 1948 93m bw
GFD / Gainsborough (A. Frank Bundy)

Four people win big prizes on the football pools.
Short story compendium; very average.

w Muriel and Sydney Box, *play* Arnold Ridley
d Bernard Knowles

Edward Rigby, Greta Gynt, Dennis Price, Jack
Warner, Mervyn Johns, Petula Clark, Marjorie
Fielding, Bill Owen, Raymond Lovell

Easy Rider* **
US 1969 94m Technicolor
Columbia / Pando / Raybert (Peter Fonda)

Two drop-outs ride across America on
motorcycles.
Happening to please hippies and motor-cycle
enthusiasts as well as amateur politicians, this
oddball melodrama drew freakishly large
audiences throughout the world and was much
imitated though never equalled in its casual
effectiveness, nor did promising careers ensue for
the actors mainly concerned.

w Peter Fonda, Dennis Hopper, Terry Southern
d Dennis Hopper *ph* Laszlo Kovacs *m* various
recordings

Peter Fonda, Dennis Hopper, *Jack Nicholson*
'Cinéma-vérité in allegory terms.'—*Peter
Fonda*
'Ninety-four minutes of what it is like to swing,
to watch, to be fond, to hold opinions and to get
killed in America at this moment.'—*Penelope
Gilliatt*
AAN: script; Jack Nicholson

Easy Street* ***
US 1916 22m approx bw silent
Mutual

In a slum street, a tramp is reformed by a dewy-
eyed missionary, becomes a policeman, and
tames the local bully.
Quintessential Chaplin, combining
sentimentality and social comment with
hilarious slapstick.

wd Charles Chaplin ph William C. Foster,
Rollie Totheroh

Charles Chaplin, Edna Purviance, Albert
Austin, Eric Campbell

Easy to Love
US 1953 96m Technicolor
MGM (Joe Pasternak)

The romances of an aqua-queen in Florida's
Cypress Gardens.
Thin, humourless and forgettable musical
vehicle sustained by spectacular water ballets.

w Laslo Vadnay, William Roberts *d* Charles
Walters *ph* Ray June *md* Lennie Hayton,
George Stoll; numbers staged by *Busby Berkeley*

Esther Williams, Tony Martin, Van Johnson

Easy to Wed*
US 1946 110m Technicolor
MGM (Jack Cummings)

A socialite threatens a newspaper editor with
libel; he postpones his own wedding and sets a
friend to compromise her.
Bright but tasteless remake of *Libelled Lady*,
with a second team cast trying hard.

w Dorothy Kingsley, Maurine Watkins, Howard
Emmett Rogers, George Oppenheimer
d Edward Buzzell *ph* Harry Stradling
m Johnny Green

Van Johnson, Esther Williams, *Lucille Ball*,
Keenan Wynn, Cecil Kellaway, Carlos Ramirez,
Ben Blue, Ethel Smith

Easy Virtue
GB 1927 73m (24 fps) bw silent
Gainsborough (Michael Balcon)

A drunkard's wife falls for a young man who

kills himself. Her past then prevents her attempts
to lead a respectable life.
Vapid social melodrama with minimal points of
interest despite its credits.

w Eliot Stannard, *play* Noël Coward *d* Alfred
Hitchcock *ph* Claude McDonnell *ed* Ivor
Montagu

Isabel Jeans, Franklyn Dyall, Eric Bransby
Williams, Ian Hunter, Violet Farebrother, Robin
Irvine

Ebb Tide**
US 1937 92m Technicolor
Paramount (Lucien Hubbard)

Sailors are stranded with a dangerous fanatic on
a South Sea island.
Interesting adaptation of Stevenson, notable
both for its early colour and its genuinely sour,
anti-romantic mood, almost unique for
Hollywood in this period.

w Bertram Millhauser, *novel* R. L. Stevenson
and Lloyd Osbourne *d* James Hogan *ph* Leo
Tover *m* Victor Young

Ray Milland, Frances Farmer, Oscar Homolka,
Barry Fitzgerald, Lloyd Nolan
† Remade 1946 as *Adventure Island*.

Echoes of a Summer
US / Canada 1975 98m Eastmancolor
Beata / Castle / Astral / Bryanston (Robert L.
Joseph)

An 11-year-old girl dying of heart disease spends
her last summer with her parents on holiday in a
Nova Scotian village.
Excruciating.

w Robert L. Joseph *d* Don Taylor *ph* John
Coquillon *m* Terry James

Jodie Foster, Richard Harris, Lois Nettleton,
Geraldine Fitzgerald, William Windom, Brad
Savage

The Eclipse*
Italy / France 1962 125m bw
Interopa-Cineriz / Paris Film (Robert and
Raymond Hakim)
original title: *L'Eclisse*

A young Roman woman breaks off one affair
and begins another.
A portrait in depth, rather tiresomely long and
with at least one totally irrelevant stock-market
sequence; but superbly done for connoisseurs.

wd Michelangelo Antonioni, Tonino Guerra,
Elio Bartolini, Ottiero Ottieri *ph* Gianni di
Venanzo *m* Giovanni Fusco

Monica Vitti, Alain Delon, Francisco Rabal

L'Ecole Buissonière*
France 1948 89m bw
UGC / CGCF
US title: *I Have a New Master*

At a provincial village school, a new teacher
introduces new methods and takes a while to win
over the locals.
Rustic comedy-drama of a kind the French do
well.

w Jean-Paul Le Chanois, Elise Freinet *d* Jean-
Paul Le Chanois *ph* Marc Fossard, Maurice
Pecqueux, André Dumaitre *m* Joseph Kosma

Bernard Blier, Juliette Fabre, Edouard Delmont

The Eddie Cantor Story
US 1953 116m Technicolor
  Cinemascope
Warner (Sidney Skolsky)

After a tough childhood on New York's east
side, Israel Iskowitz becomes a famous
entertainer.
Deliberately patterned after the success of *The
Jolson Story*, this is an unhappy example of how
close are success and failure; the elements are the
same, but this film suffers from unsure timing,
lack of humour, rather apologetic numbers, a
really dismal script and a caricature
performance in the lead.

w Jerome Weidman, Ted Sherdeman, Sidney
Skolsky *d* Alfred E. Green *ph* Edwin DuPar
md Ray Heindorf *songs* various *ch* Le Roy
Prinz

Keefe Brasselle, Marilyn Erskine, Aline
MacMahon, Arthur Franz, Alex Gerry, Gerald
Mohr, William Forrest (as Ziegfeld), Will Rogers
Jnr (as Will Rogers), and Eddie Cantor (who
also sings the songs off screen)

The Eddy Duchin Story
US 1955 123m Technicolor
  Cinemascope
Columbia (Jonie Taps, Jerry Wald)

The success story of a pianist who died of
leukemia.
Predictable, glossy, sentimental musical biopic.

w Samuel Taylor, *original story* Leo Katcher
d George Sidney *ph* Harry Stradling
md George Duning *piano* Carmen Cavallero

Tyrone Power, Kim Novak, *Victoria Shaw*,
James Whitmore, Shepperd Strudwick, Frieda
Inescort, Gloria Holden, Larry Keating

AAN: Leo Katcher; Harry Stradling; George
Duning

Edge of Darkness*
US 1943   124m   bw
Warner (Henry Blanke)

Norwegian village patriots resist the Nazis.
High-intentioned, ambitiously cast but
ultimately bathetic resistance melodrama, high
principled down to its tragic finale but
compromised by backlot shooting and the
presence of Errol Flynn.

w Robert Rossen d Lewis Milestone ph Sid
Hickox m Franz Waxman

Errol Flynn, Ann Sheridan, Walker Huston,
Judith Anderson, Ruth Gordon, Nancy
Coleman, Helmut Dantine, Morris Carnovsky,
Charles Dingle, John Beal, Richard Fraser,
Helene Thimig

Edge of Doom
US 1950   97m   bw
Samuel Goldwyn
GB title: *Stronger than Fear*

A desperate youth kills a priest and struggles
with his conscience.
A sanctimonious weirdie, extremely odd coming
from this producer, and unhappily re-edited
before release. Someone was interested enough
to want to make it, but it seems to have been
killed by the cast and the front office.

w Philip Yordan, *novel* Leo Brady d Mark
Robson ph Harry Stradling m Hugo Friedhofer

Dana Andrews, Farley Granger, Joan Evans,
Robert Keith, Paul Stewart, Mala Powers, Adele
Jergens, Harold Vermilyea, Mabel Paige

Edge of Eternity*
US 1959   80m   Technicolor
        Cinemascope
Columbia / Thunderbird (Kendrick Sweet)

A Grand Canyon sheriff traces three murders to
an ownership struggle over a disused mine.
Routine but suspenseful thriller with splendid
locations.

w Knut Swenson, Richard Collins d Don Siegel
ph Burnett Guffey m Daniele Amfitheatrof

Cornel Wilde, Victoria Shaw, Edgar Barrier,
Mickey Shaughnessy, Jack Elam

Edge of the City*
US 1957   85m   bw
MGM / Jonathan (David Susskind, Jim di
Ganci)
GB title: *A Man is Ten Feet Tall*

Racial tensions lead to tragedy in the railroad
yards of New York's waterfront.
Tense, brutal melodrama, which has historical
interest as an effective opening-up in cinematic

terms of a TV play, in its imitation of *On the
Waterfront*, and in its rebel hero and relaxed
black friend.

w Robert Alan Arthur, from his play d Martin
Ritt ph Joseph Brun m Leonard Rosenman

Sidney Poitier, John Cassavetes, Jack Warden,
Kathleen Maguire, Ruby Dee, Robert Simon,
Ruth White

Edge of the World*
GB 1937   80m   bw
GFD / Rock (Joe Rock)

Life, love and death on Foula, a remote Shetland
island.
Rare for its time, a vigorous location drama in
the Flaherty tradition; sometimes naïve, usually
exhilarating.

wd Michael Powell

Niall MacGinnis, Belle Chrystal, John Laurie,
Finlay Currie, Eric Berry

Edison the Man*
US 1940   107m   bw
MGM (John W. Considine Jnr)

Edison struggles for years in poverty before
becoming famous as the inventor of the electric
light bulb.
Standard, well-made biopic following on from
Young Tom Edison; reasonably absorbing, but
slightly suspect in its facts.

w Dore Schary, Talbot Jennings, Bradbury
Foote, Hugo Butler d Clarence Brown
m Herbert Stothart

Spencer Tracy, Rita Johnson, Lynne Overman,
Charles Coburn, Gene Lockhart, Henry
Travers, Felix Bressart

AAN: Dore Schary, Hugo Butler (original story)

Edouard et Caroline*
France 1951   99m   bw
UGC / CICC

A young pianist and his wife quarrel while
preparing for an important recital.
Gay, slight, charming comedy, a two-hander
taking place within the course of a few hours.

w Annette Wademant, Jacques Becker
d Jacques Becker ph Robert Le Fèbvre m Jean-
Jacques Grunenwald

Daniel Gélin, Anne Vernon, Jacques François,
William Tubbs, Jean Galland, Elina
Labourdette, Betty Stockfield

Edward My Son
GB 1948   112m   bw
MGM (Edwin H. Knopf)

A rich, unscrupulous man remembers the people he has made unhappy, and the son to whom he never behaved as a father should.
Unsatisfactory, rather ugly-looking adaptation of a gripping piece of theatre, with casting and direction remarkably uncertain from such professionals.

w Donald Ogden Stewart, *play* Robert Morley d George Cukor

Spencer Tracy, Deborah Kerr, Ian Hunter, James Donald, Leueen McGrath, Mervyn Johns

AAN: Deborah Kerr

The Effect of Gamma Rays on Man-in-the-Moon Marigolds
US 1972   101m   De Luxe
Newman–Foreman

A slatternly middle-aged woman dreams of better times for herself and her children.
Well-written but essentially banal and pretentious domestic drama, the kind of film that only gets made when powerful stars see in it a juicy role.

w Alvin Sargent, *play* Paul Zendel d Paul Newman ph Adam Holender m Maurice Jarre

Joanne Woodward, Nell Potts, Roberta Wallach, Judith Lowry

The Egg and I*
US 1947   104m   bw
U-I (Chester Erskine)

A city couple try to become gentleman farmers.
Mild, pleasant comedy notable chiefly for introducing a hillbilly couple, Ma and Pa Kettle, who went on, in the personae of Main and Kilbride, to make several later features. (See under Kettles.)

w Chester Erskine, Fred Finkelhoffe, *novel* Betty Macdonald d Chester Erskine ph Milton Krasner m Frank Skinner

Claudette Colbert, Fred MacMurray, *Marjorie Main, Percy Kilbride*, Louise Allbritton, Richard Long, Billy House, Ida Moore, Donald MacBride

AAN: Marjorie Main

The Egyptian*
US 1954   140m   De Luxe   Cinemascope
TCF (Darryl F. Zanuck)

In ancient Egypt an abandoned baby grows up to be physician to the pharaoh.
More risible than reasonable, sounding more like a parody than the real thing, this pretentious epic from a bestseller flounders helplessly between its highlights but has moments of good humour and makes an excellent example of the pictures they don't make 'em like any more.

w Philip Dunne, Casey Robinson, *novel* Mika Waltari d Michael Curtiz ph Leon Shamroy m Bernard Herrmann, Alfred Newman ad Lyle Wheeler, George W. Davis

Edmund Purdom, Victor Mature, *Peter Ustinov*, Bella Darvi, Gene Tierney, Michael Wilding, Jean Simmons, Judith Evelyn, Henry Daniell, John Carradine, Carl Benton Reid

'The novel . . . supplied the reader with enough occurrences and customs of Akhnaton's time . . . to hide some of the more obvious contrivances of the story. The film does not do this.'—*Carolyn Harrow, Films in Review*

AAN: Leon Shamroy

The Eiger Sanction*
US 1975   125m   Technicolor   Panavision
Universal / Malpaso (Jennings Lang)

An art teacher returns to the CIA as an exterminator, and finds himself in a party climbing the Eiger.
Silly spy melodrama with some breathtaking mountain sequences.

w Warren B. Murphy, Hal Dresner, Rod Whitaker, *novel* Trevanian d Clint Eastwood ph Frank Stanley, John Cleare, Jeff Schoolfield, Peter Pilafian, Pete White m John Williams

Clint Eastwood, George Kennedy, Vonetta McGee, Jack Cassidy, Heidi Bruhl, Thayer David

'All the villains have been constructed from prefabricated Bond models.'—*Richard Combs*

Eight and a Half**
Italy 1963   138m   bw
Cineriz (Angelo Rizzoli)
original title: *Otto e Mezzo*

A successful film director on the verge of a nervous breakdown has conflicting fantasies about his life.
A Fellini self-portrait in which anything goes.
Some of it is fascinating, some not worth the trouble of sorting out.

w Federico Fellini, Ennio Flaiano, Tullio Pinelli, Brunello Rondi d Federico Fellini ph Gianni di Venanzo m Nino Rota ad Piero Gherardi

Marcello Mastroianni, Claudia Cardinale, Anouk Aimée, Sandra Milo, Rossella Falk, Barbara Steele, Madeleine Lebeau

'The whole may add up to a magnificent folly, but it is too singular, too candid, too vividly and insistently alive to be judged as being in any way diminishing.'—*Peter John Dyer, MFB*

AAN: best foreign film; script

Eight Iron Men
US 1952   80m   bw
Columbia / Stanley Kramer

In the ruins of an Italian village, eight American infantrymen wait for relief.
Quickie war film in which everyone talks a lot and they all survive; from the time when Kramer was discovering how fast he could turn 'em out.

w Harry Brown, from his play A Sound of Hunting d Edward Dmytryk ph Roy Hunt m Leith Stevens pd Rudolph Sternad

Bonar Colleano, Lee Marvin, Arthur Franz, Richard Kiley, Nick Dennis, James Griffith, Dick Moore, George Cooper

Eight O'Clock Walk
GB 1953   87m   bw
British Lion / George King

A young barrister proves a taxi driver innocent of murder.
Minor-league courtroom stuff, an adequate time-passer.

w Katherine Strueby, Guy Morgan, story Jack Roffey, Gordon Harbord d Lance Comfort ph Brendan Stafford m George Melachrino

Richard Attenborough, Derek Farr, Cathy O'Donnell, Ian Hunter, Maurice Denham, Bruce Seton, Harry Welchman

Eighty Thousand Suspects*
GB 1963   113m   bw   Cinemascope
Rank / Val Guest

A smallpox epidemic terrorizes the city of Bath.
Predictable melodrama which adequately passes the time.

w Val Guest, novel Pillars of Midnight by Elleston Trevor d Val Guest ph Arthur Grant m Stanley Black

Claire Bloom, Richard Johnson, Yolande Donlan, Cyril Cusack, Michael Goodliffe, Mervyn Johns, Kay Walsh, Basil Dignam, Ray Barrett

El**
Mexico 1952   91m   bw
Nacional Film (Oscar Dancigers)
aka: This Strange Passion; Torments

A middle-aged aristocrat marries a beautiful young girl and falls victim to insane jealousy.
A tragi-comic case history with chilling and memorable details; not one of its director's great works, but an engaging minor one.

w Luis Bunuel, Luis Alcoriza, novel Pensamientos by Mercedes Pinto d Luis Bunuel ph Gabriel Figueroa m Luis Hernandez Breton

Arturo de Cordova, Delia Garces, Luis Beristain, Aurora Walker

El Cid*
US / Spain 1961   184m   Super Technirama
Samuel Bronston

A legendary 11th-century hero drives the Moors from Spain.
Endless glum epic with splendid action sequences as befits the high budget.

w Frederic M. Frank, Philip Yordan d Anthony Mann ph Robert Krasker m Miklos Rozsa

Charlton Heston, Sophia Loren, Raf Vallone, Geraldine Page, John Fraser, Gary Raymond, Herbert Lom, Hurd Hatfield, Massimo Serato, Andrew Cruickshank, Michael Hordern, Douglas Wilmer, Frank Thring

AAN: Miklos Rozsa; song 'The Falcon and the Dove' (m Miklos Rozsa, ly Paul Francis Webster)

El Condor
US 1970   102m   Technicolor
National General / Carthay Continental (André de Toth)

An escaped convict and a con man seek a fortune in gold believed to be hidden in a fortress in the Mexican desert.
Blood and guts western with few moments of interest.

w Larry Cohen, Steven Carabatsos d John Guillermin ph Henri Persin m Maurice Jarre

Jim Brown, Lee Van Cleef, Patrick O'Neal, Marianna Hill, Iron Eyes Cody, Elisha Cook Jnr
   'The kind of fun you can find at your friendly neighbourhood abattoir.'—Judith Crist, 1977

El Dorado*
US 1966   126m   Technicolor
Paramount / Laurel (Howard Hawks)

A gunfighter and a drunken sheriff tackle a villainous cattle baron.
Easy-going, semi-somnolent, generally likeable but disappointing western . . . an old man's movie all round.

w Leigh Brackett, novel The Stars in their Courses by Harry Joe Brown d Howard Hawks ph Harold Rosson m Nelson Riddle

John Wayne, Robert Mitchum, James Caan, Charlene Holt, Michele Carey, Ed Asner, Arthur Hunnicutt,
R. G. Armstrong, Paul Fix, Christopher George
   'A rumbustious lament for the good days of the bad old west.'—Tom Milne
   'A claustrophobic, careless and cliché-ridden

thing, wavering constantly between campy self-deprecation and pretentious pomposity.'—
Richard Schickel

El Greco

Italy / France 1964   94m   Eastmancolor
Cinemascope
(TCF) Artistiche Internazionale / Arco-Films
du Siècle (Alfredo Bini, Mel Ferrer)

In the 16th century, a Greek-Italian painter finds favour in Spain and falls in love with an aristocratic girl.
Heavily embellished history with a few good scenes.

w Guy Elmes, Massimo Franciosa, Luigi Magni, Luciano Salce *d* Luciano Salce *ph* Leonida Barboni *m* Ennio Morricone

Mel Ferrer, Rosanna Schiaffino, Adolfo Celi, °Angel Aranda

El Topo*

Mexico 1971   124m   Eastmancolor
Producciones Panic

An evil gunfighter rides through the old west and has various encounters, after which he sets himself on fire.
Curious, perverse, powerful surrealist allegory which takes in the life of Christ and the fate of man among some exceedingly unpleasant violence. A treat for connoisseurs of the unpleasantly absurd.

wd, m, ad Alexandro Jodorowsky *ph* Raphael Corkidi

Alexandro Jodorowsky, Brontis Jodorowsky, Mara Lorenzio, David Silva

Electra Glide in Blue*

US 1973   113m   De Luxe   Panavision
UA / James William Guercio / Rupert Hitzig

A small-town motor-cycle cop becomes disillusioned.
Agreeable desert melodrama in the wake of *Easy Rider*, freshly observed with mordant humour, marred by a fashionable downbeat ending.

w Robert Boris *d/m* James William Guercio *ph* Conrad Hall

Robert Blake, Billy Green Bush, Mitch Ryan, Jeannine Riley, Elisha Cook Jnr, Royal Dana

Elephant Boy**

GB 1937   80m   bw
Alexander Korda

In India, a boy elephant keeper helps government conservationists.
Documentary drama which seemed fresh and

extraordinary at the time, has dated badly since, but did make an international star of Sabu.

w John Collier, Akos Tolnay, Marcia de Sylva
d Robert Flaherty, Zoltan Korda

Sabu, Walter Hudd, Allan Jeayes, W. E. Holloway, Wilfrid Hyde White
'This is a fractured film, its skeleton is awry, its bones stick out through the skin.'—*Richard Griffith, 1941*

Elephant Walk*

US 1954   103m   Technicolor
Paramount (Irving Asher)

The owner of a Ceylon tea plantation takes back an English wife who finds the atmosphere strange and turns to a friendly overseer for comfort.
Echoes of *Jane Eyre* and *Rebecca*, with stampeding elephants instead of a mad or dead wife. Grade A fiction for ladies.

w John Lee Mahin, *novel* Robert Standish *d* William Dieterle *ph* Loyal Griggs *m* Franz Waxman

Elizabeth Taylor, Peter Finch, Dana Andrews, Abraham Sofaer
'The climactic elephant stampede's a rouser—if you're still awake.'—*Judith Crist*

Eleven Harrowhouse*

GB 1974   108m   De Luxe   Panavision
TCF / Harrowhouse (Elliott Kastner)

An American diamond merchant is robbed of a valuable jewel, and finds himself in the middle of an ingenious plot.
Amusing caper story marred by sudden changes of mood.

w Jeffrey Bloom, *novel* Gerald A. Browne
d Aram Avakian *ph* Arthur Ibbetson
m Michael J. Lewis

Charles Grodin, *James Mason*, Trevor Howard, John Gielgud, Candice Bergen, Peter Vaughan, Helen Cherry, Jack Watson, Jack Watling

Elizabeth of Ladymead

GB 1948   97m   Technicolor
BL / Imperadio (Herbert Wilcox)

Four husbands of different generations come home from war (1854, 1903, 1919, 1946) to find their wives altered.
Thin star vehicle turns into an amateur-night compendium with a few funny moments.

w Frank Harvey, from his play *d* Herbert Wilcox

Anna Neagle, Hugh Williams, Bernard Lee, Michael Laurence, Nicholas Phipps, Isobel Jeans, Michael Shepley, Jack Allen

Ellery Queen

The debonair detective created by Manfred B.
Lee and Frederic Dannay was seen in several
unremarkable second features, usually with his
secretary Nikki and his police inspector father.
The first two were made for Republic, the rest for
Columbia.

1935: THE SPANISH CAPE MYSTERY with
Donald Cook
1936: THE MANDARIN MYSTERY (Eddie
Quillan)
1940: ELLERY QUEEN MASTER
DETECTIVE (Ralph Bellamy)
1941: ELLERY QUEEN'S PENTHOUSE
MYSTERY, ELLERY QUEEN AND THE
PERFECT CRIME, ELLERY QUEEN AND
THE MURDER RING (all Bellamy)
1942: A CLOSE CALL FOR ELLERY
QUEEN, A DESPERATE CHANCE FOR
ELLERY QUEEN, ENEMY AGENTS MEET
ELLERY QUEEN (all William Gargan)
In 1971 Peter Lawford starred in a TV pilot,
Don't Look behind You, and in 1975 a one-
season series starred Jim Hutton. The books,
pseudonymously authored by Ellery Queen,
were far more popular than any of the movies.

Elmer Gantry **

US 1960   146m   Eastmancolor
UA / Bernard Smith

The exploits of an American evangelist in the
twenties.
Mainly gripping but overlong exposé of
commercialized small-town religion

wd Richard Brooks, novel Sinclair Lewis
ph John Alton m André Previn *ad Edward
Carrere*

Burt Lancaster, Jean Simmons, Arthur
Kennedy, *Shirley Jones*, Dean Jagger, Edward
Andrews, Patti Page, John McIntire

AA: Richard Brooks (as writer); Burt
Lancaster; Shirley Jones
AAN: best picture; André Previn

Elopement

US 1952   82m   bw
TCF (Fred Kohlmar)

A girl student eloping with her professor is
chased by her father.
Unconvincing domestic comedy with some lively
chase sequences.

w Bess Taffell *d* Henry Koster *ph* Joseph La
Shelle

Clifton Webb, Charles Bickford, Anne Francis,
William Lundigan, Margalo Gillmore, Evelyn
Varden, Reginald Gardiner

Elstree Calling **

GB 1930   86m   bw and colour
BIP / Wardour

A film studio mounts a television show.
Slender excuse for an all-star revue which luckily
preserves much light entertainment talent of the
time.

w Adrian Brunel, Walter C. Mycroft, Val
Valentine *d* Adrian Brunel, Alfred Hitchcock,
Jack Hulbert, André Charlot, Paul Murray

Tommy Handley, Jack Hulbert, Cicely
Courtneidge, Will Fyffe, Lily Morris, Teddy
Brown, Anna May Wong, Gordon Harker,
Donald Calthrop, John Longden, Jameson
Thomas, Bobbie Comber

The Elusive Pimpernel *

GB 1950   109m   Technicolor
BL / London Films (Michael Powell, Emeric
   Pressburger)

A foppish 18th-century London dandy is
actually the hero who rescues French aristocrats
from the guillotine.
Expensive remake of *The Scarlet Pimpernel*
which fails to please, apparently because the
talents were not congenial to the subject.
Interesting detail, though.

wd Michael Powell, Emeric Pressburger,
novel Baroness Orczy *ph* Christopher Challis
m Brian Easdale *ph* Hein Heckroth

David Niven, Margaret Leighton, Cyril Cusack,
Jack Hawkins, David Hutcheson, Robert Coote
  'The quality of excitement which should carry
the film is quite lost. *The Elusive Pimpernel* is
highly—often too highly—coloured, and has an
artificiality quite different in character from that
of the original.'—*Penelope Houston*
  'I never thought I should feel inclined to leave
a Powell and Pressburger film before the end; but
I did here.'—*Richard Mallett, Punch*

Elvira Madigan *

Sweden 1967   95m   Eastmancolor
Europa Film (Waldemar Bergendahl)

A married army officer runs off with a tightrope
dancer; when they run out of money they live in
the woods and finally commit suicide rather than
part.
A simple Victorian romantic idyll, based on a
true incident; a director's and photographer's
piece which entrances the eyes and ears while
starving the mind.

wd Bo Widerberg *ph Jorgen Persson m* Mozart

Thommy Berggren, Pia Degermark

Embassy*
US 1972   90m   colour
Hemdale / Triad / Weaver (Mel Ferrer)

At the US Embassy in Beirut, a Soviet official seeking asylum is in danger from a KGB killer.
Goodish suspenser with reasonably literate dialogue and several Hitchcockian sequences.

w William Fairchild d Gordon Hessler
ph Raoul Coutard m Jonathan Hodge

Richard Roundtree, Chuck Connors, Max Von Sydow, Broderick Crawford, Ray Milland

The Emigrants*
Sweden 1970   191m   Technicolor
Svensk Filmindustri (Bengt Forslund)
original title: Utvandrarna

A family of farmers leaves famine-stricken 19th-century Sweden for America, and builds a homestead in Minnesota.
Solemn, forceful, overlong epic which while full of trial and tribulation is sufficiently well made to cast a hypnotic spell and was a major hit among Swedish-Americans.

w Jan Troell, Bengt Forslund, from four novels by Vilhelm Moberg d, ph, ed Jan Troell m Erik Nordgren

Max Von Sydow, Liv Ullmann, Eddie Axberg, Svenolof Bern

† A sequel, The New Land, shortly appeared, and this was also the title of a short-lived TV series on the subject.

AAN: best picture; Jan Troell (direction and script); Liv Ullmann

Emil and the Detectives*
Germany 1931   80m   bw
UFA

City children discover and chase a crook, who is finally arrested.
A pleasing fable for children which has survived several subsequent versions; the original is probably the best.

w Billy Wilder, novel Erich Kästner d Gerhard Lamprecht ph Werner Brandes m Allan Grey

Fritz Rasp, Kathe Haack
† Other versions: Britain 1934, directed by Milton Rosmer, with George Hayes; West Germany 1954, directed by R. A. Stemmle, with Kurt Meisel; US 1964 (Walt Disney), directed by Peter Tewkesbury, with Walter Slezak.

Emma*
US 1932   73m   bw
MGM

A servant marries into the family.

Predictably cosy family drama tailored for its star.

w Frances Marion, Leonard Praskins, Zelda Sears d Clarence Brown ph Oliver T. Marsh

Marie Dressler, Richard Cromwell, Jean Hersholt, Myrna Loy, John Miljan, Purnell E. Pratt

AAN: Marie Dressler

Emmanuelle*
France 1974   94m   Eastmancolor
Trinacra / Orphée (Yves Rousset-Rouard)

The bored bride of a French Embassy official in Siam is initiated by well-meaning friends into various forms of sexual activity.
Not much sexier than a Sunday colour supplement, this fashionable piece of sub-eroticism took off like a bomb and spawned half-a-dozen so-called sequels. Future students may well wonder why.

w Jean-Louis Richard, novel Emmanuelle Arsan d Just Jaeckin ph Richard Suzuki, Marie Saunier m Pierre Bachelet

Sylvia Kristel, Marika Green, Daniel Sarky, Alain Cuny

'Much hazy, soft-focus coupling in downtown Bangkok.'—Michael Billington, Illustrated London News

Emperor of the North Pole*
US 1973   119m   De Luxe
TCF / Inter Hemisphere (Robert Aldrich)
GB title: Emperor of the North

In 1933 Oregon, freeloading hobos are brutally attacked by a sadistic train guard.
Unlikely melodrama with vicious but exhilarating high spots separating acres of verbiage.

w Christopher Knopf d Robert Aldrich
ph Joseph Biroc m Frank de Vol

Lee Marvin, Ernest Borgnine, Keith Carradine, Charles Tyner, Malcolm Atterbury, Elisha Cook Jnr

'It's hard, contrived, pointless in its thesis, repulsive in its people, and it's singularly joyless and contemptible in its glorification of the bum and freeloader.'—Judith Crist

The Emperor Waltz
US 1948   106m   Technicolor
Paramount (Charles Brackett)

In 1901 Austria, a countess falls for an American phonograph salesman.
Thin to the point of emaciation, this witless comedy with music, dully set-bound, proved its

director's strangest and most unsatisfactory choice.

w Charles Brackett, Billy Wilder d Billy Wilder ph George Barnes m Victor Young songs Johnny Burke, Jimmy Van Heusen ad Hans Dreier, Franz Bachelin

Bing Crosby, Joan Fontaine, Roland Culver, Lucile Watson, Richard Haydn, Harold Vermilyea, Sig Rumann, Julie Dean

The Emperor's Candlesticks *
US 1937   89m   bw
MGM (John Considine Jnr)

In old Russia, spies on opposite sides fall in love. Lavish romantic comedy drama, generally well handled; superior Hollywood moonshine.

w Monckton Hoffe, Herman J. Mankiewicz, Harold Goldman, novel Baroness Orczy d George Fitzmaurice ph Harold Rosson m Franz Waxman

William Powell, Luise Rainer, Maureen O'Sullivan, Robert Young, Frank Morgan, Douglass Dumbrille

Empire of the Ants
US 1977   89m   Movielab
AIP / Cinema 77 (Bert I. Gordon)

Giant ants menace a stretch of the Florida coast. A long way behind *Them*, but as exploitation it could be worse.

w Jack Turley, story H. G. Wells d Bert I. Gordon ph Reginald Morris m Dana Kaproff

Joan Collins, Robert Lansing, John David Carson, Albert Salmi, Jaqueline Scott

The Empty Canvas
Italy / France 1964   118m   bw
CC Champion / Concordia (Joseph E. Levine, Carlo Ponti)
original title: *La Noia*

A young painter, obsessed by his own spiritual emptiness, becomes paranoically jealous of his promiscuous young mistress.
An extraordinarily boring film version of a novel which needed Bunuel, if anybody, to handle it.

w Tonino Guerra, Ugo Liberatore, Damiano Damiani, novel Alberto Moravia d Damiano Damiani ph Roberto Gerardi m Luis Enriquez Bacalov

Horst Buchholz, Catherine Spaak, Bette Davis, Isa Miranda, Lea Padovani

En Cas de Malheur *
France / Italy 1958   120m   bw
Iena / UCIL / Incom
aka: *Love Is My Profession*

A wealthy, middle-aged lawyer leaves his wife for a worthless young wanton whom he is defending on a robbery charge.
Good solid melodrama with excellent credits: it caught all concerned on top form and had international success, but the theme is not in itself very interesting.

w Jean Aurenche, Pierre Bost, novel Georges Simenon d Claude Autant-Lara ph Jacques Natteau m René Cloërc

Jean Gabin, Edwige Feuillère, Brigitte Bardot, Franco Interlenghi

En Rade *
France 1927   60m approx   bw   silent
Neofilm

A Marseilles docker dreams of escaping his pent-in existence and fleeing with his mistress to the South Seas.
More realistic than Pagnol's *Marius* trilogy, which used the same setting, this remains an interesting slice of romantic realism, with good attention to detail.

w Alberto Cavalcanti, Claude Heymann d Alberto Cavalcanti ph Jimmy Rogers, A. Fairli, P. Enberg

Catherine Hessling, Philippe Heriat, Georges Charlia

The Enchanted Cottage *
US 1945   92m   bw
RKO

A plain girl and a disfigured man are beautiful to each other.
Wartime updating of a sentimental old play; insufficiently well considered to be more than tolerable.

w De Witt Bodeen, Herman J. Mankiewicz, play Sir Arthur Wing Pinero d John Cromwell ph Ted Tetzlaff m Roy Webb

Dorothy McGuire, Robert Young, Herbert Marshall, Mildred Natwick

The Enchanted Forest *
US 1945   77m   Cinecolor
PRC

Old John the Hermit talks to trees and animals, and rescues a lost child.
Surprising piece of Victorian whimsy, remarkably effective in its unambitious way,

especially as a product of this studio. The best known example of Cinecolor.

w Robert Lee Johnson, John Le Bar, Lou Brock d Lew Landers ph Marcel Le Picard m Alfred Hay Malotte

Harry Davenport, Edmund Lowe, Brenda Joyce, Billy Severn

Enchanted Island
US 1958 94m Technicolor
Waverly (Benedict Bogeaus)

In the 1840s two sailors jump ship and settle on what they later discover to be a cannibal island. Tame adaptation of a minor classic, with the actors all at sea.

w James Leicester, Harold Jacob Smith, novel Typee by Herman Melville d Allan Dwan ph George Stahl m Raul Lavista

Jane Powell (an unconvincing Polynesian), Dana Andrews, Don Dubbins, Arthur Shields, Ted de Corsia, Friedrich Ledebur

Enchantment **
US 1948 101m bw
Samuel Goldwyn

A London house tells the story of three generations.
Yes, a house tells the story, and the leading characters are called Rollo and Lark, but this is a very appealing piece of period romantic nonsense, with the highest possible gloss upon it.

w John Patrick, novel A Fugue in Time by Rumer Godden d Irving Reis ph Gregg Toland m Hugo Friedhofer

David Niven, Teresa Wright, Evelyn Keyes, Farley Granger, Jayne Meadows, Leo G. Carroll

Encore *
GB 1951 88m bw
GFD / Two Cities

Three more Somerset Maugham short stories introduced by the author.
The final follow-up to the success of Quartet and Trio; television playlets quickly made this kind of short story seem old-fashioned, but the standard here was high.

w T. E. B. Clarke, Arthur Macrae, Eric Ambler, stories The Ant and the Grasshopper, Winter Cruise, Gigolo and Gigolette d Pat Jackson, Anthony Pelissier, Harold French ph Desmond Dickinson m Richard Addinsell

Nigel Patrick, Roland Culver, Kay Walsh, Noel Purcell, Ronald Squire, John Laurie, Glynis Johns, Terence Morgan, David Hutcheson

The End
US 1978 100m De Luxe
UA / Lawrence Gordon (Hank Moonjean)

A selfish man finds he is dying and unsuccessfully tries to change what remains of his life.
Presumably intended as an ironic black comedy, this comes over as tasteless ham; nobody involved, least of all the director-star, has any idea how to handle it.

w Jerry Belson d Burt Reynolds ph Bobby Byrne m Paul Williams pd Jan Scott

Bert Reynolds, Dom de Luise, Sally Field, Strother Martin, David Steinberg, Joanne Woodward, Norman Fell, Myrna Loy, Pat O'Brien, Robby Benson, Carl Reiner

The End of St Petersburg **
USSR 1927 110m approx bw silent
Mezhrabpom-Russ
original title: Konyets Sankt-Peterburga
† The film was officially commissioned as part of the 10th anniversary celebrations.

The End of the Affair
GB 1954 106m bw
Columbia / Coronado (David Lewis)

In wartime London, a repressed wife has an affair with a writer but develops religious guilt which leads indirectly to her death.
Glum sinning in Greeneland; over-ambitious, miscast, and poor-looking.

w Lenore Coffee, novel Graham Greene d Edward Dmytryk ph Wilkie Cooper m Benjamin Frankel

Deborah Kerr, Van Johnson, Peter Cushing, John Mills, Stephen Murray, Nora Swinburne, Charles Goldner

The End of the River *
GB 1947 83m bw
GFD / The Archers (Michael Powell, Emeric Pressburger)

A South American Indian boy flees to the outside world and finds life in the city as dangerous as in the jungle.
Strange but oddly impressive departure for British film-makers at this time. A commercial and critical disaster.

w Wolfgang Wilhelm d Derek Twist ph Christopher Challis m Lambert Williamson

Sabu, Esmond Knight, Bibi Ferreira, Robert Douglas, Antoinette Cellier, Raymond Lovell, Torin Thatcher

The End of the Road*
GB 1954 77m bw
Group Three (Alfred Shaughnessy)

A retired engineer becomes frustrated by
idleness, and his family contemplate sending him
to an old people's home.
Reasonably absorbing study of old age, suffering
from a contrived end.

w James Forsyth, Geoffrey Orme d Wolf Rilla
ph Arthur Grant m John Addison

Finlay Currie, Duncan Lamont, Naomi Chance,
David Hannaford

Endless Night*
GB 1971 99m Eastmancolor
BL / EMI (Leslie Gilliat)

An American girl buys an English stately home
and marries a chauffeur, but is later frightened to
death.
Bumpy British thriller, structurally weak and
peopled by the dullest conceivable characters,
but with watchably scary sequences.

wd Sidney Gilliat, novel Agatha Christie
ph Harry Waxman m Bernard Herrmann

Hayley Mills, Hywel Bennett, George Sanders,
Britt Ekland, Per Oscarsson, Lois Maxwell

The Enemy Below*
US 1957 98m Technicolor
  Cinemascope
TCF (Dick Powell)

During World War II an American destroyer in
the South Atlantic is involved in a cat-and-
mouse operation with a U-boat.
Well-staged, unsurprising naval thriller with
good pace and a pat let's-not-be-nasty-to-each-
other ending.

w Wendell Mayes, novel Commander D. A.
Rayner d Dick Powell ph Harold Rosson
m Leigh Harline

Robert Mitchum, Curt Jurgens, Theodore Bikel,
David Hedison

The Enemy General
US 1960 74m bw
Columbia (Sam Katzman)

An American officer takes revenge on the
German general who executed his fiancée.
Routine World War II heroics with a plot
deserving a rather better production.

w Dan Pepper, Burt Picard d George Sherman
ph Basil Emmott md Mischa Bakaleinikoff

Van Johnson, Jean-Pierre Aumont, John Van
Dreelen, Dany Carrel, Françoise Prévost

An Enemy of the People*
US 1977 103m Metrocolor Panavision
First Artists (George Schaefer)

A small-town doctor discovers that for
commercial reasons his colleagues propose to
conceal the fact that the local spa is
contaminated by tannery waste.
Isben's plot is well intentioned but well worn – it
more or less served as the starting point for Jaws
– so in any modern version the acting is all. Here
it isn't enough, though the star so badly wanted
to do it that arguments and sulks kept him off the
screen for three years.

w Alexander Jacobs, from Arthur Miller's
version of the play by Henrik Ibsen d George
Schaefer ph Paul Lohmann

Steve McQueen, Charles Durning, Bibi
Andersson, Eric Christmas, Richard Bradford,
Richard A. Dysart

L'Enfant Sauvage*
France 1969 84m bw
UA / Films du Carrosse (Marcel Berbert)
US title: The Wild Child

In 1797, a scientist tames and studies a young
boy who has mysteriously been living wild in the
forest.
Slightly flat but generally interesting
reconstruction of a true event, the same one
which subsequently inspired TV projects such as
Stalk the Wild Child and Lucan.

w François Truffaut, Jean Gruault d François
Truffaut ph Nestor Almendros m Vivaldi

Jean-Pierre Cargol, François Truffaut, Jean
Dasté, Françoise Seigner

Les Enfants du Paradis***
France 1945 195m bw
Pathé
US title: Children of Paradise

In the 'theatre street' of Paris in the 1840s, a
mime falls in love with the elusive Garance, but
her problems with other men keep them apart.
A magnificent evocation of a place and a period,
this thoroughly enjoyable epic melodrama is
flawed only by its lack of human warmth and of
a real theme. It remains nevertheless one of the
cinema's most memorable films.

w Jacques Prévert d Marcel Carné ph Roger
Hubert m Maurice Thiriet, Joseph Kosma, G.
Mouque ad Alexandre Trauner, Léon Barsacq,
Raymond Gabutti

Arletty, Jean-Louis Barrault, Pierre Brasseur,
Marcel Herrand, Maria Casarès, Louis Salon,
Pierre Renoir, Gaston Modot, Jane Marken

AAN: Jacques Prévert

Les Enfants Terribles*
France 1950 100m bw
Jean-Pierre Melville
aka: *The Strange Ones*

The hothouse relationship of an adolescent
brother and sister leads to tragedy.
Rough-edged, stage-bound but occasionally
quite powerful exploration into familiar Cocteau
territory.

wd Jean-Pierre Melville, *novel* Jean Cocteau
ph Henri Decaë *m* Bach, Vivaldi

Nicole Stéphane, Edouard Dermithe, Renée
Cosima, Jacques Bernard

The Enforcer***
US 1950 87m bw
United States Pictures (Milton Sperling)
GB title: *Murder, Inc*

A crusading District Attorney tracks down the
leader of a gang which murders for profit.
Extremely suspenseful and well-characterized
police yarn based on fact. One of the very best of
its kind.

w Martin Rackin *d* Bretaigne Windust
ph Robert Burks *m* David Buttolph

Humphrey Bogart, Everett Sloane, Zero Mostel,
Ted de Corsia, Roy Roberts, King Donovan
'A tough, very slickly-made thriller with a host
of fine character parts.'—*NFT, 1969*
'Absorbing and exciting, with little of the
violence that so often disfigures films of this
kind.'—*Richard Mallett, Punch*

The Enforcer
US 1976 96m De Luxe Panavision
Warner / Malpaso (Robert Daley)

Brutal Inspector Callahan of the San Francisco
police redeems himself by rounding up a group
of psychopathic hoodlums.
Dirty Harry, phase three: for hardened veterans
only.

w Stirling Silliphant, Dean Riesner *d* James
Fargo *ph* Charles W. Short *m* Jerry Fielding

Clint Eastwood, Tyne Daly, Harry Guardino,
Bradford Dillman, John Mitchum, DeVeren
Brookwalter, John Crawford

England Made Me**
GB 1972 100m Eastmancolor
Hemdale / Atlantic (Jack Levin)

In 1935 a sponging Englishman becomes
involved through his sister with a German
financier.
Somewhat altered from the novel, this unusual
film remains a lively, intelligent character
melodrama.

w Desmond Cory, Peter Duffell, *novel* Graham
Greene *d* Peter Duffell *ph* Ray Parslow *m* John
Scott

Peter Finch, Michael York, Hildegarde Neil,
Michael Hordern, Joss Ackland

English without Tears*
GB 1944 89m bw
GFD / Two Cities (Anatole de Grunwald,
   Sydney Box)
US title: *Her Man Gilbey*

World War II: a rich ATS girl falls for her butler
who has become a lieutenant.
Wispy satirical comedy with amusing moments,
chiefly interesting for the pre-war League of
Nations sequences.

w Terence Rattigan, Anatole de Grunwald
d Harold French

Lilli Palmer, Michael Wilding, *Margaret
Rutherford*, Penelope Dudley Ward, Albert
Lieven, Roland Culver, Peggy Cummins

Ensign Pulver
US 1964 104m Technicolor Panavision
Warner (Joshua Logan)

Further naval misadventures of the character
from
Mr Roberts.
Threadbare naval comedy with every expected
cliché.

w Joshua Logan, Peter S. Feibleman, *play*
Joshua Logan, Thomas Heggen *d* Joshua
Logan *ph* Charles Lawton *m* George Duning

Robert Walker, Burl Ives, Walter Matthau,
Tommy Sands, Millie Perkins, Kay Medford,
Larry Hagman, James Farentino, James Coco,
Al Freeman Jnr

Enter Laughing*
US 1967 111m Technicolor
Columbia / Acre / Sajo (Carl Reiner, Joseph
   Stein)

In New York in the thirties, a young man about
to train as a pharmacist decides to become an
actor instead.
Strident Jewish comedy based on the writer-
director's own youthful experiences, which
might have been more effectively strained by
another hand. The talent is there, though.

w Joseph Stein, Carl Reiner, *play* Carl Reiner
d Carl Reiner *ph* Joseph Biroc *m* Quincy Jones

Reni Santoni, Jose Ferrer, Shelley Winters,
Elaine May, Jack Gilford, Janet Margolin,
David Opatoshu, Michael J. Pollard

Enter the Dragon **
US / Hong Kong 1973   99m   Technicolor
Panavision
Warner / Concord (Fred Weintraub, Paul
Heller)

A master of martial arts is enlisted by British
intelligence to stop opium smuggling.
The first Hollywood-based Kung Fu actioner;
not bad, on the lines of a more violent James
Bond.

w Michael Allin d Robert Clouse ph Gilbert
Hubbs m Lalo Schifrin

Bruce Lee, John Saxon, Shih Kien, Jim Kelly,
Bob Wall

The Entertainer *
GB 1960   96m   bw
BL / Bryanston / Woodfall / Holly (John
Croydon)

A faded seaside comedian reflects on his failure
as an entertainer and as a man.
Even with Olivier repeating his stage triumph, or
perhaps because of it, this tragi-comedy remains
defiantly theatrical and does not take wing on
film.

w John Osborne, Nigel Kneale, play John
Osborne d Tony Richardson ph Oswald
Morris m John Addison

Laurence Olivier, Joan Plowright, Brenda de
Banzie, Roger Livesey, Alan Bates, Shirley Anne
Field, Albert Finney, Thora Hird, Daniel
Massey

'No amount of deafening sound effects and
speciously busy cutting can remove one's feeling
that behind this distracting façade of heightened
realism lurks a basic lack of confidence.'—Peter
John Dyer

AAN: Laurence Olivier

Entertaining Mr Sloane *
GB 1969   94m   Technicolor
Pathe / Canterbury (Douglas Kentish)

A lodger attracts the amorous attention of both
the middle-aged daughter and older son of the
house.
A Gothic tour de force of bad taste which
worked better on the stage but has its moments.

w Clive Exton, play Joe Orton d Douglas
Hickox ph Wolfgang Suschitsky m Georgie
Fame

Beryl Reid, Harry Andrews, Peter McEnery,
Alan Webb

Entr'acte **
France 1924   20m approx   bw   silent
Ballets Suédois

Various eccentric characters become involved in
a crazy chase.
Hilarious nonsense short, devised originally to
be shown between the acts of a Dadaist ballet.
Very clearly the start of a famous directorial
career.

w Francis Picabia d, ed René Clair ph J. Berliet

Jean Borlin, Inge Fries, Francis Picabia, Man
Ray, Georges Auric, Marcel Achard, Marcel
Duchamps

Entre Onze Heures et Minuit *
France 1948   103m   bw
Francinex (Jacques Roitfeld)

A police detective solves his case by
impersonating one of the victims.
Twisty, elaborate murder mystery, very
competently performed but a little overlong.

w Henri Decoin, Marcel Rivet, novel Le Sosie de
la Morgue by Claude Luxel d Henri Decoin
ph Nicolas Hayer m Henri Saguet

Louis Jouvet, Madeleine Robinson, Robert
Arnoux, Gisèle Casadeus

Equus *
GB 1977   137m   colour
UA / Winkast (Denis Holt)

A middle-aged psychiatrist tries to find out why
a 17-year-old boy.blinded six horses.
Overlong film version of a play which was a
succès d'estime; it makes the fatal mistake of
showing the tragic events realistically instead of
stylistically as was done on the stage, and as a
study in abnormal psychology it is scarcely
gripping or revealing.

w Peter Shaffer, from his play d Sidney Lumet
ph Oswald Morris m Richard Rodney Bennett
pd Tony Walton

Richard Burton, Peter Firth, Colin Blakely, Joan
Plowright, Harry Andrews, Eileen Atkins, Jenny
Agutter, Kate Reid

Eroica *
Poland 1957   83m   bw
Kadr
aka: Heroism

Two ironic episodes of war; in the 1944 Warsaw
uprising and in a POW camp.
Nicely-judged little stories with a sting.

w Jerzy Stefan Stawinski, from his novels
d Andrzej Munk ph Jerzy Wojcik m Jan Krenz

Barbara Polomska, L. Niemszyk, Edward
Dziewonski, K. Rudzki, Roman Klosowski,
Josef Nowak

Erotikon*

Sweden 1920   85m approx   bw   silent
Svensk Filmindustri

When a professor discovers that his wife is
unfaithful, he consoles himself with his young
niece.

Sophisticated comedy drama filled with material
which might later have appealed to Lubitsch; a
little faded now, but it still has charm.

w Gustav Molander, Mauritz Stiller, *play* Franz
Herzeg *d Mauritz Stiller ph* Henrik Jaenzon

Lars Hanson, Karin Molander, Tora Teje,
Anders de Wahl

Erotikon*

Czechoslovakia 1929   85m approx   bw
  silent
Gem Film

A stationmaster's daughter takes a rich lover.
Atmospheric little sex drama which sufficiently
justified its title to be a big international success.

wd Gustav Machaty ph Vaclav Vich

Ita Rina, Karel Schleichert, Olaf Fjord, Theo
Pistek

The Errand Boy

US 1961   92m   bw
Paramount / Jerry Lewis

A dimwit paperhanger causes havoc in a
Hollywood studio but is eventually signed up as
a comic to rival Jerry Lewis.

Feeble comedy with the star at his self-satisfied
worst.

wd Jerry Lewis *ph* W. Wallace Kelley

Jerry Lewis, Brian Donlevy, Sig Rumann, Fritz
Feld, Isobel Elsom, Iris Adrian

Escapade

US 1935   87m   bw
MGM (Bernard Hyman)

Affairs of a Viennese artist.

Turgid romantic drama copied from the more
successful German film *Maskerade*.

w Herman J. Mankiewicz, *original* Walter
Reisch *d* Robert Z. Leonard *ph* Ernest Haller
m Bronislau Kaper, Walter Jurmann

William Powell, Luise Rainer, Virginia Bruce,
Mady Christians, Reginald Owen, Frank
Morgan, Laura Hope Crews, Henry Travers

Escapade*

GB 1955   87m   bw
Pinnacle (Daniel Angel)

Parents row with a headmaster when their three
sons steal an aeroplane, but all is well when it

turns out that they are on a peace mission.

Whimsical comedy-drama with a rather foolish
point; the cast however can hardly fail to provide
entertaining moments.

w Gilbert Holland (Donald Ogden Stewart), *play*
Roger MacDougall *d* Philip Leacock *ph* Eric
Cross *m* Bruce Montgomery

John Mills, Alastair Sim, Yvonne Mitchell,
Colin Gordon, Marie Lohr

Escapade in Florence

US 1962   80m   Technicolor
Walt Disney (Bill Anderson)

Two American students in Florence uncover art
thefts.

Cheerful adventure for children, well enough
produced on location, but quite unmemorable.

w Maurice Tombragel *d* Steve Previn *ph* Kurt
Grigoleit *m* Buddy Baker

Ivan Desny, Tommy Kirk, Annette Alliotto,
Nino Castelnuovo

Escapade in Japan

US 1957   93m   Technirama
RKO (Arthur Lubin)

An American boy survives a plane crash in
Tokyo and the crisis reunites his parents.

Nicely photographed travelogue with a thread of
plot; pleasant but hardly sustaining.

w Winston Miller *d* Arthur Lubin *ph* William
Snyder *m* Max Steiner

Cameron Mitchell, Teresa Wright, Jon Prevost,
Philip Ober

Escape

GB 1930   69m   bw
ATP

An escaped convict on Dartmoor is helped and
hindered by various chance encounters.

Episodic, unsatisfactory drama from a stilted
play.

wd Basil Dean, *play* John Galsworthy

Gerald du Maurier, Edna Best, Madeleine
Carroll, Gordon Harker, Horace Hodges, Mabel
Poulton, Lewis Casson, Ian Hunter, Felix
Aylmer

Escape**

US 1940   104m   bw
MGM

Reissue title: *When the Door Opened*

An American gets his mother out of a Nazi
concentration camp before World War II.

Ingenious but somewhat slow-moving

melodrama with an exciting climax and good production values.

w Arch Oboler, Marguerite Roberts, *novel* Ethel Vance *d Mervyn Le Roy m* Franz Waxman

Norma Shearer, Robert Taylor, *Conrad Veidt, Nazimova*, Felix Bressart, Albert Basserman, Philip Dorn, Bonita Granville

'It takes an hour to get started and makes just another feeble fable from headlines.'—*Otis Ferguson*

Escape
GB 1948 79m bw
TCF (William Perlberg)

Wholly artificial, predictable and uninteresting remake of the 1930 film.

w Philip Dunne *d* Joseph L. Mankiewicz
ph Frederick A. Young *m* William Alwyn

Rex Harrison, Peggy Cummins, William Hartnell, Norman Wooland, Jill Esmond

Escape from East Berlin
Germany / US 1962   94m   bw
MGM / Walter Wood / Hans Albin
aka: *Tunnel 28*

An East German chauffeur is persuaded to help an escape attempt by digging and tunnelling under the Berlin Wall.
Cheerless escape melodrama, thinly based on fact but without much suspense.

w Gabrielle Upton, Peter Berneis, Millard Lampell *ph* Georg Krause
m Hans-Martin Majewski

Don Murray, Christine Kaufmann, Werner Klemperer, Ingrid van Bergen

Escape from Fort Bravo*
US 1953   98m   Anscocolor
MGM (Nicholas Nayfack)

A girl helps her Confederate lover to escape from a Yankee fort in Arizona; the commander then tries to save them from Indians.
Grade A western, effectively shot in Death Valley.

w Frank Fenton *d* John Sturges *ph* Robert Surtees *m* Jeff Alexander

William Holden, Eleanor Parker, John Forsythe, William Demarest

Escape from the Dark
GB 1976   104m   Technicolor
Walt Disney (Ron Miller)

In 1909 Yorkshire, two boys save pit ponies from the slaughterhouse.

Efficient family fare with plenty of suspense and good character cameos.

w Rosemary Anne Sisson *d* Charles Jarrott
ph Paul Beeson *m* Ron Goodwin

Alastair Sim, Peter Barkworth, Maurice Colbourne, Susan Tebbs, Geraldine McEwan, Prunella Scales, Leslie Sands, Joe Gladwin

Escape from the Planet of the Apes see
Planet of the Apes

Escape from Zahrain
US 1961   93m   Technicolor   Panavision
Paramount (Ronald Neame)

Prisoners escape across the desert from an oil sheikdom.
Slow, boring adventure film; good to look at, with James Mason unbilled in a tiny part.

w Robin Estridge *d* Ronald Neame
ph Ellsworth Fredericks *m* Lyn Murray

Yul Brynner, Sal Mineo, Madlyn Rhue, Jack Warden, Jay Novello

Escape in the Desert
US 1945   81m   bw
Warner (Alex Gottlieb)

An American flier outwits renegade Nazis.
Oddball remake of *The Petrified Forest*, with Nazis sitting in for gangsters. Of no interest in itself.

w Thomas Job, *play* Robert E. Sherwood
d Edward A. Blatt *ph* Robert Burks *m* Adolph Deutsch

Philip Dorn, Helmut Dantine, Alan Hale, Jean Sullivan, Irene Manning, Samuel S. Hinds

Escape Me Never*
GB 1935   95m   bw
B and D (Herbert Wilcox)

The mother of an illegitimate baby marries a composer who loves someone else.
Archetypal romantic weepie which has probably the star's most memorable and likeable performance.

w Carl Zuckerman, Robert Cullen, *play* Margaret Kennedy *d* Paul Czinner

Elisabeth Bergner, Hugh Sinclair, Griffith Jones, Penelope Dudley Ward, Irene Vanbrugh, Leon Quartermaine, Lyn Harding

Escape Me Never
US 1947   104m   bw
Warner (Henry Blanke)

Muddled remake of the above with shifted

emphasis. So ill-conceived it's like watching through frosted glass.

w Thomas Williamson *d* Peter Godfrey *ph* Sol Polito *m* Erich Wolfgang Korngold

Errol Flynn, Ida Lupino, Eleanor Parker, Gig Young, Reginald Denny, Isobel Elsom, Albert Basserman, Ludwig Stossel, Helene Thimig

Escape to Burma

US 1955 88m Technicolor Superscope
Benedict Bogeaus

An adventurer suspected of murder hides out on the tea plantation of an indomitable American woman.
Far Eastern hokum in which the heroine has a way with elephants.

w Talbot Jennings, Herbert Donovan *d* Allan Dwan *ph* John Alton *m* Louis Forbes

Barbara Stanwyck, Robert Ryan, David Farrar, Murvyn Vye, Reginald Denny

Escape to Danger

GB 1943 92m bw
RKO (William Sistrom)

A British schoolmistress becomes a spy.
Adequate propaganda hokum.

w Wolfgang Wilhelm, Jack Whittingham *d* Lance Comfort *ph* Max Greene

Eric Portman, Ann Dvorak, Karel Stepanek, Ronald Ward, Ronald Adam, Lily Kann, David Peel, Felix Aylmer, A. E. Matthews

Escape to Glory

US 1940 74m bw
Columbia (Sam Bischoff)
aka: *Submarine Zone*

A merchant ship with a variety of passengers is stalked by a Nazi submarine.
Minor *Grand Hotel* afloat: quite brisk and watchable.

w P. J. Wolfson *d* John Brahm *ph* Franz Planer

Pat O'Brien, Constance Bennett, John Halliday, Alan Baxter, Melville Cooper, Edgar Buchanan, Marjorie Gateson

Escape to Witch Mountain*

US 1974 97m Technicolor
Walt Disney (Jerome Courtland)

Two mysterious orphan children have extraordinary powers, are chased by a scheming millionaire, and prove to come from another planet.
Mildly ingenious story frittered away by poor scripting and special effects. A stimulating change in children's films, however.

w Robert Malcolm Young, *novel* Alexander Key *d* John Hough *ph* Frank Phillips *m* Johnny Mandel *sp* Art Cruickshank, Danny Lee

Ray Milland, Donald Pleasence, Eddie Albert, Kim Richards, Ike Eisenmann, Walter Barnes, Reta Shaw, Denver Pyle

Espionage*

US 1937 67m bw
MGM (Harry Rapf)

Spies and counter spies mingle on the Orient Express.
Lively second feature on familiar lines.

w Manuel Seff, Leonard Lee, Ainsworth Morgan, *play* Walter Hackett *d* Kurt Neumann *ph* Ray June

Edmund Lowe, Madge Evans, Paul Lukas, Ketti Gallian, Skeets Gallagher, Leonid Kinskey, Barnett Parker, Frank Reicher

Espionage Agent

US 1939 83m bw
Warner (Louis F. Edelmann)

An American diplomat falls in love with a spy.
Anti-isolationist, semi-documentary exposé, a rather sketchy cross between *Foreign Correspondent* and *Confessions of a Nazi Spy*.

w Warren Duff, Michael Fessier, Frank Donaghue, Robert Buckner *d* Lloyd Bacon *ph* Charles Rosher

Joel McCrea, Brenda Marshall, Jeffrey Lynn, George Bancroft, Stanley Ridges, James Stephenson, Nana Bryant

Espoir*

France / Spain 1938–45 73m bw
Cornignion / Moligniec
aka: *Days of Hope; Man's Hope*

Events of the Spanish Civil War, recreated by surviving combatants.
Anti-fascist propaganda which seems a good deal less inspiring than on its first release, but has some vivid cinematic ideas.

wd André Malraux ph Louis Page *m* Darius Milhaud

Mejuto, Nicolas Rodriguez, Jose Lado

Esther and the King

US 1960 109m Technicolor
    Cinemascope
TCF / Galatea (Raoul Walsh)

A Persian king selects a new bride who helps defend him from his enemies.
Tedious biblical hokum with a muddled script and the usual co-production deficiencies.

w Raoul Walsh, Michael Elkins *d* Raoul Walsh
ph Mario Bava *m* Francesco Lavagnino,
Roberto Nicolosi

Richard Egan, Joan Collins, Dennis O'Dea,
Sergei Fantoni, Rik Battaglia

Esther Waters

GB 1947   108m   bw
GFD / Wessex (Ian Dalrymple)

In the 1870s, a maid is seduced by a squire but
insists on bringing up her child without help.
Faded costumer with tentative performances
and little else to recommend it.

w Michael Gordon, William Rose, Gerard
Tyrrell, *novel* George Moore *d* Ian Dalrymple,
Peter Proud
ph C. Pennington-Richards, H. E. Fowle
m Gordon Jacob

Kathleen Ryan, Dirk Bogarde, Cyril Cusack,
Ivor Barnard, Fay Compton, Mary Clare,
Morland Graham

The Eternal Sea

US 1955   96m   bw
Republic (John H. Auer)

The career of an aircraft carrier captain in World
War II and Korea.
Solemn biopic of John Hoskins: competent but
quite uninspired.

w Allen Rivkin *d* John H. Auer *ph* John L.
Russell Jnr *m* Elmer Bernstein

Sterling Hayden, Alexis Smith, Dean Jagger,
Virginia Grey

Eternally Yours*

US 1939   95m   bw
Walter Wanger

A magician's wife thinks he is too interested in
his tricks.
Slightly scatty romantic comedy, amiable if not
quite good enough to stand the test of time, but
with a great cast.

w Gene Towne, Graham Baker *d* Tay Garnett
ph Merritt Gerstad *m* Werner Janssen

Loretta Young, David Niven, Broderick
Crawford, Hugh Herbert, Billie Burke, C.
Aubrey Smith, Raymond Walburn, Zasu Pitts,
Virginia Field, Eve Arden, Herman the Rabbit

AAN: Werner Janssen

Eureka Stockade

GB 1948   103m   bw
Ealing (Leslie Norman)

In 1850, Australian gold miners revolt against a
harsh governor.

Unconvincingly made historical actioner from
Ealing's antipodean period.

w Harry Watt, Walter Greenwood, Ralph
Smart *d* Harry Watt

Chips Rafferty, Jane Barrett, Gordon Jackson,
Jack Lambert, Peter Illing, Ralph Truman, Peter
Finch

Europa 51 *

Italy 1952   110m   bw
Ponti / de Laurentiis

An American society woman living in Rome
seeks vainly for truth in the chaotic post-war
world and is committed to an asylum by her
husband.
A despairing, ironic comment on a period which
unfortunately does not convince on the personal
level.

w Roberto Rossellini and others *d* Roberto
Rossellini *ph* Aldo Tonti *m* Renzo Rossellini

Ingrid Bergman, Alexander Knox, Ettore
Giannini, Giulietta Masina

Eva

France / Italy 1962   135m   bw
Paris / Interopa (Robert and Raymond Hakim)

A raw Welsh novelist in Venice is humiliated by
a money-loving Frenchwoman who erotically
ensnares him.
Foolish story of a *femme fatale*; elegantly
Freudian at moments, it long outstays its
welcome.

w Hugo Butler, Evan Jones, *novel* James Hadley
Chase *d* Joseph Losey *ph* Gianni di Venanzo
m Michel Legrand

Stanley Baker, Jeanne Moreau, Virna Lisi,
James Villiers

The Eve of St Mark

US 1944   95m   bw
TCF

A small-town boy goes to war and his sweetheart
waits for him.
Poetic propaganda based on a sticky play which
however had a tragic ending which the film
eschews. Smartly made is all one can say.

w George Seaton, *play* Maxwell Anderson
d John M. Stahl *ph* Joseph La Shelle *m* Cyril
Mockridge

William Eythe, Anne Baxter, Michael O'Shea,
Vincent Price, Ruth Nelson, Ray Collins,
Stanley Prager, Henry Morgan

Eve Wants to Sleep*
Poland 1957 98m bw
Film Polski (Wislaw Mincer)

An innocent country girl arrives in a city overrun by subversives.
Curious yet sympathetic black farce, like a cross between *Hellzapoppin* and *M*. One on its own.

wd Tadeusz Chmielewski *ph* Stefan Matyjaskiewicz *m* Henryk Czyz

Barbara Kwiatkowska, Stanislaw Mikulski, Ludwik Benoit

Evel Knievel
US 1971 90m Metrocolor
(MGM) Fanfare (George Hamilton)

Episodes from the life of a motor-cycle stuntman.
Mildly entertaining ragbag of action sequences and fragments of philosophy which might have been more tolerable had EK played himself.

w Alan Caillou, John Milius *d* Marvin Chomsky *ph* David Walsh *m* Pat Williams

George Hamilton, Sue Lyon, Bert Freed, Rod Cameron

Evelyn Prentice
US 1934 80m bw
MGM (John W. Considine Jnr)

The wife of a criminal lawyer has an affair with a man who blackmails her.
Moderate domestic-cum-courtroom melodrama, heavily reliant on its popular stars.

w Lenore Coffee, *novel* W. E. Woodward *d* William K. Howard *ph* Charles G. Clarke *md* Oscar Radin

Myrna Loy, William Powell, Una Merkel, Harvey Stephens, Isabel Jewell, Rosalind Russell, Henry Wadsworth, Edward Brophy

Evensong*
GB 1934 84m bw
Gaumont (Michael Balcon)

At the turn of the century, an Austrian prima donna gives up her career for love.
Well-made romantic drama of its type, notable as the best of its star's few films.

w Edward Knoblock, Dorothy Farnum, *play* Beverly Nichols *d* Victor Saville

Evelyn Laye, Fritz Kortner, Carl Esmond, Alice Delysia, Emlyn Williams, Muriel Aked

Ever Since Eve
US 1937 80m bw
Warner (Earl Baldwin)

A publisher falls for a pretty girl, not realizing that she is his own plain secretary in disguise.
Silly romantic comedy which sadly lacks wit, style and believability.

w Lawrence Riley, Earl Baldwin, Lillie Hayward *d* Lloyd Bacon *ph* George Barnes *m* Heinz Roemheld

Marion Davies (her last film), Robert Montgomery, Frank McHugh, Patsy Kelly, Louise Fazenda, Barton MacLane, Mary Treen

Evergreen**
GB 1934 90m bw
Gaumont (Michael Balcon)

A star's daughter takes her mother's place, with romantic complications.
Pleasant musical with more wit and style than might be expected.

w Emlyn Williams, Marjorie Gaffney, *play* Benn W. Levy *d* Victor Saville *songs* Rodgers and Hart

Jessie Matthews, Sonnie Hale, Betty Balfour, Barry Mackay, Ivor McLaren, Hartley Power

Every Day's a Holiday*
US 1937 79m bw
Paramount (Emmanuel Cohen)

A confidence girl in the old Bowery sells Brooklyn Bridge to suckers.
The most satisfactory example of post-Legion of Decency Mae West, the smut being replaced by a lively cast of comedians.

w Mae West *d* A. Edward Sutherland *ph* Karl Struss *songs* various

Mae West, Edmund Lowe, Charles Butterworth, Charles Winninger, Walter Catlett, Lloyd Nolan, Herman Bing, Roger Imhof, Chester Conklin

Every Girl Should be Married
US 1948 84m bw
RKO (Don Hartman, Dore Schary)

A determined girl sets her cap at a bachelor pediatrician.
Woefully thin star comedy with few laughs.

w Stephen Morehouse Avery, Don Hartman *d* Don Hartman *ph* George E. Diskant *m* Leigh Harline

Cary Grant, Betsy Drake, Franchot Tone, Diana Lynn, Alan Mowbray, Elizabeth Risdon, Richard Gaines

'In the past, Cary Grant has shown a talent for quietly underplaying comedy. In this picture, he has trouble finding comedy to play.'—*Time*

Every Little Crook and Nanny
US 1972　92m　Metrocolor
MGM (Leonard J. Ackerman)

A Mafia chief finds his child's new nanny has a grudge against him.
Sporadically amusing farce.

w Cy Howard, Jonathan Axelrod, Robert Klane
d Cy Howard ph Philip Lathrop m Fred Karlin

Victor Mature, Lynn Redgrave, Paul Sand, Maggie Blye, Austin Pendleton, John Astin, Dom De Luise

Every Night at Eight
US 1935　80m　bw
Paramount (Walter Wanger)

Three sisters become a successful radio singing team.
Forgettable comedy musical with a mildly interesting cast.

w Gene Towne, Graham Baker d Raoul Walsh
ph James Van Trees songs Dorothy Fields, Jimmy McHugh

George Raft, Alice Faye, Frances Langford, Patsy Kelly, The Radio Rogues, Walter Catlett, Herman Bing

Everybody Does It
US 1949　98m　bw
TCF (Nunnally Johnson)

A stage-struck wife is chagrined to see her dull husband accidentally become an opera singer.
Very mild remake of *Wife, Husband and Friend*; everyone tries to be zany, but the result is often just silly.

w Nunnally Johnson d Edmund Goulding
ph Joseph La Shelle m Alfred Newman

Paul Douglas, Celeste Holm, Linda Darnell, Charles Coburn, Millard Mitchell, Lucile Watson, John Hoyt, George Tobias, Leon Belasco

'For sheer momentary enjoyment it would be hard to beat.'—*Richard Mallett, Punch*

Everybody Sing*
US 1937　80m　bw
MGM (Harry Rapf)

An eccentric theatrical family is upstaged by its servants, who put on a Broadway show.
Agreeably zany comedy with music.

w Florence Ryerson, Edgar Allan Woolf
d Edwin L. Marin

Allan Jones, *Fanny Brice, Judy Garland*, Reginald Owen, Billie Burke, Lynne Carver, Monty Woolley, Reginald Gardiner, Henry Armetta

Everything But the Truth
US 1956　83m　Technicolor
U-I (Howard Christie)

A small boy embarrasses his family by telling the truth at all times.
Dum-dum formula comedy made with jaded professionalism.

w Herb Meadow d Jerry Hopper ph Maury Gertsman m Milton Rosen

Maureen O'Hara, John Forsythe, Tim Hovey, Frank Faylen, Barry Atwater

Everything Happens at Night
US 1939　77m　bw
TCF (Harry Joe Brown)

Two reporters fall for the daughter of a Nobel Peace Prize winner on the run from the Gestapo.
The star's sixth American film plays down the music and skating in favour of rather jaded spy comedy. Modest entertainment.

w Art Arthur, Robert Harari d Irving Cummings ph Edward Cronjager m various

Sonja Henie, Ray Milland, Robert Cummings, Maurice Moscovitch, Leonid Kinskey, Alan Dinehart, Fritz Feld, Victor Varconi

Everything I Have Is Yours
US 1952　92m　Technicolor
MGM (George Wells)

A song and dance team is disrupted when the wife decides to become a mother.
Uninventive but lively musical vehicle for the Champions.

w George Wells d Robert Z. Leonard
ph William V. Skall md David Rose ch Nick Castle, Gower Champion

Marge and Gower Champion, Dennis O'Keefe, Eduard Franz

Everything Is Thunder*
GB 1936　76m　bw
Gaumont-British

A German girl helps a British prisoner of war to escape.
Tolerable let's-not-be-beastly melodrama, quite unusual in its time.

w Marion Dix, John Orton, novel J. B. Hardy
d Milton Rosmer ph Gunther Krampf

Constance Bennett, Douglass Montgomery, Oscar Homolka, Roy Emerton, Frederick Lloyd, George Merritt

Everything You Always Wanted to Know About Sex*

US 1972 87m De Luxe
US / Jack Rollins / Charles H. Joffe / Brodsky / Gould

Seven sketches on sexual themes.
Dishevelled revue with a reasonable number of laughs for broadminded audiences.

wd Woody Allen, *book* Dr David Reuben
ph David M. Walsh *m* Mundell Lowe *pd* Dale Hennesy

Woody Allen, Lynn Redgrave, Anthony Quayle, John Carradine, Lou Jacobi, Louise Lasser, Tony Randall, Burt Reynolds, Gene Wilder

The Evil

US 1978 89m Movielab
New World / Rangoon (Ed Carlin)

A psychologist takes a team to investigate a haunted house, and is soon sorry he meddled.
Another variation on the theme of *The Haunting* and *The Legend of Hell House*; more this time on the horror comic level, but reasonably effective.

w Donald G. Thompson *d* Gus Trikonis
ph Mario Di Leo *m* Johnny Harris

Richard Crenna, Joanna Pettet, Andrew Prine, Cassie Yates, Victor Buono, Lynne Maddy

The Evil of Frankenstein

GB 1964 94m Technicolor
U-I / Hammer (Anthony Hinds)

Frankenstein returns to his derelict castle and finds the Monster preserved in a glacier.
For their third Frankenstein film Hammer made a distribution deal with Universal and thus for the first time were able to use fragments of the old plots as well as something approximating to the Karloff make-up. Production and writing, however, are sadly dispirited except when relying on sadism.

w John Elder (Anthony Hinds) *d* Freddie Francis *ph* John Wilcox *m* Don Banks

Peter Cushing, Peter Woodthorpe, Sandor Eles, Kiwi Kingston (as the monster), Duncan Lamont, Katy Wild, David Hutcheson

The Ex-Mrs Bradford*

US 1936 87m bw
MGM (Edward Kaufman)

A doctor's scatty ex-wife involves him in solving a murder plot.
Amusing crime comedy, just a little way behind *The Thin Man.*

w Anthony Veiller, James Edward Grant
d Stephen Roberts *ph* J. Roy Hunt *m* Roy Webb

William Powell, Jean Arthur, James Gleason, Eric Blore, Robert Armstrong, Lila Lee, Grant Mitchell, Ralph Morgan

Excuse My Dust*

US 1951 82m Technicolor
MGM (Jack Cummings)

The inventor of a horseless carriage loves the daughter of a livery stable owner.
Innocuous small-town nineties comedy with a race climax. Quite pleasant.

w George Wells *d* Roy Rowland *ph* Alfred Gilks *m* Arthur Schwarz

Red Skelton, Sally Forrest, Macdonald Carey, William Demarest

The Executioner*

GB 1970 107m Technicolor Panavision
Columbia / Ameran (Charles H. Schneer)

A British spy suspects a colleague of being a double agent.
Dour espionage thriller with a reasonably holding narrative and predictable performances.

w Jack Pulman *d* Sam Wanamaker *ph* Denys Coop *m* Ron Goodwin

George Peppard, Nigel Patrick, Joan Collins, Judy Geeson, Oscar Homolka, Charles Gray, Keith Michell, George Baker, Alexander Scourby, Peter Bull, Ernest Clark, Peter Dyneley
'Does not escape from the well-worn shallow groove in which the contemporary spy film is in danger of becoming stuck.'—*Russell Campbell*

Executive Action**

US 1973 91m colour
EA Enterprises / Wakefield Orloff (Edward Lewis)

An imaginative version of the facts behind the 1963 assassination of President Kennedy.
Interesting but rather messy mixture of fact and fiction; makes one sit up while it's unreeling.

w Dalton Trumbo, *story* Mark Lane, Donald Freed *d* David Miller *ph* Robert Steadman *m* Randy Edelman

Burt Lancaster, Robert Ryan, Will Geer, Gilbert Green, John Anderson

Executive Suite***

US 1954 104m bw
MGM (John Houseman)

When the president of a big company dies, the

boardroom sees a battle for control.
First of the boardroom films of the fifties, a calculatedly commercial mixture of business ethics and domestic asides, with an all-star cast working up effective tensions.

w Ernest Lehman, novel Cameron Hawley *d Robert Wise ph* George Folsey

Fredric March, William Holden, June Allyson, *Barbara Stanwyck,* Walter Pidgeon, Shelley Winters, Paul Douglas, *Louis Calhern,* Dean Jagger, *Nina Foch,* Tim Considine
† A TV series followed in 1976.

AAN: George Folsey; Nina Foch

The Exile*
US 1948   90m   bw
U-I (Douglas Fairbanks Jnr)

The man who is to return to the English throne as Charles II hides in Holland, receives his friends and despatches his enemies.
Curious, talkative swashbuckler with only a few moments of action; the available talents are simply not used, though the director imposes a nice pictorial style.

w Douglas Fairbanks Jnr, *novel* His Majesty the King by Cosmo Hamilton *d Max Ophuls ph Franz Planer*

Douglas Fairbanks Jnr, Maria Montez, Paula Corday, Henry Daniell, Nigel Bruce, Robert Coote
† Originally released in sepia.

Exit Smiling**
US 1926   80m approx (24 fps)   bw   silent
MGM

The worst actress in a stock company saves the show.
Amusing comedy for a star who never quite made it in films: this is the best of her vehicles.

w Sam Taylor, Tim Whelan, *play* Marc Connelly *d* Sam Taylor

Beatrice Lillie, Jack Pickford, Harry Myers, Doris Lloyd, DeWitt Jennings, Louise Lorraine, Franklin Pangborn

Exodus*
US 1960   220m   Technicolor   Super Panavision 70
UA / Carlyle / Alpha (Otto Preminger)

The early years of the state of Israel, seen through various eyes.
Heavy-going modern epic, toned down from a passionate novel.

w Dalton Trumbo, *novel* Leon Uris *d* Otto Preminger *ph* Sam Leavitt *m* Ernest Gold

Paul Newman, Eva Marie Saint, Ralph Richardson, Peter Lawford, Lee J. Cobb, Sal Mineo, John Derek, Hugh Griffith, Gregory Ratoff, Felix Aylmer, David Opatoshu, Jill Haworth, Alexandra Stewart, Martin Benson, Martin Miller
'Professionalism is not enough—after three and a half hours the approach seems more exhausting than exhaustive.'—*Penelope Houston*
† Jewish comedian Mort Sahl, invited by the director to a preview, is said to have stood up after three hours and said: 'Otto—let my people go!'

AA: Ernest Gold
AAN: Sam Leavitt; Sal Mineo

The Exorcist*
US 1973   122m   Metrocolor
Warner / Hoya (William Peter Blatty)

A small girl is unaccountably possessed by the devil and turned into a repellent monster who causes several violent deaths before she is cured. Spectacularly ludicrous mishmash with uncomfortable attention to physical detail and no talent for narrative or verisimilitude. Its sensational aspects, together with a sudden worldwide need for the supernatural, assured its enormous commercial success.

w William Peter Blatty, from his novel *d* William Friedkin *ph* Owen Roizman *m* George Crumb and others *pd* Bill Malloy

Ellen Burstyn, Max Von Sydow, Jason Miller, Linda Blair, Lee J. Cobb, Kitty Winn, Jack McGowran
'No more nor less than a blood and thunder horror movie, foundering heavily on the rocks of pretension.'—*Tom Milne*
'*The Exorcist* makes no sense, [but] if you want to be shaken, it will scare the hell out of you.'—*Stanley Kauffmann*
'It exploits the subject of diabolic possession without telling you anything about it . . . just a stylistic exercise.'—*Michael Billington, Illustrated London News*
† Published 1974: *The Story Behind the Exorcist* by Peter Travers and Stephanie Reiff.

AA: William Peter Blatty
AAN: best picture; William Friedkin; Owen Roizman; Ellen Burstyn; Jason Miller; Linda Blair

Exorcist II: The Heretic
US 1977   117m   Technicolor
Warner (Richard Lederer, John Boorman)

Father Lamont, investigating the case related in *The Exorcist*, finds that the evil in Regan,

apparently exorcized, is only dormant.
Highly unsatisfactory psychic melodrama
which, far from the commercial route of the
shocker followed by its predecessor, falls flat on
its face along some wayward path of
metaphysical and religious fancy. A commercial
disaster, it was released in two versions and is
unintelligible in either.

w William Goodhart d John Boorman
ph William A. Fraker m Ennio Morricone
pd Richard MacDonald

Richard Burton, Linda Blair, Louise Fletcher,
Kitty Winn, Max Von Sydow, Paul Henried,
James Earl Jones, Ned Beatty

Experiment in Terror**

US 1962 123m bw
Columbia / Geoffrey-Kate Productions (Blake
    Edwards)
GB title: The Grip of Fear

An asthmatic stranger threatens the life of a
bank teller and her sister if she does not help him
commit a robbery.
Detailed, meticulous police thriller with San
Francisco locations. Good stuff, a bit long.

w The Gordons, from their novel Operation
Terror d Blake Edwards ph Philip Lathrop
m Henry Mancini

Glenn Ford, Lee Remick, Ross Martin

Experiment Perilous*

US 1944 91m bw
RKO (Warren Duff)

A woman's wealthy husband is killed in
mysterious circumstances, and she is suspected.
Enjoyable mystery melodrama which takes itself
with a pinch of salt.

w Warren Duff, novel Margaret Carpenter
d Jacques Tourneur ph Tony Gaudio m Roy
Webb

Hedy Lamarr, Paul Lukas, George Brent, Albert
Dekker, Margaret Wycherly

The Exploits of Elaine*

US 1914 14 episodes, each 20m approx
    bw silent
Pathé/Wharton

Detective Craig Kennedy helps his girl friend
avenge her father's murder.
Archetypal cliffhanger serial following on the
success of The Perils of Pauline. It was itself
followed within a year by The New Exploits of
Elaine and The Romance of Elaine. Chapter
headings included such now familiar clichés as
'The Clutching Hand', 'The Vanishing Jewels',
'The Poisoned Room', 'The Death Ray' and 'The

Devil Worshippers'. The films were much
praised by critics for their pace and
inventiveness.

w Charles W. Goddard, George B. Seitz, from
stories by Arthur B. Reeve d Louis Gasnier,
George B. Seitz

Pearl White, Creighton Hale, Sheldon Lewis,
Arnold Daly

Expresso Bongo*

GB 1959 111m bw Dyaliscope
BL / Britannia / Conquest (Val Guest)

A Soho agent turns a nondescript teenage singer
into an international star.
Heavily vulgarized version of a stage skit on the
Tommy Steele rock phenomenon, divested of
most of its satirical barbs and only intermittently
amusing.

w Wolf Mankowitz, from his play d Val Guest
ph John Wilcox songs David Heneker, Monty
Norman

Laurence Harvey, Sylvia Syms, Yolande
Donlan, Cliff Richard, Meier Tzelniker, Gilbert
Harding, Ambrosine Philpotts, Eric Pohlmann,
Wilfrid Lawson, Hermione Baddeley, Reginald
Beckwith, Martin Miller

Extase*

Czechoslovakia 1932 90m bw
Universal Elektra Film
aka: Ecstasy

A country girl takes a lover.
Simple love story with Freudian sequences, quite
successfully and cinematically done. It caused a
sensation at the time and was issued in various
censored versions; the star's husband later tried
to destroy all the copies.

w Gustav Machaty, story Viteslav Nezval
d Gustav Machaty ph Jan Stallich m Giuseppe
Becce

Hedy Kiesler (later Hedy Lamarr), Aribert Mog

The Exterminating Angel***

Mexico 1962 95m bw
Uninci-Films 59
original title: El Angel Exterminador

High society dinner guests find themselves
unable to leave the room, stay there for days, and
go totally to the bad before the strange spell is
broken; when they go to church to give thanks,
they find themselves unable to leave.
Fascinating surrealist fantasia on themes
elaborated with even more panache in The
Discreet Charm of the Bourgeoisie.
Nevertheless, one of its director's key films.

wd Luis Bunuel (story assistance from Luis
Alcoriza) *ph* Gabriel Figueroa *ad* Jesus Bracho

Silvia Pinal, Enrique Rambal, Jacqueline
Andere, Jose Baviera

The Extra Girl*
US 1923   69m   bw   silent
Mack Sennett

A small town girl wins a beauty contest and goes
to Hollywood.
A comparatively restrained comedy with
slapstick interludes, this charming film shows its
star at her best and admirably illustrates
Hollywood in the early twenties.

d Mack Sennett *m* Jack Ward

Mabel Normand, Max Davidson, Ralph Graves,
George Nicholls

The Extraordinary Seaman
US 1968   80m   Metrocolor   Panavision
MGM / John Frankenheimer / Edward Lewis
(John H. Cushingham, Hal Dresner)

Four stranded sailors come upon the ghostly
Royal Navy captain of a ghostly World War II
ship.
Curious sixties attempt at forties fantasy;
obviously, from its short running time and
fragmented style, something went sadly adrift
during its making, and the wide screen does not
help, but there are scattered funny moments.

w Philip Rock, Hal Dresner *d* John
Frankenheimer *ph* Lionel Lindon *m* Maurice
Jarre

David Niven, Faye Dunaway, Alan Alda,
Mickey Rooney, Jack Carter, Juano Hernandez,
Barry Kelley

Eye of the Cat*
US 1969   102m   Technicolor
Universal / Joseph M. Schenck (Bernard
Schwarz, Philip Hazelton)

A young man who hates cats goes to stay with
his crippled aunt who keeps a house full of them.
Odd, *Psycho*-like thriller (from the same screen
writer) with plenty of scary sequences but an
inadequate resolution.

w Joseph Stefano *d* David Lowell Rich
ph Russell Metty, Ellsworth Fredericks m Lalo
Schifrin *cat trainer* Ray Berwick

Eleanor Parker, Michael Sarrazin, Gayle
Hunnicutt, Tim Henry, Laurence Naismith
'Not so much a good film as an extravagantly
enjoyable one.'—*MFB*

Eye of the Devil*
GB 1967   92m   bw
MGM / Filmways (John Calley, Ben Kadish)

A French nobleman is obsessed by a family
tradition of pagan self-sacrifice.
Diabolical goings-on in a spooky castle, not
really helped by a glittering supporting cast any
more than by miscast stars, sluggish direction or
a general atmosphere of gloom rather than
suspense.

w Robin Estridge, Dennis Murphy, *novel* Day of
the Arrow by Philip Loraine *d* J. Lee-
Thompson *ph* Erwin Hillier *m* Gary
McFarland

David Niven, Deborah Kerr, Emlyn Williams,
Flora Robson, Donald Pleasence, Edward
Mulhare, David Hemmings, Sharon Tate, John
Le Mesurier, Donald Bisset
  'It is hard to say why the total effect is so
constantly hilarious.'—*MFB*
† The film had a chequered career. The first
attempt to make it was abandoned because of
Kim Novak's inadequacy; it then went through
three titles and a lot of trouble with the censor.

Eye Witness
GB 1956   82m   bw
Rank / Sydney Box

A maniacal burglar pursues a witness of his
crime into the emergency ward of a local
hospital.
Naïve but adequate suspenser with too many
character cameos getting in the way of the plot.

w Janet Green *d* Muriel Box *ph* Reg Wyer
m Bruce Montgomery

Donald Sinden, Muriel Pavlow, Belinda Lee,
Michael Craig, Nigel Stock, Susan Beaumont,
David Knight, *Ada Reeve*

The Eyes of Laura Mars
US 1978   104m   Metrocolor
Columbia / Jon Peters (Jack H. Harris)

A fashion photographer has violent
premonitions about a series of murders.
Silly and often unpleasant suspenser which
despite its chic appearance never bothers to
explain itself.

w John Carpenter, David Zelag Goodman
d Irvin Kershner *ph* Victor J. Kemper *m* Artie
Kane

Faye Dunaway, Tommy Lee Jones, Brad
Dourif, René Auberjonois, Raul Julia, Frank
Adonis

Eyes in the Night*
US 1942   80m   bw
MGM (Jack Chertok)

A blind detective sets out to discover whether a mysterious man engaged to an heiress is really a Nazi spy.

Tolerable wartime puzzler.

w Guy Trosper, Howard Emmett Rogers, *novel* Odor of Violets by Bayard Kendrick *d Fred Zinnemann ph* Robert Planck, Charles Lawton *m* Lennie Hayton

Edward Arnold, Ann Harding, Donna Reed, Allen Jenkins, John Emery, Stephen McNally, Reginald Denny, Rosemary de Camp, Stanley Ridges

† Edward Arnold appeared once more as Duncan Maclain, in *The Hidden Eye* (1944).

Eyes without a Face*

France / Italy 1959　90m　bw
Champs Elysées / Lux (Jules Borkon)
original title: *Les Yeux sans Visage*

When his daughter is mutilated in a car accident, a mad professor murders young girls in the process of grafting their faces onto hers.

Unpleasant horror film which its director seems to have made as a joke; the years have made it a cult.

w Jean Redon, from his novel　*d Georges Franju ph* Eugen Schufftan　*m* Maurice Jarre

Pierre Brasseur, Alida Valli, Edith Scob, François Guérin

Eyewitness*

GB 1970　91m　Technicolor
ITC / ABP (Paul Maslansky)

A boy is the sole witness to an assassination, but no one believes him except the assassins.

The Window all over again, the standard clichés being tricked out with fancy photography, sub-Hitchcock set-ups and Mediterranean locations, which make it all very tolerable.

w Ronald Harwood, *novel* Mark Hebden *d* John Hough *ph* David Holmes *m* Fairfield Parlour, David Whitaker

Mark Lester, Lionel Jeffries, Susan George, Tony Bonner, Jeremy Kemp, Peter Vaughan, Peter Bowles, Betty Marsden

F

F for Fake*
France / Iran / West Germany 1973   85m
   colour
Astrophore / Saco / Janus (Dominique
   Antoine, François Reichenbach)
French title: *Vérités et Mensonges*

Orson Welles, at a railway station, lectures the
audience in truth and falsehood, in art, in films
and in life.
A ragbag of an entertainment, cannibalizing as it
does more than one unsold documentary,
shredded at the editing table to match the
narrator's illusionist style. Despite the raptures
of some critics, this is an irritating effusion, and
Welles now looks more like a clever charlatan
than a master film-maker.

w Orson Welles, Oja Palinkas · *d* Orson Welles
ph Gary Graver, Christian Odasso *m* Michel
Legrand

F.P.1*
GB / Germany 1933   93m   bw
Gaumont / UFA (Erich Pommer)

Financiers try to destroy the first floating
aerodrome.
'Futuristic' melodrama about an aircraft carrier.
Very well done, and shot in two languages, but
now dated in most respects.

w Curt Siodmak, Walter Reisch, Robert
Stevenson, Peter Macfarlane *d* Karl Hartl

Conrad Veidt, Leslie Fenton, Jill Esmond,
George Merritt, Donald Calthrop, Nicholas
Hannen, Francis L. Sullivan

The Fabulous Adventures of Marco Polo
France / Italy / Yugoslavia / Egypt /
   Afghanistan 1964   115m
   Eastmancolor Franscope
Ittac / Prodi / Avala / Mounir Rafla / Italaf
   Kaboul (Raoul Lévy)
aka: *Marco the Magnificent*

In 1271 Marco Polo carries a message of peace
to Kubla Khan.
Curious mixture of melodrama and pantomime,
with a star cast half playing for laughs.

w Raoul Lévy, Denys de la Patellière *d* Denys

de la Patellière, Noel Howard *ph* Armand
Thirard *m* George Garvarentz

Horst Buchholz, Anthony Quinn, Orson Welles,
Akim Tamiroff, Robert Hossein, Omar Sharif,
Elsa Martinelli, Grégoire Aslan, Massimo
Girotti, Folco Lulli

The Fabulous Dorseys
US 1947   91m   bw
UA (Charles R. Rogers)

Two quarrelling bandleader brothers are
reunited on the death of their father.
Slight, comedic biopic with the Dorseys playing
well and trying hard.

w Richard English, Art Arthur, Curtis Kenyon
d Alfred E. Green *ph* James Van Trees *m* Leo
Shuken

Tommy Dorsey, Jimmy Dorsey (and their
bands), Janet Blair, Paul Whiteman, William
Lundigan

The Face***
Sweden 1958   103m   bw
Svensk Filmindustri
original title: *Ansiktet;* US title: *The Magician*

In 19th-century Sweden, a mesmerist and his
troupe are halted at a country post to be
examined by three officials. Partly exposed as a
fraud, he takes a frightening revenge.
A virtually indecipherable parable which may be
about the survival of Christianity (and may not),
this wholly personal Bergman fancy has to be
enjoyed chiefly for its surface frissons, for its
acting and its look, which are almost sufficient
compensation.

wd Ingmar Bergman *ph* Gunnar Fischer
m Erik Nordgren

Max Von Sydow, Ingrid Thulin, *Gunnar
Bjornstrand*, Naima Wifstrand, Ake Fridell,
Lars Ekborg, Bengt Ekerot

The Face at the Window*
GB 1939   65m   bw
Pennant / Ambassador (George King)

In 1880 Paris, a murderer uses his moronic half-
brother to distract his victims but is foiled when a
dead man apparently incriminates him.

Roistering melodrama which provided Tod
Slaughter with one of his juiciest roles and is here
effectively presented, which is more than can be
said for the screen treatments of most of his other
vehicles.

w A. R. Rawlinson, Randall Faye, *play* F.
Brooke Warren *d* George King

Tod Slaughter, Marjorie Taylor, John Warwick,
Leonard Henry, Aubrey Mallalieu

'One of the best English pictures I have seen
. . . leaves the American horror films far
behind.'—*Graham Greene*

The Face behind the Mask*
US 1941   69m   bw
Columbia (Wallace MacDonald)

When his face is disfigured in a fire, an immigrant
turns to a life of crime.
Effective second feature melodrama with a good
star performance.

w Allen Vincent, Paul Jarrico, *play* Thomas
O'Connell *d* Robert Florey *ph* Franz Planer
md Sidney Cutner

Peter Lorre, Evelyn Keyes, *Don Beddoe*, George
E. Stone

A Face in the Crowd***
US 1957   126m   bw
(Warner) Newton (Elia Kazan)

A small-town hick becomes a megalomaniac
when television turns him into a cracker-barrel
philosopher.
Brilliantly cinematic melodrama of its time
which only flags in the last lap and paints a
luridly entertaining picture of modern show
business.

w Budd Schulberg, from his story Your
Arkansas Traveller *d Elia Kazan ph Harry
Stradling, Gayne Rescher m* Tom Glazer

*Andy Griffith, Lee Remick, Walter Matthau,
Patricia Neal*, Anthony Franciosa, Percy
Waram, Marshall Neilan

'Savagery, bitterness, cutting humour.'—
Penelope Houston

A Face in the Rain*
US 1963   80m   bw
Filmways / Calvic (John Calley)

During World War II an American spy in Italy
bungles his mission, and hides in the apartment
of a professor's wife.
Offbeat, talkative melodrama with a few neat
touches.

w Hugo Butler, Jean Rouverol *d Irvin Kershner
ph Haskell Wexler m* Richard Markowitz

Rory Calhoun, Marina Berti, Niall MacGinnis

Face of a Fugitive*
US 1959   81m   Eastmancolor
Columbia / Morningside

A man falsely accused of murder makes a new
life in a frontier town.
Lively western melodrama with good
atmosphere.

w David T. Chantler *d Paul Wendkos
ph* Wilfrid M. Cline *m* Jerry Goldsmith

Fred MacMurray, Lin McCarthy, Alan Baxter,
James Coburn

The Face of Fu Manchu**
GB 1965   96m   Techniscope
Anglo–EMI / Hallam (Harry Alan Towers)

In the twenties, Nayland Smith of Scotland Yard
links an oriental crime wave with evil
mastermind Fu Manchu.
A splendidly light touch and attention to detail
make this entertaining spoof like a tuppenny
blood come to life.

w Peter Welbeck (Harry Alan Towers) *d Don
Sharp ph* Ernest Steward *m* Chris Whelan
ad Frank White

Nigel Green, Christopher Lee, Tsai Chin,
Howard Marion Crawford

Faces*
US 1968   130m   bw
Maurice McEndree

A discontented Los Angeles executive tries but
fails to go through with a divorce.
A personal, probing study of middle-aged
loneliness, made with the director's usual long-
winded relentlessness but quite frequently
compelling.

wd John Cassavetes *ph* Al Ruban *m* Jack
Ackerman

John Marley, Gena Rowlands, Lynn Carlin,
Fred Draper, Seymour Cassell

'The cast are all painfully and overpoweringly
real.'—*Jan Dawson*

AAN: John Cassavetes (as writer); Lynn Carlin;
Seymour Cassell

Faces in the Dark*
GB 1960   85m   bw
Rank /Welbeck / Penington Eady (Jon
Penington)

A blind man survives a plot against his life.
Unlikely but watchable puzzler, betrayed by
lifeless handling. Hitchcock could have worked
wonders with such a plot.

w Ephraim Kogan, John Tulley, *novel* Pierre
Boileau, Thomas Narcejac *d* David Eady
ph Ken Hodges *m* Edwin Astley

John Gregson, Mai Zetterling, Michael Denison, John Ireland, Tony Wright, Nanette Newman

The Facts of Life *
US 1960   103m   bw
(UA) HLP (Norman Panama)

Two middle-aged married suburbanites have an abortive affair.
Star comedy with muted slapstick and earnest acting, a good try, but less effective than their normal pratfalls.

w Norman Panama, Melvin Frank *d* Melvin Frank *ph* Charles Lang Jnr *m* Leigh Harline

Bob Hope, Lucille Ball, Ruth Hussey, Don Defore, Louis Nye, Philip Ober

'Random shots of mockery aimed effectively at the American middle-class way of life.'— *Peter John Dyer*

AAN: Norman Panama, Melvin Frank (script); Charles Lang Jnr; title song (*m/ly* Johnny Mercer)

Fahrenheit 451 *
GB 1966   112m   Technicolor
Rank / Anglo Enterprise / Vineyard (Lewis M. Allen)

In a fascist future state, a fireman's job is to burn books.
1984 stuff, a little lacking in plot and rather tentatively directed, but with charming moments.

w François Truffaut, Jean-Louis Richard, *novel* Ray Bradbury *d* François Truffaut *ph* Nicolas Roeg *m* Bernard Herrmann *design consultant* Tony Walton

Oskar Werner, Julie Christie, Cyril Cusack, Anton Diffring, Jeremy Spenser

Fail Safe ***
US 1964   111m   bw
Columbia / Max E. Youngstein / Sidney Lumet

An American atomic bomber is accidentally set to destroy Moscow, and the president has to destroy New York in retaliation.
Despite a confusing opening, this deadly earnest melodrama gets across the horror of its situation better than the contemporaneous *Dr Strangelove* which treated the same plot as black comedy. Here the details are both terrifying and convincing.

w Walter Bernstein, *novel* Eugene Burdick, Harvey Wheeler *d Sidney Lumet ph* Gerald Hirschfeld *m* none

Henry Fonda, Walter Matthau, Dan O'Herlihy, Frank Overton, Fritz Weaver, Edward Binns, Larry Hagman, Russell Collins

Fair Wind to Java
US 1952   92m   Trucolor
Republic (Joseph Kane)

A sailor with a mutinous crew seeks a South Sea treasure.
Routine adventure culminating in a volcanic explosion.

w Richard Tregaskis, *novel* Garland Roark *d* Joseph Kane *ph* Jack Martin *m* Victor Young

Fred MacMurray, Vera Hruba Ralston, Robert Douglas, Victor McLaglen

Faithless
US 1932   76m   bw
MGM

A spoiled rich girl and her beau both descend to working-class level and almost further.
Would-be sensational drama ruined by censorship and miscasting.

w Carey Wilson, *novel* Tinfoil by Mildred Cram *d* Harry Beaumont *ph* Oliver T. Marsh

Tallulah Bankhead, Robert Montgomery, Hugh Herbert, Maurice Murphy, Louise Closser Hale, Lawrence Grant, Henry Kolker

The Falcon
A debonair solver of crime puzzles allegedly created by Michael Arlen but owing much to The Saint and resulting from a need by RKO for more of the same. Helped by a tough/comic manservant, he flourished during the forties in sixteen second features (the last three for Film Classics). After three episodes George Sanders tired of the role and was written out by being 'shot' and having his real-life brother Tom Conway take over as his fictional one. The performances of these two actors are pleasant, though the films are now fairly unwatchable, but John Calvert who took over for the last three was not a success.

1941: THE GAY FALCON, A DATE WITH THE FALCON
1942: THE FALCON TAKES OVER (the plot was borrowed from Raymond Chandler's FAREWELL MY LOVELY), THE FALCON'S BROTHER
1943: THE FALCON STRIKES BACK, THE FALCON AND THE CO-EDS, THE FALCON IN DANGER
1944: THE FALCON IN HOLLYWOOD, THE FALCON IN MEXICO, THE FALCON OUT WEST
1945: THE FALCON IN SAN FRANCISCO
1946: THE FALCON'S ALIBI, THE FALCON'S ADVENTURE
1948: THE DEVIL'S CARGO.

APPOINTMENT WITH MURDER,
SEARCH FOR DANGER

The Fall*
Argentina 1958   86m   bw
Argentine Sono (Leopoldo Torre Nilsson)
original title: *La Caída*

A strictly brought-up college girl lodges with an
eccentric family whose strange world comes to
mean more to her than the love of a young
lawyer.
Odd, claustrophobic melodrama from a very
personal film-maker.

w Beatriz Guido, Leopoldo Torre Nilsson,
novel Beatriz Guido *d Leopoldo Torre Nilsson*
ph Alberto Etchebehere *m* Juan Carlos Paz

Elsa Daniel, Duilio Marzia, Lydia Lamaison,
Carlos Lopez Monet

The Fall of Berlin*
USSR 1949   160m   Agfacolor
Mosfilm

A steel worker turns soldier, sees all the major
Russian battles of World War II, and has his
hand shaken by Stalin.
Out-and-out propaganda, with caricatures of
famous people and magnificently staged battles.

w M. Chiaureli, P. A. Pavlenko *d* M. Chiaureli
ph L. V. Kosmatov *m* Dmitri Shostakovich

B. Andreyev, M. Gelovani (as Stalin), V.
Stanitsine (as Churchill), M. Kovaleva

The Fall of the Roman Empire**
US / Spain 1964   187m   Technicolor
   Ultra Panavision 70
Samuel Bronston

After poisoning the Emperor Marcus Aurelius
his mad son Commodus succumbs to dissipation
and allows Rome to be ravaged by pestilence and
the Barbarians.
Would-be distinguished epic with an intellectual
first hour; unfortunately the hero is a priggish
bore, the villain a crashing bore, the heroine a
saintly bore, and the only interesting character is
killed off early. A chariot race, a javelin duel,
some military clashes and a mass burning at the
stake keep one watching, and the production
values are high indeed.

w Ben Barzman, Philip Yordan *d Anthony*
Mann ph Robert Krasker, John Moore
m Dmitri Tiomkin *pd* Venerio Colasanti

Alec Guinness, Christopher Plummer, Stephen
Boyd, James Mason, Sophia Loren, John
Ireland, Eric Porter, Anthony Quayle, Mel
Ferrer, Omar Sharif
   'The film works from a restricted palette, and

the result is weirdly restraining and severe, a
dignified curb on absurdities.'—*John Coleman*
AAN: Dmitri Tiomkin

Fallen Angel*
US 1945   97m   bw
TCF (Otto Preminger)

A man plans to get rid of his wife and marry
another woman, but it is the latter who is
murdered.
Oddly sleazy melodrama, not more successful
then because it was unexpected than now
because it is miscast. Some good sequences,
though.

w Harry Kleiner, *novel* Marty Holland *d Otto*
Preminger ph Joseph La Shelle m David
Raksin

Dana Andrews, Alice Faye, Linda Darnell,
Charles Bickford, Anne Revere, Bruce Cabot,
John Carradine, Percy Kilbride
   'It holds you by its undertones of small-town
life and frustration.'—*Richard Winnington*

The Fallen Idol***
GB 1948   94m   bw
British Lion / London Films

An ambassador's small son nearly incriminates
his friend the butler in the accidental death of his
shrewish wife.
A near-perfect piece of small-scale cinema, built
up from clever nuances of acting and cinematic
technique.

w Graham Greene, from his story The Basement
Room *d Carol Reed ph Georges Périnal*
m William Alwyn

Ralph Richardson, Michèle Morgan, *Bobby*
Henrey, Sonia Dresdel, Jack Hawkins
   'A short story has become a film which is
compact without loss of variety in pace and
shape.'—*Dilys Powell*

AAN: Graham Greene; Carol Reed

The Fallen Sparrow*
US 1943   93m   bw
RKO (Robert Fellows)

An American veteran of the Spanish Civil War
finds himself hounded in New York by Nazis
seeking the Spanish flag of freedom.
Obscure melodrama, very good to look at but
hardly worth unravelling; a precursor of
Hollywood's post-war *films noirs*.

w Warren Duff, *novel* Dorothy B. Hughes
d Richard Wallace *ph Nicholas Musuraca*
md Roy Webb, Constantin Bakaleinikoff

John Garfield, Maureen O'Hara, Walter Slezak,

Martha O'Driscoll, Patricia Morison, Bruce Edwards, John Banner, John Miljan

AAN: Roy Webb, Constantin Bakaleinikoff

Falling for You*
GB 1933 88m bw
Gainsborough (Michael Balcon)

Fleet Street journalists in Switzerland try to outsmart each other.
Dated comedy very typical of the stars' extremely casual style, with immaculate set pieces.

w Jack Hulbert, Douglas Furber, Robert Stevenson, story Sidney Gilliat d Jack Hulbert, Robert Stevenson ph Bernard Knowles songs Vivian Ellis, Douglas Furber

Jack Hulbert, Cicely Courtneidge, Tamara Desni, Garry Marsh, Alfred Drayton, O. B. Clarence, Morton Selten

Fame Is the Spur*
US 1947 116m bw
GFD / Two Cities / Charter Films (John Boulting)

The rise to political eminence of a working-class socialist.
Disappointingly flat historical drama from a novel allegedly based on the career of Ramsay MacDonald. Interesting moments.

w Nigel Balchin, novel Howard Spring d Roy Boulting

Michael Redgrave, Rosamund John, Bernard Miles, Carla Lehmann, Hugh Burden, Marjorie Fielding, Seymour Hicks

A Family Affair*
US 1937 69m bw
MGM (Lucien Hubbard)

A small-town judge faces a few family problems.
The second feature that started the highly successful Hardy family series (qv under Hardy). In this case the judge and his wife were played by actors who did not persevere into the series, but the stage was otherwise set for a long run, and the town of Carvel came to mean home to many Americans abroad.

w Kay Van Riper, play Skidding by Aurania Rouverol d George B. Seitz

Lionel Barrymore, Spring Byington, Mickey Rooney, Eric Linden, Cecilia Parker, Sara Haden, Charles Grapewin, Julie Haydon

Family Honeymoon
US 1948 90m bw
U-I (John Beck, Z. Wayne Griffin)

A college professor marries a widow whose three children join them on their Grand Canyon honeymoon.
Very ordinary and predictable star comedy.

w Dane Lussier, Homer Croy d Claude Binyon ph William Daniels m Frank Skinner

Claudette Colbert, Fred MacMurray, Rita Johnson, Gigi Perreau, Peter Miles, Jimmy Hunt, Hattie McDaniel, Chill Wills

The Family Jewels
US 1965 100m Technicolor
Paramount / York / Jerry Lewis

A child heiress chooses a new father from among her five uncles.
Unfunny star farce with multiple impersonations.

w Jerry Lewis, Bill Richmond d Jerry Lewis ph W. Wallace Kelley m Pete King

Jerry Lewis, Donna Butterworth, Sebastian Cabot, Robert Strauss

Family Life**
GB 1971 108m Technicolor
EMI / Kestrel (Tony Garnett)

A 19-year-old girl is driven into a mental collapse by emotional and family problems.
A slice of suburban life and an indictment of it, put together with unknown actors and probing TV techniques. Somewhat too harrowing for fiction, but extraordinarily vivid.

w David Mercer, from his play In Two Minds d Ken Loach ph Charles Stewart m Marc Wilkinson

Sandy Ratcliff, Bill Dean, Grace Cave

Family Plot**
US 1976 126m Technicolor
Universal (Alfred Hitchcock)

A fake medium tries for easy money by producing a lost heir.
Talkative, complex, patchy, low-key but always interesting Hitchcock suspenser in an unusually friendly vein.

w Ernest Lehman, novel The Rainbird Pattern by Victor Canning d Alfred Hitchcock ph Leonard J. South m John Williams pd Henry Bumstead

Karen Black, Bruce Dern, Barbara Harris, William Devane, Ed Lauter, Cathleen Nesbitt
'Full of benign mischief, beautiful craftsmanship and that elusive sense of cinematic rhythm that has always been Hitchcock's trump card.'—Michael Billington, Illustrated London News

The Family Secret
US 1951 85m bw
Columbia / Santana (Robert Lord, Henry S. Kesler)

The son of a suburban family kills his best friend in a brawl, and his mother insists he conceal the truth even when another man is charged.
Television-style pattern play, not even very interesting at the time.

w Francis Cockrell, Andrew Solt d Henry Levin ph Burnett Guffey m George Duning

John Derek, Lee J. Cobb, Erin O'Brien Moore, Jody Lawrance, Henry O'Neill, Carl Benton Reid

'The general atmosphere is one of outward torment unbacked by inner emotion.'—*MFB*

The Family Way*
GB 1966 115m Eastmancolor
BL / Jambox (John Boulting)

There is consternation in a Lancashire family when the son can't consummate his marriage.
Overstretched domestic farce-drama. Good scenes and performances, but it was all much sharper as a one-hour TV play.

w *Bill Naughton,* from his play Honeymoon Deferred d Roy Boulting ph Harry Waxman m Paul McCartney

John Mills, *Marjorie Rhodes*, Hywel Bennett, Hayley Mills, *Avril Angers*, Murray Head, Wilfred Pickles, Barry Foster, Liz Fraser

The Fan*
US 1949 79m bw
TCF (Otto Preminger)
GB title: *Lady Windermere's Fan*

Scandal almost results when Lady Windermere loses her fan.
Reasonably polished, rather dull version of an old play, not really helped by modern bookends.

w Walter Reisch, Dorothy Parker, Ross Evans, *play* Lady Windermere's Fan by Oscar Wilde d Otto Preminger ph Joseph La Shelle m Daniele Amfitheatrof

George Sanders, Madeleine Carroll, Jeanne Crain, Richard Greene, Martita Hunt, John Sutton, Hugh Dempster, Richard Ney

Fanatic*
GB 1965 96m Technicolor
Hammer / Seven Arts (Anthony Hinds)
US title: *Die! Die! My Darling*

An American girl in England visits the mother of her dead fiancé and finds herself the prisoner of a religious maniac.
Boringly overlong Grand Guignol which even defeats its gallantly unmade-up and deathly-looking star; mildly notable however as a record of one of her last performances.

w Richard Matheson, *novel* Nightmare by Anne Blaisdell d Silvio Narizzano ph Arthur Ibbetson m Wilfrid Josephs pd Peter Proud

Tallulah Bankhead, Stefanie Powers, Peter Vaughan, Yootha Joyce, Donald Sutherland

The Fanatics*
France 1957 92m bw
Cinégraphe-Regent (Pierre Lévy)

Patriots quarrel over the assassination by bomb of a South American dictator when he travels by public plane.
Suspense melodrama with many artificial twists, but slick and well acted.

w Alex Joffé, Jean Levitte d Alex Joffé ph L. H. Burel m Paul Misraki

Pierre Fresnay, Michel Auclair, Grégoire Aslan, Betty Schneider

Fancy Pants**
US 1950 92m Technicolor
Paramount (Robert Welch)

A British actor stranded in the far west poses as a butler.
Lively western comedy remake of *Ruggles of Red Gap* (qv), one of the star's better vehicles.

w Edmund Hartman, Robert O'Brien d George Marshall ph Charles Lang Jnr m Van Cleave

Bob Hope, Lucille Ball, Bruce Cabot, Jack Kirkwood, Lea Penman, Eric Blore, John Alexander, Norma Varden

Fanfan la Tulipe*
France 1951 98m bw
Filmsonor-Ariane-Amato

Recruited into the army of Louis XV by a prophecy that he will marry the king's daughter, a young braggart does everything he can to live up to it.
Rather like a spoof Errol Flynn effort, this likeable swashbuckler can't quite summon up enough buckle or swash to be the minor classic it clearly intends.

w René Wheeler, Jean Fallet d Christian-Jaque ph Christian Matras m Georges Van Parys, Maurice Thiriet

Gérard Philipe, Gina Lollobrigida, Noel Roquevert, Marcel Herrand

Fanny (Pagnol) see Marius

Fanny*

US 1960   133m   Technicolor
Warner / Mansfield (Joshua Logan)

Life on the Marseilles waterfront, and in particular the story of two old men and two lovers.

Lumbering adaptation of three Pagnol films of the thirties (*Marius, Fanny, César*—see *Marius*) previously seen as a 1938 Hollywood film (*Port of Seven Seas*) and later as a Broadway musical. This is the dullest version despite fine photography and a couple of good performances.

w Julius J. Epstein, *play* S. N. Behrman, Joshua Logan, *films* Marcel Pagnol *d* Joshua Logan *ph* Jack Cardiff *m* Harold Rome *md* Morris Stoloff, Harry Sukman

Charles Boyer, Maurice Chevalier, Leslie Caron, Horst Buchholz, Georgette Anys, Salvatore Baccaloni, Lionel Jeffries, Raymond Bussières, Victor Francen

† The film was proudly advertised as 'Joshua Logan's *Fanny*' until the press pointed out the double meaning.

AAN: Jack Cardiff; Morris Stoloff, Harry Sukman; Charles Boyer

Fanny by Gaslight**

GB 1944   108m   bw
GFD / Gainsborough (Edward Black)
US title: *Man of Evil*

The illegitimate daughter of a cabinet minister is saved from a lustful Lord.
Highly-coloured Victorian romantic melodrama, enjoyably put over with no holds barred and a pretty high budget for the time.

w Doreen Montgomery, Aimée Stuart, *novel* Michael Sadleir *d* Anthony Asquith

James Mason, Phyllis Calvert, Stewart Granger, Wilfrid Lawson, John Laurie, Margaretta Scott, Stuart Lindsell, Jean Kent

'Seldom have I seen a film more agreeable to watch, from start to finish.'—*William Whitebait*

'Mr Asquith does not seem to have made much effort to freshen it by interesting treatment, so that the rare unusual device seems quite out of key among so much that is simple, obvious, hackneyed.'—*Richard Mallett, Punch*

† One of several costume melodramas patterned after the success of *The Man in Grey* (qv).

Fantasia****

US 1940   135m   Technicolor
Walt Disney

A concert of classical music is given cartoon interpretations. The pieces are:
    Bach: Toccata and Fugue in D Minor

    Tchaikovsky: The Nutcracker Suite
    Dukas: The Sorcerer's Apprentice
    Stravinsky: The Rite of Spring
    Beethoven: The Pastoral Symphony
    Ponchielli: Dance of the Hours
    Moussorgsky: Night on a Bare Mountain
    Schubert: Ave Maria

Brilliantly inventive for the most part, the cartoons having become classics in themselves. The least part (the Pastoral Symphony) can be forgiven.

supervisor Ben Sharpsteen *md* Edward H. Plumb

Leopold Stokowski, the Philadelphia Orchestra, Deems Taylor

'Dull as it is towards the end, ridiculous as it is in the bend of the knee before Art, it is one of the strange and beautiful things that have happened in the world.'—*Otis Ferguson*

† Multiplane cameras, showing degrees of depth in animation, were used for the first time.

Fantastic Voyage*

US 1966   100m   De Luxe   Cinemascope
TCF (Saul David)

When a top scientist is shot and suffers brain damage, a team of doctors and a boat are miniaturized and injected into his blood stream . . . but one is a traitor.
Engagingly absurd science fiction which keeps its momentum but is somewhat let down by its decor.

w Harry Kleiner *d* Richard Fleischer *ph* Ernest Laszlo *m* Leonard Rosenman *ad* Dale Hennesy, Jack Martin Smith *sp* L. B. Abbott, Art Cruickshank, Emil Kosa Jnr

Stephen Boyd, Raquel Welch, Edmond O'Brien, Donald Pleasence, Arthur Kennedy, Arthur O'Connell, William Redfield

'The process shots are so clumsily matted . . . that the actors look as if a child has cut them out with blunt scissors.'—*Pauline Kael*

AA: Ernest Laszlo

The Far Country*

US 1955   97m   Technicolor
U-I (Aaron Rosenberg)

Two cowboys on their way to the Alaska goldfields are beset by swindlers.
Sturdy star western with good production values.

w Borden Chase *d* Anthony Mann *ph* William Daniels *m* Joseph Gershenson

James Stewart, Walter Brennan, Ruth Roman, Corinne Calvet, John McIntire

Far from the Madding Crowd*
GB 1967 175m Technicolor Panavision
70
EMI / Vic / Appia (Joseph Janni)

In Victorian Wessex a headstrong girl causes
unhappiness and tragedy.
Good-looking but slackly handled version of a
melodramatic and depressing novel.

w Frederic Raphael, novel Thomas Hardy
d John Schlesinger ph Nicolas Roeg m Richard
Rodney Bennett pd Richard Macdonald

Julie Christie, Peter Finch, Alan Bates, Terence
Stamp, Prunella Ransome
  'In this rather plodding film the insufficiency of
the foreground is partly offset by the
winsomeness of the backgrounds. The very
sheep are so engaging as to entice our gaze into
some extremely amiable woolgathering.'—John
Simon

AAN: Richard Rodney Bennett

The Far Horizons
US 1955 108m Technicolor Vistavision
(Paramount) Pine–Thomas

The story of Lewis and Clark's 1803 expedition
west through the Louisiana Purchase territory.
Flabbily-handled historical hokum; potential
interest quickly dissipated.

w Winston Miller, Edmund H. North d Rudolph
Maté ph Daniel L. Fapp m Hans Salter

Fred MacMurray, Charlton Heston, Donna
Reed, Barbara Hale, William Demarest

Farewell Again*
GB 1937 85m bw
Pendennis / London Films (Erich Pommer)
US title: Troopship

Soldiers returning from India have six hours'
shore leave to sort out their problems.
Dated but sharply made compendium drama, a
solid success of its time.

w Clemence Dane, Patrick Kirwan d Tim
Whelan

Flora Robson, Leslie Banks, Robert Newton,
René Ray, Patricia Hilliard, Sebastian Shaw,
Leonora Corbett, Anthony Bushell, Edward
Lexy, Wally Patch, Edmund Willard, Martita
Hunt, John Laurie

Farewell My Lovely*
US 1944 95m bw
RKO (Adrian Scott)
aka: Murder My Sweet

A private eye searches for an ex-convict's
missing girl friend.
A revolutionary crime film in that it was the first
to depict the genuinely seedy milieu suggested by
its author. One of the first films noirs of the mid-
forties, a minor masterpiece of expressionist film
making, and a total change of direction for a
crooner who suddenly became a tough guy.

w John Paxton, novel Raymond Chandler
d Edward Dmytryk ph Harry J. Wild m Roy
Webb

Dick Powell, Claire Trevor, Anne Shirley, Mike
Mazurki, Otto Kruger, Miles Mander, Douglas
Walton, Ralf Harolde, Don Douglas, Esther
Howard
  'A nasty, draggled bit of dirty work,
accurately observed.'—C. A. Lejeune

Farewell My Lovely*
US 1975 95m Technicolor
Avco Embassy / Elliott Kastner / ITC (George
  Pappas, Jerry Bruckheimer)

A pretty sharp remake of the above, with the plot
slightly rewritten but tightened, and an excellent
performance from a rather over-age star.

w David Zelag Goodman d Dick Richards
ph John A. Alonzo m David Shire pd Dean
Tavouraris

Robert Mitchum, Charlotte Rampling, John
Ireland, Sylvia Miles, Anthony Zerbe, Jack
O'Halloran, Kate Murtagh
  'A moody, bluesy, boozy recreation of
Marlowe's tacky, neon-flashed Los Angeles of
the early forties.'—Judith Crist
  'A delicious remake with a nice, smoky 1940s
atmosphere.'—Michael Billington, Illustrated
London News

AAN: Sylvia Miles

A Farewell to Arms*
US 1932 78m bw
Paramount

In World War I, a wounded American
ambulance driver falls in love with his nurse.
Now very dated but important in its time, this
romantic drama was one of the more successful
Hemingway adaptations to be filmed.

w Benjamin Glazer, Oliver H. P. Garrett, novel
Ernest Hemingway d Frank Borzage
ph Charles Lang

Gary Cooper, Helen Hayes, Adolphe Menjou,
Mary Philips, Jack La Rue, Blanche Frederici,
Henry Armetta
  'Too much sentiment and not enough
strength.'—Mordaunt Hall, New York Times
  'Borzage has invested the war scenes with a
strange, brooding expressionist quality . . .
indeed, the overall visual style is most
impressive.'—NFT, 1974
† Remade as Force of Arms (qv) and see below.

A Farewell to Arms
US 1957   150m   De Luxe   Cinemascope
TCF / David O. Selznick

Elaborate ill-fated remake which tried to make
an adventure epic out of a low-key war drama.
Its failure caused David O. Selznick to produce
no more films.

w Ben Hecht d Charles Vidor pd Alfred Junge
ph Piero Portalupi, Oswald Morris m Mario
Nascimbene

Rock Hudson, Jennifer Jones, Vittorio de Sica,
Alberto Sordi, Kurt Kasznar, Mercedes
McCambridge, Oscar Homolka, Elaine Stritch,
Victor Francen

The Farmer Takes a Wife *
US 1935   91m   bw
TCF (Winfield Sheehan)

By the Erie Canal in the 1820s, a wandering girl
finds security with a farmer.
Pleasantly 'different' romantic drama, quite ably
executed and introducing Henry Fonda to the
screen.

w Edwin Burke, play Frank B. Elser and Marc
Connelly, novel Rome Haul by Walter D.
Edmonds d Victor Fleming ph John Seitz
m Arthur Lange

Janet Gaynor, Henry Fonda, Charles Bickford,
Slim Summerville, Andy Devine, Roger Imhof,
Jane Withers, Margaret Hamilton, Sig Rumann,
John Qualen

The Farmer Takes a Wife *
US 1953   81m   Technicolor
TCF (Frank P. Rosenberg)

Musical remake with an agreeably stylized look,
hampered by a slowish script and dull cast.

w Walter Bulloch, Sally Benson, Joseph Fields
d Henry Levin ph Arthur E. Arling m Cyril
Mockridge ad Lyle Wheeler, Addison Hehr

Betty Grable, Dale Robertson, Thelma Ritter,
Eddie Foy Jnr, John Carroll

The Farmer's Daughter
US 1940   60m   bw
Paramount (William C. Thomas)

A stage struck country girl tries to horn in on a
Broadway musical rehearsing nearby.
Feeble comedy for the sticks.

w Lewis R. Foster, Delmer Daves d James
Hogan ph Leo Tover

Martha Raye, Charles Ruggles, Richard
Denning, Gertrude Michael, William Frawley,
William Demarest, Jack Norton

The Farmer's Daughter **
US 1947   97m   bw
David O. Selznick (Dore Schary)

The Swedish maid of a congressman becomes a
political force.
Well-made Cinderella story with a touch of
asperity and top notch production values and
cast.

w Allen Rivkin, Laura Kerr d H. C. Potter
ph Milton Krasner m Leigh Harline

Loretta Young, Joseph Cotten, Ethel
Barrymore, Charles Bickford, Rose Hobart,
Rhys Williams, Harry Davenport, Tom Powers

AA: Loretta Young
AAN: Charles Bickford

The Farmer's Wife
GB 1928   67m approx   bw   silent
BIP (John Maxwell)

A farmer seeks a wife and after three
disappointments settles for his housekeeper.
A simple and not very interesting silent screen
version of a stage success which depended
largely on dialogue.

wd Alfred Hitchcock, play Eden Phillpotts
ph Jack Cox

James Thomas, Gordon Harker, Lillian Hall-
Davis

Farrebique **
France 1947   85m   bw
L'Ecran Français / Les Films Etienne Lallier

Problems of a peasant family in central France.
Superbly-filmed semi-documentary, acted by a
real family.

wd Georges Rouquier ph André Dantan
m Henri Sauguet
  'Definitely a film for posterity.'—MFB

Fashions of 1934 *
US 1934   78m   bw
Warner (Henry Blanke)

A confidence trickster conquers the French
fashion world.
Slight musical comedy with a couple of splendid
Berkeley numbers.

w F. Hugh Herbert, Carl Brickson d William
Dieterle ch Busby Berkeley ph William Rees
m/ly Sammy Fain, Irving Kahal ad Jack Okey

William Powell, Bette Davis, Verree Teasdale,
Frank McHugh, Reginald Owen, Hugh Herbert,
Henry O'Neill

Fast and Loose
US 1930   70m   bw
Paramount

A spoiled rich girl falls in love with a car mechanic.

Tiresome melodrama, dully scripted.

w Doris Anderson, Jack Kirkland, Preston Sturges, *play* The Best People by Avery Hopwood, David Gray *d* Fred Newmeyer *ph* William Steiner

Miriam Hopkins, Carole Lombard, Frank Morgan, Charles Starrett, Henry Wadsworth, David Hutcheson, Ilka Chase

Fast and Loose*
US 1939 80m bw
MGM (Frederick Stephani)

Married detectives and rare book experts solve the mystery of a missing Shakespeare manuscript.

Pleasing comedy mystery in the wake of *The Thin Man*.

w Harry Kurnitz *d* Edwin L. Marin *ph* George Folsey

Robert Montgomery, Rosalind Russell, Ralph Morgan, Reginald Owen, Etienne Girardot, Alan Dinehart, Joan Marsh, Sidney Blackmer

The Fast Lady**
GB 1962 95m Eastmancolor
Rank / Group Films (Teddy Baird)

A bashful suitor buys an old Bentley, becomes a roadhog, passes his test, captures some crooks and gets the girl.

Spirited if aimless farcical comedy which crams in all the jokes about cars anyone can think of.

w Jack Davies, Henry Blyth *d* Ken Annakin *ph* Reg Wyer *m* Norrie Paramor

Stanley Baxter, James Robertson Justice, Leslie Phillips, Julie Christie, Dick Emery

The Fastest Gun Alive*
US 1956 89m bw
MGM (Clarence Greene)

A mild-mannered western storekeeper proves to be the son of a famous gunfighter, and is put to the test.

Flimsily contrived mini-western helped by good performances.

w Frank D. Gilroy, Russel Rouse *d* Russel Rouse *ph* George Folsey *m* André Previn

Glenn Ford, Broderick Crawford, Jeanne Crain, Russ Tamblyn, Allyn Joslin, Leif Erickson, John Dehner

Fat City*
US 1972 96m Eastmancolor
Columbia / Rastar (Ray Stark)

In a small Californian town, a has-been boxer tries to get back to the top, but loses his self respect and becomes a hobo.

Vivid but over-casual exploration of failure, with more interest in the characters than the sport.

w Leonard Gardner, from his novel *d* John Huston *ph* Conrad Hall *md* Marvin Hamlisch *pd* Richard Sylbert

Stacy Keach, Jeff Bridges, Susan Tyrell

AAN: Susan Tyrell

The Fat Man
US 1950 77m bw
U-I (Aubrey Schenck)

The murder of a dentist leads to the circus.

Dense murder mystery featuring a gourmet 17-stone detective; understandably, no series resulted.

w Harry Essex, Leonard Lee *d* William Castle *ph* Irving Glassberg *m* Bernard Green

J. Scott Smart, Rock Hudson, Julie London, Clinton Sundberg, Jerome Cowan, Jayne Meadows

The Fatal Night*
GB 1948 49m bw
(Columbia) Mario Zampi

A joke haunting has unfortunate consequences.

A small, cheaply-made film which really thrilled.

w Gerald Butler, *story* The Gentleman from America by Michael Arlen *d* Mario Zampi *ph* Cedric Williams *m* Stanley Black

Lester Ferguson, Jean Short, Leslie Armstrong, Brenda Hogan, Patrick MacNee

Fate Is the Hunter
US 1964 106m bw Cinemascope
TCF / Arcola (Aaron Rosenberg)

An airline executive investigates the cause of a fatal crash in which his friend the pilot was a victim.

Watchable how-did-it happen melodrama marred by pretentious dialogue.

w Harold Medford, *novel* Ernest K. Gann *d* Ralph Nelson *ph* Milton Krasner *m* Jerry Goldsmith

Glenn Ford, Rod Taylor, Nehemiah Persoff, Nancy Kwan, Suzanne Pleshette, Jane Russell

AAN: Milton Krasner

Father Brown***
GB 1954 91m bw
(Columbia) Facet (Vivian A. Cox)
US title: *The Detective*

A Catholic clergyman retrieves a priceless church cross from master thief Flambeau.

Delightfully eccentric comedy based closely on the famous character, with a sympathetic if rather wandering script, pointed direction and some delicious characterizations. A thoroughly civilized entertainment.

w *Thelma Schnee, story* The Blue Cross by G. K. Chesterton d *Robert Hamer* ph Harry Waxman m Georges Auric

Alec Guinness, Joan Greenwood, Peter Finch, Sidney James, Cecil Parker, Bernard Lee, Ernest Thesiger, M arne Maitland

Father Came Too*
GB 1963   93m   Eastmancolor
Rank / Independent Artists

Honeymooners agree to live with her overbearing actor manager father.
Less funny sequel to *The Fast Lady*, with comic household disasters striking every couple of minutes. Easy-going, and predictably amusing in spots.

w Jack Davies, Henry Blyth d Peter Graham Scott ph Reg Wyer m Norrie Paramor

Stanley Baxter, James Robertson Justice, Sally Smith, Ronnie Barker, Timothy Bateson, Philip Locke

Father Goose*
US 1964   116m   Technicolor
U-I / Granox (Robert Arthur)

During World War II a South Seas wanderer is compelled by the Australian navy to act as sky observer on a small island, where he finds himself in charge of six refugee schoolchildren and their schoolmistress.
Eager-to-please but unsatisfactory film which wanders between farce, adventure and sex comedy, taking too long about all of them.

w Peter Stone, Frank Tarloff d Ralph Nelson ph Charles Lang Jnr m Cy Coleman

Cary Grant, Leslie Caron, Trevor Howard

AAN: Peter Stone, Frank Tarloff

Father Is a Bachelor
US 1950   85m   bw
Columbia (S. Sylvan Simon)

A young tramp cares for a family of orphaned children.
Boringly sentimental semi-western.

w Aleen Leslie, James Edward Grant d Norman Foster, Abby Berlin ph Burnett Guffey m Arthur Morton

William Holden, Coleen Gray, Charles Winninger, Stuart Erwin, Sig Ruman

Father of the Bride**
US 1950   93m   bw
MGM (Pandro S. Berman)

A dismayed but happy father surveys the cost and chaos of his daughter's marriage.
Fragmentary but mainly delightful suburban comedy which finds Hollywood in its best light vein and benefits from a strong central performance.

w *Frances Goodrich, Albert Hackett, novel Edward Streeter* d Vincente Minnelli ph John Alton m Adolph Deutsch

Spencer Tracy, Joan Bennett, Elizabeth Taylor, Don Taylor, Billie Burke, Moroni Olsen, Leo G. Carroll, Taylor Holmes, Melville Cooper

AAN: best picture; Frances Goodrich, Albert Hackett; Spencer Tracy

Father Takes a Wife*
US 1941   80m   bw
RKO (Lee S. Marcus)

A famous actress marries a shipping magnate and runs into resentment from his children.
Disappointing comedy with a script too flat for the stars to make interesting.

w Dorothy and Herbert Fields d Jack Hively ph Robert de Grasse m Roy Webb

Gloria Swanson, Adolphe Menjou, Desi Arnaz, John Howard, Helen Broderick, Florence Rice, Neil Hamilton

Father Was a Fullback
US 1949   84m   bw
TCF (Fred Kohlmar)

The coach of a college football team has domestic problems.
Thin star comedy, strictly double bill.

w Aleen Leslie, Casey Robinson, Richard Sale, Mary Loos, *play* Clifford Goldsmith d John M. Stahl ph Lloyd Ahern m Cyril Mockridge

Fred MacMurray, Maureen O'Hara, Betty Lynn, Natalie Wood, Rudy Vallee, Jim Backus

Father's Little Dividend
US 1951   81m   bw
MGM (Pandro S. Berman)

Sequel to *Father of the Bride*, in which the newlyweds have a baby.
A very flat follow-up, palatable enough at the time but quite unmemorable.

w Frances Goodrich, Albert Hackett d Vincente Minnelli ph John Alton m Albert Sandrey

Spencer Tracy, Joan Bennett, Elizabeth Taylor, Don Taylor, Billie Burke, Moroni Olsen, Frank Faylen, Marietta Canty, Russ Tamblyn

Fathom
GB 1967 99m De Luxe Franscope
TCF (John Kohn)

Adventures of a glamorous sky-diving spy.
Watchable romp with nothing memorable about
it.

w Lorenzo Semple Jnr, *novel* Larry Forrester
d Leslie Martinson *ph* Douglas Slocombe, Ken
Vos *m* Johnny Dankworth

Raquel Welch, Tony Franciosa, Clive Revill,
Ronald Fraser, Greta Chi, Richard Briers, Tom
Adams
    'Belongs not in the category of High Camp but
in that of Good Wholesome Fun.'—*MFB*

Faust**
Germany 1926 100m approx bw silent
UFA

A superbly stylish version of the legend about a
man who sells his soul to the devil. The best of
many silent versions; see also *All That Money
Can Buy*.

w Hans Kyser *d* F. W. Murnau *ph* Carl
Hoffman

Emil Jannings, Gosta Ekman, Camilla Horn,
Yvette Guilbert, William Dieterle

The FBI Story*
US 1959 149m Technicolor
Warner (Mervyn Le Roy)

An FBI agent thinks back on his career with the
bureau.
Predictable mix of domestic sentimentality (very
trying) and competent crime capsules: mad
bomber, Ku Klux Klan, thirties hoodlums, Nazi
spy rings and the cold war.

w Richard L. Breen, John Twist *d* Mervyn Le
Roy *ph* Joseph Biroc *m* Max Steiner *ad* John
Beckman

James Stewart, Vera Miles, Larry Pennell, Nick
Adams, Murray Hamilton
    'Insufferably cosy.'—*MFB*

Fear
US 1946 68m bw
Monogram

A student kills his professor, and a detective
taunts him to the point of confession.
Cheeky second feature version of *Crime and
Punishment*, with a twist ending. Not too bad in
its way.

w Alfred Zeisler, Dennis Cooper *d* Alfred
Zeisler *ph* Jackson Rose

Warren William, Peter Cookson, Anne Gwynne,
Nestor Paiva

Fear in the Night**
US 1947 72m bw
Maxwell Shane

A man suffering from a strange nightmare
discovers he has been hypnotized into
committing a murder.
Intriguing small-scale puzzler later remade to
less effect as *Nightmare* (qv). Adequate
performances and handling, but the plot's the
thing.

wd Maxwell Shane *ph* Jack Grennhalgh

Paul Kelly, De Forrest Kelley, Ann Doran, Kay
Scott

Fear in the Night*
GB 1972 85m Technicolor
Hammer (Jimmy Sangster)

A girl recovering from a nervous breakdown is
deluded into committing a murder.
Yet another variant on *Les Diaboliques*,
ingeniously worked out with good touches of
detail to produce an air of general competence.

w Jimmy Sangster, Michael Syson *d* Jimmy
Sangster *ph* Arthur Grant *m* John McCabe

Peter Cushing, Judy Geeson, Joan Collins,
Ralph Bates

Fear Is the Key*
GB 1972 108m Technicolor Panavision
EMI / KLK (Alan Ladd Jnr, Elliott Kastner)

A man conceives an elaborate plot to track down
those responsible for killing his wife and family in
a plane crash.
Reasonably absorbing, surprise-plotted thriller.

w Robert Carrington, *novel* Alistair MacLean
d Michael Tuchner *ph* Alex Thomson *m* Roy
Budd

Suzy Kendall, Barry Newman, John Vernon,
Dolph Sweet, Ben Kingsley, Ray McAnally

Fear Strikes Out
US 1957 100m bw Vistavision
Paramount / Alan Pakula

A father wants his son to become a professional
baseball player, and the son in consequence
suffers a nervous breakdown.
Rather flat biopic of Jim Piersall; well-
intentioned and careful in its psychological
insights, but too often just plain dull.

w Ted Berkman, Raphael Blau *d* Robert
Mulligan *ph* Haskell Boggs *m* Elmer Bernstein

Anthony Perkins, Karl Malden, Norma Moore,
Perry Wilson

**The Fearless Vampire Killers, or Pardon
Me, Your Teeth Are in My Neck***
US 1967   124m   Metrocolor   Panavision
MGM / Cadre Films / Filmways (Gene
    Gutowski)
aka: *Dance of the Vampires*

A professor and his assistant stake a
Transylvanian vampire.
Heavy, slow spoof of *Dracula*, most of which
shows that sense of humour is very personal; a
few effective moments hardly compensate for the
prevailing stodge.

w Gerard Brach, Roman Polanski *d* Roman
Polanski *ph* Douglas Slocombe *m* Krzystof
Komeda *pd* Wilfrid Shingleton

Jack McGowran, Roman Polanski, Alfie Bass,
Sharon Tate, *Ferdy Mayne*, Iain Quarrier, Terry
Downes

  'An engaging oddity . . . long stretches might
have been lifted intact from any Hammer
horror.'—*Tom Milne*

The Fearmakers
US 1958   85m   bw
Pacemaker (Martin H. Lancer)

A brainwashed Korean War veteran returns to
Washington and finds that his PR firm has been
taken over by communist racketeers.
Unusual but cheaply made anti-Red
propaganda, too talkative to be very
entertaining.

w Elliot West, Chris Appley, *novel* Darwin
Teilhet *d* Jacques Tourneur *ph* Sam Leavitt
m Irving Gertz

Dana Andrews, Dick Foran, Mel Tormé

A Feather in Her Hat
US 1935   72m   bw
Columbia

A London widow with delusions of grandeur
tells her son that his real mother was a famous
actress.
Outmoded mother-love drama, interestingly
cast.

w Lawrence Hazard, *story* I. A. R. Wylie
d Alfred Santell *ph* Joseph Walker

Pauline Lord, Basil Rathbone, Louis Hayward,
Billie Burke, Wendy Barrie, J. M. Kerrigan,
Victor Varconi, Nydia Westman, Thurston Hall

Feather Your Nest*
GB 1937   86m   bw
ATP (Basil Dean)

A gramophone record technician substitutes his
own voice for a star and becomes world famous.

The star in less farcical vein than usual; this is the
one in which he sings 'Leaning on a Lamp-post'.

w Austin Melford, Robert Edmunds, Anthony
Kimmins *d* William Beaudine

George Formby, Polly Ward, Enid Stamp
Taylor, Val Rosing, Davy Burnaby

Fedora*
West Germany / France 1978   110m
    Eastmancolor
Geria / SFP (Billy Wilder)

An ageing star who seems miraculously to have
kept her beauty comes out of retirement.
Sunset Boulevard revisited, with a less bitter
approach and less effectiveness; but any civilized
film is welcome in the late seventies.

w I. A. L. Diamond, Billy Wilder, from a story in
Crowned Heads by Tom Tryon *d* Billy Wilder
ph Gerry Fisher *m* Miklos Rozsa

William Holden, Marthe Keller, Hildgarde Knef,
Jose Ferrer, Mario Adorf, Henry Fonda,
Michael York

Feet First*
US 1930   88m   bw
Harold Lloyd

A shoe salesman gets entangled with crooks and
has a narrow escape when hanging from the side
of a building.
Very funny early talkie comedy, probably the
comedian's last wholly satisfactory film.

w Lex Neal, Felix Adler, Paul Gerard Smith
d Clyde Bruckman *ph* Walter Ludin, Henry
Kohler

Harold Lloyd, Robert McWade, Barbara Kent

The Female Animal
US 1957   82m   bw   Cinemascope
U-I (Albert Zugsmith)

A beach bum becomes the lover of a film star,
then falls in love with her daughter.
Dreary and humourless melodrama notable only
for the comeback appearance of one of the
screen's legendary glamour queens.

w Robert Hill *d* Harry Keller *ph* Russell Metty
m Hans Salter

Hedy Lamarr, Jan Sterling, Jane Powell, George
Nader, James Gleason

The Female on the Beach
US 1955   97m   bw
U-I (Albert Zugsmith)

A wealthy widow visits her late husband's beach
house and falls for the gigolo next door, who
later seems intent on murdering her.

Absurd and jaded melodrama, a rehash of *Love from a Stranger*, enlivened by some hilarious love-hate dialogue.

w Robert Hill, Richard Alan Simmons *d* Joseph Pevney *ph* Charles Lang *m* Joseph Gershenson

Joan Crawford, Jeff Chandler, Jan Sterling, Cecil Kellaway, Natalie Schaefer

La Femme de Nulle Part*

France 1922   70m approx   bw   silent
aka: *The Woman from Nowhere*

A woman who feels that her life has been ruined through love returns home and persuades a young girl not to do the same.

A minor atmospheric piece of some power, comparable with *Partie de Campagne* and cinematically very interesting.

wd Louis Delluc *ph* Lucas Gibory *ad* F. Jourdain

Eve Francis, Roger Karl, Gine Avril

La Femme du Boulanger**

France 1938   110m   bw
Marcel Pagnol
aka: *The Baker's Wife*

Villagers put a stop to the infidelity of the baker's wife because her husband no longer has the heart to make good bread.

Best-known of Pagnol's rustic fables, this rather obvious and long-drawn-out joke is important because international critics hailed it as a work of art (which it isn't) and because it fixed an image of the naughty bucolic French.

wd Marcel Pagnol, *novel* Jean Le Bleu by Jean Giono *ph* G. Benoit, R. Lendruz, N. Daries *m* Vincent Scotto

Raimu, Ginette Leclerc, Charles Moulin, Charpin, Maximilienne

La Femme Infidèle**

France / Italy 1968   98m   Eastmancolor
La Boétie / Cinégai (André Génovès)
aka: *The Unfaithful Wife*

A middle-aged insurance broker, set in his ways, murders his wife's lover; when she suspects the truth, they are drawn closer together.

Almost a Bunuel-like black comedy, spare and quiet, with immaculate performances.

wd Claude Chabrol *ph* Jean Rabier *m* Pierre Jansen

Stéphane Audran, Michel Bouquet, Maurice Ronet

'On any level, this bizarre murder framed by whiskies emerges as Chabrol's most flawless work to date.'—*Jan Dawson, MFB*

Femmes de Paris*

France 1954   85m approx   Agfacolor
Optimax-Lux (Edgar Bacquet)
aka: *Ah! Les Belles Bacchantes*

A touring revue is almost run out of town for indecency.

A rather crude but quite valuable record of Dhéry's stage revue, which convulsed London in the fifties.

w Robert Dhéry *d* Jean Loubignac *ph* René Colas *m* Gérard Calvi

Robert Dhéry, Colette Brosset, Louis de Funès, Raymond Bussières, the Bluebell Girls

La Ferme du Pendu*

France 1946   90m   bw
Corona
aka: *Hanged Man's Farm*

The lecherous son of a farming family brings tragedy to the lives of himself and his brothers and sister.

Cold Comfort Farm with a vengeance, appropriately played: arrant melodrama, but watchable.

w André-Paul Antoine *d* Jean Dréville *ph* André Thomas

Alfred Adam, Charles Vanel, Arlette Merry

Ferry to Hong Kong

GB 1958   113m   Eastmancolor
   Cinemascope
Rank (George Maynard)

An Austrian layabout can land at neither of the Hong Kong ferry's ports of call, but shows his true worth when a typhoon strikes.

Silly storyline and rampant bad acting ruin the Rank Organization's first attempt at an international epic.

w Vernon Harris, Lewis Gilbert *d* Lewis Gilbert *ph* Otto Heller *m* Kenneth V. Jones

Curt Jurgens, Sylvia Syms, Orson Welles, Jeremy Spenser, Noel Purcell

La Fête à Henriette*

France 1952   113m   bw
Regina-Filmsonor
aka: *Holiday for Henrietta*

Two screenwriters disagree whether or not to give their hero and heroine a happy ending.

A rather heavy-handed romantic joke which does have its moments and was later—fatally—Americanized as *Paris When It Sizzles*.

w Julien Duvivier, Henri Jeanson *d* Julien Duvivier *ph* Roger Hubert *m* Georges Auric

Dany Robin, Michel Auclair, Hildegarde Neff, Michel Roux, Saturnin Fabre, Julien Carette

Le Feu Follet*
France / Italy 1963   110m   bw
Nouvelles Editions / Arco
aka: *Will o' the Wisp; A Time to Live and a
Time to Die*

The last 24 hours, before his suicide, in the life of
an ex-alcoholic playboy.
Not quite as weary as it sounds, and full of
admirable touches, this is nevertheless a fairly
downbeat film and a pointless one.

wd Louis Malle, *novel* Pierre Drieu la Rochelle
ph Ghislain Cloquet *m* Erik Satie

Maurice Ronet, Léna Skerla, Yvonne Clech,
Hubert Deschamps, Jeanne Moreau

A Fever in the Blood
US 1960   117m   bw
Warner (Roy Huggins)

Candidates for governor sharpen their
campaigns on a murder trial.
Interestingly-cast, flabbily-written melodrama.

w Roy Huggins, Harry Kleiner, *novel* William
Pearson *d* Vincent Sherman *ph* J. Peverell
Marley *m* Ernest Gold

Efrem Zimbalist Jnr, Angie Dickinson, Don
Ameche, Herbert Marshall, Jack Kelly, Ray
Danton, Jesse White, Rhodes Reason, Robert
Colbert

Fiddler on the Roof**
US 1971   180m   Technicolor   Panavision
70
UA / Mirisch (Norman Jewison)

In a pre-revolutionary Russian village, Tevye the
Jewish milkman survives family and political
problems and when the pogroms begin
cheerfully emigrates to America.
Self-conscious, grittily realistic adaptation of the
stage musical, with slow and heavy patches in its
grossly overlong celebration of a vanished way
of life. The big moments still come off well
though the songs tend to be thrown away and the
photography is unnecessarily murky.

w Joseph Stein, from his play and Sholom
Aleichem's story Tevye and his Daughters
d Norman Jewison *ph* Oswald Morris *m* Jerry
Bock *md* John Williams *pd* Robert Boyle
ly Sheldon Harnick

Topol, Norma Crane, Leonard Frey, Molly
Picon

    'Jewison hasn't so much directed a film as
prepared a product for world consumption.'—
Stanley Kauffmann

AA: Oswald Morris; John Williams
AAN: best picture; Norman Jewison (as
director); Topol; Leonard Frey

Fiddlers Three*
GB 1944   87m   bw
Ealing (Robert Hamer)

Sailors struck by lightning on Salisbury Plain are
transported back to ancient Rome.
Sequel to *Sailors Three*; despite a harsh and
unattractive look, every conceivable joke about
old Romans is deftly mined and the good
humour flows free.

w Diana Morgan, Angus Macphail *d* Harry
Watt

Tommy Trinder, Sonnie Hale, Frances Day,
Francis L. Sullivan, Ernest Milton, Diana
Decker, Elizabeth Welch, Mary Clare

The Fiend Who Walked the West
US 1958   101m   bw   Cinemascope
TCF (Herbert B. Swope Jnr)

A sadistic killer released from prison tracks
down the associates of a cellmate and terrorizes
the district.
Western remake of *Kiss of Death*, with babyface
Robert Evans in the Widmark role. Violent and
dull.

w Harry Brown, Philip Yordan *d* Gordon
Douglas *ph* Joe MacDonald *m* Leon Klatzkin

Hugh O'Brian, Dolores Michaels, Robert Evans,
Linda Cristal, Stephen McNally, Edward
Andrews

The Fiend without a Face
GB 1957   75m   bw
Producers' Associates (John Croydon)

A scientist working on materialized thought
produces monsters from his own id.
Tepid shocker with well-organized mobile
brains.

w H. J. Leder *d* Arthur Crabtree *ph* Lionel
Banes *m* Buxton Orr *sp* Ruppel and Nordhoff

Kynaston Reeves, Terry Kilburn, Marshall
Thompson

The Fiercest Heart
US 1961   90m   De Luxe   Cinemascope
TCF (George Sherman)

A British army deserter joins a Boer trek into
South Africa.
Pioneer 'western', poorly done but with novelty
value.

w Edmund H. North, *novel* Stuart Cloete
d George Sherman *ph* Ellis Carter *m* Irving
Gertz

Stuart Whitman, Juliet Prowse, Raymond
Massey, Ken Scott, Geraldine Fitzgerald, Rafer
Johnson

Fièvre*
France 1921   50m approx   bw   silent
Alhambre

A brawl in a Marseilles bar ends in murder.
A dramatic sketch, filmed with remarkable detail
and artistry.

wd Louis Delluc *ph* A. Gibory *ad* Bécan

Eve Francis, Edmond Van Daele, Gaston
Modot

Fifi la Plume
France 1964   80m   bw
Les Films Montsouris (Albert Lamorisse)

A burglar becomes a circus bird-man, learns to
fly, and is everywhere mistaken for an angel.
A likeable fantasy idea which doesn't quite come
off, alternating uneasily between slapstick and
sentiment.

wd Albert Lamorisse *ph* Pierre Petit *m* Jean-
Michel Defaye

Philippe Avron, Mireille Nègre, Henri Lambert,
Raoul Delfosse

Fifth Avenue Girl*
US 1939   83m   bw
RKO (Gregory La Cava)

An unemployed girl is persuaded by a millionaire
to pose as a gold digger and annoy his avaricious
family.
Brightish comedy of the Cinderella kind.

w Allan Scott *d* Gregory La Cava *ph* Robert de
Grasse

Ginger Rogers, Walter Connolly, Verree
Teasdale, Tim Holt, James Ellison, Franklin
Pangborn, Kathryn Adams, Louis Calhern

55 Days at Peking*
US / Spain 1962   154m   Super
Technirama 70
Samuel Bronston

In 1900 Peking, Boxer fanatics are encouraged
by the Empress to take over the city and besiege
the international diplomatic quarter; an
American major leads the defence.
Spasmodically lively action spectacular weighed
down by romantic stretches.

w Philip Yordan, Bernard Gordon *d* Nicholas
Ray, Andrew Marton *ph* Jack Hildyard,
Manuel Berenguer *m* Dmitri Tiomkin
ad Venerio Colasanti, John Moore

Charlton Heston, David Niven, Ava Gardner,
Flora Robson, Robert Helpmann, Leo Genn,
Paul Lukas, John Ireland, Harry Andrews,
Elizabeth Sellars, Massimo Serrato, Jacques
Sernas, Geoffrey Bayldon

AAN: Dmitri Tiomkin; song 'So Little Time' (*m*
Dmitri Tiomkin, *ly* Paul Francis Webster)

The Fighter
US 1952   78m   bw
GH (Alex Gottlieb)

A Mexican fisherman whose family is murdered
by government troops becomes a prizefighter to
earn money for the rebels.
A rather glum attempt to turn a few ringside
clichés.

w Aben Kandel, Herbert Kline, *story* The
Mexican by Jack London *d* Herbert Kline
ph James Wong Howe *m* Vincente Gomez

Richard Conte, Vanessa Brown, Lee J. Cobb,
Frank Silvera

Fighter Squadron
US 1948   96m   Technicolor
Warner (Seton I. Miller)

In World War II, a dedicated flier risks his
friends' lives.
Routine aerial actioner.

w Seton I. Miller *d* Raoul Walsh *ph* Sid Hickox,
Wilfrid M. Cline *m* Max Steiner

Edmond O'Brien, Robert Stack, John Rodney,
Tom D'Andrea, Henry Hull, Walter Reed,
Shepperd Strudwick, Rock Hudson

Fighting Father Dunne
US 1948   93m   bw
RKO

A clergyman looks after unfortunate boys.
A slum melodrama which all concerned could
have made with their eyes closed, and probably
did.

w Martin Rackin, Frank Davis *d* Ted Tetzlaff
ph George E. Diskant *m* Roy Webb

Pat O'Brien, Darryl Hickman, Charles Kemper,
Una O'Connor

The Fighting Kentuckian
US 1949   100m   bw
Republic (John Wayne)

In 1810 a farmer combats land-grabbing
criminals.
Standard star western for the family.

wd George Waggner *ph* Lee Garmes *m* George
Antheil

John Wayne, Vera Ralston, Oliver Hardy, Philip
Dorn, Marie Windsor, Mae Marsh

Fighting Mad
US 1976   90m   De Luxe
TCF / Santa Fe (Roger Corman)

A rancher and his son are murdered by a local industrialist who wants their land, and the rancher's city-bred son takes revenge.
Another vigilante western in modern dress, very laborious and violent without being very exciting.

wd Jonathan Demme *ph* Bill Birch *m* Bruce Langhorne

Peter Fonda, Lynn Lowry, John Doucette, Philip Carey, Scott Glen

The Fighting O'Flynn
US 1949 94m bw
U-I (Douglas Fairbanks Jnr)

In 18th-century Ireland, a penniless young adventurer aborts Napoleon's plan for invasion.
Lively minor-league adventure.

w Douglas Fairbanks Jnr, Robert Thoeren, *novel* Justin Huntly McCarthy *d* Arthur Pierson *ph* Arthur Edeson *m* Frank Skinner

Douglas Fairbanks Jnr, Helena Carter, Richard Greene, Patricia Medina, Arthur Shields, J. M. Kerrigan
'Fairbanks plays the irrepressible O'Flynn with unflagging energy and tongue in cheek good humour; the rest of the cast stolidly refuses to see the joke.'—*MFB*

The Fighting Prince of Donegal
GB 1966 104m Technicolor
Walt Disney (Bill Anderson)

Adventures of an Irish rebel in the reign of Elizabeth I.
Adequate Boys' Own Paper romp.

w Robert Westerby, *novel* Red Hugh, Prince of Donegal by Robert T. Reilly *d* Michael O'Herlihy *ph* Arthur Ibbetson *m* George Bruns

Peter McEnery, Susan Hampshire, Tom Adams, Gordon Jackson, Andrew Keir, Norman Woolland, Richard Leech

The Fighting Seabees
US 1944 100m bw
Republic (Albert J. Cohen)

During World War II in the Pacific, construction workers attack the Japanese.
Routine, studio-staged war melodrama, heavily fleshed out with love interest.

w Borden Chase, Aeneas Mackenzie *d* Edward Ludwig *ph* William Bradford *m* Walter Scharf, Roy Webb

John Wayne, Susan Hayward, Dennis O'Keefe, William Frawley, Duncan Renaldo, Addison Richards, Leonid Kinskey, Paul Fix

AAN: Walter Scharf, Roy Webb

The Fighting 69th*
US 1940 89m bw
Warner (Hal B. Wallis)

During World War I in the trenches, a cocky recruit becomes a hero and loses his life in the process.
Recruiting poster stuff, all well enough done but bewildering in its changes of mood.

w Norman Reilly Raine, Fred Niblo Jnr, Dean Franklin *d* William Keighley *ph* Tony Gaudio

James Cagney, Pat O'Brien, George Brent, Jeffrey Lynn, Alan Hale, Frank McHugh, Dennis Morgan, Dick Foran, William Lundigan, Guinn Williams, John Litel, Henry O'Neill

Figures in a Landscape
GB 1970 110m Technicolor Panavision
Cinecrest (John Kohn)

Two men on the run are pursued by soldiers and helicopters; only one crosses the frontier.
Portentous Pinterish parable, very long-winded and relentlessly boring though good to look at. Everything is symbolic, nothing is specific, not even the country.

w Robert Shaw, *novel* Barry England *d* Joseph Losey *ph* Henri Alekan *m* Richard Rodney Bennett

Robert Shaw, Malcolm McDowell

The File of the Golden Goose
GB 1969 109m De Luxe
UA / Theme / Caralan / Dador (David E. Rose)

An American agent works with Scotland Yard to track down counterfeiters.
Incredibly predictable spy thriller which almost makes an eccentricity out of collecting so many clichés and so many tourist views of London.
Like ten TV episodes cut together.

w John C. Higgins, James B. Gordon *d* Sam Wanamaker *ph* Ken Hodges *m* Harry Robinson

Yul Brynner, Edward Woodward, Charles Gray, John Barrie, Bernard Archard, Ivor Dean, Adrienne Corri, Graham Crowden, Karel Stepanek
'The film plods wearily homewards through an exceptionally uninteresting batch of fights, intrigues and sinister encounters.'—*MFB*

The File on Thelma Jordon*
US 1949 100m bw
Paramount (Hal B. Wallis)
aka: *Thelma Jordon*

A district attorney falls for a murder suspect and has her acquitted by losing the case.

Stylishly made, murkily plotted melodrama and a superior star vehicle of its time.

w Ketti Frings *d* Robert Siodmak *ph* George Barnes *m* Victor Young

Barbara Stanwyck, Wendell Corey, Paul Kelly, Joan Tetzel, Stanley Ridges, Richard Rober, Minor Watson, Barry Kelley

La Fille du Puisatier*
France 1946 131m bw
Marcel Pagnol
aka: *The Well-Digger's Daughter*

A stern old well-digger feels bound to send his daughter away when she becomes pregnant. More country matters from Pagnol, this time with an East Lynne type plot getting in the way of some fine acting. Not much comedy.

wd Marcel Pagnol

Raimu, Fernandel, Charpin, Josette Day
  'There is a feeling in France that such films are made for the foreigner and exploit the eccentricities of French rural life rather than the realities.'—*MFB*

Film ohne Titel*
West Germany 1947 100m bw
Camera Film (Erwin Gitt)
aka: *Film without Title*

Scriptwriters discuss how it is possible to make a comedy film in post-war Germany, and evolve a story with alternative endings.
Elegantly conceived but rather humourlessly executed, this interesting film was one of the first post-war German exports, but failed to start a trend. It has similarities to *La Fête à Henriette* and *Rashomon*.

w Helmut Kautner, Ellen Fechner, Rudolf Jugert *d* Rudolf Jugert *ph* Igor Oberberg *m* Bernard Eichhorn

Hans Söhnker, Hildegarde Knef, *Irene Von Meyendorff*, Willy Fritsch

The Final Programme
GB 1973 89m Technicolor
Goodtimes / Gladiole (John Goldstone, Sanford Lieberson)
US title: *The Last Days of Man on Earth*

In the future, when the world is torn by famine and war, a scientist awaits a new messiah. Intellectualized sci-fi, hard to take as entertainment but very glossy.

wd Robert Fuest, *novel* Michael Moorcock *ph* Norman Warwick *m* Paul Beaver, Bernard Krause

Jon Finch, Jenny Runacre, Sterling Hayden, Hugh Griffith

  'Clumsy and almost incomprehensible.'—*Sight and Sound*

The Final Test
GB 1953 90m bw
Rank / ACT (R. J. Minney)

A cricketer looks forward to his last game but is out for a duck; he is however cheered by the crowd and comforted by his son.
Flat character study some way below the author's best style, cluttered up with real cricketers and stymied by lack of action.

w Terence Rattigan *d* Anthony Asquith *ph* Bill McLeod *m* Benjamin Franklin

Jack Warner, Robert Morley, George Relph

Finders Keepers
GB 1966 94m Eastmancolor
UA / Interstate (George H. Brown)

The Americans lose an atomic bomb off the Spanish coast, and it's found by a pop group. Harmless youth musical without much style. Tunes poor, comedy rather too easy-going.

w Michael Pertwee *d* Sidney Hayers *ph* Alan Hume *m* The Shadows, Norrie Paramor

Cliff Richard, The Shadows, Robert Morley, Peggy Mount, Viviane Ventura, Graham Stark, John Le Mesurier, Robert Hutton

A Fine Madness*
US 1966 104m Technicolor
Warner Seven Arts

A frustrated New York poet has outbursts of violence.
Patchy, interesting, with-it comedy which suffers from too many changes of mood.

w Elliot Baker, from his novel *d* Irvin Kershner *ph* Ted McCord *m* John Addison

Sean Connery, Jean Seberg, Joanne Woodward, Patrick O'Neal, Colleen Dewhurst, Clive Revill
  'Straddling a no man's land somewhere between the *nouvelle vague* and the crazy comedies of Old Hollywood.'—*Tom Milne*

Fingers at the Window
US 1942 90m bw
MGM (Irving Starr)

A stage magician hypnotizes lunatics into murdering all those who stand between him and an inheritance.
Slow-starting thriller which never achieves top gear.

w Rose Caylor, Lawrence P. Bachmann *d* Charles Lederer *ph* Harry Stradling, Charles Lawton

Basil Rathbone, Lew Ayres, Laraine Day, Walter Kingsford, Miles Mander, Russell Gleason

'The kind of picture actors do when they need work.'—*Lew Ayres*

Finian's Rainbow*
US 1968 140m Technicolor Panavision 70
Warner Seven Arts (Joseph Landon)

A leprechaun tries to retrieve a crock of gold from an old wanderer who has taken it to America.
Musical whimsy-whamsy, a long way after a 1947 Broadway success; in this overlong and overblown screen version the elements and the style do not jell and there is too much sentimental chat, but moments of magic shine through.

w E. Y. Harburg, Fred Saidy, from their play d Francis Ford Coppola ph Philip Lathrop m Burton Lane ly E. Y. Harburg pd Hilyard M. Brown md Ray Heindorf

Fred Astaire, Petula Clark, Tommy Steele, Don Francks, Keenan Wynn, Barbara Hancock, Al Freeman Jnr

AAN: Ray Heindorf

Finis Terrae*
France 1929 90m approx bw silent
Société Générale des Films

A re-enacted account of the lives of fishermen on remote Brittany islands.
A feature documentary which was impressive at the time; very similar to Flaherty's *Man of Aran*.

wd Jean Epstein ph Joseph Barth, Joseph Kottula

Finishing School
US 1934 73m bw
RKO (Kenneth MacGowan)

A girl at an exclusive school falls for an intern.
Modest pap for the teenage audience.

w Wanda Tuchock, Laird Doyle d Wanda Tuchock, George Nicholls Jnr ph J. Roy Hunt m Max Steiner

Frances Dee, Ginger Rogers, Billie Burke, Bruce Cabot, John Halliday, Beulah Bondi, Sara Haden

Fire Down Below
GB 1957 116m Technicolor Cinemascope
Columbia /Warwick (Irving Allen, Albert Broccoli)

Partners in a Caribbean fishing and smuggling business fall out over a woman.

Overheated melodrama with thin characters, predictable incident and ill-advised casting.

w Irwin Shaw, *novel* Max Catto d Robert Parrish ph Desmond Dickinson m Arthur Benjamin

Rita Hayworth, Robert Mitchum, Jack Lemmon, Herbert Lom, Bonar Colleano, Bernard Lee, Edric Connor, Peter Illing

A Fire Has Been Arranged
GB 1935 70m bw
Twickenham (Julius Hagen)

Ex-convicts find a building in the field where they buried the loot.
Modest star comedy. Was this the first use of this well-worn plot?

w H. Fowler Mear, Michael Barringer d Leslie Hiscott

Bud Flanagan, Chesney Allen, Alastair Sim, Robb Wilton, Mary Lawson, Harold French, C. Denier Warren

Fire Over England**
GB 1936 92m bw
Pendennis (Erich Pommer)

Elizabeth I and her navy overcome the Spanish Armada.
Though the film has a faded air and the action climax was always a bath-tub affair, the splendid cast keeps this pageant afloat and interesting.

w Clemence Dane, Sergei Nolbandov, *novel* A. E. W. Mason d William K. Howard ph James Wong Howe m Richard Addinsell

Flora Robson, Laurence Olivier, Leslie Banks, Vivien Leigh, Raymond Massey, Tamara Desni, Morton Selten, Lyn Harding, James Mason

Fire Sale*
US 1977 88m De Luxe
TCF (Marvin Worth)

Misadventures of a frantic, eccentric New York-Jewish family who own a department store.
Frenzied black farce for ethnic audiences.

w Robert Klane, from his novel d Alan Arkin ph Ralph Woolsey m Dave Grusin

Alan Arkin, Rob Reiner, Vincent Gardenia, Anjanette Comer, Kay Medford, Sid Caesar, Alex Rocco

'It moves fast enough to carry the occasional lapses from its own high standards of tastelessness.'—*Jan Dawson, MFB*

Firecreek
US 1968 104m Technicolor Panavision
Warner Seven Arts (Philip Leacock)

The people of Firecreek protect themselves from wandering gunmen.

Dour, predictable little western which does not show its stars at their best.

w Calvin Clements d Vincent McEveety
ph William Clothier m Alfred Newman

James Stewart, Henry Fonda, Gary Lockwood, Dean Jagger, Ed Begley, Jay C. Flippen, Jack Elam, James Best, Barbara Luna

'This cramped and clumsy western grinds to a standstill in its attempts to give Firecreek symbolic status . . . while the gunmen roister like mad and the townsfolk rhubarb glumly in the background.'—*MFB*

The Firefly*
US 1937 131m bw
MGM (Hunt Stromberg)

Adventures of a Spanish lady spy during the Napoleonic war.

Solid production of a romantic operetta; splendid stuff for connoisseurs.

w Frances Goodrich, Albert Hackett, Ogden Nash d Robert Z. Leonard ph Oliver Marsh *original book/ly* Otto Harbach m Rudolf Friml md Herbert Stothart

Jeanette MacDonald, *Allan Jones* (who sings the Donkey Serenade), Warren William, Billy Gilbert, Henry Daniell, George Zucco, Douglass Dumbrille

'A lavish musical monstrosity.'—*New Yorker, 1978*

Fireman Save My Child
US 1954 80m bw
U-I (Howard Christie)

In 1910 San Francisco, incompetent firemen accidentally catch a gang of crooks.

Slapstick farce intended for Abbott and Costello, taken over by a new team which did not catch on, played like the Keystone Kops. Mildly funny during the chases.

w Lee Loeb, John Grant d Leslie Goodwins
ph Clifford Stine m Joseph Gershenson

Buddy Hackett, Spike Jones and the City Slickers, Hugh O'Brian, Adèle Jergens

The Firemen's Ball*
Czechoslovakia / Italy 1967 73m
   Eastmancolor
Barrandov/ Carlo Ponti
original title: *Hori, Ma Panenko*

In a small provincial town, arrangements for the firemen's annual ball go wrong at every turn.

Vaguely amusing Tati-esque comedy with not quite enough funny moments and a prevailing atmosphere of pessimism.

w Milos Forman, Ivan Passer, Jaroslav Papousek d Milos Forman ph Miroslav Ondricek m Karel Mares

Jan Vostreil, Josef Kolb, Josef Svet, Frantisek Debelka

'A compendium of superb items.'—*Philip Strick*

Fires on the Plain**
Japan 1959 108m bw
Daiei (Masaichi Nagata)
original title: *Nobi*

In the Philippines during World War II, a half-demented Japanese private takes to the hills, becomes a cannibal, and is shot by the Americans when he tries to surrender.

Stomach-turning anti-war epic with fine scenes and performances but dubious intent.

w Natto Wada, *novel* Shohei O-oka d Kon Ichikawa ph Setsuo Kobayashi m Yasushi Akatagawa

Eiji Funakoshi, Osamu Takizawa, Micky Curtis

Fires Were Started**
GB 1942 83m bw
Crown Film Unit
aka: *I Was a Fireman*

One day and night in the life of a National Fire Service unit during the London blitz.

Thoughtful, slow-moving, poetic documentary originally intended as a training film but generally released to boost morale. Not its director's finest work, but perhaps his most ambitious.

wd Humphrey Jennings ph C. Pennington-Richards m William Alwyn

† The firemen were real firemen, but the scenes were re-enacted.

'An astonishingly intimate portrait of an isolated and besieged Britain . . . an unforgettable piece of human observation, affectionate, touching, and yet ironic.'—*Georges Sadoul*

First Comes Courage
US 1943 88m bw
Columbia (Harry Joe Brown)

During World War II, a Norwegian girl appears to be a Quisling but is really a spy getting information from the Nazis by fraternizing with them.

Doleful war drama with little to commend it except propaganda.

w Lewis Meltzer, Melvin Levy, *novel* The

Commandos by Elliott Arnold *d* Dorothy
Arzner *ph* Joseph Walker *m* Ernst Toch

Merle Oberon, Brian Aherne, Carl Esmond,
Fritz Leiber, Erik Rolf, Reinhold Schunzel,
Isobel Elsom

The First Gentleman*
GB 1948   111m   bw
Columbia (Joseph Friedman)
US title: *Affairs of a Rogue*

The affairs and foibles of the Prince Regent.
Dullish adaptation of a successful West End play
about 18th-century court life; script and
performances still entertain.

w Nicholas Phipps, Reginald Long, *play*
Norman Ginsbury d Cavalcanti

Cecil Parker, Jean-Pierre Aumont, Joan
Hopkins, Margaretta Scott, Jack Livesey,
Ronald Squire, Athene Seyler, Hugh Griffith

First Lady*
US 1937   82m   bw
Warner (Hal B. Wallis)

The President's wife is a power behind the
scenes.
Solidly entertaining Washington comedy.

w Rowland Leigh, *play* George S. Kaufman,
Katherine Dayton *d* Stanley Logan *ph* Sid
Hickox

Kay Francis, Preston Foster, Anita Louise,
Walter Connolly, Verree Teasdale, Victor Jory,
Marjorie Rambeau, Louise Fazenda

The First Legion*
US 1951   86m   bw
Sedif (Douglas Sirk)

Priests are bewildered when one of their number
is the centre of an apparent miracle.
Talkative religious drama of a peculiarly
American kind which likes to have its cake and
eat it; watchable for the performances.

w Emmet Lavery, from his play *d* Douglas Sirk
ph Robert de Grasse *m* Hans Sommer

Charles Boyer, William Demarest, Lyle Bettger,
Barbara Rush, Leo G. Carroll, Walter
Hampden, George Zucco, Taylor Holmes

First Love*
US 1939   84m   bw
Universal (Joe Pasternak)

An orphaned teenager goes to live with her uncle
and his snobbish family, and falls for a local
bigwig's son.
A vehicle carefully conceived to introduce its
star to grown-up romance. The compromises
show, but it's palatable enough.

w Bruce Manning, Lionel Houser *d* Henry
Koster *md* Charles Previn

Deanna Durbin, Robert Stack, Eugene Pallette,
Helen Parrish, Lewis Howard, Leatrice Joy
    'The most obvious Cinderella story I ever met
with, apart from *Cinderella*.'—*Richard Mallett,*
Punch

AAN: Charles Previn

First Man into Space
GB 1958   78m   bw
Producers' Associates (John Croydon)

An astronaut runs into a cloud of meteor dust
and returns to earth a vampirish killer.
Quatermass-like shocker with modest budget
but firm control.

w John C. Cooper, Lance Z. Hargreaves
d Robert Day *ph* Geoffrey Faithfull *m* Buxton
Orr

Marshall Thompson, Marla Landi, Bill Edwards

First Men in the Moon*
GB 1964   103m   Technicolor   Panavision
Columbia / Ameran (Charles H. Schneer)

A Victorian eccentric makes a voyage to the
moon and is forced to stay there.
Rather slack in plot development, but an
enjoyable schoolboy romp with a good eye for
detail and tongue firmly in cheek.

w Nigel Kneale, Jan Read, *novel* H. G. Wells
d Nathan Juran *ph* Wilkie Cooper *m* Laurie
Johnson *sp* Ray Harryhausen

Lionel Jeffries, Edward Judd, Martha Hyer
† Uncredited, Peter Finch played the bit part of a
process server.

The First of the Few**
GB 1942   117m   bw
Melbourne / British Aviation (Leslie Howard,
    George King, Adrian Brunel, John Stafford)
US title: *Spitfire*

The story of R. J. Mitchell who saw World War
II coming and devised the Spitfire.
Low-key but impressive biopic with firm acting
and good dialogue scenes. Production values
slightly shaky.

w Anatole de Grunwald, Miles Malleson, Henry
C. James, Katherine Strueby *d* Leslie Howard
m William Walton

Leslie Howard, David Niven, Rosamund John,
Roland Culver, David Horne

The First Time
US 1968   90m   De Luxe
UA / Mirisch / Rogallan (Roger Smith, Allan Carr)
GB title: You Don't Need Pajamas at Rosie's

Three teenage boys who fantasize about sex help a stranded girl under the impression that she is a prostitute.
Embarrassingly sentimental teenage sex comedy, all the more irritating by its restraint. Not a patch on Summer of '42.

w Jo Heims, Roger Smith d James Nielson ph Ernest Laszlo m Kenyon Hopkins

Jacqueline Bisset, Wes Stern, Rick Kelman, Wink Roberts, Sharon Acker

The First Texan
US 1956   82m   Technicolor
   Cinemascope
Allied Artists (Walter Mirisch)

The Governor of Tennessee helps Texas win its independence.
Generally well done biopic of Sam Houston, with the usual western excitements.

w Daniel B. Ullman d Byron Haskin ph Wilfrid Cline m Roy Webb

Joel McCrea, Felicia Farr, Jeff Morrow, Wallace Ford, Abraham Sofaer

First to Fight
US 1967   97m   Technicolor   Panavision
Warner (William Conrad)

A World War II hero is taken home and fêted, but on returning to the front he loses his nerve.
War film in the guise of a psychological study; competently done but very American in its sentiments and a bit shaky on period detail.

w Gene L. Coon d Christian Nyby ph Harold Wellman m Fred Steiner

Chad Everett, Gene Hackman, Dean Jagger, Marilyn Devon, Claude Akins

The First Travelling Saleslady
US 1956   92m   Technicolor
RKO (Arthur Lubin)

Two women set out to sell barbed wire in the old west.
Strained comedy with very few effective moments.

w Devery Freeman, Stephen Longstreet d Arthur Lubin ph William Snyder m Irving Gertz

Ginger Rogers, Carol Channing, Barry Nelson, James Arness, David Brian, Clint Eastwood

F.I.S.T. *
US 1978   145m   Technicolor
UA / Norman Jewison (Gene Corman)

The rise and fall of a union boss.
Reminiscent of All the King's Men and On the Waterfront, this much overlong melodrama has compelling passages, but the star is not quite equal to it and parts are both repetitive and obscure.

w Joe Eszterhas, Sylvester Stallone d Norman Jewison ph Laslo Kovacs m Bill Conti pd Richard MacDonald

Sylvester Stallone, Rod Steiger, Peter Boyle, Melinda Dillon, David Huffman, Tony L. Bianco, Cassie Yates, Peter Donat, Henry Wilcoxon

A Fistful of Dollars *
Italy / Germany / Spain 1964   100m
   Techniscope
UA / Jolly / Constantin / Ocean (Arrigo Colombo, Georgio Papi)

An avenging stranger, violent and mysterious, cleans up a Mexican border town.
A film with much to answer for: it began the craze for 'spaghetti westerns', took its director to Hollywood, and made a TV cowboy into a world star. In itself it is simple, noisy, brutish and actionful.

w Sergio Leone, Duccio Tessari d Sergio Leone ph Massimo Dallamano m Ennio Morricone

Clint Eastwood, Gian Maria Volonte, Marianne Koch
† Direct sequels by Leone, apart from numerous imitations, are For a Few Dollars More and The Good, the Bad and the Ugly.

A Fistful of Dynamite
Italy 1971   150m   Techniscope
UA / Rafran / San Marco / Miura (Fulvio Morsella)
aka: Duck, You Sucker

In 1913 a Mexican bandit and an ex-IRA explosives expert join forces to rob a bank.
Overblown action spectacular, far too long to be sustained by its flashes of humour and excitement. A good instance of what happens to a small talent when success goes to its head.

wd Sergio Leone ph Giuseppe Ruzzolini m Ennio Morricone

Rod Steiger, James Coburn

Fists in the Pocket *
Italy 1965   113m   bw
Doria (Ezio Passadore)
original title: I Pugni in Tasca

One of a family of epileptics murders most of the others in order to help his normal eldest brother. Complex black melodrama which makes its points, if it has any, with great style.

wd Marco Bellocchio ph Alberto Marrama *m* Ennio Morricone

Lou Castel, Paola Pitagora, Liliona Gerace
'There have been few debuts as exciting as this in recent years.'—*Tom Milne, MFB*

Fitzwilly*
US 1967 102m De Luxe Panavision
UA / Dramatic Features Inc / Walter Mirisch
GB title: *Fitzwilly Strikes Back*

A New York butler, in order to keep his lady in style, has to organize the staff into a crime syndicate.
Moderately inventive, good-looking comedy with rather too much plot and not enough funny lines.

w Isobel Lennart, *novel* A Garden of Cucumbers by Poyntz Tyler *d* Delbert Mann *ph* Joseph Biroc *m* Johnny Williams

Dick Van Dyke, Edith Evans, Barbara Feldon, John McGiver, Harry Townes, John Fiedler, Norman Fell, Cecil Kellaway, Anne Seymour, Sam Waterston, Billy Halop

Five
US 1951 89m bw
Columbia (Arch Oboler)

There are only five survivors of an atomic holocaust, and their political and racial tensions soon reduce the number to two.
Gutless talkfest which becomes interesting only when the camera moves out of doors; otherwise, too pretentious and dull by half.

wd Arch Oboler *ph* Lou Stoumen, Ed Spiegel, Sid Lubow *m* Henry Russell

William Phipps, Susan Douglas, James Anderson, Charles Lampkin, Earl Lee
'The talk leaves one with a strong impression that in this case the fittest did not survive.'—*Penelope Houston*

Five Against the House
US 1955 84m bw
Columbia (Sterling Silliphant, John Barnwell)

College students try to rob a casino.
Meandering caper melodrama with too much flabby dialogue.

w Sterling Silliphant, John Barnwell, *novel* Jack Finney *d* Phil Karlson *ph* Leslie White *m* George Duning

Guy Madison, Kim Novak, Brian Keith, Kerwin Mathews, William Conrad

Five Boys from Barska Street*
Poland 1953 115m Agfacolor
Film Polski
original title: *Piatka z Ulicy Barskiej*

Five city boys are placed on probation and gradually change their attitudes towards life and society.
Rather dated propaganda piece with a plot which surprisingly follows western models.

wd Aleksander Ford, *novel* Kazimierz Kozniewski *ph* Jaroslav Tuzar *m* Kazimierz Serocki

Tadeusz Janczar, Aleksandra Slaska, Andrzej Kozak

Five Branded Women
Italy / US 1960 100m bw
Paramount / Dino de Laurentiis

Five Yugoslav girls have their heads shaved for associating with German soldiers, and after various adventures join the partisans.
Rough, tough war adventure which makes a few boring points about love and war.

w Ivo Perelli, *novel* Ugo Pirro *d* Martin Ritt *ph* Giuseppe Rotunno *m* Francesco Lavagnino

Silvana Mangano, Van Heflin, Vera Miles, Barbara Bel Geddes, Jeanne Moreau, Richard Basehart, Harry Guardino, Steve Forrest, Alex Nicol
'For the most part the film is devoted to unexciting guerrilla action and uninviting partisan life . . . obstinately unreal despite lashings of blood, mutilation, childbirth and death.'—*MFB*

Five Came Back**
US 1939 75m bw
RKO (Robert Sisk)

A passenger plane crashlands in the jungle. It can carry back only five survivors, and headhunters are coming closer . . .
A minor film which gradually achieved cult status and was remade as *Back to Eternity* as well as being the starting point for many variations. Still gripping in its dated way.

w Jerry Cady, Dalton Trumbo, Nathanael West *d* John Farrow *ph* Nicholas Musuraca *m* Roy Webb

Chester Morris, Lucille Ball, C. Aubrey Smith, Elizabeth Risdon, Wendy Barrie, John Carradine, Joseph Calleia, Allen Jenkins, Kent Taylor, Patric Knowles

Five Card Stud
US 1968 103m Technicolor
Paramount / Hal. B. Wallis

Members of a lynching party are murdered one by one.
Would-be nonchalant murder mystery western: the stars just about hold it together, but it's an uphill fight.

w Marguerite Roberts, *novel* Ray Gaulden
d Henry Hathaway *ph* Daniel L. Fapp
m Maurice Jarre

Dean Martin, Robert Mitchum, Inger Stevens, Roddy McDowall, Katherine Justice, John Anderson, Yaphet Kotto
'Marginally watchable . . . but destined to sink without trace minutes after one leaves the cinema.'—*Gavin Millar*

'So mediocre you can't get mad at it.'—*Judith Crist*

Five Easy Pieces **
US 1970   98m   Technicolor
Columbia / Bert Schneider (Bob Rafelson, Richard Wechsler)

A middle-class drifter jilts his pregnant mistress for his brother's fiancée, but finally leaves both and hitches a ride to nowhere in particular.
Echoes of *Easy Rider*, *The Graduate* and *Charlie Bubbles* abound in this generally likeable but insubstantial modern anti-drama which at least takes place in pleasant surroundings and is firmly directed.

w Adrien Joyce, *d* Bob Rafelson *ph* Laszlo Kovacs *m* various

Jack Nicholson, Karen Black, Susan Anspach, Lois Smith, Billy 'Green' Bush, Fannie Flagg

AAN: best picture; Adrien Joyce; Jack Nicholson; Karen Black

Five Finger Exercise
US 1962   109m   bw
Columbia / Sonnis (Frederick Brisson)

A snobbish wife falls in love with a young house guest, with dire effect on her husband and son.
This West End study of a neurotic family is probably not good film material, certainly not adaptable to California, and above all not suitable to this star's whizzbang dramatics.
Numbing hysteria arrives early and stays till the end.

w Frances Goodrich, Albert Hackett, *play* Peter Shaffer *d* Daniel Mann *ph* Harry Stradling *m* Jerome Moross

Rosalind Russell, Jack Hawkins, Maximilian Schell, Richard Beymer

Five Fingers ***
US 1952   108m   bw
TCF (Otto Lang)

The valet of the British ambassador in Ankara sells military secrets to the Germans, who pay him but never use the information.
Absorbing, lightweight film adaptation of a true story of World War II; civilized suspense entertainment with all talents contributing nicely.

w Michael Wilson, book Operation Cicero by L. C. Moyzich *d Joseph L. Mankiewicz*
ph Norbert Brodine *m* Bernard Herrmann
ad Lyle Wheeler, George W. Davis

James Mason, Danielle Darrieux, Michael Rennie, Walter Hampden, Oscar Karlweis, Herbert Berghof, John Wengraf, Michael Pate
'One of the highest, fastest and most absorbing spy melodramas since Hitchcock crossed the Atlantic.'—*Arthur Knight*

AAN: Michael Wilson; Joseph L. Mankiewicz

Five Golden Hours
GB / Italy 1960   90m   bw
(Columbia) Anglofilm / Fabio Jegher (Mario Zampi)

A con man tries to murder three widows who have invested money in one of his schemes.
Ill-judged black comedy, sadly lacking style.

w Hans Wilhelm *d* Mario Zampi
ph Christopher Challis *m* Stanley Black

Ernie Kovacs, Cyd Charisse, Kay Hammond, George Sanders, Dennis Price, Reginald Beckwith, Martin Benson, Ron Moody, Finlay Currie, Avis Landone, Sidney Tafler, John Le Mesurier, Clelia Matania

Five Graves to Cairo ***
US 1943   96m   bw
Paramount (Charles Brackett)

During the North Africa campaign, British spies try to destroy Rommel's secret supply dumps.
Intriguing spy melodrama set in a desert hotel, a notable example of Hollywood's ability to snatch polished drama from the headlines.

w Charles Brackett, Billy Wilder, play Lajos Biro *d Billy Wilder m* Miklos Rozsa *ph* John Seitz

Franchot Tone, Anne Baxter, *Erich Von Stroheim* (as Rommel), Akim Tamiroff, Peter Van Eyck, Miles Mander
'Billy Wilder must have had something a little grander in mind: the cleverness lacks lustre.'—*New Yorker, 1978*

AAN: John Seitz

Five Miles to Midnight *
France / Italy 1962   110m   bw
UA / Filmsonor / Dear Film (Anatole Litvak)

A neurotic believed dead forces his terrified wife to collect his life insurance.

Hysterical melodrama, smoothly made with all the familiar expressionist devices, but far too long for its content.

w Peter Viertel, Hugh Wheeler d Anatole Litvak ph Henri Alekan m Mikis Theodorakis

Sophia Loren, Anthony Perkins, Gig Young, Jean-Pierre Aumont, Yolande Turner, Tommy Norden

'From the polished immediacy of the cars, streets, shop windows and café tables to the off-focus vertigo shots of panic, from the overhead view of neighbours on stairs . . . to the close-ups of hands in filing trays touching off the details of fear and guilt, there is a thread of colour to keep you watching.'—MFB

'A well-ordered exercise in mechanical suspense.'—Arthur Schlesinger Jnr

The Five Pennies*
US 1959 117m Technicolor Vistavision
Paramount / Dena (Jack Rose)

The rags-to-riches success story of cornet player Red Nichols.
The only touch of originality in this biopic is that the subject is given touches of irascibility. Production values reach a good standard.

w Jack Rose, Melville Shavelson d Melville Shavelson ph Daniel L. Fapp md Leith Stevens ad Hal Pereira, Tambi Larsen songs Sylvia Fine trumpet solos Red Nichols

Danny Kaye, Barbara Bel Geddes, Louis Armstrong, Bob Crosby, Harry Guardino, Tuesday Weld, Ray Anthony

AAN: Daniel L. Fapp; Leith Stevens; title song (m/ly Sylvia Fine)

Five Star Final**
US 1931 89m bw
Warner

A sensation-seeking newspaper editor causes tragedy.
Dated but still powerful melodrama which set the pattern for all the newspaper films of the thirties.

w Robert Lord, Byron Morgan, play Louis Weitzenkorn d Mervyn Le Roy ph Sol Polito md Leo F. Forbstein

Edward G. Robinson, H. B. Warner, Marian Marsh, Anthony Bushell, George E. Stone, Ona Munson, Aline MacMahon, Boris Karloff

'All the elements to make a hit attraction.'—Variety

† Remade in 1936 with Humphrey Bogart, as Two Against the World.

AAN: best picture

Five Steps to Danger
US 1956 80m bw
UA / HSK

A girl possessing secret information from her dead scientist brother has a mental breakdown, and is pursued by spies.
Lively if cliché-ridden espionage melodrama, like an old-time serial.

wd Henry S. Kesler, novel Donald Hamilton ph Kenneth Peach m Paul Sawtell, Bert Shefter

Sterling Hayden, Ruth Roman, Werner Klemperer, Richard Gaines

The Five Thousand Fingers of Doctor T**
US 1953 88m Technicolor
Columbia / Stanley Kramer

A boy who hates piano lessons dreams of his teacher as an evil genius who keeps five hundred boys imprisoned in a castle of musical instruments.
Badly scripted fantasy with gleaming sophisticated dream sequences which deserve a better frame. A real oddity to come from Hollywood at this time, even though Dr Seuss' books were and are bestsellers.

w Dr Seuss (Theodore Geisel), Alan Scott d Roy Rowland ph Franz Planer m Frederick Hollander ly Dr Seuss pd Rudolph Sternad ch Eugene Loring

Hans Conried, Tommy Rettig, Peter Lind Hayes, Mary Healy

AAN: Frederick Hollander

Five Weeks in a Balloon
US 1962 101m De Luxe Cinemascope
TCF (Irving Allen)

In 1862 a professor is financed on a balloon trip into central Africa.
Would-be humorous semi-fantasy which strives to equal Journey to the Center of the Earth but unfortunately falls flat on its face despite the interesting talent available. Limp comedy situations, poor production values.

w Charles Bennett, Irving Allen, Albert Gail, novel Jules Verne d Irving Allen ph Winton Hoch m Paul Sawtell ad Jack Martin Smith, Alfred Ybarra

Cedric Hardwicke, Peter Lorre, Red Buttons, Fabian, Richard Haydn, Billy Gilbert, Herbert Marshall, Reginald Owen, Henry Daniell

Fixed Bayonets
US 1951 93m bw
TCF (Jules Buck)

An American division in Korea fights a rearguard action.

Downbeat war melodrama of a familiar kind, with more characterization than action.

wd Samuel Fuller *ph* Lucien Ballard *m* Roy Webb

Richard Basehart, Gene Evans, Michael O'Shea, Richard Hylton, Craig Hill

The Fixer
US 1968 130m Metrocolor
MGM / Edward Lewis, John Frankenheimer

A Jew in Tsarist Russia denies his race but becomes a scapegoat for various crimes and is imprisoned without trial until he becomes a *cause célèbre*.
Worthy but extremely dreary realist melodrama.

w Dalton Trumbo, *novel* Bernard Malamud *d* John Frankenheimer *ph* Marcel Grignon *m* Maurice Jarre

Alan Bates, Dirk Bogarde, Georgia Brown, Jack Gilford, Hugh Griffith, Elizabeth Hartman, Ian Holm, David Warner, Carol White, Murray Melvin, Peter Jeffrey, Michael Goodliffe
'The kind of film in which one has to admire much of the acting simply because it is all there is to admire.'—*David Pirie*
'A totally false film, devoid of a breath of human life or truth.'—*Arthur Schlesinger Jnr*

AAN: Alan Bates

The Flag Lieutenant
GB 1933 85m bw
British and Dominions (Herbert Wilcox)

A naval lieutenant, thought to be a coward, shows his true courage when a fort is beleaguered.
Boy's Own Paper stuff from a popular play previously filmed in 1919 (with George Wynn) and 1926 (with Henry Edwards).

w W. P. Drury, Leo Tover, from their play *d* Henry Edwards

Henry Edwards, Anna Neagle, Joyce Bland, Peter Gawthorne, Sam Livesey, O. B. Clarence, Abraham Sofaer

The Flame
US 1947 97m bw
Republic (John H. Auer)

A nurse marries for money, but her ailing spouse recovers and she falls in love with him.
Turgid melodrama, ineptly presented.

w Lawrence Kimble *d* John H. Auer *ph* Reggie Lanning *m* Heinz Roemheld

Vera Hruba Ralston, John Carroll, Robert Paige, Broderick Crawford, Henry Travers, Blanche Yurka, Constance Dowling, Hattie McDaniel, Sen Yung

'A good picture to stay away from, with or without a good book.'—*Cue*

The Flame and the Arrow*
US 1950 88m Technicolor
(Warner) Harold Hecht, Frank Ross

In medieval Italy, a rebel leader seeks victory over a tyrant.
Good-humoured Robin Hood stuff with the star at his most acrobatic.

w Waldo Salt *d* Jacques Tourneur *ph* Ernest Haller *m* Max Steiner *ad* Edward Carrere

Burt Lancaster, Virginia Mayo, Robert Douglas, Aline MacMahon, Frank Allenby, Nick Cravat
'I never found a Technicolor costume picture so entertaining.'—*Richard Mallett, Punch*

AAN: Ernest Haller; Max Steiner

The Flame and the Flesh
US 1954 104m Technicolor
MGM (Joe Pasternak)

An unscrupulous American woman in Naples has a fatal fascination for the local menfolk.
Dreary remake of *Naples au Baiser du Feu* (France 1937), with the dullest possible handling all round.

w Helen Deutsch, *novel* Auguste Bailly *d* Richard Brooks *ph* Christopher Challis *m* Nicholas Brodszky

Lana Turner, Carlos Thompson, Bonar Colleano, Pier Angeli, Charles Goldner, Peter Illing

Flame in the Streets
GB 1961 93m colour Cinemascope
Rank / Somerset (Roy Baker)

A liberal-minded union man erupts when his daughter proposes to marry a black man.
Predictable East End problem picture, unconvincingly set and acted and boring into the bargain.

w Ted Willis, from his TV play Hot Summer Night *d* Roy Baker *ph* Christopher Challis *m* Phil Green

John Mills, Brenda de Banzie, Sylvia Syms, Earl Cameron, Johnny Sekka, Ann Lynn, Wilfred Brambell
'Its methods belong more to the writer's study than to life.'—*John Gillett*

The Flame of New Orleans*
US 1941 79m bw
Universal (Joe Pasternak)

A European adventuress settles in America.

Fluffy comedy romance with the exiled director scarcely in top form.

w Norman Krasna *d* René Clair *ph* Rudolph Maté *m* Frank Skinner

Marlene Dietrich, Roland Young, Bruce Cabot, Mischa Auer, Andy Devine, Frank Jenks, Eddie Quillan, Laura Hope Crews, Franklin Pangborn
† Remade as *Scarlet Angel*.

Flame of the Barbary Coast
US 1945 97m bw
Republic (Joseph Kane)

In old San Francisco, a cowboy becomes involved with a night club queen, and their fortunes are resolved by the earthquake.
Tolerable period melodrama, and the one in which Wayne played a character named Duke: the nickname stuck.

w Borden Chase *d* Joseph Kane *ph* Robert de Grasse *m* Dale Butts *sp* Howard and Theodore Lydecker

John Wayne, Ann Dvorak, Joseph Schildkraut, William Frawley, Virginia Grey, Russell Hicks, Jack Norton, Paul Fix, Marc Lawrence

AAN: Dale Butts

Flame of the Islands
US 1955 90m Trucolor
Republic (Edward Ludwig)

A girl invests a bequest in a Bahamas night club, and there becomes involved with four men.
Barely competent time-filler.

w Bruce Manning *d* Edward Ludwig *ph* Bud Thackery *m* Nelson Riddle

Yvonne de Carlo, Howard Duff, Zachary Scott, Kurt Kasznar, Barbara O'Neil, James Arness, Frieda Inescort

Flaming Star*
US 1960 92m De Luxe Cinemascope
TCF (David Weisbart)

A half-breed family is torn between two loyalties.
Solemn, unusual Civil War western with a downbeat ending.

w Clair Huffaker, Nunnally Johnson *d* Don Siegel *ph* Charles G. Clarke *m* Cyril Mockridge

Elvis Presley, Dolores del Rio, Steve Forrest, Barbara Eden, John McIntire, Rodolpho Acosta
   'Despite familiar absurdities, it has more than its share of good moments.'—*MFB*

Flamingo Road*
US 1949 94m bw
Warner (Jerry Wald)

A tough carnival dancer is stranded in a small town and soon affects the lives of the local politicians.
Standard melodrama from a bestseller, absurd but well performed.

w Robert Wilder, from his novel *d* Michael Curtiz *ph* Ted McCord *m* Max Steiner

Joan Crawford, David Brian, Sidney Greenstreet, Zachary Scott, Gladys George, Virginia Huston, Fred Clark

Flap
US 1970 106m Technicolor Panavision
Warner (Jerry Adler)
GB title: *The Last Warrior*

A drunken Indian on a dilapidated modern reservation starts a public relations war and leads a march on the city.
Unendearing comedy with a tragic end tacked on, not very entertaining as whimsy, farce or social conscience.

w Clair Huffaker, from his novel Nobody Loves a Drunken Indian *d* Carol Reed *ph* Fred Koenekamp *m* Marvin Hamlisch

   'A corny, ill-made film full of tedious movie brawls.'—*Stanley Kauffmann*

Flare Up
US 1969 98m Metrocolor
MGM / GMF (Leon Fromkes)

A man kills his wife and threatens her friends who he feels are responsible for the break-up of his marriage.
Sensationally violent melodrama with a plot that goes back to *Sudden Fear* and further.
Adequately made.

w Mark Rodgers *d* James Neilson *ph* Andrew J. McIntyre *m* Les Baxter

Raquel Welch, James Stacy, Luke Askew, Don Chastain, Ron Rifkin

Flash Gordon
The hero of the 25th century was created in comic strip form by Alex Raymond and his chief claims to film fame are three wild and woolly serials made by Universal: *Flash Gordon* (1936), *Flash Gordon's Trip to Mars* (1938), and *Flash Gordon Conquers the Universe* (1940), all starring Buster Crabbe with Charles Middleton as the wily Emperor Ming. Their cheap and cheerful futuristic sets and their non-stop action have kept them popular with film buffs through the years.
In 1974 a semi-porno spoof, *Flesh Gordon*, appeared.

Flaxy Martin
US 1948 86m bw
Warner

A lawyer falls for a racketeer's girl friend and
finds himself framed for murder.
Flatly-handled melodrama with unsympathetic
characters.

w David Lang d Richard Bare ph Carl Guthrie

Zachary Scott, Virginia Mayo, Dorothy
Malone, Tom d'Andrea, Elisha Cook Jnr

A Flea in Her Ear*
US / France 1968 94m De Luxe
Panavision
TCF (Fred Kohlmar)

Various suspicious wives and husbands
converge on the notorious Hotel Coq d'Or.
Disappointing filming of a Feydeau farce, which
needs to be much more cleverly handled to come
over with its full theatrical force.

w John Mortimer, play La Puce à l'Oreille by
Georges Feydeau d Jacques Charon
ph Charles Lang m Bronislau Kaper
pd Alexander Trauner

Rex Harrison, Rachel Roberts, Rosemary
Harris, Louis Jourdan, John Williams, Grégoire
Aslan, Edward Hardwicke, Frank Thornton,
Victor Sen Yung

'The plunge into madness never comes, and
one is left with the sight of a group of talented
players struggling with alien material.'—
Michael Billington, Illustrated London News

The Fleet's In*
US 1942 93m bw
Paramount (Paul Jones)

A sailor on leave in San Francisco takes a bet
that he can kiss the glamorous owner of a swank
nightclub.
Mindless wartime musical which happened to set
the seal of success on a number of young talents.
Previously a Clara Bow vehicle.

w Walter de Leon, Sid Silvers d Victor
Schertzinger ph William Mellor m/ly various

Dorothy Lamour, William Holden, Eddie
Bracken, Betty Hutton, Cass Daley, Gil Lamb,
Leif Erickson, Betty Jane Rhodes

The Flemish Farm
GB 1943 82m bw
Two Cities (Sydney Box)

An attempt is made to retrieve a buried flag from
occupied Belgium.
Tolerable wartime flagwaver.

w Jeffrey Dell, Jill Craigie d Jeffrey Dell

Clive Brook, Clifford Evans, Jane Baxter, Philip
Friend, Brefni O'Rourke

Flesh*
US 1932 95m bw
MGM

A German wrestler in the US falls for a street
waif.
Unusual, rather unattractive, but vivid
melodrama.

w Edmund Goulding, Moss Hart d John Ford

Wallace Beery, Ricardo Cortez, Karen Morley,
John Miljan, Jean Hersholt, Herman Bing,
Edward Brophy

Flesh and Blood
GB 1951 102m bw
BL / Harefield (Anatole de Grunwald)

Three generations of a family suffer from the
effects of heredity.
Fragmented Scottish period piece which never
settles down long enough to make an impact with
any group of characters.

w Anatole de Grunwald, play A Sleeping
Clergyman by James Bridie d Anthony
Kimmins ph Otto Heller m Charles Williams

Richard Todd, Glynis Johns, Joan Greenwood,
André Morell, Ursula Howells, Freda Jackson,
George Cole, James Hayter, Ronald Howard,
Muriel Aked

Flesh and Fantasy*
US 1943 94m bw
Universal (Charles Boyer, Julien Duvivier)

A club bore tells three strange stories.
A portmanteau with ingredients of varying
interest, attempting to emulate the success of
Tales of Manhattan. The fourth episode planned
was deleted and turned up as Destiny (qv). All
quite stylish, the best section being Lord Arthur
Savile's Crime.

w Ernest Pascal, Samuel Hoffenstein, Ellis St
Joseph,
stories Ellis St Joseph, Oscar Wilde, Laslo
Vadnay
d Julien Duvivier ph Paul Ivano, Stanley Cortez
m Alexandre Tansman

Robert Benchley, Edward G. Robinson, Barbara
Stanwyck, Charles Boyer, Betty Field, Robert
Cummings, Thomas Mitchell, C. Aubrey Smith,
Dame May Whitty, Edgar Barrier, David
Hoffman

Flesh and the Devil*
US 1926 109m bw silent
MGM

A temptress toys with three men.
Hokey but good-looking star melodrama,
climaxing with death on an ice floe. A huge
commercial success because of the off-screen
Garbo-Gilbert romance.

w Benjamin Glazer, *novel* The Undying Past by
Hermann Sudermann *d* Clarence Brown

Greta Garbo, John Gilbert, Lars Hanson, Marc
McDermott, Barbara Kent

The Flesh and the Fiends

GB 1959 97m bw Dyaliscope
Regal / Triad (Robert Baker, Monty Berman)

In 1820 Edinburgh, 'resurrection men' commit
murders to keep anatomists supplied.
Dr Robert Knox rides again, in a version more
bloody but less entertaining than *The Body
Snatcher.*

w John Gilling, Leon Griffiths *d* John Gilling

Peter Cushing, June Laverick, George Rose,
Donald Pleasence, Renée Houston, Billie
Whitelaw, Dermot Walsh

Flight Command

US 1940 116m bw
MGM (J. Walter Ruben)

A cocky recruit makes good in the naval air arm.
Routine flagwaver.

w Wells Root, Cmdr Harvey Haislip *d* Frank
Borzage *ph* Harold Rosson *m* Franz Waxman

Robert Taylor, Ruth Hussey, Walter Pidgeon,
Paul Kelly, Nat Pendleton, Red Skelton,
Shepperd Strudwick, Dick Purcell

Flight for Freedom

US 1943 101m bw
RKO (David Hempstead)

Biography of an intrepid aviatrix and her
husband.
Patchy job based on the life of Amelia Earhart,
suggesting that her final disappearance was on a
government mission. Dull production.

w Oliver H. P. Garrett, S. K. Lauren *d* Lothar
Mendes *m* Roy Webb

Rosalind Russell, Fred MacMurray, Herbert
Marshall, Eduardo Ciannelli, Walter Kingsford

Flight from Ashiya*

US / Japan 1963 102m Eastmancolor
  Panavision
UA / Harold Hecht / Daiei

When a cargo vessel sinks off the coast of Japan
during a typhoon, the helicopter rescue service
springs into action.
Conventional Grade A action thriller with

flashbacks to earlier disasters in the lives of its
heroes.

w Elliot Arnold, Waldo Salt *d* Michael
Anderson *ph* Joe MacDonald, Burnett Guffey
m Frank Cordell *pd* Eugène Lourié

Yul Brynner, Richard Widmark, George
Chakiris, Shirley Knight, Daniele Gaubert, Suzy
Parker

Flight of the Doves*

US 1971 101m colour
Columbia / Rainbow (Ralph Nelson)

Two children run away from their bullying
stepfather to join their Irish grandmother, but
are chased by a wicked uncle who knows they
are heirs to a fortune.
Pantomimish whimsy which works in fits and
starts, but has little real humour or charm.

wd Ralph Nelson, *novel* Walter Macken
ph Harry Waxman *m* Roy Budd

Ron Moody, Dorothy McGuire, Helen Raye,
Dana, Jack Wild, Stanley Holloway, William
Rushton

The Flight of the Phoenix*

US 1965 149m De Luxe
TCF / Associates and Aldrich

A cargo passenger plane crashes in the desert,
and the survivors try to avert disaster.
Achingly slow character adventure; an all-star
cast works desperately hard but the final flight of
the rebuilt plane seems almost an anti-climax
after the surfeit of personal melodramatics.

w Lukas Heller, *novel* Elleston Trevor *d* Robert
Aldrich *ph* Joseph Biroc *m* Frank de Vol

James Stewart, Richard Attenborough, Hardy
Kruger, Peter Finch, Dan Duryea, Ernest
Borgnine, Ian Bannen, Ronald Fraser, Christian
Marquand, George Kennedy

AAN: Ian Bannen

The Flight that Disappeared

US 1961 73m bw
UA / Harvard (Robert E. Kent)

Atomic scientists on an airliner find themselves
in 'heaven' being tried by people of the future.
Eccentric anti-bomb curiosity, a second feature
Outward Bound.

w Ralph Hart, Judith Hart, Owen Harris
d Reginald Le Borg *ph* Gilbert Warrenton
m Richard La Salle

Gregory Morton, Addison Richards, Craig Hill,
Paula Raymond, Dayton Lummis

Flight to Tangier
US 1953 90m Technicolor 3-D
Paramount (Nat Holt)

A female FBI agent chases a three million dollar letter of credit.
Forced and boring action romance without much of either element.

wd Charles Marquis Warren *ph* Ray Rennahan *m* Paul Sawtell

Joan Fontaine, Jack Palance, Corinne Calvet, Robert Douglas, Marcel Dalio, Jeff Morrow, Murray Matheson, John Doucette

The Flim Flam Man*
US 1967 104m De Luxe Panavision
TCF / Lawrence Turman
GB title: *One Born Every Minute*

An army deserter joins forces with an elderly con man.
Folksy comedy in a small-town setting; none of it really comes to the boil after a couple of early chase sequences.

w William Rose, *novel* Guy Owen *d* Irvin Kershner, *Yakima Canutt* *ph* Charles Lang *m* Jerry Goldsmith

George C. Scott, Michael Sarrazin, Sue Lyon, Harry Morgan, Jack Albertson, Alice Ghostley, Albert Salmi

Flipper
US 1963 87m Metrocolor
(MGM) Ivan Tors

A fisherman's son on the Florida Keys befriends a dolphin.
Harmless boy-and-animal adventure which spawned two sequels and a TV series.

w Arthur Weiss *d* James B. Clark *ph* Lamar Boren, Joseph Brun *m* Henry Vars

Chuck Connors, Luke Halpin, Kathleen Maguire, Connie Scott

Flirtation Walk*
US 1934 97m bw
Warner (Frank Borzage)

Love affairs of West Point cadets.
Light musical very typical of its period, with a few agreeable numbers.

w Delmer Daves *d* Frank Borzage *ch* Bobby Connelly *ph* Sol Polito, George Barnes *m/ly* Allie Wrubel, Mort Dixon

Dick Powell, Ruby Keeler, Pat O'Brien, Ross Alexander, John Arledge, Henry O'Neill, Guinn Williams

'A rousing recruiting poster . . . and a splendid laboratory specimen of the adolescent cinema.'—*André Sennwald, New York Times*
AAN: best picture

Floods of Fear*
GB 1958 84m bw
Rank / Sydney Box

Two escaped convicts, a warder, and a pretty girl are trapped by floods in a lonely house.
Adequate melodrama with impressively gloomy production and performances but not many surprises.

wd Charles Crichton, *novel* Joan and Ward Hawkins *ph* Christopher Challis *m* Alan Rawsthorne

Howard Keel, Anne Heywood, Harry H. Corbett, Cyril Cusack

Florian
US 1940 91m bw
MGM (Winfield Sheehan)

In 1910 Austria, a poor boy and a rich girl are united by their love of a Lippizaner stallion.
Not kinky, but strangely dull.

w Noel Langley, Geza Herczeg, James K. McGuinness *d* Edwin L. Marin

Robert Young, Helen Gilbert, Charles Coburn, Lee Bowman, Reginald Owen, S. Z. Sakall, Lucile Watson, Irina Baronova

Flower Drum Song*
US 1961 133m Technicolor Panavision
U-I / Rodgers and Hammerstein / Joseph Fields

Romantic problems among the immigrants in San Francisco's Chinatown.
A Broadway musical which on the screen seems old-fashioned, remorselessly cute, and even insulting to the Chinese characters. Within its limits, however, it is well enough staged and performed.

w Joseph Fields *m/ly* Richard Rodgers, Oscar Hammerstein II *md* Alfred Newman, Ken Darby *ph* Russell Metty *ad* Alexander Golitzen, Joseph Weight *costumes* Irene Sharaff *ch* Hermes Pan

Nancy Kwan, James Shigeta, Juanita Hall, Myoshi Umeki, James Soo, Sen Yung

AAN: Alfred Newman, Ken Darby; Russell Metty

Fluffy
US 1964 92m Eastmancolor
U-I / Scarus (Gordon Kay)

A biologist manages to tame a lion.
Mindless, cheerful animal comedy.

w Samuel Rocca *d* Earl Bellamy *ph* Clifford Stine *m* Irving Gertz

Tony Randall, Shirley Jones, Edward Andrews, Ernest Truex, Howard Morris, Jim Backus, Frank Faylen

The Flute and the Arrow*

Sweden 1957 75m Technicolor Agascope
Sandrews (Arne Sucksdorff)
original title: *En Djungelsaga*

The story of a remote Indian tribe and a prowling leopard thought to be possessed by a demon. Superbly photographed but rather dull: Sucksdorff failed to provide enough story for a feature.

wd, ph Arne Sucksdorff *m* Ravi Shankar

The Fly

US 1958 94m Eastmancolor Cinemascope
TCF (Kurt Neumann)

A scientist invents a method of transmitting and reassembling atoms. He transmits himself and does not notice a fly in the compartment . . . Unpleasant horror film which becomes ludicrous but not funny.

w James Clavell *d* Kurt Neumann *ph* Karl Struss *m* Paul Sawtell

David Hedison, Patricia Owens, Herbert Marshall, Vincent Price
† Sequels were *Return of the Fly* (1960) and *Curse of the Fly* (1965), neither worth noting in detail.

The Flying Deuces*

US 1939 67m bw
Boris Morros

Laurel and Hardy join the Foreign Legion. Patchy comedy from the end of the comedians' period of glory, and showing signs of decline.

w Ralph Spence, Harry Langdon, Charles Rogers, Alfred Schiller *d* Edward Sutherland *ph* Art Lloyd, Elmer Dyer

Stan Laurel, Oliver Hardy, Jean Parker, James Finlayson, Reginald Gardiner, Charles Middleton
'Mechanical stuff. . . seemed like *Beau Hunks* and *Bonnie Scotland* all over again.'—*William K. Everson*

Flying Down to Rio**

US 1933 89m bw
RKO (Merian C. Cooper, Lou Brock)

A dance band is a big success in Rio de Janeiro. A thin musical electrified by the finale in which

girls dance on the wings of moving airplanes, and by the teaming of Astaire and Rogers for the first time. Now an irresistible period piece.

w Cyril Hume, H. W. Hannemann, Erwin Gelsey, *play* Anne Caldwell *d* Thornton Freeland *ph* J. Roy Hunt *m* Vincent Youmans *ly* Edward Eliscu, Gus Kahn *ch* Dave Gould

Dolores del Rio, Gene Raymond, Raul Roulien, *Ginger Rogers, Fred Astaire,* Blanche Frederici, Walter Walker, Franklin Pangborn, Eric Blore

AAN: song 'The Carioca'

Flying Fortress

GB 1942 104m bw
Warner

A Canadian becomes a hero of bombing missions over Berlin.
Cardboard propaganda with silly love interest and a hilarious climax in which the hero does his stuff on the wing of a flying plane.

w Brock Williams, Gordon Wellesley, Edward Dryhurst *d* Walter Forde *ph* Gus Drisse, Basil Emmott

Richard Greene, Carla Lehmann, Betty Stockfield, Donald Stewart, Charles Heslop, Sidney King, Basil Radford, John Stuart

Flying Leathernecks

US 1951 102m Technicolor
RKO (Edmund Grainger)

Two marine officers fight the Japs and each other on Guadalcanal.
Empty, violent war actioner full of phoney heroics.

w James Edward Grant *d* Nicholas Ray *ph* William E. Snyder *m* Roy Webb

John Wayne, Robert Ryan, Janis Carter, Don Taylor, Jay C. Flippen, William Harrigan, James Bell
'Ray's treatment is depressingly second rate and does nothing to alleviate the unpleasant impression of this disturbingly violent production.'—*Penelope Houston*

The Flying Missile

US 1950 92m bw
Columbia (Jerry Bresler)

A submarine commander defies authority to prove that rockets can be launched from the deck of a submarine.
Dated semi-documentary melodrama which was pretty flat on first viewing.

w Richard English, James Gunn *d* Henry Levin *ph* William Snyder *m* George Duning

Glenn Ford, Viveca Lindfors, Henry O'Neill, Carl Benton Reid, Joe Sawyer, John Qualen

Flying Tigers
US 1942 100m bw
Republic (Edmund Grainger)

American airmen fight the Japs over World War II China.

More mock heroics with noisy but unconvincing action sequences.

w Kenneth Gamet, Barry Trivers *d* David Miller *ph* Jack Marta *m* Victor Young

John Wayne, John Carroll, Anna Lee, Paul Kelly, Mae Clarke

AAN: Victor Young

Fog over Frisco***
US 1934 68m bw
Warner (Henry Blanke)

A San Francisco heiress gets herself murdered.

Silly whodunnit highly notable for its cinematic style, all dissolves, wipes and quick takes. Probably the fastest moving film ever made, and very entertaining despite its plot inadequacy.

w Robert N. Lee, *novel* George Dyer *d* William Dieterle *ph* Tony Gaudio *md* Leo F. Forbstein *ed* Harold McLernon

Bette Davis, Donald Woods, Margaret Lindsay, Lyle Talbot, Hugh Herbert, Arthur Byron, Robert Barrat, Douglass Dumbrille, Henry O'Neill, Irving Pichel, Alan Hale

'It reveals those qualities of pace and velocity and sharpness which make the Hollywood product acceptable even when the shallow content of ideas makes you want to scream.'— *Robert Forsythe*

'Its speed is artificially created by pacing, wipes, opticals, overlapping sound, camera movement and placing of characters, and by its habit of never having time really to begin or end scenes.'—*William K. Everson*

† Remade 1942 as *Spy Ship*, a second feature.

Folies Bergère***
US 1935 84m bw
Twentieth Century (William Goetz, Raymond Griffith)
GB title: *The Man from the Folies Bergère*

A Parisian banker persuades a music hall artist to impersonate him, but the wife and girl friend become involved in the confusion.

Amusing star vehicle with inventive Berkeleyish numbers and some remarkably sexy dialogue.

w Bess Meredyth, Hal Long, *play* The Red Cat by Rudolph Lothar, Hans Adler *d* Roy del Ruth *ph* Barney McGill, Peverell Marley *md* Alfred Newman *ch* Dave Gould

Maurice Chevalier, Merle Oberon, Ann Dvorak, Eric Blore

† Remade as *That Night in Rio*, with Don Ameche, and *On the Riviera*, with Danny Kaye (both qv).

Follow a Star
GB 1959 104m bw
Rank (Hugh Stewart)

A shy amateur singer allows a fading star to mime to his voice.

Star comedy with an antique plot and a superfluity of pathos.

w Jack Davies, Henry Blyth, Norman Wisdom *d* Robert Asher *ph* Jack Asher *m* Philip Green

Norman Wisdom, Jerry Desmonde, June Laverick, Hattie Jacques, Richard Wattis, John Le Mesurier, Fenella Fielding, Ron Moody

'Such comedy as there is is mostly muffed by the lack of any sense of comic timing.'—*MFB*

Follow Me
GB 1971 93m Technicolor Panavision
Universal / Hal B. Wallis (Paul Nathan)
US title: *The Public Eye*

An eccentric private eye is hired to follow an accountant's wife, and she finds him fascinating.

Dullish, whimsical rendering of a dullish, whimsical one-act play; it never springs to life or interest.

w Peter Shaffer, from his play *d* Carol Reed *ph* Christopher Challis *m* John Barry

Topol, Michael Jayston, Mia Farrow

'An uneasy mixture of broad comedy and high romance.'—*Sight and Sound*

Follow Me Boys
US 1966 132m Technicolor
Walt Disney (Winston Hibler)

The domestic trials and tribulations of a small-town schoolmaster.

Sentimental family saga full of patriotic fervour.

w Louis Pelletier, *novel* God and My Country by Mackinlay Kantor *d* Norman Tolear *ph* Clifford Stine *m* George Bruns

Fred MacMurray, Vera Miles, Lillian Gish, Charlie Ruggles, Elliott Reid, Kurt Russell, Luana Patten, Ken Murray

'Demands an extremely strong stomach.'— *MFB*

Follow That Dream
US 1962 110m De Luxe Panavision
UA / Mirisch (David Weisbart)

A wandering family sets up house on a Florida beach.

Tiresomely cute comedy vehicle for a resistible star.

w Charles Lederer, *novel* Pioneer Go Home by Richard Powell *d* Gordon Douglas *ph* Leo Tover *m* Hans Salter

Elvis Presley, Arthur O'Connell, Joanna Moore, Anne Helm, Jack Kruschen

Follow the Boys*
US 1944   109m   bw
Universal (Charles K. Feldman)

A song and dance man organizes entertainment for the US troops during World War II.
Scrappy, unattractive propaganda tribute by the stars to the stars, enlivened only by a few guest spots.

w Lou Breslow, Gertrude Purcell *d* A. Edward Sutherland *ph* David Abel *m* Leigh Harline and others

George Raft, Vera Zorina, Charley Grapewin, Grace MacDonald, Charles Butterworth, George Macready, Elizabeth Patterson; and Orson Welles, Marlene Dietrich, Jeanette MacDonald, Dinah Shore, Donald O'Connor, Peggy Ryan, W. C. Fields, the Andrews Sisters, Artur Rubenstein, Sophie Tucker, Ted Lewis and his band, etc

AAN: song 'I'll Walk Alone' (*m* Jule Styne, *ly* Sammy Cahn)

Follow the Boys
US 1963   95m   Metrocolor   Panavision
MGM / Franmet (Laurence P. Bachmann)

An American warship is diverted from Cannes to Santa Margarita, and the waiting wives have to follow by road.
Harmless star comedy musical.

w David T. Chantler, David Osborn *d* Richard Thorpe *ph* Ted Scaife

Connie Francis, Paula Prentiss, Dany Robin, Russ Tamblyn, Richard Long

Follow the Fleet**
US 1936   110m   bw
RKO (Pandro S. Berman)

Sailors on shore leave romance a couple of girl singers.
Amiable star musical which makes heavy weather of a listless and overlong script, but has good numbers for those who can wait.

w Dwight Taylor, *play* Shore Leave by Hubert Osborne, Allan Scott *d* Mark Sandrich *ph* David Abel *m/ly* Irving Berlin

Fred Astaire, Ginger Rogers, Randolph Scott, Harriet Hilliard, Astrid Allwyn, Harry Beresford, Lucille Ball, Betty Grable, Tony Martin

Follow the Sun
US 1951   93m   bw
TCF (Samuel G. Engel)

Ben Hogan, a professional golfer, recovers slowly and painfully from a car crash and for the first time gains the affection of the crowd.
Modest sporting biopic, generally watchable but rising to no great heights.

w Frederick Hazlitt Brennan *d* Sidney Lanfield *ph* Leo Tover *m* Cyril Mockridge

Glenn Ford, Anne Baxter, Dennis O'Keefe, June Havoc, Larry Keating, Nana Bryant, Roland Winters

Folly to be Wise*
GB 1952   91m   bw
London Films / Launder and Gilliat

A brains trust at an army unit starts off a battle of the sexes.
Typical James Bridie comedy which starts brightly and whimsically, then peters out and is saved by the acting.

w Frank Launder, John Dighton, *play* It Depends What You Mean by James Bridie *d* Frank Launder *ph* Jack Hildyard *m* Temple Abady

Alastair Sim, Roland Culver, Elizabeth Allen, Martita Hunt, Colin Gordon

The Food of the Gods
US 1976   88m   Movielab
AIP (Bert I. Gordon)

A curious substance which oozes out of the ground turns common beasts into monsters.
Rather crude horror movie which has little affinity with its literary original.

wd Bert I. Gordon, *story* H. G. Wells *ph* Reginald Morris *m* Elliot Kaplan

Marjoe Gortner, Pamela Franklin, Ida Lupino, Ralph Meeker, John McLiam
   'Not only sick, but sickening.'—*Arthur Knight*
   'I wish I hadn't seen the movie, so I could avoid it like the plague.'—*John Simon*
   'More plot holes than any movie in recent memory, and enough dopey lines to make a Saturday night audience howl in all the wrong places.'—*David Sterritt, Christian Science Monitor*

A Fool There Was*
US 1914   67m (24 fps)   bw   silent
William Fox

A financier in Europe forsakes all for a *femme fatale*, and dies in her arms.
Antediluvian moral melodrama which made a

star of Bara and added the word 'vamp' to the language.

wd Frank Powell, *play* Porter Emerson Browne suggested by Rudyard Kipling's poem *The Vampire*

Theda Bara, Edward Jose, Mabel Frenyer, May Allison

Foolish Wives **

US 1921   85m approx (24 fps); originally much longer   bw   silent
Universal

In Monte Carlo, a fake count seduces and blackmails rich women.
Weird melodrama with memorable moments and a vast set; Stroheim's most vivid star performance and one of his most lavish productions.

wd Erich Von Stroheim ph Ben Reynolds, William Daniels *ad Erich Von Stroheim, Richard Day*

Erich Von Stroheim, Mae Busch, Maud George, Cesare Gravina

Fools for Scandal *

US 1938   81m   bw
Warner (Mervyn Le Roy)

A Hollywood movie star falls in love with a French nobleman.
Disappointingly leaden romantic comedy.

w Herbert and Joseph Fields, *play* Return Engagement by Nancy Hamilton, Rosemary Casey, James Shute *d* Mervyn Le Roy *ph* Ted Tetzlaff *m* Richard Rodgers, Lorenz Hart

Carole Lombard, Fernand Gravet, Ralph Bellamy, Allen Jenkins, Isabel Jeans, Marie Wilson, Ottola Nesmith

Fools Parade **

US 1971   98m   Eastmancolor
Columbia / Stanmore / Penbar (Andrew V. McLaglen)
GB title: *Dynamite Man from Glory Jail*

An ex-con has trouble cashing a cheque for his prison savings, especially as outlaws are after it.
Curious admixture of comedy, adventure and violence with a thirties setting, from the author of *Night of the Hunter*; generally gripping entertainment.

w James Lee Barrett, novel Davis Grubb
d Andrew V. McLaglen *ph* Harry Stradling Jnr *m* Henry Vars

James Stewart, George Kennedy, Strother Martin, Anne Baxter, Kurt Russell, William Windom, Mike Kellin

'A quintessentially American tribute to the

quiet heroism of the self-made man.'—*Nigel Andrews*

Footlight Parade ***

US 1933   104m   bw
Warner (Robert Lord)

A determined producer of cine-variety numbers gets the show going despite great difficulty.
Classic putting-on-a-show musical distinguished by rapid-fire dialogue, New York setting, star performances and some of the best Busby Berkeley numbers.

w Manuel Seff, James Seymour *d Lloyd Bacon ch Busby Berkeley ph* George Barnes *ad Anton Grot, Jack Okey m/ly* Harry Warren, Al Dubin, Sammy Fain, Irving Fahal

James Cagney, Joan Blondell, Ruby Keeler, Dick Powell, Frank McHugh, Guy Kibbee, Ruth Donnelly, Hugh Herbert, Claire Dodd, Herman Bing

'1,000 surprises! 300 beauties! 20 big stars!'—*publicity*
'Bevies of beauty and mere males disport themselves in a Honeymoon Hotel, by (and in) a Waterfall, and over several acres of Shanghai.'—*C. A. Lejeune*

Footlight Serenade

US 1942   80m   bw
TCF (William LeBaron)

A boxer romances a showgirl.
Indifferent star musical.

w Robert Ellis, Helen Logan, Lynn Starling *d* Gregory Ratoff *ph* Lee Garmes *md* Charles Henderson

Betty Grable, John Payne, Victor Mature, James Gleason, Phil Silvers, Jane Wyman, Cobina Wright Jnr, June Lang, Mantan Moreland

Footsteps in the Fog *

GB 1955   90m   Technicolor
Columbia / Mike Frankovich (Maxwell Setton)

A Victorian murderer plans to eliminate a blackmailing maid.
This variation on *Gaslight* turns into a black comedy without laughs, but it has effective moments and is efficiently if charmlessly made.

w Dorothy Reid, Lenore Coffee, *story* The Interruption by
W. W. Jacobs *d* Arthur Lubin *ph* Christopher Challis *m* Benjamin Frankel *ad* Wilfrid Shingleton

Stewart Granger, Jean Simmons, Bill Travers, Ronald Squire, Finlay Currie, Peter Bull

For a Few Dollars More
Italy / Spain / West Germany 1965   130m
  Techniscope
PEA / Gonzales / Constantin (Alberto
  Grimaldi)

Bounty hunters in El Paso agree to work
together.
Vague, inflated, sometimes good-looking sequel
to *A Fistful of Dollars*, with customary violence
and predictably mean performances.

wd Sergio Leone *ph* Massimo Dallamano
m Ennio Morricone

Clint Eastwood, Lee Van Cleef, Gian Maria
Volonte, Klaus Kinski

For Freedom
GB 1940
GFD / Gainsborough (Edward Black,
  Castleton Knight)

Events surrounding the Battle of the River Plate
and the sinking of the Graf Spee.
Economical wartime potboiler with much use of
newsreel.

w Miles Malleson, Leslie Arliss *d* Maurice Elvey

Will Fyffe, Anthony Hulme, E. V. H. Emmett,
Guy Middleton, Albert Lieven

For Heaven's Sake
US 1950   92m   bw
TCF (William Perlberg)

Two angels are sent to earth to mend a
Broadway producer's marriage.
Silly, flat whimsy of the *Here Comes Mr Jordan*
school, and originating from the same author.
Stale beer, but historically interesting.

w George Seaton, *play* Harry Segall *d* George
Seaton *ph* Lloyd Ahern *m* Alfred Newman

Clifton Webb, Edmund Gwenn, Robert
Cummings, Joan Bennett, Joan Blondell, Gigi
Perreau, Jack La Rue

For Love of Ivy
US 1968   100m   Perfectcolor
Cinerama / Palomar (Edgar J. Scherick, Jay
  Weston)

An invaluable coloured maid gives notice, and
the family blackmails a likeable black ne'er-do-
well to make love to her so that she will stay.
Unhappy whimsy with an extremely laboured
script and no jokes, notable only as Hollywood's
first bow towards a black love affair.

w Robert Alan Aurthur, *story* Sidney Poitier
d Daniel Mann *ph* Joseph Coffey *m* Quincy
Jones

Sidney Poitier, Abby Lincoln, Beau Bridges,
Carroll O'Connor, Nan Martin, Lauri Peters

AAN: title song (*m* Quincy Jones, *ly* Bob
Russell)

For Love or Money
US 1963   108m   Technicolor
U-I (Robert Arthur)

A rich widow hires a lawyer to look after the
affairs of her three wayward daughters; he picks
the eldest for himself.
Slow, thin, overlong comedy with a surfeit of
witless chat.

w Larry Marks, Michael Morris *d* Michael
Gordon *ph* Clifford Stine *m* Frank de Vol

Kirk Douglas, Mitzi Gaynor, Thelma Ritter,
William Bendix, Gig Young

For Me and My Gal*
US 1942   104m   bw
MGM (Arthur Freed)

Just before World War I, a girl vaudevillian
chooses between two partners.
A routine musical romance at the time of its
production, this film now stands out because of
its professional execution, its star value, and the
fact that they don't make 'em like that any more.

w Richard Sherman, Sid Silvers, Fred
Finkelhoffe *d* Busby Berkeley *ph* William
Daniels *md* Georgie Stoll, Roger Edens

Judy Garland, Gene Kelly, George Murphy,
Marta Eggerth, Ben Blue, Richard Quine,
Stephen McNally
  'A touch of imagination and a deal more than
a touch of energy.'—*The Times*

AAN: Georgie Stoll, Roger Edens

For Pete's Sake*
US 1974   90m   Eastmancolor
Columbia / Rastar / Persky–Bright–Barclay
  (Martin Erlichmann, Stanley Shapiro)

A New York taxi driver's wife borrows money
and finds herself heavily committed to work off
the debt.
Involved farcical comedy with amusing
passages.

w Stanley Shapiro, Martin Richlin *d* Peter
Yates *ph* Laszlo Kovacs *m* Artie Butler

Barbra Streisand, Michael Sarrazin, Estelle
Parsons, William Redfield, Molly Picon
  'Revives memories of how much more
inventively they used to do it thirty years ago.'—
Sight and Sound

For the First Time
US 1959   97m   Technirama
MGM / Corona / Orion (Alexander Gruter)

A famous tenor slips off incognito to Capri and falls in love with a deaf girl.

Slipshod co-production (with West Germany) with a hoary sentimental plot, a fat star, and some agreeable picture postcard views.

w Andrew Solt *d* Rudolph Maté *ph* Aldo Tonti *md* Georgie Stoll

Mario Lanza, Johanna von Koczian, Kurt Kasznar, Zsa Zsa Gabor, Hans Sohnker

For the Love of Mike*
US 1960   84m   De Luxe   Cinemascope
TCF / Shergari (George Sherman)
GB title: *None But the Brave*

An Indian boy in New Mexico is helped by a priest to care for sick animals.
Sentimental outdoor film for young people with a pleasantly light touch.

w D. D. Beauchamp *d* George Sherman *ph* Alex Phillips *m* Raul La Vista

Richard Basehart, Stuart Erwin, Arthur Shields, Armando Silvestre

For Them That Trespass
GB 1948   93m   bw
ABP

A man proves himself innocent of the crime for which he has served fifteen years in prison.
Tedious melodrama which served to introduce Richard Todd to the screen.

w J. Lee-Thompson *d* Alberto Cavalcanti *ph* Derick Williams *m* Philip Green

Richard Todd, Stephen Murray, Joan Dowling, Patricia Plunkett, Michael Laurence, Rosalyn Boulter

For Those Who Think Young
US 1964   96m   Techniscope
UA / Aubrey Schenck-Howard W. Koch
(Hugh Benson)

College students save their favourite club from closure.
Tedious beach party frolic, very typical of its day, with some odd cameo appearances.

w James and George O'Hanlon, Dan Beaumont *d* Leslie H. Martinson *ph* Harold E. Stine *m* Jerry Fielding

James Darren, Pamela Tiffin, Woody Woodbury, Nancy Sinatra, Tina Louise, Paul Lynde, Bob Denver, Jack La Rue, George Raft, Allen Jenkins, Robert Armstrong, Roger Smith

For Valour*
GB 1937   95m   bw
GFD/Capitol (Max Schach)

Adventures in two wars of a major, his shady friend, and their sons.
Agreeable adult farce with the stars each playing father and son.

w Ben Travers *d* Tom Walls

Tom Walls, Ralph Lynn, Veronica Rose, Joan Marion, Hubert Harben

For Whom the Bell Tolls**
US 1943   168m   Technicolor
Paramount (Sam Wood)

An American joins partisan fighters in the Spanish Civil War and falls in love with a refugee girl before going on a suicide mission.
Portentous, solemn adventure story based on a modern classic but without much cinematic impetus despite careful handling and useful performances. It looks expensive, though.

w Dudley Nichols, *novel* Ernest Hemingway *d* Sam Wood *ph* Ray Rennahan *m* Victor Young *pd* William Cameron Menzies

Gary Cooper, Ingrid Bergman, Akim Tamiroff, Arturo de Cordova, *Katina Paxinou*, Vladimir Sokoloff, Mikhail Rasumny, Victor Varconi, Joseph Calleia, Alexander Granach

'168 minutes of breathless thrills and romance!'—*publicity*

AA: Katina Paxinou
AAN: Ray Rennahan; Victor Young; Gary Cooper; Akim Tamiroff

Forbidden Cargo
GB 1954   85m   bw
Rank / London Independent Productions
(Sydney Box)

A customs investigator prevents a large consignment of drugs from reaching its English outlets.
Routine British thick ear.

w Sydney Box *d* Harold French *ph* C. Pennington-Richards *m* Lambert Williamson

Nigel Patrick, Elizabeth Sellars, Terence Morgan, Jack Warner

Forbidden Fruit*
France 1952   103m   bw
Gray Film
original title: *Le Fruit Défendu*

A widowered doctor marries again, then falls for a prostitute.
One of the rather solemn romantic melodramas in which the star insisted from time to time in becoming involved.

w Jacques Companeez, Henri Verneuil, Jean Manse, *novel* Lettre à Mon Juge by Georges

Simenon *d* Henri Verneuil *ph* Henri Alekan *m* Paul Durand

Fernandel, Claude Nollier, Françoise Arnoul, Sylvie

Forbidden Planet**
US 1956 98m Eastmancolor
Cinemascope
MGM (Nicholas Nayfack)

In AD 2200 a space cruiser visits the planet Altair Four to discover the fate of a previous mission.

Intriguing sci-fi with a plot derived from *The Tempest* and a Prospero who unwittingly creates monsters from his own id. High spirits and suspense sequences partially cancelled out by wooden playing from the younger actors and some leaden dialogue.

w Cyril Hume d Fred M. Wilcox ph George Folsey *m* Louis and Bebe Barron *ad* Cedric Gibbons, Arthur Lonergan

Walter Pidgeon, Anne Francis, Leslie Nielsen, Warren Stevens, Jack Kelly, Richard Anderson, Earl Holliman

'It's a pity they didn't lift some of Shakespeare's language.'—*New Yorker, 1977*

The Forbin Project**
US 1969 100m Technicolor Panavision
Universal (Stanley Chase)

An enormous computer takes over the defence of the western world; but it goes into collaboration with the Russian one.

Good-looking sci-fi for intellectual addicts.

w James Bridges, *novel* Colossus by D. F. Jones *d* Joseph Sargent *ph* Gene Polito *m* Michel Columbier

Eric Braeden, Gordon Pinsent, Susan Clark, William Schallert

Force of Arms*
US 1951 100m bw
Warner (Anthony Veiller)

A soldier in the Italian campaign falls in love with his nurse.

Routine variation on *A Farewell to Arms*, adequately but unexcitingly mounted.

w Orin Jannings, *story* Richard Tregaskis *d* Michael Curtiz *ph* Ted McCord *m* Max Steiner

William Holden, Nancy Olson, Frank Lovejoy, Gene Evans, Dick Wesson, Paul Picerni

Force of Evil***
US 1948 78m bw
MGM / Enterprise

A racketeer's lawyer finds that his boss has killed the lawyer's brother.

Involved, atmospheric melodrama about the numbers racket, moodily and brilliantly photographed in New York streets, gloweringly well acted and generally almost as hypnotic as *Citizen Kane*.

w Abraham Polonsky, Ira Wolfert, *novel* Tucker's People by Ira Wolfert *d Abraham Polonsky ph George Barnes m David Raksin*

John Garfield, *Thomas Gomez*, Beatrice Pearson, Marie Windsor

'It credits an audience with intelligence in its ears as well as its eyes.'—*Dilys Powell*

Force Ten from Navarone
GB 1978 118m colour
AIP / Guy Hamilton

During World War II, commandos are detailed to blow up a vital bridge separating the Germans and partisans in Yugoslavia.

Routine war hokum with plenty of explosions and sudden death, but not much sense. Nothing, really, to do with *The Guns of Navarone*.

w Robin Chapman, *novel* Alistair MacLean *d* Guy Hamilton *ph* Chris Challis *m* Ron Goodwin *pd* Goeffrey Drake

Robert Shaw, Edward Fox, Franco Nero, Harrison Ford, Barbara Bach, Richard Kiel

A Foreign Affair**
US 1948 116m bw
Paramount (Charles Brackett)

A deputation of American politicians goes to visit post-war Berlin and a congresswoman finds herself in an emotional triangle with a captain and his German mistress.

Bleakly sophisticated comedy from this team's headline-grabbing period; full of interest and amusement, it never quite sparkles enough to remove the doubtful taste.

w Charles Brackett, Billy Wilder, Richard Breen d Billy Wilder ph Charles Lang Jnr *m* Frederick Hollander

Jean Arthur, Marlene Dietrich, John Lund, Millard Mitchell, Peter Von Zerneck, Stanley Prager

AAN: script; Charles Lang Jnr

Foreign Affaires
GB 1935 71m bw
Gainsborough (Michael Balcon)

A gambler and a car salesman get mixed up with a phoney casino.

Mild star farce.

w Ben Travers *d* Tom Walls

Tom Walls, Ralph Lynn, Robertson Hare, Norma Varden, Marie Lohr, Diana Churchill, Cecil Parker

Foreign Correspondent ****
US 1940 120m bw
Walter Wanger

An American journalist is sent to Europe in 1938 and becomes involved with spies.
Thoroughly typical and enjoyable Hitchcock adventure with a rambling script which builds up into brilliantly managed suspense sequences: an assassination, a windmill, an attempted murder in Westminster Cathedral, a plane crash at sea. The final speech was an attempt to encourage America into the war.

w Charles Bennett, Joan Harrison, James Hilton, Robert Benchley, from Personal History by Vincent Sheean *d Alfred Hitchcock ph Rudolph Maté m* Alfred Newman *sp* Lee Zavitz *ad* Alexander Golitzen

Joel McCrea, Laraine Day, Herbert Marshall, Albert Basserman, Edmund Gwenn, George Sanders, Eduardo Ciannelli, Robert Benchley, Harry Davenport, Martin Kosleck

'If you have any interest in the true motion and sweep of pictures, watching that man work is like listening to music . . . If you would like a seminar in how to make a movie travel the lightest and fastest way, in a kind of beauty that is peculiar to movies alone, you can see this once, and then again to see what you missed, and then study it twice.'—*Otis Ferguson*

AAN: best picture; script; Rudolph Maté; Albert Basserman

Foreign Intrigue *
US 1956 100m Eastmancolor
UA / Sheldon Reynolds

A press agent investigates the death of a man who had been blackmailing potential traitors.
Location espionage melodrama of the cold war fifties, quite well done in a rather dismal vein, but a long way from *Foreign Correspondent.*

wd Sheldon Reynolds *ph* Bertil Palmgrem *m* Paul Durand

Robert Mitchum, Genevieve Page, Ingrid Thulin, Eugene Deckers

The Foreman Went to France **
GB 1941 87m bw
Ealing (Alberto Cavalcanti)
US title: *Somewhere in France*

Before Dunkirk, a Welsh foreman is sent on a mission to salvage secret French machinery.

Fresh, appealing comedy drama based on a true incident of World War II.

w John Dighton, Angus Macphail, Leslie Arliss, Roger Macdougall, Diana Morgan, *story* J. B. Priestley *d* Charles Frend *m* William Walton

Tommy Trinder, Constance Cummings, Clifford Evans, Robert Morley, Gordon Jackson, Ernest Milton

The Forest Rangers *
US 1942 85m Technicolor
Paramount (Robert Sisk)

A socialite marries a district ranger and rescues her disgruntled rival during a forest blaze.
Routine, competent, box office actioner of its time, with popular stars, adequate plot, but precious little inventiveness.

w Harold Shumate *d* George Marshall *ph* Charles Lang

Fred MacMurray, Paulette Goddard, Susan Hayward, Lynne Overman, Albert Dekker, Eugene Pallette, Regis Toomey, Rod Cameron

Forever Amber *
US 1947 137m Technicolor
TCF (William Perlberg)

Adventures of a desirable young lady during the reign of Charles II.
Much-bowdlerized version of a sensational novel of the forties; pretty but rather thin, with a colourless cast, saved by lively action sequences.

w Philip Dunne, Ring Lardner Jnr, *novel* Kathleen Winsor *d* Otto Preminger *ph* Leon Shamroy *m* David Raksin *ad Lyle Wheeler*

Linda Darnell, Cornel Wilde, *George Sanders* (as Charles II), Richard Greene, Glenn Langan, Richard Haydn, Jessica Tandy, Anne Revere, Robert Coote, John Russell, Leo G. Carroll

AAN: David Raksin

Forever and a Day **
US 1943 104m bw
RKO (Herbert Wilcox, Victor Saville)

The history of a London house from 1804 to the blitz of World War II.
Made for war charities by a combination of the European talents in Hollywood, this series of sketches was unavoidably patchy but gave good opportunities to several familiar performers and stands as a likeable quick reference to their work at this period.

w Charles Bennett, C. S. Forester, Lawrence Hazard, Michael Hogan, W. P. Lipscomb, Alice Duer Miller, John Van Druten, Alan Campbell, Peter Godfrey, S. M. Herzig, Christopher Isherwood, Gene Lockhart, R. C. Sherriff,

Claudine West, Norman Corwin, Jack Hartfield,
James Hilton, Emmet Lavery, Frederick
Lonsdale, Donald Ogden Stewart, Keith Winter
ph Robert de Grasse, Lee Garmes, Russell
Metty, Nicholas Musuraca *m* Anthony Collins
d René Clair, Edmund Goulding, Cedric
Hardwicke, Frank Lloyd, Victor Saville, Robert
Stevenson, Herbert Wilcox *ad* Albert
D'Agostino, Lawrence Williams, Al Herman

Anna Neagle, Ray Milland, *Claude Rains, C.
Aubrey Smith*, Dame May Whitty, Gene
Lockhart, Ray Bolger, Edmund Gwenn, Charles
Coburn, Ian Hunter, *Jessie Matthews, Charles
Laughton*, Montagu Love, *Cedric Hardwicke*,
Reginald Owen, *Buster Keaton*, Wendy Barrie,
Ida Lupino, *Brian Aherne*, Edward Everett
Horton, June Duprez, Eric Blore, Merle Oberon,
Una O'Connor, Nigel Bruce, *Roland Young,
Gladys Cooper*, Robert Cummings, Richard
Haydn, Elsa Lanchester, Sara Allgood, Robert
Coote, Donald Crisp, Ruth Warrick, Kent
Smith, Herbert Marshall, Victor McLaglen,
many others in bit parts
'One of the most brilliant casts of modern
times has been assembled to bolster up one of the
poorest pictures.'—*James Agate*

Forever Darling
US 1956   91m   Eastmancolor
MGM / Zanra (Desi Arnaz)

A couple's matrimonial difficulties are solved by
her guardian angel.
Cutesy-pie comedy with all concerned
embarrassed by their material.

w Helen Deutsch *d* Alexander Hall *ph* Harold
Lipstein *m* Bronislau Kaper

Lucille Ball, Desi Arnaz, James Mason (as the
angel), John Emery, Louis Calhern, John Hoyt,
Natalie Schaefer

Forever England see Brown on Resolution

Forever Female
US 1953   93m   bw
Paramount (Pat Duggan)

A young writer sells his play to a Broadway
producer who wants to transform it into a vehicle
for his ex-wife; she falls for the writer but
eventually discourages him.
Talky romantic comedy without much style or
sense of Broadway; a long way from *All About
Eve*.

w Julius J. Epstein, Philip G. Epstein, *play*
Rosalind by J. M. Barrie *d* Irving Rapper
ph Harry Stradling *m* Victor Young

Ginger Rogers, William Holden, Paul Douglas,
James Gleason, Pat Crowley

Forfaiture see The Cheat

Forget Me Not
GB 1934   72m   bw
London Films (Alexander Korda)
US title: *Forever Yours*

On board ship, a young girl falls for a widowed
tenor.
Bland romance, notable only for the star's
singing.

w Hugh Gray, Arthur Wimperis *d* Zolton
Korda, Stanley Irving

Beniamino Gigli, Joan Gardner, Ivan Brandt,
Hugh Wakefield

Forsaking All Others*
US 1934   84m   bw
MGM

A wife nearly breaks up her rather dull marriage,
but thinks better of it.
Star power carries this thin comedy drama.

w Joseph L. Mankiewicz, *play* Edward Barry
Roberts, Frank Morgan Cavett *d* W. S. Van
Dyke *ph* Gregg Toland, George Folsey

Clark Gable, Joan Crawford, Robert
Montgomery, *Charles Butterworth*, Billie Burke,
Frances Drake, Rosalind Russell, Arthur
Treacher

Fort Apache**
US 1948   127m   bw
RKO (John Ford, Merian C. Cooper)

In the old west, a military martinet has trouble
with his family as well as the Indians.
Rather stiff and unsatisfactory epic western
which yet contains sequences in its director's
best manner.

w Frank S. Nugent, *story* Massacre by James
Warner Bellah *d John Ford ph* Archie Stout
m Richard Hageman

Henry Fonda, John Wayne, Shirley Temple,
Pedro Armendariz, Ward Bond, Irene Rich,
George O'Brien, John Agar, Victor McLaglen,
Anna Lee, Dick Foran, Guy Kibbee
'A visually absorbing celebration of violent
deeds.'—*Howard Barnes*
'The whole picture is bathed in a special form
of patriotic sentimentality: scenes are held so
that we cannot fail to appreciate the beauty of
the American past.'—*New Yorker, 1976*

Fort Ti
US 1953   73m   Technicolor   3-D
Columbia (Sam Katzman)

In 1759 a platoon of Rogers' Rangers marches
north to defend their territory against Indians.

Cheap and feeble western memorable only for the amount of miscellaneous objects thrown at the audience via 3-D photography.

w Robert E. Kent d William Castle ph Lester E. White, Lathrop B. Worth md Ross di Maggio

George Montgomery, Joan Vohs, Irving Bacon, James Seay

'The lack of restraint is remarkable. To the injury of tomahawks, rifle shots, cannon balls, flaming arrows, broken bottles and blazing torches is added the insult of grubby redskins hurled judo style into one's lap.'—*David Robinson*

The Fortune
US 1975 88m Technicolor Panavision
Columbia (Hank Moonjean)

A twenties heiress elopes with her lover and his dim-witted friend but discovers that they mean to murder her for her money.
Bungled black comedy with top talent over-confident of carrying it.

w Adrien Joyce (Carole Eastman) d Mike Nichols ph John A. Alonzo m various songs pd Richard Sylbert

Jack Nicholson, Warren Beatty, Stockard Channing, Florence Stanley, Richard B. Shull, John Fiedler

'Like the ill-assorted styles of the film generally, the stars themselves frequently seem to belong in different movies.'—*Richard Combs*

'A silly, shallow, occasionally enjoyable comedy trifle . . . classy 20's production values often merit more attention than the plot.'—*Variety*

Fortune and Men's Eyes
Canada / US 1971 102m Metrocolor
MGM / Cinemex / CFD (Lester Persky, Lewis M. Allen)

Life among homosexuals in a Canadian jail.
A welter of sensational incident outweighs any point the author may have had; this prison seems to be beyond reform.

w John Herbert, from his play d Harvey Hart ph Georges Dufaux m Galt McDermot

Wendell Burton, Michael Greer

The Fortune Cookie*
US 1966 125m bw Panavision
UA / Mirisch / Phalanx / Jalem (Billy Wilder)
GB title: *Meet Whiplash Willie*

A crooked lawyer forces his slightly injured client to sue for a million dollars.
Flat, stretched-out, only occasionally effective comedy which relies too much on mordant attitudes and a single star performance.

w Billy Wilder, I. A. L. Diamond d Billy Wilder ph Joseph La Shelle m André Previn

Walter Matthau, Jack Lemmon, Ron Rich, Cliff Osmond, Lurene Tuttle

AA: Walter Matthau
AAN: Billy Wilder, I. A. L. Diamond (script); Joseph La Shelle

Fortune Is a Woman*
GB 1956 95m bw
Columbia / Frank Launder, Sidney Gilliat
US title: *She Played with Fire*

An insurance assessor investigates a fire, finds a murder, marries the victim's widow, and is blackmailed . . .
Slackly-handled mystery thriller, a disappointment from the talents involved.

w Frank Launder, Sidney Gilliat, *novel* Winston Graham d Sidney Gilliat ph Gerald Gibbs m William Alwyn

Jack Hawkins, Arlene Dahl, Dennis Price, Geoffrey Keen, Violet Farebrother, John Robinson, Bernard Miles, Greta Gynt

Forty Carats*
US 1973 109m Metrocolor
Columbia / M. J. Frankovich

A 40-year-old divorcee on holiday in Greece has a brief affair with a 22-year-old man.
Curiously miscast and mishandled comedy for the smart set; scores a laugh or two but never really takes off.

w Leonard Gershe, *play* Pierre Barillet, Jean-Pierre Gredy d Milton Katselas ph Charles Lang Jnr m Michel Legrand

Liv Ullmann, Edward Albert, Gene Kelly, Billy 'Green' Bush, Binnie Barnes, Nancy Walker, Deborah Raffin, Don Porter, Natalie Schaefer, Rosemary Murphy

The Forty First*
USSR 1927 80m approx bw silent
Mezhrabpom
original title: *Sorok Pervyi*

During the Civil War in Turkestan, a girl sniper for the Reds becomes the companion in adventure of a White lieutenant. But in the end he becomes her 41st victim.
Strong action melodrama which found an international audience.

w Boris Lavyenrov, from his novel d Yakov Protazanov ph Pyotr Yermolov

Ada Voitsik, Ivan Kovan-Samborsky
† Remade in 1956 by Grigori Chukrai, in colour.

Forty Guns
US 1957 80m bw Cinemascope
TCF / Globe (Samuel Fuller)

A powerful ranchwoman protects her hoodlum brother.
Heavily melodramatic and slow-moving western with a few effective moments.

wd Samuel Fuller *ph* Joseph Biroc *m* Harry Sukman

Barbara Stanwyck, Barry Sullivan, Dean Jagger, Gene Barry, John Ericson

Forty Little Mothers
US 1940 90m bw
MGM (Harry Rapf)

A teacher in a girls' school finds himself in charge of a baby.
Ill-advised star vehicle composed largely of whimsy . . . and no musical numbers.

w Dorothy Yost, Ernest Pagano *d* Busby Berkeley

Eddie Cantor, Judith Anderson, Bonita Granville, Rita Johnson, Diana Lewis, Nydia Westman, Martha O'Driscoll

Forty Ninth Parallel*
GB 1941 123m bw
GFD / Ortus (John Sutro, Michael Powell)
US title: *The Invaders*

In Canada, five stranded U-boat men try to escape into the US.
Episodic, effective propaganda piece which develops some nice Hitchcockian touches and allows a range of star actors to make impact.

w Emeric Pressburger, Rodney Ackland *d* Michael Powell *m* Ralph Vaughan Williams

Eric Portman, Laurence Olivier, *Anton Walbrook, Leslie Howard, Raymond Massey*, Glynis Johns, Niall MacGinnis, Finlay Currie, Raymond Lovell, John Chandos

AA: original story (Emeric Pressburger)
AAN: best picture; script

Forty Pounds of Trouble*
US 1963 105m Eastmancolor
Panavision
U-I / Curtis Enterprises (Stan Margulies)

A casino manager is chased by his ex-wife's detective for alimony payments, and also has to look after an abandoned six-year-old girl.
Standard sentimental comedy with some verve and a lively climactic chase through Disneyland.

w Marion Hargrove *d* Norman Jewison *ph* Joe MacDonald *m* Mort Lindsey

Tony Curtis, Phil Silvers, Suzanne Pleshette, Edward Andrews

Forty-Second Street**
US 1933 89m bw
Warner (Hal B. Wallis)

A Broadway musical producer has troubles during rehearsal but reaches a successful opening night.
Archetypal Hollywood putting-on-a-show musical in which the leading lady is indisposed and a chorus girl is told to get out there and come back a star. The clichés are written and performed with great zest, the atmosphere is convincing, and the numbers when they come are dazzlers.

w James Seymour, Rian James, *novel* Bradford Ropes *d* Lloyd Bacon *ch* Busby Berkeley *ph* Sol Polito *m/ly* Al Dubin, Harry Warren

Warner Baxter, Ruby Keeler, Bebe Daniels, George Brent, Una Merkel, Guy Kibbee, Dick Powell, *Ginger Rogers* (as Anytime Annie), *Ned Sparks*, George E. Stone, Allen Jenkins
   'The story has been copied a hundred times since, but never has the backstage atmosphere been so honestly and felicitously caught.'—*John Huntley, 1966*
   'It gave new life to the clichés that have kept parodists happy.'—*New Yorker, 1977*
AAN: best picture

Foul Play*
US 1978 116m Movielab
Paramount / Thomas L. Miller, Edward K. Milkis

Two innocents in San Francisco get involved in a plot to assassinate the visiting pope.
Sometimes sprightly, sometimes tired rehash of Hitchcock elements, rather on the level of the similar *Silver Streak*.

wd Colin Higgins *ph* David M. Walsh *m* Charles Fox

Goldie Hawn, Chevy Chase, Burges Meredith, Rachel Roberts, Eugene Roche, Dudley Moore, Billy Barty

The Fountain
US 1934 84m bw
RKO (Pandro S. Berman)

During World War I a British woman is tempted to forsake her mangled German air ace husband for her childhood sweetheart.
A slice of impenetrable gloom from an intractable novel.

w Jane Murfin, Samuel Hoffenstein, *novel* Charles Morgan *d* John Cromwell *ph* Henry W. Gerrard

Ann Harding, Brian Aherne, Paul Lukas, Jean Hersholt, Ralph Forbes, Violet Kemble-Cooper, Sara Haden

'One of the talkiest talkies yet.'—*Variety*

'Long and solemn and wonderfully empty.'—
Otis Ferguson

The Fountainhead**

US 1949   114m   bw

Warner (Henry Blanke)

An idealistic architect clashes with big business.
Overripe adaptation of a rather silly novel, full of
Freudian symbols and expressionist techniques
with which the star really can't cope; but an
enjoyable field day for the director and the rest of
the cast.

w Ayn Rand, from her novel d King Vidor
ph Robert Burks m Max Steiner

Gary Cooper, *Patricia Neal, Raymond Massey*,
Kent Smith, Robert Douglas, Henry Hull, Ray
Collins, Moroni Olson, Jerome Cowan

Four Daughters***

US 1938   90m   bw

Warner (Henry Blanke)

Domestic and romantic adventures of a small-
town family.
Standard small-town hearth-fire hokum,
impeccably done and really quite irresistible.

w Julius Epstein, Lenore Coffee, *novel* Sister Act
by Fannie Hurst d Michael Curtiz ph Ernest
Haller m Max Steiner

Claude Rains, John Garfield (a sensation in his
first role), Priscilla Lane, Rosemary Lane, Lola
Lane, Gale Page, Jeffrey Lynn, Frank McHugh,
May Robson, Dick Foran

'It may be sentimental, but it's grand
cinema.'—*New York Times*

† An immediate sequel was required, but the
Garfield character had been killed off, so to
accommodate him a variation was written under
the title *Daughters Courageous*; then came two
proper sequels without him, *Four Wives* and
Four Mothers. In 1955 the original was remade
as *Young at Heart* (qv).

AAN: best picture; script; Michael Curtiz; John
Garfield

The Four Days of Naples*

Italy 1962   119m   bw

Titanus-Metro (Goffredo Lombardo)

A reconstruction of the 1943 city battle in which
the Nazis were driven out by civilian fury.
A kind of update of *Open City*: much admired,
but a little ill-timed.

w Nanni Loy and others d Nanni Loy
ph Marcello Gatti m Carlo Rustichelli

Lea Massari, Frank Wolff, Domenico Formato,
Raffaele Barbato

AAN: script

The Four Feathers**

US 1929   83m   bw

Paramount (David O. Selznick)

During the Sudan campaign of the nineties, a
stay-at-home receives four white feathers as a
symbol of cowardice; but he goes undercover,
becomes a hero, and rescues his best friend.
Ambitious early talkie based on a famous
adventure novel, partly filmed in Africa;
interesting but now very stilted.

w Howard Estabrook, *novel* A. E. W. Mason
d Lothar Mendes, Merian C. Cooper, Ernest
Schoedsack ph Robert Kurlle, Merian C.
Cooper, Ernest Schoedsack m William F.
Peters

Richard Arlen, Fay Wray, Clive Brook, William
Powell, George Fawcett, Theodore Von Eltz,
Noah Beery

The Four Feathers****

GB 1939   130m   Technicolor

London (Alexander Korda, Irving Asher)

The standard version of the above, perfectly cast
and presented, with battle scenes which have
since turned up in a score of other films from
Zarak to *Master of the World*; also a triumph of
early colour.

w R. C. Sheriff, Lajos Biro, Arthur Wimperis
d Zoltan Korda ph Georges Perinal, Osmond
Borradaile, Jack Cardiff m Miklos Rozsa

*John Clements, Ralph Richardson, C. Aubrey
Smith*, June Duprez, Allan Jeayes, Jack Allen,
Donald Gray, Henry Oscar, John Laurie

'It cannot fail to be one of the best films of the
year . . . even the richest of the ham goes
smoothly down, savoured with humour and
satire.'—*Graham Greene*

† Remade 1956 as *Storm over the Nile* (qv).

Four for Texas

US 1963   124m   Technicolor

Warner / Sam Company (Robert Aldrich)

Two survivors of a stagecoach raid doublecross
each other for the loot and become rival saloon
owners.
Flabby western comedy, tediously directed and
casually performed.

w Teddi Sherman, Robert Aldrich d Robert
Aldrich ph Ernest Laszlo m Nelson Riddle

Dean Martin, Frank Sinatra, Anita Ekberg,
Ursula Andress, Charles Bronson, Victor
Buono, the Three Stooges

'The major laughs come from the Three Stooges doing an ancient routine and an old lady falling out of her wheelchair. Zowie.'—*Judith Crist*

'One suspects that the most amusing antics were those that went on off-screen.'—*Films and Filming*

Four Frightened People*
US 1934   78m   bw
Paramount / Cecil B. de Mille

A bubonic plague outbreak on board ship causes four survivors to escape via a lifeboat and trek through dangerous jungle.
Studio-bound but interesting action melodrama, of a type unusual from this director.

w Bartlett Cormack, Lenore Coffee, *novel* E. Arnot Robertson *d* Cecil B. de Mille *ph* Karl Struss *m* Karl Hajos and others

Claudette Colbert, Herbert Marshall, William Gargan, Mary Boland, Leo Carrillo, Nella Walker, Tetsu Komai, Ethel Griffies

Four Girls in Town
US 1956   85m   Technicolor
Cinemascope
U-I (Aaron Rosenberg)

Girls from various countries are chosen for Hollywood screen tests.
Formula romantic comedy adequately exposing young talent.

wd Jack Sher *ph* Irving Glassberg *m* Alex North

George Nader, Julie Adams, Marianne Cook, Elsa Martinelli, Gia Scala, Sidney Chaplin, Grant Williams, John Gavin

The Four Horsemen of the Apocalypse**
US 1921   150m approx   bw   silent
Metro

A young Argentinian fights for his father's country, France, in World War I.
Highly derivative dramatic spectacle, almost a pageant, from a fairly unreadable novel. Despite its variable if exotic style, it made a star of Rudolph Valentino.

w June Mathis, *novel* Vicente Blasco-Ibanez *d* Rex Ingram *ph* John F. Seitz

Rudolph Valentino, Alice Terry, Nigel de Brulier, Alan Hale, Jean Hersholt, Wallace Beery

'A blend of exotic settings, striking composition, dramatic lighting, and colourful if sordid atmosphere.'—*Lewis Jacobs*

The Four Horsemen of the Apocalypse*
US 1961   153m   Metrocolor
Cinemascope
MGM (Julian Blaustein)

In this ill-fated modernization, the idle grandson of an Argentinian beef tycoon finds his manhood at last as a member of the French resistance during World War II. The visionary skyriding figures of death and pestilence simply do not fit in with bombs and concentration camps. Glum acting by a too elderly company, ugly colour and the usual hindrances of Cinemascope.

w Robert Ardrey, John Gay *d* Vincente Minnelli *ph* Milton Krasner *m* André Previn

Glenn Ford, Ingrid Thulin, Charles Boyer, Paul Henreid, Lee J. Cobb, Paul Lukas, Karl Boehm, Yvette Mimieux

'An elephantine helping of hysteria and hokum.'—*Judith Crist, 1973*

Four Hours to Kill**
US 1935   74m   bw
Paramount (Arthur Hornblow Jnr)

A psychopathic gangster gets loose during an evening at the theatre.
Tense, well-handled melodrama making full use of its setting.

w *Norman Krasna*, from his play Small Miracle *d* *Mitchell Leisen* *ph* Theodor Sparkhul

Richard Barthelmess, Ray Milland, Gertrude Michael, Joe Morrison, Helen Mack, Dorothy Tree, Roscoe Karns, Henry Travers

The Four Hundred Blows**
France 1958   94m   bw   Dyaliscope
Films du Carrosse / SEDIF
original title: *Les Quatre Cents Coups*

A 12-year-old boy, unhappy at home, finds himself in a detention centre but finally escapes and keeps running.
Little more in plot terms than a piece of character observation, this engaging film is so controlled and lyrical as to be totally refreshing, and it gives a very vivid picture of the Paris streets.

wd *François Truffaut* *ph* Henri Decaë *m* Jean Constantin

Jean-Pierre Léaud, Claire Maurier, Albert Rémy
† The film is said to be based on Truffaut's own childhood.

AAN: script

Four in a Jeep*
Switzerland 1951   96m   bw
Praesensfilm (Lazar Wechsler)

In the post-war international zone of Vienna, the four nationals of a police patrol come to blows over the cases they encounter.
Historically interesting but rather bland illustration of an untenable and even tragic political situation which was treated more melodramatically in *The Third Man.*

w Richard Schweizer *d* Leopold Lindtberg *ph* Emil Barna *m* Robert Blum

Viveca Lindfors, Ralph Meeker, Yoseph Yadin, Michael Medwin

Four Jills in a Jeep
US 1944 89m bw
TCF (Irving Starr)

Four Hollywood glamour girls entertain the troops.
Condescending, dispirited 'semi-documentary' war musical.

w Robert Ellis, Helen Logan, Snag Werris *d* William A. Seiter *ph* Peverell Marley *md* Emil Newman

Kay Francis, Martha Raye, Carole Landis, Mitzi Mayfair, Jimmy Dorsey and his band, John Harvey, Phil Silvers, Dick Haymes; guest stars Alice Faye, Betty Grable, Carmen Miranda, George Jessel

'It gives the painful impression of having been tossed together in a couple of hours.'—*Bosley Crowther*

The Four Just Men*
GB 1939 85m bw
Ealing—Capad (S. C. Balcon)
US title: *The Secret Four*

To save the Empire, four stalwart Britishers agree to murder a villainous MP.
Bright, unusual but dated thriller from a popular novel.

w Roland Pertwee, Angus Macphail, Sergei Nolbandov, *novel* Edgar Wallace *d* Walter Forde

Hugh Sinclair, Francis L. Sullivan, Frank Lawton, Griffith Jones, Anna Lee, Basil Sidney, Alan Napier, Athole Stewart, Edward Chapman, Garry Marsh, Ellaline Terriss, Lydia Sherwood, George Merritt

† The TV series of the late fifties restrained its heroes from criminal acts; the men were Jack Hawkins, Richard Conte, Dan Dailey, Vittorio de Sica.

Four Men and a Prayer**
US 1938 97m bw
TCF (Kenneth MacGowan)

Four young Englishmen set out to clear the name of their dishonoured father.

Pleasantly performed mystery which improves after a slowish start.

w Richard Sherman, Sonya Levien, Walter Ferris, *novel* David Garth *d* John Ford *ph* Ernest Palmer *md* Louis Silvers

Loretta Young, Richard Greene, George Sanders, David Niven, William Henry, C. Aubrey Smith, J. Edward Bromberg, John Carradine, Alan Hale, Reginald Denny, Barry Fitzgerald, Berton Churchill, John Sutton

The Four Musketeers (The Revenge of Milady)*
Panama 1974 103m Technicolor
TCF / Film Trust / Este (Alexander Salkind, Michael Salkind)

Athos, Porthos, Aramis and D'Artagnan have a final battle with Rochefort.
Perfunctory sequel to the same team's *The Three Musketeers*; allegedly the two films were intended as one, but if so the first ten reels were by far the best, though this section has its regulation quota of high spirits and lusty action.

w George MacDonald Fraser *d* Richard Lester *ph* David Watkin *m* Lalo Schifrin *pd* Brian Eatwell

Michael York, Oliver Reed, Frank Finlay, Richard Chamberlain, Raquel Welch, Faye Dunaway, Charlton Heston, Christopher Lee, Simon Ward, Geraldine Chaplin, Jean-Pierre Cassel, Roy Kinnear

'The whole sleek formula has rolled over to reveal a very soft, very flabby underside.'—*Tony Rayns*

The Four-Poster
US 1952 103m bw
Columbia / Stanley Kramer

The history of a marriage told in a series of bedroom scenes.
Hastily shot and rather tatty looking version of a stage play; unfortunately film can't contrast the comedy of the opening and the tragedy of the close within one small set, and the UPA cartoon bridges, though smart in themselves, are merely an irritation.

w Allan Scott, *play* Jan de Hartog *d* Irving Reis *ph* Hal Mohr *m* Dmitri Tiomkin

Rex Harrison, Lilli Palmer

AAN: Hal Mohr

The Four Skulls of Jonathan Drake
US 1959 70m bw
UA / Vogue (Robert E. Kent)

A family is cursed by a head-hunting Equadorian medicine man.

Cheaply made but full-blooded occult horror, rather effectively done by a cast that knows how.

w Orville H. Hampton d Edward L. Cahn ph Maury Gertsman m Paul Dunlap

Henry Daniell, Eduard Franz, Valerie French, Grant Richards, Paul Cavanagh

'Amazonian Indians may find the plot a shade far-fetched.'—MFB

Four Sons*

US 1940   89m   bw
TCF

A Czech family is divided when the Nazis take over.

Predictable po-faced anti-Hitler melodrama released to an indifferent public well before America entered the war. A remake of a silent film set during World War I.

w John Howard Lawson d Archie Mayo ph Leon Shamroy m David Buttolph

Don Ameche, Eugenie Leontovich, Mary Beth Hughes, Alan Curtis, George Ernest, Robert Lowery, Sig Rumann, Lionel Royce, Ludwig Stossel

Four Steps in the Clouds*

Italy 1942   90m   bw
Cines Amato
original title: Quattro Passi fra le Nuvole

A travelling salesman on a bus gets involved with the problems of a pregnant girl, but misunderstandings are finally cleared up to general satisfaction.

A comedy on the American model which was a great success in wartorn Italy. Not particularly remarkable in itself, it was remade in 1957, as The Virtuous Bigamist, with Fernandel. It does show the lighter side of Italian neo-realism.

w Cesare Zavattini, Giuseppe Amato, Piero Tellini, Aldo de Benedetti d Alessandro Blasetti ph Vaclav Vich m Alessandro Cicognini

Gino Cervi, Adriana Benetti, Giuditta Rissone

Four's a Crowd

US 1938   91m   bw
Warner (Hal B. Wallis / David Lewis)

A public relations man has the job of promoting a mean-spirited millionaire, and falls in love with his daughter.

Floppy comedy, neither very witty nor as crazy as might have been expected. However, it ambles along quite engagingly.

w Casey Robinson, Sig Herzig d Michael Curtiz ph Ernest Haller m Heinz Roemheld, Ray Heindorf

Errol Flynn, Rosalind Russell, Olivia de Havilland, Patric Knowles, Walter Connolly, Hugh Herbert, Melville Cooper, Franklin Pangborn, Herman Bing, Margaret Hamilton

Fourteen Hours***

US 1951   92m   bw
TCF (Sol C. Siegel)

A man stands on the ledge of a tall building and threatens to jump.

Well-made documentary drama based on a true occurrence but given a happy ending. First class detail gives an impression of realism.

w John Paxton, article Joel Sayre d Henry Hathaway ph Joe MacDonald m Alfred Newman

Richard Basehart, Paul Douglas, Barbara Bel Geddes, Debra Paget, Agnes Moorehead, Robert Keith, Howard da Silva, Jeffrey Hunter, Martin Gabel, Jeff Corey

'A model of craftsmanship in all departments.'—Penelope Houston
'A highly enjoyable small scale picture, with a strength immensely greater than its size would suggest.'—Richard Mallett, Punch

The Fox*

US / Canada 1967   110m   De Luxe
Warner / Raymond Stross / Motion Pictures
    International (Howard Koch)

On an isolated farm, two lesbians are disturbed by the arrival of a wandering seaman.
Rather obvious sexual high jinks full of symbolism and heavy breathing.

w Lewis John Carlino, Howard Koch, novel D. H. Lawrence d Mark Rydell ph Bill Fraker m Lalo Schifrin

Anne Heywood, Sandy Dennis, Keir Dullea
AAN: Lalo Schifrin

Fox Follies of 1929

US 1929   82m   bw
Fox
GB title: Movietone Follies of 1929

An all-star review.
Every studio had its early talkie musical using up its contract stars; this was perhaps the least interesting.

wd David Butler, William K. Wells ph Charles Van Enger

Sue Carol, Lola Lane, Dixie Lee, Sharon Lynn, Stepin Fetchit

The Foxes of Harrow

US 1947   117m   bw
TCF (William A. Bacher)

In 1820 New Orleans, a philanderer seeks

advancement by breaking up his marriage.
Tolerable but rather flat adaptation of a
bestseller, stultified by central miscasting.

w Wanda Tuchock, *novel* Frank Yerby *d* John
M. Stahl *ph* Joseph La Shelle *m* Alfred
Newman

Rex Harrison, Maureen O'Hara, Richard
Haydn, Victor McLaglen, Vanessa Brown,
Patricia Medina, Gene Lockhart, Hugo Haas

Foxfire
US 1955 92m Technicolor
U-I (Aaron Rosenberg)

A rich New York girl on holiday in Arizona is
attracted to a half-Apache miner.
Romantic melodrama with action asides;
watchable for women who like that sort of thing.

w Ketti Frings, *novel* Anya Seton *d* Joseph
Pevney *ph* William Daniels *m* Frank Skinner

Jane Russell, Jeff Chandler, Frieda Inescort,
Dan Duryea

Foxhole in Cairo
GB 1960 80m bw
Omnia (Steven Pallos, Donald Taylor)

A German agent in Libya is allowed to get back
to Rommel with false information.
Interesting true spy story deflated by muddled
handling.

w Leonard Mosley, from his book The Cat and
the Mice *d* John Moxey *ph* Desmond
Dickinson *m* Wolfram Rohrig, Douglas
Gamley, Ken Jones

James Robertson Justice, Adrian Hoven, Albert
Lieven (as Rommel), Niall MacGinnis, Peter
Van Eyck, Robert Urquhart, Fenella Fielding

Fra Diavolo **
US 1933 90m bw
MGM / Hal Roach
aka: *The Devil's Brother*

Two incompetent bandits are hired as
manservants by a real bandit.
Auber's 1830 operetta becomes a vehicle for
Laurel and Hardy, setting a pattern they
followed with *Babes in Toyland* and *The
Bohemian Girl*. They have excellent sequences,
but overall the film lacks pace.

w Jeanie McPherson *d* Hal Roach, Charles
Rogers *ph* Art Lloyd, Hap Depew *md* Le Roy
Shield

Stan Laurel, Oliver Hardy, Dennis King, *James
Finlayson*, Thelma Todd

Fragment of an Empire *
USSR 1929 100m approx bw silent
Sovkino

A young man who lost his memory in World
War I regains it in 1928 and surveys the changed
social order.
Mildly satirical propaganda piece with a vivid
impression of Leningrad at the time.

w Friedrich Ermier, Katerina Vinogradskaya
d Friedrich Ermler *ph* Yevgeni Schneider

Fyoder Nikitin, Yakov Gudkin, Ludmila
Semyonova

Fragment of Fear *
GB 1970 95m Technicolor
Columbia (John R. Sloan)

A young writer investigates the murder of his
aunt, but finds that he may himself be mad.
What appears to be a whodunnit turns into a
flashy, fashionable, sub-Antonioni puzzle with
no ending, but despite the considerable irritation
this causes, the details and character cameos are
excellent.

w Paul Dehn, *novel* John Bingham *d* Richard C.
Sarafian *ph* Oswald Morris *m* Johnny Harris

David Hemmings, Gayle Hunnicutt, Roland
Culver, Daniel Massey, Flora Robson, Wilfrid
Hyde White, Adolfo Celi, Mona Washbourne

The Franchise Affair *
GB 1950 88m bw
ABP (Robert Hall)

A young girl accuses two gentlewomen of
kidnapping and ill-treating her.
Unusual and absorbing mystery based on a true
18th-century case; the treatment however is
rather too mild.

w Robert Hall, Lawrence Huntington, *novel*
Josephine Tey *d* Lawrence Huntington
ph Gunther Krampf *m* Philip Green

Michael Denison, Dulcie Gray, Anthony
Nicholls, Marjorie Fielding, Athene Seyler, Ann
Stephens, Hy Hazell, John Bailey, Kenneth
More

Francis *
US 1950 90m bw
U-I (Robert Arthur)

An army private makes friends with a talking
mule who causes him some embarrassment.
Simple-minded, quite agreeable if rather slow-
moving fantasy farce which was popular enough
to spawn several sequels and later a TV series
called *Mister Ed*.

w David Stern, from his novel *d* Arthur Lubin
ph Irving Glassberg *m* Frank Skinner

Cass, Peter Britt *d Ken
. *m* Georges Delerue

ear, Marisa Mell, Bryan

echnicolor   3-D
er)

ss finds a husband while

quite attractive light
moured star wearing -
censorable.

Sale *d* Lloyd Bacon
alter Scharf *md* Lionel

oland, Arthur Hunnicutt,

n, her clothes appear to
she agrees not to burst
a good sort, she has an
for the false, the
sh.'—*MFB*

w
(John Boulting)
tress causes havoc at a

medy with practised
w easy laughs. The
use its imperfections by
p'.

frey Dell, play Robert
d Roy Boulting

tice, Cecil Parker,
an Bannen, Agnes Laurent,
th Sharpe, Athene Seyler,

ears*
ow
ities (David E. Rose)
rench crammers fall for the
f their number.
y from a successful West

Anatole de Grunwald, Ian
ence Rattigan d Anthony

Drew, *Guy Middleton,*
id Tree, Jim Gerald, Janine
rgan

Frenchie

US 1950   80m   Technicolor
U-I (Michael Kraike)

A saloon queen sets up shop in Bottleneck, her
real aim being to track down her father's
murderers.
Modest western of the *Destry Rides Again*
school.

w Oscar Brodney *d* Louis King *ph* Maury
Gertsman *m* Hans Salter

Shelley Winters, Joel McCrea, Paul Kelly, Elsa
Lanchester, Marie Windsor, John Emery,
George Cleveland, John Russell

Frenchman's Creek**

US 1944   112m   Technicolor
Paramount (B. G. De Sylva)

In Restoration England, a lady flees from a
lascivious nobleman to her family home in
Cornwall, where she falls in love with a French
pirate.
Enjoyable Girls' Own Paper romance, dressed to
kill and entertaining despite its many palpable
absurdities.

w Talbot Jennings, *novel* Daphne du Maurier
d Mitchell Leisen *ph* George Barnes *m* Victor
Young *ad* Hans Dreier, Ernest Fegte

Joan Fontaine, Arturo de Cordova, Basil
Rathbone, Nigel Bruce, *Cecil Kellaway*, Ralph
Forbes, Moyna McGill

Frenzy*

Sweden 1944   101m   bw
Svensk Filmindustri
original title: *Hets*; aka: *Torment*

A sadistic Latin teacher and his sensitive pupil
find themselves competing for the same girl.
Hothouse melodrama of the *Blue Angel* school:
it seemed pretty powerful at the time.

w Ingmar Bergman *d Alf Sjöberg ph* Martin
Bodin *m* Hilding Rosenberg

Stig Jarrel, Alf Kjellin, Mai Zetterling

Frenzy*

GB 1972   116m   Technicolor
Universal / Alfred Hitchcock

A disillusioned and aggressive ex-RAF officer is
suspected through circumstantial evidence of
being London's 'necktie murderer'.
Has-been, unconvincing, cliché-ridden thriller,
an old man's sex suspenser, which would have
been derided if anyone but Hitchcock had made
it. As it is, a few comic and suspenseful touches
partly atone for the implausibilities and lapses of
taste.

w Anthony Shaffer, *novel* Goodbye Piccadilly,

Donald O'Connor, Patricia Medina, Zasu Pitts,
Ray Collins, John McIntyre, Eduard Franz,
Robert Warwick, and Chill Wills as Francis'
voice.

Sequels (the first six with Donald O'Connor):
1951: FRANCIS GOES TO THE RACES
1952: FRANCIS GOES TO WEST POINT
1953: FRANCIS COVERS BIG TOWN
1954: FRANCIS JOINS THE WACS
1955: FRANCIS IN THE NAVY
1956: FRANCIS IN THE HAUNTED
HOUSE (with Mickey Rooney)

Francis of Assisi

US 1961   107m   De Luxe   Cinemascope
TCF / Perseus (Plato A. Skouras)

The son of a medieval cloth merchant takes a
vow of poverty, cares for animals and dies a
hermit.
Tedious biopic.

w Eugene Vale, Jack Thomas, James Forsyth
d Michael Curtiz *ph* Piero Portalupi *m* Mario
Nascimbene

Bradford Dillman, Dolores Hart, Stuart
Whitman, Eduard Franz, Pedro Armendariz,
Cecil Kellaway, Finlay Currie, Mervyn Johns,
Athene Seyler

Frankenstein****

US 1931   71m   bw
Universal (Carl Laemmle Jnr)

A research scientist creates a living monster
from corpses, but it runs amok.
Whole books have been written about this film
and its sequels. Apart from being a fascinating if
primitive cinematic work in its own right, it set its
director and star on interesting paths and
established a Hollywood attitude towards horror
(mostly borrowed from German silents such as
The Golem). A seminal film indeed, which at
each repeated viewing belies its age.

*w Garrett Fort, Francis Edward Faragoh, John
L. Balderston,* from the play by Peggy Webling
and the novel by Mary Wollstonecraft Shelley
d James Whale, ph Arthur Edeson m David
Broekman *ad Charles D. Hall*

Boris Karloff, Colin Clive, Mae Clarke, John
Boles, *Edward Van Sloan, Frederick Kerr,
Dwight Frye*
'Still the most famous of all horror films, and
deservedly so.'—*John Baxter, 1968*
† Direct sequels by the same studio (all qv)
include *The Bride of Frankenstein, Son of
Frankenstein, Ghost of Frankenstein,
Frankenstein Meets the Wolf Man, House of
Frankenstein, House of Dracula, Abbott and
Costello Meet Frankenstein.* The later Hammer

---

series, which told the story all over again in
gorier vein, includes *The Curse of Frankenstein*
(qv), *The Revenge of Frankenstein* (qv), *The Evil
of Frankenstein, Frankenstein Created Woman,
Frankenstein Must be Destroyed, Horror of
Frankenstein, Frankenstein and the Monster
from Hell.* Other Frankenstein films date from as
early as 1908, and scores have been made in
various languages. *Young Frankenstein* (qv) is a
partly effective spoof on the Hollywood series;
The Munsters was a sixties comedy series for TV
which used the monster as its leading character
in a domestic setting.

Frankenstein Meets the Wolf Man**

US 1943   73m   bw
Universal (George Waggner)

Lawrence Talbot, the wolf man, travels to
Vasaria in the hope of a cure, and finds the
Frankenstein monster being reactivated.
Once one recovered from the bargain basement
combination of two monsters in one picture, this
was a horror comic with stylish sequences,
weakened by cuts in the script and a miscast Bela
Lugosi.

w Curt Siodmak *d Roy William Neill
ph* George Robinson *m* Hans Salter

Lon Chaney Jnr, Ilona Massey, Bela Lugosi (as
the monster), Patric Knowles, *Maria
Ouspenskaya*

Frankenstein '70

US 1958   83m   bw   Cinemascope
Allied Artists (Aubrey Schenck)

Television film-makers descend on Castle
Frankenstein; the current Count needs the
money to finance some monster making of his
own.
Boringly talkative and very silly 'futuristic' blot
on an honourable name, apart from a rather
frightening pre-credits sequence.

w Richard Landau, G. Worthing Yates
d Howard W. Koch *ph* Carl Guthrie *m* Paul
Dunlap

Boris Karloff, Tom Duggan, Jana Lund

Frankie and Johnny*

US 1966   87m   Technicolor
UA / F and J (Edward Small)

On a Mississippi riverboat, a gambling singer is
the despair of his lady partner.
Mildly amusing pastiche both of the old song and
of the various riverboat dramas.

w Alex Gottlieb *d* Frederick de Cordova
ph John Marquette *m* Fred Karger

Elvis Presley, Donna Douglas, Sue Ane

Langdon, Harry Morgan, Nancy Kovack, Audrey Christie, Jerome Cowan

Fraulein

US 1958 100m Eastmancolor
Cinemascope
TCF (Walter Reisch)

During World War II an American prisoner of war escapes and is helped by the daughter of a German professor.

Studio-bound war heroics with little conviction achieved or aimed at.

w Lee Townsend, *novel* James McGowan d Henry Koster *ph* Leo Tover *m* Daniele Amfitheatrof

Dana Wynter, Mel Ferrer, Margaret Hayes, Dolores Michaels, Theodore Bikel, Helmut Dantine

Fräulein Doktor

Italy / Yugoslavia 1968 104m
Technicolor
(Paramount) Dino de Laurentiis / Avala

In World War I, a German lady spy outwits British intelligence.

Rather glum international action melodrama.

w Diulio Coletti, H. A. L. Craig, Stanley Mann, Vittoriano Petrilli, Alberto Lattuada *d* Alberto Lattuada *ph* Luigi Kuveiller *m* Ennio Morricone

Suzy Kendall, Kenneth More, James Booth, Capucine, Alexander Knox, Nigel Green, Roberto Bisacco

† A similar story was filmed in 1936 as *Mademoiselle Docteur*.

Freaks **

US 1932 64m bw
MGM (Tod Browning)

A lady trapeze artist marries a midget, then poisons him for his money; his abnormal friends take revenge by turning her into a freak.

Made but disowned by MGM after accusations of tastelessness, this strident and silly melodrama has dated badly but has sequences of great power, especially the final massing of the freaks, slithering to their revenge in a rainstorm. It would have been better as a silent; the dialogue kills it.

w Willis Goldbeck, Leon Gordon, *novel* Spurs by Tod Robbins *d* Tod Browning *ph* Merrit B. Gerstad

Wallace Ford, Olga Baclanova, Leila Hyams, Roscoe Ates

'It is a skilfully presented production but of a character which in consideration of the

susceptibilities of mass audiences should be avoided.'—*Martin Quigley*

'For pure sensationalism it tops any picture yet produced.'—*Louella Parsons*

Freaky Friday

US 1976 100m Technicolor
Walt Disney (Ron Miller)

A 13-year-old and her mother, each discontented with their lot, express a wish to change places—and do.

A trendy update of *Vice Versa*, padded out with Disney irrelevancies and long outstaying its welcome.

w Mary Rodgers, from her novel *d* Gary Nelson *ph* Charles F. Wheeler *m* Johnny Mandel

Jodie Foster, Barbara Harris, John Astin, Patsy Kelly, Dick Van Patten, Sorrell Booke, Marie Windsor

Free and Easy *

US 1930 75m bw
MGM

A beauty contest winner is taken to Hollywood by her accident-prone manager.

Reasonably inventive vehicle for a comedian who never did quite manage talkie techniques.

w Al Boasberg, Richard Schayer *d* Edward Sedgwick

Buster Keaton, Anita Page, Robert Montgomery, Trixie Freganza

Free for All

US 1949 83m bw
U-I (Robert Buckner)

A young inventor finds a way of turning water into petrol.

Scatty comedy with mildly amusing moments.

w Robert Buckner *d* Charles T. Barton *ph* George Robinson *m* Frank Skinner

Robert Cummings, Ann Blyth, Percy Kilbride, Ray Collins, Donald Woods, Mikhail Rasumny

A Free Soul *

US 1931 91m bw
MGM

An unconventional lawyer regrets allowing his daughter to consort with a gangster.

Heavy melodrama with outdated attitudes, but an impressive example of the studio's style in the early thirties.

w John Meehan, *novel* Adela Rogers St John *d* Clarence Brown *ph* William Daniels

Lionel Barrymore, Norma Shearer, Leslie

Howard, Clark Gable, Lucy Beaumon Gleason

† Remade 1953 as *The Girl Who Had Everything*.

AA: Lionel Barrymore
AAN: Clarence Brown; Norma Sheare

Freebie and the Bean *

US 1974 113m Technicolor Par Warner (Richard Rush)

Two vaguely incompetent cops try to link mobster with the numbers racket.

Violent comedy melodrama with a high mortality rate, amoral outlook, and the us seventies reliance on incoherent plot, bum dialogue and excessive background noise. Occasionally funny all the same.

w Richard Kaufman *d* Richard Rush *ph* L Kovacs *m* Dominic Frontière

Alan Arkin, James Caan, Loretta Swit, Jac Kruschen, Mike Kellin

'It summarizes Hollywood's favourite thematic elements of the early seventies: plat male love affair, police corruption, comic violence, cynicism in high places, San Franci gay villains, the car chase. A return to the Keystone Kops, with character trimmings an lashings of sado-masochistic mayhem.'—*Cl Jeavons*

'A tasteless film from a spitball script.'—*Variety*

Freedom Radio

GB 1941 95m bw
Columbia / Two Cities (Mario Zampi)
US title: *A Voice in the Night*

In Vienna during World War II, the husband of Nazi actress runs a secret radio transmitter for Allied propaganda.

Moderate wartime flagwaver.

w Basil Wood, Gordon Wellesley, Louis Golding, Anatole de Grunwald, Jeffrey Dell, Bridget Boland, Roland Pertwee *d* Anthony Asquith

Diana Wynyard, Clive Brook, Raymond Huntley, Joyce Howard, Derek Farr, Howard Marion Crawford, Morland Graham

French Can-Can **

France / Italy 1955 105m Technicolor Franco-London / Jolly

How the can-can was launched in Paris night clubs.

A dramatically thin vehicle splendidly evoking a vision of vanished Paris: a feast for the eyes.

w Peter Myers, Ronald
Russell ph Ken Higgins

James Booth, Roy Kinn Pringle

The French Line

US 1953 102m T
RKO (Edmund Graing

A cheery Texas oil heir travelling to France.

Very thinly plotted but musical with a good-hu costumes once thought

w Mary Loos, Richard *ph* Harry J. Wild *m* W Newman *ch* Jack Col

Jane Russell, Gilbert R Mary McCarty

'A slouching Amazo stay put just as long as out of them; essentially ever-annihilating snee pretentious and the fre

A French Mistress

GB 1960 98m b
British Lion / Charter

An attractive new mis boys' school.

Sloppy, predictable c performers getting a f producers tried to exc promoting it as 'a ron

w tl *Roy Boulting; Je* Monro (Sonnie Hale)

James Robertson Jus Raymond Huntley, Thorley Walters, Ed Kenneth Griffith

French without T

GB 1939 85m
Paramount / Two C

Young Britons at a F young sister of one c Pleasant light comed End play.

w Terence Rattigan Dalrymple, *play Ter* Asquith

Ray Milland, Ellen *Ronald Culver*, Da Darcy, Kenneth M

Farewell Leicester Square by Arthur La Bern
d Alfred Hitchcock ph Gilbert Taylor m Ron
Goodwin

Jon Finch, *Alec McCowen, Barry Foster*, Vivien
Merchant, Anna Massey

'Hitchcock's most stodgy piece since *Dial M
for Murder* and possibly his least interesting film
from any period.'—*William S. Pechter*

The Freshman**
US 1925   75m (24 fps)   bw   silent
Harold Lloyd

An awkward college student accidentally
becomes a star football player.
A rather slow but striking star vehicle with
assured set-pieces. The football game climax was
later used as the first reel of *Mad Wednesday*.

w Sam Taylor, Ted Wilde, Time Whelan, John
Grey d Fred Newmeyer, Sam Taylor ph Walter
Lundin, Henry Kohler

Harold Lloyd, Jobyna Ralston, Brooks Benedict

Freud**
US 1963   140m   bw
U-I (Wolfgang Reinhardt)

Vienna 1865; Dr Sigmund Freud, a neurologist,
uses hypnotism to treat hysteria, and finds new
interest in the case of a boy whose hatred of his
father springs from incestuous love of his
mother, a failing which Freud finds in himself.
Earnest and competent biopic harking back to
Warners' similar films of the thirties, with the
addition of franker language. Generally
absorbing, but undeniably hard tack.

w Charles Kaufman, Wolfgang Reinhardt
d John Huston ph Douglas Slocombe m Jerry
Goldsmith

Montgomery Clift, Larry Parks, Susannah
York, Eileen Herlie, Susan Kohner, David
McCallum

AAN: script; Jerry Goldsmith

Friday the Thirteenth***
GB 1933   84m   bw
Gainsborough (Michael Balcon)

Several people are involved in a bus crash, and
we turn back the clock to see how they came to
be there.
Highly competent compendium of comedies and
dramas looking back to *The Bridge of San Luis
Rey* and forward to the innumerable all-star films
of the forties.

w G. H. Moresby-White, Sidney Gilliat, Emlyn
Williams d Victor Saville ph Charles Van
Enger

Sonnie Hale, Cyril Smith, *Eliot Makeham*,

Ursula Jeans, *Emlyn Williams*, Frank Lawton,
Belle Chrystal, *Max Miller*, Alfred Drayton,
Edmund Gwenn, Mary Jerrold, Gordon Harker,
Robertson Hare, Martita Hunt, Leonora
Corbett, Jessie Matthews, Ralph Richardson

Frieda*
GB 1947   97m   bw
Ealing (Michael Relph)

An RAF officer marries and takes home a girl
who helped him escape from a POW camp.
Stuffy and dated drama about how one English
family learned to love one particular German.
Timely when it appeared, however, and well
made within its conventions.

w Angus Macphail, Ronald Millar, *play* Ronald
Millar d Basil Deden ph Gordon Dines

Mai Zetterling, David Farrar, Glynis Johns,
Flora Robson, Albert Lieven

Friendly Persuasion**
US 1956   139m   De Luxe
AA (William Wyler)

At the outbreak of the Civil War, a family of
Quakers has to consider its position.
Sentimental, homespun western fare, well done
without being especially engrossing.

w Michael Wilson, *novel* Jessamyn West
d William Wyler ph Ellsworth Fredericks
m Dmitri Tiomkin

Gary Cooper, Dorothy McGuire, Anthony
Perkins, Marjorie Main, Richard Eyer, Robert
Middleton, Walter Catlett

AAN: best picture; Michael Wilson; William
Wyler; Anthony Perkins; song 'Thee I Love'
(m Dmitri Tiomkin, ly Paul Francis Webster)

Friends
US 1971   102m   Technicolor
Paramount (Lewis Gilbert)

Teenage lovers run away to a country cottage
and have a child.
Peculiar idyll given corny 'poetic' treatment: a
real non-starter.

w Jack Russell, Vernon Harris d Lewis Gilbert
ph Andrew Winding m Elton John

Sean Bury, Anicee Alvina, Toby Robbins,
Ronald Lewis

The Friends of Eddie Coyle*
US 1973   102m   Technicolor   Panavision
Paramount (Paul Monash)

An ageing hoodlum agrees to become a police
informer and is hunted down by his former
associates.

Dour gangster melodrama held together by its central performance.

w Paul Monash, *novel* George V. Higgins
d Peter Yates ph Vernon J. Kemper m Dave Grusin

Robert Mitchum, Peter Boyle, Richard Jordan, Steven Keats, Mitch Ryan, Alex Rocco

The Frisco Kid*
US 1935 77m bw
Warner (Samuel Bischoff)

A Shanghaied sailor rises to power among the riff raff of the Barbary Coast in the 1860s.
Fair melodrama with the star in action and (less interestingly) in love.

w Warren Duff, Seton I. Miller d Lloyd Bacon
ph Sol Polito md Leo F. Forbstein

James Cagney, Margaret Lindsay, Ricardo Cortez, Lili Damita, Donald Woods, Barton MacLane, George E. Stone, Addison Richards

Fritz the Cat**
US 1971 78m De Luxe
Fritz Productions / Aurica (Steve Krantz)

An alleycat student in New York seeks new and varied experience.
Carooon feature which applies the old anthropomorphism to the contemporary scene, and whips up more obscenity and violence than Disney ever dreamed of. A fast-moving orgy of outrage which could never have got by in live form.

wd/ *animator Ralph Bakshi, comic strip* R. H. Crumb
   'A bitter and snarling satire that refuses to curl up in anyone's lap.'—*Bruce Williamson*

The Frog*
GB 1937 75m bw
Herbert Wilcox

The mysterious leader of a criminal organization is unmasked.
Lively old-fashioned mystery melodrama.

w Ian Hay, Gerald Elliott, *novel* The Fellowship of the Frog by Edgar Wallace d Jack Raymond

Gordon Harker, Carol Goodner, Noah Beery, Jack Hawkins, Richard Ainley, Esmé Percy, Felix Aylmer
† Sequel 1938: *The Return of the Frog*.

The Frogmen
US 1951 96m bw
TCF (Samuel G. Engel)

Underwater demolition experts pave the way for the invasion of a Japanese-held island.
Standard, efficient war fare.

w John Tucker Battle d Lloyd Bacon
ph Norbert Brodine m Cyril Mockridge

Richard Widmark, Dana Andrews, Gary Merrill, Jeffrey Hunter, Warren Stevens, Robert Wagner, Harvey Lembeck
   'Competent, unpretentious and free from jingoism.'—*MFB*
AAN: original story (Oscar Millard); Norbert Brodine

Frogs*
US 1972 91m Movielab
AIP (George Edwards, Peter Thomas)

A remote, inhabited island in the southern States is overtaken by reptiles.
As Hitchcock might have said, the frogs is coming; instead of monsters, ordinary creepy-crawlies in their thousands devour most of the cast. Well enough done for those with strong stomachs.

w Robert Hutchison, Robert Blees d George McCowan ph Mario Tosi m Les Baxter

Ray Milland, Joan Van Ark, Sam Elliott, Adam Roarke, Judy Pace ·
   'One of the most remarkable and impressive onslaughts since *King Kong*.'—*David Pirie*

From Beyond the Grave*
GB 1973 98m Technicolor
Warner / Amicus (Milton Subotsky)

The proprietor of an East End antique shop involves his customers in horrific situations.
Reasonably lively portmanteau of tall tales from a familiar stable.

w Robin Clarke, Raymond Christodoulou
d Kevin Connor ph Alan Hume m David Gamley pd Maurice Carter

David Warner, Donald Pleasence, Ian Bannen, Diana Dors, Margaret Leighton, Ian Carmichael, Nyree Dawn Porter, Ian Ogilvy

From Headquarters
US 1933 63m bw
Warner

The police solve a murder by scientific methods.
Efficient, rather boring programmer.

w Robert N. Lee, Peter Milne d William Dieterle ph William Reese

George Brent, Margaret Lindsay, Eugene Pallette, Hugh Herbert, Hobart Cavanaugh, Robert Barrat, Henry O'Neill, Edward Ellis

From Hell to Texas

US 1958 100m Eastmancolor
 Cinemascope
TCF (Robert Buckner)
GB title: Manhunt

After accidentally killing a man, a cowboy is vengefully pursued by the victim's father. Competent chase western with a stand against violence.

w Robert Buckner, Wendell Mayes d Henry Hathaway ph Wilfrid Cline m Daniele Amfitheatrof

Don Murray, Diane Varsi, Chill Wills, Dennis Hopper,
R. G. Armstrong, Margo, Jay C. Flippen

From Here to Eternity***

US 1953 118m bw
Columbia (Buddy Adler)

Life in a Honolulu barracks at the time of Pearl Harbor.
Cleaned up and streamlined version of a bestseller in which the mainly sexual frustrations of a number of unattractive characters are laid bare. As a production, it is Hollywood in good form, and certainly took the public fancy as well as establishing Sinatra as an acting force.

w Dalton Trumbo, novel James Jones d Fred Zinnemann ph Burnett Guffey m George Duning

Burt Lancaster, Deborah Kerr, Frank Sinatra, Donna Reed, Ernest Borgnine, Montgomery Clift, Philip Ober, Mickey Shaughnessy
†The story was remade for TV in 1979 as a six-hour mini-series.

AA: best picture; Dalton Trumbo; Fred Zinnemann; Burnett Guffey; Frank Sinatra; Donna Reed
AAN: George Duning; Burt Lancaster; Deborah Kerr; Montgomery Clift

From Noon Till Three

US 1976 99m De Luxe
UA / Frankovich-Self

A bank robber becomes a local legend when he interrupts a raid to dally with an attractive widow. Later, when someone else is shot in mistake for him, he is reduced to penury, unable to prove his identity or live up to his own legend. Curious, shapeless, lumpy western satire, difficult to synopsize or analyse. Despite effort all round, it's just plain unsatisfactory.

wd Frank D. Gilroy, from his novel ph Lucien Ballard m Elmer Bernstein

Charles Bronson, Jill Ireland, Douglas Fowley, Stan Haze, Damon Douglas

'It squanders its early sparkle for a pot of message.'—Michael Billington, Illustrated London News

From Russia with Love***

GB 1963 118m Technicolor
UA / Eon (Harry Saltzman, Albert Broccoli)

A Russian spy joins an international crime organization and develops a plan to kill James Bond and steal a coding machine.
The second Bond adventure and possibly the best, with Istanbul and Venice for backdrops and climaxes involving a speeding train and a helicopter. Arrant nonsense with tongue in cheek, on a big budget.

w Richard Maibaum, Johanna Harwood, novel Ian Fleming d Terence Young ph Ted Moore m John Barry titles Robert Brownjohn

Sean Connery, Robert Shaw, Pedro Armendariz, Daniela Bianchi, Lotte Lenya, Bernard Lee, Eunice Gayson, Lois Maxwell

From the Earth to the Moon

US 1958 100m Technicolor
Waverley (Benedict Bogeaus)

In the 1880s an armaments millionaire finances a trip to the moon in a projectile fired by his own invention.
Cardboard science fiction, with an imposing cast at sea in an unspeakable script and an unseaworthy production.

w Robert Blees, James Leicester, novel Jules Verne d Byron Haskin ph Edwin DuPar m Louis Forbes ad Hal Wilson Cox

Joseph Cotten, George Sanders, Henry Daniell, Carl Esmond, Melville Cooper, Don Dubbins, Debra Paget, Patric Knowles

From the Terrace

US 1960 144m De Luxe Cinemascope
TCF / Linebrook (Mark Robson)

Life among Pennsylvania's idle rich.
Heavy-going family melodrama from a bestseller peopled with boorish characters.

w Ernest Lehman, novel John O'Hara d Mark Robson ph Leo Tover m Elmer Bernstein

Paul Newman, Joanne Woodward, Myrna Loy, Ina Balin, Leon Ames, Felix Aylmer, George Grizzard, Patrick O'Neal, Elizabeth Allen

From This Day Forward***

US 1946 95m bw
RKO (William L. Pereira)

After World War II, a New York couple think back to their early years in the poverty-stricken thirties.

Effective sentimental realism coupled with Hollywood professionalism made this film more memorable than it may sound.

w Hugo Butler, Garson Kanin, *novel* All Brides Are Beautiful by Thomas Bell *d* John Berry *ph* George Barnes *m* Leigh Harline

Joan Fontaine, Mark Stevens, Rosemary de Camp, Henry Morgan, Wally Brown, Arline Judge, Bobby Driscoll, Mary Treen

'Distinguished from the usual film about Young Love and Young Marriage by irony, poetry and realism.'—*Richard Winnington*

The Front*

US 1976 95m Metrocolor Panavision
Columbia / Persky-Bright, Devon (Martin Ritt, Charles H. Joffe)

For a small commission, a bookmaker puts his name to scripts by blacklisted writers.
Rather bland satire on the communist witch hunts of the fifties; interesting, but neither funny nor incisive enough.

w Walter Bernstein *d* Martin Ritt *ph* Michael Chapman *m* Dave Grusin

Woody Allen, Zero Mostel, Herschel Bernardi, Michael Murphy, Andrea Marcovicci, Lloyd Gough

'The pacing is off, the sequences don't flow, and the film seems sterile, unpopulated and flat.'—*New Yorker*

'A light comedy forged out of dark and authentic pain.'—*Frank Rich, New York Post*

AAN: Walter Bernstein

The Front Page***

US 1931 101m bw
Howard Hughes

A Chicago reporter wants to retire and marry, but is tricked by his scheming editor into covering one last case.
Brilliant early talkie perfectly transferring into screen terms a stage classic of the twenties. Superficially a shade primitive now, its essential power remains.

w Bartlett Cormack, Charles Lederer, *play Charles MacArthur, Ben Hecht d* Lewis Milestone *ph* Glen MacWilliams

Adolphe Menjou, Pat O'Brien, Mary Brian, Edward Everett Horton, Walter Catlett, George E. Stone, Mae Clarke, Slim Summerville, Frank McHugh

'The most riproaring movie that ever came out of Hollywood.'—*Pare Lorentz*
† Remade 1940 as *His Girl Friday* (qv).

AAN: best picture; Lewis Milestone; Adolphe Menjou

The Front Page**

US 1974 105m Technicolor Panavision
U-I (Paul Monash)

Disappointing Billy Wilder remake, relying overmuch on bad language and farcical intrusions, while tending to jettison the plot in the latter half. Some laughs nevertheless.

w Billy Wilder, I. A. L. Diamond *d* Billy Wilder *ph* Jordan S. Cronenweth *m* Billy May

Walter Matthau, Jack Lemmon, Susan Sarandon, *David Wayne*, Carol Burnett, Vincent Gardenia, Allen Garfield, Herb Edelmann, Charles Durning, *Austin Pendleton*

'The signs of coarsening in Wilder's comedy technique are unmistakable.'—*MFB*

'I can't think of a better tonic for the winter glooms.'—*Michael Billington, Illustrated London News*

Front Page Story*

GB 1953 99m bw
British Lion / Jay Lewis

A day in the life of a Fleet Street newspaper, when the editor is torn between several big stories and nearly loses his wife.
Dogged 'slice of life' drama with few excitements but some incidental entertainment and a production of routine competence.

w Jay Lewis, Jack Howells *d* Gordon Parry *ph* Gilbert Taylor *m* Jackie Brown

Jack Hawkins, Elizabeth Allan, Derek Farr, Michael Goodliffe, Martin Miller

Front Page Woman**

US 1935 82m bw
Warner (Samuel Bischoff)

Rival reporters try to outshine each other. Lively comedy-melodrama very typical of its style and time.

w Laird Doyle, Lillie Hayward, Roy Chanslor *d* Michael Curtiz *ph* Tony Gaudio *m* Leo Forbstein

Bette Davis, George Brent, Roscoe Karns, Wini Shaw, J. Carrol Naish, Walter Walker

Frontier Gal

US 1945 84m Technicolor
Universal (Michael Fessier, Ernest Pagano)
GB title: *The Bride Wasn't Willing*

An outlaw weds a saloon girl at pistol point; emerging five years later from prison, he finds he has a daughter.
Rambling western with some pretensions to humour and sentiment; not a success, but it established de Carlo as a star.

w Michael Fessier, Ernest Pagano *d* Charles
Lamont *ph* George Robinson, Charles Boyle
m Frank Skinner

Yvonne de Carlo, Rod Cameron, Sheldon
Leonard, Andy Devine, Fuzzy Knight, Andrew
Tombes, Clara Blandick

The Frozen Limits*
GB 1939   84m   bw
Gainsborough (Edward Black)

Six impecunious comedians hear of the Yukon
gold rush, and join it . . . forty years too late.
The Crazy Gang not quite at its best, but
working hard, with a few hilarious moments and
a special assist from Moore Marriott.

*w Marriott Edgar, Val Guest, J. O. C. Orton
d Marcel Varnel*

Flanagan and Allen, Nervo and Knox,
Naughton and Gold, *Moore Marriott*, Eileen
Bell, Anthony Hulme, Bernard Lee, Eric
Clavering
      'The funniest English picture yet produced . . .
it can bear comparison with *Safety Last* and *The
General*.'—*Graham Greene*

Fu Manchu
The Yellow Peril, or evil Oriental master
criminal, was created by Sax Rohmer in a 1911
novel, which led to 13 more plus some short
stories. A long series of British two-reelers was
made in the twenties, and talking films are as
follows:
1929: THE MYSTERIOUS DR FU
MANCHU, with Warner Oland (Paramount)
1930: THE RETURN OF DR FU MANCHU
(ditto)
1931: DAUGHTER OF THE DRAGON
(ditto)
1932: THE MASK OF FU MANCHU (qv)
with Boris Karloff (MGM)
1939: DRUMS OF FU MANCHU, with Henry
Brandon (Republic serial).

The remainder are British productions by Harry
Alan Towers, with Christopher Lee:
1965: THE FACE OF FU MANCHU (qv)
1966: BRIDES OF FU MANCHU
1968: THE VENGEANCE OF FU MANCHU
1969: THE BLOOD OF FU MANCHU
1970: THE CASTLE OF FU MANCHU

The Fugitive*
US 1947   104m   bw
Argosy (Merian C. Cooper, John Ford)

In an anti-clerical country, a priest is on the run.
Ford's attempt to do a Mexican *Informer* is slow
and rather boring, but the pictures are nice to
look at even though the original novel has been
totally emasculated.

w Dudley Nichols, *novel* The Power and the
Glory by Graham Greene *d John Ford*
ph Gabriel Figueroa m Richard Hageman

Henry Fonda, Dolores del Rio, Pedro
Armendariz, J. Carrol Naish, Leo Carrillo,
Ward Bond, Robert Armstrong, John Qualen
      'A symphony of light and shade, of deafening
din and silence, of sweeping movement and
repose.'—*Bosley Crowther*
      'The most pretentious travesty of a literary
work since *For Whom the Bell Tolls*.'—*Richard
Winnington*

The Fugitive Kind
US 1960   121m   bw
UA / Martin Jurow / Richard A. Shepherd /
   Pennebaker

A Mississippi drifter in a small strange town runs
into trouble with women.
Doom-laden melodrama, almost a parody of the
author's works, full of cancer patients, nympho-
dipsos, and cemetery seductions; we are
however spared the final castration.

w Tennessee Williams, Meade Roberts, *play*
Orpheus Descending by Tennessee Williams
d Sidney Lumet *ph* Boris Kaufman *m* Kenyon
Hopkins *pd* Richard Sylbert

Marlon Brando, Anna Magnani, Joanne
Woodward, Victor Jory, Maureen Stapleton, R.
G. Armstrong
      'A series of mythological engravings,
determined by a literary text and a lurid concept
of hell on earth.'—*Peter John Dyer*

Full Circle
GB / Canada 1976   97m   Eastmancolor
Paramount / Fetter-Classic (Peter Fetterman,
   Alfred Parisier)

After the death of her small daughter, a woman
leaves home to live in an old house which is
haunted by the malevolent spirit of another dead
child.
Unpleasant and incompetent supernatural
nonsense, seeking a niche somewhere between
Don't Look Now and *The Exorcist*.

w Dave Humphries, *novel* Julia by Peter Straub
d Richard Loncraine *ph* Peter Hannan *m* Colin
Towns

Mia Farrow, Keir Dullea, Tom Conti, Jill
Bennett, Robin Gammell, Cathleen Nesbitt,
Mary Morris, Edward Hardwicke

Full of Life*
US 1956   91m   bw
Columbia (Fred Kohlmar)

A poor New York/Italian couple expect a baby. Domestic comedy drama with good scenes but fatally uncertain mood.

w John Fante, from his novel *d* Richard Quine *ph* Charles Lawton Jnr *m* George Duning

Judy Holliday, Richard Conte, Esther Minciotti, Salvatore Baccaloni

The Full Treatment
GB 1960 109m bw Megascope
Columbia / Hilary / Falcon (Val Guest)
US title: *Stop Me Before I Kill*

A racing driver crashes and subsequently tries to murder his wife; psychiatric help leads to further gruesome goings-on.
Variation on *Les Diaboliques*, with very little mystery and too much talk from boring characters.

w Val Guest, Ronald Scott Thorn, *novel* Ronald Scott Thorn *d* Val Guest *ph* Gilbert Taylor *m* Stanley Black

Ronald Lewis, Diane Cilento, Claude Dauphin, Françoise Rosay, Bernard Braden

The Fuller Brush Girl*
US 1950 85m bw
Columbia (S. Sylvan Simon)
GB title: *Affairs of Sally*

A cosmetics saleslady gets involved in murder. Fairly amusing slapstick mystery with the star in good form.

w Frank Tashlin *d* Lloyd Bacon *ph* Charles Lawton *m* Heinz Roemheld

Lucille Ball, Eddie Albert, Carl Benton Reid, Gale Robbins, Jeff Connell, John Litel, Jerome Cowan, Lee Patrick

The Fuller Brush Man*
US 1948 93m bw
Columbia (S. Sylvan Simon)
GB title: *That Mad Mr Jones*

A door-to-door salesman gets involved in homicide.
Bright star comedy with slow patches.

w Frank Tashlin, Devery Freeman *d* S. Sylvan Simon *ph* Leslie White *m* Heinz Roemheld

Red Skelton, Janet Blair, Don McGuire, Adele Jergens

Fun and Fancy Free*
US 1947 73m Technicolor
Walt Disney (Ben Sharpsteen)

Cartoon stories told by and to Jiminy Cricket and Edgar Bergen.
Variable Disney ragbag including *Bongo* the

Bear, and a lengthy version of *Jack and the Beanstalk*.

w various *d* various

Fun in Acapulco
US 1963 97m Technicolor
Paramount / Hal B. Wallis

A trapeze artist becomes a lifeguard and is pursued by a lady bullfighter.
Dim comedy musical.

w Allan Weiss *d* Richard Thorpe *ph* Daniel Fapp *m* Joseph J. Lilley

Elvis Presley, Ursula Andress, Paul Lukas

Fun with Dick and Jane
US 1976 100m Metrocolor
Columbia / Peter Bart, Max Pelevsky

When an aerospace executive is fired, in order to keep up with the Joneses he and his wife embark on a life of crime.
This being a 1970s satire, they actually get away with it, providing some, but not enough, fun on the way.

w David Giler, Jerry Belson, Mordecai Richler, *story* Gerald Gaiser *d* Ted Kotcheff *ph* Fred J. Koenekamp *m* Ernest Gold

George Segal, Jane Fonda, Ed McMahon, Dick Gautier, Alan Miller

'A nitwit mixture of counterculture politics, madcap comedy and toilet humour.'—*New Yorker*

Funeral in Berlin*
GB 1967 102m Technicolor
Paramount / Harry Saltzman (Charles Kasher)

Harry Palmer is sent to Berlin to check a story that a Russian colonel wants to defect.
Initially intriguing, finally confusing, always depressing spy yarn in the sixties manner, i.e. with every character devious and no one a hero. Good production.

w Evan Jones, *novel* The Berlin Memorandum by Len Deighton *d* Guy Hamilton *ph* Otto Heller *m* Konrad Elfers *pd* Ken Adam

Michael Caine, *Oscar Homolka*, Eva Renzi, Paul Hubschmid, *Hugh Burden*, Guy Doleman, Rachel Gurney

'So many twists that even Sherlock Holmes might have been baffled . . . before long it becomes difficult to remember who is watching whom and why, or indeed whether anybody *was* watching anybody at any given moment.'—*Tom Milne*

† Second in the Harry Palmer series, of which the first was *The Ipcress File* and the third *Billion Dollar Brain* (both qv).

Funny Face**
US 1956   103m   Technicolor   Vistavision
Paramount (Roger Edens)

A fashion editor and photographer choose a shy
bookstore attendant as their 'quality woman'.
Stylish, wistful musical with good numbers but
drawn-out dialogue; finally a shade too
sophisticated and a whole lot too fey.

w Leonard Gershe d Stanley Donen ph Ray
June m/ly George and Ira Gershwin

Fred Astaire, Audrey Hepburn, Kay Thompson,
Michel Auclair, Robert Flemyng

AAN: Leonard Gershe; Ray June

Funny Girl**
US 1968   169m   Technicolor   Panavision
70
Columbia / Rastar (Ray Stark)

Fanny Brice, an ugly Jewish girl from New
York's east side, becomes a big Broadway star
but loses her husband in the process.
Interminable cliché-ridden musical drama
relieved by a few good numbers, high production
gloss and the unveiling of a new powerhouse
star.

w Isobel Lennart, from her play d William
Wyler ph Harry Stradling md Walter Scharf
m Jule Styne ly Bob Merrill pd Gene Callahan

Barbra Streisand, Omar Sharif, Walter
Pidgeon, Kay Medford, Anne Francis, Lee
Allen, Gerald Mohr, Frank Faylen

AA: Barbra Streisand
AAN: best picture; Harry Stradling; Walter
Scharf; Kay Medford; title song

Funny Lady*
US 1975   138m   Eastmancolor
Columbia / Rastar / Persky–Bright / Vista
(Ray Stark)

Fanny Brice marries Billy Rose.
Unnecessary sequel to the above, entirely
predictable and far from the truth, but with the
occasional pleasures that a high budget brings.

w Jay Presson Allen, Arnold Schulman
d Herbert Ross ph James Wong Howe
m/ly various md Peter Matz pd George Jenkins

Barbra Streisand, James Caan, Ben Vereen,
Omar Sharif, Roddy McDowall, Larry Gates
'The plot line is as slackly handled as the
milieu.'—Geoff Brown
'As Fanny Brice, Streisand is no longer
human; she's like a bitchy female impersonator
imitating Barbra Streisand.'—New Yorker

AAN: James Wong Howe; Peter Matz; song
'How Lucky Can You Get' (m/ly Fred Ebb,
John Kander)

A Funny Thing Happened on the Way to the Forum**
US 1966   99m   De Luxe
UA / Quadrangle (Melvin Frank)

In ancient Rome, a conniving slave schemes to
win his freedom.
Bawdy farce from a Broadway musical inspired
by Plautus but with a New York Jewish
atmosphere. The film pays scant attention to the
comic numbers that made the show a hit, but
adds some style of its own, including a free-for-
all slapstick climax.

w Melvin Frank, Michael Pertwee, musical
comedy Burt Shevelove, Larry Gelbart
m/ly Stephen Sondheim md Ken Thorne
d Richard Lester ph Nicolas Roeg pd Tony
Walton titles Richard Williams

Zero Mostel, Phil Silvers, Michael Crawford,
Jack Gilford, Michael Hordern, Buster Keaton,
Patricia Jessel, Leon Greene, Beatrix Lehmann
'Actors have to be very fast and very sly to
make themselves felt amid the flash and glitter of
a characteristic piece of Lester film-mosaic.'—
John Russell Taylor
'He proceeds by fits and starts and leaves
jokes suspended in mid-air . . . like coitus
interruptus going on forever.'—Pauline Kael

AA: Ken Thorne

Funnyman
US 1967   100m   bw and colour
Korty Films (Hugh McGraw, Stephen
Schmidt)

A satirical comedian seeks some better
occupation in life, but finally agrees he's best as a
comic.
One suspects Korty has seen Sullivan's Travels
several times; but even though his film tries hard,
it finally provides more yawns than appreciative
chuckles.

w John Korty, Peter Bonerz d John Korty
ph John Korty m Peter Schickele

Peter Bonerz, Sandra Archer, Carol Androsky,
Gerald Hiken
'It has its dull patches, but it made me laugh
louder and more often than any other film this
year.'—Michael Billington, Illustrated London
News

The Furies*
US 1950   109m   bw
Paramount / Hal B. Wallis

A cattle baron feuds with his tempestuous
daughter.
Interesting but heavy-going western, more
solemn than stimulating despite its Freudian
excesses.

w Charles Schnee, *novel* Niven Busch
d Anthony Mann *ph* Victor Milner *m* Franz
Waxman

Barbara Stanwyck, *Walter Huston*, Wendell
Corey, Judith Anderson, Gilbert Roland,
Thomas Gomez, Beulah Bondi, Wallace Ford,
Albert Dekker, Blanche Yurka
   'An immoral saga, capably mounted, with
some pretentious psychological trimmings.'—
MFB

AAN: Victor Milner

The Further Perils of Laurel and Hardy***
US 1967 99m bw
TCF / *Robert Youngson*

A compilation of longish extracts from the stars'
silent comedies, including *Early to Bed, The
Second Hundred Years, Should Married Men
Go Home, You're Darn Tootin', Habeas Corpus,
That's My Wife*, and *Leave 'Em Laughing*. The
producer is to be congratulated on refurbishing
so many deteriorating negatives, though the
commentary leaves much to be desired.

w, ed Robert Youngson *m* John Parker

Fury***
US 1936 94m bw
MGM (Joseph L. Mankiewicz)

A traveller in a small town is mistaken for a
murderer and apparently lynched; he escapes in
a fire but determines to have his persecutors
hanged for his murder.
Powerful drama which becomes artificial in its
latter stages but remains its director's best
American film.

w Bartlett Cormack, Fritz Lang, *story* Norman
Krasna *d* Fritz Lang *ph* Joseph Ruttenberg
m Franz Waxman

Spencer Tracy, Sylvia Sidney, Bruce Cabot,
Walter Abel, Edward Ellis, Walter Brennan,
Frank Albertson
   'The surface of American life has been rubbed
away: *Fury* gets down to the bones of the thing
and shows them for what they are.'—*C. A.
Lejeune*
   'Since the screen began to talk, no other
serious film except *The Front Page* has so clearly
shown that here is a new art and what this new
art can do.'—*John Marks*
   'Everyday events and people suddenly took on
tremendous and horrifying proportion; even the
most insignificant details had a pointed
meaning.'—*Lewis Jacobs*
   'For half its length a powerful and documented
piece of fiction about a lynching, and for the
remaining half a desperate attempt to make love,

lynching and the Hays Office come out even.'—
Otis Ferguson

AAN: Norman Krasna

The Fury*
US 1978 117m De Luxe
TCF / Frank Yablans (Ron Preissman)

The head of a government institute for psychic
research finds that his own son is wanted by
terrorists who wish to use his lethal psychic
powers.
Flashy, kaleidoscopic nonsense which never
even begins to make sense but is used as the basis
for the director's showing-off, which is
occasionally worth a glance for those with
hardened stomachs.

w John Farris, from his novel *d* Brian de Palma
ph Richard H. Kline *m* John Williams

Kirk Douglas, John Cassavetes, Carrie
Snodgress, Charles Durning, Andrew Stevens,
Amy Irving, Fiona Lewis
   'A conception of cinema that is closer to Ken
Russell than Alfred Hitchcock.'—*Richard
Combs, MFB*

Fury at Furnace Creek*
US 1948 88m bw
TCF

A westerner clears the name of his father, a
general accused of diverting a wagon train into
hostile Indian territory.
Adequate old-fashioned western with a good
story line and standard excitements.

w Charles G. Booth *d* H. Bruce Humberstone
ph Harry Jackson *m* David Raksin *md* Alfred
Newman

Victor Mature, Coleen Gray, Glenn Langan,
Reginald Gardiner

Fury at Smugglers' Bay
GB 1960 96m Eastmancolor
Panascope
(Regal) Mijo (Michael Green, Joe Vegoda)

The squire of a Cornish village is being
blackmailed by the vicious leader of a gang of
wreckers.
Watchable, then forgettable variation on
Jamaica Inn.

wd John Gilling *ph* Harry Waxman *m* Harold
Geller

Peter Cushing, John Fraser, Bernard Lee,
William Franklyn, June Thorburn, Miles
Malleson, Michele Mercier, George Coulouris

Futureworld*
US 1976 107m Metrocolor
AIP (James T. Aubrey Jnr, Paul Lazarus III)

The robot factory seen in *Westworld* (qv) now
aims at world domination by duplicating
influential figures.
Amusing and fairly suspenseful fantasy with a
bigger budget than its predecessor.

w Mayo Simon, George Schenck *d* Richard T.
Heffron *ph* Howard Schwarz, Sol Polito
m Fred Karlin

Peter Fonda, Blythe Danner, Arthur Hill, Yul
Brynner, John Ryan, Stuart Margolin, Jim
Antonio

Fuzz*
US 1972 93m De Luxe
UA / Filmways / Javelin (Jack Farren)

Detectives of Boston's 87th precinct try to catch
a rapist.

A black farce devoted to police incompetence,
though taken from a straight 'Ed McBain' story.
Brisk and sometimes funny.

w *Evan Hunter* ('Ed McBain') *d* Richard A.
Colla *ph* Jacques Marquette *m* Dave Grusin

Burt Reynolds, Raquel Welch, Jack Weston, Yul
Brynner, Tom Skerritt, James McEachin

The Fuzzy Pink Nightgown
US 1957 88m bw
UA / Russ–Field (Robert Waterfield)

A glamorous film star falls in love with her
kidnapper.
Unendurable cheap romantic farce.

w Richard Alan Simmons, *novel* Sylvia Tate
d Norman Taurog *ph* Joseph La Shelle

Jane Russell, Ralph Meeker, Keenan Wynn,
Fred Clark

G

GI Blues

US 1960 104m Technicolor
Paramount / Hal B. Wallis (Paul Nathan)

A guitar-playing gunner with the American
army in West Germany falls for a cabaret
dancer.
Routine star vehicle marking Presley's return
from military service.

w Edmund Beloin, Henry Garson d Norman
Taurog ph Loyal Griggs m Joseph J. Lilley

Elvis Presley, Juliet Prowse, Robert Ivers,
Leticia Roman, Arch Johnson

G Men***

US 1935 85m bw
Warner (Lou Edelman)

A young lawyer becomes a G-man to avenge the
murder of his best friend, and finds himself
tracking down another old friend who is a
gangster.
In the face of mounting criticism of their
melodramas making heroes of gangsters,
Warners pulled a clever switch by showing the
same crimes from a different angle, that of the
law enforcer. As an action show it became pretty
good after a slow start.

w Seton I. Miller d William Keighley ph Sol
Polito md Leo F. Forbstein

James Cagney, Ann Dvorak, Margaret Lindsay,
Robert Armstrong, Barton MacLane, Lloyd
Nolan, William Harrigan

'The gangster is back, racing madly through
one of the fastest melodramas ever made.'—
New York Sun
'The headiest dose of gunplay that Hollywood
has unleashed in recent months.'—André
Sennwald, New York Times

Gable and Lombard

US 1976 131m Technicolor
Universal (Harry Korshak)

After Carole Lombard's death in a 1942 air
crash, Clark Gable recalls their years together.
Vulgar and inaccurate representation of two
Hollywood stars of the thirties; it fails even as
titillation.

w Barry Sandler d Sidney J. Furie ph Jordan S.

Cronenweth m Michel Legrand pd Edward
Carfagno

James Brolin, Jill Clayburgh, Allen Garfield (as
Louis B. Mayer), Red Buttons, Joanne Linville

'A limply raunchy, meaningless movie with
nothing to say about the movies, about love, or
about stardom.'—New Yorker

Gabriel over the White House*

US 1933 87m bw
MGM / Walter Wanger

A crook becomes president and mysteriously
reforms.
Pleasing, dated New Deal fantasy.

w Carey Wilson, Bertram Bloch, novel Rinehard
by T. F. Tweed d Gregory La Cava ph Bert
Glennon m William Axt

Walter Huston, Karen Morley, Franchot Tone,
C. Henry Gordon, Samuel S. Hinds, Jean
Parker, Dickie Moore

Gaby

US 1956 97m Eastmancolor
  Cinemascope
MGM (Edwin H. Knopf)

†Flabby remake of Waterloo Bridge (qv);
saccharine, fussy and outmoded, despite
updated settings and a happy ending.

w Albert Hackett, Frances Goodrich, Charles
Lederer d Curtis Bernhardt ph Robert Planck
m Conrad Salinger

Leslie Caron, John Kerr, Cedric Hardwicke,
Taina Elg, Margalo Gillmore

Gaiety George

GB 1946 98m bw
Embassy (George King)

The career in the London theatre of Irish
impresario George Howard in the early part of
the century.
Tepid musical biopic.

w Katherine Strueby d George King

Richard Greene, Ann Todd, Peter Graves, Hazel
Court, Leni Lynn, Ursula Jeans, Morland
Graham, Frank Pettingell

Gaily, Gaily**
US 1969 117m De Luxe
UA / Mirisch / Cartier
GB title: *Chicago, Chicago*

The early life on a Chicago newspaper of Ben Hecht.

Busy, farcical, melodramatic, always interesting biopic of the formative years of a celebrated literary figure.

w Abram S. Ginnes, book Ben Hecht d Norman Jewison ph Richard Kline *m* Henry Mancini *pd* Robert Boyle

Beau Bridges, Melina Mercouri, *Brian Keith,* George Kennedy, Hume Cronyn, Margot Kidder, Wilfrid Hyde White, Melodie Johnson, John Randolph

Galileo*
GB 1975 145m Eastmancolor
Ely Landau / Cinevision

In the 17th century, a poor Italian mathematics teacher has trouble establishing his 'heretical' astronomical theories.

Overlong play-on-celluloid for the American Film Theatre: very decently made and acted, it lacks inspiration.

w Barbara Bray, Joseph Losey, *play* Bertolt Brecht *d* Joseph Losey *ph* Michael Reed *m* Hanns Eisler

Topol, Edward Fox, Michel Lonsdale, Richard O'Callaghan, Tom Conti, Judy Parfitt, Patrick Magee, Michael Gough, John Gielgud, Colin Blakely, Margaret Leighton, Clive Revill

The Gallant Hours*
US 1959 115m bw
UA / James Cagney / Robert Montgomery

Episodes in the career of Admiral William F. Halsey.

Adulatory but physically restrained biopic which covers World War II with barely a scene outside control room sets: interesting but finally too talky.

w Beirne Lay Jnr, Frank D. Gilroy *d* Robert Montgomery *ph* Joe MacDonald *m* Roger Wagner

James Cagney, Dennis Weaver, Richard Jaeckel, Ward Costello, Carl Benton Reid
'Imaginatively conceived but erroneously realized.'—*Robert Vas*

Gallant Journey
US 1946 86m bw
Columbia

The life of an early American aviation pioneer. Curious biopic, very tentatively done, about an inventor so obscure as to be virtually fictitious. Sentimental, artificial, but harmless.

w Byron Morgan, William A. Wellman *d* William A. Wellman *ph* Burnett Guffey *m* Martin Skiles

Glenn Ford, Janet Blair, Charles Ruggles, Henry Travers, Arthur Shields

Gallant Lady
US 1933 84m bw
Darryl F. Zanuck

A woman allows her illegitimate son to be adopted, but years later marries his stepfather. A tearjerker very typical of its time, moderately well assembled; later remade as *Always Goodbye* (qv).

w Sam Mintz, *story* Gilbert Emery, Doug Doty *d* Gregory La Cava *ph* Peverell Marley

Ann Harding, Clive Brook, Otto Kruger, Tullio Carminati, Dickie Moore, Janet Beecher

The Galloping Major*
GB 1951 82m bw
British Lion / Romulus (Monja Danischewsky)

A group of suburbanites form a syndicate to buy a racehorse.

Rather contrived and imitative sub-Ealing comedy which fails to generate much steam.

w Monja Danischewsky, Henry Cornelius *d* Henry Cornelius *ph* Stan Pavey *m* Georges Auric

Basil Radford, Janette Scott, Hugh Griffith, Jimmy Hanley, René Ray, Joyce Grenfell, Sidney Tafler, Charles Victor, A. E. Matthews

Gambit**
US 1966 109m Techniscope
Universal (Leo L. Fuchs)

A cockney thief conspires with a Eurasian girl to rob a multi-millionaire of a prize statue. An enjoyably light pattern of cross and double cross is well sustained to the end.

w Jack Davies, Alvin Sargent d Ronald Neame *ph* Clifford Stine *m* Maurice Jarre

Michael Caine, Shirley Maclaine, Herbert Lom, John Abbott, Roger C. Carmel, Arnold Moss

The Gambler**
US 1975 111m Eastmancolor
Paramount (Irwin Winkler, Robert Chartoff)

A compulsive gambler has a will to lose. Flashily made but basically uninteresting sub-Freudian study, vaguely based on Dostoievsky.

w James Tomack d Karel Reisz ph Victor J. Kemper m Mahler md Jerry Fielding

James Caan, Paul Sorvino, Lauren Hutton, Morris Carnovsky, Jacqueline Brookes, Burt Young

Gambler from Natchez
US 1954 88m Technicolor
TCF / Panoramic

A professional gambler returns to New Orleans to avenge his father's murder, and disposes of his enemies one by one.
Mildly watchable semi-western with a plot borrowed from *The Count of Monte Cristo*.

w Gerald Drayson Adams, Irving Wallace d Henry Levin ph Lloyd Ahern md Lionel Newman

Dale Robertson, Debra Paget, Thomas Gomez, Kevin McCarthy

Gambling Lady*
US 1934 66m bw
Warner

The daughter of a gambling suicide follows in father's footsteps and becomes involved in murder.
Fast-paced melodrama with a happy ending: smart entertainment of its time.

w Ralph Block, Doris Malloy d Archie Mayo ph George Barnes

Barbara Stanwyck, Joel McCrea, Pat O'Brien, Claire Dodd, C. Aubrey Smith, Robert Barrat, Philip Reed

A Game of Death
US 1945 72m bw
RKO

Cheap remake of *The Most Dangerous Game* (qv); excitement dissipated by poor handling.

w Norman Houston d Robert Wise ph J. Roy Hunt m Paul Sawtell

John Loder, Audrey Long, Edgar Barrier, Russell Wade, Russell Hicks

Games*
US 1967 100m Techniscope
Universal (George Edwards)

A sophisticated New York couple play complex games, one of which turns out to have a deadly effect.
Tedious variation on *Les Diaboliques*, with interesting moments.

w Gene Kearney d Curtis Harrington ph William A. Fraker m Samuel Matlovsky

Simone Signoret, James Caan, Katharine Ross,

Don Stroud, Kent Smith, Estelle Winwood, Marjorie Bennett

The Games*
GB 1970 97m De Luxe Panavision
TCF (Lester Linsk)

Four men in various parts of the world prepare to take part in the marathon at the Rome Olympics.
Tepid multi-drama with good locations and a well-shot and exciting climactic race.

w Erich Segal, *novel* Hugh Atkinson d Michael Winner ph Robert Paynter m Francis Lai

Stanley bbaker, Michael Crawford, Ryan O'Neal, Charles Aznavour, Jeremy Kemp, Elaine Taylor, Kent Smith, Mona Washbourne

The Gang That Couldn't Shoot Straight
US 1971 96m Metrocolor
MGM (Robert Chartoff, Irwin Winkler)

Members of the New York Mafia organize a cycle race and start antagonisms that end in mass murder.
Unfunny black comedy with all concerned gesticulating wildly.

w Waldo Salt, *novel* Jimmy Breslin d James Goldstone ph Owen Roizman m Dave Grusin

Jerry Orbach, Leigh Taylor-Young, Jo Van Fleet, Lionel Stander, Robert de Niro, Herve Villechaize, Joe Santos

The Gang's All Here*
GB 1939 77m bw
ABP (Walter C. Mycroft, Jack Buchanan)
US titleb; *The Amazing Mr Forrest*

An insurance investigator goes undercover among gangsters.
Lively comedy-melodrama.

w Ralph Spence d Thornton Freeland

Jack Buchanan, Googie Withers, Edward Everett Horton, Syd Walker, Otto Kruger, Jack La Rue, Walter Rilla

The Gang's All Here**
US 1943 103m Technicolor
TCF (William Le Baron)
GB title: *The Girls He Left Behind*

A serviceman is caught between a fiery entertainer and a Park Avenue socialite.
Frenetic wartime musical with some of Busby Berkeley's most outré choreography (e.g. The Lady in the Tutti Frutti Hat) and gleamingly effective Technicolor.

w Walter Bullock d/ch Busby Berkeley ph Edward Cronjager md Alfred Newman - t2songs Leo Robin, Harry Warren

Alice Faye, Carmen Miranda, James Ellison, Phil Baker, Benny Goodman, Charlotte Greenwood, Eugene Pallette, Edward Everett Horton

'Those who consider Berkeley a master consider this film his masterpiece.'—*New Yorker, 1976*

Gangway*
GB 1937　89m　bw
GFD / Gaumont

A girl reporter poses as a star's maid and is accused of theft.
Mildly pleasing star vehicle.

w Lesser Samuels, Sonnie Hale　*d* Sonnie Hale

Jessie Metthews, Barry Mackay, Pat Pendleton, Noel Madison, Alastair Sim

The Garden of Allah**
US 1936　80m　Technicolor
David O. Selznick

A disenchanted socialite falls in love with a renegade monk in the Algerian desert.
Arty old-fashioned romantic star vehicle; great to look at, and marking a genuine advance in colour photography, but dramatically a bit of a drag.

w W. P. Lipscomb, Lynn Riggs, *novel* Robert Hichens　*d* Richard Boleslawski　*ph* W. Howard Greene, Harotd Rosson　*m* Max Steiner
ad Sturges Carne, Lyle Wheeler, Edward Boyle

Marlene Dietrich, Charles Boyer, Basil Rathbone, Tilly Losch

'Hopelessly dated folderol.'—*J. R. Parish*
'The juiciest tale of woe ever, produced in poshly lurid colour, with a Max Steiner score poured on top.'—*Judith Crist*

Garden of Evil*
US 1954　100m　Technicolor
　Cinemascope
TCF (Charles Brackett)

En route to the Californian goldfields an ex-sheriff and a gambler help a woman to rescue her husband from a mine, but are trapped by Indians.
High-flying western melodrama with the principals glowering at each other. Stock situations quite skilfully compiled.

w Frank Fenton　*d* Henry Hathaway　*ph* Milton Krasner　*m* Bernerd Herrmann

Susan Hayward, Gary Cooper, Richard Widmark, Hugh Marlowe, Cameron Mitchell

The Garden of the Finzi-Continis**
Italy / West Germany 1970　95m
　Eastmancolor
Documento Film / CCC Filmkunst (Gianni Hecht Lucari, Arthur Cohn)

In 1938, a family of wealthy Italian Jews sees its world collapse, with a concentration camp as the next destination.
A dreamlike, poignant, and very beautiful film.

w Tullio Pinelli, Valerio Zurlini, Franco Brusati, Ugo Pirro, Vittorio Bonicelli, Alain Katz, *novel* Giorgio Bassani　*d* Vittorio de Sica
ph Ennio Guarnieri　*m* Manuel de Sica

Dominique Sanda, Lino Capolicchio, Helmut Berger, Romolo Valli, Fabio Testi

AAN: script

The Garment Jungle*
US 1957　88m　bw
Columbia (Harry Kleiner)

Union and gangster problems abound for a family in the New York clothing business.
Reasonably powerful melodrama fashioned from familiar material in the wake of *On the Waterfront*.

w Harry Kleiner　*d* Robert Aldrich, Vincent Sherman　*ph* Joseph Biroc　*m* Leith Stevens

Lee J. Cobb, Kerwin Mathews, Gia Scala, Richard Boone, Valerie French, Robert Loggia, Joseph Wiseman

Gas! or It Became Necessary to Destroy the World in Order to Save It
US 1970　79m　Movielab
AIP / San Jacinto (Roger Corman)

A gas which speeds up the ageing process is accidentally released and kills everyone over twenty-five.
Psychedelic sci-fi for the Easy Rider set. Very mildly diverting.

w Graham Armitage　*d* Roger Corman　*ph* Ron Dexter　*m* Country Joe and the Fish

Robert Corff, Elaine Giftos, Pat Patterson, Graham Armitage, Alex Wilson, Ben Vereen, Bud Cort

Gasbags*
GB 1940　77m　bw
Gainsborough (Edward Black)

Airmen stranded in Germany by a barrage balloon return in a captured secret weapon.
Fast-moving knockabout from the Crazy Gang; often inventive despite reach-me-down script and production.

w Val Guest, Marriott Edgar　*d* Marcel Varnel

Flanagan and Allen, Nervo and Knox,
Naughton and Gold, Moore Marriott, Wally
Patch, Peter Gawthorne, Frederick Valf

Gaslight****
GB 1939   88m   bw
British National (John Corfield)
US title: *Angel Street*

A Victorian schizophrenic drives his wife insane
when she seems likely to stumble on his guilty
secret of an old murder and hidden rubies.
Modest but absolutely effective film version of a
superb piece of suspense theatre.

w A. R. Rawlinson, Bridget Boland, *play Patrick
Hamilton d Thorold Dickinson*

*Anton Walbrook, Diana Wynyard, Frank
Pettingell*, Cathleen Cordell, Robert Newton,
Jimmy Hanley
   'The electric sense of tension and mid-
Victorian atmosphere are entirely cinematic.'—
Sequence, 1950

Gaslight**
US 1944   114m   bw
MGM (Arthur Hornblow Jnr)
GB title: *The Murder in Thornton Square*

Grossly overblown and less effective version of
the above, but with moments of power, effective
performances and superior production.

w John Van Druten, Walter Reisch, John L.
Balderston *d George Cukor ph Joseph
Ruttenberg m* Bronislau Kaper *ad Cedric
Gibbons*

Charles Boyer, Ingrid Bergman, Joseph Cotten,
Dame May Whitty, Barbara Everest, *Angela
Lansbury*, Edmund Breon, Halliwell Hobbes

AA: Ingrid Bergman
AAN: best picture; script; Joseph Ruttenberg;
Charles Boyer; Angela Lansbury

Gate of Hell*
Japan 1953   90m   Eastmancolor
original title: *Jigokumon*

After a 12th-century war, a soldier demands as
his prize a woman who has helped him; but she is
married.
Curious traditional Japanese saga, its emphases
strange to western eyes and ears. Its colour,
however, is devastatingly beautiful.

wd Teinosuke Kinugasa, *novel* Kan Kikuchi
ph Kohei Sugiyama m Yasushi Akutagawa

Machiko Kyo, Kazuo Hasegawa, Isao
Yamagata

A Gathering of Eagles
US 1962   115m   Eastmancolor
U-I (Sy Bartlett)

A colonel becomes unpopular when he strives to
improve the efficiency of a Strategic Air
Command base.
Tame revamp of *Twelve O'clock High* without
the justification of war; all strictly routine and
perfectly dull.

w Robert Pirosh *d* Delbert Mann *ph* Russell
Harlan *m* Jerry Goldsmith

Rock Hudson, Mary Peach, Rod Taylor, Barry
Sullivan, Kevin McCarthy

Gator
US 1976   116m   De Luxe   Todd AO 35
UA / Levy-Gardner-Laven

A convicted moonshiner is blackmailed into
becoming a government undercover man in the
organization of a hoodlum.
Shambling mixture of action, violence, and raw
humour.

w William Norton *d* Burt Reynolds *ph* William
A. Fraker *m* Charles Bernstein

Burt Reynolds, Jack Weston, Lauren Hutton,
Jerry Reed, Alice Ghostley, Dub Taylor, Mike
Douglas
   'The relentless violence, the sentimentality, the
raucous stag party humour, the inability to cut
off a scene once it has made its point, attest to the
influence of Robert Aldrich.'—*Philip French,
The Times*

The Gaunt Stranger*
GB 1938   73m   bw
Northwood / Capad (Ealing) (S. C. Balcon)
US title: *The Phantom Strikes*

A criminal master of disguise threatens to kill a
much more despicable criminal at an appointed
hour . . . and does so despite police protection.
A highly reliable suspenser of which this is
perhaps the best film version.

w Sidney Gilliat, *novel and play* The Ringer by
Edgar Wallace *d* Walter Forde *ph* Ronald
Neame

Sonnie Hale, Wilfrid Lawson, Alexander Knox,
Louise Henry, Patricia Roc, Patrick Barr, John
Longden, George Merritt
† Other versions, as *The Ringer*, appeared in
1931 and 1953.

The Gauntlet*
US 1977   109m   De Luxe   Panavision
Warner / Malpaso (Robert Daly)

A disreputable cop is assigned to escort a foul-
mouthed prostitute to a courtroom across

country, through the gauntlet of baddies who want them both dead.
The epitome of seventies violence, with no excuse except to stage one detailed shoot-up or explosion after another. Well done for those who like this sort of thing.

w Michael Butler, Dennis Shryack *d* Clint Eastwood *ph* Rexford Metz *m* Jerry Fielding

Clint Eastwood, Sondra Locke, Pat Hingle, William Prince

Gawain and the Green Knight*
GB 1973   93m   Technicolor   Panavision
UA / Sancrest (Philip Breen)

The medieval legend of a supernatural knight who challenges the king's men to kill him.
Enterprising if unsuccessful low-budget attempt to create a medieval world; too long by half.

w Philip Green, Stephen Weeks *d* Stephen Weeks *ph* Ian Wilson *m* Ron Goodwin *ad* Anthony Woollard

Murray Head, Ciaran Madden, Nigel Green, Anthony Sharp, Robert Hardy, Murray Melvin

The Gay Bride
US 1934   80m   bw
MGM

A gold-digging chorus girl marries a racketeer but soon becomes a widow.
Misfiring satirical melodrama which quickly becomes tedious.

w Bella and Samuel Spewack, *story* Repeal by Charles Francis Coe *d* Jack Conway *ph* Ray June

Carole Lombard, Chester Morris, Zasu Pitts, Nat Pendleton, Leo Carrillo

The Gay Deception*
US 1935   79m   bw
TCF (Jesse L. Lasky)

A Ruritanian prince becomes a doorman at a swank New York hotel, and marries a secretary.
Lightly-handled Cinderella story showing most of its director's accomplishment.

w Stephen Morehouse Avery, Don Hartman *d* William Wyler *ph* Joseph Valentine

Francis Lederer, Frances Dee, Benita Hume, Alan Mowbray, Akim Tamiroff, Lennox Pawle, Richard Carle, Lionel Stander

AAN: script

The Gay Desperado**
US 1936   85m   bw
Mary Pickford

An heiress is held for ransom by a romantic bandit.
Very light, quite amusing, sometimes irritatingly skittish musical spoof sparked by the director's ideas.

d Rouben Mamoulian *m* Alfred Newman

Ida Lupino, Nino Martini, Leo Carrillo, Harold Huber, Mischa Auer

'One of the best light comedies of the year . . . Mr Mamoulian's camera is very persuasive.'— *Graham Greene*

'While some of the show is fetching, the ideas mostly misfire and the spell is fitful and unsure.'—*Otis Ferguson*

The Gay Divorcee****
US 1934   107m   bw
RKO (Pandro S. Berman)
GB title: *The Gay Divorce*

A would-be divorcee in a Brighton hotel mistakes an author who loves her for a professional co-respondent.
Wildly and hilariously dated comedy musical with splendidly archaic comedy routines supporting Hollywood's great new dance team in their first big success. Not much dancing, but 'The Continental' is a show-stopper.

w George Marion Jnr, Dorothy Yost, Edward Kaufman, *musical comedy* Dwight Taylor *d* Mark Sandrich *ph* David Abel *md* Max Steiner *songs* various *sp* Vernon Walker *ad* Van Nest Polglase, Carroll Clark

Fred Astaire, Ginger Rogers, Edward Everett Horton, Alice Brady, Erik Rhodes, Eric Blore, Lillian Miles, Betty Grable

'The gayest of mad musicals!'—*publicity*
'The plot is trivial French farce, but the dances are among the wittiest and most lyrical expressions of American romanticism on the screen.'—*New Yorker, 1977*

AA: song 'The Continental' (*m* Con Conrad, *ly* Herb Magidson)
AAN: best picture; musical adaptation (Ken Webb, Samuel Hoffenstein)

Gay Purree*
US 1962   85m   Technicolor
UPA

A country cat goes to Paris and is Shanghaied.
Feature cartoon similar to Disney's later *The Aristocats* and about as good, i.e. not quite up to the best standards.

w Dorothy and Chuck Jones *d* Abe Levitow *md* Mort Lindsey

voices Judy Garland, Robert Goulet, Hermione Gingold

The Gay Sisters*
US 1942   110m   bw
Warner (Henry Blanke)

Three sisters refuse to sell their aristocratic New York mansion to make way for development. Slowish but quite interesting family drama with Chekhovian touches.

w Lenore Coffee, *novel* Stephen Longstreet d Irving Rapper ph Sol Polito m Max Steiner

Barbara Stanwyck, George Brent, Geraldine Fitzgerald, Donald Crisp, *Gig Young* (so named after his part in this film; formerly Byron Barr), Nancy Coleman, Gene Lockhart, Larry Simms, Donald Woods, Grant Mitchell

The Gazebo*
US 1959   102m   bw
MGM / Avon (Lawrence Weingarten)

A TV writer kills a blackmailer (he thinks) and hides his body in the garden.
Frenetic black comedy which must have worked better on the stage but produces a few laughs.

w George Wells, *play* Alec Coppel d George Marshall ph Paul C. Vogel m Jeff Alexander

Glenn Ford, Debbie Reynolds, Carl Reiner, John McGiver, Mabel Albertson, Doro Merande, Zasu Pitts, Martin Landau

The Geisha Boy
US 1958   98m   Technicolor   Vistavision
Paramount (Jerry Lewis)

A third-rate magician joins a USO entertainment tour in Japan.
Disconnected farce which amuses only fitfully, and actively displeases when it becomes sentimental with the star drooling over a baby.

wd Frank Tashlin ph Haskell Boggs m Walter Scharf

Jerry Lewis, Marie MacDonald, Barton MacLane, Sessue Hayakawa, Suzanne Pleshette

The Gene Krupa Story
US 1959   101m   bw
Columbia (Philip A. Waxman)
GB title: *Drum Crazy*

A successful jazz drummer is convicted on a drugs charge and falls from grace.
Dreary biopic with the expected music track.

w Orin Jannings d Don Weis ph Charles Lawton Jnr m Leith Stevens

Sal Mineo, Susan Kohner, James Darren, Susan Oliver, Yvonne Craig, Lawrence Dobkin, Celia Lovsky; and Red Nichols, Shelly Manne, Buddy Lester

The General****
US 1926   80m approx (24 fps)   bw   silent
Buster Keaton

A confederate train driver gets his train and his girl back when they are stolen by Union soldiers.
Slow-starting, then hilarious action comedy, often voted one of the best ever made. Its sequence of sight gags, each topping the one before, is an incredible joy to behold.

w Al Boasberg, Charles Smith d Buster Keaton, Clyde Bruckman ph J. Devereux Jennings, Bert Haines

Buster Keaton, Marion Mack, Glen Cavander
  'It has all the sweet earnestness in the world. It is about trains, frontier America, flower-faced girls.'—*New Yorker, 1977*
† The story is based on an actual incident of the Civil War, treated more seriously in *The Great Locomotive Chase*.
†† The screenplay with 1,400 freeze frames was issued in 1976 in the Film Classics Library (editor, Richard Anobile).

The General Died at Dawn**
US 1936   93m   bw
Paramount

A mercenary in China overcomes an evil warlord and falls in love with a spy.
Heavy-going but very decorative studio-bound intrigue which seems to take place on the old *Shanghai Express* sets with an extra infusion of dry ice. An intellectual's picture of its day.

w Clifford Odets d Lewis Milestone ph Victor Milner m Werner Janssen, Gerard Carbonara

Gary Cooper, Madeleine Carroll, *Akim Tamiroff, Dudley Digges*, Porter Hall, *William Frawley*
  'If it were not for a rather ludicrous ending, this would be one of the best thrillers for some years.'—*Graham Greene*
  'In terms of cinematic invention, a fascinating technical exercise.'—*John Baxter, 1968*
  'A curious study in exoticism.'—*NFT, 1974*

AAN: Victor Milner; Werner Janssen; Akim Tamiroff

The General Line**
USSR 1929   90m (24 fps)   bw   silent
Sovkino
original title: *Staroye i Novoye;* aka: *Old and New*

A country woman helps to start a village co-operative.
A slight piece of propaganda, put together with all of Eisenstein's magnificent cinematic resources: the cream separator demonstration is

one of the most famous montage sequences in cinema history.

wd Sergei Eisenstein co-d Grigori Alexandrov ph Edouard Tissé

Marta Lapkina and a cast of non-professionals

Il Generale della Rovere
Italy / France 1959   137m   bw
Zebra / Gaumont (Morris Ergas)

During World War II, a con man is persuaded to impersonate a dead general, and becomes so imbued with the latter's code of honour that he goes before a firing squad rather than expose a partisan.
An unlikely piece of tragic whimsy with some good acting, but imperfectly assembled and at too great length.

w Sergio Amidei, Diego Fabbri, Indro Montanelli, Roberto Rossellini *d* Roberto Rossellini *ph* Carlo Carlini *m* Renzo Rossellini

Vittorio de Sica, Hannes Messemer, Sandra Milo, Giovanna Ralli, Anne Vernon

AAN: script

Generation*
Poland 1954   90m   bw
Film Polski
original title: *Pokolenie*

In occupied Warsaw in 1942 a teenager becomes hardened by life and joins the resistance.
Heavy-going but quite striking propaganda piece, amply demonstrating its director's talents.

w Bohdan Czeszko, from his novel *d Andrzej Wajda ph* Jerzy Lipman *m* Andrzej Markowski

Tadeusz Lomnicki, Urszula Modrzynska, Roman Polanski, Zbigniew Cybulski

Genghis Khan*
US 1964   126m   Technicolor   Panavision
Columbia / Irving Allen / CCC / Avala

Temujin raises a Mongol army and revenges himself on his old enemy Jamuga.
Meandering epic in which brutality alternates with pantomimish comedy and bouts of sex.
Necessarily patchy but reasonably watchable.

w Clarke Reynolds, Beverly Cross *d* Henry Levin *ph* Geoffrey Unsworth *m* Ducan Radic

Omar Sharif, Stephen Boyd, Françoise Dorléac, *James Mason,* Robert Morley, Telly Savalas, Woody Strode, Eli Wallach, Yvonne Mitchell

Genevieve****
GB 1954   86m   Technicolor
Rank (Henry Cornelius)

Two friendly rivals engage in a race on the way back from the Brighton veteran car rally.
One of those happy films in which for no very good or expected reason a number of modest elements merge smoothly to create an aura of high style and memorable moments. A charmingly witty script, carefully pointed direction, attractive actors and locations, an atmosphere of light-hearted British sex and a lively harmonica theme turned it, after a slowish start, into one of Britain's biggest commercial hits and most fondly remembered comedies.

w William Rose d Henry Cornelius ph Christopher Challis *m Larry Adler* (who also played it) *md* Muir Mathieson *ad* Michael Stringer

Dinah Sheridan, John Gregson, Kay Kendall, Kenneth More, Geoffrey Keen, Joyce Grenfell, Reginald Beckwith, Arthur Wontner

'One of the best things to have happened to British films over the last five years.'—*Gavin Lambert*

AAN: William Rose; Muir Mathieson

The Gentle Sex**
GB 1943   93m   bw
Rank / Two Cities / Concanen (Leslie Howard, Derrick de Marney)

Seven girls from different backgrounds are conscripted into the ATS.
Unassuming war propaganda, quite pleasantly done and historically very interesting.

w Moie Charles, Aimée Stuart, Phyllis Rose, Roland Pertwee *d* Leslie Howard, Maurice Elvey

Rosamund John, Joan Greenwood, Joan Gates, Jean Gillie, Lilli Palmer, Joyce Howard, Barbara Waring, John Justin, Frederick Leister, Mary Jerrold, Everley Gregg

A Gentleman after Dark
US 1942   74m   bw
Edward Small

A jewel thief comes out of prison to pay back his vindictive wife for shopping him.
Efficient melodrama of a dated kind.

w Patterson McNutt, George Bruce, *story* A Whiff of Heliotrope by Richard Washburn Child *d* Edwin L. Marin *ph* Milton Krasner *m* Dmitri Tiomkin

Brian Donlevy, Miriam Hopkins, Preston Foster, Harold Huber, Philip Reed, Gloria Holden, Douglass Dumbrille, Ralph Morgan
† Previously filmed in 1920 as *Heliotrope* with Fred Burton; in 1928 as *Forgotten Faces* with Clive Brook; and in 1936 as *Forgotten Faces* with Herbert Marshall.

The Gentle Sergeant
US 1955   85m   bw
Columbia (Fred Kohlmar)

A Jap-hating sergeant in Tokyo falls in love with
a Japanese girl.
Efficient sentimental drama shot on the spot.

wd Richard Murphy   *ph* Burnett Guffey
m George Duning

Aldo Ray, Phil Carey, Dick York, Chuck
Connors, Mitsuko Kimura

Gentleman Jim **
US 1942   104m   bw
Warner (Robert Buckner)

The rise to fame of boxer Jim Corbett.
Cheerful biopic of a nineties show-off, mostly
played for comedy.

w Vincent Lawrence, Horace McCoy, *book* The
Roar of the Crowd by James J. Corbett   *d* Raoul
Walsh ph Sid Hickox   *m* Heinz Roemheld

Errol Flynn, Alan Hale, Alexis Smith, John
Loder, Jack Carson, *Ward Bond,* William
Frawley, Rhys Williams, Arthur Shields
'Good-natured enough, but it lacks flavour.'—
New Yorker, 1976

Gentleman's Agreement **
US 1947   118m   bw
TCF (Darryl F. Zanuck)

A journalist poses as a Jew in order to write
about anti-semitism.
Worthy melodrama which caused a sensation at
the time but as a film is alas rather dull and self-
satisfied.

w Moss Hart, *novel* Laura Z. Hobson   *d* Elia
Kazan   *ph* Arthur Miller   *m* Alfred Newman

Gregory Peck, Dorothy McGuire, *John
Garfield,* Celeste Holm, *Anne Revere,* June
Havoc, Albert Dekker, Jane Wyatt, Dean
Stockwell

AA: best picture; Elia Kazan; Celeste Holm
AAN: Moss Hart; Gregory Peck; Dorothy
McGuire; Anne Revere

Gentlemen Marry Brunettes
US 1955   95m   Technicolor
Cinemascope
UA / Russ—Field (Richard Sale, Robert
Waterfield)

Two American shopgirls seek rich husbands in
Paris, and find that their aunts were notorious
there.
Jaded sequel to *Gentlemen Prefer Blondes;* it
barely raises a smile and the numbers are dismal.

w Mary Loos, Richard Sale   *d* Richard Sale

ph Desmond Dickinson   *m* Robert Farnon
ad Paul Sheriff   *ch* Jack Cole

Jane Russell, Jeanne Crain, Alan Young, Scott
Brady, Rudy Vallee

Gentlemen Prefer Blondes *
US 1953   91m   Technicolor
TCF (Sol. C. Siegel)

A dumb blonde and a showgirl go to Paris in
search of rich husbands.
Musicalized and updated version of the twenties
satire; no real vigour, but not too bad.

w Charles Lederer, *novel* Anita Loos   *d* Howard
Hawks   *ph* Harry J. Wild   *md* Lionel Newman
songs Jule Styne, Leo Robin   *ch* Jack Cole

Jane Russell, Marilyn Monroe, Charles Coburn,
Tommy Noonan, Norma Varden, Elliott Reid,
George Winslow

Geordie *
GB 1955   99m   Technicolor
British Lion / Argonaut (Sidney Gilliat, Frank
Launder)
US title: *Wee Geordie*

A weakly Scottish boy takes a physical culture
course and becomes an Olympic hammer-
thrower.
Slight comic fable, good to look at but without
the necessary style to follow it through.

w Sidney Gilliat, Frank Launder, *novel* David
Walker   *d* Frank Launder   *ph* Wilkie Cooper
m William Alwyn

Bill Travers, Alastair Sim

George in Civvy Street
GB 1946   79m   bw
Columbia (Marcel Varnel, Ben Henry)

A soldier returns to his country pub and finds
himself in the middle of a beer war.
The star's last film was oddly lacklustre and
compared very badly with his earlier successes.

w Peter Fraser, Ted Kavanaugh, Max Kester,
Gale Pedrick   *d* Marcel Varnel

George Formby, Rosalyn Boulter, Ronald
Shiner, Ian Fleming, Wally Patch

The George Raft Story
US 1961   105m   bw
Allied Artists (Ben Schwab)
GB title: *Spin of a Coin*

In twenties New York, a dancer falls in with
gangsters, but eludes them when he goes to
Hollywood, where his acting career is harmed by
temperament.
Tepid, unconvincing biopic, rather shoddily
made but with flashes of interest.

w Crane Wilbur *d* Joseph M. Newman *ph* Carl Guthrie *m* Jeff Alexander

Ray Danton, Julie London, Jayne Mansfield, Frank Gorshin, Neville Brand (as Al Capone)

George Washington Slept Here
US 1942   93m   bw
Warner (Jerry Wald)

A New York couple move to a dilapidated country house.
Disappointingly stiff and ill-timed version of a play that should have been a natural.

w Everett Freeman, *play* George Kaufman, Moss Hart *d* William Keighley *ph* Ernest Haller *m* Adolph Deutsch

Jack Benny, Ann Sheridan, Percy Kilbride, Charles Coburn, Hattie McDaniel, William Tracy, Lee Patrick, John Emery, Charles Dingle

George White's Scandals*
US 1934   79m   bw
Fox (Winfield Sheehan)

Romance blossoms backstage during the production of a big musical.
Revue with minimum plot and some impressive numbers.

w Jack Yellen, from the Broadway show directed by George White *d* Thornton Freeland, Harry Lachman, George White *ph* Lee Garmes, George Schneiderman *songs* various

George White, Rudy Vallee, Alice Faye, Jimmy Durante, Dixie Dunbar, Adrienne Ames, Cliff Edwards, Gertrude Michael, Gregory Ratoff

George White's 1935 Scandals*
US 1935   83m   bw
Fox (Winfield Sheehan)

A small-town star is discovered by a Broadway producer.
Again, basic plot serves to introduce some pretty good acts.

w Jack Yellen, Patterson McNutt *d* George White *ph* George Schneiderman *songs* various

George White, Alice Faye, James Dunn, Eleanor Powell, Ned Sparks, Lyda Roberti, Cliff Edwards, Arline Judge

George White's Scandals*
US 1945   95m   bw
RKO (Jack J. Gross, Nat Holt, George White)

Ex-Scandals girls get together, and one disappears.
Lively comedy-musical with vaudeville orientations.

w Hugh Wedlock, Parker Levy, Howard Green

d Felix E. Feist *m* Leigh Harline *ph* Robert de Grasse *songs* various

Joan Davis, Jack Haley, Philip Terry, Martha Holliday, Ethel Smith, Margaret Hamilton, Glenn Tryon, Jane Greer, Fritz Feld, Rufe Davis

Georgy Girl*
GB 1966   100m   bw
Columbia / Everglades (Otto Plaschkes, Robert A. Goldston)

An unattractive girl is fancied by her middle-aged employer but escapes to look after the illegitimate baby of her ungrateful friend.
Frantic black farce which seems determined to shock, but has a few good scenes once you get attuned to the mood. A censorship milestone.

w Margaret Forster, Peter Nichols, *novel* Margaret Forster *d* Silvio Narizzano *ph* Ken Higgins *m* Alexander Faris

James Mason, Lynn Redgrave, Charlotte Rampling, Alan Bates, Bill Owen, Clare Kelly, Rachel Kempson

'Another swinging London story filled with people running through London late at night, dancing madly in the rain, and visiting deserted children's playgrounds to ride on the roundabouts.'—*MFB*

'So glib, so clever, so determinedly kinky that everything seems to be devalued.'—*Pauline Kael*

'Its barrage of fashionable tricks proves exhausting.'—*Sight and Sound*

AAN: Ken Higgins; James Mason; Lynn Redgrave; title song (*m* Tom Springfield, *ly* Jim Dale)

Germany Year Zero*
France / Italy 1947   78m   bw
Union Générale Cinématographique / DEFA

Life in post-war Germany is so appalling that a boy kills his father and then himself.
Both realistic and pessimistic, this depressing film has a savage power of its own but totally fails to be constructive.

wd Roberto Rossellini *ph* Robert Juillard *m* Renzo Rossellini

Franz Gruger and a cast of non-professionals

Geronimo*
US 1939   89m   bw
Paramount

The seventh cavalry gives the Indians a run for their money.
Muddled western of no discernible merit.

wd Paul H. Sloane *ph* Henry Sharp *m* Gerald Carbonara

Ellen Drew, Preston Foster, Andy Devine, Gene Lockhart, Ralph Morgan

Geronimo

US 1962   101m   Technicolor   Panavision
UA / Laven–Gardner–Levy

In 1883 Geronimo and his remaining Apaches seek peace but are betrayed.
Moderate western held back by script and performances.

w Pat Fielder d Arnold Laven ph Alex Phillips m Hugo Friedhofer

Chuck Connors, Ross Martin, Kamala Deva

Gervaise*

France 1956   116m   bw
Agnès Delahaye-Silver Films-CLCC

In 19th-century Paris, a laundrymaid is deserted by her lover, settles with another man and is able to open her own laundry, but they both take to drink.
The French equivalent of David Lean's Dickens films, superbly detailed and wonderful to look at, but with a plot which finally seems worthless and depressing.

w Jean Aurenche, Pierre Bost,
novel L'Assommoir by Emile Zola d René Clément ph René Juillard m Georges Auric decor Paul Bertrand

Maria Schell, François Périer, Suzy Delair, Mathilde Casadesus

'A tremendous tour de force of literal realism . . . a piece for the admiration of technicians, or for those whose consciences are purged and hands kept clean by the vicarious contemplation of how the other half lived—once upon a time.'—David Robinson, MFB
† Other French versions were made in 1902, 1909, 1911 and 1933.

Get Carter*

GB 1971   112m   Metrocolor
MGM / Mike Klinger

A racketeer goes to Newcastle to avenge his brother's death at the hands of gangsters. He kills those responsible but is himself shot by a sniper.
Brutal British crime melodrama with faint echoes of Raymond Chandler. Sex and thuggery unlimited, narrative disjointed, rewards few.

wd Mike Hodges, novel Jack's Return Home by Ted Lewis ph Wolfgang Suschitzky m Roy Budd

Michael Caine, John Osborne, Ian Hendry, Britt Ekland

'TV on the big screen—more sex, more

violence, but no more attention to motivation or plot logic.'—Arthur Knight

Get Cracking*

GB 1942   96m   bw
Columbia (Ben Henry)

George joins the home guard.
Adequate star comedy.

w L. DuGarde Peach d Marcel Varnel

George Formby, Edward Rigby, Frank Pettingell, Dinah Sheridan, Ronald Shiner, Wally Patch, Irene Handl

Get Off My Foot

GB 1935   83m   bw
Warner (Irving Asher)

A Smithfield porter becomes a butler, and later finds himself heir to a fortune.
The nearest Max Miller came to being a genuine film star was in this first of eight Warner comedies, but the screen simply couldn't contain him.

w Frank Launder, Robert Edmunds,
play Money By Wire by Edward Paulton d William Beaudine ph Basil Emmott

Max Miller, Chili Bouchier, Morland Graham, Jane Carr, Norma Varden, Reginald Purdell, Wally Patch

The Getaway**

US 1972   122m   Technicolor   Todd-AO 35

Solar / First Artists (David Foster, Mitchell Brower)

A convict leaves jail and promptly joins his wife in a bank robbery.
Violent, amoral, terse and fast-moving action melodrama which generally holds the interest despite its excesses.

w Walter Hill, novel Jim Thompson d Sam Peckinpah ph Lucien Ballard m Quincy Jones

Steve McQueen, Faye Dunaway, Ben Johnson, Sally Smithers, Al Lettieri, Slim Pickens

'This pair have no mission or "meaning". As in all romances, The Getaway simply extracts one element of reality and dwells on it. Nor is the violence "American". Pictures like this don't fail overseas.'—Stanley Kauffmann

Getting Straight*

US 1970   125m   Eastmancolor
Columbia / The Organization (Richard Rush)

A political activist returns to college in order to teach and discovers the foolishness of most contemporary attitudes.

Modish comedy, too long, far too pleased with itself, and now irrevocably dated.

w Robert Kaufman *novel* Ken Kolb *d* Richard Rush *ph* Laszlo Kovacs *m* Ronald Stein

Elliott Gould, Candice Bergen, Robert F. Lyons, Jeff Corey, Max Julien, Cecil Kellaway

The Ghost and Mr Chicken
US 1965   90m   Techniscope
Universal (Edward J. Montagne)

An incompetent small-town reporter finds ghosts in a local murder mansion.
Old-fashioned scare comedy starring a highly resistible comic. A big hit in American small towns.

w James Fritzell, Everett Greenbaum *d* Alan Rafkin *ph* William Margulies *m* Vic Mizzy

Don Knotts, Skip Homeier, Joan Staley, Liam Redmond, Dick Sargent, Reta Shaw

The Ghost and Mrs Muir **
US 1947   104m   bw
TCF (Fred Kohlmar)

A widow refuses to be frightened away from her seaside home by the ghost of a sea captain, with whom she falls in love.
Charming sentimental fable in Hollywood's best style.

w Philip Dunne, *novel* R. A. Dick *d* Joseph L. Mankiewicz *ph* Charles Lang *m* Bernard Herrmann *ad* Richard Day

Gene Tierney, Rex Harrison, George Sanders, Edna Best, Vanessa Brown, Anna Lee, Robert Coote, Natalie Wood, Isobel Elsom

AAN: Charles Lang

The Ghost Breakers ***
US 1940   85m   bw
Paramount (Arthur Hornblow Jnr)

A girl inherits a West Indian castle and finds herself up to her neck in ghosts, zombies and buried treasure.
Archetypal comedy horror, very well done; a follow-up to the success of *The Cat and the Canary*, and just about as entertaining.

w Paul Dickey, Walter de Leon, *play* Paul Dickey, *Charles W. Goddard d* George Marshall *ph* Charles Lang *m* Ernst Toch *ad* Hans Dreier

Bob Hope, Paulette Goddard, Paul Lukas, *Willie Best*, Richard Carlson, *Lloyd Corrigan*, Anthony Quinn, Noble Johnson, Pedro de Cordova
† Previously filmed in 1914 with H. B. Warner; in 1922 with Wallace Reid; and remade in 1953 as *Scared Stiff*.

The Ghost Goes West ***
GB 1936   85m   bw
London Films (Alexander Korda)

When a millionaire buys a Scottish castle and transports it stone by stone to America, the castle ghost goes too.
Amusing whimsy which is always pleasant but never quite realizes its full potential; fondly remembered for its star performance.

w Robert E. Sherwood, Geoffrey Kerr, *story* Eric Keown *d* René Clair *ph* Harold Rosson

Robert Donat, Jean Parker, Eugene Pallette, Elsa Lanchester, Ralph Bunker, Patricia Hilliard, Morton Selten
'Although the film is not cast in the fluid, rapidly paced style of Clair's typical work, it has a sly wit and an adroitness of manner that make it delightful.'—*André Sennwald, New York Times*

The Ghost of Frankenstein
US 1942   67m   bw
Universal (George Waggner)

Frankenstein's second son implants evil shepherd Igor's brain into the monster.
The rot set in with this flatly-handled potboiler, which had none of the literary mood or cinematic interest of *Bride* or *Son* which preceded it, and suffered from a particularly idiotic script.

w W. Scott Darling, *story* Eric Taylor *d* Erle C. Kenton *ph* Milton Krasner, Woody Bredell *m* Charles Previn *ad* Jack Otterson

Cedric Hardwicke, Lon Chaney Jnr (as the monster), Bela Lugosi, Lionel Atwill, Evelyn Ankers, Ralph Bellamy
† See *Frankenstein* for other episodes in series.

The Ghost of St Michael's **
GB 1941   82m   bw
Ealing (Basil Dearden)

A school is evacuated to the Isle of Skye, and the local ghost turns out to be an enemy agent.
The star's schoolmaster character is here at its seedy best, and he is well supported in a comedy-thriller plot.

w Angus Macphail, John Dighton *d* Marcel Varnel

Will Hay, Claude Hulbert, Felix Aylmer, Raymond Huntley, Elliot Mason, Charles Hawtrey, John Laurie, Hay Petrie, Roddy Hughes, Manning Whiley

Ghost Story *
GB 1974   89m   Fujicolor
Stephen Weeks

Former college acquaintances spend a weekend

at a country house, and one of them is drawn into tragic events of forty years before.

Overlong chiller, ingeniously shot in India but very variably acted; aims for the M. R. James style and sometimes achieves it, but badly needs cutting.

w Rosemary Sutcliff, Stephen Weeks *d* Stephen Weeks *ph* Peter Hurst *m* Ron Geesin

Murray Melvin, Larry Dann, Vivian Mackerall, Marianne Faithfull, Anthony Bate, Leigh Lawson, Barbara Shelley

The Ghost Train***
GB 1931   72m   bw
Gainsborough (Michael Balcon)

Passengers stranded at a haunted station in Cornwall include a detective posing as a silly ass in order to trap smugglers.

Excellent early sound version of a comedy-thriller play which has not only been among the most commercially successful ever written but also provided the basic plot for many another comedy: *Oh Mr Porter, The Ghost of St Michael's, Back Room Boy, Hold That Ghost*, etc. Previously filmed as a silent in 1927, with Guy Newall.

w Angus Macphail, Lajos Biro, play Arnold Ridley d Walter Forde

Jack Hulbert, Cicely Courtneidge, Donald Calthrop, Ann Todd, Cyril Raymond, Angela Baddeley, Allan Jeayes

The Ghost Train**
GB 1941   85m   bw
Gainsborough (Edward Black)

Adequate remake with the lead split into two characters, which doesn't work quite so well.

w Marriott Edgar, Val Guest, J. O. C. Orton *d* Walter Forde

Arthur Askey, Richard Murdoch, Kathleen Harrison, Morland Graham, Linden Travers, Peter Murray Hill, *Herbert Lomas*

The Ghosts of Berkeley Square*
GB 1947   89m   bw
British National (Louis H. Jackson)

Two 18th-century ghosts are doomed to haunt a London house until royalty visits.

Thin, skittish whimsy with pleasant moments.

w James Seymour, *novel* No Nightingales by S. J. Simon, Caryl Brahms *d* Vernon Sewell

Robert Morley, Claude Hulbert, Felix Aylmer, Yvonne Arnaud, Abraham Sofaer, Ernest Thesiger, Marie Lohr, Martita Hunt, A. E. Matthews, John Longden, Ronald Frankau,

Wilfrid Hyde White, Esmé Percy, Mary Jerrold, Wally Patch, Martin Miller

The Ghoul**
GB 1933   79m   bw
Gaumont (Michael Balcon)

An Egyptologist returns from the tomb to uncover stolen jewels and a murderer.

Fascinating minor horror piece reminiscent of *The Old Dark House*, with many effective moments and a ripe cast.

w Frank King, Leonard Hines, L. DuGarde Peach, Roland Pertwee, John Hastings Turner, Rupert Downing, *novel* Frank King *d T. Hayes Hunter*

Boris Karloff, Cedric Hardwicke, Ralph Richardson, Kathleen Harrison, Ernest Thesiger, Dorothy Hyson, Anthony Bushell, D. A. Clarke-Smith

† Remade after a fashion as *What A Carve Up* (1962).

The Ghoul
GB 1975   87m   Eastmancolor
Tyburn (Kevin Francis)

In the twenties, a group of stranded travellers is reduced in number when they take shelter in the house of a former clergyman.

Dismal rehash of *The Old Dark House*, with nastiness instead of wit.

w John Elder *d* Freddie Francis *ph* John Wilcox *m* Harry Robinson

Peter Cushing, Alexandra Bastedo, John Hurt, Gwen Watford, Veronica Carlson, Don Henderson

'Peter Cushing brings out his violin for a soothing spot of the classics, the local copper mutters veiled warnings before trundling off on his bike, and thick fog swirls round the exterior sets at the drop of a canister.'—*Geoff Brown*

Giant**
US 1956   197m   Warnercolor
Warner (George Stevens, Henry Ginsburg)

The life of a Texas cattle rancher through two generations.

Sprawling, overlong family saga with unconvincing acting but good visual style.

w Fred Guiol, Ivan Moffat, *novel* Edna Ferber *d George Stevens ph* William C. Mellor, Edwin DuPar *m Dmitri Tiomkin*

Rock Hudson, Elizabeth Taylor, James Dean, Mercedes McCambridge, Carroll Baker, Chill Wills, Jane Withers, Dennis Hooper, Sal Mineo, Rod Taylor, Judith Evelyn, Earl Holliman, Alexander Scourby, Paul Fix

AA: George Stevens
AAN: best picture; script; Dmitri Tiomkin;
Rock Hudson; James Dean; Mercedes
McCambridge

Gideon's Day*
GB 1958   91m   Technicolor
Columbia / John Ford (Michael Killanin)
US title: *Gideon of Scotland Yard*

A Scotland Yard Inspector has an eventful but
frustrating day.
Pleasant, ordinary little TV style police yarn
showing no evidence of its director's particular
talents.

w T. E. B. Clarke, *novel* John Creasey *d* John
Ford *ph* Frederick A. Young *m* Douglas
Gamley *ad* Ken Adam

Jack Hawkins, Dianne Foster, Anna Lee,
Andrew Ray, Anna Massey, Frank Lawton,
John Loder, Cyril Cusack

Gidget
US 1959   95m   Eastmancolor
Cinemascope
Columbia (Lewis J. Rachmil)

A 16-year-old girl falls for a surfer; her parents
disapprove until he turns out to be the son of
their best friend.
Commercial mixture of domestic comedy and
beach athletics, for nice teenagers and their
moms and pops.

w Gabrielle Upton, *novel* Frederick Kohner
d Paul Wendkos *ph* Burnett Guffey *m* George
Duning *md* Morris Stoloff

Sandra Dee, Cliff Robertson, James Darren,
Arthur O'Connell
† Sequels include *Gidget Goes Hawaiian* (1961)
with Deborah Walley; *Gidget Goes to Rome*
(1962) with Cindy Carol; and two TV movies.

The Gift Horse*
GB 1952   100m   bw
British Lion / Molton (George Pitcher)
US title: *Glory at Sea*

In 1940 an old US destroyer is given to Britain,
and an officer reluctantly takes charge of it.
Conventional, popular seafaring war adventure.

w William Fairchild, Hugh Hastings, William
Rose *d* Compton Bennett *ph* Harry Waxman
m Clifton Parker

Trevor Howard, Richard Attenborough, Sonny
Tufts, James Donald, Joan Rice, Bernard Lee,
Dora Bryan, Hugh Williams, Robin Bailey

The Gift of Love
US 1958   105m   Eastmancolor
Cinemascope
TCF (Charles Brackett)

A dying wife adopts an orphan girl so that her
husband will not be lonely.
Incredibly cloying and miscast remake of
Sentimental Journey (qv).

w Luther Davis *d* Jean Negulesco *ph* Milton
Krasner *m* Cyril Mockridge

Lauren Bacall, Robert Stack, Evelyn Rudie,
Lorne Greene

Gigi*
France 1948   109m   bw
Codo Cinema (Claude Dolbert)

In Paris in the nineties, a young girl is trained by
her aunt to be a cocotte, but when married off to
a rake she reforms him.
Charming, overlong, non-musical version of a
famous story, chiefly memorable for its local
colour.

w Pierre Laroche, *novel* Colette *d* Jacqueline
Audry *ph* Gérard Perrin *m* Marcel Landowski

Danièle Delorme, *Gaby Morlay, Yvonne de
Bray*, Frank Villard, Jean Tissier, Madeleine
Rousset

Gigi***
US 1958   119m   Metrocolor
Cinemascope
MGM (Arthur Freed)

Laundered and musicalized version; delightfully
set, costumed and performed, but oddly lacking
dance numbers.

w/ly Alan Jay Lerner *m* Frederick Loewe
d Vincente Minnelli *ph* Joseph Ruttenberg
md André Previn *pd/cost* Cecil Beaton

Leslie Caron, Louis Jourdan, Maurice
Chevalier, Hermione Gingold, Isabel Jeans,
Jacques Bergerac, Eva Gabor, John Abbott

'It has the sureness expected when a group of
the most sophisticated talents are able to work
together on material entirely suited to them.'—
Penelope Houston

AA: best picture; Alan Jay Lerner; Vincente
Minnelli; Joseph Ruttenberg; André Previn;
Cecil Beaton; Adrienne Fazan (editing); Preston
Ames and Keogh Gleason (art directors); title
song (*m* Frederick Loewe, *ly* Alan Jay Lerner);
Maurice Chevalier (special award)

Gigot
US 1962   104m   De Luxe
TCF / Seven Arts (Kenneth Hyman)

The mute caretaker of a Montmartre boarding

house looks after an ailing prostitute and her child.

From Paris, Hollywood, comes a grotesque piece of self-indulgence, the arch example of the clown who wanted to play Hamlet. Plotless, mawkish and wholly unfunny.

w John Patrick, Jackie Gleason *d* Gene Kelly *ph* Jean Bourgoin *m* Jackie Gleason *md* Michael Magne *ad* Auguste Capelier

Jackie Gleason, Katherine Kath, Gabrielle Dorziat, Jean Lefebvre, Jacques Marin

'Chaplinesque pretensions have proved fatal before to artists who will not accept their own limitations.'—*Gavin Lambert*

AAN: Michael Magne

Gilda****
US 1946   110m   bw
Columbia (Virginia Van Upp)

A gambler in a South American city resumes a love-hate relationship with an old flame . . . but she is now married to his dangerous new boss.
Archetypal Hollywood *film noir*, wholly studio-bound and the better for it, with dialogue that would seem risible if it did not happen to be dealt with in this style and with these actors, who keep the mood balanced between suspense and absurdity.

w Marion Parsonnet, story E. A. Ellington *d Charles Vidor ph Rudolph Maté md* Morris Stoloff, Marvin Skiles

Rita Hayworth, Glenn Ford, George Macready, Steve Geray, Joseph Calleia, Joe Sawyer, Gerald Mohr, Ludwig Donath

'There never was a woman like Gilda!'—*publicity*

'From a quietly promising opening the film settles into an intractable obscurity of narrative through which as in a fog three characters bite off at each other words of hate.'—*Richard Winnington*

The Gilded Lily*
US 1935   80m   bw
Paramount (Albert Lewis)

A poor stenographer who meets her reporter boy friend on a park bench is wooed by a British peer. Good depression era romantic comedy with the heroine inevitably choosing poverty.

w Claude Binyon *d* Wesley Ruggles *ph* Victor Milner

Claudette Colbert, Fred MacMurray, Ray Milland,
C. Aubrey Smith, Luis Alberni, Donald Meek

A Girl, a Guy and a Gob
US 1941   91m   bw
Harold Lloyd
GB title: *The Navy Steps Out*

A secretary and her sailor boy friend teach her stuffy boss how to enjoy life.
Did producer Lloyd intend himself for the role played by O'Brien? If so, he would have needed a stronger script to prevent this Capraesque comedy from falling flat.

w Frank Ryan, Bert Granet *d* Richard Wallace *ph* Russell Metty

Lucille Ball, Edmond O'Brien, George Murphy, George Cleveland, Henry Travers, Franklin Pangborn, Marguerite Churchill, Lloyd Corrigan

The Girl and the General
Italy / France 1967   113m   Technicolor
MGM / Champion-Corcordia

During World War I, a captured Austrian general escapes with a girl partisan.
Turgid war epic veering from melodrama to comedy.

w Luigi Malerba, Pasquale Festa Campanile *d* Pasquale Festa Campanile *ph* Ennio Guarnieri *m* Ennio Morricone

Rod Steiger, Virna Lisi, Umberto Orsini

The Girl Can't Help It*
US 1956   97m   Eastmancolor
  Cinemascope
TCF (Frank Tashlin)

A theatrical agent grooms a gangster's dumb girl friend for stardom.
Scatty, garish pop scene spoof with a plot borrowed from *Born Yesterday* and a lot of jokes about its new star's superstructure. Some scenes are funny, and it puts the first rock and roll stars in pickle for all time.

w Frank Tashlin, Herbert Baker *d* Frank Tashlin *ph* Leon Shamroy *md* Lionel Newman

Jayne Mansfield, Tom Ewell, Edmond O'Brien, Henry Jones, John Emery; and Julie London, Ray Anthony, Fats Domino, Little Richard, the Platters

Girl Crazy*
US 1943   99m   bw
MGM (Arthur Freed)
aka: *When the Girls Meet the Boys*

Romance at a desert college.
Predictable star musical with good tunes.

w Fred F. Finklehoffe, *play* Guy Bolton, Jack McGowan *d* Norman Taurog *ph* William

Daniels, Robert Planck *md* Georgie Stoll
songs George and Ira Gershwin

Judy Garland, Mickey Rooney, Guy Kibbee, Gil
Stratton, Robert E. Strickland, Rags Ragland,
June Allyson, Nancy Walker, Tommy Dorsey
and his band
† Remade 1965 as *When the Girls Meet the
Boys.*

The Girl from Manhattan
US 1948   81m   bw
UA / Benedict Bogeaus

A model returns home to help her uncle with his
mortgaged boarding house.
Mouldy comedy-drama full of kind thoughts,
charming failures and worldly priests.
Interesting for cast.

w Howard Estabrook *d* Alfred E. Green
ph Ernest Laszlo *md* David Chudnow *m* Heinz
Roemheld

Dorothy Lamour, Charles Laughton, George
Montgomery, Ernest Truex, Hugh Herbert,
Constance Collier, Sara Allgood, Frank Orth,
Howard Freeman, Adeline de Walt Reynolds,
George Chandler, Maurice Cass

The Girl from Mexico   see Mexican Spitfire

The Girl from Missouri *
US 1934   75m   bw
MGM (Bernard H. Hyman)
aka: *100% Pure*

A chorus girl determines to remain virtuous until
the right millionaire comes along.
Smart, amusing comedy very typical of its
period.

w Anita Loos, John Emerson d Jack Conway
ph Ray June *m* Dr William Axt

Jean Harlow, Franchot Tone, Lionel
Barrymore, Lewis Stone, Patsy Kelly, Alan
Mowbray, Clara Blandick, Henry Kolker
  'Noisily defiant, rip-roaring and raucous in
spots . . . fast and furious adult fare.'—
Photoplay

The Girl from Tenth Avenue
US 1935   69m   bw
Warner (Robert Lord)
GB title: *Men on Her Mind*

A jilted attorney drowns his sorrows and marries
on the rebound.
Watchable 'woman's picture'.

w Charles Kenyon, *play* Hubert Henry Davies
d Alfred E. Green *ph* James Van Trees

Bette Davis, Ian Hunter, Colin Clive, Alison

Skipworth, Katherine Alexander, John
Eldredge, Philip Reed

Girl Happy
US 1965   96m   Metrocolor   Panavision
MGM / Euterpe (Joe Pasternak)

A pop singer in Florida is forced to chaperone a
group of college girls including a gangster's
daughter.
Standard star vehicle, quite professionally made
and totally forgettable.

w Harvey Bullock, R. S. Allen *d* Boris Sagal
ph Philip Lathrop *m* George Stoll

Elvis Presley, Harold J. Stone, Shelley Fabares,
Gary Crosby, Nita Talbot

The Girl He Left Behind
US 1956   103m   bw
Warner (Frank P. Rosenberg)

The army makes a man of a spoiled youth.
Platitudinous recruiting comedy for dim
American teenagers.

w Guy Trosper, *book* Marion Hargrove
d David Butler *ph* Ted McCord *m* Ray
Heindorf

Tab Hunter, Natalie Wood, Jessie Royce
Landis, Jim Backus, Henry Jones, Murray
Hamilton, Alan King, James Garner, David
Janssen

The Girl Hunters
GB 1963   100m   bw   Panavision
Present Day (Robert Fellows)

Private eye Mike Hammer solves a few murders
plus the disappearance of his own ex-secretary.
Comic strip thuggery with the author playing his
own slouchy hero; the general incompetence
gives this cheap production an air of Kafkaesque
menace.

w Mickey Spillane, Roy Rowland, Robert
Fellows *d* Roy Rowland *ph* Ken Talbot *m* Phil
Green

Mickey Spillane, Shirley Eaton, Lloyd Nolan

The Girl in Black
Greece 1955   93m   bw
Hermes
original title: *To Koritsi me ta Mavra*

A writer holidaying on a remote fishing island
causes tension and tragedy when he falls for a
local maiden.
Watchable mood piece benefiting from its star
female performance.

wd Michael Cacoyannis *ph* Walter Lassally
m Argyris Kounadis, Manos Hadjikakis

Elle Lambetti, George Foundas, Dimitri Horna

A Girl in Every Port*

US 1928   62m (24 fps)   bw   silent
Fox

Two sailors brawl over women.
Adventure comedy with themes typical of its
director.

d Howard Hawks

Victor McLaglen, Natalie Joyce, Dorothy
Matthews, Maria Casajuana, Louise Brooks,
Francis McDonald

A Girl in Every Port

US 1951   87m   bw
RKO (Irwin Allen, Irving Cummings Jnr)

Two accident-prone sailors have trouble with a
racehorse.
Dismally mechanical farce.

wd Chester Erskine   ph Nicholas Musuraca
m Roy Webb

Groucho Marx, William Bendix, Marie Wilson,
Don Defore, Gene Lockhart

The Girl in the Headlines*

GB 1963   93m   bw
Bryanston / Viewfinder (John Davis)
US title: The Model Murder Case

Scotland Yard investigates the murder of a
model.
Standard police mystery, well enough done.

w Vivienne Knight, Patrick Campbell, novel The
Nose on My Face by Laurence Payne
d Michael Truman   ph Stan Pavey   m John
Addison

Ian Hendry, Ronald Fraser, Margaret Johnston,
Natasha Parry

The Girl in the News*

GB 1940   78m   bw
TCF (Edward Black)

A nurse is framed for the death of her employer.
Easy-going British mystery of the Agatha
Christie school.

w Sidney Gilliat, novel Roy Vickers   d Carol
Reed   ph Otto Kanturek

Margaret Lockwood, Barry K. Barnes, Emlyn
Williams, Margaretta Scott, Roger Livesey,
Basil Radford, Wyndham Goldie, Irene Handl,
Mervyn Johns, Kathleen Harrison, Richard
Bird, Michael Hordern, Roland Culver, Edward
Rigby

The Girl in the Red Velvet Swing*

US 1955   109m   De Luxe   Cinemascope
TCF (Charles Brackett)

In New York at the turn of the century, a rich
unstable man shoots his mistress's former lover.
Plushy but not very interesting recounting of a
celebrated murder case in which the victim was a
famous architect, Stanford White.

w Walter Reisch, Charles Brackett   d Richard
Fleischer   ph Milton Krasner   m Leigh Harline
ad Lyle R. Wheeler, Maurice Ransford

Ray Milland, Farley Granger, Joan Collins,
Glenda Farrell, Luther Adler, Cornelia Otis
Skinner, Philip Reed, John Hoyt
  'A needlessly long-winded piece of lush
sensationalism.'—Penelope Houston

The Girl in White*

US 1952   93m   bw
MGM (Armand Deutsch)
GB title: So Bright the Flame

The story of Dr Emily Dunning, the first woman
to become an intern in one of New York's
hospitals.
Bland biopic, modestly produced, with
predictable plot crises.

w Irmgard Von Cube, Allen Vincent, book
Bowery to Bellevue by Emily Dunning
Barringer   d John Sturges   ph Paul C. Vogel
m David Raksin

June Allyson, Arthur Kennedy, Gary Merrill,
Mildred Dunnock, Jesse White, Marilyn Erskine

The Girl Most Likely

US 1956   98m   Technicolor   RKOscope
RKO (Stanley Rubin)

A girl finds herself engaged to three men at the
same time, and envisions marriage with each.
Dully cast, quite brightly handled remake of
Tom, Dick and Harry, with modest songs and
dances.

w Devery Freeman   d Mitchell Leisen
ph Robert Planck   m Nelson Riddle

Jane Powell, Cliff Robertson, Keith Andes,
Tommy Noonan, Kaye Ballard, Una Merkel
† For Mitchell Leisen and RKO studios, their
last film.

A Girl Must Live**

GB 1939   92m   bw
Gainsborough (Edward Black)

A runaway schoolgirl falls among chorus girls
planning to marry into the nobility.
Light, peppery comedy with a strong cast.

w Frank Launder, Michael Pertwee, novel
Emery Bonnet   d Carol Reed   ph Jack Cox
md Louis Levy

Margaret Lockwood, Renée Houston, Lilli
Palmer, George Robey, Hugh Sinclair, Naunton
Wayne, Moore Marriott, Mary Clare, David

Burns, Kathleen Harrison, Martita Hunt, Helen Haye

'An unabashed display of undressed femininity, double-meaning dialogue alternating between piquancy and vulgarity, and hearty knockabout involving scantily attired young viragos who fight furiously in a whirligig of legs and lingerie.'—*Kine Weekly*

A Girl Named Tamiko
US 1962   119m   Technicolor   Panavision
Paramount / Hal B. Wallis (Paul Nathan)

A Eurasian photographer uses his women in an attempt to get American nationality.
Humdrum romantic melodrama with dim performances.

w Edward Anhalt, *novel* Ronald Kirkbride *d* John Sturges *ph* Charles Lang Jnr *m* Elmer Bernstein

Laurence Harvey, France Nuyen, Martha Hyer, Michael Wilding, Miyoshi Umeki

The Girl Next Door
US 1953   92m   Technicolor
TCF (Robert Bassler)

A Broadway musical star falls for her suburban neighbour.
Mild musical linked by UPA cartoon sequences.

w Isobel Lennart *d* Richard Sale *ph* Leon Shamroy *md* Lionel Newman *songs* Josef Myrow, Mack Gordon *ch* Richard Barstow

Dan Dailey, June Haver, Natalie Schaefer, Dennis Day, Cara Williams

The Girl of the Golden West
US 1930   81m   bw
Warner (Robert North)

A gun-toting, saloon-owning girl marries an outlaw and saves him from the sheriff.
Straight version of a dusty old Broadway success, later musicalized under the same title (see below).

w Waldemar Young, *play* David Belasco *d* John Francis Dillon *ph* Sol Polito

Ann Harding, James Rennie, Harry Bannister, Ben Hendricks Jnr, J. Farrell MacDonald

The Girl of the Golden West
US 1938   121m   bw (sepia release)
MGM (William Anthony McGuire)

In backwoods Canada, a girl loves a bandit who is being chased by the Mounties.
Solemn musical melodrama in which the stars seem miscast and a bit of pep is badly needed.
Taken from a hoary David Belasco spectacular, and looks it.

w Isobel Dawn, Boyce DeGaw *d* Robert Z. Leonard *ph* Oliver Marsh *songs* Sigmund Romberg, Gus Kahn

Jeanette MacDonald, Nelson Eddy, Walter Pidgeon, Leo Carrillo, Buddy Ebsen, Olin Howland

Girl on a Motorcycle
GB / France 1968   91m   Technicolor
Mid Atlantic / Ares (William Sassoon)
US title: *Naked under Leather;* French title: *La Motocyclette*

A married woman leaves her husband, zooms off on her motorcycle to see her lover, and crashes to her death while indulging in sexual reverie.
An incredibly plotless and ill-conceived piece of sub-porn claptrap, existing only as a long series of colour supplement photographs.

w Ronald Duncan, *novel* La Motocyclette by André Pieyre de Mandiargues *d* Jack Cardiff *ph* Jack Cardiff, René Guissart *m* Les Reed

Marianne Faithfull, Alain Delon, Roger Mutton

The Girl on the Boat
GB 1962   91m   bw
UA / Knightsbridge (John Bryan)

On a transatlantic liner in the twenties, two Englishmen fall in love.
Curious attempt to do something different with a star comic, who is clearly outclassed by the lighter talents at hand.

w Reuben Ship, *story* P. G. Wodehouse *d* Henry Kaplan *ph* Denys Coop *m* Kenneth V. Jones

Norman Wisdom, *Richard Briers*, Millicent Martin, Athene Seyler, Sheila Hancock, Philip Locke

The Girl Rosemarie
West Germany 1958   100m   bw
Roxy
original title: *Das Mädchen Rosemarie*

Corrupt industrialists and investigators alike are relieved when a girl who had been the mistress of all of them is murdered .
Slick melodrama based on an actual case; almost a documentary exposé.

w Erich Kuby, Rolf Thiele, Joe Herbst, Rolf Urich *d* Rolf Thiele *ph* Klaus von Rautenfeld *m* Norbert Schultze

Nadja Tiller, Peter Van Eyck, Carl Raddatz, Gert Frobe, Mario Adorf, Horst Frank

The Girl Rush
US 1955   85m   Technicolor   Vistavision
Paramount (Frederick Brisson, Robert Alton)

A gambler's daughter inherits a half share in a Las Vegas hotel.

Dull charmless semi-musical vehicle for a star who can't quite carry it.

w Phoebe and Henry Ephron *d* Robert Pirosh *ph* William Daniels *m* Herbert Spencer, Earle Hagen *ch* Robert Alton

Rosalind Russell, Eddie Albert, Fernando Lamas, James Gleason, Gloria de Haven, *Marion Lorne*

The Girl Who Had Everything
US 1953   69m   bw
MGM (Adolph Deutsch)

The daughter of a wealthy criminal lawyer falls in love with one of her father's crooked clients.

Glossy melodrama of purely superficial interest.

w Art Cohn, *novel* Adela Rogers St John *d* Richard Thorpe *ph* Paul Vogel *m* André Previn

Elizabeth Taylor, William Powell, Fernando Lamas, Gig Young

† Remake of *A Free Soul*.

Girlfriends*
US 1978   86m   Du Art
Cyclops (Claudia Weill, Jan Saunders)

A Jewish girl photographer in New York is ditched by her girl friend and considers men.

Mild, amusing, well-observed little comedy-drama which goes nowhere in particular and slightly outstays its welcome.

w Vicki Polon *d* Claudia Weill *ph* Fred Murphy *m* Michael Small

Melanie Mayron, Eli Wallach, Anita Skinner, Bob Balaban

Girl with Green Eyes**
GB 1963   91m   bw
UA / Woodfall (Oscar Lewenstein)

An artless young Dublin girl falls for a middle-aged writer.

Lyrical romance which just about preserves its charm by good location sense.

w Edna O'Brien, from her novel The Lonely Girl *d* Desmond Davis *ph* Manny Wynn *m* John Addison

Peter Finch, Rita Tushingham, Lynn Redgrave

Les Girls*
US 1957   114m   Metrocolor
  Cinemascope
MGM (Sol. C. Siegel)

Two members of a girl dancing troupe sue over a memoir written by the third.

Disappointing, talent-laden comedy-musical

with a *Rashomon*-like flashback plot and a curious absence of the expected wit and style.

w John Patrick, *novel* Vera Caspary *d* George Cukor *ph* Robert Surtees *m/ly* Cole Porter *ch* Jack Cole

Gene Kelly, *Kay Kendall*, Mitzi Gaynor, Taina Elg, Jacques Bergerac, Leslie Phillips, Henry Daniell, Patrick MacNee

Girls' Dormitory*
US 1936   66m   bw
TCF

A college girl falls for her headmaster.

Old-fashioned romance for nice young people, smoothly produced in the Fox mid-thirties manner.

w Gene Markey, *story* Ladislaus Fodor *d* Irving Cummings *m* Arthur Lange

Herbert Marshall, *Simone Simon*, Ruth Chatterton, Constance Collier, J. Edward Bromberg, Dixie Dunbar, Tyrone Power

Girls, Girls, Girls
US 1962   106m   Technicolor
Wallis–Hazen (Hal B. Wallis)

A nightclub singer runs a fishing boat as a hobby.

Empty-headed, lighter than air vehicle for star fans.

w Edward Anhalt, Allan Weiss *d* Norman Taurog *ph* Loyal Griggs *m* Joseph J. Lilley

Elvis Presley, Stella Stevens, Laurel Goodwin, Jeremy Slate

The Girls of Pleasure Island
US 1953   96m   Technicolor
Paramount (Paul Jones)

In 1945 the Marines land on a tiny Pacific island, disturbing the life of an English gentleman and his three inexperienced but beautiful daughters.

Tedious and wholly artificial comedy with a leaden touch, devised as a try-out for young talent.

w F. Hugh Herbert *d* F. Hugh Herbert, Alvin Ganzer *ph* Daniel Fapp *m* Lyn Murray

Leo Genn, Gene Barry, Don Taylor, Elsa Lanchester, Dorothy Bromiley, Audrey Dalton, Joan Elan

Give a Girl a Break*
US 1953   84m   Technicolor
MGM (Jack Cummings)

A Broadway star walks out on a show and three girls audition as replacements.

Minor musical vehicle for the Champions; an agreeable time-passer.

w Frances Goodrich, Albert Hackett d Stanley Donen ph William Mellor md André Previn songs Ira Gershwin, Burton Lane ch Stanley Donen, Gower Champion

Marge and Gower Champion, Debbie Reynolds, Bob Fosse, Kurt Kasznar

Give Me a Sailor
US 1938 80m bw
Paramount (Jeff Lazarus)

An ugly girl envies her sister her beaux, but ends up winning a competition for beautiful legs. One of the double bill comedies which got Bob Hope's career off to a shaky start.

w Doris Anderson, Frank Butler, play Anne Nichols d Elliott Nugent ph Victor Milner md Boris Morros

Martha Raye, Bob Hope, Betty Grable, Jack Whiting, Clarence Kolb

Give My Regards to Broadway*
US 1948 89m Technicolor
TCF

An old-time vaudevillian yearns to get back into show business.
Pleasantly performed, sentimental family musical with familiar tunes.

w Samuel Hoffenstein, Elizabeth Reinhardt d Lloyd Bacon ph Harry Jackson

Dan Dailey, Charles Winninger, Fay Bainter, Charles Ruggles, Nancy Guild

'Vaudeville is dead. I wish to God someone would bury it.'—James Agee

Give Us the Moon
GB 1944 95m bw
GFD / Gainsborough (Edward Black)

In post-war London a club is opened for idle members only.
Whimsical comedy which fell with a dull thud.

wd Val Guest, novel The Elephant is White by Caryl Brahms, S. J. Simon

Margaret Lockwood, Vic Oliver, Peter Graves, Max Bacon, Roland Culver, Frank Cellier, Jean Simmons

Give Us This Day
GB 1949 120m bw
Plantagenet (Rod E. Geiger, N. A. Bronsten)
US title: Salt to the Devil

Depression struggles of an Italian immigrant family in New York.
An unconvincing, self-pitying wallow, a very curious enterprise for a British studio.

w Ben Barzman, story Christ in Concrete by Pietro di Donato d Edward Dmytryk ph C. Pennington Richards m Benjamin Frankel

Sam Wanamaker, Lea Padovani, Kathleen Ryan, Charles Goldner, Bonar Colleano, William Sylvester, Karel Stepanek, Sidney James

'Dmytryk insisted on cutting the film himself and he has left in at least three spare reels.'—Richard Winnington

'Worth making and worth seeing, but cramped by its symbolism and its language.'—Richard Mallett, Punch

Glamorous Night
GB 1937 81m bw
ABP (Walter C. Mycroft)

An opera singer and her gypsy friends save a Ruritanian king from his scheming prime minister.
Modest transcription of a popular stage musical.

w Dudley Leslie, Hugh Brooke, William Freshman, play Ivor Novello m Ivor Novello

Mary Ellis, Otto Kruger, Victor Jory, Barry Mackay, Trefor Jones

Glamour
US 1934 74m bw
Universal

A day in the life of a Broadway star.
Competent minor entertainment.

w Doris Anderson, story Edna Ferber d William Wyler ph George Robinson

Constance Cummings, Paul Lukas, Philip Reed, Joseph Cawthorne, Doris Lloyd, Olaf Hytten

The Glass Bottom Boat
US 1966 110m Metrocolor Panavision
MGM / Arwin–Reame (Martin Melcher)

A young widow gets involved with spies.
Frantic spy spoof, pleasantly set on the Californian coast, but overflowing with pratfalls, messy slapstick and pointless guest appearances.

w Everett Freeman d Frank Tashlin ph Leon Shamroy m Frank de Vol

Doris Day, Rod Taylor, Arthur Godfrey, Paul Lynde, John McGiver, Edward Andrews, Eric Fleming, Dom De Luise

The Glass Key**
US 1935 87m bw
Paramount (E. Lloyd Sheldon)

A slightly corrupt but good-natured politician is saved by his henchman from being implicated in a murder.
Lively transcription of a zesty crime novel.

w Kathryn Scola, Kubec Glasmon, Harry Ruskin, *novel Dashiell Hammett d* Frank Tuttle *ph* Henry Sharp

Edward Arnold, George Raft, Claire Dodd, Rosalind Keith, Guinn Williams, Ray Milland

The Glass Key**

US 1942 85m bw
Paramount (Fred Kohlmar)

Nifty remake of the above which finds some limited talents in their best form, helped by a plot which keeps one watching.

w Jonathan Latimer *d Stuart Heisler ph Theodor Sparkuhl m* Victor Young

Brian Donlevy, Alan Ladd, Veronica Lake, Bonita Granville, *William Bendix,* Richard Denning, Joseph Calleia, Moroni Olsen

The Glass Menagerie**

US 1950 107m bw
Warner (Jerry Wald, Charles K. Feldman)

A shy crippled girl seeks escape from the shabby reality of life in St Louis and from her mother's fantasies.
Pleasantly moody version of one of its author's lighter and more optimistic plays; fluent and good-looking production, memorable performances.

w Tennessee Williams (with Peter Berneis) from his play *d Irving Rapper ph Robert Burks m* Max Steiner

Gertrude Lawrence, Jane Wyman, Kirk Douglas, Arthur Kennedy

The Glass Mountain

GB 1949 98m bw
Victoria (John Sutro, Joseph Janni, Fred Zelnik)

In the Dolomites, a married composer loves an Italian girl who saved his life during the war.
Tedious sudser, ineptly produced; an enormous British box office success because of its theme music.

w Joseph Janni, John Hunter, Emery Bonnet, Henry Cass, John Cousins *d* Henry Cass *m* Nino Rota

Michael Denison, Dulcie Gray, Valentina Cortèse, Tito Gobbi, Sebastian Shaw

The Glass Slipper

US 1954 94m Eastmancolor
MGM (Edwin H. Knopf)

The story of Cinderella.
To those used to the pantomime version this is dull, dreary, high-flown stuff: limbo sets, ballets,

psychological rationalization and virtually no comedy.

w/ly Helen Deutsch *d* Charles Walters *ph* Arthur E. Arling *m* Bronislau Kaper *ch* Roland Petit

Leslie Caron, Michael Wilding, Elsa Lanchester, Barry Jones, *Estelle Winwood* (as Fairy Godmother)

The Glass Web

US 1954 81m bw 3-D
U-I (A. J. Cohen)

A TV executive kills a blackmailing actress and allows a young scriptwriter to be accused.
Boring thriller set in a TV studio.

w Robert Blees, Leonard Lee *d* Jack Arnold *ph* Maury Gertsman *m* Joseph Gershenson

Edward G. Robinson, John Forsythe, Marcia Henderson, Richard Denning

The Glenn Miller Story**

US 1954 116m Technicolor
U-I (Aaron Rosenberg)

The life of the unassuming trombonist and bandleader whose plane disappeared during World War II.
Competent musical heartwarmer with a well-cast star and successful reproduction of the Miller sound. A big box office hit.

w Valentine Davies, Oscar Brodney *d Anthony Mann ph William Daniels md* Henry Mancini, Joseph Gershenson

James Stewart, June Allyson, Harry Morgan, Charles Drake, Frances Langford, Louis Armstrong, Gene Krupa

AAN: script; music direction

A Global Affair

US 1963 84m bw
Seven Arts / Hall Bartlett

A United Nations official has to look after an abandoned baby.
Flat sentimental farce which embarrassingly tries to say something about the UN.

w Arthur Marx, Bob Fisher, Charles Lederer *d* Jack Arnold *ph* Joseph Ruttenberg *m* Dominic Frontière

Bob Hope, Lilo Pulver, Michèle Mercier, Yvonne de Carlo

'Squaresville incarnate, with a side trip into Leersville.'—*Judith Crist, 1973*

Glorifying the American Girl*

US 1929 87m bw, colour sequence
Paramount (Florenz Ziegfeld)

A chorus girl rejects her boy friend for the sake of stardom.
Archetypal show-must-go-on musical.

w J. P. McEvoy, Millard Webb d Millard Webb, John Harkrider ph George Folsey md Frank Tours

Mary Eaton, Edward Crandall; and as guests Eddie Cantor, Helen Morgan, Rudy Vallee, Florenz Ziegfeld, Adolph Zukor, Otto Kahn, Texas Guinan, Mayor Jimmy Walker, Ring Lardner, Noah Beery, Johnny Weissmuller

The Glorious Adventure *
GB 1921   100m (approx)   Prizmacolor
  silent
Stoll / J. Stuart Blackton

Various lives are affected by the Great Fire of London in 1666.
Stagey costume drama, notable only as the first British film in colour.

w Felix Orman d J. Stuart Blackton

Lady Diana Manners, Victor McLaglen, Gerald Lawrence, Cecil Humphreys, Alex Crawford, Lennox Pawle (as Pepys)

Glory
US 1955   100m   Technicolor
  Superscope
RKO (David Butler)

Girl loves horse more than boy.
Conventional young love / Kentucky Derby marshmallow.

w Peter Milne d David Butler ph Wilfrid Cline m Frank Perkins

Margaret O'Brien, Walter Brennan, Charlotte Greenwood, John Lupton

Glory Alley
US 1952   79m   bw
MGM (Nicholas Nayfack)

A sullen young boxer has trouble with his girl, her father and the demon rum.
Flat, boring second feature with musical interludes.

w Art Cohn d Raoul Walsh ph William Daniels md Georgie Stoll

Leslie Caron, Ralph Meeker, Kurt Kasznar, Gilbert Roland, John McIntire, Louis Armstrong, Jack Teagarden

'This is the kind of film that contains bits of everything. New Orleans night life and an episode of the Korean war; an arty French ballet sequence and jazz from Louis Armstrong; a boxer who acquired a neurosis in childhood when his father hit him over the head and a blind old father with a French accent, who knows all about everything.'—*MFB*

The Glory Brigade
US 1953   82m   bw
TCF (William Bloom)

Greek soldiers fight in Korea alongside the Americans.
Modest war adventure with predictable racial tensions.

w Franklin Coen d Robert D. Webb ph Lucien Andriot md Lionel Newman

Victor Mature, Alexander Scourby, Lee Marvin, Richard Egan

The Glory Guys *
US 1965   112m   De Luxe   Panavision
UA / Levy–Gardner–Laven

Officers of the US cavalry disagree about dealing with the Indians.
Standard big-budget western.

w Sam Peckinpah, *novel* The Dice of God by Hoffman Birney d Arnold Laven ph James Wong Howe m Riz Ortolani

Tom Tryon, Harve Presnell, Senta Berger, Andrew Duggan, James Caan, Slim Pickens, Michael Anderson Jnr

The Gnome-Mobile *
US 1967   90m   Technicolor
Walt Disney (James Algar)

A millionaire and his family go for a forest picnic and help a colony of gnomes.
Cheerful adventures for small children, with good trick work.

w Ellis Kadison, *novel* Upton Sinclair d Robert Stevenson ph Edward Colman m Buddy Baker

Walter Brennan, Matthew Garber, Karen Dotrice, Richard Deacon, Sean McClory, Ed Wynn, Jerome Cowan, Charles Lane

The Go-Between **
GB 1970   116m   Technicolor
EMI / World Film Services (John Heyman, Norman Priggen)

Staying at a stately home around the turn of the century, 12-year-old Leo carries love letters from a farmer to his friend's sister.
A rather tiresome plot sustains a rich picture of the Edwardian gentry, a milieu with which however the director is not at home, and treats far too slowly and tricksily.

w Harold Pinter, *novel* L. P. Hartley d Joseph Losey ph *Geoffrey Fisher* m Michel Legrand ad Carmen Dillon

Alan Bates, Julie Christie, Michael Redgrave, Dominic Guard, Michael Gough, Margaret Leighton, Edward Fox

'It's an almost palpable recreation of a past environment, and that environment is the film's real achievement, not the drama enacted within it.'—*Stanley Kauffmann*

AAN: Margaret Leighton

The Go-Getter
US 1937 90m bw
Warner (Sam Bischoff)

A one-legged navy veteran is determined that his injury will not prevent him from becoming a success.
Moderate comedy-drama, agreeably played.

w Delmer Daves, Peter B. Kyne *d* Busby Berkeley *ph* Arthur Edeson *md* Leo F. Forbstein

George Brent, Charles Winninger, Anita Louise, John Eldredge, Henry O'Neill, Willard Robertson, Eddie Acuff

Go for a Take
GB 1972 90m colour
Rank / Century Films (Roy Simpson)

Two waiters in debt to a gangster take refuge in a film studio.
Painful British farce.

w Alan Hackney *d* Harry Booth *ph* Mark McDonald *m* Glen Mason

Reg Varney, Norman Rossington, Sue Lloyd, Dennis Price, Julie Ege, Patrick Newell, David Lodge

Go for Broke
US 1951 93m bw
MGM (Dore Schary)

World War II exploits of Japanese-American soldiers.
Absolutely unsurprising war film with all the anti-Japs converted by the end. Production quite good.

wd Robert Pirosh *ph* Paul C. Vogel *m* Alberto Columbo

Van Johnson, Lane Nakano, George Miki, Akira Fukunaga, Warner Anderson, Don Haggerty

AAN: Robert Pirosh (as writer)

Go into Your Dance**
US 1935 89m bw
Warner (Sam Bischoff)
GB title: *Casino de Paree*

A big-headed star gets his come-uppance and finds happiness.

Moderate backstage musical notable for the only teaming of Jolson and Keeler, who were then married.

w Earl Baldwin *d* Archie Mayo *ph* Tony Gaudio, Sol Polito *songs* Harry Warren, Al Dubin

Al Jolson, Ruby Keeler, Glenda Farrell, Benny Rubin, Phil Regan, Barton MacLane, Sharon Lynne, Akim Tamiroff, Helen Morgan, Patsy Kelly

Go Man Go
US 1954 82m bw
Alfred Palca (Anton M. Leader)

How Abe Saperstein moulded and trained the Harlem Globetrotters basketball team.
Not so much a film as an athletic demonstration with some actors round the edges.

w Arnold Becker *d James Wong Howe ph* Bill Steiner *m* Alex North

Dane Clark, Sidney Poitier, Pat Breslin, Edmond Ryan

Go Naked in the World
US 1960 103m Metrocolor
Cinemascope
MGM / Arcola (Aaron Rosenberg)

A prostitute causes a rift between son and millionaire father.
Antediluvian melodrama with overblown performances.

wd Ranald MacDougall, *novel* Tom Chanales *ph* Milton Krasner *m* Adolph Deutsch

Gina Lollobrigida, Tony Franciosa, Ernest Borgnine, Luana Patten, Will Kuluva, Philip Ober

'A good example of how the increased liberation of Hollywood can be misused.'— *MFB*

Go Tell the Spartans
US 1978 114m CFI color
Spartan Company (Allan F. Badah, Mitchell Cannold)

In Vietnam, a seasoned commander tries to get a platoon of raw soldiers out of a Vietcong ambush.
We have been here before, in other wars, and since there is little heroism to be had from Vietnam it is difficult to see why we are invited again.

w Wendell Mayes, *story* Daniel Ford *d* Ted Post *ph* Harry Stradling Jnr *m* Dick Halligan

Burt Lancaster, Craig Wasson, Jonathan Goldsmith, Marc Singer

Go to Blazes
GB 1961   84m   Technicolor
  Cinemascope
ABP (Kenneth Harper)

Ex-convicts become firemen, intending to use the
engine for smash and grab raids.
Mild comedy ruined by wide screen.

w Patrick Campbell, Vivienne Knight d Michael
Truman ph Erwin Hillier m John Addison

Dave King, Daniel Massey, Norman
Rossington, Wilfrid Lawson, Maggie Smith,
Robert Morley, Coral Browne

Go West*
US 1925   70m (24 fps)   bw   silent
Buster Keaton / Metro

A tenderfoot makes friends with a cow and takes
it everywhere.
Disappointingly slow star comedy with splendid
moments.

w Raymond Cannon d Buster Keaton ph Bert
Haines, E. Lessley

Buster Keaton, Howard Truesdall, Kathleen
Myers

Go West**
US 1940   82m   bw
MGM (Jack Cummings)

Three zanies tackle a western villain.
Minor Marx comedy with a good start (the ticket
office sketch) and a rousing finale as they take a
moving train to bits, but some pretty soggy stuff
in between.

w Irving Brecher d Edward Buzzell ph Leonard
Smith m Georgie Stoll

Groucho, Harpo, Chico, John Carroll, Diana
Lewis, Robert Barrat

Go West Young Man
US 1936   80m   bw
Paramount (Emmanuel R. Cohen)

A movie star has a car breakdown in
Pennsylvania and falls for a local lad.
Cleaned-up Mae West vehicle, all rather boring.

w Mae West, play Personal Appearance by
Lawrence Riley d Henry Hathaway ph Karl
Struss m George Stoll

Mae West, Randolph Scott, Warren William,
Lyle Talbot, Alice Brady, Isabel Jewell,
Elizabeth Patterson

God Is My Co-Pilot
US 1945   89m   bw
Warner (Robert Buckner)

Pacific air adventures during World War II.
Adequate flagwaver.

w Peter Milne, Abem Finkel, book Col. Robert
Lee Scott Jnr d Robert Florey ph Sid Hickox
m Franz Waxman

Dennis Morgan, Dane Clark, Raymond
Massey, Alan Hale, Andrea King, John Ridgely,
Stanley Ridges, Craig Stevens

The Goddess*
US 1958   105m   bw
Columbia (Milton Perlman)

A small-town girl becomes a Hollywood sex
symbol and lives to regret it.
Savage attack on the Marilyn Monroe cult, a bit
lachrymose and compromised by miscasting,
but with interesting detail.

w Paddy Chayevsky d John Cromwell
ph Arthur J. Ornitz m Virgil Thompson

Kim Stanley, Lloyd Bridges, Steven Hill, Betty
Lou Holland

AAN: Paddy Chayevsky

The Godfather***
US 1971   175m   Technicolor
Paramount / Alfran (Albert S. Ruddy)

When, after ruling for two generations, the
Mafia's New York head dies of old age, his son
takes over reluctantly but later learns how to kill.
A brilliantly-made film with all the fascination of
a snake pit: a warm-hearted family saga except
that the members are thieves and murderers.
Cutting would help, but the duller conversational
sections do heighten the cunningly judged
moments of suspense and violence.

w Francis Ford Coppola, Mario Puzo, novel
Mario Puzo d Francis Ford Coppola
ph Gordon Willis m Nino Rota pd Dean
Tavoularis

Marlon Brando (unintentionally comic in an
absurd make-up), Al Pacino, Robert Duvall,
James Caan, Richard Castellano, Diane Keaton

  'The immorality lies in his presentation of
murderers as delightful family men—the
criminal is the salt of the earth—and to our
shame we rub it into the wounds of our
Watergate-world morality and even ask for
more.'—Judith Crist, 1974

  'They have put pudding in Brando's cheeks
and dirtied his teeth, he speaks hoarsely and
moves stiffly, and these combined mechanics are
hailed as great acting . . . Like star, like film, the
keynote is inflation. The Godfather was made
from a big bestseller, a lot of money was spent on
it, and it runs over three hours. Therefore it's
important.'—Stanley Kauffmann

AA: best picture; script; Marlon Brando
AAN: Francis Ford Coppola (as director); Al
Pacino; Robert Duvall; James Caan

The Godfather, Part Two***
US 1974 200m Technicolor
Paramount / the Coppola Company (Francis
Ford Coppola)

In 1958, Michael Corleone reflects on the
problems of himself and his father before him.
Curious rehash of part of the original with new
scenes, a shade difficult to follow but full of good
scenes and performances.

w Francis Ford Coppola, Mario Puzo d *Francis
Ford Coppola* ph Gordon Willis m Nino Rota
pd Dean Tavoularis

Al Pacino, *Robert de Niro*, Diane Keaton,
Robert Duvall, John Cazale, Lee Strasberg,
Michael V. Gazzo, Talia Shire

'The complete work is an epic vision of the
corruption of America.'—*New Yorker*

AA: best picture; script; Francis Ford Coppola
(as director); Nino Rota; Robert de Niro
AAN: Al Pacino; Lee Strasberg; Michael V.
Gazzo; Talia Shire

God's Country and the Woman
US 1936 80m Technicolor
Warner (Lou Edelman)

The junior partner of a lumber company goes to
work undercover in an opponent's camp, causes
trouble, and falls in love.
Adequate outdoor melodrama in early colour.

w Norman Reilly Raine, *novel* James Oliver
Curwood d William Keighley ph Tony Gaudio

George Brent, Beverly Roberts, Barton
MacLane, Robert Barrat, Alan Hale, Addison
Richards, El Brendel, Roscoe Ates, Billy Bevan

God's Little Acre*
US 1958 110m bw
Security (Sidney Harmon)

A poor white farmer in Georgia neglects his land
in a fruitless search for gold.
Tobacco Road under another name, and not so
lively: bowdlerized and eventually tedious
despite a welter of sensational incident and
depraved characters.

w Philip Yordan, *novel* Erskine Caldwell
d Anthony Mann ph Ernest Haller m *Elmer
Bernstein*

Robert Ryan, Aldo Ray, Tina Louise, Buddy
Hackett, Jack Lord, Vic Morrow, Rex Ingram

Godspell*
US 1973 102m TVC color
Columbia / Lansbury / Duncan / Beruh (Edgar
Lansbury)

The Gospel according to St Matthew played out
musically by hippies in the streets of New York.
Wild and woolly film version of the successful
theatrical fantasy, surviving chiefly by virtue of
its gleaming photography.

w David Greene, John Michael Tebelak,
play John Michael Tebelak d *David Greene*
ph Richard G. Heimann m/ly *Stephen Schwarz*

Victor Garber, David Haskell, Jerry Sroka,
Lynne Thigpen, Robin Lamont

'A patch of terra incognita somewhere
between *Sesame Street* and the gospel according
to *Laugh-In*.'—*Bruce Williamson*

Gog*
US 1954 85m Color Corporation 3D
Ivan Tors

In an underground laboratory in New Mexico, a
giant computer controls two robots, and a spy
programmes it to kill.
Brisk, imaginative low-budget sci-fi in gleaming
colour, well staged and developed.

w Tom Taggart d Herbert B. Strock
ph Lothrop B. Worth m Harry Sukman

Richard Egan, Constance Dowling, Herbert
Marshall

Goha
France / Tunisia 1957 90m Agfacolor
Films Franco-Africains

A young Arab helps a blind musician and falls in
love with a wise man's young bride.
Curiously winning, good-looking little romance
which, apart from an unexpected sad ending,
plays like an update of the Arabian Nights.

w Georges Schéhadé, *novel* Le Livre de Goha le
Simple by A. Ades, A. Jospiovici d *Jacques
Baratier* ph Jean Bourgoin m Maurice Ohana

Omar Chérif (later Sharif), Zina Bouzaiane,
Lauro Gazzolo

Going My Way**
US 1944 126m bw
Paramount (Leo McCarey)

A young priest comes to a New York slum
parish and after initial friction charms the old
pastor he is to succeed.
Sentimental comedy which got away with it
wonderfully at the time, largely through careful
casting, though it seems thin and obvious now.

w Frank Butler, Frank Cavett, Leo McCarey
d Leo McCarey ph Lionel Lindon

songs Johnny Burke, James Van Heusen, J. R. Shannon

Bing Crosby, Barry Fitzgerald, Rise Stevens, Frank McHugh, James Brown, Gene Lockhart, Jean Heather, Porter Hall

'I should not feel safe in recommending it to anyone but a simple-hearted sentimentalist with a taste for light music.'—*Richard Mallett, Punch*
† Father O'Malley reappeared in *The Bells of St Mary's* and *Say One for Me* (both qv).

AA: best picture; script; original story (Leo McCarey); Leo McCarey (direction); Bing Crosby; Barry Fitzgerald; title song (*m* James Van Heusen, *ly* Johnny Burke)
AAN: Lionel Lindon

Goin' South
US 1978   101m   Metrocolor
Paramount (Henry Gittes, Harold Schneider)

An unwashed outlaw is saved from the rope when a young girl promises to marry and reform him . . .
. . . for no very good reason. Curious semi-comic western which might have made a good two-reeler.

w John Herman Shaner, Al Ramrus, Charles Shyer, Alan Mandel *d* Jack Nickolson *ph* Nestor Almendros *m* Van Dyke Parks, Perry Botkin Jnr

Jack Nicholson, Mary Steenburgen, Christopher Lloyd, John Belushi, Veronica Cartwright, Richard Bradford

Going to Town*
US 1935   74m   bw
Paramount (William Le Baron)

A western oil heiress moves into society.
Reasonably satisfactory Mae West vehicle, the last in fact before the censor killed her style.

w Mae West *d* Alexander Hall *ph* Karl Struss *songs* Sammy Fain, Irving Kahal

Mae West, Paul Cavanagh, Ivan Lebedeff, Tito Coral, Marjorie Gateson, Fred Kohler Snr, Monroe Owsley

Gold**
GB 1974   124m   Technicolor   Panavision
Hemdale / Avton (Michael Klinger)

A South African mining engineer falls for the boss's granddaughter and exposes a conspiracy.
Old-fashioned thick ear with spectacular underground sequences and a rousing finale.

w Wilbur Smith, Stanley Price *d* Peter Hunt *ph* Ousama Rawi *m* Elmer Bernstein

Roger Moore, Susannah York, Ray Milland, Bradford Dillman, John Gielgud, Tony Beckley

AAN: song 'Wherever Love Takes Me' (*m* Elmer Bernstein, *ly* Don Black)

Gold Diggers of Broadway*
US 1929   98m   Technicolor
Warner

Three Broadway chorus girls seek rich husbands.
Fascinating primitive musical.

w Robert Lord, *play* The Gold Diggers by Avery Hopwood *d* Roy del Ruth *ph* Barney McGill, Ray Rennahan *songs* Al Dubin, Joe Burke

Nancy Welford, Conway Tearle, Winnie Lightner, Ann Pennington, Lilyan Tashman, William Bakewell, Nick Lucas

'Exceeds in pretentiousness and beauty anything which has yet appeared on the screen!'—*publicity*
† Other versions of the play include *The Gold Diggers* (1923), *Gold Diggers of 1933* (qv), *Painting the Clouds with Sunshine* (qv).

Gold Diggers of 1933***
US 1933   96m   bw
Warner (Robert Lord)

Cheerful, competent, well-cast remake of the above; numbers include 'My Forgotten Man', 'We're in the Money' and 'Pettin' in the Park'.

w Erwin Gelsey, James Seymour, David Boehm, Ben Markson *d* Mervyn Le Roy *ch* Busby Berkeley *songs* Harry Warren, Al Dubin *ph* Sol Polito

Warren William, Joan Blondell, *Aline MacMahon*, Ruby Keeler, Dick Powell, Guy Kibbee, Ned Sparks, Ginger Rogers, Clarence Nordstrom

Gold Diggers of 1935**
US 1935   95m   bw
Warner (Robert Lord)

A socialite puts on a Broadway show at her country home, and is taken in by a swindler.
Heavy-handed but laugh-provoking comedy with familiar faces of the day, climaxed by big numbers including 'Lullaby of Broadway'.

w Manuel Seff, Peter Milne, Robert Lord *d/ch* Busby Berkeley *ph* George Barnes *songs* Al Dubin, Harry Warren

Dick Powell, Adolphe Menjou, Gloria Stuart, Alice Brady, Hugh Herbert, Glenda Farrell, Frank McHugh, Grant Mitchell, Wini Shaw

'Busby Berkeley, the master of scenic prestidigitation, continues to dazzle the eye and stun the imagination.'—*André Sennwald, New York Times*

'A decidedly heady mixture.'—*Pare Lorentz*

AA: song 'Lullaby of Broadway'

Gold Diggers of 1937*
US 1937 100m bw
Warner (Hal B. Wallis)

A group of insurance salesmen back a show.
Mild tailing-off of the Gold Diggers series,
though with the accustomed production polish.

w Warren Duff, *play* Richard Maibaum,
Michael Wallach, George Haight *d* Lloyd
Bacon *ch Busby Berkeley ph* Arthur Edeson
songs Harry Warren, Al Dubin,
E. Y. Harburg, Harold Arlen

Dick Powell, Joan Blondell, Glenda Farrell,
Victor Moore, Lee Dixon, Osgood Perkins,
Charles D. Brown

Gold Diggers in Paris*
US 1938 95m bw
Warner (Sam Bischoff)
GB title: *The Gay Imposters*

Three girls chase rich husbands abroad.
A thin end to the series, saved by an agreeable
cast.

w Earl Baldwin, Warren Duff *d* Ray Enright
ph Sol Polito, George Barnes *ch Busby
Berkeley songs* Harry Warren, Al Dubin,
Johnny Mercer

Rudy Vallee, Rosemary Lane, Hugh Herbert,
Allen Jenkins, Gloria Dickson, Melville Cooper,
Fritz Feld, Ed Brophy, Curt Bois

Gold Is Where You Find It*
US 1938 90m Technicolor
Warner (Sam Bischoff)

Gold rush miners settle as California farmers.
Agreeable western in excellent early colour.

w Warren Duff, Clements Ripley, Robert
Buckner *d* Michael Curtiz ph Sol Polito
m Max Steiner

George Brent, Olivia de Havilland, Claude
Rains, Margaret Lindsay, John Litel, Marcia
Ralston, Barton MacLane, Tim Holt, Sidney
Toler

Gold of Naples
Italy 1955 135m bw
Ponti-de Laurentiis
original title: *L'Oro di Napoli*

Six sketches, comic and tragic, give an
impression of Naples today.
A variable collection, mainly shown around the
world in abridged versions.

w Cesare Zavattini, Vittorio de Sica, Giuseppe
Marotta *d* Vittorio de Sica *ph* Otello Martelli
m Alessandro Cicognini

Vittorio de Sica, Eduardo de Filippo, Toto,
Sophia Loren, Paolo Stoppa, Silvana Mangano

Gold of the Seven Saints
US 1961 89m bw Warnerscope
Warner (Leonard Freeman)

Cowboys compete in a search for lost gold.
Adequate minor western using TV stars.

w Leigh Brackett, Leonard Freeman *d* Gordon
Douglas *ph* Joseph Biroc *m* Howard Jackson

Clint Walker, Roger Moore, Leticia Roman,
Robert Middleton, Chill Wills, Gene Evans

The Golden Age of Comedy****
US 1957 78m bw
Robert Youngson Productions

First of the scholarly compilations of silent
comedy which saved many negatives from
destruction, this is a fast-paced general survey
which despite a facetious sound track does
provide a laugh a minute. It particularly brought
Laurel and Hardy back into public notice, and
includes sections from *Two Tars* and *The Battle
of the Century*.

wd Robert Youngson narrators Dweight Weist,
Ward Wilson *m* George Steiner

Stan Laurel, Oliver Hardy, Harry Langdon, Ben
Turpin, Will Rogers, Billy Bevan, Charlie Chase,
Andy Clyde

The Golden Blade
US 1953 80m Technicolor
U-I (Richard Wilson)

With the help of a magic sword, Harun saves a
princess and captures a rebel.
Standard cut-rate Arabian Nights adventure,
very typical of its studio during the fifties.

w John Rich *d* Nathan Juran *ph* Maury
Gertsman *m* Joseph Gershenson

Rock Hudson, Piper Laurie, George Macready,
Gene Evans, Kathleen Hughes

Golden Boy*
US 1939 101m bw
Columbia (William Perlberg)

A poor boy is torn between two absorbing
interests: prizefighting and the violin.
Personalized version of a socially conscious
play; moderately effective with smooth
production and good cast.

w Lewis Meltzer, Daniel Taradash, Sarah Y.
Mason, Victor Heerman, *play* Clifford Odets

d Rouben Mamoulian *ph* Nicholas Musuraca,
Karl Freund *m* Victor Young *md* Morris
Stoloff

Barbara Stanwyck, *William Holden*, Adolphe
Menjou, Joseph Calleia, *Lee J. Cobb*, Sam
Levene, Edward Brophy, Don Beddoe
   'A slick, swift, exciting but insensitive
movie.'—*Gordon Sager*

AAN: Victor Young

The Golden Coach
Italy / France 1952   100m   Technicolor
Hoche / Panaria (Francesco Alliata)
original title: *Le Carrosse d'Or*

In Spanish South America in the 18th century,
the leading lady of a band of strolling players
turns all heads including that of the viceroy, who
scandalizes all by making her a present of his
official golden coach.
The director seems to have been chiefly
interested in the colour and the backgrounds: the
story is a bore and the leading lady ill-chosen.

w Jean Renoir, Jack Kirkland, Renzo Avanzo,
Giulio Macchi *d* Jean Renoir *ph* *Claude
Renoir* *m* Vivaldi

Anna Magnani, Duncan Lamont, Paul
Campbell, Ricardo Rioli, William Tubbs

Golden Earrings*
US 1947   95m   bw
Paramount (Harry Tugend)

A British Intelligence officer is helped by a gypsy
to sneak a poison gas formula out of Nazi
Germany.
One of the silliest stories of all time, despite the
presence of Quentin Reynolds asserting that he
believed it; also lacking in the humour which
might have saved it, but produced with polish
and interesting for the two stars at this stage in
their careers.

w Abraham Polonsky, Frank Butler, Helen
Deutsch, *novel* Yolanda Foldes *d* *Mitchell
Leisen* *ph* Daniel L. Fapp *m* Victor Young

Ray Milland, Marlene Dietrich, Murvyn Vye,
Bruce Lester, Dennis Hoey, Reinhold Schuntzel,
Ivan Triesault
   'A good deal of torso work goes on which I
can't help feeling they're a bit old for.'—*Richard
Winnington*

Golden Girl*
US 1951   108m   Technicolor
TCF (George Jessel)

The story of Lotta Crabtree, who after the Civil
War determined to become a great musical star.
Harmless semi-western biopic with good tunes.

w Walter Bullock, Charles O'Neal, Gladys
Lehman *d* Lloyd Bacon *ph* Charles G. Clarke
md Lionel Newman *ch* Seymour Felix

Mitzi Gaynor, Dale Robertson, Dennis Day,
James Barton, Una Merkel, Raymond Walburn,
Gene Sheldon

AAN: song 'Never' (*m* Lionel Newman, *ly* Eliot
Daniel)

The Golden Head
US / Hungary 1964   115m   Technirama
70
Cinerama / Hungarofilm

Passengers on a Danube pleasure boat become
involved in the theft of the golden head of St
Laszlo.
Travelogue with a thin plot, somewhat slow
moving but suitable for children.

w Stanley Boulder, Ivan Boldizsar *d* Richard
Thorpe *ph* Istvan Hildebrand *m* Peter Fenyes

George Sanders, Buddy Hackett, Douglas
Wilmer, Jess Conrad, Robert Coote

The Golden Horde
US 1951   76m   Technicolor
U-I (Howard Christie)

Crusaders meet Mongols in Samarkand, and Sir
Guy wins a princess.
Rather priceless idiocies are perpetrated in this
variation on the studio's favourite Arabian
Nights theme, but somehow they fail to make
one laugh, which should be the only possible
response to such a farrago.

w Gerald Drayson Adams *d* George Sherman
ph Russell Metty *m* Hans Salter

David Farrar, Ann Blyth, George Macready,
Henry Brandon, Richard Egan, Marvin Miller

The Golden Mistress*
US 1954   80m   Technicolor
UA / RK (Richard Kay, Harry Rybnick)

An American and his girl friend search the sea
bed for the forbidden treasure of a Haitian tribe.
Curious independent production, an adventure
in the style of silent serials; amateur in many
ways, yet with a freshness of photography and
location plus some powerful voodoo scenes.

wd Fred Judge *ph* William C. Thompson
m Raoul Kraushaar

John Agar, Rosemarie Bowe, Abner Biberman

Golden Needles
US 1974   92m   Movielab   Panavision
AIP / Sequoia (Fred Weintraub, Paul Heller)
Various factions seek a Hong Kong statue

showing seven miraculous acupuncture points.
Youth/sex/Kung Fu/James Bond action
amalgam.

w S. Lee Pogostin, Sylvia Schneble d Robert
Clouse ph Gilbert Hubbs m Lalo Schifrin

Joe Don Baker, Elizabeth Ashley, Jim Kelly,
Burgess Meredith, Ann Sothern

Golden Rendezvous
US 1977 109m colour
Film Trust / Milton Okun

Murderous mercenaries take over a freighter, but
reckon without the courageous first officer.
Blood-and-thunder hokum with many casualties
but not much sense.

w Stanley Price, novel Alistair MacLean
d Ashley Lazarus ph Ken Higgins m Jeff
Wayne

Richard Harris, Ann Turkel, David Janssen,
Burgess Meredith, John Vernon, Gordon
Jackson, Keith Baxter, Dorothy Malone, John
Carradine, Robert Flemyng, Leigh Lawson,
Robert Beatty

The Golden Salamander
GB 1949 87m bw
GFD / Pinewood (Ronald Neame, Alexander
Galperson)

An Englishman in Tunis defeats gun runners.
Boring and unconvincing action hokum.

w Lesley Storm, Victor Canning, Ronald
Neame, novel Victor Canning d Ronald Neame
ph Oswald Morris m William Alwyn

Trevor Howard, Anouk Aimée, Herbert Lom,
Miles Malleson, Walter Rilla, Jacques Sernas,
Wilfrid Hyde-White, Peter Copley

The Golden Voyage of Sinbad*
GB 1973 105m Eastmancolor
Columbia / Morningside (Charles H. Schneer)

Sinbad finds a strange map and crosses swords
with a great magician.
Routine, rather uninspired fantasy enlivened by
grotesque trick effects.

w Brian Clemens, Ray Harryhausen d Gordon
Hessler ph Ted Moore m Miklos Rozsa sp Ray
Harryhausen pd John Stoll

John Philip Law, Caroline Munro, Tom Baker,
Douglas Wilmer, Grégoire Aslan

Goldfinger***
GB 1964 112m Technicolor
UA / Eon (Harry Saltzman, Albert R. Broccoli)

James Bond prevents an international gold
smuggler from robbing Fort Knox.
Probably the liveliest and most amusing of the

Bond spy spoofs, with a fairly taut plot between
the numerous highlights. The big budget is well
used.

w Richard Maibaum, Paul Dehn, novel Ian
Fleming d Guy Hamilton ph Ted Moore
m John Barry pd Ken Adam titles Robert
Brownjohn

Sean Connery, Honor Blackman, Gert Frobe,
Harold Sakata, Shirley Eaton, Bernard Lee, Lois
Maxwell, Desmond Llewellyn

'A dazzling object lesson in the principle that
nothing succeeds like excess.'—Penelope
Gilliatt

'A diverting comic strip for grown-ups.'—
Judith Crist

The Goldwyn Follies**
US 1938 115m Technicolor
Samuel Goldwyn

A Hollywood producer seeks the average girl to
test his scripts.
Goldwyn's failure to become Ziegfeld, chiefly
due to a lack of humour in the script, still has a
soupçon of effective Hollywood satire and some
excellent numbers.

w Ben Hecht d George Marshall ph Gregg
Toland m Alfred Newman ch George
Balanchine ad Richard Day

Kenny Baker, Vera Zorina, the Ritz Brothers,
Adolphe Menjou, Edgar Bergen and Charlie
McCarthy, Helen Jepson, Phil Baker, Ella
Logan, Bobby Clark, Jerome Cowan, Nydia
Westman

AAN: Alfred Newman

The Golem***
Germany 1920 75m approx bw silent
UFA

In 16th-century Prague a Jewish Rabbi
constructs a man of clay to defend his people
against a pogrom.
There were several versions of this story
(Germany 1913, sequel 1917; Czechoslovakia
1935 and 1951), but this is almost certainly the
best, its splendid sets, performances and certain
scenes all being clearly influential on later
Hollywood films, especially Frankenstein.

w Paul Wegener, Henrik Galeen d Paul
Wegener, Carl Boese ph Karl Freund, Guido
Seeber ad Hans Poelzig

Paul Wegener, Albert Steinruck, Ernst Deutsch

Gone to Earth
GB 1948 110m Technicolor
London Films / David O. Selznick
US title: The Wild Heart

In the 1890s, a wild Shropshire girl is desired by
the local squire.
Unintentionally funny film version of an
intractable novel.

w/p/d Michael Powell and Emeric Pressburger,
novel Mary Webb *ph* Christopher Challis
m Brian Easdale *pd* Hein Heckroth

Jennifer Jones, David Farrar, Cyril Cusack,
Esmond Knight, Sybil Thorndike, Edward
Chapman, George Cole, Hugh Griffith, Beatrice
Varley

'It tries hard to be a powerful work of art, but it
is intrinsically artificial and pretentious.'—
Richard Mallett, Punch

Gone with the Wind****
US 1939   220m   Technicolor
MGM / *David O. Selznick*

An egotistic Southern girl survives the Civil War
but finally loses the only man she cares for.
The only film in history which could be
profitably revived for forty years: 'still pure
gold', said the *Daily Mirror* in 1975. Whole
books have been written about it; its essential
appeal is that of a romantic story with strong
characters and an impeccable production. The
widescreen version produced in the late sixties
ruined its composition and colour, but it is to be
hoped that the original negative still survives.

w Sidney Howard (and others), *novel Margaret
Mitchell d Victor Fleming* (and George Cukor,
Sam Wood) *ph Ernest Haller, Ray Rennahan
m Max Steiner pd William Cameron Menzies
ad Lyle Wheeler*

Clark Gable, Vivien Leigh, Olivia de Havilland,
Leslie Howard, Thomas Mitchell, Barbara
O'Neil, *Hattie McDaniel, Butterfly McQueen*,
Victor Jory, Evelyn Keyes, Ann Rutherford,
Laura Hope Crews, Harry Davenport, Jane
Darwell, Ona Munson, Ward Bond

'A major event in the history of the industry
but only a minor event in motion picture art.
There are moments when the two categories
meet on good terms, but the long stretches
between are filled with mere spectacular
efficiency.'—*Franz Hoellering, The Nation*
† The best account of the film's making is in
Gavin Lambert's 1975 book, *GWTW*.
†† In the early seventies a stage musical version
toured the world; music by Harold Rome.

AA: best picture; Sidney Howard; Victor
Fleming; Ernest Haller, Ray Rennahan; Lyle
Wheeler; Vivien Leigh; Hattie McDaniel; Hal C.
Kern and James E. Newcom (editors)
AAN: Max Steiner; Clark Gable; Olivia de
Havilland

The Good Companions***
GB 1932   113m   bw
Gaumont / Welsh–Pearson (T. A. Welsh,
George Pearson)

Three ill-assorted people take to the road and in
various capacities join the Dinky Doos pierrot
troupe.
Gallant, mini-budgeted version of Priestley's
popular picaresque novel. A little faded now, it
retains some of its vigour, and the performances
please.

w W. P. Lipscomb, Angus Macphail, Ian
Dalrymple,
novel J. B. Priestley d Victor Saville

Edmund Gwenn, Mary Glynne, John Gielgud,
Jessie Matthews, Percy Parsons, A. W.
Baskomb, Dennis Hoey, Richard Dolman,
Frank Pettingell, Finlay Currie, *Max Miller*,
Jack Hawkins, George Zucco

The Good Companions*
GB 1956   104m   Technicolor
   Cinemascope
ABP (Hamilton Inglis, J. Lee-Thompson)

Faint-hearted remake of the above, unwisely
Cinemascoped and leaving no impression.

w T. J. Morrison *d* J. Lee-Thompson *ph* Gilbert
Taylor *m* Laurie Johnson

Eric Portman, Celia Johnson, John Fraser,
Janette Scott, Hugh Griffith, Bobby Howes,
Rachel Roberts, John Salew, Thora Hird
† A stage musical version (music by André
Previn) had moderate success in London in
1974.

The Good Die Young*
GB 1954   98m   bw
Remus (Jack Clayton)

Four crooks, all with private problems, set out to
rob a mail van.
Glum all-star melodrama which set a pattern for
such things; worth waiting for is the climactic
chase through underground stations.

w Vernon Harris, Lewis Gilbert *d* Lewis
Gilbert *ph* Jack Asher *m* Georges Auric

Laurence Harvey, Margaret Leighton, Gloria
Grahame, Richard Basehart, Joan Collins, John
Ireland, Renè Ray, Stanley Baker, Robert
Morley

The Good Earth***
US 1937   138m   bw
MGM (*Irving Thalberg*)

A Chinese peasant grows rich but loses his
beloved wife.
A massive, well-meaning and fondly

remembered production which is nevertheless
artificial, unconvincing and pretty undramatic in
the second half. The star performances impress
to begin with, then wear thin, but the final locust
attack is as well done as it originally seemed.
Historically valuable as a Hollywood prestige
production of the thirties.

w Talbot Jennings, Tess Schlesinger, Claudine
West, *play* Owen and Donald Davis, *novel* Pearl
S. Buck *d Sidney Franklin ph* Karl Freund
m Herbert Stothart *montage* Slavko
Vorkapitch *ad* Cedric Gibbons

Paul Muni, Luise Rainer, Walter Connolly, Tilly
Losch, Jessie Ralph, Charley Grapewin, Keye
Luke, Harold Huber

   'One of the superb visual adventures of the
period.'—*John Baxter, 1968*

   'Prestigious boredom, and it goes on for a very
long time.'—*New Yorker, 1977*

AA: Karl Freund; Luise Rainer
AAN: best picture; Sidney Franklin

The Good Fairy*
US 1935 90m bw
Universal (Henry Henigson)

A beautiful but naïve cinema usherette ensnares
three rich men.
Unusual, rather lumpy romantic comedy using
top talent.

w Preston Sturges, play Ferenc Molnar
d William Wyler ph Norbert Brodine

Margaret Sullavan, Herbert Marshall, Frank
Morgan, Reginald Owen, Alan Hale, Beulah
Bondi, Cesar Romero, Eric Blore, Al Bridge
† Remade as *Because of Him* (qv).

Good Girls Go To Paris*
US 1939 75m bw
Columbia (William Perlberg)

After several zany adventures, a Greek professor
marries a gold digger.
Amusingly crazy comedy, one of the last of its
type.

w Gladys Lehman, Ken Englund *d* Alexander
Hall *ph* Henry Freulich *md* Morris Stoloff

Melvyn Douglas, Joan Blondell, Walter
Connolly, Alan Curtis, Joan Perry, Isabel Jeans,
Alexander D'Arcy, Clarence Kolb

The Good Guys and the Bad Guys*
US 1969 90m Technicolor Panavision
Warner (Robert M. Goldstein)

An ageing sheriff and a train robber have one last
showdown.
Good-humoured, black-flavoured western set in
the early days of automobiles.

w Ronald M. Cohen, Dennis Shyrack *d* Burt
Kennedy *ph* Harry Stradling Jnr *m* William
Lava

Robert Mitchum, George Kennedy, David
Carradine, Tina Louise, Douglas Fowley,
Martin Balsam, Lois Nettleton, John Davis
Chandler, John Carradine, Marie Windsor

Good Morning Boys**
GB 1937 79m bw
GFD / Gainsborough (Edward Black)

A schoolmaster takes his troublesome pupils to
Paris and becomes involved with an art theft.
Sprightly vehicle for the star's seedy
schoolmaster persona: it established him as a
major draw in British films.

*w Marriott Edgar, Val Guest, Anthony
Kimmins d Marcel Varnel*

Will Hay, Graham Moffatt, Lilli Palmer, Mark
Daly, Peter Gawthorne, Martita Hunt, Charles
Hawtrey, Will Hay Jnr
† Remade with Ronald Shiner as *Top of the
Form.*

Good Morning Miss Dove
US 1955 107m Eastmancolor
   Cinemascope
TCF (Samuel G. Engel)

While recovering from an operation, a small-
town schoolmistress looks back on her career.
A fairly spirited weepie with a happy ending and
a strong sense of cynicism behind the scenes.

w Eleanore Griffin, *novel* Frances Gray Patton
d Henry Koster *ph* Leon Shamroy *m* Leigh
Harline

Jennifer Jones, Robert Stack, Robert Douglas,
Kipp Hamilton, Peggy Knudsen, Marshall
Thompson, Chuck Connors, Mary Wickes

   'Mr Chips has changed sex and habitat while
preserving intact his ability to provoke epidemics
of sentimentality.'—*MFB*

Good Neighbour Sam
US 1964 130m Eastmancolor
Columbia / David Swift

A prissy suburban advertising man becomes
innocently involved in a pretence to be the
husband of the divorcee next door.
A promising comic idea is here ruined by
lengthiness, lack of funny lines, and no apparent
idea of how to film a farce. The actors are driven
to repeating every trick a dozen times.

w James Fritzell, Everett Greenbaum, David
Swift, *novel* Jack Finney *d* David Swift
ph Burnett Guffey *m* Frank de Vol

Jack Lemmon, Romy Schneider, Dorothy

Provine, Senta Berger, Edward G. Robinson,
Mike Connors, Edward Andrews, Louis Nye

Good News

US 1930   85m approx   bw
MGM

Fraternity tensions are sorted out in time for the
big football game.
Spirited early talkie musical.

w Frances Marion, Joe Farnham d Nick
Grinde, Edgar McGregor songs De Sylva,
Brown and Henderson

Bessie Love, Stanley Smith, Gus Shy, Mary
Lawlor, Lola Lane, Dorothy McNulty, Cliff
Edwards

Good News*

US 1947   83m   Technicolor
MGM (Arthur Freed)

Bright, good-humoured remake of the above.

w Betty Comden, Adolph Green d Charles
Walters ph Charles Schoenbaum md Lennie
Hayton

June Allyson, Peter Lawford, Patricia Marshall,
Joan McCracken, Mel Tormé

AAN: song 'Pass that Peace Pipe' (m/ly Ralph
Blane, Hugh Martin, Roger Edens)

The Good Old Days

GB 1939   79m   bw
Warner

A noble child is kidnapped by a chimney sweep
and saved by strolling players.
Curious Victorian vehicle for a snappy 20th-
century star.

w Austin Melford, John Dighton d Roy William
Neill

Max Miller, Hal Walters, Kathleen Gibson, H.
F. Maltby, Martita Hunt, Allan Jeayes, Roy
Emerton

Good Sam

US 1948   114m   bw
Rainbow (Leo McCarey)

A small-town business man is so charitable that
he finds himself bankrupt.
Poor, disjointed, overlong and obvious comedy
in the Capra style.

w Ken Englund d Leo McCarey ph George
Barnes m Robert Emmett Dolan

Gary Cooper, Ann Sheridan, Ray Collins,
Edmund Lowe, Joan Lorring, Ruth Roman,
Clinton Sundberg

'A bit too long, but in its incidentals often very
enjoyable.'—*Richard Mallett, Punch*

The Good, the Bad and the Ugly

Italy 1968   180m   Techniscope
PEA (Alberto Grimaldi)
original title: *Il Buono, il Bruto, il Cattivo*

During the American Civil War, three men seek
hidden loot.
Intermittently lively, very violent, and
interminably drawn out western with a number
of rather hilarious stylistic touches.

w Age Scarpelli, Luciano Vincenzoni, Sergio
Leone d Sergio Leone ph Tonino delli Colli
m Ennio Morricone

Clint Eastwood, Eli Wallach, Lee Van Cleef

Goodbye Again*

US 1961   120m   bw
UA / Mercury / Argus / Anatole Litvak

A woman of forty swaps her rich lover for a
young law student.
Melancholy romantic drama, well produced and
staged on Paris locations.

w Samuel Taylor, *novel* Aimez-vous Brahms by
Françoise Sagan d Anatole Litvak ph Armand
Thirard m Georges Auric

Ingrid Bergman, Anthony Perkins, Yves
Montand, Jessie Royce Landis, Jackie Lane
'A grey-toned Sagan novella, spread wide and
lush over two hours of screen time.'—*MFB*
'The kind of "woman's picture" that gives
women a bad name.'—*Judith Crist, 1973*

Goodbye Charlie*

US 1964   116m   De Luxe   Cinemascope
TCF / Venice (David Weisbart)

A philandering gangster, shot dead by an irate
husband, is reincarnated in his friend's house as
a dishy blonde.
Overlong but amusing Broadway comedy for
wisecrackers, uninventively adapted.

w Harry Kurnitz, *play* George Axelrod
d Vincente Minnelli ph Milton Krasner
m André Previn

Debbie Reynolds, Pat Boone, Walter Matthau,
Tony Curtis

Goodbye Columbus**

US 1969   105m   Technicolor
Paramount / Willow Tree (Stanley Jaffe)

A young Jewish librarian has an affair with the
wilful daughter of a *nouveau riche* family.
An amusing and well-observed delineation of
two kinds of Jewish life in New York; the story,
despite its frank talk of penises and diaphragms,
leaves much to be desired, and the style is post-
Graduate.

w Arnold Schulman, *novel* Philip Roth *d* Larry Peerce *ph* Gerald Hirschfeld *m* Charles Fox

Richard Benjamin, Ali MacGraw, Jack Klugman, Nan Martin, Michael Meyers, Lori Shelle

'Every father's daughter is a virgin!'— *publicity*

AAN: Arnold Schulman

The Goodbye Girl*

US 1977   110m   Metrocolor
Warner / Rastar (Ray Stark)

A misunderstanding about the lease of an apartment results in a girl dancer agreeing to share it with a would-be actor.

A very moderate script assisted by excellent acting and the usual array of Neil Simon one-liners. Nothing at all new, but enjoyable.

w Neil Simon *d* Herbert Ross *ph* David M. Walsh *m* Dave Grusin

Richard Dreyfuss, Marsha Mason, Quinn Cummings, Paul Benedict, Barbara Rhoades

Goodbye Mr Chips***

GB 1939   114m   bw
MGM (Victor Saville)

The life of a shy schoolmaster from his first job to his death.

Sentimental romance in MGM's best style, a long-standing favourite for its performances and humour; but the production seems slightly unsatisfactory these days.

w R. C. Sherriff, Claudine West, Eric Maschwitz, *novel* James Hilton *d* Sam Wood *ph* Frederick A. Young *m* Richard Addinsell

Robert Donat, Greer Garson, Paul Henreid, Lyn Harding, Austin Trevor, Terry Kilburn, John Mills, Milton Rosmer, Judith Furse

'The whole picture has an assurance, bears a glow of popularity like the face of a successful candidate on election day. And it is wrong to despise popularity in the cinema.'—*Graham Greene*

'The picture has no difficulty in using two hours to retell a story that was scarcely above short story length. *Mr Chips* is worth its time.'— *New York Times*

AA: Robert Donat
AAN: best picture; script; Sam Wood; Greer Garson

Goodbye Mr Chips*

GB 1969   147m   Metrocolor   Panavision 70
MGM / APJAC (Arthur P. Jacobs)
Elaborate musical remake of the above. Slow

and slushy, with no improvement visible whatever; but a few of the trimmings please.

w Terence Rattigan *d* Herbert Ross *ph* Oswald Morris *m* Leslie Bricusse *pd* Ken Adam *ad* John Williams

Peter O'Toole, Petula Clark, Michael Bryant, Michael Redgrave, George Baker, Jack Hedley, Sian Phillips, Alison Leggatt

'The sum total is considerably less than the parts.'—*Variety*

AAN: Leslie Bricusse; John Williams; Peter O'Toole

Goodbye My Fancy

US 1951   107m   bw
Warner (Henry Blanke)

A congresswoman returns to her old college for an honorary degree, and falls in love.
Tolerable romantic flim-flam.

w Ivan Goff, Ben Roberts, *play* Fay Kanin *d* Vincent Sherman *ph* Ted McCord *m* Daniele Amfitheatrof

Joan Crawford, Robert Young, Frank Lovejoy, Eve Arden, Janice Rule

Goodbye My Lady*

US 1956   95m   bw
Batjac

A Mississippi swamp boy finds a valuable dog but eventually returns it to its owner.
Reliable, slightly unusual family film.

w Sid Fleischman, *novel* James Street *d* William Wellman *ph* William H. Clothier, Archie Stout *m* Laurindo Almeida, George Field

Brandon de Wilde, Walter Brennan, Phil Harris, Sidney Poitier, William Hopper, Louise Beavers

Goodnight Vienna

GB 1933   76m   bw
British and Dominions (Herbert Wilcox)
US title: *Magic Night*

In 1913 Vienna, a general's son falls for a shopgirl.

Already dated when it was made, this thin musical romance nevertheless made a star of Anna Neagle and re-established Jack Buchanan on the screen.

w Holt Marvel, George Posford, from their radio play *d* Herbert Wilcox

Jack Buchanan, Anna Neagle, Gina Malo, Clive Currie, William Kendall

The Goose Steps Out*

GB 1942   79m   bw
Ealing (S. C. Balcon)

To steal a secret weapon, an incompetent teacher is sent into Germany in place of his Nazi double. Quite amusing star vehicle, not up to his best standards.

w Angus Macphail, John Dighton *d* Will Hay, Basil Dearden

Will Hay, Charles Hawtrey, Frank Pettingell, Julien Mitchell, Peter Croft, Jeremy Hawk, Peter Ustinov, Raymond Lovell, Barry Morse

The Goose Woman
US 1925   90m approx   bw   silent
Universal

A young actress falls for the son of an embittered old one.
Interesting character melodrama of which prints have survived.

w Melville Brown, *story* Rex Beach *d* Clarence Brown *ph* Milton Moore

Louise Dresser, Jack Pickford, Constance Bennett, James Barrows

Gordon's War
US 1973   90m   TVC color
TCF / Palomar (Robert L. Schaffel)

A black Vietnam veteran returns to Harlem and avenges the death of his wife.
Violent vigilante melodrama with vivid locations.

w Howard Friedlander, Ed Spielman *d* Ossie Davis *ph* Victor J. Kemper *m* Andy Bodale, Al Ellis

Paul Winfield, Carl Lee, David Downing

The Gorgeous Hussy*
US 1936   105m   bw
MGM (Joseph L. Mankiewicz)

The love life of Peggy O'Neal, protégée of President Andrew Jackson.
Bowdlerized all-star historical drama; the production values are better than the script.

w Ainsworth Morgan, Stephen Morehouse Avery, *novel* Samuel Hopkins Adams *d* Clarence Brown *ph* George Folsey *m* Herbert Stothart

Joan Crawford, Lionel Barrymore, Franchot Tone, Melvyn Douglas, Robert Taylor, James Stewart, Alison Skipworth, Louis Calhern, Beulah Bondi, Melville Cooper, Sidney Toler, Gene Lockhart

AAN: George Folsey; Beulah Bondi

Gorgo
GB 1960   78m   Technicolor
King Brothers (Wilfrid Eades)

A prehistoric monster is caught in Irish waters and brought to London, but rescued by its mother.
Amiable monster hokum with a happy ending but not much technical resource.

w John Loring, Daniel Hyatt *d* Eugene Lourié *ph* Frederick A. Young *m* Angelo Lavagnino *sp* Tom Howard

Bill Travers, William Sylvester, Vincent Winter, Christopher Rhodes, Joseph O'Conor, Bruce Seton, Martin Benson

The Gorgon*
GB 1964   83m   Technicolor
Hammer (Anthony Nelson Keys)

A castle ruin near a German village is infested by Megaera, the gorgon of ancient myth, whose gaze turns people to stone and who can take over the form of an unknowing villager.
Writhing snakes in the hair-do being too great a challenge to the make-up man, the monster is barely glimpsed and the film becomes a who-is-it, all quite suspenseful despite the central idea being too silly for words.

w John Gilling *d* Terence Fisher *ph* Michael Reed *m* James Bernard

Peter Cushing, Christopher Lee, Barbara Shelley, Richard Pasco, Patrick Troughton

The Gorilla*
US 1939   66m   bw
TCF

A murderer blames an escaped gorilla for his crimes.
Spooky house mystery comedy revamped as a Ritz Brothers vehicle; not much suspense, but it all looks good and the cast is highly satisfactory.

w Rian James, Sid Silvers, *play* Ralph Spence *d* Allan Dwan *ph* Edward Cronjager *m* David Buttolph

The Ritz Brothers, Bela Lugosi, Lionel Atwill, Patsy Kelly, Joseph Calleia, Anita Louise, Edward Norris, Wally Vernon
† There were two previous versions, in 1927 with Charlie Murray and 1931 with Joe Frisco.

Gorilla at Large
US 1954   93m   Technicolor   3-D
TCF / Panoramic (Robert L. Jacks)

A circus gorilla is used as a cover for murder.
Silly thriller with the gorilla as unconvincing as the story.

w Leonard Praskins, Barney Slater *d* Harmon Jones

Anne Bancroft, Lee J. Cobb, Cameron Mitchell,

Lee Marvin, Raymond Burr, Charlotte Austin,
Peter Whitney, Warren Stevens

The Gospel According to St Matthew*
Italy / France 1964   142m   bw
Arco / Lux (Alfredo Bini)
original title: Il Vangelo Secondo Matteo

The life of Christ seen almost as a ciné-vérité
documentary: the tone is realist but not notably
iconoclastic.

wd Pier Paolo Pasolini ph Tonino delli Colli
m Bach, Mozart, Prokofiev md Luis Enrique
Bacalov

Enrique Irazoqui, Susanna Pasolini, Mario
Socrate

AAN: Luis Enrique Bacalov

Goupi Mains Rouges*
France 1943   95m   bw
Minerva
US title: It Happened at the Inn

A French village is largely populated by
members of the same family, and one of them
murders another.
An odd little black comedy which strengthened
its director's reputation.

w Pierre Véry, Jacques Becker, novel Pierre
Véry d Jacques Becker ph Pierre Montazel,
Jean Bourgoin m Jean Alfaro

Fernand Ledoux, Georges Rollin, Blanchette
Brunoy, Robert Le.Vigan

The Gracie Allen Murder Case see Philo
Vance

The Graduate***
US 1967   105m   Technicolor   Panavision
UA / Embassy (Lawrence Turman)

A rich Californian ex-student is led into an affair
with the wife of his father's friend, then falls in
love with her daughter.
Richly reflecting the anything-goes mood of the
late sixties, this lushly-filmed sex comedy opened
a few new doors, looked ravishing, was well
acted and had a popular music score, so that few
people noticed that only the first half was any
good.

w Calder Willingham, Buck Henry, novel
Charles Webb d Mike Nichols ph Robert
Surtees songs Paul Simon singers Simon and
Garfunkel m Dave Grusin pd Richard Sylbert

Dustin Hoffman, Anne Bancroft, Katharine
Ross, Murray Hamilton, William Daniels,
Elizabeth Wilson

'Seeing The Graduate is a bit like having one's

most brilliant friend to dinner, watching him
become more witty and animated with every
moment, and then becoming aware that what
one may really be witnessing is the onset of a
nervous breakdown.'—Renata Adler

'Yes, there are weaknesses . . . But in
cinematic skill, in intent, in sheer connection with
us, The Graduate is a milestone in American film
history.'—Stanley Kauffmann

AA: Mike Nichols
AAN: best picture; script; Robert Surtees;
Dustin Hoffman; Anne Bancroft; Katharine
Ross

Grand Central Murder
US 1942   72m   bw
MGM (B. F. Zeidman)

A murder is solved in New York's giant railway
station.
Very moderate time-filler with a rather lethargic
script.

w Peter Ruric, novel Sue McVeigh d S. Sylvan
Simon

Van Heflin, Cecilia Parker, Sam Levene, Connie
Gilchrist, Millard Mitchell, Tom Conway,
Virginia Grey, Samuel S. Hinds

Grand Hotel***
US 1932   115m   bw
MGM

The lives of various hotel guests become
intertwined and reach their climaxes.
It's a little faded now, but much of the magic still
works in this first of the portmanteau movies; the
production is opulent yet somehow stiff, and the
performances have survived with varying
success.

w William A. Drake, novel Vicki Baum
d Edmund Goulding ph William Daniels
ad Cedric Gibbons

Greta Garbo, John Barrymore, Lionel
Barrymore, Joan Crawford, Wallace Beery,
Jean Hersholt, Lewis Stone
† Remade as Weekend at the Waldorf (qv).
AA: best picture

Le Grand Jeu*
France 1934   115m   bw

A young man joins the Foreign Legion to forget
a woman, meets another who reminds him of
her, and is condemned to death for murdering
the second woman's lover.
Hokey melodrama whose great interest lay in its
picture of life in the Legion.

w Charles Spaak, Jacques Feyder d Jacques

Feyder *ph* Harry Stradling, Maurice Forster *m* Hanns Eisler

Pierre-Richard Wilm, Marie Bell (in a dual role), Françoise Rosay, Charles Vanel
† A remake appeared in 1953, directed by Robert Siodmak and starring Jean-Claude Pascal, Gina Lollobrigida and Arletty. Sometimes known as *Card of Fate*, it is of little interest.

Grand National Night
GB 1953   80m   bw
Talisman (George Minter)
US title: *The Wicked Wife*

A stable owner accidentally kills his drunken wife, but fate and a complex series of events clear him.
Slightly dubious morally, but otherwise an adequate detective story with the outcome hinging on train timetables and the like.

w Dorothy and Campbell Christie, from their play *d* Bob McNaught *ph* Jack Asher *m* John Greenwood

Nigel Patrick, Moira Lister, Beatrice Campbell, Betty Ann Davies, Michael Hordern, Noel Purcell, Leslie Mitchell, Barry Mackay, Colin Gordon

Grand Prix*
US 1966   179m   Metrocolor   Super Panavision
MGM (Edward Lewis)

Motor racers converge on Monte Carlo and other European centres.
Seemingly endless montage, mostly in multi-split screens, of motor races, with some very jaded personal footage between. It looks a dream but quickly becomes a bore.

w Robert Alan Aurthur *d* John Frankenheimer *ph* Lionel Lindon *m* Maurice Jarre *pd* Richard Sylbert

James Garner, Eva Marie Saint, Brian Bedford, Yves Montand, Toshiro Mifune, Jessica Walter, Françoise Hardy, Adolfo Celi, Claude Dauphin, Genevieve Page

'The same old story with the same types we've seen flying planes and riding horses in dozens of fast, cheap, hour-and-a-quarter movies.'— *Pauline Kael*

'Nothing more nor less than a paean to the racing car . . . off the track, though, the film is firmly stuck in bottom gear.'—*MFB.*

Grand Slam
Italy / Spain / West Germany 1967   120m   Techniscope
(Paramount) Jolly-Coral-Constantin (Harry Columbo, George Papi)
original title: *Ad Ogni Costo*

A retired professor has a plan for a diamond robbery, but recruits his aides unwisely.
Long-drawn-out caper melodrama with good sequences but nothing at all new; a very poor man's *Rififi*.

w Mino Roli, Caminito, Marcello Fondato, Antonio de la Loma *d* Giuliano Montaldo *ph* Antonio Macasoli *m* Ennio Morricone

Janet Leigh, Edward G. Robinson, Klaus Kinski, Robert Hoffman, Georges Rigaud, Adolfo Celi

La Grande Illusion***
France 1937   117m   bw
RAC

During World War I, three captured French pilots have an uneasy relationship with their German commandant.
Celebrated mood piece with much to say about war and mankind; more precisely, it is impeccably acted and directed and has real tragic force.

w Jean Renoir, Charles Spaak *d* Jean Renoir *ph* Christian Matras, Claude Renoir, Bourgoin, Bourreaud *m* Joseph Kosma

Pierre Fresnay, Erich Von Stroheim, Jean Gabin, Julien Carette, Marcel Dalio, Gaston Modot, Jean Dasté, Dita Parlo

AAN: best picture

Les Grandes Manoeuvres*
France / Italy 1955   106m   Eastmancolor
Filmsonor / Rizzoli
aka: *Summer Manoeuvres*

In 1913, an army lieutenant takes a bet that he can win any woman in the town in which his regiment is quartered during manoeuvres.
An elegant, but surprisingly unwitty film from this director, saddled with a well-worn and very predictable plot.

wd René Clair *ph* Robert Le Fèbvre, Robert Juillard *m* Georges Van Parys

Gérard Philipe, Michèle Morgan, Brigitte Bardot, Yves Robert, Jean Desailly, Pierre Dux

The Grapes of Wrath****
US 1940   128m   bw
TCF (Nunnally Johnson)

After the dust-bowl disaster of the thirties,

Oklahoma farmers trek to California in the hope of a better life.

A superb film which could scarcely be improved upon. Though the ending is softened from the book, there was too much here for filmgoers to chew on. Acting, photography, direction combine to make this an unforgettable experience, a poem of a film.

w Nunnally Johnson, novel John Steinbeck *d* John Ford *ph* Gregg Toland *m* Alfred Newman

Henry Fonda, Jane Darwell, John Carradine, Charley Grapewin, Dorris Bowdon, Russell Simpson, Zeffie Tilbury, O. Z. Whitehead, John Qualen, Eddie Quillan, Grant Mitchell

   'A genuinely great motion picture which makes one proud to have even a small share in the affairs of the cinema.'—*Howard Barnes*

   'The most mature motion picture that has ever been made, in feeling, in purpose, and in the use of the medium.'—*Otis Ferguson*

AA: John Ford; Jane Darwell

AAN: best picture; Nunnally Johnson; Henry Fonda

Grass*
US 1925   50m approx   bw   silent
Famous Players-Lasky

Nomadic Iranian tribes make an annual migration in search of fresh pasture.
Striking early documentary marred by facetious sub-titles.

wd, ph Merian C. Cooper, Ernest Schoedsack *titles* Terry Ramsaye

The Grass Is Greener*
GB 1960   104m   Technirama
Grandon (Stanley Donen)

The wife of an English earl falls for an American millionaire tourist.
Heavy-going and unsuitably widescreened version of an agreeable piece of West End fluff. Performances just about save it.

w Hugh and Margaret Williams, from their play *d* Stanley Donen *ph* Christopher Challis *m/ly* Noel Coward *md* Muir Mathieson

Cary Grant, Deborah Kerr, Robert Mitchum, *Jean Simmons, Moray Watson*

   'It's too bad Coward couldn't have written the wisecracks too.'—*Philip T. Hartung*

The Grasshopper
US 1969   98m   Technicolor
NGP (Jerry Belson, Barry Marshall)

A small-town girl goes from man to man in Los Angeles and Las Vegas, finally becoming a call girl.

The road to ruin in modern dress; nicely made and quite entertaining in its gaudy way.

w Jerry Belson, *novel* The Passing of Evil by Mark MacShane *d* Jerry Paris *ph* Sam Leavitt *m* Billy Goldenberg

Jacqueline Bisset, Jim Brown, Joseph Cotten, Corbett Monica

The Gravy Train
US 1974   96m   Eastmancolor
Tomorrow (Jonathan T. Taplin)
aka: *The Dion Brothers*

A canning factory worker throws up his job to hijack a treasury van and open a seafood restaurant.
Old-hat caper story.

w David Whitney, Bill Kirby *d* Jack Starrett *ph* Jerry Hirschfeld *m* Fred Karlin

Stacy Keach, Frederic Forrest, Margot Kidder, Barry Primus

Gray Lady Down
US 1978   111m   Technicolor   Panavision
Universal / Mirisch (Walter Mirisch)

After a collision, an American submarine lodges in the neck of an underwater canyon.
A rather boring update of *Morning Departure* with added technology.

w James Whittaker, Howard Sackler, *novel* Event 1000 by David Levallee *d* David Greene *ph* Stevan Larner *m* Jerry Fielding

Charlton Heston, David Carradine, Stacy Keach, Ned Beatty, Stephen McHattie, Ronny Cox, Dorian Harewood, Rosemary Forsyth

Grease**
US 1978   110m   Metrocolor   Panavision
Paramount / Robert Stigwood, Allan Carr

The path of true love in a fifties high school does not run smoothly.
Amiable 'period' musical for teenagers: a highly fashionable exploitation of the new star John Travolta, its commercialism was undeniable, and it carefully built in appeal to older age groups.

w Bronte Woodard, *stage musical play* Jim Jacobs, Warren Casey *d* Randal Kleiser *ph* Bill Butler *pd* Phil Jefries *titles* John Wilson

John Travolta, Olivia Newton-John, Stockard Channing, Eve Arden, Frankie Avalon, Joan Blondell, Edd Byrnes, Sid Caesar, Alice Ghostley, Sha Na Na, Jeff Conaway, Barry Pearl, Michael Tucci

Greased Lightning
US 1977   96m   Movielab
Third World (Hannah Weinstein)

A black Virginian moonshiner becomes a famous stock car racer.
Fashionable action hokum based on a real character.

w Kenneth Vose, Lawrence DuKore, Melvin Van Peebles, Leon Capetanos d Michel Schultz ph George Bouillet m Fred Karlin

Richard Pryor, Beau Bridges, Pam Grier, Cleavon Little, Vincent Gardenia

The Great Adventure**
Sweden 1953   73m   bw
Arne Sucksdorff

Two boys on a farm rescue an otter and keep it as a pet.
Superbly photographed wild life film featuring a variety of small animals.

wd, ph, ed Arne Sucksdorff

Anders Norberg, Kjell Sucksdorff, Arne Sucksdorff

The Great American Broadcast*
US 1941   90m   bw
TCF (Kenneth MacGowan)

A romantic triangle set against the burgeoning years of the radio industry.
Pleasant musical, amusing if historically inaccurate.

w Don Ettlinger, Edwin Blum, Robert Ellis, Helen Logan d Archie Mayo ph Leon Shamroy, Peverell Marley songs Mack Gordon, Harry Warren

Alice Faye, John Payne, Jack Oakie, Cesar Romero, The Ink Spots, The Nicholas Brothers, The Wiere Brothers

The Great American Pastime
US 1956   89m   bw
MGM (Henry Berman)

A mild lawyer takes over a junior baseball team but incurs parental jealousy.
Thin lower-bracket comedy.

w Nathaniel Benchley d Herman Hoffman ph Arthur E. Arling m Jeff Alexander

Tom Ewell, Anne Francis, Ann Miller, Dean Jones, Raymond Bailey

The Great Bank Robbery*
US 1969   98m   colour   Panavision
Warner (Malcolm Stuart)

Would-be bank robbers turn up in a western town disguised as priests.

Western spoof without the courage of its convictions, but easy enough to watch.

w William Peter Blatty, novel Frank O'Rourke d Hy Averback ph Fred J. Koenekamp m Nelson Riddle

Kim Novak, Zero Mostel, Clint Walker, Claude Akins, Akim Tamiroff, Larry Storch, John Anderson, Sam Jaffe, Ruth Warrick, Elisha Cook Jnr

The Great Caruso**
US 1950   109m   Technicolor
MGM (Joe Pasternak)

Semi-fictional biography of the Italian tenor.
Dramatically flat but opulently staged biopic, turned into a star vehicle and a huge commercial success.

w Sonya Levien, William Ludwig d Richard Thorpe ph Joseph Ruttenberg md Johnny Green, Peter Herman Adler

Mario Lanza, Ann Blyth, Dorothy Kirsten, Jarmila Novotna, Carl Benton Reid, Eduard Franz, Richard Hageman, Ludwig Donath, Alan Napier

AAN: Johnny Green, Peter Herman Adler

Great Catherine
GB 1968   98m   Technicolor
Warner / Keep Films (Jules Buck)

An English captain visits the court of Catherine the Great.
Chaos results from the attempt to inflate an ill-considered Shavian whimsy into a feature film: the material is simply insufficient and the performances flounder in irrelevant production values.

w Hugh Leonard, play Bernard Shaw d Gordon Flemyng ph Oswald Morris m Dmitri Tiomkin pd John Bryan

Jeanne Moreau, Peter O'Toole, Zero Mostel, Jack Hawkins, Marie Lohr, Akim Tamiroff, Marie Kean, Kenneth Griffith

'All Shaw's jokes work very well, but the film has been padded out with Cossack dances, frantic chases, and unfunny slapstick.'—
Michael Billington, Illustrated London News

Great Day
GB 1945   79m   bw
RKO British (Victor Hanbury)

A village Women's Institute prepares for a visit by Mrs Roosevelt.
Modestly pleasing little drama from a successful play.

w Wolfgang Wilhelm, John Davenport, play Lesley Storm d Lance Comfort

Eric Portman, Flora Robson, Sheila Sim, Isabel Jeans, Walter Fitzgerald, Philip Friend, Marjorie Rhodes, Maire O'Neill, Beatrice Varley

Great Day in the Morning
US 1955 92m Technicolor Superscope
RKO (Edmund Grainger)

At the outbreak of the Civil War, Denver has divided loyalties.

Solemn semi-western without much excitement.

w Lesser Samuels, *novel* Robert Hardy Andrews *d* Jacques Tourneur *ph* William Snyder *m* Leith Stevens

Robert Stack, Virginia Mayo, Ruth Roman, Alex Nicol, Raymond Burr, Regis Toomey

The Great Dictator**
US 1940 129m bw
Charles Chaplin

A Jewish barber is mistaken for dictator Adenoid Hynkel.

Chaplin's satire on Hitler has a few funny moments, but the rest is heavy going, the production is cheeseparing, and the final speech to the world is a grave mistake.

wd Charles Chaplin *ph* Karl Struss, Rollie Totheroh *md* Meredith Willson *ad* J. Russell Spencer

Charles Chaplin, Paulette Goddard, *Jack Oakie* (as Napaloni), Reginald Gardiner, Henry Daniell, Billy Gilbert, Maurice Moscovitch

'For this film he takes on more than a mimed representation of common humanity; he states, and accepts, the responsibility of being one of humanity's best and most widely-known representatives.'—*Basil Wright*

'The last impassioned speech about peace and serenity still wrecks everything that has gone before: Chaplin mawkish can always overrule Chaplin the innocent mime.'—*New Yorker, 1978*

AAN: best picture; Charles Chaplin (as writer and actor); Meredith Willson; Jack Oakie

The Great Escape**
US 1963 173m De Luxe Panavision
UA / Mirisch / Alpha (John Sturges)

Allied prisoners plan to escape from a German prison camp.

Pretty good but overlong POW adventure with a tragic ending.

w James Clavell, W. R. Burnett, *book* Paul Brickhill *d* John Sturges *ph* Daniel Fapp *m* Elmer Bernstein

James Garner, *Steve McQueen*, Richard Attenborough, James Donald, Charles Bronson, Donald Pleasence, James Coburn, David McCallum, Gordon Jackson, John Leyton, Nigel Stock

Great Expectations****
GB 1946 118m bw
Rank / Cineguild (Anthony Havelock-Allan)

A boy meets an escaped convict on the Romney Marshes, with strange consequences for both of them.

Despite the inevitable simplifications, this is a superbly pictorial rendering of a much-loved novel, with all the famous characters in safe hands and masterly judgement in every department.

w Ronald Neame, David Lean, Kay Walsh, Cecil McGivern, Anthony Havelock-Allan, *novel Charles Dickens d David Lean ph Ronald Neame ad John Bryan*

John Mills, Bernard Miles, *Finlay Currie, Martita Hunt*, Valerie Hobson, *Jean Simmons*, Alec Guinness, Francis L. Sullivan, Anthony Wager, Ivor Barnard, Freda Jackson, Hay Petrie, O. B. Clarence, George Hayes, Torin Thatcher, Eileen Erskine

'The first big British film to have been made, a film that sweeps our cloistered virtues out into the open.'—*Richard Winnington*

'The best Dickens adaptation, and arguably David Lean's finest film.'—*NFT, 1969*

AA: Ronald Neame
AAN: best picture; script; David Lean (as director)

The Great Garrick**
US 1937 91m bw
Warner (Mervyn Le Roy)

When Garrick goes to act in Paris, members of the Comédie Française take over a wayside inn and try to teach him a lesson, but the plan goes awry.

A pleasant unhistorical conceit makes a rather literary film to have come from Hollywood, but it is all very winning and cast and director keep the fun simmering happily.

w Ernest Vajda *d* James Whale *ph* Ernest Haller *m* Adolph Deutsch

Brian Aherne, Edward Everett Horton, Olivia de Havilland, Lionel Atwill, *Melville Cooper, Luis Alberni, Étienne Girardot*, Marie Wilson, Lana Turner, Albert Dekker, Fritz Leiber, Dorothy Tree, Chester Clute

'As elegantly witty as anything Whale ever did.'—*Tom Milne*

'A jestful and romantic piece.'—*Frank S. Nugent, New York Times*

The Great Gatsby*
US 1949 90m bw
Paramount

Events leading to the death of a retired gangster and mysterious Long Island plutocrat.
Rather bland and uninteresting attempt to accommodate a unique author to a formula star.

w Richard Maibaum, novel F. Scott Fitzgerald
d Elliott Nugent m Robert Emmett Dolan

Alan Ladd, Macdonald Carey, Betty Field, Barry Sullivan, Howard da Silva

The Great Gatsby**
US 1974 146m Eastmancolor
Paramount / Newdon (David Merrick)

Plush version with lavish production values and pleasing period sense but not much grip on the story or characters. Overlong footage is not made to seem shorter by snail's pace and dull performances.

w Francis Ford Coppola d Jack Clayton
ph Douglas Slocombe m Nelson Riddle
pd John Box

Robert Redford, Mia Farrow, Karen Black, Scott Wilson, Sam Waterston, Lois Chiles
'Pays its creator the regrettable tribute of erecting a mausoleum over his work.'—Richard Combs
'Leaves us more involved with six-and-a-half-million dollars' worth of trappings than with human tragedy.'—Judith Crist
'A total failure of every requisite sensibility.'—Stanley Kauffmann
'Profoundly unfilmable: a poetic and ultimately pessimistic comment on the American dream is transformed by cinematic realism into pure prose.'—Michael Billington, Illustrated London News

AA: Nelson Riddle

Great Guns*
US 1941 74m bw
TCF (Sol M. Wurtzel)

A young millionaire's retainers join the army with him.
Disappointing Laurel and Hardy comedy, their first for Fox and the beginning of their decline. A few good jokes, but no overall control or inventiveness.

w Lou Breslow d Monty Banks ph Glen MacWilliams

Stan Laurel, Oliver Hardy, Sheila Ryan, Dick Nelson, Edmund Macdonald, Charles Trowbridge, Ludwig Stossel, Mae Marsh

Great Guy*
US 1936 73m bw
Grand National (Douglas Maclean)
GB title: Pluck of the Irish

An ex-prizefighter joins the bureau of weights and measures and fights corruption.
Rather tame racket film, Cagney's first independent venture away from Warners. He atones for rather thin production values.

w Henry McCarthy, Henry Johnson, James Edward Grant, Harry Ruskin d John G. Blystone ph Jack McKenzie m Merlin Skiles

James Cagney, Mae Clarke, James Burke, Edward Brophy, Henry Kolker
'It's all typical Cagney stuff, and that's the trouble with it.'—Variety

The Great Impersonation*
US 1935 81m bw
Universal (Edmund Grainger)

During World War I, a German murders an English nobleman and, being his double, takes over.
Reliable espionage melodrama with atmospheric country house asides, from a sturdily compelling novel, previously filmed in 1921 with James Kirkwood.

w Frank Wead, Eve Greene, novel E. Phillips Oppenheim d Alan Crosland ph Milton Krasner m Franz Waxman

Edmund Lowe, Valerie Hobson, Vera Engels, Henry Mollison, Lumsden Hare, Spring Byington, Charles Waldron, Dwight Frye

The Great Impersonation*
US 1942 71m bw
Universal (Paul Malvern)

Okay quickie updating of the above, serviceable rather than inventive.

w W. Scott Darling d John Rawlins ph George Robinson m Hans Salter

Ralph Bellamy, Evelyn Ankers, Aubrey Mather, Edward Norris, Karen Verne, Henry Daniell, Ludwig Stossel

The Great Imposter*
US 1961 112m bw
U-I (Robert Arthur)

The career of Ferdinand Waldo Demara, a marine and Trappist monk who also impersonated a Harvard research fellow, a prison warden, a naval doctor and a schoolteacher.
Uncertain mood hampers this biopic of a likeable fantasist.

w Liam O'Brien, book Robert Crichton

d Robert Mulligan *ph* Robert Burks *m* Henry Mancini

Tony Curtis, Raymond Massey, Karl Malden, Edmond O'Brien, Arthur O'Connell, Gary Merrill, Frank Gorshin, Joan Blackman, Robert Middleton

The Great John L.
US 1945 96m bw
UA (Frank Mastroly, James Edward Grant)
GB title: *A Man Called Sullivan*

Women in the life of prizefighter John L. Sullivan.
Very mild period biopic without the zest of *Gentleman Jim*.

w James Edward Grant *d* Frank Tuttle *ph* James Van Trees *m* Victor Young

Greg McClure, Linda Darnell, Barbara Britton, Lee Sullivan, Otto Kruger, Wallace Ford, Robert Barrat

The Great Lie***
US 1941 107m bw
Warner (Hal B. Wallis, Henry Blanke)

A determined girl loses the man she loves, believes him dead in a plane crash, and takes over the baby which his selfish wife does not want.
Absurd melodrama becomes top-flight entertainment with all concerned in cracking form and special attention on the two bitchy female leads, splendidly played. Classical music trimmings, too.

w Lenore Coffee, *novel* Polan Banks *d* Edmund Goulding *ph* Tony Gaudio *m* Max Steiner

Bette Davis, Mary Astor, George Brent, Lucile Watson, Hattie McDaniel, Grant Mitchell, Jerome Cowan

AA: Mary Astor

The Great Locomotive Chase*
US 1956 76m Technicolor
Cinemascope
Walt Disney (Lawrence Edward Watkin)

During the Civil War, Union spies steal a train and destroy track and bridges behind them.
A serious version of Buster Keaton's *The General*, based on a true incident; good sequences but no overall pace.

w Lawrence Edward Watkin *d* Francis D. Lyon *ph* Charles Boyle *m* Paul Smith

Fess Parker, Jeffrey Hunter, Jeff York, John Lupton, Kenneth Tobey

The Great Lover*
US 1949 80m bw
(Paramount) Hope Enterprises (Edmund Beloin)

On a transatlantic liner, a timid scoutmaster catches a strangler.
Amusing suspense comedy, a good star vehicle.

w Edmund Beloin, Melville Shavelson, Jack Rose *d* Alexander Hall *ph* Charles Lang *m* Joseph J. Lilley

Bob Hope, Rhonda Fleming, *Roland Young*, Jim Backus, Roland Culver, George Reeves

The Great Man**
US 1956 92m bw
U-I (Aaron Rosenberg)

A memorial programme to a much-loved TV personality turns into an exposé.
Patchy melodrama with a *Citizen Kane* framework; the best bits are very effective.

w Jose Ferrer, Al Morgan, *novel* Al Morgan *d* Jose Ferrer *ph* Harold Lipstein *m* Herman Stein

Jose Ferrer, Dean Jagger, Keenan Wynn, *Julie London*, Joanne Gilbert, *Ed Wynn*, Jim Backus

'Its distinction is in its unwavering tone—one of blunt and frequently savage irony and cynicism.'—*MFB*

'The movie is almost over before one realizes what a slick, fast sell it is (resembling nothing so much as what it is attacking).'—*Pauline Kael, 1968*

The Great Man Votes*
US 1939 72m bw
RKO

A drunken professor turns out to have the casting vote in a local election.
Slow-starting but progressively funny political comedy with some favourite talents in good form.

w John Twist, *story* Gordon Malherbe Hillman *d* Garson Kanin *ph* Russell Metty *m* Roy Webb

John Barrymore, Virginia Weidler, Peter Holden, *William Demarest, Donald MacBride*

The Great Man's Lady*
US 1942 90m bw
Paramount (William A. Wellman)

A western pioneer is inspired and encouraged by his wife.
Adequate but unsurprising flashback family drama starting with its star as a lady of 109.

w W. L. Rivers, *story* Vina Delmar *d* William L. Wellman *ph* William C. Mellor *m* Victor Young

Barbara Stanwyck, Joel McCrea, Brian Donlevy, Katharine Stevens, Thurston Hall, Lloyd Corrigan

The Great McGinty **
US 1940   83m   bw
Paramount
GB title: *Down Went McGinty*

A hobo and a crook have a hectic political career.
Lively comedy-drama which signalled the arrival as director of a new and stimulating Hollywood talent.

wd Preston Sturges m Frederick Hollander

Brian Donlevy, Akim Tamiroff, Muriel Angelus, Louis Jean Heydt, Arthur Hoyt
'This is his first directing job and where has he been all our lives? He has that sense of the incongruous which makes some of the best gaiety.'—*Otis Ferguson*
'The tough dialogue is matched by short, snappy scenes; the picture seems to have wasted no time, no money.'—*Gilbert Seldes*
'A director as adroit and inventive as any in the business . . . it starts like a five-alarm fire and never slackens pace for one moment until its unexpected conclusion.'—*Pare Lorentz*
'Sturges takes the success ethic and throws it in the face of the audience.'—*James Orsini*

The Great Mr Handel *
GB 1942   103m   Technicolor
Rank / GHW (James B. Sloan)

How the 18th-century composer came to write the Messiah.
Earnest, unlikely biopic, naïve but rather commendable.

w Gerald Elliott, Victor MacClure, *play* L. DuGarde Peach *d* Norman Walker

Wilfrid Lawson, Elizabeth Allan, Malcolm Keen, Michael Shepley, Hay Petrie, A. E. Matthews

The Great Moment **
US 1944   83m   bw
Paramount

How anaesthetics may have been invented.
Curious biopic of Dr W. T. G. Morgan, poised somewhere between utter seriousness and pratfall farce. The beginning of its director's decline, but always interesting in itself.

wd Preston Sturges, book Triumph over Pain by René Fulop-Miller *ph* Victor Milner *m* Victor Young

Joel McCrea, Betty Field, William Demarest,

Harry Carey, Franklin Pangborn, Grady Sutton, Jimmy Conlin

The Great Northfield Minnesota Raid *
US 1971   91m   Technicolor
Universal / Robertson and Associates / Jennings Lang

In 1876 a gang of bandits, technically pardoned, plan a bank robbery.
'Realistic' western in which the settings and photography have an impressively rough look but the script leaves much to be desired.

wd Philip Kaufman *ph Bruce Surtees m* Dave Grusin

Cliff Robertson, Robert Duvall, Luke Askew, Elisha Cook Jnr

The Great Profile *
US 1940   82m   bw
TCF (Raymond Griffith)

A dissipated actor disgraces his family and becomes an acrobat.
Shapeless farce in which a great talent on his last legs parodies himself.

w Milton Sperling, Hilary Lynn *d* Walter Lang *ph* Ernest Palmer *m* Cyril Mockridge

John Barrymore, Mary Beth Hughes, Gregory Ratoff, Anne Baxter, John Payne, Lionel Atwill, Edward Brophy, Willie Fung

The Great Race ***
US 1965   163m   Technicolor   Super Panavision
Warner / Patricia / Jalem / Reynard (Martin Jurow)

In 1908, the Great Leslie and Professor Fate are leading contenders in the first New York to Paris car race.
Elaborate comedy spectacular with many good moments, notably the early disasters, a western saloon brawl, and a custard pie fight. Elsewhere, there is more evidence of an oversize budget than of wit or finesse, and the entire Prisoner of Zenda spoof could have been omitted. Excellent production detail and general good humour.

w Arthur Ross *d* Blake Edwards *ph Russell Harlan m Henry Mancini pd* Fernando Carrere

Jack Lemmon, Tony Curtis, Peter Falk, Natalie Wood, George Macready, Ross Martin, Vivian Vance, Dorothy Provine

AAN: Russell Harlan; song 'The Sweetheart Tree' (*m* Henry Mancini, *ly* Johnny Mercer)

The Great Scout and Cathouse Thursday
US 1976　102m　Technicolor
AIP (Jules Buck and David Korda)
reissue title: *Wildcat*

While trying to revenge himself on an
absconding partner, an old cowboy falls for a
young prostitute.

Downright peculiar comedy western which
never seems to make up its mind what it's trying
to be, and too often is merely embarrassing.

w Richard Shapiro　*d* Don Taylor　*ph* Alex
Phillips Jnr　*m* John Cameron　*pd* Jack Martin
Smith

Lee Marvin, Oliver Reed, Kay Lenz, Robert
Culp, Elizabeth Ashley, Strother Martin, Sylvia
Miles

'It takes more than a dollop or two of
sentiment and acres of dirty talk to make a
movie.'—*Michael Billington, Illustrated
London News*

'It sounds like the latest in the cute twosome
series launched by *Butch Cassidy and the
Sundance Kid*. In fact it features not two but
seven wacky westerners who all seem addicted to
stealing, hee-hawing, falling into puddles and
punching each other in the privates.'—*Janet
Maslin, Newsweek*

The Great Sinner*
US 1949　110m　bw
MGM (Gottfried Reinhardt)

A serious young writer becomes a compulsive
gambler.

Rather pointless and heavy-handed but
extremely good-looking and splendidly cast
period drama vaguely based on Dostoievsky.

w Ladislas Fodor, Christopher Isherwood
d Robert Siodmak　*ph* George Folsey
m Bronislau Kaper　*ad Cedric Gibbons, Hans
Peck*

Gregory Peck, *Walter Huston*, Ava Gardner,
Agnes Moorehead, Ethel Barrymore, Melvyn
Douglas, Frank Morgan

The Great Sioux Massacre
US 1965　93m　Eastmancolor
　Cinemascope
Columbia / FF (Leon Fromkess)

Two officers are court-martialled after Custer's
last stand.

Fragmentary flashback western let down by
production and performances.

w Fred C. Dobbs　*d* Sidney Salkow　*ph* Irving
Lippman　*m* Emil Newman, Edward B. Powell

Joseph Cotten, Darren McGavin, Phil Carey,
Nancy Kovack, Julie Sommars, Michael Pate

The Great Sioux Uprising
US 1953　80m　Technicolor
U-I (Albert J. Cohen)

Indians rebel when their horses are stolen for sale
to the commander of Fort Laramie.
Moderate western programmer.

w Richard Breen, Gladys Atwater　*d* Lloyd
Bacon　*ph* Maury Gertsman　*m* Joseph
Gershenson

Jeff Chandler, Faith Domergue, Lyle Bettger

The Great Train Robbery***
US 1903　10m approx　bw　silent
Edison

Bandits tie up a telegraph operator and rob a
train, but are arrested.

In its day this was a real pioneer. It was among
the longest films then made, it had the most
complicated story line, it was the first western
and it used new technical tricks such as the pan
and the close-up. Needless to say, it must now be
viewed with sympathy.

wd Edwin S. Porter

Marie Murray, Broncho Billy Anderson, George
Barnes

The Great Victor Herbert*
US 1939　91m　bw
Paramount (Andrew L. Stone)

At the turn of the century a famous composer
plays cupid to two young singers.
Pleasant minor musical with excellent songs and
an infectious cheerfulness.

w Russel Crouse, Robert Lively　*d Andrew L.
Stone ph* Victor Milner　*md* Phil Boutelje,
Arthur Lange

Walter Connolly, Allan Jones, Mary Martin,
Susanna Foster, Lee Bowman

AAN: Phil Boutelje, Arthur Lange

The Great Waldo Pepper**
US 1975　108m　Technicolor　Todd-AO
　35
Universal (George Roy Hill)

In the twenties, a World War I flier becomes an
aerial stuntman.
Whimsical spectacular which concentrates less
on the mystique of flying than on a series of
splendid stunts.

w William Goldman　*d George Roy Hill
ph Robert Surtees m* Henry Mancini

Robert Redford, Bo Svenson, Bo Brundin, Susan
Sarandon, Geoffrey Lewis
'Charged with enthralling balletic
precision.'—*Tom Milne*

'One hundred per cent pure plastic adolescent male fantasy.'—*New Yorker*

The Great Waltz***
US 1938   103m   bw
MGM (Bernard Hyman)

Young Johann Strauss becomes Vienna's waltz king.
Exhilarating old-fashioned studio-set musical located in Hollywood's endearing vision of Old Vienna, assisted by streamlined production and excellent cast. Musical schmaltz.

w Walter Reisch, Samuel Hoffenstein, *story* Gottfried Reinhardt *d Julien Duvivier ph* Joseph Ruttenberg

Fernand Gravet, Luise Rainer, Miliza Korjus, Lionel Atwill, Hugh Herbert, Herman Bing, Curt Bois
   'Miliza Korjus—rhymes with gorgeous!'— *publicity*

AA: Joseph Ruttenberg
AAN: Miliza Korjus

The Great Waltz*
US 1972   134m   Metrocolor   Panavision 70
MGM (Andrew L. Stone)

Heavy-going remake set on real locations and hampered by them, styled in the manner of the same director's *Song of Norway*, i.e. with no real style at all. The music survives.

wd Andrew L. Stone *ph* David Boulton *ad* William Albert Havenmeyer *ch* Onna White

Horst Buchholz, Nigel Patrick, Mary Costa, Rossano Brazzi, Yvonne Mitchell
   'Take a box of chocolates—soft-centred, of course.'—*Michael Billington, Illustrated London News*

The Great White Hope**
US 1970   103m   De Luxe   Panavision
TCF (Lawrence Turman)

In 1910, a black boxer becomes world heavyweight champ but has trouble through his affair with a white girl.
Vivid, slightly whitewashed biopic of Jack Johnson (called Jefferson). Dramatic deficiencies outweighed by excellent period detail and a spellbinding central performance.

w Howard Sackler, from his play *d Martin Ritt ph* Burnett Guffey *m* negro traditionals *pd* John de Cuir

James Earl Jones, Jane Alexander, Lou Gilbert, Joel Fluellen, Chester Morris, Robert Webber, Hal Holbrook

AAN: James Earl Jones; Jane Alexander

The Great Ziegfeld**
US 1936   179m   bw
MGM (Hunt Stromberg)

The growth and Broadway fame of impresario Florenz Ziegfeld.
Mammoth biopic which despite a few show-stopping numbers never takes off dramatically and becomes something of an endurance test; interesting, however, as a spectacular of its time.

w William Anthony McGuire *d* Robert Z. Leonard *ph* Oliver T. Marsh, Ray June, George Folsey *md* Arthur Lange *ad* Cedric Gibbons

William Powell, Luise Rainer (as Anna Held), Myrna Loy (as Billie Burke), Frank Morgan, Reginald Owen, Nat Pendleton, Virginia Bruce, *Ray Bolger*, Harriett Hoctor, Ernest Cossart, *Fannie Brice*, Robert Greig, Gilda Gray, Leon Errol, Stanley Morner (Dennis Morgan)
   'This huge inflated gas-blown object bobs into the critical view as irrelevantly as an airship advertising somebody's toothpaste at a south coast resort. It lasts three hours. That is its only claim to special attention.'—*Graham Greene*
   'Everything should have been tightened—not in the team job of cutting those miles of negative, but in boiling down the script, saving a line here, combining two scenes into one.'—*Otis Ferguson*

AA: best picture; Luise Rainer
AAN: William Anthony McGuire; Robert Z. Leonard

The Greatest
US/GB 1977   101m   Metrocolor
Columbia/EMI (John Marshall)

The life and times of Muhammed Ali.
Bland confection of rags to riches in the boxing ring, its only plus being that Ali plays himself and offers a predictable array of enjoyable one-liners.

w Ring Lardner Jnr, from Ali's autobiography The Greatest *d* Tom Gries *ph* Harry Stradling *m* Michael Masser

Muhammed Ali, Ernest Borgnine, Roger E. Mosley, Lloyd Haynes, Malachi Throne, John Marley, Robert Duvall, David Huddleston, Ben Johnson, James Earl Jones, Dina Merrill, Paul Winfield

The Greatest Show on Earth*
US 1952   153m   Technicolor
Paramount/Cecil B. de Mille (Henry Wilcoxon)

Various dramas come to a head under the big top.
Moribund circus drama with bad acting, stilted production, an irrelevant train crash climax and a few genuinely spectacular and enjoyable moments.

w Fredric M. Frank, Theodore St John, Frank
Cavett, Barre Lyndon *d* Cecil B. de Mille
ph George Barnes, Peverell Marley, Wallace
Kelley *m* *Victor Young* *ad* Hal Pereira, Walter
Tyler

Betty Hutton, Cornel Wilde, James Stewart,
Charlton Heston, Dorothy Lamour, Gloria
Grahame, Lyle Bettger, Henry Wilcoxon,
Emmett Kelly, Lawrence Tierney, John Kellogg,
John Ringling North

AA: best picture; Cecil B. de Mille
AAN: original story (Fredric M. Frank,
Theodore St John, Frank Cavett)

The Greatest Story Ever Told**

US 1965 225m Technicolor Ultra
Panavision 70
UA / George Stevens

Solemn spectacular with an elephantine pace,
shot in Utah because allegedly it looked more
like Palestine than Palestine did. All frightfully
elegant and reverent, but totally unmoving,
partly because of the fatal casting of stars in bit
parts. (John Wayne looks in merely to say 'Truly
this man was the son of God.')

w James Lee Barrett, George Stevens, from
various sources *d tl* George Stevens *ph* William
C. Mellor, Loyal Griggs *m* Alfred Newman
ad Richard Day, William Creber

Max Von Sydow, Dorothy McGuire, Claude
Rains, Jose Ferrer, David McCallum, Charlton
Heston, Sidney Poitier, Donald Pleasence,
Roddy McDowall, Gary Raymond, Carroll
Baker, Pat Boone, Van Heflin, Sal Mineo,
Shelley Winters, Ed Wynn, John Wayne, Telly
Savalas, Angela Lansbury, Joseph Schildkraut,
Victor Buono, Nehemiah Persoff

'George Stevens was once described as a
water buffalo of film art. What this film more
precisely suggests is a dinosaur.'—*MFB*

'God is unlucky in *The Greatest Story Ever
Told*. His only begotten son turns out to be a
bore . . . the photography is inspired mainly by
Hallmark Cards . . . as the Hallelujah Chorus
explodes around us stereophonically and
stereotypically it becomes clear that Lazarus
was not so much raised from the tomb as blasted
out of it. As for pacing, the picture does not let
you forget a single second of its four hours.'—
John Simon

'No more than three minutes have elapsed
before we suspect that Stevens' name and fame
have been purchased by the Hallmark Greeting
Card Company, and that what we are looking at
is really a lengthy catalogue of greeting cards for
1965—for Those Who Care Enough to Send the
Very Best.'—*Stanley Kauffmann*

AAN: William C. Mellor, Loyal Griggs; Alfred
Newman

Greed***

US 1923 110m (24 fps) bw silent
Goldwyn / MGM

An ex-miner dentist kills his avaricious wife.
Later in Death Valley he also kills her lover, but
is bound to him by handcuffs.

This much-discussed film is often cited as its
director's greatest folly: the original version ran
eight hours. Re-edited by June Mathis, it retains
considerable power sequence by sequence, but is
necessarily disjointed in development. However,
it must be seen to be appreciated.

wd Erich Von Stroheim, *novel* McTeague by
Frank Norris *ph* Ben Reynolds, William
Daniels, Ernest B. Schoedsack *ad* Richard Day,
Cedric Gibbons, Erich Von Stroheim

Gibson Gowland, Zasu Pitts, *Jean Hersholt*,
Chester Conklin, Dale Fuller

'The end leaves one with an appalling sense of
human waste, of futility, of the drabness and
cruelty of lives stifled by genteel poverty. Every
character in the film is overwhelmed by it.'—
Gavin Lambert

† In 1972 Herman G. Weinberg published a
complete screenplay with 400 stills.

The Greed of William Hart

GB 1948 78m bw
Bushey (Gilbert Church)

In old Edinburgh, grave robbers procure corpses
for an anatomist.

Cheapie version of a much filmed subject. This
scenario was refurbished eleven years later by
the same writer as *The Flesh and the Fiends*; see
also *The Body Snatcher, Burke and Hare*.

w John Gilling *d* Oswald Mitchell

Tod Slaughter, Henry Oscar, Aubrey Woods,
Arnold Bell

The Greek Tycoon

US 1978 106m Technicolor
Universal / ABKCO (Allan Klein, Ely Landau)

A billionaire shipping tycoon marries the widow
of an American president.

Rather messy 'faction' based on Onassis and
Jacqueline Kennedy; entirely uninteresting save
for glossy backgrounds and the relentlessness
with which the characters swear at each other.

w Mort Fine *d* J. Lee Thompson *ph* Tony
Richmond *m* Stanley Myers *pd* Michael
Stringer

Anthony Quinn, Jacqueline Bisset, Raf Vallone,
Edward Albert, James Franciscus, Camilla
Sparv

The Greeks Had a Word for Them*
US 1932   77m   bw
UA

Adventures of three New York gold diggers.
Smart early talkie which helped launch the *Gold
Diggers* series and TCF's parallel *Three Little
Mice / Moon over Miami / How to Marry a
Millionaire* series.

w Sidney Howard, *play* Zoe Akins *d* Lowell
Sherman *ph* George Barnes

Joan Blondell, Madge Evans, Ina Claire, David
Manners, Lowell Sherman, Phillips Smalley,
Betty Grable

The Green Berets
US 1968   141m   Technicolor   Panavision
Warner / Batjac (Michael Wayne)

After extensive training, two tough army
detachments see service in Vietnam.
Overlong actioner criticized for unquestioningly
accepting the Vietnam cause; in itself, violent,
exhausting and dull.

w James Lee Barrett, *novel* Robin Moore *d* John
Wayne, Ray Kellogg *ph* Winton C. Hoch
m Miklos Rozsa

John Wayne, David Janssen, Jim Hutton, Aldo
Ray, Raymond St Jacques, Jack Soo, Bruce
Cabot, Patrick Wayne, Irene Tsu, Jason Evers,
Luke Askew

   'Propaganda as crude as this can only do
damage to its cause.'—*David Wilson*
   'A film best handled from a distance and with
a pair of tongs.'—*Penelope Gilliatt*

The Green Cockatoo
GB 1937   65m   bw
TCF / New World (Robert T. Kane)
aka: *Four Dark Hours; Race Gang*

A man seeks revenge on the gangsters who killed
his brother.
Sleazy little Soho-set thriller, mainly remarkable
for cast and credits.

w Edward O. Berkman, Arthur Wimperis,
story Graham Greene *d* William Cameron
Menzies

John Mills, Robert Newton, Rene Ray, Bruce
Seton, Charles Oliver

Green Dolphin Street
US 1947   141m   bw
MGM

A Channel Islander emigrates to New Zealand
and sends home for the wrong bride.
Silly 19th-century romance climaxed by rather a
good earthquake. Expensively but falsely
produced.

w Samson Raphaelson, *novel* Elizabeth Goudge
d Victor Saville *ph* George Folsey

Lana Turner, Richard Hart, Edmund Gwenn,
Van Heflin, Donna Reed

AAN: George Folsey

Green Fire
US 1954   100m   Eastmancolor
     Cinemascope
MGM

Two engineers disagree over their mining of
Columbia diamonds.
Routine adventure story with good action
highlights including landslide, flood and storm,
all deadened by dull dialogue and romantic
complications.

w Ivan Goff, Ben Roberts *d* Andrew Marton
ph Paul Vogel *m* Miklos Rozsa

Stewart Granger, Paul Douglas, Grace Kelly

Green for Danger****
GB 1946   93m   bw
Rank / Individual (Frank Launder, Sidney
     Gilliat)

A mysterious murderer strikes on the operating
table at a wartime emergency hospital.
Classic comedy-thriller, with serious detection
balanced by excellent jokes and performances,
also by moments of fright.

w Sidney Gilliat, Claud Gurney, novel
Christianna Brand *d Sidney Gilliat ph Wilkie
Cooper m* William Alwyn

*Alastair Sim, Sally Gray, Rosamund John,
Trevor Howard, Leo Genn, Megs Jenkins, Judy
Campbell,* Ronald Ward, Moore Marriott

The Green Glove
US / France 1952   89m   bw
UA / Benagoss (George Maurer)

A paratrooper against all odds returns a jewelled
relic to its proper place in a French church.
An unsatisfactory concoction by people who
have clearly seen *The Maltese Falcon* as well as
lots of Hitchcock films, this interestingly cast
and credited independent production never
really takes off.

w Charles Bennett *d* Rudolph Maté *ph* Claude
Renoir *m* Joseph Kosma

Glenn Ford, Cedric Hardwicke, Geraldine
Brooks, George Macready, Gaby Andrė, Roger
Treville

The Green Goddess*
US 1930   74m   bw
Warner

An Indian potentate holds Britishers prisoner.

Early talkie star vehicle which was also
successful on the stage and as a silent but has
little appeal now.

w Julian Josephson, *play* William Archer
d Alfred E. Green *ph* James Van Trees

George Arliss, Alice Joyce, H. B. Warner, Ralph
Forbes, David Tearle
† Remade 1942 as *Adventure in Iraq*.

AAN: George Arliss

Green Grass of Wyoming
US 1948 88m Technicolor
TCF

A rancher captures his runaway white stallion
and wins the local trotting races.
Predictable, good-looking family film shot on
location; a second sequel to *My Friend Flicka*.

w Martin Berkeley, *novel* Mary O'Hara *d* Louis
King *ph* Charles G. Clarke *m* Cyril Mockridge

Peggy Cummins, Charles Coburn, Robert
Arthur, Lloyd Nolan

AAN: Charles G. Clarke

Green Grow the Rushes
GB 1951 77m bw
ACT Films

Civil servants discover that a Kentish village is
devoted to smuggling.
Amiable but disappointingly feeble imitation of
Ealing comedy by a company formed from the
technicians' union; it simply hasn't got the right
snap in any department.

w Derek Twist, Howard Clewes, *novel* Howard
Clewes *d* Derek Twist *ph* Harry Waxman
m Lambert Williamson

Roger Livesey, Richard Burton, Honor
Blackman, Frederick Leister, John Salew, Colin
Gordon, Geoffrey Keen, Harcourt Williams,
Vida Hope

Green Hell*
US 1940 87m bw
Universal (Harry Edgington)

Explorers seek Inca treasure in the South
American Jungle.
Studio-bound potboiler unworthy of its director
but mainly enjoyable as a romp.

w Frances Marion *d* James Whale *ph* Karl
Freund

Douglas Fairbanks Jnr, Joan Bennett, George
Sanders, Vincent Price, Alan Hale, Gene
Garrick, George Bancroft, John Howard
† The temple set was re-used the same year in
The Mummy's Hand.

The Green Light*
US 1937 85m bw
Warner (Henry Blanke)

A dedicated doctor gives up his practice when a
patient dies.
Adequate star melodrama.

w Milton Krims, *novel* Lloyd C. Douglas
d Frank Borzage *ph* Byron Haskin *m* Max
Steiner

Errol Flynn, Anita Louise, Margaret Lindsay,
Cedric Hardwicke, Henry O'Neill, Spring
Byington

The Green Man*
GB 1956 80m bw
BL / Grenadier (Frank Launder, Sidney Gilliat)

A professional assassin stalks a pompous
politician.
Cheerful but not very subtle black comedy,
suffering from the attempt to make a star part
out of a very minor character.

w Sidney Gilliat, Frank Launder, from their play
Meet a Body *d* Robert Day *ph* Gerald Gibbs
m Cedric Thorpe Davie

Alastair Sim, George Cole, Jill Adams, Terry-
Thomas, Avril Angers, John Chandos, Dora
Bryan, Colin Gordon, Raymond Huntley

Green Mansions
US 1959 104m Metrocolor
Cinemascope
MGM / Avon (Edmund Grainger)

In a remote Amazon forest an adventurer
encounters Rima, a child of nature who takes
him on a quest for truth.
Absurd studio-bound Shangri-La story based on
an Edwardian fantasy that may well have suited
the printed page, but not the wide screen.
Dismally photographed in shades of green, with
all concerned looking acutely uncomfortable.

w Dorothy Kingsley, *novel* W. H. Hudson
d Mel Ferrer *ph* Joseph Ruttenberg
m Bronislau Kaper, Hector Villa-Lobos

Anthony Perkins, Audrey Hepburn, Lee J.
Cobb, Henry Silva

The Green Pastures****
US 1936 93m bw
Warner (Henry Blanke)

Old Testament stories as seen through simple-
minded negro eyes.
Though recently attacked as setting back the
cause of black emancipation, this is a brilliantly
sympathetic and humorous film, very cunningly
adapted for the screen in a series of dramatic

scenes which make the material work even better than it did on the stage.

w *Marc Connelly*, from his play and stories by Roark Bradford *d William Keighley, Marc Connelly ph Hal Mohr m Erich Wolfgang Korngold*

Rex Ingram, Oscar Polk, Eddie Anderson, Frank Wilson, George Reed

'I imagine God has a sense of humour, and I imagine that He is delighted with *The Green Pastures*.'—*Don Herold*

'That disturbance around the Music Hall yesterday was the noise of shuffling queues in Sixth Avenue and the sound of motion picture critics dancing in the street.'—*Bosley Crowther, New York Times*

The Green Scarf
GB 1954 96m bw
B and A (Bertram Ostrer, Albert Fennell)

An elderly French lawyer takes on the defence of a blind, deaf and dumb murder-suspect.
Plodding courtroom drama with familiar faces in unconvincing French guise.

w Gordon Wellesley, *novel* The Brute by Guy des Cars *d* George More O'Ferrall *ph* Jack Hildyard *m* Brian Easdale

Michael Redgrave, Ann Todd, Leo Genn, Kieron Moore

The Green Years*
US 1946 127m bw
MGM (Leon Gordon)

A young boy brought up strictly in Ireland makes friends with his mischievous grandfather.
Period family film in familiar style, sparked only by its scene-stealing star performance.

w Robert Ardrey, Sonya Levien, *novel* A. J. Cronin *d* Victor Saville *ph* George Folsey *m* Herbert Stothart *ad* Cedric Gibbons, Hans Peters

Charles Coburn, Dean Stockwell, Tom Drake, Beverly Tyler, Hume Cronyn, Gladys Cooper, Selena Royle, Jessica Tandy, Richard Haydn, Andy Clyde

'It has been described in the ads as "wonderful" by everyone within Louis B. Mayer's purchasing power except his horses, so I hesitate to ask you to take my word for it: the picture is awful.'—*James Agee*

AAN: George Folsey; Charles Coburn

The Greengage Summer*
GB 1961 99m Technicolor
Columbia / PKL (Victor Saville, Edward Small)
US title: *Loss of Innocence*

A young girl staying at a hotel falls in love with a jewel thief but is accidentally responsible for his capture.
Old-fashioned and not very interesting story with an appeal, one supposes, to well-brought-up young women. Decently made.

w Howard Koch, *novel* Rumer Godden *d* Lewis Gilbert *ph* Frederick A. Young *m* Richard Addinsell

Kenneth More, Danielle Darrieux, Susannah York, Claude Nollier, Jane Asher, Elizabeth Dear, Maurice Denham

Greenwich Village*
US 1944 82m Technicolor
TCF (William Le Baron)

In the twenties, a hick composer in New York allows his concerto to be used in a jazz musical.
Lightweight musical romp.

w Michael Fessier, Ernest Pagano *d* Walter Lang *ph* Leon Shamroy, Harry Jackson *songs* Leo Robin, Nacio Herb Brown

Carmen Miranda, Don Ameche, William Bendix, Vivian Blaine, Felix Bressart, Tony and Sally De Marco, Adolph Green, Betty Comden, Alvin Hammer, Judy Holliday

Greyfriars Bobby*
GB 1960 91m Technicolor
Walt Disney (Hugh Attwooll)

A Skye terrier keeps persistent vigil over his master's grave and is made a freeman of the city of Edinburgh.
Adequately produced film of a charming old Victorian story.

w Robert Westerby *d* Don Chaffey *ph* Paul Beeson *m* Francis Chagrin

Donald Crisp, Laurence Naismith, Alexander Mackenzie, Kay Walsh, Andrew Cruickshank, Vincent Winter, Moultrie Kelsall, Duncan Macrae

'The better Disney qualities of exact period detail and childlike directness are apparent.'—*MFB*

† The story was previously filmed as *Challenge to Lassie*.

Il Grido*
Italy 1957 102m bw
SPA Cinematografica / Robert Alexander
aka: *The Cry*

A man whose wife has left him travels across the Po Valley with his daughter in search of new happiness, but fails to find it and commits suicide.
Watchable but rather aimlessly depressing character drama.

w Michelangelo Antonioni, Elio Bartolini, Ennio de Concini *d* Michelangelo Antonioni *ph* Gianni di Venanzo *m* Giovanni Fusco

Steve Cochran, Alida Valli, Dorian Gray, Betsy Blair, Lynn Shaw

Grip of the Strangler*
GB 1958 78m bw
Producers' Associates (John Croydon)
US title: *The Haunted Strangler*

A novelist investigating an old murder case finds that he was himself the murderer.
Moderate thriller with a predictable but efficient plot.

w Jan Read *d* Robert Day *ph* Lionel Banes *m* Buxton Orr

Boris Karloff, Elizabeth Allan, Jean Kent, Vera Day, Anthony Dawson

The Grissom Gang
US 1971 128m Metrocolor
Associates and Aldrich / ABC

In 1931, a New York heiress is kidnapped by gangsters and comes to like it.
Unpleasant remake of *No Orchids for Miss Blandish* (previously filmed under that title, incredibly badly, in GB in 1948), with too much footage of lush blonde being slobbered over by psychotic thug, and an inevitable emphasis on violence.

w Leon Griffiths, *novel* James Hadley Chase *d* Robert Aldrich *ph* Joseph Biroc *m* Gerald Fried *ad* James Dowell Vance

Scott Wilson, Kim Darby, Tony Musante, Robert Lansing, Irene Dailey, Connie Stevens, Wesley Addy

'Offensive, immoral and perhaps even lascivious.'—*Vincent Canby*

Grizzly
US 1976 91m Movielab Todd AO 35
Film Ventures International
aka: *Killer Grizzly*

A mammoth bear preys upon campers in a national park.
Inept and boring shocker in the wake of *Jaws*.

w Harvey Flaxman, David Sheldon *d* William Girdler *ph* William Asman *m* Robert O. Ragland

Christopher George, Andrew Prine, Richard Jaeckel, Joan McCall

The Groundstar Conspiracy*
US 1972 96m Technicolor Panavision
Universal / Hal Roach International (Trevor Wallace)

An explosion rips apart a top secret space project, and the surviving scientist loses his memory.
Gimmicky but generally compulsive sci-fi mystery yarn, with an effective though predictable climax.

w Matthew Howard, *novel* The Alien by L. P. Davies *d* Lamont Johnson *ph* Michael Reed *m* Paul Hoffert

George Peppard, Michael Sarrazin, James Olson, Christine Belford, Tim O'Connor, James McEachin

The Group***
US 1966 152m De Luxe
UA / Famous Artists (Sidney Buchman)

The subsequent love lives of a group of girls who graduate from Vassar in 1933.
Patchy but generally fascinating series of interwoven sketches and character studies, with mainly tragic overtones; good attention to period detail, and dazzling array of new talent.

w Sidney Buchman, *novel Mary McCarthy d* Sidney Lumet *ph* Boris Kaufman *m* Charles Gross *pd* Gene Callahan

Joanna Pettet, Candice Bergen, *Jessica Walter, Joan Hackett*, Elizabeth Hartman, Mary Robin-Redd, *Kathleen Widdoes*, Shirley Knight, Larry Hagman, *Hal Holbrook, Robert Emhardt*, Robert Mulligan, James Congdon, James Broderick

'A strange, all-inclusive, no-holds-barred movie.'—*Philip T. Hartung*

Guadalcanal Diary*
US 1943 93m bw
TCF (Byron Foy)

Marines fight for a vital Pacific base.
Standard war propaganda, with good action scenes.

w Lamar Trotti, *book* Richard Tregaskis *d* Lewis Seiler *ph* Charles G. Clarke *m* David Buttolph

Preston Foster, Lloyd Nolan, William Bendix, Richard Conte, Anthony Quinn, Richard Jaeckel, Roy Roberts, Minor Watson, Ralph Byrd, Lionel Stander, Miles Mander, Reed Hadley

The Guardsman*
US 1931 83m bw
MGM

A jealous actor tests his wife's fidelity.
Theatrically effective comedy filmed for the sake of its stars; later remade as a musical, *The Chocolate Soldier* (qv).

w Ernest Vajda, Claudine West, *play* Ferenc Molnar *d* Sidney Franklin *ph* Norbert Brodine

Alfred Lunt, Lynn Fontanne, Roland Young, Zasu Pitts, Maude Eburne, Herman Bing, Ann Dvorak

AAN: Alfred Lunt; Lynn Fontanne

La Guerre Est Finie
France / Sweden 1966   122m   bw
Sofracima / Europa Film
aka: *The War Is Over*

A Spanish revolutionary maintains his ideals even though he is warned that he will be sold out. Dreary drama with romantic interludes and a fussy technique involving what appears to be the first use of flashforwards.

w Jorge Semprun *d* Alain Resnais *ph* Sacha Vierny *m* Giovanni Fusco

Yves Montand, Ingrid Thulin, Geneviève Bujold, Michel Piccoli

Guess Who's Coming to Dinner**
US 1967   112m   Technicolor
Columbia / Stanley Kramer

A well-to-do San Francisco girl announces that she is going to marry a black man, and her parents find they are less broad-minded than they thought.
The problem picture that isn't really, since everyone is so nice and the prospective bridegroom is so eligible. It looks like a photographed play, but isn't based on one; the set is unconvincing; but the acting is a dream.

w William Rose *d* Stanley Kramer *ph* Sam Leavitt *md* Frank de Vol *pd* Robert Clatworthy

Spencer Tracy, Katharine Hepburn, Kathaine Houghton (Hepburn's niece), *Sidney Poitier*, Cecil Kellaway, Roy E. Glenn Snr, Beah Richards, Isabell Sanford, Virginia Christine

'Suddenly everybody's caught up in a kind of integrated drawing-room comedy, and unable to decide whether there's anything funny in it or not.'—*Ann Birstein, Vogue*

AA: William Rose; Katharine Hepburn
AAN: best picture; Stanley Kramer; Frank de Vol; Spencer Tracy; Cecil Kellaway; Beah Richards

Guest in the House*
US 1944   121m   bw
Hunt Stromberg

A seemingly pleasant young woman is invited to stay with a family and brings tragedy and hatred to them.
Theatrical and rather unconvincing melodrama.

w Ketti Frings, *play* Dear Evelyn by Dale

Eunson, Hagar Wilde *d* John Brahm *ph* Lee Garmes *m* Werner Janssen *pd* Nicolai Remisoff

Anne Baxter, Ralph Bellamy, Aline MacMahon, Ruth Warrick, Scott McKay, Jerome Cowan, Marie McDonald, Percy Kilbride, Margaret Hamilton

AAN: Werner Janssen

Guest Wife
US 1945   90m   bw
(UA) Jack H. Skirball

For business purposes a man allows his wife to pretend to be the wife of another.
Stereotyped star farce which seemed tolerable at the time.

w Bruce Manning, John Klorer *d* Sam Wood *ph* Joseph Valentine *md* Daniele Amfitheatrof

Claudette Colbert, Don Ameche, Dick Foran, Charles Dingle, Grant Mitchell

'Mr Wood is a big gun to be trained on so trivial a target, but the result justifies the choice.'—*Richard Mallett, Punch*

AAN: Daniele Amfitheatrof

A Guide for the Married Man**
US 1967   91m   De Luxe   Panavision
TCF (Frank McCarthy)

A practised wolf explains to a perfect husband how to be unfaithful.
Generally funny revue with as many hilarious moments as flat spots.

w Frank Tarloff *d* Gene Kelly *ph* Joe Macdonald *m* Johnny Williams

Walter Matthau, Inger Stevens, *Robert Morse*, Sue Anne Langdon, Lucille Ball, Art Carney, Jack Benny, Polly Bergen, Joey Bishop, Sid Caesar, Wally Cox, Jayne Mansfield, Carl Reiner, Phil Silvers, Jeffrey Hunter, Terry-Thomas, Ben Blue

'One of the funniest films of the last several seasons . . . it has sense enough to sit down when it's through.'—*Robert Windeler*

The Guilt of Janet Ames
US 1948   83m   bw
Columbia

A paralysed war widow seeks to discover whether her husband's sacrifice was worthwhile. Embarrassing attempt by a comedienne to play Hamlet.

w Louella Macfarlane, Allen Rivkin, Devery Freeman, *story* Lenore Coffee *d* Henry Levin *ph* Joseph Walker *m* Morris Stoloff

Rosalind Russell, Melvyn Douglas, Sid Caesar,

Betsy Blair, Nina Foch, Harry Von Zell, Arthur Space

Guilty?

GB 1956   93m   bw
Grand National / Gibraltar (Charles A. Leeds)

An ex-resistance heroine is on trial for murder at the Old Bailey; her young solicitor goes to Avignon to prove her innocence.
Solidly cast old-fashioned mystery with a courtroom climax.

w Maurice J. Wilson, *novel* Death Has Deep Roots by Michael Gilbert d Edmond Greville ph Stan Pavey m Bruce Montgomery

John Justin, Barbara Laage, Donald Wolfit, Stephen Murray, Norman Wooland, Frank Villard, Sydney Tafler, Betty Stockfield

The Guinea Pig**

GB 1949   97m   bw
Pilgrim (The Boultings)
US title: *The Outsider*

The first poor boy to win a scholarship to a famous public school has a hard time.
Enjoyable though unrealistic school drama with chief interest centring on the staff. A rude word ('kick up the arse') ensured its popularity.

w Bernard Miles, Warren Chetham Strode, from the latter's play d Roy Boulting ph Gilbert Taylor m John Wooldridge

Richard Attenborough, *Robert Flemyng, Cecil Trouncer*, Sheila Sim, Bernard Miles, Joan Hickson

Gulliver's Travels**

US 1939   74m   Technicolor
(Paramount) Max Fleischer

Animated cartoon version which invents a Romeo-Juliet romance between Lilliput and Blefuscu and has the usual trouble with romantic humans. At the time it represented a genuine challenge to Disney, but has not worn well in terms of pace or inventiveness. Fleischer made one more feature cartoon, *Mr Bug Goes to Town*.

m Victor Young *songs* Ralph Rainger, Leo Robin

AAN: song 'Faithful Forever'; Victor Young

Gulliver's Travels

GB 1976   81m   Eastmancolor
EMI / Valeness-Belvision (Josef Shaftel)

An ineffective treatment, again aimed at children, in which Gulliver is the only human element and all the Lilliputians are cartooned.

w Don Black d Peter Hunt ph Alan Hume pd Michael Stringer m Michel Legrand

Richard Harris, Catherine Schell, Norman Shelley

'Bonelessly inoffensive.'—*Sight and Sound*

The Gumball Rally

US 1976   93m   Technicolor
Warner / First Artists (Chuck Bail)

A variety of vehicles take part in a crazy race from New York to Long Beach.
The stuntmen are the real stars of this good-looking but dramatically deficient chase and destruction extravaganza.

w Leon Capetanos d Chuck Bail ph Richard Glouner m Dominic Frontière stunt co-ordinator Eddie Donno

Michael Sarrazin, Normann Burton, Gary Busey, John Durren, Susan Flannery

Gumshoe**

GB 1972   85m   Eastmancolor
Columbia / Memorial (David Barber)

A Liverpool bingo caller dreams of becoming a Bogart-like private eye and finds himself in the middle of a murder case.
A likeable spoof which is never quite as funny as it means to be. Billy Liar did it better, but there's plenty of amusing detail.

w Neville Smith d Stephen Frears ph Chris Menges m Andrew Lloyd Webber

Albert Finney, Billie Whitelaw, Fulton Mackay, Frank Finlay, Janice Rule

Gun Crazy*

US 1950   87m   bw
King Brothers
reissue title: *Deadly is the Female*

A boy and girl set off on a trail of armed robbery and murder.
Modernized Bonnie and Clyde story which has become a minor cult film.

w Mackinlay Kantor, Millard Kaufman d Joseph H. Lewis ph Russell Harlan m Stuart Fryt

John Dall, Peggy Cummins, Morris Carnovsky, Barry Kroger, Annabel Shaw, Harry Lewis

Gun Fury

US 1953   80m   Technicolor   3-D
Columbia (Lewis J. Rachmil)

Outlaws rob a stagecoach and abduct a girl; her fiancé follows and takes revenge.
Adequate western programmer.

w Irving Wallace, Roy Huggins d Raoul Walsh ph Lester H. White md Mischa Bakaleinikoff

Rock Hudson, Donna Reed, Phil Carey, Lee Marvin, Neville Brand

Gun Glory

US 1957 89m Metrocolor Cinemascope
MGM (Nicholas Nayfack)

A gunfighter returns home to settle down, but finds his wife dead and his son resentful.
Dull, unexciting star western.

w William Ludwig, *novel* Man of the West by Philip Yordan d Roy Rowland ph Harold J. Marzorati m Jeff Alexander

Stewart Granger, Rhonda Fleming, Chill Wills, Steve Rowland, James Gregory

The Gun Runners*

US 1958 82m bw
UA/D DSeven Arts (Clarence Greene)

The owner of e Florida motor cruiser innocently rents it to a gun merchant.
Modestly effective action melodrama, the third version of *To Have and Have Not* (qv).

w Daniel Mainwaring, Paul Monash d Don Siegel ph Hal Mohr m Leith Stevens

Audie Murphy, Eddie Albert, Patricia Owens, Everett Sloane

A Gunfight*

US 1970 94m Technicolor
Harvest / Thoroughbred / Bryna (Ronnie Lubin, Harold Jack Bloom)

Two famous gunfighters on their uppers stage a duel for money.
Austere and anti-climactic western supposedly against popular blood lust.

w Harold Jack Bloom d Lamont Johnson ph David M. Walsh m Laurence Rosenthal

Kirk Douglas, Johnny Cash, Karen Black, Raf Vallone

Gunfight at Dodge City

US 1958 81m De Luxe Cinemascope
UA / Mirisch

After various problems, Bat Masterson is elected sheriff of Dodge City.
Fair standard western with emphasis on plot and character.

w Daniel B. Ullman, Martin M. Goldsmith d Joseph M. Newman ph Carl Guthrie m Hans Salter

Joel McCrea, Julie Adams, John McIntire, Richard Anderson, Nancy Gates

Gunfight at the OK Corral**

US 1957 122m Technicolor Vistavision
Paramount / Hal Wallis

Wyatt Earp and Doc Holliday defeat the Clanton Gang.
Watchable, ambitious, but vaguely disappointing super-western.

w Leon Uris d John Sturges ph Charles B. Lang m Dmitri Tiomkin

Burt Lancaster, Kirk Douglas, Jo Van Fleet, Rhonda Fleming, John Ireland, Frank Faylen, Kenneth Tobey, Earl Holliman

'Carefully and lavishly mounted, but overlong and overwrought.'—*John Cutts*

The Gunfighter**

US 1950 84m bw
TCF (Nunnally Johnson)

A gunfighter fails to shake off his past.
Downbeat, small-scale but very careful adult western set in a believable community.

w William Bowers, William Sellers d Henry King ph Arthur Miller m Alfred Newman

Gregory Peck, Helen Westcott, Millard Mitchell, Jean Parker, Karl Malden, Skip Homeier, Mae Marsh

'Preserves throughout a respectable level of intelligence and invention.'—*Lindsay Anderson*

AAN: original story (William Bowers)
'Not merely a good western, a good film.'—*Richard Mallett, Punch*

Gung Ho!

US 1943 88m bw
Universal / Walter Wanger

Adventures of the Marines in the Pacific War.
Trite flagwaver, popular at the time.

w Lucien Hubbard, based on the experiences of Captain W. S. LeFrancois USMC d Ray Enright

Randolph Scott, Grace MacDonald, Alan Curtis, Noah Beery Jnr, J. Carrol Naish, David Bruce, Peter Coe, Robert Mitchum

Gunga Din***

US 1939 117m bw
RKO (George Stevens)

Three cheerful army veterans meet adventure on the North-West Frontier.
Rousing period actioner with comedy asides, one of the most entertaining of its kind ever made.

w Joel Sayre, Fred Guiol, Ben Hecht, Charles MacArthur, *poem* Rudyard Kipling d George Stevens ph Joseph H. August m Alfred Newman ad Van Nest Polglase

Cary Grant, Victor McLaglen, Douglas Fairbanks Jnr, Sam Jaffe, Eduardo Ciannelli, Joan Fontaine, Montagu Love, Robert Coote, Cecil Kellaway, Abner Biberman, Lumsden Hare

'One of the most enjoyable nonsense-adventure movies of all time.'—*Pauline Kael, 1968*

'Bravura is the exact word for the performances, and Stevens' composition and cutting of the fight sequences is particularly stunning.'—*NFT, 1973*

Gunman's Walk*
US 1958   97m   Technicolor
Cinemascope
Columbia (Fred Kohlmar)

A tough westerner has two sons, one of whom follows too literally in his footsteps.
Competent action melodrama with good characterization.

w Frank Nugent *d* Phil Karlson *ph* Charles Lawton *m* George Duning

Van Heflin, Tab Hunter, James Darren, Kathryn Grant

Gunn*
US 1967   95m   Technicolor
Paramount / Geoffrey (Owen Crump)

A private eye is hired to find a gangster's killer.
Tongue-in-cheek violence from the television series, with Craig Stevens doing a Cary Grant imitation.

w Blake Edwards, William Peter Blatty *d* Blake Edwards *ph* Philip Lathrop *m* Henry Mancini

Craig Stevens, Laura Devon, Ed Asner, Sherry Jackson, Helen Traubel, J. Pat O'Malley, Regis Toomey

'Falters between parody and straight action.'—*MFB*

Guns at Batasi*
GB 1964   103m   bw   Cinemascope
TCF / George H. Brown

The headquarters of an Anglo-African regiment is threatened by rebels.
Basically the old chestnut about a group of disparate types trapped in a dangerous situation, this is given shape and stature by the star's lively performance as the martinet of an RSM.

w Robert Hollis, from his novel The Siege of Battersea *d* John Guillermin *ph* Douglas Slocombe *m* John Addison

Richard Attenborough, Flora Robson, Mia Farrow, Jack Hawkins, Cecil Parker, Percy

Herbert, Errol John, John Leyton, Earl Cameron

Guns for San Sebastian
France / Mexico / Italy 1967   111m
Eastmancolor   Franscope
MGM / Cipra / Filmes / Ernesto Enriques (Jacques Bar)

In Mexico in 1746, a rebel on the run stays to defend a besieged village.
Multi-national actioner, violent but quite undistinguished.

w Serge Ganz, Miguel Morayta, Ennio de Concini *d* Henri Verneuil *ph* Armand Thirard *m* Ennio Morricone

Anthony Quinn, Charles Bronson, Sam Jaffe, Anjanette Comer, Silvia Pinal

Guns of Darkness
GB 1962   102m   bw
ABP / Cavalcade (Thomas Clyde)

A British plantation boss in Latin America escapes with his wife when rebels strike.
Chase/escape film with a few tiny comments about violence.

w John Mortimer, *novel* Act of Mercy by Francis Clifford *d* Anthony Asquith *ph* Robert Krasker *m* Benjamin Frankel

David Niven, Leslie Caron, James Robertson Justice, David Opatoshu

The Guns of Fort Petticoat
US 1957   79m   Technicolor
Columbia / Brown-Murphy (Harry Joe Brown)

During the Civil War, a wandering Texan trains townswomen into a fighting force.
Unlikely western which passes the time.

w Walter Doniger *d* George Marshall *ph* Ray Rennahan *m* Mischa Bakaleinikoff

Audie Murphy, Kathryn Grant, Hope Emerson, Jeff Donnell, Isobel Elsom

The Guns of Loos*
GB 1927   89m (24 fps)   bw   silent
Stoll / New Era

A blinded hero of the war returns home to run an industrial empire and is confronted by a strike.
One of the better British silents, with a strong plot and an interesting cast.

w L. H. Gordon, Reginald Fogwell, Sinclair Hill *d* Sinclair Hill

Henry Victor, Madeleine Carroll, Bobby Howes, Hermione Baddeley

The Guns of Navarone **
GB 1961   157m   Technicolor
Cinemascope
Columbia / Carl Foreman (Cecil F. Ford)

In 1943 a sabotage team is sent to destroy two
giant guns on a Turkish Island.
Ambitiously produced Boy's Own Paper
heroics, with lots of noise and self-sacrifice;
intermittently exciting but bogged down by
philosophical chat.

w Carl Foreman, *novel* Alistair Maclean d J.
Lee-Thompson ph Oswald Morris m Dmitri
Tiomkin ad Geoffrey Drake

Gregory Peck, David Niven, Stanley Baker,
Anthony Quinn, Anthony Quayle, James
Darren, Gia Scala, James Robertson Justice,
Richard Harris, Irene Papas, Bryan Forbes
  'A desperate imbalance: the moral arguments
cut into the action without extending it.'—
Penelope Houston

AAN: best picture; Carl Foreman; J. Lee-
Thompson; Dmitri Tiomkin

Guns of the Timberland
US 1960   91m   Technicolor
Jaguar (Aaron Spelling)
GB title: *Stampeded*

Loggers are opposed by cattle interests.
Routine star western with tolerable production
values.

w Joseph Petracca, Aaron Spelling d Robert D.
Webb ph John Seitz m David Buttolph

Alan Ladd, Jeanne Crain, Gilbert Roland,
Frankie Avalon, Lyle Bettger, Noah Beery Jnr

The Guru
US / India 1969   112m   De Luxe
TCF / Arcadia (Ismail Merchant)

In India, an English pop singer succumbs to the
local atmosphere.
Pleasant, affectionate but forgettable anecdote of
modern India.

w Ruth Prawer Jhabvala, James Ivory d James
Ivory ph Subrata Mitra m Ustad Vilayat Khan

Michael York, Rita Tushingham, Utpal Dutt,
Aparna Sen, Barry Foster

Gus
US 1976   96m   Technicolor
Walt Disney (Ron Miller)

A football team co-opts a mule which can kick a
hundred yard ball.
Predictable Disney fantasy comedy with a direct
line back to *The Absent Minded Professor*.

w Arthur Alsberg, Don Nelson d Vincent

McEveety ph Frank Phillips m Robert F.
Brunner

Ed Asner, Don Knotts, Gary Grimes, Tim
Conway, Liberty Williams, Bob Crane, Harold
Gould, Tom Bosley, Dick Van Patten

The Guvnor
GB 1935   88m   bw
Gaumont (Michael Balcon)
US title: *Mr Hobo*

By chance a tramp becomes a bank director.
Predictable star vehicle with Arliss a most
unlikely tramp.

w Maude Howell, Guy Bolton d Milton Rosmer

George Arliss, Gene Gerrard, Viola Keats,
Patric Knowles, Frank Cellier, Mary Clare,
George Hayes
  'His admirers need not fear that he has lost
any of his usual refinement or sentiment, his
cultured English accent, his Universal
certificate.'—*Graham Greene*

A Guy Named Joe
US 1944   120m   bw
MGM (Everett Riskin)

A flier is killed but comes back as a ghost to
supervise his ex-girl's new romance.
Icky romantic comedy-drama with strong
propaganda intent; the stars make it tolerable.

w Dalton Trumbo d Victor Fleming ph George
Folsey, Karl Freund m Herbert Stothart

Spencer Tracy, Irene Dunne, Ward Bond, Van
Johnson, James Gleason, Lionel Barrymore,
Barry Nelson, Don Defore, Henry O'Neill
  'As far as I could judge, the audience loved it:
melodrama, farce, fake philosophy, swimming
eyes and all.'—*Richard Mallett, Punch*

AAN: original story (David Buchan, Chandler
Sprague)

Guys and Dolls *
US 1955   149m   Eastmancolor
Cinemascope
Samuel Goldwyn

A New York gangster takes a bet that he can
romance a Salvation Army lady.
The artifices of Runyonland are made more so
by a defiantly studio-bound production and
thoroughly flat handling; but the songs and
sometimes the performances survive.

wd Joseph L. Mankiewicz, *musical* Jo Swerling
and Abe Burrows ph Harry Stradling, *songs*
Frank Loesser md Cyril Mockridge, Jay
Blackton ch Michael Kidd ad Joseph Wright
pd Oliver Smith

Frank Sinatra, Marlon Brando, Jean Simmons,

Vivian Blaine, Stubby Kaye, B. S. Pully, Robert Keith, Sheldon Leonard, George E. Stone

'Quantity has been achieved only at the cost of quality.'—*Penelope Houston*

AAN: Harry Stradling; Cyril Mockridge, Jay Blackton

Gypsy*
US 1962 149m Technirama
Warner (Mervyn Le Roy)

The early days of stripteaser Gypsy Rose Lee, and the exploits of her ambitious mother.
A vaudeville musical that is nowhere near raucous enough, or brisk enough, for its subject, and is miscast into the bargain. The songs are great, but not here: Miss Russell is as boring as an electric drill in a role that should have been reserved for Ethel Merman.

w Leonard Spiegelgass, *book* Arthur Laurents *d* Mervyn Le Roy *m Jule Styne ly Stephen Sondheim ph* Harry Stradling *md* Frank Perkins *ad* John Beckman

Rosalind Russell, Natalie Wood, *Karl Malden*, James Milhollin

AAN: Harry Stradling; Frank Perkins

The Gypsy and the Gentleman
GB 1957 107m Eastmancolor
Rank (Maurice Cowan)

A penniless Regency rake marries a tempestuous gypsy, with melodramatic and tragic results.
Expensive and typically mistimed Rank attempt to re-do *The Man in Grey*; a barnstormer notable only for waste of talent.

w Janet Greene, *novel* Darkness I Leave You by Nina Warner Hooke *d* Joseph Losey *ph* Jack Hildyard *m* Hans May *ad* Ralph Brinton

Melina Mercouri, Keith Michell, Patrick McGoohan, June Laverick, Flora Robson, Helen Haye

The Gypsy Moths*
US 1969 110m Metrocolor
MGM (Hal Landers, Bobby Roberts)

Sky-diving stuntmen find love and death on a small-town tour.
Brilliantly breathtaking actioner which too frequently gets grounded, and does not find a reason for being so glum.

w William Hanley, *novel* James Drought *d* John Frankenheimer *p̄h* Philip Lathrop *aerial ph Carl Boenisch m* Elmer Bernstein

Burt Lancaster, Deborah Kerr, Gene Hackman, Scott Wilson, William Windom, Bonnie Bedelia, Sheree North

Gypsy Wildcat
US 1944 77m Technicolor
Universal (George Waggner)

A Transylvanian gypsy girl is really a long lost countess.
Universal's Frankenstein sets are put to lighter use in a quite incredible piece of downright hokum.

w James Hogan, Gene Lewis, James M. Cain *d* Roy William Neill *ph* George Robinson, W. Howard Greene *m* Edward Ward

Maria Montez, Jon Hall, Leo Carrillo, Gale Sondergaard, Douglass Dumbrille, Nigel Bruce, Peter Coe, Curt Bois

'The picture's so bad, it's bound to make money.'—*Cue*

Hail the Conquering Hero***
US 1944 101m bw
Paramount (Preston Sturges)

An army reject is accidentally thought a hero
when he returns to his small-town home.
Skilfully orchestrated Preston Sturges romp,
slightly marred by an overdose of sentiment but
featuring his repertory of comic actors at full
pitch.

wd Preston Sturges *ph* John Seitz *m* Werner
Heymann

Eddie Bracken, William Demarest, Ella Raines,
Franklin Pangborn, Elizabeth Patterson,
Raymond Walburn, Alan Bridge, Georgia
Caine, Freddie Steele, Jimmy Conlin, Torben
Meyer

'Mob scenes, rough-houses and sharply
serious passages are played for all the
pantomime they are worth . . . one of the
happiest, heartiest comedies in a
twelvemonth.'—*Otis L. Guernsey Jnr*

'First rate entertainment, a pattern of film
making, not to be missed.'—*Richard Mallett,
Punch*

'The energy, the verbal density, the rush of
Americana and the congestion seen periodically
in *The Miracle of Morgan's Creek* stagger the
senses in this newest film.'—*James Ursini*

'He uses verbal as well as visual slapstick, and
his comic timing is so quirkily effective that the
dialogue keeps popping off like a string of
firecrackers.'—*New Yorker, 1977*

AAN: Preston Sturges (as writer)

The Hairy Ape
US 1944 91m bw
Jules Levy

A ship's stoker aims to kill a socialite who has
insulted him.
Patchy treatment of an intractable and dated
play.

w Jules Levy, *play* Eugene O'Neill *d* Alfred
Santell *ph* Lucien Andriot *m* Michel Michelet,
Edward Paul

William Bendix, Susan Hayward, John Loder,
Dorothy Comingore, Roman Bohnen, Alan
Napier

AAN: Michel Michelet, Edward Paul

Half a Sixpence*
GB 1968 148m Technicolor Panavision
Paramount / Ameran (Charles H. Schneer,
George Sidney)

A draper's assistant inherits a fortune and moves
into society.
Mildly likeable but limp and overlong musical
which would have benefited from more intimate,
sharper treatment than the wide screen can give.
The period decor and lively numbers seem
insufficient compensation for the longueurs.

w Beverly Cross, from his play based on Kipps
by H. G. Wells *d* George Sidney *ph* Geoffrey
Unsworth *m/ly* David Heneker *pd* Ted
Haworth *ch* Gillian Lynne

Tommy Steele, Julia Foster, Cyril Ritchard,
Penelope Horner, Elaine Taylor, Hilton
Edwards, Pamela Brown, James Villiers

The Half Naked Truth*
US 1932 67m bw
RKO

A publicity agent has trouble with a
temperamental actress whose schemes are
always over the top.
Amusing wisecracking comedy.

w Bartlett Cormack, Corey Ford *d* Gregory La
Cava *ph* Bert Glennon

Lee Tracy, Lupe Velez, Eugene Pallette, Frank
Morgan, Bob McKenzie

The Halfway House*
GB 1944 99m bw
Ealing (Cavalcanti)

Overnight guests at an inn find it was bombed a
year before and they have all been given a
supernatural chance to reconsider their lives.
Interesting pattern play which would have
benefited from lighter handling.

w Angus Macphail, Diana Morgan, *play* Denis
Ogden *d* Basil Dearden

Françoise Rosay, Tom Walls, Alfred Drayton,
Sally Ann Howes, Mervyn Johns, Glynis Johns,
Esmond Knight, Richard Bird, Guy Middleton

Hallelujah!**
US 1929   106m   bw
MGM (King Vidor)

A black cotton worker accidentally kills a man
and decides to become a preacher.
Hollywood's unique black melodrama now
seems stilted because of its early talkie technique,
but at the time its picture of negro life had a
freshness and truth which was not reached again
for thirty years.

w W and Tuchock, bning Vidor *d King Vidor*
ph Gordon Avil *md Eva Jessye*

Daniel Haynes, Nina Mae McKinney, William
Fountaine, Fannie Belle De Knight, Harry Gray

Hallelujah, I'm a Bum**
US 1933   80m   bw
Lewis Milestone
GB titles: *Hallelujah I'm a Tramp; Lazy Bones*

The leader of a group of Central Park tramps
smartens himself up for love of a lady who lost
her memory. When she recovers it, he becomes a
tramp again.
Curious whimsy expressed mainly in recitative,
with embarrassing stretches relieved by
moments of visual and verbal inspiration. Very
typical of the Depression, with the tramps
knowing best how life should be lived.

*w S. N. Behrman, Ben Hecht d Lewis
Milestone ph Lucien Andriot ad Richard Day
rhymes/m/ly Richard Rodgers, Lorenz Hart*

Al Jolson, Harry Langdon, Madge Evans, Frank
Morgan, Chester Conklin

The Hallelujah Trail
US 1965   167m   Technicolor   Ultra
Panavision 70
UA / Mirisch / Kappa (John Sturges)

In 1867 a wagonload of whisky bound for
Denver is waylaid by Indians, temperance
crusaders and the civilian militia.
Absurdly inflated, prolonged, uninventive
comedy western with poor narrative grip; all
dressed up and nowhere to go.

w John Gay, *novel* Bill Gulick *d* John Sturges
ph Robert Surtees m Elmer Bernstein

Burt Lancaster, Lee Remick, Brian Keith, Jim
Hutton, Donald Pleasence, Martin Landau

The Halliday Brand*
US 1956   78m   bw
UA / Collier Young

A tough farmer/sheriff conflicts with his son over
his attitude to Indians.
Dour, reliable western melodrama with a good
cast.

w George W. George, George S. Slavin
d Joseph H. Lewis *ph* Ray Rennahan
m Stanley Wilson

Joseph Cotten, Viveca Lindfors, Ward Bond,
Betsy Blair, Bill Williams, Jay C. Flippen

Halls of Anger
US 1969   99m   De Luxe
UA / Mirisch (Herbert Hirschman)

A black basketball star goes to teach in his home
town and faces segregation problems.
Schematic melodrama, as well meaning as it is
boring.

w John Shaner, Al Ramrus *d* Paul Bogart
ph Burnett Guffey *m* Dave Grusin

Calvin Lockhart, Janet McLachlan, Jeff Bridges

Halls of Montezuma*
US 1950   113m   Technicolor
TCF (Robert Bassler)

Marines fight World War II in the Pacific.
Well-mounted, simple-minded actioner.

w Michael Blankfort *d* Lewis Milestone
ph Winton C. Hoch, Harry Jackson *m* Sol
Kaplan *md* Lionel Newman

Richard Widmark, Jack Palance, Reginald
Gardiner, Robert Wagner, Karl Malden,
Richard Hylton, Richard Boone, Skip Homeier,
Jack Webb, Bert Freed, Neville Brand, Don
Hicks, Martin Milner

'By far the noisiest war film I ever
encountered.'—*Richard Mallett, Punch*

Hamlet**
GB 1948   142m   bw
Rank / Two Cities (Laurence Olivier)

Prince Hamlet takes too long making up his
mind to revenge his father's death.
The play is sharply cut, then time is wasted
having the camera prowl pointlessly along
gloomy corridors . . . but much of the acting is
fine, some scenes compel, and the production has
a splendid brooding power.

w William Shakespeare *d* Laurence Olivier
*ph Desmond Dickinson pd Roger Furse
m* William Walton *ad Carmen Dillon*

*Laurence Olivier, Eileen Herlie, Basil Sydney,
Jean Simmons, Felix Aylmer*, Norman
Wooland, Terence Morgan, *Stanley Holloway*,
Peter Cushing, Esmond Knight, Anthony
Quayle, Harcourt Williams, John Laurie, Niall
MacGinnis, Patrick Troughton

AA: best picture; Laurence Olivier (as actor)
AAN: Laurence Olivier (as director); William
Walton; Jean Simmons

Hamlet*
USSR 1964　150m　bw　Sovscope
Lenfilm

A Russian version of the play, with lowering sets, brooding photography and strong acting.

translation Boris Pasternak *d* Grigori Kozintsev *ph* I. Gritzys *m* Dmitri Shostakovich

Innokenti Smoktunovsky, Mikhail Nazvanov, Elsa Radzin, Anastasia Vertinskaya

Hammerhead
GB 1968　99m　Technicolor
Columbia / Irving Allen

An American secret agent captures a master criminal.
Jaded James Bond imitation, full of would-be fashionable detail.

w William Bast, Herbert Baker, *novel* James Mayo *d* David Miller *ph* Kenneth Talbot, Wilkie Cooper *m* David Whitaker

Vince Edwards, Peter Vaughan, Judy Geeson, Diana Dors, Michael Bates, Beverly Adams, Patrick Cargill, Patrick Holt

Hammersmith Is Out*
US 1972　114m　Du Art Color
Cinerama / J. Cornelius Cream (Alex Lucas)

With the help of a male nurse, a homicidal mental inmate escapes and becomes the most influential man in the country.
Pretentious updating of Faust into a kind of black farce that seldom amuses but is interesting in fits and starts.

w Stanford Whitmore *d* Peter Ustinov *ph* Richard Kline *m* Dominic Frontière

Richard Burton, Elizabeth Taylor, Peter Ustinov, Beau Bridges, Leon Ames, John Schuck, George Raft

Hand in Hand*
GB 1960　80m　bw
ABP / Helen Winston

The friendship of two 7-year-olds is affected by racial prejudice because one is Catholic and the other Jewish; but after misunderstandings their friendship is confirmed by priest and rabbi.
Pleasant, well-meaning drama apparently intended for older children.

w Diana Morgan *d* Philip Leacock *ph* Frederick A. Young *m* Stanley Black

Lorette Parry, Phillip Needs, Sybil Thorndike, John Gregson, Finlay Currie

Handle with Care*
US 1958　82m　bw
MGM (Morton Fine)

Small-town college students stage a mock trial and come up with some embarrassing answers.
Interesting melodrama with a disappointing ending; a well done second feature.

w Morton Fine, David Friedkin d David Friedkin ph Harold J. Marzorati *m* Alexander Courage

Dean Jones, Joan O'Brien, Thomas Mitchell, Walter Abel, John Smith

Hands across the Table**
US 1935　81m　bw
Paramount (E. Lloyd Sheldon)

A manicurist determines to marry a rich man.
Lively romantic comedy, smoothly made and typical of its time.

w Norman Krasna, Vincent Lawrence, Herbert Fields *d Mitchell Leisen ph* Ted Tetzlaff *m* Sam Coslow, Frederick Hollander

Carole Lombard, Fred MacMurray, Ralph Bellamy, Astrid Allwyn, Ruth Donnelly, Marie Prevost, William Demarest, Ed Gargan

'A happy mixture of brainwork and horseplay and a reminder that when intelligence goes for a walk among even the oldest props, the props may come to life.'—*Otis Ferguson*

The Hands of Orlac
GB / France 1960　105m　colour
Riviera / Pendennis (Steven Pallos, Don Taylor)

A concert pianist's hands are crushed in an accident, and a mad surgeon grafts on those of an executed murderer.
Flatulent remake of the 1926 German silent and the 1935 American *Mad Love*. Stilted, hammy, threadbare and overlong.

w John Baines, Edmond T. Gréville, *novel* Maurice Renard *d* Edmond T. Gréville *ph* Desmond Dickinson *m* Claude Bolling

Mel Ferrer, Donald Wolfit, Christopher Lee

Hands of the Ripper
GB 1971　85m　Technicolor
Hammer (Aida Young)

Jack the Ripper stabs his wife to death in view of his small daughter, who grows up a sexually repressed murderess.
Gory Hammer horror with well done scenes.

w L. W. Davidson *d* Peter Sasdy *ph* Kenneth Talbot *m* Christopher Gunning *ad Roy Stannard*

Angharad Rees, Eric Porter, Dora Bryan, Jane Merrow, Derek Godfrey

Hands over the City
Italy 1963 105m bw
Galatea
original title: *Le Mani sulla Città*

A property tycoon wangles local politicians so that he gets development on the property he controls.
An angry political film which is too strident to have much entertainment value.

w Enzo Provencale, Enzo Forcella, Raffaele La Capria, Francesco Rosi d Francesco Rosi
m Piero Piccioni ph Gianni di Venanzo

Rod Steiger, Salvo Randone, and non-professionals

Handy Andy
US 1934 82m bw
Fox

A midwestern druggist is married to a snob.
Competent star vehicle overflowing with crackerbarrel philosophy.

w William Counselman, Henry Johnson, *play* Merry Andrew by Lewis Beach d David Butler
ph Arthur Miller

Will Rogers, Peggy Wood, Conchita Montenegro, Mary Carlisle, Roger Imhof, Robert Taylor (his first film), Paul Harvey

Hang 'em High
US 1967 114m De Luxe
UA / Malpaso / Leonard Freeman

A cowboy is rescued from lynching and takes revenge on his persecutors.
Hollywood's first attempt to imitate the gore and brutality of spaghetti westerns and to take back its own errant star. Emetic and interminable.

w Leonard Freeman, Mel Goldberg d Ted Post
ph Leonard South, Richard Kline m Dominic Frontière

Clint Eastwood, Inger Stevens, Ed Begley, Pat Hingle, James MacArthur, Arlene Golonka, Charles McGraw, Ben Johnson, L. Q. Jones

The Hanging Tree*
US 1958 106m Technicolor
Warner / Baroda (Martin Jurow, Richard Shepherd)

Life is tough in a Montana gold-mining camp, especially for a doctor who has killed his unfaithful wife.
Lowering western with a feeling for place and period, plus a welter of melodramatic incident.

w Wendell Mayes, Halstead Welles, *novel*

Dorothy M. Johnson d Delmer Daves ph Ted McCord m Max Steiner

Gary Cooper, Maria Schell, Karl Malden, Ben Piazza, George C. Scott

AAN: title song (m Jay Livingston, *ly* Ray Evans)

The Hangman
US 1959 86m bw
Paramount (Frank Freeman Jnr)

A marshal with a reputation for getting his man deliberately allows one to escape.
Dour, low-key western, competent but rather flat and uninteresting.

w Dudley Nichols d Michael Curtiz ph Loyal Griggs m Harry Sukman

Robert Taylor, Jack Lord, Fess Parker, Tina Louise, Mickey Shaughnessy

Hangman's House
US 1928 72m (24 fps) bw silent
Fox

To please her dying father, an Irish girl marries a wastrel instead of the man she loves, but her husband is killed in a duel.
Blarney-filled melodrama, like a sober *Quiet Man*. John Wayne can be glimpsed as an extra.

w Marion Orth, *story* Don Byrne d John Ford
ph George Schneiderman

June Collyer, Larry Kent, Earle Foxe, Victor McLaglen, Hobart Bosworth

Hangmen Also Die*
US 1943 131m bw
Fritz Lang (T. W. Baumfield)
Reissue title: *Lest We Forget*

The Nazis take revenge for the killing of Heydrich.
Disappointingly heavy-handed, though deeply felt war propaganda set in Hollywood's idea of Czechoslovakia. Only moments of interest remain.

w John Wexley, *story* Fritz Lang, Bertolt Brecht
d Fritz Lang ph James Wong Howe m Hanns Eisler

Brian Donlevy, Anna Lee, Walter Brennan, Gene Lockhart, Dennis O'Keefe, Alexander Granach, Margaret Wycherly, Nana Bryant, Hans von Twardowski (as Heydrich), Jonathan Hale, Lionel Stander
'Lang, working with American actors on an American theme, has produced *Fury*. Lang trying to recreate his own Central Europe on a Hollywood set is completely at sea.'—*Paul Rotha, 1949*

'Directed with a skill which excites and

delights . . . brilliant use of the tiny, shocking detail.'—*Dilys Powell*

AAN: Hanns Eisler

Hangover Square*
US 1944   77m   bw
TCF (Robert Bassler)

In 1903 London, a psychopathic composer murders pretty women.
This rather empty melodrama has almost nothing to do with the book from which it is allegedly taken, but the Hollywoodian evocation of gaslit London is richly entertaining and good to look at.

w Barre Lyndon, *novel* Patrick Hamilton *d John Brahm ph Joseph La Shelle m Bernard Herrmann ad Lyle Wheeler, Maurice Ransford*

Laird Cregar, Linda Darnell, George Sanders, Glenn Langan, Faye Marlowe, Alan Napier, Frederick Worlock

'Cregar lumbers around with a Karloffian glare in the spacious mists which happily blur the architectural decor.'—*Richard Winnington*

'Distinguished photography gets the last glint of fancy fright out of the pomps and vanities of the turn of the century.'—*Time*

'A half-chewed collection of reminiscences of *Dr Jekyll and Mr Hyde* and *The Lodger*.'—*Richard Mallett, Punch*

† Tragically, Laird Cregar died after slimming for this role, to which he was in any case unsuited.

Hannibal
Italy 1959   103m   Technicolor
Supercinescope
Liber Film (Ottavio Poggi)

Hannibal crosses the Alps and falls for the daughter of a Roman senator.
Unhistorical farrago which totally fails to entertain on any level.

w Mortimer Braus *d* Carlo Ludovico Bragaglia, Edgar G. Ulmer *ph* Raffaele Masciocchi *m* Carlo Rustichelli

Victor Mature, Rita Gam, Gabriele Ferzetti, Milly Vitale, Rik Battaglia

'Not even the elephants emerge with dignity.'—*MFB*

Hannibal Brooks
GB 1968   102m   De Luxe
UA / Scimitar (Michael Winner)

A British POW in Germany escapes over the Alps with an elephant.
Curious action adventure which seems undecided whether to take itself seriously. Some passable sequences.

w Dick Clement, Ian La Frenais *d* Michael Winner *ph* Robert Paynter *m* Francis Lai

Oliver Reed, Michael J. Pollard, Wolfgang Preiss, Karen Baal

Hannie Caulder
GB 1971   85m   colour   Panavision
Tigon / Curtwel (Tony Tenser)

Raped by three outlaws who murdered her husband, a western woman takes revenge.
Unintentionally comical action melodrama with the star defeating all comers.

w Z. X. Jones (Burt Kennedy, David Haft) *d* Burt Kennedy *ph* Ted Scaife *m* Ken Thorne

Raquel Welch, Robert Culp, Ernest Borgnine, Strother Martin, Jack Elam, Christopher Lee, Diana Dors

Hans Christian Andersen*
US 1952   112m   Technicolor
Samuel Goldwyn

A storytelling cobbler leaves his village to make shoes for the prima ballerina in Copenhagen.
Artificial, sugary confection with little humour and far too little magic of any kind; the star carries it nicely, but he is on his own apart from the songs.

w Moss Hart *d* Charles Vidor *ph* Harry Stradling *md* Walter Scharf *songs Frank Loesser ad Richard Day ch* Roland Petit

Danny Kaye, Zizi Jeanmaire, Farley Granger, John Qualen, Joey Walsh

AAN: Harry Stradling; Walter Scharf; song 'Thumbelina' (*m/ly* Frank Loesser)

The Happening
US 1967   101m   Technicolor
Columbia / Horizon / Dover (Jud Kinberg)

Four young hippies kidnap a wealthy businessman and don't know what to do with him; he turns the tables.
Freewheeling irresponsible comedy which even at the time of swinging cities seemed very irritating.

w Frank R. Pierson, James D. Buchanan, Ronald Austin *d* Eliot Silverstein *ph* Philip Lathrop *m* Frank de Vol *pd* Richard Day

Anthony Quinn, George Maharis, Michael Parks, Faye Dunaway, Robert Walker, Oscar Homolka, Martha Hyer, Milton Berle, Jack Kruschen

'A wacky comedy à la mode, oddly mixed and only spasmodically effective.'—*Variety*

The Happiest Days of Your Life***
GB 1950   81m   bw
British Lion / Individual (Frank Launder)

A ministry mistake billets a girls' school on a
boys' school.

Briskly handled version of a semi-classic post-
war farce, with many familiar talents in excellent
form.

w Frank Launder, John Dighton, *play John
Dighton d Frank Launder ph* Stan Pavey
m Mischa Spoliansky

*Alastair Sim, Margaret Rutherford, Joyce
Grenfell, Richard Wattis, Edward Rigby, Guy
Middleton, Muriel Aked,* John Bentley,
Bernadette O'Farrell

'Absolutely first rate fun.'—*Richard Mallett,
Punch*

The Happiest Millionaire
US 1967   159m   Technicolor
Walt Disney (Bill Anderson)

In 1916, a sporting millionaire has several
surprising interests but finds time to sort out
family problems.

Drearily inept family entertainment with a
couple of good songs and an amusing alligator
sequence but acres of yawning boredom in
between.

w A. J. Carothers, *play* Kyle Crichton, *book* My
Philadelphia Father by Cornelia Drexel Biddle
d Norman Tokar *ph* Edward Colman
m/ly Richard M. and Robert B. Sherman

Fred MacMurray, *Tommy Steele*, Greer
Garson, John Davidson, Gladys Cooper, Lesley
Anne Warren, Geraldine Page, Hermione
Baddeley

Happy Anniversary
US 1959   83m   bw
UA / Ralph Fields

A television set causes family trouble.
Marital farce designed to take a few sideswipes
at TV.

w Joseph Fields, Jerome Chodorov, from their
play Anniversary Waltz *d* David Miller *ph* Lee
Garmes *m* Sol Kaplan, Robert Allan

David Niven, Mitzi Gaynor, Carl Reiner, Loring
Smith, Patty Duke, Phyllis Povah

Happy Birthday Wanda June*
US 1971   105m   Technicolor
Columbia

An adventurer believed dead returns just as his
wife is about to choose one of two suitors.
A farcical situation becomes in this writer's
hands an investigation of the hero cult, with

many zany jokes, episodes in heaven, and bad
language. Interesting in spots, but it would have
worked better with a more fluent cinematic
technique.

w Kurt Vonnegut Jnr, from his play *d* Mark
Robson

Rod Steiger, Susannah York, George Grizzard,
Don Murray

'We can only assume that Mr Robson
deserted the filmic instincts that brought him
commercial success because here he was, finally,
in the presence of Art.'—*Hollis Alpert*

'Nothing more than a miscast film record of
the dialogue and plot outline of the stage
work.'—*Judith Crist*

The Happy Ending*
US 1969   112m   Technicolor   Panavision
UA / Pax Films (Richard Brooks)

A middle-aged woman reflects over sixteen years
of unhappy marriage.

Sometimes glib, sometimes trenchant
sophisticated drama with enough interesting
scenes to make it more than merely a 'woman's
picture'.

wd Richard Brooks ph Conrad Hall *m* Michel
Legrand

Jean Simmons, John Forsythe, Shirley Jones,
Lloyd Bridges, Teresa Wright, Dick Shawn,
Nanette Fabray, Bobby Darin, Tina Louise

'Packed with punchy little epigrams floating in
a vacuum of glossy superficiality.'—*David
Wilson*

'The truth about the process of ageing is what
binds this film together like cement.'—
Alexander Walker

AAN: Jean Simmons; song 'What Are You
Doing the Rest of Your Life' (*m* Michel Legrand,
ly Alan and Marilyn Bergman)

Happy Ever After
GB / Germany 1932   86m   bw
UFA (Erich Pommer)

Window-cleaners put a young actress on the way
to stardom.

Cheerful comedy, set and made in Germany by
mainly British talent.

w Jack Hulbert, Douglas Furber, from a story
by Walter Reisch and Billy Wilder *d* Paul
Martin, Robert Stevenson

Lilian Harvey, Jack Hulbert, Cicely
Courtneidge, Sonnie Hale, Edward Chapman

Happy Ever After*
GB 1954   87m   Technicolor
ABP / Mario Zampi
US title: *Tonight's the Night*

Irish villagers draw lots for the privilege of
murdering their rascally squire.
Fairly hilarious black comedy with a good cast
entering into the spirit of the thing.

David Niven, Yvonne de Carlo, A. E. Matthews,
Michael Shepley, George Cole, Barry Fitzgerald

Happy Go Lovely
GB 1950   97m   Technicolor
ABP (Marcel Hellman)

A chorus girl meets a millionaire during the
Edinburgh Festival.
For a semi-official contribution to the Festival of
Britain this is a lamentably unspontaneous
musical with no use of cinema techniques or
natural locales. Even allowing for the flat
handling, it is tedious.

w Val Guest d Bruce Humberstone ph Erwin
Hillier m Mischa Spoliansky

David Niven, Vera-Ellen, Cesar Romero, Bobby
Howes, Diane Hart, Gordon Jackson, Barbara
Couper, Gladys Henson, Joyce Carey

Happy Go Lucky
US 1943   81m   Technicolor
Paramount (Harold Wilson)

A cigarette girl chases a millionaire to a
Caribbean island.
Flimsy musical for those who like the stars.

w Walter de Leon, Melvin Frank, Norman
Panama d Curtis Bernhardt ph Karl Struss,
Wilfrid Cline songs Frank Loesser, Jimmy
McHugh

Mary Martin, Dick Powell, Betty Hutton
(singing 'Murder He Says'), Rudy Vallee, Eddie
Bracken, Mabel Paige, Eric Blore, Clem Bevans

Happy Gypsies*
Yugoslavia 1967   90m   Eastmancolor
Avala
aka: *I Even Knew Happy Gypsies*

A handsome, cruel-natured gypsy and his wife
have violent adventures and find themselves on
the run from the police.
The first film in the gypsy language does not
make one too sympathetic to their cause, but
some scenes are well managed and the colour is
fine.

wd Alexander Petrovic ph Tomislav Pinter
m gypsy melodies

Bekim Fehmiu, Olivera Vuco, Bata Zivojinovic

The Happy Hooker
US 1975   98m   Movielab
Double H / Cannon-Happy (Fred Caruso)

A Dutch girl in New York starts a career as a
prostitute and finds she enjoys it.
Glum sex comedy based on the supposed
exploits of a real madam; crude and not very
funny. If this is emancipation, Shirley Temple
seems more attractive by the minute.

w William Richert, *book* Xaviera Hollander
d Nicholas Sgarro ph Dick Kratina m Don
Elliott

Lynn Redgrave (hilariously miscast), Jean-
Pierre Aumont, Lovelady Powell, Nicholas
Pryor, Elizabeth Wilson, Tom Poston, Conrad
Janis, Richard Lynch

Happy Is the Bride*
GB 1957   84m   bw
British Lion / Paul Soskin

A couple planning a quiet summer wedding
reckon without the intervention of her parents.
Tame remake of *Quiet Wedding*; the right spirit
but not much sparkle.

w Jeffrey Dell, Roy Boulting, *play* Dodie Smith
d Roy Boulting ph Ted Scaife m Benjamin
Frankel

Ian Carmichael, Janette Scott, Cecil Parker,
Joyce Grenfell, Terry-Thomas, John Le
Mesurier, Eric Barker, Edith Sharpe, Athene
Seyler

Happy Land*
US 1943   75m   bw
TCF

Grandfather's ghost comes back to comfort a
family which has lost its son at war.
Sentimental flagwaver very typical of its time;
well made, it ensured not a dry eye in the house.

w Mackinlay Kantor d Irving Pichel ph Joseph
La Shelle

Don Ameche, Frances Dee, Harry Carey, Ann
Rutherford, Cara Williams, Henry Morgan,
Richard Crane, Dickie Moore

Happy Landing*
US 1938   102m   bw
TCF (David Hempstead)

A Norwegian girl falls for an American flier who
crashes near her home.
Lightweight skating musical, well put together.

w Milton Sperling, Boris Ingster d Roy del
Ruth ph John Mescall md Louis Silvers

Sonja Henie, Don Ameche, Cesar Romero,
Ethel Merman, Jean Hersholt, Billy Gilbert,
Wally Vernon, El Brendel

The Happy Road*
US / France 1956   100m   bw
MGM / Thor (Gene Kelly)

Two children run away from a Swiss school and are pursued by the American father of one of them.
Whimsical peripatetic comedy which fails to come off despite charming passages.

w Arthur Julian, Joseph Morhain, Harry Kurnitz d Gene Kelly ph Robert Juillard m Georges Van Parys

Gene Kelly, Barbara Laage, Michael Redgrave, Bobby Clark, Brigitte Fossey

The Happy Thieves
US 1962   88m   bw
UA / Hillworth (James Hill, Rita Hayworth)

A gentleman thief and his accomplice become unwittingly involved in murder.
Dreary comedy which turns into equally dreary drama and makes its European backgrounds look ugly.

w John Gay, novel The Oldest Confession by Richard Condon d George Marshall ph Paul Beeson m Mario Nascimbene

Rex Harrison, Rita Hayworth, Grégoire Aslan, Joseph Wiseman, Alida Valli

The Happy Time***
US 1952   94m   bw
Columbia / Stanley Kramer (Earl Felton)

Domestic misadventures of a family of French Canadians during the twenties.
Basically concerned with adolescent sexual stirrings, this very agreeable film has a light touch and is most deftly directed and acted.

w Earl Felton, play Samuel A. Taylor d Richard Fleischer ph Charles Lawton Jnr m Dmitri Tiomkin pd Rudolph Sternad

Charles Boyer, Louis Jourdan, Bobby Driscoll, Marsha Hunt, Marcel Dalio, Kurt Kasznar, Linda Christian, Jeanette Nolan, Jack Raine, Richard Erdman

Hara Kiri*
Japan 1962   135m   bw   Grandscope
Shochiku
original title: Seppuku

17th-century samurai often pretend to commit hara kiri so that a grand lord will have sympathy and take them on. One of them is forced to go through with it.
Strange, traditional, slow and explicitly brutal costume piece, for specialized western eyes only.

w Shinobu Hashimoto d Masaki Kobayashi

ph Yoshio Miyajima m Toru Takemitsu ad Junichi Ozumi

Tatsuya Nakadai, Shimai Iwashita, Akira Isahama

Hard Contract
US 1969   106m   De Luxe   Panavision
TCF (Marvin Schwarz)

A professional killer has sexual hang-ups.
Heavy-going modern thriller with lively scenes separated by too much self-analytical chat, not to mention a tour of Europe.

wd S. Lee Pogostin ph Jack Hildyard m Alex North

James Coburn, Lilli Palmer, Lee Remick, Burgess Meredith, Patrick Magee, Sterling Hayden, Helen Cherry, Karen Black, Claude Dauphin

'Behind it one glimpses a much better film than its surface suggests.'—MFB

'Like a flat-footed James Bond story that soaked its feet in a hot bath of existentialism.'—John Simon

A Hard Day's Night****
GB 1964   85m   bw
UA / Proscenium (Walter Shenson)

Harassed by their manager and Paul's grandpa, the Beatles embark from Liverpool by train for a London TV show.
Comic fantasia with music; an enormous commercial success with the director trying every cinematic gag in the book, it led directly to all the kaleidoscopic swinging London spy thrillers and comedies of the later sixties, and so has a lot to answer for; but at the time it was a sweet breath of fresh air, and the Beatles even seemed willing and likeable.

w Alun Owen d Richard Lester ph Gilbert Taylor songs The Beatles md George Martin

The Beatles, Wilfrid Brambell, Norman Rossington, Victor Spinetti

'A fine conglomeration of madcap clowning . . . with such a dazzling use of camera that it tickles the intellect and electrifies the nerves.'—Bosley Crowther

AAN: Alun Owen

Hard, Fast and Beautiful
US 1951   76m   bw
RKO / The Filmmakers (Collier Young)

A girl tennis player is influenced by her ambitious mother.
Unusual but not very effective melodrama.

w Martha Wilkerson, novel John R. Tunis d Ida Lupino ph Archie Stout m Roy Webb

Claire Trevor, Sally Forrest, Carleton Young, Robert Clarke, Kenneth Patterson, Joseph Kearns

Hard Steel
GB 1942   86m   bw
GFD / GHW (James B. Sloan)
reissue title: *What Shall It Profit*

A steel worker is promoted and loses his humanity, but comes to his senses when his wife leaves him.
Modest moral drama from the uplift side of the Rank empire.

w Lydia Hayward, *novel* Steel Saraband by Roger Dataller *d* Norman Walker

Wilfrid Lawson, Betty Stockfield, John Stuart, George Carney, Joan Kemp-Welch, Hay Petrie

Hard Times*
US 1975   93m   Metrocolor   Panavision
Columbia (Lawrence Gordon)
GB title: *The Streetfighter*

In New Orleans in the Depression-hit thirties, a prizefighter and a promoter help each other.
Interesting, atmospheric melodrama on the lone stranger theme.

w Walter Hill, Bryan Gindorff, Bruce Henstell *d* Walter Hill *ph* Philip Lathrop *m* Barry DeVorzon

Charles Bronson, James Coburn, Jill Ireland, Strother Martin, Maggie Blye

Hard to Handle**
US 1933   75m   bw
Warner (Robert Lord)

The success story of a cheerful public relations man.
Punchy star comedy with interesting sidelights on the social fads of the early thirties including marathon dancing, get-rich-quick schemes and grapefruit diets.

w *Wilson Mizner*, Robert Lord *d* Mervyn Le Roy *ph* Barney McGill

James Cagney, Ruth Donnelly, Mary Brian, Allen Jenkins, Claire Dodd

'A violent, slangy, down-to-the-pavement affair which has many a mirthful moment.'— *Mordaunt Hall*

The Hard Way*
US 1942   109m   bw
Warner (Jerry Wald)

A strong-willed girl pushes her reluctant sister to the heights of show business.
Unconvincing but well-mounted drama.

w Daniel Fuchs, Peter Viertel *d* Vincent

Sherman *ph* James Wong Howe *m* Heinz Roemheld *md* Leo F. Forbstein

Ida Lupino, Joan Leslie, Dennis Morgan, Jack Carson, Gladys George, Faye Emerson, Paul Cavanagh, Roman Bohnen

The Harder They Fall*
US 1956   109m   bw
Columbia (Philip Yordan)

A press agent exposes the crooked fight game.
Wearily efficient sporting melodrama.

w Philip Yordan, *novel* Budd Schulberg *d* Mark Robson *ph* Burnett Guffey *m* Hugo Friedhofer

Humphrey Bogart (his last performance), Rod Steiger, Jan Sterling, Mike Lane, Max Baer, Edward Andrews, Harold J. Stone

AAN: Burnett Guffey

The Hardy Family
America's favourite fictional characters just before and during World War II were the family of a small-town judge, who seemed to personify all that everyone was fighting for, especially as the young son was always getting into amusing scrapes. Designed by a delighted MGM as low-budgeters, they paid for many an expensive failure, and introduced, as young Andy's girl friends, a series of starlets who went on to much bigger things. The basic family was Lewis Stone, Fay Holden, Mickey Rooney, Cecilia Parker and Sara Haden (as the spinster aunt); but in the very first episode Lionel Barrymore and Spring Byington played the judge and his wife.
A FAMILY AFFAIR (1936); 69m; *d* George B. Seitz; *w* Kay Van Riper, *play* Aurania Rouverol
YOU'RE ONLY YOUNG ONCE (1938); 78m; *d* George B. Seitz; *w* Kay Van Riper; introducing Ann Rutherford (who became a regular)
JUDGE HARDY'S CHILDREN (1938); 78m; *d* George B. Seitz; *w* Kay Van Riper; *with* Ruth Hussey
LOVE FINDS ANDY HARDY (1938); 90m; *d* George B. Seitz; *w* William Ludwig; *with* Judy Garland, Lana Turner
OUT WEST WITH THE HARDYS (1938); 90m; *d* George B. Seitz; *w* Kay Van Riper, Agnes Christine Johnson, William Ludwig
THE HARDYS RIDE HIGH (1939); 81m; *d* George B. Seitz; *w* as above
ANDY HARDY GETS SPRING FEVER (1939); 85m; *d* W. S. Van Dyke II; *w* Kay Van Riper
JUDGE HARDY AND SON (1939); 90m; *d* George B. Seitz; *w* Carey Wilson; *with* June Preisser, Maria Ouspenskaya
ANDY HARDY MEETS A DEBUTANTE (1940); 89m; *d* George B. Seitz; *w* Annalee

Whitmore, Thomas Seller; *with* Judy Garland
ANDY HARDY'S PRIVATE SECRETARY
(1941); 101m; *d* George B. Seitz; *w* Jane Murfin,
Harry Ruskin; *with* Kathryn Grayson, Ian
Hunter
LIFE BEGINS FOR ANDY HARDY (1941);
100m; *d* George B. Seitz; *w* Agnes Christine
Johnson; *with* Judy Garland
THE COURTSHIP OF ANDY HARDY
(1942); 93m; *d* George B. Seitz; *w* Agnes
Christine Johnson; *with* Donna Reed
ANDY HARDY'S DOUBLE LIFE (1942);
92m; *d* George B. Seitz; *w* Agnes Christine
Johnson; *with* Esther Williams, Susan Peters
ANDY HARDY'S BLONDE TROUBLE
(1944); 107m; *d* George B. Seitz; *w* Harry
Ruskin, William Ludwig, Agnes Christine
Johnson; *with* Bonita Granville, Jean Porter,
Herbert Marshall, the Wilde twins
LOVE LAUGHS AT ANDY HARDY (1946);
94m; *d* Willis Goldbeck; *w* Harry Ruskin,
William Ludwig; *with* Bonita Granville
ANDY HARDY COMES HOME (1958); 80m;
d Howard Koch; *w* Edward Everett Hutshing,
Robert Morris Donley; *without* Lewis Stone

Harlow

US 1965 125m Technicolor Panavision
Paramount / Embassy / Prometheus (Joseph
E. Levine)

In 1929, starlet Jean Harlow is shot to fame by
her agent Arthur Landau.
Absurdly whitewashed and excruciatingly
boring rags-to-riches yarn with most of the
characters fictitious and little to do with the real
Jean Harlow. Only the studio scenes are mildly
interesting.

w John Michael Hayes *d* Gordon Douglas
ph Joseph Ruttenberg *m* Neal Hefti *ad* Hal
Pereira, Roland Anderson *costumes Edith
Head*

Carroll Baker, Peter Lawford, Mike Connors,
Red Buttons, Raf Vallone, Angela Lansbury,
Martin Balsam
'Hollywood once again succeeds in reducing
one of its few fascinating realities to the sleazy
turgid level of its more sordid fictions.'—*Judith
Crist*
† A rather better television tape drama of the
same title, starring Carol Lynley and Ginger
Rogers, was made almost simultaneously. It was
converted to film ('Electronovision') but had few
bookings.

Harmony Heaven*

GB 1930 61m colour
BIP

A composer becomes famous with the help of his
girl friend.
Unbelievably naïve musical, notable only as
British and in colour. Not tolerable today as
entertainment.

w Arthur Wimperis, Randall Faye *d* Thomas
Bentley *ph* Theodor Sparkuhl *songs* Edward
Brandt, Eddie Pola

Polly Ward, Stuart Hall, Trilby Clark, Jack
Raine

Harold and Maude**

US 1971 92m Technicolor
Paramount / Mildred Lewis / Colin Higgins

A repressed young man, fixated on death and
funerals, has an affair with an 80-year-old
woman.
Often hilarious black comedy for those who can
stand it; the epitome of bad taste, splashed
around with wit and vigour, it became a minor
cult.

w Colin Higgins *d* Hal Ashby *ph* John A.
Alonzo *m* Cat Stevens

Bud Cort, Ruth Gordon, Vivian Pickles, Cyril
Cusack

Harold Lloyd's Funny Side of Life***

US 1963 99m bw
Harold Lloyd (Duncan Mansfield)

Excerpts from twenties comedies plus a
shortened version of *The Freshman* (1925).
Excellent compilation, though the mini-feature
makes it a little unbalanced.

w Arthur Ross *m* Walter Scharf

Harold Lloyd

Harold Lloyd's World of Comedy****

US 1962 97m bw
Harold Lloyd

Generous clips from the comic climaxes of
Lloyd's best silent and sound comedies including
*Safety Last, The Freshman, Hot Water, Why
Worry, Girl Shy, Professor Beware, Movie
Crazy* and *Feet First*.
As Lloyd's work lends itself well to extract, this
can hardly fail to be a superb anthology
capsuling the appeal of one of America's greatest
silent comedians. The timing is just perfect.

m Walter Scharf *commentary* Art Ross

Harper*

US 1966 121m Technicolor Panavision
Warner / Gershwin–Kastner
GB title: *The Moving Target*

A Los Angeles private eye is hired by a rich
woman to find her missing husband.

Formula Californian detection distinguished by its cast rather than by any special talent in the writing or presentation. It seemed likely to produce a new Chandleresque school, but imitations proved very sporadic; the star repeated the role less successfully in *The Drowning Pool* (qv).

w William Goldman, *novel* The Moving Target by John Ross Macdonald d Jack Smight ph Conrad Hall m Johnny Mandel

Paul Newman, Lauren Bacall, Shelley Winters, Arthur Hill, Julie Harris, Janet Leigh, Pamela Tiffin, Robert Wagner, Robert Webber, Strother Martin

'It isn't a bad try, but it never really slips into overdrive.'—*Penelope Houston*

'Nothing needs justification less than entertainment; but when something planned only to entertain fails, it has no justification. A private-eye movie without sophistication and style is ignominious.'—*Pauline Kael, 1968*

The Harrad Experiment
US 1973 97m Eastmancolor
Cinerama / Cinema Arts (Dennis F. Stevens)

A college professor conducts a series of tests on sexual relationships.
Low-keyed Kinsey Report for the seventies, pleasantly made but not very stimulating.

w Michael Werner, Ted Cassidy, *novel* Robert H. Rimmer d Ted Post ph Richard Kline m Artie Butler

James Whitmore, Tippi Hedren, Don Johnson, Laurie Walters, Robert Middleton

'Ludicrously sober-sided amalgam of nude yoga and extra-curricular groping, which should set sex educational theory back ten years.'—*Sight and Sound*

Harriet Craig
US 1950 94m bw
Columbia (William Dozier)

A wife's only real love is her meticulously kept and richly appointed house.
Ho-hum remake of a sturdy thirties film *Craig's Wife* (qv).

w Anne Froelick, James Gunn, *play* Craig's Wife by George Kelly d Vincent Sherman ph Joseph Walker m George Duning md Morris Stoloff

Joan Crawford, Wendell Corey, Allyn Joslyn, Lucile Watson, William Bishop, K. T. Stevens, Raymond Greenleaf

Harry and Tonto*
US 1974 115m De Luxe
TCF (Paul Mazursky)

An elderly New York widower and his cat are evicted and trek to Chicago.
Amiable character study, very watchable but rather pointless.

w Paul Mazursky, Josh Greenfield d Paul Mazursky ph Michael Butler m Bill Conti

Art Carney, Ellen Burstyn, Chief Dan George, Geraldine Fitzgerald, Larry Hagman, Arthur Hunnicutt, Herbert Berghof

'A vivacious and affectionate folk tale.'—*New Yorker*

'It has a life-affirming quality as welcome contrast to the destructive delirium of most modern movies.'—*Michael Billington, Illustrated London News*

AA: Art Carney
AAN: Paul Mazursky (as writer)

Harry and Walter go to New York
US 1976 120m Metrocolor Panavision
Columbia (Don Devlin, Harry Gittes)

In oldtime New York, two carnival entertainers get involved with suffragettes and a safecracker.
Extended period romp in which the high humour soon palls and a general lack of talent makes itself felt.

w John Byrum, Robert Kaufman d Mark Rydell ph Laszlo Kovacs m David Shire pd Harry Horner

James Caan, Elliott Gould, Michael Caine, Diane Keaton, Charles Durning, Lesley Ann Warren, Jack Gilford

'A charmless mishmash.'—*Sight and Sound*

Harry Black and the Tiger
GB 1958 117m Technicolor
Cinemascope
TCF (John Brabourne)
US title: *Harry Black*

A famous tiger hunter allows his best friend to prove himself a hero, and falls in love with the friend's wife.
Lethargic melodrama with good Indian backgrounds.

w Sydney Boehm, *novel* David Walker d Hugo Fregonese ph John Wilcox m Clifton Parker

Stewart Granger, Anthony Steel, Barbara Rush, I. S. Johar

Harry in Your Pocket
US 1973 103m De Luxe Panavision
UA / Cinema Video (Bruce Geller)

Adventures of a young, a middle-aged and an old pickpocket.
Partly pleasant but rather aimless comedy

drama, agreeably set in Seattle and Salt Lake City.

w Ron Austin, James Buchanan *d* Bruce Geller *ph* Fred Koenekamp *m* Lalo Schifrin

James Coburn, *Walter Pidgeon*, Michael Sarrazin, Trish Van Devere

Harvest
France 1937　122m　bw, Marcel Pagnol
original title: *Regain*

A poacher and an itinerant girl set up house in a deserted village and bring it back to life.
Somewhat charming but interminably slow rustic parable.

wd Marcel Pagnol, *novel* Jean Giono *ph* Willy *m* Arthur Honegger

Gabriel Gabrio, Fernandel, Orane Demazis, E. Delmont

Harvey***
US 1950　104m　bw
U-I (John Beck)

A middle-aged drunk has an imaginary white rabbit as his friend, and his sister tries to have him certified.
An amiably batty play with splendid lines is here transferred virtually intact to the screen and survives superbly thanks to understanding by all concerned, though the star is as yet too young for a role which he later made his own.

w Mary Chase (with Oscar Brodney) from her play *d* Henry Koster *ph* William Daniels

James Stewart, Josephine Hull, Victoria Horne, Peggy Dow, *Cecil Kellaway*, Charles Drake, *Jesse White*, Nana Bryant, Wallace Ford

AA: Josephine Hull
AAN: James Stewart

The Harvey Girls**
US 1946　101m　Technicolor
MGM (Arthur Freed)

A chain of 19th-century restaurants hires young ladies to go out west as waitresses.
Sprightly if overlong musical based on fact; a good example of an MGM middle-budget extravaganza.

w Edmund Beloin, Nathaniel Curtis *d* George Sidney *ph* George Folsey *md* Lennie Hayton *songs* Johnny Mercer, Harry Warren

Judy Garland, Ray Bolger, John Hodiak, Preston Foster, Virginia O'Brien, Angela Lansbury, Marjorie Main, Chill Wills, Kenny Baker, Selena Royle

'Anybody who did anything at all in America up to 1900 is liable to be made into a film by MGM.'—*Richard Winnington*

AA: song 'On the Atcheson, Topeka and the Santa Fe'
AAN: Lennie Hayton

Harvey Middleman Fireman*
US 1965　76m　Eastmancolor
Columbia (Robert L. Lawrence)

A frustrated middle-aged fireman begins an affair; the resulting guilt complex drives him to a psychiatrist.
Grotesque satirical comedy from one of the sixties' most fashionable cartoonists. Mild, quite pleasing, occasionally crude.

wd/m Ernest Pintoff ph Karl Malkames

Gene Troobnick, Hermione Gingold, Pat Harty

Has Anybody Seen My Gal?**
US 1952　89m　Technicolor
U-I (Ted Richmond)

A multi-millionaire pretends to be poor and moves in with distant relatives to test their worthiness.
Very agreeable comedy set in the twenties and centring on a satisfying star performance.

w Joseph Hoffman *d Douglas Sirk ph* Clifford Stine *m* Joseph Gershenson *ad Bernard Herzbrun, Hilyard Brown*

Charles Coburn, Piper Laurie, Rock Hudson, Gigi Perreau, Lynn Bari, Larry Gates, William Reynolds, Skip Homeier, James Dean

The Hasty Heart*
GB 1949　104m　bw
ABP (Vincent Sherman)

At an army hospital in Burma, attitudes to an arrogant young Scot change when it is learned that he has only a few weeks to live.
Flat, adequate filming of a successful sentimental stage play.

w Ranald MacDougall, *play* John Patrick *d* Vincent Sherman *ph* Wilkie Cooper *m* Jack Beaver

Richard Todd, Patricia Neal, Ronald Reagan, Orlando Martins, Howard Marion-Crawford

AAN: Richard Todd

Hatari!*
US 1962　158m　Technicolor
Paramount / Malabar (Howard Hawks)

International hunters in Tanganyika catch game to send to zoos.
Plotless adventure film with good animal sequences but no shape or suspense; a typical folly of its director, whose chief interest is seeing smart men and women in tough action. The elephants steal this overlong show.

w Leigh Brackett *d* Howard Hawks *ph Russell Harlan m Henry Mancini*

John Wayne, Elsa Martinelli, Red Buttons, Hardy Kruger

AAN: Russell Harlan; Elmer Bernstein, Jocelyn La Garde; song 'My Wishing Doll' (*m* Elmer Bernstein, *ly* Mack David)

The Hatchet Man
US 1932   74m   bw
Warner
GB title: *The Honourable Mr Wong*

The executioner of a San Francisco tong dutifully kills his best friend but promises to care for his daughter.
Unconvincing Chinese-American melodrama.

w J. Grubb Alexander, *play* Achmed Abdullah, David Belasco *d* William A. Wellman *ph* Sid Hickox

Edward G. Robinson, Loretta Young, Dudley Digges, Leslie Fenton, Edmund Breese, Tully Marshall, J. Carrol Naish, Noel Madison, Blanche Frederici

A Hatful of Rain*
US 1957   108m   bw   Cinemascope
TCF / (Buddy Adler)

A war veteran becomes a drug addict and upsets his wife and family.
One of the first drug dramas: straightforward, well acted, and quite powerful.

w Michael V. Gazzo (with Alfred Hayes), from his play *d* Fred Zinnemann *ph* Joe Macdonald *m* Bernard Herrmann

Eva Marie Saint, Don Murray, Anthony Franciosa, Lloyd Nolan, Howard da Silva

AAN: Anthony Franciosa

Hatter's Castle**
GB 1941   102m   bw
Paramount British (Isadore Goldsmith)

In the nineties, a megalomaniac Scottish hatter ruins the lives of his wife and daughter.
Enjoyable period melodrama with a rampant star performance and pretty good detail.

w Rodney Ackland, *novel* A. J. Cronin *d* Lance Comfort *ph* Max Greene *m* Horace Shepherd

Robert Newton, Deborah Kerr, James Mason, Beatrice Varley, Emlyn Williams, Henry Oscar, Enid Stamp-Taylor, Brefni O'Rourke

The Haunted Palace
US 1963   85m   Pathecolor   Panavision
AIP / Alta Vista (Roger Corman)

In 1875 a New Englander claims an old mansion as his inheritance and is haunted by his vicious ancestor.
Plodding horror comic, too slow to give opportunities to its stalwart cast.

w Charles Beaumont, from material by H. P. Lovecraft and Edgar Allan Poe *d* Roger Corman *ph* Floyd Crosby *m* Ronald Stein

Vincent Price, Lon Chaney Jnr, Debra Paget, Frank Maxwell, Leo Gordon, Elisha Cook Jnr, John Dierkes
'For those of ghoulish bent, or lovers of the perfectly awful.'—*Judith Crist*

The Haunting*
GB 1963   112m   bw   Panavision
MGM / Argyle (Robert Wise)

An anthropologist, a sceptic and two mediums spend the weekend in a haunted Boston mansion. Quite frightening but exhausting and humourless melodrama with a lot of suspense, no visible spooks, and not enough plot for its length. The wide screen is a disadvantage.

w Nelson Gidding, *novel* The Haunting of Hill House by Shirley Jackson *d* Robert Wise *ph* David Boulton *m* Humphrey Searle *pd* Elliot Scott

Richard Johnson, Claire Bloom, Russ Tamblyn, Julie Harris, Lois Maxwell, Valentine Dyall

Having Wonderful Time
US 1938   70m   bw
RKO (Pandro S. Berman)

A New York girl falls in love at a summer camp. Mild comedy which, robbed of its original Jewish milieu, falls resoundingly flat.

w Arthur Kober, from his play *d* Alfred Santell *ph* Robert de Grasse *m* Roy Webb

Ginger Rogers, Douglas Fairbanks Jnr, Peggy Conklin, Lucille Ball, Lee Bowman, Eve Arden, Red Skelton, Donald Meek, Jack Carson

Hawaii*
US 1966   186m   De Luxe   Panavision
UA / Mirisch (Lewis J. Rachmil)

In 1820 a pious Yale divinity student becomes a missionary to the Hawaiian islands.
Ambitious attempt to contrast naïve dogma with native innocence, ruined by badly handled sub-plots, storms, a childbirth sequence and other distractions, all fragments of an immense novel. Heavy going.

w Daniel Taradash, Dalton Trumbo, *novel* James A. Michener *d* George Roy Hill *ph* Russell Harlan *m* Elmer Bernstein *2nd unit Richard Talmadge pd* Cary Odell

Max Von Sydow, Julie Andrews, Richard

Harris, *Jocelyn la Garde*, Carroll O'Connor, Torin Thatcher, Gene Hackman

'Consistently intelligent humanism gives it a certain stature among the wide screen spectacles.'—*Brenda Davies*

The Hawaiians

US 1970   132m   De Luxe   Panavision
UA / Mirisch (Walter Mirisch)
GB title: *Master of the Islands*

A young scion of a shipping business leaves after an argument and strikes oil in terrain supposedly barren.

More fragments from Michener, covering 1870 to 1900 and comprising an absolutely uninteresting family chronicle with moments of spectacle.

w James R. Webb *d* Tom Gries *ph* Philip Lathrop *m* Henry Mancini *pd* Cary Odell

Charlton Heston, Tina Chen, Geraldine Chaplin, John Philip Law, Alec McCowen, Mako, Ann Knight, Lyle Bettger, Keye Luke

'A quickfire succession of corruption, revolution, plague, fire and questions of moral responsibility.'—*MFB*

'Total relaxation—preferably of the brain—is recommended.'—*Judith Crist*

Hazard

US 1948   95m   bw
Paramount (Mel Epstein)

A compulsive lady gambler agrees to marry the winner of a dice game, but runs away and is chased by a private detective.

Silly, unamusing romantic comedy-drama.

w Arthur Sheekman, Roy Chanslor *d* George Marshall *ph* Daniel L. Fapp *m* Frank Skinner

Paulette Goddard, Macdonald Carey, Fred Clark, Stanley Clemens, Maxie Rosenbloom, Charles McGraw

'A good bit this side of inspired.'—*New York Times*

He Laughed Last*

US 1956   77m   Technicolor
Columbia (Jonie Taps)

In the twenties, New York gangsters battle for control of a night club.

Small-scale gangster burlesque which comes off rather better than its credits suggest.

wd Blake Edwards *ph* Henry Freulich *m* Arthur Morton

Frankie Laine, Lucy Marlow, Anthony Dexter, *Jesse White*

He Ran All the Way*

US 1951   78m   bw
UA / Bob Roberts

A hoodlum on the run from the police virtually picks up a girl and hides in her family's apartment.

Uninteresting situation melodrama helped by intelligent acting and handling.

w Guy Endore, Hugo Butler, *novel* Sam Ross *d* John Berry *ph* James Wong Howe *m* Franz Waxman

John Garfield, Shelley Winters, Wallace Ford, Selena Royle, Gladys George, Norman Lloyd, Bobby Hyatt

He Snoops to Conquer

GB 1944   103m   bw
Columbia (Ben Henry, Marcel Varnel)

A local handyman exposes a corrupt council.

Spotty star comedy with insufficient zest for its great length.

w Stephen Black, Howard Irving Young, Norman Lee, Michael Vaughan, Langford Reed *d* Marcel Varnel

George Formby, Robertson Hare, Elizabeth Allen, Aubrey Mallalieu

He Stayed for Breakfast

US 1940   89m   bw
Columbia (B. P. Schulberg)

A Parisian communist waiter hides out in the apartment of American capitalists, and learns from them.

Post-*Ninotchka* comedy, not bad but somehow rather uninteresting and mechanical.

w P. J. Wolfson, Michael Fessier, Ernest Vajda, *play* Liberté Provisoire by Michel Duran *d* Alexander Hall *ph* Joseph Walker

Melvyn Douglas, Loretta Young, Alan Marshal, Eugene Pallette, Una O'Connor, Curt Bois, Leonid Kinskey

He Walked by Night*

US 1948   80m   bw
Eagle—Lion / Bryan Foy

A burglar becomes a cop-killer and is hunted down by the police.

Interesting if rather flatly handled documentary melodrama in clear imitation of *Naked City*.

w John C. Higgins, Crane Wilbur *d* Alfred Werker *ph* John Alton *m* Leonid Raab

Richard Basehart, Scott Brady, Roy Roberts, White Bissell

He Who Gets Slapped*
US 1924   80m approx (24 fps)   bw   silent
MGM

A scientist starts a new life as a circus clown.
Odd poetic tragedy, Metro-Goldwyn-Mayer's
very first production; the public took to it
surprisingly well.

w Victor Sjostrom, Carey Wilson, play Leonid
Andreyev d Victor Sjostrom

Lon Chaney, Norma Shearer, John Gilbert,
Tully Marshall, Ford Sterling

He Who Must Die*
France / Italy 1957   126m   bw
    Cinemascope
original title: Celui Qui Doit Mourir

In a Greek village in 1921, preparations for a
passion play are interrupted by the arrival of
refugees from the mountains.
Occasionally striking, but mainly arty and
pretentious parable; however well meant, a bore
to watch.

w Ben Barzman, Jules Dassin, novel Nikos
Kazantzakis d Jules Dassin ph Jacques
Natteau m Georges Auric

Jean Servais, Carl Mohner, Pierre Vaneck,
Melina Mercouri, Fernand Ledoux

He Who Rides a Tiger
GB 1965   103m   bw
British Lion / David Newman

A feckless burglar comes out of prison and
returns to the old life.
Cliché crime yarn which tries rather desperately
after fresh detail but bogs down in romantic
asides.

w Trevor Peacock d Charles Crichton ph John
Von Kotze m Alexander Faris

Tom Bell, Judi Dench, Paul Rogers, Kay Walsh,
Ray McAnally, Jeremy Spenser

Head*
US 1968   85m   Technicolor
Columbia (Bert Schneider)

Fantasia on the life of a sixties pop group.
A psychedelic trip of a movie which does for the
Monkees what A Hard Day's Night and Yellow
Submarine did for the Beatles, and what Monty
Python did for us all. Sometimes funny, slick and
clever; often just plain silly.

w Jack Nicholson, Bob Rafaelson d Bob
Rafaelson ph Michael Hugo m Ken Thorne
sp Chuck Gaspar

The Monkees, Victor Mature, Annette
Funicello, Timothy Carey

'Random particles tossed around in some

demented jester's wind machine.'—Richard
Combs, MFB, 1978

Head Over Heels*
GB 1937   81m   bw
Gaumont (S. C. Balcon)

A singing star can't make up her mind between
two men.
Interestingly dated light star vehicle.

w Dwight Taylor, Fred Thompson, Marjorie
Gaffney, play Francois de Croisset d Sonnie
Hale

Jessie Matthews, Robert Flemyng, Louis Borell,
Romney Brent, Helen Whitney Bourne, Eliot
Makeham

The Heart is a Lonely Hunter*
US 1968   123m   Technicolor
Warner Seven Arts (Joel Freeman)

Incidents in the life of a gentle deaf mute in a
small southern town.
Wispy film of a wistful novel; quite well done but
overlong and hard to cheer at.

w Thomas C. Ryan, novel Carson McCullers
d Robert Ellis Miller ph James Wong Howe
m Dave Grusin

Alan Arkin, Sondra Locke, Stacy Keach,
Laurinda Barrett, Chuck McCann, Biff
McGuire, Percy Rodriguez, Cicely Tyson

AAN: Alan Arkin; Sondra Locke

Heart of Glass*
West Germany 1976   94m   Eastmancolor
Werner Herzog

A wandering herdsman with special powers
supplies a factory owner with the secret of
making a very precious glass.
Apocalyptic visionary parable which may mean
everything, or nothing, but amuses fitfully while
it's on the screen.

wd Werner Herzog, text Herbert Achternbusch
ph Jorg Schmidt-Reitwin m Popol Vuh

Josef Bierbichler, Stefan Guttler, Clemens
Scheitz, Sepp Müller

The Heart of the Matter*
GB 1953   105m   bw
British Lion / London Films (Ian Dalrymple)

In 1942 in an African colony a police officer has
an affair while his wife is away, is blackmailed,
and plans suicide despite his staunch Catholic
belief.
Rather stodgy attempt to film Graham Greene;
perhaps everyone tries a little too hard, and in
any case the ending is compromised.

w Ian Dalrymple, Lesley Storm, novel Graham

Greene *d* George More O'Ferrall *ph* Jack Hildyard *m* Brian Easdale

Trevor Howard, Maria Schell, Elizabeth Allan, Denholm Elliott, Peter Finch, Gérard Oury, George Coulouris, Earl Cameron, Michael Hordern, Colin Gordon, Cyril Raymond, Orlando Martins

'A curious choice for commercial filming.'— *Lindsay Anderson*

Heartbeat

US 1946 102m
RKO / Robert and Raymond Hakim

A French gamin released from reform school becomes a professional pickpocket.
Unamusing remake of *Battement de Coeur*, with script and most performances very strained.

w Hans Wilhelm, Max Kolpe, Michel Druan, Morrie Ryskind *d* Sam Wood *ph* Joe Valentine *m* Paul Misraki

Ginger Rogers, Jean-Pierre Aumont, Adolphe Menjou, *Basil Rathbone*, Mikhail Rasumny, Melville Cooper, Mona Maris, Henry Stephenson

'The heartbeat is irregular and sadly ailing.'— *Photoplay*

The Heartbreak Kid*

US 1972 106m De Luxe
(TCF) Palomar (Edgar J. Scherick)

Disappointed with his honeymoon, a sporting goods salesman promptly sets his cap at a richer, prettier prospective spouse.
Heartless modern comedy reminiscent of *The Graduate*; quite well done but unsympathetic and somehow too American to export satisfactorily.

w Neil Simon, *story* A Change of Plan by Bruce Jay Friedman *d* Elaine May *ph* Owen Roizman *m* Garry Sherman

Charles Grodin, Cybill Shepherd, Jeannie Berlin, Eddie Albert, Audra Lindley, William Prince, Art Metrano

'The latest in a relatively new kind of American film—glittery trash.'—*Stanley Kauffmann*

AAN: Jeannie Berlin; Eddie Albert

Hearts of the West*

US 1975 103m Metrocolor
MGM / Bill–Zieff (Tony Bill)
GB title: *Hollywood Cowboy*

In the early thirties a naïve mid-westerner almost accidentally becomes a Hollywood star.
Overstretched comedy poking gentle fun at old

Hollywood: likeable but finally disappointing, as it obviously needed a Buster Keaton.

w Rob Thompson *d* Howard Zieff *ph* Mario Tosi *m* Ken Lauber

Jeff Bridges, Alan Arkin, Andy Griffith, Blythe Danner, Donald Pleasence, Richard B. Shull, Herb Edelman

The Heat's On

US 1943 79m bw
Columbia (Milton Carter)
GB title: *Tropicana*

A star seeks financial backing from an elderly angel whose sister runs the Legion of Purity. Dim musical vehicle for a fading star; her last film for twenty-seven years.

w Fitzroy Davis, George S. George, Fred Schiller *d* Gregory Ratoff *ph* Franz Planer *md* Yasha Bunchuk

Mae West, Victor Moore, William Gaxton, Almira Sessions, Lester Allan, Mary Roche, Hazel Scott, Alan Dinehart, Lloyd Bridges, Xavier Cugat and his Orchestra

Heaven Can Wait***

US 1943 112m Technicolor
TCF (Ernst Lubitsch)

On arrival in Hades, an elderly playboy reports his peccadilloes to Satan, who sends him Upstairs.
Charming period piece with fantasy bookends; the essence of the piece is its evocation of American society in the nineties, and in its director's waspish way with a funny scene.

w Samson Raphaelson, play Birthday by Lazlo Bus-Fekete *d Ernst Lubitsch ph Edward Cronjager m* Alfred Newman *ad James Basevi, Leland Fuller*

Don Ameche, Gene Tierney, *Laird Cregar, Charles Coburn, Marjorie Main*, Eugene Pallette, *Allyn Joslyn*, Spring Byington, Signe Hasso, Louis Calhern

'It was so good I half believed Lubitsch could still do as well as he ever did, given half a chance.'—*James Agee*

AAN: best picture; Ernst Lubitsch; Edward Cronjager

Heaven Can Wait*

US 1978 100m Movielab
Paramount / Warren Beatty (Howard W. Koch Jnr, Charles H. McGuire)

A football star finds himself accidentally in heaven after a car accident; when he is allowed to return, his body has been cremated, so he has to find another.

Unexpectedly commercially successful (the late seventies clearly need religion) remake of 1941's *Here Comes Mr Jordan*. It lacks the sharpness and style of its predecessor, and despite amusing moments is often merely tacky.

w Warren Beatty, Elaine May, *play* Harry Segall *d* Warren Beatty, Buck Henry *ph* William A. Fraker *m* Dave Grusin *pd* Paul Sylbert

Warren Beatty, Julie Christie, James Mason (as Mr Jordan), Jack Warden, Charles Grodin, *Dyan Cannon*, Buck Henry, Vincent Gardenia, Joseph Maher

Heaven Fell That Night
France / Italy 1958   90m   Eastmancolor
    Cinemascope
IENA / CEIAP (Raoul Levy)
original title: *Les Bijoutiers du Clair de Lune*

A young girl becomes involved in a revenge plot and finds herself on the run with a killer.
Heavy going sex-and-violence hokum.

w Roger Vadim, Peter Viertel, *novel* Albert Vidalie *d* Roger Vadim *ph* Armand Thirard *m* Georges Auric

Brigitte Bardot, Alida Valli, Stephen Boyd, Pepe Nieto

Heaven Knows Mr Allison*
US 1957   105m   Technicolor
    Cinemascope
TCF (Buddy Adler, Eugene Franks)

Marooned on a small Pacific island during World War II, a marine and a nun, antagonistic to each other, combine to outwit the Japs.
Silly adventure story with predictably well-handled action sequences separated by even more predictable dialogue, lots of it.

w John Lee Mahin, John Huston, *novel* Charles Shaw *d* John Huston *ph* Oswald Morris *m* Georges Auric

Robert Mitchum, Deborah Kerr

AAN: script; Deborah Kerr

Heaven Only Knows
US 1947   98m   bw
(UA)

An angel is sent to the old west to reform a bad man.
Whimsical comedy-drama which doesn't work at all, even as a distant cousin of *Here Comes Mr Jordan*.

w Art Arthur, Rowland Leigh *d* Albert S. Rogell *ph* Karl Struss *m* Heinz Roemheld

Robert Cummings, Brian Donlevy, Marjorie

Reynolds, Bill Goodwin, John Litel, Stuart Erwin

The Heavenly Body
US 1943   93m   bw
MGM (Arthur Hornblow Jnr)

An astronomer is too busy to notice his wife, so she takes up astrology and meets a dark handsome stranger as predicted.
Thin romantic comedy which despite crazy touches never actually makes one laugh.

w Michael Arlen, Walter Reisch *d* Alexander Hall *ph* Robert Planck *m* Bronislau Kaper

William Powell, Hedy Lamarr, James Craig, Fay Bainter, Henry O'Neill, Spring Byington, Morris Ankrum, Connie Gilchrist

Heavens Above*
GB 1963   118m   bw
British Lion / Charter (Roy Boulting)

A northern parson with proletarian sympathies is accidentally appointed to a snobby village where he converts the dowager aristocrat to works of absurd charity. Eventually he has the whole country in an uproar and takes the place of an astronaut.
Patchy satirical comedy which takes unsteady aim at too many targets but scores some predictable laughs.

w Frank Harvey, John Boulting *d* John Boulting *ph* Max Greene *m* Richard Rodney Bennett

Peter Sellers, Isabel Jeans, Cecil Parker, Brock Peters, Ian Carmichael, Irene Handl, Eric Sykes, Bernard Miles

Hedda*
GB 1975   102m   Technicolor
Brut (Robert Enders)

A selfish pregnant woman is bored by her husband and revolted at the idea of carrying his child. She takes an opportunity to revenge herself on an old lover, but the scheme rebounds on herself.
Rather flat rendering of a play which has received more than its due share of attention.

wd Trevor Nunn, *play* Henrik Ibsen *ph* Douglas Slocombe *m* Laurie Johnson

Glenda Jackson, Peter Eyre, Timothy West, Jennie Linden, Patrick Stewart

AAN: Glenda Jackson

Heidi*
US 1937   88m   bw
TCF (Raymond Griffith)

An orphan is sent to stay with her crusty grandfather in a mountain village.
Star-tailored version of a favourite children's story; just what the box office ordered at the time.

w Walter Ferris, Julian Josephson, *novel* Johanna Spyri *d* Allan Dwan *ph* Arthur Miller *md* Louis Silvers

Shirley Temple, Jean Hersholt, Arthur Treacher, Helen Westley, Pauline Moore, Mary Nash, Thomas Beck, Sidney Blackmer, Mady Christians, Sig Rumann, Marcia Mae Jones, Christian Rub

The Heiress **
US 1949 115m bw
Paramount (William Wyler)

A plain but rich young woman takes revenge on her fortune-seeking lover.
Richly-decorated and generally pleasing version of a stage success based on a Henry James story set in the nineties.

w Ruth and Augustus Goetz, from their play and Henry James's Washington Square *d William Wyler ph* Leo Tover *m* Aaron Copland *ad John Meehan*

Olivia de Havilland, Ralph Richardson, Montgomery Clift, Miriam Hopkins, Vanessa Brown, Mona Freeman, Ray Collins

AA: Aaron Copland; Olivia de Havilland
AAN: best picture; William Wyler; Leo Tover; Ralph Richardson

The Helen Morgan Story
US 1957 118m bw Cinemascope
Warner (Martin Rackin)
GB title: *Both Ends of the Candle*

A young singer rises from vaudeville to Broadway but becomes an alcoholic.
Moderately truthful biopic with effective twenties trimmings.

w Oscar Saul, Dean Riesner, Stephen Longstreet, Nelson Gidding *d* Michael Curtiz *ph* Ted McCord *m* various *ad* John Beckman

Ann Blyth, Paul Newman, Richard Carlson, Gene Evans, Alan King, Cara Williams, Walter Woolf King (as Ziegfeld)

Helen of Troy
US / Italy 1955 118m Warnercolor
Cinemascope
Warner (Robert Wise)

Helen is kidnapped by Paris and regained by use of the Trojan Horse.
Dingy historical spectacular, stultifyingly boring until the final spectacle, with the actors obviously wishing themselves doing anything but mouthing the doggerel dialogue.

w John Twist, Hugh Gray *d* Robert Wise *ph* Harry Stradling *m* Max Steiner

Rosanna Podesta, Jacques Sernas, Cedric Hardwicke, Niall MacGinnis, Stanley Baker, Nora Swinburne, Robert Douglas, Torin Thatcher, Harry Andrews, Janette Scott, Ronald Lewis, Brigitte Bardot

Hell and High Water
US 1954 103m Technicolor
Cinemascope
TCF (Raymond A. Klune)

A privately-financed anti-Red scientific expedition sets off for Alaska to prevent a Chinese anti-American plot.
Early scoper which mixes deviously plotted schoolboy fiction with submarine spectacle and cold war heroics.

wd Samuel Fuller *ph* Joe MacDonald *m* Alfred Newman

Richard Widmark, Bella Darvi, Victor Francen, David Wayne, Cameron Mitchell, Gene Evans

Hell Below
US 1933 105m bw
MGM

Tensions mount at a Mediterranean submarine base during World War I.
Adequate war actioner with appropriate trimmings of heroism, tragedy, comedy and romance.

w John Lee Mahin, John Meehan, Laird Doyle, Raymond Schrock, *novel* Pigboats by Commander Edward Ellsberg *d* Jack Conway *ph* Harold Rosson

Robert Montgomery, Walter Huston, Madge Evans, Jimmy Durante, Eugene Pallette, Robert Young, Edwin Styles, John Lee Mahin, Sterling Holloway

Hell below Zero
GB 1954 91m Technicolor
Columbia / Warwick (Irving Allen, Albert Broccoli)

An American adventurer accompanies the daughter of a whaling captain to the Antarctic to discover who killed her father.
Adequate outdoor thick ear with an unusual setting and lively cast.

w Alec Coppel, Max Trell, *novel* The White South by Hammond Innes *d* Mark Robson *ph* John Wilcox *m* Clifton Parker

Alan Ladd, Joan Tetzel, Basil Sydney, Stanley Baker, Jill Bennett, Niall MacGinnis

Hell Divers*

US 1931 113m bw
MGM

Friendly rivalry exists between two officers in the
Naval Air Force.
Routine romantic melodrama with action
highlights; a crowdpuller of its day.

w Harvey Gates, Malcolm Stuart Boylan, *story*
Spig Wead *d* George Hill *ph* Harold Wenstrom

Wallace Beery, Clark Gable, Conrad Nagel,
Dorothy Jordan, Marjorie Rambeau, Marie
Prévost, Cliff Edwards

'It's a matter of squadron after squadron of
planes, the mechanics attached thereto, the
cutting in and around newsreel material, which
Metro does so well, and Beery's excellent
personal performance.'—*Hollywood Reporter*

Hell Drivers*

GB 1957 108m bw Vistavision
Rank / Aqua (Ben Fisz)

Fast driving on death-trap roads is required of
rival lorry drivers for a cheapjack haulage firm.
Absurd, violent, hilarious and constantly
surprising melodrama with the silliest of
premises backed by a good cast and well handled
thrill sequences.

w John Kruse, C. Raker Endfield *d* C. Raker
Endfield *ph* Geoffrey Unsworth *m* Hubert
Clifford

Stanley Baker, Patrick McGoohan, Herbert
Lom, Peggy Cummins, William Hartnell,
Wilfrid Lawson, Sidney James, Jill Ireland, Alfie
Bass, Gordon Jackson

'This extraordinary film may interest future
historians for its description of road haulage and
masculine social behaviour in the mid-20th
century . . . though produced with efficiency and
assurance it is disagreeable and occasionally
vicious.'—*MFB*

Hell in the Pacific*

US 1969 104m Technicolor Panavision
Cinerama / Selmur (Reuben Bercovitch)

During World War II, an American pilot and a
Japanese naval officer who are stranded on the
same tiny Pacific island almost become friends.
Highly artificial and pretentious allegorical two-
parter which is occasionally well acted and good
to look at.

w Alexander Jacobs, Eric Bercovici *d* John
Boorman *ph* Conrad Hall *m* Lalo Schifrin

Lee Marvin, Toshiro Mifune

'No real reverberation and no real excitement,
intellectual or physical.'—*Tom Milne*

Hell Is a City*

GB 1959 93m bw Hammerscope
ABP / Hammer (Michael Carreras)

A jewel thief breaks jail and is hunted by the
Manchester police.
Lively semi-documentary, cameo-filled cop
thriller filmed on location.

wd Val Guest, *novel* Maurice Proctor *ph* Arthur
Grant *m* Stanley Black

Stanley Baker, John Crawford, Donald
Pleasence, Maxine Audley, Billie Whitelaw,
Joseph Tomelty, George A. Cooper, Vanda
Godsell

'A hectic pace, with frequent scene changes,
mobility of camera and performers, and much
rapid, loud, intense dialogue.'—*MFB*

Hell Is for Heroes*

US 1962 90m bw
Paramount (Henry Blanke)

In 1944, embittered GIs fight and die while
taking a German pillbox near the Siegfried line.
Fairly routine anti-war film with a strong cast
and effectively-directed moments battling a
generally artificial look.

w Robert Pirosh, Richard Carr *d* Don Siegel
ph Harold Lipstein *m* Leonard Rosenman

Steve McQueen, Bobby Darin, Fess Parker,
James Coburn, Bob Newhart, Harry Guardino

Hell on Frisco Bay

US 1955 98m Warnercolor
    Cinemascope
Jaguar (George Berthelon)

An ex-cop sets out to find the man who framed
him for manslaughter.
Tedious actioner enlivened by the character
parts and a violent climax.

w Sidney Boehm, Martin Rackin, *novel* William
P. McGivern *d* Frank Tuttle *ph* John Seitz
m Max Steiner

Alan Ladd, Edward G. Robinson, Joanne Dru,
Paul Stewart, William Demarest, Fay Wray

Hell to Eternity

US 1960 132m bw
Allied Artists / Atlantic (Irving H. Levin)

Marine Guy Gabaldon, brought up by Japanese
foster parents, has divided loyalties after Pearl
Harbor.
Battle-strewn biopic which after two hours
seems to lose its point, if it ever had one, but is
efficiently made.

w Ted Sherdeman, Walter Roeber Schmidt
d Phil Karlson *ph* Burnett Guffey *m* Leith
Stevens

Jeffrey Hunter, David Janssen, Vic Damone,
Patricia Owens, Richard Eyer, Sessue
Hayakawa

The Hell with Heroes
US 1968 102m Techniscope
Universal (Stanley Chase)

Air cargo experts find themselves unwittingly
smuggling cigarettes into France, and American
counter-intelligence steps in.
Unremarkable, totally predictable action
melodrama.

w Halsted Welles, Harold Livingston d Joseph
Sargent ph Bud Thackery m Quincy Jones

Rod Taylor, Claudia Cardinale, Harry
Guardino, Kevin McCarthy, Pete Deuel,
William Marshall

Heller in Pink Tights*
US 1960 100m Technicolor Vistavision
Paramount / Ponti–Girosi

Adventures of a dramatic company touring the
west in the 1880s.
Genteel spoof western which does not quite
come off.

w Dudley Nichols, Walter Bernstein, novel Louis
L'Amour d George Cukor ph Harold Lipstein
m Daniele Amfitheatrof ad Hal Pereira, Eugene
Allen

Sophia Loren, Anthony Quinn, Steve Forrest,
Eileen Heckart, Edmund Lowe, Margaret
O'Brien, Ramon Novarro

'It has a welcome individuality which is never
quite smothered by its lapses into convention.'—
Penelope Houston

Hellfighters
US 1969 120m Technicolor Panavision
Universal (Robert Arthur)

Oil well fire-fighting specialists have problems
among themselves and with their womenfolk.
Ham-fisted story line and performances are
slightly, but only slightly, compensated by
excellent special effects.

w Clair Huffaker d Andrew V. McLaglen
ph William H. Clothier m Leonard Rosenman

John Wayne, Jim Hutton, Katharine Ross, Vera
Miles, Jay C. Flippen, Bruce Cabot, Barbara
Stuart

'The overall effect is unpardonably tedious.'—
MFB

The Hellfire Club*
GB 1960 93m Eastmancolor
Dyaliscope
Regal / New World (Robert S. Baker, Monty
Berman)

In the 18th century, a nobleman's child escapes
from his degenerate father, joins a travelling
circus, and later returns to claim his inheritance.
Sprightly historical romantic melodrama lightly
based on the nefarious activities of the real
Hellfire Club; energetic and entertaining if
slightly too jokey.

w Leon Griffiths, Jimmy Sangster d/ph Robert
S. Baker, Monty Berman m Clifton Parker

Keith Michell, Peter Arne, Adrienne Corri, Kai
Fischer, Bill Owen, Peter Cushing, David Lodge,
Francis Matthews

The Hellions
GB 1961 80m Technirama
Columbia / Irving Asher

In the 1860s, a family of South African outlaws
starts a reign of terror in a small village.
A British attempt to restage the OK Corral; it
goes sadly awry.

w Harold Swanton, Patrick Kirwan, Harold
Huth d Ken Annakin ph Ted Moore m Larry
Adler

Richard Todd, Lionel Jeffries, James Booth,
Jamie Uys, Ronald Fraser, Anne Aubrey, Zena
Walker, Marty Wilde, Colin Blakely

'Unconvincingly staged and plotted, tediously
violent, uncertainly directed and very badly
acted.'—MFB

Hello Dolly**
US 1969 129m De Luxe Todd-AO
TCF / Chenault (Ernest Lehman)

In 1890 New York, a widowed matchmaker has
designs on a wealthy grain merchant.
Generally agreeable but overblown musical
based on a slight but much worked-over farce,
fatally compromised by the miscasting of a too-
young star. Some exhilarating moments.

w Ernest Lehman, musical Jerry Herman (m/ly)
and Michael Stewart (book), from Thornton
Wilder's play The Matchmaker d Gene Kelly
ph Harry Stradling md Lennie Hayton, Lionel
Newman pd John de Cuir ch Michael Kidd

Barbra Streisand, Walter Matthau, Michael
Crawford, Marianne McAndrew, E. J. Peaker,
Tommy Tune, David Hurst

'The film leaves an oddly negative impression;
a good deal of synthetic effervescence . . . but
very little real vitality.'—David Wilson

AAN: best picture; Harry Stradling; Lennie
Hayton, Lionel Newman

Hello Frisco Hello*
US 1943 98m Technicolor
TCF (Milton Sperling)

On the Barbary Coast, a girl singer becomes a star.
Moderately pleasing period musical with plenty going on but nothing very striking.

w Robert Ellis, Helen Logan, Richard Macauley *d* Bruce Humberstone *ph* Charles Clarke, Allen Davey *songs* various *ad* James Basevi, Boris Leven

Alice Faye, John Payne, Jack Oakie, Lynn Bari, Laird Cregar, June Havoc, Ward Bond, Aubrey Mather, George Barbier, Frank Orth

AA: song 'You'll Never Know' (*m* Harry Warren, *ly* Mack Gordon)
AAN: Charles Clarke, Allen Davey

Hello Goodbye
US 1970   101m   De Luxe
TCF (André Hakim)

A cheerful young Englishman falls for a mysterious Frenchwoman who turns out to be the wife of a Baron.
Modest, aimless, forgettable romantic comedy, full of old-fashioned clichés imperfectly remembered.

w Roger Marshall *d* Jean Negulesco *ph* Henri Decaë *m* Francis Lai *pd* John Howell *ad* Auguste Capelier

Michael Crawford, Geneviève Gilles, Curt Jurgens, Ira Furstenberg

Hello Sister*
US 1933   62m   bw
Fox (Winfield Sheehan)
aka: *Walking down Broadway*

Boy meets girl in New York.
A mild little romance, only notable because it was edited down from an original by Erich Von Stroheim, and touches of his work remain.

w Erich Von Stroheim, Leonard Spiegelgass, *novel* Dawn Powell *d* Erich Von Stroheim, Alfred Werker *ph* James Wong Howe

James Dunn, Boots Mallory, Zasu Pitts, Minna Gombell

Hell's Angels****
US 1930   135m   bw (some scenes in colour)
Howard Hughes

Two Americans become fliers in World War I. Celebrated early talkie spectacular, with zeppelin and flying sequences that still thrill. The dialogue is another matter, but all told this expensive production, first planned as a silent, is a milestone of cinema history.

w Howard Estabrook, Harry Behn *d* Howard Hughes *ph* Tony Gaudio, Harry Perry, E. Burton Steene

Ben Lyon, James Hall, Jean Harlow, John Darrow, Lucien Prival

  'It is not great, but it is as lavish as an eight-ring circus, and when you leave the theatre you will know you have seen a movie and not a tinny reproduction of a stage show.'—*Pare Lorentz*

AAN: Tony Gaudio, Harry Perry, E. Burton Steene

Hell's Heroes
US 1930   65m   bw
Universal

Three cowboys find an abandoned baby.
Yet another version of *Three Godfathers*; maybe not the best but the shortest.

w Tom Reed, *novel* Peter Kyne *d* William Wyler *ph* George Robinson

Charles Bickford, Raymond Hatton, Fred Kohler, Fritzi Ridgeway

Hell's Island*
US 1955   84m   Technicolor   Vistavision
Paramount / Pine–Thomas

Crooks congregate on a Caribbean island in search of a famous ruby.
Cheeky rehash of *The Maltese Falcon*, not bad in its own routine way.

w Maxwell Shane *d* Phil Karlson *ph* Lionel Lindon *md* Irvin Talbot

John Payne, Mary Murphy, *Francis L. Sullivan*, Arnold Moss

Hellzapoppin***
US 1942   84m   bw
Universal / Mayfair (Glenn Tryon, Alex Gottlieb)

Two incompetent comics make a picture.
Zany modification of a smash burlesque revue; the crazy jokes are toned down and a romantic interest is added (and tentatively sent up). The result is patchy but often hilarious, and the whole is a handy consensus of forties humour and pop music.

w Nat Perrin, Warren Wilson *d* H. C. Potter *ph* Woody Bredell *md* Charles Previn

Ole Olsen, Chic Johnson, Hugh Herbert, Martha Raye, Mischa Auer, Robert Paige, Jane Frazee, Shemp Howard, Elisha Cook Jnr, Richard Lane

AAN: song 'Pig Foot Pete' (*m* Gene de Paul, *ly* Don Raye)

Help!*

GB 1965   92m   Eastmancolor
UA / Walter Shenson / Suba Films

An oriental high priest chases the Beatles around the world because one of them has a sacred ring.

Exhausting attempt to outdo *A Hard Day's Night* in lunatic frenzy, which goes to prove that some talents work better on low budgets. The humour is a frantic cross between *Hellzapoppin*, the Goons, Bugs Bunny and the shade of Monty Python to come. It looks good but becomes too tiresome to entertain.

w Charles Wood, Marc Behm *d* Dick Lester
ph David Watkin m The Beatles ad Ray Simm

The Beatles, Leo McKern, Eleanor Bron, Victor Spinetti

Helter Skelter

GB 1949   75m   bw
GFD / Gainsborough

A heiress with hiccups is helped by the staff of the BBC.

Scatty comedy which tries everything, from custard pies and guest stars to a clip from a silent Walter Forde comedy. It isn't the British *Hellzapoppin* it sets out to be, but hardened buffs will find it worth a look.

w Patrick Campbell *d* Ralph Thomas *ph* Jack Asher *m* Francis Chagrin

Carol Marsh, David Tomlinson, Mervyn Johns, Peter Hammond, Jimmy Edwards, Richard Hearne, Jon Pertwee, Terry-Thomas

Hemingway's Adventures of a Young Man*

US 1962   145m   De Luxe   Cinemascope
TCF (Jerry Wald)
aka: *Adventures of a Young Man*

The son of a weak doctor and a religious mother breaks away from his family circle on a voyage of discovery.

Curious mélange of ill-assimilated Hemingway stories based on his Nick Adams character. The film has good intentions but no shape or style, and the guest stars don't help.

w A. E. Hotchner, *stories* Ernest Hemingway
d Martin Ritt *ph* Lee Garmes *m* Franz Waxman

Richard Beymer, Diane Baker, Corinne Cálvet, Fred Clark, Dan Dailey, James Dunn, Juano Hernandez, Arthur Kennedy, Ricardo Montalban, Susan Strasberg, Paul Newman, Jessica Tandy, Eli Wallach

Hennessy

GB 1975   104m   colour
AIP / Marseilles (Peter Snell)

Angered at the death of his family in the Belfast troubles, an Irish revolutionary hurries to London to blow up the Houses of Parliament.

Unattractive, uninventive thriller with a silly script and not an ounce of real suspense.

w John Gay, *story* Richard Johnson *d* Don Sharp *ph* Ernest Steward *m* John Scott *pd* Ray Simm

Rod Steiger, Richard Johnson, Lee Remick, Trevor Howard, Eric Porter, Peter Egan, David Collings

Henry Aldrich

Henry was originally a radio character created by Ezra Stone, an awkward small-town youth who like Andy Hardy was always getting into scrapes. Clifford Goldsmith wrote the original play which hit Broadway as well as the radio waves before starting a Hollywood series of amiable Paramount second features, most of them starring Jimmy Lydon with Charles Smith as his friend Dizzy.

1939: WHAT A LIFE (with Jackie Cooper)
1941: LIFE WITH HENRY (with Jackie Cooper). HENRY ALDRICH FOR PRESIDENT
1942: HENRY AND DIZZY, HENRY ALDRICH EDITOR
1943: HENRY ALDRICH GETS GLAMOUR, HENRY ALDRICH SWINGS IT, HENRY ALDRICH HAUNTS A HOUSE
1944: HENRY ALDRICH BOY SCOUT, HENRY ALDRICH PLAYS CUPID, HENRY ALDRICH'S LITTLE SECRET

Henry V****

GB 1944   137m   Technicolor
Rank / Two Cities (Laurence Olivier)

Shakespeare's historical play is seen in performance at the Globe Theatre in 1603; as it develops, the scenery becomes more realistic.

Immensely stirring, experimental and almost wholly successful production of Shakespeare on film, sturdy both in its stylization and its command of more conventional cinematic resources for the battle.

w Laurence Olivier, Alan Dent, *play* William Shakespeare *d Laurence Olivier ph Robert Krasker m William Walton ad Paul Sheriff*

Laurence Olivier, *Robert Newton, Leslie Banks, Esmond Knight*, Renée Asherson, George Robey, *Leo Genn*, Ernest Thesiger, Ivy St Helier, Ralph Truman, Harcourt Williams, Max Adrian, Valentine Dyall, Felix Aylmer, John Laurie, Roy Emerton

AAN: William Walton; Laurence Olivier (as actor)

Henry VIII and His Six Wives*
GB 1972   125m   Technicolor
EMI (Roy Baird)

Dullish historical account of the king's reign,
staged as recollections from his deathbed but
lacking any of the sparkle of *The Private Life of
Henry VIII* made forty years previously.
Accurate sets and costumes fail to compensate
for lack of film flair.

w Ian Thorne *d* Waris Hussein *ph* Peter
Suschitsky *m* David Munro

Keith Michell, Frances Cuka (Aragon),
Charlotte Rampling (Boleyn), Jane Asher
(Seymour), Jenny Bos (Cleves), Lynne Frederick
(Howard), Barbara Leigh-Hunt (Parr), Donald
Pleasence (Thomas Cromwell)
† The production was stimulated by a highly
successful BBC TV series, *The Six Wives of
Henry VIII*

Her Cardboard Lover*
US 1942   93m   bw
MGM (J. Walter Ruben)

A flirtatious lady hires a lover to make her fiancé
jealous.
Paper-thin comedy previously filmed in silent
days as *The Passionate Plumber* (with Buster
Keaton). It did nobody any good, but preserves
some style despite a witless script.

w Jacques Deval, John Collier, Anthony Veiller,
William H. Wright, *play* Jacques Deval
d George Cukor *ph* Harry Stradling, Robert
Planck

Norma Shearer, Robert Taylor, George
Sanders, Frank McHugh, Elizabeth Patterson,
Chill Wills

Her Highness and the Bellboy
US 1945   112m   bw
MGM (Joe Pasternak)

A hotel bellboy forsakes his crippled sweetheart
to woo a visiting princess.
Glutinous sentimental mishmash; one waits for
musical numbers which never happen.

w Richard Connell, Gladys Lehmann *d* Richard
Thorpe *ph* Harry Stradling *m* Georgie Stoll

Hedy Lamarr, Robert Walker, June Allyson,
Rags Ragland, Agnes Moorehead, Carl
Esmond, Warner Anderson, Ludwig Stossel

Her Husband's Affairs*
US 1947   83m   bw
Columbia (Raphael Hakim)

A husband and wife team of advertising agents
promote a depilatory which turns out to grow
hair instead.

Mildly amiable crazy comedy.

w Ben Hecht *d* S. Sylvan Simon *ph* Charles
Lawton Jnr

Lucille Ball, Franchot Tone, Edward Everett
Horton, Mikhail Rasumny, Gene Lockhart,
Nana Bryant, Jonathan Hale, Mabel Paige

Her Jungle Love*
US 1938   81m   Technicolor
Paramount (George M. Arthur)

An aviator crashlands in the jungle, where he is
comforted by a lovely lady, a chimp and a lion
but distressed by an earthquake, a volcano and
assorted villains.
Second of Dorothy Lamour's jungle hokum
shows, and the first in colour; despite its fair
technical proficiency, the fact that it once packed
'em in is tribute to the changing tastes of
mankind.

w Joseph M. March, Lillie Hayward, Eddie
Welch *d* George Archainbaud *ph* Ray
Rennahan *m* Gregory Stone

Dorothy Lamour, Ray Milland, Lynne
Overman, J. Carrol Naish, Dorothy Howe

Her Twelve Men
US 1954   91m   Anscocolor
MGM (John Houseman)

A woman teacher in a boys' school reforms a
difficult class.
Predictable, sugary and artificial school story
with the star exuding sweetness and light.

w William Roberts, Laura Z. Hobson *d* Robert
Z. Leonard *ph* Joseph Ruttenberg *m* Bronislau
Kaper

Greer Garson, Robert Ryan, Richard Haydn,
Barry Sullivan

Herbie Goes to Monte Carlo
US 1977   105m   Technicolor
Walt Disney (Ron Miller)

The Volkswagen with a mind of its own enters
the Monte Carlo rally and routs a gang of
thieves.
Utterly predictable, patchily made family
comedy.

w Arthur Alsberg, Don Nelson *d* Vincent
McEveety *ph* Leonard J. South *m* Frank de Vol

Dean Jones, Don Knotts, Julie Sommars,
Jacques Marin, Roy Kinnear, Bernard Fox
† Second sequel to *The Love Bug*.

Hercules
Italy 1957 105m Eastmancolor
Dyaliscope
Oscar / Galatea
original title: *Le Fatiche di Ercole*

Hercules helps Jason find the golden fleece.
The strong man epic which started a genre; of
little interest in itself.

w Pietro Francisci, Ennio de Concini, Gaio
Frattini *d* Pietro Francisci *ph* Mario Bava
m Enzo Masetti

Steve Reeves, Sylva Koscina, Gianna Maria
Canale, Fabrizio Mione

Hercules Unchained
Italy / France 1959 105m Eastmancolor
Dyaliscope
Lux / Galatea
original title: *Ercole e la Regina di Lidia*

Hercules has problems with the king of Thebes
and the queen of Lidia.
More comic-strip versions of old legends. This
item had more spent on it in publicity than in
production cost, and consequently was seen by
vast audiences around the world. It isn't very
good.

w Pietro Francisci, Ennio di Concini *d* Pietro
Francisci *ph* Mario Bava *m* Enzo Masetti

Steve Reeves, Sylva Koscina, Sylvia Lopez,
Primo Carnera

† Many sequels followed, the hero sometimes
being known as Ursus or Goliath.

Here Come the Coeds
US 1945 88m bw
Universal (John Grant)

Janitors help to forestall a mortgage foreclosure
on a college for women.
Routine star vehicle with few highlights.

w Arthur T. Horman, John Grant *d* Jean
Yarbrough *ph* George Robinson *songs* Jack
Brooks, Edgar Fairchild

Bud Abbott, Lou Costello, Lon Chaney Jnr,
Peggy Ryan, Martha O'Driscoll, Donald Cook,
June Vincent, Charles Dingle

Here Come the Girls *
US 1953 78m Technicolor
Paramount (Paul Jones)

In the nineties an ageing chorus boy traps a
mysterious murderer.
Spotty, ineptly titled star comedy with music; in
fact among the last of his passable vehicles, with
excellent production backing.

w Edmund Hartmann, Hal Kanter *d* Claude

Binyon *ph* Lionel Lindon *md* Lyn Murray
ad Hal Pereira, Roland Anderson

Bob Hope, Rosemary Clooney, Tony Martin,
Arlene Dahl, Millard Mitchell, Fred Clark,
William Demarest, Robert Strauss

Here Come the Huggetts *
GB 1948 93m bw
Rank / Gainsborough (Betty Box)

A suburban family has its ups and downs.
Cosy domestic comedy drama, a presage of TV
soap operas to come, or Britain's answer to the
Hardys, depending how you look at it. Tolerable
at the time.

w Mabel and Denis Constanduros, Muriel and
Sydney Box, Peter Rogers *d* Ken Annakin

Jack Warner, Kathleen Harrison, Jane Hylton,
Susan Shaw, Petula Clark, Jimmy Hanley,
David Tomlinson, Diana Dors, Peter
Hammond, John Blythe

† The Huggetts had actually originated in
Holiday Camp the previous year, and appeared
again in *Vote for Huggett* and *The Huggetts
Abroad*; Warner and Harrison became an
inseparable duo for many years.

Here Come the Waves
US 1944 98m bw
Paramount (Mark Sandrich)

A sailor falls in love with identical twin Waves.
Empty-headed, professionally executed musical
recruiting poster.

w Allen Scott, Ken Englund, Zion Myers
d Mark Sandrich *ph* Charles Lang *md* Robert
Emmett Dolan *songs* Harold Arlen, Johnny
Mercer

Bing Crosby, Betty Hutton, Sonny Tufts, Ann
Doran, Gwen Crawford

AAN: song 'Accentuate the Positive' (*m* Harold
Arlen, *ly* Johnny Mercer)

Here Comes Mr Jordan ***
US 1941 93m bw
Columbia (Everett Riskin)

A prizefighter who is also an amateur
saxophonist crashes in his private plane and goes
to heaven by mistake: he was supposed to
survive and live another forty years.
Unfortunately when he goes back for his body it
has been cremated, so he has to find another one,
recently deceased . . .
Weird heavenly fantasy which succeeded
because of its novelty and because heaven in
wartime was a comforting vision. As a movie
taken on its own merits, it suffers from
illogicalities, a miscast star and a wandering plot,

but scene for scene there is enough firmness and control to make it memorable. It certainly had many imitations, including *Angel on My Shoulder, Down to Earth, A Guy Named Joe, Heaven Only Knows, The Horn Blows at Midnight* and *That's the Spirit.*

w *Seton I. Miller, Sidney Buchman, play* Halfway to Heaven by Harry Segall
d *Alexander Hall* ph Joseph Walker
m Frederick Hollander md Morris Stoloff

Robert Montgomery, Evelyn Keyes, Rita Johnson, *Claude Rains, James Gleason, Edward Everett Horton,* John Emery, *Donald MacBride,* Halliwell Hobbes, Don Costello
† Remade 1978 as *Heaven Can Wait.*

AA: original story (Harry Segall)
AAN: Seton I. Miller, Sidney Buchman; Alexander Hall; Joseph Walker; Robert Montgomery; James Gleason

Here Comes the Groom*
US 1951 114m bw
Paramount (Frank Capra)

A journalist adopts war orphans and reforms his selfish fiancée.
Tired attempt by Capra to recapture his pre-war mood; despite intermittent pleasures it has neither the right style nor the topical substance.

w Virginia Van Upp, Myles Connelly, Liam O'Brien, *story* Robert Riskin d *Frank Capra*
ph George Barnes md Joseph Lilley songs Jay Livingston, Ray Evans

Bing Crosby, Jane Wyman, Franchot Tone, Alexis Smith, James Barton, Connie Gilchrist, Robert Keith, Anna Maria Alberghetti
'The general impression is of a loud, strident, rather vulgar comedy in which technique is used to disappointingly mechanical ends, and which a few bright lines of dialogue cannot rescue from tedium.'—*Penelope Houston*

AA: song 'In the Cool Cool Cool of the Evening' (m Hoagy Carmichael, ly Johnny Mercer)
AAN: Robert Riskin

Here Comes the Navy*
US 1934 86m bw
Warner

An aggressive young naval rating fights with his former friend, now Petty Officer.
Breezy comedy melodrama teaming Cagney and O'Brien for the first time and offering star heroics as a sop to the Legion of Decency.

w Ben Markson, Earl Baldwin d *Lloyd Bacon*
ph Arthur Edeson m Leo F. Forbstein

James Cagney, Pat O'Brien, Dorothy Tree, Gloria Stuart, Frank McHugh, Robert Barrat

'Rapid and reasonably authentic, a satisfactory addition to a series of cinema cartoons which, because their colour and mood are indigenous and timely, may be more interesting twenty years from now.'—*Time*

AAN: best picture

Here We Go round the Mulberry Bush*
GB 1967 96m Technicolor
UA / Giant (Larry Kramer, Clive Donner)

A school-leaver is obsessed by sex and determines to lose his virginity.
Repetitive comedy which certainly opened new avenues in British humour and seemed pretty permissive at the time (pre-*Graduate*). In itself, however, more modish than sympathetic.

w Hunter Davies (with Larry Kramer), from his novel d *Clive Donner* ph Alex Thomson
m various groups

Barry Evans, Judy Geeson, Angela Scoular, Adrienne Posta, Sheila White, Vanessa Howard, Denholm Elliott, Maxine Audley, Moyra Fraser, Michael Bates
'The only incongruity is that it should have been made by adults, so completely does it enter into the teenager's view of himself.'—*MFB*

A Hero Ain't Nothing but a Sandwich
US 1977 107m CFI color
New World / Radnitz-Mattel (Robert B. Radnitz)

Problems for an urban family in the black ghetto.
Well-intentioned but ultimately wearisome and cliché-strewn melodrama.

w Alice Childress, from her novel d *Ralph Nelson* ph Frank Stanley m Tom McIntosh

Cicely Tyson, Paul Winfield, Larry B. Scott, Helen Martin, Glynn Turman
'The sort of dreaded wholesome film that cultural and societal groups heavily endorse but nobody pays money to go see.'—*Variety*

Heroes
US 1977 113m Technicolor
Universal (David Foster, Lawrence Turman)

A Vietnam veteran, made slightly kooky by his experiences, settles down after several adventures when he falls in love.
Just plain awful: a would-be star vehicle that doesn't work.

w James Carabatsos (and, uncredited, David Freeman) d *Jeremy Paul Kagan* ph Frank Stanley m Jack Nitzche, Richard Hazard

Henry Winkler, Sally Field, Harrison Ford, Val Avery

The Heroes Are Tired

France 1955   101m   bw
Cila-Terra
original title: *Les Héros Sont Fatigués*

Two ex-wartime pilots, one Free French and the other German, set up an air charter service in Liberia but come to grief over stolen diamonds. Gloomy post-war *film noir* set in a peculiarly depressing atmosphere, and not really sharp enough to overcome its squalid plot.

w Yves Ciampi, Jacques-Laurent Bost, *novel* Christine Garnier   *d* Yves Ciampi *ph* Henri Alekan   *m* Louiguy

Yves Montand, Maria Félix, Jean Servais, Curt Jurgens, Gérard Oury

The Heroes of Telemark*

GB 1965   131m   Technicolor   Panavision
Rank / Benton (Ben Fisz)

Norwegian resistance workers in World War II help the Allies to smash a heavy water plant. Ambling narrative with big action sequences which often seem irrelevant, so that the story as a whole fails to excite.

w Ivan Moffat, Ben Barzman   *d* Anthony Mann *ph* Robert Krasker   *m* Malcolm Arnold

Kirk Douglas, Richard Harris, Ulla Jacobsson, Roy Dotrice, Anton Diffring

Hero's Island*

US 1962   94m   Technicolor   Panavision
UA / Daystar / Portland (James Mason, Leslie Stevens)

In 1718 bondslaves settle on a Carolina island, are attacked by fishermen and protected by Blackbeard the Pirate.
An oddly personal, patchy, rather mysterious film with a rhetorical script and rather good action sequences.

wd Leslie Stevens   *ph* Ted McCord   *m* Dominic Frontière

James Mason, Kate Manx, Neville Brand, Rip Torn

Herr Puntila and his Servant Matti*

Austria 1955   95m   Agfacolor
Bauerfilm

A rich landowner, usually drunk, is rescued from scrapes by his patient valet.
A cogent comedy which its author is said to have approved in this version.

w Alberto Cavalcanti, Vladimir Pozner, Ruth Wieden, *play* Bertolt Brecht   *d* Alberto Cavalcanti   *ph* André Bac, Arthur Hämmerer *m* Hanns Eisler

Curt Bois, Hans Engelmann, Maria Emo, Edith Prager

Hers to Hold

US 1943   94m   bw
Universal (Felix Jackson)

A girl decides whether or not to marry a serviceman.
Limp star vehicle, a sequel to *Three Smart Girls* (qv).

w Lewis R. Foster   *d* Frank Ryan   *ph* Elwood Bredell   *md* Charles Previn   *m* Frank Skinner

Deanna Durbin, Joseph Cotten, Charles Winninger, Nella Walker, Gus Schilling, Ludwig Stossel

AAN: song 'Say a Prayer for the Boys Over There' (*m* Jimmy McHugh, *ly* Herb Magidson)

Hester Street*

US 1974   89m   bw
Midwest Films (Raphael D. Silver)

How Jewish immigrants settled in East Side New York in the nineties.
Modest, humorous, but not always smooth or dramatically emphatic chronicle of a familiar background; the detail however is excellent.

wd Joan Micklin Silver, *story* Yeki by Abraham Cahan   *ph* Kenneth Van Sickle   *m* William Bolcom

Steven Keats, Carol Kane, Mel Howard, Dorrie Kavanaugh, Doris Roberts
   'A small, beautifully detailed, slightly shaggy independent film of charm and substance.'— *Judith Crist*
   'For old diehards who still go to the cinema seeking humanity, tenderness and insight.'— *Michael Billington, Illustrated London News*

AAN: Joan Micklin Silver (as writer)

Hi Diddle Diddle*

US 1943   72m   bw
Columbia / Andrew Stone
aka: *Try and Find It*

Young lovers are hampered by con artist parents.
Scatty comedy with amusing patches and some zest in the telling.

w Edmund L. Hartmann   *d* Andrew L. Stone *ph* Charles Van Enger   *m* Phil Boutelje

Adolphe Menjou, Pola Negri, Dennis O'Keefe, Billie Burke, Martha Scott, June Havoc

AAN: Phil Boutelje

Hi Gang

GB 1941   100m   bw
Rank / Gainsborough (Edward Black)

American expatriates in London get involved in a case of mistaken identity.

Icky farce based faintly on a wartime radio variety series, notable only for preserving the three stars involved.

w Val Guest, Marriott Edgar, J. O. C. Orton, Howard Irving Young *d* Marcel Varnel

Bebe Daniels, Ben Lyon, Vic Oliver, Graham Moffatt, Moore Marriott, Felix Aylmer, Sam Browne

Hi Nellie*
US 1934   79m   bw
Warner (Robert Presnell)

An ex-editor is demoted to advice to the lovelorn and gets involved in city rackets.

Minor, effective star comedy-melodrama.

w Abem Finkel, Sidney Sutherland *d* Mervyn Le Roy *ph* Sol Polito

Paul Muni, Glenda Farrell, Ned Sparks, Robert Barrat, Hobart Cavanaugh, Berton Churchill, Donald Meek, Douglass Dumbrille, Edward Ellis

† Remade in 1935 as *Front Page Woman*; 1937 as *Love Is on the Air*; 1942 as *You Can't Escape Forever*; 1949 as *The House across the Street*.

Hickey and Boggs
US 1972   111m   De Luxe
UA / Film Guarantors Ltd (Fouad Said)

Two down and out private eyes, hired to find a girl, keep falling over dead bodies.

Extraordinarily confused thriller with moments of humour and well staged action sequences.

w Walter Hill *d* Robert Culp *ph* Wilmer Butler *m* Ted Ashford

Robert Culp, Bill Cosby, Rosalind Cash

The Hidden Fortress*
Japan 1958   123m   bw   Tohoscope
Toho (Masumi Fujimoto)
original title: *Kakushi Toride No San-Akunin*

In medieval Japan, the heiress of a feudal lord is saved from a bandit by a samurai.

Roistering eastern western.

w Ryuzo Kikushima, Hideo Oguni, Shinobu Hashimoto, Akira Kurosawa *d* Akira Kurosawa *ph* Ichio Yamazaki *m* Masaru Sato

Toshiro Mifune, Misa Uehara, Minoru Chiaki

High and Low*
Japan 1963   142m   bw   Tohoscope
Toho (Tomoyuki Tanaka)

A wealthy shoe manufacturer's chauffeur's son is kidnapped in mistake for his own, and he faces a moral dilemma.

Interesting, rather gloomy Japanese version of a light American thriller with all the style expected of the director.

w Hideo Oguni, Ryuzo Kikushima, Eijiro Hisaito, Akira Kurosawa, *novel* The King's Ransom by Ed McBain *d* Akira Kurosawa *ph* Asakazu Makai, Takao Saito *m* Masaru Sato

Toshiro Mifune, Kyoko Kagawa, Tatsuya Nakadai

The High and the Mighty*
US 1954   147m   Warnercolor
    Cinemascope
Wayne–Fellows

A big passenger plane is in trouble over the Pacific, and its occupants react in various ways to the prospect of a crash landing.

Compendium fiction with even the pilot having a personal problem which could cloud his judgment. Tolerable, well made hokum.

w Ernest K. Gann, from his novel *d* William Wellman *ph* William Clothier *m* Dmitri Tiomkin

John Wayne, Robert Newton, Robert Stack, Doe Avedon, Claire Trevor, Laraine Day, Jan Sterling, Phil Harris, Sidney Blackmer, John Howard

AA: Dmitri Tiomkin
AAN: William Wellman; Claire Trevor; Jan Sterling; title song (*m* Dmitri Tiomkin, *ly* Ned Washington)

High Anxiety*
US 1977   94m   De Luxe
TCF / Crossbow (Mel Brooks)

A psychologist taking up a new appointment suspects that his predecessor may have been murdered.

Elementary but somewhat entertaining spoof of various Hitchcock movies (*Spellbound, North by Northwest, The Birds*), with the level of humour as unsubtle and lavatorial as one has come to expect.

w Mel Brooks, Ron Clark, Rudy DeLuca, Barry Levinson *d* Mel Brooks *ph* Paul Lohmann *m* John Morris

Mel Brooks, Madeline Kahn, Cloris Leachman, Harvey Korman, Ron Carey, Howard Morris, Dick Van Patten

'It basically just shambles along, in search of the next big set-piece to send up.'—*Richard Combs, MFB*

High-Ballin'
US 1978   100m   Movielab
AIP / Stanley Chase / Pando (Jan Slan)

An independent trucker battles hijackers as well
as pressures from a giant trucking firm.
Routine action hokum, a long way behind 1948's
Theives' Highway and even less entertaining
than TV's *Movin' On*.

w Paul Edwards *d* Peter Carter *ph* René
Verzier *m* Paul Hoffert

Peter Fonda, Jerry Reed, Helen Shaver, Chris
Wiggins

High Barbaree
US 1947   91m   bw
MGM

A pilot crashlands in the Pacific and finds
himself drifting towards a Utopian island
fancifully described by his favourite uncle.
Thin Hollywood mysticism on Shangri-La lines
but without the solid virtues of plot, dialogue and
imagination.

w Anne Morrison Chapin, Whitfield Cook, Cyril
Hume *d* Jack Conway *ph* Sidney Wagner

Van Johnson, June Allyson, Thomas Mitchell,
Marilyn Maxwell

The High Bright Sun
GB 1965   114m   Technicolor
Rank (Betty Box)
US title: *McGuire Go Home*

In 1957 Cyprus the British army is beleaguered
by partisans, and an officer tries to contact a
leading rebel.
Confused and boring attempt to make romantic
drama out of an intractably sad situation.

w Ian Stuart Black, from his novel *d* Ralph
Thomas *ph* Ernest Steward *m* Angelo
Lavagnino

Dirk Bogarde, Susan Strasberg, George
Chakiris, Denholm Elliott

The High Command*
GB 1936   88m   bw
ABFD / Fanfare / Wellesley (Gordon
   Wellesley)

The general of a West African garrison has a
guilty secret known to his young medical officer.
Dated melodrama, rather interestingly
performed and directed.

w Katherine Strueby, *novel* The General Goes
Too Far by Lewis Robinson *d* Thorold
Dickinson *ph* Otto Heller *m* Ernest Irving

James Mason, Lionel Atwill, Lucie Mannheim,
Steve Geray, Leslie Perrins

The High Cost of Loving*
US 1958   87m   bw
MGM (Milo O. Frank Jnr)

A happily married middle class couple have
doubts about their future.
Pleasant, mildly satirical romantic comedy
which doesn't really get anywhere.

w Rip Van Ronkel *d* Jose Ferrer *ph* George J.
Folsey *m* Jeff Alexander

Jose Ferrer, Gena Rowlands, Joanne Gilbert,
Jim Backus, Bobby Troup, Philip Ober, Edward
Platt, Werner Klemperer

High Flight
GB 1958   102m   Technicolor
Columbia / Warwick (Phil C. Samuel)

Cadets train at the Royal Air Force College.
Simple-minded peacetime flagwaver.

w Joseph Landon, Ken Hughes *d* John Gilling
ph Ted Moore *md* Muir Mathieson *m* Kenneth
V. Jones, Douglas Gamley *title march* Eric
Coates

Ray Milland, Bernard Lee, Kenneth Haigh,
Anthony Newley, Kenneth Fortescue, Sean
Kelly, Helen Cherry

High Flyers
US 1937   70m   bw
RKO (Lee Marcus)

Two incompetents are duped into smuggling
contraband gems.
Feeble finale to the career of two comedians.

w Benny Rubin, Bert Granet, *play* Victor
Mapes *d* Edward Cline *ph* Jack Mackenzie
songs Herman Ruby, Dave Dreyer

Bert Wheeler, Robert Woolsey, Lupe Velez,
Marjorie Lord, Margaret Dumont, Jack Carson,
Paul Harvey

High Noon**
US 1952   85m   bw
Stanley Kramer

A marshal gets no help when he determines to
defend his town against revengeful badmen.
A minor western with a soft-pedalled message
for the world, this turned out to be a classic
simply because it was well done, with every scene
and performance clearly worked out.
Cinematically it was pared to the bone, and the
theme tune helped.

*w Carl Foreman d Fred Zinnemann ph Floyd
Crosby m Dmitri Tiomkin singer* Tex Ritter

Gary Cooper, Grace Kelly, Thomas Mitchell,
Lloyd Bridges, Katy Jurado, Otto Kruger, Lon
Chaney, Henry Morgan

'When the hands point up . . . the excitement starts!'—*publicity*

'Like nearly all the Kramer productions, this is a neat, well-finished and literate piece of work, though its limitations are more conventional than most.'—*Gavin Lambert*

'A western to challenge *Stagecoach* for the all-time championship.'—*Bosley Crowther*

'A series of crisp and purposeful scenes that interpret each other like the pins on a strategist's war map.'—*Robert L. Hatch*

AA: Dmitri Tiomkin; Gary Cooper; title song (*m* Dmitri Tiomkin, *ly* Ned Washington)
AAN: best picture; Carl Foreman; Fred Zinnemann

High Plains Drifter*
US 1972   105m   Technicolor   Panavision
Universal / Malpaso (Robert Daley)

A mysterious stranger rides into town and terrifies the inhabitants.
Semi-supernatural, mystical revenge western with an overplus of violence. Very watchable, but irritating.

w Ernest Tidyman *d* Clint Eastwood *ph* Bruce Surtees *m* Dee Barton *ad* Henry Bumstead

Clint Eastwood, Verna Bloom, Marianna Hill, Mitch Ryan, Jack Ging

'Ritualized violence and plodding symbolism make for heavy going.'—*Sight and Sound*

'A nervously humorous, self-conscious near-satire on the prototype Eastwood formula.'—*Variety*

High Sierra*
US 1941   96m   bw
Warner (Hal. B. Wallis, Mark Hellinger)

An ex-con gangster plans one last heist in the Californian mountains, but is mortally wounded through his involvement with two women.
Rather dreary action melodrama which gave Bogart his first real star part (after George Raft turned it down). Remade 1955 as *I Died a Thousand Times* (qv); also in 1949 as a western, *Colorado Territory*.

w John Huston, W. R. Burnett, *novel* W. R. Burnett *d* Raoul Walsh *ph* Tony Gaudio *m* Adolph Deutsch

Humphrey Bogart, Ida Lupino, Joan Leslie, Alan Curtis, Arthur Kennedy, Henry Hull, Henry Travers, Jerome Cowan

'The last swallow, perhaps, of the gangsters' summer.'—*William Whitebait*

'Like it or not, I'll be damned if you leave before the end, or go to sleep.'—*Otis Ferguson*

'As gangster pictures go, this one has everything—speed, excitement, suspense, and

that ennobling suggestion of futility which makes for irony and poetry.'—*New York Times*

High Society
US 1956   107m   Technicolor   Vistavision
MGM (Sol C. Siegel)

A haughty rich girl chooses between several suitors.
Cold, flat, dull musical reworking of *The Philadelphia Story* (qv), with ill-cast performers and just a few bright moments.

w John Patrick *d* Charles Walters *ph* Paul C. Vogel *m/ly* Cole Porter *md* Johnny Green, Saul Chaplin *ad* Cedric Gibbons, Hans Peters

Bing Crosby, Grace Kelly, Frank Sinatra, Celeste Holm, Louis Armstrong, Sidney Blackmer, Margalo Gillmore, Louis Calhern, Lydia Reed, John Lund

AAN: Johnny Green, Saul Chaplin; song 'True Love'

High Society Blues
US 1930   102m   bw
Fox

A girl ditches a French count in favour of an all-American hero.
Frothy musical romance which did nothing for its stars and is now unwatchable.

w Howard J. Green *d* David Butler *ph* Charles Van Enger *songs* Joe McCarthy, James Hanley

Janet Gaynor, Charles Farrell, William Collier Snr, Hedda Hopper, Louise Fazenda, Lucien Littlefield, Joyce Compton

High Tide at Noon
GB 1957   111m   bw
Rank (Julian Wintle)

Passions run high among lobster fishermen in Nova Scotia.
Neat, clean romantic melodrama in agreeable surroundings.

w Neil Paterson *d* Philip Leacock *ph* Eric Cross *m* John Veale

Betta St John, Michael Craig, Patrick McGoohan, William Sylvester, Flora Robson, Alexander Knox, Peter Arne, Patrick Allen, Susan Beaumont

High Time
US 1960   103m   De Luxe   Cinemascope
TCF / Bing Crosby

A middle-aged widower goes back to college.
Flaccid comedy-musical with some undergraduatish jokes.

w Tom and Frank Waldman *d* Blake Edwards

ph Ellsworth Fredericks *m* Henry Mancini
songs Sammy Cahn, Jimmy Van Heusen

Bing Crosby, Tuesday Weld, Fabian, Richard
Beymer, Nicole Maurey

AAN: song 'The Second Time Around'
(*m* Jimmy Van Heusen, *ly* Sammy Cahn)

High Treason*

GB 1951   93m   bw
GFD / Conqueror (Paul Soskin)

Saboteurs are routed by the London police.
Unconvincing documentary melodrama which
moves fast enough to be entertaining.

w Frank Harvey, Roy Boulting   *d* Roy Boulting
ph Gilbert Taylor   *m* John Addison

Liam Redmond, André Morell, Anthony
Bushell, Kenneth Griffith, Patric Doonan, Joan
Hickson, Anthony Nicholls, Mary Morris,
Geoffrey Keen, Dora Bryan

High Wall

US 1948   99m   bw
MGM

A war veteran is put in an asylum after
confessing to killing his wife, but later events
prove that he was drugged into saying so.
Adequately entertaining, supremely
unconvincing mystery melodrama.

w Sydney Boehm   *d* Curtis Marshall   *ph* Paul C.
Vogel   *m* Bronislau Kaper

Robert Taylor, Herbert Marshall, Audrey
Totter, Dorothy Patrick, H. B. Warner, Warner
Anderson

High, Wide and Handsome*

US 1937   110m   bw
Paramount (Arthur Hornblow Jnr)

Pennsylvania 1859: a travelling showgirl falls in
love with a farmer.
Disappointingly stilted period musical with most
of the talent ill at ease until the final reel.

w Oscar Hammerstein II   *d* Rouben Mamoulian
ph Victor Milner, Theodore Sparkuhl   *ch* LeRoy
Prinz   *songs* Jerome Kern, Oscar Hammerstein
II   *md* Boris Morros   *ad* Hans Dreier, John
Goodman

Irene Dunne, Randolph Scott, Dorothy Lamour,
Raymond Walburn, Alan Hale, Elizabeth
Patterson, Charles Bickford, William Frawley,
Akim Tamiroff, Ben Blue, Irving Pichel, Lucien
Littlefield

A High Wind in Jamaica*

GB 1965   104m   De Luxe   Cinemascope
TCF (John Croydon)

In Victorian days, English children en route
home from Jamaica are captured by pirates and
influence their lives.
Semi-serious adventure story with a highly
unlikely ending in which the chief pirate allows
himself to be executed for a murder committed
by a child. There are however pleasures along the
way.

w Stanley Mann, Ronald Harwood, Denis
Cannan, *novel* Richard Hughes   *d* Alexander
Mackendrick   *ph* Douglas Slocombe   *m* Larry
Adler

Deborah Baxter, Anthony Quinn, James
Coburn, Isabel Dean, Nigel Davenport, Gert
Frobe, Lila Kedrova

Higher and Higher*

US 1943   90m   bw
RKO (Tim Whelan)

Servants have an elaborate plan to restore the
family fortune.
Unamusing musical which undernourishes
several talents.

w Jay Dratler, Ralph Spence, *play* Gladys
Hurlbut, Joshua Logan   *d* Tim Whelan
ph Robert de Grasse   *md* Constantin
Bakaleinikoff   *songs* Jimmy McHugh, Harold
Adamson

Michele Morgan, Jack Haley, *Frank Sinatra*,
Leon Errol, Marcy McGuire, *Victor Borge*,
Mary Wickes, Barbara Hale, Elizabeth Risdon

AAN: Constantin Bakaleinikoff; song 'I
Couldn't Sleep a Wink Last Night (*m* Jimmy
McHugh, *ly* Harold Adamson)

The Highwayman

US 1951   82m   Cinecolor
Allied Artists / Jack Dietz (Hal. E. Chester)

A 17th-century nobleman disguises himself as a
Quaker and becomes a highwayman to right
wrongs.
Curious Poverty Row period actioner with ideas
generally above its station, not to mention an
unexpected tragic ending.

w Jan Jeffries, *poem* Alfred Noyes   *d* Lesley
Selander   *ph* Harry Neumann   *m* Herschel
Burke Gilbert

Philip Friend, Charles Coburn, Victor Jory,
Wanda Hendrix, Cecil Kellaway, Scott Forbes,
Virginia Huston, Dan O'Herlihy

Hilda Crane

US 1956   87m   Technicolor
   Cinemascope
TCF (Herbert B. Swope Jnr)

An unhappy woman marries for the third time
and convinces herself it won't work.

Emotional melodrama of the old school: very moderate in all departments.

wd Philip Dunne, *play* Samson Raphaelson *ph* Joe MacDonald *m* David Raksin

Jean Simmons, Guy Madison, Jean-Pierre Aumont, *Evelyn Varden*, Judith Evelyn, Peggy Knudsen

The Hill**
GB 1965   122m   bw
MGM / Seven Arts (Kenneth Hyman)

Prisoners rebel against the harsh discipline of a British military detention centre in North Africa during World War II.
Lurid melodrama which descends fairly quickly into black farce with a number of sweaty actors outshouting each other. Enjoyable on this level when you can hear the dialogue through the poor sound recording.

w Ray Rigby, from his TV play *d* Sidney Lumet *ph* Oswald Morris *m* none

Sean Connery, Harry Andrews, Michael Redgrave, Ian Bannen, Alfred Lynch, *Ossie Davis*, Roy Kinnear, Jack Watson, Ian Hendry

A Hill in Korea
GB 1956   81m   bw
British Lion / Wessex (Anthony Squire)

During the Korean war, a small patrol guards a hill.
Minor war talk-piece, shot in Surrey and looking it.

w Ian Dalrymple, Anthony Squire, Ronald Spencer, *novel* Max Catto *d* Julian Amyes *ph* Freddie Francis *m* Malcolm Arnold

George Baker, Harry Andrews, Stanley Baker, Michael Medwin, Ronald Lewis, Stephen Boyd, Victor Maddern, Harry Landis
  'Character is adequately sketched into a suitably laconic script.'—*MFB*

Hill 24 Doesn't Answer
Israel 1954   101m   bw
Sikor (Thorold Dickinson, Peter Frye)

Four friends defend Hill 24 against the Arabs on the eve of the cease-fire, and are all killed.
Israel's first feature film, a curious amalgam of the slick and the amateur, with long flashbacks which make it resemble *The Bridge of San Luis Rey*.

w Zvi Kolitz, Peter Frye, Joanna and Thorold Dickinson *d* Thorold Dickinson *ph* Gerald Gibbs *m* Paul Ben-Haim

Michael Wager, Edward Mulhare, Haya Hararit, Arie Lavi, Michael Shilo

The Hindenberg*
US 1975   125m   Technicolor   Panavision
Universal / Filmmakers (Robert Wise)

In 1937, sabotage causes the airship Hindenberg to crash on arrival at New York.
An extremely uninteresting guess at the cause of this famous disaster. The plot and dialogue are leaden, and such actors as have more than a couple of lines look extremely glum. The special effects, however, are fine despite curious blue-rinse photographic processing.

w Nelson Gidding, *novel* Michael M. Mooney *d* Robert Wise *ph* Robert Surtees *pd* Edward Carfagno *sp* Albert Whitlock *m* David Shire

George C. Scott, Anne Bancroft, Burgess Meredith, William Atherton, Roy Thinnes, Gig Young, Charles Durning, Robert Clary, René Auberjonois
  'The tackiest disaster movie yet—a cheap and chaotic collage of painted drops, wooden actors and not-so-special effects that manages to make one of this century's most sensational real-life catastrophes seem roughly as terrifying as a badly stubbed toe.'—*Frank Rich*

AAN: Robert Surtees

The Hired Hand
US 1971   93m   Technicolor
Universal / Pando (William Hayward)

Two western drifters avenge the killing of their friend and settle down to work on a farm; but violence follows them.
A potentially enjoyable small-scale western is spoiled by pretentious direction and effects which bore the spectator to death.

w Alan Sharp *d* Peter Fonda *ph* Vilmos Zsigmond *m* Bruce Langhorne

Peter Fonda, Warren Oates, Verna Bloom, Severn Darden
  'The first slow-motion western, with endless artsy photography not quite succeeding in obscuring the rambling plot.'—*Judith Crist, 1973*
  'When a film begins with a "lyrical" shot, your heart has a right to sink.'—*Stanley Kauffman*

The Hireling*
GB 1973   108m   colour
Columbia / World Film Services (Ben Arbeid)

In the twenties, a lady's chauffeur falls in love with her.
Talkative drama, elegant but not much fun.

w Wolf Mankowitz, *novel* L. P. Hartley *d* Alan Bridges *ph* Michael Reed *m* Marc Wilkinson *pd* Natasha Kroll

Sarah Miles, Robert Shaw, Peter Egan, Elizabeth Sellars, Caroline Mortimer

Hiroshima Mon Amour*
France / Japan 1959 91m bw
Argos / Comei / Pathé / Daiei

A French actress working in Hiroshima falls for a Japanese architect and remembers her tragic love for a German soldier during the occupation. Jumbled mixture of flashbacks and flashforwards which can now be recognized as typical of this director and on its first appearance was hailed as a work of art in an innovative new style.

w Marguerite Duras d Alain Resnais ph Sacha Vierny, Takahashi Michio m Giovanni Fusco, Georges Delerue

Emmanuele Riva, Eiji Okada

AAN: Marguerite Duras

His Brother's Wife
US 1936 91m bw
MGM (Lawrence Weingarten)

A young scientist is helped out of trouble by his brother, on condition he disappears; the brother then weds the scientist's girl friend.
Heavy romantic melodrama containing everything including jungle fever, flung together to take advantage of the stars' real-life romance.

w Leon Gordon, John Meehan, story George Auerbach
d W. S. Van Dyke II ph Oliver T. Marsh m Franz Waxman

Robert Taylor, Barbara Stanwyck, Joseph Calleia, John Eldredge, Jean Hersholt, Samuel S. Hinds, Leonard Mudie, Jed Prouty

His Butler's Sister*
US 1943 94m bw
Universal (Felix Jackson)

A temporary maid falls for her sophisticated boss.
Pleasant comedy musical: no great shakes, but the principals give the air of enjoying themselves.

w Samuel Hoffenstein, Betty Reinhardt d Frank Borzage ph Elwood Bredell m Hans Salter

Deanna Durbin, Franchot Tone, Pat O'Brien, Evelyn Ankers, Walter Catlett, Alan Mowbray, Akim Tamiroff, Else Janssen, Iris Adrian

His Girl Friday****
US 1940 92m bw
Columbia (Howard Hawks)

A remake of *The Front Page* (qv), with Hildy Johnson turned into a woman.
Frantic, hilarious black farce with all participants at their best; possibly the fastest comedy ever filmed, and one of the funniest.

w Charles Lederer, play The Front Page by Charles MacArthur, Ben Hecht d Howard Hawks ph Joseph Walker m Sydney Cutner md Morris Stoloff

Rosalind Russell, Cary Grant, Ralph Bellamy, Gene Lockhart, Porter Hall, Ernest Truex, Cliff Edwards, Clarence Kolb, Roscoe Karns, Frank Jenks, Abner Biberman, Frank Orth, John Qualen, Helen Mack, Billy Gilbert, Alma Kruger

'The kind of terrific verbal slam-bang that has vanished from current film-making.'—New Yorker, 1975

'One of the fastest of all movies, from line to line and from gag to gag.'—Manny Farber, 1971

'Overlapping dialogue carries the movie along at breakneck speed; word gags take the place of the sight gags of silent comedy, as this vanished race of brittle, cynical, childish people rush around on corrupt errands.'—Pauline Kael, 1968

'The main trouble is that when they made The Front Page the first time, it stayed made.'—Otis Ferguson

His Glorious Night
US 1929 85m bw
MGM
GB title: Breath of Scandal

A princess falls in love with a commoner. Soporific early talkie, remade in 1960 as A Breath of Scandal. The movie which first exposed its star's high-pitched voice, it is credited with killing his career.

w Willard Mack, play Olimpia by Ferenc Molnar d Lionel Barrymore

John Gilbert, Catherine Dale Owen, Hedda Hopper, Gustav von Seyffertitz, Nance O'Neil

His Kind of Woman*
US 1951 120m bw
RKO (Howard Hughes, Robert Sparks)

At a remote Mexican ranch resort, a gangster on the run holds up residents including a fortune-hunting girl and a fading matinee idol. Agreeable tongue-in-cheek melodrama which slightly outstays its welcome but is generally good fun.

w Frank Fenton, d John Farrow ph Harry J. Wild m Leigh Harline md Constantin Bakaleinikoff

Robert Mitchum, Jane Russell, Vincent Price,

Raymond Burr, Tim Holt, Charles McGraw, Marjorie Reynolds, Jim Backus

His Lordship*
GB 1936   71m   bw
Gaumont (S. C. Balcon)
US title: Man of Affairs

A politician's twin takes his place to expose an old murder.
Comfortable star comedy-drama.

w Maude Howell, Edwin Greenwood, L. DuGard Peach, play The Nelson Touch by Neil Grant d Herbert Mason

George Arliss, Rene Ray, Romilly Lunge, Jessie Winter, Allan Jeayes

His Majesty O'Keefe
GB 1954   90m   Technicolor
Warner / Harold Hecht

Native islanders are taught by an easygoing mariner how to exploit their natural resources and defend themselves against pirates.
Thin adventure romance with too little for its star to do.

w Borden Chase, James Hill d Byron Haskin ph Otto Heller m Robert Farnon

Burt Lancaster, Joan Rice, André Morell, Abraham Sofaer, Benson Fong, Archie Savage

His Woman
US 1931   80m   bw
Paramount

The captain of a tramp freighter finds himself in charge of an abandoned baby and a runaway girl.
Slow, indifferent comedy drama, previously filmed in 1929 as Sal of Singapore.

w Adelaide Heilbron, Melville Baker, novel The Sentimentalist by Dale Collins ph Arthur Ellis

Gary Cooper, Claudette Colbert, Averill Harris, Richard Spiro, Douglass Dumbrille, Joseph Calleia, Harry Davenport

Une Histoire D'Amour*
France 1951   95m   bw
Jacques Roitfeld / Cité Films
GB title: Love Story

A police inspector discovers that a young couple killed themselves because of parental opposition.
A rather soggy little drama made watchable by its careful detail and immaculate leading performance.

w Michel Audiard d Robert Clavel ph Louis Page m Paul Misraki

Louis Jouvet, Daniel Gélin, Dany Robin

History Is Made at Night*
US 1937   97m   bw
Walter Wanger

A divorcee and her new love have trouble from her ex-husband.
Atmospheric, artificial, generally entertaining romantic comedy-drama of a kind which went out of fashion long ago.

w Gene Towne, Graham Baker d Frank Borzage ph Gregg Toland m Alfred Newman

Charles Boyer, Jean Arthur, Leo Carrillo, Colin Clive

'So souped up with demonic passions and tender glances and elegant photography that it's rather fun.'—New Yorker, 1978

The History of Mr Polly*
GB 1949   94m   bw
GFD / Two Cities (John Mills)

A draper's assistant buys a small shop but tires of his nagging wife and decides the time has come for a change.
Patchy but generally amusing version of a popular comic novel, very English and rather appealingly done.

w Anthony Pelissier, novel H. G. Wells d Anthony Pelissier ph Desmond Dickinson m William Alwyn

John Mills, Sally Ann Howes, Megs Jenkins, Finlay Currie, Betty Ann Davies, Edward Chapman

Hit!
US 1973   134m   Technicolor   Panavision
Paramount (Harry Korshak)

A federal agent takes personal action against a drug ring which caused his daughter's death.
Black vigilante melodrama, very violent and interminably padded out with irrelevancies.

w Alan Trustman, David M. Wolf d Sidney J. Furie ph John A. Alonzo m Lalo Schifrin

Billy Dee Williams, Richard Pryor, Paul Hampton, Gwen Welles

'No more under-the-armpit shots, but obscurity is still the keynote of this Sidney Furie effort in the urban vigilante genre.'—Sight and Sound

Hit the Deck
US 1954   112m   Eastmancolor   Cinemascope
MGM (Joe Pasternak)

Romantic adventures of three sailors on shore leave in San Francisco.
Boring situations and performances reduce the

temperature of this youth musical which is not another *On the Town*.

w Sonya Levien, William Ludwig, *musical play* Herbert Fields, *novel* Shore Leave by Hubert Osborn *ph* George Folsey *m* Vincent Youmans *ly* Leo Robin *ch* Hermes Pan

Tony Martin, Jane Powell, Ann Miller, Debbie Reynolds, Walter Pidgeon, Vic Damone, Gene Raymond

Hitler
US 1961   107m   bw
Three Crown / E. Charles Straus

A sex-oriented, semi-fictional biopic of the German dictator, from the murder of his niece to his final madness and suicide.
Enterprising sensationalism which deserves a nod for sheer audacity.

w Sam Neuman *d* Stuart Heisler *ph* Joseph Biroc *m* Hans Salter

Richard Basehart, Maria Emo, Martin Kosleck, John Banner

The Hitler Gang**
US 1944   101m   bw
Paramount (B. G. De Sylva)

The rise to power of Hitler and his henchmen. Though at the time it seemed rather like a serious cabaret turn, this fictionalization of historical fact has some good impersonations and dramatically effective scenes.

w Frances Goodrich, Albert Hackett *d John Farrow ph* Ernest Laszlo *m* David Buttolph

Robert Watson, Martin Kosleck (Goebbels), Victor Varconi (Hess), Luis Van Rooten (Himmler), Alexander Pope (Goering), Roman Bohnen, Ivan Triesault, Helene Thimig, Reinhold Schunzel, Sig Rumann, Alexander Granach

Hitler—The Last Ten Days
GB / Italy 1973   104m   Technicolor
MGM / Wolfgang Reinhardt / Westfilm

With Adolf and Eva in the bunker.
Claustrophobic historical reconstruction with an uncomfortable star.

w Ennio de Concini, Maria Pia Fusco, Wolfgang Reinhardt, Ivan Moffat *d* Ennio de Concini *ph* Ennio Guarnieri *m* Mischa Spoliansky

Alec Guinness, Simon Ward, Doris Kunstmann, Adolfo Celi, Diane Cilento, Eric Porter, Joss Ackland

Hitler's Children*
US 1943   83m   bw
RKO (Edward A. Golden)

A family reacts to Hitler and the Hitler Youth. Artificial melodrama set in an unlikely Germany but successful at the time because of its topicality and its refusal to play the Nazis as idiots, which was the usual Hollywood line.

w Emmet Lavery, *book* Education for Death by Gregor Ziemer *d* Edward Dmytryk *m* Roy Webb

Tim Holt, Bonita Granville, Otto Kruger, Kent Smith, H. B. Warner, Lloyd Corrigan, Erford Gage, Gavin Muir, Hans Conried

H. M. Pulham Esquire**
US 1940   120m   bw
MGM (King Vidor)

A moderately successful Bostonian businessman looks back over his rather stuffy life and has a fling.
Solidly upholstered drama which does not quite do justice to the book on which it is based.

w King Vidor, Elizabeth Hill, *novel* John P. Marquand *d* King Vidor

Robert Young, Ruth Hussey, Hedy Lamarr, Charles Coburn, Van Heflin, Fay Holden, Bonita Granville

HMS Defiant*
GB 1962   101m   Technicolor
 Cinemascope
Columbia / GW (John Brabourne)
US title: *Damn the Defiant*

Mutiny erupts on an 18th-century British sailing ship.
Rather unpleasant and unenterprising sea fare reminiscent of the goings-on aboard the *Bounty*. Well enough staged and acted but not very remarkable or memorable.

w Nigel Kneale, Edmund H. North, *novel* Mutiny by Frank Tilsley *d* Lewis Gilbert *ph* Christopher Challis *m* Clifton Parker

Alec Guinness, Dirk Bogarde, Anthony Quayle, Tom Bell, Nigel Stock, Murray Melvin, Victor Maddern, Maurice Denham, Walter Fitzgerald

'It authentically if superficially recreates the days of press gangs, maggots and the cat.'— *Peter John Dyer*

Hobson's Choice***
GB 1953   107m   bw
British Lion / London (Norman Spencer)

In the 1890s a tyrannical Lancashire bootmaker is brought to heel by his plain-speaking daughter and her simple-minded husband.
Brilliantly played version of a famous working-class comedy, memorably set and

photographed; one regrets only the slight decline of the predictable third act.

w Norman Spencer, Wynard Browne, *play* Harold Brighouse *d* David Lean *ph* Jack Hildyard *m* Malcolm Arnold *ad* Wilfrid Shingleton

Charles Laughton, Brenda de Banzie, John Mills, Richard Wattis, Helen Haye, Daphne Anderson, Prunella Scales

Hoffman
GB 1970   113m   Technicolor
ABP / Longstone (Ben Arbeid)

A middle-aged misfit blackmails a typist into spending a week with him.
Interminable sex comedy padded out from a short TV play; it quickly becomes claustrophobic, tasteless, and boring.

w Ernest Gebler, from his novel and play *d* Alvin Rakoff *ph* Gerry Turpin *m* Ron Grainer

Peter Sellers, Sinead Cusack, Jeremy Bulloch, Ruth Dunning

Hold Back the Dawn*
US 1941   115m   bw
Paramount (Arthur Hornblow Jnr)

A would-be immigrant into the US via Mexico marries a schoolteacher he does not love.
Surprisingly effective romantic melodrama with a nice style and some mordant lines in the script.

w *Charles Brackett, Billy Wilder* d *Mitchell Leisen* ph *Leo Tover* m Victor Young

Charles Boyer, Olivia de Havilland, Paulette Goddard, Victor Francen, Walter Abel, Curt Bois, Rosemary de Camp, Nestor Paiva, Mitchell Leisen

AAN: best picture; Charles Brackett, Billy Wilder; Leo Tover; Victor Young; Olivia de Havilland

Hold That Blonde
US 1945   75m   bw
Paramount (Paul Jones)

A psychiatrist suggests that romance may cure a kleptomaniac, but the patient unfortunately chooses a jewel thief.
Thin comedy which erupts into frantic farce, with some energetic slapstick and a Harold Lloyd style finale.

w Walter de Leon, Earl Baldwin, E. Edwin Moran *d* George Marshall *ph* Daniel L. Fapp *m* Werner Heymann

Eddie Bracken, Veronica Lake, Albert Dekker, Frank Fenton, George Zucco, Donald MacBride, Norma Varden, Willie Best

Hold That Co-Ed*
US 1938   80m   bw
TCF (David Hempstead)
GB title: *Hold That Girl*

A girl dressed as a boy wins a university football match and thereby helps a governor get re-elected.
Intriguingly-cast crazy comedy which works up into a fine frenzy.

w Karl Tunberg, Don Ettinger, Jack Yellen *d* George Marshall *ph* Robert Planck *md* Arthur Lange

John Barrymore, Joan Davis, George Murphy, Marjorie Weaver, Jack Haley, George Barbier, Donald Meek, Johnny Downs, Guinn Williams

Hold That Ghost*
US 1941   86m   bw
Universal (Burt Kelly, Glenn Tryon)

A group of strangers are stranded in an apparently haunted house.
Long thought of as Abbott and Costello's best comedy, this now seems pretty strained and slow to start, but it has its classic moments.

w Robert Lees, Fred Rinaldo, John Grant *d* Arthur Lubin *ph* Elwood Bredell, Joe Valentine *m* Hans Salter

Bud Abbott, Lou Costello, Joan Davis, the Andrews Sisters, Richard Carlson, *Ted Lewis* and his band, Evelyn Ankers, Marc Lawrence, Mischa Auer

Hold Your Man*
US 1933   89m   bw
MGM (Sam Wood)

A hard-boiled young woman falls for a confidence man, has his baby, and waits for him to emerge from prison.
Briskly-fashioned star comedy-drama with entertaining moments.

w Anita Loos, Howard Emmett Rogers *d* Sam Wood *ph* Harold Rosson

Jean Harlow, Clark Gable, Stuart Erwin, Dorothy Burgess, Muriel Kirkland, Paul Hurst
   'The sudden transition from wise-cracking romance to sentimental penitence provides a jolt.'—*Frank S. Nugent*

The Hole*
France / Italy 1959   123m   bw
Play-Art / Filmsonor / Titanus (Serge Silberman)
original title: *Le Trou*

Four convicts in a Paris prison dig a tunnel to freedom and almost make it.
Meticulous escape drama nicely shot in very

limited sets: hypnotic for those with the patience to adjust to its pace.

w Jacques Becker, José Giovanni, Jean Aurel, *novel* José Giovanni *d* Jacques Becker *ph* Ghislain Cloquet

Philippe Leroy, Mark Michel, Jean Kéraudy, Michel Constantine

A Hole in the Head*

US 1959   120m   De Luxe   Cinemascope
Sincap (Frank Capra)

A Miami hotelier is threatened with foreclosure and tries to raise the money from his provident elder brother.
Easy-going comedy without much point, but various amusing facets artfully deployed.

w Arnold Shulman, from his TV and stage play *d* Frank Capra *ph* William H. Daniels *m* Nelson Riddle

Frank Sinatra, Edward G. Robinson, Eleanor Parker, Eddie Hodges, Carolyn Jones, Thelma Ritter, Keenan Wynn, Joi Lansing

AA: song 'High Hopes' (*m* Jimmy Van Heusen, *ly* Sammy Cahn)

The Hole in the Wall

US 1929   73m   bw
Paramount

A gangster falls for a phony fortune teller intent on a revenge scheme.
Involved melodrama, a primitive talkie notable chiefly for its stars.

w Pierre Collings, *play* Fred Jackson *d* Robert Florey *ph* George Folsey

Edward G. Robinson, Claudette Colbert, David Newell, Nelly Savage, Donald Meek, Louise Closser Hale

Holiday*

US 1930   99m   bw
Pathe (E. B. Derr)

A bright-minded rich girl steals her sister's fiancé, a struggling young lawyer.
Competent early talkie version of a hit play.

w Horace Jackson, *play* Philip Barry *d* Edward H. Griffith *ph* Norbert Brodine *m* Josiah Zuro

Ann Harding, Robert Ames, Mary Astor, Edward Everett Horton, Hedda Hopper, Monroe Owsley, William Holden

AAN: Horace Jackson; Ann Harding

Holiday***

US 1938   93m   bw
Columbia (Everett Riskin)
GB titles: *Free to Live; Unconventional Linda*

Elegant, highly successful remake of the above; still a stage play on film, but subtly devised to make the very most of the lines and performances.

w Donald Ogden Stewart *d* George Cukor *ph* Franz Planer *m* Sidney Cutner

Katharine Hepburn, Cary Grant, Doris Nolan, *Edward Everett Horton* (same role), *Ruth Donnelly, Lew Ayres*, Henry Kolker, Binnie Barnes

Holiday Affair

US 1949   87m   bw
RKO (Don Hartman)

A young widow falls for an easy-going boat builder.
Flimsy star-shaped romantic comedy with nice touches.

w Isobel Lennart *d* Don Hartman *ph* Milton Krasner *m* Roy Webb

Robert Mitchum, Janet Leigh, Wendell Corey, Griff Barnett, Esther Dale, Gordon Gebert, Henry O'Neill, Harry Morgan

Holiday Camp*

GB 1947   97m   bw
GFD / Gainsborough (Sydney Box)

At a summer holiday camp, a murderer on the prowl affects people's enjoyment in various ways.
Seminal compendium comedy drama, a bore in itself but establishing several post-war norms of the British cinema, including the Huggetts.

w Muriel and Sydney Box, Ted Willis, Peter Rogers, Mabel and Denis Constanduros *d* Ken Annakin

Jack Warner, Kathleen Harrison, Flora Robson, Dennis Price, Hazel Court, Emrys Jones, Yvonne Owen, Esmond Knight, Jimmy Hanley, Peter Hammond, Esma Cannon, John Blythe, Susan Shaw

Holiday for Lovers

US 1959   103m   De Luxe   Cinemascope
TCF (David Weisbart)

To distract his teenage daughter from boys, a Boston psychiatrist organizes a family holiday in South America.
Frail old-fashioned family comedy with entirely predictable situations culminating in a drunk scene for stuffy father.

w Luther Davis *d* Henry Levin *ph* Charles G. Clarke *m* Leigh Harline

Clifton Webb, Jane Wyman, Paul Henreid, Carol Lynley, Jill St John, Gary Crosby, José Greco

Holiday for Sinners

US 1952 72m bw
MGM (John Houseman)

In New Orleans during the Mardi Gras three old friends meet crises in their lives.
Slightly curious but not very interesting portmanteau drama.

w A. I. Bezzerides, *novel* Hamilton Basso
d Gerald Mayer ph Paul Vogel md Alberto Columbo

Gig Young, Keenan Wynn, Janice Rule, Richard Anderson, William Campbell, Michael Chekov, Sandro Giglio, Edith Barrett, Porter Hall

'It gives an impression of blurred, rather heavy-going sincerity.'—MFB

Holiday in Mexico

US 1946 127m Technicolor
MGM

The daughter of the American Ambassador to Mexico falls for Jose Iturbi.
Travel brochure musical in which the occasional plums do not redeem the sogginess of the pudding.

w Isobel Lennart d George Sidney ph Harry Stradling

Walter Pidgeon, Ilona Massey, Jane Powell, Jose Iturbi, Roddy McDowall

Holiday Inn**

US 1942 101m bw
Paramount (Mark Sandrich)

The joint proprietors of a roadhouse hotel love the same girl.
Plain, simple-minded musical which provided a peg for pleasant performances and good numbers. It hit the box office spot, especially as it introduced 'White Christmas'.

w Claude Binyon, Elmer Rice d Mark Sandrich ph David Abel m/ly Irving Berlin md Robert Emmett Dolan

Bing Crosby, Fred Astaire, Walter Abel, Marjorie Reynolds, Virginia Dale, Louise Beavers, Irving Bacon, James Bell

AA: song 'White Christmas'
AAN: original story (Irving Berlin); Robert Emmett Dolan

The Holly and the Ivy*

GB 1952 83m bw
British Lion / London (Anatole de Grunwald)

Christmas brings family revelations in a remote Norfolk rectory.
A badly-filmed stage success which succeeds because of its performances.

w Anatole de Grunwald, *play* Wynard Browne
d George More O'Ferrall ph Ted Scaife
m Malcolm Arnold

Ralph Richardson, Celia Johnson, Margaret Leighton, Denholm Elliott, John Gregson, Hugh Williams, Margaret Halstan, Maureen Delany, William Hartnell, Robert Flemyng, Roland Culver

'This type of direct translation to the screen, using none of the cinema's resources, can only do harm to the play itself.'—*Penelope Houston*

Hollywood Boulevard*

US 1936 75m bw
Paramount (A. M. Botsford)

A washed-up Hollywood actor writes a sensational memoir for publication, but lives to regret it.
Entertaining melodrama with famous names in bit parts.

w Marguerite Roberts d Robert Florey ph Karl Struss m Gregory Stone

John Halliday, Marsha Hunt, Robert Cummings, C. Henry Gordon, Frieda Inescort, Esther Dale; and Gary Cooper, Francis X. Bushman, Maurice Costello, Mae Marsh, Charles Ray, Jane Novak, Bryant Washburn, Jack Mulhall, Creighton Hale, Bert Roach

Hollywood Canteen*

US 1944 123m bw
Warner (Alex Gottlieb)

The stars give their evenings to entertaining soldiers.
Shoddily made but sociologically fascinating record of Hollywood doing its bit in World War II.

wd Delmer Daves ph Bert Glennon m Ray Heindorf md Leo F. Forbstein

Joan Leslie, Robert Hutton, Dane Clark, Janis Paige; and The Andrews Sisters, Jack Benny, Joe E. Brown, Eddie Cantor, Joan Crawford, Bette Davis, John Garfield, Sidney Greenstreet, Paul Henreid, Peter Lorre, Ida Lupino, Dennis Morgan, Roy Rogers, S. Z. Sakall, Alexis Smith, Barbara Stanwyck, Jane Wyman, etc etc

'The corporal steps slowly backwards, in his eyes that look of glazed ecstasy which Jennifer Jones wore all through *The Song of Bernadette*. He has just been kissed by Joan Leslie.'—*Richard Winnington*

AAN: Ray Heindorf; song 'Sweet Dreams, Sweetheart' (m M. K. Jerome, ly Ted Koehler)

Hollywood Cavalcade**

US 1939 96m Technicolor
TCF (Harry Joe Brown)

The career of an old-time Hollywood producer.
A lively first half with amusing re-staging of
early slapstick comedies gives way depressingly
to personal melodrama, but there is enough
historical interest to preserve the balance.

w Ernest Pascal *d* Irving Cummings *ph* Allen
M. Davey, Ernest Palmer *ad* Richard Day,
Wiard B. Ihnen *md* Louis Silvers

Don Ameche, Alice Faye, *J. Edward Bromberg*,
Alan Curtis, Stuart Erwin, Jed Prouty, Buster
Keaton, Donald Meek, and the original
Keystone Kops

Hollywood Hotel

US 1937   109m   bw
Warner (Sam Bischoff)

A Hollywood radio show has its problems.
Half-hearted, overlong Warner musical with
little of the expected zip.

w Jerry Wald, Maurice Leo, Richard Macauley
d Busby Berkeley *ph* Charles Rosher, George
Barnes *m/ly* Johnny Mercer, Richard Whiting

Dick Powell, Rosemary Lane, Lola Lane, Hugh
Herbert, Ted Healy, Glenda Farrell, Louella
Parsons, Alan Mowbray, Frances Langford,
Allyn Joslyn, Benny Goodman, Edgar Kennedy

Hollywood or Bust

US 1956   95m   Technicolor   Vistavision
(Paramount) Hal Wallis

Two halfwits win a car and drive across country
to Hollywood.
Dopey comedy with more misses than hits; the
last film of Martin and Lewis as a team.

w Erna Lazarus *d* Frank Tashlin *ph* Daniel
Fapp *m* Walter Scharf

Dean Martin, Jerry Lewis, Pat Crowley, Maxie
Rosenbloom, Anita Ekberg

Hollywood Party

US 1934   68m   bw (Technicolor
sequence)
MGM

A mad Russian throws a party which ends in
disaster.
Dismal 'all-star' comedy relieved by guest
appearances.

w Howard Dietz, Arthur Kober *d* (uncredited)
Richard Boleslawski, Allan Dwan, Roy
Rowland *ph* James Wong Howe

Laurel and Hardy, Jimmy Durante, Lupe Velez,
Charles Butterworth, Eddie Quillan, Ted Healy
and the Stooges, Polly Moran

The Hollywood Revue of 1929**

US 1929   116m   part-Technicolor
MGM (Harry Rapf)

A variety show featuring most of MGM's talent
in slightly surprising acts, this is something of a
bore to sit through but an archival must; and just
occasionally it boasts surprising vitality.

w Al Boasberg, Robert E. Hopkins *d* Charles F.
Reisner *ph* John Arnold, Irving Ries,
Maximillian Fabian *ch* Sammy Lee
m/ly various

Jack Benny, Buster Keaton, Joan Crawford,
John Gilbert, Norma Shearer, Laurel and
Hardy, Marion Davies, Marie Dressler, William
Haines, Lionel Barrymore, Conrad Nagel,
Bessie Love, Cliff Edwards, Nils Asther

Hollywood Story*

US 1951   76m   bw
U-I (Leonard Goldstein)

A young producer solves a 20-year-old studio
murder mystery.
Adequate potboiler with a reasonably absorbing
plot and glimpses of silent stars.

w Frederick Kohner, Fred Brady *d* William
Castle *ph* Carl Guthrie *m* Joseph Gershenson

Richard Conte, Julia Adams, Richard Egan,
Henry Hull, Fred Clark, Jim Backus, Paul
Cavanagh; and Francis X. Bushman, William
Farnum, Betty Blythe, Helen Gibson, Joel
McCrea

Holocaust 2000

GB/Italy 1977   102m   Technicolor
   Technovision
(Rank) Aston / Embassy (Edmondo Amati)

The executive in charge of a thermonuclear plant
in the Middle East is drawn into a legend about
the rebirth of the anti-Christ, and discovers that
the evil one is his own son.
Extraordinary mishmash of horror, religiosity
and social conscience which scarcely works on
any level.

w Sergio Donati, Alberto de Martino, Michael
Robson *d* Alberto de Martino *ph* Erico
Menczer *m* Ennio Morricone

Kirk Douglas, Simon Ward, Agostina Belli,
Anthony Quayle, Virginia McKenna, Spiros
Focas, Alexander Knox, Adolfo Celi
   'The wildest farrago yet to have come out of
the demonology genre.'—*Richard Combs, MFB*

Holy Matrimony*

US 1943   87m   bw
TCF

A famous painter comes back from exile for a

knighthood; but when his valet dies of pneumonia, has him buried as himself in Westminster Abbey.

Slightly stilted but generally warmly amusing version of a favourite novel, with excellent star performances.

w Nunnally Johnson, *novel* Arnold Bennett d John Stahl ph Lucien Ballard

Monty Woolley, Gracie Fields, Laird Cregar, Eric Blore, Una O'Connor

'A pleasant hour and a half, very well produced and acted.'—*James Agate*

AAN: Nunnally Johnson

Hombre**

US 1967   111m   De Luxe   Panavision
TCF / Hombre Productions (Martin Ritt, Irving Ravetch)

Stagecoach passengers at the mercy of a robber are helped by a despised half-caste.

Slow but suspenseful western melodrama which works up to a couple of good climaxes but falls away in an unnecessary tragic ending.

w Irving Ravetch, Harriet Frank, *novel* Elmore Leonard d Martin Ritt ph James Wong Howe m David Rose

Paul Newman, *Diane Cilento, Fredric March*, Richard Boone, Martin Balsam, Barbara Rush, Cameron Mitchell

'A fine array of quirkish characters . . . and some unusually literate dialogue.'—*Tom Milne*

Home at Seven

GB 1952   85m   bw
British Lion / London (Maurice Cowan)
US title: *Murder on Monday*

A clerk suffers a 24-hour loss of memory and may have been involved in a murder.

Intriguing suburban mystery, well acted but all too flatly transferred from the stage.

w Anatole de Grunwald, *play* R. C. Sherriff d Ralph Richardson ph Jack Hildyard, Edward Scaife

Ralph Richardson, Margaret Leighton, Jack Hawkins, Campbell Singer, Michael Shepley, Margaret Withers, Meriel Forbes, Frederick Piper

'A film with a notable absence of imagination in conception, direction and acting is not vindicated because it was made very cheaply in fifteen days . . . it seems ominous that the technique closely resembles that of television.'—*MFB*

Home before Dark

US 1958   137m   bw
Warner (Mervyn Le Roy)

A college professor brings his wife home after a year in a mental hospital, but trouble starts again as the circumstances are unchanged.

Overlong, heavygoing, well-made soap opera, quite unconvincing despite firm performances and a suitably gloomy *mise-en-scène*.

w Eileen and Robert Bassing d Mervyn Le Roy ph Joseph Biroc md Ray Heindorf

Jean Simmons, Efrem Zimbalist Jnr, Dan O'Herlihy, Rhonda Fleming, Mabel Albertson

Home from the Hill

US 1959   150m   Metrocolor
Cinemascope
MGM / Sol C. Siegel (Edmund Grainger)

A southern landowner with a voracious sexual appetite has trouble with his two sons, legitimate and illegitimate.

Shades of *Cold Comfort Farm* and *Tobacco Road* . . . and this solemn family saga does go on a bit.

w Irving Ravetch, Harriet Frank, *novel* William Humphrey d Vincente Minnelli ph Milton Krasner m Bronislau Kaper

Robert Mitchum, George Hamilton, George Peppard, Eleanor Parker, Luana Patten, Everett Sloane, Constance Ford, Ray Teal

Home in Indiana

US 1944   103m   Technicolor
TCF (André Daven)

Farmers compete in trotting races and their progeny fall in love.

Archetypal homespun Americana, well enough made according to its lights, but now like something from another world . . . an innocent one.

w Winston Miller, *novel* The Phantom Filly by George Agnew Chamberlain d Henry Hathaway ph Edward Cronjager m Hugo Friedhofer md Emil Newman

Jeanne Crain, June Haver, Lon McCallister, Walter Brennan, Charlotte Greenwood, Ward Bond, Charles Dingle, Willie Best
† Remade as *April Love*.

AAN: Edward Cronjager

Home of the Brave*

US 1949   86m   bw
Stanley Kramer

During World War II, a black man finds himself the butt of racist behaviour from the rest of his platoon.

One of the first films to touch the subject of anti-black bias, this now seems pretty tame and dated, and in fact never was much more than a filmed play (in which the butt was originally a Jew).

w Carl Foreman, *play* Arthur Laurents *d* Mark Robson *ph* Robert de Grasse *m* Dmitri Tiomkin

Frank Lovejoy, Lloyd Bridges, Douglas Dick, James Edwards, Steve Brodie, Jeff Corey, Cliff Clark

Home Sweet Homicide
US 1946 90m bw
TCF

Children solve a murder mystery with the help of their mother, a detective novelist.
Mild family fare.

w F. Hugh Herbert, *novel* Craig Rice *d* Lloyd Bacon *ph* John Seitz

Lynn Bari, Randolph Scott, Peggy Ann Garner, Connie Marshall, Dean Stockwell, Barbara Whiting

Homecoming
US 1948 113m bw
MGM (Sidney Franklin)

A ruthless society doctor is called up in World War II and has his life changed by a brief affair with a nurse who is killed in action.
Ho-hum romantic melodrama which stumbles most badly when it aims to be serious.

w Paul Osborn *d* Mervyn Le Roy *ph* Harold Rosson *md* Charles Previn *m* Bronislau Kaper

Clark Gable, Lana Turner, Anne Baxter, John Hodiak, Ray Collins, Gladys Cooper, Cameron Mitchell, Marshall Thompson

'Its basic substance, like the base of a perfume, has a terrible smell; but to many moviegoers the end-product will seem quite pleasant.'—*Time*

The Homecoming*
GB 1973 114m colour
American Express / Ely Landau

Tensions mount and sexual revelations abound in the house of a retired London butcher.
Plain treatment of an anything-but-plain Pinter play. The result is a record of a performance rather than a film.

w Harold Pinter, from his play *d* Peter Hall *ph* David Watkin *m* Thelonious Monk *pd* John Bury

Paul Rogers, Cyril Cusack, Michael Jayston, Ian Holm, Vivien Merchant, Terence Rigby

'Shocking in its own lucidity, and fascinating as an arrangement of mutually reflecting prisms . . . the remarkable control of Pinter's language

guarantees that the dramatic situations are revealed to be even *more* abstract and diagrammatic as they steadily accumulate psychological density.'—*Jonathan Rosenbaum*

Homicidal
US 1961 87m bw
Columbia / William Castle

A murderous blonde and a very strange young man both live in the house of a paralysed old lady.
Transvestite horror comic allegedly based on a true case; made on a low budget and played for cheap shocks.

w Robb White *d* William Castle *ph* Burnett Guffey *m* Hugo Friedhofer

Jean Arless, Glenn Corbett, Patricia Breslin, Eugenie Leontovitch, Alan Bunce, Richard Rust
† The film was played with a 'fright break' during which faint-hearted members of the audience might leave before the final onslaught.

L'Homme au Chapeau Rond*
France 1946 91m bw
Alcina

When his wife dies, a man becomes obsessed with causing the downfall of her two lovers.
Heavy-going melodrama without much in the way of light relief; chiefly memorable for its central performance.

w Charles Spaak, Jean Loubignic, *novel* The Eternal Husband by Dostoevsky *d* Pierre Billon *ph* Nicolas Torporkoff *m* Maurice Thiriet

Raimu, Aimé Clariond, Lucy Valnor

Hondo*
US 1954 93m Warnercolor 3-D
Wayne–Fellows

In 1874 New Mexico a cavalry despatch rider stops to defend a lonely widow and her son against Indians.
Overwritten but pleasant-looking western, clearly patterned after *Shane*.

w James Edward Grant *d* John Farrow *ph* Robert Burks, Archie Stout *m* Emil Newman, Hugo Friedhofer

John Wayne, Geraldine Page, Ward Bond, Michael Pate

AAN: Geraldine Page

The Honey Pot*
US 1966 150m Technicolor
UA / Famous Artists (Charles K. Feldman) (Joseph L. Mankiewicz)

A millionaire pretends to be dying in order to trick three former mistresses; but one of them is murdered.

Uneasy variation, via two other variations, on Ben Jonson's *Volpone*; despite bright moments, the mood is fatally inconsistent, and a cloud of pseudo-sophisticated dialogue hangs over the whole thing like a pall.

wd Joseph L. Mankiewicz, *play* Mr Fox of Venice by Frederick Knott, *novel* The Evil of the Day by Thomas Sterling *ph* Gianni di Venanzo *m* John Addison *pd* John De Cuir

Rex Harrison, Susan Hayward, *Maggie Smith*, Cliff Robertson, Capucine, Edie Adams, Adolfo Celi, Herschel Bernardi

'One of the talkiest pictures ever made.'—
Stephen Farber

Honeymoon
US 1947   74m   bw
RKO (Warren Duff)
GB title: *Two Men and a Girl*

An 18-year-old elopes to Mexico City with an army corporal but meets a sophisticated older man.

Emaciated comedy, one of the reasons for Shirley Temple's early retirement.

w Michael Kanin, *story* Vicki Baum *d* William Keighley *ph* Edward Cronjager *m* Leigh Harline

Shirley Temple, Franchot Tone, Guy Madison, Lina Romay, Gene Lockhart, Grant Mitchell

Honeymoon
Spain / GB 1959   109m   Technicolor
Technirama / Dimension 180
Suevia / Everdene (Cesario Gonzalez, Michael Powell)
Spanish title: *Luna de Miel*

An ex-ballerina in Spain with her new husband is tempted to return to the boards.

Incredibly shapeless travel poster with some dancing and two interpolated ballets to provide moments of musical interest. An unbelievable disaster from the co-creator of *The Red Shoes*.

w Michael Powell, Luis Escobar *d* Michael Powell *ph* Georges Périnal, Gerry Turpin *m* Mikis Theodorakis

Anthony Steel, Ludmilla Tcherina, Antonio, Leonide Massine

Honeymoon Hotel
US 1964   98m   Metrocolor
Cinemascope
MGM / Avon (Lawrence Weingarten)

A jilted swain goes off with a philandering friend on what was to have been his honeymoon trip . . . only to be followed by his repentant fiancée.
Rather unattractive farce with insufficient funny moments.

w R. S. Allen, Harvey Bulloch *d* Henry Levin *ph* Harold Lipstein *m* Walter Scharf

Nancy Kwan, Robert Goulet, Robert Morse, Jill St John, Elsa Lanchester, Keenan Wynn

The Honeymoon Machine
US 1961   91m   Metrocolor
Cinemascope
MGM / Avon (Lawrence Weingarten)

A naval lieutenant uses the ship's computer to break the bank at the Venice casino.
Stolid, expensive-looking comedy which barely raises a laugh.

w George Wells, *play* The Golden Fleecing by Lorenzo Semple Jnr *d* Richard Thorpe *ph* Joseph La Shelle *m* Leigh Harline

Steve McQueen, Brigid Bazlen, Jim Hutton, Paula Prentiss, Dean Jagger, Jack Weston, Jack Mullaney

The Honkers*
US 1971   102m   De Luxe
UA / Levy–Gardner–Laven

An ageing rodeo rider has trouble with his wife.
Quiet, carefully accomplished study of a man and his milieu.

w Steve Ihnat, Stephen Lodge *d* Steve Ihnat *ph* John Crabe *m* Jimmie Haskell

James Coburn, Lois Nettleton, Slim Pickens, Richard Anderson

Honky Tonk*
US 1941   104m   bw
MGM (Pandro S. Berman)

A western con man meets his match in the daughter of a fake judge.
Generally amusing comedy melodrama that ambles along between two styles but leaves a pleasant after-effect.

w Marguerite Roberts, John Sandford *d* Jack Conway *ph* Harold Rosson *m* Franz Waxman

Clark Gable, Lana Turner, Frank Morgan, Claire Trevor, Marjorie Main, Albert Dekker, Henry O'Neill, Chill Wills, Betty Blythe
'A lively, lusty western that makes you wish you had been there.'—*Variety*

Honolulu
US 1938   83m   bw
MGM (Jack Cummings)

A movie star is mistaken for his double.
Sloppy comedy with a few musical numbers.

w Herbert Fields, Frank Partos *d* Edward
Buzzell *ph* Joseph Ruttenberg

Robert Young, Eleanor Powell, George Burns,
Gracie Allen, Rita Johnson, Ruth Hussey,
Clarence Kolb, Sig Rumann, Eddie Anderson

'The whole thing seems to have been thrown
together so that Eleanor Powell can do a frenetic
hula.'—*New Yorker, 1977*

An Honourable Murder*
GB 1959 70m bw
Danziger

Boardroom executives scheme to be rid of their
chairman.
Oddball, interesting attempt to play *Julius
Caesar* in modern dress. Not entirely successful,
but full marks for trying.

w Brian Clemens, Eldon Howard *d* Godfrey
Grayson

Norman Wooland, Margaretta Scott, Lisa
Daniely, Douglas Wilmer, Philip Saville, John
Longden

Hoodlum Empire
US 1952 98m bw
Republic (Joseph Kane)

A Congressional committee investigates a
racketeer.
Moderate semi-documentary potboiler inspired
by the Kefauver investigations.

w Bruce Manning, Bob Considine *d* Joseph
Kane *ph* Reggie Lanning *m* Nathan Scott

Brian Donlevy, Forrest Tucker, Claire Trevor,
Vera Ralston, Luther Adler, John Russell, Gene
Lockhart, Grant Withers, Taylor Holmes

'Familiar gangster melodramatics and
repentances, played out in a rigmarole of
flashbacks.'—*MFB*

The Hoodlum Priest*
US 1961 100m bw
UA / Don Murray–Walter Wood

A Jesuit teacher tries to help young criminals,
especially a condemned murderer.
Moderately well done, very depressing and
downbeat chunk of social conscience based on
the life of Charles Dismas Clark.

w Don Mankiewicz, Joseph Landon *d* Irvin
Kershner *ph* Haskell Wexler *m* Richard
Markowitz

Don Murray, Keir Dullea, Larry Gates, Cindi
Wood, Logan Ramsey

The Hoodlum Saint
US 1946 93m bw
MGM (Cliff Reid)

A cynical newspaperman turns to religion and
succours thieves.
Hard-boiled sentimentality, a downright peculiar
and doleful comedy drama in deflated post-war
mood.

w Frank Wead, James Hill *d* Norman Taurog
ph Ray June *m* Nathaniel Shilkret

William Powell, Esther Williams, Angela
Lansbury, James Gleason, Lewis Stone, Rags
Ragland, Frank McHugh, Slim Summerville,
Roman Bohnen, Louis Jean Heydt, Charles
Arnt, Charles Trowbridge, Henry O'Neill

The Hook
US 1962 98m bw Panavision
MGM / Perlberg–Seaton

Three GIs escaping from Korea are ordered to
execute a prisoner but cannot bring themselves
to do it.
Predictable, claustrophobic drama which
becomes a slick exercise in morality.

w Henry Denker, from his novel Vahe Katcha
d George Seaton *ph* Joe Ruttenberg

Kirk Douglas, Robert Walker, Nick Adams,
Nehemiah Persoff

Hook, Line and Sinker
US 1968 92m Technicolor
Columbia / Jerry Lewis

A salesman who thinks he is dying goes on a
spending spree; when he learns the truth, he has
to disappear because of his huge debts.
Miserable comedy with frantic slapstick
interludes. The plot might have served Preston
Sturges.

w Rod Amateau *d* George Marshall *ph* W.
Wallace Kelley *m* Dick Stabile

Jerry Lewis, Peter Lawford, Anne Francis,
Pedro Gonzales Gonzales

Hooper*
US 1978 99m Metrocolor
Warner / Burt Reynolds, Lawrence Gordon
(Hank Moonjean)

An ageing stunt man decides on one last
sensational stunt before retiring.

There are some agreeably striking moments,
but you can't make a movie out of stunts and
loud cameraderie. This one palls half way
through.

w Thomas Rickman, Bill Kerby *d* Hal
Needham *ph* Bobby Byrne *m* Bill Justis

Burt Reynolds, Sally Field, Brian Keith, Jan-Michael Vincent, John Marley, Robert Klein, James Best, Adam West

Hopalong Cassidy

Cassidy, a creation of Clarence E. Mulford, was a fictitious gentleman cowboy who oddly enough wore black; 26 books about him were published between 1912 and 1956 when Mulford died. 66 films were made starring William Boyd as Hoppy, with either George Gabby Hayes or Andy Clyde as comic sidekick: Harry Sherman produced them, first for Paramount and then for UA, and they were later edited down for TV, in which medium Boyd became a folk hero and eventually made a further series. The films were easy-going, slow-moving second features which always pointed an admirable moral for children; their main directors were Howard Bretherton, Nate Watt, Lesley Selander and George Archainbaud.

1935: HOPALONG CASSIDY, THE EAGLE'S BROOD, BAR 20 RIDES AGAIN
1936: CALL OF THE PRAIRIE, THREE ON THE TRAIL, HEART OF THE WEST, HOPALONG CASSIDY RETURNS, TRAIL DUST
1937: BORDERLAND, HILLS OF OLD WYOMING, NORTH OF THE RIO GRANDE, RUSTLERS' VALLEY, HOPALONG RIDES AGAIN, TEXAS TRAIL
1938: HEART OF ARIZONA, BAR 20 JUSTICE, PRIDE OF THE WEST, SUNSET TRAIL, THE FRONTIERSMAN, PARTNERS OF THE PLAINS, CASSIDY OF BAR 20
1939: RANGE WAR, LAW OF THE PAMPAS, SILVER ON THE SAGE, RENEGADE TRAIL
1940: SANTA FE MARSHAL, THE SHOWDOWN, HIDDEN GOLD, STAGECOACH WAR, THREE MEN FROM TEXAS
1941: DOOMED CARAVAN, IN OLD COLORADO, BORDER VIGILANTES, PIRATES ON HORSEBACK, WIDE OPEN TOWN, OUTLAWS OF THE DESERT, RIDERS OF THE TIMBERLINE, SECRETS OF THE WASTELAND, STICK TO YOUR GUNS, TWILIGHT ON THE TRAIL
1942: UNDERCOVER MAN
1943: COLT COMRADES, BAR 20, LOST CANYON, HOPPY SERVES A WRIT, BORDER PATROL, THE LEATHER BURNERS, FALSE COLOURS, RIDERS OF THE DEADLINE
1944: MYSTERY MAN, FORTY THIEVES, TEXAS MASQUERADE, LUMBERJACK
1946: THE DEVIL'S PLAYGROUND
1947: FOOL'S GOLD, HOPPY'S HOLIDAY, MARAUDERS, UNEXPECTED GUEST, DANGEROUS VENTURE
1948: SINISTER JOURNEY, SILENT CONFLICT, STRANGE GAMBLE, BORROWED TROUBLE, THE DEAD DON'T DREAM, FALSE PARADISE

Horizons West

US 1952   81m   Technicolor
U-I (Albert J. Cohen)

After the Civil War, a rancher builds an empire on greed and ruthlessness, and his brother has to bring him to trial.
Rather lugubrious western with the usual quota of effective action scenes.

w Louis Stevens d Budd Boetticher
ph Charles P. Boyle md Joseph Gershenson

Rock Hudson, Robert Ryan, Julia Adams, John McIntire, Raymond Burr, Dennis Weaver, Judith Braun

The Horizontal Lieutenant

US 1962   90m   Metrocolor
  Cinemascope
MGM / Euterpe (Joe Pasternak)

World War II Hawaii; an amorous intelligence officer accidentally captures a Japanese guerrilla.
Very moderate army farce of no great skill or memorability.

w George Wells d Richard Thorpe ph Richard Bronner m George Stoll

Jim Hutton, Paula Prentiss, Jim Backus, Miyoshi Umeki, Jack Carter

The Horn Blows at Midnight

US 1945   80m   bw
Warner (Mark Hellinger)

An angel is sent to earth to destroy the planet with Gabriel's horn.
Wacky comedy inspired by *Here Comes Mr Jordan,* but on a broader slapstick level; much better than its star always pretended.

w Sam Hellman, James V. Kern d Raoul Walsh
ph Sid Hickox m Franz Waxman

Jack Benny, Alexis Smith, Dolores Moran, Allyn Joslyn, Guy Kibbee, Reginald Gardiner,

Franklin Pangborn, John Alexander, Margaret
Dumont

Hornet's Nest
US 1969   109m   De Luxe
UA / Triangle (Stanley S. Kanter)

In World War II Italy, a wounded US army
demolitions expert is nursed back to health by
child partisans, who help him destroy a German-
held dam.

Overlong war exploits with the children used as a
tiresome gimmick.

w S. S.Schweitzer *d* Phil Karlson *ph* Gabor
Pogani *m* Ennio Morricone

Rock Hudson, Sergio Fantoni, Sylva Koscina,
Jacques Sernas

Horse Feathers****
US 1932   69m   bw
Paramount

A college needs to win at football, and its corrupt
new president knows just how to do it.

Possibly the Marxes' wildest yet most
streamlined kaleidoscope of high jinks and
irreverence, with at least one bright gag or line to
the minute and lively musical interludes to boot.
A classic of zany comedy.

w Bert Kalmar, Harry Ruby, S. J. Perelman,
Will B. Johnstone *d* Norman Z. McLeod
ph Ray June *m/ly* Bert Kalmar, Harry Ruby

Groucho, Chico, Harpo, Zeppo, *Thelma Todd,*
Robert Greig

'The current Marx comedy is the funniest
talkie since the last Marx comedy, and the record
it establishes is not likely to be disturbed until the
next Marx comedy comes along. As for
comparisons, I was too busy having a good time
to make any.'—*Philip K. Scheuer*

The Horse Soldiers*
US 1959   119m   De Luxe
UA / Mirisch (John Lee Mahin, Martin Rackin)

In 1863 a Union cavalry officer is sent three
hundred miles into Confederate territory to
demolish a railroad junction.

Typically sprawling John Ford cavalry western
with not too many high spots and more sombre
ingredients than usual.

w John Lee Mahin, Martin Rackin *d* John Ford
ph William Clothier *m* David Buttolph

John Wayne, William Holden, Constance
Towers, Hoot Gibson

The Horse without a Head**
GB 1963   89m   Technicolor
Walt Disney (Hugh Attwooll)

Stolen money is hidden in an old toy horse, and
crooks trying to get it back clash with police and
children.

Excellent children's adventure with scenes on
trains and in a toy factory.

w T. E. B. Clarke *d* Don Chaffey *ph* Paul
Beeson *m* Eric Rogers

Leo McKern, Jean-Pierre Aumont, Herbert
Lom, Pamela Franklin, Vincent Winter

The Horsemen
US 1970   109m   colour   Super
   Panavision
Columbia / John Frankenheimer—Edward
   Lewis

An Afghan tribesman is determined to rival his
father at horsemanship.

Rather tedious variant on *Taras Bulba*; plenty of
action but not much characterization, or taste, or
interest.

w Dalton Trumbo, *novel* Joseph Kessel *d* John
Frankenheimer *ph* Claude Renoir *m* Georges
Delerue

Omar Sharif, Jack Palance, Leigh Taylor-
Young, Peter Jeffrey, Eric Pohlmann, Despo,
David De Keyser

The Horse's Mouth*
GB 1958   93m   Technicolor
UA / Knightsbridge (John Bryan)

An obsessive painter is a liability to his friends.

Thin but fitfully amusing light study of a social
outcast, with a background of London river and
streets. Too slight for real success.

w Alec Guinness, *novel* Joyce Cary *d* Ronald
Neame *ph* Arthur Ibbetson *m* K. V. Jones from
Prokofiev *paintings* John Bratby

Alec Guinness, Kay Walsh, Renée Houston,
Robert Coote, Arthur Macrae, Michael Gough,
Ernest Thesiger

AAN: Alec Guinness (as actor)

The Hospital**
US 1971   101m   De Luxe   Panavision
UA / Simcha (Howard Gottfried)

A city hospital is beset by weird mishaps, and it
transpires that a killer is on the loose.

Black comedy with the emphasis on sex and
medical ethics; in the same genre as *M*A*S*H*,
and very funny if you can take it.

w Paddy Chayevsky d Arthur Hiller *ph* Victor Kemper *m* Morris Surdin

George C. Scott, Diana Rigg, Barnard Hughes, Nancy Marchand, Richard Dysart

AA: Paddy Chayevsky
AAN: George C. Scott

Hostages
US 1943   88m   bw
Paramount

In occupied Prague, the Nazis seize a variety of hostages and threaten them with death as a reprisal for underground activities.
Modest morale-builder, unfortunately padded out with melodramatics and overacting.

w Lester Cole, Frank Butler, *novel* Stefan Heym *d* Frank Tuttle

Luise Rainer, Paul Lukas, William Bendix, Oscar Homolka, Arturo de Cordova, Katina Paxinou, Roland Varno

Hostile Witness
GB 1968   101m   De Luxe
UA / Caralan / Dador (David E. Rose)

A barrister suffers a nervous breakdown after the death of his daughter and finds himself accused of murder.
Complex courtroom thriller, filmed in a flatly boring way with stagey sets and performances. The plot is the only interest.

w Jack Roffey, from his play *d* Ray Milland *ph* Gerry Gibbs

Ray Milland, Sylvia Sims, Felix Aylmer, Raymond Huntley, Geoffrey Lumsden, Norman Barrs, Percy Marmont, Ewan Roberts

Hot Blood
US 1955   85m   Technicolor
   Cinemascope
Columbia (Howard Welsch)

A dying gypsy king wants his young brother to get married and succeed him.
What promises to be a boring musical proves to be a boring melodrama. Artificial Romany hokum.

w Jesse Lasky Jnr *d* Nicholas Ray *ph* Ray June *m* Les Baxter

Cornel Wilde, Jane Russell, Joseph Calleia, Helen Westcott, Mikhail Rasumny

Hot Enough for June
GB 1963   98m   Eastmancolor
Rank (Betty E. Box)
US title: *Agent 8¾*

A penniless writer is sent to Czechoslovakia on a goodwill mission and finds himself being used as a spy.
Very moderate spoof, neither very funny nor very thrilling.

w Lukas Heller, *novel* The Night before Wenceslas by Lionel Davidson *d* Ralph Thomas *ph* Ernest Steward *m* Angelo Lavagnino

Dirk Bogarde, Sylva Koscina, Robert Morley, Leo McKern, John Le Mesurier

Hot Millions*
US 1968   106m   colour
MGM / Mildred Freed Alberg

A confidence trickster makes a fortune out of fictitious companies.
Elaborate, talky, overlong comedy with irresistible star performances.

w Ira Wallach, Peter Ustinov *d* Eric Till

Peter Ustinov, Maggie Smith, Bob Newhart, Karl Malden, Robert Morley, Cesar Romero

AAN: Ira Wallach, Peter Ustinov (script)

Hot Pepper
US 1933   76m   bw
Fox

Ex-Marines Flagg and Quirt become bootleggers and quarrel over a fiery South American entertainer.
Fourth and last in the comedy-melodrama series stemming from *What Price Glory?* Mild, stereotyped entertainment.

w Barry Connors, Philip Klein, Dudley Nichols *d* John G. Blystone *ph* Charles G. Clarke

Edmund Lowe, Victor McLaglen, Lupe Velez, El Brendel, Lillian Bond

The Hot Rock***
US 1972   105m   De Luxe   Panavision
TCF (Hal Landers, Bobby Roberts)
GB title: *How to Steal a Diamond in Four Uneasy Lessons*

Four crooks plan to rob the Brooklyn Museum of a priceless diamond.
Enjoyable variation on the caper theme, with relaxed comic performances and highly skilled technical back-up. It's refreshing to come across a film which hits its targets so precisely.

w William Goldman, novel Donald E. Westlake *d* Peter Yates *ph* Ed Brown *m* Quincy Jones

Robert Redford, George Segal, Zero Mostel, Paul Sand, Ron Leibman, Moses Gunn, William Redfield

'A funny, fast-paced, inventive and infinitely clever crime comedy, almost as if *The French Connection* had been remade as a piece of urban humour.'—*Michael Korda*

Hot Spell*
US 1958　86m　bw　Vistavision
Paramount / Hal Wallis

In a small southern town, a husband seeks to leave his wife and family for a 20-year-old girl. Overwrought domestic drama slipping perilously close to farce at times, but a good theatrical vehicle for its stars.

w James Poe, *play* Next of Kin by Lonnie Coleman　*d* Daniel Mann　*ph* Loyal Griggs
m Alex North

Anthony Quinn, Shirley Booth, Shirley Maclaine, Earl Holliman, Eileen Heckart

Hot Summer Night*
US 1957　85m　bw
MGM (Morton S. Fine)

A foolhardy reporter determines on an interview with a notorious outlaw, and has to be rescued. Interesting but disappointing low-budget experiment.

w Morton S. Fine, David Friedkin　*d* David Friedkin　*ph* Harold S. Marcorati　*m* André Previn

Leslie Nielsen, Colleen Miller, Edward Andrews, Jay C. Flippen, James Best, Paul Richards, Robert Wilke, Claude Akins

Hotel*
US 1967　124m　Technicolor
Warner (Wendell Mayes)

Guests at a luxurious New Orleans hotel have various problems.
Old-fashioned omnibus drama from a bestseller, quite brightly done.

w Wendell Mayes, *novel* Arthur Hailey
d Richard Quine　*ph* Charles Lang　*m* Johnny Keating

Rod Taylor, Catherine Spaak, Karl Malden, Melvyn Douglas, Merle Oberon, Richard Conte, Michael Rennie, Kevin McCarthy, Alfred Ryder

Hotel Berlin*
US 1945　98m　bw
Warner (Louis F. Edelman)

Various lives intertwine in a Berlin hotel towards the end of the war.
After five years of total war this view of life on the other side can hardly fail to be unconvincing,

but the actors gleefully seize on moments of melodrama.

w Thomas Job, *novel* Vicki Baum　*d* Peter Godfrey　*ph* Carl Guthrie　*m* Franz Waxman

Raymond Massey, Peter Lorre, Faye Emerson, Helmut Dantine, Andrea King, Alan Hale, George Coulouris, Henry Daniell, Helene Thimig, Kurt Kreuger, Steve Geray, Frank Reicher

Hotel for Women
US 1939　83m　bw
TCF (Raymond Griffith)

Young city gold diggers are encouraged by a matron.
Slight comedy drama notable for the acting debut of hostess Elsa Maxwell.

w Katherine Scola, Darrell Ware　*d* Gregory Ratoff　*ph* Peverell Marley

Elsa Maxwell, Linda Darnell, Ann Sothern, James Ellison, John Halliday, Lynn Bari, Alan Dinehart

Hotel Haywire
US 1937　66m　bw
Paramount (Harold Hurley)

An astrologer makes eyes at a dentist's wife, and causes much confusion in a hotel.
Frantic farce which might have been funnier if it had stuck to the original script and cast (it was intended for Burns and Allen).

w Preston Sturges (before studio revision)
d George Archainbaud　*ph* Henry Sharp

Leo Carrillo, Lynne Overman, Mary Carlisle, Benny Baker, Spring Byington, George Barbier, Porter Hall, Lucien Littlefield

Hotel Imperial
US 1939　67m　bw
Paramount

Balkans, 1916: a Polish dancer suspects a Hungarian officer of being responsible for her sister's death.
Dim romantic melodrama with espionage trimmings.

w Gilbert Gabriel, Robert Thoeren, *play* Lajos Biro　*d* Robert Florey　*ph* William Mellor

Ray Milland, Isa Miranda, Reginald Owen, Gene Lockhart, J. Carrol Naish, Curt Bois, Henry Victor, Albert Dekker

Hotel Paradiso*
US 1966　99m　Metrocolor　Panavision
MGM (Peter Glenville)

Various romantic affairs come to a head one evening at a seedy hotel.

A famous boulevard farce seems jellied in aspic in this good-looking but very flatly handled film version, in which famous artists are left to caper about on an unsuitable wide screen with no help from the director.

w Peter Glenville, Jean-Claude Carrière, *play* Georges Feydeau *d* Peter Glenville *ph Henri Decaë m* Laurence Rosenthal *pd François de Lamothe*

Alec Guinness, Gina Lollobrigida, Robert Morley, Peggy Mount, Douglas Byng, Akim Tamiroff, Robertson Hare

Hotel Reserve
GB 1944   89m   bw
RKO (Victor Hanbury)

An Austrian refugee in the south of France is asked by the police to track down a spy among his fellow hotel guests.

Slow, obvious and poorly made suspenser from a good novel.

w John Davenport, *novel* Epitaph for a Spy by Eric Ambler *d* Victor Hanbury, Lance Comfort, Max Greene *ph* Max Greene

James Mason, Lucie Mannheim, Raymond Lovell, Julien Mitchell, Martin Miller, Herbert Lom, Frederick Valk, Valentine Dyall

Hotel Sahara*
GB 1951   96m   bw
GFD / Tower (George H. Brown)

In North Africa during World War II, a small hotel changes its loyalties to suit its occupiers. Overstretched, studio-bound, fitfully amusing comedy.

w George H. Brown, Patrick Kirwan *d* Ken Annakin *ph* David Harcourt *m* Benjamin Franklin

Peter Ustinov, Yvonne de Carlo, David Tomlinson, Roland Culver, Albert Lieven, Bill Owen, Sidney Tafler, Ferdy Mayne

'Cheerful, uncomplicated empty stuff... no more subtle than a music hall sketch.'—*Richard Mallett, Punch*

Houdini*
US 1953   106m   Technicolor
Paramount (George Pal)

In the 1890s a fairground magician shows a passionate talent for escapology and finally kills himself by undertaking increasingly impossible tricks.

Superficial biopic with more attention to

romance than to interesting detail. Some zest in the playing is killed by claustrophobic studio sets.

w Philip Yordan *d* George Marshall *ph* Ernest Laszlo *m* Roy Webb

Tony Curtis, Janet Leigh, Torin Thatcher, Sig Rumann, Angela Clarke

The Hound Dog Man
US 1959   87m   bw
TCF / Company of Artists (Jerry Wald)

An irresponsible country boy gets his come-uppance.

Mild, competent backwoods comedy drama introducing a teenage rave.

w Fred Gipson, Winston Miller *d* Don Siegel *ph* Charles G. Clarke *m* Cyril Mockridge

Fabian, Stuart Whitman, Carol Lynley, Arthur O'Connell, Betty Field, Royal Dano, Jane Darwell, Edgar Buchanan, Claude Akins

The Hound of the Baskervilles**
US 1939   80m   bw
(TCF) Gene Markey

Sherlock Holmes solves the mystery of a supernatural hound threatening the life of a Dartmoor baronet.

Basil Rathbone's first appearance as Sherlock Holmes is in a painstaking studio production which achieves good atmosphere and preserves the flavour if not the letter of the book but is let down by a curious lack of pace.

w Ernest Pascal, *novel* Arthur Conan Doyle *d* Sidney Lanfield *ph* Peverell Marley *m* Cyril Mockridge *ad* Thomas Little

Basil Rathbone, Nigel Bruce, Richard Greene, Wendy Barrie, Lionel Atwill, Morton Lowry, John Carradine, Barlowe Borland, Beryl Mercer, Ralph Forbes, E. E. Clive, Eily Malyon, Mary Gordon

† For Rathbone's other appearances as Holmes see under *Sherlock Holmes*.

The Hound of the Baskervilles*
GB 1959   86m   Technicolor
UA / Hammer (Anthony Hinds)

Spirited remake let down by dogged Hammer insistence on promises of horror and sex; good atmosphere also let down by poor colour.

w Peter Bryan *d* Terence Fisher *ph* Jack Asher *m* James Bernard

Peter Cushing, André Morell, Christopher Lee, Marla Landi, Ewen Solon, Francis de Wolff

Hound of the Baskervilles
GB 1977 85m Technicolor
Hemdale / Michael White Ltd (John
  Goldstone)

A pointless, pitiful and vulgar spoof of an
enjoyable original.

W Dudley Moore, Peter Cook, Paul Morrissey
d Paul Morrissey *ph* Dick Bush, John Wilcox
M Dudley Moore

Peter Cook (Sherlock Holmes), Dudley Moore
(Watson), Denholm Elliot (Stapleton), Terry
Thomas (Mortimer), Joan Greenwood, Max
Wall. Irene Handl, Kenneth Williams, Hugh
Griffith, Roy Kinnear, Penelope Keith, Dana
Gillespie, Prunella Scales, Jessie Matthews,
Spike Milligan

The Hour before the Dawn
US 1944 75m bw
Paramount (William Dozier)

When a pacifist English nobleman discovers
during World War II that he has married a Nazi
spy, he strangles her and joins the forces.
Stultifyingly absurd, badly made and acted
melodrama which its author clearly wished he
had never written, as it was later withdrawn from
his canon.

w Michael Hogan, Lester Samuels, *novel* W.
Somerset Maugham *d* Frank Tuttle *ph* John F.
Seitz *m* Miklos Rozsa

Franchot Tone, Veronica Lake, John Sutton,
Binnie Barnes, Henry Stephenson, Philip
Merivale, Nils Asther, Edmund Breon

Hour of the Gun**
US 1967 101m De Luxe Panavision
UA / Mirisch / Kappa (John Sturges)

After the gunfight at the OK corral, Wyatt Earp
tracks down the rest of the Clanton gang.
Vividly set, slowly developed western which
makes an ambiguous but forceful figure of Earp.
Generally confident and interesting.

*w Edward Anhalt d John Sturges ph Lucien
Ballard m* Jerry Goldsmith

James Garner, Jason Robards Jnr, Robert
Ryan, Steve Ihnat, Michael Tolan, Frank
Converse, Sam Melville, Monte Markham,
Albert Salmi, Jon Voight, William Windom,
Charles Aidman

The Hour of the Wolf*
Sweden 1967 89m bw
Svensk Filmindustri (Lars-Owe Carlberg)
original title: *Vargtimmen*

A painter, at his summer island home with his
wife, is terrorized by monstrous nightmares and
by memories of his own adulterous past.
Rather like the gloomy side of *Smiles of a
Summer Night*, this very typical Bergman
melodrama doesn't quite flow as intended, and
whatever its meaning may be, its surface is less
entertaining than usual.

wd Ingmar Bergman *ph* Sven Nykvist *m* Mars
Johan Werle

Max Von Sydow, Liv Ullmann, Ingrid Thulin,
Erland Josephson

The Hour of Thirteen
GB 1952 78m bw
MGM (Hayes Goetz)

Edwardian London is shocked when policemen
are stabbed one by one.
Jaded Hollywood-English thriller, a remake of
The Mystery of Mr X (qv).

w Leon Gordon, Howard Emmett Rogers, *novel*
X vs Rex by Philip MacDonald *d* Harold
French *ph* Guy Green *m* John Addison

Peter Lawford, Dawn Addams, Roland Culver,
Derek Bond, Leslie Dwyer, Michael Hordern,
Colin Gordon, Heather Thatcher

The House across the Bay
US 1940 88m bw
(UA) Walter Wanger

To protect her racketeer husband from his
enemies, his wife has him convicted of income
tax evasion.
Unpersuasive melodrama, a star potboiler.

w Kathryn Scola *d* Archie Mayo *ph* Merritt
Gerstad *m* Werner Janssen

Joan Bennett, George Raft, Lloyd Nolan, Walter
Pidgeon, Gladys George, June Knight

House Calls*
US 1978 98m Technicolor
Universal (Alex Winitsky, Arlene Sellers)

A middle-aged doctor finds himself widowed and
seeks a new mate.

Spotty comedy which tries to combine
conventional romantic spats with medical satire,
and comes off only in fits and starts.

w Max Shulman, Julius J. Epstein, Alan Mandel,
Charles Shyer *d* Howard Zieff *ph* David M.
Walsh *m* Henry Mancini

Walter Matthau, Glenda Jackson, Art Carney,
Richard Benjamin, Candice Azzara, Thayer
David, Dick O'Neill

A House Divided*
US 1931   70m   bw
Universal (Paul Kohner)

A tough widowed fisherman seeks a new wife,
but she falls in love with his son.
Glum variation on *Desire under the Elms*,
interesting for early Wyler touches.

w John P. Clymer, Dale Van Every, John
Huston, *story* Heart and Hand by Olive Edens
d William Wyler ph Charles Stumar

Walter Huston, Kent Douglass, Helen
Chandler, Vivian Oakland, Frank Hagney,
Mary Foy

The House in Nightmare Park*
GB 1973   95m   Technicolor
EMI / Associated London Films

In 1907, a ham actor is asked to perform at an
old dark house in the country where an axe
murderer prowls during the night.
Standard creepy house comedy thriller, well
enough done though it would have been better
with Bob Hope.

w Clive Exton, Terry Nation *d* Peter Sykes
ph Ian Wilson *m* Harry Robinson

Frankie Howerd, Ray Milland, Hugh Burden,
Kenneth Griffith, John Bennett, Rosalie
Crutchley, Ruth Dunning

The House in the Square*
GB 1951   91m   Technicolor (b/w
  endpieces)
TCF (Sol C. Siegel)
US title: *I'll Never Forget You*

An American atomic chemist living in London
becomes his own ancestor of two hundred years
ago, and falls in love.
Slow-starting but thereafter quite acceptable
remake of *Berkeley Square* (qv), with some
interesting dialogue and a genuinely affecting
fade-out.

w Ranald MacDougall, play John L. Balderston
d Roy Baker *ph* Georges Périnal *m* William
Alwyn *ad* C. P. Norman

Tyrone Power, Ann Blyth, Michael Rennie,
Beatrice Campbell, Dennis Price, Raymond
Huntley, Irene Browne, Robert Atkins (as Dr
Johnson)

A House Is Not a Home
US 1964   98m   bw
(Paramount) Embassy (Clarence Greene)

The life story of New York's most famous
madam, Polly Adler.

Dismal, unappealing, laundered biopic, cheaply
made in an unconvincing period setting.

w Russel Rouse, Clarence Greene *d* Russel
Rouse *ph* Harold Stine *m* Joseph Weiss

Shelley Winters, Robert Taylor, Cesar Romero,
Ralph Taeger, Broderick Crawford

House of Bamboo
US 1955   102m   De Luxe   Cinemascope
TCF (Buddy Adler)

Japanese and American authorities move into
undercover action against Tokyo gangsters.
Routine big-budget crime drama with only the
location in its favour; a time passer, vaguely
adapted from *The Street with No Name* (qv).

w Harry Kleiner *d* Samuel Fuller *ph* Joe
MacDonald *m* Leigh Harline

Robert Stack, Robert Ryan, Shirley Yagamuchi,
Cameron Mitchell, Sessue Hayakawa

House of Cards
US 1968   100m   Techniscope
Universal / Westward (Dick Berg)

An American becomes tutor in the Paris
household of a French general's widow, and
finds himself a pawn in a high-powered game of
international intrigue.
Good-looking location thriller which after an
intricate opening settles into a *39 Steps*-style
chase, but makes little of it.

w James P. Bonner, *novel* Stanley Ellin *d* John
Guillermin *ph* Piero Portalupi *m* Francis Lai

George Peppard, Inger Stevens, Orson Welles,
Keith Michell, William Job, Maxine Audley,
Peter Bayliss

House of Dracula*
US 1945   67m   bw
U–I (Paul Malvern)

As a result of being visited in one evening by
Count Dracula, the Wolf Man and the
Frankenstein monster, a sympathetic doctor
goes on the rampage.
Mind-boggling finale to the first Universal
monster cycle, with a happy ending for the Wolf
Man. Cheaply made and not really inventive, but
has to be seen to be believed.

w Edward T. Lowe *d* Erle C. Kenton
ph George Robinson *m* Edgar Fairchild

Onslow Stevens, John Carradine, Lon Chaney
Jnr, Glenn Strange, Lionel Atwill, Martha
O'Driscoll, Jane Adams

The House of Fear see The Last Warning (1929)

House of Frankenstein*
US 1944 71m bw
U–I (Paul Malvern)

A mad doctor thaws out the monster and the Wolf Man (frozen at the end of *Frankenstein Meets the Wolf Man*) but comes to a sticky end. Originally called *Chamber of Horrors*, this was the studio's first attempt to package its monsters (the first two reels are about Dracula). It could have been pacier in view of the possibilities, but it has its interest.

w Edward T. Lowe, Curt Siodmak d Erle C. Kenton ph George Robinson m Hans Salter

Boris Karloff, John Carradine, Lon Chaney Jnr, George Zucco, J. Carrol Naish, Anne Gwynne, Elena Verdugo, Lionel Atwill, Sig Rumann, Glenn Strange

House of Numbers
US 1957 92m bw Cinemascope
MGM (Charles Schnee)

A man helps his thuggish twin brother escape from prison.
An original melodramatic idea is frittered away through slow pacing.

w Russel Rouse, Don M. Mankiewicz, *novel* Jack Finney d Russel Rouse ph George J. Folsey m André Previn

Jack Palance, Barbara Lang, Harold J. Stone, Edward Platt

The House of Rothschild*
US 1934 87m bw (Technicolor sequence)
Twentieth Century (Darryl F. Zanuck)

The chronicles of the famous banking family at the time of the Napoleonic Wars.
Lavish historical pageant with interesting scenes and performances.

w Nunnally Johnson, *play* George Hembert Westley d Alfred Werker ph Peverell Marley m Alfred Newman

George Arliss, Loretta Young, Boris Karloff, Robert Young, C. Aubrey Smith, Arthur Byron, Helen Westley, Reginald Owen, Florence Arliss, Alan Mowbray, Holmes Herbert

AAN: best picture

House of Secrets
GB 1956 97m Technicolor Vistavision
Rank / Julian Wintle (Vivian A. Cox)

A naval officer is asked to impersonate a lookalike counterfeiter and work undercover to expose the gang.
Old-hat Boys' Own Paper adventure story, mindlessly watchable.

w Robert Buckner, Bryan Forbes d Guy Green ph Harry Waxman m Hubert Clifford

Michael Craig, Julia Arnall, Brenda de Banzie, David Kossoff, Barbara Bates, Gerard Oury, Geoffrey Keen, Anton Diffring

The House of Seven Gables
US 1940 89m bw
Universal

In 17th-century New England, a jealous brother sends his sister's fiancé to prison.
Flat adaptation of a grim, brooding novel; it never grips.

w Lester Cole, *novel* Nathaniel Hawthorne d Joe May ph Milton Krasner m Frank Skinner

George Sanders, Margaret Lindsay, Vincent Price, Alan Napier, Nan Grey, Cecil Kellaway, Dick Foran, Miles Mander

AAN: Frank Skinner

The House of the Angel**
Argentina 1957 73m bw
Argentina Sono Film (Leopoldo Torre Nilsson)
original title: *La Casa del Angel*

A repressed girl is obsessed for life by the shame of her first love affair.
Fascinating minor classic in a heavily Wellesian style.

w Beatriz Guido, Leopoldo Torre Nilsson, Martin Rodriguez Mentasti, *novel* Beatriz Guido d *Leopoldo Torre Nilsson* ph Anibal Gonzalez Paz m Juan Carlos Paz

Elsa Daniel, Lautaro Murua, Guillermo Battaglia
'The first major work of a director of individual vision and strongly national style.'—*Robert Vas, MFB*

House of the Damned*
US 1963 63m bw
TCF / Associated Producers (Maury Dexter)

An architect is asked to make a survey of an old empty castle, but he and his wife find that someone or something is in hiding there.
Corny but mildly effective second feature with a few neat touches.

w Harry Spalding d *Maury Dexter* ph John Nickolaus Jnr m Henry Vars

Ronald Foster, Merry Anders

House of the Seven Hawks

GB 1959   92m   bw
MGM / David E. Rose

An American adventurer becomes involved in a
search by criminals for buried Nazi loot.
Cliché-ridden thick ear, adequately produced
but of no interest.

w Jo Eisinger, *novel* The House of Seven Flies by
Victor Canning d Richard Thorpe ph Ted
Scaife m Clifton Parker

Robert Taylor, Nicole Maurey, Linda Christian,
Donald Wolfit, David Kossoff, Eric Pohlmann,
Gerard Heinz

House of Strangers**

US 1949   101m   bw
TCF (Sol C. Siegel)

An Italian-American banker who rigidly
controls his three sons is arrested for illegal
practices, and the family ties slacken.
Interesting ethnic melodrama with good script
and performances; much remade, e.g. as *Broken
Lance*.

w Philip Yordan, *novel* Jerome Weidman
d Joseph L. Mankiewicz ph Milton Krasner
m Daniele Amfitheatrof

Edward G. Robinson, Richard Conte, Susan
Hayward, *Luther Adler*, Paul Valentine, Efrem
Zimbalist Jnr, Debra Paget, Hope Emerson,
Esther Minciotti, Diana Douglas

House of Usher*

US 1960   85m   Eastmancolor
  Cinemascope
AIP / Alta Vista (Roger Corman)
GB title: *The Fall of the House of Usher*

The last of the Usher line, prone to catalepsy, is
buried alive by her brother and returns to wreak
vengeance.
Stylish but grottily-coloured low-budget horror
which started the Poe cycle of the sixties. A bit
slow, it would have worked better in the standard
screen ratio, but there is a tense and spectacular
finale.

w Richard Matheson, *story* Edgar Allan Poe
d Roger Corman ph Floyd Crosby m Les
Baxter ad Daniel Haller

Vincent Price, Myrna Fahey, Mark Damon,
Harry Ellerbe

House of Wax**

US 1953   88m   Warnercolor   3-D
Warner (Bryan Foy)

Mutilated in a fire at his wax museum, a
demented sculptor arranges a supply of dead
bodies to be covered in wax for exhibition at his
new showplace.
Spirited remake of *The Mystery of the Wax
Museum* (qv); as a piece of screen narrative it
leaves much to be desired, but the sudden shocks
are well managed, perhaps because this is the
first Grade-A 3-D film, packed with gimmicks
irrelevant to the story and originally shown with
stereophonic sound.

w Crane Wilbur d André de Toth ph Bert
Glennon m David Buttolph

Vincent Price (whose horror career began here),
Carolyn Jones, Paul Picerni, Phyllis Kirk, Frank
Lovejoy
†The director could not see the 3-D effect, being
blind in one eye.

House of Women see Caged

House on Haunted Hill

US 1958   75m   bw
Allied Artists / William Castle

An old house which has seen several murders is
the setting for a millionaire's party.
Gimmick ghost story with some (unexplained)
gruesome moments; the most outlandish of its
producer's cheapjack trick films (*Thirteen
Ghosts, The Tingler, Macabre*, etc), it was
originally billed as being in Emergo, which
meant that at an appropriately horrific moment
an illuminated skeleton on wires was suddenly
trundled over the heads of the audience.

w Robb White d William Castle ph Carl
Guthrie m Von Dexter

Vincent Price, Richard Long, Carol Ohmart,
Alan Marshal, Elisha Cook Jnr

The House on 92nd Street****

US 1945   88m   bw
TCF (*Louis de Rochemont*)

During World War II in New York, the FBI
routs Nazi spies after the atomic bomb formula.
Highly influential documentary-style 'now it can
be told' spy drama, which borrowed the feel of its
producer's *March of Time* series and applied
them to a fairly true story set on genuine
locations though with a modicum of fictional
mystery and suspense.
Highly effective in its own right, it looked
forward to *The Naked City* three years later; the
later film unaccountably got most of the credit
for taking Hollywood out into the open air.

w Barre Lyndon, Charles G. Booth, John Monks
Jnr d Henry Hathaway ph Norbert Brodine
m David Buttolph

William Eythe, Lloyd Nolan, Signe Hasso, *Leo G. Carroll*, Gene Lockhart, Lydia St Clair, Harry Bellaver

AAN: original story (Charles G. Booth)

The House on Telegraph Hill
US 1951 93m bw
TCF (Robert Bassler)

A woman in a concentration camp assumes her dead friend's identity so that on release she can be sent to America; but murder threatens there. Modernized amalgam of *Gaslight* and *Suspicion*, not as good as either, but the complexities of the story hold adequate interest.

w Elick Moll, Frank Partos, *novel* Dana Lyon d Robert Wise ph Lucien Ballard m Sol Kaplan

Richard Basehart, Valentina Cortesa, William Lundigan, Fay Baker, Gordon Gebert, Steve Geray

The House that Dripped Blood *
GB 1970 102m Eastmancolor
Amicus (Milton Subotsky)

A Scotland Yard man investigating a disappearance is led to a house with a murderous history.
Quartet of stories in *Dead of Night* style, neatly made and generally pleasing despite a low level of originality in the writing.

w Robert Bloch d Peter John Duffell ph Robert Parslow m Michael Dress

John Bennett, Christopher Lee, Peter Cushing, Denholm Elliott, Joanna Dunham, Nyree Dawn Porter, Jon Pertwee, Ingrid Pitt

Houseboat
US 1958 110m Technicolor Vistavision
Paramount / Scribe (Jack Rose)

A widower with three children engages a maid who is really a socialite, and they all set up house on a boat.
Artificial sentimental comedy with A-1 credits but little style or bite.

w Melville Shavelson, Jack Rose d Jack Rose ph Ray June m George Duning

Cary Grant, Sophia Loren, Martha Hyer, Eduardo Ciannelli, Harry Guardino

AAN: script; song 'Almost In Your Arms' (m/ly Jay Livingston, Ray Evans)

The Housekeeper's Daughter *
US 1939 71m bw
Hal Roach

A gangster's moll returns to mama for a visit and falls in love with the stuffy son of the household. Zany crime farce which too often lets its zip fade, but atones in a crazy firework finale.

w Rian James, Gordon Douglas, *novel* Donald Henderson Clarke d Hal Roach ph Norbert Brodine m Amedeo de Filippi

Joan Bennett, John Hubbard, Adolphe Menjou, William Gargan, George E. Stone, Peggy Wood, Donald Meek, Marc Lawrence, Lilian Bond, Victor Mature, Luis Alberni

Housemaster *
GB 1938 95m bw
ABPC (Walter C. Mycroft)

A schoolmaster sides with his boys against the new headmaster's dictatorial methods.
Pleasing photographed play with all concerned in good form.

w Dudley Leslie, Elizabeth Meehan, *play* Bachelor Born by Ian Hay d Herbert Brenon

Otto Kruger, Diana Churchill, Phillips Holmes, Joyce Barbour, Kynaston Reeves, Rene Ray, Walter Hudd, John Wood, Cecil Parker, Michael Shepley, Jimmy Hanley

Housewife
US 1934 69m bw
Warner

For an advertising copywriter, success almost brings divorce.
Modestly efficient romantic programmer of its day.

w Manuel Seff, Lillie Hayward d Alfred E. Green ph William Rees m Leo F. Forbstein

Bette Davis, George Brent, Ann Dvorak, John Halliday, Ruth Donnelly, Hobart Cavanaugh, Robert Barrat, Phil Regan

'The dramatic punches are not merely telegraphed, but radioed.' —*Frank S. Nugent*

How Do I Love Thee
US 1970 109m Metrocolor
ABC (Robert Enders, Everett Freeman)

A philosophy professor recalls the odd career of his atheist father.
Curious comedy about an eccentric and his family relationships, a kind of *Cheaper by the Dozen* with religion added. Not on in 1970.

w Everett Freeman, *novel* Let Me Count the Ways by Peter De Vries d Michael Gordon ph Russell Metty m Randy Sparks

James Gleason, Maureen O'Hara, Shelley Winters, Rick Lenz, Rosemary Forsyth

How Green Was My Valley***
US 1941 118m bw
TCF (Darryl F. Zanuck)

Memories of childhood in a Welsh mining village.

Prettified and unconvincing but dramatically very effective tearjerker in the style which lasted from Cukor's *David Copperfield* to *The Green Years*. High production values here add a touch of extra class, turning the result into a Hollywood milestone despite its intrinsic inadequacies.

w Philip Dunne, *novel* Richard Llewellyn d John Ford ph Arthur Miller m Alfred Newman

Walter Pidgeon, Maureen O'Hara, Roddy McDowall, Donald Crisp, Sara Allgood, Anna Lee, John Loder, Barry Fitzgerald, Patric Knowles, Morton Lowry, Arthur Shields, Frederic Worlock

'Perfection of cinematic narrative . . . pure visual action, pictures powerfully composed, dramatically photographed, smoothly and eloquently put together.'—*James Shelley Hamilton*

AA: best picture; John Ford; Arthur Miller; Donald Crisp

AAN: Philip Dunne; Alfred Newman; Sara Allgood

How I Won the War
GB 1967 110m Eastmancolor
UA / Petersham (Richard Lester)

During World War II an earnest young man becomes an officer and survives many tribulations including the death of his comrades. Appalling kaleidoscope of black comedy and the director's own brand of uncontrolled cinematic zaniness, with echoes of *Candide* and *Oh What a Lovely War!* Just the way to alienate a paying audience.

w Charles Wood, *novel* Patrick Ryan d Richard Lester ph David Watkin m Ken Thorne

Michael Crawford, John Lennon, Roy Kinnear, Lee Montague, Jack McGowran, Michael Hordern, Jack Hedley, Karl Michael Vogler, Ronald Lacey, James Cossins, Alexander Knox

'Pretentious tomfoolery.'—*John Simon*

'One feels that Lester has bitten off more than he can chew . . . the ideas misfire, lost somewhere between the paper on which they were conceived and the celluloid on which they finally appear.'—*MFB*

How Sweet It Is*
US 1968 98m Technicolor Panavision
Warner / Cherokee / National General (Garry Marshall, Jerry Belson)

Suspicious of their son's intentions towards his girl friend on a European holiday, a middle-aged American couple decide to follow.

Good-looking, rather silly comedy, plain spoken in the modern manner but without much entertainment value except when farce gets the upper hand.

w Garry Marshall, Jerry Belson, *novel* The Girl in the Turquoise Bikini by Muriel Resnik d Jerry Paris ph Lucien Ballard m Pat Williams

James Garner, Debbie Reynolds, Maurice Ronet, Paul Lynde, Marcel Dalio, Terry-Thomas, Donald Losby, Hilarie Thompson

'One of those slender marital farces in which the behaviour of the adults is consistently more juvenile than that of the teenagers.'—*MFB*

How the West Was Won*
US 1962 162m Technicolor Cinerama
MGM / Cinerama (Bernard Smith)

Panoramic western following the daughter of a pioneering family from youth (1830) to old age, with several half-relevant stories along the way. Muddled spectacular with splendid set-pieces but abysmal dullness in between, especially if not seen in three-strip Cinerama (the Cinemascope prints are muddy and still show the dividing lines). An all-star fairground show of its time.

w James R. Webb d Henry Hathaway (first half), John Ford (Civil War), George Marshall (train) ph William Daniels, Milton Krasner, Charles Lang Jnr, Joseph La Shelle m Alfred Newman ad George W. Davis, William Ferrari, Addison Hehr

Debbie Reynolds, Carroll Baker, Lee J. Cobb, Henry Fonda, Carolyn Jones, Karl Malden, Gregory Peck, George Peppard, Robert Preston, James Stewart, Eli Wallach, John Wayne, Richard Widmark, Brigid Bazlen, Walter Brennan, David Brian, Andy Devine, Raymond Massey, Agnes Moorehead, Henry Morgan, Thelma Ritter, Russ Tamblyn, Spencer Tracy (narrator)

'That goddamned Cinerama . . . do you know a waist shot is as close as you could get with that thing?'—*Henry Hathaway*

AA: James R. Webb

AAN: best picture; photography; music

How to Be Very Very Popular
US 1955 89m De Luxe Cinemascope
TCF (Nunnally Johnson)

Two belly dancers on the run from gangsters hide out in a co-ed college.

Wacky remake of *She Loves Me Not* (qv); tries hard for a vein of freewheeling lunacy but only occasionally achieves it. A few numbers might have helped.

wd Nunnally Johnson *ph* Milton Krasner *m* Cyril Mockridge

Betty Grable, Sheree North, *Charles Coburn*, Robert Cummings, Orson Bean, Fred Clark, Tommy Noonan

How to Commit Marriage
US 1969 98m Technicolor
Cinerama / Naho (Bill Larence)

A couple decide to divorce, with repercussions on their family and in-laws.
Tiresome generation-gap comedy.

w Ben Starr, Michael Kanin *d* Norman Panama *ph* Charles Lang *m* Joseph J. Lilley

Bob Hope, Jackie Gleason, Jane Wyman, Leslie Nielsen, Maureen Arthur, Paul Stewart, Tina Louise

How to Marry a Millionaire **
US 1953 96m Technicolor
Cinemascope
TCF (Nunnally Johnson)

Three girls rent an expensive New York apartment and set out to trap millionaires. Cinemascope's first attempt at modern comedy was not quite as disastrous as might have been expected, largely because of the expensiveness of everything and the several stars still brightly twinkling, but the handling of this variation on the old *Golddiggers* theme, while entirely amiable, is dramatically very slack.

w Nunnally Johnson *d* Jean Negulesco *ph* Joe MacDonald *md* Alfred Newman *m* Cyril Mockridge

Lauren Bacall, Marilyn Monroe, Betty Grable, *William Powell*, Cameron Mitchell, David Wayne, Rory Calhoun, Alex D'Arcy, Fred Clark

How to Murder a Rich Uncle
GB 1957 80m bw Cinemascope
Columbia / Warwick (Ronald Kinnoch)

An impoverished nobleman decides to murder his rich old uncle.
Feebly-handled black comedy which does not come off at all despite a highly talented cast.

w John Paxton, *play* Il faut tuer Julie by Dider Daix *d* Nigel Patrick *ph* Ted Moore

Nigel Patrick, Charles Coburn, *Katie Johnson*, Wendy Hiller, Anthony Newley, Athene Seyler, Michael Caine, Noel Hood, Kenneth Fortescue

How to Murder Your Wife *
US 1964 118m Technicolor
UA / Murder Inc (George Axelrod)

A strip cartoonist tests out his violent scenes in real life; when his wife disappears he finds himself accused of murder.
Amusing preliminaries give way to dreary plot complications and an overlong courtroom scene. Leave after the first hour.

w George Axelrod *d* Richard Quine *ph* Harry Stradling *m* Neal Hefti *pd Richard Sylbert*

Jack Lemmon, Virna Lisi, *Terry-Thomas, Eddie Mayehoff*, Sidney Blackmer, Claire Trevor

How to Save a Marriage and Ruin Your Life
US 1968 102m Technicolor Panavision
Columbia / Nob Hill (Stanley Shapiro)

An attorney takes it upon himself to convince his friend of the infidelity of the friend's mistress . . .
Tedious sex antics without any sex; a few smiles are not enough to endear it.

w Stanley Shapiro, Nate Monaster *d* Fielder Cook *ph* Lee Garmes *m* Michel Legrand

Dean Martin, Eli Wallach, Stella Stevens, Anne Jackson, Betty Field, Jack Albertson, Katharine Bard

'Another variation on Hollywood's patent version of the Restoration comedy, which as usual abandons the lustiness of its 17th-century prototype in favour of guilt-ridden lechery and a fundamental respect for the married state.'— *MFB*

How to Steal a Million *
US 1966 127m De Luxe Panavision
TCF / World Wide (Fred Kohlmar)

The daughter of an art forger mistakenly involves a private detective in a robbery. High-class but rather boring romantic comedy; the credits promise much but interest wanes quickly owing to uncertain handling.

w Harry Kurnitz *d* William Wyler *ph* Charles Lang *m* Johnny Williams

Audrey Hepburn, Peter O'Toole, Charles Boyer, Hugh Griffith, Eli Wallach, Fernand Gravet, Marcel Dalio

'Terribly wordy and slow . . . Wyler hasn't got the touch nowadays.'—*Sight and Sound*

How to Succeed in Business without Really Trying **
US 1967 121m De Luxe Panavision
UA / Mirisch (David Swift)

A window cleaner cajoles his way to the top of a New York company.

Cinematically uninventive but otherwise brisk and glowing adaptation of a sharp, slick Broadway musical.

w David Swift, *musical book* Abe Burrows, Jack Weinstock, Willie Gilbert, *book* Shepherd Mead *d* David Swift *ph* Burnett Guffey *m/ly Frank Loesser ch* Dale Moreda after Bob Fosse

Robert Morse, Rudy Vallee, Michele Lee, Anthony Teague, Maureen Arthur, Murray Matheson

'Shows how taste and talent can succeed in bringing a stage musical to the screen with its virtues intact.'—*John Cutts*

The Howards of Virginia

US 1940   117m   bw
Columbia (Frank Lloyd)
GB title: *The Tree of Liberty*

A Virginian surveyor finds himself involved in the Revolutionary War.

Historical cavalcade in which central miscasting seems to cast a shadow of artifice over the whole. Interesting but seldom stimulating.

w Sidney Buchman, *novel* The Tree of Liberty by Elizabeth Page *d* Frank Lloyd *ph* Bert Glennon *m* Richard Hageman

Cary Grant, Martha Scott, Cedric Hardwicke, Alan Marshal, Richard Carlson, Paul Kelly, Irving Bacon, Elizabeth Risdon

AAN: Richard Hageman

Huckleberry Finn

US 1931   71m   bw
Paramount

The river adventures of Mark Twain's scapegrace hero.
Adequate early talkie family film.

d Norman Taurog

Jackie Coogan, Junior Durkin, Mitzi Green, Jackie Searl, Eugene Pallette

Huckleberry Finn**

US 1939   90m   bw
MGM (Joseph L. Mankiewicz)

Solidly competent remake with excellent production values and several entertaining sequences.

w Hugo Butler *d* Richard Thorpe *ph* John Seitz

Mickey Rooney, Walter Connolly, William Frawley, Rex Ingram

Huckleberry Finn*

US 1960   107m   Metrocolor
MGM
aka: *The Adventures of Huckleberry Finn*

Another patchy remake.

w James Lee *d* Michael Curtiz

Eddie Hodges, Tony Randall, Archie Moore, Neville Brand, Judy Canova, Buster Keaton, Andy Devine

Huckleberry Finn

US 1974   118m   De Luxe   Panavision
UA / Apjac / Readers Digest (Robert Greenhut)

Ambitious but lustreless version of the famous story, with songs.

w/ly/m Richard M. Sherman, Robert B. Sherman *d* J. Lee-Thompson *ph* Laszlo Kovacs *pd* Philip Jeffries

Jeff East, Paul Winfield, David Wayne, Harvey Korman, Arthur O'Connell, Gary Merrill, Natalie Trundy

'It expires in a morass of treacle.'—*Tom Milne*

'It transforms a great work of fiction into something bland, boring and tasteless.'—*Michael Billington, Illustrated London News*

The Hucksters**

US 1947   115m   bw
MGM (Arthur Hornblow Jnr)

Back from the war, an advertising executive finds it difficult to put up with his clients' tantrums.

Good topical entertainment which still entertains and gives a good impression of its period.

w Luther Davis, *novel* Frederic Wakeman *d* Jack Conway *ph* Harold Rosson *m* Lennie Hayton

Clark Gable, Deborah Kerr, Ava Gardner, *Sidney Greenstreet*, Adolphe Menjou, Keenan Wynn, Edward Arnold, Aubrey Mather

'A good picture, quick and to the point.'—*Photoplay*

Hud***

US 1963   112m   bw   Panavision
Paramount / Salem / Dover (Martin Ritt, Irving Ravetch)

Life is hard on a Texas ranch, and the veteran owner is not helped by his sexually arrogant ne'er-do-well son, who is a bad influence on the household.

Superbly set in an arid landscape, this incisive

character drama is extremely well directed and acted but somehow lacks the touch of greatness.

w Irving Ravetch, Harriet Frank, novel Horseman Pass By by Larry McMurty *d Martin Ritt ph James Wong Howe m* Elmer Bernstein

Paul Newman, Patricia Neal, Melvyn Douglas, Brandon de Wilde

AA: James Wong Howe; Patricia Neal; Melvyn Douglas
AAN: script; Martin Ritt; Paul Newman

Hudson's Bay**
US 1940 95m bw
TCF (Kenneth MacGowan)

Pierre Radisson, a French Canadian trapper, opens up millions of acres of northern wilderness for England.
Well-made historical saga with good production and performances.

w Lamar Trotti d Irving Pichel ph Peverell Marley, George Barnes *m* Alfred Newman *ad* Richard Day, Wiard B. Ihnen

Paul Muni, Laird Cregar, Gene Tierney, John Sutton, Virginia Field, Vincent Price (as King Charles II), Nigel Bruce, Morton Lowry, Robert Greig, Frederic Worlock, Montagu Love

Hue and Cry***
GB 1946 82m bw
Ealing

East End boys discover that their favourite boys' paper is being used by crooks to pass information.
The first 'Ealing comedy' uses vivid London locations as background for a sturdy comic plot with a climax in which the criminals are rounded up by thousands of boys swarming over dockland.

w T. E. B. Clarke d Charles Crichton ph Douglas Slocombe, John Seaholme

Alastair Sim, Jack Warner, Harry Fowler, Valerie White, Frederick Piper
  'Refreshing, bloodtingling and disarming.'— *Richard Winnington*

Hugo the Hippo
US 1975 78m colour
Brut (Robert Halmi)

An independently-minded hippo combats a Zanzibar magician.
Uninventive cartoon feature, endearing neither in characterization nor in draughtsmanship.

w Thomas Baum *d* William Feigenbaum *md* Bert Keyes

Hugs and Kisses*
Sweden 1966 96m bw
Sandrews (Göran Lindgren)
original title: *Puss och Kram*

A destitute bohemian takes over the house and the wife of the old executive friend who shelters him out of pity.
Rather like a comedy version of the Dirk Stroeve section of *The Moon and Sixpence,* this sophisticated film came under censorship fire for depicting the first full frontal female.

wd Jonas Cornell *ph* Lars Swanberg *m* Bengt Ernryd

Sven-Bertil Taube, Agneta Ekmanner, Hakan Serner
  'The brilliance of the film lies in the way humour and sadness are kept in perfect equilibrium.'—*MFB*

Huis Clos*
France 1954 99m bw
Films Marceau

Two women and a man die, go to hell, and are locked up for ever in an elegant room.
Rather flat intellectual fantasy from a play which made great waves when first performed.

w Pierre Laroche, *play* Jean-Paul Sartre *d* Jacqueline Audry *ph* Robert Juillard *m* Joseph Kosma

Arletty, Frank Villard, Gaby Sylvia
  'Without the ecstasy, terror and poetic imagination of a Cocteau, the subject becomes a fatally stationary one.'—*Peter John Dyer, MFB*

The Human Comedy*
US 1943 117m bw
MGM (Clarence Brown)

In a small town during the war, a telegram boy brings tragedy to others and is touched by it himself.
Gooey, sentimental morale booster in the best MGM tradition, a variant on the Hardy family series but with all the pretensions of its author.

w Howard Estabrook, *novel* William Saroyan *d Clarence Brown ph* Harry Stradling

Mickey Rooney, Frank Morgan, James Craig, Marsha Hunt, Jackie Jenkins, Fay Bainter, Ray Collins, Van Johnson, Donna Reed
  'The dignity and simplicity of the ideas shade off into cheap pretentiousness.'—*Bosley Crowther*

'The best one can say of it . . . is that it tries on the whole to be "faithful" to Saroyan; not invariably a good idea.'—*James Agee*

AAN: best picture; Clarence Brown; Harry Stradling; Mickey Rooney

Human Desire
US 1954   90m   bw
Columbia (Lewis J. Rachmil)

A jealous railway official forces his wife to help him murder her suspected lover.
Drab and unattractive remake of *La Bête Humaine*.

w Alfred Hayes *d* Fritz Lang *ph* Burnett Guffey *m* Daniele Amfitheatrof

Gloria Grahame, Glenn Ford, Broderick Crawford, Edgar Buchanan

Humoresque**
US 1947   125m   bw
Warner (Jerry Wald)

An ambitious violinist gets emotionally involved with his wealthy patroness.
Lush soaper about suffering in high society, complete with tragic end and lashings of classical music (Isaac Stern on the sound track).

w Clifford Odets, Zachary Gold, *novel* Fannie Hurst *d* Jean Negulesco *ph* Ernest Haller *md* Franz Waxman

Joan Crawford, John Garfield, Oscar Levant, J. Carrol Naish, Joan Chandler, Tom D'Andrea, Craig Stevens, Ruth Nelson

AAN: Franz Waxman

The Hunchback of Notre Dame**
US 1923   120m approx (24 fps)   bw
   silent
Universal

The deformed Notre Dame bellringer rescues a gypsy girl from the evil intentions of her guardian.
Victorian gothic version with a riveting star performance.

w Percy Poore Sheehan, Edward T. Lowe Jnr, *novel* Notre Dame de Paris by Victor Hugo *d* Wallace Worsley *ph* Robert S. Newhard, Tony Kornman

Lon Chaney, Patsy Ruth Miller, Norman Kerry, Ernest Torrence, Gladys Brockwell, Kate Lester, Brandon Hurst, Tully Marshall

The Hunchback of Notre Dame****
US 1939   117m   bw
RKO (Pandro S. Berman)

This superb remake is one of the best examples of Hollywood expertise at work: art direction, set construction, costumes, camera, lighting and above all direction brilliantly support an irresistible story and bravura acting.

w Sonya Levien, Bruno Frank d William Dieterle ph Joseph H. August m Alfred Newman ad Van Nest Polglase

Charles Laughton, Cedric Hardwicke, Maureen O'Hara, Edmond O'Brien, Thomas Mitchell, Harry Davenport, Walter Hampden, Alan Marshal, George Zucco, Katherine Alexander, Fritz Leiber, Rod la Rocque

'Has seldom been bettered as an evocation of medieval life.'—*John Baxter, 1968*

'It exceeds in sheer magnificence any similar film in history. Sets are vast and rich in detail, crowds are immense, and camera uses of both are versatile, varied and veracious.'—*Motion Picture Herald*

† Other versions: *Esmeralda* (1906, French); *Notre Dame de Paris* (1911, French); *The Darling of Paris* (1917, US, with Theda Bara); and see above and below.

AAN: Alfred Newman

The Hunchback of Notre Dame
France / Italy 1956   107m   Eastmancolor
   Cinemascope
Paris Films / Panitalia (Robert and Raymond Hakim)

Crude international rehash with nothing to commend it, though the script before dubbing may have been interesting.

w Jacques Prévert, Jean Aurenche *d* Jean Delannoy *ph* Michel Kelber *m* Georges Auric

Anthony Quinn, Gina Lollobrigida, Jean Danet, Alain Cuny, Robert Hirsch

The Hundred Pound Window
GB 1943   84m   bw
Warner

A racecourse clerk becomes involved with gamblers who bribe him to rig the totalizator, but he finally exposes them.
Routine programmer notable only for giving a leading role to an old character actor.

w Abem Finkel, Brock Williams, Rodney Ackland *d* Brian Desmond Hurst

Frederick Leister, Mary Clare, Anne Crawford, Richard Attenborough, David Farrar, Niall MacGinnis, David Hutcheson

Hungry Hill

GB 1946   92m   bw
GFD / Two Cities (William Sistrom)

An Irish family feud spans three generations.
Rather uninteresting costume melodrama.

*w Daphne du Maurier, Terence Young, Francis
Crowdy d Brian Desmond Hurst*

Margaret Lockwood, Dennis Price, Cecil
Parker, Michael Denison, F. J. McCormick,
Dermot Walsh, Jean Simmons, Eileen Herlie,
Siobhan McKenna, Eileen Crowe, Dan
O'Herlihy

Hunted*

GB 1952   84m   bw
GFD / Independent Artists (Julian Wintle)
US title: *The Stranger in Between*

A runaway boy joins forces with a runaway
murderer, and the latter sacrifices himself for the
boy's safety.
Predictable pattern melodrama, nicely made and
acted.

*w Jack Whittingham d Charles Crichton
ph Eric Cross m Hubert Clifford*

Dirk Bogarde, Jon Whiteley, Kay Walsh,
Elizabeth Sellars, Frederick Piper, Geoffrey
Keen, Julian Somers

Hunted Men*

US 1938   67m   bw
Paramount

A killer on the run moves into a private home
and is outwitted by the head of the house.
Competent second feature which sticks in the
memory.

*w Horace McCoy, William R. Lipman d Louis
King ph Victor Milner*

Lloyd Nolan, Lynne Overman, Mary Carlisle, J.
Carrol Naish, Anthony Quinn, Dorothy
Peterson

The Hunters

US 1958   108m   De Luxe   Cinemascope
TCF (Dick Powell)

A fearless American pilot is sent to Korea on a
special mission.
Standard war thriller, good to look at when
airborne but pretty boring on the ground;
propaganda element very strong.

*w Wendell Mayes d Dick Powell ph Charles G.
Clarke m Paul Sawtell*

Robert Mitchum, Robert Wagner, Richard
Egan, Mai Britt

The Hunting Party

US 1971   108m   De Luxe
UA / Brighton / Levy–Gardner–Levy

A sadistic Texas baron sets out to shoot one by
one the outlaws who have kidnapped his wife.
Crude, brutish and repellent melodrama: the
epitome of permissiveness, replete with gore,
rape and sadism.

*w William Norton, Gilbert Alexander, Lou
Morheim d Don Medford ph Cecilio Paniagua
m Riz Ortolani*

Gene Hackman, Candice Bergen, Oliver Reed

The Hurricane**

US 1937   110m   bw
Samuel Goldwyn (Merritt Hulburd)

The simple life on a South Pacific island is
disrupted, not only by a vindictive governor but
by a typhoon.
Tolerable island melodrama with a spectacular
climax and a generally good cast.

w Dudley Nichols, Oliver H. P. Garrett, novel
Charles Nordhof, James Norman Hall *d John
Ford, Stuart Heisler ph Bert Glennon m Alfred
Newman*

Dorothy Lamour, Jon Hall, *C. Aubrey Smith,
Mary Astor, Raymond Massey, Thomas
Mitchell*, John Carradine, Jerome Cowan
†Remade in 1979.

AAN: Alfred Newman; Thomas Mitchell

Hurricane Smith

US 1952   90m   Technicolor
Paramount / Nat Holt

An adventurer charters a boat to find a South
Sea treasure but the boat owner turns the tables
on him.
Standard thick ear with plenty of action.

*w Frank Gruber d Jerry Hopper ph Ray
Rennahan m Paul Sawtell*

John Ireland, Yvonne de Carlo, James Craig,
Forrest Tucker

Hurry Sundown

US 1967   146m   Technicolor   Panavision
Paramount / Sigma (Otto Preminger)

Post-war racial problems in Georgia farmland,
with degenerate whites and noble blacks.
Incredibly cliché-ridden epic melodrama with
action and sex asides, from a rock bottom
bestseller. It long outstays its welcome even for
unintentional hilarity.

w Thomas C. Ryan, Horton Foote, novel K. B.

Gilden *d* Otto Preminger *ph* Loyal Griggs, Milton Krasner *m* Hugo Montenegro

Jane Fonda, Michael Caine, Rex Ingram, Diahann Carroll, Burgess Meredith, John Philip Law, Robert Hooks, Faye Dunaway, Beah Richards, George Kennedy, Madeleine Sherwood

'Critic Wilfrid Sheed wrote recently that no film is ever so bad that you can't find some virtue in it. He must not have seen *Hurry Sundown*.'— *Rex Reed*

'To criticize it would be like tripping a dwarf.'—*Wilfrid Sheed*

'A pantomime version of Greek tragedy.'— *MFB*

Husbands*
US 1970   154m   De Luxe
Columbia / Faces Music Inc (Al Ruban)

Three married men, shocked by the death of their friend, impulsively get drunk, fly to London and set out on a weekend of dissipation.
Irritatingly rough hewn and insanely overlong, this half-improvised tragi-comedy forces three good actors to overplay embarrassingly; but its best moments are memorable.

wd John Cassavetes *ph* Victor Kemper *m* none

Peter Falk, John Cassavetes, Ben Gazzara

Hush Hush Sweet Charlotte**
US 1964   133m   bw
TCF / Associates and Aldrich

A southern belle lives thirty-seven years in a lonely mansion tormented by nightmarish memories of her fiancé's murder. Suddenly, after a series of apparent hauntings and other strange events, she finds she didn't do it.
Padded but generally enjoyable replay of elements from *Whatever Happened to Baby Jane*, with a large helping of *Les Diaboliques*. The stars help more than the director.

w Henry Farrell, Lukas Heller *d* Robert Aldrich *ph* Joseph Biroc *m* Frank de Vol *ad* William Glasgow

Bette Davis, Olivia de Havilland, Joseph Cotten, Cecil Kellaway, Victor Buono, William Marshall, Mary Astor, Agnes Moorehead

'The blood is on the cleaver, the madwoman is on the loose, the headless corpse is on the prowl and the Guignol is about as grand as it can get.'—*Judith Crist*

AAN: Joseph Biroc; Frank de Vol; Agnes Moorehead; title song (*m* Frank de Vol, *ly* Mack David)

Hustle
US 1975   118m   Eastmancolor
Paramount / RoBurt (Robert Aldrich)

A police lieutenant lives with a call girl and is drawn into her corrupt life.
Doleful crime melodrama with both eyes in the gutter.

w Steve Shagan *d* Robert Aldrich *ph* Joseph Biroc *m* Frank de Vol

Burt Reynolds, Catherine Deneuve, Ben Johnson, Paul Winfield, Eileen Brennan, Eddie Albert, Ernest Borgnine, Catherine Bach, Jack Carter

'A fine companion piece to *Kiss Me Deadly* in its vision of a journey to the end of the night in quest of a myth.'—*Tim Milne*

'Even with such a meandering script as this, one expects more than the paltry fare Aldrich offers.'—*Paul Coleman*

The Hustler**
US 1961   135m   bw   Cinemascope
TCF / Robert Rossen

A pool room con man comes to grief when he falls in love.
Downbeat melodrama with brilliantly handled and atmospheric pool table scenes; the love interest is redundant.

w Robert Rossen, Sidney Carroll, *novel* Walter Tevis *d* Robert Rossen *ph* Eugen Schufftan *m* Kenyon Hopkins

Paul Newman, Jackie Gleason, George C. Scott, Piper Laurie, Myron McCormick, Murray Hamilton, Michael Constantine

'There is an overall impression of intense violence, and the air of spiritual decadence has rarely been conveyed so vividly.'—*David Robinson*

AA: Eugen Schufftan
AAN: best picture; script; Robert Rossen (as director); Paul Newman; Jackie Gleason; George C. Scott; Piper Laurie

Hysteria
GB 1964   85m   bw
MGM / Hammer (Jimmy Sangster)

An American suffering from amnesia is discharged from a London clinic and walks into a murder plot.

Complicated and rather unsympathetic Hammer twister.

w Jimmy Sangster *d* Freddie Francis *ph* John Wilcox *m* Don Banks

Robert Webber, Lelia Goldoni, Anthony Newlands, Jennifer Jayne, *Maurice Denham, Peter Woodthorpe*

I

I Accuse*
GB 1958 99m bw Cinemascope
MGM (Sam Zimbalist)

In 1894 Paris, Alfred Dreyfus is tried for treason and later defended by Emile Zola.
A well tried historical incident is stolidly retold and unsuitably wide-screened; the star cast tends to flounder for lack of assistance.

w Gore Vidal *d* Jose Ferrer *ph* Frederick A. Young *m* William Alwyn

Jose Ferrer (Dreyfus), *Anton Walbrook* (Esterhazy), Emlyn Williams (Zola), Viveca Lindfors, David Farrar, Leo Genn, Herbert Lom, Harry Andrews, Felix Aylmer, George Coulouris, Donald Wolfit

I Aim at the Stars
US 1960 107m bw
Columbia / Morningside / Fama (Charles H. Schneer)

The story of German rocket expert Wernher Von Braun and his later work on American space vehicles.
Shaky biopic of a controversial scientist who changed sides.

w Jay Dratler *d* J. Lee-Thompson *ph* Wilkie Cooper *m* Laurie Johnson

Curt Jurgens, Herbert Lom, James Daly, Gia Scala, Victoria Shaw, Adrian Hoven, Karel Stepanek

'Mannered panning shots and crafty cutting abound, leading to a stylistic St Vitus' Dance.'—
John Gillett

I Am a Camera
GB 1955 99m bw
Romulus (Jack Clayton)

A young English writer observes life in Berlin in the early thirties, and has a platonic relationship with an amoral and reckless young English girl.
A rather flat and flabby treatment of the stories by Christopher Isherwood and the play by John Van Druten, all better known these days in the form of *Cabaret*. Disappointingly unstylish.

w John Collier *d* Henry Cornelius *ph* Guy Green *m* Malcolm Arnold

Julie Harris, Laurence Harvey, Shelley Winters, Ron Randell, Anton Diffring

I Am a Fugitive from a Chain Gang****
US 1932 90m bw
Warner (Hal B. Wallis)

An innocent man is convicted and after brutal treatment with the chain gang becomes a vicious criminal on the run.
Horrifying story in the semi-documentary manner; a milestone in Hollywood history and still a fairly compelling piece of shock entertainment.

w *Sheridan Gibney, Brown Holmes, Robert E. Burns* *d* Mervyn Le Roy *ph* Sol Polito

Paul Muni, Glenda Farrell, Helen Vinson, Preston Foster, Allen Jenkins, Edward J. Macnamara, Berton Churchill, Edward Ellis

'To be enthusiastically commended for its courage, artistic sincerity, dramatic vigour, high entertainment concept and social message.'—
Wilton A. Barrett

AAN: best picture; Paul Muni

I Am the Law*
US 1938 83m bw
Columbia (Everett Riskin)

A law professor is asked by a civic leader to become a special prosecutor cleaning up rackets. Adequate star potboiler, quite enjoyable.

w Jo Swerling *d* Alexander Hall *ph* Henry Freulich *md* Morris Stoloff

Edward G. Robinson, Otto Kruger, John Beal, Barbara O'Neil, Wendy Barrie, Arthur Loft, Marc Lawrence

I Believe in You*
GB 1952 95m bw
Ealing (Michael Relph)

Interwoven stories of probation officers; watchable and reasonable but not very compelling.

w Michael Relph, Basil Dearden, Jack Whittingham, Nicholas Phipps *d* Basil Dearden

Celia Johnson, Cecil Parker, Godfrey Tearle, Harry Fowler, George Relph, Joan Collins,

Laurence Harvey, Ernest Jay, Ursula Howells,
Sidney James, Katie Johnson, Ada Reeve,
Brenda de Banzie

I Can Get It for You Wholesale*
US 1951 89m bw
TCF (Sol C. Siegel)
GB title: This Is My Affair
American TV title: Only the Best

An ambitious young mannequin starts her own
dressmaking firm and sets her sights high.
Watchable comedy-drama which quickly sheds
the edge of satire which might have made it the
dressmaker's All About Eve.

w Abraham Polonsky, novel Jerome Weidman
d Michael Gordon ph Milton Krasner m Sol
Kaplan md Lionel Newman

Susan Hayward, Dan Dailey, George Sanders,
Sam Jaffe, Randy Stuart, Marvin Kaplan, Harry
Von Zell

I Confess**
US 1953 94m bw
Warner / Alfred Hitchcock

A priest hears the confession of a murderer and
cannot divulge it to the police even though he is
himself suspected.
Hitchcock is always worth watching, and
although this old chestnut gives him very
restricted scope he imbues the story with a
strong feeling for its setting (Quebec) and an
overpowering sense of doom.

w George Tabori, William Archibald, play Paul
Anthelme d Alfred Hitchcock ph Robert Burks
m Dmitri Tiomkin

Montgomery Clift, Anne Baxter, Brian Aherne,
Karl Malden, Dolly Haas, O. E. Hasse
  'Whatever its shortcomings, it has the
professional concentration of effect, the
narrative control, of a story teller who can still
make most of his rivals look like amateurs.'—
MFB

I Could Go on Singing*
GB 1963 99m Eastmancolor
  Panavision
UA / Barbican (Lawrence Turman)

An American singing star in Britain looks up an
old lover and tries to take over their illegitimate
son, but the call of the footlights proves stronger.
The star enjoys her last specially-tailored role; a
banal, old-fashioned agreeable one-woman
show.

w Mayo Simon d Ronald Neame ph Arthur
Ibbetson m Mort Lindsey

Judy Garland, Dirk Bogarde, Aline MacMahon,
Jack Klugman

I Cover the Waterfront*
US 1933 75m bw
(UA)

A reporter uses a girl's friendship to expose her
father's smuggling activities.
In its time a tough, even daring melodrama, this
plot has now become the stuff of every other TV
series episode.

w Wells Root, Jack Jevne, Max Miller d James
Cruze ph Ray June

Claudette Colbert, Ben Lyon, Ernest Torrence,
Hobart Cavanaugh
  'A bit raw and a bit sentimental and a bit
routine, the film does let life in through the
cracks.'—Graham Greene

I Didn't Do It
GB 1945 97m bw
Columbia (Ben Henry, Marcel Varnel)

Murder in a theatrical boarding house, with
suspicion pointing at Our George.
One of the star's last vehicles: not too bad at all,
but without the sweet smell of success.

w Howard Irving Young, Stephen Black,
Norman Lee, Peter Fraser, Michael Vaughan
d Marcel Varnel

George Formby, Billy Caryll, Hilda Mundy,
Gaston Palmer, Jack Daly, Carl Jaffe, Marjorie
Browne, Wally Patch

I Died a Thousand Times
US 1955 109m Warnercolor
  Cinemascope
Warner (Willis Goldbeck)

An ex-convict plans a big hotel robbery, but
things go wrong within his gang.
Overlong, heavygoing, tedious gangster
melodrama with too much talk.

w W. R. Burnett d Stuart Heisler ph Ted
McCord m David Buttolph

Jack Palance, Shelley Winters, Lori Nelson, Lon
Chaney Jnr, Lee Marvin, Gonzales Gonzales,
Earl Holliman, Perry Lopez
  'This remake of High Sierra is scarcely more
inspired than its title.'—MFB
  'It is an insult to the intelligence to pull this old
mythological hero out of the archives and set
him on a mountaintop again.'—New York
Times

The I Don't Care Girl*
US 1953 78m Technicolor
TCF (George Jessel)

The life of musical entertainer Eva Tanguay, at
her height during World War I, as told by three
men in her life.
Breezy, conventional backstage musical biopic.

w Walter Bullock *d* Lloyd Bacon *ph* Arthur Arling *md* Lionel Newman *ch* Jack Cole, Seymour Felix

Mitzi Gaynor, David Wayne, Oscar Levant, *George Jessel*, Warren Stevens

I Don't Want to be Born
GB 1975   94m   Eastmancolor
(Rank) Unicapital (Norma Corney)
US title: *The Devil within Her*

An ex-stripper gives birth to a monstrous baby which goes on a murderous rampage.
Sick horror stuff with a high death rate and no notable credits.

w Stanley Price *d* Peter Sasdy *ph* Ken Talbot *m* Ron Grainer

Joan Collins, Ralph Bates, Donald Pleasence, Eileen Atkins, George Claydon

I Dood It!
US 1943   102m   bw
MGM (Jack Cummings)
GB title: *By Hook or by Crook*

A tailor falls for a Hollywood star.
Boring star comedy with interpolated musical numbers.

w Sig Herzig, Fred Saidy *d* Vincente Minnelli *ph* Ray June *md* Georgie Stoll

Red Skelton, Eleanor Powell, John Hodiak, Lena Horne, Jimmy Dorsey and his Orchestra, Hazel Scott, Richard Ainley

I Dream Too Much
US 1935   95m   bw
RKO (Pandro S. Berman)

A French girl singer marries an American composer.
Forgettable vehicle for an operatic star.

w Edmund North, James Gow *d* John Cromwell *ph* David Abel *songs* Jerome Kern, Dorothy Fields

Lily Pons, Henry Fonda, Eric Blore, Osgood Perkins, Lucien Littlefield, Lucille Ball, Esther Dale, Mischa Auer, Paul Porcasi

I Escaped from Devil's Island
US 1973   81m   De Luxe
UA / Roger Corman, Gene Corman

In 1918, a black convict makes his plans for escape.
Rough, brutish melodrama which plainly aimed to beat *Papillon* to the box office.

w Richard L. Adams *d* William Witney *ph* Rosalio Solano *m* Les Baxter

Jim Brown, Christopher George, Rick Ely, James Luisi, Richard Rust

'Exploitation's own *Papillon*, mercifully free from big brother's pretentiousness.'—*Sight and Sound*

I Killed Rasputin
France / Italy 1967   100m   Eastmancolor
Franscope
Copernic / CGC (Raymond Danon)

The evil monk of the Russian court is killed by Prince Yusopov.
Dull version of a much told story. One of the big international films that never seems to get shown anywhere.

w Alain Decaux, Claude Desailly, Robert Hossein *d* Robert Hossein *ph* Henri Persin *m* André Hossein

Gert Frobe, Peter McEnery, Robert Hossein, Geraldine Chaplin, Ira Furstenberg, Patrick Balkany

† The script was authorized by Prince Yusopov.
'A tedious illustrated history lesson which actually manages to obscure the motivation behind the murder.'—*MFB*

I Killed the Count
GB 1939   89m   bw
Grafton (Isadore Goldschmidt)

Four people confess to the murder of a philanderer.
Inept version of a West End success.

w Alec Coppel, Lawrence Huntington, *play* Alec Coppel *d* Fred Zelnik

Syd Walker, Ben Lyon, Terence de Marney, Barbara Blair, Antoinette Cellier, Kathleen Harrison, Athole Stewart, Leslie Perrins, Ronald Shiner

I Know Where I'm Going**
GB 1945   91m   bw
GFD / The Archers (Michael Powell, Emeric Pressburger)

A determined girl travels to the Hebrides to marry a wealthy old man, but is stranded on Mull and marries a young naval officer instead.
A strange assembling of attractive but disparate elements: romance, comedy, bleak scenery, a trained hawk and a dangerous whirlpool. At the time it seemed to represent the Elizabethan age of the British cinema, and remains entertaining for its parts though a bit of a puzzle as a whole.

wd Michael Powell, Emeric Pressburger ph Erwin Hillier

Wendy Hiller, Roger Livesey, Pamela Brown,

Nancy Price, Finlay Currie, John Laurie,
George Carney, Walter Hudd
'Continuously fresh and interesting,
intelligently written and played, and full of
beautiful photography.'—*Richard Mallett,
Punch*

I Live for Love
US 1935   83m   bw
Warner (Bryan Foy)
GB title: *I Live For You*

A socialite has show business leanings.
Minor musical.

w Jerry Wald, Julius Epstein, Robert Andrews
d/ch Busby Berkeley *ph* George Barnes
md Leo F. Forbstein

Dolores del Rio, Everett Marshall, Allen
Jenkins, Eddie Conrad, Guy Kibbee, Berton
Churchill

I Live in Grosvenor Square
GB 1945   113m   bw
ABP (Herbert Wilcox)
US title: *A Yank in London*

A duke's daughter falls in love with an American
air force sergeant.
Sloppily-made topical romance which was hot
box office at the time and started the producer's
'London' romances: *Piccadilly Incident, Spring
in Park Lane, Maytime in Mayfair,* etc.

w Nicholas Phipps, William D. Bayles, Maurice
Cowan *d* Herbert Wilcox *ph* Max Greene

Anna Neagle, *Dean Jagger*, Rex Harrison,
Robert Morley, Jane Darwell, Nancy Price,
Irene Vanbrugh, Edward Rigby, Walter Hudd

I Live My Life
US 1935   85m   bw
MGM (Bernard H. Hyman)

A bored society girl falls for a working class
archaeologist.
Standard star romance.

w Joseph L. Mankiewicz, *story* Claustrophobia
by A. Carter Goodloe *d* W. S. Van Dyke II
ph George Folsey

Joan Crawford, Brian Aherne, Frank Morgan,
Aline MacMahon, Eric Blore, Jessie Ralph,
Arthur Treacher, Hedda Hopper, Etienne
Girardot, Ed Brophy

I'll Take Romance
US 1937   85m   bw
Columbia (Everett Riskin)

When an opera singer refuses to fulfil a South
American contract, her impresario kidnaps her.
Moderate star vehicle.

w George Oppenheimer, Jane Murfin *d* Edward
H. Griffith *ph* Lucien Andriot *songs* various

Grace Moore, Melvyn Douglas, Helen Westley,
Stuart Erwin, Margaret Hamilton, Walter
Kingsford, Esther Muir

I Love a Mystery*
US 1945   68m   bw
Columbia

An eastern secret society offers a businessman a
large sum for his head when he dies, as he
resembles their founder whose embalmed head is
deteriorating.
Start of a short series of mysteries from a radio
series; the production was never up to the
ingenious plots.

w Charles O'Neal *d* Henry Levin *ph* Burnett
Guffey

George Macready, Jim Bannon, Nina Foch

I Love a Soldier
US 1944   106m   bw
Paramount (Mark Sandrich)

A San Francisco girl thinks hard before
embarking on a wartime marriage.
Glossy, insubstantial sudser chiefly memorable
for casting its leading lady as a welder.

w Allan Scott *d* Mark Sandrich *ph* Charles
Lang *m* Robert Emmett Dolan

Paulette Goddard, Sonny Tufts, Beulah Bondi,
Walter Sande, Mary Treen, Ann Doran, Barry
Fitzgerald

I Love Melvin*
US 1953   77m   Technicolor
MGM (George Wells)

A photographer's assistant falls for a high-born
chorus girl.
Zippy little musical with all concerned working
hard with thin material.

w George Wells *d* Don Weis *ph* Harold
Rosson *md* George Stoll *ch* Robert Alton

Donald O'Connor, Debbie Reynolds, Una
Merkel, Allyn Joslyn

I Love My Wife
US 1970   95m   Technicolor
Universal (Robert Kaufman)

The affairs of a successful doctor with a guilt
complex about sex.
Frantic, fashionable comedy drama with wildly
erratic treatment and performances.

w Robert Kaufman *d* Mel Stuart *ph* Vilis
Lapenieks *m* Lalo Schifrin

Elliott Gould, Brenda Vaccaro, Angel Tompkins

'A leer-laden, anti-feminist tract disguised as a comedy.'—*Judith Crist*

I Love You Again*
US 1940 99m bw
MGM (Lawrence Weingarten)

A much married man gets amnesia and turns into a gay Lothario.
Sprightly romantic comedy with all concerned letting rip until the pace slows.

w Charles Lederer, George Oppenheimer, Harry Kurnitz *d* W. S. Van Dyke II *ph* Oliver T. Marsh *m* Franz Waxman

William Powell, Myrna Loy, Frank McHugh, Edmund Lowe, Donald Douglas, Nella Walker, Pierre Watkin

I Love You, Alice B. Toklas*
US 1968 93m Technicolor
Warner Seven Arts / Paul Mazursky, Larry Tucker

An asthmatic Los Angeles lawyer escapes his bullying fiancée by joining the flower people.
Quite amusing satirical farce about the dangers of marijuana, Gertrude Stein and Jewish mothers, thrown together with no great sense of style but achieving hilarious moments among the longueurs.

w Paul Mazursky, Larry Tucker d Hy Averback *ph* Philip Lathrop *m* Elmer Bernstein *pd* Pato Guzman

Peter Sellers, Jo Van Fleet, Joyce Van Patten, Leigh Taylor-Young, David Arkin, Herb Edelman

I Loved a Woman*
US 1933 90m bw
Warner (Henry Blanke)

The career of a Chicago meat packer is hampered by his social-climbing wife.
Potboiling star melodrama which still holds some interest.

w Charles Kenyon, Sidney Sutherland *d* Alfred E. Green *ph* James Van Trees

Edward G. Robinson, Kay Francis, Genevieve Tobin,
J. Farrell MacDonald, Henry Kolker, Robert Barrat

I Married a Monster from Outer Space*
US 1958 78m bw
Paramount / Gene Fowler Jnr

A young man is taken over by alien invaders but his wife helps to destroy them and bring him back to normal.
Decent, plodding, reasonably effective low-budget science fiction on a well-trampled theme; its minor virtues have been effaced by its silly title.

w Louis Vittes *d* Gene Fowler Jnr *ph* Haskell Boggs *sp* John P. Fulton

Tom Tryon, Gloria Talbott, Robert Ivers

I Married a Witch****
US 1942 82m bw
(UA) Cinema Guild / René Clair

A Salem witch and her sorcerer father come back to haunt the descendant of the Puritan who had them burned.
Delightful romantic comedy fantasy which shows all concerned at the top of their form. Hollywood moonshine, impeccably distilled.

w Robert Pirosh, Marc Connelly, novel The Passionate Witch by Thorne Smith *d René Clair ph* Ted Tetzlaff *m* Roy Webb

Fredric March, Veronica Lake, Cecil Kellaway, Robert Benchley, Susan Hayward, Elizabeth Patterson, Robert Warwick

'She knows all about love potions . . . and lovely motions!'—*publicity*

AAN: Roy Webb

I Married a Woman
US 1956 85m bw RKOscope
RKO

A nervous young advertising executive neglects his wife, who determines to make him jealous.
Simple-minded comedy tailored to unsympathetic stars.

w Goodman Ace *d* Hal Kanter *ph* Lucien Ballard *m* Cyril Mockridge

George Gobel, Diana Dors, Adolphe Menjou, Jessie Royce Landis, Nita Talbot

I Married an Angel
US 1942 84m bw
MGM (Hunt Stromberg)

An attractive angel lures a playboy from his earthly girl friends.
Silly musical fantasy which spelled the end of a great musical star partnership.

w Anita Loos, *play* Vilismary Janos *d* W. S. Van Dyke *m/ly* Richard Rodgers, Lorenz Hart

Jeanette MacDonald, Nelson Eddy, Edward Everett Horton, Binnie Barnes, Reginald Owen, Douglass Dumbrille

'As bland as operetta but without its energy.'—*New Yorker, 1978*

I Met a Murderer*
GB 1939   78m   bw
Grand National / Gamma (Roy Kellino,
    Pamela Kellino, James Mason)

A murderer on the run meets a girl novelist who
is touring in her motor caravan.
Semi-professional location melodrama which
won commendation at the time but now seems
very faded.

w Pamela Kellino, James Mason d Roy Kellino
ph Roy Kellino m Eric Ansell

James Mason, Pamela Kellino, Sylvia Coleridge,
William Devlin, Peter Coke
    'Graceful, gallant, resourceful . . . better and
more enjoyable than most studio pictures.'—
James Agee
    'That it has a number of defects does not mean
that it is not worthy of serious consideration.'—
Basil Wright

I Met Him in Paris*
US 1937   86m   bw
Paramount (Wesley Ruggles)

A fashion designer spends five years' savings on
a fling in Paris and finds herself pursued to
Switzerland by two philanderers.
Not very witty but likeable romantic comedy
with polished performers near their best.

w Claude Binyon d Wesley Ruggles ph Leo
Tover m John Leopold md Boris Morros

*Claudette Colbert, Melvyn Douglas, Robert
Young*, Lee Bowman, Mona Barrie
    'At least half the footage is a perfect scream,
and if you miss it you are an old sobersides, and
who cares.'—*Otis Ferguson*

I Met My Love Again
US 1937   77m   bw
Walter Wanger

A small-town girl marries a drunken writer, but
on his death returns to her first love, a biology
professor.
Mildly pleasing, rather dated romantic drama
with good local colour.

w David Hertz, *novel* Summer Lightning by
Aileen Corliss d Joshua Logan, Arthur Ripley
ph Hal Mohr

Henry Fonda, Joan Bennett, Alan Marshal,
Dorothy Stickney, Dame May Whitty, Alan
Baxter, Louise Platt, Tim Holt, Florence Lake

I, Mobster
US 1958   80m   bw   Cinemascope
Edward L. Alperson

A slum teenager becomes a top gangster.
Routine gangland thriller.

w Steve Fisher, *novel* Joseph Hilton Smith
d Roger Corman ph Floyd Crosby m Gerald
Fried

Steve Cochran, Lita Milan, Robert Strauss,
Celia Lovsky, Grant Withers

I, Monster*
GB 1970   75m   Eastmancolor
Amicus (Milton Subotsky)

A straight remake of *Dr Jekyll and Mr Hyde*,
holding closely to the original novel but
mysteriously using different names.
Interesting minor work.

w Milton Subotsky d Stephen Weeks ph Moray
Grant m Carl Davis ad Tony Curtis

Christopher Lee, Peter Cushing, Richard
Hurndall, George Merritt

I Never Sang for My Father*
US 1969   92m   Technicolor
Columbia / Jamel (Gilbert Cates)

When his mother dies, a middle-aged widower is
saddled with his cantankerous father, who tries
to prevent him from remarrying.
Literal transcription of a Eugene O'Neillish play,
a fascinating if depressing character study.

w *Robert Anderson*, from his play d Gilbert
Cates ph Morris Hartzband, George Stoetzel
m Al Gorgoni, Barry Mann

*Melvyn Douglas, Gene Hackman, Dorothy
Stickney*, Estelle Parsons

AAN: Robert Anderson; Melvyn Douglas;
Gene Hackman

I Passed for White
US 1960   92m   bw
Allied Artists (Fred M. Wilcox)

A light-skinned negress comes to New York but
fails to achieve happiness by pretending to be
white.
Earnest, rather dreary social drama which
doesn't get anywhere.

d Fred M. Wilcox

Sonya Wilde, James Franciscus, Pat Michon,
Elizabeth Council

I Remember Mama**
US 1948   134m   bw
RKO (George Stevens)

A novelist remembers some of the adventures of
growing up with her Swedish–American family.
Overlong, but well-upholstered nostalgia: warm-
hearted, sentimental, nicely detailed, richly acted
but just a little boring in spots.

w De Witt Bodeen, *play* John Van Druten, *book* Mama's Bank Account by Kathryn Forbes *d* George Stevens *ph* Nicholas Musuraca *m* Roy Webb

Irene Dunne, Barbara Bel Geddes, Oscar Homolka, Edgar Bergen, Philip Dorn, Ellen Corby, Florence Bates, Cedric Hardwicke, Barbara O'Neil, Rudy Vallee

AAN: Nicholas Musuraca; Irene Dunne; Barbara Bel Geddes; Oscar Homolka; Ellen Corby

I Saw What You Did
US 1965   82m   bw
Universal / William Castle

A murderer thinks that two playful teenagers have witnessed his deed, and sets out to kill them too.
Predictable and long-winded suspenser, very short of inventive detail.

w William McGivern, *novel* Ursula Curtiss *d* William Castle *ph* Joseph Biroc *m* Van Alexander

John Ireland, Joan Crawford, Leif Erickson

I See a Dark Stranger **
GB 1945   112m   bw
GFD / Individual
US title: *The Adventuress*

An Irish colleen who hates the English comes to England to spy for the Germans but falls in love with a young English officer.
Slipshod plotting does not quite destroy the jolly atmosphere of this comedy-thriller which has the cheek to take an IRA member as its heroine. Good fun, very well staged.

w Frank Launder, Sidney Gilliat, Wolfgang Wilhelm d Frank Launder ph Wilkie Cooper m William Alwyn

Deborah Kerr, Trevor Howard, Raymond Huntley, Norman Shelley, Michael Howard, Brenda Bruce, Liam Redmond, Brefni O'Rourke
'It is the cinematic equivalent of Irish blarney which inspires most of this picture.'—*MFB*

I Stole a Million
US 1939   89m   bw
Universal (Burt Kelly)

A cab driver cheated by a finance company becomes a criminal to support his family.
Ho-hum star melodrama.

w Nathanael West, *story* Lester Cole *d* Frank Tuttle *ph* Milton Krasner

George Raft, Claire Trevor, Dick Foran, Henry Armetta, Victor Jory, Joe Sawyer, Stanley Ridges

I Take This Woman
US 1931   74m   bw
Paramount

A reckless society girl falls for a cowhand and agrees to live in his ramshackle house.
Patchy romantic comedy–drama of little remaining interest.

w Vincent Lawrence, *novel* Lost Ecstasy by Mary Roberts Rinehart *d* Marion Gering, Slavko Vorkapitch *ph* Victor Milner

Gary Cooper, Carole Lombard, Helen Ware, Lester Vail, Charles Trowbridge, Clara Blandick

I Take This Woman
US 1939   97m   bw
MGM (Louis B. Mayer)

A doctor marries a beautiful European and decides too late that he does not love her.
Thin comedy–drama which Louis B. Mayer unaccountably took it into his head to produce personally. The results had to be re-shot so much and so often that Hollywood dubbed the film *I Re-Take This Woman*. It offers little in the way of entertainment.

w James Kevin McGuinness, *story* Charles MacArthur
d W. S. Van Dyke *m* Bronislau Kaper

Spencer Tracy, Hedy Lamarr, Verree Teasdale, Kent Taylor, Laraine Day, Mona Barrie, Jack Carson, Paul Cavanagh, Marjorie Main

I Thank a Fool
GB 1962   100m   Metrocolor
  Cinemascope
MGM (Anatole de Grunwald)

A woman found guilty of the murder of her lover is offered a fresh start in the home of the prosecutor's family . . . but another nightmare situation builds up.
Jane Eyre melodrama of the loonier type, with good actors struggling through a wild but unrewarding script.

w Karl Tunberg, *novel* Audrey Erskine Lindop *d* Robert Stevens *ph* Harry Waxman *m* Ron Goodwin

Peter Finch, Susan Hayward, Diane Cilento, Cyril Cusack, Kieron Moore, Athene Seyler

I the Jury
US 1953   87m   bw   3-D
Parklane (Victor Saville)

Private eye Mike Hammer avenges the murder of his friend.
Charmless toughie, roughly made and devoid of plot or character interest.

wd Harry Essex *ph* John Alton *m* Franz Waxman

Biff Elliott, Peggie Castle, Preston Foster, Elisha Cook Jnr, John Qualen

I Wake Up Screaming**

US 1941 79m bw

TCF (Milton Sperling)

GB and alternative title: *Hot Spot*

A model is murdered and her sister joins forces with the chief suspect to find the real killer.
Moody thriller with plenty going for it including one memorable performance.

w Dwight Taylor, *novel* Steve Fisher *d* H. Bruce Humberstone *ph* Edward Cronjager *m* Cyril Mockridge

Betty Grable, Victor Mature, Carole Landis, *Laird Cregar*, William Gargan, Alan Mowbray, Allyn Joslyn, Elisha Cook Jnr
† Remade as *Vicki* (qv).

I Walk Alone*

US 1948 98m bw

Paramount (Hal B. Wallis)

An ex-smuggler comes out seeking vengeance after fourteen years in prison.
Dreary gangster drama unworthy of its stars.

w Charles Schnee, *play* Beggars Are Coming to Town by Theodore Reeves *d* Byron Haskin *ph* Leo Tover *m* Victor Young

Burt Lancaster, Kirk Douglas, Lizabeth Scott, Wendell Corey, Kristine Miller, George Rigaud, Marc Lawrence, Mike Mazurki

I Walk the Line*

US 1970 97m Eastmancolor
Panavision

Columbia / Frankenheimer / Lewis / Halcyon / Atticus (Harold D. Cohen)

A Tennessee sheriff protects moonshiners for the favours of their daughter; when an investigator arrives, bloodshed results.
Competent but uninteresting hothouse melodrama in which only the plot twists compel attention.

w Alvin Sargent, *novel* An Exile by Madison Jones *d* John Frankenheimer *ph* David M. Walsh *md* Robert Johnson

Gregory Peck, Tuesday Weld, Estelle Parsons, Ralph Meeker

I Walked with a Zombie*

US 1943 68m bw

RKO (*Val Lewton*)

A nurse is retained by a Caribbean planter to care for his voodoo-sick wife.

Mild horror from the famous Lewton package; some style, but generally thin stuff, the plot having been mirthfully borrowed from *Jane Eyre*.

w Curt Siodmak, Ardel Wray *d* Jacques Tourneur *ph* J. Roy Hunt *m* Roy Webb

Frances Dee, James Ellison, Tom Conway, Christine Gordon, Edith Barrett, James Bell, Sir Lancelot

I Wanna Hold Your Hand

US 1978 104m Technicolor

Universal / Steven Spielberg (Tamara Asseyev, Alex Rose)

A day in 1964 finds assorted New Jersey teenagers eagerly awaiting the Beatles' appearance on the Ed Sullivan Show. Modest period comedy utilizing fresh young talent.

w Robert Zemeckis, Bob Gale *d* Robert Zemeckis *ph* Donald M. Morgan *md*

Nancy Allen, Bobby diCicco, Marc McClure, Susan Kendall Newman

I Want a Divorce

US 1940 74m bw

Paramount

A young law student marries rashly, but is prevented from doing anything about it by examples of the unhappiness brought by divorce. Peculiar comedy-drama which never seems to make up its mind to any particular course.

w Frank Butler, *story* Adela Rogers St John *d* Ralph Murphy

Dick Powell, Joan Blondell, Frank Fay, Gloria Dickson, Jessie Ralph, Conrad Nagel, Harry Davenport, Sidney Blackmer, Louise Beavers

I Want to Live*

US 1958 120m bw

(UA) Walter Wanger

A vagrant prostitute is executed in the gas chamber despite growing doubt as to her guilt. Sober, harrowing treatment of the Barbara Graham case, uneasily adapted to provide a star role amid the tirade against capital punishment.

w Nelson Gidding, Don Mankiewicz *d* Robert Wise *ph* Lionel Lindon *m* John Mandel

Susan Hayward, Simon Oakland, Virginia Vincent, Theodore Bikel, Wesley Lau, Philip Coolidge

'An inconclusive amalgam of variously unexplored themes.'—*Peter John Dyer*

AA: Susan Hayward
AAN: Nelson Gidding, Don Mankiewicz; Robert Wise; Lionel Lindon

I Want What I Want
GB 1971   105m   Eastmancolor
Marayan (Raymond Stross)

Roy has a sex change operation and becomes Wendy.

Although based on an actual trans-sexual experience, this film confuses more than it informs, and provokes unintentional mirth when its glamorous star is playing a boy.

w Gillian Freeman, novel Geoff Brown d John Dexter ph Gerry Turpin m Johnny Harris

Anne Heywood, Paul Rogers, Harry Andrews, Jill Bennett

I Want You
US 1951   101m   bw
Samuel Goldwyn

A family reacts to the Korean war.
Glossy small-town flagwaver; no Best Years of Our Lives.

w Irwin Shaw d Mark Robson ph Harry Stradling m Leigh Harline ad Richard Day

Dorothy McGuire, Dana Andrews, Farley Granger, Peggy Dow, Robert Keith, Ray Collins, Mildred Dunnock, Martin Milner, Jim Backus

'A recruiting picture which seems to accept a third world war almost as a present reality.'— Penelope Houston
'Below the entertaining surface it has very little of value to offer.'—Richard Mallett, Punch

I Wanted Wings*
US 1941   131m   bw
Paramount (Arthur Hornblow Jnr)

The fortunes of three recruits to the American Air Force.
Cheerful, overlong recruiting poster with concessions to melodrama.

w Richard Maibaum, Beirne Lay Jnr, Sig Herzig d Mitchell Leisen ph Leo Tover, Elmer Dyer m Victor Young

Ray Milland, William Holden, Brian Donlevy, Wayne Morris, Veronica Lake, Constance Moore, Harry Davenport, Phil Brown

I Was a Communist for the FBI
US 1951   83m   bw
Warner (Bryan Foy)

Matt Cvetic, a Pittsburgh steel worker, is actually an FBI agent working undercover to trap communists.
Crude and shoddy Red-baiting melodrama, a kind of updating of Confessions of a Nazi Spy but using a sadly deteriorated technique.

w Crane Wilbur, Matt Cvetic d Gordon Douglas ph Edwin DuPar

Frank Lovejoy, Dorothy Hart, Phil Carey, James Millican, Richard Webb, Paul Picerni, Konstantin Shayne

'It seems that this is a subject which Hollywood is incapable of tackling even at its customary level of journalistic efficiency.'— Penelope Houston

I Was a Male War Bride**
US 1949   105m   bw
TCF (Sol C. Siegel)
GB title: You Can't Sleep Here

A WAC in Europe marries a French officer and can't get him home.
High-spirited farce against realistic backgrounds of war-torn Europe, which scarcely accord with Cary Grant's pretending to be a Frenchman (and later a Frenchwoman). Funny, though.

w Charles Lederer, Hagar Wilde, Leonard Spiegelgass d Howard Hawks ph Norbert Brodine, Osmond Borradaile m Cyril Mockridge md Lionel Newman

Cary Grant, Ann Sheridan, Marion Marshall, Randy Stuart

I Was Happy Here*
GB 1965   91m   bw
Partisan (Roy Millichip)
US title: Time Lost and Time Remembered

A girl leaves her husband in London and returns to the little Irish port of her childhood.
Nicely made, over-mannered study in nostalgia and lost illusions.

w Edna O'Brien, Desmond Davis d Desmond Davis ph Manny Wynn m John Addison

Sarah Miles, Cyril Cusack, Julian Glover, Sean Caffrey, Marie Kean

I Was Monty's Double**
GB 1958   100m   bw
ABP / Maxwell Setton
US title: Hell, Heaven and Hoboken

To distract the Nazis in Africa, an actor is hired to pose as General Montgomery.
An amusing and intriguing first hour gives way to spy chases, but the overall provides solid entertainment.

w Bryan Forbes, book M. E. Clifton-James d John Guillermin ph Basil Emmott m John Addison

John Mills, Cecil Parker, M. E. Clifton-James, Patrick Allen, Leslie Phillips, Michael Hordern, Marius Goring

I Was a Spy**
GB 1933   89m   bw
Gaumont (Michael Balcon)

In Belgium 1914, a nurse is trained as a spy.
Good standard war espionage melodrama.

w W. P. Lipscomb, Ian Hay, *book* Marthe
McKenna   d Victor Saville

Madeleine Carroll, Conrad Veidt, Herbert
Marshall, Gerald du Maurier, Edmund Gwenn,
Donald Calthrop, Nigel Bruce, Anthony
Bushell, Martita Hunt

I Was a Teenage Werewolf
US 1957   76m   bw
AIP / Sunset (Herman Cohen)

A scientist experiments on an aggressive student
and turns him into a werewolf.
Hilarious farrago with a title which achieved a
splendour of its own.

w Ralph Thornton   d Gene Fowler Jnr
ph Joseph La Shelle   m Paul Dunlap

Michael Landon, Whit Bissell, Yvonne Leslie

I Wonder Who's Kissing Her Now*
US 1947   104m   Technicolor
TCF (George Jessel)

The career of nineties songwriter Joseph E.
Howard.
Routine biopic, quite pleasantly handled.

w Lewis R. Foster   d Lloyd Bacon   ph Ernest
Palmer   md Alfred Newman   ad Richard Day,
Boris Leven   ch Hermes Pan

Mark Stevens, June Haver, Martha Stewart,
Reginald Gardiner, Lenore Aubert, William
Frawley, Gene Nelson

Ice Cold in Alex**
GB 1958   132m   bw
ABP (W. A. Whittaker)
US title: *Desert Attack*

In 1942 Libya, the commander of a motor
ambulance gets his vehicle and passengers to
safety despite the hazards of minefields and a
German spy.
Engrossing desert adventure with plenty of
suspense sequences borrowed from *The Wages
of Fear*; long, but very well presented.

w T. J. Morrison, Christopher Landon   d J. Lee-
Thompson   ph Gilbert Taylor   m Leighton Lucas

John Mills, Sylvia Sims, Anthony Quayle, Harry
Andrews

Ice Follies of 1939
US 1939   82m   bw (Technicolor
sequence)
MGM (Harry Rapf)

A Hollywood star goes east to help her old ice-
skating friends put on a show.
The downright peculiar sight of these particular
stars on ice is backed by good turns and
practically no story.

w Florence Ryerson, Edgar Allan Woolf
d Reinhold Schunzel   ph Joseph Ruttenberg,
Oliver T. Marsh   m Roger Edens

Joan Crawford, James Stewart, Lew Ayres,
Lewis Stone, Lionel Stander, Bess Ehrhardt,
Charles D. Brown, the International Ice Follies

Ice Palace
US 1960   143m   Warnercolor
   Cinemascope
Warner (Henry Blanke)

After World War I, two men set up a fishery
business in Alaska, and their subsequent lives are
tied up with the political development of the
state.
Tedious saga from a bestseller, with entertaining
incidents but no real grip.

w Harry Kleiner, *novel* Edna Ferber   d Vincent
Sherman   ph Joseph Biroc   m Max Steiner
ad Malcolm Bert

Richard Burton, Robert Ryan, Martha Hyer,
Carolyn Jones, Jim Backus, Ray Danton, Diane
McBain, Karl Swenson

Ice Station Zebra
US 1968   148m   Metrocolor   Super
Panavision
MGM / Filmways (James C. Pratt)

Russian and American agents speed towards the
North Pole to recover a lost capsule containing
vital military information.
Talky and unconvincingly staged spy adventure
with a disappointing lack of action and a great
many cold war platitudes.

w Douglas Heyes, Harry Julian Fink, *novel*
Alistair MacLean   d John Sturges   ph Daniel L.
Fapp   m Michel Legrand

Rock Hudson, Patrick McGoohan, Ernest
Borgnine, Jim Brown, Tony Bill, Lloyd Nolan,
Gerald S. O'Loughlin, Alf Kjellin
   'It's terrible in such a familiar way that at some
level it's pleasant. We learn to settle for so little,
we moviegoers.'—*Pauline Kael*

AAN: Daniel L. Fapp

Ichabod and Mr Toad**
US 1949   68m   Technicolor
Walt Disney

Cartoon versions of stories by Washington
Irving and Kenneth Grahame.
An uncomfortable double bill; the story of

Ichabod, though well narrated by Basil Rathbone, is macabre without being very interesting; *The Wind in the Willows*, however, is charmingly pictured, and Mr Toad is splendidly voiced by Eric Blore.

d Jack Kinney, Clyde Geronimi, James Algar *supervisor* Ben Sharpsteen

I'd Climb the Highest Mountain*
US 1951 88m Technicolor
TCF (Lamar Trotti)

A Methodist preacher and his wife face the problems of life in a remote part of North Georgia.
Pleasant, rambling, adequately serious and old-fashioned family entertainment, well presented in Hollywood's medium style.

w Lamar Trotti, *novel* Corra Harris d Henry King ph Edward Cronjager m Sol Kaplan md Lionel Newman

Susan Hayward, William Lundigan, Rory Calhoun, Barbara Bates, Gene Lockhart, Lynn Bari, Ruth Donnelly, Alexander Knox

I'd Rather Be Rich*
US 1964 96m Eastmancolor
U–I / Ross Hunter

To comfort her dying grandfather, an heiress introduces an eligible stranger as her fiancé . . . but the old man recovers and begins matchmaking.
Reasonably zesty remake of *It Started with Eve*, kept afloat by Chevalier's performance.

w Oscar Brodney, Leo Townsend, Norman Krasna d Jack Smight ph Russell Metty m Percy Faith

Maurice Chevalier, Sandra Dee, Robert Goulet, Andy Williams, Gene Raymond, Hermione Gingold, Charles Ruggles

An Ideal Husband*
GB 1947 96m Technicolor
British Lion / London Films (Alexander Korda)

In the nineties, the career of a London diplomat is threatened by the reappearance of an old flame.
A slight, stiff play is swamped by the cast, the decor, and very garish colour, but there are moments of enjoyment along the way.

w Lajos Biro, *play* Oscar Wilde d Alexander Korda ph Georges Périnal m Arthur Benjamin ad Vincent Korda cost Cecil Beaton

Paulette Goddard, Hugh Williams, Michael Wilding, Diana Wynyard, *C. Aubrey Smith, Constance Collier*, Glynis Johns, Christine Norden

'The composing and cutting of this fine raw material is seldom above medium grade.'— *James Agee*

Idiot's Delight*
US 1939 105m bw
MGM (Hunt Stromberg)

At the outbreak of World War II, in a hotel on the Swiss border, a hoofer with an all-girl troupe meets an old flame masquerading as a Russian countess.
Interesting but quite unsuccessful film version of a highly artificial play which had been carried off superbly by the Lunts but was now somewhat less well cast, though it did represent an early Hollywood challenge to Hitler. The flagwaving in fact made it more than a little boring.

w Robert E. Sherwood, from his play d Clarence Brown ph William Daniels

Clark Gable, Norma Shearer, Edward Arnold, Charles Coburn, Burgess Meredith, Joseph Schildkraut, Laura Hope Crews, Skeets Gallagher, Pat Patterson, Fritz Feld
'The fun and excitement are still there, however filtered it may be.'—*Film Daily*
'The mood of the whole thing is forced and cheap—the coming world war staged by Maurice Chevalier.'—*Otis Ferguson*

The Idle Class*
US 1922 20m approx bw silent
First National / Charles Chaplin

A tramp dreams of the rich life and is mistaken for the husband of a lady.
Rather slight later Chaplin without the full-blooded farcical elements which made him so popular around 1917.

wd Charles Chaplin ph Rollie Totheroh

Charles Chaplin, Edna Purviance, Mack Swain

The Idol
GB 1966 111m bw
Embassy (Leonard Lightstone)

A divorced woman falls in love with her son's friend.
Stupefyingly boring generation-gap sex drama.

w Millard Lampell d Daniel Petrie ph Ken Higgins m Johnny Dankworth

Jennifer Jones, Michael Parks, John Leyton, Jennifer Hilary, Guy Doleman, Natasha Pyne

Idol of Paris
GB 1948 105m bw
Premier (R. J. Minney)

In old Paris, a ragman's daughter becomes queen of the demi-mondaines.

Unintentionally hilarious copy of the
Gainsborough period romances which had been
so popular; much criticized because the leading
ladies fight a duel with whips, but that's the least
of its faults.

w Norman Lee, Stafford Dickens, Henry Ostrer,
novel Paiva Queen of Love by Alfred Shirkauer
d Leslie Arliss

Beryl Baxter, Christine Norden, Michael Rennie,
Margaretta Scott, Keneth Kent, Henry Oscar,
Miles Malleson, Andrew Osborn, Andrew
Cruickshank

If . . .***
GB 1968   111m   Eastmancolor
Paramount / Memorial (Lindsay Anderson,
   Michael Medwin)

Discontent at a boys' public school breaks out
into rebellion.
Allegorical treatment of school life with much
fashionable emphasis on obscure narrative,
clever cutting, variety of pace, even an
unaccountable changing from colour to
monochrome and vice versa. Intelligence is
clearly at work, but it seems to have suffered
from undigested gobs of Pinter, and the film as a
whole makes no discernible point.

w David Sherwin d Lindsay Anderson
ph Miroslav Ondricek m Marc Wilkinson
pd Jocelyn Herbert

Malcolm McDowell, David Wood, Richard
Warwick, Robert Swann, Christine Noonan,
Peter Jeffrey, Arthur Lowe, Anthony Nicholls
   'The school . . . is the perfect metaphor for the
established system all but a few of us continue to
accept.'—David Wilson
   'It's something like the Writing on the
Wall.'—Lindsay Anderson
   'Combines a cold and queasy view of youth
with a romantic view of violence.'—New Yorker

If I Had a Million**
US 1932   88m   bw
Paramount

Various people each receive a million dollars
from an eccentric who wants to test their
reactions.
Interesting, dated multi-part comedy drama
remembered chiefly for the brief sequence in
which Laughton blows a raspberry to his boss
and Fields chases road hogs. As an
entertainment it's patchy, lacking an overall
style.

w Claude Binyon, Whitney Bolton, Malcolm
Stuart Boylan, John Bright, Sidney Buchman,
Lester Cole, Isabel Dawn, Boyce DeGaw,
Walter de Leon, Oliver H. P. Garrett, Harvey
Gates, Grover Jones, Ernst Lubitsch, Lawton
Mackaill, Joseph L. Mankiewicz, William
Slavens McNutt, Seton I. Miller, Tiffany Thayer,
story Robert D. Andrews d Ernst Lubitsch,
Norman Taurog, Stephen Roberts, Norman Z.
McLeod, James Cruze, William A. Seiter, H.
Bruce Humberstone

W. C. Fields, Charles Laughton, May Robson,
Richard Bennett, Alison Skipworth, Gary
Cooper, Wynne Gibson, George Raft, Jack
Oakie, Frances Dee, Charles Ruggles, Mary
Boland, Roscoe Karns, Gene Raymond, Lucien
Littlefield

If I Had My Way*
US 1940   82m   bw
Universal (David Butler)

Two vaudevillians help an orphan girl and open a
new night club.
Quite likeable and very typical star vehicle of its
period.

w William Conselman, James V. Kern d David
Butler

Bing Crosby, Charles Winninger, Gloria Jean,
El Brendel, Allyn Joslyn, Donald Woods, Eddie
Leonard, Claire Dodd, Blanche Ring

If I Were King*
US 1938   101m   bw
Paramount

The 14th-century poet and rascal François
Villon matches wits with Louis XI and leads an
uprising of the people.
A story which we have grown used to seeing with
music as The Vagabond King is here well
presented but somehow rings hollow, with
insufficient derring-do; it is the wrong kind of
swashbuckling for its star, who is for once
outacted by Rathbone in an unusual wily
characterization.

w Preston Sturges d Frank Lloyd m Richard
Hageman

Ronald Colman, Basil Rathbone, Frances Dee,
Ellen Drew, C. V. France, Heather Thatcher,
Henry Wilcoxon, Sidney Toler

AAN: Richard Hageman; Basil Rathbone

If I'm Lucky
US 1945   79m   bw
TCF (Brian Foy)

A singer runs for state governor and exposes
corruption.
Lacklustre remake of Thanks a Million, with
decidedly dispirited elements.

w Snag Werris, Robert Ellis, Helen Logan,

George Bricker *d* Lewis Seiler *ph* Glen
MacWilliams

songs Edgar de Lange, Joseph Myrow *md* Emil
Newman

Vivian Blaine, Perry Como, Carmen Miranda,
Harry James, Phil Silvers, Edgar Buchanan,
Reed Hadley

If It's Tuesday, This Must Be Belgium*
US 1969   98m   De Luxe
UA / Wolper (Stan Margulies)

A group of American tourists have various
adventures during a lightning tour of Europe.
Amusing comedy which does pretty well by a
good idea.

w David Shaw *d* Mel Stuart *ph* Vilis Lapenieks
m Walter Scharf

Suzanne Pleshette, Ian McShane, Mildred
Natwick, Murray Hamilton, Michael
Constantine, Sandy Baron, Norman Fell, Peggy
Cass, Marty Ingels, Pamela Britton, Luke
Halpin, Aubrey Morris

If Winter Comes
US 1948   97m   bw
MGM (Victor Saville)

A sentimental idealist, unhappily married, finds
himself at the mercy of village gossip when he
takes in a pregnant girl.
Artificial romantic nonsense, unconvincingly
staged and modernized from a very dated
bestseller.

w Marguerite Roberts, Arthur Wimperis,
novel A. S. M. Hutchinson *d* Victor Saville
ph George Folsey *m* Herbert Stothart

Walter Pidgeon, Deborah Kerr, Janet Leigh,
Angela Lansbury, Binnie Barnes, Dame May
Whitty, Reginald Owen

If You Knew Susie*
US 1948   90m   bw
RKO

A vaudeville couple retire to his ancestral home
in New England.
Mild family comedy capitalizing on the team
established in *Show Business*.

w Warren Wilson, Oscar Brodney *d* Gordon
Douglas *ph* Frank Redman

Eddie Cantor, Joan Davis, Allyn Joslyn, Bobby
Driscoll, Charles Dingle

Ikiru*
Japan 1952   143m   bw
Toho
aka: *Living; Doomed*

A clerk learns that he is dying and spends his last
months creating a children's playground.
A moving and beautifully made personal drama
which also gives an interesting background of
modern Japan.

w Hideo Oguni, Shinobu Hashimoto, Akira
Kurosawa *d Akira Kurosawa ph* Asaishi
Nakai *m* Fumio Hayasaka

Takashi Shimura, Nobuo Kaneko, Kyoko Seki

I'll Be Seeing You**
US 1944   85m   bw
David O. Selznick (Dore Schary)

A lady convict at home on parole for Christmas
meets and falls for a shell-shocked soldier.
Schmaltzy, middle-American romantic drama
with some nicely handled moments and plenty of
talent on hand. In the Hollywood mainstream.

w Marion Parsonnet, *novel* Charles Martin
d William Dieterle ph Tony Gaudio m Daniele
Amfitheatrof

Ginger Rogers, Joseph Cotten, Shirley Temple,
Spring Byington, Tom Tully, Chill Wills

'A sentimental, improbable picture, but
unexpectedly rewarding in detail.'—*Richard
Mallett, Punch*

I'll Cry Tomorrow*
US 1955   119m   bw
MGM (Lawrence Weingarten)

Lillian Roth, a Broadway/Hollywood star of the
early thirties, becomes an alcoholic.
Fictionalized biopic, pretty well done of the True
Confessions kind.

w Helen Deutsch, Jay Richard Kennedy, *book*
Lillian Roth, Gerold Frank *d* Daniel Mann
ph Arthur E. Arling *m* Alex North

Susan Hayward, Richard Conte, Eddie Albert,
Jo Van Fleet, Don Taylor, Ray Danton, Margo

'By emphasizing physical degradation in
almost every frame, the film makes her less an
object of acutely personal concern than a street
casualty seen remotely from the top of a bar.'—
Alexander Walker

AAN: Arthur E. Arling; Susan Hayward

Ill Met by Moonlight
GB 1956   104m   bw   Vistavision
Rank / Vega (Michael Powell, Emeric
   Pressburger)
US title: *Night Ambush*

In Crete during the German occupation, British
agents work with partisans to capture a German
general.
Disappointingly dreary war adventure with too
many night locations, too little suspense and

characterization, and photography which seems to be deliberately unattractive.

wd Michael Powell, Emeric Pressburger, *book* W. Stanley Moss *ph* Christopher Challis *m* Mikis Theodorakis

Dirk Bogarde, Marius Goring, David Oxley, Cyril Cusack, John Cairney, Laurence Payne, Wolfe Morris, Michael Gough

I'll Never Forget Whatshisname*
GB 1967   96m   Technicolor
Universal / Scimitar (Michael Winner)

An advertising executive gives up power and money for integrity on a small literary magazine, but is won back by a mogul.
Vivid yet muddled tragi-comedy of the sixties, with splashes of sex and violence in trendy settings, a hero one really doesn't believe in, and a title which seems to have no meaning whatsoever.

w Peter Draper *d* Michael Winner *ph* Otto Heller *m* Francis Lai

Oliver Reed, Orson Welles, Carol White, Harry Andrews, Michael Hordern, Wendy Craig, Marianne Faithfull

I'll See You in My Dreams*
US 1952   112m   bw
Warner (Louis F. Edelman)

The domestic and professional life of songwriter Gus Kahn.
Quiet-toned, well made, quite forgettable musical.

w Melville Shavelson, Jack Rose *d* Michael Curtiz *ph* Ted McCord *md* Ray Heindorf *ch.* Le Roy Prinz

Doris Day, Danny Thomas, Frank Lovejoy, Patrice Wymore, James Gleason

I'll Take Sweden
US 1965   96m   Technicolor
UA / Edward Small

A widowed oil company executive accepts a Stockholm posting to remove his teenage daughter from an unsuitable attachment.
Feeble comedy which unwisely attempts to be with it, but is bogged down by amateurish handling and wit-wise is sadly without it.

w Nat Perrin, Bob Fisher, Arthur Marx *d* Frederick de Cordova *ph* Daniel L. Fapp *m* Jimmy Haskell

Bob Hope, Tuesday Weld, Frankie Avalon, Dina Merrill, Jeremy Slate, John Qualen, Walter Sande

Illegal*
US 1955   88m   bw
Warner (Frank P. Rosenberg)

A disillusioned District Attorney becomes a racketeer's lawyer but finally denounces him at the cost of his own life.
Competent remake of *The Mouthpiece* (qv), a good star melodrama.

w W. R. Burnett, James R. Webb, *story* Frank J. Collins *d* Lewis Allen *ph* Peverell Marley *m* Max Steiner

Edward G. Robinson, Nina Foch, Albert Dekker, Hugh Marlowe, Jayne Mansfield, Howard St John, Ellen Corby
'Hard-hitting stuff in the old gangster tradition.'—*MFB*

The Illustrated Man*
US 1969   103m   Technicolor   Panavision
Warner / SKM (Howard B. Kreitsek, Ted Mann)

A strange wanderer tells weird stories based on the tattooed pictures which cover him from tip to toe.
Oddball compendium based rather insecurely on Ray Bradbury stories; in this form they don't amount to much but the presentation is assured.

w Howard B. Kreitsek *d* Jack Smight *ph* Philip Lathrop *m* Jerry Goldsmith *ad* Joel Schiller

Rod Steiger, Claire Bloom, Robert Drivas, Don Dubbins, Jason Evers
'A curiously passionless affair – efficient enough, meaty enough, but without poetry, without charm, without beauty.'—*Philip Strick*
'A pretentious comic strip of maudlin and muddled fantasies.'—*Judith Crist*

Illustrious Corpses*
Italy / France 1975   120m   Technicolor
PEA / UA (Alberto Grimaldi)
original title: *Cadaveri Eccellenti*

A right-wing conspiracy to arouse feelings against dissidents is found to be behind the murders of public figures.
Elegant police melodrama on an unlikely political thesis.

w Francesco Rosi, Tonino Guerra, Lino Jannuzzi, *novel* Il Contesto by Leonardo Sciascia *d* Francesco Rosi *ph* Pasqualino de Santis *m* Piero Piccioni

Lino Ventura, Alain Cuny, Maolo Bonacelli, Marcel Bozzuffi, Max Von Sydow, Fernando Rey, Charles Vanel, Tina Aumont
'Like watching layer after layer peeled off some diseased flower until the poisoned root is reached.'—*Michael Billington, Illustrated London News*

I'm All Right Jack***
GB 1960   104m   bw
British Lion / Charter (Roy Boulting)

A world-innocent graduate takes a job in
industry; by starting at the bottom he provokes a
national strike.
Satirical farce which manages to hit most of its
widespread targets and finds corruption in high,
low and middle places. A not inaccurate picture
of aspects of British life in the fifties, and a
presage of the satire boom to come with *Beyond
the Fringe* and *That Was the Week That Was*.

w Frank Harvey, John Boulting, *novel* Private
Life by *Alan Hackney* *d* John Boulting *ph* Max
Greene *m* Ken Hare

Ian Carmichael, Peter Sellers, Irene Handl,
Richard Attenborough, *Terry-Thomas*, Dennis
Price, Margaret Rutherford, Liz Fraser, *John Le
Mesurier*, Sam Kydd

I'm No Angel***
US 1933   88m   bw
Paramount (William Le Baron)

A carnival dancer gets off a murder charge,
moves into society and sues a man for breach of
promise.
The star's most successful vehicle, credited with
saving the fortunes of Paramount, remains a
highly diverting side show with almost a laugh a
minute. Released before the Legion of Decency
was formed, it also contains some of Mae's
fruitiest lines.

w Mae West *d* Wesley Ruggles *ph* Leo Tover

Mae West, Edward Arnold, Cary Grant,
Gregory Ratoff, Ralf Harolde, Kent Taylor,
Gertrude Michael

'The most freewheeling of all Mae's screen
vehicles, and the most satisfying of the lot.'—
James Robert Parish

Images
Eire 1972   101m   Technicolor
   Panavision
Lions Gate / Hemdale (Tommy Thompson)

A semi-hysterical woman is confronted by the
images of her former lovers.
Pretentious psycho-drama which might have
made a good half-hour.

wd Robert Altman *ph* Vilmos Zsigismond
m John Williams

Susannah York, René Auberjonois, Marcel
Bozzuffi

Imitation General
US 1958   88m   bw
MGM (William Hawks)

France 1944: when a general is killed, a sergeant
takes his place to preserve morale.
Odd, rather unpalatable war comedy-drama.

w William Bowers *d* George Marshall
ph George Folsey

Glenn Ford, Red Buttons, Taina Elg, Dean
Jones, Kent Smith

Imitation of Life**
US 1934   109m   bw
Universal

A woman becomes rich through the pancake
recipe of her black servant, but the latter has a
tragic life because her daughter passes for white.
Monumentally efficient tearjerker, generally well
done.

w William Hurlbut, *novel* Fannie Hurst *d John
Stahl ph* Merritt Gerstad *m* Heinz Roemheld

Claudette Colbert, Warren William, *Louise
Beavers*, Ned Sparks, Rochelle Hudson, Fredi
Washington, Alan Hale, Henry Armetta

'Classic, compulsively watchable rags-to-
riches-and-heartbreak weeper.'—*New Yorker,
1977*

AAN: best picture

Imitation of Life*
US 1959   124m   Eastmancolor
U-I (Ross Hunter)

Glossy remake of the above with its heroine now
an actress; stunningly produced but dully acted,
making its racially sensitive plot seem insincere.

w Eleanore Griffin, Allan Scott *d Douglas Sirk
ph* Russell Metty *m* Frank Skinner

Lana Turner, Juanita Moore, John Gavin, Susan
Kohner, Dan O'Herlihy, Sandra Dee, Robert
Alda

AAN: Juanita Moore; Susan Kohner

The Immigrant**
US 1917   20m approx   bw   silent
Mutual

A penniless immigrant befriends a girl on the
boat and later helps her in a café.
One of the most inventive early Chaplins, with
touches of sentiment and social comment which
for once only strengthen and do not antagonize.

wd Charles Chaplin ph William C. Foster,
Rollie Totheroh

Charles Chaplin, Edna Purviance, Albert
Austin, Henry Bergman

Immoral Tales
France 1974   103m   Eastmancolor
Argos (Anatole Dauman)

Four bawdy stories, ranging from 1498 to 1970.
The usual sex portmanteau with a little more
strength in the detail and interest in human
behaviour than usual.

wd Walerian Borowczyk *ph* Bernard
Daillencourt, Guy Durban, Michel Zolat, Noel
Véry *m* Maurice Le Roux

Lise Danvers, Charlotte Alexandra, Paloma
Picasso, Florence Bellamy

'You come out having learned something
about the waywardness of life and love and
having been taken on a mystery tour into the
present, the past, and the enigmatic strangeness
of womanhood.'—*Michael Billington,
Illustrated London News*

The Immortal Sergeant*
US 1943 90m bw
TCF (Lamar Trotti)

In the North African campaign, a battle-
toughened sergeant is killed after inspiring the
raw recruits under his command.
'Inspirational' war adventure, quite neatly done
but a shade embarrassed by its own poetic
leanings.

w Lamar Trotti, *novel* John Brophy *d* John
Stahl *ph* Arthur Miller *m* David Buttolph

Henry Fonda, Thomas Mitchell, Maureen
O'Hara, Allyn Joslyn, Reginald Gardiner,
Melville Cooper, Branwell Fletcher, Morton
Lowry

Impact
US 1949 111m bw
(UA) Harry M. Popkin

A woman and her lover plan the murder of her
rich industrialist husband, but things go wrong
and the husband survives under another
name . . .
Curiously elongated but watchable melodrama,
with the impression of a second team doing its
best.

w Dorothy Reid *d* Arthur Lubin *ph* Ernest
Laszlo

Brian Donlevy, Ella Raines, Charles Coburn,
Helen Walker

The Impatient Years
US 1944 91m bw
Columbia

A soldier finds difficulty in adjusting to his
civilian matrimonial state.
Thin star comedy.

w Virginia Van Upp *d* Irving Cummings
ph Joseph Walker *m* Marlin Skiles

Jean Arthur, Lee Bowman, Charles Coburn,
Edgar Buchanan, Harry Davenport, Grant
Mitchell, Jane Darwell

The Imperfect Lady
US 1947 97m bw
Paramount (Karl Tunberg)
GB title: *Mrs Loring's Secret*

In nineties London, an MP marries a lady with a
past.
Dusty melodrama, adequately produced.

w Karl Tunberg, *story* Ladislas Fodor *d* Lewis
Allen *ph* John F. Seitz *m* Victor Young

Ray Milland, Teresa Wright, Cedric Hardwicke,
Virginia Field, Anthony Quinn, Reginald Owen,
Melville Cooper, George Zucco, Rhys Williams,
Charles Coleman, Miles Mander, Edmund
Breon, Frederick Worlock

The Impersonator*
GB 1961 64m bw
Bryanston / Herald (Anthony Perry)

Americans at a British air base are suspected
when a murderous prowler strikes.
Well made second-feature thriller with effective
locations, suspense sequences and village
atmosphere.

wd Alfred Shaughnessy *ph* John Coquillon
m de Wolfe

John Crawford, Jane Griffith, Patricia Burke,
John Salew

The Importance of Being Earnest**
GB 1952 95m Technicolor
Rank / Javelin / Two Cities (Teddy Baird)

Two wealthy and eligible bachelors of the
nineties have problems with their marriage
prospects.
Disappointingly stagey rendering (when
compared, say, with *Occupe-toi d'Amélie*) of
Britain's most wondrously witty lighter-than-air
comedy of manners. As a record of a theatrical
performance, however, it is valuable.

w Anthony Asquith, *play* Oscar Wilde
d Anthony Asquith *ph* Desmond Dickinson
m Benjamin Frankel *ad* Carmen Dillon

*Michael Redgrave, Michael Denison, Edith
Evans, Margaret Rutherford, Joan Greenwood,
Miles Malleson, Dorothy Tutin, Walter Hudd*

'A more positive decision on style should have
been taken. A film of this kind must be either an
adaptation or a piece of filmed theatre. This one,
being partially both, is not wholly either.'—
Gavin Lambert

The Impossible Years
US 1968   98m   Metrocolor   Panavision
MGM / Marten (Lawrence Weingarten)

A university psychiatrist has trouble controlling
his nubile 17-year-old daughter.
Wacky farce which veers between the tasteless
and the ludicrous, and is never more than
momentarily entertaining.

w George Wells, *play* Bob Fisher, Arthur Marx
d Michael Gordon *ph* William H. Daniels
m Don Costa

David Niven, Lola Albright, Chad Everett,
Ozzie Nelson, Cristina Ferrare, Don Beddoe

In a Lonely Place*
US 1950   93m   bw
Columbia / Santana (Robert Lord)

An embittered Hollywood scriptwriter escapes a
murder charge but loses his girl friend through
his violent temperament.
Curious character melodrama which intrigues
without satisfying.

w Andrew Solt, *novel* Dorothy B. Hughes
d Nicholas Ray *ph* Burnett Guffey *m* George
Antheil

Humphrey Bogart, Gloria Grahame, Frank
Lovejoy, Carl Benton Reid, Art Smith, Jeff
Donnell

'It remains better than average, but lacks the
penetration which would make it really
interesting.'—*Gavin Lambert*

In Celebration
GB 1974   131m   Eastmancolor
Ely Landau / Cinevision

Three sons travel north for their miner father's
fortieth wedding anniversary.
Sharply observant but fairly predictable
dramatics, plainly filmed.

w David Storey, from his play d Lindsay
Anderson *ph* Dick Bush *m* Christopher
Gunning

Alan Bates, James Bolam, Brian Cox,
Constance Chapman, Bill Owen

In Cold Blood*
US 1967   134m   bw   Panavision
Columbia / Richard Brooks

An account of a real life crime in which an entire
family was brutally murdered by wandering
gunmen.
Unnecessarily complicated as narrative, and
uncompromisingly brutal in treatment, this well-
meaning film is hard to take in many ways.

wd Richard Brooks, *book* Truman Capote
ph Conrad Hall *m* Quincy Jones

Robert Blake, Scott Wilson, John Forsythe, Paul
Stewart, Gerald S. O'Loughlin, Jeff Corey

'It marks a slight step up for its director, best
remembered for reducing *Lord Jim* to pablum
and *The Brothers Karamazov* to pulp.'—*John
Simon*

AAN: Richard Brooks (as writer); Richard
Brooks (as director); Conrad Hall; Quincy Jones

In Enemy Country
US 1968   107m   Techniscope
Universal (Harry Keller)

In 1939 Paris, the French secret service evolves
an elaborate four-year undercover plan.
Standard, overlong espionage melodrama with
no surprises.

w Edward Anhalt, *story* Sy Bartlett *d* Harry
Keller *ph* Loyal Griggs *m* William Lava

Tony Franciosa, Anjanette Comer, Guy
Stockwell, Paul Hubschmid, Tom Bell, Harry
Townes, Michael Constantine, John Marley

In Harm's Way*
US 1965   167m   bw   Panavision
Paramount / Sigma (Otto Preminger)

The American navy retaliates after Pearl
Harbor.
Odd mix of all-star action, spectacle (mostly
models) and personal romances, with a few
interesting scenes; shorn of colour it seems
rather half-hearted.

w Wendell Mayes, *novel* James Bassett *d* Otto
Preminger *ph* Loyal Griggs *m* Jerry Goldsmith
titles Saul Bass

John Wayne, Kirk Douglas, Patricia Neal, Tom
Tryon, Paula Prentiss, Brandon de Wilde,
Stanley Holloway, Burgess Meredith, Henry
Fonda, Dana Andrews, Franchot Tone, Jill
Haworth, George Kennedy, Hugh O'Brian,
Carroll O'Connor, Patrick O'Neal, Slim
Pickens, Bruce Cabot, Larry Hagman, James
Mitchum

'Lacks even a touch of the touch.'—*Stanley
Kauffmann*

AAN: Loyal Griggs

In Like Flint
US 1967   107m   De Luxe   Cinemascope
TCF (Saul David)

Top agent Derek Flint unmasks a subversive
female spy ring which has kidnapped the
President.
This sequel to *Our Man Flint* (qv) is silly rather
than funny, a spy spoof which becomes
irritatingly hard to take.

w Hal Fimberg *d* Gordon Douglas *ph* William
Daniels *m* Jerry Goldsmith

James Coburn, Lee J. Cobb, Jean Hall, Andrew
Duggan, Anna Lee

'It gently founders in yards of flat dialogue,
lavishly uninteresting sets, fuzzy colour
processing, and a supporting cast in which all the
girls look alarmingly mass produced.'—*MFB*

In Love and War
US 1958   111m   Eastmancolor
Cinemascope
TCF (Jerry Wald)

Three men from different backgrounds join the
US Marines and see service in the Pacific.
Self-conscious propaganda concoction of bare
routine interest.

w Edward Anhalt, *novel* Anton Myrer *d* Philip
Dunne *ph* Leo Tover *m* Hugo Friedhofer

Jeffrey Hunter, Robert Wagner, Bradford
Dillman, Dana Wynter, Hope Lange, Sheree
North, France Nuyen

In Name Only*
US 1939   94m   bw
RKO (Pandro S. Berman)

A rich man falls in love but his wife refuses a
divorce. The stars seem unhappy in this sombre
matrimonial drama, but of its kind it's
surprisingly well made.

w Richard Sherman, *novel* Memory of Love by
Bessie Brewer *d* John Cromwell *ph* J. Roy
Hunt *m* Roy Webb

Cary Grant, Carole Lombard, Kay Francis,
Charles Coburn, Helen Vinson

'Shot with a refined taste for interior
decoration . . . it is oversweetened with the
material for tears.'—*Graham Greene*

In Old Arizona**
US 1929   95m   bw
Fox

Adventures of the Cisco Kid.
Primitive sound western, a sensation in its day
but now of purely historical interest.

w Tom Barry, *stories* O. Henry *d* Raoul Walsh,
Irving Cummings *ph* Arthur Edeson

Warner Baxter, Edmund Lowe, Dorothy
Burgess, J. Farrell MacDonald
†See also *The Cisco Kid.*

AA: Warner Baxter
AAN: best picture; Tom Barry; Raoul Walsh,
Irving Cummings; Arthur Edeson

In Old Chicago***
US 1938   115m   bw
TCF (Kenneth MacGowan)

Events leading up to the great Chicago fire
include a torrid romance between a gambler and
a café singer.
Spectacular melodrama which with its two-
million-dollar budget was a deliberate attempt to
outdo *San Francisco*, and only failed because
the cast was less interesting. A splendid studio
super-production.

w Lamar Trotti, Sonya Levien, *novel* We the
O'Learys by Niven Busch *d* Henry King,
ph Peverell Marley *m* Louis Silvers *sp* H. Bruce
Humberstone, Daniel B. Clark, Fred Sersen,
Louis J. Witte *ad* William Darling

Tyrone Power, Alice Faye, Don Ameche, *Alice
Brady,* Andy Devine, Brian Donlevy, Phyllis
Brooks, Tom Brown, Sidney Blackmer, Berton
Churchill, Paul Hurst, Rondo Hatton, Eddie
Collins

AA: Alice Brady
AAN: Niven Busch (original story); Louis
Silvers

In Our Time*
US 1944   110m   bw
Warner (Jerry Wald)

English girl marries Polish count and helps defy
the Nazis.
Ambitious, would-be meaningful melodrama
that doesn't quite come off.

w Ellis St Joseph, Howard Koch *d* Vincent
Sherman *ph* Carl Guthrie *m* Franz Waxman

Ida Lupino, Paul Henreid, Nancy Coleman,
Nazimova, Mary Boland, Victor Francen,
Michael Chekhov

'The story starts a good many hares but
prudently refrains from following them.'—
Richard Mallett, Punch

In Person
US 1935   85m   bw
RKO (Pandro S. Berman)

A glamorous but exhausted film star tries to
escape her public by fleeing incognito to the
country.
Mild star comedy.

w Allan Scott, *novel* Samuel Hopkins Adams
d William A. Seiter *ph* Edward Cronjager

Ginger Rogers, George Brent, Alan Mowbray,
Grant Mitchell, Samuel S. Hinds, Spencer
Charters

In Search of Gregory
GB 1969   90m   Technicolor
Universal / Vic Films / Vera Films (Joe Janni,
   Daniele Senatore)

A girl attends her father's wedding to meet a
mysterious guest named Gregory, whom she
never quite contacts.
Irritatingly pretentious Pinterish puzzle-drama
with apparently no hidden depths except the urge
to be clever.

w Tonino Guerra, Lucile Laks d Peter Wood
ph Otto Heller, Giorgio Tonti m Ron Grainer

Julie Christie, Michael Sarrazin, John Hurt,
Adolfo Celi, Roland Culver, Tony Selby
   'Moments in a vacuum: however lively the
surface, the centre remains depressingly inert.'—
MFB

In Search of the Castaways***
GB 1961   100m   Technicolor
Walt Disney (Hugh Attwooll)

With the aid of an eccentric professor, three
children seek their lost explorer father in some
geographically fantastic regions of South
America.
Engaging Victorian fantasy which starts
realistically and builds up to sequences in the
manner of The Wizard of Oz and concludes in
Treasure Island vein. Jaunty juvenile fare.

w Lowell S. Hawley, novel Captain Grant's
Children by Jules Verne d Robert Stevenson
ph Paul Beeson m William Alwyn ad Michael
Stringer

Maurice Chevalier, Hayley Mills, George
Sanders, Wilfrid Hyde White, Wilfrid Brambell

In Society*
US 1944   74m   bw
U-I

Two incompetent plumbers ruin a mansion.
One of the better A & C romps, with little
padding between the comedy highlights, though
the trimmings are fearsomely dated.

w John Grant, Hal Finberg, Edmund L.
Hartmann d Jean Yarbrough ph Jerome Ash
m Edgar Fairchild

Bud Abbott, Lou Costello, Kirby Grant, Ann
Gillis, Arthur Treacher, Steve Geray, George
Dolenz, Marion Hutton

In the Cool of the Day
US 1962   91m   Metrocolor   Panavision
MGM (John Houseman)

The frail wife of a New York publisher dies in
Greece after an affair with his colleague.
Travelogue with romantic asides; a pretty glum
business.

w Meade Roberts, novel Susan Ertz d Robert
Stevens ph Peter Newbrook m Francis
Chagrin ad Ken Adam

Jane Fonda, Peter Finch, Arthur Hill, Angela
Lansbury, Constance Cummings

In the French Style*
US / France 1962   105m   bw
Columbia / Casanna / Orsay (Robert Parrish,
   Irwin Shaw)

An American girl in Paris has affairs with a
young boy and with a divorced newspaperman.
Smooth, episodic, romantic character study, well
made but with no perceptible dramatic point.

w Irwin Shaw d Robert Parrish ph Michel
Kelber m Josef Kosma

Jean Seberg, Stanley Baker, Philippe Fouquet

In the Good Old Summertime*
US 1949   102m   Technicolor
MGM (Joe Pasternak)

In a Chicago music store in 1906, a salesgirl
corresponds through a dating service with a man
who turns out to be the manager she detests.
Cheerful remake of The Shop around the Corner
(qv), with agreeable music, garish colour and not
much style.

w Albert Hackett, Frances Goodrich, Ivan Tors,
play Miklos Laszlo d Robert Z. Leonard
ph Harry Stradling md George Stoll ad Randell
Duell ch Robert Alton

Judy Garland, Van Johnson, S. Z. Sakall, Spring
Byington, Clinton Sundberg, Buster Keaton,
Lilian Bronson

In the Heat of the Night**
US 1969   109m   De Luxe
UA / Mirisch (Walter Mirisch)

In a small southern town, the bigoted and
bombastic sheriff on a murder hunt grudgingly
accepts the help of a black detective.
Overrated policier in which the personality clash
is amusing (and was timely) but the murder
puzzle is a complete throwaway.

w Sterling Silliphant d Norman Jewison
ph Haskell Wexler m Quincy Jones

Sidney Poitier, Rod Steiger, Warren Oates,
Quentin Dean, William Schallert
† Poitier subsequently starred in a couple of very
inferior sequels, They Call Me Mister Tibbs and
The Organization (both qv).

AA: best picture; Sterling Silliphant; Rod Steiger
AAN: Norman Jewison

In the Navy*
US 1941   86m   bw
Universal (Alex Gottlieb)

Two incompetents and a singing heart-throb are
naval recruits.
A basically feeble follow-up to *Buck Privates*
which outgrossed its predecessor and now
stands as an interesting pointer to how mass
entertainment has changed since 1941.

w John Grant, Arthur T. Horman *d* Arthur
Lubin *ph* Joseph Valentine *songs* Gene de Paul,
Don Raye

Bud Abbott, Lou Costello, Dick Powell, The
Andrews Sisters, Claire Dodd, Dick Foran,
Shemp Howard

In This Our Life**
US 1942   101m   bw
Warner (David Lewis)

A neurotic girl steals her sister's husband, leaves
him in the lurch, dominates her hapless family
and is killed while on the run from the police.
Splendid star melodrama with good supporting
acting and background detail.

w Howard Koch, novel Ellen Glasgow *d* John
Huston *ph* Ernest Haller *m* Max Steiner

Bette Davis, Charles Coburn, Olivia de
Havilland, Frank Craven, George Brent, Dennis
Morgan, Billie Burke, Hattie McDaniel, Lee
Patrick, Walter Huston (uncredited)

In Which We Serve****
GB 1942   114m   bw
Rank / Two Cities (Noel Coward)

Survivors from a torpedoed destroyer recall their
life at sea and on leave.
Dated but splendid flagwaver; an archetypal
British war film of almost limitless propaganda
value.

w Noel Coward *d* Noel Coward, David Lean
m Noel Coward

Noel Coward, Bernard Miles, *John Mills,*
Richard Attenborough, *Celia Johnson,* Kay
Walsh, Joyce Carey, Michael Wilding, Penelope
Dudley Ward, Kathleen Harrison, Philip Friend,
George Carney, Geoffrey Hibbert, James
Donald

'One of the screen's proudest achievements at
any time and in any country.'—*Newsweek*

AAN: best picture; Noel Coward (as writer)

Inadmissible Evidence**
GB 1968   96m   bw
Paramount / Woodfall (Ronald Kinnoch)

A frustrated 40-year-old solicitor is on the verge
of a nervous breakdown.

Interesting and surprisingly successful
transcription of a difficult play which was
virtually an anti-humanity soliloquy.

w John Osborne, from his play *d Anthony Page*
ph Kenneth Hodges *m* Dudley Moore
ad Seamus Flannery

Nicol Williamson, Eleanor Fazan, Jill Bennett,
Peter Sallis, Eileen Atkins, Isobel Dean

'A play that was conceived as an increasingly
bad dream has been made into a grittily detailed,
naturalistic film.'—*Stanley Kauffmann*

Incendiary Blonde*
US 1945   112m   Technicolor
Paramount (Joseph Sistrom)

The life of twenties nightclub queen Texas
Guinan.
Laundered biopic with guns, girls and gangsters
as well as songs.

w Claude Binyon, Frank Butler *d* George
Marshall *ph Ray Rennahan m* Robert Emmett
Dolan

Betty Hutton, Arturo de Cordova, Charles
Ruggles, Albert Dekker, Barry Fitzgerald, Mary
Phillips, Bill Goodwin, Eduardo Ciannelli,
Maurice Rocco

'It runs its noisy but high-minded course
through steamy emotion, painful
misunderstanding and dramatic self-sacrifice,
winding up in the snow among the blood of dead
gangsters. Have we ever seen gangsters in
Technicolor before?'—*Richard Mallett, Punch*

AAN: Robert Emmett Dolan

Les Inconnus dans la Maison*
France 1941   94m   bw
Continental

An embittered ex-barrister saves his teenage
daughter from a murder charge.
Unlikely melodrama remade as *Stranger in the
House*; this version has more compelling writing
and acting.

w Henri-Georges Clouzot, novel Georges
Simenon *d* Henri Decoin *ph* Jules Kruger
m Roland Manuel

Raimu, Juliette Faber, Jacques Baumer, Jean
Tissier

The Incredible Journey**
US 1963   80m   Technicolor
Walt Disney (James Algar)

Two dogs and a cat, separated from their
owners, escape and travel 250 miles home.
A novelty attraction which keeps going purely
on its animal interest, which is considerable.

w James Algar, *book* Sheila Burnford *d* Fletcher

Markle *ph* Kenneth Peach, Jack Couffer, Lloyd Beebe *m* Oliver Wallace

The Incredible Melting Man
US 1977   84m   Movielab
AIP / Quartet (Max J. Rosenberg)

The survivor of a space flight is rushed to hospital with radiation burns and an infection which causes his flesh to melt.
Unpleasant and nonsensical horror film with a few unintentional laughs and a plot borrowed from *The Quatermass Experiment*.

wd William Sachs *ph* Willy Curtis *m* Arlon Ober

Alex Rebar, Burr DeBenning, Myron Healey, Myron Aldredge

The Incredible Mr Limpet
US 1964   102m   Technicolor
Warner (John C. Rose)

A meek but patriotic clerk is turned down by the navy and turns into a fish. In this form he becomes a radar assistant to a warship.
Sentimental sub-Disney goo, part animated.

w Jameson Bewer, John C. Rose, *novel* Theodore Pratt *d* Arthur Lubin *ph* Harold Stine *m* Frank Perkins

Don Knotts, Andrew Duggan, Larry Keating, Jack Weston

The Incredible Sarah*
GB 1976   105m   Technicolor
Readers Digest (Helen M. Strauss)

The career of French actress Sarah Bernhardt up to the age of thirty-five.
Mildly pleasing old-fashioned biopic with remarkably unreliable detail and a regrettably bland approach to its fascinating subject.

w Ruth Wolff *d* Richard Fleischer *ph* Christopher Challis *m* Elmer Bernstein *pd* Elliot Scott

Glenda Jackson, Daniel Massey, Yvonne Mitchell, Douglas Wilmer, David Langton, Simon Williams, John Castle, Edward Judd, Peter Sallis

The Incredible Shrinking Man**
US 1957   81m   bw
U-I (Albert Zugsmith)

After being caught in a radioactive mist, a man shrinks inexorably to micro-size.
Horrifyingly inevitable sci-fi with imaginative touches gracing a cheap production.

w Richard Matheson *d* Jack Arnold *ph* Ellis W. Carter *m* Joseph Gershenson *sp* Clifford Stine, Roswell A. Hoffman, Everett H. Bronssard

Grant Williams, Randy Stuart, April Kent, Paul Langton
'It opens up new vistas of cosmic terror.'— *Peter John Dyer*

The Indian Fighter
US 1955   88m   Technicolor Cinemascope
UA / Bryna (William Schorr)

An Indian fighter protects a wagon train from the Sioux.
Simple-minded western with touches of philosophy and not much drive.

w Frank Davis, Ben Hecht *d* André de Toth *ph* Wilfrid M. Cline *m* Franz Waxman

Kirk Douglas, Elsa Martinelli, Walter Abel, Walter Matthau, Diana Douglas, Eduard Franz, Lon Chaney Jnr, Alan Hale Jnr, Elisha Cook Jnr

Indiscreet**
GB 1958   100m   Technicolor
Grandon (Stanley Donen)

An American diplomat in London falls in love with an actress but protects himself by saying he is married.
Affairs among the ultra rich, amusing when played by these stars but with imperfect production values which the alarmingly thin plot allows one too much time to consider.

w Norman Krasna, from his play Kind Sir *d* Stanley Donen *ph* Frederick A. Young *m* Richard Bennett, Ken Jones

Cary Grant, Ingrid Bergman, Phyllis Calvert, Cecil Parker, David Kossoff, Megs Jenkins
'One is often on the point of being bored, but one never is, quite.'—*Richard Roud*
'A film to which you would not hesitate to take your jeweller, your architect, your home decorator, your dressmaker and your domestic staff.'—*Alexander Walker*

Indiscretion of an American Wife*
Italy / US 1954   75m   bw
David O. Selznick (Vittorio de Sica)
Alternative titles: *Terminus Station, Indiscretion*

An American woman and an Italian professor say goodbye in Rome's terminal station.
Strained attempt to re-do *Brief Encounter* against the busy background of a great railway station; moments of interest, but artificiality prevails, and the plot never gets up enough steam.

w Cesare Zavattini, Truman Capote, etc *d* Vittorio de Sica *ph* G. R. Aldo *m* Aldo Cicognini

Jennifer Jones, Montgomery Clift, Gino Cervi, Richard Beymer

Inferno**

US 1953 83m Technicolor 3-D
TCF (William Bloom)

When a millionaire breaks his leg in the desert, his wife and her lover leave him to die; but he contrives to catch up with them.

An outdoor melodrama which made better use of 3-D than any other film, suggesting the lone handicapped figure in the vast spaces; but the lovers are dull and the fire climax perfunctory.

w Francis Cockrell d Roy Baker ph Lucien Andriot m Paul Sawtell

Robert Ryan, William Lundigan, Rhonda Fleming

The Informer****

US 1935 91m bw
RKO (Cliff Reid)

An IRA leader is betrayed by a simple-minded hanger-on who wants money to emigrate; he is hounded by fellow rebels and his own conscience.

A tedious plot is turned into brilliant cinema by full-blooded acting and a highly stylized yet brilliantly effective mise en scène which never attempts reality.

w Dudley Nichols, novel Liam O'Flaherty d John Ford ph Joseph H. August m Max Steiner ad Van Nest Polglase

Victor McLaglen, Heather Angel, Margot Grahame, Una O'Connor, Wallace Ford, Preston Foster, J. M. Kerrigan, Joe Sawyer, Donald Meek

'As impressive as Scarface, or anything in the whole powerful literature redolent of fog and grime and dreariness which the Germans gave to the Americans.'—Bardèche and Brasillach

AA: Dudley Nichols; John Ford; Max Steiner; Victor McLaglen
AAN: best picture

The Informers

GB 1963 104m bw
Rank (William MacQuitty)
US title: Underworld Informers

A police informer is murdered and his brother takes revenge.

Basic police melodrama, with clumsy script and jaded direction.

w Alun Falconer, novel Death of a Snout by Douglas Warner d Ken Annakin ph Reg Wyer m Clifton Parker

Nigel Patrick, Colin Blakely, Derren Nesbitt

L'Ingénue Libertine

France 1950 88m approx bw
Codo-Cinéma (Jean Velter)

A romantic girl lives in an imaginary world of affairs, but can't bring herself to consummate her marriage.

Minor period sex comedy which has the distinction of being Britain's first 'X' film, though the naughtiness is more implied than stated.

w P. Laroche, novel Colette d Jacqueline Audry ph Grignon m Vincent Scotto

Daniele Delorme, Frank Villard, Jean Tissier

Inherit the Wind***

US 1960 127m bw
UA / Lomitas (Stanley Kramer)

A fictionalized account of the 1925 Scopes 'monkey trial', when a schoolmaster was accused of teaching the theory of evolution.

Splendid theatrics with fine performances, marred by boring subplots but enhanced by a realistic portrait of a sweltering southern town.

w Nathan E. Douglas, Harold Jacob Smith, play Jerome Lawrence, Robert E. Lee d Stanley Kramer ph Ernest Laszlo m Ernest Gold

Spencer Tracy, Fredric March, Florence Eldridge, Gene Kelly, Dick York, Donna Anderson, Harry Morgan, Elliott Reid, Claude Akins

AAN: script; Ernest Laszlo; Spencer Tracy

The Inn of the Sixth Happiness**

GB 1958 158m De Luxe Cinemascope
TCF (Mark Robson)

An English servant girl becomes a missionary and spends many arduous years in China.

Romanticized biopic of Gladys Aylward, with lots of children, a happy ending, and everyone sensationally miscast. Somehow it all works, even North Wales standing in for China.

w Isobel Lennart, book The Small Woman by Alan Burgess d Mark Robson ph Frederick A. Young m Malcolm Arnold

Ingrid Bergman, Curt Jurgens, Robert Donat, Athene Seyler, Ronald Squire, Richard Wattis, Moultrie Kelsall

AAN: Mark Robson

Inner Sanctum

The title was taken from a radio show featuring mystery stories with a last minute twist. The films were introduced rather oddly by a misshapen head in a crystal ball on the empty table of a boardroom. The head belonged to David Hoffman, and he introduced each film: 'This . . . is the inner sanctum . . .' (The original

reference was presumably to the innermost working of the human mind.) The films, made for Universal, all starred Lon Chaney Jnr (who alternated as hero and villain); they were among the most boring and badly made second feature thrillers of the forties.
1943: CALLING DR DEATH
1944: WEIRD WOMAN, DEAD MAN'S EYES
1945: STRANGE CONFESSION (remake of THE MAN WHO RECLAIMED HIS HEAD), THE FROZEN GHOST
1946: PILLOW OF DEATH

Innocent Bystanders*
GB 1972   110m   Eastmancolor
Sagittarius (George H. Brown)

The British secret service sends three agents to trace a Russian traitor.
Confused and violent espionage thriller; rather a waste of good production.

w James Mitchell d Peter Collinson ph Brian Probyn m John Keating

Stanley Baker, Geraldine Chaplin, Dana Andrews, Donald Pleasence

Innocent Sinners**
GB 1957   95m   bw
Rank (Hugh Stewart)

A 13-year-old London girl builds a garden in the rubble of a bombed church, and gets into trouble with the police.
Likeable, slightly unfinished, mildly astringent little human drama full of well-observed character sketches.

w Neil Paterson, novel An Episode of Sparrows by Rumer Godden d Philip Leacock ph Harry Waxman m Philip Green

Flora Robson, Catherine Lacey, David Kossoff, Barbara Mullen, June Archer

The Innocents**
GB 1961   99m   bw   Cinemascope
TCF / Achilles (Jack Clayton)

In Victorian times, a spinster governess in a lonely house finds her young charges possessed by evil demons of servants now dead.
Elaborate revamping of Henry James' The Turn of the Screw, the ghosts being now (possibly) the figments of a frustrated woman's imagination. The frissons would have worked better on a normal-shaped screen, but the decor, lighting and general handling are exceptional.

w William Archibald, Truman Capote d Jack Clayton ph Freddie Francis ad Wilfrid Shingleton

Deborah Kerr, Megs Jenkins, Pamela Franklin, Martin Stephens, Michael Redgrave, Peter Wyngarde

Innocents in Paris
GB 1953   102m   bw
Romulus (Anatole de Grunwald)

British tourists spend a weekend in the gay city.
Strained compendium of anecdotes which misses an easy target.

w Anatole de Grunwald d Gordon Parry ph Gordon Lang m Josef Kosma

Alastair Sim, Margaret Rutherford, Jimmy Edwards, Claire Bloom, Laurence Harvey, Ronald Shiner

Innocents of Paris
US 1929   69m   bw
Paramount

A Parisian junk dealer saves a boy's life and falls for his aunt.
Heavygoing and dated musical comedy which introduced Chevalier to world audiences.

w Ethel Doherty, Ernest Vajda d Richard Wallace ph Charles Lang songs Leo Robin, Richard A. Whiting

Maurice Chevalier, Sylvia Beecher, Russell Simpson, George Fawcett

Inserts*
GB 1975   117m   De Luxe
UA / Film and General (Davina Belling, Clive Parsons)

In 1930 Hollywood, a fading silent queen and a has-been director take to drugs.
Curious, interesting semi-porno melodrama with Pinterish asides and an inaccurate but stimulating feel of the film city at its height.

wd John Byrum ph Denys Coop md Jessica Harper

Richard Dreyfuss, Jessica Harper, Veronica Cartwright, Bob Hoskins, Stephen Davies

Inside Daisy Clover*
US 1965   128m   Technicolor   Panavision
Warner / Pakula–Mulligan (Alan J. Pakula)

Tribulations of an adolescent movie star in thirties Hollywood.
Amusing, rather hysterical variant on A Star Is Born; agreeably wacky in spots, glum in others. Would have benefited from the greater permissiveness possible a few years later.

w Gavin Lambert, from his novel d Robert Mulligan ph Charles Lang Jnr m André Previn ch Herbert Ross ad Robert Clatworthy

Natalie Wood, Robert Redford, Ruth Gordon, Christopher Plummer, Roddy MacDowall

'The movie is short on characters, detail, activity, dialogue, even music; it's as if it's so determined to be stylish and sophisticated that rather than risk vulgarity or banality, it eliminates almost everything.'—*Pauline Kael, 1968*

AAN: Ruth Gordon

Inside Out*

GB / West Germany 1975 97m Technicolor
Warner / Kettledrum (Judd Bernard)

A German ex-commandant of a POW camp enlists the aid of Americans in a daring plan to kidnap a Nazi war criminal from East Germany and find buried Nazi loot.
Entertaining but very silly actioner with too many changes of mood, though some sequences please.

w Judd Bernard, Stephen Schneck *d* Peter Duffell *ph* John Coquillon *m* Konrad Elfers

Telly Savalas, James Mason, Robert Culp, Aldo Ray, Gunter Meisner, Adrian Hoven, Charles Korvin, Richard Warner

The Inspector*

GB 1961 111m De Luxe Cinemascope
TCF (Mark Robson)
US title: *Lisa*

In 1946 a Dutch policeman rescues a Jewish girl from an ex-Nazi and helps smuggle her to Palestine.
Peripatetic melodrama with surface suspense and subdued thoughts of ideology and race. Moments of interest, but generally dully developed and acted.

w Nelson Gidding, *novel* Jan de Hartog *d* Philip Dunne *ph* Arthur Ibbetson *m* Malcolm Arnold

Stephen Boyd, Dolores Hart, Leo McKern, *Hugh Griffith*, Donald Pleasence, Harry Andrews, Robert Stephens, Marius Goring

'A sluggish mélange of melodrama, romance, mystery and what the inactive might call action.'—*Judith Crist*

An Inspector Calls**

GB 1954 79m bw
British Lion / Watergate

In 1912 a prosperous Yorkshire family is visited by a mysterious inspector who proves that each of them was partly responsible for the death of a young girl.
Tactful, enjoyable record of a celebrated play in its author's most typical manner.

w Desmond Davis, *play J. B. Priestley d* Guy Hamilton *ph* Ted Scaife *m* Francis Chagrin *ad* Joseph Bato

Alastair Sim, Jane Wenham, Arthur Young, Olga Lindo, Brian Worth, Eileen Moore, Bryan Forbes

Inspector Clouseau

GB 1968 105m Eastmancolor Panavision
UA / Mirisch (Lewis J. Rachmil)

An incompetent French policeman is brought to London to investigate the aftermath of the Great Train Robbery.
Tiresome charade with all the jokes well telegraphed, and a background of swinging London.

w Tom and Frank Waldman *d* Bud Yorkin *ph* Arthur Ibbetson *m* Ken Thorne

Alan Arkin, Delia Boccardo, Frank Finlay, Patrick Cargill, Beryl Reid, Barry Foster

The Inspector General**

US 1949 101m Technicolor
Warner (Jerry Wald)
aka: *Happy Times*

An assistant elixir salesman with a travelling fair is mistaken by villagers for the dreaded inspector general.
Well wrought but basically boring version of a basically boring classic farce full of rhubarbing Old Russians. Nice production and hilarious moments do not quite atone for the dull stretches.

w Philip Rapp, Harry Kurnitz, *play* Nikolai Gogol *d* Henry Koster *ph* Elwood Bredell *songs* Sylvia Fine *m* John Green *ad* Robert Haas

Danny Kaye, Walter Slezak, Barbara Bates, Elsa Lanchester, Gene Lockhart, Alan Hale, Benny Baker, Walter Catlett

Inspector Hornleigh*

GB 1938 87m bw
TCF (Robert T. Kane)

The Chancellor of the Exchequer's bag is stolen. First of three police comedy-dramas based on a character created for the radio series Monday Night at Eight by Hans Priwin. Not bad, but the thinnest of the trio.

w Bryan Wallace, Gerald Elliott, Richard Llewellyn *d* Eugene Forde

Gordon Harker, Alastair Sim, Hugh Williams, Steve Geray, Wally Patch, Edward Underdown, Gibb McLaughlin, Ronald Adam

Inspector Hornleigh Goes to It*
GB 1940 87m bw
TCF (Edward Black)
US title: *Mail Train*

Hornleigh and Bingham track down a fifth
columnist.
Zestful comedy thriller climaxing on an express
train: good fun for addicts of the genre.

*w Val Guest, J. O. C. Orton, Frank Launder
d Walter Forde ph John Cox md Louis Levy*

Gordon Harker, Alastair Sim, Phyllis Calvert,
Edward Chapman, Charles Oliver, Raymond
Huntley, Percy Walsh, David Horne, Peter
Gawthorne

Inspector Hornleigh on Holiday*
GB 1939 87m bw
TCF (Edward Black)

The inspector and his sergeant solve the death of
a fellow boarder at a seaside hotel.
Lively Hitchcockian comedy-thriller romp with
an excellent script and plenty of variety of
location.

*w Frank Launder, Sidney Gilliat, J. O. C. Orton
d Walter Forde ph John Cox md Louis Levy*

Gordon Harker, Alastair Sim, Linden Travers,
Wally Patch, Edward Chapman, Philip Leaver,
Kynaston Reeves

Inspiration
US 1930 74m bw
MGM

A French artists' model renounces her lover in
case she harms his career.
Inane romantic melodrama.

*w Gene Markey d Clarence Brown ph William
Daniels*

Greta Garbo, Robert Montgomery, Lewis
Stone, Marjorie Rambeau, Beryl Mercer, John
Miljan

The Intelligence Men
GB 1965 104m Eastmancolor
Rank / Hugh Stewart
US title: *Spylarks*

Two incompetent spies blunder through a series
of adventures.
Inept and rather embarrassing big-screen debut
for two excellent television comedians.

*w S. C. Green, R. M. Hills d Robert Asher
ph Jack Asher m Phillip Green*

Eric Morecambe, Ernie Wise, William Franklyn,
April Olrich, Richard Vernon, David Lodge,
Warren Mitchell, Francis Matthews

Intent to Kill*
GB 1958 89m bw Cinemascope
TCF / Zonic (Adrian Worker)

In a Montreal hospital, attempts are made on the
life of a South American dictator recovering
from a brain operation.
Solidly entertaining suspenser.

*w Jimmy Sangster d Jack Cardiff ph Desmond
Dickinson m Kenneth V. Jones*

Richard Todd, Betsy Drake, Herbert Lom,
Warren Stevens, Alexander Knox

Interiors*
US 1978 95m Technicolor
UA / Jack Rollins-Charles H. Joffe

Everybody in a well-heeled American family has
problems.

Curious attempt by Woody Allen to make his
own version of the Bergmanesque psycho-dramas
he usually satirizes. Apparently this is the real
Woody, and the comedian was a mask. Oh, well.

wd Woody Allen ph Gordon Willis m none

Kristin Griffith, Marybelle Hurt, Richard
Jordan, Diane Keaton, E. G. Marshall,
Geraldine Page, Maureen Stapleton, Sam
Waterston

Interlude
US 1958 89m Technicolor
  Cinemascope
U-I (Ross Hunter)

An American girl in Munich falls in love with an
orchestral conductor but leaves him because of
his insane wife.
Dull remake of *When Tomorrow Comes* (qv),
with poor script and performances.

*w Daniel Fuchs, Franklin Coen d Douglas Sirk
ph R. F. Schoengarth m Frank Skinner*

Rossano Brazzi, June Allyson, Françoise
Rosay, Marianne Cook, Keith Andes, Jane
Wyatt
   'Contains every cliché known to romantic
fiction.'—*MFB*

Interlude*
GB 1968 113m Technicolor
Columbia / Domino (David Deutsch, Jack
  Hanbury)

A girl reporter falls for a celebrated orchestral
conductor; they have an affair but he finally goes
back to his wife.
Intermezzo remade for the swinging London set,
quite agreeable in parts because of the acting but
generally rather soggy.

w Lee Langley, Hugh Leonard d Kevin

Billington *ph Gerry Fisher m* Georges Delerue *pd* Tony Woolard

Oskar Werner, Barbara Ferris, *Virginia Maskell, John Cleese,* Donald Sutherland, Nora Swinburne, Alan Webb

'If you laughed at *Brief Encounter* you will roar over this one.'—*Wilfrid Sheed*

'It's got all the schmaltz and none of the style of the tearjerkers of yesteryear.'—*Judith Crist, 1973*

Intermezzo***
US 1939   69m   bw
David O. Selznick
GB title: *Escape to Happiness*

A renowned, married violinist has an affair with his musical protégée.
Archetypal cinema love story, Hollywoodized from a Swedish original but quite perfect in its brief, sentimental way.

w George O'Neil, *original scenario* Gosta Stevens, Gustav Molander *d Gregory Ratoff ph* Gregg Toland *m Robert Henning, Heinz Provost m (score)* Lou Forbes

Leslie Howard, Ingrid Bergman, John Halliday, Edna Best, Cecil Kellaway

AAN: Lou Forbes

International House*
US 1932   73m   bw
Paramount

A weird variety of travellers are quarantined in a Shanghai hotel where a local doctor has perfected television.
Madcap farce which succeeds in hits and misses.

w Francis Martin, Walter de Leon, Lou Heifetz, Neil Brant *d* Edward Sutherland *ph* Ernest Haller

W. C. Fields, George Burns, Gracie Allen, Peggy Hopkins Joyce, Stuart Erwin, Sari Matitza, Bela Lugosi, Edmund Breese, Lumsden Hare, Rose Marie, Rudy Vallee, Sterling Holloway, Cab Calloway and his band, Colonel Stoopnagle and Budd

'Constructed along the lines of a mammoth vaudeville show, the motivating story often is sidetracked entirely to permit a lot of unrelated hokum comedy.'—*Motion Picture Herald*

International Lady*
US 1941   102m   bw
Edward Small

An FBI man falls for the lady Axis agent he is chasing.
Cliché-ridden melodrama partially saved by light comedy touches.

w Howard Estabrook *d* Tim Whelan *ph* Hal Mohr *m* Lucien Moraweck

George Brent, Basil Rathbone, Ilona Massey, Gene Lockhart, George Zucco, Francis Pierlot, Martin Kosleck, Marjorie Gateson

International Squadron*
US 1941   87m   bw
Warner (Edmund Grainger)

A playboy becomes a fighting air ace.
Standard war story, quite well done; remake of *Ceiling Zero* (qv).

w Barry Trivers, *story* Frank Wead *d* Lothar Mendes *ph* Arthur Edeson

Ronald Reagan, James Stephenson, Julie Bishop, Cliff Edwards, Reginald Denny, Olympe Bradna, William Lundigan, John Ridgely

International Velvet
GB 1978   125m   Metrocolor
MGM (Bryan Forbes)

A hostile orphan becomes an international horsewoman. Disappointing attempt to produce a sequel to 1944's *National Velvet*; none of it coheres, one is not clear to whom it is intended to appeal, and some of the dialogue is fearsome.

wd Bryan Forbes *ph* Tony Imi *m* Francis Lai *pd* Keith Wilson

Nanette Newman, Tatum O'Neal, Anthony Hopkins, Christopher Plummer, Peter Barkworth, Dinsdale Landen

The Internecine Project*
GB 1974   89m   Eastmancolor
Maclean and Co / Lion International / Hemisphere
   (Barry Levinson, Andrew Donally)

A Harvard professor arranges the mutual extermination of four people who could spoil a politician's presidential chances.
Coldly murderous romp with plenty of style.

w Barry Levinson, Jonathan Lynn, *novel* Mort W. Elkind *d Ken Hughes ph* Geoffrey Unsworth *m* Roy Budd

James Coburn, Lee Grant, Harry Andrews, Ian Hendry, Michael Jayston, Keenan Wynn

Internes Can't Take Money*
US 1937   75m   bw
Paramount (Benjamin Glazer)
GB title: *You Can't Take Money*

A hospital doctor persuades a gangster friend to help a woman find her missing child.
Quite interesting minor melodrama, first of the Dr Kildare series which was subsequently recast and restyled by MGM.

w Rian James, Theodore Reed, *story* Max
Brand *d Alfred Santell ph* Theodor Sparkuhl
m Gregory Stone

Joel McCrea, Barbara Stanwyck, Lloyd Nolan,
Stanley Ridges, Lee Bowman, Irving Bacon

The Interns*
US 1962   130m   bw
Columbia / Interns Co. / Robert Cohn

In an American hospital, newly qualified doctors
have personal and career problems.
Birth, abortion, sudden death, drugs and
women's lib all figure in this melodramatic
compendium which succeeds well enough on its
own level and spawned a sequel (*The New
Interns*) and an unsuccessful TV series.

w Walter Newman, David Swift, *novel* Richard
Frede *d* David Swift *ph* Russell Metty *m* Leith
Stevens

Cliff Robertson, Michael Callan, James
MacArthur, Nick Adams, Suzy Parker, Buddy
Ebsen, Telly Savalas

Interpol
GB 1957   92m   bw   Cinemascope
Columbia / Warwick (Irving Allen, Albert R.
   Broccoli)
US title: *Pickup Alley*

The US Anti-Narcotics Squad trails across
Europe the insane and ruthless leader of a drug
ring.
Drearily routine thick ear electrified by one
performance but not helped by wide screen.

w John Paxton *d* John Gilling *ph* Ted Moore
m Richard Bennett

Victor Mature, Anita Ekberg, *Trevor Howard,*
Bonar Colleano, Marne Maitland, Eric
Pohlmann, Alec Mango, Peter Illing, Sidney
Tafler

The Interrupted Journey
GB 1949   80m   bw
Valiant (Anthony Havelock-Allan)

An author leaves his wife for another woman,
changes his mind on the journey, pulls the
communication cord and causes a train crash.
Or does he?
Minor melodrama with expressionist tendencies
and a dream explanation. Interesting for its parts
rather than its whole.

w Michael Pertwee *d* Daniel Birt *ph* Erwin
Hillier

Richard Todd, Valerie Hobson, Christine
Norden, Tom Walls, Ralph Truman, Vida Hope

Interrupted Melody
US 1955   106m   Eastmancolor
   Cinemascope
MGM (Jack Cummings)

The story of Marjorie Lawrence, an Australian
opera singer who fell victim to polio.
Standard biopic which jells less well than some.

w William Ludwig, Sonya Levien *d* Curtis
Bernhardt *ph* Joe Ruttenberg, Paul Vogel
music supervisor Saul Chaplin

Eleanor Parker, Glenn Ford, Roger Moore,
Cecil Kellaway, Stephen Bekassy

AA: script
AAN: Eleanor Parker

Intimacy*
US 1965   87m   bw
Goldstone (David Heilwell)

A businessman in need of a government contract
tries to compromise the official concerned.
Unusual minor melodrama, interesting but not
quite successful.

w Eva Wolas *d* Victor Stoloff *ph* Ted Saizis
m Geordie Hormel

Barry Sullivan, Nancy Malone, Jack Ging, Joan
Blackman, Jackie Shannon

Intimate Relations see Les Parents
Terribles

The Intimate Stranger*
GB 1956   95m   bw
Anglo–Guild (Alec Snowden)
US title: *Finger of Guilt*

An American film producer in England is
plagued by a strange girl who claims to have
been his mistress.
Acceptable mystery thriller which holds the
interest and has good detail.

w Peter Howard *d* Joseph Walton (Joseph
Losey) *m* Trevor Duncan *ph* Gerald Gibbs

Richard Basehart, Mary Murphy, Mervyn
Johns, Constance Cummings, Roger Livesey,
Faith Brook

The Intruder*
GB 1953   84m   bw
British Lion / Ivan Foxwell

An ex-army officer surprises a burglar and
recognizes his old commander who has been ill-
served by society.
Watchable but rather mechanical compendium
drama in which a series of cameos supposedly
sum up the problems of life in post-war Britain.

w Robin Maugham, John Hunter, *novel* Line on

Ginger by Robin Maugham *d* Guy Hamilton
ph Ted Scaife *m* Francis Chagrin

Jack Hawkins, Michael Medwin, Hugh
Williams, George Cole, Dennis Price, Dora
Bryan

The Intruder*
US 1961   84m   bw
Filmgroup (Roger Corman)
GB title: *The Stranger*

A mild-mannered stranger arrives in a southern
town and stirs up racist trouble.
Cheaply-made social melodrama with many
effective moments.

w Charles Beaumont, from his novel *d* Roger
Corman *ph* Taylor Byars *m* Herman Stein

William Shatner, Frank Maxwell, Beverly
Lunsford, Robert Emhardt, Jeanne Cooper, Leo
Gordon, Charles Beaumont

Intruder in the Dust***
US 1951   87m   bw
MGM (Clarence Brown)

In a southern town, a boy and an old lady solve a
mystery and prevent a black man from being
lynched.
Excellent character drama which also offers
vivid local colour, a murder puzzle and social
comment. A semi-classic.

w Ben Maddow, novel William Faulkner
d Clarence Brown ph Robert Surtees
m Adolph Deutsch

Juano Hernandez, Elizabeth Patterson, David
Brian, Claude Jarman Jnr, *Porter Hall*, Will
Geer

'It is surely the years of range and experience
which have given him a control of the medium so
calm, sure and—apparently—easy that he can
make a complex story seem simple and
straightforward.'—*Pauline Kael*

'A really good movie that is also and
incidentally the first honestly worked out
"racial" film I have seen.'—*Richard Winnington*

Invaders from Mars
US 1953   82m   Cinecolor   3D
Edward L. Alperson

Martian invaders use hypnotized humans as
saboteurs.
Poverty Row sci-fi partly redeemed by its erratic
but talented designer who provides flashes of
visual imagination.

w Richard Blake *d/pd William Cameron
Menzies ph* John Seitz *m* Raoul Kraushaar

Helena Carter, Arthur Franz, Leif Erickson,
Hillary Brooke

Invasion**
GB 1966   82m   bw
AA / Merton Park (Jack Greenwood)

An English village is beset one night by invaders
from outer space.
Understated, effective little suspenser, well done
in all departments.

w Roger Marshall *d Alan Bridges ph* James
Wilson *m* Bernard Ebbinghouse

Edward Judd, Valerie Gearon, Lyndon Brook,
Yoko Tani, Tsai Chin, Barrie Ingham, Arthur
Sharp

Invasion of the Body Snatchers****
US 1956   80m   bw   Superscope
Allied Artists / Walter Wanger

A small American town is imperceptibly taken
over by an alien force.
Persuasive, thoroughly satisfying, low-budget
science fiction, put across with subtlety and
intelligence in every department.

w Daniel Mainwaring, *novel Jack Finney d Don
Siegel ph* Ellsworth Fredericks *m* Carmen
Dragon

Kevin McCarthy, Dana Wynter, Larry Gates,
King Donovan, Carolyn Jones, Virginia
Christine, Sam Peckinpah

Invasion of the Body Snatchers**
US 1978   115m   Technicolor
UA / Robert H. Solo

Superior updating of the 1956 classic, with
excellent and careful work all round, even to
having Kevin McCarthy repeating his original
role in a cameo.

w W. D. Richter d Philip Kaufman ph Michael
Chapman *m* Denny Zeitlin *pd* Charles Rosen

Donald Sutherland, Brooke Adams, Leonard
Nimoy, Veronica Cartwright, Jeff Goldblum,
Art Hindle, Lelia Goldoni, Kevin McCarthy,
Don Siegel

Invasion Quartet
GB 1961   87m   bw
MGM (Ronald Kinnoch)

An ill-assorted foursome of officers and a boffin
take on the dangerous mission of silencing a
Nazi gun trained on Dover.
A plot which could have been handled any way is
played unsatisfactorily for farce, and all
concerned are understandably uneasy.

w Jack Trevor Story, John Briley, *story* Norman
Collins *d* Jay Lewis *ph* Geoffrey Faithfull,
Gerald Moss *m* Ron Goodwin

Bill Travers, Spike Milligan, Grégoire Aslan,

John Le Mesurier, Thorley Walters, Maurice Denham, Millicent Martin, Cyril Luckham

Invasion USA

US 1952 70m bw
Columbia (Albert Zugsmith)

A hypnotist in a New York bar gives a group of people a foretaste of what might happen to them under atomic attack.
Ludicrous, dangerous, hilarious low-budget exploitationer composed mainly of rubber rocks and old newsreels.

w Robert Smith d Alfred E. Green ph John L. Russell m Albert Glasser

Dan O'Herlihy, Gerald Mohr, Peggie Castle

Investigation of a Citizen above Suspicion*

Italy 1970 115m Technicolor
Vera (Daniele Senatore)

A successful police inspector kills his mistress and, paranoically considering himself above suspicion, plants clues leading to himself and even confesses the crime.
Fairly engrossing character study with political undertones; cinematically quite striking, too.

w Ugo Pirro, Elio Petri d Elio Petri ph Luigi Kuveiller m Ennio Morricone

Gian Maria Volonte, Florinda Bolkan, Salvo Randone, Gianni Santuccio

Invisible Boy

US 1957 89m bw
MGM / Pan (Nicholas Nayfack)

A scientist allows his 10-year-old son to repair a robot, which comes under the control of an alien force.
Minor sci-fi utilizing the robot from Forbidden Planet.

w Cyril Hume d Herman Hoffman ph Harold Wellman m Les Baxter

Richard Eyer, Philip Abbott, Harold J. Stone, Diane Brewster

The Invisible Man****

US 1933 71m bw
Universal (Carl Laemmle Jnr)

A scientist discovers a means of making himself invisible, but in the process becomes a megalomaniac.
Superb blend of eccentric character comedy, melodrama and trick photography in a Hollywood English setting; remarkably faithful to the spirit of the book. It made a star of Claude Rains in his first film, even though he is seen for only a couple of seconds.

w R. C. Sheriff, Philip Wylie, novel H. G. Wells d James Whale ph Arthur Edeson sp John P. Fulton

Claude Rains, Gloria Stuart, William Harrigan, Henry Travers, E. E. Clive, Una O'Connor, Forrester Harvey, Dudley Digges, Holmes Herbert

'Taken either as a technical exercise or as a sometimes profoundly moving retelling of the Frankenstein fable, it is one of the most rewarding of recent films.'—William Troy
† Sequels, successively less interesting, were The Invisible Man Returns (1939), Invisible Woman (qv) (1940), Invisible Agent (1942), The Invisible Man's Revenge (1944) and Abbott and Costello Meet the Invisible Man (qv) (1951). A short-lived TV series followed in 1975: it was restructured as Gemini Man in 1976.

The Invisible Ray*

US 1936 79m bw
Universal

A scientist discovers a superpowerful element which makes him homicidal.
Slow-moving science fiction with a touch of horror, and the pattern for its star's many later roles as a sympathetic man who turns into a monster. Interesting rather than stimulating.

w John Colton, story Howard Higgin, Douglas Hodges d Lambert Hillyer ph George Robinson m Franz Waxman sp John P. Fulton

Boris Karloff, Bela Lugosi, Frances Drake, Frank Lawton, Walter Kingsford, Beulah Bondi, Violet Kemble Cooper, Nydia Westman

Invisible Stripes

US 1940 82m bw
Warner (Hal B. Wallis)

An ex-con finds it difficult to go straight.
By 1940 Warners must have been able to make rip-offs of Angels with Dirty Faces in their sleep, and this one, despite its cast, suggests that they did.

w Warren Duff, book Warden Lewis E. Lawes d Lloyd Bacon ph Ernest Haller m Heinz Roemheld

George Raft, Humphrey Bogart, William Holden, Flora Robson, Jane Bryan, Paul Kelly, Lee Patrick, Henry O'Neill, Moroni Olson

The Invisible Woman*

US 1941 72m bw
Universal (Burt Kelly)

A mad scientist turns a model invisible.
Screwball comedy with a deteriorating star at his hammiest: generally very laboured, but with some funny moments.

w Robert Lees, Fred Rinaldo, Gertrude Purcell d A. Edward Sutherland ph Elwood Bredell

John Barrymore, Charles Ruggles, Virginia Bruce, John Howard, Oscar Homolka, Donald MacBride, Edward Brophy, Shemp Howard, Margaret Hamilton, Maria Montez

Invitation

US 1952 81m bw
MGM (Lawrence Weingarten)

When a millionaire's daughter believes she is dying, revelations ensue about her beloved husband's original intentions.
Competently idiotic weepie with a happy ending.

w Paul Osborn, story Jerome Weidman d Gottfried Reinhardt ph Ray June m Bronislau Kaper

Dorothy McGuire, Van Johnson, Ruth Roman, Louis Calhern, Ray Collins, Michael Chekhov

'The dialogue is stagey and the treatment indeterminate, with overmuch reliance on the dubious emotional reinforcement of loud background music.'—Penelope Houston

Invitation to a Gunfighter*

US 1964 92m De Luxe
UA / Stanley Kramer (Richard Wilson)

A small-town tyrant hires a smooth gunfighter to keep down the farmers he has cheated.
Predictable, rather self-satisfied little western with a studio look. Smart script and performances.

w Elizabeth and Richard Wilson d Richard Wilson ph Joseph MacDonald m David Raksin

Yul Brynner, George Segal, Janice Rule, Pat Hingle

Invitation to Happiness

US 1939 95m bw
Paramount (Wesley Ruggles)

A society girl marries a prizefighter.
Routine star romantic drama.

w Claude Binyon d Wesley Ruggles ph Leo Tover m Frederick Hollander

Irene Dunne, Fred MacMurray, Charles Ruggles, Billy Cook, William Collier Snr, Marion Martin

Invitation to the Dance**

GB 1954 92m Technicolor
MGM (Arthur Freed)

Three stories in dance and mime.
Unsuccessful ballet film which closed its star's great period and virtually ended the heyday of the Hollywood musical. The simple fact emerged that European ballet styles were not Kelly's

forte; yet there was much to enjoy in Circus, Ring around the Rosy and The Magic Lamp.

w/ch/d Gene Kelly ph Frederick A. Young m Jacques Ibert, André Previn, Rimsky-Korsakov ad Alfred Junge

Gene Kelly, Igor Youskevitch, Tommy Rall, Belita, Tamara Toumanova

The Ipcress File**

GB 1965 109m Techniscope
Rank / Steven / Lowndes (Harry Saltzman)

An intelligence man traces a missing scientist and finds that one of his own superiors is a spy. The attempt to present a low-key James Bond (glasses, good at cookery, supermarket shopper) is frustrated by flashy direction and a confused plot. It did herald a new genre though the whole ambiance is now sadly dated, like an old copy of The Sunday Times Colour Supplement.

w Bill Canaway, James Doran, novel Len Deighton d Sidney J. Furie ph Otto Heller m John Barry ad Ken Adam

Michael Caine, Nigel Green, Guy Doleman, Sue Lloyd, Gordon Jackson

† Two sequels appeared starring 'Harry Palmer' (never named in the books): Funeral in Berlin and Billion Dollar Brain (both qv).

Irene

US 1940 101m bw (colour sequence)
RKO / Imperator (Herbert Wilcox)

A New York Irish shopgirl moves into society. Fairly dim picturization of the old musical: the cast does its best.

w Alice Duer Miller, play James H. Montgomery d Herbert Wilcox ph Russell Metty md Anthony Collins songs Harry Tierney, Joseph McCarthy

Anna Neagle, Ray Milland, Roland Young, Alan Marshal, May Robson, Billie Burke, Arthur Treacher, Marsha Hunt, Isabel Jewell, Ethel Griffies

'This pre-camp version tries to be innocuously charming, and the effort is all too evident.'—New Yorker, 1976

† Previously filmed in 1926 with Colleen Moore.

AAN: Anthony Collins

Irish Eyes Are Smiling**

US 1944 90m Technicolor
TCF (Damon Runyon)

The life and times of a nineties songwriter, Ernest R. Ball.
Standard musical biopic, handsomely mounted.

w Earl Baldwin, John Tucker Battle d Gregory

Ratoff *ph* Harry Jackson *md* Alfred Newman,
Charles Henderson

Dick Haymes, June Haver, Monty Woolley,
Anthony Quinn, Beverly Whitney, Maxie
Rosenbloom, Veda Ann Borg, Clarence Kolb

AAN: Alfred Newman, Charles Henderson

The Irish in Us
US 1935   84m   bw
Warner (Samuel Bischoff)

Adventures of three New York brothers.
Routine, good-natured star action frolic.

w Earl Baldwin *d* Lloyd Bacon *ph* George
Barnes *md* Leo F. Forbstein

James Cagney, Pat O'Brien, Olivia de Havilland,
Mary Gordon, Frank McHugh, Allen Jenkins, J.
Farrell MacDonald, Thomas Jackson

Irma La Douce*
US 1963   146m   Technicolor   Panavision
UA / Phalanx / Mirisch / Edward L. Alperson
    (Billy Wilder)

A Paris policeman falls for a prostitute and
becomes her pimp.
A saucy yarn originally presented inventively as
a small-scale stage musical becomes a tasteless
yawn on the big screen, especially when
presented at such length and without the songs.
Minor compensations abound but are
insufficient.

w Billy Wilder, I. A. L. Diamond *d* Billy Wilder
ph Joseph La Shelle *md* André Previn *musical
themes* Marguerite Monnot *ad* Alexander
Trauner

Shirley Maclaine, Jack Lemmon, Lou Jacobi,
Herschel Bernardi, Joan Shawlee, Bruce Yarnell

AA: André Previn
AAN: Joseph La Shelle; Shirley Maclaine

The Iron Curtain
US 1948   87m   bw
TCF (Sol C. Siegel)

A Russian official in Ottawa becomes
disillusioned and reveals to the US authorities
details of a spy ring.
Cold war biopic of Igor Gouzenko; not badly
done in the semi-documentary mould.

w Milton Krims *d* William Wellman *ph* Charles
G. Clarke *md* Alfred Newman, using Russian
themes

Dana Andrews, Gene Tierney, Berry Kroeger,
Edna Best

The Iron Duke*
GB 1934   88m   bw
Gaumont (Michael Balcon)

After Waterloo, the Duke of Wellington defeats
a French scheme to discredit him.
A popular historical star vehicle of its time and a
good example of British pre-war production in
the Korda mould.

w Bess Meredith, play H. M. Harwood *d* Victor
Saville

George Arliss, Gladys Cooper, Emlyn Williams,
Ellaline Terriss, A. E. Matthews, Edmund
Willard, Felix Aylmer

The Iron Horse*
US 1924   119m (24 fps)   bw   silent
Fox

A man seeking to avenge his father's murder
works on the first transcontinental railroad.
Archetypal western, very slow to start but with
an authentic cast of thousands.

w Charles Kenyon, John Russell *d* John Ford
ph George Schneidermann

George O'Brien, Madge Bellamy, Cyril
Chadwick, Fred Kohler

The Iron Maiden
GB 1962   98m   Eastmancolor
AA / GHW (Peter Rogers)

An aircraft designer gets into trouble because of
his affection for traction engines.
Feeble attempt to duplicate the success of
Genevieve, this time starring a steamroller. Very
English.

w Vivian Cox, Leslie Bricusse *d* Gerald
Thomas *ph* Alan Hume *m* Eric Rogers

Michael Craig, Alan Hale Jnr, Jeff Donnell,
Cecil Parker, Noel Purcell, Roland Culver, the
Duke of Bedford, Anne Helm

The Iron Man
US 1931   73m   bw
Universal (Carl Laemmle Jnr)

A prizefighter is spurred on by his money-
hungry wife.
Competent, routine, ringside melodrama.

w Francis Edward Faragoh, *novel* W. R.
Burnett *d* Tod Browning *ph* Percy Hilburn

Lew Ayres, Jean Harlow, Robert Armstrong,
John Miljan, Eddie Dillon, Ned Sparks

The Iron Mask*
US 1929   97m   bw   talking sequences,
    sound and music score
(UA) Douglas Fairbanks

The true prince of France is kidnapped and
imprisoned, but the villains reckon without
D'Artagnan and the three musketeers.

Spirited star rendition of Dumas, the last big silent costume drama of the twenties.

w W. Elton Thomas (Douglas Fairbanks), *novel* Ten Years After by Alexandre Dumas *d* Allan Dwan *ph* Henry Sharp *pd* Maurice Leloir

Douglas Fairbanks, Nigel de Brulier, Belle Bennett, Marguerite de la Motte

The Iron Mistress
US 1952   107m   Technicolor
Warner (Henry Blanke)

The life of westerner Jim Bowie and his famous knife.
Stolid actioner with uninspired script and performances.

w James R. Webb, *novel* Paul I. Wellman *d* Gordon Douglas *ph* John Seitz *m* Max Steiner

Alan Ladd, Virginia Mayo, Joseph Calleia, Phyllis Kirk, Alf Kjellin, Douglas Dick, Tony Caruso, George Voskovec

The Iron Petticoat
GB 1956   96m   Technicolor   Vistavision
Remus / Harry Saltzman (Betty E. Box)

An American air force officer persuades a Russian lady flier of the advantages of the western way of life.
Feeble imitation of *Ninotchka* with a saucy star team which simply doesn't jell.

w Ben Hecht *d* Ralph Thomas *ph* Ernest Steward

Bob Hope, Katharine Hepburn, James Robertson Justice, Robert Helpmann, David Kossoff, Alan Gifford, Paul Carpenter, Noelle Middleton

Is Paris Burning?
France / US 1965   165m   Panavision   bw
Paramount / Transcontinental / Marianne (Paul Graetz)

A multi-storied account of the 1944 liberation of Paris.
Muddled, scribbled, tedious and confusing attempt at a thinking man's all-star war epic.

w Francis Ford Coppola, Gore Vidal *d* René Clément *ph* Marcel Grignon *m* Maurice Jarre

Leslie Caron, Gert Frobe, Charles Boyer, Yves Montand, Orson Welles, Alain Delon, Jean-Pierre Cassel, Jean-Paul Belmondo, Kirk Douglas, Glenn Ford, Claude Dauphin, Daniel Gélin, Anthony Perkins, Simone Signoret, Robert Stack, George Chakiris

AAN: Marcel Grignon

Isadora*
GB 1968   138m   Eastmancolor   Panavision
Universal (Robert and Raymond Hakim)
US title: *The Loves of Isadora*

Eccentric character dancer Isadora Duncan reflects on her crowded and unconventional life.
Ambitious and expensive but finally unsatisfactory biopic of a controversial figure of the twenties.

w Melvyn Bragg, Clive Exton *d* Karel Reisz *ph* Larry Pizer *m* Maurice Jarre *pd* Jocelyn Herbert *ad* Michael Seymour, Ralph Brinton

Vanessa Redgrave, Jason Robards Jnr, James Fox, Ivan Tchenko, John Fraser, Bessie Love

'A brave attempt at a daunting task.'—*Tom Milne*

The Island*
Japan 1961   92m   bw
Kindai Eiga Kyokai (Kaneto Shindo)
original title: *Hadaka no Shima*

The quiet tenor of life for the only family inhabiting a tiny island is eventually broken by illness and death.
Slow, controlled, beautiful film in which not a single word of dialogue is spoken. The artificiality of this concept eventually diminishes its stature.

wd Kaneto Shindo ph Kiyoshi Kuroda *m* Hikaru Hayashi

Nobuko Otowa, Taiji Tonoyama, Shinji Tanaka, Masanori Horimoto

'A visual poem which mirrors tedium without ever inducing it.'—*MFB*

The Island at the Top of the World**
US 1974   93m   Technicolor
Walt Disney (Winston Hibler)

In 1907, a rich Englishman commissions an airship to take him to a mythical arctic Shangri-La in search of his lost son.
Generally brisk and effective adventure fantasy whose trick effects are sufficiently splendid to redeem a sag in the middle and an overplus of Viking chatter which has to be laboriously translated.

w John Whedon, *novel* The Lost Ones by Ian Cameron *d* Robert Stevenson *ph* Frank Phillips *m* Maurice Jarre *pd Peter Ellenshaw sp Art Cruickshank, Danny Lee*

Donald Sinden, David Hartman, Jacques Marin, Mako

Island in the Sky*
US 1953   109m   bw
Wayne–Fellows (Robert Fellows)

A transport plane makes a forced landing north of Greenland, and the crew must survive till help comes.

Well made outdoor suspenser shot in the California Sierras.

w Ernest K. Gann, from his novel d William Wellman ph Archie Stout m Emil Newman ad James Basevi

John Wayne, Lloyd Nolan, Walter Abel, Allyn Joslyn, Andy Devine, James Arness

Island in the Sun*
GB 1957   119m   Technicolor
  Cinemascope
TCF (Darryl F. Zanuck)

Sexual and racial problems erupt on a West Indian island.

Portmanteau romantic melodrama which generally misfires, especially in an attempt to parallel Crime and Punishment; but the cast is interesting.

w Alfred Hayes, novel Alec Waugh d Robert Rossen ph Frederick A. Young m Malcolm Arnold

James Mason, Joan Fontaine, Harry Belafonte, John Williams, Dorothy Dandridge, Joan Collins, Michael Rennie, Patricia Owens, Stephen Boyd, Basil Sydney, Diana Wynyard, Ronald Squire, John Justin

Island of Lost Souls*
US 1932   74m   bw
Paramount

On a remote South Sea island, mad Dr Moreau transforms animals into humans by vivisection. Unchilling but interesting thriller with a rolling-eyed star performance.

w Waldemar Young, Philip Wylie, story The Island of Dr Moreau by H. G. Wells d Erle C. Kenton ph Karl Struss

Charles Laughton, Bela Lugosi, Richard Arlen, Kathleen Burke, Leila Hyams

Island of Love
US 1963   101m   Technicolor   Panavision
Warner / Belgrave (Morton da Costa)

A gangster finances a film providing his girl friend stars, but when it flops he chases the producers to a Greek island.

Dismally unfunny comedy wasting a talented cast.

w David R. Schwarz d Morton da Costa ph Harry Stradling m George Duning

Robert Preston, Tony Randall, Walter Matthau, Giorgia Moll

Island of Terror
GB 1966   89m   Eastmancolor
Planet (Tom Blakeley)

On an Irish island, a scientist makes monsters who thrive on bone.

Horror hokum, moderately done.

w Edward Andrew Mann, Alan Ramsen d Terence Fisher ph Reg Wyer m Malcolm Lockyer sp John St John Earl

Peter Cushing, Edward Judd, Carole Gray, Eddie Byrne, Sam Kydd, Niall MacGinnis

Island of the Blue Dolphins
US 1964   93m   Eastmancolor
U-I / Robert B. Radnitz

Two orphaned children grow up alone on a Californian island, protected by wild dogs. Pleasant if unconvincing family film based on a true story.

w Ted Sherdeman, Jane Klove, novel Scott O'Dell d James B. Clark ph Leo Tover m Paul Sawtell

Celia Kaye, Larry Dornasin, George Kennedy

Islands in the Stream
US 1976   105m   Metrocolor   Panavision
Paramount (Peter Bart, Max Palevsky)

On a Bahamian island in 1940, an expatriate American artist welcomes his three sons and reflects on the futility of life.

Shapeless semi-autobiographical fragments culminating unpersuasively in an action climax of heroic self-sacrifice. A film on which no expense has been spared and which doesn't work at all.

w Denne Bart Petitclerc, novel Ernest Hemingway d Franklin Schaffner ph Fred J. Koenekamp m Jerry Goldsmith

George C. Scott, David Hemmings, Gilbert Roland, Susan Tyrell, Richard Evans, Claire Bloom, Hart Bochner, Julius Harris

Isle of the Dead**
US 1945   72m   bw
RKO (Val Lewton)

On a Balkan island in 1912 a group of people shelter from the plague and fear that one of their number is a vampire.

Glum, ghoulish melodrama with some neatly handled shocks; quite different from any other horror film.

w Ardel Wray, Josef Mischel d Mark Robson ph Jack Mackenzie m Leigh Harline

Boris Karloff, Ellen Drew, Helene Thimig, Marc Cramer, Katherine Emery, Alan Napier, Jason Robards

Isn't It Romantic *
US 1948 87m bw
Paramount (Daniel Dare)

Romance hits the household of an ex-Civil War colonel in Indiana.
Pleasant but forgettable period semi-musical.

w Theodore Strauss, Josef Mischel, Richard Breen d Norman Z. McLeod ph Lionel Lindon m Joseph J. Lilley

Veronica Lake, Mona Freeman, Mary Hatcher, Roland Culver, Billy de Wolfe, Patric Knowles, Richard Webb, Kathryn Givney, Pearl Bailey

Isn't Life Wonderful? *
US 1924 88m (24 fps) bw silent
(UA) David Wark Griffith

The life of a family in post-war Germany.
An unpopular subject, and a grey-looking film, but the director shows a lot of his strength in it.

wd D. W. Griffith, story Geoffrey Moss

Carol Dempster, Neil Hamilton, Helen Lowell, Frank Puglia, Marcia Harris

Isn't Life Wonderful? *
GB 1952 83m Technicolor
ABP (Warwick Ward)

In 1902, drunken Uncle Willie runs a bicycle shop and manages to reconcile a lovers' quarrel.
Engaging, well cast family comedy.

w Brock Williams d Harold French ph Erwin Hillier m Philip Green ad Terence Verity

Donald Wolfit, Eileen Herlie, Cecil Parker, Eleanor Summerfield, Robert Urquhart, Cecil Trouncer

Istanbul
US 1956 84m Technicolor
Cinemascope
U-I (Albert J. Cohen)

Various adventurers and an amnesiac girl seek stolen diamonds in Istanbul.
Dim remake of a flat-footed piece of thick ear called *Singapore*.

w Seton I. Miller, Barbara Gray, Richard Alan Simmons d Joseph Pevney ph William Daniels m Joseph Gershenson

Errol Flynn, Cornell Borchers, John Bentley, Torin Thatcher, Leif Erickson, Martin Benson, Vladimir Sokoloff, Werner Klemperer, Nat King Cole, Peggy Knudsen

It *
US 1927 72m (24 fps) bw silent
Famous Players-Lasky

A shopgirl tries to live by the tenets of Elinor Glyn's book, and finally marries her boss.
In its day a fast and funny spoof, and the years have not dealt too unkindly with it.

w Hope Loring, Louis D. Lighton, adaptation Elinor Glyn d Clarence Badger ph H. Kinley Martin

Clara Bow, Antonio Moreno, William Austin, Jacqueline Gadson, Gary Cooper, Elinor Glyn

It Ain't Hay
US 1943 79m bw
Universal (Alex Gottlieb)
GB title: *Money for Jam*

When a racehorse dies, a New York cabbie and his friend try to find a new one for the impecunious owners.
Formula Abbott and Costello with a small injection of sentiment and Runyonese. Not their best by a mile.

w Allen Boretz, John Grant, story Princess O'Hara by Damon Runyon d Erle C. Kenton ph Charles Von Enger songs Harry Revel, Paul Francis Webster

Bud Abbott, Lou Costello, Grace McDonald, Cecil Kellaway, Patsy O'Connor, Eugene Pallette, Shemp Howard, Eddie Quillan

It All Came True *
US 1940 97m bw
Warner (Mark Hellinger)

A gangster hides out in a boarding house and puts it back on its feet.
Competent New York fairy story full of sweetness and light.

w Michael Fessier, Lawrence Kimble, story Better Than Life by Louis Bromfield d Lewis Seiler ph Ernest Haller m Heinz Roemheld

Humphrey Bogart, Ann Sheridan, Jeffrey Lynn, Zasu Pitts, Una O'Connor, Jessie Busley, John Litel, Grant Mitchell, Felix Bressart

It Always Rains on Sunday ***
GB 1947 92m bw
Ealing

An escaped convict takes refuge in his married mistress's house in East London.
Influential slumland melodrama, now dated—the stuff of every other television play—but at the time electrifyingly vivid and very well done.

w Angus Macphail, Robert Hamer, Henry Cornelius, novel Arthur La Bern d Robert

Hamer ph Douglas Slocombe m Georges Auric

Googie Withers, John McCallum, Jack Warner, Edward Chapman, Susan Shaw, Sidney Tafler

It Came from beneath the Sea
US 1955   80m   bw
Columbia / Sam Katzman (Charles Schneer)

A giant octopus half destroys San Francisco.
Tepid monster movie; special effects only fair.

w George Worthing Yates, Hal Smith d Robert Gordon ph Henry Freulich md Mischa Bakaleinikoff

Kenneth Tobey, Faith Domergue, Donald Curtis, Ian Keith

It Came from Outer Space**
US 1953   80m   bw   3-D
U-I (William Alland)

A young astronomer sees a space ship land in the Arizona desert and tracks down the occupants who can adopt human appearance at will.
Quite bright science fiction, the first to use this theme of borrowing bodies and the first to utilize the western desert locations. 3-D adds a shock moment or two.

w Harry Essex, story Ray Bradbury d Jack Arnold ph Clifford Stine m Herman Stein md Joseph Gershenson

Richard Carlson, Barbara Rush, Charles Drake, Kathleen Hughes

It Grows on Trees
US 1952   84m   bw
U-I (Leonard Goldstein)

A housewife finds a money tree in her backyard.
Protracted fantasy comedy.

w Leonard Praskins, Barney Slater d Arthur Lubin ph Maury Gertsman m Frank Skinner

Irene Dunne (her last film), Dean Jagger, Joan Evans, Richard Crenna, Edith Meiser, Dee Pollock

It Had To Be You
US 1947   98m   bw
Columbia / Don Hartman

A dizzy dame runs out on three prospective husbands and is pursued by an Indian.
Weak sex farce without the courage of its lack of convictions.

w Norman Panama, Melvin Frank d Don Hartman, Rudolph Maté ph Rudolph Maté m Heinz Roemheld md Morris Stoloff

Ginger Rogers, Cornel Wilde, Percy Waram, Spring Byington, Thurston Hall, Ron Randell

It Happened at the World's Fair
US 1962   104m   Metrocolor   Panavision
MGM / Ted Richmond

At the Seattle World's Fair, two crop-dusting pilots have romantic intrigues.
Routine star vehicles.

w Si Rose, Seaman Jacobs d Norman Taurog ph Joseph Ruttenberg m Leith Stevens

Elvis Presley, Gary Lockwood, Joan O'Brien, Yvonne Craig, Ginny Tiu

It Happened Here**
GB 1963   99m   bw
UA / Kevin Brownlow, Andrew Mollo

What might have happened if the Germans had invaded England in 1940.
A remarkable semi-professional reconstruction which took seven years to film and is totally convincing in detail, but unfortunately rather confused and padded as drama.

wd Kevin Brownlow, Andrew Mollo ph Peter Suschitsky m Jack Beaver

Sebastian Shaw, Pauline Murray, Fiona Lekland, Honor Fehrson

It Happened in Athens
US 1961   100m   De Luxe
TCF (James S. Elliott)

At the first revival of the Olympic Games in 1896 a publicity-seeking actress announces that she will marry whoever wins the Marathon.
Witless extravagant romp, well mounted but adding up to zero.

w Laszlo Vadnay d Andrew Marton ph Curt Courant

Jayne Mansfield, Trax Colton, Bob Mathias

It Happened in Brooklyn*
US 1947   103m   bw
MGM

Young New Yorkers with musical talents find their way to fame.
Well-handled routine musical of its time.

w Isobel Lennart d Richard Whorf ph Robert Planck

Frank Sinatra, Jimmy Durante, Kathryn Grayson, Peter Lawford, Gloria Grahame

It Happened on Fifth Avenue*
US 1947   115m   bw
AA

A child of divorce finds amiable squatters in her millionaire father's house.
Curious, overlong, cheerful Capraesque comedy with the mildest of social pretensions.

w Everett Freeman, Frederick Stephani, Herbert Clyde Lewis *d* Roy del Ruth *ph* Henry Sharp

Gale Storm, Ann Harding, Victor Moore, Charles Ruggles, Don Defore

AAN: script

It Happened One Night****
US 1934 105m bw
Columbia (Frank Capra)

A runaway heiress falls in love with the reporter who is chasing her across America.
Highly successful and influential romantic comedy, the first to use buses and motels as background and still come up sparkling; it remains superlative in patches, but overall has a faded, dated air.

w Robert Riskin, story Night Bus by Samuel Hopkins Adams *d Frank Capra ph* Joseph Walker *md* Louis Silvers

Clark Gable, Claudette Colbert, Walter Connolly, Roscoe Karns, Alan Hale, Ward Bond, Jameson Thomas, Arthur Hoyt

'It will be a long day before we see so little made into so much.'—*Otis Ferguson*
'Something to revive your faith in a medium which could belong among the great arts.'—*Robert Forsythe*
† Remade 1956 (badly) as *You Can't Run away From It.*

AA: best picture; Robert Riskin; Frank Capra; Clark Gable; Claudette Colbert

It Happened to Jane
US 1959 98m Technicolor
  Cinemascope
Columbia / Arwin (Richard Quine)

A lady lobster dealer becomes involved in a battle with the railroad whose inefficiency affects her business.
Witless, wholesome farce which promises more than it delivers.

w Norman Karkov *d* Richard Quine *ph* Charles Lawton Jnr *m* George Duning

Doris Day, Jack Lemmon, *Ernie Kovacs*, Steve Forrest

It Happened Tomorrow***
US 1944 84m bw
(UA) Arnold Pressburger

A reporter meets an old man with the power to show him tomorrow's newspaper headlines, so that he always gets scoops—including his own death . . .
Engaging fantasy, flawlessly made and quietly very entertaining.

w Dudley Nichols, René Clair d René Clair ph Archie Stout m Robert Stolz

Dick Powell, Linda Darnell, Jack Oakie, *John Philliber,* Edgar Kennedy, Ed Brophy, George Cleveland, Sig Rumann

AAN: Robert Stolz

It Happens Every Spring
US 1949 80m bw
TCF (William Perlberg)

A chemistry teacher discovers a formula that makes baseballs repellent to wood.
Smartly produced but rather desperate fantasy comedy.

w Valentine Davies *d* Lloyd Bacon *ph* Joe MacDonald *m* Leigh Harline

Ray Milland, Jean Peters, Paul Douglas, Ed Begley, Ted de Corsia, Ray Collins, Jessie Royce Landis, Alan Hale Jnr

AAN: original story (Shirley W. Smith, Valentine Davies)

It Happens Every Thursday*
US 1953 80m bw
U-I (Anton Leader)

The new owner of a small-town newspaper becomes unpopular through his attempts to boost the circulation.
Pleasant comedy with amusing scenes.

w Dane Lussier *d* Joseph Pevney *ph* Russell Metty *m* Joseph Gershenson

Loretta Young, John Forsythe, Jimmy Conlin, Frank McHugh, Edgar Buchanan, Jane Darwell

It Should Happen to You**
US 1954 87m bw
Columbia (Fred Kohlmar)

A slightly daffy New York model with an urge to be famous rents a huge billboard and puts her name on it.
Likeable comedy which starts brightly and slowly falls apart, disappointing considering the credentials of the talents involved and the satiric possibilities of the plot.

w Ruth Gordon, Garson Kanin d George Cukor ph Charles Lang *m* Frederick Hollander

Judy Holliday, Jack Lemmon, Peter Lawford, Michael O'Shea

It Shouldn't Happen to a Vet
GB 1976 93m Technicolor
EMI / Talent Associates / Readers Digest

Adventures of a Yorkshire vet just before World War II.

Competent sequel to *All Creatures Great and Small* (qv).

w Alan Plater, *books* James Herriot *d* Eric Till *ph* Arthur Ibbetson *m* Laurie Johnson

John Alderton, Colin Blakely, Lisa Harrow, Bill Maynard, Richard Pearson, Raymond Francis, John Barrett, Paul Shelley

It Started in Naples*
US 1960   100m   Technicolor   Vistavision
Paramount / Capri (Jack Rose)

A Philadelphia lawyer goes to Naples to settle his dead brother's affairs, and falls for his nephew's aunt.
Nicely made, formula romantic comedy which started life as a vehicle for Gracie Fields.

w Melville Shavelson, Jack Rose, Susi Cecchi d'Amico *d* Melville Shavelson *ph* Robert Surtees *m* Alessandro Cicognini

Clark Gable, Sophia Loren, Vittorio de Sica, Marietto, Paulo Carlini

It Started in Paradise
GB 1952   94m   Technicolor
GFD / British Film Makers (Leslie Parkyn, Sergei Nolbandov)

The career of an ambitious dress designer.
Stilted and garishly coloured but often amusing backstage melodrama of the fashion world: a Hollywood-style star vehicle which seems faintly surprising as a British product.

w Marghanita Laski *d* Compton Bennett *ph* Jack Cardiff *m* Malcolm Arnold *ad* Edward Carrick

Jane Hylton, Ian Hunter, Terence Morgan, Muriel Pavlow, Brian Worth, *Martita Hunt*, *Ronald Squire, Harold Lang*, Joyce Barbour, Kay Kendall

It Started with a Kiss
US 1959   104m   Metrocolor
Cinemascope
MGM / Arcola (Aaron Rosenberg)

An army sergeant posted to Spain is embarrassed when his wife follows him.
Flabby comedy with the emphasis on sex and pratfalls.

w Charles Lederer *d* George Marshall *ph* Robert Bronner *m* Jeff Alexander

Glenn Ford, Debbie Reynolds, Fred Clark, Edgar Buchanan, Eva Gabor

It Started with Eve**
US 1941   93m   bw
Universal (Joe Pasternak)

A dying millionaire wants to see his grandson engaged, so a waitress obliges for an hour . . . but the old man recovers.
Charming comedy which was probably the star's best film; remade as *I'd Rather be Rich* (qv).

w Norman Krasna, Leo Townsend *d* Henry Koster *md* Charles Previn, Hans Salter

Deanna Durbin, Charles Laughton, Robert Cummings, Margaret Tallichet, Guy Kibbee, Walter Catlett, Catherine Doucet

AAN: Charles Previn, Hans Salter

The Italian Job**
GB 1969   100m   Eastmancolor
Panavision
Paramount / Oakhurst (Michael Deeley)

Crooks stage a traffic jam in Turin in order to pull off a bullion robbery.
Lively caper comedy which provides a good measure of entertainment.

w Troy Kennedy Martin *d* Peter Collinson *ph* Douglas Slocombe, Norman Warwick *m* Quincy Jones

Michael Caine, Noel Coward, Benny Hill, Raf Vallone, Tony Beckley, Rossano Brazzi, Maggie Blye, Irene Handl, John Le Mesurier, Fred Emney

It's a Big Country
US 1952   89m   bw
MGM (Robert Sisk)

Seven stories show the diversity of the US and the glory of being one of its citizens.
Stultifying flagwaver memorable chiefly as a waste of good actors.

w William Ludwig, Helen Deutsch, George Wells, Allen Rivkin, Dorothy Kingsley, Isobel Lennart *d* Richard Thorpe, Don Weis, John Sturges, Don Hartman, William Wellman, Charles Vidor, Clarence Brown *ph* John Alton, Ray June, William Mellor, Joseph Ruttenberg *m* Bronislau Kaper, Rudolph G. Kopp, David Raksin, David Rose

Ethel Barrymore, Keefe Brasselle, Nancy Davis, Van Johnson, Gene Kelly, Janet Leigh, Marjorie Main, Fredric March, George Murphy, William Powell, S. Z. Sakall, Lewis Stone, James Whitmore

It's a Gift**
US 1934   73m   bw
Paramount (William Le Baron)

A general store proprietor buys an orange ranch by mail and transports his family to California.
Roughly assembled comedy of disasters which

happens to show the star more or less at his best, though the expected climax is lacking.

w Jack Cunningham, *story* W. C. Fields, J. P. McEvoy *d* Norman Z. McLeod *ph* Henry Sharp

W. C. Fields, Kathleen Howard, Jean Rouverol, Julian Madison, Tommy Bupp, Baby LeRoy

It's a Great Feeling*

US 1949 85m Technicolor
Warner (Alex Gottlieb)

No one will direct a Jack Carson movie, so he has to do it himself.
Amiable studio farce with plenty of guest appearances.

w Jack Rose, Mel Shavelson *d* David Butler *ph* Wilfrid M. Cline *m/ly* Jule Styne, Sammy Cahn

Jack Carson, Doris Day, Dennis Morgan, Bill Goodwin, Gary Cooper, Joan Crawford, Errol Flynn, Sidney Greenstreet, Danny Kaye, Patricia Neal, Edward G. Robinson, Jane Wyman, Eleanor Parker, Ronald Reagan

AAN: title song

It's a Mad Mad Mad Mad World**

US 1963 192m Technicolor Ultra Panavision 70
UA / Stanley Kramer

An assortment of people including a frustrated cop are overcome by greed when they hear of buried loot.
Three hours of frantic chasing and violent slapstick is too much even when done on this scale and with this cast, but one must observe that scene for scene it is extremely well done and most of the players are in unusually good form though they all outstay their welcome and are upstaged by the stunt men.

w William and Tania Rose *d* Stanley Kramer *ph* Ernest Laszlo *m* Ernest Gold *stunts* Carey Loftin *titles* Saul Bass

Spencer Tracy, Jimmy Durante, *Milton Berle*, Sid Caesar, Ethel Merman, Buddy Hackett, Mickey Rooney, Dick Shawn, *Phil Silvers, Terry-Thomas*, Jonathan Winters, Edie Adams, Dorothy Provine, Eddie Anderson, Jim Backus, William Demarest, Peter Falk, Paul Ford, Leo Gorcey, Ben Blue, Edward Everett Horton, Buster Keaton, Joe E. Brown, Carl Reiner, the Three Stooges, Zasu Pitts, Sterling Holloway, Jack Benny, Jerry Lewis

'To watch on a Cinerama screen in full colour a small army of actors inflict mayhem on each other with cars, planes, explosives and other devices for more than three hours with stereophonic sound effects is simply too much

for the human eye and ear to respond to, let alone the funny bone.'—*Dwight MacDonald*

AAN: Ernest Laszlo; Ernest Gold; title song (*m* Ernest Gold, *ly* Mack David)

It's a 2'6" above the Ground World

GB 1972 96m Eastmancolor
British Lion / Welbeck / Betty E. Box—Ralph Thomas
Also known as: *The Love Ban*

A Roman Catholic couple go on the pill.
Smutty, not very funny sex comedy.

w Kevin Laffan, from his play *d* Ralph Thomas *ph* Tony Imi *m* Stanley Myers

Nanette Newman, Hywel Bennett, Russell Lewis, Simon Henderson, Milo O'Shea

It's a Wonderful Life****

US 1946 129m bw
RKO / Liberty Films (Frank Capra)

A man is prevented from committing suicide by an elderly angel, who takes him back through his life to show him what good he has done.
Superbly assembled small-town comedy drama in a fantasy framework; arguably Capra's best and most typical work.

w *Frances Goodrich, Albert Hackett, Frank Capra d Frank Capra ph Joseph Walker, Joseph Biroc m Dmitri Tiomkin*

James Stewart, Henry Travers, Donna Reed, Lionel Barrymore, Thomas Mitchell, Beulah Bondi, Frank Faylen, Ward Bond, Gloria Grahame, H. B. Warner, Frank Albertson, Samuel S. Hinds, Mary Treen

'One of the most efficient sentimental pieces since *A Christmas Carol.'*—*James Agee*

'The most brilliantly made motion picture of the 1940s, so assured, so dazzling in its use of screen narrative.'—*Charles Higham*

'In its own icky, bittersweet way, it's terribly effective.'—*New Yorker, 1977*

AAN: best picture; Frank Capra; James Stewart

It's a Wonderful World**

US 1939 86m bw
MGM (Frank Davis)

Kidnapped by a suspected murderer, a girl helps him track down the real criminal.
Madcap comedy mystery which now seems much fresher and funnier than it did at the time. A highlight of the crazy comedy cycle.

w Ben Hecht, Herman J. Mankiewicz *d* W. S. Van Dyke II *ph* Oliver Marsh

Claudette Colbert, James Stewart, Guy Kibbee, Nat Pendleton, Frances Drake, Edgar Kennedy,

Ernest Truex, Richard Carle, Sidney Blackmer, Andy Clyde, Cliff Clark, Hans Conried
'One of the few genuinely comic pictures in a dog's age.'—*Otis Ferguson*

It's Alive
US 1974   91m   Technicolor
Warner / Larco (Larry Cohen)

A new-born baby turns out to be a vicious monster. Exploitation horror flick in the worst of taste, with a good central performance.

wd Larry Cohen *ph* Fenton Hamilton *m* Bernard Herrmann

John Ryan, Sharon Farrell, Andrew Duggan, Guy Stockwell, James Dixon, Michael Ansara

It's Always Fair Weather**
US 1955   101m   Eastmancolor
Cinemascope
MGM (Arthur Freed)

In 1945 three army veterans vow to meet ten years on, but they find each other dull failures until they go on a wild spree.
Rather dejected New Yorkish comedy with musical sequences; some of it works very well, but the colour is crude and the wide screen doesn't help.

w/ly/m Betty Comden, Adolph Green *d* Gene Kelly, Stanley Donen *ph* Robert Bronner *md* André Previn

Gene Kelly, Dan Dailey, Michael Kidd, Dolores Gray, Cyd Charisse

AAN: Betty Comden, Adolph Green (as writers); André Previn

It's Hard to Be Good
GB 1948   93m   bw
GFD / Two Cities

A demobbed war hero determines to spread peace and goodwill, but comes one cropper after another.
Well intended but somehow unprofessional comedy which irritates more than it amuses.

wd Jeffrey Dell *ph* Laurie Friedman *m* Anthony Hopkins

Jimmy Hanley, Anne Crawford, Raymond Huntley

It's in the Air*
GB 1938   86m   bw
ABFD

Adventures of an accident-prone RAF recruit. Amiable star comedy with good situations and songs.

wd Anthony Kimmins

George Formby, Garry Marsh, Polly Ward, Julien Mitchell, Jack Hobbs, Hal Gordon

It's in the Bag**
US 1945   87m   bw
(UA) Manhattan Productions
GB title: *The Fifth Chair*

The owner of a flea circus seeks a legacy hidden in one of five chairs which have been sold to a variety of people.
Patchily amusing, star-studded comedy which was also filmed as *Keep Your Seats Please* and *The Twelve Chairs*. Full enjoyment requires some knowledge of American radio characters.

w Jay Dratler, Alma Reville *d* Richard Wallace *ph* Russell Metty *m* Werner Heymann

Fred Allen, Binnie Barnes, *Jack Benny*, Robert Benchley, Don Ameche, Victor Moore, Rudy Vallee, William Bendix, Jerry Colonna
'An untidy piece that doesn't make the most of itself but is full of fun.'—*Richard Mallett, Punch*

It's Love Again*
GB 1936   83m   bw
Gaumont (Michael Balcon)

A chorus girl poses as a socialite who has hit the headlines without ever existing.
Delightfully dated comedy musical.

w Lesser Samuels, Marian Dix, Austin Melford *d* Victor Saville

Jessie Matthews, Robert Young, Sonnie Hale, Ernest Milton, Robb Wilton, Sara Allgood, Athene Seyler, Cyril Raymond.

It's Love I'm After*
US 1937   90m   bw
Warner

A beloved stage star couple fight like cat and dog behind the scenes.
Amusing romantic farce which has worn rather less well than might have been expected but does present two stars at their peak.

w Casey Robinson *d* Archie Mayo *ph* James Van Trees *m* Heinz Roemheld

Bette Davis, Leslie Howard, Olivia de Havilland, Patric Knowles, Eric Blore, George Barbier, Spring Byington, Bonita Granville, E. E. Clive
'One of the most delightful and diverting comedies the madcap cinema has yet turned out.'—*New York World Telegram*
'Proceeds like a somewhat deranged *Taming of the Shrew* . . . [BD and LH] are surrounded by that set of millionaires, valets and heiresses that were at one time as much of a convention in American comedy as the fops of Restoration theatre.'—*American Film Institute*

It's Not Cricket
GB 1948 77m bw
GFD / Gainsborough

Bowler-hatted officers catch a Nazi spy.
Over-spoofed comedy which barely allows the
stars a real chance.

w Lyn Lockwood, Bernard MacNab d Alfred
Roome ph Gordon Lang m Arthur Wilkinson

Basil Radford, Naunton Wayne, Maurice
Denham, Susan Shaw, Nigel Buchanan

It's Only Money
US 1962 84m bw
Paramount / York / Jerry Lewis Productions
(Paul Jones)

A TV repair mechanic hampers his detective
friend in a search for a missing heir, which turns
out to be himself.
Patchy mystery spoof with the star in rather
better form than usual, and a memorable scene in
which he is chased by an army of lawnmowers.

w John Fenton Murray d Frank Tashlin ph W.
Wallace Kelley m Walter Scharf

Jerry Lewis, Zachary Scott, Joan O'Brien, Jesse
White, Jack Weston

It's That Man Again**
GB 1942 84m bw
GFD / Gainsborough (Edward Black)

The Mayor of Foaming-at-the-Mouth puts on a
show to save a bombed theatre.
Smart, fast-moving comedy which no longer
seems particularly funny in itself but is an
invaluable record of the characters and
wisecracks of a radio show which proved a prime
morale booster during World War II.

w Howard Irving Young, Ted Kavanagh
d Walter Forde

Tommy Handley, Jack Train, Greta Gynt, Dino
Galvani, Dorothy Summers, Horace Percival,
Sidney Keith, Clarence Wright

Ivan the Terrible**
USSR 1942–6 100m (part one), 88m (part
two) bw
   (some Agfacolor in part two)
Mosfilm
original title: Ivan Groznyi

The life of a 16th-century tsar.
A heavy-going film overflowing with grim,
gloomy and superbly composed images: the plot
is by the way, and part two (also known as The
Boyars' Plot) is not up to the standard of part
one, in which the coronation sequence alone is a
masterpiece of cinema.

wd, ed Sergei Eisenstein ph Edouard Tissé
(exteriors), Andrei Moskvin (interiors) m Sergei
Prokoviev ad Isaac Shpinel, L. Naumova

Nikolai Cherkassov, Ludmilla Tselikovskaya,
Serafima Birman

Ivanhoe*
GB 1953 106m Technicolor
MGM (Pandro S. Berman)

Derring-do among the knights of medieval
England.
Tolerable, big-budget spectacular based on Sir
Walter Scott's novel.

w Noel Langley, Aeneas Mackenzie d Richard
Thorpe
ph F. A. Young m Miklos Rozsa

Robert Taylor, Joan Fontaine, Elizabeth Taylor,
Emlyn Williams, George Sanders, Robert
Douglas, Finlay Currie, Felix Aylmer, Francis
de Wolff, Guy Rolfe, Norman Wooland, Basil
Sydney

AAN: best picture; F. A. Young; Miklos Rozsa

I've Lived Before
US 1956 82m bw
U–I (Howard Christie)

After a plane crash, the pilot recovers but
believes himself to be another airman who died in
1918.
Dullish, talky drama which wastes its interesting
reincarnation theme.

w Norman Jolley, William Talman d Richard
Bartlett ph Maury Gertsman m Herman Stein

Jock Mahoney, Leigh Snowden, Ann Harding,
John McIntire, Raymond Bailey, Jerry Paris

Ivy*
US 1947 99m bw
Universal (William Cameron Menzies)

In Edwardian society England, a lady poisoner
gets her come-uppance.
Curiously ineffective period thriller in which the
star is the elegant but artificial production
design: the script is deadly dull.

w Charles Bennett, novel Mrs Belloc Lowndes
d Sam Wood ph Russell Metty m Daniele
Amfitheatrof pd William Cameron Menzies

Joan Fontaine, Herbert Marshall, Patric
Knowles, Richard Ney, Cedric Hardwicke,
Lucile Watson, Sara Allgood, Henry
Stephenson, Rosalind Ivan, Lilian Fontaine,
Una O'Connor, Isobel Elsom, Alan Napier, Paul
Cavanagh, Gavin Muir, Norma Varden

J

J. W. Coop*
US 1971   112m   Eastmancolor
Columbia / Robertson and Associates (Cliff Robertson)

After ten years in prison, a rodeo rider returns to his home town.
Well-made but rather inconsequential drama with attractive locations.

w Cliff Robertson, Gary Cartwright, Bud Shrake d Cliff Robertson ph Frank Stanley m Don Randi, Louie Shelton

Cliff Robertson, Cristina Ferrare, Geraldine Page,
R. G. Armstrong

Jabberwocky
GB 1977   101m   Technicolor
Umbrella (John Goldstone, Sandy Lieberson)

A medieval cooper's apprentice is mistaken for a prince and slays the dragon which is terrorizing the neighbourhood.
An intellectual Carry On film, with very little more taste and a great deal more unpleasant imagery. Despite much re-editing, the laughs are very intermittent.

w Charles Alverson, Terry Gilliam d Terry Gilliam ph Terry Bedford m De Wolfe pd Roy Smith

Michael Palin, Max Wall, Deborah Fallender, Warren Mitchell, John Le Mesurier, Harry H, Corbett, Rodney Bewes, Bernard Bresslaw

'The constant emphasis on blood, excrement, dismemberment and filth ultimately becomes rather wearing.'—*Michael Billington, Illustrated London News*

Jack the Giant Killer**
US 1961   94m   Technicolor
Zenith / Edward Small (Robert E. Kent)

Demon Pendragon kidnaps the princess of Cornwall but she is rescued by a farmer's son.
Very creditable fairy tale, with the right style and atmosphere assisted by vigorous acting, good pace and excellent trick effects. Unfortunately it turned out rather scary for a child audience and so fell between two stools.

w Orville Hampton, Nathan Juran d Nathan

Juran ph David S. Horsley m Paul Sawtell, Bert Shefter sp Howard Anderson ad Fernando Carere, Frank McCoy

Kerwin Mathews, Judi Meredith, *Torin Thatcher*, Don Beddoe, Walter Burke, Barry Kelley

Jack the Ripper
GB 1958   84m   bw
Mid Century (Baker and Berman)

In Victorian London the Ripper murders are finally attributed to a demented surgeon.
Flat and rather flabby treatment of a *cause célèbre*, saved by a reasonably convincing period look.

w Jimmy Sangster d/ph Robert S. Baker, Monty Berman m Stanley Black

Ewen Solon, Lee Patterson, Eddie Byrne, Betty McDowell, John Le Mesurier

Jackass Mail
US 1942   80m   bw
MGM (John Considine Jnr)

A horse thief marries the proprietress of a gambling saloon in the hope of hijacking her mail line, but she reforms him.
Boisterously conceived but anaemically scripted western comedy with the stars in full throttle.

w Lawrence Hazard d Norman Z. McLeod ph Clyde de Vinna m David Snell, Earl Brent

Wallace Beery, Marjorie Main, J. Carrol Naish, Darryl Hickman, William Haade, Hobart Cavanaugh

'This time at least they are repeating their variation on the Min-and-Bill routine among companions whose resemblance to burlesque is as unabashed as their own.'—*Bosley Crowther, New York Times*

Jackboot Mutiny
Germany 1955   77m   bw
Arca-Ariston
original title: *Es Geschah am 20 Juli*

An account of the army officers' plot to assassinate Hitler.
Documentary-like treatment without much

attempt at characterization. An important
historical document nevertheless.

w W. P. Zibaso, Gustav Machaty *d* G. W.
Pabst *ph* Kurt Hasse *m* Johannes Weissenbach
Bernhard Wicki, Karl Ludwig Diehl, Carl Wery

The Jackpot **
US 1950 85m bw
TCF (Samuel G. Engel)

A suburban husband finds that life becomes
complicated when winning the jackpot on a
radio quiz makes him a celebrity.
Modest, skilful comedy in Hollywood's best
manner.

*w Phoebe and Henry Ephron d Walter Lang
ph* Joseph La Shelle *md* Lionel Newman

James Stewart, Barbara Hale, James Gleason,
Fred Clark, Alan Mowbray, Patricia Medina,
Natalie Wood, Tommy Rettig, Robert Gist, Lyle
Talbot

Jack's the Boy*
GB 1932 91m bw
Gainsborough (Michael Balcon)

The police commissioner's son proves his worth
in rounding up a smash-and-grab gang.
Dated but lively farce which established its star
as a British box office attraction of the thirties.

w W. P. Lipscomb *d* Walter Forde *ph* Leslie
Rowson

Jack Hulbert, Cicely Courtneidge, Francis
Lister, Winifred Shotter, Peter Gawthorne, Ben
Field
'A riotously funny, good, clean, honest British
picture.'—*Sydney Carroll, Sunday Times*
† The film in which Hulbert sang 'The Flies
Crawled Up the Window' (*m* Vivian Ellis,
ly Douglas Furber). ·

Jackson County Jail
US 1976 84m Metrocolor
(UA) New World (Roger Corman)

A lady driver is hijacked, attacked, disbelieved
by the local police, thrown into jail and raped by
the jailer, whom she brains with a stool.
An exploitation piece with social pretensions
which it in no way justifies: it is however quite
competently entertaining in its mindlessly violent
way.

w Donald Stewart *d* Michael Miller *ph* Bruce
Logan *m* Loren Newkirk

Yvette Mimieux, Tommy Lee Jones, Robert
Carradine, Frederic Cook, Severn Darden,
Howard Hesseman

Jacqueline*
GB 1957 93m bw
Rank (George H. Brown)

A Belfast shipyard worker cannot stand heights,
takes to drink, and is helped by his small
daughter.
Convincing, well-made, realistically set domestic
comedy-drama.

w Patric Kirwan, Liam O'Flaherty *d* Roy
Baker *ph Geoffrey Unsworth m* Cedric Thorpe
Davie

John Gregson, Kathleen Ryan, Jacqueline
Ryan, Noel Purcell, Cyril Cusack, Marie Kean,
Liam Redmond, Maureen Delany

Jailhouse Rock*
US 1957 96m bw Cinemascope
MGM (Pandro S. Berman)

An ex-convict becomes a pop star.
Reasonably competent star vehicle, sourer in
tone than most.

w Guy Trosper *d* Richard Thorpe *ph* Robert
Bronner *md* Jeff Alexander

Elvis Presley, Judy Tyler, Mickey Shaughnessy,
Vaughn Taylor, Dean Jones

Jamaica Inn*
GB 1939 107m bw
Mayflower (Erich Pommer)

In old Cornwall, an orphan girl becomes
involved with smugglers.
Stagey, stilted adventure story which never loses
its studio feel or takes fire as a Hitchcock picture.
The cast keeps it interesting.

w Sidney Gilliat, Joan Harrison, J. B. Priestley,
novel Daphne du Maurier *d Alfred Hitchcock
ph* Harry Stradling, Bernard Knowles *m* Eric
Fenby

Charles Laughton, Maureen O'Hara, Leslie
Banks, Robert Newton, Emlyn Williams, Wylie
Watson, Marie Ney, Morland Graham
'I was irresistibly reminded of an all-star
charity matinee.'—*Graham Greene*

Jamaica Run
US 1953 92m Technicolor
Paramount Pine–Thomas

A search for documents, which may apportion a
great house to another branch of the family,
leads to murder.
Plot-bound romantic mystery in period, with
elements of a Caribbean *Rebecca*. Watchable
medium-budget hokum.

wd Lewis R. Foster, *novel* Max Murray
ph Lionel Lindon *m* Lucien Cailliet

Ray Milland, Arlene Dahl, Wendell Corey, Patric Knowles

Jane Eyre***

US 1944 96m bw
TCF (William Goetz)

In Victorian times, a harshly treated orphan girl becomes governess in a mysterious Yorkshire mansion with a brooding master.
Sharply paced, reasonably faithful and superbly staged Hollywood version of Charlotte Brontë's archetypal romantic novel which stimulated so many imitations, including *Rebecca*.

w Aldous Huxley, Robert Stevenson, John Houseman d Robert Stevenson ph George Barnes m Bernard Herrmann sp Fred Sersen ad Wiard B. Ihnen, James Basevi

Joan Fontaine, Orson Welles, Margaret O'Brien, *Henry Daniell,* John Sutton, Agnes Moorehead, Elizabeth Taylor, Peggy Ann Garner, Sara Allgood, Aubrey Mather, Hillary Brooke, Edith Barrett, Ethel Griffies, Barbara Everest, *John Abbott*

'A careful and tame production, a sadly vanilla-flavoured Joan Fontaine, and Orson Welles treating himself to road operatic sculpturings of body, cloak and diction, his eyes glinting in the Rembrandt gloom, at every chance, like side orders of jelly.'—*James Agee*

'The essentials are still there; and the non-essentials, such as the gloom, the shadows, the ground mist, the rain and the storms, have been expanded and redoubled and magnified to fill up the gaps.'—*Richard Mallett, Punch*

Janice Meredith

US 1925 153m bw silent
Metro-Goldwyn / Cosmopolitan

Vicissitudes of the coquettish daughter of a New Jersey family through the War of Independence.
Marathon melodrama not unlike *Gone with the Wind* in subject matter, but of no remaining interest.

w Lilly Hayward, novel Paul Leicester Ford d E. Mason Hopper ad Joseph Urban music score Deems Taylor

Marion Davies, Harrison Ford, Macklyn Arbuckle, Joseph Kilgour, George Nash, Tyrone Power Snr, May Vokes, W. C. Fields, Olin Howland

Janie

US 1944 106m bw
Warner (Brock Pemberton)

The teenage daughter of a middle-class American household gets into innocent scrapes with the army.

Deafening tomboy farce.

w Agnes Christine Johnson, Charles Hoffman, play Josephine Bentham, Herschel V. Williams Jnr d Michael Curtiz ph Carl Guthrie songs Lee David, Sammy Cahn, Jule Styne

Joyce Reynolds, Robert Hutton, Ann Harding, Edward Arnold, Robert Benchley, Claire Foley, Hattie McDaniel

† *Janie Gets Married*, made the following year and running 89m, had almost identical credits except that Joan Leslie replaced Joyce Reynolds and Dorothy Malone joined the cast.

Japanese War Bride*

US 1952 94m bw
TCF / Bernhard (Joseph Bernhard)

An officer wounded in Korea marries his Japanese nurse and takes her home to California.
Predictable domestic drama very similar to the British *Frieda*, marginally interesting for sociological reasons.

w Catherine Turney d King Vidor ph Lionel Lindon m Emil Newman

Shirley Yamaguchi, Don Taylor, Cameron Mitchell, Marie Windsor, James Bell, Louise Lorimer

Jason and the Argonauts***

GB 1963 104m Technicolor
Columbia / Charles H. Schneer

With help and hindrance from the gods, Jason voyages in search of the Golden Fleece and meets all kinds of monsters.
Rambling semi-classic mythological fantasy which keeps its tongue firmly in its cheek and provides a framework for some splendid stop-frame animation.

w Jan Read, Beverly Cross d Don Chaffey ph Wilkie Cooper m Bernard Herrmann sp Ray Harryhausen

Todd Armstrong, Honor Blackman, Niall MacGinnis, Andrew Faulds, Nancy Kovack

Jassy

GB 1947 102m Technicolor
GFD / Gainsborough (Sydney Box)

A gypsy servant girl falls in love with her master but is accused of murder.
Period romantic melodrama of the *Man in Grey* school; poor of its kind despite high production values.

w Dorothy and Campbell Christie, Geoffrey Kerr, novel Norah Lofts d Bernard Knowles ph Geoffrey Unsworth

Margaret Lockwood, Patricia Roc, Dennis

Price, Basil Sydney, Dermot Walsh, Nora
Swinburne, Linden Travers, Ernest Thesiger,
Cathleen Nesbitt, John Laurie, Jean Cadell,
Clive Morton

Java Head*

GB 1934   85m   bw
ATP (Basil Dean)

In 1850 Bristol, a shipbuilder forsakes his
Manchu wife for an English girl.
Rather obvious period melodrama with full-
blooded acting.

w Martin Brown, Gordon Wellesley d J. Walter
Ruben

Anna May Wong, John Loder, Ralph
Richardson, Elizabeth Allan, Edmund Gwenn,
Herbert Lomas, George Curzon, Roy Emerton

Jaws**

US 1975   125m   Technicolor   Panavision
Universal / Zanuck–Brown (William S.
   Gilmore Jnr)

A man-eating shark causes havoc off the Long
Island coast.
In the exploitation-hungry seventies this film
took more money than any other. In itself,
despite genuinely suspenseful and frightening
sequences, it is a slackly narrated and sometimes
flatly handled thriller with an over-abundance of
dialogue and, when it finally appears, a pretty
unconvincing monster.

w Peter Benchley, Carl Gottlieb, *novel* Peter
Benchley d *Steven Spielberg* ph Bill Butler
m John Williams

Robert Shaw, Roy Scheider, *Richard Dreyfuss*,
Lorraine Gary, Murray Hamilton, Carl Gottlieb
   'A mind-numbing repast for sense-sated
gluttons. Shark stew for the stupefied.'—
William S. Pechter

AA: John Williams
AAN: best picture

Jaws 2

US 1978   117m   Technicolor   Panavision
Universal / Richard Zanuck, David Brown (Joe
Alves)

Another man-eating shark menaces teenagers in
the Long Island resort of Amity.
Repetitive and feeble sequel aimed directly at the
popcorn market.

w Carl Gottlieb, Howard Sackler, Dorothy
Tristan d Jeannot Szwarc ph Michael Butler,
David Butler, Michael McGowan m John
Williams

Roy Scheider, Lorraine Gary, Murray
Hamilton, Joseph Mascolo, Colin Wilcox

The Jayhawkers

US 1959   110m   Technicolor   Vistavision
Paramount / Panama and Frank

Before the Civil War, a farmer defeats a militant
posse of private raiders.
Unconvincing but rather unusual western, flat
patches alternating with striking ones.

w Melvin Frank, Joseph Petracca, Frank
Fenton,
A. I. Bezzerides d Melvin Frank ph Loyal
Griggs m Jerome Moross

Fess Parker, Jeff Chandler, Nicole Maurey,
Henry Silva, Herbert Rudley

Jazz Comedy*

USSR 1934   93m   bw
Mosfilm
original title: *Vesolye Rebyata*

A shepherd is frequently mistaken for a famous
conductor.
Peripatetic comedy with many sight gags and
western slapstick: Russian comedy being still a
rare thing, it seems something of a revelation.

w Grigori Alexandrov, Nikolai Erdman, V.
Mass d *Grigori Alexandrov* ph Vladimir
Nilsen m Isaac Dunayevsky

Lubov Orlova, Leonid Utyosov, Maria
Strelkova

The Jazz Singer****

US 1927   89m   bw
Warner

A cantor's son makes it big in show business.
Archetypal Jewish weepie which became of
absorbing interest as the first talkie film (songs
and a few fragments of speech) and in its way,
surprisingly, is not half bad.

w Alfred A. Cohn, *play* Samson Raphaelson
d *Alan Crosland* ph Hal Mohr m & md Ray
Heindorf, Max Steiner

Al Jolson, May McAvoy, Warner Oland,
Eugenie Besserer, Otto Lederer
   'A beautiful period piece, extravagantly
sentimental . . . yet entirely compelling in its own
conviction.'—*NFT, 1969*

AAN: Alfred A. Cohn; Ray Heindorf, Max
Steiner

The Jazz Singer

US 1953   107m   Technicolor
Warner (Louis F. Edelman)

Ill-considered, schmaltzy remake of the above.

w Frank Davis, Leonard Stern, Lewis Meltzer
d Michael Curtiz ph Carl Guthrie md Ray
Heindorf

Danny Thomas, Peggy Lee, Mildred Dunnock, Eduard Franz

Jeanne Eagels*
US 1957   114m   bw
Columbia (George Sidney)

A sideshow dancer becomes a Broadway star of the twenties but dies of drugs.
Well-upholstered but basically too conventional showbiz biopic.

w Daniel Fuchs, Sonya Levien, John Fante d George Sidney ph Robert Planck m George Duning

Kim Novak, Jeff Chandler, Agnes Moorehead, Charles Drake, Larry Gates, *Virginia Grey*

Jeannie*
GB 1941   101m   bw
GFD / Tansa (Marcel Hellman)
US title: *Girl in Distress*

A Scots girl comes into money and takes a European holiday.
Mildly astringent, generally amusing comedy which overcomes shaky production. Remade as *Let's Be Happy* in 1952.

w Anatole de Grunwald, Roland Pertwee, *play* Aimée Stuart d Harold French

Barbara Mullen, Michael Redgrave, *Albert Lieven*, Wilfrid Lawson, Kay Hammond, Edward Chapman, Googie Withers, Gus MacNaughton

Jennie Gerhardt
US 1933   85m   bw
Paramount (B. P. Schulberg)

An unmarried mother is hard done by but gets the man she loves in the end.
Archetypal weepie, adequately put across.

w Josephine Lovett, Joseph M. March, S. K. Lauren, Frank Portos d Marion Gering ph Leon Shamroy

Sylvia Sidney, Donald Cook, Mary Astor, Edward Arnold, H. B. Warner, Theodor Von Eltz

Jennifer
US 1953   73m   bw
AA (Berman Swarttz)

The lady housekeeper of a California mansion broods on the mysterious disappearance of her predecessor.
Slight, quietly effective suspenser with a let-down ending.

w Virginia Myers d Joel Newton ph James Wong Howe m Ernest Gold

Ida Lupino, Howard Duff, Robert Nicholas, Mary Shipp

Jeopardy
US 1952   69m   bw
MGM (Sol Baer Fielding)

A man on a camping holiday falls off a jetty and gets stuck in the timbers while the water rises; his wife frantically seeks help from an escaped convict.
Panic melodrama enjoyable for its clichés.

w Mel Dinelli d John Sturges ph Victor Milner m Dmitri Tiomkin

Barbara Stanwyck, Barry Sullivan, Ralph Meeker

Jeremiah Johnson*
US 1972   107m   Technicolor   Panavision
Warner (Joe Wizan)

In the 1850s an ex-soldier becomes a mountain trapper.
Splendidly made if rather desultorily plotted adventure story with the feel of raw reality.

w John Milius, Edward Anhalt d Sydney Pollack ph Andrew Callaghan m John Rubinstein, Tim McIntire

Robert Redford, Will Geer, Allyn McLerie

Jeremy
US 1973   90m   De Luxe
UA / Kenasset

A music student falls in love with a ballet dancer.
Sentimental love story with nothing positive to commend it, chiefly interesting because for commercial release it was blown up from 16mm.

wd Arthur Barron ph Paul Goldsmith m Lee Holdridge

Robby Benson, Glynnis O'Connor, Len Bari, Leonardo Cimino

Jericho
GB 1937   77m   bw
Buckingham (Walter Futter, Max Schach)

A court-martialled officer pursues a murderous deserter across Africa.
Lively star vehicle of its day.

w Frances Marion, George Barraud, Peter Ruric, Robert N. Lee d Thornton Freeland

Paul Robeson, Henry Wilcoxon, Wallace Ford, John Laurie, James Carew

The Jerusalem File
US / Israel 1971   96m   Metrocolor
MGM / Sparta (Ram Ben Efraim)

American archaeologists in Jerusalem become involved in Arab/Israeli espionage.
Muddled mixture of action and politics.

w Troy Kennedy Martin *d* John Stoll *ph* Raoul Coutard *m* John Scott

Bruce Davison, Nicol Williamson, Donald Pleasence, Ian Hendry

Jesse James**
US 1939   106m   Technicolor
TCF (Nunnally Johnson)

After the Civil War, two brothers take to train robbing when railroad employees harass their family.
The life of an outlaw turns into family entertainment when Hollywood bathes it in sentiment, soft colour, family background and warm humour. It works dangerously well, and the action sequences are splendid.

w Nunnally Johnson d Henry King ph George Barnes md Louis Silvers ad William Darling, George Dudley

Tyrone Power, Henry Fonda, Nancy Kelly, Jane Darwell, Randolph Scott, Henry Hull, Slim Summerville, Brian Donlevy, J. Edward Bromberg, John Carradine, Donald Meek
   'An authentic American panorama.'—*New York Times*
* Sequel 1940: *The Return of Frank James.*
Remake 1957: *The True Story of Jesse James.*

Jessica
France / Italy / US 1962   105m
   Technicolor
   Panavision
UA / Ariane / Dear Film (Jean Negulesco)

The attractive midwife in a Sicilian village causes the women to go on a sex strike.
Synthetic rustic naughtiness showing several influences imperfectly assimilated.

w Edith Sommer, *novel* The Midwife of Pont Clery by Flora Sundstrom *d* Jean Negulesco *ph* Piero Portalupi *m* Mario Nascimbene

Angie Dickinson, Maurice Chevalier, Noel Noel, Gabriele Ferzetti, Sylva Koscina, Agnes Moorehead, Marcel Dalio

Jesus Christ Superstar*
US 1973   107m   Technicolor   Todd-AO
35
Universal (Norman Jewison, Robert Stigwood)

Young tourists in Israel re-enact episodes of the life of Christ.
Location-set fantasia based on the phenomenally successful rock opera; some of it

works, but the original concept was a theatrical one.

w Melvyn Bragg, Norman Jewison, *book* Tim Rice *d* Norman Jewison *m Andrew Lloyd Webber ph* Douglas Slocombe *md* André Previn

Ted Neeley, Carl Anderson, Yvonne Elliman, Barry Dennen
   'One of the true fiascos of modern cinema.'—*Paul D. Zimmerman*

AAN: André Previn

Jet over the Atlantic
US 1958   95m   bw
Warner / Inter Continental (Benedict Bogeaus)

A noble British passenger on a plane from Madrid to New York has planted a gas bomb in the luggage compartment.
Mechanical airborne suspenser with the usual assortment of unconvincing types making unconvincing gestures.

w Irving H. Cooper *d* Byron Haskin *ph* George Stahl *m* Lou Forbes

Guy Madison, Virginia Mayo, George Raft, George Macready, Ilona Massey, Anna Lee, Margaret Lindsay, Venetia Stevenson, Mary Anderson, Brett Halsey, Frederic Worlock

Jet Pilot
US 1950–57   112m   Technicolor
Howard Hughes (Jules Furthman)

A Russian lady spy falls for an American pilot.
Lamentably dull and stupid romantic actioner of which all concerned should be thoroughly ashamed, especially as it took seven years to complete and is not even technically competent.

w Jules Furthman *d* Josef Von Sternberg (and others) *ph* Winton C. Hoch *m* Bronislau Kaper

John Wayne, Janet Leigh, Jay C. Flippen, Paul Fix, Richard Rober, Roland Winters, Ivan Triesault, Hans Conried
   'One of the most childish, tedious and futile cold war spy dramas yet concocted by a Hollywood screenwriter.'—*John Gillett*

Jet Storm*
GB 1959   99m   bw
British Lion / Britannia / Pendennis (Steven Pallos)

An airliner in flight from London to New York is discovered to have a bomb on board.
All-star slice-of-life suspenser with competently handled dialogue and situations.

w Cy Endfield, Sigmund Miller *d* Cy Endfield *ph* Jack Hildyard *m* Thomas Rajna

Richard Attenborough, George Rose, Hermione Baddeley, Mai Zetterling, Diane Cilento, Stanley Baker, Harry Secombe, Virginia Maskell, Elizabeth Sellars, Sybil Thorndike, Bernard Braden, Cec Linder, David Kossoff

Les Jeux Interdits***
France 1952   84m   bw
Robert Dorfmann (Paul Joly)
aka: *Forbidden Games; The Secret Game*

In 1940, the little daughter of refugee parents sees her parents killed, and takes refuge with a peasant family, the small son of which helps her bury her dead puppy. They make a game of building a cemetery, which leads to a village feud . . .

Poignant anti-war tract which seemed a masterpiece at the time and is full of marvellous moments, but no longer holds up as a whole.

w Jean Aurenche, Pierre Bost, novel François Boyer *d René Clément ph* Robert Julliard *m* Narciso Yepes

Brigitte Fossey, Georges Poujouly, Amédée, Laurence Badie, Jacques Marin, Suzanne Courtal, Lucien Hubert

AAN: François Boyer (original story)

Les Jeux Sont Faits*
France 1947   91m   bw
Films Gibe

Falling in love in Purgatory, two murdered people get a second chance to return to earth, but spend their time quarrelling.
Somewhat despondent romantic fantasy with morsels of wit.

w Jean-Paul Sartre *d* Jean Delannoy *ph* Christian Matras *m* Georges Auric

Micheline Presle, Marcel Pagliero, Marguerite Moreno, Charles Dullin

Jew Suss**
GB 1934   109m   bw
Gaumont (Michael Balcon)
US title: *Power*

In old Wurttemberg, a Jew gains power to help his people, then finds he is Gentile.
Interesting, heavy-handed historical satire on the pointlessness of race distinctions, made partly in answer to Nazi oppression in Germany.

w Dorothy Farnum, A. R. Rawlinson, *novel* Leon Feuchtwangler *d* Lothar Mendes

Conrad Veidt, Benita Hume, Frank Vosper, Cedric Hardwicke, Gerald du Maurier, Pamela Ostrer

Jew Suss*
Germany 1940   85m   bw
Terra

Celebrated travesty of the above, in which the Jew is wholly evil and rapes Aryan girls.

w Ludwig Metzger, Veit Harlan, Eberhard Wolfgang Möller *d* Veit Harlan *ph* Bruno Mondi *m* Wolfgang Zeller

Ferdinand Marian, Werner Krauss, Heinrich George, Kristina Söderbaum

'The epitome of anti-semitic propaganda . . . the most notorious film of the Third Reich and one which brought disgrace on almost everyone connected with it.'—*Georges Sadoul*

'Highly recommended for its artistic value and, to serve the politics of the State, recommended for young people.'—*Josef Goebbels*

Jewel Robbery*
US 1932   68m   bw
Warner

A jewel thief and a millionaire's wife fall in love in Vienna.
Good sparkling fun in the shadow of *Trouble in Paradise* (qv).

w Erwin Gelsey, *play* Ladislaus Fodor *d* William Dieterle *ph* Robert Kurrle

William Powell, Kay Francis, Hardie Albright, André Luguet, Henry Kolker, Spencer Charters, Alan Mowbray, Helen Vinson, Lawrence Grant

Jezebel***
US 1938   104m   bw
Warner (Henry Blanke)

Before the Civil War, a southern belle stirs up trouble among the menfolk by her wilfulness and spite, but atones when a plague strikes.
Superb star melodrama, tossed to her in compensation for losing *Gone with the Wind*, and dealt with in high style by all concerned.

w Clements Ripley, Abem Finkel, John Huston, *play* Owen Davis Snr *d* William Wyler *ph* Ernest Haller *m* Max Steiner

Bette Davis, Henry Fonda, George Brent, Margaret Lindsay, Fay Bainter, Richard Cromwell, Donald Crisp, Henry O'Neill, John Litel, Spring Byington, Eddie Anderson, Gordon Oliver, Irving Pichel

'Its excellences come from many sources— good plotting and writing, a director and photographer who know how to make the thing flow along with dramatic pictorial effect, and a cast that makes its story a record of living people.'—*James Shelley Hamilton*

'Without the zing Davis gave it, it would have

looked very mossy indeed.'—*Pauline Kael,
1968*

AA: Bette Davis; Fay Bainter
AAN: best picture; Ernest Haller; Max Steiner

Jigsaw
US 1949 72m bw
(UA) Tower (The Danzigers)

An assistant District Attorney uncovers a mob
stirring up racial hatred.
Undistinguished piece of do-goodery, curiously
decorated by guest stars doing bit parts as a
gesture of goodwill.

w Fletcher Markle, Vincent McConnor
d Fletcher Markle *ph* Don Malkames *m* Robert
Stringer

Franchot Tone, Jean Wallace, Myron
McCormick, Marc Lawrence, Marlene Dietrich,
Henry Fonda, John Garfield, Marsha Hunt,
Leonard Lyons, Burgess Meredith

Jigsaw**
GB 1962 107m bw Cinemascope
British Lion / Britannia / Figaro (Val Guest)

Brighton policemen track down the murderer of
a woman found in a lonely house on the beach.
Absorbing and entertaining little murder
mystery which sustains its considerable length
with interesting detail and plays as fair as can be
with the audience. Excellent unassuming
entertainment.

wd Val Guest, play Sleep Long My Love by
Hilary Waugh *ph* Arthur Grant *m* none

Jack Warner, Ronald Lewis, *Michael Goodliffe*,
Yolande Donlan, John Barron

Jim Thorpe, All-American
US 1951 105m bw
Warner (Everett Freeman)
GB title: *Man of Bronze*

A Red Indian becomes a star footballer, but later
succumbs to drink.
Adequate sporting biopic.

w Douglas Morrow, Everett Freeman
d Michael Curtiz *ph* Ernest Haller *m* Max
Steiner

Burt Lancaster, Charles Bickford, Steve
Cochran, Phyllis Thaxter, Dick Wesson

Jimmy the Gent*
US 1934 67m bw
Warner (Robert Lord)

A racketeer supplies heirs for unclaimed estates.
Adequate star crime comedy.

w Bertram Millhauser *d* Michael Curtiz *ph* Ira
Morgan *md* Leo F. Forbstein

Jimmy Cagney, Bette Davis, Alice White, Allen
Jenkins, Arthur Hohl, Mayo Methot, Alan
Dinehart, Hobart Cavanaugh, Ralf Harolde,
Philip Reed, Joe Sawyer

'Fast and flip, rough and rowdy.'—*New York
American*

Jitterbugs*
US 1943 75m bw
TCF (Sol M. Wurtzel)

Laurel and Hardy help a nightclub singer to fight
off gangsters.
The last Laurel and Hardy film to contain any
good scenes, and almost the only one of their
TCF films that did.

w Scott Darling *d* Mal St Clair *ph* Lucien
Andriot

Stan Laurel, Oliver Hardy, Vivian Blaine, Bob
Bailey, Douglas Fowley, Noel Madison, Lee
Patrick

Jivaro
US 1953 91m Technicolor 3D
Paramount / William H. Pine, William
  C. Thomas
GB title: *Lost Treasure of the Amazon*

A mixed party of Americans follows a drunken
treasure seeker into the jungle.
Elementary treasure hunt adventure, hampered
by studio foliage, bad script and half-hearted
acting.

w Winston Miller, *story* David Duncan
d Edward Ludwig *ph* Lionel Lindon *m* Gregory
Stone

Fernando Lamas, Rhonda Fleming, Brian
Keith, Lon Chaney Jnr, Marvin Miller, Richard
Denning

Joan of Arc
US 1948 145m Technicolor
Walter Wanger

The last campaign of the Maid of Orleans.
Strictly from Dullsville; one studio-set piece
follows another, and a group of talented people
clearly thought that prestige would sell itself
without the hard work that goes into more
commercial productions.

w Maxwell Anderson, Andrew Solt, *play* Joan of
Lorraine by Maxwell Anderson *d* Victor
Fleming *ph* Joe Valentine *m* Hugo Friedhofer
md Emil Newman *ad* Richard Day

Ingrid Bergman, Jose Ferrer, George Coulouris,
Francis L. Sullivan, Gene Lockhart, Ward
Bond, John Ireland, Hurd Hatfield, Cecil
Kellaway, George Zucco, J. Carrol Naish

'A bad film with one or two good things. It is

childishly oversimplified, its battles *papier maché,* its heroine far too worldly, its spiritual content that of a chromo art calendar.'— *Herman G. Weinberg*

AA: Joe Valentine
AAN: Ingrid Bergman; Jose Ferrer

Joan of Paris
US 1942   95m   bw
TCF

A French resistance leader sacrifices herself so that Allied pilots can escape.
Well-made propaganda adventure dignified by excellent cast.

w Charles Bennett, Ellis St. Joseph, *story* Jacques Thery, Georges Kessel *d* Robert Stevenson *m* Roy Webb

Michele Morgan, Paul Henreid, Thomas Mitchell, Laird Cregar, May Robson, Alexander Granach, Alan Ladd

AAN: Roy Webb

Joanna
GB 1968   122m   De Luxe   Panavision
TCF / Laughlin (Michael S. Laughlin)

A girl art student comes to London and quickly finds the road to ruin.
Antediluvian rubbish tarted up with swinging London settings.

wd Michael Sarne *ph* Walter Lassally *m* Rod McKuen

Genevieve Waite, Christian Doermer, Calvin Lockhart, Donald Sutherland

'An unnecessarily protracted punishing of a very dead quadruped.'—*MFB*

The Job**
Italy 1961   90m   bw
24 Horses Films (Alberto Soffientini)
original title; *Il Posto*

A teenage boy gets his first job, and progresses from office boy to clerk when a senior man dies.
Appealingly observant social comedy, very simple and extremely effective.

wd Ermanno Olmi ph Lamberto Caimi

Sandro Panzeri, Loredana Detto

'Rueful and funny and honest . . . the players have been encouraged not so much to act as to behave. Olmi stalks them like a naturalist, and the result is a small, unique and perfect achievement in film-making.'—*Penelope Houston, MFB*

Joe*
US 1970   107m   De Luxe
Cannon (David Gil)

A construction worker in a bar meets a businessman who has just killed his daughter's drug addicted lover; they become buddies in their hatred of hippies.
Highly successful in America as a backlash against permissiveness, this rough-hewn opportunistic melodrama is vivid enough but moves in fits and starts.

w Norman Wexler *d/ph* John G. Avildsen *m* Bobby Scott

Peter Boyle, Dennis Patrick, Audrey Caire, Susan Sarandon

'A bad film disfigured by brute strokes of tendentiousness.'—*Penelope Gilliatt*
AAN: Norman Wexler

Joe Butterfly
US 1957   90m   Technicolor
   Cinemascope
U-I (Aaron Rosenberg)

Shortly after World War II, American occupying troops are conned by a Japanese interpreter.
Dull comedy intent on healing old wounds.

w Sy Gomberg, Jack Sher, Marion Hargrove *d* Jesse Hibbs *ph* Irving Glassberg *m* Joseph Gershenson

Burgess Meredith, Audie Murphy, George Nader, Keenan Wynn, Fred Clark, John Agar, Charles McGraw

Joe Dakota
US 1957   90m   Technicolor
   Cinemascope
U-I (Howard Christie)

A stranger appears in a western town in search of his Indian friend, who turns out to have been murdered by the townspeople so that they can share the profits from his oil well.
Feeble rip-off of *Bad Day at Black Rock*.

w William Talman, Norman Jolley *d* Richard Bartlett *ph* George Robinson *md* Joseph Gershenson

Jock Mahoney, Luana Patten, Charles McGraw, Barbara Lawrence, Claude Akins, Lee Van Cleef

Joe Kidd
US 1972   87m   Technicolor   Panavision
Universal / Malpaso (Sidney Beckerman)

A disreputable bounty hunter tracks down the leader of a tribe of Mexican bandits.
Rough and tumble star western with untenable moral attitudes.

w Elmore Leonard *d* John Sturges *ph* Bruce Surtees *m* Lalo Schifrin

Clint Eastwood, Robert Duvall, John Saxon, Don Stroud, James Wainwright

Joe Macbeth
GB 1955 90m bw
Columbia / Frankovich (George Maynard)

A gangster is urged by his wife to rub out his boss.
Almost too bad to be funny, this effort to update Shakespeare has actors behaving as though they were stuck in treacle, and its gimmick quality is quickly dissipated by an indifferent production.

w Philip Yordan *d* Ken Hughes *ph* Basil Emmott *m* Trevor Duncan

Paul Douglas, Ruth Roman, Grégoire Aslan, Bonar Colleano, Sidney James

Joe Smith American*
US 1942 63m bw
MGM (Jack Chertok)
GB title: *Highway to Freedom*

An aircraft factory worker with special knowledge is kidnapped by Nazis but leads the FBI to his captors.
Watchable propaganda thriller credited with easing Americans into a war mood.

w Allen Rivkin, *story* Paul Gallico *d* Richard Thorpe *ph* Charles Lawton Jnr

Robert Young, Marsha Hunt, Darryl Hickman, Harvey Stephens, Jonathan Hale, Noel Madison, Joseph Anthony
'Not a high-powered movie, it is a first rate die for the new propaganda models which Hollywood is readying for mass production.'—*Time*

Joey Boy
GB 1965 91m bw
British Lion / Launder–Gilliat

In 1941, a group of petty crooks join the army. Abysmal service comedy, incredibly cheap and tatty and the nadir of several of the talents involved.

wd Frank Launder *ph* Arthur Lavis *m* Philip Green

Harry H. Corbett, Stanley Baxter, Bill Fraser, Reg Varney, Percy Herbert, Lance Percival
'As visually shoddy as it is unfunny . . . the final shot (Corbett pulling a lavatory chain) is all too crudely apt.'—*MFB*

John and Julie
GB 1955 82m Eastmancolor
Group Three (Herbert Mason)

Two children run away to see the coronation.
Genial little family comedy full of stock comic characters.

wd William Fairchild *ph* Arthur Grant *m* Philip Green

Colin Gibson, Leslie Dudley, Peter Sellers, Moira Lister, Wilfrid Hyde White, Sidney James, Andrew Cruickshank

John and Mary*
US 1969 92m De Luxe Panavision
TCF / Debrod (Ben Kadish)

Two New Yorkers have a one-night affair and cannot decide whether to continue.
Slight, disappointing sex comedy vehicle for two stars who were very hot at the time.

w John Mortimer, *novel* Mervyn Jones *d* Peter Yates *ph* Gayne Rescher *m* Quincy Jones *pd* John Robert Lloyd

Dustin Hoffman, Mia Farrow, Michael Tolan, Sunny Griffin, Tyne Daly
'The emphasis is not on action but on acting, which although skilful and subtly nuanced does not in this case amount to the same thing as character.'—*Jan Dawson*
'Despite all the "now" sets and surfaces, it's like an old comedy of the thirties—minus the comedy.'—*Judith Crist*

John Goldfarb Please Come Home
US 1965 96m De Luxe Cinemascope
TCF / Steve Palmer / J. Lee-Thompson

An American spy pilot crashlands near the palace of a Middle Eastern potentate at the same time as a girl reporter arrives for an interview.
Would-be satire on the cold war, anti-feminism, American football, American/Arab relations, etc. None of it works for a minute, and the actors' desperation can be plainly seen.

w William Peter Blatty *d* J. Lee-Thompson *ph* Leon Shamroy *m* Johnny Williams

Shirley Maclaine, Richard Crenna, Peter Ustinov, Fred Clark, Wilfrid Hyde White, Jim Backus

John Loves Mary
US 1948 87m bw
Warner

A GI returns home to get married, but unfortunately, to help a friend, he has already entered into a marriage of convenience.
Moderately amusing comedy with an excess of complications.

w Phoebe and Henry Ephron, *play* Norman Krasna *d* David Butler *ph* Peverell Marley

Ronald Reagan, Patricia Neal, Jack Carson, Virginia Field

John Paul Jones
US 1959   126m   Technirama
Warner / Samuel Bronston

At the time of the American revolution a young Scotsman rises to great heights in the American navy.

Fragmented biopic with a succession of guest stars which turn it into a charade almost as silly as *The Story of Mankind*. On that level it is not unentertaining.

wd John Farrow *ph* Michel Kelber *m* Max Steiner

Robert Stack, Charles Coburn (as Benjamin Franklin), Bette Davis (as Catherine the Great), Marisa Pavan, Jean-Pierre Aumont, Peter Cushing, Bruce Cabot, Macdonald Carey

Johnny Allegro*
US 1949   81m   bw
Columbia (Irving Starr)
GB title: *Hounded*

A private eye eliminates a counterfeiter and marries his wife.

Cheeky variation on the plot of *Gilda*, with Macready repeating his role; later stages borrow from *The Most Dangerous Game*. All mildly diverting.

w Karen de Wolf, Guy Endore, James Edward Grant *d* Ted Tetzlaff *ph* Joseph Biroc *m* George Duning

George Raft, George Macready, Nina Foch, Will Geer, Ivan Triesault

'Without any particular distinction, but certainly not boring.'—*Richard Mallett, Punch*

Johnny Angel*
US 1945   79m   bw
RKO

A seaman solves the mystery of his father's ship, found empty and adrift in the Gulf of Mexico. Very watchable mystery with plenty of plot twists and efficient presentation.

w Steve Fisher *d* Edwin L. Marin *ph* Harry J. Wild

George Raft, Claire Trevor, Signe Hasso, Lowell Gilmore, Hoagy Carmichael, Marvin Miller

Johnny Apollo
US 1940   93m   bw
TCF (Harry Joe Brown)

A well-heeled young man turns crook.
Moderate crime melo, impeccably turned out.

w Philip Dunne, Rowland Brown *d* Henry

Hathaway *ph* Arthur Miller *m* Cyril Mockridge *md* Alfred Newman

Tyrone Power, Dorothy Lamour, Edward Arnold, Lloyd Nolan, Charles Grapewin, Lionel Atwill, Marc Lawrence, Jonathan Hale

Johnny Belinda**
US 1948   103m   bw
Warner (Jerry Wald)

In a remote fishing community, a deaf mute girl is raped and the sympathetic local doctor is suspected of being the father of her baby.
Melodrama of the old school which in 1948 seemed oddly to mark a new permissiveness and made a big star of Jane Wyman; the production and locations were also persuasive.

w Irmgard Von Cube, Allen Vincent, *play* Elmer Harris *d* Jean Negulesco *ph* Ted McCord *m* Max Steiner *md* Leo F. Forbstein

Jane Wyman, Lew Ayres, Charles Bickford, Agnes Moorehead, Stephen McNally, Jan Sterling, Rosalind Ivan, Mabel Paige

AA: Jane Wyman
AAN: best picture; script; Jean Negulesco; Ted McCord; Max Steiner; Lew Ayres; Charles Bickford; Agnes Moorehead

Johnny Come Lately*
US 1943   97m   bw
William Cagney
GB title: *Johnny Vagabond*

A travelling newspaperman is jailed for vagrancy in a small town and stays to expose corrupt politicians.

A turn-of-the-century folksy drama seemed an odd choice for a Cagney independent production, and it was not very persuasively made, but the star produced moments of his old charisma.

w John Van Druten, *novel* McLeod's Folly by Louis Bromfield *d* William K. Howard *ph* Theodor Sparkuhl *m* Leigh Harline

James Cagney, *Grace George*, Marjorie Main, Marjorie Lord, Hattie McDaniel, Edward McNamara, Bill Henry, Robert Barrat, George Cleveland, Margaret Hamilton, Lucien Littlefield, Irving Bacon

'The kind of business that might result if Jimmy Cagney, the immortal Hollywood movie star, had returned to play the lead in the annual production of his old high school's Masque and Film Club.'—*John T. McManus*

AAN: Leigh Harline

Johnny Concho
US 1956   84m   bw
UA / Kent (Frank Sinatra)

A coward runs Cripple Creek because he has a gunfighter brother, but when the latter is shot another gunman takes over.

Unexpected small-scale western, pleasantly made but no *High Noon*.

w David P. Harmon, Don McGuire *d* Don McGuire *ph* William Mellor *m* Nelson Riddle

Frank Sinatra, *William Conrad*, Phyllis Kirk, Wallace Ford, John Qualen

Johnny Cool*

US 1963   101m   bw
UA / Chrislaw (William Asher)

A Sicilian bandit is sent to the US on a mission of vengeance.

Chilling gangster thriller, the callousness of which is apparently meant to be counterpointed by the humorous cameo appearances of several well-known faces. This does not work.

w John McPartland, *novel* Joseph Landon *d* William Asher *ph* Sam Leavitt *m* Billy May

Henry Silva, Elizabeth Montgomery, Jim Backus, Marc Lawrence, John McGiver, Sammy Davis Jnr, Mort Sahl, Telly Savalas, Joseph Calleia, Robert Armstrong, Douglass Dumbrille, Elisha Cook Jnr

Johnny Dark

US 1954   85m   Technicolor
U-I (William Alland)

A motor company produces a new sports car designed by an employee, who drives it in a race.
Competent, unremarkable action melodrama tailor-made for its star.

w Franklin Coen *d* George Sherman *ph* Carl Guthrie *m* Joseph Gershenson

Tony Curtis, Piper Laurie, Don Taylor, Paul Kelly, Ilka Chase, Sidney Blackmer

Johnny Eager*

US 1941   107m   bw
MGM (John W. Considine)

A gangster makes a play for a society girl.
Well-made, rather unattractive gangster melodrama.

w John Lee Mahin, James Edward Grant *d* Mervyn Le Roy *ph* Harold Rosson

Robert Taylor, *Van Heflin*, Lana Turner, Edward Arnold, Robert Sterling, Patricia Dane, Glenda Farrell, Henry O'Neill

AA: Van Heflin

Johnny Frenchman

GB 1945   111m   bw
Ealing (S. C. Balcon)

Rivalry between the fishermen of Cornwall and Brittany prevents the course of true love from running smooth.

Rhubarbing extras and studio sets make this an unreal and disappointing Ealing melodrama, and all the actors look helpless.

w T. E. B. Clarke *d* Charles Frend *ph* Roy Kellino

Françoise Rosay, Tom Walls, Patricia Roc, Paul Dupuis, Ralph Michael, Frederick Piper, Arthur Hambling

Johnny Got His Gun

US 1971   111m   colour
World Entertainments Ltd (Bruce Campbell)

In 1918 a soldier is so badly wounded as to lose arms, legs, eyes, ears, mouth and nose, and begs his doctors to kill him.

A horrifying and fascinating premise turns out to have nowhere to go, at least not in this talky treatment which the author has nurtured too long.

wd Dalton Trumbo *ph* Jules Brenner *m* Jerry Fielding

Timothy Bottoms, Jason Robards Jnr, Marsha Hunt, Donald Sutherland, Kathy Fields, Diane Varsi

Johnny Guitar*

US 1953   110m   Trucolor
Republic (Nicholas Ray)

In old Arizona, the proprietress of a gambling saloon stakes a claim to valuable land and incurs the enmity of a lady banker.

Weird Freudian western notable for a running catfight between its lady protagonists; the title character is decidedly secondary. Not exactly a good movie, but memorable because it's almost always over the top.

w Philip Yordan, *novel* Roy Chanslor *d* Nicholas Ray *ph* Harry Stradling *m* Victor Young

Joan Crawford, Mercedes McCambridge, Sterling Hayden, Ernest Borgnine, Ward Bond, John Carradine, Scott Brady

'A very rum western, with cockeyed feminist attitudes.'—*New Yorker, 1975*

Johnny Nobody

GB 1960   88m   bw   Warwickscope
Columbia / Viceroy (Irving Allen, Albert Broccoli)

A drunken Irish author challenges God to strike him dead for blasphemy. When an amnesiac shoots him, a nationwide religious controversy

begins, but the deed is found to have a mercenary motive.
A mysterious rigmarole which irritates more than it entertains.

w Patrick Kirwan, *story* The Trial of Johnny Nobody by Albert Z. Carr d Nigel Patrick ph Ted Moore m Ron Goodwin

Nigel Patrick, Aldo Ray, Yvonne Mitchell, William Bendix, Cyril Cusack, Niall MacGinnis, Bernie Winters, Noel Purcell, Jimmy O'Dea

'The more one thinks of it, the more one is amazed that anyone should have thought a plot and players as uniformly unlikely as these could have worked out satisfactorily.'—*Peter John Dyer, MFB*

Johnny Stool Pigeon
US 1949 75m bw
U-I (Aaron Rosenberg)

A detective releases a convict on condition that he leads him to a drug smuggling gang.
Competent low budget addition to the documentary police cycle.

w Robert L. Richards d William Castle ph Maury Gertsman m Milton Schwarzwald

Howard Duff, Shelley Winters, Dan Duryea, Gary Moore, Tony Curtis, John McIntire, Barry Kelley, Leif Erickson

Johnny Tremain
US 1957 81m Technicolor
Walt Disney

In 1773 Boston an apprentice silversmith joins the Sons of Liberty and helps start the War of Independence.
Schoolbook history with little vitality.

w Tom Blackburn, *novel* Esther Forbes d Robert Stevenson ph Charles B. Boyle m George Bruns

Hal Stalmaster, Luana Patten, Jeff York, Sebastian Cabot, Richard Beymer, Walter Sande

Johnny Trouble
US 1956 88m bw
Clarion (John H. Auer)

An elderly widow becomes involved with a boys' college and thinks she has found her lost grandson.
Sentimental, whimsical star vehicle.

w Charles O'Neal, David Lord d John H. Auer ph Peverell Marley m Frank de Vol

Ethel Barrymore, Stuart Whitman, Cecil Kellaway, Carolyn Jones, Jesse White

The Johnstown Flood*
US 1926 70m approx (24 fps) bw silent
Fox

A construction worker is warned by his girl friend of an approaching flood, in which she dies.
Curious melodrama with mild spectacle.

w Efrid Bingham, Robert Lord d Irving Cummings

George O'Brien, Janet Gaynor (her first film), Paul Panzer, George Harris

The Joker Is Wild*
US 1957 126m bw Vistavision
Paramount / Charles Vidor

Joe E. Lewis, a twenties nightclub singer, loses his voice after an attack by gangsters, and becomes a comedian.
Reasonably lively showbiz biopic in jaundiced vein; good atmosphere but far too long.

w Oscar Saul, *book* Art Cohn d Charles Vidor ph Daniel L. Fapp m Walter Scharf

Frank Sinatra, Mitzi Gaynor, Eddie Albert, Jeanne Crain, Beverly Garland, Jackie Coogan, Ted de Corsia

AA: song 'All the Way' (m Jimmy Van Heusen, ly Sammy Cahn)

The Jokers**
GB 1967 126m Technicolor
Universal / Adastra / Gildor / Scimitar (Maurice Foster, Ben Arbeid)

Two young brothers in London society plan to create a sensation by borrowing (and replacing) the crown jewels.
Bright suspense comedy which sums up the swinging London era pretty well and is generally amusing though it finally lacks aplomb.

w *Dick Clement, Ian La Frenais d Michael Winner ph* Ken Hodges m Johnny Pearson

Michael Crawford, Oliver Reed, Harry Andrews, *James Donald*, Daniel Massey, Michael Hordern, Gabriella Licudi, Frank Finlay, Warren Mitchell, Rachel Kempson, Peter Graves

A Jolly Bad Fellow*
GB 1964 95m bw
British Lion / Pax / Tower / Michael Balcon (Donald Taylor)
US title: *They All Died Laughing*

A brash chemistry don tries a new poison on his enemies.
Interesting but finally irritating comedy of murders with a punnish rather than a donnish

script and only moments of genuine sub-Ealing hilarity.

w Robert Hamer, Donald Taylor, *novel* Don Among the Dead Men by C. E. Vulliamy *d* Robert Hamer *ph* Gerald Gibbs *m* John Barry

Leo McKern, Janet Munro, Maxine Audley, Duncan Macrae, Dennis Price, Miles Malleson, Leonard Rossiter

Jolson Sings Again**

US 1949 96m Technicolor
Columbia (Sidney Buchman)

Al Jolson's later career and second marriage to a nurse he met while entertaining troops in World War II.

Breezy, routine, rather empty sequel to the following.

w Sidney Buchman *d* Henry Levin *ph* William Snyder *md* Morris Stoloff, George Duning

Larry Parks, Barbara Hale, William Demarest, Ludwig Donath, Bill Goodwin, Tamara Shayne, Myron McCormick

AAN: Sidney Buchman; William Snyder; Morris Stoloff, George Duning

The Jolson Story****

US 1946 129m Technicolor
Columbia (Sidney Skolsky)

Asa Yoelson, son of a cantor, becomes Al Jolson, the great entertainer of the twenties; but showbiz success brings marital difficulties. Whitewashed biopic in impeccable Hollywood style, with everything working shamelessly right, a new star in the leading role, perfect if unambitious production values, and a deluge of the best songs ever written.

w *Stephen Longstreet d Alfred E. Green, Joseph H. Lewis ph* Joseph Walker *md* Morris Stoloff

Larry Parks (using Jolson's own voice), *William Demarest, Evelyn Keyes, Ludwig Donath, Tamara Shayne,* Bill Goodwin, *Scotty Beckett,* John Alexander

AA: Morris Stoloff
AAN: Joseph Walker; Larry Parks; William Demarest

Jonathan Livingston Seagull*

US 1973 114m De Luxe Panavision
Paramount / JLS Partnership / Hall Bartlett

The life of a seagull who aims to fly faster than any of his peers and eventually arrives in a perfect world.

Weird 'family' fantasy based on a phenomenally successful book which clearly could not translate

easily to the screen. The bird photography is much more successful than the mysticism.

w Richard Bach, from his book *d* Hall Bartlett *ph Jack Couffer m* Neil Diamond, Lee Holdridge *ph* Boris Leven

'A parable couched in the form of a nature film of overpowering beauty and strength in which, perhaps to our horror, we are forced to recognize ourselves in a seagull obsessed with the heights.'—*Michael Korda*

The Jones Family

Less human, more farcical than the Hardy films (qv), this series was TCF's second feature answer to MGM's money-makers, and pleased a lot of people at the time. Pop was Jed Prouty, Mom was Spring Byington, Grandma was Florence Roberts, and the youngsters included Kenneth Lake, George Ernest, Billy Mahan, June Carlson and June Lang. The first script was from a play by Katharine Cavanaugh, and the principal director was Frank Strayer.

1936: EVERY SATURDAY NIGHT, EDUCATING FATHER, BACK TO NATURE
1937: OFF TO THE RACES, BORROWING TROUBLE, HOT WATER
1938: LOVE ON A BUDGET, TRIP TO PARIS, SAFETY IN NUMBERS, DOWN ON THE FARM
1939: EVERYBODY'S BABY, QUICK MILLIONS, THE JONES FAMILY IN HOLLYWOOD, TOO BUSY TO WORK
1940: ON THEIR OWN
† An earlier series with different actors was abandoned after two episodes: *Young as You Feel* (1931), *Business and Pleasure* (1932).

Joseph Andrews

GB 1977 104m Eastmancolor
UA/Woodfall (Neil Hartley)

Adventures of a naïve 18th-century footman. Woebegone attempt to restage *Tom Jones.*

w Allan Scott, Chris Bryant *d* Tony Richardson *ph* David Watkin *m* John Addison *pd* Michael Annals

Peter Firth, Ann-Margret, Michael Hordern, Beryl Reid, Jim Dale, Peter Bull, John Gielgud, Hugh Griffith, Timothy West, Wendy Craig, Peggy Ashcroft, James Villiers, Karen Dotrice, Ronald Pickup

'Even the incidental pleasures cannot offset the sense of *déjà vu* which pervades this musty enterprise.'—*John Pym, MFB*

Josephine and Men

GB 1955 98m Eastmancolor
Charter (John and Roy Boulting)

The three romances of a determined young woman.
Alarmingly thin, old-fashioned romantic comedy with all resolved in a country cottage.
Nothing quite works, especially the colour.

w Nigel Balchin, Roy Boulting, Frank Harvey d Roy Boulting ph Gilbert Taylor m John Addison

Glynis Johns, *Jack Buchanan*, Donald Sinden, Peter Finch, Heather Thatcher, Ronald Squire

Josette
US 1938   73m   bw
TCF (Gene Markey)

A New Orleans coquette teases two men.
Very minor musical, well enough presented but adding up to almost nothing.

w James Edward Grant d Allan Dwan ph John Mescall *songs* Harry Revel, Mack Gordon

Simone Simon, Don Ameche, Robert Young, Joan Davis, Bert Lahr, Paul Hurst, William Collier Snr, Lynn Bari, William Demarest

Jour de Fête***
France 1948   87m   bw
Francinex

A village postman sees a film about the efficiency of the American postal service and decides to smarten himself up.
First, and some say best, of Tati's comedy vehicles: two-thirds superb local colour, one-third hilarious slapstick.

w Jacques Tati, Henri Marquet d *Jacques Tati* ph Jacques Mercanton m Jean Yatove

Jacques Tati, Guy Decomble, Paul Fankeur, Santa Relli

Le Jour Se Lève***
France 1939   85m   bw
Sigma
aka: *Daybreak*

A murderer is besieged by police in his attic room, remembers his past through the night, and shoots himself.
A model of French poetic realism, and a much-praised film which was almost destroyed when it was bought for an American remake (*The Long Night*).

w Jacques Viot, Jacques Prévert d Marcel Carné ph Curt Courant, Philippe Agostini, André Bac m Maurice Jaubert ad Alexander Trauner

Jean Gabin, Jules Berry, Arletty, Jacqueline Laurent

'The man walks about his room, moves a few things, lies on his bed, looks out of the window,

chain-smokes . . . and one is genuinely interested in him all the time (remembering afterwards that there exist directors who contrive to be boring even when they use fifteen characters in a motor car chase crackling with revolver shots).'— *Richard Mallett, Punch*

The Journey
US 1959   125m   Technicolor
MGM / Alby (Anatole Litvak)

During the 1956 Hungarian uprising, a busload of international passengers is detained overnight by a Russian major.
Pretentious, predictable and dull multi-melodrama peopled by uninteresting characters; different handling might have made a *Casablanca* of it.

w George Tabori d Anatole Litvak ph Jack Hildyard m Georges Auric

Yul Brynner, Deborah Kerr, Jason Robards Jnr, Anouk Aimée, Robert Morley, E. G. Marshall, Anne Jackson, David Kossoff, Kurt Kasznar, Gerard Oury

'Ten minutes of this and we know where we are: we are back in the 1930s with Alfred Hitchcock and that glamorous band of international characters trapped in Mitteleuropa.'—*Steven Marcus*

Journey for Margaret*
US 1942   81m   bw
MGM (B. P. Fineman)

An American correspondent brings home an orphan from the London blitz.
Efficient tearful propaganda which coincidentally made a star of little Margaret O'Brien.

w David Hertz, William Ludwig, *book* William L. White d W. S. Van Dyke ph Ray June m Franz Waxman

Robert Young, Laraine Day, *Margaret O'Brien*, Billy Severn, Fay Bainter, Signe Hasso, Nigel Bruce, Halliwell Hobbes

Journey into Autumn*
Sweden 1954   86m   bw
Sandrews (Rune Waldekrantz)
original title: *Kvinnodrom*

Two business women visiting Gothenburg have difficult relationships to settle.
Moody, impressionist sex drama which succeeds by fits and starts.

wd Ingmar Bergman ph Hilding Bladh

Eva Dahlbeck, Harriet Andersson, Gunnar Bjornstrand, Ulf Palme, Inga Landgre, Naima Wifstrand

'Scenes of austere anti-romanticism and painful irony.'—*Peter John Dyer, MFB*

Journey into Fear***
US 1942 71m bw
RKO (Orson Welles)

A munitions expert finds himself in danger from assassins in Istanbul, and has to be smuggled home.

Highly enjoyable impressionist melodrama supervised by Orson Welles and full of his touches and excesses.

w Joseph Cotten, Orson Welles, novel Eric Ambler d Norman Foster (and *Orson Welles*) *ph Karl Struss m* Constantin Bakaleinikoff

Joseph Cotten, Dolores del Rio, Jack Moss, Orson Welles, Ruth Warrick, Agnes Moorehead

'Brilliant atmosphere, the nightmare of pursuit, eccentric encounters on the way, and when the shock comes it leaps at eye and ear.'—*William Whitebait*

Journey to the Center of the Earth***
US 1959 132m De Luxe Cinemascope
TCF (Charles Brackett)

An Edinburgh professor and assorted colleagues follow an explorer's trail down an extinct Icelandic volcano to the earth's centre.
Enjoyable hokum which gets more and more fantastic but only occasionally misses its footing; it ends splendidly with the team being catapulted out of Stromboli on a tide of lava.

w Walter Reisch, Charles Brackett, novel Jules Verne *d Henry Levin ph* Leo Tover *m Bernard Herrmann ad* Lyle R. Wheeler, Franz Bachelin, Herman A. Blumenthal

James Mason, Arlene Dahl, Pat Boone, Peter Ronson, Diane Baker, Thayer David

'The attraction of a Jules Verne fantasy . . . is in the endearing contrast between the wildest adventures and the staidest Victorian propriety on the part of those undergoing them . . . There is about the whole film a good-natured enjoyment of its own excesses.'—*Penelope Houston*

Journey to the Far Side of the Sun*
GB 1969 99m De Luxe Cinemascope
Universal / Century 21 Productions (Gerry Anderson)
    Alternative title: *Doppelganger*

An astronaut on a mission to a hitherto undetected planet discovers it to be an exact duplicate of Earth, and his own double returns in his place.

Intriguing, impeccably produced, but rather dull science fiction.

w Gerry and Sylvia Anderson, Donald James *d* Robert Parrish *ph* John Read *m* Barry Gray *sp* Harry Oakes *models* Derek Meddings

Ian Hendry, Roy Thinnes, Patrick Wymark, Lynn Loring, Herbert Lom, George Sewell, Ed Bishop

Journey Together*
GB 1944 95m bw
RAF Film Unit

Trainee pilots receive instruction in England and America before going on their first bombing mission.

Modest wartime semi-documentary, pleasingly done.

w Terence Rattigan *d* John Boulting *ph* Harry Waxman *m* Gordon Jacob *pd* John Howell

Richard Attenborough, Jack Watling, David Tomlinson, Edward G. Robinson, Hugh Wakefield, Sebastian Shaw, Ronald Adam, Bessie Love

Journey's End*
GB 1930 120m bw
Gainsborough–Welsh–Pearson–Tiffany (George Pearson)

France 1917: personal tensions mount as men die in the trenches.

Primitive early sound version (made in Hollywood because of better equipment) of a justly celebrated play first performed a year earlier. Cinematically uninteresting, with acting generally over the top, but it kept Whale and Clive in Hollywood where they shortly collaborated on *Frankenstein*.

w Joseph Moncure March, Gareth Gundrey, *play R. C. Sheriff d* James Whale *ph* Benjamin Kline

Colin Clive, Ian MacLaren, David Manners, Billy Bevan, Anthony Bushell, Robert Adair

'It has been transferred to the screen with the greatest possible tact and discretion.'—*James Agate*

'Hollywood has produced its first sex-appeal-less film. Mr George Pearson is to be congratulated on his restraint.'—*Punch*

Joy in the Morning
US 1965 103m Metrocolor
MGM (Henry T. Weinstein)

Early episodes in the marriage of a poor teenage student.

Glutinous romantic drama, quite well made.

w Sally Benson, Alfred Hayes, Norman Lessing, *novel* Betty Smith *d* Alex Segal *ph* Ellsworth Fredericks *m* Bernard Herrmann

Richard Chamberlain, Yvette Mimieux, Arthur Kennedy, Oscar Homolka, Joan Tetzel, Sidney Blackmer

Joy of Living*
US 1938 90m bw
RKO (Felix Young)

A practical-minded Broadway songstress succumbs to the charms of an aristocratic freewheeler.
Zany romantic comedy, not quite zippy enough to make one forget its irritating archness, but socio-historically very interesting, in the mould of *You Can't Take It with You.*

w Gene Towne, Allan Scott, Graham Baker *d* Tay Garnett *ph* Joseph Walker *md* Frank Tours

Irene Dunne, Douglas Fairbanks Jnr, Alice Brady, Guy Kibbee, Lucille Ball, Eric Blore, Jean Dixon, Warren Hymer, Billy Gilbert

Joyless Street*
Germany 1925 139m (24 fps) bw silent
Sofar Film
original title: *Die Freudlose Gasse*

Problems of the inhabitants of a street in Vienna after World War I.
Realistic but studio-set melodrama which brought its director and Greta Garbo to international fame. In itself the film begins by stimulating and ends by boring.

w Willy Haas, *novel* Hugo Bettauer *d* G. W. Pabst *ph* Guido Seeber, Curt Oertel, Robert Lach

Asta Nielsen, Werner Krauss, *Greta Garbo*, Valeska Gert, Agnes Esterhazy
'Moments of searing pain, of mental anguish, of sheer unblemished beauty.'—*Paul Rotha, The Film Till Now*

Juarez**
US 1939 132m bw
Warner (Hal. B. Wallis, Henry Blanke)

A revolutionary leader causes the downfall of Emperor Maximilian of Mexico.
Spectacular historical drama with many fine moments which do not quite coalesce into a dramatic whole, chiefly owing to the lack of a single viewpoint.

w John Huston, Wolfgang Reinhardt, Aeneas Mackenzie *d William Dieterle ph Tony Gaudio m Erich Wolfgang Korngold*

Brian Aherne, Bette Davis, Paul Muni, Claude Rains, John Garfield, Donald Crisp, Gale Sondergaard, Joseph Calleia, Gilbert Roland, Henry O'Neill, Pedro de Cordoba, Montagu Love, Harry Davenport
'A million dollars' worth of ballroom sets, regimentals, gauze shots and whiskers.'—*Otis Ferguson*
'Dramatically by far the most effective of Warners' biographical films of the thirties.'—*Graham Greene*
'Muni's big-star solemn righteousness is like a dose of medicine.'—*New Yorker, 1977*

AAN: Brian Aherne

Jubal
US 1955 101m Technicolor
   Cinemascope
Columbia (William Fadiman)

A rancher's wife causes trouble when she falls in love with a wandering cowhand.
Solid sex western, moderately interestingly done.

w Russell S. Hughes, Delmer Daves, *novel* Jubal Troop by Paul Wellman *d* Delmer Daves *ph* Charles Lawton *m* David Raksin

Glenn Ford, Ernest Borgnine, Felicia Farr, Rod Steiger, Valerie French, Charles Bronson, Noah Beery Jnr

Jubilee*
GB 1978 104m colour
Whaley-Malin/Megalovision

Queen Elizabeth I is transported by her astrologer into the latter part of the 20th century, and is appalled by what she sees.
Outrageous dissection of modern urban life, full of black jokes: it has the right attitudes but is not free of a determination to shock at all costs.

w Derek Jarman and others *d* Derek Jarman *ph* Peter Middleton *m* Brian Eno

Jenny Runacre, Little Nell, Toyah Willcox, Jordan, Hermine Demoriane
'One of the most intelligent and interesting films to be made in Britain in a long time.'—*Scott Meek, MFB*

Jubilee Trail*
US 1954 103m Trucolor
Republic (Joseph Kane)

Jealousy and murder by covered wagon en route from New Orleans to the California gold fields.
Bumpy adventure melodrama, generally quite entertaining.

w Bruce Manning, *novel* Gwen Bristow *d* Joseph Kane *ph* Jack Marta *m* Victor Young

Vera Hruba Ralston, Forrest Tucker, Joan
Leslie, Pat O'Brien, John Russell, Ray
Middleton ·

Judex**

France 1916   12 episodes totalling 5 hours
     approx   bw   silent

A Robin Hood type crimefighter destroys the
empire of an evil banker.
Stylishly enjoyable serial from the maker of *Les
Vampires* and *Fantômas*.

w Arthur Bernade, Louis Feuillade *d* Louis
Feuillade

René Creste, Musidora, Yvette Andreyor, Louis
Leubas
† Another *Judex* serial was made in 1917, and in
1933 came a feature version directed by Maurice
Champreux, with René Ferte. In 1963 Georges
Franju directed another feature remake with
Channing Pollock, and this was extremely well
received.

The Judge Steps Out*

US 1947   91m   bw
RKO
GB title: *Indian Summer*

A middle-aged judge leaves his wife and sets off
on an aimless journey in the course of which he
falls in love with a café proprietress.
A pleasing human story, simply told in a manner
which at the time seemed more French than
American.

w Boris Ingster, Alexander Knox *d* Boris
Ingster

Alexander Knox, Ann Sothern, George Tobias,
Sharyn Moffett

Judgment at Nuremberg**

US 1961   190m   bw
UA / Roxlom (Stanley Kramer)

A fictionalized version of the 1948 trial of the
Nazi leaders for crimes against humanity.
Interminable, heavy-going dramatic
documentary expanded from a succinct TV play
into a courtroom marathon with philosophical
asides. All good stuff, but too much of it.

w Abby Mann, from his play *d* Stanley Kramer
ph Ernest Laszlo *m* Ernest Gold *pd* Rudolph
Sternad   •

Spencer Tracy, Marlene Dietrich, Burt
Lancaster, Richard Widmark, *Maximilian
Schell*, Judy Garland, Montgomery Clift,
William Shatner, Edward Binns, Werner

Klemperer, Torben Meyer, Alan Baxter, Ray
Teal

'Some believe that by tackling such themes
Kramer earns at least partial remission from
criticism. How much? 20 per cent off for
effort?'—*Stanley Kauffmann*

AA: Abby Mann; Maximilian Schell
AAN: best picture; Stanley Kramer; Ernest
Laszlo; Spencer Tracy; Judy Garland;
Montgomery Clift

Judgment Deferred

GB 1951   88m   bw
Group Three (John Baxter)

A collection of Dorset eccentrics brings to book
the head of a dope smuggling ring who has
framed one of their associates.
An unusual story can't compensate for stagey
handling in this first disappointing production of
a company set up by the National Film Finance
Corporation to make low budget films with top
talent.

w Geoffrey Orme, Barbara Emary, Walter
Meade *d* John Baxter *ph* Arthur Grant

Hugh Sinclair, Helen Shingler, Abraham
Sodaer, Leslie Dwyer, Joan Collins, Harry
Locke, Elwyn Brook Jones, Bransby Williams,
Maire O'Neill, Harry Welchman

Judith

US 1965   109m   Technicolor   Panavision
Paramount / Cumulus / Command

In 1947 Israel, loyalists rescue the wife of an
escaped war criminal and ask her to identify him,
but she takes her own revenge.
Glowering kibbutz adventures, well enough
made but adding up to neither one thing nor the
other, and rather confusing to non-Jews.

w Jon Michael Hayes, *story* Lawrence Durrell
d Daniel Mann *ph* John Wilcox *m* Sol Kaplan
pd Wilfrid Shingleton

Sophia Loren, Peter Finch, Jack Hawkins, Hans
Verner, André Morell

Judith of Bethulia

US 1913   42m (24 fps)   bw   silent
D. W. Griffith for Biograph

A widow in a city attacked by the Assyrians
courts their leader and beheads him.
Semi-biblical melodrama in Griffith's most
Victorian style.

w Frank Woods *d* D. W. Griffith *ph* Billy Bitzer

Blanche Sweet, Henry B. Walthall, Lillian Gish,

Dorothy Gish, Lionel Barrymore, Mae Marsh, Robert Harron

Juggernaut
GB 1936 64m bw
Ambassador

A scientist lacking funds for his experiments agrees to commit murder.
Tedious melodrama which wastes Karloff's time.

w Cyril Campion, H. Fowler Mear, H. Fraenkel
d Henry Edwards ph Sidney Blythe

Boris Karloff, Mona Goya, Joan Wyndham, Arthur Margetson, Anthony Ireland, Morton Selten

Juggernaut **
US 1974 110m De Luxe Panavision
UA / Richard Alan Simmons

A transatlantic liner is threatened by a mad bomber.
Elaborate suspense spectacular, most of which works pretty well.

w Richard Alan Simmons d Richard Lester
ph Gerry Fisher m Ken Thorne pd Terence Marsh

Richard Harris, David Hemmings, Omar Sharif, Anthony Hopkins, Ian Holm, Shirley Knight, Roy Kinnear, Cyril Cusack, Freddie Jones
  'However unoriginal its basic ingredients, it hardly ever slackens its pace or diverts attention from its central premise.'—*Jonathan Rosenbaum*
  'Jaunty, cynical slapstick.'—*New Yorker*

The Juggler
US 1953 88m bw
Columbia / Stanley Kramer

A Jewish refugee in Palestine has a horror of being imprisoned, and runs away from a transit camp with a small wandering boy.
Well-meaning cheapie, a curiously aimless topical drama which fails to make any of its several points.

w Michael Blankfort, from his novel d Edward Dmytryk ph Roy Hunt m Georges Antheil

Kirk Douglas, Milly Vitale, Paul Stewart, Joey Walsh

Juke Girl
US 1942 90m bw
Warner (Jack Saper, Jerry Wald)

Fruit workers in Florida get involved in murder.
Hokum melodrama with all concerned treading water.

w A. I. Bezzerides, *novel* Theodore Pratt

d Curtis Bernhardt ph Bert Glennon m Adolph Deutsch

Ann Sheridan, Ronald Reagan, Richard Whorf, Gene Lockhart, Faye Emerson, George Tobias, Alan Hale, Howard da Silva, Donald McBride, Fuzzy Knight, Willie Best

Jules et Jim **
France 1961 105m bw Franscope
Films du Carrosse / SEDIF (Marcel Berbert)

Before World War I, in Paris, a girl alternates between a French and a German student, and after the war they meet again to form a constantly shifting triangle.
The plot bores before the end, but the treatment is consistently interesting and the acting almost equally so.

w François Truffaut, Jean Gruault, *novel* Henri-Pierre Roche d François Truffaut ph Raoul Coutard m Georges Delerue

Oskar Werner, Jeanne Moreau, Henri Serre
  'The sense is of a director intoxicated with the pleasure of making films.'—*Penelope Houston, MFB*

Julia **
US 1977 117m Technicolor
TCF (Julien Derode)

Lillian Hellman reflects on the fortunes of her friend Julia, filled with enthusiasm for European causes and finally killed by the Nazis.
Thoughtful, elegant patchwork of thirties memories, a vehicle for actors and a subtle, self-effacing director.

w Alvin Sargent, *book* Pentimento by Lillian Hellman d Fred Zinnemann ph Douglas Slocombe m Georges Delerue ph Carmen Dillon, Gene Callahan, Willy Holt

Jane Fonda, Vanessa Redgrave, Jason Robards Jnr, Maximilian Schell, Hal Holbrook, Rosemary Murphy, Cathleen Nesbitt, Maurice Denham

Julia Misbehaves
US 1948 99m bw
MGM (Everett Riskin)

An actress returns to her stuffy husband when her daughter is about to marry.
Desperate attempt to find a vehicle for a fading star team.

w William Ludwig, Arthur Wimperis, Harry Ruskin, *novel* The Nutmeg Tree by Margery Sharp d Jack Conway ph Joseph Ruttenberg m Adolph Deutsch

Greer Garson, Walter Pidgeon, Elizabeth Taylor, Peter Lawford, Cesar Romero, Lucile

Watson, Nigel Bruce, Mary Boland, Reginald Owen, Ian Wolfe, Edmund Breon, Fritz Feld, Aubrey Mather, Henry Stephenson

Julie*

US 1956 97m bw
MGM / Arwin (Marty Melcher)

A concert pianist plans to murder his wife.
Wildly improbable but entertaining suspenser in which the lady finally has to assume control of an airplane.

wd Andrew Stone ph Fred Jackman Jnr
m Leith Stevens

Doris Day, Louis Jourdan, Barry Sullivan, Frank Lovejoy, John Gallaudet
'Some of the dialogue reaches a fine pitch of banality.'—MFB

AAN: Andrew Stone (as writer); title song
(m Leith Stevens, ly Tom Adair)

Juliet of the Spirits*

Italy / France 1965 145m Technicolor
Federiz / Francoriz (Clemente Fracassi)
original title: Giulietta degli Spiriti

A bored middle-aged woman finds she can conjure up spirits who lead her into a life of sensual gratification.
A fascinating patchwork of autobiographical flashbacks, the distaff side of Eight and a Half.

w Federico Fellini, Tullio Pinnelli, Brunello Rondi, Ennio Flaiano d Federico Fellini
ph Gianni di Venanzo m Nino Rota

Giulietta Masina, Mario Pisu, Sandra Milo, Valentina Cortese, Sylva Koscina
'A kaleidoscope of fantasy, a series of cerebral inventions, of which only a few are artistically justified . . . an extravagant illusion, a huge confidence trick, with little new to say and an often pedantic way of saying it.'—David Wilson, MFB

Julius Caesar**

US 1953 121m bw
MGM (John Houseman)

Cassius and Brutus lead the conspirators who murder Caesar, but are themselves routed by Mark Antony.
Straightforward, rather leaden presentation of Shakespeare's play, lit by effective moments in the acting, but the sudden change from talk to battle is not smoothed over.

wd Joseph L. Mankiewicz ph Joseph Ruttenberg m Miklos Rozsa ad Cedric Gibbons, Edward Carfagno

John Gielgud, James Mason, Marlon Brando, Greer Garson, Deborah Kerr, Louis Calhern,

Edmond O'Brien, George Macready, Michael Pate, John Hoyt, Alan Napier

AAN: best picture; Joseph Ruttenberg; James Mason

Julius Caesar

GB 1969 116m Technicolor Panavision
Commonwealth United (Peter Snell)

Elementary production with a surprising number of faults and very few merits.

w Robert Furnival d Stuart Burge ph Ken Higgins m Michael Lewis pd Julia Trevelyan Oman

Richard Johnson, Jason Robards Jnr, John Gielgud, Charlton Heston, Robert Vaughn, Richard Chamberlain, Diana Rigg, Jill Bennett, Christopher Lee, Alan Browning, Andrew Crawford

AAN: Michael Lewis

Jumbo*

US 1962 124m Metrocolor Panavision
MGM (Joe Pasternak, Martin Melcher)
aka: Billy Rose's Jumbo

In 1910, the daughter of the owner of a shaky circus prevents a take-over bid.
Hoary circus story with music. General effect disappointing: the elephant steals the show.

w Sidney Sheldon, play Ben Hecht, Charles MacArthur d Charles Walters ph William H. Daniels m/ly Richard Rodgers, Lorenz Hart md George Stoll ch Busby Berkeley

Doris Day, Jimmy Durante, Stephen Boyd, Martha Raye, Dean Jagger

AAN: George Stoll

Jump for Glory

GB 1937 89m bw
Criterion (Douglas Fairbanks Jnr, Marcel Hellman)
US title: When Thief Meets Thief

Adventures of a cat burglar who accidentally kills his ex-partner.
Curious star comedy drama with pleasing scenes.

w John Meehan Jnr, Harold French, novel Gordon MacDonnell d Raoul Walsh

Douglas Fairbanks Jnr, Valerie Hobson, Alan Hale, Edward Rigby, Barbara Everest, Jack Melford, Anthony Ireland

Jump into Hell

US 1955 93m bw
Warner (David Weisbart)

Paratroops relieve a fort in Indo-China.
Mediocre semi-documentary war heroics.

w Irving Wallace d David Butler ph Peverell Marley m David Buttolph

Jacques Sernas, Kurt Kasznar, Arnold Moss, Peter Van Eyck, Pat Blake

Jumping Jacks*
US 1952 96m bw
Paramount / Hal B. Wallis

Two cabaret comedians join the paratroops.
Standard star farce, one of Martin and Lewis' best.

w Robert Lees, Fred Rinaldo, Herbert Baker d Norman Taurog ph Daniel L. Fapp m Joseph J. Lilley

Dean Martin, *Jerry Lewis*, Mona Freeman, Robert Strauss, Don Defore

June Bride
US 1948 97m bw
Warner (Henry Blanke)

Two bickering reporters are sent to cover a small-town wedding.
Sloppily structured romantic farce in which nothing ever comes together.

w Ranald MacDougall, *play* Feature for June by Eileen Tighe, Graeme Lorimer d Bretaigne Windust ph Ted McCord m David Buttolph

Bette Davis, Robert Montgomery, Fay Bainter, Tom Tully, Betty Lynn, Barbara Bates, Jerome Cowan, Mary Wickes, Debbie Reynolds

The Jungle Book*
US 1942 109m Technicolor
Alexander Korda (W. Howard Greene)
aka: *Rudyard Kipling's Jungle Book*

Growing up with animals in an Indian forest, a boy forestalls the getaway of three thieves.
High-budgeted but rather boring live action version with stiff-jointed model animals.

w Laurence Stallings, *stories* Rudyard Kipling d Zoltan Korda, André de Toth ph W. Howard Greene m Miklos Rozsa

Sabu, Joseph Calleia, John Qualen, Frank Puglia, Rosemary de Camp

AAN: W. Howard Greene; Miklos Rozsa

Jungle Book*
US 1967 78m Technicolor
Walt Disney

Cartoon version relying less on action than on songs and voices; patchily successful but no classic.

d Wolfgang Reitherman m/ly Richard and

Robert Sherman, Terry Gilkyson *voices* George Sanders, Phil Harris, Louis Prima, Sebastian Cabot, Sterling Holloway

AAN: song 'The Bare Necessities' (m/ly Terry Gilkyson)

Jungle Jim
When Johnny Weissmuller began to show his middle-age spread, Columbia put him in a jacket and more or less redid his Tarzan thing in a series of second features which appeared to be shot in producer Sam Katzman's back garden and gradually indulged in wilder and wilder plots.
None of them has more than curiosity value.
Main scriptwriters were Carroll Young, Dwight Babcock, Sam Newman; main directors William Berke, Lee Sholem, Spencer G. Bennet.

1948: JUNGLE JIM
1949: THE LOST TRIBE
1950: CAPTIVE GIRL, MARK OF THE GORILLA, PYGMY ISLAND
1951: FURY OF THE CONGO, JUNGLE MANHUNT
1952: JUNGLE JIM IN THE FORBIDDEN LAND, VOODOO TIGER
1953: SAVAGE MUTINY, VALLEY OF THE HEADHUNTERS, KILLER APE
1954: JUNGLE MANEATERS, CANNIBAL ATTACK
1955: JUNGLE MOON MEN, DEVIL GODDESS

The Jungle Princess*
US 1936 84m bw
Paramount (E. Lloyd Sheldon)

A British hunter is injured on a tropical island and rescued by a native girl and her animal retinue.
Dorothy Lamour's first film role cast her as the female Tarzan she was to play (in a sarong, of course) a dozen times again. This is strictly a programmer, but after its success it was all done again, rather better, as *Her Jungle Love*.

w Cyril Hume, Gerald Geraghty, Gouverneur Morris d William Thiele ph Harry Fischbeck md Boris Morros

Dorothy Lamour, Ray Milland, Akim Tamiroff, Lynne Overman, Molly Lamont, Hugh Buckler

'Poor Mr Lynne Overman is expected to lend humorous relief to a film already richly comic.'—*Graham Greene*

Junior Bonner*
US 1972 105m Movielab Todd-AO 35
Joe Wizan / Booth—Gardner / Solar / ABC

An ageing rodeo star returns to his home town and finds his family in trouble.

Well-made, rather downcast and not very interesting drama, remarkably gentle from this director.

w Jeb Rosebrook *d* Sam Peckinpah *ph* Lucien Ballard *m* Jerry Fielding

Steve McQueen, Ida Lupino, Robert Preston, Joe Don Baker, Ben Johnson

Juno and the Paycock*
GB 1930 85m bw
British International (John Maxwell)

During the Irish troubles of the early twenties, tragedy comes to a poor Dublin family.
A plainly done film version of a modern classic whose changes of mood would not in any case have worked well on the screen.

w Alfred Hitchcock, Alma Reville, *play* Sean O'Casey *d* Alfred Hitchcock *ph* Jack Cox

Sara Allgood, Edward Chapman, Maire O'Neill, Sidney Morgan, John Laurie
  'A film which completely justifies the talkies.'—*James Agate*

Jupiter's Darling*
US 1954 96m Eastmancolor
  Cinemascope
MGM (George Wells)

Advancing on Rome, Hannibal falls in love with the dictator's fiancée.
A splendid example of the higher lunacy, with coloured elephants decorating an MGM musical about the fall of the Roman Empire. Small elements can be salvaged, and the gall is enough to be divided into three parts.

w Dorothy Kingsley, *play* The Road to Rome by Robert E. Sherwood *d* George Sidney *ph* Paul C. Vogel, Charles Rosher *m* Burton Lane *ly* Harold Adamson *ch* Hermes Pan *ad* Cedric Gibbons, Uric McCleary

Esther Williams, Howard Keel, George Sanders, Marge and Gower Champion, Richard Haydn, William Demarest

Just for You
US 1952 104m Technicolor
Paramount (Paul Duggan)

A successful songwriter finds that his troublesome teenage son is in love with his own fiancée.
Tiresomely scripted, pleasantly played romantic comedy with music.

w Robert Carson, *novel* Famous by Stephen Vincent Benet *d* Elliott Nugent *ph* George Barnes *md* Emil Newman *songs* Harry Warren, Leo Robin

Bing Crosby, Jane Wyman, Bob Arthur, Ethel Barrymore, Natalie Wood, Cora Witherspoon, Regis Toomey

AAN: song 'Zing a Little Zong'

Just Imagine
US 1930 102m bw
Fox

A man who dies in 1930 is revived in 1980 and can't get used to the pace of life.
Famous fantasy which doesn't live up to its reputation and can now be seen as hampered by poor sets, script and acting. Futuristic sets are few but choice.

d David Butler *w, songs* De Sylva, Brown, Henderson *ch* Seymour Felix

El Brendel, Maureen O'Sullivan, John Garrick, Frank Albertson, Marjorie White, Hobart Bosworth, Mischa Auer, Wilfred Lucas

Just My Luck
US 1957 86m bw
Rank (Hugh Stewart)

A jeweller's assistant becomes involved in horse racing.
Flat star vehicle.

w Alfred Shaughnessy *d* John Paddy Carstairs *ph* Jack Cox *m* Philip Green

Norman Wisdom, Leslie Phillips, Margaret Rutherford, Delphi Lawrence

Justice Est Faite*
France 1950 105m bw
Silver Films

The personal lives of jurors in a mercy killing case affect their verdict.
Absorbing courtroom drama with a message.

w Charles Spaak, André Cayatte *d* André Cayatte *ph* Jean Bourgoin *m* Raymond Legrand

Valentine Tessier, Claude Nollier, Jacques Castelot, Michel Auclair

Justine
US 1969 116m De Luxe Panavision
TCF / Pandro S. Berman

In Alexandria in the thirties, the beautiful wife of a wealthy banker influences the lives of all who meet her.
Disastrous condensed version of a very unusual set of novels whose atmosphere has not translated at all well. The result is like a bad rehearsal for a film, which is not surprising in view of the number of producers variously involved. The author feared 'a sort of *Peyton Place* with camels', and got it.

w Lawrence B. Marcus, *novels* The Alexandria Quartet by Lawrence Durrell *d* George Cukor *ph* Leon Shamroy *m* Jerry Goldsmith

Anouk Aimée, Michael York, Dirk Bogarde, Anna Karina, John Vernon, George Baker, Philippe Noiret, Robert Forster, Jack Albertson, Michael Dunn, Barry Morse, Cliff Gorman, Severn Darden

'Could well stand as a model of what can happen when Hollywood gets to grips with a celebrated literary property.'—*David Wilson*

'Despite leaden forays into homosexuality, transvestitism, incest, and child prostitution, it remains as naively old-fashioned in its emotional and intellectual vocabulary as in its actual verbiage and cinematic technique.'—*John Simon*

K

Kaleidoscope*
GB 1966 103m Technicolor
Warner / Winkast (Elliott Kastner)
Reissue title: *The Bank Breaker*

An American playboy breaks into a playing card
factory and marks the designs so that he can win
in every European casino.
Would-be swinging comedy-thriller which in fact
is entertaining only when it stops trying to
dazzle.

w Robert and Jane Howard-Carrington d Jack
Smight ph Christopher Challis m Stanley
Myers ad Maurice Carter

Warren Beatty, Susannah York, Clive Revill,
Eric Porter, Murray Melvin

'A "groovie movie" it certainly is, with a
battery of fashionable camera tricks,
kaleidoscopic dissolves, and virtually every
scene introduced from behind an irrelevant piece
of furniture.'—*David Wilson*

Kameradschaft*
Germany 1931 92m bw
Nerofilm
aka: *Comradeship*

On the Franco-German border French miners
are imprisoned below ground and Germans
burrow to free them.
Salutary message film with good dramatic
pointing.

w Laszlo Vajda, Karl Otten, Peter Martin
Lampel d G. W. Pabst ph Fritz Arno Wagner,
Robert Baberski

Ernst Busch, Alexander Granach, Fritz
Kampers, Gustav Puttjer

Kanal*
Poland 1956 97m bw
Film Polski (Stanislaw Adler)
aka: *They Loved Life*

In 1944, an anti-Nazi resistance group is trapped
in a sewer.
A suffocatingly unpleasant film to watch; its
message and technical excellence are undoubted.

w Jerzy Stawinski, from his novel Kloakerne
d Andrzej Wajda ph Jerzy Lipman m Jan
Krenz

Teresa Izewska, Tadeusz Janczar, Emil
Kariewicz, Wienczylaw Glinski

Kangaroo
US 1952 84m Technicolor
TCF (Robert Bassler)

In old Australia, a con man pretends to be a
rancher's long lost heir, then complicates things
by falling in love with the rancher's daughter.
Standard romantic action hokum.

w Harry Kleiner d Lewis Milestone ph Charles
G. Clarke m Sol Kaplan

Maureen O'Hara, Peter Lawford, Finlay Currie,
Richard Boone, Chips Rafferty, Charles
Tingwell

Kansas City Bomber
US 1972 99m Metrocolor
MGM / Levy–Gardner–Laven / Raquel Welch
(Marty Elfand)

A roller skating star finds time between affairs to
beat her rival in a big match.
Vulgar melodrama with good action scenes.

w Thomas Rickman, Calvin Clements d Jerrold
Freedman ph Fred Koenekamp m Don Ellis

Raquel Welch, Kevin McCarthy, Norman
Alden, Jeanne Cooper

Kapo
Italy / France 1960 115m bw
Vides / Zebra / Francinex

A French Jewess survives the horrors of a Nazi
concentration camp and becomes camp guard.
Curious exploitation piece which turns tragedy
into melodrama, and doesn't even do that with
much flair.

w Franco Solinas, Gillo Pontecorvo d Gillo
Pontecorvo ph Goffredo Bellisario, Alexander
Sekulovic m Carlo Rustichelli

Susan Strasberg, Laurent Terzieff, Emmanuelle
Riva

Kate Plus Ten
GB 1938 81m bw
Wainwright (Richard Wainwright)

A police inspector falls for the attractive female leader of a bullion gang.
Curious comedy thriller with insufficient of either commodity.

w Jack Hulbert, Jeffrey Dell, *novel* Edgar Wallace *d* Reginald Denham

Jack Hulbert, Genevieve Tobin, Noel Madison, Francis L. Sullivan, Arthur Wontner, Frank Cellier, Googie Withers, Peter Haddon, Felix Aylmer, Leo Genn, Edward Lexy

Kathleen
US 1941   88m   bw
MGM (George Haight)

A neglected daughter finds a new wife for her widowed father.
One of the reasons for Shirley Temple's early retirement.

w Mary McCall Jnr, *story* Kay Van Riper *d* Harold S. Bucquet *ph* Sidney Wagner *m* Franz Waxman

Shirley Temple, Herbert Marshall, Laraine Day, Gail Patrick, Felix Bressart, Nella Walker, Lloyd Corrigan

Kathy O
US 1958   99m   Eastmancolor
    Cinemascope
U-I (Sy Gomberg)

A temperamental child star befriends a lonely columnist.
Overlong Hollywood comedy drama with amusing moments.

w Jack Sher, Sy Gomberg *d* Jack Sher *ph* Arthur E. Arling *m* Frank Skinner *songs* Charles Tobias, Ray Joseph

Patty McCormack, Dan Duryea, Jan Sterling, Sam Levene

Keep 'Em Flying
US 1941   86m   bw
Universal (Glenn Tryon)

Two incompetents in the Army Air Corps get mixed up with identical twin girls.
A big moneymaker of its day, this comedy now seems especially resistible.

w True Boardman, Nat Perrin, John Grant *d* Arthur Lubin *ph* Joseph Valentine

Bud Abbott, Lou Costello, Martha Raye, Carol Bruce, William Gargan, Dick Foran, Charles Lang

Keep Fit*
GB 1937   82m   bw
ATP (Basil Dean)

A barber mistaken for an athlete finally excels at sport and also catches a thief.
Good star vehicle with snappy songs and fast comedy scenes.

w Anthony Kimmins, Austin Melford *d Anthony Kimmins*

George Formby, Kay Walsh, Guy Middleton, Gus McNaughton, Edmund Breon, George Benson, C. Denier Warren, Hal Gordon, Hal Walters, Leo Franklyn

Keep Smiling*
GB 1938   91m   bw
TCF (Robert T. Kane)
US title: *Smiling Along*

Problems of a touring concert party.
Pretty good star vehicle, though with unfortunate signs of an attempt to glamorize Our Gracie.

w Val Valentine, Rodney Ackland *d* Monty Banks

Gracie Fields, Roger Livesey, Mary Maguire, Peter Coke, Jack Donohue, Tommy Fields, Eddie Gray, Edward Rigby, Hay Petrie

Keep Your Powder Dry
US 1945   93m   bw
MGM (George Haight)

Three girls from different backgrounds join the WACS.
Totally uninteresting and unconvincing female flagwaver.

w Mary C. McCall Jnr, George Bruce *d* Edward Buzzell *ph* Ray June *m* David Snell

Lana Turner, Laraine Day, Susan Peters, Agnes Moorehead, Bill Johnson, Natalie Schaefer, June Lockhart, Lee Patrick

Keep Your Seats Please*
GB 1936   82m   bw
ATP (Basil Dean)

A prospective heir seeks a fortune hidden in one of six chairs.
Good star comedy on a theme later reworked in *It's in the Bag* (qv) and *The Twelve Chairs* (qv).

w Tom Geraghty, Ian Hay, Anthony Kimmins, *play* Twelve Chairs by Elie Ilf, Eugene Petrov *d* Monty Banks

George Formby, Florence Desmond, Alastair Sim, Gus McNaughton, Harry Tate

Keeper of the Flame*
US 1942   100m   bw
MGM (Victor Saville)

A reporter befriends the widow of a politician

and forces her to disclose her husband's guilty secret.

Well-acted but over-solemn melodrama which badly needs a sting in the tail.

w Donald Ogden Stewart, *novel* I. A. R. Wylie d George Cukor *ph* William Daniels m Bronislau Kaper

Spencer Tracy, Katharine Hepburn, Richard Whorf, Margaret Wycherly, Donald Meek, Stephen McNally, Audrey Christie, Frank Craven

Keepers of Youth

GB 1931 70m bw
BIP

A young schoolmaster finds his fresh ideas make him unpopular, especially when he is found in a compromising position with the assistant matron.

Old-fashioned drama with a few lively scenes.

w Frank Launder, *play* Arnold Ridley d Thomas Bentley *ph* James Wilson, Bert Ford

Garry Marsh, Ann Todd, Robin Irvine, John Turnbull, O. B. Clarence, Mary Clare

Kelly and Me

US 1956 86m Technicolor
Cinemascope
U-I (Robert Arthur)

The ups and downs of a song and dance man and the dog who shares his act.

Mild vaudeville saga with totally predictable twists.

w Everett Freeman d Robert Z. Leonard *ph* Maury Gertsman *m* Joseph Gershenson

Van Johnson, Piper Laurie, Martha Hyer, Onslow Stevens

Kelly's Heroes

US / Yugoslavia 1970 143m Metrocolor
Panavision
MGM / The Warriors / Avala (Irving Leonard)

During World War II, an American platoon abducts a German general and accidentally discovers the whereabouts of a fortune in gold.

Crude slam-bang actioner for the obvious market.

w Troy Kennedy Martin d Brian G. Hutton *ph* Gabriel Figueroa *m* Lalo Schifrin *2nd unit* Andrew Marton

Clint Eastwood, Telly Savalas, Don Rickles, Donald Sutherland, Carroll O'Connor, Stuart Margolin, Dick Davalos

'Over two hours of consistently devastating explosions, pyrotechnics and demolition.'— *MFB*

'Made for no possible reason other than a chance to use the Yugoslav army at cut rates.'— *Judith Crist, 1973*

The Kennel Murder Case*

US 1933 73m bw
Warner

Philo Vance proves that an apparent suicide is really murder.

Complex murder mystery, very smartly handled and often cited as a classic of the genre; later remade as *Calling Philo Vance*.

w Robert N. Lee, Peter Milner, *novel* S. S. Van Dine d *Michael Curtiz* *ph* William Reese

William Powell, Mary Astor, Eugene Pallette, Ralph Morgan, Helen Vinson, Jack La Rue, Paul Cavanagh, Robert Barrat

'Players are cast so inevitably to type that the film is like a demonstration of the principles of running a stock company.'—*New Yorker, 1978*
† See also *Philo Vance*.

The Kentuckian

US 1955 104m Technicolor
Cinemascope
UA / Hecht–Lancaster

A Kentucky backwoodsman takes his small son to settle in Texas.

Ambling mid-western with moments of interest.

w A. B. Guthrie Jnr, *novel* The Gabriel Horn by Felix Holt d Burt Lancaster *ph* Ernest Laszlo m Bernard Herrmann

Burt Lancaster, Dianne Foster, Diana Lynn, *Walter Matthau*, John McIntire, Una Merkel, John Carradine

Kentucky*

US 1938 95m Technicolor
TCF (Gene Markey)

Horse-breeding rivalry prevents the smooth running of true love.

Harmless family entertainment, more professionally handled than its innumerable later imitations. Remade as *April Love*.

w Lamar Trotti, *novel* The Look of Eagles by John Taintor Foote d David Butler *ph* Ernest Palmer *md* Louis Silvers

Loretta Young, Richard Greene, Walter Brennan, Douglass Dumbrille, Karen Morley, Moroni Olsen, Russell Hicks

AA: Walter Brennan

La Kermesse Héroique**

France 1935 115m bw
Tobis
aka: *Carnival in Flanders*

When Spaniards invade a Flemish town in 1616, the men make themselves scarce and the women find other ways of conquering.

Sprightly though overlong comedy which seemed risqué at the time and therefore enjoyed international success.

w Charles Spaak, Jacques Feyder, novel Charles Spaak *d Jacques Feyder ph* Harry Stradling *m* Louis Beydts *ad* Lazare Meerson

Françoise Rosay, Louis Jouvet, Jean Murat, Alfred Adam, André Alerme

'A mixture of gay absurdity and shrewd comment, selecting its own pitch and holding it—comedy, you might say, self-contained.'—*Otis Ferguson*

Kes*

GB 1969 109m Technicolor
UA / Woodfall (Tony Garnett)

In a northern industrial town, a boy learns about life from the fate of his pet bird.

'Realistic' family drama, full of the kind of merit that does not equate with entertainment: hard to take and harder to hear.

w Barry Hines, Ken Loach, Tony Garnet, *novel* A Kestrel for a Knave by Barry Hines *d* Ken Loach *ph* Chris Menges *m* John Cameron

David Bradley, Lynne Perrie, Colin Welland, Freddie Fletcher, Brian Glover

'There emerges a most discouraging picture of life in the industrial north . . . infinitely sad in its total implications, it is also immensely funny in much of its detail.'—*Brenda Davies*

The Kettles

The rustic couple evolved from characters in *The Egg and I* (qv); Marjorie Main and Percy Kilbride went on to play them in a cheap but very popular series for Universal, variously scripted and directed.

1949: MA AND PA KETTLE
1950: MA AND PA KETTLE GO TO TOWN?
1951: MA AND PA KETTLE BACK ON THE FARM
1952: MA AND PA KETTLE AT THE FAIR
1953: MA AND PA KETTLE ON VACATION
1954: MA AND PA KETTLE AT HOME
1955: MA AND PA KETTLE AT WAIKIKI
1956: THE KETTLES IN THE OZARKS (Arthur Hunnicutt instead of Kilbride)
1957: THE KETTLES ON OLD MACDONALD'S FARM (Parker Fennelly instead of Kilbride)

The Key*

GB 1958 134m bw Cinemascope
Columbia / Open Road (Carl Foreman)

World War II tugboat skippers, about to embark on dangerous missions, pass on the key to an apartment and a girl to go with it.

Rather foolish symbolic melodrama which never makes its purpose clear but along the way provides fragments of love story, chunks of the supernatural and dollops of war action, rather languidly assembled with great technical competence but little real feeling. The talent occasionally shows through.

w Carl Foreman, *novel* Stella by Jan de Hartog *d* Carol Reed *ph* Oswald Morris *m* Malcolm Arnold

William Holden, Sophia Loren, *Trevor Howard,* Oscar Homolka, Kieron Moore

Key Largo***

US 1948 101m bw
Warner (Jerry Wald)

A returning war veteran fights gangsters on the Florida keys.

Moody melodrama on similar lines to *To Have and Have Not:* it sums up the post-war mood of despair, allows several good acting performances, and builds up to a pretty good action climax.

w Richard Brooks, John Huston, play Maxwell Anderson *d John Huston ph Karl Freund m* Max Steiner

Humphrey Bogart, Lauren Bacall, *Claire Trevor, Edward G. Robinson, Lionel Barrymore,* Thomas Gomez, Marc Lawrence

'It's a confidently directed, handsomely shot movie, and the cast go at it as if the nonsense about gangsters and human dignity were high drama.'—*New Yorker, 1977*

AA: Claire Trevor

Key to the City

US 1950 101m bw
MGM (Z. Wayne Griffin)

At a San Francisco convention, two mayors get involved in several escapades and fall in love. Routine romantic comedy.

w Robert Riley Crutcher *d* George Sidney *ph* Harold Rosson *m* Bronislau Kaper

Clark Gable, Loretta Young, Frank Morgan, James Gleason, Marilyn Maxwell, Raymond Burr, Lewis Stone, Raymond Walburn, Pamela Britton

'A comedy made to measure . . . the script concerns itself with wringing every possible

laugh from a number of stock situations.'—
Variety

The Keys of the Kingdom*
US 1944   137m   bw
TCF (Joseph L. Mankiewicz)

The life of a 19th-century Scottish priest in
China.
Studio-made missionary melodrama, a big hit
for its new star but otherwise an undistinguished
piece of work with a shuffling pace and not much
by way of climax.

w Joseph L. Mankiewicz, Nunnally Johnson,
novel A. J. Cronin *d* John M. Stahl *ph* Arthur
Miller *m* Alfred Newman *ad* James Basevi,
William Darling.

Gregory Peck, Thomas Mitchell, Vincent Price,
Rose Stradner, Roddy McDowall, Edmund
Gwenn, Cedric Hardwicke, Peggy Ann Garner,
James Gleason, Anne Revere

'Long, earnest, long, worthy, interesting and
long.'—*Richard Mallett, Punch*

AAN: Arthur Miller; Alfred Newman; Gregory
Peck

Khartoum*
GB 1966   134m   Technicolor   Ultra
   Panavision
UA / Julian Blaustein

The last years of General Gordon.
Dullish history book stuff which fails to explain
Gordon the man but occasionally erupts into
glowing action.

w Robert Ardrey *d* Basil Dearden *ph* Edward
Scaife, Harry Waxman m Frank Cordell

Charlton Heston, Laurence Olivier, Ralph
Richardson, Richard Johnson, Hugh Williams,
Alexander Knox, Johnny Sekka, Nigel Green,
Michael Hordern

'Academic accuracy and spectacular battles
are unhappy partners.'—*MFB*

'Beautifully photographed, lavishly mounted,
intelligently acted, but ultimately dull.'—*Sight
and Sound*

AAN: Robert Ardrey

Kicking the Moon Around
GB 1938   78m   bw
Vogue (Howard Welsch)
US titles: *The Playboy; Millionaire Merry Go
Round*

A millionaire goes into show business to
establish a career for his singing protégée.
Mild, frothy comedy, dated but quite fluent.

w Angus McPhail, Roland Pertwee, Michael

Hogan, Harry Fowler Mear *d* Walter Forde
ph Francis Carver

Ambrose and his Orchestra, Evelyn Dall, Hal
Thompson, Florence Desmond, Harry
Richman, C. Denier Warren, Max Bacon

The Kid***
US 1921   52m approx (24 fps)   bw   silent
First National / Charles Chaplin

A tramp brings up an abandoned baby, and later
loses him to his mother; but there is a happy
ending.
Sentimental comedy set in the slums. The
comedy is very sparingly laid on, but the effect of
the whole is much less painful than the synopsis
would suggest, the production is comparatively
smooth, the child actor is sensational, and the
film contains much of the quintessential Chaplin.

wd Charles Chaplin ph Rollie Totheroh

Charles Chaplin, Jackie Coogan, Edna
Purviance

Kid Auto Races at Venice
US 1914   6m approx   bw   silent
Keystone

This much mentioned film is no more than a few
candid camera shots of a children's car race on
the California beach. It so happened that the
young Charles Chaplin was called upon to liven
up proceedings by causing a nuisance, and
hastily conceived his tramp costume to do so.
His fragments of comedy, primitive though they
now seem, made him a star.

w Henry Lehrman

Kid Blue
US 1973   100m   De Luxe   Panavision
TCF / Marvin Schwarz Productions

In 1902 Texas a young outlaw tries to go
straight.
Deliberately myth-deflating western with
agreeably rich detail.

w Edwin Shrake *d* James Frawley *ph* Billy
Williams *m* Tim McIntyre, John Rubenstein
pd Joel Schiller

Dennis Hopper, Warren Oates, Peter Boyle, Ben
Johnson, Lee Purcell, Janice Rule, Clifton James

A Kid for Two Farthings*
GB 1955   96m   Eastmancolor
London Films (Carol Reed)

Among the colourful characters of London's
Petticoat Lane market moves a boy whose pet
goat seems to have the magical power of a
unicorn.

Whimsical character comedy-drama made with
some style but too insubstantial and
unconvincing to be affectionately remembered.

w Wolf Mankowitz d Carol Reed ph Ted
Scaife m Benjamin Frankel

Celia Johnson, Diana Dors, David Kossoff,
Brenda de Banzie, Sidney Tafler, Primo
Carnera, Joe Robinson

The Kid from Brooklyn

US 1946   114m   Technicolor
Samuel Goldwyn

A timid milkman becomes a prizefighter.
Yawn-provoking comedy, a remake of Harold
Lloyd's *The Milky Way*; the first indication that
Danny Kaye could be a bore.

w Grover Jones, Frank Butler, Richard Connell
d Norman Z. McLeod ph Gregg Toland
md Carmen Dragon

Danny Kaye, Virginia Mayo, Vera-Ellen, Steve
Cochran, Eve Arden, Walter Abel, Lionel
Stander, Fay Bainter, Clarence Kolb

The Kid from Spain**

US 1932   90m   bw
Samuel Goldwyn

A simpleton is mistaken for a celebrated
bullfighter.
Charmingly dated star musical which, though
primitive in some respects, is a splendid reminder
of its period.

w William Anthony McGuire, Bert Kalmar,
Harry Ruby d Leo McCarey ph Gregg Toland
ch Busby Berkeley

Eddie Cantor, Lyda Roberti, Robert Young,
Ruth Hall, John Miljan, Noah Beery, J. Carrol
Naish, Stanley Fields, Betty Grable, Paulette
Goddard

Kid Galahad*

US 1937   101m   bw
Warner (Samuel Bischoff)

A bellhop is groomed as a prizefighter, and his
trainer grows jealous.
Good standard prizefight melodrama, remade as
The Wagons Roll at Night and later as *Kid
Galahad* with Elvis Presley (see below).

w Seton I. Miller, *novel* Francis Wallace
d Michael Curtiz ph Tony Gaudio m Heinz
Roemheld, Max Steiner

Edward G. Robinson, Bette Davis, Wayne
Morris, Jane Bryan, Humphrey Bogart, Harry
Carey

Kid Galahad

US 1962   96m   De Luxe
UA / Mirisch (David Weisbart)

Tolerable light-hearted musical remake of the
above.

w William Fay d Phil Karlson ph Burnett
Guffey m Jeff Alexander

Elvis Presley, Lola Albright, Gig Young, Joan
Blackman, Charles Bronson, Ned Glass, David
Lewis, Robert Emhardt

Kid Glove Killer*

US 1942   73m   bw
MGM (Jack Chertok)

A police laboratory scientist tracks down the
murderer of the mayor and finds his best friend is
the culprit.
Professional police suspenser of the kind now
tackled by television.

w John Higgins, Allen Rivkin d Fred
Zinnemann

Van Heflin, Lee Bowman, Marsha Hunt, Samuel
S. Hinds, Eddie Quillan

Kid Millions

US 1935   90m   bw (Technicolor
sequence)
Samuel Goldwyn

An East Side kid inherits a fortune and has the
time of his life.
Dated star musical with moments which still
please.

w George Oppenheimer, William Anthony
McGuire d Roy del Ruth ph Gregg Toland
m/ly Bert Kalmar, Harry Ruby ad Richard
Day

Eddie Cantor, Ethel Merman, Ann Sothern,
George Murphy, Warren Hymer

Kidnapped*

US 1938   90m   bw
TCF

During the Jacobite rebellion a young boy is sold
by his wicked uncle as a slave, and is helped by
an outlaw.
Much altered version of a classic adventure
story, exciting enough in its own right, and well
made in the thirties tradition.

w Sonya Levien, Richard Sherman, Walter
Ferris, *novel* Robert Louis Stevenson d Alfred
L. Werker m Arthur Lange

Warner Baxter, Freddie Bartholemew, Arleen
Whelan, John Carradine, C. Aubrey Smith,
Nigel Bruce, Reginald Owen

Kidnapped*
GB 1971 107m Movielab Panavision
Omnibus (Frederick H. Brogger)

Remake incorporating sections of *Catriona*. Not particularly exciting, but the acting helps.

w Jack Pulman *d* Delbert Mann *ph* Paul Beeson *m* Roy Budd

Michael Caine, Lawrence Douglas, Trevor Howard, Jack Hawkins, Donald Pleasence, Gordon Jackson, Freddie Jones, Jack Watson

The Kidnappers*
GB 1953 95m bw
Rank / Nolbandov–Parkyn
US title: *The Little Kidnappers*

In a Nova Scotian village at the turn of the century a stern old man denies his young grandchildren a pet, so they borrow a baby and hide it in the woods.
Fairly pleasing and popular whimsy for family audiences.

w Neil Paterson *d* Philip Leacock *ph* Eric Cross *m* Bruce Montgomery

Duncan Macrae, Vincent Winter, Jon Whiteley, Theodore Bikel, Jean Anderson

Kiki
US 1931 96m bw
UA / Mary Pickford (Joseph M. Schenck)

Long unseen star musical.

w Sam Taylor, *play* David Belasco *d* Sam Taylor *ph* Karl Struss

Mary Pickford, Reginald Denny, Joseph Cawthorne, Margaret Livingston

Kill or Cure
GB 1962 88m bw
MGM (George H. Brown)

A series of murders at a nature clinic are solved by a bumbling private detective.
Flatfooted and unprofessional murder farce whose only pace is slow.

w David Pursall, Jack Seddon *d* George Pollock *ph* Geoffrey Faithfull *m* Ron Goodwin

Terry-Thomas, Eric Sykes, Dennis Price, Lionel Jeffries, Moira Redmond, David Lodge, Ronnie Barker

The Killer Elite
US 1975 120m De Luxe Panavision
UA / Exeter–Persky Bright (Martin Baum, Arthur Lewis)

A private crime fighting organization handles cases which the CIA prefers not to.

Smooth, fashionable violence which seems to proclaim the end of a cycle.

w Marc Norman, Stirling Silliphant, *novel* Monkey in the Middle by Robert Rostand *d* Sam Peckinpah *ph* Philip Lathrop *m* Jerry Fielding

James Caan, Robert Duvall, Arthur Hill, Gig Young, Mako, Bo Hopkins, Burt Young, Tom Clancy

'Merely a commercial chore.'—*Tom Milne*
'A mysterious, elliptical, visually triumphant film about personal survival in a world of mean-minded machination.'—*Michael Billington, Illustrated London News*

Killer McCoy
US 1947 104m bw
MGM (Sam Zimbalist)

A prizefighter becomes involved in a murder. Grade A production applied to a grade B script.

w Frederick Hazlitt Brennan, Thomas Lennon, George Bruce, George Oppenheimer *d* Roy Rowland

Mickey Rooney, Ann Blyth, Brian Donlevy, James Dunn, Tom Tully, Sam Levene, James Bell, Gloria Holden

The Killer That Stalked New York
US 1950 75m bw
Columbia (Robert Cohn)
GB title: *Frightened City*

New York is on the alert for a girl smallpox carrier.
Absurdly-titled minor thriller, quite competent but wholly unsurprising.

w Harry Essex *d* Earl McEvoy *ph* Joseph Biroc *m* Hans Salter

Charles Korvin, Evelyn Keyes, William Bishop, Dorothy Malone, Lola Albright, Barry Kelley, Carl Benton Reid, Ludwig Donath

The Killers*
US 1946 105m bw
U-I (Mark Hellinger)
TV title: *A Man Alone*

In a small sleazy town a gangster waits for two assassins to kill him, and we later find out why.
Elaborate tale of cross and double-cross, stunningly executed.

w Anthony Veiller, *story* Ernest Hemingway *d* Robert Siodmak *ph* Elwood Bredell *m* Miklos Rozsa

Burt Lancaster, Edmond O'Brien, Ava Gardner, Albert Dekker, Sam Levene, John Miljan, Virginia Christine, Vince Barnett, Charles D.

Brown, Donald MacBride, Phil Brown, Charles McGraw, William Conrad

'About one tenth is Hemingway's, the rest is Universal-International's.'—*Richard Winnington*

'Seldom does a melodrama maintain the high tension that distinguishes this one.'—*Variety*
† John Huston contributed to the script but is not credited.

AAN: Anthony Veiller; Robert Siodmak; Miklos Rozsa

The Killers*
US 1964   95m   Pathecolor
U-I (Don Siegel)

Zesty, brutal remake intended for TV, but released theatrically because of its violence.

w Gene L. Coon *d* Don Siegel *ph* Richard L. Rawlings *m* Johnny Williams

John Cassavetes, Lee Marvin, Clu Gulager, Angie Dickinson, Ronald Reagan, Claude Akins

Killer's Kiss
US 1955   64m   bw
UA / Stanley Kubrick

A prizefighter rescues a girl from her gangster lover, and is marked for death.
Tedious low-budget indie which first brought its director into notice.

w/d/ph Stanley Kubrick *m* Gerald Fried

Frank Silvera, Irene Kane, Jamie Smith

The Killers of Kilimanjaro
GB 1959   91m   Technicolor
  Cinemascope
Columbia / Warwick
US title: *Adamson of Africa*

A railroad engineer helps a girl find her lost father and fiancé.
Old-fashioned safari adventure full of action and animals.

w Richard Maibaum, Cyril Hume *d* Richard Thorpe *ph* Ted Moore *m* William Alwyn

Robert Taylor, Anne Aubrey, Grégoire Aslan, Anthony Newley

The Killing**
US 1956   83m   bw
UA / Harris–Kubrick (J. B. Harris)

An ex-convict recruits helpers to steal two million dollars from a racetrack.
Incisive, entertaining, downbeat caper movie clearly influenced by *The Asphalt Jungle* and *Rififi*.

wd Stanley Kubrick, *novel* Clean Break by Lionel White *ph* Lucien Ballard *m* Gerald Fried

Sterling Hayden, Marie Windsor, Jay C. Flippen, Elisha Cook Jnr, Coleen Gray, Vince Edwards, Ted de Corsia, Joe Sawyer, Tim Carey

'The visual authority constantly dominates a flawed script.'—*Arlene Croce*

'The camera watches the whole shoddy show with the keen eye of a terrier stalking a pack of rats.'—*Time*

The Killing of Sister George*
US 1969   138m   Metrocolor
Associates and Aldrich / Palomar

An ageing lesbian actress is fired from a TV serial and her life collapses around her.
Heavily handled film version of an amusing and moving play; everything is clumsily spelt out, including the love scenes, and the actresses are forced to repeat themselves.

w Lukas Heller, *play Frank Marcus d* Robert Aldrich *ph* Joseph Biroc *m* Gerald Fried

Beryl Reid, Susannah York, *Coral Browne*, Roland Fraser, Patricia Medina, Hugh Paddick, Cyril Delevanti

'The play was second-rate, but with its nice blend of the homely and the chilling, the absurdist and the perverse, it had the quality of a Kraft-Ebbing comic book. Aldrich and Heller have turned this material into a crawling tear-jerker, the lines spoken at a speed adjusted to non-English or non-language-speaking audiences.'—*John Simon*

Kim*
US 1951   112m   Technicolor
MGM (Leon Gordon)

The orphaned son of a British soldier in India has adventures with his horseman friend who belongs to the British secret service.
Colourful Boys' Own Paper high jinks, quite lively but never convincing.

w Leon Gordon, Helen Deutsch, Richard Schayer, *novel* Rudyard Kipling *d* Victor Saville *ph* William Skall *m* André Previn

Errol Flynn, Dean Stockwell, Paul Lukas, Robert Douglas, Thomas Gomez, Cecil Kellaway, Arnold Moss, Reginald Owen

'Ornate, lavish, but curiously lacking in genuine atmosphere, vitality or period sense.'—*Penelope Houston*

Kind Hearts and Coronets***
GB 1949   106m   bw
Ealing

An impecunious heir eliminates eight D'Ascoynes who stand between him and the family fortune.
Witty, genteel black comedy well set in the

stately Edwardian era and quite deserving of its reputation for wit and style; yet the effect is curiously muffled and several opportunities missed.

w Robert Hamer, John Dighton d Robert Hamer ph Douglas Slocombe

Dennis Price, Alec Guinness (in eight roles), *Valerie Hobson, Joan Greenwood,* Miles Malleson, Arthur Lowe

'A brilliant misfire for the reason that its plentiful wit is literary and practically never pictorial.'—*Richard Winnington*

'Enlivened with cynicism, loaded with dramatic irony and shot through with a suspicion of social satire.'—*Daily Telegraph*

Kind Lady*
US 1935   76m   bw
MGM / Lucien Hubbard
aka: *House of Menace*

A confidence trickster insinuates himself and his criminal friends into the house of an invalid lady. Unusual but unconvincing melodrama with overwrought leading performances.

w Bernard Schubert, *play* Edward Chodorov, *story* Hugh Walpole *d* George B. Seitz *ph* George Folsey *m* Edward Ward

Basil Rathbone, Aline MacMahon, Mary Carlisle, Frank Albertson, Dudley Digges, Doris Lloyd

Kind Lady*
US 1951   78m   bw
MGM (Armand Deutsch)

Edwardian-set remake of the above, rather more subtly acted but failing to extract all possible frissons.

w Jerry Davis, Edward Chodorov, Charles Bennett *d* John Sturges *ph* Joseph Ruttenberg *m* David Raksin

Maurice Evans, Ethel Barrymore, Angela Lansbury, Keenan Wynn, Betsy Blair, John Williams

'A curiously tame melodrama whose shocks, when they do come, are muffled and ineffectual.'—*Penelope Houston*

A Kind of Loving***
GB 1962   112m   bw
Anglo-Amalgamated / Vic Films / Waterhall

A young north country draughtsman is forced into marriage, has to live with his dragon-like mother in law, and finally sorts out a relationship with his unhappy wife.
Blunt melodrama with strong kinship to *Saturday Night and Sunday Morning*, strikingly directed and photographed amid urban grime and suburban conformity.

w Keith Waterhouse, Willis Hall, *novel* Stan Barstow *d* John Schlesinger *ph* Denys Coop *m* Ron Grainer

Alan Bates, June Ritchie, Thora Hird, Bert Palmer, Gwen Nelson

King and Country*
GB 1964   86m   bw
BHE (Norman Priggen, Joseph Losey)

In the trenches during World War I, a private is courtmartialled and shot for desertion.
Neat cinematic treatment of a very downbeat play.

w Evan Jones, *play* Hamp by John Wilson *d* Joseph Losey *ph Denys Coop m* Larry Adler *pd* Richard Macdonald

Tom Courtenay, *Dirk Bogarde*, Leo McKern, Barry Foster, James Villiers, Peter Copley

The King and Four Queens
US 1956   86m   De Luxe   Cinemascope
UA / Russ / Field / Gabco (David Hempstead)

A cowboy braves the wrath of a lady sharpshooter to gain gold and the hand of one of her four daughters.
Tawdry sex western sporadically enlivened by good-humoured playing.

w Margaret Fitts, Richard Alan Simmons *d* Raoul Walsh *ph* Lucien Ballard *m* Alex North

Clark Gable, Eleanor Parker, Jo Van Fleet, Jean Willes, Barbara Nichols, Sara Shane, Roy Roberts

'A superficially cynical exercise in the rival attractions of sex and money.'—*MFB*

The King and I**
US 1956   133m   Eastmancolor
   Cinemascope 55
TCF (Charles Brackett)

Musical remake of *Anna and the King of Siam* (qv), from the highly successful stage production. The film is opulent in lush detail but quite lacking in style.

w Ernest Lehman *d* Walter Lang *ph* Leon Shamroy *m Richard Rodgers book/ly* Oscar Hammerstein II *md* Alfred Newman, Ken Darby *ad* Lyle Wheeler, John de Cuir

Deborah Kerr, Yul Brynner, Rita Moreno, Martin Benson, Alan Mowbray, Geoffrey Toone, Terry Saunders

'Gaiety has something of a struggle to survive.'—*Penelope Houston*
   AA: Yul Brynner

AAN: best picture; Walter Lang; Leon
Shamroy; Alfred Newman, Ken Darby;
Deborah Kerr

The King and the Chorus Girl
US 1937   94m   bw
Warner (Mervyn Le Roy)

A European prince on the spree falls for a New
York chorine.
Reasonably lively romantic comedy.

w Norman Krasna, Groucho Marx, from their
story Grand Passion d Mervyn Le Roy
 ph Tony Gaudio

Joan Blondell, Fernand Gravet, Edward Everett
Horton, Jane Wyman

King Arthur Was a Gentleman
GB 1942   99m   bw
GFD / Gainsborough (Edward Black)

A soldier becomes a hero when he believes he has
King Arthur's sword.
Not-too-successful attempt to turn a music hall
comedian into a figure of Chaplinesque pathos.

w Val Guest, Marriott Edgar d Marcel Varnel

Arthur Askey, Evelyn Dall, Anne Shelton, Max
Bacon, Jack Train, Peter Graves, Vera Frances,
Ronald Shiner, Brefni O'Rourke

King Creole
US 1958   116m   bw   Vistavision
(Paramount) Hal B. Wallis

A failed graduate becomes a singer in a New
Orleans night club, and gets involved with
gangsters.
Disagreeable crook melodrama turned into a
musical star vehicle.

w Herbert Baker, Michael V. Gazzo, novel A
Stone for Danny Fisher by Harold Robbins
d Michael Curtiz

Elvis Presley, Carolyn Jones, Dean Jagger,
Walter Matthau, Dolores Hart, Paul Stewart

A King in New York*
GB 1957   109m   bw
Attica (Charles Chaplin)

A penniless European king finds himself at odds
with the American way of life.
Feeble Chaplin comedy from his anti-American
period; tedious dialogue and poor physical
production allow only momentary flashes of the
satire intended.

wd/m Charles Chaplin ph Georges Périnal

Charles Chaplin, Michael Chaplin, Oliver
Johnson, Dawn Addams, Jerry Desmonde,
Harry Green, Maxine Audley, Sid James

'Unhappily he is a sadder and an older man;

the real punch is gone. His dethroned king is an
ironically apt image.'—Marvin Felheim

'Maybe the worst film ever made by a
celebrated film artist.'—New Yorker, 1977

'It shows how the coming of sound was a curse
to Chaplin; how its freedoms dissipated his
strengths; how his attempts to exploit it
intellectually and ideologically played to his
weaknesses; how, in short, he was much more
grievously hurt by history in art than by history
in politics.'—Stanley Kauffmann

King Kong****
US 1933   100m   bw
RKO (Merian C. Cooper)

A film producer on safari brings back a giant ape
which terrorizes New York.
The greatest monster movie of all, a miracle of
trick work and suspense, with some of the most
memorable moments in film history.

w James Creelman, Ruth Rose, story Edgar
Wallace d Merian C. Cooper, Ernest
Schoedsack ph Edward Linden, Verne Walker,
J. O. Taylor sound effects Murray Spivak chief
technician Willis J. O'Brien m Max Steiner

Robert Armstrong, Fay Wray, Bruce Cabot,
Frank Reicher

AAN: photography

King Kong
US 1976   135m   metrocolor   Panavision
Dino de Laurentiis

Semi-spoof remake with added sexual overtones;
though launched on a massive wave of publicity,
it lacks both the charm and the technical
resources of its predecessor.

w Lorenzo Semple Jnr d John Guillermin
ph Richard H. Kline m John Barry pd Dale
Hennesy, Mario Chiari

Jeff Bridges, Charles Grodin, Jessica Lange,
John Randolph, René Auberjonois, Julius
Harris, Ed Lauter

King Lear*
GB / Denmark 1970   137m   bw
Columbia / Filmways—Laterna (Michael
Birkett)

Tragedy ensues when an old king prematurely
divides his kingdom between his daughters.
Miserably photographed in freezing Jutland, this
is a deliberately downbeat version which despite
its varied points of interest is extremely hard to
sit through.

w William Shakespeare (a cut text) d Peter
Brook ph Henning Kristiansen m none
pd Georges Wakhevitch

Paul Scofield, Irene Worth, Alan Webb, Tom Fleming, Susan Engel, Cyril Cusack, Patrick Magee, Jack MacGowran

King of Alcatraz*
US 1938 56m bw
Paramount (William C. Thomas)

Convicts escape on a freighter, but one needs surgery. Pacy programmer with a stalwart cast.

w Irving Reis *d* Robert Florey *ph* Harry Fischbeck *md* Boris Morros

Gail Patrick, J. Carrol Naish, Lloyd Nolan, Harry Carey, Robert Preston, Anthony Quinn, Dennis Morgan, Porter Hall

King of Burlesque*
US 1936 88m bw
TCF (Kenneth MacGowan)

A vaudeville impresario overcomes his troubles. Well-written musical with plenty of variety talent.

w James Seymour, Gene Markey, Harry Tugend *d* Sidney Lanfield *ph* Peverell Marley *songs* various

Warner Baxter, Alice Faye, Jack Oakie, Mona Barrie, Arline Judge, Dixie Dunbar, Gregory Ratoff, Herbert Mundin, *Fats Waller*, Kenny Baker

† Remade as *Hello Frisco Hello*.

King of Gamblers
US 1937 79m bw
Paramount
aka: *Czar of the Slot Machines*

A ruthless gangster loves a singer who loves a reporter who is out to expose him.
A muddled script mars this pacy lower-birth item.

w Doris Anderson *d* Robert Florey *ph* Harry Fischbeck *md* Boris Morros

Akim Tamiroff, Claire Trevor, Lloyd Nolan, Buster Crabbe, Porter Hall

King of Hearts
France / Italy 1966 110m Eastmancolor
UA / Fildebroc / Montoro (Philippe de Broca)
original title: *Le Roi de Coeur*

In World War I, a Scottish soldier finds a war-torn town occupied only by lunatics who have escaped from the asylum and who want to make him their king.
Heavy-handed whimsy which never catches fire despite the talents involved.

w Daniel Boulanger *d* Philippe de Broca *ph* Pierre Lhomme *m* Georges Delerue

Alan Bates, Geneviève Bujold, Jean-Claude Brialy, Françoise Christophe, Pierre Brasseur, Micheline Presle, Adolfo Celi, Julien Guiomar

King of Jazz***
US 1930 101m Technicolor
Universal (Carl Laemmle Jnr)

Musical revue.
Stylish, spectacular, revelatory early musical: a treasure trove.

devised/d John Murray Anderson w Harry Ruskin, Charles MacArthur *pd* Hal Mohr, Ray Rennahan, Jerome Ash *ad Herman Rose*

Paul Whiteman and his orchestra, John Boles, Bing Crosby (with the Rhythm Boys), Laura la Plante, Glenn Tryon, Slim Summerville, Walter Brennan

King of Kings**
US 1927 155m approx (24 fps) (various versions) bw silent
(Pathé) Cecil B. de Mille

The life of Jesus, seen more or less from the viewpoint of Mary Magdalene.
A patchy but frequently moving and pictorially effective work, ranging from the sublime (the first view of Jesus as a blind man regains his sight) to the ridiculous ('Harness my zebras, gift of the Nubian king!' says Mary Magdalene in a subtitle).

w Jeanie Macpherson *d* Cecil B. de Mille *ph* J. Peverell Marley

H. B. Warner, Jacqueline Logan, Joseph Schildkraut (Judas), Ernest Torrence (Peter), Victor Varconi (Pilate), Dorothy Cumming (Mary, mother of Jesus), Rudolph Schildkraut (Caiaphas)

'The most impressive of all motion pictures.'—*Mordaunt Hall, New York Times*

King of Kings*
US 1961 161m Super Technirama
MGM / Samuel Bronston

The life of Jesus Christ.
Known in the trade as *I Was a Teenage Jesus*, this good-looking but rather tedious film is neither vulgar nor very interesting; a solemn, decent, bible-in-pictures pageant.

w Philip Yordan *d* Nicholas Ray *ph* Franz Planer, Manuel Berenger *m* Miklos Rozsa *ad* Georges Wakhevitch

Jeffrey Hunter, Robert Ryan, Siobhan McKenna, Frank Thring, Hurd Hatfield, Rip Torn, Harry Guardino, Viveca Lindfors, Rita Gam

The King of Marvin Gardens*

US 1972　104m　Eastmancolor
Columbia / BBS (Bob Rafaelson)

The host of a late night radio talk show gets
embroiled in his brother's schemes.
Thoughtful tragi-comedy overweighted by talk,
but with good performances.

w Jacob Brackman d Bob Rafaelson ph Laszlo
Kovacs

Jack Nicholson, Bruce Dern, Ellen Burstyn,
Julia Anne Robinson

'Indecipherable dark nonsense about brothers
and goals and the American dream. An
unqualified disaster.'—New Yorker

'Glum news from the people who made Five
Easy Pieces, which had a lot of good work in it
along with some pretentious flab. In their new
picture the flab has taken over.'—Stanley
Kauffmann

King of the Damned*

GB 1935　76m　bw
Gaumont (Michael Balcon)

On a South Seas convict settlement, harsh
treatment leads to mutiny.
A downright peculiar project for a British studio
at this time, but technically very competent for
those who like this kind of thing.

w Charles Bennett, Sidney Gilliat, Noel Langley,
play John Chancellor d Walter Forde
ph Bernard Knowles md Louis Levy

Conrad Veidt, Helen Vinson, Noah Beery, Cecil
Ramage, Edmund Willard, Raymond Lovell,
Allan Jeayes, Percy Parsons

King of the Khyber Rifles

US 1954　100m　Technicolor
Cinemascope
TCF (Frank Rosenberg)

In 1857 a British garrison in India is threatened
by the forces of Kuuram Khan but saved by a
half-caste officer.
Standard North-West Frontier adventure, old-
fashioned and rather dull.

w Ivan Goff, Ben Roberts d Henry King
ph Leon Shamroy m Bernard Herrmann

Tyrone Power, Terry Moore, Michael Rennie,
Guy Rolfe, John Justin

King of the Roaring Twenties

US 1961　106m　bw
Warner / AA / Bischoff—Diamond
GB title: The Big Bankroll

A gambler, Arnold Rothstein, becomes powerful
among twenties gangsters.
Routine crime drama, shoddily made.

w Jo Swerling d Joseph M. Newman ph Carl
Guthrie m Franz Waxman

David Janssen, Dianne Foster, Mickey Rooney,
Mickey Shaughnessy, Diana Dors, Dan
O'Herlihy, Jack Carson, Keenan Wynn, William
Demarest, Joseph Schildkraut, Regis Toomey,
Murvyn Vye

'Superficial, shopworn biography of an
infamous bookie.'—MFB

King, Queen, Knave*

US / West Germany 1972　92m
Eastmancolor
Wolper / Maran (Lutz Hengst)

The wife of a Munich bookseller falls for his
adolescent nephew.
Amusing, capriciously directed sex comedy.

w David Shaw, David Seltzer, novel Vladimir
Nabokov d Jerzy Skolomowski ph Charly
Steinberger m Stanley Myers

Gina Lollobrigida, David Niven, John Moulder-
Brown, Mario Adorf, Carl Fox-Duering

King Rat*

US 1965　134m　bw
Columbia / Coleytown (James Woolf)

In Singapore's Changi Gaol during World War
II an American corporal lives more comfortably
than the other prisoners by shabby dealings with
the camp guards.
Overlong but generally gripping character
melodrama—'not a story of escape but a story
of survival'.

wd Bryan Forbes, novel James Clavell
ph Burnett Guffey m John Barry

George Segal, Tom Courtenay, John Mills,
James Fox, Denholm Elliott, Todd Armstrong,
Patrick O'Neal, James Donald, Alan Webb,
Leonard Rossiter, Geoffrey Bayldon

AAN: Burnett Guffey

King Richard and the Crusaders

US 1954　113m　Warnercolor
Cinemascope
Warner (Henry Blanke)

During the Crusades, the dreaded Saladin
arrives in England in disguise and falls in love
with Lady Edith . . .
Crudely confected comic strip version of Sir
Walter Scott's The Talisman, ineptly written and
cast, with poor production values.

w John Twist d David Butler ph Peverell
Marley m Max Steiner

Rex Harrison (as Saladin), Virginia Mayo,
George Sanders, Laurence Harvey, Robert
Douglas

'Do not adjust your set—the sound you hear is Sir Walter Scott turning in his grave.'—*Sunday Express*

King Solomon's Mines*
GB 1938 80m bw
Gainsborough (Geoffrey Barkas)

Explorers in Africa persuade an exiled chief to help them find a diamond mine.
Rather somnolent though well-cast version of a favourite adventure novel, with a splendid final reel.

w Michael Hogan, A. R. Rawlinson, Roland Pertwee, Ralph Spence, Charles Bennett, *novel* H. Rider Haggard *d* Robert Stevenson *ph* Glen MacWilliams *m* Mischa Spoliansky

Cedric Hardwicke, *Paul Robeson*, Roland Young, John Loder, Anna Lee, Sydney Fairbrother, Robert Adams

'They kept the eye of the camera open for every form of wild and savage life and crammed it all into the picture, so one gets the impression that Allan Quartermain is delivering a lecture with illustrations rather than taking part in an adventure.'—*Richard Mallett, Punch*

King Solomon's Mines*
US 1950 102m Technicolor
MGM (Sam Zimbalist)

A remake which is largely travelogue with the merest trimmings of story.

w Helen Deutsch *d* Compton Bennett *ph* Robert Surtees

Stewart Granger, Deborah Kerr, Richard Carlson, Hugo Haas, Lowell Gilmore

AAN: best picture; Robert Surtees

The King Steps Out*
US 1936 85m bw
Columbia (William Perlberg)

Emperor Franz Josef falls in love with the sister of the princess to whom he is betrothed.
Rather heavy-handed romance with music, not in its director's best style but showing flashes of his decorative talent.

w Sidney Buchman, *operetta* Cissy by Herbert and Ernst Marischka *d* Josef Von Sternberg *ph* Lucien Ballard *songs* Fritz Kreisler, Dorothy Fields *ad* Stephen Goossen

Grace Moore, Franchot Tone, Walter Connolly, Raymond Walburn, Herman Bing, Victor Jory, Elizabeth Risdon, Nana Bryant, Frieda Inescort, Thurston Hall

'Josef Von Sternberg asked that it not be included in retrospectives of his work, but he really did make the damned thing.'—*New Yorker, 1977*

Kingdom of the Spiders
US 1977 95m colour
Arachnid / Dimension (Henry Fownes)

In an Arizona valley the death rate soars when tarantulas begin preying in groups on humans instead of singly on each other.
The spiders is coming, as Hitch might have remarked, and not even giant-size. Standard shudders, efficiently presented.

w Richard Robinson, Alan Caillou *d* John Cardos *ph* John Morrill, John Wheeler *md* Igo Kantor

William Shatner, Tiffany Bolling, Woody Strode, David MacLean

Kings Go Forth
US 1958 109m bw
UA / Ross–Eton (Frank Ross)

August 1944: two American soldiers fall out over a black French woman who is torn between them.
Heavy-going war melodrama, well enough done for those who can take it.

w Merle Miller, *novel* Joe David Brown *d* Delmer Daves *ph* Daniel Fapp *m* Elmer Bernstein

Frank Sinatra, Tony Curtis, Natalie Wood, Leora Dana, Karl Swenson

Kings of the Sun
US 1963 108m De Luxe Panavision
UA / Mirisch (Lewis J. Rachmil)

A Mayan tribe emigrates from Mexico to Texas and makes peace with the local Indian chief.
Ponderous dark age epic replete with human sacrifice, high-mindedness and solemn pauses. The actors and sets carry it as far as it will go.

w Elliot Arnold, James R. Webb *d* J. Lee-Thompson *ph* Joe MacDonald *m* Elmer Bernstein *ad* Alfred Ybarra

Yul Brynner, George Chakiris, Shirley Anne Field, Richard Basehart, Brad Dexter, Barry Morse

King's Rhapsody
GB 1955 93m Eastmancolor
Cinemascope
Everest (Herbert Wilcox)

An exiled Ruritanian king leaves his mistress to return home to a political marriage.
Love versus duty in a ludicrously inept film of Ivor Novello's highly theatrical musical drama,

cheaply made and killed stone dead by casting and wide screen.

w Pamela Bower, Christopher Hassall, A. P. Herbert d Herbert Wilcox ph Max Greene

Errol Flynn, Anna Neagle, Patrice Wymore, Martita Hunt, Finlay Currie

King's Row****
US 1941   127m   bw
Warner (David Lewis)

In a small American town during the early years of the century, three children grow up into a world of cruelty and madness.
Superb Hollywood melodrama, a Peyton Place with great visual strength, haunting music and a wholly absorbing if incredible plot.

w Casey Robinson, novel Henry Bellamann d Sam Wood ph James Wong Howe m Erich Wolfgang Korngold pd William Cameron Menzies

Ann Sheridan, Robert Cummings, Ronald Reagan, Claude Rains, Betty Field, Charles Coburn, Nancy Coleman, Maria Ouspenskaya, Harry Davenport, Judith Anderson, Karen Verne

AAN: best picture; Sam Wood; James Wong Howe

The King's Thief
US 1955   79m   Eastmancolor
   Cinemascope
MGM (Edwin H. Knopf)

The Duke of Brampton plots treason against Charles II but a highwayman robs him of an incriminating notebook.
Dismal swashbuckler with neither zest nor style, just a cast of unhappy-looking actors.

w Charles Knopf d Robert Z. Leonard ph Robert Planck

David Niven, Edmund Purdom, Ann Blyth, George Sanders, Roger Moore

Kipps***
GB 1941   112m   bw
TCF (Edward Black)
US title: The Remarkable Mr Kipps

In 1906, a draper's assistant comes into money and tries to crash society.
Charming, unassuming film of a well-loved novel, later musicalized as Half a Sixpence.

w Sidney Gilliat, novel H. G. Wells d Carol Reed ph Arthur Crabtree m Charles Williams

Michael Redgrave, Phyllis Calvert, Diana Wynyard, Arthur Riscoe, Max Adrian, Helen Haye, Michael Wilding, Lloyd Pearson, Edward Rigby, Hermione Baddeley, Frank Pettingell, Beatrice Varley, Kathleen Harrison, Felix Aylmer

Kismet
US 1930   90m   bw
Warner

An Oriental magician overcomes a wicked vizier.
Rather tame filming of a spectacular which belongs on the stage.

w Howard Estabrook, play Edward Knoblock d John Francis Dillon ph John Seitz

Otis Skinner, Loretta Young, David Manners, Mary Duncan, Sidney Blackmer, Fred Sterling, Edmund Breese, Montagu Love

Kismet*
US 1944   100m   Technicolor
MGM (Everett Riskin)

Hollow and humourless but striking-looking remake of the above.

w John Meehan, d William Dieterle ph Charles Rosher m Herbert Stothart ad Cedric Gibbons, Daniel B. Cathcart

Ronald Colman, Marlene Dietrich, James Craig, Edward Arnold, Hugh Herbert, Joy Ann Page, Florence Bates, Harry Davenport, Hobart Cavanaugh, Robert Warwick

AAN: Charles Rosher; Herbert Stothart

Kismet
US 1955   113m   Eastmancolor
   Cinemascope
MGM (Arthur Freed)

Unlucky musical remake from the stage show with Borodin music.

w Charles Lederer, Luther Davis, from their musical play d Vincente Minnelli ph Joseph Ruttenberg ch Jack Cole ad Cedric Gibbons, Preston Ames

Howard Keel, Ann Blyth, Dolores Gray, Vic Damone, Monty Woolley, Sebastian Cabot, Jay C. Flippen, Mike Mazurki, Jack Elam

The Kiss*
US 1929   70m approx (24 fps)   bw   silent
MGM

A woman is accused of the murder of her jealous husband.
A wisp of a melodrama, enlivened by its star; otherwise only notable as MGM's last silent picture.

w Hans Kraly d Jacques Feyder

Greta Garbo, Lew Ayres, Conrad Nagel,
Holmes Herbert, Anders Randolf

Kiss and Make Up
US 1934 80m bw
Paramount (B. P. Schulberg)

A Parisian beauty specialist forsakes a rich client
for his loyal secretary.
Forgettable romantic comedy.

w Harlan Thompson, George Marion Jnr, *play*
Stephen Bekeffi d Harlan Thompson *ph* Leon
Shamroy

Cary Grant, Genevieve Tobin, Helen Mack,
Edward Everett Horton, Lucien Littlefield,
Mona Maris

Kiss and Tell*
US 1945 92m bw
Columbia (Sol C. Siegel)

To protect another girl, an irrepressible teenager
pretends to be pregnant.
Good-humoured farcical comedy which at the
time was thought pretty shocking, especially
with the infant darling of the thirties in the lead.

w F. Hugh Herbert, from his play d Richard
Wallace *ph* Charles Lawton *m* Werner
Heymann

Shirley Temple, Robert Benchley, Walter Abel,
Jerome Courtland, Katherine Alexander, Porter
Hall, Tom Tully

'All brilliantly characteristic of the worst
anyone could think of American life.'—*James
Agee*

A Kiss before Dying*
US 1956 94m De Luxe Cinemascope
UA / Crown (Robert Jacks)

A college boy kills women who get in his way.
Reasonably absorbing exercise in
psychopathology which would have been more
effective on a smaller screen.

w Lawrence Roman, *novel* Ira Levin d Gerd
Oswald *ph* Lucien Ballard *m* Lionel Newman

Jeffrey Hunter, Joanne Woodward, Robert
Wagner, Virginia Leith, *Mary Astor*, George
Macready

A Kiss for Corliss
US 1949 88m bw
UA / James Nasser
aka: *Almost a Bride*

A teenager develops a crush on a middle-aged
roué.
Dismal sequel to *Kiss and Tell* in the shadow of
The Bachelor and the Bobby Soxer.

w Howard Dimsdale d Richard Wallace
ph Robert de Grasse *m* Werner Heymann

David Niven, Shirley Temple, Tom Tully,
Darryl Hickman, Virginia Welles

A Kiss in the Dark
US 1949 87m bw
Warner (Harry Kurnitz)

A concert pianist finds romance in a boarding
house peopled with zany characters.
Paper-thin romantic comedy.

w Harry Kurnitz d Delmer Daves *ph* Robert
Burks *m* Max Steiner

David Niven, Jane Wyman, Broderick
Crawford, Maria Ouspenskaya, Victor Moore,
Wayne Morris, Joseph Buloff, Curt Bois

Kiss Me Again**
US 1925 77m approx (24 fps) bw silent
Warner

A bored wife is tempted to stray, but doesn't.
Excellent silent comedy from an old boulevard
farce, remade to less effect in the forties as *That
Uncertain Feeling*.

w Hans Kraly, *play* Divorcons by Victorien
Sardou, Emile de Najac d Ernst Lubitsch
ph Charles Von Enger

Marie Prévost, Monte Blue, John Roche, Willard
Louis, Clara Bow

'Another sex masterpiece from the Attila of
Hollywood . . . Continental high comedy done in
the central European manner with Germanic
harshness and irony of attack.'—*Ted Shane,
New Yorker*

'Perhaps the most exquisite light screen
comedy ever made on the subject of l'amour.'—
Herman G. Weinberg

Kiss Me Deadly
US 1955 105m bw
UA / Parklane (Robert Aldrich)

By helping a girl who is nevertheless murdered,
Mike Hammer prevents crooks from stealing a
case of radio-active material.
Curiously arty and excruciatingly boring private
eye thriller, a ripe piece of cinematic cheese full
of tilt shots and symbols: even the titles read
from down to up.

w A. I. Bezzerides, d Robert Aldrich *ph* Ernest
Laszlo *m* Frank de Vol

Ralph Meeker, Albert Dekker, Cloris
Leachman, Paul Stewart, Juano Hernandez,
Wesley Addy, Maxene Cooper

Kiss Me Kate**

US 1953 111m Anscocolor 3-D
MGM (Jack Cummings)

The married leading players of a musical version
of *The Taming of the Shrew* lead an equally
tempestuous life backstage.
Brisk, bright screen version of the Broadway
musical hit.

w Dorothy Kingsley, *play* Samuel and Bella
Spewack *d* George Sidney *ph* Charles Rosher
m/ly Cole Porter *md* André Previn, Saul
Chaplin *ch* Hermes Pan

Howard Keel, Kathryn Grayson, Ann Miller,
Keenan Wynn, Bobby Van, Tommy Rall, James
Whitmore, Bob Fosse, Kurt Kasznar

AAN: André Previn, Saul Chaplin

Kiss Me Stupid*

US 1964 124m bw Panavision
UA / Mirisch / Phalanx / (Billy Wilder)

A womanizing pop singer stops overnight in a
small California desert town and shows interest
in an unsuccessful songwriter in order to get at
his wife.

Draggy, tasteless, surprisingly unamusing
smoking room story, with the actors behaving as
though driven against their will (apart from Dean
Martin, ideally cast as the idol who gets a
headache if he doesn't have sex every night).
Some good wisecracks, but it should have been
much faster and funnier.

w Billy Wilder, I. A. L. Diamond, *play* L'oro
della fantasia by Anna Bonacci *d* Billy Wilder
ph Joseph La Shelle *m* André Previn
pd Alexander Trauner *songs* George and Ira
Gershwin

Dean Martin, Kim Novak, Ray Walston, Cliff
Osmond

'A work of ferocious tastelessness . . . Swiftian
in its relentless disgust.'—*Peter Barnes*

Kiss of Death**

US 1947 98m bw
TCF

A captured thief informs on his own gang, and a
psychopathic killer is sent to extract vengeance.
Gloomy, well-made semi-location thriller which
descends into heavy melodrama. Remade as *The
Fiend Who Walked the West.*

w Ben Hecht, Charles Lederer *d* Henry
Hathaway *ph* Norbert Brodine *m* David
Buttolph

Victor Mature, Richard Widmark, Brian
Donlevy, Coleen Gray, Karl Malden, Taylor
Holmes

AAN: original story (E. Lipsky); Richard
Widmark

Kiss of the Vampire*

GB 1962 88m Eastmancolor
U-I / Hammer (Anthony Hinds)
US title: *Kiss of Evil*

In 1910 a Bavarian disciple of Dracula lures a
British honeymoon couple.
This unsubtle variation on *Dracula* is handled in
lively fashion, with a splendid climax in which
assorted white-robed vampires are destroyed by
bats.

w John Elder *d* Don Sharp *ph* Alan Hume
m James Bernard

Noel Willman, Clifford Evans, Edward De
Souza, Jennifer Daniel, Isobel Black

Kiss the Blood Off My Hands

US 1948 80m bw
Universal (Harold Hecht)
GB title: *Blood on My Hands*

A nurse helps a seaman on the run for murder.
Risible romantic melodrama in never-was
London docks setting, with Newton large as life
and twice as villainous.

w Leonardo Bercovici, *novel* Gerald Butler
d Norman Foster *ph* Russell Metty *m* Miklos
Rozsa

Joan Fontaine, Burt Lancaster, Robert Newton,
Lewis Russell, Aminta Dyne

Kiss the Boys Goodbye*

US 1941 85m bw
Paramount

A Broadway producer falls for one of his
chorines.
Moderately smart musical entertainment of its
time.

w Harry Tugend, Dwight Taylor, *play* Clare
Boothe *d* Victor Schertzinger *m/ly* Victor
Schertzinger, Frank Loesser

Don Ameche, Mary Martin, Oscar Levant,
Rochester, Raymond Walburn, Connie Boswell,
Virginia Dale, Barbara Jo Allen, Elizabeth
Patterson

Kiss the Girls and Make Them Die

Italy 1966 106m Technicolor
Dino de Laurentiis
original title: *Si Tutte le Donne del Mondo . . .*

A rich industrialist has a plan to sterilize the
whole male population of the world and restock
it with his own mistresses, whom he keeps in
suspended animation.
Patchy James Bond spoof.

w Jack Pulman, Dino Maiuri *d* Henry Levin, Dino Maiuri *ph* Aldo Tonti *m* Mario Nascimbene

Michael Connors, Dorothy Provine, Raf Vallone, Terry-Thomas

Kiss Them for Me
US 1957 105m Eastmancolor
Cinemascope
TCF (Jerry Wald)

Three navy pilots spend a weekend's unofficial leave in San Francisco, and get into various kinds of trouble.
Based on a novel which also served as source for the musical *Hit the Deck*, this very heavy-footed comedy with serious asides is most unsuitably cast and generally ill-timed and unattractive.

w Julius Epstein, *novel* Shore Leave by Frederick Wakeman *d* Stanley Donen *ph* Milton Krasner *m* Lionel Newman

Cary Grant, Jayne Mansfield, Suzy Parker, Ray Walston, Larry Blyden, Leif Erickson, Werner Klemperer

Kiss Tomorrow Goodbye
US 1950 102m bw
(Warner) William Cagney

A violent criminal breaks jail and plans several daring robberies.
Surprisingly brutal star melodrama which failed to repeat the success of *White Heat*.

w Harry Brown, *novel* Horace McCoy *d* Gordon Douglas *ph* Peverell Marley *m* Carmen Dragon

James Cagney, Barbara Payton, Ward Bond, Luther Adler, Helena Carter, Steve Brodie, Rhys Williams, Barton MacLane, Frank Reicher, John Litel

'The mixture as before without an ingredient changed.'—*Otis Guernsey Jnr*

Kisses for My President
US 1964 113m bw
Warner / Pearlayne (Curtis Bernhardt)

America's first woman president causes problems for her husband.
Solidly-carpentered comedy with too few ideas for its length.

w Claude Binyon, Robert G. Kane *d* Curtis Bernhardt *ph* Robert Surtees *m* Bronislau Kaper

Polly Bergen, Fred MacMurray, Arlene Dahl, Eli Wallach, Edward Andrews

Kissin' Cousins
US 1963 96m Metrocolor Panavision
MGM / Four Leaf (Sam Katzman)

The USAF wants to build a missile base on Smokey Mountain, and their PR man discovers that one of the hillbillies is his double.
A feeble production in every sense, even below its star's usual standard.

w Gerald Drayson Adams, Gene Nelson *d* Gene Nelson *ph* Ellis W. Carter *md* Fred Karger

Elvis Presley, Arthur O'Connell, Glenda Farrell, Jack Albertson

The Kissing Bandit
US 1948 102m Technicolor
MGM (Joe Pasternak)

In old California, a young businessman finds he is expected to keep up his bandit father's criminal and romantic reputation.
Silly, witless musical which never settles into gear; mocked by its star as Benny mocked *The Horn Blows at Midnight*.

w Isabel Lennart, John Briard Harding *d* Laslo Benedek *ph* Robert Surtees *m* Georgie Stoll

Frank Sinatra, Kathryn Grayson, J. Carrol Naish, Mildred Natwick, Mikhail Rasumny, Billy Gilbert, Clinton Sundberg

Kitty
GB 1928 90m (24 fps) bw silent
BIP / Burlington (Victor Saville)

A shopgirl loves a paralysed amnesiac, but his mother interferes.
Uninteresting romantic melodrama, notable only as Britain's first sound film: a few dialogue sequences were quickly added for a reissue in 1929.

w Violet Powell, Benn W. Levy, *novel* Warwick Deeping *d* Victor Saville

John Stuart, Estelle Brody, Dorothy Cumming, Marie Ault, Olaf Hytten

Kitty***
US 1945 103m bw
Paramount (Karl Tunberg)

In 18th-century London, an aristocrat makes a duchess of a guttersnipe.
Well-detailed period *Pygmalion* which works much better than one would expect.

w Darrell Ware, Karl Tunberg, *novel* Rosamund Marshall *d* Mitchell Leisen *ph* Daniel L. Fapp *m* Victor Young

Paulette Goddard, Ray Milland, Cecil Kellaway, Constance Collier, Reginald Owen,

Patric Knowles, Dennis Hoey, Sara Allgood,
Eric Blore, Gordon Richards, Michael Dyne

Kitty Foyle**
US 1940   108m   bw
RKO (Harry E. Edgington, David Hempstead)

A white-collar girl has a troubled love life.
Solid entertainment of its time, especially aimed
at ambitious young ladies.

w Dalton Trumbo, Donald Ogden Stewart, *novel*
Christopher Morley d Sam Wood ph Robert de
Grasse m Roy Webb

Ginger Rogers, Dennis Morgan, James Craig,
Eduardo Ciannelli, Ernest Cossart, Gladys
Cooper, Mary Treen

AA: Ginger Rogers
AAN: best picture; Dalton Trumbo, Donald
Ogden Stewart; Sam Wood

The Klansman
US 1974   112m   Technicolor
Paramount / Atlanta (William Alexander)

An Alabama sheriff confronts the Ku Klux
Klan.
Violent melodrama, all noise, brutality and bad
acting.

w Millard Kaufman, Samuel Fuller, *novel*
William Bradford Huie d Terence Young
ph Lloyd Ahern, Aldo Tonti m Stax
Organisation

Lee Marvin, Richard Burton, Cameron Mitchell,
O. J. Simpson, Lola Falana, David Huddleston,
Luciana Paluzzi, Linda Evans
    'There's not a shred of quality, dignity,
relevance or impact in this yahoo-oriented
bunk.'—*Variety*

Klondike Annie
US 1936   83m   bw
Paramount (William Le Baron)

A torch singer on the run disguises herself as a
missionary and revivifies a Klondike mission.
Laundered Mae West vehicle, from her fading
period but not too bad.

w Mae West, Marion Morgan, George B.
Dowell d Raoul Walsh ph George Clemer

Mae West, Victor McLaglen, Philip Reed, Helen
Jerome Eddy, Harry Beresford, Harold Huber,
Esther Howard

Klute***
US 1971   114m   Technicolor   Panavision
Warner (Alan J. Pakula)

A policeman leaves the force to investigate the
disappearance of a research scientist, and takes
up with a call girl who is involved.

Excellent adult thriller with attention to detail
and emphasis on character.

w Andy K. Lewis, Dave Lewis d Alan J. Pakula
ph Gordon Lewis m Michael Small

Jane Fonda, Donald Sutherland, Charles Cioffi,
Roy Scheider, Rita Gam

AA: Jane Fonda
AAN: Andy K. Lewis, Dave Lewis

The Knack***
GB 1965   84m   bw
UA / Woodfall (Oscar Lewenstein)

A sex-starved young teacher lets one room of his
house to a successful womanizer, another to an
innocent girl from the north.
An excuse for an anarchic series of visual gags, a
kaleidoscope of swinging London in which
anything goes. Brilliantly done in the style of *A
Hard Day's Night*.

w Charles Wood, *play* Ann Jellicoe d Richard
Lester ph David Watkin m John Barry

*Michael Crawford, Ray Brooks, Rita
Tushingham*, Donal Donnelly

Knave of Hearts*
GB 1954   103m   bw
Transcontinental (Paul Graetz)
aka: *Monsieur Ripois et Son Nemesis*

A born philanderer confesses all his affairs to his
wife.
Well-observed though strangely flat and
disappointing sex comedy, something of a
pioneer in its time and therefore perhaps too
diffident in its approach.

w René Clément, Hugh Mills d René Clément
ph Oswald Morris m Roman Vlad

Gérard Philipe, Margaret Johnston, Joan
Greenwood, Natasha Parry, Valerie Hobson

Knickerbocker Holiday
US 1944   84m   bw
UA / Harry Joe Brown / PCA

In old New Amsterdam, a one-legged tyrant
finally sees the light.
Artificial musical from a famous stage original,
with engaging moments including Charles
Coburn singing 'September Song'.

w Thomas Lennon, from the 1938 stage musical
(m Kurt Weill, ly Maxwell Anderson) based on
Father Knickerbocker's History of New York
by Washington Irving d Harry Joe Brown
ph Phil Tammura m Werner Heymann

Charles Coburn, Nelson Eddy, Constance
Dowling, Ernest Cossart, Shelley Winters, Otto
Kruger

AAN: Werner Heymann

Knife in the Water*
Poland 1962   94m   bw
ZRF Kamera (Stanislaw Zylewicz)
original title: *Noz w Wodzie*

A young couple ask a hitchhiker to spend a
weekend on their yacht, and regret it.
Detached little melodrama in which the sex and
violence hover beneath the surface. All very
watchable, but in a minor key.

w Jerzy Skolimowski, Roman Polanski, Jakub
Goldberg *d Roman Polanski ph* Jerzy Lipman
m Krzystof Komeda

Leon Niemczyk, Jolanta Umecka, Zygmunt
Malanowicz

Knight without Armour**
GB 1937   107m   bw
London Films (Alexander Korda)

During the Russian Revolution of 1917, a
widowed countess is helped to safety by a British
translator.
Underrated romantic adventure with big
production values and some splendid moments.

w Lajos Biro, Arthur Wimperis, Frances
Marion, *novel* James Hilton *ph Harry
Stradling d Jacques Feyder m* Miklos Rozsa

Robert Donat, Marlene Dietrich, Irene
Vanbrugh, Herbert Lomas, Austin Trevor, Basil
Gill, David Tree, John Clements, Lawrence
Hanray
'A first class thriller, beautifully directed, with
spare and convincing dialogue and a nearly
watertight scenario.'—*Graham Greene*

Knights of the Round Table*
GB 1953   115m   Eastmancolor
        Cinemascope
MGM (Pandro S. Berman)

Lancelot, banished from King Arthur's court for
loving Guinevere, returns to defeat the evil
Modred.
Disappointingly flat, pageant-like adaptation of
the legends, with a few lively strands
insufficiently firmly drawn together.

w Talbot Jennings, Jan Lustig, Noel Langley
d Richard Thorpe *ph* Frederick A. Young,
Stephen Dade *m* Miklos Rozsa *ad* Alfred
Junge, Hans Peters

Robert Taylor, Mel Ferrer, Ava Gardner, Anne
Crawford, Stanley Baker, Felix Aylmer, Robert
Urquhart, Niall MacGinnis

Knights of the Teutonic Order*
Poland 1960   180m   Eastmancolor
        Dyaliscope
Studio Unit (Zygmunt Krol)

Teutonic knights pillage Poland on the pretext of
converting the inhabitants to Christianity; when
they kill a noblewoman, her daughter swears
revenge.
Medieval epic differing little from those of
Hollywood, but splendid to look at.

w Jerzy Stafan Stawinski, Aleksander Ford,
novel Henryk Sienkiewicz *d* Aleksander Ford
ph Mieczyslaw Jahoda *m* Kazimierz Serocki

Urszula Modrzynska, Grazyna Staniszewska,
Andrzej Szalawski

Knock on Any Door*
US 1949   100m   bw
Columbia (Nicholas Ray)

A defence lawyer pleads with the jury for the life
of a slum boy on a murder charge.
Smartly-made but empty melodrama making
facile social points.

w Daniel Taradash, John Monks Jnr, *novel*
Willard Motley *d* Nicholas Ray *ph* Burnett
Guffey *m* George Antheil

Humphrey Bogart, John Derek, George
Macready, Allene Roberts

Knock on Wood**
US 1954   103m   Technicolor
Paramount (Norman Panama, Melvin Frank)

Stolen plans are hidden inside the dummy of an
unsuspecting ventriloquist.
Excellent star comedy with good script and
production (but some strange ideas of London's
geography).

wd Norman Panama, Melvin Frank ph Daniel
Fapp *songs* Sylvia Fine *m* Leith Stevens
ch Michael Kidd

Danny Kaye, Mai Zetterling, David Burns,
Torin Thatcher, Leon Askin, Abner Biberman,
Steve Geray

AAN: Norman Panama, Melvin Frank (script)

Knute Rockne, All American
US 1940   98m   bw
Warner (Robert Fellows)

The career of a famous Notre Dame football
coach.
Standard sporting biopic.

w Robert Buckner *d* Lloyd Bacon *ph* Tony
Gaudio

Pat O'Brien, Ronald Reagan, Gale Page,
Donald Crisp, Albert Basserman, John Qualen,
John Sheffield

Kongo
US 1932   86m   bw
MGM

An embittered African recluse takes revenge on the daughter of his former enemy.

No-holds-barred melodrama which never really exerts the right grip; a remake of the Lon Chaney silent *West of Zanzibar*.

w Leon Gordon, *play* Chester de Vonde, Kilbourn Gordon *d* William Cowen *ph* Harold Rosson

Walter Huston, Lupe Velez, Virginia Bruce, Conrad Nagel, C. Henry Gordon

Kotch*
US 1971 114m Metrocolor
ABC / Kotch Company (Richard Carter)

An eccentric 72-year-old widower is at odds with his family and helps a pregnant babysitter.

Variously amusing, moving and sentimental, this generally likeable film about a crotchety grandpa is sustained by its star performance.

w John Paxton, *novel* Katherine Topkins *d* Jack Lemmon *ph* Richard H. Kline *m* Marvin Hamlisch

Walter Matthau, Deborah Watts, Felicia Farr, Charles Aidman

AAN: Walter Matthau; song 'Life Is What You Make It' (*m* Marvin Hamlisch, *ly* Johnny Mercer)

Krakatoa, East of Java
US 1968 136m Technicolor Cinerama
ABC / Cinerama (Lester A. Sansom)

In 1883 the SS *Batavia Queen* leaves Singapore and is engulfed by the Krakatoa eruption.

Mindless spectacular, technically quite impressive but with no dramatic interest whatsoever.

w Clifford Newton Gould, Bernard Gordon *d* Bernard Kowalski *ph* Manuel Berenguer *m* Frank de Vol *pd/sp* Eugene Lourié

Maximilian Schell, Diane Baker, Brian Keith, Rossano Brazzi, Barbara Werle, John Leyton, Sal Mineo,
J. D. Cannon, Marc Lawrence

'Apparently designed to disprove the old adage, "they don't make them like that any more". At a conservative count it includes such sure-fire cinematic ingredients as hidden treasure, deep-sea divers with shattered lungs and claustrophobia, mutiny *and* fire on board ship, nuns, convicts, a lost orphan boy, girl divers and even a little striptease, climaxing in the biggest explosion and the greatest tidal wave known to history.'—*MFB*

The Kremlin Letter
US 1970 122m De Luxe Panavision
TCF (Carter de Haven, Sam Wiesenthal)

An American intelligence team is sent undercover to Moscow to retreive an arms treaty mistakenly signed.

Tediously violent cold war mystifier: a few good performances do not make it worth unravelling.

w John Huston, Gladys Hill, *novel* Noel Behn *d* John Huston *ph* Ted Scaife *m* Robert Drasnin *pd* Ted Haworth

Richard Boone, Orson Welles, Bibi Andersson, Max Von Sydow, Patrick O'Neal, Ronald Radd, George Sanders, Dean Jagger, Nigel Green, Barbara Parkins, Lila Kedrova, Michael MacLiammoir, Sandor Eles, Niall MacGinnis, John Huston

'One of those all-star international spy sagas that trick out an indecipherably tortuous plot with a series of vignettes in which the pleasures of star-spotting are expected to compensate for any narrative longueurs.'—*Nigel Andrews*

Kwaidan*
Japan 1964 164m Eastmancolor
  Tohoscope
Ninjin Club / Bungei

Four elegant ghost stories by Lafcadio Hearn.

Visually a superb production; all the stories have merit, but *en masse* prove a bit much at one sitting.

w Yoko Mizuki *d* Masaki Kobayashi *ph* Yoshio Miyajima *m* Toru Takemitsu *ad* Shigemasa Toda

Rentaro Mikuni, Ganjiro Nakamura, Katsuo Nakamura

L

The L-Shaped Room*

GB 1962 142m bw

British Lion / Romulus (James Woolf, Richard Attenborough)

A girl intending to have an abortion takes a room in a London suburban house which is none too clean but full of characters.

Watchable, mildly sensational low-life-melodrama of the pre-swinging London era when well-to-dos thought it amusing to live in garrets. Hellishly overlong but enjoyable in patches because of the professionalism with which it is made.

w Bryan Forbes, *novel* Lynne Reid Banks
d Bryan Forbes ph Douglas Slocombe
m Brahms, John Barry

Leslie Caron, Tom Bell, *Brock Peters, Cicely Courtneidge,* Bernard Lee, *Avis Bunnage, Patricia Phoenix, Emlyn Williams*

'It would be hard to imagine a more unlikely, or commercially more sure-fire group of lodgers living under a single roof than this pregnant French girl, maladjusted negro, lesbian actress, couple of prostitutes, and unpublished writer who finally commits it all to paper—shades of *I Am a Camera* as well as *A Taste of Honey*.'— *MFB*

AAN: Leslie Caron

Laburnum Grove**

GB 1936 73m bw

ATP (Basil Dean)

A suburban father reveals he is a forger. Agreeable worm-turns comedy melodrama, much copied since.

w Gordon Wellesley, Anthony Kimmins, *play J. B. Priestley* d Carol Reed

Cedric Hardwicke, Edmund Gwenn, Victoria Hopper, Ethel Coleridge, Katie Johnson, Francis James

'Here at last is an English film one can unreservedly praise.'—*Graham Greene*

The Lacemaker

France / Switzerland / West Germany 1977
107m Eastmancolor

Action / FR3 / Citel / Janus (Yves Gasser)

original title: *La Dentellière*

An 18-year-old girl becomes ill and withdrawn when her first affair breaks up.

Careful social character study, witty and observant but in memory insufficiently differentiated from numerous exploitation pieces with similar plots.

w Pascal Lainé, Claude Goretta, *novel* Pascal Lainé d Claude Goretta ph Jean Boffety
m Pierre Jansen

Isabelle Huppert, Yves Beneyton, Florence Giorgetti, Anne Marie Düringer

Ladies Courageous

US 1944 88m bw

Universal (Walter Wanger)

Girls ferry war planes from base to base for the USAF. Absolutely predictable propaganda potboiler.

w Norman Reilly Raine, Doris Gilbert d John Rawlins ph Hal Mohr

Loretta Young, Geraldine Fitzgerald, Diana Barrymore, Evelyn Ankers, Anne Gwynne, Philip Terry, David Bruce, Lois Collier, Samuel S. Hinds

Ladies in Love*

US 1936 97m bw

TCF (B. G. De Sylva)

Man-hunting girls in Budapest form a joint plan. Amusing romantic nonsense.

w Melville Baker, *play* Ladislaus Bus-Fekete
d Edward H. Griffith ph Hal Mohr md Louis Silvers

Janet Gaynor, Loretta Young, Constance Bennett, Simone Simon, Don Ameche, Paul Lukas, Tyrone Power, Alan Mowbray, Wilfred Lawson, J. Edward Bromberg, Virginia Field

Ladies in Retirement**

US 1941 92m bw

Columbia

A housekeeper murders her employer for the sake of her two mentally disturbed sisters. Splendidly effective Grand Guignol, from a well-written play but filmically quite interesting. Remade with lots of gore as *The Mad Room* (qv).

w Reginald Denham, Edward Percy, Garrett Fort, *play* Reginald Denham, Edward Percy *d Charles Vidor ph* George Barnes *m* Ernst Toch

Ida Lupino, Louis Hayward, Isobel Elsom, Edith Barrett, Elsa Lanchester, Emma Dunn

AAN: Ernst Toch

Ladies Love Brutes
US 1930   83m   bw
Paramount

A gangster tries to improve himself to marry a socialite.

Uneasy comedy-drama with good moments.

w Waldemar Young, Herman J. Mankiewicz, *play* Pardon My Glove by Zoe Akins *d* Rowland V. Lee *ph* Harry Fischbeck

George Bancroft, Mary Astor, Fredric March, Margaret Quimby, Stanley Fields

Ladies' Man*
US 1931   70m   bw
Paramount

A man of the world preys successfully on rich women until one grows jealous when her daughter falls for him.

Vivid, hard melodrama showing the blacker side of early thirties high society living.

w Herman J. Mankiewicz d Lothar Mendes *ph* Victor Milner

William Powell, Kay Francis, Carole Lombard, Gilbert Emery, Olive Tell

Ladies' Man
US 1961   106m   Technicolor
Paramount / York (Jerry Lewis)

The adventures of an accident-prone houseboy at a Hollywood hotel for aspiring actresses.

Hit-or-miss collection of comic scraps which might have benefited from being put together on a less grandiose scale.

w Jerry Lewis, Bill Richmond *Jerry Lewis m* Walter Scharf

Jerry Lewis, Helen Traubel, Jack Kruschen, Doodles Weaver, Gloria Jean

'Regression into infantilism cannot be carried much further than this.'—*MFB*

Ladies of the Big House
US 1931   77m   bw
Paramount

A married couple are framed on a murder charge and sent to prison.

Melodramatic nonsense in the wake of *The Big House.*

w Louis Weitzenkorn *d* Marion Gering *ph* David Abel

Sylvia Sidney, Gene Raymond, Wynne Gibson, Rockcliffe Fellows, Earle Foxe

Ladies Should Listen
US 1934   63m   bw
Paramount (Douglas MacLean)

A knowledgeable switchboard operator helps a financier with his problems.

Moderately beguiling, instantly forgettable romantic frou-frou.

w Claude Binyon, Frank Butler, Guy Bolton *d* Frank Tuttle *ph* Harry Sharp

Cary Grant, Frances Drake, Edward Everett Horton, Rosita Morena, George Barbier, Nydia Westman, Charles Ray

Ladies They Talk About*
US 1933   69m   bw
Warner

Trouble in a women's prison.

Entertaining comedy-melodrama which had some brushes with the Hays Office because of its frankly man-hungry characters.

w Sidney Sutherland, Brown Holmes, *play* Women in Prison by Dorothy Mackaye, Carlton Miles *d* Howard Bretherton, William Keighley *ph* John Seitz

Barbara Stanwyck, Lyle Talbot, Preston Foster, Dorothy Burgess, Lillian Roth, Maude Eburne, Ruth Donnelly, Harold Huber

Ladies Who Do
GB 1963   85m   bw
British Lion / Bryanston / Fanfare (George H. Brown)

Charladies form a successful company from tips they salvage from wastepaper baskets.

Mild farce sustained by familiar actors.

w Michael Pertwee *d* C. M. Pennington-Richards *ph* Geoffrey Faithfull *m* Ron Goodwin

Peggy Mount, Miriam Karlin, Robert Morley, Harry H. Corbett, Dandy Nichols

The Lady and the Mob
US 1939   65m   bw
Columbia (Fred Kohlmar)

A lady bank owner menaced by gangsters forms her own mob.

Weak comedy.

w Richard Maibaum, Gertrude Purcell *d* Ben Stoloff *ph* John Stumar

Fay Bainter, Ida Lupino, Lee Bowman, Henry Armetta, Warren Hymer, Harold Huber

The Lady and the Monster
US 1944   86m   bw
Republic (George Sherman)
aka: *Tiger Man*
GB title: *The Lady and the Doctor*

A scientist keeps alive the brain of a mortally injured financier, and it comes to dominate him.
Fair, over-padded version of a much filmed thriller (see also *Donovan's Brain, Vengeance*).

w Dane Lussier, Frederick Kohner, *novel* Donovan's Brain by Curt Siodmak *d* George Sherman *ph* John Alton *m* Walter Scharf

Erich Von Stroheim, Richard Arlen, Vera Hruba Ralston, Mary Nash, Sidney Blackmer, Helen Vinson

Lady and the Tramp**
US 1955   76m   Technicolor
Cinemascope
Walt Disney (Erdmann Penner)

A pedigree spaniel falls foul of two stray cats and has a romantic adventure with a mongrel who helps her.
Pleasant cartoon feature in Disney's cutest and most anthropomorphic vein.

d Hamilton Luske, Clyde Geronomi, Wilfred Jackson *m* Oliver Wallace

Lady Be Good*
US 1941   111m   bw
MGM (Arthur Freed)

Married songwriters produce a musical.
Thin musical with good talent and tunes; very little connection with the 1924 musical show.

w Jack McGowan, Kay Van Riper, John McClain *d* Norman Z. McLeod *ph* George J. Folsey, Oliver T. Marsh *songs* various

Eleanor Powell, Robert Young, Ann Sothern, Red Skelton, Dan Dailey, Virginia O'Brien, Reginald Owen, John Carroll, Lionel Barrymore, Jimmy Dorsey and his Orchestra

AA: song 'The Last Time I Saw Paris'
(*m* Jerome Kern, *ly* Oscar Hammerstein II)

Lady By Choice*
US 1934   78m   bw
Columbia

A publicity-mad dancer adopts an old rummy as a Mother's Day stunt.
Amusing sentimental comedy in the wake of *Lady for A Day*.

w Jo Swerling, Dwight Taylor *d* David Burton *ph* Ted Tetzlaff

Carole Lombard, May Robson, Walter Connolly, Roger Pryor, Arthur Hohl, Raymond Walburn, James Burke, Henry Kolker

Lady Caroline Lamb*
GB 1972   123m   Eastmancolor
Panavision
EMI / GEC / Pulsar / Video Cinematographica
(Fernando Ghia)

In 1805, impulsive Lady Caroline Ponsonby marries William Lamb, later Lord Melbourne, and then disgraces him by her wildness.
Pale, disappointing historical fiction with good spots but no reverence for fact; slackly written and handled, and not helped by the wide screen.

wd Robert Bolt *ph* Oswald Morris *m* Richard Rodney Bennett *ad* Carmen Dillon

Sarah Miles, Jon Finch, Richard Chamberlain (as Byron), Margaret Leighton, John Mills (as Cobbett), *Ralph Richardson* (as George III), *Laurence Olivier* (as Wellington)

Lady Chatterley's Lover
France 1955   101m / 84m (English version)
bw
Regie du Film / Orsay Film (Gilbert Cohen-Séat)

The wife of a crippled and impotent mine-owner has an affair with a coarse gamekeeper and enjoys it.
Hilariously-po-faced transcription of a notorious novel, of no cinematic interest whatever.

w Gaston Bonheur, Philippe de Rothschild, Marc Allégret, *novel* D. H. Lawrence *d* Marc Allégret *ph* Georges Périnal *m* Joseph Kosma

Danielle Darrieux, Leo Genn, Erno Crisa

The Lady Consents
US 1936   76m   bw
RKO (Edward Kaufman)

When a doctor's wife sees that he is in love with another woman, she makes it easy for him to get a divorce; but he finally comes back to her.
Unbelievable matinée drama for star fans.

w P. J. Wolfson, Anthony Veiller, *play* The Indestructible Mrs Talbot by P. J. Wolfson *d* Stephen Roberts *ph* J. Roy Hunt

Ann Harding, Herbert Marshall, Margaret Lindsay, Walter Abel, Edward Ellis, Hobart Cavanaugh, Ilka Chase

The Lady Eve***
US 1941   97m   bw
Paramount (Paul Jones)

A lady cardsharper and her father are outsmarted on a transatlantic liner by a millionaire simpleton; she plans an elaborate revenge.

Hectic romantic farce, the first to show its director's penchant for mixing up sexual innuendo, funny men and pratfalls. There are moments when the pace drops, but in general it's scintillating entertainment, especially after viewing its weak remake *The Birds and the Bees* (qv).

wd Preston Sturges, play Monckton Hoffe *ph* Victor Milner *m* Leo Shuken, Charles Bradshaw

Barbara Stanwyck, Henry Fonda, Charles Coburn, Eugène Pallette, William Demarest, Eric Blore, Melville Cooper, Martha O'Driscoll, Janet Beecher, Robert Greig, Luis Alberni, Jimmy Conlin

'The whole theme, with all its variations of keys, is played to one end, to get laughs, and at several different levels it gets them.'—*National Board of Review*

'Preston Sturges, they tell me, is known in Hollywood as "the streamlined Lubitsch". This needn't put you off, because if he goes on producing films as lively as this one he will one day come to be known as Preston Sturges.'—*William Whitebait*

'This time Preston Sturges has wrapped you up another package that is neither very big nor very flashy, but the best fun in months.'—*Otis Ferguson*

'A mixture of visual and verbal slapstick, of high artifice and pratfalls . . . it represents the dizzy high point of Sturges' writing.'—*New Yorker, 1977*

AAN: Monckton Hoffe (original story)

Lady for a Day***
US 1933 95m bw
Columbia

Gangsters help an old apple seller to pose as a rich woman when her daughter visits.
Splendid sentimental comedy full of cinematic resource; the best translation of Runyon to the screen.

w Robert Riskin, story Madame La Gimp by Damon Runyon *d Frank Capra ph* Joseph Walker

May Robson, Warren William, Guy Kibbee, Glenda Farrell, Ned Sparks, Jean Parker, Walter Connolly, Nat Pendleton

AAN: best picture; Robert Riskin; Frank Capra; May Robson

Lady for a Night
US 1941 87m bw
Republic (Albert J. Cohen)

The lady owner of a gambling boat determines to break into society.
Moderate period comedy with a belated murder plot.

w Isabel Dawn, Boyce DeGaw *d* Leigh Jason *ph* Norbert Brodine *m* David Buttolph

Joan Blondell, John Wayne, Ray Middleton, Philip Merivale, Blanche Yurka, Edith Barrett, Leonid Kinskey, Montagu Love

The Lady from Cheyenne
US 1949 87m bw
Universal (Frank Lloyd)

In 1860 Wyoming, a schoolmistress fights for women's rights.
Mild western star romance.

w Kathryn Scola, Warren Duff *d* Frank Lloyd *ph* Milton Krasner *m* Frank Skinner

Loretta Young, Robert Preston, Gladys George, Edward Arnold, Frank Craven, Jessie Ralph, Spencer Charters, Alan Bridge

Lady from Louisiana
US 1941 84m bw
Republic (Bernard Vorhaus)

In old Mississippi, a lottery-owner's daughter falls in love with a lawyer employed to make her father's business illegal.
Curious pot-boiler containing everything but the kitchen stove, including murder and a raging storm.

w Vera Caspary, Guy Endore, Michael Hogan *d* Bernard Vorhaus *ph* Jack Marta *m* Cy Feuer

John Wayne, Ona Munson, Ray Middleton, Henry Stephenson, Helen Westley, Dorothy Dandridge, Jack Pennick

The Lady from Shanghai**
US 1948 87m bw
Columbia (Richard Wilson, William Castle)

A seaman becomes involved in the maritime wanderings of a crippled lawyer and his homicidal frustrated wife.
Absurd, unintelligible, plainly much cut and rearranged, this thriller was obviously left too much in Welles' hands and then just as unfairly taken out of them; but whole sequences of sheer brilliance remain, notably the final shoot-out in the hall of mirrors.

wd Orson Welles, novel If I Die Before I Wake by Sherwood King *ph Charles Lawton Jnr m* Heinz Roemheld

Orson Welles, Rita Hayworth, *Everett Sloane, Glenn Anders,* Ted de Corsia, Erskine Sanford, Gus Schilling

'The slurred social conscience of the hero

leads him to some murky philosophizing, all of which with many individualities of diction clog the issue and the sound track. Sub-titles, I fear, would have helped.'—*Richard Winnington*

The Lady Gambles

US 1949 99m bw
U-I (Michael Kraike)

A happy woman destroys her marriage when she becomes addicted to gambling.
Boring, overwrought, underplotted fiction for women.

w Lewis Meltzer, Oscar Saul *d* Michael Gordon *ph* Russell Metty *m* Frank Skinner

Barbara Stanwyck, Robert Preston, Stephen McNally, Edith Barrett, John Hoyt
  'A kind of *Lost Weekend* of the gaming tables.'—*Ella Smith*

Lady Godiva

US 1955 89m Technicolor
U-I (Robert Arthur)

Lord Leofric tames a Saxon shrew but she suspects his motives and rides naked through the streets of Coventry to prove the loyalty of the Saxons.
Comic strip historical legend, reliably turned out for midwestern family audiences.

w Oscar Brodney, Harry Ruskin *d* Arthur Lubin *m* Joseph Gershenson

George Nader, Maureen O'Hara, Vic Morrow, Eduard Franz, Torin Thatcher

Lady Godiva Rides Again

GB 1951 90m bw
British Lion / London Films / Sidney Gilliat, Frank Launder

A waitress wins a local beauty contest and becomes a charm school starlet and later a stripteaser.
Disappointing satirical comedy with good credentials.

w Frank Launder, Val Valentine *d* Frank Launder *ph* Wilkie Cooper *m* William Alwyn

Pauline Stroud, Stanley Holloway, Diana Dors, Alastair Sim, George Cole, Dennis Price, John McCallum, Bernadette O'Farrell, Kay Kendall, Dora Bryan

The Lady Has Plans

US 1942 77m bw
Paramount (Fred Kohlmar)

A lady reporter in Lisbon is mistaken for a Nazi spy.
Competent fluff which veers between comedy and melodrama.

w Harry Tugend *d* Sidney Lanfield *ph* Charles Lang

Paulette Goddard, Ray Milland, Albert Dekker, Roland Young, Margaret Hayes, Cecil Kellaway, Addison Richards, Edward Norris

Lady Ice

US 1973 92m Technicolor Panavision
Tomorrow Entertainment (Harrison Starr)

An insurance investigator steals a diamond and goes into partnership with a gangster's daughter.
Unamusing Miami-based thriller.

w Alan Trustman, Harold Clemins *d* Tom Gries *ph* Lucien Ballard *m* Perry Botkin Jnr

Donald Sutherland, Jennifer O'Neil, Robert Duvall, Patrick Magee

Lady in a Cage

US 1964 97m bw
American Entertainments Corp. (Luther Davis)

A rich widow is trapped by roving marauders in her private elevator.
Unpleasant and boring suspenser with nasty details.

w Luther Davis *d* Walter Grauman *ph* Lee Garmes *m* Paul Glass *pd* Rudolf Sternad

Olivia de Havilland, James Caan, Ann Sothern, Jeff Corey
  'The film parades its pretensions on a note of high-pitched hysteria.'—*MFB*

Lady in Cement

US 1968 93m De Luxe Panavision
TCF / Arcola / Millfield (Aaron Rosenberg)

A Florida private eye on his morning swim finds a dead blonde.
Routine private eye stuff with fashionable sex and violence added.

w Marvin H. Albert, Jack Guss *d* Gordon Douglas *ph* Joseph Biroc *m* Hugo Montenegro

Frank Sinatra, Raquel Welch, Richard Conte, Martin Gabel, Lainie Kazan, Pat Henry, Steve Peck
  'While *Tony Rome* seemed to herald a return to the forties thriller, *Lady in Cement* marks nothing more exciting than a return to *Tony Rome*.'—*MFB*

The Lady in Question*

US 1940 81m bw
Columbia

A Parisian shopkeeper on a jury is responsible for getting a girl acquitted of a murder charge, but begins to worry when his son falls in love with her.

Stagey but quite satisfying Hollywood remake of the French drama *Gribouille,* with Raimy and Michele Morgan.

w Lewis Meltzer, *story* Marcel Achard *d* Charles Vidor *ph* Lucien Andriot *m* Lucien Moraweck

Brian Aherne, Rita Hayworth, Glenn Ford, Irene Rich, George Coulouris, Lloyd Corrigan, Evelyn Keyes, Edward Norris, Curt Bois, Frank Reicher

The Lady in the Car with Glasses and a Gun
France / US 1969   105m   Eastmancolor Panavision
Lira Film / Columbia (Anatole Litvak)

An English secretary in Paris decides to drive to the coast but has various adventures which make her believe she is either mad or amnesiac.
Muddled, tedious suspenser with a totally implausible 'explanation'.

w Richard Harris, Eleanor Perry *d* Anatole Litvak *ph* Claude Renoir *m* Michel Legrand

Samantha Eggar, Oliver Reed, John McEnery, Stéphane Audran

Lady in the Dark**
US 1944   100m   Technicolor
Paramount (Richard Blumenthal)

The editress of a fashion magazine is torn between three men, has worrying dreams, and takes herself to a psychoanalyst.
Lush, stylish and frequently amusing version of a Broadway musical, lacking most of the songs; despite its faults, an excellent example of studio spectacle and a very typical forties romantic comedy.

w Frances Goodrich, Albert Hackett, *play* Moss Hart *d Mitchell Leisen ph Ray Rennahan m Kurt Weill ly* Ira Gershwin *md* Robert Emmett Dolan *sp* Gordon Jennings *ad Hans Dreier*

Ginger Rogers, Warner Baxter, Ray Milland, Jon Hall, *Mischa Auer,* Mary Phillips, Barry Sullivan

AAN: Ray Rennahan; Robert Emmett Dolan

Lady in the Lake*
US 1947   103m   bw
MGM (George Haight)

A private eye is assigned to find a missing wife . . .
Complex private eye yarn which makes the original Chandler dialogue sound childish by over-reliance on the subjective camera method: we see the hero's face only when he looks in a

mirror. An experiment that failed because it was not really understood.

w Steve Fisher, *novel* Raymond Chandler *d* Robert Montgomery *ph* Paul C. Vogel *m* David Snell

Robert Montgomery, Audrey Totter, Lloyd Nolan, Tom Tully, Leon Ames

Lady in the Morgue*
US 1938   70m   bw
Universal (Irving Starr)
GB title: *The Case of the Missing Blonde*

A private eye investigates a suicide and finds three murders.
Bright second feature thriller produced under the Crime Club banner.

w Eric Taylor, Robertson White, *novel* Jonathan Latimer *d Otis Garrett ph* Stanley Cortez *md* Charles Previn

Preston Foster, Frank Jenks, Patricia Ellis, Barbara Pepper, Thomas Jackson, Gordon Elliott

The Lady Is a Square
GB 1958   99m   bw
ABP / Wilcox–Neagle

An impoverished socialite widow tries to keep her husband's symphony orchestra going and is helped by a pop singer.
Strained attempt to carry on the *Spring in Park Lane* tradition, with a few inspirations from Joe Pasternak and *One Hundred Men and a Girl.* Earnest performances, obvious jokes.

w Harold Purcell, Pamela Bower, Nicholas Phipps *d* Herbert Wilcox *ph* Gordon Dines *md* Wally Stott

Anna Neagle, Frankie Vaughan, Anthony Newley, Janette Scott, Wilfrid Hyde White

The Lady Is Willing
US 1942   91m   bw
Columbia (Mitchell Leisen)

A musical comedy star adopts a baby and falls in love with its pediatrician.
Dull mixture of light drama and heavy comedy, with all concerned ill at ease.

w James Edward Grant, Albert McCleery *d* Mitchell Leisen *ph* Ted Tetzlaff *m* W. Frank Harling

Marlene Dietrich, Fred MacMurray, Aline MacMahon, Stanley Ridges, Arline Judge, Marietta Canty

Lady Killer***
US 1933   76m   bw
Warner (Henry Blanke)

A cinema usher turns to crime, flees to
Hollywood, and becomes a movie star.
Hectic slam-bang action comedy with
melodramatic moments. Great fun.

w Ben Markson, *novel* The Finger Man by
Rosalind Keating Shaffer d Roy del Ruth
ph Tony Gaudio md Leo F. Forbstein

James Cagney, Mae Clarke, Leslie Fenton,
Margaret Lindsay, Henry O'Neill, Willard
Robertson, Raymond Hatton, Russell Hopton
  'A kind of résumé of everything he has done to
date in the movies.'—*New York Evening Post*

Lady L
France / Italy / US 1965   124m
  Eastmancolor   Panavision
Concordia / Champion / MGM (Carlo Ponti)

An 80-year-old lady recalls her romantic life
from her youth as a Paris laundress.
Unhappy, lumbering, styleless attempt to
recapture several old forms, indifferently though
expensively made and acted.

wd Peter Ustinov, *novel* Romain Gary ph Henri
Alekan m Jean Françaix ad Jean D'Eaubonne,
Auguste Capelier

Sophia Loren, David Niven, Paul Newman,
Peter Ustinov, Claude Dauphin, Philippe Noiret,
Michel Piccoli, Marcel Dalio, Cecil Parker,
Eugène Deckers

Lady Luck
US 1946   97m   bw
RKO (Warren Duff)

The daughter of a long line of ill-fated gamblers
marries one and tries to reform him, but the
reverse happens.
Tedious comedy drama.

w Lynn Root, Frank Fenton d Edwin L. Marin
ph Lucien Andriot m Leigh Harline

Robert Young, Barbara Hale, Frank Morgan,
James Gleason, Don Rice, Harry Davenport,
Lloyd Corrigan

Lady of Burlesque*
US 1943   91m   bw
Hunt Stromberg
GB title: *Striptease Lady*

A burlesque dancer solves a number of
backstage murders.
Agreeable murder mystery with strong
injections of comedy.

w James Gunn, *novel* The G-String Murders by
Gypsy Rose Lee d William A. Wellman
ph Robert de Grasse m Arthur Lange

Barbara Stanwyck, Michael O'Shea, J. Edward
Bromberg, Iris Adrian, Gloria Dickson, Charles
Dingle

AAN: Arthur Lange

Lady of the Tropics
US 1939   92m   bw
MGM (Sam Zimbalist)

An American playboy in Saigon marries a half-
caste girl but her former admirer prevents her
from getting a passport.
Interminable romantic melodrama with stars
apparently straight from the taxidermist.

w Ben Hecht d Jack Conway ph George
Folsey m Franz Waxman

Robert Taylor, Hedy Lamarr, Joseph
Schildkraut, Gloria Franklin, Ernest Cossart

Lady on a Train*
US 1945   84m   bw
Universal (Felix Jackson)

A girl arriving in New York by train sees a
murder committed and can't make anyone
believe her.
Cheerful mystery which starts in the right spirit
but does not progress too satisfactorily.

w Edmund Beloin, Robert O'Brien, *novel* Leslie
Charteris d Charles David m Miklos Rozsa

Deanna Durbin, Ralph Bellamy, David Bruce,
Edward Everett Horton, George Coulouris,
Allen Jenkins, Dan Duryea, Patricia Morison

Lady Possessed
US 1952   86m   bw
Republic / Portland (James Mason)

An unbalanced woman imagines she is destined
to take the place of a pianist's dead wife.
Weary melodramatic nonsense dating from
Hollywood's first obsession with psychiatry.

w Pamela Kellino, James Mason, *novel* Del
Palma by Pamela Kellino d William Spier, Roy
Kellino ph Karl Struss m Nathan Scott

James Mason, June Havoc, Stephen Dunne, Fay
Compton, Pamela Kellino, Steven Geray

Lady Scarface
US 1941   69m   bw
RKO (Cliff Reid)

A police lieutenant captures a dangerous female
gangster.
Weird gangster second feature with too many
domestic comedy asides; notable only for the
appearance in it of its dignified lead, fresh from
Rebecca.

w Armand D'Usseau, Richard Collins d Frank
Woodruff ph Nicholas Musuraca

Judith Anderson, Dennis O'Keefe, Frances
Neal, Mildred Coles, Eric Blore, Marc Lawrence

Lady Sings the Blues **
US 1972   144m   Eastmancolor
Panavision
Paramount / Motown / Weston / Furie (Jay
Weston, James S. White)

The disastrous private life of blues singer Billie
Holliday.
Old-fashioned showbiz biopic with new-
fashioned drugs, sex and squalor.

w Terence McCloy, Chris Clark, Suzanne de
Passe d Sidney J. Furie ph John Alonzo
m Michel Legrand md Gil Askey

Diana Ross, Billy Dee Williams, Richard Pryor,
James Callahan, Sid Melton

AAN: script; Gil Askey; Diana Ross

A Lady Takes a Chance
US 1943   86m   bw
RKO (Frank Ross)
aka: The Cowboy and the Girl

A New York office girl on holiday in Oregon falls
for a rodeo rider.
Slender star action romance.

w Robert Ardrey d William A. Seiter ph Frank
Redman m Roy Webb

Jean Arthur, John Wayne, Charles Winninger,
Phil Silvers, Mary Field, Don Costello, John
Philliber, Grady Sutton, Hans Conried

A Lady to Love
US 1930   92m   bw
MGM

An ageing grape grower spots an attractive
waitress, sends her a marriage proposal by mail,
but encloses a photo of his handsome foreman.
Rather primitive but well acted version of a
subject later filmed more fluently under the title
of the original play.

w Sidney Howard, from his play They Knew
What They Wanted d Victor Seastrom
ph Merritt B. Gerstad

Edward G. Robinson, Vilma Banky, Robert
Ames, Richard Carle

The Lady Vanishes ****
GB 1938   97m   bw
Gaumont British (Edward Black)

En route back to England by train from
Switzerland, an old lady disappears and two
young people investigate.
The disappearing lady trick brilliantly
refurbished by Hitchcock and his screenwriters,
who even get away with a horrid model shot at

the beginning. Superb, suspenseful, brilliantly
funny, meticulously detailed entertainment.

w Sidney Gilliat, Frank Launder, novel The
Wheel Spins by Ethel Lina White d Alfred
Hitchcock ph Jack Cox md Louis Levy

Margaret Lockwood, Michael Redgrave, Dame
May Whitty, Paul Lukas, Basil Radford,
Naunton Wayne, Catherine Lacey, Cecil
Parker, Linden Travers, Googie Withers, Mary
Clare, Philip Leaver

'If it were not so brilliant a melodrama, we
should class it as a brilliant comedy.'—Frank S.
Nugent

'No one can study the deceptive effortlessness
with which one thing leads to another without
learning where the true beauty of this medium is
to be mined.'—Otis Ferguson
† Hitchcock was actually second choice as
director. The production was ready to roll as
Lost Lady, directed by Roy William Neill, with
Charter and Caldicott already in place, when
Neill became unavailable and Hitch stepped in.

Lady Windermere's Fan *
US 1925   80m (24 fps)   bw   silent
Warner

The mysterious Mrs Erlynne almost causes a
scandal in London society.
Oscar Wilde's play transposed to the twenties,
with the Lubitsch touch daringly displacing
Wildean epigrams. Still more amusing than the
sound remake, The Fan.

w Julien Josephson d Ernst Lubitsch
ph Charles Van Enger

Ronald Colman, May McAvoy, Irene Rich, Bert
Lytell, Edward Martindel

'Lubitsch's best silent film, full of incisive
details, discreet touches, nuances of gestures,
where behaviour betrays the character and
discloses the sentiment of the personages.'—
Georges Sadoul

The Lady with a Lamp *
GB 1951   110m   bw
British Lion / Imperadio (Herbert Wilcox)

The life of Florence Nightingale and her work in
reforming the nursing service in 19th-century
England.
Solid biopic, not quite in accord with history.

w Warren Chetham Strode, play Reginald
Berkeley d Herbert Wilcox ph Max Greene
m Anthony Collins ad William C. Andrews

Anna Neagle, Michael Wilding, Gladys Young,
Felix Aylmer, Julian D'Albie, Arthur Young,
Edwin Styles, Barbara Couper, Cecil Trouncer,
Rosalie Crutchley

'A slow, sedate, refined chronicle . . . Herbert

Wilcox is a good deal more at ease with the balls and dinners, than with anything that happens later.'—*Penelope Houston*

'It may please fans of Anna Neagle and Michael Wilding, but not fans of Florence Nightingale.'—*Richard Mallett, Punch*

Lady with a Past*
US 1932 80m bw
RKO (Charles R. Rogers)
GB title: *Reputation*

A wealthy but shy girl almost accidentally finds herself with a reputation as a scarlet woman, and the men flock around her.
Moderately enjoyable star comedy drama.

w Horace Jackson, *novel* Harriet Henry *d* Edward H. Griffith *ph* Hal Mohr *m* Max Steiner

Constance Bennett, Ben Lyon, David Manners, Astrid Allwyn, Merna Kennedy, Blanche Frederici, Nella Walker

Lady with Red Hair*
US 1940 78m bw
Warner (Edmund Grainger)

The life of actress Mrs Leslie Carter and her association with impresario David Belasco.
Mildly interesting but unsatisfying biopic of a lady scarcely remembered.

w Charles Kenyon, Milton Krims, N. Brewster Morse, Norbert Faulkner *d* Curtis Bernhardt *ph* Arthur Edeson *m* Heinz Roemheld

Miriam Hopkins, Claude Rains, Richard Ainley, John Litel, Laura Hope Crews, Helen Wesley, Mona Barrie, Victor Jory, Cecil Kellaway, Fritz Leiber, Halliwell Hobbes

The Lady with the Little Dog*
USSR 1959 90m bw
Lenfilm
original title: *Dama s Sobachkoi*

In Yalta at the turn of the century, an unhappily married woman and a married man start an affair which lasts secretly over the years.
Modestly pleasing, subtly acted anecdote.

wd Josef Heifits, story Anton Chekhov *ph* Andrei Moskvin, D. Meschiev *m* Jiri Sternwald

Ya Savvina, Alexei Batalov, Ala Chostakova

A Lady without Passport*
US 1950 84m bw
MGM (Samuel Marx)

A secret service undercover man tracks down aliens being smuggled into the US, and falls in love with one of them.

Routine material, very well handled.

w Howard Dimsdale *d Joseph H. Lewis* *ph* Paul C. Vogel *m* David Raksin

Hedy Lamarr, John Hodiak, James Craig, George Macready, Steve Geray

The Ladykillers*
GB 1955 97m Technicolor
Ealing (Seth Holt)

An old lady takes in a sinister lodger, who with his four friends commits a robbery. When she finds out, they plot to kill her, but are hoist with their own petards.
Overrated comedy in poor colour; those who made it quite clearly think it funnier than it is.

w William Rose *d* Alexander Mackendrick *ph* Otto Heller *m* Tristam Cary

Alec Guinness, *Katie Johnson*, Peter Sellers, Cecil Parker, Herbert Lom, Danny Green, Jack Warner, Frankie Howerd, Kenneth Connor

AAN: William Rose

A Lady's Morals
US 1930 75m bw
MGM
GB title: *Jenny Lind*

The 'Swedish nightingale' learns that love is more important than a singing career.
Cliché-strewn romance with music.

w Hans Kraly, Claudine West, John Meehan, Arthur Richman *d* Sidney Franklin

Grace Moore, Reginald Denny, Wallace Beery, Jobyna Howland

Lafayette
France / Italy 1961 158m Super
   Technirama 70
Copernic / Cosmos (Maurice Jacquin)

French officers help America in the revolutionary war of 1776.
Nerveless international epic, interesting only for its star cameos.

w Jean-Bernard Luc, Suzanne Arduini, Jacques Sigurd, François Ponthier, Jean Dréville, Maurice Jacquin *d* Jean Dréville *ph* Claude Renoir, Roger Hubert *m* Steve Laurent, Pierre Duclos

Michel Le Royer, Jack Hawkins, Orson Welles, Howard St John, Vittorio de Sica, Edmund Purdom, Jacques Castelot, Folco Lulli

'It looks, sounds and smells like nothing so much as the same old indigestible, ill-dubbed, co-produced continental spectaculars which have already turned the stomach in a whole range of lesser screen ratios.'—*MFB*

Lafayette Escadrille
US 1957   93m   bw
Warner (William Wellman)
GB title: *Hell Bent for Glory*

Early in World War I, a young American joins
the French air force.
The director's valedictory film, on a subject close
to his heart, is a curiously disappointing, flat and
disjointed affair, partly salvaged by a good
period feel.

w A. S. Fleischmann *d* William A. Wellman
ph William Clothier *m* Leonard Rosenman

Tab Hunter, David Janssen, Clint Eastwood,
Will Hutchins, Paul Fix

The Lambeth Walk
GB 1939   84m   bw
CAPAD / Pinebrook (Anthony Havelock-
    Allan)

A cockney bloke inherits a dukedom.
Mild screen version of a popular musical play
and a song which became a nationwide hit.

w Clifford Grey, John Paddy Carstairs, Robert
Edmunds, *play* Me and My Girl by Louis Rose,
Douglas Furber, Noel Gay *d* Albert de
Courville

Lupino Lane, Sally Gray, Seymour Hicks, Enid
Stamp Taylor, Wilfrid Hyde White, Charles
Heslop, Norah Howard

The Lamp Still Burns
GB 1943   90m   bw
GFD / Two Cities (Leslie Howard)

Adventures of wartime probationary nurses.
Understated wartime morale-builder, no longer
very interesting.

w Elizabeth Baron, Roland Pertwee, *novel* One
Pair of Feet by Monica Dickens *d* Maurice
Elvey

Rosamund John, Stewart Granger, Godfrey
Tearle, Sophie Stewart, John Laurie, Margaret
Vyner, Cathleen Nesbitt, Joyce Grenfell

Lancelot and Guinevere*
GB 1962   117m   Eastmancolor
    Panavision
Emblem (Cornel Wilde)
US title: *Sword of Lancelot*

Sir Lancelot covets the wife of his beloved King
Arthur, but after Arthur's death she takes the
veil.
Decently made, rather tame transcription of the
legends, with all concerned doing quite
creditably but not brilliantly.

w Richard Schayer, Jefferson Pascal *d* Cornel
Wilde *ph* Harry Waxman *m* Ron Goodwin

Cornel Wilde, Jean Wallace, Brian Aherne,
George Baker, John Barrie

Lancer Spy*
US 1937   80m   bw
TCF

A German spy is captured and his English
double is sent back to replace him.
World War I yarn on the lines of *The Great
Impersonation* (qv). Excellent production and a
good beginning and end, but a slow middle.

w Philip Dunne, *novel* Marthe McKenna
d Gregory Ratoff *ph* Barney McGill *m* Arthur
Lange

George Sanders, Dolores del Rio, Peter Lorre,
Joseph Schildkraut, Virginia Field, Sig Rumann,
Fritz Feld

Land of the Pharaohs*
US 1955   105m   Warnercolor
    Cinemascope
Warner / Continental (Howard Hawks)

Pharaoh is obsessed with life after death and
builds a great pyramid for himself and his
treasures . . . but his wife is ambitious . . .
Unexpected, interesting excursion into Ancient
Egypt, distended by Cinemascope; basically a
macabre melodrama with a final spectacular
twist. The engineering details would make a
fascinating documentary.

w William Faulkner, Harry Kurnitz, H. Jack
Bloom *d* Howard Hawks *ph Lee Garmes,
Russell Harlan m Dmitri Tiomkin
ad Alexander Trauner*

Jack Hawkins, Joan Collins, Alexis Minotis,
James Robertson Justice, Sidney Chaplin

The Land That Time Forgot*
GB 1974   91m   Technicolor
Amicus (John Dark)

In 1916, survivors from a torpedoed supply ship
find themselves on a legendary island full of
prehistoric monsters.
Lively old-fashioned adventure fantasy with
good technical credits.

w James Cawthorne, Michael Moorcock, *novel*
Edgar Rice Burroughs *d* Kevin Connor
ph Alan Hume *m* Douglas Gamley *pd Maurice
Carter sp* Derek Meddings, Roger Dicken

Doug McClure, John McEnery, Susan
Penhaligon, Keith Barron, Anthony Ainley

The Land Unknown*
US 1957   78m   bw   Cinemascope
U-I (William Alland)

A plane is forced down into a strange Antarctic valley where dinosaurs still roam.
Efficient adventure fantasy on *King Kong* lines but without any of that film's panache.

w Laslo Gorog *d* Virgil Vogel *ph* Ellis Carter *m* Joseph Gershenson *sp* Roswell Hoffman, Fred Knoth, Orien Ernest, Jack Kevan

Jock Mahoney, Shawn Smith, William Reynolds, Henry Brandon

Land without Bread*
Spain 1932 27m bw
Ramon Acin
aka: *Las Hurdes*

A famous documentary showing the poorest region of northern Spain, notable for some stunningly unpleasant images impeccably staged.

wd, ed Luis Bunuel *ph* Eli Lotar

Land without Music*
GB 1936 80m bw
Capitol Films (Max Schach)
US title: *Forbidden Music*

The ruler of a Ruritanian country bans music because her subjects are too busy singing to make money. A revolutionary singer however wins the duchess's hand and reverses her decision.
Artless but attractively played operetta with the star in excellent form.

w Marian Dix, L. Du Garde Peach *d* Walter Forde *ph* John Boyle *m* Oscar Straus

Richard Tauber, Jimmy Durante, Diana Napier, June Clyde, Derrick de Marney, Esme Percy, George Hayes, Edward Rigby

Landfall
GB 1949 88m bw
ABPC (Victor Skuzetzky)

A test pilot mistakenly believes that he accidentally sank a British submarine.
Second rate transcription of a popular novel.

w Talbot Jennings, Gilbert Gunn, Anne Burnaby, *novel* Nevil Shute *d* Ken Annakin

Michael Denison, Patricia Plunkett, Kathleen Harrison, David Tomlinson, Joan Dowling, Maurice Denham, A. E. Matthews, Margaretta Scott, Sebastian Shaw, Laurence Harvey

The Landlord*
US 1970 110m De Luxe
UA / Mirisch / Carter

A tycoon's son buys a tenement in Brooklyn's black ghetto, and conscience diverts him into improving the lot of his tenants.

Overlong satirical comedy, good on detail but short on structure.

w Bill Gunn, *novel* Kristin Hunter *d* Hal Ashby *ph* Gordon Willis *m* Al Kooper *pd* Robert Boyle

Beau Bridges, Lee Grant, Pearl Bailey, Diana Sands

'Bad taste from start to finish . . . not an avenue of offensiveness to any race is left unexplored.'—*Judith Crist*

AAN: Lee Grant

Landru
France / Italy 1962 115m Eastmancolor
Rome-Paris / CC Champion (Carlo Ponti, Georges de Beauregard)
aka: *Bluebeard*

The true story of a furniture dealer who murdered women for financial gain, also treated by Chaplin in *Monsieur Verdoux*.

A curious artificial style has been adopted, making a tragi-comedy look like a farce which isn't very funny, and falls on very stony ground indeed despite the all star cast.

w Françoise Sagan *d* Claude Chabrol *ph* Jean Rabier *m* Pierre Jansen

Charles Denner, Michèle Morgan, Danielle Darrieux, Hildegarde Knef, Stéphane Audran, Catherine Rouvel

Larceny
US 1948 89m bw
Universal (Aaron Rosenberg)

A con man fleeces a war widow into paying for a memorial to her husband, but falls in love with her.
Drearily predictable melodrama.

w Herbert F. Margolis, Louis Markein, William Bowers *novel* The Velvet Fleece by Lois Ely, John Fleming *d* George Sherman *ph* Irving Glassberg *m* Leith Stevens

Joan Caulfield, John Payne, Dan Duryea, Shelley Winters, Dorothy Hart, Richard Rober, Dan O'Herlihy

Larceny Inc.
US 1942 95m bw
Warner (Jack Saper, Jerry Wald)

An ex-convict tries to rob a bank but finds that honesty pays best.
Tepid comedy-drama from the period when Warners were taming their gangster image.

w Everett Freeman, Edwin Gilbert, *play* The Night before Christmas by Laura and S. J. Perelman *d* Lloyd Bacon *ph* Tony Gaudio

Edward G. Robinson, Jane Wyman, Broderick Crawford, Anthony Quinn, Jack Carson, Edward Brophy, Harry Davenport, John Qualen, Barbara Jo Allen, Jackie Gleason, Grant Mitchell, Andrew Tombes

The Las Vegas Story
US 1952 88m bw
RKO (Robert Sparks)

When an investment broker and his new wife stop at Las Vegas, her shady past begins to emerge.
So-so programmer with some eccentric talents in average form, capped by a desert helicopter chase.

w Earl Felton, Harry Essex d Robert Stevenson ph Harry J. Wild m Constantin Bakaleinikoff

Jane Russell, Victor Mature, Vincent Price, Hoagy Carmichael, Colleen Miller, Brad Dexter, Jay C. Flippen

Lassie
The official Lassie series, made by MGM, was as follows:

1943: LASSIE COME HOME (qv)
1945: SON OF LASSIE (d S. Sylvan Simon with Peter Lawford, Donald Crisp, Nigel Bruce)
1946: COURAGE OF LASSIE (d Fred M. Wilcox with Elizabeth Taylor, Frank Morgan, Tom Drake)
1948: THE HILLS OF HOME[1] (d Fred M. Wilcox with Edmund Gwenn, Donald Crisp, Tom Drake)
1949: THE SUN COMES UP (d Richard Thorpe with Jeanette MacDonald, Lloyd Nolan)
1949: CHALLENGE TO LASSIE (d Richard Thorpe with Edmund Gwenn, Donald Crisp)
1951: THE PAINTED HILLS (d Harold F. Kress with Paul Kelly, Bruce Cowling)

† Later 'Lassie' features were taken from episodes of the long-running TV series.

[1] (GB title: *Master of Lassie*)

Lassie Come Home *
US 1943 88m Technicolor
MGM (Samuel Marx)

A poor family is forced to sell its beloved dog, but she makes a remarkable journey to return to them.
First of the Lassie films and certainly the best: an old-fashioned heartwarmer.

w Hugo Butler, *novel* Eric Knight d Fred M. Wilcox ph Leonard Smith m Daniele Amfitheatrof

Roddy McDowall, Elizabeth Taylor, Donald Crisp, Edmund Gwenn, Dame May Whitty, Nigel Bruce, Elsa Lanchester, J. Pat O'Malley

'The late Eric Knight wrote this immortal essay in Doggery-Woggery. MGM finished it off.'—*Richard Winnington*

AAN: Leonard Smith

The Last American Hero *
US 1973 95m De Luxe Panavision
TCF / Wizan / Rojo (John Cutts, William Roberts)

The adventures of an illicit whisky distiller with a passion for fast cars.
Observant, amusing hillbilly comedy drama based on the early life of racing driver Junior Johnson.

w William Roberts d Lamont Johnson ph George Silano m Charles Fox

Jeff Bridges, Valerie Perrine, Geraldine Fitzgerald, Ned Beatty, Art Lund, Gary Busey
† Reissue title: *Hard Driver*.

The Last Angry Man *
US 1959 100m bw
Columbia (Fred Kohlmar)

An old doctor in a Brooklyn slum is made the subject of a TV documentary.
Self-confidently sentimental wallow which just about works.

w Gerald Green d Daniel Mann ph James Wong Howe m George Duning

Paul Muni, David Wayne, Betsy Palmer, Luther Adler, Dan Tobin, Robert F. Simon

AAN: Paul Muni

The Last Blitzkrieg
US 1959 84m bw
Columbia / Sam Katzman

During the Battle of the Bulge a German leads a squad of American saboteurs.
Weakly pacifist, technically incompetent war adventure.

w Lou Morheim d Arthur Dreifuss ph Ted Scaife m Hugo de Groot

Van Johnson, Kerwin Mathews, Dick York, Larry Storch

The Last Bridge
Austria / Yugoslavia 1953 95m bw
Cosmopol / UFUS (Carl Szokoll)

During World War II, a German nurse in Yugoslavia is captured by partisans and turns to their point of view.
Message melodrama, very ably put together with a bleakly tragic climax; but nothing at all new.

w Helmut Kautner, Norbert Kunze *d* Helmut Kautner *ph* Elio Carniel *m* Carl de Groof

Maria Schell, Bernhard Wicki, Barbara Rütting, Carl Möhner

The Last Chance*
Switzerland 1945   105m   bw
Praesens Film

In 1943 an Englishman and an American escape from a fascist camp in northern Italy and with the help of refugees cross the mountains into Switzerland.
Earnest propaganda piece which struck the spot at the time: cinematically rather plodding, but with some exciting scenes.

w Richard Schweitzer *d* Leopold Lindtberg *ph* Emil Berna *m* Robert Blum

E. G. Morrison, Ray Reagan, John Hoy, Luisa Rossi

The Last Command*
US 1955   110m   Trucolor
Republic (Frank Lloyd)

Jim Bowie returns to Texas in the 1830s and dies at the Alamo alongside other famous men.
Reasonably interesting western on a subject which has often figured but seldom worked.

w Warren Duff *d* Frank Lloyd *ph* Jack Marta *m* Max Steiner

Ernest Borgnine, Sterling Hayden, Anna Maria Alberghetti, Arthur Hunnicutt, Richard Carlson, J. Carrol Naish

The Last Days of Dolwyn*
GB 1949   95m   bw
London / BLPA (Anatole de Grunwald)
US title: *Woman of Dolwyn*

A Welsh valley is flooded to make a reservoir and a village has to be evacuated.
Interesting but rather stagey drama based on an actual 19th-century event, with personal melodrama added.

wd Emlyn Williams *ph* Otto Heller *m* John Greenwood

Edith Evans, Emlyn Williams, Richard Burton, Hugh Griffith, Barbara Couper, Allan Aynesworth
'The conventionally picturesque Welsh flavour and mounting probabilities apart, the treatment is stiff and episodic.'—*MFB*

The Last Days of Pompeii**
US 1935   96m   bw
RKO (Merian C. Cooper)

In ancient Pompeii, various personal dramas are submerged in the eruption of Vesuvius.
Starchy melodrama capped by a reel of spectacular disaster.

w Ruth Rose, Boris Ingster, *novel* Lord Lytton *d* Merian C. Cooper, Ernest Schoedsack *ph* Eddie Linden Jnr, Ray June *m* Roy Webb *sp Vernon Walker, Harry Redmond*

Preston Foster, Basil Rathbone, Alan Hale, Dorothy Cooper

The Last Detail**
US 1973   104m   Metrocolor
Columbia / Acrobat / Persky—Bright (Gerald Ayres)

Two hardened naval petty officers escort a young recruit, sentenced for thieving, from Virginia to a New Hampshire jail, and give him a wild last night.
Foul-mouthed weekend odyssey, with a few well-observed moments for non-prudes. Technically the epitome of Hollywood's most irritating seventies fashion, with fuzzy sound recording, dim against-the-light photography, and a general determination to show up the ugliness of everything around us.

w Robert Towne, *novel* Darryl Ponicsan *d* Hal Ashby *ph* Michael Chapman *m* Johnny Mandel

Jack Nicholson, Otis Young, Randy Quaid, Clifton James, Carol Kane
'Visually it is relentlessly lower-depths gloomy, and the material, though often very funny, is programmed to wrench your heart.'—*New Yorker*

AAN: Robert Towne; Jack Nicholson; Randy Quaid

The Last Dinosaur
US 1977   100m   colour
Rankin-Bass Productions

An oil-drilling team discovers a *tyrannosaurus rex* while probing the polar oil-cap.
Inept monster saga with poorish special effects from a Japanese team.

w William Overgard *d* Alex Grasshof, Tom Kotani *ph* Shoshi Ueda *m* Maury Laws

Richard Boone, Joan Van Ark, Steven Keats

The Last Flight****
US 1931   80m   bw
Warner

In 1919, four veteran American fliers stay on in Paris in the hope of calming their shattered physical and emotional states.
Fascinatingly offhand study on post-war cynicism and the faint hope of a better world, beautifully written and directed in a manner

more effective than *The Sun Also Rises*.

w John Monk Saunders, from his novel Single Lady *d* William Dieterle *ph* Sid Hickox

Richard Barthelmess, Helen Chandler, David Manners, John Mack Brown, *Elliott Nugent*, Walter Byron

'A narrative as tight and spare as a Racine tragedy . . . unique in Hollywood of that time in its persistent, calculated understatement.'—*Tom Milne, 1975*

The Last Gangster*
US 1937 81m bw
MGM

A gangster is released from Alcatraz and plans vengeance on his wife for deserting him.
Clean-cut star melodrama which suddenly turns sentimental.

w John Lee Mahin *d* Edward Ludwig
ph William Daniels *montage Slavko Vorkapitch*

Edward G. Robinson, Rose Stradner, James Stewart, Lionel Stander, Douglas Scott, John Carradine, Sidney Blackmer, Edward Brophy

'A lot of water has flowed under the bridge since *Little Caesar*, but Mr Robinson has breasted the tides to make his impersonation of a 1937 thug as persuasive as was his portrait of a killer in that earlier classic of rats and rackets.'—*Frank Nugent*

The Last Grenade
GB 1969 93m Eastmancolor
Panavision
Cinerama / Dimitri de Grunwald / Josef Shaftel

An army mercenary is betrayed by an ex-friend in the Congo and pursues him to Hong Kong.
Violent action melodrama with few redeeming qualities.

w Kenneth Ware, *novel* The Ordeal of Major Grigsby by John Sherlock *d* Gordon Flemyng *ph* Alan Hume *m* Johnny Dankworth

Stanley Baker, Alex Cord, Honor Blackman, Richard Attenborough, Rafer Johnson, Andrew Keir, Ray Brooks, Julian Glover, John Thaw

The Last Hard Men
US 1976 97m De Luxe Panavision
TCF / Belasco–Seltzer–Thatcher

A train robber breaks jail and sets out to revenge himself on the now-retired lawman who committed him.
Tough action adventure without much sense except to paint the end of the golden days of the west.

w Guerdon Trueblood, *novel* Gun Down by

Brian Garfield *d* Andrew V. McLaglen
ph Duke Callaghan *m* Jerry Goldsmith

Charlton Heston, James Coburn, Barbara Hershey, Christopher Mitchum, Michael Parks, Jorge Rivero, Thalmus Rasulala

'Script and direction seem equally tired.'—*Sight and Sound*

Last Holiday*
GB 1950 88m bw
ABPC / Watergate (Stephen Mitchell, A. D. Peters, J. B. Priestley)

A man with a short time to live has a thoroughly enjoyable and useful final fling.
Slight, amusing and moving comedy drama spoiled by an unnecessary double twist.

w J. B. Priestley *d* Henry Cass *ph* Ray Elton *m* Francis Chagrin

Alec Guinness, Kay Walsh, Beatrice Campbell, Grégoire Aslan, Bernard Lee, Wilfrid Hyde White, Helen Cherry, Sidney James, Muriel George

The Last Hunt*
US 1955 103m Eastmancolor
Cinemascope
MGM (Dore Schary)

Buffalo hunters fall out with each other.
Terse, brutish outdoor western with something to say about old western myths and a famous ending in which the bad guy freezes to death while waiting to gun down the hero.

wd Richard Brooks ph Russell Harlan
m Daniele Amfitheatrof

Stewart Granger, Robert Taylor, Debra Paget, Lloyd Nolan, Russ Tamblyn, Constance Ford

The Last Hurrah***
US 1958 125m bw
Columbia (John Ford)

The political boss of a New England town fights his last campaign.
Enjoyable if disjointed melodrama, an old man's film crammed with cameo performances from familiar faces: important as one of Hollywood's great sentimental reunions.

w Frank Nugent, novel Edwin O'Connor *d John Ford ph* Charles Lawton Jnr

Spencer Tracy, Jeffrey Hunter, Dianne Foster, *Pat O'Brien, Basil Rathbone, Edward Brophy, Donald Crisp, James Gleason, John Carradine, Ricardo Cortez, Wallace Ford, Frank McHugh*, Frank Albertson, Anna Lee, Jane Darwell, Willis Bouchey, Basil Ruysdael

The Last Journey*
GB 1935 66m bw
Twickenham (Julius Hagen)

The driver of an express train, driven mad with
jealousy, goes berserk.
Workmanlike little train suspenser with an
exciting climax.

w John Soutar, H. Fowler Mear, *story* J.
Jefferson Farjeon d Bernard Vorhaus

Godfrey Tearle, Hugh Williams, Julien Mitchell,
Judy Gunn, Nelson Keys, Frank Pettingell, Olga
Lindo, Sydney Fairbrother

The Last Laugh*
Germany 1924 73m approx (24 fps) bw
  silent
UFA
original title: *Der Letzte Mann*

The old doorman of a luxury hotel is given the
job of lavatory attendant but comes into a
fortune and gets his revenge.
Ironic anecdote made important by its virtual
abandonment of dialogue and whole-hearted
adoption of the camera eye technique which
gives some thrilling dramatic effects.

w *Carl Mayer* d *F. W. Murnau* ph Karl Freund
Emil Jannings, Max Hiller, Maly Delschaft,
Hans Unterkirchen
† A German remake of 1955 had Hans Albers in
the lead and was of no interest.

The Last Mile*
US 1932 84m bw
World Wide (E. W. Hammons)

Tensions mount in jail as the execution of Killer
Mears approaches.
Strident melodrama which works up quite a head
of hysteria.

w Seton I. Miller, *play* John Wexley d Sam
Bischoff ph Arthur Edeson

Preston Foster, Howard Phillips, George E.
Stone, Noel Madison

The Last Mile
US 1959 81m bw
UA / Vanguard (Milton Subotsky)

Even more hysterical remake, retaining the
original period. A cheerless, though literally
electrifying, entertainment.

w Milton Subotsky, Seton I. Miller d Howard
W. Koch ph Joseph Brun m Van Alexander

Mickey Rooney, Clifford David, Frank Conroy,
Frank Overton, Leon Janney

The Last of Mrs Cheyney
US 1929 94m bw
MGM

A confidence woman in British high society falls
in love.
Old theatrical warhorse, much filmed but never
very satisfactorily. (See below.)

w Hans Kraly, Claudine West, *play* Frederick
Lonsdale d Sidney Franklin ph William
Daniels

Norma Shearer, Basil Rathbone, George
Barraud, Hedda Hopper, Maude Turner
Gordon, Herbert Bunston

The Last of Mrs Cheyney
US 1937 98m bw
MGM (Lawrence Weingarten)

Adequate, unexciting remake.

w Leon Gordon, Samson Raphaelson,
Monckton Hoffe d Richard Boleslawski
ph George Folsey m William Axt

Joan Crawford, Robert Montgomery, William
Powell, Frank Morgan, Jessie Ralph, Nigel
Bruce, Benita Hume, Melville Cooper, Sara
Haden
† A further remake was *The Law and the Lady*
(qv).

The Last of Sheila*
US 1973 123m Technicolor
Warner (Herbert Ross)

A Hollywood star is killed by a hit-and-run
driver; a year later her husband invites six friends
to his yacht, and murders begin.
Confused, in-jokey showbiz whodunnit with
flashes of interest.

w Stephen Sondheim, Anthony Perkins
d Herbert Ross ph Gerry Turpin m Billy
Goldenberg ad Ken Adam

Richard Benjamin, Dyan Cannon, James
Coburn, James Mason, Joan Hackett, Ian
MacShane, Raquel Welch
'The most teasing riddles for an audience are
likely to be the real identities of the personalities
being satirized.'—*MFB*

The Last of the Comanches*
US 1953 85m Technicolor
Columbia (Buddy Adler)
GB title: *The Sabre and the Arrow*

Survivors of an Indian raid take refuge in an
abandoned mission until help arrives.
Competent western remake of *Sahara* (which
was a remake of *The Lost Patrol*).

w Kenneth Gamet d André de Toth ph Charles
Lawton Jnr m George Duning

Broderick Crawford, Barbara Hale, Lloyd Bridges, Martin Milner

The Last of the Mohicans
US 1936 91m bw
Edward Small

Incidents during colonial America's French–Indian war.
Vigorous if rough-and-ready western, later remade (poorly) as *Last of the Redmen* and as a Canadian TV series.

w Philip Dunne, John Balderston, Paul Perez, Daniel Moore, *novel* James Fenimore Cooper *d* George B. Seitz *ph* Robert Planck *m* Roy Webb

Randolph Scott, Binnie Barnes, Bruce Cabot, Henry Wilcoxon, Heather Angel, Hugh Buckler

Last of the Red Hot Lovers*
US 1972 98m Technicolor
Paramount (Howard W. Koch)

A middle-aged fish restaurateur feels the need for an extra-marital spree.
Modest, plainly-filmed sex comedy from a reliable stable.

w Neil Simon, from his play *d* Gene Saks *ph* Victor J. Kemper *m* Neal Hefti

Alan Arkin, Paula Prentiss, Sally Kellerman, Renée Taylor

The Last Outpost*
US 1935 75m bw
Paramount (E. Lloyd Sheldon)

A British officer is captured by the Kurds and freed by an adventurer whose wife he covets.
Patchy, unusual adventure story with good moments.

w Philip MacDonald, *story* F. Britten Austin *d* Charles Barton, Louis Gasnier *ph* Theodor Sparkuhl

Cary Grant, Claude Rains, Gertrude Michael, Kathleen Burke, Colin Tapley, Akim Tamiroff, Billy Bevan, Jameson Thomas

The Last Picture Show***
US 1971 118m bw
Columbia / LPS / BDS (Stephen J. Friedman)

Teenage affairs in a small Texas town in 1951, ending with the hero's embarkation for Korea and the closing of the tatty cinema.
Penetrating nostalgia with over-emphasis on sex; the detail is the attraction.

w Larry McMurty, Peter Bogdanovich *d* Peter Bogdanovich *ph* Robert Surtees *m* original recordings *pd* Polly Platt

Timothy Bottoms, Jeff Bridges, Cybill Shepherd, Ben Johnson, Cloris Leachman, Ellen Burstyn
'The most important work by a young American director since *Citizen Kane*.'—*Paul D. Zimmerman*
'So many things in it are so good that I wish I liked it more.'—*Stanley Kauffmann*

AA: Ben Johnson; Cloris Leachman
AAN: best picture; script; Peter Bogdanovich (as director); Robert Surtees; Jeff Bridges; Ellen Burstyn

The Last Remake of Beau Geste
US 1977 85m Technicolor
Universal (William S. Gilmore Jnr)

The Geste brothers find themselves in the Foreign Legion after the theft of the Blue Water sapphire.
Woebegone spoof of a romantic original, with most of the jokes totally irrelevant to the purpose and seldom at all funny.

w Marty Feldman, Chris J. Allen *d* Marty Feldman *ph* Gerry Fisher *m* John Morris

Marty Feldman, Michael York, Ann-Margret, Peter Ustinov, Trevor Howard, James Earl Jones, Henry Gibson, Terry-Thomas, Roy Kinnear, Spike Milligan, Hugh Griffith, Irene Handl
'A ragbag of a film which looks like nothing so much as a Monty Python extravaganza in which inspiration has run dry and the comic timing gone sadly awry.'—*Tom Milne, MFB*

The Last Run*
US 1971 92m Metrocolor Panavision
MGM (Carter de Haven)

An ex-Chicago gangster retired to a Portuguese fishing village undertakes one last fatal job.
Well-made, rather uninteresting downbeat melodrama.

w Alan Sharp *d* Richard Fleischer *ph* Sven Nykvist *m* Jerry Goldsmith

George C. Scott, Tony Musante, Trish Van Devere

The Last Safari
GB 1967 110m Technicolor
Paramount (Henry Hathaway)

A disillusioned white hunter takes on one last safari.
Dullsville adventure story with good animal photography redeeming some of the clichés.

w John Gay, *novel* Gilligan's Last Elephant by Gerald Hanley *d* Henry Hathaway *ph* Ted Moore *m* Johnny Dankworth

Stewart Granger, K az Garas, Gabriella Licudi, Johnny Sekka, Liam Redmond, Eugene Deckers

The Last Stage*
Poland 1947   110m   bw
Film Polski
original title: *Ostatni Etap*

Women suffer but one is finally rescued from the Nazi concentration camp at Auschwitz.
A dour, obsessive, horrifying record of human inhumanity, set in the actual camp and made by two former inmates.

w Wanda Jakubowska, Gerda Schneider
d Wanda Jakubowska *ph* Borys Monastyrskį
m R. Palester

Huguette Faget, W. Bartowna, T. Gorecka

Last Summer*
US 1969   97m   Eastmancolor
Alsid / Francis (Alfred Crown, Sidney Beckerman)

Well-to-do teenagers have sexual adventures on a summer seaside holiday.
Striking off-beat melodrama with vividly sketched characters.

w Eleanor Perry, *novel* Evan Hunter *d* Frank Perry *ph* Gerald Hirschfeld *m* John Simon

Barbara Hershey, Richard Thomas, Bruce Davison, Cathy Burns, Ernesto Gonzales, Ralph Waite

AAN: Cathy Burns

The Last Sunset
US 1961   112m   Eastmancolor
U-I (Brynaprod)

A killer and his hunter learn a lot about each other before the final showdown.
Slow psycho-western with pretensions to tragedy.

w Dalton Trumbo, *novel* Showdown at Crazy Horse by Howard Grigsby *d* Robert Aldrich *ph* Ernest Laszlo *m* Ernest Gold

Rock Hudson, Kirk Douglas, Dorothy Malone, Carol Lynley, Joseph Cotten, Regis Toomey, Neville Brand

Last Tango in Paris*
France / Italy / US 1972   129m
  Technicolor
Les Artistes Associés / PEA / UA (Alberto Grimaldi)

A middle-aged man and a young French girl have a doomed love affair.
Pretentious sex melodrama mainly notable for being banned.

w Bernardo Bertolucci, Franco Arcalli
d Bernardo Bertolucci *ph* Vittorio Storaro
m Gato Barbieri

Marlon Brando, Maria Schneider, Jean-Pierre Léaud

AAN: Bernardo Bertolucci (as director); Marlon Brando

The Last Time I Saw Archie
US 1961   98m   bw
UA / Mark VII / Manzanita / Talbot (Jack Webb)

Adventures of a con man amid overage civilian pilots at an army/air force base.
Patchy service comedy.

w William Bowers *d* Jack Webb *ph* Joe MacDonald *m* Frank Comstock

Jack Webb, Robert Mitchum, Martha Hyer, France Nuyen, Louis Nye, Jimmy Lydon, Richard Arlen, Don Knotts, Robert Strauss, Joe Flynn

The Last Time I Saw Paris
US 1954   116m   Technicolor
MGM

A writer recalls his romance with a wealthy American girl in Paris.
Dull romantic drama which very deadeningly and predictably updates F. Scott Fitzgerald's *Babylon Revisited*.

w Julius J. and Philip G. Epstein, Richard Brooks *d* Richard Brooks *ph* Joseph Ruttenberg *m* Conrad Salinger

Elizabeth Taylor, Van Johnson, Walter Pidgeon, Donna Reed, Eva Gabor

Last Train from Gun Hill*
US 1959   98m   Technicolor Vistavision
(Paramount) Hal B. Wallis / Bryna

A marshal tracks down the man who raped and murdered his wife; it turns out to be the son of an old friend.
Good suspense and action western culminating in a *High Noon* situation.

w James Poe *d* John Sturges *ph* Charles Lang Jnr *m* Dmitri Tiomkin

Kirk Douglas, Anthony Quinn, Earl Holliman, Carolyn Jones, Brian Hutton

The Last Train from Madrid
US 1937   85m   bw
Paramount (George M. Arthur)

A variety of people escape the fighting in the Spanish Civil War.

Tawdry topical melodrama with cliché characters and situations.

w Louis Stevens, Robert Wyler *d* James Hogan *ph* Harry Fischbeck *md* Boris Morros

Dorothy Lamour, Lew Ayres, Gilbert Roland, Karen Morley, Lionel Atwill, Helen Mack, Robert Cummings, Olympe Bradna, Anthony Quinn, Lee Bowman, George Lloyd

'It is probably the worst film of the decade and should have been the funniest.'—*Graham Greene*

'Simply a topical and different background for a glib little fiction.'—*Frank S. Nugent*

The Last Tycoon

US 1976   124m   Technicolor
Paramount / Academy / Sam Spiegel

The production head of a Hollywood studio in the thirties has his troubles complicated when he falls in love with a girl who reminds him of his dead wife.

Astonishingly inept and boring big budget all-star melodrama which doesn't even begin promisingly (the scenes from supposed thirties films are woefully inaccurate in style); it then bogs down in interminable dialogue scenes, leaving its famous cast all at sea.

w Harold Pinter, *novel* F. Scott Fitzgerald *d* Elia Kazan *ph* Victor Kemper *m* Maurice Jarre *pd* Eugene F. Callahan

Robert de Niro, Robert Mitchum, Tony Curtis, Jeanne Moreau, Jack Nicholson, Ingrid Boulting, Donald Pleasence, Ray Milland, Dana Andrews, John Carradine

'So enervated it's like a vampire movie after the vampires have left.'—*New Yorker*

'That the result is incoherent is no surprise; that it is so hollow and visually graceless adds a kind of wonder to the disappointment.'—*Sight and Sound*

'The breathless reverence that informs the movie kills it stone dead.'—*Michael Billington, Illustrated London News*

The Last Valley

GB 1970   128m   Eastmancolor   Todd-AO
ABC / Season / Seamaster (James Clavell)

In 1641 during the Thirty Years War a scholar tries to defend a remote and prosperous Swiss valley against a horde of mercenaries.

Big-scale historical action picture crammed with pillage, torture, rape, death at the stake, throat cutting and general carnage; reasonably literate for all that, and convincingly set.

wd James Clavell, *novel* J. B. Pick *ph* Norman Warwick *m* John Barry *ad* Peter Mullins

Michael Caine, Omar Sharif, Florinda Bolkan, Nigel Davenport, Per Oscarsson, Arthur O'Connell, Brian Blessed

The Last Voyage*

US 1960   91m   Metrocolor
MGM / Andrew and Virginia Stone

A boiler room explosion causes an old passenger liner to sink.

Spectacular if dramatically deficient actioner for which a genuine liner (awaiting scrapping) was sunk.

wd Andrew L. Stone *ph* Hal Mohr *m* Rudy Schrager

Robert Stack, Dorothy Malone, Edmond O'Brien, George Sanders, Woody Strode, Jack Kruschen

'A prolonged nerve stretcher.'—*MFB*

The Last Wagon

US 1960   99m   Eastmancolor
Cinemascope
TCF (William B. Hawks)

A half breed wanted for murder joins an 1875 wagon train.

Heavy-going big-scale western.

w James Edward Grant, Delmer Daves, Gwen Bagni *d* Delmer Daves *ph* Wilfrid Cline *m* Lionel Newman

Richard Widmark, Felicia Farr, Tommy Rettig, Susan Kohner, Ray Stricklyn, Nick Adams, Carl Benton Reid

The Last Waltz

US 1978   115m   De Luxe
UA / Martin Scorsese, Jonathan Taplin

Rock documentary featuring the last concert of The Band.

An occasion for specialists, very adequately packaged.

d Martin Scorsese *pd* Boris Leven

The Last Warning*

US 1929   88m   bw
Universal

Murder backstage.

Shot as a silent film, with sound hurriedly added, this remains a stylish comedy-thriller with all the familiar ingredients of the whodunnit.

w Alfred A. Cohn *d* Paul Leni *ph* Hal Mohr

Laura La Plante, Montagu Love, Roy D'Arcy, John Boles, Mack Swain, Slim Summerville, Margaret Livingston

† Remade in 1938 as *The House of Fear*, a William Gargan second feature.

The Last Warning
US 1938 62m bw
Universal

A private eye mystery.
Better-than-average second feature.

w Edmund L. Hartmann, *novel* The Dead Don't
Care by Jonathan Latimer d Albert S. Rogell

Preston Foster, Joyce Compton, Frank Jenks

The Last Wave*
Australia 1977 106m Atlab
(UA) Ayer / MacElroy / Derek Power

During a spell of freak weather, a lawyer has
recurrent dreams which give him the key to an
Aborigine prophecy about the world being
destroyed by flood . . .
Curious supernatural drama successfully played
as a mystery, with excellent atmosphere and
special effects.

w Peter Weir, Tony Morphett, Petru Popescu
d Peter Weir ph Russell Boyd m Charles Wain
pd Goran Warff

Richard Chamberlain, Olivia Hamnet,
Frederick Parslow

'A Hitchcockian sense of minatory
dislocation.'—*Tim Pulleine, MFB*

Last Year at Marienbad**
France / Italy 1961 94m bw Dyaliscope
Terra / Tamara / Cormoran / Precitel / Como /
   Argos / Cinetel / Silver / Cineriz

In a vast old-fashioned hotel, a man meets a
woman who may or may not have had an affair
with him the previous year in Marienbad—or
was it Frederiksbad?
A dreamy, elegant film which presents a puzzle
with no solution. It has its attractions for film
buffs and cryptogram addicts, but is not for
anyone who simply wants to be told a story.

w *Alain Robbe-Grillet* d *Alain Resnais*
ph Sacha Vierny m Francis Seyrig ad Jacques
Saulnier

Delphine Seyrig, Giorgio Albertazzi, Sacha
Pitoeff

'Clearly the film's creators know exactly what
they want to do and have done it with complete
success. Whether one responds to the result is
entirely a matter of temperament.'—*John
Russell Taylor, MFB*

AAN: Alain Robbe-Grillet

The Late Edwina Black*
GB 1951 78m bw
IFD / Elvey—Gartside
US title: *Obsessed*

When a schoolteacher's wife is found dead, the
police have three suspects.
Adequately suspenseful Victorian thriller from a
successful play.

w Charles Frank, David Evans, *play* William
Dinner, William Morum d Maurice Elvey
ph Stephen Dade m Allan Gray

Geraldine Fitzgerald, David Farrar, *Roland
Culver*, Jean Cadell; Mary Merrall, Harcourt
Williams, Charles Heslop, Ronald Adam

The Late George Apley*
US 1946 96m bw
TCF (Joseph L. Mankiewicz)

The uneventful family life of a Boston blueblood.
Pleasant but tame family comedy-drama, solidly
carpentered.

w Philip Dunne, *novel* John P. Marquand
d Joseph L. Mankiewicz ph Joseph La Shelle
m Cyril Mockridge

Ronald Colman, Edna Best, Vanessa Brown,
Richard Haydn, Peggy Cummins, Charles
Russell

The Late Show*
US 1977 93m Metrocolor
Warner (Robert Altman)

An ageing private eye in Los Angeles finds that
his ex-partner's death and a lost cat have a
complex connection.
A more-or-less engaging spoof of, or perhaps a
valediction to, the private eye genre, with
engaging scenes marred by poor colour and
occasional excesses of violent action.

wd Robert Benton ph Chuck Rosher m Ken
Wannberg

Art Carney, Lily Tomlin, Bill Macy, Ruth
Nelson, Howard Duff, Joanna Cassidy, Eugene
Roche

Latin Lovers
US 1953 104m Technicolor
MGM (Joe Pasternak)

An heiress on holiday in Brazil looks for a man
who will love her for herself alone.
Barren romantic drama, flatfooted and drawn
out.

w Isobel Lennart d Mervyn Le Roy ph Joseph
Ruttenberg m George Stoll

Lana Turner, Ricardo Montalban, John Lund,
Louis Calhern, Jean Hagen

Latin Quarter*
GB 1945 80m bw
British National
US title: *Frenzy*

In nineties Paris a mad sculptor murders his
fiancée and hides her inside his latest exhibit.
Artificial-looking but melodramatically effective
thriller with a chilling climax and a detailed
Dégas-period background.

wd Vernon Sewell ph Gunther Krampf, play
l'Angoisse by Pierre Mills, Charles Vylars

Derrick de Marney, Joan Greenwood, Beresford
Egan, Frederick Valk, Lily Kann, Martin Miller

Laugh with Max Linder**
France 1963   88m   bw
Films Max Linder
original title: *En Compagnie de Max Linder*

Excerpts from three of the dapper comedian's
most famous American comedies: *Be My Wife*
(1921), *The Three Must Get Theres* (1922),
Seven Years' Bad Luck (1923)
A compilation which must serve as a consensus
of this almost forgotten comedian's work. The
gag with a broken mirror in particular was
borrowed by innumerable other comedians,
notably the Marx Brothers in *Duck Soup.*
Audiences new to Linder's work will find him not
especially sympathetic but capable of many
felicities. He wrote, produced and directed all
three films.

compiler Maud Max Linder

Laughing Anne
GB 1953   90m   Technicolor
Republic / Wilcox—Neagle

French Anne and her boxing lover are
characters of the Javanese waterfront; he kills
her after she has fallen for a sea captain.
Cheap and turgid adaptation of a Joseph Conrad
story; the author would not recognize it. Studio
settings put the lid on hilariously bad work all
round.

w Pamela Bower *d* Herbert Wilcox *ph* Max
Greene *m* Anthony Collins

Margaret Lockwood, Forrest Tucker, Ronald
Shiner, Wendell Corey, Robert Harris

The Laughing Policeman*
US 1973   112m   De Luxe
TCF (Stuart Rosenberg)
GB title: *An Investigation of Murder*

A mad machine-gunner eludes the San
Francisco police.
Downbeat, semi-documentary police thriller
with pretensions. Too complex by half, with an
overplus of characterization, but the location
work is excellent.

w Thomas Rickman, *novel* Maj Sjowall, Per
Wahloo *d* Stuart Rosenberg *ph* David Walsh
m Charles Fox

Walter Matthau, Bruce Dern, Lou Gossett,
Albert Paulsen, Anthony Zerbe

Laughter**
US 1930   99m   bw
Paramount

An ex-Follies girl marries a millionaire but later
goes on a spree with the composer she once
loved.
Sharply observed, before its time romantic
comedy reminiscent now of the later
Philadelphia Story in its attitudes to wealth and
love. A precursor of the smart crazy comedies of
the mid-thirties.

*w Donald Ogden Stewart d Harry d'Abbabie
d'Arrast ph* George Folsey

Fredric March, Nancy Carroll, Frank Morgan,
Glen Anders, Diane Ellis

'One of the best talking pictures I have ever
seen.'—*James Agate*

'A talkie with so fast a pace that it crowds the
comprehension of half the customers . . . marked
at intervals by superb dialogue and the quick
hand of a smart director.'—*Pare Lorentz*

'A lovely sophisticated comedy.'—*New
Yorker, 1977*

AAN: Donald Ogden Stewart

Laughter in Paradise*
GB 1951   93m   bw
ABPC (*Mario Zampi*)

An eccentric leaves in his will a fortune for each
of his relations providing they will perform
certain embarrassing or criminal acts.
A funny idea gets half-hearted treatment, but the
good bits are hilarious.

w Michael Pertwee, Jack Davies *d* Mario
Zampi *ph* William McLeod *m* Stanley Black

Alastair Sim, Joyce Grenfell, Hugh Griffith, Fay
Compton, John Laurie, George Cole, Guy
Middleton, Ronald Adam, Leslie Dwyer, A. E.
Matthews, Beatrice Campbell
† Remade 1972 as *Some Will, Some Won't.*

Laughter in the Dark*
GB / France 1969   104m   De Luxe
UA / Woodfall / Winkast / Marceau (Neil
    Hartley)

A wealthy art dealer is taken in by an ambitious
usherette and her lover, and after being blinded
in a car accident tries to kill them.
Unsatisfactory adaptation of a novel with a very
specialized appeal: conventional swinging
London and Riviera settings only confuse the
spectator. Moments do work, though.

w Edward Bond, *novel* Vladimir Nabokov

d Tony Richardson *ph* Dick Bush *m* Raymond Leppard *ad* Julia Trevelyan Oman

Nicol Williamson, Anna Karina, Jean-Claude Drouot, Peter Bowles, Sian Phillips

'It fails to create the slightest interest in its trio of repulsive characters.'—*Philip Strick*

Laura****

US 1944 85m bw
TCF (Otto Preminger)

A beautiful girl is murdered . . . or is she? A cynical detective investigates.
A quiet, streamlined little murder mystery that brought a new adult approach to the genre and heralded the mature *film noir* of the later forties. A small cast responds perfectly to a classically spare script, and in Clifton Webb a new star is born.

w Jay Dratler, Samuel Hoffenstein, Betty Reinhardt, *novel* Vera Caspary *d* Otto Preminger *ph* Joseph La Shelle *m* David Raksin

Dana Andrews, Clifton Webb, Gene Tierney, Judith Anderson, *Vincent Price*, Dorothy Adams, James Flavin

'Everybody's favourite chic murder mystery.'—*New Yorker, 1977*
† Rouben Mamoulian directed some scenes before handing over to Preminger.

AA: Joseph La Shelle
AAN: script; Otto Preminger; Clifton Webb

Laurel and Hardy's Laughing Twenties**

US 1965 90m bw
MGM / Robert Youngson

Excerpts from lesser comedians of the period—Max Davidson, Charlie Chase—are interspersed with highlights from Laurel and Hardy's silent two reelers.
A hilarious and craftsmanlike compilation, perhaps a little too long for its own good.

w, ed Robert Youngson *commentator* Jay Jackson *m* Skeets Alquist

† Films extracted include *Putting Pants on Philip, From Soup to Nuts, Wrong Again, The Finishing Touch, Liberty, Double Whoopee, Leave 'Em Laughing, You're Darn Tooting* and the custard pie climax from *The Battle of the Century*.

The Lavender Hill Mob****

GB 1951 78m bw
Ealing (Michael Truman)

A timid bank clerk conceives and executes a bullion robbery.
Superbly characterized and inventively detailed comedy, one of the best ever made at Ealing or in Britain.

w T. E. B. Clarke *d* Charles Crichton *ph* Douglas Slocombe *m* Georges Auric

Alec Guinness, Stanley Holloway, Sidney James, Alfie Bass, Marjorie Fielding, Edie Martin, John Gregson, Gibb McLaughlin

'Amusing situations and dialogue are well paced and sustained throughout: the climax is delightful.'—*MFB*

AA: T. E. B. Clarke
AAN: Alec Guinness

Law and Disorder

GB 1940 73m bw
British Consolidated (K. C. Alexander)

A solicitor unmasks saboteurs using portable radios to direct bombers.
Thin, tolerable comedy thriller using most of the talents of *This Man is News*.

w Roger MacDonald *d* David MacDonald

Barry K. Barnes, Alastair Sim, Diana Churchill, Edward Chapman, Austin Trevor, Leo Genn

Law and Disorder*

GB 1958 76m bw
British Lion / Hotspur (Paul Soskin)

Crooks rally round a confederate about to be arrested, to prevent his son from learning of his father's real career.
Amusing, well-pointed caper on sub-Ealing lines.

w T. E. B. Clarke, *novel* Smuggler's Circuit by Denys Roberts *d* Charles Crichton *ph* Ted Scaife *m* Humphrey Searle

Michael Redgrave, Robert Morley, Joan Hickson, Lionel Jeffries, Ronald Squire, Elizabeth Sellars

Law and Disorder*

US 1975 102m Technicolor Panavision
Memorial / Leroy Street / Ugo Fadsin (William Richert)

New York suburbanites aghast at escalating violence form themselves into a vigilante patrol.
Bewilderingly uneven comedy drama which starts as satirical comedy and ends with one of the heroes dead and the other moralizing. Sporadically interesting, and certainly topical.

w Ivan Passer, William Richert, Kenneth Harris Fishman *d* Ivan Passer *ph* Arthur J. Ornitz *m* Andy Badale

Ernest Borgnine, Carroll O'Connor, Karen Black, Ann Wedgeworth, Leslie Ackerman, David Spielberg

The Law and Jake Wade*

US 1958   86m   Metrocolor
Cinemascope
MGM (William Hawks)

A marshal helps an old outlaw friend to escape
from jail, and lives to regret it.
Good standard western, enjoyable throughout
but with no outstanding merits.

w William Bowers d John Sturges ph Robert
Surtees

Robert Taylor, Richard Widmark, Patricia
Owens, Robert Middleton, Henry Silva

The Law and the Lady

US 1951   104m   bw
MGM (Edwin H. Knopf)

A couple of confidence tricksters inveigle
themselves into the house of a vulgar
millionairess, but one of them has an attack of
conscience.
Dreary remake of *The Last of Mrs Cheyney* (qv)
with the locale altered, the plot simplified, and
the level of wit diluted.

w Leonard Spiegelgass, Karl Tunberg d Edwin
H. Knopf ph George Folsey m Carmen Dragon

Greer Garson, Michael Wilding, Fernando
Lamas, Marjorie Main, Hayden Rorke, Margalo
Gillmore, Ralph Dumke

Law of the Lawless

US 1963   87m   Techniscope
Paramount / A. C. Lyles

A judge arrives in a small western town to
conduct the murder trial of a former friend.
Jaded western of interest only for the producer's
custom of packing the bit roles with former stars.

w Steve Fisher d William F. Claxton ph Lester
Shorr

Dale Robertson, Yvonne de Carlo, William
Bendix, Bruce Cabot, Barton MacLane, John
Agar, Richard Arlen, Kent Taylor, Lon Chaney
Jnr

Law of the Tropics

US 1941   76m   bw
Warner (Ben Stoloff)

A café singer on the run from a murder charge
marries a South American rubber plantation
owner.
Hackneyed melodrama born from a mating of
Oil for the Lamps of China and *Tropic Zone*.

w Charles Grayson d Ray Enright ph Sid
Hickox m Howard Jackson

Constance Bennett, Jeffrey Lynn, Regis

Toomey, Mona Maris, Frank Puglia, Thomas
Jackson, Craig Stevens

The Lawless

US 1949   83m   bw
Paramount / Pine–Thomas
GB title: *The Dividing Line*

The editor of a California small-town newspaper
defends a Spanish boy who is being victimized
by the racist element.
Well-meaning 'realistic' melodrama,
unfortunately among the dullest of the socially
conscious movies of this period.

w Geoffrey Homes d Joseph Losey ph Roy
Hunt m Mahlon Merrick

Macdonald Carey, Gail Russell, John Sands,
John Hoyt, Lee Patrick, Lalo Rios

The Lawless Breed

US 1952   83m   Technicolor
U-I (William Alland)

The adventures and repentance of badman John
Wesley Hardin.
Standard western programmer with the star in
an unlikely role.

w Bernard Gordon d Raoul Walsh ph Irving
Glassberg m Joseph Gershenson

Rock Hudson, Julie Adams, John McIntire,
Dennis Weaver, Hugh O'Brian

A Lawless Street

US 1955   78m   Technicolor
Columbia (Harry Joe Brown)

A marshal marries a dance hall entertainer, and
loses interest in his job when she leaves him.
Enjoyable minor western.

w Kenneth Gamet, *novel* Marshal of Medicine
Bend by Brad Ward d Joseph H. Lewis ph Ray
Rennahan m Paul Sawtell

Randolph Scott, Angela Lansbury, Warner
Anderson, Jean Parker, Wallace Ford, John
Emery, James Bell, Ruth Donnelly, Michael
Pate, Jeanette Nolan, Don Megowan

Lawman*

US 1970   99m   Technicolor
UA / Scimitar (Michael Winner)

When a marshal tracks down drunken cowboys
who have killed an old man, the townsfolk's
resistance leads to a bloodbath.
Terse, violent western with a good cast.

w Gerald Wilson d Michael Winner ph Bob
Paynter m Jerry Fielding

Burt Lancaster, Robert Ryan, Lee J. Cobb,

Sheree North, Robert Duvall, Joseph Wiseman, John McGiver, Albert Salmi, J. D. Cannon

Lawrence of Arabia***
GB 1962 221m Technicolor Super Panavision 70
Columbia / Horizon (Sam Spiegel)

An adventurer's life with the Arabs, told in flashbacks after his accidental death in the thirties.
Sprawling epic which manages after four hours to give no insight whatever into the complexities of character of this mysterious historic figure, but is often spectacularly beautiful and exciting along the way.

w Robert Bolt *d David Lean ph Frederick A. Young m Maurice Jarre pd John Box ad John Stoll*

Peter O'Toole, Omar Sharif, Arthur Kennedy, Jack Hawkins, Donald Wolfit, Claude Rains, Anthony Quayle, *Alec Guinness*, Anthony Quinn, Jose Ferrer, Michel Ray, Zia Mohyeddin
'Grandeur of conception is not up to grandeur of setting.'—*Penelope Houston*

AA: best picture; David Lean; Frederick A. Young; Maurice Jarre
AAN: Robert Bolt; Peter O'Toole; Omar Sharif

The Lawyer*
US 1970 120m Technicolor
Paramount (Brad Dexter)

An ambitious young Italian-American defence lawyer takes on a murder case.
Smartly-scripted, perfectly ordinary courtroom drama in a well-detailed western setting. The star subsequently played the same character in a TV series, *Petrocelli*.

w Sidney J. Furie, Harold Buchman *d Sidney J. Furie ph* Ralph Woolsey *m* Malcolm Dodds

Barry Newman, Harold Gould, Diana Muldaur, Robert Colbert, Kathleen Crowley, Booth Colman

Lawyer Man
US 1932 68m bw
Warner

An honest lawyer becomes corrupted by success.
Smart, cynical melodrama, dated but sufficiently fast-paced to remain interesting.

w Rian James, James Seymour, *novel* Max Trell *d* William Dieterle *ph* Robert Kurrle

William Powell, Joan Blondell, Helen Vinson, Alan Dinehart, Allen Jenkins, David Landau, Claire Dodd

Laxdale Hall
GB 1952 77m bw
Group Three (Alfred Shaughnessy)
US title: *Scotch on the Rocks*

MPs are sent to investigate a tiny Hebridean island which refuses to pay road tax.
Thin rehash of *Whisky Galore* put together without the Ealing style. Minor compensations can be found.

w John Eldridge, Alfred Shaughnessy *d* John Eldridge *ph* Arthur Grant *m* Frank Spencer

Raymond Huntley, Ronald Squire, Sebastian Shaw, Fulton Mackay, Kathleen Ryan, Kynaston Reeves

Le Mans*
US 1971 108m De Luxe Panavision
Solar / Cinema Center (Jack N. Reddish)

A sullen American enters for the 24-hour race. Almost no plot and little documentary examination; what's left is a multitude of racing shots with Steve McQueen at the wheel. For some this may be enough.

w Harry Kleiner *d* Lee H. Katzin *ph* Robert B. Hauser, René Gruissart Jnr *m* Michel Legrand

Steve McQueen, Siegfried Rauch, Elga Andersen, Ronald Leigh-Hunt

The League of Gentlemen***
GB 1960 112m bw
Rank / Allied Film Makers (Michael Relph)

An ex-army officer recruits high-class misfits with guilty secrets to help him in a bank robbery. Delightfully handled comedy adventure, from the days (alas) when crime did not pay; a lighter ending would have made it a classic.

w *Bryan Forbes, novel* John Boland *d Basil Dearden ph* Arthur Ibbetson *m* Philip Green

Jack Hawkins, Richard Attenborough, *Roger Livesey, Nigel Patrick*, Bryan Forbes, Kieron Moore, Terence Alexander, *Norman Bird*, Robert Coote, Melissa Stribling, Nanette Newman, Gerald Harper, Patrick Wymark, David Lodge, Doris Hare, Lydia Sherwood

Lease of Life*
GB 1954 94m Eastmancolor
Ealing (Jack Rix)

A poor clergyman is given a year to live, and puts it to good use.
Somewhat depressing but well-acted drama with excellent village atmosphere.

w Eric Ambler *d* Charles Frend *ph* Douglas Slocombe *m* Alan Rawsthorne

Robert Donat, Kay Walsh, Adrienne Corri, Denholm Elliott

The Leather Boys *
GB 1963   108m bw   Cinemascope
British Lion / Garrick (Raymond Stross)

Two working-class teenagers marry for sex; she
becomes a drudge and he develops a relationship
with a homosexual motorcyclist.
Sharply-observed slice of low life which now
seems quite dated, the central figures no longer
being of the 'heroic' interest given them at the
time. Technically the film is tediously and
fashionably flashy.

w Gillian Freeman, *novel* Elliot George d Sidney
J. Furie ph Gerald Gibbs m Bill McGuffie

Rita Tushingham, Dudley Sutton, Colin
Campbell, Gladys Henson

The Leather Saint
US 1955   86m bw   Vistavision
Paramount (Norman Retchin)

To provide his parish hospital with medical
equipment, a Catholic priest becomes a
commercial prizefighter.
Unlikely piece of religiosity, not too badly done.

w Norman Retchin, Alvin Ganzer d Alvin
Ganzer ph Haskell Boggs md Irvin Talbot

Paul Douglas, John Derek, Cesar Romero,
Ernest Truex, Jody Lawrance

Leathernecking
US 1930   80m bw
RKO (Louis Sarecky)

A Honolulu socialite falls for a marine, but
grows cool when she discovers that he is a
private and not an officer as he pretended.
Curiously cast, spasmodically funny non-
musical version of a Rodgers and Hart
Broadway hit.

w Alfred Jackson, Jane Murfin, *play* Present
Arms by Herbert Fields, Rodgers and Hart
d Edward Cline ph J. Roy Hunt m Oscar
Levant

Irene Dunne (her first role), Ken Murray, Eddie
Foy Jnr, Louise Fazenda, Ned Sparks, Lilyan
Tashman

Leave Her to Heaven
US 1945   111m Technicolor
TCF (William A. Bacher)

A selfish, jealous woman causes unhappiness for
those around her, even in her suicide.
No-holds-barred melodrama of the old school;
what seemed lush production at the time now
looks tatty.

w Jo Swerling, *novel* Ben Ames Williams d John
M. Stahl ph Leon Shamroy m Alfred Newman

Gene Tierney, Cornel Wilde, Jeanne Crain,

Vincent Price, Mary Phillips, Ray Collins, Gene
Lockhart, Reed Hadley, Chill Wills

AA: Leon Shamroy
AAN: Gene Tierney

Leaves from Satan's Book *
Denmark 1919   80m approx (24 fps)   bw
  silent
Nordisk

Episodes from the activities of Satan through the
ages: with Christ, the Inquisition, the French
Revolution and the Russian Revolution.
Vaguely propagandist short-story compilation
with effective moments.

w Edgar Hoyer, Carl Dreyer, *novel* The Sorrows
of Satan by Marie Corelli d Carl Dreyer
ph George Schneevoigt

The Left Hand of God
US 1955   87m   De Luxe   Cinemascope
TCF (Buddy Adler)

China, 1947: a Catholic priest newly arrived in a
small village proves to be an American flier on
the run from a warlord; but he contrives to work
a small 'miracle'.
Hollywood religiosity at its most contrived, put
together without distinction; the players have a
wary look.

w Alfred Hayes, *novel* William E. Barrett
d Edward Dmytryk ph Franz Planer m Victor
Young

Humphrey Bogart, Gene Tierney, Lee J. Cobb,
E. G. Marshall, Agnes Moorehead

The Left Handed Gun *
US 1958   102m bw
Warner / Haroll (Fred Coe)

Billy the Kid sets out to shoot four men who have
killed his friend.
'Method'-oriented western, efficiently made but
somewhat downcast.

w Leslie Stevens, *TV play* Gore Vidal d Arthur
Penn ph Peverell Marley m Alexander Courage

Paul Newman, John Dehner, Lita Milan, Hurd
Hatfield

Left Right and Centre *
GB 1959   95m bw
British Lion / Launder and Gilliat

A TV personality becomes Tory candidate at a
by-election.
Scrappy political comedy with the saving grace
of a large number of comic talents.

w Sidney Gilliat, Val Valentine d Sidney Gilliat
ph Gerald Gibbs m Humphrey Searle

Ian Carmichael, Alastair Sim, Patricia Bredin,

Richard Wattis, Eric Barker, Gordon Harker, George Benson, Frederick Leister

The Legacy
GB 1978   102m   colour
Columbia / Pethurst / Turman-Foster (David Foster)

An American designer goes to stay with her employer and finds herself in the middle of an occult murder plot.
Cliché-ridden screamer which will please the easily pleased.

w Jimmy Sangster, Patrick Tilley, Paul Wheeler d Richard Marquand ph Dick Bush, Alan Hume m Michael J. Lewis

Katharine Ross, Sam Elliot, John Standing, Ian Hogg, Margaret Tyzack, Charles Gray, Lee Montaque, Hidegard Neil

The Legend of Hell House *
GB 1973   94m   De Luxe
TCF / Academy (James H. Nicholson)

Four people arrive at a haunted house in which several psychic investigators have been killed.
Harrowing thriller, a less solemn but more frightening version of *The Haunting*.

w Richard Matheson, from his novel d John Hough ph Alan Hume m Brian Hodgson, Delia Derbyshire

Pamela Franklin, Roddy McDowall, Clive Revill, Gayle Hunnicutt, Roland Culver, Peter Bowles, Michael Gough
'One of the most absorbing, goose-fleshing and mind-pleasing ghost breaker yarns on film.'—*Judith Crist, 1977*

The Legend of Lobo *
US 1962   67m   Technicolor
Walt Disney (James Algar)

The life of a forest wolf.
Anthropomorphic entertainment in which a dreaded animal becomes something of a hero and finally saves his mate from bounty hunters.
Impeccably contrived, like a live-action *Bambi*.

w Dwight Hauser, James Algar, *story* Ernest Thompson Seton d James Algar ph Jack Couffer, Lloyd Beebe m Oliver Wallace

The Legend of Lylah Clare *
US 1968   130m   Metrocolor   Panavision
MGM / Robert Aldrich

A mad director brings an unknown actress to Hollywood because of her resemblance to a former star, his creation, who had died mysteriously.
Unintentionally risible melodrama with echoes

of *Svengali* and *Sunset Boulevard*; not to the public's taste, or anyone else's, in the late sixties.

w Hugo Butler, Jean Rouverol, *TV play* Robert Thom, Edward de Blasio d Robert Aldrich ph Joseph Biroc m Frank de Vol

Peter Finch, Kim Novak, Ernest Borgnine, Coral Browne, Milton Seltzer, Rossella Falk, Gabriele Tinti, Valentina Cortesa, George Kennedy

Legend of the Lost
US 1957   107m   Technirama
UA / Batjac / Robert Haggiag / Dear (Henry Hathaway)

Two adventurers and a slave girl seek a lost city in the Sahara.
Tediously vague and underplotted desert adventure with a few attractive moments.

w Robert Presnell Jnr, Ben Hecht d Henry Hathaway ph Jack Cardiff m A. F. Lavagnino

John Wayne, Sophia Loren, Rossano Brazzi

The Legend of the Seven Golden Vampires
GB / Hong Kong 1974   89m
  Eastmancolor   Panavision
Hammer–Shaw (Don Houghton, Vee King Shaw)

In 1904 Chungking, Professor Van Helsing finds his old enemy Dracula behind a Chinese vampire cult.
Hectic, outlandish mix of Hammer horror and Kung Fu; plenty of gusto but not much sense.

w Don Houghton d Roy Ward Baker ph John Wilcox, Roy Ford m James Bernard

Peter Cushing, David Chiang, Julie Ege, Robin Stewart, John Forbes Robertson

The Legend of Tom Dooley
US 1959   77m   bw
Columbia / Shpetner

At the end of the Civil War, Confederate youths take the law into their own hands and attack Unionists.
Youthful rebellion in historical mould, decently but rather dully delivered, based on a folk ballad.

w Stan Shpetner d Ted Post ph Gilbert Warrenton m Ronald Stein

Michael Landon, Richard Rust, Jo Morrow

The Lemon Drop Kid *
US 1951   91m   bw
Paramount (Robert A. Welch)

A gangster forces a bookie to find the money which he has lost on a horse through the bookie's incompetence.

Amusing Bob Hope/Runyon vehicle despite heavy sentiment about an old folks' home. The Santa Claus sequences are memorable.

w Edmund Hartman, Frank Tashlin, Robert O'Brien, *story* Damon Runyon *d* Sidney Lanfield *ph* Daniel L. Fapp

Bob Hope, Marilyn Maxwell, Lloyd Nolan, Jane Darwell, Andrea King, Fred Clark, Jay C. Flippen, William Frawley, Harry Bellaver

Lenin in October*
USSR 1937   111m   bw
Mosfilm
original title: *Lenin v Octiabrye*

The activities of Lenin during the revolution. Stalwart propaganda piece, of solid but not outstanding cinematic interest.

w Alexei Kapler *d Mikhail Romm* ph Boris Volchok *m* Anatoli Alexandrov

Boris Shchukin
† The success of this film provoked *Lenin in 1918*, made in the following year (132m) by the same talents, with Cherkassov as Gorky. Many other Russian films on Lenin have followed.

Lenny**
US 1974   111m   bw
UA (Marvin Worth)

The career of obscene comedian Lenny Bruce and his struggles with the law.
Old-fashioned rags-to-riches-to-rags story, rampant with the new permissiveness. Filmically extremely clever, emotionally hollow.

w Julian Barry, from his play *d Bob Fosse* ph Bruce Surtees *md* Ralph Burns *pd* Joel Schiller

Dustin Hoffman, Valerie Perrine, Jan Miner, Stanley Beck, Gary Morton
'For audiences who want to believe that Lenny Bruce was a saintly gadfly who was martyred for having lived before his time.'—*New Yorker*

AAN: best picture; Julian Barry; Bob Fosse; Bruce Surtees; Dustin Hoffman; Valerie Perrine

Leo the Last
GB 1969   104m   De Luxe
UA / Char / Wink / Boor (Irwin Winkler, Robert Chartoff)

An alienated aristocrat brings his retinue to a London slum and has an effect on most of the inhabitants.
Infuriating symbolic fantasy; only the writer-director (presumably) has any idea what it is about.

w William Stair, John Boorman *d* John Boorman *ph* Peter Suschitsky *m* Dred Myrow *pd* Tony Woollard

Marcello Mastroianni, Billie Whitelaw, Calvin Lockhart, Glenna Forster Jones, Graham Crowden, Gwen Ffrangcon Davies, David de Keyser, Vladek Sheybal, Kenneth J. Warren

Léon Morin, Priest*
France / Italy 1961   117m   bw
Rome-Paris Films (Georges de Beauregard)

During the German occupation of France a young widow finds herself falling in love with the young priest who is converting her to religion. An intellectual romance, sharp and witty for the most part, with vivid wartime backgrounds.

wd Jean-Pierre Melville, *novel* Béatrix Beck *ph* Henri Decaë *m* Martial Solal, Albert Raisner

Jean-Paul Belmondo, Emmanuele Riva, Irène Tunc, Marielle Gozzi

The Leopard***
US / Italy 1963   205m   Technirama
Fox / Titanus / SNPC / GPC (Goffredo Lombardo)
original title: *Il Gattopardo*

The family life of an Italian nobleman at the time of Garibaldi.
Elaborate, complex family saga, painted like an old master with great care and attention to detail, but with not much chance outside Italy of delivering its original dramatic force. Visconti had asked for Lancaster, so TCF picked up the international release but couldn't make head or tail of it commercially; they even ruined its high quality by releasing a dubbed, shortened version in Cinemascope and De Luxe colour of poor standard.

wd Luchino Visconti, *novel* Giuseppe de Lampedusa *ph Giuseppe Rotunno* m Nino Rota *ad Mario Garbuglia*

Burt Lancaster, Claudia Cardinale, Alain Delon, Paolo Stoppa, Serge Reggiani, Leslie French

Leopard in the Snow
GB / Canada 1977   94m   Technicolor
Seastone / Leopard in the Snow (W. Laurence Heisey)

A girl caught in a Cumberland blizzard is rescued by a mysterious stranger with a pet leopard. He turns out to be a disfigured racing driver, and she falls in love with him.
A deliberate cross between *Jayne Eyre* and a shopgirl's romance, adequately produced for its intended audience.

w Anne Mather, Jill Hyem, *novel* Anne Mather *d* Gerry O'Hara *ph* Alfie Hicks *m* Kenneth V. Jones

Keir Dullea, Susan Penhaligon, Jeremy Kemp,
Kenneth More, Billie Whitelaw

The Leopard Man **
US 1943   59m   bw
RKO (Val Lewton)

Murders in a Mexican border town are attributed
to an escaped leopard.
Effective minor piece in the Lewton horror
gallery; poor plot countered by highly effective
suspense sequences.

w Ardel Wray, Edward Dein, novel Black Alibi
by Cornell Woolrich d Jacques Tourneur
ph Robert de Grasse

Dennis O'Keefe, Jean Brooks, Margo, James
Bell, Isabel Jewell

Lepke
US 1974   110m   De Luxe   Panavision
Warner / AmeriEuro Pictures (Menaham
   Golan)

After World War I a small-time crook becomes
head of Murder Incorporated.
Violent but totally uninteresting gangster
melodrama; fidelity to fact is not enough.

w Wesley Hau, Tamor Hoffs d Menahem
Golan ph Andrew Davis m Ken Wannberg
pd Jack Degovia

Tony Curtis, Anjanette Comer, Michael Callan,
Warren Berlinger, Milton Berle, Gianni Russo
   'A kosher version of The Godfather.'—Verina
Glaessner

A Lesson in Love
Sweden 1953   95m   bw
Svensk Filmindustri

A gynaecologist and his wife grow bored and
turn to other partners, but are reconciled.
Slight comedy, surprisingly unsubtle for its
creator, but passable.

wd Ingmar Bergman ph Martin Bodin, Bengt
Nordwal m Dag Wiren

Gunnar Bjornstrand, Eba Dahlbeck, Harriet
Andersson, Yvonne Lombard, Ake Grönberg

Let 'Em Have It *
US 1935   90m   bw
Edward Small
GB title: False Faces

The FBI go after criminals on a terror spree.
Lively cops and robbers with some starkly
effective moments.

w Joseph Moncure March, Elmer Harris d Sam
Wood
ph J. Peverell Marley, Robert Planck

Richard Arlen, Virginia Bruce, Alice Brady,
Bruce Cabot, Harvey Stephens, Eric Linden,
Joyce Compton, J. Farrell MacDonald

Let Freedom Ring
US 1939   100m   bw
MGM (Harry Rapf)

A westerner returns to his home town and clears
it of corruption.
Elementary Hollywood actioner with curious
credits, climaxed by Eddy singing The Star
Spangled Banner.

w Ben Hecht d Jack Conway

Nelson Eddy, Victor McLaglen, Virginia Bruce,
Lionel Barrymore, H. B. Warner, Raymond
Walburn, Edward Arnold, Guy Kibbee, Charles
Butterworth, Billy Bevan

Let George Do It **
GB 1940   82m   bw
Ealing (Basil Dearden)

A ukelele player accidentally goes to Bergen
instead of Blackpool and is mistaken for a spy.
Generally thought to be the best George Formby
vehicle, with plenty of pace, good situations and
catchy tunes.

w John Dighton, Austin Melford, Angus
MacPhail, Basil Dearden d Marcel Varnel

George Formby, Phyllis Calvert, Garry Marsh,
Romney Brent, Bernard Lee, Coral Browne,
Torin Thatcher, Hal Gordon

Let No Man Write My Epitaph
US 1960   106m   bw
Columbia / Boris D. Kaplan

A slum boy wants to become a concert pianist
but falls in with gangsters.
Squalid, predictable melodrama without many
redeeming features.

w Robert Presnell Jnr, novel Willard Motley
d Philip Leacock ph Burnett Guffey m George
Duning

James Darren, Shelley Winters, Burl Ives, Sal
Mineo, Jean Seberg, Jeanne Cooper, Ricardo
Montalban, Ella Fitzgerald

Let the People Sing *
GB 1942   105m   bw
British National (John Baxter)

An out-of-work comedian persuades a drunken
nobleman to join a protest against the closing of
a village hall.
A development of The Good Companions which
compares quite nicely with the Capra films from
across the water: naïve but entertaining, with
good star performances.

w John Baxter, Barbara K. Emery, Geoffrey Orme,
novel J. B. Priestley d John Baxter

Alastair Sim, Fred Emney, Edward Rigby,
Patricia Roc, Oliver Wakefield, Marian Spencer,
Olive Sloane, Gus McNaughton, Charles
Hawtrey

Let's Be Happy
GB 1957   107m   Technicolor
ABP / Marcel Hellman

Footling musical remake of *Jeannie* (qv).

w Diana Morgan *d* Henry Levin

Vera-Ellen, Tony Martin, Robert Flemyng,
Zena Marshall, Guy Middleton, Katherine
Kath, Jean Cadell, Gordon Jackson
   'Success still eludes the Anglo-American
musical.'—*MFB*

Let's Be Famous
GB 1939   83m   bw
Ealing (Michael Balcon)

A stage struck Irish lad and Lancashire lass have
various adventures in London.
Easy-going comedy introducing radio
personalities of the day.

w Roger MacDougall, Allan MacKinnon
d Walter Forde *ph* Ronald Neame, Gordon
Dines *md* Ernest Irving

Jimmy O'Dea, Betty Driver, Sonnie Hale,
Patrick Barr, Basil Radford, Milton Rosmer,
Garry Marsh

Let's Dance
US 1950   112m   Technicolor
Paramount (Robert Fellows)

Show business partners reunite after five years of
private life.
Tediously plotted musical with a couple of good
numbers.

w Allan Scott, *story* Maurice Zolotow
d Norman Z. McLeod *ph* George Barnes
songs Frank Loesser

Fred Astaire, Betty Hutton, Roland Young,
Ruth Warrick, Lucile Watson, Barton
MacLane, Shepperd Strudwick, Melville
Cooper, Harold Huber, George Zucco

Let's Do It Again
US 1953   95m   Technicolor
Columbia (Oscar Saul)

A songwriter and his wife plan a divorce but call
it off in the nick of time.
Tame musical remake of *The Awful Truth* (qv),
pleasant enough but lacking style and punch.

w Mary Loos, Richard Sale *d* Alexander Hall
ph Charles Lawton Jnr *m* George Duning
md Morris Stoloff *songs* Lester Lee, Ned
Washington

Jane Wyman, Ray Milland, Aldo Ray, Leon
Ames

Let's Do It Again
US 1975   113m   Technicolor
Warner / First Artists / Verdon (Melville
   Tucker, Pembroke J. Herring)

Three Atlanta workers conceive a zany plan to
raise money for their church by hypnotizing a
boxer into winning a big fight.
Lively but overlong farce reassembling the black
talents of *Uptown Saturday Night.*

w Richard Wesley *d* Sidney Poitier *ph* Donald
M. Morgan *m* Curtis Mayfield

Sidney Poitier, Bill Cosby, Calvin Lockhart,
John Amos, Denise Nicholas, Ossie Davis,
Jimmy Walker

Let's Face It
US 1943   76m   bw
Paramount (Fred Kohlmar)

A smart-alec soldier has a plot involving a ladies'
health camp, but finds himself up to his neck in
spies.
Tepid star comedy which unaccountably ditches
almost all the numbers from the musical on
which it was based.

w (uncredited) from the musical play by
Dorothy and Herbert Fields and Cole Porter,
based on the play Cradle Snatchers by Norma
Mitchell and Russell Medcraft *d* Sidney
Lanfield *ph* Lionel Lindon *songs* Cole Porter

Bob Hope, Betty Hutton, Eve Arden, Phyllis
Povah, Dona Drake, Zasu Pitts, Marjorie
Weaver, Raymond Walburn, Joe Sawyer

Let's Kill Uncle
US 1966   92m   colour
Universal / William Castle

A boy is threatened by his wicked uncle, and
retaliates.
Mildly intriguing black comedy, leadenly
handled.

w Mark Rodger, *novel* Rohan O'Grady
d William Castle *ph* Harold Lipstein
m Herman Stein

Nigel Green, Mary Badham, Pat Cardi, Robert
Pickering

Let's Live a Little
US 1948   85m   bw
Eagle-Lion / United California Productions

An advertising agent falls for his lady
psychiatrist, and after many vicissitudes they
and their former partners make it to the altar.
Mild comedy which just about bubbles along
despite a rather uncomfortable cast.

w Albert J. Cohen, Jack Harvey *d* Richard
Wallace *ph* Ernest Laszlo *m* Werner Heymann

Hedy Lamarr, Robert Cummings, Anna Sten,
Robert Shayne, Mary Treen

Let's Make Love*

US 1960   118m   De Luxe   Cinemascope
TCF

A multi-millionaire, learning that he is to be
burlesqued in a Broadway show, joins the cast as
an actor.

Complex, moderately sophisticated,
occasionally funny musical inspired by *On the
Avenue* (qv); lively characterizations but poor
numbers.

w Norman Krasna *d* George Cukor *ph* Daniel
L. Fapp *ch* Jack Cole *md* Lionel Newman, Earl
H. Hagen *songs* Sammy Cahn, Jimmy Van
Heusen

Yves Montand, Marilyn Monroe, Tony Randall,
Wilfrid Hyde White, Frankie Vaughan, David
Burns, and guests Bing Crosby, Gene Kelly,
Milton Berle

AAN: Lionel Newman, Earl H. Hagen

Let's Scare Jessica to Death

US 1971   89m   colour
Paramount / Jessica Co

Back home after a nervous breakdown, our
heroine is troubled by voices and visions, not to
mention an ambulant corpse and a vampire or
two.

Competent screamie.

w Norman Jonas, Ralph Rose *d* John Hancock
ph Bob Baldwin *m* Orville Stoeber

Zohra Lampert, Barton Heyman

The Letter*

US 1929   61m   bw
Paramount

Early talkie version of a solid piece of theatre.
See below.

story and play W. Somerset Maugham *d* Jean
de Limur

Jeanne Eagels, O. P. Heggie, Reginald Owen,
Herbert Marshall, Irene Browne

AAN: Jeanne Eagels

The Letter****

US 1940   95m   bw
Warner (Robert Lord)

A rubber plantation owner's wife kills a man in
what seems to have been self-defence; but a letter
from her proves it to have been a crime of
passion, and becomes an instrument of
blackmail.

Excellent performances and presentation make
this the closest approximation on film to reading
a Maugham story of the Far East, though
censorship forced the addition of an infuriating
moral ending.

w Howard Koch, story *W. Somerset Maugham*
d William Wyler ph Tony Gaudio m Max
Steiner

Bette Davis, Herbert Marshall, James
Stephenson, Sen Yung, Frieda Inescort, Gale
Sondergaard, Bruce Lester, Tetsu Komai
† Herbert Marshall played the lover in the first
version and the husband in the second.

AAN: best picture; William Wyler; Tony
Gaudio; Max Steiner; Bette Davis; James
Stephenson

Letter from an Unknown Woman****

US 1948   89m   bw
Universal (John Houseman)

A woman wastes her life in unrequited love for a
rakish pianist.

Superior 'woman's picture' which gave its
director his best chance in America to recreate
his beloved Vienna of long ago. Hollywood
production magic at its best.

w Howard Koch, novel *Stefan Zweig* *d Max*
Ophuls ph Franz Planer m Daniele
Amfitheatrof *ad Alexander Golitzen*

Joan Fontaine, Louis Jourdan, Mady Christians,
Art Smith, Marcel Journet

'A film full of snow, sleigh bells, lights
gleaming in ornamental gardens and trysts at
night.'—*Charles Higham, 1972*

'It is fascinating to watch the sure deft means
by which Ophuls sidetracks seemingly inevitable
clichés and holds on to a shadowy, tender mood,
half buried in the past. Here is a fragile filmic
charm that is not often or easily
accomplished.'—*Richard Winnington*

Letter of Introduction*

US 1938   100m   bw
Universal (John M. Stahl)

A young actress is encouraged by an ageing star
whom she does not know is her father.
Commercial melodrama with luxury trimmings,
all very neatly packaged.

w Sheridan Gibney, Leonard Spiegelgass
d John M. Stahl *ph* Karl Freund

Adolphe Menjou, Andrea Leeds, Edgar Bergen
(and Charlie McCarthy), George Murphy, Eve
Arden, Rita Johnson, Ernest Cossart, Ann
Sheridan

A Letter to Three Wives **
US 1949   102m   bw
TCF (Sol C. Siegel)

Three wives on a picnic receive word from a
friend that she has run off with one of their
husbands.
Amusing short-story compendium which
seemed more revelatory at the time than it does
now, and paved the way for its writer-director's
heyday.

wd Joseph L. Mankiewicz, *novel* John
Klempner *ph* Arthur Miller *m* Alfred Newman

Jeanne Crain, Ann Sothern, Linda Darnell,
Jeffrey Lynn, Kirk Douglas, *Paul Douglas*,
Barbara Lawrence, Connie Gilchrist, Florence
Bates, Hobart Cavanaugh, and the voice of
Celeste Holm
   'A peek into the other woman's male!'—
publicity
   'A mere shadow of those acid Hollywood
comedies of the thirties . . . over-written and
under-directed . . . but it has a supply of ironies
and makes a certain alkaline comment on
present-day American customs and manners.'—
Richard Winnington

AA: Joseph L. Mankiewicz (as writer); Joseph
L. Mankiewicz (as director)
AAN: best picture

Les Liaisons Dangereuses *
France 1959   106m   bw
Films Marceau

Valmont and his wife compare notes on each
other's affairs.
Showy modernization of a notorious minor
classic.

w Roger Vailland, Roger Vadim, Claude Brûlé,
novel Choderlos de Laclos *d* Roger Vadim
ph Marcel Grignon *m* Jack Murray, Thelonius
Monk

Gérard Philipe, Jeanne Moreau, Annette Vadim,
Jeanne Valerie, Simone Renant, Jean-Louis
Trintignant
   'A woman's picture par excellence.'—*John
Russell Taylor, MFB*

Libel *
GB 1959   100m   bw
MGM / Comet (Anatole de Grunwald)

An ex-POW baronet is accused of being an
impostor.
Old-fashioned courtroom spellbinder, quite
adequately done though occasionally creaky.

w Anatole de Grunwald, Karl Tunberg, *play*
Edward Wooll *d* Anthony Asquith *ph* Robert
Krasker *m* Benjamin Frankel

Dirk Bogarde, Olivia de Havilland, Paul Massie,
Wilfrid Hyde White, Robert Morley, Anthony
Dawson, Richard Wattis, Martin Miller,
Millicent Martin

Libeled Lady **
US 1936   98m   bw
MGM (Lawrence Weingarten)

An heiress sues a newspaper, and the editor hires
a friend to compromise her.
Lively four-star romantic comedy which sums
up its era as well as any.

w Maurine Watkins, Howard Emmett Rogers,
George Oppenheimer *d* Jack Conway
ph Norbert Brodine

*Jean Harlow, Myrna Loy, Spencer Tracy,
William Powell, Walter Connolly,* Charley
Grapewin, Cora Witherspoon,
E. E. Clive, Charles Trowbridge
† Remade as *Easy to Wed* (qv); central situation
borrowed for *Man's Favorite Sport* (qv).

AAN: best picture

The Liberation of L. B. Jones *
US 1970   102m   Technicolor
Columbia / Liberation Co (Ronald Lubin)

Racial murder is the result when a black
undertaker wants a divorce in a small Tennessee
town.
Violent, pointless but well-made melodrama
which really does not take matters much further
than *Intruder in the Dust*.

w Stirling Silliphant, Jesse Hill Ford, from
Ford's novel *d* William Wyler *ph* Robert
Surtees *m* Elmer Bernstein

Lee J. Cobb, Anthony Zerbe, Roscoe Lee
Browne, Lola Falana, Lee Majors, Barbara
Hershey, Yaphet Kotto, Arch Johnson, Chill
Wills
   'With its genuinely ferocious climax it adds up
to probably the most powerful, if not the most
sophisticated, race-war film the commercial
studios have yet produced.'—*Nigel Andrews*

Licensed to Kill
GB 1965   97m   Eastmancolor
Alistair Films (Estelle E. Richmond)
US title: *The Second Best Secret Agent in the
Whole Wide World*

The Foreign Office calls in agent Charles Vine to protect a top international scientist.
Cheap copy of James Bond which wins no laurels but produces a few efficient routine thrills.

w Howard Griffiths, Lindsay Shonteff d Lindsay Shonteff ph Terry Maher m Bertram Chappell

Tom Adams, Veronica Hurst, Karel Stepanek, Felix Felton, Peter Bull

Liebelei *
Austria 1932 85m bw
Fred Lissa

A young army officer falls in love; but he is killed in a duel and his girl commits suicide.
Semi-classic romantic novelette, like a warm-up for *Letter from an Unknown Woman*.

w Hans Wilhelm, Kurt Alexander, *story* Arthur Schnitzler d *Max Ophuls* ph Franz Planer m Theo Macheber

Magda Schneider, Wolfgang Liebeneiner, Luise Ullrich, Willy Eichberger, Gustaf Gruendgens, Paul Hoerbiger

† A revised French version played as *Une Histoire d'Amour*. The story had previously been shot under the same title in Germany in 1927; and in the sixties Romy Schneider and Alain Delon appeared in a French remake called *Christine*.

Lies My Father Told Me
Canada 1975 102m colour
Columbia / Pentimento / Pentacle (Anthony Bedrich, Harry Gulkin)

Adventures of a poor Jewish boy and his grandfather in Montreal in the twenties.
Effectively if rather dishonestly sentimental, this is the kind of family picture for which critics are always clamouring but which few people in the seventies will pay to see.

w Ted Allan, from his book d Jan Kadar ph Paul Van der Linden m Sol Kaplan

Yossi Yadin, Len Birman, Marilyn Lightstone, Jeffrey Lynas

† A British low-budgeter was made from the same story in 1940, changing the venue to Ireland and the race to Irish.

AAN: Ted Allan

Lt Robin Crusoe USN
US 1966 114m Technicolor
Walt Disney (Bill Walsh, Ron Miller)

A navy pilot parachutes on to a Pacific island and gets involved in the local women's lib movement.

Slow-paced family comedy with very few laughs.

w Bill Walsh, Don da Gradi d Byron Paul ph William Snyder m Bob Brunner

Dick Van Dyke, Nancy Kwan, Akim Tamiroff

The Lieutenant Wore Skirts
US 1955 99m Eastmancolor
Cinemascope
TCF (Buddy Adler)

When a TV writer joins the service, his wife enlists to be near him; but he is rejected on medical grounds.
Raucous, tasteless farce which tries far too hard to raise laughs.

w Albert Beich, Frank Tashlin d Frank Tashlin ph Leo Tover m Cyril Mockridge

Tom Ewell, Sheree North, Rita Moreno, Rick Jason, Les Tremayne

The Life and Death of Colonel Blimp ***
GB 1943 163m Technicolor
GFD / Archers (Michael Powell, Emeric Pressburger)
US title: *Colonel Blimp*

A British soldier survives three wars and falls in love with three women.
Not the Blimp of the cartoon strip, but a sympathetic figure in a warm, consistently interesting if idiosyncratic love story against a background of war. The Archers as usual provide a sympathetic German lead (friend of the hero); quite a coup in wartime.

wd *Michael Powell, Emeric Pressburger* ph Jack Cardiff m Allan Gray ad Alfred Junge

Roger Livesey, Anton Walbrook, Deborah Kerr, Roland Culver, James McKechnie, Albert Lieven, Arthur Wontner, A. E. Matthews, David Hutcheson, Ursula Jeans, John Laurie, Harry Welchman

The Life and Times of Judge Roy Bean *
US 1972 124m Technicolor Panavision
National General / Famous Artists (John Foreman)

A fantasia on the famous outlaw judge of the old west.
Sporadically entertaining but schematically messy mixture of burlesqued folklore and violent action, not in the same league as *Butch Cassidy*.

w John Milius d John Huston ph Richard Moore m Maurice Jarre

Paul Newman, Ava Gardner, Jacqueline Bisset, Tab Hunter, Stacy Keach, Roddy McDowall, Anthony Perkins, John Huston

AAN: song 'Marmalade, Molasses and Honey'
(*m* Maurice Jarre, *ly* A. and M. Byrne)

Life at the Top*
GB 1965   117m   bw
Columbia / Romulus (James Woolf)

Ten years after marrying into money, Joe
Lampton is dissatisfied, and he and his wife both
have affairs.

Rough-talking but basically predictable and old-
fashioned sequel to *Room at the Top*, a bit
compromised by having to reflect the sixties
London scene; the early Yorkshire sequences are
the best.

w Mordecai Richler *d* Ted Kotcheff *ph* Oswald
Morris *m* Richard Addinsell

Laurence Harvey, Jean Simmons, Honor
Blackman, Michael Craig, Donald Wolfit,
Margaret Johnston, Allan Cuthbertson,
Ambrosine Philpotts, Robert Morley, Nigel
Davenport, George A. Cooper

  'Another thoroughly mean-spirited film of a
kind which has been taking root in the British
cinema.'—*Tom Milne*

†The character of Joe Lampton was later used in
a long running TV series called *Man at the Top*,
which sprouted a film of its own under that title.

Life Begins
US 1932   72m   bw
Warner (Ray Griffith)

A night in a maternity hospital.
Multi-melodrama later remade as *A Child Is
Born*. Passable.

w Earl Baldwin, *play* Mary McDougal Axelson
d James Flood *ph* James Van Trees

Loretta Young, Eric Linden, Aline MacMahon,
Preston Foster, Glenda Farrell, Frank McHugh,
Clara Blandick, Elizabeth Patterson, Gilbert
Roland

Life Begins at Eight Thirty*
US 1942   85m   bw
TCF (Nunnally Johnson)
GB title: *The Light of Heart*

A distinguished actor is reduced through drink to
being a street corner Santa Claus.
Diluted and sentimentalized version of an
agreeable play.

w Nunnally Johnson, *play* Emlyn Williams
d Irving Pichel *ph* Edward Cronjager *m* Alfred
Newman

Monty Woolley, Ida Lupino, Cornel Wilde, Sara
Allgood, Melville Cooper, J. Edward Bromberg

Life for Ruth*
GB 1962   91m   bw
Rank / Allied Film Makers (Michael Relph,
  Basil Dearden)

A little girl dies because her parents' religion
forbids blood transfusions.
Dramatized from the headlines, this little case
history is small beer as film-making, and not
exactly entertainment, but absorbing as a
comment on human behaviour.

w Janet Green, John McCormick *d* Basil
Dearden *ph* Otto Heller *m* William Alwyn
md Muir Mathieson

Michael Craig, Patrick McGoohan, Janet
Munro

A Life in the Balance*
US 1954   75m   bw
TCF / Panoramic (Leonard Goldstein)

A Mexican widower springs into action when his
young son is kidnapped by a murderer.
Taut little melodrama taking place during one
night in Mexico City; made with vigour on a low
budget.

w Robert Presnell Jnr, Leo Townsend *d Harry
Horner*

ph J. Gomez Urquiza *m* Raul Lavista

Ricardo Montalban, Anne Bancroft, Lee Marvin

The Life of Emile Zola***
US 1937   116m   bw
Warner (Henry Blanke)

The French writer intervenes in the case of
Alfred Dreyfus, condemned unjustly to Devil's
Island.
The box office success of this solidly-carpentered
piece of Hollywood history was compounded in
equal parts of star power and the sheer novelty of
having such a thing turn up at the local Odeon.

w Heinz Herald, Geza Herczeg, Norman Reilly
Raine *d William Dieterle ph Tony Gaudio
m* Max Steiner *ad Anton Grot*

Paul Muni, Joseph Schildkraut, Gale
Sondergaard, Gloria Holden, Donald Crisp,
Erin O'Brien Moore, John Litel, Henry O'Neill,
Morris Carnovsky, Ralph Morgan, Louis
Calhern, Robert Barrat, Vladimir Sokoloff,
Harry Davenport, Robert Warwick, Walter
Kingsford

  'Along with *Louis Pasteur*, it ought to start a
new category—the Warner crusading films,
costume division.'—*Otis Ferguson*

  'A grave story told with great dignity and
superbly played and produced.'—*Pare Lorentz*

  'One of the fine ones which begin as a film and
end as an experience.'—*John Grierson*

AA: best picture; Joseph Schildkraut
AAN: script; William Dieterle; Max Steiner;
Paul Muni

A Life of Her Own
US 1950   108m   bw
MGM (Voldemar Vetluguin)

An innocent girl from Kansas becomes one of
New York's top models.
Road to ruin, American style, from the pages of
a women's magazine.

w Isabel Lennart d George Cukor ph George
Folsey m Bronislau Kaper

Lana Turner, Ray Milland, Tom Ewell, Louis
Calhern, Ann Dvorak, Barry Sullivan, Jean
Hagen

   'This story belongs to the realms of soap
opera—extremely artificial, highly moral in
tone, and deliberately concocted to combine
luxurious settings with an elementary assault on
the audience's emotions.'—MFB

The Life of Jimmy Dolan
US 1933   85m   bw
Warner (Hal B. Wallis)
GB title: The Kid's Last Fight

An amiable wanderer is mistaken for a prize-
fighter wanted for murder.
Modest character romance, later remade as
They Made Me a Criminal.

w David Boehm, Erwin Gelsey, play Bertram
Millhauser, Beulah Marie Dix d Archie Mayo
ph Arthur Edeson

Douglas Fairbanks Jnr, Loretta Young, Aline
MacMahon, Guy Kibbee, Lyle Talbot, Fifi
D'Orsay, Harold Huber, George Meeker

The Life of Vergie Winters
US 1934   82m   bw
RKO (Pandro S. Berman)

A rising politician marries for position but keeps
watch over his mistress and their child.
Archetypal soap opera, a cross between Stella
Dallas and Back Street.

w Jane Murfin, novel Louis Bromfield d Alfred
Santell ph Lucien Andriot

Ann Harding, John Boles, Helen Vinson, Frank
Albertson, Lon Chaney Jnr, Sara Haden, Ben
Alexander, Donald Crisp

Life Upside Down*
France 1964   92m   bw
A.J. Films
original title: La Vie à l'Envers

A pleasant, ordinary young man discovers the
joy of being absolutely alone, and begins to
detach himself from his surroundings, ending up
in a barren flat and a private hospital ward.
Engaging semi-comic case history which
generates much sympathy for its eccentric hero.

wd Alain Jessua ph Jacques Robin m Jacques
Loussier

Charles Denner, Anna Gaylor, Guy Saint-Jean,
Nicole Gueden

   'The tone is civilized, quiet, infinitely peaceful
and often brilliantly funny.'—Brenda Davies,
MFB

Life with Father*
US 1947   118m   Technicolor
Warner (Robert Buckner)

Turn-of-the-century anecdotes of an irascible
well-to-do paterfamilias who won't be baptized.
Well-upholstered screen version of a long
running play; oddly tedious considering the
talent involved.

w Donald Ogden Stewart, play Howard
Lindsay, Russel Crouse d Michael Curtiz
ph Peverell Marley, William V. Skall m Max
Steiner ad Robert Hass

William Powell, Irene Dunne, Edmund Gwenn,
Zasu Pitts, Elizabeth Taylor, Martin Milner,
Jimmy Lydon, Emma Dunn, Moroni Olsen,
Elizabeth Risdon

   'Everybody seems to be trying too hard . . . the
director is totally out of his element in this
careful, deadly version.'—New Yorker, 1978
* Censorship of the day absurdly clipped
Father's famous last line: 'I'm going to be
baptized, damn it!'

AAN: Peverell Marley, William V. Skall; Max
Steiner; William Powell

Lifeboat**
US 1944   96m   bw
TCF (Kenneth MacGowan)

Survivors from a torpedoed passenger ship
include the U-Boat commander responsible.
Propaganda gimmick melodrama interesting for
the casting and for Hitchcock's response to the
challenge of filming in one cramped set.

w Jo Swerling, story John Steinbeck d Alfred
Hitchcock ph Glen MacWilliams m Hugo
Friedhofer

Tallulah Bankhead, Walter Slezak, Henry Hull,
John Hodiak, Canada Lee, William Bendix,
Mary Anderson, Heather Angel, Hume Cronyn

AAN: John Steinbeck; Alfred Hitchcock; Glen
MacWilliams

Lift to the Scaffold*
France 1957   89m   bw
Nouvelles Editions de Films (Jean Thuillier)
original title: *Ascenseur pour l'Echafaud*

An executive murders his employer but is
trapped in the building all night; meanwhile his
car is stolen and he is arrested for a murder
committed by the thief.
Complex, watchable suspenser with pretensions.

w Roger Nimier, Louis Malle, *novel* Noel Calef
d Louis Malle ph Henri Decaë m Miles Davis

Maurice Ronet, Jeanne Moreau, Georges
Poujouly, Yori Bertin, Lino Ventura
  'Cold, clever and rather elegant.'—*Penelope
Houston, MFB*

The Light across the Street
France 1955   99m   bw
EGC / Fernand Rivers (Jacques Gauthier)
original title: *La Lumière d'en Face*

A lorry driver, injured in an accident, becomes
insanely jealous of his young wife.
Low-life melodrama tailored for the sultry
attractions of its new star.

w Louis Cahavance, René Masson, René
Lefèvre d Georges Lacombe ph Louis Page
m Norbert Glanzberg

Brigitte Bardot, Raymond Pellégrin, Roger
Pigaut, Claude Romain

The Light at the Edge of the World
US / Spain / Lichtenstein 1971   120m
   Eastmancolor   Panavision
Bryna / Jet / Triumfilm (Kirk Douglas, Ilya
   Salkind)

A lighthouse keeper near Cape Horn resists a
band of wreckers.
Pretentious, disaster-prone version of a simple
adventure story; one wonders not so much what
went wrong as whether anything went right in
this international venture.

w Tom Rowe, *novel* Jules Verne d Kevin
Billington ph Henri Decaë m Piero Piccioni
Kirk Douglas, Yul Brynner, Samantha Eggar,
Jean-Claude Drouot, Fernando Rey, Renato
Salvatori

The Light in the Forest
US 1958   92m   Technicolor
Walt Disney

Kidnapped by Indians as an infant, a teenager is
returned to his parents but finds the white man's
ways disturbing.
Modest frontier drama with a moral.

w Lawrence Edward Watkin, *novel* Conrad

Richter d Herschel Daugherty ph Ellsworth
Fredericks m Paul Smith

James MacArthur, Carol Lynley, Jessica Tandy,
Wendell Corey, Fess Parker, Joanne Dru,
Joseph Calleia

The Light in the Piazza
GB 1962   101m   Metrocolor
   Cinemascope
MGM (Arthur Freed)

An American matron in Florence tries to marry
off her mentally retarded daughter to a wealthy
Italian.
Puzzling romantic drama in which one is never
quite sure why the characters behave as they do;
in the end all one appreciates is the tour of
northern Italy.

w Julius J. Epstein, *novel* Dorothy Spencer
d Guy Green ph Otto Heller m Mario
Nascimbene

Olivia de Havilland, Yvette Mimieux, George
Hamilton, Rossano Brazzi, Barry Sullivan

The Light that Failed*
US 1939   97m   bw
Paramount

A London artist is going blind as the result of a
war wound, and must finish the portrait of the
little cockney whom he loves.
Nicely-made but rather boring star romance; no
surprises in plot or performance.

w Robert Carson, *story* Rudyard Kipling
d William Wellman ph Theodor Sparkuhl
m Victor Young

Ronald Colman, Walter Huston, Ida Lupino,
Dudley Digges, Muriel Angelus, Fay Helm
† Previously filmed in 1916 and 1923.

The Light Touch
US 1951   107m   bw
MGM (Pandro S. Berman)

An elegant art thief tries to doublecross the
gangster who employs him.
Elongated and witless romantic charade on
European locations.

wd Richard Brooks, *story* Jed Harris, Tom
Reed ph Robert Surtees m Miklos Rozsa

Stewart Granger, George Sanders, Pier Angeli,
Kurt Kasznar, Larry Keating, Rhys Williams,
Norman Lloyd, Mike Mazurki
  'A comedy thriller which moves far too slowly
for its imperfections to be overlooked.'—
Penelope Houston, MFB

Light Up the Sky
GB 1960   90m   bw
British Lion / Bryanston (Lewis Gilbert)

Life on a searchlight battery during World War
II.

Wartime comedy-drama with accent on the
laughs but adding dollops of tragedy and
sentiment. A very patchy entertainment.

w Vernon Harris, *play* Touch It Light by Robert
Storey d Lewis Gilbert ph John Wilcox
m Douglas Gamley

Ian Carmichael, Tommy Steele, Benny Hill,
Sydney Tafler, Victor Maddern, Harry Locke,
Johnny Briggs, Dick Emery

Lightning Strikes Twice
US 1951   91m   bw
Warner (Henry Blanke)

A woman decides to clear her lover of suspicion
of murder, but later has her own doubts.
Silly melodrama with no credibility, little
suspense, and too much talk.

w Lenore Coffee, *novel* Margaret Echard
d King Vidor ph Sid Hickox m Max Steiner

Richard Todd, Ruth Roman, Mercedes
McCambridge, Zachary Scott, Darryl
Hickman, Frank Conroy, Kathryn Givney

Lights of New York***
US 1928   57m   bw
Warner

A chorus girl becomes involved with gangsters.
The first '100 per cent all-talking' film,
dramatically primitive but historically
important.

w F. Hugh Herbert, Murray Roth d Bryan Foy
ph E. B. DuPar

Helene Costello, Cullen Landis, Wheeler
Oakman, Eugene Pallette, Tom Dugan, Gladys
Brockwell, Mary Carr

'100 per cent crude.'—*Variety*

Lights of Variety*
Italy 1950   94m   bw
Film Capitolium (Alberto Lattuada)

A stage-struck young girl forsakes the manager
of the troupe in which she found stardom for the
bright lights of the city.
Tragi-comical backstage story in which the bits
of detail are more entertaining than the plot.

w Federico Fellini d Alberto Lattuada
ph Otello Martelli m Felice Lattuada

Peppino de Filippo, Carla del Poggio, Giulietta
Masina, John Kitzmiller, Folco Lulli

The Likely Lads*
GB 1976   90m   bw
EMI (Aida Young)

Two Geordie friends, with wife and mistress, go
on a touring holiday.
Valuable as a record of an excellent and long-
running TV series, this big screen version finds
most of the humour regrettably broadened.

w Dick Clement, Ian La Frenais d Michael
Tuchner ph Tony Imi m Mike Hugg

Rodney Bewes, James Bolam, Brigit Forsyth,
Mary Tamm, Sheila Fern, Zena Walker

A Likely Story
US 1947   88m   bw
RKO (Richard H. Berger)

A man thinks he has only a short time to live, and
in trying to do his best for a girl friend gets mixed
up with gangsters.
Even a star cast could not have made much of
this zany comedy script.

w Bess Taffel d H. C. Potter ph Roy Hunt
m Leigh Harline md Constantin Bakaleinikoff

Barbara Hale, Bill Williams, Lanny Rees, Sam
Levene, Dan Tobin, Nestor Paiva

Lil Abner*
US 1959   113m   Technicolor   Vistavision
Paramount / Panama–Frank (Norman
  Panama)

The hillbilly town of Dogpatch, tagged the most
useless community in America, fights being used
as a test site for
A-bombs.
Set-bound, intrinsically American, but bright
and cheerful film of a stage show about Al
Capp's famous comic strip characters.

wd Norman Panama, Melvin Frank from the
musical show (*ly* Johnny Mercer, *words* Gene de
Paul) ph Daniel L. Fapp m Gene de Paul
md Joseph Lilley, Nelson Riddle ch Dee Dee
Wood, Michael Kidd

Peter Parrish, Billie Hayes, Howard St John,
Stubby Kaye, Stella Stevens, Julie Newmar,
Robert Strauss

AAN: Joseph Lilley, Nelson Riddle

Lilacs in the Spring
GB 1954   94m   Trucolor
Republic / Everest (Herbert Wilcox)
US title: *Let's Make Up*

During the London blitz a young actress is
knocked unconscious and dreams of herself as
Nell Gwyn, Queen Victoria and her own mother
before waking up to deal with her personal
problems.

Good-humoured theatrical charade deadened by
poorish production and colour, strengthened by
the star's game run-through of her staple
characters. How Mr Flynn came to be involved
is anybody's guess.

w Harold Purcell, from his play The Glorious
Days d Herbert Wilcox ph Max Greene
m Robert Farnon

Anna Neagle, Errol Flynn, Peter Graves, David
Farrar, Kathleen Harrison

Lili*
US 1952   81m   Technicolor
MGM (Edwin H. Knopf)

A 16-year-old orphan girl joins a carnival and
falls in love with the magician.
Romantic whimsy dependent entirely on
treatment, which is sometimes heavy-handed.
Charm, ballet and puppets are provided, but a
little cheerful song and dance would not have
been amiss.

w Helen Deutsch, novel Paul Gallico
d/ch Charles Walters ph Robert Planck
m Bronislau Kaper ad Cedric Gibbons, Paul
Stroesse

Leslie Caron, Jean-Pierre Aumont, Mel Ferrer,
Kurt Kasznar

AA: Bronislau Kaper
AAN: Helen Deutsch; Charles Walters; Robert
Planck; Leslie Caron

Lilies of the Field*
US 1963   94m   bw
UA / Rainbow / Ralph Nelson

An itinerant black workman in New Mexico
helps a group of German nuns to build a chapel.
Liberal, sentimental, under-dramatized little
comedy with everyone coming to understand
each other's point of view, so that the audience
feels improved if not especially entertained.

w James Poe, novel William E. Barrett d Ralph
Nelson ph Ernest Haller m Jerry Goldsmith

Sidney Poitier, Lilia Skala

AA: Sidney Poitier
AAN: best picture; James Poe; Ernest Haller;
Lilia Skala

Liliom*
US 1930   94m   bw
Fox

A Budapest carnival man is killed in a fight but
later comes back from heaven to see how his
family is doing.
Ingeniously-staged fantasy, very dated but a lot
more interesting than its musical remake
Carousel (qv).

w S. N. Behrman, play Ferenc Molnar d Frank
Borzage ph Chester Lyons m Richard Fall

Charles Farrell, Rose Hobart, Estelle Taylor,
Lee Tracy, Walter Abel, Guinn Williams, H. B.
Warner, Dawn O'Day (Anne Shirley)

Lilith*
US 1964   126m   bw
Columbia / Centaur (Robert Rossen)

A trainee therapist at an asylum falls in love with
a patient.
Strange, wistful, poetic and rather soporific
character melodrama.

wd Robert Rossen, novel J. R. Salamanca
ph Eugen Schufftan m Kenyon Hopkins
pd Richard Sylbert

Warren Beatty, Jean Seberg, Peter Fonda, Kim
Hunter, Anne Meacham, James Patterson,
Jessica Walter, Gene Hackman
  'A remarkable attempt to dig a little deeper in
an almost untilled field, and to throw some light
on the relationship between madness and the
creative imagination.'—Tom Milne

Lillian Russell**
US 1940   130m   bw
TCF (Gene Markey)

The life and loves of the famous nineties
entertainer.
Whitewashed biopic, extremely well made of its
kind, and very typical.

w William Anthony McGuire d Irving
Cummings ph Leon Shamroy md Alfred
Newman

Alice Faye, Don Ameche, Edward Arnold,
Warren William, Henry Fonda, Leo Carrillo,
Helen Westley, Dorothy Peterson, Ernest Truex,
Nigel Bruce, Claud Allister, Lynn Bari, Weber
and Fields, Eddie Foy Jnr, Una O'Connor

Limbo*
US 1972   111m   Technicolor
Universal (Linda Gottlieb)
aka: Chained to Yesterday

Women wait for their husbands to return from
Vietnam.
Worthy but dramatically uninteresting multi-
storied semi-propaganda piece with an untried
cast.

w Joan Silver, James Bridges d Mark Robson
ph Charles Wheeler m Anita Kerr

Kate Jackson, Katherine Justice, Stuart
Margolin, Hazel Medina, Kathleen Nolan

Limehouse Blues*
US 1935 65m bw
Paramount
aka: *East End Chant*

In London's shady quarter, an oriental
roustabout tries to leave his jealous mistress for a
girl with a shady past.
Artificial, atmospheric melodrama set in a never-
never Limehouse redolent of *Broken Blossoms*.
Interesting for its very excesses.

w Arthur Phillips, Cyril Hume, Grover Jones
d Alexander Hall *ph* Harry Fischbeck

George Raft, Anna May Wong, Jean Parker,
Kent Taylor, Billy Bevan

Limelight
GB 1935 80m bw
GFD / Herbert Wilcox

A chorus girl helps a street singer to become a
star.
Highly predictable backstage musical drama
which made a nine days wonder of 'The Street
Singer'.

w Laura Whettier *d* Herbert Wilcox

Anna Neagle, *Arthur Tracy*, Jane Winton, Ellis
Jeffreys, Muriel George

Limelight*
US 1952 144m bw
Charles Chaplin

A broken-down music hall comedian is
stimulated by a young ballerina to a final hour of
triumph.
Sentimental drama in a highly theatrical London
East End setting. In other hands it would be very
hokey, but Chaplin's best qualities, as well as his
worst, are in evidence, and in a way the film sums
up his own career.

*wd/m Charles Chaplin ph Karl Struss
ad Eugene Lourié photographic
consultant* Rollie Totheroh

Charles Chaplin, Claire Bloom, Buster Keaton,
Sydney Chaplin, Nigel Bruce, Norman Lloyd
'From the first reel it is clear that he now wants
to talk, that he *loves* to talk . . . where a
development in the story line might easily be
conveyed by a small visual effect, he prefers to
make a speech about it . . . it is a disturbing
rejection of the nature of the medium itself.'—
Walter Kerr

AA: Charles Chaplin (for music)

The Lineup*
US 1958 86m bw
Columbia (Frank Cooper)

San Francisco police trap a gunman who is also
a drug contact.
Energetic, polished movie version of a popular
TV series, *San Francisco Beat*.

w Stirling Silliphant *d Don Siegel ph* Hal Mohr
m Mischa Bakaleinikoff

Warren Anderson, Robert Keith, Eli Wallach

The Lion
GB 1962 96m De Luxe Cinemascope
TCF (Samuel G. Engel)

An American lawyer goes to Africa to visit his
ex-wife and their child.
Unabsorbing marital drama with child and
animal interest.

w Irene and Louis Kamp, *novel* Joseph Kessel
d Jack Cardiff *ph* Ted Scaife *m* Malcolm
Arnold

William Holden, Trevor Howard, Capucine,
Pamela Franklin
'The main fault must be attributed to the
spiritless direction of Jack Cardiff, whose recent
change of métier has resulted in the industry
losing a great lighting cameraman.'—*John
Gillett*

The Lion Has Wings*
GB 1939 76m bw
Alexander Korda

A documentary drama tracing the steps leading
up to the outbreak of war.
Once-inspiring propaganda piece, now
regrettably hilarious. Valuable social history,
though.

w Adrian Brunel, E. V. H. Emmett *d* Michael
Powell, Brian Desmond Hurst, Adrian Brunel

Merle Oberon, Ralph Richardson, June Duprez,
Robert Douglas, Anthony Bushell, Derrick de
Marney, Brian Worth, Austin Trevor

The Lion in Winter*
GB 1968 134m Eastmancolor
Panavision
Avco Embassy / Haworth (Martin Poll)

Henry II and Eleanor of Aquitaine celebrate
Christmas together and have a family row.
An acting feast for two principals and assorted
supports, a talking marathon in which not all the
talk is good, a smart comedy with sudden lapses
into melodrama; stimulating in parts but all
rather tiresome by the end, especially as there is
not much medieval splendour.

w James Goldman, from his play *d* Anthony
Harvey *ph* Douglas Slocombe *m* John Barry

Katharine Hepburn, Peter O'Toole, Jane

Merrow, John Castle, Anthony Hopkins, Nigel Terry, Timothy Dalton

'He is not writing a factual movie about the Plantagenets but an interpretation in which he combines their language and ours.'—*Philip T. Hartung*

AA: James Goldman; John Barry; Katharine Hepburn
AAN: best picture; Anthony Harvey; Peter O'Toole

A Lion Is in the Streets*
US 1953   88m   Technicolor
Warner / William Cagney

An itinerant confidence trickster becomes a defender of the people, is nominated for governor, and becomes corrupt.
Busy melodrama which came a bit soon after *All the King's Men* but now seems at least its equal.

w Luther Davis, *novel* Adria Locke Langley *d* Raoul Walsh *ph* Harry Stradling *m* Franz Waxman *pd* Wiard Ihnen

James Cagney, Barbara Hale, Anne Francis, Warner Anderson, John McIntire, Jeanne Cagney, Lon Chaney Jnr, Frank McHugh, Larry Keating, Onslow Stevens, James Millican, Sara Haden

'A headlong and dynamic drama which offers Mr Cagney one of his most colourful and meaningful roles.'—*Bosley Crowther*

Lipstick
US 1976   90m   Technicolor
Paramount / Dino de Laurentiis

A girl is raped but gets nowhere in court until her sister lures the man to rape her too.
Franker but not very interesting extension of a fifties co-feature, with all the developments well telegraphed.

w David Rayfiel *d* Lamont Johnson *ph* Bill Butler *m* Michel Polnareff

Margaux Hemingway, Perry King, Anne Bancroft, Chris Sarandon, Mariel Hemingway, Robin Gammell

The Liquidator*
GB 1965   104m   Metrocolor   Panavision
MGM / Leslie Elliott (Jon Pennington)

An ex-war hero is recruited by the secret service as an eliminator of security risks.
Fairly lively James Bond spoof which is never quite as funny as it imagines.

w Peter Yeldham, *novel* John Gardner *d* Jack Cardiff *ph* Ted Scaife *m* Lalo Schifrin

Rod Taylor, Trevor Howard, *David Tomlinson*,

Jill St John, Wilfrid Hyde White, Derek Nimmo, Eric Sykes, Akim Tamiroff

Lisbon
US 1956   90m   Trucolor   Naturama
Republic (Ray Milland)

An international crook negotiates an Iron Curtain prisoner's release, but the man's wife has other ideas.
Glossy international intriguer with smart performances.

w John Tucker Battle *d* Ray Milland *ph* Jack Marta *m* Nelson Riddle

Ray Milland, *Claude Rains*, Maureen O'Hara, Yvonne Furneaux, Francis Lederer, Percy Marmont, Edward Chapman

The List of Adrian Messenger**
US 1963   98m   bw
U-I / Joel (Edward Lewis)

An intelligence officer traps a mass murderer with a penchant for disguise.
Old-fashioned mystery thriller, as though Holmes and Watson were combatting a modern Moriarty (and a rough-hewn production). The whole thing is camped up like an end-of-term treat, and as a further gimmick four guest stars allegedly appear under heavy disguise in cameo parts.

w Anthony Veiller, *novel* Philip MacDonald *d* John Huston *ph* Joe MacDonald *m* Jerry Goldsmith

George C. Scott, Kirk Douglas, Clive Brook, Dana Wynter, Jacques Roux, Walter Tony Huston, Herbert Marshall, Bernard Archard, Gladys Cooper; and Robert Mitchum, Frank Sinatra, Burt Lancaster, Tony Curtis

Listen Darling
US 1938   70m   bw
MGM (Jack Cummings)

Children try to find their widowed mother a new husband.
Slight domestic comedy chiefly notable for its young talent.

w Elaine Ryan, Anne Morrison Chapin, *story* Katherine Brush *d* Edwin L. Marin *ph* Charles Lawton Jnr *m* George Axt *md* George Stoll

Mary Astor, Judy Garland, Freddie Bartholomew, Walter Pidgeon, Alan Hale, Scotty Beckett, Charley Grapewin, Barnett Parker, Gene Lockhart

Lisztomania

GB 1975   104m   colour   Panavision
Warner / VPS / Goodtimes (Roy Baird, David
    Puttnam)

The life of Liszt seen in terms of a modern pop
performer.
The most excessive and obscene of all this
director's controversial works, incapable of
criticism on normal terms except that it seems
unusually poor in production values.

wd Ken Russell *ph* Peter Suschitsky *md* John
Forsyth

Roger Daltrey, Sara Kestelman, Paul Nicholas,
Fiona Lewis, John Justin, Ringo Starr

'Ken Russell's first completely unmitigated
catastrophe in several years . . . a welter of
arbitrary gags, manic self-references and frantic
exploitation-movie clichés.'—*Tony Rayns*

'Oscar Wilde once said "Each man kills the
thing he loves", and the remark perfectly suits
Ken Russell's film treatments of classical
composers . . . he has bludgeoned into pulp some
of the finest music civilization has produced.'—
Patrick Snyder

The Little Ark

US 1971   86m   De Luxe   Panavision
Cinema Center / Robert B. Radnitz

Two war orphans and their pets, trapped in a
flood, sail to safety in a houseboat.
Well-meaning, somewhat allegorical family film,
too desultory to maintain interest and rather too
frightening for children.

w Joanna Crawford, *novel* Jan de Hartog
d James B. Clark *ph* Austin Dempster, Denys
Coop *m* Fred Karlin

Theodore Bikel, Philip Frame, Genevieve
Ambas

Little Big Horn*

US 1951   86m   bw
Lippert (Carl K. Hittleman)
GB title: *The Fighting Seventh*

A cavalry squad sets out to warn Custer about
Little Big Horn, but all the men are massacred
before Custer arrives.
Dour, impressive low-budget western.

wd Charles Marquis Warren ph Ernest Miller
m Paul Dunlap

Lloyd Bridges, John Ireland, Marie Windsor,
Reed Hadley, Hugh O'Brian, Wally Cassell,
King Donovan

Little Big Man*

US 1970   147m   Technicolor   Panavision
Stockbridge / Hiller / Cinema Center (Stuart
    Millar)

An aged veteran of the old west recounts his life
story—with elaborations.
A number of episodes varying from stark
tragedy to satirical farce are framed for no good
reason by the star in heavy disguise; the intention
is hard to guess but there are goodies along the
way.

w Calder Willingham, *novel* Thomas Berger
d Arthur Penn *ph Harry Stradling m* John
Hammond *pd* Dean Tavoularis

Dustin Hoffman, Martin Balsam, Faye
Dunaway, *Chief Dan George*, Richard
Mulligan, Jeff Corey

'A hip epic, with an amiable first hour. Then
the massacres and messages take over.'—*New
Yorker, 1976*

'A tangy and, I think, unique film with
American verve, about some of the things
American verve has done.'
—*Stanley Kauffmann*

A Little Bit of Heaven

US 1940   87m   bw
Universal (Joe Pasternak)

A 12-year-old girl becomes a singing sensation
but runs into family opposition.
Predictable vehicle for a young star being built
up as a stop-gap Deanna Durbin.

w Daniel Taradash, Gertrude Purcell, Harold
Goldman, *story* Grover Jones *d* Andrew
Marton

Gloria Jean, Robert Stack, Hugh Herbert, C.
Aubrey Smith, Stuart Erwin, Nan Grey, Eugene
Pallette, Billy Gilbert, Butch and Buddy

Little Boy Lost

US 1953   95m   bw
Paramount (William Perlberg)

An American returns to Paris after the war to
find his wife dead and his small son missing.
Rather dull tearjerker.

wd George Seaton, *novel* Marghanita Laski
ph George Barnes *m* Victor Young

Bing Crosby, Claude Dauphin, Christian
Fourcade, Gabrielle Dorziat, Nicole Maurey

Little Caesar****

US 1930   77m   bw
Warner

The rise and fall of a vicious gangster.
Its central character clearly modelled on Al
Capone, this also has historical interest as
vanguard of a spate of noisy gangster films. The
star was forever identified with his role, and the
film, though technically dated, moves fast
enough to maintain interest nearly fifty years
later.

w Francis Faragoh, Robert E. Lee, *novel* W. R. Burnett *d* Mervyn Le Roy *ph* Tony Gaudio

Edward G. Robinson, Douglas Fairbanks Jnr, Glenda Farrell, William Collier Jnr, Ralph Ince, George E. Stone, Thomas Jackson, Stanley Fields, Sidney Blackmer

'It has irony and grim humour and a real sense of excitement and its significance does not get in the way of the melodrama.'—*Richard Dana Skinner*

AAN: Francis Faragoh, Robert E. Lee

The Little Colonel**
US 1935   80m   bw (colour sequence)
TCF (B. G. De Sylva)

In a southern household after the Civil War, a little girl ends a family feud, plays Cupid to her sister, routs a few villains and mollifies her cantankerous grandfather.
First-class Temple vehicle, the first to boast an expensive production.

w William Conselman, *novel* Annie Fellows Johnson *d* David Butler *ph* Arthur Miller *md* Arthur Lange

Shirley Temple, Lionel Barrymore, Evelyn Venable, John Lodge, Bill Robinson, Hattie McDaniel, Sidney Blackmer

Little Fauss and Big Halsy
US 1970   99m   Movielab   Panavision
Paramount / Alfran / Furie (Albert S. Ruddy)

Two motor cycle track racers team up and have violent adventures round the country.
Rather pointless capers in the wake of *Easy Rider*, neither interesting nor well done.

w Charles Eastman *d* Sidney J. Furie *ph* Ralph Woolsey

Robert Redford, Michael J. Pollard, *Noah Beery Jnr*, Lauren Hutton

'A sort of *Batman and Robin* on wheels.'—*Rex Reed*

The Little Foxes***
US 1941   116m   bw
Samuel Goldwyn

A family of schemers in post-Civil War days will stop at nothing to outwit each other.
Superb film of a brilliant play; excellent to look at and listen to, with a compelling narrative line and memorable characters.

w Lillian Hellman, *from her play* *d* William Wyler *ph* Gregg Toland *m* Meredith Willson

Bette Davis, Herbert Marshall, Teresa Wright, Richard Carlson, Charles Dingle, Dan Duryea, Carl Benton Reid, Patricia Collinge, Jessica Grayson, Russell Hicks

'One of the really beautiful jobs in the whole range of movie making.'—*Otis Ferguson*

AAN: best picture; Lillian Hellman; William Wyler; Meredith Willson; Bette Davis; Teresa Wright; Patricia Collinge

The Little Giant
US 1933   74m   bw
Warner

At the end of Prohibition, a beer baron moves to California and tries to break into society.
Disappointingly unfunny gangster comedy which never really gets going.

w Robert Lord, Wilson Mizner *d* Roy del Ruth *ph* Sid Hickox *md* Leo F. Forbstein

Edward G. Robinson, Mary Astor, Helen Vinson, Kenneth Thompson, Russell Hopton, Donald Dillaway

Little Giant
US 1946   91m   bw
Universal (Joseph Gershenson)
GB title: *On the Carpet*

Misadventures of a vacuum cleaner salesman.
Curious, unsatisfactory Abbott and Costello comedy in which the boys play separate characters instead of working as a team. They should have waited for a better script before experimenting.

w Paul Jarrico, Richard Collins, Walter de Leon *d* William A. Seiter *ph* Charles van Enger *m* Edgar Fairchild

Bud Abbott, Lou Costello, Brenda Joyce, George Cleveland, Elena Verdugo

The Little Girl Who Lives Down the Lane
US / Canada / France 1976   94m   colour
Zev Braun / ICL / Filmedis-Filmel (Zev Braun)

A 13-year-old girl, when her father dies, is discovered to be keeping her mother's corpse in the cellar, and doesn't stop at more murders to keep her secret.
Tasteless piece of grand guignol, badly directed and over-acted.

w Laird Koenig, from his novel *d* Nicolas Gessner *ph* Pene Verzier *m* Christian Gaubert

Jodie Foster, Alexis Smith, Martin Sheen, Scott Jacoby

† Originally intended as a TV movie.

The Little Hut
US 1957   90m   Eastmancolor
MGM / Herbson S A

A man, his wife and her lover are shipwrecked on a desert island.
Sophisticated French farce which falls

resoundingly flat in this bowdlerized Hollywood version in bilious colour, fatally compromising itself at the beginning with a 'realistic' London prologue.

w F. Hugh Herbert, *play* André Roussin and Nancy Mitford *d* Mark Robson *ph* Frederick A. Young *m* Robert Farnon *ad* Elliot Scott

Stewart Granger, David Niven, Ava Gardner, Walter Chiari, Finlay Currie, Jean Cadell

Little Man, What Now?*

US 1934 90m bw
Universal

Problems of Germany in the grip of unemployment.
One of the studio's several 'sequels' to *All Quiet on the Western Front*, poignant at the time but now very dated.

w William Anthony McGuire, *novel* Hans Fallada *d* Frank Borzage *ph* Norbert Brodine

Margaret Sullavan, Douglass Montgomery, Alan Hale, Muriel Kirkland, Alan Mowbray, Mae Marsh

The Little Minister

US 1934 110m bw
RKO (Pandro S. Berman)

In 1840 Scotland, the gypsy girl with whom the new pastor falls unsuitably in love is really the local earl's wayward daughter.
Tedious film version of a cloyingly whimsical play.

w Jane Murfin, Sarah Y. Mason, Victor Heerman, *play* J. M. Barrie *d* Richard Wallace *ph* Henry Gerrard *m* Max Steiner

Katharine Hepburn, John Beal, Alan Hale, Donald Crisp, Lumsden Hare, Andy Clyde, Beryl Mercer, Dorothy Stickney, Frank Conroy, Reginald Denny

Little Miss Broadway

US 1938 70m bw
TCF (David Hempstead)

A small girl is adopted by the owner of a hotel for vaudeville artistes.
One of the child star's more casual vehicles, but quite pleasing.

w Harry Tugend, Jack Yellen *d* Irving Cummings *ph* Arthur Miller *md* Louis Silvers

Shirley Temple, George Murphy, Jimmy Durante, Edna May Oliver, Phyllis Brooks, George Barbier, Edward Ellis, Jane Darwell, El Brendel, Donald Meek, Claude Gillingwater, Russell Hicks

'It can't be old age, but it does look like weariness.'—*New York Times*

Little Miss Marker**

US 1934 80m bw
Paramount (B. P. Schulberg)
GB title: *The Girl in Pawn*

A cynical racetrack gambler is forced to adopt a little girl, who not only softens him but saves him from his enemies.
The twin appeals of Temple (a new hot property) and Runyon made this a big hit of its time.

w William R. Lipman, Sam Hellman, Gladys Lehman, *story* Damon Runyon *d* Alexander Hall *ph* Alfred Gilks

Shirley Temple, Adolphe Menjou, Dorothy Dell, Charles Bickford, Lynne Overman, Frank McGlynn Snr, Willie Best
† Remade as *Sorrowful Jones* (qv).

Little Murders

US 1971 108m De Luxe
TCF / Brodsky–Gould (Jack Brodsky)

A young photographer rises above all the urban horror of New York life, but when his wife is killed by a sniper he takes to violence.
This adaptation of an ultrablack comedy would have worked better as a comic strip, for its characters are satirical puppets, and when played by human beings the whole thing seems violently silly.

w Jules Feiffer, from his play *d* Alan Arkin *ph* Gordon Willis *m* Fred Kaz

Elliot Gould, Marcia Rodd, Elizabeth Wilson, Vincent Gardenia, Alan Arkin

Little Nellie Kelly*

US 1940 100m bw
MGM (Arthur Freed)

The daughter of a New York Irish cop makes good on the stage.
Sentimental nostalgic vehicle for young Judy Garland, who plays both wife and daughter and sings plenty of standard melodies.

w Jack McGowan, *play* George M. Cohan *d* Norman Taurog *songs* George M. Cohan, Roger Edens, Lew Brown, Arthur Freed *ph* Ray June

Judy Garland, George Murphy, Charles Winninger, Douglas McPhail, Arthur Shields, Forrester Harvey

A Little Night Music

Austria 1977 102m Technicolor
Sacha Wien / Elliott Kastner

A stuffy lawyer with a young wife nearly restarts an affair with an old flame.
Uneasy Viennese adaption of the fascinating Broadway musical by Stephen Sondheim based

on Bergman's *Smiles of a Summer Night*. The
Swedish atmosphere is missed, direction is
insecure, and no substitute has been found for
the stylization of the original. And the leading
lady is a bore.

w Hugh Wheeler *d* Harold Prince *m/ly* Stephen
Sondheim

Elizabeth Taylor, *Len Cariou, Diana Rigg,
Hermione Gingold,* Lesley-Anne Down,
Laurence Guiltard, Christopher Guard, Lesley
Dunlop

Little Old New York
US 1940   100m   bw
TCF (Raymond Griffith)

The story of Robert Fulton and his invention of
the steamboat.
Romantic hokum with a veneer of fact; good
production.

w Harry Tugend, *play* Rida Johnson Young
d Henry King *ph* Leon Shamroy *m* Alfred
Newman

Alice Faye, Richard Greene, Fred MacMurray,
Henry Stephenson, Brenda Joyce, Andy Devine,
Fritz Feld, Ward Bond

The Little Prince
US 1974   89m   Technicolor
Paramount / Stanley Donen   *

A small boy leaves the asteroid he rules to learn
of life on earth.
A whimsical bestseller turns into an arch musical
which falls over itself early on and never
recovers; in any case it fatally lacks the common
touch, though it has pleasing moments.

w Alan Jay Lerner, *novel* Antoine de St-
Exupery *d* Stanley Donen *ph Christopher
Challis m/ly* Frederick Loewe, Alan Jay Lerner
pd John Barry

Richard Kiley, Steven Warner, *Bob Fosse,* Gene
Wilder, Joss Ackland, Clive Revill, Victor
Spinetti, Graham Crowden

'Handsome production cannot obscure
limited artistic achievement.'—*Variety*

AAN: title song; musical adaptation (Angela
Morley, Douglas Gamley)

The Little Princess**
US 1939   93m   Technicolor
TCF (Gene Markey)

In Victorian London a little girl is left at a harsh
school when her father goes abroad.
One of the child star's plushest vehicles, a
charming early colour film complete with dream
sequence and happy ending.

w Ethel Hill, Walter Ferris, *novel* Frances

Hodgson Burnett *d* Walter Lang *ph Arthur
Miller, William Skall md* Louis Silvers

Shirley Temple, Richard Greene, Anita Louise,
Ian Hunter, Cesar Romero, Arthur Treacher,
Mary Nash, Sybil Jason, Miles Mander, Marcia
Mae Jones, Beryl Mercer, E. E. Clive

Little Women***
US 1933   115m   bw
RKO / David O. Selznick (Kenneth
   MacGowan)

The growing up of four sisters in pre-Civil War
America.
Charming 'big picture' of its day, with excellent
production and performances.

w Sarah Y. Mason, Victor Heerman, *novel*
Louisa May Alcott *d George Cukor ph* Henry
Gerrard *m* Max Steiner

Katharine Hepburn, Paul Lukas, Joan Bennett,
Frances Dee, Jean Parker, *Spring Byington*,
Edna May Oliver, Douglass Montgomery,
Henry Stephenson, Samuel S. Hinds, John
Lodge, Nydia Westman

'If to put a book on the screen with all the
effectiveness that sympathy and good taste and
careful artifice can devise is to make a fine
motion picture, then *Little Women* is a fine
picture.'—*James Shelley Hamilton*

'One of the most satisfactory pictures I have
ever seen.'—*E. V. Lucas, Punch*

AA: script
AAN: best picture; George Cukor

Little Women*
US 1949   122m   Technicolor
MGM

Syrupy Christmas-card remake, notably lacking
the light touch.

w Andrew Solt, Sarah Y. Mason, Victor
Heerman *d* Mervyn Le Roy *ph* Franz Planer
m Adolph Deutsch (after Max Steiner)

June Allyson, Elizabeth Taylor, Peter Lawford,
Margaret O'Brien, Janet Leigh, Mary Astor

'It will raise a smile and draw a tear from the
sentimental.'—*MFB*

AAN: Franz Planer

The Little World of Don Camillo*
France / Italy 1952   106m   bw
Rizzoli-Amato-Francinex (Giuseppe Amato)

In a small Italian village the parish priest and the
communist mayor are in a constant state of
amiable feud.
Slightly lethargic character comedy with a mild
message for its times, popular enough to warrant
several sequels.

w Julien Duvivier, René Barjavel, *novel* Giovanni Guareschi *d* Julien Duvivier *ph* Nicolas Hayer *m* Alessandro Cicognini

Fernandel, Gino Cervi, Sylvie, Manara, Vera Talqui, Franco Interlenghi
'Cute and cosy.'—*MFB*

The Littlest Rebel*
US 1935 70m bw
TCF (B. G. De Sylva)

A small southern girl persuades President Lincoln to release her father.
Charming, archetypal early Temple vehicle, very well produced.

w Edwin Burke, *play* Edward Peple *d* David Butler *ph* John Seitz *m* Cyril Mockridge

Shirley Temple, John Boles, Jack Holt, Karen Morley, *Bill Robinson*, Guinn Williams, Willie Best, Frank McGlynn Snr

Live a Little, Steal a Lot
US 1974 102m CFI
American International (Dominick Galate)

Jewel thieves go from success to success, but the police finally force them to strike a bargain and return the gems.
Elaborate but rather unattractive caper story based on the exploits of two real criminals.

w E. Arthur Kuhn *d* Marvin Chomsky *ph* Michael Hugo *m* Philip Lambro

Robert Conrad, Don Stroud, Donna Mills, Robyn Miller, Luther Adler, Paul Stewart

Live and Let Die*
GB 1973 121m Eastmancolor
UA / Eon (Harry Saltzman)

James Bond chases a black master criminal and becomes involved in West Indian Voodoo. Standard tongue-in-cheek spy adventure with a new lightweight star and an air of *déjà vu*. Professional standards high.

w Tom Mankiewicz, *novel* Ian Fleming *d* Guy Hamilton *ph* Ted Moore *m* George Martin *titles* Maurice Binder

Roger Moore, Yaphet Kotto, Jane Seymour, Clifton James, David Hedison, Bernard Lee, Lois Maxwell
'Plot lines have descended further to the level of the old Saturday afternoon serial, and the treatment is more than ever like a cartoon.'— *Variety*

'A Bond movie is not made. It is packaged. Like an Almond Joy. So much coconut to this much chocolate and a dash of raisins.'—*Joseph Gelmis*

AAN: title song (*m/ly* Paul and Linda McCartney)

Live for Life
France / Italy 1967 130m Eastmancolor
UA / Ariane / Vides
original title: *Vivre pour Vivre*

A news reporter forsakes his wife for a fashion model.
Interminable and unoriginal romantic drama against Sunday supplement backgounds.

w Pierre Uytterhoeven, Claude Lelouch *d,* *ph* Claude Lelouch *m* Francis Lai

Yves Montand, Candice Bergen, Annie Forardot, Irene Tunc
'The overall effect is of *Gone with the Wind* remade by Jacopetti.'—*New Yorker*

Live, Love and Learn
US 1937 78m bw
MGM (Harry Rapf)

A bohemian painter is tamed by marriage. Tiresome romantic trifle.

w Charles Brackett, Cyril Hume, Richard Maibaum *d* George Fitzmaurice *ph* Ray June

Robert Montgomery, Rosalind Russell, Robert Benchley, Helen Vinson, Mickey Rooney, Monty Woolley, E. E. Clive, Maude Eburne

Live Now, Pay Later
GB 1962 104m bw
(Regal) Woodlands / Jay Lewis (Jack Hanbury)

A credit store salesman is himself heavily in debt, and his private life is in ruins; but even after a chapter of unexpected and tragic events he remains irrepressibly optimistic.
A satirical farce melodrama which lets fly in too many directions at once and has a cumulatively cheerless effect despite funny moments.

w Jack Trevor Story, *novel* All on the Never Never by Jack Lindsay *d* Jay Lewis *ph* Jack Hildyard *m* Ron Grainer

Ian Hendry, John Gregson, June Ritchie, Geoffrey Keen, Liz Fraser

Lives of a Bengal Lancer**
US 1935 119m bw
Paramount (Louis D. Lighton)

Adventures on the North-West Frontier. British army heroics are here taken rather solemnly, but the film is efficient and fondly remembered.

w Waldemar Young, John F. Balderston, Achmed Abdullah, Grover Jones, William

Slavens McNut, *book* Francis Yeats-Brown
d Henry Hathaway *ph* Charles Lang

Gary Cooper, *Franchot Tone, Richard Barthelmess, Sir Guy Standing*, C. Aubrey Smith, Monte Blue, Kathleen Burke, Colin Tapley, *Douglass Dumbrille*, Akim Tamiroff, Noble Johnson

AAN: best picture; script; Henry Hathaway

The Living Desert**

US 1953   72m   Technicolor
Walt Disney (James Algar)

A light-hearted documentary showing the animals and insects which live in American desert areas. The aim is entertainment and Disney is not above faking, i.e. the famous sequence in which scorpions appear to do a square dance, but on its level the thing is brilliantly done.

w James Algar, Winston Hibler, Ted Sears
d James Algar ph N. Paul Kenworthy Jnr,
Robert H. Grandall *m* Paul Smith *special processes* Ub Iwerks

'The film has the same cosy anthropomorphism as a Disney cartoon and its facetious commentary and vulgar music score are typical of others in the series.'—*Georges Sadoul*

† The other 'Free Life Adventures' were: *Seal Island* 49 (3 reels), *Beaver Valley* 50 (3 reels), *Nature's Half Acre* 51 (3 reels), *Water Birds* 52 (3 reels), *Prowlers of the Everglades* 53 (3 reels), *The Vanishing Prairie* 154, *The African Lion* 55, *Secrets of Life* 56, *White Wilderness* 58, Jungle Cat 60.

Living Free

GB 1972   92m   colour
Columbia / Open Road / High Road

On the death of Elsa the lioness, George and Joy Adamson capture her three cubs and transfer them for their own safety to Serengeti.
Sloppy sequel to *Born Free*, depending very heavily on the appeal of the cubs.

w Maurice Kaufman *d* Jack Couffer
ph Wolfgang Suschitzky *m* Sol Kaplan

Susan Hampshire, Nigel Davenport, Geoffrey Keen

The Living Idol

Mexico / US 1956   100m   Eastmancolor
Cinemascope
MGM (Albert Lewin)

A Mexican girl becomes possessed by the spirit of the jaguar to whom local maidens were once sacrificed.
Pretentious but rather enjoyable highbrow

hokum of the heady kind expected from this producer.

wd Albert Lewin ph Jack Hildyard
m Rodolpho Halffter

James Robertson Justice, Steve Forrest, Liliane Montevecchi

Living in a Big Way

US 1947   103m   bw
MGM

A demobbed GI finds he can't get on with his rich selfish wife and opens up a charity home for the families of war casualties.
Odd mixture of comedy, drama and a few songs and dances, not forgetting a message or two. It mostly falls flat on its face.

w Gregory La Cava, Irving Ravetch *d* Gregory La Cava *ph* Harold Rosson *m* Lennie Hayton

Gene Kelly, Marie McDonald, Charles Winninger, Phyllis Thaxter, Spring Byington, Clinton Sundberg

Living It Up*

US 1954   95m   Technicolor
Paramount / Hal B. Wallis (Paul Jones)

A suspected victim of radium poisoning is played up by the press into a national hero.
Remake of *Nothing Sacred* with Lewis as Carole Lombard; deserves a mark for cheek.

w Jack Rose, Mel Shavelson *d* Norman Taurog *ph* Daniel Fapp

Dean Martin, Jerry Lewis, Janet Leigh, Edward Arnold, Fred Clark, Sheree North, Sig Rumann

Living on Velvet*

US 1935   77m   bw
Warner (Edward Chodorov)

A happy-go-lucky aviator changes his life style when he narrowly escapes death in a crash.
Reasonably interesting 'serious' drama of its period.

w Jerry Wald, Julius Epstein *d* Frank Borzage *ph* Sid Hickox *md* Leo F. Forbstein

George Brent, Kay Francis, Warren William, Helen Lowell, Henry O'Neill, Samuel S. Hinds, Russell Hicks, Edgar Kennedy

Lizzie

US 1957   81m   bw
MGM / Bryna (Jerry Bresler)

Murder and rape turn a girl into a triple personality.
Preposterous cash-in on *The Three Faces of Eve*, too silly to be even funny.

w Mel Dinelli, *novel* The Bird's Nest by Shirley

Jackson *d* Hugo Haas *ph* Paul Ivano *m* Leith
Stevens

Eleanor Parker, Richard Boone, Joan Blondell,
Hugo Haas
'Ruddy peculiar.'—*MFB*

Lloyd's of London**
US 1936 115m bw
TCF (Kenneth MacGowan)

A young messenger boy in the 18th century
grows up to found a great insurance company.
Thoroughly well mounted, if unconvincing and
slightly boring, historical charade in which the
Prince of Wales, Lord Nelson, Dr Johnson and
other personages make guest appearances. An
archetypal prestige film of its time which also
turned out to be box office.

w Ernest Pascal, Walter Ferris, *book* Curtis
Kenyon *d Henry King ph* Bert Glennon
md Louis Silvers

Tyrone Power, Madeleine Carroll, George
Sanders, Freddie Bartholomew, C. Aubrey
Smith, Guy Standing, Virginia Field, Montagu
Love, Gavin Muir, Miles Mander, Una
O'Connor, E. E. Clive
'The name of England is so freely on the
characters' lips that we recognize at once an
American picture. These people live, make love,
bear children all from the most patriotic motives,
and it's all rather like London in coronation
week.'—*Graham Greene*

Lock Up Your Daughters
GB 1969 103m Technicolor
Columbia./ Domino (David Deutsch)

In 18th-century London an aristocratic rake and
various lower orders are all in search of female
companionship and get their wires crossed.
Noisy, vulgar, ill-acted version (without music)
of a successful musical based on two old
theatrical warhorses.

w Keith Waterhouse, Willis Hall, *play* Bernard
Miles based on Rape upon Rape by Henry
Fielding and The Relapse by John Vanbrugh
d Peter Coe *ph* Peter Suschitsky *m* Ron
Grainer *pd* Tony Woollard

Christopher Plummer, Roy Kinnear, Georgia
Brown, Susannah York, Glynis Johns, Ian
Bannen, Tom Bell, Elaine Taylor, Jim Dale,
Kathleen Harrison, Roy Dotrice, Vanessa
Howard, Fenella Fielding, Peter Bayliss,
Richard Wordsworth, Peter Bull, Fred Emney
'Subtlety is neither required nor displayed.'—
Jack Ibberson

The Locket
US 1946 85m bw
RKO

A *femme fatale* is bent on destroying men, and
eventually we discover why.
Dark, confusing melodrama very typical of the
immediate post-war years; it has little to say but
says it dourly, even achieving flashbacks within
flashbacks within flashbacks.

w Sheridan Gibney *d* John Brahm *ph* Nicholas
Musuraca *m* Roy Webb

Laraine Day, Robert Mitchum, Brian Aherne,
Gene Raymond, Ricardo Cortez

The Lodger*
GB 1932 85m bw
Twickenham (Julius Hagen)
US title: *The Phantom Fiend*

The upstairs lodger is suspected of being Jack the
Ripper . . .
Modernized version of a story already tackled by
Hitchcock as a silent and to be done again in
costume in 1944. Not bad, for a minor British
film of the time.

w Ivor Novello, Miles Mander, Paul Rotha, H.
Fowler Mear, *novel* Mrs Belloc Lowndes
d Maurice Elvey

Ivor Novello, Elizabeth Allan, A. W. Baskomb,
Jack Hawkins, Barbara Everest, Peter
Gawthorne, Kynaston Reeves

The Lodger*
US 1944 84m bw
TCF (Robert Bassler)

1880s version of the above in which the lodger *is*
Jack the Ripper.
Nicely mounted apart from some anachronisms,
but a little dull.

w Barre Lyndon *d* John Brahm *ph* Lucien
Ballard m Hugo Friedhofer

Laird Cregar, Merle Oberon, George Sanders,
Cedric Hardwicke, Sara Allgood, Aubrey
Mather, Queenie Leonard, Helena Pickard,
Lumsden Hare, Frederick Worlock

Logan's Run*
US 1976 118m Metrocolor Todd-AO
MGM (Saul David)

In the future, people try to escape from a society
which dooms everyone to death at thirty.
Interesting and quite exciting fantasy
melodrama which mercifully moves instead of
preaching.

w David Zelag Goodman, novel William F.
Nolan *d* Michael Anderson *ph* Ernest Laszlo
m Jerry Goldsmith *pd* Dale Hennesy

Michael York, Richard Jordan, Jenny Agutter, Roscoe Lee Browne, Farrah Fawcett-Majors, Peter Ustinov, Michael Anderson Jnr

'A science fiction film made by people who don't understand science fiction for the amusement of people who don't care one way or the other.'—*S. Frank, L. A. Panorama*

AAN: Ernest Laszlo

Lola*

France / Italy 1960   91m   bw   Franscope
Rome-Paris / Euro-International

A cabaret dancer in Nantes chooses between three men.

A slight romance which was much admired for its decoration and visual style, which reminded many of Max Ophuls.

wd Jacques Demy ph Raoul Coutard *m* Michel Legrand

Anouk Aimée, Jacques Harden, Marc Michel, Elina Labourdette

Lola Montes*

France / Germany 1955   140m
   Eastmancolor   Cinemascope
Gamma / Florida / Oska

The life of the famous courtesan and her romance with the King of Bavaria, told in diverting fragments by a circus ringmaster.
An elaborate, expensive and trickily presented historical charade which confused the public and bankrupted its production company; but the various shorter versions released didn't help.

w Max Ophuls, Annette Wademant, Franz Geiger, *novel* Cécil Saint-Laurent *d Max Ophuls ph* Christian Matras *m* Georges Auric *ad* Jean d'Aubonne, Willy Schatz

Martine Carol, Anton Walbrook, Peter Ustinov, Ivan Desny, Oskar Werner, Will Quadflieg

Lolita**

GB 1962   152m   bw
MGM / Seven Arts / AA / Anya / Transworld
   (James B. Harris)

A middle-aged lecturer falls for a 14-year-old girl and marries her mother to be near her.
Fitfully amusing but slightly plotted and very lengthy screen version of a sensational novel in which the heroine is only twelve, which makes a difference. The flashback introduction and various comic asides are pretentious and alienating.

w Vladimir Nabokov, from his novel *d* Stanley Kubrick *ph* Oswald Morris *m* Nelson Riddle

James Mason, Shelley Winters, Sue Lyon, Peter Sellers

'The director's heart is apparently elsewhere. Consequently, we face the problem without the passion, the badness without the beauty, the agony without the ecstasy.'—*Andrew Sarris*

'A diluted *Blue Angel* with a teenage temptress instead of a tart.'—*Stanley Kauffmann*

AAN: Vladimir Nabokov

Lolly Madonna XXX

US 1973   105m   Metrocolor
MGM (Rodney Carr-Smith)
GB title: *The Lolly Madonna War*

Tennessee hillbilly farmers fight over a meadow.
Violent feudin' melodrama, technically accomplished but of limited interest to non-hillbillies.

w Rodney Carr-Smith, Sue Grafton, from her novel *d* Richard C. Sarafian *ph* Philip Lathrop *m* Fred Myrow

Rod Steiger, Robert Ryan, Scott Wilson, Jeff Bridges, Season Hubley

London After Midnight*

US 1927   approx 75m   bw   silent
MGM

A creepy house murder is solved by hypnotism, and a grinning monster proves to be a red herring.
Famous star thriller of which lamentably no prints survive; remade as *Mark of the Vampire*.

w Tod Browning, Waldemar Young   *d* Tod Browning

Lon Chaney, Marceline Day, Conrad Nagel, Henry B. Walthall, Polly Moran

London Belongs to Me**

GB 1948   112m   bw
GFD / Individual (Frank Launder, Sidney
   Gilliat)
US title: *Dulcimer Street*

A young boy is arrested on a murder charge and his boarding-house friends rally to his defence.
Unconvincing but highly entertaining sub-Dickensian comedy-drama with a rousing finish and an abundance of character roles.

w Sidney Gilliat, J. B. Williams, *novel* Norman Collins *d Sidney Gilliat ph* Wilkie Cooper *m* Benjamin Frankel

Alastair Sim, Stephen Murray, Richard Attenborough, Fay Compton, Wylie Watson, Susan Shaw, Ivy St Helier, Joyce Carey, Andrew Crawford, Eleanor Summerfield, Hugh Griffith, Gladys Henson

London Melody
GB 1937   75m   bw
GFD / Herbert Wilcox
US title: *Girls in the Street*

A diplomat falls for a dancer.
Light but rather humourless musical drama.

w Florence Tranter, Monckton Hoffe *d* Herbert
Wilcox

Anna Neagle, Tullio Carminati, Robert
Douglas, Horace Hodges

London Town*
GB 1947   126m   Technicolor
GFD / Wesley Ruggles
US title: *My Heart Goes Crazy*

An understudy finally achieves stardom thanks
to his daughter's schemes.
Disastrous and expensive attempt to make a
major British musical without a single new idea.
Tasteless, tawdry and sluggish, but it does record
for posterity four of the star's sketches.

w Elliot Paul, Siegfried Herzig, Val Guest
d Wesley Ruggles

Sid Field, Greta Gynt, Kay Kendall, Tessie
O'Shea, Claude Hulbert, Sonnie Hale, Mary
Clare, Petula Clark, Jerry Desmonde

'I can't see the point of importing an American
director and giving him all the time and money in
the world to play with when we can make bad
musicals on our own, and quicker.'—*Richard
Winnington*

Lone Star
US 1952   90m   bw
MGM (Z. Wayne Griffin)

Andrew Jackson enlists the aid of a Texas
adventurer to persuade Sam Houston to change
his mind about an agreement with Mexico.
Slow-moving semi-western, hard to follow for
non-Americans. Production values quite high.

w Borden Chase, Howard Estabrook *d* Vincent
Sherman *ph* Harold Rosson *m* David Buttolph

Clark Gable, Ava Gardner, Lionel Barrymore,
Broderick Crawford, Ed Begley, Beulah Bondi,
James Burke, William Farnum, Lowell Gilmore,
Moroni Olsen, Russell Simpson, William
Conrad

The Lone Wolf
The jewel thief turned sleuth was created by
Louis Joseph Vance and turned up in several
silent films. During the talkie period several
actors played Michael Lanyard; the role of his
valet passed from Raymond Walburn to Eric
Blore to Alan Mowbray. All the films were made
for Columbia, but only the first was anything like
a main feature.

1935: THE LONE WOLF RETURNS (*d* Roy
William Neill with Melvyn Douglas)
1938: THE LONE WOLF IN PARIS (*d* Albert
S. Rogell with Francis Lederer)
1939: THE LONE WOLF SPY HUNT (*d* Peter
Godfrey with Warren William)
1940: THE LONE WOLF STRIKES (*d* Sidney
Salkow with Warren William)
1941: THE LONE WOLF MEETS A LADY,
THE LONE WOLF TAKES A CHANCE,
THE LONE WOLF KEEPS A DATE (all as
above), SECRETS OF THE LONE WOLF
(*d* Edward Dmytryk; WW)
1943: ONE DANGEROUS NIGHT
(*d* Michael Gordon: WW), PASSPORT TO
SUEZ (*d* André de Toth: WW)
1946: THE NOTORIOUS LONE WOLF (*d* D.
Ross Lederman; with Gerald Mohr)
1947: THE LONE WOLF IN LONDON
(*d* Leslie Goodwins: GM), THE LONE WOLF
IN MEXICO (*d* D. Ross Lederman: GM)
1949: THE LONE WOLF AND HIS LADY
(*d* John Hoffman: GM)

**The Loneliness of the Long Distance
Runner***
GB 1962   104m   bw
British Lion / Bryanston / Woodfall (Tony
   Richardson)

The only thing a Borstal boy does well is run, and
as he trains he thinks back to his depressing life.
Rather pale study of a social outcast; interesting
scenes do not quite form a compelling whole.

w Alan Sillitoe, from his short story *d* Tony
Richardson *ph* Walter Lassally *m* John
Addison

Tom Courtenay, Michael Redgrave, James
Bolam, Avis Bunnage, Alec McCowen, Joe
Robinson, Julia Foster

Lonely Are the Brave*
US 1962   107m   bw   Panavision
U-I / Joel (Edward Lewis)

The last of the cowboy rebels is no match for
pursuit by jeep and helicopter.
A strange, sad, rather moving fable, with very
good performances and action scenes, but a
shade too unrelenting in its downbeat tone to
become a popular classic.

w Dalton Trumbo, *novel* Brave Cowboy by
Edward Abbey *d* David Miller *ph* Philip
Lathrop *m* Jerry Goldsmith

Kirk Douglas, Walter Matthau, Gena
Rowlands, Michael Kane, Carroll O'Connor,
Karl Swenson, George Kennedy, Bill Raisch

The Lonely Man
US 1957   87m   bw   Vistavision
Paramount (Pat Duggan)

An outlaw hopes to regain social recognition and contacts the son who abhors him.
Dullish psycho western.

w Harry Essex, Robert Smith d Henry Levin
ph Lionel Lindon m Van Cleave

Jack Palance, Anthony Perkins, Elaine Aiken, Neville Brand, Lee Van Cleef, Elisha Cook Jnr, Robert Middleton

Lonelyhearts*
US 1958   103m   bw
UA / Dore Schary

A young journalist finds himself engrossed, appalled and sickened by his work on the agony column.
Episodic, occasionally interesting but generally too vaguely liberal; an intellectual reshaping of a despairing novel. The producer as usual is well meaning but doesn't quite make it.

w Dore Schary, novel Nathanael West
d Vincent J. Donehue ph John Alton m Conrad Salinger

Montgomery Clift, Robert Ryan, Myrna Loy, Dolores Hart, Maureen Stapleton

AAN: Maureen Stapleton

Lonesome*
US 1928   69m (24 fps)   bw   silent
Universal

Young lovers lose each other at Luna Park but later discover that they are neighbours.
Amiable exploration of the life of city workers, comparable with The Crowd but showing a lighter touch.

w Edmund T. Lowe d Paul Fejos ph Gilbert Warrenton

Glenn Tryon, Barbara Kent

The Long and the Short and the Tall*
GB 1960   105m   bw
ABP / Michael Balcon
US title: Jungle Fighters

In Malaya during World War II a Japanese scout is captured by a British patrol.
Stark war melodrama with the emphasis on character. Vivid at the time, it now seems very routine.

w Wolf Mankowitz, play Willis Hall d Leslie Norman
ph Erwin Hillier m Stanley Black

Laurence Harvey, Richard Todd, David McCallum, Richard Harris, Ronald Fraser, John Meillon, John Rees, Kenji Takaki

The Long Arm**
GB 1956   96m   bw
Ealing (Tom Morahan)
US title: The Third Key

A Scotland Yard superintendent solves a series of robberies.
Good straightforward police thriller with careful detail.

w Janet Green, Robert Barr d Charles Frend
ph Gordon Dines m Gerbrand Schurmann

Jack Hawkins, Dorothy Alison, John Stratton, Michael Brooke, Geoffrey Keen, Sidney Tafler, Meredith Edwards, Ralph Truman, Ursula Howells
'A generally efficient example of popular British film-making.'—MFB

The Long Dark Hall
GB 1951   86m   bw
British Lion / Five Oceans (Anthony Bushell)

A chorus girl is murdered and her married lover is accused.
Miserable mystery with a trick ending, most inappropriately cast.

w Nunnally Johnson, W. E. C. Fairchild
d Anthony Bushell, Reginald Beck ph Wilkie Cooper m Benjamin Frankel

Rex Harrison, Lilli Palmer, Raymond Huntley, Denis O'Dea, Anthony Bushell, Henry Longhurst, Patricia Wayne, Meriel Forbes, Brenda de Banzie, Anthony Dawson

The Long Day's Dying
GB 1968   95m   Techniscope
Paramount / Junction Films

Three British paratroopers in Europe are cut off from their unit and die pointlessly.
Violent, irritating anti-war film which resurrects all the clichés and makes itself unpleasant into the bargain.

w Charles Wood, novel Alan White d Peter Collinson ph Brian Probyn m Malcolm Lockyer pd Disley Jones

David Hemmings, Tom Bell, Tony Beckley, Alan Dobie
'It is typical of all that is wrong with the film that it should end on a frozen frame of a soldier in the act of dying while heavily ironic patriotic music swells on the sound track.'—David Wilson

Long Day's Journey into Night **
US 1961   174m   bw
Ely Landau

Connecticut 1912: days in the life of an ageing actor, his drug addicted wife and their sons, one of whom is an alcoholic and the other Eugene O'Neill.
Heavy going, nicely handled, superbly acted version of a play which can be a player's triumph and certainly is here; but it still has more effect in the theatre.

w Eugene O'Neill d Sidney Lumet ph Boris Kaufman m André Previn pd Richard Sylbert

Ralph Richardson, Katharine Hepburn, Jason Robards Jnr, Dean Stockwell

'Letting his players have their head, lighted miraculously so that every flicker of emotion is preserved, and pursuing them with Kaufman's unobtrusive camera, Lumet illuminates the play, line by line, and gives it all the impact of a live performance.'—Brenda Davies

'A very great play has been not translated to the screen but reverently put behind glass.'—John Simon

The Long Duel
GB 1967   115m   Technicolor   Panavision
Rank (Ken Annakin)

On the North-West Frontier in the twenties, British officers disagree about handling the natives, and one of them forms a strong regard for the native leader.
Unconvincing cut-price Indian adventure with little cohesion and less entertainment value.

w Peter Yeldham d Ken Annakin ph Jack Hildyard m Patrick John Scott

Trevor Howard, Yul Brynner, Harry Andrews, Charlotte Rampling, Virginia North, Andrew Keir, Laurence Naismith, Maurice Denham

'The dialogue seems to have been written by a computer fed a programme of execrable films on the same theme.'—MFB

The Long Goodbye
US 1973   111m   Technicolor   Panavision
UA / Lions Gate (Jerry Bick)

Philip Marlowe helps an eccentric friend who is suspected of murdering his wife.
Ugly, boring travesty of a well-respected detective novel, the apparent intention being to reverse the author's attitudes completely and to substitute dullness and incomprehensibility.

w Leigh Brackett, novel Raymond Chandler d Robert Altman ph Vilmos Zsigmond m John T. Williams

Elliott Gould, Nina Van Pallandt, Sterling Hayden, Mark Rydell, Henry Gibson

'Altman's fragmentation bomb blows up itself rather than the myths he has said he wants to lay to rest.'—Sight and Sound

'The trouble is that this Marlowe is an untidy, unshaven, semi-literate dimwit slob who could not locate a missing skyscraper and who would be refused service at a hot dog stand.'—Charles Champlin

'A spit in the eye to a great writer.'—Michael Billington, Illustrated London News

The Long Gray Line *
US 1955   138m   Technicolor   Cinemascope
Columbia (Robert Arthur)

The career of an athletics trainer at West Point. Dim biopic, the kind of true life yarn that Americans like, produced in the cheerful, sentimental, sparring way that John Ford likes.

w Edward Hope, book Bring Up the Brass by Merty Maher d John Ford ph Charles Lawton Jnr m George Duning md Morris Stoloff

Tyrone Power, Maureen O'Hara, Donald Crisp, Ward Bond, Robert Francis, Betsy Palmer, Phil Carey, Harry Carey Jnr, Patrick Wayne, Sean McClory

'Its celebration of the codes and ideals of West Point vexatiously combines sentimental cosiness and a kind of religious awe.'—Gavin Lambert

The Long Hot Summer *
US 1958   118m   Eastmancolor   Cinemascope
TCF (Jerry Wald)

Conflict arises between a Mississippi town boss and a tenant farmer.
Busy Peyton Place-style family brawling saga with sex on the side, flabby as narrative but compulsive as character study.

w Irving Ravetch, Harriet Frank, stories William Faulkner d Martin Ritt ph Joseph La Shelle m Alex North

Orson Welles, Paul Newman, Joanne Woodward, Tony Franciosa, Lee Remick, Angela Lansbury

Long John Silver
Australia 1953   106m   Eastmancolor   Cinemascope
TI Pictures (Joseph Kaufman)

Back from Treasure Island, Silver and Hawkins plan a return visit with fresh clues to the treasure. Cheaply produced, bitsy-piecy adventure fragments with no one to restrain the star from eye-rolling.

w Martin Rackin *d* Byron Haskin *ph* Carl Guthrie *m* David Buttolph

Robert Newton, Connie Gilchrist, Kit Taylor, Rod Taylor

The Long Long Trailer*
US 1954   96m   Anscocolor
MGM (Pandro S. Berman)

A construction engineer and his bride buy a trailer for their honeymoon, and wish they hadn't.
Disaster comedy with long bright periods and the inevitable saggy bits.

w Frances Goodrich, Albert Hackett, *novel* Clinton Twiss *d* Vincente Minnelli *ph* Robert Surtees *m* Adolph Deutsch

Lucille Ball, Desi Arnaz, Marjorie Main, Keenan Wynn, Moroni Olsen

Long Lost Father
US 1934   63m   bw
RKO

A restaurant owner saves his daughter from a theft charge.
Competent minor star drama.

w Dwight Taylor, *novel* G. B. Stern *d* Ernest B. Schoedsack

John Barrymore, Helen Chandler, Donald Cook, Alan Mowbray, Claude King

The Long Memory
GB 1952   96m   bw
Rank (Hugh Stewart)

An ex-con, framed for a murder he did not commit, plots revenge but instead uncovers a fresh crime.
Slow and dreary melodrama set largely on a barge, never rising to anything like excitement.

w Robert Hamer, Frank Harvey, *novel* Winston Clewes *d* Robert Hamer *ph* Harry Waxman *m* William Alwyn

John Mills, John McCallum, Elizabeth Sellars, Geoffrey Keen

The Long Night*
US 1947   97m   bw
(RKO) Anatole Litvak

A young man shoots the seducer of his sweetheart and barricades himself in a room against the police.
Good-looking but empty remake of *Le Jour se Lève.*

w John Wexley, *story* Jacques Viot *d* Anatole Litvak *ph* Sol Polito *m* Dmitri Tiomkin

Henry Fonda, Barbara Bel Geddes, Vincent Price, Ann Dvorak, Queenie Smith
'This film faithfully reproduces the letter while altering the spirit of the original almost beyond recognition.'—*MFB*

Long Pants*
US 1927   58m (24 fps)   bw   silent
First National / Harry Langdon

A country bumpkin has trouble in the city.
Far from the best Langdon comedy, but funny in flashes.

w Arthur Ripley *d* Frank Capra *ph* Elgin Lessley

Harry Langdon, Gladys Brockwell, Alan Roscoe, Alma Bennett

The Long Ships
GB / Yugoslavia 1963   126m   Technirama
Columbia / Warwick / Avila (Irving Allen)

A Viking adventurer and a Moorish prince fall out over a golden bell.
Stilted medieval epic with some visual compensations but more chat than action.

w Berkely Mather, Beverly Cross, *novel* Frank G. Bengtsson *d* Jack Cardiff *ph* Christopher Challis *m* Dusan Radic

Richard Widmark, Sidney Poitier, Russ Tamblyn, Rosanna Schiaffino, Oscar Homolka, Colin Blakely

The Long Voyage Home**
US 1940   104m   bw
Walter Wanger

Merchant seamen on shore leave get drunk, philosophical and have adventures.
Stagey-looking but dramatically interesting amalgam of four one-act plays by Eugene O'Neill, with talent abounding.

w Dudley Nichols *d* John Ford *ph* Gregg Toland *m* Richard Hageman

John Wayne, Thomas Mitchell, Ian Hunter, Ward Bond, Barry Fitzgerald, Wilfrid Lawson, Mildred Natwick, John Qualen, Arthur Shields, Joe Sawyer

AAN: best picture; Dudley Nichols; John Ford; Richard Hageman

The Long Wait
US 1954   93m   bw
UA / Parklane (Lesser Samuels)

An amnesia victim returns home to solve a murder in which he was involved.
Flatulent version of a Mickey Spillane novel, over-plotted and inadequately motivated.

w Alan Green, Lesser Samuels *d* Victor Saville
ph Franz Planer *m* Mario Castelnuovo Tedesco

Anthony Quinn, Charles Coburn, Gene Evans,
Peggie Castle, Dolores Donlan

The Longest Day **
US 1972 169m bw Cinemascope
TCF *(Darryl F. Zanuck, Elmo Williams)*

A multi-faceted account of the landings in
Normandy in June 1944.

Extraordinarily noisy war spectacular,
enjoyable as a violent entertainment once one
has caught all the threads, but emotionally
unaffecting because every part is played by a
star.

w Cornelius Ryan, Romain Gary, James Jones,
David Pursall, Jack Seddon, *book* Cornelius
Ryan *d* Andrew Marton, Ken Annakin,
Bernhard Wicki *ph* Henri Persin, Walter
Wottitz, Pierre Levent, Jean Bourgoin
m Maurice Jarre, Paul Anka

John Wayne, Robert Mitchum, Henry Fonda,
Robert Ryan, Rod Steiger, Robert Wagner, Paul
Anka, Fabian, Tommy Sands, Richard Beymer,
Mel Ferrer, Jeffrey Hunter, Sal Mineo, Roddy
McDowall, Stuart Whitman, Steve Forrest,
Eddie Albert, Edmond O'Brien, Red Buttons,
Tom Tryon, Alexander Knox, Ray Danton, Ron
Randell, Richard Burton, Donald Houston,
Kenneth More, Peter Lawford, Richard Todd,
Leo Genn, John Gregson, Sean Connery,
Michael Medwin, Leslie Phillips, Irina Demich,
Bourvil, Jean-Louis Barrault, Christian
Marquand, Arletty, Curt Jurgens, Paul
Hartmann, Gert Frobe, Wolfgang Preiss, Peter
Van Eyck, Christopher Lee, Eugene Deckers,
Richard Wattis

AAN: best picture; photography

The Longest Yard
US 1974 122m Technicolor
Paramount / Long Road (Albert S. Ruddy)
GB title: *The Mean Machine*

Imprisoned for drunkenness and car theft, a
football star is blackmailed into training a prison
football team of hulking misfits.

Violent, meandering comedy-drama with
murderous jokes but no narrative grip.

w Tracy Keenan Wynn *d* Robert Aldrich
ph Joseph Biroc *m* Frank de Vol

Burt Reynolds, Eddie Albert, Ed Lauter,
Michael Conrad, Jim Hampton

Look Back in Anger *
GB 1959 99m bw
ABP / Woodfall (Gordon L. T. Scott)

A bad-tempered young man with a grudge
against life and the government runs a market
stall, lives in a squalid flat, and has an affair with
his wife's best friend.

Well-made version of a play whose sheer
dreariness was theatrically stimulating but in
terms of film realism becomes only depressing
and stupid despite competence all round. It also
set shoddy standards for its many less proficient
imitators.

w Nigel Kneale, *play John Osborne* *d* Tony
Richardson *ph Oswald Morris* *m* Chris Barber

*Richard Burton, Mary Ure, Claire Bloom, Edith
Evans, Gary Raymond,* Glen Byam Shaw,
Phyllis Neilson-Terry, Donald Pleasence,
George Devine

Look for the Silver Lining *
US 1949 106m Technicolor
Warner (William Jacobs)

The life story of twenties stage star Marilyn
Miller.

Harmless musical biopic with a sense of humour.

w Phoebe and Henry Ephron, Marian Spitzer,
Bert Kalmar, Harry Ruby *d* David Butler
ph Peverell Marley *md* Ray Heindorf

June Haver, *Ray Bolger, Charles Ruggles,*
Gordon Macrae, Rosemary de Camp, S. Z.
Sakall, Walter Catlett

AAN: Ray Heindorf

Look Up and Laugh *
GB 1935 82m bw
ATP (Basil Dean)

Market stallholders defy a big chain store.
Good star comedy with music.

w Gordon Wellesley, *story* J. B. Priestley *d* Basil
Dean

Gracie Fields, Douglas Wakefield, Harry Tate,
Alfred Drayton, Morris Harvey, Vivien Leigh,
Robb Wilton

Looking for Mr Goodbar
US 1977 136m Metrocolor
Paramount (Freddie Fields)

A teacher of deaf children leads a sordid secret
night life.

Exploitative and very boring sex melodrama
which doesn't even make one believe in its
central character.

wd Richard Brooks, *novel* Judith Rossner
ph William A. Fraker *m* Artie Kane *ad* Edward
Carfagno

Diane Keaton, Tuesday Weld, William
Atherton, Richard Kiley

The Looking Glass War
GB 1969 107m Technicolor Panavision
Columbia / M. J. Frankovich

The British secret service sends a young Pole into East Germany to find a top secret film. Jaundiced spy story which aims for irony and tragedy but becomes merely verbose and irritating.

wd Frank R. Pierson, *novel* John Le Carré
ph Austin Dempster *m* Wally Scott

Christopher Jones, Pia Degermark, Ralph Richardson, Anthony Hopkins, Paul Rogers, Susan George, Ray McAnally, Robert Urquhart, Maxine Audley, Anna Massey

'There are a lot of incidental pleasures, but in the final analysis they only add up to half a film.'—*Nigel Andrews*

Looking on the Bright Side*
GB 1931 81m bw
ATP (Basil Dean)

A songwriter gets ideas above his station but eventually returns to the manicurist who loves him.
Dated but lively musical which helped confirm Gracie's stardom.

w Basil Dean, Archie Pitt, Brock Williams
d Basil Dean

Gracie Fields, Richard Dolman, Julian Rose, Wyn Richmond

Loot*
GB 1970 101m Eastmancolor
Performing Arts Ltd (Arthur Lewis)

A crook hides his mother's body and uses the coffin to carry the proceeds of a robbery.
Breakneck black farce which still can't move quite fast enough to cover up its bad taste, though well done by all concerned.

w Ray Galton, Alan Simpson, *play* Joe Orton
d Silvio Narizzano *ph* Austin Dempster
m Keith Mansfield, Richard Willing-Denton
ad Anthony Pratt

Richard Attenborough, Lee Remick, Hywel Bennett, Milo O'Shea, Dick Emery

Lord Jeff
US 1938 78m bw
MGM (Frank Davis)
GB title: *The Boy from Barnardo's*

A well-brought-up boy gets into trouble and is sent under supervision to a naval school.
Adequate family film with absolutely no surprises.

w Bradford Roper, Val Burton, André Boehm
d Sam Wood *ph* John Seitz *m* Edward Ward

Freddie Bartholomew, Mickey Rooney, Charles Coburn, Herbert Mundin, Terry Kilburn, Gale Sondergaard, Peter Lawford

Lord Jim*
GB 1964 154m Technicolor Super Panavision
Columbia / Keep (René Dupont)

Adventures of a sailor who prowls the Far East looking for truth; he helps enslaved natives, is raped by a tribal chief, and finally sacrifices his life.
Lush and very boring farrago of miscellaneous incident, with a central character about whose fate no one can care. However, an expensive production must have its points of interest, and the belated introduction of a gentleman villain gives a little edge.

wd Richard Brooks, *novel* Joseph Conrad
ph Frederick A. Young *m* Bronislau Kaper
pd Geoffrey Drake

Peter O'Toole, *James Mason*, Eli Wallach, Paul Lukas, Jack Hawkins, Daliah Lavi, Curt Jurgens, Akim Tamiroff

Lord Love a Duck*
US 1966 105m bw
UA / Charleston (George Axelrod)

A senior Los Angeles student practises hypnotism on his girl friend.
Rather sloppy satire on American culture and fancies, dressed up as crazy comedy; occasional laughs.

w Larry H. Johnson, George Axelrod, *novel* Al Hine *d* George Axelrod *ph* Daniel Fapp
m Neal Hefti

Roddy McDowall, Tuesday Weld, Lola Albright, Ruth Gordon, Harvey Korman, Max Showalter

Lord of the Flies
GB 1963 91m bw
Allen–Hogdon Productions / Two Arts (Lewis M. Allen)

After a plane crash, a party of English schoolboys are stranded on an uncharted tropical island and gradually turn savage.
Semi-professional production of a semi-poetic novel which worked well on the printed page but on screen seems crude and unconvincing.

wd Peter Brook, *novel* William Golding *ph* Tom Hollyman, Gerald Feil *m* Raymond Leppard

James Aubrey, Tom Chapin, Hugh Edwards, Roger Elwin, Tom Gaman

Lorna Doone**

GB 1934   90m   bw
ATP (Basil Dean)

In 1625 on Exmoor, a farmer comes to love an
outlaw's daughter who proves to be in reality a
kidnapped heiress.
Simple, straightforward, effective version of the
famous romance, with refreshing use of
exteriors.

w Dorothy Farnum, Miles Malleson, Gordon
Wellesley, *novel* R. D. Blackmore d Basil Dean

Victoria Hopper, John Loder, Margaret
Lockwood, *Roy Emerton,* Edward Rigby, Mary
Clare, Roger Livesey, George Curzon, D. A.
Clarke-Smith, Lawrence Hanray, Amy Veness,
Eliot Makeham

Lorna Doone

US 1951   89m   Technicolor
Columbia (Edward Small)

Grotesque remake which treats the story like a
cheap western.

w Jesse L. Lasky Jnr, Richard Schayer d Phil
Karlson ph Charles Van Enger m George
Duning

Barbara Hale, Richard Greene, Anne Howard,
William Bishop, Carl Benton Reid, Ron Randell,
Sean McClory, Onslow Stevens, Lester
Matthews, John Dehner

Lost*

GB 1955   89m   Technicolor
Rank (Vivian A. Cox)
US title: *Tears for Simon*

The police go on the trail of a stolen child.
Mildly effective semi-documentary police story,
with good use of locations.

w Janet Green d Guy Green ph Harry
Waxman m Benjamin Frankel

David Farrar, David Knight, Julia Arnall,
Anthony Oliver, Thora Hird, Eleanor
Summerfield, Marjorie Rhodes, Joan Sims

Lost Angel*

US 1946   91m   bw
MGM (Robert Sisk)

A lost little girl is adopted by a reporter.
Good star vehicle for the sentimentally-inclined,
with solid production and casting back-up.

w Isabel Lennart d Roy Rowland ph Robert
Surtees m Daniele Amfitheatrof

Margaret O'Brien, James Craig, Marsha Hunt,
Philip Merivale, Henry O'Neill, Donald Meek,
Keenan Wynn

'A beautiful opportunity for true satire is
offered and, I regret to say, thrown away. For

our little Gulliver is rapidly decivilized by all the
familiar bromidic palliatives: love, crooning,
fairies and night clubs.'—*Richard Winnington*

Lost Boundaries*

US 1949   105m   bw
Film Classics (Louis de Rochemont)

In a New Hampshire town in the forties, a
beloved doctor and his wife are found to have
negro blood.
Well-meaning but dramatically ineffective racial
drama which meanders along allowing an
occasional burst of genuine feeling to come
through.

w Virginia Shaler, Eugene Ling d Alfred
Werker ph William J. Miller m Louis
Applebaum

Mel Ferrer, Beatrice Pearson, Richard Hylton,
Susan Douglas, Canada Lee, Grace Coppin

'It cannot be said to betray its subject, but is,
rather, unequal to it.'—*Gavin Lambert*

Lost Command

US 1966   128m   Technicolor   Panavision
Columbia / Red Lion (Mark Robson)

Adventures of a French paratroop regiment in
Indo-China and Algeria.
Anti-war war adventure; noisy but scarcely
inspired.

w Nelson Gidding, *novel* The Centurions by Jean
Larteguy d Mark Robson ph Robert Surtees
m Franz Waxman

Anthony Quinn, Alain Delon, George Segal,
Michèle Morgan, Maurice Ronet, Claudia
Cardinale, Grégoire Aslan, Jean Servais

The Lost Continent*

GB 1968   98m   Technicolor
Hammer (Michael Carreras)

The captain of a tramp steamer illegally carries
dynamite, and he and his passengers are
stranded in a weird Sargasso Sea colony run by
the Spanish Inquisition.
Hilariously imaginative hokum with splendid art
direction and some of the grottiest monsters on
film; but memorable moments do not quite add
up to a classic of the genre.

w Michael Nash, *novel* Uncharted Seas by
Dennis Wheatley d Michael Carreras ph Paul
Beeson m Gerard Schurmann sp Robert A.
Mattey, Cliff Richardson ad Arthur Lawson

Eric Porter, Hildegarde Neff, Suzanna Leigh,
Tony Beckley, Nigel Stock, Neil McCallum,
Jimmy Hanley, James Cossins, Victor Maddern

'One of the most ludicrously enjoyable bad
films since *Salome Where She Danced.*'—*MFB*

Lost Horizon****

US 1937　130m (released at 118m)　bw
Columbia (Frank Capra)

Escaping from an Indian revolution, four people are kidnapped by plane and taken to an idyllic civilization in a Tibetan valley, where the weather is always kind and men are not only gentle to each other but live to a very advanced age.

Much re-cut romantic adventure which leaves out some of the emphasis of a favourite Utopian novel but stands up pretty well on its own, at least as a supreme example of Hollywood moonshine, with perfect casting, direction and music. If the design has a touch of Ziegfeld, that's Hollywood.

w *Robert Riskin, novel James Hilton* d *Frank Capra* ph Joseph Walker m *Dmitri Tiomkin* ad Stephen Goosson

Ronald Colman, H. B. Warner, Thomas Mitchell, Edward Everett Horton, Sam Jaffe, Isabel Jewell, Jane Wyatt, Margo, John Howard

'One of the most impressive of all thirties films, a splendid fantasy which, physically and emotionally, lets out all the stops.'—*John Baxter, 1968*

'One is reminded of a British critic's comment on *Mary of Scotland*, "the inaccuracies must have involved tremendous research".'—*Robert Stebbins*

†A 1943 reissue trimmed down the negative still further, to 109 minutes; but in 1979 the American Film Institute was busily restoring a print of the original length.

AAN: Dmitri Tiomkin; H. B. Warner

Lost Horizon*

US 1972　143m Panavision Technicolor
Columbia / Ross Hunter

Torpid remake with a good opening followed by slabs of philosophizing dialogue and an unbroken series of tedious songs.

w *Larry Kramer* d *Charles Jarrott* ph Robert Surtees m Burt Bacharach ad Preston Ames

Peter Finch, Liv Ullmann, Sally Kellerman, *Bobby Van,* George Kennedy, Michael York, Olivia Hussey, James Shigeta, John Gielgud, Charles Boyer

Lost in a Harem**

US 1944　89m　bw
MGM

Two travelling entertainers in the Middle East get mixed up with a conniving sultan, who hypnotizes them.

Lively, well-staged romp which shows the comedians at their best and uses astute borrowings from burlesque, pantomime, and Hollywood traditions of fantasy and running jokes.

w *Harry Ruskin, John Grant, Harry Crane* d *Charles Reisner* ph Lester White m David Snell

Bud Abbott, Lou Costello, Douglass Dumbrille, Marilyn Maxwell, John Conte, Jimmy Dorsey and his Orchestra

The Lost Man

US 1969　113m Technicolor Panavision
Universal (Ernest B. Wehmeyer)

After a robbery, a crook is pursued by the police and goes into hiding.

Odd Man Out made over as a vehicle for polemics about civil rights for blacks: too shiny, too long, too talky to have any grip.

w Robert Alan Aurthur ph Jerry Finnerman m Quincy Jones

Sidney Poitier, Joanna Shimkus, Al Freeman Jnr, Michael Tolan, Leon Bibb, Richard Dysart, David Steinberg, Paul Winfield

The Lost Moment*

US 1947　89m　bw
U-I (Martin Gabel)

An American publisher goes to Venice to recover love letters written by a famous poet to a lady now aged 105.

Slightly absurd but memorable period drama with a guilty secret eventually coming to light, all put across with apparently deliberate artificiality.

w Leonardo Bercovici, *novel* The Aspern Papers by Henry James d Martin Gabel ph Hal Mohr m Daniele Amfitheatrof

Robert Cummings, Susan Hayward, *Agnes Moorehead,* Joan Lorring, Eduardo Ciannelli

'A compelling piece, highly stylized and very personal, with a beautifully photographed studio recreation of Venice.'—*NFT, 1973*

The Lost Patrol***

US 1934　74m　bw
RKO (Cliff Reid)

A small British army group is lost in the Mesopotamian desert under Arab attack.
Much-copied adventure story of a small patrol under attack (compare *Sahara, Bataan* and *The Last of the Comanches* for a start). The original now seems pretty starchy but retains moments of power.

w *Dudley Nichols, story* Patrol by Philip MacDonald d *John Ford* ph Harold Wenstrom m Max Steiner

Victor McLaglen, Boris Karloff, Wallace Ford, Reginald Denny, J. M. Kerrigan, Billy Bevan, Alan Hale

AAN: Max Steiner

The Lost People
GB 1949 89m bw
GFD / Gainsborough (Gordon Wellesley)

Displaced persons gather for comfort in a disused German theatre.
Once again a very flat film has been unsuitably made from an effective piece of theatre, with all possible types present and all views represented. Not on.

w Bridget Boland, from her play Cockpit d Bernard Knowles ph Jack Asher m John Greenwood

Richard Attenborough, Mai Zetterling, Siobhan McKenna, Dennis Price, Maxwell Reed, William Hartnell, Gerard Heinz, Harcourt Williams, Marcel Poncin

The Lost Squadron*
US 1932 72m bw
RKO

World War I pilots find work stunting for a movie studio.
Unusual comedy-drama with several points of interest.

w Herman J. Mankiewicz, Wallace Smith d George Archainbaud ph Leo Tover, Edward Cronjager

Richard Dix, Mary Astor, Erich Von Stroheim, Joel McCrea, Dorothy Jordan, Hugh Herbert, Robert Armstrong

The Lost Weekend****
US 1945 101m bw
Paramount *(Charles Brackett)*

Two days in the life of a young dipsomaniac writer.
Startlingly original on its release, this stark little drama keeps its power, especially in the scenes on New York streets and in a dipso ward. It could scarcely have been more effectively filmed.

w *Charles Brackett, Billy Wilder, novel* Charles Jackson *d Billy Wilder ph John F. Seitz m* Miklos Rozsa

Ray Milland, Jane Wyman, Philip Terry, *Howard da Silva, Frank Faylen*

AA: best picture; script; Billy Wilder (as director); Ray Milland
AAN: Frank Faylen

The Lost World
US 1960 98m De Luxe Cinemascope
TCF / Saratoga (Irwin Allen)

Professor Challenger is financed by a newspaper to confirm the report of prehistoric life on a South African plateau.
Pitiful attempt to continue the success of *Journey to the Center of the Earth*, with the story idiotically modernized, unconvincing monsters, a script which inserts conventional romance and villainy, and fatal miscasting of the central part.

w Irwin Allen, Charles Bennett, *novel* Sir Arthur Conan Doyle *d* Irwin Allen *ph* Winton C. Hoch *m* Bert Shefter, Paul Sawtell

Claude Rains, *Michael Rennie*, David Hedison, *Richard Haydn*, Fernando Lamas, Jill St John, Ray Stricklyn

'Resembles nothing so much as a ride on a rundown fairground Ghost Train.'—*MFB*

Louisiana Purchase*
US 1941 98m Technicolor
Paramount (Harold Wilson)

Efforts are made to compromise a politician. Quite lively transcription of a Broadway musical success with elements of political satire including a climactic filibuster scene.

w Jerome Chodorov, Joseph Fields, *play* Morrie Ryskind *songs* Irving Berlin *d* Irving Cummings *ph* Harry Hallenberger, Ray Rennahan

Bob Hope, Vera Zorina, *Victor Moore,* Irene Bordoni, Dona Drake, Raymond Walburn, Maxie Rosenbloom, Frank Albertson, Donald MacBride, Andrew Tombes

AAN: Harry Hallenberger, Ray Rennahan

Louisiana Story*
US 1948 77m bw
Standard Oil Company (Robert Flaherty)

In the Louisiana bayous a young native boy watches as oil drillers make a strike.
Quite beautiful but over-extended semi-documentary.

w Robert and Frances Flaherty *d* Robert Flaherty *ph* Richard Leacock *m* Virgil Thompson

Joseph Boudreaux, Lionel Leblanc, Frank Hardy

AAN: original story

Love*
US 1927 82m (24 fps) bw silent
MGM (Edmund Goulding)

Anna Karenina leaves her husband and child for Count Vronsky.

Marginally interesting first shot at a famous subject by a star who came back to it in 1935.

w Frances Marion, Lorna Moon, *novel* Leo Tolstoy *d* Edmund Goulding *ph* William Daniels *m* Ernst Luz *ad* Cedric Gibbons, Alexander Toluboff

Greta Garbo, John Gilbert, Brandon Hurst, Philippe de Lacy, George Fawcett, Emily Fitzroy

† An alternative happy ending was provided for exhibitors who wanted it.

Love Affair
US 1932   68m   bw
Columbia

An heiress falls for a flying instructor.
Mild romantic comedy drama.

w Jo Swerling, *story* Ursula Parrott *d* Thornton Freeland *ph* Ted Tetzlaff

Dorothy Mackaill, Humphrey Bogart, Jack Kennedy, Astrid Allwyn, Halliwell Hobbes, Barbara Leonard

Love Affair***
US 1939   89m   bw
Paramount (Leo McCarey)

On a transatlantic crossing, a European man of the world meets a New York girl, but their romance is flawed by misunderstanding and physical accident.
The essence of Hollywood romance, and one of the most fondly remembered films of the thirties, perhaps because of the easy comedy sense of the first half.

w Delmer Daves, Donald Ogden Stewart, *story* Mildred Cram, Leo McCarey *d* Leo McCarey *ph* Rudolph Maté

Charles Boyer, Irene Dunne, Maria Ouspenskaya, Lee Bowman, Astrid Allwyn, Maurice Moscovitch

'Those excited over the mastery of form already achieved in pictures, will like to follow this demonstration of the qualities of technique and imagination the films must always have and keep on recruiting to their service . . . Clichés of situation and attitude are lifted almost beyond recognition by a morning freshness of eye for each small thing around.'—*Otis Ferguson*

'McCarey brought off one of the most difficult things you can attempt with film. He created a mood, rather than a story; he kept it alive by expert interpolations; he provided comedy when he needed comedy and poignancy when he needed substance; and he did it with the minimum of effort.'—*Pare Lorentz*

† Remade as *An Affair to Remember* (qv).

AAN: best picture; original story; Irene Dunne; Maria Ouspenskaya; song 'Wishing' (*m/ly* Buddy de Sylva)

Love and Death*
US 1975   85m   De Luxe
UA / Jack Rollins, Charles H. Joffe

In 1812 Russia, a man condemned reviews the follies of his life.
Personalized comedy fantasia inspired by *War and Peace*, Ingmar Bergman and S. J. Perelman. Basically only for star fans.

wd Woody Allen *ph* Ghislain Cloquet *m* Prokofiev

Woody Allen, Diane Keaton, Georges Adel, Despo, Frank Adu

Love and Hisses*
US 1937   84m   bw
TCF (Kenneth MacGowan)

A gossip columnist and a bandleader continue their feud.
Moderate sequel to *Wake Up and Live* (qv); it got by.

w Art Arthur, Curtis Kenyon *d* Sidney Lanfield *ph* Robert Planck

Walter Winchell, Ben Bernie and his orchestra, Joan Davis, Bert Lahr, Simone Simon, Ruth Terry

Love and Pain and the Whole Damn Thing
US 1972   113m   Eastmancolor
Columbia / Gus (Alan J. Pakula)

An asthmatic young American on holiday in Spain has an affair with an older woman suffering from an incurable disease.
Dreary doomed romance studiously treated as tourist comedy.

w Alvin Sargent *d* Alan J. Pakula *ph* Geoffrey Unsworth *m* Michael Small

Maggie Smith, Timothy Bottoms

The Love Bug**
US 1968   107m   Technicolor
Walt Disney (Bill Walsh)

An unsuccessful racing driver finds that his small private Volkswagen has a mind of its own.
Amusing, pacy period fantasy in the best Disney style.

w Bill Walsh, Don da Gradi *d* Robert Stevenson *ph* Edward Colman *m* George Bruns *sp* Eustace Lycett

David Tomlinson, Dean Jones, Michele Lee,

Buddy Hackett, Joe Flynn, Benson Fong, Joe E. Ross

Love Crazy*
US 1941 100m bw
MGM (Pandro S. Berman)

When his wife threatens to divorce him, a businessman hatches all manner of crazy schemes, including disguising himself as his own sister.

Zany romantic comedy, over-stretched but with a fair share of hilarity.

w William Ludwig, Charles Lederer, David Hertz d Jack Cummings ph Ray June m David Snell

William Powell, Myrna Loy, Gail Patrick, Jack Carson, Florence Bates, Sidney Blackmer, Vladimir Sokoloff, Donald MacBride, Sig Rumann, Sara Haden, Elisha Cook Jnr, Kathleen Lockhart

Love Eternal*
France 1943 111m bw
André Paulvé
original title: *L'Eternel Retour*

The love story of Tristan and Isolde. This modernized version had a Teutonic look and was respected rather than admired.

w Jean Cocteau d Jean Delannoy ph Roger Hubert m Georges Auric ad Wakhevitch

Jean Marais, Madeleine Sologne, Jean Murat, Yvonne de Bray

Love from a Stranger*
GB 1937 90m bw
Trafalgar (Max Schach)

A young woman realizes she may have married a maniac.

Stalwart suspenser from a popular novel and play.

w Frances Marion, *play* Frank Vosper, *story* Philomel Cottage by Agatha Christie d Rowland V. Lee ph Philip Tannura m Benjamin Britten

Ann Harding, Basil Rathbone, Binnie Hale, Bruce Seton, Jean Cadell, Bryan Powley, Joan Hickson, Donald Calthrop

Love from a Stranger
US 1947 81m bw
Eagle Lion (James J. Geller)
GB title: *A Stranger Walked In*

Stilted period remake.

w Philip MacDonald d Richard Whorf ph Tony Gaudio m Hans Salter

Sylvia Sidney, John Hodiak, Ann Richards, John Howard, Isobel Elsom, Frederick Worlock

The Love Goddesses**
US 1965 87m bw
Paramount / Walter Reade / Sterling

A light-hearted account of female sexuality on the Hollywood screen.

Sharp-eyed compilation film which is worth a dozen books on the subject.

pd Saul J. Turell, Graeme Ferguson m Percy Faith narrator Carl King
† Clips include *Blonde Venus, Morocco, True Heart Susie, Cleopatra* (1934), *Intolerance, The Cheat, The Sheik, Blood and Sand, The Sorrows of Satan, The Loves of Sunya, Diary of a Lost Girl, Ecstasy, L'Atlantide, Peter the Tramp, Cabin in the Cotton, Platinum Blonde, Gold Diggers of 1933, No Man of Her Own, Professional Sweetheart, Love Me Tonight, I'm No Angel, Baby Face, They Won't Forget, College Swing, Her Jungle Love, Gilda, A Place in the Sun, Some Like it Hot.*

Love Happy*
US 1949 85m bw
Lester Cowan / Mary Pickford

A group of impoverished actors accidentally gets possession of the Romanov diamonds.
The last dismaying Marx Brothers film, with Harpo taking the limelight and Groucho loping in for a couple of brief, tired appearances. A roof chase works, but Harpo tries too hard for sentiment, and the production looks shoddy.

w Ben Hecht, Frank Tashlin, Mac Benoff d David Miller ph William Mellor

Groucho, Harpo, Chico, Eric Blore, Ilona Massey, Marilyn Monroe

Love Has Many Faces
US 1964 104m Eastmancolor
Columbia / Jerry Bresler

A rich woman marries a beach boy and has an affair with another, who is murdered.
Hilarious but unentertaining sex melodrama built around an overage star.

w Marguerite Roberts d Alexander Singer ph Joseph Ruttenberg m David Raksin

Lana Turner, Cliff Robertson, Hugh O'Brian, Stefanie Powers, Ruth Roman, Virginia Grey
'For connoisseurs of perfectly awful movies.'—*Judith Crist*

Love in the Afternoon
US 1957 126m bw
AA (Billy Wilder)

The daughter of a private detective warns an American philanderer in Paris that an enraged husband is en route to shoot him.

Tired and dreary romantic sex comedy, miscast and far too long. With the talent around, there are of course a few compensations.

w Billy Wilder, I. A. L. Diamond, *novel* Claude Anet d Billy Wilder ph William Mellor m Franz Waxman ad Alexander Trauner

Gary Cooper, Audrey Hepburn, Maurice Chevalier, John McGiver

Love Is a Ball

US 1962 112m Technicolor Panavision
UA / Oxford / Gold Medal (Martin H. Poll)
GB title: *All This and Money Too*

A Riviera matchmaker recruits instructors to train his star pupil, but one of them walks away with the lady.

Forgettable comedy in which more effort goes into the glamorous background than the script.

w David Swift, Tom and Frank Waldman, *novel* The Grand Duke and Mr Pimm by Lindsay Hardy d David Swift
ph Edmond Séchan m Michel Legrand

Glenn Ford, Charles Boyer, Hope Lange, Ricardo Montalban, Telly Savalas, Ruth McDevitt, Ulla Jacobsson

Love Is a Many Splendored Thing*

US 1955 102m De Luxe Cinemascope
TCF (Buddy Adler)

During the Korean War, a Eurasian lady doctor in Hong Kong falls in love with a war correspondent. Self-admittedly sentimental soaper with a tragic ending; the theme tune kept it popular for years.

w John Patrick, *novel* Han Suyin d Henry King
ph Leon Shamroy m Alfred Newman

Jennifer Jones, William Holden, Torin Thatcher, Isobel Elsom, Murray Matheson, Virginia Gregg, Richard Loo

AA: Alfred Newman; title song (*m* Sammy Fain, *ly* Paul Francis Webster)
AAN: best picture; Leon Shamroy; Jennifer Jones

Love Is News*

US 1937 78m bw
TCF (Earl Carroll, Harold Wilson)

An heiress marries a scoop-hunting reporter just to show him how embarrassing publicity can be. Silly romantic comedy with plenty of laughs.

w Harry Tugend, Jack Yellen d Tay Garnett
ph Ernest Palmer

Tyrone Power, Loretta Young, Don Ameche, Slim Summerville, Dudley Digges, Walter Catlett, Jane Darwell, Stepin Fetchit, George Sanders, Frank Conroy, Elisha Cook Jnr
† Remade as *Sweet Rosie O'Grady* and *That Wonderful Urge.*

Love Letters*

US 1945 101m bw
Paramount (Hal B. Wallis)

A girl who has lost her memory through war shock is threatened by more physical danger. Oddly unexciting romantic melodrama directed and designed in heavy but satisfying style. Typical post-war depressive fare.

w Ayn Rand, *novel* Pity My Simplicity by Chris Massie d William Dieterle ph Lee Garmes
m Victor Young

Jennifer Jones, Joseph Cotten, Ann Richards, Gladys Cooper, Anita Louise, Cecil Kellaway, Robert Sully, Byron Barr, Reginald Denny, Lumsden Hare

AAN: Jennifer Jones; title song (*m* Victor Young, *ly* Edward Heyman)

Love, Life and Laughter*

GB 1934 83m bw
ATP (Basil Dean)

A film actress catches the eye of a Ruritanian prince.

Lively star vehicle ranging from sentiment to slapstick.

w Robert Edmunds d Maurice Elvey

Gracie Fields, John Loder, Norah Howard, Allan Aynesworth, Esme Percy, Robb Wilton, Fred Duprez, Horace Kenney, Veronica Brady

The Love Lottery

GB 1953 83m Technicolor
Ealing (Monja Danischewsky)

A British film star is persuaded to offer himself as first prize in a lottery.

Satirical farce which doesn't come off, mainly owing to paucity of comedy ideas.

w Harry Kurnitz d Charles Crichton
ph Douglas Slocombe m Benjamin Frankel
pd Tom Morahan

David Niven, Herbert Lom, Peggy Cummins, Anne Vernon, Charles Victor, Gordon Jackson, Felix Aylmer, Hugh McDermott

The Love Machine

US 1971 110m Eastmancolor
Columbia / Mike Frankovich

Megalomaniac TV reporter progresses to

network programme controller but is finally
undone by his vivid sex life.
Stodgy, silly melodrama from a bestseller whose
inspiration was well known in TV circles.

w Samuel Taylor, *novel* Jacqueline Susann
d Jack Haley Jnr *ph* Charles Lang Jnr *m* Artie
Butler

John Philip Law, Dyan Cannon, Robert Ryan,
Jackie Cooper, David Hemmings, Shecky
Greene

Love Me Forever
US 1936 92m bw
Columbia

A down and out singer makes good.
Fair star vehicle.

w Jo Swerling, Sidney Buchman *d* Victor
Schertzinger *ph* Joe Walker *md* Louis Silvers

Grace Moore, Leo Carillo, Robert Allen, Spring
Byington, Michael Bartlett, Thurston Hall,
Douglas Dumbrille, Luis Alberni

Love Me or Leave Me**
US 1955 122m Eastmancolor
  Cinemascope
MGM (Joe Pasternak)

Twenties singer Ruth Etting is befriended by a
racketeer who pushes her to the top but drives
her to drink and despair in the process.
Agreeably bitter showbiz biopic which gives the
impression of being not too far from the truth.

w Daniel Fuchs, Isabel Lennart *d* Charles
Vidor *ph* Arthur E. Arling *md* George Stoll
ad Cedric Gibbons, Urie McCleary

Doris Day, James Cagney, Cameron Mitchell,
Robert Keith, Tom Tully, Harry Bellaver,
Richard Gaines

AAN: original story (Daniel Fuchs); George
Stoll; James Cagney; song 'I'll Never Stop
Loving You' (*m* Nicholas Brodszky, *ly* Sammy
Cahn)

Love Me Tender
US 1959 95m bw Cinemascope
TCF (David Weisbart)

Three brothers fall out over loot they have
brought home from the Civil War.
Odd western designed (perhaps after shooting
began) as Presley's introductory vehicle; he sings
four songs before getting shot, and reappears in
ghostly form at the end.

w Robert Buckner *d* Robert D. Webb *ph* Leo
Tover *m* Lionel Newman

Richard Egan, Debra Paget, Elvis Presley,
Robert Middleton, William Campbell, Neville

Brand, Mildred Dunnock, Bruce Bennett, James
Drury, Ken Clark, Barry Coe

Love Me Tonight****
US 1932 104m bw
Paramount (Rouben Mamoulian)

A Parisian tailor accidentally moves into the
aristocracy.
The most fluently cinematic comedy musical
ever made, with sounds and words, lyrics and
music, deftly blended into a compulsively and
consistently laughable mosaic of sophisticated
nonsense; one better than the best of Lubitsch
and Clair.

w Samuel Hoffenstein, Waldemar Young,
George Marion Jnr *d* Rouben Mamoulian
ph Victor Milner *songs* Rodgers and Hart

Maurice Chevalier, Jeanette MacDonald,
Charles Butterworth, Charles Ruggles, Myrna
Loy, C. Aubrey Smith, Elizabeth Patterson,
Ethel Griffies, Blanche Frederici, Robert Greig

'Gay, charming, witty, it is everything that the
Lubitsch musicals should have been but never
were.'—*John Baxter, 1968*
'With the aid of a pleasant story, a good
musician, a talented cast and about a million
dollars, he has done what someone in Hollywood
should have done long ago—he has illustrated a
musical score.'—*Pare Lorentz*
'It has that infectious spontaneity which
distinguishes the American musical at its
best.'—*Peter Cowie, 1970*
'A rich amalgam of filmic invention, witty
decoration and wonderful songs.'—*NFT, 1974*

Love on the Dole***
GB 1941 100m bw
British National (John Baxter)

Life among unemployed cotton workers in
industrial Lancashire between the wars.
Vividly characterized, old-fashioned social
melodrama, well made on a low budget; a rare
problem picture for Britain at this time.

w Walter Greenwood, Barbara K. Emery, Rollo
Gamble, *novel* Walter Greenwood *d* John
Baxter

Deborah Kerr, Clifford Evans, *George Carney*,
Joyce Howard, Frank Cellier, Geoffrey Hibbert,
Mary Merrall, Maire O'Neill, *Marjorie Rhodes*,
A. Bromley Davenport, Marie Ault, Iris
Vandeleur, Kenneth Griffith

Love on the Run*
US 1936 81m bw
MGM (Joseph L. Mankiewicz)

Rival newspapermen help an heiress to escape an

unwanted wedding and in the process uncover a ring of spies.
Harebrained star farce, smoothly assembled and still fairly funny.

w John Lee Mahin, Manuel Seff, Gladys Hurlbut d W. S. Van Dyke ph Oliver T. Marsh

Clark Gable, Joan Crawford, Franchot Tone, Reginald Owen, Mona Barrie, Ivan Lebedeff, William Demarest

'A slightly daffy cinematic item of absolutely no importance.'—*New York Times*

The Love Parade**
US 1929 112m bw
Paramount (Ernst Lubitsch)

The prince of Sylvania marries.
Primitive sound operetta set among the idle European rich, with clear but faded instances of the Lubitsch touch.

w Ernest Vajda, Guy Bolton, *play* The Prince Consort by Leon Xanrof and Jules Chancel d Ernst Lubitsch ph Victor Milner *songs* Victor Schertzinger, Clifford Grey

Maurice Chevalier, Jeanette MacDonald, Lupino Lane, Lillian Roth, Edgar Norton, Lionel Belmore, Eugene Pallette

'The first truly cinematic screen musical in America.'—*Theodore Huff*

AAN: best picture; Ernst Lubitsch; Victor Milner; Maurice Chevalier

Love, Soldiers and Women
France / Italy 1953 96m bw
Franco-London / Continental
original title: *Destinées*; US title: *Daughters of Destiny*

Three stories of women in war: Joan of Arc, Lysistrata, and a modern American war widow visiting her husband's grave.
Uninteresting patchwork with Lysistrata predictably stealing the show.

'Jeanne': w Jean Aurenche, Pierre Bost d Jean Delannoy *with* Michèle Morgan
'Elizabeth': w Sergio Amedei d Marcel Pagliero *with* Claudette Colbert, Eleanora Rossi Drago
'Lysistrata': w Jean Ferry, Henri Jeanson, Carlo Rim, *play* Aristophanes d Christian-Jaque *with* Martine Carol, Raf Vallone, Paolo Stoppa

Love Story
GB 1944 112m bw
GFD / Gainsborough (Harold Huth)
US title: *A Lady Surrenders*

In Cornwall during World War II, a half-blind airman falls for a pianist with a weak heart.

Novelettish love story which became popular because of its Cornish Rhapsody.

w Leslie Arliss, Doreen Montgomery, Rodney Ackland, *novel* J. W. Drawbell d Leslie Arliss m Hubert Bath

Margaret Lockwood, Stewart Granger, Patricia Roc, Tom Walls, Reginald Purdell, Moira Lister
'A splendid, noble and fatuous piece.'—*C. A. Lejeune*
'In psychology and dialogue this is straight out of *Mabel's Weekly*.'—*Richard Winnington*

Love Story*
US 1970 100m Movielab
Paramount (David Golden)

Two students marry; she dies.
A barrage of ripe old Hollywood clichés spiced with new-fangled bad language. In the circumstances, well enough made, and certainly astonishingly popular.

w Erich Segal, from his novelette d Arthur Hiller ph Dick Kratina m Bach, Mozart, Handel md Francis Lai

Ali MacGraw, Ryan O'Neal, Ray Milland, John Marley
'Camille with bullshit.'—*Alexander Walker*

AAN: best picture; Erich Segal; Arthur Hiller; Francis Lai; Ali MacGraw; Ryan O'Neal; John Marley

Love That Brute
US 1950 85m bw
TCF (Fred Kohlmar)

A ruthless Chicago gangleader is actually a softy, leaving his supposedly rubbed-out enemies in a comfortable cellar; a young governess persuades him to reform.
Rickety, dully-scripted gangster farce.

w Darrell Ware, John Lee Mahin, Karl Tunberg d Alexander Hall ph Lloyd Ahern m Cyril Mockridge

Paul Douglas, Jean Peters, Cesar Romero, Joan Davis, Arthur Treacher

Love Thy Neighbour
GB 1973 85m Technicolor
EMI / Hammer (Roy Skeggs)

A prejudiced white worker has coloured neighbours.
Elongated screen version of the popular TV series in which the West Indians smile through all the insults and come out top in the end. It might have been worse, but not much.

w Vince Powell, Harry Driver d John Robins ph Moray Grant m Albert Elms

Jack Smethurst, Kate Williams, Rudolph
Walker, Nina Baden-Semper, Bill Fraser,
Charles Hyatt, Keith Marsh, Patricia Hayes,
Arthur English

Love under Fire

US 1937   75m   bw
TCF (Nunnally Johnson)

A detective catches up with a lady jewel thief in
Madrid during the Spanish Civil War.
Adequately entertaining but rather tasteless
adventure comedy.

w Gene Fowler, Allen Rivkin, Ernest Pascal,
play Walter Hackett d George Marshall
ph Ernest Palmer m Arthur Lange

Loretta Young, Don Ameche, Frances Drake,
Walter Catlett, John Carradine, Borrah
Minevitch and his Rascals, Sig Rumann, Harold
Huber, E. E. Clive, Katherine de Mille

Love with the Proper Stranger**

US 1964   100m   bw
Paramount / Boardwalk (Alan J. Pakula)

A musician tries to help his pregnant shopgirl
friend get an abortion, but they decide to get
married instead.
Oddly likeable comedy drama set on New
York's Italian East Side, with an excellent
location sense.

w Arnold Schulman d Robert Mulligan
ph Milton Krasner m Elmer Bernstein

Steve McQueen, Natalie Wood, Tom Bosley,
Edie Adams, Herschel Bernardi

AAN: Arnold Schulman; Milton Krasner;
Natalie Wood

The Loved One*

US 1965   118m   bw
MGM / Filmways (Neil Hartley)

A young English poet in California gets a job at a
very select burial ground.
A pointed satire on the American way of death
has been allowed to get out of hand, with writer
and actors alike laying it on too thick; but there
are pleasantly waspish moments in a movie
advertised as 'the motion picture with something
to offend everybody'.

w Terry Southern, Christopher Isherwood, novel
Evelyn Waugh d Tony Richardson ph Haskell
Wexler m John Addison pd Rouben Ter-
Arutunian

Robert Morse, John Gielgud, Rod Steiger,
Liberace, Anjanette Comer, Jonathan Winters,
Dana Andrews, Milton Berle, James Coburn,
Tab Hunter, Margaret Leighton, Roddy
McDowall, Robert Morley, Lionel Stander

'Even a chaotic satire like this is cleansing, and
it's embarrassing to pan even a bad movie that
comes out against God, mother and country.'—
Pauline Kael, 1968

'A spineless farrago of collegiate gags.'—
Stanley Kauffmann

'A sinking ship that makes it to port because
everyone on board is too giddy to panic.'—New
Yorker, 1978

Lovely to Look At*

US 1952   102m   Technicolor
MGM (Jack Cummings)

Three Broadway producers inherit a Paris
fashion house.
Lavish but dullish remake of Roberta (qv), in
itself no great shakes as a storyline; again the
fashions and the numbers are the thing.

w George Wells, Harry Ruby d Mervyn Le
Roy ph George J. Folsey m Jerome Kern
ad Cedric Gibbons, Gabriel Scognamillo

Howard Keel, Kathryn Grayson, Ann Miller,
Red Skelton

A Lovely Way to Die

US 1968   98m   Techniscope
Universal (Richard Lewis)
GB title: A Lovely Way to Go

An ex-cop becomes bodyguard to a suspected
murderess, but proves her innocent.
Offbeat mélange of caper comedy, black farce,
private eye detection, courtroom drama,
spectacular action and routine thick ear. Doesn't
work.

w A. J. Russell d David Lowell Rich ph Morris
Hartzband m Kenyon Hopkins

Kirk Douglas, Sylva Koscina, Eli Wallach,
Martyn Green, Kenneth Haigh, Sharon Farrell

'The net result is rather as though Philip
Marlowe had met Doris Day on his not very
inspiring way to the forum.'—MFB

Lover Come Back**

US 1961   107m   Eastmancolor
U-I / Seven Pictures / Nob Hill / Arwin

Rival executives find themselves advertising a
non-existent product.
Fairly sharp advertising satire disguised as a
romantic comedy; the most entertaining of the
Day-Hudson charmers.

w Stanley Shapiro, Paul Henning d Delbert
Mann ph Arthur E. Arling m Frank de Vol

Doris Day, Rock Hudson, Tony Randall, Jack
Oakie, Edie Adams

AAN: Stanley Shapiro, Paul Henning

The Lovers

GB 1972   89m   Eastmancolor
British Lion / Gildor (Maurice Foster)

A Manchester bank clerk with a prim girl friend
finds it difficult to lose his virginity.
Well-written but rather arch comedy which
seemed much funnier and fresher as a TV series.

w Jack Rosenthal d Herbert Wise ph Bob
Huke m Carl Davis

Richard Beckinsale, Paula Wilcox, Joan Scott,
Susan Littler, John Comer, Stella Moray,
Nikolas Simmonds

Lovers and Other Strangers***

US 1969   104m   Metrocolor
ABC / David Susskind

After living together for eighteen months, Susan
and Mike decide to get married, and find their
parents have sex problems of their own.
Wise, witty and well acted sex farce, with many
actors making the most of ample chances under
firm directoral control.

w Renée Taylor, Joseph Bologna, David Zelag
Goodman d Cy Howard ph Andrew Laszlo
m Fred Karlin

Gig Young, Anne Jackson, Richard Castellano,
Bonnie Bedelia, Michael Brandon, Beatrice
Arthur, Robert Dishy, Harry Guardino, Diane
Keaton, Cloris Leachman, Anne Meara, Marian
Hailey

'An extremely engaging comedy.'—Gillian
Hartnoll

AA: song 'For All We Know' (m Fred Karlin,
ly Robb Wilson, Arthur James)
AAN: script; Richard Castellano

The Lovers of Lisbon*

France 1954   112m   bw
EGC / Hoche / Fides (Jacques Gauthier)
original title: Les Amants du Tage

A man who has killed his unfaithful wife is
acquitted of murder, gets a job as a taxi driver in
Lisbon, and falls for a rich Englishwoman who
has killed her husband and is being pursued by a
police inspector.
Pretentious tosh with a few compensations.

w Marcel Rivet, novel Joseph Kessel d Henri
Verneuil ph Roger Hubert m Lucien Legrand

Daniel Gélin, Françoise Arnoul, Trevor
Howard, Ginette Leclerc, Marcel Dalio

The Lovers of Toledo

Italy / France / Spain 1952   82m   bw
EGE / Lux / Athenea (Raymond Eger)

In 1825 a cruel police chief releases a political

prisoner in return for the hand in marriage of his
mistress.
Curiously unpersuasive period melodrama with
good credits but too many international cooks.

w Claude Vermorel, story Le Coffre et le
Revenant by Stendhal d Henri Decoin
ph Michel Kelber m Jean-Jacques Grunenwald

Pedro Armendariz, Alida Valli, Gérard Landry,
Françoise Arnoul

Loves of a Blonde**

Czechoslovakia 1965   82m   bw
Barrandov Studios
original title: Lasky Jedne Plavovlasky
aka: A Blonde in Love

A factory girl falls for a visiting musician but
meets suspicion from his family when she
pursues him.
Mild anecdote with excellent humorous detail
which endeared it to international critics.

w Milos Forman, Jaroslav Papousek, Ivan
Passer d Milos Forman ph Miroslav Ondricek
m Evzen Illin

Hanna Brejchova, Vladimir Pucholt

'It depends on an instinctive sense of timing
and a consistent vision of life and people.'—
Georges Sadoul

The Loves of Carmen

US 1948   99m   Technicolor
Columbia (Charles Vidor)

In 1820s Seville, a dragoon corporal is enslaved
by a gypsy, kills her husband and becomes an
outlaw.
Unrewarding version of the original much-filmed
story, with both stars plainly wishing they were
elsewhere.

w Helen Deutsch, novel Prosper Mérimée
d Charles Vidor ph William Snyder m Mario
Castelnuovo-Tedesco

Rita Hayworth, Glenn Ford, Victor Jory, Ron
Randell, Luther Adler, Arnold Moss, Margaret
Wycherly, Bernard Nedell

AAN: William Snyder

The Loves of Joanna Godden

GB 1947   89m   bw
Ealing (Sidney Cole)

On Romney Marsh at the turn of the century, a
woman farmer has three suitors.
Dullish 'woman's picture'.

w H. E. Bates, Angus Macphail, novel Sheila
Kaye-Smith d Charles Frend

Googie Withers, John McCallum, Jean Kent,

Derek Bond, Chips Rafferty, Henry Mollison,
Sonia Holm, Edward Rigby, Josephine Stuart

The Loves of Sunya
US 1927   80m (24 fps)   bw   silent
Swanson Producing Corporation

A yogi recognizes two young lovers as people he
wronged in a previous existence, and warns them
of impending disaster.
Star tosh of its period, unthinkable now as a
screen attraction.

w Earle Brown, *play* The Eyes of Youth by Max
Marcin, Charles Guernon d Albert Parker
ph Dudley Murphy ad Hugo Ballin

Gloria Swanson, John Boles, Anders Randolph,
Hush Miller, Florbelle Fairbanks, Raymond
Hackett

† Previously filmed as *Eyes of Youth* with Clara
Kimball Young.

Lovin' Molly*
US 1973   98m   Movielab
Stephen Friedman (David Golden)

In Texas between 1925 and 1945, two men
friends and an accommodating lady have a
shifting relationship.
Odd little drama compendium, with fragments
told by each in turn; too slight in structure and
substance for complete success, but interesting
most of the way.

w Stephen Friedman, *novel* Leaving Cheyenne
by Larry McMurtry d *Sidney Lumet*
ph Edward Brown m Fred Hellerman

Blythe Danner, Anthony Perkins, Beau Bridges,
Edward Binns, Susan Sarandon

Loving**
US 1970   90m   Eastmancolor
Columbia / Brooks Ltd (Don Devlin)

A commercial artist reaches crisis point with
both his wife and his mistress.
Smart New Yorkish sex comedy, typical of
many but better than most.

w *Don Devlin, novel* Brooks Wilson Ltd by J. M.
Ryan d *Irvin Kershner* ph Gordon Willis
m Bernardo Segall pd Walter Scott Herndon

George Segal, Eva Marie Saint, Sterling
Hayden, Keenan Wynn, Nancie Phillips, Janis
Young, David Doyle

Loving Couples*
Sweden 1964   118m   bw
Sandrew (Rune Waldekranz)
original title: *Alskande Par*

Three expectant mothers think back over their
sex lives.

Superbly made, rather hollow diatribe against
sex, presented as a series of intricate flashbacks.
Along the way, there is much to enjoy, but the
result is not really a film of importance.

w Mai Zetterling, David Hughes,
novel Froknarna von Pahlen by Agnes von
Krusenstjerna d *Mai Zetterling* ph Sven
Nykvist m Rodger Wallis

Harriet Andersson, Gunnel Lindblom, Anita
Bjork, Gunnar Bjornstrand, Eva Dahlbeck,
Frank Sundstrom, Inga Landgre

'. . . that air of packaged neurosis so peculiar
to the Swedish cinema.'—*Tom Milne, MFB*

Loving You
US 1957   101m   Technicolor   Vistavision
Paramount / Hal B. Wallis

A press agent signs a young hillbilly singer to
give zest to her husband's band.
Empty-headed, glossy star vehicle.

w Herbert Baker, Hal Kanter d Hal Kanter
ph Charles Lang Jnr

Elvis Presley, Lizabeth Scott, Wendell Corey,
Dolores Hart, James Gleason

The Luck of Ginger Coffey*
Canada / US 1964   100m   bw
Crawley / Roth–Kershner (Leon Roth)

An Irish layabout in Canada finds it difficult to
keep a job or protect his family.
Mildly interesting character study with good
background detail of Montreal.

w Brian Moore, from his novel d Irvin
Kershner ph Manny Wynn m Bernardo Segall

Robert Shaw, Mary Ure, Liam Redmond

The Luck of the Irish*
US 1947   99m   bw
TCF (Fred Kohlmar)

A New York newsman's love life is complicated
by a helpful leprechaun he meets in Ireland.
Hollywood moonshine, second class: the will
and the players are there, but the script is not
funny enough.

w Philip Dunne, *novel* There Was a Little Man
by Constance and Guy Jones d Henry Koster
ph Joseph La Shelle m Cyril Mockridge

Tyrone Power, *Cecil Kellaway*, Anne Baxter,
Lee J. Cobb, James Todd, Jayne Meadows, J. M.
Kerrigan, Phil Brown

AAN: Cecil Kellaway

Lucky Jim**
GB 1958   95m   bw
British Lion / Charter (Roy Boulting)

At a provincial university, an accident-prone junior lecturer has a disastrous weekend with his girl friend and his professor.

Quite funny in its own right, this is a vulgarization of a famous comic novel which got its effects more subtly, with more sense of place, time and character.

w Jeffrey Dell, Patrick Campbell, *novel* Kingsley Amis d John Boulting ph Max Greene

Ian Carmichael, Hugh Griffith, Terry-Thomas, Sharon Acker, Jean Anderson, Maureen Connell, Clive Morton, John Welsh, Reginald Beckwith, Kenneth Griffith

Lucky Jordan

US 1942 83m bw
Paramount (Fred Kohlmar)

A con man is drafted and overcomes Nazi agents.

Forgettable star cheapie.

w Darrell Ware, Karl Tunberg d Frank Tuttle ph John F. Seitz

Alan Ladd, Helen Walker, Sheldon Leonard, Marie McDonald, Mabel Paige, Lloyd Corrigan, Dave Willock, Miles Mander

Lucky Lady

US 1975 · 118m De Luxe
TCF / Gruskoff / Venture (Michael Gruskoff)

A cabaret girl in 1930 Tijuana joins two adventurers in smuggling liquor into the US by boat.

Whatever can be done wrong with such a story has been done, including irritatingly washed out photography, kinky sex, and sudden switches from farce to gore. None of it holds the interest for a single moment.

w Willard Huyck, Gloria Katz d Stanley Donen ph Geoffrey Unsworth m Ralph Burns pd John Barry

Liza Minnelli, Gene Hackman, Burt Reynolds, Michael Hordern, Geoffrey Lewis, Robby Benson

'A manic mess that tries to be all things to all people and ends up offering nothing to anyone.'—*Frank Rich*

'It sports its calculations on its sleeve like rhinestones.'—*Sight and Sound*

Lucky Me*

US 1954 100m Warnercolor Cinemascope
Warner (Henry Blanke)

Theatrical entertainers stranded in Florida get a lucky break.

Watchable, forgettable musical.

w James O'Hanlon, Robert O'Brien, Irving Elinson d Jack Donohue ph Wilfrid M. Cline md Ray Heindorf

Doris Day, Robert Cummings, Phil Silvers, Eddie Foy Jnr, Nancy Walker, Martha Hyer, Bill Goodwin, Marcel Dalio

'The first Cinemascope musical . . . pleasant, light-hearted, frothy entertainment.'—*MFB*

Lucky Night

US 1939 90m bw
MGM (Louis D. Lighton)

An heiress goes out into the world to make a life for herself, and falls for a man she finds on a park bench.

Tedious pattern romance which did neither of its stars any good.

w Vincent Laurence, Grover Jones d Norman Taurog ph Ray June

Myrna Loy, Robert Taylor, Joseph Allen, Henry O'Neill, Douglas Fowley, Marjorie Main, Charles Lane, Bernard Nedell

Lucky Partners*

US 1940 101m bw

Two strangers share a sweepstake ticket and fall in love.

A very thin comedy kept afloat by its stars.

w Allan Scott, John Van Druten, *story* Bonne Chance by Sacha Guitry d Lewis Milestone ph Robert de Grasse m Dmitri Tiomkin

Ronald Colman, Ginger Rogers, Jack Carson, Spring Byington, Cecilia Loftus, Harry Davenport

Lucretia Borgia

France / Italy 1952 105m approx Technicolor
Ariane / Filmsonor / Rizzoli

Cesare Borgia uses his beautiful sister as a political pawn.

Well-mounted but rather boring period barnstormer.

w Cecil Saint-Laurent, Jacques Sigurd, Christian-Jaque d Christian-Jaque ph Christian Matras m Maurice Thiriet

Martine Carol, Pedro Armendariz, Massimo Serato, Ventine Tessier

Lucy Gallant*

US 1955 104m Technicolor Vistavision
Paramount / Pine—Thomas

The success story of a dressmaker who comes to run a group of fashion shops but neglects her love life.

Efficient, smartly-handled woman's picture.

w John Lee Mahin, Winston Miller, *novel* The Life of Lucy Gallant by Margaret Cousins *d* Robert Parrish *ph* Lionel Lindon *m* Van Cleave

Jane Wyman, Charlton Heston, Claire Trevor, Thelma Ritter, William Demarest, Wallace Ford, Tom Helmore, Mary Field

Ludwig*

Italy / France / West Germany 1972   186m Technicolor   Panavision
Mega / Cinetel / Dieter Gessler / Divina (Robert Gordon Edwards)

The 19th-century King of Bavaria becomes involved in scandal and goes mad.
A stylish but historically questionable and highly coloured view of events; it drags its heels long before history did.

w Luchino Visconti, Enrico Medioli *d* Luchino Visconti *ph* Armando Nannuzzi *md* Franco Nannino

Helmut Berger, Romy Schneider, Trevor Howard, Silvana Mangano, Helmut Griem, Nora Ricci, Gert Frobe, John Moulder Brown

Lullaby of Broadway*

US 1951   92m   Technicolor
Warner (William Jacobs)

The daughter of a faded Broadway star becomes the new toast of the town.
Reasonably lively musical with solid production values but little style or wit.

w Earl Baldwin *d* David Butler *ph* Wilfrid Cline *md* Ray Heindorf

Doris Day, Billy de Wolfe, Gene Nelson, Gladys George, Florence Bates, S. Z. Sakall

Lumière D'Eté*

France 1943   112m   bw
Discina (Andre Paulvé)

The idle and decadent rich in a mountain hotel are affected in various ways by workmen in the valley below.
Unusual and generally interesting character melodrama.

w Jacques Prévert, Pierre Laroche *d* Jean Grémillion *ph* Louis Page *m* Roland Manuel

Madeleine Renaud, Pierre Brasseur, Madeleine Robinson, Paul Bernard, Jane Marken, Georges Marchal

Lunch on the Grass**

France 1959   91m   Eastmancolor
Compagnie Jean Renoir
original title: *Déjeuner sur l'Herbe*

An international scientist hears the pipes of pan, embarks on a country idyll and impregnates a housemaid whom he later marries.
Charming if overlong frolic with ideas, a harking back to earlier Renoir themes such as in *Boudu Sauvé des Eaux*.

wd Jean Renoir *ph* Georges Leclerc *m* Joseph Kosma

Paul Meurisse, Catherine Rouvel, Fernand Sardou, Ingrid Nordine
'A warm, loving, garrulous, undisciplined film.'—*Penelope Houston, MFB*

Lure of the Wilderness

US 1952   92m   Technicolor
TCF (Robert L. Jacks)

A man falsely accused of murder hides for eight years in Georgia's Okefenokee swamp.
Remake of *Swamp Water*, with Walter Brennan playing the same part. The plot works fairly well still, but colour doesn't suit the scenery.

w Louis Lantz, *story* Vereen Bell *d* Jean Negulesco *ph* Edward Cronjager *m* Franz Waxman

Jeffrey Hunter, Jean Peters, Walter Brennan, Constance Smith, Jack Elam

Lured*

US 1947   102m   bw
(UA) James Nasser
GB title: *Personal Column*

An American dancer stranded in London helps Scotland Yard catch a killer.
Minor murder mystery with a pleasing cast.

w Leo Rosten, from the French film *Pièges* *d* Douglas Sirk *ph* William Daniels *m* Michel Michelet *pd* Nicolai Remisoff

Lucille Ball, George Sanders, Charles Coburn, Boris Karloff, Cedric Hardwicke, Alan Mowbray, George Zucco, Joseph Calleia, Robert Coote, Alan Napier

Lust for a Vampire

GB 1970   95m   Technicolor
Hammer (Harry Fine, Michael Style)

In 1830 an English writer discerns that a pupil in an exclusive mid-European girls' school is a reincarnated vampire.
Moderate Hammer horror.

w Tudor Gates, based on J. Sheridan Le Fanu's Carmilla *d* Jimmy Sangster *ph* David Muir *m* Harry Robinson

Ralph Bates, Michael Johnson, Barbara Jefford, Suzanna Leigh, Yutte Stensgaard, Mike Raven, Helen Christie

Lust for Gold

US 1949   90m   bw
Columbia (S. Sylvan Simon)

A young man goes to Arizona to search for a lost gold mine discovered by his grandfather. Moderate western drama consisting largely of flashback.

w Ted Sherdeman, Richard English, *novel* Thunder God's Gold by Barry Storm *d* S. Sylvan Simon *ph* Archie Stout *m* George Duning

Ida Lupino, Glenn Ford, Gig Young, William Prince, Edgar Buchanan, Will Geer, Paul Ford

Lust for Life**

US 1956   122m   Metrocolor
Cinemascope
MGM (John Houseman)

The life of Vincent Van Gogh.
Fairly absorbing, not inaccurate, but somehow uninspiring biopic, probably marred by poor colour and wide screen; despite good work all round, it simply doesn't fall into a classic category.

w Norman Corwin, *book* Irving Stone *d* Vincente Minnelli *ph* F. A. Young, Russell Harlan *m* Miklos Rozsa *ad* Cedric Gibbons, Hans Peters, Preston Ames

Kirk Douglas, Anthony Quinn (as Gauguin), James Donald, Pamela Brown, Everett Sloane, Niall MacGinnis, Noel Purcell, Henry Daniell, Lionel Jeffries, Madge Kennedy, Jill Bennett, Laurence Naismith

  'Two hours of quite shattering and exciting entertainment.'—*Alan Dent, Illustrated London News*

AA: Anthony Quinn
AAN: Norman Corwin; Kirk Douglas

The Lusty Men*

US 1952   113m   bw
RKO / Wald–Krasna (Jerry Wald)

Tensions lead to the death of one of a pair of rider friends on a rodeo tour.
Standard melodrama with semi-documentary detail and star performances.

w Horace McCoy, David Dortort *d* Nicholas Ray *ph* Lee Garmes *m* Roy Webb

Robert Mitchum, Arthur Kennedy, Susan Hayward, Arthur Hunnicutt

Luther*

US 1973   112m   Eastmancolor
American Express / Ely Landau / Cinevision

In 1525, the teachings of Luther culminate in the Peasants' Revolt.

Hard-to-watch filming by the American Film Theatre of a singularly theatrical play, and not a very good one at that. Some good acting.

w Edward Anhalt, *play* John Osborne *d* Guy Green *ph* Freddie Young *m* John Addison *pd* Peter Mullins

Stacy Keach, Patrick Magee, Hugh Griffith, Robert Stephens, Alan Badel, Julian Glover, Judi Dench, Leonard Rossiter, Maurice Denham

Luv

US 1967   95m   Technicolor   Panavision
Columbia / Jalem (Martin Manulis)

When a man prevents an old friend from jumping off the Brooklyn Bridge and brings him home, a sexual square dance develops.
A modern comedy that should have stayed in the theatre.

w Elliott Baker, *play* Murray Shisgal *d* Clive Donner *ph* Ernest Laszlo *m* Gerry Mulligan

Jack Lemmon, Peter Falk, Elaine May, Nina Wayne, Eddie Mayehoff, Paul Hartman, Severn Darden

  'A light but incisive comedy about the patterns and language of love in a Freud-ridden society has become an inept and lethally unamusing film farce.'—*MFB*

Luxury Liner

US 1933   72m   bw
Paramount

Stories of various passengers on a liner bound from New York to Bremerhaven.
Interesting minor multi-drama, like a rough sketch for *Ship of Fools* (qv).

w Gene Markey, Kathryn Scola, *novel,* Gina Kaus *d* Lothar Mendes *ph* Victor Milner

George Brent, Zita Johann, Vivienne Osborne, Alice White, Verree Teasdale, C. Aubrey Smith, Frank Morgan, Henry Wadsworth, Billy Bevan

Luxury Liner

US 1948   98m   Technicolor
MGM (Joe Pasternak)

The captain of a liner has trouble with his teenage daughter.
Minor shipboard musical with pleasing talents applied.

w Gladys Lehmann, Richard Connell *d* Richard Whorf *ph* Ernest Laszlo *md* George Stoll

George Brent, Jane Powell, Lauritz Melchior, Frances Gifford, Marina Koshetz, Xavier Cugat, Richard Derr, Connie Gilchrist

Lydia*

US 1941 104m bw

Alexander Korda (Lee Garmes)

An ageing lady recalls her former beaux. Pleasing remake of *Carnet du Bal*, with excellent production values.

w Ben Hecht, Samuel Hoffenstein, *story* Julien Duvivier, Laszlo Bus-Fekete *d Julien Duvivier ph Lee Garmes m* Miklos Rozsa *pd Vincent Korda*

Merle Oberon, Joseph Cotten, Alan Marshal, Edna May Oliver, Hans Yaray, George Reeves, John Halliday, Sara Allgood

AAN: Miklos Rozsa

Lydia Bailey

US 1952 89m Technicolor

TCF (Jules Schermer)

In 1802 a Boston lawyer visits Haiti to obtain the signature of a wayward heiress, and becomes involved in the negro fight against the French. Standard adventure romance with plenty of excitements.

w Michael Blankfort, Philip Dunne, *novel* Kenneth Roberts *d* Jean Negulesco *ph* Harry Jackson *m* Hugo Friedhofer

Dale Robertson, Anne Francis, Charles Korvin, William Marshall, Adeline de Walt Reynolds

M

M ***
Germany 1930   118m   bw
Nero Film

A psychopathic murderer of children evades the police but is caught by the city's criminals who find his activities getting them a bad name. An unmistakable classic whose oddities are hardly worth criticizing, this is part social melodrama and part satire, but entirely unforgettable, with most of its sequences brilliantly staged.

w Thea Von Harbou, Paul Falkenberg, Adolf Jansen, Karl Vash d Fritz Lang ph Fritz Arno Wagner m Adolf Jansen ad Karl Vollbrecht, Emil Hasler

Peter Lorre, Otto Wernicke, Gustav Grundgens
  'Visual excitement, pace, brilliance of surface and feeling for detail.'—New Yorker, 1977
† Of Lang's later work, Fury comes closest to the feeling and style of M.

M *
US 1951   82m   bw
Columbia (Seymour Nebenzal)

Faithful but fated remake; without the heavy expressionist techniques, the story seems merely silly and the atmosphere is all wrong.

w Norman Reilly Raine, Leo Katcher d Joseph Losey ph Ernest Laszlo m Michel Michelet

David Wayne, Howard da Silva, Luther Adler, Martin Gabel, Glenn Anders, Karen Morley, Norman Lloyd, Walter Burke

Ma and Pa Kettle *
US 1949   75m   bw
U-I (Leonard Goldstein)

Pa Kettle wins a house in a contest and is accused of cheating.
First of a series of low-budget comedies which, based on characters from The Egg and I (qv), had astonishing commercial success in America. The standard varied from adequate to painful.

w Herbert Margolis, Louis Morheim, Al Lewis d Charles Lamont ph Maury Gertsman m Milton Schwarzwald

Marjorie Main, Percy Kilbride, Richard Long, Meg Randall
  'Not exactly Noel Coward.'—Leonard Maltin
† For others in the series, see under The Kettles.

Ma Nuit chez Maud *
France 1969   110m   bw
Films du Losange
aka: My Night at Maud's

A Catholic clerk in a small town falls in love with an elegant divorcee but can't bring himself to court her openly and marries someone else. Subdued, literate talk-piece which finally exhausts rather than stimulates.

wd Eric Rohmer ph Nestor Almendros

Jean-Louis Trintignant, Françoise Fabian, Marie-Christine Barault

AAN: Eric Rohmer (as writer)

Macabre
US 1958   73m   bw
AA (William Castle)

When a small-town doctor's daughter is kidnapped, he fears she may have been buried alive in the cemetery.
Genuine but unsuccessful attempt to film a horror comic; incredibly stodgy writing, acting and direction put the lid on it.

w Robb White d William Castle ph Carl Guthrie m Les Baxter

William Prince, Jim Backus, Jacqueline Scott, Philip Tonge, Ellen Corby
  'A ghoulish but totally ineffective horror piece, set mainly in undertakers' offices and an atmosphere of graveyards and swirling fog.'—MFB
† When first released, admission carried insurance against death by fright. Some said it should have been death by boredom.

Macao
US 1952   81m   bw
RKO (Alex Gottlieb)

A wandering American in the Far East helps a detective catch a gangster.

A few flashy decorative touches show the director's hand, otherwise this is routine, murky thick ear.

w Bernard C. Schoenfeld, Stanley Rubin *d* Josef Von Sternberg (and Nicholas Ray) *ph* Harry J. Wild *m* Anthony Collins

Robert Mitchum, Jane Russell, William Bendix, Gloria Grahame, Thomas Gomez

MacArthur the Rebel General*
US 1977   130m   Technicolor
Universal / Richard D. Zanuck, David Brown

The exploits of General MacArthur during the Pacific wars and his strained relationships with two presidents.

Sober, earnest political biography with war sequences; very well done but somehow unsympathetic.

w Hal Barwood, Matthew Robbins *d* Joseph Sargent *ph* Mario Tosi *m* Jerry Goldsmith

Gregory Peck, Dan O'Herlihy (as Roosevelt), Ed Flanders (as Truman), Ward Costello, Marj Dusay, Ivan Bonar

Macbeth*
US 1948   89m   bw
Republic (Orson Welles)

A famous—or infamous—attempt to film Shakespeare in twenty-one days in papier mâché settings running with damp; further hampered by the use of a form of unintelligible bastard Scots. A few striking moments at the beginning remain; the rest should be silence.

d Orson Welles *ph* John L. Russell *m* Jacques Ibert *ad* Fred Ritter

Orson Welles, Jeanette Nolan, Dan O'Herlihy, Roddy McDowall, Edgar Barrier, Robert Coote

Macbeth*
GB 1971   140m   Technicolor   Todd-AO 35
Playboy / Caliban (Andrew Braunsberg)

A sharpened and brutalized version; the blood swamps most of the cleverness and most of the poetry.

d Roman Polanski *ph* Gilbert Taylor *m* the Third Ear Band *pd* Wilfrid Shingleton

Jon Finch, Francesca Annis, Martin Shaw, Nicholas Selby, John Stride

McCabe and Mrs Miller
US 1971   120m   Technicolor   Panavision
Warner (David Foster, Mitchell Brower)

At the turn of the century a gambling gunfighter comes to a northwest mining town and uses his money to set up lavish brothels.

Obscurely scripted, muddy-coloured and harshly recorded western melodrama whose squalid 'realism' comes as close to fantasy as does *The Wizard of Oz*.

w Robert Altman, Brian Mackay, *novel* McCabe by Edmund Naughton *d* Robert Altman *ph* Vilmos Zsigmond *pd* Leon Ericksen

Warren Beatty, Julie Christie, René Auberjonois, Shelley Duvall, John Schuck

'A fleeting, diaphanous vision of what frontier life might have been.'—*Pauline Kael*

'Altman directed *M*A*S*H*, which wandered and was often funny; then *Brewster McCloud*, which wandered and was not funny; now this, which wanders and is repulsive. The thesis seems to be that if you take a corny story, fuzz up the exposition, vitiate the action, use a childishly ironic ending, and put in lots of profanity and nudity, you have Marched On with Time.'—*Stanley Kauffmann*

AAN: Julie Christie

The McConnell Story
US 1955   107m   Warnercolor Cinemascope
Warner (Henry Blanke)
GB title: *Tiger in the Sky*

The career and accidental death of a jet ace of the Korean war.

Crude, obvious and saccharine biopic.

w Ted Sherdeman, Sam Rolfe *d* Gordon Douglas *ph* John Seitz, Ted McCord *m* Max Steiner

Alan Ladd, June Allyson, James Whitmore, Frank Faylen, Willis Bouchey

Macho Callahan
US 1970   100m   Movielab   Panavision
Avco / Felicidad (Bernard Kowalski, Martin C. Schute)

A vengeful cowboy annihilates all who stand in his way.

Squalid Mexican-made western with unremitting emphasis on violence.

w Clifford Newton Gould *d* Bernard Kowalski *ph* Gerry Fisher *m* Pat Williams

David Janssen, Lee J. Cobb, David Carradine, James Booth

MacKenna's Gold*
US 1969   136m   Technicolor   Super Panavision
Columbia / Highroad (Carl Foreman, Dmitri Tiomkin)

A dying Indian entrusts a sheriff with a map of

the legendary Valley of Gold, and when the news breaks the map is in demand.

Curious serial-like western melodrama packed with stars and pretensions above its station. On a lower level, it is quite enjoyable.

w Carl Foreman, *novel* Will Henry *d* J. Lee-Thompson *ph* Joseph MacDonald, Harold Wellman *m* Quincy Jones *pd* Geoffrey Drake

Gregory Peck, Omar Sharif, Telly Savalas, Camilla Sparv, Keenan Wynn, Julie Newmar, Ted Cassidy, Eduardo Ciannelli, Eli Wallach, Edward G. Robinson, Raymond Massey, Burgess Meredith, Anthony Quayle, Lee J. Cobb

'Preposterous hotch-potch of every cliché known to the gold lust book.'—*MFB*

'Twelve-year-olds of all ages might tolerate it.'—*Judith Crist*

'A western of truly stunning absurdity, a thriving example of the old Hollywood maxim about how to succeed by failing big.'—*Vincent Canby*

The McKenzie Break*
GB 1970   106m   De Luxe
UA / Levy–Gardner–Laven

During World War II, German prisoners at a Scottish camp stage an escape.
Effective little action suspenser.

w William Norton *d* Lamont Johnson *ph* Michael Reed *m* Riz Ortolani

Brian Keith, Helmut Griem, Ian Hendry, Jack Watson, Patrick O'Connell, Horst Janson

The Mackintosh Man*
GB 1973   99m   Technicolor
Warner / Newman–Foreman / John Huston

A government agent is sent to prison to contact a criminal gang.
Convoluted but entertaining spy thriller with good performances and action sequences.

w Walter Hill, *novel* The Freedom Trap by Desmond Bagley *d* John Huston *ph* Oswald Morris *m* Maurice Jarre

Paul Newman, James Mason, Dominique Sanda, Nigel Patrick, Harry Andrews, Michael Hordern, Ian Bannen, Peter Vaughan, Roland Culver, Percy Herbert, Robert Lang, Leo Genn

McLintock*
US 1963   127m   Technicolor   Panavision
UA / Batjac (Michael Wayne)

A cattle baron can control a whole town but not his termagant wife.
Sub-Ford western farce borrowed from *The Taming of the Shrew*, with much fist-fighting and

mud-splattering, and rather too much chat in between.

w James Edward Grant *d* Andrew V. McLaglen *ph* William H. Clothier *m* Frank de Vol

John Wayne, Maureen O'Hara, Yvonne de Carlo, Patrick Wayne, Stefanie Powers, Chill Wills, Bruce Cabot, Jack Kruschen

The McMasters
US 1969   90m   Technicolor
JayJen (Dimitri de Grunwald)

A black man returning home from the Civil War gets unexpected help from a tough landowner.
Racial western with black, white and red points of view, all very violently expressed.

w Harold Jacob Smith *d* Alf Kjellin *ph* Lester Shorr *m* Coleridge-Taylor Parkinson

Brock Peters, Burl Ives, David Carradine, Nancy Kwan, Jack Palance, Dane Clark, John Carradine, I. Q. Jones, R. G. Armstrong

The Macomber Affair*
US 1947   89m   bw
(UA) Benedict Bogeaus (Casey Robinson)

The wife of a bullying big game hunter falls for their guide.
Safari melodrama with a plot which has become a cliché but seemed fresh enough at the time.
Goodish writing and acting.

w Casey Robinson, *story* The Short Happy Life of Francis Macomber by Ernest Hemingway *d* Zoltan Korda *ph* Karl Struss *m* Miklos Rozsa

Gregory Peck, Joan Bennett, Robert Preston, Reginald Denny, Carl Harbord, Jean Gillie

Macon County Line
US 1973   89m   Eastmancolor
Sam Arkoff / Max Baer

In mid-fifties Louisiana, a couple of hell-raisers are harassed by a local sheriff, and much bloodshed results.
Shapeless melodrama more or less in the wake of *Easy Rider*; an unattractive film which unaccountably had great box-office success.

w Max Baer, Richard Compton *d* Richard Compton *ph* Daniel Lacambre *m* Stu Phillips

Alan Vint, Cheryl Waters, Geoffrey Lewis, Joan Blackman, Jesse Vint, Max Baer

McQ
US 1974   111m   Technicolor   Panavision
Warner / Batjac / Levy–Gardner

A Seattle police detective goes after the gangster who killed his friend.

Rambling, violent thriller with good sequences but no cohesion.

w Lawrence Roman *d* John Sturges *ph* Harry Stradling Jnr *m* Elmer Bernstein

John Wayne, Eddie Albert, Diana Muldaur, Colleen Dewhurst, Clu Gulager, David Huddleston, Julie Adams

Mad About Men

GB 1954 90m Technicolor
GFD / Group Films (Betty Box)

By mutual agreement, a sports mistress and a mermaid change places for a while.
Laborious rehash of *Miranda* with familiar jokes.

w Peter Blackmore *d* Ken Annakin *ph* Ernest Steward *m* Benjamin Frankel

Glynis Johns, Donald Sinden, Anne Crawford, Margaret Rutherford, Dora Bryan, Nicholas Phipps, Irene Handl

Mad about Music *

US 1938 98m bw
Universal (Joe Pasternak)

A girl at a Swiss school adopts a personable visitor as her father.
Pleasing star vehicle with charm and humour; badly remade as *Toy Tiger* (qv).

w Bruce Manning, Felix Jackson *d* Norman Taurog *ph* Joseph Valentine *m/ly* Harold Adamson, Jimmie McHugh *m* Frank Skinner, Charles Previn

Deanna Durbin, Herbert Marshall, Gail Patrick, Arthur Treacher, Helen Parrish, Marcia Mae Jones, William Frawley

AAN: original story (Marcella Burke, Frank Kohner); Joseph Valentine; Frank Skinner, Charles Previn

The Mad Doctor

US 1941 90m bw
Paramount (George Arthur)

A doctor marries wealthy women and then murders them.
Naïve melodrama of little interest except as a vehicle for its star.

w Howard J. Green *d* Tim Whelan *ph* Ted Tetzlaff

Basil Rathbone, Ellen Drew, John Howard, Barbara Allen, Ralph Morgan, Martin Kosleck

The Mad Genius

US 1931 81m bw
Warner

A crippled puppeteer adopts a boy and makes him into a great dancer.
Curious variation on *Trilby*, filmed as *Svengali* the previous year with much the same cast. Not a great success: the script is dreadful.

w J. Grubb Alexander, Harvey Thew, *play* The Idol by Martin Brown *d* Michael Curtiz *ph* Barney McGill *ad* Anton Grot

John Barrymore, Marian Marsh, Donald Cook, Luis Alberni, Carmel Myers, Charles Butterworth, Boris Karloff, Frankie Darro

The Mad Ghoul

US 1943 65m bw
Universal

A mad scientist needs fresh hearts to keep alive the victims of his experiments with a poison vapour.
Stagey, tasteless horror melodrama.

w Hans Kraly *d* James Hogan

George Zucco, David Bruce, Evelyn Ankers, Turhan Bey

Mad Love **

US 1935 83m bw
MGM (John Considine Jnr)
GB title: *The Hands of Orlac*

A pianist loses his hands in an accident; a mad surgeon, in love with the pianist's wife, grafts on the hands of a murderer.
Absurd Grand Guignol done with great style which somehow does not communicate itself in viewer interest, only in cold admiration.

w Guy Endore, P. J. Wolfson, John Balderston, *novel* The Hands of Orlac by Maurice Renard *d* Karl Freund *ph* Chester Lyons, Gregg Toland *m* Dmitri Tiomkin

Colin Clive, Peter Lorre, Frances Drake, Ted Healy, Edward Brophy, Isabel Jewell, Sara Haden

The Mad Magician

US 1954 72m bw
Columbia (Bryan Foy)

A magician's star-struck inventor murders his employer and several others who stand between him and the big time.
Hokey horror flick set in the eighties and originally shown in 3-D.

w Crane Wilbur *d* John Brahm *ph* Bert Glennon *m* Emil Newman

Vincent Price, Mary Murphy, Eva Gabor, John Emery, Patrick O'Neal

The Mad Miss Manton*
US 1938 80m bw
RKO (Pandro S. Berman)

A zany socialite involves her friends in a murder mystery.
Mildly funny comedy-thriller without too much of either, but a good example of the style of thirties craziness at its zenith.

w Philip G. Epstein d Leigh Jason ph Nicholas Musuraca m Roy Webb

Barbara Stanwyck, Henry Fonda, Sam Levene, Frances Mercer, Stanley Ridges, Whitney Bourne, Hattie McDaniel, Miles Mander

The Mad Room
US 1969 92m Berkey Pathecolor
Columbia / Norman Mauer

A companion kills her wealthy employer so that her mentally retarded brother and sister will have a home.
Tasteless remake of Ladies in Retirement, in the brutalized vein which audiences are supposed by producers to want. In modern dress and sharp locations, it succeeds only in being nauseating.

w Bernard Girard, A. Z. Martin d Bernard Girard ph Harry Stradling Jnr m Dave Grusin

Stella Stevens, Shelley Winters, Skip Ward, Carol Cole, Severn Darden

Mad Wednesday*
US 1947 77m bw
Howard Hughes

A middle-aged book-keeper is sacked and goes on the town.
Woolly and unattractive farce which proved something of a disaster for all the talents concerned but historically is of considerable interest. It begins with an excerpt from The Freshman and continues to comic adventures with a lion.

wd/pd Preston Sturges (re-edited by others)
ph Robert Pittack m Werner Richard Heymann

Harold Lloyd, Jimmy Conlin, Raymond Walburn, Franklin Pangborn, Al Bridge, Margaret Hamilton, Edgar Kennedy

Madame Bovary
US 1949 114m bw
MGM (Pandro S. Berman)

A passionate girl marries a dull husband, takes a lover, and commits suicide.
Dull, emasculated version of a classic.

w Robert Ardrey, novel Gustave Flaubert
d Vincente Minnelli m Miklos Rozsa

Jennifer Jones, Van Heflin, James Mason, Louis Jourdan, Christopher Kent, Gene Lockhart,
Gladys Cooper, John Abbott, George Zucco
† Previously filmed in 1932 as Unholy Love.

Madame Butterfly
US 1932 88m bw
Paramount

A Japanese geisha commits hara kiri when an American lieutenant passes her up for a western girl.
Drearily modernized version of the opera without its music; an odd idea to say the least.

w Josephine Lovett, Joseph M. March, play David Belasco, John Luther Long d Marion Gering ph David Abel md W. Franke Harling

Sylvia Sidney, Cary Grant, Charlie Ruggles, Sandor Kallay, Irving Pichel, Helen Jerome Eddy

Madame Curie*
US 1944 124m bw
MGM (Sidney Franklin)

The life and marriage of the woman who discovered radium.
Dignified and rather dull biopic which well exemplifies MGM's best production style of the forties.

w Paul Osborn, Paul H. Rameau, book Eve Curie d Mervyn Le Roy ph Joseph Ruttenberg m Herbert Stothart ad Cedric Gibbons, Paul Groesse

Greer Garson, Walter Pidgeon, Henry Travers, Albert Basserman, Robert Walker, C. Aubrey Smith, Dame May Whitty, Victor Francen, Elsa Basserman, Reginald Owen, Van Johnson
'It achieves a notable triumph in making the discovery of a new element seem almost as glamorous as an encounter with Hedy Lamarr.'—C. A. Lejeune

AAN: best picture; Joseph Ruttenberg; Herbert Stothart; Greer Garson; Walter Pidgeon

Madame De*
France / Italy 1953 102m bw
Franco-London / Indus / Rizzoli
US title: The Earrings of Madame de

Tragic misunderstandings arise when a society wife sells her earrings and tells her husband she has lost them.
Elegant, rather heavy-handed but superbly glossy extension of a fashionable novelette.

w Marcel Achard, Max Ophuls, Annette Wademant, novel Louise de Vilmorin d Max Ophuls ph Christian Matras m Oscar Straus, Georges Van Parys ad Jean d'Eaubonne

Charles Boyer, Danielle Darrieux, Vittorio de Sica, Lea di Lea, Jean Debucourt

Madame Dubarry**
Germany 1919   85m (24 fps)   bw   silent
Union-UFA
US title: *Passion*

The life and times of the glamorous courtesan of
Louis XV.
Milestone silent film which introduced to the
cinemas of America and Britain not only the
subtleties of the European cinema but the more
adaptable subtleties of a key director, here
dealing rather heavy-handedly with material
which he should later have re-used.

w Fred Orbing, Hans Kraly *d* Ernst Lubitsch
ph Theodor Sparkuhl

Pola Negri, Emil Jannings, Harry Liedtke,
Reinhold Schunzel

Madame Satan*
US 1930   105m   bw
MGM (C. B. de Mille)

When her husband strays, a socialite disguises
herself as a mysterious *femme fatale* and wins
him back.
Abysmal comedy in which both director and
principals appear frozen until the closing reels
present a crazy, spectacular party on a dirigible
which crashes but allows a happy ending.

w Jeanie Macpherson *d* C. B. de Mille
ph Harold Rosson

Kay Johnson, Reginald Denny, Lillian Roth,
Roland Young

Madame X*
US 1929   95m   bw
MGM

After an accidental death, a wealthy woman
disappears and goes down in the world; at a
subsequent murder trial she is defended by her
unrecognizing son.
Two silent versions (with Dorothy Donnelly and
Pauline Frederick) had been made of this old
theatrical warhorse; two sound versions
followed this one. The thing defies criticism.

w Willard Mack, *play* Alexandre Bisson
d Lionel Barrymore

Ruth Chatterton, Raymond Hackett, Mitchell
Lewis, Sidney Toler, Carroll Nye, Lewis Stone,
Richard Carle
'Works like this confound the reformers,
elevate the name of pictures, and tell the world
that there is an art in film making.'—*Variety*

AAN: Lionel Barrymore; Ruth Chatterton

Madame X*
US 1937   72m   bw
MGM (James K. McGuinness)

Competent remake with an excellent cast.

w John Meehan *d* Sam Wood *m* David Snell

Gladys George, John Beal, Warren William,
Reginald Owen, Lynne Carver, Henry Daniell,
Emma Dunn, Ruth Hussey, George Zucco
'A fine old play, dated and outmoded.
Audiences will leave the theatre expecting to find
the coachman with horse and buggy.'—*Variety*

Madame X
US 1965   100m   Technicolor
Universal / Ross Hunter / Eltee

An elaborately dressed remake which suffered
from a wooden lead; the more expensive the
production, the more obvious the holes in the
plot and the psychology.

w Jean Holloway *d* David Lowell Rich
ph Russell Metty *m* Frank Skinner

Lana Turner, John Forsythe, Ricardo
Montalban, *Constance Bennett*, Burgess
Meredith, Keir Dullea, Virginia Grey, Warren
Stevens
'One is free to enjoy a luxurious wallow in
emotions that are all the more enjoyable for
having no connection whatever with reality.'—
Brenda Davies

Made for Each Other*
US 1938   90m   bw
David O. Selznick

Problems of a lawyer and his new wife culminate
in the near-death of their infant son.
Smooth star tearjerker.

w Jo Swerling *d* John Cromwell *ph* Leon
Shamroy *m* Hugo Friedhofer, David Buttolph,
theme Oscar Levant *pd* William Cameron
Menzies

Carole Lombard, James Stewart, Charles
Coburn, Lucile Watson, Harry Davenport,
Eddie Quillan, Esther Dale, Louise Beavers

Made for Each Other*
US 1971   107m   De Luxe
TCF / Roy Townshend

Romance between two New Yorkers with
inferiority complexes.
Elongated cabaret sketch, a Brooklynesque
comedy of flashy brilliance but limited general
interest.

w Renée Taylor, Joe Bologna *d* Robert B. Bean
ph William Storz

Renée Taylor, Joe Bologna

Madeleine*

GB 1949   114m   bw
GFD / David Lean / Cineguild (Stanley
Haynes)

In Victorian Glasgow a well-to-do young woman
is accused of murdering her lover, but the verdict
is 'not proven'.
Dramatically dead because of its ambiguous
ending, this lavish and good-looking treatment of
a *cause célèbre* was a mistake for all concerned,
but its incidental pleasures are considerable.

w Nicholas Phipps, Stanley Haynes *d David
Lean ph Guy Green w* William Alwyn *pd John
Bryan costumes* Margaret Furse

Ann Todd, Leslie Banks, Elizabeth Sellars, Ivor
Barnard, Ivan Desny, Norman Wooland,
Edward Chapman, Barbara Everest, André
Morell, Barry Jones, Jean Cadell, John Laurie,
Eugene Deckers

Mademoiselle Docteur*

GB 1937   84m   bw
Grafton / Trafalgar (Max Schach)

A German lady spy falls for a British agent.
War melodrama vaguely based on fact and later
remade as *Fraulein Doktor*.

w Jacques Natanson, Marcel Achard, Ernest
Betts *d* Edmond Greville

Dita Parlo, John Loder, Erich Von Stroheim,
Claire Luce, Gyles Isham, Clifford Evans, John
Abbott

Mademoiselle Fifi*

US 1944   69m   bw
RKO (Val Lewton)

During the Franco-Prussian war a stagecoach is
held up because a prostitute, despite the urging of
her fellow passengers, refuses to sleep with a
Prussian officer. When she gives in, they shun
her, and she kills him.
Interesting low budget version of a story which
inspired many films.

w Josef Mischel, Peter Ruric, *stories* Boule de
Suif/Mademoiselle Fifi by Guy de Maupassant
d Robert Wise *ph* Harry Wild *m* Werner
Heymann

Simone Simon, Kurt Kreuger, John Emery, Alan
Napier, Jason Robards Sr, Norma Varden,
Helen Freeman, Fay Helm

Madhouse*

GB 1974   92m   Eastmancolor
AIP / Amicus (Milton Subotsky)

A reluctant horror actor makes a comeback and
finds himself involved in a series of grisly
murders.

In-jokey horror piece with clips from old AIP
chillers; quite likeable.

w Greg Morrison, *novel* Devilday by Angus
Hall *d Jim Clark ph* Ray Parslow *m* Douglas
Gamley

Vincent Price, Peter Cushing, Robert Quarry,
Adrienne Corri, Natasha Pyne, Linda Hayden,
Barry Dennen

Madigan*

US 1968   100m   Techniscope
Universal (Frank P. Rosenberg)

A Brooklyn police detective brings in a
dangerous escaped criminal at the cost of his
own life.
Lively, well-characterized police thriller with
excellent locations.

w Henri Simoun, Abraham Polonsky, *novel* The
Commissioner by Richard Dougherty *d Don
Siegel ph* Russell Metty *m* Don Costa

Richard Widmark, Henry Fonda, Michael
Dunn, Inger Stevens, Harry Guardino, James
Whitmore, Susan Clark, Steve Ihnat, Don
Stroud, Sheree North, Warren Stevens,
Raymond St Jacques
† The character was later resurrected for a TV
series also starring Richard Widmark.

Madison Avenue

US 1961   94m   bw   Cinemascope
TCF (Bruce Humberstone)

An advertising executive plans to revenge
himself on his treacherous boss.
Predictable melodrama with an adequate plot
but dismal acting and presentation.

w Norman Corwin, *novel* The Build-Up Boys by
Jeremy Kirk *d* Bruce Humberstone *ph* Charles
G. Clarke *m* Harry Sukman

Dana Andrews, Jeanne Crain, Eleanor Parker,
Eddie Albert, Howard St John, Henry Daniell,
Kathleen Freeman
    'Simply nowhere near grand enough.'—*MFB*

Madness of the Heart

GB 1949   105m   bw
GFD / Two Cities (Richard Wainright)

A blind girl marries a French aristocrat and has
to cope with a jealous neighbour.
Heavily disguised version of the *Rebecca* theme,
with a happy ending after many alarums and
excursions, most of them irrelevant. As film-
making, very thin.

wd Charles Bennett, *novel* Flora Sandstrom
ph Desmond Dickinson *m* Allan Gray

Margaret Lockwood, Paul Dupuis, Kathleen
Byron, Maxwell Reed

Madonna of the Seven Moons

GB 1944   110m   bw

GFD / Gainsborough (R. J. Minney)

Affected by childhood rape, a demure lady has a second life as a daring gypsy.

Novelettish balderdash killed stone dead by stilted presentation; but highly successful in its day.

w Roland Pertwee, Brock Williams, *novel* Margery Lawrence d Arthur Crabtree

Phyllis Calvert, Stewart Granger, Patricia Roc, Peter Glenville, John Stuart, Jean Kent, Nancy Price, Peter Murray Hill, Reginald Tate

The Madwoman of Chaillot*

GB 1969   142m   Technicolor   Panavision

Warner / Commonwealth United (Ely Landau)

An eccentric Parisian lady has equally eccentric friends, but her real life is in the past.

A highly theatrical whimsy which somewhat lacks humour, this should never have been considered as a film, certainly not as an all-star extravaganza; but it was, and it falls flat on its face in the first reel of tedious conversation.

w Edward Anhalt, *play* Jean Giraudoux d Bryan Forbes *ph* Claude Renoir, Burnett Guffey m Michael J. Lewis *pd* Ray Simm

Katharine Hepburn, Yul Brynner, Danny Kaye, Edith Evans, Charles Boyer, Claude Dauphin, John Gavin, Paul Henreid, Nanette Newman, Oscar Homolka, Margaret Leighton, Giulietta Masina, Richard Chamberlain, Donald Pleasence, Fernand Gravet

'One finds oneself too often longing for the drop of the curtain.'—*Brenda Davies*

'The intentions are honourable—defeat is inevitable.'—*Rex Reed*

'One of Giraudoux's less good and most fragile plays has been rewritten, bloated with inept contemporary references, drawn out to gigantic proportions of humourless vacuity, and peopled with a barrelful of nonacting stars.'—*John Simon*

Maedchen in Uniform*

Germany 1931   90m   bw

Deutsche Film- Gemeinschaft

aka: *Girls in Uniform*

A girl at a strict boarding school falls in love with one of the teachers and commits suicide.

Famous early stab at lesbianism, remade in 1958 with Romy Schneider and Lilli Palmer. Interesting for content, not style.

w F. D. Andam, Christa Winsloe, *play* Gestern und Heute by Christa Winsloe d Leontine Sagan *ph* Reimar Kuntze m Hansen Milde-Meissner

Dorothea Wieck, Ellen Schwannecke, Hertha Thiele, Emilie Lunde

The Maggie*

GB 1953   93m   bw

Ealing (Michael Truman)

US title: *High and Dry*

An American businessman is tricked into sending his private cargo to a Scottish island on an old puffer in need of repair.

Mildly amusing comedy about the wily Scots; not the studio at its best, but pretty fair.

w *William Rose* d *Alexander Mackendrick* *ph* Gordon Dines m John Addison

Paul Douglas, *Alex Mackenzie*, James Copeland, Abe Barker, Dorothy Alison, Hubert Gregg, Geoffrey Keen, Andrew Keir, Tommy Kearins

The Magic Bow

GB 1946   106m   bw

GFD / Gainsborough

Episodes in the life of the violin virtuoso Paganini.

Poor costumer, dramatically and historically unpersuasive.

w Norman Ginsbury, Roland Pertwee d Bernard Knowles *ph* Jack Cox *violin solos Yehudi Menuhin*

Stewart Granger, Jean Kent, Phyllis Calvert, Dennis Price, Cecil Parker, Felix Aylmer, Frank Cellier, Marie Lohr, Henry Edwards

The Magic Box*

GB 1951   118m   Technicolor

Festival Films (Ronald Neame)

The life of William Friese-Greene, a British cinema pioneer who died in poverty.

A joint British film industry venture to celebrate the Festival of Britain, this rather downbeat and uneventful story takes on the nature of a pageant or a series of charades, with well-known people appearing to no good purpose. But it means well.

w Eric Ambler d John Boulting *ph* Jack Cardiff m William Alwyn *pd* John Bryan

Robert Donat, Margaret Johnson, Maria Schell, John Howard Davies, Renée Asherson, Richard Attenborough, Robert Beatty, Michael Denison, Leo Genn, Marius Goring, Joyce Grenfell, Robertson Hare, Kathleen Harrison, Jack Hulbert, Stanley Holloway, Glynis Johns, Mervyn Johns, Barry Jones, Miles Malleson, Muir Mathieson, A. E. Matthews, John McCallum, Bernard Miles, Laurence Olivier, Cecil Parker, Eric Portman, Dennis Price, Michael Redgrave, Margaret

Rutherford, Ronald Shiner, Sybil Thorndike,
David Tomlinson, Cecil Trouncer, Peter
Ustinov, Kay Walsh, Emlyn Williams,
Harcourt Williams, Googie Withers

The Magic Christian
GB 1970 95m Technicolor
Commonwealth United / Grand Films (Dennis
O'Dell)

An eccentric millionaire spends his wealth
deflating those who pursue money or power.
A series of variably funny but always unpleasant
sketches, climaxing with citizens delving for
spoils in a vat of blood and manure. In its aim to
be satirical, very typical of its time.

w Terry Southern, Joseph McGrath, Peter
Sellers, novel Terry Southern d Joseph
McGrath ph Geoffrey Unsworth m Ken
Thorne pd Assheton Gorton

Peter Sellers, Ringo Starr, Richard
Attenborough, Laurence Harvey, Christopher
Lee, Spike Milligan, Yul Brynner, Roman
Polanski, Raquel Welch, Wilfrid Hyde White,
Fred Emney, John Le Mesurier, Dennis Price,
Patrick Cargill, John Cleese, Graham Chapman

The Magic Face
US 1951 90m bw
Columbia (Mort Briskin, Robert Smith)

A brilliant German impersonator kills Hitler,
takes his place, and leads Germany deliberately
into defeat.
Hilariously unlikely anecdote 'as told to William
Shirer', performed with vigour but handicapped
by a shoddy production.

w Mort Briskin, Robert Smith d Frank Tuttle
ph Tony Braun m Herschel Burke Gilbert

Luther Adler, Patricia Knight, Ilka Windish,
William L. Shirer

'If Shirer believed this story, then he must be
the only person in the world to do so.'—Gavin
Lambert

Magic Fire
US 1954 94m Trucolor
Republic (William Dieterle)

The life and loves of Richard Wagner.
Remarkably boring biopic with much music but
little story or characterization. Ugly colour
minimizes German locations.

w Bertita Harding, E. A. Dupont, David
Chantler d William Dieterle ph Ernest Haller
md Erich Wolfgang Korngold

Alan Badel, Yvonne de Carlo, Peter Cushing,
Frederick Valk, Carlos Thompson, Valentina
Cortesa

The Magic of Lassie
US 1978 99m colour
Jack Wrather (Bonita Granville)

A collie dog is sold but makes its way back
home.
Downright peculiar revamp of Lassie Come
Home with music and an ageing all-star cast.

w Jean Holloway, Richard B. Sherman, Robert
M. Sherman d Don Chaffey

James Stewart, Alice Faye, Mickey Rooney,
Pernell Roberts, Stephanie Zimbalist, Gene
Evans

The Magic Sword
US 1962 80m Eastmancolor
UA / Bert I. Gordon

The son of a well-meaning witch rescues a
princess from the clutches of an evil sorcerer.
Shaky medieval fantasy on too low a budget.

w Bernard Schoenfeld d Bert I. Gordon ph Paul
Vogel m Richard Markowitz sp Milt Rice

Basil Rathbone, Estelle Winwood, Gary
Lockwood, Anne Helm

Magic Town
US 1947 103m bw
William A. Wellman

An opinion pollster discovers a small town which
exactly mirrors the views of the USA at large.
A bright Capraesque idea is extraordinarily
dully scripted, the production looks dim, and all
concerned are operating one degree under.

w Robert Riskin d William A. Wellman
ph Joseph Biroc m Roy Webb

James Stewart, Jane Wyman, Kent Smith, Regis
Toomey, Donald Meek

The Magician*
US 1926 approx 80m bw silent
MGM

A dabbler in the occult comes to grief when he
tries to influence a young girl.
A melodrama with interesting credits;
unfortunatley no prints remain.

from the novel by Somerset Maugham d Rex
Ingram

Paul Wegener, Ivan Petrovitch, Alice Terry

The Magnet
GB 1950 79m bw
Ealing (Sidney Cole)

A small boy steals a magnet and accidentally
becomes a hero.
Very mild Ealing comedy, not really up to snuff.

w T. E. B. Clarke *d* Charles Frend *ph* Lionel Banes *m* William Alwyn

Stephen Murray, Kay Walsh, William Fox, Meredith Edwards, Gladys Henson, Thora Hird, Wylie Watson

The Magnetic Monster*

US 1953   75m   bw
UA / Ivan Tors

A new radio-active element causes 'implosions' of increasing size by drawing energy from the area around it.
Well-told low-budget sci-fi with the audience kept abreast of all developments; the undersea lab scenes are borrowed from an old German film, *Gold*.

w Curt Siodmak, Ivan Tors *d* Curt Siodmak *pd* George Van Marter

Richard Carlson, King Donovan, Jean Byron, Byron Foulger

The Magnificent Ambersons****

US 1942   88m   bw
RKO (Orson Welles)

A proud family loses its wealth and its control of the neighbourhood, and its youngest male member gets his come-uppance.
Fascinating period drama told in brilliant cinematic snippets; owing to studio interference the last reels are weak, but the whole is a treat for connoisseurs, and a delight in its fast-moving control of cinematic narrative.

wd Orson Welles, *novel* Booth Tarkington *ph* Stanley Cortez *m* Bernard Herrmann *ad* Mark-Lee Kirk

Joseph Cotten, Dolores Costello, Agnes Moorehead, Tim Holt, Anne Baxter, Ray Collins, Richard Bennett, Erskine Sanford, Donald Dillaway

'Rich in ideas that many will want to copy, combined in the service of a story that few will care to imitate.'—*C. A. Lejeune.*
† Previously filmed in 1925 as *Pampered Youth*.

AAN: best picture; Stanley Cortez; Agnes Moorehead

Magnificent Doll

US 1946   95m   bw
Universal (Jack H. Skirball, Bruce Manning)

Dolly Madison, wife of the President, finds that traitor Aaron Burr is a memory from her own past.
Uneasy historical semi-fiction, badly cast and rather boring, yet with some sense of period style.

w Irving Stone *d* Frank Borzage *ph* Joseph Valentine *m* Hans Salter

Ginger Rogers, David Niven, Burgess Meredith, Stephen McNally, Peggy Wood, Robert Barrat

The Magnificent Dope

US 1942   83m   bw
TCF (William Perlberg)

As a publicity stunt a success school brings the nation's most complete failure to New York, and he outsmarts them all.
Dim sub-Capra comedy.

w George Seaton *d* Walter Lang *ph* Peverell Marley *md* Emil Newman

Henry Fonda, Lynn Bari, Don Ameche, Edward Everett Horton, George Barbier, Frank Orth, Hobart Cavanaugh

The Magnificent Matador

US 1955   94m   Eastmancolor
  Cinemascope
Edward L. Alperson
GB title: *The Brave and the Beautiful*

A matador trains his illegitimate son to follow in his footsteps but has a premonition of his death in the ring.
Dreary bullfighting drama with romantic interludes.

w Charles Lang *d* Budd Boetticher *ph* Lucien Ballard *m* Raoul Kraushaar

Anthony Quinn, Maureen O'Hara, Manuel Rojas, Richard Denning, Thomas Gomez, Lola Albright

Magnificent Obsession**

US 1935   112m   bw
Universal (John M. Stahl)

The playboy who is half-responsible for the death of a woman's husband and for her own blindness becomes a surgeon and cures her.
Absurd soaper which was phenomenally popular and is certainly well done.

w George O'Neil, Sarah Y. Mason, Victor Heerman, *novel* Lloyd C. Douglas *d* John M. Stahl *ph* John Mescall

Irene Dunne, Robert Taylor, Ralph Morgan, Sara Haden, Charles Butterworth, Betty Furness, Arthur Hoyt, Gilbert Emery, Arthur Treacher

Magnificent Obsession**

US 1954   108m   Technicolor
Universal (*Ross Hunter*)

Glossy remake which sent Ross Hunter to the commercial heights as a remaker of thirties weepies. This one worked best.

w Robert Blees *d Douglas Sirk ph* Russell Metty *m* Frank Skinner

Jane Wyman, Rock Hudson, Agnes Moorehead, Barbara Rush, Otto Kruger, Gregg Palmer, Paul Cavanagh, Sara Shane

AAN: Jane Wyman

The Magnificent Rebel

US 1960   94m   Technicolor
Walt Disney (Peter V. Herald)

Episodes in the life of the young Beethoven.
Solid Disney biopic, shot in Vienna with good period detail.

w Joanne Court *d* Georg Tressler *ph* Goran Strindberg *md* Frederick Stark

Karl Boehm, Ernst Nadhering, Ivan Desny, Gabriele Porks

The Magnificent Seven**

US 1960   138m   De Luxe   Panavision
UA / Mirisch–Alpha (John Sturges)

A Mexican village hires seven American gunmen for protection against bandits.
Popular western based on the Japanese *Seven Samurai*; good action scenes, but the rest is verbose and often pretentious.

w William Roberts *d* John Sturges *ph* Charles Lang Jnr *m Elmer Bernstein*

Yul Brynner, Steve McQueen, Robert Vaughn, *James Coburn, Charles Bronson,* Horst Buchholz, Eli Wallach, Brad Dexter, Vladimir Sokoloff

AAN: Elmer Bernstein

The Magnificent Seven Deadly Sins

GB 1971   107m   colour
Tigon (Graham Stark)

Compendium of comedy sketches, a very variable ragbag of old jokes.

w Bob Larbey, John Esmonde, Dave Freeman, Barry Cryer, Graham Chapman, Graham Stark, Marty Feldman, Alan Simpson, Ray Galton, Spike Milligan *d* Graham Stark *ph* Harvey Harrison Jnr *m* Roy Budd

Bruce Forsyth, Joan Sims, Roy Hudd, Harry Secombe, Leslie Phillips, Julie Ege, Harry H. Corbett, Ian Carmichael, Alfie Bass, Spike Milligan, Ronald Fraser

The Magnificent Seven Ride

US 1972   100m   De Luxe
UA / Mirisch (William A. Calihan)

Tired finale to a patchy series (*Return of the Seven, Guns of the Magnificent Seven*) in which the original leader returns to save a Mexican village once again from bandits. Very modest.

w Arthur Rowe *d* George McCowan *ph* Fred Koenekamp *m* Elmer Bernstein

Lee Van Cleef, Stefanie Powers, Mariette Hartley, Pedro Armendariz Jnr, Luke Askew

The Magnificent Two

GB 1967   100m   Eastmancolor
Rank (Hugh Stewart)

One of two incompetent travelling salesmen in a Latin American banana republic is persuaded to pose as a dead rebel leader.
More or less a Bob Hope vehicle, adapted for the less realistic Morecambe and Wise with unhappy results: too few sight gags and a curious emphasis on violence. The third and last of their attempts to find film vehicles.

w S. C. Green, R. M. Hills, Michael Pertwee, Peter Blackmore *d* Cliff Owen *ph* Ernest Steward *m* Ron Goodwin

Eric Morecambe, Ernie Wise, Margit Saad, Cecil Parker, Virgilio Teixeira, Isobel Black, Martin Benson

The Magnificent Yankee*

US 1951   88m   bw
MGM (Armand Deutsch)
GB title: *The Man with Thirty Sons*

Episodes in the later life of Judge Oliver Wendell Holmes.
Vaguely well-meaning biopic without much dramatic sense.

w Emmet Lavery, from his play *d* John Sturges *ph* Joseph Ruttenberg *m* David Raksin

Louis Calhern, Ann Harding, Eduard Franz, Philip Ober, Richard Anderson, Edith Evanson

AAN: Louis Calhern

Magnum Force*

US 1973   124m   Technicolor   Panavision
Warner / Malpaso (Robert Daley)

Inspector Harry Callahan has to track down his partner who is slaughtering gangsters in cold blood.
Toned-down sequel to *Dirty Harry*; the violence is still there but the hero no longer commits it. Proficient, exciting and immoral.

w John Milius *d* Ted Post *ph* Frank Stanley *m* Lalo Schifrin

Clint Eastwood, Hal Holbrook, Mitch Ryan, Felton Perry, David Soul

'A ragbag of western mythology and head-on thuggery.'—*Sight and Sound*

The Magus

GB 1968   116m   De Luxe   Panavision
TCF / Blazer (John Kohn, Jud Kinberg)

An English schoolmaster on a Greek island is influenced by the local magician.
Fashionable philosophical nonsense, an elaborate mystery with no solution; the kind of film that all concerned begin to wish they had never thought of, especially as the presentation has nothing like the panache required, so that not even the critics liked it.

w John Fowles, from his novel *d* Guy Green *ph* Billy Williams *m* Johnny Dankworth *pd* Don Ashton

Michael Caine, Anthony Quinn, Candice Bergen, Anna Karina, Paul Stassino, Julian Glover, George Pastell

'Faintly ludicrous some of the time and painfully unexciting all of the time.'—*MFB*

'This may not be the most misguided movie ever made, but it's in there pitching.'—*Rex Reed*

'There's enough incoherence pretending to be enigma, sex play and chat about existentialism and self-discovery to make teenagers think they're having an experience; for grown-ups it's an ordeal.'—*Judith Crist*

'It has much of the fascination of a Chinese puzzle, but it would have been infinitely more enthralling if it hadn't been quite so flatly acted and directed.'—*Michael Billington, Illustrated London News*

Mahler*

GB 1974   115m   Technicolor
Goodtimes Enterprises (Roy Baird)

Fantasia on the life and times of the Jewish composer.
Fairly successful Ken Russell musical biopic on the lines of his early BBC specials.

wd Ken Russell ph Dick Bush

Robert Powell, Georgiana Hale, Richard Morant, Lee Montague, Rosalie Crutchley, Benny Lee, David Collings

'A piece of movie making that sets my pulses racing.'—*Michael Billington, Illustrated London News*

Mahogany

US 1975   109m   colour   Panavision
Paramount / Nikor (Rob Cohen, Jack Ballard)

The love life of a model and fashion designer.
Virtually a Joan Crawford vehicle redesigned for a black heroine who creates her own clothes.
Fairly hilarious.

w John Byrum *d* Berry Gordy *ph* David Watkin *m* Michael Masser

Diana Ross, Billy Dee Williams, Anthony Perkins, Jean-Pierre Aumont, Nina Foch, Beah Richards, Marisa Mell

'The level of silliness rises steadily.'—*Geoff Brown*

'Movies as frantically bad as *Mahogany* can be enjoyed on at least one level; the spectacle of a lot of people making fools of themselves.'—*Time*

'What *Mahogany* does so fascinatingly and sometimes hilariously is to pilfer certain stock clichés of 50's Hollywood and adapt them to a black milieu.'—*Molly Haskell*

AAN: song 'Do You Know Where You're Going To?' (*m* Michael Masser, *ly* Gerry Goffin)

Maid of Salem*

US 1937   86m   bw
Paramount (Frank Lloyd)

In 1692 Salem, a young girl is accused of witchcraft but saved by her lover.
Remarkably solemn period melodrama, unfortunately betrayed by amiable but miscast leads.

w Bradley King, Walter Ferris, Durward Grinstead *d* Frank Lloyd *ph* Leo Tover *m* Victor Young

Claudette Colbert, Fred MacMurray, Harvey Stephens, Gale Sondergaard, Louise Dresser, Edward Ellis, Beulah Bondi, Bonita Granville

The Maids

GB 1974   95m   Technicolor
Ely Landau / Cinevision

Two Paris maids evolve a sado-masochistic ritual involving the death of their employer, but never go through with it.
Unbalanced and dreary film version of an essentially theatrical play.

w Robert Enders, Christopher Miles, *play* Jean Genet *d* Christopher Miles *ph* Douglas Slocombe *m* Laurie Johnson

Glenda Jackson, Susannah York, Vivien Merchant, Mark Burns

Maigret Sets a Trap*

France / Italy 1957   119m   bw
Intermondia / J. P. Guibert / Jolly Film

Maigret sets a policewoman as decoy for a knife murderer . . .
Probably the best Maigret film, with excellent Parisian atmosphere and excellent acting.

w Michel Audiard, novel Georges Simenon *d* Jean Delannoy *ph* Louis Page *m* Paul Misraki *ad* René Renoux

Jean Gabin, Annie Girardot, Jean Desailly, Oliver Hussenot, Alfred Adam, Lino Ventura

Mail Order Bride

US 1963   83m   Metrocolor   Panavision
MGM (Richard E. Lyons)
GB title: *West of Montana*

An old westerner tries to find a bride for a wild
young man in his charge.
Mild western comedy drama; quite tolerable.

wd Burt Kennedy *ph* Paul C. Vogel *m* George
Bassman

Buddy Ebsen, Lois Nettleton, Keir Dullea,
Warren Oates, Marie Windsor

The Main Attraction

US 1962   90m   Metrocolor
Seven Arts (John Patrick)

A wandering singer causes emotional problems
backstage at a circus.
Limp melodrama with the star miscast as a fatal
charmer.

w John Patrick *d* Daniel Petrie *ph* Geoffrey
Unsworth *m* Andrew Adorian

Pat Boone, Mai Zetterling, Nancy Kwan,
Yvonne Mitchell, John Le Mesurier

Main Street to Broadway*

US 1953   102m   bw
Lester Cowan Productions

After several reverses a young playwright sees
his work through to a Broadway opening night;
it fails, but he has learned several lessons.
Curious, flat attempt to show the public how
Broadway works, with big stars playing
themselves in cameo roles.

w Samson Raphaelson *d* Tay Garnett
ph James Wong Howe

Tom Morton, Mary Murphy, Ethel Barrymore,
Lionel Barrymore, Shirley Booth, Rex Harrison,
Lilli Palmer, Helen Hayes, Henry Fonda,
Tallulah Bankhead, Mary Martin, Louis
Calhern, John Van Druten, Cornel Wilde,
Joshua Logan, Agnes Moorehead, Gertrude
Berg

Les Mains Sales

France 1951   103m   bw
Fernand Rivers
aka: *Dirty Hands*

A young communist intellectual, required to kill
a traitor, finds he can do so only when he
suspects the man of making love to his wife.
Verbose and dull version of a play which had
some international success as *Crime Passionel*.

wd Fernand Rivers, *play* Jean-Paul Sartre
ph Jean Bachelet

Pierre Brasseur, Daniel Gélin, Claude Nollier

Maisie

US 1939   74m   bw
MGM (J. Walter Ruben)

Adventures of a Brooklyn showgirl.
Acceptable programmer which led to a series, all
quite watchable and absolutely forgettable.

w Mary McCall Jnr, *novel* Dark Dame by
Wilson Collinson *d* Edwin L. Marin
ph Leonard Smith

Ann Sothern, Robert Young, Ian Hunter, Ruth
Hussey, Anthony Allan (John Hubbard), Cliff
Edwards

The succeeding titles, mostly written by Mary
McCall and directed by Marin or Harry
Beaumont or Roy del Ruth, were:

1940: CONGO MAISIE (with John Carroll; a
remake of RED DUST), GOLD RUSH
MAISIE (with Lee Bowman), MAISIE WAS A
LADY (with Lew Ayres, Maureen O'Sullivan)
1941: RINGSIDE MAISIE (with George
Murphy; GB title CASH AND CARRY)
1942: MAISIE GETS HER MAN (with Red
Skelton; GB title SHE GOT HER MAN)
1943: SWING SHIFT MAISIE (with James
Craig; GB title THE GIRL IN OVERALLS)
1944: MAISIE GOES TO RENO (with John
Hodiak; GB title YOU CAN'T DO THAT TO
ME)
1946: UP GOES MAISIE (with George
Murphy; GB title UP SHE GOES)

The Major and the Minor**

US 1942   100m   bw
Paramount (Arthur Hornblow Jnr)

A girl poses as a child in order to travel half fare
on a train, and is helped by an officer who falls
for her.
Moderately smart comedy showing the writer-
director's emergent style. Remade as *You're
Never Too Young* (qv).

w Charles Brackett, Billy Wilder *d Billy Wilder*
ph Leo Tover *m* Robert Emmett Dolan

Ginger Rogers, Ray Milland, Rita Johnson,
Robert Benchley, Diana Lynn, Edward Fielding,
Frankie Thomas, Charles Smith
   'The script seems to have been concocted after
the title.'—*New Yorker, 1977*

Major Barbara***

GB 1941   121m   bw
Gabriel Pascal

The daughter of an armaments millionaire joins
the Salvation Army but resigns when it accepts
her father's donation.
Stagey but compulsive version of a play in which
the author takes typical side swipes at anything
and everything within reach, allowing for some

gorgeous acting (and overacting) by an impeccable cast.

w Anatole de Grunwald, Gabriel Pascal, *play Bernard Shaw d* Gabriel Pascal, Harold French, David Lean

Wendy Hiller, Rex Harrison, Robert Morley, Robert Newton, Marie Lohr, Emlyn Williams, Sybil Thorndike, Deborah Kerr, David Tree, Felix Aylmer, Penelope Dudley Ward, Walter Hudd, Marie Ault, Donald Calthrop

'Shaw's ebullience provides an unslackening fount of energy . . . his all-star cast of characters are outspoken as no one else is in films except the Marx Brothers.'—*William Whitebait*

Major Dundee*
US 1965   134m   Eastmancolor
Panavision
Columbia (Jerry Bresler)

A small group of men from a US cavalry post sets out to annihilate marauding Indians.
Large-scale, rough and ready western which rambles along in humourless vein but rises to some spectacularly bloodthirsty climaxes.

w Harry Julian Fink, Oscar Saul, Sam Peckinpah *d* Sam Peckinpah *ph* Sam Leavitt *m* Daniele Amfitheatrof

Charlton Heston, Richard Harris, Jim Hutton, James Coburn, Michael Anderson Jnr, Warren Oates, Senta Berger, Slim Pickens

A Majority of One
US 1961   156m   Technicolor
Warner (Mervyn Le Roy)

A Jewish widow has a shipboard romance with a Japanese businessman.
Interminable stage-bound comedy-drama, boringly assembled and fatally compromised by the casting of stars who are neither Jewish nor Japanese.

w Leonard Spiegelgass, from his play *d* Mervyn Le Roy *ph* Harry Stradling *m* Max Steiner

Rosalind Russell, Alec Guinness, Ray Danton, Madlyn Rhue

AAN: Harry Stradling

Make a Wish
US 1937   75m   bw
(RKO) Sol Lesser

A composer discovers a boy singer at a summer camp.
Acceptable family entertainment.

w Gertrude Berg, Bernard Schubert, Earle Snell *d* Kurt Neumann *ph* John Mescall *songs* Oscar Strauss *m* Hugo Riesnfeld

Basil Rathbone, Bobby Breen, Marion Claire,

Leon Errol, Henry Armetta, Ralph Forbes, Donald Meek

Make Me a Star
US 1932   80m   bw
Paramount

A grocery clerk goes to Hollywood and becomes a film star.
Modest remake of a silent success; see also *Merton of the Movies.*

w Sam Wintz, Walter de Leon, Arthur Kober, *novel* Merton of the Movies by Harry Leon Wilson *d* William Beaudine *ph* Allen Siegler

Stuart Erwin, Joan Blondell, Zasu Pitts, Ben Turpin, Florence Roberts; and Tallulah Bankhead, Clive Brook, Garry Cooper, Maurice Chevalier, Claudette Colbert, Fredric March, Jack Oakie, Charlie Ruggles, Sylvia Sidney

Make Me an Offer*
GB 1954   88m   Eastmancolor
Group Three (W. P. Lipscomb)

An antique dealer has an ambition to own a famous vase.
Mildly pleasant Jewish comedy with interesting sidelights on the antique business.

w W. P. Lipscomb, *novel* Wolf Mankowitz *d* Cyril Frankel *ph* Denny Densham *m* John Addison

Peter Finch, Adrienne Corri, *Meier Tzelniker,* Rosalie Crutchley, Finlay Currie, *Ernest Thesiger,* Wilfrid Lawson, Alfie Bass

Make Mine Music**
US 1946   74m   Technicolor
Walt Disney (Joe Grant)

A programme of cartoon shorts: JOHNNY FEDORA, ALL THE CATS JOIN IN, WITHOUT YOU, TWO SILHOUETTES, CASEY AT THE BAT, THE MARTINS AND THE COYS, BLUE BAYOU, AFTER YOU'VE GONE, WILLIE THE SINGING WHALE.
An insubstantial banquet, sometimes arty and sometimes chocolate boxy, which occasionally rises to the expected heights.

w various *d* various

Make Way for Tomorrow**
US 1937   94m   bw
Paramount (Leo McCarey)

An elderly couple are in financial difficulty and have to be parted because their children will not help.
Sentimental drama which had a devastating

effect at the time but now seems oversimplified and exaggerated.

w Vina Delmar, *novel* The Years Are So Long by Josephine Lawrence *d* Leo McCarey *m* George Antheil

Victor Moore, Beulah Bondi, Thomas Mitchell, Fay Bainter, Porter Hall, Barbara Read, Maurice Moscovitch, Elizabeth Risdon, Gene Lockhart

'The most brilliantly directed and acted film of the year.'—*John Grierson*

Malaya*
US 1949   95m   bw
MGM (Pandro S. Berman)
GB title: *East of the Rising Sun*

An adventurer attempts to smuggle rubber out of Japanese occupied Malaya.
Dour action melodrama, unworthy of its considerable cast but watchable.

w Frank Fenton *d* Richard Thorpe *ph* George Folsey *m* Bronislau Kaper

Spencer Tracy, James Stewart, Sidney Greenstreet, John Hodiak, Valentina Cortesa, Lionel Barrymore, Gilbert Roland

The Male Animal*
US 1942   101m   bw
Warner (Wolfgang Reinhardt)

A dry college professor emancipates himself when his wife becomes attracted to a football star.
Stagebound but amusing college comedy with pleasant humour and good performances.
Remade as *She's Working Her Way through College* (qv).

w Julius J. and Philip G. Epstein, Stephen Morehouse Avery, *play* James Thurber and Elliott Nugent *d* Elliott Nugent *ph* Arthur Edeson *m* Heinz Roemheld

Henry Fonda, Olivia de Havilland, Jack Carson, Joan Leslie, Eugene Pallette, Don Defore, Herbert Anderson, Hattie McDaniel

The Malta Story
GB 1953   103m   bw
GFD / British Film Makers (Peter de Sarigny)

An English flier is involved in the defence of Malta during World War II.
Glib propaganda piece which is not very excitingly written or characterized, and fails to convince on any but the most elementary level.

w William Fairchild, Nigel Balchin *d* Brian Desmond Hurst *ph* Robert Krasker *m* William Alwyn

Alec Guinness, Anthony Steel, Muriel Pavlow,
Jack Hawkins, Flora Robson, Renée Asherson, Ralph Truman, Reginald Tate, Hugh Burden

The Maltese Falcon**
US 1931   80m   bw
Warner

After the death of his partner, private eye Sam Spade is dragged into a quest for a priceless statuette.
Excellent crime melodrama with smart pace and performances. Remade as *Satan Met a Lady* (1936); and see below.

w Maude Fulton, Lucien Hubbard, Brown Holmes, *novel Dashiell Hammett d* Roy del Ruth *ph* William Rees

Ricardo Cortez, Bebe Daniels, *Dudley Digges*, Dwight Frye, Robert Elliott, Thelma Todd, Oscar Apfel

'The best mystery thriller of the year.'—*New York Times*

The Maltese Falcon****
US 1941   101m   bw
Warner (Henry Blanke)

A remake which shows the difference between excellence and brilliance; here every nuance is subtly stressed, and the cast is perfection.

wd John Huston *ph* Arthur Edeson *m* Adolph Deutsch

Humphrey Bogart, Mary Astor, Sidney Greenstreet, Elisha Cook Jnr, Barton MacLane, Lee Patrick, Peter Lorre, Gladys George, *Ward Bond, Jerome Cowan*

'The first crime melodrama with finish, speed and bang to come along in what seems like ages.'—*Otis Ferguson*

'A work of entertainment that is yet so skilfully constructed that after many years and many viewings, it has the same brittle explosiveness—and some of the same surprise—that it had in 1941.'—*Pauline Kael, 1968*

'The trick which Mr Huston has pulled is a combination of American ruggedness with the suavity of the English crime school—a blend of mind and muscle—plus a slight touch of pathos.'—*Bosley Crowther, New York Times*

AAN: best picture; John Huston (as writer); Sidney Greenstreet

Mambo
Italy / USA 1954   92m (English version), 107m (Italian version)   bw

A Venetian shopgirl loves a worthless gambler, is romanced by a haemophiliac count, and joins a dance troupe.

Patchy melodrama with plenty going on but no grip.

w Guido Piovene, Ivo Perelli, Ennio de Concini, Robert Rossen *d* Robert Rossen *ph* Harold Rosson *m* Nino Rota, Francesco Lavagnino *sets* Andrei Andrejew *ch* Katherine Dunham

Silvana Mangano, Michael Rennie, Shelley Winters, Vittorio Gassman, Eduardo Cianelli, Mary Clare, Katherine Dunham and her troupe

Mame*
US 1974 131m Technicolor Panavision
Warner / ABC (Robert Fryer, James Cresson)

In 1928, a 10-year-old boy goes to live with his eccentric, sophisticated aunt.
Old-fashioned and rather bad film of a much overrated Broadway musical, inept in most departments but with occasional show-stopping moments.

w Paul Zandel, *play* Jerome Lawrence, Robert E. Lee, *book* Patrick Dennis *d* Gene Saks *ph* Philip Lathrop *m/ly* Jerry Herman *pd* Robert F. Boyle

Lucille Ball, Beatrice Arthur, Robert Preston, Bruce Davison, Jane Connell, Joyce Van Patten, John McGiver

'It makes one realize afresh the parlous state of the Hollywood musical, fighting to survive against misplaced superstars and elephantine budgets matched with minuscule imagination.'—*Geoff Brown*

'The cast seem to have been handpicked for their tone-deafness, and Lucille Ball's close-ups are shot blatantly out of focus.'—*Sight and Sound*

'So terrible it isn't boring; you can get fixated staring at it and wondering what Lucille Ball thought she was doing.'—*New Yorker, 1977*

Mammy*
US 1930 84m bw
Warner

Murder backstage at a minstrel show.
One of the star's better musicals.

w L. G. Rigby, Joseph Jackson *d* Michael Curtiz *ph* Barney McGill *m* Irving Berlin

Al Jolson, Lowell Sherman, Hobart Bosworth, Louise Dresser, Lee Moran

A Man About the House
GB 1947 95m bw
British Lion (Edward Black)

Two English ladies inherit an Italian villa and fall under the spell of the handsome handyman, who marries one of them and proceeds slowly to poison her.

Now clearly dull, at the time this seemed a fairly enterprising rehash of *Gaslight*, *Kind Lady* and *Rebecca*.

w J. B. Williams, Leslie Arliss *d* Leslie Arliss *ph* Tom Day

Margaret Johnston, Dulcie Gray, Kieron Moore, Felix Aylmer, Lilian Braithwaite

A Man About the House
GB 1974 90m colour
EMI / Hammer (Roy Skeggs)

Two young women, their male flatmate and their landlords combine forces to prevent the terrace from being razed for redevelopment.
Mild and rather exhausting sex comedy from the TV series, as relentlessly single-minded as a 'Carry On'.

w Johnnie Mortimer, Brian Cooke *d* John Robins *ph* Jimmy Allen *m* Christopher Gunning

Richard O'Sullivan, Paula Wilcox, Sally Thomsett, Yootha Joyce, Brian Murphy, Peter Cellier, Patrick Newell, Spike Milligan, Arthur Lowe

Man about Town*
US 1939 85m bw
Paramount (Arthur Hornblow Jnr)

A Broadway producer in London makes his girlfriend jealous.
Fairly amusing comedy-musical programmer.

w Morrie Ryskind *d* Mark Sandrich *ph* Ted Tetzlaff *md* Victor Young

Jack Benny, Dorothy Lamour, Edward Arnold, Binnie Barnes, Phil Harris, Eddie Anderson, Monty Woolley, Isabel Jeans, Betty Grable, E. E. Clive

A Man Alone*
US 1955 96m Trucolor
Republic

A wandering gunman is framed by other badmen.
Solemn, slow-moving but generally interesting western, the star's first attempt at direction.

w John Tucker Battle *d Ray Milland ph* Lionel Lindon *m* Victor Young

Ray Milland, Mary Murphy, Ward Bond, Raymond Burr, Arthur Space, Lee Van Cleef, Alan Hale Jnr

A Man and a Woman**
France 1966 102m Eastmancolor
Les Films 13
aka: *Un Homme et une Femme*

A racing driver and a script girl, both of whose

spouses are dead, meet while visiting their children, and an affair leads to marriage. Slight romantic drama so tricked out with smart images that it looks like a series of expensive commercials. A great box office success, but its director never again succeeded in this vein which he made his own.

w Claude Lelouch, Pierre Uytterhoven
d Claude Lelouch ph Claude Lelouch
m Francis Lai

Anouk Aimée, Jean-Louis Trintignant

'When in doubt, Lelouch's motto seems to be, use a colour filter or insert lyrical shots of dogs and horses; when in real doubt, use both.'—*Tom Milne, MFB*

AA: Claude Lelouch, Pierre Uytterhoven
AAN: Claude Lelouch (as director); Anouk Aimée

Man at the Top*
GB 1973   87m   Technicolor
Hammer / Dufton (Peter Charlesworth)

A pharmaceutical executive finds that his firm is marketing an unsafe drug.
Further adventures of the belligerent hero of *Room at the Top* (qv), this time following a popular television series. All very fashionable and predictable.

w Hugh Whitemore d Mike Vardy ph Bryan Probyn m Roy Budd

Kenneth Haigh, Nanette Newman, Harry Andrews, John Quentin, Charlie Williams

The Man Between*
GB 1953   101m   bw
British Lion / London Films (Carol Reed)

Ivo Kern operates successfully as a West Berlin racketeer; love causes a softening of his attitudes and leads to his death.
Imitation *Third Man* with an uninteresting mystery and a solemn ending. Good acting and production can't save it.

w Harry Kurnitz d Carol Reed ph Desmond Dickinson m John Addison ad André Andreiev

James Mason, Hildegarde Neff, Claire Bloom, Geoffrey Toone, Ernst Schroeder
'A cold-hearted film about people with cold feet.'—*Daily Express*

A Man Called Horse*
US 1970   114m   Technicolor   Panavision
Cinema Center / Sanford Howard

In 1825 an English aristocrat is captured by Indians, lives with them and eventually becomes their leader.
Harrowing account of tribal life and customs,

with much bloodshed and torture and most of the dialogue in Indian. Occasionally impressive but not exactly entertaining.

w Jack di Witt, *story* Dorothy M. Johnson
d Elliot Silverstein ph Robert Hauser
m Leonard Rosenman

Richard Harris, Judith Anderson, Jean Gascon, Manu Tupou
† Sequel 1976: *The Return of a Man Called Horse.*

The Man Called Noon
GB / Spain / Italy 1973   95m   Technicolor
Frontier / Montana / Finarco (Euan Lloyd)

A western gunslinger loses his memory.
Childish western melodrama in the violent manner.

w Scot Finch, *novel* Louis L'Amour d Peter Collinson ph John Cabrera m Luis Bacalov

Richard Crenna, Stephen Boyd, Rosanna Schiaffino, Farley Granger

A Man Called Peter*
US 1955   119m   De Luxe   Cinemascope
TCF (Samuel G. Engel)

The life of Peter Marshall, a Scottish clergyman who became chaplain to the US Senate.
Careful but rather dreary biopic.

w Eleanore Griffin, *book* Catherine Marshall
d Henry Koster ph Harold Lipstein m Alfred Newman

Richard Todd, Jean Peters, Marjorie Rambeau, Jill Esmond, Les Tremayne, Robert Burton

AAN: Harold Lipstein

A Man Could Get Killed*
US 1966   98m   Technicolor   Panavision
Universal / Cherokee (Ernest Wehmeyer)

An American businessman in Lisbon is mistaken for a secret agent.
Minor thrill comedy with a confused plot and a willing cast.

w T. E. B. Clarke, Richard Breen, *novel* Diamonds Are Danger by David Walker
d Ronald Neame, Cliff Owen ph Gabor Pogany
m Bert Kaemfert

James Garner, Melina Mercouri, Sandra Dee, Tony Franciosa, Robert Coote, Roland Culver, Cecil Parker, Grégoire Aslan, Dulcie Gray, Martin Benson, Niall MacGinnis

A Man for All Seasons****
GB 1966   120m   Technicolor
Columbia / Highland (Fred Zinnemann)

Sir Thomas More opposes Henry VIII's divorce, and events lead inexorably to his execution. Irreproachable film version of a play which has had its narrative tricks removed but stands up remarkably well. Acting, direction, sets, locations and costumes all have precisely the right touch.

w Robert Bolt, from his play *d Fred Zinnemann ph Ted Moore m Georges Delerue pd John Box*

Paul Scofield, Wendy Hiller, Susannah York, *Robert Shaw,* Orson Welles, Leo McKern, Nigel Davenport, John Hurt, Corin Redgrave, Cyril Luckham, Jack Gwyllim

AA: best picture; Robert Bolt; Fred Zinnemann; Ted Moore; Paul Scofield
AAN: Wendy Hiller; Robert Shaw

Man Friday
GB 1975   115m   Eastmancolor
  Panavision
Avco-Embassy / ITC / ABC / Keep Films
  (Jules Buck)

The story of Robinson Crusoe told so that Friday appears the more intelligent.
A pointless and not very entertaining exercise which wears out its welcome very early.

w Adrian Mitchell d Jack Gold ph Alex Phillips m Carl Davis

Peter O'Toole, Richard Roundtree

'Liberal intentions trail sadly through every sequence and cause absurd fluctuations of tone, since no one seems to have decided whether laborious slapstick, heavy portentousness or method acting is the best vehicle for the message.'—*Jill Forbes*

The Man from Blankley's
US 1930   67m   bw
Warner

A drunken aristocrat goes to the wrong party and teaches those present, and himself, a thing or two.
Amusing star trifle, previously filmed as a silent.

w Harvey Thew, Joseph Jackson, story F. Anstey d Alfred E. Green ph James Van Trees

John Barrymore, Loretta Young, William Austin, Albert Gran, Emily Fitzroy

The Man from Colorado
US 1949   99m   Technicolor
Columbia (Jules Schermer)

A maladjusted Civil War veteran becomes a western judge and rules by the gun.
Slightly unusual, watchable star western.

w Robert D. Andrews, Ben Maddow, Borden Chase d Henry Levin ph William Snyder m George Duning

Glenn Ford, William Holden, Ellen Drew, Ray Collins, Edgar Buchanan, Jerome Courtland, James Millican, Jim Bannon

Man from Del Rio
US 1956   82m   bw
UA / Robert L. Jacks

A Mexican hobo becomes sheriff and forces the local badman to leave town.
Modest, efficient, rather brutal little western.

w Richard Carr d Harry Horner ph Stanley Cortez m Fred Steiner

Anthony Quinn, Katy Jurado, Peter Whitney, Douglas Fowley

The Man from Laramie**
US 1955   104m   Technicolor
  Cinemascope
Columbia (William Goetz)

A wandering cowman seeks revenge on those who killed his brother.
Grade A western with new-fangled touches of brutality touching off the wide screen spectacle.

w Philip Yordan, Frank Burt d Anthony Mann ph Charles Lang Jnr m George Duning md Morris Stoloff

James Stewart, Arthur Kennedy, Donald Crisp, Cathy O'Donnell, Alex Nicol, Aline MacMahon, Wallace Ford, Jack Elam

The Man from Morocco
GB 1944   116m   bw
ABP

Members of the international brigade are captured and later sent by Vichy to build a Sahara railway for the Germans; one escapes to London with vital information.
Stilted, meandering and extremely unconvincing melodrama with a star ill at ease.

w Warwick Ward, Edward Dryhurst, Marguerite Steen, story Rudolph Cartier d Max Greene ph Basil Emmott

Anton Walbrook, Margaretta Scott, Mary Morris, Reginald Tate, Peter Sinclair, David Horne

The Man from the Alamo*
US 1953   79m   Technicolor
U-I (Aaron Rosenberg)

A survivor of the Alamo is thought to be a deserter but proves his story and exposes a villain.
Satisfying western programmer.

w Steve Fisher, D. D. Beauchamp *d* Budd
Boetticher *ph* Russell Metty *m* Frank Skinner

Glenn Ford, Victor Jory, Julia Adams, Hugh
O'Brian

The Man from the Diners' Club*
US 1963   96m   bw
Columbia / Dena / Ampersand

A clerk accidentally lets a credit card go to a
notorious gangster, and makes desperate efforts
to retrieve it.
Minor star comedy with funny moments
surviving a slapdash script.

w Bill Blatty *d* Frank Tashlin *ph* Hal Mohr
m Stu Philips

Danny Kaye, Telly Savalls, Martha Hyer, Cara
Williams, Everett Sloane, George Kennedy

The Man from Uncle
This long-running one-hour TV series (1964–8)
began as a spoof of James Bond, which was itself
a spoof. Not much more serious or convincing
than *Batman*, they caused a lot of people to
suspend their disbelief. Robert Vaughn played
Napoleon Solo, David McCallum Ilya
Kuryakin, and Leo G. Carroll Mr Waverly.
Several feature films were made up from various
episodes, and did well in cinemas in some
countries. They were: TO TRAP A SPY, THE
SPY WITH MY FACE, THE KARATE
KILLERS, THE SPY IN THE GREEN HAT,
ONE OF OUR SPIES IS MISSING, THE
HELICOPTER SPIES, HOW TO STEAL
THE WORLD and ONE SPY TOO MANY.

The Man from Yesterday
US 1932   71m   bw
Paramount

A man is reported missing in World War I, but
years later his wife and her new fiancé find him in
Switzerland, dying of gas poisoning.
Enoch Arden rides again, and very boringly.

w Oliver H. P. Garrett *d* Berthold Viertel
ph Karl Struss

Claudette Colbert, Clive Brook, Charles Boyer,
Andy Devine, Alan Mowbray, Christian Rub

Man Hunt**
US 1941   98m   bw
TCF (Kenneth MacGowan)

A big game hunter misses a shot at Hitler and is
chased back to England by the Gestapo.
Despite hilariously inaccurate English
backgrounds, this is perhaps its director's most
vivid Hollywood thriller, though watered down
in tone from the original novel.

w Dudley Nichols, *novel* Rogue Male by
Geoffrey Household *d* Fritz Lang *ph* Arthur
Miller *m* Alfred Newman

Walter Pidgeon, Joan Bennett, *George Sanders*,
John Carradine, Roddy McDowall, Ludwig
Stossel, Heather Thatcher, Frederick Worlock

'A tense and intriguing thriller that is both
propaganda and exciting entertainment.'—*Paul
M. Jensen, 1969*

'In its manipulation of these dark and intent
forces on a checkerboard, it manages to take
your breath away.'—*Otis Ferguson*
† Remade for TV in 1976 as *Rogue Male*.

The Man I Love
US 1946   76m   bw
Warner (Arnold Albert)

A nightclub singer is involved with a mobster.
Dreary little melodrama which never really gets
going.

w Catherine Turney *d* Raoul Walsh *ph* Sid
Hickox *m* Max Steiner

Ida Lupino, Robert Alda, Andrea King, Martha
Vickers, Bruce Bennett, Alan Hale, Dolores
Moran, John Ridgely

The Man I Married*
US 1940   79m   bw
TCF (Raymond Griffith)
aka: *I Married a Nazi*

When an American couple take a European
vacation, the wife is horrified to find her
husband, who is of German parentage, agreeing
with the Nazis.
Naïve but striking melodrama exploring
attitudes of its time.

w Oliver H. P. Garrett, *novel* Swastika by Oscar
Shisgall *d* Irving Pichel *ph* Peverell Marley
m David Buttolph

Joan Bennett, Francis Lederer, Lloyd Nolan,
Anna Sten, Otto Kruger, Maria Ouspenskaya,
Ludwig Stossel, Johnny Russell

The Man in Grey**
GB 1943   116m   bw
GFD / Gainsborough (Edward Black)

In Regency times, an aristocratic girl's love for
her less fortunate friend is repaid by jealousy,
treachery and murder.
Rather dully performed flashback costume
melodrama which caught the public imagination
in the middle of a dreary world war, especially as
its evil leading characters were played by stars
who rapidly went right to the top. The several
imitations which followed, including *The Wicked
Lady, Jassy* and *Hungry Hill*, became known as
the Gainsborough school.

w Margaret Kennedy, Leslie Arliss, Doreen Montgomery, *novel* Lady Eleanor Smith d Leslie Arliss *ph* Arthur Crabtree *m* Cedric Mallabey *ad* Walter Murton

James Mason, Margaret Lockwood, Phyllis Calvert, Stewart Granger, Helen Haye, Nora Swinburne, Raymond Lovell, Martita Hunt

'There was not a moment when I would not gladly have dived for my hat.'—*James Agate*

'All the time-tested materials: gypsy fortune-teller; scowling, black-browed villain; gushy diary kept by a doe-eyed girl who munches candied violets; fire-breathing adventuress who dotes on discord and low-cut gowns . . .'—*Time*

The Man in Half Moon Street
US 1944 91m bw
Paramount

A mysteriously handsome young scientist is actually a 90-year-old who has discovered a surgical method of preserving youth.
Boring screen version of a play which was conceived in an almost romantic vein; Hollywood has taken it too literally.

w Charles Kenyon, *play* Barre Lyndon d Ralph Murphy *ph* Henry Sharp *m* Miklos Rozsa

Nils Asther, Helen Walker, Brandon Hurst, *Reinhold Schunzel*

† Remade in straight horror vein as *The Man Who Could Cheat Death (qv)*.

The Man in the Back Seat*
GB 1961 57m bw
Independent Artists (Julian Wintle, Leslie Parkyn)

Two robbers fail to separate a bookie from the locked bag chained to his wrist; at first taking him with them they finally kill him and are apparently haunted by him.
Taut, downbeat little crime thriller which won a few critical plaudits.

w Malcolm Hulke, Eric Paice d Vernon Sewell *ph* Reg Wyer *m* Stanley Black

Derren Nesbitt, Keith Faulkner, Carol White, Harry Locke

Man in the Dark*
US 1953 70m bw 3-D
Columbia (Wallace Macdonald)

A convict submits to a brain operation which will remove his criminal tendencies. Unfortunately it also removes his memory, and on his release he is bewildered when gangsters expect him to know where the loot is hidden.
Silly low-budgeter which is only notable as the 3-D film which most exploited the short-lived

medium. Apart from a roller coaster ride, objects hurled at the audience include scissors, spiders, knives, forceps, fists and falling bodies.

w George Bricker, Jack Leonard d Lew Landers *ph* Floyd Crosby *md* Ross de Maggio

Edmond O'Brien, Audrey Totter, Ted de Corsia, Horace MacMahon

The Man in the Gray Flannel Suit*
US 1956 152m Eastmancolor
Cinemascope
TCF (Darryl F. Zanuck)

A young New York executive is offered a demanding job but decides that his first loyalty is to his wife and children.
An amusingly accurate novel of Madison Avenue mores becomes a marathon emotional melodrama in which the mordant bits quickly give way to domestic problems and a guilt complex about a wartime affair, shown in lengthy flashback. It's all too much.

w Nunnally Johnson, *novel* Sloan Wilson d Nunnally Johnson *ph* Charles G. Clarke *m* Bernard Herrmann

Gregory Peck, Fredric March, Jennifer Jones, Ann Harding, *Arthur O'Connell, Henry Daniell*, Marisa Pavan, Lee J. Cobb, Keenan Wynn, Gene Lockhart, Gigi Perreau, Connie Gilchrist, Joseph Sweeney

The Man in the Iron Mask***
US 1939 119m bw
Edward Small

King Louis XIV keeps his twin brother prisoner. Exhilarating swashbuckler based on a classic novel, with a complex plot, good acting and the three musketeers in full cry.

w George Bruce, *novel* Alexandre Dumas d James Whale *ph* Robert Planck *m* Lucien Moraweck

Louis Hayward, Warren William (as D'Artagnan), Alan Hale, Bert Roach, Miles Mander, Joan Bennett, *Joseph Schildkraut*, Walter Kingsford, Marion Martin, Montagu Love, Albert Dekker

'A sort of combination of *The Prisoner of Zenda* and *The Three Musketeers*, with a few wild west chases thrown in . . . not unentertaining.'—*Richard Mallett, Punch*
* Remade 1976 as a TV movie.

AAN: Lucien Moraweck

The Man in the Middle*
GB 1964 94m bw Cinemascope
TCF / Pennebaker / Belmont (Walter Seltzer)
In India during World War II, an American

lieutenant is indicted for murder and the defence counsel is instructed to lose the case.

Courtroom melodrama with unusual angles; quite intriguing, though the wide screen doesn't help.

w Keith Waterhouse, Willis Hall, *novel* The Winston Affair by Howard Fast *d* Guy Hamilton *ph* Wilkie Cooper *m* John Barry

Robert Mitchum, Trevor Howard, Keenan Wynn, Barry Sullivan, France Nuyen, Alexander Knox

'For once Mitchum seems to have an excuse for keeping his eyes at half mast.'—*Judith Crist*

The Man in the Mirror
GB 1936 82m bw
JH Productions / Wardour (Julius Hagen)

A timid man's reflection steps out of the mirror and organizes him.

Modest comedy with a pleasing star.

w F. McGrew Willis, Hugh Mills, *novel* William Garrett *d* Maurice Elvey

Edward Everett Horton, Geneviève Tobin, Garry Marsh, Ursula Jeans, Alastair Sim, Aubrey Mather, Felix Aylmer

Man in the Moon
GB 1960 99m bw
Allied Film Makers / Excalibur (Michael Relph)

A man who earns his living as Mr Normal, a human guinea pig for scientific research, is chosen as the first astronaut.

Dated comedy which rather dismayingly turns from mild satire to outright farce and fantasy.

w Michael Relph, Bryan Forbes *d* Basil Dearden *ph* Harry Waxman *m* Philip Green

Kenneth More, Shirley Anne Field, Michael Hordern, John Phillips, John Glyn-Jones, Charles Gray, Norman Bird

The Man in the Net
US 1958 96m bw
UA / Mirisch-Jaguar (Walter Mirisch)

When a painter is accused of murdering his wife, he goes into hiding and is helped by children. Extremely tedious and inept mystery, doubly disappointing in view of the credits.

w Reginald Rose, *novel* Patrick Quentin *d* Michael Curtiz *ph* John Seitz *m* Hans Salter

Alan Ladd, Carolyn Jones, Diane Brewster, John Lupton, Charles McGraw, Tom Helmore, John Alexander

Man in the Shadow *
US 1957 80m bw   Cinemascope
U-I (Albert Zugsmith)
GB title: *Pay the Devil*

The sheriff of a small western town investigates a murder against the wishes of a powerful local rancher.

Mini-social drama in which the honest man wins out at last . . . and who would expect anything different. A brooding melodrama which delivers less than it promises.

w Gene L. Coon *d* Jack Arnold *ph* Arthur E. Arling *m* Joseph Gershenson

Jeff Chandler, Orson Welles, Colleen Miller, John Larch, Joe Schneider, Leo Gordon

The Man in the Sky *
GB 1956 87m bw
Ealing (Seth Holt)
US title: *Decision against Time*

A test pilot refuses to bale out when an engine catches fire; his plight is interwoven with scenes of his family, friends and associates.

Thin suspense drama with some effective moments but too many irrelevant asides.

w William Rose, John Eldridge *d* Charles Crichton *ph* Douglas Slocombe *m* Gerbrand Schurmann

Jack Hawkins, Elizabeth Sellars, Walter Fitzgerald, Eddie Byrne, John Stratton, Victor Maddern, Lionel Jeffries, Donald Pleasence

The Man in the White Suit ****
GB 1951 81m bw
Ealing (Sidney Cole)

A scientist produces a fabric that never gets dirty and never wears out. Unions and management are equally aghast.

Brilliant satirical comedy played as farce and put together with meticulous cinematic counterpoint, so that every moment counts and all concerned give of their very best.

w Roger Macdougall, John Dighton, Alexander Mackendrick *d* Alexander Mackendrick *ph* Douglas Slocombe *m* Benjamin Frankel

Alec Guinness, Joan Greenwood, Cecil Parker, Vida Hope, *Ernest Thesiger*, Michael Gough, Howard Marion Crawford, Miles Malleson, George Benson, Edie Martin

'The combination of an ingenious idea, a bright, funny and imaginative script, skilful playing and perceptive brisk direction has resulted once more in a really satisfying Ealing comedy.'—*Richard Mallett, Punch*

AAN: script

Man in the Wilderness*
US 1971 105m Technicolor Panavision
Warner / Wilderness (Sanford Howard)

In 1820 in the Canadian northwest, a fur trapper
is mauled by a grizzly and left for dead, but he
learns to survive and sets out for revenge.
Endurance melodrama modelled after *A Man
Called Horse*; a bit stretched and only for the
hardened, but taking an agreeably unromantic
view of nature.

w Jack di Witt *d* Richard Sarafian *ph* Gerry
Fisher *m* Johnny Harris

Richard Harris, John Huston, John Bindon,
Prunella Ransome, Henry Wilcoxon, Ben
Carruthers

Man Made Monster*
US 1940 57m bw
Universal
GB title: *The Electric Man*

A scientist experiments with a man who is
impervious to electric shock, and turns him into
a walking robot.
A smart little semi-horror originally planned for
Karloff and Lugosi.

w Joseph West *d* George Waggner *ph* Elwood
Bredell *m* Hans Salter *md* Charles Previn
sp John P. Fulton

Lon Chaney Jnr, Lionel Atwill, Anne Gwynne,
Frank Albertson, Samuel S. Hinds

Man of a Thousand Faces**
US 1957 122m bw Cinemascope
U-I (Robert Arthur)

The rise to fame of silent screen character actor
Lon Chaney.
Moderately commendable biopic with a strong
sense of period Hollywood, an excellent star
performance, but too much sudsy emoting about
deaf mute parents and an ungrateful wife.

w R. Wright Campbell, Ivan Goff, Ben Roberts
d Joseph Pevney *ph* Russell Metty *m* Frank
Skinner *ad* Alexander Golitzen

James Cagney, Dorothy Malone, Robert Evans
(as Irving Thalberg), Roger Smith, *Marjorie
Rambeau,* Jane Greer, Jim Backus

AAN: script

Man of Aran**
GB 1934 75m bw
Gainsborough (Michael Balcon)

The primitive life of crofting and fishing folk in
the west of Ireland.
A lowering documentary very typical of its
maker: highly impressive scene for scene, but

tedious as a whole; still, highly remarkable that it
was made at all for the commercial cinema.

w Robert and Frances Flaherty *d* Robert
Flaherty

Colman King, Maggie Dirane (amateurs)
'In so far as it is a rendering of the efforts of the
Atlantic to overwhelm and demolish a wall of
rock, it is magnificent; but the human note is
inadequate and unnecessary.'—*E. V. Lucas,
Punch*

Man of Conquest
US 1939 99m bw
Republic (Sol C. Siegel)

The life of western hero Sam Houston, who
became president of Texas.
Competent action/domestic biopic.

w Wells Root, E. E. Paramore Jnr *d* George
Nicholls Jnr *ph* Joseph H. August *m* Victor
Young

Richard Dix, Joan Fontaine, Gail Patrick,
Edward Ellis, Victor Jory, Robert Barrat,
George Hayes, Ralph Morgan, Robert
Armstrong, C. Henry Gordon, Janet Beecher

AAN: Victor Young

Man of La Mancha*
US 1972 132m De Luxe
UA / PEA (Arthur Hiller)

Arrested by the Inquisition and thrown into
prison, Miguel de Cervantes relates the story of
Don Quixote.
Unimaginative but generally good-looking
attempt to recreate on the screen an essentially
theatrical experience.

w Dale Wasserman, from his play *d* Arthur
Hiller *ph* Goffredo Rotunno *m* Mitch Leigh
ly Joe Darion *md* Laurence Rosenthal
ad Luciano Damiani

Peter O'Toole, Sophia Loren, James Coco,
Harry Andrews, John Castle, Brian Blessed
'Needful of all the imagination the spectator
can muster.'—*Variety*

AAN: Laurence Rosenthal

Man of the West
US 1958 100m De Luxe Cinemascope
UA / Ashton (Walter M. Mirisch)

In 1874 Arizona, a reformed gunman is cajoled
by his old buddies to help them rob a bank.
Talkative, set-bound, cliché-ridden star western
with minor compensations.

w Reginald Rose, *novel* Will C. Brown
d Anthony Mann *ph* Ernest Haller *m* Leigh
Harline

Gary Cooper, Lee J. Cobb, Julie London,
Arthur O'Connell, Jack Lord, John Dehner,
Royal Dano, Robert Wilke

Man on a String
US 1960   92m   bw
Columbia / Louis de Rochemont
GB title: Confessions of a Counterspy

A Russian-born Hollywood producer is asked
by the Russians to work as a spy but becomes a
double agent.
Slightly unbelievable biopic about Boris Morros,
rather childlike in its simplicity and not too
entertaining either.

w John Kafka, Virginia Shaler, book Ten Years a
Counterspy by Boris Morros d André de Toth
ph Charles Lawton Jnr and others m George
Duning

Ernest Borgnine, Kerwin Mathews, Colleen
Dewhurst, Alexander Scourby, Glenn Corbett,
Vladimir Sokoloff

Man on a Swing
US 1975   108m   Technicolor
Paramount (Howard B. Jaffe)

Investigations into a murder are helped by a
would-be medium.
Overlong and confused psycho-mystery with
one stand-out performance.

w David Zelag Goodman d Frank Perry
ph Adam Holender m Lalo Schifrin

Cliff Robertson, Joel Grey, Dorothy Tristan,
Peter Masterson
  'Runs out of interest long before it runs out of
film.'—Variety

Man on a Tightrope*
US 1953   105m   bw
TCF (Robert L. Jacks)

A Czech circus owner has trouble with the
communist authorities and tries to escape.
Adventure story with cold war pretensions
which virtually kill it.

w Robert Sherwood d Elia Kazan ph Georg
Krause m Franz Waxman

Fredric March, Cameron Mitchell, Adolphe
Menjou, Richard Boone, John Dehner,
Dorothea Wieck

Man on Fire
US 1957   95m   bw
MGM (Sol C. Siegel)

When his wife divorces him, a middle-aged man
refuses to hand over their son.
Low-key personal drama of very moderate
interest and modest budget.

wd Ranald MacDougall ph Joseph Ruttenberg
m David Raksin

Bing Crosby, Inger Stevens, Mary Fickett, E. G.
Marshall

The Man on the Eiffel Tower*
US 1948   82m   Anscocolor
A & T (Irving Allen)

A crazy killer defies Inspector Maigret to
discover his identity.
Early independent production, an unsatisfactory
crime melodrama with international talent and
Paris locations. Some quirky acting carries it
through.

w Harry Brown, novel A Battle of Nerves by
Simenon d Burgess Meredith ph Stanley Cortez

Charles Laughton, Burgess Meredith, Franchot
Tone, Robert Hutton, Jean Wallace, Patricia
Roc, Wilfrid Hyde White, Belita

The Man on the Flying Trapeze*
US 1935   65m   bw
Paramount (William Le Baron)
GB title: The Memory Expert

Adventures of an oppressed family man who is
useful to his boss because of his prodigious
memory.
Plotless rigmarole of shapeless comedy sketches,
for star fans.

w Ray Harris, Sam Hardy, Jack Cunningham,
Bobby Vernon, story Charles Bogle (W. C.
Fields) d Clyde Bruckman ph Al Gilks

W. C. Fields, Kathleen Howard, Mary Brian,
Grady Sutton, Vera Lewis, Lucien Littlefield,
Oscar Apfel

The Man on the Roof*
Sweden 1976   109m   Eastmancolor
Svensk Filmindustri (Per Berglund)
original title: Mannen pa Taket

A brutal policeman is murdered, and a rooftop
sniper turns out to be the culprit.
Alternately vivid and lumbering police thriller
with a regrettable tendency to moralize.

wd Bo Widerberg, novel The Abominable Man
by Max Sjöwall, Max Wahlöös ph Odd Geir
Saether, Per Kallberg, others m Björn Lindh

Carl Gustav Lindstedt, Gunnel Wadner, Hakan
Serner Sven Wollter

Man Proof
US 1938   74m   bw
MGM (Louis D. Lighton)

In trying to win back her man a woman
discovers she really loves someone else.

Modest romantic comedy which leaves its stars at sea.

w Vincent Lawrence, Waldemar Young, George Oppenheimer, *novel* The Four Marys by Fanny Heaslip Lea d Richard Thorpe *ph* Karl Freund m Franz Waxman

Myrna Loy, Franchot Tone, Walter Pidgeon, Rosalind Russell, Nana Bryant, Ruth Hussey

The Man They Could Not Hang
US 1939   65m   bw
Columbia

A scientist working on a mechanical heart causes the death of a volunteer student. He is executed, but his assistant restores him to life and he determines to murder those who convicted him.
Predictable horror hokum which set Karloff on his mad doctor cycle.

w Karl Brown d Nick Grinde *ph* Benjamin Kline

Boris Karloff, Lorna Gray, Robert Wilcox, Roger Pryor, Don Beddoe, Byron Foulger

A Man to Remember*
US 1938   80m   bw
RKO (Robert Sisk)

At a small-town doctor's funeral, his life is remembered by mourners.
Modestly effective family film.

w Dalton Trumbo, *novel* Failure by Katharine Haviland-Taylor d Garson Kanin ph J. Roy Hunt m Roy Webb

Edward Ellis, Anne Shirley, Lee Bowman, William Henry, Granville Bates

The Man Upstairs*
GB 1959   88m   bw
British Lion / ACT (Robert Dunbar)

A mild-mannered lodger becomes violent, injures a policeman, and barricades himself in his room.
Character melodrama reminiscent of both *Fourteen Hours* and *Le Jour se Lève*, but not so interesting as either.

w Alun Falconer d Don Chaffey *ph* Gerald Gibbs

Richard Attenborough, Bernard Lee, Donald Houston, Dorothy Alison, Maureen Connell, Kenneth Griffith, Virginia Maskell, Patricia Jessel

The Man Who Broke the Bank at Monte Carlo*
US 1935   67m   bw
TCF (Nunnally Johnson)

A Russian émigré becomes a taxi driver, wins a fortune at roulette, loses it all again, and returns happily to his cab.
Very mild, unconvincing and not very entertaining malarkey which rested squarely on its star, who carried it with aplomb.

w Nunnally Johnson d Stephen Roberts *ph* Ernest Palmer

Ronald Colman, Joan Bennett, Colin Clive, Nigel Bruce, Montagu Love, Frank Reicher, Ferdinand Gottschalk

The Man Who Came to Dinner***
US 1941   112m   bw
Warner (Jack Saper, Jerry Wald)

An acid-tongued radio celebrity breaks his hip while on a lecture tour, and terrorizes the inhabitants of the suburban home where he must stay for several weeks.
Delightfully malicious caricature of Alexander Woolcott which, though virtually confined to one set, moves so fast that one barely notices the lack of cinematic variety, and certainly provides more than a laugh a minute, especially for those old enough to understand all the references.

w Julius J. and Philip G. Epstein, *play George S. Kaufman, Moss Hart* d William Keighley *ph* Tony Gaudio m Frederick Hollander

Monty Woolley, Bette Davis, Ann Sheridan, *Jimmy Durante* (spoofing Harpo Marx), *Reginald Gardiner* (spoofing Noel Coward), Richard Travis, *Billie Burke, Grant Mitchell, Ruth Vivian, Mary Wickes*, George Barbier, Elisabeth Fraser

The Man Who Cheated Himself
US 1950   81m   bw
TCF (Jack M. Warner)

A woman shoots her husband and her homicide detective lover covers up for her.
Efficient crime melodrama.

w Seton I. Miller, Philip MacDonald d Felix Feist *ph* Russell Harlan m Louis Forbes

Lee J. Cobb, Jane Wyatt, John Dall, Terry Frost

The Man Who Could Cheat Death
GB 1959   83m   Technicolor
Paramount / Hammer (Anthony Nelson-Keys)

A surgeon looks 35 but is really 104, having had a series of gland operations performed on himself.
Vulgar, gory, gruesomely coloured Hammer version of a rather attractive play, previously filmed under its original title *The Man in Half*

Moon Street (qv). The shocks are routine, and entertainment value is minimal.

w Jimmy Sangster, *play* Barre Lyndon *d* Terence Fisher *ph* Jack Asher *m* Richard Rodney Bennett

Anton Diffring, Hazel Court, Christopher Lee, Arnold Marle, Delphi Lawrence, Francis de Wolff

The Man Who Could Work Miracles***
GB 1936   82m   bw
London (Alexander Korda)

A city clerk discovers he has the power to work miracles (given him by sportive gods) and nearly causes the end of the earth.
Slow-moving but rather pleasing variation on a simple theme.

w Lajos Biro, *story* H. G. Wells *d* Lothar Mendes *ph* Harold Rosson

Roland Young, Ralph Richardson, Ernest Thesiger, Edward Chapman, Joan Gardner, Sophie Stewart, Robert Cochrane, George Zucco, Lawrence Hanray, George Sanders

The Man Who Cried Wolf
US 1937   66m   bw
Universal (E. M. Asher)

A distinguished actor confesses to several murders he did not do so that he will be ignored when he does commit the one he intends.
Ingenious but dated crime suspenser.

w Charles Grayson, Sy Bartlett, *story* Too Clever to Live by Arthur Rothsfel *d* Lewis R. Foster *ph* George Robinson

Lewis Stone, Tom Brown, Barbara Read, Marjorie Main, Jameson Thomas

The Man Who Fell to Earth*
GB 1976   138m   colour   Panavision
British Lion (Michael Deeley, Barry Spikings)

A visitor from another planet tries to colonize Earth, but his powers are destroyed and he ends an alcoholic cripple.
A weird piece of intellectual science fiction made weirder by longueurs of all varieties: obscure narrative, voyeuristic sex, pop music and metaphysics. Not an easy film or a likeable one, despite its great technical skill.

w Paul Mayersburg, *novel* Walter Tevis *d* Nicolas Roeg *ph* Anthony Richmond *md* John Phillips

David Bowie, Rip Torn, Candy Clark, Buck Henry

'Once you have pierced through its glittering veneer, you find only another glittering veneer

underneath.'—*Michael Billington, Illustrated London News*

'There is a punch line, but it takes forever, and great expectations slump away.'—*Charles Champlin, L.A. News*

The Man Who Finally Died
GB 1962   100m   bw   Cinemascope
British Lion / Magna / White Cross (Norman Williams)

A German-born Englishman returns to Bavaria for news of his father, and becomes involved in a spy plot.
Busy adaptation of a TV serial with a convoluted plot which might have been more pacily developed and better explained.

w Lewis Greifer, Louis Marks *d* Quentin Lawrence *ph* Stephen Dade *m* Philip Green

Stanley Baker, Peter Cushing, Mai Zetterling, Eric Portman, Niall MacGinnis, Nigel Green, Barbara Everest, Harold Scott

The Man Who Found Himself
US 1937   67m   bw
RKO (Cliff Reid)

A nurse helps a downcast doctor face his problems and renew his enthusiasm for life.
Simple-minded programmer.

w J. Robert Bren, Edmund Hartman, G. V. Atwater *d* Lew Landers *ph* Roy Hunt

John Beal, Joan Fontaine, Philip Huston, Jane Walsh, George Irving

The Man Who Had His Hair Cut Short*
Belgium 1966   94m   bw
Belgian Cultural Ministry

A frustrated law clerk has an aberration after attending an autopsy and meeting again an old love.
Pessimistic case history with unpleasant details often brilliantly recorded.

w Anna de Pagter, André Delvaux *d* André Delvaux *ph* Ghislain Cloquet *m* Freddy Devreese

Seene Rouffaer, Beata Tyszkiewicz, Hector Camerlynck

The Man Who Had Power over Women
US 1959   105m   Eastmancolor   Cinemascope
TCF (Nunnally Johnson)

An arrogant, exhibitionist film producer finally alienates his long-suffering wife.
Something of an aberration, with good scenes submerged in an unholy mixture of sharp comedy and sentimental melodrama.

wd Nunnally Johnson, *novel* Colours of the Day by Romain Gary *ph* Milton Krasner *m* Robert Emmett Dolan

Henry Fonda, Leslie Caron, Myron McCormick, Cesare Danova, Marcel Dalio, Conrad Nagel, Harry Ellerbe

'A pretentious extravaganza on a romantic theme.'—*MFB*

The Man Who Haunted Himself
GB 1970 94m Technicolor
ABP / Excalibur (Michael Relph)

After recovering from a road accident, a staid businessman finds that he has an evil doppelganger who steals his wife and his job. Mildly effective if inexplicable story idea which served more suitably as a Hitchcock TV half hour and here, despite adequate production, outstays its welcome.

w Basil Dearden, Michael Relph, *story* The Case of Mr Pelham by Anthony Armstrong *d* Basil Dearden *ph* Tony Spratling *m* Michael Lewis

Roger Moore, Hildegarde Neil, Olga-Georges Picot, Anton Rodgers, Freddie Jones, Thorley Walters, John Carson, John Welsh

The Man Who Knew Too Much***
GB 1934 84m bw
GFD / Gaumont British (Ivor Montagu)

A child is kidnapped by spies to ensure her father's silence, but he springs into action. Splendid early Hitchcock which after a faded start moves into memorable sequences involving a dentist, an East End mission and the Albert Hall. All very stagey by today's standards, but much more fun than the expensive remake.

w A. R. Rawlinson, Charles Bennett, D. B. Wyndham Lewis, Edwin Greenwood, Emlyn Williams *d* Alfred Hitchcock *ph* Curt Courant *m* Arthur Benjamin

Leslie Banks, Edna Best, *Peter Lorre*, Nova Pilbeam, Frank Vosper, Hugh Wakefield, Pierre Fresnay

'The film's mainstay is its refined sense of the incongruous.'—*Peter John Dyer, 1964*

The Man Who Knew Too Much*
US 1956 120m Technicolor Vistavision
(Paramount) Alfred Hitchcock

Flaccid remake of the above, twice as long and half as entertaining, though it does improve after a very slow start.

w John Michael Hayes, Angus MacPhail *d* Alfred Hitchcock *ph* Robert Burks *m* Bernard Herrmann

James Stewart, Doris Day, Bernard Miles,

Brenda de Banzie, Daniel Gelin, Ralph Truman, Mogens Wieth, Alan Mowbray, Hillary Brooke

AAN: song 'Que Sera Sera' (*m/ly* Jay Livingston, Ray Evans)

The Man Who Loved Cat Dancing
US 1973 114m Metrocolor Panavision
MGM (Martin Poll, Eleanor Perry)

A runaway wife is kidnapped by train thieves and comes to love one of them.
Outdoor variation on *No Orchids for Miss Blandish*, remarkably lacking in any kind of entertainment value.

w Eleanor Perry, *novel* Marilyn Dunham *d* Richard Sarafian *ph* Harry Stradling Jnr *m* John Williams

Sarah Miles, Burt Reynolds, Lee J. Cobb, Jack Warden, George Hamilton, Bo Hopkins, Robert Donner, Jay Silverheels

'Any number of things have gone wrong with this peculiarly dreary western.'—*Tom Milne*

'Sarah Miles undergoes more perils than Pauline.'—*Variety*

The Man Who Loved Redheads
GB 1954 90m Eastmancolor
British Lion / London Films (Josef Somlo)

Throughout his career, a diplomat seeks women who resemble the redhead with whom in youth he had had an idyllic affair.
West End theatrical moonshine, poorly filmed in ugly colour but saved by the cast.

w Terence Rattigan, from his play Who Is Sylvia? *d* Harold French *ph* Georges Périnal *m* Benjamin Frankel

John Justin, Moira Shearer, *Roland Culver*, Gladys Cooper, Denholm Elliott, Harry Andrews, Patricia Cutts, Moira Fraser, *Joan Benham*, Jeremy Spenser

The Man Who Never Was**
GB 1955 102m De Luxe Cinemascope
TCF / André Hakim

In 1943, the British secret service confuses the Germans by dropping a dead man into the sea with false documents.
Mainly enjoyable true life war story marred by an emotional romantic sub-plot with a double twist but helped by an equally fictitious spy hunt which cheers up the last hour.

w Nigel Balchin, *book* Ewen Montagu *d* Ronald Neame *ph* Oswald Morris *m* Alan Rawsthorne

Clifton Webb, Robert Flemyng, Gloria Grahame, *Stephen Boyd*, Laurence Naismith, Josephine Griffin

The Man Who Played God*
US 1932 81m bw
Warner
GB title: *The Silent Voice*

A musician goes deaf but finds satisfaction in
helping a young student.
Stagey but effective star vehicle which Arliss also
played as a silent film. Remade as *Sincerely
Yours* (qv).

w Julian Josephson, Maude Howell, *play* The
Silent Voice by Jules Eckert Goodman *d* John
G. Adolfi *ph* James Van Trees

George Arliss, Violet Heming, Ivan Simpson,
Bette Davis, Louise Closser Hale, Donald Cook,
Ray Milland

The Man Who Reclaimed His Head*
US 1934 81m bw
Universal (Henry Henigson)

A writer who feels he has been betrayed and his
brain sapped by his publisher takes a gruesome
revenge.
Oddball period melodrama tailored rather
unsuccessfully for a new star. Remade as
Strange Confession (see *Inner Sanctum*).

w Jean Bart, Samuel Ornitz, *play* Jean Bart
d Edward Ludwig

Claude Rains, Joan Bennett, Lionel Atwill,
Juanita Quigley, Henry O'Neill, Lawrence
Grant

The Man Who Shot Liberty Valance*
US 1962 122m bw
Paramount / John Ford (Willis Goldbeck)

A tenderfoot becomes a hero for shooting a bad
man, but the shot was really fired by his friend
and protector.
Clumsy, obvious western with the director over-
indulging himself but providing some good
scenes in comedy vein.

w James Warner Bellah, Willis Goldbeck
d John Ford *ph* William H. Clothier *m* Cyril
Mockridge

James Stewart, John Wayne, Vera Miles, Lee
Marvin, Edmond O'Brien, Andy Devine,
Jeanette Nolan, John Qualen, Ken Murray,
Woody Strode, Lee Van Cleef, Strother Martin,
John Carradine

'Like Queen Victoria, John Wayne has
become lovable because he stayed in the saddle
into a new era.'—*Pauline Kael*

'A heavy-spirited piece of nostalgia.'—*Judith
Crist, 1975*

The Man Who Talked Too Much
US 1940 75m bw
Warner (Edmund Grainger)

A smart defence attorney gets the goods on a
gangster and decides to turn him in.
Below-par remake of *The Mouthpiece* (qv), later
filmed again as *Illegal* (qv).

w Walter de Leon, Tom Reed, *play* The
Mouthpiece by Frank J. Collins / Vincent
Sherman *ph* Sid Hickox

George Brent, Brenda Marshall, Richard
Barthelmess, Virginia Bruce, William Lundigan,
John Litel, George Tobias, Henry Armetta, Alan
Baxter

The Man Who Watched Trains Go By
GB 1952 80m Technicolor
Raymond Stross
aka: *Paris Express*

A clerk steals money in order to fulfil his wish of
world travel, and this leads to murder.
Miscast minor Simenon, not exactly badly made
but with no spark of excitement or suspense.

wd Harold French, *novel* Georges Simenon
ph Otto Heller *m* Benjamin Frankel

Claude Rains, Marius Goring, Marta Toren,
Anouk Aimée, Herbert Lom, Ferdy Mayne

The Man Who Would Be King*
US 1975 129m colour Panavision
Columbia / Allied Artists / Persky-Bright /
   Devon (John Foreman)

In India in the 1880s, two adventurers find
themselves accepted as kings by a remote tribe,
but greed betrays them.
After an ingratiating start this ambitious fable
becomes more predictable, and comedy gives
way to unpleasantness. Despite its sporadic high
quality, one does not remember it with
enthusiasm.

w John Huston, Gladys Hill, *story* Rudyard
Kipling *d* John Huston *ph* Oswald Morris
m Maurice Jarre *pd* Alexander Trauner

Sean Connery, Michael Caine, Christopher
Plummer (as Kipling), Saeed Jaffrey, Jack May,
Shakira Caine

AAN: script

The Man with a Cloak*
US 1951 81m bw
MGM (Stephen Ames)

In 1848 New York, a mysterious stranger (who
turns out to be Edgar Allan Poe) helps a young
French girl to keep her inheritance.
Curious domestic melodrama set on MGM's

choicest sets; its playful literary allusion causes it
to fall between suspense thriller and character
drama, but the acting keeps one watching.

w Frank Fenton, *story* John Dickson Carr
d Fletcher Markle *ph* George Folsey *m* David
Raksin

Joseph Cotten, Barbara Stanwyck, Leslie
Caron, Louis Calhern, Joe de Santis, Jim
Backus, Margaret Wycherly

The Man with Nine Lives *
US 1940 73m bw
Columbia
GB title: *Behind the Door*

A scientist believes he can cure cancer by
freezing, but accidentally locks himself and his
patients in an underground ice chamber for
seven years, and goes berserk when thawed out.
Interesting, rather prophetic science fiction
thriller which rather lacks the style required to
put it over.

w Karl Brown, *story* Harold Shumate *d* Nick
Grinde *ph* Benjamin Kline

Boris Karloff, Byron Foulger, Roger Pryor, Jo
Ann Sayers

The Man with the Golden Arm *
US 1956 119m bw
Otto Preminger

A Chicago poker dealer finally kicks the drug
habit.
Sensational on its first release, with its cold
turkey scenes, this now seems a muddled
impressionist melodrama with echoes of the
silent German cinema and much over-acting and
miscasting all round. But Sinatra is good; and it
is different . . .

w Walter Newman, Lewis Meltzer, *novel* Nelson
Algren *d* Otto Preminger *ph* Sam Leavitt
m Elmer Bernstein *pd* Joe Wright *titles* Saul
Bass

Frank Sinatra, Kim Novak, Eleanor Parker,
Darren McGavin, Arnold Stang, Robert
Strauss, John Conte, Doro Merande, George E.
Stone
   'Nothing very surprising or exciting . . . a
pretty plain and unimaginative look-see at a
lower depths character.'—*Bosley Crowther*
   'A very inferior film . . . the script is
inexcusably clumsy, the sets are unbelievable
and the casting is ridiculous.'—*Diana Willing,
Films in Review*
   'It has the same running time as *Citizen Kane*
but it seems a whole lot longer.'—*Robert James*
AAN: Elmer Bernstein; Frank Sinatra

The Man with the Golden Gun *
GB 1974 125m Eastmancolor
UA / Eon (Harry Saltzman, Albert R. Broccoli)

James Bond goes to the Far East to liquidate a
professional assassin named Scaramanga.
Thin and obvious Bond extravaganza with
conventional expensive excitements.

w Richard Maibaum, Tom Mankiewicz, *novel*
Ian Fleming *d* Guy Hamilton *ph* Ted Moore,
Oswald Morris *m* John Barry *pd* Peter Murton

Roger Moore, Christopher Lee, Britt Ekland,
Maud Adams, Hervé Villechaize, Clifton James,
Richard Loo, Marc Lawrence
   'The script lacks satiric insolence and the
picture grinds on humourlessly.'—*New Yorker*

The Man with the Gun *
US 1955 84m bw
UA / Formosa (Sam Goldwyn Jnr)
GB title: *The Trouble Shooter*

A gunfighter in search of his estranged wife
becomes lawman of a lawless town.
Modest, watchable western.

w N. B. Stone Jnr, Richard Wilson *d* Richard
Wilson *ph* Lee Garmes *m* Alex North

Robert Mitchum, Jan Sterling, Karen Sharpe,
Henry Hull, Emile Meyer, John Luplon

The Man with the Movie Camera **
USSR 1928 60m approx bw silent
VUFKU
original title: *Chelovek s Kinoapparatom*

A 'camera eye' documentary without any plot,
showing, through a succession of street and
interior scenes, all the tricks of which the
instrument is capable; it takes a bow at the end.
Unique documentary which was understandably
a sensation when it first appeared but now often
seems merely quaint.

wd, ed Dziga Vertov *ph* Mikhail Kaufman

The Man with Two Faces *
US 1934 72m bw
Warner

An actor takes revenge on a scoundrel who had
preyed on his sister.
Pleasing melodrama hinging on disguise; the
Hays Office surprisingly allowed the hero to get
away with it.

w Tom Reed, Niven Busch, *play* The Dark
Tower by George S. Kaufman, Alexander
Woolcott *d* Archie Mayo *ph* Tony Gaudio

Edward G. Robinson, Mary Astor, Ricardo
Cortez, Louis Calhern, Mae Clarke, John
Eldredge

The Man Within*
GB 1947   88m   Technicolor
GFD / Production Film Service
US title: *The Smugglers*

An orphan boy discovers that his mysterious
new guardian is a smuggler.
Unconvincing period yarn which has managed
to drain every vestige of subtlety from the novel,
but at least looks good.

w Muriel and Sydney Box, *novel* Graham
Greene *d* Bernard Knowles *ph* Geoffrey
Unsworth *m* Clifton Parker

Michael Redgrave, Richard Attenborough, Jean
Kent, Joan Greenwood

The Man without a Star*
US 1955   89m   Technicolor
U-I (Aaron Rosenberg)

A wandering cowboy helps settlers to put up
barbed wire against an owner of vast cattle
herds.
Conventional but entertaining star western.

w Borden Chase, D. D. Beauchamp, *novel* Dee
Linford *d* King Vidor *ph* Russell Metty
m Joseph Gershenson

Kirk Douglas, Jeanne Crain, Claire Trevor,
William Campbell, Jay C. Flippen, Mara
Corday, Richard Boone
† Remade for TV as *A Man Called Gannon*.

The Manchurian Candidate***
US 1962   126m   bw
UA / MC (Howard W. Koch)

A Korean war 'hero' comes back a brainwashed
zombie triggered to kill a liberal politician, his
control being his own monstrously ambitious
mother.
Insanely plotted but brilliantly handled spy
thriller, a mixture of Hitchcock, Welles and *All
the King's Men*.

w George Axelrod, *novel* Richard Condon
d John Frankenheimer *ph* Lionel Lindon
m David Amram *pd* Richard Sylbert

Frank Sinatra, Laurence Harvey, Janet Leigh,
James Gregory, Angela Lansbury, Henry Silva,
John McGiver
   'The unAmerican film of the year.'—*Penelope
Houston*
   'An intelligent, funny, superbly written,
beautifully played, and brilliantly directed study
of the all-embracing fantasy in everyday social,
emotional and political existence.'—*Philip
Strick, 1973*

AAN: Angela Lansbury

Mandingo
US 1975   126m   Technicolor
Dino de Laurentiis (Peter Herald)

On a slave breeding plantation in 1840
Louisiana, passions ride high.
Like *Gone with the Wind* with all the characters
on heat, this exuberant and unpleasant
melodrama goes several points over the top from
start to finish but proved to have wide appeal for
the groundlings, in the *Tobacco Road* tradition
of a wallow in other people's depravities.

w Norman Wexler, *play* Jack Kirkland, *novel*
Kyle Onstott *d* Richard Fleischer *ph* Richard
H. Kline *m* Maurice Jarre *pd* Boris Leven

James Mason, Susan George, Perry King,
Richard Ward, Brenda Sykes, Ken Norton

Mandy***
GB 1952   93m   bw
Ealing (Leslie Norman)
US title: *The Crash of Silence*

A little girl, born deaf, is sent to a special school.
Carefully wrought and very sympathetic little
semi-documentary film in which all the adults
underplay in concession to a new child star who
alas did not last long at the top.

w Nigel Balchin, Jack Whittingham, *novel* This
Day Is Ours by Hilda Lewis *d* Alexander
Mackendrick *ph* Douglas Slocombe *m* William
Alwyn

Jack Hawkins, Terence Morgan, Phyllis
Calvert, *Mandy Miller*, Godfrey Tearle,
Dorothy Alison

Manèges*
France 1950   90m   bw
Films Modernes-Discina (Emil Natan)
GB title: *The Wanton*

A scheming girl marries the middle-aged owner
of a riding school and, with her greedy mother,
milks him of his money.
A neat little melodrama with flashbacks so
arranged that the girl, paralysed in an accident,
seems for the first half to have an angelic
character.

w Jacques Sigurd *d* Yves Allégret *ph* Jean
Bourgoin

Simone Signoret, Bernard Blier, *Frank Villard*,
Jane Marken

Manhandled
US 1949   97m   bw
Paramount / Pine–Thomas

The secretary of a bogus psychiatrist becomes
involved in a murder and finds herself in danger
from all comers.

Modest, overlong suspenser with adequate production values.

w Lewis R. Foster, Whitman Chambers, *novel* The Man Who Stole a Dream by L. S. Goldsmith *d* Lewis R. Foster *ph* Ernest Laszlo *m* David Chudnow

Dorothy Lamour, Dan Duryea, Sterling Hayden, Irene Hervey, Harold Vermilyea, Philip Reed, Alan Napier, Art Smith, Irving Bacon

Manhattan Melodrama**
US 1934 93m bw
MGM (David O. Selznick)

Two slum boys grow up friends, one as district attorney and the other as a gangster.
Archetypal American situation drama (cf *Angels with Dirty Faces, Cry of the City*, etc), with the bad guy inevitably indulging in self-sacrifice at the end. An all-star cast makes it palatable in this case, though the film is inevitably dated.

w Oliver H. P. Garrett, Joseph L. Mankiewicz, *story* Arthur Caesar *d* W. S. Van Dyke *ph* James Wong Howe

William Powell, Clark Gable, Myrna Loy, Leo Carrillo, Nat Pendleton, George Sidney, Isabel Jewell, Thomas E. Jackson
† *Manhattan Melodrama* gained some irrelevant fame as the movie John Dillinger was watching when he was cornered and shot.

AAN: Arthur Caesar

Maniac
GB 1963 86m bw Hammerscope
Columbia / Hammer (Jimmy Sangster)

Murders by oxyacetelyne torch in the Camargue, with the wrong lunatic going to the asylum.
Hammer's mark two plot, the shuddery murder mystery in which someone is not quite what he seems; feebly done in this case, with a fatally slow start.

w Jimmy Sangster *d* Michael Carreras *ph* Wilkie Cooper

Kerwin Mathews, Donald Houston, Nadia Gray, Justine Lord

The Manitou
US 1978 104m CFI Color
Herman Weist / Melvin Simon (William Girdler)

A fake spiritualist finds his girl friend is possessed by the demon of a 400-year-old Indian.
Boring retread of *The Exorcist*.

w William Girdler, Jon Cedar, Tom Pope, *novel*

Graham Masterton *d* William Girdler *ph* Michel Hugo *m* Lalo Schifrin

Tony Curtis, Susan Strasberg, Michael Ansara, Stella Stevens, Jon Cedar, Ann Sothern, Burgess Meredith, Paul Mantee

Mannequin
US 1937 95m bw
MGM (Joseph L. Mankiewicz)

The wife of a small-time crook gets a modelling job and falls for a shipping magnate.
Competent star melodrama about a working girl's harassments.

w Lawrence Hazard *d* Frank Borzage *ph* George Folsey *m* Edward Ward

Joan Crawford, Spencer Tracy, Alan Curtis, Ralph Morgan, Mary Philips, Elizabeth Risdon, Leo Gorcey

AAN: song 'Always and Always' (*m* Edward Ward, *ly* Chet Forrest, Bob Wright)

Manon*
France 1949 96m bw
Alcina (P. E. Decharme)

After the liberation, a girl who has been a collaborator becomes involved in the black market, passes from man to man, and ends up being shot by Arabs in the Sahara desert.
Oddball modernized version of *Manon Lescaut*, with post-war pessimism and the glamour of sin going hand in hand. Worth comparing with *Gilda*.

w H. G. Clouzot, J. Ferry, *novel* L'Abbé Prévost *d* H. G. Clouzot *ph* Armand Thirard *m* Paul Misraki

Michel Auclair, Cécile Aubry, Serge Reggiani, Gabrille Dorziat
'A clever idea, handled cleverly, but without depth of feeling.'—*Penelope Houston*

Manon des Sources
France 1952 190m bw
Films Marcel Pagnol

A Provençal girl who lives in the hills with her goats is thought to be a witch, and takes her revenge on the populace by stopping the water supply.
Insanely long idyll of the countryside with the writer-director unintentionally caricaturing himself.

wd Marcel Pagnol *ph* Willy *m* Raymond Legrand

Jacqueline Pagnol, Raymond Péllegrin, Henri Vibert
'Something of an endurance test for all but the

most enthusiastic Pagnol admirers.'—*John Gillett, MFB*

Manpower*
US 1941   103m   bw
Warner (Mark Hellinger)

Power linesmen fall out over a nightclub hostess. Yet another variation on *Tiger Shark*, with vivid fisticuff and storm sequences supporting the star performers.

w Richard Macaulay, Jerry Wald *d* Raoul Walsh *ph* Ernest Haller *m* Adolph Deutsch

Edward G. Robinson, George Raft, Marlene Dietrich, Alan Hale, Frank McHugh, Eve Arden, Barton MacLane, Walter Catlett, Joyce Compton, Ward Bond

'The pace and cutting are those of the best gangster films . . . the climax outdoes anything the Lyceum may have known.'—*William Whitebait*

Man's Castle*
US 1933   75m   bw
Columbia

Romance blooms among the unemployed who live in a shanty town on the banks of the East River.
Depression moonshine which at the time was taken for realism; sociologically very interesting but very faded as entertainment.

w Jo Swerling, *play* Lawrence Hazard *d* Frank Borzage *ph* Joseph August

Spencer Tracy, Loretta Young, Glenda Farrell, Walter Connolly, Arthur Hohl, Marjorie Rambeau, Dickie Moore

'Heavily sentimental yet magically romantic.'—*New Yorker, 1977*

Man's Favourite Sport?*
US 1963   120m   Technicolor
Universal / Gibraltar / Laurel (Howard Hawks)

A star salesman of fishing tackle finds his bluff called when he has to enter a fishing competition.
Over-extended romantic farce drawn by the director from memories of older and better films, such as *Libeled Lady* and his own *Bringing Up Baby*.

w John Fenton Murray *d* Howard Hawks *ph* Russell Harlan *m* Henry Mancini

Rock Hudson, Paula Prentiss, Maria Perschy, Charlene Holt, John McGiver, Roscoe Karns

'Hawks' deadpan documentation of a physical gag is as effective as ever, but the overall pace of his direction is curiously contemplative, as though he were savoring all his past jokes for the last time.'—*Andrew Sarris*

Mantrap
US 1961   93m   bw   Panavision
Paramount / Tiger (Edmond O'Brien, Stanley Frazen)

An honest man is lured by an old Marine friend into a hi-jack attempt which leads to the death of his wife.
Rather uninteresting melodrama, played and directed for more than it's worth.

w Ed Waters, *novel* Taint of the Tiger by John D. Macdonald *d* Edmond O'Brien *ph* Loyal Griggs *m* Leith Stevens

Jeffrey Hunter, David Janssen, Stella Stevens, Hugh Sanders

Manuela*
GB 1957   95m   bw
British Lion / Ivan Foxwell
US title: *Stowaway Girl*

In a South American port, the engineer of a tramp steamer smuggles aboard a half caste girl, but it is the disillusioned captain who falls in love with her.
Downbeat seafaring melodrama, fine for those seeking a mood piece.

w William Woods, from his novel *d* Guy Hamilton *ph* Otto Heller *m* William Alwyn

Trevor Howard, Elsa Martinelli, Pedro Armendariz, Donald Pleasence

The Manxman
GB 1929   90m (24 fps)   bw   silent
British International (John Maxwell)

A fisherman thought drowned comes back to find that his girl is expecting his best friend's baby.
Stern romantic melodrama of virtually no interest despite its director.

w Eliot Stannard, *novel* Hall Caine *d* Alfred Hitchcock *ph* Jack Cox

Carl Brisson, Malcolm Keen, Anny Ondra, Randle Ayrton, Clare Greet
† Previously filmed in 1916 with Henry Ainley and Elizabeth Risdon.

Many Rivers to Cross*
US 1955   94m   Eastmancolor
  Cinemascope
MGM (Jack Cummings)

A trapper bound for Canada is helped by a sharp-shooting girl, and in return he saves her from marauding Indians.
Simple-minded, cheerful, quite refreshing western compounded of equal parts comedy and action.

w Harry Brown, Guy Trosper *d* Roy Rowland *ph* John Seitz *m* Cyril Mockridge

Robert Taylor, Eleanor Parker, Victor McLaglen, Josephine Hutchinson, Jeff Richards, Russ Tamblyn, James Arness, Alan Hale Jnr

Mara Maru
US 1952 98m bw
Warner (David Weisbart)

A Manila salvage expert locates a sunken treasure and defeats crooks who are also in pursuit of it.
Lethargic but pleasant-looking star vehicle with a plot borrowed from *The Maltese Falcon*.

w N. Richard Nash, Philip Yordan, Sidney Harmon, Hollister Noble *d* Gordon Douglas *ph Robert Burks m* Max Steiner

Errol Flynn, Ruth Roman, Raymond Burr, Paul Picerni, Richard Webb

The Marat/Sade*
GB 1966 116m De Luxe
UA / Marat Sade (Michael Birkett)
aka: *The Persecution and Assassination of Jean-Paul Marat as performed by the inmates of the Asylum of Charenton under the direction of the Marquis de Sade*

The title tells all, except that at the end the inmates go berserk.
Fairly plain filming of an Old Vic *succès d'estime* which it became fashionable to announce that one had seen and understood. The film makes no effort to attract the unbeliever.

w Adrian Mitchell, *play* Peter Weiss *d* Peter Brook *ph* David Watkin *m* Richard Peaslee

Glenda Jackson, Patrick Magee, Ian Richardson, Michael Williams, Robert Lloyd, Clifford Rose, Freddie Jones

March or Die
GB 1977 107m Technicolor
ITC / Associated General (Dick Richards, Jerry Bruckheimer)

In 1918, tensions rise at a Foreign Legion outpost threatened by Arabs.
Incredibly old-hat romantic melodrama of the kind that was being spoofed forty years ago. The considerable talent involved seems unfortunately under instruction to take it seriously.

w David Zelag Goodman *d* Dick Richards *ph* John Alcott *m* Maurice Jarre

Gene Hackman, Terence Hill, Catherine Deneuve, Max Von Sydow, Ian Holm, Marcel Bozzuffi
† The writer and director more successfully revived a different set of clichés in *Farewell My Lovely*.

Marco the Magnificent
France / Italy / Yugoslavia / Egypt / Afghanistan 1964 115m Eastmancolor Franscope
Ittac / Prodi / Avala / Mounir Rafla / Italaf Kaboul (Raoul Lévy)
aka: *The Fabulous Adventures of Marco Polo*

In 1271, Marco Polo carries a message of peace from the Pope to Kubla Khan.
Patchwork epic produced under the usual international difficulties: the result is just as often boring as entertaining, and varies between straight adventures and spoof.

w Raoul Lévy, Denys de la Patellière *d* Denys de la Patellière, Noel Howard *ph* Armand Thirard *m* Georges Garvarentz

Horst Buchholz, Anthony Quinn, Akim Tamiroff, Orson Welles, Robert Hossein, Omar Sharif, Elsa Martinelli, Grégoire Aslan, Massimo Girotti, Folco Lulli

Mardi Gras
US 1958 107m De Luxe Cinemascope
TCF (Jerry Wald)

In New Orleans at holiday time, a film star falls for a cadet.
Mindless musical using up available talent.

w Winston Miller, Hal Kanter *d* Edmund Goulding *ph* Wilfrid M. Cline *md* Lionel Newman

Pat Boone, Christine Carere, Sheree North, Tommy Sands, Gary Crosby, Fred Clark, Richard Sargent, Barrie Chase

AAN: Lionel Newman

Mare Nostrum*
US 1925 approx 110m bw silent
MGM

A Spanish captain loves a German spy.
Tragic romantic melodrama, a major attraction of its time.

w Willis Goldbeck, *novel* Vicente Blasco Ibanez *d* Rex Ingram

Antonio Moreno, Alice Terry

Margie***
US 1946 94m Technicolor
TCF (Walter Morosco)

A married woman reminisces about her college days, when she married the French teacher despite her tendency to lose her bloomers at the most embarrassing moments.
Wholly pleasing nostalgia, very smartly and brightly handled.

w F. Hugh Herbert, *stories* Ruth McKinney,

Richard Bransten *d Henry King ph* Charles
Clarke *md* Alfred Newman

Jeanne Crain, Glenn Langan, *Alan Young*, Lynn
Bari, Barbara Lawrence, Conrad Janis, Esther
Dale

Margin for Error*

US 1943   74m   bw
TCF (Ralph Dietrich)

Just before World War II, the Nazi consul in
New York is murdered in his own office.
Mildly intriguing whodunnit with the case solved
by a Jewish cop.

w Lillie Hayward, *play* Clare Boothe Luce
d Otto Preminger *ph* Edward Cronjager
m Leigh Harline

Milton Berle, Joan Bennett, Otto Preminger,
Carl Esmond, Howard Freeman, Poldy Dur,
Hans Von Twardowski

Marguerite de la Nuit*

France / Italy 1955   126m   Technicolor
SNEG / Gaumont Actualités / Cino del Duca
(Léon Carré)

An octogenarian signs a pact with the devil in
return for his lost youth; but when he has it he
causes the death of the woman he loves.
Expensive, sporadically interesting, but
unpersuasive updating of *Faust*.

w Ghislaine Autant-Lara, Gabriel Arout
d Claude Autant-Lara *ph* Jacques Natteau
m René Cloërc

Michèle Morgan, Yves Montand, Jean-François
Calvé, Massimo Girotti

Maria Marten, or The Murder in the Red Barn

GB 1935   67m   bw
George King

A wicked Victorian squire kills his pregnant
mistress and is haunted.
Stilted melodrama, ripely played, from a real-life
case. (The villain's scalp is still exhibited in a
museum at Bury St Edmunds.)

w Randall Faye *d* George King

Tod Slaughter, Sophie Stewart, Eric Portman,
Clare Greet

† Several versions had been made in silent days.

Marie Antoinette*

US 1938   149m   bw
MGM (Hunt Stromberg)

The last days of the French court before the
revolution.
Too slow by half, and so glamorized and
fictionalized as to lack all interest, this long

delayed production stands only as an example of
MGM's expensive prestige movies of the thirties.

w Claudine West, Donald Ogden Stewart,
Ernest Vajda *d* W. S. Van Dyke *ph* William
Daniels *montage* Slavko Vorkapitch
m Herbert Stothart *ad* Cedric Gibbons

Norma Shearer, Tyrone Power, John
Barrymore, Robert Morley, Gladys George,
Anita Louise, Joseph Schildkraut, Henry
Stephenson, Reginald Gardiner, Peter Bull,
Albert Dekker, Cora Witherspoon, Barnett
Parker, Joseph Calleia, Henry Kolker, George
Zucco, Henry Daniell, Harry Davenport, Barry
Fitzgerald, Mae Busch, Robert Barrat

'A resplendent bore.'—*New Yorker, 1977*

AAN: Herbert Stothart; Norma Shearer;
Robert Morley

La Marie du Port

France 1949   95m   bw
Sacha Gordine

A Cherbourg restaurateur takes his mistress
home for her father's funeral, and falls in love
with her younger sister.
Slight romantic drama, well enough put over but
not very memorable except for its slightly
cynical mood.

w Louis Chavance, Marcel Carné,
novel Georges Simenon *d* Marcel Carné
ph Henri Alekan *m* Joseph Kosma

Jean Gabin, Blanchette Brunoy, Nicole Courcel,
Claude Romain, Louis Cseigner, Jeanne
Marken, Carette

Marie Octobre

France 1958   102m   bw
Orex / SF / Abbey / Doxa (Lucien Viard)

At a reunion dinner of a wartime resistance
group, a traitor is exposed and killed.
Stultifying one-set talkfest employing
Hitchcock's long-discarded ten-minute take.

w Julien Duvivier, Jacques Robert,
novel Jacques Robert *d* Julien Duvivier
ph Robert Le Fèbvre *m* Jean Yatove
ad Georges Wakhevitch

Danielle Darrieux, Serge Reggiani, Bernard
Blier, Paul Meurisse, Noel Roquevert, Lino
Ventura, Paul Guers, Paul Frankeur

Marines Let's Go

US 1961   103m   De Luxe   Cinemascope
TCF (Raoul Walsh)

Marines fighting in Korea are granted leave in
Japan.
Brawling tragi-farce with predictable characters,
a long way after *What Price Glory*.

w John Twist, *story* Raoul Walsh *d* Raoul
Walsh *ph* Lucien Ballard *m* Irving Gertz

Tom Tryon, David Hedison, Tom Reese, Linda
Hutchins, William Tyler

'A typically noisy, insensitive and maudlin
tribute to the American Marines.'—*MFB*

Marius**

France 1931   125m   bw
Marcel Pagnol / Paramount

The son of a Marseilles waterfront café owner
gives up his sweetheart to go to sea.
Celebrated character drama which succeeds
through the realism and vitality of its people and
their dialogue.

w Marcel Pagnol, from his play *d* Alexander
Korda *ph* Ted Pahle *m* Francis Grammon

Raimu, Pierre Fresnay, Charpin, Orane
Demazis

† Two sequels with the same players and from
the same pen made this a famous trilogy. In
Fanny (1932, 128m, *d* Marc Allégret) the
heroine marries an old widower to give her baby
a father. In *César* (1936, 117m, *d* Marcel
Pagnol) Marius comes back twenty years later
and is reunited with his family.
†† *Port of Seven Seas* (MGM 1938) was a
hammy and stagey Hollywood compression of
the trilogy. See also *Fanny* (1960) a dull version
of the stage musical, with the songs removed.

Marjorie Morningstar

US 1958   123m   Warnercolor
(Warner) United States Pictures (Milton
Sperling)

A New York Jewish girl has great ambitions for
herself but ends up a suburban housewife.
Stodgy 'woman's picture' with all talents
somewhat uneasy in their assignments, mainly
because the Jewish quality is imperfectly
conveyed.

w Everett Freeman, *novel* Herman Wouk
d Irving Rapper *ph* Harry Stradling *m* Max
Steiner

Natalie Wood, Gene Kelly, Claire Trevor,
Everett Sloane, Ed Wynn, Martin Milner,
Carolyn Jones, George Tobias, Jesse White,
Martin Balsam

AAN: song 'A Very Private Love' (*m* Sammy
Fain, *ly* Paul Francis Webster)

The Mark*

GB 1961   127m   bw   Cinemascope
TCF / Raymond Stross / Sidney Buchman

A sexual psychopath finds on emerging from

prison that his past still haunts him despite the
help of his psychiatrist.
Worthy but evasive social drama which outstays
its welcome but provides good performances.

w Sidney Buchman, Stanley Mann *d* Guy
Green *ph* Douglas Slocombe *m* Richard
Rodney Bennett

Stuart Whitman, Maria Schell, *Rod Steiger*,
Brenda de Banzie, Maurice Denham, Donald
Wolfit, Paul Rogers, Donald Houston

'There is seriousness and care, but neither
boldness nor passion . . . no hint of the truly
sordid is allowed to seep through.'—*MFB*

AAN: Stuart Whitman

The Mark of Cain

GB 1947   88m   bw
GFD / Two Cities (W. P. Lipscomb)

The attractive housekeeper of a Manchester
businessman is blamed when his brother
accidentally poisons him.
Turgid period melodrama in which few
opportunities are offered and none taken.

w Francis Crowdy, Christianna Brand, W. P.
Lipscomb, *novel* Airing in a Closed Carriage by
Joseph Shearing *d* Brian Desmond Hurst
ph Erwin Hillier *m* Bernard Stevens

Sally Gray, Eric Portman, Patrick Holt, Dermot
Walsh, Denis O'Dea, Edward Lexy, Miles
Malleson

Mark of the Vampire*

US 1935   61m   bw
MGM (E. J. Mannix)

A policeman tries to solve an old murder in an
eerie house by hiring vaudeville performers to
pose as vampires.
Semi-spoof horror which is flawed by lack of
pace and a patchy script, but contains splendid
visual moments. A remake of the Lon Chaney
silent, *London After Midnight*.

w Guy Endore, Bernard Schubert *d* Tod
Browning *ph* James Wong Howe

Lionel Barrymore, Jean Hersholt, Elizabeth
Allan, Bela Lugosi, Carol Borland, Lionel
Atwill, Henry Wadsworth, Donald Meek, Jessie
Ralph, Ivan Simpson, Holmes Herbert

The Mark of Zorro*

US 1920   90m (24 fps)   bw   silent
Douglas Fairbanks

A Mexican Robin Hood carves his initial
wherever he turns up to harass the Spanish
invaders.
A little faded now, but this swashbuckler opened

up a whole new career for its star; the 1940 version clearly has more style.

w from the novel The Curse of Capistrano by Johnston McCulley d Fred Niblo m William Perry

Douglas Fairbanks, Marguerite de la Motte, Noah Beery

The Mark of Zorro***
US 1940 94m bw
TCF (Raymond Griffith)

After being educated in Spain, Diego de Vega returns to California and finds the country enslaved and his father half-corrupted by tyrants. Disguising himself as a masked bandit, he leads the country to expel the usurpers.
Splendid adventure stuff for boys of all ages, an amalgam of *The Scarlet Pimpernel* and *Robin Hood* to which in this version the director adds an overwhelming pictorial sense which makes it stand out as the finest of all.

w John Tainton Foote, Garrett Fort, Bess Meredyth d Rouben Mamoulian ph Arthur Miller m Alfred Newman ad Richard Day, Joseph C. Wright

Tyrone Power, Basil Rathbone, J. Edward Bromberg, Linda Darnell, Eugene Pallette, Montagu Love, Janet Beecher, Robert Lowery

AAN: Alfred Newman

Marked Woman*
US 1937 96m bw
Warner (Lou Edelman)

A nightclub girl is persuaded to testify against an underworld boss.
A twist on the usual run of gangster melodramas, performed with the star's accustomed intensity and presented with the studio's usual panache.

w Robert Rossen, Abem Finkel d Lloyd Bacon ph George Barnes md Leo F. Forbstein

Bette Davis, Humphrey Bogart, Jane Bryan, Eduardo Ciannelli, Isabel Jewell, Allen Jenkins, Mayo Methot, Lola Lane, Henry O'Neill
† Remade as *Lady Gangster*.

Marlowe*
US 1969 95m Metrocolor
MGM / Katzka–Berne–Cherokee / Beckerman (Sergei Petchnikoff)

Private eye Philip Marlowe is hired by a nervous girl to find her missing brother.
The authentic Chandler atmosphere is caught by this busy thriller, but there seems to be a deliberate attempt to make a confusing plot even more obscure, so that the end result is more tiresome than amusing.

w Stirling Silliphant, *novel* The Little Sister by Raymond Chandler d Paul Bogart ph William H. Daniels m Peter Matz

James Garner, Rita Moreno, Sharon Farrell, Bruce Lee, Gayle Hunnicutt, Carroll O'Connor, William Daniels, Jackie Coogan
'One does wonder whether the simple human squalor of the Bogart–Chandler era can ever be recaptured by an increasingly meretricious Hollywood.'—*MFB*

Marnie*
US 1964 130m Technicolor
Universal / Geoffrey Stanley Inc (Alfred Hitchcock)

A rich man marries a kleptomaniac and cures her, but a nightmare in her past makes her still sexually frigid.
Psychodrama with background crime and suspense, lethargically handled by the old master, who alone knows what he saw in it in the first place, as this heroine does not even have fire under her ice. The production is curiously artificial in many ways, from dummy horses to backcloths to back projection.

w Jay Presson Allen, *novel* Winston Graham d Alfred Hitchcock ph Robert Burks m Bernard Herrmann pd Robert Boyle

Tippi Hedren, Sean Connery, Martin Gabel, Diane Baker, Louise Latham

Marooned*
US 1969 134m Technicolor
Panavision 70
Columbia / Frankovich–Sturges (Frank Capra Jnr)

Three astronauts are stranded in space, and a rescue mission gets under way.
Very heavy-going space suspenser with all possible technical accomplishment but little life of its own.

w Mayo Simon, *novel* Martin Caidin d John Sturges ph Daniel Fapp pd Lyle R. Wheeler

Gregory Peck, Richard Crenna, David Janssen, James Franciscus, Gene Hackman, Lee Grant, Nancy Kovack, Mariette Hartley, Scott Brady
'In something like the plight of Ironman One, Sturges' work seems on the point of slowing to a standstill as it drifts further into projects of ever-increasing, self-effacing size and anonymous technical dexterity.'—*Richard Combs*
'It has all the zip, zest and zing of a moon walk, and I suspect a computer fed a dictionary could come up with better dialogue.'—*Judith Crist, 1973*

AAN: Daniel Fapp

The Marriage Circle **

US 1924   78m (24 fps)   bw   silent
Warner

A bachelor on the loose becomes amorously
involved in two marriages.
Feather-light comedy of manners which began a
whole new American school, heavily influenced
by various European masters.

w Paul Bern, *play* Only a Dream by Lothar
Schmidt d *Ernst Lubitsch* ph Charles Van
Enger

Monte Blue, Florence Vidor, Marie Prevost,
Adolphe Menjou, Creighton Hale

'A vanished world of roses, kisses and
embraces, of whispers and sighs, of a woman's
shadowed arm encased in georgette beckoning
across a moonlit garden . . . and hand-kissing all
over the place.'—*Herman G. Weinberg*
† Remade as *One Hour with You*, also by
Lubitsch.

The Marriage Go Round

US 1961   98m   De Luxe   Cinemascope
TCF (Leslie Stevens)

A Swedish girl suggests to a married American
professor that she borrow his body for mating
purposes, believing they would produce the
perfect child.
Silly, unfunny sex comedy.

w Leslie Stevens d Walter Lang ph Leo Tover
m Dominic Frontière

James Mason, Susan Hayward, Julie Newmar,
Robert Paige, June Clayworth

'As tedious as it is tasteless.'—*Evening
Standard*

Marriage Is a Private Affair

US 1943   116m   bw
MGM (Pandro S. Berman)

A spoilt rich girl becomes a petulant wife.
Abysmally slow, uninvolving and poorly acted
star fodder.

w David Hertz, Lenore Coffee, *novel* Judith
Kelly d Robert Z. Leonard ph Ray June
m Bronislau Kaper

Lana Turner, James Craig, John Hodiak,
Frances Gifford, Keenan Wynn, Nataiie
Schaefer, Hugh Marlowe, Paul Cavanagh

The Marriage of a Young Stockbroker **

US 1971   95m   De Luxe
TCF / Laurence Turman

A stockbroker who finds his life and his marriage
dull tries voyeurism and extra-marital sex.
Sardonic adult comedy of the battle between the
sexes, pretty lively from start to finish.

w *Lorenzo Semple Jnr, novel* Charles Webb
d Laurence Turman ph Laszlo Kovacs m Fred
Karlin

Richard Benjamin, Joanna Shimkus, Elizabeth
Ashley, Adam West, Patricia Barry

Marriage on the Rocks

US 1965   109m   Technicolor   Panavision
Warner / A-C / Sinatra (William H. Daniels)

An ad man and his wife decide to go to Mexico
for a divorce but once there change their minds;
she ends up accidentally married to his best
friend.
All this talent retreats fearfully from a witless,
tasteless script and slow handling. A dismal
comedy.

w Cy Howard d Jack Donohue ph William H.
Daniels m Nelson Riddle

Frank Sinatra, Dean Martin, Deborah Kerr,
Cesar Romero, Hermione Baddeley, Tony Bill,
Nancy Sinatra, John McGiver

'A long, coarse, and nearly always unfunny
comedy, hammered together for no apparent
reason except to make money.'—*New Yorker*

The Marriage Playground

US 1929   70m   bw
Paramount

Children of divorced rich parents wander round
Europe in a group.
Slightly unusual drama of its day; sound
technique very thin.

w J. Walter Rubin, Doris Anderson, *novel* The
Children by Edith Wharton d Lothar Mendes
ph Victor Milner

Fredric March, Kay Francis, Mary Brian,
Lilyan Tashman, Huntley Gordon, Anita Louise

Marry Me

GB 1949   97m   bw
GFD / Gainsborough (Betty Box)

Four stories of a marriage bureau.
A styleless portmanteau of anecdotes put over
by a clear second team.

w Lewis Gilbert, Denis Waldock d Terence
Fisher ph Ray Elton d Clifton Parker

Derek Bond, Susan Shaw, Patrick Holt, Carol
Marsh, David Tomlinson, Zena Marshall, Guy
Middleton, Nora Swinburne, Jean Cadell, Mary
Jerrold

The Marrying Kind **

US 1952   93m   bw
Columbia (Bert Granet)

A couple seeking divorce tell their troubles to a
judge, and change their minds.

Smart, New Yorkish, tragi-comic star vehicle
which works pretty well.

w Ruth Gordon, Garson Kanin *d* George
Cukor *ph* Joseph Walker *m* Hugo Friedhofer

Judy Holliday, Aldo Ray, Madge Kennedy,
Mickey Shaughnessy

La Marseillaise*

France 1937   145m   bw
Films La Marseillaise (Jean Renoir)

The story of the French revolution of 1789.
A rather disconnected epic which, despite a few
splendid scenes, never moved its audiences to
enthusiasm.

wd Jean Renoir *ph* Jean Bourgoin and others
md Joseph Kosma

Pierre Renoir, Lise Delemare, Louis Jouvet,
Leon Larive, Georges Spanelly, Elisa Ruis,
William Aguet

The Marseilles Contract

GB / France 1974   89m   Eastmancolor
Warner / AIP / Kettledrum / PECF (Judd
    Bernard)

US title: *The Destructors*

An American narcotics agent in Paris hires an
assassin to dispose of a drug smuggler.
Routine action melodrama with a jokey
atmosphere not sustained by a downbeat script.

w Judd Bernard *d* Robert Parrish *ph* Douglas
Slocombe *m* Roy Budd

Michael Caine, Anthony Quinn, James Mason,
Alexandra Stewart, Marcel Bozzufi, Maurice
Ronet

Martin Luther*

US / Germany 1953
Louis De Rochemont / Lutheran Church
    Productions (Lothar Wolff)

The career and doubts of Martin Luther.
Frequently vivid, occasionally boring, small-
scale account of the first Protestant.

w Allan Sloane, Lothar Wolff, others *d* Irving
Pichel *ph* Joseph C. Brun *m* Mark Lothar

Niall MacGinnis, John Ruddock, Pierre Lefèvre,
Guy Verney, David Horne, Philip Leaver, Irving
Pichel, Alexander Gauge

AAN: Joseph C. Brun

Martin Roumagnac

France 1946   99m   bw
Alcina (Marc Le Pelletier)

The trial, with flashbacks, of a small-town
businessman who has murdered his mistress.

Wholly unabsorbing and ordinary story of a
crime passionnel, totally wasting its stars.

wd Georges Lacombe *ph* Roger Hubert
m Marcel Mirouze

Jean Gabin, Marlene Dietrich, Margo Lion,
Marcel Herrand

Marty****

US 1955   91m   bw
UA / Hecht–Hill–Lancaster (Harold Hecht)

A 34-year-old Brooklyn butcher fears he will
never get a girl because he is unattractive, but at
a Saturday night dance he meets a girl with
similar fears. Unfortunately she is not
Italian . . .

The first of the filmed teleplays which in the mid-
fifties seemed like a breath of spring to
Hollywood (they were cheap) and also brought
in a new wave of talent. This is one of the best, its
new naturalistic dialogue falling happily on the
ear; but it has been so frequently imitated since
that its revolutionary appearance is hard to
imagine.

w Paddy Chayevsky, from his play *d Delbert
Mann ph Joseph La Shelle m* Roy Webb

*Ernest Borgnine, Betsy Blair, Esther Minciotti,
Joe Mantell*, Karen Steele, Jerry Paris

    'Something rare in the American cinema
today: a subtle, ironic and compassionate study
of ordinary human relationships.'—*Gavin
Lambert*

AA: best picture; Paddy Chayevsky; Delbert
Mann; Ernest Borgnine
AAN: Joseph La Shelle; Betsy Blair; Joe
Mantell

Mary Burns Fugitive*

US 1935   84m   bw
Paramount (Walter Wanger)

The innocent girl friend of a gangster is
convicted through circumstantial evidence,
escapes from prison and finds true love.
Competent meshing of well-tried thirties
elements, a good typical wish-fulfilment
melodrama of its time.

w Gene Towne, Graham Baker, Louis Stevens
d William K. Howard *ph* Leon Shamroy

Sylvia Sidney, Melvyn Douglas, Alan Baxter,
Pert Kelton, Wallace Ford, Brian Donlevy,
Esther Dale

Mary Mary

US 1963   126m   Technicolor
Warner (Mervyn Le Roy)

A publisher falls in love again with his ex-wife
but finds she is being pursued by a film star.

Feeble film version of a lighter-than-air Broadway success, with the actors paralysed behind the footlights and the camera asleep in the stalls.

w Richard L. Breen, *play* Jean Kerr *d* Mervyn Le Roy *ph* Harry Stradling *m* Frank Perkins

Debbie Reynolds, Barry Nelson, Michael Rennie, Diane McBain

Mary of Scotland*
US 1936   123m   bw
RKO (Pandro S. Berman)

Mary Stuart refuses to give up her claim to the English throne, and is eventually executed. Sombre historical charade with splendid sets and atmosphere but suffering from script and performances that don't quite make it despite effort all round.

w Dudley Nichols, *play* Maxwell Anderson *d* John Ford *ph* Joseph H. August *m* Nathaniel Shilkret *ad* Van Nest Polglase, Carroll Clark

Katharine Hepburn, Fredric March, Donald Crisp, Florence Eldridge, Douglas Walton, John Carradine, Robert Barrat, Monte Blue, Moroni Olsen, Frieda Inescort, Alan Mowbray

'An unpromising and stagey play is fleshed out into a rich and confident exercise in filmcraft.'— *John Baxter, 1968*

'Events are walked through as though they were rooms in a museum, and closing time at three.'—*Otis Ferguson*

Mary Poppins***
US 1964   139m   Technicolor
Walt Disney (Bill Walsh)

In Edwardian London a magical nanny teaches two slightly naughty children to make life enjoyable for themselves and others. Sporadically a very pleasant and effective entertainment for children of all ages, with plenty of brightness and charm including magic tricks, the mixing of live with cartoon adventures, and just plain fun. It suffers, however, from a wandering narrative in the second half (when Miss Poppins scarcely appears) and from Mr Van Dyke's really lamentable attempt at Cockney.

w Bill Walsh, Don da Gradi, *novel* P. L. Travers *d* Robert Stevenson *ph* Edward Colman *m/ly* Richard M. and Robert B. Sherman *pd* Tony Walton *sp* Eustace Lycett, Peter Ellenshaw, Robert A. Mattey

Julie Andrews, David Tomlinson, Glynis Johns, Dick Van Dyke, Reginald Owen, Ed Wynn, Matthew Garber, Karen Dotrice, Hermione Baddeley, Elsa Lanchester, Arthur Treacher, Jane Darwell

AA: Richard M. and Robert B. Sherman; Julie Andrews; song 'Chim Chim Cheree'
AAN: best picture; script; Robert Stevenson; Edward Colman

Mary Queen of Scots
GB 1971   128m   Technicolor   Panavision
Universal / Hal B Wallis

The story of Mary Stuart's opposition to Elizabeth I, her imprisonment and execution. Schoolbook history in which none of the characters comes to life; dramatic movement is almost entirely lacking despite the liberties taken with fact.

w John Hale *ph* Christopher Challis *d* Charles Jarrott *m* John Barry

Vanessa Redgrave, Glenda Jackson, Trevor Howard, Patrick McGoohan

AAN: John Barry; Vanessa Redgrave

M*A*S*H***
US 1970   116m   De Luxe   Panavision
TCF / Aspen (Ingo Preminger, Leon Ericksen)

Surgeons at a mobile hospital in Korea spend what spare time they have chasing women and bucking authority.
Savage comedy of man's rebellion in the face of death, alternating sex farce with gory operation scenes; hailed as the great anti-everything film, and certainly very funny for those who can take it. It led to a television series which for once did not disgrace its original.

w Ring Lardner Jnr, *novel* Richard Hooker *d* Robert Altman *ph* Harold E. Stine *m* Johnny Mandel

Donald Sutherland, Elliott Gould, Tom Skerritt, Sally Kellerman, Robert Duvall, Jo Ann Pflug, René Auberjonois, Gary Burghof

'Bloody funny. A hyper-acute wiretap on mankind's death wish.'—*Joseph Morgenstern*

'The laughter is blood-soaked and the comedy cloaks a bitter and terrible truth.'—*Judith Crist*

AA: Ring Lardner Jnr
AAN: best picture; Robert Altman; Sally Kellerman

The Mask of Dimitrios***
US 1944   99m   bw
Warner (Henry Blanke)

A timid Dutch novelist is drawn into a Middle-Eastern intrigue with money at the centre of it. Generally successful international intriguer, moodily shot in evocative sets, and remarkable for its time in that the story is not distorted to fit romantic stars: character actors bear the entire burden.

w Frank Gruber, novel Eric Ambler *d Jean Negulesco ph Arthur Edeson m* Adolph Deutsch

Peter Lorre, Sidney Greenstreet, Zachary Scott, Faye Emerson, Victor Francen, Steven Geray, Florence Bates, Eduardo Ciannelli, Kurt Katch, John Abbott, Monte Blue

The Mask of Fu Manchu**

US 1932   70m   bw
MGM

Nayland Smith and his party are caught and threatened with torture by the yellow terror. Highly satisfactory episode in the nefarious adventures of the master criminal, fast moving, humorous and very good to look at.

w John Willard, Edgar Woolf, Irene Kuhn, *stories* Sax Rohmer *d Charles Brabin, Charles Vidor ph Tony Gaudio*

Boris Karloff, Myrna Loy, Lewis Stone, Karen Morley, Charles Starrett, Jean Hersholt, Lawrence Grant

The Masque of the Red Death**

GB 1964   89m   Pathecolor   'Scope
AIP / Alta Vista (George Willoughby)

A medieval Italian prince practises devil worship while the plague rages outside, but when he holds a ball, death is an uninvited guest.
Languorous, overstretched, often visually striking horror piece with some extremely effective touches among its longueurs.

w Charles Beaumont, R. Wright Campbell, *story* Edgar Allan Poe *d Roger Corman ph Nicolas Roeg m* David Lee *ad Robert Jones costumes Laura Nightingale*

Vincent Price, Hazel Court, Jane Asher, Patrick Magee, John Westbrook

Masquerade*

GB 1965   101m   Eastmancolor
UA / Novus (Michael Relph)

To avert friction between Arab states the young heir to one of them is abducted by a British secret service agent; but one of the plotters has other fish to fry.
Quite a lively spy romp with a spectacular action climax, but the plot is simply too complicated.

w Michael Relph, William Goldman, *novel* Castle Minerva by Victor Canning *d* Basil Dearden *ph* Otto Heller *m* Philip Green *pd* Don Ashton

Cliff Robertson, Jack Hawkins, Charles Gray, Bill Fraser, Marisa Mell, Michel Piccoli, John Le Mesurier

Masquerade in Mexico

US 1945   96m   bw
Paramount (Karl Tunberg)

A stranded showgirl is hired by a Mexican banker to entice a gigolo away from his wife. Talent-starved remake of *Midnight* (qv), which seems second-hand even if you don't know why.

w Karl Tunberg *d* Mitchell Leisen *ph* Lionel Lindon *m* Victor Young

Dorothy Lamour, Arturo de Cordova, Patric Knowles, Ann Dvorak, George Rigaud, Natalie Schafer, Mikhail Rasumny, Billy Daniels

The Master of Ballantrae

GB 1953   89m   Technicolor
Warner

Two brothers toss to decide which shall join Bonnie Prince Charlie's 1745 rebellion.
Half-hearted version of a classic adventure novel.

w Herb Meadow, *novel* R. L. Stevenson *d* William Keighley *ph* Jack Cardiff *m* William Alwyn

Errol Flynn, Anthony Steel, Roger Livesey, Beatrice Campbell, Felix Aylmer, Mervyn Johns, Jacques Berthier, Yvonne Furneaux, Ralph Truman

'All that can be salvaged from this rather unforgivable Anglo-American junket are some pleasant exteriors.'—*Gavin Lambert*

Master of Bankdam*

GB 1947   105m   bw
GFD / Holbein (Nat Bronsten, Walter Forde, Edward Dryhurst)

19th-century chronicles of a mill-owning Yorkshire family.
Archetypal 'trouble at t'mill' saga with moderate production, good acting and undeniably compulsive story.

w Edward Dryhurst, Moie Charles, *novel* Thomas Armstrong *d* Walter Forde

Tom Walls, Anne Crawford, Dennis Price, Stephen Murray, Linden Travers, Jimmy Hanley, Nancy Price, David Tomlinson, Herbert Lomas

Master of the World

US 1961   104m   Magnacolor
AIP / Alta Vista (James H. Nicholson, Anthony Carras)

In 1848 a mad inventor takes to the air in his magnificent flying machine in the hope of persuading men to stop war.
Aerial version of *Twenty Thousand Leagues under the Sea*, with cheap sets and much use of

stock footage; some scenes however have a certain vigour.

w Richard Matheson, *novels* Jules Verne d William Witney *ph* Gil Warrenton *m* Les Baxter

Vincent Price, Charles Bronson, Henry Hull, Mary Webster, David Frankham

Mata Hari**
US 1932   92m   bw
MGM

The career of the famous lady spy of World War I.
Elaborate melodrama, pictorially satisfying and generally more entertaining than might be supposed, with both star and supporting cast in rich thespian form.

w Benjamin Glazer, Leo Birinski, Doris Anderson, Gilbert Emery *d George Fitzmaurice ph* William Daniels

Greta Garbo, Ramon Novarro, Lionel Barrymore, Lewis Stone, C. Henry Gordon, Karen Morley, Blanche Frederici

The Matchmaker*
US 1958   101m   bw   Vistavision
Paramount (Don Hartman)

In New York at the turn of the century, a rich merchant decides to marry again but the matchmaker he consults has her own eye on him. Cold and lifeless version of an amusing play which also served as the basis for the musical *Hello Dolly* (qv).

w John Michael Hayes, *play* Thornton Wilder d Joseph Anthony *ph* Charles Lang *m* Adolph Deutsch

Shirley Booth, Paul Ford, Anthony Perkins, Shirley Maclaine, Wallace Ford, Robert Morse, Perry Wilson

'Long static dialogue exchanges are further extended by frequent confidences expressed directly to the audience . . . but in spite of the general lack of pace, lightness and dimension there is still a great deal to enjoy.'—*Peter John Dyer*

Matilda
US 1978   105m   Movielab
AIP / Albert S. Ruddy

A down-at-heel theatrical agent finds success with a boxing kangaroo.
Damon Runyon meets Walt Disney in an old-fashioned family audience picture for which there may no longer be an audience.

w Albert S. Ruddy, Timothy Galfas, *novel* Paul

Gallico *d* Daniel Mann *ph* Jack Woolf *pd* Boris Leven

Elliott Gould, Robert Mitchum, Harry Guardino, Clive Revill, Karen Carlson, Lionel Stander, Art Metrano, Roy Clark

La Maternelle*
France 1932   89m   bw
Photosonor

A maid in a nursery school becomes devoted to the children and in particular to one who causes trouble when her friend decides to marry.
A touching drama of its day which now seems rather primitive.

w Jean Benoit-Lévy *d* Jean Benoit-Lévy, Marie Epstein *ph* Georges Asselin *m* Edouard Flament

Madeleine Renaud, Paulette Elambert, Alice Tissot, Mady Berry

The Mating Game
US 1959   96m   Metrocolor
  Cinemascope
MGM (Philip Barry Jnr)

An income-tax inspector becomes involved in the affairs of an unorthodox farming family.
Dismally unfunny adaptation for Americans of a very English novel; everyone works hard to no avail.

w William Roberts, *novel* The Darling Buds of May by H. E. Bates *d* George Marshall *ph* Robert Bronner *m* Jeff Alexander

Debbie Reynolds, Tony Randall, Paul Douglas, Fred Clark, Una Merkel, Philip Ober, Charles Lane, Philip Coolidge

'Every joke is driven past the point of exhaustion.'—*MFB*

The Mating Season
US 1950   101m   bw
Paramount (Charles Brackett)

A factory draughtsman marries an ambassador's daughter; his mother loses her job and comes incognito to work for them as a cook. Uninteresting mechanical domestic comedy in which the young folk are dull and the older ones overplay.

w Walter Reisch, Charles Brackett, Richard Breen *d* Mitchell Leisen *ph* Charles Lang

Gene Tierney, John Lund, Miriam Hopkins, Thelma Ritter, Jan Sterling

A Matter of Dignity*
Greece 1957   104m   bw
Finos (Anis Nohra)
original title: *To Telefteo Psemma*

The daughter of a bankrupt family reluctantly agrees to marry a millionaire, and the family's false values lead to tragedy.

Rather offbeat melodrama with the director in good form.

wd Michael Cacoyannis *ph* Walter Lassally *m* Manos Hadjidakis

Ellie Lambetti, Georges Pappas, Athena Michaelidou

A Matter of Life and Death****

GB 1946   104m   Technicolor

GFD / Archers (Michael Powell, Emeric Pressburger)

US title: *Stairway to Heaven*

A pilot with brain damage after bailing out is torn between this world and the next, but an operation puts things to rights.

Outrageous fantasy which seemed more in keeping after the huge death toll of a world war, and in any case learned the Hollywood lesson of eating its cake and still having it, the supernatural elements being capable of explanation. A mammoth technical job in the heavenly sequences, it deserves full marks for its sheer arrogance, wit, style and film flair.

wd Michael Powell, Emeric Pressburger ph Jack Cardiff m Allan Gray pd Hein Heckroth

David Niven, Roger Livesey, Kim Hunter, Marius Goring, Raymond Massey, Abraham Sofaer

'Powell and Pressburger seem to have reached their heaven at last . . . an illimitable Wembley stadium, surrounded by tinkly music and mists, from which all men of insight, if they were ever careless enough to get there, would quickly blaspheme their way out.'—*Richard Winnington*

A Matter of Who

GB 1961   92m   bw

MGM / Foray (Walter Shenson, Milton Holmes)

The World Health Organization tracks down a smallpox outbreak.

Curious blend of semi-documentary with suspense and comedy; not really a starter.

w Milton Holmes *d* Don Chaffey *ph* Erwin Hillier *m* Edwin Astley

Terry-Thomas, Sonja Ziemann, Alex Nicol, Guy Deghy, Richard Briers, Clive Morton, Geoffrey Keen, Martin Benson, Honor Blackman, Carol White

Maya

US 1966   91m   Technicolor   Panavision

MGM / King Brothers (Mary P. Murray, Herman King)

A teenage American boy arrives in India to visit his disillusioned father, who finally comes to understand him only after he has run away.

Good-looking but otherwise uninteresting animal drama which served as the pilot for a TV series.

w John Fante *d* John Berry *ph* Gunter Senftleben *m* Riz Ortolani

Clint Walker, Jay North, I. S. Johar, Sajid Kahn

Mayerling

France / GB 1968   141m   Eastmancolor   Panavision

Corona / Winchester (Robert Dorfmann)

In 1888 the heir to the Habsburg Empire is forced into a suicide pact with his mistress.

Tedious dramatization of historical events which in 1936 had made a delicate French film but in these hands seems an endless and boring manipulation of doubtful events into turgid romance.

wd Terence Young, *novel* Claude Anet *ph* Henri Alekan *m* Francis Lai *pd* Georges Wakhevitch

Omar Sharif, Catherine Deneuve, James Mason, Ava Gardner, James Robertson Justice, Genevieve Page, Ivan Desny, Maurice Teynac

The Mayor of 44th Street

US 1942   86m   bw

RKO (Cliff Reid)

Dance bands are threatened by hooligans demanding protection money.

Boring melodrama with music.

w Lewis R. Foster *d* Alfred E. Green *ph* Robert de Grasse *songs* Mort Greene, Harry Revel

George Murphy, Anne Shirley, Richard Barthelmess, William Gargan, Joan Merrill, Millard Mitchell, Mary Wickes, Freddie Martin and band

AAN: song 'There's a Breeze on Lake Louise'

The Mayor of Hell*

US 1933   90m   bw

Warner

A racketeer becomes superintendent of a reform school, and it changes his life.

Moderate star vehicle with a plot that did yeoman service thereafter in Dead End Kids films.

w Edward Chodorov *d* Archie Mayo *ph* Barney McGill *m* Leo F. Forbstein

James Cagney, Madge Evans, Allen Jenkins, Dudley Digges, Frankie Darro

'Propaganda for nothing: like most of what comes out of Hollywood, it is entertaining trash.'—*Time*

† Remade in 1938 as *Crime School* with Humphrey Bogart, 1939 as *Hell's Kitchen* with Ronald Reagan.

Maytime **
US 1937 132m bw (sepia sequence)
MGM (Hunt Stromberg)

An opera star falls in love with a penniless singer but her jealous impresario shoots him.
Lush romantic musical which turns gradually into melodrama and ends in a ghostly reunion for the lovers. If that's what you like, it could scarcely be better done.

w Noel Langley, *operetta* Rida Johnson Young *d* Robert Z. Leonard *ph* Oliver T. Marsh *m* Sigmund Romberg *md* Herbert Stothart

Jeanette MacDonald, Nelson Eddy, John Barrymore, Herman Bing, Lynne Carver, Rafaela Ottiano, Paul Porcasi, Sig Rumann

AAN: Herbert Stothart

The Maze
US 1953 81m bw 3-D
Allied Artists

The heir to a title also inherits a family curse and turns into a giant frog.
Rather splendidly idiotic horror film which raises plenty of laughs but no frissons.

w Dan Ullman, *story* Maurice Sandoz *d* William Cameron Menzies *ph* Harry Neumann *m* Marlin Skiles

Richard Carlson, Veronica Hurst, Katherine Emery, Michael Pate, Lillian Bond, Hillary Brooke, Owen McGiveney

Me and Marlborough *
GB 1935 84m bw
GFD / Gainsborough (Michael Balcon)

In Marlborough's army, a woman takes the place of her soldier husband to prove his innocence of spying.
Curious period service farce, not quite a success but an interesting attempt at something different.

w Ian Hay, Marjorie Gaffney, *story* W. P. Lipscomb, Reginald Pound *d* Victor Saville

Cicely Courtneidge, Tom Walls, Barry McKay, Alfred Drayton

Me and My Gal *
US 1932 79m bw
Fox
GB title: *Pier 13*

A cop on the beat romances a hashslinger and catches a crook.
Pleasant little programmer, very evocative of its period.

w Arthur Kober *d* Raoul Walsh *ph* Arthur Miller

Spencer Tracy, Joan Bennett, George Walsh, Marion Burns, J. Farrell MacDonald, Noel Madison, Henry B. Walthall

† Remade in 1949 as *Pier 13*.

Me and the Colonel
US 1958 110m bw
Columbia / Court–Goetz (William Goetz)

In 1940 an anti-semitic Polish colonel is obliged to flee from France in the company of a Jewish refugee.
Rather obvious war comedy with predictable but not very entertaining situations, sentiment, action and pathos. The stars cope well enough but the picture never picks up steam.

w S. N. Behrman, George Froeschel, *play* Franz Werfel *d* Peter Glenville *ph* Burnett Guffey *m* George Duning

Danny Kaye, Curt Jurgens, Nicole Maurey, Françoise Rosay, Akim Tamiroff, Martita Hunt, Alexander Scourby, Liliane Montevecchi, Ludwig Stossel

Me, Natalie *
US 1969 111m De Luxe
Cinema Center (Stanley Shapiro)

An unattractive 18-year-old girl moves into Greenwich Village and learns to accept herself as she is.
Basically very predictable but rather well done character study with excellent detail.

w A. Martin Zweiback *d* Fred Coe *ph* Arthur J. Ornitz *m* Henry Mancini

Patty Duke, James Farentino, Martin Balsam, Elsa Lanchester, Salome Jens, Nancy Marchand, Al Pacino

Mean Streets **
US 1973 110m Technicolor
Taplin–Perry–Scorsese (Jonathan T. Taplin)

Four young Italian-Americans use Tony's Bar as a base for drinking, brawling and hustling.
Relentlessly sordid melodrama with a good eye for realistic detail.

w Martin Scorsese, Mardik Martin *d* Martin Scorsese *ph* Norman Gerard

Harvey Keitel, Robert de Niro, David Proval, Amy Robinson, Richard Romanus

'A thicker-textured rot than we have ever had in an American movie, and a deeper sense of evil.'—*New Yorker*

'Lacks a sense of story and structure . . . unless a film-maker respects the needs of his audience, he can't complain if that audience fails to show up.'—*Variety*

'Extraordinarily rich and distinguished on many levels.'—*Joseph Gelmis*

The Mechanic

US 1972   100m   Technicolor
UA / Chartoff / Winkler / Carlino

A professional assassin under contract to the Mafia makes his missions look like accidents.
Violent thriller with a few pretensions, but too flashily made to be taken seriously.

w Lewis John Carlino *d* Michael Winner *ph* Richard Kline, Robert Paynter *m* Jerry Fielding

Charles Bronson, Jan-Michael Vincent, Keenan Wynn, Jill Ireland

A Medal for Benny*

US 1945   77m   bw
Paramount (Paul Jones)

An old rustic is the centre of small town celebrations in honour of his dead war hero son.
Satirical-sentimental location drama, effective but not memorable.

w Frank Butler, *original story* John Steinbeck, Jack Wagner *d* Irving Pichel *ph* Lionel Lindon *m* Victor Young

Dorothy Lamour, Arturo de Cordova, *J. Carrol Naish*, Mikhail Rasumny, Charles Dingle, Frank McHugh, Grant Mitchell

AAN: original story; J. Carrol Naish

Medea*

Italy / France / West Germany 1970   118m
   Eastmancolor
San Marco / Number One / Janus (Franco
   Rossellini, Marina Cicogna)

Jason brings back as his wife the high priestess of the Golden Fleece, but her adjustment is to say the least uncomfortable.
In modern terms the case history of a psychopath, this weird production plays like an opera without music, and seems to have been designed as a vehicle for its charismatic star.

wd Pier Paolo Pasolini, *play* Euripides *ph* Ennio Guarnieri

Maria Callas, Giuseppe Gentile, Laurent Terzieff, Massimo Girotti

The Medium*

Italy 1951   80m   bw
Transfilm (Walter Lowendahl)

A fake medium feels a genuine manifestation, shoots at it and kills her assistant, but is still not sure whether he was responsible.
A filmic but not entirely satisfactory treatment of a modest but popular modern opera.

wd, m Gian-Carlo Menotti, his opera
co-d Alexander Hammid *ph* Enzo Serafin

Marie Powers, Anna Maria Alberghetti, Leo Coleman

AAN: Gian-Carlo Menotti (for music)

Medium Cool**

US 1969   111m   Technicolor
Paramount / H & J Pictures (Tully Friedman)

A TV news cameraman is made apathetic by the events around him.
Stimulating if overlong comment on the quality of life in the sixties, immaculately made and with a rather effective though obvious twist ending.

wd, ph Haskell Wexler *m* Mike Bloomfield *ad* Leon Ericksen

Robert Forster, Verna Bloom, Peter Bonerz, Marianna Hill, Sid McCoy

'A deeply moving questioning of America's violence and voyeurism.'—*Jan Dawson*

'I can't think of any film that tells one more about the texture of American life today.'—*Michael Billington, Illustrated London News*

The Medusa Touch*

GB / France 1978   109m   Technicolor
ITC / Bulldog / Citeca (Arnon Milchan, Elliott Kastner)

A novelist is haunted by the belief that he can cause disaster.
And he does, very predictably, while any intellectual excitement in the script is rapidly replaced by mere mayhem.
Different, but not exciting.

w John Briley, *novel* Peter Van Greenway *d* Jack Gold *ph* Arthur Ibbetson *m* Michael J. Lewis *sp* Doug Ferris

Richard Burton, Lee Remick, Lino Ventura, Harry Andrews, Alan Badel, Jeremy Brett, Michael Hordern, Gordon Jackson

Meet Danny Wilson

US 1952   83m   bw
U-I (Leonard Goldstein)

An overbearing crooner gets to the top with the help of gangsters.
Fairly abrasive star vehicle, almost amounting to self-parody.

w Don McGuire *d* Joseph Pevney *ph* Maury
Gertsman *md* Joseph Gershenson

Frank Sinatra, Shelley Winters, Alex Nicol,
Raymond Burr

Meet John Doe***
US 1941 123m bw
Liberty Films (Frank Capra)

A tramp is hired to embody the common man in
a phony political drive, and almost commits
suicide.
Vividly staged but over-sentimental Capra
extravaganza with high spots outnumbering low.

w Robert Riskin d Frank Capra ph George
Barnes *m* Dmitri Tiomkin

Gary Cooper, *Barbara Stanwyck*, Edward
Arnold, Walter Brennan, James Gleason, Spring
Byington, Gene Lockhart, Rod la Rocque,
Irving Bacon, Regis Toomey, Ann Doran,
Warren Hymer, Andrew Tombes

  'For the sake of a happy ending that would
keep Gary Cooper alive, the meanings were so
distorted that the original authors sued.'—*New
Yorker, 1978*

AAN: original story (Richard Connell, Robert
Presnell)

Meet Me after the Show*
US 1951 88m Technicolor
TCF (George Jessel)

A musical star thinks she has discovered an
affair between her husband and his glamorous
backer.
Surprisingly bright routine musical.

w Mary Loos, Richard Sale *d Richard Sale
ph Arthur E. Arling md* Lionel Newman
songs Jule Styne, Leo Robin

Betty Grable, Macdonald Carey, Rory Calhoun,
Eddie Albert, Irene Ryan

Meet Me at Dawn
GB 1946 99m bw
TCF / Marcel Hellman
US title: *The Gay Duellist*

A professional duellist is commissioned to
provoke a duel with a senator, but unwittingly
hires the senator's daughter to play the injured
party.
A totally laborious and artificial period comedy
which never seems even to aspire to the style
required.

w Lesley Storm, James Seymour, Maurice
Cowan, *story* Le Tueur by Anatole Litvak,
Marcel Achard *d* Thornton Freeland
ph Gunther Krampf *m* Mischa Spoliansky

Hazel Court, William Eythe, Stanley Holloway,

Margaret Rutherford, Basil Sydney, Irene
Browne

Meet Me at the Fair
US 1952 87m Technicolor
U-I (Albert J. Cohen)

In 1900, an orphan joins a travelling medicine
show.
Mildly pleasing open-air comedy drama.

w Irving Wallace, *novel* The Great Companions
by Gene Markey *d* Douglas Sirk *ph* Maury
Gertsman *md* Joseph Gershenson

Diana Lynn, Dan Dailey, Hugh O'Brian, Chet
Allen, Rhys Williams

Meet Me in Las Vegas
US 1956 112m Eastmancolor
  Cinemascope
MGM (Joe Pasternak)
GB title: *Viva Las Vegas!*

A gambler's luck changes when he grabs the
hand of a passing ballerina.
Listless song-and dance extravaganza which
wastes a great deal of talent.

w Isabel Lennart *d* Roy Rowland *ph* Robert
Bronner *m* Georgie Stoll, Johnny Green
ly Sammy Cahn *ch* Eugène Loring, Hermes Pan

Dan Dailey, Cyd Charisse, Agnes Moorehead,
Lili Darvas, Paul Henreid, Oscar Karlweis, Lena
Horne, Jerry Colonna, Frankie Laine

  'A large-scale musical of almost stupefying
banality.'—*MFB*

AAN: Georgie Stoll, Johnny Green

Meet Me in St Louis***
US 1944 113m Technicolor
MGM (Arthur Freed)

Scenes in the life of an affectionate family at the
turn of the century.
Patchy but generally highly agreeable musical
nostalgia with an effective sense of the passing
years and seasons.

w Irving Brecher, Fred F. Finklehoffe, *novel*
Sally Benson *d Vincente Minnelli ph* George
Folsey *md* Georgie Stoll

Judy Garland, Margaret O'Brien, Tom Drake,
Leon Ames, Mary Astor, Lucille Bremer, June
Lockhart, *Harry Davenport*, Marjorie Main,
Joan Carroll, Hugh Marlowe, Robert Sully,
Chill Wills

  'A family group framed in velvet and tinsel . . .
it has everything a romantic musical should
have.'—*Dilys Powell, 1955*

AAN: script; George Folsey; Georgie Stoll;
song 'The Trolley Song' (*m/ly* Ralph Blane,
Hugh Martin)

Meet Me Tonight
GB 1952   85m   Technicolor
Rank / Anthony Havelock Allan

Three short Noel Coward plays: *Red Peppers, Fumed Oak, Ways and Means.*
Regrettably bald treatment of three playlets which have not lasted well. A thoroughly artificial evening.

w/m Noel Coward *d* Anthony Pelissier *ph* Desmond Dickinson

Ted Ray, Kay Walsh, Stanley Holloway, Betty Ann Davies, Nigel Patrick, Valerie Hobson

Meet Mr Lucifer*
GB 1953   81m   bw
Ealing (Monja Danischewsky)

The Demon King in a tatty provincial pantomime dreams he is the devil preventing people from wasting time watching television. Clean and occasionally amusing piece of topical satire on tellymania; but the prologue is funnier than the sketches.

w Monja Danischewsky, *play* Beggar My Neighbour by Arnold Ridley *d* Anthony Pelissier *ph* Desmond Dickinson *m* Eric Rogers

Stanley Holloway, Peggy Cummins, Jack Watling, Barbara Murray, Joseph Tomelty, Gordon Jackson, Jean Cadell, Kay Kendall, Ian Carmichael, Gilbert Harding, Charles Victor, Humphrey Lestocq

Meet Nero Wolfe*
US 1936   73m   bw
Columbia

A corpulent stay-at-home sleuth solves a disappearance and a murder.
The film debut of an engaging crime character, who oddly never made it to a series.

w Howard J. Green, Bruce Manning, Joseph Anthony, *novel* Fer de Lance by Rex Stout *d* Herbert Biberman *ph* Henry Freulich

Edward Arnold, Lionel Stander, Joan Perry, Rita Hayworth, Victor Jory, Nana Bryant, Walter Kingsford, John Qualen

Meet the People
US 1944   100m   bw
MGM (E. Y. Harburg)

A Broadway musical star proves she isn't snooty by taking a job in a shipyard.
Thin propaganda musical which wastes a fair amount of talent.

w S. M. Herzig, Fred Saidy, *play* Louis Lantz, Sol and Ben Barzman *d* Charles Reisner *ph* Robert Surtees *songs* various

Lucille Ball, Dick Powell, Virginia O'Brien, Bert Lahr, Rags Ragland, June Allyson, Steve Geray, Phil Regan, Spike Jones and his City Slickers, Vaughn Monroe and his Orchestra

Melba
GB 1953   113m   Technicolor
Horizon (Sam Spiegel)

The life of the internationally famous Australian opera singer of Victorian days.
Moderately interesting recreation of a woman and an era, though dramatically rather stodgy.

w Harry Kurnitz *d* Lewis Milestone *md* Muir Mathieson *ad* André Andreiev

Patrice Munsel, Robert Morley, Alec Clunes, Martita Hunt, Sybil Thorndike, John McCallum

Melody
GB 1971   106m   Eastmancolor
Hemdale / Sagittarius / Goodtimes
aka: *S.W.A.L.K.*

Calf love at school causes jealousy between two boys.
Tough-sentimental teenage comedy-drama of little interest to adults.

w Alan Parker *d* Waris Hussein *ph* Peter Suschitsky *m* Richard Hewson

Jack Wild, Mark Lester, Tracy Hyde

Melody Time*
US 1948   75m   Technicolor
Walt Disney (Ben Sharpsteen)

An unlinked variety show of cartoon segments. A mainly mediocre selection with the usual moments of high style: *Once upon a Wintertime, Bumble Boogie, Johnny Appleseed, Little Toot, Trees, Blame it on the Samba, Pecos Bill.*

w various *d* various

The Member of the Wedding*
US 1953   91m   bw
Columbia / Stanley Kramer

A 12-year-old girl learns something about life when her sister gets married and a young boy dies.
Boringly contained in a kitchen set, this filmed play has interesting characters but is really not good enough for the talent involved.

w Edna and Edward Anhalt, *play* and *novel* Carson McCullers *d* Fred Zinnemann *ph* Hal Mohr *m* Alex North

Julie Harris, *Ethel Waters,* Brandon de Wilde, Arthur Franz, Nancy Gates, James Edwards

AAN: Julie Harris

The Men*
US 1950   85m   bw
Stanley Kramer
reissue title: *Battle Stripe*

Paraplegic war veterans are prepared for civilian
life; the fiancée of one of them helps overcome
his problems.
Vivid semi-documentary melodrama, at the time
rather shocking in its no-holds-barred treatment
of sexual problems.

w Carl Foreman d Fred Zinnemann ph Robert
de Grasse *m* Dmitri Tiomkin

Marlon Brando, Teresa Wright, Everett Sloane,
Jack Webb, Howard St John
'A completely new experience between men
and women!'—*publicity*
'Don't be misled into feeling that to see this
film is merely a duty; it is, simply, an experience
worth having.'—*Richard Mallett, Punch*

AAN: Carl Foreman

Men Are Not Gods
GB 1937   92m   bw
London (Alexander Korda)

An actor playing Othello nearly strangles his
wife.
Tepid melodramatic attempt at a theme later
used in
A Double Life.

w G. B. Stern, Iris Wright *d* Walter Reisch

Miriam Hopkins, Sebastian Shaw, Rex
Harrison, Gertrude Lawrence, A. E. Matthews,
Val Gielgud, Laura Smithson

The Men in Her Life
US 1941   90m   bw
Columbia (Gregory Ratoff)

A former circus rider becomes a ballerina.
Well-worn rags-to-riches romance of little
interest.

w Frederick Kohner, Michael Wilson, Paul
Trivers, *novel* Ballerina by Lady Eleanor Smith
d Gregory Ratoff *ph* Harry Stradling, Arthur
Miller *md* David Raksin

Loretta Young, Conrad Veidt, Dean Jagger,
Eugenie Leontovich, Shepperd Strudwick, Otto
Kruger, Paul Baratoff

Men in War
US 1957   104m   bw
Security (Sidney Harmon)

Korea 1950: an infantry platoon is cut off from
HQ and tries to take an enemy-occupied hill.
Stereotyped small-scale war heroics; the film
makes its points but fails to entertain.

w Philip Yordan *d* Anthony Mann *ph* Ernest
Haller *m* Elmer Bernstein

Robert Ryan, Robert Keith, Aldo Ray, Vic
Morrow, James Edwardes, Sen Yung

Men in White
US 1934   80m   bw
MGM

An ambitious intern is in love with an attractive
socialite who resents his devotion to duty.
Popular but obvious star drama.

w Waldemar Young, *play* Sidney Kingsley
d Richard Boleslawski *ph* George Folsey

Clark Gable, Myrna Loy, Jean Hersholt,
Elizabeth Allan, Otto Kruger, C. Henry Gordon,
Wallace Ford

Men of Boys' Town
US 1941   106m   bw
MGM (John W. Considine Jnr)

Further adventures of Father Flanagan.
Mushy sequel to *Boys' Town* (qv).

w James Kevin McGuinness *d* Norman Taurog
ph Harold Rosson

Spencer Tracy, Mickey Rooney, Bobs Watson,
Larry Nunn, Lee J. Cobb, Mary Nash, Henry
O'Neill, Darryl Hickman, Anne Revere

Men of the Fighting Lady
US 1954   80m   Anscocolor
MGM (Henry Berman)

Adventures of an aircraft carrier during the
Korean War.
Tepid war actioner with a few effective semi-
documentary sequences of naval tactics.

w Art Cohn *d* Andrew Marton *ph* George
Folsey *m* Miklos Rozsa

Van Johnson, Walter Pidgeon, Louis Calhern,
Dewey Martin, Keenan Wynn, Frank Lovejoy,
Robert Horton

Men of Tomorrow
GB 1932   88m   bw
Paramount (Alexander Korda)

Oxford students have more than academic work
on their minds.
Dim comedy-drama with an interesting cast.

w Arthur Wimperis, Anthony Gibbs, *play*
Young Apollo by Anthony Gibbs *d* Leontine
Sagan

Maurice Braddell, Joan Gardner, Emlyn
Williams, Merle Oberon, Robert Donat

Men of Two Worlds

GB 1946   109m · Technicolor
GFD / Two Cities (John Sutro)
US title: *Witch Doctor*
aka: *Kisenga, Man of Africa*

In Tanganyika, an educated native helps white
men to counter the force of witch doctors and
persuade tribes to leave an infected area.
Earnest but totally unpersuasive semi-
documentary shot in unconvincing sets and
garish colour.

w Thorold Dickinson, Joyce Cary, E. Arnot
Robertson, Herbert Victor *d* Thorold
Dickinson *m* Arthur Bliss

Eric Portman, Phyllis Calvert, Robert Adams,
Orlando Martins, Arnold Marle, Cathleen
Nesbitt, David Horne, Cyril Raymond

Men with Wings

US 1938   106m   Technicolor
Paramount (William Wellman)

Civil aviation pioneers fall out over a girl.
Disappointing epic from the maker of *Wings*,
with highly predictable story line, modest acting
and ho-hum spectacle.

w Robert Carson *d* William Wellman *ph* W.
Howard Greene *m* W. Franke Harling, Gerald
Carbonara

Fred MacMurray, Ray Milland, Louise
Campbell, Andy Devine, Lynne Overman,
Porter Hall, Walter Abel, Virginia Weidler,
Donald O'Connor

Men without Women

US 1932   77m   bw
Fox

Men in a submarine are trapped on the ocean
bed.
Early talkie action drama noted more for its
credits than its accomplishment.

w Dudley Nichols *d* John Ford *ph* Joseph H.
August

Kenneth MacKenna, Frank Albertson, Paul
Page, Pat Somerset, Stuart Erwin, Warren
Hymer, John Wayne

The Mephisto Waltz*

US 1971   109m   De Luxe
TCF / QM Productions

A satanic concert pianist on the point of death
wills his soul into the body of a journalist.
Complex diabolical mumbo-jumbo with plenty
of style.

w Ben Maddow, *novel* Fred Mustard Stewart
d Paul Wendkos *ph* William W. Spencer
m Jerry Goldsmith

Alan Alda, Jacqueline Bisset, Curt Jurgens,
Barbara Parkins

The Mercenaries

GB 1968   100m   Metrocolor   Panavision
MGM / George Englund
US title: *Dark of the Sun*

In the Belgian Congo in 1960 a mercenary
officer is ordered to bring back a fortune in
diamonds by armoured train.
Basically an old-fashioned thriller about the
hazards of a journey beset by brutish villains and
damsels in distress, this unpleasant film is
notable for the amount of sadistic action it crams
into its running time.

w Quentin Werty, Adrian Spies, *novel* Dark of
the Sun by Wilbur Smith *d* Jack Cardiff
ph Edward Scaife *m* Jacques Loussier

Rod Taylor, Yvette Mimieux, Kenneth More,
Jim Brown, Peter Carsten, André Morell, Guy
Deghy, Calvin Lockhart, Alan Gifford

'The violence done to the human body is
matched by violence done to the intelligence by a
stock adventure story given a gloss of topicality
and social insult.'—*Judith Crist*

Merrill's Marauders

US 1962   98m   Technicolor
Cinemascope
Warner / US Pictures (Milton Sperling)

Adventures of a crack US army unit in 1942
Burma.
Physically exhausting war adventure with
emphasis on hand-to-hand fighting and much
bloodshed.

w Samuel Fuller, Milton Sperling *d* Samuel
Fuller *ph* William Clothier *m* Howard Jackson

Jeff Chandler, Ty Hardin, Andrew Duggan,
Peter Brown, Will Hutchins

Merrily We Go to Hell

US 1932   78m   bw
Paramount

A socialite marries a dipsomaniac journalist.
Glum problem drama.

w Edwin Justin Mayer, *novel* I Jerry Take Thee
Joan by Cleo Lucas *d* Dorothy Arzner
ph David Abel

Sylvia Sidney, Fredric March, Adrienne Allen,
Richard Gallagher, Florence Burton, Esther
Howard, Kent Taylor

Merrily We Live*

US 1938   90m   bw
Hal Roach

A zany family hires a chauffeur who is actually a famous writer posing as a tramp.
Quite likeable compound of *My Man Godfrey* and *You Can't Take It with You.*

w Eddie Moran, Jack Jevne *d* Norman Z. McLeod *ph* Norbert Brodine *md* Marvin Hatley

Constance Bennett, Brian Aherne, Billie Burke, Alan Mowbray, Patsy Kelly, Ann Dvorak, Tom Brown, Bonita Granville, Marjorie Rambeau, Clarence Kolb

AAN: Norbert Brodine; Billie Burke; title song (*m* Phil Craig, *ly* Arthur Quenzer)

Merry Andrew
US 1958 103m Metrocolor Cinemascope
MGM / Sol C. Siegel

A stuffy teacher in search of an ancient statue joins a travelling circus.
Deliberately charming star comedy which plumps too firmly for whimsy and, despite its professionalism, provokes barely a smile, let alone a laugh.

w Isabel Lennart, I. A. L. Diamond, *story* Paul Gallico *d/ch* Michael Kidd *ph* Robert Surtees *m* Saul Chaplin *ly* Johnny Mercer

Danny Kaye, Pier Angeli, Baccaloni, Noel Purcell, Robert Coote, Patricia Cutts, Rex Evans, Walter Kingsford, Tommy Rall, Rhys Williams

The Merry Monahans
US 1944 90m bw
Universal (Michael Fessier, Ernest Pagano)

Adventures of a family of vaudeville performers. Acceptable backstage comedy drama with good atmosphere.

w Michael Fessier, Ernest Pagano *d* Charles Lamont *ph* Charles Van Enger *m* Hans Salter

Donald O'Connor, Jack Oakie, Rosemary de Camp, Peggy Ryan, Ann Blyth, Isabel Jewell, John Miljan

AAN: Hans Salter

The Merry Widow*
US 1925 111m (24 fps) bw silent
MGM (Irving Thalberg)

A bankrupt king orders a nobleman to woo a wealthy American widow.
An operetta without music (or dialogue) is usually a poor thing, but the director added a few unpredictable touches.

w Erich Von Stroheim, Benjamin Glazer, *operetta* Victor Leon, Leo Stein *d* Erich Von Stroheim

Mae Murray, John Gilbert, Roy D'Arcy, Tully Marshall

† The story goes that when reproved by Thalberg for wasting film stock on, for instance, endless shots of a wardrobe full of shoes, Von Stroheim remarked: 'The character has a foot fetish.' 'And you,' said Thalberg, 'have a footage fetish!'

The Merry Widow**
US 1934 99m bw
MGM

Patchy, but sometimes sparkling version.

w Samson Raphaelson, Ernest Vajda *d* Ernst Lubitsch *ph* Oliver T. Marsh *m* Franz Lehar

Maurice Chevalier, Jeanette MacDonald, Edward Everett Horton, Una Merkel, George Barbier, Donald Meek, Sterling Holloway, Shirley Ross

The Merry Widow
US 1952 105m Technicolor
MGM (Joe Pasternak)

Chill, empty remake.

w Sonya Levien, William Ludwig *d* Curtis Bernhardt *ph* Robert Surtees

Fernando Lamas, Lana Turner, Richard Haydn, Una Merkel, Thomas Gomez, John Abbott
'Nothing has been omitted (except the spirit of the original).'—*MFB*

Merton of the Movies*
US 1947 82m bw
MGM

An innocent young man in Hollywood becomes a star.
The plot and characterizations of this old chestnut are resistible, but the Hollywood background is well managed and convincing.

w George Wells, Lou Breslow, *novel* Henry Leon Wilson *d* Robert Alton *m* David Snell

Red Skelton, Virginia O'Brien, Alan Mowbray

A Message to Garcia*
US 1936 86m bw
TCF (Raymond Griffith)

During the Spanish–American war a Cuban girl helps an American agent get through to the rebel leader with a diplomatic message.
Agreeable embroidery of a historical incident: good production values and entertaining star performances.

w W. P. Lipscomb, Gene Fowler, *book* Andrew S. Rohan *d* George Marshall *ph* Rudolph Maté *m* Louis Silvers

Wallace Beery, Barbara Stanwyck, John Boles,
Alan Hale, Herbert Mundin, Mona Barrie

Metropolis***

Germany 1926   120m approx (24 fps)   bw
silent
UFA

In the year 2000, the workers in a modernistic
city live underground and unrest is quelled by the
persuasion of a saintly girl, Maria; but a mad
inventor creates an evil Maria to incite them to
revolt.

Always somewhat overlong, and certainly
heavy-going in places, this futuristic fantasy not
only has many brilliant sequences which created
genuine excitement and terror, but it inspired a
great many Hollywood clichés to come, notably
the Frankenstein theme. The BBC's version of
the seventies, with an electronic music sound
track, is the most satisfactory.

w *Thea Von Harbou* d *Fritz Lang* ph *Karl
Freund, Günther Rittau* sp Eugen Schufftan
ad *Otto Hunte, Erich Kettelhut, Karl Vollbrecht*

Brigitte Helm, Alfred Abel, Gustav Fröhlich,
Rudolf Klein-Rogge, Fritz Rasp

'It goes too far and always gets away with
it.'—*New Yorker, 1978*

Mexican Spitfire

A series of second feature comedies nominally
about a young businessman and his
temperamental Mexican wife (Donald Woods
and Lupe Velez), whose interest shifted firmly to
the young man's accident-prone uncle Matt and
his aristocratic boss Lord Epping, both of whom
were played by the rubber-legged Ziegfeld comic
Leon Errol at something near the top of his form.
The plots made little sense, but the hectic
situations provoked hearty roars of laughter.
The films were all made by RKO, and all
directed by Leslie Goodwins.

1939: THE GIRL FROM MEXICO,
MEXICAN SPITFIRE
1940: MEXICAN SPITFIRE OUT WEST
1941: MEXICAN SPITFIRE'S BABY,
MEXICAN SPITFIRE AT SEA
1942: MEXICAN SPITFIRE SEES A
GHOST, MEXICAN SPITFIRE'S
ELEPHANT
1943: MEXICAN SPITFIRE'S BLESSED
EVENT

Michael Shayne

The private eye created by Brett Halliday was
featured in several second features starring
Lloyd Nolan, mostly directed by Eugene Forde
for Fox. They were adequate time-passers
without too much sparkle.

1940: MICHAEL SHAYNE PRIVATE
DETECTIVE
1941: DRESSED TO KILL, JUST OFF
BROADWAY, THE MAN WHO
WOULDN'T DIE
1942: TIME TO KILL (a version of Chandler's
FAREWELL MY LOVELY), BLUE WHITE
AND PERFECT

Mickey One*

US 1965   93m   bw
Columbia / Florin / Tatira (Arthur Penn,
Harrison Starr)

A nightclub entertainer runs away after an orgy
to find some meaning in his life.
Obscure symbolic melodrama whose flashes of
talent and interest needed firmer control.

w Alan Surgal d Arthur Penn ph Ghislain
Cloquet m Eddie Sauter pd George Jenkins

Warren Beatty, Hurd Hatfield, Alexandra
Stewart, Franchot Tone, Teddy Hart, Jeff Corey

'Arresting at first, it becomes more and more
bogged down by its own pretensions, until one's
main interest is simply in seeing it through.'—
MFB

Midas Run

US 1969   104m   Technicolor
Raymond Stross / MPI (Leon Chooluck)
GB title: *A Run on Gold*

An ageing secret service chief plans to hi-jack a
bullion shipment.
Incompetently handled caper story with interest
unwisely shifted for romantic purposes to the
plotter's recruits.

w James D. Buchanan, Ronald Austin, Berne
Giler d Alf Kjellin ph Ken Higgins m Elmer
Bernstein

Fred Astaire, Richard Crenna, Anne Heywood,
Ralph Richardson, Roddy McDowall, Adolfo
Celi, Maurice Denham, Cesar Romero

Middle of the Night**

US 1959   118m   bw
Columbia (George Justin)

An elderly garment manufacturer falls in love
with a young girl.
Serious and moving examination of a human
predicament, shot against beautifully observed
New York backgrounds.

w *Paddy Chayevsky*, from his TV play d Delbert
Mann ph *Joseph Brun* m George Bassman

Fredric March, Kim Novak, Glenda Farrell, Jan
Norris, Lee Grant

'A work of greater cogency than his New York

play script and of deeper maturity than his
Marty.'—*Time*

'The best of the TV transformations into
film.'—*Stanley Kauffmann*

Midnight

US 1934 80m bw
Universal / All Star (Chester Erskine)
aka: *Call It Murder*

A District Attorney finds his own daughter on
the wrong side of the law.
Tepid family melodrama.

wd Chester Erskine, *play* Paul and Claire Sifton

Sidney Fox, O. P. Heggie, Henry Hull,
Humphrey Bogart, Margaret Wycherly, Lynne
Overman, Richard Whorf, Cora Witherspoon

Midnight***

US 1939 95m bw
Paramount (Arthur Hornblow Jnr)

A girl stranded in Paris is hired by an aristocrat
to seduce the gigolo paying unwelcome attention
to his wife.
Sparkling sophisticated comedy which barely
flags until a slightly disappointing ending; all the
talents involved are in excellent form.

w Billy Wilder, Charles Brackett, story Edwin
Justus Mayer, Franz Schultz *d Mitchell Leisen*
ph Charles Lang *m* Frederick Hollander

*Claudette Colbert, Don Ameche, John
Barrymore,* Francis Lederer, Mary Astor,
Elaine Barrie, Hedda Hopper, Rex O'Malley
'Leisen's masterpiece, one of the best
comedies of the thirties.'—*John Baxter, 1968*
'One of the authentic delights of the
thirties.'—*New Yorker, 1976*

Midnight Cowboy***

US 1969 113m De Luxe
UA / Jerome Hellman

A slightly dim-witted Texan comes to New York
to offer his services as a stud for rich ladies, but
spends a hard winter helping a tubercular con
man.
Life in the New York gutter, brilliantly if not too
accurately observed by a master showman with
no heart.

w Waldo Salt, *novel* James Leo Herlihy *d John
Schlesinger ph Adam Holender md* John
Barry *pd* John Robert Lloyd

Jon Voight, Dustin Hoffman, Brenda Vaccaro,
Sylvia Miles, John McGiver
'If only Schlesinger's directorial self-discipline
had matched his luminous sense of scene and his
extraordinary skill in handling actors, this would
have been a far more considerable film.'—
Arthur Schlesinger Jnr (no relation)

'A great deal besides cleverness, a great deal of
good feeling and perception and purposeful
dexterity.'—*Stanley Kauffmann*

AA: best picture; Waldo Salt; John Schlesinger
AAN: Dustin Hoffman; Jon Voight; Sylvia
Miles

Midnight Episode

GB 1950 78m bw
Columbia / Triangle (Thomas Lageard)

An old busker stumbles over a dead body and a
lot of money.
Tame British version of Raimu's French success
Monsieur La Souris, saved only by its star
performance.

w Rita Barisse, Reeve Taylor, Paul Vincent
Carroll, David Evans, William Templeton
d Gordon Parry *ph* Hone Glendining

Stanley Holloway, Natasha Parry, Leslie
Dwyer, Reginald Tate, Meredith Edwards,
Wilfrid Hyde White, Joy Shelton

Midnight Express*

GB 1978 121m Eastmancolor
Columbia / Casablanca (Alan Marshall, David
Puttnam)

Tribulations of an American student arrested in
Turkey for carrying hashish.
Misleadingly-titled wallow in prison atrocities,
extremely well made but certainly not
entertaining and with little discernible point.

w Oliver Stone, *memoir* Billy Hayes *d* Alan
Parker *ph* Michael Seresin *m* Giorgio Moroder

Brad Davis, Randy Quaid, John Hurt, Irene
Miracle, Bo Hopkins

Midnight Lace*

US 1960 108m Eastmancolor
Universal (Ross Hunter, Martin Melcher)

The wife of a rich Londoner is terrorized by
threatening phone calls and voices in the fog.
Thoroughly silly rehash of *Gaslight* and *The Boy
Who Cried Wolf*; its glamorous accoutrements
can't fight a lack of humour or predictable plot
development.

w Ivan Goff, Ben Roberts, *play* Matilda Shouted
Fire by Janet Green *d* David Miller *ph* Russell
Metty *m* Frank Skinner

Doris Day, Rex Harrison, John Gavin, Myrna
Loy, Roddy McDowall, Herbert Marshall,
Natasha Parry, John Williams, Anthony
Dawson, Hermione Baddeley, Richard Ney,
Rhys Williams, Doris Lloyd

The Midnight Man

US 1974 117m Technicolor
Universal / Norlan (Roland Kibbee, Burt
    Lancaster)

An ex-cop, paroled after killing his wife's lover,
takes a job as security guard and runs into a
murder case.

Muddled mystery with pretentious
characterization and bouts of violence.

wd Roland Kibbee, Burt Lancaster, *novel* The
Midnight Lady and the Mourning Man by David
Anthony *ph* Jack Priestley *m* Dave Grusin

Burt Lancaster, Susan Clark, Cameron Mitchell,
Morgan Woodward, Harris Yulin, Robert
Quarry, Joan Lorring, Lawrence Dobin, Ed
Lauter

'A thriller that has the impenetrability of
Chandler but none of the flavour.'—*Tom Milne*

'Efficient enough but lifeless, and burdened
with portentous sentiments about solitude,
violence and the nature of the beast.'—*Sight and
Sound*

Midshipman Easy

GB 1935 77m bw
ABP (Basil Dean, Thorold Dickinson)
US title: *Men of the Sea*

In 1790, young naval officers rescue a girl from
Spanish bandits.

Stilted adventure story with interesting credits.

w Anthony Kimmins, *novel* Frederick Marryat
d Carol Reed

Hughie Green, Margaret Lockwood, Harry
Tate, Robert Adams, Roger Livesey, Lewis
Casson

A Midsummer Night's Dream***

US 1935 117m bw
Warner (Max Reinhardt)

Two pairs of lovers sort out their problems with
fairy help at midnight in the woods of Athens.

Shakespeare's play is treated with remarkable
respect in this super-glamorous Hollywood
adaptation based on the Broadway production
by Max Reinhardt. Much of it comes off, and
visually it's a treat.

w Charles Kenyon, Mary McCall Jnr, *play*
William Shakespeare *d Max Reinhardt,
William Dieterle ph Hal Mohr, Fred Jackman,
Byron Haskin, H. F. Koenekamp*
m Mendelssohn *md Erich Wolfgang Korngold
ch Bronislawa Nijinska ad Anton Grot*

James Cagney, Dick Powell, Jean Muir, Ross
Alexander, Olivia de Havilland, Joe E. Brown,
Hugh Herbert, Arthur Treacher, Frank
McHugh, Otis Harlan, Dewey Robinson, *Victor
Jory*, Verree Teasdale, *Mickey Rooney*, Anita

Louise, Grant Mitchell, Ian Hunter, Hobart
Cavanaugh

'The publicity push behind the film is
tremendous—it is going to be a success or
everyone at Warner Brothers is going to get
fired.'—*Robert Forsythe*

'Its assurance as a work of film technique is
undoubted.'—*John Baxter, 1968*

'Its worst contradiction lies in the way
Warners first ordered up a whole batch of
foreign and high-sounding names to handle
music, dances, general production—and then
turned around and handed them empty vessels
for actors.'—*Otis Ferguson*

AA: photography
AAN: best picture

Midway*

US 1976 131m Technicolor Panavision
    Sensurround
Universal / Mirisch Corporation (Walter
    Mirisch)
GB title: *The Battle of Midway*

The tide turns for the Americans when the
Japanese attack the Pacific island of Midway in
1942.

Noisy flagwaver with confused strategy and too
many stars in small parts.

w Donald S. Sanford *d* Jack Smight *ph* Harry
Stradling Jnr *m* John Williams

Charlton Heston, Henry Fonda, Robert
Mitchum, Glenn Ford, Edward Albert, James
Coburn, Hal Holbrook, Toshiro Mifune, Robert
Wagner, Robert Webber, Ed Nelson, James
Shigeta, Monte Markham, Chris George, Glenn
Corbett

'We are over-informed about the movements
of every ship and plane, under-informed about
how the battle was finally won, and positively
swamped with tedious human interest.'—*Sight
and Sound*

Mighty Joe Young*

US 1949 94m bw
RKO (Merian C. Cooper)

A little girl brings back from Africa a pet gorilla
which grows to enormous size and causes a city
to panic.

Rather tired comic-sentimental follow-up to
King Kong, with a tedious plot and variable
animation but a few endearing highlights.

w Ruth Rose *d* Ernest Schoedsack *ph* J. Roy
Hunt *m* Roy Webb *sp* Willis O'Brien, Ray
Harryhausen

Terry Moore, Ben Johnson, Robert Armstrong,
Frank McHugh, Douglas Fowley

The Mikado*

GB 1939 91m Technicolor
GFD / G and S (Geoffrey Toye, Victor Somlo)

In Japan, a timid official is appointed Lord High
Executioner and finds that his first intended
victim is the Emperor's son, travelling incognito.
Agreeable film version of the classic Gilbert and
Sullivan comic opera, with some of the D'Oyly
Carte Company's most celebrated members in
excellent form.

w Geoffrey Toye, *opera* W. S. Gilbert *m* Arthur
Sullivan *d* Victor Schertzinger

Martyn Green, John Barclay, Sydney Granville,
Kenny Baker, Jean Colin, Constance Willis
† The 1966 version by British Home
Entertainment featured a later D'Oyly Carte
company including John Reed but suffered from
a frozen camera and flat lighting, so that little of
the original vivacity and charm came over.

Mildred Pierce**

US 1945 113m bw
Warner (Jerry Wald)

A dowdy housewife leaves her husband,
becomes the owner (through hard work) of a
restaurant chain, and survives a murder case
before true love comes her way.
A woman's picture par excellence, glossily and
moodily photographed, with a star suffering in
luxury on behalf of the most ungrateful daughter
of all time.

w Ranald MacDougall, Catherine Turney,
novel James M. Cain *d Michael Curtiz
ph Ernest Haller m Max Steiner ad Anton
Grot*

Joan Crawford, Jack Carson, Zachary Scott,
Eve Arden, Ann Blyth, Bruce Bennett, George
Tobias, Lee Patrick, Moroni Olsen
  'The kind of woman most men want—but
shouldn't have!'—*publicity*

AA: Joan Crawford
AAN: best picture; script; Ernest Haller; Eve
Arden; Ann Blyth

The Milkman

US 1950 87m bw
Universal-International (Ted Richmond)

Two milkmen tangle with gangsters.
Odd little comedy which gets the benefit of the
doubt more by bringing its stars together than by
giving them anything to do.

w Albert Beich, James O'Hanlon, Martin
Ragaway, Leonard Stern *d* Charles Barton
ph Clifford Stine *m* Milton Rosen

Donald O'Connor, Jimmy Durante, Joyce
Holden, Piper Laurie, William Conrad, Paul
Harvey, Henry O'Neill

The Milky Way*

US 1936 88m bw
Paramount / Harold Lloyd (Edward Sheldon)

A milkman becomes a prizefighter and
overcomes a gang of crooks.
Modest Harold Lloyd comedy towards the end
of his career; remade as *The Kid from Brooklyn*
(qv).

w Grover Jones, Frank Butler, Richard Connell,
play Lynn Root, Harry Clark *ph* Alfred Gilks
d Leo McCarey

Harold Lloyd, Adolphe Menjou, Verree
Teasdale, Helen Mack, William Gargan, George
Barbier, Lionel Stander
  'The work of many hands, all laid on
expertly.'—*Otis Ferguson*

The Milky Way*

France / Italy 1968 102m Eastmancolor
Greenwich / Medusa (Serge Silberman)

Two tramps set off on pilgrimage from Paris to a
Spanish shrine, and have various surprising
encounters.
A picaresque examination of Catholic doctrine,
full of surface interest but requiring special
knowledge for full appreciation.

w Luis Bunuel, Jean-Claude Carrière *d Luis
Bunuel ph* Christian Matras *m* Luis Bunuel

Laurent Terzieff, Paul Frankeur, Delphine
Seyrig, Edith Scon

Le Million****

France 1931 89m bw
Tobis (Frank Clifford)

An artist and an ingratiating crook search Paris
for a lost lottery ticket.
With its delicate touch, perfect sense of comedy
timing and infectious use of recitative and song,
this is superb screen entertainment using most of
the medium's resources.

wd René Clair, musical comedy Georges Berr,
M. Guillemaud *ph* Georges Périnal *m Georges
Van Parys, Armand Bernard, Philippe Parès
ad* Lazare Meerson

Annabella, René Lefèvre, *Paul Olivier*, Louis
Allibert, Vanda Gréville, Raymond Cordy
  'René Clair at his exquisite best; no one else
has ever been able to make a comedy move with
such delicate inevitability.'—*New Yorker, 1978*
† The style of this film was developed and
expanded in Hollywood by Lubitsch in *One
Hour with You* and by Mamoulian in *Love Me
Tonight.*

Million Dollar Baby
US 1941   100m   bw
Warner (Hal B. Wallis, David Lewis)

A girl inherits a fortune and a lot of problems.
Very predictable but sometimes sprightly
comedy with a hard-working cast.

w Richard Macaulay, Jerry Wald, Casey
Robinson, *story* Miss Wheelwright Discovers
America by Leonard Spiegelgass *d* Curtis
Bernhardt *ph* Charles Rosher

Priscilla Lane, Jeffrey Lynn, Ronald Reagan,
May Robson, Lee Patrick, Helen Westley,
George Barbier, John Qualen, Walter Catlett,
Nan Wynn

Million Dollar Duck
US 1971   92m   Technicolor
Walt Disney (Bill Anderson)

A duck lays eggs with solid gold yolks, which
provoke interest from gangsters as well as the
government.
Minor Disney fantasy borrowed without
permission from
Mr Drake's Duck (qv).

w Roswell Rogers *d* Vincent McEveety
ph William Snyder *m* Buddy Baker

Dean Jones, Sandy Dennis, Joe Flynn

Million Dollar Legs *
US 1932   64m   bw
Paramount

A mythical sport-ridden country decides to enter
the Olympic Games.
The good gags in this film are weighted down by
plodding treatment, and the general effect is
more doleful than funny.

w Harry Myers, Nick Barrows, Joseph L.
Mankiewicz *d* Edward Cline *ph* Arthur Todd

W. C. Fields, Jack Oakie, Andy Clyde, Lyda
Roberti, Ben Turpin, Hugh Herbert, Billy
Gilbert, George Barbier, Susan Fleming

'One of the silliest and funniest pictures ever
made.'—*New Yorker, 1977*

Million Dollar Legs
US 1939   59m   bw
Paramount

College students back a favourite horse.
Very modest collegiate comedy.

w Lewis Foster, Richard English *d* Nick
Grinde *ph* Harry Fischbeck

Betty Grable, John Hartley, Donald O'Connor,
Jackie Coogan, Buster Crabbe, Thurston Hall

Million Dollar Mermaid *
US 1952   115m   Technicolor
MGM (Arthur Hornblow Jnr)
GB title: *The One Piece Bathing Suit*

The story of Australian swimmer Annette
Kellerman.
Inaccurate biopic with a *raison d'être* in its
spectacular aquashow scenes, but nothing at all
new in its script.

w Everett Freeman *d* Mervyn Le Roy
ph George J. Folsey *md* Adolph Deutsch
ch Busby Berkeley

Esther Williams, Victor Mature, Walter
Pidgeon, David Brian, Jesse White, Maria
Tallchief, Howard Freeman

AAN: George J. Folsey

The Million Pound Note *
GB 1954   91m   Technicolor
GFD / Group Films (John Bryan)
US title: *Man with a Million*

A man inherits a million dollars in the form of a
single banknote and finds it difficult to spend.
Fairly pleasing period comedy which wears its
one joke pretty thin but is nicely decorated and
acted.

w Jill Craigie, *story* Mark Twain *d* Ronald
Neame *ph* Geoffrey Unsworth *m* William
Alwyn

Gregory Peck, Jane Griffiths, Ronald Squire,
Joyce Grenfell, A. E. Matthews, Reginald
Beckwith, Hartley Power, Wilfrid Hyde White

A Millionaire for Christy
US 1951   91m   bw
TCF (Bert Friedlob)

A lawyer's secretary is sent to Los Angeles to
inform an heir of his good fortune, and decides to
marry him.
Modest romantic comedy with plenty to be
modest about.

w Ken Englund *d* George Marshall *ph* Harry
Stradling *m* Victor Young

Eleanor Parker, Fred MacMurray, Richard
Carlson, Douglass Dumbrille

The Millionairess *
GB 1960   90m   De Luxe   Cinemascope
TCF / Dimitri de Grunwald (Pierre Rouve)

The richest woman in the world falls for a poor
Indian doctor.
Messy travesty of a Shavian comedy that was
never more than a star vehicle to begin with.
Hardly any of it works despite the star cast, who
are mostly miscast.

w Wolf Mankowitz, *play* Bernard Shaw
d Anthony Asquith *ph* Jack Hildyard
m Georges Van Parys

Sophia Loren, Peter Sellers, Alastair Sim,
Vittorio de Sica, Dennis Price, Gary Raymond,
Alfie Bass, Miriam Karlin, Noel Purcell

'The result, lacking any sort of dramatic
cohesion or continuity and seemingly planned
less as a film than as a series of haphazard
effects, is merely tiring.'—*Peter John Dyer*

Millions like Us **
GB 1943   103m   bw
GFD / Gainsborough (Edward Black)

The tribulations of a family in wartime,
especially of the meek daughter who goes into
war work and marries an airman, who is killed.
Fragmentary but reasonably accurate picture of
the Home Front during World War II; a little
more humour would not have been out of place,
but as propaganda it proved an effective weapon.

wd Frank Launder, Sidney Gilliat ph Jack Cox
md Louis Levy

Patricia Roc, Gordon Jackson, Moore Marriott,
Eric Portman, Anne Crawford, Basil Radford,
Naunton Wayne, Joy Shelton, Megs Jenkins

'There is an unsentimental warmheartedness
which I hope we shall cling to and extend in
filmed representations of the British scene.'—
Richard Winnington
† The only picture Launder and Gilliat directed
side by side on the floor.

Min and Bill **
US 1930   69m   bw
MGM

A boozy old waterfront character and his wife
try to keep her daughter from being placed in
care.
Well-remembered and much-loved character
comedy which led to the even more successful
Tugboat Annie with the same team.

w Frances Marion, Marion Jackson, *play* Dark
Star by Lorna Moon *d* George Hill *ph* Harold
Wenstrom

Marie Dressler, Wallace Beery, Dorothy
Jordan, Marjorie Rambeau, Donald Dillaway,
Russell Hopton

AA: Marie Dressler

The Mind Benders *
GB 1963   113m   bw
Anglo–Amalgamated / Novus (Michael
Relph)

A scientist undergoes an experiment aimed at
depriving him of all sensation. It works too well;

he becomes a sadist; and his colleagues can't
reverse the process.
Matter-of-factly played hocus-pocus with spy
asides; quite gripping while it's on, but in no way
memorable.

w James Kennaway *d* Basil Dearden *ph* Denys
Coop *m* Georges Auric

Dirk Bogarde, John Clements, Mary Ure,
Michael Bryant

The Mind of Mr Soames
GB 1970   98m   Technicolor
Columbia / Amicus (Teresa Bolland)

A man who has lived in a coma for thirty years is
cured but faces the world as a new-born infant.
Ill-advised attempt at science fiction with
meaning; its earnestness becomes a bore.

w John Hale, Edward Simpson, *novel* Charles
Eric Maine *d* Alan Cooke *ph* Billy Williams
m Michael Dress

Terence Stamp, Robert Vaughn, Nigel
Davenport, Donal Donnelly, Christian Roberts,
Vickery Turner, Scott Forbes

Mine Own Executioner ***
GB 1947   108m   bw
London Films

A lay psychiatrist undertakes the care of a
mentally disturbed war veteran, but fails to
prevent him from murdering his wife.
When this film first appeared it seemed like the
first adult drama featuring sophisticated people
to emerge from a British studio. Time and
television have blunted its impact, but it remains
a well told suspense melodrama with memorable
characters.

w Nigel Balchin, from his novel *d Anthony
Kimmins ph* Wilkie Cooper *m* Benjamin
Frankel

Burgess Meredith, Kieron Moore, Dulcie Gray,
Barbara White, Christine Norden

'The first psychoanalytical film that a grown-
up can sit through without squirming.'—
Richard Winnington

Ministry of Fear ***
US 1944   85m   bw
Paramount (Seton I. Miller)

During World War II in England, a man just out
of a mental hospital wins a cake at a village fair
and finds himself caught up in bewildering
intrigues.
Little to do with the novel, but a watchable, well-
detailed little thriller on Hitchcock lines, once
you forgive the usual phoney Hollywood
England.

w Seton I. Miller, *novel* Graham Greene *d* Fritz
Lang *ph* Henry Sharp *m* Victor Young

Ray Milland, Marjorie Reynolds, Carl Esmond,
Hillary Brooke, Dan Duryea, Percy Waram,
Alan Napier, Erskine Sanford

'A crisp and efficiently made thriller with no
pretension to intellectual content.'—*Paul Jensen*

The Miniver Story
GB 1950   104m   bw
MGM (Sidney Franklin)

Mrs Miniver faces the tribulations of post-war
Britain.
Glum sequel to *Mrs Miniver*, with the dauntless
heroine finally succumbing to a glossy but fatal
disease. Well enough made, but very hard to
take.

w Ronald Millar, George Froeschel *d* H. C.
Potter *ph* Joseph Ruttenberg *m* Herbert
Stothart

Greer Garson, Walter Pidgeon, Cathy
O'Donnell, John Hodiak, Leo Genn, Reginald
Owen, Henry Wilcoxon, William Fox, Anthony
Bushell

Minnie and Moskowitz*
US 1971   115m   Technicolor
Universal (Al Rubin)

Two lonely Los Angeles misfits have a bumpy
courtship.
Enjoyably aimless character comedy.

wd John Cassavetes *ph* Arthur J. Ornitz *m* Bob
Harwood

Gena Rowlands, Seymour Cassel

The Miracle
Italy 1948   40m   bw
Tania Film (Roberto Rossellini)

A simple-minded peasant woman is seduced by a
shepherd but believes her baby has been
immaculately conceived.
Curious, rather unsatisfactory parable originally
intended as part of a two-item tribute to the
power of a star actress. (The other section,
Cocteau's *The Human Voice*, was withdrawn for
copyright reasons.)

w Tullio Pinelli, Roberto Rossellini, Federico
Fellini *d* Roberto Rossellini *ph* Aldo Tonti
m Renzo Rossellini

Anna Magnani, Federico Fellini

The Miracle
US 1959   121m   Technirama
Warner (Henry Blanke)

In Spain during the Peninsular War, a nun
breaks her vows in order to follow a British

soldier, and a statue of the Virgin Mary steps
down to take her place.
And that's only the beginning in this very tall
tale, full of heavy breathing, violent action and
religiosity, from the old Max Reinhardt pageant.
Quite incredible, and sloppily done.

w Frank Butler, *play* Karl Vollmoeller *d* Irving
Rapper *ph* Ernest Haller *m* Elmer Bernstein

Carroll Baker, Roger Moore, Walter Slezak,
Vittorio Gassman, Katina Paxinou, Dennis
King, Isobel Elsom, Torin Thatcher

Miracle in Milan**
Italy 1951   101m   bw
PDS / ENIC

A foundling goes to live with the poor on the
outskirts of Milan, and his erstwhile guardian
returns from heaven to help them repel
capitalists and fly away on broomsticks to a
better land.
An unlikely fable which manages to avoid all the
obvious pitfalls and sends one out of the cinema
in a warm glow.

w Cesare Zavattini, Vittorio de Sica, *novel* Toto
il Buono by Cesare Zavattini *d Vittorio de Sica*
ph G. R. Aldo *m* Alessandro Cicognini

Francesco Golisano, Brunella Bovo, Emma
Gramatica, Paolo Stoppa

Miracle in Soho
GB 1957   93m   Eastmancolor
Rank (Emeric Pressburger)

A Soho roadworker falls for a barmaid.
Rudimentary romantic whimsy in an
unconvincing street set, with characters either
too voluble or just plain dull.

w Emeric Pressburger *d* Julian Amyes
ph Christopher Challis *m* Brian Easdale

John Gregson, Belinda Lee, Cyril Cusack

Miracle in the Rain**
US 1954   107m   bw
Warner (Frank P. Rosenberg)

A plain New York girl falls for a soldier; when he
is killed in action, he keeps their appointment on
the church steps as a ghost.
Archetypal Hollywood schmaltz, half acute
observation of amusing types, half sentimental
whimsy, with a final supernatural touch of eating
your cake and having it.

*w Ben Hecht d Rudolph Maté ph Russell
Metty m Franz Waxman*

Janey Wyman, Van Johnson, Fred Clark, Eileen
Heckart, William Gargan

The Miracle Man
US 1932 85m bw
Paramount

A gang of crooks is reformed by a faith healer they have exploited.
Adequate remake of the silent Lon Chaney vehicle; no sparks this time.

w Waldemar Young, Samuel Hoffenstein, *play* Frank L. Packard, George M. Cohan *d* Norman Z. McLeod *ph* David Abel

Sylvia Sidney, Chester Morris, Irving Pichel, John Wray, Robert Coogan, Hobart Bosworth, Boris Karloff, Ned Sparks, Virginia Bruce

The Miracle of Morgan's Creek****
US 1944 99m bw
Paramount (Preston Sturges)

Chaos results when a stuttering hayseed tries to help a girl accidentally pregnant by a soldier she met hazily at a dance.
Weird and wonderful one-man assault on the Hays Office and sundry other American institutions such as motherhood and politics; an indescribable, tasteless, roaringly funny mêlée, as unexpected at the time as it was effective, like a kick in the pants to all other film comedies.

wd Preston Sturges *ph* John Seitz *m* Leo Shuken, Charles Bradshaw

Betty Hutton, Eddie Bracken, William Demarest, Diana Lynn, Porter Hall, Akim Tamiroff, Brian Donlevy, Alan Bridge
'Like taking a nun on a roller coaster.'—*James Agee*
'This film moves in a fantastic and irreverent whirl of slapstick, nonsense, farce, sentiment, satire, romance, melodrama—is there any ingredient of dramatic entertainment except maybe tragedy and grand opera that hasn't been tossed into it?'—*National Board of Review*
'Bad taste or no bad taste, I thoroughly enjoyed it.'—*Richard Mallett, Punch*
AAN: Preston Sturges (as writer)

The Miracle of Our Lady of Fatima
US 1952 102m Warnercolor
Warner (Bryan Foy)

An account of the 1917 appearance of the Virgin Mary to three Portuguese peasant children.
Poorly staged religious film which manages to be less pro-Catholic than anti-communist, and was clearly seen by Jack L. Warner as a means of atoning for *Mission to Moscow*. A real cold war piece.

w Crane Wilbur, James O'Hanlon *d* John Brahm *ph* Edwin DuPar *m* Max Steiner *ad* Edward Carrere

Gilbert Roland, Frank Silvera, Angela Clarke, Jay Novello
AAN: Max Steiner

The Miracle of the Bells
US 1948 120m bw
Jesse L. Lasky

The death of a glamorous film star causes a small-town miracle and a nationwide publicity stunt.
One hopes that this oddity was intended as a satire; as a straight entertainment it's more than a little icky, and good production values scarcely help.

w Ben Hecht, *novel* Russell Janney *d* Irving Rapper *ph* Robert de Grasse *m* Leigh Harline

Fred MacMurray, Alida Valli, Frank Sinatra, Lee J. Cobb
'An offensive exhibition of vulgar insensitivity.'—*MFB*
'I hereby declare myself the founding father of the Society for the Prevention of Cruelty to God.'—*James Agee*

The Miracle of the White Stallions*
US 1962 118m Technicolor
Walt Disney (Peter V. Herald)
GB title: *The Flight of the White Stallions*

During World War II the Nazis occupy Vienna and the owner of the Spanish Riding School guides his stallions to safety.
Adequate family adventure fare with a dull hero but interesting backgrounds.

w A. J. Carothers *d* Arthur Hiller *ph* Gunther Anders *m* Paul Smith

Robert Taylor, Lilli Palmer, Eddie Albert, Curt Jurgens

Miracle on Main Street*
US 1936 76m bw
RKO / Jack Skirball

A cabaret dancer finds an abandoned baby but her plans are thwarted by the return of her husband.
Odd, interesting but flatly handled melodrama.

w Sam Ornitz, Boris Ingster, *story* Felix Jackson *d* Steve Sekely *ph* Charles Van Enger

Walter Abel, Margo, William Collier, Jane Darwell, Lyle Talbot, Wynne Gibson

Miracle on 34th Street***
US 1947 94m bw
TCF (William Perlberg)
GB title: *The Big Heart*

A department store Santa Claus claims to be the real thing.

Mainly charming comedy fantasy which quickly became an American classic but does suffer from a few dull romantic stretches.

wd George Seaton, *story* Valentine Davies *ph* Charles Clarke, Lloyd Ahern *m* Cyril Mockridge

Edmund Gwenn, Maureen O'Hara, John Payne, Natalie Wood, Gene Lockhart, Porter Hall, William Frawley, Jerome Cowan, Thelma Ritter

AA: George Seaton (as writer); Valentine Davies; Edmund Gwenn
AAN: best picture

The Miracle Woman*
US 1932 90m bw
Columbia (Harry Cohn)

A lady evangelist turns confidence trickster. Mild satirical drama inspired by the career of Aimée Semple Macpherson.

w Jo Swerling, *play* Bless You Sister by Robert Riskin, John Meehan *d* Frank Capra *ph* Joseph Walker *m* uncredited

Barbara Stanwyck, Sam Hardy, David Manners, Beryl Mercer, Russell Hopton
'Such a beauty, well staged and handsomely lighted.'—*New Yorker, 1977*

The Miracle Worker*
US 1962 106m bw
UA / Playfilms (Fred Coe)

The childhood of Helen Keller, taught by Annie Sullivan after being left blind, deaf and dumb in an illness.
A moving real-life story is given hysterical treatment and the good scenes have a hard task winning through; in any case a documentary might have been more persuasive.

w William Gibson, from his play *d* Arthur Penn *ph* Ernest Caparros *m* Laurence Rosenthal *ad* George Jenkins

Anne Bancroft, Patty Duke, Victor Jory, Inga Swenson, Andrew Prine, Beah Richards

AA: Anne Bancroft; Patty Duke
AAN: William Gibson; Arthur Penn

Mirage***
US 1965 109m bw
U-I (Harry Keller)

During a New York power blackout, an executive falls to his death from a skyscraper and a cost accountant loses his memory.
Striking puzzler, rather slowly developed but generally effective and with a strong sense of place and timing.

w Peter Stone, *novel* Howard Fast *d* Edward Dmytryk *ph* Joe MacDonald *m* Quincy Jones

Gregory Peck, Diane Baker, Walter Abel, *Walter Matthau*, Leif Erickson, Kevin McCarthy

Miranda*
GB 1947 80m bw
GFD / Gainsborough

A doctor on holiday in Cornwall catches a mermaid and takes her to London disguised as an invalid.
Simple-minded comedy which scores a few easy laughs on obvious targets.

w Peter Blackmore, from his play *d* Ken Annakin *ph* Ray Elton *m* Temple Abady

Glynis Johns, Griffith Jones, Googie Withers, *Margaret Rutherford*, David Tomlinson, Sonia Holm, John McCallum
† Sequel 1949, *Mad about Men.*

Les Misérables****
US 1935 109m bw
Twentieth Century (Darryl F. Zanuck)

Unjustly convicted and sentenced to years in the galleys, Jean Valjean emerges to build up his life again but is hounded by a cruel and relentless police officer.
Solid, telling, intelligent version of a much-filmed classic novel; in adaptation and performance it is hard to see how this film could be bettered.

w W. P. Lipscomb, *novel* Victor Hugo *d* Richard Boleslawski *ph* Gregg Toland *m* Alfred Newman

Fredric March, Charles Laughton, Cedric Hardwicke, Rochelle Hudson, Frances Drake, John Beal, Jessie Ralph, Florence Eldridge
'A superlative effort, a thrilling, powerful, poignant picture.'—*New York Evening Post*
'Deserving of rank among the cinema's finest achievements.'—*New York World Telegram*
† Other versions of the story: 1909, 1913 (French); 1917 (William Farnum); 1923 (French: Gabriel Gabrio); 1929 as *The Bishop's Candlesticks* (Walter Huston); 1934 (French: Harry Baur); 1946 (Italian: Gino Cervi); 1952 (see below); 1956 (French: Jean Gabin); 1978 (British: Richard Jordan).

AAN: best picture; Gregg Toland

Les Misérables**
US 1952 106m bw
TCF (Fred Kohlmar)

Solemn remake, well done but lacking the spark of inspiration.

w Richard Murphy *d* Lewis Milestone *ph* Joseph La Shelle *m* Alex North

Michael Rennie, Robert Newton, Edmund

Gwenn, Debra Paget, Cameron Mitchell, Sylvia Sidney, Elsa Lanchester, James Robertson Justice, Joseph Wiseman, Rhys Williams

The Misfits *
US 1961   124m   bw
UA / Frank E. Taylor

Cowboys gather in the Nevada desert to rope wild mustangs, and a divorcee becomes involved with one of them.
Ill-fated melodrama whose stars both died shortly afterwards; a solemn, unattractive, pretentious film which seldom stops wallowing in self-pity.

w Arthur Miller d John Huston ph Russell Metty m Alex North

Clark Gable, Marilyn Monroe, Montgomery Clift, Eli Wallach, Thelma Ritter, James Barton, Estelle Winwood, Kevin McCarthy

Miss Annie Rooney
US 1942   86m   bw
Edward Small

Poor Irish girl loves rich boy.
A totally routine offering for a teenage star; no wonder she didn't make it.

w George Bruce d Edwin L. Marin ph Lester White md Edward Paul

Shirley Temple, William Gargan, Guy Kibbee, Dickie Moore, Peggy Ryan, Gloria Holden, Jonathan Hale, Mary Field

Miss Grant Takes Richmond *
US 1949   87m   bw
Columbia (S. Sylvan Simon)
GB title: *Innocence Is Bliss*

A dumb secretary helps defeat crooks and improve the local housing situation.
Mildly amusing star comedy.

w Nat Perrin, Devery Freeman, Frank Tashlin d Lloyd Bacon ph Charles Lawton Jnr m Heinz Roemheld md Morris Stoloff

Lucille Ball, William Holden, Janis Carter, James Gleason, Gloria Henry, Frank McHugh, George Cleveland

Miss London Ltd
GB 1943   99m   bw
GFD / Gainsborough (Edward Black)

An escort agency is formed to assist soldiers on leave.
Flagwaving light entertainment with popular performers of the time.

w Val Guest, Marriott Edgar d Val Guest

Arthur Askey, Anne Shelton, Evelyn Dall,

Richard Hearne, Max Bacon, Jack Train, Peter Graves, Jean Kent

Miss Marple
Agatha Christie's inquisitive spinster detective was brought to the screen by director George Pollock and star Margaret Rutherford in four increasingly disappointing films for MGM.

1962: MURDER SHE SAID (qv)
1963: MURDER AT THE GALLOP
1964: MURDER MOST FOUL, MURDER AHOY

Miss Pinkerton *
US 1932   66m   bw
Warner

A private nurse helps a police detective to solve a murder case.
Pleasing little mystery comedy.

w Lilyan Hayward, Niven Busch, *story* Mary Roberts Rinehart d Lloyd Bacon ph Barney McGill

Joan Blondell, George Brent, Mae Madison, John Wray, Ruth Hall, C. Henry Gordon, Elizabeth Patterson
† Remade as *The Nurse's Secret* (1946).

Miss Sadie Thompson *
US 1953   91m   Technicolor   3-D
Columbia (Lewis J. Rachmil)

Vigorous semi-musical remake of *Rain* (qv); a good star vehicle, but not otherwise notable.

w Harry Kleiner d Curtis Bernhardt ph Charles Lawton md George Duning

Rita Hayworth, Jose Ferrer, Aldo Ray, Russell Collins, Harry Bellaver

AAN: song 'Blue Pacific Blues' (m Lester Lee, ly Ned Washington)

Miss Susie Slagle's
US 1946   88m   bw
Paramount (John Houseman)

Romances of nursing students in 1910 Baltimore.
Modest melodramatic potboiler.

w Anne Froelich, Hugo Butler, *novel* Augusta Tucker d John Berry ph Charles Lang Jnr m Daniele Amfitheatrof

Veronica Lake, Joan Caulfield, Sonny Tufts, Lillian Gish, Ray Collins, Billy de Wolfe, Bill Edwards, Roman Bohnen, Morris Carnovsky, Lloyd Bridges

Miss Tatlock's Millions *
US 1948   101m   bw
Paramount (Charles Brackett)

A stunt man impersonates the idiot heir to a fortune.

Tasteless but quite funny comedy with a cast of eccentrics indulging in enjoyable fooling.

w Charles Brackett, Richard L. Breen
d Richard Haydn ph Charles Lang Jnr
m Victor Young

John Lund, Wanda Hendrix, Monty Woolley, Barry Fitzgerald, Robert Stack, Ilka Chase, Dorothy Stickney

Mission to Moscow**
US 1943 112m bw
Warner (Robert Buckner)

The Russian career of US Ambassador Joseph E. Davies.

Stodgy but fascinating wartime propaganda piece viewing the Russians as warm-hearted allies; in the later days of the McCarthy witch hunt, Jack L. Warner regretted he had ever allowed it to be made.

w Howard Koch, book Joseph E. Davies
d Michael Curtiz ph Bert Glennon m Max Steiner

Walter Huston, Ann Harding, Oscar Homolka, George Tobias, Gene Lockhart, Eleanor Parker, Richard Travis, Helmut Dantine, Victor Francen, Henry Daniell, Barbara Everest, Dudley Field Malone, Roman Bohnen, Maria Palmer, Moroni Olsen, Minor Watson

Mississippi*
US 1935 80m bw
Paramount (Arthur Hornblow Jnr)

A showboat singer has a cloud on his reputation. Mild period musical with occasional stops for comedy.

w Herbert Fields, Claude Binyon, story Booth Tarkington d Edward A. Sutherland
ph Charles Lang m/ly Rodgers and Hart

Bing Crosby, W. C. Fields, Joan Bennett, Gail Patrick, Claude Gillingwater, John Miljan, Queenie Smith

Mississippi Gambler
US 1953 98m Technicolor
U-I (Ted Richmond)

A showboat gambler has trouble with a bad loser, but finally marries his sister.
Picturesque star melodrama with period settings and not much meat in the story.

w Seton I. Miller d Rudolph Maté ph Irving Glassberg m Frank Skinner

Tyrone Power, Piper Laurie, John McIntyre, Julia Adams, Dennis Weaver

The Missouri Breaks
US 1976 126m De Luxe
UA / Elliott Kastner / Robert B. Sherman

Montana ranchers and rustlers fight over land and livestock, and a hired killer shoots it out with a horse thief.
Savage, dislikeable western with both stars over the top.

w Thomas McGuane d Arthur Penn
ph Michael Butler m John Williams

Marlon Brando, Jack Nicholson, Randy Quaid, Kathleen Lloyd, Frederic Forrest, Harry Dean Stanton

'It is typical of the film's richness and ambiguity that the title has about five possible punning meanings.'—Michael Billington, Illustrated London News

Mr Ace
US 1946 84m bw
Benedict Bogeaus

A rich, spoiled congresswoman is backed by a gangster but gets religion.
Odd star drama, perfunctorily made.

w Fred Finklehoffe d Edwin L. Marin ph Karl Struss m Heinz Roemheld

Sylvia Sidney, George Raft, Stanley Ridges, Sara Haden, Jerome Cowan

Mr and Mrs Smith*
US 1941 95m bw
RKO (Harry E. Edington)

A much-married couple discover that their marriage wasn't legal.
Smartish matrimonial comedy, surprisingly but not obviously directed by the master of suspense.

w Norman Krasna d Alfred Hitchcock
ph Harry Stradling m Edward Ward

Carole Lombard, Robert Montgomery, Gene Raymond, Jack Carson, Philip Merivale, Lucile Watson, William Tracy

'I doubt that your interest or amusement will last as long as the picture.'—Otis Ferguson

Mr Belvedere Goes to College*
US 1949 88m bw
TCF (Samuel G. Engel)

A self-styled genius goes back to school and helps a college widow.
Flat follow up to Sitting Pretty (qv), with only a few laughs.

w Richard Sale, Mary Loos, Mary McCall Jnr
d Elliott Nugent ph Lloyd Ahern m Alfred Newman

Clifton Webb, Shirley Temple, Alan Young,

Tom Drake, Jessie Royce Landis, Kathleen
Hughes, Taylor Holmes

Mr Belvedere Rings the Bell*
US 1951   87m   bw
TCF (André Hakim)

Imperturbable Mr Belvedere enters an old folks'
home under false pretences to test his theories of
ageing.
A not unagreeable star vehicle for those who can
stand the sentiment.

w Ranald MacDougall, *play* The Silver Whistle
by Robert E. McEnroe *d* Henry Koster
ph Joseph La Shelle *m* Cyril Mockridge

Clifton Webb, Joanne Dru, Hugh Marlowe,
Zero Mostel, Doro Merande

Mr Billion*
US 1977   93m   De Luxe
TCF / Pantheon Gabriel Katzka, Steve Bach,
   Ken Friedman)

An Italian garage mechanic becomes heir to a
vast estate, providing he can get to San
Francisco in time for the signing ceremony and
outwit the villains trying to stop him.
Moderately engaging old-fashioned comedy-
adventure.

w Ken Friedman, Jonathan Kaplan *d* Jonathan
Kaplan *ph* Matthew F. Leonetti *m* Dave
Grusin

Terence Hill, Valerie Perrine, Jackie Gleason,
Slim Pickens, William Redfield, Chill Wills

Mr Blandings Builds His Dream House***
US 1948   84m   bw
RKO (Norman Panama, Melvin Frank)

A New York advertising man longs to live in the
Connecticut countryside, but finds the way to
rural satisfaction is hard.
It hasn't the lightness and brightness of the book,
but this is a fun film for the middle-aged who like
to watch three agreeable stars doing their thing.

w *Norman Panama, Melvin Frank, novel* Eric
Hodgkin
d H. C. Potter *ph* James Wong Howe *m* Leigh
Harline *md* Constantin Bakaleinikoff

*Cary Grant, Myrna Loy, Melvyn Douglas,
Reginald Denny,* Louise Beavers, Ian Wolfe,
Harry Shannon, Nestor Paiva, Jason Robards
   'A bulls-eye for middle-class middlebrows.'—
James Agee
   'I loved it. That was really a pleasure to
make.'—*H. C. Potter, 1973*

Mister Buddwing
US 1966   99m   bw
MGM / DDD / Cherokee (Douglas Laurence,
   Delbert Mann)
GB title: *Woman without a Face*

An amnesiac wakes up in Central Park and goes
in search of his identity.
Rather muddled melodrama in which the
characters are so dull that by the time the
flashbacks fall into place we scarcely care.

w Dale Wassermann, *novel* Buddwing by Evan
Hunter *d* Delbert Mann *ph* Ellsworth
Fredericks *m* Kenyon Hopkins

James Garner, Jean Simmons, Angela
Lansbury, Suzanne Pleshette, Katharine Ross,
George Voskovec, Jack Gilford, Joe Mantell,
Raymond St Jacques

Mister Cory
US 1957   92m   Eastmancolor
   Cinemascope
U-I (Robert Arthur)

A small-time gangster leaves the Chicago slums
to seek fame and fortune among the country-
club set.
Modest star comedy drama.

wd Blake Edwards *ph* Russell Metty *m* Joseph
Gershenson

Tony Curtis, Martha Hyer, Charles Bickford,
Kathryn Grant

Mr Deeds Goes to Town***
US 1936   118m   bw
Columbia (Frank Capra)

A small-town poet inherits a vast fortune and
sets New York on its heels by his honesty.
What once was fresh and charming now seems
rather laboured in spots, and the production is
parsimonious indeed, but the courtroom scene
still works, and the good intentions conquer all.

w *Robert Riskin, story* Opera Hat by Clarence
Budington Kelland *d Frank Capra ph* Joseph
Walker *md* Howard Jackson

Gary Cooper, Jean Arthur, Raymond Walburn,
Lionel Stander, Walter Catlett, George
Bancroft, Douglass Dumbrille, H. B. Warner,
Ruth Donnelly, *Margaret Seddon, Margaret
McWade*
   'I have an uneasy feeling he's on his way out.
He's started to make pictures about themes
instead of people.'—*Alistair Cooke*
   'Everywhere the picture goes, from the
endearing to the absurd, the accompanying
business is carried through with perfect zip and
relish.'—*Otis Ferguson*

AA: Frank Capra

AAN: best picture; Robert Riskin; Gary Cooper

Mr Denning Drives North

GB 1951   93m   bw

London Films (Anthony Kimmins, Stephen
   Mitchell)

A wealthy man accidentally kills a criminal in
love with his daughter; he hides the body, which
then disappears.

Initially suspenseful but finally disappointing
melodrama which seems to lack a twist or two.

w Alec Coppel d Anthony Kimmins ph John
Wilcox m Benjamin Frankel

John Mills, Phyllis Calvert, Sam Wanamaker,
Freda Jackson

Mr Dodd Takes the Air

US 1937   78m   bw

Warner (Mervyn Le·Roy)

A country cousin becomes a hit as a crooner.
Modest comedy for small towns.

w William Wister Haines, Elaine Ryan,
story Clarence Budington Kelland d Alfred E.
Green ph Arthur Edeson songs Al Dubin,
Harry Warren

Kenny Baker, Jane Wyman, Alice Brady,
Gertrude Michael, Frank McHugh, Luis
Alberni, Henry O'Neill, Harry Davenport

AAN: Al Dubin and Harry Warren for
'Remember Me'

Mr Drake's Duck**

GB 1950   85m   bw

Daniel M. Angel / Douglas Fairbanks

A duck lays a uranium egg, and a gentleman
farmer finds himself at the centre of international
military disagreement.

Brisk and amusing minor comedy deploying
British comic types to good purpose.

wd Val Guest, radio play Ian Messiter ph Jack
Cox

Douglas Fairbanks Jnr, Yolande Donlan,
Wilfrid Hyde White, A. E. Matthews, Jon
Pertwee, Reginald Beckwith, Howard Marion-
Crawford, Peter Butterworth, Tom Gill

Mister 880**

US 1950   90m   bw

TCF (Julian Blaustein)

An elderly counterfeiter perplexes the US Secret
Service.

Whimsical star comedy which moves along
cheerfully enough to be a good example of the
Hollywood programmer at its prime.

w Robert Riskin d Edmund Goulding
ph Joseph La Shelle m Sol Kaplan

Edmund Gwenn, Burt Lancaster, Dorothy
McGuire, Millard Mitchell

AAN: Edmund Gwenn

Mr Emmanuel*

GB 1944   97m   bw

Two Cities (William Sistrom)

In 1936 an elderly Jew visits Germany in search
of the mother of an orphan boy.

Simply made but quite effective and unusual
story giving Aylmer his only star part.

w Gordon Wellesley, Norman Ginsburg, novel
Louis Golding d Harold French

Felix Aylmer, Greta Gynt, Walter Rilla, Peter
Mullins, Ursula Jeans, Elspeth March, Meier
Tzelniker

Mr Forbush and the Penguins*

GB 1971   101m   Technicolor

EMI / PGI / Henry Trettin

A biologist is sent to the Antarctic to study
penguins, and gets a new understanding of life.
Rather broken-backed animal film with a moral;
pleasant enough, its two halves don't fit together.

w Anthony Shaffer, novel Graham Billey d Roy
Boulting, Arne Sucksdorff ph Harry Waxman,
Ted Scaife m John Addison

John Hurt, Hayley Mills, Tony Britton

Mr Hobbs Takes a Vacation*

US 1962   116m   De Luxe   Cinemascope

TCF (Jerry Wald)

A city dweller takes a seaside house for a family
holiday, but it turns out to be a crumbling ruin.

Overlong, sloppy comedy which devotes too
much time to teenage romance but manages
occasional smiles.

w Nunnally Johnson, novel Edward Streeter
d Henry Koster ph.W. C. Mellor m Henry
Mancini

James Stewart, Maureen O'Hara, Fabian, John
Saxon, Marie Wilson, Reginald Gardiner, John
McGiver

Mr Imperium

US 1951   87m   Technicolor

MGM (Edwin H. Knopf)

GB title: You Belong to My Heart

An exiled king in Hollywood meets a famous film
star with whom he once had a romance.

Minor romantic drama with songs.

w Edwin Knopf, Don Hartman d Don

Hartman *ph* George J. Folsey *songs* Harold Arlen *m* Bronislau Kaper

Lana Turner, Ezio Pinza, Marjorie Main, Barry Sullivan, Cedric Hardwicke, Debbie Reynolds

Mr Klein*

France / Italy 1976 123m Eastmancolor
Lira / Adel / Nova / Mondial Te-Fi (Raymond Danon, Alain Delon)

In 1942 Paris, a prosperous antique dealer is mistaken for a mysterious Jew of the same name, and despite the danger gradually assumes his identity.
Complex Kafkaesque character study: occasionally arresting but generally rather glum.

w Franco Solinas *d* Joseph Losey *ph* Gerry Fisher *m* Egisto Macchi, Pierre Porte

Alain Delon, Jeanne Moreau, Suzanne Flon, Michael Lonsdale, Lous Seigner, Juliet Berto

Mr Lucky*

US 1943 98m bw
RKO (David Hempstead)

During World War II a gambling ship owner goes straight and instigates Bundles for Britain. Unconvincing mixture of comedy and drama with the actors looking somewhat bewildered.

w Milton Holmes, Adrian Scott *d* H. C. Potter *ph* George Barnes *m* Roy Webb

Cary Grant, Laraine Day, Charles Bickford, Gladys Cooper, Alan Carney, Henry Stephenson, Paul Stewart, Walter Kingsford
† Remade 1950 as *Gambling House.*

Mr Majestyk*

US 1974 103m De Luxe
UA / Mirisch (Walter Mirisch)

A Colorado melon grower crosses swords with the local Mafia.
Violent but unexpectedly enjoyable action melodrama.

w Elmore Leonard *d* Richard Fleischer *ph* Richard Kline *m* Charles Bernstein

Charles Bronson, Al Lettieri, Linda Cristal, Lee Purcell, Paul Keslo

Mister Moses*

GB 1965 103m Technicolor Panavision
UA / Frank Ross / Talbot

A quack doctor is the only person who can persuade an African tribe to move before their land is flooded, and he leads them to their promised land.
Adventure spectacle with naïve biblical parallels; quite agreeable.

w Charles Beaumont, Monja Danischewsky,

novel Max Catto *d* Ronald Neame *ph* Oswald Morris *m* John Barry

Robert Mitchum, Carroll Baker, Ian Bannen, Alexander Knox, Reginald Beckwith, Raymond St Jacques

Mr Moto

The Japanese detective created by John P. Marquand and played by Peter Lorre figured in several above-average second features of the late thirties, but the outbreak of war caused him to vanish. The casts were interesting, the TCF production excellent, and the director usually Norman Foster. The 1965 attempt to revive the character with Henry Silva was painfully boring.

1937: THINK FAST MR MOTO (with Virginia Field, Sig Rumann), THANK YOU MR MOTO (with Pauline Frederick, Sidney Blackmer)
1938: MR MOTO'S GAMBLE (with Keye Luke, Lynn Bari), MR MOTO TAKES A CHANCE (with Rochelle Hudson, J. Edward Bromberg), MYSTERIOUS MR MOTO (with Henry Wilcoxon, Erik Rhodes)
1939: MR MOTO'S LAST WARNING (with Ricardo Cortez, George Sanders, Robert Coote, John Carradine), MR MOTO IN DANGER ISLAND (with Jean Hersholt, Warren Hymer), MR MOTO TAKES A VACATION (with Joseph Schildkraut, Lionel Atwill)
1965: THE RETURN OF MR MOTO

Mr Music*

US 1950 113m bw
Paramount (Robert L. Welch)

A college girl is employed to keep an idle middle-aged songwriter's nose to the grindstone.
Bland musical remake of *Accent on Youth* (qv); pleasant performances, moments of comedy, guest stars.

w Arthur Sheekman *d* Richard Haydn *ph* George Barnes *songs* Johnny Burke, James Van Heusen *ad* Hans Dreier, Earl Hedrick

Bing Crosby, Nancy Olson, Charles Coburn, Ruth Hussey, Marge and Gower Champion, Peggy Lee, Groucho Marx

Mr Peabody and the Mermaid

US 1948 89m bw
U-I (Nunnally Johnson)

A middle-aged husband imagines an affair with a mermaid.
Bone-headed quick-cash-in on *Miranda* (qv); it never begins to work.

w Nunnally Johnson, *novel* Guy and Constance Jones *d* Irving Pichel *ph* Russell Metty *m* Robert Emmett Dolan

William Powell, Ann Blyth, Irene Hervey, Andrea King, Clinton Sundberg

Mr Perrin and Mr Traill*
GB 1948   92m   bw
GFD / Two Cities

A handsome young master at a boys' school incurs the jealousy of an embittered colleague. Flat, over-acted but mildly watchable picturization of a well-known story.

w L. A. G. Strong, *novel* Hugh Walpole d Lawrence Huntington *ph* Erwin Hillier m Alan Gray

Marius Goring, David Farrar, Greta Gynt, Edward Chapman, Raymond Huntley, Mary Jerrold, Finlay Currie, Ralph Truman

Mister Quilp
GB 1975   119m   Technicolor   Panavision
Reader's Digest (Helen M. Straus)
aka: *The Old Curiosity Shop*

In 1840 London, an antique-shop owner is in debt to a hunchback moneylender who has designs on his business.
The novel, with its villainous lead, is a curious choice for musicalizing, and in this treatment falls desperately flat, with no sparkle of imagination visible anywhere.

w Louis Kamp, Irene Kamp, *novel* The Old Curiosity Shop by Charles Dickens d Michael Tuchner *ph* Christopher Challis m Anthony Newley *pd* Elliot Scott *md* Elmer Bernstein *ch* Gillian Lynne

Anthony Newley, Michael Hordern, David Hemmings, Sarah-Jane Varley, David Warner, Paul Rogers, Jill Bennett
   'Another soggy piece of family entertainment from Reader's Digest, who produced the toothless screen musicals of *Tom Sawyer* and *Huckleberry Finn.*'—*Philip French*
   'Dickens shorn of sentiment, melodrama or love . . . Mr Newley's Quilp, a galvanized Quasimodo on a permanent high, is something of a strain to watch.'—*Michael Billington, Illustrated London News*

Mr Ricco
US 1975   98m   Panavision   colour
MGM (Douglas Netter)

A defence counsel risks his life to prove his black client innocent.
Complex urban action thriller with a tired, ageing hero and impenetrable plot.

w Robert Hoban d Paul Bogart *ph* Frank Stanley m Chico Hamilton

Dean Martin, Eugene Roche, Thalmus Rasulala,

Denise Nicholas, Cindy Williams, *Geraldine Brooks*, Frank Puglia

Mister Roberts**
US 1955   123m   Warnercolor
   Cinemascope
Warner / Leland Hayward

Life aboard a World War II cargo ship yearning for action.
A mixture of comedy and sentimentality which has become an American minor classic as a play; this film version is a shambling affair but gets most of the effects over.

w Frank Nugent, Joshua Logan, *play* Thomas Heggen and Joshua Logan, *novel Thomas Heggen* d John Ford, Mervyn Le Roy *ph* Winton Hoch m Franz Waxman

Henry Fonda, James Cagney, William Powell, Jack Lemmon, Betsy Palmer, Ward Bond, Phil Carey, Ken Curtis, Harry Carey Jnr

AA: Jack Lemmon
AAN: best picture

Mr Robinson Crusoe
US 1932   76m   bw
Douglas Fairbanks

A playboy takes a bet that he could live alone on a desert island . . . but a girl turns up.
Mild adventure comedy with the star in subdued form.

w Douglas Fairbanks d Edward Sutherland m Alfred Newman

Douglas Fairbanks, William Farnum, Earle Browne, Maria Alba

Mr Sardonicus
US 1961   90m   bw
Columbia / William Castle

A surgeon is lured to an ex-girl friend's remote home to cure her sadistic husband's crippled face.
Flatly handled, boring semi-horror.

w Robb White d William Castle

Ronald Lewis, Guy Rolfe, Audrey Dalton, Oscar Homolka

Mr Scoutmaster
US 1953   87m   bw
TCF

A TV personality wants to understand children and is persuaded to take over a scout troop.
A star vehicle which starts promisingly enough in the *Sitting Pretty* vein but quickly falls headlong into an abyss of sentimentality.

w Leonard Praskins, Barney Slater d Henry

Levin *ph* Joseph La Shelle *m* Cyril Mockridge
md Lionel Newman

Clifton Webb, Edmund Gwenn, George
Winslow, Frances Dee, Veda Ann Borg

Mr Skeffington***
US 1944   127m   bw
Warner (Julius J. and Philip G. Epstein)

A selfish beauty finally turns to her discarded
dull husband; when he is blind, he doesn't mind
her faded looks.

Long, patchily made, but thoroughly enjoyable
star melodrama.

w Julius J. and Philip G. Epstein, *novel*
'Elizabeth' *d* Vincent Sherman *ph* Ernest
Haller *m* Franz Waxman

Bette Davis, Claude Rains, Walter Abel,
Richard Waring, George Coulouris, John
Alexander, Jerome Cowan

'An endless woman's page dissertation on
What To Do When Beauty Fades.'—*James
Agee*

'To call the film a good one would be to
exaggerate; but entertaining and interesting, I
insist, it is.'—*Richard Mallett, Punch*

AAN: Bette Davis; Claude Rains

Mr Smith Goes to Washington****
US 1939   130m   bw
Columbia (Frank Capra)

Washington's youngest senator exposes
corruption in high places, almost at the cost of
his own career.

Archetypal high-flying Capra vehicle, with the
little man coming out top as he seldom does in
life. Supreme gloss hides the corn, helter-skelter
direction keeps one watching, and all concerned
give memorable performances. A cinema classic.

w Sidney Buchman, *story* Lewis R. Foster
d Frank Capra *ph* Joseph Walker *m* Dmitri
Tiomkin *montage* Slavko Vorkapich

*James Stewart, Claude Rains, Jean Arthur,
Thomas Mitchell, Edward Arnold*, Guy Kibbee,
Eugene Pallette, Beulah Bondi, *Harry Carey*, H.
B. Warner, Astrid Allwyn, Ruth Donnelly,
Charles Lane, Porter Hall

'More fun, even, than the Senate itself . . . not
merely a brilliant jest, but a stirring and even
inspiring testament to liberty and freedom.'—
Frank S. Nugent, New York Times

'A totally compelling piece of movie-making,
upholding the virtues of traditional American
ideals.'—*NFT, 1973*

'Very good, beautifully done and extremely
entertaining; long, but worth the time it takes.'—
Richard Mallett, Punch

'More of the heartfelt than is good for the
stomach.'—*New Yorker, 1977*

AA: Lewis R. Foster
AAN: best picture; Sidney Buchman; Frank
Capra; Dmitri Tiomkin; James Stewart; Claude
Rains; Harry Carey

Mr Topaze
GB 1961   84m   Eastmancolor
Cinemascope
TCF / Dimitri de Grunwald (Pierre Rouve)
US title: *I Like Money*

An honest ex-schoolmaster becomes prosperous
when he joins some shady businessmen.
Predictable, sluggish character comedy, with a
good actor unable to make it as a star. Or as a
director.

w Pierre Rouve, *play* Topaze by Marcel Pagnol
d Peter Sellers *ph* John Wilcox *m* Georges Van
Parys

Peter Sellers, Herbert Lom, Leo McKern, Nadia
Gray, Martita Hunt, John Neville, Billie
Whitelaw, Michael Gough, Joan Sims, John Le
Mesurier, Michael Sellers

'A film of minor pleasures and major
inadequacies.'—*Penelope Houston, MFB*

* See also *Topaze* (1933).

Mr Winkle Goes to War
US 1944   80m   bw
Columbia (Jack Moss)
GB title: *Arms and the Woman*

A middle-aged bank clerk joins the army and
becomes a hero.
Agreeable, forgettable propaganda comedy-
drama.

w Waldo Salt, George Corey, Louis Solomon,
novel Theodore Pratt *d* Alfred E. Green
ph Joseph Walker *m* Carmen Dragon, Paul
Sawtell

Edward G. Robinson, Ruth Warrick, Ted
Donaldson, Bob Haymes, Richard Lane, Robert
Armstrong, Walter Baldwin

Mr Wong
A cheeseparing set of second features from
Monogram, based on stories by Hugh Wiley.
Boris Karloff was unsuitably cast as a Chinese
detective, and in the last film he was replaced by
Keye Luke. The films were directed by William
Nigh.

1938: MR WONG DETECTIVE
1939: THE MYSTERY OF MR WONG, MR
WONG IN CHINATOWN
1940: THE FATAL HOUR, DOOMED TO

DIE (GB title: THE MYSTERY OF THE
WENTWORTH CASTLE)
1941: PHANTOM OF CHINATOWN

Mr Wu *
US 1927   80m approx (24 fps)   bw   silent
MGM

A Chinese villain kills his daughter when she
wants to marry an Englishman.
Turgid outmoded melodrama from a stage
success: purely a star vehicle.

w Lorna Moon, *play* Maurice Vernon, Harold
Owen d William Nigh

Lon Chaney, Louise Dresser, Anna May Wong,
Ralph Forbes, Renee Adoree, Holmes Herbert

Mrs Fitzherbert
GB 1947   99m   bw
British National

The Prince Regent secretly marries a Catholic
widow.
Stilted, ill-cast historical charade.

w Montgomery Tully, *novel* Winifred Carter
d Montgomery Tully ph James Wilson m Hans
May

Peter Graves, Joyce Howard, Leslie Banks,
Margaretta Scott

Mrs Mike
US 1949   99m   bw
Nassour / Huntingdon Hartford (Edward
   Gross)

A Mountie takes his new wife to live in the frozen
northwest.
Predictable sentimental drama, well enough
done to keep interest, but only just.

w Lewis Levitt, De Witt Bodeen d Louis King
ph Joseph Biroc m Max Steiner

Dick Powell, Evelyn Keyes, J. M. Kerrigan,
Angela Clarke

Mrs Miniver **
US 1942   134m   bw
MGM (Sidney Franklin)

An English housewife survives World War II.
This is the rose-strewn English village,
Hollywood variety, but when released it proved a
beacon of morale despite its false sentiment,
absurd rural types and melodramatic situations.
It is therefore beyond criticism, except that some
of the people involved should have known better.

w Arthur Wimperis, George Froeschel, James
Hilton, Claudine West d William Wyler
ph Joseph Ruttenberg m Herbert Stothart

Greer Garson, Walter Pidgeon, Teresa Wright,

Richard Ney, Dame May Whitty, Henry
Travers, Reginald Owen, Henry Wilcoxon,
Helmut Dantine, Rhys Williams, Aubrey
Mather

AA: best picture; William Wyler; Joseph
Ruttenberg; Greer Garson; Teresa Wright
AAN: script; Walter Pidgeon; Dame May
Whitty; Henry Travers

Mrs O'Malley and Mr Malone *
US 1950   69m   bw
MGM (William H. Wright)

On a train to New York, a radio contest winner
and a lawyer help solve a murder.
Lively second feature farce.

w William Powers d Norman Taurog ph Ray
June

Marjorie Main, James Whitmore, Ann Dvorak,
Fred Clark, Dorothy Malone, Phyllis Kirk

Mrs Parkington
US 1944   124m   bw
MGM (Leon Gordon)

A lady's maid marries a miner who becomes
wealthy, and pushes her way into society.
Thoroughly unconvincing three-generation
drama, with a bewigged and powdered star
giving the boot to her conniving relations. It has
production values and nothing else.

w Robert Thoeren, Polly James, *novel* Louis
Bromfield d Tay Garnett ph Joseph
Ruttenberg m Bronislau Kaper

Greer Garson, Walter Pidgeon, Edward Arnold,
Agnes Moorehead, Cecil Kellaway, Gladys
Cooper, Frances Rafferty, Tom Drake, Peter
Lawford, Dan Duryea, Hugh Marlowe, Selena
Royle
† The heroine is shown having a romance with
Edward VII when Prince of Wales; special
scenes were shot for the European version
substituting Cecil Kellaway, who played
Edward, by Hugo Haas who played a European
king of indeterminate origin.

AAN: Greer Garson; Agnes Moorehead

Mrs Pollifax—Spy
US 1970   110m   De Luxe
UA / Mellor (Frederick Brisson)

A respectable American matron offers her
services to the CIA and sees active service in
Albania.
Incredible comedy-dramatic vehicle for a star
who won't give up. An obvious failure from the
word go.

w C. A. McKnight, *novel* Dorothy Gilman

d Leslie Martinson *ph* Joseph Biroc *m* Lalo Schifrin

Rosalind Russell, Darren McGavin

Mrs Wiggs of the Cabbage Patch*
US 1934 80m bw
Paramount (Douglas MacLean)

Adventures of a poor family who live on the wrong side of the tracks in a broken down old shack.

A Depression fantasy of respectability and optimism, almost incredible to see now, although it plumbed the same never-never milieu as did Chaplin. Moments of comedy still please, but one does long for Mr Fields' delayed entry.

w William Slavens McNutt, Jane Storm, *novel* Alice Hegan Rice *d* Norman Taurog *ph* Charles Lang

Pauline Lord, *Zasu Pitts, W. C. Fields*, Evelyn Venable, Kent Taylor, Charles Middleton, Donald Meek, Edith Fellows, Virginia Weidler, George Breakston

'A nasty all's-right-with-the-world burlesque of poverty, with emotions to tug at such heartstrings as are worn dangling from the mouth.'—*Otis Ferguson*

Mrs Wiggs of the Cabbage Patch
US 1942 80m bw
Paramount

Curiously quick remake, almost word for word, but without the moments of inspiration.

w Doris Anderson, Jane Storm, William Slavens McNutt *d* Ralph Murphy

Fay Bainter, Hugh Herbert, Vera Vague, Barbara Britton, Carl Switzer, Moroni Olsen, Billy Lee

Mix Me a Person
GB 1961 116m bw
Wessex (Sergei Nolbandov)

A barrister's psychiatrist wife takes on one of his failures, a client condemned to death for murder. Once it gets started, a routine suspense thriller with the wrong man convicted and an espresso bar background. Not a very good one, though.

w Ian Dalrymple, *novel* Jack Trevor Story *d* Leslie Norman *ph* Ted Moore *songs* Johnny Worth *md* Muir Mathieson

Anne Baxter, Donald Sinden, Adam Faith, Walter Brown, Glyn Houston

Mixed Company
US 1974 109m De Luxe
UA / Cornell (Melville Shavelson)

A basketball coach and his wife adopt several children of different races.

Room for One More and then some, but not very interesting.

w Melville Shavelson, Mort Lachman *d* Melville Shavelson *ph* Stan Lazan *m* Fred Karlin *pd* Stan Jolley

Barbara Harris, Joseph Bologna, Lisa Gerritson, Arianne Heller

The Mob*
US 1951 87m bw
Columbia (Jerry Bresler)
GB title: *Remember That Face*

A policeman works undercover to catch a dockside racketeer.

Tough, lively thriller with effectively sustained mystery and a serial-like finale.

w William Bowers *d* Robert Parrish *ph* Joseph Walker *m* George Duning

Broderick Crawford, Richard Kiley, Ernest Borgnine, Neville Brand, Charles Bronson

Moby Dick*
US 1930 75m bw
Warner

Captain Ahab returns minus a leg from fighting the white whale, and finds that his fiancée is too shocked to love him.

Mangled remake of a fine novel filmed in silent form as *The Sea Beast*.

w J. Grubb Alexander, *novel* Herman Melville *d* Lloyd Bacon *ph* Robert Kurrie

John Barrymore, Joan Bennett, Lloyd Hughes, May Boley, Walter Long

Moby Dick**
GB 1956 116m Technicolor
John Huston

A whaling skipper is determined to harpoon the white whale which robbed him of a leg.

Pretentious period adventure, rather too obsessed with symbolism and certainly too slowly developed, but full of interesting detail which almost outweighs the central miscasting.

w Ray Bradbury, John Huston, *novel* Herman Melville *d* John Huston *ph* Oswald Morris *m* Philip Stainton

Gregory Peck, Richard Basehart, Friedrich Ledebur, Leo Genn, Orson Welles, James Robertson Justice, Harry Andrews, Bernard Miles, Noel Purcell, Edric Connor, Joseph Tomelty, Mervyn Johns

'Interesting more often than exciting.'—*Variety*

The Model and the Marriage Broker
US 1952   103m   bw
TCF (Charles Brackett)

A broker conceals her profession from a friend
but gets the friend fixed up.
Moderate, unsurprising comedy somewhat
overweighted by talent which can't express itself.

w Charles Brackett, Walter Reisch, Richard
Breen d George Cukor ph Milton Krasner
m Cyril Mockridge

Thelma Ritter, Jeanne Crain, Scott Brady, Zero
Mostel, Michael O'Shea, Nancy Kulp

Modern Times*
US 1936   87m   bw
Charles Chaplin

An assembly-line worker goes berserk but can't
get another job.
Silent star comedy produced in the middle of the
sound period; flashes of genius alternate with
sentimental sequences and jokes without punch.

wd/m Charles Chaplin ph Rollie Totheroh, Ira
Morgan

Charles Chaplin, Paulette Goddard, Henry
Bergman, Chester Conklin, Tiny Sandford
 'A feature picture made out of several one- and
two-reel shorts, proposed titles being *The Shop,
The Jailbird, The Singing Waiter*.'—*Otis
Ferguson*

Modesty Blaise
GB 1966   119m   Technicolor
TCF / Modesty Blaise Ltd (Joseph Janni)

Female arch-agent Modesty Blaise defends a
shipload of diamonds against a sadistic master
criminal.
Comic-strip adventures made by people with no
sense of humour; Fu Manchu was much more
fun.

w Evan Jones, *comic strip* Peter O'Donnell, Jim
Holdaway d Joseph Losey ph Jack Hildyard
m Johnny Dankworth

Monica Vitti, Dirk Bogarde, Terence Stamp,
Harry Andrews, Michael Craig, Scilla Gabel,
Clive Revill, Rossella Falk, Joe Melia

Mogambo*
GB 1954   116m   Technicolor
MGM (Sam Zimbalist)

The headquarters of a Kenyan white hunter is
invaded by an American showgirl and a British
archaeologist and his wife, and they all go off on
a gorilla hunt.
Amiable, flabby remake of *Red Dust*, with

direction scarcely in evidence and the gorillas
out-acting a genial cast.

w John Lee Mahin d John Ford ph Robert
Surtees, F. A. Young

Clark Gable, Ava Gardner, Grace Kelly,
Donald Sinden, Laurence Naismith, Philip
Stainton
† The story was also made as *Congo Maisie* in
1940.

AAN: Ava Gardner; Grace Kelly

Molly and Me
US 1945   76m   bw
TCF

A cantankerous old man is tamed by his new
housekeeper.
Sentimental little star vehicle.

d Lewis Seiler

Gracie Fields, Monty Woolley, Reginald
Gardiner, Roddy McDowall, Natalie Schaefer,
Edith Barrett
† This followed the more successful teaming of
the stars in *Holy Matrimony*.

The Molly Maguires
US 1970   123m   Technicolor   Panavision
Paramount / Tamm (Martin Ritt, Walter
 Bernstein)

In the Pennsylvania coalmining district in the
1870s, an undercover detective exposes the
leaders of a secret society.
Sober-sided and slow-moving account of actual
events which also formed the basis for Conan
Doyle's rather more entertaining *The Valley of
Fear*. Expensive, nicely photographed, but
unpersuasive and empty.

w Walter Bernstein d Martin Ritt ph James
Wong Howe m Henry Mancini

Richard Harris, Sean Connery, Samantha
Eggar, Frank Finlay, Anthony Zerbe, Bethel
Leslie, Art Lund
 'The film's vague sense of grievance and
harrowing circumstances hangs in the air like the
smoky pall cast up by the anthracite
workings.'—*Richard Combs*
 'A cold, dry and rather perfunctory film.'—
Arthur Schlesinger Jnr

Moment to Moment
US 1966   108m   Technicolor
Universal (Mervyn Le Roy)

A housewife finds herself with a body on her
hands.
Incredibly old-fashioned romantic/
melodramatic malarkey set on the French
Riviera but scarcely moving a step out of

Hollywood. Lush settings made it marketable to women.

w John Lee Mahin, Alec Coppel *d* Mervyn Le Roy *ph* Harry Stradling *m* Henry Mancini

Jean Seberg, *Honor Blackman*, Sean Garrison, Arthur Hill, Grégoire Aslan

Mon Oncle*
France 1956   116m   Eastmancolor
Specta / Gray / Alterdel—Centaure (Louis Dolivet)

A small boy has less affection for his parents than for his vague, clumsy uncle.
Tiresomely long star vehicle, with Tati harping on his theory of detachment, ie keeping his comic character on the fringes of the action. It really doesn't work in a film of this length, and the jokes are thin.

w Jacques Tati, Jacques Lagrange *d* Jacques Tati *ph* Jean Bourgoin *m* Alain Romains, Franck Barcellini

Jacques Tati, Jean-Pierre Zola, Adrienne Servatie, Alain Becourt, Yvonne Arnaud
'Deft, elusive, full of heart.'—*Brenda Davies, MFB*

Mondo Cane*
Italy 1961   105m   Technicolor
Cineriz
aka: *A Dog's Life*

A documentary of thirty sequences of violently eccentric human behaviour, including cannibalism, pig killing, a dog meal restaurant, etc.
Emetic exploitation piece, quite glibly assembled. Its huge commercial success made one worry for the world.

wd Gualtiero Jacopetti *ph* Antonio Climati, Benito Frattari

AAN: song 'More' (*m* Riz Ortolani, Nino Oliviero, *ly* Norman Newell)

The Money Trap
US 1966   92m   bw   Panavision
MGM (Max E. Youngstein, David Karr)

A hard-up policeman turns to crime.
A cheap thriller decorated with waning stars; competent at the lowest level.

w Walter Bernstein, *novel* Lionel White *d* Burt Kennedy *ph* Paul C. Vogel *m* Hal Schaefer

Glenn Ford, Rita Hayworth, Elke Sommer, Ricardo Montalban, Joseph Cotten, Tom Reese, James Mitchum

Monkey Business***
US 1931   81m   bw
Paramount

Four ship's stowaways crash a society party and catch a few crooks.
The shipboard part of this extravaganza is one of the best stretches of Marxian lunacy, but after the Chevalier impersonations it runs out of steam. Who's grumbling?

w S. J. Perelman, *Will B. Johnstone, Arthur Sheekman d* Norman Z. McLeod *ph* Arthur L. Todd

Groucho, Chico, Harpo, Zeppo, Thelma Todd, Rockcliffe Fellowes, Ruth Hall, Harry Woods

Monkey Business*
US 1952   97m   bw
TCF (Sol C. Siegel)

A chimpanzee in a research lab accidentally concocts an elixir of youth.
Remarkably laboured comedy by and with top people; it can't fail to have funny moments, but they are few and far between.

w Ben Hecht, Charles Lederer, I. A. L. Diamond *d* Howard Hawks *ph* Milton Krasner *m* Leigh Harline

Cary Grant, Ginger Rogers, *Charles Coburn, Marilyn Monroe*, Hugh Marlowe

A Monkey in Winter*
France 1962   103m   bw   Totalvision
CIPRA / Cité (Jacques Bar)
aka: *Une Singe en Hiver; It's Hot in Hell*

In a small Normandy resort, a hotel owner and a literary guest get drunk together and plan great fantasies, but finally return to their responsibilities.
Amiable, meandering star character comedy.

w François Boyer, *novel* Antoine Blondin *d* Henri Verneuil *ph* Louis Page *m* Michel Magne

Jean Gabin, Jean-Paul Belmondo, Suzanne Flon, Noel Roquevert, Paul Frankeur, Gabrielle Dorziat

Monkey on My Back
US 1957   93m   bw
UA / Imperial / Edward Small

A Guadalcanal hero is given morphine to relieve malaria and becomes addicted.
Dreary case history sold as exploitation.

w Crane Wilbur, Anthony Veiller, Peter Dudley, from the experiences of Barney Ross *d* André de Toth *ph* Maury Gertsman

Cameron Mitchell, Dianne Foster, Jack Albertson, Paul Richards

Monkeys Go Home
US 1966   101m   Technicolor
Walt Disney (Ron Miller)

An American inherits a French olive farm and
trains chimpanzees to harvest the crop.
Footling comedy with not much of an idea, let
alone a plot.

w Maurice Tombragel, novel The Monkeys by
G. K. Wilkinson d Andrew V. McLaglen
ph William Snyder m Robert F. Brunner

Maurice Chevalier, Dean Jones, Yvette
Mimieux, Bernard Woringer, Jules Munshin,
Alan Carney

'Innocuous, extrovertly cheerful and good-
humoured—and very dull.'—MFB

The Monolith Monsters
US 1957   77m   bw
U–I (Howard Christie)

A meteorite lands in the desert and causes rocks
to rise and expand, becoming toppling pillars
which threaten a local community.
Dully-written science fiction with moderate
special effects.

w Norman Jolley, Robert M. Fresco d John
Sherwood ph Ellis Carter md Joseph
Gershenson

Lola Albright, Grant Williams, Les Tremayne,
Phil Harvey

Monsieur Beaucaire*
US 1946   93m   bw
Paramount (Paul Jones)

King Louis XV's bumbling barber impersonates
a court dandy.
What seemed a lively period burlesque has faded
somewhat with age, but it still has its moments.
Any relation between this and the silent
Valentino film is quite accidental.

w Melvin Frank, Norman Panama d George
Marshall ph Lionel Lindon md Robert Emmett
Dolan

Bob Hope, Joan Caulfield, Patric Knowles,
Marjorie Reynolds, Cecil Kellaway, Joseph
Schildkraut, Reginald Owen, Constance Collier,
Hillary Brooke, Douglass Dumbrille, Mary
Nash

'Whether you yawn or rather wearily laugh
depends chiefly on your chance state of mind.'—
James Agee

Monsieur Hulot's Holiday***
France 1953   91m   bw
Cady / Discina (Fred Orain)
original title: Les Vacances de Monsieur Hulot

An accident-prone bachelor arrives at a seaside
resort and unwittingly causes havoc for himself
and everyone else.
Despite lame endings to some of the jokes, this is
a film to set the whole world laughing, Hulot
himself being an unforgettable character and
some of the timing magnificent. One feels that it
could very nearly happen.

w Jacques Tati, Henri Marquet d Jacques Tati
ph Jacques Mercanton, Jean Mouselle m Alain
Romans

Jacques Tati, Nathalie Pascaud, Michèle Rolla,
Valentine Camax

'The casual, amateurish air of his films clearly
adds to their appeal: it also appears to explain
their defects.'—Penelope Houston, MFB

AAN: script

Monsieur Verdoux**
US 1947   125m   bw
Charles Chaplin

A bank cashier marries and murders rich women
to support his real wife.
Interesting but unsatisfactory redrafting of the
Landru case; the star is more dapper than funny,
the moral is unconvincing, and the slapstick
sequences too often raise yawns.

wd/m Charles Chaplin ph Rollie Totheroh

Charles Chaplin, Martha Raye, Isobel Elsom

AAN: Charles Chaplin (as writer)

Monsieur Vincent*
France 1947   113m   bw
EDIC/UGC

The life of 17th-century St Vincent de Paul, who
gave up all worldly goods to devote his life to the
poor.
Earnest, realistic Catholic biopic.

w Jean-Bernard Luc, Jean Anouilh d Leon
Carré ph Claude Renoir m J. J. Grunenwald

Pierre Fresnay, Aimé Clairiond, Jean
Debucourt, Lise Delemare

The Monster and the Girl
US 1940   64m   bw
Paramount

A man is wrongfully executed and his brain is
implanted in a gorilla, which goes on the
rampage.
Curiously ineffectual considering its plot and
cast, this little horror thriller seems to have been
the first to use this particular situation, which
became very well worn later.

w Stuart Anthony d Stuart Heisler ph Victor
Milner

Paul Lukas, Ellen Drew, Joseph Calleia, George

Zucco, Robert Paige, Rod Cameron, Phillip Terry, Onslow Stevens, Gerald Mohr

Monte Carlo*
US 1930 94m bw
Paramount

A count passes himself off as a hairdresser to win a gambling lady.

Faded but charming romantic comedy with music, the first to show its director's sound style in full throttle, notably in the final 'Beyond the Blue Horizon' sequence.

w Ernest Vajda, *play* The Blue Coast by Hans Muller, *novel* Monsieur Beaucaire by Booth Tarkington *d* Ernst Lubitsch *ph* Victor Milner *ad* Hans Dreier

Jack Buchanan, Jeanette MacDonald, Zasu Pitts, Tyler Brooke, Claud Allister, Lionel Belmore

'Very stylish and sly, not to be missed.'—*New Yorker, 1978*

The Monte Carlo Story
Italy / US 1956 101m Technirama
Tatanus (Marcello Girosi)

A gambler looks for a rich wife, and finds instead a glamorous woman as penniless as himself: they become confidence tricksters but suffer a change of heart.

Lubitsch might have made something of it, but this is a flavourless pudding of a film and the stars can do nothing with it.

wd Samuel Taylor, *story* Marcello Girosi, Dino Risi *ph* Giuseppe Rotunno *m* Renzo Rossellini

Marlene Dietrich, Vittorio de Sica, Arthur O'Connell, Mischa Auer, Natalie Trundy, Jane Rose, Renato Rascel

Monte Walsh*
US 1970 108m Technicolor
Cinema Center (Hal Landis, Bobby Roberts)

Two ageing cowboys find life increasingly hard and hopeless; an old acquaintance kills one and is shot by the other.

'Realistic' western developed in leisurely style with the emphasis on character and on the real drudgery of frontier life.

w David Z. Goodman, Lukas Heller, *novel* Jack Schaefer *d* William A. Fraker *ph* David M. Walsh *m* John Barry

Lee Marvin, Jack Palance, Jeanne Moreau, Mitch Ryan, Jim Davis

'As boring a western as ever involved a bronco-busting scene that alone cost almost half a million dollars.'—*Judith Crist*

Monty Python and the Holy Grail**
GB 1975 90m Technicolor
EMI / Python (Monty) Pictures / Michael White (Mark Forstater)

King Arthur and his knights seek the Holy Grail. Hellzapoppin-like series of linked sketches on a medieval theme; some slow bits, but often uproariously funny and with a remarkable visual sense of the middle ages.

w Graham Chapman, John Cleese, Terry Gilliam, Eric Idle, Michael Palin *d* Terry Gilliam, Terry Jones *ph* Terry Bedford *animation* Terry Gilliam *m* Neil Innes *pd* Roy Smith

Graham Chapman, John Cleese, Terry Gilliam, Eric Idle, Michael Palin

'The team's visual buffooneries and verbal rigmaroles are piled on top of each other with no attention to judicious timing or structure, and a form which began as a jaunty assault on the well-made revue sketch and an ingenious misuse of television's fragmented style of presentation, threatens to become as unyielding and unfruitful as the conventions it originally attacked.'—*Geoff Brown*

The Moon and Sixpence***
US 1943 85m bw (colour sequence)
Albert Lewin / David L. Loew (Stanley Kramer)

A stockbroker leaves his wife and family, spends some selfish years painting in Paris and finally dies of leprosy on a South Sea island.

Pleasantly literary adaptation of an elegant novel based on the life of Gauguin; a little stodgy in presentation now, but much of it still pleases.

w Albert Lewin, *novel* W. Somerset Maugham *d* Albert Lewin *ph* John Seitz *m* Dmitri Tiomkin

George Sanders, Herbert Marshall (as Maugham), *Steve Geray*, Doris Dudley, Elena Verdugo, Florence Bates, Heather Thatcher, Eric Blore, Albert Basserman

'An admirable film until the end, when it lapses into Technicolor and techni-pathos.'—*James Agate*

AAN: Dmitri Tiomkin

The Moon Is Blue*
US 1953 99m bw
Otto Preminger

A spry young girl balances the attractions of a middle-aged lover against her young one.

Paper-thin comedy partly set on top of the Empire State Building (and thereafter in a dowdy set); mildly amusing in spots, it gained notoriety,

and a Production Code ban, by its use of such
naughty words as 'virgin' and 'mistress'.

w F. Hugh Herbert, from his play d Otto
Preminger ph Ernest Laszlo

Maggie McNamara, David Niven, William
Holden, Tom Tully, Dawn Addams

'It adds nothing to the art of cinema and
certainly does not deserve the attention it will get
for flouting the Production Code.'—*Philip T.
Hartung*

AAN: Maggie McNamara; title song
(*m* Herschel Burke Gilbert, *ly* Sylvia Fine)

The Moon Is Down**
US 1943   90m   bw
TCF

A Norwegian village resists the Nazis.
Sombre, talkative, intelligent little drama, the
best of the resistance films, shot on the set of
How Green Was My Valley (with snow
covering).

w *Nunnally Johnson*, *novel* John Steinbeck
d *Irving Pichel* ph Arthur Miller m Alfred
Newman

Henry Travers, Cedric Hardwicke, Lee J. Cobb,
Dorris Bowden, Margaret Wycherly, Peter Van
Eyck, John Banner

Moon over Burma
US 1940   76m   bw
Paramount

Jungle lumbermen fight over a standard
American entertainer.
Routine adventure romance climaxing in a forest
fire.

w Frank Wead, W. P. Lipscomb, Harry Clark
d Louis King ph William Mellor

Dorothy Lamour, Robert Preston, Preston
Foster, Doris Nolan, Albert Basserman,
Frederick Worlock, Addison Richards

Moon over Miami*
US 1941   92m   Technicolor
TCF (Harry Joe Brown)

Two sisters seek rich husbands in Florida.
Musical remake of *Three Blind Mice*, which was
suspiciously similar to *Golddiggers of
Broadway*, *The Greeks Had a Word for Them*,
etc., and the later *How to Marry a Millionaire*
and *Three Little Girls in Blue*. In short, a
Hollywood standard, not too badly done.

w Vincent Lawrence, Brown Holmes d Walter
Lang ph Peverell Marley, Leon Shamroy
md Alfred Newman

Don Ameche, Betty Grable, Carole Landis,
Charlotte Greenwood, Jack Haley, Cobina
Wright Jnr, Robert Greig

Moon Pilot**
US 1961   98m   Technicolor
Walt Disney (Ron Miller)

A reluctant astronaut falls in love with a girl
from outer space, who finally accompanies him
on his mission.
Engaging science-fiction spoof with good
performances.

w Maurice Tombragel, *serial* Robert Buckner
d James Neilson ph William Snyder m Peter
Smith sp Eustace Lycett

Edmond O'Brien, Tom Tryon, Brian Keith

The Moon Spinners*
GB 1964   119m   Technicolor
Walt Disney (Bill Anderson)

A young girl holidaying in Crete becomes
involved with jewel robbers.
Teenage adventure against attractive locations;
quite agreeable but overlong.

w Michael Dyne, *novel* Mary Stewart d James
Neilson ph Paul Beeson m Ron Grainer

Hayley Mills, Peter McEnery, Eli Wallach, Joan
Greenwood, John Le Mesurier, *Pola Negri*

Moon Zero Two
GB 1969   100m   Technicolor
Hammer (Michael Carreras)

In 2021, the moon is being colonized and crooks
are trying to get control of an asteroid.
A self-acknowledged 'space western' which has a
few bright ideas but suffers from a childish script.

w Michael Carreras, *story* Gavin Lyall, Frank
Hardman, Martin Davidson d Roy Ward
Baker ph Paul Beeson m Don Ellis

James Olson, Catherina Von Schell, Warren
Mitchell, Ori Levy, Adrienne Corri, Dudley
Foster, Bernard Bresslaw, Neil McCallum

'It's all just about bad enough to fill older
audiences with nostalgia for the inspired
innocence of Flash Gordon, or even the good old
days of Abbott and Costello in outer space.'—
MFB

Moonfleet*
US 1955   87m   Eastmancolor
Cinemascope
MGM (John Houseman)

In Dorset in 1770 an orphan boy finds that his
elegant guardian leads a gang of smugglers.
Period gothic melodrama which nearly, but not
quite, comes off; the script simply doesn't build
to the right climax, and too many characters

come to nothing. But there are splendid moments.

w Margaret Fitts, Jan Lustig, *novel* J. Meade Faulkner *d* Fritz Lang *ph* Robert Planck *m* Miklos Rozsa

Stewart Granger, Jon Whiteley, George Sanders, Joan Greenwood, Viveca Lindfors, Liliane Montevecchi, Melville Cooper, Sean McClory, John Hoyt, Alan Napier

Moonlight Sonata*
GB 1937 90m bw
Pall Mall (Lothar Mendes)

Stranded victims of a plane crash are affected by the art of a famous pianist.
Curious, slight, unexpected play-on-film designed to showcase the talent of Paderewski.

w Edward Knoblock, E. M. Delafield *d* Lothar Mendes

Ignace Paderewski, Eric Portman, *Marie Tempest,* Charles Farrell, Barbara Greene, Binkie Stuart

The Moonlighter
US 1953 77m bw 3-D
Warner (Joseph Bernhard)

A cattle rustler moves towards reforming.
Ho-hum western which offers its stars little to work with and was not even very exciting in 3-D.

w Niven Busch *d* Roy Rowland *ph* Bert Glennon *m* Heinz Roemheld

Fred MacMurray, Barbara Stanwyck, Ward Bond, William Ching, John Dierkes, Morris Ankrum

The Moonraker*
GB 1958 82m Technicolor
ABPC (Hamilton Inglis)

During the English Civil War, a noble highwayman smuggles the king's son into France.
Likeable swashbuckler which confines its second half to suspense at an inn, a who-is-it rather than a whodunnit. Good fun.

w Robert Hall, Wilfred Eades, Alistair Bell, *play* Arthur Watkyn *d* David MacDonald

George Baker, Sylvia Syms, Marius Goring, Peter Arne, Richard Leech, Clive Morton, Paul Whitsun-Jones, Gary Raymond, John Le Mesurier (as Cromwell), Patrick Troughton, Michael Anderson Jnr

Moonrise*
US 1948 90m bw
Republic

A murderer's son is driven into violence by memories and fears of his childhood.
Broody melodrama set against a remote village and swamp background; not a very interesting story, but memorable detail.

w Charles Haas *d Frank Borzage ph* John L. Russell *m* William Lava

Gail Russell, Dane Clark, Ethel Barrymore, Allyn Joslyn, Rex Ingram

The Moon's Our Home*
US 1936 80m bw
Paramount (Walter Wanger)

A headstrong actress marries an adventurer on impulse, and they both try to work it out.
Light, bright romantic comedy with the zany tinge then in fashion.

w Isabel Dawn, Boyce DeGaw, *novel* Faith Baldwin *d* William A. Seiter *ph* Joseph Valentine

Margaret Sullavan, Henry Fonda, Beulah Bondi, Charles Butterworth, Margaret Hamilton, Dorothy Stickney, Lucien Littlefield

The Moonshine War
US 1970 100m Metrocolor Panavision
MGM / Filmways (James C. Pratt, Leonard Blair)

In Kentucky just before the repeal of prohibition, a corruptible revenue agent regrets bringing in a sadistic crook to help confiscate illegal whisky.
Downright peculiar hillbilly melodrama, neither straight nor satirical; interesting only in fits and starts.

w Elmore Leonard, from his novel *d* Richard Quine *ph* Richard H. Kline *m* Fred Karger

Patrick McGoohan, Richard Widmark, Alan Alda, Melodie Johnson, Will Geer

The Moonspinners see The Moon Spinners

Moontide*
US 1942 94m bw
TCF (Mark Hellinger)

A seaman cares for an unhappy waif.
A Hollywood attempt at romantic melodrama in the French manner. It looks good, and the cast is fine, but everything is just a bit too glum.

w John O'Hara, *novel* Willard Robertson *d* Archie Mayo *ph* Charles G. Clarke *m* Cyril Mockridge, David Buttolph

Jean Gabin, Ida Lupino, Claude Rains, Thomas Mitchell, Jerome Cowan, Sen Yung, Tully Marshall, Helen Reynolds

AAN: Charles G. Clarke

The Morals of Marcus

GB 1936   75m   bw
Gaumont British (W. J. Locke)

A girl escapes from a Middle Eastern harem by
stowing away with a British aristocrat.
Feeble 'naughty' comedy, killed by lack of wit
and pace.

w Guy Bolton, Miles Mander, play W. J. Locke
d Miles Mander

Lupe Velez, Ian Hunter, Adrienne Allen, Noel
Madison,
J. H. Roberts, H. F. Maltby

The More the Merrier***

US 1943   104m   bw
Columbia (George Stevens)

In crowded Washington during World War II, a
girl allows two men to share her apartment and
falls in love with the younger one.
Thoroughly amusing romantic comedy with
bright lines and situations; remade less
effectively as *Walk Don't Run* (qv).

w Robert Russell, Frank Ross, Richard
Flournoy, Lewis R. Foster d George Stevens
ph Ted Tetzlaff m Leigh Harline md Morris
Stoloff

Jean Arthur, Joel McCrea, Charles Coburn,
Richard Gaines, Bruce Bennett

'The gayest comedy that has come from
Hollywood in a long time. It has no more
substance than a watermelon, but is equally
delectable.'—*Howard Barnes*

AA: Charles Coburn

AAN: best picture; script; original story (Frank
Ross, Robert Russell); George Stevens; Jean
Arthur

Morgan—A Suitable Case for Treatment**

GB 1966   97m   bw
British Lion / Quintra (Leon Clore)

A young woman determines to leave her talented
but half-mad artist husband, who has a fixation
on gorillas and behaves in a generally uncivilized
manner.
Archetypal sixties marital fantasy, an extension
of *Look Back in Anger* in the mood of swinging
London. As tiresome as it is funny—but it *is*
funny.

w David Mercer, from his play d Karel Reisz
ph Larry Pizer, Gerry Turpin m Johnny
Dankworth

Vanessa Redgrave, *David Warner*, Robert
Stephens, Irene Handl, Newton Blick, Nan
Munro

'Poor Morgan: victim of a satire that doesn't

bite, lost in a technical confusion of means and
ends, and emerging like an identikit photograph,
all bits and pieces and no recognizable face.'—
Penelope Houston

'The first underground movie made above
ground.'—*John Simon*

'I think *Morgan* is so appealing to college
students because it shares their self-view: they
accept this mess of cute infantilism and
obsessions and aberrations without expecting
the writer and director to resolve it and without
themselves feeling a necessity to sort it out.'—
Pauline Kael

AAN: Vanessa Redgrave

Morning Departure*

GB 1950   102m   bw
Rank / Jay Lewis (Leslie Parkyn)
US title: *Operation Disaster*

Twelve men are caught in a trapped submarine,
and only eight can escape.
Archetypal stiff-upper-lip service tragedy, which
moves from briskness to a slow funereal ending.

w William Fairchild, play Kenneth Woolard
d Roy Baker ph Desmond Dickinson

John Mills, Richard Attenborough, Nigel
Patrick, Lana Morris, Peter Hammond, Helen
Cherry, James Hayter, Andrew Crawford,
George Cole, Michael Brennan, Wylie Watson,
Bernard Lee, Kenneth More

Morning Glory***

US 1933   74m   bw
RKO (Pandro S. Berman)

A young actress comes to New York determined
to succeed.
Marvellously evocative theatrical drama which
provided a strong star part for a fresh young
actress and surrounded her with accomplished
thespians. Remade to much less effect as *Stage
Struck* (qv).

w Howard J. Green, play Zoe Akins d Lowell
Sherman ph Bert Glennon

Katharine Hepburn, Douglas Fairbanks Jnr,
Adolphe Menjou, Mary Duncan, C. Aubrey
Smith, Don Alvarado ·

AA: Katharine Hepburn

Morocco***

US 1930   97m   bw
Paramount

A cabaret singer arrives in Morocco and
continues her wicked career by enslaving all the
men in sight; but true love reaches her at last.
The star's first American film reveals her
quintessence, and although wildly dated in

subject matter remains a perversely enjoyable entertainment.

w Jules Furthman, *novel* Amy Jolly by Benno Vigny *d Josef Von Sternberg ph* Lee Garmes

Marlene Dietrich, Gary Cooper, Adolphe Menjou, Ullrich Haupt, Juliette Compton, Francis McDonald

'A cinematic pattern brilliant, profuse, subtle, and at almost every turn inventive.'—*Wilton A. Barrett*

AAN: Josef Von Sternberg; Lee Garmes; Marlene Dietrich

The Mortal Storm**
US 1940   100m   bw
MGM

A German family in the thirties is split by Nazism.
Solid anti-Nazi melodrama typical of the period before America entered the war; good performances outweigh unconvincing studio sets.

w Claudine West, George Froeschel, Andersen Ellis, *novel* Phyllis Bottome *d Frank Borzage ph* William Daniels *m* Edward Kane

Margaret Sullavan, Robert Young, James Stewart, Frank Morgan, Robert Stack, Bonita Granville, Irene Rich, Maria Ouspenskaya

Moss Rose
US 1947   82m   bw
TCF

A Victorian chorus girl suspects her aristocratic admirer of being a murderer.
Absurd, stilted mystery melodrama with a better-looking production than it deserves.

w Jules Furthman, Tom Reed *d* Gregory Ratoff *ph* Joe MacDonald *m* David Buttolph

Peggy Cummins, Victor Mature, Ethel Barrymore, Vincent Price

The Most Dangerous Game***
US 1932   63m   bw
(RKO) Merian C. Cooper
GB title: *The Hounds of Zaroff*

A mad hunter lures guests on to his island so that he can hunt them down like animals.
Dated but splendidly shivery melodrama with moments of horror and mystery and a splendidly photographed chase sequence. Much imitated in curious ways, and not only by direct remakes such as *A Game of Death* and *Run for the Sun* (qv).

w James Creelman, *story* Richard Connell *d* Ernest B. Schoedsack, Irving Pichel *ph* Henry Gerrard *m* Max Steiner

Leslie Banks, Joel McCrea, Fay Wray, Robert Armstrong, Noble Johnson

The Most Dangerous Man in the World
GB 1969   99m   De Luxe   Panavision
TCF / APJAC (Mort Abrahams)
US title: *The Chairman*

A top scientist is sent by western intelligence on a mission into Red China, with a transmitter and a detonator implanted in his skull.
Wild Boys' Own Paper adventure which regrettably slows down in the middle for political philosophizing.

w Ben Maddow, *novel* The Chairman by Jay Richard Kennedy *d* J. Lee-Thompson *ph* Ted Moore *m* Jerry Goldsmith

Gregory Peck, Anne Heywood, Arthur Hill, Conrad Yama, Francisca Tu, Keye Luke, Alan Dobie, Ori Levy

Mother***
USSR 1926   90m approx (24 fps)   bw
silent
Mezhrabpom–Russ
original title: *Mat*

A mother incriminates her strike-breaking son, but realizes her error.
Propagandist social melodrama which is also brilliantly conceived and edited, with sequences matching those of Eisenstein.

w N. Zarkhi, V. I. Pudovkin, *novel* Maxim Gorky *d V. I. Pudovkin ph* A. Golovnia

Vera Baranovskaya, Nikolai Batalov
† Other versions appeared in 1920 and (*d* Mark Donskoi) 1955.

Mother Carey's Chickens
US 1938   82m   bw
RKO (Pandro S. Berman)

The tribulations of a small-town family in the nineties.
Modest domestic drama, not totally unpleasing.

w S. K. Lauren, Gertrude Purcell, *novel* Kate Douglas Wiggin *d* Rowland V. Lee *ph* Roy Hunt

Anne Shirley, Ruby Keeler, Fay Bainter, James Ellison, Walter Brennan, Donnie Dunagan, Frank Albertson, Alma Kruger, Jackie Moran, Virginia Weidler, Margaret Hamilton
† Remade 1963 as *Summer Magic*.

Mother Didn't Tell Me
US 1950   88m   bw
TCF (Fred Kohlmar)

A working girl marries a doctor and their off duty hours don't coincide.

Thin comedy.

wd Claude Binyon, *novel* The Doctor Wears Three Faces by Mary Baird *ph* Joseph La Shelle

Dorothy McGuire, William Lundigan, June Havoc, Gary Merrill, Jessie Royce Landis

Mother, Jugs and Speed
US 1976   98m   De Luxe   Panavision
TCF (Joseph R. Barbera)

Comic and tragic events in the lives of Los Angeles drivers of private commercial ambulances.
Black comedy of incidents ranging from farcical to sentimental, sometimes funny but basically unacceptable in either vein.

w Tom Mankiewicz *d* Peter Yates *ph* Ralph Woolsey *m* various *md* Joel Sill

Bill Cosby, Raquel Welch, Harvey Keitel, *Allen Garfield*, Bruce Davison, Larry Hagman

Mother Riley Meets the Vampire
GB 1952   74m   bw
Renown (John Gilling)

An old washerwoman accidentally catches a robot-wielding crook called The Vampire.
Childish farce notable for Lucan's last appearance in his dame role, and Lugosi's last substantial appearance of any kind—two pros at the end of their tether.

w Val Valentine *d* John Gilling *ph* Stan Pavey

Arthur Lucan, Bela Lugosi, Dora Bryan, Richard Wattis

'Stupid, humourless and repulsive.'—*MFB*

Mother Wore Tights*
US 1947   109m   Technicolor
TCF (Lamar Trotti)

Recollections of a vaudeville team and their growing family.
Well-mounted, reasonably charming family musical, one of the best of the many TCF examples of this genre.

w Lamar Trotti, *book* Miriam Young *d* Walter Lang *ph* Harry Jackson *md* Alfred Newman, Charles Henderson

Betty Grable, Dan Dailey, Mona Freeman, Connie Marshall, Vanessa Brown, Robert Arthur, Sara Allgood, William Frawley, Ruth Nelson

AA: Alfred Newman, Charles Henderson
AAN: Harry Jackson; song 'You Do' (*m* Josef Myrow, *ly* Mack Gordon)

Moulin Rouge
US 1934   69m   bw
(UA) Darryl F. Zanuck

The wife of a songwriter impersonates her own sister in order to revitalize her marriage and her stage career.
Predictable minor star vehicle, quite competently done.

w Nunnally Johnson, Henry Lehrman, *play* Lyon de Bri *d* Sidney Lanfield *ph* Charles Rosher *md* Alfred Newman

Constance Bennett, Franchot Tone, Tullio Carminati, Helen Westley, Andrew Tombes, Hobart Cavanaugh

Moulin Rouge**
GB 1952   119m   Technicolor
Romulus (Jack Clayton)

Fictional biopic of Toulouse Lautrec.
The dramatic emphasis is on the love affairs of the dwarfish artist, but the film's real interest is in its evocation of 19th-century Montmartre, and especially in the first twenty-minute can can sequence. Nothing later can stand up to the exhilaration of this, and the film slowly slides into boredom.

w John Huston, Anthony Veiller, *novel* Pierre La Mure *d* John Huston *ph* Oswald Morris *m* Georges Auric *ad* Paul Sheriff

Jose Ferrer, Zsa Zsa Gabor, Katherine Kath, Colette Marchand

AAN: best picture; John Huston (as director); Jose Ferrer; Colette Marchand

The Mountain*
US 1956   105m   Technicolor   Vistavision
Paramount (Edward Dmytryk)

After an airplane crash the wreck is difficult to reach. A young man sets off alone to loot it, and his elder brother follows to stop him.
An indeterminate production in which one believes neither the setting, the plot nor the characters, especially not with Vistavision making everything sharply unreal and the brothers seeming two generations apart.

w Ranald MacDougall, *novel* Henri Troyat *d* Edward Dmytryk *ph* Franz Planer *m* Daniele Amfitheatrof

Spencer Tracy, Robert Wagner, Claire Trevor, William Demarest, E. G. Marshall

The Mountain Eagle
GB 1926   72m approx (24 fps)   bw   silent
Gainsborough / Emelka (Michael Balcon)
US title: *Fear o'God*

A young schoolmistress resists the attentions of

a businessman, escapes to the mountains, and marries a recluse.

Unremarkable romantic drama; one of the lost Hitchcock films.

w Eliot Stannard *d* Alfred Hitchcock *ph* Baron Ventigmilia

Nita Naldi, Bernard Goetzke, Malcolm Keen

The Mountain Road

US 1960 102m bw
Columbia / William Goetz

In 1944 China, an American officer helps peasants against the Japanese.

Confused and rather dreary war adventure with pretensions.

w Alfred Hayes, *novel* Theodore White *d* Delbert Mann *ph* Burnett Guffey *m* Jerome Moross *md* Morris Stoloff

James Stewart, Lisa Lu, Glenn Corbett, Henry Morgan, Frank Silvera, James Best, Mike Kellin, Frank Maxwell, Alan Baxter

Mourning Becomes Electra*

US 1947 170m bw
RKO / Theatre Guild (Dudley Nichols)

Murder, doom and guilt affect a New England family at the end of the Civil War.

A mark for trying is all. This is a clearly fated attempt to film the unfilmable, a long and lugubrious updating of Sophocles with more than its share of risible moments.

wd Dudley Nichols, *play* Eugene O'Neill *m* Richard Hagemann *ph* George Barnes *ad* Albert D'Agostino

Michael Redgrave, Rosalind Russell, Katina Paxinou, Kirk Douglas, Raymond Massey, Nancy Coleman, Leo Genn

'A star cast fumbles with helpless and sometimes touching ineptitude.'—*Gavin Lambert*

AAN: Michael Redgrave; Rosalind Russell

The Mouse on the Moon

GB 1963 85m Eastmancolor
UA / Walter Shenson

The tiny duchy of Grand Fenwick discovers that its home-made wine makes excellent rocket fuel.

Piddling sequel to *The Mouse that Roared*, suffering from a hesitant script, too few jokes, and overacting.

w Michael Pertwee *d* Richard Lester *ph* Wilkie Cooper *m* Ron Grainer

Margaret Rutherford, Ron Moody, Bernard Cribbins, David Kossoff, Terry-Thomas, Michael Crawford

The Mouse that Roared**

GB 1959 85m Technicolor
Columbia / Open Road (Carl Foreman)

The tiny duchy of Grand Fenwick is bankrupt, and its minister decides to declare war on the United States, be defeated, and receive Marshall Aid.

Lively comedy which sounds rather better than it plays, but has bright moments.

w Roger Macdougall, Stanley Mann, *novel* Leonard Wibberley *d* Jack Arnold *ph* John Wilcox *m* Edwin Astley

Peter Sellers (playing three parts), Jean Seberg, David Kossoff, William Hartnell, Leo McKern, Macdonald Parke, Harold Kasket

'The kind of irrepressible topical satire whose artistic flaws become increasingly apparent but whose merits outlast them.'—*Peter John Dyer*

Mousey*

GB 1973 74m colour TVM
RSO (Beryl Vertue, Aida Young)
GB theatrical title: *Cat and Mouse*

An unhinged schoolteacher taunts his ex-wife with murder threats.

Unusual psychological thriller.

w John Peacock *d* Daniel Petrie *ph* Jack Hildyard *m* Ron Grainer

Kirk Douglas, Jean Seberg, John Vernon, Sam Wanamaker, James Bradford, Bessie Love

The Mouthpiece**

US 1932 90m bw
Warner (Lucien Hubbard)

A prosecuting counsel successfully turns to defence but becomes corrupt.

A hard-hitting and entertaining melodrama allegedly based on the career of William Fallon, a New York lawyer.

w Joseph Jackson, Earl Baldwin *d* James Flood, Elliott Nugent *ph* Barney McGill

Warren William, Sidney Fox, Aline MacMahon, John Wray, Ralph Ince, Guy Kibbee

Move Over Darling**

US 1963 103m De Luxe Cinemascope
TCF / Arcola / Arwin (Aaron Rosenberg, Marty Melcher)

A wife who has spent five years shipwrecked on a desert island returns to find that her husband has just remarried.

Thin but fitfully amusing remake of *My Favorite Wife*; sheer professionalism gets it by.

w Hal Kanter, Jack Sher *d* Michael Gordon *ph* Daniel L. Fapp *m* Lionel Newman

Doris Day, James Garner, Polly Bergen, Thelma Ritter, Chuck Connors, Fred Clark

Movie Crazy***
US 1932   82m   bw
Harold Lloyd

A filmstruck young man is mistakenly invited to Hollywood for a film test.

The silent comedian is not quite at his best in this early sound comedy, but it contains his last really superb sequences and its picture of Hollywood is both amusing and nostalgic.

w Harold Lloyd and others d Clyde Bruckman ph Walter Lundin

Harold Lloyd, Constance Cummings

Moving Violation*
US 1976   91m   De Luxe
TCF / Roger Corman

Small-town teenagers are pursued by the sheriff because they saw him commit a murder.
Old hat suspenser with a smart new line in thrills.

w David R. Osterhout, William Norton d Charles S. Dubin ph Charles Correll m Don Leake

Stephen McHattie, Kay Lenz, Eddie Albert, Lonnie Chapman, Will Geer
  'Probably the most hair-raising pursuit sequences in the history of film.'—*Cleveland Amory*

Much Too Shy
GB 1942   92m   bw
Columbia (Ben Henry)

A gormless handyman gets into trouble when the portraits of his lady clients are sold to an advertising agency with nude bodies added to them.
A slightly vulgar and talkative farce which restricts the star.

w Ronald Frankau d Marcel Varnel

George Formby, Kathleen Harrison, Hylda Bayley, Eileen Bennett, Joss Ambler, Jimmy Clitheroe

The Mudlark**
GB 1951   98m   bw
TCF (Nunnally Johnson)

A scruffy boy from the docks breaks into Windsor Castle to see Queen Victoria and ends her fifteen years of seclusion.
A pleasant whimsical legend which could have done without the romantic interest, but which despite an air of unreality provides warm-hearted, well upholstered entertainment for family audiences.

w Nunnally Johnson, novel Theodore Bonnet d Jean Negulesco ph Georges Périnal m William Alwyn ad C. P. Norman

Alec Guinness, Irene Dunne, Andrew Ray, Anthony Steel, Constance Smith, Finlay Currie, Edward Rigby

The Mummy**
US 1932   72m   bw
Universal

An Egyptian mummy comes back to life and covets a young girl.
Strange dreamlike horror film with only fleeting frissons but plenty of narrative interest despite the silliest of stories and some fairly stilted acting.

w John I. Balderston d Karl Freund ph Charles Stumar

Boris Karloff, Zita Johann, David Manners, Arthur Byron, Edward Van Sloan
  'It beggars description . . . one of the most unusual talkies ever produced.'—*New York Times*
  'Editing very much in the Germanic style, magnificent lighting and a superb performance from Karloff make this a fantasy almost without equal.'—*John Baxter, 1968*

The Mummy*
GB 1959   88m   Technicolor
Hammer

A mummy brought back to England by archaeologists wakes up and goes on the rampage.
Typical Hammer vulgarization of a Hollywood legend; starts slowly and unpleasantly, but picks up speed and resource in the last half hour.

w Jimmy Sangster d Terence Fisher ph Jack Asher m Frank Reizenstein

Peter Cushing, Christopher Lee, Yvonne Furneaux, Eddie Byrne, Felix Aylmer, Raymond Huntley, John Stuart
† Hammer sequels, of little interest, were *Curse of the Mummy's Tomb* (1964), *The Mummy's Shroud* (1967) and *Blood from the Mummy's Tomb* (1971).

The Mummy's Hand**
US 1940   67m   bw
Universal

The high priest of an evil sect revivifies an Egyptian mummy and uses it to kill off members of an archaeological expedition.
Semi-sequel to 1932's *The Mummy*, economically using the same flashback. It starts off in comedy vein, but the last half hour is among the most scary in horror film history.

w Griffin Jay, Maxwell Shane *d Christy
Cabanne ph* Elwood Bredell

Dick Foran, Wallace Ford, *George Zucco*, Cecil
Kellaway, Peggy Moran, *Tom Tyler, Eduardo
Ciannelli*

† Sequels, of decreasing merit, were *The
Mummy's Tomb* (1942) (in which the heroes of
The Mummy's Hand are killed off), *The
Mummy's Ghost* (1944) and *The Mummy's
Curse* (1944). See also *Abbott and Costello Meet
the Mummy*.

Murder**
GB 1930 92m bw
British International (John Maxwell)

A girl is convicted of murder, but one of the
jurors sets out to prove her innocent.
Interesting early Hitchcock, a rare whodunnit
for him.

w Alma Reville, *novel* Enter Sir John by
Clemence Dane and Helen Simpson *d Alfred
Hitchcock ph* Jack Cox

Herbert Marshall, Nora Baring, Phyllis
Konstam, Edward Chapman, Miles Mander,
Esmé Percy, Donald Calthrop

Murder at Monte Carlo
GB 1934 70m bw
Warner (Irving Asher)

A professor is murdered for his roulette system.
Modest second feature notable only as a
springboard for the career of its star.

w John Hastings Turner, Michael Barringer,
novel Tom Van Dyke *d* Ralph Ince

Errol Flynn, Eve Gray, Paul Graetz, Molly
Lamont, Ellis Irving

Murder at the Vanities*
US 1934 89m bw
Paramount (E. Lloyd Sheldon)

Murder backstage at the first night of Earl
Carroll's Vanities.
Curious, stylish mixture of musical numbers,
broad comedy and mystery. Dated, but fun.

w Carey Wilson, Joseph Gollomb, Sam
Hellman *d Mitchell Leisen ph* Leo Tover

Jack Oakie, Victor McLaglen, Carl Brisson,
Kitty Carlisle, Dorothy Stickney, Gertrude
Michael, Jessie Ralph, Gail Patrick

Murder by Contract*
US 1958 81m bw
Columbia / Orbin (Leon Chooluck)

A professional killer makes a fatal mistake and is
shot down by police.

Low-budgeter which seemed stark and original
at the time, but television has familiarized its
contents. Moody, contrasty photography and
restrained style give it a minor distinction.

w Ben Simcoe *d Irving Lerner ph* Lucien
Ballard m Perry Borkin

Vince Edwards, Philip Pine, Herschel Bernardi,
Caprice Toriel

'Ice cold and completely unsentimental.'—
John Gillett

Murder by Death*
US 1976 94m Metrocolor
Columbia / Ray Stark

Several (fictional) detectives are invited to stay at
the home of a wealthy recluse, and mystery and
murder follow.
Sometimes thin but generally likeable spoof of a
longstanding genre; the stars seize their
opportunities avidly, and the film does not
outstay its welcome

w Neil Simon *d* Robert Moore *ph* David M.
Walsh *m* Dave Grusin *pd* Stephen Grimes

Peter Falk, Alec Guinness, Peter Sellers,
Truman Capote, Estelle Winwood, Elsa
Lanchester, Eileen Brennan, James Coco, David
Niven, Maggie Smith, Nancy Walker

'Plenty of scene-stealing actors but not many
scenes worth stealing.'—*Michael Billington,
Illustrated London News*

'Polished performances fail to compensate for
a vacuous and frustratingly tortuous plot.'—
Sight and Sound

Murder by the Clock
US 1931 76m bw
Paramount

Creepy goings on in an old house after the death
of a dowager who has built herself a tomb from
which she can escape if buried alive.
Tasteless chiller which had the distinction of
being withdrawn from British circulation after
public protests.

w Henry Myers, Rufus King, Charles Beahan,
play Charles Beahan, *novel* Rufus King
d Edward Sloman

Lilyan Tashman, William 'Stage' Boyd, Regis
Toomey, Irving Pichel, Blanche Frederici,
Walter McGrail

Murder He Says**
US 1945 91m bw
Paramount (E. D. Leshin)

An insurance salesman stays with a homicidal
family of hillbillies.
A curious black farce which seems to be

compounded of *Cold Comfort Farm* and *The Red Inn*. Very funny, and ahead of its time.

w Lou Breslow *d* George Marshall *ph* Theodor Sparkuhl

Fred MacMurray, Marjorie Main, Helen Walker, Peter Whitney, Jean Heather, Porter Hall, Mabel Paige

Murder in the Cathedral
GB 1951   136m   bw
George Hoellering

The 12th-century struggle between Henry II and his archbishop culminates in the assassination of Becket in Canterbury Cathedral.
Plainly filmed, slightly amateur version of the celebrated verse play; scarcely a rewarding cinematic experience.

wd George Hoellering, *play* T. S. Eliot *ph* David Kosky *m* Laszlo Lajtha *ad* Peter Pendrey

Father John Grosner, Alexander Gauge, David Ward, George Woodbridge, Basil Burton, Paul Rogers, Niall MacGinnis, Mark Dignam, Leo McKern

'A curious ordeal for the audience . . . a no-man's-land between cinema and drama has been discovered, rather than any extension of either.'—*Gavin Lambert*

Murder in the Fleet
US 1935   70m   bw
MGM (Lucien Hubbard)

Sabotage on a navy cruiser turns out to be the work of a mad inventor.
Weak and confused mixture of melodrama and comedy.

wd Edward Sedgwick *ph* Milton Krasner

Robert Taylor, Jean Parker, Jean Hersholt, Ted Healy, Una Merkel, Nat Pendleton, Raymond Hatton, Donald Cook, Mischa Auer

Murder, Incorporated
US 1960   103m   bw   Cinemascope
TCF (Burt Balaban)

In the thirties, Anastasia and Lepke build up their crime syndicate which spreads terror through New York.
Tedious and poorly made gangster thriller, unforgivable faults considering the many admirable models it has to follow.

w Irve Tunick, Mel Barr *d* Burt Balaban, Stuart Rosenberg *ph* Gayne Rescher *m* Frank de Vol

Stuart Whitman, Mai Britt, Henry Morgan, Peter Falk, David J. Stewart, Simon Oakland, Morey Amsterdam

AAN: Peter Falk

The Murder Man*
US 1935   84m   bw
MGM (Harry Rapf)

A reporter commits murder and frames someone else.
Good low-key melodrama with an interesting cast.

w Tim Whelan, John C. Higgins *d* Tim Whelan

Spencer Tracy, Virginia Bruce, Lionel Atwill, James Stewart, Harvey Stephens, William Collier Snr

Murder on the Orient Express**
GB 1974   131m   Technicolor
EMI / GW Films (John Brabourne, Richard Goodwin)

In the early thirties, Hercule Poirot solves a murder on a snowbound train.
Reasonably elegant but disappointingly slackly-handled version of a classic mystery novel. Finney overacts and his all-star support is distracting, while as soon as the train chugs into its snowdrift the film stops moving too, without even a dramatic 'curtain'.

w Paul Dehn, *novel* Agatha Christie *d* Sidney Lumet *ph* Geoffrey Unsworth *m* Richard Rodney Bennett *pd* Tony Walton

Albert Finney, *Ingrid Bergman*, Lauren Bacall, Wendy Hiller, Sean Connery, Vanessa Redgrave, Michael York, Martin Balsam, Richard Widmark, Jacqueline Bisset, Jean-Pierre Cassel, Rachel Roberts, George Coulouris, *John Gielgud*, Anthony Perkins, Colin Blakely, Jeremy Lloyd, Denis Quilley

'Audiences appear to be so hungry for this type of entertainment that maybe it hardly matters that it isn't very good.'—*Judith Crist*

AA: Ingrid Bergman
AAN: Paul Dehn; Geoffrey Unsworth; Richard Rodney Bennett; Albert Finney

Murder She Said*
GB 1962   87m   bw
MGM (George H. Brown)

An elderly spinster investigates after seeing a woman strangled in a passing train.
Frightfully British and disappointingly tame adaptation of an Agatha Christie character, with only the star (who is somewhat miscast) holding one's attention.

w David Pursall, Jack Seddon, *novel* 4.50 from Paddington by Agatha Christie *d* George Pollock *ph* Geoffrey Faithfull *m* Ron Goodwin

Margaret Rutherford, Charles Tingwell, Muriel Pavlow, Arthur Kennedy, James Robertson

Justice, Thorley Walters, Gerald Cross, Conrad Phillips

† Thanks to Miss Rutherford's popularity, three increasingly poor sequels were made: *Murder at the Gallop* (1963), *Murder Most Foul* (1964), *Murder Ahoy* (1964).

The Murderers Are Among Us*
Germany 1947   87m   bw
Defa
original title: *Die Mörder Sind Unter Uns*
In the ruins of Berlin several post-war characters indulge in gloomy self-examination.
Almost a caricature of what one would expect from a defeated people, this now-curious item has a certain power of its own.

wd Wolfgang Staudte *ph* Friedl Behn-Grund, Eugen Klagemann *m* Ernst Roters

Hildegard Knef, Ernst Fischer, Arno Paulsen

Murderer's Row
US 1966   108m   Technicolor
Columbia / Meadway–Claude / Euan Lloyd
Matt Helm tracks down an international villain who has kidnapped an inventor.
Witless and uninventive spy spoof which drags itself wearily along but never attempts an explanation of its own title.

w Herbert Baker, *novel* Donald Hamilton *d* Henry Levin *ph* Sam Leavitt *m* Lalo Schifrin

Dean Martin, Ann-Margret, Karl Malden, Camilla Sparv, James Gregory, Beverly Adams, Tom Reese

Murders in the Rue Morgue*
US 1932   62m   bw
Universal
A series of grisly murders prove to be the work of a trained ape.
A distant relation of the original story, mildly interesting for its obvious Caligari influences, but not very good in any way.

w Tom Reed, Dale Van Avery, John Huston, *story* Edgar Allan Poe *d* Robert Florey *ph* Karl Freund

Bela Lugosi, Sidney Fox, Leon Ames, Bert Roach, Brandon Hurst

Murders in the Rue Morgue*
US 1971   86m   Foto Film Color
AIP
Poe's story is being presented at a Grand Guignol theatre in Paris, and when murders happen within the company Inspector Vidocq comes to investigate.
Playfully plotted chiller which has more to do with *The Phantom of the Opera* than with Poe. A good time waster for addicts.

w Charles Wicking, Henry Slesar *d* Gordon Hessler *ph* Manuel Berengier *m* Waldo de Los Rios

Jason Robards Jnr, Herbert Lom, Lilli Palmer, Adolfo Celi, Michael Dunn

Muriel*
France / Italy 1963   116m   Eastmancolor
Argos / Alpha / Eclair / Films de la Pléiade / Dear Films (Anatole Dauman)
aka: *Muriel, ou le Temps d'un Retour*
A widow and her stepson are both misled by memories of past loves.
Elusive character drama which, though over-generous in length, fails to satisfy.

w Jean Cayrol *d* Alain Resnais *ph* Sacha Vierny *m* Hans Werner Henze

Delphine Seyrig, Jean-Pierre Kérien, Nita Klein, Jean-Baptiste Thierrée
'One has to watch and listen with every nerve alert.'—*Tom Milne, MFB*

Murphy's War*
GB 1971   108m   Eastmancolor
Panavision
Hemdale / Yates–Deeley (Michael Deeley)
A torpedoed British merchantman in Venezuela devotes himself to bombing a U-boat from a home-made plane.
Modest adventure story with the star in better form than the script.

w Stirling Silliphant, *novel* Max Catto *d* Peter Yates *ph* Douglas Slocombe *m* John Barry

Peter O'Toole, Sian Phillips, Philippe Noiret, Horst Janson

Music for Millions*
US 1944   117m   bw
MGM
A small girl helps her pregnant sister who is a member of Jose Iturbi's orchestra.
Dewy-eyed wartime musical, full of popular classics, sentimentality and child interest, all smoothly packaged. As an example of what the public wanted in 1944, quite an eye-opener.

w Myles Connelly *d* Henry Koster *ph* Robert Surtees

Margaret O'Brien, June Allyson, Jose Iturbi, Jimmy Durante, Marsha Hunt, Hugh Herbert, Henry Davenport, Connie Gilchrist

AAN: Myles Connelly

Music Hath Charms*
GB 1935 70m bw
BIP (Walter C. Mycroft)

A dance band's broadcast has various effects on listeners.

Pleasing, modest portmanteau of sketches with music.

w Jack Davies, Courtney Territt, L. Du Garde Peach d Thomas Bentley, Alexander Esway, Walter Summers, Arthur Woods

Henry Hall and his Orchestra, Carol Goodner, W. H. Berry, Arthur Margetson, Antoinette Cellier, Billy Milton

Music in the Air
US 1934 85m bw
Fox

An opera singer is torn between two men. Heavy-going light entertainment.

w Howard Young, Billy Wilder, play Oscar Hammerstein II, Jerome Kern ph Ernest Palmer d Joe May

Gloria Swanson, John Boles, Douglass Montgomery, June Lang, Al Shean, Reginald Owen, Joseph Cawthorn, Hobart Bosworth

The Music Lovers*
GB 1970 123m Eastmancolor
Panavision
UA / Rossfilms (Roy Baird)

Homosexual composer Tchaikovsky is impelled to marry, loses his sponsor, drives his wife into an asylum and dies of cholera.

Absurd fantasia on the life of a great composer, produced in a manner reminiscent of MGM's sillier musicals; up to a point hysterically (and unintentionally) funny, then rather sickening.

w Melvyn Bragg, book Beloved Friend by C. D. Bowen, Barbara Van Meck d Ken Russell ph Douglas Slocombe md André Previn

Richard Chamberlain, Glenda Jackson, Christopher Gable, Max Adrian, Isabella Telezynska, Maureen Pryor, Andrew Faulds

'Tchaikovsky has been made the excuse for a crude melodrama about sex.'—Konstantin Bazarov

The Music Man***
US 1962 151m Technirama
Warner (Morton da Costa)

A confidence trickster persuades a small-town council to start a boys' band, with himself as the agent for all the expenses.

Reasonably cinematic, thoroughly invigorating transference to the screen of a hit Broadway

musical. Splendid period 'feel', standout performances, slight sag in second half.

w Marion Hargrove, book Meredith Willson d Morton da Costa ph Robert Burks md Ray Heindorf ch Onna White songs Meredith Willson

Robert Preston, Shirley Jones, Buddy Hackett, Hermione Gingold, Pert Kelton, Paul Ford

AA: Ray Heindorf
AAN: best picture

Mustang Country
US 1976 79m Technicolor
Universal (John Champion)

In 1925 Montana, a rancher comes out of retirement to help to round up a wild stallion. Mild outdoor yarn for family audiences.

wd John Champion ph J. Barry Herron m Lee Holdridge

Joel McCrea, Nika Mina, Robert Fuller, Patrick Wayne

The Mutations
GB 1974 92m Eastmancolor
Columbia / Getty (Robert D. Weinbach)

A bio-chemist uses circus freaks in his experiments to find the perfect synthesis of plant and animal.

Tasteless horror film with little style of any kind.

w Robert D. Weinbach, Edward Mann d Jack Cardiff ph Paul Beeson m Basil Kirchin

Donald Pleasence, Tom Baker, Brad Harris, Julie Ege, Michael Dunn, Scott Antony, Jill Haworth, Lisa Collings

Mutiny on the Bounty***
US 1935 135m bw
MGM (Irving Thalberg, Albert Lewin)

An 18th-century British naval vessel sets off for South America but during a mutiny the captain is cast adrift and the mutineers settle in the Pitcairn Islands.

A still-entertaining adventure film which seemed at the time like the pinnacle of Hollywood's achievement but can now be seen to be slackly told, with wholesale pre-release editing very evident. Individual scenes and performances are however refreshingly well-handled.

w Talbot Jennings, Jules Furthman, Carey Wilson, book Charles Nordhoff, James Hall d Frank Lloyd ph Arthur Edeson m Herbert Stothart

Charles Laughton, Clark Gable, Franchot Tone, Movita, Dudley Digges, Henry Stephenson, Donald Crisp, Eddie Quillan, Francis Lister, Spring Byington, Ian Wolfe

AA: best picture
AAN: script; Frank Lloyd; Herbert Stothart;
Charles Laughton; Clark Gable; Franchot Tone

Mutiny on the Bounty
US 1962 185m Technicolor Ultra
    Panavision 70
MGM / Arcola (Aaron Rosenberg)

Overlong and unattractive remake marred
principally by Brando's English accent and
various production follies, not to mention his
overlong and bloody death scene. The shipboard
sadism still works pretty well, but after the
landing in Tahiti boredom takes over.

w Charles Lederer d Lewis Milestone
ph Robert Surtees m Bronislau Kaper

Trevor Howard, Marlon Brando, Richard
Harris, Hugh Griffith, Tarita, Richard Haydn,
Percy Herbert, Duncan Lamont, Gordon
Jackson, Chips Rafferty, Noel Purcell

AAN: best picture; Robert Surtees; Bronislau
Kaper; song 'Follow Me' (m Bronislau Kaper,
ly Paul Francis Webster)

My Blood Runs Cold
US 1965 108m bw Panavision
Warner (William Conrad)

A spoilt heiress meets a strange young man who
claims she is the reincarnation of a long dead
charmer; he turns out to be a madman who has
come across an old diary.
Initially intriguing but eventually exhausting
melodrama with a weak solution.

w John Mantley d William Conrad ph Sam
Leavitt m George Duning

Troy Donahue, Joey Heatherton, Barry
Sullivan, Jeanette Nolan

    'Not all that bad, but not worth missing I Love
Lucy for either.'—Leonard Maltin

My Blue Heaven
US 1950 96m Technicolor
TCF (Sol C. Siegel)

A pair of troupers want a family, by adoption if
not otherwise.
Routine musical drenched in sentimentality.

w Lamar Trotti, Claude Binyon d Henry
Koster ph Alfred E. Arling songs Harold Arlen

Betty Grable, Dan Dailey, Mitzi Gaynor, David
Wayne, Jane Wyatt, Una Merkel

My Brother Jonathan
GB 1947 108m bw
ABP

The life of a small-town doctor who wanted to be
a great surgeon.

Unobjectionable, unexciting novel-on-film with
the typically British artificial studio look of the
time.

w Leslie Landau, Adrian Alington,
novel Francis Brett Young d Harold French
ph Derick Williams m Hans May

Michael Denison, Dulcie Gray, Ronald Howard,
Stephen Murray

My Brother Talks to Horses
US 1946 93m bw
MGM (Samuel Marx)

A boy who can talk to horses finds himself in
demand by racetrack gamblers.
Well-mounted but uninspired whimsy with a
fatal lack of pace.

w Morton Thomson, from his novel Joe the
Wounded Tennis Player d Fred Zinnemann
ph Joseph Ruttenburg

Butch Jenkins, Peter Lawford, Charlie Ruggles,
Edward Arnold, Beverly Tyler, Spring Byington

My Brother's Keeper
GB 1948 91m bw
GFD / Gainsborough (Antony Darnborough)

Two convicts escape, handcuffed together; one is
violent, the other innocent.
Pre-Defiant Ones social melodrama, quite well
made but suffering from miscasting.

w Frank Harvey, story Maurice Wiltshire
d Alfred Roome, Roy Rich

Jack Warner, George Cole, Jane Hylton, David
Tomlinson, Bill Owen, Raymond Lovell,
Yvonne Owen, Beatrice Varley

My Cousin Rachel*
US 1953 98m bw
TCF (Nunnally Johnson)

A Cornish gentleman dies in Italy after marrying
a mysterious lady; when she comes to England
she arouses the hostility, and love, of her
husband's foster son.
Well-wrought but dramatically unsatisfactory
Victorian melodrama from a bestseller; plenty of
suspicion but no solution makes Rachel a dull
girl.

w Nunnally Johnson, novel Daphne du Maurier
d Henry Koster ph Joseph La Shelle m Franz
Waxman

Olivia de Havilland, Richard Burton, John
Sutton, Audrey Dalton, Ronald Squire

AAN: Joseph La Shelle; Richard Burton

My Daughter Joy
GB 1950   81m   bw
Columbia / Gregory Ratoff
US title: *Operation X*

In order to cement a new trade pact, an international financier plans to marry his daughter to the son of an African sultan.

Turgid melodrama swamping some good actors.

w Robert Thoeren, William Rose, *novel* David Golder by Irene Neirowsky *d* Gregory Ratoff *ph* Georges Périnal

Edward G. Robinson, Peggy Cummins, Nora Swinburne, Richard Greene, Finlay Currie, Gregory Ratoff, Ronald Adam, Walter Rilla, James Robertson Justice, David Hutcheson

My Darling Clementine***
US 1946   98m   bw
TCF (Samuel G. Engel)

Wyatt Earp cleans up Tombstone and wipes out the Clanton gang at the OK corral.

Archetypal western mood piece, full of nostalgia for times gone by and crackling with memorable scenes and characterizations.

w Samuel G. Engel, Winston Miller, *book* Wyatt Earp, Frontier Marshal by Stuart N. Lake *d* John Ford *ph* Joe MacDonald *m* Cyril Mockridge

Henry Fonda, Victor Mature, Walter Brennan, Linda Darnell, Cathy Downs, Tim Holt, Ward Bond, *Alan Mowbray*, John Ireland, Jane Darwell

'Every scene, every shot is the product of a keen and sensitive eye.'—*Bosley Crowther*

'Considerable care has gone to its period reconstruction, but the view is a poetic one.'—*Lindsay Anderson*

My Dream Is Yours
US 1949   101m   Technicolor
Warner

A Hollywood talent scout discovers a new singer.

Competent, forgettable musical.

w Harry Kurnitz, Dane Lussier *d* Michael Curtiz *ph* Ernest Haller *m* Harry Warren *ly* Ralph Blane *ch* Le Roy Prinz.

Doris Day, Jack Carson, Lee Bowman, Adolphe Menjou, Eve Arden, S. Z. Sakall

My Fair Lady***
US 1964   175m   Technicolor
Super Panavision 70
CBS / Warner (Jack L. Warner)

Musical version of *Pygmalion*, about a flower girl trained by an arrogant elocutionist to pass as a lady.

Careful, cold transcription of a stage success; cinematically quite uninventive when compared with *Pygmalion* itself, but a pretty good entertainment.

w Alan Jay Lerner, *play* Pygmalion by Bernard Shaw *d* George Cukor *ph* Harry Stradling *m* Frederick Loewe *ch* Hermes Pan *ad* Gene Allen *costumes Cecil Beaton*

Rex Harrison, Audrey Hepburn, *Stanley Holloway*, Wilfrid Hyde White, Gladys Cooper, Jeremy Brett, Theodore Bikel, Isobel Elsom, Mona Washbourne, Walter Burke

'The property has been not so much adapted as elegantly embalmed.'—*Andrew Sarris*

AA: best picture; George Cukor; Harry Stradling; Rex Harrison
AAN: Alan Jay Lerner; Stanley Holloway; Gladys Cooper

My Favorite Blonde***
US 1942   78m   bw
Paramount (Paul Jones)

A burlesque comic travelling by train helps a lady in distress and lives to regret it.

Smartly paced spy comedy thriller, one of its star's best vehicles.

w Don Hartman, Frank Butler, Melvin Frank, Norman Panama *d* Sidney Lanfield *ph* William Mellor *m* David Buttolph

Bob Hope, Madeleine Carroll, Gale Sondergaard, George Zucco, Lionel Royce, Walter Kingsford, Victor Varconi

My Favorite Brunette*
US 1947   87m   bw
Paramount (Daniel Dare)

A photographer gets mixed up with mobsters.

Pretty fair star vehicle which half-heartedly spoofs *Farewell My Lovely*.

w Edmund Beloin, Jack Rose *d* Elliott Nugent *ph* Lionel Lindon *m* Robert Emmett Dolan

Bob Hope, Dorothy Lamour, Peter Lorre, Lon Chaney Jnr, John Hoyt, Charles Dingle, Reginald Denny

My Favorite Spy*
US 1951   93m   bw
Paramount (Paul Jones)

A burlesque comic is asked by the US government to pose as an international spy who happens to be his double.

Moderately funny star vehicle with more willing hands than good ideas. The chase finale however is worth waiting for.

w Edmund Hartmann, Jack Sher *d* Norman Z.
McLeod *ph* Victor Milner *m* Victor Young

Bob Hope, Hedy Lamarr, Francis L. Sullivan,
Arnold Moss, Mike Mazurki, Luis Van Rooten

My Favorite Wife***
US 1940   88m   bw
RKO (Leo McCarey)

A lady explorer returns after several
shipwrecked years to find that her husband has
married again.
A well-worn situation gets its brightest treatment
in this light star vehicle.

*w Sam and Bella Spewack, Leo McCarey
d Garson Kanin ph* Rudolph Maté *m* Roy
Webb

Cary Grant, Irene Dunne, Randolph Scott, Gail
Patrick, Ann Shoemaker, Donald MacBride
    'One of those comedies with a glow on it.'—
Otis Ferguson
† Other variations (qv): *Too Many Husbands,
Our Wife, Three for the Show, Move Over
Darling.*

AAN: script; Roy Webb

My Foolish Heart*
US 1949   98m   bw
Samuel Goldwyn

A woman deceives her husband into thinking her
forthcoming child is his.
A 'woman's picture' par excellence, and among
the first to benefit from commercial plugging of a
schmaltzy theme tune.

w Julius J. and Philip G. Epstein, *story* J. D.
Salinger *d* Mark Robson *ph* Lee Garmes
m Victor Young

Susan Hayward, Dana Andrews, Kent Smith,
Robert Keith, Gigi Perreau, Lois Wheeler, Jessie
Royce Landis

AAN: Susan Hayward; title song (*m* Victor
Young, *ly* Ned Washington)

My Forbidden Past
US 1951   81m   bw
RKO (Polan Banks)

A New Orleans beauty seeks vengeance when
her cousin prevents her marriage.
Stuffy period melodrama with vigorous
performances.

w Marion Parsonnet, *novel* Polan Banks
d Robert Stevenson *ph* Harry J. Wild
m Frederick Hollander *ad* Albert S. D'Agostino

Ava Gardner, Melvyn Douglas, Robert
Mitchum, Janis Carter, Lucile Watson

My Friend Flicka*
US 1943   89m   Technicolor
TCF

Adventures of a young boy and his pet colt.
Winsome boy-and-horse story, one of the most
popular family films of the forties. Sequel 1945
with virtually the same cast: *Green Grass of
Wyoming.*

w Mary O'Hara from her novel *d* Harold
Schuster *m* Alfred Newman

Roddy McDowall, Preston Foster, Rita
Johnson, James Bell, Jeff Corey

My Friend Irma*
US 1949   103m   bw
Paramount / Hal B. Wallis

Dumb blonde Irma deserts her crooked boy
friend and marries a singing soda jerk.
Comic strip humour responsible for the screen
debut of Martin and Lewis. Sequel 1950: *My
Friend Irma Goes West.*

w Cy Howard, Parke Levy, *radio show* Cy
Howard *d* George Marshall *ph* Leo Tover
m Roy Webb

Marie Wilson, John Lund, Diana Lynn, *Dean
Martin, Jerry Lewis*, Don Defore, Hans
Conried, Kathryn Givney

My Gal Sal*
US 1942   103m   Technicolor
TCF (Robert Bassler)

The career and romances of songwriter Paul
Dreiser.
Conventional nineties musical biopic, more
vigorous and likeable than most.

w Seton I. Miller, Darrell Ware, Karl Tunberg,
book My Brother Paul by Theodore Dreiser
d Irving Cummings *ph* Ernest Palmer
md Alfred Newman

Rita Hayworth, Victor Mature, John Sutton,
Carole Landis, James Gleason, Phil Silvers,
Walter Catlett, Mona Maris, Frank Orth

AAN: Alfred Newman

My Geisha
US 1962   120m   Technirama
Paramount / Steve Parker

A director makes a film in Japan; his wife
disguises herself as a geisha and gets the leading
role.
Silly, overstretched comedy with pretty
locations.

w Norman Krasna *d* Jack Cardiff
ph Shunichuro Nakao *m* Franz Waxman

Shirley Maclaine, Yves Montand, Robert
Cummings, Edward G. Robinson, Yoko Tani

My Girl Tisa***
US 1948   95m   bw
United States Pictures (Milton Sperling)

An immigrant girl in New York in the nineties
falls for an aspiring politician, is threatened with
deportation but saved by the intervention of
Theodore Roosevelt.
Charming period fairy tale with excellent
background detail and attractive performances.

w Allen Boretz, play Lucille S. Prumbs, Sara B.
Smith d Elliott Nugent ph Ernest Haller
m Max Steiner

Lilli Palmer, Sam Wanamaker, Alan Hale,
Stella Adler, Akim Tamiroff

My Learned Friend***
GB 1943   76m   bw
Ealing (Robert Hamer)

A shady lawyer is last on a mad ex-convict's
murder list of those who helped get him
convicted.
Madcap black farce, plot-packed and generally
hilarious; the star's last vehicle, but one of his
best, with superbly timed sequences during a
pantomime and on the face of Big Ben.

w John Dighton, Angus Macphail d Basil
Dearden, Will Hay

Will Hay, Claude Hulbert, Mervyn Johns,
Ernest Thesiger, Charles Victor, Lloyd Pearson,
Maudie Edwards,
G. H. Mulcaster, Gibb McLaughlin

My Life with Caroline*
US 1941   81m   bw
RKO (Lewis Milestone)

An understanding husband thinks his high-
spirited wife may be having an affair.
Very minor romantic comedy with an agreeable
air but no substance whatever.

w John Van Druten, Arnold Belgard d Lewis
Milestone ph Victor Milner m Werner
Heymann

Ronald Colman, Anna Lee, Reginald Gardiner,
Charles Winninger, Gilbert Roland

My Little Chickadee*
US 1939   83m   bw
Universal (Lester Cowan)

A shady lady and an incompetent cardsharp
unmask a villain in the old west.
A clash of comedy personalities which is
affectionately remembered but in truth does not
play very well apart from the odd line.

w Mae West, W. C. Fields d Edward Cline
ph Joseph Valentine m Frank Skinner
md Charles Previn

Mae West, W. C. Fields, Joseph Calleia, Dick
Foran, Margaret Hamilton
  'It obstinately refuses to gather
momentum.'—The Times
  'A classic among bad movies . . . the satire
never really gets off the ground. But the ground is
such an honest mixture of dirt, manure and corn
that at times it is fairly aromatic.'—Pauline
Kael, 1968

My Lucky Star*
US 1938   84m   bw
TCF (Harry Joe Brown)

A shopgirl is innocently caught in a
compromising situation with the owner's son.
Fluffy comedy, acceptable as a background for
skating sequences.

w Harry Tugend, Jack Yellen d Roy del Ruth
ph John Mescall songs Mack Gordon, Harry
Revel

Sonja Henie, Richard Greene, Joan Davis,
Buddy Ebsen, Cesar Romero, Arthur Treacher,
George Barbier, Louise Hovick, Billy Gilbert

My Man and I
US 1952   99m   bw
MGM (Stephen Ames)

A Mexican farm labourer, proud of his
American citizenship, is drawn into trouble.
Eccentric melodrama in which all the native
Americans are whores, cheats or murderers; well
enough made but not very interesting.

w John Fante, Jack Leonard d William
Wellman ph William Mellor m David Buttolph

Ricardo Montalban, Shelley Winters, Claire
Trevor, Wendell Corey

My Man Godfrey***
US 1936   90m   bw
Universal (Gregory La Cava)

A zany millionaire family invite a tramp to be
their butler and find he is richer than they are.
Archetypal Depression concept which is also
one of the best of the thirties crazy sophisticated
comedies, though its pacing today seems
somewhat unsure.

w Morrie Ryskind, Eric Hatch, Gregory La
Cava d Gregory La Cava ph Ted Tetzlaff

Carole Lombard, William Powell, Alice Brady,
Mischa Auer, Eugene Pallette, Gail Patrick,
Alan Mowbray, Jean Dixon

AAN: best picture; script; Gregory La Cava (as

director); Carole Lombard; William Powell; Alice Brady; Mischa Auer

My Man Godfrey
US 1957 92m Technicolor
Cinemascope
U-I (Ross Hunter)

Tepid remake which without the period background, and in unsuitable wide screen, raises very few laughs.

w Everett Freeman, Peter Berneis, William Bowers *d* Henry Koster *ph* William Daniels *m* Frank Skinner

June Allyson, David Niven, Jessie Royce Landis, Jay Robinson, Robert Keith, Martha Hyer, Eva Gabor

My Name Is Julia Ross **
US 1945 65m bw
Columbia

A girl is kidnapped and forced to impersonate an heiress.
A very good second feature which has been culted into a reputation beyond its worth, though it is undeniably slick and entertaining.

w Muriel Roy Bolton, *novel* The Woman in Red by Anthony Gilbert *d* Joseph H. Lewis *ph* Burnett Guffey *md* Mischa Bakaleinikoff

Nina Foch, Dame May Whitty, George Macready, Roland Varno, Doris Lloyd
'A superior, well-knit thriller.'—*Don Miller*

My Own True Love
US 1948 84m bw
Paramount

A lonely man home from the war quarrels with his son over a girl twenty years younger than himself.
Minor romantic drama, competently but coldly presented.

w Arthur Kober, *novel* Yolanda Foldes *d* Compton Bennett *ph* Charles Lang *m* Robert Emmett Dolan

Phyllis Calvert, Melvyn Douglas, Philip Friend, Wanda Hendrix, Binnie Barnes

My Pal Gus
US 1952 84m bw
TCF (Stanley Rubin)

A business man has a five-year-old problem son and in sorting him out falls in love with his schoolteacher.
Unrewarding domestic drama with actors who look as though they would rather be somewhere else.

w Fay and Michael Kanin *d* Robert Parrish *ph* Leo Tover *m* Leigh Harline

Richard Widmark, Joanne Dru, Audrey Totter, George Winslow, Joan Banks, Regis Toomey, Ludwig Donath

My Reputation
US 1946 96m bw
Warner (Henry Blanke)

A widow is talked about for dispensing too soon with her weeds.
Dim drama, hastily shot on familiar sets with a reach-me-down script.

w Catherine Turney, *novel* Instruct My Sorrows by Clare Jaynes *d* Curtis Bernhardt *ph* James Wong Howe *m* Max Steiner

Barbara Stanwyck, George Brent, Warner Anderson, Lucile Watson, John Ridgely, Eve Arden, Jerome Cowan, Esther Dale, Scotty Beckett

My Sister Eileen *
US 1942 96m bw
Columbia (Max Gordon)

Two Ohio girls come to New York and live with some zany friends in a Greenwich Village basement apartment.
Rather strained high jinks which were, not surprisingly, later musicalized.

w Ruth McKinney, Joseph Fields, Jerome Chodorov, *book* Ruth McKinney *d* Alexander Hall *ph* Joseph Walker *md* Morris Stoloff

Rosalind Russell, Janet Blair, Brian Aherne, Allyn Joslyn, George Tobias, Elizabeth Patterson, June Havoc

AAN: Rosalind Russell

My Sister Eileen *
US 1955 108m Technicolor
Cinemascope
Columbia (Fred Kohlmar)

Musical version of the above, via a Broadway show. Watchable but hardly stimulating.

w Blake Edwards, Richard Quine, *play* Joseph Fields, Jerome Chodorov *d* Richard Quine *ph* Charles Lawton Jnr *m* George Duning *md* Morris Stoloff *ch* Bob Fosse *songs* Jule Styne, Leo Robin

Betty Garrett, Janet Leigh, Jack Lemmon, Bob Fosse, Kurt Kasznar, Horace MacMahon, Dick York

My Six Convicts *
US 1952 104m bw
Columbia / Stanley Kramer

A psychologist joins the staff of an American prison and gains the trust of six inmates. Moderately interesting semi-documentary melodrama marred by a conventional prison break climax.

w Michael Blankfort, *book* Donald Powell Wilson d Hugo Fregonese ph Guy Roe m Dmitri Tiomkin

John Beal, *Millard Mitchell, Gilbert Roland*, Marshall Thompson, Regis Toomey

My Six Loves
US 1965   101m   Technicolor   Vistavision
Paramount / Gant Gaither

A musical comedy star goes to the country for a rest and with the help of the local minister adopts six scruffy children.

Icky sentimental comedy for the easily pleased.

w John Fante, Joseph Calvelli, William Wood d Gower Champion ph Arthur E. Arling m Walter Scharf

Debbie Reynolds, David Janssen, Cliff Robertson, Eileen Heckart

  'Enough to make you settle for cyclamates—or cyanide.'—*Judith Crist, 1973*

My Son John
US 1952   122m   bw
Paramount (Leo McCarey)

An American Catholic family is horrified when its eldest son is revealed as a communist.

The lower depths of Hollywood's witch hunt cycle are marked by this Goldwynesque family saga, all sweetness and light, in which the commie son is treated as though he had rabies. Purely as entertainment the plot is pretty choppy and defeats all attempts at acting.

w Myles Connelly, Leo McCarey d Leo McCarey ph Harry Stradling m Robert Emmett Dolan

Helen Hayes, Robert Walker, Dean Jagger, Van Heflin, Minor Watson, Frank McHugh, Richard Jaeckel

AAN: Leo McCarey (original story)

My Son My Son*
US 1940   117m   bw
Edward Small

A man who becomes rich spoils his son and lives to regret it.

Solid narrative from a bestseller.

w Lenore Coffee, *novel* Howard Spring d Charles Vidor

Brian Aherne, Madeleine Carroll, Louis Hayward, Laraine Day, Henry Hull

My Teenage Daughter
GB 1956   100m   bw
British Lion / Everest (Herbert Wilcox)
US title: *Teenage Bad Girl*

A widow's seventeen-year-old daughter meets an aggressive young man and ends up in court.

Predictable domestic drama, a tame British version of *Rebel without a Cause*.

w Felicity Douglas d Herbert Wilcox ph Max Greene

Anna Neagle, Sylvia Syms, Kenneth Haigh, Norman Wooland, Wilfrid Hyde White, Julia Lockwood, Helen Haye

My Wife's Best Friend
US 1952   87m   bw
TCF (Robert Bassler)

A wife assumes different personalities in an effort to keep her wayward husband.

Moderately lively comedy.

w Isabel Lennart d Richard Sale ph Leo Tover m Leigh Harline

Anne Baxter, Macdonald Carey, Cecil Kellaway, Leif Erickson

My Wild Irish Rose
US 1947   101m   Technicolor
Warner

The ups and downs of Irish tenor Chauncey Olcott and his encounters with Lillian Russell. Inoffensive but not very exciting period musical, rather lacking in humour.

w Peter Milne, *book* Rita Ilcott d David Butler ph Arthur Edeson m Ray Heindorf, Max Steiner ch Le Roy Prinz

Dennis Morgan, Arlene Dahl, Andrea King, Alan Hale, George Tobias

AAN: Ray Heindorf, Max Steiner

Myra Breckinridge
US 1970   94m   De Luxe   Panavision
TCF (Robert Fryer)

After a sex change operation a film critic goes to Hollywood to accomplish the deflation of the American male.

A sharply satirical novel has been turned into a sleazy and aimless picture which became a watershed of permissiveness; after international outcry it was shunned even by its own studio. A few good laughs do emerge from the morass, but even the old clips are misused.

w Mike Sarne, David Giler, *novel* Gore Vidal d Mike Sarne ph Richard Moore m Lionel Newman

Mae West, Raquel Welch, John Huston, Rex

Reed, Jim Backus, John Carradine, Andy
Devine

'At last, the book that couldn't be written is
now the motion picture that couldn't be
made!'—*publicity*

Mysterious Island*
GB 1961   101m   Technicolor
Columbia / Ameran (Charles Schneer)

Confederate officers escape by balloon and join
shipwrecked English ladies on a strange island
where they are menaced by prehistoric monsters
and helped by Captain Nemo.
Rambling, lively juvenile adventure with good
moments and excellent monsters.

w John Prebble, Dan Ullman, Crane Wilbur,
novel Jules Verne *d* Cy Endfield *ph* Wilkie
Cooper *m* Bernard Herrmann *sp* Ray
Harryhausen

Joan Greenwood, Michael Craig, Herbert Lom,
Michael Callan, Gary Merrill

The Mysterious Lady
US 1928   84m (24 fps)   bw   silent
MGM

A glamorous Russian spy has to save her lover
from execution as a traitor.
Threadbare star melodrama.

w Bess Meredyth *d* Fred Niblo

Greta Garbo, Conrad Nagel, Gustav Von
Seyffertitz

The Mystery of Edwin Drood*
US 1935   85m   bw
Universal

In a cathedral town, a drug-addicted choirmaster
is his nephew's rival for the hand of Rosa Bud.
Fairly creditable attempt to deal with a famous
unfinished novel. Slightly stilted, but good
visuals and performances.

w John L. Balderston, Gladys Unger, Bradley
King, Leopold Atlas, *novel* Charles Dickens
d Stuart Walker

Claude Rains, Douglass Montgomery, Heather
Angel, David Manners, E. E. Clive, Valerie
Hobson

The Mystery of Marie Roget
US 1942   61m   bw
Universal (Paul Malvern)

A Parisian music hall star plots to kill her sister
but herself disappears.
Ham-fisted, stilted mystery drama relying hardly
at all on its original.

w Michael Jacoby, *story* Edgar Allan Poe *d* Phil
Rosen *ph* Elwood Bredell

Maria Montez, Patric Knowles, *Maria
Ouspenskaya*, Lloyd Corrigan, John Litel,
Edward Norris, Frank Reicher

The Mystery of Mr X
US 1934   84m   bw
MGM

In foggy London, a jewel thief protects himself
by finding the murderer of several policemen.
Passable mystery, later remade as *The Hour of
Thirteen*.

w Howard Emmett Rogers, Philip MacDonald,
Monckton Hoffe, *novel* X vs Rex by Philip
MacDonald *d* Edgar Selwyn *ph* Oliver T.
Marsh

Robert Montgomery, Elizabeth Allan, Lewis
Stone, Ralph Forbes, Henry Stephenson,
Forrester Harvey

The Mystery of the Wax Museum****
US 1933   77m   Technicolor
Warner (Henry Blanke)

A sculptor disfigured in a fire builds a wax
museum by covering live victims in wax.
Archetypal horror material is augmented by a
sub-plot about drug-running and an
authoritative example of the wisecracking
reporter school of the early thirties. The film is
also notable for its highly satisfactory use of two-
colour Technicolor and for its splendid art
direction. Remade 1953 as *House of Wax* (qv).

w Don Mullally, Carl Erickson, *play* Charles S.
Belden *d* Michael Curtiz *ph* Ray Rennahan
ad Anton Grot

Lionel Atwill, Fay Wray, *Glenda Farrell, Frank
McHugh*, Gavin Gordon, Allen Vincent, Edwin
Maxwell

'Marvellously grisly chiller.'—*Judith Crist,
1977*

Mystery Street*
US 1950   93m   bw
MGM (Frank E. Taylor)

Harvard medical scientists help solve a murder
by examining the victim's bones.
Standard semi-documentary police thriller; well
paced and quite entertaining.

w Sidney Boehm, Richard Brooks *d* John
Sturges *ph* John Alton *m* Rudolph Kopp

Ricardo Montalban, Sally Forrest, Elsa
Lanchester, Bruce Bennett, Marshall
Thompson, Jan Sterling

AAN: Leonard Speigelgass (original story)

Mystery Submarine
GB 1962   92m   bw
British Lion / Britannia / Bertram Ostrer
US title: *Decoy*

A Nazi submarine is captured and sent out again
with a British crew.

Routine war adventure.

w Hugh Woodhouse, Bertram Ostrer, Jon
Manchip White   *d* C. M. Pennington-Richards
ph Stan Pavey   *m* Clifton Parker

Edward Judd, James Robertson Justice,
Laurence Payne, Albert Lieven

N

Naked Alibi
US 1954 85m bw
U-I (Ross Hunter)

The police track a homicidal baker to a Mexican
border town.
Modest police thriller which sags after it crosses
the border.

w Lawrence Roman d Jerry Hopper ph Russell
Metty m Joseph Gershenson

Sterling Hayden, Gene Barry, Gloria Grahame,
Marcia Henderson, Casey Adams, Chuck
Connors

The Naked and the Dead
US 1958 131m Technicolor RKOscope
RKO Teleradio / Gregjac (Paul Gregory)

Adventures of an army platoon in the Pacific
war.
Shorn of the four letter words which made the
novel notorious, this is a routine war film, neither
very good nor very bad.

w Denis and Terry Sanders, novel Norman
Mailer d Raoul Walsh ph Joseph La Shelle
m Bernard Herrmann

Aldo Ray, Cliff Robertson, Raymond Massey,
William Campbell, Richard Jaeckel, James Best,
Joey Bishop, Robert Gist, Jerry Paris, L. Q.
Jones

The Naked City****
US 1948 96m bw
Universal (Mark Hellinger)

New York police track down a killer.
Highly influential documentary thriller which,
shot on location in New York's teeming streets,
claimed to be giving an impression of city life;
actually its real mission was to tell an ordinary
murder tale with an impressive accumulation of
detail and humour. The narrator's last words
became a cliché: 'There are eight million stories
in the naked city. This has been one of them.'

w Malvin Wald, Albert Maltz d Jules Dassin
ph William Daniels m Frank Skinner, Miklos
Rozsa md Milton Schwarzwald

Barry Fitzgerald, Don Taylor, Howard Duff,
Dorothy Hart, Ted de Corsia, Adelaide Klein

AA: William Daniels
AAN: original story (Malvin Wald)

Naked Earth
GB 1958 96m bw Cinemascope
TCF / Foray Films (Adrian Worker)

In 1895 a young Irish farmer goes to Africa to
grow tobacco, but moves on to crocodile
hunting.
Predictable and uninteresting epic of endurance;
not very convincing either.

w Milton Holmes d Vincent Sherman ph Erwin
Hillier

Richard Todd, Juliette Greco, John Kitzmiller,
Finlay Currie, Laurence Naismith, Christopher
Rhodes, Orlando Martins

The Naked Edge
GB 1961 100m bw
US / Pennebaker / Baroda (Walter Seltzer,
George Glass)

A successful executive is suspected by his wife of
an old murder in which he testified against the
man who was convicted.
Dreary thriller which piles up red herrings in
shoals, then abandons them all for a razor-and-
bathroom finale.

w Joseph Stefano, novel First Train to Babylon
by Max Ehrlich d Michael Anderson ph Erwin
Hillier m William Alwyn

Gary Cooper, Deborah Kerr, Peter Cushing,
Eric Portman, Diane Cilento, Hermione
Gingold, Michael Wilding, Ronald Howard

The Naked Hills
US 1955 73m Pathecolor
Allied Artists / La Salle (Josef Shaftel)

Starting in 1849, a young prospector spends his
life looking for gold.
Curious, mildly interesting saga with an
obsession instead of a plot.

wd Josef Shaftel ph Frederick Gately
m Herschel Burke Gilbert

David Wayne, Marcia Henderson, Keenan
Wynn, James Barton, Jim Backus, Denver Pyle

The Naked Jungle*

US 1954 95m Technicolor
Paramount / George Pal (Frank Freeman Jnr)

In 1901 a young woman is married by proxy to a South American cocoa planter, and when she arrives at his jungle home she has to conquer not only him but an army of soldier ants.
Mixture of *Rebecca* elements with a more unusual kind of thrill; all quite watchable, and the ant scenes very effective.

w Philip Yordan, Ranald MacDougall, *story* Leiningen Versus the Ants by Carl Stephenson d George Pal ph Ernest Laszlo m Daniele Amfitheatrof

Charlton Heston, Eleanor Parker, William Conrad, Abraham Sofaer, John Dierkes, Douglas Fowley

The Naked Maja

Italy / US 1959 112m Technirama
MGM / Titanus (Goffredo Lombardo)

Peasant Francisco Goya becomes a famous painter through the influence of the Duchess of Alba.
Boring and unconvincing biopic.

w Giorgio Prosperi, Norman Corwin, Albert Lewin, Oscar Saul d Henry Koster ph Giuseppe Rotunno m Francesco Lavagnino

Anthony Franciosa, Ava Gardner, Amedeo Nazzari, Gino Cervi, Lea Padovani, Massimo Serrato
'This travesty of Goya's life, country and period adds up to nothing more entertaining than a perfunctory, heavy-handed pageant.'—*MFB*

The Naked Prey*

US 1964 94m Technicolor Panavision
Paramount / Theodora / Sven Persson
(Cornel Wilde)

In 1840, a white hunter becomes brutalized when a tribe hunts him down as though he were a lion.
Savage adventure story with bloodthirsty detail; unusual and certainly effective.

w Clint Johnston, Don Peters d Cornel Wilde ph I. A. R. Thompson md Andrew Tracy, from African folk music

Cornel Wilde, Gert Van Den Berg, Ken Gampu
'Overtones pretentious, but it tries.'—*Sight and Sound*

AAN: script

The Naked Runner

GB 1967 104m Techniscope
Warner / Artanis (Brad Dexter)

British intelligence conceive a plan to turn an innocent businessman into a spy killer.

Silly espionage thriller further marred by its director's penchant for making a zany composition of every frame.

w Stanley Mann, *novel* Francis Clifford d Sidney J. Furie ph Otto Heller m Harry Sukman

Frank Sinatra, Peter Vaughan, Derren Nesbitt, Nadia Gray, Toby Robins, Cyril Luckham, Edward Fox, Inger Stratton
'It might be a good movie to read by if there were light in the theatre.'—*Pauline Kael*

The Naked Spur*

US 1952 91m Technicolor
MGM (William H. Wright)

A bounty hunter has trouble getting his quarry back to base.
Standard big studio western shot in Colorado, with all characters motivated by greed.

w Sam Rolfe, Harold Jack Bloom d Anthony Mann ph William Mellor m Bronislau Kaper

James Stewart, Robert Ryan, Janet Leigh, Millard Mitchell

AAN: script

The Naked Street

US 1955 83m bw
Edward Small

A racketeer's daughter marries a worthless crook: her father saves him from the electric chair but he murders again.
Semi-documentary exposé melodrama about unpleasant people; reasonably proficient on its level.

w Maxwell Shane, Leo Katcher d Maxwell Shane ph Floyd Crosby m Emil Newman

Anthony Quinn, Anne Bancroft, Farley Granger, Peter Graves

The Naked Truth*

GB 1957 92m bw
Rank / Mario Zampi
US title: *Your Past is Showing*

Celebrities band together to kill a blackmailer who threatens to expose unsavoury aspects of their lives.
Frenzied black farce, quite a lot of which comes off.

w Michael Pertwee d Mario Zampi ph Stan Pavey m Stanley Black

Peter Sellers, Terry-Thomas, Peggy Mount, Dennis Price, Shirley Eaton, Georgina Cookson

Nana*

US 1934 89m bw
Samuel Goldwyn

The high life and subsequent degradation of a
Parisian demi-mondaine in the nineties.
Stylish yet stolid slice of *le beau monde*, intended
to create a new star.

w Willard Mack, Harry Wagstaff Gribble, *novel*
Emile Zola *d Dorothy Arzner ph Gregg Toland*

Anna Sten, Lionel Atwill, Phillips Holmes,
Richard Bennett, Mae Clarke, Muriel Kirkland,
Reginald Owen, Jessie Ralph

Nancy Drew

This series of second features starring Bonita
Granville as a teenage small-town detective was
moderately well received but quickly forgotten.
The character was created in novels by Edward
Stratemeyer and his daughter Harriet Evans; the
films were all directed by William Clemens for
Warners.

1938: NANCY DREW, DETECTIVE
1939: NANCY DREW, REPORTER:
NANCY DREW. TROUBLE SHOOTER:
NANCY DREW AND THE HIDDEN
STAIRCASE

Nancy Goes to Rio

US 1950 99m Technicolor
MGM (Joe Pasternak)

Two actresses, mother and daughter, are both
after the same part.
Mild shipboard musical.

w Sidney Sheldon *d* Robert Z. Leonard *ph* Ray
June

Jane Powell, Ann Sothern, Carmen Miranda,
Barry Sullivan, Louis Calhern, Fortunio
Bonanova, Hans Conried

Nancy Steele Is Missing*

US 1938 85m bw
TCF (Nunnally Johnson)

Crooks try to pass off a girl as the long lost heir
to a fortune.
Slightly unusual, well cast melodrama.

w Charles Francis Coe *d* George Marshall

Victor McLaglen, Peter Lorre, June Lang, Jane
Darwell, John Carradine

The Nanny*

GB 1965 93m bw
ABP / Hammer (Jimmy Sangster)

A ten-year-old boy hates his nanny, and with
good reason, for she is a neurotic murderess.
Muted Hammer experiment in
psychopathology, with too much equivocation

before the dénouement; the star's role allows few
fireworks, and the plot is rather unpleasant.

w Jimmy Sangster, *novel* Evelyn Piper *d Seth
Holt ph* Harry Waxman *m* Richard Rodney
Bennett

Bette Davis, Jill Bennett, William Dix, James
Villiers, Wendy Craig, Pamela Franklin,
Maurice Denham

Nanook of the North*

US 1921 57m (1947 sound version) bw
silent
Revillon Freres

The life of an Eskimo and his family.
Primitive but trail-blazing documentary, hard to
sit through for modern audiences.

wd, ph, ed Robert Flaherty
† Nanook himself died of hunger on the ice
shortly after the film was released.

Napoleon**

France 1927 130m approx (24 fps) bw
(some colour) silent
WESTI / Société Générale de Films

The early life of Napoleon.
An epic which, although generally well done in
most particulars, owes its great interest to its use
of triptych screens which at the end combine to
show one giant picture, the clear precursor of
Cinerama. In 1934 Gance revised his film and
added stereophonic sound.

wd, ed Abel Gance ph various *m* Arthur
Honegger

Albert Dieudonné, Antonin Artaud, Pierre
Batcheff

Napoleon and Samantha

US 1972 91m Technicolor
Walt Disney (Winston Hibler)

When his old guardian dies, a small boy and his
girl friend run away with their pet lion.
Patchy, episodic action drama for older children,
with a very sleepy lion.

w Stewart Raffil *d* Bernard McEveety
ph Monroe Askins *m* Buddy Baker

Michael Douglas, Will Geer

AAN: Buddy Baker

The Narrow Margin***

US 1950 70m bw
RKO (Stanley Rubin)

Police try to guard a prosecution witness on a
train from Chicago to Los Angeles.
Tight little thriller which takes every advantage
of its train setting. What the trade used to call a

sleeper, it gave more satisfaction than many a
top feature.

w Earl Felton d Richard Fleischer ph George
E. Diskant

Charles McGraw, Marie Windsor, Jacqueline
White, Queenie Leonard

AAN: original story (Martin Goldsmith, Jack
Leonard)

Nashville **
US 1975   161m   Metrocolor   Panavision
Paramount / ABC (Robert Altman)

A political campaign in Nashville organizes a
mammoth pop concert to gain support.
Kaleidoscopic, fragmented, multi-storied
musical melodrama, a mammoth movie which
can be a bore or an inspiration according to
taste. Certainly many exciting moments pass by,
but the length is self-defeating.

w Joan Tewkesbury d Robert Altman ph Paul
Lohmann md Richard Baskin

Geraldine Chaplin, David Arkin, Barbara
Baxley, Ned Beatty, Karen Black, Keith
Carradine, Henry Gibson, Keenan Wynn, Lily
Tomlin, Ronee Blakley

'A gigantic parody . . . crammed with samples
taken from every level of Nashville society,
revealed in affectionate detail bordering on
caricature in a manner that would surely delight
Norman Rockwell.'—Philip Strick

AA: song 'I'm Easy' (m/ly Keith Carradine)
AAN: best picture; Robert Altman; Lily
Tomlin; Ronee Blakley

Nasty Habits *
GB 1976   92m   Technicolor
Brut / Bowden (Robert Enders)

An abbess dies and the nuns vie for succession.
Satirical comedy rather obviously based on the
Watergate scandals; initially amusing, but very
tiresome by the end.

w Robert Enders, novel The Abbess of Crewe by
Muriel Spark d Michael Lindsay-Hogg
ph Douglas Slocombe m John Cameron

Glenda Jackson, Melina Mercouri, Genevieve
Page, Sandy Dennis, Anne Jackson, Anne
Meara, Edith Evans, Susan Penhaligon, Rip
Torn, Eli Wallach, Jerry Stiller

'The sort of material just about fit for a half-
hour TV sketch.'—Richard Combs, MFB

The National Health *
GB 1973   97m   Eastmancolor
Columbia (Ned Sherrin, Terry Glinwood)

Life in the general men's ward of a large
antiquated hospital.

Acerbic comedy from a National Theatre play
which mixes tragedy and farce into a kind of
Carry on Dying.

w Peter Nichols, from his play d Jack Gold
ph John Coquillon m Carl David pd Ray Simm

Jim Dale, Lynn Redgrave, Eleanor Bron, Sheila
Scott-Wilkinson, Donald Sinden, Colin Blakely,
Clive Swift

National Lampoon's Animal House *
GB 1978   109m   Technicolor
Universal (Matty Simmons, Ivan Reitman)

On an American campus around 1962, scruffy
newcomers challenge the elegant elite.
A ragbag of college gags, of interests only to
whose who have had the experience; but its
success caused much imitation, especially in
American television.

w Harold Ramis, Douglas Kenney, Chris Miller
d John Landis ph Charles Correll m Elmer
Bernstein

John Belushi, Tim Matheson, John Vernon,
Donald Sutherland, Verna Bloom, Cesare
Danova, Mary Louise Weller

National Velvet *
US 1944   125m   Technicolor
MGM (Pandro S. Berman)

Children train a horse to win the Grand
National.

A big bestseller from another era; its flaws of
conception and production quickly became
evident.

w Theodore Reeves, Helen Deutsch, novel Enid
Bagnold d Clarence Brown ph Leonard Smith
m Herbert Stothart

Mickey Rooney, Elizabeth Taylor, Anne Revere,
Donald Crisp, Angela Lansbury, Jackie Jenkins,
Reginald Owen, Terry Kilburn, Norma Varden,
Alec Craig, Arthur Shields, Dennis Hoey
† Sequel 1978: International Velvet.

AA: Anne Revere
AAN: Clarence Brown; Leonard Smith

Naughty But Nice
US 1939   90m   bw
Warner (Sam Bischoff)

A professor of classical music accidentally
writes a popular song.
Mildly amusing comedy musical with all the
tunes adapted from the classics (cf That Night
with You).

w Jerry Wald, Richard Macaulay d Ray
Enright ph Arthur L. Todd songs Harry
Warren, Johnny Mercer

Dick Powell, Ann Sheridan, Ronald Reagan,
Gale Page, Zasu Pitts, Jerry Colonna

Naughty Marietta**
US 1935   106m   bw
MGM (Hunt Stromberg)

A French princess goes to America and falls in
love with an Indian scout.
Period operetta which set the seal of success on
the MacDonald-Eddy team. In itself, dated but
quite pleasing for those who like the genre.

w John Lee Mahin, Frances Goodrich, Albert
Hackett, *operetta* Rida Johnson Young *d* W. S.
Van Dyke *ph* William Daniels *m* Victor
Herbert *ad* Cedric Gibbons

Jeanette MacDonald, Nelson Eddy, Frank
Morgan, Elsa Lanchester, Douglass Dumbrille,
Joseph Cawthorn, Cecelia Parker, Walter
Kingsford

  'When these two profiles come together to sing
Ah Sweet Mystery of Life, it's beyond camp, it's
in a realm of its own.'—*Judith Crist, 1977*
AAN: best picture

The Naughty Nineties
US 1945   72m   bw
Universal (Edward L. Hartmann, John Grant)

Two incompetents help an old showboat owner.
Dim star comedy apart from the team's rendition
of their most famous routine, 'Who's On First'.

w Edmund L. Hartmann, John Grant, Edmund
Joseph, Hal Fimburg *d* Jean Yarborough
ph George Robinson

Bud Abbott, Lou Costello, Henry Travers, Alan
Curtis, Rita Johnson, Joe Sawyer

The Navigator***
US 1924   63m approx (24 fps)   bw   silent
MGM

A millionaire and his girl are the only people on a
transatlantic liner marooned in mid-ocean.
A succession of hilarious sight gags: the star in
top form.

w Jean Havez, Clyde Bruckman, J. A. Mitchell
d Buster Keaton, Donald Crisp *ph* Elgin
Lessley, Byron Houck

Buster Keaton, Kathryn McGuire

Navy Blues
US 1941   109m   bw
Warner (Jerry Wald)

Naval ratings get into trouble in Honolulu.
Undernourished musical comedy with not too
much of either commodity.

w Jerry Wald, Richard Macaulay, Arthur T.

Horman *d* Lloyd Bacon *ph* Tony Gaudio
ch Seymour Felix
songs Arthur Scwarz, Johnny Mercer

Ann Sheridan, Jack Oakie, Martha Raye, Jack
Haley, Herbert Anderson, Jack Carson, Richard
Lane, Jackie Gleason, Howard da Silva

Nazarin*
Mexico 1958   94m   bw
Barbachano Ponce

A Catholic priest tries to take the teachings of
Christ literally, but is drastically misunderstood.
A black atheistic satire pretty typical of its
director, but not among his most enjoyable
works.

w Julio Alejandro, Luis Bunuel, *novel* Benito
Perez Galdos *d Luis Bunuel ph* Gabriel
Figueroa

Francisco Rabal, Marga Lopez, Rita Macedo,
Ignacio Lopez Tarso

Nazi Agent*
US 1942   84m   bw
MGM (Irving Asher)

A German-American is forced by his Nazi twin
to help a group of German spies.
Modest suspenser with a plot twist similar to *The
Great Impersonation* and *Dead Ringer*.

w Paul Gangelin, John Meehan Jnr *d Jules
Dassin*

Conrad Veidt, Ann Ayars, Frank Reicher,
Dorothy Tree, Martin Kosleck

Necromancy
US 1973   83m   colour
Cinerama (Bert I. Gordon)

Two young people become involved in small-
town witchcraft.
Low-key, low-talent thriller overbalanced by its
star.

wd Bert I. Gordon *m* Fred Karger

Orson Welles, Pamela Franklin, Michael
Onthean, Lee Purcell

Ned Kelly
GB 1970   103m   Technicolor
UA / Woodfall (Neil Hartley)

The career of a 19th-century Australian outlaw.
Obstinately unlikeable action picture with some
kind of message which never becomes clear amid
all the cleverness.

w Tony Richardson, Ian Jones *d* Tony
Richardson *ph* Gerry Fisher *m* Shel Silverstein
pd Jocelyn Herbert

Mick Jagger, Allen Bickford, Geoff Gilmour, Mark McManus

Negatives*

GB 1968   98m   Eastmancolor
Crispin / Kettledrum (Judd Bernard)

Three people indulge in sexual fantasies involving Dr Crippen and Baron Von Richthofen.
Smoothly done but impenetrable psychological poppycock: what is fact and what is fancy, only the author knows.

w Peter Everett, Roger Lowry, *novel* Peter Everett d Peter Medak ph Ken Hodges m Basil Kirchin

Glenda Jackson, Peter McEnery, Diane Cilento, Maurice Denham, Steven Lewis, Norman Rossington

Nell Gwyn**

GB 1934   85m   bw
B and D (Herbert Wilcox)

The affair of Charles II and an orange seller.
Naïve, vivid account of a famous couple; physically cheap and rather faded, but the best film on the subject and one of the best covering this period.

w *Miles Malleson* d *Herbert Wilcox*

Anna Neagle, Cedric Hardwicke, Jeanne de Casalis, Muriel George, Miles Malleson, Esmé Percy, Moore Marriott

The Neptune Factor

Canada 1972   98m   De Luxe   Panavision
TCF / Quadrant / Bellevue–Pathe (Sanford Howard)
Later retitled: *The Neptune Disaster*

American oceanologists conduct an experiment in underwater living.
Wet 'actioner' in which very little happens except a few porthole views of magnified fish.

w Jack de Witt d Daniel Petrie ph Harry Makin m Lalo Schifrin

Ben Gazzara, Walter Pidgeon, Yvette Mimieux, Ernest Borgnine, Chris Wiggins

Neptune's Daughter*

US 1949   93m   Technicolor
MGM (Jack Cummings)

A lady bathing suit designer has a South American romance.
Generally thought one of the better aquatic musicals, and certainly very typical of them and its studio at this time.

w Dorothy Kingsley d Edward Buzzell ph Charles Rosher m George Stoll

Esther Williams, Red Skelton, Ricardo Montalban, Betty Garrett, Keenan Wynn, Xavier Cugat and his Orchestra, Mike Mazurki, Ted de Corsia, Mel Blanc

The Net

GB 1953   86m   bw
Rank / Two Cities (Anthony Darnborough)
US title: *Project M 7*

Tension among boffins in an aviation research station leads to murder and the discovery of a spy.
Low-key suspenser, quite adequately presented.

w William Fairchild, *novel* John Pudney d Anthony Asquith ph Desmond Dickinson m Benjamin Frankel

Phyllis Calvert, Noel Willman, Herbert Lom, James Donald, Robert Beatty, Muriel Pavlow, Walter Fitzgerald, Maurice Denham

Network**

US 1976   121m   Metrocolor
MGM / UA (Howard Gottfried, Fred Caruso)

A network news commentator begins to say what he thinks about the world and becomes a new messiah to the people and an embarrassment to his sponsors.
Overheated satire which in between its undoubted high points becomes noisy and tiresome, not helped by fuzzy photography. Its very existence in a commercial system, however, is as remarkable as its box-office success.

w *Paddy Chayevsky* d Sidney Lumet ph Owen Roizman m Elliot Lawrence

Peter Finch, William Holden, Faye Dunaway, Robert Duvall, Wesley Addy, Ned Beatty, Beatrice Straight, John Carpenter
  'The cast of this messianic farce take turns yelling at us soulless masses.'—*New Yorker*
  'Too much of this film has the hectoring stridency of tabloid headlines.'—*Michael Billington, Illustrated London News*
† The theme was taken up a year later in the shortlived TV series *W.E.B.*

AA: Peter Finch; Beatrice Straight
AAN: Sidney Lumet; William Holden; Ned Beatty

Nevada Smith*

US 1966   131m   Eastmancolor
  Panavision
Avco / Solar (Joe Levine, Henry Hathaway)

A cowboy takes a long revenge on the outlaws who murdered his parents.
Violent, sour, occasionally lively but frequently boring western melodrama on a well worn theme.

w John Michael Hayes, from the 'early life' of a character in The Carpetbaggers by Harold Robbins *d* Henry Hathaway *ph* Lucien Ballard *m* Alfred Newman

Steve McQueen, Karl Malden, Brian Keith, Suzanne Pleshette, Arthur Kennedy, Janet Margolin, Howard da Silva, Raf Vallone, Pat Hingle

Never a Dull Moment

US 1950   89m   bw
RKO (Harriet Parsons)

A lady music critic marries a rodeo cowboy and finds life hard down on the ranch.
Very mild star programmer.

w Lou Breslow, Doris Anderson, *novel* Who Could Ask for Anything More? by Kay Swift *d* George Marshall *ph* Joseph Walker *m* Constantin Bakaleinikoff

Irene Dunne, Fred MacMurray, William Demarest, Andy Devine, Gigi Perreau, Natalie Wood, Philip Ober, Jack Kirkwood

Never a Dull Moment

US 1967   100m   Technicolor
Walt Disney (Ron Miller)

An unsuccessful actor is mistaken for a notorious gangster.
Slapstick romp with vigour but not much flair.

w A. J. Carothers, *novel* John Godey *d* Jerry Paris *ph* William Snyder *m* Robert F. Brunner

Dick Van Dyke, Edward G. Robinson, Dorothy Provine, Henry Silva, Joanna Moore, Tony Bill, Slim Pickens, Jack Elam

Never Give a Sucker an Even Break*

US 1941   70m   bw
Universal
GB title: What a Man

W. C. Fields dives off an aeroplane into the lap of a young woman who has never seen a man; she falls in love with him.
Stupefyingly inept in its scripting and pacing, this comedy is often irresistibly funny because of the anti-everything personality of its writer-star. No one else could have got away with it, or would have been likely to try.

w John T. Neville, Prescott Chaplin, *story* Otis Criblecoblis (W. C. Fields) *d* Edward Cline *ph* Charles Van Enger *m* Frank Skinner

W. C. Fields, Gloria Jean, Leon Errol, Butch and Buddy, Franklin Pangborn, Anne Nagel, Mona Barrie, Ann Miller, Margaret Dumont

Never Let Go

GB 1960   91m   bw
Rank / Julian Wintle—Leslie Parkin (Peter de Sarigny)

A travelling salesman has his car stolen and stands up to the sadistic gang boss responsible.
Brutishly unattractive thriller, apparently designed for the sole purpose of giving Peter Sellers a villainous part.

w Alun Falconer *d* John Guillermin *ph* Christopher Challis *m* John Barry

Richard Todd, Peter Sellers, Elizabeth Sellars, Adam Faith, Carol White, Mervyn Johns, Noel Willman

Never Let Me Go

GB 1953   94m   bw
MGM (Clarence Brown)

After World War II an American correspondent marries a Russian ballerina but is later deported by the authorities.
Ho-hum romantic melodrama, quite interestingly cast.

w Roland Millar, George Froeschel, *novel* Came the Dawn by Roger Bax *d* Delmer Daves *ph* Robert Krasker *m* Hans May

Clark Gable, Gene Tierney, Richard Haydn, Belita, Bernard Miles, Kenneth More, Karel Stepanek, Theodore Bikel, Frederick Valk

Never Love a Stranger

US 1958   93m   bw
Harold Robbins / Allied Artists (Peter Gettlinger)

A Catholic boy who has become a gangster helps his Jewish friend who has become assistant district attorney to trap a vicious hoodlum.
The old *Manhattan Melodrama* theme is dusted off once again, this time to very little effect.

w Harold Robbins, Richard Day, *novel* Harold Robbins *d* Robert Stevens *ph* Lee Garmes *m* Raymond Scott

John Drew Barrymore, Steve McQueen, Robert Bray, Lita Milan, R. G. Armstrong, Salem Ludwig

Never on Sunday*

Greece 1959   97m   bw
Lopert / Melinafilm (Jules Dassin)
original title: Pote tin Kyriaki

An American scholar in Greece is infatuated by a prostitute and sets about improving her.
Amiable if rather shoddy variation on *Pygmalion*: the star performance and the music carried it, along with its own naughtiness, to success.

wd Jules Dassin ph Jacques Natteau m Manos Hadjidakis

Melina Mercouri, Jules Dassin, Georges Foundas, Tito Vandis, Despo Diamantidou
  'It barely stands scrutiny, but it communicates cheerfulness, and this in itself is no mean achievement.'—Penelope Houston, MFB

AAN: Jules Dassin (as director); Manos Hadjidakis for title song

Never Put it in Writing*
GB 1963   93m   bw
MGM / Andrew Stone

A young executive tries to recover from the mails an indiscreet letter he has written to his boss. Frantic hit-or-miss farcical comedy distinguished by Dublin locations and cast.

wd Andrew Stone ph Martin Curtis m Frank Cordell

Pat Boone, Fidelma Murphy, Reginald Beckwith, John Le Mesurier, Colin Blakely

Never Say Die*
US 1939   80m   bw
Paramount (Paul Jones)

A millionaire hypochondriac is convinced he is dying.
Thin farce with Hope on the very brink of stardom; some bright moments.

w Don Hartman, Frank Butler, Preston Sturges d Elliott Nugent ph Leo Tover md Boris Morros

Martha Raye, Bob Hope, Andy Devine, Alan Mowbray, Gale Sondergaard, Sig Rumann, Ernest Cossart, Monty Woolley, Christian Rub

Never Say Goodbye
US 1956   96m   Technicolor
U-I (Albert J. Cohen)

In 1945 Berlin an American army doctor marries a pianist who is later trapped in the Russian zone; they meet years later in America. Romantic drama aimed at a female audience, remade from This Love of Ours (qv).

w Charles Hoffman d Jerry Hopper ph Maury Gertsman

Rock Hudson, George Sanders, Cornell Borchers, Ray Collins, David Janssen

Never So Few
US 1959   124m   Metrocolor
  Cinemascope
MGM / Canterbury (Edmund Grainger)

Adventures of World War II Americans commanding Burmese guerrillas.

Jungle actioner with pauses for philosophizing; well enough made but not very interesting.

w Millard Kaufman, novel Tom Chamales d John Sturges ph William H. Daniels m Hugo Friedhofer

Frank Sinatra, Gina Lollobrigida, Peter Lawford, Steve McQueen, Paul Henreid, Richard Johnson, Brian Donlevy, Charles Bronson, Dean Jones

Never Steal Anything Small
US 1958   94m   Eastmancolor
  Cinemascope
U-I (Aaron Rosenberg)

The reformation of a corrupt but sympathetic dockers' union boss.
Curious semi-musical which doesn't come off at all despite excellent credentials.

wd Charles Lederer, play The Devil's Hornpipe by Rouben Mamoulian, Maxwell Anderson ph Harold Lipstein m Allie Wrubel ly Maxwell Anderson ch Hermes Pan

James Cagney, Shirley Jones, Roger Smith, Cara Williams, Nehemiah Persoff, Royal Dano, Anthony Caruso

Never Take No for an Answer*
GB 1951   82m   bw
Anthony Havelock-Allan

A small boy goes to Rome to get permission from the Pope to take his sick donkey to be blessed in the church.
Slight, easy-going whimsy with attractive sunlit locations.

w Paul and Pauline Gallico, novel The Small Miracle by Paul Gallico d Maurice Cloche, Ralph Smart ph Otto Heller m Nino Rota

Vittorio Manunta, Denis O'Dea, Guido Cellano, Nerio Bernardi
  'The main pleasures of this slender film are visual ones.'—MFB
† Remade as a TV movie Small Miracle.

Never Too Late
US 1965   104m   Technicolor   Panavision
Warner / Lear–Yorkin (Norman Lear)

A well-to-do middle-aged housewife discovers she is pregnant.
Predictable, rather hysterical domestic comedy, flatly developed from a successful play which offered two star parts for old stagers.

w Sumner Arthur Long, from his play d Bud Yorkin ph Philip Lathrop m David Rose

Paul Ford, Maureen O'Sullivan, Connie Stevens, Jim Hutton, Lloyd Nolan, Henry Jones, Jane Wyatt

Never Wave at a WAC
US 1952   87m   bw
Independent Artists (Frederick Brisson)
GB title: *The Private Wore Skirts*

A Washington hostess joins the WACs and finds
she can't get beyond the rank of private.
Pattern comedy, unconvincing in all respects but
with a smattering of funny moments.
Flagwaving takes over towards the end.

w Ken Englund   *d* Norman Z. McLeod
ph William Daniels   *m* Elmer Bernstein

Rosalind Russell, Paul Douglas, Marie Wilson,
William Ching, Leif Erickson, Arleen Whelan,
Charles Dingle

The New Babylon*
USSR 1929   80m approx (24 fps)   bw
  silent
Sovkino
original title: *Novyi Vavilon*

The rise and fall of the 1871 French commune,
seen through the eyes of a girl department store
worker.
Propagandist socio-historical melodrama, most
interesting now for its sub-Eisenstein technique.

wd Leonid Trauberg, Grigori Kozintsev
ph Andrei Moskvin, Yevgeni Mikhailov
m Dmitri Shostakovich   *ad* Yevgeni Enei

Yelena Kuzmina, Pyotr Sobelevsky, Sophie
Magarill

The New Centurions*
US 1972   103m   Eastmancolor
  Panavision
Columbia / Chartoff—Winkler
GB title: *Los Angeles Precinct 45*

An old cop teaches a new one.
'Realistic' crime prevention saga which spawned
the TV series *Police Story* and *Police Woman*.
Well done within its limits.

w Stirling Silliphant, *novel* Joseph Wambaugh
d Richard Fleischer   *ph* Ralph Woolsey
m Quincy Jones

George C. Scott, Stacy Keach, Jane Alexander,
Rosalind Cash, Scott Wilson

New Faces*
US 1954   99m   Eastmancolor
  Cinemascope
Edward L. Alperson (Leonard Sillman)

A revue goes on despite money problems.
Five minutes of plot, ninety-five minutes of revue
from the Broadway stage; mostly quite amusing,
and chiefly notable for introducing Eartha Kitt
with all her standards.

w various   *d* Harry Horner   *ph* Lucien Ballard
revue deviser John Murray Anderson

Eartha Kitt, Ronny Graham, Alice Ghostley,
Robert Clary, Paul Lynde

The New Interns
US 1964   123m   bw
Columbia (Robert Cohn)

Young doctors at a city hospital have trouble
saving a rapist and his victim.
Unnecessary sequel to *The Interns*, its 'realism'
requiring large pinches of salt.

w Wilton Schiller   *d* John Rich   *ph* Lucien
Ballard   *m* Earle Hagen

George Segal, Telly Savalas, Michael Callan,
Dean Jones, Inger Stevens, Stefanie Powers, Lee
Patrick

A New Kind of Love
US 1963   110m   Technicolor
Paramount / Llenroc (Melville Shavelson)

An American dress designer in Paris is softened
by a boorish newspaper columnist.
Very thin sex comedy, dressed to kill but with
nowhere to go.

wd Melville Shavelson   *ph* Daniel Fapp   *m* Leith
Stevens

Paul Newman, Joanne Woodward, Maurice
Chevalier, Thelma Ritter, George Tobias

AAN: Leith Stevens

The New Land see The Emigrants

A New Leaf*
US 1970   102m   Movielab
Paramount / Aries / Elkins (Joe Manduke)

A middle-aged playboy, close to bankruptcy,
thinks of acquiring a wealthy wife.
Agreeably mordant comedy which sparkles in
patches rather than as a whole.

wd Elaine May, story The Green Heart by Jack
Ritchie   *ph* Gayne Rescher   *m* John Mandel,
Neal Hefti   *pd* Richard Fried

Walter Matthau, Elaine May, Jack Weston,
George Rose, William Redfield, James Coco

'Unashamedly a thirties fairy tale in modern,
but not fashionable, dress.'—*Jan Dawson*

New Moon*
US 1940   105m   bw
MGM (Robert Z. Leonard)

Romance in old French Louisiana.
Stalwart adaptation of an operetta previously
filmed in 1931 with Lawrence Tibbett and Grace
Moore.

w Jacques Deval, Robert Arthur *d* Robert Z. Leonard *ph* William Daniels *m/ly* Sigmund Romberg, Oscar Hammerstein

Jeanette MacDonald, Nelson Eddy, Mary Boland, George Zucco, H. B. Warner, Stanley Fields, Grant Mitchell

New Orleans*

US 1947 89m bw
Jules Levey

How jazz was born, according to the movies.
Routine low-budgeter enlivened by a splendid array of guest musicians.

w Elliot Paul, Dick Irving Hyland *d* Arthur Lubin *ph* Lucien Andriot *md* Nathaniel Finston

Louis Armstrong and his All Stars, Arturo de Cordova, Dorothy Patrick, *Billie Holiday, Meade Lux Lewis, Woody Herman* and his Orchestra

New York Confidential

US 1955 87m bw
Warner / Russel Rouse, Clarence Greene

The head of a crime syndicate is assassinated by his own hired killer.
Unexciting 'realistic' thriller with the gangsters presented as family and businessmen; seventeen years later *The Godfather* did it rather better.

w Clarence Greene, Russel Rouse *d* Russel Rouse *ph* Edward Fitzgerald *m* Joseph Mullendore *pd* Fernando Carrere

Broderick Crawford, Richard Conte, Anne Bancroft, Marilyn Maxwell, Onslow Stevens, J. Carrol Naish, Barry Kelley, Mike Mazurki, Celia Lovsky

The New York Hat*

US 1912 10m approx (24 fps) bw silent
D. W. Griffith

A small-town minister is gossiped about when he buys a hat for a young girl.
Influential early short story film with good local backgrounds.

w Anita Loos *d* D. W. Griffith *ph* Billy Bitzer

Mary Pickford, Lionel Barrymore, Lillian Gish, Dorothy Gish, Robert Harron, Mack Sennett, Mae Marsh

New York, New York*

US 1977 153m Technicolor Panavision
UA / Chartoff–Winkler (Gene Kirkwood)

In the late forties in New York, a single-minded saxophonist fails to do right by his girl friend, who becomes a Hollywood star.
A clever recreation of the big band era, hampered by gross overlength, unattractive characters and a pessimistic plot.

w Earl Mac Rauch, Mardik Martin *d* Martin Scorsese *ph* Laszlo Kovacs *pd* Boris Leven *md* Ralph Burns

Liza Minnelli, Robert de Niro, Lionel Stander, Barry Primus

Newman's Law

US 1974 99m Technicolor
Universal (Richard Irving)

A cop uses unconventional methods to trap drug smugglers.
Very routine police actioner, just above TV movie level.

w Anthony Wilson *d* Richard Heffron *ph* Vilis Lapenieks *m* Robert Prince

George Peppard, Roger Robinson, Eugene Roche, Gordon Pinsent, Abe Vegoda

The Next of Kin***

GB 1942 102m bw
Ealing (S. C. Balcon)

Careless talk causes loss of life in a commando raid.
A propaganda instructional film which was made so entertainingly that it achieved commercial success and remains an excellent example of how to make a bitter pill palatable.

w Thorold Dickinson, Basil Bartlett, Angus Macphail, John Dighton *d* Thorold Dickinson

Mervyn Johns, Nova Pilbeam, Stephen Murray, Reginald Tate, Basil Radford, Naunton Wayne, Geoffrey Hibbert, Philip Friend, Mary Clare, Basil Sydney

'The detail everywhere is curious and surprising, with something of the fascination of a Simenon crime being unravelled.'—*William Whitebait*

Next Stop Greenwich Village*

US 1975 111m Movielab
TCF (Paul Mazursky, Tony Ray)

In 1953 in a poor quarter of New York, a young Jew tries to stretch his wings.
A bumper bundle of Jewish clichés dressed up as autobiography, and switching abruptly from comedy to tragedy and back. Vivid, but not exactly entertaining.

wd Paul Mazursky *ph* Arthur Ornitz *m* Bill Conti

Lenny Baker, Shelley Winters, Ellen Greene, Lois Smith, Dori Brenner

'Some tartly comic observation, but the fragmented structure keeps the mixture inert.'—*Sight and Sound*

Next Time We Love

US 1936   87m   bw
Universal (Paul Kohner)
GB title: *Next Time We Live*

The wife of a war-correspondent has plenty of time for romance.
Romantic drama which badly needs an injection of comedy.

w Melville Baker, *stories* Ursula Parrott
d Edward H. Griffith   ph Joseph Valentine

Margaret Sullavan, Ray Milland, James Stewart, Grant Mitchell, Robert McWade

The Next Voice You Hear*

US 1950   83m   bw
MGM (Dore Schary)

God speaks to mankind on the radio, and the life of Joe Smith American is changed.
Soppy parable, the archetypal instance of Schary's reign of do-goodery at MGM. (He wrote a book about it, *Case History of a Movie*.) The idea is handled with deadly reverence, and falls quite flat, while the depiction of the inhabitants of American suburbia is depressing.

w Charles Schnee   d William Wellman
ph William Mellor   m David Raksin

James Whitmore, Nancy Davis, Lillian Bronson, Jeff Corey

'The sins of the American working man are singularly uninteresting and their obliteration seems scarcely to require the very voice of God.'—*Henry Hart*

Niagara***

US 1952   89m   Technicolor
TCF (Charles Brackett)

While visiting Niagara Falls, a faithless wife is plotting to murder her husband, but he turns the tables.
Excellent suspenser with breathtaking locations; in the best Hitchcock class though slightly marred by the emphasis on Monroe's wiggly walk (it was her first big part).

w Charles Brackett, Walter Reisch, Richard Breen   d Henry Hathaway   ph Joe MacDonald
m Sol Kaplan

Joseph Cotten, Jean Peters, *Marilyn Monroe*, Don Wilson, Casey Adams

'A masterly example of fluid screen narrative.'—*Charles Higham*

'It would have turned out a much better picture if James Mason had played the husband as I wanted. He has that intensity, that neurotic edge. He was all set to do it, but his daughter Portland said she was sick of seeing him die in his pictures.'—*Henry Hathaway*

Nice Girl?*

US 1941   95m   bw
Universal

A teenager finds herself in demand by two older men.
Amusing romantic trifle supposed to mark the growing up of Universal's great teenage star.

w Richard Connell, Gladys Lehman   d William A. Seiter   ph Joseph Valentine   md Charles Previn

Deanna Durbin, Franchot Tone, Robert Stack, Walter Brennan, Robert Benchley, Helen Broderick, Ann Gillis

A Nice Girl Like Me

GB 1969   91m   Eastmancolor
Anglo Embassy / Partisan (Roy Millichip)

A sheltered young lady sets out to see life but keeps getting pregnant.
Insufferable romantic whimsy, made to look like a marathon TV commercial but never so interesting.

w Anne Piper, Desmond Davis   d Desmond Davis   ph Gil Taylor, Manny Wynn   m Pat Williams

Barbara Ferris, Harry Andrews, Gladys Cooper, Joyce Carey, Bill Hinnant, James Villiers, Christopher Guinee, Fabia Drake

'High-toned woman's magazine nostalgia.'—*MFB*

A Nice Little Bank that should be Robbed

US 1958   87m   bw   Cinemascope
TCF (Anthony Muto)
GB title: *How to Rob a Bank*

Two incompetent crooks rob a bank and buy a racehorse.
Feeble comedy, a sad waste of its stars.

w Sidney Boehm   d Henry Levin   ph Leo Tover

Mickey Rooney, Tom Ewell, Mickey Shaugnessy, Dina Merrill

Nicholas and Alexandra*

US 1971   189m   Eastmancolor
Panavision
Columbia / Horizon (Sam Spiegel)

The life of Tsar Nicholas II from 1904 to the execution of the family in 1918.
Inflated epic of occasional interest, mainly for its sets; generally heavy going.

w James Goldman, *book* Robert K. Massie
d Franklin Schaffner   ph *Frederick A. Young*
m Richard Rodney Bennett   pd John Box

Michael Jayston, Janet Suzman, Laurence Olivier, Jack Hawkins, Tom Baker, Harry Andrews, Michael Redgrave, Alexander Knox

AAN: best picture; Frederick A. Young; Richard Rodney Bennett; Janet Suzman

Nicholas Nickleby **
GB 1947 108m bw
Ealing

The adventures of a Victorian schoolmaster, deprived of his rightful fortune, who joins a band of travelling entertainers.
Quite tasteful and expert but too light-handed potted version of Dickens, which suffered by comparison with the David Lean versions.

w John Dighton, novel Charles Dickens d Alberto Cavalcanti ph Gordon Dines

Derek Bond, Cedric Hardwicke, Alfred Drayton, Sybil Thorndike, Stanley Holloway, James Hayter, Sally Ann Howes, Jill Balcon, Cyril Fletcher, Fay Compton

Nickelodeon *
US/GB 1976 122m Metrocolor
Columbia / EMI / Chartoff–Winkler (Frank Marshall)

In 1910, various characters come together to make movies, finally attending the 1915 opening in Hollywood of The Birth of a Nation.
What should have been a hugely entertaining chunk of comic nostalgia is killed stone dead by embarrassed acting, poor timing, and a general lack of funny ideas, despite having so much to borrow from.

w W. D. Richter, Peter Bogdanovich d Peter Bogdanovich ph Laszlo Kovacs md Richard Hazard

Ryan O'Neal, Burt Reynolds, Tatum O'Neal, Brian Keith, Stella Stevens, John Ritter, Jane Hitchcock

'Ponderous slapstick and a pathetic parody of Harold Lloyd.'—Sight and Sound

The Niebelungen ***
Germany 1924 bw silent
Decla–Bioscop
Part One: 'Siegfried': 115m approx (24 fps)
Part Two: 'Kriemheld's Revenge': 125m approx (24 fps)

Siegfried kills a dragon and marries a princess of Burgundy but the fierce queen Brunhilde arranges his death. His widow marries Attila the Hun and they massacre the Burgundians.
Stately, warlike legends are transformed into a slow, chilling, awe-inspiring sequence of films, the décor being of special interest. The films were conceived as a tribute to the German nation, and were among Hitler's favourites.

w Thea Von Harbou d Fritz Lang ph Carl

Hoffman, Gunther Rittau ad Otto Hunte, Karl Vollbrecht, Erich Kettelhut

Paul Richter, Marguerite Schön, Theodor Loos, Hannah Ralph, Rudolph Klein-Rogge

Night after Night *
US 1932 70m bw
Paramount

An ex-boxer seeking refinement buys a night club and falls for a socialite.
Dim little drama which is remembered for introducing Mae West to the screen with her famous line, 'Goodness had nothing to do with it'.

w Vincent Laurence, novel Single Night by Louis Bromfield d Archie Mayo ph Ernest Haller

George Raft, Constance Cummings, Wynne Gibson, Mae West, Alison Skipworth, Roscoe Karns, Louis Calhern

Night and Day *
US 1946 132m Technicolor
Warner (Arthur Schwarz)

The life of Cole Porter.
Or rather, a fictitious story about a composer who happens to be called Cole Porter. A careful but undistinguished musical with pleasant moments.

w Charles Hoffman, Leo Townsend, William Bowers d Michael Curtiz ph Peverell Marley, William V. Skall m/ly Cole Porter md Max Steiner, Ray Heindorf ch Le Roy Prinz

Cary Grant, Alexis Smith, Monty Woolley, Mary Martin, Ginny Simms, Jane Wyman, Eve Arden, Victor Francen, Alan Hale, Dorothy Malone

AAN: Max Steiner, Ray Heindorf

Night and the City
GB 1950 101m bw
TCF (Samuel G. Engel)

A crooked wrestling promoter is tracked down by an underworld gang.
A fated attempt to extend the success of Naked City in a London setting; the surface is accomplished enough, but the plot and characters are just plain dull, especially as little is seen of the police.

w Jo Eisinger, novel Gerald Kersh d Jules Dassin ph Max Greene m Benjamin Frankel

Richard Widmark, Gene Tierney, Googie Withers, Hugh Marlowe, Herbert Lom

'Brilliantly photographed, it is an example of neo-expressionist techniques at their most potent.'—Richard Roud, 1964

A Night at the Opera****
US 1935 96m bw
MGM (Irving Thalberg)

Three zanies first wreck, then help an opera company.

Certainly among the best of the Marxian extravaganzas, and the first to give them a big production to play with as well as musical interludes by other than themselves for a change of pace. The mix plays beautifully.

w George S. Kaufman, Morrie Ryskind d Sam Wood ph Merritt Gerstad md Herbert Stothart

Groucho, Chico, Harpo (Zeppo absented himself from here on), Margaret Dumont, Kitty Carlisle, Allan Jones, Walter Woolf King, Sig Rumann

Night Boat to Dublin
GB 1945 99m bw
ABP (Hamilton Inglis)

An MI5 man saves an atom scientist from kidnapping.
Generally watchable low key thriller with familiar British ingredients.

w Lawrence Huntington, Robert Hall
d Lawrence Huntington

Robert Newton, Raymond Lovell, Muriel Pavlow, Guy Middleton, Herbert Lom, Martin Miller, Marius Goring

Night Club Scandal
US 1937 74m bw
Paramount

A society doctor murders his wife and incriminates her lover.
Smooth second feature remake of Guilty as Hell, chiefly notable for its star's last controlled performance.

w Lillie Hayward, play Riddle Me This by Daniel Rubin d Ralph Murphy

John Barrymore, Lynne Overman, Charles Bickford, Elizabeth Patterson, Evelyn Brent, Louise Campbell, J. Carrol Naish

Night Flight*
US 1933 84m bw
MGM

The president of a civil airline insists that dangerous night flights must continue as a mark of progress.
Spurious, unsatisfactory, multi-star air melodrama lacking both narrative flow and the common touch.

w Oliver H. P. Garrett, stories Antoine de St Exupèry d Clarence Brown ph Oliver T. Marsh, Elmer Dyer, Charles Marshall

John Barrymore, Helen Hayes, Lionel Barrymore, Clark Gable, Robert Montgomery, Myrna Loy, William Gargan, C. Henry Gordon

'It is in the sense it conveys of human beings caught in the swift machinery of modern living that Night Flight soars above other pictures of its kind.'—James Shelley Hamilton

Night Games*
Sweden 1966 105m bw
Sandrews (Lena Malmsjö)
original title: Nattlek

A 35-year-old man is sexually inhibited by memories of his dead mother's passions and perversions.
Curious Freudian parable apparently intended as a comment on the state of Europe. Audiences found it merely peculiar.

wd Mai Zetterling, from her novel ph Rune Ericson m Jan Johansson, George Riedel

Ingrid Thulin, Keve Hjelm, Lena Brundin, Naima Wifstrand

'The best one can say is that it never lets up for a moment.'—David Wilson, MFB

Night Hair Child
GB 1971 89m Movielab
Leander / Harry Alan Towers (Graham Harris)

A 12-year-old boy makes sexual advances to his stepmother.
Corrupt voyeuristic weirdie which has to be seen to be believed.

w Trevor Preston d James Killy ph Harry Waxman m Stelvio Cipriani

Mark Lester, Britt Ekland, Hardy Kruger, Harry Andrews, Lilli Palmer

Night Has a Thousand Eyes
US 1948 80m bw
Paramount (André Boehm)

A vaudeville mentalist finds that he really does have the power to predict the future.
Predictable supernatural melodrama closely modelled on The Clairvoyant (qv); quite nicely made but simply not exciting.

w Barre Lyndon, Jonathan Latimer, novel Cornell Woolrich d John Farrow ph John F. Seitz m Victor Young

Edward G. Robinson, Gail Russell, John Lund, Virginia Bruce, William Demarest, Richard Webb, Jerome Cowan

The Night Has Eyes*
GB 1942 79m bw
ABP (John Argyle)
US title: Terror House

A young teacher disappears on the Yorkshire moors; her friend goes in search, and comes under the influence of a strange young man and his sinister housekeeper.

Stagey but effective little thriller, with oodles of fog and bog to help the suspense.

w Alan Kennington *d* Leslie Arliss *ph* Gunther Krampf

James Mason, Joyce Howard, *Wilfrid Lawson, Mary Clare*, Tucker McGuire, John Fernald
'Some ingenuity and not a little style.'—*The Times*

The Night Holds Terror*
US 1955   86m   bw
Columbia (Andrew Stone)

Three gunmen on the run kidnap a factory worker and hold him to ransom.

Effective, detailed, low-budget police melodrama; its plot may be over familiar now, but at the time it was refreshing and the whole film an intelligent exercise in suspense.

wd Andrew Stone ph Fred Jackman Jnr *m* Lucien Calliet

Jack Kelly, Hildy Parks, John Cassavetes, David Cross, Edward Marr, Jack Kruschen

A Night in Casablanca**
US 1946   85m   bw
David L. Loew

Three zanies rout Nazi refugees in a North African hotel.

The last authentic Marxian extravaganza; it starts uncertainly, builds to a fine sustained frenzy, then peters out in some overstretched airplane acrobatics.

w Joseph Fields, Roland Kibbee, Frank Tashlin *d* Archie Mayo *ph* James Van Trees *m* Werner Janssen *pd* Duncan Cramer

Groucho, Chico, Harpo, Sig Rumann, Lisette Verea, Charles Drake, Lois Collier, Dan Seymour

A Night in Paradise
US 1946   84m   Technicolor
(Universal) Walter Wanger

Aesop falls in love at the court of King Croesus.

Deadly boring, unintentionally funny Arabian Nights farrago without the saving grace of action.

w Ernest Pascal, Emmet Lavery, *novel* Peacock's Feather by George S. Hellman *d* Arthur Lubin *ph* Hal Mohr *m* Frank Skinner

Merle Oberon, Turhan Bey, Thomas Gomez, Gale Sondergaard, Ray Collins, George Dolenz,

John Litel, Ernest Truex, Jerome Cowan, Douglass Dumbrille

Night into Morning
US 1951   86m   bw
MGM (Edwin H. Knopf)

A college professor loses his wife and son in an accident; despair drives him to drink and attempted suicide.

Well-made and well meaning melodrama whose virtual absence of plot makes it seem by the end merely maudlin.

w Karl Tunberg, Leonard Spiegelgass *d* Fletcher Markle *ph* George Folsey *m* Carmen Dragon

Ray Milland, Nancy Davis, John Hodiak, Lewis Stone, Jean Hagen, Rosemary de Camp

Night Key
US 1937   67m   bw
Universal

An inventor's idea is stolen by his former partner, and he takes an appropriate revenge. Low-key star melodrama: competent, but no great shakes.

w Tristam Tupper, John C. Moffit *d* Lloyd Corrigan *ph* George Robinson *make up* Jack Pierce

Boris Karloff, Jean Rogers, Warren Hull, Samuel S. Hinds, Alan Baxter, Ward Bond, Edwin Maxwell

Night Mail***
GB 1936   24m   bw
GPO Film Unit

A 'film poem' showing the journey of the mail train from London to Glasgow.

One of the best and most influential of British documentaries: despite a few absurdities, it remains a pleasure to watch.

wd Basil Wright, Harry Watt ph J. Jones, H. E. Fowle *m Benjamin Britten* poem W. H. Auden *sound arrangements* Alberto Cavalcanti

Night Monster
US 1942   73m   bw
Universal
GB title: *House of Mystery*

Murders are committed in a spooky house by a cripple who produces synthetic legs by self-hypnotism.

Stilted, creaky would-be thriller with a good cast and an impertinent plot.

w Charles Upson Young *d* Ford Beebe *ph* Charles Van Enger

Ralph Morgan, Don Porter, Irene Hervey, Bela Lugosi, Lionel Atwill, Nils Asther, Leif Erickson, Frank Reicher

Night Moves*
US 1975 99m Technicolor
Warner / Hillier / Layton (Robert M. Sherman)

A private eye is engaged to find a runaway teenager.
Apparently a Chandlerish mystery, this is really a Pinterish audience-teaser with obsessions about communication and the meaning of life. A smart-ass entertainment for eager trendies.

w Alan Sharp d Arthur Penn ph Bruce Surtees m Michael Small pd George Jenkins

Gene Hackman, Jennifer Warren, Edward Binns, Harris Yulin, Kenneth Mars

'Beneath the complicated unravelling of a mystery, an anti-mystery, with the hero's detection registering as an evasion of his own problems; beneath a densely charted intrigue of betrayals and cross purposes, a cryptic void . . .'—*Jonathan Rosenbaum*

'A suspenseless suspenser . . . there's very little rhyme or reason for the plot's progression.'—*Variety*

'Rich and dense enough to set up reverberations long after one has left the cinema.'—*Michael Billington, Illustrated London News*

Night Must Fall**
US 1937 117m bw
MGM (Hunt Stromberg)

A bland young bellboy who is really a psychopathic murderer attaches himself to the household of a rich old lady.
Unconvincing but memorable Hollywood expansion of an effective British chiller.

w John Van Druten, play Emlyn Williams d Richard Thorpe ph Ray June m Edward Ward

Robert Montgomery, Rosalind Russell, *May Whitty*, Alan Marshal, Merle Tottenham, Kathleen Harrison, Matthew Boulton, E. E. Clive

'A pretty little murder play has made a long dim film.'—*Graham Greene*

AAN: Robert Montgomery; May Whitty

Night Must Fall
GB 1964 105m bw
MGM (Albert Finney, Karel Reisz)

Dreary remake with a mannered star performance and the emphasis on axe murders. A mistake from beginning to end.

w Clive Exton d Karel Reisz ph Freddie Francis m Ron Grainer

Albert Finney, Susan Hampshire, Mona Washbourne, Sheila Hancock, Michael Medwin, Joe Gladwin, Martin Wyldeck

'Not so much a thriller as a typically humourless example of that overworked genre known as psychological drama . . . (Finney) constantly recalls a ventriloquist's dummy.'—*MFB*

The Night My Number Came Up*
GB 1954 94m bw
Ealing (Tom Morahan)

A man dreams that his plane will crash, and the dream begins to come true.
Intriguing little melodrama which badly lacks a twist ending and foxes itself by a flashback construction which leaves very little open to doubt. Production generally good.

w R. C. Sheriff d Leslie Norman ph Lionel Banes m Malcolm Arnold

Michael Redgrave, Alexander Knox, Sheila Sim, Denholm Elliott, Ursula Jeans, George Rose, Nigel Stock, Michael Hordern, Ralph Truman, Victor Maddern, Bill Kerr, Alfie Bass

Night Nurse*
US 1931 72m bw
Warner

A nurse uncovers a plot by other members of the household against her patient's children.
Fast-moving melodrama with solid star performances; just what the public wanted in 1931.

w Oliver H. P. Garrett, novel Dora Macy d William Wellman ph Chick McGill

Barbara Stanwyck, Ben Lyon, Joan Blondell, Clark Gable, Charles Winninger, Vera Lewis, Blanche Frederici, Charlotte Merriam

'A conglomeration of exaggerations, often bordering on serial dramatics.'—*Hollywood Reporter*

Night of the Demon*
GB 1957 82m bw
Columbia / Sabre (Frank Bevis)
US title: *Curse of the Demon*

An occultist despatches his enemies by raising a giant medieval devil.
Despite dim work from the leads, this supernatural thriller is intelligently scripted and achieves several frightening and memorable sequences in the best Hitchcock manner.

w *Charles Bennett, Hal E. Chester, story Casting the Runes by M. R. James d Jacques*

Tourneur ph Ted Scaife *m* Clifton Parker
ad Ken Adam

Dana Andrews, Peggy Cummins, *Niall MacGinnis, Athene Seyler,* Brian Wilde, Maurice Denham, Ewan Roberts, Liam Redmond, Reginald Beckwith

Night of the Eagle**
GB 1961   87m   bw
Independent Artists (Albert Fennell)

At a medical school, a jealous witch sets an evil force on her rival.
Pretty good supernatural thriller, let down by leading performances and sustained by character roles and solid production values in creepy sequences.

w Charles Beaumont, Richard Matheson, George Baxt, *novel* Conjure Wife by Fritz Leiber Jnr *d Sidney Hayers ph* Reg Wyer *m* William Alwyn

Margaret Johnston, Janet Blair, Peter Wyngarde, Anthony Nicholls, Reginald Beckwith, Kathleen Byron

The Night of the Following Day*
US 1969   100m   Technicolor
Universal / Gina (Hubert Cornfield)

A young girl arriving in Paris to stay with her father is kidnapped and held to ransom by an eccentric gang.
Straightforward suspense thriller with delusions of grandeur; the second half bogs down in pretentious talk and the end suggests that the whole thing was a dream.

w Hubert Cornfield, Robert Phippeny, *novel* The Snatchers by Lionel White *d Hubert Cornfield ph* Willy Kurant *m* Stanley Myers

Marlon Brando, Richard Boone, Rita Moreno, Pamela Franklin, Jess Hahn

The Night of the Generals**
GB 1967   148m   Technicolor   Panavision
Columbia / Horizon / Filmsonor (Sam Spiegel)

A German intelligence agent tracks down a psychopathic Nazi general who started killing prostitutes in Warsaw during World War I.
A curiously bumpy narrative which is neither mystery nor character study but does provide a few effective sequences and impressive performances. The big budget seems well spent.

w Joseph Kessel, Paul Dehn, *novel* Hans Helmut Hirst *d* Anatole Litvak *ph* Henri Decaë *m* Maurice Jarre *pd* Alexander Trauner

Peter O'Toole, *Omar Sharif, Tom Courtenay,* Donald Pleasence, Joanna Pettet, *Philippe Noiret,* Charles Gray, Coral Brown, John

Gregson, Harry Andrews, Nigel Stock, Christopher Plummer, Juliette Greco
'The "who" is obvious from the first and the "dunnit" interminable.'—*Judith Crist, 1973*
'Lurid and vivid, if nothing else.'—*Robert Windeler*

The Night of the Grizzly
US 1966   102m   Techniscope
Paramount (Burt Dunne)

A Wyoming ex-sheriff kills a marauding bear and earns the respect of his son.
Stout-hearted family film, rather sluggishly made.

w Warren Douglas *d* Joseph Pevney *ph* Harold Lipstein, Loyal Griggs *m* Leith Stevens

Clint Walker, Martha Hyer, Keenan Wynn, Leo Gordon, Kevin Brodie, Nancy Kulp, Ellen Corby, Jack Elam, Ron Ely

The Night of the Hunter***
US 1955   93m   bw
UA / Paul Gregory

A psychopathic preacher goes on the trail of hidden money, the secret of which is held by two children.
Weird, manic fantasy in which evil finally comes to grief against the forces of sweetness and light (the children, an old lady, water, animals). Although the narrative does not flow smoothly there are splendidly imaginative moments, and no other film has ever quite achieved its texture.

w James Agee, novel Davis Grubb *d Charles Laughton ph Stanley Cortez m* Walter Schumann

Robert Mitchum, Shelley Winters, Lillian Gish, Don Beddoe, Evelyn Varden, Peter Graves, James Gleason
'One of the most frightening movies ever made.'—*Pauline Kael, 1968*
'A genuinely sinister work, full of shocks and over-emphatic sound effects, camera angles and shadowy lighting.'—*NFT, 1973*
'One of the most daring, eloquent and personal films to have come from America in a long time.'—*Derek Prouse*

The Night of the Iguana***
US 1964   125m   bw
MGM / Seven Arts (Ray Stark)

A disbarred clergyman becomes a travel courier in Mexico and is sexually desired by a teenage nymphomaniac, a middle-aged hotel owner and a frustrated itinerant artist.
The author is most tolerable when poking fun at his own types, and this is a sharp, funny picture with a touch of poetry.

w Anthony Veiller, *play Tennessee Williams*
d John Huston *ph Gabriel Figueroa*
m Benjamin Frankel *ad* Stephen Grimes

Richard Burton, Deborah Kerr, Ava Gardner,
Sue Lyon, *Grayson Hall, Cyril Delevanti*

AAN: Gabriel Figueroa; Grayson Hall

Night of the Lepus
US 1972   88m   Metrocolor
MGM (A. C. Lyles)

A serum meant to control a surplus of rabbits
instead produces monster varieties four feet tall.
Tolerable sci-fi tailored to a very tired formula.

w Don Holiday, Gene R. Kearney *d* William F.
Claxton *ph* Ted Voigtlander *m* Jimmie Haskell

Stuart Whitman, Rory Calhoun, Janet Leigh,
Paul Fix,
De Forrest Kelley

'For insomniacs with lax standards.'—*Judith
Crist*

Night Passage*
US 1957   90m   Technirama
U-I (Aaron Rosenberg)

A railroad worker entrusted with a payroll finds
that the bandits trying to rob it are led by his own
brother.
Obscurely titled and rather empty western
providing standard excitements.

w Borden Chase *d* James Neilson *ph* William
Daniels *m* Dmitri Tiomkin

James Stewart, Audie Murphy, Dan Duryea,
Brandon de Wilde, Dianne Foster

Night People*
US 1954   93m   Technicolor
   Cinemascope
TCF (Nunnally Johnson)

When a US corporal stationed in Berlin is
kidnapped by the Russians, his influential father
flies into action.
Curiously titled cold war suspenser which would
have been more memorable if not in
Cinemascope; the pace and talent are visible, but
the wide screen and poor colour dissipate them.

wd Nunnally Johnson ph Charles G. Clarke
m Cyril Mockridge

Gregory Peck, Broderick Crawford, Anita
Bjork, Walter Abel, Rita Gam, Buddy Ebsen, Jill
Esmond, Peter Van Eyck

AAN: original story (Jed Harris, Tom Reed)

Night Plane from Chungking
US 1942   69m   bw
Paramount

Assorted international passengers are flown
from Chungking to India, but one of their
number is a German spy who will kill to get his
hands on vital information.
A lower-case 'who is it' based on *Shanghai
Express*. Not bad according to its lights.

w Earl Felton, Theodore Reeves, Lester Cole
d Ralph Murphy

Ellen Drew, Robert Preston, Otto Kruger, Steve
Geray, Ernest Dorian, Tamara Geva, Sen Yung

Night Song
US 1947   101m   bw
RKO (Harriet Parsons)

A wealthy socialite falls for a blind pianist and
pretends to be blind also, and poor to boot.
Silly, pretentious soaper, moodily photographed.

w Frank Fenton, Irving Hyland, De Witt
Bodeen *d* John Cromwell *ph Lucien Ballard*
m Leith Stevens

Dana Andrews, Merle Oberon, Hoagy
Carmichael, Ethel Barrymore, Artur
Rubenstein, Eugene Ormandy

The Night They Raided Minsky's**
US 1968   99m   De Luxe
UA / Tandem (Norman Lear)
GB title: *The Night They Invented Striptease*

Various human problems are posed and solved
during a night at a burlesque theatre.
Marvellous kaleidoscopic ragbag of brilliant
fragments which unfortunately don't cohere in
the mind into a really memorable film, though it
gives detailed pleasure on every viewing.

w Arnold Schulman, Sidney Michaels, Norman
Lear, *book* Rowland Barber *d William
Friedkin ph Andrew Laszlo m Charles
Strouse pd William Eckar, Jean Eckar
ch* Danny Daniels *narrator* Rudy Vallee

Jason Robards, Britt Ekland, *Norman Wisdom*,
Forrest Tucker, Joseph Wiseman, Bert Lahr,
Harry Andrews, Denholm Elliott, Elliot Gould,
Jack Burns

'The Fanny Brice country stunningly brought
to life—every face a snapshot of yesterday.'—
Alexander Walker

A Night to Remember*
US 1941   91m   bw
Columbia (Samuel Bischoff)

A Greenwich Village mystery-writing couple try
to solve a murder.
Reasonably sparkling comedy whodunnit with a
zany tinge.

w Richard Flournoy, Jack Henley *d* Richard

Wallace *ph* Joseph Walker *m* Werner Heymann *md* Morris Stoloff

Loretta Young, Brian Aherne, Jeff Donnell, William Wright, Sidney Toler, Gale Sondergaard, Donald MacBride, Lee Patrick, Blanche Yurka

A Night to Remember***
GB 1958   123m   bw
Rank (William Macquitty)

The story of the 1912 sea disaster when the *Titanic* struck an iceberg.
A major film enterprise featuring hundreds of cameos, none discernibly more important than the other. On this account the film seems alternately stiff and flabby as narrative, but there is much to enjoy and admire along the way, though the sense of awe is dissipated by the final model shots.

w Eric Ambler, book Walter Lord *d Roy Baker ph Geoffrey Unsworth m* William Alwyn

Kenneth More, Honor Blackman, Michael Goodliffe, David McCallum, George Rose, Anthony Bushell, Ralph Michael, John Cairney, Kenneth Griffith, Frank Lawton, Michael Bryant

'A worthy, long-drawn-out documentary, with noticeably more honesty about human nature than most films, but little shape or style.'—*Kenneth Cavender*

Night Train to Munich***
GB 1940   93m   bw
TCF (Edward Black)
aka: *Gestapo; Night Train*

A British agent poses as a Nazi in order to rescue a Czech inventor.
First-rate comedy suspenser obviously inspired by the success of *The Lady Vanishes* and providing much the same measure of thrills and laughs.

w Frank Launder, Sidney Gilliat, novel Report on a Fugitive by Gordon Wellesley *d Carol Reed ph* Otto Kanturek *m* Charles Williams *md* Louis Levy

Margaret Lockwood, *Rex Harrison, Basil Radford, Naunton Wayne*, Paul Henreid, Keneth Kent, Felix Aylmer, Roland Culver, *Eliot Makeham, Raymond Huntley*, Wyn'dham Goldie

'A very nice triumph of skill and maturity in films, and thus a pleasure to have.'—*Otis Ferguson*

AAN: Gordon Wellesley

Night unto Night*
US 1949   85m   bw
Warner (Owen Crump)

An epileptic scientist falls for a girl hallucinated by the ghost of her dead husband.
Cheerless nuthouse melodrama, one of the well-meant aberrations which Hollywood studios used to produce as a sop to conscience.

w Kathryn Scola, *novel* Philip Wylie *d Don Siegel ph* Peverell Marley *m* Franz Waxman

Ronald Reagan, Viveca Lindfors, Rosemary de Camp, Broderick Crawford, Osa Massen, Craig Stevens, Erskine Sanford

The Night Walker*
US 1964   86m   bw
U-I / William Castle

The widow of a tough executive, killed and disfigured in an explosion, is haunted in her dreams not only by him but by a mysterious lover who turns up in reality.
Stiff and unconvincing but still fairly frightening low-budget shocker with a plot twist or two.

w Robert Bloch d William Castle *ph* Harold Stine *m* Vic Mizzy

Robert Taylor, *Barbara Stanwyck*, Lloyd Bochner, Rochelle Hudson, Judi Meredith, Hayden Rorke

Night Watch
GB 1973   98m   Technicolor
Avco / Brut (David White)

A widow recovering from a nervous breakdown keeps seeing bodies in the night. Her friends try to help, but things are not quite what they seem.
Predictable coiled-spring shocker which goes curiously flat despite a star cast and lashings of blood. Perhaps we have all been here once too often.

w Tony Williamson, *play* Lucille Fletcher *d* Brian G. Hutton *ph* Billie Williams *m* John Cameron

Elizabeth Taylor, Laurence Harvey, Billie Whitelaw, Robert Lang, Tony Britton, Bill Dean

'It has all the trappings of a Joan Crawford vehicle of the forties, with numerous elegant dresses for Miss Taylor, an appropriately unbecoming wardrobe for Miss Whitelaw, and a set which is an art director's dream.'—*Brenda Davies*

'Elizabeth Taylor's gowns are by Valentino, her jewellery is by Van Cleef and Arpels, even her kitchen is by Westinghouse. And she is *still* going out of her mind.'—*Alexander Walker*

Night without Sleep
US 1952 77m bw
TCF (Robert Bassler)

A man reconstructs his drunken actions the
night before, and fears he has committed a
murder.
Dreary melodrama, all frayed tempers,
drunkenness and cigarette smoke.

w Frank Partos, Elick Moll d Roy Baker
ph Lucien Ballard

Gary Merrill, Linda Darnell, Hildegarde Neff,
Hugh Beaumont, Mae Marsh

The Nightcomers*
GB 1971 96m Technicolor
Scimitar / Kastner–Kanter–Ladd (Michael
Winner)

How the ghost-ridden children in *The Turn of the
Screw* became evil; they became involved in
aberrant sexual activities between the gardener
and the housekeeper, and finally murdered the
former.
Despite its unexpected literariness this is
unpleasant and unconvincing nonsense with a
boring script punctuated by shock cuts and very
little period feel.

w Michael Hastings d Michael Winner
ph Robert Paynter m Jerry Fielding

Stephanie Beacham, Marlon Brando, Thora
Hird, Harry Andrews, Verna Harvey,
Christopher Ellis

Nightfall*
US 1957 78m bw
Columbia (Ted Richmond)

The police and two bank robbers chase an
innocent artist who happens to know that the
loot is hidden in a Wisconsin snowdrift.
Occasionally stylish but obscurely narrated
suspenser.

w Stirling Silliphant, *novel* David Goodis
d Jacques Tourneur ph Burnett Guffey
m George Duning

Anne Bancroft, Aldo Ray, Brian Keith, James
Gregory, Jocelyn Brando, Frank Albertson

Nightmare
US 1942 81m bw
Universal

A gambler in wartime London helps a beautiful
girl escape from Nazi spies.
Thin espionage thriller with a good sequence or
two and a smooth villain.

w Dwight Taylor, *novel* Escape by Philip
MacDonald d Tim Whelan

Brian Donlevy, Diana Barrymore, *Gavin Muir*,
Henry Daniell, Hans Conried, Arthur Shields

Nightmare*
US 1956 89m bw
UA / Pine–Thomas / Shane (Maxwell Shane)

A young musician is hypnotized into committing
a murder, and reconstructs his actions with the
help of his policeman brother-in-law.
Lethargic remake of the ingenious *Fear in the
Night* (qv). Watchable.

wd Maxwell Shane, *novel* Cornell Woolrich
ph Joseph Biroc m Herschel Burke Gilbert

Edward G. Robinson, Kevin McCarthy, Virginia
Christine, Connie Russell

Nightmare*
GB 1964 82m bw Hammerscope
U-I / Hammer (Jimmy Sangster)

18-year-old Janet still has nightmares after
seeing her mad mother kill her father six years
ago; brought home, even more frightening
visions afflict her.
Genuinely scary *Diabolique*-type mystery with
the usual Hammer borrowings put to good use.

w Jimmy Sangster d Freddie Francis ph John
Wilcox m Don Banks

Moira Redmond, David Knight, Brenda Bruce,
John Welsh, *Jennie Linden*

Nightmare Alley**
US 1947 112m bw
TCF

A fairground barker becomes a successful
confidence trickster dealing with the
supernatural, but finally sinks to the depths.
Unusual road to ruin melodrama, a striking
oddity from Hollywood at the time, and still
quite interesting and well done.

w Jules Furthman, *novel* William Lindsay
Gresham d Edmund Goulding ph Lee Garmes
m Cyril Mockridge

Tyrone Power, Coleen Gray, Joan Blondell,
Taylor Holmes, Helen Walker, Mike Mazurki,
Ian Keith

Nightmare in the Sun*
US 1963 81m De Luxe
Afilmco (Marc Lawrence, John Derek)

A rich man kills his wife and blames a hitch-hiker
who has had a brief affair with her.
Modest independent melodrama, quite
interestingly made though not entirely effective.

w Ted Thomas d Marc Lawrence ph Stanley
Cortez m Paul Glass

John Derek, Ursula Andress, Arthur O'Connell,
Aldo Ray

Nikki, Wild Dog of the North*
US 1961   74m   Technicolor
Walt Disney (Winston Hibler)

The life of a Canadian trapper's wolf dog.
Pleasing 'true life fiction' which didn't quite
reach top feature status.

w Ralph Wright, Winston Hibler, *novel* James
Oliver Curwood d Jack Couffer m Oliver
Wallace

Emile Genest, Jean Coutu

Nine Girls
US 1944   78m   bw
Columbia (Burt Kelly)

College girls are murdered in a sorority house.
Cheapjack whodunnit with a cardboard look
and feel.

w Karen de Wolff, Connie Lee, *play* Wilfred H.
Pettit d Leigh Jason ph James Van Trees
m John Leopold

Ann Harding, Evelyn Keyes, Jinx Falkenberg,
Anita Louise, Leslie Brooks, Lynn Merrick, Jeff
Donnell, Nina Foch, Marcia Mae Jones, William
Demarest

Nine Hours to Rama
GB 1962   125m   De Luxe   Cinemascope
TCF / Red Lion (Mark Robson)

Events leading to the assassination of Mahatma
Gandhi.
Fictionalized, sensationalized and very dull, this
multi-character drama holds interest only for
snatches of acting and location backgrounds.

w Nelson Gidding, *novel* Stanley Wolpert
d Mark Robson ph Arthur Ibbetson
m Malcolm Arnold

Jose Ferrer, Diane Baker, Robert Morley, J. S.
Casshyap, Horst Buchholz, Harry Andrews

'The only interesting line in the movie is the
thick brown one visible on the inside of every
white collar.'—*John Simon*

1984*
GB 1955   91m   bw
Holiday (N. Peter Rathvon)

Europe has become the fascist state of Oceania,
ruled by Big Brother; Winston Smith yearns for
the old days, and is brainwashed.
The famous prophecy of a dehumanized future is
followed with reasonable fidelity apart from the
defiant ending, but the novel is too literary for
cinematic success and the result is too often both
downbeat and boring.

w William P. Templeton, Ralph Bettinson, *novel*
George Orwell d *Michael Anderson* ph C.
Pennington Richards m Malcolm Arnold

Michael Redgrave, Edmond O'Brien, Jan
Sterling, David Kossoff, Mervyn Johns, Donald
Pleasence

1900*
Italy / France / West Germany 1976   320m
Technicolor
TCF / PEA / Artistes Associés / Artemis
(Alberto Grimaldi)
original title: *Novecento*

The political and personal vicissitudes of a noble
Italian family between 1900 and 1945.
Immensely long and heavy-going study of the
rise of fascism in the form of a family saga. For
specialists only.

w Bernardo Bertolucci, Franco Arcalli,
Giuseppe Bertolucci d Bernardo Bertolucci
ph Vittorio Stovaro m Ennio Morricone
ad Enzo Frigiero

Burt Lancaster, Robert de Niro, Gerard
Depardieu, Dominique Sanda, Donald
Sutherland, Sterling Hayden

'Exasperatingly uneven, but its most powerful
moments can't be matched by any movie since
Godfather Two.'—*Time*

'Bertolucci tried to write a 19th-century novel
on film: the result is appalling, yet it has the
grandeur of a classic visionary folly.'—*New*
Yorker

† The film was normally shown in two separate
parts.

99 and 44/100 Per Cent Dead
US 1974   98m   De Luxe   Panavision
Joe Wizan / Vashon
aka: *Call Harry Crown*

A losing gang boss hires a trouble shooter.
Violent gangster melodrama apparently
intended as a black comedy; if so, as clumsy as
its title.

w Robert Dillon d John Frankenheimer
ph Ralph Woolsey m Henry Mancini

Richard Harris, Edmond O'Brien, Bradford
Dillman, Ann Turkel, Chuck Connors,
Constance Ford

'Esthetically, commercially and morally, a
quintessential fiasco.'—*Variety*

99 River Street*
US 1953   83m   bw
UA / Edward Small

A taxi driver becomes involved in a diamond
robbery.

Adequate thick ear with quite good detection and action sequences.

w Robert Smith d Phil Karlson ph Franz Planer

John Payne, Evelyn Keyes, Frank Faylen, Brad Dexter, Peggie Castle

Ninotchka***
US 1939 110m bw
MGM (Ernst Lubitsch)

A Paris playboy falls for a communist emissary sent to sell some crown jewels.
Sparkling comedy on a theme which has been frequently explored; delicate pointing and hilarious character comedy sustain this version perfectly until the last half hour, when it certainly sags; but it remains a favourite Hollywood example of this genre.

w Charles Brackett, Billy Wilder, Walter Reisch, story Melchior Lengyel d Ernst Lubitsch ph William Daniels m Werner Heymann

Greta Garbo, Melvyn Douglas, Sig Rumann, Alexander Granach, Felix Bressart, Ina Claire, Bela Lugosi

'The Lubitsch style, in which much was made of subtleties—glances, finger movements, raised eyebrows—has disappeared. Instead we have a hard, brightly lit, cynical comedy with the wisecrack completely in control.'—John Baxter, 1968

AAN: best picture; script; story; Greta Garbo

No Blade of Grass
GB 1970 97m Metrocolor Panavision
MGM (Cornel Wilde)

Industrial pollution sets a destructive virus ruining the crops of the world; anarchy spreads through Britain and one family takes refuge in the Lake District.
Apocalyptic sci-fi, moderately well done though so humourless as to be almost funny.

w Sean Forestal, Jefferson Pascal, novel John Christopher d Cornel Wilde ph H. A. R. Thompson m Burnell Whibley

Nigel Davenport, Jean Wallace, Patrick Holt, John Hamill

No Deposit, No Return
US 1976 112m Technicolor
Walt Disney (Ron Miller)

Airport confusion causes crooks to abduct (unwittingly) a millionaire's grandchildren; the millionaire gives chase.
Overlong and tedious action comedy which makes little sense.

w Arthur Alsberg, Don Nelson d Norman Tokar ph Frank Phillips m Buddy Baker

David Niven, Darren McGavin, Don Knotts, Herschel Bernardi, Barbara Feldon, John Williams, Vic Tayback, Kim Richards

No Down Payment**
US 1957 105m bw Cinemascope
TCF (Jerry Wald)

Tension among smart suburban couples in a Los Angeles housing development.
Lively domestic melodrama, very useful to sociologists as a mirror of its times.

w Philip Yordan, novel John McPartland d Martin Ritt ph Joseph La Shelle m Leigh Harline

Joanne Woodward, Tony Randall, Sheree North, Jeffrey Hunter, Cameron Mitchell, Patricia Owens, Barbara Rush, Pat Hingle

No Funny Business
GB 1933 75m bw
John Stafford

Two professional co-respondents are sent to the Riviera; each mistakes the other as his client.
Stagey farce, notable for its unlikely star teaming and its hilariously dated style.

w Victor Hanbury, Frank Vosper, Dorothy Hope d John Stafford, Victor Hanbury

Gertrude Lawrence, Laurence Olivier, Jill Esmond, Edmund Breon, Gibb McLaughlin, Muriel Aked

No Highway**
GB 1951 98m bw
TCF (Louis D. Lighton)
US title: No Highway in the Sky

During a transatlantic flight, a boffin works out that the plane's tail is about to fall off from metal fatigue.
The central premise of this adaptation from a popular novel is fascinating, but the romantic asides are a distraction and the characters cardboard; the film still entertains through sheer professionalism.

w R. C. Sheriff, Oscar Millard, Alec Coppel, novel Nevil Shute d Henry Koster ph Georges Périnal

James Stewart, Marlene Dietrich, Glynis Johns, Jack Hawkins, Janette Scott, Elizabeth Allan, Kenneth More, Niall MacGinnis, Ronald Squire

No Leave, No Love
US 1946 118m bw
MGM (Joe Pasternak)

Sailors on leave meet an English girl.
Witless, overlong musical extravaganza.

w Charles Martin, Leslie Karkos *d* Charles
Martin *ph* Harold Rosson, Robert Surtees
md Georgie Stoll

Van Johnson, Pat Kirkwood, Keenan Wynn,
Guy Lombardo and his Orchestra, Edward
Arnold, Marie Wilson, Leon Ames

No Limit*
GB 1935 79m bw
ATP (Basil Dean)

A motor mechanic enters for the TT Races.
Lively star comedy with Isle of Man locations.

w Tom Geraghty, Fred Thompson, *story* Walter
Greenwood *d* Monty Banks

George Formby, Florence Desmond, Edward
Rigby, Jack Hobbs, Peter Gawthorne, Alf
Goddard

No Love for Johnnie*
GB 1960 111m bw Cinemascope
Rank / Five Star (Betty E. Box)

The personal and political problems of a Labour
MP.
Predictable but quite lively study of ambition
and frustration, with good cameos;
Cinemascope all but ruins its impact.

w Nicholas Phipps, Mordecai Richler, *novel*
Wilfred Fienburgh *d* Ralph Thomas *ph* Ernest
Steward *m* Malcolm Arnold

Peter Finch, Mary Peach, *Stanley Holloway*,
Donald Pleasence, Billie Whitelaw, Hugh
Burden, Rosalie Crutchley, Michael Goodliffe,
Mervyn Johns, Geoffrey Keen, Paul Rogers,
Dennis Price, Peter Barkworth, Fenella Fielding,
Gladys Henson

No Man Is an Island
US 1962 114m Eastmancolor
U-I / Gold Coast (John Monks Jnr, Richard
Goldstone)
GB title: *Island Escape*

After the Japanese attack on Guam, a radioman
finds refuge in a leper colony and sets up his own
resistance unit.
Unexceptionable war adventure in the jungle.

wd John Monks Jnr, Richard Goldstone
ph Carl Kayser *m* Restie Umali

Jeffrey Hunter, Marshall Thompson, Barbara
Perez, Ronald Remy

'Good clean fun for right-minded
teenagers.'—*MFB*

No Man of Her Own*
US 1932 98m bw
Paramount

A big-time gambler marries a local girl on a bet
and tries to keep her innocent of his activities.
Star romantic comedy drama, quite
professionally assembled and played.

w Maurine Watkins, Milton H. Gropper
d Wesley Ruggles *ph* Leo Tover

Clark Gable, Carole Lombard, Dorothy
Mackail, Grant Mitchell, George Barbier,
Elizabeth Patterson, J. Farrell MacDonald

'Just about everything that the ordinary
picture fan looks for: drama, romance, comedy,
strong build-ups, exciting climaxes, a fine line of
human interest.'—*Film Daily*

No Man of Her Own*
US 1949 98m bw
Paramount (Richard Maibaum)

A pregnant wanderer is involved in a train crash
and assumes the identity of the wife of a dead
passenger.
Glossy star melodrama, very watchable.

w Catherine Turney, Sally Benson, Mitchell
Leisen *d Mitchell Leisen ph* Daniel L. Fapp
m Hugo Friedhofer

Barbara Stanwyck, John Lund, Lyle Bettger,
Jane Cowl, Phyllis Thaxter, Henry O'Neill,
Richard Denning

No Minor Vices
US 1948 96m bw
(MGM) Enterprise

A doctor brings home an artist friend who
proceeds to wreck his household.
Interminable thin comedy which gives no clue as
to what the talent involved thought it was doing.

w Arnold Manoff *d* Lewis Milestone *ph* George
Barnes *m* Franz Waxman

Dana Andrews, Lilli Palmer, Louis Jourdan,
Jane Wyatt, Norman Lloyd

No More Ladies
US 1935 79m bw
MGM

A society girl thinks that by marrying a rake she
can reform him.
Breezy sophisticated comedy which doesn't
quite maintain its impetus.

w Donald Ogden Stewart, Horace Jackson, *play*
A. E. Thomas *d* Edward H. Griffith, George
Cukor *ph* Oliver T. Marsh

Joan Crawford, Robert Montgomery, Franchot
Tone, Charles Ruggles, Edna May Oliver, Gail
Patrick, Reginald Denny, Arthur Treacher

No Orchids for Miss Blandish
GB 1948   102m   bw
Renown (A. R. Shipman, Oswald Mitchell)

An heiress is kidnapped by gangsters and falls for their psychopathic leader.
Hilariously awful gangster movie from a bestselling shocker.
Everyone concerned is all at sea, and the result is one of the worst films ever made.

wd St John L. Clowes, *novel* James Hadley Chase *ph* Gerald Gibbs

Jack La Rue, Linden Travers, Hugh McDermott, Walter Crisham, Lily Molnar, Zoe Gail

'This must be the most sickening exhibition of brutality, perversion, sex and sadism ever to be shown on a cinema screen . . . with pseudo-American accents the actors literally battle their way through a script laden with suggestive dialogue.'—*MFB*
† Remade as *The Grissom Gang* (qv).

No Parking
GB 1938   72m   bw
Herbert Wilcox

A car park attendant is mistaken for an American killer.
Modest, entertaining star comedy.

w Gerald Elliott, *story* Carol Reed *d* Jack Raymond

Gordon Harker, Leslie Perrins, Irene Ware, Cyril Smith

No Peace among the Olives
Italy 1950   99m   bw
Lux (Domenico Davanzati)

A young shepherd goes home after the war and finds himself at war again—against a local racketeer.
A rather crude melodrama comparable with the American *Thieves' Highway* and other *films noirs* of the time.

w Giuseppe de Santis and others *d* Giuseppe de Santis *ph* Pietro Portalupi *m* Goffredo Petrassi

Lucia Bose, Raf Vallone, Folco Lulli, Dante Maggio

No Questions Asked
US 1951   80m   bw
MGM (Nicholas Nayfack)

A young lawyer undertakes shady business and finds himself framed for murder.
Well made second feature on conventional lines.

w Sidney Sheldon *d* Harold Kress *ph* Harold Lipstein *m* Leith Stevens

Barry Sullivan, George Murphy, Arlene Dahl, Jean Hagen, William Reynolds, Mari Blanchard

No Resting Place
GB 1951   77m   bw
Colin Lesslie

A wandering Irish tinker accidentally kills a man and is hounded by a Civil Guard.
Interesting attempt at realistic location drama, suffering from a dejected plot and unsympathetic characters.

w Paul Rotha, Colin Lesslie, Michael Orrom, *novel* Ian Niall *ph* Wolfgang Suschitsky *m* William Alwyn

Michael Gough, Noel Purcell, Jack McGowran

No Room at the Inn
GB 1948   82m   bw
British National (Ivan Foxwell)

A monstrous woman half-starves evacuees and turns her house into a brothel.
Absurd melodrama from a play which was popular because it offered a full-blooded star performance. The film is less convincing but works pretty well on its level.

w Ivan Foxwell, Dylan Thomas, *play* Joan Temple *d* Dan Birt

Freda Jackson, Joy Shelton, Hermione Baddeley, Joan Dowling, Harcourt Williams, Sydney Tafler, Frank Pettingell, Niall MacGinnis

No Sad Songs for Me
US 1950   89m   bw
Columbia (Buddy Adler)

A young wife discovers she has only eight months to live, and spends it planning her husband's future.
Well-meant but rather icky melodrama featuring one of those beautiful illnesses that appear to have no physical effect.

w Howard Koch, *novel* Ruth Southard *d* Rudolph Maté *ph* Joseph Walker *m* George Duning

Margaret Sullavan, Wendell Corey, Viveca Lindfors, Natalie Wood, John McIntire

AAN: George Duning

No Sex Please, We're British*
GB 1973   91m   Technicolor
Columbia / BHP (John R. Sloan)

A wrongly addressed parcel of dirty postcards causes chaos when it arrives at a bank.
Archetypal British farce with less plot than one might expect, but quite brightly performed.

w Anthony Marriott, Johnnie Mortimer, Brian Cooke,
play Anthony Marriott, Alistair Foot d Cliff Owen ph Ken Hodges m Eric Rogers

Ronnie Corbett, Beryl Reid, *Arthur Lowe*, Ian Ogilvy, Susan Penhaligon, David Swift, Michael Bates, Gerald Sim

No Time for Comedy*
US 1940 93m bw
Warner (Robert Lord)

A playwright is depressed by the times and has lost the knack of making people laugh.
Smooth film version of a thoughtful romantic comedy play.

w Julius J. and Philip G. Epstein, play S. N. Behrman d William Keighley ph Ernest Haller m Heinz Roemheld

James Stewart, Rosalind Russell, Charles Ruggles, Genevieve Tobin, Allyn Joslyn, Clarence Kolb, Louise Beavers

No Time for Love*
US 1943 83m bw
Paramount (Mitchell Leisen)

A lady photographer falls for the foreman of a crew digging a tunnel under the Hudson.
Agreeable romantic slapstick farce.

w Claude Binyon d Mitchell Leisen ph Charles Lang Jnr m Victor Young

Claudette Colbert, Fred MacMurray, Ilka Chase, Richard Haydn, June Havoc, Marjorie Gateson, Bill Goodwin

No Time for Sergeants
US 1958 111m bw
Warner (Mervyn Le Roy)

Adventures of a hillbilly army conscript.
Heavy-handed adaptation of the stage success, a real piece of filmed theatre with not much sparkle to it.

w John Lee Mahin, play Ira Levin, novel Mac Hyman d Mervyn Le Roy ph Harold Rosson m Ray Heindorf

Andy Griffith, William Fawcett, Murray Hamilton, Nick Adams, Myron McCormick, Bartlett Robinson

No Trees in the Street
GB 1958 96m bw
ABP / Allegro (Frank Godwin)

Problems of a London slum family in the thirties.
Artificial and unconvincing attempt at a London *Love on the Dole*, dragged up and redigested in a later era when 'realism' was thought to be fashionable.

w Ted Willis, from his play d J. Lee-Thompson ph Gilbert Taylor m Laurie Johnson

Sylvia Syms, Herbert Lom, Joan Miller, Melvyn Hayes, Stanley Holloway, Liam Redmond, Ronald Howard, Carole Lesley, Lana Morris, Lily Kann

'Nothing remains but crude sensationalism and several moments of unconscious humour.'—*MFB*

No Way Out*
US 1950 106m bw
TCF (Darryl F. Zanuck)

A crook stirs up racial feeling against a black doctor in whose hands his brother has died.
Vivid, hard-hitting melodrama with a hospital background and a strong sociological flavour.

w Joseph L. Mankiewicz, Lesser Samuels d Joseph L. Mankiewicz ph Milton Krasner m Alfred Newman

Richard Widmark, Sidney Poitier, Linda Darnell, Stephen McNally, Harry Bellaver, Stanley Ridges, Ossie Davis, Ruby Dee

AAN: script

No Way to Treat a Lady*
US 1968 108m Technicolor
Paramount / Sol C. Siegel

A mass murderer of women who is also a master of disguise has a running battle with a police detective.
Curious mixture of star show-off piece, murder mystery, black farce, suspense melodrama and Jewish comedy. Bits of it come off very well, but it's a bumpy ride.

w John Gay, novel William Goldman d Jack Smight ph Jack Priestley m Stanley Myers

Rod Steiger, George Segal, Lee Remick, Eileen Heckart, Murray Hamilton, Michael Dunn

Nob Hill*
US 1945 95m Technicolor
TCF (André Daven)

In the gay nineties, a San Francisco saloon owner tries to step into society and win one of its most eligible young ladies.
Engaging period musical drama with all talents working well.

w Wanda Tuchock, Norman Reilly Raine d Henry Hathaway ph Edward Cronjager md Emil Newman, Charles Henderson

George Raft, Joan Bennett, Peggy Ann Garner, Vivian Blaine, Alan Reed, B. S. Pully, Edgar Barrier

Nobody Lives Forever
US 1946   100m   bw
Warner (Robert Buckner)

A con man fleeces a rich widow, then falls in love with her.

Forgettable romantic melodrama.

w W. R. Burnett d Jean Negulesco ph Arthur Edeson m Adolph Deutsch

John Garfield, Geraldine Fitzgerald, Walter Brennan, Faye Emerson, George Coulouris, George Tobias

Nobody Runs Forever*
GB 1968   101m   Eastmancolor
Rank / Selmur (Betty E. Box)
US title: *The High Commissioner*

An Australian detective is sent to arrest the high commissioner in London on a charge of murdering his first wife.
Sub-Hitchcock thriller which comes to life in patches but has a plot and dialogue which obviously embarrass the actors.

w Wilfred Greatorex, *novel* The High Commissioner by Jon Cleary ph Ernest Steward m Georges Delerue

Rod Taylor, Christopher Plummer, Lilli Palmer, Camilla Sparv, Daliah Lavi, Clive Revill, Lee Montague, Calvin Lockhart, Derren Nesbitt, Leo McKern, Franchot Tone

Nobody's Perfect
US 1968   103m   Techniscope
Universal (Howard Christie)

An ex-naval officer returns to Japan to make amends for stealing a buddha.
Flatfooted comedy adventure.

w John D. F. Black, *novel* The Crows of Edwina Hill by Allan R. Bosworth d Alan Rafkin ph Robert H. Wyckoff m Irving Gertz

Doug McClure, Nancy Kwan, Steve Carlson, James Whitmore, David Hartman, Gary Vinson, James Shigeta

Nocturne*
US 1946   87m   bw
RKO (Joan Harrison)

A police detective investigates the death of a composer.
Amusingly self-mocking crime thriller, quite smoothly done in all departments.

w *Jonathan Latimer d Edwin L. Marin* ph Harry J. Wild m Leigh Harline

George Raft, Lynn Bari, Virginia Huston, Joseph Pevney, Myrna Dell, Edward Ashley, Walter Sande, Mabel Paige

Non Stop New York
GB 1937   71m   bw
GFD / Gaumont

In 1940, gangsters on a transatlantic airliner try to kill a key witness.
Slightly futuristic thriller of its time, now hilariously dated but quite entertaining as well as giving a rare picture of air travel in the thirties.

w Curt Siodmak, Roland Pertwee, J. O. C. Orton, Derek Twist, *novel* Sky Steward by Ken Attiwill d Robert Stevenson

John Loder, Anna Lee, Francis L. Sullivan, Frank Cellier, Desmond Tester, Athene Seyler, Jerry Verno

None But the Brave
US 1965   105m   Technicolor   Panavision
Warner / Eiga / Toho / Artanis (Frank Sinatra)

During World War II a plane carrying US Marines to the Pacific front crashlands on an island held by Japanese.
Anti-war melodrama in which the action scenes are more memorable than the admirable sentiments.

w John Twist, Katsuya Susaki d Frank Sinatra ph Harold Lipstein m Johnny Williams

Frank Sinatra, Clint Walker, Tommy Sands, Tony Bill, Brad Dexter

None But the Lonely Heart*
US 1944   113m   bw
RKO (David Hempstead)

In the thirties, a cockney drifter finds himself when he learns that his mother is dying.
Wildly astonishing moodpiece to come from Hollywood during World War II; its picture of East End low life is as rocky as its star performance, but it started Miss Barrymore on the west coast career which sustained her old age.

wd Clifford Odets, *novel* Richard Llewellyn ph George Barnes m Hanns Eisler md Constantin Bakaleinikoff

Cary Grant, *Ethel Barrymore*, June Duprez, Barry Fitzgerald, Jane Wyatt, George Coulouris, Dan Duryea, Konstantin Shayne, Morton Lowry, Helene Thimig

AA: Ethel Barrymore
AAN: Hanns Eisler; Cary Grant

None Shall Escape*
US 1945   85m   bw
Columbia (Sam Bischoff)

The career of a Nazi officer shown as flashbacks from his trial as a war criminal.

Taut topical melodrama reflecting the mood of the time.

w Lester Cole d André de Toth ph Lee Garmes m Ernst Toch

Alexander Knox, Marsha Hunt, Henry Travers, Dorothy Morris, Richard Crane

AA: Lester Cole; original story (Alfred Neumann, Joseph Thau)

Noose
GB 1948   98m   bw
ABPC/Edward Dryhurst

A Soho black market gang is exposed.
Vivid though rather tatty film version of a West End play success.

w Richard Llewellyn, from his play d Edmond T. Greville ph Hone Glendining m Charles Williams

Nigel Patrick, Carole Landis, Derek Farr, Joseph Calleia, Stanley Holloway, Hay Petrie, John Slater

Non Stop New York
GB 1937   71m   bw
GFD / Gaumont

In 1940, gangsters on a transatlantic airliner try to kill a key witness.
Slightly futuristic thriller of its time, now hilariously dated but quite entertaining as well as giving a rare picture of air travel in the thirties.

w Curt Siodmak, Roland Pertwee, J. O. C. Orton, Derek Twist, novel Sky Steward by Ken Attiwill d Robert Stevenson

John Loder, Anna Lee, Francis L. Sullivan, Frank Cellier, Desmond Tester, Athene Seyler, Jerry Verno

Nora Prentiss*
US 1946   117m   bw
Warner (William Jacobs)

A doctor falls for a café singer who ruins his life.
Standard star melodrama aimed at women, and appreciated by them.

w N. Richard Nash, story Paul Webster, Jack Sobell d Vincent Sherman ph James Wong Howe m Franz Waxman

Ann Sheridan, Kent Smith, Bruce Bennett, Robert Alda, Rosemary de Camp, John Ridgely, Wanda Hendrix

The Norseman
US 1978   90m   Movielab
AIP / Charles B. Pierce / Fawcett Majors

A Viking heads across the sea to America in search of his long lost father.

Low grade hokum for the easily pleased.

wd Charles B. Pierce ph Robert Bethard m Jaime Mendoza-Nava

Lee Majors, Cornel Wilde, Mel Ferrer, Jack Elam, Chris Connelly

North by Northwest****
US 1959   136m   Technicolor   Vistavision
MGM (Alfred Hitchcock)

A businessman is mistaken for a spy, and enemy agents then try to kill him because he knows too much.
Delightful chase comedy-thriller with a touch of sex, a kind of compendium of its director's best work, with memories of The 39 Steps, Saboteur and Foreign Correspondent among others.

w Ernest Lehman d Alfred Hitchcock ph Robert Burks m Bernard Herrmann

Cary Grant, Eva Marie Saint, James Mason, Leo G. Carroll, Martin Landau, Jessie Royce Landis, Adam Williams

AAN: Ernest Lehman

North Star*
US 1943   105m   bw
Samuel Goldwyn (William Cameron Menzies)
aka: Armored Attack

A Russian village defends itself against the Nazi onslaught.
Highly artificial propaganda piece later disowned by its makers and retitled. Good acting can't make its mark when the Russian steppes become a never-never land.

w Lillian Hellmann d Lewis Milestone ph James Wong Howe m Aaron Copland

Anne Baxter, Farley Granger, Jane Withers, Dana Andrews, Walter Brennan, Erich Von Stroheim, Dean Jagger, Ann Harding, Carl Benton Reid, Walter Huston

'Putting American villagers into Russian costumes and calling them by Russian names is never going to deceive this old bird.'—James Agate

'Its failure is the case history of every Hollywood film that steps out of its scope.'—Richard Winnington

AAN: Lillian Hellmann; James Wong Howe; Aaron Copland

North to Alaska*
US 1960   122m   De Luxe   Cinemascope
TCF (Henry Hathaway)

In 1900, two successful gold prospectors have woman trouble.
Good-natured brawling adventure story which

could do with cutting but is certainly the type of action movie they don't make 'em like any more.

w John Lee Mahin, Martin Rackin, Claude Binyon, *play* Birthday Gift by Ladislas Fodor *d* Henry Hathaway *ph* Leon Shamroy *m* Lionel Newman

John Wayne, Stewart Granger, Fabian, Capucine, Ernie Kovacs, Mickey Shaughnessy, Karl Swenson, Joe Sawyer, John Qualen

Northern Pursuit*
US 1943 94m bw
Warner (Jack Chertok)

A Mountie tracks a stranded Nazi pilot through the Canadian wastes.

Rather unusual star actioner, not badly done.

w Frank Gruber, Alvah Bessie *d* Raoul Walsh *ph* Sid Hickox *m* Adolph Deutsch

Errol Flynn, Helmut Dantine, Julie Bishop, John Ridgely, Gene Lockhart, Tom Tully, Bernard Nedell

Northwest Frontier***
GB 1959 129m Eastmancolor
  Cinemascope
Rank / Marcel Hellman
US title: *Flame Over India*

In 1905 an English officer during a rebellion escorts a young Hindu prince on a dangerous train journey.

Thoroughly enjoyable Boys' Own Paper adventure story with excellent set pieces and a spot-the-villain mystery.

w Robin Estridge *d* J. Lee-Thompson *ph* Geoffrey Unsworth *m* Mischa Spoliansky

Kenneth More, Lauren Bacall, Herbert Lom, Ursula Jeans, Wilfrid Hyde White, I. S. Johar, Eugene Deckers, Ian Hunter

'*Northwest Frontier* seems to have borrowed its eccentric engine from *The General*, its hazardous expedition from *Stagecoach* and its background of tribal violence from *The Drum*.'—*Penelope Houston*

Northwest Mounted Police*
US 1940 125m Technicolor
Paramount (Cecil B. de Mille)

A Texas Ranger seeks a fugitive in Canada.

Typical big-scale action concoction by de Mille, but in this case none of it's very memorable and the detail is poor.

w Alan Le May, Jesse Lasky Jnr, C. Gardner Sullivan *d* Cecil B. de Mille *ph* Victor Milner, Duke Green *m* Victor Young

Gary Cooper, Paulette Goddard, Madeleine Carroll, Preston Foster, Robert Preston, George Bancroft, Lynne Overman, Akim Tamiroff, Walter Hampden, Lon Chaney Jnr, Montagu Love, George E. Stone

'Two hours of colour, killing, kindness and magnificent country.'—*Otis Ferguson*

AAN: Victor Milner, Duke Green; Victor Young

Northwest Outpost
US 1940 91m bw
Republic (Allan Dwan)
GB title: *End of the Rainbow*

Adventures of California cavalrymen.
Milk-and-water adventures in a forgettable operetta.

w Elizabeth Meehan, Richard Sale *d* Allan Dwan *ph* Reggie Lanning *m* Rudolf Friml

Nelson Eddy, Ilona Massey, Hugo Haas, Elsa Lanchester

Northwest Passage***
(Part One, Rogers' Rangers)
US 1940 126m Technicolor
MGM (Hunt Stromberg)

Colonial rangers fight it out with hostile Indians. Part Two was never made, but no one seemed to mind that the characters in Part One never got round to seeking the titular sea route. The adventures depicted had the feel of historical actuality, and the star was well cast.

w Lawrence Stallings, Talbot Jennings, *novel* Kenneth Roberts *d* King Vidor *ph* Sidney Wagner, William V. Skall *m* Herbert Stothart

Spencer Tracy, Robert Young, Ruth Hussey, Walter Brennan, Nat Pendleton, Robert Barrat, Lumsden Hare, Donald MacBride

AAN: Sidney Wagner, William V. Skall

Norwood
US 1969 95m Technicolor
Paramount / Hal B. Wallis

A Vietnam veteran returns to his Texas home but feels restless and decides to become a radio singer.

A rather ordinary film about an innocent abroad, neither very funny nor very moving.

w Marguerite Roberts *d* Jack Haley Jnr *ph* Robert B. Hauser *m* Al de Lory

Glen Campbell, Kim Darby, Joe Namath, Carol Lynley, Pat Hingle, Tisha Sterling, Dom De Luise, Jack Haley, Cass Daley, Gil Lamb

Nosferatu***
Germany 1921 72m approx (24 fps) bw
Prana

Count Dracula goes to Bremen and is destroyed by sunlight.
An unofficial treatment of the Bram Stoker novel, with a terrifying count and several splendid moments. It took its director to Hollywood.

w Henrik Galeen d F. W. Murnau ph Fritz Arno Wagner ad Albin Grau

Max Schreck, Gustav Von Wangenheim, Greta Schroeder, Alexander Granach

Not as a Stranger **
US 1955   135m   bw
UA / Stanley Kramer

A medical student has professional and personal struggles.
Earnest filming of a bestseller, with all the actors too old for their parts.

w Edna and Edward Anhalt, novel Morton Thompson d Stanley Kramer ph Franz Planer m George Antheil pd Rudolph Sternad

Robert Mitchum, Olivia de Havilland, Broderick Crawford, Frank Sinatra, Gloria Grahame, Charles Bickford, Myron McCormick, Lon Chaney Jnr, Jesse White, Henry Morgan, Lee Marvin, Virginia Christine

Not of This Earth **
US 1957   72m   bw
AA (Roger Corman)

An alien comes to earth in human form in search of blood which may save his planet.
Modestly budgeted minor sci-fi; ruthless, original and competent.

w Charles Griffith, Mark Hanna d Roger Corman ph John Mescall m Ronald Stein

Paul Birch, Beverly Garland, Morgan Jones

Not with My Wife You Don't
US 1966   119m   Technicolor
Warner / Fernwood / Reynard (Norman Panama, Joel Freeman)

A Korean war veteran is furious when an old rival turns up in London and again makes eyes at his wife.
Extraordinarily flat star comedy of cross and double cross among friends.

w Norman Panama, Larry Gelbart, Peter Barnes d Norman Panama ph Charles Lang, Paul Beeson m Johnny Williams

Tony Curtis, George C. Scott, Virna Lisi, Carroll O'Connor, Richard Eastham

'About as frothy as a tin of dehydrated milk.'—MFB

'It has all the verve, subtlety and sophistication of its title.'—Judith Crist

Nothing But the Best **
GB 1964   99m   Eastmancolor
Anglo Amalgamated / Domino (David Deutsch)

An ambitious clerk learns to fight his way to the top by cheek and one-upmanship.
Hard, skilful, rather unattractive comedy with interesting social comments on its time.

w Frederic Raphael d Clive Donner ph Nicolas Roeg m Ron Grainer ad Reece Pemberton

Alan Bates, Denholm Elliott, Harry Andrews, Millicent Martin, Pauline Delany

Nothing But the Night *
GB 1972   90m   Eastmancolor
Rank / Charlemagne (Anthony Nelson Keys)

The trustees of an orphanage die off mysteriously, and it seems that the orphans themselves are responsible.
Convoluted murder mystery with horror elements and a twist hardly worth waiting for; earnest performances help.

w Brian Hayles, novel John Blackburn d Peter Sasdy ph Ken Talbot m Malcolm Williamson

Christopher Lee, Peter Cushing, Diana Dors, Georgia Brown, Keith Barron, John Robinson

Nothing But Trouble
US 1945   70m   bw
MGM (B. F. Ziedman)

A chef and butler accidentally prevent a poison plot against a young king.
Feebly-devised star comedy, their last for a big studio.

w Russel Rouse, Ray Golden d Sam Taylor ph Charles Salerno Jnr m Nathaniel Shilkret

Stan Laurel, Oliver Hardy, Mary Boland, Henry O'Neill, David Leland

Nothing Sacred ****
US 1937   77m   Technicolor
David O. Selznick

A girl thought to be dying of a rare disease is built up by the press into a national heroine; but the diagnosis was wrong.
Hollywood's most bitter and hilarious satire, with crazy comedy elements and superb wisecracks; a joy.

w Ben Hecht d William Wellman ph W. Howard Greene m Oscar Levant

Carole Lombard, Fredric March, Walter Connolly, Charles Winninger, Sig Rumann, Frank Fay, Maxie Rosenbloom, Margaret Hamilton, Hedda Hopper, Monty Woolley, Hattie McDaniel, Olin Howland, John Qualen

† Refashioned in 1953 as a stage musical, *Hazel Flagg*, with music by Jule Styne; this in turn became a Martin and Lewis comedy *Living It Up* (Jerry Lewis in the Carole Lombard part).

Notorious***

US 1946 101m bw

David O. Selznick (Barbara Keon)

In Rio, a notorious lady marries a Nazi renegade to help the US government but finds herself falling in love with her contact.

Superb romantic suspenser containing some of Hitchcock's best work.

w Ben Hecht *d* Alfred Hitchcock *ph* Ted Tetzlaff *m* Roy Webb

Cary Grant, Ingrid Bergman, Claude Rains, Louis Calhern, Leopoldine Konstantin, Reinhold Schunzel

'Velvet smooth in dramatic action, sharp and sure in its characters, and heavily charged with the intensity of warm emotional appeal.'— *Bosley Crowther*

'The suspense is terrific.'—*New Yorker, 1976*

AAN: Ben Hecht; Claude Rains

The Notorious Landlady

GB 1962 127m bw

Columbia / Kohlmar / Quine (Fred Kohlmar)

An American diplomat in London takes rooms with a murder suspect; after many mysterious happenings he helps to clear her.

Flatly whimsical goings on in comical old London, complete with fog and eccentrics. The actors all try hard but are deflated by the script.

w Larry Gelbart, Richard Quine *d* Richard Quine *ph* Arthur E. Arling *m* George Duning

Kim Novak, Jack Lemmon, Fred Astaire, Lionel Jeffries, Estelle Winwood, Maxwell Reed

La Notte*

Italy / France 1960 121m bw

Nepi / Sofitedip / Silver

A moderately successful novelist and his wife begin to question their marriage and their life. Slow but engaging character drama set during one night in Milan.

w Michelangelo Antonioni, Ennio Flaiano, Antonio Guerra *d* Michelangelo Antonioni *ph* Gianni di Venanzo *m* Giorgio Gaslini

Marcello Mastroianni, Jeanne Moreau, Monica Vitti, Bernhard Wicki

Nous Sommes Tous les Assassins*

France 1952 108m bw

UGC

aka: *Are We All Murderers?*

An illiterate youth is taught to kill during the war; afterwards he kills again for money and is sent for execution.

A solemn sermon on capital punishment, and a powerful though rather glib one.

w André Cayatte, Charles Spaak *d* André Cayatte *ph* Jean Bourgoin

Marcel Mouloudji, Raymond Pellégrin, Antoine Balpêtre, Claude Laydu

Les Nouveaux Messieurs*

France 1928 135m approx (24 fps) bw silent

Albatros / Séquance

A glamorous dancer forsakes a count for a rising trade union official.

Lengthy political satire which caused a few headlines when first released.

w Charles Spaak, Jacques Feyder, *play* Robert de Flers, Francis de Grosset *d* Jacques Feyder *ph* Georges Perinal, Maurice Defassiaux *ad* Lazare Meerson

Albert Prejean, Gaby Morlay, Henri Roussel

Now About these Women . . .*

Sweden 1964 80m Eastmancolor

Svensk Filmindustri

aka: *All These Women*

A critic comes to stay with a famous cellist whose biography he is writing, but his efforts are hampered by all the women in the house.

Virtually indescribable black farce comedy which doesn't really work, yet, as always with this director, is continually of interest.

w Erland Josephson, Ingmar Bergman *d* Ingmar Bergman *ph* Sven Nykvist *m* Erik Nordgren

Jarl Kulle, Georg Funkquist, Eva Dahlbeck, Karen Kavli, Harriet Andersson, Bibi Andersson, Gertrud Fridh

Now and Forever*

US 1934 82m bw

Paramount (Louis D. Lighton)

A jewel thief and his mistress are taught a thing or two by his small daughter.

Odd mixture of comedy and drama which was box office at the time but seems pretty dated after forty years, though technically very smooth.

w Vincent Lawrence, Sylvia Thalberg *d* Henry Hathaway *ph* Harry Fischbeck

Gary Cooper, Carole Lombard, Shirley Temple, Guy Standing, Charlotte Granville, Gilbert Emery, Henry Kolker

777 **The Nun's Story**

Now Barabbas . . .
GB 1949 87m bw
Warner / Anatole de Grunwald
aka: *Now Barabbas Was a Robber*

Stories of men in prison.
Thinly intercut dramas; from a stage success.

w Anatole de Grunwald, *play* William Douglas
Home *d* Gordon Parry *ph* Otto Heller

Richard Greene, Cedric Hardwicke, William
Hartnell, Kathleen Harrison, Leslie Dwyer,
Richard Burton, Kenneth More, Ronald
Howard, Stephen Murray, Beatrice Campbell,
Betty Ann Davies, Alec Clunes

Now I'll Tell
US 1934 72m bw
Fox (Winfield Sheehan)
GB title: *When New York Sleeps*

The story of Arnold Rothstein, gambler-
racketeer of the twenties, as told by his widow.
Competent crime/domestic programmer.

wd Edwin Burke *ph* Ernest Palmer *m* Hugo
Friedhofer

Spencer Tracy, Helen Twelvetrees, Hobart
Cavanaugh, Alice Faye, G. P. Huntley Jnr,
Shirley Temple, Leon Ames

'In spite of the breezy sequences with which it
starts, it quickly gets improbable and goes from
bad to maudlin.'—*Otis Ferguson*

Now Voyager***
US 1942 117m bw
Warner (Hal B. Wallis)

A dowdy frustrated spinster takes the
psychiatric cure and embarks on a doomed love
affair.
A basically soggy script still gets by, and how,
through the romantic magic of its stars, who
were all at their best; and suffering in mink went
over very big in wartime.

w Casey Robinson, *novel* Olive Higgins Prouty
d Irving Rapper *ph* Sol Polito *m* Max Steiner

Bette Davis, Claude Rains, Paul Henreid,
Gladys Cooper, John Loder, Bonita Granville,
Ilka Chase, Lee Patrick, Charles Drake,
Franklin Pangborn

'If it were better, it might not work at all. This
way, it's a crummy classic.'—*New Yorker, 1977*

AA: Max Steiner
AAN: Bette Davis; Gladys Cooper

Now You See Him Now You Don't
US 1972 88m Technicolor
Walt Disney

Two students discover an elixir of invisibility and
help prevent a gangster from taking over the
college.
Flat Disney frolic with fair trick effects.

w Joseph L. McEveety *d* Robert Butler
ph Frank Phillips *m* Robert F. Brunner
sp Eustace Lycett, Danny Lee

Kurt Russell, Cesar Romero, Joe Flynn, Jim
Backus, William Windom, Edward Andrews,
Richard Bakalyan

Number Seventeen*
GB 1932 63m bw
BIP (John Maxwell)

A girl jewel thief reforms and helps the police
track down her former gang.
Minor Hitchcock thriller largely confined to a
single interior until the final train chase, which
despite obvious models remains exhilarating.

w Alfred Hitchcock, Alma Reville, Rodney
Ackland, *play* J. Jefferson Farjeon *d* Alfred
Hitchcock *ph* Jack Cox

Leon M. Lion, Anne Grey, John Stuart, Donald
Calthrop, Barry Jones, Garry Marsh
† The same play had been filmed as a silent in
1928 by Geza Bolvary, with Guy Newall; it was
shot in Germany.

The Nun and the Sergeant
US 1962 74m bw
UA / Springfield

In Korea, a tough sergeant commanding a 'dirty
dozen' mission is joined by a schoolgirl and a
nun.
Minor war adventure, moderately well done but
highly unconvincing.

w Don Cerveris *d* Franklin Adreon *ph* Paul
Ivano *m* Jerry Fielding

Anna Sten, Robert Webber, Leo Gordon, Hari
Rhodes

The Nun's Story***
US 1959 151m Technicolor
Warner (Henry Blanke)

A Belgian girl joins a strict order, endures
hardship in the Congo, and finally returns to
ordinary life.
The fascinating early sequences of convent
routine are more interesting than the African
adventures, but this is a careful, composed and
impressive film with little Hollywood
exaggeration.

w Robert Anderson, *book* Kathryn C. Hulme
d Fred Zinnemann *ph* Franz Planer *m* Franz
Waxman

Audrey Hepburn, Peter Finch, Edith Evans,

Peggy Ashcroft, Dean Jagger, Mildred
Dunnock, Patricia Collinge, Beatrice Straight

AAN: best picture; Robert Anderson; Fred
Zinnemann; Franz Planer; Franz Waxman;
Audrey Hepburn

Nurse on Wheels
GB 1963   86m   bw
Anglo Amalgamated / GHW (Peter Rogers)

Adventures of a young District Nurse.
Part sentimental, part Carry On; watchable of its
curious kind.

w Norman Hudis, *novel* Nurse Is a Neighbour
by Joanna Jones d Gerald Thomas ph Alan
Hume m Eric Rogers

Juliet Mills, Ronald Lewis, Joan Sims, Raymond
Huntley, Athene Seyler

The Nutty Professor
US 1963   107m   Technicolor
Paramount / Jerry Lewis (Ernest D.
   Glucksman)

An eccentric chemistry professor discovers an
elixir which turns him into a pop idol.
Long dreary comedy which contains patches of
its star at somewhere near his best; but even *Dr
Jekyll and Mr Hyde* is funnier.

w Jerry Lewis, Bill Richmond d Jerry Lewis
ph W. Wallace Kelley m Walter Scharf

Jerry Lewis, Stella Stevens, Howard Morris,
Kathleen Freeman

O

O. Henry's Full House **
US 1952   117m   bw
TCF (André Hakim)
GB title: *Full House*

John Steinbeck introduces five stories by O.
Henry.
Modelled on the success of *Quartet* (qv), this
compendium was less successful because these
turn-of-the century tales of New York depend
less on character than on the sting in the tail; but
the cast and production were lavish.

m Alfred Newman

THE COP AND THE ANTHEM *w* Lamar
Trotti *d* Henry Koster *ph* Lloyd Ahern
Charles Laughton, David Wayne, Marilyn
Monroe
THE CLARION CALL *w* Richard Breen
d Henry Hathaway *ph* Lucien Ballard
Dale Robertson, Richard Widmark
THE LAST LEAF *w* Ivan Goff, Ben Roberts
d Jean Negulesco *ph* Joe MacDonald
Anne Baxter, Jean Peters, Gregory Ratoff
THE RANSOM OF RED CHIEF
w uncredited *d* Howard Hawks *ph* Milton
Krasner
Fred Allen, Oscar Levant
THE GIFT OF THE MAGI *w* Walter Bullock
d Henry King *ph* Joe MacDonald
Jeanne Crain, Farley Granger

O.H.M.S.
GB 1936   86m   bw
Gaumont (Geoffrey Barkas)
US title: *You're in the Army Now*

British forces fighting in China are joined by an
American gangster on the run, who dies a hero.
Stiff-upper-lip adventure of no particular
interest.

w Bryan Edgar Wallace, Austin Melford, A. R.
Rawlinson, Lesser Samuels, Ralph Bettinson
d Raoul Walsh

John Mills, Wallace Ford, Anna Lee, Frank
Cellier, Grace Bradley, Frederick Leister

O Lucky Man **
GB 1973   174m   Eastmancolor
Warner / Memorial / Sam

The odyssey of a trainee salesman who after a
while as an international financier settles down to
be a do-gooder.
Modern revue-style version of *Candide/Decline
and Fall*; very hit or miss in style and effect, and
hellishly overlong, but with good things along the
way.

w David Sherwin *d* Lindsay Anderson
ph Miroslav Ondricek *m Alan Price pd* Jocelyn
Herbert

*Malcolm McDowell, Arthur Lowe, Ralph
Richardson*, Rachel Roberts, Helen Mirren,
Mona Washbourne, Dandy Nichols
  'A sort of mod *Pilgrim's Progress*.'—*New
Yorker*

O.S.S. *
US 1946   107m   bw
Paramount

American spies are parachuted into France in
1943.
Espionage heroics with an unhappy ending and a
slight documentary flavour. Not bad of its kind.

w Richard Maibaum *d Irving Pichel ph* Lionel
Lindon

Alan Ladd, Geraldine Fitzgerald, Patric
Knowles, John Hoyt, Don Beddoe

Oasis
France / Germany 1956   100m approx
  Eastmancolor   Cinemascope
TCF / Roxy / Criterion (Gerd Oswald, Luggi
  Waldleitner)

An ex-pilot gets involved with two attractive
women who are smuggling gold across the
Sahara.
Glum romantic adventure.

w Joseph and Georges Kessel *d* Yves Allégret
ph Roger Hubert *m* Paul Misraki

Pierre Brasseur, Michèle Morgan, Cornell
Borchers, Grégoire Aslan

Objective Burma *
US 1944   142m   bw
Warner (Jerry Wald)

Exploits of an American platoon in the Burma
campaign.

Overlong but vivid war actioner which caused a diplomatic incident by failing to mention the British contribution.

w Ranald MacDougall, Lester Cole, Alvah Bessie *d* Raoul Walsh *ph* James Wong Howe *m* Franz Waxman

Errol Flynn, James Brown, William Prince, George Tobias, Henry Hull, Warner Anderson, John Alwin

The Oblong Box

GB 1969 95m Eastmancolor
AIP (Gordon Hessler)

One of two 19th-century brothers is mysteriously disfigured and buried alive; he recovers and runs amok.
Nastily effective horror film with a frail story but good background detail.

w Lawrence Huntington *d* Gordon Hessler *ph* John Coquillon *m* Harry Robinson

Vincent Price, Christopher Lee, Alastair Williamson, Hilary Dwyer, Peter Arne, Maxwell Shaw, Rupert Davies

'A pervasive aura of evil.'—*MFB*

Obsession

GB 1948 98m bw
GFD / Independent Sovereign
US title: *The Hidden Room*

A doctor decides to kill his wife's lover by imprisoning him in a lonely cellar while he accumulates enough acid to destroy all traces of his body.
Implausible, overstretched thriller, carefully enough done to be bearable.

w Alec Coppel, from his play A Man About a Dog *d* Edward Dmytryk *ph* C. Pennington Richards *m* Nino Rota

Robert Newton, Sally Gray, Phil Brown, Naunton Wayne

Obsession**

US 1976 98m Technicolor Panavision
Columbia (Robert S. Bremson)

A widower with guilt feelings meets the double of his dead wife and is drawn into a strange plot.
Hitchcockian adventure with a few unwise attempts at seriousness, à la *Don't Look Now*.
Generally entertaining, skilled and quite rewarding.

w Paul Schrader *d* Brian de Palma *ph* Vilmos Zsigmond *m* Bernard Herrmann

Cliff Robertson, Geneviève Bujold, John Lithgow, Sylvia Williams, Wanda Blackman, Patrick McNamara

AAN: Bernard Herrmann

Occupe-Toi d'Amélie***

France 1949 95m bw
Lux (Louis Wipf)
aka: *Keep an Eye on Amelia*

A Parisian cocotte agrees to go through a mock marriage ceremony with her lover's best friend to fool his uncle: but the ceremony turns out to be real.
Hilarious and superbly stylized adaptation of a period boulevard farce: the play starts in a theatre, showing the audience, but gradually cinema technique takes over. Acting, timing and editing are all impeccable, and the production stands as a model of how such things should be done.

w Jean Aurenche, Pierre Bost, play Georges Feydeau *d* Claude Autant-Lara *ph* André Bac *m* René Cloërc

Danielle Darrieux, Jean Desailly, Bourvil, Carette, Grégoire Aslan

'Even those who do not respond to the artificialities of French vaudeville will admire the ingenuity and elegance of treatment.'—*Gavin Lambert, MFB*

'Most people, I think, could see it with considerable enjoyment even twice on the same evening.'—*Richard Mallett, Punch*

Ocean's Eleven*

US 1960 128m Technicolor Panavision
Warner (Lewis Milestone)

A gang of friends plan to rob a Las Vegas casino.
Self-indulgent and overlong caper comedy which marked Hollywood's entry into a subsequently much overworked field. In this case the plot stops all too frequently for guest spots and in-jokes.

w Harry Brown, Charles Lederer *d* Lewis Milestone *ph* William H. Daniels *m* Nelson Riddle

Frank Sinatra, Peter Lawford, Sammy Davis Jnr, Richard Conte, Dean Martin, Angie Dickinson, Cesar Romero, Joey Bishop, Patrice Wymore, Akim Tamiroff, Henry Silva, Ilka Chase

The October Man**

GB 1947 98m bw
GFD / Two Cities (Eric Ambler)

After an accident which causes a head injury and subsequent depression, a lonely man staying at a small hotel is suspected of a local murder.
Nice blend of character study, mystery and suspense, with excellent attention to suburban detail.

w Eric Ambler *d* Roy Baker *ph* Erwin Hillier

John Mills, Joan Greenwood, Edward

Chapman, Kay Walsh, Catherine Lacey, Joyce Carey, Adrianne Allen, Felix Aylmer

The Odd Couple**
US 1968 105m Technicolor Panavision
Paramount (Howard W. Koch)

A fussy divorce-shocked newswriter moves in with his sloppy sportscaster friend, and they get on each other's nerves.
Straight filming of a funny play which sometimes seems lost on the wide screen, but the performances are fine.

w Neil Simon, from his play *d* Gene Saks
ph Robert B. Hauser *m* Neal Hefti

Jack Lemmon, Walter Matthau, John Fiedler, Herb Edelman, David Sheiner, Larry Haines, Monica Evans, Carole Sheely, Iris Adrian

AAN: Neil Simon

Odd Man Out***
GB 1946 115m bw
GFD / Two Cities (Carol Reed)
US title: *Gang War*

An IRA gunman, wounded and on the run in Belfast, is helped and hindered by a variety of people.
Superbly crafted but rather empty dramatic charade, visually and emotionally memorable but with nothing whatever to say.

w F. L. Green, R. C. Sheriff, *novel* F. L. Green *d* Carol Reed *ph* Robert Krasker *m* William Alwyn

James Mason, Robert Newton, Kathleen Ryan, F. J. McCormick, Cyril Cusack, Robert Beatty, Fay Compton, Dan O'Herlihy, Denis O'Dea, Maureen Delany, Joseph Tomelty, William Hartnell

'The story seems to ramify too much, to go on too long, and at its unluckiest to go arty. Yet detail by detail *Odd Man Out* is made with great skill and imaginativeness and with a depth of ardour that is very rare.'—*James Agee*

Odds against Tomorrow*
US 1959 96m bw
UA / Harbel (Robert Wise)

Three crooks plan to rob a bank, but two of them cause the enterprise to fail because of their own racist hatreds.
Sour, glossy crime thriller with elementary social significance.

w John O. Killens, Nelson Gidding, *novel* John P. McGivern *d* Robert Wise *ph* Joseph Brun *m* John Lewis

Robert Ryan, Harry Belafonte, *Ed Begley,*

Shelley Winters, Gloria Grahame, Will Kuluva, Kim Hamilton

'An efficient but unnecessarily portentous thriller.'—*Penelope Houston*

The Odessa File**
GB 1974 129m Eastmancolor
  Panavision
Columbia / Domino / Oceanic (John Woolf)

In 1963, a young German reporter tracks down a gang of neo-Nazis.
Elaborate but uninvolving suspenser with several excellent cliffhanging sequences and a let-down climax.

w Kenneth Ross, George Markstein, *novel* Frederick Forsyth *d* Ronald Neame *ph* Oswald Morris *m* Andrew Lloyd Webber *pd* Rolf Zeherbauer

Jon Voight, Maria Schell, Maximilian Schell, Mary Tamm, Derek Jacobi, Peter Jeffrey, *Noel Willman*

Odette*
GB 1950 123m bw
Herbert Wilcox

A Frenchwoman with an English husband spies for the French resistance, is caught and tortured.
Deglamorized true life spy story with emotional moments let down by generally uninspired handling, also by the too well-known image of its star, who however gives a remarkable performance.

w Warren Chetham Strode, *book* Jerrard Tickell *d* Herbert Wilcox *ph* Max Greene

Anna Neagle, Trevor Howard, Peter Ustinov, Marius Goring

'As a work of art, pretty flat . . . though innumerable people will find it moving and impressive, they will have done the work themselves.'—*Richard Mallett, Punch*

Of Human Bondage**
US 1934 83m bw
(RKO)

A well-to-do Englishman is brought down by his infatuation with a sluttish waitress.
This version of the famous novel brought Bette Davis to prominence but is not otherwise any better than the others.

w Lester Cohen, *novel* W. Somerset Maugham *d* John Cromwell *ph* Henry W. Gerrard

Leslie Howard, Bette Davis, Frances Dee, Reginald Owen, Reginald Denny, Kay Johnson, Alan Hale

Of Human Bondage*
US 1946 105m bw
Warner (Henry Blanke)

Good-looking but thoroughly dull remake.

w Catherine Turney d Edmund Goulding
ph Peverell Marley m Erich Wolfgang
Korngold

Paul Henreid, Eleanor Parker, Alexis Smith,
Edmund Gwenn, Patric Knowles, Janis Paige,
Henry Stephenson

Of Human Bondage
GB 1964 99m bw
Seven Arts / MGM (James Woolf)

Disastrous remake with both star roles miscast.

w Bryan Forbes d Henry Hathaway, Ken
Hughes ph Oswald Morris m Ron Goodwin
pd John Box

Laurence Harvey, Kim Novak, Nanette
Newman, Roger Livesey, Jack Hedley, Robert
Morley, Siobhan McKenna, Ronald Lacey

Of Human Hearts*
US 1938 100m bw
MGM (John Considine Jnr)

A 19th-century idyll of middle America and
especially of a preacher and his wayward son.
Curious all-American moral fable, splendidly
made and acted.

w Bradbury Foote, novel Benefits Forgot by
Honoré Morrow d Clarence Brown ph Clyde
de Vinna m Herbert Stothart

Walter Huston, James Stewart, Beulah Bondi,
Gene Reynolds, Charles Coburn, Guy Kibbee,
John Carradine, Gene Lockhart, Ann
Rutherford

AAN: Beulah Bondi

Of Love and Desire
US 1963 97m De Luxe
New World (Victor Stoloff)

An engineer in Mexico takes up with the boss's
nymphomaniac sister.
Unwise sensationalist vehicle for an ageing
leading lady who is past such carryings on.

w Laslo Gorag, Richard Rush d Richard Rush
ph Alex Phillips m Ronald Stein

Merle Oberon, Steve Cochran, John Agar, Curt
Jurgens

Of Mice and Men***
US 1939 107m bw
Hal Roach (Lewis Milestone)

An itinerant worker looks after his mentally
retarded cousin, a giant who doesn't know his
own strength.
A strange and unexpected tragedy which has
strength and is very persuasively made but seems
somehow unnecessary.

w Eugene Solow, novel John Steinbeck d Lewis
Milestone ph Norbert Brodine m Aaron
Copland

Burgess Meredith, Lon Chaney Jnr, Betty Field,
Charles Bickford, Roman Bohnen, Bob Steele,
Noah Beery Jnr

AAN: best picture; Aaron Copland

Off Limits
US 1953 89m bw
Paramount
GB title: Military Policemen

A boxing manager trains a young fighter in the
military police.
Flat star comedy.

w Hal Kanter, Jack Sher d George Marshall
ph Peverell Marley m Van Cleave

Bob Hope, Mickey Rooney, Marilyn Maxwell,
Marvin Miller

The Offence*
GB 1972 113m De Luxe
UA / Tantallon

A tough police inspector bullies a suspected child
molester.
Tortuous psychological study on the fringe of
hysteria; good performances.

w John Hopkins, from his play This Story of
Yours d Sidney Lumet ph Gerry Fisher
m Harrison Birtwhistle

Sean Connery, Trevor Howard, Ian Bannen,
Vivien Merchant

Oh Dad, Poor Dad, Mamma's Hung You
in the Closet and I'm Feelin' So Sad
US 1966 86m Technicolor
Paramount / Seven Arts (Ray Stark, Stanley
Rubin)

A dead father helps his son to get married despite
his mother's influence to the contrary.
Zany black comedy which never really worked
on the stage, let alone the screen.

w Ian Bernard, play Arthur Kopit d Richard
Quine ph Geoffrey Unsworth m Neal Hefti

Rosalind Russell, Jonathan Winters, Robert
Morse, Hugh Griffith, Barbara Harris, Lionel
Jeffries, Cyril Delevanti, Hiram Sherman

Oh, God*
US 1977 104m Technicolor
Warner (Jerry Weintraub)

A bewildered supermarket manager is enlisted by God to prove to the world that it can only work if people try.

Overlong but generally amiable reversion to the supernatural farces of the forties: its success seems to show that people again need this kind of comfort.

w Larry Gelbart, *novel* Avery Corman *d* Carl Reiner *ph* Victor Kemper *m* Jack Elliott

George Burns, John Denver, Ralph Bellamy, Donald Pleasence, Teri Garr, William Daniels, Barnard Hughes, Paul Sorvino, Barry Sullivan, Dinah Shore, Jeff Corey, David Ogden Stiers

'Undeniably funny and almost impossible to dislike.'—*Tom Milne, MFB*

Oh Men! Oh Women!

US 1957   90m   Eastmancolor
   Cinemascope
TCF (Nunnally Johnson)

A psychoanalyst discovers that his wife is involved with two of his patients.
Scatty Broadway comedy which strains the patience.

wd Nunnally Johnson, *play* Edward Chodorov *ph* Charles G. Clarke *m* Cyril Mockridge

David Niven, Ginger Rogers, Dan Dailey, Barbara Rush, Tony Randall

Oh Mr Porter****

GB 1937   84m   bw
GFD / Gainsborough (Edward Black)

The stationmaster of an Irish halt catches gun-runners posing as ghosts.
Marvellous star comedy showing this trio of comedians at their best, and especially Hay as the seedy incompetent. The plot is borrowed from *The Ghost Train*, but each line and gag brings its own inventiveness. A delight of character comedy and cinematic narrative.

w Marriott Edgar, Val Guest, J. O. C. Orton, *story* Frank Launder *d Marcel Varnel* *ph* Arthur Crabtree *md* Louis Levy

Will Hay, Moore Marriott, Graham Moffatt, Dave O'Toole, Dennis Wyndham

'That rare phenomenon: a film comedy without a dud scene.'—*Peter Barnes, 1964*

'Behind it lie the gusty uplands of the British music hall tradition, whose rich soil the British film industry is at last beginning to exploit.'—*Basil Wright*

Oh Rosalinda!

GB 1955   105m   Technicolor
   Cinemascope
ABP / Powell and Pressburger

A playboy in four-power Vienna plays a practical joke on four officers and the flirtatious wife of one of them.
Lumbering attempt to modernize *Die Fledermaus*, unsuitably wide-screened and totally lacking the desired Lubitsch touch. A monumental step in the decline of these producers, and a sad stranding of a brilliant cast.

wd Michael Powell, Emeric Pressburger *ph* Christopher Challis *m* Johann Strauss *ad* Hein Heckroth

Anton Walbrook, Michael Redgrave, Anthony Quayle, Mel Ferrer, Dennis Price, Ludmilla Tcherina

Oh What a Lovely War**

GB 1969   144m   Technicolor   Panavision
Paramount / Accord (Brian Duffy, Richard
   Attenborough)

A fantasia with music on World War I.
A brave all-star attempt which comes off only in patches; the pier apparatus from the stage show really doesn't translate, the piece only works well when it becomes cinematic, as in the recruiting song and the final track-back from the graves. But there are many pleasures, as well as yawns, along the way.

w Len Deighton, *stage show* Joan Littlewood, Charles Chilton *d* Richard Attenborough *ph Gerry Turpin m* various *md* Alfred Ralston *pd Don Ashton*

Ralph Richardson, Meriel Forbes, John Gielgud, Kenneth More, John Clements, Paul Daneman, Joe Melia, Jack Hawkins, John Mills, Maggie Smith, Michael Redgrave, Laurence Olivier, Susannah York, Dirk Bogarde, Phyllis Calvert, Vanessa Redgrave

'This musical lampoon is meant to stir your sentiments, evoke nostalgia, and make you react to the obscenity of battles and bloodshed, and apparently it does all that for some people.'—*New Yorker, 1977*

Oh You Beautiful Doll*

US 1949   93m   Technicolor
TCF (George Jessel)

Fred Fisher wants to write opera but is more successful with pop songs.
Standard turn of the century biopic, very pleasantly handled and performed.

w Albert and George Lewis *d* John M. Stahl *ph* Harry Jackson *md* Alfred Newman

S. Z. Sakall, Mark Stevens, June Haver, *Charlotte Greenwood*, Jay C. Flippen, Gale Robbins

Oil for the Lamps of China*
US 1935 98m bw
Warner (Robert Lord)

The career in China of an American oil company representative.

Adequate general audience picture from a bestseller.

w Laird Doyle, *novel* Alice Tisdale Hobart
d Mervyn Le Roy *ph* Tony Gaudio *m* Heinz Roemheld *md* Leo F. Forbstein

Pat O'Brien, Josephine Hutchinson, Jean Muir, Lyle Talbot, Arthur Byron, John Eldredge, Henry O'Neill, Donald Crisp

'Far above average in performance, direction and content.'—*John Baxter, 1968*
† Remade 1941 as *Law of the Tropics*.

Okay for Sound*
GB 1937 85m bw
GFD / Gainsborough (Edward Black)

The Crazy Gang runs amok in a film studio.
Patchy farce with music hall talents of the time.

w Marriott Edgar, Val Guest, R. P. Weston, Bert Lee *d* Marcel Varnel *ph* Jack Cox *md* Louis Levy

Bud Flanagan, Chesney Allen, Jimmy Nervo, Teddy Knox, Charlie Naughton, Jimmy Gold, Fred Duprez, Enid Stamp-Taylor, Graham Moffatt, Meinhart Maur, H. F. Maltby, Peter Dawson, The Radio Three, The Sherman Fisher Girls

Oklahoma!**
US 1955 143m Technicolor Todd-AO
Rodgers and Hammerstein (Arthur Hornblow Jnr)

A cowboy wins his girl despite the intervention of a sinister hired hand.

Much of the appeal of the musical was in its simple timeworn story and stylized sets; the film makes the first merely boring and the latter are replaced by standard scenery, not even of Oklahoma. The result is efficient rather than startling or memorable.

w Sonya Levien, William Ludwig, *'book'* Oscar Hammerstein, *play* Green Grow the Rushes by Lynn Riggs *d* Fred Zinnemann *ph* Robert Surtees *songs* Richard Rodgers, Oscar Hammerstein II *m* Robert Russell Bennett, Jay Blackton, Adolph Deutsch *pd* Oliver Smith

Gordon Macrae, Shirley Jones, Rod Steiger, Gloria Grahame, Charlotte Greenwood, Gene Nelson, Eddie Albert

AAN: Robert Surtees; Robert Russell Bennett, Jay Blackton, Adolph Deutsch

Oklahoma Crude*
US 1973 111m Technicolor
Columbia / Stanley Kramer

In 1913, a drifting oil man stops to help a girl develop her rig.

Dour, downbeat melodrama with restricted action and much bad language; within its lights quite entertaining, but odd.

w Marc Norman *d* Stanley Kramer *ph* Robert Surtees *m* Henry Mancini *pd* Alfred Sweeney

Faye Dunaway, George C. Scott, John Mills, Jack Palance, Woodrow Parfrey

The Oklahoma Kid**
US 1939 80m bw
Warner (Samuel Bischoff)

During the settlement of the Cherokee Strip a cowboy avenges the unjust lynching of his father.

Competent but slightly disappointing star western memorable for the clash in this guise of its protagonists, more usually seen as gangsters.

w Warren Duff, Robert Buckner, Edward E. Paramore *d* Lloyd Bacon *ph* James Wong Howe *m* Max Steiner

James Cagney, Humphrey Bogart, Rosemary Lane, Donald Crisp, Harvey Stephens, Charles Middleton, Edward Pawley, Ward Bond

'There's something entirely disarming about the way he has tackled horse opera, not pretending for a minute to be anything but New York's Jimmy Cagney all dressed up as a Robin Hood of the old west.'—*Frank Nugent*

Old Acquaintance**
US 1943 110m bw
Warner (Henry Blanke)

Two jealous lady novelists interfere in each other's love lives.

A dated but rather splendid battle of the wild cats, with two stars fighting their way through a plush production and a rather overlong script.

w John Van Druten, Lenore Coffee, *play* John Van Druten *d* Vincent Sherman *ph* Sol Polito *m* Franz Waxman

Bette Davis, Miriam Hopkins, Gig Young, John Loder, Dolores Moran, Philip Reed, Roscoe Karns, Anne Revere

'The odd thing is that on the screen such trash can seem mature and even adventurous.'—*James Agee*

'Trashy fun, on an unusually literate level.'—*New Yorker, 1978*

Old Bones of the River*
GB 1938   90m   bw
GFD / Gainsborough (Edward Black)

A teacher in Africa accidentally quells a native rising.

Tediously funny star comedy; enough said.

w Marriott Edgar, Val Guest, J. O. C. Orton character Edgar Wallace d Marcel Varnel ph Arthur Crabtree m Louis Levy ad Vetchinsky

Will Hay, Moore Marriott, Graham Moffatt, Robert Adams, Jack Livesey

The Old Curiosity Shop*
GB 1934   95m   bw
BIP / Wardour

The lives of a gambler and his granddaughter are affected by a miserly dwarf.

Heavy-going Dickens novel given reasonably rich production and well enough acted; sentimentality prevented a remake until the unsuccessful *Mister Quilp* (qv) in 1975.

w Margaret Kennedy, Ralph Neale, *novel* Charles Dickens d Thomas Bentley

Hay Petrie, Ben Webster, Elaine Benson, Beatrice Thompson, Gibb McLaughlin, Reginald Purdell, Polly Ward

The Old Dark House ****
US 1932   71m   bw
Universal

Stranded travellers take refuge in the house of a family of eccentrics.

Marvellous horror comedy filled with superb grotesques and memorable lines, closely based on a Priestley novel but omitting the more thoughtful moments. A stylist's and connoisseur's treat.

w Benn W. Levy, R. C. Sherriff, *novel* Benighted by *J. B. Priestley* d James Whale ph Arthur Edeson

Melvyn Douglas, Charles Laughton, Raymond Massey, Boris Karloff, Ernest Thesiger, Eva Moore, Gloria Stuart, Lilian Bond, Brember Wills, John Dudgeon (Elspeth Dudgeon)

'An unbridled camp fantasy directed with great wit.'—*Charles Higham*

'Each threat as it appears is revealed to be burlap and poster paint . . . despite storm, attempted rape and a remarkable final chase, the film is basically a confidence trick worked with cynical humour by a brilliant technician.'—*John Baxter, 1968*

†The 1963 Hammer 'remake' is best forgotten.

The Old-Fashioned Way*
US 1934   74m   bw
Paramount / (William Le Baron)

Adventures of The Great McGonigle and his troupe of travelling players.

Period comedy tailored for its star and incorporating fragments of *The Drunkard.* Not so funny as it might be, but essential for students.

w Garnett Weston, Jack Cunningham, Charles Bogle (W. C. Fields) d William Beaudine ph Benjamin Reynolds m Harry Revel

W. C. Fields, Joe Morrison, Judith Allen, Jan Duggan, Jack Mulhall, Baby Leroy

The Old Maid**
US, 1939   95m   bw
Warner (Henry Blanke)

When her suitor is killed in the Civil War, an unmarried mother lets her childless cousin bring up her daughter as her own.

A 'woman's picture' par excellence, given no-holds-barred treatment by all concerned but a little lacking in surprise.

w Casey Robinson, *play* Zoe Akins, *novel* Edith Wharton d Edmund Goulding ph Tony Gaudio m Max Steiner md Leo F. Forbstein

Bette Davis, Miriam Hopkins, George Brent, Jane Bryan, Donald Crisp, Louise Fazenda, Henry Stephenson, Jerome Cowan, William Lundigan, Rand Brooks

'It is better than average and sticks heroically to its problem, forsaking all delights and filling a whole laundry bag with wet and twisted handkerchiefs.'—*Otis Ferguson*

'The picture isn't bad, but it trudges along and never becomes exciting.'—*New Yorker, 1977*

The Old Man and the Sea*
US 1958   89m   Technicolor
Warner / Leland Hayward

An old fisherman dreams of hooking a great fish. Expensive but poor-looking and stultifyingly dull one-character drama with variable production effects, a low key *Moby Dick.* Interesting but not effective.

w Ernest Hemingway, from his novel d John Sturges ph James Wong Howe, Floyd Crosby, Tom Tutweiler, Lamar Boren m Dmitri Tiomkin

Spencer Tracy, Felipe Pazos, Harry Bellaver

'A literary property about as suited for the movie medium as *The Love Song of J. Alfred Prufrock.'*—*Time*

AA: Dmitri Tiomkin
AAN: James Wong Howe; Spencer Tracy

Old Mother Riley

This Irish washerwoman with flailing arms and a nice line in invective was a music hall creation of Arthur Lucan, a variation of a pantomime dame. His wife Kitty Macshane played Mother Riley's daughter, and despite personal difficulties they were top of the bill for nearly 30 years. The films were very cheaply made and the padding is difficult to sit through, but Lucan at his best is a superb comedian: they were made for small independent companies such as Butcher's and usually directed by Maclean Rogers.

1937: OLD MOTHER RILEY
1938: OLD MOTHER RILEY IN PARIS
1939: OLD MOTHER RILEY MP, OLD MOTHER RILEY JOINS UP
1940: OLD MOTHER RILEY IN BUSINESS, OLD MOTHER RILEY'S GHOSTS
1941: OLD MOTHER RILEY'S CIRCUS
1942: OLD MOTHER RILEY IN SOCIETY
1943: OLD MOTHER RILEY DETECTIVE
1944: OLD MOTHER RILEY AT HOME
1945: OLD MOTHER RILEY HEADMISTRESS
1947: OLD MOTHER RILEY'S NEW VENTURE
1949: OLD MOTHER RILEY'S JUNGLE TREASURE
1952: MOTHER RILEY MEETS THE VAMPIRE

Old Yeller*

US 1957 83m Technicolor
Walt Disney

The love of a boy for his dog.
Archetypal family movie set in a remote rural area.

w Fred Gipson, William Tubberg, *novel* Fred Gipson d Robert Stevenson ph Charles P. Boyle m Oliver Wallace

Dorothy McGuire, Fess Parker, Tommy Kirk, Kevin Corcoran, Jeff York, Chuck Connors

Oliver!***

GB 1968 146m Technicolor Panavision 70

Columbia / Warwick / Romulus (John Woolf)

A musical version of *Oliver Twist*.
The last, perhaps, of the splendid film musicals which have priced themselves out of existence; it drags a little in spots but on the whole it does credit both to the show and the original novel, though eclipsed in style by David Lean's straight version.

w Vernon Harris, *play* Lionel Bart, *novel* Charles Dickens d Carol Reed ph Oswald Morris m Lionel Bart md John Green pd John Box ch Onna White

Ron Moody, Oliver Reed, Harry Secombe, *Mark Lester*, Shani Wallis, *Jack Wild*, Hugh Griffith, Joseph O'Conor, Leonard Rossiter, Hylda Baker, Peggy Mount, Megs Jenkins

'Only time will tell if it is a great film but it is certainly a great experience.'—*Joseph Morgenstern*

'There is a heightened discrepancy between the romping jollity with which everyone goes about his business and the actual business being gone about . . . such narrative elements as the exploitation of child labour, pimping, abduction, prostitution and murder combine to make *Oliver!* the most non-U subject ever to receive a U certificate.'—*Jan Dawson*

AA: best picture; Carol Reed; John Green
AAN: Vernon Harris; Oswald Morris; Ron Moody; Jack Wild

Oliver Twist****

GB 1948 116m bw
GFD / Cineguild

A foundling falls among thieves but is rescued by a benevolent old gentleman.
Simplified, brilliantly cinematic version of a voluminous Victorian novel, beautiful to look at and memorably played, with every scene achieving the perfect maximum impact.

w David Lean, Stanley Haynes, *novel* Charles Dickens d David Lean ph Guy Green m Arnold Bax pd John Bryan

Alec Guinness, Robert Newton, Francis L. Sullivan, John Howard Davies, Kay Walsh, Anthony Newley, Henry Stephenson, Mary Clare, Gibb McLaughlin, Diana Dors

'A thoroughly expert piece of movie entertainment.'—*Richard Winnington*

Oliver's Story

US 1978 92m Technicolor
Paramount (David V. Picker)

A sequel to *Love Story*, showing how Oliver succumbed to depression but finally found another girl friend.
Love means never having to watch this trendy rubbish.

w Erich Segal, John Korty d John Korty ph Arthur Ornitz m Francis Lai, Lee Holdridge

Ryan O'Neal, Candice Bergen, Nicola Pagett, Edward Binns, Ray Milland

Olly Olly Oxen Free
US 1978   93m   Metrocolor
Rico Lion (Richard A. Colla)

A junkyard proprietress helps two young
children to launch a decrepit-hot-air balloon.
Simpleminded children's adventure with a
surprising star.

w Eugene Poinc d Richard A. Colla ph Gayne
Rescher m Bob Alcivar pd Peter Wooley

Katherine Hepburn, Kevin McKenzie, Dennis
Dimster

Los Olvidados*
Mexico 1951   88m   bw
Utramar / Oscar Dancigers
aka: *The Young and the Damned*

A good boy is contaminated by the young thugs
in Mexico City's slums, and both he and his
tormentor die violently.
Sober but penetrating analysis of social
conditions leading to violence. The film was
widely acclaimed, yet its very proficiency and
excellent photography tend to glamorize its
subject. Compare, however, the Hollywood
resolutions of *Dead End*, on a similar subject.

w Luis Bunuel, Luis Alcoriza, Oscar Dancigers
d Luis Bunuel ph Gabriel Figueroa m Gustavo
Pitaluga

Alfonso Mejia, Miguel Inclan, Estela Inda,
Roberto Cobo

Olympische Spiele*
Germany 1936   Part 1, 118m; Part 2, 107m
    bw

Leni Riefenstahl

An account of the Berlin Olympic Games.
This magnificent film is in no sense a mere
reporting of an event. Camera movement,
photography and editing combine with music to
make it an experience truly olympian, especially
in the introductory symbolic sequence
suggesting the birth of the games. It was also,
dangerously, a hymn to Nazi strength.

d, ed Leni Riefenstahl assistant Walter
Ruttman ph Hans Ertl, Walter Franz and 42
others m Herbert Windt

Omar Khayyam
US 1956   101m   Technicolor   Vistavision
Paramount (Frank Freeman Jnr)

The Persian poet and philosopher defends his
Shah against the Assassins.
Clean but dull Arabian Nights fantasy with
pantomime sets and no humour.

w Barre Lyndon d William Dieterle ph Ernest
Laszlo m Victor Young

Cornel Wilde, Michael Rennie, Raymond
Massey, John Derek, Yma Sumac, Sebastian
Cabot, Debra Paget

The Omega Man*
US 1971   98m   Technicolor   Panavision
Warner / Walter Seltzer

In 1977 a plague resulting from germ warfare
has decimated the world's population; in Los
Angeles, one man wages war against loathsome
carriers of the disease.
'Realistic' version of a novel which was about
vampires taking over, and was previously filmed
unsatisfactorily as *The Last Man on Earth*. This
nasty version rises to a few good action
sequences but is bogged down by talk in
between.

w John William Corrington and Joyce M.
Corrington, *novel* I Am Legend by Richard
Matheson d Boris Sagal ph Russell Metty
m Ron Grainer

Charlton Heston, Rosalind Cash, Anthony
Zerbe

The Omen**
US 1976   111m   De Luxe   Panavision
TCF (Harvey Bernhard)

The adopted child of an ambassador to Great
Britain shows unnerving signs of being
diabolically inspired.
Commercially successful variation on *The
Exorcist*, quite professionally assembled and
more enjoyable as entertainment than its
predecessor.

w David Seltzer d *Richard Donner* ph Gil
Taylor m Jerry Goldsmith

Gregory Peck, Lee Remick, David Warner,
Billie Whitelaw, Leo McKern, Harvey Stevens,
Patrick Troughton, Anthony Nicholls, Martin
Benson

AA: Jerry Goldsmith

On a Clear Day You Can See For Ever*
US 1970   129m   Technicolor   Panavision
Paramount (Howard Koch)

A psychiatric hypnotist helps a girl to stop
smoking, and finds that in trances she
remembers previous incarnations.
Romantic musical which tries, and fails, to
substitute wispy charm for its original Broadway
vitality. There are compensations.

w Alan Jay Lerner, from his play d Vincente
Minnelli ph Harry Stradling m Burton Lane

Barbra Streisand, Yves Montand, Bob Newhart,
Larry Blyden, Jack Nicholson, Simon Oakland

On an Island with You

US 1948 104m Technicolor
MGM

A film actress on location in the South Seas is chased by a naval officer.
Below par musical which far outstays its welcome.

w Dorothy Kingsley, Dorothy Cooper, Charles Martin, Hans Wilhelm d Richard Thorpe ph Charles Rosher

Esther Williams, Peter Lawford, Jimmy Durante, Ricardo Montalban, Cyd Charisse, Xavier Cugat and his Orchestra

On Approval***

GB 1943 80m bw
(GFD) Clive Brook

An Edwardian duke and an American heiress plan a chaperoned trial marriage in a remote Scottish castle.
Sparkling comedy of manners made even more piquant by careful casting and mounting; a minor delight.

w Clive Brook, Terence Young, play Frederick Lonsdale d Clive Brook

Clive Brook, Beatrice Lillie, Googie Withers, Roland Culver, O. B. Clarence, Lawrence Hanray, Hay Petrie

'Totally diverting, highly cinematic.'—NFT, 1974

'There has probably never been a richer, funnier anthology of late-Victorian mannerisms.'—Time

On Borrowed Time*

US 1939 98m bw
MGM (Sidney Franklin)

An old man refuses to die and chases Death up the apple tree.
Amiable, very American fantasy with much sentiment and several effective moments.

w Alice Duer Miller, Frank O'Neill, Claudine West, novel Lawrence Edward Watkin d Harold S. Bucquet m Franz Waxman

Lionel Barrymore, Bobs Watson, Beulah Bondi, Cedric Hardwicke (as Mr Brink), Una Merkel, Ian Wolfe, Philip Terry, Eily Malyon

'A weird, wild, totally unpredictable fantasy with dream sequences more like Bunuel than anything in the cinema.'—John Russell Taylor, 1965

On Dangerous Ground

US 1951 82m bw
RKO (John Houseman)

A tough cop falls in love with the blind sister of a mentally defective murderer.
Pretentious Hollywood film noir in the Gabin manner, partly redeemed by its glossy surface.

w A. I. Bezzerides, novel George Butler d Nicholas Ray ph George E. Diskant m Bernard Herrmann

Robert Ryan, Ida Lupino, Ward Bond, Ed Begley, Cleo Moore, Charles Kemper

On Her Majesty's Secret Service**

GB 1969 140m Technicolor Panavision
UA / Eon / Danilaq (Harry Saltzman, Albert R. Broccoli)

James Bond tracks down master criminal Blofeld in Switzerland.
Perhaps to compensate for no Sean Connery and a tragic ending, the producers of this sixth Bond opus shower largesse upon us in the shape of no fewer than four protracted and spectacular climaxes. Splendid stuff, but too much of it, and the lack of a happy centre does show.

w Richard Maibaum, novel Ian Fleming d Peter Hunt ph Michael Reed, Egil Woxholt, Roy Ford, John Jordan m John Barry pd Syd Cain

George Lazenby, Diana Rigg, Telly Savalas, Ilse Steppat, Gabriele Ferzetti, Yuri Borienko, Bernard Lee, Lois Maxwell

On Moonlight Bay**

US 1951 95m Technicolor
Warner (William Jacobs)

Family crises, to do with growing up and young love, in a 1917 Indiana town.
Pleasant musical, competently made, from the Penrod stories, with the emphasis switched to big sister.

w Melville Shavelson, Jack Rose, stories Booth Tarkington d Roy del Ruth ph Ernest Haller md Ray Heindorf

Doris Day, Gordon Macrae, Leon Ames, Rosemary de Camp, Billy Gray
† See also By the Light of the Silvery Moon, a companion piece.

On Our Merry Way*

US 1948 107m bw
Benedict Bogeaus, Burgess Meredith

A reporter is urged by his wife to dig up some human interest stories.
Frail compendium of anecdotes which barely work.

w Laurence Stallings, story Arch Oboler d King Vidor, Leslie Fenton ph Joseph August, Gordon Avil, John Seitz, Edward Cronjager m Heinz

Roemheld *md* David Chudnow, Skitch
Henderson

Burgess Meredith, Paulette Goddard, Fred
MacMurray, Hugh Herbert, James Stewart,
Dorothy Lamour, Victor Moore, Henry Fonda,
William Demarest

On the Avenue**
US 1937 89m bw
TCF (Gene Markey)

An heiress rages because she is being satirized in
a revue, but later falls in love with the star.
Bright musical which keeps moving and uses its
talents wisely.

*w Gene Markey, William Conselman d Roy del
Ruth ph Lucien Andriot m/ly Irving Berlin
ch Seymour Felix*

*Dick Powell, Madeleine Carroll, The Ritz
Brothers,* George Barbier, Alice Faye, Walter
Catlett, Joan Davis, E. E. Clive
† Revamped as *Let's Make Love* (qv).

On the Beach**
US 1959 134m bw
US / Stanley Kramer

When most of the world has been devastated by
atomic waste, an American atomic submarine
sets out to investigate.
Gloomy prophecy which works well in spasms
but is generally too content to chat rather than
imagine. A solid prestige job nevertheless.

*w John Paxton, James Lee Barrett, novel Nevil
Shute d Stanley Kramer ph Giuseppe Rotunno,
Daniel Fapp m Ernest Gold pd Rudolph
Sternad*

Gregory Peck, Ava Gardner, *Fred Astaire,*
Anthony Perkins, Donna Anderson, John Tate,
Lola Brooks

'Its humanism is clearly of the order that seeks
the support of a clamorous music score. The
characters remain little more than spokesmen for
timid ideas and Salvation Army slogans, their
emotions hired from a Hollywood prop room;
which is all pretty disturbing in a film about
nothing less than the end of the world.'—*Robert
Vas*

AAN: Ernest Gold

On the Beat
GB 1962 105m bw
Rank (Hugh Stewart)

A Scotland Yard car park attendant manages to
capture some crooks and become a policeman.
Busy but flat comedy vehicle, never very
likeable.

*w Jack Davies d Robert Asher ph Geoffrey
Faithfull m Philip Green*

Norman Wisdom, Jennifer Jayne, Raymond
Huntley, David Lodge

On the Buses
GB 1971 88m Technicolor
EMI / Hammer (Ronald Woolfe, Ronald
  Chesney)

Women drivers cause trouble at a bus depot.
Grotesque, ham-handed farce from a TV series
which was sometimes funny; this is merely
vulgar.

*w Ronald Woolfe, Ronald Chesney d Harry
Booth ph Mark MacDonald m Max Harris*

Reg Varney, Doris Hare, Anna Karen, Michael
Robbins, Stephen Lewis

On the Double*
US 1961 92m Technicolor Panavision
Paramount / Dena–Capri (Jack Rose)

During World War II, an American private is
asked to impersonate a British intelligence
officer.
From the plot and the talents it seems one might
start laughing at this while still in the queue, but
in fact most of it goes sadly awry and it never
quite comes to the boil.

*w Jack Rose, Melville Shavelson d Melville
Shavelson ph Harry Stradling, Geoffrey
Unsworth m Leith Stevens*

Danny Kaye, Dana Wynter, Wilfrid Hyde
White, Diana Dors, Margaret Rutherford, Allan
Cuthbertson, Jesse White

On the Fiddle*
GB 1961 97m bw
Anglo-Amalgamated / S. Benjamin Fisz
US title: *Operation Snafu*

A wide boy and a slow-witted gypsy have comic
and other adventures in the RAF.
Curious mixture of farce and action, more on
American lines than British, but quite
entertainingly presented.

*w Harold Buchman, novel Stop at a Winner by
R. F. Delderfield d Cyril Frankel ph Ted Scaife
m Malcolm Arnold*

Alfred Lynch, Sean Connery, Cecil Parker,
Wilfrid Hyde White, Kathleen Harrison, Alan
King, Eleanor Summerfield, Eric Barker,
Terence Longdon, John Le Mesurier, Harry
Locke

On the Night of the Fire *

GB 1939 94m bw
GFD / G & S (Josef Somlo)
US title: *The Fugitive*

A barber kills the blackmailer of his wife.
Dour little drama, rather unusual for pre-war British studios.

w Brian Desmond Hurst, Terence Young, *novel* F. L. Green *d* Brian Desmond Hurst

Ralph Richardson, Diana Wynyard, Romney Brent, Mary Clare, Henry Oscar, Frederick Leister

On the Riviera **

US 1951 90m Technicolor
TCF (Sol C. Siegel)

A cabaret artist is persuaded to pose as a philandering businessman.
Remake of *Folies Bergère* and *That Night in Rio* (see also *On the Double*); disliked at the time and accused of tastelessness, it now seems smarter and funnier than comparable films of its era.

w Valentine Davies, Phoebe and Henry Ephron *d* Walter Lang *ph* Leon Shamroy

Danny Kaye, Corinne Calvet, Gene Tierney, Marcel Dalio, Jean Murat

On the Threshold of Space

US 1956 96m Eastmancolor
  Cinemascope
TCF (William Bloom)

The USAF medical corps explores human reactions at high altitudes.
Semi-documentary flagwaver with dreary domestic asides; very dated now, and of no particular nostalgic interest.

w Simon Wincelberg, Francis Cockrill *d* Robert D. Webb *ph* Joe MacDonald

Guy Madison, Virginia Leith, John Hodiak, Dean Jagger, Warren Stevens

On the Town ****

US 1949 98m Technicolor
MGM (*Arthur Freed*)

Three sailors enjoy twenty-four hours' leave in New York.
Most of this brash location musical counts as among the best things ever to come out of Hollywood; the serious ballet towards the end tends to kill it, but it contains much to be grateful for.

w Betty Comden, Adolph Green, *ballet* Fancy Free by Leonard Bernstein *d/ch* Gene Kelly, Stanley Donen *ph* Harold Rosson *md* Lennie Hayton, Roger Edens *songs* various

Gene Kelly, Frank Sinatra, Jules Munshin,

Vera-Ellen, Betty Garrett, Ann Miller, Tom Dugan, Florence Bates, Alice Pearce

'A film that will be enjoyed more than twice.'—*Lindsay Anderson*
'So exuberant that it threatens at moments to bounce right off the screen.'—*Time*
'The speed, the vitality, the flashing colour and design, the tricks of timing by which motion is fitted to music, the wit and invention and superlative technical accomplishment make it a really exhilarating experience.'—*Richard Mallett, Punch*

AA: Lennie Hayton, Roger Edens

On the Waterfront ***

US 1954 108m bw
Columbia / Sam Spiegel

After the death of his brother, a young stevedore breaks the hold of a waterfront gang boss.
Intense, broody dockside thriller with 'method' performances; very powerful of its kind, and much imitated.

w Budd Schulberg, from his novel *d* Elia Kazan *ph* Boris Kaufman *m* Leonard Bernstein

Marlon Brando, Eva Marie Saint, *Lee J. Cobb*, Rod Steiger, Karl Malden, Pat Henning, Leif Erickson, James Westerfield, John Hamilton

'An uncommonly powerful, exciting and imaginative use of the screen by gifted professionals.'—*New York Times*

AA: best picture; Budd Schulberg; Boris Kaufman; Marlon Brando; Eva Marie Saint
AAN: Leonard Bernstein; Lee J. Cobb; Rod Steiger; Karl Malden

On with the Show

US 1929 98m Technicolor (two-colour)
Warner

Crude early talkie musical revue with historical interest.

w Robert Lord, *play* Shoestring by Humphrey Pearson *d* Alan Crosland *ph* Tony Gaudio *songs* Grant Clarke, Harry Akst

Betty Compson, Louise Fazenda, Sally O'Neil, Joe E. Brown, Ethel Waters, Arthur Lake

On Your Toes *

US 1939 94m bw
Warner (Robert Lord)

Backstage jealousies at the ballet.
Smooth film version of a top Broadway show of its time.

w Jerry Wald, Richard Macaulay, *play* George Abbott *d* Ray Enright *ph* James Wong Howe, Sol Polito *m/ly* Richard Rodgers, Lorenz Hart

Vera Zorina, Eddie Albert, Alan Hale, Frank

McHugh, James Gleason, Donald O'Connor, Gloria Dickson

Once a Jolly Swagman*
GB 1948   100m   bw
GFD / Wessex (Ian Dalrymple)
US title: *Maniacs on Wheels*

A factory worker becomes a speedway rider. Competent sporting drama of no particular interest.

w William Rose, Jack Lee d Jack Lee ph H. E. Fowle m Bernard Stevens

Dirk Bogarde, Renée Asherson, Bonar Colleano, Bill Owen

Once a Thief
US 1965   107m   bw   Panavision
MGM / Cipra / RN / Fred Engel (Jacques Bar)

An ex-convict is hounded by a vengeful cop. Glum crime melodrama gleamingly photographed but otherwise quite routine.

w Zekial Marko d Ralph Nelson ph Robert Burks m Lalo Schifrin

Alain Delon, Ann-Margret, Van Heflin, Jack Palance, John David Chandler

Once in a Lifetime**
US 1933   80m approx   bw
Universal

How a script was sold in old-time Hollywood. Half good-humoured, half-scathing satire on Hollywood; technique dated, content still amusing.

w Seton I. Miller, *play* Moss Hart, George S. Kaufman d Russell Mack ph George Robinson

Jack Oakie, Sidney Fox, Aline MacMahon, Russell Hopton, Zasu Pitts, Louise Fazenda, Gregory Ratoff, Onslow Stevens

Once Is Not Enough
US 1975   122m   Movielab   Panavision
Paramount / Sujac / Aries (Howard W. Koch)
aka: *Jacqueline Susann's Once Is Not Enough*

The daughter of a movie producer is corrupted by his circle.
Old-fashioned jet-set melodrama with new-fashioned sexual novelties.

w Julius J. Epstein, *novel* Jacqueline Susann d Guy Green ph John A. Alonzo m Henry Mancini pd John de Cuir

Kirk Douglas, Alexis Smith, David Janssen, George Hamilton, Melina Mercouri, Gary Conway, Brenda Vaccaro, Deborah Raffin

AAN: Brenda Vaccaro

Once More My Darling
US 1949   92m   bw
Universal (Joan Harrison)

A young girl is romantically pursued by an older man.
Tame comedy.

w Robert Carson d Robert Montgomery ph Franz Planer m Elizabeth Firestone

Robert Montgomery, Ann Blyth, Jane Cowl, Taylor Holmes, Charles McGraw

Once More with Feeling
GB 1960   92m   Technicolor
Columbia / Stanley Donen

The volatile private life of an orchestral conductor.
Thin comedy from a West End play, something between a shouting match and a fashion show.

w Harry Kurnitz, from his play d Stanley Donen ph Georges Périnal md Muir Mathieson pd Alexander Trauner

Yul Brynner, Kay Kendall, Geoffrey Toone, Maxwell Shaw, Mervyn Johns, Martin Benson, Gregory Ratoff

Once Upon a Honeymoon*
US 1942   116m   bw
RKO (Leo McCarey)

An American radio correspondent and an ex-burlesque queen cheat the Nazis—and her husband—in Europe during World War II. Smooth but curious mixture of comedy and drama, a satisfactory but unmemorable star vehicle.

w Sheridan Gibney, Leo McCarey d Leo McCarey ph George Barnes m Robert Emmett Dolan

Cary Grant, Ginger Rogers, Walter Slezak, Albert Dekker, Albert Bassermann, Ferike Boros, Harry Shannon

'The attempt to play for both laughs and significance against a terrifying background of Nazi aggression is on the whole a little disappointing.'—*Newsweek*

Once Upon a Time*
US 1944   89m   bw
Columbia (Louis Edelman)

A luckless producer makes a sensation out of a boy and his dancing caterpillar.
Thin whimsical comedy, too slight to come off given such standard treatment, but with nice touches along the way.

w Lewis Meltzer, Oscar Saul, *radio play* My Client Curley by Norman Corwin, Lucille F.

Herrmann *d* Alexander Hall *ph* Franz Planer *m* Frederick Hollander

Cary Grant, Janet Blair, James Gleason, Ted Donaldson, Howard Freeman, William Demarest, Art Baker, John Abbott

'There just isn't enough material here for a full-length feature.'—*Philip T. Hartung*

Once Upon a Time in the West *

Italy / US 1969   165m   Techniscope
Paramount / Rafran / San Marco (Fulvio Morsella)

A lonely woman in the old west is in danger from a band of gunmen.

Immensely long and convoluted epic western marking its director's collaboration with an American studio and his desire to make serious statements about something or other. Beautifully made, empty, and very violent.

w Sergio Leone, Sergio Donati *d* Sergio Leone *ph* Tonino Delli Colli *m* Ennio Morricone

Henry Fonda, Claudia Cardinale, Jason Robards, Charles Bronson, Gabriele Ferzetti, Keenan Wynn, Paolo Stoppa, Lionel Stander, Jack Elam, Woody Strode

The One and Only

US 1978   98m   Movielab
Paramount / First Artists (Steve Gordon, David V. Picker)

A stage-struck egomaniac finds success at the expense of happiness with his wife.

Uneasy mixture of farce and sentiment intended as a star vehicle, but not a very successful one.

w Steve Gordon *d* Carl Reiner *ph* Victor J. Kemper *m* Patrick Williams

Henry Winkler, Kim Darby, Gene Saks, William Daniels, Polly Holiday, Herve Villechaize, Harold Gould, Richard Lane

One Day in the Life of Ivan Denisovich *

GB 1971   105m   Eastmancolor
Group W (Caspar Wrede)

Life in a Siberian labour camp in 1950.

A fairly successful book adaptation, as far as mere pictures can cope with the harrowing detail.

w Ronald Harwood, *novel* Alexander Solzhenitsyn *d* Caspar Wrede *ph* Sven Nykvist *m* Arne Nordheim

Tom Courtenay, Espen Skjonberg, James Maxwell, Alfred Burke, Eric Thompson, Matthew Guinness

'The film's general air of earnestness deflects rather than stimulates involvement.'—*David Wilson*

One Desire

US 1955   94m   Technicolor
U-I (Ross Hunter)

The romantic career of the lady owner of a gambling saloon.

Tawdry nineties drama which never really gets going.

w Lawrence Roman, Robert Blees, *novel* Tacey Cromwell by Conrad Richter *d* Jerry Hopper *ph* Maury Gertsman *m* Frank Skinner *md* Joseph Gershenson

Anne Baxter, Rock Hudson, Julia Adams, Natalie Wood, Barry Curtis, William Hopper, Carl Benton Reid

'The standards of writing and characterization belong to a Victorian servant girl's paper-covered romance.'—*MFB*

One Eyed Jacks

US 1961   141m   Technicolor   Vistavision
Paramount (Frank P. Rosenberg)

An outlaw has a running battle with an old friend.

Grossly self-indulgent western controlled (unwisely) by its star, full of solemn pauses and bouts of violence.

w Guy Trosper, Calder Willingham, *novel* The Authentic Death of Hendry Jones by Charles Neider *d* Marlon Brando *ph* Charles Lang Jnr *m* Hugo Friedhofer

Marlon Brando, Karl Malden, Pina Pellicier, Katy Jurado, Slim Pickens, Ben Johnson, Timothy Carey, Elisha Cook Jnr

AAN: Charles Lang Jnr

One Flew over the Cuckoo's Nest ***

US 1975   134m   De Luxe
UA / Fantasy Films (Paul Zaentz, Michael Douglas)

A cheerful immoralist imprisoned for rape is transferred for observation to a state mental hospital.

Wildly and unexpectedly commercial film of a project which had lain dormant for fourteen years, this amusing and horrifying film conveniently sums up anti-government attitudes as well as make love not war and all that. It's certainly impossible to ignore.

w Laurence Hauben, Bo Goldman, *novel Ken Kesey d Milos Forman ph* Haskell Wexler *m* Jack Nitzche *pd* Paul Sylbert

Jack Nicholson, Louise Fletcher, William Redfield, Will Sampson, Brad Dourif, Christopher Lloyd

'Lacks the excitement of movie art, but the

story and the acting make the film emotionally powerful.'—*New Yorker*

AA: best picture; script; Milos Forman; Jack Nicholson; Louise Fletcher
AAN: Haskell Wexler; Jack Nitzche; Brad Dourif

One Foot in Heaven*
US 1941   108m   bw
Warner (Robert Lord, Irving Rapper)

The small-town doings of a methodist minister. Slow but pleasing chronicle, nicely assembled.

w Casey Robinson, *biography* (of his father) Hartzell Spence *d* Irving Rapper *ph* Charles Rosher *m* Max Steiner

Fredric March, Martha Scott, Beulah Bondi, Gene Lockhart, Elizabeth Fraser, Harry Davenport, Laura Hope Crews, Grant Mitchell, Moroni Olsen, Ernest Cossart, Jerome Cowan
    'A clean, sweet, decent picture.'—*Cecilia Ager*

AAN: best picture

One Foot in Hell
US 1960   89m   De Luxe   Cinemascope
TCF (Sydney Boehm)

The sheriff of a small western town is secretly plotting revenge on the townsfolk for their long-ago treatment of his wife.
Unusual western suspenser with plenty of violent action and an extremely equivocal hero.

w Aaron Spelling, Sydney Boehm *d* James B. Clark *ph* William C. Mellor *m* Dominic Frontière

Alan Ladd, Dan O'Herlihy, Don Murray, Dolores Michaels, Barry Coe, Larry Gates, John Alexander

One Hour with You***
US 1932   84m   bw
Paramount (*Ernst Lubitsch*)

The affairs of a philandering Parisian doctor. Superbly handled comedy of manners in Lubitsch's most inventive form, handled by a most capable cast. Unique entertainment of a kind which is, alas, no more.

w *Samson Raphaelson, play* Only a Dream by Lothar Schmidt *d* *George Cukor, Ernst Lubitsch ph* Victor Milner *m* *Oscar Straus, Richard Whiting 'ly Leo Robin ad Hans Dreier*

Maurice Chevalier, Jeanette MacDonald, Genevieve Tobin, Roland Young, Charles Ruggles, George Barbier
    'A brand new form of musical entertainment . . . he has mixed verse, spoken and sung, a smart and satiric musical background, asides to the

audience, and sophisticated dialogue, as well as lilting and delightful songs . . . The result is something so delightful that it places the circle of golden leaves jauntily upon the knowing head of Hollywood's most original director.'— *Philadelphia Inquirer*
† A remake of Lubitsch's silent success *The Marriage Circle*.

AAN: best picture

One Hundred and One Dalmatians***
US 1961   79m   Technicolor
Walt Disney

The dogs of London help save puppies which are being stolen for their skins by a cruel villainess. Disney's last really splendid feature cartoon, with the old flexible style cleverly modernized and plenty of invention and detail in the story line. The London backgrounds are especially nicely judged.

w Bill Peet, *novel* Dodie Smith *d* Wolfgang Reitherman, Hamilton S. Luske, Clyde Geronimi

One Hundred Men and a Girl***
US 1937   84m   bw
Universal (*Joe Pasternak*)

A young girl persuades a great conductor to form an orchestra of unemployed musicians. Delightful and funny musical fable, an instance of the Pasternak formula of sweetness and light at its richest and best.

w *Bruce Manning, Charles Kenyon, Hans Kraly d Henry Koster ph* Joseph Valentine *m* Charles Previn *songs* various

Deanna Durbin, Adolphe Menjou, Leopold Stokowski, Alice Brady, Mischa Auer, Eugene Pallette, Billy Gilbert, Alma Kruger, Jed Prouty, Frank Jenks, Christian Rub

AA: Charles Previn
AAN: original story (Hans Kraly)

100 Rifles*
US 1969   109m   De Luxe
TCF / Marvin Schwartz

In war-torn Mexico, a black American sheriff and his prisoner become involved in a girl's fight for vengeance after her father's death. Blood-soaked adventure with plenty of tough action and tight pace. A little too purposeful in its unpleasantness to be very entertaining.

w Clair Huffaker, Tom Gries, *novel* Robert MacLeod *d Tom Gries ph* Cecilio Paniagua *m* Jerry Goldsmith

Jim Brown, Raquel Welch, Burt Reynolds,

Fernando Lamas, Dan O'Herlihy, Hans Gudegast

One in a Million*

US 1937 94m bw
TCF (Raymond Griffith)

The daughter of a Swiss innkeeper becomes an Olympic ice-skating champion.
Sonja Henie's film debut shows Hollywood at its most professional, making entertainment out of the purest moonshine with considerable injections of novelty talent.

w Lenore Praskins, Mark Kelly d Sidney Lanfield ph Edward Cronjager md Louis Silvers

Sonja Henie, Don Ameche, The Ritz Brothers, Jean Hersholt, Ned Sparks, Arline Judge, Dixie Dunbar, Borrah Minnevitch and his Rascals, Montagu Love

One Is a Lonely Number*

US 1972 97m Metrocolor
MGM (Stan Margulies)

When her husband leaves her, a woman tries to develop new interests.
Satirical sentimental view of American divorce, with interesting moments.

w David Seltzer, novel Rebecca Morris d Mel Stuart ph Michel Hugo m Michel Legrand

Trish Van Devere, Monte Markham, Michael Douglas, Janet Leigh

One Little Indian

US 1973 91m Technicolor
Walt Disney (Winston Hibler)

A cavalry corporal escapes from jail and falls in with a ten-year-old Indian.
Sentimental semi-western, a bit dull for Disney apart from a camel.

w Harry Spalding d Bernard McEveety ph Charles F. Wheeler m Jerry Goldsmith

James Garner, Vera Miles, Pat Hingle, Morgan Woodward, John Doucette

One Million BC*

US 1940 80m bw
Hal Roach
GB title: Man and His Mate
aka: The Cave Dwellers

Life between warring tribes of primitive man in the stone age.
Impressive-looking but slow-moving grunt-and-groan epic originally based on D. W. Griffith's Man's Genesis and on which Griffith did some work. The totally unhistoric dinosaurs (which

had disappeared long before man arrived) are impressively concocted by magnifying lizards.

w Mickell Novak, George Baker, Joseph Frickert d Hal Roach, Hal Roach Jnr, D. W. Griffith ph Norbert Brodine m Werner R. Heymann

Victor Mature, Carole Landis, Lon Chaney Jnr, John Hubbard, Nigel de Brulier, Conrad Nagel

AAN: Werner R. Heymann

One Million Years BC*

GB 1966 100m Technicolor
Hammer (Michael Carreras)

A vague remake of the above, with animated monsters. Not badly done, with some lively action.

w Michael Carreras d Don Chaffey ph Wilkie Cooper m Mario Nascimbene

John Richardson, Raquel Welch, Robert Brown, Percy Herbert, Martine Beswick

'Very easy to dismiss the film as a silly spectacle; but Hammer production finesse is much in evidence and Don Chaffey has done a competent job of direction. And it is all hugely enjoyable.'—David Wilson

One Minute to Zero

US 1952 105m bw
RKO (Edmund Grainger)

In Korea a US colonel is evacuating American civilians but is forced to bomb refugees.
Flat war film with Something To Say and the star at his most humourless.

w Milton Krims, William Haines d Tay Garnett ph William E. Snyder m Constantin Bakaleinikoff

Robert Mitchum, Ann Blyth, William Talman, Charles McGraw, Richard Egan

One More River*

US 1934 88m bw
Universal (James Whale)
GB title: Over the River

A wife runs away from her husband, and he sets detectives on her and her lover.
Old-fashioned, well made picturization of a novel.

w R. C. Sheriff, novel John Galsworthy d James Whale ph John Mescall m W. Franke Harling

Colin Clive, Diana Wynyard, C. Aubrey Smith, Jane Wyatt, Lionel Atwill, Mrs Patrick Campbell, Frank Lawton, Reginald Denny, C. Aubrey Smith, Henry Stephenson, Alan Mowbray, E. E. Clive

'Taste, elegance, narrative drive and a

deliberate nostalgia for the Galsworthy
period.'—*Peter John Dyer, 1966*

One More Spring*
US 1935   87m   bw
Fox (Winfield Sheehan)

Three strangers, in reduced circumstances due to
the Depression, meet in Central Park and pool
their resources.
Topical serio-comedy which looks pretty dated
but still serves as a summation of American mid-
thirties attitudes.

w Edwin Burke, novel Robert Nathan *d* Henry
King *ph* John Seitz *md* Arthur Lange

Janet Gaynor, Warner Baxter, Walter Woolf
King, Grant Mitchell, Jane Darwell, Roger
Imhof, John Qualen, Dick Foran, Stepin Fetchit

One More Time
GB 1969   93m   De Luxe
UA / Chrislaw–Tracemark (Milton Ebbins)

More crime-solving adventures of Salt and
Pepper.
Even less funny than before; see *Salt and
Pepper*.

w Michael Pertwee *d* Jerry Lewis *ph* Ernest
Steward *m* Les Reed

Peter Lawford, Sammy Davis Jnr, Esther
Anderson, Maggie Wright

One More Tomorrow*
US 1946   89m   bw
Warner (Henry Blanke)

A wealthy playboy marries a left-wing
photographer and buys up her magazine.
An interesting but dated play fails to come to life
because neither cast nor director seem to
understand what it's about.

w Charles Hoffman, Catherine Turney, Julius J.
and Philip G. Epstein, *play* The Animal
Kingdom by Philip Barry *d* Peter Godfrey
ph Bert Glennon *d* Max Steiner

Ann Sheridan, Dennis Morgan, Jack Carson,
Alexis Smith, Jane Wyman, Reginald Gardiner,
John Loder, Marjorie Gateson

One More Train to Rob
US 1971   108m   Technicolor
Universal (Robert Arthur)

A train robber comes out of prison and warily
takes up with his old partners.
Undistinguished western which tries to be funny
and serious at the same time.

w Don Tait, Dick Nelson *d* Andrew V.
McLaglen *ph* Alric Edens *m* David Shire

George Peppard, Diana Muldaur, John Vernon,
France Nuyen, Steve Sandor

One Night in Lisbon
US 1941   97m   bw
Paramount (Edward H. Griffith)

During World War II an American flier falls for
a British socialite who is being used by the
government as a decoy for spies.
Flabby romantic comedy-drama which mostly
wastes a good cast.

w Virginia Van Upp *d* Edward H. Griffith

Madeleine Carroll, Fred MacMurray, Edmund
Gwenn, Patricia Morison, Billie Burke, John
Loder, Dame May Whitty, Reginald Denny,
Billy Gilbert

One Night in the Tropics
US 1940   69m   bw
Universal (Leonard Spiegelgass)

Holidays on a Caribbean island lead to a double
wedding.
Very lightweight comedy-musical notable only
for introducing Abbott and Costello.

w Gertrude Purcell, Charles Grayson, *play* Love
Insurance by Earl Derr Biggers *d* A. Edward
Sutherland *ph* Joseph Valentine *md* Charles
Previn *songs* Oscar Hammerstein II, Jerome
Kern, Otto Harbach, Dorothy Fields

Allan Jones, Nancy Kelly, Bud Abbott, Lou
Costello, Robert Cummings, Leo Carillo, Peggy
Moran, Mary Boland

One Night of Love**
US 1934   95m   bw
Columbia (Harry Cohn)

An opera star rebels against her demanding
teacher.
Light classical musical which was a surprising
box office success and brought Hollywood
careers for Lily Pons, Gladys Swarthout, Miliza
Korjus, etc.

w Dorothy Speare, Charles Beahan, S. K.
Lauren, James Gow, Edmund North *d Victor
Schertzinger ph* Joseph Walker *songs* Victor
Schertzinger, Gus Kahn *md* Pietro Cimini

Grace Moore, Tullio Carminati, Lyle Talbot,
Mona Barrie, Nydia Westman, Jessie Ralph,
Luis Alberni, Jane Darwell

AAN: best picture; Victor Schertzinger (as
director); Victor Schertzinger, Gus Kahn; Grace
Moore

One of Our Aircraft Is Missing*

GB 1941 102m bw

British National (Michael Powell, Emeric
 Pressburger)

A bomber is grounded after a raid and its crew is
helped by the Dutch resistance.
Efficient propaganda piece which starts
vigorously but gets bogged down in talk.

wd Michael Powell, Emeric Pressburger

Godfrey Tearle, Eric Portman, Hugh Williams,
Bernard Miles, Hugh Burden, Emrys Jones,
Googie Withers, Pamela Brown, Peter Ustinov,
Joyce Redman, Hay Petrie, Robert Helpmann,
Alec Clunes

AAN: original story (Emeric Pressburger)

One of Our Dinosaurs Is Missing*

US 1975 94m Technicolor

Walt Disney (Bill Walsh)

In the 1920s a strip of secret microfilm is
smuggled out of China and hidden in a
dinosaur's skeleton in the Natural History
Museum.
Unexceptionable family comedy with everyone
trying hard; somehow it just misses, perhaps
because it is told through talk rather than
cinematic narrative.

w Bill Walsh, novel The Great Dinosaur
Robbery by David Forrest d Robert Stevenson
ph Paul Beeson m Ron Goodwin

Helen Hayes, Peter Ustinov, Derek Nimmo,
Clive Revill, Joan Sims, Bernard Bresslaw, Roy
Kinnear, Deryck Guyler, Richard Pearson

One Sunday Afternoon**

US 1933 93m bw

Paramount (Louis D. Lighton)

In 1910, a Brooklyn dentist feels he has married
the wrong girl, but discovers that his choice was
the right one.
Pleasant period comedy drama which was twice
remade; as The Strawberry Blonde (qv) and see
below.

w William Slavens McNutt, Grover Jones, play
James Hagan d Stephen Roberts ph Victor
Milner

Gary Cooper, Frances Fuller, Fay Wray, Neil
Hamilton, Roscoe Karns

 'Still pitched in stage tempo and unfolds
haltingly.'—Variety

One Sunday Afternoon

US 1948 90m Technicolor

Warner (Jerry Wald)

Pleasant but undistinguished musical remake of
the above.

w Robert L. Richards d Raoul Walsh ph Sid
Hickox, Wilfrid M. Cline md Ray Heindorf
ad Anton Grot

Dennis Morgan, Dorothy Malone, Janis Paige,
Don Defore, Ben Blue

 'A lackadaisical and uninspired jaunt down
memory lane.'—New Yorker, 1978

The One That Got Away**

GB 1957 111m bw

Rank (Julian Wintle)

A German flier, Franz Von Werra, is captured
and sent to various British prisoner-of-war
camps, from all of which he escapes.
True-life biopic, developed in a number of
suspense and action sequences, all very well
done.

w Howard Clewes, book Kendal Burt, James
Leasor d Roy Baker ph Eric Cross m Hubert
Clifford

Hardy Kruger, Michael Goodliffe, Colin
Gordon, Alec McCowen

One Third of a Nation*

US 1939 79m bw

Federal Theatre (Dudley Murphy)

A shopgirl persuades a landlord to tear down his
dangerous slums and put up good buildings.
Naïve do-goodery, not too persuasively
managed.

w Dudley Murphy, Oliver H. P. Garrett, play
Arthur Arent d Dudley Murphy ph William
Miller

Sylvia Sidney, Leif Erickson, Myron
McCormick, Hiram Sherman, Sidney Lumet,
Percy Waram

One Touch of Venus*

US 1948 82m bw

Universal / Lester Cowan

In a fashionable department store, a statue of
Venus comes to life and falls for a window
dresser.
Pleasant satirical comedy, watered down from
the Broadway original.

w Harry Kurnitz, Frank Tashlin, play S. J.
Perelman, Ogden Nash d William A. Seiter
ph Franz Planer songs Kurt Weill ad Bernard
Herzbrun, Emrich Nicholson

Ava Gardner, Robert Walker, Eve Arden, Dick
Haymes, Olga San Juan, Tom Conway

One, Two, Three***

US 1961 115m bw Panavision

UA / Mirisch / Pyramid

An executive in West Berlin is trying to sell Coca

Cola to the Russians while preventing his boss's daughter from marrying a communist.

Back to *Ninotchka* territory, but this time the tone is that of a wild farce which achieves fine momentum in stretches but also flags a lot in between, teetering the while on the edge of taste.

w Billy Wilder, I. A. L. Diamond, *play* Ferenc Molnar *d Billy Wilder ph* Daniel Fapp *m* André Previn

James Cagney, Horst Buchholz, Arlene Francis, Pamela Tiffin, Lilo Pulver, Howard St John, Leon Askin

'A sometimes bewildered, often wonderfully funny exercise in nonstop nuttiness.'—*Time*

'This first-class featherweight farce is a serious achievement.'—*Stanley Kauffmann*

AAN: Daniel Fapp

One Way Passage *
US 1932   69m   bw
Warner (Robert Lord)

On an ocean voyage, a dying girl falls in love with a crook going home to face a life sentence. Pattern melodrama which stood Hollywood in good stead.

w Wilson Mizner, Joseph Jackson, Robert Lord *d* Tay Garnett *ph* Robert Kurrie

William Powell, Kay Francis, Frank McHugh, Aline MacMahon, Warren Hymer, Herbert Mundin, Roscoe Karns, Stanley Fields
† Remade as *'Til We Meet Again* (qv).

AAN: original story (Robert Lord)

One Way Pendulum
GB 1964   85m   bw
UA / Woodfall (Michael Deeley)

A suburban clerk leads a dream existence; his son teaches speak-your-weight machines to sing, while he sets an imaginary murder trial in motion.

A nonsense play (which has many adherents) resists the literalness of the camera eye.

w N. F. Simpson, from his play *d* Peter Yates *ph* Denys Coop *m* Richard Rodney Bennett

Eric Sykes, George Cole, Peggy Mount, Alison Leggatt, Mona Washbourne

One Way Street
US 1950   79m   bw
U-I / Leonard Goldstein (Sam Goldwyn Jnr)

A disillusioned doctor steals a fortune and hides out in a Mexican village, where he regains his self-respect.

Thin and pointless melodrama.

w Lawrence Kimble *d* Hugo Fregonese *ph* Maury Gertsman *m* Frank Skinner

James Mason, Marta Toren, Dan Duryea, William Conrad, King Donovan, Jack Elam

'It is reported that James Mason chooses his own parts, and if this is true I have to report that he is a glutton for punishment.'—*Daily Herald*

'One of the dullest, most stupid films of the year.'—*Sunday Pictorial*

Onibaba *
Japan 1964   104m   bw   Tohoscope
Kindai Eiga Kyokai / Tokyo Eiga
aka: *The Hole*

In medieval times on a remote marshy plain, mother and daughter live by killing stray soldiers and selling their armour, until daughter takes one for a lover and mother becomes jealous.

A kind of original horror legend is told by this strange, compelling piece with its frequent moments of nastiness. It remains, perhaps mercifully, unique.

wd Kaneto Shindo *ph* Kiyomi Juroda *m* Hikaru Hayashi

Nobuko Otowa, Jitsuko Yoshimura, Kei Sato

Onionhead
US 1958   110m   bw
Warner (Jules Schermer)

Adventures of a ship's cook in the US Coastguard.

Service comedy that must have seemed funnier in the US than in Britain.

w Nelson Gidding, *novel* Weldon Hill *d* Norman Taurog *ph* Harold Rosson *md* Ray Heindorf

Andy Griffith, Felicia Farr, Walter Matthau, Erin O'Brien, Joe Mantell, Ray Danton, Roscoe Karns, James Gregory, Tige Andrews
† An attempt to cash in on the success of *No Time for Sergeants*.

Only Angels Have Wings **
US 1939   121m   bw
Columbia (Howard Hawks)

Tension creeps into the relationships of the men who fly cargo planes over the Andes when a stranded showgirl sets her cap at the boss.

For an action film this is really too restricted by talk and cramped studio sets, and its theme was more entertainingly explored in *Red Dust*. Still, it couldn't be more typical of the Howard Hawks film world, where men are men and women have to be as tough as they are.

wd Howard Hawks ph Joseph Walker, Elmer Dyer *m* Dmitri Tiomkin *md* Morris Stoloff

Cary Grant, Jean Arthur, Rita Hayworth,

Richard Barthelmess, Thomas Mitchell, Sig Rumann, Victor Kilian, John Carroll, Allyn Joslyn

'All these people did the best they could with what they were given—but look at it.'—*Otis Ferguson*

The Only Game in Town
US 1969 113m De Luxe
TCF (Fred Kohlmar)

A Las Vegas chorus girl and a piano player have an unhappy life because of his gambling fever. Uninteresting two-header from a play that didn't make it; no light relief, no action, and not even very good acting.

w Frank D. Gilroy, from his play *d* George Stevens *ph* Henri Decaë *m* Maurice Jarre

Elizabeth Taylor, Warren Beatty, Charles Braswell, Hank Henry

'It epitomizes the disaster the studio and star systems foist on films . . . the only two-character tale around to cost $11 million.'—*Judith Crist*

Only the Valiant
US 1950 105m bw
William Cagney

A tough cavalry officer in a lonely fort wins a battle against Indians.
Standard top-of-the-bill western; competent but not very gripping.

w Edmund H. North, Harry Brown *d* Gordon Douglas *ph* Lionel Lindon *m* Franz Waxman

Gregory Peck, Ward Bond, Gig Young, Lon Chaney Jnr, Barbara Payton, Neville Brand

Only Two Can Play***
GB 1962 106m bw
British Lion / Vale (Launder and Gilliat)

A much married assistant librarian in a Welsh town has an abortive affair with a councillor's wife.
Well characterized and generally diverting 'realistic' comedy which slows up a bit towards the end but contains many memorable sequences and provides its star's last good character performance.

w *Bryan Forbes, novel* That Uncertain Feeling by *Kingsley Amis d Sidney Gilliat ph* John Wilcox *m* Richard Rodney Bennett *ad* Albert Witherick

Peter Sellers, Mai Zetterling, Virginia Maskell, Richard Attenborough, Raymond Huntley, John Le Mesurier, *Kenneth Griffith*

Only When I Larf*
GB 1968 103m Eastmancolor
Paramount / Beecord (Len Deighton, Brian Duffy, Hugh Attwooll)

The adventures of three confidence tricksters. Quite likeable but unmemorable 'with it' comedy of the sixties; the tricks are more amusing than the characterization.

w John Salmon, *novel* Len Deighton *d* Basil Dearden *ph* Anthony Richmond *m* Ron Grainer

Richard Attenborough, David Hemmings, Alexandra Stewart, Nicholas Pennell, Melissa Stribling, Terence Alexander, Edric Connor, Calvin Lockhart, Clifton Jones

Ooh, You Are Awful*
GB 1972 97m Eastmancolor
British Lion / Quintain (E. M. Smedley Aston)
US title: *Get Charlie Tully*

A London con man seeks a fortune, the clue to which is tattooed on the behind of one of several girls.
Amusing star vehicle with plenty of room for impersonations and outrageous jokes.

w John Warren, John Singer *d Cliff Owen ph* Ernest Stewart *m* Christopher Gunning

Dick Emery, Derren Nesbitt, Ronald Fraser, Pat Coombs, William Franklyn, Brian Oulton, Norman Bird

Open City**
Italy 1945 101m bw
Minerva
original title: *Roma, Città Aperta*

Italian underground workers defy the Nazis in Rome towards the end of the war.
A vivid newsreel quality is achieved by this nerve-stretching melodrama in which all the background detail is as real as care could make it.

w Sergio Amidei, Federico Fellini *d* Roberto *Rossellini ph* Ubaldo Arata *m* Renzo Rossellini

Aldo Fabrizzi, *Anna Magnani,* Marcello Pagliero, Maria Michi

AAN: script

Open Season
US / Spain / Switzerland 1974 104m
Eastmancolor Panavision
Impala / Arpa (George H. Brown, Jose S. Vicuna)

Three young criminals hunt human prey, but one of their victims takes his own revenge.
Rough, flashy, violent melodrama which

pretends to have something to say but in fact is merely sensationalist.

w David Osborn, Liz Charles Williams *d* Peter Collinson *ph* Fernando Arribas *m* Ruggero Cini

Peter Fonda, Cornelia Sharp, John Phillip Law, Richard Lynch, Albert Mendoza, William Holden

'Both patience and the plot line are severely strained by the artiness Collinson frequently indulges, with frozen shots to mark the moments of truth and a meaningless punctuation throughout of long shots, angles and flashes.'— *Tom Milne*

'An offensive, gamy potboiler.'—*Variety*

Opening Night

US 1978   144m   Metrocolor
Faces Distribution (Al Ruban)

A Broadway actress is on the point of a nervous breakdown.
Interminable addition to the director's list of unwatchable personal films.

wd John Cassavetes *ph* Al Ruban *m* Bo Horwood

Gena Rowlands, Ben Gazzara, John Cassavetes, Joan Blondell, Paul Stewart, Zohra Lampert, Laura Johnson

'Shrill, puzzling, depressing and overlong.'— *Variety*

L'Opéra de Quat' Sous see Die Dreigroschenoper

Operation Amsterdam*

GB 1958   104m   bw
Rank / Maurice Cowan

In 1940 spies are sent into Holland to prevent the invading Germans from finding Amsterdam's stock of industrial diamonds.
Semi-documentary war adventure, well mounted and played.

w Michael McCarthy, John Eldridge, *book* Adventure in Diamonds by David Walker *d* Michael McCarthy *ph* Reg Wyer, *m* Philip Green

Peter Finch, Tony Britton, Eva Bartok, Alexander Knox, Malcolm Keen, Tim Turner, John Horsley, Melvyn Hayes, Christopher Rhodes

Operation Crossbow*

GB 1965   116m   Metrocolor   Panavision
MGM / Carlo Ponti
aka: *The Great Spy Mission*

In World War II, trained scientists are parachuted into Europe to destroy the Nazi

rocket-making plant at Peenemunde.
Unlikely, star-packed war yarn with more passing tragedy than most, all obliterated by a shoot-em-up James Bond finale.

w Robert Imrie (Emeric Pressburger), Derry Quinn, Ray Rigby *d* Michael Anderson *ph* Erwin Hillier *m* Ron Goodwin

George Peppard, Tom Courtenay, John Mills, Sophia Loren, Lilli Palmer, Anthony Quayle, Patrick Wymark, Jeremy Kemp, Paul Henreid, Trevor Howard, Sylvia Sims, Richard Todd

Operation Daybreak

US 1975   119m   Technicolor
Warner / Howard R. Schuster / American Allied (Carter de Haven)

In 1941, Czech patriots kill the hated Nazi Heydrich and are hunted down.
Curiously-timed evocation of wartime resistance adventures, too realistic for the squeamish and certainly not very entertaining despite a fair level of professionalism.

w Ronald Harwood, *novel* Seven Men at Daybreak by Alan Burgess *d* Lewis Gilbert *ph* Henri Decaë *m* David Hentschel

Timothy Bottoms, Martin Shaw, Joss Ackland, Nicola Pagett, Anthony Andrews, Anton Diffring, Carl Duering, Diana Coupland

Operation Mad Ball*

US 1957   105m   bw
Columbia (Jed Harris)

American troops in Normandy are forbidden to fraternize with nurses, but a clandestine dance is arranged.
Madcap army farce which keeps promising to be funnier than it is.

w Arthur Carter, Jed Harris, Blake Edwards, *play* Arthur Carter *d* Richard Quine *ph* Charles Lawton Jnr *m* George Duning

Jack Lemmon, Ernie Kovacs, Kathryn Grant, Mickey Rooney, James Darren, Arthur O'Connell

Operation Pacific

US 1950   109m   bw
Warner (Louis F. Edelmann)

Adventures of a submarine commander in the Pacific war.
Routine war heroics, tolerably done but overstretched.

wd George Waggner *ph* Bert Glennon *m* Max Steiner

John Wayne, Patricia Neal, Ward Bond, Scott Forbes, Phil Carey, Paul Picerni, William Campbell, Martin Milner

Operation Petticoat*
US 1959 124m Eastmancolor
Universal / Granart (Robert Arthur)

During World War II, a crippled submarine is refloated by fair means and foul, and a party of nurses is taken aboard.
Flabby comedy with good moments, but not many.

w Stanley Shapiro, Maurice Richlin d Blake Edwards ph Russell Harlan m David Rose

Cary Grant, Tony Curtis, Joan O'Brien, Dina Merrill, Gene Evans, Arthur O'Connell, Richard Sargent

'Grant is a living lesson in getting laughs without lines.'—*Variety*

AAN: script

Operation Secret
US 1952 108m bw
Warner (Henry Blanke)

A traitor in the French resistance movement shoots a colleague, and the wrong man is accused.
Belated World War II adventure which gives the impression of having been discarded by Errol Flynn.

w James R. Webb, Harold Medford d Lewis Seiler ph Ted McCord m Roy Webb

Cornel Wilde, Steve Cochran, Paul Picerni, Karl Malden

Operation Thunderbolt*
Israel 1977 117m Eastmancolor
Panavision
GS Films (Menahem Golan, Yoram Globus)
aka: *Entebbe: Operation Thunderbolt*

An account of the rescue of Israeli hostages from terrorists who have hijacked their plane to Entebbe.
Victory at Entebbe and *Raid on Entebbe* were made with all-star casts for American television. This home-grown account of a famous deed is more modest yet more authoritative.

w Clarke Reynolds d Menahem Golan ph Adam Greenberg m Dov Seltzer

Klaus Kinski, Assaf Dayan, Ori Levy, Yehoram Geon, Mark Heath

Operator 13
US 1933 86m bw
MGM / Cosmopolitan (Lucien Hubbard)
GB title: *Spy 13*

During the Civil War an actress becomes a Union spy.
Elaborate period romance with action highlights.

w Harry Thew, Zelda Sears, Eve Greene

d Richard Boleslawski ph George Folsey m William Axt

Marion Davies, Gary Cooper, Jean Parker, Katherine Alexander, Ted Healy, Russell Hardie, Henry Wadsworth, Douglass Dumbrille

AAN: George Folsey

The Opposite Sex
US 1956 116m Metrocolor
Cinemascope
MGM (Joe Pasternak)

A New York socialite divorces her unfaithful husband but finally takes him back.
Softened, musicalized version of *The Women* (qv); very patchy, shapeless, and not nearly sharp enough.

w Fay and Michael Kanin, *play* Clare Boothe d David Miller m George Stoll songs Nicholas Brodsky, Sammy Cahn

June Allyson, Dolores Gray, Joan Collins, Ann Sheridan, Agnes Moorehead, Joan Blondell, Barbara Jo Allen, Charlotte Greenwood

The Optimists of Nine Elms*
GB 1973 110m Eastmancolor
Cheetah / Sagittarius (Adrian Gaye, Victor Lyndon)

Children of a London slum make friends with an old busker.
Gentle, sentimental, quite well-observed piece of wistful melancholia, falsified by its star performance.

wd *Anthony Simmons*, from his novel co-w Tudor Gates ph Larry Pizer m George Martin

Peter Sellers, Donna Mullane, John Chaffey, David Daker, Marjorie Yates

The Oracle
GB 1952 83m bw
Group Three (Colin Lesslie)

A reporter discovers that a village well in Ireland contains an oracle which can predict the future.
Weak sub-Ealing comedy which aims to please and gets a few laughs. All very British.

w Patrick Campbell d C. M. Pennington-Richards ph Wolfgang Suschitsky m Temple Abady

Robert Beatty, Virginia McKenna, Mervyn Johns, Gilbert Harding

Orca—Killer Whale
US 1977 92m Technicolor Panavision
Famous Films / Dino de Laurentiis

Off Newfoundland, a killer whale takes revenge for its mate's death.

A rather unpleasant attempt to mix horror and thrills with ecology: not very entertaining, and not for the squeamish.

w Luciano Vincenzoni, Sergio Donati
d Michael Anderson ph Ted Moore, J. Barry Herron m Ennio Morricone

Richard Harris, Charlotte Rampling, Will Sampson, Keenan Wynn
'The biggest load of cod imaginable.'—*Philip Bergson, Sunday Times*
'There are more thrills to be had in the average dolphinarium.'—*Sight and Sound*

Orchestra Wives**
US 1942 97m bw
TCF (William Le Baron)

A small-town girl marries the singer of a travelling swing band.
Fresh and lively musical of its period, full of first-class music and amusing backstage backbiting.

w Karl Tunberg, Darrell Ware d Archie Mayo
ph Lucien Ballard md Alfred Newman

Ann Rutherford, George Montgomery, Lynn Bari, *Glenn Miller and his Orchestra*, Carole Landis, Jackie Gleason

AAN: song 'I've Got a Girl in Kalamazoo' (m Harry Warren, ly Mack Gordon)

Orders Are Orders
GB 1954 78m bw
Group 3 (Donald Taylor)

Flabby update of *Orders Is Orders* with an interesting cast below par.

w Donald Taylor, Geoffrey Orme d David Paltenghi ph Arthur Grant m Stanley Black

Peter Sellers, Brian Reece, Sid James, Tony Hancock, Margot Grahame, Raymond Huntley, Maureen Johnson, June Thorburn, Bill Fraser

Orders Is Orders
GB 1933 88m bw
Gaumont British (Michael Balcon)

An army barracks is disrupted when an American film company gets permission to work there.
Breezy farce which pleased at the time.

w Leslie Arliss, Sidney Gilliat, *play* Ian Hay, Anthony Armstrong d Walter Forde ph Glen MacWilliams

Charlotte Greenwood, James Gleason, Cedric Hardwicke, Cyril Maude, Ian Hunter, Ray Milland, Jane Carr, Donald Calthrop, Eliot Makeham, Wally Patch, Finlay Currie

Orders to Kill*
GB 1958 111m bw
British Lion / Lynx (Anthony Asquith, Anthony Havelock-Allan)

During World War II a bomber pilot undertakes a mission to parachute into occupied France and kill a double agent, who turns out afterwards to have been innocent.
Strong, hard-to-take but well made war story about the effect of war on conscience.

w Paul Dehn d Anthony Asquith ph Desmond Dickinson m Benjamin Frankel

Paul Massie, Irene Worth, James Robertson Justice, *Leslie French*, Eddie Albert, Lillian Gish, John Crawford, Jacques Brunius, Lionel Jeffries

The Organization
US 1971 108m De Luxe
UA / Mirisch (Walter Mirisch)

San Francisco policemen combat an international drug smuggling organization.
The third and weakest adventure of Virgil Tibbs, black policeman of *In the Heat of the Night*. Absolutely routine.

w James R. Webb d Don Medford ph Joseph Biroc m Gile Melle

Sidney Poitier, Barbara McNair, Sheree North, Gerald S. O'Loughlin

Orphans of the Storm*
US 1921 124m (24 fps) bw silent
D. W. Griffith

Two sisters are caught up in the French revolution of 1789.
Half melodrama, half epic, this celebrated film survives chiefly by its careful attention to historical detail and by the excitement of its crowd scenes.

w D. W. Griffith, *play* Adolph Ennery d D. W. Griffith ph Henrick Sartov

Lillian Gish, Dorothy Gish, Joseph Schildkraut, Lucille La Verne, Morgan Wallace, Frank Puglia, Creighton Hale

Orphée***
France 1949 112m bw
André Paulvé 1 / Films du Palais Royal

Death, represented by a princess, falls in love with Orpheus, a poet, and helps him when he goes into hell in pursuit of his dead love.
Fascinating poetic fantasy which may have been finally unintelligible but was filled to overflowing with memorable scenes and cinematic tricks, from the entry to the hereafter through a mirror to intercepted code messages such as 'L'oiseau

compte avec ses doigts'. The closest the cinema
has got to poetry.

wd Jean Cocteau, from his play *ph Nicolas
Hayer m Georges Auric ad Jean d'Eaubonne*

*Jean Marais, François Périer, Maria Casarès,
Marie Déa, Edouard Dermithe, Juliette Greco*

'It is a drama of the visible and the invisible . . .
I interwove many myths. Death condemns
herself in order to help the man she is duty bound
to destroy. The man is saved but Death dies: it is
the myth of immortality.'—*Jean Cocteau*
† See the sequel *Le Testament d'Orphée*.

The Oscar*
US 1966 118m Pathecolor
Paramount / Greene–Rouse

On the night of the Academy Awards his friend
recalls a heel's rise to stardom.
Squalid, sensationalist account of Hollywood
mores; one hopes it isn't quite true.

w Harlan Ellison, Russel Rouse, Clarence
Greene, *novel* Richard Sale *d* Russel Rouse
ph Joseph Ruttenberg *m* Percy Faith

Stephen Boyd, Elke Sommer, Tony Bennett,
Eleanor Parker, Milton Berle, Joseph Cotten, Jill
St John, Edie Adams, Ernest Borgnine, Ed
Begley, Walter Brennan, Broderick Crawford,
James Dunn, Peter Lawford, Edith Head, Hedda
Hopper, Merle Oberon, Bob Hope, Frank
Sinatra

'This is the sort of film that only Hollywood
could make, and on that level it is preposterously
enjoyable.'—*David Wilson*

'That true movie rarity—a picture that attains
a perfection of ineptitude quite beyond the power
of words to describe.'—*Richard Shickel*

Oscar Wilde**
GB 1959 96m bw
Vantage (William Kirby)

Scandal strikes Oscar Wilde through his
involvement with Lord Alfred Douglas.
Competent, well acted version of well-known
events of the nineties, with Morley in his original
stage role; generally more satisfactory than *The
Trials of Oscar Wilde* which was shot
simultaneously.

w Jo Eisinger *d* Gregory Ratoff *ph* Georges
Périnal *m* Kenneth V. Jones

Robert Morley, John Neville, Phyllis Calvert,
Ralph Richardson, Dennis Price, Alexander
Knox, Edward Chapman, Martin Benson,
Robert Harris, Henry Oscar, William Devlin

Ossessione*
Italy 1942 135m bw
ICI

A wanderer falls for the wife of an innkeeper and
they murder him, but fate takes a hand.
Unofficial remake of *The Postman Always Rings
Twice*, barely released outside Italy. A powerful
melodrama credited with starting the neo-realist
school.

w Antonio Pietrangeli, Giuseppe de Santis,
Gianni Puccini, Luchino Visconti, Mario
Alicata *d Luchino Visconti ph* Aldo Tonti,
Domenico Scala *m* Giuseppe Rosati

Massimo Girotti, Clara Calamai, Elio Marcuzzo
† Other versions: *Le Dernier Tournant* (France
1939); *The Postman Always Rings Twice* (US
1945).

Othello*
US / France 1951 91m bw
Mercury / Films Marceau

Shakespeare's play as rearranged by Orson
Welles at the start of his European wanderings;
modest budget, flashes of brilliance, poor
technical quality, variable acting. Not really the
best way to film Shakespeare.

w Orson Welles, *play* William Shakespeare
d Orson Welles *ad* Alexander Trauner

Orson Welles, Micheal MacLiammoir, Fay
Compton, Robert Cook, Suzanne Cloutier,
Michael Laurence, Hilton Edwards, Doris
Dowling

Othello*
GB 1965 166m Technicolor Panavision
BHE (Richard Godwin)

A record of the National Theatre production,
disappointing in terms of cinema but a valuable
record of a famous performance.

d Stuart Burge *ph* Geoffrey Unsworth
md Richard Hampton

Laurence Olivier, Frank Finlay, Joyce Redman,
Maggie Smith, Derek Jacobi, Robert Lang,
Anthony Nicholls

AAN: Laurence Olivier; Frank Finlay; Joyce
Redman; Maggie Smith

The Other*
US 1972 100m De Luxe
TCF / Rex-Benchmark (Tom Tryon)

A boy insists that his dead twin is responsible for
several unexplained deaths.
Subtle family ghost story for intellectuals; a bit
pretentious and restrained for popular success.

w Tom Tryon, from his novel *d* Robert
Mulligan *ph* Robert Surtees *m* Jerry
Goldsmith *pd* Albert Brenner

Uta Hagen, Diana Muldaur, Chris Connelly, Victor French

The Other Love
US 1947   96m   bw
Enterprise (David Lewis)

At a Swiss sanatorium, a lady concert pianist who is dying falls in love with her doctor.
Fairly icky 'woman's picture' with uncomfortable performances.

w Ladislas Fodor, Harry Brown, *story* Erich Maria Remarque d André de Toth ph Victor Milner m Miklos Rozsa

Barbara Stanwyck, David Niven, Richard Conte, Gilbert Roland, Joan Lorring, Lenore Aubert

The Other Side of Midnight
US 1977   166m   De Luxe   Panavision
TCF / Frank Yablans, Martin Ransohoff (Howard W. Koch Jnr)

Before and after World War II a young Parisienne courts an American flyer, but her tycoon husband eventually exacts a grim revenge on both of them.
Turgid and interminable adaptation of a best-seller, with no likeable characters and several unpleasant sequences.

w Herman Raucher, Daniel Taradash, *novel* Sidney Sheldon d Charles Jarrott ph Fred J. Koenekamp m Michel Legrand pd John De Cuir

Marie-France Pisier, John Beck, Susan Sarandon, Raf Vallone, Clu Gulager, Christian Marquand

'After 166 minutes the feeling that one has actually lived through it all is a little too real for comfort.'—*David Badder, MFB*

'A fatuous, money-spinning film from the fatuous, money-spinning book.'—*New Yorker*

'Right down to the nonsense title, this epic of schlock restores the era of *Now Voyager* . . . the movie equivalent of a good bad read.'—*Time Out*

The Other Side of the Mountain
US 1975   102m   Technicolor
Universal / Filmways / Larry Peerce (Edward S. Feldman)
GB title: *A Window to the Sky*

A girl skiing champion is paralysed by polio.
Maudlin tearjerker based on a real case; altogether too much of a good thing.

w David Seltzer, *book* A Long Way Up by E. G. Valens d Larry Peerce ph David M. Walsh m Charles Fox

Marilyn Hassett, Beau Bridges, Belinda Montgomery, Nan Martin, William Bryant, Dabney Coleman

AAN: song 'Richard's Window' (*m* Chales Fox, *ly* Norman Gimbel)

The Other Side of the Mountain Part Two
USS 1977   99m   Technicolor
Universal / Filmways (Edward S. Feldman)

Crippled skier Jill Kinmont becomes a teacher and falls in love again.
More true-life weepie material spun out from the first successful film; the sequel is quickly forgettable.

w Douglas Day Stewart d Larry Peerce ph Ric Waite m Lee Holdridge

Marilyn Hassett, Timothy Bottoms, Nan Martin, Belinda J. Montgomery

Otley**
GB 1968   91m   Technicolor
Columbia / Open Road (Bruce Cohn Curtis)

An inoffensive Londoner falls in with spies and murderers.
Semi-spoof comedy thriller taking in James Bondery and the swinging London set. Generally pretty funny, but not entirely certain of its own motives.

w Ian La Frenais, Dick Clement, *novel* Martin Waddell d Dick Clement ph Austin Dempster m Stanley Myers

Tom Courtenay, Romy Schneider, Alan Badel, James Villiers, Leonard Rossiter, Freddie Jones, James Bolam, Fiona Lewis

Our Betters*
US 1933   83m   bw
RKO (David O. Selznick)

An American woman in London finds her titled husband is unfaithful and sets about causing society scandals.
Dimly adapted West End success makes an interesting but unamusing film.

w Jane Murfin, Harry Wagstaff Gribble, *play* W. Somerset Maugham d George Cukor ph Charles Rosher md Max Steiner

Constance Bennett, Violet Kemble Cooper, Alan Mowbray, Gilbert Roland, Phoebe Foster, Charles Starrett, Grant Mitchell, Anita Louise, Minor Watson, Hugh Sinclair

'One of those familiar dreams of high life in which we are asked to admire even while we condemn the superb immorality of our almost godlike betters.'—*The Times*

Our Blushing Brides see Our Dancing
Daughters

Our Daily Bread*
US 1934 80m bw
King Vidor

A young couple in the depression inherit a
broken-down farm and make it work.
A rather drab sequel to *The Crowd*, with an
irrigation ditch finale in clear imitation of
Eisenstein.

w Elizabeth Hill, *story* King Vidor *d* King
Vidor *ph* Robert Planck *m* Alfred Newman

Karen Morley, Tom Keene, John Qualen,
Barbara Pepper, Addison Richards
† Vidor so desperately wanted to make the film
that, discovering its theme to be unpopular with
sponsors, he pawned everything he owned to
finance it.

Our Dancing Daughters*
US 1928 86m approx (24 fps) bw silent
MGM / Cosmopolitan

A wild young socialite knows when to stop, and
makes a good marriage; her friend doesn't and
falls to her death while drunk.
Mild exploitation piece of its time which swept
Joan Crawford to stardom after her dance in her
underwear.

w Josephine Lovett *d* Harry Beaumont
ph George Barnes

Joan Crawford, Johnny Mack Brown, Dorothy
Sebastian, Anita Page, Nils Asther
† Sequels: *Our Modern Maidens* (silent, 1929)
with JC, Rod La Rocque, Douglas Fairbanks
Jnr, Anita Page, *w* Josephine Lovett; *Our
Blushing Brides* (sound, 1930) with JC, Robert
Montgomery, Anita Page, Dorothy Sebastian,
Raymond Hackett, *w* Bess Meredyth and John
Howard Lawson. Neither was remarkable.

AAN: Josephine Lovett

Our Hearts Were Young and Gay*
US 1944 81m bw
Paramount (Sheridan Gibney)

Two well-to-do flappers of the twenties find fun
and romance in Paris.
A pleasant, undemanding piece of nostalgia
based on a popular biography; in 1946 a less
successful sequel, *Our Hearts Were Growing
Up*, involved the young ladies with bootleggers at
Princeton.

w Sheridan Gibney, *book* Cornelia Otis Skinner,
Emily Kimbrough *d* Lewis Allen *ph* Theodor
Sparkuhl *m* Werner Heymann

Gail Russell, Diana Lynn, Charles Ruggles,

Dorothy Gish, Beulah Bondi, James Brown, Bill
Edwards, Jean Heather

Our Hospitality**
US 1923 70m approx (24 fps) bw silent
Metro / Buster Keaton

Around 1850, a southerner returns home to
claim his bride and finds himself in the middle of
a blood feud.
Charming rather than hilarious star comedy
with a splendid ancient train and at least one
incredible stunt by the star.

w Jean Havez, Joseph Mitchell, Clyde
Bruckman *d* Buster Keaton, Jack Blystone
ph Elgin Lessley, Gordon Jennings

Buster Keaton, Natalie Talmadge, Joe Keaton,
Buster Keaton Jnr

Our Little Girl
US 1935 63m bw
TCF (Edward Butcher)

A doctor's daughter brings her parents together.
One of the child star's thinner and more
sentimental vehicles.

w Stephen Morehouse Avery, Allen Rivkin, Jack
Yellen, *story* Heaven's Gate by Florence
Leighton Pfalzgraf *d* John Robertson *ph* John
Seitz *md* Oscar Bradley

Shirley Temple, Joel McCrea, Rosemary Ames,
Lyle Talbot, Erin O'Brien-Moore

Our Man Flint*
US 1965 108m De Luxe Cinemascope
TCF (Saul David)

An American secret agent and super stud fights
an organization bent on controlling the world
through its weather.
Comic strip imitation of James Bond; in its wild
way the first instalment scored a good many
laughs, but the sequel, *In Like Flint* (qv), quickly
ended the series.

w Hal Fimberg, Ben Starr *d* Daniel Mann
ph Daniel L. Fapp *m* Jerry Goldsmith

James Coburn, Lee J. Cobb, Gila Golan,
Edward Mulhare, Benson Fong, Sigrid Valdis
'Despite the fact that everyone from designers
to actors seems to be having a ball, the film
somehow goes over the edge of parody—
ultimately it looks suspiciously like a case of
wish-fulfilment.'—*John Gillett*

Our Man in Havana*
GB 1959 112m bw Cinemascope
Columbia / Kingsmead (Carol Reed)

A British vacuum cleaner salesman in Havana

allows himself to be recruited as a spy, and wishes he hadn't.

The wry flavour of the novel does not really translate to the screen, and especially not to the wide screen, but a few lines and characters offer compensation.

w Graham Greene, from his novel d Carol Reed ph Oswald Morris m Hermanos Deniz Cuban Rhythm Band

Alec Guinness, *Noel Coward*, Burl Ives, Maureen O'Hara, Ernie Kovacs, *Ralph Richardson*, Jo Morrow, Paul Rogers, Grègoire Aslan, Duncan Macrae

'The main weakness is the absence of economic, expressive cutting and visual flow. As a result . . . stretches of dialogue become tedious to watch; and the essential awareness of the writer's shifting tensions yields disappointingly to the easier mannerisms of any conventional comedy-thriller.'—*Peter John Dyer*

Our Miss Fred *
GB 1972   96m   Technicolor
EMI / Willis WorldWide (Josephine Douglas)

In World War II France, an actor escapes in women's clothes when his troupe is captured by the Nazis.

A carefully nurtured vehicle for Britain's top female impersonator somehow doesn't come off; celluloid both constrains his range and reveals his inadequacies.

w Hugh Leonard d Bob Kellett ph Dick Bush m Peter Greenwell

Danny La Rue, Alfred Marks, Lance Percival, Lally Bowers, Frances de la Tour, Walter Gotell

Our Modern Maidens see Our Dancing Daughters

Our Mother's House *
GB 1967   105m   Metrocolor
MGM / Filmways (Jack Clayton)

When mother dies, seven children, who don't want to go to an orphanage, bury her in the garden. Then their ne'er-do-well father turns up. Unpleasant and rather boring melodrama, too silly to have much dramatic impact.

w Jeremy Brooks, Haya Harareet, *novel* Julian Gloag d Jack Clayton ph Larry Pizer m Georges Delerue

Dirk Bogarde, Margaret Brooks, Pamela Franklin, Mark Lester, Yootha Joyce, Anthony Nicholls

'The children begin to display an alarming variety of accents . . . and when Dirk Bogarde enters, doing a rich Bill Sykes act as the long lost wicked father to a predominantly genteel family, the whole structure collapses.'—*Tom Milne*

Our Relations ***
US 1936   65m   bw
Hal Roach / Stan Laurel Productions

Two sailors entrusted with a diamond ring get mixed up with their long lost and happily married twin brothers.

A fast-moving comedy which contains some of Laurel and Hardy's most polished work as well as being their most satisfying production.

w Richard Connell, Felix Adler, Charles Roger, Jack Jevne, *story* The Money Box by W. W. Jacobs d Harry Lachman ph Rudolph Mate

Stan Laurel, Oliver Hardy, James Finlayson, Alan Hale, Sidney Toler, Daphne Pollard, Iris Adrian, Noel Madison, Ralf Harolde, *Arthur Housman*

Our Town **
US 1940   90m   bw
Principal Artists / Sol Lesser

Birth, life and death in a small New Hampshire community.

One of the main points of the play, the absence of scenery, is abandoned in this screen version, and the graveyard scene has to be presented as a dream, but the film retains the narrator and manages to make points of its own while absorbing the endearing qualities which made the play a classic.

w Thornton Wilder, Frank Craven, Harry Chantlee, *play* Thornton Wilder d Sam Wood ph Bert Glennon m Aaron Copland pd William Cameron Menzies

Frank Craven, William Holden, *Martha Scott, Thomas Mitchell, Fay Bainter, Guy Kibbee, Beulah Bondi*, Stuart Erwin

'You can nearly smell things cooking, and feel the night air.'—*Otis Ferguson*

AAN: best picture; Aaron Copland; Martha Scott

Our Very Own
US 1950   93m   bw
Samuel Goldwyn

A girl is shocked to discover that she is adopted. Another Goldwyn foray into chintzy, middle-class, small-town America, but not a winning example.

w F. Hugh Herbert d David Miller ph Lee Garmes m Victor Young ad Richard Day

Ann Blyth, Farley Granger, Joan Evans, Jane Wyatt, Ann Dvorak, Donald Cook, Natalie Wood, Gus Schilling, Phyllis Kirk

Our Vines Have Tender Grapes*

US 1945 105m bw
MGM (Robert Sisk)

Life in a Norwegian farm community in southern Wisconsin.

Unexceptionable family picture produced in MGM's best manner.

w Dalton Trumbo, *novel* George Victor Martin d Roy Rowland *ph* Robert Surtees *m* Bronislau Kaper

Edward G. Robinson, Margaret O'Brien, James Craig, Agnes Moorehead, Jackie 'Butch' Jenkins, Morris Carnovsky, Frances Gifford, Sara Haden

Our Wife

US 1941 95m bw
Columbia (John M. Stahl)

A composer is romantically torn between a lady scientist and his own ex-wife.

Middling romantic comedy of a kind very familiar at the time.

w P. J. Wolfson, *play* Lillian Day by Lyon Mearson d John M. Stahl *ph* Franz Planer *m* Leo Shuken

Melvyn Douglas, Ruth Hussey, Ellen Drew, Charles Coburn, John Hubbard, Harvey Stephens

Out of Season*

GB 1975 90m Technicolor
EMI / Lorimar

One winter in an English seaside resort, an old love is rekindled.

Restrained sexual fireworks in the old French manner, well enough done with excellent atmosphere but a shade overlong and marred by the need to indulge in modern tricks such as a deliberately ambiguous ending.

w Reuben Bercovitch, Eric Bercovici d *Alan Bridges* ph Arthur Ibbetson *m* John Cameron

Cliff Robertson, Vanessa Redgrave, Susan George, Edward Evans

Out of the Clouds*

GB 1954 88m Eastmancolor
Ealing (Michael Relph, Basil Dearden)

Several personal stories mesh against a background of London airport during a fog.
A dull compendium of stories with a background of documentary detail which is now fascinating because it's so dated.

w John Eldridge, Michael Relph d Michael Relph, Basil Dearden *ph* Paul Beeson *m* Richard Addinsell

Anthony Steel, Robert Beatty, David Knight,

Margo Lorenz, James Robertson Justice, Eunice Gayson, Isabel Dean, Gordon Harker, Bernard Lee, Michael Howard, Marie Lohr, Esme Cannon, Abraham Sofaer

'The film relies considerably on small-time players and marginal incidents; the detail, however, never looks like adding up to a satisfactory whole.'—*Penelope Houston*

Out of the Fog*

US 1941 86m bw
Warner (Henry Blanke)

Gangsters move in to terrorize an innocent Brooklyn family.
Standard exploration of a situation which became routine.

w Robert Rossen, Jerry Wald, Richard Macaulay, *play* The Gentle People by Irwin Shaw d Anatole Litvak *ph* James Wong Howe

Ida Lupino, John Garfield, Thomas Mitchell, Eddie Albert, George Tobias, Aline MacMahon, Jerome Cowan, John Qualen, Leo Gorcey

Out of the Past**

US 1947 97m bw
RKO (Warren Duff)
GB title: *Build My Gallows High*

A private detective is hired by a hoodlum to find his homicidal girl friend; he does, and falls in love with her.

Moody *film noir* with Hollywood imitating French models; plenty of snarling and a death-strewn climax.

w Geoffrey Homes, from his novel Build My Gallows High d *Jacques Tourneur* ph Nicholas Musuraca *m* Roy Webb

Robert Mitchum, Jane Greer, Kirk Douglas, Rhonda Fleming, Richard Webb, Steve Brodie, Virginia Huston, Dickie Moore

'Is this not an outcrop of the national masochism induced by a quite aimless, newly industrialized society proceeding rapidly on its way to nowhere?'—*Richard Winnington*

Out of this World

US 1945 96m bw
Paramount (Sam Coslow)

A Western Union messenger becomes a hit crooner and a national phenomenon.
Very mild comedy with the gimmick that Bing Crosby dubbed the singing.

w Walter de Leon, Arthur Phillips d Hal Walker *ph* Stuart Thompson *m* Victor Young

Eddie Bracken, Veronica Lake, Diana Lynn, Cass Daley, Parkyakarkus, Donald MacBride, Florence Bates, Carmen Cavallero

The Out of Towners*

US 1970　98m　Movielab
Paramount / Jalem (Paul Nathan)

An executive and his wife fly into New York for
an interview, but their encounter with the city is a
mounting series of traumatic disasters.
A love-hate relationship with a city
demonstrated by a resident is something of an in-
joke and becomes increasingly hysterical and
unsympathetic, but there are bright moments in
this company.

w Neil Simon　d Arthur Hiller　ph Andrew
Laszlo　m Quincy Jones

Jack Lemmon, Sandy Dennis

Outback*

Australia 1970　109m　Technicolor
NIT / Group W (George Willoughby)

A young teacher becomes involved in the
rougher side of life in a remote Australian village.
A convincingly brutal picture of a community
whose interests range from homosexuality to a
bloody kangaroo hunt.

w Evan Jones, novel Wake in Fright by Kenneth
Cook　d Ted Kotcheff ph Brian West　m John
Scott

Gary Bond, Donald Pleasence, Chips Rafferty

An Outcast of the Islands**

GB 1951　102m　bw
London Films (Carol Reed)

A shiftless trader finds a secret Far Eastern
trading post where he can be happy – but even
here he becomes an outcast.
An interesting but not wholly successful attempt
to dramatize a complex character study. It looks
great and is well acted.

w William Fairchild, novel Joseph Conrad
d Carol Reed ph John Wilcox m Brian Easdale

Trevor Howard, Ralph Richardson, Kerima,
Robert Morley, Wendy Hiller, George
Coulouris, Frederick Valk, Wilfrid Hyde White,
Betty Ann Davies

'The script is so overwhelmed by the narrative
itself that the characters and relationships fail to
crystallize . . . while the handling is often
intelligent, ingenious, and has its effective
moments, no real conception emerges.'—Gavin
Lambert

The Outcasts of Poker Flat

US 1937　68m　bw
RKO (Robert Sisk)

Four undesirables are run out of town and stuck
in a mountain cabin during a snowstorm.

Overstretched anecdote with a predictably
downbeat finale and not much action.

w John Twist, Harry Segall, story Bret Harte
d Christy Cabanne ph Rudolph Maté

Preston Foster, Jean Muir, Van Heflin

The Outcasts of Poker Flat

US 1952　80m　bw
TCF (Julian Blaustein)

Good-looking but equally undramatic remake of
the above.

w Edmund H. North d Joseph M. Newman
ph Joseph La Shelle m Hugo Friedhofer

Dale Robertson, Anne Baxter, Cameron
Mitchell, Miriam Hopkins

The Outfit

US 1973　103m　Metrocolor
MGM (Carter de Haven)

A criminal just out of prison finds himself in
danger from the Syndicate.
Unattractive rehash of Point Blank with much
gratuitous violence.

wd John Flynn, novel Richard Stark ph Bruce
Surtees m Jerry Fielding

Robert Duvall, Karen Black, Robert Ryan, Joe
Don Baker, Timothy Carey, Richard Jaeckel,
Sheree North, Marie Windsor, Jane Greer,
Elisha Cook Jnr

'A nice profusion of Hollywood character
actors makes up for the overall lack of drive.'—
Sight and Sound

The Outlaw*

US 1943　126m　bw
Howard Hughes

Billy the Kid, Doc Holliday and Pat Garrett
meet up at a way station and quarrel over a half-
breed girl.
Half-baked western with much pretentious chat
and the main interest squarely focused on the
bosom of the producer's new discovery. This
aspect kept censorship ballyhoo going for six
years before the film was finally released in
truncated form, and audiences found it not worth
the wait, though it does look good.

w Jules Furthman d Howard Hughes ph Gregg
Toland md Victor Young

Jack Beutel, Jane Russell, Thomas Mitchell,
Walter Huston

Outlaw Blues

US 1977　101m　Technicolor
Warner / Fred Weintraub – Paul Heller (Steve
　Tisch)

An ex-con finds that a singing star has stolen his song.
Fashionable comedy-melodrama with no great entertainment value despite action scenes towards the end.

w B. W. L. Norton d Richard T. Heffron ph Jules Brenner m Charles Bernstein

Peter Fonda, Susan Saint James, John Crawford, James Callahan, Michael Lerner

The Outlaw Josey Wales*
US 1976 135m De Luxe Panavision
Warner (Robert Daley)

A westerner gradually avenges the death of his wife at the hands of bandits.
Bloodthirsty actioner in the star's usual mould; likely to prove unintentionally funny for hardened addicts.

w Phil Kaufman, Sonia Chernus, *novel* Gone to Texas by Forrest Carter d Clint Eastwood ph Bruce Surtees m Jerry Fielding

Clint Eastwood, Chief Dan George, Sondra Locke, John Vernon, Bill McKinney

AAN: Jerry Fielding

Outpost in Morocco
US 1949 92m bw
Joseph N. Ermolieff

A romantic Foreign Legion officer falls for the daughter of an enemy Arab.
Despite authentic locations and the co-operation of the Legion this is a stolid piece of work, too dull even for children's matinees.

w Charles Grayson, Paul de St Columbe d Robert Florey ph Lucien Andriot

George Raft, Akim Tamiroff, Marie Windsor, John Litel, Eduard Franz

Outrage
US 1950 75m bw
Filmmakers (Collier Young)

A girl who has been raped is almost unhinged by the experience.
Well-meaning low-budgeter, thin in entertainment value.

w Ida Lupino, Collier Young, Marvin Wald d Ida Lupino ph Archie Stout m Paul Sawtell md Constantin Bakaleinikoff pd Harry Horner

Mala Powers, Tod Andrews, Robert Clarke, Raymond Bond, Lilian Hamilton

'An unconvincing mixture of sensationalism, sentiment and half-baked sociology.'—*MFB*

The Outrage*
US 1964 97m bw Panavision
MGM / Harvest / February / Ritt / Kayos (A. Ronald Lubin)

Conflicting views of a western murder.
Wildly ineffective remake of *Rashomon*, with everyone strangely overacting and little sense of the west as it is normally depicted.

w Michael Kanin d Martin Ritt ph James Wong Howe m Alex North

Paul Newman, Edward G. Robinson, Laurence Harvey, Claire Bloom, William Shatner, Albert Salmi

The Outriders
US 1950 93m Technicolor
MGM (Richard Goldstone)

Three Confederate soldiers escape from a yankee prison camp.
Competent star western with solid production values.

w Irving Ravetch d Roy Rowland ph Charles Schoenbaum m André Previn

Joel McCrea, Arlene Dahl, Barry Sullivan, Claude Jarman Jnr, Ramon Novarro

The Outsider
US 1961 108m bw
U-I (Sy Bartlett)

Ira Hayes, a simple Red Indian, becomes a war hero but cannot reconcile himself to living in a white society.
Prolonged biopic which proves a shade too much for an eager star; it's all earnest and mildly interesting but not cinematically compulsive.

w Stewart Stern d Delbert Mann ph Joseph La Shelle m Leonard Rosenman

Tony Curtis, James Franciscus, Bruce Bennett, Gregory Walcott, Vivian Nathan, Edmund Hashim, Stanley Adams

Outward Bound*
US 1930 82m bw
Warner

Passengers on a strange liner discover that they are all dead and heading for purgatory.
Early sound version of a popular twenties play which does not translate too well to cinematic forms and now seems very dated apart from a couple of performances; remade as *Between Two Worlds* (qv).

w J. Grubb Alexander, *play* Sutton Vane d Robert Milton ph Hal Mohr

Leslie Howard, Douglas Fairbanks Jnr, Alec B. Francis, Helen Chandler, Beryl Mercer, Alison Skipworth, Montagu Love, Dudley Digges

Over the Moon
GB 1937   78m   Technicolor
London Films (Alexander Korda)

A poor girl comes into a fortune but this does not help her romance with a proud young doctor.
Insubstantial comedy which turns itself into a European travelogue before petering out.

w Anthony Pelissier, Arthur Wimperis, Alec Coppel d Thornton Freeland ph Harry Stradling m Mischa Spoliansky

Merle Oberon, Rex Harrison, Ursula Jeans, Robert Douglas, Louis Borell, Zena Dare, Peter Haddon, David Tree

Over Twenty-One
US 1945   102m   bw
Columbia (Sidney Buchman)

A famous lady screenwriter copes with wartime domestic problems while her husband is off at the war.
Thin star comedy based on Ruth Gordon's play about her own predicament; not for the wider audience, and not very good anyway.

w Sidney Buchman, play Ruth Gordon d Alexander Hall ph Rudolph Maté m Marlin Skiles

Irene Dunne, Alexander Knox, Charles Coburn, Jeff Donnell, Lee Patrick, Phil Brown, Cora Witherspoon

The Overlanders**
Australia 1946   91m   bw
Ealing

In 1943 a drover saves a thousand head of cattle from the Japanese by taking them two thousand miles across country.
Attractive, easy-going semi-western, the first and best of several films made by Ealing Studios in Australia.

wd Harry Watt ph Osmond Borradaile

Chips Rafferty, John Heyward, Daphne Campbell

Overlord*
GB 1975   83m   bw
EMI / Jowsend (James Quinn)

An eighteen-year-old is called up in early 1944 and killed in the D-Day landings.
Semi-documentary recreating a time in history (with much aid from newsreels) but making no discernible point. Interesting, though.

w Stuart Cooper, Christopher Hudson d Stuart Cooper ph John Alcott m Paul Glass

Brian Stirner, Davyd Harries, Nicholas Ball, Julie Neesam

Owd Bob*
GB 1938   78m   bw
GFD / Gainsborough (Edward Black)
US title: To the Victor

A Cumberland farmer's faithful dog is accused of killing sheep.
Sentimental yarn with good location backgrounds; the plot was later reused as Thunder in the Valley.

w Michael Hogan, J. B. Williams, novel Alfred Olivant d Robert Stevenson ph Jack Cox md Louis Levy

Will Fyffe, John Loder, Margaret Lockwood, Moore Marriott, Graham Moffatt, Wilfred Walter, Elliot Mason

The Owl and the Pussycat*
US 1970   96m   Eastmancolor
Panavision
Columbia / Rastar (Ray Stark)

A bookstore assistant reports a fellow tenant for prostitution, and when she is evicted she moves in with him.
Wacky, bawdy double act which starts promisingly but outstays its welcome. A solid step forward in permissiveness, with kinky behaviour as well as four-letter words.

w Buck Henry, play Bill Manhoff d Herbert Ross ph Harry Stradling, Andrew Laszlo m Richard Halligan

Barbra Streisand, George Segal, Robert Klein, Allen Garfield

'If computers ever turn out romantic comedies, the results will look like this.'—Stanley Kauffmann

The Ox-Bow Incident**
US 1943   75m   bw
TCF (Lamar Trotti)
GB title: Strange Incident

A cowboy is unable to prevent three wandering travellers being unjustly lynched for murder.
Stark lynch law parable, beautifully made but very depressing.

w Lamar Trotti, novel Walter Van Tilburg Clark d William Wellman ph Arthur Miller m Cyril Mockridge

Henry Fonda, Henry Morgan, Jane Darwell, Anthony Quinn, Dana Andrews, Mary Beth Hughes, William Eythe, Harry Davenport, Frank Conroy

'Realism that is as sharp and cold as a knife.'—Frank S. Nugent, New York Times

AAN: best picture

P

P.J.
US 1967   109m   Techniscope
Universal (Edward J. Montagne)
GB title: *New Face in Hell*

A down-at-heel private eye takes a job as
bodyguard to a boorish businessman.
Routine thick-ear with a predictable turnabout
plot.

w Philip Reisman Jnr   *d* John Guillermin
ph Loyal Griggs   *m* Neal Hefti

George Peppard, Gayle Hunnicutt, Raymond
Burr, Susan St James, Coleen Gray, Jason
Evers, Wilfrid Hyde White, Severn Darden
  'Enough action to keep you from noticing that
the plot doesn't make any sense.'—*Judith Crist*

Pacific Blackout
US 1942   76m   bw
Paramount (Sol C. Siegel)

An inventor escapes from jail and proves his
innocence during a practice air raid blackout.
Minor melo which proved profitably topical,
being released shortly after the Japanese attack
on Pearl Harbor.

w Lester Cole, W. P. Lipscomb   *d* Ralph
Murphy   *ph* Theodor Sparkuhl

Robert Preston, Martha O'Driscoll, Philip
Merivale, Eva Gabor, Louis Jean Heydt,
Thurston Hall

Pacific Destiny
GB 1956   97m   Eastmancolor
  Cinemascope
James Lawrie

Experiences of a British colonial servant in the
South Seas.
Pleasant episodic drama which needed a firmer
hand all round.

w Richard Mason, *autobiography* A Pattern of
Islands by Sir Arthur Grimble   *d* Wolf Rilla
ph Martin Curtis   *m* James Bernard

Denholm Elliott, Susan Stephen, Michael
Hordern

Pack Up Your Troubles*
US 1931   68m   bw
Hal Roach

Two World War I veterans try to look after their
late pal's orphan daughter.
Patchy comedy vehicle in which too many gags
are not fully thought out or timed.

w H. M. Walker   *d* George Marshall, Ray
McCarey   *ph* Art Lloyd

Stan Laurel, Oliver Hardy, Donald Dillaway,
Mary Carr, Charles Middleton, Dick Cramer,
James Finlayson, Tom Kennedy, Billy Gilbert

The Pad, and How to Use It*
US 1966   86m   Technicolor
Universal (Ross Hunter)

A shy young man has his first date.
Pleasant, odd little comedy apparently made in
emulation of *The Knack*.

w Thomas C. Ryan, Benn Starr, *play* The
Private Ear by Peter Shaffer   *d* Brian C. Hutton
ph Ellsworth Fredericks   *m* Russ Garcia

Brian Bedford, James Farentino, Julie Sommars,
Edy Williams, Nick Navarro

Paddy the Next Best Thing
US 1933   75m   bw
Fox

Adventures of an Irish tomboy in New York.
Modest star comedy from a popular play.

w Edwin Burke, *play* Gertrude Page   *d* Harry
Lachman   *ph* John Seitz

Janet Gaynor, Warner Baxter, Walter Connolly,
Harvey Stephens, Margaret Lindsay

Padre Padrone**
Italy 1977   113m   Eastmancolor
Radiotelevisione Italia (Tonino Paoletti)
aka: *Father and Master*

The author recounts how he grew up with a
violent and tyrannical father.
A vivid chunk of autobiography with food for
thought on several levels, and a clever piece of
film-making to boot.

wd Paolo Taviani, Vittorio Taviani,
book Gavino Ledda   *ph* Mario Masini
md Egisto Macchi

Omero Antonutti, Saverio Marconi, Marcella
Michelangeli

Pagan Love Song
US 1950   76m   Technicolor
MGM (Arthur Freed)

An American schoolteacher marries a Tahitian girl.
Very mild musical potboiler using familiar talents.

w Robert Nathan, Jerry Davis d Robert Alton ph Charles Rosher m Harry Warren ly Arthur Freed

Esther Williams, Howard Keel, Rita Moreno, Minna Gombell

Page Miss Glory*
US 1935   90m   bw
Warner / Cosmopolitan

A con man wins a beauty contest with a composite photograph of a non-existent girl. Amusing comedy-musical, unjustly forgotten.

w Delmer Daves, Robert Lord, play Joseph Schrank, Philip Dunning d Mervyn Le Roy ph George Folsey m/ly Harry Warren, Al Dubin

Dick Powell, Marion Davies, Frank McHugh, Pat O'Brien, Mary Astor, Lyle Talbot, Patsy Kelly, Allen Jenkins, Barton MacLane

Paid*
US 1930   80m   bw
MGM
GB title: *Within the Law*

A woman sent to prison unjustly plots revenge on those responsible.
Reliable melodrama with the heroine eventually forgiving and forgetting.

w Charles MacArthur, Lucien Hubbard, *play* Within the Law by Bayard Veiller d Sam Wood ph Charles Rosher

Joan Crawford, Kent Douglass, Robert Armstrong, Marie Prévost, John Miljan, Polly Moran

Paid in Full
US 1950   105m   bw
Paramount / Hal B. Wallis

A woman is responsible for the death of her sister's child, and becomes pregnant herself in the knowledge that giving birth will be fatal to her.
Stolid, contrived tearjerker.

w Robert Blees, Charles Schnee d William Dieterle ph Leo Tover m Victor Young

Lizabeth Scott, Diana Lynn, Robert Cummings, Eve Arden, Ray Collins, Frank McHugh, Stanley Ridges, Louis Jean Heydt

Paint Your Wagon*
US 1969   164m   Technicolor   Panavision 70
Paramount / Alan Jay Lerner (Tom Shaw)

During the California Gold Rush, two prospectors set up a Mormon menage with the same wife.
Good-looking but uncinematic and monumentally long version of an old musical with a new plot and not much dancing. There are minor pleasures, but it really shouldn't have been allowed.

w Paddy Chayevsky, *musical play* Alan Jay Lerner, Frederick Loewe d Joshua Logan ph William A. Fraker md Nelson Riddle pd John Truscott

Lee Marvin, Clint Eastwood, Jean Seberg, Harve Presnell, Ray Walston
'One of those big movies in which the themes are undersized and the elements are juggled around until nothing fits together right and even the good bits of the original show you started with are shot to hell.'—*Pauline Kael*

AAN: Nelson Riddle

The Painted Veil*
US 1934   84m   bw
MGM

In China, a doctor's wife gives up her lover to join her husband fighting an epidemic.
Soulful melodrama which seemed much more acceptable in this version than in the summer stock style remake *The Seventh Sin*.

w John Meehan, Salka Viertel, Edith Fitzgerald, *novel* W. Somerset Maugham d Richard Boleslawski ph William Daniels

Greta Garbo, George Brent, Herbert Marshall, Warner Oland, Jean Hersholt

Painting the Clouds with Sunshine
US 1951   86m   Technicolor
Warner (William Jacobs)

Three singing sisters go to Las Vegas in search of rich husbands.
Yet another revamp of the original *Gold Diggers* (qv), and not a very lively one.

w Henry Clark, Roland Kibbee, Peter Milne d David Butler ph Wilfred Cline

Virginia Mayo, Gene Nelson, Dennis Morgan, S. Z. Sakall, Lucille Norman, Tom Conway

Paisà*
Italy 1946   115m   bw
Foreign Film Productions / OFI

Six episodes in the Battle of Italy between 1943 and 1945.

More important historically than dramatically, *Paisà* was always a somewhat disappointing experience, especially as the earlier episodes are stronger than the later ones. Like *Open City*, it was partly improvised and had a gritty documentary quality.

w Federico Fellini, Roberto Rossellini *d* Roberto Rossellini *ph* Otello Martelli *m* Renzo Rossellini

William Tubbs, Gar Moore, Maria Michi and non-professionals

AAN: script

The Pajama Game ***
US 1957   101m   Warnercolor
Warner / George Abbott

Workers in a pajama factory demand a pay rise, but their lady negotiator falls for the new boss. Brilliantly conceived musical on an unlikely subject, effectively concealing its Broadway origins and becoming an expert, fast-moving, hard-hitting piece of modern musical cinema.

w George Abbott, Richard Bissell, book Seven and a Half Cents by Richard Bissell *d* Stanley Donen, *ph* Harry Stradling *songs Richard Adler, Jerry Ross ch Bob Fosse*

Doris Day, John Raitt, *Eddie Foy Jnr*, Reta Shaw, Carol Haney

Pal Joey **
US 1957   109m   Technicolor
Columbia / Essex–Sidney (Fred Kohlmar)

The rise of a nightclub entertainer who is also a heel.
Smart musical which begins very brightly indeed but slides off alarmingly into conventional sentiment.

w Dorothy Kingsley, *play* John O'Hara, *stories* John O'Hara *d* George Sidney *ph* Harold Lipstein *songs Richard Rodgers, Lorenz Hart*

Frank Sinatra, Rita Hayworth, Kim Novak, Bobby Sherwood, Hank Henry, Elizabeth Patterson, Barbara Nichols

The Paleface ***
US 1948   91m   Technicolor
Paramount (Robert L. Welch)

Calamity Jane undertakes an undercover mission against desperadoes, and marries a timid dentist as a cover.
Splendid wagon train comedy western with the stars in excellent form. Sequel, *Son of Paleface* (qv); remake, *The Shakiest Gun in the West* (1968).

w Edmund Hartman, Frank Tashlin d Norman Z. McLeod *ph* Ray Rennahan *m* Victor Young

Bob Hope, Jane Russell, Robert Armstrong, Iris Adrian, Robert Watson, Jack Searle, Joe Vitale, Clem Bevans, Charles Trowbridge

AA: song 'Buttons and Bows' (*m* Jay Livingston, *ly* Ray Evans)

The Palm Beach Story ***
US 1942   88m   bw
Paramount (Paul Jones)

The wife of a penurious engineer takes off for Florida to set her sights on a millionaire. Flighty comedy, inconsequential in itself, but decorated with scenes, characters and zany touches typical of its creator, here at his most brilliant if uncontrolled.

wd Preston Sturges ph Victor Milner

Claudette Colbert, Joel McCrea, Rudy Vallee, Mary Astor, Sig Arno, Robert Warwick, Torben Meyer, Jimmy Conlin, William Demarest, Jack Norton, Robert Greig, Roscoe Ates, Chester Conklin, Franklin Pangborn, Alan Bridge, *Robert Dudley*

'Surprises and delights as though nothing of the kind had been known before . . . farce and tenderness are combined without a fault.'— *William Whitebait*

Palm Springs Weekend
US 1963   100m   Technicolor
Warner (Michael Hoey)

Various holidaymakers at Palm Springs get romantically involved.
Youth-oriented farce, better produced than most but basically a depressing experience.

w Earl Hanmer Jnr *d* Norman Taurog *ph* Harold Lipstein *m* Frank Perkins

Troy Donahue, Ty Hardin, Connie Stevens, Stefanie Powers, Robert Conrad, Jack Weston, Andrew Duggan

Palmy Days
US 1932   77m   bw
Samuel Goldwyn

Shady fortune tellers find a willing stooge. Dated star comedy.

w Eddie Cantor, Mornie Ryskind, David Greenman *d* A. Edward Sutherland *ph* Gregg Toland *ch* Busby Berkeley

Eddie Cantor, Charlotte Greenwood, Charles Middleton, George Raft, Walter Catlett

Pan-Americana *
US 1945   85m   bw
RKO (Sid Rogell)

A New York magazine sends editors around South America to choose the prettiest girl of each nation.
Slick, mindless musical with good numbers.

w Laurence Kimble d John H. Auer ph Frank Redman md Constantin Bakaleinikoff ch Charles O'Curran

Audrey Long, Philip Terry, Robert Benchley, Eve Arden, Ernest Truex, Marc Cramer

Panama Hattie
US 1942   79m   bw
MGM (Arthur Freed)

A showgirl in Panama helps to capture Nazis.
Dim film version of a Broadway musical, stripped of most of its music and more like a *Maisie* comedy.

w Jack McGowan, Wilkie Mahoney, *musical play* Herbert Fields, B. G. De Sylva, Cole Porter d Norman Z. McLeod ph George Folsey md George Stoll

Ann Sothern, Dan Dailey, Red Skelton, Marsha Hunt, Rags Ragland, Virginia O'Brien, Alan Mowbray, Ben Blue, Carl Esmond

Pancho Villa
Spain 1972   93m   Technicolor
Granada Films (Bernard Gordon)

In 1916 Villa is rescued from execution and starts a reign of terror.
Mexican banditry played half for laughs and half for real; not a successful compromise.

w Julian Halevy d Eugenio Martin ph Allejandro Ulloa m Anton Garcia-Abril

Telly Savalas, Clint Walker, Chuck Connors

Pandora and the Flying Dutchman*
GB 1950   122m   Technicolor
Romulus (Albert Lewin)

A cold but beautiful American woman in Spain falls for a mystery man who turns out to be a ghostly sea captain; she dies so as to be with him.
Pretentious, humourless, totally unpersuasive fantasy of the kind much better done in *Portrait of Jennie*. The writer-director wears Omar Khayyam's moving finger to the bone, and the actors look thoroughly unhappy; even the colour is a bit thick.

wd Albert Lewin ph Jack Cardiff m Alan Rawsthorne ad John Bryan

James Mason, Ava Gardner, Harold Warrender, Nigel Patrick, Sheila Sim, Mario Cabre, John Laurie, Pamela Kellino, Marius Goring
'Conspicuous in its confident assumption of scholarship and its utter poverty of imagination and taste.'—C. A. Lejeune

'It might have been enjoyably silly but for Lewin's striving to be classy and an air of third-rate decadence that hangs about it. This is an Anglo-American co-production and one of the occasions, I think, when we might be generous and let Hollywood have all the credit.'—Richard Winnington

Pandora's Box*
Germany 1929   97m approx (24 fps)   bw silent
Nero Film
original title: *Die Büchse der Pandora*
aka: *Lulu*

A woman murders her lover, becomes a prostitute, and is murdered in London by Jack the Ripper.
Oddball fantasy on a few favourite German themes: very watchable, and benefiting from its star performance.

w G. W. Pabst, Laszlo Wajda, *plays* Erdgeist and Pandora's Box by Franz Wedekind d G. W. Pabst ph Günther Krampf

Louise Brooks, Fritz Kortner, Franz Lederer, Gustav Diessl
† Remade in Austria in 1962 as *No Orchids for Lulu*, with Nadja Tiller.

The Panic in Needle Park
US 1971   110m   De Luxe
Gadd Productions (Dominick Dunne)

Drug addiction problems in a New York ghetto.
Vivid, intimate but overlong and unsympathetic account of a junkie and his mistress.

w Joan Didion, John Gregory Dunne, *novel* James Mills d Jerry Schatzberg ph Adam Holender m none

Al Pacino, Kitty Winn, Adam Vint, Richard Bright, Kiel Martin

Panic in the Streets***
US 1950   96m   bw
TCF (Sol C. Siegel)

On the New Orleans waterfront, public health officials seek a carrier of bubonic plague.
Semi-documentary suspenser in the *Naked City* manner; location Hollywood at its best.

w Richard Murphy, Edward and Edna Anhalt d Elia Kazan ph Joe MacDonald m Alfred Newman

Richard Widmark, Jack Palance, Paul Douglas, Barbara Bel Geddes, Zero Mostel
'A model of what an action story should be . . . every department is admirably handled.'—Richard Mallett, Punch

AAN: original story (Edward and Edna Anhalt)

Panic in Year Zero*

US 1962 93m bw Cinemascope
AIP (Lou Rusoff, Arnold Houghland)

Adventures of a family on a fishing trip in the mountains when Los Angeles is blasted by a nuclear attack.

Mildly interesting catalogue of predictable events—thugs, looting, fear of fall-out—in a simple-minded script finishing with a hopeful meeting of the UN.

w Jay Simms, John Morton d Ray Milland
ph Gil Warrenton m Les Baxter

Ray Milland, Jean Hagen, Frankie Avalon, Joan Freeman

Panique*

France 1946 98m bw
Filmsonor

A respectable man knows who committed a murder, and the murderer cunningly swings the blame onto him.

Careful suspenser with a twist ending.

w Charles Spaak, Julien Duvivier, novel Georges Simenon d Julien Duvivier ph Nicolas Hayer

Michel Simon, Viviane Romance, Paul Bernard

Papa's Delicate Condition

US 1963 98m Technicolor
Paramount / Amro (Jack Rose)

At the turn of the century in a small Texas town an amiable family man gets into scrapes when he drinks too much.

Basically pleasing period comedy which suffers from slow, stiff treatment.

w Jack Rose, book Corinne Griffith d George Marshall ph Loyal Griggs m Joseph J. Lilley

Jackie Gleason, Glynis Johns, Charles Ruggles, Charles Lane, Laurel Goodwin, Juanita Moore, Elisha Cook Jnr, Murray Hamilton

AA: song 'Call Me Irresponsible' (m James Van Heusen, ly Sammy Cahn)

The Paper Chase*

US 1973 111m De Luxe Panavision
TCF (Robert C. Thompson, Rodrick Paul)

A Harvard law graduate falls in love with the divorced daughter of his tetchiest professor. A thoughtful analysis of attitudes to learning turns into just another youth movie.

wd James Bridges, novel John Jay Osborn Jnr
ph Gordon Willis m John Williams

Timothy Bottoms, Lindsay Wagner, John Houseman, Graham Bickel

'A slightly unfocused account of conformism and milk-mild rebellion on the campus.'—Sight and Sound

AA: John Houseman
AAN: James Bridges (as writer)

Paper Moon**

US 1973 103m bw
Paramount / Saticoy (Peter Bogdanovich)

In the American midwest in the thirties, a bible salesman and a plain little girl make a great con team.

Unusual but overrated comedy, imperfectly adapted from a very funny book, with careful but disappointing period sense and photography. A lot more style and gloss was required.

w Alvin Sargent, novel Addie Pray by Joe David Brown d Peter Bogdanovich ph Laszlo Kovacs m popular songs and recordings

Ryan O'Neal, Tatum O'Neal, Madeleine Kahn, John Hillerman

'I've rarely seen a film that looked so unlike what it was about.'—Stanley Kauffmann

'At its best the film is only mildly amusing, and I'm not sure I could recall a few undeniable highlights if pressed on the point.'—Gary Arnold

AA: Tatum O'Neal
AAN: Alvin Sargent, Madeleine Kahn

Paper Tiger

GB 1975 99m Technicolor
Maclean and Co (Euan Lloyd)

An ageing Englishman becomes tutor to the son of the Japanese ambassador in a Pacific state, and finds he has to live his heroic fantasies in reality.

Uneasy adventure comedy drama which might, given more skilled handling, have been much better than it is.

w Jack Davies d Ken Annakin ph John Cabrera m Roy Budd

David Niven, Toshiro Mifune, Hardy Kruger, Ando, Ivan Desny, Irene Tsu, Miiko Taka, Ronald Fraser, Jeff Corey

'Makes no demands, except on 99 minutes of our time.'—Michael Billington, Illustrated London News

Papillon*

US 1973 150m Technicolor Panavision
Papillon Partnership / Corona / General Production Co (Robert Dorfmann)

Filmed autobiography of life on Devil's Island. Overlong and rather dreary film of a bestseller; it determinedly rubs the audience's nose in ordure from the start, and the final successful escape is one try too many.

w Dalton Trumbo, Lorenzo Semple Jnr, book

Henri Charrière *d* Franklin Schaffner *ph* Fred Koenekamp *m* Jerry Goldsmith

Steve McQueen, Dustin Hoffman, Don Gordon, Anthony Zerbe, George Coulouris, Woodrow Parfrey

'A 2½-hour epic trampling the corn growing round the theme of man's inhumanity to man.'— *Sight and Sound*

'Papillon offers torture as entertainment but winds up making entertainment a form of torture . . . a tournament of brutality unrelieved by imagination.'—*Paul D. Zimmermann*

'So overloaded with details that the stars are almost lost in exposition, repetition and unfocused drama.'—*Judith Crist, 1977*

AAN: Jerry Goldsmith

The Paradine Case**

US 1947   115m   bw
Selznick

A barrister falls in love with his client, a murder suspect who, it turns out, is actually guilty. A stodgy and old-fashioned script is given gleaming treatment; this and the acting make it seem better thirty years later than it did on release.

w David O. Selznick, *novel* Robert Hichens *d Alfred Hitchcock ph* Lee Garmes *m* Franz Waxman

Gregory Peck, *Alida Valli*, Ann Todd, Louis Jourdan, *Charles Laughton*, Charles Coburn, Ethel Barrymore, Leo G. Carroll

'This is the wordiest script since the death of Edmund Burke.'—*James Agee*

'The characters and their problems don't make much imprint on a viewer; if you can't remember whether you've seen the picture or not, chances are you did and forgot it.'—*New Yorker, 1976*

AAN: Ethel Barrymore

Paradise Alley

US 1978   107m   Technicolor
Universal / Force Ten (John F. Roach, Ronald A. Suppa)

The adventures of three wrestling brothers in New York's Hell's Kitchen during the forties. Fashionable update of the *City for Conquest* school, not in itself very interesting despite amusing bits.

wd Sylvester Stallone *ph* Laszlo Kovacs *m* Bill Conti *pd* John W. Corso

Sylvester Stallone, Kevin Conway, Anne Archer, Joe Spinell, Armand Assante, Lee Canalito

The Parallax View*

US 1974   102m   Technicolor   Panavision
Paramount / Gus / Harbour / Doubleday

Witnesses to a political assassination are systematically killed, despite the efforts of a crusading journalist.
Stylish, persuasive political thriller with a downbeat ending; the villains win.

w David Giler, Lorenzo Semple Jnr, *novel* Loren Singer *d* Alan J. Pakula *ph* Gordon Willis *m* Michael Small

Warren Beatty, Paula Prentiss, William Daniels, Hume Cronyn, Walter McGinn

Paramount on Parade*

US 1930   102m   bw   (Technicolor sequence)
Paramount (Elsie Janis)

A revue featuring Paramount contract stars. A ragged affair by any standard, but worth a look for a couple of Chevalier's numbers.

w various *d* Dorothy Arzner, Otto Brower, Edmund Goulding, Victor Heerman, Edwin H. Knopf, Rowland V. Lee, Ernst Lubitsch, Lothar Mendes, Victor Schertzinger, Edward Sutherland, Frank Tuttle *ph* Harry Fischbeck, Victor Milner *m* various

Richard Arlen, Jean Arthur, George Bancroft, Clara Bow, Nancy Carroll, Ruth Chatterton, Maurice Chevalier, Gary Cooper, Leon Errol, Kay Francis, Harry Green, Mitzi Green, Dennis King, Fredric March, Nino Martini, Jack Oakie, Charles 'Buddy' Rogers, Lillian Roth, Fay Wray, Clive Brook, Warner Oland, Eugene Pallette, William Powell

Paranoiac*

GB 1963   80m   bw   Cinemascope
U-I / Hammer (Anthony Hinds)

An heiress is saved from a suicide attempt by a young man claiming to be her dead brother. A complex maze of disguise, mistaken identity, family curses and revelations of something nasty in the woodshed, out of *Psycho* by *Taste of Fear*. Not very good in itself, but interesting in its borrowings.

w Jimmy Sangster *d* Freddie Francis *ph* Arthur Grant *m* Elisabeth Lutyens

Oliver Reed, Janette Scott, Alexander Davion, Sheila Burrell, Liliane Brousse, Maurice Denham, John Bonney

Les Parapluies de Cherbourg**

France / West Germany 1964   92m
Eastmancolor
Parc / Madeleine / Beta
aka: *The Umbrellas of Cherbourg*

A shopgirl loves a gas station attendant. He goes on military service; she finds she is pregnant and marries for security. Years later they meet briefly by accident.

Unexpected, charming, pretty successful screen operetta with only sung dialogue. Careful acting and exquisite use of colour and camera movement paste over the thinner sections of the plot.

wd Jacques Demy ph Jean Rabier m Michel Legrand ad Bernard Evein

Catherine Deneuve, *Anne Vernon*, Nino Castelnuovo

'Poetic neo-realism.'—*Georges Sadoul*

AAN: script

Pardners

US 1956 88m Technicolor Vistavision
Paramount (Paul Jones)

An incompetent idiot goes west and accidentally cleans up the town.

Stiff western star burlesque, a remake of *Rhythm on the Range.*

w Sidney Sheldon *d* Norman Taurog *ph* Daniel Fapp *songs* Sammy Cahn, Jimmy Van Heusen

Dean Martin, Jerry Lewis, Agnes Moorehead, Lori Nelson, John Baragrey, Jeff Morrow, Lon Chaney Jnr

Pardon My Past*

US 1945 88m bw
Columbia

A man unwittingly takes on the problems of his double, a shady playboy.

Amusing mistaken identity comedy.

w Earl Felton, Karl Kamb *d* Leslie Fenton *ph* Russell Metty

Fred MacMurray, Marguerite Chapman, Akim Tamiroff, Rita Johnson, William Demarest, Harry Davenport

Pardon Us*

US 1931 55m bw
Hal Roach
aka: *Jailbirds*

Two zany bootleggers find themselves in and out of prison.

Patchy star comedy which finds the boys on the whole not in quite their best form.

w H. M. Walker *d* James Parrott *ph* Jack Stevens

Stan Laurel, Oliver Hardy, Wilfred Lucas, Walter Long, James Finlayson

The Parent Trap*

US 1961 129m Technicolor
Walt Disney (George Golitzen)

Twin daughters of separated parents determine to bring the family together again.

Quite bright but awesomely extended juvenile romp.

wd David Swift, *novel* Das Doppelte Lottchen by Erich Kastner *ph* Lucien Ballard *m* Paul Smith

Hayley Mills, Maureen O'Hara, Brian Keith, Charles Ruggles, Leo G. Carroll, Una Merkel, Joanna Barnes, Cathleen Nesbitt, Ruth McDevitt, Nancy Kulp

Les Parents Terribles**

France 1948 98m bw
Sirius

Life with a family in which the children are as neurotic as the parents.

Alternately hilarious and tragic, this is a fascinating two-set piece of filmed theatre, with every performance a pleasure.

wd Jean Cocteau from his play *ph* Michel Kelber *m* Georges Auric *ad* Christian Bérard, Guy de Gastyne

Jean Marais, Yvonne de Bray, Gabrielle Dorziat, Marcel André, Josette Day
† In 1953 a curious and unsatisfactory British version was made by Charles Frank under the title *Intimate Relations*, with Marian Spencer, Russell Enoch, Ruth Dunning, Harold Warrender and Elsy Albiin.

Paris Blues*

US 1961 98m Technicolor
UA / Pennebaker / Diane / Jason / Monica / Monmouth (Sam Shaw)

Two jazz musicians have romantic problems in Paris.

Semi-serious mini-drama with emphasis on the music; one is not quite sure what the actors thought they were up to.

w Jack Sher, Irene Kamp, Walter Bernstein, *novel* Harold Flender *d* Martin Ritt *ph* Christian Matras *m* Duke Ellington

Paul Newman, Joanne Woodward, Sidney Poitier, Louis Armstrong, Diahann Carroll, Serge Reggiani, Barbara Laage

AAN: Duke Ellington

Paris Calling

US 1941 95m bw
Universal / Charles K. Feldman

When the Nazis invade Paris, a woman discovers that her husband is a traitor.

Totally predictable flagwaver.

w Benjamin Glazer, Charles Kaufmann
d Edwin L. Marin ph Milton Krasner
m Richard Hageman

Elisabeth Bergner, Basil Rathbone, Randolph
Scott, Gale Sondergaard, Lee J. Cobb, Eduardo
Ciannelli, Charles Arnt

Paris Holiday*
US 1957 101m Technirama
UA / Tolda (Bob Hope)

An American comedian meets a French one in
Paris, and both have narrow escapes because
their script contains the clue to a gang of
counterfeiters.
Amiable location romp with the stars in pretty
good form.

w Edmund Beloin, Dean Riesner d Gerd
Oswald ph Roger Hubert m Joseph J. Lilley

Bob Hope, Fernandel, Anita Ekberg, Martha
Hyer, André Morell, Maurice Teynac, Jean
Murat, Preston Sturges

Paris Qui Dort*
France 1923 40m approx (24 fps) bw
  silent
Films Diamant
aka: The Crazy Ray

A mad scientist invents a ray which brings
everyone but six people in Paris to a halt.
Mildly entertaining semi-professional comedy
showing several of its director's most engaging
traits.

wd, ed René Clair ph Maurice Défassiaux, Paul
Guichard

Henri Rollan, Albert Préjean, Marcel Vallée,
Madeleine Rodrigue

Paris Underground
US 1945 97m bw
(UA) Constance Bennett
GB title: Madame Pimpernel

Two women caught in Paris when the Nazis
invade continue their resistance activities.
Artificial and not very exciting flagwaver.

w Boris Ingster, Gertrude Purcell, novel Etta
Shiber d Gregory Ratoff ph Lee Garmes
m Alexander Tansman

Constance Bennett, Gracie Fields, George
Rigaud, Kurt Kreuger, Leslie Vincent

Paris When It Sizzles
US 1963 110m Technicolor
Paramount (Richard Quine, George Axelrod)

A film writer tries out several script ideas with his
secretary as heroine and himself as hero or
villain.
As a French film called La Fête à Henriette this
was a charming whimsy, but Hollywood made it
heavy-handed and boring, especially as no one in
it seems to be having much fun.

w George Axelrod, screenplay Julien Duvivier,
Henri Jeanson d Richard Quine ph Charles
Lang Jnr m Nelson Riddle

William Holden, Audrey Hepburn, Grégoire
Aslan, Noel Coward, Raymond Bussières

Park Row
US 1952 83m bw
UA / Samuel Fuller

Conflict breaks out between two newspapers in
1886 New York.
Earnest but flat low-budgeter of a rather unusual
kind.

wd Samuel Fuller ph Jack Russell ad Ray
Robinson

Gene Evans, Mary Welch, Herbert Hayes,
Forrest Taylor

Parnell*
US 1937 96m bw
MGM

A 19th-century Irish politician comes to grief
through his love for a married woman.
Well made but miscast biopic, a resounding thud
at the box office.

w John Van Druten, S. N. Behrman, play Elsie
T. Schauffler d John M. Stahl ph Karl Freund
m William Axt

Clark Gable, Myrna Loy, Edmund Gwenn,
Edna May Oliver, Alan Marshal, Donald Crisp,
Billie Burke, Berton Churchill, Donald Meek,
Montagu Love, George Zucco
  'A singularly pallid, tedious and unconvincing
drama.'—Frank Nugent

Parrish
US 1961 137m Technicolor
Warner (Delmer Daves)

A young tobacco plantation worker has an
ample sex life and the luck to become boss.
Predictable trudge through scenes from a
bestselling novel, less offensive than most such
adaptations.

wd Delmer Daves, novel Mildred Savage
ph Harry Stradling m Max Steiner

Troy Donahue, Claudette Colbert, Karl Malden,
Dean Jagger, Connie Stevens, Diane McBaine,
Sharon Hugueny

The Parson of Panamint
US 1941 84m bw
Paramount (Harry Sherman)

A gold rush mountain town is corrupted by
success until a two-fisted parson puts things
right.
Middling western morality play.

w Harold Shumate, Adrian Scott, *novel* Peter B.
Kyne *d* William McGann

Charles Ruggles, Ellen Drew, Philip Terry,
Joseph Schildkraut, Henry Kolker, Janet
Beecher, Paul Hurst

Une Partie de Campagne*
France 1936 40m bw
Pierre Braunberger
aka: *A Day in the Country*

Around 1880, a Parisian tradesman and his
family picnic one Sunday in the country, and one
of the daughters falls in love.
An unfinished film which was much admired for
its local colour, like an impressionist picture
come to life.

wd Jean Renoir, *story* Guy de Maupassant
ph Claude Renoir, Jean Bourgoin *m* Joseph
Kosma

Sylvie Bataille, Georges Darnoul, Jane Marken,
Paul Temps

The Party*
US 1968 98m De Luxe Panavision
UA / Mirisch / Geoffrey (Blake Edwards)

An accident-prone Indian actor is accidentally
invited to a swank Hollywood party and wrecks
it.
Would-be Tatiesque comedy of disaster,
occasionally well-timed but far too long for all its
gloss.

w Blake Edwards, Tom and Frank Waldman
d Blake Edwards *ph* Lucien Ballard *m* Henry
Mancini *pd* Fernando Carrere

Peter Sellers, Claudine Longet, Marge
Champion, Fay McKenzie, Steve Franken,
Buddy Lester

'One thing the old movie makers did know is
that two reels is more than enough of this
stuff.'—*Wilfred Sheed*
'It is only rarely that one laughs or even
smiles; mostly one just chalks up another point
for ingenuity.'—*Tom Milne*

Party Girl
US 1958 98m Metrocolor
  Cinemascope
MGM / Euterpe (Joe Pasternak)

In twenties Chicago, a lawyer wins a girl from a
gangster.
Heavy-handed Scarface-style saga which at one
time won a curious reputation for being a satire.

w George Wells *d* Nicholas Ray *ph* Robert
Bronner *m* Jeff Alexander

Robert Taylor, Cyd Charisse, Lee J. Cobb, John
Ireland, Kent Smith, Claire Kelly, Corey Allen

The Party's Over
GB 1963 94m bw
Tricastle (Anthony Perry)

An American girl joins a group of Chelsea
beatniks and dies in a fall from a balcony; her
father investigates.
Tasteless and boring swinging London trash
which became notorious when its producers
(Rank) disowned it because it features a party at
which a man makes love to a dead girl. An
unattractive display of moral squalor.

w Marc Behm *d* Guy Hamilton *ph* Larry Pizer
m John Barry

Oliver Reed, Eddie Albert, Ann Lynn, Louise
Sorel

Passage Home
GB 1955 102m bw
GFD / Group Films (Julian Wintle)

In 1931, tensions run high on a merchant ship
when the captain accepts an attractive girl as
passenger from South America.
Obvious melodrama complete with drunken
captain and storm at sea; not badly done if it
must be done at all.

w William Fairchild, *novel* Richard Armstrong
d Roy Baker *ph* Geoffrey Unsworth *m* Clifton
Parker

Peter Finch, Anthony Steel, Diane Cilento, Cyril
Cusack, Geoffrey Keen, Hugh Griffith, Duncan
Lamont, Bryan Forbes, Gordon Jackson,
Michael Craig

Passage to Marseilles*
US 1944 110m bw
Warner (Hal B. Wallis)

Convicts escape from Devil's Island and join the
Free French.
The only known film to have flashbacks within
flashbacks within flashbacks, this confusing if
sometimes entertaining all-star saga is done to
death by its unconvincing flagwaving endpapers
which prevent it from being at all comparable
with *Casablanca*, as was clearly intended.

w Casey Robinson, Jack Moffitt, *story* Charles
Nordhoff, James Hall *ph* James Wong Howe
d Michael Curtiz *m* Max Steiner

Humphrey Bogart, Michèle Morgan, Claude
Rains, Philip Dorn, Sidney Greenstreet, Peter
Lorre, Helmut Dantine, George Tobias, John
Loder, Victor Francen, Eduardo Ciannelli
  'Invincibly second rate.'—*Richard Mallet,
Punch*

Passenger*
Poland 1963   63m   bw   Dyaliscope
Kadr
original title: *Pasazerka*

A German woman on a liner sees a woman she
thinks she recognizes, and realizes that it is one
of her charges when she was an official in a
concentration camp.
Minor but effective character drama, in essence
an investigation of guilt. The director died during
its making, so some scenes are replaced by still
photographs.

wd Andrzej Munk, play Zofia Posmysz-
Piasecka *ph* Krzysztof Winiewicz

Aleksandra Slaska, Anna Ciepielewska

The Passenger*
Italy / France / Spain 1975   119m
  Metrocolor
MGM / CCC / Concordia / CIPI (Carlo Ponti)
aka: *Profession: Reporter*

A TV reporter in a desert hotel changes identities
with a dead man and finds he is now an African
gun runner being drawn irresistibly towards his
own death.
Pretty much in the style of *Blow Up*, but this time
with no frills of fashion or nudity to bring the
public in. After this, Antonioni was given up by
the commercial cinema.

w Mark Peploe, Peter Wollen, Michelangelo
Antonioni *d* Michelangelo Antonioni
ph Luciano Tovoli *md* Ivan Vandor

Jack Nicholson, Maria Schneider, Jenny
Runacre, Ian Hendry
  'A film of real romance, depth and power . . .
the very quintessence of cinema.'—*Michael
Billington, Illustrated London News*

The Passing of the Third Floor Back*
GB 1935   90m   bw
Gaumont (Ivor Montagu)

A Christ-like visitor stays at a London boarding
house and changes the lives of the inmates.
Competent film version of a famous,
sentimental, dated play.

w Michael Hogan, Alma Reville, *play* Jerome
K. Jerome *d* Berthold Viertel

Conrad Veidt, Renè Ray, Anna Lee, Frank

Cellier, Mary Clare, Beatrix Lehmann, Cathleen
Nesbitt, Sara Allgood

The Passionate Friends**
GB 1948   91m   bw
GFD / Cineguild (Eric Ambler)
US title: *One Woman's Story*

A woman marries an older man, then meets
again her young lover.
A simple and obvious dramatic situation is
tricked out with flashbacks and the inimitable
high style of its director to make a satisfying
entertainment.

w Eric Ambler, *novel* H. G. Wells *d* David
Lean *ph Guy Green m* Richard Addinsell

Ann Todd, Trevor Howard, Claude Rains, Betty
Ann Davies, Isabel Dean, Arthur Howard,
Wilfrid Hyde White

The Passionate Stranger
GB 1956   97m   part bw, part
  Eastmancolor
British Lion / Beaconsfield (Peter Rogers,
  Gerald Thomas)
US title: *A Novel Affair*

A lady novelist bases a character on her virile
chauffeur; he reads the book and thinks she
fancies him.
Feeble comedy, half of it consisting of a
dramatization of the heroine's very dull novel.

w Muriel and Sydney Box *d* Muriel Box
ph Otto Heller *m* Humphrey Searle

Ralph Richardson, Margaret Leighton, Carlo
Justini, Patricia Dainton, Marjorie Rhodes,
Thorley Walters, Frederick Piper

Passionate Summer
GB 1958   104m   Eastmancolor
Rank / Kenneth Harper

A divorced headmaster at a Jamaican school is
loved by three women.
Silly melodrama with splendid backgrounds
ruined by poor colour.

w Joan Henry, *novel* The Shadow and the Peak
by Richard Mason *d* Rudolph Cartier
ph Ernest Steward *m* Angelo Lavagnino

Virginia McKenna, Bill Travers, Yvonne
Mitchell, Alexander Knox, Ellen Barrie, Carl
Mohner.
  'The climactic hurricane does little to dispel
the overall feeling of emotional suffocation.'—
MFB

Passport to Pimlico****
GB 1949   84m   bw
Ealing (E. V. H. Emmett)

Part of a London district is discovered to belong to Burgundy, and the inhabitants find themselves free of rationing restrictions.
A cleverly detailed little comedy which inaugurated the best period of Ealing, its preoccupation with suburban man and his foibles. Not exactly satire, but great fun, and kindly with it.

w T. E. B. Clarke d Henry Cornelius ph Lionel Banes *m Georges Auric*

Stanley Holloway, *Margaret Rutherford,* Basil Radford, Naunton Wayne, Hermione Baddeley, John Slater, Paul Dupuis, Jane Hylton, Raymond Huntley, Betty Warren, Barbara Murray, Sidney Tafler

AAN: T. E. B. Clarke

The Password Is Courage*
GB 1962 116m bw
MGM / Andrew and Virginia Stone

In Europe during World War II, Sgt-Major Charles Coward has a career of escapes and audacious anti-Nazi exploits.
Lively, slightly over-humorous account of one man's war, well mounted and shot entirely on location.

wd Andrew L. Stone, *biography* John Castle *ph* David Boulton

Dirk Bogarde, Maria Perschy, Alfred Lynch, Nigel Stock, Reginald Beckwith
'The experiences are, it seems, mainly true but they do not seem so.'—*Guardian*

Pastor Hall*
GB 1940 97m bw
Charter (John Boulting)

The story of German village pastor Niemoller, who in 1934 was shot for denouncing the Nazis. A courageous film of its time, not very interesting dramatically or cinematically.

w Leslie Arliss, Haworth Bromley, Anna Reiner, *play* Ernst Toller *d* Roy Boulting

Wilfrid Lawson, Nova Pilbeam, Seymour Hicks, Marius Goring, Percy Walsh, Brian Worth, Peter Cotes, Hay Petrie

Pat and Mike**
US 1952 95m bw
MGM (Lawrence Weingarten)

A small-time sports promoter takes on a female intellectual multi-champion.
A comedy which amuses because of its star playing, but doesn't really develop. All very easy going, with guest appearances from sporting personalities.

w Ruth Gordon, Garson Kanin *d* George Cukor *ph* William Daniels *m* David Raksin

Spencer Tracy, Katharine Hepburn, Aldo Ray, William Ching, Sammy White, Jim Backus, Phyllis Povah

AAN: script

Pat Garrett and Billy the Kid
US 1973 106m Metrocolor Panavision
MGM (Gordon Carroll)

Blood-spattered version of a western legend, with violence always to the fore, accentuated by the impossibility of listening to the dialogue because of poor direction and recording.

w Rudolph Wurlitzer *d* Sam Peckinpah *ph* John Coquillon *m* Bob Dylan

James Coburn, Kris Kristofferson, Bob Dylan, Richard Jaeckel, Katy Jurado, Slim Pickens, Chill Wills, Jason Robards Jnr
'A sombre, intense, downbeat essay on the truth behind the legend and the legend behind the the truth.'—*Sight and Sound*
'Shows what Peckinpah can do when he doesn't put his mind to it.'—*Stanley Kauffmann*
'A rash adventure in inadvertent self-parody.'—*William S. Pechter*

A Patch of Blue*
US 1966 105m bw Panavision
MGM / Pandro S. Berman

A blind girl who lives in a slum is helped by a negro with whom she falls in love without realizing his colour.
Polished tearjerker with racial overtones; nicely done for those who can take it.

wd Guy Green, *novel* Be Ready with Bells and Drums by Elizabeth Kata *ph* Robert Burks *d* Jerry Goldsmith

Sidney Poitier, Elizabeth Hartman, Shelley Winters, Wallace Ford, Ivan Dixon, Elizabeth Fraser, John Qualen

AA: Shelley Winters
AAN: Robert Burks; Jerry Goldsmith; Elizabeth Hartman

Pather Panchali**
India 1955 115m bw
Government of West Bengal

In a small Bengal village, the son of a would-be writer grows up in poverty and tragedy before setting off with what remains of the family to seek a living in Benares.
A remarkable first film of a director now famous, showing that people are much the same though the details of their daily lives may be different.

The pace may be slow but the content is mainly absorbing.

wd Satyajit Ray, novels Bhibuti Bashan Bannerjee *ph* Subrata Mitra *m* Ravi Shankar

Kanu Bannerjee, Karuna Bannerjee, Uma Das Gupta, Subir Bannerjee, Chunibala

Paths of Glory****
US 1957 86m bw
UA / Bryna (James B. Harris)

In 1916 in the French trenches, three soldiers are courtmartialled for cowardice.
Incisive melodrama chiefly depicting the corruption and incompetence of the high command; the plight of the soldiers is less interesting. The trench scenes are the most vivid ever made, and the rest is shot in genuine castles, with resultant difficulties of lighting and recording; the overall result is an overpowering piece of cinema.

w Stanley Kubrick, Calder Willingham, Jim Thompson, *novel* Humphrey Cobb *d Stanley Kubrick ph Georg Krause m* Gerald Fried

Kirk Douglas, Adolphe Menjou, George Macready, Wayne Morris, Richard Anderson, Ralph Meeker, Timothy Carey
 'A bitter and biting tale, told with stunning point and nerve-racking intensity.'—*Judith Crist*
 'Beautifully performed, staged, photographed, cut and scored.'—*Colin Young*

Patrick the Great*
US 1945 88m bw
Universal (Howard Benedict)

An actor whose career is waning is jealous of his young son.
Slick teenage family comedy, virtually a one-man show for O'Connor.

w Jane Hall, Bertram Millhauser, Dorothy Bennett, Frederick and Ralph Block *d* Frank Ryan *ph* Frank Redman *m* Hans Salter

Donald O'Connor, Donald Cook, Peggy Ryan, Frances Dee, Eve Arden, Thomas Gomez, Gavin Muir, Andrew Tombes

The Patriot**
US 1928 110m approx (24 fps) bw silent
Paramount

Mad Czar Paul I is assassinated by his chief adviser for the good of the state.
Historical melodrama with a good many comedy touches: the director makes the most of both aspects, but they don't in the end hang together despite bravura acting.

w Hans Kraly, novel Alfred Neumann *d Ernst Lubitsch ph* Bert Glennon *ad* Hans Dreier

Emil Jannings, Lewis Stone, Florence Vidor, Neil Hamilton

AA: Hans Kraly
AAN: best picture; Emil Jannings; Ernst Lubitsch

The Patsy
US 1964 101m Technicolor
Paramount

Hollywood executives try to mould a bellboy to replace a deceased comedian.
A few mildly funny scenes scarcely atone for a long raucous comedy in which the star upstages his betters.

wd Jerry Lewis *ph* Wallace Kelley *m* David Raksin

Jerry Lewis, Everett Sloane, Peter Lorre, John Carradine, Phil Harris, Hans Conried

Patterns***
US 1956 88m bw
UA / Jed Harris, Michael Myerberg
GB title: *Patterns of Power*

The tough boss of a New York corporation forces a showdown between a young executive and the older ineffectual man who he hopes will resign.
Tense little boardroom melodrama with domestic asides, one of the best of the filmed TV plays of the mid-fifties.

w Rod Serling, from his play *d Fielder Cook ph* Boris Kaufman

Van Heflin, Everett Sloane, Ed Begley, Beatrice Straight, Elizabeth Wilson

Patton***
US 1969 171m De Luxe Dimension 150
TCF (Frank McCarthy)
GB title: *Patton—Lust for Glory*

World War II adventures of an aggressive American general.
Brilliantly handled wartime character study which is also a spectacle and tries too hard to have it both ways, but as a piece of film-making is hard to beat.

w Francis Ford Coppola, Edmund H. North *d Franklin Schaffner ph Fred Koenekamp m Jerry Goldsmith*

George C. Scott, Karl Malden, Michael Bates, Stephen Young, Michael Strong, Frank Latimore
 'Here is an actor so totally immersed in his

part that he almost makes you believe he is the man himself.'—*John Gillett*

AA: best picture; script; Franklin Schaffner; George C. Scott

AAN: Fred Koenekamp; Jerry Goldsmith

Paula
US 1952 80m bw
Columbia (Buddy Adler)
GB title: *The Silent Voice*

A barren wife causes a boy's deafness in an accident; she cures and adopts him.
Adequate woman's picture, a vehicle for a star and a luxuriant wardrobe.

w James Poe, William Sackheim *d* Rudolph Maté *ph* Charles Lawton Jnr *m* George Duning

Loretta Young, Kent Smith, Alexander Knox, Tommy Rettig

The Pawnbroker**
US 1965 114m bw
Landau–Unger (Worthington Miner)

A Jew in slummy New York is haunted by his experiences in Nazi prison camps.
Engrossing, somewhat over-melodramatic character study, generally well done.

w David Friedkin, Morton Fine, *novel* Edward Lewis Wallant *d* Sidney Lumet *ph* Boris Kaufman *m* Quincy Jones

Rod Steiger, Brock Peters, Geraldine Fitzgerald, Jaime Sanchez, Thelma Oliver, Juano Hernandez

AAN: Rod Steiger

Pay or Die!*
US 1960 109m bw
Allied Artists (Richard Wilson)

In 1906, a New York Italian police detective forms a special squad to combat the Black Hand.
Tough, convincing period melodrama.

w Richard Wilson, Bertram Millhauser *d* Richard Wilson *ph* Lucien Ballard *m* David Raksin *ad* Fernando Carrere

Ernest Borgnine, Alan Austin, Zohra Lampert, Robert F. Simon, Renata Vanni

Payday
US 1972 103m colour
Cinerama / Pumice / Fantasy (Ralph J. Gleason)

An over-age pop singer has personal problems which erupt into violence.
Well made, dislikeable melodrama.

w Don Carpenter *d* Daryl Duke *ph* Richard C. Glouner *md* Ed Bogas

Rip Torn, Ahna Capri, Elayne Heilveil, Michael C. Gwynn

Payment Deferred*
US 1932 75m bw
MGM

A man desperate for money poisons his wealthy nephew.
Watchable photographed play.

w Ernest Vajda, Claudine West, *play* Jeffrey Dell *d* Lothar Mendes *ph* Merritt Gerstad

Charles Laughton, Maureen O'Sullivan, Ray Milland, Dorothy Peterson, Veree Teasdale, Billy Bevan, Halliwell Hobbes

Payment on Demand*
US 1951 90m bw
RKO / Jack H. Skirball

A happy wife and mother is appalled when her husband asks for a divorce.
A star suffers her way through luxury to a happy ending; good enough stuff for its intended audience.

w Bruce Manning, Curtis Bernhardt *d* Curtis Bernhardt *ph* Leo Tover *m* Victor Young

Bette Davis, Barry Sullivan, Jane Cowl, Kent Taylor, Betty Lynn, John Sutton, Frances Dee, Otto Kruger

'An absolutely typical Joan Crawford picture except that Bette Davis happens to be in the Joan Crawford part.'—*Richard Mallett, Punch*

Payroll*
GB 1961 105m bw
Anglo Amalgamated / Lynx (Norman Priggen)

Small-time crooks snatch £100,000, but after the getaway things begin to go wrong.
Tense, vivid, thoroughly predictable *Rififi*-style thriller, handled with solid professionalism.

w George Baxt, *novel* Derek Bickerton *d* Sidney Hayers *ph* Ernest Steward *m* Reg Owen

Michael Craig, Billie Whitelaw, Françoise Prévost, Kenneth Griffith, William Lucas, Tom Bell, Barry Keegan, Joan Rice, Glyn Houston

Peeper
US 1975 87m De Luxe Panavision
TCF / Chartoff–Winkler (Ron Buck)

In 1947 Los Angeles, a poor British private eye gets into trouble when he seeks a man's lost daughter.
Semi-spoofing Chandleresque caper which is never quite funny or quite thrilling enough.

w W. D. Richter, *novel* Deadfall by Keith Laumer *d* Peter Hyams *ph* Earl Rath *m* Richard Clements

Michael Caine, Natalie Wood, Kitty Winn,
Thayer David, Liam Dunn
  'Flimsy whimsy.'—*Variety*

Peeping Tom

GB 1959   109m   Eastmancolor
Anglo Amalgamated / Michael Powell

A film studio focus puller is obsessed by the lust
to murder beautiful women and photograph the
fear on their faces.
Thoroughly disagreeable suspenser, a kind of
compendium of the bad taste the director
showed in flashes during his career.

w Leo Marks *d* Michael Powell *ph* Otto Heller
m Brian Easdale

Carl Boehm, Moira Shearer, Anna Massey,
Maxine Audley, Esmond Knight, Michael
Goodliffe, Shirley Ann Field, Jack Watson

Peg of Old Drury*

GB 1935   76m   bw
Herbert Wilcox / B & D

The romance of 18th-century actress Peg
Woffington with David Garrick.
Primitive but vivacious historical romp with
adequate star performances.

w Miles Malleson, *play* Masks and Faces by
Charles Reade, Tom Taylor *d* Herbert Wilcox

Anna Neagle, Cedric Hardwicke, Jack Hawkins,
Margaretta Scott, Hay Petrie

Peking Express

US 1951   90m   bw
Paramount / Hal B. Wallis

In communist China, an assortment of people
are aboard a train which is diverted by outlaws.
Pot-boiling remake of *Shanghai Express* (qv);
an adequate time-passer.

w John Meredyth Lucas *d* William Dieterle
ph Charles Lang *m* Dmitri Tiomkin

Joseph Cotten, Corinne Calvet, Edmund
Gwenn, Marvin Miller
  'Lacks flavour or distinction.'—*Leonard
Maltin*

The Penalty

US 1941   81m   bw
MGM (Jack Chertok)

The son of a gangster is regenerated by farm life
and turns against his father.
Antediluvian sweetness and light which wastes a
good cast.

w Harry Ruskin, John C. Higgins *d* Harold S.
Bucquet

Edward Arnold, Lionel Barrymore, Marsha
Hunt, Robert Sterling, Gene Reynolds

Pendulum*

US 1969   102m   Technicolor
Columbia / Pendulum (Stanley Niss)

A convicted murderer and rapist is freed on
appeal and kills the wife of the detective who
arrested him.
Heavy-going police melodrama, efficient but not
very interesting.

w Stanley Niss *d* George Schaefer *ph* Lionel
Lindon *m* Walter Scharf

George Peppard, Jean Seberg, Richard Kiley,
Charles McGraw, Robert F. Lyons, Madeleine
Sherwood

Penelope

US 1966   98m   Metrocolor   Panavision
MGM / Euterpe (Joe Pasternak, Arthur Loew
Jnr)

The wife of a bank vice-president is a bank
robber and kleptomaniac.
Would be cute comedy which only sickens one
for wasting its talent.

w George Wells, *novel* E. V. Cunningham
d Arthur Hiller *ph* Harry Stradling *m* Johnny
Williams

Natalie Wood, Ian Bannen, Dick Shawn, Peter
Falk, Jonathan Winters, Lila Kedrova, Lou
Jacobi, Norma Crane, Arthur Malet, Jerome
Cowan

Penn of Pennsylvania

GB 1941   79m   bw
British National (Richard Vernon)
US title: *The Courageous Mr Penn*

Persecuted Quakers leave England for America.
Stodgily fictionalized history.

w Anatole de Grunwald, *book* William Penn by
C. E. Vulliamy *d* Lance Comfort

Clifford Evans, Deborah Kerr, Denis Arundell,
Aubrey Mallalieu, Henry Oscar, Max Adrian

Penny Princess

GB 1952   94m   Technicolor
Rank / Conquest (Frank Godwin)

A New York shopgirl inherits a tiny European
state and boosts its economy by marketing a
mixture of cheese and schnapps.
Thin, spoofy comedy with mild moments of fun.

wd Val Guest *ph* Geoffrey Unsworth *m* Ronald
Hamner

Dirk Bogarde, Yolande Donlan, A. E.
Matthews, Anthony Oliver, Edwin Styles,
Reginald Beckwith, Kynaston Reeves, Peter
Butterworth, Laurence Naismith, Mary Clare,
Desmond Walter-Ellis

Penny Serenade*
US 1941 120m bw
Columbia (Fred Guiol)

Courtship, marriage and the death of two
children are recollected by a woman
contemplating divorce.
Well-played but uneasy film which veers
suddenly and disconcertingly from light comedy
into tragedy.

w Morrie Ryskind d George Stevens ph Joseph
Walker m W. Franke Harling

Cary Grant, Irene Dunne, Beulah Bondi, Edgar
Buchanan, Ann Doran

'To make something out of very little, and that
so near at hand, is one of the tests of artistry.'—
Otis Ferguson

AAN: Cary Grant

The Penthouse
GB 1967 96m Eastmancolor
Paramount / Tahiti (Harry Fine)

Illicit lovers in an unfinished block of flats are
terrorized by intruders.
Thoroughly objectionable and unpleasant
melodrama with no attractive characters and no
attempt to explain itself.

wd Peter Collinson, play The Meter Man by J.
Scott Forbes ph Arthur Lavis m John
Hawkesworth

Suzy Kendall, Terence Morgan, Tony Beckley,
Norman Rodway, Martine Beswick

'Pornography in Pinter's clothing.'—MFB

The People against O'Hara*
US 1952 102m bw
MGM (William H. Wright)

An ex-alcoholic defence lawyer sacrifices himself
to prove his client's innocence.
Formula drama, well made and entertainingly
performed, with snatches of bright dialogue.

w John Monks Jnr, novel Eleanor Lipsky d John
Sturges ph John Alton m Carmen Dragon

Spencer Tracy, Diana Lynn, Pat O'Brien, John
Hodiak, James Arness, Arthur Shields, Eduardo
Ciannelli, Louise Lorimer

The People Next Door
US 1970 93m De Luxe
Avco Embassy (Herb Brodkin)

Suburban parents have trouble with their drug-
addicted teenage daughter.
Hysterical melodrama with good credentials.

w J. P. Miller, from his TV play d David Greene
ph Gordon Willis m Don Sebesky

Eli Wallach, Julie Harris, Hal Holbrook, Cloris
Leachman, Stephen McHattie, Nehemiah
Persoff

'As unlovely a picture of suburban living as
one is likely to see.'—Judith Crist

People on Sunday*
Germany 1929 72m approx (24 fps) bw
silent
Filmstudio 1929
original title: Menschen am Sonntag

Two couples spend a day in Berlin's countryside.
Influential semi-documentary with fascinating
credits.

w Billy Wilder, Curt Siodmak d Robert
Siodmak, Fred Zinnemann, Edgar G. Ulmer
ph Eugen Schüfftan

Brigitte Borchert, Christl Ehlers, Annie Schreyer

The People That Time Forgot
GB 1977 90m Technicolor
AIP / Amicus (John Dark)

Major McBride tries to rescue his old friend from
a prehistoric island on which he disappeared in
1916.
Tepid sequel to The Land That Time Forgot:
even the dinosaurs don't rise to the occasion.

w Patrick Tilley d Kevin Connor ph Alan
Hume m John Scott pd Maurice Carter

Patrick Wayne, Sarah Douglas, Dana Gillespie,
Doug McClure, Thorley Walters, Shane
Rimmer, Tony Britton

People Will Talk**
US 1951 110m bw
TCF (Darryl F. Zanuck)

A surgeon's unorthodox psychological methods
cause jealousy among his colleagues, especially
when he falls in love with a pregnant patient.
Oddly entertaining jumble of melodrama,
comedy, romance, speeches and a little mystery,
all quite typical of its director.

wd Joseph L. Mankiewicz, play Dr Praetorius
by Curt Goetz ph Milton Krasner md Alfred
Newman

Cary Grant, Jeanne Crain, Finlay Currie, Hume
Cronyn, Walter Slezak, Sidney Blackmer, Basil
Ruysdael

'A picture so mature and refreshingly frank as
to hold that an erring young woman might be
rewarded with a wise and loving mate is most
certainly a significant milestone in the moral
emancipation of American films.'—New York
Times

Pepe
US 1960   195m   Eastmancolor
  Cinemascope
Columbia / George Sidney (Jacques Gelman)

A Mexican peasant in Hollywood gets help from
the stars.
Feeble and seemingly endless extravaganza in
which the boring stretches far outnumber the
rest, and few of the guests have anything
worthwhile to do.

w Dorothy Kingsley, Claude Binyon d George
Sidney ph Joe MacDonald md Johnny Green

Cantinflas, Dan Dailey, Shirley Jones, Ernie
Kovacs, Jay North, William Demarest, Michael
Callan, Maurice Chevalier, Bing Crosby,
Richard Conte, Bobby Darin, Sammy Davis
Jnr, Jimmy Durante, Zsa Zsa Gabor, Hedda
Hopper, Joey Bishop, Peter Lawford, Janet
Leigh, Jack Lemmon, Kim Novak, André
Previn, Donna Reed, Debbie Reynolds, Greer
Garson, Edward G. Robinson, Cesar Romero,
Frank Sinatra, Billie Burke, Tony Curtis, Dean
Martin, Charles Coburn

AA: song 'Faraway Part of Town' (m André
Previn, ly Dory Langdon)
AAN: Joe MacDonald; Johnny Green

Pépé le Moko**
France 1936   90m   bw
Paris Film

A Parisian gangster lives in the Algerian casbah
where the police can't get at him; but love causes
him to emerge and be shot.
Romantic melodrama modelled on the
American gangster film but with a decided poetic
quality of its own: the Americans promptly paid
it the compliment of remaking it as the not-too-
bad *Algiers*.

w Henri Jeanson, Roger d'Ashelbe, *novel* Roger
d'Ashelbe (Henri La Barthe) d *Julien Duvivier*
ph Jules Kruger m Vincent Scotto ad Jacques
Krauss

Jean Gabin, Mireille Ballin Gabriel Gabrio,
Lucas Gridoux
  'One of the most compelling of all French
films.'—*New Yorker, 1977*

Percy
GB 1971   103m   Eastmancolor
Anglo EMI / Welbeck (Betty E. Box)

After an unfortunate accident, a young man
undergoes a successful penis transplant, and sets
out to discover who the donor was.
Barrage of phallic jokes, some quite funny, but
mostly as witless as the whole idea.

w Hugh Leonard, *novel* Raymond Hitchcock

d Ralph Thomas ph Ernest Steward m Ray
Davies

Hywel Bennett, Elke Sommer, *Denholm Elliott*,
Britt Ekland, Cyd Hayman

Percy's Progress
GB 1974   101m   Eastmancolor
EMI (Betty E. Box)

A chemical causes impotence in all males except
the owner of the first transplanted penis.
Percy dug deep, but this is really the bottom of
the barrel.

w Sid Colin d Ralph Thomas ph Tony Imi
m Tony Macauley

Leigh Lawson, Elke Sommer, Denholm Elliott,
Judy Geeson, Harry H. Corbett, Vincent Price,
Adrienne Posta, Julie Ege, James Booth

Perfect Friday*
GB 1970   95m   Eastmancolor
London Screenplays / Sunnymede (Dimitri de
  Grunwald)

A bank manager engages aristocratic help to rob
his own bank.
Middling comedy caper.

w Anthony Greville-Bell, J. Scott Forbes
d Peter Hall ph Alan Hume m Johnny
Dankworth pd Terence Marsh

Stanley Baker, Ursula Andress, David Warner,
Patience Collier, T. P. McKenna, David Waller,
Joan Benham, Julian Orchard

The Perfect Furlough
US 1958   93m   Eastmancolor
  Cinemascope
U-I (Robert Arthur)
GB title: *Strictly for Pleasure*

To help morale at a remote Arctic army unit, one
of the men is selected to enjoy the perfect leave in
Paris on behalf of the others.
Amiable farce which entertains while it's on but
is quickly forgotten.

w Stanley Shapiro d Blake Edwards ph Philip
Lathrop m Frank Skinner

Tony Curtis, Janet Leigh, Elaine Stritch, Keenan
Wynn, Troy Donahue, King Donovan, Linda
Cristal

The Perfect Marriage
US 1946   88m   bw
Paramount / Hal B. Wallis

On their tenth wedding anniversary, a happy
couple have a row and start divorce proceedings.
Wispy comedy, unmemorable and rather
tiresome.

w Leonard Spiegelgass, *play* Samson Raphaelson *d* Lewis Allen *ph* Russell Metty *m* Frederick Hollander

David Niven, Loretta Young, Eddie Albert, Nona Griffith, Virginia Field, Jerome Cowan, Rita Johnson, Charles Ruggles, Nana Bryant, Zasu Pitts

'Another film about disillusionment and reconciliation in a mansion with constant evening dress.'—*Sunday Times*

The Perfect Specimen
US 1937   98m   bw
Warner (Harry Joe Brown)

The grandmother of a rich young man brings him up uncontaminated by the world, but when a girl crashes her car into his fence he proves fitted to deal with the situation.
Fantasticated comedy a long way after *Mr Deeds* and too slow by half.

w Norman Reilly Raine, Lawrence Riley, Brewster Morse, Fritz Falkenstein, Samuel Hopkins Adams *d* Michael Curtiz *ph* Charles Rosher

Errol Flynn, Joan Blondell, Hugh Herbert, Edward Everett Horton, May Robson, Dick Foran, Beverly Roberts, Allen Jenkins

Perfect Strangers**
GB 1947   102m   bw
MGM / London Films (Alexander Korda)
US title: *Vacation from Marriage*

A downtrodden clerk and his dowdy wife go to war, and come back unrecognizably improved.
Pleasant comedy with good actors; but the turnabout of two such caricatures really strains credibility.

w Clemence Dane, Anthony Pelissier *d* Alexander Korda

Robert Donat, Deborah Kerr, Glynis Johns, Ann Todd, Roland Culver, Elliot Mason, Eliot Makeham, Brefni O'Rourke, Edward Rigby

AA: original story (Clemence Dane)

Perfect Strangers
US 1950   87m   bw
Warner (Jerry Wald)
GB title: *Too Dangerous to Love*

Two jurors on a murder case fall in love.
Talkative, unlikely, and rather boring potboiler.

w Edith Sommer, *play* Ladies and Gentlemen by Charles MacArthur, Ben Hecht *d* Bretaigne Windust *ph* Peverell Marley *m* Leigh Harline

Ginger Rogers, Dennis Morgan, Thelma Ritter, Margalo Gillmore, Howard Freeman, Alan Reed, Paul Ford, George Chandler

Perfect Understanding*
GB 1933   80m   bw
Gloria Swanson British Pictures Ltd

A couple agree to marry on condition that they will never disagree with each other.
Silly comedy with a unique star combination looking acutely uncomfortable.

w Miles Malleson, Michael Powell *d* Cyril Gardner *ph* Curt Courant

Gloria Swanson, Laurence Olivier, John Halliday, Nigel Playfair, Michael Farmer, Genevieve Tobin, Nora Swinburne

The Perfect Woman*
GB 1949   89m   bw
GFD / Two Cities

A girl changes places with her inventor uncle's robot woman.
Described as a romp, this is in fact a pretty good farce, very fast moving and well played after the usual expository start.

w George Black, Bernard Knowles, J. B. Boothroyd, *play* Wallace Geoffrey, Basil Mitchell *d* Bernard Knowles *ph* Jack Hildyard *m* Arthur Wilkinson

Patricia Roc, Nigel Patrick, Stanley Holloway, David Hurst, Miles Malleson, Irene Handl

Performance*
GB 1970   105m   Technicolor
Warner / Goodtimes (Donald Cammell)

A vicious gangster moves in with an ex-pop star.
Dense, Pinterish melodrama about alter egos; not really worth the trouble it takes, but superficially very flashily done.

w Donald Cammell *d Nicolas Roeg, Donald Cammell ph Nicolas Roeg m* Jack Nitzche *md* Randy Newman

James Fox, Mick Jagger, Anita Pallenberg, Michèle Breton, Stanley Meadows, Allan Cuthbertson

A Perilous Journey
US 1953   87m   bw
Republic (W. J. O'Sullivan)

A party of women sail to the California goldfields to sell themselves into marriage.
Reasonably lively action drama.

w Richard Wormser, *novel* The Golden Tide by Virgie Roe *d* R. G. Springsteen *ph* Jack Marta *m* Victor Young

Vera Ralston, David Brian, Charles Winninger, Scott Brady, Virginia Grey, Ben Cooper

The Perils of Pauline*
US 1947   96m   Technicolor
Paramount (Sol C. Siegel)

The career of silent serial queen Pearl White. An agreeable recreation of old time Hollywood, with plenty of slapstick chases but a shade too much sentiment also.

w P. J. Wolfson d George Marshall ph Ray Rennahan md Robert Emmett Dolan

Betty Hutton, John Lund, Billy de Wolfe, William Demarest, Constance Collier, Frank Faylen, William Farnum, Paul Panzer, Snub Pollard, Creighton Hale, Chester Conklin, James Finlayson, Hank Mann, Bert Roach, Francis McDonald, Chester Clute

AAN: song 'I Wish I Didn't Love You So' (m/ly Frank Loesser)

Period of Adjustment
US 1962   122m   bw   Panavision
MGM / Marton (Lawrence Weingarten)

A Korean War veteran has the shakes and his sexual adequacy is effected, as his wife furiously discovers.
Comedy of maladjustment, tolerably witty but unsuitably widescreened.

w Isabel Lennart, play Tennessee Williams d George Roy Hill ph Paul bc. Vogel m Lyn Murray

Tony Franciosa, Jane Fonda, Jim Hutton, Lois Nettleton

Permission to Kill
US / Austria 1975   97m   Technicolor Panavision
Warner / Sascha (Paul Mills)

British agents try to stop a communist returning home from the west.
Prolonged, confusing and boring spy melodrama in which everyone looks understandably glum.

w Robin Estridge, from his novel d Cyril Frankel ph Freddie Young m Richard Rodney Bennett

Bekim Fehmiu, Dirk Bogarde, Ava Gardner, Timothy Dalton, Frederic Forrest
    'Pretentious political mishmash.'—MFB

Perri*
US 1957   75m   Technicolor
Walt Disney (Winston Hibler)

The life of a squirrel.
Disney's first True Life Fantasy, in which live footage of animals is manipulated against artificial backgrounds to produce an effect as charming and unreal as a cartoon.

w Ralph Wright, Winston Hibler, novel Felix

Salten d Ralph Wright ph various m Paul Smith

AAN: Paul Smith

Persecution
GB 1974   96m   Eastmancolor
Fanfare / Tyburn (Kevin Francis)

A rich American woman in England is hated by her son and fearful that her murky past will be revealed.
Rich but not engrossing nonsense, somewhat à la Baby Jane, with hazy script and stolid production.

w Robert B. Hutton, Rosemary Wootten d Don Chaffey ph Ken Talbot m Paul Ferris

Lana Turner, Ralph Bates, Olga Georges-Picot, Trevor Howard, Suzan Farmer, Ronald Howard, Patrick Allen
    'Gives off the unmistakable odour of damp mothballs.'—Michael Billington, Illustrated London News

Persona**
Sweden 1966   81m   bw
Svensk Filmindustri (Lars-Owe Carlberg)

A nurse begins to identify with her mentally ill patient, and herself has a nervous breakdown.
Intense clinical study presented in a very complex cinematic manner which tends to obscure the main theme while providing endless fascination for cinéastes.

wd Ingmar Bergman ph Sven Nykvist m Lars Johan Werle, Liv Ullmann, Bibi Andersson, Gunnar Bjornstrand
    'Reactions have ranged from incomprehension to irritation with what is dismissed as a characteristic piece of self-indulgence on Bergman's part—Bergman talking to himself again.'—David Wilson, MFB
    'A puzzling, obsessive film that Bergman seems not so much to have worked out as to have torn from himself.'—New Yorker, 1977

Personal Affair
GB 1953   83m   bw
Rank / Two Cities (Anthony Darnborough)

A schoolmaster and his neurotic wife run into trouble when a girl pupil develops a crush on him.
Preposterous domestic drama making much ado about nothing.

w Lesley Storm, from her play d Anthony Pelissier ph Reg Wyer m William Alwyn

Leo Genn, Gene Tierney, Glynis Johns, Pamela Brown

Personal Property*

US 1937 84m bw
MGM (John W. Considine Jnr)
GB title: *The Man in Possession*

An American widow in England, in financial straits, falls for the bailiff sent to keep an eye on her.

Moderate star comedy which still amuses.

w Hugh Mills, Ernest Vajda, *play* The Man in Possession by H. M. Harwood *d* W. S. Van Dyke II *ph* William Daniels *m* Franz Waxman

Jean Harlow, Robert Taylor, Reginald Owen, Una O'Connor, Henrietta Crosman, E. E. Clive, Cora Witherspoon, Barnett Parker

Persons in Hiding*

US 1939 71m bw
Paramount

A bored girl absconds with gangsters and becomes a public enemy.

Interesting programmer which led to several sequels using the same book as source; this one was vaguely inspired by the story of Bonnie and Clyde.

w William R. Lipman, Horace McCoy, *book* J. Edgar Hoover *d* Louis King *ph* Harry Fischbeck *m* Boris Morros

Patricia Morison, J. Carrol Naish, Lynne Overman, William Henry, Helen Twelvetrees, William Frawley

Persons Unknown*

Italy 1958 105m bw
Lux / Vides / Cinecittà (Franco Cristaldi)
original title: *I Soliti Ignoti;* US title: *Big Deal on Madonna Street*

Adventures of a gang of incompetent thieves, who get arrested more often than they get away, and finally, elaborately drill through a wall into the bank . . . only to find it's the wrong wall and they are in another room of the same flat.

Spoof black comedy working up to an elaborate take-off of *Rififi*; a great success in Italy and the USA, mildly received elsewhere.

w Age Scarpelli, Suso Cecchi d'Amico, Mario Monicelli *d* Mario Monicelli *ph* Gianni di Venanzo *m* Piero Umiliani

Vittorio Gassman, Renato Salvatori, Toto, Marcello Mastroianni, Memmo Carotenuto, Carla Gravina, Rosanna Rory

Pete 'n Tillie*

US 1972 100m Technicolor Panavision
Universal (Julius J. Epstein)

The tragi-comic marriage of two eccentrics. Curious: plain drama treated as comedy, with surprisingly satisfactory results, but not an example to be followed.

w Julius J. Epstein, *novel* Witch's Milk by Peter de Vries *d* Martin Ritt *ph* John Alonzo *m* John T. Williams

Walter Matthau, Carol Burnett, Geraldine Page, René Auberjonois, Barry Nelson, Henry Jones

'For the most part an amusing, moving, sentimental comedy. The wisecracks stay on this side of human possibility – that is, we don't feel, as we do so often with Neil Simon, that the characters have private gag writers in their homes.'—*Stanley Kauffmann*

AAN: Julius J. Epstein; Geraldine Page

Pete Kelly's Blues*

US 1955 95m Warnercolor
Cinemascope
Warner (Jack Webb)

Jazz musicians in the twenties get involved with gangsters.

Minor cult film, mainly for the score; dramatically it is not exactly compelling.

w Richard L. Breen *d* Jack Webb *ph* Hal Rosson *ph* Harper Goff *m* Sammy Cahn, Ray Heindorf, Arthur Hamilton, Matty Matlock

Jack Webb, Edmond O'Brien, Janet Leigh, Peggy Lee, Andy Devine, *Ella Fitzgerald,* Lee Marvin, Martin Milner

'Concerned with striking attitudes and establishing an atmosphere rather than developing anything very coherent in the way of narrative . . . one remains aware of an over-deliberate straining after effect.'—*Penelope Houston*

AAN: Peggy Lee

Peter Ibbetson*

US 1935 85m bw
Paramount (Louis D. Lighton)

Childhood sweethearts meet again as adults, are separated when he is imprisoned for her husband's murder, but are reunited in heaven. Downright peculiar romantic fantasy, even more oddly cast, but extremely well produced.

w Vincent Lawrence, Waldemar Young, Constance Collier, *novel* George du Maurier *d* Henry Hathaway *ph* Charles Lang *m* Ernst Toch

Gary Cooper, Ann Harding, Ida Lupino, John Halliday, Douglass Dumbrille, Virginia Weidler, Dickie Moore, Doris Lloyd

AAN: Ernst Toch

Peter Pan***
US 1953   76m   Technicolor
Walt Disney

Three London children are taken into fairyland
by a magic flying boy who cannot grow up.
Solidly crafted cartoon version of a famous
children's play; not Disney's best work, but still
miles ahead of the competition.

supervisor Ben Sharpsteen *d* Wilfred Jackson,
Clyde Geronomi, Hamilton Luske

The Peterville Diamond
GB 1942   85m   bw
Warner (A. H. Salomon)

A bored wife revives her husband's interest by
cultivating the advances of a jewel thief.
Modest comedy-drama, smoothly presented: the
same play formed the basis of Dieterle's *Jewel
Robbery*.

w Brock Williams, Gordon Wellesley, *play* Jewel
Robbery by Ladislas Fodor *d* Walter Forde
ph Basil Emmott *md* Jack Beaver

Anne Crawford, Donald Stewart, Renee
Houston, Oliver Wakefield, Charles Heslop,
William Hartnell, Felix Aylmer, Charles Victor

Pete's Dragon
US 1977   127m   Technicolor
Walt Disney (Ron Miller, Jerome Courtland)

In Maine in 1900, a nine-year-old boy escapes
from grasping foster-parents with his pet dragon,
which no one but himself can see.
A kind of juvenile rewrite of *Harvey*. The dragon
is drawn (rather poorly) and the human
characters are not exactly three-dimensional. A
long way from *Mary Poppins*.

w Malcolm Marmorstein, *story* Seton I. Miller,
S. S. Field *d* Don Chaffey *ph* Frank Phillips
anim Ken Anderson *md* Irwin Kostal *songs* Al
Kasha, Joel Hirschhorn *ch* Onna White

Sean Marshall, Mickey Rooney, Jim Dale, Helen
Reddy, Red Buttons, Shelley Winters, Jim
Backus, Joe E. Ross, Ben Wrigley

The Petrified Forest**
US 1936   83m   bw
Warner (Henry Blanke)

Travellers at a way station in the Arizona desert
are held up by gangsters.
Rather faded melodrama (it always was), which
is important to Hollywood for introducing such
well used figures as the poet idealist hero and the
gangster anti-hero, and for giving Bogart his first
meaty role. Otherwise, the settings are artificial,
the acting theatrical, the development
predictable and the dialogue pretentious.

w Charles Kenyon, Delmer Daves, *play* Robert
E. Sherwood *d* Archie Mayo *ph* Sol Polito
md Leo F. Forbstein

Leslie Howard, Bette Davis, *Humphrey Bogart,*
Genevieve Tobin, Dick Foran, Joe Sawyer,
Porter Hall, Charley Grapewin
  'Drama slackens under the weight of Mr
Sherwood's rather half-baked philosophy.'—
Alistair Cooke
†Remade as *Escape in the Desert* (qv).

Petticoat Fever
US 1936   80m   bw
MGM (Frank Davis)

A girl and her stuffy fiancé crash land their plane
in sub-Arctic Labrador and are helped by a
wireless operator who has not seen a woman for
two years.
Pert, slightly unusual comedy which comes off
pretty well.

w Harold Goldman, *play* Mark Reed *d* George
Fitzmaurice *ph* Ernest Haller

Robert Montgomery, Myrna Loy, Reginald
Owen, Winifred Shotter

The Petty Girl
US 1950   88m   Technicolor
Columbia (Nat Perrin)
GB title: *Girl of the Year*

A calendar artist takes a staid college professor
as his model, and causes a scandal.
Witless comedy musical which barely lingers in
the memory.

w Nat Perrin, *story* Mary McCarthy *d* Henry
Levin *ph* William Snyder *songs* Harold Arlen,
Johnny Mercer

Robert Cummings, Joan Caulfield, Melville
Cooper, Elsa Lanchester, Audrey Long, Mary
Wickes, Frank Orth·

Petulia*
US 1968   105m   Technicolor
Warner / Petersham (Raymond Wagner)

A doctor's life is disrupted by his meeting and
loving a kooky girl who has family problems.
Swinging London melodrama which happens to
be set in San Francisco. All very flashy, and
occasionally arresting or well acted, but adding
up to nothing.

w Lawrence B. Marcus, *novel* Me and the Arch
Kook Petulia by John Haase *d* Richard Lester
ph Nicolas Roeg *m* John Barry

George C. Scott, Julie Christie, Richard
Chamberlain, Joseph Cotten, Arthur Hill,
Shirley Knight, Kathleen Widdoes, Pippa Scott
  'A sad and savage comment on the ways we

waste our time and ourselves in upper-middle-class America.'—*Richard Schickel*

'A soulless, arbitrary, attitudinizing piece of claptrap.'—*John Simon*

Peyton Place**
US 1957   157m   De Luxe   Cinemascope
TCF (Jerry Wald)

Sex, frustration and violence ferment under the placid surface of a small New England town.
Well-made film of what was at the time a scandalous bestseller, one of the first to reveal those nasty secrets of 'ordinary people'.

w John Michael Hayes, *novel* Grace Metalious *d* Mark Robson *ph* William Mellor *m* Franz Waxman

Lana Turner, Arthur Kennedy, Hope Lange, Lee Philips, Lloyd Nolan, Diane Varsi, RussTamblyn, Terry Moore, Barry Coe, David Nelson, Betty Field, Mildred Dunnock, Leon Ames, Lorne Greene

AAN: best picture; John Michael Hayes; Mark Robson; William Mellor; Lana Turner; Arthur Kennedy; Hope Lange; Diane Varsi; Russ Tamblyn

Phaedra*
US / Greece 1961   116m   bw
UA / Melinafilm (Jules Dassin)

A tycoon's wife falls in love with her stepson.
Ludicrous, awesomely folly-filled attempt to modernize and sex up Greek tragedy.

wd Jules Dassin *ph* Jacques Natteau *m* Mikis Theodorakis

Melina Mercouri, Anthony Perkins, Raf Vallone, Elizabeth Ercy

'Unfortunately unforgettable.'—*John Simon*

Phantom Lady**
US 1944   87m   bw
Universal

A man is accused of murder and his only alibi is a mysterious lady he met in a bar.
Odd little thriller which doesn't really hold together but is made for the most part with great style.

w Bernard C. Schoenfeld, *novel* William Irish *d* Robert Siodmak

Franchot Tone, Alan Baxter, Ella Raines, Elisha Cook Jnr, Fay Helm, Andrew Tombes

Phantom of Crestwood*
US 1932   77m   bw
RKO (David O. Selznick)

Murder strikes when a blackmailer assembles her victims.

Lively mystery with spoof elements.

w Bartlett Cormack, J. Walter Ruben *d* J. Walter Ruben

Ricardo Cortez, H. B. Warner, Anita Louise, Karen Morley, Pauline Frederick, Robert McWade, Skeets Gallagher

Phantom of the Opera***
US 1926   94m (24 fps)   bw (Technicolor
   sequence)   silent
Universal

A disfigured man in a mask abducts the prima donna of the Paris Opera House to his lair in the sewers below.
Patchy but often splendid piece of Grand Guignol which not only provided its star with a famous role but was notable for its magnificent visual style.

w Raymond Shrock, Elliot Clawson, *novel* Gaston Leroux *d* Rupert Julian *ph* Charles Van Enger, Virgil Miller *ad* Dan Hall

Lon Chaney, Mary Philbin, Norman Kerry, Gibson Gowland

The Phantom of the Opera**
US 1943   92m   Technicolor
Universal (George Waggner)

This version is more decorous and gentlemanly, with much attention paid to the music, but it certainly has its moments.

w Erich Taylor, Samuel Hoffenstein, *d* Arthur Lubin *ph* Hal Mohr, W. Howard Greene *m* Edmund Ward *ad* John B. Goodman, Alexander Golitzen

Claude Rains, Nelson Eddy, Susanna Foster, Edgar Barrier, Leo Carrillo, J. Edward Bromberg, Jane Farrar, Hume Cronyn

AAN: Hal Mohr, W. Howard Greene; Edmund Ward

Phantom of the Opera
GB 1962   90m   Technicolor
U-I / Hammer (Anthony Hinds)

Stodgy remake with the accent on shock.

w John Elder *d* Terence Fisher *ph* Arthur Grant *m* Edwin Astley

Herbert Lom, Edward de Souza, Heather Sears, Thorley Walters, Michael Gough, Ian Wilson, Martin Miller, John Harvey, Miriam Karlin

'The only shock is that the British, who could have had a field day with this antique, have simply wafted it back with a lick and a promise.'—*New York Times*

Phantom of the Paradise *
US 1974   91m   Movielab
TCF / Pressman Williams (Edward R.
  Pressman)

A modern satirical remake of *Phantom of the
Opera* in rock opera terms, set in a pop music
palace. Not bad in spots, but it doesn't really
know where it's going.

wd Brian de Palma *ph* Larry Pizer *m* Paul
Williams *pd* Jack Fisk

Paul Williams, William Finley, Jessica Harper,
George Memmoli, Gerrit Graham
   'Too broad in its effects and too bloated in
style to cut very deeply as a parody . . . closer to
the anything goes mode of a *Mad* magazine
lampoon.'—*Richard Combs*
AAN: Paul Williams

Phantom of the Rue Morgue
US 1954   84m   Warnercolor   3-D
Warner (Henry Blanke)

In old Paris, a killer of pretty girls turns out to be
an ape.
Dull revamping of a rather dull story, with
boring characters and little horror.

w Harold Medford, James R. Webb,
story Murders in the Rue Morgue by Edgar
Allan Poe *d* Roy del Ruth *ph* Peverell Marley
m David Buttolph

Karl Malden, Claude Dauphin, Steve Forrest,
Patricia Medina, Allyn McLerie, Dolores Dorn

The Phantom President *
US 1932   78m   bw
Paramount

A fast-talking quack doubles for a lacklustre
presidential candidate.
A likely but in fact unsuccessful film debut for a
famous Broadway star: many points of interest.

w Walter de Leon, Harlan Thompson
d Norman Taurog *ph* David Abel
songs Richard Rodgers, Lorenz Hart

George M. Cohan, Claudette Colbert, Jimmy
Durante, George Barbier, Sidney Toler,
Jameson Thomas, Paul Hurst, Alan Mowbray
   'For anyone who cares about American
theatrical history, it's an indispensable record of
Cohan's style.'—*New Yorker, 1978*

The Phantom Tollbooth **
US 1969   90m   Metrocolor
MGM / Animation Visual Arts

A bored boy goes through a magic tollbooth to
land beyond his wildest imagination, rescues
Rhyme and Reason, and defeats the Demons of
Ignorance.

Ambitious and well-devised, though rather slow-
starting, cartoon feature which falls in style
somewhere between *Alice in Wonderland* and
The Wizard of Oz but is more intellectual than
either and would be beyond the reach of most
children. Discerning adults may have a ball.

w Chuck Jones, Sam Rosen, *novel* Norton
Juster *d* Chuck Jones, Abe Levitow *ph* Maurice
Noble

Butch Patrick

Phase IV
GB 1973   84m   Technicolor
Paramount / Alced (Paul B. Radin)

In the Arizona desert, ants attack a scientific
installation.
Oddly effective if repulsive science fiction; the
ants are all the more unpleasant because they
stay the normal size.

w Mayo Simon *d* Saul Bass *ph* Dick Bush
m Brian Gascoyne

Nigel Davenport, Lynne Frederick, Michael
Murphy, Alan Gifford

The Phenix City Story *
US 1955   100m   bw
Allied Artists (Sam Bischoff, David Diamond)

A young lawyer fights the racketeers who
control his town.
Goodish example of the semi-documentary
melodramas of small-town corruption which
swarmed out of Hollywood following the
Kefauver investigations.

w Crane Wilbur, Dan Mainwaring *d* Phil
Karlson *ph* Harry Neumann *m* Harry Sukman

Richard Kiley, *Edward Andrews*, John
McIntire, Kathryn Grant

Phfft
US 1954   91m   bw
Columbia (Fred Kohlmar)

The title refers to the sound of an expiring match;
the story tells of a couple who get divorced and
try to find out what they have been missing.
Champagne comedy with no bubbles.

w George Axelrod *d* Mark Robson *ph* Charles
Lang *m* Frederick Hollander

Jack Lemmon, Judy Holliday, Kim Novak, Jack
Carson, Luella Gear, Donald Randolph, Donald
Curtis, Merry Anders

The Philadelphia Story ****
US 1940   112m   bw
MGM (Joseph L. Mankiewicz)

A stuffy heiress, about to be married for the

second time, turns human and returns gratefully to number one.

Hollywood's most wise and sparkling comedy, with a script which is even an improvement on the original play. Cukor's direction is so discreet you can hardly sense it, and all the performances are just perfect.

w Donald Ogden Stewart, play Philip Barry d George Cukor ph Joseph Ruttenberg m Franz Waxman ad Cedric Gibbons

Katharine Hepburn, Cary Grant, James Stewart, Ruth Hussey, Roland Young, John Halliday, Mary Nash, Virginia Weidler, John Howard, Henry Daniell

'There are just not enough superlatives sufficiently to appreciate this show.'— *Hollywood Reporter*

AA: Donald Ogden Stewart; James Stewart AAN: best picture; George Cukor; Katharine Hepburn; Ruth Hussey

Philo Vance

The smooth sleuth created by S. S. Van Dine was a popular film hero of the thirties, for several different companies and with several different actors. As a series it was very variable indeed.

1929: THE CANARY MURDER CASE (Paramount: William Powell); THE GREENE MURDER CASE (Paramount: William Powell) 1930: THE BISHOP MURDER CASE (MGM: Basil Rathbone); THE BENSON MURDER CASE (Paramount: William Powell) 1933: THE KENNEL MURDER CASE (qv) (Warner: William Powell) 1934: THE DRAGON MURDER CASE (Warner: Warren William) 1935: THE CASINO MURDER CASE (MGM: Paul Lukas) 1936: THE GARDEN MURDER CASE (MGM: Edmund Lowe) 1937: NIGHT OF MYSTERY (Paramount: Grant Richards) 1937: THE SCARAB MURDER CASE (British: Wilfrid Hyde White) 1939: THE GRACIE ALLEN MURDER CASE (Paramount: Warren William); CALLING PHILO VANCE (Warner: James Stephenson) 1947: PHILO VANCE RETURNS (PRC: William Wright); PHILO VANCE'S GAMBLE (PRC: Alan Curtis); PHILO VANCE'S SECRET MISSION (PRC: Alan Curtis)

Phone Call from a Stranger

US 1952 96m bw
TCF (Nunnally Johnson)

Of four airplane acquaintances, only one

survives a crash; he visits the families of the others.

Four stories with an unlikely link. (The compendium craze, which had started in 1948 with *Quartet*, was now straining itself.) Nothing to remember except Miss Davis.

w Nunnally Johnson d Jean Negulesco ph Milton Krasner m Franz Waxman

Bette Davis, Gary Merrill, Michael Rennie, Shelley Winters, Keenan Wynn, Evelyn Varden, Warren Stevens, Craig Stevens

'A cinematic party line on which several conversations are going at once, none of them coming across very distinctly.'—*Time*

Piccadilly*

GB 1929 105m (24 fps) bw silent
BIP (E. A. Dupont)

A club owner's fiancée is accused of killing his Chinese mistress.

Sub-Edgar Wallace melodrama, no longer watchable with a straight face.

w Arnold Bennett d E. A. Dupont

Gilda Gray, Anna May Wong, Jameson Thomas, Cyril Ritchard, Ellen Pollock, Charles Laughton, Debroy Somers and his Band

Piccadilly Incident*

GB 1946 102m bw
ABP (Herbert Wilcox)

During World War II, a girl believed drowned returns from the front to find her husband remarried.

The Enoch Arden theme again, and the first of the Wilcox-Neagle 'London' films, though untypically a melodrama with a sad ending. Efficient enough for its chosen audience.

w Nicholas Phipps d Herbert Wilcox ph Max Greene

Anna Neagle, Michael Wilding, Michael Laurence, Frances Mercer, Coral Browne, A. E. Matthews, Edward Rigby, Brenda Bruce

Piccadilly Jim*

US 1936 100m bw
MGM (Harry Rapf)

A cartoonist helps his father to marry by making the bride's stuffy family objects of ridicule. Amiable comedy with a diverting London setting.

w Charles Brackett, Edwin Knopf, novel P. G. Wodehouse d Robert Z. Leonard ph Joseph Ruttenberg m William Axt

Robert Montgomery, Madge Evans, Frank Morgan, Billie Burke, Eric Blore, Robert

Benchley, Ralph Forbes, Cora Witherspoon, E. E. Clive

Piccadilly Third Stop
GB 1960   90m   bw
Rank / Sydney Box / Ethiro (Norman Williams)

A smooth crook seduces the daughter of an eastern ambassador in London to gain entry to the embassy and rob it.
Boring and rather unpleasant thriller partly redeemed by a final chase through the Underground.

w Leigh Vance d Wolf Rilla ph Ernest Steward m Philip Green

Terence Morgan, Yoko Tani, John Crawford, William Hartnell, Mai Zetterling, Dennis Price, Ann Lynn

Pick a Star
US 1937   67m   bw
Hal Roach / MGM

An innocent girl in Hollywood achieves stardom with the help of a publicity man.
Perfectly awful Cinderella story with interesting glimpses behind the studio scenes and (if you can wait that long) a couple of good Laurel and Hardy sequences.

w Richard Flournoy, Arthur Vernon Jones, Thomas J. Dugan d Edward Sedgwick ph Norbert Brodine

Rosina Lawrence, Jack Haley, Patsy Kelly, Mischa Auer, *Stan Laurel, Oliver Hardy,* Charles Halton, Lyda Roberti

Pick Up
US 1951   78m   bw
Columbia (Hugo Haas)

A lonely middle-aged man falls for a tart who is interested only in his money.
Modest variation on *The Blue Angel*, the first of several second features made by Haas to feature himself as a second Emil Jannings. They got progressively more maudlin.

wd Hugo Haas ph Paul Ivano

Hugo Haas, Beverly Michaels, Allan Nixon, Howard Chamberlin

Pickup on South Street*
US 1953   80m   bw
TCF (Jules Schermer)

A pickpocket steals a girl's wallet and finds himself up to his neck in espionage.
Over-rich mixture of crime, violence and anti-communism, smartly made without being very interesting.

wd Samuel Fuller ph Joe MacDonald m Leigh Harline

Richard Widmark, Jean Peters, *Thelma Ritter*, Richard Kiley
† Remade 1968 as *Capetown Affair*.
AAN: Thelma Ritter

The Pickwick Papers*
GB 1952   115m   bw
George Minter (Bob McNaught)

Various adventures of the Pickwick Club culminate in Mrs Bardell's suit for breach of promise.
Flatly conceived and loosely constructed Dickensian comedy; good humour and lots of well-known faces do not entirely atone for lack of artifice.

wd Noel Langley ph Wilkie Cooper m Anthony Hopkins ad Fred Pusey

James Hayter, James Donald, Donald Wolfit, Hermione Baddeley, Hermione Gingold, Kathleen Harrison, *Nigel Patrick*, Alexander Gauge, Lionel Murton

Picnic***
US 1956   113m   Technicolor Cinemascope
Columbia (Fred Kohlmar)

A brawny wanderer causes sexual havoc one summer in a small American town.
Seminal melodrama setting new directions for Hollywood and illustrating the side of life the Hardy family never showed. Generally quite compulsive despite some overacting.

w Daniel Taradash, *play William Inge* d Joshua Logan ph James Wong Howe m George Duning pd Jo Mielziner ad William Flannery

William Holden, Kim Novak, Rosalind Russell, *Susan Strasberg*, Arthur O'Connell, Cliff Robertson, Betty Field, Verna Felton, Reta Shaw

AAN: best picture; Joshua Logan; George Duning; Arthur O'Connell

Picnic at Hanging Rock*
Australia 1975   115m   Eastmancolor
Picnic Productions / Australia Film Corporation (Hal and Jim McElroy)

In 1900, schoolgirls set out for a picnic; some disappear and are never found.
An intriguing but finally irritating puzzle with no answer; the atmosphere is nicely calculated, but as in *L'Avventura* the whole thing outstays its welcome.

w Cliff Green, *novel* Joan Lindsay d Peter Weir ph Russell Boyd m Bruce Smeaton

Rachel Roberts, Dominic Guard, Helen Morse, Jacki Weaver, Vivean Gray, Kirsty Child

'Atmospherically vivid, beautifully shot, and palpably haunting.'—*Michael Billington, Illustrated London News*

Picture Mommy Dead

US 1966   88m   Pathecolor
Embassy / Berkeley (Bert I. Gordon)

A girl who has been hospitalized following the death of her mother in a fire returns home to find, apparently, that her father's new wife is trying to kill her.

Twist-ending shocker with tired stars, from the tag end of the *Baby Jane* cycle.

w Robert Sherman   *d* Bert I. Gordon
ph Ellsworth Fredericks   *m* Robert Drasnin

Don Ameche, Martha Hyer, Zsa Zsa Gabor, Susan Gordon, Maxwell Reed, Signe Hasso, Wendell Corey

The Picture of Dorian Gray***

US 1945   110m   bw   (Technicolor inserts)
MGM

A Victorian gentleman keeps in the attic a picture of himself, which shows his age and depravity while he stays eternally young. Elegant variation on *Dr Jekyll and Mr Hyde*, presented in portentous style which suits the subject admirably.

wd Albert Lewin, novel Oscar Wilde   *ph* Harry Stradling   *m* Herbert Stothart

George Sanders, Hurd Hatfield, Donna Reed, Angela Lansbury, Peter Lawford

'Respectful, earnest, and, I'm afraid, dead.'—*James Agee*

'Loving and practised hands have really improved Wilde's original, cutting down the epigrammatic flow . . . and rooting out all the preciousness which gets in the way of the melodrama.'—*Richard Winnington*

AA: Harry Stradling
AAN: Angela Lansbury

The Picture Snatcher**

US 1933   77m   bw
Warner

An ex-racketeer just out of prison becomes a scandal photographer.
Lively star vehicle, interesting for period detail.

w Allen Rivkin, P. J. Wolfson   *d* Lloyd Bacon
ph Sol Polito   *md* Leo F. Forbstein

James Cagney, Ralph Bellamy, Patricia Ellis, Alice White, Ralf Harolde, Robert Emmett O'Connor, Robert Barrat

'A vulgar but generally funny collection of blackouts.'—*Time*

'Fast, snappy, tough and packed with action.'—*New York Herald Tribune*
† Remade 1947 as *Escape from Crime*, with Richard Travis.

A Piece of the Action

US 1977   135m   Metrocolor
Warner / First Artists / Verdon (Melville Tucker)

Crooks are blackmailed into helping rebellious adolescents.
A black version, at immense length, of the hoodlum comedies in which the Dead End Kids so often featured. Not badly made, but out of date without being nostalgic.

w Charles Blackwell, *story* Timothy March
d Sidney Poitier   *ph* Don Morgan   *m* Curtis Mayfield

Sidney Poitier, James Earl Jones, Bill Cosby, Denise Nicholas, Hope Clarke, Tracy Reed, Jason Evers, Marc Lawrence

The Pied Piper**

US 1942   86m   bw
TCF (Nunnally Johnson)

An elderly man who hates children finds himself smuggling several of them out of occupied France.
Smart, sentimental, occasionally funny war adventure.

w Nunnally Johnson, *novel* Nevil Shute   *d* Irving Pichel   *ph* Edward Cronjager   *m* Alfred Newman

Monty Woolley, Anne Baxter, Roddy McDowall, Otto Preminger, J. Carrol Naish, Lester Matthews, Jill Esmond, Peggy Ann Garner

AAN: best picture; Edward Cronjager; Monty Woolley

The Pied Piper

GB 1971   90m   Eastmancolor Panavision
Sagittarius / Goodtimes (David Puttnam, Sanford Lieberson)

In 1349 a strolling minstrel rids Hamelin of a plague of rats.
Paceless, slightly too horrific, and generally disappointing fantasy, especially from this director; poor sets and restricted action.

w Jacques Demy, Mark Peploe, Andrew Birkin
d Jacques Demy   *ph* Peter Suschitsky
m Donovan   *pd* Assheton Gorton

Donovan, Donald Pleasence, Michael Hordern, Jack Wild, Diana Dors, John Hurt

The Pigeon That Took Rome
US 1962   101m   bw   Panavision
Paramount / Llenroc (Melville Shavelson)

American undercover agents are smuggled into Rome during the German occupation.
Heavy-going war comedy-drama with bright sequences countered by too little wit and too many voluble Italians.

wd Melville Shavelson, *novel* The Easter Dinner by Donald Downes *ph* Daniel Fapp *m* Alessandro Cicognini

Charlton Heston, Elsa Martinelli, Brian Donlevy, Harry Guardino, Baccaloni

Pigskin Parade
US 1936   93m   bw
TCF (Bogart Rogers)
GB title: *Harmony Parade*

A country farmer becomes a college football hero.
Livelier-than-average college comedy.

w Harry Tugend, Jack Yellen, William Conselman *d* David Butler *ph* Arthur Miller *md* David Buttolph

Stuart Erwin, Patsy Kelly, Jack Haley, Johnny Downs, Betty Grable, Arline Judge, Dixie Dunbar, Judy Garland, Tony Martin, Elisha Cook Jnr

AAN: Stuart Erwin

The Pilgrim*
US 1923   38m approx (24 fps)   bw   silent
First National

An escaped convict disguises himself as a minister and does a few good deeds.
Star comedy with more sentiment than laughter.

wd Charles Chaplin *ph* Rollie Totheroh

Charles Chaplin, Edna Purviance, Kitty Bradbury, Mack Swain

Pillars of the Sky
US 1956   95m   Technicolor
   Cinemascope
U-I (Robert Arthur)
GB title: *The Tomahawk and the Cross*

An indian scout and a missionary help bring peace between cavalry and indians.
Modest western, adequately done.

w Sam Rolfe *d* George Marshall *ph* Harold Lipstein *m* Joseph Gershenson

Jeff Chandler, Dorothy Malone, Ward Bond,

Keith Andes, Lee Marvin, Sydney Chaplin, Michael Ansara, Willis Bouchey

Pillow Talk**
US 1959   110m   Eastmancolor
   Cinemascope
U-I (Ross Hunter, Martin Melcher)

Two people who can't stand each other fall in love via a party line.
Slightly elephantine romantic comedy which nevertheless contains a number of funny scenes and was notable for starting off the Hudson-Day partnership and a run of similar comedies which survived the sixties.

w Stanley Shapiro, Maurice Richlin *d* Michael Gordon *ph* Arthur E. Arling *m* Frank de Vol

Doris Day, Rock Hudson, Tony Randall, Thelma Ritter, Nick Adams, Julia Meade, Allen Jenkins, Marcel Dalio, Lee Patrick

AAN: Frank de Vol; Doris Day; Thelma Ritter

Pillow to Post
US 1945   96m   bw
Warner (Alex Gottlieb)

A girl poses as a soldier's wife to get a hotel room.
World War II comedy on a familiar theme (*The More the Merrier, Standing Room Only, The Doughgirls,* etc). Uninspired.

w Charles Hoffman, *play* Pillar to Post by Rose Simon Kohn *d* Vincent Sherman *ph* Wesley Anderson *m* Frederick Hollander

Ida Lupino, Sidney Greenstreet, William Prince, Stuart Erwin, Ruth Donnelly, Barbara Brown, Frank Orth

Pilot Number Five
US 1943   71m   bw
MGM (B. P. Fineman)

A pilot in the South Pacific volunteers for a desperate mission because—we learn in flashback—he hates fascists.
Rather unpalatable propaganda encased in dim drama.

w David Hertz *d* George Sidney

Franchot Tone, Gene Kelly, Marsha Hunt, Van Johnson, Alan Baxter, Dick Simmons, Steve Geray

Pimpernel Smith**
GB 1941   121m   bw
British National (Leslie Howard)
US titles: *Mister V; The Fighting Pimpernel*

A professor of archaeology goes into war-torn Europe to rescue refugees.
The Scarlet Pimpernel unassumingly and quite

effectively brought up to date, with memorable scenes after a slow start.

w Anatole de Grunwald, Roland Pertwee, Ian Dalrymple *d* Leslie Howard

Leslie Howard, Mary Morris, Francis L. Sullivan, Hugh McDermott, Raymond Huntley, Manning Whiley, Peter Gawthorne, David Tomlinson

Pin Up Girl
US 1944   83m   Technicolor
TCF (William Le Baron)

A Washington secretary becomes a national celebrity when she meets a navy hero.
Adequate star flagwaver, mildly interesting for its new streamlined set designs.

w Robert Ells, Helen Logan, Earl Baldwin *d* Bruce Humberstone *ph* Ernest Palmer *md* Emil Newman, Charles Henderson *ch Hermes Pan ad James Basevi, Joseph C. Wright*

Betty Grable, John Harvey, Martha Raye, Joe E. Brown, Eugene Pallette, Dave Willcock, Charles Spivak and his Orchestra
   'A spiritless blob of a musical, and a desecration of a most inviting theme.'—*Bosley Crowther*

The Pink Jungle
US 1968   104m   Techniscope
Universal / Cherokee (Stan Margulies)

A photographer and his model are stranded in a South American village and become involved in a diamond hunt.
Curious mixture of adventure and light comedy that works only in patches.

w Charles Williams, *novel* Snake Water by Alan Williams *d* Delbert Mann *ph* Russell Metty *m* Ernie Freeman

James Garner, Eva Renzi, George Kennedy, Nigel Green, Michael Ansara, George Rose
   'Another backlot cheapie.'—*Robert Windeler*

The Pink Panther **
US 1963   113m   Technirama
UA / Mirisch (Martin Jurow)

An incompetent *sureté* inspector is in Switzerland on the trail of a jewel thief called The Phantom.
Sporadically engaging mixture of pratfalls, Raffles, and Monsieur Hulot, all dressed to kill and quite palatable for the uncritical. Inspector Clouseau later became a cartoon character and also provoked four sequels, *Inspector Clouseau, The Return of the Pink Panther, The Pink*

Panther Strikes Again and *The Revenge of the Pink Panther.*

w Maurice Richlin, Blake Edwards *d* Blake Edwards *ph* Philip Lathrop *m* Henry Mancini *ad* Fernando Carrere *animation* De Patie-Freleng

David Niven, Peter Sellers, Capucine, Claudia Cardinale, Robert Wagner, Brenda de Banzie, Colin Gordon

The Pink Panther Strikes Again*
GB 1976   103m   De Luxe   Panavision
United Artists / Amjo (Blake Edwards)

After a nervous breakdown, Chief Inspector Dreyfus builds up a vast criminal organization devoted to the extermination of Inspector Clouseau.
Zany pratfall farce with signs of overconfidence since the success of *The Return of the Pink Panther*. But some gags are funny, despite a rather boring star.

w Frank Waldman, Blake Edwards *d* Blake Edwards *ph* Harry Waxman *m* Henry Mancini

Peter Sellers, Herbert Lom, Colin Blakely, Leonard Rossiter, Lesley-Anne Down, Burt Kwouk

AAN: song, 'Come To Me' (*ly* Don Black, *m* Henry Mancini)

Pink String and Sealing Wax*
GB 1945   89m   bw
Ealing (S. C. Balcon)

In 1880 Brighton, a publican's wife plans to have her husband poisoned.
Unusual, carefully handled period crime melodrama which needed a slightly firmer grip.

w Diana Morgan, Robert Hamer, *play* Roland Pertwee *d* Robert Hamer

Googie Withers, Mervyn Johns, Gordon Jackson, Sally Ann Howes, Mary Merrall, John Carol, Catherine Lacey, Gary Marsh

Pinky**
US 1949   102m   bw
TCF (Darryl F. Zanuck)

In the American south, a negro girl who passes for white has romantic problems.
Rather blah problem picture which seemed brave at the time; a highly professional piece of work nevertheless.

w Philip Dunne, Dudley Nichols, *novel* Quality by Cid Ricketts Summer *d* Elia Kazan *ph* Joe MacDonald *m* Alfred Newman

Jeanne Crain, Ethel Barrymore, Ethel Waters, William Lundigan, Basil Ruysdael, Nina Mae McKinney, Frederick O'Neal, Evelyn Varden

AAN: Jeanne Crain; Ethel Barrymore; Ethel Waters

Pinocchio**
US 1940   77m   Technicolor
Walt Disney

The blue fairy breathes life into a puppet, which has to prove itself before it can turn into a real boy.
Charming, fascinating, superbly organized and streamlined cartoon feature without a single second of boredom.

supervisors Ben Sharpsteen, Hamilton Luske *m/ly* Leigh Harline, Ned Washington, Paul J. Smith

'A film of amazing detail and brilliant conception.'—*Leonard Maltin*
'A work that gives you almost every possible kind of pleasure to be got from a motion picture.'—*Richard Mallett, Punch*
'The limits of the animated cartoon have been blown so wide open that some of the original wonder of pictures has been restored.'—*Otis Ferguson*

AA: Leigh Harline (*m*); song 'When You Wish Upon a Star' (*m* Leigh Harline, *ly* Ned Washington)

Piranha*
US 1978   92m   Metrocolor
New World (Roger Corman, Jeff Schechtman, Jon Davison)

A mad doctor's stock of man-eating fish is accidentally released into the local rivers.
Slightly spoofy thriller with a high death rate and a better than usual script. On the whole, an improvement on *Jaws*.

w John Sayles *d* Joe Dante *ph* Jamie Anderson *m* Pino Danaggio *sp* Jon Berg

Bradford Dillman, Heather Menzies, Kevin McCarthy, Bruce Gordon, Barbara Steele, Keenan Wynn, Dick Miller

The Pirate**
US 1948   102m   Technicolor
MGM (Arthur Freed)

In a West Indian port, a girl imagines that a wandering player is a famous pirate, who in fact is her despised and elderly suitor.
Minor MGM musical with vivid moments and some intimation of the greatness shortly to come; all very set-bound, but the star quality is infectious.

w Albert Hackett, Frances Goodrich, *play* S. N. Behrman *d* Vincente Minnelli *ph* Harry Stradling *m/ly* Cole Porter *md* Lennie Hayton

Gene Kelly, Judy Garland, Walter Slezak, Gladys Cooper, Reginald Owen, George Zucco, the Nicholas Brothers

AAN: Lennie Hayton

Pirates of Blood River*
GB 1961   84m   Technicolor
   Hammerscope
Hammer (Anthony Nelson Keys)

Pirates in search of gold terrorize a Huguenot settlement.
Land-locked blood and thunder for tough schoolboys.

w John Hunter, John Gilling *d* John Gilling *ph* Arthur Grant

Christopher Lee, Andrew Keir, Kerwin Mathews, Glenn Corbett, Peter Arne, Oliver Reed, Marla Landi, Michael Ripper

The Pit and the Pendulum*
US 1961   85m   Pathecolor   Panavision
AIP / Alta Vista (Roger Corman)

Lovers plan to drive her brother mad; he responds by locking them in his torture chamber.
The centrepiece only is borrowed from Poe; the rest is lurid but mostly ineffective. Still, its commercial success started the Poe cycle of the sixties.

w Richard Matheson *d* Roger Corman *ph* Floyd Crosby *m* Les Baxter

Vincent Price, Barbara Steele, John Kerr

'As in *House of Usher*, the quality of the film is its full-blooded feeling for Gothic horror— storms and lightning, mouldering castles and cobwebbed torture chambers, bleeding brides trying to tear the lids from their untimely tombs.'—*David Robinson*

Pitfall
US 1948   85m   bw
Samuel Bischoff

An insurance investigator proves easy prey for a grasping woman.
Modest suspenser, quite efficiently made.

w Jay Dratler, from his novel *d* André de Toth *ph* Harry Wild *md* Louis Forbes

Dick Powell, Lizabeth Scott, Jane Wyatt, Raymond Burr, John Litel, Byron Barr, Ann Doran

Pittsburgh
US 1942   91m   bw
Universal (Charles K. Feldman)

A coal miner's daughter has two loves, all of them trying to improve their social status as

Pittsburgh becomes a world centre of steel production.

Routine melodrama ending as a flagwaver, and allowing none of its stars any opportunity.

w Kenneth Gamet, Tom Reed d Lewis Seiler ph Robert de Grasse m Hans Salter

Marlene Dietrich, Randolph Scott, John Wayne, Frank Craven, Louise Allbritton, Shemp Howard, Ludwig Stossel, Thomas Gomez

A Place in the Sun **
US 1951 122m bw
Paramount / George Stevens

A poor young man, offered the chance of a rich wife, allows himself to be convicted and executed for the accidental death of his former fiancée. Overblown, overlong and over-praised melodrama from a monumental novel of social guilt; sometimes visually striking, this version alters the stresses of the plot and leaves no time for sociological detail. A film so clearly intended as a masterpiece could hardly fail to be boring.

w Maurice Wilson, Harry Brown, *novel* An American Tragedy by Theodore Dreiser d George Stevens ph William C. Mellor m Franz Waxman ad Hans Dreier, Walter Tyler

Montgomery Clift, Elizabeth Taylor, Shelley Winters, Anne Revere, Keefe Brasselle, Fred Clark, Raymond Burr, Frieda Inescort, Shepperd Strudwick, Kathryn Givney, Walter Sande

'An almost incredibly painstaking work . . . mannered enough for a very fancy Gothic murder mystery. This version gives the story a modern setting, but the town is an arrangement of symbols of wealth, glamour and power versus symbols of poor, drab helplessness—an arrangement far more suitable to the thirties than to the fifties.'—*Pauline Kael*

AA: script; George Stevens; William C. Mellor; Franz Waxman

AAN: best picture; Montgomery Clift; Shelley Winters

A Place of One's Own **
GB 1944 92m bw
GFD / Gainsborough (R. J. Minney)

In Edwardian times, an old house is taken over by an elderly couple, and their young companion is possessed by the spirit of a murdered girl. Charming little ghost story, not quite detailed enough to be totally effective.

w Brock Williams, *novel* Osbert Sitwell d Bernard Knowles ph Stephen Dade m Hubert Bath md Louis Levy

James Mason, Barbara Mullen, Margaret Lockwood, Dennis Price, Helen Haye, Michael Shepley, Dulcie Gray, Moore Marriott

'A fine piece of work . . . gripping, marvellous, outstanding, eerie, perky, beautiful, lovely and different.'—*C. A. Lejeune*

'One comes away with an impression of elegance which has not so far been frequent in the British cinema.'—*Dilys Powell*

A Place to Go
GB 1963 86m bw
British Lion / Excalibur (Michael Relph, Basil Dearden)

A young man depressed by his urban environment turns to crime.

Panorama of London low life, efficiently varied and well made but not in any way memorable. *It Always Rains on Sunday*, fifteen years earlier, wears better.

w Michael Relph, Clive Exton, *novel* Bethnal Green by Michael Fisher d Basil Dearden ph Reg Wyer m Charles Blackwell

Rita Tushingham, Mike Sarne, Doris Hare, John Slater, Bernard Lee, Barbara Ferris, Roy Kinnear

The Plague of the Zombies *
GB 1965 91m Technicolor
Hammer (Anthony Nelson Keys)

A voodoo-practising Cornish squire raises zombies from the dead and uses them to work his tin mine.

They don't explain why he didn't simply hire the living; apart from that this is Hammer on its better side, with a charming elderly hero and good suspense sequences.

w Peter Bryan d John Gilling ph Arthur Grant m James Bernard

André Morell, John Carson, Diane Clare, Brook Williams, Jacqueline Pearce, Alex Davion, Michael Ripper

'Visually the film is splendid . . . the script manages several offbeat strokes.'—*MFB*

The Plainsman **
US 1936 113m bw
Paramount / Cecil B. de Mille

The life of Wild Bill Hickok and his friends Buffalo Bill and Calamity Jane.

Standard big-scale thirties western; narrative lumpy, characters idealized, spectacle impressive, technical credits high.

w Waldemar Young, Lynn Riggs, Harold Lamb d Cecil B. de Mille ph Victor Milner, George Robinson m George Antheil md Boris Morros

Gary Cooper, James Ellison, Jean Arthur, Charles Bickford, Helen Burgess, Porter Hall, Paul Harvey, Victor Varconi

Le Plaisir*
France 1952   97m   bw
Stera / CCFC

Three stories by Guy de Maupassant, about the search for pleasure: 'Le Masque', 'La Maison Tellier', 'Le Modèle'.
Stylish but rather subdued compendium, with no highlights to stay in the memory.

w Jacques Natanson, Max Ophuls d Max Ophuls ph Christian Matras, Philippe Agostini m Joe Hajos

Claude Dauphin, Gaby Morlay; Madeleine Renaud, Danielle Darrieux, Ginette Leclerc, Jean Gabin, Pierre Brasseur; Simone Simon, Daniel Gélin

'An attractive theme tune, good performances, and the pleasure itself of virtuosity.'—*Gavin Lambert, MFB*

Planet of the Apes***
US 1968   119m   De Luxe   Panavision
TCF / Apjac (Mort Abrahams)

Astronauts caught in a time warp land on a planet which turns out to be Earth in the distant future, when men have become beasts and the apes have taken over.
Stylish, thoughtful science fiction which starts and finishes splendidly but suffers from a sag in the middle. The ape make-up is great.

w *Michael Wilson, Rod Serling, novel* Monkey Planet by Pierre Boulle d *Franklin Schaffner ph Leon Shamroy m* Jerry Goldsmith

Charlton Heston, Roddy McDowall, *Kim Hunter,* Maurice Evans, James Whitmore, James Daly, Linda Harrison

'One of the most telling science fiction films to date.'—*Tom Milne*
†Sequels, in roughly descending order of interest, were BENEATH THE PLANET OF THE APES (1969), ESCAPE FROM THE PLANET OF THE APES (1970), CONQUEST OF THE PLANET OF THE APES (1972) and BATTLE FOR THE PLANET OF THE APES (1973). A TV series followed in 1974, and a cartoon series in 1975.

AAN: Jerry Goldsmith

The Planter's Wife
GB 1952   91m   bw
Rank / Pinnacle (John Stafford)
US title: *Outpost in Malaya*

Malaya under the terrorists. A wife is planning to leave but changes her mind after she and her husband defend their home in a siege.
Superficial studio-bound melodrama unworthy of its subject but a good star vehicle.

w Peter Proud, Guy Elmes d Ken Annakin ph Geoffrey Unsworth m Allan Gray

Claudette Colbert, Jack Hawkins, Ram Gopal, Jeremy Spenser, Tom Macauley, Helen Goss

Platinum Blonde*
US 1931   92m   bw
Columbia

A newspaper reporter falls for an heiress.
Limp romantic comedy with interesting performances: the film which established Jean Harlow.

w Robert Riskin, Jo Swerling, *story* Harry E. Chandler, Doug Churchill d Frank Capra ph Joseph Walker

Robert Williams, Loretta Young, Jean Harlow, Halliwell Hobbes, Reginald Owen

Play Dirty*
GB 1969   118m   Technicolor   Panavision
UA / Lowndes (Harry Saltzman)

During World War II, a squad of ex-criminals is given the job of destroying an enemy oil depot in North Africa.
Small-scale Dirty Dozen with would-be ironic twists; well made entertainment for the stout-hearted.

w Lotte Colin, Melvyn Bragg d André de Toth ph Edward Scaife m Michel Legrand

Michael Caine, Nigel Davenport, Nigel Green, Harry Andrews, Bernard Archard, Daniel Pilon

Play It Again Sam*
US 1972   86m   Technicolor   Panavision
Paramount / Apjac

A neurotic film critic is abandoned by his wife and seeks fresh companionship, with help from the shade of Humphrey Bogart.
Random comedy for star fans, mainly quite lively and painless.

w Woody Allen, from his play d Herbert Ross ph Owen Roizman m Billy Goldenberg

Woody Allen, Diane Keaton, Jerry Lacy, Susan Anspach

Play Misty for Me*
US 1971   102m   Technicolor
Universal / Malpaso (Robert Daley)

A radio disc jockey is pestered by a girl who turns out to be homicidally jealous.
Smartly made if over-extended psycho

melodrama with good suspense sequences and a fair quota of shocks.

w Jo Heims, Dean Reisner *d* Clint Eastwood *ph* Bruce Surtees *m* Dee Barton

Clint Eastwood, Jessica Walter, Donna Mills, John Larch

Playmates*
US 1941 96m bw
RKO (Cliff Reid)

For the sake of a lucrative radio contract, John Barrymore agrees to turn bandleader Kay Kyser into a Shakespearian actor.
Barrymore's last film is a weird comedy concoction, awesome in its waste of his talents but fairly funny in a high school kind of way.

w James V. Kern *d* David Butler *ph* Frank Redman *songs* James Van Heusen, Johnny Burke

Kay Kyser and his Band, *John Barrymore,* Ginny Simms, Lupe Velez, May Robson, Patsy Kelly, Peter Lind Hayes, George Cleveland

Playtime*
France 1960 152m Eastmancolor 70mm
Specta Films (René Silvera)

Hulot and a group of American tourists are bewildered by life in an airport, a business block and a restaurant.
Incredibly extended series of sketches, none of which is devastatingly funny, The irritation is that the talent is clearly there but needs control.

w Jacques Tati, Jacques Lagrange *d* Jacques Tati *ph* Jean Badal, Andreas Winding *m* Francis Lemarque *pd* Eugene Roman

Jacques Tati, Barbara Dennek, Jacqueline Lecomte, Henri Piccoli

'Tati still seems the wrong distance from his audience: not so far that we cannot see his gifts, not close enough so that they really touch.'— *Stanley Kauffmann*

'How sad that the result of all this, though it includes a great deal of intermittent pleasure, comes at times so dangerously close to boredom.'—*Brenda Davies, MFB*

'A series of brilliant doodles by an artist who has earned the right to indulge himself on such a scale.'—*Alexander Walker*

Plaza Suite*
US 1971 114m Technicolor
Paramount (Howard B. Koch)

Three sketches set in the same suite at New York's Plaza Hotel, with Walter Matthau appearing in all three but in different character.

A highly theatrical entertainment which was bound to seem flattened on the screen, but emerges with at least some of its laughs intact.

w Neil Simon, from his play *d* Arthur Hiller *ph* Jack Marta *m* Maurice Jarre

Walter Matthau, Maureen Stapleton, Barbara Harris, Lee Grant, Louise Sorel

Please Believe Me
US 1950 87m bw
MGM (Val Lewton)

An English girl inherits an American ranch and is chased by a millionaire, a con man and a lawyer.
Dullsville comedy which failed to establish its star in America.

w Nathaniel Curtis *d* Norman Taurog *ph* Robert Planck

Deborah Kerr, Robert Walker, Mark Stevens, Peter Lawford, James Whitmore, Spring Byington

Please Don't Eat the Daisies
US 1960 111m Metrocolor Panavision
MGM (Joe Pasternak)

The family of a drama critic move to the country. Thin, obvious comedy, all dressed up but with nowhere to go.

w Isobel Lennart, *book* Jean Kerr *d* Charles Walters *ph* Robert Bronner *m* David Rose

Doris Day, David Niven, Janis Paige, Spring Byington, Patsy Kelly, Richard Haydn, Jack Weston, John Harding, Margaret Lindsay

Please Murder Me
US 1956 78m bw
DCA (Donald Hyde)

An attorney defends an accused murderess, at great cost to himself.
Adequate Poverty Row suspenser with a foreseeable trick ending.

w Al C. Ward, Donald Hyde *d* Peter Godfrey *ph* Allen Stensvold

Angela Lansbury, Raymond Burr, Dick Foran, John Dehner, Lamont Johnson, Denver Pyle

Please Sir
GB 1971 101m Eastmancolor
Rank / LWL / Leslie Grade (Andrew Mitchell)

The masters and pupils of Fenn Street school go on an annual camp.
Grossly inflated, occasionally funny big-screen version of the TV series.

w John Esmonde, Bob Larbey *d* Mark Stuart *ph* Wilkie Cooper *m* Mike Vickers

John Alderton, Deryck Guyler, Joan Sanderson, Noel Howlett, Eric Chitty, Richard Davies

The Pleasure Garden
GB / Germany 1925   74m approx (24 fps)
   bw   silent
Gainsborough / Emelka (Michael Balcon, Erich Pommer)

A chorus girl marries a rich colonial who goes native.
Boring melodrama with a few touches typical of its director, whose first film it is.

w Eliot Stannard, *novel* Oliver Sandys *d* Alfred Hitchcock *ph* Baron Ventigmilia

Virginia Valli, John Stuart, Miles Mander, Carmelita Gerghty

The Pleasure Girls
GB 1965   88m   bw
Compton Tekli

Girl flatmates in London have trouble with their boy friends.
The road to ruin sixties style, hackneyed but quite well observed.

wd Gerry O'Hara ph Michael Reed *m* Malcolm Lockyer

Ian McShane, Francesca Annis, Tony Tanner, Klaus Kinski, Mark Eden, Suzanna Leigh

The Pleasure of His Company
US 1961   114m   Technicolor
Paramount / Perlberg–Seaton

An ageing playboy arrives unexpectedly in San Francisco for his daughter's wedding.
Tame family comedy, very flatly adapted from the stage; dressed to kill, but with no narrative or cinematic drive.

w Samuel Taylor, *play* Samuel Taylor, Cornelia Otis Skinner *d* George Seaton *ph* Robert Burks *m* Alfred Newman

Fred Astaire, Lilli Palmer, Debbie Reynolds, Charles Ruggles, Tab Hunter, Gary Merrill, Harold Fong
   'Smart comedy in its most diluted form.'—
MFB

The Pleasure Seekers
US 1964   107m   De Luxe   Cinemascope
TCF (David Weisbart)

Three girls in Madrid find boy friends.
Dim remake of *Three Coins in the Fountain,* adequate but unstimulating on all levels.

w Edith Sommer *d* Jean Negulesco *ph* Daniel L. Fapp *m* Lionel Newman, Alexander Courage

Ann-Margret, Tony Franciosa, Carol Lynley,

Gene Tierney, Brian Keith, Gardner McKay, Isobel Elsom

AAN: Lionel Newman, Alexander Courage

The Plough and the Stars*
US 1936   72m   bw
RKO (Cliff Reid, Robert Sisk)

In 1916, a Dublin marriage is threatened by the husband's appointment as commander of the citizen army.
Rather elementary film version of the play about the Troubles; interesting for effort rather than performance, and for the talent involved.

w Dudley Nichols, *play* Sean O'Casey *d* John Ford *ph* Joseph August *m* Roy Webb

Barbara Stanwyck, Preston Foster, Barry Fitzgerald, Denis O'Dea, Eileen Crowe, F. J. McCormick, Arthur Shields, Una O'Connor, Moroni Olsen, J. M. Kerrigan, Bonita Granville

Plunder of the Sun*
US 1953   81m   bw
Warner (Robert Fellows)

Various criminal elements seek buried treasure among the Mexican Aztec ruins.
Interestingly located, well made, unconvincingly scripted melodrama, yet another borrowing from *The Maltese Falcon.*

w Jonathan Latimer, *novel* David Dodge *d* John Farrow *ph* Jack Draper *m* Antonio D. Conde

Glenn Ford, Diana Lynn, Francis L. Sullivan, Patricia Medina, Sean McClory, Douglass Dumbrille, Eduardo Noriega

The Plunderers
US 1960   94m   bw
Allied Artists / August (Joseph Pevney)

In the old west, four juvenile delinquents take over a town.
The Wild One in period dress. Nothing in particular.

w Bob Barbash *d* Joseph Pevney *ph* Eugene Polito *m* Leonard Rosenman

Jeff Chandler, John Saxon, Ray Sticklyn, Roger Torrey, Dee Pollock, Marsha Hunt, Dolores Hart, Jay C. Flippen, James Westerfield

Plymouth Adventure*
US 1952   105m   Technicolor
MGM (Dore Schary)

The Pilgrim Fathers sail from Plymouth on the Mayflower and spend their first months ashore on the coast of America.
Well-meaning schoolbook history, totally unconvincing and very dull despite obvious

effort all round. One or two of the actors have their moments.

w Helen Deutsch, *novel* Ernest Gebler
d Clarence Brown *ph* William Daniels
m Miklos Rozsa

Spencer Tracy, Gene Tierney, Van Johnson, Leo Genn, Dawn Addams

'It demonstrates how Hollywood can dull down as well as jazz up history.'—*Judith Crist, 1973*

Pocket Money

US 1972   100m   Technicolor
First Artists / Coleytown

Two slow-thinking Arizona cowboys try to make money herding cattle.
Peculiar modern western comedy drama which doesn't work.

w Terry Malick, *novel* Jim Kane by J. K. S. Brown d Stuart Rosenberg *ph* Laszlo Kovacs m Alex North

Paul Newman, Lee Marvin, Strother Martin, Kelly Jean Peters, Wayne Rogers

Pocketful of Miracles

US 1961   136m   Technicolor   Panavision
UA / Franton (Frank Capra)

Kindly gangsters help an old apple seller to persuade her long-lost daughter that she is a lady of means.
Boring, overlong remake of *Lady for a Day*, showing that Capra's touch simply doesn't work on the wide screen, that his themes are dated anyway, and that all the fine character actors in Hollywood are a liability unless you find them something to do.

w Hal Kanter, Harry Tugend, *scenario* Robert Riskin, *story* Damon Runyon d Frank Capra *ph* Robert Bronner m Walter Scharf

Bette Davis, Glenn Ford, Hope Lange, Arthur O'Connell, Peter Falk, Thomas Mitchell, Edward Everett Horton, Sheldon Leonard, Barton MacLane, Jerome Cowan, Fritz Feld, Snub Pollard, David Brian, Ann-Margret, John Litel, Jay Novello, Willis Bouchey, George E. Stone, Mike Mazurki, Jack Elam, Mickey Shaughnessy, Peter Mann, Frank Ferguson

'The effect is less one of whimsy than of being bludgeoned to death with a toffee apple.'—*Peter John Dyer*

'The story has enough cracks in it for the syrup to leak through.'—*Playboy*

AAN: title song (*m* James Van Heusen, *ly* Sammy Cahn); Peter Falk

Poet's Pub

GB 1949   79m   bw
GFD / Aquila

A rowing blue takes over a Tudor inn and discovers a priceless jewelled gauntlet, the wearer of which is kidnapped during the performance of a pageant.
Very thin, naive treatment of a whimsical novel. The last film to use the Independent Frame process.

w Diana Morgan, *novel* Eric Linklater
d Frederick Wilson *ph* George Stretton
m Clifton Parker

Derek Bond, Rona Anderson, Barbara Murray, Leslie Dwyer, Joyce Grenfell

Poil de Carotte*

France 1932   94m   bw

A small boy is picked on by his ageing mother to the point where he attempts suicide.
Country melodrama which made its director's name but seems a little faded now despite bravura sequences.

w Jules Renard d Julien Duvivier *ph* Thirard Monniot

Harry Baur, Robert Lynen, Catherine Fontenoy

Point Blank*

US 1967   92m   Metrocolor   Panavision
MGM / Judd Bernard, Irwin Winkler

A gangster takes an elaborate revenge on his cheating partner.
Extremely violent gangster thriller, well shot on location and something of a cult, but with irritating pretentiousness and obscure plot points.

w Alexander Jacobs, David Newhouse, Rafe Newhouse, *novel* The Hunter by Richard Stark d John Boorman *ph* Philip Lathrop m Johnny Mandel

Lee Marvin, Angie Dickinson, Keenan Wynn, Carroll O'Connor, Lloyd Bochner, Michael Strong, John Vernon, Sharon Acker
†*The Outfit* (qv) is a kind of sequel / reprise.

Poison Pen*

GB 1939   79m   bw
ABP (Walter C. Mycroft)

A village community is set at odds by a writer of vindictive anonymous letters.
Effective minor drama, with good location atmosphere.

w Doreen Montgomery, William Freshman, N. C. Hunter, Esther McCracken, *play* Richard Llewellyn d Paul Stein

Flora Robson, Reginald Tate, Robert Newton, Ann Todd, Geoffrey Toone, Belle Chrystal, Edward Chapman, Edward Rigby
  'A lamentably artificial piece.'—*Richard Mallett, Punch*

Polly of the Circus
US 1932   72m   bw
MGM

A trapeze artiste falls for the local minister, but incurs disapproval from his bishop.
Elementary romance reminiscent of silent drama.

w Carey Wilson, *play* Margaret Mayo *d* Alfred Santell *ph* George Barnes

Marion Davies, Clark Gable, C. Aubrey Smith, Raymond Hatton, David Landau, Maude Eburne, Guinn Williams, Ray Milland

Pollyanna*
US 1960   134m   Technicolor
Walt Disney (George Golitzen)

A 12-year-old orphan girl cheers up the grumps of the small town where she comes to live.
Well cast but overlong and rather humourless remake of a children's classic from an earlier age.

wd David Swift, *novel* Eleanor Porter
ph Russell Harlan *m* Paul Smith *ad* Carroll Clark, Robert Clatworthy

Hayley Mills, Jane Wyman, Karl Malden, Nancy Olson, Adolphe Menjou, Donald Crisp, Agnes Moorehead, Richard Egan, Kevin Corcoran, James Drury, Reta Shaw, Leora Dana
  'Even Hayley Mills can neither prevent one from sympathizing with the crusty aunts, hermits, vicars and hypochondriacs who get so forcibly cheered up, nor from feverishly speculating whether films like this don't run the risk of inciting normally kind and gentle people into certain excesses of violent crime – child murder, for instance.'—*MFB*

Pony Express*
US 1953   101m   Technicolor
Paramount (Nat Holt)

In 1860 Buffalo Bill Cody and Wild Bill Hickok are sent to establish pony express stations across California.
Standard western which tells a factual tale adequately if rather slowly.

w Charles Marquis Warren *d* Jerry Hopper
ph Ray Rennahan *m* Paul Sawtell

Charlton Heston, Forrest Tucker, Rhonda Fleming, Jan Sterling

Pony Soldier
US 1952   82m   Technicolor
TCF (Samuel G. Engel)
GB title: *MacDonald of the Canadian Mounties*

The mounties settle the hash of Canadian Indian renegades who have been causing trouble on the American border.
Mediocre outdoor adventure.

w John C. Higgins *d* Joseph M. Newman
ph Harry Jackson *m* Alex North

Tyrone Power, Cameron Mitchell, Robert Horton, Thomas Gomez, Penny Edwards, *Adeline de Walt Reynolds*

Pool of London
GB 1950   85m   bw
Ealing (Michael Relph)

A smuggling sailor gets involved in murder.
Routine semi-documentary police thriller with locations in London docks decorating a standard piece of thick ear.

w Jack Whittingham, John Eldridge *d* Basil Dearden *ph* Gordon Dines

Bonar Colleano, Susan Shaw, Earl Cameron, Renée Asherson, Moira Lister, Max Adrian, James Robertson Justice, Joan Dowling
  'Done with such imagination, humour and visual attractiveness as to hold the pleased attention of all who like to use their eyes and their ears.'—*Richard Mallett, Punch*

Poor Cow*
GB 1967   101m   Eastmancolor
Anglo Amalgamated / Vic / Fenchurch (Joe Janni)

The dismal life of a young London mother who lives in squalor with her criminal husband.
Television-style fictional documentary determined to rub one's nose in the mire.
Innovative and occasionally striking but not very likeable.

w Nell Dunn, Ken Loach, *novel* Nell Dunn
d Ken Loach *ph* Brian Probyn *m* Donovan

Carol White, Terence Stamp, John Bindon, Kate Williams, Queenie Watts
  'A superficial, slightly patronizing excursion into the nether realms of social realism.'—*Jan Dawson*

Poor Little Rich Girl*
US 1936   79m   bw
TCF (Darryl F. Zanuck)

A child is separated from her father and joins a radio singing act.
Pleasing star vehicle with all the expected

elements, adapted from a Mary Pickford vehicle of 1917.

w Sam Hellman, Gladys Lehman, Harry Tugend d Irving Cummings ph John Seitz songs Mack Gordon, Harry Revel

Shirley Temple, Jack Haley, Alice Faye, Gloria Stuart, Michael Whalen, Sara Haden, Jane Darwell, Claude Gillingwater, Henry Armetta

Pope Joan
GB 1972   132m   Eastmancolor
Panavision
Big City Productions / Kurt Unger
aka: *The Devil's Imposter*

The legend of a 9th-century German semi-prostitute who discovered a vocation to preach and was made Pope.
Uninspiring pageant, brutish and rather silly, full of would-be medieval sensationalism.

w John Briley d Michael Anderson ph Billy Williams m Maurice Jarre pd Elliott Scott

Liv Ullmann, Trevor Howard, Olivia de Havilland, Maximilian Schell, Keir Dullea, Robert Beatty, Franco Nero, Patrick Magee

Popi*
US 1969   113m   De Luxe
UA / Leonard Films (Herbert B. Leonard)

Adventures of a cheerful inhabitant of New York's Puerto Rican ghetto.
Ethnic comedy-drama of the kind that has since found its way in abundance into American TV series. Very competently done for those who like it, e.g. Puerto Ricans.

w Tina and Lester Pine d Arthur Hiller ph Ross Lowell m Dominic Frontière

Alan Arkin, Rita Moreno, Miguel Alejandro, Ruben Figuero
   'An appropriately disenchanted view of an immigrant's struggling ambitions in the Promised Land.'—*Richard Combs*

Poppy*
US 1936   74m   bw
Paramount (Paul Jones)

An itinerant medicine-seller sets up his stall in a small town where his daughter falls in love with the mayor's son.
Clumsily but heavily plotted vehicle for W. C. Fields, who as usual has great moments but seems to rob the show of its proper pace.

w Waldemar Young, Virginia Van Upp, *play* Dorothy Donnelly d A. Edward Sutherland ph William Mellor

W. C. Fields, Rochelle Hudson, Richard

Cromwell, Granville Bates, Catherine Doucet, Lynne Overman, Maude Eburne
   'Antique hokum trussed up for a Fields vehicle.'—*Literary Digest*

Porgy and Bess*
US 1959   138m   Technicolor   Todd-AO
Samuel Goldwyn

A slum girl falls in love with a crippled beggar.
Negro opera about the inhabitants of Catfish Row; full of interest for music lovers, but not lending itself very readily to screen treatment.

w N. Richard Nash, *libretto* Du Bose Heyward, *play* Porgy by Du Bose and Dorothy Heyward d Otto Preminger ph Leon Shamroy m George Gershwin m André Previn, Ken Darby ch Hermes Pan

Sidney Poitier, Dorothy Dandridge, Sammy Davis Jnr, Pearl Bailey, Brock Peters, Diahann Carroll, Clarence Muse

AA: André Previn, Ken Darby
AAN: Leon Shamroy

Pork Chop Hill*
US 1959   97m   bw
UA / Lewis Milestone

The Americans in Korea take a vital hill but the colonel in command finds it difficult to hold.
Ironic war film with vivid spectacle separated by much talk.

w James R. Webb d Lewis Milestone ph Sam Leavitt m Leonard Rosenman pd Nicolai Remisoff

Gregory Peck, Harry Guardino, George Shibata, Woody Strode, James Edwards, Rip Torn, George Peppard, Barry Atwater, Robert Blake

Port of New York*
US 1949   82m   bw
Eagle Lion (Aubrey Schenck)

A woman narcotics smuggler determines to betray her colleagues to the authorities.
Good routine semi-documentary thick ear, notable for an early appearance by Yul Brynner as villain-in-chief.

w Eugene Ling d Laslo Benedek ph George E. Diskant

Scott Brady, Richard Rober, K. T. Stevens, Yul Brynner

Port of Seven Seas*
US 1938   81m   bw
MGM (Henry Henigson)
Love on the Marseilles waterfront.

Stagey Hollywoodization of Pagnol's *Marius* trilogy: some vigour shows through.

w Preston Sturges *d* James Whale *ph* Karl Freund

Wallace Beery, Frank Morgan, Maureen O'Sullivan, John Beal, Jessie Ralph, Cora Witherspoon

Porte des Lilas*
France / Italy 1957   95m   bw
Filmsonor / Rizzoli (Jacques Plante)
aka: *Gate of Lilacs*

A gangster on the run shelters in a poor quarter of Paris, but his treachery is his undoing.
Atmospheric comedy-drama put across with the expected style but providing very little to smile at.

w René Clair, Jean Aurel, *novel* La Grande Ceinture by René Fallet *d* René Clair *ph* Robert Le Fèbvre *m* Georges Brassens

Pierre Brasseur, Georges Brassens, Henri Vidal, Dany Carrel, Raymond Bussières, Amedée, Alain Bouvette

Les Portes de la Nuit*
France 1946   106m   bw
Pathé Cinema
aka: *Gates of Night*

Various people in post-war Paris are drawn into a pattern woven by Destiny—who appears as a melancholy tramp.
A polished piece of post-war gloom, and the archetype of all *films noirs* of the period. The beginning, also, of its director's decline.

w Jacques Prévert *d* Marcel Carné *ph* Philippe Agostini *m* Joseph Kosma *ad* Alexander Trauner

Pierre Brasseur, Yves Montand, Nathalie Nattier, Serge Reggiani, Jean Vilar, Saturnin Fabre, Mady Berry, Dany Robin
† One of the few films to have been based on a ballet—*Le Rendezvous* by Prévert. Oddly enough its realistic scenes of daily life are among its most successful elements.

Portnoy's Complaint
US 1972   101m   Technicolor   Panavision
Warner / Chehnault (Ernest Lehman)

A young New York Jewish boy has mother and masturbation problems.
Foolhardy attempt to film a fashionably sensational literary exercise; one of Hollywood's last attempts – thank goodness – to be 'with it'.

wd Ernest Lehman, *novel* Philip Roth *ph* Philip Lathrop *m* Michel Legrand

Richard Benjamin, Karen Black, Lee Black, Jack Somack, Jill Clayburgh, Jeannie Berlin

'The spectator is forced into the doubly uncomfortable position of a voyeur who can't actually see anything.'—*Jan Dawson*

Portrait from Life
GB 1948   90m   bw
GFD / Gainsborough

In an art gallery, a German professor recognizes a portrait as that of his daughter, lost during the war in Germany, and after a search discovers her to have been an amnesiac under the protection of a leading Nazi.
Tolerable melodrama with similarities to *The Seventh Veil* (the girl has to choose between four men).

w Frank Harvey Jnr, Muriel and Sydney Box *d* Terence Fisher *ph* Jack Asher *m* Benjamin Frankel

Mai Zetterling, Robert Beatty, Guy Rolfe, Herbert Lom, Patrick Holt

Portrait in Black*
US 1960   113m   Eastmancolor
U-I / Ross Hunter

An elderly shipping tycoon is murdered by his wife and doctor, but they are blackmailed.
Absurd old-fashioned melodrama of dark doings among the idle rich. Quite entertaining for addicts.

w Ivan Goff, Ben Roberts *d* Michael Gordon *ph* Russell Metty *m* Frank Skinner

Lana Turner, Anthony Quinn, Richard Basehart, Anna May Wong, Lloyd Nolan, Sandra Dee, John Saxon, Ray Walston, Virginia Grey

'Connoisseurs of the higher tosh should find it irresistible.'—*Penelope Houston*

Portrait of a Mobster
US 1961   108m   bw
Warner

The career of twenties gangster Dutch Schultz. Over-familiar, warmed over racketeering stuff with no particular edge or style.

w Howard Browne *d* Joseph Pevney *ph* Eugene Polito *m* Max Steiner

Vic Morrow, Leslie Parrish, Peter Breck, Ray Danton (repeating as Legs Diamond), Norman Alden, Ken Lynch

Portrait of Clare
GB 1950   98m   bw
ABPC (Leslie Landau)

In 1900, a woman looks back on her three
marriages.
High school novelette for easily pleased female
audiences.

w Leslie Landau, Adrian Arlington,
novel Francis Brett Young *d* Lance Comfort
ph Gunther Krampf *ad* Don Ashton

Margaret Johnston, Richard Todd, Robin
Bailey, Ronald Howard, Mary Clare, Marjorie
Fielding, Anthony Nicholls, Lloyd Pearson

Portrait of Jennie***
US 1948 86m bw (tinted sequence)
David O. Selznick
GB title: *Jennie*

A penniless artist meets a strange girl who seems
to age each time he sees her; they fall in love and
he discovers that she has long been dead, though
she finally comes to life once more during a sea
storm like the one in which she perished.
A splendid example of the higher Hollywood
lunacy: a silly story with pretensions about life
and death and time and art, presented with
superb persuasiveness by a first-class team of
actors and technicians.

w Peter Berneis, Paul Osborn, Leonard
Bernovici, *novel* Robert Nathan *d William
Dieterle ph Joseph August m Dmitri Tiomkin,*
after Debussy

Jennifer Jones, Joseph Cotten, Ethel Barrymore,
David Wayne, Lillian Gish, Henry Hull,
Florence Bates

'Though the story may not make sense, the
pyrotechnics, joined to the dumbfounded
silliness, keeps one watching.'—*New Yorker
1976*

AAN: Joseph August

The Poseidon Adventure**
US 1972 117m De Luxe Panavision
TCF / Kent (Irwin Allen)

A luxury liner is capsized, and trapped
passengers have to find their way to freedom via
an upside down world.
Tedious disaster movie which caught the public
fancy and started a cycle. Spectacular moments,
cardboard characters, flashes of imagination.

w Stirling Silliphant, Wendell Mayes, *novel* Paul
Gallico *ph* Harold Stine *d* Ronald Neame
m John Williams *pd* William Creber

Gene Hackman, Ernest Borgnine, Shelley
Winters, Red Buttons, Carol Lynley, Leslie
Nielson, Arthur O'Connell

'The script is the only cataclysm in this
waterlogged *Grand Hotel.*'—*New Yorker*

AA: song 'The Morning After' (*m/ly* Al Kasha,
Joel Hirschhorn)

Posse**
US 1975 93m Technicolor Panavision
Paramount / Bryna (Kirk Douglas)

A US marshal seeking higher office vows to
capture a railroad bandit, but the tables are
smartly turned.
Unusual minor western, quite pleasing in all
departments and neither mindless nor violent.

*w William Roberts, Christopher Knopf d Kirk
Douglas ph* Fred Koenekamp *m* Maurice Jarre

Kirk Douglas, Bruce Dern, Bo Hopkins, James
Stacy, Luke Askey, David Canary

Possessed*
US 1931 76m bw
MGM

A factory girl goes to New York in search of
riches.
Reasonably gutsy Depression melodrama which
moves at a fair pace.

w Lenore Coffee, *play* The Mirage by Edgar
Selwyn *d* Clarence Brown *ph* Oliver T. Marsh

Joan Crawford, Clark Gable, Wallace Ford,
Skeets Gallagher, Frank Conroy, Marjorie
White, John Miljan

'Lots of luxury; lots of charm; lots of smooth
talk about courage and marriage and what
women want.'—*James R. Quirk*

Possessed*
US 1947 108m bw
Warner (Jerry Wald)

An emotionally unstable nurse marries her
employer but retains a passionate love for an
engineer whom she kills when he does not
respond.
Extremely heavy, almost Germanic, flashback
melodrama with everyone tearing hammer and
tongs at the rather ailing script. Fun if you're in
that mood, and an interesting example of the
American *film noir* of the forties.

w Silvia Richards, Ranald MacDougall,
novel One Mán's Secret by Rita Weiman
*d Curtis Bernhardt ph Joseph Valentine
m* Franz Waxman

Joan Crawford, Raymond Massey, Van Heflin,
Geraldine Brooks, Stanley Ridges, John
Ridgely, Moroni Olsen

'Acting with bells on.'—*Richard Winnington*
'Miss Crawford performs with the passion and
intelligence of an actress who is not content with
just one Oscar.'—*James Agee*

AAN: Joan Crawford

The Possession of Joel Delaney*

US 1971 108m Eastmancolor
ITC / Haworth (George Justin)

A wealthy New York divorcee tries to save her brother from death at the hands of a Puerto Rican occult group who believe in ritual murder and demonic possession.

Unpleasant, frightening and overlong horror film with some kind of message struggling to get out but precious little entertainment value.

w Matt Robinson, Grimes Grice, *novel* Ramona Stewart d Waris Hussein ph Arthur J. Ornitz m Joe Ragoso

Shirley Maclaine, Perry King, Lisa Kohane, David Ellacott

'Some see the film as a political allegory; I see it as a piece of political tosh.'—*Michael Billington, Illustrated London News*

The Postman Always Rings Twice*

US 1946 113m bw
MGM (Carey Wilson)

A guilty couple murder her husband but get their come-uppance.

Pale shadow of *Double Indemnity,* efficient but not interesting or very suspenseful.

w Harry Ruskin, Niven Busch, *novel* James M. Cain d Tay Garnett ph Sidney Wagner m George Basserman

Lana Turner, John Garfield, Cecil Kellaway, Hume Cronyn, Leon Ames, Audrey Totter, Alan Reed

Postman's Knock*

GB 1961 88m bw
MGM (Ronald Kinnoch)

A village postman is transferred to London, finds life and work bewildering, but captures some crooks and ends up a hero.

Mildly amusing star vehicle rising to good comic climaxes.

w John Briley, Jack Trevor Story d Robert Lynn ph Gerald Moss m Ron Goodwin

Spike Milligan, Barbara Shelley, Wilfrid Lawson

Pot O'Gold

US 1941 87m bw
(UA) James Roosevelt
GB title: *The Golden Hour*

A radio giveaway show finds work for idle musicians.

Thin Capraesque comedy which needed more determined handling.

w Walter de Leon d George Marshall ph Hal Mohr md Lou Forbes

James Stewart, Paulette Goddard, Horace Heidt, Charles Winninger, Mary Gordon, Frank Melton, Jed Prouty

The Power*

US 1967 109m
Metrocolor Cinemascope
MGM / George Pal

Scientists researching into human endurance are menaced by one of their number who has developed the ability to kill by will power.

Interesting but finally unexciting and exasperating science fiction which badly lacks a gimmick one can actually see.

w John Gay, *novel* Frank M. Robinson d Byron Haskin ph Ellsworth Fredericks m Miklos Rozsa

Michael Rennie, George Hamilton, Suzanne Pleshette, Nehemiah Persoff, Earl Holliman, Arthur O'Connell, Aldo Ray, Barbara Nichols, Yvonne de Carlo, Richard Carlson, Gary Merrill, Ken Murray, Miiko Taka, Celia Lovsky

'The movie takes itself very seriously. We don't have to.'—*Robert Windeler*

The Power and the Glory*

US 1933 76m bw
Fox (Jesse L. Lasky)

The flashback story of a tycoon who rose from nothing and was corrupted by power.

Often noted as a forerunner of *Citizen Kane,* this is in fact a disappointing film with a very thin script and a general sense of aimlessness. 'Presented in narratage' meant that the characters voice their unspoken thoughts. Most interesting for its credits.

w Preston Sturges d William K. Howard

Spencer Tracy, Colleen Moore, Ralph Morgan, Helen Vinson

The Power and the Prize*

US 1956 98m bw Cinemascope
MGM (Nicholas Nayfack)

An ambitious company executive is criticized by his president for wanting to marry a European refugee, but the other executives support him.

Unconvincing big business fairy tale which passes the time competently enough, though Taylor is a humourless hero.

w Robert Ardrey, *novel* Howard Swiggett d Henry Koster ph George Folsey m Bronislau Kaper

Robert Taylor, Elizabeth Mueller, Mary Astor, Burl Ives, Charles Coburn, Cedric Hardwicke

Power Play

GB / Canada 1978   109m   colour
Robert Cooper / Canada United Kingdom
    (Christopher Dalton)

In a mythical country, a tank commander joins
the leaders of a coup d' ètat only to doublecross
them.
Uninteresting mixture of violent action and
verbosity.

wd Martyn Burke   *ph* Ousama Rawi   *m* Ken
Thorne

Peter O'Toole, David Hemmings, Donald
Pleasence, Barry Morse

The Powers Girl

US 1942   92m   bw
UA / Charles R. Rogers
GB title: *Hello Beautiful*

Girls come to New York to become models for
John Robert Powers.
Extremely thin and forgettable musical.

w Edwin Moran, Harry Segall, *book* John
Robert Powers   *d* Norman Z. McLeod
ph Stanley Cortez   *md* Louis Silvers

George Murphy, Anne Shirley, Carole Landis,
Alan Mowbray (as Powers), Dennis Day, Benny
Goodman and his Orchestra, Mary Treen

Practically Yours

US 1944   89m   bw
Paramount (Mitchell Leisen)

A war hero comes back after being supposed
dead, and finds himself with a fiancée he never
met.
Silly romantic comedy which never gets going.

w Norman Krasna   *d* Mitchell Leisen
ph Charles Lang Jnr   *m* Victor Young

Claudette Colbert, Fred MacMurray, Gil Lamb,
Cecil Kellaway, Robert Benchley, Rosemary de
Camp, Tom Powers, Jane Frazee

Prelude to Fame

GB 1950   88m   bw
Rank / Two Cities (Donald B. Wilson)

The health of a child musical prodigy is
endangered by an ambitious woman who pushes
him to the top.
Banal drama with classical music, generally
overacted by the adults.

w Robert Westerby, *story* Young Archimedes
by Aldous Huxley   *d* Fergus McDonell
ph George Stretton

Jeremy Spenser, Guy Rolfe, Kathleen Ryan,
Kathleen Byron, James Robertson Justice,
Henry Oscar, Rosalie Crutchley

The Premature Burial

US 1961   81m   Eastmancolor
    Panavision
AIP (Roger Corman)

A man afraid of being buried alive suffers just
that fate, but later comes to and wreaks revenge
on his tormentors.
Gloomy Gothic horror based vaguely on Edgar
Allan Poe: the ultimate in graveyard
ghoulishness.

w Charles Beaumont, Ray Russell   *d* Roger
Corman   *ph* Floyd Crosby   *m* Ronald Stein
ad Daniel Haller

Ray Milland, Heather Angel, Hazel Court,
Richard Ney, Alan Napier, John Dierkes

Presenting Lily Mars*

US 1943   104m   bw
MGM (Joe Pasternak)

A girl from the sticks hits it big on Broadway.
No, the plot wasn't new, but some of the
numbers were nice.

w Richard Connell, Gladys Lehman,
novel Booth Tarkington   *d* Norman Taurog
ph Joseph Ruttenberg   *md* George Stoll

Judy Garland, Van Heflin, Fay Bainter, Richard
Carlson, Martha Eggerth, Spring Byington, Bob
Crosby and his band, Tommy Dorsey and his
band

The President's Analyst*

US 1967   104m   Technicolor Panavision
Paramount / Panpiper (Stanley Rubin)

A psychiatrist who has been asked to treat the
President is pursued by spies of every
nationality.
Wild political satirical farce which finally
unmasks as its chief villain the telephone
company. Laughs along the way, but it's all
rather too much.

wd Theodore J. Flicker   ph William A. Fraker
m Lalo Schifrin   *ph* Pato Guzman

James Coburn, Godfrey Cambridge, Severn
Darden, Joan Delaney, Pat Harrington, Eduard
Franz, Will Geer

The President's Lady*

US 1953   96m   bw
TCF (Sol C. Siegel)

An account of the early career of Andrew
Jackson, a lawyer whose frail wife died shortly
after he became president.
Well-produced political historical romance.

w John Patrick, *novel* Irving Stone   *d* Henry
Levin   *ph* Leo Tover   *m* A lfred Newman

Charlton Heston, Susan Hayward, John McIntire, Fay Bainter, Carl Betz

Pressure Point*
US 1962   89m   bw
UA / Larcas / Stanley Kramer

A black prison psychiatrist has longstanding trouble with a violent racist inmate.
Curious, quite compelling case history, told in pointless and confusing flashback; sharply made and photographed, melodramatically acted.

w Hubert Cornfield, S. Lee Pogositin d Hubert Cornfield ph Ernest Haller m Ernest Gold

Sidney Poitier, Bobby Darin, Peter Falk, Carl Benton Reid

Pretty Baby*
US 1950   92m   bw
Warner (Harry Kurnitz)

A girl finds it easier to get a seat on the subway if she is carrying a (dummy) baby, but gets into complications when she meets a baby food king.
Silly but quite pleasant comedy variation on Bachelor Mother.

w Everett Freeman, Harry Kurnitz d Bretaigne Windust ph Peverell Marley m David Buttolph

Betsy Drake, Edmund Gwenn, Dennis Morgan, Zachary Scott, William Frawley

Pretty Baby
US 1978   109m   Metrocolor
Paramount (Louis Malle)

A 12-year-old girl grows up in a New Orleans brothel.
Tedious elaboration of a sensational subject; neither good art nor good commerce.

w Polly Platt, Louis Malle d Louis Malle ph Sven Nykvist md Jerry Wexler

Keith Carradine, Susan Sarandon, Brooke Shields, Francis Faye, Antonio, Fargas

Pretty Maids All in a Row*
US 1971   95m   Metrocolor
MGM (Gene Roddenbury)

High school girl students are being murdered by their guidance counsellor.
Uneasy murder comedy with few laughs, casting its star as a most unlikely villain. An interesting if unsuccessful attempt to be different.

w Gene Roddenberry, novel Francis Pollini d Roger Vadim ph Charles Rosher m Lalo Schifrin

Rock Hudson, Angie Dickinson, Telly Savalas, Roddy McDowall, Keenan Wynn

Pretty Poison**
US 1968   89m   De Luxe
TCF / Lawrence Turman / Mollino (Marshal Backlar, Noel Black)

A psychotic arsonist enlists the aid of a teenager but soon discovers she is kinkier than he and has murder in mind.
Bizarre black comedy-melodrama, quite successfully mixed and served.

w Lorenzo Semple Jnr, novel She Let Him Continue by Stephen Geller d Noel Black ph David Quaid m Johnny Mandel

Anthony Perkins, Tuesday Weld, Beverly Garland, John Randolph, Dick O'Neill, Clarice Blackburn

Pretty Polly
GB 1967   102m   Techniscope
Universal / George W. George, Frank Granat
US title: A Matter of Innocence

On a world tour with her vulgar aunt, a timid maiden finds romance in Singapore.
Slight romantic fable decked out with travel guide backgrounds and at odds with the cynicism of the short story from which it originates.

w Keith Waterhouse, Willis Hall, story Noel Coward d Guy Green ph Arthur Ibbetson m Michel Legrand

Hayley Mills, Trevor Howard, Shashi Kapoor, Brenda de Banzie, Dick Patterson, Peter Bayliss, Patricia Routledge, Dorothy Alison

'It came and went this winter, leaving a slight trace of camphor and old knitting needles.'— Wilfrid Sheed

Pride and Prejudice***
US 1940   116m   bw
MGM (Hunt Stromberg)

An opinionated young lady of the early 19th-century wins herself a rich husband she had at first despised for his pride.
A pretty respectable version of Jane Austen's splendid romantic comedy, with a generally excellent cast; full of pleasurable moments.

w Aldous Huxley, Jane Murfin, play Helen Jerome, novel Jane Austen d Robert Z. Leonard

Laurence Olivier, Greer Garson, Edmund Gwenn, Mary Boland, Melville Cooper, Edna May Oliver, Karen Morley, Frieda Inescort, Bruce Lester, Edward Ashley, Ann Rutherford, Maureen O'Sullivan, E. E. Clive, Heather Angel, Marsha Hunt

'The most deliciously pert comedy of old manners, the most crisp and crackling satire in costume that we in this corner can remember ever having seen on the screen.'—*Frank S. Nugent, New York Times*

The Pride and the Passion*

US 1957   131m   Technicolor   Vistavision
UA / Stanley Kramer

In 1810 Spain a British naval officer helps Spanish guerrillas, by reactivating an old cannon, to win their fight against Napoleon.
Stolid, miscast adventure spectacle, its main interest being the deployment of the gun across country by surging throngs of peasants.

w Edna and Edward Anhalt, *novel* The Gun by C. S. Forester *d* Stanley Kramer *ph* Franz Planer *m* Georges Antheil

Cary Grant, Sophia Loren, Frank Sinatra, Theodore Bikel, John Wengraf, Jay Novello, Philip Van Zandt

'The whirr of the cameras often seems as loud as the thunderous cannonades. It evidently takes more than dedication, co-operative multitudes and four million dollars to shoot history in the face.'—*Time*

The Pride of St Louis

US 1952   93m   bw
TCF (Jules Schermer)

The life of baseball star Dizzy Dean, who injured himself and became a commentator.
Sporting biopic of clearly restricted interest; modestly well done.

w Herman J. Mankiewicz *d* Harmon Jones *ph* Leo Tover *m* Arthur Lange

Dan Dailey, Joanne Dru, Richard Haydn, Richard Crenna, Hugh Sanders

AAN: original story (Guy Trosper)

Pride of the Marines*

US 1945   120m   bw
Warner (Jerry Wald)
GB title: *Forever in Love*

The story of Marine Al Schmid, blinded while fighting the Japanese.
Over-dramatic, sudsy biopic which is well enough mounted to carry quite an impact in the flagwaving Hollywood style.

w Albert Maltz *d* Delmer Daves *ph* Peverell Marley *m* Franz Waxman

John Garfield, Eleanor Parker, Dane Clark, John Ridgely, Rosemary de Camp, Ann Doran, Warren Douglas, Tom D'Andrea

AAN: Albert Maltz

The Pride of the Yankees*

US 1942   128m   bw
Samuel Goldwyn

The story of baseball star Lou Gehrig, who died of leukemia at the height of his powers.
Standard sporting biopic ending on Gehrig's famous speech to the crowd; emotion covers the film's other deficiencies.

w Jo Swerling, Herman J. Mankiewicz, *story* Paul Gallico *d* Sam Wood *ph* Rudolph Maté *m* Leigh Harline *pd* William Cameron Menzies

Gary Cooper, Teresa Wright, Babe Ruth, Walter Brennan, Dan Duryea, Elsa Janssen, Ludwig Stossel, Virginia Gilmore

AAN: best picture; script; Rudolph Maté; Leigh Harline; Gary Cooper; Teresa Wright

Prime Cut

US 1972   91m   Technicolor   Panavision
Cinema Center (Joe Wizan)

A Kansas gangster incurs the wrath of his Chicago bosses, and a hired killer is sent to eliminate him.
Gory cat-and-mouse chase melodrama with no interest save its excesses.

w Robert Dillon *d* Michael Ritchie *ph* Gene Polito *m* Lalo Schifrin

Gene Hackman, Lee Marvin, Angel Tompkins, Sissy Spacek

The Prime Minister*

GB 1940   109m   bw
Warner (Max Milder)

Episodes in the life of Disraeli.
Modestly budgeted historical pageant notable only for performances.

w Brock Williams, Michael Hogan *d* Thorold Dickinson

John Gielgud, Diana Wynyard, Will Fyffe, Stephen Murray, Owen Nares, Fay Compton (as Queen Victoria), Lyn Harding, Leslie Perrins

The Prime of Miss Jean Brodie*

GB 1969   116m   De Luxe
TCF (Robert Fryer)

A sharp-minded Edinburgh schoolmistress of the thirties is a bad influence on her more easily-swayed pupils.
Interesting but slackly handled and maddeningly played character drama.

w Jay Presson Allen, *novel* Muriel Spark *d* Ronald Neame *ph* Ted Moore *m* Rod McKuen *pd* John Howell

Maggie Smith, Robert Stephens, Pamela Franklin, Celia Johnson, Gordon Jackson, Jane Carr

'The novel lost a good deal in its stage

simplification, and loses still more in its movie reduction of that stage version.'—*John Simon*

AA: Maggie Smith
AAN: song 'Jean' (*m/ly* Rod McKuen)

The Primrose Path
US 1940 92m bw
RKO (Gregory La Cava)

The youngest of a family of shanty-town prostitutes falls in love with an honest hamburger stand proprietor.
Downright peculiar melodrama for its day and age, and not very entertaining either, spending most of its time being evasive.

w Allan Scott, Gregory La Cava, *play* Robert Buckner, Walter Hart, *novel* February Hill by Victoria Lincoln *d* Gregory La Cava *ph* Joseph H. August *m* Werner Heymann

Ginger Rogers, Joel McCrea, Marjorie Rambeau, Henry Travers, Miles Mander, Queenie Vassar, Joan Carroll

'The story isn't good enough, the direction isn't sincere enough, to give any pain to the lumps in the throat which its designers obviously had in mind.'—*Richard Mallett, Punch*

AAN: Marjorie Rambeau

The Prince and the Pauper*
US 1937 118m bw
Warner (Robert Lord)

In Tudor London, young Edward VI changes places with a street urchin who happens to be his double.
Well-produced version of a famous story; it never quite seems to hit the right style or pace, but is satisfying in patches.

w Laird Doyle, *novel* Mark Twain *d* William Keighley *ph* Sol Polito *m* Erich Wolfgang Korngold

Errol Flynn, Claude Rains, Billy and Bobby Mauch, Henry Stephenson, Barton MacLane, Alan Hale, Eric Portman, Montagu Love (as Henry VIII), Lionel Pape, Halliwell Hobbes, Fritz Leiber

The Prince and the Pauper*
Panama 1977 121m Technicolor Panavision
International Film Production / Ilya and Alexander Salkind
US title: *Crossed Swords*

Young Edward VI changes place with a beggar, who helps to expose a traitor.
Moderately well-made swashbuckler with an old-fashioned air, not really helped by stars in

cameo roles or by the poor playing of the title roles.

w George MacDonald Fraser, *novel* Mark Twain *d* Richard Fleischer *ph* Jack Cardiff *m* Maurice Jarre *pd* Anthony Pratt

Mark Lester, Oliver Reed, Raquel Welch, Ernest Borgnine, George C. Scott, Rex Harrison, David Hemmings, Charlton Heston (as Henry VIII), Harry Andrews, Murray Melvin, Julian Orchard

The Prince and the Showgirl*
GB 1957 117m Technicolor
Warner / Marilyn Monroe Productions (Laurence Olivier)

In London for the 1911 coronation, a Ruritanian prince picks up a chorus girl and they come to understand and respect each other.
Heavy-going comedy, rich in production values but weak in dramatic style and impact.

w Terence Rattigan, from his play The Sleeping Prince *d* Laurence Olivier *ph* Jack Cardiff *m* Richard Addinsell *pd* Roger Furse *ad* Carmen Dillon

Laurence Olivier, Marilyn Monroe, Sybil Thorndike, Richard Wattis, Jeremy Spenser, Esmond Knight, Rosamund Greenwood, Maxine Audley

Prince of Foxes*
US 1949 107m bw
TCF (Sol. C. Siegel)

A wandering adventurer in medieval Italy gets mixed up with the Borgias.
Good-looking historical fiction with a slight edge to it.

w Milton Krims, *novel* Samuel Shellabarger *d* Henry King *ph* Leon Shamroy *m* Alfred Newman

Tyrone Power, Orson Welles, Wanda Hendrix, Felix Aylmer, Everett Sloane, Katina Paxinou, Marina Berti

'Plot, counterplot, action and vengeance.'—*MFB*

'This pretentious chapter of pseudo-history never rises above the merely spectacular, hovers mostly around the conventionally banal, and descends once to the unpardonably crude.'—*Richard Mallett, Punch*

AAN: Leon Shamroy

Prince of Players*
US 1955 102m De Luxe Cinemascope
TCF (Philip Dunne)

Episodes in the life of actor Edwin Booth, brother of the man who killed Abraham Lincoln.
Earnest but ham-fisted biopic more notable, as a

Hollywood entertainment, for its dollops of straight Shakespeare than for any dramatic interest.

w Moss Hart, *book* Eleanor Ruggles *d* Philip Dunne *ph* Charles G. Clarke *m* Bernard Herrmann

Richard Burton, Eva Le Gallienne, Maggie McNamara, John Derek, Raymond Massey, Charles Bickford, Elizabeth Sellars, Ian Keith

Prince Valiant*
US 1954 100m Technicolor
Cinemascope
TCF (Robert L. Jacks)

The son of the exiled king of Scandia seeks King Arthur's help against the usurper, and becomes involved in a court plot.
Agreeable historical nonsense for teenagers, admittedly and sometimes hilariously from a comic strip.

w Dudley Nichols, *comic strip* Harold Foster *d* Henry Hathaway *ph* Lucien Ballard *m* Franz Waxman

Robert Wagner, James Mason, Debra Paget, Sterling Hayden, Victor McLaglen, Donald Crisp, Brian Aherne, Barry Jones, Primo Carnera

The Prince Who Was a Thief
US 1951 88m Technicolor
U-I (Leonard Goldstein)

An Arabian Nights prince is lost as a baby and brought up by thieves, but finally fights back to his rightful throne.
Given the synopsis, any viewer can write the script himself. Standard eastern western romp.

w Gerald Drayson Adams, Aeneas Mackenzie, *story* Theodore Dreiser *d* Rudolph Maté *ph* Irving Glassberg *m* Hans Salter

Tony Curtis, Piper Laurie, Everett Sloane, Jeff Corey

The Princess and the Pirate*
US 1944 94m Technicolor
Samuel Goldwyn (Don Hartman)

An impostor is on the run from a vicious pirate. Typical star costume extravaganza with fewer laughs than you'd expect.

w Don Hartman, Melville Shavelson, Everett Freeman *d* David Butler *ph* William Snyder, Victor Milner *m* David Rose

Bob Hope, Virginia Mayo, Victor McLaglen, Walter Slezak, Walter Brennan, Marc Lawrence, Hugo Haas, Maude Eburne

AAN: David Rose

The Princess Comes Across*
US 1936 76m bw
Paramount (Arthur Hornblow Jnr)

A starstruck Brooklyn girl makes a transatlantic liner voyage disguised as a princess, and finds herself involved in a murder mystery.
Zany comedy thriller with plenty of jokes.

w Walter de Leon, Frances Martin, Frank Butler, Don Hartman, Philip MacDonald, *novel* Louis Lucien Rogger *d* William K. Howard *ph* Ted Tetzlaff

Carole Lombard, Fred MacMurray, Alison Skipworth, Douglass Dumbrille, William Frawley, Porter Hall, George Barbier, Lumsden Hare, Sig Rumann, Mischa Auer, Tetsu Komai

Princess O'Rourke
US 1943 94m bw
Warner (Hal B. Wallis)

An ace pilot falls for a princess and causes diplomatic complications.
Very thin wartime comedy with a propaganda ending involving Franklin Roosevelt.

wd Norman Krasna *ph* Ernest Haller *m* Frederick Hollander

Olivia de Havilland, Robert Cummings, Charles Coburn, Jack Carson, Jane Wyman, Harry Davenport, Gladys Cooper, Minor Watson, Curt Bois

AA: Norman Krasna (as writer)

The Prisoner*
GB 1955 91m bw
(Columbia) Facet / London Independent Producers (Vivian A. Cox)

In a European totalitarian state, a Cardinal is tortured and brainwashed.
Virtually a two-character talkpiece from an offbeat play which should have stayed in the theatre.

w Bridget Boland, from her play *d* Peter Glenville *ph* Reg Wyer *m* Benjamin Frankel

Alec Guinness, Jack Hawkins, Wilfrid Lawson, Kenneth Griffith, Ronald Lewis, Raymond Huntley

The Prisoner of Second Avenue*
US 1975 98m Technicolor Panavision
Warner (Melvin Frank)

A New York clerk and his wife are driven to distraction by the problems of urban living.
Gloomier-than-usual (from this author) collection of one-liners which almost turns into a psychopathic melodrama and causes its amiable leading players to overact horrendously.

w Neil Simon, from his play *d* Melvin Frank
ph Philip Lathrop *m* Marvin Hamlisch

Jack Lemmon, Anne Bancroft, Gene Saks,
Elizabeth Wilson

The Prisoner of Shark Island**
US 1936 95m bw
TCF (Darryl F. Zanuck)

The story of the doctor who treated the assassin
of President Lincoln.
Well-mounted historical semi-fiction with
excellent detail.

*w Nunnally Johnson d John Ford ph Bert
Glennon md Louis Silvers*

Warner Baxter, Gloria Stuart, Joyce Kay,
Claude Gillingwater, Douglas Wood, Harry
Carey, Paul Fix, John Carradine

'A powerful film, rarely false or slow,
maintaining the relentless cumulative pressure,
the logical falling of one thing into another, until
the audience is included in the movement and
carried along with it in some definite emotional
life that is peculiar to the art of motion pictures at
its best.'—*Otis Ferguson*

Prisoner of War
US 1954 81m bw
MGM (Henry Berman)

Life in a communist prison camp in Korea.
Sensational propaganda, reduced to comic strip
level.

w Allen Rivkin *d* Andrew Marton *ph* Robert
Planck
m Jeff Alexander

Ronald Reagan, Steve Forrest, Dewey Martin,
Oscar Homolka, Robert Horton, Paul Stewart,
Henry Morgan, Stephen Bekassy

'It presents its catalogue of horrors in a
manner unworthy of the cause it attempts to
uphold.'—*John Gillett*

The Prisoner of Zenda****
US 1937 101m bw
David O. Selznick

An Englishman on holiday in Ruritania finds
himself helping to defeat a rebel plot by
impersonating the kidnapped king at his
coronation.
A splendid schoolboy adventure story is
perfectly transferred to the screen in this
exhilarating swashbuckler, one of the most
entertaining films to come out of Hollywood.

*w John Balderston, Wills Root, Donald Ogden
Stewart, novel Anthony Hope d John Cromwell
ph James Wong Howe m Alfred Newman*

Ronald Colman, Douglas Fairbanks Jnr,

Madeleine Carroll, David Niven, Raymond
Massey, Mary Astor, *C. Aubrey Smith*, Byron
Foulger, Montagu Love

† Previously filmed in 1913 and 1922.

'The most pleasing film that has come along in
ages.'—*New York Times*

AAN: Alfred Newman

The Prisoner of Zenda*
US 1952 100m Technicolor
MGM (Pandro S. Berman)

A costly scene-for-scene remake which only
goes to show that care and discretion are no
match for the happy inspiration of the original.

w John Balderston, Noel Langley *d* Richard
Thorpe *ph* Joseph Ruttenberg *m Alfred
Newman*

Stewart Granger, James Mason, Deborah Kerr,
Robert Coote, Robert Douglas, Jane Greer,
Louis Calhern, Francis Pierlot, Lewis Stone

The Private Affairs of Bel Ami*
US 1947 119m bw
UA / David L. Loew (Ray Heinz)

In nineties Paris, a career journalist climbs to
fame over the ruined lives of his friends.
Tame and stuffy adaptation of an incisive novel,
rather poorly produced.

wd Albert Lewin, *novel* Guy de Maupassant
ph Russell Metty *m* Darius Milhaud

George Sanders, Angela Lansbury, Ann
Dvorak, Frances Dee, John Carradine, Hugo
Haas, Marie Wilson, Albert Basserman, Warren
William

Private Angelo
GB 1949 106m bw
Pilgrim (Peter Ustinov)

An Italian soldier hates war and spends World
War II on the run from both sides.
Listless satirical comedy that just isn't funny
enough.

w Peter Ustinov, Michael Anderson, *novel* Eric
Linklater *d* Peter Ustinov *ph* Erwin Hillier

Peter Ustinov, Godfrey Tearle, Robin Bailey,
Maria Denis, Marjorie Rhodes, James
Robertson Justice, Moyna McGill

The Private Files of J. Edgar Hoover*
US 1978 112m Movielab
AIP / Larco (Larry Cohen)

The supposedly true facts of the career of the
longtime head of the FBI.
Unreliable exposé with some interesting bits.

wd Larry Cohen *ph* Paul Glickman *m* Miklos Rosza

Broderick Crawford, Jose Ferrer, Michael Parks, Ronee Blakely, Rip Torn, Celeste Holm, Dan Dailey, Raymond St Jacques, Howard Da Silva, June Havoc, John Marley, Andrew Duggan, Lloyd Nolan

The Private Life of Don Juan

GB 1934 90m bw
London Films (Alexander Korda)

In 17th-century Spain, the famous lover fakes death and makes a comeback in disguise.
Lacklustre frolic by an overage star through dismal sets. The production was meant to extend the success of *The Private Life of Henry VIII*, but totally failed to do so.

w Lajos Biro, Frederick Lonsdale, *play* Henri Bataille *d* Alexander Korda *ph* Georges Périnal *m* Ernst Toch

Douglas Fairbanks, Merle Oberon, Binnie Barnes, Benita Hume, Joan Gardner, Melville Cooper, Athene Seyler, Owen Nares
'One of those ideas that never really take off.'—*New Yorker, 1977*

The Private Life of Henry VIII***

GB 1933 97m bw
London Films (*Alexander Korda*)

How Henry beheaded his second wife and acquired four more.
This never was a perfect film, but certain scenes are very funny and its sheer sauciness established the possibility of British films making money abroad, as well as starting several star careers. It now looks very dated and even amateurish in parts.

w Lajos Biro, Arthur Wimperis *d* Alexander Korda *ph* Georges Périnal *m* Kurt Schroeder

Charles Laughton, Elsa Lanchester, Robert Donat, Merle Oberon, Binnie Barnes, Franklin Dyall, Miles Mander, Wendy Barrie, Claud Allister, Everly Gregg

AA: Charles Laughton
AAN: best picture

The Private Life of Sherlock Holmes***

GB 1970 125m De Luxe Panavision
UA / Phalanx / Mirisch / Sir Nigel (Billy Wilder)

A secret Watson manuscript reveals cases in which Sherlock Holmes became involved with women.
What started as four stories is reduced to two, one brightly satirical and the other no more than a careful and discreet recreation, with the occasional jocular aside, of the flavour of the stories themselves. A very civilized and pleasing entertainment except for the hurried rounding-off which is a let-down.

w Billy Wilder, I. A. L. Diamond *d* Billy Wilder *ph* Christopher Challis *m* Miklos Rozsa *ad* Alexander Trauner

Robert Stephens, Colin Blakely, Genevieve Page, Clive Revill, Christopher Lee, Catherine Lacey, Stanley Holloway
'Affectionately conceived and flawlessly executed.'—*NFT, 1974*

Private Lives*

US 1931 92m bw
MGM

Ex-marrieds desert their intended new spouses to try each other again.
An essentially theatrical comedy, and a great one, seems somewhat slow-witted on film.

w Hans Kraly, Richard Schayer, *play* Noel Coward *d* Sidney Franklin *ph* Ray Binger

Norma Shearer, Robert Montgomery, Reginald Denny, Una Merkel, Jean Hersholt

The Private Lives of Elizabeth and Essex**

US 1939 106m Technicolor
Warner (Robert Lord)

Elizabeth I falls in love with the Earl of Essex, but events turn him into a rebel and she has to order his execution.
Unhistorical history given the grand treatment; a Hollywood picture book, not quite satisfying dramatically despite all the effort.

w Norman Reilly Raine, Aeneas Mackenzie, *play* Elizabeth the Queen by Maxwell Anderson *d* Michael Curtiz *ph* Sol Polito *m* Erich Wolfgang Korngold

Bette Davis, Errol Flynn, Olivia de Havilland, Donald Crisp, Vincent Price, Alan Hale, Henry Stephenson, Henry Daniell, Leo G. Carroll, Nanette Fabray, Robert Warwick, John Sutton
'A rather stately, rigorously posed and artistically technicolored production.'—*Frank S. Nugent*

AAN: Sol Polito; Erich Wolfgang Korngold

Private Number

US 1936 80m bw
TCF (Raymond Griffith)

A wealthy young man keeps a secret of his marriage to a housemaid.
Warmed-over class melodrama previously filmed in 1930 as *Common Clay*. Adequate within its lights.

w Gene Markey, William Conselman, *play*
Common Clay by Cleves Kinkead *d* Roy del
Ruth *ph* Peverell Marley

Loretta Young, Robert Taylor, Basil Rathbone,
Patsy Kelly, Marjorie Gateson, Paul Harvey,
Monroe Owsley, John Miljan

Private Potter
GB 1962 89m bw
MGM / Ben Arbeid

A young soldier is court-martialled for
cowardice but claims he had a vision of god.
Stilted morality play, unpersuasively made and
acted.

w Ronald Harwood, from his TV play *d* Caspar
Wrede *ph* Arthur Lavis *m* George Hall

Tom Courtenay, Mogens Wieth, Ronald Fraser,
James Maxwell, Ralph Michael, Brewster
Mason

The Private War of Major Benson
US 1955 105m Technicolor
Cinemascope
U-I (Howard Pine)

A soldier with outspoken views is sent to cool off
as commander of a military academy run by an
order of nuns.
Cute and sentimental nonsense with unlikely
situations, a martinet becoming soft-centred and
a happy-ever-after finale.

w William Roberts, Richard Alan Simmons
d Jerry Hopper *ph* Harold Lipstein *m* Joseph
Gershenson

Charlton Heston, Julie Adams, Tim Hovey,
William Demarest, Tim Considine, Sal Mineo,
Nana Bryant, Milburn Stone, Mary Field

AAN: original story (Bob Mosher, Joe
Connelly)

Private Worlds*
US 1935 84m bw
Paramount (Walter Wanger)

Romance among the doctors at a mental
hospital.
Melodrama treated with what was at the time
unexpected seriousness.

w Lynn Starling, *novel* Phyllis Bottome
d Gregory La Cava *ph* Leon Shamroy

Claudette Colbert, Charles Boyer, Joel McCrea,
Joan Bennett, Helen Vinson, Esther Dale,
Samuel S. Hinds

AAN: Claudette Colbert

A Private's Affair
US 1959 92m De Luxe Cinemascope
TCF (David Weisbart)

Three army recruits form a close harmony trio
and get into various scrapes.
Thin service comedy for the 'new' youth
audience.

w Winston Miller *d* Raoul Walsh *ph* Charles G.
Clarke *m* Cyril Mockridge

Sal Mineo, Christine Carere, Barry Coe,
Barbara Eden, Gary Crosby, Terry Moore, Jim
Backus, Jessie Royce Landis

Private's Progress***
GB 1956 97m bw
British Lion / Charter (Roy Boulting)

An extremely innocent young national
serviceman is taught a few army dodges and
becomes a dupe for jewel thieves.
Celebrated army farce with satirical pretensions;
when released it had something to make
everyone in Britain laugh.

w Frank Harvey, John Boulting, novel Alan
Hackney *d John Boulting ph* Eric Cross
m John Addison

Ian Carmichael, Terry-Thomas, Richard
Attenborough, *Dennis Price,* Peter Jones,
William Hartnell, Thorley Walters, Ian Bannen,
Jill Adams, Victor Maddern, Kenneth Griffith,
Miles Malleson, *John Le Mesurier*

Privilege*
GB 1967 103m Technicolor
Universal /Worldfilm / Memorial (John
Heyman)

The publicity campaign for a pop star turns him
into a religious messiah.
Rather hysterical fable for our time, undeniably
forceful in spots and yawnful in others.

w Norman Bogner, *story* Johnny Speight
d Peter Watkins ph Peter Suschitsky *m* Mike
Leander

Paul Jones, Jean Shrimpton, Mark London, Max
Bacon, Jeremy Child, James Cossins, Victor
Henry
   'Everything in it goes wrong, and one can do
little but catalogue the failures.'—*MFB*

The Prize***
US 1963 135m Metrocolor Panavision
MGM / Roxbury (Pandro S. Berman)

In Stockholm during the Nobel Prize awards, a
drunken American author stumbles on a spy
plot.
Whatever the original novel is like, the film is a
Hitchcock pastiche which works better than

most Hitchcocks: suspenseful, well characterized, fast moving and funny from beginning to end.

w Ernest Lehman, novel Irving Wallace *d Mark Robson ph* William Daniels *m* Jerry Goldsmith

Paul Newman, Elke Sommer, *Edward G. Robinson,* Diane Baker, Kevin McCarthy, *Leo G. Carroll,* Micheline Presle

A Prize of Arms
GB 1961 105m bw
British Lion / Interstate (George Maynard)

An ex-army officer and an explosives expert plan to steal an army payroll.
Standard, pacy caper melodrama offering nothing at all new.

w Paul Ryder *d* Cliff Owen *ph* Gilbert Taylor *m* Robert Sharples

Stanley Baker, Tom Bell, Helmut Schmid, John Phillips

A Prize of Gold
GB 1955 100m Technicolor
Columbia / Warwick (Phil C. Samuel)

An American army sergeant in Berlin decides to steal a cargo of Nazi loot.
Routine caper thriller with sentimental leanings.

w Robert Buckner, John Paxton, *novel* Max Catto *d* Mark Robson *ph* Ted Moore *m* Malcolm Arnold

Richard Widmark, Mai Zetterling, Nigel Patrick, George Cole, Donald Wolfit, Andrew Ray, Joseph Tomelty, Karel Stepanek

The Prizefighter and the Lady
US 1933 102m bw
MGM (Hunt Stromberg)
GB title: *Every Woman's Man*

A boxer falls for a high class gangster's girl.
Plodding romantic melodrama, popular because it starred a real boxer.

w John Meehan, John Lee Mahin *d* W. S. Van Dyke

Myrna Loy, Max Baer, Otto Kruger, Walter Huston, Jack Dempsey, Primo Carnera

AAN: original story (Frances Marion)

The Prodigal
US 1955 115m Eastmancolor
Cinemascope
MGM (Charles Schnee)

The son of a Hebrew farmer falls for the high priestess of a pagan cult.

Wildly apocryphal 'biblical' story of obvious expensiveness but no merit.

w Maurice Zimm *d* Richard Thorpe *ph* Joseph Ruttenberg *m* Bronislau Kaper

Lana Turner, Edmund Purdom, Louis Calhern, James Mitchell, Walter Hampden, Francis L. Sullivan, Joseph Wiseman, Audrey Dalton, Taina Elg, Neville Brand, Cecil Kellaway

'A few lines of dialogue derive from the Bible; the rest is pure Hollywood, but Hollywood in its mood of sham solemnity when even the unintentional jokes are not funny.'—*MFB*

The Producers*
US 1967 88m Pathecolor
Avco / Springtime / MGM / Crossbow (Sidney Glazier)

A Broadway producer seduces elderly widows to obtain finance for his new play, sells 25000 per cent in the expectation that it will flop, and is horrified when it succeeds.
Dismally unfunny satire except for the play itself, *Springtime for Hitler,* which is neatly put down. This has, however, become a cult film, so that criticism is pointless.

wd Mel Brooks *ph* Joseph Coffey *m* John Morris

Zero Mostel, Gene Wilder, Kenneth Mars, Estelle Winwood, Renee Taylor, Dick Shawn

'Over and over again promising ideas are killed off, either by over-exposure or bad timing.'—*Tom Milne*

'An almost flawless triumph of bad taste, unredeemed by wit or style.'—*Arthur Schlesinger Jnr*

AA: Mel Brooks (as writer)
AAN: Gene Wilder

Professional Soldier
US 1936 75m bw
TCF (Darryl F. Zanuck)

A kidnapper befriends the young prince who is his victim.
Predictable, polished family film.

w Gene Fowler, Howard Willis Smith, *story* Damon Runyon *d* Tay Garnett *ph* Rudolph Maté *m* Louis Silvers

Victor McLaglen, Freddie Bartholemew, Constance Collier, Gloria Stuart, Michael Whalen

Professional Sweetheart
US 1933 70m bw
RKO (Merian C. Cooper)
GB title: *Imaginary Sweetheart*

A radio 'purity girl' seeks some real life romance. Modestly smart comedy of no lasting merit.

w Maurine Watkins *d* William Seiter
ph Edward Cronjager

Ginger Rogers, Betty Furness, Gregory Ratoff, Sterling Holloway, Frank McHugh, Zasu Pitts, Allen Jenkins, Norman Foster, Edgar Kennedy, Franklin Pangborn

The Professionals**
US 1966   123m   Technicolor   Panavision
Columbia / Pax (Richard Brooks)

Skilled soldiers of fortune are hired by a millionaire rancher to get back his kidnapped wife.
Strong-flavoured star western with good suspense sequences.

wd Richard Brooks, *novel* A Mule for the Marquesa by Frank O'Rourke *ph* Conrad Hall *m* Maurice Jarre

Burt Lancaster, Lee Marvin, Robert Ryan, Jack Palance, Ralph Bellamy, Claudia Cardinale, Woody Strode

'After the *Lord Jim* excursion, it is good to see Brooks back on his own professional form, filming the tight, laconic sort of adventure which usually seems to bring out the best in Hollywood veterans.'—*Penelope Houston*

'It has the expertise of a cold old whore with practised hands and no thoughts of love.'—*Pauline Kael, 1968*

AAN: Richard Brooks (as writer and as director); Conrad Hall

Professor Beware*
US 1938   93m   bw
Paramount

A staid professor finds himself on the run across America in pursuit of an Egyptian artefact.
Slow-starting comedy with only moments of the comedian at his best.

w Delmer Daves, Jack Cunningham, *story* Crampton Harris, Francis M. and Marian B. Cockrell *d* Elliott Nugent

Harold Lloyd, Phyllis Welch, Raymond Walburn, Lionel Stander, William Frawley, Thurston Hall, Cora Witherspoon, Sterling Holloway

Project X*
US 1968   97m   Technicolor
Paramount / William Castle

In the year 2118, a man is scientifically induced to think he lives in the 1960s so that he can recover a lost secret.

Fearsomely complex science fiction, cheaply made but on the whole intriguingly imagined.

w Edmund Morris, *novels* Leslie P. Davies *d* William Castle *ph* Harold Stine *m* Van Cleave

Christopher George, Greta Baldwin, Henry Jones, Monte Markham, Harold Gould

Promise at Dawn
US / France 1970   102m   De Luxe
Avco / Nathalie (Jules Dassin)

The boyhood of novelist Romain Gary and the last years of his fearsome Russian Jewish actress mother with whom he traipses around Europe.
Scrappy star vehicle and unnecessary biopic in a variety of indulgent styles.

w Jules Dassin, *play* First Love by Samuel Taylor *d* Jules Dassin *ph* Jean Badal *m* Georges Delerue

Melina Mercouri, Assef Dayan

Promise Her Anything
GB 1966   97m   Technicolor
Seven Arts (Stanley Rubin)

A mail order movie maker falls for a young French widow in the next flat.
Scatty comedy set in Greenwich Village and aiming in vain for a kind of frantic bohemian charm, with a baby as deus ex machina.

w William Peter Blatty *d* Arthur Hiller *ph* Douglas Slocombe *m* Lynn Murray

Warren Beatty, Leslie Caron, Hermione Gingold, Lionel Stander, Robert Cummings, Keenan Wynn, Cathleen Nesbitt

The Proud and Profane
US 1956   112m   bw   Vistavision
Paramount (William Perlberg)

In the Pacific War a Roman Catholic widow fall for a tough Lieutenant Colonel. ('My pleasure is physical; my men call me The Beast.')
Unlikely romantic melodrama with a certain amount of plain speaking, otherwise routine.

wd George Seaton, *novel* The Magnificent Bastards by Lucy Herndon Crockett *ph* John F Warren *m* Victor Young

William Holden, Deborah Kerr, Thelma Ritter, Dewey Martin, William Redfield

The Proud Ones
US 1956   94m   Eastmancolor
   Cinemascope
TCF (Robert L. Jacks)

A marshal cleans up a crooked town despite the

hazards of his own physical disability and a deputy who hates him.

Entertaining though rather foolishly scripted western.

w Edmund North, Joseph Patracca d Robert D. Webb ph Lucien Ballard m Lionel Newman

Robert Ryan, Jeffrey Hunter, Virginia Mayo, Robert Middleton

The Proud Rebel

US 1958   103m   Technicolor
MGM / Sam Goldwyn Jnr

After the Civil War, a southerner wanders the Yankee states in search of a doctor to cure his mute son; he falls for a lady farmer and his son finds his voice at a crucial moment.

Pretty dim family western for pretty dim families; everything happens precisely according to plan.

w Joseph Patracca, Lillie Hayward d Michael Curtiz ph Ted McCord m Jerome Moross

Alan Ladd, Olivia de Havilland, David Ladd, Dean Jagger, Cecil Kellaway, Dean Stanton, Henry Hull, John Carradine, James Westerfield

The Proud Valley*

GB 1939   76m   bw
Ealing (Sergei Nolbandov)

A black stoker helps unemployed Welsh miners reopen their pits.

Neat little propaganda drama.

w Roland Pertwee, Louis Golding, Jack Jones d Pen Tennyson

Paul Robeson, Edward Chapman, Edward Rigby, Rachel Thomas, Simon Lack, Clifford Evans, Allan Jeayes

Providence*

France / Switzerland 1977   107m
Eastmancolor
Action Film / Société Francaise de Production / FR3 / Citel (Philippe Dussart)

A famous writer, dying, spends a painful night in unpleasant and sometimes fantastic recollections of his sons and their women; but the reality, when they come to lunch next day, is somewhat different.

Despite its cast and other credits, this is a repellent and not too well acted study in the lack of communication, told at undue length and in turgid colour.

w David Mercer d Alain Resnais ph Ricardo Aronovitch m Miklos Rozsa ad Jacques Saulnier

John Gielgud, Dirk Bogarde, Ellen Burstyn, David Warner, Elaine Stritch

The Prowler*

US 1951   92m   bw
Horizon (Sam Spiegel)

A discontented wife thinks she sees a prowler and calls a cop; they have an affair and murder her husband.

Another variant on Double Indemnity and The Postman Always Rings Twice; the script is terse and the actors well-handled.

w Hugo Butler d Joseph Losey ph Arthur Miller

Van Heflin, Evelyn Keyes, John Maxwell, Katharine Warren

'A rivetingly cool, clean thriller.'—NFT, 1973

Prudence and the Pill*

GB 1968   92m   De Luxe
TCF / Kenneth Harper, Ronald Kahn

A girl borrows her mother's contraceptive pills and replaces them with aspirin, causing no end of complications.

Self-consciously naughty sex comedy with a long denouement and some stiff patches to affect one's enjoyment of the brighter moments.

w Hugh Mills, from his play d Fielder Cook ph Ted Moore m Bernard Ebbinghouse

David Niven, Deborah Kerr, Edith Evans, Keith Michell, Robert Coote, Irina Demick, Joyce Redman, Judy Geeson

'Everybody winds up pregnant to clutter the earth, apparently, with people as obnoxious as their progenitors.'—Judith Crist

Psyche 59

GB 1964   94m   bw
Columbia / Troy / Schenck (Philip Hazelton)

A wife recovering from blindness realizes that her husband is in love with her sister.

Pretentious melodrama with stuffy dialogue, pompous direction and irritating characters.

w Julian Halevy, novel Françoise de Ligneris d Alexander Singer ph Walter Lassally m Kenneth V. Jones

Patricia Neal, Curt Jurgens, Samantha Eggar, Ian Bannen, Beatrix Lehmann

Psycho***

US 1960   109m   bw
Shamley / Alfred Hitchcock

At a lonely motel vicious murders take place and are attributed to the manic mother of the young owner.

Curious shocker devised by Hitchcock as a tease and received by most critics as an unpleasant horror piece in which the main scene, the shower stabbing, was allegedly directed not by

Hitchcock but by Saul Bass. After enormous commercial success it achieved classic status over the years; despite effective moments of fright, it has a childish plot and script, and its interest is that of a tremendously successful confidence trick, made for very little money by a TV crew.

w Joseph Stefano, *novel* Robert Bloch *d Alfred Hitchcock* (and *Saul Bass*) *ph* John L. Russell *m* Bernard Herrmann

Anthony Perkins, Vera Miles, John Gavin, Janet Leigh, John McIntire, Martin Balsam, Simon Oakland

'Probably the most visual, most cinematic picture he has ever made.'—*Peter Bogdanovich*
†When asked by the press what he used for the blood in the bath, Mr Hitchcock said: 'Chocolate sauce'.

AAN: Alfred Hitchcock; John L. Russell; Janet Leigh

Psychomania
GB 1972   91m   Technicolor
Benmar (Andrew Donally)

A Hells Angels motor cyclist commits suicide and returns from the dead an invulnerable monster.
Arrant nonsense of the macabre sort, sometimes irresistibly amusing.

w Armand d'Usseau *d* Don Sharp *ph* Ted Moore *m* David Whitaker

George Sanders, Nicky Henson, Beryl Reid, Robert Hardy

The Psychopath
GB 1966   83m   Techniscope
Paramount / Amicus (Milton Subotsky)

Men are found dead in London, each with a doll beside him.
Complicated horror thriller in which the actors go further over the top the more the plot winds down.

w Robert Bloch *d* Freddie Francis *ph* John Wilcox *m* Philip Martell

Patrick Wymark, Margaret Johnston, John Standing, Alexander Knox, Judy Huxtable, Don Borisenko, Thorley Walters, Colin Gordon

PT 109
US 1963   140m   Technicolor   Panavision
Warner (Brian Foy)

Adventures of president-to-be John F. Kennedy when he was a naval lieutenant in the Pacific during World War II.
Extraordinarily protracted and very dull action

story which seems to have been overawed by its subject.

w Richard L. Breen *d* Leslie H. Martinson *ph* Robert Surtees *m* William Lava, David Buttolph

Cliff Robertson, Ty Hardin, James Gregory, Robert Blake

The Public Enemy***
US 1931   84m   bw
Warner
GB title: *Enemies of the Public*

Two slum boys begin as bootleggers, get too big for their boots, and wind up dead.
Although it doesn't flow as a narrative, this early gangster film still has vivid and startling scenes and was most influential in the development of the urban American crime film.

w Kubec Glasmon, John Bright *d William Wellman ph* Dev Jennings

James Cagney, Edward Woods, Jean Harlow, Joan Blondell, Beryl Mercer, Donald Cook, Mae Clarke, Leslie Fenton

'The real power of *The Public Enemy* lies in its vigorous and brutal assault on the nerves and in the stunning acting of James Cagney.'—*James Shelley Hamilton*

AAN: Kubec Glasmon, John Bright

Public Enemy's Wife
US 1935   78m   bw
Warner (Sam Bischoff)
GB title: *G-Man's Wife*

Lower-berth gangster thrills culminating in a chase climax; neatly enough done.

w Abem Finkel, Harold Buckley, *story* David O. Selznick,
P. J. Wolfson *ph* Ernest Haller *d* Nick Grinde

Pat O'Brien, Margaret Lindsay, Robert Armstrong, Cesar Romero, Dick Foran, Dick Purcell
† Remade as *Bullets for O'Hara* (1942).

Public Hero Number One
US 1935   89m   bw
MGM (Lucien Hubbard)

A G-man goes undercover to track down the Purple Gang.
Moderate thick ear dating from the time when studios tried to smother public outcry against gangster films by presenting the cop as the hero.

w Wells Root *d* J. Walter Ruben *ph* Gregg Toland

Chester Morris, Jean Arthur, Joseph Calleia, Lionel Barrymore, Paul Kelly, Lewis Stone, Paul Hurst

'The best picture on criminal life I've seen.'—
Otis Ferguson

Pufnstuf
US 1970   98m   Technicolor
Universal / Krofft Enterprises

A dejected boy is led by his talking flute on a
talking boat to Living Island, full of strange but
friendly animals in fear of an incompetent witch.
Amalgam of a TV series using life-size puppets
to project a mildly pleasing variation on *The
Wizard of Oz*, without quite achieving the right
blend of wit and charm.

w John Fenton Murray, Si Rose
d Hollingsworth Morse *ph* Kenneth Peach
m Charles Fox *ad* *Alexander Golitzen*

Jack Wild, Billie Hayes, Martha Raye, Mama
Cass

Pulp*
GB 1972   95m   colour
UA / Klinger–Caine–Hodges (Michael
   Klinger)

An ex-funeral director now living in the
Mediterranean as a successful pulp fiction writer
gets involved with gangsters and weirdos.
Occasionally funny pastiche which sorely lacks
shape and is sustained by guest appearances and
zany ideas.

wd *Mike Hodges* *ph* Ousama Rawi *m* George
Martin

Michael Caine, *Mickey Rooney*, Lizabeth Scott,
Lionel Stander, Nadia Cassini, Al Lettieri,
Dennis Price

'Various eccentrics act out their "turns", but
never quite lift a light comedy-thriller through
the more playful and productive inversions of
parody.'—*Richard Combs*

The Pumpkin Eater***
GB 1964   118m   bw
Columbia / Romulus (James Woolf)

A compulsive mother (of eight children) finds her
third marriage rocking when she gets evidence of
her husband's affairs.
Brilliantly made if basically rather irritating
kaleidoscope of vivid scenes about silly people,
all quite recognizable as sixties Londoners; very
well acted.

w Harold Pinter, *novel* Penelope Mortimer
d *Jack Clayton* *ph* *Oswald Morris* *m* Georges
Delerue

Anne Bancroft, Peter Finch, James Mason,
Maggie Smith, Cedric Hardwicke, Richard
Johnson, Eric Porter

'There never was a film so rawly
memorable.'—*Evening Standard*
'It is solid, serious, intelligent, stylish. It is also,
for the most part, quite dead.'—*The Times*
AAN: Anne Bancroft

The Punch and Judy Man*
GB 1962   96m   bw
(ABP) Macconkey (Gordon L. T. Scott)

A seashore children's entertainer tries and fails
to establish himself as an important citizen.
Melancholy comedy of failure which did not
please its star's adherents and indeed just missed
the style it was seeking.

w Philip Oakes, Tony Hancock *d* Jeremy
Summers *ph* Gilbert Taylor *m* Derek Scott,
Don Banks

Tony Hancock, Sylvia Syms, Ronald Fraser,
Barbara Murray, John Le Mesurier, Hugh Lloyd

Puppet on a Chain*
GB 1970   98m   Technicolor
Big City (Kurt Unger)

An American Interpol agent hunts down drug
smugglers in Amsterdam.
Sadistic adventure thriller, a toughened version
of James Bond, climaxing in a splendid boat
chase through Amsterdam.

.w Alistair MacLean, Don Sharp, Paul Wheeler,
novel Alistair MacLean *d* Geoffrey Reeve, *Don
Sharp ph* Jack Hildyard, Skeets Kelly *m* Piero
Piccioni

Sven Bertil Taube, Barbara Parkins, Patrick
Allen, Alexander Knox, Vladek Sheybal
'One suspects that a marionette also sat in for
Alistair MacLean.'—*Judith Crist*

The Purple Heart*
US 1944   99m   bw
TCF (Darryl F. Zanuck)

American prisoners of war in Japan are tried and
executed.
Relentlessly sombre flagwaver, extremely
persuasively presented.

w Jerome Cady, Darryl F. Zanuck *d* Lewis
Milestone *ph* Arthur Miller *m* Alfred Newman

Dana Andrews, Richard Conte, Farley Granger,
Kevin O'Shea, Sam Levene, Don Barry, Richard
Loo

The Purple Mask
US 1955   82m   Technicolor
   Cinemascope
U-I (Howard Christie)

In 1802 Paris the Royalist resistance to
Napoleon is led by the mysterious Purple Mask,

who also disguises himself as a foppish dandy.
Cheeky rewrite of *The Scarlet Pimpernel*, with
plenty of gusto but not much style.

w Oscar Brodney *d* Bruce Humberstone
ph Irving Glassberg *m* Joseph Gershenson

Tony Curtis, Dan O'Herlihy, Colleen Miller,
Gene Barry, Angela Lansbury, George Dolenz,
John Hoyt

'Sir Percy, one feels, would have personally
conducted this lot to the guillotine.'—*MFB*

The Purple Plain*
GB 1954   100m   Technicolor
GFD / Two Cities (John Bryan)

During the Burma campaign, a Canadian
squadronleader regains his shattered nerves
during an arduous trek across country.
Psychological study and eastern adventure
combined; not the best of either, but a potent
crowd-puller.

w Eric Ambler, *novel* H. E. Bates *d* Robert
Parrish *ph* Geoffrey Unsworth *m* John Veale

Gregory Peck, Maurice Denham, Win Min
Than, Lyndon Brook, Brenda de Banzie,
Bernard Lee, Anthony Bushell, Ram Gopal

Pursued*
US 1947   101m   bw
(Warner) United States (Milton Sperling)

A revenge-seeking cowboy accidentally causes a
tragedy in his adopted family.
Glum, good-looking revenge western.

w Niven Busch *d* Raoul Walsh *ph* *James Wong
Howe* *m* Max Steiner

Robert Mitchum, Teresa Wright, Judith
Anderson, Dean Jagger, Alan Hale, Harry
Carey Jnr

The Pursuit of Happiness
US 1934   75m   bw
Paramount (Arthur Hornblow Jnr)

In 1776 Connecticut a Puritan maid falls for a
Hessian soldier.
Mildly pleasing romantic comedy centring on
the ancient practice of 'bundling' in which
betrothed couples might sleep together fully
clothed.

w Stephen Morehouse Avery, Jack
Cunningham, J. P. McEvoy, Virginia Van Upp,
play Lawrence Langner, Armina Marshall
d Alexander Hall *ph* Karl Struss

Francis Lederer, Joan Bennett, Charles Ruggles,
Mary Boland, Walter Kingsford, Minor Watson

The Pursuit of Happiness*
US 1970   98m   Eastmancolor
Columbia / TA Films / Norton–Simon (David
Susskind)

A New York college dropout is sent to prison
after a hit and run accident.
Smooth, watchable but empty youth movie.

w Sidney Carroll, George L. Sherman *d* Robert
Mulligan *ph* Dick Kratina *m* Dave Grusin

Michael Sarrazin, Barbara Hershey, Robert
Klein, Ruth White, E. G. Marshall, Arthur Hill

Pushover*
US 1954   91m   bw
Columbia (Jules Schermer)

An honest policeman involves himself in murder
for loot.
Another variation on *Double Indemnity*,
smoothly carpentered as the first appearance of
newly-groomed star Kim Novak. The events of a
night were familiar and watchable.

w Roy Huggins, *novels* The Night Watch by
Thomas Walsh, Rafferty by William S.
Ballinger *d Richard Quine* *ph* Lester B. White
m Arthur Morton

Fred MacMurray, Kim Novak, Phil Carey,
Dorothy Malone, E. G. Marshall

Puzzle of a Downfall Child
US 1970   104m   Technicolor
Universal / Newman–Foreman

Fantasy reminiscences of a top fashion model.
Pretentious, fashionable, seemingly interminable
collage of sex and high living.

w Adrian Joyce *d Jerry Schatzberg* *ph* Adam
Holender *m* Michael Small

Faye Dunaway, Barry Primus, Viveca Lindfors,
Barry Morse, Roy Scheider

Pygmalion****
GB 1938   96m   bw
Gabriel Pascal

A professor of phonetics takes a bet that he can
turn a cockney flower seller in six months into a
lady who can pass as a duchess.
Perfectly splendid Shavian comedy of bad
manners, extremely well filmed and containing
memorable lines and performances;
subsequently turned into the musical *My Fair
Lady* (qv). One of the most heartening and adult
British films of the thirties.

w Anatole de Grunwald, W. P. Lipscomb, Cecil
Lewis, Ian Dalrymple, *play Bernard Shaw
d Anthony Asquith, Leslie Howard* *m Arthur
Honegger*

*Leslie Howard, Wendy Hiller, Wilfrid Lawson,
Scott Sunderland, Marie Lohr, David Tree,
Esmé Percy, Everley Gregg, Jean Cadell*

'An exhibition of real movie-making – of a
sound score woven in and out of tense scenes,
creating mood and tempo and
characterization.'—*Pare Lorentz*

AA: script; Bernard Shaw; Leslie Howard;
Wendy Hiller

Q

Q Planes**
GB 1939   82m   bw
Harefield / London Films (Irving Asher,
   Alexander Korda)
US title: Clouds over Europe

A secret ray helps spies to steal test aircraft
during proving flights.
Lively comedy thriller distinguished by a droll
leading performance.

w Brock Williams, Jack Whittingham, Arthur
Wimperis d Tim Whelan

Ralph Richardson, Laurence Olivier, Valerie
Hobson, George Merritt, George Curzon, Gus
McNaughton, David Tree

Quackser Fortune Has a Cousin in the Bronx*
US 1970   90m   Eastmancolor
UMC (John H. Cushingham)

An Irish layabout strikes up an acquaintance
with an American student.
Likeable if plotless Dublin comedy, pleasantly
photographed.

w Gabriel Walsh d Waris Hussein ph Gil
Taylor m Michael Dress

Gene Wilder, Margot Kidder, Eileen Colgen,
Seamus Ford

Quai des Brumes***
France 1938   89m   bw
Rabinovitch
US title: Port of Shadows

An army deserter rescues a girl from crooks but
is killed before they can escape.
Artificial, set-bound, but at the time wholly
persuasive melodrama which became one of the
archetypal French films of the thirties, its
doomed lovers syndrome not being picked up by
Hollywood until after World War II.

w Jacques Prévert, novel Pierre MacOrlan
d Marcel Carné ph Eugen Schüfftan
m Maurice Jaubert ad Alexander Trauner

Jean Gabin, Michèle Morgan, Michel Simon,
Pierre Brasseur

'Unity of space, time and action give the film a
classical finish.'—Georges Sadoul
† The plot was in fact almost identical with that

of Pépé le Moko. The romantic pessimism of
these films, plus Le Jour Se Lève, so suited the
mood of France that Vichy officials later said: 'If
we have lost the war it is because of Quai des
Brumes.'

Quai des Orfèvres*
France 1947   105m   bw
Majestic

A music hall artiste is accused of murdering the
man he took to be seducing his mistress.
The equivalent of many a British Scotland Yard
thriller, but a good one, with excellent acting,
atmosphere and suspense.

w Henri-Georges Clouzot, Jean Ferry,
novel Legitime Défense by Stanislas-André
Steeman d Henri-Georges Clouzot ph Armand
Thirard m Francis Lopez

Louis Jouvet, Bernard Blier, Suzy Delair, Pierre
Larquey, Simone Rennant

Quality Street*
US 1937   84m   bw
RKO (Pandro S. Berman)

When an officer returns from the Napoleonic
wars, he does not recognize his sweetheart,
whose beauty has faded, so she masquerades as
her own capricious niece.
Fairly successful attempt to capture on screen
the essence of Barrie whimsy; everyone tries
hard, anyway.

w Mortimer Offner, Allan Scott, play J. M.
Barrie d George Stevens ph Robert de Grasse
m Roy Webb

Katharine Hepburn, Franchot Tone, Fay
Bainter, Eric Blore, Cora Witherspoon, Estelle
Winwood, Florence Lake, Joan Fontaine

AAN: Roy Webb

The Quare Fellow
GB 1962   90m   bw
Anthony Havelock-Allan

Life in a Dublin prison when two men are to be
hanged, as experienced by a new young warder.
Watered-down version of a rumbustious stage
tragi-comedy, with not much but the gloom left.

wd Arthur Dreifuss, *play* Brendan Behan
ph Peter Hennessey *m* Alexander Faris

Patrick McGoohan, Sylvia Syms, Walter
Macken, Dermot Kelly, Hilton Edwards

Quartet***
GB 1948 120m bw
GFD / Gainsborough (Anthony Darnborough)

Four stories introduced by the author.

This entertaining production began the
compendium fashion (*Full House, Phone Call
from a Stranger*, etc) and is fondly remembered,
though all the stories had softened endings and
the middle two did not work very well as drama.
Subsequent Maugham compilations were *Trio*
and *Encore* (both qv).

*w R. C. Sherriff, stories W. Somerset
Maugham m* John Greenwood

THE FACTS OF LIFE *d* Ralph Smart
ph Ray Elton

*Basil Radford, Naunton Wayne, Mai Zetterling,
Jack Watling,* James Robertson Justice

THE ALIEN CORN *d* Harold French
ph Ray Elton

Dirk Bogarde, Françoise Rosay, Raymond
Lovell, Honor Blackman, Irene Browne

THE KITE *d* Arthur Crabtree *ph* Ray Elton

George Cole, Hermione Baddeley, Susan Shaw,
Mervyn Johns, Bernard Lee

THE COLONEL'S LADY *d* Ken Annakin
ph Reg Wyer

Cecil Parker, Linden Travers, Nora Swinburne,
Ernest Thesiger, Felix Aylmer, Henry Edwards,
Wilfrid Hyde White

Quatermass and the Pit**
GB 1967 97m Technicolor
Hammer / Anthony Nelson Keys
US title: *Five Million Years to Earth*

Prehistoric skulls are unearthed during London
Underground excavations, and a weird and
deadly force makes itself felt.

The third film of a Quatermass serial is the most
ambitious, and in many ways inventive and
enjoyable, yet spoiled by the very fertility of the
author's imagination: the concepts are simply
too intellectual to be easily followed in what
should be a visual thriller. The climax, in which
the devil rears over London and is 'earthed', is
satisfactorily harrowing.

w Nigel Kneale, from his TV serial *d Roy Ward
Baker ph* Arthur Grant *m* Tristam Cary

Andrew Keir, James Donald, Barbara Shelley,

Julian Glover, Duncan Lamont, Edwin
Richfield, Peter Copley

The Quatermass Experiment**
GB 1955 82m bw
Exclusive / Hammer (Anthony Hinds)
US title: *The Creeping Unknown*

When a rocketship returns from space, two of its
three crew members have disappeared and the
third is slowly taken over by a fungus which
thrives on blood.

Intelligent science fiction based on a highly
successful BBC TV serial; the film version is
generally workmanlike despite its obvious low
budget.

w Richard Landau, Val Guest, *serial Nigel
Kneale d* Val Guest *ph* Jimmy Harvey

Brian Donlevy, Jack Warner, Margia Dean,
Richard Wordsworth, David King Wood, Thora
Hird, Gordon Jackson

Quatermass II**
GB 1957 85m bw
Hammer (Anthony Hinds)
US title: *Enemy from Space*

A research station operating under military
secrecy is supposed to be making synthetic
foods, but is in fact an acclimatization centre for
invaders from outer space.

Simplified version of a TV serial, a bit stodgy in
the talk scenes, but building into sequences of
genuine alarm and based on an idea of lingering
persuasiveness.

w Nigel Kneale, Val Guest, *serial Nigel Kneale
d Val Guest ph* Gerald Gibbs *m* James Bernard

Brian Donlevy, John Longden, Sidney James,
Bryan Forbes, William Franklyn, Charles Lloyd
Pack, Percy Herbert, Tom Chatto

Queen Bee*
US 1955 95m bw
Columbia (Jerry Wald)

A wealthy woman has a compulsion to dominate
everyone around her.

Claustrophobic southern-set melodrama
obviously created for its star.

wd Ranald MacDougall, *novel* Edna Lee
ph Charles Lang *m* George Duning *md* Morris
Stoloff

Joan Crawford, Barry Sullivan, Betsy Palmer,
John Ireland, Lucy Marlow, William Leslie, Fay
Wray

AAN: Charles Lang

Queen Christina****
US 1933   101m   bw
MGM (Walter Wanger)

The queen of 17th-century Sweden, distressed at the thought of a political marriage, goes wandering through her country in men's clothes and falls in love with the new Spanish ambassador.
The star vehicle par excellence, superb to look at and one of its star's most fondly remembered films. Historically it's nonsense, but put across with great style.

w Salka Viertel, H. M. Harwood, S. N. Behrman d Rouben Mamoulian ph William Daniels m Herbert Stothart

Greta Garbo, John Gilbert, Ian Keith, Lewis Stone,
C. Aubrey Smith, Reginald Owen, Elizabeth Young

'Garbo, as enchanting as ever, is still enveloped by her unfathomable mystery.'— *Photoplay*

Queen Elizabeth*
France 1912   35m approx (24 fps)   bw
silent
Histrionic Film
original title: *Les Amours de la Reine Elisabeth*

Scenes from the life of the queen.
Abysmally boring now, this film is important in several ways. It is our best record of Sarah Bernhardt. It was immensely successful throughout the world. It made cinema interesting to all classes, not just the hoi polloi. It made the fortunes of Adolph Zukor, who bought it cheaply and went on to found Paramount Pictures. (Bernhardt is said to have remarked to him: 'You have put me in pickle for all time!')

w Eugene Moreau d Henri Desfontaines, Louis Mercanton, Sarah Bernhardt, Lou Tellegen

Queen Kelly**
US 1928   100m approx (24 fps) (unfinished version)
   bw   silent
United Artists / Joseph Kennedy

A convent girl goes to the bad, is ill-used by a prince, becomes a white slave in Africa but finally inherits a fortune.
Sexually-oriented extravaganza, the last great folly of its director but never finished by him. Various versions exist: in all of them individual scenes are more entertaining than the whole. Extracts were shown in *Sunset Boulevard*.

wd Erich Von Stroheim ph Gordon Pollock,

Paul Ivano, Ben Reynolds *m Adolf Tandler ad Harry Miles*

Gloria Swanson, Walter Byron, Seena Owen

Queen of Atlantis see L'Atlantide

Queen of Hearts*
GB 1936   80m   bw
ATP (Basil Dean)

A working girl poses as a socialite and wins a matinee idol.
Stalwart romantic comedy with its star slightly more glamorized than usual.

w Clifford Grey, H. F. Maltby, Douglas Furber, Anthony Kimmins, Gordon Wellesley d Monty Banks

Gracie Fields, John Loder, Enid Stamp Taylor, Fred Duprez, Edward Rigby, Hal Gordon

The Queen of Spades***
GB 1948   96m   bw
ABP / World Screen Plays

A Russian officer tries to wrest from an ancient countess the secret of winning at cards, in return for which he has sold her soul to the devil; but she dies of fright and haunts him.
Disappointingly slow-moving but splendidly atmospheric recreation of an old Russian story with all the decorative stops out; the chills when they come are quite frightening, the style is impressionist and the acting suitably extravagant.

w Rodney Ackland, Arthur Boys, novel Alexander Pushkin d Thorold Dickinson ph Otto Heller m Georges Auric ad Oliver Messel

Anton Walbrook, Edith Evans, Ronald Howard, Yvonne Mitchell, Mary Jerrold

Queen of the Mob*
US 1940   61m   bw
Paramount

A murderess and her three sons are captured by the FBI.
Pacy crime melodrama from the *Persons in Hiding* series, based on the exploits of Ma Barker.

w Horace McCoy, William R. Lippmann d James Hogan ph Theodor Sparkuhl

Blanche Yurka, Ralph Bellamy, Jack Carson, Richard Denning, Paul Kelly, J. Carrol Naish, Jeanne Cagney, William Henry, James Seay, Hedda Hopper

The Queen's Guards
GB 1960   112m   Technicolor
   Cinemascope
TCF / Imperial (Michael Powell)

Reminiscences during trooping the colour of
father and son guardsmen.
Incredibly old-fashioned family melodrama
complete with skeleton in family closet; despite
its date it has a decidedly pre-war air, except that
it might have been more smartly done then.

w Roger Milner d Michael Powell ph Gerald
Turpin m Brian Easdale

Raymond Massey, Daniel Massey, Robert
Stephens, Ursula Jeans, Judith Stott, Elizabeth
Shepherd, Duncan Lamont, Ian Hunter, Jack
Watling

   'This flagwaving museum piece would be
distressing if it weren't so inept . . . [the actors]
battle manfully with dialogue and characters as
dated as a Crimean cavalry charge. The film
could scarcely be taken as a tribute to the
Guards except, just possibly, by elderly aunts in
Cheltenham.'—*MFB*

Queimada!
France / Italy 1968   132m   De Luxe
PEA / PPA (Alberto Grimaldi)
aka: *Burn!*

A diplomat is sent to a Caribbean island to break
the Portuguese sugar monopoly and becomes
involved with revolutionaries.
An indigestible attempt to combine adventure
with the film of ideas; very tedious.

w Franco Solinas, Giorgio Arlorio d Gillo
Pontecorvo ph Marcello Gatti m Ennio
Morricone

Marlon Brando, Renato Salvatori, Norman Hill,
Evaristo Marquez

Quentin Durward*
GB 1955   101m   Eastmancolor
   Cinemascope
MGM (Pandro S. Berman)
aka: *The Adventures of Quentin Durward*

An elderly English lord sends his nephew to woo
a French lady on his behalf; but the boy falls in
love with her himself.
Haphazardly constructed and produced, but
quite enjoyable, period romp, with a bold black
villain and several rousing set pieces including a
final set-to on bell ropes.

w Robert Ardrey, *novel* Sir Walter Scott
d Richard Thorpe ph Christopher Challis
m Bronislau Kaper

Robert Taylor, Kay Kendall, Robert Morley,
Alec Clunes, Marius Goring, Wilfrid Hyde

White, Ernest Thesiger, Duncan Lamont,
Harcourt Williams, Laya Raki, George Cole

Quest for Love*
GB 1971   90m   Eastmancolor
Rank / Peter Rogers Productions (Peter Eton)

After an explosion during an experiment, a
young physicist finds himself living a different
life, in love with a dying girl; returning to normal,
he finds the girl and saves her.
Pleasing variation on *Berkeley Square,* quite
well staged and played.

w Terence Feely, *story* Random Quest by John
Wyndham, Ralph Thomas ph Ernest Steward
m Eric Rogers

Tom Bell, Joan Collins, Denholm Elliott,
Laurence Naismith, Lyn Ashley

Quick before It Melts
US 1964   97m   Metrocolor   Panavision
MGM / Biography (Douglas Lawrence,
   Delbert Mann)

A journalist is sent to cover a naval enterprise in
the Antarctic, and gets a scoop despite his
shyness.
Noisy service comedy with precious little plot.

w Dale Wasserman, *novel* Philip Benjamin
d Delbert Mann ph Russell Harlan m David
Rose

George Maharis, Robert Morse, Anjanette
Comer, James Gregory, Howard St John, Janine
Gray, Michael Constantine

   'The combination of romantic dalliance,
service high jinks and hectic journalism remains
uniformly flat all through.'—*MFB*

Quick Let's Get Married
US 1965   100m   colour
Golden Eagle (William Marshall)
aka: *The Confession, Seven Different Ways*

The voice of a sneak thief in a ruined church is
taken by an unwed mother as a miracle.
Downright peculiar mishmash wasting
interesting stars; an independent production by
Rogers and husband in Jamaica.

w Allen Scott d William Dieterle ph Robert
Bronner m Michael Colicchio

Ginger Rogers, Ray Milland, Barbara Eden,
Walter Abel, Cecil Kellaway, Elliott Gould,
Michael Ansara, David Hurst

Quick Millions**
US 1931   69m   bw
Fox

An ambitious truck driver becomes a ruthless
racketeer.

Fast-moving, otherwise naïve early gangster melodrama notable for Tracy's first star performance.

w Courtney Terrett, Rowland Brown, John Wray *d Rowland Brown* ph Joseph August

Spencer Tracy, Marguerite Churchill, Sally Eilers, Robert Burns, John Wray, George Raft

The Quiet American**
US 1957　122m　bw
UA / Figaro (Joseph L. Mankiewicz)

An American in Saigon has naïve ideas for ending the war; he saves the life of a journalist who for various reasons becomes jealous and is duped into betraying the American to the communists.
Semi-successful excursion into the territory of Graham Greene, who as in *Brighton Rock* has allowed his ironic ending to be totally re-emphasized, here making the film anti-communist instead of anti-American.

wd Joseph L. Mankiewicz, novel Graham Greene ph Robert Krasker *m* Mario Nascimbene

Michael Redgrave, Audie Murphy, Claude Dauphin, Giorgia Moll, Bruce Cabot, Fred Sadoff, Richard Loo

The Quiet Man***
US 1952　129m　Technicolor
Republic / Argosy (John Ford, Merian C. Cooper)

An Irish village version of *The Taming of the Shrew*, the tamer being an ex-boxer retired to the land of his fathers and in need of a wife.
Archetypal John Ford comedy, as Irish as can be, with everything but leprechauns and the Blarney Stone on hand. Despite some poor sets the film has a gay swing to it, much brawling vigour and broad comedy, while the actors all give their roistering best.

w Frank Nugent, story Maurice Walsh *d John Ford ph Winton C. Hoch, Archie Stout m Victor Young*

John Wayne, Maureen O'Hara, Barry Fitzgerald, Victor McLaglen, Ward Bond, Mildred Natwick, Francis Ford, Arthur Shields, Eileen Crowe, Sean McClory, Jack McGowran

AA: John Ford; Winton C. Hoch, Archie Stout
AAN: best picture; Frank Nugent; Victor McLaglen

Quiet Please, Murder*
US 1943　70m　bw
TCF (Ralph Dietrich)

Nazis and art thieves cause a high death rate in a public library.
Unusual, stylish second feature.

wd John Larkin ph Joe MacDonald

George Sanders, Kurt Katch, Gail Patrick, Richard Denning, Lynne Roberts, Sidney Blackmer, Byron Foulger

Quiet Wedding***
GB 1940　80m　bw
Paramount / Conqueror (Paul Soskin)

Middle-class wedding preparations are complicated by family guests.
A semi-classic British stage comedy is admirably filmed with a splendid cast.

w Terence Rattigan, Anatole de Grunwald, play Esther McCracken d Anthony Asquith

Margaret Lockwood, Derek Farr, *A. E. Matthews, Marjorie Fielding, Athene Seyler, Peggy Ashcroft*, Margaretta Scott, Frank Cellier, Roland Culver, Jean Cadell, David Tomlinson, Bernard Miles
†Remade as *Happy is The Bride* (qv).

Quiet Weekend
GB 1946　92m　bw
Associated British

The Royds spend a weekend at their country cottage and get involved with poachers.
Trivial and poorly-made sequel, not up to the standard of *Quiet Wedding* as a comic study of British types.

w Victor Skuzetsky, *play* Esther McCracken *d* Harold French *ph* Eric Cross

Derek Farr, Marjorie Fielding, George Thorpe, Frank Cellier

The Quiller Memorandum*
GB 1966　105m　Eastmancolor
　　Panavision
Rank / Ivan Foxwell / Carthay

A British secret service man is sent to Berlin to combat a neo-Nazi organization.
Disappointingly thin but smooth and watchable spy story.

w Harold Pinter, *novel* The Berlin Memorandum by Adam Hall (Elleston Trevor) *d* Michael Anderson *ph Erwin Hillier m* John Barry

George Segal, Max Von Sydow, Alec Guinness, Senta Berger, George Sanders, Robert Helpmann, Robert Flemyng
'In disposing of most of the storyline Pinter has virtually thrown out the baby with the bathwater; all that remains is a skeleton plot which barely makes sense and is totally lacking in excitement.'—*Brenda Davies*

'Harold Pinter wrote the screenplay and for each word of dialogue there has to be a separate scene involving several different camera angles, which is perhaps why they asked him to do it as the story is pretty thin.'—*J. A., Illustrated London News*

Quo Vadis **
US 1951   171m   Technicolor
MGM (Sam Zimbalist)

A Roman commander under Nero falls in love with a Christian girl and jealous Poppea has them both thrown to the lions.
Spectacular but stagey and heavy-handed Hollywood version of a much-filmed colossus which shares much of its plot line with *The Sign of the Cross*. Three hours of solemn tedium with flashes of vigorous acting and a few set pieces to take the eye; but the sermonizing does not take away the bad taste of the emphasis on physical brutality.

w John Lee Mahin, S. N. Behrman, Sonya Levien *d* Mervyn Le Roy *ph* Robert Surtees, William V. Skall *m* Miklos Rozsa *ad* Cedric Gibbons, Edward Carfagno, William Horning

Robert Taylor, Deborah Kerr, *Peter Ustinov, Leo Genn, Patricia Laffan,* Finlay Currie, Abraham Sofaer, Marina Berti, Buddy Baer, Felix Aylmer, Nora Swinburne, Ralph Truman, Norman Wooland

AAN: best picture; Robert Surtees, William V. Skall; Miklos Rozsa; Peter Ustinov; Leo Genn

R

RPM (Revolutions Per Minute)
US 1970 97m colour
Columbia / Stanley Kramer

At an American college, a middle-aged professor teaches liberal ideas.
Dim, thankfully forgotten addition to the *Strawberry Statement* cycle.

w Erich Segal *d* Stanley Kramer *ph* Michel Hugo, Perry Botkin Jnr *m* Barry de Vorzon

Anthony Quinn, Ann-Margret, Gary Lockwood, Paul Winfield, Alan Hewitt

Rabbit, Run
US 1970 94m Technicolor Panavision
Warner

A man leaves his pregnant wife for a prostitute. Uninteresting sex melodrama without any of the wit which distinguishes the book; hard to sit through.

w Howard B. Kreitsek, *novel* John Updike *d* Jack Smight *ph* Philip Lathrop *m* Ray Burton, Brian King

James Caan, Anjanette Comer, Arthur Hill, Jack Albertson, Carrie Snodgress

The Rabbit Trap*
US 1959 76m bw
UA / Canon (Harry Kleiner)

A hardworking draughtsman finally defies his boss and completes his holiday with his family. Watchable minor drama just about marking the end of Hollywood's infatuation with TV plays which had begun with *Marty*; the moral and family problems of ordinary people were beginning to prove a shade lacking in excitement.

w J. P. Miller, from his TV play *d* Philip Leacock *ph* Irving Glassberg *m* Jack Marshall

Ernest Borgnine, Bethel Leslie, David Brian, Kevin Corcoran

Race with the Devil
US 1975 88m De Luxe
TCF / Saber / Maslansky (Wes Bishop)

Holidaymakers witness a black mass and are pursued by the diabolists.

Silly melodrama which resolves into a wild car chase and much violence.

w Lee Frost, Wes Bishop *d* Jack Starrett *ph* Robert Jessup *m* Leonard Rosenman

Peter Fonda, Warren Oates, Loretta Swit, Lara Parker, R. G. Armstrong

The Racers
US 1955 112m De Luxe Cinemascope
TCF (Julian Blaustein)
GB title: *Such Men Are Dangerous*

A Monte Carlo Rally contestant is financed by an attractive lady gambler.
Routine racing car melodrama, totally unmemorable but impersonally efficient.

w Charles Kaufman, *novel* Hans Ruesch *d* Henry Hathaway *ph* Joe MacDonald *m* Alex North

Kirk Douglas, Bella Darvi, Gilbert Roland, Cesar Romero, Lee J. Cobb, Katy Jurado, Charles Goldner, George Dolenz

Rachel and the Stranger*
US 1948 92m bw
RKO (Richard H. Berger)

A western farmer feels real love for his wife for the first time when an attractive stranger seems likely to take her away from him.
Modestly appealing romantic drama in a western setting.

w Martin Rackin, *novel* Howard Fast *d* Norman Foster *ph* Maury Gertsman *m* Roy Webb *md* Constantin Bakaleinikoff

Loretta Young, Robert Mitchum, William Holden, Gary Gray, Tom Tully, Sara Haden, Frank Ferguson

Rachel, Rachel**
US 1968 101m Eastmancolor
Warner / Kayos (Paul Newman)

Events in the life of a middle-aged schoolmistress in a small New England town.
Appealing and freshly observed study of a limited personality in a small community.

w Stewart Stern, novel A Jest of God by

Margaret Laurence *d Paul Newman ph Gayne Rescher m* Jerome Moross

Joanne Woodward, Estelle Parsons, James Olson, Kate Harrington, Donald Moffat, Geraldine Fitzgerald, Bernard Barrow

'It could all very easily degenerate into a woman's weepy; and the fact that it doesn't is due largely to Newman's refusal to treat Manawaka as another Peyton Place.'—*Jan Dawson*

AA: Stewart Stern

AAN: best picture; Joanne Woodward; Estelle Parsons

The Rack
US 1956   100m   bw
MGM (Arthur M. Loew Jnr)

A veteran of the Korean War is courtmartialled for collaborating with the enemy under torture.
Dullish courtroom melodrama overstretched from a TV play.

w Stewart Stern, from his TV play *d* Arnold Laven *ph* Paul Vogel *m* Adolph Deutsch

Paul Newman, Walter Pidgeon, Edmond O'Brien, Lee Marvin, Cloris Leachman, Wendell Corey

The Racket*
US 1951   88m   bw
RKO / Edmund Grainger

Police break up the empire of a powerful gangster.
Oddly timed and rather weak remake of the 1928 film; glossy but very old-fashioned in treatment.

w William Wister Haines, *play* Bartlett Cormack *d* John Cromwell *ph* George E. Diskant *m* Constantin Bakaleinikoff

Robert Ryan, Robert Mitchum, Ray Collins, Lizabeth Scott, William Talman

Raffles*
US 1940   72m   bw
Samuel Goldwyn

Raffles the famous cricketer is also a compulsive and daring amateur thief.
Slight, modernized version of the turn-of-the-century stories; very palatable, but it could have been better.

w John Van Druten, Sydney Howard, *novel* Raffles the Amateur Cracksman by E. W. Hornung *d* Sam Wood *ph* Gregg Toland *m* Victor Young

David Niven, Olivia de Havilland, *Dudley Digges*, May Whitty, Douglas Walton, Lionel Pape, E. E. Clive, Peter Godfrey

Rage
US 1966   103m   Technicolor
Columbia / Joseph M. Schenck / Cinematografico Jalisco (Gilberto Gazcon)

A drunken doctor finds a new will to live during a difficult journey to avert a rabies epidemic.
Pattern melodrama with no surprises, but gripping most of the way.

w Teddi Sherman, Gilberto Gazcon, Fernando Mendez *d* Gilberto Gazcon *ph* Rosalio Solano *m* Gustavo Cesar Carreon

Glenn Ford, Stella Stevens, David Reynoso, Armando Silvestre

Rage
US 1972   99m   De Luxe   Panavision
Warner (Fred Weintraub)

A father takes revenge when his son dies after a chemical warfare accident.
Well-meaning but turgid and boring melodrama.

w Philip Friedman, Dan Kleinman *d* George C. Scott *ph* Fred Koenekamp *m* Lalo Schrifrin

George C. Scott, Richard Basehart, Martin Sheen, Barnard Hughes, Stephen Young
'Sluggish, tired and tiring.'—*Variety*

Rage in Heaven
US 1941   82m   bw
MGM (Gottfried Reinhardt)

An unstable millionaire becomes jealous of his wife and arranges his own death so that her supposed lover will be suspected.
Stilted melodrama with the stars more or less at sea.

w Christopher Isherwood, Robert Thoeren, *novel* James Hilton *d* W. S. Van Dyke II *ph* Oliver T. Marsh *m* Bronislau Kaper

Robert Montgomery, Ingrid Bergman, George Sanders, Lucile Watson, Oscar Homolka, Philip Merivale, Matthew Boulton, Aubrey Mather
'Nothing happens but the obvious, and that only after a long and confused struggle.'—*Otis Ferguson*

A Rage to Live
US 1965   101m   bw   Panavision
UA / Mirisch (Lewis J. Rachmil)

The unhappy college and married life of a nymphomaniac.
Well made but deliberately 'daring' case history which becomes too obvious and silly.

w John T. Kelley, *novel* John O'Hara *d* Walter Grauman *ph* Charles Lawton *m* Nelson Riddle

Suzanne Pleshette, Bradford Dillman, Ben Gazzara, Peter Graves, Bethel Leslie, James Gregory, Ruth White

'Stuff like this needs the exuberance of grand opera; sadly, all it gets here is a blue note.'— *MFB*

Raggedy Ann and Andy*
US 1977 85m Movielab Panavision
Lester Osterman (Richard Horner)

Toys come to life and have their own adventures while their owner is absent.
Attractive fully animated cartoon feature in which only the central story is lacking in pace and humour.

w Patricia Thackray, Max Wilk, *stories* Johnny Gruelle *d Richard Williams*

The Raging Moon*
GB 1970 111m Technicolor
EMI (Bruce Cohn Curtis)
aka: *Long Ago Tomorrow*

A love affair develops between two inmates of a home for the physically handicapped.
Appealing romantic drama which nearly became a big commercial success.

wd Bryan Forbes, novel Peter Marshall *ph* Tony Imi *m* Stanley Myers

Malcolm McDowell, Nanette Newman, Georgia Brown, Bernard Lee, Gerald Sim, Michael Flanders

The Raging Tide
US 1951 93m bw
U-I (Aaron Rosenberg)

A San Francisco gangster stows away on a fishing trawler and redeems himself when he perishes saving the life of a fisherman.
Fearfully old-fashioned seafaring melodrama, rather well made.

w Ernest K. Gann, from his novel Fiddler's Green *d* George Sherman *ph Russell Metty m* Frank Skinner

Richard Conte, Charles Bickford, Shelley Winters, Stephen McNally, Alex Nicol, Jesse White, John McIntire

The Ragman's Daughter
GB 1972 94m Technicolor
TCF / Penelope (Harold Becker)

A Nottingham layabout falls in love with an exciting middle-class girl; they fail to overcome parental opposition and she is killed in a road accident.
Wispy drama framed in pointless flashbacks; done on the cheap, it never seems to get anywhere and even fails to use its locations to advantage.

w Alan Sillitoe, from his short story *d* Harold Becker *ph* Michael Seresin *m* Kenny Clayton

Simon Rouse, Victoria Tennant, Patrick O'Connell, Leslie Sands

The Raid*
US 1954 83m Technicolor
TCF (Robert L. Jacks)

In 1864 six confederate soldiers escape from a union prison, and from a Canadian refuge carry out a revenge raid on a small Vermont town.
Interesting little action drama, crisply characterized and plotted, and based on a historical incident.

w Sidney Boehm, story Affair at St Albans by Herbert Ravenal Sass *d Hugo Fregonese ph Lucien Ballard m* Roy Webb

Van Heflin, Anne Bancroft, Richard Boone, Lee Marvin, Tommy Rettig, Peter Graves, Douglas Spencer, Will Wright, John Dierkes

Raid on Rommel
US 1971 99m Technicolor
Universal (Harry Tatelman)

In North Africa during World War II, a British officer releases prisoners of war and leads them in an assault on Tobruk.
Dispirited low-budget actioner apparently first intended for television.

w Richard Bluel *d* Henry Hathaway *ph* Earl Rath *m* Hal Mooney

Richard Burton, John Colicos, Clinton Greyn, Wolfgang Preiss

The Railway Children***
GB 1971 108m Technicolor
EMI (Robert Lynn)

Three Edwardian children and their mother move into Yorkshire when their father is imprisoned as a spy, and have adventures on the railway line while helping to prove his innocence.
Fresh and agreeable family film with many pleasing touches to compensate for its meandering plot.

wd Lionel Jeffries, novel E. Nesbit *ph Arthur Ibbetson m* Johnny Douglas

Dinah Sheridan, William Mervyn, Jenny Agutter, Bernard Cribbins, Iain Cuthbertson, Gary Warren

Rain*
US 1932 92m bw
(UA)

Stranded passengers in Pago Pago during an epidemic include a prostitute and a missionary who lusts after her.

Early talkie version of a much filmed story; interesting but not very entertaining now that the sensational aspects have worn off.

w Maxwell Anderson, *play* John Colton, Clemence Randolph, *story* W. Somerset Maugham *d* Lewis Milestone *ph* Oliver T. Marsh

Joan Crawford, Walter Huston, William Gargan, Beulah Bondi, Matt Moore, Guy Kibbee, Walter Catlett

† Other versions: *Sadie Thompson* (1928) with Gloria Swanson; *Miss Sadie Thompson* (1953) (qv).

Rainbow Island
US 1944   95m   Technicolor
Paramount (I. D. Leshin)

A white girl brought up by her doctor father on a Pacific island is pursued by three sailors escaping from the Japanese.
Cheerful spoof of the sarong cycle with the star seeing the joke; otherwise a silly service farce with South Sea trimmings.

w Walter de Leon, Seena Owen, Arthur Phillips *d* Ralph Murphy *ph* Karl Struss *m* Roy Webb

Dorothy Lamour, Eddie Bracken, Gil Lamb, Barry Sullivan, Forrest Orr, Anne Revere, Reed Hadley, Marc Lawrence

The Rainbow Jacket
GB 1954   99m   Technicolor
Ealing (Michael Relph)

A boy jockey is blackmailed into losing a big race.
Disappointing racecourse drama which packs in all the expected ingredients.

w T. E. B. Clarke *d* Basil Dearden

Kay Walsh, Bill Owen, Edward Underdown, Robert Morley, Wilfrid Hyde White, Charles Victor, Honor Blackman, Sidney James

The Rainmaker
US 1956   121m   Technicolor   Vistavision
Paramount / Hal B. Wallis (Paul Nathan)

In 1913 Kansas, a fake rainmaker has more success melting the heart of a confirmed spinster.
Such a whimsical play is too talky to make a good movie, especially as the actors are over-age, their performances are mannered, the dialogue seems interminable and the production is too stagey.

w N. Richard Nash, from his play *d* Joseph Anthony *ph* Charles Lang Jnr *m* Alex North

Katharine Hepburn, Burt Lancaster, Wendell Corey, Lloyd Bridges, Earl Holliman, Cameron Prud'homme, Wallace Ford

AAN: Alex North; Katharine Hepburn

The Rains Came ***
US 1939   103m   bw
TCF

High-class parasites in India during the Raj redeem themselves when a flood disaster strikes.
Wholly absorbing disaster spectacular in which the characterization and personal plot development are at least as interesting as the spectacle, and all are encased in a glowingly professional production.

w Philip Dunne, Julien Josephson, *novel* Louis Bromfield *d* Clarence Brown *ph* Arthur Miller *m* Alfred Newman *sp* Fred Sersen

Myrna Loy, *George Brent*, Tyrone Power, Brenda Joyce, *Maria Ouspenskaya, Joseph Schildkraut*, H. B. Warner, Nigel Bruce, Mary Nash, Jane Darwell, Marjorie Rambeau, Henry Travers

'It would be difficult to improve on the direction, the outbreak of the monsoon, a curtain billowing in the breeze, a lamp casting the shadow of latticework against white silk, servants scattering for cover . . .'—*Charles Higham, 1972*

AAN: Alfred Newman

The Rains of Ranchipur
US 1955   104m   Eastmancolor   Cinemascope
TCF (Frank Ross)

Dismal remake of *The Rains Came*, with bored actors and inferior production, all the character of the original being wiped out by badly processed wide-screen spectacle.

w Merle Miller *d* Jean Negulesco *ph* Milton Krasner *m* Hugo Friedhofer

Lana Turner, Fred MacMurray, Richard Burton, Joan Caulfield, Eugenie Leontovich, Michael Rennie

Raintree County
US 1958   166m   Technicolor   Panavision (Camera 65)
MGM (David Lewis)

During the Civil War a southern belle gets the man she thinks she wants, but subsequently finds life as a schoolmaster's wife boring.
Dreary attempt by MGM to out-do *Gone with the Wind*, with neither characters nor plot one third as interesting and the production values merely expensive.

w Millard Kaufman, *novel* Ross Lockridge

d Edward Dmytryk *ph* Robert Surtees
m Johnny Green

Montgomery Clift, Elizabeth Taylor, Eva Marie
Saint, Nigel Patrick, Lee Marvin, Rod Taylor,
Agnes Moorehead, Walter Abel, Jarma Lewis,
Tom Drake, Gardner McKay, Rhys Williams

AAN: Johnny Green; Elizabeth Taylor

A Raisin in the Sun*
US 1961   128m   bw
Columbia / Paman–Doris (David Susskind,
   Philip Rose)

The life of a struggling black family in a cramped
Chicago flat.
Earnest but claustrophobic play-on-film which
long outstays its welcome but contains good
performances.

w Lorraine Hansberry, from her play *d* Daniel
Petrie *ph* Charles Lawton Jnr *m* Laurence
Rosenthal

Sidney Poitier, Ruby Dee, Claudia McNeil,
Diana Sands, Ivan Dixon, John Fielder, Lou
Gossett

The Rake's Progress*
GB 1945   123m   bw
GFD / Individual (Frank Launder, Sidney
   Gilliat)
US title: *Notorious Gentleman*

The career of a cheerful ne'er-do-well playboy of
the thirties.
The road to ruin played for light comedy, with
silly endpapers in which, quite out of character,
the rake becomes a war hero. Generally good
production, witty script.

w Frank Launder, Sidney Gilliat, *story* Val
Valentine *d* Sidney Gilliat *ph* Wilkie Cooper
m William Alwyn *pd* David Rawnsley

Rex Harrison, Lilli Palmer, Margaret Johnston,
Godfrey Tearle, Griffith Jones, Guy Middleton,
Jean Kent, Marie Lohr, Garry Marsh, David
Horne, Alan Wheatley

Rally Round the Flag Boys
US 1958   106m   De Luxe   Cinemascope
TCF (Leo McCarey)

A small community protests at the siting nearby
of a missile base.
Raucous service and sex comedy which becomes
frenetic without ever being very funny.

w Claude Binyon, Leo McCarey, *novel* Max
Shulman *d* Leo McCarey *ph* Leon Shamroy
m Cyril Mockridge

Paul Newman, Joanne Woodward, Joan Collins,
Jack Carson, Dwayne Hickman, Tuesday Weld,
Gale Gordon, Murvyn Vye

Ramona
US 1936   90m   Technicolor
TCF (Sol M. Wurtzel)

A half-breed girl and an Indian chief's son
combat the greed of white pioneers.
Old-fashioned, stuffy adventure romance, much
filmed in silent days.

w Lamar Trotti, *novel* Helen Hunt Jackson
d Henry King *ph* William Skall, Chester Lyons
m Alfred Newman

Loretta Young, Don Ameche, Kent Taylor,
Pauline Frederick, Jane Darwell, Katherine de
Mille, Victor Kilian, John Carradine

Rampage
US 1963   98m   Technicolor
Warner Seven Arts / Talbot (William
   Fadiman)

Two white hunters love the same girl; one
releases a tiger to harm the other, but it escapes.
Silly, unconvincing, old-style melodrama in
which even the animals seem to overact.

w Robert Holt, Marguerite Roberts, *novel* Alan
Caillou *d* Phil Karlson *ph* Harold Lipstein
m Elmer Bernstein

Robert Mitchum, Jack Hawkins, Elsa Martinelli,
Sabu, Emile Genest

Ramrod
US 1947   94m   bw
UA (Harry Sherman)

A predatory lady ranch owner hires a tough
foreman and her ruthlessness causes several
deaths and a stampede.
Ho-hum minor western with fading stars.

w Jack Moffit, Graham Baker, Cecile Kramer,
story Luke Short *d* André de Toth *ph* Russell
Harlan *m* Adolph Deutsch

Veronica Lake, Joel McCrea, Preston Foster,
Charles Ruggles, Donald Crisp, Arleen Whelan,
Lloyd Bridges

Rancho De Luxe
US 1974   95m   De Luxe
UA / EK (Anthony Ray)

Cheerful cattle rustlers go on a binge and end up
in prison.
Modern anti-everything western; it's anti-
entertainment as well.

w Thomas McGuane *d* Frank Perry
ph William A. Fraker *m* Jimmy Buffett

Sam Waterston, Jeff Bridges, Elizabeth Ashley,
Charlene Dallas, Clifton James, Slim Pickens

Rancho Notorious
US 1952   89m   Technicolor
RKO / Fidelity (Howard Welsch)

A cowboy seeking revenge for his girl friend's
murder follows a clue to a lonely ranch run by a
saloon singer.
Curious western which seems to have been
intended as another *Destry Rides Again* but is
made in a hard inflexible style which prevents it
from appealing.

w Daniel Taradash d Fritz Lang ph Hal Mohr
m Emil Newman

Marlene Dietrich, Arthur Kennedy, Mel Ferrer,
Gloria Henry, William Frawley, Jack Elam

Random Harvest ***
US 1942   126m   bw
MGM (Sidney Franklin)

A shell-shocked officer in the 1914–18 war
escapes from an asylum, marries a music hall
singer and is idyllically happy until a shock
makes him remember that he is the head of a
noble family. His wife, whom he does not now
remember, dutifully becomes his secretary and
years later another shock brings memory and
happiness back.
A silly enough story works remarkably well in
this rather splendid, no holds barred, roses round
the door romance in Hollywood's best style with
incomparable stars. A triumph of the Peg's
Paper syndrome, and hugely enjoyable because
it is done so enthusiastically.

w Claudine West, George Froeschel, Arthur
Wimperis, *novel* James Hilton d Mervyn Le
Roy ph Joseph Ruttenberg m Herbert Stothart

Ronald Colman, Greer Garson, Susan Peters,
Philip Dorn, Reginald Owen, Edmund Gwenn,
Henry Travers, Margaret Wycherly, Bramwell
Fletcher, Arthur Margetson

'I would like to recommend this film to those
who can stay interested in Ronald Colman's
amnesia for two hours and who could with
pleasure eat a bowl of Yardley's shaving soap for
breakfast.'—*James Agee*

AAN: best picture; script; Mervyn Le Roy;
Herbert Stothart; Ronald Colman; Susan Peters

Ransom *
US 1955   104m   bw
MGM (Nicholas Nayfack)

A rich man takes desperate measures to rescue
his son from a kidnapper.
Solid but overlong suspenser, virtually a vehicle
for a star at his twitchiest and most dogged.

w Cyril Hume, Richard Maibaum d Alex Segal
ph Arthur E. Arling m Jeff Alexander

Glenn Ford, Donna Reed, Leslie Nielsen, Juano
Hernandez, Robert Keith

Ransom *
GB 1975   98m   Eastmancolor
Lion International (Peter Rawley)

A British ambassador to Scandinavia is
kidnapped by terrorists and a Norwegian
security chief gives chase.
Topical but unconvincing action thriller with
unfamiliar detail; builds up to exciting sequences
but is quickly forgotten.

w Paul Wheeler d Caspar Wrede ph Sven
Nykvist m Jerry Goldsmith

Sean Connery, Ian McShane, Norman Bristow,
John Cording, Isabel Dean, William Fox, Robert
Harris

Rapture
US / France 1965   104m   bw
International Classics / TCF (Christian Ferry)

A mentally unstable girl has a tragic romance
with a fugitive murderer.
Gloomy all the way, and if it's art it needs
explaining.

w Stanley Mann, *novel* Rapture in My Rags by
Phyllis Hastings d John Guillermin ph Marcel
Grignon

Patricia Gozzi, Dean Stockwell, Melvyn
Douglas, Gunnel Lindblom

The Rare Breed
US 1966   97m   Technicolor   Panavision
Universal (William Alland)

An English bull is taken by its woman owner to
St Louis to breed with American longhorns, and
various frictions are caused among the ranchers.
Amusing western idea which misses fire by not
coming down firmly as either drama or comedy;
it does however pass the time amiably enough.

w Ric Hardman d Andrew V. McLaglen
ph William H. Clothier m Johnny Williams

James Stewart, Maureen O'Hara, Brian Keith,
Juliet Mills, Don Galloway, David Brian, Jack
Elam, Ben Johnson

Rashomon ***
Japan 1951   83m   bw
Daiei
aka: *In the Woods*

In medieval Japan, four people have different
versions of a violent incident when a bandit
attacks a nobleman in the forest.
Indescribably vivid in itself, and genuinely
strange (one of the versions is told by a ghost),
Rashomon reintroduced Japanese films to the

world market and was remade (badly) in Hollywood as *The Outrage*.

wd Akira Kurosawa, story Inside a Bush by Ryunosuke Akutagawa *ph* Kazuo Matsuyama *m* Takashi Matsuyama

Toshiro Mifune, Machiko Kyo, Masayuki Mori, Takashi Shimura

'A masterpiece, and a revelation.'—*Gavin Lambert, MFB*

Rasputin and the Empress*
US 1932   133m   bw
MGM (Irving Thalberg)
GB title: *Rasputin the Mad Monk*

The story of the last years of the Russian court, when a sinister monk gained influence over the empress.

An unhappy film which was besieged by lawsuits and never generated much drama of its own despite starring the three Barrymores, who all seemed to be acting in separate rooms. Production values are the most impressive thing about it.

w Charles MacArthur *d* Richard Boleslawski *ph* William Daniels *m* Herbert Stothart

John Barrymore, Ethel Barrymore, Lionel Barrymore, Diana Wynyard, Ralph Morgan, C. Henry Gordon, Edward Arnold, Jean Parker, Gustav Von Seyffertitz, Anne Shirley (Dawn O'Day)

AAN: Charles MacArthur

The Rat Race*
US 1960   105m   Technicolor
Paramount / Perlberg–Seaton

A young jazz musician and a dance hall hostess share a flat and face the adversities of New York. A kind of sour fairy tale of the big city which has neither enough jokes nor enough incident but purveys the kind of charm that grows on one despite oneself.

w Garson Kanin, from his play *d* Robert Mulligan *ph* Robert Burks *m* Elmer Bernstein

Tony Curtis, Debbie Reynolds, Jack Oakie, Kay Medford, Don Rickles

'The New Yorkers of *The Rat Race* – noisy soft-hearted landlady, philosophical bartender, backchatting taxi driver – are as familiar as the settings of shabby apartment house and quiet little bar across the street. Film makers no longer need to invent here – they simply move in for a few weeks.'—*Penelope Houston*

Rattle of a Simple Man
GB 1964   95m   bw
Sydney Box (William Gell)

A shy football supporter in London spends the night with a tart for a bet.

Archetypal farcical situation with sentiment added to string it out to twice its proper length. Production values modest but adequate.

w Charles Dyer, from his play *d* Muriel Box *ph* Reg Wyer *m* Stanley Black

Harry H. Corbett, *Diane Cilento*, Thora Hird, Charles Dyer

The Raven*
US 1935   61m   bw
Universal

A doctor obsessed by Poe-inspired torture devices transforms a gangster on the run into a hideous mutant.

Silly but quite effective horror film with memorable sequences.

w David Boehm *d* Lew Landers *ph* Charles Stumar

Bela Lugosi, Boris Karloff, Samuel S. Hinds, Irene Ware, Lester Matthews

The Raven*
US 1963   86m   Pathecolor   Panavision
AIP / Alta Vista (Roger Corman)

Two 15th-century conjurors fight a deadly duel of magic.

The rather splendid duel is a long time coming; the preliminaries are largely confined to chat in a single set, and the random jokes do not quite atone for the boredom.

w Richard Matheson *d* Roger Corman *ph* Floyd Crosby *m* Les Baxter

Vincent Price, Peter Lorre, Boris Karloff, Hazel Court, Jack Nicholson

Raw Wind in Eden
US 1958   93m   Eastmancolor
Cinemascope
U-I (William Alland)

A model is stranded on a Sardinian island, and falls in love with a mysterious American who turns out to be a disillusioned millionaire. Wish-fulfilment woman's picture with the occasional relief of a smart line.

w Elizabeth and Richard Wilson *d* Richard Wilson *ph* Enzo Serafin *m* Hans Salter

Esther Williams, Jeff Chandler, Carlos Thompson, Rossana Podesta, Eduardo de Filippo, Rik Battaglia

Rawhide**
US 1950   86m   bw
TCF (Samuel G. Engel)
TV title: *Desperate Siege*

Four escaped convicts terrorize a stagecoach stop.

Good suspense western with excellent technical credits.

w Dudley Nichols d Henry Hathaway ph Milton Krasner m Sol Kaplan

Tyrone Power, Susan Hayward, Hugh Marlowe, Jack Elam, Dean Jagger, George Tobias, Edgar Buchanan, Jeff Corey

The Razor's Edge *
US 1947 146m bw
TCF (Darryl F. Zanuck)

A well-to-do young man spends the years between the wars first idling, then looking for essential truth.

The novel was an empty parable with amusing trimmings. In the film the trimmings seem less amusing, but the presentation is glossy.

w Lamar Trotti, novel W. Somerset Maugham *d* Edmund Goulding *ph* Arthur Miller *m* Alfred Newman *ad* Richard Day, Nathan Juran

Tyrone Power, Gene Tierney, *Clifton Webb, Herbert Marshall,* John Payne, Anne Baxter, Lucile Watson, Frank Latimore, Elsa Lanchester, Fritz Kortner

'I like Somerset Maugham when he's looking through keyholes or down cracks, not at vistas.'—*Richard Winnington*

AA: Anne Baxter
AAN: best picture; Clifton Webb

Reach for Glory *
GB 1962 86m bw
Columbia / Blazer (John Kohn, Jud Kinberg)

During World War II, evacuee boys play war games and a German refugee is accidentally killed.

Grim and unpalatable parable, competently rather than excitingly made.

w John Rae, from his novel The Custard Boys *d* Philip Leacock *ph* Bob Huke *m* Bob Russell

Kay Walsh, Harry Andrews, Michael Anderson Jnr, Oliver Grimm, Alexis Kanner, Martin Stephenson, Richard Vernon

Reach for the Sky *
GB 1956 135m bw
Rank / Pinnacle (Daniel M. Angel)

Douglas Bader loses both legs in a 1931 air crash, learns to walk on artificial limbs and flies again in World War II.

Box office exploitation of one man's personal heroism, adequately but not inspiringly put together with many stiff upper lips and much jocular humour.

wd Lewis Gilbert, *book* Paul Brickhill *ph* Jack Asher *m* John Addison

Kenneth More, Muriel Pavlow, Lyndon Brook, Lee Patterson, Alexander Knox, Dorothy Alison, Sydney Tafler, Howard Marion Crawford

Ready Willing and Able
US 1937 93m bw
Warner (Samuel Bischoff)

Two songwriters import an English leading lady for their new show.

Lightweight star musical with no outstanding qualities.

w Sig Herzig, Jerry Wald, Warren Duff *d* Ray Enright *ph* Sol Polito *ch* Bobby Connelly *songs* Johnny Mercer, Richard Whiting

Ruby Keeler, Ross Alexander, Lee Dixon, Wini Shaw, Jane Wyman, Allen Jenkins

The Real Glory *
US 1939 96m bw
Samuel Goldwyn

Soldiers of fortune help the American Army to quell a terrorist uprising in the Philippines just after the Spanish-American War.

Well made Gunga Dinnery.

w Jo Swerling, Robert R. Presnell *d* Henry Hathaway *ph* Rudolph Maté *m* Alfred Newman *ad* James Basevi

Gary Cooper, David Niven, Broderick Crawford, Andrea Leeds, Reginald Owen, Kay Johnson, Russell Hicks, Vladimir Sokoloff

'The same sort of picture as *Gunga Din.*'—*Richard Mallett, Punch*

Reap the Wild Wind **
US 1942 124m Technicolor
Paramount / Cecil B. de Mille

Seafaring salvage engineers fight over a southern belle.

Georgia-set period adventure; intended as another *Gone with the Wind,* it simply doesn't have the necessary, but on its level it entertains solidly, climaxing with the famous giant squid fight.

w Alan le May, Jesse Lasky Jnr *d* Cecil B. de Mille *ph* Victor Milner, Dewey Wrigley, William V. Skall *m* Victor Young *ad* Hans Dreier, Roland Anderson

Ray Milland, John Wayne, *Paulette Goddard,* Raymond Massey, Robert Preston, Lynne Overman, Susan Hayward, Charles Bickford, Walter Hampden, Louise Beavers, Martha O'Driscoll, Hedda Hopper

AAN: photography

Rear Window***
US 1954   112m   Technicolor
Alfred Hitchcock

A news photographer, confined to his room by a broken leg, sees a murder committed in a room on the other side of the court.

Artificial but fairly gripping suspenser of an unusual kind; with such restricted settings, all depends on the script and the acting, and they generally come up trumps.

w *John Michael Hayes, novel* Cornell Woolrich d *Alfred Hitchcock ph* Robert Burks *m* Franz Waxman

James Stewart, Grace Kelly, Raymond Burr, Judith Evelyn, Wendell Corey, Thelma Ritter

AAN: John Michael Hayes; Alfred Hitchcock; Robert Burks

Rebecca****
US 1940   130m   bw
David O. Selznick

The naïve young second wife of a Cornish landowner is haunted by the image of his glamorous first wife Rebecca.

The supreme Hollywood entertainment package, set in Monte Carlo and Cornwall, with generous helpings of romance, comedy, suspense, melodrama and mystery, all indulged in by strongly-drawn characters, and directed by the new English wizard for the glossiest producer in town, from a novel which sold millions of copies. It really couldn't miss, and it didn't.

w *Robert E. Sherwood, Joan Harrison, novel Daphne du Maurier* d *Alfred Hitchcock ph* George Barnes *m* Franz Waxman

Laurence Olivier, Joan Fontaine, George Sanders, Judith Anderson, Nigel Bruce, Gladys Cooper, Florence Bates, Reginald Denny, C. Aubrey Smith, Melville Cooper, Leo G. Carroll, Leonard Carey

AA: best picture; George Barnes
AAN: script; Alfred Hitchcock; Franz Waxman; Laurence Olivier; Joan Fontaine; Judith Anderson

Rebecca of Sunnybrook Farm
US 1938   80m   bw
TCF (Raymond Griffith)

A child performer becomes a pawn in the fight to exploit her talents on radio.

Unrecognizable revamping of a famous story makes a very thin star vehicle.

w Karl Tunberg, Don Ettlinger, *novel* Kate Douglas Wiggin *d* Allan Dwan *ph* Arthur Miller *songs* various

Shirley Temple, Randolph Scott, Jack Haley,
Gloria Stuart, Phyllis Brooks, Helen Westley, Slim Summerville, Bill Robinson

The Rebel*
GB 1960   105m   Technicolor
Associated British (W. A. Whitaker)
US title: *Call Me Genius*

A suburban businessman goes to Paris to become an artist.

A kind of farcical *The Moon and Sixpence,* insufficiently well tailored to the requirements of a very specialized comic, but occasionally diverting none the less.

w Alan Simpson, Ray Galton *d* Robert Day *ph* Gilbert Taylor *m* Frank Cordell

Tony Hancock, George Sanders, Paul Massie, Margit Saad, Grégoire Aslan, Dennis Price, Irene Handl, Mervyn Johns, Peter Bull, John Le Mesurier, Nanette Newman, Oliver Reed, John Wood

'The more prosaic the setting, the funnier Hancock seems; transplanted into a conventionally silly screen art world, he is submerged among the other grotesques.'— *Penelope Houston*

Rebel without a Cause**
US 1955   111m   Warnercolor
   Cinemascope
Warner (David Weisbart)

The adolescent son of a well-to-do family gets into trouble with other kids and the police.

The first film to suggest that juvenile violence is not necessarily bred in the slums, this somewhat dreary melodrama also catapulted James Dean to stardom as the prototype fifties rebel.

w Stewart Stern *d* Nicholas Ray *ph* Ernest Haller *m* Leonard Rosenman

James Dean, Natalie Wood, Jim Backus, Sal Mineo, Ann Doran, Dennis Hopper, Nick Adams

AAN: original story (Nicholas Ray); Natalie Wood; Sal Mineo

Reckless
US 1935   96m   bw
MGM (David O. Selznick)

A theatrical agent loves the glamorous star he represents, but she marries a drunken millionaire.

Remarkably flat backstage melodrama with music, based on the life of Libby Holman.

w P. J. Wolfson *d* Victor Fleming *ph* George Folsey *songs* various

Jean Harlow, William Powell, Franchot Tone,

May Robson, Ted Healy, Nat Pendleton,
Rosalind Russell, Henry Stephenson

The Reckless Moment *
US 1949 82m bw
Columbia (Walter Wanger)

A woman accidentally kills her daughter's
would-be seducer, and is then trailed by a
blackmailer.
Uninteresting melodrama electrified by Ophuls'
direction, which might have been applied to
something more worthwhile.

w Henry Garson, R. W. Soderborg, *novel* The
Blank Wall by Elizabeth Sanxay Holding
d Max Ophuls ph Burnett Guffey *m* Hans
Salter *md* Morris Stoloff

Joan Bennett, James Mason, Geraldine Brooks,
Henry O'Neill, Shepperd Strudwick
  'Swift, sure narrative and solidly pleasurable
detail.'—*Richard Winnington*

The Reckoning **
GB 1969 108m Technicolor
Columbia / Ronald Shedlo (Hugh Perceval)

A tough London executive with a Liverpool-
Irish background has a brutal streak and a self-
destructive urge, but goes on narrowly averting
misfortune.
Interesting melodrama of a man disgusted with
both bourgeois and working-class values; slickly
made and fast-moving.

w John McGrath, novel The Harp That Once by
Patrick Hall *d Jack Gold ph Geoffrey
Unsworth m* Malcolm Arnold

Nicol Williamson, Rachel Roberts, Paul Rogers,
Zena Walker, Ann Bell, Gwen Nelson, J. G.
Devlin

The Red Badge of Courage **
US 1951 69m bw
MGM (Gottfried Reinhardt)

A youth called up during the Civil War gets his
first taste of battle.
Fresh, poetic, but dramatically unsatisfactory
filming of a classic American novel. The story of
its production is fascinatingly told in *Picture*, a
book by Lillian Ross.

wd John Huston, novel Stephen Crane
ph Harold Rosson m Bronislau Kaper

Audie Murphy, Bill Mauldin, Douglas Dick,
Royal Dano, John Dierkes, Andy Devine,
Arthur Hunnicutt

Red Ball Express
US 1952 83 bw
U-I (Aaron Rosenberg)

A supply column runs from the Normandy
beachhead to Patton's army on the outskirts of
Paris.
Standard war adventure, not too convincingly
mounted but providing the usual excitements.

w John Michael Hayes *d* Budd Boetticher
ph Maury Gertsman

Jeff Chandler, Sidney Poitier, Alex Nicol, Judith
Braun, Hugh O'Brian, Jack Kelly, Jack Warden

The Red Beret
GB 1953 88m Technicolor
Warwick (Irving Allen, Albert R. Broccoli)
US title: *Paratrooper*

In 1940, an American with a guilt complex joins
the British paratroopers.
Routine war action flagwaver; good battle
scenes, rubbish in between.

w Richard Maibaum, Frank Nugent,
book Hilary St George Saunders *d* Terence
Young *ph* John Wilcox *m* John Addison

Alan Ladd, Susan Stephen, Leo Genn, Harry
Andrews, Donald Houston, Anthony Bushell,
Patric Doonan, Stanley Baker, Lana Morris

The Red Danube
US 1950 119m bw
MGM (Carey Wilson)

In occupied Vienna, citizens are being returned
to Russia against their will.
Tedious and silly Red-baiting cold war charade.

w Gina Kaus, Arthur Wimperis, *novel* Vespers
in Vienna by Bryan Marshall *d* George Sidney
ph Charles Rosher *m* Miklos Rozsa

Ethel Barrymore, Walter Pidgeon, Janet Leigh,
Peter Lawford, Francis L. Sullivan, Angela
Lansbury, Louis Calhern, Melville Cooper

The Red Desert *
Italy / France 1964 116m Eastmancolor
Duemila / Federiz (Angelo Rizzoli)
original title: *Il Deserto Rosso*

A wife suffers from depression, and a brief affair
with her husband's friend doesn't help.
Elongated character study, very talkative but
rather decoratively designed with the same
subtle use of colour in an urban landscape as was
seen later in *Blow Up*.

w Michelangelo Antonioni, Tonino Guerra
d Michelangelo Antonioni ph Carlo di Palma
m Giovanni Chionetti

Monica Vitti, Richard Harris, Carlos Chionetti

Red Dust ***
US 1932 86m bw
MGM

On a rubber plantation in Indo-China, the overseer is pursued by his engineer's bride but himself falls for a stranded prostitute.
Vigorous romantic melodrama with echoes of *Rain;* remade as *Congo Maisie* (1940) and *Mogambo* (1954).

w John Lee Mahin, *play* Wilson Collison *d* Victor Fleming *ph* Harold Rosson

Clark Gable, Jean Harlow, Mary Astor, Gene Raymond, Donald Crisp, Tully Marshall, Forrester Harvey

'Gable and Harlow have full play for their curiously similar sort of good-natured toughness.'—*Time*

'Sure fire fun. Done so expertly it almost overcomes the basic script shortcomings.'—*Variety*

Red Garters**
US 1954   91m   Technicolor
Paramount (Pat Duggan)

Various familiar types congregate in the western town of Paradise Lost, and settle matters by the Code of the West.
Amusing western musical spoof slightly deadened by its pretty but finally boring theatrically stylized scenery. Songs are catchy, performances good natured.

w *Michael Fessier d* George Marshall *ph Arthur E. Arling m* Joseph J. Lilley *songs* Jay Livingston, Ray Evans

Rosemary Clooney, Guy Mitchell, Gene Barry, Jack Carson, Pat Crowley, Cass Daley, Frank Faylen, Reginald Owen

'A musical of considerable freshness and gaiety.'—*MFB*

Red Headed Woman*
US 1932   74m   bw
MGM

A shopgirl marries the boss but is rejected in his social circles.
Unconvincing but occasionally entertaining melodrama.

w Anita Loos, *novel* Katharine Brush *d* Jack Conway *ph* Harold Rosson

Jean Harlow, Chester Morris, Lewis Stone, Leila Hyams, Una Merkel, Henry Stephenson, Charles Boyer, May Robson

The Red House*
US 1947   100m   bw
Sol Lesser

A moody farmer's guilty obsession with an old house in the woods is that he murdered his parents in it.

Psycho-like suspense melodrama, too extended for comfort and too restricting for the actors, but effective in spurts.

wd Delmer Daves, *novel* George Agnew Chamberlain *ph* Bert Glennon *m* Miklos Rozsa

Edward G. Robinson, Judith Anderson, Lon McCallister, Allene Roberts, Rory Calhoun, Julie London, Ona Munson

The Red Inn*
France 1951   95m   bw
Memnon
original title: *L'Auberge Rouge*

In 1833, stagecoach travellers stay at a remote inn, where the owners intend to rob and murder them.
Extreme black farce which manages to be pretty funny for those who can take this kind of thing: even the survivors of the night's massacre fall down a ravine.

w *Jean Aurenche, Pierre Bost d* Claude Autant-Lara *ph* André Bac *m* René Cloërc *ad* Max Douy

Fernandel, Françoise Rosay, Carette, Grégoire Aslan

Red Line 7000
US 1965   110m   Technicolor
Paramount / Laurel (Howard Hawks)

The career and loves of a stock car racer.
Very routine romantic actioner full of the director's favourite situations but failing to find any fresh slant.

w George Kirgo *d* Howard Hawks *ph* Milton Krasner *m* Nelson Riddle

James Caan, Laura Devon, Gail Hire, Charlene Holt, John Robert Crawford

Red Mountain
US 1951   84m   Technicolor
Paramount / Hal B. Wallis

A Confederate captain joins Quantrell's Raiders but is horrified by their brutality.
Fast-moving action western.

w John Meredyth Lucas, George W. George, George F. Slavin *d* William Dieterle *ph* Charles Lang Jnr *m* Franz Waxman

Alan Ladd, Lizabeth Scott, Arthur Kennedy, John Ireland, Jeff Corey, James Bell

Red Planet Mars
US 1952   87m   bw
UA / Donald Hyde, Anthony Veiller

Americans and Russians both tune in to Mars and learn that it is a powerful Christian planet;

the news causes first panic, then a religious revival and a determination to live more harmoniously on earth.

Lunatic farrago that has to be seen to be believed.

w Anthony Veiller, John L. Balderston *d* Harry Horner *ph* Joseph Biroc *m* Mahlon Merrick *md* David Chudnow *ad* Charles D. Hall

Herbert Berghof, Peter Graves, Andrea King, Marvin Miller

The Red Pony
US 1949   88m   Technicolor
Republic (Lewis Milestone)

When his pet pony dies after an illness, a farmer's son loses faith in his father.
Sincere but rather obvious little fable which although capably made does not make inspiring film drama.

w John Steinbeck *d* Lewis Milestone *ph* Tony Gaudio *m* Aaron Copland *pd* Nicolai Remisoff

Myrna Loy, Robert Mitchum, Peter Miles, Louis Calhern, Shepperd Strudwick, Margaret Hamilton

Red River**
US 1948   133m   bw
UA / Monterey (Howard Hawks)

How the Chisholm Trail was developed as a cattle drive.
Brawling western, a bit serious and long drawn out but with splendid action sequences.

w Borden Chase, Charles Schnee *d* Howard Hawks *ph* Russell Harlan *m* Dmitri Tiomkin

John Wayne, Montgomery Clift, Joanne Dru, Walter Brennan, Colleen Gray, John Ireland, Noah Beery Jnr, Harry Carey Jnr

AAN: original story (Borden Chase)

Red Salute*
US 1935   78m   bw
Edward Small
aka: *Runaway Daughter*; GB title: *Arms and the Girl*

A college girl with communist leanings takes a cross country trip with an American soldier.
Odd little romantic comedy modelled on *It Happened One Night*; it was picketed for its inconsequential attitude to politics.

w Humphrey Pearson, Manuel Seff *d* Sidney Lanfield *ph* Robert Planck

Barbara Stanwyck, Robert Young, Hardie Albright, Cliff Edwards, Ruth Donnelly, Gordon Jones, Henry Kolker

The Red Shoes****
GB 1948   136m   Technicolor
GFD / The Archers *(Michael Powell, Emeric Pressburger)*

A girl student becomes a great ballet star but commits suicide when torn between love and her career.

Never was a better film made from such a penny plain story so unpersuasively written and performed; the splendour of the production is in the intimate view it gives of life backstage in the ballet world with its larger-than-life characters. The ballet excerpts are very fine, and the colour discreet; the whole film is charged with excitement.

wd Michael Powell, Emeric Pressburger *ph* Jack Cardiff *m* Brian Easdale *pd* Hein Heckroth

Anton Walbrook, Moira Shearer, Marius Goring, Robert Helpmann, Albert Basserman, Frederick Ashton, Leonide Massine, Ludmilla Tcherina, Edmond Knight

AA: Brian Easdale
AAN: best picture; original story (Michael Powell, Emeric Pressburger)

Red Skies of Montana
US 1952   99m   Technicolor
TCF (Samuel G. Engel)
aka: *Smoke Jumpers*

Tension among firefighting crews in the mountains of Montana.
Adequate, routine action melodrama with semi-documentary touches.

w Harry Kleiner *d* Joseph M. Newman *ph* Charles G. Clarke *m* Sol Kaplan

Richard Widmark, Jeffrey Hunter, Constance Smith, Richard Boone, Richard Crenna

Red Sky at Morning
US 1970   113m   Technicolor
Universal / Hal Wallis

During World War II the family of an officer on active service find life in New Mexico not what they've been used to.
Peyton Place by any other name, well produced but of little real interest.

w Marguerite Roberts, *novel* Richard Bradford *d* James Goldstone *ph* Vilmos Zsigismond *m* Billy Goldenberg

Claire Bloom, Richard Thomas, Richard Crenna, Catherine Burns, Desi Arnaz Jnr, John Colicos, Harry Guardino

Red Sun
France / Italy / Spain 1971   108m
   Eastmancolor
Corona / Oceania / Balcazar (Robert Dorfman)

In 1870 Arizona, an outlaw is forced to
accompany a Japanese samurai to recover a
ceremonial sword which his partner has stolen.
Unusual but generally ineffective western with a
fashionable international cast.

w Lair Koenig, D. B. Peitclerc, W. Roberts, L.
Roman d Terence Young ph Henri Alekan
m Maurice Jarre

Charles Bronson, Toshiro Mifune, Alain Delon,
Ursula Andress, Capucine
   'A nice exotic item ruined by suburban
direction.'—Sight and Sound

The Red Tent*
Italy / USSR 1970   121m   Technicolor
Paramount / Vides / Mosfilm (Franco
   Cristaldi)

The story of General Nobile's ill-fated 1928
expedition by dirigible to the Arctic.
Stiffly-conceived international spectacular with
one striking sequence but not much good cheer.

w Ennio de Concini, Richard Adams d Mikhail
Kalatozov ph Leonid Kalashnikov m Ennio
Morricone

Peter Finch, Sean Connery, Hardy Kruger,
Claudia Cardinale, Mario Adorf, Massimo
Girotti

Redbeard*
Japan 1965   165   bw   Tohoscope
Toho-Kurosawa
original title: Akahige

Problems of a 19th-century doctor.
Almost a Japanese version of The Citadel:
Kurosawa himself called it 'a monument to
goodness in man'. Rather heavy-going, but
sporadically compelling.

w Masato Ide, Hideo Oguni, Akira Kurosawa,
novel Shugoro Yamamoto d Akira Kurosawa
ph A. Nakai, T. Saito m M. Sato

Toshiro Mifune, Yuzo Kayama

Reflection of Fear
US 1971   90m   Eastmancolor
Columbia (Howard B. Jaffe)

A retarded teenage girl kills her mother and her
grandmother.
Psycho thriller of little interest or suspense.

w Edward Hume, Lewis John Carlino, novel Go
to Thy Deathbed by Stanton Forbes d William
A. Fraker ph Laszlo Kovacs m Fred Myrow

Robert Shaw, Mary Ure, Signe Hasso, Sondra
Locke, Mitch Ryan

Reflections in a Golden Eye*
US 1967   108m   Technicolor
Warner Seven Arts (Ray Stark)

Repressions at a peacetime army camp in
Georgia. A private soldier rides nude on
horseback, a major has the hots for him, the
major's wife has an affair with their neighbour,
whose wife has cut off her nipples with garden
shears.
A film as idiotic as its story line, but smoothly
marshalled so that at least it's more amusing
than boring.

w Chapman Mortimer, Gladys Hill,
novel Carson McCullers d John Huston
ph Aldo Tonti pd Stephen Grimes m Toshiro
Mayuzumi

Marlon Brando, Elizabeth Taylor, Brian Keith,
Julie Harris, Robert Forster, Zorro David
   'One feels trapped in a huge overheated
hothouse containing nothing but common
snapdragons.'—John Simon
   'Nothing more than nutty people and pseudo
porn.'—Judith Crist
   'Pedestrian, crass, and uninvolving to the
point of repellence.'—John Simon
   'Too much expressionistic foliage on the
screen and too much declamatory thunder on the
sound track.'—Pauline Kael

The Reformer and the Redhead*
US 1950   90m   bw
MGM (Norman Panama, Melvin Frank)

A small-town reform candidate abandons his
crooked protector and wins under his own
steam, helped by the daughter of the zoo
superintendent.
Scatty sub-Capra comedy with a lightweight
script but good production and playing.

wd Norman Panama, Melvin Frank ph Ray
June m David Raksin

Dick Powell, June Allyson, Cecil Kellaway,
David Wayne, Ray Collins, Robert Keith,
Marvin Kaplan

La Règle du Jeu***
France 1939   113m   bw
La Nouvelle Edition Française
aka: The Rules of the Game

A count organizes a weekend shooting party
which results in complex love intrigues among
servants as well as masters.
Celebrated satirical comedy with a uniquely
bleak outlook.

w Jean Renoir, Carl Koch d Jean Renoir

ph Jean Bachelet, Alain Renoir *m* Joseph Kosma, Roger Desormières *ad* Eugène Lourié, Max Douy

Marcel Dalio, Nora Gregor, Jean Renoir, Mila Parély, Julien Carette, Gaston Modot, Roland Toutain

† The film was originally banned as indicating the corruption of France, and during the war the negative was destroyed during an air raid; but eventually a full version was pieced together from various materials.

Reign of Terror*
US 1949 88m bw
Universal-International
aka: *The Black Book*

During the French Revolution, a secret organization strives to overthrow Robespierre.
Unhistorical but quite stylish melodrama with an unusual cast and flavour.

w Philip Yordan, Aeneas Mackenzie *d Anthony Mann ph* John Alton *m* Sol Kaplan

Robert Cummings, Arlene Dahl, Richard Basehart, Richard Hart, Arnold Moss, Beulah Bondi

The Reincarnation of Peter Proud
US 1974 104m Technicolor
Avco Embassy / Bing Crosby (Frank P. Rosenberg)

A history professor is troubled by recurring dreams of his former existence.
Hysterical psychic melodrama which pretty well ruins its own chances by failing to explain its plot.

w Max Ehrlich, from his novel *d* J. Lee-Thompson *ph* Victor J. Kemper *m* Jerry Goldsmith

Michael Sarrazin, Jennifer O'Neill, Margot Kidder, Cornelia Sharpe, Paul Hecht

'It may well be the silliest approach to the subject in any medium . . . all flashbacks trampling the action with the finesse of a rogue elephant.'—*Tom Milne*

The Reivers*
US 1970 111m Technicolor Panavision
Cinema Center / Duo / Solar (Irving Ravetch)

In Mississippi at the turn of the century a hired hand borrows the new family auto for a trip into Memphis with the grandson of the family and a black stablehand.
Pleasant but insubstantial yarn of more gracious days; most attractive to look at, it entertains gently without ever reaching a point.

w Irving Ravetch, Harriet Frank Jnr, *novel* William Faulkner *d* Mark Rydell

ph Richard Moore m John Williams

Steve McQueen, Sharon Farrell, Will Geer, Rupert Crosse, Mitch Vogel, Michael Constantine, Juano Hernandez, Clifton James

AAN: John Williams; Rupert Crosse

The Reluctant Debutante*
US 1958 96m Metrocolor Cinemascope
MGM / Avon (Pandro S. Berman)

A noble couple have difficulty in steering their American-educated daughter through the intricacies of the London season.
A slight but pleasing British comedy has become a rather strident example of lend-lease, but still affords minor pleasures.

w William Douglas Home, from his play *d* Vincente Minnelli *ph* Joseph Ruttenberg *md* Eddie Warner *ad* Jean d'Aubonne

Rex Harrison, Kay Kendall, Sandra Dee, Peter Myers, Angela Lansbury, John Saxon, Diane Clare

The Reluctant Dragon**
US 1941 72m Technicolor
Walt Disney

A tour of the Disney Studios affords some glimpses of how cartoons are made.
Amiable pot-pourri of cartoon shorts *(Baby Weems, How to Ride a Horse* and the title story) linked by a studio tour of absorbing interest.

w various *d* Alfred Werker (live action), various

Robert Benchley, Frances Gifford, Nana Bryant

Reluctant Heroes*
GB 1951 80m bw
Byron (Henry Halstead)

Comedy of national servicemen and their misdemeanours.
Simple-minded army farce which was popular for years as play and film.

w Colin Morris, from his play *d* Jack Raymond

Brian Rix, Ronald Shiner, Derek Farr, Christine Norden, Larry Noble

The Reluctant Widow
GB 1950 91m bw
Rank / Two Cities (Gordon Wellesley)

During the Napoleonic wars a governess is co-opted as a spy.
Thin romantic drama which despite nice art direction never really sparks into life.

w Gordon Wellesley, J. B. Boothroyd, *novel* Georgette Heyer *d* Bernard Knowles *ph* Jack Hildyard *ad Carmen Dillon*

Jean Kent, Guy Rolfe, Kathleen Byron, Paul

Dupuis, Lana Morris, Julian Dallas, Peter Hammond, Andrew Cruickshank

Remains to be Seen
US 1953 88m bw
MGM (Arthur Hornblow Jnr)

The manager of an apartment house finds a dead body, and before the police arrive someone sticks a knife into it.
Flabby comedy-thriller giving the cast little to work on.

w Sidney Sheldon, play Howard Lindsay, Russel Crouse d Don Weis ph Robert Planck md Jeff Alexander

June Allyson, Van Johnson, Angela Lansbury, Louis Calhern, John Beal, Dorothy Dandridge

The Remarkable Andrew*
US 1942 80m bw
Paramount (Richard Blumenthal)

A young municipal bookkeeper is framed by local politicians but helped by the ghost of Andrew Jackson and friends.
Pleasant, rather faded, whimsical comedy which also managed to be propaganda for the war effort.

w Dalton Trumbo d Stuart Heisler ph Theodor Sparkuhl

William Holden, Ellen Drew, Brian Donlevy, Rod Cameron, Richard Webb, Porter Hall, Frances Gifford, Nydia Westman, Montagu Love

The Remarkable Mr Pennypacker
US 1959 87m Technicolor
    Cinemascope
TCF

A Pennsylvania businessman leads two lives with two separate families.
Feeble and obvious period comedy of bigamy; very few laughs.

w Walter Reisch, play Liam O'Brien d Henry Levin ph Milton Krasner m Leigh Harline

Clifton Webb, Dorothy McGuire, Charles Coburn, Ray Stricklyn, Jill St John, Ron Ely, David Nelson

Rembrandt****
GB 1937 85m bw
London Films (Alexander Korda)

Episodes in the life of the 17th-century painter. Austerely comic, gently tragic character piece, superbly staged and photographed, with a great performance at its centre.

w Lajos Biro, June Head, Carl Zuckmayer d Alexander Korda

Charles Laughton, Elsa Lanchester, Gertrude Lawrence, Edward Chapman, Walter Hudd, Roger Livesey, Herbert Lomas, Allan Jeayes, Sam Livesey, Raymond Huntley, John Clements
'Amazingly full of that light which the great master of painting subdued to his supreme purpose.'—James Agate

Remember?
US 1939 83m bw
MGM (Milton Bren)

A newly married couple do not get on, so a friend gives them a potion which makes them lose their memories and fall in love all over again.
Silly, witless comedy which did no good for anyone concerned.

w Corey Ford, Norman Z. McLeod d Norman Z. McLeod ph George Folsey

Robert Taylor, Greer Garson, Lew Ayres, Billie Burke, Reginald Owen, George Barbier, Henry Travers, Richard Carle, Laura Hope Crews, Halliwell Hobbes, Sig Rumann

Remember Last Night?**
US 1936 80m bw
Universal

Socialites with hangovers find that murder was committed during their party.
Ingenious but overlong mixture of styles: farce, Thin Man comedy, murder mystery, satire, fantasy. Very well worth looking at.

w Harry Clark, Dan Totheroh, Doris Malloy, novel The Hangover Murders by Adam Hobhouse d James Whale ph Joseph Valentine

Robert Young, Edward Arnold, Arthur Treacher, Constance Cummings, Robert Armstrong, Sally Eilers, Reginald Denny, Ed Brophy, Jack La Rue, Gustav Von Seyffertitz, Gregory Ratoff

Remember the Day*
US 1941 86m bw
TCF (William Perlberg)

An elderly schoolteacher recollects her past life. Pleasant sentimental drama, very well mounted.

w Tess Schlesinger, Frank Davis, Allan Scott, play Philo Higley d Henry King ph George Barnes

Claudette Colbert, John Payne, Shepperd Strudwick, Jane Seymour, Anne Revere, Frieda Inescort

Remember the Night*
US 1940 94m bw
Paramount (Mitchell Leisen)

An assistant district attorney takes a lady

shoplifter home with him for Christmas.
Eccentric but winning blend of comedy,
romance and drama, deftly mixed by master
chefs.

w Preston Sturges d Mitchell Leisen ph Ted
Tetzlaff *m* Frederick Hollander

Barbara Stanwyck, Fred MacMurray, Beulah
Bondi, Elizabeth Patterson, Sterling Holloway,
Paul Guilfoyle, Willard Robertson

Remorques*
France 1941   80m   bw
MAIC
US title: *Stormy Waters*

A tugboat captain falls in love with a mysterious
woman but remains faithful to his invalid wife.
Effective, minor, romantic melodrama.

w Jacques Prévert, André Cayatte, *novel* Roger
Vercel *d* Jean Grémillion *ph* Armand Thirard,
Louis Née *m* Roland Manuel

Jean Gabin, Michèle Morgan, Madeleine
Renaud, Fernand Ledoux

Rendezvous
US 1935   106m   bw
MGM (Lawrence Weingarten)

A decoding expert breaks an enemy spy ring.
Agreeable light romantic comedy drama with an
espionage plot.

w Bella and Samuel Spewack, *novel* Black
Chamber by Herbert Yardley *d* William K.
Howard *ph* William Daniels *m* William Axt

William Powell, Rosalind Russell, Binnie
Barnes, Lionel Atwill, Cesar Romero, Samuel S.
Hinds, Henry Stephenson, Frank Reicher

Rentadick
GB 1972   94m   Eastmancolor
Rank / Paradise / Virgin (Ned Sherrin)

Incompetent private eyes become involved in the
battle for a deadly nerve gas.
Ineffective crazy comedy which never takes
shape, preferring to aim barbs of satire in all
directions.

w John Cleese, Graham Chapman *d* Jim Clark
ph John Coquillon *m* Carl Davis

James Booth, Richard Briers, Julie Ege, Donald
Sinden, Roy Kinnear

Repeat Performance*
US 1947   93m   bw
Eagle / Lion

People in trouble find they can repeat the
previous year.
Adequate flashback fantasy, very dated now.

w Walter Bullock *d* Alfred L. Werker *ph* Lew
O'Connell

Louis Hayward, Joan Leslie, Tom Conway,
Richard Basehart, Virginia Field

Report to the Commissioner
US 1974   112m   Metrocolor
UA / M. J. Frankovich
GB title: *Operation Undercover*

A policeman's son follows in father's footsteps
but finds life around Times Square dismaying.
Realistic, concerned crime melodrama with
nothing very new to say.

w Abby Mann, Ernest Tidyman, *novel* James
Mills *d* Milton Katselas *ph* Mario Tosi
m Elmer Bernstein

Michael Moriarty, Yaphet Kotto, Susan Blakely,
Hector Elizondo, Tony King, Michael McGuire
'A clear also-ran in the police thriller
stakes.'—*Verina Glaessner*
'A bit too full of sweat and frenzy.'—*Michael
Billington, Illustrated London News*

The Reptile*
GB 1966   90m   Technicolor
Hammer (Anthony Nelson Keys)

A Cornish village is terrified by several
mysterious and unpleasant deaths; it turns out
that the daughter of the local doctor, victim of a
Malayan sect, periodically turns into a deadly
snake.
Silly horror story most effectively filmed as a
mixture of chills, detection and good
characterization.

w John Elder d John Gilling ph Arthur Grant
m Don Banks

Noel Willman, Jennifer Daniel, Ray Barrett,
Jacqueline Pearce, Michael Ripper, John Laurie,
Marne Maitland

Repulsion**
GB 1965   105m   bw
Compton / Tekli (Gene Gutowski)

A Belgian manicurist in London is driven by
pressures into neurotic withdrawal; terrified
above all by sex, she locks herself up in her
gloomy flat and murders her boy friend and
landlord when they try to approach her.
Weird, unmotivated but undeniably effective
Grand Guignol in the form of a case history;
little dialogue, which is just as well as the director
at that time clearly had no ear for the language.

w Roman Polanski, Gerard Brach *d Roman
Polanski ph Gilbert Taylor m* Chico Hamilton

Catherine Deneuve, Ian Hendry, John Fraser,
Patrick Wymark, Yvonne Furneaux

Requiem for a Heavyweight*
US 1962   87m   bw
Columbia (David Susskind)
GB title: *Blood Money*

The last bouts of a prizefighter who will not
realize his career is over.
Tough, effective melodrama, extremely well
acted.

w Rod Serling, from his TV play d Ralph
Nelson ph Arthur J. Ornitz m Laurence
Rosenthal

Anthony Quinn, *Jackie Gleason, Mickey
Rooney,* Julie Harris, Stan Adams, Madame
Spivy, Jack Dempsey, Cassius Clay

The Rescuers*
US 1977   77m   Technicolor
Walt Disney (Ron Miller)

The Mouse Rescue Aid Society volunteer to
bring back a girl lost in a swamp.
Feature-length cartoon which, while by no
means as bad as some of Disney's very routine
seventies product, still seems light years away
from his classics of the thirties.

w various, from stories by Margery Sharp
d Wolfgang Reitherman, John Lounsbery, Art
Stevens

   'The people who really need rescuing are the
Disney animators and cameramen.'—*Time Out*

Resurrection
US 1931   81m   bw
Universal

In 1870s Russia, a peasant girl is seduced by a
prince and bears his child.
Unremarkable version of a much-filmed
melodrama.

w Finis Fox, *novel* Leo Tolstoy d Edwin
Carewe ph Robert B. Kurrie, Al Green
m Dmitri Tiomkin

Lupe Velez, John Boles, Nance O'Neil, William
Keighley, Rose Tapley
† See also: *We Live Again*.

Retreat, Hell!
US 1952   95m   bw
(Warner) United States (Milton Sperling)

Adventures of a Marine unit in the Korean War.
Standard war film.

w Milton Sperling, Ted Sherdeman d Joseph H.
Lewis ph Warren Lynch m William Lava

Frank Lovejoy, Richard Carlson, Anita Louise,
Russ Tamblyn

Return from the Ashes*
GB 1965   104m   bw   Panavision
UA / Mirisch (J. Lee-Thompson)

A woman returns from Dachau to find that her
husband is living with her step-daughter and that
they plan to murder her.
Broken-backed thriller melodrama, the first half
of which is quite irrelevant to the second. The
whole is modestly inventive for those who don't
mind a mixture of *Enoch Arden, Psycho* and
Dial M for Murder with a touch of the
concentration camps and a background of post-
war misery.

w Julius J. Epstein, *novel* Hubert Monteilhet
d J. Lee-Thompson ph Christopher Challis
m Johnny Dankworth

Ingrid Thulin, Maximilian Schell, Samantha
Eggar, Herbert Lom

Return from Witch Mountain
US 1978   93m   Technicolor
Walt Disney (Ron Miller, Jerome Courtland)

A brother and sister from outer space come back
to earth for a vacation and are used by crooks for
their own purposes.
Acceptable sequel to *Escape from Witch
Mountain,* with improved special effects.

w Malcolm Marmorstein d John Hough
ph Frank Phillips m Lalo Schifrin sp Eustace
Lycett, Art Cruickshank, Danny Lee

Bette Davis, Christopher Lee, Ike Eisenmann,
Kim Richards, Jack Soo

The Return of a Man Called Horse*
US 1976   125m   De Luxe   Panavision
UA / Sandy Howard / Richard Harris

The English nobleman of *A Man Called Horse*
goes back to the west to save his adopted Indian
tribe from extinction.
Another 'realistic' action adventure with torture
highlights; nicely made, but not for the
squeamish.

w Jack de Witt d Irvin Kershner ph Owen
Roizman m Laurence Rosenthal

Richard Harris, Gale Sondergaard, Geoffrey
Lewis, Bill Lucking, Jorge Luke
†At 17 minutes, this pre-title sequence must be
the longest so far.

The Return of Dr X*
US 1939   62m   bw
Warner (Bryan Foy)

A modern vampire terrorizes the city.
Minor thriller which doesn't get going till the last
reel; only notable for Bogart's appearance as the
monster. Nothing to do with *Dr X*.

w Lee Katz, *novel* The Doctor's Secret by William J. Makin d Vincent Sherman ph Sid Hickox

Dennis Morgan, Rosemary Lane, Wayne Morris, Humphrey Bogart, Olin Howland, John Litel

The Return of Dracula*

US 1958 77m bw
UA / Gramercy (Jules V. Levy, Arthur Gardner)
GB title: *The Fantastic Disappearing Man*

A European vampire makes his way to an American small town in the guise of a refugee Iron Curtain painter.
Quite nicely made low-budget horror film with a good balance of the supernatural and the ordinary.

w Pat Fielder d *Paul Landres* ph Jack McKenzie m Gerald Fried

Francis Lederer, Norma Eberhardt, Ray Stricklyn, Jimmie Baird, John Wengraf

The Return of Frank James*

US 1940 92m Technicolor
TCF (Darryl F. Zanuck)

A sequel to *Jesse James (*qv).
Moody, nicely photographed western in which Jesse's brother avenges his murder.

w Sam Hellman d *Fritz Lang* ph George Barnes, William V. Skall m David Buttolph

Henry Fonda, Gene Tierney, Jackie Cooper, Henry Hull, John Carradine, J. Edward Bromberg, Donald Meek, Eddie Collins, George Barbier

  'I doubt if any character was ever as lily white as that of Frank James here, but that is a present from the Hays Office to you, and anyway the part is played by Henry Fonda. Durn if I don't like that boy.'—*Otis Ferguson*

The Return of the Bad Men

US 1948 90m bw
RKO (Nat Holt)

A farmer tries to reform the female leader of a terrorist outlaw gang, but she is killed in a bank . raid.
Standard, well shot western which contrives to introduce a number of well-known historical bandits.

w Charles O'Neal, Jack Netteford, Luci Ward d Ray Enright ph J. Roy Hunt m Roy Webb md Constantin Bakaleinikoff

Randolph Scott, Robert Ryan, Anne Jeffreys, Jacqueline White, Steve Brodie

The Return of the Pink Panther*

GB 1974 113m De Luxe Panavision
UA / Jewel / Pimlico / Mirisch / Geoffrey (Blake Edwards)

When the Pink Panther diamond – national treasure of the Eastern state of Lugash – is once again stolen, bungling Inspector Clouseau is called in.
Rehash of jokes from *The Pink Panther* (qv), not bad in parts but a rather tedious whole.

w Frank Waldman, Blake Edwards d Blake Edwards ph Geoffrey Unsworth m *Henry Mancini*

Peter Sellers, Christopher Plummer, Herbert Lom, Catherine Schell, Peter Arne, Peter Jeffrey, Grégoire Aslan, David Lodge, Graham Stark

  'The film never comes fully to the boil, but simmers in a series of self-contained, self-destructing little set pieces.'—*Richard Combs*

The Return of the Scarlet Pimpernel*

GB 1937 94m bw
London Films (Alexander Korda, Arnold Pressburger)

Sir Percy Blakeney saves his wife and other French aristos from the guillotine.
Predictable, stylish revolutionary romance, much thinner in plot and performance than its predecessor.

w Lajos Biro, Arthur Wimperis, Adrian Brunel d Hans Schwarz

Barry K. Barnes, Sophie Stewart, Margaretta Scott, James Mason, *Henry Oscar*, Francis Lister, Anthony Bushell

The Return of the Seven

US 1966 95m Technicolor Panavision
UA / Mirisch / CB (Ted Richmond)

The seven gunmen, slightly reconstituted, fight again to rescue some kidnapped farmers.
The mixture as before (see *The Magnificent Seven*); adequate but scarcely inspired.

w Larry Cohen d Burt Kennedy ph Paul Vogel m Elmer Bernstein

Yul Brynner, Robert Fuller, Julian Mateos, Warren Oates, Claude Akins, Virgilio Texeira, Emilio Fernandez, Jordan Christopher

AAN: Elmer Bernstein

The Return of the Vampire*

US 1943 69m bw
Columbia

Dracula reappears amid the London blitz.
Surprisingly well made and complexly plotted horror film; it looks good and only lacks

humour. The wolf man, however, is a regrettable intrusion.

w Griffin Jay *d* Lew Landers *ph* John Stumar, L. J. O'Connell *m* Mario Castelnuovo-Tedesco *md* Morris Stoloff

Bela Lugosi, Nina Foch, Frieda Inescort, Miles Mander, Matt Willis, Roland Varno, Ottola Nesmith

Return to Macon County

US 1975   89m   Movielab
AIP / Macon Service Company (Eliot Schick)

In the fifties, two wandering youths pick up a waitress and have serious trouble with a manic policeman in America's unfriendliest area.
Slam-bang sequel to *Macon County Line,* rather unintentionally comic.

wd Richard Compton *ph* Jacques Marquette *m* Robert O. Ragland

Nick Nolte, Don Johnson, Robin Mattson, Robert Viharo

Return to Paradise*

US 1953   109m   Technicolor
UA / Aspen (Theron Warth)

A peace seeker settles on a tiny South Sea island and leaves when his wife dies; he returns after World War II with his daughter.
Curious idyll, slow but not displeasing.

w Charles Kaufman, *novel* James Michener *d* Mark Robson *ph* Winton Hoch *m* Dmitri Tiomkin

Gary Cooper, Barry Jones, Roberta Haynes, Moira MacDonald

Return to Peyton Place*

US 1961   122m   De Luxe   Cinemascope
TCF / API (Jerry Wald)

Constance Mackenzie's daughter writes a novel about Peyton Place and falls in love with the publisher.
More closets are unlocked, more skeletons fall out; for addicts, the sequel does not disappoint, and it's all very glossy.

w Ronald Alexander *d* Jose Ferrer *ph* Charles G. Clarke *m* Franz Waxman

Jeff Chandler, Carol Lynley, Eleanor Parker, *Mary Astor,* Robert Sterling, Luciana Paluzzi, Brett Halsey, Tuesday Weld
   'Enough soap suds to pollute the Mississippi along with the mind.'—*Judith Crist, 1973*

Reunion in France

US 1943   104m   bw
MGM (Joseph L. Mankiewicz)
GB title: *Mademoiselle France*

A selfish Parisian dress designer gradually realizes that her world has changed when the Nazis invade and she is asked to help an American flier.
Action flagwaver which tries also to be a woman's picture and goes pretty soppily about it.

w Jan Lustig, Marvin Borowsky, Marc Connelly, *story* Ladislas Bus-Fekete *d* Jules Dassin *ph* Robert Planck *m* Franz Waxman

Joan Crawford, John Wayne, Philip Dorn, Reginald Owen, Albert Basserman, John Carradine, Ann Ayars, J. Edward Bromberg, Henry Daniell, Moroni Olsen, Howard da Silva
   'Miss Crawford isn't making all the sacrifices implied in the script . . . Dressing like a refugee is certainly not in her contract.'—*New York Herald Tribune*

Reunion in Vienna*

US 1933   100m   bw
MGM

A long-exiled nobleman tries to take up an old romance even though the lady is married.
Lacklustre adaptation of a play which must have style; the performances remain interesting.

w Ernest Vajda, Claudine West, *play* Robert E. Sherwood *d* Sidney Franklin *ph* George Folsey

John Barrymore, Diana Wynyard, Frank Morgan, May Robson, Eduardo Ciannelli, Una Merkel, Henry Travers

AAN: George Folsey

Revenge

GB 1971   89m   Eastmancolor
Rank / Peter Rogers Productions (George H. Brown)

When children are raped and murdered in a north country town, two men take the law into their own hands.
Crude melodrama set in Cold Comfort Farm country; efficient but unrewarding.

w John Kruse *d* Sidney Hayers *ph* Ken Hodges *m* Eric Rodgers

Joan Collins, Sinead Cusack, James Booth, Ray Barrett, Kenneth Griffith

The Revenge of Frankenstein

GB 1958   89m   Technicolor
Columbia / Hammer (Anthony Hinds)

Baron Frankenstein evades the guillotine and makes a new creature with the brain of a homicidal dwarf.
Dullish horror farrago with a few indications of quirkish humour.

w Jimmy Sangster, Hurford Janes d Terence Fisher ph Jack Asher m Leonard Salzedo

Peter Cushing, Michael Gwynn, Oscar Quitak, Francis Matthews, Eunice Gayson, John Welsh, Lionel Jeffries, Richard Wordsworth, Charles Lloyd Pack, John Stuart, Arnold Diamond
† This second Hammer Frankenstein set the tone for the rest; see The Curse of Frankenstein.

The Revenge of the Pink Panther
US 1978   98m   Technicolor   Panavision
UA / Blake Edwards

Inspector Clouseau tracks down a drug-smuggling industrialist.
Feeble addition to a series which was always too pleased with itself.

w Frank Waldman, Ron Clarke, Blake Edwards d Blake Edwards ph Ernie Day m Henry Mancini

Peter Sellers, Herbert Lom, Robert Webber, Dyan Cannon, Burt Kwouk, Paul Stewart, Robert Loggia, Graham Stark

The Revengers
US 1972   108m   De Luxe   Panavision
Cinema Center / Martin Rackin

A rancher gathers a posse to hunt down the Indians who have allegedly murdered his wife and family.
Standard major western with a dismal script which echoes The Dirty Dozen and The Wild Bunch: sometimes repulsive, seldom exciting.

w Wendell Mayes d Daniel Mann ph Gabriel Torres m Pino Calvi

William Holden, Ernest Borgnine, Susan Hayward, Woody Strode, Roger Hanin

The Revolt of Mamie Stover
US 1956   93m   Eastmancolor
Cinemascope
TCF (Buddy Adler)

A dance hall girl leaves San Francisco for Honolulu, makes money there but reforms for love of a rich novelist.
Absurdly bowdlerized and boring film version of a novel about a sleazy prostitute; hardly worth making at all in this form, especially as the cast seems well capable of a raunchier version.

w Sidney Boehm, novel William Bradford Huie d Raoul Walsh ph Leo Tover m Hugo Friedhofer

Jane Russell, Agnes Moorehead, Richard Egan, Joan Leslie

The Revolutionary
US 1970   101m   Technicolor
(UA) Pressman–Williams (Edward R. Pressman)

Episodes in the life of a revolutionary, from distributing leaflets to attempted assassination.
A rather casual study of one man's radicalism, in no particular time or place; no doubt of great interest to other revolutionaries.

w Hans Konigsberger d Paul Williams ph Brian Probyn m Michael Small

Jon Voight, Jennifer Salt, Robert Duvall

The Reward
US 1965   92m   De Luxe   Cinemascope
TCF / Aaron Rosenberg

A mixed group of adventurers set out across the desert to capture a murderer; but thieves fall out.
Pretentious and talky melodrama which quickly scuttled its director's chances in Hollywood. Little action, obvious outcome, attractive Death Valley locations.

w Serge Bourgignon, Oscar Mullard, novel Michael Barrett d Serge Bourgignon ph Joe MacDonald m Elmer Bernstein

Max Von Sydow, Efrem Zimbalist Jnr, Yvette Mimieux, Gilbert Roland, Emilio Fernandez, Henry Silva

Rhapsody
US 1954   116m   Technicolor
MGM (Lawrence Weingarten)

A wealthy woman affects the lives of two quite different musicians, each of whom has his weakness.
Tedious romantic drama which vainly attempted a smart veneer but boasted a splendid musical sound track.

w Fay and Michael Kanin, novel Maurice Guest by Henry Handel Richardson d Charles Vidor ph Robert Planck md Johnny Green, Bronislau Kaper pianist Claudio Arrau violinist Michael Rabin

Elizabeth Taylor, Vittorio Gassman, John Ericson, Louis Calhern, Michael Chekhov, Barbara Bates, Celia Lovsky, Richard Hageman

Rhapsody in Blue**
US 1945   139m   bw
Warner (Jesse L. Lasky)

The life story of composer George Gershwin. No more trustworthy on factual matters than other Hollywood biopics of its era, this rather glum saga at least presented the music and the performers to excellent advantage.

w Howard Koch, Elliot Paul *d Irving Rapper*
ph Sol Polito md Ray Heindorf, Max Steiner
ch Le Roy Prinz *ad* Anton Grot, John Hughes

Robert Alda, Joan Leslie, Alexis Smith, Charles
Coburn, Julie Bishop, *Albert Basserman, Oscar
Levant, Herbert Rudley*, Rosemary de Camp,
Morris Carnovsky, *Al Jolson, Paul Whiteman*,
George White, Hazel Scott

AAN: Ray Heindorf, Max Steiner

Rhino
US 1964   91m   Metrocolor
MGM / Ivan Tors (Ben Chapman)

A scientist working with white rhinos is joined by
an unscrupulous big game hunter.
Inoffensive African adventure.

w Art Arthur, Arthur Weiss *d* Ivan Tors
ph Sven Persson, Lamar Boren *m* Lalo Schifrin

Harry Guardino, Robert Culp, Shirley Eaton

Rhodes of Africa *
GB 1936   91m   bw
Gaumont (Geoffrey Barkas)
US title: *Rhodes*

A rough-hewn diamond miner becomes Prime
Minister of Cape Colony.
Heavy-going but generally interesting historical
drama shot on location.

w Michael Barringer, Leslie Arliss, Miles
Malleson, *book* Sarah Millin *d* Berthold Viertel

Walter Huston, Oscar Homolka, Basil Sydney,
Peggy Ashcroft, Frank Cellier, Bernard Lee,
Lewis Casson

Rhubarb
US 1951   94m   bw
Paramount (Perlberg–Seaton)

A millionaire leaves his fortune, including a
baseball team, to a wild ginger cat, which means
problems for his publicity agent.
Typical scatty farce of the early fifties, held
together by the splendid performance of the
disdainful feline in the title role rather than by
any special merit in the handling.

w Dorothy Reid, Francis Cockrill, *novel* H.
Allen Smith *d* Arthur Lubin *ph* Lionel Lindon
m Van Cleave

Ray Milland, Jan Sterling, Gene Lockhart,
William Frawley

Rhythm on the Range *
US 1936   87m   bw
Paramount (Benjamin Glazer)

A hired hand saves the boss's daughter when she
is kidnapped by local badmen.

Easy-going musical comedy with a western
background, later remade as *Pardners* (qv).

w John C. Moffett, Sidney Salkow, Walter de
Leon, Francis Martin *d* Norman Taurog
ph Karl Struss *songs* various

Bing Crosby, Martha Raye, Frances Farmer,
Bob Burns, Lucile Watson, Samuel S. Hinds,
George E. Stone, Warren Hymer

Rhythm on the River *
US 1940   92m   bw
Paramount (William Le Baron)

A song writer employs 'ghosts' to produce his
music and lyrics; they discover this fact and go
into business for themselves.
Cheerful musical with strong billing.

w Dwight Taylor, Billy Wilder, Jacques Théry
d Victor Schertzinger *ph* Ted Tetzlaff
m Johnny Burke, James V. Monaco

*Bing Crosby, Mary Martin, Basil Rathbone,
Oscar Levant*, Oscar Shaw, Charley Grapewin,
William Frawley

AAN: song 'Only Forever'

Rich and Strange *
GB 1932   83m   bw
BIP (John Maxwell)
US title: *East of Shanghai*

A young couple come into money and take a trip
around the world.
Slight, agreeable early talkie with a few
Hitchcock touches.

w Alma Reville, Val Valentine, Alfred
Hitchcock *d Alfred Hitchcock ph* Jack Cox,
Charles Martin *m* Hal Dolphe

Henry Kendall, Joan Barry, Percy Marmont,
Betty Amann, Elsie Randolph

The Rich Are Always with Us
US 1932   73m   bw
Warner (Sam Bischoff)

A socialite determines on a divorce but her new
love is annoyed by her concern for her ex-
husband.
Cocktail drama of a kind which totally
disappeared from the screen.

w Austin Parker, *novel* E. Pettit *d* Alfred E.
Green *ph* Ernest Haller *m* W. Franke Harling

Ruth Chatterton, George Brent, John Miljan,
Bette Davis, Adrienne Dore, Mae Madison,
Robert Warwick

Rich Man's Folly
US 1931   80m   bw
Paramount

A rich man has no time for his children.
Curious updating of Dickens' *Dombey and Son*;
not really a success.

w Grover Jones, Edward Paramore Jnr *d* John
Cromwell *ph* David Abel

George Bancroft, Frances Dee, Robert Ames,
Juliette Compton, Dorothy Peterson

Rich, Young and Pretty
US 1951 95m Technicolor
MGM (Joe Pasternak)

A Texas rancher takes his young daughter to
Paris, where she meets her real mother.
Moderate musical.

w Dorothy Cooper, Sidney Sheldon *d* Norman
Taurog *ph* Robert Planck *m* Nicholas
Brodszky *ly* Sammy Cahn *ch* Nick Castle

Danielle Darrieux, Wendell Corey, Jane Powell,
Fernando Lamas, Vic Damone

AAN: song 'Wonder Why' (*m* Nicholas
Brodszky, *ly* Sammy Cahn)

Richard III***
GB 1956 161m Technicolor Vistavision
London Films (Laurence Olivier)

Shakespeare's play about Richard Crookback,
his seizure of the throne and his defeat at
Bosworth.
Theatrical but highly satisfying filming of a
splendidly melodramatic view of history.
Interesting but not fussy camera movement,
delightful sets (followed by a disappointingly
'realistic' battle) and superb performances.

w William Shakespeare (adapted by Laurence
Olivier, Alan Dent, with additions) *d Laurence
Olivier ph Otto Heller ph Roger Furse
m William Walton ad Carmen Dillon*

Laurence Olivier, Claire Bloom, *Ralph
Richardson, Cedric Hardwicke*, Stanley Baker,
Alec Clunes, John Gielgud, Mary Kerridge,
Pamela Brown, Michael Gough, Norman
Wooland, Helen Haye, Patrick Troughton, Clive
Morton, Andrew Cruickshank

AAN: Laurence Olivier

The Ride Back*
US 1957 79m bw
UA / Associates and Aldrich (William Conrad)

A lawman arrests an outlaw wanted for murder,
but has the problem of getting him back to base.
Slightly offbeat low-budget western, well enough
done if it had to be done at all.

w Anthony Ellis *d* Allen H. Miner *ph* Joseph
Biroc *m* Frank de Vol

Anthony Quinn, William Conrad, George
Trevino, Lita Milan

Ride beyond Vengeance
US 1966 100m Technicolor
Columbia / Tiger / Goodson / Todman /
Sentinel / Fenady

A young westerner, accused of cattle rustling
and branded, vows revenge.
Dourly brutal but studio-bound and very padded
western; if there is any entertainment value it
doesn't emerge for more than a few moments.

w Andrew J. Fenady, *novel* The Night of the
Tiger by Al Dewlen *d* Bernard McEveety
ph Lester Shorr *m* Richard Markowitz

Chuck Connors, Michael Rennie, Kathryn
Hays, Claude Akins, Bill Bixby, Paul Fix, Gary
Merrill, Joan Blondell, Gloria Grahame, Ruth
Warrick, Arthur O'Connell, Frank Gorshin,
James MacArthur

† Probably intended as a TV movie and found
too violent.

Ride 'Em Cowboy
US 1941 82m bw
Universal (Alex Gottlieb)

Two hot dog vendors find themselves working on
an Arizona dude ranch.
Slick but routine comedy star vehicle with no
outstanding sequences.

w True Boardman, John Grant *d* Arthur Lubin
ph John W. Boyle *songs* Don Raye, Gene de
Paul

Bud Abbott, Lou Costello, Dick Foran, Anne
Gwynne, Samuel S. Hinds, Richard Lane,
Johnny Mack Brown, Ella Fitzgerald

Ride the High Country**
US 1962 94m Metrocolor
Cinemascope
MGM (Richard E. Lyons)
GB title: *Guns in the Afternoon*

Two retired lawmen help transport gold from a
mining camp to the bank, but one has ideas of his
own.
Thoughtful western graced by ageing star
presences; generally well done.

w N. B. Stone Jnr *d Sam Peckinpah ph* Lucien
Ballard *m* George Bassman

Joel McCrea, Randolph Scott, Edgar Buchanan,
Mariette Hartley, James Drury
  'A nice little conventional unconventional
western.'—*Stanley Kauffmann*

Ride the Pink Horse*.
US 1947   101m   bw
U-I

An ex-serviceman visits a New Mexican town in
search of the gangster who killed his buddy.
Dour, complex melodrama with a certain
amount of style but not enough substance.

w Charles Lederer, *novel* Dorothy B. Hughes
d Robert Montgomery *ph* Russell Metty
m Frank Skinner

Robert Montgomery, Wanda Hendrix, Andrea
King, Thomas Gomez, Fred Clark, Art Smith

AAN: Thomas Gomez

Ride the Wild Surf
US 1964   101m   Eastmancolor
Columbia / Jana (Jo and Art Napoleon)

Surf riders go to Hawaii and find romance.
Pleasant, overlong, open air fun and games.

w Jo and Art Napoleon d Don Taylor
ph Joseph Biroc m Stu Phillips

Fabian, Shelley Fabares, Tab Hunter, Barbara
Eden

Ride, Vaquero
US 1953   90m   Anscocolor
MGM (Stephen Ames)

Ranchers settling in New Mexico after the Civil
War cause some natives to turn bandit; one of
them has a mysterious American associate
called Rio.
Very mildly interesting western with the stars
rather swamping a humourless script.

w Frank Fenton d John Farrow ph Robert
Surtees m Bronislau Kaper

Robert Taylor, Ava Gardner, Howard Keel,
Anthony Quinn, Charlita

Riders to the Stars*
US 1954   81m   Color Corporation
UA / Ivan Tors

Rocket scientists investigate the problems of
cosmic bombardment.
Enjoyably straightforward science fiction with
no monsters or political problems; it has decided
historic interest as a record of what scientists in
1954 thought rocket travel would be like.

w Curt Siodmak d Richard Carlson ph Stanley
Cortez m Harry Sukman

Richard Carlson, Herbert Marshall, William
Lundigan, Dawn Addams, Martha Hyer, Robert
Karnes, Lawrence Dobkin

Riding High
US 1943   88m   Technicolor
Paramount (Fred Kohlmar)
GB title: *Melody Inn*

A burlesque queen goes home to Arizona and
helps ranchers by performing at a dude ranch.
Dim formula musical with exuberance but
neither wit nor style.

w Walter de Leon, Arthur Phillips, Art Arthur,
play Ready Money by James Montgomery
d George Marshall ph Karl Struss, Harry
Hallenberger md Victor Young

Dorothy Lamour, Dick Powell, Victor Moore,
Gil Lamb, Cass Daley, Bill Goodwin, Rod
Cameron, Glenn Langan, Andrew Tombes, Tim
Ryan, Douglas Fowley, Milt Britton and his
Band

Riding High*
US 1950   112m   bw
Paramount (Frank Capra)

An easygoing racing man forsakes the chance of
wealth to train his beloved horse for the Imperial
Derby.
The director's familiar ingredients—farce,
sentimentality, fast cutting, nice people and a lot
of noise—seem a shade too tried and tested in
this remake of his 1934 success *Broadway Bill*.
Despite the cast, the result is only moderately
entertaining.

w Robert Riskin d Frank Capra ph George
Barnes, Ernest Laszlo m James Van Heusen
ly Johnny Burke

Bing Crosby, Coleen Gray, Charles Bickford,
Raymond Walburn, James Gleason, Oliver
Hardy, Frances Gifford, William Demarest,
Ward Bond, Clarence Muse, Percy Kilbride,
Harry Davenport, Margaret Hamilton,
Douglass Dumbrille, Gene Lockhart

Riff Raff
US 1935   90m   bw
MGM (Irving Thalberg)

A con man and his wife end up on the wrong side
of the law.
Modest comedy drama that never quite sparks.

w Frances Marion, H. W. Haneman, Anita
Loos d Robert Z. Leonard

Jean Harlow, Spencer Tracy, Joseph Calleia,
Una Merkel, Mickey Rooney, Victor Kilian, J.
Farrell MacDonald

Riff Raff*
US 1947   80m   bw
RKO

A dying man hands a Panama City con man a

map to valuable oil deposits, and various shady people are after it.

Rather heavy but well made comedy-drama with some striking scenes.

w Martin Rackin *d* Ted Tetzlaff *ph* George E. Diskant *m* Roy Webb

Pat O'Brien, Walter Slezak, Anne Jeffreys, Percy Kilbride, Jerome Cowan

Rififi **

France 1955   116m   bw
Indus / Pathé / Prima
original title: *Du Rififi chez les Hommes*

After an elaborate raid on a jewellery store, thieves fall out and the caper ends in bloodshed.

A film with much to answer for, in the form of hundreds of imitations showing either detailed accounts of robberies (*Topkapi, Gambit*) or gloomy looks at the private lives of criminals. At the time it seemed crisp and exciting, and the 25-minute silent robbery sequence is quite something.

w René Wheeler, Jules Dassin, Auguste le Breton, *novel* Auguste le Breton *d* Jules Dassin *ph* Philippe Agostini *m* Georges Auric

Jean Servais, Carl Mohner, Robert Manuel, Marie Sabouret, Perlo Vita (Jules Dassin)
† Several 'sequels' were made using the word *rififi* (criminal argot for 'trouble') in the title, but in plot terms they were entirely unrelated.

The Right Approach

US 1961   92m   bw   Cinemascope
TCF (Oscar Brodney)

A Hollywood opportunist tries to make it as a star.

A potentially witty Hollywood story is sabotaged by a style which is as naïve as it is dismal; and Mr Vaughan's hopes of stardom unfairly ended right here.

w Fay and Michael Kanin, *play* Garson Kanin *d* David Butler *ph* Sam Leavitt *m* Dominic Frontière

Frankie Vaughan, Martha Hyer, Juliet Prowse, Gary Crosby, David MacLean, Jesse White, Jane Withers

Right Cross

US 1950   90m   bw
MGM (Armand Deutsch)

A boxing champion injures his hand and has to abandon his career.

Rather dull sporting melodrama with a Mexican background, saved by good production values.

w Charles Schnee *d* John Sturges *ph* Norbert Brodine *m* David Raksin

Dick Powell, June Allyson, Lionel Barrymore, Ricardo Montalban

The Ring

US 1952   79m   bw
King Brothers

A young Mexican becomes a prizefighter in the hope of winning greater respect for Mexican-Americans.

Well-meant low-budget programmer.

w Irving Shulman *d* Kurt Neumann *ph* Russell Harlan *m* Herschel Burke Gilbert

Gerald Mohr, Lalo Rios, Rita Moreno, Robert Arthur

Ring of Bright Water *

GB 1969   107m   Technicolor
Palomar / Brightwater (Joseph Strick)

A civil servant buys a pet otter and moves to a remote cottage in the western Highlands.

Disneyesque fable for animal lovers, from a bestselling book.

w Jack Couffer, Bill Travers, *book* Gavin Maxwell *d* Jack Couffer *ph* Wolfgang Suschitsky *m* Frank Cordell

Bill Travers, Virginia McKenna, Peter Jeffrey, Roddy McMillan, Jameson Clark

Ring of Fear

US 1954   88m   Warnercolor
   Cinemascope
Warner / Wayne—Fellows (Robert M.
   Fellowes)

A homicidal maniac returns to the circus where he used to work and causes various 'accidents'. Tediously predictable circus melodrama with a curious but not very likeable cast.

w Paul Fix, Philip MacDonald, James Edward Grant *d* James Edward Grant *ph* Edwin DuPar *m* Emil Newman, Arthur Lange

Clyde Beatty, Pat O'Brien, Mickey Spillane, Sean McClory, Marion Carr, John Bromfield, Pedro Gonzalez Gonzalez, Emett Lynn

Ring of Fire

US 1961   90m   Metrocolor
MGM / Andrew and Virginia Stone

An Oregon sheriff is kidnapped by teenage delinquents but manages to lead them into both a police trap and a forest fire.

Outdoor action thriller with a plot which is ludicrously unconvincing in detail, though the fire scenes impress.

wd Andrew L. Stone *ph* William H. Clothier *m* Duane Eddy

David Janssen, Joyce Taylor, Frank Gorshin, Joel Marston

Ring of Spies*
GB 1963   90m   bw
British Lion (Leslie Gilliatt)
US title: *Ring of Treason*

How the Portland spy ring was tracked down. Documentary drama, rather less intriguing, somehow, than the actual facts; but the sheer thought of spies in the suburbs keeps interest going.

w Frank Launder, Peter Barnes *d* Robert Tronson *ph* Arthur Lavis

Bernard Lee, Margaret Tyzack, David Kossoff, Nancy Nevinson, William Sylvester

The Ringer*
GB 1952   78m   bw
BL / London (Hugh Perceval)

A dangerous criminal known only as The Ringer threatens to kill the crooked lawyer responsible for his sister's death.
Artful old-fashioned mystery, quite well restaged, and in fact the best extant example of filmed Wallace.

w Val Valentine, *novel* and *play* Edgar Wallace *d* Guy Hamilton *ph* Ted Scaife *m* Malcolm Arnold

Donald Wolfit, Mai Zetterling, Herbert Lom, Greta Gynt, William Hartnell, Norman Wooland

Rings on Her Fingers*
US 1942   85m   bw
TCF (Milton Sperling)

The front girl for a couple of confidence tricksters falls in love with their first victim. Lively comedy which drags into drama in its second half.

w Ken Englund *d* Rouben Mamoulian *ph* George Barnes *m* Cyril Mockridge

Gene Tierney, Henry Fonda, Laird Cregar, Spring Byington, Shepperd Strudwick, Frank Orth, Henry Stephenson, Marjorie Gateson

Rio
US 1939   78m   bw
Universal

A crooked financier escapes from Devil's Island to join his wife in Rio, only to find she has been unfaithful.
Modest but well made melodrama.

w Stephn Morehouse Avery, Frank Partos, Edwin Justus Mayer, Abem Kandel, Jean

Negulesco *d John Brahm ph* Hal Mohr
md Charles Previn

Basil Rathbone, Victor McLaglen, Sigrid Gurie, Robert Cummings, Leo Carrillo, Billy Gilbert, Irving Bacon, Irving Pichel

Rio Bravo**
US 1959   141m   Technicolor
Warner (Howard Hawks)

A wandering cowboy and a drunken sheriff hold a town against outlaws.
Cheerfully overlong and slow-moving western in which everybody, including the director, does his thing. All very watchable for those with time to spare, but more a series of revue sketches than an epic.

w Jules Furthman, Leigh Brackett *d Howard Hawks ph* Russell Harlan *m* Dmitri Tiomkin

John Wayne, Dean Martin, Ricky Nelson, Angie Dickinson, Walter Brennan, Ward Bond, John Russell, Pedro Gonzalez Gonzalez, Claude Akins, Harry Carey Jnr, Bob Steele
† More or less remade in 1966 as *El Dorado* and in 1970 as *Rio Lobo.*

Rio Conchos*
US 1964   107m   De Luxe   Cinemascope
TCF (David Weisbart)

Two thousand rifles are stolen from an army command port and traced to the hide-out of a former Confederate colonel who wants to continue the Civil War.
Good standard western which shares much of its story line with *The Comancheros.*

w Clair Huffaker, Joseph Landon *d* Gordon Douglas *ph* Joe MacDonald *m* Jerry Goldsmith

Richard Boone, Edmond O'Brien, Stuart Whitman, Tony Franciosa

Rio Grande*
US 1950   105m   bw
Republic (John Ford, Merian C. Cooper)

A Cavalry unit on the Mexican border in the 1880s conducts a vain campaign against marauding Indians.
Thin Ford western on his favourite theme, with too many pauses for song, too many studio sets, and too little plot. *Aficionados,* however, will find much to admire.

w James Kevin McGuinness, *story* James Warner Bellah *d* John Ford *ph* Bert Glennon, Archie Stout *m* Victor Young

John Wayne, Maureen O'Hara, Ben Johnson, Claude Jarman Jnr, Harry Carey Jnr, Chill Wills, J. Carrol Naish, Victor McLaglen

Rio Lobo*
US 1970   114m   Technicolor
Cinema Center (Howard Hawks)

A union colonel near the end of the Civil War
recovers a gold shipment and exposes a traitor.
Rambling western with traces of former glory,
enjoyable at least for its sense of humour.

w Leigh Brackett, Burton Wohl d Howard
Hawks ph William Clothier m Jerry Goldsmith

John Wayne, Jorge Rivero, Jennifer O'Neill,
Jack Elam, Victor French, Chris Mitchum, Mike
Henry

Rio Rita
US 1929   135m   bw and Technicolor
RKO (William Le Baron)

Romance on a ranch near the Mexican border.
Very early talkie version of a popular Broadway
operetta of the twenties; historical interest only.

w Luther Reed, Russell Mack, *book* Guy Bolton,
Fred Thomson, as produced by Florenz
Ziegfeld d Luther Reed ph Robert Kurle, Lloyd
Knetchel md Victor Baravalle *songs* Harry
Tierney, Joe McCarthy

Bebe Daniels, John Boles, Bert Wheeler, Robert
Woolsey, Dorothy Lee, Don Alvarado, George
Renavent

Rio Rita
US 1942   91m   bw
MGM (Pandro S. Berman)

Flat-footed remake bringing in Nazi spies; poor
comedy even by Abbott and Costello standards.

w Richard Connell, Gladys Lehman d S. Sylvan
Simon ph George J. Folsey

Bud Abbott, Lou Costello, John Carroll,
Kathryn Grayson, Tom Conway, Barry Nelson

Riot
US 1968   98m   Technicolor
Paramount / William Castle

While the warden is away, thirty-five convicts
take over a state penitentiary and are violently
subdued.
Strikingly bloody melodrama set in an actual
prison in Arizona; well made, but less
entertaining than Cagney and Raft used to be.

w James Poe, *novel* Frank Elli d Buzz Kulik
ph Robert B. Hauser m Christopher Komeda

Gene Hackman, Jim Brown, Ben Carruthers,
Mike Kellin, Gerald O'Loughlin, Clifford David

Riot in Cell Block Eleven*
US 1954   80m   bw
Allied Artists / Walter Wanger

In a big American prison three convicts seize
their guards, free the other prisoners and
barricade themselves in their block.
Socially concerned low-budgeter, quite nicely
made and persuasive of the need for prison
reform.

w Richard Collins d Don Siegel ph Russell
Harlan m Herschel Burke Gilbert

Neville Brand, *Emile Meyer,* Frank Faylen, Leo
Gordon, Robert Osterloh, Paul Frees, Don
Keefer

'As a compassionate, angry, unsensational
account of an episode of violence it makes
considerably more impact than many of the
overblown melodramas currently in fashion.'—
Penelope Houston

Riptide*
US 1934   90m   bw
MGM (Irving Thalberg)

A British diplomat weds a Manhattan chorus
girl, but she later falls for an old flame.
Elegantly set, star-packed drawing-room drama
which somehow didn't click.

wd Edmund Goulding ph Ray June m Herbert
Stothart

Norma Shearer, Robert Montgomery, Herbert
Marshall, Mrs Patrick Campbell, Skeets
Gallagher, Ralph Forbes, Lilyan Tashman,
Helen Jerome Eddy, George K. Arthur,
Halliwell Hobbes

The Rise and Fall of Legs Diamond
US 1960   101m   bw
Warner / United States (Milton Sperling)

The career of a New York hoodlum of the
twenties.
Inspired, like *King of the Roaring Twenties,* by
the TV success of *The Untouchables,* this was
part of a brief attempt by Warners to recapture
its pre-war gangster image. Alas, stars and style
were equally lacking.

w Joseph Landon d Budd Boetticher ph Lucien
Ballard m Leonard Rosenman

Ray Danton, Karen Steele, Elaine Stewart, Jesse
White, Simon Oakland, Robert Lowery, Warren
Oates, Judson Pratt

The Rise and Rise of Michael Rimmer
GB 1970   101m   Technicolor
Warner / David Frost (Harry Fine)

An efficiency expert takes over an advertising
agency and is soon an MP, a cabinet minister,
and PM.
Satirical comedy which quickly goes overboard
and is only occasionally funny; it does, however,

mark the final death throes of the swinging sixties, and the changeover to *Monty Python*.

w Peter Cook, John Cleese, Kevin Billington, Graham Chapman *d* Kevin Billington *ph* Alex Thompson *m* John Cameron

Peter Cook, John Cleese, Arthur Lowe, Denholm Elliott, Ronald Fraser, Vanessa Howard, George A. Cooper, Harold Pinter, James Cossins, Roland Culver, Dudley Foster, Julian Glover, Dennis Price, Ronnie Corbett

Rise and Shine

US 1941 93m bw
TCF (Mark Hellinger)

A dumb but brilliant football player is kidnapped by the other side.
Drab collegiate comedy, disappointing considering the credits.

w Herman J. Mankiewicz, *novel* My Life and Hard Times by James Thurber *d* Allan Dwan *ph* Edward Cronjager *m* Emil Newman

Linda Darnell, Jack Oakie, George Murphy, Walter Brennan, Milton Berle, Sheldon Leonard, Donald Meek, Ruth Donnelly, Donald MacBride, Raymond Walburn, Emma Dunn

The Rising of the Moon

Eire 1957 81m bw
Warner / Four Provinces (Lord Killanin)

Three Irish short stories.
Curiously dull John Ford portmanteau with the Abbey players.

w Frank Nugent, *stories* Frank O'Connor, Malcolm J. McHugh, Lady Gregory *d* John Ford *ph* Robert Krasker *m* Eamonn O'Gallagher *narrator* Tyrone Power

Maureen Connell, Eileen Crowe, Cyril Cusack, Maureen Delany, Donal Donelly, Frank Lawton, Edward Lexy, Jack MacGowran, Denis O'Dea, Jimmy O'Dea, Noel Purcell

The Ritz*

US 1976 90m Technicolor
Warner (Denis O'Dell)

A comedy of mistaken identities in a gay New York turkish bath.
An adaptation of a stage success which doesn't seem nearly as funny as it thinks it is; but some of it does work.

w Terrance McNally, from his play *d* Richard Lester *ph* Paul Wilson *m* Ken Thorne *pd* Phillip Harrison

Jack Weston, Rita Moreno, Jerry Stiller, Kaye Ballard, Bessie Love, George Coulouris, F. Murray Abrahams, Treat Williams

The River*

India 1951 87m Technicolor
Oriental / International / Theatre Guild
 (Kenneth McEldowney)

Episodes in the life of a small English community living on the banks of the Ganges.
A slight and surprising work from this director, superbly observed and a pleasure to watch but dramatically very thin.

w Rumer Godden, Jean Renoir, *novel* Rumer Godden *d Jean Renoir ph Claude Renoir m* M. A. Partha Sarathy
ph Eugene Lourie

Nora Swinburne, Esmond Knight, Arthur Shields, Adrienne Corri
† Renoir's assistant was Satyajit Ray

River of No Return*

US 1954 91m Technicolor
 Cinemascope
TCF (Stanley Rubin)

During the California gold rush a widower and his 10-year-old son encounter a saloon singer with a gold claim.
Cheerful, clichéd star western designed to exploit the splendours of early Cinemascope, and very adequate for this purpose.

w Frank Fenton *d* Otto Preminger *ph* Joseph La Shelle *m* Cyril Mockridge *md* Lionel Newman

Robert Mitchum, Marilyn Monroe, Tommy Rettig, Rory Calhoun, Murvyn Vye

The River's Edge

US 1956 87m Eastmancolor
 Cinemascope
TCF (Benedict Bogeaus)

A fugitive bank robber forces a farmer to guide him over the mountains into Mexico.
Sluggish open-air character melodrama.

w Harold J. Smith *d* Allan Dwan *ph* Harold Lipstein *m* Lou Forbes

Ray Milland, Anthony Quinn, Debra Paget, Byron Foulger

The Road Back**

US 1937 97m bw
Universal (James Whale)

After World War I, German soldiers go home to problems and disillusion.
A major work, intended as a sequel to *All Quiet on the Western Front*. Despite impressive sequences, it doesn't quite reach inspiring heights.

w R. C. Sherriff, Charles Kenyon, *novel* Erich Maria Remarque *d James Whale ph* John

Mescall, George Robinson m Dmitri Tiomkin
ad Charles D. Hall

Richard Cromwell, John King, Slim
Summerville, Andy Devine, Barbara Read,
Louise Fazenda, Noah Beery Jnr, Lionel Atwill,
John Emery, Etienne Girardot, Spring Byington,
Laura Hope Crews
† The film is said to have been extensively reshot
after protests from the German consul in Los
Angeles. No 35mm negative now exists, as it
reverted to Remarque and was lost.

Road House*
US 1948 95m bw
TCF

A road house owner is jealous of his manager
and frames him for murder.
Dated but watchable *film noir* of its era, with all
characters cynical or homicidal.

w Edward Chodorov *d* Jean Negulesco
ph Joseph La Shelle *m* Cyril Mockridge

Richard Widmark, Ida Lupino, Cornel Wilde,
Celeste Holm

Road Show*
US 1941 86m bw
Hal Roach

A young man wrongly committed to an insane
asylum escapes with other inmates and joins a
travelling circus.
Engaging scatty comedy on familiar Roach lines
which suffers from lame pacing but manages
some likeable moments.

w Arnold Beldard, Harry Langdon, Mickell
Novak, *novel* Eric Hatch *d* Gordon Douglas

John Hubbard, Adolphe Menjou, Carole Landis,
Patsy Kelly, George E. Stone

The Road to Glory*
US 1936 103m bw
TCF (Darryl F. Zanuck)

Adventures of a French regiment in World
War I.
Meticulously produced war movie which bears
comparison with *All Quiet on the Western Front*.

w Joel Sayre, William Faulkner *d* Howard
Hawks *ph* Gregg Toland *m* Louis Silvers

Fredric March, Warner Baxter, Lionel
Barrymore, June Lang, Gregory Ratoff, Victor
Kilian, John Qualen, Julius Tannen, Leonid
Kinskey

Road to Singapore*
US 1940 84m bw
Paramount (Harlan Thompson)

Two rich playboys swear off women until they
quarrel over a Singapore maiden.
The first Hope–Crosby–Lamour 'road' picture
is basically a light romantic comedy and quite
forgettable; the series got zanier as it progressed.

w Don Hartman, Frank Butler, *story* Harry
Hervey *d* Victor Schertzinger *ph* William C.
Mellor *m* Victor Young

Bing Crosby, Bob Hope, Dorothy Lamour,
Charles Coburn, Judith Barrett, Anthony
Quinn, Jerry Colonna

Road to Zanzibar**
US 1941 92m bw
Paramount (Paul Jones)

The trio on safari in Africa, with *Hellzapoppin*
gags breaking in and an anything-goes
atmosphere.

w Frank Butler, Sy Bartlett *d* Victor
Schertzinger *ph* Ted Tetzlaff *songs* Johnny
Burke, Jimmy Van Heusen

Hope, Crosby, Lamour, Una Merkel, Eric Blore,
Luis Alberni, Douglass Dumbrille
'The funniest thing I've seen on the screen in
years. Years.'—*Otis Ferguson*

Road to Morocco**
US 1942 83m bw
Paramount (Paul Jones)

Hollywood Arab palaces, a captive princess,
topical gags and talking camels.

w Frank Butler, Don Hartman *d* David Butler
ph William C. Mellor *md* Victor Young
songs Johnny Burke, Jimmy Van Heusen

Hope, Crosby, Lamour, Anthony Quinn, Dona
Drake

AAN: script

Road to Utopia**
US 1945 89m bw
Paramount (Paul Jones)

The California gold rush, with all the previous
gag styles in good order, capped by a cheeky
epilogue and constant explanatory narration by
Robert Benchley.

w Norman Panama, Melvin Frank *d* Hal
Walker *ph* Lionel Lindon *m* Leigh Harline
songs Johnny Burke, Jimmy Van Heusen

Hope, Crosby, Lamour, Douglass Dumbrille,
Hillary Brooke, Jack La Rue

AAN: script

Road to Rio**
US 1947 100m bw
Paramount (Daniel Dare)

Guest stars are given their head, plot intrudes again in the shape of a hypnotized heiress, and the style is more constrained (but still funny).

w Edmund Beloin, Jack Rose d Norman Z. McLeod ph Ernest Laszlo md Robert Emmett Dolan songs Johnny Burke, Jimmy Van Heusen

Hope, Crosby, Lamour, Gale Sondergaard, Frank Faylen, the Wiere Brothers, the Andrews Sisters

AAN: Robert Emmett Dolan

Road to Bali*
US 1952   91m   Technicolor
Paramount (Harry Tugend)

In and around the South Seas, with colour making the sets obvious and the gags only tediously funny. The team's zest was also flagging.

w Frank Butler, Hal Kanter, William Morrow d Hal Walker ph George Barnes md Joseph J. Lilley songs Johnny Burke, Jimmy Van Heusen

Hope, Crosby, Lamour, Murvyn Vye, Peter Coe

Road to Hong Kong
GB 1962   91m   bw
UA / Melnor (Norman Panama)

Curious, slightly dismal-looking attempt to continue the series in a British studio and on a low budget. A few good gags, but it's all very tired by now, and the space fiction plot makes it seem more so.

w Norman Panama, Melvin Frank d Melvin Frank ph Jack Hildyard m Robert Farnon pd Roger Furse

Hope, Crosby, Lamour, Joan Collins, Robert Morley, Walter Gotell, Felix Aylmer and guests Peter Sellers, David Niven, Frank Sinatra, Dean Martin, Jerry Colonna

Roadhouse Nights*
US 1930   71m   bw
Paramount

A reporter exposes a gangster operating from a country nightclub.
Experimental mingling of elements which later become very familiar.

w Garrett Fort, story Ben Hecht d Hobart Henley ph William Steiner

Helen Morgan, Charles Ruggles, Fred Kohler, Jimmy Durante, Fuller Mellish Jnr

The Roaring Twenties***
US 1939   106m   bw
Warner (Hal B. Wallis)

A World War I veteran returns to New York,

innocently becomes involved in bootlegging, builds up an empire and dies in a gang war.
Among the last of the Warner gangster cycle, this was perhaps the best production of them all, despite the familiar plot line: stars and studio were in cracking form.

w Jerry Wald, Richard Macaulay, Robert Rossen, story Mark Hellinger d Raoul Walsh, Anatole Litvak ph Ernest Haller

James Cagney, Humphrey Bogart, Priscilla Lane, Jeffrey Lynn, Gladys George, Frank McHugh, Paul Kelly, Elizabeth Risdon

Rob Roy the Highland Rogue
GB 1953   81m   Technicolor
Walt Disney (Perce Pearce)

After the defeat of the clans in the 1715 rebellion, their leader escapes and after several adventures is granted a royal pardon.
A kind of Scottish Robin Hood, so stiffly acted and made that it might as well—or better—be a cartoon.

w Lawrence E. Watkin d Harold French ph Guy Green m Cedric Thorpe Davie

Richard Todd, Glynis Johns, James Robertson Justice, Michael Gough, Finlay Currie, Geoffrey Keen, Archie Duncan

Robbery*
GB 1967   113m   Eastmancolor
Joseph E. Levine / Oakhurst (Michael Deeley, Stanley Baker)

Criminals conspire to rob the night mail train from Glasgow.
Heavy-going fictionalized account of the famous train robbery of 1963; best seen as standard cops and robbers, with some good chase sequences.

w Edward Boyd, Peter Yates, George Markstein d Peter Yates ph Douglas Slocombe m Johnny Keating

Stanley Baker, James Booth, Frank Finlay, Joanna Pettet, Barry Foster, William Marlowe, Clinton Greyn, George Sewell

Robbery under Arms
GB 1957   99m   Eastmancolor
Rank (Joe Janni)

In 19th-century Australia, two farming brothers join the notorious outlaw Captain Starlight.
Howlingly dull film version of a semi-classic adventure novel; a rambling story with no unity of viewpoint is saved only by excellent photography.

w Alexander Baron, W. P. Lipscomb, novel Rolf Boldrewood d Jack Lee ph Harry Waxman m Matyas Seiber

Peter Finch, David McCallum, Ronald Lewis,
Maureen Swanson, Jill Ireland, Laurence
Naismith, Jean Anderson

The Robe **
US 1953   135m   Technicolor
  Cinemascope
TCF (Frank Ross)

Followers and opponents of Jesus are affected by
the robe handed down by him at his crucifixion.
The first film in Cinemascope was, surprisingly,
a biblical bestseller, but the crowded Roman sets
hid most of the flaws in the process. The film
itself was competent and unsurprising in the well-
tried *Sign of the Cross* manner.

w Philip Dunne, *novel* Lloyd C. Douglas
d Henry Koster *ph* Leon Shamroy *m* Alfred
Newman

Richard Burton, Jean Simmons, Michael
Rennie, *Victor Mature*, Jay Robinson, Torin
Thatcher, Dean Jagger, Richard Boone, Betta St
John, Jeff Morrow, Ernest Thesiger, Dawn
Addams

AAN: best picture; Leon Shamroy; Richard
Burton

Roberta *
US 1935   105m   bw (Technicolor
  sequence)
RKO (Pandro S. Berman)

An American inherits a Parisian fashion house.
Thin and remarkably flatly-handled musical
romance of the old school, charged only by the
occasional appearances in supporting roles of
Astaire and Rogers, then on the brink of
stardom.

w Jane Murfin, Sam Mintz, Allan Scott, *play*
Otto Harbach, *book* Gowns by Roberta by Alice
Duer Miller *d* William A. Seiter *ph* Edward
Cronjager *m Jerome Kern md* Max Steiner
ch Fred Astaire *ad* Van Nest Polglase

Irene Dunne, *Fred Astaire, Ginger Rogers*,
Randolph Scott, Helen Westley, Claire Dodd,
Victor Varconi, Torben Meyer
† Remade as *Lovely to Look At* (qv).

AAN: song 'Lovely to Look At'

Robin and Marian *
US 1976   107m   Technicolor
Columbia / Rastar (Dennis O'Dell)

Robin Hood returns from the Crusades and finds
conditions in Britain depressing; he finally
conquers the evil Sheriff but dies in the attempt.
A kind of serious parody of medieval life, after
the fashion of *The Lion in Winter* but much
glummer; in fact, nothing to laugh at at all.

w James Goldman *d* Richard Lester *ph* David
Watkin *m* John Barry *pd* Michael Stringer

Sean Connery, Audrey Hepburn, Robert Shaw,
Ronnie Barker, Nicol Williamson, Richard
Harris, Denholm Elliott, Kenneth Haigh, Ian
Holm, Bill Maynard, Esmond Knight, Peter
Butterworth

'Surface realism only hides a core of mush,
suddenly revealed when the hero and heroine
settle down for love-making in a field of corn.'—
Geoff Brown

'Whimsical jokiness is a bit hard to reconcile
with the final plunge into sacrificial romance.'—
Michael Billington, Illustrated London News

Robin and the Seven Hoods *
US 1964   123m   Technicolor   Panavision
Warner / PC (Howard W. Koch, William H.
  Daniels)

A spoof of the Robin Hood legend set in
gangland Chicago of the twenties.
Too flabby by far to be as funny as it thinks it is,
this farrago of cheerful jokes has effective
moments and lively routines, but most of them
are nearly swamped by flat treatment and the
wide screen.

w David Schwartz *d* Gordon Douglas
ph William H. Daniels *m* Nelson Riddle
songs Sammy Cahn, James Van Heusen

Frank Sinatra, Dean Martin, Bing Crosby,
Sammy Davis Jnr, Peter Falk, Barbara Rush,
Edward G. Robinson, Victor Buono, Barry
Kelley, Jack La Rue, Allen Jenkins, Sig
Rumann, Hans Conried

AAN: Nelson Riddle; song 'My Kind of Town'
(*m* James Van Heusen, *ly* Sammy Cahn)

Robin Hood **
US 1922   127m approx   (24 fps)   bw
  silent
Douglas Fairbanks

Robin Hood combats Prince John and the
Sheriff of Nottingham.
An elaborate version of the legend which
featured some of Hollywood's most celebrated
sets and allowed the star to perform a selection of
exhilarating stunts.

w Douglas Fairbanks *d* Allan Dwan *ph* Arthur
Edeson *ad* Wilfrid Buckland, Irvin J. Martin

Douglas Fairbanks, Wallace Beery, Alan Hale,
Enid Bennett

'The high water mark of film production. It did
not grow from the bankroll, it grew from the
mind.'—*R. E. Sherwood*

† See also *The Adventures of Robin Hood* and
The Story of Robin Hood and his Merrie Men.

Robin Hood
US 1973   83m   Technicolor
Walt Disney (Wolfgang Reitherman)

Alarmingly poor cartoon feature with all the
characters 'played' by animals; songs especially
dim and treatment quite lifeless.

w Larry Clemmons, Ken Anderson, others
d Wolfgang Reitherman *voices* Brian Bedford,
Peter Ustinov, Terry-Thomas, Phil Harris, Andy
Devine, Pat Buttram

AAN: song 'Love' (m George Bruns, ly Floyd
Huddleston)

Robinson Crusoe on Mars **
US 1964   110m   Techniscope
Paramount / Devonshire (Aubrey Schenck)

An astronaut lands on Mars and learns to
survive until rescue comes.
Remarkably close to Defoe (Man Friday being a
refugee in an interplanetary war) this is an
absorbing, entertaining and well-staged piece of
science fiction, strikingly shot in Death Valley.

w Ib Melchior, John C. Higgins d Byron
Haskin ph Winton C. Hoch m Van Cleave
sp Lawrence Butler ad Hal Pereira, Arthur
Lonergan

Paul Mantee, Adam West, Vic Lundin

Robinson Crusoeland
France / Italy 1950   98m   bw
Sirius / Franco-London / Fortezza
aka: Atoll K; Escapade; Utopia

Stan and Ollie inherit an island in the Pacific, but
uranium is discovered on it.
Laurel and Hardy's last film is a dispiriting mess,
and the less said about it the better.

w unknown Leo Joannon, John Berry
ph Armand Thirard, Louis Née

Stan Laurel, Oliver Hardy, Suzy Delair

Rocco and his Brothers **
Italy / France 1960   180m   bw
Titanus / Les Films Marceau (Goffredo
    Lombardo)

A peasant family moves into Milan, and each of
its five brothers has his problems.
Massive portmanteau of realistic stories, a bit
hard to take despite its undoubted brilliance.

w Luchino Visconti, Suso Cecchi d'Amico,
Vasco Pratolini d Luchino Visconti
ph Giuseppe Rotunno m Nino Rota

Alain Delon, Renato Salvatori, Annie Girardot,
Katina Paxinou, Roger Hanin, Paolo Stoppa,
Suzy Delair, Claudia Cardinale

Rock a Bye Baby
US 1958   107m   Technicolor   Vistavision
Paramount (Jerry Lewis)

A film star asks her devoted schoolday admirer
to look after her triplets by a secret marriage.
Tasteless jazzing-up of The Miracle of Morgan's
Creek by talents distinctly unsympathetic.

wd Frank Tashlin ph Haskell Boggs m Walter
Scharf

Jerry Lewis, Marilyn Maxwell, Reginald
Gardiner, Salvatore Baccaloni, Hans Conried,
Isobel Elsom, James Gleason, Isa Moore,
Connie Stevens

Rock around the Clock *
US 1956   74m   bw
Columbia (Sam Katzman)

A band playing a new form of jive—rock 'n
roll— becomes a nationwide sensation.
A cheap second feature with guest artists, this
cheerful little movie deserved at least a footnote
in the histories because it spotlights the origins
and the leading purveyors of rock 'n roll. It also
caused serious riots in several countries. A
sequel in 1957, Don't Knock the Rock, was
merely cheap.

w Robert E. Kent, James B. Gordon d Fred F.
Sears ph Benjamin H. Kline

Bill Haley and the Comets, the Platters, Little
Richard, Tony Martinez and his Band, Freddie
Bell and the Bellboys, Johnny Johnson, Alan
Freed, Lisa Gaye, Alix Talton

Rockets Galore
GB 1958   94m   Technicolor
Rank / Relph and Dearden
US title: Mad Little Island

The Scottish island of Todday resists the
installation of a rocket-launching site.
Amiable but disappointingly listless sequel to
Whisky Galore.

w Monja Danischewsky d Michael Relph
ph Reg Wyer m Cedric Thorpe Davie

Jeannie Carson, Donald Sinden, Roland Culver,
Noel Purcell, Ian Hunter, Duncan Macrae, Jean
Cadell, Carl Jaffe, Gordon Jackson, Catherine
Lacey

Rocketship XM *
US 1950   79m   bw
Lippert (Kurt Neumann)

An expedition to the moon lands by accident on
Mars.
The first post-war space adventure is sheer
hokum, quite likeable for its cheek though not for
its cheap sets.

wd Kurt Neumann *ph* Karl Struss *m* Ferde Grofe

Lloyd Bridges, Osa Massen, John Emery, Hugh O'Brian

The Rocking Horse Winner*
GB 1949 90m bw
Rank / Two Cities (John Mills)

A boy discovers he can predict winners while riding an old rocking horse; his mother's greed has fatal results.

A very short story is fatally over-extended and becomes bathetic; but the production is solid and the film deserves a mark for trying.

wd Anthony Pelissier, *story* D. H. Lawrence *ph* Desmond Dickinson *m* William Alwyn *ad* Carmen Dillon

John Mills, Valerie Hobson, John Howard Davies, Ronald Squire, Hugh Sinclair, Cyril Smith

Rocky**
US 1976 119m Technicolor
UA / Chartoff-Winkler (Gene Kirkwood)

A slightly dimwitted Philadelphia boxer makes good.

Pleasantly old-fashioned comedy-drama with rather unattractive characters in the modern manner. Despite the freshness, on the whole *Marty* is still preferable.

w Sylvester Stallone *d* John G. Avildsen *ph* James Crabe *m* Bill Conti

Sylvester Stallone, Burgess Meredith, Talia Shire, Burt Young, Carl Weathers, Thayer David

AA: best picture; John G. Avildsen; Sylvester Stallone (as actor)

AAN: Sylvester Stallone (as writer); song 'Gotta Fly Now' (*m* Bill Conti, *ly* Carol Connors, Ayn Robbins); Burgess Meredith; Talia Shire; Burt Young

Rocky Mountain
US 1950 83m bw
Warner (William Jacobs)

A Confederate horseman gets involved in an Indian war.

Routine star western with unusual tragic ending.

w Winston Miller, Alan le May *d* William Keighley *ph* Ted McCord *m* Max Steiner

Errol Flynn, Patrice Wymore, Scott Forbes, Guinn Williams, Slim Pickens

Rogue Cop
US 1954 92m bw
MGM (Nicholas Nayfack)

A police detective is on the payroll of a crime syndicate.

Uncompelling star melodrama.

w Sidney Boehm, *novel* William P. McGivern *d* Roy Rowland *ph* John Seitz *m* Jeff Alexander

Robert Taylor, George Raft, Janet Leigh, Steve Forrest, Anne Francis

'Another of the sour, disillusioned crime stories which have recently been coming into fashion.'—*Penelope Houston*

AAN: John Seitz

The Rogue Song*
US 1930 115m Technicolor
MGM (Lionel Barrymore)

A bandit wins the hand of a Russian princess.

Primitive early sound operetta, not salvaged by a few Laurel and Hardy scenes added as an afterthought.

w Frances Marion, John Colton, *operetta* Gypsy Love by Franz Lehar, Robert Bodansky *d* Lionel Barrymore, Hal Roach *ph* Percy Hilburn, C. Edgar Schoenbaum

Laurence Tibbett, Catherine Dale Owen, Florence Lake, Judith Voselli, Nance O'Neill, Stan Laurel, Oliver Hardy

AAN: Laurence Tibbett
† No print is known to exist.

Rogue's March
US 1953 84m bw
MGM (Leon Gordon)

A British army officer is unjustly accused of espionage but becomes a hero in India.

Victorian comedy adventure set on a never-never frontier. Not much.

w Leon Gordon *d* Allan Davis *ph* Paul C. Vogel *m* Alberto Columbo

Peter Lawford, Richard Greene, Janice Rule, Leo G. Carroll, John Abbott, Patrick Aherne

Rogues of Sherwood Forest*
US 1950 80m Technicolor
Columbia (Fred M. Packard)

Robin Hood's son helps the barons to force the signing of Magna Carta.

Satisfactory action adventure.

w George Bruce *d* Gordon Douglas *ph* Charles Lawton Jnr *m* Heinz Roemheld, Arthur Morton

John Derek, Diana Lynn, George Macready, Alan Hale, Paul Cavanagh, Lowell Gilmore, Billy House

Rogues' Regiment
US 1948   86m   bw
U-I

An intelligence man joins the French Foreign
Legion in Saigon to track down an ex-Nazi.
Keen but rather muddled actioner.

w Robert Buckner d Robert Florey ph Maury
Gertsman m Daniele Amfitheatrof

Dick Powell, Marta Toren, Vincent Price,
Stephen McNally

Rollerball*
US 1975   129m   Technicolor   Scope
UA / Norman Jewison

In the 21st century an ultra-violent game is used
to release the anti-social feelings of the masses.
A one-point parable, and an obvious point at
that, is stretched out over more than two hours of
violence in which the rules of the game are not
even explained. A distinctly unlikeable film.

w William Harrison d Norman Jewison
ph Douglas Slocombe md André Previn
pd John Box

James Caan, John Houseman, Ralph
Richardson, Maud Adams, John Beck, Moses
Gunn

'A classic demonstration of how several
millions of dollars can be unenjoyably
wasted.'—Jonathan Rosenbaum

Rollercoaster
US 1977   118m   Technicolor   Panavision
  Sensurround
Universal (Jennings Lang)

A saboteur blows up rollercoasters if his
blackmail demands are not met.
Limp, unsuspenseful, would-be spectacular in
which a stalwart cast struggles with inane
dialogue and situations.

w Richard Levinson, William Link d James
Goldstone ph David M. Walsh m Lalo Schifrin

George Segal, Timothy Bottoms, Richard
Widmark, Susan Strasberg, Harry Guardino,
Henry Fonda

Le Roman d'un Tricheur*
France 1936   83m   bw
Cinéas
aka: The Story of a Cheat

A reformed elderly cardsharp writes his
memoirs.
First person singular comedy, a tour de force in
which only the narrator speaks, the rest use
pantomime only.

wd Sacha Guitry ph Marcel Lucien
Sacha Guitry, Marguerite Moreno, Serge Grave

Roman Holiday**
US 1953   118m   bw
Paramount (William Wyler)

A princess on an official visit to Rome slips away
incognito and falls in love with a newspaperman.
Wispy, charming, old-fashioned romantic
comedy shot in Rome and a little obsessed by the
locations; one feels that a studio base would have
resulted in firmer control of the elements. The
stars, however, made it memorable.

w Ian McLellan Hunter, John Dighton
d William Wyler ph Franz Planer, Henri
Alekan m Georges Auric

Gregory Peck, Audrey Hepburn, Eddie Albert,
Hartley Power, Harcourt Williams

AA: best picture; Audrey Hepburn
AAN: script; William Wyler; photography;
Eddie Albert

Roman Scandals**
US 1933   93m   bw
Samuel Goldwyn

A troubled young man dreams himself back in
ancient Rome.
Musical farce which is not only pretty
entertaining on its own account but remains
interesting for a number of reasons; as its star's
best vehicle, for its Depression bookends, as a
spoof on The Sign of the Cross and the
inspiration of scores of other comedies in which
the heroes dreamed themselves back into other
times. Note also the musical numbers, the
chariot race finale, and the rare appearance of
Ruth Etting.

w William Anthony McGuire, George
Oppenheimer, Arthur Sheekman, Nat Perrin,
story George S. Kaufman, Robert E. Sherwood
d Frank Tuttle chariot sequence Ralph Cedar
ph Gregg Toland ch Busby Berkeley
songs various

Eddie Cantor, Gloria Stuart, Ruth Etting,
Edward Arnold, Alan Mowbray, Verree
Teasdale

The Roman Spring of Mrs Stone*
GB 1961   104m   Technicolor
Warner Seven Arts / AA (Louis de
  Rochemont)

A widowed American actress in Rome begins to
drift into lassitude and moral decline.
Vivien Leigh gets degraded again in this
rambling novella complete with mysterious dark
stranger waiting at the end. Nice to look at, and
occasionally compelling, but unsuccessful as a
whole.

w Gavin Lambert, novel Tennessee Williams

d José Quintero *ph* Harry Waxman *m* Richard Addinsell *pd* Roger Furse *ad* Herbert Smith

Vivien Leigh, Warren Beatty, Lotte Lenya, Jeremy Spenser, Coral Browne, Ernest Thesiger

AAN: Lotte Lenya

Romance*
US 1930 76m bw
MGM

A clergyman falls in love with the opera singer mistress of an industrialist.
Simple-minded romantic drama with the star not at her best; but an interesting example of 'high class' romance of the time.

w Bess Meredyth, Edwin Justus Mayer, *play* Edward Sheldon *d* Clarence Brown *ph* William Daniels

Greta Garbo, Lewis Stone, Gavin Gordon, Elliott Nugent, Clara Blandick, Florence Lake, Henry Armetta

AAN: Clarence Brown; Greta Garbo

Romance of a Horse Thief
US / Yugoslavia 1971 100m Technicolor
Allied Artists / Jadran / Emmanuel L. Wolf (Gene Gutowski)

In a Polish village in 1904 there is dismay when horses are commandeered by Cossacks for service in the Russo-Japanese war.
Nostalgic Jewish drama which ends up rather like *Fiddler on the Roof* without the music.

w David Opatoshu, based on his father's novel *d* Abraham Polonsky *ph* Piero Portalupisisic *m* Mort Shuman

Yul Brynner, Eli Wallach, Jane Birkin, Oliver Tobias, Lainie Kazan, David Opatoshu

The Romance of Rosy Ridge
US 1947 103m bw
MGM (Jack Cummings)

After the Civil War, farmers make their own peace.
Mild period romance with everything settled by a betrothal.

w Lester Cole, *novel* Mackinlay Kantor *d* Roy Rowland

Van Johnson, Thomas Mitchell, Janet Leigh, Selena Royle, Marshall Thompson, Dean Stockwell

'Rustic charm spread through it like molasses.'—*Douglas Eames*

Romance on the High Seas*
US 1948 99m Technicolor
Warner (Alex Gottleib, George Amy)
GB title: *It's Magic*

Various romances mesh on an ocean voyage.
Lightweight musical which introduces Doris Day and generally manages to keep afloat.

w Julius J. and Philip G. Epstein, I. A. L. Diamond *d* Michael Curtiz *ph* Elwood Bredell *m* Ray Heindorf *songs* Jule Styne, Sammy Cahn

Jack Carson, Janis Paige, Don Defore, Doris Day, Oscar Levant, S. Z. Sakall, Eric Blore, Franklin Pangborn, Fortunio Bonanova

AAN: Ray Heindorf; song 'It's Magic' (*m* Jule Styne, *ly* Sammy Cahn)

Romanoff and Juliet*
US 1961 103m Technicolor
U-I / Pavla (Peter Ustinov)

Both Americans and Russians woo the tiny country of Concordia, and war threatens while the ambassadors' children fall in love.
Despite the author's wit this pattern comedy became something of a bore as a stylized stage piece, and the film is not smartly enough handled to be anything but a yawn; the humour never becomes cinematic.

wd Peter Ustinov, from his play *ph* Robert Krasker *m* Mario Nascimbene *ad* Alexander Trauner

Peter Ustinov, Sandra Dee, John Gavin, Akim Tamiroff, Tamara Shayne, John Phillips, Alix Talton, Peter Jones

The Romantic Englishwoman*
GB 1975 116m Eastmancolor
Dial / Meric–Matalon (Daniel M. Angel)

A discontented woman, holidaying at Baden Baden, falls in love with a stranger while her husband completes a novel on the same theme.
Almost as ambiguous as *Last Year in Marienbad,* this annoying film wastes good actors in a script which hovers uncertainly between fantasy, melodrama and reality, intending one supposes to make humourless and obvious comparisons between romance and life.

w Tom Stoppard, Thomas Wiseman, *novel* Thomas Wiseman *d* Joseph Losey *ph* Gerry Fisher *m* Richard Hartley

Glenda Jackson, Michael Caine, Helmut Berger, Marcus Richardson, Kate Nelligan, René Kolldehoff, Michel Lonsdale

'The central trio bite off their lines, play deviously with hypocrisies and humiliations, and seem slightly aware that they're creations by artifice out of artificiality.'—*Penelope Houston*

'An itsy-bitsy, fragmented film that seems less than the sum of its parts.'—*Michael Billington, Illustrated London News*

Rome Express***
GB 1932   94m   bw
Gaumont (Michael Balcon)

Thieves and blackmail victims are among the
passengers on an express train.

Just a little faded now as sheer entertainment,
this remains the prototype train thriller from
which *The Lady Vanishes, Murder on the Orient
Express* and a hundred others are all borrowed;
it also spawned a myriad movies in which
strangers are thrown together in dangerous
situations. Technically it still works very well,
though the script needs modernizing.

w Clifford Grey, Sidney Gilliat, Frank Vosper,
Ralph Stock   *d* Walter Forde

Conrad Veidt, Gordon Harker, Esther Ralston,
Joan Barry, Harold Huth, Cedric Hardwicke,
Donald Calthrop, Hugh Williams, Finlay
Currie, Frank Vosper, Muriel Aked, Eliot
Makeham

  'A first class craftsman's job.'—*Basil Wright*
†Remade 1948 as *Sleeping Car to Trieste* (qv).

Romeo and Juliet*
US 1936   127m   bw
MGM (Irving Thalberg)

Hollywood Shakespeare with a super production
and a rather elderly cast. Not entertaining in the
strict sense, but full of interest.

w Talbot Jennings   *d* George Cukor   *ph* William
Daniels   *m* Herbert Stothart   *ad* Cedric Gibbons

Leslie Howard, Norma Shearer, John
Barrymore, Basil Rathbone, Edna May Oliver,
Henry Kolker, C. Aubrey Smith, Violet Kemble-
Cooper, Robert Warwick, Virginia Hammond,
Reginald Denny, Ralph Forbes, Andy Devine,
Conway Tearle

AAN: best picture; Norma Shearer; Basil
Rathbone

Romeo and Juliet
GB 1954   138m   Technicolor
Rank / Verona (Joe Janni, Sandro Ghenzi)

Good-looking but extremely boring version shot
on Italian locations with quite unacceptable
leads.

wd Renato Castellani   *ph* Robert Krasker
m Roman Vlad

Laurence Harvey, Susan Shentall, Aldo Zollo,
Enzo Fiermonte, Flora Robson, Mervyn Johns,
Sebastian Cabot, Lydia Sherwood, Giulio
Garbinetti, Nietta Zocchi, Bill Travers, Norman
Wooland, John Gielgud as prologue speaker

Romeo and Juliet*
GB 1968   152m   Technicolor
Paramount / BHE / Verona / Dino de
    Laurentiis (Anthony Havelock-Allan, John
    Brabourne, Richard Goodwin)

The with-it version for modern youngsters;
unfortunately the admirably rapid style does not
suit the verse, and long before the much-deferred
end the thing becomes just as tiresome as the
other versions.

w Franco Brusati, Masolino D'Amico   *d* Franco
Zeffirelli   *ph* Pasquale de Santis   *m* Nino Rota

Leonard Whiting, Olivia Hussey, John
McEnery, Michael York, Pat Heywood, Milo
O'Shea, Paul Hardwick, Natasha Parry,
Antonio Pierfederici, Esmeralda Ruspoli, Bruce
Robinson, Roberto Bisacco, Laurence Olivier as
prologue speaker

AA: Pasquale de Santis
AAN: best picture; Franco Zeffirelli

La Ronde***
France 1950   100m   bw
Sacha Gordine

In 1900 Vienna, an elegant compère shows that
love is a merry-go-round: prostitute meets
soldier meets housemaid meets master meets
married woman meets husband meets midinette
meets poet meets actress meets officer meets
prostitute meets soldier . . .

Superb stylized comedy with a fine cast, subtle
jokes, rich decor and fluent direction; not to
mention a haunting theme tune.

w Jacques Natanson, Max Ophuls, *novel* Arthur
Schnitzler   *d* Max Ophuls   *ph* Christian Matras
m Oscar Straus

Anton Walbrook, Simone Signoret, Serge
Reggiani, Simone Simon, Daniel Gélin, Danielle
Darrieux, Fernand Gravey, Odette Joyeux,
Jean-Louis Barrault, Isa Miranda, Gérard
Philipe

  'One of the most civilized films to have come
from Europe in a long time.'—*Gavin Lambert,
MFB*

AAN: script

La Ronde
France 1964   110m   Eastmancolor
    Franscope
Robert and Raymond Hakim

Vulgarization of the above, reset in Paris in
1913. The lack of a compère vastly reduces the
number of jokes.

w Jean Anouilh   *d* Roger Vadim   *ph* Henri
Decaë   *m* Michel Magne

Marie Dubois, Claude Giraud, Anna Karina,

Jean-Claude Brialy, Jane Fonda, Maurice Ronet, Catherine Spaak, Bernard Noel, Francine Bergé, Jean Sorel

Rookery Nook**

GB 1930   76m   bw
British and Dominions (Herbert Wilcox)

A nervous husband on holiday tries to hide a runaway girl who has asked for protection against her stepfather.
Primitive talkie technique cannot entirely conceal the brilliance of the original Aldwych farce team in their most enduring vehicle.

w Ben Travers, from his play d Tom Walls

Ralph Lynn, Tom Walls, Robertson Hare, Winifred Shotter, Mary Brough, Ethel Coleridge, Griffith Humphreys, Margot Grahame

Room at the Top***

GB 1958   117m   bw
Remus (John and James Woolf)

An ambitious young clerk causes the death of his real love but manages to marry into a rich family.
Claimed as the first British film to take sex seriously, and the first to show the industrial north as it really was, this melodrama actually cheats on both counts but scene for scene is vivid and entertaining despite a weak central performance.

w Neil Paterson, novel John Braine d Jack Clayton ph Freddie Francis m Mario Nascimbene

Laurence Harvey, Simone Signoret, Heather Sears, Donald Wolfit, Ambrosine Philpotts, Donald Houston, Raymond Huntley, John Westbrook, Allan Cuthbertson, Hermione Baddeley, Mary Peach

'A drama of human drives and torments told with maturity and precision.'—Stanley Kauffmann

AA: Neil Paterson; Simone Signoret
AAN: best picture; Jack Clayton; Freddie Francis; Hermione Baddeley

Room for One More

US 1952   95m   bw
Warner (Henry Blanke)

A married couple adopt several underprivileged children.
Slightly mawkish family movie redeemed by star performances.

w Jack Rose, Melville Shavelson d Norman Taurog ph Robert Burks m Max Steiner

Cary Grant, Betsy Drake, Lurene Tuttle, Randy Stuart, George Winslow

Room Service*

US 1938   78m   bw
RKO (Pandro S. Berman)

Penniless theatricals find ways of staying in a hotel until they can find a backer.
Claustrophobic Broadway farce unsuitably adapted for the Marx Brothers, who are constrained by having to play characters with a passing resemblance to human beings.

w Morrie Ryskind, play John Murray, Allen Boretz d William A. Seiter ph Russell Metty m Roy Webb

Groucho, Chico, Harpo, Lucille Ball, Donald MacBride, Frank Albertson, Ann Miller, Philip Loeb

'It should also be noted . . . that there is a scene in which a turkey is chased around a room. Not everybody will care for this.'—MFB
† Remade as Step Lively (qv).

Rooney*

GB 1958   88m   bw
Rank (George H. Brown)

Adventures of a bachelor Irish dustman.
Moderately charming, though unconvincing, Dublin comedy.

w Patrick Kirwan, novel Catherine Cookson d George Pollock ph Christopher Challis m Philip Green

John Gregson, Barry Fitzgerald, Muriel Pavlow, June Thorburn, Noel Purcell, Marie Kean, Liam Redmond, Jack MacGowan, Eddie Byrne

Rooster Cogburn*

US 1975   108m   Technicolor   Panavision
Universal (Paul Nathan)

An elderly marshal after a gang of outlaws is helped by the Bible-thumping daughter of a priest.
Disappointing western too obviously patterned after True Grit and The African Queen. Having had the idea for outrageous star casting, the producers obviously decided erroneously that the film would make itself.

w Martin Julien d Stuart Millar ph Harry Stradling Jnr m Laurence Rosenthal

John Wayne, Katharine Hepburn, Anthony Zerbe, Richard Jordan, John McIntyre, Strother Martin

'Like one of those infuriating exhibition bouts in which two resilient old pros bob, weave and spar without ever landing any punches.'—Michael Billington, Illustrated London News

† 'Martin Julien' allegedly covers the writing talents of Hal Wallis, his wife Martha Hyer, and some friends.

The Roots of Heaven*
US 1958   125m   Eastmancolor
Cinemascope
TCF / Darryl F. Zanuck

A white man in central Africa dedicates himself to prevent the slaughtering of elephants.
Curiously patchy version of a novel which was a strange choice for filming; so many side issues are introduced that at times it takes on the look of another jolly safari adventure.

w Romain Gary, Patrick Leigh-Fermor, *novel* Romain Gary *d* John Huston *ph* Oswald Morris *m* Malcolm Arnold

Trevor Howard, Juliette Greco, Errol Flynn, Eddie Albert, Orson Welles, Paul Lukas, Herbert Lom, Grégoire Aslan, Friedrich Ledebur, Edric Connor
'The Huston who did *Sierra Madre* would have lighted his cigar with this script.'—*Stanley Kauffmann*

Rope**
US 1948   80m   Technicolor
Transatlantic (Sidney Bernstein, Alfred Hitchcock)

Two homosexuals murder a friend for the thrill of it and conceal his body in a trunk from which they serve cocktails to a party including his father and girl friend.
An effective piece of Grand Guignol on the stage, this seemed rather tasteless when set in a New York skyscraper, especially when the leading role of the investigator was miscast and Hitch had saddled himself with the ten-minute take, a short-lived technique which made the entire action (set in one room) cinematically continuous (and dizzy-making). Of considerable historic interest, nevertheless.

w Arthur Laurents, *play* Patrick Hamilton *d* Alfred Hitchcock *ph* Joseph Valentine, William V. Skall *md* Leo F. Forbstein *theme* François Poulenc

James Stewart, John Dall, Farley Granger, Joan Chandler, Cedric Hardwicke, Constance Collier, Edith Evanson, Douglas Dick

Rope of Sand*
US 1949   105m   bw
Paramount (Hal B. Wallis)

Various factions seek hidden diamonds in a prohibited South African area.
Ham-fisted adventure story which suggests at times that a violent parody of *Casablanca* was intended. The stars carry it through.

w Walter Doniger *d* William Dieterle *ph* Charles Lang *m* Franz Waxman

Burt Lancaster, Paul Henreid, Claude Rains, Peter Lorre, Corinne Calvet, Sam Jaffe

Rosalie*
US 1938   118m   bw
MGM (William Anthony McGuire)

A college football hero falls for an incognito Balkan princess.
Ambitious light musical with a wispy plot but satisfying numbers.

w William Anthony McGuire, *play* William Anthony McGuire, Guy Bolton *d* W. S. Van Dyke *ph* Oliver T. Marsh *songs* Cole Porter

Nelson Eddy, Eleanor Powell, Frank Morgan, Ray Bolger, Ilona Massey, Reginald Owen, Edna May Oliver, Jerry Colonna

Rose Marie*
US 1936   113m   bw
MGM (Hunt Stromberg)

A Canadian Mountie gets his man—and a lady.
Backwoods romance from a stage success, filmed mostly on location and quite successfully.

w Frances Goodrich, Albert Hackett, Alice Duer Miller, *play* Otto Harbach, Oscar Hammerstein II *d* W. S. Van Dyke *ph* William Daniels *md* Herbert Stothart *songs* various

Nelson Eddy, Jeanette MacDonald, James Stewart, Reginald Owen, Allan Jones, Gilda Gray, George Regas, Alan Mowbray, Robert Greig, Una O'Connor, David Niven, Herman Bing
† Previously filmed in 1928—and see below.

Rose Marie
US 1954   115m   Technicolor
Cinemascope
MGM (Mervyn Le Roy)

Dull remake with stodgy handling and poor sets.

w Ronald Millar *d* Mervyn Le Roy *ph* Paul C. Vogel *md* Georgie Stoll *ch* Busby Berkeley

Howard Keel, Ann Blyth, Fernando Lamas, Bert Lahr, Marjorie Main, Ray Collins

Rose of Washington Square**
US 1939   86m   bw
TCF (Nunnally Johnson)

Tribulations of a Broadway singer in love with a worthless husband.
Revamping of the Fanny Brice story; smartly done, but the material interpolated for Jolson is what makes the film notable.

w Nunnally Johnson *d* Gregory Ratoff *ph* Karl
Freund *m* Louis Silvers *songs* various

Alice Faye, Tyrone Power, *Al Jolson, Hobart
Cavanaugh,* William Frawley, Joyce Compton,
Louis Prima and his band

The Rose Tattoo
US 1955   117m   bw   Vistavision
Paramount / Hal B. Wallis

A Sicilian woman on the gulf coast is tormented
by the infidelity of her dead husband, but a
brawny truckdriver makes her forget him.
Heavily theatrical material, unsuited to the big
screen for all the powerful acting (or perhaps
because of it).

w Tennessee Williams, from his play *d* Daniel
Mann *ph* James Wong Howe *m* Alex North

Anna Magnani, Burt Lancaster, Marisa Pavan,
Ben Cooper, Virginia Grey, Jo Van Fleet

   'The boldest story of love you have ever been
permitted to see!'—*publicity*

AA: Tennessee Williams; James Wong Howe;
Anna Magnani

AAN: best picture; Alex North; Marisa Pavan

Roseanna McCoy
US 1949   89m   bw
Samuel Goldwyn

In old Virginia the Hatfields and the McCoys
continue their feud with tragic results.
Hillbilly Romeo and Juliet saga, a shade too
cornfed despite the credits.

w John Collier *d* Irving Reis *ph* Lee Garmes
m David Buttolph

Joan Evans, Farley Granger, Charles Bickford,
Raymond Massey, Richard Basehart, Aline
MacMahon

Rosebud
US 1975   126m   Eastmancolor
   Panavision
UA / Otto Preminger

Five girls of wealthy families are kidnapped by
the Palestine Liberation Army.
Overlong topical suspenser which goes awry by
not being very suspenseful, and by packing in too
many irrelevant satirical jibes.

w Erik Lee Preminger, *novel* Joan Hemingway,
Paul Bonnecarrere *d* Otto Preminger *ph* Denys
Coop *m* Laurent Petitgerard *titles* Saul Bass

Peter O'Toole, Richard Attenborough, Cliff
Gorman, Claude Dauphin, John V. Lindsay,
Peter Lawford, Raf Vallone, Adrienne Corri

Roseland*
US 1977   103m   color
Cinema Shares / Merchant Ivory (Ismail
   Merchant)

Generation after generation, the lonely and the
loving come to a New York ballroom.
Pleasantly intentioned slice-of-life drama which
is rather slackly written and handled, with
unprofessionalism showing through at several
points.

w Ruth Prawer Jhabvala *d* James Ivory
ph Ernest Vincze *m* Michael Gibson

Geraldine Chaplin, Teresa Wright, Lou Jacobi,
Don de Natale, Louise Kirkland, Helen
Gallagher, Joan Copeland, Conrad Janis, Lilia
Skala, Christopher Walken

Rosemary's Baby**
US 1968   137m   Technicolor
Paramount / William Castle

After unwittingly becoming friendly with
diabolists, an actor's wife is impregnated by the
Devil.
Seminal gothic melodrama which led in due
course to the excesses of *The Exorcist*; in itself
well done in a heavy-handed way, the book being
much more subtle.

wd Roman Polanski, *novel Ira Levin*
ph William Fraker *m* Krzysztof Komeda
pd Richard Sylbert

Mia Farrow, John Cassavetes, Ruth Gordon,
Sidney Blackmer, Patsy Kelly, Ralph Bellamy,
Maurice Evans, Angela Dorian, Elisha Cook,
Charles Grodin

AA: Ruth Gordon
AAN: Roman Polanski (as writer)

Rosie
US 1967   98m   Techniscope
Universal / Ross Hunter (Jacque Mapes)

A rich woman spends wildly and her daughters
try to have her committed to safeguard their
inheritance.
Hopelessly muddled comedy drama which flits
from one mood to the other without making a
success of either.

w Samuel Taylor, *play* Ruth Gordon, *French
original* Les Joies de la Famille by Philippe
Heriat *d* David Lowell Rich *ph* Clifford Stine
m Lyn Murray

Rosalind Russell, Brian Aherne, Sandra Dee,
Vanessa Brown, Audrey Meadows, James
Farentino, Leslie Nielsen, Margaret Hamilton,
Reginald Owen, Juanita Moore, Virginia Grey
   'A mawkish mixture of *Auntie Mame* and
King Lear.'—*MFB*

Rotten to the Core
GB 1965   88m   bw   Panavision
BL / Tudor (The Boulting Brothers)

Ex-convicts plan an army payroll robbery.
Routine caper comedy, unsuitably
widescreened, with a few good jokes along the
way.

w Jeffrey Dell, Roy Boulting, John Warren, Len
Heath d John Boulting ph Freddie Young
m Michael Dress

Anton Rodgers, *Thorley Walters*, Eric Sykes,
Kenneth Griffith, Charlotte Rampling, Ian
Bannen, Avis Bunnage, Raymond Huntley
†The original title, *Rotten to the Corps*, was
more apt but plainly seemed too subtle.

Le Rouge et le Noir*
France / Italy 1954   170m approx
   Eastmancolor
Franco London / Documento
aka: *Scarlet and Black*

A carpenter's son becomes a private tutor,
seduces his master's wife and is sent to study for
the priesthood . . .
Massive attempt to conquer an unfilmable novel.
Some enjoyable scenes and decor are the best it
can offer.

w Jean Aurenche, Pierre Bost, Claude Autant-
Lara, *novel* Stendhal d Claude Autant-Lara
ph Michel Kelber m René Cloërc ad Max Douy

Gérard Philipe, Danielle Darrieux, Antonella
Lualdi, Jean Martinelli

The Rough and the Smooth
GB 1959   99m   bw
Renown (George Minter)

An archaeologist about to marry the niece of a
press lord falls for a mysterious nymphomaniac.
Preposterous melodrama about unreal people;
its very excesses become enjoyable for those who
can stay the course.

w Audrey Erskine-Lindop, Dudley Leslie,
novel Robin Maugham d Robert Siodmak
ph Otto Heller md Muir Mathieson

Tony Britton, Najda Tiller, William Bendix,
Natasha Parry, Norman Wooland, Donald
Wolfit, Tony Wright, Adrienne Corri, Joyce
Carey

   'The script is never even on nodding terms
with life, and tries to make up for this deficiency
by a candidly explosive vocabulary which gives
the production a weirdly old-fashioned air.'—
MFB

Rough Night in Jericho
US 1967   97m   Techniscope
Universal (Martin Rackin)

A stagecoach man rids a cattle town of a villain.
Totally uninteresting star western with glum
performances.

w Sidney Boehm, Marvin H. Albert, *novel* The
Man in Black by Marvin H. Albert d Arnold
Laven ph Russell Metty m Don Costa

George Peppard, Dean Martin, Jean Simmons,
John McIntire, Slim Pickens, Don Galloway,
Brad Weston

Rough Shoot*
GB 1952   86m   bw
Raymond Stross
US title: *Shoot First*

A retired US officer in Dorset thinks he has shot
a poacher—but the dead man is a spy, and
someone else shot him.
Minor Hitchcock-style thriller with a climax in
Madame Tussaud's. Generally efficient and
entertaining.

w *Eric Ambler, novel* Geoffrey Household
d Robert Parrish ph Stan Pavey m Hans May

Joel McCrea, Evelyn Keyes, Marius Goring,
Roland Culver, Frank Lawton, Herbert Lom

Roughly Speaking*
US 1945   117m   bw
Warner (Henry Blanke)

Oddball, overlong domestic comedy drama
about father's wild and impractical schemes.

w Louise Randall Pierson, from her book
d Michael Curtiz ph Joseph Walker m Max
Steiner

Rosalind Russell, Jack Carson, Robert Hutton,
Jean Sullivan, Alan Hale, Donald Woods,
Andrea King, Ray Collins, Kathleen Lockhart

The Rounders
US 1965   85m   Metrocolor   Panavision
MGM (Richard E. Lyons)

Two modern cowboys mean to settle down but
never get around to it.
Pale comedy western which never gets going.

wd Burt Kennedy, *novel* Max Evans ph Paul C.
Vogel m Jeff Alexander

Henry Fonda, Glenn Ford, Chill Wills, Sue
Anne Langdon, Edgar Buchanan

Roustabout
US 1964   101m   Techniscope
Hal B. Wallis

A wandering tough guy joins a travelling carnival.

Dreary star vehicle momentarily salvaged by its co-star.

w Allan Weiss, Anthony Lawrence *d* John Rich *ph* Lucien Ballard *m* Joseph L. Lilley

Elvis Presley, Barbara Stanwyck, Sue Ann Langdon, Joan Freeman, Leif Erickson

Roxie Hart**
US 1942 72m bw
TCF (Nunnally Johnson)

A twenties showgirl confesses for the sake of publicity to a murder of which she is innocent.

Crowded Chicago burlesque which now seems less funny than it did but is full of smart moments.

w Nunnally Johnson, play Chicago by Maurine Watkins *d* William Wellman *ph* Leon Shamroy

Ginger Rogers, George Montgomery, *Adolphe Menjou,* Lynne Overman, Nigel Bruce, Spring Byington, Sara Allgood, William Frawley

'A masterpiece of form, of ensemble acting, of powerhouse comedy and scripting.'—*NFT, 1974*

† The play was also filmed in 1927 under its original title, with Phyllis Haver.

The Royal Family of Broadway*
US 1930 82m bw
Paramount
GB title: *Theatre Royal*

The off-stage escapades of a famous family of actors.

Fairly funny lampoon of the Barrymores, primitively staged and very talky but still entertaining for those in the joke.

w Herman J. Mankiewicz, Gertrude Purcell, *play* George S. Kaufman, Edna Ferber *d* George Cukor, Cyril Gardner *ph* George Folsey

Fredric March, Henrietta Crosman, Ina Claire, Mary Brian, Charles Starrett, Frank Conroy

'Lionel does not come into the burlesque at all, and I can quite believe that he is the most damaged of the entire family.'—*James Agate*

'Stagebound and awkward, but great fun anyway.'—*New Yorker, 1977*

AAN: Fredric March

Royal Flash
GB 1975 118m Technicolor
TCF / Two Roads (David V. Picker, Denis O'Dell)

A Victorian bully and braggart has various adventures in Europe and Ruritania.

A rather unsatisfactory romp which takes pot shots at every 19th-century person and object in the encyclopaedia, but is never as funny as it intends to be.

w George Macdonald Fraser, from his novel *d* Richard Lester *ph* Geoffrey Unsworth *m* Ken Thorpe *ph* Terence Marsh

Malcolm McDowall, Oliver Reed, Alan Bates, Florinda Bolkan, Britt Ekland, Lionel Jeffries, Tom Bell, Joss Ackland, Leon Greene, Richard Hurndall, Alastair Sim, Michael Hordern

A Royal Scandal
US 1945 94m bw
TCF (Ernst Lubitsch)
GB title: *Czarina*

The illicit loves of Catherine the Great.

Censored romps around some chilly court sets; very few moments of interest, and none of the style of the silent version *Forbidden Paradise.*

w Edwin Justus Mayer, *play* Lajos Biro, Melchior Lengyel *d* Otto Preminger *ph* Arthur Miller *m* Alfred Newman

Tallulah Bankhead, Charles Coburn, Anne Baxter, William Eythe, Vincent Price, Mischa Auer, Sig Rumann, Vladimir Sokoloff

Royal Wedding
US 1951 93m Technicolor
MGM (Arthur Freed)
GB title: *Wedding Bells*

Journalists congregate in London for the royal wedding.

Thin musical with acceptable numbers.

w Alan Jay Lerner *d* Stanley Donen *ph* Robert Planck *md* Johnny Green *songs* Alan Jay Lerner, Burton Lane

Fred Astaire, Jane Powell, Sarah Churchill, Peter Lawford, Keenan Wynn

AA: song 'Too Late Now' (*m* Burton Lane, *ly* Alan Jay Lerner)

Ruby Gentry ——
US 1952 82m bw
Joseph Bernhard / King Vidor

A tempestuous girl, brought up as a boy in the Carolina swamps, has a love-hate relationship with a local aristocrat, revenges herself on the people who scorn her, loses her lover in a swamp shooting, and becomes a sea captain.

Richly absurd sex melodrama typical of its director and star yet not very entertaining.

w Sylvia Richards *d* King Vidor *ph* Russell Harlan *m* Heinz Roemheld *ad* Dan Hall

Jennifer Jones, Charlton Heston, Karl Malden, Josephine Hutchinson

Ruggles of Red Gap**
US 1935   90m   bw
Paramount (Arthur Hornblow Jnr)

A British butler has a startling effect on the family of an American rancher who takes him out west.
A famous comedy which seemed hilarious at the time but can now be seen as mostly composed of flat spots; the performances however are worth remembering.

w Walter de Leon, Harlan Thompson, Humphrey Pearson, *novel* Harry Leon Wilson d Leo McCarey ph Alfred Gilks

Charles Laughton, Mary Boland, Charles Ruggles, Zasu Pitts, Roland Young, Leila Hyams, James Burke, Maude Eburne, Lucien Littlefield
'A sane, witty, moving and quite unusual picture of Anglo-American relations.'—*C. A. Lejeune*
† Remade as *Fancy Pants* (qv).

AAN: best picture

Rulers of the Sea*
US 1939   96m   bw
Paramount (Frank Lloyd)

Problems surround the first steamship voyage across the Atlantic.
Well-made period action drama.

w Talbot Jennings, Frank Cavett, Richard Collins d Frank Lloyd

Douglas Fairbanks Jnr, Margaret Lockwood, Will Fyffe, Montagu Love, George Bancroft, Mary Gordon, Alan Ladd

The Ruling Class*
GB 1971   155m   De Luxe
Keep Films (Jules Buck, Jack Hawkins)

The fetishistic Earl of Gurney is succeeded by his mad son Jack who believes he is God.
An overlong satirical play with brilliant patches is hamfistedly filmed but boasts some bright performances. The hits are as random as the misses, however.

w Peter Barnes, from his play d Peter Medak ph Ken Hodges m John Cameron

Peter O'Toole, Harry Andrews, *Arthur Lowe, Alastair Sim,* Coral Browne, Michael Bryant
'This irritating and unsatisfying film is worth being irritated and unsatisfied by.'—*Stanley Kauffmann*

Rumba*
US 1935   71m   bw
Paramount (William Le Baron)

A society girl has a yen for a Broadway hoofer.
Streamlined star vehicle which attempts to recapture the success of *Bolero* (qv).

w Howard J. Green d Marion Gering ph Ted Tetzlaff

Carole Lombard, George Raft, Margo, Lynne Overman, Monroe Owsley, Iris Adrian, Gail Patrick, Samuel S. Hinds, Jameson Thomas

Run for Cover*
US 1955   92m   Technicolor   Vistavison
Paramount (William H. Pine)

An ex-convict becomes innocently involved in a train robbery.
Adequate star western.

w William C. Thomas, *story* Harriet Frank Jnr, Irving Ravetch d Nicholas Ray ph Daniel Fapp md Howard Jackson

James Cagney, Viveca Lindfors, John Derek, Jean Hersholt, Grant Withers, Ernest Borgnine, Jack Lambert

Run for the Sun
US 1956   99m   Technicolor   Superscope
UA / Russ–Field (Harry Tatelman)

Crashlanding in the Mexican jungle, a disillusioned author and a lady journalist find themselves at the mercy of renegade Nazis.
Tame remake of *The Most Dangerous Game* with Count Zaroff replaced by Lord Haw-Haw.
Sluggish plot development mars the action.

w Dudley Nichols, Roy Boulting d Roy Boulting ph Joseph La Shelle m Fred Steiner

Richard Widmark, Jane Greer, Trevor Howard, Peter Van Eyck

A Run for Your Money*
GB 1949   83m   bw
Ealing (Leslie Norman)

Welsh Rugby supporters have various adventures on their one day in London.
Slight, bright, British chase comedy with characterizations as excellent as they are expected.

w Richard Hughes, Charles Frend, Leslie Norman d Charles Frend ph Douglas Slocombe m Ernest Irving

Alec Guinness, Meredith Edwards, Moira Lister, Donald Houston, Hugh Griffith, Clive Morton, Joyce Grenfell

Run of the Arrow
US 1956 85m Technicolor RKOscope
Global (Samuel Fuller)

An ex-Civil War soldier is captured by Indians
and accepted by them, but sickened by their
violence.
Bloody little western in the accustomed Fuller
vein of unpleasantness.

wd Samuel Fuller *ph* Joseph Biroc *m* Victor
Young

Rod Steiger, Sarita Montiel, Charles Bronson,
Tim McCoy, Ralph Meeker

Run Silent Run Deep*
US 1958 93m bw
UA / Hecht–Hill–Lancaster (William Schorr)

Antagonisms flare up between the officers of a
US submarine in Tokyo Bay during World
War II.
Competent, unsurprising war actioner trading
on its stars.

w John Gay *d* Robert Wise *ph* Russell Harlan
m Franz Waxman

Clark Gable, Burt Lancaster, Jack Warden,
Brad Dexter, Nick Cravat, Joe Maross, H. M.
Wynant
'Mostly good sea fights. Otherwise it's damn
the torpedoes, half speed ahead.'—*Time*

Run Wild, Run Free*
GB 1969 98m Technicolor
Columbia / Irving Allen (John Danischewsky)

A mute boy living on Dartmoor gains self-
confidence through the love of animals.
Rather vaguely developed family film with
agreeable sequences.

w David Rook, from his novel The White Colt
d Richard C. Sarafian *ph* Wilkie Cooper
m David Whitaker

John Mills, Sylvia Syms, Mark Lester, Bernard
Miles, Gordon Jackson, Fiona Fullerton

The Runaway Bus*
GB 1954 78m bw
Eros / Conquest–Guest (Val Guest)

Passengers at London Airport are fogbound,
and a relief bus driver takes some of them to
Blackbushe. Incognito among them are robbers
and detectives . . .
Vaguely plotted variation on *The Ghost Train*,
with fair production, a good smattering of jokes,
and a hilarious view of a great airport in its
earlier days.

wd Val Guest *ph* Stan Pabey *m* Ronald Binge

Frankie Howerd, Margaret Rutherford, George
Coulouris, Petula Clark, Terence Alexander,
Toke Townley, Belinda Lee

The Running Man*
GB 1963 103m Technicolor Panavision
Columbia / Peet (Carol Reed, John R. Sloan)

A private airline pilot fakes an accident and
disappears, leaving his wife to collect the
insurance and meet him in Spain.
Flabby, expensive suspenser; both plot and
character take a back seat to scenic views.

w John Mortimer, *novel* The Ballad of the
Running Man by Shelley Smith *d* Carol Reed
ph Robert Krasker *m* William Alwyn

Laurence Harvey, Alan Bates, Lee Remick,
Felix Aylmer, Eleanor Summerfield, Allan
Cuthbertson
'There seems to be something about the
panoramic screen that seduces film-makers into
filling it with irrelevant local colour and drawing
the whole proceedings out to a length that
matches its width.'—*Brenda Davies*

Running Scared
GB 1972 98m Technicolor Panavision
Paramount / Wigan / Hemmings / O'Toole
  (Gareth Wigan)

A university student is generally condemned for
allowing his friend to commit suicide; eventually
he takes his own life.
Depressing and rather pointless exercise in death
wish complicated by a doomed love affair.

w Clive Exton, David Hemmings, *novel* Gregory
MacDonald *d* David Hemmings *ph* Ernest
Day *m* Michael J. Lewis

Robert Powell, Gayle Hunnicutt, Barry Morse,
Stephanie Bidmead, Edward Underdown,
Maxine Audley, Georgia Brown

Russian Roulette
US 1975 90m Eastmancolor
ITC / Elliott Kastner / Bulldog

Real and fake secret agents shoot it out when the
Russian premier is about to visit Vancouver.
Fast-moving but impossible to follow location
thriller which resolves itself into a series of
chases.

w Tom Ardies, Stanley Mann, Arnold Margolin,
novel Kosygin is Coming by Tom Ardies *d* Lou
Lombardo *ph* Brian West *m* Michael J. Lewis

George Segal, Gordon Jackson, Denholm
Elliott, Cristina Raines, Richard Romanus,
Louise Fletcher, Nigel Stock
'A stale, mechanical espionage caper that
wastes its star.'—*Kevin Thomas*

The Russians Are Coming, The Russians Are Coming*

US 1966 126m De Luxe Panavision
UA / Mirisch (Norman Jewison)

Russian submariners make a forced landing on a Connecticut holiday island and cause panic.
'Daring' cold war comedy which turns out to be of the most elementary and protracted nature, saved from boredom only by a few cameos.

w William Rose, *novel* The Off-Islanders by Nathaniel Benchley d Norman Jewison ph Joseph Biroc m Johnny Mandel

Carl Reiner, Eva Marie Saint, Alan Arkin, John Philip Law, Paul Ford, Tessie O'Shea, Brian Keith, Jonathan Winters, Theodore Bikel, Ben Blue

'Rather amiable, though the film, like its title, seems to repeat most things twice.'—*Sight and Sound*

AAN: best picture; William Rose; Alan Arkin

Ruthless*

US 1948 104m bw
Eagle Lion / Arthur S. Lyons

A conniver breaks several lives on his way to the top.
Rich melodrama with some entertaining moments.

w S. K. Lauren, Gordon Kahn, *novel* Prelude to Night by Dayton Stoddert d Edgar G. Ulmer ph Bert Glennon m Werner Janssen

Zachary Scott, Sidney Greenstreet, Diana Lynn, Louis Hayward, Martha Vickers, Lucille Bremer, Edith Barrett, Raymond Burr, Dennis Hoey

Ryan's Daughter**

GB 1971 206m Metrocolor Panavision 70
MGM / Faraway (Anthony Havelock-Allan)

1916 Ireland: a village schoolmaster's wife falls for a British officer.
A modestly effective pastoral romantic melodrama, stretched on the rack of its director's meticulous film-making technique and unnecessarily big budget. A beautiful, impressive, well-staged and well-acted film, but not really four hours' worth of drama.

w Robert Bolt d David Lean ph Frederick A. Young m Maurice Jarre pd Stephen Grimes (who created an entire village)

Sarah Miles, Robert Mitchum, Chris Jones, John Mills, Trevor Howard, Leo McKern

'Instead of looking like the money it cost to make, the film feels like the time it took to shoot.'—*Alexander Walker*

AA: Frederick A. Young; John Mills
AAN: Sarah Miles

S

SOS Pacific*
GB 1959 91m bw
Rank / Sydney Box (John Nasht, Patrick Filmer-Sankey)

Survivors of a Pacific plane crash await rescue on a small island which is the site of an imminent H-bomb test.

Satisfactory open-air thick ear with strongly deployed types and a suspense climax.

w Robert Westerby d Guy Green ph Wilkie Cooper

Eddie Constantine, Pier Angeli, John Gregson, Richard Attenborough, Eva Bartok, Clifford Evans, Jean Anderson, Cec Linder

Saadia
US 1953 87m Technicolor
MGM (Albert Lewin)

A young French doctor in the Sahara has trouble with the local witch doctor.

Pretentious and ill-considered multi-national romance from the champion of Omar's Rubaiyat.

wd Albert Lewin, novel Echec au Destin by Francis D'Autheville ph Christopher Challis m Bronislau Kaper

Cornel Wilde, Mel Ferrer, Rita Gam, Michel Simon, Wanda Rotha, Cyril Cusack, Marcel Poncin, Peter Bull

Sabotage***
GB 1936 76m bw
Gaumont British (Michael Balcon, Ivor Montagu)
US title: A Woman Alone

The proprietor of a small London cinema is a dangerous foreign agent.

Unattractively plotted but fascinatingly detailed Hitchcock suspenser with famous sequences and a splendidly brooding melodramatic atmosphere.

w Charles Bennett, Ian Hay, Helen Simpson, E. V. H. Emmett, novel The Secret Agent by Joseph Conrad d Alfred Hitchcock ph Bernard Knowles md Louis Levy

Oscar Homolka, Sylvia Sidney, John Loder, Desmond Tester, Joyce Barbour, Matthew Boulton

'Tightly packed, economical, full of invention and detail.'—NFT, 1961

Saboteur***
US 1942 108m bw
Universal (Frank Lloyd, Jack H. Skirball)

A war worker unjustly suspected of sabotage flees across the country and unmasks a spy ring.

Flawed Hitchcock action thriller, generally unsatisfactory in plot and pace but with splendid sequences at a ball, in Radio City Music Hall, and atop the Statue of Liberty.

w Peter Viertel, Joan Harrison, Dorothy Parker, story Alfred Hitchcock d Alfred Hitchcock ph Joseph Valentine m Frank Skinner md Charles Previn

Robert Cummings, Patricia Lane, Otto Kruger, Alan Baxter, Alma Kruger, Norman Lloyd

The Saboteur, Code Name Morituri*
US 1965 122m bw
TCF / Arcola / Colony (Aaron Rosenberg)

In 1942 a German pacifist working for the allies is actually a German spy.

Dreary as a whole, suspenseful in snatches, this shipboard melodrama is full of irrelevancies and is in any case played much more seriously than the matter demands.

w Daniel Taradash, novel Werner Jeorg Kosa d Bernhard Wicki ph Conrad Hall m Jerry Goldsmith

Yul Brynner, Marlon Brando, Trevor Howard, Janet Margolin

AAN: Conrad Hall

Sabrina*
US 1954 113m bw
Paramount (Billy Wilder)
GB title: Sabrina Fair

The chauffeur's daughter is wooed by both her brother employers.

Superior comedy, rather uneasily cast.

w Billy Wilder, play Samuel Taylor d Billy

Wilder *ph* Charles Lang Jnr *m* Frederick Hollander

Humphrey Bogart, William Holden, Audrey Hepburn, Walter Hampden, John Williams, Martha Hyer, Joan Vohs, Marcel Dalio

AAN: Billy Wilder (as writer and director); Charles Lang Jnr; Audrey Hepburn

The Sad Sack
US 1957 98m bw Vistavision
Paramount (Paul Nathan)

Adventures of an army misfit.
Resistible star comedy.

w Edmund Beloin, Nate Monaster, *cartoon* George Baker *d* George Marshall *ph* Loyal Griggs *m* Walter Scharf

Jerry Lewis, David Wayne, Phyllis Kirk, Peter Lorre, Joe Mantell, Gene Evans, George Dolenz, Liliane Montvecchi, Shepperd Strudwick

Saddle the Wind*
US 1958 84m Metrocolor
Cinemascope
MGM (Armand Deutsch)

A reformed gunman's young brother gets into bad company.
Modestly effective, humourless western drama.

w Rod Serling *d* Robert Parrish *ph* George J. Folsey *m* Jeff Alexander

Robert Taylor, John Cassavetes, Julie London, Donald Crisp, Charles McGraw, Royal Dano, Richard Erdman

Sadie McKee*
US 1934 88m bw
MGM (Lawrence Weingarten)

A maid at various times loves her master, a young ne'er-do-well, and a middle-aged millionaire.
Solidly carpentered millgirl's romance of the period.

w John Meehan, *story* Vina Delmar *d* Clarence Brown *ph* Oliver T. Marsh

Joan Crawford, Franchot Tone, Gene Raymond, Edward Arnold, Esther Ralston, Jean Dixon, Leo Carrillo, Akim Tamiroff
 'The stuff the fans cry for.'—*Hollywood Reporter*

Sadie Thompson*
US 1928 95m (24 fps) bw silent
Gloria Swanson

In the South Seas, a fire-and-brimstone missionary is attracted to a prostitute.
Steamy, much-filmed melodrama (see *Rain,*

Miss Sadie Thompson). This version has long been unavailable for revaluation.

w G. Gardner Sullivan, *story* Rain by W. Somerset Maugham *d* Raoul Walsh *ph* George Barnes, Robert Kurrle *ad* William Cameron Menzies

Gloria Swanson, Lionel Barrymore, Blanche Frederici, Charles Lane, Florence Midgley, Raoul Walsh

AAN: George Barnes; Gloria Swanson

Safari
GB 1956 91m Technicolor
Cinemascope
Warwick (Adrian Worker)

A white hunter falls in love with the wife of his employer and luckily the latter is killed by the Mau Mau.
Feeble adventure story exploiting political tensions.

w Anthony Veiller *d* Terence Young *ph* John Wilcox, Fred Ford, Ted Moore *m* William Alwyn

Victor Mature, Janet Leigh, Roland Culver, John Justin, Earl Cameron, Liam Redmond, Orlando Martins

The Safecracker
GB 1958 96m bw
MGM / Coronado (David E. Rose)

A safecracker is released to help in a commando raid during World War II.
One-twelfth of a dirty dozen, with a long indecisive lead-up and not much pull as drama or comedy.

w Paul Monash, *story* Rhys Davies *d* Ray Milland *ph* Gerald Gibbs *m* Richard Rodney Bennett

Ray Milland, Barry Jones, Jeanette Sterke, Victor Maddern, Ernest Clark, Cyril Raymond, Melissa Stribling

Safety Last***
US 1923 70m (24 fps) bw silent
Harold Lloyd

A small-town boy goes to the big city and to impress his girl friend enters a contest to climb a skyscraper.
Marvellous star comedy which set a new standard not only in sight gags but in the comedy-thrill stunts which became Lloyd's stock-in-trade.

w Harold Lloyd, Sam Taylor, Tim Whelan, Hal Roach *d* Sam Taylor, Fred Newmeyer *ph* Walter Lundin

Harold Lloyd, Mildred Davis, Noah Young

Sahara **
US 1943   97m   bw
Columbia

During the retreat from Tobruk a group of men
of mixed nationality find water for themselves
and harass the Nazis.
Good, simple war actioner with a realistic feel
and strong characters deployed in melodramatic
situations.

w John Howard Lawson, Zoltan Korda
d *Zoltan Korda* *ph* Rudolph Maté *m* Miklos
Rozsa

Humphrey Bogart, Bruce Bennett, Lloyd
Bridges, Rex Ingram, J. Carrol Naish, Dan
Duryea, Kurt Kreuger

AAN: Rudolph Maté; J. Carrol Naish

Saigon
US 1948   93m   bw
Paramount (P. J. Wolfson)

Veteran airmen in Saigon are offered half a
million to help in a robbery.
Tired studio-set star actioner.

w P. J. Wolfson, Arthur Sheekman *d* Leslie
Fenton *ph* John Seitz *m* Robert Emmett Dolan

Alan Ladd, Veronica Lake, Douglas Dick,
Wally Cassell, Luther Adler, Morris Carnovsky,
Mikhail Rasumny

Sail a Crooked Ship
US 1961   88m   bw
Columbia / Philip Barry Jnr

A shipowner unwittingly takes on a crew of
crooks intending to use the boat as a getaway
after a bank robbery.
Flimsy comedy sustained by a star comedian.

w Ruth Brooks Flippen, Bruce Geller,
novel Nathaniel Benchley *d* Irving Brecher
ph Joseph Biroc *m* George Duning

Robert Wagner, *Ernie Kovacs*, Dorothy Hart,
Carolyn Jones, Frank Gorshin

Sailor Beware
US 1952   103m   bw
Paramount / Hal B. Wallis

Martin and Lewis in the navy.
Unlovable star antics.

w James Allardice, Martin Rackin,
play Kenyon Nicholson, Charles Robinson
d Hal Walker *ph* Daniel L. Fapp *m* Joseph J.
Lilley

Dean Martin, Jerry Lewis, Corinne Calvet,
Marion Marshall, Robert Strauss, Leif Erickson

Sailor Beware *
GB 1956   80m   bw
Romulus (Jack Clayton)
US title: *Panic in the Parlor*

A young sailor has trouble with his mother-in-
law-to-be.
Plain but adequate film version of a successful
lowbrow stage farce about an archetypal female
dragon.

w Philip King and Falkland L. Cary, from their
play *d* Gordon Parry *ph* Douglas Slocombe
m Peter Akister

Peggy Mount, Esma Cannon, Cyril Smith,
Shirley Eaton, Ronald Lewis

**The Sailor Who Fell from Grace with the
Sea**
GB 1976   105m   Technicolor
AVCO / Sailor Company (Martin Poll)

A precocious boy interferes with his widowed
mother's affair with a sailor by castrating the
latter.
Weird and unattractive sex fantasy set in
Dartmouth of all places and not helped by
tiresome sex scenes.

wd Lewis John Carlino, *novel* Gogo No Eiko by
Mishima Yukio *ph* Douglas Slocombe *m* John
Mandel

Sarah Miles, Kris Kristofferson, Jonathan Kahn,
Margo Cunningham, Earl Rhodes

Sailors Three **
GB 1940   86m   bw
Ealing (Culley Forde)
US title: *Three Cockeyed Sailors*

Drunken sailors capture a German battleship by
mistake.
Low service comedy which keeps moving, is
brightly played and reaches a good standard.
Sequel: *Fiddlers Three* (qv).

w Angus Macphail, John Dighton, Austin
Melford *d* Walter Forde

Tommy Trinder, Claude Hulbert, Michael
Wilding, Carla Lehmann, Jeanne de Casalis,
James Hayter, John Laurie

The Saint
Leslie Charteris' famous character, the reformed
British gentleman crook who becomes a Robin
Hood of crime, has been most popular in the
long-running sixties TV series starring Roger
Moore. The films which featured him never
seemed to hit quite the right note, and now seem
slow. All but one were made for RKO, who later
switched allegiance to THE FALCON (qv).

1938: THE SAINT IN NEW YORK

1939: THE SAINT STRIKES BACK, THE
SAINT IN LONDON
1940: THE SAINT'S DOUBLE TROUBLE,
THE SAINT TAKES OVER
1941: THE SAINT IN PALM SPRINGS, THE
SAINT'S VACATION
1943 (Republic): THE SAINT MEETS THE
TIGER
1954: THE SAINT'S GIRL FRIDAY

Louis Hayward played the role in the first and
last; Hugh Sinclair in VACATION and TIGER;
George Sanders in the rest.

St Benny the Dip

US 1951   79m   bw
Danzigers

Gamblers learn to escape the law by dressing as
priests, but circumstance converts them to good
works.
Unfunny comedy notable only for its cast.

w John Roeburt d Edgar G. Ulmer ph Don
Malkames m Robert Stringer

Freddie Bartholemew, Roland Young, Dick
Haymes, Lionel Stander, Nina Foch

St Ives

US 1973   93m   Technicolor
Warner (Pancho Kohner, Stanley Kanter)

An ex-police reporter gets involved in a complex
murder puzzle.
Soporific suspenser with every tired situation in
the book.

w Barry Beckerman, novel The Procane
Chronicle by Oliver Bleeck d J. Lee-Thompson
ph Lucien Ballard m Lalo Schifrin

Charles Bronson, Harry Guardino, John
Houseman, Jacqueline Bisset, Maximilian
Schell, Harris Yulin, Dana Elcar, Elisha Cook
Jnr

Saint Joan

GB 1957   110m   bw
Otto Preminger

Glumly assembled screen version of the
brilliantly argumentative play about the Maid of
Orleans. Plenty of talent, but neither wit nor
style.

w Graham Greene, play Bernard Shaw d Otto
Preminger ph Georges Périnal m Mischa
Spoliansky pd Roger Furse

Jean Seberg, Anton Walbrook, Richard
Widmark, John Gielgud, Felix Aylmer, Harry
Andrews, Richard Todd

St Louis Blues*

US 1939   92m   bw
Paramount (Jeff Lazarus)

A Broadway musical star finds new fame down
south.
Moderate star entertainment with good guest
artists.

w John C. Moffitt, Malcolm Stuart Boylan,
Frederick Hazlitt Brennan d Raoul Walsh
ph Theodor Sparkuhl songs Frank Loesser,
Burton Lane

Dorothy Lamour, Lloyd Nolan, Tito Guizar,
Jerome Cowan, Jessie Ralph, William Frawley,
the King's Men, Matty Melneck and his
Orchestra

St Martin's Lane**

GB 1938   85m   bw
Mayflower (Erich Pommer)
US title: Sidewalks of London

A middle-aged busker falls in love with a brilliant
girl dancer who becomes a star.
Well-made romantic drama with star
performances and interesting theatrical
background.

w Clemence Dane d Tim Whelan

Charles Laughton, Vivien Leigh, Rex Harrison,
Tyrone Guthrie, Larry Adler, Gus
MacNaughton

The St Valentine's Day Massacre

US 1967   99m   De Luxe   Panavision
TCF / Los Altos (Roger Corman)

The twenties gang war between Al Capone and
Bugs Moran.
The director's first big studio film is
disappointing; stagey, poorly developed,
unconvincing-looking and overacted.

w Howard Browne d Roger Corman ph Milton
Krasner m Fred Steiner md Lionel Newman

Jason Robards Jnr, George Segal, Ralph
Meeker, Jean Hale, Clint Ritchie, Joseph
Campanella, Richard Bakalyan, David Canary,
Bruce Dern, Harold J. Stone, Kurt Kreuger,
John Agar, Alex D'Arcy

The Sainted Sisters

US 1948   89m   bw
Paramount (Richard Maibaum)

Two New York con girls find themselves taken in
by the inhabitants of the small town in which
they are hiding out.
Unfunny period comedy which misses on all
cylinders.

w Harry Clark d William D. Russell ph Lionel
Lindon m Van Cleave

Veronica Lake, Joan Caulfield, Barry
Fitzgerald, William Demarest, George Reeves,
Beulah Bondi, Chill Wills, Darryl Hickman

Sally and St Anne

US 1952   90m   bw
U-I (Leonard Goldstein)

When an Irish-American family is threatened
with eviction, the daughter appeals to St Anne
for help.

Whimsical comedy, quite nimbly performed.

w James O'Hanlon, Herb Meadow d Rudolph
Maté ph Irving Glassberg m Frank Skinner

Ann Blyth, Edmund Gwenn, Hugh O'Brian,
John McIntire, Jack Kelly

Sally in Our Alley*

GB 1931   77m   bw
Basil Dean

Poor girl loves wounded soldier.
Early talkie drama with music which made
Gracie Fields a star and gave her a theme song.

w Miles Malleson, Archie Pitt, Alma Reville,
play The Likes of 'Er by Charles McEvoy
d Maurice Elvey

Gracie Fields, Ian Hunter, Florence Desmond,
Ivor Barnard

Sally, Irene and Mary

US 1938   72m   bw
TCF (Gene Markey)

Three girls try to break into show business.
Simple-minded romantic comedy-musical, well
enough done.

w Harry Tugend, Jack Yellen d William A.
Seiter ph Peverell Marley md Arthur Lange

Alice Faye, Tony Martin, Fred Allen, Jimmy
Durante, Gregory Ratoff, Joan Davis, Marjorie
Weaver, Gypsy Rose Lee

Salome

US 1953   103m   Technicolor
Columbia (Buddy Adler)

Princess Salome of Galilee eludes her licentious
stepfather, falls in love with a secret Christian,
and leaves home when her dancing fails to save
the life of John the Baptist.
Distorted biblical hokum with an interesting cast
frozen into unconvincing attitudes.

w Harry Kleiner, Jesse Lasky Jnr d William
Dieterle ph Charles Lang m George Duning
md Daniele Amfitheatrof ad John Meehan

Rita Hayworth, Charles Laughton, Stewart
Granger, Judith Anderson, Cedric Hardwicke,

Alan Badel, Basil Sydney, Maurice Schwartz,
Rex Reason, Arnold Moss

Salome Where She Danced*

US 1945   90m   Technicolor
Universal (Walter Wanger, Alexander
Golitzen)

During the Austro-Prussian war a dancer is
suspected of being a spy and flees to Arizona,
where she affects the lives of the citizenry.
Absurdly plotted and stiffly played romantic
actioner whose sheer creakiness made it a minor
cult film.

w Laurence Stallings, story Michael J. Phillips
d Charles Lamont· ph Hal Mohr, W. Howard
Green m Edward Ward

Yvonne de Carlo, Rod Cameron, Albert Dekker,
David Bruce, Walter Slezak, Marjorie
Rambeau, J. Edward Bromberg, Abner
Biberman, John Litel, Kurt Katch

Saloon Bar*

GB 1940   76m   bw
Ealing (Michael Balcon)

A murder is solved during an evening in a pub.
Amusing, well-made little suspenser from a West
End success.

w Angus MacPhail, John Dighton, play Frank
Harvey d Walter Forde ph Ronald Neame
md Ernest Irving

Gordon Harker, Elizabeth Allen, Mervyn Johns,
Joyce Barbour, Anna Konstam, Judy Campbell,
Norman Pierce, Alec Clunes, Felix Aylmer,
Mavis Villiers, Torin Thatcher, O. B. Clarence

Salt and Pepper

GB 1968   101m   De Luxe
UA / Chrislaw / Tracemark (Milton Ebbins)

Soho nightclub proprietors solve a murder.
Infuriating throwaway star vehicle set in the
dregs of swinging London. The sequel, One
More Time (1970), was quite unnecessary.

w Michael Pertwee d Richard Donner ph Ken
Higgins m Johnny Dankworth

Sammy Davis Jnr, Peter Lawford, Michael
Bates, Ilona Rodgers, John Le Mesurier,
Graham Stark, Ernest Clark

Salute John Citizen

GB 1942   98m   bw
British National (Wallace Orton)

A clerk and his family suffer cheerfully through
the blitz.
Modest, competent propaganda piece.

w Clemence Dane, Elizabeth Baron, novel Mr

Bunting at War by Robert Greenwood
d Maurice Elvey

Edward Rigby, Stanley Holloway, George
Robey, Mabel Constanduros, Jimmy Hanley,
Dinah Sheridan, Peggy Cummins, Stewart
Rome

Salute to the Marines
US 1943   101m   Technicolor
MGM (John Considine Jnr)

A sergeant-major struggles to get his family out
of the Philippines when the Japs attack.
Recruiting poster heroics with comedy
interludes.

w Wells Root, George Bruce, *story* Robert
Andrews d S. Sylvan Simon

Wallace Beery, Fay Bainter, Marilyn Maxwell,
William Lundigan, Keye Luke, Reginald Owen,
Ray Collins, Noah Beery, Russel Gleason

The Salvation Hunters**
US 1925   65m (24 fps)   bw   silent
Academy Photoplays (Josef Von Sternberg,
   George K. Arthur)

Among the mud flats of San Pedro, a boy wins
his girl from a brute.
Mini-budgeted minor classic whose very artiness
and pretentiousness were keys to its director's
later development.

wd *Josef Von Sternberg* ph Josef Von
Sternberg, Edward Gheller

George K. Arthur, Georgia Hale, Bruce Guerin

Salvatore Giuliano*
Italy 1961   125m   bw
Lux / Vides / Galatea (Franco Cristaldi)

The bullet-ridden body of key Sicilian Mafia
leader Giuliano triggers flashbacks to his
complex and brutal career.
Vivid, sometimes obscure, politically oriented
melodrama based on fact. Undoubtedly a local
classic, but not an easy film to appreciate.

w Francesco Rosi, Suso Cecchi d'Amico, Enzo
Provenzale, Franco Solinas d Francesco Rosi
ph Gianni di Venanzo m Piero Piccioni

Frank Wolff, Salvo Randone, Federico Zardi
   'Epic reportage in the twentieth-century
manner of a society reminiscent of some
backward corner of the nineteenth century.'—
Peter John Dyer, MFB

The Salzburg Connection
US 1972   93m   De Luxe   Panavision
TCF (Ingo Preminger)

An American lawyer on holiday in Salzburg
finds himself suspected by spies of both sides.

Turgid, routine action thriller with attractive
locations.

w Oscar Millard, *novel* Helen MacInnes d Lee
H. Katzin ph Wolfgang Treu md Lionel
Newman

Barry Newman, Anna Karina, Maria
Brandauer, Karen Jensen, Wolfgang Preiss
   'So dull you can't tell the CIA agents from the
neo-Nazis or double agents—or the inept actors
from the blocks and stones in the handsome
Austrian locales.'—*Judith Crist*

Sam Whiskey
US 1969   96m   De Luxe
UA / Brighton (Jules Levy, Arthur Gardner,
   Arnold Laven)

An itinerant gambler is paid to recover a fortune
in gold bars from the bottom of a Colorado river.
Easy-going but rather slackly-handled western.

w William W. Norton d Arnold Laven
ph Robert Moreno m Herschel Burke Gilbert

Burt Reynolds, Clint Walker, Ossie Davis,
Angie Dickinson, Rick Davis, William Schallert

Same Time, Next Year*
US 1978   119m   colour
Universal / Walter Mirisch, Robert Mulligan

An illicit affair is carried on for twenty-five years,
the couple confining themselves to one annual
meeting in a hotel.
Careful film version of a smash Broadway
comedy; the flimsiness of the premise is
concealed, but it remains a one-set play.

w Bernard Slade, from his play d Robert
Mulligan ph Robert Surtees m Marvin
Hamlisch pd Henry Bumstead

Ellen Burstyn, Alan Alda

Sammy Going South*
GB 1963   128m   Eastmancolor
   Cinemascope
Bryanston (Hal Mason)
US title: *A Boy Ten Feet Tall*

A 10-year-old boy is orphaned in Port Said and
hitch-hikes to his aunt in Durban.
Disappointing family-fodder epic in which the
mini-adventures follow each other too
predictably.

w Denis Cannan, *novel* W. H. Canaway
d Alexander Mackendrick ph Erwin Hillier
m Tristam Cary

Fergus McClelland, Edward G. Robinson,
Constance Cummings, Harry H. Corbett

Samson and Delilah
US 1949 128m Technicolor
Paramount / Cecil B. de Mille

Delilah, rejected by religious strong man Samson, cuts his hair and delivers him to his enemies.
Absurd biblical hokum, stodgily narrated and directed, monotonously photographed and edited, and notable only for the 30-second destruction of the temple at the end.

w Jesse L. Lasky Jnr, Fredric M. Frank d Cecil B. de Mille ph George Barnes m Victor Young ad Hans Dreier, Walter Tyler

Hedy Lamarr, Victor Mature, Angela Lansbury, George Sanders, Henry Wilcoxon, Olive Deering, Fay Holden, Russ Tamblyn

'To ignore so enormous, over-coloured, over-stuffed, flamboyant an "epic" would be almost as absurd as taking it seriously.'—*Richard Mallett, Punch*

AAN: George Barnes; Victor Young

San Antonio*
US 1945 109m Technicolor
Warner (Robert Buckner)

A cowboy incurs the jealousy of a saloon owner.
Typically thinly-plotted Warner star western which works well enough sequence by sequence, climaxing with a fight in the deserted Alamo.

w Alan le May, W. R. Burnett d David Butler ph Bert Glennon m Max Steiner

Errol Flynn, Alexis Smith, Paul Kelly, Victor Francen, S. Z. Sakall, John Litel, Florence Bates, Robert Shayne, Monte Blue, Robert Barrat

AAN: song 'Some Sunday Morning' (m Ray Heindorf, M. K. Jerome, ly Ted Koehler)

San Demetrio London*
GB 1943 105m bw
Ealing (Robert Hamer)

In 1940, the survivors of a crippled tanker bring it back home.
Rather flat and dated propaganda piece which seemed much more vivid at the time.

w Robert Hamer, Charles Frend, story F. Tennyson Jesse d Charles Frend

Walter Fitzgerald, Mervyn Johns, Ralph Michael, Robert Beatty, Charles Victor, Frederick Piper, Gordon Jackson

San Diego I Love You*
US 1944 83m bw
Universal (Michael Fessier, Ernest Pagano)

A family travels to San Diego to promote father's inventions.
Pleasing, easy-come-easy-go comedy full of memorable incident and characterization.

w Michael Fessier, Ernest Pagano d Reginald Le Borg

Louise Allbritton, Edward Everett Horton, Jon Hall, Eric Blore, *Buster Keaton*, Irene Ryan

San Francisco****
US 1936 117m bw
MGM (John Emerson, Bernard Hyman)

The loves and career problems of a Barbary Coast saloon proprietor climax in the 1906 earthquake.
Incisive, star-packed, superbly-handled melodrama which weaves in every kind of appeal and for a finale has some of the best special effects ever conceived.

w Anita Loos, story Robert Hopkins d W. S. Van Dyke ph Oliver T. Marsh md Herbert Stothart montage John Hoffman

Clark Gable, Spencer Tracy, Jeanette MacDonald, Jack Holt, Jessie Ralph, Ted Healy, Shirley Ross, Al Shean, Harold Huber

'Prodigally generous and completely satisfying.'—*Frank S. Nugent*

AAN: best picture; Robert Hopkins; W. S. Van Dyke; Spencer Tracy

The San Francisco Story*
US 1952 90m bw
Warner / Fidelity–Vogue (Howard Welsch)

In 1856, a wanderer bound for China stops in San Francisco to get involved in politics.
Lively melodrama with good period feel.

w D. D. Beauchamp, novel Richard Summers d Robert Parrish ph John Seitz m Emil Newman

Joel McCrea, Yvonne de Carlo, Sidney Blackmer, Florence Bates

San Quentin*
US 1937 70m bw
Warner (Sam Bischoff)

A convict's sister loves the warden.
Standard tough prison melodrama, competently done.

w Peter Milne, Humphrey Cobb, story John Bright, Robert Tasker d Lloyd Bacon ph Sid Hickox

Pat O'Brien, Ann Sheridan, Humphrey Bogart, Barton MacLane, Joseph Sawyer, Veda Ann Borg

Sanctuary
US 1960   90m   bw   Cinemascope
TCF (Richard D. Zanuck)

The governor's daughter is seduced by a
bootlegger, and her life goes from one tragedy to
another.
Confused adaptation of unadaptable material,
full of pussyfoot daring but little sense.

w James Poe, *novel* William Faulkner d Tony
Richardson *ph* Ellsworth Fredericks *m* Alex
North

Lee Remick, Bradford Dillman, Yves Montand,
Odetta, Harry Townes, Howard St John, Reta
Shaw, Strother Martin

The Sand Pebbles*
US 1966   193m   De Luxe   Panavision
TCF / Argyle / Solar (Robert Wise)

In 1926 an American gunboat patrolling the
Yangtze river gets involved with Chinese
warlords.
Confused action blockbuster with Vietnam
parallels for those who care to pick them up;
pretty thinly stretched entertainment despite the
tons of explosive.

w Robert Anderson, *novel* Richard McKenna
d Robert Wise *ph* Joseph MacDonald *m* Jerry
Goldsmith

Steve McQueen, Candice Bergen, Richard
Attenborough, Richard Crenna, Marayat
Andriane, Mako, Larry Gates. Simon Oakland
'If it had been done twenty years ago, it would
have been fast and unpretentious, with some
ingeniously faked background shots . . . and we
would never have asked for larger historical
meanings.'—*Pauline Kael*

AAN: best picture; Joseph MacDonald; Jerry
Goldsmith; Steve McQueen; Mako

Sanders of the River*
GB 1935   98m   bw
London (Alexander Korda)

Problems of a British colonial servant in keeping
peace among the tribes.
Much-caricatured African adventure of the very
old school, helped by Robeson's personality.

w Lajos Biro, Jeffrey Dell, Arthur Wimperis
d Zoltan Korda

Leslie Banks, Paul Robeson, Nina Mae
McKinney, Robert Cochran

The Sandpiper
US 1965   116m   Metrocolor   Panavision
MGM / Filmways (John Calley)

An artist lives with her illegitimate son in a

Monterey beach shack; when she is forced to
send the boy to school he attracts the attention of
the minister in charge.
Absurd novelettish love story basically copied
from *The Garden of Allah;* pretty seascapes are
the most rewarding aspect.

w Dalton Trumbo, Michael Wilson d Vincente
Minnelli *ph* Milton Krasner *m* Johnny Mandel

Elizabeth Taylor, Richard Burton, Eva Marie
Saint, Charles Bronson, Robert Webber
'Straight Louisa May Alcott interlarded with
discreet pornographic allusions.'—*John Simon*
'Sex-on-the-sand soap opera.'—*Robert
Windeler*

AA: song 'The Shadow of Your Smile'
(*m* Johnny Mandel, *ly* Paul Francis Webster)

Sands of Iwo Jima*
US 1949   109m   bw
Republic (Edmund Grainger)

During World War II in the Pacific, a tough
sergeant of marines moulds raw recruits into
fighting men but is himself shot by a sniper.
Celebrated star war comic, still quite hypnotic in
its flagwaving way.

w Harry Brown, James Edward Grant d Allan
Dwan *ph* Reggie Lanning *m* Victor Young

John Wayne, John Agar, Adele Mara, Forrest
Tucker, Arthur Franz, Julie Bishop, Richard
Jaeckel
'The battle sequences are terrifyingly real . . .
but the personal dramatics make up a
compendium of war-picture clichés.'—*Variety*
'Say what you like about the sentimental
flavour of war pictures such as this, there's no
denying they keep you in your seat.'—*Richard
Mallett, Punch*

AAN: John Wayne

Sands of the Kalahari
GB 1965   119m   Technicolor   Panavision
Pendennis (Cy Endfield, Stanley Baker)

Survivors of a plane crash trek across the desert
and are menaced by baboons and each other.
Hysterical melodrama with predictable heebie-
jeebies by all concerned and the baddie finally
left to the mercy of the monkeys. For hardened
sensationalists.

wd Cy Endfield, *novel* William Mulvihill
ph Erwin Hillier *m* Johnny Dankworth

Stanley Baker, Stuart Whitman, Harry
Andrews, Susannah York, Theodore Bikel,
Nigel Davenport, Barry Lowe

Sangaree
US 1953 95m Technicolor 3-D
Paramount / Pine–Thomas

Trouble ensues when a plantation owner wills his
wealth to the son of a slave.
Period skullduggery rather hammily presented.

w David Duncan, *novel* Frank G. Slaughter
d Edward Ludwig ph Lionel Lindon, W.
Wallace Kelley m Lucien Caillet

Fernando Lamas, Arlene Dahl, Patricia Medina,
Francis L. Sullivan, Charles Korvin, Tom
Drake, John Sutton, Willard Parker, Lester
Matthews

Santa Fe Trail **
US 1940 110m bw
Warner (Robert Fellows)

A cavalry officer is responsible for the final
capture of John Brown.
The most solemn western from star or studio has
impressive patches amid routine excitements.

w Robert Buckner *d Michael Curtiz* ph Sol
Polito m Max Steiner

Errol Flynn, Olivia de Havilland, Raymond
Massey, Ronald Reagan, Alan Hale, Van Heflin,
Gene Reynolds, Henry O'Neill
   'A thousand miles of danger with a thousand
thrills a mile!'—*publicity*

Santee
US 1972 93m colour
Vagabond (Deno Paoli, Edward Platt)

A boy goes west to find his father and befriends
the bounty hunter who has killed him.
Personable, violent western with adequate style
and performances.

w Brand Bell d Gene Nelson ph Donald
Morgan m Don Randi

Glenn Ford, Michael Burns, Dana Wynter, Jay
Silverheels, Harry Townes, John Larch

Santiago
US 1956 92m Warnercolor
   Cinemascope
Warner (Martin Rackin)
GB title: *The Gun Runner*

A Mississippi paddle-boat sets out for Cuba with
a consignment of guns for the rebels.
Stiff period actioner of no particular merit.

w Martin Rackin, John Twist d Gordon
Douglas ph John Seitz m David Buttolph

Alan Ladd, Rossana Podesta, Lloyd Nolan,
Chill Wills, Paul Fix, L. Q. Jones, Frank de
Kova

The Saphead*
US 1920 70m (24 fps) bw silent
Buster Keaton (Winchell Smith)

A shy young man reads a manual on how to win
the modern girl.
Interesting early star comedy: quite winning in
its way, but without the spectacular moments
which were a feature of his later films.

w Winchell Smith d Herbert Blache

Buster Keaton, Beula Booker, William H.
Crane, Irving Cummings

Sapphire **
GB 1959 92m Eastmancolor
Rank / Artna (Michael Relph)

Scotland Yard solves the murder of a coloured
music student.
Efficient police thriller with a strong race angle.

w Janet Green d Basil Dearden ph Harry
Waxman m Philip Green

Nigel Patrick, Michael Craig, Yvonne Mitchell,
Paul Massie, Bernard Miles, Olga Lindo, Earl
Cameron, Gordon Heath, Robert Adams

Saps at Sea
US 1940 60m bw
Hal Roach

Olly needs a rest after working in a horn factory,
so he and Stan take a boating holiday but are
kidnapped by a gangster.
Disappointing star comedy with gags too few
and too long drawn out.

w Charles Rogers, Harry Langdon, Gil Pratt,
Felix Adler d Gordon Douglas ph Art Lloyd

Stan Laurel, Oliver Hardy, James Finlayson,
Dick Cramer, Ben Turpin

Saraband for Dead Lovers*
GB 1948 96m Technicolor
Ealing (Michael Relph)
US title: *Saraband*

The tragic love affair of Konigsmark and Sophie
Dorothea, wife of the Elector of Hanover who
later became George I of England.
Gloomy but superb-looking historical love story;
it just misses being a memorable film.

w John Dighton, Alexander Mackendrick,
novel Helen Simpson d Basil Dearden, Michael
Relph ph Douglas Slocombe m Alan
Rawsthorne

Stewart Granger, Joan Greenwood, Françoise
Rosay, Flora Robson, Peter Bull
   'Suspense, romance, interest and excitement in
full measure.'—*MFB*

Sarah and Son
US 1930   85m   bw
Paramount

A widow seeks the baby her husband took away from her.
Mother love saga; soppy but with good credits.

w Zoe Akins, *novel* Timothy Shea *d* Dorothy Arzner *ph* Charles Lang

Ruth Chatterton, Fredric March, Fuller Mellish Jnr, Gilbert Emery, Doris Lloyd

AAN: Ruth Chatterton

Saratoga*
US 1937   102m   bw
MGM (Bernard H. Hyman)

A bookmaker helps the daughter of a horse breeder.
Forgettable racetrack drama notable chiefly as the last film of Jean Harlow who died before it was completed.

w Anita Loos, Robert Hopkins *d* Jack Conway *ph* Ray June *m* Edward Ward

Clark Gable, Jean Harlow, Lionel Barrymore, Frank Morgan, Walter Pidgeon, Una Merkel, Cliff Edwards, George Zucco, Jonathan Hale
'Glib, forthright, knowing and adroit.'—*Time*

Saratoga Trunk*
US 1943   135m   bw
Warner (Hal B. Wallis)

A notorious woman comes back to New Orleans and falls for a cowboy helping a railroad combine against their rivals.
Curious, unsatisfactory, miscast and overlong film version of a bestseller; there are enjoyable sequences, but it simply fails to come alive.

w Casey Robinson, *novel* Edna Ferber *d* Sam Wood *ph* Ernest Haller *m* Max Steiner *ph* Joseph St Amaad

Ingrid Bergman, Gary Cooper, Flora Robson, Jerry Austin, Florence Bates, John Warburton, John Abbott, Curt Bois, Ethel Griffies
'It lacks a logical pattern of drama and character . . . a piece of baggage labelled solely for the stars.'—*Bosley Crowther*

Saskatchewan
US 1954   87m   Technicolor
U-I (Aaron Rosenberg)
GB title: *O'Rourke of the Royal Mounted*

A mountie helps the lady survivor of an Indian attack.
Standard star actioner.

w Gil Doud *d* Raoul Walsh *ph* John Seitz *m* Joseph Gershenson

Alan Ladd, Shelley Winters, J. Carrol Naish, Hugh O'Brian, Robert Douglas, Richard Long, Jay Silverheels

The Satan Bug*
US 1965   114m   De Luxe   Panavision
UA / Mirisch / Kappa (John Sturges)

At a top-secret desert research station, one scientist is a traitor, and a deadly virus has been stolen for use by a mad millionaire.
Slow-moving, portentous, gadget-filled actioner which looks good but seldom stimulates.

w James Clavell, Edward Anhalt, *novel* Alistair MacLean *d* John Sturges *ph* Robert Surtees *m* Jerry Goldsmith

George Maharis, Richard Basehart, Anne Francis, Dana Andrews, Ed Asner

Satan Met a Lady*
US 1936   74m   bw
Warner (Henry Blanke)

Various crooks and a private detective pursue a rare artifact.
Perversely rewritten version of *The Maltese Falcon* (qv). Fascinating but not really successful

w Brown Holmes *w* William Dieterle *ph* Arthur Edeson *m* Leo F. Forbstein

Bette Davis, Warren William, Alison Skipworth, Arthur Treacher, Wini Shaw, Marie Wilson, Porter Hall
'One lives through it in constant expectation of seeing a group of uniformed individuals appear suddenly from behind the furniture and take the entire cast into protective custody.'—*Bosley Crowther*

Satan Never Sleeps
US / GB 1962   126m   De Luxe
   Cinemascope
TCF / Leo McCarey
GB title: *The Devil Never Sleeps*

In the late forties in China, Catholic missionaries defy the communists.
Failed anti-Red imitation of *Inn of the Sixth Happiness* with the priests from *Going My Way*. Has to be seen to be believed.

w Claude Binyon, Leo McCarey *d* Leo McCarey *ph* Oswald Morris *m* Richard Rodney Bennett

Clifton Webb, William Holden, France Nuyen, Weaver Lee, Athene Seyler, Martin Benson

The Satanic Rites of Dracula
GB 1973   88m   Technicolor
Hammer (Roy Skeggs)
US title: *Dracula is Alive and Well and
Living in London*

When vampires infest London, a property
speculator proves to be Dracula himself.
Intriguingly plotted screamer with more mystery
than horror.

w Don Houghton *d* Alan Gibson *ph* Brian
Probyn *m* John Cacavas

Peter Cushing, Christopher Lee, Michael Coles,
William Franklyn, Freddie Jones, Richard
Vernon, Patrick Barr

Satan's Skin
GB 1970   93m   Eastmancolor
Tigon / Chilton (Tony Tenser)
aka: *Blood on Satan's Claw*

In 1670 a farmer unearths a skull with one eye
intact, and a devil creature subsequently terrifies
the village.
Implausible, unpleasant but occasionally rather
stylish horror picture.

w Robert Wynne-Simmons *d* Piers Haggard
ph Dick Bush *m* Marc Wilkinson

Patrick Wymark, Linda Hayden, Barry
Andrews, Avice Landon, Tamara Ustinov

Satellite in the Sky
GB 1956   85m   Warnercolor
Cinemascope
Warner / Tridelta / Danziger

A rocketship is ordered to lose a tritonium bomb
in space, but the device attaches itself to the side
of the ship.
Boringly talkative low-budget science fiction
with ideas beyond its station but not enough
talent to put them over.

w John Mather, J. T. McIntosh, Edith Dell
d Paul Dickson *ph* Georges Périnal *m* Albert
Elms

Kieron Moore, Lois Maxwell, Donald Wolfit,
Bryan Forbes, Jimmy Hanley, Alan Gifford

Saturday Island
GB 1951   102m   Technicolor
Coronado (David E. Rose)
US title: *Island of Desire*

In 1943 a supply boat is torpedoed and a
Canadian nurse finds romance on a desert island
with a US marine and a one-armed RAF pilot.
Unlikely, conversational, old-fashioned love
story.

wd Stuart Heisler, *novel* Hugh Brooke

ph Oswald Morris *m* William Alwyn

Linda Darnell, Tab Hunter, Donald Gray

Saturday Night and Sunday Morning****
GB 1960   89m   bw
Bryanston / Woodfall (Harry Salzman, Tony
Richardson)

A Nottingham factory worker is dissatisfied with
his lot, gets into trouble through an affair with a
married woman, but finally settles for
convention.
Startling when it emerged, this raw working-
class melodrama, with its sharp detail and strong
comedy asides, delighted the mass audience
chiefly because of its strong central character
thumbing his nose at authority. Matching the
mood of the times, and displaying a new attitude
to sex, it transformed British cinema and was
much imitated.

w Alan Sillitoe, from his novel *d* Karel Reisz
ph Freddie Francis *m* Johnny Dankworth

Albert Finney, Shirley Anne Field, *Rachel
Roberts*, Bryan Pringle, Norman Rossington,
Hylda Baker

Saturday Night Fever*
US 1978   119m   Movielab
Paramount / Robert Stigwood (Milt Felsen)

Italian roughnecks in Brooklyn live for their
Saturday night disco dancing, and one of them
falls in love with a girl who makes him realize
there are better things in life.
Foul-mouthed, fast-paced slice of life which
plays like an updated version of *Marty* except
that all the characters seem to have crawled from
under stones. The slick direction, fast editing and
exciting dance numbers do something to take
away the sour taste.

w Norman Wexler, *story* Nik Cohn *d* John
Badham *ph* Ralf D. Bode *songs* Barry, Robin
and Maurice Gibb (and others), performed by
the Bee Gees *ed* David Rawlins *pd* Charles
Bailey

John Travolta, Karen Lynn Gorney, Barry
Miller, Joseph Cali, Paul Pape, Bruce Ornstein

Saturday's Children
US 1940   101m   bw
Warner (Henry Blanke)

An impractical young inventor marries an
ambitious young woman, but depressed finances
lead to discord.
Glum, dated rehash of a 1929 silent; watchable
but not compelling.

w Julius J. and Philip G. Epstein, *play* Maxwell

Anderson d Vincent Sherman ph James Wong Howe

John Garfield, Claude Rains, Anne Shirley, Lee Patrick, George Tobias, Roscoe Karns, Elizabeth Risdon, Berton Churchill

Satyricon*

Italy / France 1969   129m   De Luxe Panavision
UA / PAA / PEA (Alberto Grimaldi)
aka: *Fellini Satyricon*

Sexual adventures of a Roman student. Garish, sporadically enjoyable sketches on a very thin thread of plot: a more benevolent version of the usual Fellini nightmare.

w Federico Fellini, Bernandino Zapponi d Federico Fellini ph Giuseppe Rotunno m Nino Rota, Ilhan Mimaroglu, Tod Dockstader, Andrew Rudin pd Danilo Donati

Martin Potter, Hiram Keller, Salvo Randone, Max Born

'A picaresque satire in fragments . . . a series of tableaux which carry the poetry visually at the price of coherence.'—*Mike Wallington, MFB*

AAN: Federico Fellini (as director)

The Savage

US 1952   95m   Technicolor
Paramount (Mel Epstein)

A white boy grows up with Indians and later suffers from divided loyalties.
Solemn, rather tedious but well produced western.

w Sidney Boehm, *novel* L. L. Foreman d George Marshall ph John F. Seitz m Paul Sawtell

Charlton Heston, Susan Morrow, Peter Hanson, Joan Taylor, Richard Rober, Don Porter

The Savage Eye*

US 1959   68m   bw
City Film Corporation (Ben Maddow, Joseph Strick, Sidney Meyers)

An unhappily married young woman takes a jaundiced view of life around her in Los Angeles. The wisp of plot is merely an excuse to present a documentary exposé of the seamier side of life in America's most eccentric city, with its faith healers and revellers. Much of it is fascinating, though the film is not a cohesive whole and the would-be poetic commentary falls on its face.

wd, ed Ben Maddow, Joseph Strick, Sidney Meyers m Leonard Rosenman

Barbara Baxley, Gary Merrill, Herschel Bernardi

The Savage Innocents

GB / France / Italy 1960   107m   Super Technirama 70
Joseph Janni / Magic Film / Playart / Gray Films (Maleno Malenotti)

Trials of an Eskimo and his wife in Canada's frozen north.
Conscientious, determined and very boring account of Eskimo life played by actors talking pidgin English. Not a success despite the magnificent photography.

w Nicholas Ray, *novel* Top of the World by Hans Ruesch d Nicholas Ray, Baccio Bandini ph Aldo Tonti, Peter Hennessy m Angelo Lavagnino

Anthony Quinn, Yoko Tani, Marie Yang, Peter O'Toole, Carlo Justini, Anna May Wong, Lee Montague, Ed Devereaux

Savage Messiah*

GB 1972   103m   Metrocolor
MGM / Russ–Arts (Ken Russell)

The life together (1910–14) of the 18-year-old painter Gaudier and 38-year-old Sophie Brzeska.
Intense, fragmentary art film about two eccentrics; would have better suited TV.

w Christopher Logue, *book* H. S. Ede d Ken Russell ph Dick Bush m Michael Garrett pd Derek Jarman

Dorothy Tutin, Scott Anthony, Helen Mirren, Lindsay Kemp, Michael Gough, John Justin

Savage Pampas

Spain / Argentina / US 1967   108m
Eastmancolor   Superpanorama
Jaime Prados–Dasa–Sam Bronston

In 19th-century Argentina the commander of an isolated fort finds that a bandit is bribing his men to desert.
Densely plotted semi-western, sometimes good to look at but slow and lugubrious.

w Hugo Fregonese, John Melson d Hugo Fregonese ph Marcel Berenguer m Waldo de los Rios

Robert Taylor, Ron Randell, Ty Hardin, Rosenda Monteros, Marc Lawrence

Savage Sam*

US 1962   104m   Technicolor
Walt Disney (Bill Anderson)

The youngest son of a homesteading family has a troublesome dog which redeems itself by tracking down Apaches.
Folksy boy-and-dog western, good of its kind, with adequate suspense and scenery.

w Fred Gipson, William Tunberg *d* Norman Tokar *ph* Edward Colman *m* Oliver Wallace

Brian Keith, Tommy Kirk, Kevin Corcoran, Dewey Martin, Jeff York

'A cadet edition of the best of Ford.'—*MFB*

Savages
US 1972 106m colour
Angelika / Merchant—Ivory (Joseph Saleh)

Forest wanderers take over a deserted mansion and begin to feel its civilizing influence.
Mild fable which needed a Bunuel to do it justice; a few lively moments.

w George Swift Trow, Michael O'Donoghue *d* James Ivory *ph* Walter Lassally *m* Joe Raposo

Louis Stadlen, Anne Francine, Thayer David, Salome Jens, Neil Fitzgerald

Save the Tiger*
US 1972 100m Movielab
Paramount / Jalem / Filmways / Cirandinha (Steve Shagan)

A middle-aged businessman regrets the slack morality of modern America.
Self-adulatory drama which really has little point but gets a few marks for meaning well and for vivid scenes.

w Steve Shagan *d* John G. Avildsen *ph* Jim Crabe *m* Marvin Hamlisch

Jack Lemmon, Jack Gilford, Laurie Heineman, Norman Burton, Thayer David

'A scathing indictment of the US, of materialism, war, marriage—the works. Wordy, literate and deeply felt.'—*NFT, 1974*

AA: Jack Lemmon
AAN: Steve Shagan; Jack Gilford

Sawdust and Tinsel*
Sweden 1953 95m bw
Svensk Filmindustri
aka: *The Naked Night;* original title: *Gycklarnas Afton*

The owner of a travelling circus leaves his mistress for his separated wife, and is challenged to fight by the mistress's new lover.
Powerfully-made yet rather pointless melodrama about unpleasant people.

wd Ingmar Bergman ph Sven Nykvist *m* Karl-Birger Blomdahl

Harriet Andersson, Ake Grönberg, Hasse Ekman, Annika Tretow

The Saxon Charm
US 1948 88m bw
Universal (Joseph Sistrom)

A Broadway impresario dominates the lives of those around him.
Rather heavy-going comedy drama which could have done with more malicious wit; allegedly based on Jed Harris.

wd Claude Binyon, *novel* Frederick Wakeman *ph* Milton Krasner *m* Walter Scharf

Robert Montgomery, Susan Hayward, John Payne, Audrey Totter, Henry Morgan, Harry Von Zell, Cara Williams, Chill Wills, Heather Angel

Say Hello to Yesterday
GB 1970 92m Eastmancolor
Josef Shaftel (William Hill)

A middle-aged married woman goes to London for shopping and is pursued by a strange young man whom she allows to seduce her.
Unattractive 'with it' romantic drama with a swinging London setting, a long way after *Brief Encounter.*

w Alvin Rakoff, Peter King *d* Alvin Rakoff *ph* Geoffrey Unsworth *m* Riz Ortolani

Jean Simmons, Leonard Whiting, *Evelyn Laye*, John Lee, Jack Woolgar

Say One for Me
US 1959 117m De Luxe Cinemascope
TCF / Bing Crosby (Frank Tashlin)

Adventures of a parish priest in New York's theatrical quarter.
Unconvincing, unattractive imitation of *Going My Way* which counters bad taste with religiosity.

w Robert O'Brien *d* Frank Tashlin *ph* Leo Tover *songs* Sammy Cahn, James Van Heusen *md* Lionel Newman

Bing Crosby, Robert Wagner, Debbie Reynolds, Ray Walston, Les Tremayne, Connie Gilchrist, Frank McHugh, Joe Besser, Sebastian Cabot

AAN: Lionel Newman

Sayonara**
US 1957 147m Technirama
Goetz Pictures—Pennebaker (William Goetz)

An American air force major in Tokyo after the war falls in love with a Japanese actress.
A lush travelogue interrupted by two romances, one tragic and one happy. A great success at the time, though mainly of interest to Americans; now vaguely dated.

w Paul Osborn, *novel* James A. Michener *d* Joshua Logan *ph* Ellsworth Fredericks *m* Franz Waxman *ad* Ted Haworth

Marlon Brando, Miyoshi Umeki, Miiko Taka,

Red Buttons, Ricardo Montalban, Patricia
Owens, Kent Smith, Martha Scott, James
Garner

AA: Miyoshi Umeki; Red Buttons
AAN: best picture; Paul Osborn; Ellsworth
Fredericks; Marlon Brando

Scalawag
US / Italy 1973   93m   Technicolor
Bryna / Inex–Oceania (Anne Douglas)

Mexico 1840: a one-legged pirate and a boy try
to trace a hidden treasure.
Flagrant reworking of *Treasure Island*, heavily
overdone by stars and rhubarbing extras alike.

w Albert Maltz, Sid Fleischman *d* Kirk
Douglas *ph* Jack Cardiff *m* John Cameron

Kirk Douglas, Mark Lester, Neville Brand,
David Stroud, Lesley-Anne Down, Phil Brown

The Scalphunters*
US 1968   102m   De Luxe   Panavision
UA / Bristol / Norlan (Levy–Gardner–Laven)

An old cowboy and a black ex-slave track down
a gang who kill Indians for their scalps.
Vigorous, aimless, likeable comedy western with
the emphasis on brawling.

w William Norton *d* Sydney Pollack *ph* Duke
Callaghan, Richard Moore *m* Elmer Bernstein

Burt Lancaster, Ossie Davis, Telly Savalas,
Shelley Winters, Nick Cravat, Paul Picerni

'It is the sort of frolic where bodies litter the
ground, but you know they'll get up and draw
their pay. And where even a villain can crack a
joke without losing face.'—*Robert Ottaway*

Scandal at Scourie
US 1953   90m   Metrocolor
MGM (Edwin H. Knopf)

The wife of the Protestant reeve of a Scottish-
Canadian Protestant community adopts a
Catholic child.
Sentimental whimsy with no holds barred, but
with rather jaded acting and production.

w Norman Corwin, Leonard Spiegelgass, Karl
Tunberg *d* Jean Negulesco *ph* Robert Planck
m Daniele Amfitheatrof

Greer Garson, Walter Pidgeon, Agnes
Moorehead, Arthur Shields, Philip Ober, Donna
Corcoran

A Scandal in Paris*
US 1946   100m   bw
UA / Arnold Pressburger
aka: *Thieves' Holiday*

Adventures of Vidocq, a 19th-century rogue
who became Paris chief of police.

The actors look uneasy in their costumes, and
the sets are cardboard, but there is fun to be had
from this light comedy-drama.

w Ellis St Joseph *d* Douglas Sirk *ph* Guy Roe

George Sanders, Signe Hasso, Carole Landis,
Akim Tamiroff, Gene Lockhart

Scandal Sheet
US 1952   81m   bw
Columbia (Edward Small)
GB title: *The Dark Page*

An editor has to allow his star reporter to expose
a murderer—himself.
Obvious, reasonably holding melodrama with
familiar characters.

w Ted Sherdeman, Eugene Ling, James Poe,
novel Samuel Fuller *d* Phil Karlson *ph* Burnett
Guffey *m* George Duning

Broderick Crawford, John Derek, Donna Reed,
Rosemary de Camp, Henry O'Neill, Henry
Morgan

Scandalous John
US 1971   117m   Technicolor
Walt Disney (Bill Walsh)

The elderly owner of a derelict ranch resists all
efforts to close him up.
Unsatisfactory Disney attempt to capture a
more adult audience than usual; overlong,
repetitious and dreary.

w Bill Walsh, Don da Gradi, *novel* Richard
Gardner *d* Robert Butler *ph* Frank Phillips
m Rod McKuen

Brian Keith, Alfonso Arau, Michele Carey, Rick
Lenz, Henry Morgan, Simon Oakland

The Scapegoat*
GB 1959   92m   bw
MGM / Du Maurier–Guinness (Dennis Van
Thal)

A quiet bachelor on a French holiday is tricked
into assuming the identity of a lookalike
aristocrat who wants to commit a murder.
Disappointing adaptation of a good story, with
much evidence of re-cutting and an especially
slack middle section.

w Gore Vidal, Robert Hamer, *novel* Daphne du
Maurier *d* Robert Hamer *ph* Paul Beeson
m Bronislau Kaper

Alec Guinness, Bette Davis, Irene Worth, Nicole
Maurey, Pamela Brown, Geoffrey Keen

The Scar
US 1948   83m   bw
Eagle–Lion (Bryan Foy, Paul Henreid)
aka: *Hollow Triumph*

A fugitive kills his psychoanalyst double and takes his place, but is caught for the double's crimes.

Cheap suspense thriller with no suspense and no surprises.

w Daniel Fuchs, *novel* Murray Forbes d Steve Sekely ph John Alton m Sol Kaplan

Joan Bennett, Paul Henreid, Eduard Franz, Leslie Brooks, John Qualen, Mabel Paige, Herbert Rudley

Scaramouche**
US 1952   115m   Technicolor
MGM (Carey Wilson)

A young man disguises himself as an actor to avenge the death of his friend at the hands of a wicked marquis.

Cheerful swashbuckler set in French revolutionary times, first filmed in the twenties with Ramon Novarro. MGM costume production at somewhere near its best.

w Ronald Millar, George Froeschel, *novel* Rafael Sabatini d George Sidney ph Charles Rosher m Victor Young ad Cedric Gibbons, Hans Peters

Stewart Granger, Mel Ferrer, Eleanor Parker, Janet Leigh, Henry Wilcoxon, Nina Foch, Lewis Stone, Robert Coote, Richard Anderson

Scarecrow*
US 1973   112m   Technicolor   Panavision
Warner (Robert M. Sherman)

Two of the world's losers hitch-hike across America.

Well-shot but eventually dreary parable of friendship, a pedestrian *Easy Rider*.

w Garry Michael White d Jerry Schatzberg ph Vilmos Zsigmond m Fred Myrow

Gene Hackman, Al Pacino

'Here's a picture that manages to abuse two American myths at once—the Road and the Male Pair.'—*Stanley Kauffmann*

Scared Stiff
US 1953   108m   bw
Paramount (Hal B. Wallis)

Nightclub entertainers get involved with a girl who has inherited a spooky castle off the Cuban coast.

Stretched-out remake of *The Ghost Breakers*; the last half hour, being closest to the original, is the most nearly funny.

w Herbert Baker, Walter de Leon d George Marshall, Ed Simmons, Norman Lear ph Ernest Laszlo md Joseph J. Lilley

Dean Martin, Jerry Lewis, Lizabeth Scott,

Carmen Miranda, George Dolenz, Dorothy Malone, William Ching, Jack Lambert

The Scarf
US 1951   86m   bw
UA / Gloria (I. G. Goldsmith)

A man escapes from a lunatic asylum and proves himself innocent of the crime for which he was committed.

Glum and pretentious murder mystery with a pictorial style to match its flowery dialogue.

wd E. A. Dupont ph Franz Planer m Herschel Burke Gilbert

John Ireland, Mercedes McCambridge, Emlyn Williams, James Barton, Lloyd Gough, Basil Ruysdael

Scarface****
US 1932   99m   bw
Howard Hughes
aka: *The Shame of a Nation*

The life and death of a Chicago gangster of the twenties.

Obviously modelled on Al Capone, with an incestuous sister thrown in, this was perhaps the most vivid film of the gangster cycle, and its revelling in its own sins was not obscured by the subtitle, *The Shame of a Nation*.

w Ben Hecht, Seton I. Miller, John Lee Mahin, W. R. Burnett, Fred Pasley, *novel* Armitage Traill d Howard Hawks ph Lee Garmes, L. W. O'Connell

Paul Muni, Ann Dvorak, George Raft, Boris Karloff, Osgood Perkins, Karen Morley, C. Henry Gordon, Vince Barnett, Henry Armetta, Edwin Maxwell

'More brutal, more cruel, more wholesale than any of its predecessors.'—*James Shelley Hamilton*

The Scarface Mob*
US 1958   96m   bw
Desilu (Quinn Martin)

Al Capone's empire thrives while he is in Alcatraz, and prohibition agent Eliot Ness recruits a tough squad to fight the gangsters.

Though released theatrically, this was in effect a pilot film for the successful TV series *The Untouchables*, well enough done within its limits.

w Paul Monash, *novel* The Untouchables by Eliot Ness d Phil Karlson ph Charles Straumer m Wilbur Hatch

Robert Stack, Neville Brand, Keenan Wynn, Barbara Nichols, Joe Mantell, Pat Crowley, Bruce Gordon, Paul Picerni, Abel Fernandez

Scarlet Angel

US 1952   81m   Technicolor
U-I (Leonard Goldstein)

A saloon hostess presents herself to a wealthy family as their dead son's wife.
Modest, satisfactorily plotted woman's picture with action interludes.

w Oscar Brodney d Sidney Salkow ph Russell Metty m Joseph Gershenson

Yvonne de Carlo, Rock Hudson, Richard Denning, Henry O'Neill, Amanda Blake

The Scarlet Blade*

GB 1963   82m   Technicolor
    Hammerscope
Hammer (Anthony Nelson Keys)
US title: *The Crimson Blade*

In 1648, a Cromwellian colonel plans to hang every royalist rebel.
Adequate swashbuckler.

wd John Gilling ph Jack Asher m Gary Hughes

Lionel Jeffries, Oliver Reed, Jack Hedley, June Thorburn, Duncan Lamont

The Scarlet Coat

US 1955   99m   Eastmancolor
    Cinemascope
MGM (Nicholas Nayfack)

During the American War of Independence, an American officer deserts to the British in order to unmask a traitor.
Rather talky historical actioner with too much time spent on friendship and romance.

w Karl Tunberg d John Sturges ph Paul C. Vogel m Conrad Salinger

Cornel Wilde, Michael Wilding, George Sanders, Anne Francis, Robert Douglas, Bobby Driscoll, John McIntire

The Scarlet Empress***

US 1934   109m   bw
Paramount

A fantasia on the love life of Catherine the Great. A marvellous, overwhelming, dramatically insubstantial but pictorially brilliant homage to a star; not to everyone's taste, but a film to remember.

w Manuel Komroff d Josef Von Sternberg ph Bert Glennon md W. Franke Harling, John M. Leipold, Milan Roder ad Hans Dreier, Peter Ballbusch, Richard Kollorsz

Marlene Dietrich, John Lodge, Sam Jaffe, Louise Dresser,
C. Aubrey Smith, Gavin Gordon, Jameson Thomas

'She's photographed behind veils and fishnets,

while dwarfs slither about and bells ring and everybody tries to look degenerate.'—*New Yorker, 1975*

'A ponderous, strangely beautiful, lengthy and frequently wearying production.'—*Mordaunt Hall, New York Times*

The Scarlet Hour

US 1955   93m   bw   Vistavision
Paramount (Michael Curtiz)

A bored wife persuades her lover to turn thief; her husband misconstrues the situation and is accidentally killed.
Complex suspenser designed to introduce new talent; rather too smooth, and pretty boring.

w Rip van Ronkel, Frank Tashlin, Meredyth Lucas d Michael Curtiz ph Lionel Lindon m Leith Stevens

Carol Ohmart, Tom Tryon, James Gregory, Jody Lawrance, E. G. Marshall, *Elaine Stritch*

The Scarlet Letter*

US 1926   90m (24 fps)   bw   silent
MGM / Jury

In Puritan New England, the mother of an illegitimate child wears the scarlet A (for adulteress) for years rather than reveal that her lover was the village priest.
Celebrated 17th-century melodrama, quite powerfully made in the best silent tradition, but of little intrinsic interest for modern audiences.

w Frances Marion, *novel* Nathaniel Hawthorne d Victor Sjostrom ph Henrik Sartov ad Cedric Gibbons

Lillian Gish, Lars Hanson, Karl Dane, Henry B. Walthall
† Other versions include the following: US 1910, US 1911, US 1913, US 1917, US 1920, GB 1922, US 1934, Germany 1971, US (TV) 1979

The Scarlet Pimpernel***

GB 1934   98m   bw
London Films (Alexander Korda)

In the early days of the French revolution, an apparently foppish Englishman leads a daring band in rescuing aristocrats from the guillotine.
First-class period adventure with a splendid and much imitated plot, strong characters, humour and a richly detailed historical background.

w Robert E. Sherwood, Sam Berman, Arthur Wimperis, Lajos Biro, *novel* Baroness Orczy d Harold Young

Leslie Howard, Merle Oberon, Raymond Massey, Nigel Bruce, Bramwell Fletcher, Anthony Bushell, Joan Gardner, Walter Rilla

'One of the most romantic and durable of all swashbucklers.'—*New Yorker, 1976*

'A triumph for the British film world.'—*Sunday Times*

Scarlet Street**
US 1946   103m   bw
Universal / Diana (Walter Wanger)

A prostitute is murdered by her client and her pimp is executed for the crime.

Daring but rather gloomy Hollywood melodrama, the first in which a crime went unpunished (though the culprit was shown suffering remorse). Interesting and heavily Teutonic, but as entertainment not a patch on the similar but lighter *The Woman in the Window*, which the same team had made a year previously.

w Dudley Nichols, *play* La Chienne by George de la Fouchardière (filmed by Jean Renoir in 1932) *d Fritz Lang ph* Milton Krasner *m* Hans Salter *ad* Alexander Golitzen

Edward G. Robinson, Joan Bennett, Dan Duryea, Jess Barker, Margaret Lindsay, Rosalind Ivan, Samuel S. Hinds, Arthur Loft

'The director unerringly chooses the right sound and image to assault the spectator's sensibilities.'—*C. A. Lejeune*

Scars of Dracula
GB 1970   96m   Technicolor
Hammer / EMI (Aida Young)

A young man on the run finds himself an unwitting guest of Count Dracula.

Overpadded vampire saga, its few effective moments stemming directly from the original novel.

w John Elder *d* Roy Ward Baker *ph* Moray Grant *m* James Bernard

Christopher Lee, Dennis Waterman, Christopher Matthews, Jenny Hanley, Patrick Troughton, Michael Gwynn, Bob Todd

School for Husbands
GB 1937   71m   bw
Wainwright (Richard Wainwright)

A romantic novelist annoys the husbands of his adoring fans.

Would-be champagne comedy which bubbles pretty well for most of its length.

w Frederick Jackson, Gordon Aherry, Austin Melford, *play* Frederick Jackson *d* Andrew Marton *ph* Phil Tannura

Rex Harrison, Henry Kendall, Romney Brent, Diana Churchill, June Clyde

School for Scoundrels*
GB 1960   94m   bw
ABP / Guardsman (Hal E. Chester)

A failure reports to the College of One-Upmanship and his life is transformed.

Amusing trifle, basically a series of sketches by familiar comic actors.

w Patricia Mayes, Hal E. Chester, *books* Stephen Potter *d* Robert Hamer *ph* Erwin Hillier *m* John Addison

Ian Carmichael, Alastair Sim, Terry-Thomas, Janette Scott, Dennis Price, Peter Jones, Edward Chapman, John Le Mesurier

School for Secrets
GB 1946   108m   bw
Rank / Two Cities (George H. Brown, Peter Ustinov)
US title: *Secret Flight*

The boffins who invented radar find themselves in a little war action of their own.

An unsatisfactory entertainment which, with the best intentions, shuffles between arch comedy, character drama, war action and documentary, doing less than justice to any of these aspects.

wd Peter Ustinov

Ralph Richardson, Raymond Huntley, Richard Attenborough, Marjorie Rhodes, John Laurie, Ernest Jay, David Tomlinson, Finlay Currie

Scorpio
US 1972   114m   Technicolor
UA / Scimitar (Walter Mirisch)

CIA agents doublecross each other.

Incredibly complex spy thriller in which it's difficult to know, or care, who's following whom. The brutalities, however, are capably staged.

w David W. Rintels, Gerald Wilson *d* Michael Winner *ph* Robert Paynter *m* Jerry Fielding

Burt Lancaster, Alain Delon, Paul Scofield, John Colicos, Gayle Hunnicutt, J. D. Cannon

'Strictly zoom and thump.'—*Sight and Sound*

Scotland Yard
US 1941   68m   bw
TCF (Sol M. Wurtzel)

The Nazis capture a London banker and use his double to turn funds over to them.

Outlandish spy melodrama which certainly keeps the interest.

w Samuel G. Engel, John Balderston, *play* Deniston Clift *d* Norman Foster *ph* Virgil Miller

Nancy Kelly, Edmund Gwenn, Henry Wilcoxon, John Loder, Melville Cooper, Gilbert Emery, Norma Varden

Scott of the Antarctic **
GB 1948   111m   Technicolor
Ealing (Sidney Cole)

After long preparation, Captain Scott sets off on
his ill-fated 1912 expedition to the South Pole.
The stiff-upper-lip saga par excellence; inevitable
knowledge of the end makes it pretty downbeat,
and the actors can only be sincere; but the
snowscapes, most of them artificial, are fine.

w Ivor Montagu, Walter Meade, Mary Hayley
Bell d Charles Frend m Ralph Vaughan
Williams

John Mills, James Robertson Justice, Derek
Bond, Harold Warrender, Reginald Beckwith,
Kenneth More, James McKechnie, John
Gregson

The Scoundrel **
US 1935   74m   bw
Paramount (Ben Hecht, Charles MacArthur)

A famous writer dies; his ghost comes back to
find the meaning of love.
Unique thirties supernatural melodrama with
barbs of dated wit despatched by a splendid cast.
Nonsense, but great nonsense.

wd Ben Hecht, Charles MacArthur

Noel Coward, Alexander Woolcott, Julie
Haydon, Stanley Ridges, Eduardo Ciannelli

'An unmistakeable whiff from a gossip column
world which tries hard to split the difference
between an epigram and a wisecrack.'—William
Whitebait

AAN: script

Scream and Scream Again *
GB 1969   94m   Eastmancolor
AIP / Amicus (Milton Subotsky)

Murders are traced to superhuman composite
beings created by a mad scientist.
Energetic and well-staged though rather
humourless shocker.

w Christopher Wicking, novel The Disorientated
Man by Peter Saxon d Gordon Hessler ph John
Coquillon m David Whittaker ad Don
Mingaye

Vincent Price, Christopher Lee, Peter Cushing,
Alfred Marks, Anthony Newlands, David Lodge

Scrooge *
GB 1935   78m   bw
Twickenham (Julius Hagen, Hans Brahm)

A miser reforms after ghosts haunt him on
Christmas Eve.
Acceptable unambitious version with interesting
performances.

w Seymour Hicks, H. Fowler Mear,
novel Charles Dickens d Henry Edwards

Seymour Hicks, Donald Calthrop (Cratchit),
Athene Seyler, Oscar Asche, Barbara Everest,
Maurice Evans, C. V. France, Marie Ney

Scrooge ***
GB 1951   86m   bw
Renown (Brian Desmond Hurst)

By far the best available version of the classic
parable; casting, art direction, pace and general
handling are as good as can be.

w Noel Langley d Brian Desmond Hurst ph C.
Pennington-Richards m Richard Addinsell

Alastair Sim, Mervyn Johns, Kathleen
Harrison, Jack Warner, Michael Hordern,
Hermione Baddeley, George Cole, Miles
Malleson

Scrooge *
GB 1970   113m   Technicolor   Panavision
Cinema Center / Waterbury

Dim musical version, darkly coloured and quite
lost on the wide screen; but it has its macabre
moments of trick photography.

w/m/ly Leslie Bricusse d Ronald Neame
ph Oswald Morris pd Terry Marsh

Albert Finney, Michael Medwin, Alec Guinness,
Edith Evans, Kenneth More, David Collings,
Laurence Naismith, Kay Walsh

AAN: song 'Thank You Very Much'
(m/ly Leslie Bricusse); music

Scudda Hoo, Scudda Hay
US 1948   98m   Technicolor
TCF (Walter Morosco)
GB title: Summer Lightning

A farmer's son is less interested in girls than in
the welfare of his two mules.
Antediluvian rural romance for the simple-
minded.

wd F. Hugh Herbert, novel George Aghew
Chamberlain ph Ernest Palmer m Cyril
Mockridge

June Haver, Lon McCallister, Walter Brennan,
Anne Revere, Natalie Wood, Robert Karnes,
Henry Hull, Tom Tully, Marilyn Monroe

The Sea Chase *
US 1955   117m   Warnercolor
    Cinemascope
Warner (John Farrow)

In 1939 a German freighter tries to make it from
Sydney harbour back to Germany.
Unusual but not very compelling naval

melodrama, chiefly because the leads are miscast.

w James Warner Bellah, John Twist, *novel* Andrew Geer *d* John Farrow *ph* William Clothier *m* Roy Webb

John Wayne, Lana Turner, David Farrar, Lyle Bettger, Tab Hunter, James Arness, Dick Davalos, John Qualen

'A film compounded of monotonously familiar ingredients.'—*Penelope Houston*

Sea Devils

GB 1953   90m   Technicolor
Coronado (David E. Rose)

Spies prevent Napoleon's invasion of England.
Cheerful, forgettable swashbuckler.

w Borden Chase *d* Raoul Walsh *ph* Wilkie Cooper *m* Richard Addinsell

Yvonne de Carlo, Rock Hudson, Maxwell Reed, Denis O'Dea, Michael Goodliffe, Bryan Forbes, Ivor Barnard, Arthur Wontner

Sea Fury

GB 1958   97m   bw
Rank (Benjamin Fisz)

Rivalry strikes up between an old and a young sailor on tugboats plying between Spain and England.
Shapeless, leery melodrama with strong performances and an exciting storm-at-sea climax.

w John Kruse, Cy Endfield *d* Cy Endfield *ph* Reg Wyer *m* Philip Green

Stanley Baker, Victor McLaglen, Luciana Paluzzi, Grégoire Aslan, Francis de Wolff, David Oxley, Rupert Davies, Robert Shaw

The Sea Gull*

GB 1968   141m   Technicolor
Warner / Sidney Lumet

Loves and hates on a 19th-century Russian estate.
Rather heavily star-studded, but certainly proficient film version of a Chekhov favourite.

w Moura Budberg, *play* Anton Chekhov *d* Sidney Lumet *ph* Gerry Fisher *m* none *pd* Tony Walton

James Mason, Simone Signoret, Vanessa Redgrave, David Warner, Harry Andrews, Ronald Radd, Eileen Herlie, Kathleen Widdoes, Denholm Elliott, Alfred Lynch

The Sea Hawk***

US 1940   122m   bw
Warner (Hal B. Wallis, Henry Blanke)

Elizabeth I encourages one of her most able captains to acts of piracy against the Spanish.
Wobbly-plotted but stirring and exciting seafaring actioner, with splendid battle and duel scenes.

w Seton I. Miller, Howard Koch *d* Michael Curtiz *ph* Sol Polito *m* Erich Wolfgang Korngold *ad* Anton Grot

Errol Flynn, Flora Robson, Brenda Marshall, *Henry Daniell*, Claude Rains, Donald Crisp, Alan Hale, Una O'Connor, James Stephenson, Gilbert Roland, William Lundigan

'Endless episodes of court intrigue tend to diminish the effect of the epic sweep of the high seas dramatics.'—*Variety*

AAN: Erich Wolfgang Korngold

The Sea of Grass

US 1947   131m   bw
MGM (Pandro S. Berman)

A cattle tycoon is so obsessed by his work that he alienates his family.
Brooding, overlong semi-western with an unexpected cast.

w Marguerite Roberts, Vincent Lawrence, *novel* Conrad Richter *d* Elia Kazan *ph* Harry Stradling *m* Herbert Stothart

Spencer Tracy, Katharine Hepburn, Melvyn Douglas, Phyllis Thaxter, Robert Walker, Edgar Buchanan, Harry Carey, Ruth Nelson, James Bell

'An epically dreary film.'—*Time*

Sea of Sand*

GB 1958   98m   bw
Rank / Tempean (Robert Baker, Monty Berman)

Just before Alamein an Eighth Army desert group plans to destroy one of Rommel's last petrol dumps.
Good standard war suspenser.

w Robert Westerby *d* Guy Green *ph* Wilkie Cooper *m* Clifton Parker

Richard Attenborough, John Gregson, Vincent Ball, Percy Herbert, Michael Craig, Barry Foster, Andrew Faulds, Dermot Walsh

The Sea Shall Not Have Them

GB 1954   93m   bw
Eros / Daniel M. Angel

Survivors of a seaplane crash await rescue in a dinghy.
Rather dim computerized compendium of flashback mini-dramas.

w Lewis Gilbert, Vernon Harris *d* Lewis Gilbert *ph* Stephen Dade *m* Malcolm Arnold

Dirk Bogarde, Michael Redgrave, Bonar Colleano, Jack Watling, Anthony Steel, Nigel Patrick, James Kenney, Sidney Tafler, George Rose

Sea Wife
GB 1957   82m   De Luxe   Cinemascope
TCF / Sumar (André Hakim)

Survivors of a shipwreck near Singapore in 1942 are rescued, not before the bosun has fallen in love with the only lady, not knowing she is a nun.
Flashbacked, uncertain, intermittently effective film of a popular minor novel.

w George K. Burke, *novel* Sea Wyf and Biscuit by J. M. Scott *d* Bob McNaught *ph* Ted Scaife *m* Kenneth v. Jones, Leonard Salzedo

Richard Burton, Joan Collins, Basil Sydney, Cy Grant

The Sea Wolf**
US 1941   90m   bw
Warner (Henry Blanke)

Survivors of a ferry crash in San Francisco Bay are picked up by a psychopathic freighter captain who keeps them captive.
Much filmed action suspenser which in this version looks great but overdoes the talk.

w Robert Rossen, *novel* Jack London *d* Michael Curtiz *ph* Sol Polito *m* Erich Wolfgang Korngold
Edward G. Robinson, Alexander Knox, Ida Lupino, John Garfield, Gene Lockhart, Barry Fitzgerald, Stanley Ridges, David Bruce, Howard da Silva

'A Germanic, powerful work almost devoid of compromise.'—*Charles Higham, 1972*
† Other versions appeared in 1913, with Hobart Bosworth; in 1920, with Noah Beery; in 1925, with Ralph Ince; in 1930, with Milton Sills; in 1950 (as *Barricade*, turned into a western), with Raymond Massey; in 1958 (as *Wolf Larsen*), with Barry Sullivan; and in 1975 (Italian), as *Wolf of the Seven Seas*, with Chuck Connors.

Seagulls over Sorrento
GB 1954   92m   bw
MGM (John and Roy Boulting)
US title: *Crest of the Wave*

Life on a naval research station on a small Scottish island.
A long-running British service comedy has been Americanized to little effect, but it remains just about watchable.

w Frank Harvey, Roy Boulting, *play* Hugh Hastings *d* John and Roy Boulting *ph* Gilbert Taylor *m* Miklos Rozsa

Gene Kelly, John Justin, Bernard Lee, Sidney James, Jeff Richards, Patric Doonan, Patrick Barr

Seal Island see The Living Desert

The Seashell and the Clergyman*
France 1928   30m approx (24 fps)   bw
silent
(Producer unknown)

A clergyman is afflicted by sexual torments.
Celebrated surrealist short with memorable images amid a great deal of confusion.

w Antonin Artaud *d Germaine Dulac* *ph* Paul Guichard

Alix Allin
† In GB the film was banned by the censor with the famous comment: 'It is so cryptic as to have no apparent meaning. If there is a meaning, it is doubtless objectionable.'

Sealed Verdict
US 1948   83m   bw
Paramount (Robert Fellows)

An American officer in Germany falls in love with the ex-girl friend of a Nazi war criminal.
Routine melodrama, as boring as it sounds.

w Jonathan Latimer, *novel* Lionel Shapiro *d* Lewis Allen *ph* Leo Tover *m* Hugo Friedhofer

Ray Milland, Florence Marly, Broderick Crawford, John Hoyt, John Ridgely, Ludwig Donath

Seance on a Wet Afternoon*
GB 1964   121m   bw
Rank / Allied Film Makers (Richard Attenborough, Bryan Forbes, Jack Rix)

A fake medium persuades her husband to kidnap a child so that she can become famous by revealing its whereabouts in a trance.
Overlong character melodrama in which the suspense is better than the psychopathology. A mannered performance from the lady, a false nose from the gentleman, and a general air of gloom.

wd Bryan Forbes *ph* Gerry Turpin *m* John Barry

Kim Stanley, Richard Attenborough, Nanette Newman, Patrick Magee

AAN: Kim Stanley

The Search*
US / Switzerland 1948   105m   bw
MGM / Praesens Film (Lazar Wechsler)

An American soldier in Germany cares for a war orphan.

Vivid semi-documentary post-war drama which falls down in its elementary dramatics but sent audiences home wiping away tears.

w Richard Schweizer, David Wechsler, Paul Jarrico *d* Fred Zinnemann *ph* Emil Berna *m* Robert Blum

Montgomery Clift, Aline MacMahon, Ivan Jandl, Wendell Corey

AA: script
AAN: Fred Zinnemann; Montgomery Clift

The Search for Bridey Murphy*
US 1956   84m   bw   Vistavision
Paramount (Pat Duggan)

A Colorado businessman and amateur hypnotist finds a lady neighbour so good a subject that he is able to delve into her previous incarnation as a long-dead Irish peasant.

Adequately presented with alienation effects, but mainly consisting of two-shots and fuzzy flashbacks, this treatment of an actual case (subsequently discredited) works up to a fine pitch of frenzy when the subject seems unable to come back from her previous life.

wd Noel Langley, *book* Morey Bernstein *ph* John F. Warren *m* Irving Talbot

Teresa Wright, Louis Hayward, Kenneth Tobey, Nancy Gates, Richard Anderson

The Searchers**
US 1956   119m   Technicolor   Vistavision
Warner / C. V. Whitney (Merian C. Cooper)

A Confederate war veteran tracks down the Indians who have slaughtered his brother and sister-in-law and carried off their daughter.

Desultory, easy-going, good-looking western in typical Ford style; a bit more solemn than usual.

w Frank S. Nugent, *novel* Alan le May *d* John Ford *ph* Winton C. Hoch *m* Max Steiner

John Wayne, Jeffrey Hunter, Natalie Wood, Vera Miles, Ward Bond, John Qualen, Henry Brandon, Antonio Moreno

The Searching Wind*
US 1946   107m   bw
Paramount (Hal B. Wallis)

Affairs of an American diplomat in Europe during the thirties.

Earnest melodrama which would have been better timed six years earlier. Excellent production, though.

w Lillian Hellman, from her play *d* William Dieterle *ph* Lee Garmes *m* Victor Young *ad* Hans Dreier, Franz Bachelin

Robert Young, Sylvia Sidney, Ann Richards, Douglas Dick, Dudley Digges, Albert Basserman, Dan Seymour

Sebastian
GB 1968   100m   Eastmancolor
Paramount / Maccius (Herb Brodkin, Michael Powell)

An Oxford professor and code expert is appointed to the secret service.

Mildly spoofy spy yarn: style but not much substance.

w Gerald Vaughan-Hughes *d* David Greene *ph* Gerry Fisher *m* Jerry Goldsmith *pd* Wilfred Shingleton

Dirk Bogarde, *John Gielgud,* Lilli Palmer, Susannah York, Janet Munro, Margaret Johnston, Nigel Davenport, Ronald Fraser

'One of the problems with this kind of movie is the enormous pressure put on the audience to have a good time over practically nothing.'— *Renata Adler*

Second Chance
US 1953   82m   Technicolor   3-D
RKO (Edmund Grainger)

In South America, a professional killer stalks a gangster's moll.

Comic strip antics with a climax on a stalled cable car.

w Oscar Millard, Sidney Boehm, *story* D. M. Marshman Jnr *d* Rudolph Maté *ph* William Snyder *m* Roy Webb

Robert Mitchum, Linda Darnell, Jack Palance, Reginald Sheffield, Roy Roberts

Second Chorus
US 1941   84m   bw
Paramount (Boris Morros)

Two trumpeters and their lady manager hit Broadway.

Mild musical.

w Elaine Ryan, Ian McClellan Hunter, Frank Cavett
d H. C. Potter *ph* Theodor Sparkuhl *songs* various *m* Artie Shaw

Fred Astaire, Burgess Meredith, Paulette Goddard, Charles Butterworth, Artie Shaw and his Band, Frank Melton, Jimmy Conlon

AAN: Artie Shaw; song 'Love of my Life' (*m* Artie Shaw, *ly* Johnny Mercer)

Second Fiddle
US 1939   86m   bw
TCF (Gene Markey)

A Minnesota skating schoolteacher goes to
Hollywood and becomes a star.
Routine star vehicle.

w Harry Tugend *d* Sidney Lanfield *ph* Leon
Shamroy *md* Louis Silvers

Sonja Henie, Tyrone Power, Edna May Oliver,
Rudy Vallee, Mary Healy, Lyle Talbot, Alan
Dinehart

AAN: song 'I Poured My Heart into a Song'
(*m/ly* Irving Berlin)

The Second Greatest Sex
US 1955   87m   Technicolor
  Cinemascope
U-I (Albert J. Cohen)

Western women emulate Lysistrata to stop their
men from feuding.
Flat attempt to cash in on *Seven Brides for
Seven Brothers*; some good acrobatic dancing
but no style.

w Charles Hoffman *d* George Marshall
ph Wilfrid M. Cline *md* Joseph Gershenson
ch Lee Scott

Jeanne Crain, George Nader, Bert Lahr, Kitty
Kallen, Paul Gilbert, Keith Andes, Mamie Van
Doren, Tommy Rall

Second Honeymoon
US 1937   79m   bw
TCF (Raymond Griffith)

A man tries to win back his ex-wife.
Moderate star romantic comedy.

w Kathryn Scola, Darrell Ware, *story* Philip
Wylie *d* Walter Lang *ph* Ernest Palmer

Tyrone Power, Loretta Young, Stuart Erwin,
Claire Trevor, Marjorie Weaver, Lyle Talbot, J.
Edward Bromberg

The Second Mrs Tanqueray
GB 1952   75m   bw
Vandyke (Roger Proudlock)

A Victorian society widower marries a notorious
lady.
Stiff-backed penny-pinching version of an
interestingly antiquated play.

play Arthur Wing Pinero *d* Dallas Bower

Pamela Brown, Hugh Sinclair, Ronald Ward,
Virginia McKenna, Andrew Osborn

The Second Time Around
US 1961   99m   De Luxe   Cinemascope
TCF / Cummings / Harman (Jack Cummings)

In 1912 Arizona, a widow stands for sheriff and
has plenty of choice for a husband.

Light-hearted western fun mixed with family
sentimentality.

w Oscar Saul, Cecil Van Heusen, *novel* Richard
Emery Roberts *d* Vincent Sherman *ph* Ellis W.
Carter *m* Gerald Fried

Debbie Reynolds, Steve Forrest, Andy Griffith,
Juliet Prowse, Thelma Ritter, Ken Scott, Isobel
Elsom
  'Keep a lemon handy for sucking to ward off
an attack of the terminal cutesies.'—*Judith
Crist, 1973*

Seconds**
US 1966   106m   bw
Paramount / Joel / Gibraltar (Edward Lewis)

A secret organization sells a special service to the
jaded rich; apparent death followed by physical
rejuvenation.
An intriguing half-hour is followed by a glum
new life for our hero, capped by a horrifying
finale in which, dissatisfied, he learns he is to
become one of the corpses necessary to the
organization's continuance.

w Lewis John Carlino, *novel* David Ely *d John
Frankenheimer ph James Wong Howe m* Jerry
Goldsmith *titles* Saul Bass

Rock Hudson, *John Randolph, Will Geer,*
Salome Jens, Jeff Corey, Richard Anderson,
Murray Hamilton, Wesley Addy

AAN: James Wong Howe

The Secret Agent**
GB 1936   83m   bw
Gaumont British (Michael Balcon, Ivor
  Montagu)

A reluctantly recruited spy is ordered to kill a
man.
Unsatisfactory in casting and writing, this
Hitchcock suspenser nevertheless has many
typically amusing moments.

w Charles Bennett, *play* Campbell Dixon, *story*
Ashenden by Somerset Maugham *d Alfred
Hitchcock ph* Bernard Knowles *md* Louis Levy

John Gielgud, Robert Young, *Peter Lorre,*
Madeleine Carroll, Percy Marmont, Lilli
Palmer, Florence Kahn
  'As uncommon as it is unsentimentally
cruel.'—*Peter John Dyer, 1964*
  'Many sequences which show Hitchcock at his
very best: the fake funeral, the murder on the
mountainside, the riverside café, and the climax
in a chocolate factory.'—*NFT, 1961*

The Secret beyond the Door
US 1948   98m   bw
Universal / Walter Wanger (Fritz Lang)

An heiress marries a moody millionaire with a death fixation, and comes to think of herself as his next potential victim.

Silly melodrama with much chat and little suspense.

w Sylvia Richards, *story* Rufus King *d* Fritz Lang *ph* Stanley Cortez *m* Miklos Rozsa

Joan Bennett, Michael Redgrave, Anne Revere, Barbara O'Neil, Natalie Schaefer, Paul Cavanagh

'A dog-wagon *Rebecca* with a seasoning of psychiatrics.'—*Otis L. Guernsey Jnr*

The Secret Bride
US 1935   63m   bw
Warner

A District Attorney is secretly married to the daughter of the politician he is trying to convict.
Dismal melodrama, tritely scripted.

w Tom Buckingham, F. Hugh Herbert, Mary McCall Jnr, *play* Concealment by Leonard Ide *d* William Dieterle *ph* Ernest Haller

Barbara Stanwyck, Warren William, Glenda Farrell, Grant Mitchell, Arthur Byron, Henry O'Neill, Douglass Dumbrille

Secret Ceremony
GB 1969   109m   Eastmancolor
Universal / World Films / Paul M. Heller (John Heyman, Norman Priggen)

A prostitute mothers a young girl with a strange past.
Nuthouse melodrama for devotees of the director.

w George Tabori, *short story* Marco Denevi *d* Joseph Losey *ph* Gerry Fisher *m* Richard Rodney Bennett

Elizabeth Taylor, Robert Mitchum, Mia Farrow, Pamela Brown, Peggy Ashcroft

'This piece of garbage is so totally ridiculous that I can't imagine why anyone would want to be in it, let alone see it.'—*Rex Reed*

Secret Command
US 1944   92m   bw
Columbia (Phil L. Ryan)

An ex-foreign correspondent goes undercover at a shipyard to track down saboteurs.
Routine wartime thick ear.

w Roy Chanslor, *story* The Saboteurs by John and Ward Hawkins *d* Eddie Sutherland *ph* Franz Planer *m* Paul Sawtell

Pat O'Brien, Carole Landis, Chester Morris, Ruth Warrick, Barton MacLane, Tom Tully, Wallace Ford, Howard Freeman

The Secret Fury
US 1950   86m   bw
RKO (Jack H. Skirball, Bruce Manning)

A successful pianist is deliberately driven insane by her fiancé.
Derivative melodrama of no great interest.

w Lionel House *d* Mel Ferrer *ph* Leo Tover *m* Roy Webb *md* Constantin Bakaleinikoff

Claudette Colbert, Robert Ryan, Jane Cowl, Paul Kelly, Philip Ober, Elizabeth Risdon, Doris Dudley

The Secret Garden*
US 1949   92m   bw (Technicolor sequence)
MGM

An orphan girl goes to stay with her moody uncle and brightens up the lives of those around her.
Subdued, richly produced, rather likeable Victorian fable with the same moral as *The Bluebird* and *The Wizard of Oz*: happiness is in your own back yard.

w Robert Ardrey, *novel* Frances Hodgson Burnett *d* Fred M. Wilcox *ph* Ray June *m* Bronislau Kaper

Margaret O'Brien, Herbert Marshall, Gladys Cooper, Elsa Lanchester, Dean Stockwell, Brian Roper

'Uneven, but oddly and unexpectedly interesting.'—*Richard Mallett, Punch*

The Secret Heart
US 1946   97m   bw
MGM (Edwin H. Knopf)

A widow has problems with her emotionally disturbed daughter.
Old-fashioned woman's picture.

w Rose Franken, William Brown Meloney *d* Robert Z. Leonard *ph* George Folsey *m* Bronislau Kaper

Claudette Colbert, Walter Pidgeon, June Allyson, Robert Sterling, Marshall Thompson, Elizabeth Patterson, Richard Derr, Patricia Medina

' "There are three things you can't hide," says Walter Pidgeon in one of his bantering moments; "love, smoke, and a man riding a camel." I would add a fourth—that old MGM touch.'—*Richard Winnington*

The Secret Invasion
US 1964   98m   De Luxe   Panavision
UA / San Carlos (Gene Corman)

During World War II five convicted criminals become commandos.

Cut price *Dirty Dozen*, quite well made and
exciting.

w R. Wright Campbell *d* Roger Corman
ph Arthur E. Arling *m* Hugo Friedhofer

Stewart Granger, Raf Vallone, Henry Silva,
Mickey Rooney, Edd Byrnes, William
Campbell, Peter Coe

The Secret Life of an American Wife **
US 1968   92m   De Luxe
TCF / Charlton (George Axelrod)

A bored suburban housewife sets out to seduce a
movie star.
Sympathetic comedy of sixties suburban
manners.

wd George Axelrod ph Leon Shamroy *m* Billy
May

Walter Matthau, Anne Jackson, Patrick O'Neal,
Edy Williams

  'Both a first-class satire on American mores
and a compassionate study of wish-
fulfilment.'—*NFT, 1970*

The Secret Life of Walter Mitty **
US 1947   110m   Technicolor
Samuel Goldwyn

A mother's boy dreams of derring-do, and
eventually life catches up with fiction.
This pleasantly remembered star comedy,
though it never had much to do with Thurber,
can now be seen to have missed most of its
opportunities, though the nice moments do tend
to compensate.

w Ken Englund, Everett Freeman, *story* James
Thurber *d* Norman Z. McLeod *ph* Lee
Garmes *m* David Raksin

Danny Kaye, Virginia Mayo, Boris Karloff,
Florence Bates, Fay Bainter, *Thurston Hall*,
Ann Rutherford, Gordon Jones, Reginald
Denny

Secret Mission
GB 1942   94m   bw
GFD / Marcel Hellman / Excelsior

During World War II four British Intelligence
officers are landed in occupied France to
discover the truth about German defences.
Stilted war suspenser.

w Anatole de Grunwald, Basil Bartlett, Terence
Young *d* Harold French *ph* Bernard Knowles
m Mischa Spoliansky

Hugh Williams, Carla Lehmann, James Mason,
Roland Culver, Nancy Price, Michael Wilding,
Percy Walsh

The Secret of Blood Island
GB 1964   84m   Technicolor
U-I / Hammer

A girl parachutist secret agent is smuggled into a
Japanese POW camp and out again.
Absurd blood and thunder, almost perversely
enjoyable—but not quite.

w John Gilling *d* Quentin Lawrence *ph* Jack
Asher *m* James Bernard

Barbara Shelley, Jack Hedley, Charles Tingwell,
Bill Owen, Lee Montague

The Secret of Convict Lake *
US 1951   83m   bw
TCF (Frank P. Rosenberg)

In the 1870s, escaped convicts take over a
California town.
Brooding, snowy, set-bound western
melodrama; predictable but watchable.

w Oscar Saul *d* Michael Gordon *ph* Leo Tover
m Sol Kaplan *md* Lionel Newman

Glenn Ford, Gene Tierney, Ann Dvorak, Ethel
Barrymore, Zachary Scott, Barbara Bates, Cyril
Cusack, Jeanette Nolan, Ruth Donnelly

The Secret of My Success
GB 1965   105m   Metrocolor   Panavision
MGM / Andrew and Virginia Stone

A village policeman follows his mother's dictum
that he should not think ill of others, and
accidentally goes from success to success.
Flabby portmanteau comedy full of in-jokes and
flat-footed farce; satire is not evident.

wd Andrew L. Stone *ph* David Boulton
m Lucien Caillet and others *md* Roland Shaw

James Booth, Lionel Jeffries, *Amy Dalby*, Stella
Stevens, Honor Blackman, Shirley Jones, Joan
Hickson

The Secret of Santa Vittoria *
US 1969   140m   Technicolor   Panavision
UA / Stanley Kramer

In 1945 an Italian village hides its wine from the
occupying Germans.
Expected, exhausting epic comedy with
everyone talking at once.

w William Rose, Ben Maddow, *novel* Robert
Crichton *d* Stanley Kramer *ph* Giuseppe
Rotunno *m* Ernest Gold

Anthony Quinn, Anna Magnani, Virna Lisi,
Hardy Kruger, Sergio Franchi, Renato Rascel

  'A brainless farrago of flying rolling pins and
rotten vegetables, filled with the kind of
screaming, belching, eye-rolling fictional Italians
only Stanley Kramer could invent.'—*Rex Reed*

AAN: Ernest Gold

The Secret of the Incas
US 1954   101m   Technicolor
Paramount (Mel Epstein)

Various adventurers seek a priceless Inca jewel.
Boys' Own Paper yarn which sounds a good deal
more exciting than it is: too much talk and a few
choice studio backcloths drop the tension
alarmingly, and the script lacks humour and
conciseness.

w Ranald MacDougall, Sidney Boehm d Jerry
Hopper ph Lionel Lindon m David Buttolph

Charlton Heston, Robert Young, Thomas
Mitchell, Nicole Maurey, Yma Sumac, Glenda
Farrell, Michael Pate

The Secret of the Loch
GB 1934   80m   bw
ABFD / Bray Wyndham

A diver thinks he finds a prehistoric monster in
Loch Ness.
Mildly amusing exploitation item following the
1934 rebirth of interest in the old legend.

w Charles Bennett, Billie Bristow d Milton
Rosmer

Seymour Hicks, Nancy O'Neil, Gibson
Gowland, Frederick Peisley, Rosamund John,
Ben Field

The Secret Partner*
GB 1961   91m   bw
MGM (Michael Relph)

A blackmailing dentist is visited by a mysterious
hooded stranger who forces him to rob one of his
businessman victims.
Complex puzzle thriller, neatly made in sub-
Hitchcock style.

w David Pursall, Jack Seddon d Basil Dearden
ph Harry Waxman m Philip Green

Stewart Granger, Haya Harareet, Bernard Lee,
Hugh Burden, Melissa Stribling, Norman Bird,
Conrad Philips

The Secret People*
GB 1951   96m   bw
Ealing (Sidney Cole)

European refugees in London during the thirties
become members of a ring of anarchists.
Downbeat political melodrama which pleased
neither the masses nor the highbrows, despite
plaudits for sensitive direction and
performances.

w Thorold Dickinson, Wolfgang Wilhelm
d Thorold Dickinson ph Gordon Dines
m Roberto Gerhard

Valentina Cortese, Serge Reggiani, Audrey
Hepburn, Charles Goldner, Megs Jenkins, Irene
Worth, Athene Seyler, Reginald Tate

'The tension and power of the film make it one
of the most remarkable British productions for
some time.'—*Penelope Houston*

'That *Secret People*, despite the creative
agonies recorded by Mr Lindsay Anderson [in a
book on the making of the film] should turn out
to be a confused, unco-ordinated spy thriller
concealing a tentative message deep down below
some strained effects of style is another tragedy
of British film hopes.'—*Richard Winnington*

The Secret Six*
US 1931   83m   bw
MGM

A syndicate of businessmen finance two
reporters to get evidence against a gang of
bootleggers.
Solidly carpentered gangster thriller.

w Frances Marion d George Hill ph Harold
Wenstrom

Wallace Beery, Lewis Stone, Clark Gable, John
Mack Brown, Jean Harlow, Marjorie Rambeau,
Paul Hurst, Ralph Bellamy, John Miljan

The Secret War of Harry Frigg
US 1967   109m   Techniscope
Universal / Albion (Hal E. Chester)

In 1943 a private engineers the escape of five
captured generals.
Unattractive war comedy; slow, uninventive and
overlong.

w Peter Stone, Frank Tarloff d Jack Smight
ph Russell Metty m Carlo Rustichelli

Paul Newman, *John Williams*, Sylva Koscina,
Andrew Duggan, Tom Bosley, Charles D. Gray,
Vito Scotti, James Gregory

The Secret Ways*
US 1961   112m   bw
U-I / Heath (Richard Widmark)

An American reporter is recruited to rescue a
scholar from communist Hungary.
Pretentious Iron Curtain melodrama, quite good
to look at but overlong and no *Third Man*.

w Jean Hazelwood, *novel* Alistair MacLean
d Phil Karlson ph Max Greene m Johnny
Williams

Richard Widmark, Sonja Ziemann, Charles
Regnier, Walter Rilla, Howard Vernon, Senta
Berger

See Here Private Hargrove*
US 1944   102m   bw
MGM (George Haight)

Adventures of a raw recruit in the US army.
Standard transcription of a humorous bestseller
which did its best to make the war painless for
Americans.

w Harry Kurnitz, *book* Marion Hargrove
d Wesley Ruggles *ph* Charles Lawton *m* David
Snell

Robert Walker, Donna Reed, Robert Benchley,
Keenan Wynn, Bob Crosby, Ray Collins, Chill
Wills, Grant Mitchell

† Sequel 1945: *What Next, Corporal Hargrove?*

The Seekers
GB 1954   90m   Eastmancolor
GFD / Fanfare (George H. Brown)
US title: *Land of Fury*

In 1820 a British sailor and his family emigrate
to New Zealand.
Stilted epic which never gains the viewer's
sympathy or interest.

w William Fairchild d Ken Annakin
ph Geoffrey Unsworth *m* William Alwyn

Jack Hawkins, Glynis Johns, Inia Te Wiata,
Noel Purcell, Kenneth Williams, Laya Raki

The Sellout
US 1951   82m   bw
MGM (Nicholas Nayfack)

A newspaper editor exposes a corrupt
administration.
Competent melodrama with no surprises.

w Charles Palmer d Gerald Mayer ph Paul
Vogel m David Buttolph

Walter Pidgeon, John Hodiak, Audrey Totter,
Thomas Gomez, Everett Sloane, Cameron
Mitchell, Karl Malden, Paula Raymond

Semi-Tough*
US 1977   107m   De Luxe
UA / David Merrick

The manager's daughter decides between two
star members of a football team.
Rambling satiric comedy which takes jabs at
various states of mind in America today, notably
the fashionable forms of self-help therapy. Much
of it comes off quite well.

w Walter Bernstein, *novel* Dan Jenkins
d Michael Ritchie ph Charles Rosher Jnr
m Jerry Fielding

Burt Reynolds, Kris Kristofferson, Jill
Clayburgh, Bert Convy, Robert Preston, Lotte
Lenya, Roger E. Mosley

The Senator Was Indiscreet*
US 1947   95m   bw
U-I (Nunnally Johnson)
GB title: *Mr Ashton Was Indiscreet*

A foolish politician determines to become
president and hires a press agent.
Satirical political farce which hurls its shafts
wide and doesn't seem to mind how few of them
hit.

w Charles MacArthur, *story* Edwin Lanham
d George S. Kaufman *ph* William Mellor
m Daniele Amfitheatrof

William Powell, Ella Raines, Peter Lind Hayes,
Ray Collins, Arleen Whelan, Allen Jenkins,
Hans Conried, Charles D. Brown

Send Me No Flowers*
US 1964   100m   Technicolor
U-I / Martin Melcher (Harry Keller)

A hypochondriac mistakenly thinks he is dying
and tries to provide another spouse for his wife.
A timeworn farcical situation is handled in the
glossy Doris Day manner; it all starts quite
brightly but gradually fizzles out.

w Julius Epstein, *play* Norman Barrasch, Carroll
Moore d Norman Jewison ph Daniel Fapp
m Frank de Vol ad Alexander Golitzen, Robert
Clatworthy

Doris Day, Rock Hudson, Tony Randall, Paul
Lynde, Clint Walker, Hal March, Edward
Andrews

Sensations of 1945
US 1944   87m   bw
Andrew L. Stone

Father and son disagree over the handling of
their publicity agency.
Slim plot holds together a ragbag of variety acts,
some quite choice.

w Dorothy Bennett d Andrew L. Stone
ph Peverell Marley, John Mescall md Mahlon
Merrick

Eleanor Powell, W. C. Fields, Sophie Tucker,
Dennis O'Keefe, Eugene Pallette, C. Aubrey
Smith, Lyle Talbot, Dorothy Donegan, Cab
Calloway and his band, Woody Herman and his
band

AAN: Mahlon Merrick

Senso*
Italy 1953   115m   Technicolor
Lux
aka: *The Wanton Countess* (cut version)

In 1866 Venice a noblewoman falls in love with
an officer of the invading Austrian army, but
finally denounces him.

The melodramatic plot is less important than the portrait of a period, for this is an expensive film in the grand style, often breathtaking to look at.

w Luchino Visconti, Suso Cecchi d'Amico and others *story* Camilla Botto *d Lucino Visconti ph* G. R. Aldo, Robert Krasker *m* Anton Bruckner *ad* Ottavio Scotti

Alida Valli, Farley Granger, Massimo Girotti, Christian Marquand

Sentimental Journey
US 1946 94m bw
TCF (Walter Morosco).

An actress who knows she is dying arranges for a little orphan girl to take her place in her husband's affections.
Hollywood's most incredible three-handkerchief picture; nicely made, but who dared to write it?

w Samuel Hoffenstein, Elizabeth Reinhardt, *story* Nelia Gardner White *d* Walter Lang *ph* Norbert Brodine *m* Cyril Mockridge

Maureen O'Hara, John Payne, William Bendix, Cedric Hardwicke, Glenn Langan, Mischa Auer, Connie Marshall, Kurt Kreuger

'In twenty years of filmgoing I can't remember being so slobbered at: the apotheosis of the weepie.'—*Richard Winnington*
† Remade as *The Gift of Love* (qv).

The Sentinel
US 1976 92m Technicolor
Universal / Jeffrey Konvitz

A disturbed girl in an old apartment house is haunted by walking corpses: the house turns out to be the gateway to hell and her boy friend its appointed sentinel.
Vulgarly modish rip-off of several fashionable themes, notably *Rosemary's Baby* and *The Exorcist*.

w Michael Winner, Jeffrey Konvitz, *novel* Jeffrey Konvitz *d* Michael Winner *ph* Dick Kratina *m* Gil Melle

Chris Sarandon, Cristina Raines, Martin Balsam, John Carradine, Jose Ferrer, Ava Gardner, Arthur Kennedy, Burgess Meredith, Sylvia Miles, Deborah Raffin, Eli Wallach, Jerry Orbach

'Moral or ironic points are hard to discern in the eye-wrenching flux of a Michael Winner movie, which drifts and zooms across its polished people and places in a continual caressing motion, as crudely excitatory as any sex movie when the climaxes are approaching.'—*Richard Combs, MFB*

Separate Tables **
US 1958 98m bw
UA / Hecht–Hill–Lancaster (Harold Hecht)

Emotional tensions among the boarders at a British seaside guest house.
The genteel melodramas seem less convincing on the Hollywood screen than they did on the London stage, but the handling is thoroughly professional.

w Terence Rattigan, John Gay, *play* Terence Rattigan *d* Delbert Mann *m* David Raksin *ph* Charles Lang

Burt Lancaster, Rita Hayworth, *David Niven*, Deborah Kerr, *Wendy Hiller, Gladys Cooper, Cathleen Nesbitt, Felix Aylmer,* Rod Taylor, Audrey Dalton, *May Hallatt*

AA: David Niven; Wendy Hiller
AAN: best picture; script; Charles Lang; David Raksin; Deborah Kerr

September Affair
US 1950 104m bw
Paramount (Hal B. Wallis)

Two married people fall in love and a plane crash in which they are reported dead gives them their chance.
Turgid romantic melodrama, not very well made despite the background tour of Capri; what made it a hit was the playing of the old Walter Huston record of the title song.

w Robert Thoeren *d* William Dieterle *ph* Charles B. Lang *m* Victor Young

Joseph Cotten, Joan Fontaine, Françoise Rosay, Jessica Tandy, Robert Arthur, Jimmy Lydon

'A smooth surface mirrors the film's essential superficiality.'—*Penelope Houston*

September Storm
US 1960 110m De Luxe Cinemascope 3-D
TCF / Alco (Edward L. Alperson)

A New York model and two adventurers search for sunken treasure off an uncharted Mediterranean island.
Thin actioner originally intended to marry 3-D and Cinemascope, but failed to do so.

w W. R. Burnett, *novel* The Girl in the Red Bikini by Steve Fisher *d* Byron Haskin *ph* Jorge Stahl Jnr, Lamar Boren *m* Edward L. Alperson Jnr

Joanne Dru, Mark Stevens, Robert Strauss

Serenade
US 1956 121m Warnercolor
Warner (Henry Blanke)

A vineyard worker becomes a successful opera singer and is desired by two women.

Cliché success story with plot taking second place to singing.

w Ivan Goff, Ben Roberts, John Twist, *novel* James M. Cain *d* Anthony Mann *ph* Peverell Marley *md* Ray Heindorf *songs* Nicholas Brodszky

Mario Lanza, Joan Fontaine, Sarita Montiel, Vincent Price, Joseph Calleia, Harry Bellaver, Vince Edwards, Silvio Minciotti

The Sergeant
US 1968   108m   Technicolor
Warner / Robert Wise (Richard Goldstone)

France, 1952. In a dreary army camp, a tough army sergeant with a guilt complex is brought face to face with his own homosexuality.
Well-made but very ponderous and limited melodrama which could have been told in half the time.

w Dennis Murphy, from his novel *d* John Flynn *ph* Henri Persin *m* Michel Mayne

Rod Steiger, John Philip Law, Frank Latimore, Ludmila Mikael

Sergeant Madden
US 1939   90m   bw
MGM (J. Walter Ruben)

A policeman's son becomes a gangster.
Routine crime melodrama with sentimental trimmings, quite untypical of its director.

w Wells Root, *story* A Gun in His Hand by William A. Ulman *d* Josef Von Sternberg *ph* John Seitz *m* William Axt

Wallace Beery, Tom Brown, Alan Curtis, Laraine Day, Fay Holden, Marc Lawrence, Marion Martin

Sgt Pepper's Lonely Hearts Club Band
US 1978   111m   Technicolor   Panavision
Universal / Robert Stigwood (Dee Anthony)

A family band finds a new sound despite the activities of villains.
Oddball hotch-potch of middle-aged comedy and youth nostalgia with an American small-town setting. Some moments please, but most of it simply doesn't gell.

w Henry Edwards *d* Michael Schultz *ph* Owen Roizman *m* various (mostly the Beatles) *pd* Brian Eatwell

Peter Frampton, Barry Gibb, Robin Gibb, Maurice Gibb, George Burns, Frankie Howerd, Donald Pleasence, Paul Nicholas, Sandy Farina, Alice Cooper, Steve Martin, Earth Wind and Fire

'Another of those films which serve as feature-length screen advertising for an album.'—*Variety*

Sergeant Rutledge *
US 1960   111m   Technicolor
Warner / John Ford (Willis Goldbeck, Patrick Ford)

In 1881 a black army sergeant is on trial for rape and murder, but his defence counsel reveals the real culprit.
Flashback western; not the director's best, but generally of some interest.

w James Warner Bellah, Willis Goldbeck *d* John Ford *ph* Bert Glennon *m* Howard Jackson

Woody Strode, Jeffrey Hunter, Constance Towers, Willis Bouchey, Billie Burke, Carleton Young, Juano Hernandez, Mae Marsh

Sergeant York **
US 1941   134m   bw
Warner (Jesse L. Lasky)

The story of a gentle hillbilly farmer who became a hero of World War I.
Standard real-life fiction given the big treatment; a key Hollywood film of its time in several ways.

w Abem Finkel, Harry Chandler, Howard Koch, John Huston *d Howard Hawks ph Sol Polito m Max Steiner*

Gary Cooper, Joan Leslie, Walter Brennan, George Tobias, David Bruce, Stanley Ridges, Margaret Wycherly, Dickie Moore, Ward Bond

'I hardly think the effect is any different from that of a parade, with colours and a band; it is stirring and it is too long; there are too many holdups and too many people out of step, and your residue of opinion on the matter is that it will be nice to get home and get your shoes off.'—*Otis Ferguson*

AA: Gary Cooper
AAN: best picture; script; Howard Hawks; Sol Polito; Max Steiner; Walter Brennan; Margaret Wycherly

Sergeants Three
US 1961   112m   Technicolor   Panavision
(UA) Essex–Claude (Frank Sinatra)

Just after the Civil War three cavalry sergeants, with the help of an ex-slave bugler, dispose of some hostile Indians.
High-spirited but exhausting parody of *Gunga Din*, with bouts of unfunny bloodthirstiness separated by tedious slabs of dialogue.

w W. R. Burnett *d* John Sturges *ph* Winton Hock, Carl Guthrie *m* Billy May

Frank Sinatra, Dean Martin, Peter Lawford,

Sammy Davis Jnr, Joey Bishop, Henry Silva, Ruta Lee

'The participants have a better time than the onlookers.'—*Judith Crist, 1973*

Serious Charge

GB 1959 99m bw
Alva (Mickey Delamar)

A small-town troublemaker, accused by his priest of being responsible for the death of a young girl, amuses himself by accusing the priest of making homosexual advances.
A sensational play of its time makes a dull film despite earnest performances.

w Guy Elmes, Mickey Delamar, *play* Philip King *d* Terence Young *ph* Georges Périnal *m* Leighton Lucas

Anthony Quayle, Andrew Ray, Sarah Churchill, Irene Browne, Percy Herbert, Cliff Richard

The Serpent

France / Italy / Germany 1974 124m colour
Films La Boetie (Henri Verneuil)

A top KGB official defects to the west.
Complicated, humourless, multi-lingual spy capers.

w Henri Verneuil, Gilles Perrault, *novel* Pierre Nord *d* Henri Verneuil *ph* Claude Renoir *m* Ennio Morricone

Yul Brynner, Henry Fonda, Dirk Bogarde, Philippe Noiret, Farley Granger, Virna Lisi

The Serpent's Egg*

West Germany / US 1977 120m Eastmancolor
Rialto-Dino de Laurentiis

An American trapeze artist has a hard time in Berlin at the time of Hitler's rise to power.
More of a curate's egg, really, with a poor leading performance and too many lapses into nastiness, but much incidental interest of the kind one associates with the director.

wd Ingmar Bergman *ph* Sven Nykvist *m* Rolf Wilhelm *pd* Rolf Zehetbauer

David Carradine, Liv Ullmann, Gert Frobe, James Whitmore, Heinz Bennent

Serpico*

US 1973 130m Technicolor
Paramount / Artists Entertainment Complex / Dino de Laurentiis (Martin Bregman)

A New York cop reveals police corruption and is eventually forced to leave the country.
A harrowing true story played with authentic gloom and violence.

w Waldo Salt, Norman Wexler, *book* Peter Maas *d Sidney Lumet ph* Arthur J. Ornitz *m* Mikis Theodorakis

Al Pacino, John Randolph, Jack Kehoe, Biff McGuire

'There's nothing seriously wrong with *Serpico* except that it's unmemorable, and not even terribly interesting while it's going on.'—*Stanley Kauffmann*

AAN: script; Al Pacino

The Servant**

GB 1963 116m bw
Elstree / Springbok (Joseph Losey, Norman Priggen)

A rich, ineffectual young man is gradually debased and overruled by his sinister manservant and his sexy 'sister'.
Acclaimed in many quarters on its first release, this downbeat melodrama now seems rather naïve and long drawn out; its surface gloss is undeniable, but the final orgy is more risible than satanic.

w Harold Pinter, *novel* Robin Maugham *d* Joseph Losey *ph Douglas Slocombe m* Johnny Dankworth

Dirk Bogarde, James Fox, Sarah Miles, Wendy Craig, Catherine Lacey, Richard Vernon

'Moodily suggestive, well acted, but petering out into a trickle of repetitious unmeaningful nastiness.'—*John Simon*

Servants' Entrance

US 1934 88m bw
Fox

A maid falls in love with a chauffeur.
Upstairs downstairs style comedy drama; passable.

w Samson Raphaelson, *novel* Sigrid Boo *d* Frank Lloyd *ph* Hal Mohr

Janet Gaynor, Lew Ayres, Walter Connolly, G. P. Huntley Jnr, Sig Rumann, Louise Dresser, Astrid Allwyn, Ned Sparks

Service for Ladies

GB 1932 93m bw
Paramount (Alexander Korda)
US title: *Reserved for Ladies*

A waiter has a way with his rich lady clients.
Tenuous satirical comedy, a variation on the American silent *The Grand Duchess and the Waiter.*

w Eliot Crawshay-Williams, Lajos Biro, *novel* The Head Waiter by Ernst Vajda *d* Alexander Korda

Leslie Howard, George Grossmith, Benita

Hume, Elizabeth Allan, Morton Selten, Cyril Ritchard, Martita Hunt, Merle Oberon

The Set Up***
US 1949 72m bw
RKO (Richard Goldstone)

An ageing boxer refuses to pull his last fight, and is beaten up by gangsters.
One of the most brilliant little *films noirs* of the late forties; thoroughly studio-bound, yet evoking a brilliant feeling for time and place. Photography, direction, editing, acting are all of a piece.

w Art Cohn, *poem* Joseph Moncure March
d Robert Wise ph Milton Krasner
md Constantin Bakaleinikoff

Robert Ryan, Audrey Totter, George Tobias, Alan Baxter, Wallace Ford

Seven Angry Men*
US 1954 90m bw
Allied Artists (Vincent M. Fennelly)

In Kansas, John Brown determines to abolish slavery by violence.
Low-budget, intensely felt little biopic of the celebrated 19th-century fanatic and his sons.

w Daniel B. Ullman *d* Charles Marquis Warren
ph Ellsworth Fredericks *m* Carl Brandt

Raymond Massey, Jeffrey Hunter, Larry Pennell, Debra Paget, Leo Gordon, John Smith, James Best, Dennis Weaver

Seven Beauties*
Italy 1975 115m Technicolor
Medusa (Lina Wertmuller, Giancarlo Giannini, Arrigo Colombo)
original title: *Pasqualino Settebellezze*

An incorrigible survivor manages to get through the rigours of World War II and scarcely notices the damage to his honour.
Candide-like mixture of farce and satire with the addition of a good deal of unpleasantness. Less meaningful abroad than on its home ground.

wd Lina Wertmuller *ph* Tonino delli Colli
m Enzo Jannacci

Giancarlo Giannini, Fernando Rey, Shirley Stoler, Piero di Iorio

AAN: Lina Wertmuller (as writer and as director); Giancarlo Giannini

Seven Brides for Seven Brothers**
US 1954 104m Anscocolor
Cinemascope
MGM (Jack Cummings)

In the old west, seven hard-working brothers

decide they need wives, and carry off young women from the villages around.
Disappointingly studio-bound western musical, distinguished by an excellent score and some brilliant dancing, notably the barn-raising sequence.

w Frances Goodrich, Albert Hackett, *story* Sobbin' Women by Stephen Vincent Benet
d Stanley Donen ph George Folsey *ch Michael Kidd songs Johnny Mercer, Gene de Paul
m* Adolph Deutsch, Saul Chaplin

Howard Keel, Jane Powell, Jeff Richards, Russ Tamblyn, Tommy Rall, Howard Petrie, Marc Platt, Jacques d'Amboise, Matt Mattox

AAN: best picture; script; George Folsey; Adolph Deutsch, Saul Chaplin

Seven Cities of Gold*
US 1955 103m De Luxe Cinemascope
TCF (Robert D. Webb, Barbara McLean)

In 1796, a Spanish expedition sets out from Mexico to annex California, but with it goes Father Junipero Serra . . .
A semi-historical, semi-religious western which ends up not being much of anything but has interesting sequences.

w Richard L. Breen, John C. Higgins, *novel* Isabelle Gibson Ziegler *d* Robert D. Webb
ph Lucien Andriot *m* Hugo Friedhofer

Michael Rennie, Richard Egan, Anthony Quinn, Rita Moreno, Jeffrey Hunter, Eduardo Noriega, John Doucette

Seven Days in May***
US 1964 120m bw
Seven Arts / Joel / John Frankenheimer (Edward Lewis)

An American general's aide discovers that his boss intends a military takeover because he considers the President's pacifism traitorous. Absorbing political mystery drama marred only by the unnecessary introduction of a female character. Stimulating entertainment.

w Rod Serling, novel Fletcher Knebel, Charles W. Bailey II *d John Frankenheimer*
ph Ellsworth Fredericks m Jerry Goldsmith

Kirk Douglas, Burt Lancaster, *Fredric March*, Ava Gardner, Martin Balsam, *Edmond O'Brien*, George Macready, John Houseman
  'A political thriller which grips from start to finish.'—*Penelope Houston*
  'It is to be enjoyed without feelings of guilt, there should be more movies like it, and there is nothing first class about it.'—*John Simon*

AAN: Edmond O'Brien

Seven Days Leave
US 1929   83m   bw
Paramount (Louis D. Lighton)
GB title: *Medals*

A London charlady 'adopts' a soldier, and both
their lives are changed.
Sentimental melodrama which suited the times
and confirmed Cooper's stardom.

w John Farrow, Dan Totheroh, *play* The Old
Lady Shows Her Medals by J. M. Barrie
d Richard Wallace *ph* Charles Lang

Gary Cooper, Beryl Mercer, Daisy Belmore,
Nora Cecil, Tempe Piggott, Arthur Hoyt, Basil
Radford

Seven Days Leave
US 1942   87m   bw
RKO (Tim Whelan)

In order to inherit a hundred thousand dollars, a
soldier must marry within a week.
Cheerful frivolity featuring radio stars of the
time.

w William Bowers, Ralph Spence, Curtis
Kenyon, Kenneth Earl *d* Tim Whelan
ph Robert de Grasse *md* Roy Webb

Lucille Ball, Victor Mature, Harold Peary, Mary
Cortes, Ginny Simms, Ralph Edwards, Peter
Lind Hayes, Marcy McGuire, Wallace Ford

Seven Days to Noon**
GB 1950   94m   bw
London Films (The Boulting Brothers)

A professor engaged on atomic research
threatens to blow up London unless his work is
brought to an end.
Persuasively understated suspense piece which
was subsequently much copied, so that it now
seems rather obvious.

*w Frank Harvey, Roy Boulting, Paul Dehn,
James Bernard d John Boulting ph* Gilbert
Taylor *m* John Addison

*Barry Jones, Olive Sloane, André Morell, Joan
Hickson,* Sheila Manahan, Hugh Cross, Ronald
Adam, Marie Ney

'A first rate thriller that does not pretend to a
serious message, but yet will leave a query in the
mind.'—*Richard Winnington*

AA: script

The Seven Deadly Sins*
France / Italy 1952   150m   bw
Franco London / Costellazione

The master of ceremonies introduces seven
stories and an epilogue.
Among the most successful compendiums of its
kind, partly because of cast and credits and

partly because it came when French naughtiness
was appealing to a wide international audience.

w Jean Aurenche, Pierre Bost, Roberto
Rossellini, Leo Joannon, Carlo Rim, Diego
Fabbri, Liana Ferri, Eduardo de Filippo,
Charles Spaak, Turi Vaselle, René Wheeler
d Eduardo de Filippo, Jean Drèville, Yves
Allègret, Roberto Rossellini, Carlo Rim, Claude
Autant-Lara, Georges Lacombe

Gérard Philipe, Isa Miranda, Eduardo de
Filippo, Noel-Noel, Louis de Funès, Viviane
Romance, Frank Villard, Henri Vidal, Michèle
Morgan, Françoise Rosay

711 Ocean Drive*
US 1950   102m   bw
Columbia (Frank N. Seltzer)

A wireless expert is drawn into the bookie racket.
Overlong but vigorous crime exposé melodrama
with excellent location sequences, notably a
climax on Hoover Dam.

w Richard English, Francis Swann *d Joseph H.
Newman ph* Franz Planer *m* Sol Kaplan

Edmond O'Brien, Joanne Dru, Otto Kruger,
Don Porter, Sammy White, Dorothy Patrick,
Barry Kelley, Howard St John

Seven Faces of Dr Lao*
US 1964   100m   Metrocolor
MGM / George Pal

An elderly Chinaman with a penchant for
spectacular disguise solves the problems of a
western desert town.
A pleasant idea and excellent production are
submerged in a sloppily sentimental and verbose
script.

w Charles G. Finney, from his novel *d* George
Pal *ph* Robert Bronner *m* Leigh Harline *make
up* William Tuttle

Tony Randall, Arthur O'Connell, John Ericson,
Barbara Eden, Noah Beery Jnr, Lee Patrick,
Minerva Urecal, John Qualen

Seven Hills of Rome
US / Italy 1957   104m   Technirama
MGM / Titanus (Lester Welch)

An American singer in Italy is pursued by the
fiancée with whom he has quarrelled.
Thin travelogue with several halts for the star to
sing; production very patchy.

w Art Cohn, Giorgio Prosperi *d* Roy Rowland
ph Tonino Delli Colli *md* George Stoll

Mario Lanza, Renato Rascel, Marisa Allasio,
Peggie Castle

Seven Keys to Baldpate*

US 1935   69m   bw
RKO

An old theatrical warhorse also filmed in 1926 and 1947. None is as amusing as a good stage production.

play George M. Cohan, *story* Earl Derr Biggers *d* William Hamilton, Edward Killy *ph* Robert de Grasse

Gene Raymond, Margaret Callahan, Eric Blore, Grant Mitchell, Moroni Olsen, Henry Travers

The Seven Little Foys*

US 1955   95m   Technicolor   Vistavision
Paramount (Jack Rose)

The story of a family vaudeville act.
Routine showbiz biopic, a little heavy on the syrup.

w Melville Shavelson, Jack Rose *d* Melville Shavelson *ph* John F. Warren *md* Joseph J. Lilley

Bob Hope, Milly Vitale, George Tobias, Angela Clarke, Herbert Heyes, *James Cagney* as George M. Cohan

AAN: script

Seven Men from Now

US 1956   78m   Warnercolor
Batjac (Andrew V. McLaglen, Robert E. Morrison)

A sheriff seeks revenge when his wife is killed by bandits.
Good western programmer.

w Burt Kennedy *d* Budd Boetticher *ph* William H. Clothier *m* Henry Vars

Randolph Scott, Gail Russell, Lee Marvin, Walter Reed, Don Barry, John Larch

The Seven Minutes

US 1971   102m   De Luxe
TCF (Russ Meyer)

A bookseller is arrested for distributing an obscene novel, and many people are unexpectedly involved in the court case.
A fascinating piece of old-fashioned hokum, full of 'daring' words and cameo performances.

w Richard Warren Lewis, *novel* Irving Wallace *d* Russ Meyer *ph* Fred Mandl *m* Stu Philips

Wayne Maunder, Marianne MacAndrew, Yvonne de Carlo, Phil Carey, Jay C. Flippen, Edy Williams, Lyle Bettger, Ron Randell, David Brian, Charles Drake, John Carradine, Harold J. Stone

Seven Nights in Japan

GB / France 1976   104m   Eastmancolor
EMI–Marianne (Lewis Gilbert)

The heir to the British throne has shore leave in Tokyo and falls in love with a geisha.
Tediously daring romance with a banal script which seems over impressed by its own barely-existent controversial qualities.

w Christopher Wood *d* Lewis Gilbert *ph* Henri Decaë *m* David Hentschel

Michael York, Hidemi Aoki, James Villiers, Peter Jones, Charles Gray

The Seven Per Cent Solution

US 1976   114m   Technicolor
Universal (Herbert Ross)

Dr Watson lures Sherlock Holmes to Vienna so that Professor Freud can cure him of persecution complex and cocaine addiction.
Drearily serious spoof with only a glimmer of the required style and a totally miscast Holmes.

w Nicholas Meyer, from his novel *d* Herbert Ross *ph* Oswald Morris *m* John Addison *pd* Ken Adam

Nicol Williamson, Robert Duvall, Alan Arkin, Vanessa Redgrave, Laurence Olivier, Jeremy Kemp, Samantha Eggar, Joel Grey, Charles Gray, Georgia Brown, Regine

'Sorrily botched all-star extravaganza.'—
Sight and Sound

'Comes into the category of hit and myth . . .
A heavyweight spoof in which Sherlock Holmes is placed under hypnosis by Sigmund Freud. The audience is then placed under hypnosis by director Herbert Ross.'—*Michael Billington, Illustrated London News*

AAN: script

Seven Samurai ***

Japan 1954   200m   bw
Toho (Shojiro Motoki)
original title: *Shichi-nin no Samurai*

16th-century villagers hire samurai to defend their property against an annual raid by bandits.
Superbly strange, vivid and violent medieval adventure which later served as the basis for the western *The Magnificent Seven*.

w Akira Kurosawa, Shinobu Hashimoto, Hideo Oguni *d* Akira Kurosawa *ph* Asaichi Nakai *m* Fumio Hayasaka

Toshiro Mifune, Takashi Shimura, Kuninori Kodo

'It is as sheer narrative, rich in imagery, incisiveness and sharp observation, that it makes its strongest impact . . . It provides a fascinating display of talent, and places its director in the

forefront of creative film-makers of his
generation.'—*Gavin Lambert, Sight and Sound*

Seven Seas to Calais

US / Italy 1962   103m   Eastmancolor
  Cinemascope
MGM / Adelphia

In 1577, Sir Francis Drake follows the Spanish
treasure route.
Ho-hum swashbuckler with a background of
schoolboy history.

w Filippo Sanjust *d* Rudolph Maté *ph* Giulio
Gianini *m* Franco Mannino

Rod Taylor, Keith Michell, Irene Worth,
Anthony Dawson, Basil Dignam

Seven Sinners*

GB 1936   70m   bw
Gaumont (Michael Balcon)
US title: *Doomed Cargo*

Gunrunners wreck trains to cover traces of
murder.
Fascinatingly dated comedy suspenser with
excellent sub-Hitchcock sequences, the whole
thing having a strong flavour of *The 39 Steps*.

w Frank Launder, Sidney Gilliat, L. DuGarde
Peach, Austin Melford, *play* The Wrecker by
Arnold Ridley, Bernard Merivale *d Albert de
Courville*

Edmund Lowe, Constance Cummings, Thomy
Bourdelle, Henry Oscar, Felix Aylmer, Allan
Jeayes, O. B. Clarence

Seven Sinners*

US 1940   86m   bw
Universal (Joe Pasternak)
GB title: *Café of Seven Sinners*

A cabaret singer is deported from several South
Sea islands for causing too many fights among
the naval officers.
Ho-hum hokum with an amiable cast and a
good-natured final free-for-all.

w John Meehan, Harry Tugend *d* Tay Garnett
ph Rudolph Maté *m* Frank Skinner

Marlene Dietrich, John Wayne, Albert Dekker,
Broderick Crawford, Mischa Auer, Billy Gilbert,
Oscar Homolka, Anne Lee, Samuel S. Hinds
  'Nothing to worry about, unless you happen to
be in the theatre, watching it go from fairly good
to worse than worse.'—*Otis Ferguson*

Seven Sweethearts

US 1942   98m   bw
MGM (Joe Pasternak)

Seven daughters must marry in sequence, eldest
first.

Period musical frou-frou inspired by *Pride and
Prejudice*. So light it almost floats.

w Walter Reisch, Leo Townsend *d* Frank
Borzage *ph* George Folsey *m* Franz Waxman

Kathryn Grayson, Marsha Hunt, Van Heflin,
Cecelia Parker, S. Z. Sakall, Peggy Moran,
Isobel Elsom, Diana Lewis, Donald Meek,
Louise Beavers

Seven Thieves*

US 1960   102m   bw   Cinemascope
TCF (Sidney Boehm)

An elderly crook conceives a last plan to rob the
Monte Carlo casino.
Routine caper story, efficiently presented with
some humour.

w Sidney Boehm, *novel* Lions at the Kill by Max
Catto *d* Henry Hathaway *ph* Sam Leavitt
m Dominic Frontière

Edward G. Robinson, Rod Steiger, Joan Collins,
Eli Wallach, Michael Dante, Alexander
Scourby, Berry Kroeger, Sebastian Cabot
  'Christ, it was supposed to be a fun film, and
Steiger is far, far from having a sense of
humour.'—*Henry Hathaway*

The Seven-Ups

US 1973   103m   TVC   De Luxe
TCF / Philip D'Antoni

Gangsters are hunted down by a secret force of
the New York police.
Formulary realistic rough stuff in the wake of
The French Connection.

w Albert Ruben, Alexander Jacobs *d* Philip
D'Antoni *ph* Urs Furrer *m* Don Ellis

Roy Scheider, Victor Arnold, Jerry Leon, Tony
Lo Bianco, *Richard Lynch*

Seven Waves Away

GB 1956   95m   bw
Columbia / Copa (John R. Sloan)
US title: *Abandon Ship*

After the sinking of a luxury liner, the officer in
charge of a lifeboat has to make life or death
decisions.
Initially gripping but finally depressing open sea
melodrama derived from *Souls at Sea* and later
remade for TV as *The Last Survivors*.

wd Richard Sale *ph* Wilkie Cooper *m* Arthur
Bliss

Tyrone Power, Mai Zetterling, Lloyd Nolan,
Stephen Boyd, Moira Lister, James Hayter,
Marie Lohr, Moultrie Kelsall, Noel Willman,
Gordon Jackson, Clive Morton, John Stratton
  'Eventually one is bludgeoned into a grudging

admiration for the film's staying power.'—*Peter John Dyer*

Seven Women*
US 1966   100m   Metrocolor   Panavision
MGM / John Ford / Bernard Smith

In 1935, an isolated Chinese mission staffed by American women is overrun by bandits.
Dusty melodrama which might have appealed in the thirties but was quite out of tune with the sixties. Well enough made and acted, but a strange choice for Ford's last film.

w Janet Green, John McCormick, *story* Chinese Finale by Norah Lofts *d John Ford ph* Joseph La Shelle *m* Elmer Bernstein

Anne Bancroft, Flora Robson, Margaret Leighton, Sue Lyon, Mildred Dunnock, Betty Field, Anna Lee, Eddie Albert, Mike Mazurki, Woody Strode, Irene Tsu

The Seven Year Itch*
US 1955   105m   De Luxe   Cinemascope
TCF (Charles K. Feldman, Billy Wilder)

A married man has a fling with the girl upstairs.
An amusing theatrical joke, with dream sequences like revue sketches, is really all at sea on the big screen, especially as the affair remains unconsummated, but direction and performances keep the party going more or less.

w Billy Wilder, George Axelrod, *play* George Axelrod *d Billy Wilder ph* Milton Krasner *m* Alfred Newman

Tom Ewell, Marilyn Monroe, Sonny Tufts, Evelyn Keyes, Robert Strauss, Oscar Homolka, Marguerite Chapman, Victor Moore

1776*
US 1972   141m   Eastmancolor
Panavision
Columbia / Jack L. Warner

The thirteen American colonies prepare to declare their independence of Great Britain.
Plain, low-key filming of the successful Broadway musical showing the domestic lives of the historical figures concerned. Splendid moments alternate with stretches of tedium.

w Peter Stone, from his play *d* Peter Hunt *ph* Harry Stradling Jnr *m/ly* Sherman Edwards *ad* George Jenkins

William Daniels, Howard da Silva, Ken Howard, Donald Madden, Blythe Danner

AAN: Harry Stradling Jnr

Seventh Cavalry
US 1956   75m   Technicolor
Columbia / Scott-Brown

An officer accused of cowardice volunteers to bring back General Custer's body after Little Big Horn.
Lively co-feature with a good traditional action climax.

w Peter Packer *d* Joseph H. Lewis *ph* Ray Rennahan *m* Mischa Bakaleinikoff

Randolph Scott, Barbara Hale, Jay C. Flippen, Jeanette Nolan, Frank Faylen

The Seventh Cross**
US 1944   112m   bw
MGM (Pandro S. Berman)

Seven Germans escape from a concentration camp, and the Nazis threaten to execute them all. Just one escapes.
Impressive melodrama, brilliantly limiting its escape/suspense story to studio sets. Old-style Hollywood production at its best; but a rather obviously contrived story.

w Helen Deutsch, *novel* Anna Seghers *d* Fred Zinnemann *ph* Karl Freund *m* Roy Webb *ad* Cedric Gibbons, Leonid Vasian

Spencer Tracy, Signe Hasso, Hume Cronyn, Jessica Tandy, Agnes Moorehead, Felix Bressart, George Macready, George Zucco

AAN: Hume Cronyn

The Seventh Dawn
GB 1964   123m   Technicolor
UA / Holden / Charles K. Feldman (Karl Tunberg)

In the early fifties a Malayan rubber planter finds that his best friend is a leading terrorist.
Doom-laden romantic adventure drama with a lot of suffering and too little entertainment value.

w Karl Tunberg, *novel* The Durian Tree by Michael Keon *d* Lewis Gilbert *ph* Freddie Young *m* Riz Ortolani

William Holden, Tetsuro Tamba, Capucine, Susannah York, Michael Goodliffe, Allan Cuthbertson, Maurice Denham

'Echoes of *The Ugly American, Love Is a Many-Splendored Thing*, and many another adventure East of Sumatra, with every character running absolutely true to form.'—*MFB*

'An interminable melange of political, racial and romantic clichés, with performances and dialogue as overripe as the jungle setting.'—*Judith Crist, 1973*

Seventh Heaven**
US 1927   93m approx (24 fps)   bw   silent
Fox

A Paris sewer worker shelters a street waif,

marries her and after idyllic happiness goes off to war, returning blinded.

All softness, sweetness and light, a very typical – and attractive – film of its director and a big influence on Hollywood's European period.

w Benjamin Glazer, *play* Austin Strong *d* Frank Borzage *ph* Ernest Palmer, J A. Valentine

Janet Gaynor, Charles Farrell, Gladys Brockwell, David Butler

AA: Benjamin Glazer; Frank Borzage; Janet Gaynor
AAN: best picture

Seventh Heaven*
US 1937 102m bw
TCF (Raymond Griffith)

Dewy-eyed remake; the mood is antediluvian but the production impresses.

w Melville Baker *d* Henry King *ph* Merritt Gerstad *m* Louis Silvers *ad* William Darling

James Stewart, Simone Simon, Jean Hersholt, Gale Sondergaard, J. Edward Bromberg, Gregory Ratoff, John Qualen, Victor Kilian, Sig Rumann, Mady Christians

The Seventh Seal***
Sweden 1957 95m bw
Svensk Filmindustri (Allan Ekelund)
original title: *Det Sjunde Inseglet*

Death comes for a knight, who challenges him to a game of chess while he tries to show illustrations of goodness in mankind; but Death takes them all away in the end.

A modestly budgeted minor classic which, because of its international success and its famous shots, is seldom analysed in detail. In fact its storyline is meandering and apparently pointless, and it is kept going by its splendid cinematic feel and its atmosphere is that of a dark world irrationally sustained by religion.

wd Ingmar Bergman *ph* Gunnar Fischer *m* Erik Nordgren

Max Von Sydow, Bengt Ekerot, Gunnar Bjornstrand, Nils Poppe, Bibi Andersson, Gunnel Lindblom

'The most extraordinary mixture of beauty and lust and cruelty, Odin-worship and Christian faith, darkness and light.'—*Alan Dent, Illustrated London News*

The Seventh Sin
US 1957 94m bw Cinemascope
MGM (David Lewis)

A faithless wife accompanies her bacteriologist husband to fight a Chinese cholera epidemic, and regains her self-respect.

Tatty remake of a Garbo vehicle which was dated even in 1934. (See *The Painted Veil.)*

w Karl Tunberg, *novel* The Painted Veil by Somerset Maugham *d* Ronald Neame *ph* Ray June *m* Miklos Rozsa

Eleanor Parker, Bill Travers, George Sanders, Jean-Pierre Aumont, Françoise Rosay

The Seventh Veil***
GB 1945 94m bw
Theatrecraft / Sydney Box / Ortus

A concert pianist is romantically torn between her psychiatrist, her guardian, and two other fellows.

A splendid modern melodrama in the tradition of *Jane Eyre* and *Rebecca*; it set the seal of moviegoing approval on psychiatry, classical music, and James Mason, and it is the most utter tosh.

w Muriel and Sydney Box *d* Compton Bennett *ph* Reg Wyer *m* Benjamin Frankel

James Mason, Ann Todd, Herbert Lom, Albert Lieven, Hugh McDermott, Yvonne Owen, David Horne, Manning Whiley

'An example of the intelligent, medium-priced picture made with great technical polish which has represented for Hollywood the middle path between the vulgar and the highbrow.'—*Spectator*

'A popular film that does not discard taste and atmosphere.'—*Daily Mail*

'A rich, portentous mixture of Beethoven, Chopin, Kitsch and Freud.'—*Pauline Kael, 1968*

'An odd, artificial, best sellerish kind of story, with reminiscences of *Trilby* and *Jane Eyre* and all their imitations down to *Rebecca.*'—*Richard Mallett, Punch*

AA: script

The Seventh Victim*
US 1943 71m bw
RKO (*Val Lewton*)

A girl goes to New York in search of her sister, who is under the influence of Satanists.

Much praised but in effect rather boring little thriller, with rather stately acting and ponderous direction and dialogue. Censorship made the plot so obscure that it's difficult to follow.

w Charles O'Neal, De Witt Bodeen *d* Mark Robson *ph* Nicholas Musuraca *m* Constantin Bakaleinikoff

Kim Hunter, Tom Conway, Jean Brooks, Hugh Beaumont, Erford Gage, Isabel Jewell, Evelyn Brent

'It is the almost oppressive mood, the romantic

obsession with death-in-life, which dominates the film.'—*NFT, 1973*

† Note the use in the first scene of the staircase from *The Magnificent Ambersons.*

The Seventh Voyage of Sinbad*
US 1958   89m   Technicolor
Columbia / Morningside (Charles Schneer)

Sinbad seeks a roc's egg which will restore his fiancée from the midget size to which an evil magician has reduced her.
Lively fantasy with narrative drive and excellent effects.

w Kenneth Kolb *d* Nathan Juran *ph* Wilkie Cooper *m* Bernard Herrmann *sp Ray Harryhausen*

Kerwin Mathews, Kathryn Grant, Torin Thatcher, Richard Eyer, Alec Mango

A Severed Head*
GB 1970   98m   Technicolor
Columbia / Winkast (Alan Ladd Jnr)

A wine merchant has a long-standing affair which he thinks is secret, but is annoyed when his wife tries the same game.
Unwisely boisterous screen version of a slyly academic novel; tolerably sophisticated for those who don't know the original.

w Frederic Raphael, *novel* Iris Murdoch *d* Dick Clement *ph* Austin Dempster *m* Stanley Myers *pd* Richard Macdonald

Lee Remick, Richard Attenborough, Ian Holm, Claire Bloom, Jennie Linden, Clive Revill

Sex and the Single Girl
US 1964   114m   Technicolor
Warner / Richard Quine / Reynard (William T. Orr)

A journalist worms his way into the life of a lady sexologist in order to unmask her—but guess what.
Coy sex comedy with noise substituting for wit and style, all pretence being abandoned in a wild chase climax.

w Joseph Heller, David R. Schwarz, *book* Helen Gurley Brown *d* Richard Quine *ph* Charles Lang Jnr *m* Neal Hefti

Natalie Wood, Tony Curtis, Henry Fonda, Lauren Bacall, Mel Ferrer, Fran Jeffries, Edward Everett Horton, Otto Kruger
'For those willing to devote two hours of their lives to a consideration of Natalie Wood's virginity.'—*Judith Crist, 1973*

Sextette*
US 1978   91m   Metrocolor
Briggs and Sullivan (Warren G. Toub)

The honeymoon of a Hollywood film star is interrupted by her previous husbands.
An amazing last stab at her old métier by an 86-year-old ex-star. It doesn't work, of course, and most of it is embarrassing, but the attempt is in itself remarkable.

w Herbert Baker, *play* Mae West *d* Ken Hughes *ph* James Crabe *m* Artie Butler

Mae West, Tony Curtis, Ringo Starr, Dom de Luise, Timothy Dalton, George Hamilton, Alice Cooper, Rona Barrett, Walter Pidgeon, George Raft

Shack Out on 101*
US 1955   80m   bw
AA / William F. Broidy

A waitress at a café near a research establishment unmasks two spies.
Modest suspenser which seemed at the time to have some fresh and realistic attitudes.

w Ed and Mildred Dein *d* Ed Dein *ph* Floyd Crosby *m* Paul Dunlap

Frank Lovejoy, Lee Marvin, Keenan Wynn, Terry Moore, Whit Bissell

Shadow in the Sky
US 1951   78m   bw
MGM (William H. Wright)

A shell-shocked marine moves from a psychiatric hospital to live with his sister.
Low-key drama, plainly but quite well done, though of little continuing interest.

w Ben Maddow *d* Fred M. Wilcox *ph* George Folsey *m* Bronislau Kaper

Ralph Meeker, Nancy Davis, James Whitmore, Jean Hagen

Shadow of a Doubt***
US 1943   108m   bw
Universal (Jack H. Skirball)

A favourite uncle comes to visit his family in a small Californian town. He is actually on the run from police, who know him as the Merry Widow murderer.
Hitchcock's quietest film is memorable chiefly for its depiction of small-town life; but the script is well written and keeps the suspense moving slowly but surely.

w Thornton Wilder, Sally Benson, Alma Reville, story Gordon McDonell *d Alfred Hitchcock ph* Joe Valentine *m* Dmitri Tiomkin

Joseph Cotten, Teresa Wright, Hume Cronyn,
Macdonald Carey, Patricia Collinge, Henry
Travers, Wallace Ford
† Remade in 1958 as *Step Down to Terror*, with
Charles Drake.

Shadow of the Cat
GB 1961   79m   bw
U-I / BHP

A cat appears to wreak vengeance on those who
murdered its mistress.
Tolerable old dark house shocker with an
amusing theme not too well sustained.

w George Baxt *d* John Gilling *ph* Alec Grant
m Mikis Theodorakis

André Morell, William Lucas, Barbara Shelley,
Conrad Phillips, Alan Wheatley, Vanda Godsell,
Richard Warner, Freda Jackson

Shadow on the Wall
US 1949   84m   bw
MGM (Robert Sisk)

A child is traumatized by the accidental
witnessing of the murder of her unpleasant
stepmother.
Forgettable melodramatic suspenser.

w William Ludwig *d* Pat Jackson *ph* Ray June
m André Previn

Ann Sothern, Zachary Scott, Gigi Perreau,
Nancy Davis, Kristine Miller, John McIntire

The Shadow on the Window
US 1957   73m   bw
Columbia (Jonie Taps)

Three teenage thugs break into a lonely house,
murder its owner and hold a girl hostage.
Routine crime programmer, rather boringly
unravelled.

w Leo Townsend, David Harmon *d* William
Asher *ph* Kit Carson *m* George Duning

Betty Garrett, Phil Carey, John Barrymore Jnr,
Corey Allen, Gerald Saracini

Shadows*
US 1959   81m   bw
Cassavetes / Cassel / Maurice McEndree

Two blacks and their sister find their identities in
Manhattan.
16mm realistic drama which began a new and
essentially dreary trend of grainily true-life
pictures with improvised dialogue and little
dramatic compression.

w the cast *d* John Cassavetes *ph* Erich Kollmar
m Charles Mingus

Ben Carruthers, Leila Goldoni, Hugh Hurd,
Rupert Crosse, Anthony Ray

Shaft*
US 1971   100m   Metrocolor
MGM / Shaft Productions (Joel Freeman)

A black private eye finds himself at odds with a
powerful racketeer.
Violent, commercial action thriller which
spawned two sequels and a tele-series as well as
stimulating innumerable even more violent
imitations.

w Ernest Tidyman, John D. F. Black *d* Gordon
Parks *ph* Urs Furrer *m* Isaac Hayes

Richard Roundtree, Moses Gunn, Charles
Cioffi, Christopher St John
  'Relentlessly supercool dialogue, all
throwaway colloquialisms and tough
Chandlerian wisecracks.'—*MFB*

AA: title song (*m/ly* Isaac Hayes)
AAN: Isaac Hayes (musical score)

Shaft in Africa
US 1973   112m   Metrocolor   Panavision
(MGM) Shaft Productions (Roger Lewis)

Shaft is kidnapped by an Ethiopian emir who
wants him to track down a gang of slavers.
More miscellaneous violence, rather shoddily
assembled, with a few good jokes.

w Stirling Silliphant *d* John Guillermin
ph Marcel Grignon *m* Johnny Pate

Richard Roundtree, Frank Finlay, Vonetta
McGee

Shaft's Big Score
US 1972   105m   Metrocolor   Panavision
MGM / Shaft Productions (Richard Lewis,
  Ernest Tidyman)

Shaft avenges the death of a friend and comes up
against the numbers racket.
Violent footage and an incomprehensible plot.

w Ernest Tidyman *d* Gordon Parks *ph* Urs
Furrer *m* Gordon Parks

Richard Roundtree, Moses Gunn, Drew Bundini
Brown, Joseph Mascolo

The Shaggy DA
US 1976   92m   Technicolor
Walt Disney (Ron Miller)

A magic ring enables a young lawyer to become
a talking dog and thus expose corruption.
Rather feeble sequel to *The Shaggy Dog*, with
overtones of Watergate.

w Don Tait *d* Robert Stevenson *ph* Frank
Phillips *m* Buddy Baker *sp* Eustace Lycett, Art
Cruickshank, Danne Lee

Dean Jones, Tim Conway, Suzanne Pleshette, Jo Anne Worley, Vic Tayback, Keenan Wynn, Dick Van Patten

The Shaggy Dog*
US 1959   101m   bw
Walt Disney (Bill Walsh)

A small boy turns into a big shaggy dog and catches some crooks.
Simple-minded, overlong Disney comedy for kids and their indulgent parents; good laughs in the chase scenes.

w Bill Walsh, Lillie Hayward, *novel* The Hound of Florence by Felix Salten *d* Charles Barton *ph* Edward Colman *m* Paul Smith

Fred MacMurray, Jean Hagen, Tommy Kirk, Cecil Kellaway, Annette Funicello, Tim Considine, Kevin Corcoran, Alexander Scourby

Shake Hands with the Devil*
Eire 1959   110m   bw
UA / Troy / Pennebaker (Michael Anderson)

In 1921 Dublin a surgeon is the secret leader of the IRA, and comes to cherish violence as an end rather than a means.
Downbeat action melodrama, politically very questionable but well made.

w Ivan Goff, Ben Roberts, *novel* Rearden Connor *d* Michael Anderson *ph* Erwin Hillier *m* William Alwyn

James Cagney, Glynis Johns, Don Murray, Dana Wynter, Michael Redgrave, Sybil Thorndike, Cyril Cusack, Niall MacGinnis, Richard Harris, Ray McAnally, Noel Purcell

Shakedown
US 1950   80m   bw
U-I (Ted Richmond)

A ruthless press photographer becomes a blackmailer.
Routine crime melodrama, adequately done.

w Alfred Lewis, Martin Goldsmith *d* Joseph Pevney *ph* Irving Glassberg *m* Joseph Gershenson

Howard Duff, Brian Donlevy, Anne Vernon, Peggy Dow, Lawrence Tierney, Bruce Bennett

The Shakedown
GB 1959   92m   bw
Rank / Alliance / Ethiro (Norman Williams)

A Soho vice boss photographs prominent people in compromising situations and blackmails them.
A semi-remake set in the squalid London so beloved of film makers at the time, before it

became 'swinging'. Of no interest or entertainment value.

w Leigh Vance *d* John Lemont *ph* Brendan J. Stafford *m* Philip Green

Terence Morgan, Hazel Court, Donald Pleasence, Bill Owen, Robert Beatty, Harry H. Corbett, Gene Anderson, Eddie Byrne

The Shakiest Gun in the West
US 1967   101m   Techniscope
Universal (Edward J. Montagne)

A cowardly dentist becomes a western hero.
Dreary farce, an unsubtle remake of *The Paleface.*

w Jim Fritzell, Everett Greenbaum *d* Alan Rafkin *ph* Andrew Jackson *m* Vic Mizzy

Don Knotts, Barbara Rhoades, Jackie Coogan, Don Barry

Shalako
GB 1968   118m   Technicolor   Franscope
Kingston / Dimitri de Grunwald (Euan Lloyd)

New Mexico, 1880: a cowboy acts as guide to European aristocratic big game hunters, but the Indians become annoyed and attack.
A cute idea is given routine treatment; though packed with stars, the action never becomes very exciting despite incidental brutalities.

w J. J. Griffith, Hal Hopper, Scot Finch, *novel* Louis L'Amour *d* Edward Dmytryk *ph* Ted Moore *m* Robert Farnon

Sean Connery, Brigitte Bardot, Jack Hawkins, Stephen Boyd, Peter Van Eyck, Honor Blackman, Eric Sykes, Alexander Knox, Woody Strode, Victor French

Shall We Dance?**
US 1937   116m   bw
RKO (Pandro S. Berman)

Dancing partners pretend to be married but are not; until they both get the same idea.
A light musical which was full of good things but nevertheless began the decline of Astaire-Rogers films; repetition was obvious, as was ostentation for its own sake, and the audience was expecting too much.

w Allan Scott, Ernest Pagano *d* Mark Sandrich *ph* David Abel *m/ly* George and Ira Gershwin *md* Nathaniel Shilkret *ad* Van Nest Polglase

Fred Astaire, Ginger Rogers, Edward Everett Horton, Eric Blore, Harriet Hoctor, Jerome Cowan, Ketti Gallian, Ann Shoemaker

AAN: song 'They Can't Take That Away From Me'

Shampoo*
US 1975 110m Technicolor
Columbia / Persky–Bright / Vista (Warren
Beatty)

A Beverly Hills hairdresser seduces his most
glamorous clients.
Ugly little sex farce with few laughs but much
dashing about and bad language. Its setting on
election eve 1968 has made some people think it
a political satire.

w Robert Towne, Warren Beatty d Hal Ashby
ph Laszlo Kovacs m Paul Simon

Warren Beatty, Julie Christie, Lee Grant, Goldie
Hawn, Jack Warden, Tony Bill, Jay Robinson

'It has the bursting-with-talent but fuzziness-
of-effect aspect of a movie made by a group of
friends for their own amusement.'—*Richard
Combs*

AA: Lee Grant
AAN: script; Jack Warden

Shamus
US 1972 98m Eastmancolor
Columbia / Robert M. Weitman

A private eye is hired by a wealthy man to
recover stolen jewels and find a murderer.
A forties retread with seventies violence; junky
stuff, with a few laughs for buffs who can spot the
in-jokes.

w Barry Beckerman d Buzz Kulik ph Victor J.
Kemper m Jerry Goldsmith

Burt Reynolds, Dyan Cannon, John Ryan, Joe
Santos, Giorgio Tozzi, Ron Weyland

'Very hectic, very vividly New York and as
idiotic as Reynolds' physical resiliency.'—
Judith Crist

Shane***
US 1953 118m Technicolor
Paramount (George Stevens, Ivan Moffat)

A mysterious stranger helps a family of
homesteaders.
Archetypal family western, but much slower and
statelier than most, as though to emphasize its
own quality, which is evident anyway.

w A. B. Guthrie Jnr, *novel* Jack Schaefer
d George Stevens ph Loyal Griggs m Victor
Young

Alan Ladd, Jean Arthur, Van Heflin, *Jack
Palance*, Brandon de Wilde, Ben Johnson, Edgar
Buchanan, Emile Meyer, Elisha Cook Jnr, John
Dierkes

'A kind of dramatic documentary of the
pioneer days of the west.'—*MFB*

'Westerns are better when they're not too self-
importantly self-conscious.'—*New Yorker,
1975*

AA: Loyal Griggs
AAN: best picture; A. B. Guthrie Jnr; George
Stevens; Jack Palance

Shanghai
US 1935 77m bw
Paramount (Walter Wanger)

A visiting American lady falls in love with a half
caste.
Romantic drama programmer.

w Gene Towne, Graham Baker, Lynn Starling
d James Flood ph James Van Trees

Loretta Young, Charles Boyer, Warner Oland,
Alison Skipworth, Fred Keating, Charles
Grapewin, Walter Kingsford

Shanghai Express***
US 1932 84m bw
Paramount

A British officer and his old flame meet on a train
which is waylaid by Chinese bandits.
Superbly pictorial melodrama which set the
pattern for innumerable train movies to come,
though none matched its deft visual quality and
few sketched in their characters so neatly. Plot
and dialogue are silent style, but refreshingly so.

w Jules Furthman d Josef Von Sternberg
ph Lee Garmes ad Hans Dreier

Marlene Dietrich, Clive Brook, Warner Oland,
Anna May Wong, Eugene Pallette, Lawrence
Grant, Louise Closser Hale, Gustav Von
Seyffertitz

'A limited number of characters, all
meticulously etched, highly atmospheric sets and
innumerable striking photographic
compositions.'—*Curtis Harrington, 1964*

AA: Lee Garmes
AAN: best picture; Josef Von Sternberg

The Shanghai Gesture*
US 1941 90m bw
Arnold Pressburger (Albert de Courville)

The proprietress of a Shanghai gambling casino
taunts her ex-husband by showing him his
daughter in a state of degradation; but he proves
that the girl is her daughter also.
An ancient theatrical shocker was completely
bowdlerized and chopped into nonsense for the
screen; but the director's hand showed in the
handling of the vast casino set.

w Josef Von Sternberg, Geza Herczeg, Karl
Vollmoeller, Jules Furthman, *play* John Colton
d Josef Von Sternberg ph Paul Ivano
m Richard Hageman ad Boris Leven

Ona Munson, Victor Mature, Walter Huston, Gene Tierney, Albert Basserman, Phyllis Brooks, Maria Ouspenskaya, Eric Blore, Ivan Lebedeff, Mike Mazurki

'The effect of a descent into a maelstrom of iniquity.'—*Curtis Harrington, 1962*

'In spite of all the changes necessitated by the Hays Office, seldom have decadence and sexual depravity been better suggested on the screen.'—*Richard Roud, 1966*

'Hilariously, awesomely terrible.'—*New Yorker, 1977*

AAN: Richard Hageman

The Sharkfighters
US 1956 72m Technicolor
Cinemascope
(UA) Formosa (Samuel Goldwyn Jnr)

To save the lives of fliers forced down into the sea, navy scientists experiment with a shark repellent.
Straightforward semi-documentary with suspenseful action sequences.

w Lawrence Roman, John Robinson *d* Jerry Hopper *ph* Lee Garmes *m* Jerome Moross

Victor Mature, Karen Steele, James Olson, Claude Akins

Shark's Treasure*
US 1974 95m De Luxe
UA / Symbol (Cornel Wilde)

Treasure hunters seek buried gold in the Caribbean where sharks abound.
Fairly thrilling action hokum.

wd Cornel Wilde *ph* Jack Atcheler, Al Giddings *m* Robert O. Ragland

Cornel Wilde, Yaphet Kotto, John Neilson, David Canary, Cliff Osmond

'Wilde maintains his reputation for making the most likeable bad movies around.'—*Tom Milne*

She*
US 1935 89m bw
RKO (Merian C. Cooper)

Ancient papers lead a Cambridge professor and his friends to the lost city where dwells a queen who cannot die—until she falls in love.
The producers have the right spirit for this Victorian fantasy, but tried too hard to emulate the mood of their own *King Kong*, and it was a mistake to transfer the setting from Africa to the Arctic. One for connoisseurs, though.

novel H. Rider Haggard *d* Ernest Schoedsack *m* Max Steiner

Randolph Scott, Nigel Bruce, Helen Gahagan

'To an unrepentant Haggard fan it does sometimes seem to catch the thrill as well as the childishness of his invention.'—*Graham Greene*

She
GB 1965 105m Technicolor
Hammerscope
ABP / Hammer (Aida Young)

Flat, uninventive and tedious remake which reverts to Africa but does nothing else right; it ignores the essential Cambridge prologue and ignores all suggestions of fantasy.

w David T. Chantler *d* Robert Day *ph* Harry Waxman *m* James Bernard

Peter Cushing, Ursula Andress, Christopher Lee, John Richardson, Bernard Cribbins, André Morell, Rosenda Monteros

'The stagey decor of Kor is in the art deco style of Radio City Music Hall, and you keep expecting the Rockettes to turn up . . . the picture is deadly slow, and the lovebirds could try anyone's patience, but camp like this is a rarity.'—*New Yorker, 1976*

She Couldn't Say No
US 1952 89m bw
RKO (Robert Sparks)
GB title: *Beautiful But Dangerous*

An heiress returns to the town of her childhood to distribute anonymous gifts to those who had helped her.
Moderate Capraesque comedy which doesn't quite come off.

w D. D. Beauchamp, William Bowers, Richard Flournoy *d* Lloyd Bacon *ph* Harold J. Wild *m* Roy Webb

Jean Simmons, Robert Mitchum, Arthur Hunnicutt, Edgar Buchanan, Wallace Ford, Raymond Walburn

She Didn't Say No!
GB 1958 97m Technicolor
ABP (Sergei Nolbandov)

A young Irish widow has five illegitimate children, each by a different father.
Coyly daring comedy full of stage Oirishisms and obvious jokes, a few of which work.

w T. J. Morison, Una Troy, from her novel We Are Seven *d* Cyril Frankel *ph* Gilbert Taylor *m* Tristam Cary

Eileen Herlie, Jack MacGowran, Perlita Neilson, Niall MacGinnis, Ian Bannen

She Done Him Wrong***
US 1933 68m bw
Paramount (William Le Baron)

A lady saloon keeper of the Gay Nineties falls

for the undercover cop who is after her.
As near undiluted Mae West as Hollywood ever
came: fast, funny, melodramatic and pretty
sexy; also a very atmospheric and well-made
movie.

w Mae West, from her play Diamond Lil (with
help on the scenario from Harry Thew, John
Bright) *d Lowell Sherman ph* Charles Lang
songs Ralph Rainger

Mae West, Cary Grant, Owen Moore, Gilbert
Roland, Noah Beery, David Landau, Rafaela
Ottiano, Rochelle Hudson, Dewey Robinson

AAN: best picture

She Gets Her Man*
US 1945 73m bw
Universal (Warren Wilson)

A country girl in New York tracks down a
blowgun murderer.
Disarming mystery farce which tries every
slapstick situation known to gag writers, and
gets away with it.

w Warren Wilson, Clyde Bruckman *d* Erle C.
Kenton *ph* Jerry Ash

Joan Davis, William Gargan, Leon Errol,
Milburn Stone, Russell Hicks

She Loves Me Not*
US 1934 85m bw
Paramount (Benjamin Glazer)

A showgirl murder witness takes refuge in a
men's college.
Larky musical farce later remade as *True to the
Army* and *How to be Very Very Popular*; this
first version is perhaps the most nearly amusing.

w Ben Glazer, *novel* Edward Hope, *play* Howard
Lindsay *d* Elliott Nugent *ph* Charles Lang
songs various

Bing Crosby, Miriam Hopkins, Kitty Carlisle,
Edward Nugent, Lynne Overman, Henry
Stephenson, Warren Hymer, George Barbier

AAN: song 'Love in Bloom'

She Wore a Yellow Ribbon**
US 1949 103m Technicolor
RKO

Problems of a cavalry officer about to retire.
Fragmentary but very enjoyable western with all
Ford ingredients served piping hot.

w Frank Nugent, Laurence Stallings, *story*
James Warner Bellah *d John Ford ph Winton
C. Hoch m* Richard Hageman

John Wayne, Joanne Dru, John Agar, Ben

Johnson, Harry Carey Jnr, Victor McLaglen,
Mildred Natwick, George O'Brien, Arthur
Shields

AA: Winton C. Hoch

The Sheep Has Five Legs*
France 1954 96m bw
Raoul Ploquin
original title: *Le Mouton a Cinq Pattes*

A town seeking publicity tries to bring together
the five quintuplet grandsons of its oldest
inhabitant.
Mildly saucy star vehicle which was in fact most
notable for introducing Fernandel to an
international audience.

w Albert Valentin *d* Henri Verneuil *ph* Armand
Thirard *m* Georges Van Parys

Fernandel, Françoise Arnoul, Delmont, Paulette
Dubost, Louis de Funès

AAN: original story

The Sheepman*
US 1958 91m Metrocolor
Cinemascope
MGM (Edmund Grainger)

A tough sheep farmer determines to settle in a
cattle town.
Easy-going western with humorous moments.

w William Bowers, James Edward Grant
d George Marshall *ph* Robert Bronner *m* Jeff
Alexander

Glenn Ford, Shirley Maclaine, Leslie Nielsen,
Mickey Shaughnessy, Edgar Buchanan

AAN: script

The Sheik*
US 1921 73m (24 fps) bw silent
Famous Players-Lasky / George Melford

An English heiress falls for a desert chieftain.
Archetypal romantic tosh which set the seal on
Valentino's superstardom.

w Monte M. Katterjohn, *novel* E. M. Hull
d George Melford *ph* William Marshall

Rudolph Valentino, Agnes Ayres, Adolphe
Menjou, Walter Long, Lucien Littlefield
† *Son of the Sheik*, released in 1926, was even
more popular.

The Sheik Steps Out
US 1937 68m bw
Republic (Herman Schlom)

A modern sheik has a riotous time in the big city.
Uninventive spoof of the Valentino myth.

w Adele Buffington, Gordon Kahn *d* Irving
Pichel *ph* Jack Marta *md* Alberto Columbo

Ramon Novarro, Lola Lane, Gene Lockhart, Kathleen Burke, Stanley Fields

Shenandoah**
US 1965　105m　Technicolor
Universal (Robert Arthur)

How the American Civil War affected the lives of a Virginia family.
Surprisingly hard-centred and moving semi-western for the family; excellent performances and well-controlled mood.

w James Lee Barrett d Andrew V. McLaglen ph William Clothier m Frank Skinner md Joseph Gershenson

James Stewart, Rosemary Forsyth, Doug McClure, Glenn Corbett, Katharine Ross, Philip Alford

The Sheriff of Fractured Jaw
GB 1959　103m　Eastmancolor
　Cinemascope
TCF / Daniel M. Angel

A London gunsmith in the old west accidentally becomes a hero.
Tame, predictable comedy with a clear lack of invention.

w Arthur Dales d Raoul Walsh ph Otto Heller m Robert Farnon

Kenneth More, Jayne Mansfield, Robert Morley, Ronald Squire, David Horne, Henry Hull, Eynon Evans, Bruce Cabot, William Campbell

Sherlock Holmes
The innumerable Sherlock Holmes films are noted in Filmgoer's Companion, and in this volume the appropriate films are listed under their own titles with the exception of the modernized dozen made in the forties by Universal, starring Basil Rathbone as Holmes and Nigel Bruce as Watson. These followed on from Fox's two period pieces, THE HOUND OF THE BASKERVILLES and THE ADVENTURES OF SHERLOCK HOLMES (qv). The series started and ended somewhat lamely but several of the episodes remain highly enjoyable, for performances and dialogue rather than plot or pacing. All but the first were directed by Roy William Neill.

1942: SHERLOCK HOLMES AND THE VOICE OF TERROR (d John Rawlins with Reginald Denny, Thomas Gomez); SHERLOCK HOLMES AND THE SECRET WEAPON* (with Lionel Atwill as Moriarty) 1943: SHERLOCK HOLMES IN WASHINGTON* (with Henry Daniell, George Zucco); SHERLOCK HOLMES FACES DEATH** (with Halliwell Hobbes, Dennis Hoey)
1944: SHERLOCK HOLMES AND THE SPIDER WOMAN** (with Gale Sondergaard, Dennis Hoey); THE SCARLET CLAW** (with Gerald Hamer); THE PEARL OF DEATH** (with Miles Mander, Dennis Hoey, Rondo Hatton)
1945: THE HOUSE OF FEAR* (with Aubrey Mather, Dennis Hoey); THE WOMAN IN GREEN* (with Henry Daniell as Moriarty); PURSUIT TO ALGIERS (with Martin Kosleck)
1946: TERROR BY NIGHT* (with Alan Mowbray), DRESSED TO KILL (GB title: SHERLOCK HOLMES AND THE SECRET CODE; with Patricia Morison)

Sherlock Holmes*
US 1932　68m　bw
Fox

Moriarty brings Chicago gangsters into London. Interesting but rather unsatisfactory Holmes adventure.

w Bertram Milhauser d William K. Howard ph George Barnes

Clive Brook, Reginald Owen, Ernest Torrence, Miriam Jordan, Alan Mowbray, Herbert Mundin

Sherlock Junior**
US 1924　45m (24 fps)　bw　silent
MGM

A film projectionist, unjustly accused of stealing a watch, has dreams of being a great detective. Fast-moving, gag-filled comedy which ranks among its star's best.

w Clyde Bruckman, Jean Haves, Joseph Mitchell d, ed Buster Keaton ph Elgin Lessley, Bryon Houck

Buster Keaton, Kathryn McGuire, Ward Crane, Joseph Keaton

She's Working Her Way through College
US 1952　101m　Technicolor
Warner (William Jacobs)

A burlesque queen goes to college and brings out the beast in an English professor.
Limp and vulgar musical remake of a well-liked play and film; just about gets by as a lowbrow timekiller.

w Peter Milne, play The Male Animal by James Thurber, Elliott Nugent d Bruce Humberstone ph Wilfrid Cline md Ray Heindorf ch Le Roy Prinz songs Sammy Cahn, Vernon Duke

Virginia Mayo, Ronald Reagan, Don Defore,

Gene Nelson, Phyllis Thaxter, Patrice Wymore
† Sequel 1953: *She's Back on Broadway*.

Shine on Harvest Moon*
US 1944   112m   bw (Technicolor sequence)
Warner (William Jacobs)

The life and times of vaudeville singer Nora Bayes.

Standard ragtime biopic, very adequately made.

w Sam Hellman, Richard Weil, Francis Swan, James Kern d David Butler ph Arthur Edeson md Heinz Roemheld

Ann Sheridan, Dennis Morgan, Jack Carson, Irene Manning, S. Z. Sakall, Marie Wilson, Robert Shayne

Shining Victory
US 1941   80m   bw
Warner (Robert Lord)

A psychiatrist is torn between love and duty.
Adequate romantic programmer.

w Howard Koch, Ann Froelick, play Jupiter Laughs by A. J. Cronin d Irving Rapper ph James Wong Howe

James Stephenson, Geraldine Fitzgerald, Donald Crisp, Barbara O'Neil, Montagu Love, Sig Rumann

Ship Ahoy
US 1942   95m   bw
MGM (Jack Cummings)

On a trip to Puerto Rico, a tap dancer is enlisted as a spy.
Tepid musi-comedy.

w Harry Clark d Eddie Buzzell ph Leonard Smith md George Stoll ad Merrill Pye

Eleanor Powell, Red Skelton, Bert Lahr, Virginia O'Brien, William Post Jnr, James Cross

Ship of Fools***
US 1965   150m   bw
Columbia / Stanley Kramer

In 1933 a German liner leaves Vera Cruz for Bremerhaven with a mixed bag of passengers. Ambitious, serious, quite fascinating slice-of-life shipboard multi-melodrama. Capable mounting, memorable performances and a bravura finale erase memories of padding and symbolic pretensions.

w Abby Mann, novel Katherine Anne Porter d Stanley Kramer ph Ernest Laszlo m Ernest Gold

Vivien Leigh, Simone Signoret, Oskar Werner, Heinz Ruhmann, Jose Ferrer, Lee Marvin,

Elizabeth Ashley, *Michael Dunn*, George Segal, Jose Greco, Charles Korvin, Alf Kjellin, Werner Klemperer, John Wengraf, Lilia Skala, Karen Verne

AA: Ernest Laszlo
AAN: best picture; Abby Mann; Simone Signoret; Oskar Werner; Michael Dunn

The Ship That Died of Shame
GB 1955   91m   bw
Ealing (Michael Relph, Basil Dearden)

The wartime crew of a motor gunboat buy the vessel and go into postwar business as smugglers.
Thin and rather obvious melodramatic fable.

w John Whiting, Michael Relph, Basil Dearden, novel Nicholas Monsarrat d Michael Relph, Basil Dearden ph Gordon Dines m William Alwyn

Richard Attenborough, George Baker, Bill Owen, Virginia McKenna, Roland Culver, Bernard Lee, Ralph Truman, John Chandos
   'A sentimental fantasy tacked on to a basically conventional thriller.'—*Penelope Houston*

Ships with Wings*
GB 1941   103m   bw
Ealing (S. C. Balcon)

Aircraft carriers prepare for World War II.
Historically interesting, dramatically insubstantial flagwaver.

w Sergei Nolbandov, Patrick Kirwan, Austin Melford, Diana Morgan d Sergei Nolbandov

John Clements, Leslie Banks, Jane Baxter, Ann Todd, Basil Sydney, Edward Chapman, Hugh Williams, Frank Pettingell, Michael Wilding

The Shiralee*
GB 1957   99m   bw
Ealing (Jack Rix)

An Australian swagman leaves his wife and takes to the road with his small daughter. Episodic character comedy-drama throwing a fairly sharp light on the Australian scene.

w Neil Paterson, Leslie Norman, novel D'Arcy Niland d Leslie Norman ph Paul Beeson m John Addison

Peter Finch, Dana Wilson, Elizabeth Sellars, George Rose, Russell Napier, Nial MacGinnis, Tessie O'Shea

Shock
US 1946   70m   bw
TCF

A girl in a hotel sees a murder committed, and an

elaborate plan is concocted to silence her.
Flat treatment ruins a good suspense situation.

w Eugene Ling *d* Alfred Werker *ph* Glen
MacWilliams, Joe MacDonald

Vincent Price, Lynn Bari, Frank Latimore,
Annabel Shaw

'Extreme improbabilities and a general lack of
finish.'—*MFB*

Shock Corridor

US 1963 101m Technicolor
Leon Fromkess / Sam Firks (Samuel Fuller)

A journalist gets himself admitted to a mental
asylum to solve the murder of an inmate.
Sensational melodrama, a cinematic equivalent
of the yellow press, and on that level quite lively.

wd Samuel Fuller

Peter Breck, Constance Towers, Gene Evans,
James Best, Hari Rhodes, Philip Ahn

Shock Treatment

US 1964 94m bw
Warner (Aaron Rosenberg)

Murders are committed in a mental institution.
Tasteless thriller, not even very arresting as a
yarn.

w Sidney Boehm *d* Denis Sanders *ph* Sam
Leavitt *m* Jerry Goldsmith

Lauren Bacall, Roddy MacDowall, Carol
Lynley, Ossie Davis, Stuart Whitman, Douglass
Dumbrille

The Shocking Miss Pilgrim

US 1946 85m Technicolor
TCF (William Perlberg)

In 1894 Boston, a lady typist (stenographer)
fights for women's rights.
Period comedy with music; not nearly as sharp
as it thinks it is.

wd George Seaton *ph* Leon Shamroy *ad* James
Basevi, Boris Leven *songs* George and Ira
Gershwin

Betty Grable, Dick Haymes, Anne Revere,
Allyn Joslyn, Gene Lockhart, Elizabeth
Patterson, Arthur Shields, Elizabeth Risdon

The Shoes of the Fisherman**

US 1968 157m Metrocolor Panavision
MGM (George Englund)

After twenty years as a political prisoner, a
Russian bishop becomes Pope.
Predigested but heavy-going picturization of a
bestseller; big budget, big stars, big hopes. In fact
a commercial dud, with plenty of superficial
interest but more dramatic contrivance than
religious feeling.

w John Patrick, James Kennaway, *novel* Morris
West *d* Michael Anderson *ph* Erwin Hiller
m Alex North *ad* Edward Carfagno, George W.
Davis

Anthony Quinn, David Janssen, Laurence
Olivier, Oskar Werner, John Gielgud, Barbara
Jefford, Leo McKern, Vittorio de Sica, Clive
Revill, Paul Rogers

'A splendidly decorated curate's egg.'—*MFB*

AAN: Alex North

Shoeshine**

Italy 1946 90m bw
Paolo W. Tamburella
original title: *Sciuscià*

In Nazi-occupied Rome two shoeshine boys
become involved in black marketeering, with
tragic consequences.
Not especially rewarding to watch now, this was
a key film in the development of Italian neo-
realism.

w Cesare Zavattini, Sergio Amidei, Adolfe
Franci, C. G. Viola *d* Vittorio de Sica
ph Anchise Brizzi, Elio Paccara

Franco Interlenghi, Rinaldo Smordoni

AAN: script

Shoot the Pianist*

France 1960 80m bw Dyaliscope
Films de la Pléiade (Pierre Braunberger)
original title: *Tirez sur le Pianiste*

A bar-room piano player becomes involved with
gangsters and his girl friend is killed.
Fair copy of an American *film noir*, not
especially interesting except for its sharp
observation.

w Marcel Moussy, François Truffaut,
novel Down There by David Goodis
d François Truffaut *ph* Raoul Coutard *m* Jean
Constantin, Georges Deleru

Charles Aznavour, Nicole Berger, Marie
Dubois, Michèle Mercier, Albert Rémy

'Pictorially it is magnificent, revealing
Truffaut's brilliant control over his images;
emotionally, it is all a little jejeune.'—*John
Gillett, MFB*

The Shooting

US 1966 82m De Luxe
Santa Clara (Jack Nicholson, Monte Hellman)

An ex-bounty hunter is trailed by a hired killer.
Simplistic semi-professional western which
achieves some power despite poor technical
quality and a deliberately obscure ending.

w Adrien Joyce *d* Monte Hellman *ph* Gregory
Sandor *m* Richard Markowitz

Warren Oates, Will Hutchins, Jack Nicholson,
Millie Perkins

Shooting Stars*
GB 1928 80m (24 fps) bw silent
British Instructional (H. Bruce Woolf)

The wife of a film star puts real bullets in a prop
gun but her lover is killed by mistake.
Late silent drama with comedy touches: its main
interest lies in its behind-the-scenes background
and in the emergence of a new director.

w John Orton, Anthony Asquith *d* Anthony
Asquith, A. V. Bramble

Annette Benson, Brian Aherne, Donald
Calthrop, Wally Patch, Chili Bouchier

The Shootist**
US 1976 100m Technicolor Panavision
Paramount / Frankovich-Self

In 1901, a dying ex-gunfighter arrives in a small
town to set his affairs in order.
Impressive semi-western melodrama, very well
written and acted all round; the kind of solidly
entertaining and thoughtful movie one imagined
they didn't make any more.

w Miles Hood Swarthout, Scott Hale, *novel*
Glendon Swarthout *d* Don Siegel *ph* Bruce
Surtees *m* Elmer Bernstein

John Wayne, Lauren Bacall, James Stewart,
Ron Howard, Bill McKinney, Richard Boone,
John Carradine, Scatman Crothers, Harry
Morgan, Hugh O'Brian, Sheree North

'Just when it seemed that the western was an
endangered species, due for extinction because it
had repeated itself too many times, Wayne and
Siegel have managed to validate it once more.'—
Arthur Knight

Shootout
US 1971 94m Technicolor
Universal (Hal B. Wallis)

After seven years in prison, a bank robber seeks
out his betrayer.
Routine, flatly-handled revenge western.

w Marguerite Roberts, *novel* The Lone Cowboy
by Will James *d* Henry Hathaway *ph* Earl
Rath *m* Dave Grusin

Gregory Peck, Pat Quinn, Robert F. Lyons,
Susan Tyrell, Jeff Corey, James Gregory, Rita
Gam

The Shop around the Corner**
US 1940 97m bw
MGM (Ernst Lubitsch)

In a Budapest shop, the new floorwalker and a
girl who dislikes him find they are pen pals.
Pleasant period romantic comedy which holds
no surprises but is presented with great style.

w Samson Raphaelson, *play* Nikolaus Laszlo
d Ernst Lubitsch *ph* William Daniels *m* Werner
Heymann

James Stewart, Margaret Sullavan, *Frank
Morgan*, Joseph Schildkraut, Sara Haden, *Felix
Bressart*, William Tracy

'It's not pretentious but it's a beautiful job of
picture-making, and the people who did it seem
to have enjoyed doing it just as much as their
audiences will enjoy seeing it.'—*James Shelley
Hamilton*

'An agreeably bittersweet example of light
entertainment.'—*Charles Higham, 1972*

'One of the most beautifully acted and paced
romantic comedies ever made in this country.'—
New Yorker, 1978

† Remade as *In The Good Old Summertime*
(qv).

The Shop at Sly Corner
GB 1946 92m bw
Pennant (George King)
US title: *Code of Scotland Yard*

An antique dealer who is also a fence kills a
blackmailer in order to shield his daughter.
Competent but stagey version of a West End
success, giving full rein to a bravura star
performance.

w Katherine Strueby, *play* Edward Percy
d George King

Oscar Homolka, Muriel Pavlow, Derek Farr,
Manning Whiley, Kenneth Griffith, Kathleen
Harrison, Garry Marsh, Irene Handl

The Shop on Main Street*
Czechoslovakia 1965 128m bw
Ceskoslovensky Film
original title: *Obchod na Korze*; aka: *The Shop
on the High Street*

During the German invasion of Czechoslovakia,
a well-meaning carpenter tries to shield an old
Jewish lady, but his own rough treatment kills
her.
A rather obvious sentimental fable, developed at
too great length, but with bravura acting.

w Ladislav Grosman, Jan Kadar, Einar Klos
d Jan Kadar, Einar Klos *ph* Vladimir Novotny
m Zdenek Liska

Ida Kaminska, Jozef Kroner, Hana Slivkova,
Martin Holly

AAN: Ida Kaminska

Shopworn Angel*
US 1928   90m approx   bw   part-talkie
Paramount (Louis D. Lighton)

A showgirl meets a naïve young soldier off to war
and forsakes her man about town.
Hard-boiled, soft-centred romantic drama
remade as below and later as *That Kind of
Woman* (qv).

w Howard Estabrook, Albert Shelby Le Vino,
play Private Pettigrew's Girl by Dana Burnet
d Richard Wallace *ph* Charles Lang

Nancy Carroll, Gary Cooper, Paul Lukas,
Emmett King

Shopworn Angel*
US 1938   85m   bw
MGM (Joseph L. Mankiewicz)

Smooth, close remake of the above.

w Waldo Salt *d* H. C. Potter *ph* Joseph
Ruttenberg *montage* Slavko Vorkapitch

Margaret Sullavan, James Stewart, Walter
Pidgeon, Hattie McDaniel, Sam Levene

Short Cut to Hell
US 1957   89m   bw   Vistavision
Paramount (A. C. Lyles)

A racketeer hires a gunman to commit a double
murder, then doublecrosses him.
Rough and ready remake of *This Gun for Hire*
(qv), less arresting than the original.

w Ted Berkeman, Raphael Blau, W. R. Burnett,
novel A Gun for Sale by Graham Greene
d James Cagney *ph* Haskell Boggs *md* Irvin
Talbot

Robert Ivers, Georgeann Johnson, William
Bishop, Murvyn Vye

A Shot in the Dark*
US 1964   101m   De Luxe   Panavision
UA / Mirisch / Geoffrey (Blake Edwards)

A woman is accused of shooting her lover;
accident-prone Inspector Clouseau investigates.
Further adventures of the oafish, Tatiesque
clodhopper from *The Pink Panther*; mildly
funny for those in the mood for pratfalls.

w Blake Edwards, William Peter Blatty *d* Blake
Edwards *ph* Christopher Challis *m* Henry
Mancini *pd* Michael Stringer

Peter Sellers, Elke Sommer, George Sanders,
Herbert Lom, Tracy Reed, Graham Stark

Shoulder Arms*
US 1918   24m (24 fps)   bw   silent
Charles Chaplin / First National

A soldier in the trenches dreams of winning the
war single-handedly.
A comedy which meant a great deal at the time
of its release but now provides precious little to
laugh at.

wd Charles Chaplin *ph* Rollie Totheroh

Charles Chaplin, Edna Purviance, Sydney
Chaplin, Henry Bergman, Albert Austin

The Shout*
GB 1978   87m   colour
Rank / Recorded Picture (Jeremy Thomas)

A man who may be mad claims that, like the old
aborigine magicians, he can kill by shouting.
Curiously gripping but ultimately pointless fable,
very well done to little purpose.

w Michael Austin, Jerzy Skolimovsky, *story*
Robert Graves *d* Jerzy Skolimovsky *ph* Mike
Molloy *m* Rupert Hine, Anthony Banks,
Michael Rutherford

Alan Bates, Susannah York, John Hurt, Robert
Stephens, Tim Curry

Shout at the Devil*
GB 1976   147m   Technicolor   Panavision
Tonav (Michael Klinger)

In 1913 Zanzibar, a hard-drinking American
and an old Etonian Englishman join forces to
rout a brutal German commissioner who resents
their poaching ivory in his territory.
The main characters are respectively repellent,
effete, and just plain nasty, but the action scenes
are vivid and the production is mainly notable as
an expensive old-fashioned British film made at a
time when there were few British films of any
kind.

w Wilbur Smith, Stanley Price, Alastair Reid,
novel Wilbur Smith *d* Peter Hunt *ph* Mike
Reed *m* Maurice Jarre

Lee Marvin, Roger Moore, Barbara Parkins,
Renè Kolldehoff, Ian Holm, Karl Michael
Vogler, Maurice Denham, Jean Kent, Robert
Lang, Murray Melvin, George Coulouris
  'Elephantine plod through the action
highlights of a best seller.'—*Sight and Sound*

Show Business***
US 1944   92m   bw
RKO (Eddie Cantor)

The careers of four friends in vaudeville.
Lively low-budget period musical which
probably presents the best picture of what old-
time vaudeville was really like; a lot of fun when
the plot doesn't get in the way.

w Joseph Quillan, Dorothy Bennett *d* Edwin L.

Marin ph Robert de Grasse, Vernon L. Walker *md* Constantin Bakaleinikoff *ch Nick Castle*

Eddie Cantor, Joan Davis, George Murphy, Constance Moore, Don Douglas, Nancy Kelly

'Bits of archaic vaudeville which give off a moderately pleasant smell of peanuts and cigar smoke.'—*James Agee*

The Show Goes On
GB 1937 93m bw
ABFD (Basil Dean)

A mill girl becomes a star singer with the help of a dying composer.
An attempt to turn Gracie Fields into a serious performer, this was not much enjoyed by her fans.

w Austin Melford, Anthony Kimmins, E. G. Valentine *d* Basil Dean

Gracie Fields, Owen Nares, Edward Rigby, John Stuart, Horace Hodges, Amy Veness, Cyril Rutchard

Show of Shows**
US 1929 128m Technicolor
Warner (Darryl F. Zanuck)

A big musical show put on by Warner contract artists.
Primitive early talkie, of vital historical interest but mostly photographed from a seat in the stalls.

w/m various *d* John G. Adolfi *ph* Barney McGill

Frank Fay, H. B. Warner, Monte Blue, Lupino Lane, Ben Turpin, Chester Morris, Ted Lewis and his band, Georges Carpentier, Patsy Ruth Miller, Beatrice Lillie, Winnie Lightner, Irene Bordoni, Myrna Loy, Douglas Fairbanks Jnr, John Barrymore, Betty Compson

'Colour photography of the crudest, most garish kind, the resulting impression being that a child of seven has been let loose with a shilling box of paints.'—*James Agate*

Show Them No Mercy*
US 1935 76m bw
TCF (Raymond Griffith)
GB title: *Tainted Money*

Kidnappers are rounded up by G-men.
Lively crime thriller typical of its time.

w Kubec Glasmon, Henry Lehrman *d* George Marshall *ph* Bert Glennon

Rochelle Hudson, Cesar Romero, Bruce Cabot, Edward Norris, Edward Brophy, Warren Hymer

'Direct, surely dramatic, inevitable and full of terror.'—*Otis Ferguson*

Showboat***
US 1936 110m bw
Universal (Carl Laemmle Jnr)

Lives and loves of the personnel on an old-time Mississippi showboat.
Great style and excellent performances mark this version, which still suffers from longueurs in the middle followed by the rapid passage of many years to provide a happy ending.

w Oscar Hammerstein II, from his book for the Broadway musical from Edna Ferber's novel *d* James Whale *ph* John Mescall *m* Jerome Kern *ly* Oscar Hammerstein II

Irene Dunne, Allan Jones, Helen Morgan, Paul Robeson, Charles Winninger, Hattie McDaniel, Donald Cook, Sammy White
† A primitive talkie version of *Showboat*, now lost, was made in 1929.

Showboat**
US 1951 108m Technicolor
MGM (Arthur Freed)

Vigorous remake with good ensemble dancing; otherwise inferior to the 1936 version.

w John Lee Mahin *d* George Sidney *ph* Charles Rosher *md* Conrad Salinger, Adolph Deutsch *ch Robert Alton*

Kathryn Grayson, *Howard Keel*, Ava Gardner, William Warfield, *Joe E. Brown*, Robert Sterling, Marge and Gower Champion, Agnes Moorehead

AAN: Charles Rosher; Conrad Salinger, Adolph Deutsch

Showdown
US 1972 99m Technicolor Todd-AO 35
Universal (George Seaton)

A sheriff finds that his old friend is leader of an outlaw gang.
Routine star western adequately done.

w Theodore Taylor *d* George Seaton *ph* Ernest Laszlo *m* David Shire

Rock Hudson, Dean Martin, Susan Clark, Donald Moffat, Don McLiam

The Shrike
US 1955 88m bw
U-I (Aaron Rosenberg)

A brilliant theatre man has a nervous breakdown because his wife is a vindictive harpy.
Theatrical two-hander, aridly filmed, of little interest except to show that both stars are capable of sustained emotional acting.

w Ketti Frings, *play* Joseph Kramm *d* Jose

Ferrer *ph* William Daniels *m* Frank Skinner
titles Saul Bass

Jose Ferrer, June Allyson, Joy Page, Jacqueline
de Wit, Kendall Clark

'The film is unvaryingly paced, the result, one
feels, of a respectable but far from invigorating
honesty of purpose.'—*MFB*

The Shuttered Room
GB 1967   110m   Technicolor
Warner / Troy–Schenck (Philip Hazelton)

Returning to her childhood home on an island off
the New England coast, a girl and her husband
are subjected to terror and violence.
Stretched out suspenser which looks good and is
carefully made but fails in its effort to combine
the menace of teenage yobboes with that of the
monster lurking upstairs.

w D. B. Ledrov, Nathaniel Tanchuck, *story* H.
P. Lovecraft, August Derleth *d David Greene
ph Ken Hodges m* Basil Kirchin

Gig Young, Carol Lynley, Flora Robson, Oliver
Reed, William Devlin

Une Si Jolie Petite Plage*
France 1948   91m   bw
CICC (Emile Darbon)
aka: *Such a Pretty Little Beach*

A murderer returns to the small seaside town
where he spent his childhood, befriends the maid
at the hotel, and after a few days kills himself.
A melancholy anecdote which works both as a
character study and pictorially.

w Jacques Sigurd *d* Yves Allégret *ph* Henri
Alekan *m* Maurice Thiriet

Gérard Philipe, Jean Servais, *Madeleine
Robinson*, Jane Marken, Carette

'Shows fine craftsmanship and is beautifully
sensitive to place and atmosphere.'—*Gavin
Lambert, MFB*

Side Street
US 1950   83m   bw
MGM (Sam Zimbalist)

A petty thief finds himself involved with big-time
crooks.
Well-made but rather boring crime melodrama
with an excellent car chase finale.

w Sidney Boehm *d* Anthony Mann *ph* Joseph
Ruttenberg *m* Lennie Hayton

Farley Granger, Cathy O'Donnell, James Craig,
Paul Kelly, Jean Hagen, Edmon Ryan, Paul
Harvey

Sidewalks of New York*
US 1931   73m   bw
MGM (Lawrence Weingarten)

The playboy owner of some tenement
apartments falls in love with the daughter of one
of the tenants.
Interesting rather than wholly successful early
sound comedy which marked the beginning of
Keaton's decline; he was not allowed full control
and the comedy scenes are thinly spaced.

w George Landy, Paul Gerard Smith, Eric
Hatch, Robert E. Hopkins *d* Jules White, Zion
Myers *ph* Leonard Smith

Buster Keaton, Anita Page, Cliff Edwards,
Frank Rowan

The Siege of Pinchgut
GB 1959   104m   bw
Ealing (Eric Williams)

Escaped convicts take over a small island in
Sydney harbour.
Disappointingly obvious location melodrama
with routine excitements.

w Harry Watt, Jon Cleary *d* Harry Watt
ph Gordon Dines *m* Kenneth V. Jones

Aldo Ray, Heather Sears, Neil McCallum,
Victor Maddern, Carlo Justini

The Siege at Red River
US 1954   86m   Technicolor
TCF / Panoramic (Leonard Goldstein)

During the American Civil War a Confederate
agent behind northern lines defeats a treacherous
helper and escapes to the south.
Modest, generally watchable, and quite
forgettable western.
w Sidney Boehm *d* Rudolph Maté *ph* Edward
Cronjager *m* Lionel Newman

Van Johnson, Joanne Dru, Richard Boone,
Milburn Stone, Jeff Morrow, Craig Hill

The Siege of Sidney Street*
GB 1960   92m   bw   Dyaliscope
Midcentury (Robert S. Baker, Monty Berman)

An account of the anarchists who infiltrated
London in 1912.
Detailed but not dramatically absorbing
historical reconstruction with unsatisfactory
fictional trimmings.

w Jimmy Sangster, Alexander Baron
d/ph Robert S. Baker, Monty Berman
m Stanley Black

Peter Wyngarde, Donald Sinden, Nicole Berger,
Kieron Moore, Leonard Sachs, Tutte Lemkow

The Siege of the Saxons
GB 1963   85m   Technicolor
Columbia / Ameran (Jud Kinberg)

When King Arthur is ill, the Saxons plot his overthrow but are foiled by a handsome outlaw. Comic strip adventure with action highlights borrowed from older and better films.

w John Kohn, Jud Kinberg *d* Nathan Juran *ph* Wilkie Cooper, Jack Willis

Ronald Lewis, Janette Scott, Ronald Howard, Mark Dignam, John Laurie, Richard Clarke, Jerome Willis

The Sign of the Cross***
US 1932   123m   bw
Paramount (Cecil B. de Mille)

In the days of Nero, a Roman officer is converted to Christianity.
A heavily theatrical play becomes one of de Mille's most impressive films, the genuine horror of the arena mingling with the debauched humour of the court. A wartime prologue added in 1943 prolongs the film without improving it.

w Waldemar Young, Sidney Buchman, *play* Wilson Barrett *d* Cecil B. de Mille *ph* Karl Struss

Fredric March, Elissa Landi, *Charles Laughton, Claudette Colbert,* Ian Keith, Harry Beresford, Arthur Hohl, Nat Pendleton

'A beautiful film to watch . . . a triumph of popular art.'—*Charles Higham, 1972*

'However contemptible one may find de Mille's moralizing, it is impossible not to be impressed by *The Sign of the Cross*.'—*John Baxter, 1968*

'De Mille's bang-them-on-the-head-with-wild-orgies-and-imperilled-virginity style is at its ripest.'—*New Yorker, 1976*

'Preposterous, but the laughter dies on the lips.'—*NFT, 1974*

'A picture which will proudly lead all the entertainment the screen has ever seen.'—*publicity*

AAN: Karl Struss

The Sign of the Pagan
US 1954   92m   Technicolor
   Cinemascope
U-I (Albert J. Cohen)

Attila the Hun is defeated by the Romans.
Historic horse opera, rather cheaply done.

w Oscar Brodney, Barre Lyndon *d* Douglas Sirk *ph* Russell Metty *m* Frank Skinner, Hans Salter

Jeff Chandler, Jack Palance, Rita Gam,

Ludmilla Tcherina, Jeff Morrow, George Dolenz, Eduard Franz, Alexander Scourby

The Sign of the Ram
US 1948   84m   bw
Columbia

A selfish invalid interferes in her family's affairs. Stultifying melodrama in the wake of *Guest in the House*, devised for the unfortunate Miss Peters who was crippled after an accident. Poor production values don't help.

w Charles Bennett *d* John Sturges *ph* Burnett Guffey

Susan Peters, Alexander Knox, Peggy Ann Garner, May Whitty

Signpost to Murder
US 1967   74m   bw   Panavision
MGM / Martin (Lawrence Weingarten)

A convicted murderer escapes after ten years and a lonely wife promises to help him.
Tricksy mystery set in a never-never English village.

w Sally Benson, *play* Monte Doyle *d* George Englund *ph* Paul C. Vogel *m* Lyn Murray

Joanne Woodward, Stuart Whitman, Edward Mulhare, Alan Napier, Murray Matheson

The Silence*
Sweden 1963   96m   bw
Svensk Filmindustri
original title: *Tystnaden*

Of two women in a large hotel in a foreign city where the military are dominant, one masturbates while the other sleeps with a barman.
Bergman may know what this was all about, but it's a certainty that no one else did: so everyone thought it must be very clever and went to see it. Superficially, as usual, it is careful and fascinating.

wd Ingmar Bergman *ph* Sven Nykvist *m* from Bach

Ingrid Thulin, Gunnel Lindblom

Le Silence est d'Or*
France 1947   99m   bw
Pathé / RKO Radio

In 1906 a comedian becomes a film producer and as a result falls into an affair with a young girl.
Somehow not an important film, but quite a delightful one, especially for its local colour and for the combination of Clair and Chevalier up to their old tricks.

wd René Clair ph Armand Thirard *m* Georges Van Parys

Maurice Chevalier, François Périer, Marcelle Derrien

The Silencers*
US 1966   103m   Technicolor
Columbia / Irving Allen (Jim Schmerer)

Adventures of a sexy secret agent.
Or, James Bond sent up rotten. Plenty of fun along the way, with in-jokes and characters like Lovey Kravezit, but the plot could have done with more attention, and the sequels (*Murderers Row, The Ambushers, Wrecking Crew*) were uncontrolled disaster areas.

w Oscar Saul, *novel* Donald Hamilton *d* Phil Karlson *ph* Burnett Guffey *m* Elmer Bernstein

Dean Martin, Stella Stevens, Victor Buono, Daliah Lavi, Cyd Charisse, Robert Webber, James Gregory, Nancy Kovack

Silent Dust*
GB 1947   82m   bw
ABP / Independent Sovereign

A baronet builds a memorial to his son who has apparently been killed in action, but the son turns up and proves to be an absolute bounder.
Effective stage melodrama, quite neatly filmed.

w Michael Pertwee, *play* The Paragon by Roland and Michael Pertwee *d* Lance Comfort *ph* Wilkie Cooper *m* Georges Auric

Sally Gray, Derek Farr, Stephen Murray, Nigel Patrick, Seymour Hicks

The Silent Enemy
GB 1958   112m   bw
Romulus (Bertram Ostrer)

The World War II exploits of a naval frogman in the Mediterranean.
Stereotyped naval underwater adventures, adequately presented.

wd William Fairchild *ph* Egil Woxholt, Otto Heller *m* William Alwyn

Laurence Harvey, John Clements, Michael Craig, Dawn Addams, Sidney James, Alec McCowen, Nigel Stock

The Silent Flute
US 1978   95m   colour
Volare (Richard St Johns)

In a martial arts tournament, a hero is chosen to challenge the wizard Zetan.
Curiously mystical adventure allegory with an unhelpful title. Not too bad for those in the mood.

w Stirling Silliphant, Stanley Mann *d* Richard Moore *ph* Ronnie Taylor *m* Bruce Smeaton

Jeff Cooper, David Carradine, Roddy McDowall, Christopher Lee, Eli Wallach

Silent Movie*
US 1976   87m   De Luxe
TCF (Michael Hertzberg)

An alcoholic producer gets the idea that a silent movie would be a great novelty, and tries to get stars to take part.
Fairly lively spoof with the talents concerned in variable form. The shortage of laughter made it a hit in the seventies, but at no time does it approach the Keaton or Laurel and Hardy level.

w Mel Brooks, Ron Clark, Rudy de Luca, Barry Levinson *d* Mel Brooks *ph* Paul Lohmann *m* John Morris

Mel Brooks, Marty Feldman, Dom De Luise, Bernardette Peters, Sid Caesar, Harold Gould, Fritz Feld, Harry Ritz, Henny Youngman *guest stars* Anne Bancroft, Paul Newman, Burt Reynolds, James Caan, Liza Minnelli, Marcel Marceau

The Silent Partner
US 1978   105m   colour
Carolco (Garth H. Drabinsky)

A bank teller foils an attempted raid and steals the money himself.
A suspense thriller of a familiar kind; it might have been entertaining but elects instead to be unpleasant.

w Curtis Hanson, *novel* Think of a Number by Anders Bodelson *d* Daryl Duke *ph* Stephen Katz *m* Oscar Peterson

Christopher Plummer, Elliott Gould, Susannah York, Celine Lomez, Michael Kirby

Silent Running*
US 1971   90m   Technicolor
Universal / Michel Gruskoff / Douglas Trumbull

Members of a space station crew in 2001 are space gardening to replenish nuclear-devasted earth.
Sombre futuristic fantasy, well made but slow and muddled in development.

w Deric Washburn, Mike Cimino, Steve Bocho *d* Douglas Trumbull *ph* Charles F. Wheeler *m* Peter Schickele

Bruce Dern, Cliff Potts, Ron Rifkin, Jesse Vint

Silk Stockings*
US 1957 116m Metrocolor
  Cinemascope
MGM (Arthur Freed)

A Russian composer in Paris agrees to write
music for a Hollywood film; a lady commissar is
sent to get him back.
Musical rewrite of *Ninotchka* via a Broadway
show; good moments but generally very
stretched.

w Leonard Gershe, Leonard Spiegelgass, *play*
George S. Kaufman, Leueen McGrath, Abe
Burrows, *original play* Melchior Lengyel
d Rouben Mamoulian *ph* Robert Bronner
m/ly Cole Porter *md* André Previn

Fred Astaire, Cyd Charisse, Peter Lorre, Janis
Paige, George Tobias, Jules Munshin, Joseph
Buloff

The Silken Affair
GB 1956 96m bw
Dragon (Fred Feldkamp)

An accountant decides to live it up, and finds
himself on trial for manipulating the firm's
books.
Unsatisfactory mix of comedy and fantasy, with
a dim plot and virtually no comic ideas.

w Robert Lewis Taylor *d* Roy Kellino
ph Gilbert Taylor *m* Peggy Stuart

David Niven, Genevieve Page, Wilfrid Hyde
White, Ronald Squire, Beatrice Straight,
Howard Marion Crawford, Dorothy Alison

Silken Skin*
France 1964 118m bw
Films du Carrosse / SEDIF
original title: *La Peau Douce*

A middle-aged married man leaves his wife for
an attractive young girl, but the latter leaves him
and his wife shoots him.
Carefully balanced mixture of comedy and
melodrama which rings almost every possible
change on the theme of adultery and does so with
wit.

w François Truffaut, Jean-Louis Richard
d François Truffaut *ph* Raoul Coutard
m Georges Delerue

Jean Desailly, Françoise Dorléac, Nelly
Benedetti

Silver Bears
GB 1977 113m Technicolor
EMI / Raleigh (Martin Schute)

A Las Vegas money man invests money in
various European outlets and makes a killing.

Extraordinarily complex financial jape which
tries the patience of all but financiers.

w Peter Stone, *novel* Paul Erdman *d* Ivan
Passer *ph* Anthony Richmond *m* Claude
Bolling

Michael Caine, Louis Jourdan, Cybill Shepherd,
Stephane Audran, David Warner, Tom
Smothers, Martin Balsam, Charles Gray

The Silver Chalice
US 1955 142m Warnercolor
  Cinemascope
Warner (Victor Saville)

Adventures of a slave freed by Luke the apostle
to fashion a chalice to hold the cup used at the
Last Supper.
Po-faced biblical hokum, slower and deadlier
than most, with howlingly bad casting and
direction. On reflection, interesting things are
being attempted with limbo set design, but in this
sea of boredom the attempt only raises an
eyebrow.

w Lesser Samuels, *novel* Thomas B. Costain
d Victor Saville *ph* William V. Skall *m* Franz
Waxman *pd* Rolf Gerard

Paul Newman, Pier Angeli, Jack Palance,
Virginia Mayo, Walter Hampden, Joseph
Wiseman, Alexander Scourby, Lorne Greene,
Michael Pate, E. G. Marshall

AAN: William V. Skall; Franz Waxman

The Silver Fleet*
GB 1943 87m bw
GFD / Archers (Michael Powell, Emeric
  Pressburger, Ralph Richardson)

In occupied Holland, a shipping magnate
destroys his new U-boat and himself and his
Nazi mentors with it. Slow-starting, rather stilted
melodrama which when it gets into its stride
provides good acting and gripping propaganda.

wd Vernon Sewell, Gordon Wellesley

Ralph Richardson, Esmond Knight, Googie
Withers, Beresford Egan, Frederick Burtwell,
Kathleen Byron

Silver Queen
US 1942 80m bw
UA / Harry Sherman

A chivalrous western gambler rescues a girl from
the wiles of a villain.
Standard romantic melodrama mainly set in
saloons.

w Bernard Schubert, Cecile Kramer *d* Lloyd
Bacon *ph* Russell Harlan *m* Victor Young

George Brent, Priscilla Lane, Bruce Cabot,

Lynne Overman, Eugene Pallette, Janet Beecher,
Guinn Williams, Roy Barcroft

AAN: Victor Young

Silver Streak*

US 1976   113m   De Luxe
TCF / Martin Ransohoff, Frank Yablans

On a trans-continental train, a young publisher
discovers a murder and is at the mercy of the
culprits.
Rather like an update of a Bob Hope comedy-
thriller with a whiff of sex, this amiable spoof
goes on too long, brings in a second comic too
late, and ends with fashionable but irrelevant
violence.

w Colin Higgins d Arthur Hiller ph David M.
Walsh m Henry Mancini pd Alfred Sweeney

Gene Wilder, Jill Clayburgh, Richard Pryor,
Patrick McGoohan, Ned Beatty, Clifton James,
Ray Walston, Richard Kiel

 'Nineteen-seventies performers are trapped in
this fake thirties mystery comedy, which is so
inept you can't even get angry.'—New Yorker

Simba

GB 1955   99m   Eastmancolor
GFD / Group Film (Peter de Sarigny)

An English farmer in Kenya fights the Mau Mau.
Savagely topical melodrama which tends to
cheapen a tragic situation.

w John Baines d Brian Desmond Hurst
ph Geoffrey Unsworth m Francis Chagrin

Dirk Bogarde, Donald Sinden, Virginia
McKenna, Basil Sydney, Marie Ney, Joseph
Tomelty, Earl Cameron, Orlando Martins

Simon and Laura*

GB 1955   91m   Technicolor   Vistavision
GFD / Group Films (Teddy Baird)

The actors who play husband and wife in a TV
series are married in reality and hate each other,
a fact that shows in the live Christmas episode.
Adequate film of a reasonably sophisticated
West End comedy; good lines and
performances.

w Peter Blackmore, play Alan Melville d Muriel
Box ph Ernest Steward m Benjamin Frankel

Peter Finch, Kay Kendall, Ian Carmichael, Alan
Wheatley, Richard Wattis, Muriel Pavlow,
Maurice Denham, Hubert Gregg

The Sin of Madelon Claudet

US 1931   74m   bw
MGM
GB title: The Lullaby

A mother is separated from her illegitimate baby.
Sob stuff for a rising star: hilarious now.

w Charles MacArthur, play Edgar Selwyn
d Edgar Selwyn

Helen Hayes, Robert Young, Neil Hamilton,
Lewis Stone, Marie Prevost, Cliff Edwards, Jean
Hersholt, Karen Morley

AA: Helen Hayes

Sinbad and the Eye of the Tiger

GB 1977   113m   Metrocolor
Columbia / Andor (Charles H. Schneer, Ray
  Harryhausen)

Sinbad frees a city from a wicked woman's spell.
Lumpish sequel to a sequel: even the animated
monsters raise a yawn this time.

w Beverly Cross d Sam Wanamaker ph Ted
Moore m Roy Budd sp Ray Harryhausen

Patrick Wayne, Taryn Power, Jane Seymour,
Margaret Whiting, Patrick Troughton

Sinbad the Sailor

US 1947   117m   Technicolor
RKO (Stephen Ames)

Sinbad sets off on his eighth voyage to find the
lost treasure of Alexander.
Well-staged but humourless Arabian Nights
swashbuckler.

w John Twist d Richard Wallace ph George
Barnes m Roy Webb

Douglas Fairbanks Jnr, Walter Slezak, Maureen
O'Hara, Anthony Quinn, George Tobias, Jane
Greer, Mike Mazurki, Sheldon Leonard

Since You Went Away***

US 1944   172m   bw
David O. Selznick

When hubby is away at the war, his wife and
family adopt stiff upper lips.
Elaborate flagwaving investigation of the well-
heeled American home front in World War II,
with everyone brimming with goodwill and not a
dry eye in the place. Absolutely superbly done, if
it must be done at all, and a symposium of
Hollywood values and techniques of the time.

w David O. Selznick, book Margaret Buell
Wilder d John Cromwell ph Stanley Cortez,
Lee Garmes m Max Steiner pd William L.
Pereira

Claudette Colbert, Joseph Cotten, Jennifer
Jones, Shirley Temple, Agnes Moorehead,
Monty Woolley, Lionel Barrymore, Guy
Madison, Robert Walker, Hattie McDaniel,
Craig Stevens, Keenan Wynn, Albert
Basserman, Nazimova, Lloyd Corrigan

'A deft, valid blend of showmanship, humour, and yard-wide Americanism.'—*James Agee*

'The whole litany of that middle-class synthetic emotionalism, meticulously annotated over a decade by tough and sentimental experts, has been procured for us.'—*Richard Winnington*

'A rather large dose of choking sentiment.'—*Bosley Crowther*

'It is not an average US reality. It is an average US dream.'—*Time*

AA: Max Steiner

AAN: best picture; Stanley Cortez; Claudette Colbert; Jennifer Jones; Monty Woolley

Sincerely Yours

US 1955 115m Warnercolor
Warner (Henry Blanke)

A concert pianist goes deaf and retires to his penthouse, but with the help of binoculars lipreads the humble folk below. Helping them anonymously gives him courage to have an operation.

Absurd updating for a modern non-star of a creaky old George Arliss vehicle *The Man Who Played God*.

w Irving Wallace *d* Gordon Douglas *ph* William H. Clothier *m adviser* George Liberace

Liberace, Joanne Dru, Dorothy Malone, Alex Nicol, William Demarest

Sinful Davey

GB 1968 95m Eastmancolor
Panavision
UA / Mirisch / Webb (William N. Graf)

In 1821 a young Scotsman determines to become a criminal like his father, but falls in love. Thin imitation of *Tom Jones*, highly implausible but played with some zest.

w James R. Webb, based on the autobiography of David Haggart *d* John Huston *ph* Ted Scaife, Freddie Young *m* Ken Thorne *pd* Stephen Grimes

John Hurt, Pamela Franklin, Nigel Davenport, Ronald Fraser, Robert Morley, Maxine Audley, Noel Purcell

Sing As We Go***

GB 1934 80m bw
ATP (Basil Dean)

An unemployed millgirl gets various holiday jobs in Blackpool.

A splendid, pawky star vehicle which is also the best picture we have of industrial Lancashire in the thirties. Great fun.

w J. B. Priestley, Gordon Wellesley d Basil Dean

Gracie Fields, John Loder, Frank Pettingell, Dorothy Hyson, Stanley Holloway

'We have an industrial north that is bigger than Gracie Fields running around a Blackpool fun fair.'—*C. A. Lejeune*

Sing Baby Sing*

US 1936 87m bw
TCF (Darryl F. Zanuck)

A drunken Shakespearian actor sets his sights on a night club singer.

Reasonably hilarious take-off on the John Barrymore-Elaine Barrie affair, with several Fox contractees fooling to the top of their bent with the help of good musical numbers.

w Milton Sperling, Jack Yellen, Harry Tugend *d* Sidney Lanfield *ph* Peverell Marley *songs* various *md* Louis Silvers

Alice Faye, Adolphe Menjou, Gregory Ratoff, Patsy Kelly, Ted Healy, The Ritz Brothers, Montagu Love, Dixie Dunbar

AAN: song 'When Did You Leave Heaven?' (*ly* Walter Bullock, *m* Richard Whiting)

Sing You Sinners**

US 1938 88m bw
Paramount (Wesley Ruggles)

The adventures of a happy-go-lucky family and their racehorse.

Cheerful family musical with amiable cast and good tunes.

w Claude Binyon *d* Wesley Ruggles *ph* Karl Struss *md* Boris Morros

Bing Crosby, Donald O'Connor, Fred MacMurray, Elizabeth Patterson, Ellen Drew, John Gallaudet

The Singer Not the Song

GB 1960 132m colour Cinemascope
Rank (Roy Baker)

In an isolated Mexican town a priest defies an outlaw who oddly respects him.

Lengthy character drama with little action or humour but a great deal of moody introspection and a suggestion of homosexuality.

w Nigel Balchin, *novel* Audrey Erskine Lindop *d* Roy Baker *ph* Otto Heller *m* Philip Green

John Mills, Dirk Bogarde, Mylene Demongeot, John Bentley, Laurence Naismith, Eric Pohlmann

'A rewarding film, as startling as a muffled scream from the subconscious.'—*Peter John Dyer*

The Singing Fool**
US 1928   110m   bw
Warner

A successful singer goes on the skids when his
small son dies.
Early talkie musical, a sensation because of its
star's personality, but a pretty maudlin piece of
drama.

w C. Graham Baker, *play* Leslie S. Barrows
d Lloyd Bacon ph Byron Haskin *songs* Lew
Brown, Ray Henderson, B. G. De Sylva

Al Jolson, Davey Lee, Betty Bronson, Josephine
Dunn, Arthur Housman

'Obvious and tedious as the climax is, when
the black-faced comedian stands before the
camera and sings "Sonny Boy" you know the
man is greater, somehow, than the situation, the
story or the movie.'—*Pare Lorentz*

Singin' in the Rain****
US 1952   102m   Technicolor
MGM (Arthur Freed)

When talkies are invented, the reputation of one
female star shrivels while another grows.
Brilliant comic musical, the best picture by far of
Hollywood in transition, with the catchiest tunes,
the liveliest choreography, the most engaging
performances and the most hilarious jokes of
any musical.

w *Adolph Green, Betty Comden* d/*ch* Gene
Kelly, Stanley Donen ph Harold Rosson
m Nacio Herb Brown md Lennie Hayton
ly Arthur Freed

*Gene Kelly, Donald O'Connor, Debbie
Reynolds, Millard Mitchell, Jean Hagen,* Rita
Moreno, Cyd Charisse, *Douglas Fowley*

'Perhaps the most enjoyable of all movie
musicals.'—*New Yorker, 1975*

AAN: Lennie Hayton; Jean Hagen

The Singing Kid
US 1936   83m   bw
Warner (Robert Lord)

A cocky night club singer takes a talented
juvenile under his wing.
Routine star vehicle most notable for a string of
standards sung by him right after the credits.

w Warren Duff, Pat C. Flick d William
Keighley ph George Barnes md Leo F.
Forbstein *songs* E. Y. Harburg, Harold Arlen

Al Jolson, Sybil Jason, Allen Jenkins, Lyle
Talbot, Edward Everett Horton, Beverly
Roberts, Claire Dodd

The Singing Nun
US 1966   98m   Metrocolor   Panavision
MGM (Jon Beck)

Adventures of a nun who takes her music to the
outside world.
Icky musical drama based on a true character.

w Sally Benson, John Furia d Henry Koster
ph Milton Krasner md Harry Sukman
songs Soeur Sourire

Debbie Reynolds, Greer Garson, Ricardo
Montalban, Agnes Moorehead, Chad Everett,
Katharine Ross, Ed Sullivan, Juanita Moore

AAN: Harry Sukman

Sink the Bismarck**
GB 1960   97m   bw   Cinemascope
TCF / John Brabourne

In 1941, Britain's director of naval operations
arranges the trapping and sinking of Germany's
greatest battleship.
Tight little personal drama which would have
been better on a standard screen, as its ships are
plainly models and much of the footage
stretched-out newsreel. Nevertheless, a good
example of the stiff-upper-lip school.

w Edmund H. North d Lewis Gilbert
ph Christopher Challis m Clifton Parker
md Muir Mathieson

Kenneth More, Dana Wynter, Karel Stepanek,
Carl Mohner, Laurence Naismith, Geoffrey
Keen, Michael Hordern, Maurice Denham,
Esmond Knight

The Sins of Rachel Cade
US 1960   123m   Technicolor
Warner (Henry Blanke)

An American missionary nurse in the Belgian
Congo falls in love with a crashed flier and has a
baby.
Romantic melodrama which starts like *The
Nun's Story* and ends like Peg's Paper;
competent on its level.

w Edward Anhalt, *novel* Charles Mercer
d Gordon Douglas ph Peverell Marley m Max
Steiner

Angie Dickinson, Roger Moore, Peter Finch,
Errol John, Woody Strode, Juano Hernandez,
Frederick O'Neal, Mary Wickes

Siren of Atlantis see L'Atlantide

Sirocco
US 1951   98m   bw
Columbia / Santana (Robert Lord)

In 1925 Damascus, an American runs guns for
the rebels.

Tedious romantic drama in the *Casablanca* vein but with none of the magic.

w A. I. Bezzerides, Hans Jacoby, *novel* Coup de Grâce by Joseph Kessel *d* Curtis Bernhardt *ph* Burnett Guffey *m* George Antheil

Humphrey Bogart, Marta Toren, Lee J. Cobb, Everett Sloane, Gerald Mohr, Zero Mostel, Onslow Stevens

Sister Kenny*
US 1946 116m bw
RKO

The career of a nurse who instigated treatment for polio.
Standard, well-done biopic.

w Dudley Nichols, Alexander Knox, Mary McCarthy *d* Dudley Nichols *ph* George Barnes

Rosalind Russell, Alexander Knox, Dean Jagger, Philip Merivale, Beulah Bondi, Dorothy Peterson

AAN: Rosalind Russell

The Sisters*
US 1938 98m bw
Warner (Hal B. Wallis)

The marriages of three sisters from a small Montana town.
Well-made potboiler for women; it even brings in the San Francisco earthquake, and the star teaming is piquant to say the least.

w Milton Krims, *novel* Myron Brinig *d* Anatole Litvak *ph* Tony Gaudio *m* Max Steiner

Bette Davis, Errol Flynn, Anita Louise, Ian Hunter, Donald Crisp, Beulah Bondi, Jane Bryan, Alan Hale, Dick Foran, Henry Travers, Patric Knowles, Lee Patrick, Harry Davenport

Sitting Pretty*
US 1933 85m bw
Paramount (Charles R. Rogers)

Two songwriters strike it rich in Hollywood.
Cheerful comedy musical, interesting for its backgrounds.

w Jack McGowan, S. J. Perelman, Lou Breslow *d* Harry Joe Brown *ph* Milton Krasner *songs* Mack Gordon, Harry Revel

Jack Oakie, Jack Haley, Ginger Rogers, Thelma Todd, Gregory Ratoff, Lew Cody, Harry Revel, Mack Gordon

Sitting Pretty*
US 1948 84m bw
TCF (Samuel G. Engel)

A young couple acquire a most unusual male baby sitter, a self-styled genius who sets the neighbourhood on its ears by writing a novel about it.
Out of the blue, a very funny comedy which entrenched Clifton Webb as one of Hollywood's great characters and led to two sequels, *Mr Belvedere Goes to College* and *Mr Belvedere Rings the Bell* (qv).

w F. Hugh Herbert, *novel* Belvedere by Gwen Davenport *d* Walter Lang *ph* Norbert Brodine *m* Alfred Newman

Clifton Webb, Robert Young, Maureen O'Hara, *Richard Haydn*, Louise Allbritton, Ed Begley, Randy Stuart, Larry Olsen

AAN: Clifton Webb

Sitting Target
GB 1972 92m Metrocolor
MGM (Barry Kulick)

A violent killer escapes from jail and seeks revenge on those who 'shopped' him.
Rough, tough action thriller; passes the time for hardened addicts.

w Alexander Jacobs, *novel* Lawrence Henderson *d* Douglas Hickox *ph* Ted Scaife *m* Stanley Myers *pd* Jonathan Barry

Oliver Reed, Jill St John, Edward Woodward, Frank Finlay, Ian McShane, Freddie Jones, Robert Beatty

Situation Hopeless But Not Serious
US 1965 97m bw
Paramount / Castle (Gottfried Reinhardt)

In 1944, two American fliers are captured by a friendly, lonely mild-mannered German, who keeps them in his cellar and hasn't the heart to tell them when the war is over . . .
Flat little comedy which leaves a talented cast no room for manoeuvre.

w Silvia Reinhardt, *novel* The Hiding Place by Robert Shaw *d* Gottfried Reinhardt *ph* Kurt Hasse *m* Harold Byrne

Alec Guinness, Robert Redford, Mike Connors, Anita Hoefer

Six Bridges to Cross
US 1955 96m bw
U-I (Aaron Rosenberg)

The criminal career of a young hoodlum in Boston in the thirties.
Public Enemy reprise with a sentimental veneer, smooth but uninteresting.

w Sidney Boehm, *novel* They Stole Two and a Half Million Dollars and Got Away with It by Joseph F. Dineen *d* Joseph Pevney *ph* William Daniels *m* Joseph Gershenson

Tony Curtis, George Nader, Julie Adams, Jay C. Flippen, Sal Mineo, Jan Merlin

Six Day Bike Rider

US 1934   69m   bw
Warner (Sam Bischoff)

One of life's failures impresses his girl by entering a cycling contest.
One of the star's stronger comedy vehicles.

w Earl Baldwin d Lloyd Bacon ph Warren Lynch

Joe E. Brown, Maxine Doyle, Frank McHugh, Gordon Westcott

Six of a Kind *

US 1934   69m   bw
Paramount

Comic adventures of six people driving across America.
Minor comedy which doesn't come off as a whole but adequately displays the talents of its stars.

w Walter de Leon, Harry Ruskin d Leo McCarey ph Henry Sharp m Ralph Rainger

Charles Ruggles, Mary Boland, W. C. Fields, Alison Skipworth, George Burns, Gracie Allen
'Another pleasing film . . . it reminds the Englishman of *Three Men in a Boat*.'—*E. V. Lucas, Punch*

633 Squadron *

GB 1964   94m   Technicolor   Panavision
UA / Mirisch (Cecil F. Ford)

In 1944 Mosquito aircraft try to collapse a cliff overhanging a munitions factory in a Norwegian fjord.
Standard war heroics with enough noise and disorder to keep most audiences hypnotized.

w James Clavell, Howard Koch, *novel* Frederick E. Smith d Walter Grauman ph Ted Scaife, John Wilcox m Ron Goodwin

Cliff Robertson, George Chakiris, Maria Perschy, Harry Andrews, Donald Houston, Michael Goodliffe

Sixty Glorious Years **

GB 1938   95m   Technicolor
Imperator (Herbert Wilcox)
US title: *Queen of Destiny*

Scenes from the life of Queen Victoria.
A stately pageant apparently composed of material which couldn't be fitted into the previous year's black-and-white success *Victoria the Great*. Fascinating, though the camerawork is not very nimble.

w Robert Vansittart, Miles Malleson, Charles de Grandcourt d Herbert Wilcox ph Frederick A. Young

Anna Neagle, Anton Walbrook, C. Aubrey Smith, Walter Rilla, Charles Carson, Felix Aylmer, Lewis Casson
† The two films were edited together in 1943 to make a new selection called *Queen Victoria*, and in the process the original negatives were accidentally destroyed, so that both films now have to be printed from unattractive dupes.

The Ski Raiders

US 1972   90m   Technicolor   Panavision
Warner (Edward L. Rissien)
aka: *Snow Job*

An alpine ski instructor devises a scheme to rob a bank.
Very medium caper thriller with a breathtaking opening sequence.

w Ken Kolb, Jeffrey Bloom d George Englund ph Gabor Pogany, Willy Bogner m Jacques Loussier

Jean Claude Killy, Cliff Potts, Vittorio de Sica, Daniele Gaubert

Skidoo

US 1968   98m   Technicolor   Panavision
Paramount / Sigma (Otto Preminger)

Active and reformed gangsters get involved with hippies and preach universal love.
Abysmal mishmash with top talent abused; clearly intended as satirical farce, but in fact one of the most woebegone movies ever made.

w Doran William Cannon d Otto Preminger ph Leon Shamroy m Harry Nilsson

Jackie Gleason, Carol Channing, Groucho Marx, Frankie Avalon, Fred Clark, Michael Constantine, Frank Gorshin, John Philip Law, Peter Lawford, Burgess Meredith, George Raft, Cesar Romero, Mickey Rooney
'Unspeakable.'—*Michael Billington, Illustrated London News*

The Skin Game *

US 1971   102m   Technicolor   Panavision
Warner / Cherokee (Harry Keller)

A white and a black con man have near escapes in many a western town.
Amusing comedy western with good pace and a few shafts of wit.

w Peter Stone, Richard Alan Simmons d Paul Bogart ph Fred Koenekamp m David Shire

James Garner, Lou Gossett, Susan Clark, Brenda Sykes, Ed Asner, Andrew Duggan, Henry Jones, Neva Patterson

Skippy*

US 1931   88m   bw

Paramount

The young son of a local health inspector makes friends in the slums.

Standard, blameless family entertainment.

w Joseph L. Mankiewicz, Norman McLeod, comic strip Percy Crosby d Norman Taurog ph Karl Struss

Jackie Cooper, Robert Coogan, Mitzi Green, Jackie Searl, Willard Robertson

AA: Norman Taurog

AAN: best picture; script; Jackie Cooper

Skirts Ahoy

US 1952   105m   Technicolor

MGM (Joe Pasternak)

Three girls join the navy and get their men.

Musical recruiting poster, quite devoid of interest.

w Isobel Lennart d Sidney Lanfield ph William Mellor m Harry Warren ly Ralph Blane ch Nick Castle

Esther Williams, Vivian Blaine, Joan Evans, Barry Sullivan, Keefe Brasselle, Dean Miller, Debbie Reynolds, Bobby Van, Billy Eckstine

The Skull

GB 1965   83m   Techniscope

Paramount / Amicus (Milton Subotsky)

The skull of the Marquis de Sade haunts two antiquarians.

Clodhopping horror with very visible wires.

w Milton Subotsky, story Robert Bloch d Freddie Francis ph John Wilcox m Elisabeth Lutyens

Peter Cushing, Christopher Lee, Patrick Wymark, Jill Bennett, Nigel Green, Michael Gough, George Coulouris

Skullduggery

US 1969   105m   Technicolor   Panavision

Universal (Saul David)

Archaeologists and adventurers clash on a trek in New Guinea.

Fashionable oddball adventure about the discovery of an unspoiled primitive tribe; the elements don't jell.

w Nelson Gidding d Gordon Douglas ph Robert Moreno m Oliver Nelson

Burt Reynolds, Susan Clark, Roger C. Carmel, Paul Hubschmid, Chips Rafferty, Alexander Knox, Edward Fox, Wilfrid Hyde White, Rhys Williams

Sky Full of Moon

US 1952   73m   bw

MGM (Sidney Franklin Jnr)

A rodeo cowboy wins money and a showgirl in Las Vegas.

Ambling comedy with an agreeable air of innocence.

wd Norman Foster ph Ray June m Paul Sawtell

Carleton Carpenter, Jan Sterling, Keenan Wynn

Sky Riders*

US 1976   91m   De Luxe   Todd-AO 35

TCF (Terry Morse Jnr)

In Athens, the family of an American businessman is kidnapped by terrorists and rescued by hang gliders led by a soldier of fortune.

Old-fashioned actioner with new-fashioned political concern.

w Jack de Witt, Stanley Mann, Gary Michael White, Hall T. Sprague, Bill McGaw d Douglas Hickox ph Ousama Rawi m Lalo Schifrin

James Coburn, Susannah York, Robert Culp, Charles Aznavour, Werner Pochath, Kenneth Griffith, Harry Andrews

Sky West and Crooked

GB 1965   102m   Eastmancolor

Rank / John Mills

US title: *Gypsy Girl*

A mentally retarded girl falls in love with a gypsy.

Eccentric rural melodrama with echoes of *Cold Comfort Farm* and *Les Jeux Interdits*. Interesting, but scarcely a runaway success.

w Mary Hayley Bell, John Prebble d John Mills ph Arthur Ibbetson m Malcolm Arnold

Hayley Mills, Ian McShane, Laurence Naismith, *Geoffrey Bayldon*, Annette Crosbie, Norman Bird

'Behind the overwhelming feyness of it all lurk assumptions which in cold blood look almost sinister.'—*MFB*

Skyjacked*

US 1972   101m   Metrocolor   Panavision

MGM / Walter Seltzer

A Boeing 707 on a flight from Los Angeles to Minneapolis is forced by a mad bomber to fly to Moscow.

Shamelessly hackneyed aeroplane adventure with quite enjoyable elements.

w Stanley R. Greenberg, novel Hijacked by David Harper d John Guillermin ph Harry Stradling Jnr m Perry Botkin Jnr

Charlton Heston, Yvette Mimieux, James
Brolin, Claude Akins, Jeanne Crain, Rosey
Grier, Walter Pidgeon, Leslie Uggams

Skylark
US 1941   94m   bw
Paramount (Mark Sandrich)

A wife decides on her fifth anniversary that she is
tired of being secondary to her husband's career,
and needs a fling.
Formula matrimonial comedy; plenty of talent
but no sparkle.

w Z. Myers, *play* Samson Raphaelson *d* Mark
Sandrich *ph* Charles Lang

Claudette Colbert, Ray Milland, Brian Aherne,
Binnie Barnes, Walter Abel, Grant Mitchell,
Mona Barrie, Ernest Cossart

The Sky's the Limit*
US 1943   89m   bw
RKO (David Hempstead)

A flier on leave meets and falls for a news
photographer.
Thin musical with incidental compensations.

w Frank Fenton, Lynn Root *d* Edward H.
Griffith *ph* Russell Metty *m* Leigh Harline
md Leo F. Forbstein *songs* Harry Warren, Al
Dubin

Fred Astaire, Joan Leslie, *Robert Benchley*,
Robert Ryan, Elizabeth Patterson

AAN: Leigh Harline; song 'My Shining Hour'
(*m* Harold Arlen, *ly* Johnny Mercer)

Slander
US 1956   81m   bw
MGM (Armand Deutsch)

Revelations about a film star in a scandal
magazine lead to blackmail and murder.
Unlikely melodrama, routinely assembled, based
on the Confidential Magazine lawsuits.

w Jerome Weidman *d* Roy Rowland *ph* Harold
J. Marzerati *m* Jeff Alexander

Van Johnson, Ann Blyth, Steve Cochran,
Marjorie Rambeau, Harold J. Stone

Slap Shot*
US 1977   124m Technicolor
Universal / Robert J. Wunsch, Stephen
   Friedman

The wily player-coach of a fading ice hockey
team finds ways, including dirty play, of keeping
it going.
Violent, foul-mouthed comedy which works as it
goes but leaves a bad taste in the mouth.

w Nancy Dowd *d* George Roy Hill *ph* Victor
Kemper, Wallace Worsley *md* Elmer Bernstein

Paul Newman, Michael Ontkean, Lindsay
Crouse, Jennifer Warren, Strother Martin

'Fast, noisy, profane . . . gets you laughing, all
right, but you don't necessarily enjoy
yourself.'—*New Yorker*

'Both indulgent and moralizing, the self-
consciously racy script ends up looking merely
opportunistic.'—*Time Out*

Slattery's Hurricane
US 1949   87m   bw
TCF (William Perlberg)

Loves of a storm-spotting pilot with the US
Weather Bureau in Florida.
Forgettable programmer with good storm
sequences.

w Herman Wouk, Richard Murphy, *novel*
Herman Wouk *d* André de Toth *ph* Charles G.
Clarke *m* Lionel Newman

Richard Widmark, Linda Darnell, Veronica
Lake, John Russell, Gary Merrill, Walter
Kingsford

Slaughter
US 1972   90m   De Luxe   Todd-AO 35
AIP / Slaughter United (Monroe Sachson)

A black Vietnam veteran hunts down the
underworld syndicate which killed his mother
and father.
Hectic crime yarn with a pitilessly violent hero
and not enough style to relieve the unappetizing
monotony.

w Mark Hanna, Don Williams *d* Jack Starrett
ph Rosanio Solano *m* Luchi de Jesus

Jim Brown, Rip Torn, Don Gordon, Cameron
Mitchell

'The cast perform their trigger-happy tasks
with all the passionate conviction of a team of
well-oiled robots.'—*Jan Dawson*

Slaughter on Tenth Avenue
US 1957   103m bw
U-I (Albert Zugsmith)

The New York DA's office investigates union
murders on the docks.
Uninteresting imitation of *On the Waterfront*.

w Lawrence Roman, *novel* The Man Who
Rocked the Boat by William J. Keating, Richard
Carter *d* Arnold Laven *ph* Fred Jackman
m Richard Rodgers

Richard Egan, Jan Sterling, Dan Duryea, Julie
Adams, Walter Matthau, Charles McGraw,
Sam Levene, Mickey Shaughnessy, Harry
Bellaver

Slaughter's Big Rip-Off

US 1973   93m   Movielab   Todd-AO 35
AIP (Monroe Sachson)

Still on the run from gangsters who have killed
his best friend, Slaughter violently disposes of a
number of adversaries.

More routine black violence, a rampage of
senseless brutality against sunny Los Angeles
backgrounds.

w Charles Johnson d Gordon Douglas
ph Charles Wheeler m Jim Brown, Fred Wesley

Jim Brown, Ed MacMahon, Brock Peters, Don
Stroud

Slaughterhouse Five*

US 1972   104m   Technicolor
Universal / Vanadas (Paul Monash)

A suburban optometrist has nightmare
space/time fantasies involving Nazi POW
camps and a strange futuristic planet.
Interesting but infuriating anti-war fantasy for
intellectuals.

w Stephen Geller, novel Kurt Vonnegut Jnr
d George Roy Hill ph Miroslav Ondricek m J.
S. Bach, performed by Glen Gould pd Henry
Bumstead

Michael Sacks, Ron Leibman, Eugène Roche,
Sharon Gans, Valerie Perrine, Sorrell Booke,
John Dehner

'A lot of good makings in this picture; but very
little is made.'—Stanley Kauffmann

Slave Girl

US 1947   79m   Technicolor
U-I (Michael Fessier, Ernest Pagano)

In the early 1800s, a diplomat is sent to Tripoli to
ransom sailors held by the power-mad potentate.
Criticism would be superfluous: when the film
was finished it was obviously so bad that
executives ordered the addition of a talking
camel and other Hellzapoppin-type jokes in
order to turn it into a comedy.

w Michael Fessier, Ernest Pagano d Charles
Lamont ph George Robinson, W. Howard
Greene m Milton Rosen

George Brent' Yvonne de Carlo, Albert Dekker,
Broderick Crawford, Lois Collier, Andy Devine,
Carl Esmond, Arthur Treacher

Slave Girls

GB 1966   95m   Technicolor
Cinemascope
Hammer (Aida Young)

A hunter seeking white rhinoceros finds himself
in a lost valley ruled by a tribe of women.

Feebly preposterous comic strip farrago without
the saving grace of humour.

wd Michael Carreras ph Michael Reed m Carlo
Mantelli

Michael Latimer, Martine Beswick, Edina
Ronay

Slaves

US 1969   110m   Eastmancolor
Slaves Company / Theatre Guild / Walter
Reade (Philip Langner)

In 1850 Kentucky a slave stands up for his rights
and plans escape.

Well-meaning but muddled and old-fashioned
melodrama, hardly well enough done to raise
comparison with Gone with the Wind.

wd Herbert J. Biberman ph Joseph Brun
m Bobby Scott

Stephen Boyd, Ossie Davis, Dionne Warwick,
Shepperd Strudwick, Nancy Coleman, David
Huddleston, Gale Sondergaard

Sleep My Love*

US 1948   96m   bw
(UA) Mary Pickford (Charles 'Buddy' Rogers)

A man plots to murder his wife, but is foiled.
Thin suspenser, rather splendidly photographed
in the expressionist manner.

w St Clair McKelway, novel Leo Rosten
d Douglas Sirk ph Joseph Valentine m Rudy
Schrager

Claudette Colbert, Don Ameche, Robert
Cummings, Rita Johnson, George Coulouris,
Hazel Brooks, Keye Luke

Sleeper*

US 1973   88m   De Luxe
UA / Charles Rollins, Charles Joffe (Jack
Greenberg)

A health food store owner is deep frozen after an
operation and wakes two hundred years in the
future.

Predictable star vehicle with an agreeable string
of bright gags.

w Woody Allen, Marshall Brickman d Woody
Allen ph David M. Walsh m Woody Allen
pd Dale Hennesy

Woody Allen, Diane Keaton, John Beck, Mary
Gregory

'Verbal and visual gags rain down like
hailstones.'—Michael Billington, Illustrated
London News

The Sleeping Beauty*

US 1959   75m   Technirama 70
Walt Disney (Ken Peterson)

Rather stodgy, unwisely Cinemascoped feature cartoon of the old legend; very fashionable and detailed, but somehow lifeless.

d Clyde Geronomi *md* George Bruns *pd* Don da Gradi, Ken Anderson

AAN: George Bruns

The Sleeping Car Murders*
France 1965 95m bw Cinemascope
PECF (Julien Derode)
original title: *Compariment Tueurs*

When the overnight express from Marseilles reaches Paris, a girl is found dead in the sleeping car.
Rather long-winded whodunnit with an unlikely solution: a good pace helps, however, as do skilful borrowings from American police films of the forties.

wd Costa-Gavras, *novel* Sebastien Japrisot *ph* Jean Tournier *m* Michel Magne

Yves Montand, Simone Signoret, Pierre Mondy, Catherine Allégret, Jacques Pérrin, Jean-Louis Trintignant, Michel Piccoli

Sleeping Car to Trieste*
GB 1948 95m bw
GFD / Two Cities

Spy melodrama, a slow-starting but generally entertaining remake of *Rome Express* (qv).

w Allan Mackinnon *d* John Paddy Carstairs *ph* Jack Hildyard *m* Benjamin Frankel

Albert Lieven, Jean Kent, David Tomlinson, David Hutcheson, Rona Anderson, Paul Dupuis, Finlay Currie, *Alan Wheatley*, Derrick de Marney, Grégoire Aslan, Hugh Burden

The Sleeping City**
US 1950 85m bw
U-I (Leonard Goldstein)

A policeman disguises himself as a medical student to learn more about a murder in a general hospital.
A location melodrama of modest excellence.

w Jo Eisinger d George Sherman ph William Miller m Frank Skinner

Richard Conte, Richard Taber, Coleen Gray, John Alexander, Peggy Dow, Alex Nicol

The Sleeping Tiger
GB 1954 89m bw
Anglo-Amalgamated / Insignia (Victor Hanbury)

A psychiatrist overpowers a criminal and takes him home as a guinea pig; the criminal then falls in love with the psychiatrist's wife.

Turgid and unconvincing melodrama, a thoroughgoing bore.

w Harold Buchman, Carl Foreman, *novel* Maurice Moiseiwitch *d* Joseph Losey *ph* Harry Waxman *m* Malcolm Arnold

Dirk Bogarde, Alexander Knox, Alexis Smith, Hugh Griffith, Maxine Audley, Glyn Houston, Billie Whitelaw

The Slender Thread*
US 1966 98m bw
Paramount / Athene (Stephen Alexander)

A volunteer social worker tries to prevent a woman from committing suicide while police track her down from their phone conversations.
Acceptable star melodrama, curiously artificially styled.

w Stirling Silliphant *d* Sydney Pollack *ph* Loyal Griggs *m* Quincy Jones

Anne Bancroft, Sidney Poitier, Steven Hill, Telly Savalas

Sleuth**
GB 1972 139m colour
Palomar (Morton Gottlieb)

A successful thriller writer invents a murder plot which rebounds on himself.
Well-acted version of a highly successful piece of stage trickery; despite hard work all round it seems much less clever and arresting on the screen, and the tricks do show.

w Anthony Shaffer, from his play *d* Joseph L. Mankiewicz *ph* Oswald Morris *m* John Addison

Laurence Olivier, Michael Caine

AAN: Joseph L. Mankiewicz; John Addison; Laurence Olivier; Michael Caine

A Slight Case of Murder***
US 1938 85m bw
Warner (Sam Bischoff)

When a beer baron tries to go legitimate his colleagues attempt to kill him, but end up shooting each other.
Amusing black farce, remade to less effect as *Stop, You're Killing Me* (qv).

w Earl Baldwin, Joseph Schrank, *play* Damon Runyon, Howard Lindsay *d Lloyd Bacon ph* Sid Hickox
m M. K. Jerome, Jack Scholl

Edward G. Robinson, Jane Bryan, Willard Parker, *Ruth Donnelly,* Allen Jenkins, John Litel, Harold Huber, Edward Brophy, Bobby Jordan

'The complications crazily mount, sentiment never raises its ugly head, a long nose is made at violence and death.'—*Graham Greene*

Slightly Honorable
US 1940 85m bw
UA (Tay Garnett)

Lawyer partners set out to break a crime syndicate.
Fair crime thriller which can't decide whether it's comedy or drama.

w John Hunter Lay, Robert Tallman, Ken Englund, *novel* Send Another Coffin by F. G. Presnell *d* Tay Garnett *ph* Merritt Gerstad *m* Werner Janssen

Pat O'Brien, Broderick Crawford, Edward Arnold, Eve Arden, Claire Dodd, Ruth Terry, Bernard Nedell, Alan Dinehart, Douglass Dumbrille, Ernest Truex

Slightly Scarlet
US 1956 92m Technicolor Superscope
(RKO) Benedict Bogeaus

The mayor's secretary loves the leader of a criminal gang.
Competent but uninteresting crime romance.

w Robert Blees, *novel* James A. Cain *d* Allan Dwan *ph* John Alton *m* Louis Forbes

Arlene Dahl, John Payne, Rhonda Fleming, Kent Taylor, Ted de Corsia

'So complicated that it is difficult to sort out which characters are supposed to be sympathetic.'—*MFB*

The Slipper and the Rose*
GB 1976 146m Technicolor Panavision
Paradine Co-Productions (David Frost, Stuart Lyons)

The story of Cinderella.
The elements are charming, but the treatment is fussy yet uninventive and the film is immensely overlong and lacking in magic and wit. Alas, not the renaissance of the family film that was hoped for.

w Bryan Forbes, Robert and Richard Sherman *d* Bryan Forbes *ph* Tony Imi *songs* Robert and Richard Sherman *pd* Ray Simm

Richard Chamberlain, Gemma Craven, Kenneth More, Michael Hordern, Edith Evans, Annette Crosbie, Margaret Lockwood, *Christopher Gable*, Julian Orchard, Lally Bowers, John Turner

'The tunes, I'm afraid, go in one ear and out the other; and, as Dr Johnson said of *Paradise Lost*, no man wished it a minute longer.'—*Michael Billington, Illustrated London News*

Slither*
US 1972 96m Metrocolor
MGM / Talent Associates / Jack Sher

An ex-con, some gangsters, and a few mobile homes are involved in a chase across California for some hidden loot.
Wackily with-it comedy-thriller ranging from violence to slapstick, the former always undercut into the latter. Pretty funny, once you get the idea.

w W. D. Richter *d* Howard Zieff *ph* Laszlo Kovacs *m* Tom McIntosh

James Caan, Peter Boyle, Sally Kellerman, Louise Lasser

The Small Back Room**
GB 1949 106m bw
London Films / The Archers
US title: *Hour of Glory*

A bomb expert with a lame foot and a drink problem risks his life dismantling a booby bomb and returns to his long-suffering girl friend.
Rather gloomy suspense thriller with ineffective personal aspects but well-made location sequences and a fascinating background of boffins at work in post-war London.

wd Michael Powell, Emeric Pressburger *ph* Christopher Challis *m* Brian Easdale

David Farrar, Kathleen Byron, Jack Hawkins, Leslie Banks, Robert Morley, Cyril Cusack

Small Change*
France 1976 105m Eastmancolor
Films du Carosse / Artistes Associés (Marcel Berbert, Roland Thenot)
original title: *L'Argent de Poche*

Linked incidents affecting a class of small boys in provincial France.
Competent if rather ordinary little portmanteau which one can't imagine adults actually paying to see.

w François Truffaut, Susan Schiffman *d* François Truffaut *ph* Pierre-William Glenn *m* Maurice Jaubert

Geory Desmouceaux, Philippe Goldman, Claudio Deluca

Small Town Girl*
US 1936 90m bw
MGM (Hunt Stromberg)

A girl traps a handsome stranger into offering marriage when he's drunk, then sets out to win him when he's sober.
Thin but adequate romantic comedy, a good example of MGM's production line of the mid-thirties, with established star and character players helping upcoming talents.

w John Lee Mahin, Edith Fitzgerald, *novel* Ben

Ames Williams *d* William A. Wellman
ph Charles Rosher

Janet Gaynor, Robert Taylor, James Stewart,
Binnie Barnes, Frank Craven, Elizabeth
Patterson, Lewis Stone, Andy Devine, Isabel
Jewell, Charley Grapewin, Robert Greig, Agnes
Ayres

Small Town Girl*
US 1953 93m Technicolor
MGM (Joe Pasternak)

Musical remake of the above.
Willing hands make the most of it, but the songs
are not the best.

w Dorothy Cooper, Dorothy Kingsley *d* Leslie
Kardos *ph* Joseph Ruttenberg *songs* Leo
Robin, Nicholas Brodszky *md* André Previn

Jane Powell, Farley Granger, *Bobby Van,* Ann
Miller, Robert Keith, Billie Burke, S. Z. Sakall,
Fay Wray, Nat King Cole

The Small Voice*
GB 1948 83m bw
British Lion / Constellation (Anthony
  Havelock-Allan)
US title: *Hideout*

Escaped convicts hold up a playwright and his
wife in their country cottage.
Gripping, well-characterized version of a very
well worn plot.

w Derek Neame, Julian Orde, *novel* Robert
Westerby *d* Fergus McDonell

James Donald, Valerie Hobson, Howard Keel,
David Greene, Michael Balfour, Joan Young

The Small World of Sammy Lee
GB 1962 107m bw
Bryanston / Seven Arts / Ken Hughes (Frank
  Godwin)

A small-time Soho crook tries desperately to
raise money to pay off threatening bookies.
Overlong 'realist' comedy-melodrama based on
a TV play and filled with low-life 'characters';
vivid but cursed with a tedious hero.

wd Ken Hughes, from his TV play *ph* Wolfgang
Suschitzky *m* Kenny Graham *ad* Seamus
Flannery

Anthony Newley, Julia Foster, Robert Stephens,
Wilfrid Brambell, Warren Mitchell, Miriam
Karlin, Kenneth J. Warren

The Smallest Show on Earth*
GB 1957 81m bw
British Lion / Launder and Gilliat (Michael
  Relph)
US title: *Big Time Operators*

Two young marrieds inherit a decayed cinema
and make it pay.
Amiable caricature comedy with plenty of
obvious jokes and a sentimental attachment to
old cinemas but absolutely no conviction, little
plot, and a very muddled sense of the line
between farce and reality.

w William Rose, John Eldridge *d* Basil Dearden
ph Douglas Slocombe *m* William Alwyn

Bill Travers, Virginia McKenna, Margaret
Rutherford, Bernard Miles, Peter Sellers, Leslie
Phillips, Francis de Wolff

Smart Money
US 1931 90m bw
Warner

A gambler hits the big time but finally goes to
jail.
Rather ordinary crime drama, a distinct letdown
for its star after *Little Caesar.*

w Kubec Glasmon, John Bright, Lucien
Hubbard, Joseph Jackson *d* Alfred E. Green
ph Robert Kurrie

Edward G. Robinson, James Cagney, Evalyn
Knapp, Ralf Harolde, Noel Francis, Margaret
Livingstone, Boris Karloff, Billy House
† This film marks the only teaming of Robinson
and Cagney.

AAN: script

Smart Woman
US 1948 93m bw
Monogram (Hal E. Chester)

A crafty lady lawyer becomes romantically
involved with a crusading district attorney.
What to Monogram was a high-class production
would have been a very routine programmer
from anyone else.

w Alvah Bessie, Louise Morheim, Herbert
Margolis *d* Edward A. Blatt *ph* Stanley Cortez
m Louis Gruenberg *md* Constantin
Bakaleinikoff

Constance Bennett, Brian Aherne, Barry
Sullivan, Michael O'Shea, James Gleason, Otto
Kruger, Isobel Elsom, Taylor Holmes, John
Litel

Smash-up, The Story of a Woman
US 1947 113m bw
U-I
GB title: *A Woman Destroyed*

The story of a lady alcoholic.
Tedious distaff side of *The Lost Weekend.*

w John Howard Lawson *d* Stuart Heisler
ph Stanley Cortez

Susan Hayward, Lee Bowman, Eddie Albert, Marsha Hunt, Carl Esmond, Carleton Young, Charles D. Brown

AAN: original story (Dorothy Parker, Frank Cavett); Susan Hayward

Smashing Time
GB 1967   96m   Eastmancolor
Paramount / Partisan / Carlo Ponti (Ray Millichip)

Two north country girls have farcical adventures in swinging London, including paint squirting and pie throwing.
Horrendous attempt to turn two unsuitable actresses into a female Laurel and Hardy; plenty of coarse vigour but no style or sympathy.

w George Melly d Desmond Davis ph Manny Wynn m John Addison

Rita Tushingham, Lynn Redgrave, Ian Carmichael, Anna Quayle, Michael York, Irene Handl, Jeremy Lloyd

Smile*
US 1975   113m   De Luxe
UA (Michael Ritchie)

A bird's eye view of the Young Miss America pageant in a small California town.
A witty series of sketches in the form of a drama-documentary or satirical mosaic.
Highly polished fun for those who can stay the course.

w Jerry Belson d Michael Ritchie ph Conrad Hall m various

Bruce Dern, Barbara Feldon, Michael Kidd, Geoffrey Lewis, Nicholas Pryor

'A beady, precise, technically skilful movie.'— Michael Billington, Illustrated London News

Smiles of a Summer Night**
Sweden 1955   105m   bw
Svensk Filmindustri
original title: Sommarnattens Leende

A country lawyer meets again a touring actress who was once his mistress, and accepts an invitation for him and his young wife to stay at her mother's country home for a weekend.
Comedy of high period manners with an admirable detached viewpoint and elegant trappings. It later formed the basis of Stephen Sondheim's A Little Night Music, a stage musical which was later filmed.

wd Ingmar Bergman ph Gunnar Fischer m Erik Nordgren

Gunnar Bjornstrand, Eva Dahlbeck, Ulla Jacobsson, Harriet Andersson, Margit Carlquist, Naima Wifstrand, Jarl Kulle

Smiley*
GB 1957   97m   Technicolor Cinemascope
TCF / London Films (Anthony Kimmins)

An adventurous Australian boy has various adventures and finally gets the bicycle he wants.
An open-air 'William'-type story for children, quite nicely made and generally refreshing.
Smiley Gets a Gun was a less effective sequel.

w Moore Raymond, Anthony Kimmins d Anthony Kimmins ph Ted Scaife, Russ Wood m William Alwyn

Colin Petersen, Ralph Richardson, Chips Rafferty, John McCallum

Smilin' Through**
US 1932   97m   bw
MGM (Irving Thalberg)

Three generations of complications follow when a Victorian lady is accidentally killed by a jealous lover on her wedding day.
Archetypal sentimental romantic drama, wholly absorbing to the mass audience and extremely well done; originally a 1922 Norma Talmadge vehicle.

w Ernest Vajda, Claudine West, Donald Ogden Stewart,
J. B. Fagan, play Jane Cowl, Jane Murfin d Sidney Franklin ph Lee Garmes

Norma Shearer, Leslie Howard, Fredric March, O. P. Heggie, Ralph Forbes, Beryl Mercer

'A sensitive and beautiful production distinguished by excellent settings and rich photography.'—New York Mirror

AAN: best picture

Smilin' Through*
US 1941   100m   Technicolor
MGM (Victor Saville)

Flat but adequate remake of the above.

w Donald Ogden Stewart, John Balderston d Frank Borzage

Jeanette MacDonald, Gene Raymond, Brian Aherne, Ian Hunter, Frances Robinson, Patrick O'Moore

The Smiling Lieutenant***
US 1931   88m   bw
Paramount (Ernst Lubitsch)

A Viennese guards officer leaves his mistress to become consort to a visiting princess.
A sophisticated soufflé in Lubitsch's best style, naughty but quite nice, with visual effects largely replacing dialogue.

w Ernest Vajda, Samson Raphaelson, operetta

A Waltz Dream *d Ernst Lubitsch ph* George
Folsey *m* Oscar Straus *md* Adolph Deutsch

Maurice Chevalier, Miriam Hopkins, Claudette
Colbert, Charles Ruggles, George Barbier,
Elizabeth Patterson

' All the shrewd delights that were promised in
The Love Parade all realized with an economy
and sureness that give it a luster which no other
American-made comedy satire has achieved.
One must look to *Le Million* to find its peer.'—
Richard Watts, New York Post

AAN: best picture

Smokey and the Bandit*
US 1977　97m　Technicolor
Universal / Rastar (Robert L. Levy)

A Georgia bootlegger on a mission picks up a
girl in distress and is chased by her irate sheriff
fiancé.
Frantic chase comedy full of car crashes and low
lines: a surprise box office smash.

w James Lee Barrett, Charles Shyer, Alan
Mandel *d* Hal Needham *ph* Bobby Byrne
m Bill Justis, Jerry Reed, Art Feller

Burt Reynolds, Jackie Gleason, Sally Field,
Jerry Reed, Mike Henry, Pat McCormick, Paul
Williams

Smoky
US 1946　87m　Technicolor
TCF (Robert Bassler)

An especially independent horse virtually runs
the ranch on which he lives.
Family saga of the great outdoors, well enough
assembled.

w Dwight Cummings, Lillie Hayward, Dorothy
Yost, *novel* Will James *d* Louis King
ph Charles Clarke *md* Emil Newman

Fred MacMurray, Anne Baxter, Burl Ives, Bruce
Cabot, Esther Dale
† The story was also made by Fox in 1934 and
1966.

SNAFU
US 1945　85m　bw
Columbia
GB title: *Welcome Home*

Middle-class parents rescue their difficult
15-year-old son from the army, then wish they
hadn't.
Predictable, well-greased comedy of a rebellious
teenager.

w Louis Solomon, Harold Buchman, from their
play *d* Jack Moss *ph* Franz Planer

Robert Benchley, Vera Vague, Conrad Janis,
Nanetta Parks

† The title can be bowdlerized as 'Situation
Normal, All Fouled Up'.

The Snake Pit**
US 1948　108m　bw
TCF (Anatole Litvak, Robert Bassler)

A girl becomes mentally deranged and has
horrifying experiences in an institution.
A headline-hitting film which made a stirring
plea for more sympathetic treatment of mental
illness. Very well made, and arrestingly acted,
but somehow nobody's favourite movie.

w Frank Partos, Millen Brand, *novel* Mary Jane
Ward *d* Anatole Litvak *ph* Leo Tover *m* Alfred
Newman

Olivia de Havilland, Leo Genn, Mark Stevens,
Celeste Holm, Glenn Langan, Leif Erickson,
Beulah Bondi, Lee Patrick, Natalie Schaefer

AAN: best picture; script; Anatole Litvak;
Alfred Newman; Olivia de Havilland

The Sniper**
US 1952　87m　bw
Columbia / Stanley Kramer (Edna and
Edward Anhalt)

A psychopath kills a succession of blondes with
a high-powered rifle.
Semi-documentary police drama which was
quite startling and influential when released but
seems quite routine now.

w Harry Brown *d* Edward Dmytryk *ph* Burnett
Guffey *m* George Antheil

Adolphe Menjou, Arthur Franz, Gerald Mohr,
Richard Kiley, Frank Faylen, Marie Windsor

AAN: original story (Edna and Edward Annalt)

The Snorkel
GB 1958　80m　bw
Columbia / Hammer (Michael Carreras)

A man murders his wife and is given away by his
observant young stepdaughter.
Tenuous suspenser which outstays its welcome.

w Peter Myers, Jimmy Sangster, Anthony
Dawson *d* Guy Green *ph* Jack Asher

Peter Van Eyck, Mandy Miller, William
Franklyn, Grègoire Aslan

Snow Treasure
US 1968　95m　Eastmancolor
Sagittarius (Irving Jacoby)

In Nazi-occupied Norway a teenage boy finds
gold hidden in the snow; an underground agent
helps him get it to safety.
Curiously undernourished but attractively made
adventure film.

w Irving Jacoby, Peter Hansen, *novel* Marie McSwigan *d* Irving Jacoby *ph Sverre Bergli m* Egil Monn-Iversen

James Franciscus, Paul Anstad, Paoul Oyen, Randi Borch

Snow White and the Seven Dwarfs****
US 1937 82m Technicolor
Walt Disney

In Disney's first feature cartoon, a mammoth enterprise which no one in the business thought would work. The romantic leads were wishy-washy but the splendid songs and the marvellous comic and villainous characters turned the film into a world-wide box office bombshell which is almost as fresh today as when it was made.

w Ted Sears, Otto Englander, Earl Hurd, Dorothy Ann Blank, Richard Creedon, Dick Richard, Merrill de Maris, Webb Smith, from the fairy tale by the brothers Grimm *supervising director David Hand m* Frank Churchill, Leigh Harline, Paul Smith *songs Larry Morey, Frank Churchill*

'The first full-length animated feature, the turning point in Disney's career, a milestone in film history, and a great film.'—*Leonard Maltin*
'Sustained fantasy, the animated cartoon grown up.'—*Otis Ferguson*
AAN: Frank Churchill, Leigh Harline, Paul Smith

Snow White and the Three Stooges*
US 1961 107m De Luxe Cinemascope
(TCF) Chanford (Charles Wick)
GB title: *Snow White and the Three Clowns*

The old story retold as a vehicle for a champion skater and three veteran clowns. Surprisingly tolerable as a holiday attraction, once you get over the shock.

w Noel Langley, Elwood Ullman *d* Walter Lang *ph* Leon Shamroy *m* Lyn Murray *ad* Jack Martin Smith, Maurice Ransford

Carol Heiss, Moe Howard, Larry Fine, Joe de Rita, Edson Stroll, Patricia Medina, Guy Rolfe, Buddy Baer, Edgar Barrier

Snowball Express
US 1972 99m Technicolor
Walt Disney (Ron Miller)

An insurance accountant inherits a dilapidated skiing hotel in the Colorado Rockies. Uninspired family comedy with slapstick on the snow slopes.

w Don Tait, Jim Parker, Arnold Margolin, *novel* Château Bon Vivant by Frankie and John O'Rear *d* Norman Tokar *ph* Frank Phillips *m* Robert F. Brunner

Dean Jones, Nancy Olson, Henry Morgan, Keenan Wynn, Mary Wickes, Johnny Whittaker
'As wholesome and bland as that old American favourite the peanut butter and jelly sandwich.'—*MFB*

The Snows of Kilimanjaro**
US 1952 117m Technicolor
TCF (Darryl F. Zanuck)

A hunter lies wounded in Africa and while waiting for help looks back over his life and loves.
Hollywood version of a portable Hemingway, with reminiscences of several novels stirred into a lush and sprawling mix of action and romance, open spaces and smart salons. A big popular star film of its time, despite constricted and unconvincing characters.

w Casey Robinson, *story* Ernest Hemingway *d Henry King ph* Leon Shamroy *m* Bernard Herrmann

Gregory Peck, Susan Hayward, Ava Gardner, Hildegard Neff, Leo G. Carroll, Torin Thatcher, Marcel Dalio
'A naïve kind of success story with a conventional boy-meets-lots-of-girls plot.'—*Karel Reisz*
AAN: Leon Shamroy

So Big*
US 1932 80m bw
Warner (Lucien Hubbard)

A schoolteacher marries a farmer, has trouble with her son, falls in love with a sculptor. Watchable, superficial, top-talented adaptation of a best-seller, first filmed in 1925 with Colleen Moore.

w J. Grubb Alexander, Robert Lord, *novel* Edna Ferber *d* William Wellman *ph* Sid Hickox

Barbara Stanwyck, George Brent, Dickie Moore, Guy Kibbee, Bette Davis, Hardie Albright

So Big
US 1953 101m bw
Warner (Henry Blanke)

By the time this inflated remake came along, the story was just too corny despite careful production.

w John Twist *d* Robert Wise *ph* Ellsworth Fredericks *m* Max Steiner

Jane Wyman, Sterling Hayden, Richard Beymer, Nancy Olson, Steve Forrest, Elizabeth Fraser, Martha Hyer

So Dear to My Heart*
US 1948   84m   Technicolor
Walt Disney

Life on a country farm in 1903.
Live action nostalgia with a few cartoon
segments; well enough done, but mainly
appealing to well brought up children.

w John Tucker Battle, *novel* Midnight and
Jeremiah by Sterling North d Harold Schuster
ph Winton C. Hoch m Paul Smith

Burl Ives, Beulah Bondi, Harry Carey, Luana
Patten, Bobby Driscoll

AAN: song 'Lavender Blue' (m Eliot Daniel,
ly Larry Morey)

So Ends Our Night*
US 1941   120m   bw
(UA) David L. Loew, Albert Lewin

Refugees from Nazi Germany are driven from
country to country and meet persecution
everywhere.
Worthy but rather drab and unfocused
melodrama from the headlines.

w Talbot Jennings, *novel* Flotsam by Erich
Maria Remarque d John Cromwell ph William
Daniels m Louis Gruenberg

Fredric March, Margaret Sullavan, Glenn Ford,
Frances Dee, Anna Sten, Erich Von Stroheim,
Joseph Cawthorn, Leonid Kinskey, Alexander
Granach, Sig Rumann
  'It ought to be a great picture but it isn't.'—
Archer Winsten, New York Post

AAN: Louis Gruenberg

So Evil My Love*
US 1948   100m   bw
Paramount (Hal B. Wallis)

A missionary's widow is enticed into a life of
crime and immorality by a scoundrelly artist.
Curious Victorian melodrama with a Wildean
flavour; doesn't quite come off.

w Leonard Spiegelgass, Ronald Miller, *novel*
Joseph Shearing d Lewis Allen ph Max Greene
m Victor Young, William Alwyn

Ray Milland, Ann Todd, Geraldine Fitzgerald,
Leo G. Carroll, Raymond Huntley, Martita
Hunt, Moira Lister, Raymond Lovell, Muriel
Aked, Finlay Currie, Hugh Griffith

So Goes My Love
US 1946   88m   bw
(U-I) Jack H. Skirball / Bruce Manning
GB title: *A Genius in the Family*

The domestic life of inventor Hiram Maxim.
Formula period family film with pleasant
moments.

w Bruce Manning, James Clifden d Frank Ryan
ph Joseph Valentine

Myrna Loy, Don Ameche, Rhys Williams,
Bobby Driscoll, Richard Gaines

So Little Time
GB 1952   88m   bw
ABP / Mayflower (Aubrey Baring, Maxwell
Setton)

In occupied Belgium an aristocratic lady falls in
love with a Nazi colonel.
Doomed love story with musical
accompaniment; tolerable but slow.

w John Cresswell d Compton Bennett
ph Oswald Morris m Robert Gill

Marius Goring, Maria Schell, Gabrielle Dorziat,
Barbara Mullen

So Long at the Fair*
GB 1950   86m   bw
Rank / Gainsborough / Sydney Box (Betty E.
Box)

During the 1889 Paris Exposition a girl books
into a hotel with her brother, and next day finds
that he has totally disappeared and his existence
is denied by all concerned.
Straightforward version of an old yarn which has
turned up in such varied forms as *The Lady
Vanishes* and *Bunny Lake is Missing*. This
modest production is pleasant enough but badly
lacks drive.

w Hugh Mills, Anthony Thorne d Terence
Fisher, Anthony Darnborough ph Reginald
Wyer m Benjamin Frankel ad Cedric Dawe

Jean Simmons, Dirk Bogarde, David Tomlinson,
Marcel Poncin, Cathleen Nesbitt, Honor
Blackman, Betty Warren, Felix Aylmer, André
Morell

So Proudly We Hail*
US 1943   125m   bw
Paramount (Mark Sandrich)

The self-sacrifice of war nurses in the Pacific.
Fairly harrowing and well-meant but studio-
bound and unconvincing flagwaver.

w Allan Scott d Mark Sandrich ph Charles
Lang m Miklos Rosza

Claudette Colbert, Paulette Goddard, Veronica
Lake, George Reeves, Barbara Britton, Walter
Abel, Sonny Tufts, John Litel
  'Probably the most deadly accurate picture
ever made of what war looks like through the
lenses of a housewives' magazine romance.'—
James Agee
  'The stars are devotedly, almost gallantly,
deglamorized and dishevelled but they cannot

escape the smell of studio varnish.'—*Richard Winnington*

AAN: Allan Scott; Charles Lang; Paulette Goddard

So Red the Rose*
US 1935 82m bw
Paramount (Douglas MacLean)

The life of a southern family during the Civil War.
Quiet, pleasing historical romance.

w Laurence Stallings, Maxwell Anderson, Edwin Justus Mayer, *novel* Stark Young *d* King Vidor *ph* Victor Milner *m* W. Franke Harling

Margaret Sullavan, Randolph Scott, Walter Connolly, Elizabeth Patterson, Janet Beecher, Robert Cummings

So This Is Love
US 1953 101m Technicolor
Warner (Henry Blanke)
GB title: *The Grace Moore Story*

Events leading up to Grace Moore's debut at the Metropolitan Opera in 1928.
Acceptable musical biopic full of the usual Hollywood contrivances.

w John Monks Jnr, from Grace Moore's autobiography *d* Gordon Douglas *ph* Robert Burks *md* Ray Heindorf, Max Steiner *ch* Le Roy Prinz *ad* Edward Carrere

Kathryn Grayson, Merv Griffin, Joan Weldon, Walter Abel, Rosemary de Camp, Jeff Donnell, Douglas Dick, Mabel Albertson, Fortunio Bonanova

So This Is New York*
US 1948 78m bw
Stanley Kramer / Enterprise

In 1919 some country cousins who have come into money have a big time in the gay city.
Curious, sporadically effective, silent-style comedy which doesn't quite come off.

w Carl Foreman, Herbert Baker, *novel* The Big Town by Ring Lardner *d* Richard Fleischer *ph* Jack Russell

Henry Morgan, Rudy Vallee, Hugh Herbert, Bill Goodwin, Virginia Grey, Dona Drake, Leo Gorcey

So This Is Paris
US 1955 96m Technicolor
U-I (Albert J. Cohen)

Three American sailors on leave in Paris meet girls and help war orphans.
Very thin imitation of *On the Town*, bogged down by sentimentality and lack of sparkle. The musical numbers, however, are not bad.

w Charles Hoffman *d* Richard Quine *ph* Maury Gertsman *md* Joseph Gershenson *ch* Gene Nelson, Lee Scott

Tony Curtis, Gloria de Haven, Gene Nelson, *Corinne Calvet*, Paul Gilbert, Mara Corday, Allison Hayes

So Well Remembered*
GB 1947 114m bw
(RKO) Alliance (Adrian Scott)

The ambitious daughter of a mill-owner marries a rising politician but almost ruins his life.
Rather routine treatment of a three-decker north country novel; humdrum incident and unsympathetic characters, but full of minor British virtues.

w John Paxton, *novel* James Hilton *d* Edward Dmytryk *ph* Frederick A. Young

John Mills, Martha Scott, Trevor Howard, Patricia Roc, Richard Carlson

Soak the Rich*
US 1935 74m bw
Paramount (Ben Hecht, Charles MacArthur)

A rebellious rich girl is cured when she is rescued from kidnapping.
Smartly written social comedy-melodrama.

wd Ben Hecht, Charles MacArthur *ph* Leon Shamroy

Walter Connolly, John Howard, Mary Taylor, Lionel Stander, Ilka Chase

Society Doctor
US 1935 63m bw
MGM (Lucien Hubbard)

A doctor's modern ideas incur hostility: he goes into private practice, but returning to the hospital is wounded by a gangster and supervises his own operation under spinal anaesthetic.
Melodramatic hokum with most attention going to the second male lead, the young and rising Robert Taylor.

w Sam Marx, Michael Fessier, *novel* The Harbor by Theodore Reeves *d* George B. Seitz *ph* Lester White *m* Oscar Radin

Chester Morris, Virginia Bruce, Robert Taylor, Billie Burke, Raymond Walburn, Henry Kolker, William Henry

Sodom and Gomorrah
Italy / France 1962 154m colour
Titanus / S. N. Pathe (Gottfredo Lombardo)

Lot and the Hebrews become involved in a

Helamite plan to take over the rich sinful cities of Sodom and Gomorrah.

Dreary biblical blood-and-thunder; an international muddle, tedious in the extreme outside a few hilariously misjudged moments.

w Hugo Butler, Giorgio Prosperi *d* Robert Aldrich *ph* Silvano Ippoliti, Cyril Knowles *m* Miklos Rozsa *ad* Ken Adam

Stewart Granger, Stanley Baker, Pier Angeli, Anouk Aimée, Rossana Podesta

Soft Beds, Hard Battles

GB 1973 107m colour
Rank / Charter (John Boulting)

Inhabitants of a Paris brothel help to win World War II.

Ragbag of poor sketches and dirty jokes, with the star in several ineffective roles including Hitler.

w Leo Marks, Roy Boulting *d* Roy Boulting *ph* Gil Taylor *m* Neil Rhoden

Peter Sellers, Lila Kedrova, Curt Jurgens, Gabriella Licudi, Jenny Hanley

Sol Madrid

US 1968 90m Metrocolor Panavision
MGM / Gershwin–Kastner (Hall Bartlett)
GB title: *The Heroin Gang*

An undercover narcotics agent is assigned to track down an elusive Mafia executive.
Humdrum, predictable, brutishly violent international crime caper.

w David Karp, *novel* Fruit of the Poppy by Robert Wilder *d* Brian G. Hutton *ph* Fred Koenekamp *m* Lalo Schifrin

David McCallum, Telly Savalas, Stella Stevens, Ricardo Montalban, Rip Torn, Pat Hingle, Paul Lukas, Perry Lopez, Michael Ansara.

Solaris **

USSR 1972 165m Sovcolor Scope
Mosfilm

A psychologist is sent to investigate the many deaths in a space station orbiting a remote planet.
Heavy-going but highly imaginative space fiction in which the menaces are ghosts materialized from the subjects' guilty pasts. The technology is superbly managed, but the whole thing is rather humourless.

w Andrei Tarkovsky, Friedrich Gorenstein, *novel* Stanislaw Lem *d* Andrei Tarkovsky *ph* Vadim Yusov *m* Eduard Artemyev

Natalya Bondarchuk, Donatas Banionis, Yuri Yarvet

Soldier Blue *

US 1970 114m Technicolor Panavision
Avco (Gabriel Katzka, Harold Loeb)

A paymaster's detachment of the US cavalry is attacked by Indians seeking gold, and two white survivors trek through the desert.
Extremely violent 'anti-violence' western with a particularly nauseating climax following clichés all the way. From a director with pretensions.

w John Gay, *novel* Arrow in the Sun by Theodore V. Olsen *d* Ralph Nelson *ph* Robert Hauser *m* Roy Budd

Candice Bergen, Peter Strauss, Donald Pleasence

'One is more likely to be sickened by the film itself than by the wrongs it tries to right.'—*Tom Milne*

Soldier in the Rain

US 1963 87m bw
AA / Cedar / Solar (Martin Jurow)

Two army sergeants have wild plans for their demob, but one dies.
Curious sentimental tragi-comedy which misfires on all cylinders.

w Blake Edwards, Martin Richlin, *novel* William Goldman *d* Ralph Nelson *ph* Philip Lathrop *m* Henry Mancini

Steve McQueen, Jackie Gleason, Tuesday Weld, Tony Bill, Tom Poston, Ed Nelson, John Hubbard

Soldier of Fortune *

US 1955 96m De Luxe Cinemascope
TCF (Buddy Adler)

When a photographer disappears in Red China, his wife comes to Hong Kong to institute a search, enlists the aid of an amiable smuggler.
Cheerful Boys' Own Paper adventure romance with attractive locations and some silly anti-Red dialogue.

w Ernest K. Gann, from his novel *d* Edward Dmytryk *ph* Leo Tover *m* Hugo Friedhofer

Clark Gable, Susan Hayward, Gene Barry, Alex D'Arcy, Michael Rennie, Tom Tully, Anna Sten, Russell Collins, Leo Gordon

'A very good adventure film but not one of the Gable smashes.'—*Hollywood Reporter*

Soldiers Three

US 1951 87m bw
MGM (Pandro S. Berman)

Adventures of three roistering British officers on the North-West Frontier.
A kind of unofficial remake of *Gunga Din* without the title character; one suspects it was

meant seriously and found to be so bad that the only way out was strenuously to play it for laughs.

w Marguerite Roberts, Tom Reed, Malcolm Stuart Boylan *d* Tay Garnett *ph* William Mellor *m* Adolph Deutsch

Stewart Granger, David Niven, Robert Newton, Walter Pidgeon, Cyril Cusack, Greta Gynt, Frank Allenby, Robert Coote, Dan O'Herlihy

The Solid Gold Cadillac **
US 1956 99m bw
Columbia (Fred Kohlmar)

A very minor stockholder upsets the crooked board of a large corporation.
Vaguely Capraesque comedy which begins brightly but peters out; performances sustain passing interest.

w Abe Burrows, *play* George S. Kaufman, Howard Teichmann *d* Richard Quine *ph* Charles Lang *m* Cyril Mockridge

Judy Holliday, Paul Douglas, *John Williams, Fred Clark*, Hiram Sherman, Neva Patterson, Ralph Dumke, Ray Collins, Arthur O'Connell

Solomon and Sheba *
US 1959 142m Super Technirama 70
UA / Edward Small (Ted Richmond)

When David names his younger son as heir, his older son plots revenge.
Dullish biblical spectacle, alternating between pretentiousness and cowboys and Indians.

w Anthony Veiller, Paul Dudley, George Bruce *d* King Vidor *ph* Frederick A. Young *m* Mario Nascimbene *ad* Richard Day, Alfred Sweeney

Yul Brynner, Gina Lollobrigida, George Sanders, Marisa Pavan, David Farrar, John Crawford, Laurence Naismith, Alejandro Rey, Harry Andrews

Sombrero
US 1953 103m Technicolor
MGM (Jack Cummings)

Two Mexican villages feud over the burial place of a famous poet.
Rather self-consciously unusual musical which never catches fire but certainly keeps one watching its incredible mixture of music and melodrama.

w Norman Foster, Josefina Niggli, from her novel *A Mexican Village* *d* Norman Foster *ph* Ray June *m* Leo Arnaud

Ricardo Montalban, Pier Angeli, Yvonne de Carlo, Nina Foch, Cyd Charisse, Rick Jason,

Jose Greco, Thomas Gomez, Kurt Kasznar, Walter Hampden, John Abbott
'Staggering is the only word for the hokum of this extraordinary film.'—*Gavin Lambert*

Some Call It Loving
US 1973 103m Technicolor
Pleasant Pastures / James B. Harris

A young man buys a 'sleeping beauty' at a fair but is sorry when he wakes her up.
Fashionable fantasy, amplified from a slender, winning short story.

wd James B. Harris, *story* Sleeping Beauty by John Collier *ph* Mario Tosi *m* Richard Hazard

Zalman King, Carol White, Tisa Farrow, Richard Pryor, Veronica Anderson

Some Came Running
US 1959 136m Metrocolor
  Cinemascope
MGM / Sol C. Siegel

A disillusioned writer returns after service to his home town and takes up with a gambler and a prostitute.
Strident and rather pointless melodrama with solid acting and production values.

w John Patrick, Arthur Sheekman, *novel* James Jones *d* Vincente Minnelli *ph* William H. Daniels *m* Elmer Bernstein

Frank Sinatra, Dean Martin, Shirley Maclaine, Martha Hyer, Arthur Kennedy, Nancy Gates, Leora Dana

AAN: song 'To Love and Be Loved' (*m* James Van Heusen, *ly* Sammy Cahn); Shirley Maclaine; Martha Hyer; Arthur Kennedy

Some Girls Do
GB 1969 93m Eastmancolor
Rank / Ashdown (Betty E. Box)

Bulldog Drummond traces the sabotage of a supersonic airliner to a gang of murderous women.
Abysmal spoof melodrama in the swinging sixties mould; a travesty of a famous character.

w David Osborn, Liz Charles-Williams *d* Ralph Thomas *ph* Ernest Steward *m* Charles Blackwell

Richard Johnson, Daliah Lavi, Bebi Loncar, James Villiers, Sydne Rome, Robert Morley, Maurice Denham, Florence Desmond, Ronnie Stevens

Some Kind of a Nut
US 1969 89m De Luxe
UA / Mirisch / TFT / DFI (Walter Mirisch)

When a bank teller grows a beard because of an

unsightly bee sting, he is thought to be flouting authority and his whole life changes.
Laboured, cliché-ridden anti-establishment comedy, a waste of the talent involved.

wd Garson Kanin *ph* Burnett Guffey, Gerald Hirschfeld *m* Johnny Mandel

Dick Van Dyke, Angie Dickinson, Rosemary Forsyth, Zohra Lampert, Elliot Reid, Dennis King

Some Like It Hot
US 1939   65m   bw
Paramount

A sideshow owner runs out of money.
Very mild comedy, one of several which helped to establish Hope's star potential.

w Lewis R. Foster, *play* Wilkie C. Mahoney, Ben Hecht, Gene Fowler *d* George Archainbaud *ph* Karl Struss

Bob Hope, Shirley Ross, Una Merkel, Gene Krupa, Richard Denning

Some Like It Hot***
US 1959   122m   bw
UA / Mirisch (Billy Wilder)

Two unemployed musicians accidentally witness the St Valentine's Day Massacre and flee to Miami disguised as girl musicians.
Overstretched but sporadically very funny comedy which constantly flogs its central idea to death and then recovers with a smart line or situation. It has in any case become a milestone of film comedy.

w Billy Wilder, I. A. L. Diamond *d* Billy Wilder *ph* Charles Lang Jnr *m* Adolph Deutsch

Jack Lemmon, Tony Curtis, Marilyn Monroe, Joe E. Brown, George Raft, Pat O'Brien, Nehemiah Persoff, George E. Stone, Joan Shawlee

AAN: script; Billy Wilder (as director); Charles Lang Jnr; Jack Lemmon

Some People
GB 1962   93m   Eastmancolor
Vic Films (James Archibald)

Troublesome teenage factory workers are helped by a church organist and become model citizens.
Bland propaganda for the Duke of Edinburgh's Award scheme for young people, quite acceptably presented, with pop music ad lib.

w John Eldridge *d* Clive Donner *ph* John Wilcox *m* Ron Grainer

Kenneth More, Ray Brooks, Annika Wells,

David Andrews, Angela Douglas, David Hemmings, Harry H. Corbett

Some Will, Some Won't
GB 1969   90m   Technicolor
ABP / Transocean (Giulio Zampi)

In order to inherit under an eccentric will, four people have to perform tasks out of character.
Thin remake of *Laughter in Paradise* (qv); funny moments extremely few.

w Lew Schwarz *d* Duncan Wood *ph* Harry Waxman *m* Howard Blake

Ronnie Corbett, Thora Hird, Michael Hordern, Leslie Phillips, Barbara Murray, James Robertson Justice, Dennis Price, Wilfrid Brambell, Eleanor Summerfield, Arthur Lowe

Somebody Killed Her Husband
US 1978   96m   Movielab
Columbia / Melvin Simon (Martin Poll)

The title tells what happened when an unhappily married young mother falls in love.
Very thin suspense comedy which starts as it ends, uncertainly.

w Reginald Rose *d* Lamont Johnson *ph* Andrew Laszlo, Ralf D. Bode *m* Alex North *ph* Ted Haworth

Farrah Fawcett-Majors, Jeff Bridges, John Wood, Tammy Grimes, John Glover, Patricia Elliott

Somebody Loves Me
US 1952   97m   Technicolor
Paramount / Perlberg–Seaton

First successful in San Francisco at earthquake time, Blossom Seeley climbs to Broadway success with her partner Benny Fields, then retires to become his wife.
Adequate, unsurprising star musical of the second or third rank.

wd Irving Brecher *ph* George Barnes *songs* Jay Livingston, Ray Evans

Betty Hutton, Ralph Meeker, Robert Keith, Adele Jergens, Billie Bird, Sid Tomack, Ludwig Stossel

Somebody Up There Likes Me*
US 1956   112m   bw
MGM (Charles Schnee)

An East Side kid with reform school experience becomes middleweight boxing champion of the world.
A sentimental fantasia on the life of Rocky Graziano, expertly blending violence, depression, prizefight sequences and fake uplift.

w Ernest Lehman *d* Robert Wise *ph* Joseph Ruttenberg *m* Bronislau Kaper

Paul Newman, Pier Angeli, Everett Sloane, Eileen Heckart, Sal Mineo, Joseph Buloff, Harold J. Stone, Robert Loggia

AA: Joseph Ruttenberg

Something Big

US 1971   108m   Technicolor
Cinema Center / Stanmore and Penbar
   (Andrew V. McLaglen)

A retiring cavalry colonel has a last battle with his old enemy.
Wry serio-comic western in the Ford tradition.

w James Lee Barrett *d* Andrew V. McLaglen *ph* Harry Stradling Jnr *m* Marvin Hamlisch

Dean Martin, Brian Keith, Honor Blackman, Carol White, Ben Johnson, Albert Salmi, Denver Pyle

Something for Everyone*

US 1970   110m   colour
National General (John Flaxman)
GB title: *Black Flowers for the Bride*

A young con man insinuates himself into the household of a widowed Austrian countess.
Unusual black comedy which doesn't quite come off.

w Hugh Wheeler, *novel* The Cook by Harry Kressing *d* Harold Prince *ph* Walter Lassally *m* John Kander

Angela Lansbury, Michael York, Anthony Corlan, Heidelinde Weis

'Nothing much for anyone, actually.'—*New Yorker*

Something for the Birds

US 1952   81m   bw
TCF (Samuel G. Engel)

An elderly fraud is of help to a Washington girl trying to save a bird sanctuary.
Derivative, competent but slightly boring political whimsy on Capra lines.

w I. A. L. Diamond, Boris Ingster *d* Robert Wise *ph* Joseph La Shelle *m* Sol Kaplan

Edmund Gwenn, Victor Mature, Patricia Neal, Larry Keating, Christian Rub

Something for the Boys

US 1944   87m   Technicolor
TCF (Irving Starr)

A southern plantation is turned into a retreat for army wives.
Modest musical, vaguely based on a Broadway success.

w Robert Ellis, Helen Logan, Frank Gabrielson, *musical comedy* Cole Porter, Herbert and Dorothy Fields *d* Lewis Seiler *ph* Ernest Palmer *songs* Cole Porter

Carmen Miranda, Michael O'Shea, Vivian Blaine, Phil Silvers, Sheila Ryan, Perry Como, Glenn Langan, Cara Williams

Something in the Wind

US 1946   89m   bw
U-I (Joseph Sistrom)

A lady disc jockey is mistaken for her aunt, who has been seeing too much for the heirs' liking of a wealthy old man.
Poorish star musical comedy.

w Harry Kurnitz, William Bowers *d* Irving Pichel

Deanna Durbin, Donald O'Connor, John Dall, Charles Winninger, Helena Carter

Something Money Can't Buy

GB 1952   82m   bw
Rank / Vic (Joe Janni)

After World War II a young couple find civilian life difficult and dreary, but finally start a catering and secretarial business.
Weakly contrived comedy which makes nothing of its possibilities and is limply handled all round.

w Pat Jackson, James Lansdale Hodson *d* Pat Jackson *ph* C. Pennington-Richards *m* Nino Rota

Patricia Roc, Anthony Steel, A. E. Matthews, Moira Lister, David Hutcheson, Michael Trubshawe, Diane Hart, Charles Victor, Henry Edwards

Something of Value

US 1957   113m   bw
MGM (Pandro S. Berman)

A young African with many English friends is initiated into the Kikuyu.
An attempt to see all sides in the case of the African ritual murders of the fifties; bloodthirsty and unconvincing as well as dull.

wd Richard Brooks, *novel* Robert Ruark *ph* Russell Harlan *m* Miklos Rozsa

Rock Hudson, Sidney Poitier, Dana Wynter, Wendy Hiller, Robert Beatty, Juano Hernandez, William Marshall, Walter Fitzgerald, Michael Pate

Something to Live For

US 1952   89m   bw
Paramount (George Stevens)

A commercial artist member of Alcoholics

Anonymous falls for a dipsomaniac actress but refuses to break up his marriage.
Glossy romantic melodrama with some style but no depth; the casting makes it seem like a sequel to *The Lost Weekend*.

w Dwight Taylor *d* George Stevens *ph* George Barnes *m* Victor Young

Ray Milland, Joan Fontaine, Teresa Wright, Richard Derr, Douglas Dick

'The victory over alcohol becomes a somewhat woebegone business.'—*Penelope Houston*

Something Wild
US 1961 112m bw
(UA) Prometheus (George Justin)

A girl's life and attitudes change after she is raped, and she moves in with a garage mechanic. A bit of a wallow, with much method acting but no clear analysis of the central relationship.

w Jack Garfein, Alex Karmel, *novel* Mary Ann by Alex Karmel *d* Jack Garfein *ph* Eugene Schufftan *m* Aaron Copland *ad* Richard Day

Carroll Baker, Ralph Meeker, Mildred Dunnock, Charles Watts, Martin Kosleck, Jean Stapleton

Sometimes a Great Notion*
US 1971 114m Technicolor Panavision
Universal / Newman–Foreman
GB title: *Never Give an Inch*

In a small Oregon township, trouble is caused by an independent family of lumberjacks. Freewheeling but unsatisfactorily eccentric comedy-melodrama which never quite jells but has flashes of individuality.

w John Gay, *novel* Ken Kesey *d Paul Newman* *ph* Richard Moore *m* Henry Mancini

Paul Newman, Henry Fonda, Lee Remick, Michael Sarrazin, Richard Jaeckel, Linda Lawson, Cliff Potts

AAN: song 'All His Children' (*m* Henry Mancini, *ly* Alan and Marilyn Bergman); Richard Jaeckel

Somewhere I'll Find You*
US 1942 108m bw
MGM (Pandro S. Berman)

Brother war correspondents quarrel over a girl and later find her in Indo-China smuggling Chinese babies to safety.
Absurd but satisfactory star vehicle of the second rank, with the theme designed to prepare America for war.

w Marguerite Roberts, *story* Charles Hoffman

d Wesley Ruggles *ph* Harold Rosson *m* Bronislau Kaper

Clark Gable, Lana Turner, Robert Sterling, Patricia Dane, Reginald Owen, Lee Patrick, Charles Dingle, Rags Ragland, William Henry

Somewhere in England
GB 1940 79m bw
Mancunian (John E. Blakeley)

High jinks among army recruits staging a show. One of a series of misshapen and badly made regional comedies which afflicted British cinemas in the forties and should be mentioned for their immense popularity, their new-style vulgarity (later to be refined by the Carry On series) and their highly popular stars.

w Arthur Mertz, Rodney Parsons *d* John E. Blakeley

Frank Randle, Harry Korris, Robbie Vincent, Winki Turner, Dan Young
† Subsequently released, or allowed to escape, between 1941 and 1949 were *Somewhere in Camp, Somewhere on Leave, Somewhere in Civvies* and *Somewhere in Politics*.

Somewhere in the Night*
US 1946 111m bw
TCF

An amnesiac war veteran tries to discover his true identity and discovers he is a crook with much-wanted information. ·
Overlong suspenser with a tentative *film noir* atmosphere. A few nice touches partly atone for a tediously conversational plot.

w Howard Dimsdale, Joseph L. Mankiewicz *d* Joseph L. Mankiewicz *ph* Norbert Brodine *m* David Buttolph

John Hodiak, Nancy Guild, Lloyd Nolan, Richard Conte, Josephine Hutchinson, *Fritz Kortner*

Son of Ali Baba
US 1952 75m Technicolor
U-I (Leonard Goldstein)

A cadet of the military academy outwits a wicked caliph.
Routine Arabian Nights hokum.

w Gerald Drayson Adams *d* Kurt Neumann *ph* Maury Gertsman *m* Joseph Gershenson

Tony Curtis, Piper Laurie, Susan Cabot, Victor Jory

Son of Dracula*
US 1943 80m bw
Universal

A mysterious stranger named Alucard, with a

penchant for disappearing in puffs of smoke, turns up on a southern plantation.
Stolid series entry with a miscast lead; nicely handled moments.

w Eric Taylor *d* Robert Siodmak *ph* George Robinson *m* Hans Salter

Lon Chaney Jnr, Louise Allbritton, Robert Paige, Samuel S. Hinds, Evelyn Ankers, Frank Craven, J. Edward Bromberg
† The title cheats: he isn't the son of, but the old man himself . . .

Son of Frankenstein***
US 1939 99m bw
Universal (Rowland V. Lee)

The old baron's son comes home and starts to dabble, with the help of a broken-necked and vindictive shepherd.
Handsomely mounted sequel to *Bride of Frankenstein* and the last of the classic trio. The monster is less interesting, but there are plenty of other diversions, including the splendid if impractical sets.

w Willis Cooper *d* Rowland V. Lee *ph* George Robinson *m* Frank Skinner *ad* Jack Otterson

Basil Rathbone, Boris Karloff, Bela Lugosi, Lionel Atwill, Josephine Hutchinson, Donnie Dunagan, Emma Dunn, *Edgar Norton,* Lawrence Grant

Son of Fury*
US 1942 102m bw
TCF (William Perlberg)

An 18th-century Englishman is deprived of his inheritance, flees to a South Sea island but comes back seeking restitution.
Elaborate costumer which suffers from loss of suspense during the central idyll. Much to enjoy along the way.

w Philip Dunne, *novel* Benjamin Blake by Edison Marshall *d John Cromwell ph* Arthur Miller *m* Alfred Newman

Tyrone Power, Gene Tierney, George Sanders, Frances Farmer, Roddy McDowall, John Carradine, Elsa Lanchester, *Dudley Digges,* Harry Davenport, Halliwell Hobbes
† Remade as *Treasure of the Golden Condor* (qv).

Son of Kong*
US 1933 69m bw
RKO (Merian C. Cooper)

After Kong has wrecked New York, producer Carl Denham flees from his creditors and finds more monsters on the old island.

Hasty sequel to the splendid *King Kong*; the results were so tame and unconvincing that the film was sold as a comedy, but it does have a few lively moments after four reels of padding.

w Ruth Rose *d* Ernest B. Schoedsack *ph* Eddie Linden, Vernon Walker, J. O. Taylor *m* Max Steiner *sp Willis O'Brien*

Robert Armstrong, Helen Mack, Frank Reicher, John Marston, Victor Wong

Son of Monte Cristo*
US 1940 102m bw
(UA) Edward Small

The masked avenger who quashes a dictatorship in 1865 Lichtenstein is none other than the son of Edmond Dantes.
Cheerful swashbuckler of the second class.

w George Bruce *d* Rowland V. Lee *ph* George Robinson *m* Edward Ward

Louis Hayward, Joan Bennett, George Sanders, Florence Bates, Lionel Royce, Montagu Love, Clayton Moore, Ralph Byrd

Son of Paleface*
US 1952 95m Technicolor
(Paramount) Bob Hope (Robert L. Welch)

A tenderfoot and a government agent compete for the attentions of a lady bandit.
Gagged-up sequel to *The Paleface*; much of the humour now seems self-conscious and dated in the *Road* tradition which it apes, but there are still moments of delight.

w Frank Tashlin, Joseph Quillan, Robert L. Welch *d* Frank Tashlin *ph* Harry J. Wild *m* Lyn Murray

Bob Hope, Roy Rogers, Jane Russell, Trigger, Douglass Dumbrille, Harry Von Zell, Bill Williams, Lloyd Corrigan

AAN: song 'Am I in Love' (*m/ly* Jack Brooks)

Son of Robin Hood
GB 1958 77m Eastmancolor
Cinemascope
TCF / Argo (George Sherman)

Robin's daughter joins with the Regent's brother to overthrow the Black Duke.
Empty-headed romp, more or less in the accepted tradition.

w George George, George Slavin *d* George Sherman *ph* Arthur Grant *m* Leighton Lucas

David Hedison, June Laverick, David Farrar, Marius Goring, Philip Friend, Delphi Lawrence, George Coulouris, George Woodbridge

Son of Sinbad*
US 1955 88m Technicolor Superscope
RKO (Robert Sparks)

Sinbad and Omar Khayyam are imprisoned by
the Caliph but escape with the secret of green
fire.
Arabian Nights burlesque, mainly quite bright,
with the forty thieves played by harem girls.

w Aubrey Wisberg, Jack Pollexfen d Ted
Tetzlaff ph William Snyder m Victor Young

Dale Robertson, Vincent Price, Sally Forrest,
Lili St Cyr, Mari Blanchard, Leon Askin, Jay
Novello

A Song Is Born*
US 1948 113m Technicolor
Samuel Goldwyn

Flat remake of *Ball of Fire* (qv), graced by an
array of top-flight musical talent.

w Harry Tugend d Howard Hawks ph Gregg
Toland md Emil Newman

Danny Kaye, Virginia Mayo, Hugh Herbert,
Steve Cochran, Felix Bressart, J. Edward
Bromberg, Mary Field, Ludwig Stossel, Louis
Armstrong, Charlie Barnet, Benny Goodman,
Lionel Hampton, Tommy Dorsey, Mel Powell

The Song of Bernadette*
US 1943 156m bw
TCF (William Perlberg)

A peasant girl has a vision of the Virgin Mary at
what becomes the shrine of Lourdes.
Hollywood religiosity at its most commercial;
but behind the lapses of taste and truth is an
excellent production which was phenomenally
popular and created a new star.

w George Seaton, novel Franz Werfel d Henry
King ph Arthur Miller m Alfred Newman
ad James Basevi, William Darling

Jennifer Jones, William Eythe, Charles
Bickford, Vincent Price, Lee J. Cobb, Gladys
Cooper, Anne Revere, Roman Bohnen, Patricia
Morison, Aubrey Mather, Charles Dingle, Mary
Anderson, Edith Barrett, Sig Rumann

'A tamed and pretty image, highly varnished,
sensitively lighted, and exhibited behind
immaculate glass, the window at once of a shrine
and of a box office.'—*James Agee*

'It contains much to conciliate even the
crustiest and most prejudiced objector.'—
Richard Mallett, Punch

AA: Alfred Newman; Jennifer Jones
AAN: George Seaton; Henry King; Charles
Bickford; Gladys Cooper; Anne Revere

Song of Ceylon**
GB 1934 40m bw
Ceylon Tea Board (John Grierson)

A pictorial, almost sensuous, but not very
informative documentary in four sections: 'The
Buddha', 'The Virgin Island', 'The Voices of
Commerce', 'The Apparel of a God'. Its
influence was immense.

wd, ph Basil Wright m Walter Leigh

Song of Freedom*
GB 1936 80m bw
Hammer (J. Fraser Passmore)

A black London docker becomes an opera
singer, then goes to Africa to free the tribe of
which he has discovered himself to be the head.
A weird fable but a good star vehicle and a
surprisingly smart production for the time.

w Fenn Sherie, Ingram d'Abbes, Michael
Barringer, Philip Lindsay d J. Elder Wills

Paul Robeson, Elizabeth Welch, George Mosart,
Esmé Percy

Song of Love*
US 1947 118m bw
MGM (Clarence Brown)

The story of Clara and Robert Schumann and
their friend Johannes Brahms.
Dignified musical biopic which unfortunately
falls into most of the pitfall clichés of the genre.
Dull it may be, but it looks good and the music is
fine.

w Ivan Tors, Irmgard Von Cube, Allen Vincent,
Robert Ardrey d Clarence Brown ph Harry
Stradling md Bronislau Kaper ad Cedric
Gibbons piano Artur Rubenstein

Katharine Hepburn, Paul Henreid, Robert
Walker, Henry Daniell, Leo G. Carroll, Else
Janssen, Gigi Perreau

'This is how Brahms and the Schumanns
might very possibly have acted if they had
realized that later on they would break into the
movies.'—*Time*

Song of Norway*
US 1970 141m De Luxe
   Super Panavision 70
ABC / Andrew and Virginia Stone

A fantasia on the life of Grieg.
Multinational hodgepodge, mostly in the *Sound
of Music* style but with everything from cartoons
to Christmas cracker backgrounds. Quite
watchable, and the landscapes are certainly
splendid.

wd Andrew Stone ph Davis Boulton stage

musical Milton Lazarus *(book)* Robert Wright, George Forrest *(m/ly)*

Toralv Maurstad, Florence Henderson, Christina Schollin, Frank Poretta, Harry Secombe, Edward G. Robinson, Robert Morley, Elizabeth Larner, Bernard Archard, Oscar Homolka, Richard Wordsworth

Song of Russia
US 1944   107m   bw
MGM (Joe Pasternak)

An American symphony conductor is in Russia when hostilities begin, and watches the citizens' war effort with admiration.
A terrible big-budget film which followed the wartime propaganda line but five years later was heavily criticized by the Unamerican Activities Committee (for the wrong reasons).

w Paul Jarrico, Richard Collins *d* Gregory Ratoff *m* Herbert Stothart

Robert Taylor, Susan Peters, John Hodiak, Robert Benchley, Felix Bressart, Michael Chekhov, Darryl Hickman

'Film makers have evolved a new tongue—the broken accent deriving from no known language to be used by foreigners on all occasions.'— *Richard Winnington*

Song of Scheherazade
US 1947   107m   Technicolor
Universal (Edward Kaufman)

In 1865 naval cadet Rimsky-Korsakov falls in love with a dancer.
Yet another composer takes a drubbing in this dull and unconvincing hodgepodge.

wd Walter Reisch *ph* Hal Mohr, William V. Skall *md* Miklos Rozsa *ch* Tilly Losch *ad* Jack Otterson

Yvonne de Carlo, Jean-Pierre Aumont, Brian Donlevy, Eve Arden, Charles Kullman, John Qualen, Richard Lane, Terry Kilburn

Song of Songs*
US 1933   89m   bw
Paramount (Rouben Mamoulian)

A German peasant girl falls for a sculptor but marries a lecherous baron.
Pretentious romantic nonsense, made fairly palatable by the director's steady hand.

wd Rouben Mamoulian, *play* Edward Sheldon, *novel* Das hohe Lied by Hermann Sudermann *ph* Victor Milner *m* Karl Hajos, Milien Rodern *ad* Hans Dreier

Marlene Dietrich, Brian Aherne, Lionel Atwill, Alison Skipworth, Hardie Albright

'An ornate and irresistible slice of outright hokum.'—*Peter John Dyer, 1966*

Song of Surrender
US 1949   93m   bw
Paramount (Richard Maibaum)

In turn-of-the-century New England, a sophisticated visitor from New York falls for the wife of the museum curator.
Ho-hum romantic drama, well enough presented.

w Richard Maibaum *d* Mitchell Leisen *ph* Daniel L. Fapp *m* Victor Young

Wanda Hendrix, Claude Rains, Macdonald Carey, Andrea King, Henry Hull, Elizabeth Patterson, Art Smith

Song of the Islands*
US 1942   75m   Technicolor
TCF (William Le Baron)

On a South Sea island, the daughter of an Irish beachcomber falls for the son of an American cattle king.
Wispy musical with agreeable settings and lively songs.

w Joseph Schrank, Robert Pirosh, Robert Ellis, Helen Logan *d* Walter Lang *ph* Ernest Palmer *md* Alfred Newman *songs* various

Betty Grable, Victor Mature, Jack Oakie, Thomas Mitchell, *Hilo Hattie*, Billy Gilbert, George Barbier

Song of the South*
US 1947   94m   Technicolor
Walt Disney (Perce Pearce)

On a long-ago southern plantation, small boys listen to the Brer Rabbit stories from an elderly black servant.
Too much Uncle Remus and not enough Brer Rabbit, we fear, but children liked it. The cartoons were actually very good.

w Dalton Raymond *d* Harve Foster *ph* Gregg Toland *m* Daniele Amfitheatrof, Paul J. Scott, Charles Wolcott *cartoon credits* various

Ruth Warrick, Bobby Driscoll, James Baskett, Luana Patten, Lucile Watson, Hattie McDaniel

'The ratio of live to cartoon action is approximately two to one, and that is the ratio of the film's mediocrity to its charm.'—*Bosley Crowther*

AA: song 'Zip a Dee Do Dah' (*m* Allie Wrubel, *ly* Ray Gilbert)
AAN: Daniele Amfitheatrof, Paul J. Scott, Charles Wolcott

A Song to Remember **
US 1945   113m   Technicolor
Columbia (Louis F. Edelman)

The life and death of Chopin and his liaison with
George Sand.

Hilarious classical musical biopic which was
unexpectedly popular and provoked a flood of
similar pieces. As a production, not at all bad,
but the script . . .

w Sidney Buchman d Charles Vidor ph Tony
Gaudio md Miklos Rozsa, Morris Stoloff
piano José Iturbi ad Lionel Banks, Van Nest
Polglase

Cornel Wilde, Merle Oberon, Paul Muni,
Stephen Bekassy, Nina Foch, George Coulouris,
Sig Arno, Howard Freeman, George Macready
  'It is the business of Hollywood to shape the
truth into box-office contours.'—Richard
Winnington

AAN: original story (Ernest Marischka); Tony
Gaudio; Miklos Rozsa, Morris Stoloff; Cornel
Wilde

Song without End
US 1960   142m   Eastmancolor
   Cinemascope
Columbia (William Goetz)

The life and loves of Franz Liszt.
What worked at the box office for Chopin failed
disastrously for Liszt; famous people are turned
into papier maché dullards. Again, the
production is elegance itself.

w Oscar Millard d Charles Vidor, George
Cukor ph James Wong Howe md Morris
Stoloff, Henry Sukman piano Jorge Bolet
ad Walter Holscher

Dirk Bogarde, Capucine, Genevieve Page,
Patricia Morison, Ivan Desny, Martita Hunt,
Lyndon Brook, Alex Davion (as Chopin)

AA: Morris Stoloff, Henry Sukman

Sons and Lovers ***
GB 1960   103m   bw   Cinemascope
TCF / Company of Artists / Jerry Wald

A Nottingham miner's son learns about life and
love.

Well-produced and generally absorbing, if
unsurprising, treatment of a famous novel.

w Gavin Lambert, T. E. B. Clarke, novel D. H.
Lawrence d Jack Cardiff ph Freddie Francis
m Mario Nascimbene

Dean Stockwell, Trevor Howard, Wendy Hiller,
Mary Ure, Heather Sears, William Lucas,
Donald Pleasence, Ernest Thesiger
  'An album of decent Edwardian snapshots.'—
Peter John Dyer

AA: Freddie Francis
AAN: best picture; script; Jack Cardiff; Trevor
Howard; Mary Ure

The Sons of Katie Elder *
US 1965   122m   Technicolor   Panavision
Paramount / Hal B. Wallis (Paul Nathan)

At Katie Elder's funeral, her four troublesome
wandering sons find themselves on the verge of
further trouble.

Sluggish all-star western with predictable
highlights.

w Allan Weiss, William H. Wright, Harry Essex
d Henry Hathaway ph Lucien Ballard m Elmer
Bernstein

John Wayne, Dean Martin, Michael Anderson
Jnr, Earl Holliman, Martha Hyer, Jeremy Slate,
James Gregory, George Kennedy, Paul Fix

Sons of the Desert ****
US 1934   68m   bw
Hal Roach
GB title: Fraternally Yours

Stan and Ollie want to go to a Chicago
convention, but kid their wives that they are
going on a cruise for health reasons.
Archetypal Laurel and Hardy comedy,
unsurpassed for gags, pacing and sympathetic
characterization.

w Frank Craven, Byron Morgan d William A.
Seiter ph Kenneth Peach

Stan Laurel, Oliver Hardy, Charlie Chase, Mae
Busch, Dorothy Christie

Sorcerer
US 1977   121m   Technicolor
Universal / Film Properties International
   (William Friedkin)
GB title: Wages of Fear

Volunteers are needed to drive nitro-glycerine to
an outpost in the South American jungle.
Why anyone should have wanted to spend
twenty million dollars on a remake of The Wages
of Fear, do it badly, and give it a misleading title
is anybody's guess. The result is dire.

w Walon Green, novel Georges Arnaud (and the
film by Henri-Georges Clouzot) d William
Friedkin ph John M. Stephens, Dick Bush
m various pd John Box

Roy Scheider, Bruno Cremer, Francisco Rabal,
Amidou, Ramon Bieri

Sorrowful Jones
US 1949   88m   bw
Paramount (Robert L. Welch)

A racetrack tout unofficially adopts an orphan girl.
Heavy-going sentimental comedy peopled by comic gangsters, a remake of *Little Miss Marker* with the emphasis changed.

w Melville Shavelson, Edmund Hartmann, Jack Rose, *story* Damon Runyon *d* Sidney Lanfield *ph* Daniel L. Fapp *m* Robert Emmett Dolan

Bob Hope, Lucille Ball, William Demarest, Bruce Cabot, Thomas Gomez, Tom Pedi, Houseley Stevenson, Mary Jane Saunders

Sorry Wrong Number**
US 1948   89m   bw
Paramount (Hal B. Wallis, Anatole Litvak)

A bedridden neurotic woman discovers she is marked for murder and tries to summon help.
Artificial but effective suspenser, extended from a radio play.

w Lucille Fletcher, from her play *d* Anatole Litvak *ph* Sol Polito *m* Franz Waxman

Barbara Stanwyck, Burt Lancaster, Ann Richards, Wendell Corey, Ed Begley, Harold Vermilyea, Leif Erickson, William Conrad

AAN: Barbara Stanwyck

Souls at Sea*
US 1937   93m   bw
Paramount

In a 19th-century shipwreck an intelligence officer must save himself, and his mission, at the cost of other lives, and is courtmartialled.
A lively seafaring melodrama produced on a fairly impressive scale.

w Grover Jones, Dale Van Every *d* Henry Hathaway *ph* Charles Lang Jnr *m* Milan Roder, W. Franke Harling *md* Morris Stoloff

Gary Cooper, George Raft, Frances Dee, Henry Wilcoxon, Harry Carey, Olympe Bradna, Robert Cummings, Porter Hall, George Zucco, Virginia Weidler, Joseph Schildkraut, Gilbert Emery

AAN: Milan Roder, W. Franke Harling

The Sound and the Fury
US 1959   117m   Eastmancolor
Cinemascope
TCF / Jerry Wald

A once proud southern family has sunk low in finance and moral stature, and a stern elder son tries to do something about it.
Heavy melodrama with performances to match.

w Irving Ravetch, Harriet Frank Jnr, *novel* William Faulkner *d* Martin Ritt *ph* Charles G. Clarke *m* Alex North

Yul Brynner, Joanne Woodward, Margaret Leighton, Stuart Whitman, Ethel Waters, Jack Warden, Françoise Rosay, John Beal, Albert Dekker

'A fourth carbon copy of Chekhov in Dixie.'—*Stanley Kauffmann*

The Sound Barrier**
GB 1952   118m   bw
London Films (David Lean)
US title: *Breaking the Sound Barrier*

An aircraft manufacturer takes risks with the lives of his family and friends to prove that the sound barrier can be broken.
Riveting, then topical, melodrama with splendid air sequences; a bit upper crust, but with well-drawn characters.

w Terence Rattigan *d* David Lean *ph* Jack Hildyard *m* Malcolm Arnold

Ralph Richardson, Nigel Patrick, Ann Todd, John Justin, Dinah Sheridan, Joseph Tomelty, Denholm Elliott

AAN: Terence Rattigan

The Sound of Music***
US 1965   172m   De Luxe   Todd-AO
TCF / Argyle (Robert Wise)

In 1938 Austria, a trainee nun becomes governess to the Trapp family, falls in love with the widower father, and helps them all escape from the Nazis.
Slightly muted, very handsome version of an enjoyably old-fashioned stage musical with splendid tunes.

w Ernest Lehman, *book* Howard Lindsay, Russel Crouse *d* Robert Wise *ph* Ted McCord *m/ly* Richard Rodgers, Oscar Hammerstein II *md* Irwin Kostal *pd* Boris Leven

Julie Andrews, Christopher Plummer, Richard Haydn, Eleanor Parker, *Peggy Wood*, Anna Lee, Marni Nixon

'. . . sufficient warning to those allergic to singing nuns and sweetly innocent children.'—*John Gillett*

AA: best picture; Robert Wise; Irwin Kostal
AAN: Ted McCord; Julie Andrews; Peggy Wood

Sound Off
US 1952   83m   Supercinecolor
Columbia (Jonie Taps)

An entertainer is recruited into the army and has predictable difficulties.
Dishevelled service farce with funny moments.

w Blake Edwards, Richard Quine *d* Richard Quine *ph* Ellis Carter *m* Morris Stoloff

Mickey Rooney, Anne James, Sammy White, John Asher, Gordon Jones

Sounder*
US 1972   105m   De Luxe   Panavision
TCF / Radnitz–Mattel (Robert B. Radnitz)

During the thirties Depression, black sharecroppers in the deep south endure various tribulations.
Well made liberated family movie . . . but not very exciting.

w Lonnie Elder III, *novel* William H. Armstrong *d* Martin Ritt *ph* John Alonzo *m* Taj Mahal

Paul Winfield, Cicely Tyson, Kevin Hooks, Carmen Mathews, James Best, Taj Mahal

AAN: best picture; Lonnie Elder III; Paul Winfield; Cicely Tyson

Sous les Toits de Paris*
France 1930   92m   bw
Tobis (Frank Clifford)

A Parisian street singer falls in love with a girl, fights her lover, and proves himself innocent of theft.
Surprisingly serious and darkly lit little comedy-drama which, while well enough directed, hardly seems to merit its classic status.

wd René Clair ph Georges Périnal *m* Armand Bernard *pd* Lazare Meerson

Albert Préjean, Pola Illery, Gaston Modot, Edmond Gréville

South of Algiers
GB 1952   95m   Technicolor
ABP / Mayflower (Aubrey Baring, Maxwell Setton)
US title: *The Golden Mask*

Archaeologists and thieves search the Sahara for a priceless mask.
Schoolboy adventure story with a straightforward plot and plenty of local colour.

w Robert Westerby *d* Jack Lee *ph* Oswald Morris *m* Robert Gill

Van Heflin, Wanda Hendrix, Eric Portman, Charles Goldner, Jacques François, Jacques Brunius, Alec Mango, Marne Maitland

South Pacific**
US 1958   170m   Technicolor   Todd-AO
Magna / S. P. Enterprises (Buddy Adler)

In 1943 an American navy nurse on a South Pacific island falls in love with a middle-aged French planter who becomes a war hero.
Overlong, solidly produced film of the musical stage hit, with great locations, action climaxes and lush photography (also a regrettable

tendency to use alarming colour filters for dramatic emphasis).

w Paul Osborn, Richard Rodgers, Oscar Hammerstein II, Joshua Logan, *stories* Tales of the South Pacific by James A. Michener *d* Joshua Logan *ph* Leon Shamroy *m/ly Richard Rodgers, Oscar Hammerstein II md* Alfred Newman, Ken Darby *ch* Le Roy Prinz

Mitzi Gaynor, Rossano Brazzi, Ray Walston, John Kerr, France Nuyen, Juanita Hall

AAN: Leon Shamroy; Alfred Newman, Ken Darby

South Riding**
GB 1937   91m   bw
London Films (Alexander Korda, Victor Saville)

A schoolmistress in a quiet Yorkshire dale exposes crooked councillors and falls for the depressed local squire.
Dated but engrossing multi-drama from a famous novel; a good compact piece of film-making.

w Ian Dalrymple, Donald Bull, novel Winifred Holtby d Victor Saville

Ralph Richardson, Edna Best, Edmund Gwenn, Ann Todd, Glynis Johns, John Clements, Marie Lohr, Milton Rosmer, Edward Lexy

South Sea Woman
US 1953   89m   bw
Warner (Sam Bischoff)

Adventures of a fight-loving marine in the Pacific war.
Unlovable mixture of brawling, romancing and war-winning.

w Edwin Blum, *play* William M. Rankin *d* Arthur Lubin *ph* Ted McCord *m* David Buttolph

Burt Lancaster, Virginia Mayo, Chuck Connors, Arthur Shields, Barry Kelley, Leon Askin

The Southern Star*
GB / France 1968   105m   Techniscope
Columbia / Eurofrance / Capitole

In French West Africa in 1912, a penniless American finds a huge diamond which several crooks are after.
Quite a likeable adventure romp, with good suspense sequences and convincing jungle settings.

w David Pursall, Jack Seddon, *novel* Jules Verne *d* Sidney Hayers *ph* Raoul Coutard *m* Georges Garvarentz

George Segal, Ursula Andress, Orson Welles,

Ian Hendry, Michael Constantine, Johnny
Sekka, Harry Andrews

A Southern Yankee*
US 1948 90m bw
MGM (Paul Jones)
GB title: *My Hero*

During the Civil War a southern bellboy
masquerades as a spy and finds himself behind
enemy lines.
A rather feeble reworking of Buster Keaton's
The General, with some excellent gags
supervised by the master himself.

w Harry Tugend *d* Edward Sedgwick *ph* Ray
June *m* David Snell

Red Skelton, Brian-Donlevy, Arlene Dahl,
George Coulouris, Lloyd Gough, John Ireland,
Minor Watson, Charles Dingle

The Southerner***
US 1945 91m bw
(UA) David Loew, Robert Hakim

Problems of penniless farmers in the deep south.
Impressive, highly pictorial outdoor drama,
more poetic than *The Grapes of Wrath* and
lacking the acting strength.

wd Jean Renoir, *novel* Hold Autumn in Your
Hand by George Sessions Perry *ph* Lucien
Andriot *m* Werner Janssen

Zachary Scott, Betty Field, *Beulah Bondi*, J.
Carrol Naish, Percy Kilbride, Blanche Yurka,
Norman Lloyd

  'I cannot imagine anybody failing to be
spellbound by this first successful essay in
Franco-American screen collaboration.'—
Richard Winnington

AAN: Jean Renoir (as director); Werner
Janssen

Soylent Green*
US 1973 97m Metrocolor Panavision
MGM (Walter Seltzer, Russell Thatcher)

In 2022, the population of New York exists in
perpetual heat on synthetic foods; a policeman
hears from his elderly friend about an earlier time
when things were better.
Lively futuristic yarn with a splendid climax
revealing the nature of the artificial food; marred
by narrative incoherence and by direction which
fails to put plot points clearly across.

w Stanley R. Greenberg, *novel* Make Room,
Make Room by Harry Harrison *d* Richard
Fleischer *ph* Richard H. Kline *m* Fred Myrow

Charlton Heston, *Edward G. Robinson*, Leigh
Taylor-Young, Chuck Connors, Brock Peters,
Joseph Cotten

Spanish Affair
US 1958 92m Technicolor Vistavision
Paramount / Nomad (Bruce Odlum)

An American architect in Madrid falls in love
with his interpreter and is pursued by her lover.
Curiously plotless excuse for a travelogue, lushly
photographed but not exactly gripping.

w Richard Collins *d* Don Siegel *ph* Sam Leavitt
m Daniele Amfitheatrof

Richard Kiley, Carmen Sevilla, Jose Guardiola

The Spanish Gardener
GB 1956 97m Technicolor Vistavision
Rank (John Bryan)

The British consul in Spain is annoyed when his
young son develops a strong friendship with the
gardener.
Slow, understated study in human relationships
which doesn't come off; any sexual relevance is
well concealed.

w Lesley Storm, John Bryan, *novel* A. J. Cronin
d Philip Leacock *ph* Christopher Challis
m John Veale

Dirk Bogarde, Michael Hordern, Jon Whiteley,
Cyril Cusack, Geoffrey Keen, Maureen
Swanson, Lyndon Brook, Josephine Griffin,
Bernard Lee, Rosalie Crutchley

The Spanish Main*
US 1945 101m Technicolor
RKO (Robert Fellows)

In the Caribbean, the fiancée of the Spanish
viceroy is kidnapped by a pirate who determines
to tame her before marrying her.
Slightly tongue-in-cheek pirate hokum; generally
good value for the easily amused.

w George Worthing Yates, Herman J.
Mankiewicz *d* Frank Borzage *ph* George
Barnes *m* Hanns Eisler *md* Constantin
Bakaleinikoff

Paul Henreid, Maureen O'Hara, Binnie Barnes,
Walter Slezak, John Emery, Barton MacLane, J.
M. Kerrigan, Nancy Gates, Fritz Leiber, Jack
La Rue, Mike Mazurki, Victor Kilian

AAN: George Barnes

Spare the Rod
GB 1961 93m bw
British Lion / Bryanston /Weyland (Victor
Lyndon)

At an East End school, a novice master wins the
confidence of tough pupils.
A British *Blackboard Jungle*, paving the way for
To Sir with Love; not exciting on its own
account.

w John Cresswell, *novel* Michael Croft *d* Leslie Norman *ph* Paul Beeson *m* Laurie Johnson

Max Bygraves, Geoffrey Keen, Donald Pleasence, Richard O'Sullivan, Betty McDowall, Eleanor Summerfield, Mary Merrall

Sparrows Can't Sing
GB 1962   94m   bw
Elstree / Carthage

Returning after two years at sea, a sailor searches for his wife and threatens vengeance on her lover.

Relentlessly caricatured cockney comedy melodrama, too self-conscious to be effective, and not at all likeable anyway.

w Stephen Lewis, Joan Littlewood *d* Joan Littlewood *ph* Mac Greene *m* James Stevens

James Booth, Barbara Windsor, Roy Kinnear, Avis Bunnage, George Sewell, Barbara Ferris, Murray Melvin, Arthur Mullard

Spartacus**
US 1960   196m   Super Technirama 70
U-I / Bryna (Edward Lewis)

The slaves of ancient Rome revolt and are quashed.

Long, well-made, downbeat epic with deeper than usual characterization and several bravura sequences.

w Dalton Trumbo, *novel* Howard Fast *d* Stanley Kubrick *ph* Russell Metty *m* Alex North *pd* Alexander Golitzen

Kirk Douglas, Laurence Olivier, Charles Laughton, Tony Curtis, Jean Simmons, Peter Ustinov, John Gavin, Nina Foch, Herbert Lom, John Ireland, John Dall, Charles McGraw, Woody Strode

'Everything is depicted with a lack of imagination that is truly Marxian.'—*Anne Grayson*

'A lot of first-rate professionals have pooled their abilities to make a first-rate circus.'—*Stanley Kauffmann*

'One comes away feeling rather revolted and not at all ennobled.'—*Alan Dent, Illustrated London News*

AA: Russell Metty; Peter Ustinov
AAN: Alex North

Spawn of the North**
US 1938   110m   bw
Paramount (Albert Lewin)

In 1890s Alaska, American fishermen combat Russian poachers.

Solidly carpentered all-star action melodrama, a sizzler of its day. Remade 1953 as *Alaska Seas*.

w Talbot Jennings, Jules Furthman *d* Henry Hathaway *ph* Charles Lang *m* Dmitri Tiomkin

George Raft, Henry Fonda, Dorothy Lamour, *John Barrymore*, Akim Tamiroff, Louise Platt, Lynne Overman, Fuzzy Knight, Vladimir Sokoloff, Duncan Renaldo, John Wray

Speak Easily*
US 1932   83m   bw
MGM

A professor inherits a Broadway musical and falls for the lure of the bright lights.

Interesting Keaton talkie at the point of his decline.

w Ralph Spence, Lawrence E. Johnson, *novel* Footlights by Clarence Budington Kelland *d* Edward Sedgwick *ph* Harold Wentstrom

Buster Keaton, Jimmy Durante, Hedda Hopper

Special Delivery
US 1976   99m   De Luxe
TCF / Bing Crosby Productions (Richard Berg)

Three disabled Vietnam veterans rob a bank, and the consequences are complicated.

Unremarkable suspenser which takes itself too seriously.

w Don Gazzaniga *d* Paul Wendkos *ph* Harry Stradling Jnr *m* Lalo Schifrin

Bo Svenson, Cybill Shepherd, Michael C. Gwynne, Vic Tayback, Sorrell Booke

The Specter of the Rose*
US 1946   90m   bw
Republic

A schizophrenic ballet dancer lives his role and nearly murders his wife.

A rather hilarious bid for culture: hard to sit through without laughing, but unique.

wd Ben Hecht *ph* Lee Garmes *m* Georges Antheil

Viola Essen, Ivan Kirov, Michael Chekhov

Spellbound
GB 1940   82m   bw
Pyramid Amalgamated (R. Murray Leslie)
aka: *Passing Clouds*; US title: *The Spell of Amy Nugent*

A young man is in despair when his fiancée dies, and nearly goes mad when a medium materializes her from the dead.

Very odd, very naïve, but somehow rather winning.

w Miles Malleson, *novel* The Necromancers by Robert Benson *d* John Harlow

Derek Farr, Vera Lindsay, Frederick Leister, Hay Petrie, Diana King, Felix Aylmer

Spellbound***
US 1945   111m   bw
David O. Selznick

The new head of a mental institution is an impostor and an amnesiac; a staff member falls in love with him and helps him recall the fate of the real Dr Edwardes.

Enthralling and rather infuriating psychological mystery; the Hitchcock touches are splendid, and the stars shine magically, but the plot could have stood a little more attention.

w Ben Hecht, Angus MacPhail, *novel* The House of Dr Edwardes by Francis Beeding *d Alfred Hitchcock ph George Barnes dream sequence Salvador Dali m Miklos Rozsa ad* James Basevi

Ingrid Bergman, Gregory Peck, Leo G. Carroll, Michael Chekhov, Rhonda Fleming, John Emery, Norman Lloyd, Steve Geray

'Just about as much of the id as could be safely displayed in a Bergdorf Goodman window.'— *James Agee*

'Bergman's apple-cheeked sincerity has rarely been so out of place as in this confection whipped up by jaded chefs.'—*New Yorker, 1976*

AAN: best picture; Alfred Hitchcock; George Barnes; Miklos Rozsa; Michael Chekhov

Spencer's Mountain*
US 1963   121m   Technicolor   Panavision
Warner (Delmer Daves)

Life in rural America in the thirties with a poor quarry worker and his family of nine.

Sentimental rose-tinted hokum which later became TV's *The Waltons*. Expertly concocted, Hollywood style.

wd Delmer Daves, *novel* Earl Hanmer Jnr *ph* Charles Lawton, H. F. Koenekamp *m* Max Steiner

Henry Fonda, Maureen O'Hara, James MacArthur, Donald Crisp, Wally Cox, Mimsy Farmer, Lilian Bronson

The Spider and the Fly
GB 1949   95m   bw
GFD / Maxwell Setton, Aubrey Baring

In 1913 a Parisian safecracker constantly outwits an inspector of the Sûreté, but war brings changes.

Coldly ironic comedy drama which really, regrettably, doesn't work.

w Robert Westerby *d* Robert Hamer· *ph* Geoffrey Unsworth *m* Georges Auric

Eric Portman, Guy Rolfe, Nadia Gray, George Cole, Edward Chapman, John Carol, Maurice Denham

'Not sufficiently exciting for a thriller, not quite sharp enough for a real drama of character.'—*Gavin Lambert, MFB*

The Spider's Stratagem*
Italy 1970   97m   Eastmancolor
Radiotelevisione Italiana / Red Film (Giovanni Bertolucci)

Revisiting the village in the Po valley where his father was murdered by fascists in 1936, our gradually disillusioned hero learns that his father was really a traitor executed by his own men.

Elaborately mysterious puzzle play for intellectuals, with infinite shades of meaning which few will bother to explore. The atmosphere, however, is superbly caught.

w Bernardo Bertolucci, Eduardo de Gregorio, Marilu Parolini, *story* The Theme of the Traitor and the Hero by Jorge Luis Borges *d* Bernardo Bertolucci *ph* Vittorio Storaro, Franco di Giacomo

Giulio Brogi, Alida Valli, Tino Scotti, Pino Campanini

The Spikes Gang
US 1974   96m   De Luxe
UA / Mirisch / Duo / Sanford

Three boys shelter a bank robber and join his gang.

Doom-laden, violent western with a few comic lines.

w Irving Ravetch, Harriet Frank Jnr, *novel* The Bank Robber by Giles Tippette *d* Richard Fleischer *ph* Brian West *m* Fred Karlin

Lee Marvin, Gary Grimes, Ron Howard, Charles Martin Smith, Arthur Hunnicutt, Noah Beery Jnr

Spinout
US 1966   93m   Metrocolor   Panavision
MGM / Euterpe (Joe Pasternak)
GB title: *California Holiday*

A carefree touring singer agrees to drive an experimental car in a road race.

Mild star musical which at least stays in the open air.

w Theodore J. Flicker, George Kirgo *d* Norman Taurog *ph* Daniel L. Fapp *md* Georgie Stoll

Elvis Presley, Shelley Fabares, Carl Betz, Cecil Kellaway, Diane McBain, Deborah Walley, Jack Mullaney, Will Hutchins, Una Merkel

The Spiral Road
US 1962   145m   Eastmancolor
U-I (Robert Arthur)

In 1936 Java, an atheist medical man fights a
leprosy epidemic and eventually becomes a
missionary.
A long slog through jungle/religious clichés, with
a hilariously miscast star and an almost
Victorian script.

w John Lee Mahin, Neil Paterson, *novel* Jan de
Hartog *d* Robert Mulligan *ph* Russell Harlan
m Jerry Goldsmith

Rock Hudson, Burl Ives, Geoffrey Keen, Gena
Rowlands, Will Kuluva, Neva Patterson, Philip
Abbott

The Spiral Staircase***
US 1946 83m bw
David O. Selznick

A small town in 1906 New England is terrorized
by a psychopathic killer of deformed girls.
Archetypal old dark house thriller, superbly
detailed and set during a most convincing
thunderstorm. Even though the identity of the
villain is pretty obvious, this is a superior
Hollywood product.

w *Mel Dinelli, novel* Some Must Watch by Ethel
Lina White *d Robert Siodmak ph Nicholas
Musuraca m Roy Webb ad Albert S.
D'Agostino, Jack Okey*

Dorothy McGuire, George Brent, Kent Smith,
Ethel Barrymore, Rhys Williams, Rhonda
Fleming, Gordon Oliver, Sara Allgood, James
Bell

'A nice, cosy and well-sustained atmosphere
of horror.'—*C. A. Lejeune*

AAN: Ethel Barrymore

The Spiral Staircase
GB 1975 89m Technicolor
Warner / Raven (Peter Shaw)

Modernized remake of the above using virtually
the same script, and apparently determined to
prove how badly it can be presented.

w Allan Scott, Chris Bryant *d* Peter Collinson
ph Ken Hodges *m* David Lindup

Jacqueline Bisset, Christopher Plummer, Sam
Wanamaker, Mildred Dunnock, Gayle
Hunnicutt, Sheila Brennan, Elaine Stritch, John
Ronane, Ronald Radd

'I don't think this needless remake is going to
set anyone's flesh creeping, except at the vulgar
flashiness of the whole enterprise.'—*Michael
Billington, Illustrated London News*

The Spirit Is Willing
US 1966 100m Technicolor
Paramount / William Castle

A family finds that its holiday home is haunted
by the ghosts of a *crime passionel*.

Overlong, overlayed and witless farce with
virtually no opportunity well taken.

w Ben Starr, *novel* The Visitors by Nathaniel
Benchley *d* William Castle *ph* Hal Stine *m* Vic
Mizzy

Sid Caesar, Vera Miles, John McGiver, Cass
Daley, John Astin, Mary Wickes, Jesse White

The Spirit of St Louis*
US 1957 135m Warnercolor
Cinemascope
Warner (Leyland Hayward)

In 1927 Charles Lindbergh flies a specially
constructed plane 3,600 miles nonstop New
York to Paris in 33½ hours.
Impeccably in its period, this needlessly
Cinemascoped reconstruction can scarcely
avoid dull patches since for long stretches its
hero is on screen solo apart from a fly, and his
monologues become soporific.

w Billy Wilder, Wendell Mayes, *book* Charles
Lindbergh *d* Billy Wilder *ph* Robert Burks,
Peverell Marley *m* Franz Waxman

James Stewart, Murray Hamilton, Marc
Connelly

Spite Marriage*
US 1929 77m (24 fps) bw silent
MGM / Buster Keaton (Lawrence
Weingarten)

A tailor's assistant loves an actress, who marries
him to spite someone else.

For a Keaton comedy from his great period, this
is remarkably thin on invention, and its
pleasures, though undeniable, are minor.

w Richard Schayer, Lew Lipton *d* Edward
Sedgwick *ph* Reggie Lanning

Buster Keaton, Dorothy Sebastian, Edward
Earle, Leila Hyams

Spitfire*
US 1934 88m bw
RKO (Pandro S. Berman)

An Ozark mountain girl believes herself to be a
faith healer and is driven from the community.
Curious star melodrama with effective moments.

w Jane Murfin, *play* Trigger by Lula Vollmer
d John Cromwell *ph* Edward Cronjager *m* Max
Steiner

Katharine Hepburn, Robert Young, Ralph
Bellamy, Martha Sleeper, Louis Mason

Splendor
US 1935 77m bw
Samuel Goldwyn

The son of a once-wealthy Park Avenue family marries a poor girl.
Dated romantic drama.

w Rachel Crothers, from her play *d* Elliott Nugent *ph* Gregg Toland *md* Alfred Newman

Joel McCrea, Miriam Hopkins, Helen Westley, Katherine Alexander, David Niven, Paul Cavanagh, Billie Burke, Arthur Treacher

Splendor in the Grass*
US 1961 124m Technicolor
Warner / NBI (Elia Kazan)

Adolescent love in a small Kansas town in the twenties.
Impressive though curiously unmemorable addition to a nostalgic young sex cycle which was already played out; production and performances well up to scratch.

w Wiliam Inge *d* Elia Kazan *ph* Boris Kaufman *m* David Armran

Natalie Wood, Warren Beatty, Pat Hingle, Audrey Christie, Barbara Loden, Zohra Lampert, Sandy Dennis
'Less like a high-school version of *Summer and Smoke* than [like] an Andy Hardy story with glands.'—*Stanley Kauffmann*

AA: William Inge
AAN: Natalie Wood

The Split
US 1968 90m Metrocolor Panavision
MGM / Spectrum (Robert Chartoff, Irwin Winkler)

A black criminal plans to rob the Los Angeles Coliseum during a football match.
Busy, brutal crime thriller, well enough done but totally unsympathetic.

w Robert Sabarpff, *novel* The Seventh by Richard Stark *d* Gordon Flemyng *ph* Burnett Guffey *m* Quincy Jones

Jim Brown, Diahann Carroll, Ernest Borgnine, Julie Harris, Gene Hackman, Jack Klugman, Warren Oates, James Whitmore, Donald Sutherland

Split Second
US 1953 85m bw
RKO (Edmund Grainger)

An escaped convict hides out with four hostages in an Arizona ghost town which has been cleared in preparation for an atom bomb test.
Routine suspenser.

w William Bowers, Irving Wallace *d* Dick Powell *ph* Nicholas Musuraca *m* Roy Webb

Stephen McNally, Alexis Smith, Jan Sterling,

Keith Andes, Arthur Hunnicutt, Paul Kelly, Richard Egan, Robert Paige

The Spoilers*
US 1930 86m bw
Paramount

In Alaska during the gold rush, crooked government officials begin despoiling the richest claims.
Early talkie version of a famous brawling saga.

w Bartlett Cormack, Agnes Brand Leahy, *novel* Rex Beach *d* Edward Carewe *ph* Harry Fischbeck

Gary Cooper, William 'Stage' Boyd, Betty Compson, Kay Johnson, Harry Green, Slim Summerville

The Spoilers**
US 1942 87m bw
Universal (Frank Lloyd)

Two adventurers in the Yukon quarrel over land rights and a saloon entertainer.
Well-packaged mixture of saloon brawls, romance and adventure, much filmed as a silent.

w Lawrence Hazard, Tom Reed *d* Ray Enright *ph* Milton Krasner *m* Hans Salter *ad* Jack Otterson

Marlene Dietrich, Randolph Scott, John Wayne, Margaret Lindsay, Harry Carey, Richard Barthelmess, George Cleveland, Samuel S. Hinds

The Spoilers*
US 1955 82m Technicolor
U-I (Ross Hunter)

Adequate, unmemorable remake of the above.

w Oscar Brodney, Charles Hoffman *d* Jesse Hibbs *ph* Maury Gertsman *m* Joseph Gershenson

Anne Baxter, Jeff Chandler, Rory Calhoun, Barbara Britton, Carl Benton Reid, Ray Danton, John McIntire, Raymond Walburn, Wallace Ford

Spring and Port Wine
GB 1970 101m Technicolor
EMI / Memorial (Michael Medwin)

A Lancashire family runs into trouble when stern father insists that teenage daughter should eat a meal she refuses.
A popular old-fashioned stage comedy which simply doesn't work on film, partly from being set in a too-real town (Bolton) and partly because of a miscast lead.

w Bill Naughton, from his play *d* Peter

Hammond *ph* Norman Warwick *m* Douglas Gamley *pd* Reece Pemberton

James Mason, Diana Coupland, Susan George, Rodney Bewes, Hannah Gordon, Adrienne Posta, Arthur Lowe

Spring in Park Lane**
GB 1948　92m　bw
British Lion / Herbert Wilcox

A diamond merchant's niece falls for a footman who just happens to be an impoverished lord in disguise.
Flimsy but highly successful romantic comedy which managed to get its balance right and is still pretty entertaining, much more so than its sequel *Maytime in Mayfair*.

w Nicholas Phipps, *play* Come Out of the Kitchen by Alice Duer Miller *d Herbert Wilcox ph* Max Greene

Anna Neagle, Michael Wilding, Tom Walls, Nicholas Phipps, Peter Graves, Marjorie Fielding, *Nigel Patrick*, Lana Morris
'A never-failing dream of Olde Mayfaire and its eternally funny butlers and maids, its disguised lords and ladies.'—*Richard Winnington*

Spring Parade*
US 1940　89m　bw
Universal (Joe Pasternak)

A single baker's assistant falls for a prince.
Pleasing, artificial Austrian frou-frou with star and support in good escapist form.

w Bruce Manning, Felix Jackson, *story* Ernst Marischka *d* Henry Koster *ph* Joseph Valentine *m* Robert Stolz *md* Charles Previn

Deanna Durbin, Robert Cummings, S. Z. Sakall, Mischa Auer, Henry Stephenson, Anne Gwynne, Butch and Buddy

AAN: Joseph Valentine; Charles Previn; song 'Waltzing in the Clouds' (*m* Robert Stolz, *ly* Gus Kahn)

Spring Reunion
US 1957　79m　bw
UA / Bryna (Jerry Bresler)

College classmates fall in love all over again at a reunion fifteen years later.
Romantic fiction for the middle-aged, performed with bare competence.

wd Robert Pirosh *ph* Harold Lipstein *m* Herbert Spencer, Earle Hagen

Betty Hutton, Dana Andrews, Jean Hagen, Robert Simon, James Gleason, Laura La Plante, Irene Ryan

Springfield Rifle
US 1952　93m　Warnercolor
Warner (Louis E. Edelman)

A Union officer gets himself cashiered, joins the Confederates as a spy, and unmasks a traitor.
Stolid Civil War western with Grade A production but not much individuality.

w Charles Marquis Warren, Frank Davis *d* André de Toth *ph* Edwin DuPar *m* Max Steiner

Gary Cooper, Phyllis Thaxter, David Brian, Lon Chaney Jnr, Paul Kelly, Phil Carey, James Millican, Guinn Williams

Springtime in the Rockies
US 1942　91m　Technicolor
TCF (Darryl F. Zanuck)

Romances blossom on a mountain holiday.
Flimsily-plotted, studio-bound, absolutely routine musical.

w Walter Bullock, Ken Englund *d* Irving Cummings *ph* Ernest Palmer *songs* Mack Gordon, Harry Warren

Betty Grable, John Payne, Carmen Miranda, Edward Everett Horton, Cesar Romero, Charlotte Greenwood, Frank Orth, Harry James and his Music Makers

Spy Hunt*
US 1950　74m　bw
Universal (Ralph Dietrich)
GB title: *Panther's Moon*

Secret microfilm is stowed in the collar of one of two panthers being transported out of Europe by train for circus use.
Slick minor espionage thriller.

w George Zuckerman, Leonard Lee, *novel* Panther's Moon by Victor Canning *d* George Sherman, *ph* Irving Glassberg *m* Walter Scharf *md* Joseph Gershenson

Howard Duff, Marta Toren, Philip Friend, Robert Douglas, Philip Dorn, Walter Slezak, Kurt Kreuger

The Spy in Black**
GB 1939　82　bw
Harefield / Alexander Korda (Irving Asher)
US title: *U-Boat 29*

In the Orkneys in 1917, German spies don't trust each other.
Unusual romantic melodrama which provided an unexpectedly interesting romantic team.

w Emeric Pressburger, Roland Pertwee, *novel* J. Storer Clouston *d* Michael Powell

Conrad Veidt, Valerie Hobson, Hay Petrie,

Helen Haye, Sebastian Shaw, Marius Goring,
June Duprez, Athole Stewart, Cyril Raymond

The Spy Who Came in from the Cold**

GB 1966 112m bw
Paramount / Salem (Martin Ritt)

A British master spy is offered a chance to get
even with his East German opponent by being
apparently sacked, disillusioned, and open for
recruitment.

The old undercover yarn with trimmings of such
sixties malaises as death wish, anti-
establishmentism and racial problems. As a
yarn, quite gripping till it gets too downbeat, but
very harshly photographed.

w Paul Dehn, Guy Trosper, *novel* John Le
Carré *d* Martin Ritt *ph* Oswald Morris *m* Sol
Kaplan *pd* Tambi Larsen

Richard Burton, Claire Bloom, *Oskar Werner*,
Peter Van Eyck, Sam Wanamaker, Rupert
Davies, George Voskovec, Cyril Cusack,
Michael Hordern, Robert Hardy, Bernard Lee,
Beatrix Lehmann
AAN: Richard Burton

The Spy Who Loved Me

GB 1977 125m Eastmancolor
    Panavision
UA / Eon (Albert R. Broccoli)

James Bond and a glamorous Russian spy
combine forces to track down and eliminate a
megalomaniac shipping magnate with an
undersea missile base.

Witless spy extravaganza in muddy colour, with
the usual tired chases and pussyfoot violence but
no new gimmicks except a seven-foot villain with
steel teeth.

w Christopher Wood, Richard Maibaum,
novel Ian Fleming *d* Lewis Gilbert *ph* Claude
Renoir *m* Marvin Hamlisch *pd* Ken Adam

Roger Moore, Barbara Bach, Curt Jurgens,
Richard Kiel, Caroline Munro, Walter Gotell,
Bernard Lee, Lois Maxwell, George Baker,
Desmond Llewellyn, Edward De Souza, Sydney
Tafler

'The film, bearing no relation to its nominal
source, seems to do nothing more than
anthologize its forerunners.'—*Tim Pulleine,
MFB*

The Spy with a Cold Nose

GB 1966 93m Eastmancolor
Paramount / Associated London / Embassy
    (Robert Porter)

A fashionable vet is blackmailed by MI5 into
inserting a radio transmitter into a bulldog.

Rather painful, overacted and overwritten farce
full of obvious jokes masquerading as satire.

w Ray Galton, Alan Simpson *d* Daniel Petrie
ph Kenneth Higgins *m* Riz Ortolani

Lionel Jeffries, Laurence Harvey, Daliah Lavi,
Eric Sykes, Eric Portman, Colin Blakely,
Denholm Elliott, Robert Flemyng, Paul Ford,
Bernard Lee, June Whitfield, Bernard Archard

S*P*Y*S

GB 1974 100m Technicolor
Dymphana / C-W / American Film Properties
    (Irwin Winkler, Robert Chartoff)

Clumsy CIA agents in Paris come across a list of
KGB agents in China.

Surprisingly dull and unfashionable parade of
comic spy clichés; the talents involved obviously
intended something closer to M*A*S*H.

w Malcolm Marmorstein, Lawrence J. Cohen,
Fred Freeman *d* Irwin Kershner *ph* Gerry
Fisher *m* John Scott

Elliott Gould, Donald Sutherland, Zouzou, Joss
Ackland, Kenneth Griffith, Vladek Sheybal

'Seems to have arrived several years too late to
find its true niche.'—*Sight and Sound*

Squadron Leader X

GB 1942 100m bw
RKO (Victor Hanbury)

A Nazi hero poses as a British pilot but has
difficulty getting back home.

Tall war story with dreary romantic trimmings.

w Wolfgang Wilhelm, Miles Malleson *d* Lance
Comfort

Eric Portman, Ann Dvorak, Walter Fitzgerald,
Barry Jones, Henry Oscar, Beatrice Varley

The Square Jungle

US 1955 85m bw
U-I (Albert Zugsmith)

A conceited boxer gets his come-uppance.
Tailor-made studio co-feature.

w George Zuckerman *d* Jerry Hopper
ph George Robinson *m* Heinz Roemheld

Tony Curtis, Ernest Borgnine, Pat Crowley, Jim
Backus, Paul Kelly

The Square Peg*

GB 1958 89m bw
Rank (Hugh Stewart)

An army recruit finds he is the double of a
German general.
Slam-bang star slapstick, shorter than usual and
with a few jokes that can't fail.

w Jack Davies *d* John Paddy Carstairs *ph* Jack Cox *m* Philip Green

Norman Wisdom, Edward Chapman, Campbell Singer, Hattie Jacques, Brian Worth, Terence Alexander

The Squaw Man
US 1931   106m   bw
MGM (Cecil B. de Mille)
GB title: *The White Man*

An Indian maiden saves the life of a British aristocrat, bears his child and commits suicide.
Third outing for a hoary miscegenation drama filmed in 1914 with Dustin Farnum and Red Wing, and in 1918 with Elliott Dexter and Ann Little. This talkie version sank without trace.

w Lucien Hubbard, Lenore Coffee, *play* Edwin Milton Royle *d* Cecil B. de Mille *ph* Harold Rosson

Warner Baxter, Lupe Velez, Charles Bickford, Eleanor Boardman, Roland Young, Paul Cavanagh, Raymond Hatton

The Squeaker*
GB 1937   77m   bw
London Films (Alexander Korda)
US title: *Murder on Diamond Row*

A dangerous diamond fence is unmasked by a discredited policeman.
Typical Edgar Wallace who-is-it, performed with old-fashioned bravura.

w Edward O. Berkman, Bryan Wallace, *novel* Edgar Wallace *d* William K. Howard

Edmund Lowe, Sebastian Shaw, Ann Todd, Tamara Desni, Alastair Sim, Robert Newton, Allan Jeayes, Stewart Rome

The Squeeze
GB 1977   107m   Technicolor
Warner / Martinat (Stanley O'Toole)

An alcoholic ex-cop rescues his ex-wife from kidnappers.
Sleazy action thriller which despite efficient production goes over the top in its search for unpleasant detail.

w Leon Griffiths, *novel* David Craig *d* Michael Apted *ph* Dennis Lewiston *m* David Hentschel

Stacy Keach, David Hemmings, Stephen Boyd, Edward Fox, Carol White, Freddie Starr

Squirm
US 1976   92m   Movielab
AIP / The Squirm Company (Edgar Lansbury, Joseph Beruh)

A power cable cut in a storm turns worms into maneaters.

Revolting shocker with a few funny moments for those who can take it.

wd Jeff Lieberman *ph* Joseph Mangine *m* Robert Prince

John Scardino, Patricia Pearcy, R. A. Dow, Jean Sullivan

Stage Door***
US 1937   93m   bw
RKO (Pandro S. Berman)

Life in a New York theatrical boarding house for girls.
Melodramatic, sharply comedic, always fascinating slice of stagey life from a Broadway hit; the performances alone make it worth preserving.

w Morrie Ryskind, Anthony Veiller, play Edna Ferber, George S. Kaufman d Gregory La Cava ph Robert de Grasse *m* Roy Webb *ad* Van Nest Polglase

Katharine Hepburn, Ginger Rogers, Adolphe Menjou, Gail Patrick, Constance Collier, Andrea Leeds, Lucille Ball, Samuel S. Hinds, Jack Carson, Franklin Pangborn, Eve Arden

'It is a long time since we have seen so much feminine talent so deftly handled.'—*Otis Ferguson*

'Zest and pace and photographic eloquence.'—*Frank S. Nugent, New York Times*

'A rare example of a film substantially improving on a stage original and a remarkably satisfying film on all levels.'—*NFT, 1973*

AAN: best picture; Gregory La Cava; Andrea Leeds

Stage Door Canteen*
US 1963   132m   bw
Sol Lesser (Barnett Briskin)

How the stars in New York entertained the armed forces during World War II.
Nothing as a film, mildly interesting as sociology and for some rarish appearances.

w Delmer Daves *d* Frank Borzage *ph* Harry Wild *m* Freddie Rich *pd* Harry Horner

Cheryl Walker, Lon McCallister, Judith Anderson, Tallulah Bankhead, Ray Bolger, Katherine Cornell, Helen Hayes, George Jessel, Alfred Lunt, Harpo Marx, Yehudi Menuhin, Elliott Nugent, Cornelia Otis Skinner, Ethel Waters, May Whitty, William Demarest, Gracie Fields, Katharine Hepburn, Gertrude Lawrence, Ethel Merman, Merle Oberon, Johnny Weissmuller, Edgar Bergen, Jane Cowl, Lynn Fontanne, Paul Muni, Gypsy Rose Lee, George Raft, etc; Count Basie, Benny Goodman, Xavier

Cugat, Guy Lombardo, Kay Kyser and their bands

AAN: Freddie Rich; song 'We Mustn't Say Goodbye' (*m* Johnny Monaco, *ly* Al Dubin)

Stage Fright*
GB 1950   110m   bw
Warner (Alfred Hitchcock)

A man is on the run for a backstage murder, and his girl friend takes a job as maid to the great star he says is responsible.

Creaky Hitchcock thriller in which you can see all the joins and the stars seem stuck in treacle; but a few of the set pieces work well enough.

w Whitfield Cook, *novel* Man Running by Selwyn Jepson *d* Alfred Hitchcock *ph* Wilkie Cooper *m* Leighton Lucas

Marlene Dietrich, Jane Wyman, Richard Todd, Alastair Sim, Michael Wilding, Sybil Thorndike, Kay Walsh, Miles Malleson

Stage Struck
US 1936   95m   bw
Warner (Robert Lord)

Young people put on a show and become instant hits.

Dim musical oddly shorn of production numbers.

w Tom Buckinham, Pat C. Flick, Robert Lord *d/ch* Busby Berkeley *ph* Byron Haskin *m* Leo F. Forbstein *songs* Harold Arlen, E. Y. Harburg

Dick Powell, Joan Blondell, Jeanne Madden, the Yacht Club Boys, Warren William, Frank McHugh

Stage Struck**
US 1957   95m   Technicolor
RKO (Stuart Millar)

A young actress comes to New York intent on stardom . . .

Careful, slightly arid remake of *Morning Glory* marred by a tiresome central performance; good theatrical detail.

w Ruth and Augustus Goetz, *play* Zoe Akins *d* Sidney Lumet *ph* Franz Planer *m* Alex North *ad* Kim Edgar Swados

Susan Strasberg, Henry Fonda, Herbert Marshall, *Joan Greenwood*, Christopher Plummer

Stage to Thunder Rock
US 1964   89m   Techniscope
Paramount / A. C. Lyles

An ageing sheriff takes a bank robber back to jail by stagecoach.

Acceptable lower-berth western with the producer's usual roster of half-forgotten character actors.

w Charles Wallace *d* William F. Claxton *ph* W. Wallace Kelley *m* Paul Dunlap

Barry Sullivan, Marilyn Maxwell, Scott Brady, Keenan Wynn, Allan Jones, Lon Chaney Jnr, John Agar, Wanda Hendrix, Anne Seymour, Robert Lowery

Stagecoach****
US 1939   99m   bw
(UA) Walter Wanger

Various western characters board a stagecoach in danger from an Indian war party.

What looked like a minor western, with a plot borrowed from Maupassant's *Boule de suif*, became a classic by virtue of the firm characterization, restrained writing, exciting climax and the scenery of Monument Valley. Whatever the reasons, it damn well works.

w Dudley Nichols, *story* Stage to Lordsburg by Ernest Haycox *d* John Ford *ph* Bert Glennon, Ray Binger *m* Richard Hageman, W. Franke Harling, John Leopold, Leo Shuken, Louis Gruenberg *md* Boris Morros

Claire Trevor, John Wayne, Thomas Mitchell, George Bancroft, Andy Devine, *Berton Churchill,* Louise Platt, *John Carradine, Donald Meek,* Tim Holt, Chris-Pin Martin

'Grand Hotel on wheels.'—*New Yorker, 1975*

'The basic western, a template for everything that followed.'—*John Baxter, 1968*

'A motion picture that sings a song of camera.'—*Frank S. Nugent, New York Times*

AA: Thomas Mitchell
AAN: best picture; John Ford; Bert Glennon; Ray Binger

Stagecoach
US 1966   114m   De Luxe   Cinemascope
TCF / Martin Rackin

Absolutely awful remake of the above; costly but totally spiritless, miscast and uninteresting.

w Joseph Landon *d* Gordon Douglas *ph* William H. Clothier *m* Jerry Goldsmith

Ann-Margret, Alex Cord, Bing Crosby, Van Heflin, Slim Pickens, Robert Cummings, Stefanie Powers, Michael Connors, Red Buttons, Keenan Wynn

Staircase*
US /France 1969   101m   De Luxe
Panavision
TCF / Stanley Donen

The problems of two ageing homosexual hairdressers.

Unsatisfactorily opened-out and over-acted version of an effective two-hander play. Oddly made in France, so that the London detail seems all wrong.

w Charles Dyer, from his play d Stanley Donen ph Christopher Challis m Dudley Moore

Richard Burton, Rex Harrison, Cathleen Nesbitt, Beatrix Lehmann

'The shape is smashed . . . no longer a graceful duet, it becomes a waddling tale, spattered with ugliness, that falls into the biggest sentimental trap for homosexual material: it pleads for pity.'—*Stanley Kauffmann*

Stakeout on Dope Street *
US 1958 83m bw
Warner (Andrew J. Fenady)

Three young men find a briefcase containing heroin and are attacked by the gangsters who lost it.
Lively little crime morality, uneven but worth a look.

w Irwin Schwartz, Irvin Kershner, Andrew J. Fenady d *Irvin Kershner* ph *Mark Jeffrey* m Richard Markowitz

Yale Wexler, Jonathon Haze, Morris Miller, Abby Dalton

Stalag 17 **
US 1953 120m bw
Paramount (Billy Wilder)

Comedy and tragedy for American servicemen in a Nazi prisoner-of-war camp.
High jinks, violence and mystery in a sharply calculated mixture; an atmosphere quite different from the understated British films on the subject.

w *Billy Wilder, Edwin Blum, play* Donald Bevan, Edmund Trzinski d Billy Wilder ph Ernest Laszlo m Franz Waxman

William Holden, Don Taylor, Otto Preminger, *Robert Strauss*, Harvey Lembeck, Richard Erdman, Peter Graves, Neville Brand, Sig Rumann

'A facility for continuous rapid-fire action which alternately brings forth the laughs and tingles the spine.'—*Otis L. Guernsey Jnr*

AA: William Holden
AAN: Billy Wilder (as director), Robert Strauss

The Stalking Moon *
US 1968 109m Technicolor Panavision
National General / Stalking Moon Company (Alan J. Pakula)

An ageing scout escorts home a white woman who has escaped from the Indians, and kills a murderous Apache.
Slow, thoughtful western with effective moments.

w Alvin Sargent, *novel* Theodore V. Olsen d Robert Mulligan ph Charles Lang m Fred Karlin

Gregory Peck, Eva Marie Saint, Robert Forster, Frank Silvera

Stallion Road
US 1947 97m bw
Warner (Alex Gottlieb)

An outbreak of anthrax threatens a racing stable.
Routine romantic drama with sporting background.

w Stephen Longstreet d James V. Kern ph Arthur Edeson m Frederick Hollander

Ronald Reagan, Alexis Smith, Zachary Scott, Peggy Knudsen, Patti Brady, Harry Davenport, Frank Puglia

Stamboul Quest
US 1934 88m bw
MGM

During World War I, Germany's most notorious lady spy falls for an American medical student.
Modest variation on the true story twice filmed as *Fräulein Doktor*; standard Hollywood values.

w Herman J. Mankiewicz d Sam Wood ph James Wong Howe

Myrna Loy, George Brent, Lionel Atwill, C. Henry Gordon, Douglass Dumbrille, Mischa Auer

Stand by for Action
US 1943 109m bw
MGM (Robert Z. Leonard, Orville O. Dull)
GB title: *Cargo of Innocents*

A Harvard graduate learns the realities of war on an old destroyer.
Studio-bound war heroics slurping into sentiment.

w George Bruce, Herman J. Mankiewicz, John L. Balderston d Robert Z. Leonard ph Charles Rosher

Robert Taylor, Charles Laughton, Brian Donlevy, Walter Brennan, Marilyn Maxwell, Henry O'Neill

Stand In *
US 1937 90m bw
Walter Wanger

An efficiency expert is sent to save a Hollywood studio from bankruptcy.
Amusing satire which could have done with sharper scripting and firmer control but is pleasantly remembered.

w Gene Towne, Graham Baker, *serial* Clarence Budington Kelland *d* Tay Garnett *ph* Charles G. Clarke *m* Heinz Roemheld

Leslie Howard, Joan Blondell, Humphrey Bogart, Alan Mowbray, Marla Shelton, C. Henry Gordon, Jack Carson, Tully Marshall

Stand Up and Be Counted*
US 1971   99m   Eastmancolor
Columbia / Mike Frankovich

An international woman journalist returns to Denver and becomes involved in women's lib.
A glamoured-up flirtation with a fashionable theme, quite nicely done but instantly dated— and sociologically interesting.

w Bernard Slade *d* Jackie Cooper *ph* Fred Koenekamp *m* Ernie Wilkins

Jacqueline Bisset, Stella Stevens, Steve Lawrence, Gary Lockwood, *Loretta Swit,* Lee Purcell, Madlyn Rhue

Stand Up and Cheer*
US 1934   80m   bw
Fox (Winfield Sheehan)

The new US Secretary of Amusement attempts to shake the country's Depression blues by staging a mammoth revue.
Naïve propaganda, but the whole world was swept away to cloud nine—by Shirley Temple.

w Will Rogers, Philip Klein *d* Hamilton McFadden *ph* Ernest Palmer *md* Arthur Lange

Warner Baxter, Madge Evans, Nigel Bruce, Stepin Fetchit, Frank Melton, Lila Lee, Ralph Morgan, James Dunn, *Shirley Temple,* John Boles, George K. Arthur

'Impossible to file it away in an ordinary drawer marked 'Stinkers'. This one is extra, it is super, and it butters itself very thickly with the most obvious sort of topical significance.'—*Otis Ferguson*

Stand Up and Fight*
US 1939   99m   bw
MGM (Mervyn Le Roy)

A southern aristocrat comes into conflict with a stagecoach operator used as transportation for stolen slaves.
Superior star action piece with plenty of vigorous brawls.

w James M. Cain, Jane Murfin, Harvey Ferguson
d W. S. Van Dyke II *ph* Leonard Smith *m* William Axt

Wallace Beery, Robert Taylor, Florence Rice, Helen Broderick, Robert Bickford, Barton MacLane, Charley Grapewin, John Qualen

Stand Up Virgin Soldiers
GB 1977   90m   Technicolor
Warner / Greg Smith / Maidenhead

More sexual adventures of National Servicemen in Singapore in 1950.
The Virgin Soldiers had a certain authenticity behind the fooling; this is a bawdy romp, and not a very efficient one.

w Leslie Thomas, from his novel *d* Norman Cohen *ph* Ken Hodges *m* Ed Welch

Nigel Davenport, Robin Askwith, George Layton, Robin Nedwell, Warren Mitchell, John Le Mesurier, Edward Woodward, Irene Handl

Standing Room Only*
US 1944   83m   bw
Paramount (Paul Jones)

Hotel rooms being hard to find in wartime Washington, a resourceful secretary hires out herself and her boss as a servant couple.
Moderate romantic farce with a few good laughs.

w Darrell Ware, Karl Tunberg *d* Sidney Lanfield *ph* Charles Lang *m* Robert Emmett Dolan

Paulette Goddard, Fred MacMurray, Edward Arnold, Roland Young, Hillary Brooke, Porter Hall, Clarence Kolb, Anne Revere

Stanley and Livingstone***
US 1939   101m   bw
TCF (Kenneth MacGowan)

An American journalist goes to Africa to find a lost Victorian explorer.
A prestige picture which played reasonably fair with history and still managed to please the masses.

w Philip Dunne, Julien Josephson *d* Henry King *ph* George Barnes *m* Alfred Newman *ad* Thomas Little

Spencer Tracy, Cedric Hardwicke, Richard Greene, Nancy Kelly, Walter Brennan, Charles Coburn, Henry Hull, Henry Travers, Miles Mander, Holmes Herbert

'Sound, worthy, interesting.'—*Richard Mallett, Punch*

The Star*
US 1952   91m   bw
TCF / Bert E. Friedlob

A once famous Hollywood star is financially and
psychologically on her uppers.
A movie apparently tailor-made for its star turns
out to be a disappointingly plotless wallow.

w Katherine Albert, Dale Eunson d Stuart
Heisler ph Ernest Laszlo m Victor Young

Bette Davis, Sterling Hayden, Natalie Wood,
Warner Anderson, Minor Watson

AAN: Bette Davis
 'The story of every woman who ever climbed
the stairway to the stars—and found herself at
the bottom looking up!'—*publicity*

Star!*
US 1968   194m   De Luxe   Todd-AO
TCF / Robert Wise (Saul Chaplin)

Revue artist Gertrude Lawrence rises from
poverty to international stardom and a measure
of happiness.
Elephantiasis finally ruins this patient, detached,
generally likeable recreation of a past theatrical
era. In the old Hollywood style, it would
probably have been even better on a smaller
budget; but alas the star would still have been ill
at ease with the drunken termagant scenes.

w William Fairchild d Robert Wise ph Ernest
Laszlo md Lennie Hayton ch Michael Kidd
pd Boris Leven

Julie Andrews, Richard Crenna, Michael Craig,
Daniel Massey (as Noel Coward), John Collin,
Robert Reed, Bruce Forsyth, Beryl Reid, Jenny
Agutter
† Short version: *Those Were the Happy Days*.

AAN: Ernest Laszlo; Lennie Hayton; title song
(*m* James Van Heusen, *ly* Sammy Cahn); Daniel
Massey

Star Dust*
US 1940   85m   bw
TCF (Kenneth MacGowan)

A talent scout discovers a new Hollywood star.
Light, amusing studio comedy, a pleasing
addition to Hollywood mythology.

w Robert Ellis, Helen Logan d Walter Lang
ph Peverell Marley m David Buttolph

Linda Darnell, John Payne, Roland Young,
Charlotte Greenwood, William Gargan, Mary
Beth Hughes, Donald Meek, Jessie Ralph

A Star Is Born***
US 1937   111m   Technicolor
David O. Selznick

A young actress meets Hollywood success and
marries a famous leading man, whose star wanes
as hers shines brighter.
Abrasive romantic melodrama which is also the
most accurate study of Hollywood ever put on
film.

w Dorothy Parker, Alan Campbell, Robert
Carson, story William A. Wellman, based partly
on *What Price Hollywood* (1932)(qv)
d William A. Wellman ph W. Howard Greene
m Max Steiner

Janet Gaynor, Fredric March, Adolphe Menjou,
Lionel Stander, Andy Devine, May Robson,
Owen Moore, Franklin Pangborn
 'Good entertainment by any standards.'—
Frank S. Nugent, New York Times
 'A peculiar sort of masochistic self-
congratulatory Hollywood orgy.'—*New
Yorker, 1975*
 'The first colour job that gets close to what
colour must eventually come to: it keeps the
thing in its place, underlining the mood and
situation of the story rather than dimming
everything else out in an iridescent razzle-
dazzle.'—*Otis Ferguson*

AA: script
AAN: best picture; William A. Wellman; Janet
Gaynor; Fredric March

A Star Is Born**
US 1954   181m   Technicolor
   Cinemascope
Warner (Sidney Luft)

Musical version of the above which begins very
strongly and has two splendid performances, but
suffers in the second half from a lack of writing
strength and heavy post-production cutting. The
numbers add very little except length.

w Moss Hart d George Cukor ph Sam Leavitt
md Ray Heindorf

Judy Garland, James Mason, Charles Bickford,
Jack Carson, Tommy Noonan, Amanda Blake,
Lucy Marlow
 'Maintains a skilful balance between the
musical and the tear jerker.'—*Penelope Houston*

AAN: Ray Heindorf; song 'The Man that Got
Away' (*m* Harold Arlen, *ly* Ira Gershwin); Judy
Garland; James Mason

A Star Is Born*
US 1976   140m   Metrocolor
Warner / Barwood / First Artists (Barbra
   Streisand, Jon Peters)

Interminable remake set in the pop world amid
screaming crowds and songs at high decibel
level; also an insufferable piece of showing off by
the star. But some of the handling has style.

w John Gregory Dunne, Joan Didion, Frank Pierson *d* Frank Pierson *ph* Robert Surtees *md* Paul Williams *pd* Polly Platt

Barbra Streisand, Kris Kristofferson, Paul Mazursky, Gary Busey

'A clear case for the monopolies commission.'—*Michael Billington, Illustrated London News*

'A bore is starred.'—*Village Voice*

AA: song 'Evergreen' (*m* Barbra Streisand, *ly* Paul Williams)

AAN: Roger Surtees; Roger Kellaway (music underscoring)

The Star Maker*
US 1939 94m bw
Paramount (Charles R. Rodgers)

A songwriter makes the big time by organizing kid acts.
Pleasant minor musical based on the career of Gus Edwards.

w Frank Butler, Don Hartman, Arthur Caesar *d* Roy del Ruth

Bing Crosby, Louise Campbell, Linda Ware, Ned Sparks, Laura Hope Crews, Janet Waldo, Walter Damrosch

Star of Midnight**
US 1935 90m bw
RKO (Pandro S. Berman)

A New York attorney solves the disappearance of a leading lady.
Wisecracking, debonair murder mystery modelled on *The Thin Man*.

w Howard J. Green, Anthony Veiller, Edward Kaufman *d* Stephen Roberts *ph* J. Roy Hunt *m* Max Steiner

William Powell, Ginger Rogers, Paul Kelly, Gene Lockhart, Ralph Morgan, Leslie Fenton, J. Farrell MacDonald

'It is all suavity and amusement; pistol shots and cocktails.'—*Graham Greene*

'One of the best sophisticated comedy-mysteries in a period full of such films.'—*NFT, 1973*

The Star Spangled Girl
US 1971 92m colour
Paramount (Howard W. Koch)

A sweet old-fashioned girl is fought for by two young radicals.
Unamusingly 'with it' comedy from an unsuccessful play.

w Arnold Margolin, Jim Parker, *play* Neil Simon *d* Jerry Paris *ph* Sam Leavitt *m* Charles Fox

Sandy Duncan, Tony Roberts, Todd Susman, Elizabeth Allen

Star Spangled Rhythm***
US 1942 99m bw
Paramount (Joseph Sistrom)

The doorman of Paramount Studios pretends to his sailor son that he is a big producer. Frenetic farce involving most of the talent on Paramount's payroll and culminating in an 'impromptu' show staged for the navy. A good lighthearted glimpse of wartime Hollywood.

w Harry Tugend *d* George Marshall *ph* Leo Tover, Theodor Sparkuhl *md* Robert Emmett Dolan *songs* Johnny Mercer, Harold Arlen

Betty Hutton, Eddie Bracken, *Victor Moore, Walter Abel*, Anne Revere, Cass Daley, Gil Lamb, Macdonald Carey, Bob Hope, Bing Crosby, Paulette Goddard, Veronica Lake, Dorothy Lamour, Vera Zorina, Fred MacMurray, Ray Milland, Lynne Overman, Franchot Tone, Dick Powell, *Walter Dare Wahl and Co, Cecil B. de Mille, Preston Sturges,* Alan Ladd, Rochester, Katherine Dunham, Susan Hayward

AAN: Robert Emmett Dolan; song 'Black Magic' (*m* Harold Arlen, *ly* Johnny Mercer)

Star Wars***
US 1977 121m Technicolor Panavision
TCF/Lucasfilm (Gary Kurtz)

A rebel princess in a distant galaxy escapes, and with the help of her robots and a young farmer overcomes the threatening forces of evil.
Flash Gordon rides again, but with timing so impeccably right that the movie became a phenomenon and one of the top grossers of all time. In view of the hullaballoo, some disappointment may be felt with the actual experience of watching it . . . but it's certainly good harmless fun, put together with style and imagination.

wd George Lucas ph Gilbert Taylor *m* John Williams *pd* John Barry *sp* many and various

Mark Hamill, Harrison Ford, Carrie Fisher, Peter Cushing, Alec Guinness, Anthony Daniels (See Threepio), Kenny Baker (Artoo Detoo), Dave Prowse (Darth Vader)

'A great work of popular art, fully deserving the riches it has reaped.'—*Time*

'Acting in this movie I felt like a raisin in a giant fruit salad. And I didn't even know who the coconuts or the canteloups were.'—*Mark Hamill*

The Star Witness*
US 1931   68m   bw
Warner

An old man witnesses a crime and is threatened
by gangsters.
Pacy melodrama with good performances.

w Lucien Hubbard d William Wellman
ph James Van Trees

Walter Huston, Chic Sale, Grant Mitchell,
Frances Starr, Sally Blane

AAN: Lucien Hubbard

Stars and Stripes Forever*
US 1952   89m   Technicolor
TCF (Lamar Trotti)
GB title: Marching Along

In the 1890s John Philip Sousa, a bandmaster
who wants to write ballads, finds success as a
writer of marches.
Low-key musical biopic with predictably noisy
numbers.

w Lamar Trotti, from Sousa's autobiography
d Henry Koster ph Charles G. Clarke
md Alfred Newman

Clifton Webb, Debra Paget, Robert Wagner,
Ruth Hussey, Finlay Currie, Roy Roberts,
Lester Matthews

The Stars Are Singing
US 1952   99m   Technicolor
Paramount (Irving Asher)

A Polish refugee girl illegally enters the US and
becomes an opera star.
Painless Cinderella fantasy in which everybody
sings.

w Liam O'Brien d Norman Taurog ph Lionel
Lindon md Victor Young

Anna Maria Alberghetti, Lauritz Melchior,
Rosemary Clooney, Fred Clark, Mikhail
Rasumny

Stars in My Crown*
US 1950   89m   bw
MGM (William H. Wright)

A two-gun parson brings peace to a Tennessee
town after the Civil War.
Sentimental family western, quite pleasantly
made and performed.

w Margaret Pitts, novel Joe David Brown
d Jacques Tourneur ph Charles Schoenbaum
m Adolph Deutsch

Joel McCrea, Ellen Drew, Dean Stockwell,
Juano Hernandez, James Mitchell, Lewis Stone,
Alan Hale, Amanda Blake

The Stars Look Down*
GB 1939   110m   bw
Grafton (Isadore Goldschmidt)

The son of a coal miner struggles to become an
MP.
Economically but well made social drama from a
popular novel, with good pace and backgrounds.

w J. B. Williams, A. J. Cronin, novel A. J. Cronin
d Carol Reed

Michael Redgrave, Margaret Lockwood,
Edward Rigby, Emlyn Williams, Nancy Price,
Allan Jeayes, Cecil Parker, Linden Travers

Stars over Broadway
US 1935   89m   bw
Warner (Sam Bischoff)

Unremarkable musical, with unusual talent.

w Jerry Wald, Julius J. Epstein, Pat C. Flick
d William Keighley ph George Barnes md Leo
F. Forbstein ch Busby Berkeley, Bobby
Connolly songs Harry Warren, Al Dubin

James Melton, Jane Froman, Pat O'Brien, Jean
Muir, Frank McHugh, Marie Wilson, Frank Fay

Start the Revolution without Me*
US 1969   90m   Technicolor
Warner / Norbud

Two sets of twins get mixed up at the court of
Louis XVI.
Historical spoof of the kind subsequently made
familiar by Mel Brooks; the script might have
suited Abbott and Costello better than these two
actors.

w Fred Freeman, Lawrence J. Cohen d Bud
Yorkin ph Jean Tournier m John Addison

Donald Sutherland, Gene Wilder, Hugh Griffith,
Jack McGowran, Billie Whitelaw, Victor
Spinetti, Ewa Aulin

State Fair*
US 1933   98m   bw
Fox (Winfield Sheehan)

Dad wants his prize pig to win at the fair, but the
younger members of his family have romance in
mind.
Archetypal family film, much remade but never
quite so pleasantly performed.

w Paul Green, Sonya Levien, novel Phil Stong
d Henry King ph Hal Mohr md Louis de
Francesco

Will Rogers, Janet Gaynor, Lew Ayres, Sally
Eilers, Norman Foster, Louise Dresser, Frank
Craven, Victor Jory, Hobart Cavanaugh

'A pungent, good-humoured motion
picture.'—Pare Lorentz

'Vigour, freshness and sympathy abound in its admittedly idealized fantasy treatment of small-town life.'—*Charles Higham, 1972*

AAN: best picture; script

State Fair **

US 1945 100m Technicolor
TCF (William Perlberg)
TV title: *It Happened One Summer*

Musical remake with an amiable cast and a rousing score.

w/ly Oscar Hammerstein II *d* Walter Lang
ph Leon Shamroy *m Richard Rodgers*
md Alfred Newman

Charles Winninger, Jeanne Crain, Dana Andrews, Vivian Blaine, Dick Haymes, Fay Bainter, Frank McHugh, Percy Kilbride, Donald Meek

'Surely the sort of theme that clamours for movie treatment. But no, say Twentieth Century Fox: let's make the fair look like a night club. Let's look around for stars of pristine nonentity. Let's screw the camera down to the studio floor. The result, "an epic that sings to the skies . . . with glorious, glamorous new songs".'—*Richard Winnington*

AA: song 'It Might As Well Be Spring'; Alfred Newman (with Charles Henderson)

State Fair

US 1962 118m De Luxe Cinemascope
TCF (Charles Brackett)

Dullsville modernized version, condescending towards the rurals and peopled by unattractive youngsters.

w Richard Breen *d* Jose Ferrer *ph* William C. Mellor *md* Alfred Newman

Pat Boone, Alice Faye, Tom Ewell, Pamela Tiffin, Ann-Margret, Bobby Darin, Wally Cox

State of the Union ***

US 1948 110m bw
(MGM) Liberty Films (Frank Capra)
GB title: *The World and His Wife*

An estranged wife rejoins her husband when he is running for president.
Brilliantly scripted political comedy which unfortunately goes soft at the end but offers stimulating entertainment most of the way.

w Anthony Veiller, Myles Connelly, *play* Howard Lindsay, Russel Crouse *d* Frank Capra *ph* George J. Folsey *m* Victor Young

Spencer Tracy, Katharine Hepburn, Adolphe Menjou, Van Johnson, Angela Lansbury, Lewis Stone, Howard Smith, Raymond Walburn, Charles Dingle

'A triumphant film, marked all over by Frank Capra's artistry.'—*Howard Barnes*

State Secret **

GB 1950 104m bw
British Lion / London (Frank Launder, Sidney Gilliat)
US title: *The Great Manhunt*

In a Ruritanian country, spies pursue a surgeon, the only man who knows that the dictator is dead.
Hitchcockian chase comedy-thriller which is well detailed and rises to the heights on occasion.

wd Sidney Gilliat *ph* Robert Krasker
m William Alwyn

Douglas Fairbanks Jnr, Glynis Johns, Herbert Lom, Jack Hawkins, Walter Rilla, Karel Stepanek, Carl Jaffe

'An admirably fast-moving diversion in the Hitchcock tradition.'—*Richard Mallett, Punch*

Station Six Sahara

GB 1962 101m bw
British Lion / CCC / Artur Brauner (Victor Lyndon)

Five men working on a remote Saharan pipeline quarrel over the favours of an American girl whose car crashes nearby.
Raging old-fashioned melodrama with the courage of its lack of convictions.

w Bryan Forbes, Brian Clemens *d* Seth Holt
ph Gerald Gibbs *m* Ron Grainer

Carroll Baker, Ian Bannen, Peter Van Eyck, Denholm Elliott, Mario Adorf, Jorg Felmy, Biff McGuire

Station West

US 1948 91m bw
RKO (Robert Sparks)

A saloon queen is the secret head of a gang of gold robbers.
Predictable but well made western patterned after *Destry Rides Again*.

w Frank Fenton, Winston Miller, *novel* Luke Short *d* Sidney Lanfield *ph* Harry J. Wild
m Heinz Roemheld

Dick Powell, Jane Greer, Agnes Moorehead, Burl Ives, Tom Powers, Gordon Oliver, Steve Brodie, Guinn Williams, Raymond Burr, Regis Toomey

The Statue

US 1970 89m Eastmancolor
Cinerama / Josef Shaftel (Anis Nohra)

A languages professor is embarrassed when his

sculptress wife makes an immense nude statue of him—with someone else's private parts.
Strained phallic comedy which doesn't even make the most of its one joke.

w Alec Coppel, Denis Norden *d* Rod Amateau *ph* Piero Portalupi *m* Riz Ortolani

David Niven, Virna Lisi, Robert Vaughn, Ann Bell, John Cleese, Hugh Burden

Stay Away Joe
US 1968 102m Metrocolor Panavision
MGM (Douglas Lawrence)

An Indian rodeo rider returns to his reservation, makes several romantic conquests, and helps a government rehabilitation scheme.
Thin if surprising vehicle for a singing star; all rather tedious.

w Michael A. Hoey, *novel* Dan Cushman *d* Peter Tewkesbury *ph* Fred Koenekamp *m* Jack Marshall

Elvis Presley, Burgess Meredith, Joan Blondell, Katy Jurado, Thomas Gomez, Henry Jones, L. Q. Jones

Stay Hungry
US 1976 102m De Luxe
UA / Outov (Harold Schneider, Bob Rafaelson)

The heir to an Alabama estate annoys the locality by assembling a curious bunch of friends and making unexpected use of his money.
Rather obvious and pointless fable; well made but not very stimulating.

w Charles Gaines, Bob Rafaelson, *novel* Charles Gaines *d* Bob Rafaelson *ph* Victor Kemper *m* Bruce Langhorne, Byron Berline

Jeff Bridges, Sally Field, Arnold Schwarzenegger, R. G. Armstrong, Robert Englund, Roger E. Mosley

Steamboat Bill Jnr*
US 1928 71m (24 fps) bw silent
UA / Buster Keaton / Joseph Schenck

A student takes over his father's old Mississippi steamboat, and wins the daughter of his rival.
Rather flat comedy redeemed by a magnificent cyclone climax.

w Carl Harbaugh, Buster Keaton *d* Charles Riesner *ph* J. Devereaux Jennings, Bert Haines

Buster Keaton, Ernest Torrence, Marion Byron

Steamboat Round the Bend*
US 1935 80m bw
TCF (Sol M. Wurtzel)

A Mississippi steamboat captain defeats his rival

and finds evidence to clear his nephew of a murder charge.
Rather heavily-scripted star vehicle which sacrifices fun for atmosphere but is often good to look at.

w Dudley Nichols, Lamar Trotti, *novel* Ben Lucien Berman *d John Ford ph* George Schneiderman *m* Samuel Kaylin

Will Rogers, Anne Shirley, Eugene Pallette, John McGuire, Irvin S. Cobb, Berton Churchill, Stepin Fetchit, Roger Imhof, Raymond Hatton

The Steel Bayonet
GB 1957 85m bw Hammerscope
(UA) Hammer (Michael Carreras)

During the assault on Tunis a battle-weary platoon holds a farm against enemy attack.
Dreary cliché-ridden war melodrama peopled by all the usual types.

w Howard Clewes *d* Michael Carreras *ph* Jack Asher *m* Leonard Salzedo

Leo Genn, Kieron Moore, Michael Medwin, Robert Brown, Michael Ripper, John Paul, Bernard Horsfall

Steel Town
US 1952 84m Technicolor
U-I (Leonard Goldstein)

A steel president's nephew joins the company as a furnace hand.
Routine drama with an unusual background.

w Gerald Drayson Adams, Lou Breslow *d* George Sherman *ph* Charles P. Boyle *m* Joseph Gershenson

Ann Sheridan, John Lund, Howard Duff, James Best, Nancy Kulp

The Steel Trap*
US 1952 85m bw
TCF / Thor (Bert E. Friedlob)

An assistant bank manager steals half a million dollars from the vault but is troubled by conscience and manages to put it back before the loss is discovered.
Solidly competent little suspenser with plenty of movement.

wd Andrew Stone ph Ernest Laszlo *m* Dmitri Tiomkin

Joseph Cotten, Teresa Wright, Jonathan Hale, Walter Sande

Steelyard Blues
US 1972 92m Technicolor
Warner / S. B. Productions (Tony Bill, Michael and Julia Phillips)

An ex-con and his call-girl friend are an embarrassment to his DA brother.
Bits and pieces of anti-establishment comedy are tacked on to a thin plot; a few of them work.

w David S. Ward *d* Alan Myerson *ph* Laszlo Kovacs, Steven Larner *m* Nick Gravenites

Donald Sutherland, Jane Fonda, Peter Boyle, Howard Hesseman

Stella Dallas*
US 1925 110m approx (24 fps) bw
silent
Samuel Goldwyn

An uncouth woman loses both husband and daughter.
Standard weepie complete with 'out into the cold cold snow' ending, but handled here with tact and discretion. A seminal film of its time.

w Frances Marion, *novel* Olive Higgins Prouty *d* Henry King *ph* Arthur Edeson

Belle Bennett, Ronald Colman, Lois Moran, Jean Hersholt, Douglas Fairbanks Jnr, Alice Joyce

Stella Dallas*
US 1937 106m bw
Samuel Goldwyn

Fashionable remake with excellent talent; 1937 audiences came to sneer and stayed to weep.

w Victor Heerman, Sara Y. Mason *d King Vidor ph* Rudolph Maté *m* Alfred Newman

Barbara Stanwyck, John Boles, Anne Shirley, Barbara O'Neil, Alan Hale, Marjorie Main, Tim Holt

AAN: Barbara Stanwyck; Anne Shirley

Step Down to Terror
US 1959 76m bw
U-I (Joseph Gershenson)
GB title: *The Silent Stranger*

A man returns to his home town and is discovered to be a psychopathic killer on the run.
Dismal reworking of *Shadow of a Doubt*; strictly second feature stuff.

w Mel Dinelli, Czenzi Ormonde, Chris Cooper *d* Harry Keller *ph* Russell Metty *m* Joseph Gershenson

Charles Drake, Coleen Miller, Rod Taylor, Josephine Hutchinson, Jocelyn Brando

Step Lively*
US 1944 88m bw
RKO (Robert Fellows)

Gleaming musical remake of *Room Service* (qv); all very efficient if witless.

w Warren Duff, Peter Milne *d* Tim Whelan *ph* Robert de Grasse *md* Constantin Bakaleinikoff *songs* Jule Styne, Sammy Cahn

Frank Sinatra, George Murphy, Adolphe Menjou, Gloria de Haven, Anne Jeffreys, Walter Slezak, Eugene Pallette

The Stepford Wives*
US 1974 115m TVC
Fadsin / Palomar (Edgar J. Sherick)

A new wife in a commuter village outside New York finds all her female friends too good to be true . . . because their husbands have had them replaced by computerized models.
An attractive idea which needs a much lighter and pacier touch but entertains in patches and shows agreeable sophistication.

w William Goldman, *novel* Ira Levin *d* Bryan Forbes *ph* Owen Roizman *m* Michael Small *pd* Gene Callahan

Katharine Ross, Paula Prentiss, Nanette Newman, Peter Masterson, Patrick O'Neal, Tina Louise, William Prince

Steptoe and Son
GB 1972 98m Technicolor
EMI / Associated London Films (Aida Young)

Harold gets married, mislays his wife but thinks he is a father.
Strained attempt to transfer the TV rag-and-bone comedy (which in the US became *Sanford and Son*) to the big screen. Not the same thing at all.

w Ray Galton, Alan Simpson *d* Cliff Owen *ph* John Wilcox *m* Roy Budd, Jack Fishman

Wilfrid Brambell, Harry H. Corbett, Carolyn Seymour, Arthur Howard, Victor Maddern
† *Steptoe and Son Ride Again*, which followed in 1973, was even more crude and out of character.

The Sterile Cuckoo
US 1969 107m Technicolor
Paramount / Boardwalk (Alan J. Pakula)
GB title: *Pookie*

A talkative but insecure college girl has her first sexual adventures.
Rather tiresome comedy drama with good scenes; general handling far too restrained.

w Alvin Sargent, *novel* John Nicholson *d* Alan J. Pakula *ph* Milton Krasner *m* Fred Karlin

Liza Minnelli, Tim McIntire, Wendell Burton, Austin Green, Sandra Faison

AAN: song 'Come Saturday Morning' (*m* Fred Karlin, *ly* Dory Previn); Liza Minnelli

Stevie*
US/GB 1978   102m   Technicolor
First Artists / Grand Metropolitan (Robert
Enders)

An account of the uneventful life of poetess
Stevie Smith, lived out mainly in a London
suburb under the fear of death.
Claustrophobic showcase for a whimsical lady;
interesting for some specialized audiences.

w Hugh Whitemore, from his play d Robert
Enders ph Freddie Young m Marcus Gowers

Glenda Jackson, Mona Washbourne, Trevor
Howard, Alec McCowen

Stiletto
US 1969   99m   Berkey–Pathe
Avco / Harold Robbins

A wealthy playboy racing driver is in fact a
Mafia executioner.
Dreary, violent, fashionable Mafioso melodrama
with international jet set trimmings.

w A. J. Russsell, novel Harold Robbins
d Bernard Kowalski ph Jack Priestly m Sid
Ramin

Alex Cord, Britt Ekland, Barbara McNair,
Patrick O'Neal, Joseph Wiseman, John Dehner,
Eduardo Ciannelli, Roy Scheider

The Sting*
US 1973   129m   Technicolor
Universal / Richard Zanuck, David Brown
  (Tony Bill, Michael S. Phillips)

In twenties Chicago, two con men stage an
elaborate revenge on a big time gangster who
caused the death of a friend.
Bright, likeable, but overlong, unconvincingly
studio-set and casually developed comedy
suspenser cashing in on star charisma but riding
to enormous success chiefly on its tinkly music
and the general lack of simple entertainment.

w David S. Ward d George Roy Hill ph Robert
Surtees m Scott Joplin (arranged by Marvin
Hamlisch) ad Henry Bumstead

Paul Newman, Robert Redford, Robert Shaw,
Charles Durning, Ray Walston, Eileen Brennan

'A visually claustrophobic, mechanically
plotted movie that's meant to be a roguishly
charming entertainment.'—New Yorker

'It demonstrates what can happen when a
gifted young screenwriter has the good fortune to
fall among professionals his second time out.'—
Judith Crist

AA: best picture; David S. Ward; George Roy
Hill; Marvin Hamlisch

AAN: Robert Surtees; Robert Redford

A Stitch in Time
GB 1963   94m   bw
Rank (Hugh Stewart)

A butcher's boy goes into hospital and falls for a
nurse.
Thin star slapstick; all one can say is that it's
marginally preferable to Jerry Lewis.

w Jack Davies d Robert Asher ph Jack Asher
m Philip Green

Norman Wisdom, Edward Chapman, Jerry
Desmonde, Jeanette Sterke, Jill Melford

Stolen Hours
GB 1963   97m   De Luxe
UA / Mirisch / Barbican (Denis Holt)

An American divorcee with only a year to live
falls in love with her surgeon.
Tired remake of Dark Victory; pleasant Cornish
backgrounds.

w Jessamyn West d Daniel Petrie ph Harry
Waxman m Mort Lindsey

Susan Hayward, Michael Craig, Diane Baker,
Edward Judd, Paul Rogers

Stolen Kisses*
France 1968   91m   Eastmancolor
Films du Carrosse / Artistes Associés (Marcel
  Berbert)

original title: Baisers Volés

An ineffective young man can find neither work
nor love.
A pleasing, rather sad little comedy which has
almost the feel of a Keaton; but one is not quite
sure at the end what its creator intended.

w François Truffaut, Claude de Givray, Bernard
Revon d François Truffaut ph Denys Clerval
m Antoine Duhamel

Jean-Pierre Léaud, Delphine Seyrig, Michel
Lonsdale, Claude Jade

A Stolen Life*
GB 1938   91m   bw
(Paramount) Orion (Anthony Havelock-Allan)

In Brittany, a woman deceives her husband by
exchanging identities with her dead twin.
An actress's showcase, quite satisfactorily
mounted.

w Margaret Kennedy, George Barraud, novel
Karel J. Benes d Paul Czinner m William
Walton

Elisabeth Bergner, Michael Redgrave, Wilfrid
Lawson, Richard Ainley, Mabel Terry-Lewis,
Clement McCallin

A Stolen Life*
US 1946   107m   bw
Warner (Bette Davis)

Enjoyable if slightly disappointing remake with
New England backgrounds.

w Catherine Turney d Curtis Bernhardt ph Sol
Polito, Sid Hickox m Max Steiner

Bette Davis, Glenn Ford, Dane Clark, Walter
Brennan, Charles Ruggles, Bruce Bennett,
Peggy Knudsen, Esther Dale

'A distressingly empty piece of show-off.'—
Bosley Crowther

'What I'm waiting for is a film about beautiful
identical quintuplets who all love the same
man.'—*Richard Winnington*

The Stone Killer*
US 1973   96m   Technicolor
Columbia / Dino de Laurentiis (Michael
   Winner)

A brutal Los Angeles police detective takes on
the Mafia.
Fast-moving amalgam of chases and violence
with a downbeat hero.

w Gerald Wilson, *novel* A Complete State of
Death by John Gardner d Michael Winner
ph Richard Moore m Roy Budd

Charles Bronson, Martin Balsam, Ralph Waite,
David Sheiner, Norman Fell

'Film-making as painting by numbers.'—
Sight and Sound

The Stooge
US 1951   100m   bw
Paramount / Hal B. Wallis

In 1930 a conceited song and dance man fails to
realize that his moronic stooge is the act's real
attraction.
Typical, and particularly resistible, Martin and
Lewis concoction: whenever one thinks of
laughing, a dollop of sentimentality comes along
and promptly quashes the idea.

w Fred Finkelhoffe, Martin Rackin d Norman
Taurog ph Daniel L. Fapp m Joseph J. Lilley

Dean Martin, Jerry Lewis, Polly Bergen, Marie
McDonald, Eddie Mayehoff, Marion Marshall,
Richard Erdman

Stop You're Killing Me
US 1953   86m   Warnercolor
Warner (Louis F. Edelman)

At the end of prohibition a beer baron decides to
go straight, but finds his house filled with the
corpses of rival gangsters.
Frantic remake of *A Slight Case of Murder* with

a few musical numbers added; all rather messy.

w James O'Hanlon d Roy del Ruth ph Ted
McCord md Ray Heindorf

Broderick Crawford, Claire Trevor, Virginia
Gibson, Bill Hayes, Sheldon Leonard, Joe Vitale,
Howard St John, Henry Morgan, Margaret
Dumont

Stopover Tokyo
US 1957   100m   Eastmancolor
   Cinemascope
TCF (Walter Reisch)

An American spy in Tokyo seeks to capture a
communist undercover man.
Sprawling espionage stuff with frequent halts for
scenic tours.

w Richard L. Breen, Walter Reisch, *novel* John
P. Marquand d Richard L. Breen ph Charles G.
Clarke m Paul Sawtell

Robert Wagner, Joan Collins, Edmond O'Brien,
Ken Scott, Larry Keating

The Stork Club
US 1945   98m   bw
Paramount (B. G. De Sylva)

A nightclub hat-check girl saves an elderly
millionaire from drowning.
Very light comedy with music, a great ad for a
once famous night haunt.

w B. G. De Sylva, John McGowan d Hal
Walker ph Charles Lang Jnr md Robert
Emmett Dolan

Betty Hutton, Barry Fitzgerald, Don Defore,
Robert Benchley, Bill Goodwin, Iris Adrian,
Mary Young, Mikhail Rasumny

Storm Center
US 1956   87m   bw
Columbia / Phoenix (Julian Blaustein)

A small-town librarian is dismissed when she
refuses to remove a communist book from the
shelves.
Formula anti-McCarthy melodrama originally
designed for Mary Pickford's comeback; not
very absorbing and rather dingily produced.

w Daniel Taradash Elick Moll d Daniel
Taradash ph Burnett Guffey m George Duning

Bette Davis, Brian Keith, Kim Hunter, Paul
Kelly, Joe Mantell

Storm Fear
US 1955   88m   bw
(UA) Theodora (Cornel Wilde)

Three fugitives from justice hide in a mountain
cabin, but all meet violent deaths.

Gloomy, strenuous melodrama, partly shot outdoors.

w Horton Foote, *novel* Clinton Seeley *d* Cornel Wilde *ph* Joseph La Shelle *m* Elmer Bernstein

Cornel Wilde, Jean Wallace, Dan Duryea, Lee Grant, Steven Hill, Dennis Weaver

Storm in a Teacup*
GB 1936   87m   bw
Alexander Korda / Victor Saville

A national sensation ensues when a Scottish provost fines an old lady for not licensing her dog, and she refuses to pay.
Early Ealing-type comedy, a bit emaciated by later standards.

w Ian Dalrymple, Donald Bull, *play* Sturm in Wasserglass by Bruno Frank *d* Ian Dalrymple, Victor Saville *ph* Max Greene

Vivien Leigh, Rex Harrison, Cecil Parker, Sara Allgood, Ursula Jeans, Gus McNaughton, Arthur Wontner

Storm over Asia*
USSR 1928   93m approx (24 fps)   bw silent
Mezhrabpomfilm
original title: *Potomok Chingis-Khana*; aka: *The Heir to Genghis Khan*

A Mongolian trapper is discovered to be descended from Genghis Khan and made puppet emperor of a Soviet province.
Curious yarn without much discernible point though with the usual patches of propagandizing. It certainly looks good.

w Osip Brik *d* V. I. Pudovkin *ph* A. L. Golovnya

I. Inkizhinov, Valeri Inkizhinov, A. Dedintsev

Storm over Lisbon
US 1944   86m   bw
Republic (George Sherman)

An international spy mastermind runs a Lisbon night club and sells documents to the highest bidder.
Feeble copy of *Casablanca*.

w Doris Gilbert, Dane Lussier *d* George Sherman *ph* John Alton *m* Walter Scharf

Vera Hruba Ralston, Erich Von Stroheim, Richard Arlen, Eduardo Ciannelli, Otto Kruger, Robert Livingston, Mona Barrie, Frank Orth

Storm over the Nile
GB 1955   107m   Technicolor Cinemascope
Independent / London (Zoltan Korda)

Feeble remake of *The Four Feathers* (qv), using most of that film's action highlights stretched out to fit the wide screen.

w R. C. Sheriff *d* Terence Young *ph* Ted Scaife, Osmond Borradaile *m* Benjamin Frankel

Anthony Steel, Laurence Harvey, Ronald Lewis, Ian Carmichael, James Robertson Justice, Mary Ure, Geoffrey Keen, Jack Lambert, Ferdy Mayne, Michael Hordern

'The material appears not so much dated as fossilized within its period.'—*Penelope Houston*

Storm over Tibet
US 1951   87m   bw
Columbia / Summit (Ivan Tors, Laslo Benedek)

An explorer steals a holy mask which brings bad luck.
Slight adventure yarn ingeniously built around an old German documentary.

w Ivan Tors, Sam Mayer *d* Andrew Marton *ph* George E. Diskant, Richard Angst *m* Arthur Honegger

Rex Reason, Diana Douglas, Myron Healey

Storm Warning*
US 1950   93m   bw
Warner (Jerry Wald)

A New York model goes south to visit her sister, and finds that her brother-in-law is an oversexed brute and a Ku Klux Klan killer.
Heavy melodrama disguised as a social document; sufficiently arresting for its purposes.

w Daniel Fuchs, Richard Brooks *d* Stuart Heisler *ph* Carl Guthrie *m* Daniele Amfitheatrof

Ginger Rogers, Doris Day, *Steve Cochran*, Ronald Reagan, Hugh Sanders, Raymond Greenleaf, Ned Glass

Stormy Weather***
US 1943   77m   bw
TCF (Irving Mills)

A backstage success story lightly based on the career of Bill Robinson.
Virtually a high-speed revue with all-black talent, and what talent! The production is pretty slick too.

w Frederick Jackson, Ted Koehler *d Andrew Stone ph Leon Shamroy, Fred Sersen md Benny Carter ch* Clarence Robinson

Bill Robinson, Lena Horne, Fats Waller, Ada Brown, Cab Calloway, Katherine Dunham and her Dancers, Eddie Anderson, Flournoy Miller, *The Nicholas Brothers,* Dooley Wilson

The Story of a Woman

US / Italy 1969   101m   Technicolor
Universal / Westward (Leonardo Bercovici)

A Swedish girl pianist in Rome falls in love with a
fashionable doctor, then back in Sweden meets
an American diplomat.

Intermezzo-type romantic drama with colour
supplement trappings. Tolerable of its kind.

wd Leonardo Bercovici *ph* Piero Portalupi
m John Williams

Robert Stack, Bibi Andersson, James Farentino,
Annie Girardot, Frank Sundstrom

The Story of Adèle H*

France 1975   98m   Eastmancolor
Films du Carrosse / Artistes Associés (Marcel
    Berbert, Claude Miller)

In 1863, the daughter of Victor Hugo follows her
lover to Nova Scotia.

Surprisingly slow and stilted version of a true
story, though with a few of the expected
subtleties.

w François Truffaut, Jean Gruault, Suzanne
Schiffman *d* François Truffaut *ph* Nestor
Almendros *m* Maurice Jaubert

Isabelle Adjani, Bruce Robinson, Sylvia
Marriott

AAN: Isabelle Adjani

The Story of Alexander Graham Bell**

US 1939   97m   bw
TCF (Kenneth MacGowan)
GB title: *The Modern Miracle*

The inventor of the telephone marries a deaf girl.
Acceptable history lesson with dullish principals
but excellent production.

w Lamar Trotti *d* Irving Cummings *ph* Leon
Shamroy

Don Ameche, Henry Fonda, Loretta Young,
Charles Coburn, Gene Lockhart, Spring
Byington, Bobs Watson

The Story of Dr Wassell*

US 1944   140m   Technicolor
Paramount / Cecil B. de Mille

The adventures of a naval doctor who heroically
saved men during the Pacific war.

Long, slogging, glamorized account of real
events which is typical de Mille and very
unconvincing physically, but keeps one watching
simply as a story.

w Alan le May, Charles Bennett, *book* James
Hilton *d* Cecil B. de Mille *ph* Victor Milner,
William Snyder *m* Victor Young

Gary Cooper, Laraine Day, Signe Hasso,

Dennis O'Keefe, Carol Thurston, Carl Esmond,
Paul Kelly, Stanley Ridges

'The director has taken a true story of heroism
. . . and jangled it into a cacophony of dancing
girls, phoney self-sacrifice and melodramatic
romance.'—*Howard Barnes*

The Story of Esther Costello*

GB 1957   103m   bw
Columbia / Romulus (James Woolf)
US title: *The Golden Virgin*

A blind Irish deaf mute girl is adopted by an
American socialite and her plight becomes an
international cause.

Rich melodrama develops from this unlikely
premise and the star enjoys it hugely.

w Charles Kaufman, *novel* Nicholas Monsarrat
d David Miller *ph* Raoul Kraushaar *m* Georges
Auric

Joan Crawford, Heather Sears, Rossano Brazzi,
Ron Randell, Lee Patrick, Fay Compton, John
Loder, Denis O'Dea, Sidney James, Maureen
Delany

The Story of GI Joe**

US 1945   108m   bw
(UA) Lester Cowan (David Hall)
aka: *War Correspondent*

Journalist Ernie Pyle follows fighting men into
the Italian campaign.

Slow, convincing, sympathetic war film with
good script and performances; not by any means
the usual action saga.

w Leopold Atlas, Guy Endore, Philip Stevenson,
book Ernie Pyle d William A. Wellman
ph Russell Metty m Ann Ronell, Louise
Applebaum

Burgess Meredith, Robert Mitchum, Freddie
Steele, Wally Cassell, Jimmy Lloyd, Jack Reilly

'It is humorous, poignant and tragic, an
earnestly human reflection of a stern life and the
dignity of man.'—*Thomas M. Pryor*

'A tragic and eternal work of art.'—*James
Agee*

'One of the best films of the war.'—*Richard
Mallett, Punch*

AAN: script; music score; song 'Linda'
(*m/ly* Ann Ronell); Robert Mitchum

The Story of Gilbert and Sullivan*

GB 1953   109m   Technicolor
British Lion / London Films (Frank Launder,
    Sidney Gilliat)

In 1875 a young composer named Arthur
Sullivan and a librettist named William Gilbert
come together under the auspices of Rupert

D'Oyly Carte and write the Savoy Operas.
Light, accurate, well-cast and well-produced
Victorian musical which somehow fails to ignite
despite the immense talent at hand.

w Sidney Gilliat, Leslie Baily *d* Sidney Gilliat
ph Christopher Challis *md* Sir Malcolm Sargent
pd Hein Heckroth

Robert Morley, Maurice Evans, Peter Finch,
Eileen Herlie, Dinah Sheridan, Isabel Dean,
Wilfrid Hyde White, Muriel Aked

The Story of Louis Pasteur***
US 1935   85m   bw
Warner (Henry Blanke)

How the eminent 19th-century French scientist
overcomes obstacles in finding cures for various
diseases.
Adequate biopic which caused a sensation and
started a trend; some of the others were better
but this was the first example of Hollywood
bringing schoolbook history to box office life.

w Sheridan Gibney, Pierre Collins *d* William
Dieterle *ph* Tony Gaudio *m* Bernhard Kaun,
Heinz Roemheld

Paul Muni, Josephine Hutchinson, Anita
Louise, Donald Woods, Fritz Leiber, Henry
O'Neill, Porter Hall, Akim Tamiroff, Walter
Kingsford

'What should be vital and arresting has been
made hollow and dull . . . we are tendered
something that is bright and stagey for
something out of life.'—*Otis Ferguson*

'More exciting than any gangster
melodrama.'—*C. A. Lefeune*

AA: script; Paul Muni
AAN: best picture

The Story of Mankind
US 1957   100m   Technicolor
Warner / Cambridge (Irwin Allen)

A heavenly tribunal debates whether to allow
man to destroy himself, and both the Devil and
the Spirit of Man cite instances from history.
Hilarious charade, one of the worst films ever
made, but full of surprises, bad performances,
and a wide range of stock shots.

w Irwin Allen, Charles Bennett, *book* Henrik
Van Loon *d* Irwin Allen *ph* Nicholas
Musuraca *m* Paul Sawtell

Ronald Colman, Vincent Price, Cedric
Hardwicke, the Marx Brothers, Hedy Lamarr,
Agnes Moorehead, Reginald Gardiner, Peter
Lorre, Virginia Mayo, Charles Coburn, Francis
X. Bushman

The Story of Robin Hood and his Merrie Men
GB 1952   84m   Technicolor
Walt Disney (Perce Pearce)

When Prince John starts a ruthless taxation
campaign, Robert Fitzooth turns outlaw.
Fairly competent but quite forgettable version of
the legend, softened for children.

w Laurence E. Watkin *d* Ken Annakin *ph* Guy
Green *m* Clifton Parker

Richard Todd, Joan Rice, James Hayter, Hubert
Gregg, James Robertson Justice, Martita Hunt,
Peter Finch

The Story of Ruth
US 1960   132m   De Luxe   Cinemascope
TCF (Samuel G. Engel)

Ruth becomes the favourite of a pagan king but
eventually flees to Israel.
Tedious, portentous bible-in-pictures, of
virtually no interest or entertainment value.

w Norman Corwin *d* Henry Koster *ph* Arthur
E. Arling *m* Franz Waxman

Elana Eden, Peggy Wood, Viveca Lindfors,
Stuart Whitman, Tom Tryon, Jeff Morrow,
Thayer David, Eduard Franz

The Story of Seabiscuit
US 1949   98m   Technicolor
Warner (William Jacobs)
GB title: *Pride of Kentucky*

The success story of a racehorse.
Blue grass vapidities, the kind of family
entertainment that drove the families away.

w John Taintor Foote *d* David Butler
ph Wilfrid Cline *md* David Buttolph

Shirley Temple, Barry Fitzgerald, Lon
McCallister, Rosemary de Camp, Donald
McBride, Pierre Watkin

The Story of Temple Drake*
US 1933   71m   bw
Paramount

A neurotic southern flapper is abducted by
gangsters, and likes it.
Deliberately shocking melodrama of its time,
restructured from a notorious book later filmed
under its own title. Very dated, but interesting.

w Oliver H. P. Garrett, *novel* Sanctuary by
William Faulkner *d* Stephen Roberts *ph* Karl
Struss

Miriam Hopkins, Jack La Rue, William Gargan,
William Collier Jnr, Irving Pichel, Guy Standing,
Elizabeth Patterson, Florence Eldridge

The Story of Three Loves
US 1953 122m Technicolor
MGM (Sidney Franklin)

Three love stories concerning the passengers on a transatlantic liner.
Three bits of old-fashioned kitsch, one tragic, one whimsical, one melodramatic, all rather slow and dull though well produced.

w John Collier, Jan Lustig, George Froeschel *d* Gottfried Reinhardt, Vincente Minnelli *ph* Charles Rosher, Harold Rosson *m* Miklos Rozsa

Ethel Barrymore, James Mason, Moira Shearer, Pier Angeli, Leslie Caron, Kirk Douglas, Farley Granger, Agnes Moorehead, Zsa Zsa Gabor

The Story of Vernon and Irene Castle **
US 1939 93m bw
RKO (George Haight, Pandro S. Berman)

The story of a husband and wife dance team who had their first success in Paris and became influential international celebrities before he was killed as a flier in World War I.
Pleasant understated musical with very agreeable dance sequences and a firm overall style. The last of the main stream of Astaire-Rogers musicals.

w Richard Sherman, Oscar Hammerstein II, Dorothy Yost, *books* Irene Castle *d* H. C. Potter *ph* Robert de Grasse *md* Victor Baravalle *ch* Hermes Pan *ad* Van Nest Polglase

Fred Astaire, Ginger Rogers, Edna May Oliver, Walter Brennan, Lew Fields, Etienne Girardot, Donald MacBride

The Story of Will Rogers
US 1950 109m Technicolor
Warner (Robert Arthur)

A wild west performer becomes a Ziegfeld star and pop philosopher.
Bland, unshaped biopic of one of American show business's best loved figures, who died in an air crash in 1935.

w Frank Davis, Stanley Roberts *d* Michael Curtiz *ph* Wilfrid M. Cline *md* Victor Young

Will Rogers Jnr, Jane Wyman, James Gleason, Eddie Cantor (as himself), Carl Benton Reid

The Story on Page One
US 1960 123m bw Cinemascope
TCF / Company of Artists

A lawyer undertakes the defence of a woman who with her lover is charged with the murder of her husband.
Long drawn out and not very interesting

courtroom drama, performed and presented with some style.

wd Clifford Odets *ph* James Wong Howe *m* Elmer Bernstein

Rita Hayworth, Tony Franciosa, Gig Young, Mildred Dunnock, Hugh Griffith, Sanford Meisner, Alfred Ryder

Stowaway *
US 1936 86m bw
TCF (Earl Carroll, Harold Wilson)

The orphan daughter of a Shanghai missionary stows away on an American pleasure ship.
Very good star vehicle in which Shirley performs some of her best musical numbers.

w William Conselman, Arthur Sheekman, Nat Perrin *d* William A. Seiter *ph* Arthur Miller *md* Louis Silvers

Shirley Temple, Robert Young, Alice Faye, Eugene Pallette, Helen Westley, Arthur Treacher, J. Edward Bromberg, Astrid Allwyn

La Strada *
Italy 1954 94m bw
Ponti / de Laurentiis
aka: *The Road*

A half-witted peasant girl is sold to an itinerant strong man and ill-used by him.
Curious attempt at a kind of poetic neo-realism, saved by style and performances.

w Federico Fellini, Ennio Flaiano, Tullio Pinelli *d* Federico Fellini *ph* Otello Martelli *m* Nino Rota

Giulietta Masina, Anthony Quinn, Richard Basehart

AAN: script

Straight on Till Morning
GB 1972 96m Technicolor
EMI / Hammer (Roy Skeggs)

A Liverpool girl in London meets a dangerous psychotic.
Unattractive suspenser, wildly directed.

w Michael Peacock *d* Peter Collinson *ph* Brian Probyn *m* Roland Shaw

Rita Tushingham, Shane Briant, Tom Bell, Annie Ross, James Bolam

Straight Time
US 1978 114m Technicolor
Warner / First Artists / Sweetwall (Stanley Beck, Tim Zinnemann)

A psychotic parolee fails to go straight.
Unappetizing social melodrama with an irresolute leading performance.

w Alvin Sargent, Edward Bunker, Jeffrey Boam,
novel No Beast So Fierce by Edward Bunker
d Ulu Grosbard *ph* Owen Roizman *m* David
Shire

Dustin Hoffman, Theresa Russell, Gary Busey,
Harry Dean Stanton

'One leaves the theatre hoping the character
will die painfully and slowly in a hail of
bullets.'—*Variety*

Strait Jacket
US 1963 92m bw
Columbia / William Castle

A woman who murdered her faithless husband
with an axe is released twenty years later, and
more axe murders occur.
Dull and unattractive shocker in which all
concerned lean over backwards to conceal the
trick ending.

w Robert Bloch *d* William Castle *ph* Arthur E.
Arling *m* Van Alexander

Joan Crawford, Diane Baker, Leif Erickson,
Howard St John, Rochelle Hudson, George
Kennedy

The Strange Affair
GB 1968 106m Techniscope
Paramount (Howard Harrison, Stanley Mann)

A young London policeman finds that his
superiors are almost as corrupt as the villains.
Stylishly made melodrama of despair, with a
sexy nymphet heroine straight from swinging
London. It all leaves a sour taste in the mouth.

w Stanley Mann, *novel* Bernard Toms *d* David
Greene *ph* Max Thompson *m* Basil Kirchin

Michael York, Jeremy Kemp, Susan George,
Jack Watson, George A. Cooper

Strange Bedfellows
US 1965 99m Technicolor
U-I / Panama—Frank (Melvin Frank)

An American executive in London nearly
divorces his fiery Italian wife.
Frantic sex comedy with picture postcard
background; fatiguing rather than funny, but
with minor compensations.

w Melvin Frank, Michael Pertwee *d* Melvin
Frank *ph* Leo Tover

Rock Hudson, Gina Lollobrigida, Gig Young,
Edward Judd, Howard St John, Arthur Haynes,
Dave King, Terry-Thomas

'The grind of predictable situations is further
afflicted by considerable lapses in taste.'—*MFB*

Strange Boarders*
GB 1938 79m bw
GFD / Gainsborough (Edward Black)

A police detective postpones his honeymoon to
book into a boarding house and discover which
of the guests is a spy.
Quite engaging comedy-thriller in the Hitchcock
mould, with entertaining performances and
incidents.

w A. R. Rawlinson, Sidney Gilliatt, *novel* The
Strange Boarders of Paradise Crescent by E.
Phillips Oppenheim *d* Herbert Mason *ph* Jack
Cox

Tom Walls, Renee Saint-Cyr, Leon M. Lion,
Googie Withers, C. V. France, Ronald Adam,
Irene Handl, George Curzon, Martita Hunt

Strange Cargo*
US 1940 105m bw
MGM (Joseph L. Mankiewicz)

Eight convicts escape from Devil's Island and
are influenced by a Christ-like fugitive.
One of Hollywood's occasional lunacies; one
doubts whether even the author knew the point
of this cockamamy parable, but it was well
produced and acted.

w Lawrence Hazard, *novel* Not Too Narrow,
Not Too Deep by Richard Sale *d* Frank
Borzage *ph* Robert Planck *m* Franz Waxman

Clark Gable, Joan Crawford, Ian Hunter, Peter
Lorre, Paul Lukas, Albert Dekker, J. Edward
Bromberg, Eduardo Ciannelli, Frederick
Worlock

'Even the most hardened mystics may
blush.'—*New Yorker, 1978*

The Strange Door*
US 1951 81m bw
U-I (Ted Richmond)

A young nobleman, passing through the one-
way door of a castle, finds himself the prisoner of
a madman.
Torture-chamber suspenser, adequately if rather
tediously developed, with most of its interest
reposing in the cast.

w Jerry Sackheim, *story* The Sire de Maletroit's
Door by Robert Louis Stevenson *d* Joseph
Pevney *ph* Irving Glassberg *m* Joseph
Gershenson

Charles Laughton, Boris Karloff, Michael Pate,
Sally Forrest, Richard Stapley, Alan Napier

Strange Interlude**
US 1932 110m bw
MGM (Irving Thalberg)
GB title: *Strange Interval*

Problems of an unfulfilled wife and her lover. Surprising film version of a very heavy modern classic, complete with asides to the audience; very dated now, but a small milestone in Hollywood's development.

w Bess Meredyth, C. Gardner Sullivan, *play* Eugene O'Neill *d* Robert Z. Leonard *ph* Lee Garmes

Norma Shearer, Clark Gable, May Robson, Alexander Kirkland, Ralph Morgan, Robert Young, Maureen O'Sullivan, Henry B. Walthall
'A cinematic novelty to be seen by discerning audiences.'—*Film Weekly*
'More exciting than a thousand "action" movies.'—*Pare Lorentz*

Strange Intruder
US 1957 78m bw
AA (Lindsley Parsons)

A psychopathic ex-POW menaces the children of his dead friend's wife.
Gloomy second feature melodrama, rather well presented.

w David Evans, Warren Douglas, *novel* Helen Fowler *d* Irving Rapper *ph* Ernest Haller *m* Paul Dunlap

Edmund Purdom, Ida Lupino, Ann Harding, Jacques Bergerac, Carl Benton Reid

Strange Lady in Town
US 1955 118m Warnercolor
Cinemascope
Warner (Mervyn Le Roy)

Adventures of a woman doctor in 1880 Santa Fe.
Quaint western drama which is never any more convincing than its star.

w Frank Butler *d* Mervyn Le Roy *ph* Harold Rosson *m* Dmitri Tiomkin

Greer Garson, Dana Andrews, Cameron Mitchell, Lois Smith, Walter Hampden

The Strange Love of Martha Ivers**
US 1946 116m bw
Paramount / Hal B. Wallis

A murderous child becomes a wealthy woman with a spineless lawyer husband; the melodrama starts when an ex-boy friend returns to town.
Irresistible star melodrama which leaves no stone unturned; compulsive entertainment of the old school.

w Robert Rossen *d* Lewis Milestone *ph* Victor Milner *m* Miklos Rozsa

Barbara Stanwyck, Van Heflin, Kirk Douglas, Lizabeth Scott, Judith Anderson, Roman Bohnen

'Fate drew them together and only murder can part them!'—*publicity*
AAN: original story (Jack Patrick)

The Strange One*
US 1957 99m bw
Columbia / Sam Spiegel
GB title: *End as a Man*

A sadistic cadet causes trouble at a southern military college.
A weird and unsavoury but rather compelling melodrama which unreels like a senior version of *Tom Brown's Schooldays*.

w Calder Willingham, from his novel End as a Man *d* Jack Garfein *ph* Burnett Guffey *m* Kenyon Hopkins

Ben Gazzara, George Peppard, Mark Richman, Pat Hingle, Arthur Storch, Paul Richards, Geoffrey Horne, James Olson
'The film's brilliance is in its persuasive depiction of a highly controversial, artificially organized world; its failure is to make any dramatic statement about it.'—*MFB*

The Strange Woman
US 1946 100m bw
(UA) Hunt Stromberg (Jack Chertok)

A scheming woman plays with the lives of three men.
Star wish-fulfilment; otherwise a hammy costume piece.

w Herb Meadows, *novel* Ben Ames Williams *d* Edgar G. Ulmer *ph* Lucien Andriot *m* Carmen Dragon

Hedy Lamarr, George Sanders, Louis Hayward, Gene Lockhart, Hillary Brooke

The Stranger*
US 1946 95m bw
(RKO) Sam Spiegel

An escaped Nazi criminal marries an American woman and settles in a Connecticut village.
Highly unconvincing and artificial melodrama enhanced by directorial touches, splendid photography and no-holds-barred climax involving a church clock.

w Anthony Veiller, *story* Victor Trivas, Decia Dunning *d* Orson Welles *ph* Russell Metty *m* Bronislau Kaper

Edward G. Robinson, Orson Welles, Loretta Young, Philip Merivale, Richard Long, Konstatin Shayne
'Some striking effects, with lighting and interesting angles much relied on.'—*Bosley Crowther*

AAN: original story

Stranger at My Door
US 1956 85m bw
Republic (Sidney Picker)

A gunman takes refuge in the house of a
preacher who tries to convert him.
Odd, sentimental little western morality play, not
badly presented.

w Barry Shipman d William Witney ph Bud
Thackery m Dale Butts

Macdonald Carey, Skip Homeier, Patricia
Medina, Louis Jean Heydt

A Stranger in My Arms
US 1958 88m bw Cinemascope
U-I (Ross Hunter)

A test pilot falls in love with his dead friend's
widow and helps her face up to her in-laws.
Dreary romantic drama.

w Peter Berneis, novel And Ride a Tiger by
Robert Wilder d Helmut Kautner ph William
Daniels m Joseph Gershenson

June Allyson, Jeff Chandler, Mary Astor, Sandra
Dee, Charles Coburn, Conrad Nagel, Peter
Graves

Stranger on the Third Floor*
US 1940 64m bw
RKO

A reporter finds that he was wrong in the well-
intentioned testimony which helps convict an
innocent man for murder.
Stylish B feature with a striking dream scene and
a curious fleeting performance by Lorre as the
real murderer.

w Frank Partos d Boris Ingster ph Nicholas
Musuraca m Roy Webb

Margaret Tallichet, Peter Lorre, John McGuire,
Charles Waldron, Elisha Cook Jnr, Charles
Halton, Ethel Griffies

The Stranger's Hand
GB 1953 85m bw
British Lion / John Stafford, Peter Moore
aka: Mano della Straniero

A schoolboy is due to meet his father in Venice,
but the father is kidnapped by enemy agents.
Rather tentative suspense thriller with a vague
plot which seems to defeat an excellent cast.

w Guy Elmes, Giorgio Bassani, story Graham
Greene d Mario Soldati ph Enzo Serafin
m Nino Rota

Trevor Howard, Richard O'Suliivan, Francis L.
Sullivan, Alida Valli, Eduardo Ciannelli,
Richard Basehart, Stephen Murray

Strangers May Kiss
US 1931 82m bw
MGM

A sophisticated wife takes love and fidelity lightly.
Dated romantic drama.

w John Meehan, novel Ursula Parrott d George
Fitzmaurice ph William Daniels

Norma Shearer, Robert Montgomery, Neil
Hamilton, Marjorie Rambeau, Irene Rich

Strangers on a Train*
US 1951 101m bw
Warner (Alfred Hitchcock)

A tennis star is pestered on a train by a psychotic
who wants to swap murders, and proceeds to
carry out his part of the bargain.
This quirky melodrama has the director at his
best, sequence by sequence, but the story is
basically unsatisfactory. It makes superior
suspense entertainment, however.

w Raymond Chandler, Czenzi Ormonde, novel
Patricia Highsmith d Alfred Hitchcock
ph Robert Burks m Ray Heindorf

Farley Granger, Robert Walker, Ruth Roman,
Leo G. Carroll, Patricia Hitchcock, Marion
Lorne, Howard St John, Jonathan Hale, Laura
Elliott
'You may not take it seriously, but you
certainly don't have time to think about anything
else.'—Richard Mallett, Punch

† Remade 1970 as Once You Kiss A Stranger.
AAN: Robert Burks

Strangers When We Meet*
US 1960 117m Technicolor
     Cinemascope
Columbia / Bryna (Richard Quine)

A successful architect starts an affair with a
beautiful married neighbour.
Beverly Hills soap opera with lots of romantic
suffering in luxury. Lumpy but generally
palatable.

w Evan Hunter, from his novel d Richard
Quine ph Charles Lang Jnr m George Duning

Kirk Douglas, Kim Novak, Ernie Kovacs,
Walter Matthau, Barbara Rush, Virginia Bruce,
Helen Gallagher, Kent Smith

The Strangler
US 1963 80m bw
AA

An obese lab technician murders nurses who
help his hated mother.
Modest, lively shocker.

w Bill S. Ballinger d Burt Topper ph Jacques
Marquette m Martin Skiles

Victor Buono, David McLean, Ellen Corby, Diane Sayer

The Stranglers of Bombay

GB 1959 81m bw Megascope
Columbia / Hammer (Anthony Hinds)

In 1826 travellers are waylaid and sacrificially killed by a cult of stranglers.
Semi-historical parade of atrocities, repellent but scarcely exciting.

w David Z. Goodman *d* Terence Fisher *ph* Arthur Grant *m* James Bernard

Guy Rolfe, Allan Cuthbertson, Andrew Cruickshank, Marne Maitland, Jan Holden, George Pastell, Paul Stassino

Strategic Air Command

US 1955 114m Technicolor Vistavision
Paramount (Samuel J. Briskin)

A baseball player is recalled to air force duty.
Sentimental flagwaver featuring the newest jets of the fifties.

w Valentine Davies, Beirne Lay Jnr *d* Anthony Mann *ph* William Daniels *m* Victor Young

James Stewart, June Allyson, Frank Lovejoy, Barry Sullivan, Alex Nicol, Bruce Bennett, Jay C. Flippen, James Millican, James Bell

AAN: original story (Beirne Lay Jnr)

The Stratton Story

US 1949 106m bw
MGM (Sam Wood)

An amateur baseball enthusiast becomes a famous professional, but suffers an accident which involves the amputation of a leg.
Mild sentimental biopic, well made but not very interesting.

w Douglas Morrow, Guy Trosper *d* Sam Wood *ph* Harold Rosson *m* Adolph Deutsch

James Stewart, June Allyson, Frank Morgan, Agnes Moorehead, Bill Williams

AAN: original story (Douglas Morrow)

Straw Dogs

GB 1971 118m Eastmancolor
Talent Associates / Amerbroco (Daniel Melnick)

In a Cornish village, a mild American university researcher erupts into violence when taunted by drunken villagers who commit sustained assaults on himself and his wife.
Totally absurd, poorly contrived, hilariously overwritten Cold Comfort Farm melodrama with farcical violence.

w David Zelag Goodman, Sam Peckinpah, *novel*

The Siege of Trencher's Farm by Gordon M. Williams *d* Sam Peckinpah *ph* John Coquillon, *m* Jerry Fielding

Dustin Hoffman, Susan George, Peter Vaughan, David Warner, T. P. McKenna, Colin Welland

AAN: Jerry Fielding

The Strawberry Blonde**

US 1941 97m bw
Warner (William Cagney)

A dentist in turn-of-the-century Brooklyn wonders whether he married the right woman.
Pleasant period comedy drama, a remake of *One Sunday Afternoon* (qv).

w Julius J. and Philip G. Epstein *d* Raoul Walsh *ph* James Wong Howe *m* Heinz Roemheld

James Cagney, Olivia de Havilland, *Rita Hayworth, Alan Hale,* George Tobias, Jack Carson, Una O'Connor, George Reeves

'It not only tells a very human story, it also creates an atmosphere, recreates a period.'— *New York Sun*

AAN: Heinz Roemheld

The Strawberry Statement

US 1970 109m Metrocolor
MGM / Robert Chartoff, Irwin Winkler

Student rebels occupy a university administration building.
One of a short-lived group of student anti-discipline films of the early seventies, and about the most boring.

w Israel Horowitz, *novel* James Simon Kunen *d* Stuart Hagmann *ph* Ralph Woolsey *m* Ian Freebairn Smith

Bruce Davison, Kim Darby, Bud Cort, Murray MacLeod

Street Corner

GB 1953 94m bw
Rank / LIP / Sydney Box
US title: *Both Sides of the Law*

Days in the lives of the women police of Chelsea.
Patter-plotted female *Blue Lamp*; just about watchable.

w Muriel and Sydney Box *d* Muriel Box *ph* Reg Wyer *m* Temple Abady

Rosamund John, Anne Crawford, Peggy Cummins, Terence Morgan, Barbara Murray, Sarah Lawson, Ronald Howard, Eleanor Summerfield, Michael Medwin

Street of Chance

US 1930 78m bw
Paramount

A New York gambler gets his come-uppance.
Dullish family melodrama with gangsters as *dei
ex machina*.

w Howard Estabrook, Lenore Coffee *d* John
Cromwell *ph* Charles Lang

William Powell, Kay Francis, Regis Toomey,
Jean Arthur

AAN: script

Street of Shame*
Japan 1956 85m bw
Daiei (Masaichi Nagata)
original title: *Akasen Chitai*

Stories of women in a Tokyo brothel.
Unremarkable material executed with the style
expected of the director.

w Masashige Narusawa *d* Kenji Mizoguchi
ph Kazuo Miyagawa *m* Toshiro Mayazumi

Machiko Kyo, Ayako Wakao, Aiko Mimasu

Street Scene*
US 1931 80m bw
Samuel Goldwyn

In a New York slum street on a hot summer
night, an adulterous woman is shot by her
husband.
Slice-of-life drama from an influential play;
never much of a film, and very dated.

w Elmer Rice, from his play *d* King Vidor
ph George Barnes

Sylvia Sidney, William Collier Jnr, Max Mantor,
David Landau, Estelle Taylor, Russell Hopton

The Street with No Name*
US 1948 93m bw
TCF

An FBI man goes undercover to unmask a
criminal gang.
The oldest crime plot in the world, applied with
vigour to the documentary realism of *The House
on 92nd Street* and built around the *Kiss of
Death* psychopathic character created by
Richard Widmark.

w Harry Kleiner *d* William Keighley *ph* Joe
MacDonald *m* Lionel Newman

Richard Widmark, Mark Stevens, Lloyd Nolan,
Barbara Lawrence, Ed Begley
† Remade 1955 as *House of Bamboo*.

A Streetcar Named Desire**
US 1951 122m bw
Charles K. Feldman / Elia Kazan

A repressed southern widow is raped and driven
mad by her brutal brother-in-law.
Reasonably successful, decorative picture from

a highly theatrical but influential play; unreal
sets and atmospheric photography vaguely
Sternbergian.

w Tennessee Williams, from his play *d* Elia
Kazan *ph* Harry Stradling *m* Alex North
ad Richard Day

Vivien Leigh, Marlon Brando, Kim Hunter,
Karl Malden

AA: Vivien Leigh; Kim Hunter; Karl Malden
AAN: best picture; Tennessee Williams; Elia
Kazan; Harry Stradling; Alex North; Marlon
Brando

Streets of Laredo
US 1949 92m Technicolor
Paramount

Two of three bandit friends become Texas
Rangers.
Adequate star western, a remake of *The Texas
Rangers*.

w Charles Marquis Warren *d* Leslie Fenton
ph Ray Rennahan *m* Victor Young

William Holden, William Bendix, Macdonald
Carey, Mona Freeman

Strictly Dishonourable
US 1951 94m bw
MGM (Melvin Frank, Norman Panama)

A young girl falls in love with a rakish Italian
opera star; he is such a sentimentalist that he
marries her.
Emasculated sentimental version of the sharp
Preston Sturges comedy.

wd Norman Panama, Melvin Frank *ph* Ray
June

Ezio Pinza, Janet Leigh, Millard Mitchell, Maria
Palmer

Strike***
USSR 1924 70m approx (24 fps) bw
silent
Goskino / Proletkult

A 1912 strike of factory workers is brutally put
down by the authorities.
Brilliant propaganda piece with superbly
cinematic sequences.

wd Sergei M. Eisenstein ph Edouard Tissé,
Vassili Khvatov

Grigori Alexandrov, Maxim Strauch, Mikhail
Gomarov

Strike Me Pink*
US 1936 104m bw
Samuel Goldwyn

A timid amusement park owner is threatened by crooks.
Acceptable star comedy with music.

w Frank Butler, Walter de Leon, Francis Martin *d* Norman Taurog *ph* Gregg Toland, Merritt Gerstad

Eddie Cantor, Sally Eilers, Ethel Merman, William Frawley, Parkyakarkus

Strike Up the Band *
US 1940 120m bw
MGM (Arthur Freed)

A high-school band takes part in a nationwide radio contest.
Rather tiresomely high-spirited musical with the stars at the top of their young form.

w Fred Finklehoffe, John Monks Jnr
d/ch Busby Berkeley *ph* Ray June *md* Georgie Stoll, Roger Edens

Judy Garland, Mickey Rooney, Paul Whiteman and his Orchestra, June Preisser, William Tracy, Larry Nunn

AAN: Georgie Stoll, Roger Edens; song 'Our Love Affair' (*m/ly* Roger Edens, Georgie Stoll)

The Strip *
US 1951 85m bw
MGM (Joe Pasternak)

A band drummer is accused of the murder of a racketeer.
Minor mystery melodrama intriguingly set on Sunset Strip, with jazz accompaniment.

w Allen Rivkin *d* Leslie Kardos *ph* Robert Surtees *m* George Stoll

Mickey Rooney, Sally Forrest, William Demarest, James Craig, Kay Brown; and Louis Armstrong, Earl Hines, Jack Teagarden

AAN: song 'A Kiss To Build a Dream On (*m/ly* Bert Kalmar, Harry Ruby, Oscar Hammerstein II)

The Stripper *
US 1963 95m bw Cinemascope
TCF (Jerry Wald)
GB title: *Woman of Summer*

An ageing beauty queen returns to her Kansas hometown and has an affair with a 19-year-old garage hand.
Downbeat character melodrama typical of its time and its author; competent but sterile and rather tedious.

w Meade Roberts, *play* A Loss of Roses by William Inge *d* Franklin Schaffner
ph Ellsworth Fredericks *m* Jerry Goldsmith

Joanne Woodward, Richard Beymer, *Claire Trevor,* Carol Lynley, Robert Webber, Louis Nye, Gypsy Rose Lee, Michael J. Pollard

The Strong Man *
US 1926 75m approx (24 fps) bw (colour sequence) silent
Harry Langdon

A war veteran returns and searches the city for his female penfriend.
Quite charming star comedy, probably Langdon's best.

w Frank Capra, Arthur Ripley, Hal Conklin, Robert Eddy *d* Frank Capra *ph* Elgin Lessley, Glenn Kershner

Harry Langdon, Gertrude Astor, Tay Garnett

The Strongest Man in the World
US 1976 92m Technicolor
Walt Disney (Bill Anderson)

An accident in a science lab gives a student superhuman strength.
Formula comedy for older children.

w Joseph L. McEveety, Herman Groves
d Vincent McEveety *ph* Andrew Jackson
m Robert F. Brunner

Kurt Russell, Joe Flynn, Eve Arden, Cesar Romero, Phil Silvers, Dick Van Patten, Harold Gould, William Schallert, James Gregory, Roy Roberts, Fritz Feld, Raymond Bailey, Eddie Quillan, Burt Mustin

Strongroom *
GB 1961 80m bw
Bryanston / Theatrecraft (Guido Coen)

Two car breakers plan a once-for-all bank robbery but get involved with potential murder when their hostages get locked in.
Suspenseful second feature with gloss and pace.

w Max Marquis, René Harris *d* Vernon Sewell
ph Basil Emmott *m* Johnny Gregory

Colin Gordon, Ann Lynn, Derren Nesbitt, Keith Faulkner

The Struggle *
US 1931 88m bw
UA / D. W. Griffith

A New Yorker goes to the bad on bootleg liquor.
The director's last film reveals many of his old skills allied to a Victorian tract.

w Anita Loos, John Emerson *d* D. W. Griffith

Hal Skelly, Zita Johann, Charlotte Wynters, Jackson Halliday

The Stud

GB 1978   90m   colour
Brent Walker / Artoc (Edward D. Simons)

A millionaire's wife installs her lover as manager
of a discotheque, but he becomes bored and
wants a place of his own.
Life among the unpleasant rich. A surprise box
office success, richly undeserved.

w Jackie Collins, from her novel d Quentin
Masters ph Peter Hannan m Biddu

Joan Collins, Oliver Tobias, Sue Lloyd, Mark
Burns, Doug Fisher, Walter Gotell
   'Watching it is rather like being buried alive in
a coffin stuffed with back numbers of *Men
Only.*'—*Alan Brien*

The Student Prince

US 1954   107m   Anscocolor
   Cinemascope
MGM (Joe Pasternak)

A prince studies in Heidelberg and falls for a
barmaid.
Ruritanian operetta, lumpishly filmed, with
Mario Lanza providing only the voice of the hero
as he got too fat to play the part.

w William Ludwig, Sonya Levien, play Old
Heidelberg by Wilhelm Meyer-Foerster
operetta Dorothy Donnelly d Richard Thorpe
ph Paul C. Vogel m Sigmund Romberg
md George Stoll

Edmund Purdom, Ann Blyth, John Williams,
Edmund Gwenn, S. Z. Sakall, John Ericson,
Louis Calhern, Betta St John, Evelyn Varden

A Study in Terror*

GB 1965   95m   Eastmancolor
Compton–Tekli / Sir Nigel (Henry E. Lester)

Sherlock Holmes discovers the identity of Jack
the Ripper.
A reasonably good Holmes pastiche marred by a
surfeit of horror and over-riotous local colour;
quite literate, but schizophrenic.

w Donald and Derek Ford, novel Ellery Queen
d James Hill ph Desmond Dickinson m John
Scott ad Alex Vetchinsky

John Neville, Donald Houston, John Fraser,
Robert Morley, Cecil Parker, Anthony Quayle,
Barbara Windsor, Adrienne Corri, Judi Dench,
Frank Finlay, Barry Jones, Kay Walsh, Georgia
Brown

The Subject Was Roses*

US 1968   107m   Metrocolor
MGM (Edgar Lansbury)

A young war veteran finds he can't communicate
with his parents, and vice versa.
Photographed play notable for its performances.

w Frank D. Gilroy, from his play d Ulu
Grosbard

Patricia Neal, Jack Albertson, Martin Sheen,
Don Saxon, Elaine Williams

AA: Jack Albertson
AAN: Patricia Neal

Submarine Command

US 1951   87m   bw
Paramount (John Farrow, Joseph Sistrom)

A submarine officer who considers himself a
coward becomes a hero in Korea.
Very routine soul-searching actioner.

w Jonathan Latimer d John Farrow ph Lionel
Lindon m David Buttolph

William Holden, Don Taylor, Nancy Olsen,
William Bendix, Moroni Olsen, Peggy Webber

Submarine X-I

GB 1967   90m   Eastmancolor
UA / Mirisch (John C. Champion)

A submarine commander in World War II trains
men to attack the *Lindendorf* in midget
submarines.
Belated quota quickie, routine in every
department.

w Donald S. Sanford, Guy Elmes d William
Graham ph Paul Beeson

James Caan, Norman Bowler, David Sumner

The Subterraneans

US 1960   89m   Metrocolor
   Cinemascope
MGM (Arthur Freed)

The love affairs of San Francisco bohemians.
A boring oddity with lashings of eccentric
behaviour and sexual hang-ups; MGM
venturing very timidly outside its field.

w Robert Thom, novel Jack Kerouac d Ranald
MacDougall ph Joseph Ruttenberg m André
Previn

George Peppard, Leslie Caron, Janice Rule,
Roddy McDowall, Anne Seymour, Jim Hutton

Subway in the Sky

GB 1958   87m   bw
Sydney Box (John Temple-Smith, Patrick
   Filmer-Sankey)

A Berlin cabaret star finds her landlady's ex-
husband, a deserter, hiding in her apartment and
sets out to prove his innocence of drug
smuggling.
Tedious photographed play with precious few
points of dramatic interest.

w Jack Andrews, *play* Ian Main *d* Muriel Box
ph Wilkie Cooper *m* Mario Nascimbene

Hildegarde Neff, Van Johnson, Katherine Kath,
Cec Linder, Albert Lieven, Edward Judd

Such Good Friends*
US 1971   102m   Movielab
Paramount / Sigma (Otto Preminger)

A successful man has a mysterious illness and
his wife enlists help from his friends.
Satirical parable which alternates between sex
comedy and medical exposé; generally heavy-
going but with good moments.

w Elaine May, *novel* Louis Gould *d* Otto
Preminger *ph* Gayne Rescher *m* Thomas Z.
Shepherd

Dyan Cannon, James Coco, Jennifer O'Neil,
Nina Foch, Laurence Luckinbill, Ken Howard,
Burgess Meredith, Louise Lasser, Sam Levene,
Rita Gam, Nancy Guild

Sudden Fear**
US 1952   111m   bw
RKO / Joseph Kaufman

A playwright heiress finds that her husband is
plotting to kill her.
Archetypal star suspenser, glossy and effectively
climaxed.

w Lenore Coffee, Robert Smith *d David Miller*
ph Charles Lang Jnr *m* Elmer Bernstein

Joan Crawford, Jack Palance, Gloria Grahame,
Bruce Bennett, Mike Connors

AAN: Charles Lang Jnr; Joan Crawford; Jack
Palance

Suddenly*
US 1954   75m   bw
UA / Robert Bassler

Gunmen take over a suburban house and plan to
assassinate the President who is due to pass by.
Moderately effective minor suspenser with rather
too much psychological chat.

w Richard Sale *d* Lewis Allen *ph* Charles G.
Clarke *m* David Raksin

Frank Sinatra, Sterling Hayden, James
Gleason, Nancy Gates, Kim Charney

Suddenly It's Spring
US 1947   87m   bw
Paramount (Claude Binyon)

A WAC captain comes home to find that her
husband wants a divorce.
Tired romantic comedy with no fizz at all.

w Claude Binyon *d* Mitchell Leisen *ph* Daniel
L. Fapp *m* Victor Young

Paulette Goddard, Macdonald Carey, Fred
MacMurray, Arleen Whelan, Lillian Fontaine,
Frank Faylen, Victoria Horne

Suddenly Last Summer*
GB 1959   114m   bw
Columbia / Horizon (Sam Spiegel)

A homosexual poet's young cousin goes mad
when she sees him raped and murdered by beach
boys.
Arty flashback talk-piece from a one-act play,
padded out with much sub-poetic mumbo
jumbo; it takes too long to get to the revelation,
which is ambiguously presented anyway.

w Gore Vidal, *play* Tennessee Williams
d Joseph L. Mankiewicz *ph Jack Hildyard*
m Buxton Orr, Malcolm Arnold *pd Oliver*
Messel

Katharine Hepburn, Elizabeth Taylor,
Montgomery Clift, Albert Dekker, Mercedes
McCambridge, Gary Raymond
  'A short play turns into a ludicrous, lumbering
horror movie.'—*New Yorker, 1978*

AAN: Katharine Hepburn; Elizabeth Taylor

Suez*
US 1938   104m   bw
TCF (Darryl F. Zanuck)

The career of French engineer Ferdinand de
Lesseps, who built the Suez Canal.
Superbly mounted but rather undramatic
fictionalized biopic.

w Philip Dunne, Julien Josephson *d* Allan
Dwan *ph* Peverell Marley *md* Louis Silvers

Tyrone Power, Annabella, Loretta Young, J.
Edward Bromberg, Joseph Schildkraut, Henry
Stephenson, Sidney Blackmer, Maurice
Moscovitch, Sig Rumann, Nigel Bruce, Miles
Mander, George Zucco, Leon Ames, Rafaela
Ottiano

AAN: Peverell Marley; Louis Silvers

Sugarland Express**
US 1974   110m   Technicolor   Panavision
Universal (Richard Zanuck, David Brown)

A convict's wife persuades him to escape
because their baby is being adopted, and they
inadvertently leave behind them a trail of
destruction, ending in tragedy.
Mainly comic adventures with a bitter aftertaste,
very stylishly handled.

w Hal Barwood, Matthew Robbins *d Steven*
Spielberg ph Vilmos Zsigmond *m* John
Williams

Goldie Hawn, Ben Johnson, Michael Sacks,
William Atherton

'*Ace in the Hole* meets *Vanishing Point*.'—
Sight and Sound

The Suitor*
France 1962 85m bw
CAPAC
original title: *Le Soupirant*

A nervous young man makes several attempts to
get married.
The most successful feature of Pierre Etaix, a
student of Tati: his jokes are more polished but in
the end his own personality seems rather lacking.

w Pierre Etaix, Jean-Claude Carrière *d* Pierre
Etaix *m* Pierre Levant

Pierre Etaix, Laurence Lignères, France Arnell

The Sullivans*
US 1944 111m bw
TCF (Sam Jaffe)
Reissue title: *The Fighting Sullivans*

Five sons of the same family are killed in World
War II.
Inspirational true story which had a wide appeal.

w Mary C. McCall Jnr *d* Lloyd Bacon
ph Lucien Andriot *m* Alfred Newman

Anne Baxter, Thomas Mitchell, Selena Royle,
Edward Ryan, Trudy Marshall, John Campbell,
James Cardwell, John Alvin, George Offerman
Jnr, Roy Roberts

AAN: original story (Jules Schermer, Edward
Doherty)

Sullivan's Travels****
US 1941 90m bw
Paramount (Paul Jones)

A Hollywood director tires of comedy and goes
out to find real life.
Marvellously sustained tragi-comedy which
ranges from pratfalls to the chain gang and never
loses its grip or balance.

wd Preston Sturges *ph* John Seitz *m* Leo
Shuken

Joel McCrea, Veronica Lake, Robert Warwick,
William Demarest, Franklin Pangborn, Porter
Hall, Byron Foulger, Eric Blore, Robert Greig,
Torben Meyer, *Jimmy Conlin*, Margaret Hayes

'A brilliant fantasy in two keys—slapstick
farce and the tragedy of human misery.'—*James
Agee*

Summer and Smoke
US 1961 118m Technicolor Vistavision
Paramount / Hal B. Wallis

In a small Mississippi town in 1916, the
minister's spinster daughter nurses an
unrequited love for the local rebel.

Wearisome screen version, in hothouse settings,
of a pattern play about earthly and spiritual love.

w James Poe, Meade Roberts, *play* Tennessee
Williams *d* Peter Glenville *ph* Charles Lang
Jnr *m* Elmer Bernstein *ad* Walter Tyler

Geraldine Page, Laurence Harvey, Una Merkel,
John McIntire, Pamela Tiffin, Rita Moreno,
Thomas Gomez, Casey Adams, Earl Holliman,
Lee Patrick, Malcolm Atterbury

AAN: Elmer Bernstein; Geraldine Page; Una
Merkel

Summer Holiday**
US 1948 92m Technicolor
MGM (Arthur Freed)

Life for a small-town family at the turn of the
century.
Musical version of a famous play: excellent
individual numbers, warm playing and
sympathetic scenes, but a surprising lack of
overall style.

w Frances Goodrich, Albert Hackett, Ralph
Blane, *play* Ah Wilderness by Eugene O'Neill
d Rouben Mamoulian *ph* Charles Schoenbaum
md Lennie Hayton *ch* Charles Walters

Walter Huston, Mickey Rooney, Frank
Morgan, Agnes Moorehead, Butch Jenkins,
Selena Royle, Marilyn Maxwell, Gloria de
Haven, Anne Francis

Summer Holiday*
GB 1962 109m Technicolor
          Cinemascope
ABP / Ivy (Kenneth Harper)

Four young London Transport mechanics
borrow a double decker bus for a continental
holiday.
Pacy, location-filmed youth musical with plenty
of general appeal.

w Peter Myers, Ronnie Cass *d* Peter Yates
ph John Wilcox *md* Stanley Black

Cliff Richard, Lauri Peters, Melvyn Hayes, Una
Stubbs, Teddy Green, Ron Moody, Lionel
Murton, David Kossoff

Summer Interlude*
Sweden 1950 97m bw
Svensk Filmindustri (Alan Ekelund)
original title: *Sommarlek*

A prima ballerina remembers a happy summer
she spent with a boy who was tragically killed.
Melancholy romance quite typical of its creator
but with less density of meaning than usual.

w Ingmar Bergman, Herbert Grevenius

d Ingmar Bergman *ph* Gunnar Fischer, Bengt Jarnmark *m* Erik Nordgren

Maj-Britt Nilsson, Birger Malmsten, Alf Kjellin

Summer Magic*
US 1963   104m   Technicolor
Walt Disney (Ron Miller)

Children help their widowed mother in 1912 Boston.

Amiable remake of *Mother Carey's Chickens*, irreproachably presented.

w Sally Benson *d* James Neilson *ph* William Snyder *m* Buddy Baker *songs* the Sherman Brothers

Hayley Mills, Burl Ives, Dorothy McGuire, Darren McGavin, Deborah Walley, Una Merkel, Eddie Hodges, Michael J. Pollard

AAN: William Snyder

Summer of '42*
US 1971   103m   Technicolor
Warner (Richard Alan Roth)

Adolescents make sexual explorations on a New England island in 1942.

Well-observed indulgence in the new permissiveness.

w Herman Raucher *d* Robert Mulligan *ph* Robert Surtees *m* Michel Legrand

Jennifer O'Neill, Gary Grimes, Jerry Houser, Oliver Conant, Lou Frizell

AA: Michel Legrand
AAN: Herman Raucher

Summer of the Seventeenth Doll
US / Australia 1959   94m   bw
UA / Hecht–Hill–Lancaster (Leslie Norman)
US title: *Season of Passion*

Two cane-cutters on their annual city lay-off have woman trouble.

Miscast and unsatisfactory rendering of a good play; the humour has evaporated.

w John Dighton, *play* Ray Lawler *d* Leslie Norman *ph* Paul Beeson *m* Benjamin Frankel

Ernest Borgnine, John Mills, Angela Lansbury, Anne Baxter, Vincent Ball

A Summer Place
US 1959   130m   Technicolor
Warner (Delmer Daves)

Romantic summer adventures of teenagers and their elders on an island off the coast of Maine.

Sex among the idle rich: a routine piece of Hollywood gloss, bowdlerized from a bestseller.

wd Delmer Daves, *novel* Sloan Wilson *ph* Harry Stradling *m* Max Steiner

Richard Egan, Dorothy McGuire, Sandra Dee, Arthur Kennedy, Troy Donahue, Constance Ford, Beulah Bondi

Summer Stock*
US 1950   109m   Technicolor
MGM (Joe Pasternak)
GB title: *If You Feel Like Singing*

A theatre troupe takes over a farm for rehearsals, and the lady owner gets the bug.

Likeable but halting musical with the star's weight problems very obvious.

w George Wells, Sy Gomberg *d* Charles Walters *ph* Robert Planck *md* Johnny Green *ch* Nick Castle

Judy Garland, Gene Kelly, Gloria de Haven, Carleton Carpenter, Eddie Bracken, Phil Silvers, Hans Conried

Summer Storm*
US 1944   106m   bw
UA (Seymour Nebenzal)

In 1912 Russia, a provincial judge falls for a local mancatcher.

One of Hollywood's occasional aberrations, an attempt to do something very European in typical west coast style. An interesting failure.

w Rowland Lee, *story* The Shooting Party by Anton Chekhov *d* Douglas Sirk *ph* Archie Stout *md* Karl Hajos

George Sanders, Linda Darnell, *Edward Everett Horton*, Anna Lee, Hugo Haas, John Philiber, Sig Rumann, André Charlot

AAN: Karl Hajos

Summer Wishes, Winter Dreams*
US 1973   88m   Technicolor
Columbia / Rastar (Jack Brodsky)

A neurotic New York housewife goes to pieces when her mother dies but finds a new understanding of her husband when she accompanies him on a trip to the World War II battlefields.

Menopausal melodrama, well observed but disappointingly wispy and underdeveloped.

w Stewart Stern *d* Gilbert Cates *ph* Gerald Hirschfeld *m* Johnny Mandel

Joanne Woodward, Martin Balsam, Sylvia Sidney, Dori Brenner, Win Forman

AAN: Joanne Woodward; Sylvia Sidney

Summer with Monika*
Sweden 1952   97m   bw
Svensk Filmindustri (Allan Ekelund)

A wild, restless girl defies her parents and goes off with her boy friend for an island holiday. Her subsequent pregnancy and motherhood don't in the least suit her, and the father is left alone with the baby.

Probably truthful but rather glum and unsophisticated drama of young love; not among Bergman's most interesting films.

w Ingmar Bergman, *novel* Per Anders Fogelstrom *ph* Gunnar Fischer *m* Erik Nordgren

Harriet Andersson, Lars Ekborg

Summertime***

US 1955 99m Eastmancolor
Ilya Lopert / Alexander Korda
GB title: *Summer Madness*

An American spinster has a holiday in Venice and becomes romantically involved.
Delightful, sympathetic travelogue with dramatic asides, great to look at and hinging on a single superb performance.

w David Lean, H. E. Bates, *play* The Time of the Cuckoo by Arthur Laurents *d David Lean ph Jack Hildyard m* Sandro Cicogini

Katharine Hepburn, Rossano Brazzi, Isa Miranda, Darren McGavin, Mari Aldon, André Morell

'The eye is endlessly ravished.'—*Dilys Powell*

AAN: David Lean; Katharine Hepburn

Summertree

US 1971 88m Eastmancolor
Warner / Bryna (Kirk Douglas)

A bored student learns about life and becomes a Vietnam casualty.
Well-made, rather tedious character study; good social observation.

w Edward Hume, Stephen Yafa, *play* Ron Cowen *d* Anthony Newley *ph* Richard C. Glouner *m* David Shire

Michael Douglas, Brenda Vaccaro, Jack Warden, Barbara Bel Geddes

The Sun Also Rises**

US 1957 129m Eastmancolor
Cinemascope
TCF (Darryl F. Zanuck)

In Paris after World War I an impotent journalist meets a nymphomaniac lady of title, and they and their odd group of friends have various saddening adventures around Europe. Not a bad attempt to film a difficult novel, though Cinemascope doesn't help and the last half hour becomes turgid. *The Last Flight* (qv)

conveyed the same atmosphere rather more sharply.

w Peter Viertel, *novel* Ernest Hemingway *d Henry King ph* Leo Tover *m* Hugo Friedhofer

Tyrone Power, Ava Gardner, *Errol Flynn*, Eddie Albert, Mel Ferrer, Robert Evans, Juliette Greco, Gregory Ratoff, Marcel Dalio, Henry Daniell

The Sun Never Sets

US 1939 98m bw
Universal (Rowland V. Lee)

Two brothers in the African colonial service prevent a munitions baron from plunging the world into war.
Stiff upper lip melodrama, very dated.

w W. P. Lipscomb *d* Rowland V. Lee *ph* George Robinson *m* Frank Skinner *md* Charles Previn

Basil Rathbone, Douglas Fairbanks Jnr, Virginia Field, Lionel Atwill, Barbara O'Neil, C. Aubrey Smith, Melville Cooper

The Sun Shines Bright**

US 1953 92m bw
Republic / Argosy (John Ford, Merian C. Cooper)

Forty years after the Civil War, the judge of a Kentucky town still has trouble quelling the Confederate spirit.
Mellow anecdotes of time gone by, scrappily linked but lovingly polished; a remake of a Will Rogers vehicle *Judge Priest*.

w Lawrence Stallings, *stories* Irwin S. Cobb *d John Ford ph Archie Stout m Victor Young*

Charles Winninger, Arleen Whelan, John Russell, Stepin Fetchit, Milburn Stone, Grant Withers, Russell Simpson

'Passages of quite remarkable poetic feeling ... alive with affection and truthful observation.'—*Lindsay Anderson*

Sun Valley Serenade*

US 1941 86m bw
TCF (Milton Sperling)

The band manager at an Idaho ice resort takes care of a Norwegian refugee.
Simple-minded musical which still pleases because of the talent involved.

w Robert Ellis, Helen Logan *d* H. Bruce Humberstone *ph* Edward Cronjager *songs* Mack Gordon, Harry Warren *m* Emil Newman

Sonja Henie, *Glenn Miller and his Orchestra*, John Payne, *Milton Berle*, Lynn Bari, Joan

Davis, *The Nicholas Brothers*, Dorothy Dandridge

AAN: Edward Cronjager; Emil Newman; song 'Chattanooga' (*m* Harry Warren, *ly* Mack Gordon)

Sunday, Bloody Sunday***
GB 1971   110m   De Luxe
UA / Vectia (Joseph Janni)

A young designer shares his sexual favours equally between two loves of different sexes, a Jewish doctor and a lady executive.
Stylishly made character study with melodramatic leanings, rather self-conscious about its risky subject but, scene by scene, both adult and absorbing, with an overpowering mass of sociological detail about the way we live.

w Penelope Gilliatt *d* John Schlesinger *ph* Billy Williams *m* Ron Geesin *pd* Luciana Arrighi

Glenda Jackson, Peter Finch, Murray Head, Peggy Ashcroft, Maurice Denham, Vivian Pickles, Frank Windsor, Tony Britton, Harold Goldblatt

AAN: Penelope Gilliatt; John Schlesinger; Glenda Jackson; Peter Finch

Sunday Dinner for a Soldier*
US 1944   86m   bw
TCF (Walter Morosco)

A poor family living on a derelict Florida houseboat scrape together enough money to invite a soldier for a meal.
Sentimental little flagwaving romance, quite sympathetically presented and agreeably underacted.

w Wanda Tuchock, Melvin Levy *d* Lloyd Bacon *ph* Joe MacDonald *m* Alfred Newman

Anne Baxter, John Hodiak, Charles Winninger, Anne Revere, Connie Marshall, Chill Wills, Bobby Driscoll, Jane Darwell

'Simple, true and tender, the best propaganda America has put out in the current year.'— *Richard Winnington*

Sunday in New York*
US 1963   105m   Metrocolor
MGM / Seven Arts (Everett Freeman)

Complications in the love life of a brother and sister, each of whom thinks the other is very moral.
Fresh, fairly adult sex comedy with New York backgrounds.

w Norman Krasna, from his play *d* Peter Tewkesbury *ph* Leo Tover *m* Peter Nero

Cliff Robertson, Rod Taylor, Jane Fonda, Robert Culp, Jo Morrow, Jim Backus

Sundays and Cybèle*
France 1962   110m   bw   Franscope
Terra / Fides / Orsa / Trocadéro (Romain Pinès)
original title: *Cybèle ou les Dimanches de Ville d'Avray*

An amnesiac ex-pilot strikes up a friendship with an abandoned 12-year-old girl, but the relationship is misunderstood and ends in tragedy.
A fashionable film of its time which now has little to offer: its director's reputation sagged alarmingly when he went to Hollywood.

w Serge Bourgignon, Antoine Tudal, *novel* Bernard Echasseriaux *d* Serge Bourgignon *ph* Henri Decaë *m* Maurice Jarre

Hardy Kruger, Nicole Courcel, Patricia Gozzi, Daniel Ivernel

'Studied charm and a creakingly melodramatic dénouement take the place of any serious attempt to probe the characters or situation . . . the film is so busily preoccupied with being as attractive, visually and sentimentally, as it possibly can, that it never has time to consider what it is being attractive about.'—*Tom Milne, MFB*

AAN: script: Maurice Jarre

Sundown
US 1941   91m   bw
Walter Wanger

The adopted daughter of an Arab trader assists British troops in Africa during World War II.
Artificial-looking romantic actioner with good cast.

w Barre Lyndon *d* Henry Hathaway *ph* Charles Lang *m* Miklos Rozsa

Gene Tierney, Bruce Cabot, George Sanders, Harry Carey, Joseph Calleia, Cedric Hardwicke, Carl Esmond, Reginald Gardiner

AAN: Charles Lang; Miklos Rozsa

The Sundowners**
GB / Australia 1960   133m   Technicolor
Warner (Gerry Blatner)

In the twenties an Irish sheepdrover and his family travel from job to job in the Australian bush.
Easygoing, often amusing but lethargically developed family film with major stars somewhat ill at ease. Memorable sequences.

w Isabel Lennart, *novel* Jon Cleary *d* Fred Zinnemann *ph* Jack Hildyard *m* Dmitri Tiomkin

Robert Mitchum, Deborah Kerr, *Glynis Johns*,

Peter Ustinov, Michael Anderson Jnr, Dina
Merrill, *Wylie Watson*, Chips Rafferty

'For all Zinnemann's generous attention to
character, the hints of longing, despair and
indomitable spirit, the overall impression
remains one of sheer length and repetition and
synthetic naturalism.'—*Richard Winnington*

AAN: best picture; Isabel Lennart; Fred
Zinnemann; Deborah Kerr; Glynis Johns

Sunny*
US 1930   81m   bw
Warner

A showgirl falls for a rich young man.
Tinny early musical notable for its star.

w Humphrey Pearson, Henry McCarthy,
musical play Otto Harbach, Oscar Hammerstein
II, Jerome Kern *ph* Ernest Haller *d* William A.
Seiter

Marilyn Miller, Lawrence Grey, Jack Donahue,
Mackenzie Ward, O. P. Heggie

Sunny*
US 1941   97m   bw
RKO / Imperator (Herbert Wilcox)

Adequate remake of the above.

w Sig Herzig *d* Herbert Wilcox *ph* Russell
Metty *m* Anthony Collins

Anna Neagle, Ray Bolger, John Carroll, Edward
Everett Horton, Frieda Inescort, Grace and Paul
Hartman

AAN: Anthony Collins

Sunny Side Up*
US 1929   80m   bw
Fox

A slum girl falls for the son of a rich
Southampton family.
Typical early musical of the softer kind;
rewarding for those who can project themselves
back.

w/m/ly B. G. De Sylva, Lew Brown, Ray
Henderson *d* David Butler *ph* Ernest Palmer

Janet Gaynor, Charles Farrell, El Brendel,
Marjorie White, Sharon Lynn

Sunnyside*
US 1919   27m approx (24 fps)   bw   silent
First National / Charles Chaplin

The overworked odd job man at a country hotel
has a pastoral dream.
Very mildly funny star comedy which was
intended as a satire on the D. W.
Griffith/Charles Ray type of rural drama then
popular. It doesn't work in this vein either.

wd Charles Chaplin *ph* Rollie Totheroh

Charles Chaplin, Edna Purviance, Tom Wilson,
Albert Austin, Henry Bergman

Sunrise**
US 1927   97m (24 fps)   bw   silent
Fox

A villager in love with a city woman tries to kill
his wife but then repents and spends a happy day
with her.
Lyrical melodrama, superbly handled: generally
considered among the finest Hollywood
productions of the twenties.

w Carl Meyer. *novel* A Trip to Tilsit by
Hermann Sudermann *d* F. W. Murnau *ph* Karl
Struss, Charles Rosher *m* (sound version) Hugo
Riesenfeld

Janet Gaynor, George O'Brien, Margaret
Livingston

AA: Karl Struss, Charles Rosher; Janet Gaynor

Sunrise at Campobello*
US 1960   143m   Technicolor
Warner / Dore Schary

The early life of Franklin Roosevelt, including
his battle against polio and return to politics.
Static filming of a rather interesting Broadway
success and of a memorable performance.

w Dore Schary, from his play *d* Vincent J.
Donehue *ph* Russell Harlan *m* Franz Waxman

Ralph Bellamy, Greer Garson, Ann Shoemaker,
Hume Cronyn, Jean Hagen

AAN: Greer Garson

Sunset Boulevard***
US 1950   110m   bw
Paramount (Charles Brackett)

A luckless Hollywood scriptwriter goes to live
with a wealthy older woman, a slightly dotty and
extremely possessive relic of the silent screen.
Incisive melodrama with marvellous moments
but a tendency to overstay its welcome; the first
reels are certainly the best, though the last scene
is worth waiting for and the malicious
observation throughout is a treat.

*w Charles Brackett, Billy Wilder, D. M.
Marshman Jnr d Billy Wilder ph John F. Seitz
m Franz Waxman*

*Gloria Swanson, William Holden, Erich Von
Stroheim, Fred Clark, Nancy Olson,* Jack
Webb, Lloyd Gough, *Cecil B. de Mille,* H. B.
Warner, Anna Q. Nilsson, Buster Keaton,
Hedda Hopper

'That rare blend of pungent writing, expert
acting, masterly direction and unobtrusively

artistic photography which quickly casts a spell over an audience and holds it enthralled to a shattering climax.'—*New York Times (T.M.P.)*

'Miss Swanson's performance takes her at one bound into the class of Boris Karloff and Tod Slaughter.'—*Richard Mallett, Punch*

AA: script; Franz Waxman

AAN: best picture; Billy Wilder (as director); John F. Seitz; Gloria Swanson; William Holden; Erich Von Stroheim; Nancy Olson

The Sunshine Boys*

US 1975 111m Metrocolor
MGM / Rastar (Ray Stark)

Two feuding old vaudeville comedians come together for a television spot, and ruin it.

Over-extended sketch in which one main role is beautifully underplayed, the other hammed up, and the production lacks any kind of style. The one-liners are good, though.

w Neil Simon, from his play *d* Herbert Ross
ph David M. Walsh *md* Harry V. Lojewski

Walter Matthau, George Burns, Richard Benjamin, Carol Arthur

'It's just shouting, when it needs to be beautifully timed routines.'—*New Yorker*

'They feud with ill-matched resources, and the movie's visual delights vanish with the title sequence.'—*Sight and Sound*

AA: George Burns
AAN: Neil Simon; Walter Matthau

Sunstruck

Australia 1972 92m Eastmancolor
Immigrant (Jack Neary, James Grafton)

A shy Welsh schoolmaster emigrates to the Australian outback.

Simple-minded, uninspired, predictable family comedy for star fans.

w Stan Mars *d* James Gilbert *ph* Brian West
m Peter Knight

Harry Secombe, Maggie Fitzgibbon, John Meillon, Dawn Lake

Superfly

US 1972 98m Technicolor
Warner (Sig Shore)

The New York adventures of black cocaine peddlers.

'Sensational' comedy with violence in which the pushers exit laughing. Tedious and deplorable.

w Philip Fenty *d* Gordon Parks *ph* James Signorelli *m* Jeff Alexander .

Ron O'Neal, Carl Lee, Sheila Frazier

'It suggests that New York is now nothing more than a concrete junkieyard.'—*Philip Strick*

Superman

US / GB 1978 142m colour Panavision
Warner / Alexander Salkind (Pierre Spengler)

A baby saved from the planet Krypton when it explodes grows up as a newspaperman and uses his tremendous powers to fight evil and support the American way.

Long, lugubrious and only patchily entertaining version of the famous comic strip, with far too many irrelevant preliminaries and misguided sense of its own importance.

w Mario Puzo, David Newman, Robert Benton, Leslie Newman *d* Richard Donner *ph* Geoffrey Unsworth *m* John Williams *pd* John Barry
sp various

Christopher Reeve, Marlon Brando, Margot Kidder, Jackie Cooper, Glenn Ford, Phyllis Thaxter, Trevor Howard, Gene Hackman, Ned Beatty, Susannah York, Valerie Perrine

† Reprehensible records were set by Brando getting three million dollars for a ten-minute performance (and then suing for a share of the gross); and by the incredible $7\frac{1}{2}$-minute credit roll at the end.

Supernatural*

US 1933 67m bw
Paramount

A girl is possessed by the soul of a dead murderess.

Mad doctor nonsense, interestingly but not very successfully styled.

w Harvey Thew, Brian Marlow *d* Victor Halperin *ph* Arthur Martinelli

Carole Lombard, H. B. Warner, Randolph Scott, Vivienne Osborne, Alan Dinehart

Support Your Local Gunfighter

US 1971 92m De Luxe
UA / Cherokee / Brigade (Burt Kennedy)

A con man jumps a train at a small mining town and is mistaken for a dreaded gunfighter.

Disappointing sequel to the following; just a couple of good jokes.

w James Edward Grant *d* Burt Kennedy
ph Harry Stradling Jnr *m* Jack Elliott, Allyn Ferguson

James Garner, Suzanne Pleshette, Joan Blondell, Jack Elam, Chuck Connors, Harry Morgan, Marie Windsor, Henry Jones, John Dehner

Support Your Local Sheriff**
US 1968　92m　Technicolor
UA / Cherokee (William Bowers)

Gold is found near a western village, and the resulting influx of desperate characters causes problems for the sheriff.
Amusing comedy, drawing on many western clichés.

w William Bowers d Burt Kennedy ph Harry Stradling Jnr *m* Jeff Alexander

James Garner, Joan Hackett, Walter Brennan, Jack Elam, Henry Morgan, Bruce Dern, Henry Jones

'It rejuvenates a stagnating genre by combining just the right doses of parody and affectionate nostalgia.'—*Jan Dawson*

Suppose They Gave a War and Nobody Came
US 1969　114m　De Luxe
Engel–Auerbach / ABC (Fred Engel)

Three accident-prone PROs try to give the army a good name in a town which wishes it would go away; they eventually cause panic by arriving at a dance in a tank.
Muddled farce which may have hoped to be satire.

w Don McGuire, Hal Captain *d* Hy Averback *ph* Burnett Guffey *m* Jerry Fielding

Tony Curtis, Brian Keith, Ernest Borgnine, Ivan Dixon, Suzanne Pleshette, *Tom Ewell*, Bradford Dillman, Arthur O'Connell, Robert Emhardt, John Fiedler, Don Ameche

Surprise Package
GB 1960　100m　bw
Columbia / Stanley Donen

An American gangster is deported to the same Mediterranean island as an exiled European king, whose crown gets stolen.
Flat and feeble comedy which defeats its stars.

w Harry Kurnitz, *novel* Art Buchwald *d* Stanley Donen *ph* Christopher Challis *m* Benjamin Frankel

Yul Brynner, Noel Coward, Mitzi Gaynor, Bill Nagy, Eric Pohlmann, George Coulouris, Warren Mitchell

Susan and God*
US 1940　117m　bw
MGM (Hunt Stromberg)
GB title: *The Gay Mrs Trexel*

A flighty society woman gets religion but fails to practise what she preaches.
Unusual comedy-drama for MGM to tackle, but a fairly successful one for high class audiences.

w Anita Loos, play Rachel Crothers *d George Cukor ph* Robert Planck *m* Herbert Stothart

Joan Crawford, Fredric March, Ruth Hussey, John Carroll, Rita Hayworth, Nigel Bruce, Bruce Cabot, Rita Quigley, Rose Hobart, Constance Collier, Gloria de Haven, Marjorie Main

Susan Lenox, Her Fall and Rise*
US 1931　76m　bw
MGM
GB title: *The Rise of Helga*

A farm girl flees to the city when her father tries to marry her off to a brute.
Moderate star melodrama with the star somewhat miscast.

w Wanda Tuchock, novel David Graham Phillips *d* Robert Z. Leonard *ph* William Daniels

Greta Garbo, Clark Gable, Jean Hersholt, John Miljan, Alan Hale

Susan Slade
US 1961　116m　Technicolor
Warner (Delmer Daves)

An engineer brings his family back to San Francisco from Chile, and his teenage daughter runs into problems of the heart.
Stilted, busy sudser.

w Delmer Daves, novel Doris Hume *d* Delmer Daves *ph* Lucien Ballard *m* Max Steiner

Connie Stevens, Troy Donahue, Dorothy McGuire, Lloyd Nolan, Brian Aherne, Natalie Schaefer, Grant Williams, Bert Convy, Kent Smith

Susan Slept Here
US 1954　98m　Technicolor
RKO (Harriet Parsons)

The Hollywood scriptwriter of a film about youth problems agrees to look after a delinquent teenage girl.
Skittish, would-be piquant comedy; quite unattractive.

w Alex Gottlieb *d* Frank Tashlin *ph* Nicholas Musuraca *md* Leigh Harline

Dick Powell, Debbie Reynolds, Anne Francis, Glenda Farrell, Alvy Moore, Horace MacMahon

AAN: song 'Hold My Hand'

Susannah of the Mounties*
US 1939　78m　bw
TCF (Kenneth MacGowan)

A little girl who is the only survivor of a wagon

train massacre is looked after by the Canadian Mounties.

Adequate star action romance, Shirley's last real success.

w John Taintor Foote, Philip Dunne *d* Sidney Lanfield *ph* Bert Glennon *m* Louis Silvers

Shirley Temple, Randolph Scott, Margaret Lockwood,
J. Farrell MacDonald, Maurice Moscovitch, Moroni Olsen, Victor Jory

The Suspect*
US 1944 84m bw
Universal

A henpecked husband kills his wife and is blackmailed.
Efficient studio-bound suspenser with theatrically effective acting.

w Bertram Millhauser, *novel* James Ronald *d* Robert Siodmak *ph* Paul Ivano

Charles Laughton, Henry Daniell, Rosalind Ivan, Ella Raines, Molly Lamont, Dean Harens
'High marks for tension, local colour, story.'—*William Whitebait*

Suspect*
GB 1960 81m bw
The Boulting Brothers / British Lion

Government research chemists find a traitor in their midst.
Entertaining but fairly routine spy melodrama, shot on an experimental low budget but confined to lower berth bookings.

w Nigel Balchin, from his novel Sort of Traitors *d* Roy and John Boulting *ph* Max Greene *m* John Wilkes

Tony Britton, Virginia Maskell, Peter Cushing, Ian Bannen, Raymond Huntley, Donald Pleasence, Thorley Walters, Spike Milligan, Kenneth Griffith
'A better standard of second feature film is badly needed, but the way to do it is not by making pictures which look as though they have strayed from TV.'—*Penelope Houston*

Suspicion**
US 1941 99m bw
RKO

A sedate young girl marries a playboy, and comes to suspect that he is trying to murder her.
Rather artificial and stiff Hitchcock suspenser, further marred by an ending suddenly switched to please the front office. Full of the interesting touches one would expect.

w Samson Raphaelson, Alma Reville, Joan Harrison, *novel* Before the Fact by Francis Iles

d Alfred Hitchcock *ph* Harry Stradling *m* Franz Waxman

Joan Fontaine, Cary Grant, Nigel Bruce, Cedric Hardwicke, May Whitty, Isabel Jeans, Heather Angel, Leo G. Carroll

AA: Joan Fontaine
AAN: best picture; Franz Waxman

Suspiria*
Italy 1976 97m Eastmancolor Technovision
Seda Spettacoli (Claudio Argento)

A young American dance student arrives at dead of night at a continental academy where murder is the order of the day.
Psycho meets *The Exorcist*, with no holds barred: a genuinely scary thriller with gaudy visuals and a screaming sound track. A pyrotechnic display for those who can take it.

w Dario Argento, Dario Nicolodi *d* Dario Argento *ph* Luciano Tovoli *m* Dario Argento

Jessica Harper, Alida Valli, Joan Bennett, Stefania Casini, Udo Kier
'Thunderstorms and explicitly grotesque murders pile up as Argento happily abandons plot mechanics to provide a bravura display of his technical skill.'—*Time Out*

Suzy*
US 1936 95m bw
MGM (Maurice Revnes)

A French air ace of World War I marries an American showgirl; they then find that her former husband, thought dead, is still alive.
Proficient star comedy-drama with romance, action, comedy and a complex plot. A showcase for its stars.

w Dorothy Parker, Alan Campbell, Horace Jackson, Lenore Coffee, *novel* Herbert Gorman *d* George Fitzmaurice *ph* Ray June *m* William Axt

Jean Harlow, Cary Grant, Franchot Tone, Benita Hume, Lewis Stone

AAN: song 'Did I Remember' (*m* Walter Donaldson, *ly* Harold Adamson)

Svengali**
US 1931 81m bw
Warner

In nineties Paris, a hypnotist turns a girl into a great opera singer but she does not reciprocate his love.
Victorian fantasy melodrama with a great grotesque part for the star and interesting artwork.

w J. Grubb Alexander, *novel* Trilby by George
du Maurier *d Archie Mayo ph* Barney McGill

John Barrymore, Marian Marsh, Luis Alberni,
Lumsden Hare, Donald Crisp, Paul Porcasi

'Barrymore never needed occult powers to be
magnetic, but interest flags when he's
offscreen.'—*New Yorker, 1978*

AAN: Barney McGill

Svengali
GB 1954   82m   Eastmancolor
Renown / Alderdale (Douglas Pierce)

Flatulent remake which does have the virtue of
following the original book illustrations but is
otherwise unpersuasive.

wd Noel Langley *ph* Wilkie Cooper *m* William
Alwyn *ad Fred Pusey*

Donald Wolfit, Hildegarde Neff, Terence
Morgan, Derek Bond, Paul Rogers, David
Kossoff, Hubert Gregg, Noel Purcell, Alfie Bass,
Harry Secombe

Swallows and Amazons
GB 1974   92m   Eastmancolor
EMI / Theatre Projects

In the twenties four children have adventures in
the Lake District.
Mild family film, great to look at but lacking in
real excitement or style.

w David Wood, *novel* Arthur Ransome
d Claude Whatham *ph* Denis Lewiston
m Wilfred Josephs

Virginia McKenna, Ronald Fraser, Simon West,
Sophie Neville, Zanna Hamilton, Stephen
Grenville

Swamp Water**
US 1941   90m   bw
TCF (Irving Pichel)
GB title: *The Man Who Came Back*

A fugitive holds out for years in the Okenfenokee
swamp, and affects the lives of the local
township.
A strange little story, not very compelling as
drama but with striking photography and
atmosphere. Remade more straightforwardly as
Lure of the Wilderness (qv).

w Dudley Nicholas, *story* Vereen Bell *d Jean
Renoir ph Peverell Marley m* David Buttolph

Walter Huston, Walter Brennan, Anne Baxter,
Dana Andrews, Virginia Gilmore, John
Carradine, Eugene Pallette, Ward Bond, Guinn
Williams

'So bad it's terrific.'—*Otis Ferguson*

The Swan*
US 1956   108m   Eastmancolor
  Cinemascope
MGM (Dore Schary)

In 1910 Hungary, a girl of noble stock is
groomed to marry the crown prince.
Interesting chiefly for a typical Hollywood
reaction to a news event; about to lose their top
star to a real life prince, MGM dusted off this old
and creaky property for her last film. The star
cast can't make much of it and the treatment is
very heavy.

w John Dighton, *play* Ferenc Molnar *d* Charles
Vidor *ph* Robert Surtees *m* Bronislau Kaper
ad Cedric Gibbons, Randall Duell

Grace Kelly, Alec Guinness, Louis Jourdan,
Agnes Moorehead, Jessie Royce Landis, Brian
Aherne, Leo G. Carroll, *Estelle Winwood,*
Robert Coote

'Balancing between artificial comedy and a no
less artificial romantic theme, the film ultimately
requires considerably greater finesse and
subtlety in the handling.'—*Penelope Houston*

Swanee River**
US 1939   84m   Technicolor
TCF (Darryl F. Zanuck)

The life and loves of Stephen Foster.
Attractive, unsurprising family film in rich early
colour, sparked by Jolson as E. P. Christy.

w John Taintor Foote, Philip Dunne *d* Sidney
Lanfield *md* Louis Silvers

Don Ameche, *Al Jolson*, Andrea Leeds, Felix
Bressart, Russell Hicks

AAN: Louis Silvers

The Swarm
US 1978   116m   Technicolor   Panavision
  Warner (Irwin Allen)

African killer bees menace the US.
Very obvious all-star disaster movie with risible
dialogue. A box office flop, probably because
several TV movies had already tackled the same
subject.

w Stirling Silliphant, *novel* Arthur Herzog
d Irwin Allen *ph* Fred J. Koenekamp *m* Jerry
Goldsmith *sp* L. B. Abbott, Van Der Veer,
Howard Jensen

Michael Caine, Katharine Ross, Richard
Widmark, Richard Chamberlain, Olivia de
Havilland, Fred MacMurray, Ben Johnson, Lee
Grant, Jose Ferrer, Patty Duke Astin, Slim
Pickens, Bradford Dillman, Henry Fonda,
Cameron Mitchell

Swashbuckler*
US 1976 101m Technicolor
Universal / Elliott Kastner (Jennings Lang)
GB title: *The Scarlet Buccaneer*

Rival pirates help a wronged lady.
Uninspired reworking of some old Errol Flynn
ideas; the idea was pleasant, but the old style is
sadly lacking.

w Jeffrey Bloom *d* James Goldstone *ph* Philip
Lathrop *m* John Addison *pd* John Lloyd

Robert Shaw, James Earl Jones, Peter Boyle,
Geneviève Bujold, Beau Bridges, Geoffrey
Holder
   'This tacky pastepot job can't make up its
mind whether it's serious, tongue-in-cheek,
satirical, slapstick, burlesque, parody or
travesty; but be assured it is all of the
above.'—*Variety*

Sweeney!*
GB 1976 89m Technicolor
EMI / Euston (Tom Childs)

Scotland Yard's Flying Squad investigates a
suicide and uncovers an elaborate political
blackmail scheme.
Enjoyable big screen version of a pacy, violent
TV cop show.

w Ranald Graham *d* David Wickes *ph* Dusty
Miller *m* Denis King

John Thaw, Denis Waterman, Barry Foster, Ian
Bannen, Colin Welland, Michael Coles, Joe
Melia

**Sweeney Todd, the Demon Barber of
Fleet Street***
GB 1936 68m bw
George King

A barber kills his customers and makes them
into 'mutton pies' for sale at the shop next door.
Decent version of a famous old melodrama;
stilted as film-making, but preserving a
swaggering star performance.

w Frederick Hayward, H. F. Maltby, *play*
George Dibdin-Pitt

Tod Slaughter, Bruce Seton, Eve Lister, Stella
Rho, Ben Soutten

Sweet Adeline
US 1935 85m bw
Warner (Edward Chodorov)

In the nineties, the daughter of a beer garden
owner attracts the attention of a composer and
becomes a Broadway star.
Unexceptionable, and quite forgotten,
adaptation of a pleasant, old-fashioned
Broadway musical.

w Erwin S. Gelsey, *play* Jerome Kern, Oscar
Hammerstein II, Harry Armstrong, Dick
Gerard *d* Mervyn Le Roy *m/ly* Jerome Kern,
Oscar Hammerstein II *ph* Sol Polito *ch* Bobby
Connolly *ad* Robert Haas

Irene Dunne, Donald Woods, Ned Sparks, Hugh
Herbert, Wini Shaw, Louis Calhern, Nydia
Westman, Joseph Cawthorn

Sweet Bird of Youth*
US 1961 120m Metrocolor
   Cinemascope
MGM / Roxbury (Pandro S. Berman)

A Hollywood drifter brings an ageing glamour
star back to his home town, but runs into revenge
from the father of a girl he had seduced.
Emasculated version of an overwrought play
with the author's usual poetic squalor; comatose
patches alternate with flashes of good acting and
diverting dialogue, but the wide screen and heavy
colour don't direct the attention.

wd Richard Brooks, *play* Tennessee Williams
ph Milton Krasner *md* Robert Armbruster

Paul Newman, Geraldine Page, *Ed Begley*,
Mildred Dunnock, Rip Torn, Shirley Knight,
Madeleine Sherwood

AA: Ed Begley
AAN: Geraldine Page; Shirley Knight

Sweet Charity*
US 1969 149m Technicolor Panavision
   70
Universal (Robert Arthur)

A New York taxi dancer dreams of love.
A revue-type musical bowdlerized from Fellini's
Le notti di Cabiria accords ill with real New
York locations, especially as its threads of plot
come to nothing; but behind the camera are
sufficient stylists to ensure striking success with
individual numbers.

w Peter Stone, *play* Neil Simon *d* Robert Fosse
ph Robert Surtees *md* Cy Coleman *ly* David
Fields

Shirley Maclaine, Ricardo Montalban, John
McMartin, *Chita Rivera*, Paula Kelly, Stubby
Kaye, Sammy Davis Jnr
   'The kind of platinum clinker designed to send
audiences flying towards the safety of their
television sets.'—*Rex Reed*

AAN: Cy Coleman (as music director)

Sweet November
US 1968 113m Technicolor
Warner Seven Arts / Jerry Gershwin, Elliott
   Kastner

An English tycoon in New York meets a girl who

takes a new lover every month because she
hasn't long to live.
Irritating exercise in eccentric sentimentality, not
helped by twitchy stars.

w Herman Raucher d Robert Ellis Miller
ph Daniel L. Fapp m Michel Legrand

Anthony Newley, Sandy Dennis, Theodore
Bikel, Burr de Benning

The Sweet Ride
US 1967 110m De Luxe Panavision
TCF (Joe Pasternak)

Surfers and drop-outs on a California beach
have woman trouble.
Teenage melodrama, well produced but abysmal
of content.

w Tom Mankiewicz, novel William Murray
d Harvey Hart ph Robert B. Hauser m Pete
Rugolo

Jacqueline Bisset, Tony Franciosa, Michael
Sarrazin, Bob Denver, Michael Wilding

Sweet Rosie O'Grady*
US 1943 79m Technicolor
TCF (William Perlberg)

A Police Gazette reporter tries to uncover the
past of a musical comedy star.
Pleasant nineties musical with plenty of zest but
a lack of good numbers. A typical success of the
war years.

w Ken Englund d Irving Cummings ph Ernest
Palmer ch Hermes Pan songs Mack Gordon,
Harry Warren ad James Basevi, Joseph C.
Wright

Betty Grable, Robert Young, Adolphe Menjou,
Reginald Gardiner, Virginia Grey, Phil Regan,
Sig Rumann, Hobart Cavanaugh, Alan
Dinehart
† Remake of Love Is News; remade as That
Wonderful Urge.

Sweet Smell of Success***
US 1957 96m bw
UA / Norma / Curtleigh (James Hill)

A crooked press agent helps a megalomaniac
New York columnist break up his sister's
marriage.
Moody, brilliant, Wellesian melodrama put
together with great artificial style; the plot
matters less than the photographic detail and the
skilful manipulation of decadent characters,
bigger than life-size.

w Clifford Odets, Ernest Lehman d Alexander
Mackendrick ph James Wong Howe m Elmer
Bernstein ad Edward Carrere

Burt Lancaster, Tony Curtis, Martin Milner,
Sam Levene, Susan Harrison, Barbara Nichols,
Emile Meyer

Sweethearts**
US 1938 120m Technicolor
MGM (Hunt Stromberg)

Two stars of the musical stage never stop
fighting each other.
The lightest and most successful of the
MacDonald/Eddy musicals, with an excellent
script, production and cast.

w Dorothy Parker, Alan Campbell d W. S. Van
Dyke ph Oliver Marsh m Victor Herbert
md Herbert Stothart

Jeanette MacDonald, Nelson Eddy, Frank
Morgan, Ray Bolger, Florence Rice, Mischa
Auer, Fay Holden, Reginald Gardiner, Herman
Bing, Allyn Joslyn, Raymond Walburn, Lucile
Watson, Gene Lockhart

AAN: Herbert Stothart

The Swimmer**
US 1968 94m Technicolor
Columbia / Horizon / Dover (Frank Perry,
    Roger Lewis)

A man clad only in trunks swims his way home
via the pools of his rich friends, and arrives home
to find that his success is a fantasy.
Strange but compelling fable, too mystifying for
popular success, about the failure of the
American dream. Annoyingly inexplicit, but well
made and sumptuously photographed in a
variety of Connecticut estates.

w Eleanor Perry, short story John Cheever
d Frank Perry, Sydney Pollack ph David L.
Quaid m Marvin Hamlisch

Burt Lancaster, Janice Rule, Kim Hunter,
Diana Muldaur, Cornelia Otis Skinner, Marge
Champion

Swing High Swing Low**
US 1937 97m bw
Paramount (Arthur Hornblow Jnr)

A talented trumpeter goes on a bender but is
rescued by his wife.
Backstage comedy-drama, a beautifully
cinematic version of a very tedious story also
filmed as Dance of Life (1929) and When My
Baby Smiles at Me (1948).

w Virginia Van Upp, Oscar Hammerstein II,
play Burlesque by George Manker Walters,
Arthur Hopkins d Mitchell Leisen ph Ted
Tetzlaff m Victor Young md Boris Morros

Carole Lombard, Fred MacMurray, Charles Butterworth, Jean Dixon, Dorothy Lamour, Harvey Stephens, Franklin Pangborn, Anthony Quinn

'Enough concentrated filmcraft to fit out half a dozen of those gentlemen who are always dashing around in an independent capacity making just the greatest piece of cinema ever.'—*Otis Ferguson*

Swing Time**
US 1936   103m   bw
RKO (Pandro S. Berman)

A dance team can't get together romantically because he has a commitment to a girl back home.
Satisfactory but unexciting musical vehicle for two stars at the top of their professional and box-office form.

w Howard Lindsay, Allan Scott d George Stevens ph David Abel md Nathaniel Shilkret songs Jerome Kern, Dorothy Fields

Fred Astaire, Ginger Rogers, Victor Moore, Helen Broderick, Eric Blore, Betty Furness, Georges Metaxa

AA: song 'The Way You Look Tonight'

Swing Your Lady*
US 1937   77m   bw
Warner (Sam Bischoff)

A promoter gets involved in the problems of a hillbilly wrestler.
Minor comedy with some laughs.

w Joseph Scrank, Maurice Leo, *story* Toehold on Artemus by H. R. Marsh d Ray Enright ph Arthur Edeson m Adolph Deutsch

Humphrey Bogart, Louise Fazenda, Nat Pendleton, Frank McHugh, Penny Singleton, Allen Jenkins, Ronald Reagan, The Weaver Brothers and Elviry

The Swinger
US 1966   81m   Technicolor
Paramount / George Sidney

When a girl writer's wholesome stories are rejected, she pretends to have a naughty past. With-it comedy which audiences preferred to be without.

w Lawrence Roman d George Sidney ph Joseph Biroc m Marty Paich

Ann-Margret, Tony Franciosa, Robert Coote, Yvonne Romain, Horace MacMahon, Nydia Westman

'A hectically saucy mixture of lechery,

depravity, perversion, voyeurism and girlie magazines . . . a heavy, witless pudding.'—*MFB*

The Swiss Family Robinson
US 1940   93m   bw
(RKO) Gene Towne, Graham Baker

A shipwrecked family builds a new home on a desert island.
Pleasing low-budgeter.

w Gene Towne, Graham Baker, Walter Ferris, *novel* Johann Wyss d Edward Ludwig ph Nicholas Musuraca

Thomas Mitchell, Edna Best, Freddie Bartholemew, Tim Holt, Terry Kilburn

'In outlook, dialogue and manner it is frankly old-fashioned.'—*MFB*

The Swiss Family Robinson*
GB 1960   126m   Technicolor   Panavision
Walt Disney (Bill Anderson, Basil Keys)

Quite pleasing comedy adventure from the children's classic.

w Lowell S. Hawley d Ken Annakin ph Harry Waxman m William Alwyn

John Mills, Dorothy McGuire, James MacArthur, Tommy Kirk, Kevin Corcoran, Janet Munro, Sessue Hayakawa, Cecil Parker

Swiss Miss*
US 1938   73m   bw
(MGM) Hal Roach

Two mousetrap salesmen in Switzerland run into trouble with a cook, a gorilla and two opera singers.
Operetta style vehicle which constrains its stars, since their material is somewhat below vintage anyway. Not painful to watch, but disappointing.

w James Parrott, Felix Adler, Charles Nelson d John G. Blystone ph Norbert Brodine

Stan Laurel, Oliver Hardy, Walter Woolf King, Della Lind, Eric Blore

The Sword and the Rose
GB 1952   91m   Technicolor
Walt Disney (Perce Pearce)

The romantic problems of young Mary Tudor. Unhistorical charade not quite in the usual Disney vein, and not very good.

w Laurence E. Watkin, *novel* When Knighthood Was in Flower by Charles Major d Ken Annakin ph Geoffrey Unsworth m Clifton Parker

Richard Todd, Glynis Johns, James Robertson

Justice, Michael Gough, Jane Barrett, Peter Copley, Rosalie Crutchley, Jean Mercure, D. A. Clarke-Smith

The Sword in the Stone**
US 1963 80m Technicolor
Walt Disney (Ken Peterson)

In the Dark Ages, a young forest boy named Wart becomes King Arthur.
Feature cartoon with goodish sequences but disappointingly showing a flatness and economy of draughtsmanship.

w Bill Peet, *novel* The Once and Future King by T. H. White d Wolfgang Reitherman m George Bruns *songs* The Sherman Brothers

AAN: George Bruns

Sword of Sherwood Forest
GB 1960 80m Technicolor Megascope
Columbia / Hammer / Yeoman (Richard Greene, Sidney Cole)

Robin Hood reveals the villainy of the Sheriff of Nottingham and the Earl of Newark.
This big-screen version of a popular TV series makes a rather feeble addition to the legend, but the actors try hard.

w Alan Hackney d Terence Fisher ph Ken Hodges m Alan Hoddinott

Richard Greene, Peter Cushing, Richard Pasco, Niall MacGinnis, Jack Gwyllim, Sarah Branch, Nigel Green

Sylvia
US 1964 115m bw
Paramount / Joseph E. Levine

A millionaire with a mysterious fiancée hires a detective to discover the truth about her past.
Improbable story of a high-minded prostitute, sluggishly narrated and variably acted.

w Sidney Boehm, *novel* E. V. Cunningham d Gordon Douglas ph Joseph Ruttenberg m David Raksin

Carroll Baker, George Maharis, Peter Lawford, Joanne Dru, Ann Sothern, Viveca Lindfors, Edmond O'Brien, Aldo Ray

Sylvia Scarlett*
US 1935 94m bw
RKO (Pandro S. Berman)

A girl masquerades as a boy in order to escape to France with her crooked father.
Strange, peripatetic English comedy-adventure which failed to ring any bells but preserves aspects of interest.

w Gladys Unger, John Collier, Mortimer Offner, *novel* Compton Mackenzie d George Cukor ph Joseph August m Roy Webb

Katharine Hepburn, Cary Grant, Edmund Gwenn, Brian Aherne, Lennox Pawle

'It seems to go wrong in a million directions, but it has unusually affecting qualities.'—*New Yorker, 1978*

La Symphonie Pastorale*
France 1946 105m bw
Les Films Gibe

A Swiss pastor takes in an orphan child who grows up to be a beautiful girl and causes jealousy between himself and his son.
Curious mountain tragedy, a great visual pleasure with its symbolic use of snow and water.

w Jean Delannoy, Jean Aurenche, *novel* André Gide d Jean Delannoy ph Armand Thirard m Georges Auric

Pierre Blanchar, Michèle Morgan

Symphony of Six Million
US 1932 94m bw
RKO (Pandro S. Berman)
GB title: *Melody of Life*

A doctor drags himself from New York's slums to Park Avenue, but feels guilty and demoralized when he can't save the life of his own father.
Monumental tearjerker, not badly done.

w Bernard Schubert, J. Walter Ruben, *novel* Fannie Hurst d Gregory La Cava ph Leo Tover m Max Steiner

Irene Dunne, Ricardo Cortez, Gregory Ratoff, Anna Appel, Noel Madison, Julie Haydon

The System
US 1953 90m bw
Warner (Sam Bischoff)

A crime leader is softened by love, and allows himself to be convicted.
Strange nonsense inspired by the Kefauver investigations into American society; neither edifying nor entertaining.

w Jo Eisinger d Lewis Seiler ph Edwin DuPar m David Buttolph

Frank Lovejoy, Joan Weddon, Bob Arthur, Paul Picerni, Don Beddoe

The System
GB 1964 90m bw
British Lion / Bryanston / Kenneth Shipman
US title: *The Girl-Getters*

Seaside layabouts have a system for collecting

and sharing rich girl visitors, but one of the latter traps the leader at his own game.

Adequate sexy showcase for some looming talents; all very unattractive, but smoothly directed in a number of imitated styles.

w Peter Draper *d Michael Winner ph Nicolas Roeg m* Stanley Black

Oliver Reed, Jane Merrow, Barbara Ferris, Julia Foster, Ann Lynn, Guy Doleman, Andrew Ray, David Hemmings, John Alderton, Derek Nimmo, Harry Andrews

T

Tabu*
US 1931 80m bw
Colorart Synchrotone

The life of a young Tahitian pearl fisherman.
The plot is used only to bring together the
elements of a superb travelogue, but the conflicts
between the aims of the two directors are clearly
seen.

wd F. W. Murnau, Robert Flaherty *ph* Floyd
Crosby, Robert Flaherty *m* Hugo Riesenfeld

AAN: Floyd Crosby

Tail Spin
US 1938 83m bw
TCF (Harry Joe Brown)

The interwoven private lives of lady civilian air
pilots.
Predictable romantic goings on; a tear, a smile, a
song, etc.

w Frank Wead *d* Roy del Ruth *ph* Karl Freund
m Louis Silvers

Alice Faye, Constance Bennett, Joan Davis,
Nancy Kelly, Charles Farrell, Jane Wyman,
Kane Richmond, Wally Vernon, Harry
Davenport

Take a Giant Step
US 1958 100m bw
UA / Sheila / Hecht–Hill–Lancaster (Julius J.
    Epstein)

A young black person brought up in a white
town feels ill at ease and runs into adolescent
troubles.
Well-meaning racial drama with good detail but
no real feeling.

w Louis S. Peterson, Julius J. Epstein *d* Philip
Leacock *ph* Arthur Arling *m* Jack Marshall

Johnny Nash, Estelle Hemsley, Ruby Dee,
Frederick O'Neal

Take a Girl Like You
GB 1970 101m Eastmancolor
Columbia / Albion (Hal E. Chester)

A north country girl comes to teach in London
and has man trouble.

Old-fashioned novelette with sex trimmings and
neither zest nor humour.

w George Melly, *novel* Kingsley Amis
d Jonathan Miller *ph* Dick Bush *m* Stanley
Myers

Hayley Mills, Oliver Reed, Noel Harrison,
Sheila Hancock, John Bird, Aimi MacDonald

Take a Letter, Darling*
US 1942 94m bw
Paramount (Fred Kohlmar)
GB title: *Green-Eyed Woman*

A woman executive hires a male secretary.
Smartish romantic comedy.

w Claude Binyon d Mitchell Leisen ph John
Mescall *m* Victor Young

Rosalind Russell, Fred MacMurray, Macdonald
Carey, Constance Moore, Cecil Kellaway,
Charles Arnt, Kathleen Howard, Dooley Wilson

AAN: John Mescall; Victor Young

Take Care of My Little Girl
US 1951 93m Technicolor
TCF (Julian Blaustein)

A university freshwoman gets into trouble with
her sorority.
Ho-hum exposé of college conventions, of
routine interest at best.

w Julius J. and Philip G. Epstein, *novel* Peggy
Goodwin *d* Jean Negulesco *ph* Harry Jackson
m Alfred Newman

Jeanne Crain, Mitzi Gaynor, Dale Robertson,
Jean Peters, Jeffrey Hunter

'As is customary in college pictures, it appears
that Tri U recruits most of its strength from the
chorus.'—*Penelope Houston*

Take Her, She's Mine*
US 1963 98m De Luxe Cinemascope
TCF (Henry Koster)

A lawyer protects his teenage daughter from
boys and causes.
Routine Hollywood family comedy with some
laughs and an agreeable cast.

w Nunnally Johnson, *play* Phoebe and Henry

Ephron *d* Henry Koster *ph* Lucien Ballard *m* Jerry Goldsmith

James Stewart, Sandra Dee, Robert Morley, Audrey Meadows, Philippe Forquet, John McGiver

Take Me High

GB 1973 90m Technicolor
EMI (Kenneth Harper)

A bank manager helps an unsuccessful restaurant to launch a new hamburger.
Jaded youth musical with no dancing but some zip and bounce to commend it to mums and dads if not to its intended young audience.

w Christopher Penfold *d* David Askey *ph* Norman Warwick *m/songs* Tony Cole

Cliff Richard, Debbie Watling, Hugh Griffith, George Cole, Anthony Andrews, Richard Wattis

Take Me Out to the Ball Game ***

US 1949 93m Technicolor
MGM (Arthur Freed)
GB title: *Everybody's Cheering*

A woman takes over a baseball team and the players are antagonistic.
Lively, likeable nineties comedy musical which served as a trial run for *On the Town* and in its own right is a fast-moving, funny, tuneful delight with no pretensions.

w Harry Tugend, George Wells *d* Gene Kelly, Stanley Donen *ph* George Folsey *md* Adolph Deutsch *songs* Betty Comden, Adolph Green, Roger Edens

Gene Kelly, Frank Sinatra, Esther Williams, *Betty Garrett*, Jules Munshin, Edward Arnold, Richard Lane, Tom Dugan

Take Me to Town

US 1953 81m Technicolor
U-I (Ross Hunter)

The three sons of a backwoods widower import a vaudeville artiste as their new mother.
Old-fashioned family schmaltz containing every known cliché professionally stitched into the plot.

w Richard Morris *d* Douglas Sirk *ph* Russell Metty *m* Joseph Gershenson

Ann Sheridan, Sterling Hayden, Philip Reed, Lee Patrick, Lee Aaker, Harvey Grant, Dusty Henley

Take My Life **

GB 1947 79m bw
GFD / Cineguild (Anthony Havelock-Allan)

A man is suspected of murdering an ex-girl friend, and his wife journeys to Scotland to prove him innocent.
Hitchcock-style thriller with excellent detail and performances.

w Winston Graham, Valerie Taylor *d* Ronald Neame *ph* Guy Green *m* William Alwyn

Hugh Williams, Greta Gynt, Marius Goring, Francis L. Sullivan, Rosalie Crutchley, Henry Edwards, Ronald Adam

Take My Tip

GB 1937 74m bw
Gaumont-British

Lord Pilkington gets his revenge on a confidence trickster when they meet at a Dalmatian hotel.
Reasonably lively comedy musical adapted for the stars.

w Sidney Gilliat, Michael Hogan, Jack Hulbert *d* Herbert Mason *ph* Bernard Knowles *songs* Sam Lerner, Al Goodheart, Al Hoffman

Jack Hulbert, Cicely Courtneidge, Frank Cellier, Harold Huth, Frank Pettingell, Robb Wilton, H. F. Maltby

Take One False Step *

US 1949 94m bw
U-I (Chester Erskine)

An innocent middle-aged man who has befriended a girl is hunted by the police when she is murdered.
Fairly absorbing and well-cast chase thriller in a minor key.

w Irwin Shaw, Chester Erskine, *story* Night Call by Irwin and David Shaw *d* Chester Erskine *ph* Franz Planer *m* Walter Scharf

William Powell, Shelley Winters, Marsha Hunt, Dorothy Hart, James Gleason, Felix Bressart, Art Baker, Sheldon Leonard

Take the High Ground

US 1953 101m Anscocolor
MGM (Dore Schary)

A tough sergeant trains army conscripts for action in Korea.
Very routine flagwaver.

w Millard Kaufman *d* Richard Brooks *ph* John Alton *m* Dmitri Tiomkin

Richard Widmark, Karl Malden, Carleton Carpenter, Elaine Stewart, Russ Tamblyn, Jerome Courtland, Steve Forrest, Robert Arthur

AAN: Millard Kaufman

Take the Money and Run
US 1968   85m   Technicolor
Palomar (Charles H. Joffe)

A social misfit becomes a bungling crook.
A torrent of middling visual gags, not the star's
best vehicle.

wd Woody Allen ph Lester Shorr m Marvin
Hamlisch

Woody Allen, Janet Margolin, Marcel Hillaire

The Taking of Pelham 123*
US 1974   104m   Technicolor   Panavision
UA / Palomar / Palladium (Gabriel Katzka)

Four ruthless gunmen hold a New York subway
train to ransom and have an ingenious plan for
escape.
Entertaining crime caper made less enjoyable by
all the fashionable faults; the script is
deliberately hard to follow and full of four letter
words, the sound track hard to hear, and the
visuals ugly.

w Peter Stone, novel John Godey d Joseph
Sargent ph Owen Roizman m David Shire

Walter Matthau, Robert Shaw, Martin Balsam,
Hector Elizondo, Earl Hindman, James
Broderick
     'Full of noise and squalling and dirty words
used for giggly shock effects.'—New Yorker

Taking Off*
US 1971   92m   Movielab
Universal (Alfred W. Crown, Michael
   Hausman)

Suburban parents seek their errant daughter
among the hippies, and gradually lose their own
inhibitions.
Slight, formless, but amusing revue-style
comment by a Czech director on the American
scene.

w Milos Forman, John Guare, Jean-Claude
Carrière, John Klein d Milos Forman
ph Miroslav Ondricek

Lynn Carlin, Buck Henry, Linnea Heacock

A Tale of Five Cities
GB 1951   99m   bw
Grand National (Alexander Paal)
US title: A Tale of Five Women

An amnesiac American seeks clues to his past in
Rome, Vienna, Paris, Berlin and London.
Tedious pattern drama remarkable only for its
then untried cast.

w Patrick Kirwan, Maurice J. Wilson
d Montgomery Tully ph Gordon Lang m Hans
May

Bonar Colleano, Gina Lollobrigida, Barbara
Kelly, Lana Morris, Anne Vernon, Eva Bartok

A Tale of Two Cities*
US 1936   121m   bw
MGM (David O. Selznick)

A British lawyer sacrifices himself to save
another man from the guillotine.
Richly detailed version of the classic melodrama,
with production values counting more than the
acting.

w W. P. Lipscomb, S. N. Behrman, novel
Charles Dickens d Jack Conway ph Oliver T.
Marsh m Herbert Stothart

Ronald Colman, Elizabeth Allan, Basil
Rathbone, Edna May Oliver, Blanche Yurka,
Reginald Owen, Henry B. Walthall, Donald
Woods, Walter Catlett, H. B. Warner, Claude
Gillingwater, Fritz Leiber

AAN: best picture

A Tale of Two Cities*
GB 1958   117m   bw
Rank (Betty E. Box)

Modest but still costly remake with good
moments but a rather slow pace.

w T. E. B. Clarke d Ralph Thomas ph Ernest
Steward m Richard Addinsell

Dirk Bogarde, Dorothy Tutin, Christopher Lee,
Athene Seyler, Rosalie Crutchley, Ernest Clark,
Stephen Murray, Paul Guers, Donald Pleasence,
Ian Bannen, Cecil Parker, Alfie Bass
     'Serviceable rather than imaginative.'—MFB

Tales from the Crypt*
GB 1972   92m   Eastmancolor
Metromedia / Amicus (Milton Subotsky)

Five people get lost in catacombs and are shown
the future by a sinister monk who turns out to be
Satan.
Fair ghoulish fun; a quintet of stories with a
recognizable Amicus link.

w Milton Subotsky, from comic strips by
William Gaines d Freddie Francis ph Norman
Warwick m Douglas Gamley

Ralph Richardson, Geoffrey Bayldon, Peter
Cushing, Joan Collins, Ian Hendry, Robin
Phillips, Richard Greene, Barbara Murray, Roy
Dotrice, Nigel Patrick, Patrick Magee

Tales of Beatrix Potter*
GB 1971   90m   Technicolor
EMI (Richard Goodwin)
US title: Peter Rabbit and the Tales of Beatrix
   Potter

Children's stories danced by the Royal Ballet in animal masks.

A charming entertainment for those who can appreciate it, though hardly the most direct way to tell these stories.

w Richard Goodwin, Christine Edward *d* Reginald Mills *ph* Austin Dempster *m* John Lanchbery *ch Frederick Ashton masks Rotislav Doboujinsky pd* Christine Edward

The Tales of Hoffman**

GB 1953 127m Technicolor
British Lion / London / Michael Powell, Emeric Pressburger

The poet Hoffman, in three adventures, seeks the eternal woman and is beset by eternal evil. Overwhelming combination of opera, ballet, and rich production design, an indigestible hodgepodge with flashes of superior talent.

wd Michael Powell, Emeric Pressburger *ph* Christopher Challis *m Jacques Offenbach pd Hein Heckroth*

Robert Rounseville, Robert Helpmann, Pamela Brown, Moira Shearer, Frederick Ashton, Leonide Massine, Ludmilla Tcherina, Ann Ayars, Mogens Wieth; music conducted by Sir Thomas Beecham with the Royal Philharmonic Orchestra

'The most spectacular failure yet achieved by Powell and Pressburger, who seem increasingly to dissipate their gifts in a welter of aimless ingenuity.'—*Gavin Lambert*

'An art director's picnic: I marvelled without being enthralled.'—*Richard Mallett, Punch*

Tales of Manhattan**

US 1942 118m bw
TCF (Boris Morros, Sam Spiegel)

Separate stories of a tail coat, which passes from owner to owner.

The stories are all rather disappointing in their different veins, but production standards are high and a few of the stars shine. A sequence starring W. C. Fields was deleted before release.

w Ben Hecht, Ferenc Molnar, Donald Ogden Stewart, Samuel Hoffenstein, Alan Campbell, Ladislas Fodor, Laslo Vadnay, Laszlo Gorog, Lamar Trotti, Henry Blankfort *d Julien Duvivier ph* Joseph Walker *m* Sol Kaplan

Charles Boyer, Rita Hayworth, Thomas Mitchell, Eugene Pallette; Ginger Rogers, Henry Fonda, Cesar Romero, Gail Patrick, Roland Young; *Charles Laughton*, Elsa Lanchester, Victor Francen, Christian Rub; *Edward G. Robinson*, George Sanders, James Gleason,

Harry Davenport; Paul Robeson, Ethel Waters, Eddie Anderson

† Duvivier was clearly chosen to make this film because of his success with the similar *Carnet de Bal*; he and Boyer went on to make the less successful *Flesh and Fantasy* on similar lines.

Tales of Terror*

US 1962 90m Pathecolor Panavision
AIP (Roger Corman)

'Morella': a dying girl discovers the mummified body of her mother. 'The Black Cat': a henpecked husband kills his wife and walls up the body. 'The Facts in the Case of M Valdemar': an old man is hypnotized at the moment of death.

Tolerable short story compendium, rather short on subtlety and style.

w Richard Matheson, *stories* Edgar Allan Poe *d* Roger Corman *ph* Floyd Crosby *m* Les Baxter

Vincent Price, *Peter Lorre*, Basil Rathbone, Debra Paget

Tales That Witness Madness

GB 1973 90m colour
Paramount / Amicus (Milton Subotsky, Norman Priggen)

Five ghostly tales linked by an old bookshop. Average example of the Amicus compendiums.

w Jay Fairbank *d* Freddie Francis *ph* Norman Warwick *m* Bernard Ebbinghouse

Jack Hawkins, Donald Pleasence, Georgia Brown, Donald Houston, Suzy Kendall, Peter McEnery, Joan Collins, Michael Jayston, Kim Novak, Michael Petrovitch, Mary Tamm

Talk About a Stranger*

US 1952 65m bw
MGM (Richard Goldstone)

In a small town, gossip is unjustly aroused over a mysterious stranger who is suspected of various crimes.

Unusual though rather naïve second feature, directed for more than its worth.

w Margaret Fitts, *novel* Charlotte Armstrong *d* David Bradley *ph* John Alton *m* David Buttolph

George Murphy, Nancy Davis, Lewis Stone, Billy Gray, Kurt Kasznar

The Talk of the Town***

US 1942 118m bw
Columbia (George Stevens, Fred Guiol)

A girl loves both a suspected murderer and the lawyer who defends him.

Unusual mixture of comedy and drama, delightfully handled by three sympathetic stars.

w Irwin Shaw, Sidney Buchman d George Stevens ph Ted Tetzlaff *m* Frederick Hollander

Roland Colman, Cary Grant, Jean Arthur, Edgar Buchanan, Glenda Farrell, Charles Dingle, Emma Dunn, Rex Ingram

'A rip-roaring, knock-down-and-drag-out comedy about civil liberties.'—*John T. McManus*

AAN: best picture; original story (Sidney Harmon); script; Ted Tetzlaff

The Tall Headlines
GB 1952   100m   bw
Grand National / Raymond Stross
aka: *The Frightened Bride*

A family is affected when the eldest son is executed for murder.
Glum, boring, badly cast, badly written and generally inept melodrama.

w Audrey Erskine Lindop (from her novel), Dudley Leslie *d* Terence Young *ph* C. M. Pennington-Richards *m* Hans May

Flora Robson, Michael Denison, Mai Zetterling, Jane Hylton, André Morell, Dennis Price, Mervyn Johns, Naunton Wayne

'A falsity which will surely surprise even those familiar with the conventions of British middle-class cinema.'—*Lindsay Anderson*

Tall in the Saddle
US 1944   87m   bw
RKO (Robert Fellows)

The newly-arrived ranch foreman finds that his boss has been murdered.
Quite a watchable, and forgettable, mystery western.

w Michael Hogan, Paul J. Fix *d* Edwin L. Marin *ph* Robert de Grasse *m* Roy Webb *md* Constantin Bakaleinikoff

John Wayne, Ella Raines, Ward Bond, George 'Gabby' Hayes, Audrey Long, Elizabeth Risdon, Don Douglas, Paul Fix, Russell Wade

The Tall Men*
US 1955   122m   De Luxe   Cinemascope
TCF (William A. Bacher, William B. Hawks)

After the Civil War, two Texans head north for the Montana goldfields.
Solid star western.

w Sidney Boehm, Frank Nugent, *novel* Clay Fisher *d* Raoul Walsh *ph* Leo Tover *m* Victor Young

Clark Gable, Jane Russell, Robert Ryan,

Cameron Mitchell, Juan Garcia, Harry Shannon, Emile Meyer

'A big action feast and value for anyone's money.'—*Newsweek*

Tall Story
US 1960   91m   bw
Warner / Mansfield (Joshua Logan)

A college basketball player faces various kinds of trouble when he marries.
Dislikeable campus comedy with leading players miscast.

w Julius J. Epstein, *novel* The Homecoming Game by Howard Nemoor *d* Joshua Logan *ph* Ellsworth Fredericks *m* Cyril Mockridge

Anthony Perkins, Jane Fonda, Ray Walston, Anne Jackson, Marc Connelly, Murray Hamilton, Elizabeth Patterson

The Tall T*
US 1957   78m   Technicolor
Columbia / Scott–Brown (Harry Joe Brown)

Three bandits hold up a stagecoach and take a hostage, but are outwitted by a rancher.
Good small-scale suspense western with plenty of action and a blood-spattered finale.

w Burt Kennedy d Budd Boetticher ph Charles Lawton Jnr

Randolph Scott, Richard Boone, Maureen O'Sullivan, Arthur Hunnicutt, Skip Homeier, John Hubbard, Henry Silva

The Tall Target**
US 1951   78m   bw
MGM (Richard Goldstone)

A discredited police officer tries to stop the assassination of Abraham Lincoln on a train to Washington.
Lively period suspenser with excellent attention to detail and much of the attraction of *The Lady Vanishes*. The plot slightly relaxes its hold before the end.

w George Worthing Yates, Art Cohn d Anthony Mann ph Paul C. Vogel ad Cedric Gibbons, Eddie Imazu

Dick Powell, *Adolphe Menjou*, Paula Raymond, Marshall Thompson, *Ruby Dee*, Richard Rober, Will Geer, Florence Bates

'An intelligent minor picture which makes good use of its material.'—*MFB*

Tamahine
GB 1962   95m   Technicolor
Cinemascope
ABP (John Bryan)

The headmaster of a boys' school is visited by his glamorous half-caste Polynesian cousin.
Simple-minded school comedy with predictable situations.

w Denis Cannan, *novel* Thelma Niklaus d Philip Leacock m Malcolm Arnold

John Fraser, Nancy Kwan, Dennis Price, Derek Nimmo, Justine Lord, James Fox, Coral Browne, Michael Gough, Allan Cuthbertson

The Tamarind Seed*
GB 1974 125m Eastmancolor
Panavision
Jewel / Lorimar / Pimlico (Ken Wales)

While holidaying in Barbados, a British widow falls for a Russian military attaché.
Old-fashioned romance which turns into a mild spy caper. A well-heeled time-passer.

w Blake Edwards, *novel* Evelyn Anthony
d Blake Edwards ph Frederick A. Young
m John Barry

Julie Andrews, Omar Sharif, Sylvia Syms, Dan O'Herlihy, Anthony Quayle, Oscar Homolka

'A painless timekiller, but one wishes Miss Andrews didn't always give the impression that she had just left her horse in the hallway.'— *Michael Billington, Illustrated London News*

The Taming of the Shrew*
US 1967 122m Technicolor Panavision
Columbia / Royal / FAI (Richard McWhorter)

Petruchio violently tames his shrewish wife.
Busy version of one of Shakespeare's more proletarian comedies; the words in this case take second place to violent action and rioting colour.

w Suso Cecchi d'Amico, Paul Dehn, Franco Zeffirelli d Franco Zeffirelli ph Oswald Morris, Luciano Trasatti m Nino Rota

Richard Burton, Elizabeth Taylor, Michael York, Michael Hordern, Cyril Cusack, Alfred Lynch, Natasha Pyne, Alan Webb, Victor Spinetti

'As entertainment *Kiss Me Kate* is infinitely better but then Cole Porter was a real artist and Burton is a culture vulture.'— *Wilfrid Sheed*

'The old warhorse of a comedy has been spanked into uproarious life.'— *Hollis Alpert*

Tammy*
US 1957 89m Technicolor
Cinemascope
U-I (Ross Hunter)

A backwoods tomboy falls for a stranded flier.
Whimsical romance for middle America, which started Hollywood's last series of proletarian

family appeal before the family was entirely forsaken for four letter words.

w Oscar Brodney d Joseph Pevney ph Arthur E. Arling m Frank Skinner md Joseph Gershenson

Debbie Reynolds, Walter Brennan, Leslie Nielsen, Mala Powers, Fay Wray, Sidney Blackmer, Mildred Natwick

Tammy and the Doctor
US 1963 88m Eastmancolor
U-I / Ross Hunter

Tammy leaves her riverboat to accompany an old lady who needs an operation in the big city.
More artless family fodder.

w Oscar Brodney d Harry Keller ph Russell Metty m Frank Skinner

Sandra Dee, Peter Fonda, Macdonald Carey, Beulah Bondi, Margaret Lindsay, Reginald Owen, Adam West

'The aura of simple religion and naïve philosophy remains singularly charmless.'— *MFB*

Tammy Tell Me True
US 1961 97m Eastmancolor
U-I (Ross Hunter)

Tammy gets a college education and charms all comers.
Sugar-coated sequel to the above.

w Oscar Brodney d Harry Keller ph Clifford Stine m Percy Faith

Sandra Dee, John Gavin, Charles Drake, Virginia Grey, *Beulah Bondi*, Julia Meade, Cecil Kellaway, Edgar Buchanan

'The heroine appears to be not so much old-fashioned as positively retarded.'— *MFB*

Tampico
US 1944 75m bw
TCF (Robert Bassler)

A tanker captain picks up survivors from a torpedoed ship and finds himself involved with spies.
Very minor action melodrama, efficiently made.

w Kenneth Gamet, Fred Niblo Jnr, Richard Macaulay d Lothar Mendes ph Charles G. Clarke

Edward G. Robinson, Lynn Bari, Victor McLaglen, Marc Lawrence, E. J. Ballentine, Mona Maris

Tap Roots
US 1948 109m Technicolor
U-I

A southern family tries to remain neutral in the Civil War.

Minor *Gone with the Wind* saga, quite expensively produced but not very exciting.

w Alan le May, *novel* James Street *d* George Marshall *ph* Winton C. Hoch, Lionel Lindon *m* Frank Skinner

Susan Hayward, Van Heflin, Boris Karloff, Julie London, Whitfield Connor

Tarantula
US 1955   80m   bw
U-I (William Alland)

Scientists working on an artificial food become grossly misshapen, and an infected spider escapes and grows to giant size.

Moderate monster hokum with the desert setting which became a cliché; the grotesque faces are more horrific than the spider, which seldom seems to touch the ground.

w Robert M. Fresco, Martin Berkeley *d* Jack Arnold *ph* George Robinson *m* Joseph Gershenson

Leo G. Carroll, John Agar, Mara Corday, Nestor Paiva

Taras Bulba*
US 1962   124m   Eastmancolor
Panavision
UA / H-H / Avala (Harold Hecht)

A cossack leader has bitter disagreements with his rebellious son.

Violent action epic based on a well-worn story; plenty of spectacular highlights.

w Waldo Salt, Karl Tunberg, *novel* Nicolai Gogol *d* J. Lee-Thompson *ph* Joe MacDonald *m* Franz Waxman *pd* Edward Carrere

Yul Brynner, Tony Curtis, Christine Kaufmann, Sam Wanamaker, Guy Rolfe, George Macready, Vladimir Sokoloff, Abraham Sofaer

AAN: Franz Waxman

Target Zero
US 1955   93m   bw
Warner (David Weisbart)

An infantry patrol in Korea is cut off behind enemy lines.

Routine battle exploits with a highly unlikely superimposed romance.

w Sam Rolfe *d* Harmon Jones *ph* Edwin DuPar *m* David Buttolph

Richard Conte, Charles Bronson, Richard Stapley, Chuck Connors, L. Q. Jones, Peggie Castle

Targets*
US 1967   90m   Pathecolor
(Paramount) Peter Bogdanovich

An elderly horror film star confronts and disarms a mad sniper at a drive-in movie.

Oddball melodrama apparently meant to contrast real and fantasy violence; it doesn't quite work despite effective moments, and the low budget shows.

wd Peter Bogdanovich *ph* Laszlo Kovacs

Boris Karloff, Tim O'Kelly, James Brown, Sandy Baron

The Tarnished Angels
US 1957   91m   bw   Cinemascope
U-I (Albert Zugsmith)

A reporter falls in with a self-torturing family of circus air aces.

Unsatisfactory attempt to reunite the talents of *Written on the Wind*; a dull story, very boringly presented.

w George Zuckerman, *novel* Pylon by William Faulkner *d* Douglas Sirk *ph* Irving Glassberg *m* Frank Skinner *md* Joseph Gershenson

Rock Hudson, Robert Stack, Dorothy Malone, Jack Carson, Robert Middleton

Tarzan
The talkie *Tarzans* began with Johnny Weissmuller and tailed off from there. (See *Filmgoer's Companion* for the silents.) The 1932 version more or less followed the original Edgar Rice Burroughs novel, and all the MGM entries had a special vivid quality about them, but subsequently the productions, usually produced under the aegis of Sol Lesser, tailed off towards the standard of the TV series of the sixties starring Ron Ely.

1932: TARZAN THE APE MAN** (MGM: Weissmuller with Maureen O'Sullivan: *d* W. S. Van Dyke: 99m)

1933: TARZAN THE FEARLESS (Principal: Buster Crabbe: *d* Robert Hill: 73m)

1934: TARZAN AND HIS MATE*** (MGM: Weissmuller with Maureen O'Sullivan: *d* Cedric Gibbons: 105m)

'Certainly one of the funniest things you'll ever see.'—*Otis Ferguson*

1935: THE NEW ADVENTURES OF TARZAN (Burroughs: Herman Brix: *d* Edward Kull: 75m)

1936: TARZAN ESCAPES** (MGM: Weissmuller with Maureen O'Sullivan: *d* Richard Thorpe: 95m)

1938: TARZAN'S REVENGE (Sol Lesser: Glenn Morris: *d* D. Ross Lederman: 70m);

TARZAN AND THE GREEN GODDESS
(Principal: Herman Brix: *d* Edward Kull: 72m:
largely a re-edit of NEW ADVENTURES)
1939: TARZAN FINDS A SON (MGM:
Weissmuller with O'Sullivan: Richard Thorpe:
90m)
1941: TARZAN'S SECRET TREASURE
(MGM: Weissmuller with O'Sullivan: *d* Richard
Thorpe: 81m)
1942: TARZAN'S NEW YORK
ADVENTURE (MGM: Weissmuller with
O'Sullivan: *d* Richard Thorpe: 71m)
1943: TARZAN ESCAPES (RKO:
Weissmuller: *d* William Thiele: 78m);
TARZAN'S DESERT MYSTERY (RKO:
Weissmuller: *d* William Thiele: 70m)
1945: TARZAN AND THE AMAZONS
(RKO: Weissmuller: *d* Kurt Neumann: 76m)
1946: TARZAN AND THE LEOPARD
WOMAN (RKO: Weissmuller: *d* Kurt
Neumann: 72m)
1947: TARZAN AND THE HUNTRESS
(RKO: Weissmuller: *d* Kurt Neumann: 72m)
1948: TARZAN AND THE MERMAIDS
(RKO: *d* Robert Florey: Weissmuller: 68m)
1949: TARZAN'S MAGIC FOUNTAIN
(RKO: Lex Barker: *d* Lee Sholem: 73m)
1950: TARZAN AND THE SLAVE GIRL
(RKO: Lex Barker: *d* Lee Sholem: 74m)
1951: TARZAN'S PERIL (RKO: Lex Barker:
d Byron Haskin: 79m)
1952: TARZAN'S SAVAGE FURY (RKO:
Lex Barker: *d* Cy Endfield: 80m)
1953: TARZAN AND THE SHE-DEVIL
(RKO: Lex Barker: *d* Kurt Neumann: 76m)
1955: TARZAN'S HIDDEN JUNGLE (RKO:
Gordon Scott: *d* Harold Schuster: 73m)
1957: TARZAN AND THE LOST SAFARI
(colour) (MGM: Gordon Scott: *d* Bruce
Humberstone: 84m)
1958: TARZAN'S FIGHT FOR LIFE (colour)
(MGM: Gordon Scott: *d* Bruce Humberstone:
86m)
1959: TARZAN'S GREATEST
ADVENTURE (colour) (MGM: Gordon Scott:
d John Guillermin: 90m)
1959: TARZAN THE APE MAN (colour:
remake of the original story) (MGM: Denny
Miller: *d* Joseph Newman: 82m)
1960: TARZAN THE MAGNIFICENT
(colour) (Paramount: Gordon Scott: *d* Robert
Day: 88m)
1962: TARZAN GOES TO INDIA (colour)
(MGM: Jock Mahoney: *d* John Guillermin:
86m)
1963: TARZAN'S THREE CHALLENGES
(colour) (MGM: Jock Mahoney: *d* Robert Day:
92m)
1966: TARZAN AND THE VALLEY OF

GOLD (colour) (NatGen: Mike Henry: Robert
Day: 90m)
1967: TARZAN AND THE GREAT RIVER
(colour) (Paramount: Mike Henry: *d* Robert
Day: 88m)
1968: TARZAN AND THE JUNGLE BOY
(colour) (Paramount: Mike Henry: *d* Robert
Day: 90m)

The Tartars
Italy 1960 105m Technicolor
Totalscope
Lux (Riccardo Gualino)

Viking settlers on the Russian steppes fight
Tartar invaders.
Action-packed comic strip.

d Richard Thorpe *ph* Amerigo Genarelli

Orson Welles, Victor Mature, Folco Lulli,
Arnoldo Foa

Task Force
US 1949 116m bw (Technicolor
sequences)
Warner (Jerry Wald)

An admiral about to retire recalls his struggle to
promote the cause of aircraft carriers.
Stilted and long-drawn-out flagwaver with too
much chat and action highlights borrowed from
wartime newsreel.

wd Delmer Daves *ph* Robert Burks, Wilfrid M.
Cline *m* Franz Waxman

Gary Cooper, Walter Brennan, Jane Wyatt,
Wayne Morris, Julie London, Bruce Bennett,
Stanley Ridges, Jack Holt

A Taste of Excitement
GB 1968 99m Eastmancolor
Trio Films (George Willoughby)

An English girl holidaying on the Riviera
suspects that someone is trying to kill her.
Standard frightened lady/'they won't believe me'
mystery with enough twists to satisfy addicts.

w Brian Carton, Don Sharp, *novel* Waiting for a
Tiger by Ben Healey *d* Don Sharp *ph* Paul
Beeson

Eva Renzi, David Buck, Peter Vaughan, Sophie
Hardy, Paul Hubschmid, Kay Walsh

Taste of Fear**
GB 1961 82m bw
Columbia / Hammer (Jimmy Sangster)
US title: *Scream of Fear*

A crippled heiress visits her long-lost father and
is haunted by his corpse.
Smartly tricked-out sub-Hitchcock screamer

with sudden shocks among the Riviera settings and a plot which Hammer borrowed from *Les Diaboliques* and used again and again.

w Jimmy Sangster *d* Seth Holt *ph* Douglas Slocombe *m* Clifton Parker

Susan Strasberg, Ann Todd, Ronald Lewis, Christopher Lee, Leonard Sachs

'All those creaking shutters, flickering candles, wavering shadows and pianos playing in empty rooms still yield a tiny frisson.'—*Penelope Houston*

A Taste of Honey***
GB 1961   100m   bw
British Lion / Bryanston / Woodfall (Tony Richardson)

Adventures of a pregnant Salford teenager, her sluttish mother, black lover and homosexual friend.
Fascinating offbeat comedy drama with memorable characters and sharply etched backgrounds.

w Shelagh Delaney, Tony Richardson, *play* Shelagh Delaney *d* Tony Richardson *ph* Walter Lassally *m* John Addison

Rita Tushingham, Dora Bryan, Murray Melvin, Robert Stephens, Paul Danquah

'Tart and lively around the edges and bitter at the core.'—*Peter John Dyer*

Taste the Blood of Dracula
GB 1969   95m   Technicolor
Hammer (Aida Young)

A depraved peer involves three Victorian businessmen in the reactivation of Dracula. Latterday vampire saga, initially lively but mainly dreary.

w John Elder *d* Peter Sasdy *ph* Arthur Grant *m* James Bernard

Christopher Lee, Geoffrey Keen, Gwen Watford, Linda Hayden, Peter Sallis, Anthony Corlan, John Carson, Ralph Bates

The Tattered Dress
US 1957   93m   bw   Cinemascope
U-I (Albert Zugsmith)

While conducting a murder defence, a criminal lawyer annoys a vindictive small-town sheriff, who plots revenge.
Silly melodrama which rapidly loses interest after a promising start.

w George Zuckerman *d* Jack Arnold *ph* Carl Guthrie *m* Frank Skinner

Jeff Chandler, Jack Carson, Jeanne Crain, Gail Russell, George Tobias, Edward Andrews, Philip Reed

Tawny Pipit*
GB 1944   85m   bw
GFD / Two Cities (Bernard Miles)

The life of a village in wartime is disrupted when two rare birds nest in a local meadow.
Pleasant, thin little comedy, a precursor of the Ealing school.

w Bernard Miles *d* Bernard Miles, Charles Saunders

Bernard Miles, Rosamund John, Niall MacGinnis, Jean Gillie, Christopher Steele, Lucie Mannheim, Brefni O'Rourke, Marjorie Rhodes

'Almost unimaginably genteel.'—*James Agee*
'Not quite dry enough for the epicures nor sweet enough for the addicts.'—*C. A. Lejeune*

Taxi
US 1952   77m   bw
TCF (Samuel G. Engel)

A taxi driver helps a young mother find her husband, and falls for her herself.
Practised sentimental guff, Hollywoodized from the French film *Sans Laisser d'Adresse*.

w D. M. Marshman Jnr, Daniel Fuchs *d* Gregory Ratoff *ph* Milton Krasner *m* Leigh Harline

Dan Dailey, Constance Smith, Neva Patterson, Blanche Yurka, Walter Woolf King

Taxi Driver***
US 1976   114m   Metrocolor
Columbia / Italo—Judeo (Michael and Julia Philips)

A lonely Vietnam veteran becomes a New York taxi driver and allows the violence and squalor around him to explode in his mind.
The epitome of the sordid realism of the seventies, this unlovely but brilliantly made film haunts the mind and paints a most vivid picture of a hell on earth. Unfortunately the plot in the latter stages makes no sense.

w Paul Schraeder *d* Martin Scorsese *ph* Michael Chapman *m* Bernard Herrmann

Robert de Niro, Jodie Foster, Cybill Shepherd, Peter Boyle, Leonard Harris, Harvey Keitel

'I don't question the truth of this material. I question Scorse's ability to lift it out of the movie gutters into which less truthful directors have trampled it.'—*Stanley Kauffmann*

AAN: best picture; Bernard Herrmann; Robert de Niro; Jodie Foster

Tea and Sympathy
US 1956   122m   Metrocolor
 Cinemascope
MGM (Pandro S. Berman)

A sensitive teenage schoolboy is scorned by his
tougher classmates, but his housemaster's wife
takes him in hand . . .
Overblown and bowdlerized version of a quiet
little Broadway play: impeccable production
values, but no spark.

w Robert Anderson (and the Hays office), from
his play d Vincente Minnelli ph John Alton
m Adolph Deutsch

Deborah Kerr, *John Kerr*, Leif Erickson,
Edward Andrews, Darryl Hickman
 'Even the most daring story can be brought
onto the screen when done with courage, honesty
and good taste.'—*publicity*

Tea for Two*
US 1950   97m   Technicolor
Warner (William Jacobs)

A nearly bankrupt financier promises his niece
25,000 dollars for her new musical show if she
can say no to every question for twenty-four
hours.
Tinkly, quite amusing light musical which has
little to do with *No No Nanette* on which it is
allegedly based.

w Henry Clark d David Butler ph Wilfrid
Cline md Ray Heindorf

Doris Day, Gordon Macrae, Gene Nelson, Eve
Arden, Billy de Wolfe, S. Z. Sakall, Bill
Goodwin, Patrice Wymore

Teacher's Pet*
US 1957   120m   bw   Vistavision
Paramount / Perlberg–Seaton (William
Perlberg)

A tough city editor falls for a lady professor of
journalism and enrols as a student.
Overlong one-joke comedy which quickly
reneges on its early promise; but the principals
play up divertingly.

w Fay and Michael Kanin d George Seaton
ph Haskell Boggs m Roy Webb

Clark Gable, Doris Day, Gig Young, Mamie
Van Doren, Nick Adams

AAN: Fay and Michael Kanin; Gig Young

The Teahouse of the August Moon*
US 1956   123m   Metrocolor
 Cinemascope
MGM (Jack Cummings)

Okinawa 1944: a wily interpreter helps
American troops succumb to the oriental way of
life.

Adequate, well-acted screen version of a
Broadway comedy which succeeded largely
because of its theatricality. A few good jokes
remain.

w John Patrick, from his play d Daniel Mann
ph John Alton m Saul Chaplin

Marlon Brando, Glenn Ford, Eddie Albert, *Paul
Ford*, Michiko Kyo, Henry Morgan

The Teckman Mystery
GB 1954   90m   bw
British Lion / London Films / Corona (Josef
Somlo)

An author commissioned to write the biography
of a dead airman finds him very much alive and
his own life in danger.
Peripatetic spy story with the twists expected of
this author; all quite enjoyable.

w Francis Durbridge, James Matthews, *BBC
serial* Francis Durbridge d Wendy Toye
ph Jack Hilyard m Clifton Parker

Margaret Leighton, John Justin, Michael
Medwin, Meier Tzelniker, Roland Culver,
George Coulouris, Raymond Huntley, Duncan
Lamont

Teenage Rebel
US 1956   94m   bw   Cinemascope
TCF (Charles Brackett)

A wealthy California woman is visited by her
teenage daughter from a former marriage; the
girl proceeds to make difficulties for everyone.
The first film in black-and-white Cinemascope is
a tedious drama of unreal people.

w Walter Reisch, Charles Brackett, *play* Edith
Sommer d Edmund Goulding ph Joe
MacDonald m Leigh Harline

Ginger Rogers, Michael Rennie, Mildred
Natwick, Betty Lou Keim, Warren Berlinger,
Louise Beavers, Irene Hervey

Telefon
US 1977   103m   Metrocolor
MGM (James B. Harris)

A Russian agent is instructed to seek out and
destroy a ring of hard liners who are opposing
detente with the west.
Moderately watchable espionage capers with a
slightly new twist.

w Peter Hyams, Stirling Silliphant, *novel* Walter
Wager d Don Siegel ph Michael Butler m Lalo
Schifrin

Charles Bronson, Lee Remick, Donald
Pleasence, Tyne Daly, Alan Badel, Patrick
Magee, Sheree North

Tell Me That You Love Me, Junie Moon
US 1969   113m   Technicolor
Paramount / Sigma (Otto Preminger)

A disfigured girl, a homosexual paraplegic and an introvert epileptic set up house together. Absurd tragicomedy which remains disturbingly icky in conception and execution.

w Marjorie Kellogg, from her novel d Otto Preminger ph Boris Kaufman m Philip Springer

Liza Minnelli, Ken Howard, Robert Moore, Kay Thompson, Leonard Frey, James Coco, Fred Williamson

'Like seeing a venerated senior citizen desperately trying to show he's in love with today by donning see-through clothes.'— *Michael Billington, Illustrated London News*

Tell No Tales**
US 1938   68m   bw
MGM (Edward Chodorov)

A managing editor seeks a big scoop to save his newspaper, and solves a kidnap-murder case. Intriguingly written and handled second feature, with excellent pace, performance and entertainment value.

w *Lionel Houser* d *Leslie Fenton* ph Joseph Ruttenberg m William Axt

Melvyn Douglas, Louise Platt, Gene Lockhart, Douglass Dumbrille, Zeffie Tilbury, Halliwell Hobbes

'Full of excellent detail, and the smallest part is a genuine character. Add these qualities to its pace and excitement and you have something well worth seeing.'—*Richard Mallett, Punch*

Tell Them Willie Boy is Here*
US 1969   97m   Technicolor
Universal (Philip A. Waxman)

In 1909 an Indian turned cowboy comes up against old prejudices and is pursued into the desert after an accidental death. Boringly predictable story of white man's guilt, very professionally made.

wd *Abraham Polonsky, novel* Willie Boy by Harry Lawton ph *Conrad Hall* m Dave Grusin

Robert Redford, Robert Blake, Katharine Ross, Susan Clark, Barry Sullivan, Charles McGraw, Charles Aidman, John Vernon

Tempest
Italy / France / Yugoslavia 1958   123m   Technirama
(Paramount) Dino de Laurentiis / Gray / S. N Pathe / Bosnia

Adventures of a Russian ensign banished by Catherine the Great. Expensive but sloppy epic which fails to generate much interest.

w Louis Peterson, Alberto Lattuada, Ivo Perelli, *novel* The Captain's Daughter by Alexander Pushkin d Alberto Lattuada ph *Aldo Tonti* m Piero Piccioni

Van Heflin, Geoffrey Horne, Silvana Mangano, Oscar Homolka, Viveca Lindfors, Robert Keith, Vittorio Gassman, Finlay Currie, Agnes Moorehead, Helmut Dantine, Laurence Naismith

Temptation
US 1946   92m   bw
Universal (Edward Small)

An archaeologist's wife takes to poisoning both her husband and her blackmailing lover. Hoary Edwardian melodrama, unpersuasively restaged.

w Robert Thoeren, *novel* Bella Donna by Robert Hichens d Irving Pichel ph Lucien Ballard m Daniele Amfitheatrof

Merle Oberon, George Brent, Charles Korvin, Paul Lukas, Lenore Ulric, Arnold Moss, Ludwig Stossel, Gavin Muir, Ilka Gruning, André Charlot

Temptation Harbour
GB 1946   104m   bw
ABP (Victor Skutesky)

A railway signalman finds and keeps stolen money. Well-presented but boringly predictable melodrama with an overwrought leading performance set against yards of studio fog.

w Victor Skutesky, Frederic Gotfurt, Rodney Ackland, *novel* Newhaven–Dieppe by Georges Simenon d Lance Comfort

Robert Newton, Simone Simon, William Hartnell, Marcel Dalio, Margaret Barton, Edward Rigby, Joan Hopkins, Charles Victor, Kathleen Harrison

The Ten Commandments**
US 1923   150m approx (24 fps)
   part Technicolor   silent
Paramount / Famous Players–Lasky (Cecil B. de Mille)

Moses leads the Israelites into the promised land in modern San Francisco; a story of two brothers shows the power of prayer and truth. The two halves in fact are totally disconnected; but this is a de Mille spectacular and therefore beyond reproach, while as a Hollywood milestone it cannot be denied a place in the Hall of Fame.

w Jeanie MacPherson *d* Cecil B. d Mille *ph* Bert Glennon and others (*colour,* Ray Renahan)

Theodore Roberts, Richard Dix, Rod la Rocque, Edythe Chapman, Leatrice Joy, Nita Naldi

'It will last as long as the film on which it is recorded.'—*James R. Quirk, Photoplay*

The Ten Commandments*
US 1956 219m Technicolor Vistavision
Paramount / Cecil B. de Mille (Henry Wilcoxon)

The life of Moses and his leading of the Israelites to the Promised Land.
Popular but incredibly stilted and verbose bible-in-pictures spectacle. A very long haul along a monotonous route, with the director at his pedestrian worst.

w Aeneas Mackenzie, Jesse L. Lasky Jnr, Jack Gariss, Frederic M. Frank *d* Cecil B. de Mille *ph* Loyal Griggs *m* Elmer Bernstein

Charlton Heston, Yul Brynner, Edward G. Robinson, Anne Baxter, Nina Foch, Yvonne de Carlo, John Derek, H. B. Warner, Henry Wilcoxon, Judith Anderson, John Carradine, Douglass Dumbrille, Cedric Hardwicke, Martha Scott, Vincent Price

AAN: best picture; Loyal Griggs

Ten Days in Paris
GB 1939 82m bw
Columbia (Jerome J. Jackson)
US titles: *Missing Ten Days/Spy in the Pantry*

An amnesiac wakes up in Paris and finds he has been involved in espionage activities.
Modest, quite likeable little comedy suspenser.

w John Meehan Jnr, James Curtis, *novel* The Disappearance of Roger Tremayne by Bruce Graeme *d* Tim Whelan *ph* Otto Kanturek

Rex Harrison, Karen Verne, Leo Genn, Joan Marion, Anthony Holles, John Abbott, Hay Petrie

Ten Gentlemen from West Point**
US 1942 104m bw
TCF (William Perlberg)

Adventures in Indian territory, and back at West Point, of the first recruits to that military academy in the early 1800s.
Likeable mixture of comedy and flagwaving adventure, with excellent production values and a dominating performance.

w Richard Maibaum, George Seaton *d* Henry

Hathaway *ph* Leon Shamroy *m* Alfred Newman

Laird Cregar, George Montgomery, Maureen O'Hara, John Sutton, Shepperd Strudwick, Victor Francen, Harry Davenport, Ward Bond, Douglass Dumbrille, Ralph Byrd, Louis Jean Heydt

AAN: Leon Shamroy

Ten Little Indians*
GB 1966 91m bw
Tenlit (Harry Alan Towers)

Ten people, including two servants invited to a remote house in the Austrian Alps are murdered one by one.
Fair copy of a classic whodunnit.

w Peter Yeldham, Harry Alan Towers, *novel* Agatha Christie *d* George Pollock *ph* Ernest Steward *m* Malcolm Lockyer

Wilfrid Hyde White, Dennis Price, Stanley Holloway, Leo Genn, Shirley Eaton, Hugh O'Brian, Daliah Lavi, Fabian, Mario Adorf, Marianne Hoppe
† Made also in 1945 and 1975, as *And Then There Were None* (qv).

Ten North Frederick*
US 1958 102m bw Cinemascope
TCF (Charles Brackett)

At the funeral of a local politico, his family and friends think back to the events of his life.
Small beer, but a generally adult and entertaining family drama despite a miscast lead.

wd Philip Dunne, novel John O'Hara *ph* Joe MacDonald *m* Leigh Harline

Gary Cooper, Geraldine Fitzgerald, Diane Varsi, Stuart Whitman, Suzy Parker, Tom Tully, Ray Stricklyn, John Emery

Ten Rillington Place*
GB 1970 111m Eastmancolor
Columbia / Filmways (Basil Appleby)

An account of London's sordid Christie murders of the forties.
Agreeably seedy reconstruction of a *cause célèbre,* carefully built around the star part of a murderous aberrant landlord. Too long, however, and finally too lacking in detail.

w Clive Exton, *book* Ludovic Kennedy *d* Richard Fleischer *ph* Denys Coop

Richard Attenborough, *John Hurt,* Judy Geeson, Pat Heywood, Isobel Black, Geoffrey Chater, André Morell, Robert Hardy

Ten Seconds to Hell
US 1959   93m   bw
Hammer / Seven Arts (Michael Carreras)

Bomb disposal experts in post-war Berlin quarrel over a girl.

Boring, harsh, hollow melodrama, so artificially constructed that no one can possibly care who gets exploded.

w Robert Aldrich, Teddi Sherman, *novel* The Phoenix by Lawrence Bachmann d Robert Aldrich ph Ernest Laszlo m Kenneth V. Jones

Jack Palance, Jeff Chandler, Martine Carol, Robert Cornthwaite, Dave Willock, Wesley Addy

Ten Tall Men
US 1951   97m   Technicolor
Columbia / Norma (Harold Hecht)

A Foreign Legion patrol prevents a Riff attack. Comic strip adventures, efficiently handled.

w Roland Kibbee, Frank Davis d Willis Goldbeck ph William Snyder m David Buttolph

Burt Lancaster, Gilbert Roland, Kieron Moore, John Dehner, Jody Lawrance, George Tobias, Mike Mazurki

10.30 pm Summer
US / Spain 1966   85m   Technicolor
UA / Jorill / Argos (Jules Dassin, Anatole Litvak)

The neurotic Greek wife of an Englishman travelling in Spain becomes obsessed with a murderer on the run.
Preposterously overwrought romantic melodrama.

w Jules Dassin, Marguerite Duras, *novel* Marguerite Duras d Jules Dassin ph Gabor Pogany m Christobel Hallfter

Peter Finch, Melina Mercouri, Romy Schneider, Julian Mateos

Ten Thousand Bedrooms
US 1956   114m   Metrocolor
   Cinemascope
MGM (Joe Pasternak)

An American millionaire finds romance when he buys a Rome hotel.
Old-fashioned, unfunny comedy sadly lacking pace and style.

w Laslo Vadnay, Art Cohn, William Ludwig, Leonard Spiegelgass d Richard Thorpe ph Robert Bronner m George Stoll *songs* Nicholas Brodszky, Sammy Cahn

Dean Martin, Eva Bartok, Anna Maria

Alberghetti, Walter Slezak, Paul Henreid, Jules Munchin, Marcel Dalio

Ten Who Dared
US 1960   92m   Technicolor
Walt Disney (James Algar)

In 1869 a scientific expedition sets out to chart the Colorado River.
Tedious and unconvincing adventures.

w Lawrence E. Watkin, from the journal of Major John Wesley Powell d William Beaudine

Brian Keith, John Beal, James Drury, R. G. Armstrong, Ben Johnson, L. Q. Jones

Tender Comrade
US 1943   101m   bw
RKO (David Hempstead)

Lady welders whose husbands are fighting men keep their chins up during World War II.
Dim tearjerker.

w Dalton Trumbo d Edward Dmytryk ph Russell Metty m Leigh Harline

Ginger Rogers, Robert Ryan, Ruth Hussey, Patricia Collinge, Mady Christians, Kim Hunter, Jane Darwell

Tender Is the Night*
US 1961   146m   De Luxe   Cinemascope
TCF (Henry T. Weinstein)

Adventures around Europe between the wars of a rich American psychiatrist who has married his patient.
Patchy, fairly literal transcription of a patently unfilmable novel about defiantly unreal people in what would now be the jet set. About half the result is superficially entertaining.

w Ivan Moffat, *novel* F. Scott Fitzgerald d Henry King ph Leon Shamroy m Bernard Herrmann

Jennifer Jones, Jason Robards Jnr, *Joan Fontaine, Tom Ewell*, Cesare Danova, Jill St John, Paul Lukas

AAN: title song (m Sammy Fain, ly Paul Francis Webster)

The Tender Trap*
US 1955   111m   Eastmancolor
   Cinemascope
MGM (Lawrence Weingarten)

A smart New York agent has a way with women which annoys his friend; but Casanova gets his come-uppance when he sets his sights on an apparently naïve young actress.
Thin comedy with agreeable moments, not helped by the wide screen.

w Julius J. Epstein, *play* Max Shulman, Robert Paul Smith *d* Charles Walters *ph* Paul Vogel *m* Jeff Alexander

Frank Sinatra, Debbie Reynolds, David Wayne, Celeste Holm, Lola Albright, Carolyn Jones

AAN: title song (*m* James Van Heusen, *ly* Sammy Cahn)

Tennessee Johnson*
US 1943 102m bw
MGM (J. Walter Ruben)
GB title: *The Man on America's Conscience*

The rise and the problems of President Andrew Johnson.
Sincere, straightforward, well-produced historical drama which failed to set the Thames—or the Hudson—on fire.

w John Balderston, Wells Root *d* William Dieterle *ph* Harold Rosson *m* Herbert Stothart

Van Heflin, Ruth Hussey, Lionel Barrymore, Marjorie Main, Regis Toomey, Montagu Love, Porter Hall, Charles Dingle, J. Edward Bromberg

'Dieterle's customary high-minded, high-polished mélange of heavy touches and intelligent performances.'—*James Agee*

Tension
US 1950 91m bw
MGM (Robert Sisk)

A chemist plans the perfect murder of his wife's lover, loses his nerve, then finds himself suspected when the man is murdered after all.
Disappointing suspenser which starts well but outstays its welcome.

w Allen Rivkin *d* John Berry *ph* Harry Stradling *m* André Previn

Richard Basehart, Audrey Totter, Barry Sullivan, Cyd Charisse, Lloyd Gough, Tom d'Andrea

Tentacles
Italy 1976 102m Technicolor
Technovision
Esse Cinematografica (E. F. Doria)

A deadly menace which leaves its victims as skeletons washed up on the California beach turns out to be a giant octopus . . .
Dreary *Jaws* rehash. Sadly there is no element of spoofing, it's all deadly serious.

w Jerome Max, Tito Carpi, Steve Carabatsos, Sonia Molteni *d* Oliver Hellman (Sonia Assonitis) *ph* Roberto d'Ettore Piazzoli *m* S. W. Cipriani

Shelley Winters, John Huston, Bo Hopkins, Henry Fonda, Claude Akins, Cesare Danova, Delia Boccardo

Tenth Avenue Angel
US 1948 74m bw
MGM (Ralph Wheelwright)

The little daughter of poor parents loses her faith in life.
Icky sentimental piece for a waning child star.

w Angna Enters, Craig Rice, Harry Ruskin, Eleanore Griffin *d* Roy Rowland *ph* Robert Surtees *m* Rudolph G. Kopp

Margaret O'Brien, Angela Lansbury, George Murphy, Phyllis Thaxter, Rhys Williams, Warner Anderson, Audrey Totter, Connie Gilchrist

The Tenth Victim
Italy / France 1965 92m Technicolor
Avco / CC Champion / Concordia (Carlo Ponti)

In the 21st century murder is legalized to avoid birth control and war, and ten killings bring a fabulous prize.
Science fiction satire which just about gets by.

w Tonina Guerra, Giorgio Salvioni, Ennio Flaiano, Elio Petri, *story* The Seventh Victim by Robert Sheckley *d* Elio Petri *ph* Gianni di Venanzo *m* Piero Piccioni

Ursula Andress, Marcello Mastroianni, Elsa Martinelli, Massimo Serato

Teresa**
US 1951 101m bw
MGM (Arthur M. Loew)

A soldier with mother problems brings home an Italian bride.
Careful, sensitive, intelligent variation on a problem frequently considered by films of this period (*Frieda, Fräulein, Japanese War Bride*).

w Stewart Stern *d* Fred Zinnemann *ph* William J. Miller *m* Louis Applebaum

Pier Angeli, John Ericson, Patricia Collinge, Richard Bishop, Peggy Ann Garner, Ralph Meeker, Bill Mauldin

AAN: original story (Arthur Hayes, Stewart Stern)

Term of Trial*
GB 1962 130m bw
Romulus (James Woolf)

An unsuccessful schoolmaster is accused of rape by a nymphomaniac schoolgirl he has scorned.
Rather flabby 'adult' drama, too schematic to be really interesting despite the best that acting can do.

wd Peter Glenville, *novel* The Burden of Proof by James Barlow *ph* Oswald Morris *m* Jean-Michel Demase *ad* Antony Woolard

Laurence Olivier, Sarah Miles, Simone Signoret, Hugh Griffith, Terence Stamp, Roland Culver, Frank Pettingell, Thora Hird, Dudley Foster, Norman Bird

La Terra Trema*
Italy 1948   160m   bw
Universalia

The life of a Sicilian fisherman and his family. Seriously intended, carefully composed semi-documentary stressing the economic problems of the simple life. A commercial disaster: even the Italians couldn't understand the accents of the local actors.

wd Luchino Visconti *ph* G. R. Aldo *m* Luchino Visconti, Willy Ferrero

A Terrible Beauty
GB 1960   90m   bw
UA / Raymond Stross
US title: *Night Fighters*

In a north Irish village, the IRA revive their activities on the outbreak of World War II. Heavily Oirish melodrama with a muddled message.

w Robert Wright Campbell, *novel* Arthur Roth *d* Tay Garnett *ph* Stephen Dade *m* Cedric Thorpe Davie

Robert Mitchum, Anne Heywood, Dan O'Herlihy, Cyril Cusack, Richard Harris, Marianne Benet

The Terror
US 1928   82m approx   bw
Warner

A mysterious killer lurks in the cellars of a country house.
Primitive talkie which attempted a few new styles but showed that more were needed, also that some silent actors could not make the transfer.

w Harvey Gates, *novel* and *play* Edgar Wallace *d* Roy del Ruth

May McAvoy, Edward Everett Horton, Louise Fazenda, Alec B. Francis

'The only terrible thing about this talkie Terror is its unnatural slowness . . . the characters speak as if they were dictating important letters.'—*A. P. Herbert, Punch*
† *Return of the Terror* (US 1934) has little to do with it.

The Terror
US 1963   81m   Pathecolor
AIP / Filmgroup (Roger Corman, Francis Ford Coppola)

A baron lives for twenty years in a creepy castle, mourning the death of his wife . . .
Shoddy horror improvised over a weekend on the set of *The Raven*. It looks it.

w Leo Gordon, Jack Hill *d* Roger Corman *ph* John Nickolaus *m* Ronald Stein

Boris Karloff, Jack Nicholson, Sandra Knight, Dorothy Neumann

Terror in a Texas Town*
US 1958   81m   bw
UA / Frank N. Seltzer

A Swedish seaman arrives in a small western town and avenges the death of his brother. Stylish second feature western, a genuine sleeper which holds the interest throughout.

w Ben L. Perry *d* *Joseph H. Lewis* *ph* Ray Rennahan *m* Gerald Fried

Sterling Hayden, Sebastian Cabot, Carol Kelly, Eugene Martin, Ned Young

Terror in the Wax Museum
US 1973   94m   De Luxe
Bing Crosby Productions / Fenady Associates (Andrew J. Fenady)

In Victorian London a waxworks owner is murdered . . .
Cheaply produced murder mystery (even the waxworks can't stand still) with horror asides and a cast of elderly hams.

w Jameson Brewer *d* George Fenady *ph* William Jurgensen *m* George Duning

Ray Milland, Broderick Crawford, Elsa Lanchester, Louis Hayward, John Carradine, Shani Wallis, Maurice Evans, Patric Knowles

The Terror of the Tongs
GB 1960   79m   Technicolor
Hammer / Merlin

In 1910 Hong Kong a merchant avenges the death of his daughter at the hands of a villainous secret society.
Gory melodrama with dollops of screams, torture and vaguely orgiastic goings-on.

w Jimmy Sangster *d* Anthony Bushell *ph* Arthur Grant *m* James Bernard

Geoffrey Toone, Christopher Lee, Yvonne Monlaur, Brian Worth, Richard Leech

Tess of the Storm Country
US 1932   80m   bw
Fox

A retired sea captain's daughter loves the lord of the manor.
Antiquated tushery first filmed as a Mary Pickford silent.

w S. N. Behrman, Sonya Levien, Rupert Hughes, *novel* Grace Miller White *d* Alfred Santell *ph* Hal Mohr

Janet Gaynor, Charles Farrell, Dudley Digges, June Clyde, George Meeker

Test Pilot**
US 1938 118m bw
MGM (Louis D. Lighton)

A brilliant but unpredictable test pilot is helped by his wife and his self-sacrificing friend.
A big box-office star vehicle of its time, still interesting as a highly efficient product.

w Waldemar Young, Vincent Lawrence, *story* Frank Wead *d* Victor Fleming *ph* Ray June *m* Franz Waxman

Clark Gable, Myrna Loy, Spencer Tracy, Lionel Barrymore, Samuel S. Hinds, Marjorie Main, Gloria Holden

'The picture is so noisy with sure-fire elements—box office cast, violent excitement, glycerine tears and such—that it may be hard to keep the ear attuned to the quieter, more authentically human things in it.'—*James Shelley Hamilton*

AAN: best picture; Frank Wead

Le Testament d'Orphée*
France 1959 83m bw
Éditions Cinégraphiques (Jean Thullier)
aka: *The Testament of Orpheus*

The poet, an 18th-century man, dies, enters space time, is revived, and seeks his identity.
Rather like a melancholy madman's *Alice in Wonderland*, this bizarre jumble has its fascinations but misses by a mile the arresting qualities of *Orphée*.

wd Jean Cocteau *ph* Roland Pointoizeau *m* Georges Auric and others

Jean Cocteau, Edouard Dermithe, Maria Casarès, François Périer, Henri Crémieux, Yul Brynner, Jean-Pierre Léaud, Daniel Gélin, Jean Marais, Pablo Picasso, Charles Aznavour

The Testament of Dr Mabuse**
Germany 1933 122m bw
Nero

A sequel to *Dr Mabuse the Gambler*: the criminal mastermind dies in an asylum, and his assistant takes over his identity.
Fast-moving penny dreadful, alleged by its director to be a denouncing of the doctrines of Hitler, but showing little evidence of being more than a very slick entertainment.

w Thea Von Harbou, Fritz Lang *d* Fritz Lang *ph* Fritz Arno Wagner *ad* Karl Vollbrecht, Emil Hassler

Rudolf Klein-Rogge, Otto Wernicke, Gustav Diesl

† On arrival in America Lang claimed that 'slogans of the Third Reich have been put into the mouths of criminals in the film'. Yet his wife, who co-scripted it, stayed behind as a confirmed Nazi.

The Texan
US 1930 79m bw
Paramount

The Llano Kid absolves his bandit past.
Early sound western, an interesting curiosity.

w Daniel Nathan Rufin, *story* The Double-Dyed Deceiver by O. Henry *d* John Cromwell *ph* Victor Milner

Gary Cooper, Fay Wray, Emma Dunn, Oscar Apfel

The Texans
US 1938 92m bw
Paramount (Lucien Hubbard)

Problems of the post-Civil War years include new railroads, the Ku Klux Klan, and the new cattle drive routes.
Formula western with fairly well staged excitements backing a routine romantic triangle.

w Bertram Millhauser, Paul Sloane, William Wister Haines *d* James Hogan *ph* Theodor Sparkuhl *m* Gerard Carbonara

Joan Bennett, Randolph Scott, May Robson, Walter Brennan, Robert Cummings, Raymond Halton, Robert Barrat, Francis Ford

Texas
US 1941 94m bw (released in sepia)
Columbia (Sam Bischoff)

Two veteran Civil War southerners head for Texas to set up a cattle business.
Western vehicle for two young stars, now very ordinary-looking.

w Horace McCoy, Lewis Meltzer, Michael Blankfort *d* George Marshall *ph* George Meehan

William Holden, Glenn Ford, Claire Trevor, George Bancroft, Edgar Buchanan, Don Beddoe, Andrew Tombes, Addison Richards

Texas across the River
US 1966 101m Techniscope
Universal (Harry Keller)

A Texan, an Indian and a Spanish nobleman on
the run from jealous rivals have various
adventures.
Sloppy western which seems to have had jokes
added when someone realized it wasn't good
enough to be taken seriously.

w Wells Root, Harold Greene, Ben Starr
d Michael Gordon ph Russell Metty m Frank
de Vol md Joseph Gershenson

Dean Martin, Alain Delon, Joey Bishop,
Rosemary Forsyth, Tina Marquand, Peter
Graves, Andrew Prine, Michael Ansara

Texas Carnival
US 1951   77m   Technicolor
MGM (Jack Cummins)

A fairground showman is mistaken for a
millionaire and runs up debts.
Very thin comedy musical relying entirely on its
stars.

w Dorothy Kingsley d Charles Walters
ph Robert Planck m Harry Warren ly Dorothy
Fields ch Hermes Pan

Esther Williams, Red Skelton, Howard Keel,
Ann Miller, Paula Raymond, Keenan Wynn,
Tom Tully

Texas Lady
US 1955   85m   Technicolor   Superscope
RKO (Nat Holt)

A lady newspaper owner runs an anti-corruption
campaign.
Mild family western.

w Horace McCoy d Tim Whelan ph Ray
Rennahan m Paul Sawtell

Claudette Colbert, Barry Sullivan, Grey
Walcott, James Bell, Horace MacMahon, Ray
Collins, Walter Sande, Douglas Fowley

The Texas Rangers*
US 1936   95m   bw
Paramount (King Vidor)

Three wandering ne'er-do-wells break up; two
join the Texas Rangers and hunt down the third,
who is an outlaw.
Pleasantly remembered star western, later
remade as *The Streets of Laredo* (qv).

w Louis Stevens d King Vidor ph Edward
Cronjager

Fred MacMurray, Jack Oakie, Lloyd Nolan,
Jean Parker, Edward Ellis

Thank God It's Friday
US 1978   89m   Metrocolor
Columbia / Motown / Casablanca (Rob
Cohen)

Problems of a disc jockey in a Hollywood disco.
Routine youth programmer, rather like *Rock
Around the Clock* twenty years after.

w Barry Armyan Bernstein d Robert Klane
ph James Crabe pd Tom H. John m various

Valerie Landsburg, Terri Nunn, Chick Vennera,
Donna Summer, The Commodores

Thank You, Jeeves*
US 1936   57m   bw
TCF (Sol M. Wurtzel)

A valet helps prevent his master from becoming
involved in gun-running.
Competent second feature notable as Niven's
first leading role; also one of the very few
attempts to film Wodehouse.

w Joseph Hoffman, Stephen Gross, story P. G.
Wodehouse d Arthur Greville Collins
ph Barney McGill

David Niven, Arthur Treacher, Virginia Field,
Lester Matthews, Colin Tapley

Thank Your Lucky Stars***
US 1943   127m   bw
Warner (Mark Hellinger)

Eddie Cantor and his double get involved in
planning a patriotic show.
All-star wartime musical with some unexpected
turns and a generally funny script.

w Norman Panama, Melvin Frank, James V.
Kern d David Butler ph Arthur Edeson
md Leo F. Forbstein ch Le Roy Prinz
songs Frank Loesser, Arthur Schwartz

*Eddie Cantor, Dennis Morgan, Joan Leslie,
Edward Everett Horton, S. Z. Sakall,
Humphrey Bogart, Jack Carson, Bette Davis,
Olivia de Havilland, Errol Flynn, John Garfield,
Alan Hale, Ida Lupino, Ann Sheridan, Dinah
Shore, George Tobias, Spike Jones and his City
Slickers, Willie Best, Hattie McDaniel*

AAN: song 'They're Either Too Young or Too
Old'

Thanks a Million**
US 1935   87m   bw
TCF (Darryl F. Zanuck)

A crooner runs for governor.
Smart, amusing political musical.

w Nunnally Johnson d Roy del Ruth
ph Peverell Marley songs Arthur Johnston, Gus
Kahn

Dick Powell, Fred Allen, Ann Dvorak, Patsy
Kelly, Phil Baker, Paul Whiteman and his band,
the Yacht Club Boys, Benny Baker, Raymond
Walburn, Alan Dinehart

Thanks for the Memory*
US 1938 75m bw
Paramount

A smart novelist has trouble with his marriage.
Light, agreeable domestic comedy on familiar
lines.

w Lynn Starling, play Up Pops the Devil by
Frances Goodrich, Albert Hackett d George
Archainbaud

Bob Hope, Shirley Ross

Thark*
GB 1932 79m bw
British and Dominion (Herbert Wilcox)

The heir to an old mansion spends a night in it to
prove it is not haunted.
Very funny Aldwych farce, plainly transferred to
the screen with the original stage team intact.
One's only regret is that it peters out at the end.

w Ben Travers, from his play d Herbert Wilcox

Ralph Lynn, Tom Walls, Robertson Hare, Mary
Brough, Claude Hulbert, Gordon James

That Certain Age*
US 1938 95m bw
Universal (Joe Pasternak)

A girl gets a crush on an older man.
Pleasant, well-cast star musical for the family.

w Bruce Manning d Edward Ludwig ph Joseph
Valentine songs Jimmy McHugh, Harold
Adamson

Deanna Durbin, Melvyn Douglas, Jackie
Cooper, Irene Rich, Nancy Carroll, John
Halliday, Juanita Quigley, Jackie Searl, Charles
Coleman

AAN: song 'My Own'

That Certain Feeling
US 1956 102m Technicolor Vistavision
Paramount (Melvin Frank, Norman Panama)

An arrogant comic strip artist loses his touch
and hires a 'ghost'—the ex-husband of his
secretary/fiancée.
Arid comedy from a mild Broadway play, totally
miscast and lacking any kind of interest.

w Norman Panama, Melvin Frank, I. A. L.
Diamond, William Altman, play King of Hearts
by John Kerr, Eleanor Brooke d Norman
Panama, Melvin Frank ph Loyal Griggs
m Joseph J. Lilley

Bob Hope, George Sanders, Eva Marie Saint,
Pearl Bailey, Al Capp

That Certain Woman*
US 1937 91m bw
Warner (Hal B. Wallis)

A gangster's widow goes straight but runs into
complex marriage trouble.
Self-sacrifice and mother love are rewarded by
two convenient deaths and a happy ending in this
routine romantic melodrama remade from a
silent success.

wd Edmund Goulding, from his original screen
play The Trespasser ph Ernest Haller m Max
Steiner

Bette Davis, Henry Fonda, Ian Hunter, Anita
Louise, Donald Crisp, Katherine Alexander,
Mary Philips, Minor Watson

That Cold Day in the Park
Canada 1969 115m Eastmancolor
(Commonwealth United) Donald Factor /
    Robert Altman / Leon Mirrell

A spinster invites a lonely wandering boy into
her home, makes him a prisoner and becomes
possessively jealous.
A companion piece to The Collector, rather
better done for those who like morbid
psychology.

w Gillian Freeman, novel Richard Miles
d Robert Altman ph Laszlo Kovacs m Johnny
Mandel

Sandy Dennis, Michael Burns, Suzanne Benton,
Luana Anders, John Garfield Jnr
    'About as pretentious, loathsome and stupid
as a film can get.'—John Simon

That Darn Cat!*
US 1965 116m Technicolor
Walt Disney (Bill Walsh, Ron Miller)

A troublesome cat inadvertently helps to trail
bank robbers.
Overlong but generally pleasing small-town
comedy with well-paced sequences and a
fascinating feline hero.

w The Gordons, Bill Walsh, novel Undercover
Cat by the Gordons d Robert Stevenson
ph Edward Colman m Bob Brunner

Hayley Mills, Dean Jones, Dorothy Provine,
Roddy McDowall, Neville Brand, Elsa
Lanchester, William Demarest, Frank Gorshin,
Grayson Hall, Ed Wynn

That Forsyte Woman*
US 1949 114m Technicolor
MGM (Leon Gordon)
GB title: The Forsyte Saga

The wife of an Edwardian man of property falls
in love with her niece's fiancé.

Moderately successful American attempt to film the first part of a very British novel sequence; so genteel, however, that it becomes dull.

w Jan Lustig, Ivan Tors, James B. Williams, *novel* A Man of Property by John Galsworthy d Compton Bennett *ph* Joseph Ruttenberg m Bronislau Kaper

Greer Garson, *Errol Flynn*, Robert Young, Janet Leigh, Walter Pidgeon, Harry Davenport, Aubrey Mather

That Funny Feeling
US 1965   92m   Technicolor
U-I (Harry Keller)

A maid pretends she lives in her boss's apartment.
Makeshift romantic comedy which barely takes the attention even while it's on.

w David R. Schwarz d Richard Thorpe *ph* Clifford Stine m Joseph Gershenson

Sandra Dee, Bobby Darin, Donald O'Connor, Nita Talbot, Larry Storch, Leo G. Carroll, James Westerfield

That Girl from Paris
US 1936   105m   bw
RKO (Pandro S. Berman)

A Paris opera singer falls for a swing band leader and stows away on a transatlantic liner to be near him.
Comedy-accented musical romance: not bad but not memorable.

w P. J. Wolfson, Dorothy Yost, Jane Murfin d Leigh Jason *ph* J. Roy Hunt *md* Nathaniel Shilkret

Lily Pons, Gene Raymond, Jack Oakie, Herman Bing, Lucille Ball, Mischa Auer, Frank Jenks

That Hagen Girl
US 1947   83m   bw
Warner (Alex Gottlieb)

A girl is convinced she is the illegitimate daughter of her teacher.
Stale teenage drama with odd anti-establishment overtones.

w Charles Hoffman, *novel* Edith Kneipple Roberts d Peter Godfrey *ph* Karl Freund m Franz Waxman

Shirley Temple, Ronald Reagan, Rory Calhoun, Lois Maxwell, Dorothy Peterson, Charles Kemper, Conrad Janis, Harry Davenport

That Hamilton Woman **
US 1942   128m   bw
London Films (Alexander Korda)
GB title: *Lady Hamilton*

The affair of Lord Nelson and Emma Hamilton. Bowdlerized version of a famous misalliance; coldly made but quite effective scene by scene, with notable performances.

w Walter Reisch, R. C. Sherriff d Alexander Korda *ph* Rudolph Maté m Miklos Rozsa

Laurence Olivier, Vivien Leigh, Gladys Cooper, Alan Mowbray, Sara Allgood, Henry Wilcoxon, Halliwell Hobbes

AAN: Rudolph Maté

That Kind of Woman
US 1953   92m   bw
Paramount / Ponti–Girosi

World War II remake of *Shopworn Angel* (qv); rather well made but basically dated and dull.

w Walter Bernstein d Sidney Lumet *ph* Boris Kaufman m Daniele Amfitheatrof

Sophia Loren, Tab Hunter, George Sanders, Jack Warden, Barbara Nicholas, Keenan Wynn
   'The romantic reunion of Tab Hunter and Sophia Loren resembles nothing so much as a sea scout given a luxury liner for Christmas.'— *Peter John Dyer*

That Lady
GB 1955   100m   Eastmancolor
   Cinemascope
TCF / Atlanta (Sy Bartlett)

A noble widow at the court of Philip II of Spain loves a minister but incurs the king's jealous hatred.
Tepid historical romance which never flows as a film should.

w Anthony Veiller, Sy Bartlett, *novel* Kate O'Brien d Terence Young *ph* Robert Krasker m John Addison

Olivia de Havilland, Gilbert Roland, *Paul Scofield*, Françoise Rosay, Dennis Price, Anthony Dawson, Robert Harris, Peter Illing, Christopher Lee
   'Somehow, somewhere, one feels, something went very wrong.'—*MFB*

That Lady in Ermine
US 1948   89m   Technicolor
TCF (Ernst Lubitsch)

Two generations of European noblewomen learn to repel invaders.
Cheerless musical comedy which never gets started, what with the director dying during production and unsuitable stars lost in tinselly sets; the result can have appealed to no one.

w Samson Raphaelson d Ernst Lubitsch, Otto Preminger *ph* Leon Shamroy *songs* Leo Robin, Frederick Hollander

Betty Grable, Douglas Fairbanks Jnr, Cesar Romero, Walter Abel, Reginald Gardiner, Harry Davenport

AAN: song 'This Seems to be the Moment' (*m* Frederick Hollander, *ly* Leo Robin)

That Lucky Touch
GB 1975 93m Technicolor
Rank / Gloria (Dimitri de Grunwald)

During NATO war games in Brussels, a lady correspondent falls for an arms dealer.
Dim romantic farce which gives the impression of emanating from a dog-eared script written for the kind of stars who no longer shine.

w John Briley, *story* Moss Hart *d* Christopher Miles *ph* Douglas Slocombe *m* John Scott

Roger Moore, Susannah York, Lee J. Cobb, Shelley Winters, Jean-Pierre Cassel, Raf Vallone, Sydne Rome, Donald Sinden

That Man Bolt
US 1973 103m Technicolor
Universal (Bernard Schwarz)

Adventures of a professional black courier skilled in the martial arts.
Black Kung Fu hokum from a major company; tolerable of its debased kind.

w Quentin Werty, Charles Johnson *d* Henry Levin,
David Lowell Rich *ph* Gerald Perry Finnerman *m* Charles Bernstein

Fred Williamson, Bryon Webster, Miko Mayama, Teresa Graves
  'Gives every indication of having been devised by a computer fed with a variety of ingredients currently thought to guarantee box office success.'—*John Raisbeck, MFB*

That Man from Rio
France / Italy 1964 120m Eastmancolor
Ariane / Artistes Associés / Dear Film / Vides (Alexander Mnouchkine, Georges Danciger)
original title: *L'Homme de Rio*

An airforce pilot finds himself helping his girl friend in a worldwide search for stolen statuettes.
Elaborate mock thriller which is never quite as much fun as those involved seem to think. It provoked several inferior sequels.

w J. P. Rappeneau, Ariane Mnouchkine, Daniel Boulanger, Philippe de Broca *d* Philippe de Broca *ph* Edmond Séchan *m* Georges Delerue

Jean-Paul Belmondo, Jean Servais, Françoise Dorléac, Adolfo Celi, Simone Renant
  'Fantasy takes over, with Belmondo outdoing Fairbanks in agility, Lloyd in cliffhanging, and

Bond in indestructibility.'—*Brenda Davies, MFB*

AAN: script

That Midnight Kiss
US 1949 98m Technicolor
MGM (Joe Pasternak)

An unknown becomes a great singing star.
Simple-minded vehicle for the first appearance of Mario Lanza.

w Bruce Manning, Tamara Hovey *d* Norman Taurog *ph* Robert Surtees *m* Bronislau Kaper

Kathryn Grayson, Ethel Barrymore, Jose Iturbi, Mario Lanza, Keenan Wynn, J. Carrol Naish, Jules Munshin, Thomas Gomez, Marjorie Reynolds

That Night*
US 1957 88m bw
Galahad (Himan Brown)

An overwhelmed TV writer has a heart attack, and recovers after a series of medical setbacks.
Impressive minor case history, hardly entertainment but quite arresting.

w Robert Wallace, Burton J. Rowles *d* John Newland *ph* Maurice Hartzband *m* Mario Nascimbene

John Beal, Augusta Dabney, Shepperd Strudwick, Ralph Murphy

That Night in Rio*
US 1941 90m Technicolor
TCF (Fred Kohlmar)

A nightclub entertainer is paid to impersonate a lookalike count, but this causes complications with the countess.
Zippy musical based on a story first used in *Folies Bergère* (qv) and later in *On the Riviera* (qv).

w George Seaton, Bess Meredyth, Hal Long, *play* Rudolph Lothar, Hans Adler *d* Irving Cummings *ph* Leon Shamroy *songs* Mack Gordon, Harry Warren

Don Ameche, Alice Faye, Carmen Miranda, S. Z. Sakall,
J. Carrol Naish, Curt Bois, Leonid Kinskey, Maria Montez

That Obscure Object of Desire*
France / Spain 1978 103m Eastmancolor
Greenwich / Galaxie / In Cine (Serge Silberman)

A middle-aged gentleman suffers continual humiliations from the girl he loves.
Unrecognizable remake of a novel previously filmed as a vehicle for Dietrich and Bardot.

Despite the tricking out with surrealist touches (the girl is played by two different actresses) it is not one of Bunuel's best, and amuses only on the surface.

w Luis Bunuel, Jean-Claude Carrière, *novel* La Femme et le Pantin by Pierre Louys *d* Luis Bunuel *ph* Edmond Richard *m* from Richard Wagner

Fernando Rey, Carole Bouquet, Angela Molina, Julien Bertheau

That Riviera Touch
GB 1966   98m   Eastmancolor
Rank (Hugh Stewart)

Two tourists in the south of France get mixed up with jewel thieves.
Disappointing star comedy ending in a surfboard chase.

w S. C. Green, R. M. Hills, Peter Blackmore *d* Cliff Owen *ph* Otto Heller *m* Ron Goodwin

Eric Morecambe, Ernie Wise, Suzanne Lloyd, Paul Stassino, Armand Mestral

That Touch of Mink**
US 1962   99m   Eastmancolor
Panavision
U-I / Granley / Arwin / Nob Hill (Stanley Shapiro, Martin Melcher)

Bachelor tycoon pursues virginal secretary.
Jaded sex comedy (or what passed for it in nudge-nudge 1962) enlivened by practised star performances and smart timing.

w Stanley Shapiro, Nate Monaster *d* Delbert Mann *ph* Russell Metty *m* George Duning

Cary Grant, Doris Day, Gig Young, Audrey Meadows, Dick Sargent, *John Astin*

AAN: script

That Uncertain Feeling*
US 1941   84m   bw
Ernst Lubitsch

A wife with insomnia and hiccups befriends a wacky concert pianist who proceeds to move into her home.
Although Lubitsch had made this story before, as the silent *Kiss Me Again*, the elements didn't really jell in this version, which seemed silly rather than funny.

w Donald Ogden Stewart, Walter Reisch, *play* Divorçons by Victorien Sardou, Emile de Najac *d* Ernst Lubitsch *ph* George Barnes *m* Werner Heymann *pd* Alexander Golitzen

Merle Oberon, Melvyn Douglas, Burgess Meredith, Alan Mowbray, Olive Blakeney, Harry Davenport, Eve Arden, Sig Rumann

That Way With Women
US 1947   84m   bw
Warner (Charles Hoffman)

A millionaire amuses himself by playing Cupid to a young couple.
Routine remake of *The Millionaire*: just about watchable.

w Leo Townsend *d* Frederick de Cordova *ph* Ted McCord *m* Frederick Hollander

Sidney Greenstreet, Dane Clark, Martha Vickers, Alan Hale, Craig Stevens, Barbara Brown

That Woman Opposite
GB 1957   83m   bw
Monarch (William Gell)
US title: *City after Midnight*

In a small French town, a killer returns to silence a witness.
Slow-paced semi-mystery, reasonably well done.

wd Compton Bennett, *story* The Emperor's Snuff Box by John Dickson Carr *ph* Lionel Banes *m* Stanley Black

Phyllis Kirk, Dan O'Herlihy, Wilfrid Hyde White, Petula Clark, Jack Watling, William Franklyn, Margaret Withers

That Wonderful Urge
US 1948   82m   bw
TCF (Fred Kohlmar)

A newspaperman is forced into marriage with a publicity-shy heiress.
Tepid romantic comedy, a remake of *Love Is News* (qv).

w Jay Dratler *d* Robert B. Sinclair *ph* Charles Clarke *m* Cyril Mockridge

Gene Tierney, Tyrone Power, Reginald Gardiner, Arleen Whelan, Lucile Watson, Gene Lockhart, Porter Hall, Taylor Holmes

That'll Be the Day*
GB 1973   91m   Technicolor
EMI / Goodtimes (David Puttnam, Sanford Lieberson)

In 1958, a young drifter becomes a fairground worker, and eventually walks out on his wife and family to become a pop star.
Spirited return to British realism, with well-sketched cameos, a likeable dour viewpoint, and a cheerful pop music background.

w Ray Connolly *d* Claude Whatham *ph* Peter Suschitsky *md* Neil Aspinall, Keith Moon

David Essex, Ringo Starr, Rosemary Leach, James Booth, Billy Fury, Keith Moon, Rosalind Ayres

'As insubstantial as one of its own attempts at a statement.'—*Tony Rayns*

That's Entertainment**
US 1974   137m   Metrocolor   70mm
(blown up) / scope
MGM (Daniel Melnick, Jack Haley Jnr)

Fred Astaire, Gene Kelly, Elizabeth Taylor, James Stewart, Bing Crosby, Liza Minnelli, Donald O'Connor, Debbie Reynolds, Mickey Rooney and Frank Sinatra introduce highlights from MGM's musical past.
A slapdash compilation which was generally very big at the box office and obviously has fascinating sequences, though the narration is sloppily sentimental and the later wide-screen sequences let down the rest.

wd Jack Haley Jnr *ph* various *m* various

principal stars as above plus Judy Garland, Esther Williams, Eleanor Powell, Clark Gable, Ray Bolger
'While many ponder the future of MGM, none can deny that it has one hell of a past.'—*Variety*
'It is particularly gratifying to get the key sequences from certain movies without having to sit through a fatuous storyline.'—*Michael Billington, Illustrated London News*

That's Entertainment Part Two**
US 1976   133m   Metrocolor   70mm
(blown up) / scope
MGM (Saul Chaplin, Daniel Melnick)

More of the above, introduced by Fred Astaire and Gene Kelly, with comedy and drama sequences as well as musical.

d Gene Kelly *titles* Saul Bass *ph* various

principal stars as above plus Jeanette MacDonald, Nelson Eddy, the Marx Brothers, Laurel and Hardy, Jack Buchanan, Judy Garland, Ann Miller, Mickey Rooney, Oscar Levant, Louis Armstrong, etc.

That's My Boy
US 1951   98m   bw
Paramount / Hal B. Wallis (Cy Howard)

An athletic father tries to press his hypochondriac teenage son into the same mould. American college comedy of no international interest.

w Cy Howard *d* Hal Walker *ph* Lee Garmes *m* Leigh Harline

Dean Martin, Jerry Lewis, Eddie Mayehoff, Ruth Hussey, Polly Bergen, John McIntire

That's Right, You're Wrong*
US 1939   91m   bw
RKO (David Butler)

A band leader gets a Hollywood contract but is hated by the studio head.
Typical of the nonsense musicals featuring Kay Kyser and his radio Kollege of Musical Knowledge. The movie background and self-spoofing made this first attempt one of the best.

w William Conselman, James V. Kern *d* David Butler *ph* Russell Metty *songs* various

Kay Kyser, Adolphe Menjou, Lucille Ball, Dennis O'Keefe, May Robson, Edward Everett Horton, Ish Kabibble, Ginny Simms, Roscoe Karns, Moroni Olsen, Hobart Cavanaugh, Sheilah Graham, Hedda Hopper

Theatre of Blood*
GB 1973   102m   De Luxe
UA / Cineman (John Kohn, Stanley Mann)

A Shakespearean actor uses appropriate murder methods on the various critics who have ridiculed his performances.
Spoof horror picture which goes too far with some sick visuals; the idea and some of the performances are fine.

w Anthony Greville-Bell *d* Douglas Hickox *ph* Wolfgang Suschitzky *m* Michael J. Lewis *pd* Michael Seymour

Vincent Price, Diana Rigg, Ian Hendry, Harry Andrews, Coral Browne, Robert Coote, Jack Hawkins, Michael Hordern, Arthur Lowe, Robert Morley, Dennis Price, Diana Dors, Joan Hickson, Renée Asherson, Milo O'Shea, Eric Sykes

Them!***
US 1954   94m   bw
Warner (David Weisbart)

Atomic bomb radiation causes giant ants to breed in the New Mexico desert.
Among the first, and certainly the best, of the post-atomic monster animal cycle, this durable thriller starts with several eerie desert sequences and builds up to a shattering climax in the Los Angeles sewers. A general air of understatement helps a lot.

w Ted Sherdeman, *story* George Worthing Yates *d* Gordon Douglas *ph* Sid Hickox *m* Bronislau Kaper

Edmund Gwenn, James Whitmore, Joan Weldon, James Arness, Onslow Stevens
'I asked the editor: How does it look? And he said: Fine. I said: Does it look honest? He said: As honest as twelve foot ants can look.'—*Gordon Douglas*

Theodora Goes Wild*
US 1936   94m   bw
Columbia (Everett Riskin)

A small-town girl writes a titillating bestseller.
Mildly crazy comedy which helped develop the
trend for stars performing undignified antics but
today seems rather slow and dated.

w *Sidney Buchman, story* Mary McCarthy
d Richard Boleslawski ph Joseph Walker
m Morris Stoloff

Irene Dunne, Melvyn Douglas, Thomas
Mitchell, Thurston Hall, Rosalind Keith, Spring
Byington, Elizabeth Risdon, Nana Bryant

There Goes My Heart
US 1938   91m   bw
Hal Roach

A reporter is assigned to track down a runaway
heiress.
Very pale imitation of *It Happened One Night.*

w Jack Jevne, Eddie Moran d Norman Z.
McLeod ph Norbert Brodine m Marvin Hatley

Fredric March, Virginia Bruce, Patsy Kelly,
Nancy Carroll, Eugene Pallette, Claude
Gillingwater, Arthur Lake, Harry Langdon,
Etienne Girardot

AAN: Marvin Hatley

There Was a Crooked Man*
GB 1960   107m   bw
UA / Knightsbridge (John Bryan)

An ex-safecracker outwits the crooked mayor of
an industrial town.
Semi-happy attempt to humanize a knockabout
clown; good supporting performances and
production.

w Reuben Ship d Stuart Burge ph Arthur
Ibbetson m Kenneth V. Jones

Norman Wisdom, Andrew Cruickshank, Alfred
Marks, Susannah York, Reginald Beckwith

There Was a Crooked Man*
US 1970   126m   Technicolor   Panavision
Warner Seven Arts (Joseph L. Mankiewicz)

In 1883 Arizona a murderer tries to escape from
jail and recover hidden loot but is constantly
thwarted by the sheriff who arrested him, now a
warden.
Curious black comedy melodrama with lots of
talent going nowhere in particular; hard to
endure as a whole but with entertaining scenes.

w David Newman, Robert Benton d Joseph L.
Mankiewicz ph Harry Stradling Jnr m Charles
Strouse ad Edward Carrere

Kirk Douglas, Henry Fonda, Hume Cronyn,
Warren Oates, Burgess Meredith, John
Randolph, Arthur O'Connell, Martin Gabel,
Alan Hale

There's a Girl in My Soup*
GB 1970   96m   Eastmancolor
Columbia / Ascot (John Boulting)

A randy TV personality finds himself outplotted
by a waif he picks up.
Flimsy screen version of a long-running sex
comedy; some laughs, but the star is
uncomfortably miscast.

w Terence Frisby, from his play d Roy Boulting
ph Harry Waxman m Mike D'Abo

Peter Sellers, Goldie Hawn, Tony Britton, Nicky
Henson, John Comer, Diana Dors, Judy
Campbell

There's Always Tomorrow
US 1956   84m   bw
Universal (Ross Hunter)

A married man falls for another woman.
Very flat variation on *Brief Encounter*, with stars
going through mechanical paces.

w Bernard Schoenfeld, *story* Ursula Parrott
d Douglas Sirk ph Russell Metty m Herman
Stein, Heinz Roemheld

Barbara Stanwyck, Fred MacMurray, Joan
Bennett, Pat Crowley, William Reynolds, Gigi
Perreau, Jane Darwell

There's No Business like Show Business**
US 1954   117m   De Luxe   Cinemascope
TCF (Sol C. Siegel)

The life and times of a family of vaudevillians.
Mainly entertaining events and marvellous tunes
make up this very Cinemascoped musical, in
which the screen is usually filled with six people
side by side.

w Phoebe and Henry Ephron d *Walter Lang*
ph Leon Shamroy m/ly Irving Berlin ad John
de Cuir, Lyle Wheeler m Lionel Newman,
Alfred Newman

*Ethel Merman, Dan Dailey, Marilyn Monroe,
Donald O'Connor,* Johnny Ray, Mitzi Gaynor,
Hugh O'Brian, Frank McHugh

AAN: original story (Lamar Trotti); Lionel
Newman, Alfred Newman

These Dangerous Years
GB 1957   92m   bw
British Lion / Anna Neagle

A Liverpool teenage gang leader is called up and
becomes a better guy.

Dim drama with music marking the debut of a
singing star.

w John Trevor Story *d* Herbert Wilcox
ph Gordon Dines *m* Stanley Black

Frankie Vaughan, George Baker, Carole Lesley,
Jackie Lane, Katherine Kath, Eddie Byrne,
Kenneth Cope

These Thousand Hills
US 1958 96m Eastmancolor
  Cinemascope
TCF (David Weisbart)

A successful cattle rancher finds that his best
friend is a rustler.
Large-scale but somehow unimpressive western
variant on *The Virginian*, cluttered with sub-
plots.

w Alfred Hayes, *novel* A. B. Guthrie Jnr
d Richard Fleischer *ph* Charles G. Clarke
m Leigh Harline

Richard Egan, Stuart Whitman, Don Murray,
Lee Remick, Albert Dekker, Harold J. Stone,
Patricia Owens

These Three**
US 1936 93m bw
Samuel Goldwyn

A lying schoolgirl accuses two schoolmistresses
of scandalous behaviour.
Bowdlerized version of a famous play (instead of
lesbianism we have extra-marital affairs). It
worked well enough at the time but now seems
dated; oddly enough when the play was filmed
full strength in 1962 it didn't work at all.

w Lillian Hellman, from her play *The Children's
Hour* *d* William Wyler *ph* Gregg Toland
m Alfred Newman

Merle Oberon, Miriam Hopkins, Joel McCrea,
Bonita Granville, Catherine Doucet, Alma
Kruger, Marcia Mae Jones, Margaret Hamilton,
Walter Brennan

AAN: Bonita Granville

These Wilder Years
US 1956 91m bw
MGM (Jules Schermer)

A wealthy industrialist returns to his home town
to trace his illegitimate son.
Modest sentimental drama with practised stars.

w Frank Fenton *d* Roy Rowland *ph* George
Folsey *m* Jeff Alexander

James Cagney, Barbara Stanwyck, Walter
Pidgeon, Betty Lou Keim, Don Dubbins,
Edward Andrews

They All Kissed the Bride
US 1942 86m bw
Columbia (Edward Kaufman)

A woman executive falls in love with the
crusading writer who is out to expose working
conditions in her company.
No surprises are expected or provided in this
very ho-hum romantic comedy.

w P. J. Wolfson *d* Alexander Hall *ph* Joseph
Walker *md* Morris Stoloff

Joan Crawford, Melvyn Douglas, Roland
Young, Billie Burke, Allen Jenkins, Andrew
Tombes, Helen Parrish, Mary Treen

AAN: Joan Crawford

They Call Me Mister Tibbs!
US 1970 108m De Luxe
UA / Mirisch (Herbert Hirshman)

A San Francisco police lieutenant suspects a
crusading local minister of murder.
Flat, dispirited police melodrama with irrelevant
domestic asides, a long way after *In the Heat of
the Night* which introduced the main character.
(*The Organization* was the third and last in the
so-called series.)

w Alan R. Trustman, James R. Webb *d* Gordon
Douglas *ph* Gerald Finnerman *m* Quincy Jones

Sidney Poitier, Martin Landau, Barbara
McNair, Anthony Zerbe, Jeff Corey, Juano
Hernandez, Ed Asner

They Came to a City*
GB 1944 77m bw
Ealing (Sidney Cole)

Assorted people find themselves outside the
gates of a mysterious city.
The *Outward Bound* format applied to post-war
reconstruction, with characters deciding what
kind of a world they want. Good talk and good
acting, but not quite cinema.

w Basil Dearden, Sidney Cole, *play J. B.
Priestley* *d* Basil Dearden

Googie Withers, John Clements, Raymond
Huntley, Renée Gadd, A. E. Matthews, Mabel
Terry-Lewis, *Ada Reeve*, Norman Shelley,
Frances Rowe

They Came to Cordura*
US 1959 123m Technicolor
  Cinemascope
Columbia / Goetz–Baroda (William Goetz)

In 1916 Mexico, six American military heroes
are recalled to base, but the hardships of the
journey reveal their true colours.

Watchable adventure epic, not so arresting as was intended but quite professional.

w Ivan Moffat, Robert Rossen, *novel* Glendon Swarthout d Robert Rossen ph Burnett Guffey m Elie Siegmeister

Gary Cooper, Rita Hayworth, Van Heflin, Richard Conte, Tab Hunter, Michael Callan, Dick York, Robert Keith

They Came to Rob Las Vegas*

Spain / France / Germany / Italy 1969 128m Techniscope
Warner / Isasi / Capitoli / Eichberg / Franca

Criminals ambush a security truck in the Nevada desert.
Long-winded, flashily directed, gleamingly photographed, occasionally lively, frequently violent, finally tedious caper melodrama with a multi-lingual cast.

w Anthony Isasi, Jo Eisinger d Anthony Isasi ph *Juan Gelpi* m Georges Gavarentz

Jack Palance, Lee J. Cobb, Elke Sommer, Gary Lockwood, Georges Geret, Jean Servais

They Dare Not Love

US 1941 76m bw
Columbia (Sam Bischoff)

An Austrian prince flees the Nazis, but they force him to return and he has to leave his fiancée in America.
Curiously naïve romantic propaganda from this director; not at all memorable.

w Charles Bennett, Ernest Vajda d James Whale ph Franz Planer m Morris Stoloff

George Brent, Martha Scott, Paul Lukas, Egon Brecher, Roman Bohnen, Edgar Barrier, Frank Reicher

They Died with Their Boots On**

US 1941 140m bw
Warner (Robert Fellows)

The life of General Custer and his death at Little Big Horn.
It seems it all happened because of an evil cadet who finished up selling guns to the Indians. Oh, well! The first half is romantic comedy, the second steels itself for the inevitable tragic outcome, but it's all expertly mounted and played in the best old Hollywood style.

w Wally Kline, Aeneas Mackenzie d Raoul Walsh ph Bert Glennon m Max Steiner

Errol Flynn, Olivia de Havilland, Arthur Kennedy, Charles Grapewin, Anthony Quinn, Sidney Greenstreet, Gene Lockhart, Stanley Ridges, John Litel, Walter Hampden, Regis Toomey, Hattie McDaniel

They Drive by Night**

GB 1938 84m bw
Warner (Jerome Jackson)

An ex-convict is helped by lorry drivers to solve the silk stocking murders of which he is suspected.
Excellent, little-seen British suspenser of the Hitchcock school.

w Derek Twist, *novel* James Curtis d Arthur Woods

Emlyn Williams, Ernest Thesiger, Anna Konstam, Allan Jeayes, Antony Holles, Ronald Shiner
  'Dialogue, acting and direction put this picture on a level with the French cinema.'—*Graham Greene*

They Drive by Night**

US 1940 97m bw
Warner (Mark Hellinger)
GB title: *The Road to Frisco*

A truck driver loses his brother in an accident, and in an attempt to improve his lot becomes involved with a scheming murderess.
Solid melodramatic entertainment which borrows the second half of its plot from *Bordertown*.

w Jerry Wald, Richard Macaulay, *novel* Long Haul by A. I. Bezzerides d Raoul Walsh md Adolph Deutsch

George Raft, Humphrey Bogart, *Ann Sheridan, Ida Lupino*, Gale Page, Alan Hale, Roscoe Karns, John Litel, Henry O'Neill, George Tobias

They Flew Alone*

GB 1941 103m bw
RKO / Imperator (Herbert Wilcox)
US title: *Wings and the Woman*

The story of Amy Johnson and Jim Mollison, married flying pioneers of the thirties.
Adequate fictionalized history with interesting historical detail.

w Miles Malleson d Herbert Wilcox

Anna Neagle, Robert Newton, Edward Chapman, Nora Swinburne, Joan Kemp-Welch, Charles Carson, Brefni O'Rourke

They Gave Him a Gun

US 1937 94m bw
MGM (Harry Rapf)

Despite the efforts of his friend, a war-hardened veteran turns to crime and comes to a sticky end.
Dullish moral melodrama with its stars looking as though stuck in glue.

w Cyril Hume, Richard Maibaum, Maurice Rapf,
novel William Joyce Cowan *d* W. S. Van Dyke II *ph* Harold Rosson

Spencer Tracy, Franchot Tone, Gladys George, Edgar Dearing, Mary Treen, Cliff Edwards

They Got Me Covered**
US 1943 93m bw
Samuel Goldwyn

An incompetent foreign correspondent inadvertently breaks up a spy ring in Washington.
One of Hope's better and most typical comedy-thriller vehicles.

w Harry Kurnitz *d* David Butler *ph* Rudolph Maté *m* Leigh Harline

Bob Hope, Dorothy Lamour, Otto Preminger, Lenore Aubert, Eduardo Ciannelli, Marion Martin, Donald Meek, Donald MacBride, Walter Catlett, John Abbott, Florence Bates, Philip Ahn

They Knew What They Wanted**
US 1940 96m bw
RKO (Erich Pommer)

A waitress agrees by mail to marry a California-Italian vineyard owner, but is aghast when she arrives to discover that he sent his handsome foreman's photograph.
First-rate minor drama, expertly handled by stars and production team alike.

w Robert Ardrey, *play* Sidney Howard *d* Garson Kanin *ph* Harry Stradling *m* Alfred Newman

Charles Laughton, Carole Lombard, William Gargan, Harry Carey, Frank Fay
'For dialogue, acting, background and film creation it's a honey.'—*Otis Ferguson*

AAN: William Gargan

They Live by Night*
US 1948 96m bw
RKO

A young man imprisoned for an accidental killing escapes with two hardened criminals and is forced to take part in their crimes.
Well-made if basically uninteresting melodrama with a draggy romantic interest; its 'realistic' yet impressionist style drew attention on its first release, and it was remade in the seventies as *Thieves like Us* (qv).

w Charles Schnee *d* Nicholas Ray *ph* George E. Diskant

Farley Granger, Cathy O'Donnell, Howard da Silva

They Made Me a Criminal*
US 1939 92m bw
Warner (Benjamin Glazer)

When he thinks he has killed a boxing opponent, a young man flees to the west and settles on a farm.
Competent remake of *The Life of Jimmy Dolan*, a tribute to the American way.

w Sig Herzig *d* Busby Berkeley *ph* James Wong Howe

John Garfield, Claude Rains, Gloria Dickson, May Robson, Billy Halop, Bobby Jordan, Leo Gorcey, Huntz Hall, Gabriel Dell, Ann Sheridan

They Made Me a Fugitive*
GB 1947 104m bw
Warner / Alliance (Nat Bransten, James Carter)
US title: *I Became a Criminal*

An ex-RAF pilot is drawn into black marketeering. Framed for a killing, he escapes from Dartmoor and takes revenge on the gang leader.
Deliberately squalid thriller which began a fashion for British realism, but now seems only momentarily entertaining.

w Noel Langley, *novel* A Convict Has Escaped by Jackson Budd *d* Alberto Cavalcanti *ph* Otto Heller

Trevor Howard, Sally Gray, *Griffith Jones*, René Ray, Mary Merrall, Vida Hope, Ballard Berkeley, Phyllis Robins

They Met in Bombay*
US 1941 86m bw
MGM (Hunt Stromberg)

Jewel thieves on the run in the East fall in love.
A rather unusual romantic comedy chase which provides pretty satisfactory star entertainment.

w Edwin Justus Mayer, Anita Loos, Leon Gordon *d* Clarence Brown *ph* William Daniels *m* Herbert Stothart

Clark Gable, Rosalind Russell, Peter Lorre, Reginald Owen, Jessie Ralph, Matthew Boulton, Eduardo Ciannelli, Luis Alberni

They Might be Giants*
US 1972 88m Technicolor
Universal / Paul Newman, John Foreman

A lawyer imagines he is Sherlock Holmes, and is taken in hand by Dr Mildred Watson.
Curious fantasy comedy which rather

tentatively satirizes modern life and the need to retreat into unreality. Mildly pleasing entertainment for intellectuals.

w James Goldman, from his play *d* Anthony Harvey *ph* Victor Kemper *m* John Barry

George C. Scott, Joanne Woodward, Jack Gilford, Lester Rawlins

They Only Kill Their Masters*
US 1972 98m Metrocolor
MGM (William Belasco)

A village police chief doggedly solves a series of murders.
Atmospheric, serio-comic murder mystery with a cast of old hands.

w Lane Slate *d* James Goldstone *ph* Michel Hugo *m* Perry Botkin Jnr

James Garner, Katharine Ross, Hal Holbrook, June Allyson, Harry Guardino, Tom Ewell, Peter Lawford, Ann Rutherford, Chris Connelly, Edmond O'Brien, Art Metrano, Arthur O'Connell

They Shall Have Music
US 1939 105m bw
Samuel Goldwyn
GB title: *Melody of Youth*

Jascha Heifetz conducts a charity concert to help a music school for slum children.
Formula family film given the best possible production.

w John Howard Lawson, Irmgard Von Cube *d* Archie Mayo *ph* Gregg Toland *md* Alfred Newman

Joel McCrea, Jascha Heifetz, Andrea Leeds, Gene Reynolds, Walter Brennan, Porter Hall, Terry Kilburn, Diana Lynn (Dolly Loehr)

AAN: Alfred Newman

They Shoot Horses, Don't They?*
US 1969 129m De Luxe Panavision
Palomar / Chartoff–Winkler–Pollack

Tragedy during a six-day marathon dance contest in the early thirties.
An unrelievedly harrowing melodrama about dreary people, confused by 'flashforwards' but full of skilled technique, entertaining detail, and one brilliant performance.

w James Poe, Robert E. Thompson, *novel* Horace McCoy *d* Sydney Pollack *ph* Philip Lathrop *m* John Green *md* John Green, Albert Woodbury *pd* Harry Horner

Gig Young, Jane Fonda, Susannah York, Michael Sarrazin, Red Buttons, Bonnie Bedelia, Bruce Dern

AAN: script; John Green, Albert Woodbury; Sydney Pollack; Jane Fonda; Susannah York

They Were Expendable*
US 1945 135m bw
MGM (John Ford, Cliff Reid)

Life in and around motor torpedo boats in the Pacific War.
Long drawn out flagwaver with some nice moments.

w Frank Wead, *book* William L. White *d* John Ford *ph* Joseph H. August *m* Herbert Stothart

John Wayne, Robert Montgomery, Donna Reed, Jack Holt, Ward Bond, Marshall Thompson, Leon Ames, Cameron Mitchell, Jeff York

They Were Not Divided*
GB 1951 102m bw
Rank / Two Cities (Earl St John)

The life of a Guards officer is paralleled with that of his American friend; they both die on a reconnaissance during the advance on Berlin.
Odd mixture of barrack room comedy, semi-documentary action, propaganda and the most appalling sentimentality. No one questioned it at the box office, though.

wd Terence Young *ph* Harry Waxman *m* Lambert Williamson

Edward Underdown, Ralph Clanton, Helen Cherry, Stella Andrews, Michael Brennan, Michael Trubshaw, R.S.M. Brittain

'It is a rather curious experience to see a film made with all the best trappings of realism containing so many of the clichés of the studio.'—*Gavin Lambert*

They Were Sisters
GB 1945 115m bw
GFD / Gainsborough (Harold Huth)

The problems of three married sisters.
Flatly handled multi-melodrama, the chief attraction being 'wicked' James Mason as a sadist.

w Roland Pertwee, *novel* Dorothy Whipple *d* Arthur Crabtree *ph* Jack Cox *m* Louis Levy

James Mason, Phyllis Calvert, Dulcie Gray, Hugh Sinclair, Anne Crawford, Peter Murray Hill, Pamela Kellino

They Who Dare
GB 1953 107m Technicolor
British Lion / Mayflower

During World War II a group of British soldiers are sent on a raiding expedition to Rhodes.

Grimmish war actioner with plenty of noise but not much holding power.

w Robert Westerby *d* Lewis Milestone *ph* Wilkie Cooper *m* Robert Gill

Dirk Bogarde, Denholm Elliott, Akim Tamiroff, Gerard Oury, Eric Pohlmann, Alec Mango

They Won't Believe Me *
US 1947 95m bw
RKO (Joan Harrison)

A playboy finds himself on trial for murder because of his philandering with three women.
Unusual suspenser with Hitchcock touches; quite neatly packaged, complete with twist ending.

w Jonathan Latimer *d* Irving Pichel *ph* Harry J. Wild *m* Roy Webb

Robert Young, Susan Hayward, Rita Johnson, Jane Greer, Tom Powers, Don Beddoe, Frank Ferguson

They Won't Forget ***
US 1937 94m bw
Warner (Mervyn Le Roy)

The murder of a girl in a southern town leads to a lynching.
Finely detailed social drama, a classic of American realism; harrowing to watch.

w Robert Rossen, Aben Kandel, *novel* Death in the Deep South by Ward Greene *d* Mervyn Le Roy *ph* Arthur Edeson, Warren Lynch *m* Adolph Deutsch *md* Leo F. Forbstein

Claude Rains, Gloria Dickson, Edward Norris, Otto Kruger, Allyn Joslyn, Linda Perry, Elisha Cook Jnr, Lana Turner, Cy Kendall, Elizabeth Risdon

'Not only an honest picture, but an example of real movie-making.'—*Pare Lorenz*

The Thief *
US 1952 86m bw
Harry M. Popkin (Clarence Greene)

A nuclear physicist is on the run from the FBI, who suspect him of being a spy.
Curious attempt to produce a thriller with no dialogue whatever; parts are well done, but the strain eventually shows, as the makers are not quite clever enough to flesh out the trickery with human interest.

w Clarence Greene, Russel Rouse *d* Russel Rouse *ph* Sam Leavitt *m* Herschel Gilbert

Ray Milland, Martin Gabel, Rita Gam, Harry Bronson, John McKutcheon

AAN: Herschel Gilbert

The Thief of Baghdad ****
GB 1940 109m Technicolor
London Films (Alexander Korda)

A boy thief helps a deposed king thwart an evil usurper.
Marvellous blend of magic, action and music, the only film to catch on celluloid the overpowering atmosphere of the Arabian Nights.

w Miles Malleson, Lajos Biro *d* Michael Powell, Ludwig Berger, Tim Whelan *ph* Georges Périnal, Osmond Borradaile *m* Miklos Rozsa *sp* Lawrence Butler

Conrad Veidt, Sabu, John Justin, June Duprez, Morton Selten, Miles Malleson, Rex Ingram, Mary Morris

'The true stuff of fairy tale.'—*Basil Wright*
'Both spectacular and highly inventive.'—*NFT, 1969*

AA: Georges Périnal, Osmond Borradaile
AAN: Miklos Rozsa

Thief of Damascus
US 1952 78m Technicolor
Columbia / Sam Katzman

The wicked ruler of Damascus is deposed by his own general, in league with Sinbad, Aladdin, and Scheherezade.
Mindless bosh, interesting only for its liberal use of scenes from *Joan of Arc*; the mind boggles at the costume compromise.

w Robert E. Kent *d* Will Jason *ph* Ellis W. Carter *m* Mischa Bakaleinikoff

Paul Henreid, Lon Chaney Jnr, Jeff Donnell, John Sutton, Elena Verdugo

The Thief Who Came to Dinner
US 1973 105m De Luxe
Warner / Tandem (Bud Yorkin)

A computer analyst determines to become a jewel thief.
Tedious comedy aping the *Raffles* school but saddled with a complex plot and listless script.

w Walter Hill, *novel* Terence L. Smith *d* Bud Yorkin *ph* Philip Lathrop *m* Henry Mancini

Ryan O'Neal, Jacqueline Bisset, Warren Oates, Jill Clayburgh, Charles Cioffi

Thieves' Highway **
US 1949 94m bw
TCF (Robert Bassler)

A truck driver tracks down the racketeers who cheated and maimed his father.
Glossy, highly professional thick ear shedding a convincing light into one of America's less salubrious corners.

w A. I. Bezzerides, from his novel Thieves' Market *d Jules Dassin ph Norbert Brodine m* Alfred Newman

Richard Conte, Valentina Cortesa, Lee J. Cobb, Jack Oakie, Millard Mitchell, Joseph Pevney, Barbara Lawrence, Hope Emerson

Thin Ice*
US 1937 78m bw
TCF (Raymond Griffith)
GB title: *Lovely to Look At*

A skating instructress at an Alpine resort falls in love with a visiting prince.
Light-hearted musical vehicle for Hollywood's newest novelty – a skating star.

w Boris Ingster, Milton Sperling, *novel* Der Komet by Attila Orbok *d* Sidney Lanfield *ph* Robert Planck, Edward Cronjager *md* Louis Silvers

Sonja Henie, Tyrone Power, Arthur Treacher, Raymond Walburn, Joan Davis, Sig Rumann, Alan Hale, Melville Cooper

The Thin Man****
US 1934 93m bw
MGM (Hunt Stromberg)

In New York over Christmas, a tipsy detective with his wife and dog solves the murder of an eccentric inventor.
Fast-moving, alternately comic and suspenseful mystery drama developed in brief scenes and fast wipes. It set a sparkling comedy career for two stars previously known for heavy drama, it was frequently imitated, and it showed a wisecracking, affectionate married relationship almost for the first time.

w Frances Goodrich, Albert Hackett, novel Dashiell Hammett d W. S. Van Dyke ph James Wong Howe *m* William Axt

William Powell, Myrna Loy, Maureen O'Sullivan, Nat Pendleton, Minna Gombell, Edward Ellis, Porter Hall, Henry Wadsworth, William Henry, Harold Huber, Cesar Romero, Edward Brophy

'A strange mixture of excitement, quips and hard-boiled sentiment . . . full of the special touches that can come from nowhere but the studio, that really make the feet a movie walks on.'—*Otis Ferguson*
† Sequels, on the whole of descending merit, included the following, all made at MGM with the same star duo: 1936: *After the Thin Man* (110m). 1939: *Another Thin Man* (102m). 1941: *Shadow of the Thin Man* (97m). 1944: *The Thin Man Goes Home* (100m). 1947: *Song of the Thin Man* (86m).

AAN: best picture; script; W. S. Van Dyke; William Powell

The Thin Red Line
US 1964 99m bw Cinemascope
Security / ACE (Sidney Harmon)

Raw recruits land on Guadalcanal and most of them are killed.
Weary, routine, realistic war drama.

w Bernard Gordon, *novel* James Jones *d* Andrew Marton *ph* Manuel Berenguer *m* Malcolm Arnold

Keir Dullea, Jack Warden, James Philbrook, Kieron Moore

The Thing from Another World**
US 1951 87m bw
RKO / Winchester (Howard Hawks)

A US scientific expedition in the Arctic is menaced by a ferocious being they inadvertently thaw out from a spaceship.
Curiously drab suspense shocker mainly set in corridors, with insufficient surprises to sustain its length. It does, however, contain the first space monster on film, and is quite nimbly made, though it fails to use the central gimmick from its original story.

w Charles Lederer, *story* Who Goes There by J. W. Campbell Jnr *d* Christian Nyby (with mysterious help, either Hawks or Orson Welles) *ph* Russell Harlan *m* Dmitri Tiomkin

Robert Cornthwaite, Kenneth Tobey, Margaret Sheridan, Bill Self, Dewey Martin, James Arness (as the thing)

'There seems little point in creating a monster of such original characteristics if he is to be allowed only to prowl about the North Pole, waiting to be destroyed by the superior ingenuity of the US Air Force.'—*Penelope Houston*
'A monster movie with pace, humour and a collection of beautifully timed jabs of pure horror.'—*NFT, 1967*

Things to Come****
GB 1936 113m bw
London Films (Alexander Korda)

War in 1940 is followed by plague, rebellion, a new glass-based society, and the first rocketship to the moon.
Fascinating, chilling and dynamically well-staged vignettes tracing mankind's future. Bits of the script and acting may be wobbly, but the sets and music are magnificent, the first part of the prophecy chillingly accurate, and the whole mammoth undertaking almost unique in film history.

w H. G. Wells, from his book The Shape of
Things to Come *d/pd William Cameron
Menzies ph Georges Périnal m Arthur Bliss
sp Harry Zech, Ned Mann ad Vincent Korda*

Raymond Massey, Edward Chapman, Ralph
Richardson, Margaretta Scott, Cedric
Hardwicke, Sophie Stewart, Derrick de Marney,
John Clements

    'An amazingly ingenious technical
accomplishment, even if it does hold out small
hope for our race . . . the existence pictured is as
joyless as a squeezed grapefruit.'—*Don Herold*

    'A leviathan among films . . . a stupendous
spectacle, an overwhelming, Dorean, Jules
Vernesque, elaborated *Metropolis,* staggering to
eye, mind and spirit, the like of which has never
been seen and never will be seen again.'—*The
Sunday Times*

The Third Day
US 1965   119m   Technicolor   Panavision
Warner (Jack Smight)

An amnesiac learns that he is a rich unpopular
tycoon facing a major crisis.
Glum melodrama which suggests domestic
mystery but provides only interminable chat.

w Burton Wohl, Robert Presnell Jnr, *novel*
Joseph Hayes *d* Jack Smight *ph* Robert
Surtees *m* Percy Faith

George Peppard, Elizabeth Ashley, Roddy
McDowall, Herbert Marshall, Mona
Washbourne, Robert Webber, Charles Drake,
Sally Kellerman, Arte Johnson, Vincent
Gardenia

Third Finger Left Hand
US 1940   96m   bw
MGM (John W. Considine Jnr)

A lady fashion editor fends off unwanted suitors
by saying she is already married, but a
commercial artist trumps this card by claiming
to be the long lost husband of her invention.
Cheerful but overstretched romantic comedy.

w Lionel Houser *d* Robert Z. Leonard
ph George Folsey *m* David Snell

Myrna Loy, Melvyn Douglas, Lee Bowman,
Bonita Granville, Raymond Walburn, Felix
Bressart, Sidney Blackmer

The Third Man**
GB 1949   100m   bw
British Lion / London Films / David O.
    Selznick / Alexander Korda (Carol Reed)

An unintelligent but tenacious writer of westerns
arrives in post-war Vienna to join his old friend
Harry Lime, who seems to have met with an
accident . . . or has he?

Totally memorable and irresistible romantic
thriller. Stylish from the first to the last, with
inimitable backgrounds of zither music and war-
torn buildings pointing up a then-topical black
market story full of cynical characters but not
without humour. Hitchcock with feeling, if you
like.

*w Graham Greene d Carol Reed ph Robert
Krasker m Anton Karas*

*Joseph Cotten, Trevor Howard, Alida Valli,
Orson Welles, Bernard Lee, Wilfrid Hyde
White,* Ernst Deutsch, Siegfried Breuer, Erich
Ponto, Paul Hoerbiger

    'Sensitive and humane and dedicated, [Reed]
would seem to be enclosed from life with no
specially strong feelings about the stories that
come his way other than that they should be
something he can perfect and polish with a
craftsman's love.'—*Richard Winnington*

    'Crammed with cinematic plums which could
do the early Hitchcock proud.'—*Time*

AA: Robert Krasker
AAN: Carol Reed

Third Man on the Mountain
GB 1959   103m   Technicolor
Walt Disney (Bill Anderson)

In 1865 a Swiss dishwasher dreams of
conquering the local mountain, and befriends a
distinguished mountaineer.
Handsomely photographed boys' adventure
story.

w Eleanore Griffin, *novel* Banner in the Sky by
James Ramsay Ullman *d* Ken Annakin
ph Harry Waxman, *George Tairraz m* William
Alwyn

James MacArthur, Michael Rennie, Janet
Munro, James Donald, Herbert Lom, Laurence
Naismith, Walter Fitzgerald, Nora Swinburne

The Third Secret
GB 1964   103m   bw   Cinemascope
TCF / Hubris (Robert L. Joseph)

A psychiatrist apparently commits suicide; a
patient who has relied on his strength finds the
truth by interviewing other patients.
Pretentious package of short stories, only one of
which is relevant to the frame (yet another one
featuring Patricia Neal was shot but discarded);
full of philosophical conversations on a Thames
mudbank and other absurdities, but well enough
put together.

*w Robert L. Joseph d Charles Crichton
ph* Douglas Slocombe *m* Richard Arnell

Stephen Boyd, *Pamela Franklin,* Jack Hawkins,

Richard Attenborough, Rachel Kempson, Diane
Cilento, Paul Rogers, Freda Jackson

'An unappealing and irritatingly muddled
scribble of a film, thoroughly lacking in
suspense, veracity and justification.'—*MFB*

The Third Voice **
US 1959 80m bw Cinemascope
TCF (Maury Dexter, Hubert Cornfield)

A woman kills her wealthy lover and an
accomplice impersonates him through a series of
complex negotiations.
Superstylish minor thriller, with a plot
fascinating as it unfolds and a climax which is
only a slight letdown.

wd Hubert Cornfield, *novel* All the Way by
Charles Williams *ph* Ernest Haller *m* Johnny
Mandel

Edmond O'Brien, Laraine Day, Julie London

Thirteen Ghosts
US 1960 88m Technicolor
Columbia / William Castle

A penniless scholar inherits a haunted house.
Childish thriller for which the audience was
issued with a 'ghost viewer' (anaglyph
spectacles) so that they could see the 'spirits'.
The gimmick was called Illusion-O.

w Robb White *d* William Castle *ph* Joseph
Biroc *m* Von Dexter

Charles Herbert, Jo Morrow, Martin Milner,
Rosemary de Camp, Donald Woods, Margaret
Hamilton

Thirteen Hours by Air *
US 1936 80m bw
Paramount (E. Lloyd Sheldon)

A transcontinental plane is hijacked by an ex-
convict.
Solidly carpentered minor thriller which is also
an interesting record of the early days of
commercial aviation.

w Bogart Rogers, Kenyon Nicholson *d Mitchell
Leisen ph* Theodor Sparkhul

Fred MacMurray, Joan Bennett, Zasu Pitts,
Alan Baxter, Fred Keating, Brian Donlevy, John
Howard, Ruth Donnelly, Dean Jagger

13 Rue Madeleine *
US 1946 95m bw
TCF (Louis de Rochemont)

Four trained American espionage agents locate
a Nazi rocket site in France.
Semi-documentary spy stuff in the tradition of
The House on 92nd Street but rather less
satisfactory despite excellent technique.

w John Monks Jnr, Sy Bartlett *d* Henry
Hathaway *ph* Norbert Brodine *m* David
Buttolph *md* Alfred Newman

James Cagney, Annabella, Richard Conte,
Frank Latimore, Walter Abel, Melville Cooper,
Sam Jaffe, Blanche Yurka

'Far and away the roughest, toughest spy
chase yet gleaned from the bulging files of the
OSS.'—*Time*

'I stole the plot of *The Virginian* and used it.
I'd always wanted to make that story
anyway.'—*Henry Hathaway*

13 West Street *
US 1962 80m bw
Columbia / Ladd Enterprises

An engineer is attacked on the street by teenage
hoodlums and becomes obsessed by revenge.
Competent, darkly photographed, rather
dislikeable little thriller, a kind of trial run for
Death Wish.

w Bernard Schoenfeld, Robert Presnell Jnr
d Philip Leacock *ph* Charles Lawton Jnr
m George Duning

Alan Ladd, Rod Steiger, Dolores Dorn, Michael
Callan, Kenneth MacKenna, Margaret Hayes

The Thirteenth Guest *
US 1932 70m bw
Monogram (M. H. Hoffman)

A haunted house, a will at midnight, and a
frightened lady.
Archetypal comedy thriller, shot on Poverty
Row but still watchable.

w Francis Hyland, Arthur Hoerl, *novel*
Armitage Traill *ph* Albert Ray *ph* Harry
Neumann, Tom Galligan

Ginger Rogers, Lyle Talbot, J. Farrell
MacDonald, James Eagles, Eddie Phillips,
Erville Alderson

The Thirteenth Letter *
US 1951 85m bw
TCF (Otto Preminger)

A small French-Canadian town suffers from an
outbreak of poison pen letters.
Moderate transcription of a memorable French
film, *Le Corbeau*; in this version the events seem
all too predictable and the performances dull.

w Howard Koch *d* Otto Preminger *ph* Joseph
La Shelle *m* Alex North

Charles Boyer, Linda Darnell, Constance Smith,
Michael Rennie, Françoise Rosay, Judith
Evelyn

–30–
US 1959 96m bw
Warner / Mark VII (Jack Webb)
GB title: *Deadline Midnight*

A night in the newsroom of a paper preoccupied with scoops.
Not very dramatic, oddly titled and rather pretentious newspaper melodrama confined largely to one set.

w William Bowers *d* Jack Webb *ph* Edward Colman *m* Ray Heindorf

Jack Webb, William Conrad, David Nelson, Whitney Blake, James Bell, Nancy Valentine

Thirty Day Princess*
US 1934 74m bw
Paramount (B. P. Schulberg)

An actress is hired to impersonate a princess who gets mumps while visiting New York in hope of a loan.
Modest comedy which needed a wittier script but is stylishly played.

w Preston Sturges, Frank Partos, *novel* Clarence Budington Kelland *d* Marion Gering *ph* Leon Shamroy

Sylvia Sidney, Cary Grant, Edward Arnold, Henry Stephenson, Vince Barnett, Edgar Norton, Lucien Littlewood

Thirty Is a Dangerous Age, Cynthia
GB 1967 84m Technicolor
Columbia / Walter Shenson

A timid nightclub pianist has trouble with women but sells his first musical.
Mild star vehicle for a very mild star, basically a few thin sketches, frantically overdirected.

w Dudley Moore, Joe McGrath, John Wells *d* Joe McGrath *ph* Billy Williams *m* Dudley Moore *titles* Richard Williams

Dudley Moore, Eddie Foy Jnr, Suzy Kendall, John Bird, Duncan Macrae, Patricia Routledge, John Wells

The Thirty-Nine Steps***
GB 1935 81m bw
Gaumont British (Ivor Montagu)

A spy is murdered; the man who has befriended her is suspected, but eludes the police until a chase across Scotland produces the real villains.
Marvellous comedy thriller with most of the gimmicks found not only in Hitchcock's later work but in anyone else's who has tried the same vein. It has little to do with the original novel, and barely sets foot outside the studio, but it makes every second count, and is unparalleled in its use of timing, atmosphere and comedy relief.

w Charles Bennett, Alma Reville, *novel* John Buchan *d* Alfred Hitchcock *ph* Bernard Knowles *m* Hubert Bath, Jack Beaver *md* Louis Levy

Robert Donat, Madeleine Carroll, Godfrey Tearle, Lucie Mannheim, Peggy Ashcroft, John Laurie, *Wylie Watson, Helen Haye*, Frank Cellier

'A narrative of the unexpected – a humorous, exciting, dramatic, entertaining, pictorial, vivid and novel tale told with a fine sense of character and a keen grasp of the cinematic idea.'— *Sydney W. Carroll*

'A miracle of speed and light.'—*Otis Ferguson*

The Thirty-Nine Steps*
GB 1960 93m Eastmancolor
Rank (Betty E. Box)

Just to show that stars and story aren't everything, this scene-for-scene remake muffs every opportunity for suspense or general effectiveness, and is practically a manual on how not to make a thriller.

w Frank Harvey *d* Ralph Thomas *ph* Ernest Steward *m* Clifton Parker

Kenneth More, Taina Elg, Barry Jones, Faith Brook, Brenda de Banzie, Duncan Lamont, James Hayter, Michael Goodliffe, Reginald Beckwith

The Thirty-Nine Steps*
GB 1978 102m Eastmancolor
Rank / Norfolk International (James Kenelm Clarke)

Eager-to-please remake which goes back to the original period and more or less the original story, but rather spoils itself by a cliffhanger climax on the face of Big Ben, absurdly borrowed from Will Hay's *My Learned Friend*.

w Michael Robson, *d* Don Sharp *ph* John Coquillon *m* Ed Welch *ph* Harry pottle

Robert Powell, Karen Dotrice, John Mills, Eric Porter, David Warner, George Baker, Ronald Pickup, Timothy West, Donald Pickering, Andrew Keir, Robert Flemyng, Miles Anderson

Thirty Seconds over Tokyo*
US 1944 138m bw
MGM (Sam Zimbalist)

How the first American attack on Japan was planned.
Sturdy World War II action flagwaver, with Tracy guesting as Colonel Dolittle.

w Dalton Trumbo d Mervyn Le Roy ph Harold Rosson, Robert Surtees m Herbert Stothart

Spencer Tracy, Van Johnson, Robert Walker, Phyllis Thaxter, Tim Murdock, Don Defore, Robert Mitchum

AAN: Harold Rosson, Robert Surtees

Thirty-Six Hours*
US 1964   115m   bw   Panavision
MGM / Perlberg–Seaton / Cherokee (William Perlberg)

In 1944 an American major is kidnapped by the Nazis and after drugging is made to think that the war is over.
Well-detailed spy suspenser.

wd George Seaton, stories Roald Dahl, Carl K. Hittleman ph Philip Lathrop m Dmitri Tiomkin

James Garner, Rod Taylor, Eva Marie Saint, Werner Peters, John Banner

This above All*
US 1942   110m   bw
TCF (Darryl F. Zanuck)

A surgeon's daughter on active service during World War II falls in love with a conscientious objector who is also an army deserter: he proves his bravery during an air raid.
Superior studio-set war romance.

w R. C. Sheriff, novel Eric Knight d Anatole Litvak ph Arthur Miller m Alfred Newman

Tyrone Power, Joan Fontaine, Thomas Mitchell, Henry Stephenson, Nigel Bruce, Gladys Cooper, Philip Merivale, Alexander Knox, Melville Cooper

AAN: Arthur Miller

This Could Be the Night
US 1957   104m   bw   Cinemascope
MGM (Joe Pasternak)

A schoolteacher becomes secretary to a gangster in his Broadway night club.
Unlikely romantic melodrama with music, like a more solemn Guys and Dolls.

w Isabel Lennart, story Cornelia Baird Gross d Robert Wise ph Russell Harlan m George Stoll

Jean Simmons, Paul Douglas, Tony Franciosa, Julie Wilson, Joan Blondell, J. Carrol Naish, Zasu Pitts

This Day and Age*
US 1933   98m   bw
Paramount / Cecil B. de Mille

During a youth week, boys put a gangster on trial and by his own methods force him to confess to murder.
A curious aberration for de Mille, this fairly powerful movie was condemned in some quarters as an incitement to fascism.

w Bartlett Cormack d Cecil B. de Mille ph Peverell Marley m Howard Jackson, L. W. Gilbert, Abel Baer

Charles Bickford, Richard Cromwell, Judith Allen, Harry Green, Ben Alexander
'Loaded with that power which excites emotional hysteria . . . should stimulate audiences to the same pitch of enthusiasm as it did the preview crowd.'—Motion Picture Herald

This Earth Is Mine
US 1959   124m   Technicolor Cinemascope
U-I / Vintage (Casey Robinson, Claude Heilman)

A French-American vineyard owner in California brings out his granddaughter from England in the hope that she will consolidate his dynasty.
Solidly efficient film of a solidly efficient novel.

w Casey Robinson, novel The Cup and the Sword by Alice Tisdale Hobart d Henry King ph Winton Hoch, Russell Metty m Hugo Friedhofer

Jean Simmons, Claude Rains, Rock Hudson, Dorothy McGuire, Kent Smith, Anna Lee, Ken Scott

This Gun for Hire***
US 1942   81m   bw
Paramount (Richard M. Blumenthal)

A professional killer becomes involved in a fifth columnist plot.
Efficient Americanization of one of its author's more sombre entertainments. The melodrama has an authentic edge and strangeness to it, and it established the star images of both Ladd and Lake, as well as being oddly downbeat for a Hollywood product of this jingoistic time.

w Albert Maltz, W. R. Burnett, novel A Gun for Sale by Graham Greene d Frank Tuttle ph John Seitz m David Buttolph

Alan Ladd, Veronica Lake, Robert Preston, Laird Cregar, Tully Marshall, Mikhail Rasumny, Marc Lawrence

This Happy Breed**
GB 1944   114m   Technicolor
GFD / Two Cities / Cineguild (Noel Coward,
    Anthony Havelock-Allan)

Life between the wars for a London suburban
family.
Coward's domestic epic is unconvincingly
written and largely miscast, but sheer
professionalism gets it through, and the decor is
historically interesting.

w David Lean, Ronald Neame, Anthony
Havelock-Allan, *play* Noel Coward *d David
Lean*

Robert Newton, Celia Johnson, Stanley
Holloway, John Mills, Kay Walsh, Amy Veness,
Alison Leggatt
    'Nearly two hours of the pleasure of
recognition, which does not come very far up the
scale of aesthetic values.'—*Richard Mallett,
Punch*

This Happy Feeling
US 1958   92m   Eastmancolor
    Cinemascope
U-I (Ross Hunter)

An ageing actor is invigorated by a mild affair
with his secretary.
Flat romantic comedy: the bubbles obstinately
refuse to rise.

wd Blake Edwards, *play* For Love or Money by
F. Hugh Herbert *ph* Arthur E. Arling *m* Frank
Skinner

Curt Jurgens, Debbie Reynolds, John Saxon,
Alexis Smith, *Mary Astor, Estelle Winwood*

This Is My Affair**
US 1937   102m   bw
TCF (Kenneth MacGowan)
GB title: *His Affair*

When President McKinley is assassinated, one
of his top undercover agents is suspected of
being a criminal, and threatened with execution.
Jolly good romantic melodrama with excellent
period trappings; Hollywood of the thirties at its
routine best.

*w Allen Rivkin, Lamar Trotti d William A.
Seiter ph Robert Planck md* Arthur Lange

Robert Taylor, Barbara Stanwyck, Victor
McLaglen, Brian Donlevy, Sidney Blackmer,
John Carradine, Sig Rumann, Alan Dinehart,
Douglas Fowley
    'The best American melodrama of the year . . .
admirable acting, quick and cunning direction
. . . a sense of doom, of almost classic
suspense.'—*Graham Greene*

This Is My Street
GB 1963   94m   bw
Anglo-Amalgamated / Adder (Jack Hanbury)

A Battersea wife has a fling with her mother's
lodger.
Unremarkable low-life drama.

w Bill MacIlwraith, *novel* Nan Maynard
d Sidney Hayers *ph* Alan Hume *m* Eric Rogers

June Ritchie, Ian Hendry, Avice Landon,
Meredith Edwards, Madge Ryan, John Hurt,
Mike Pratt, Tom Adams

This Is the Army**
US 1943   121m   Technicolor
Warner (Jack L. Warner, Hal B. Wallis)

Army recruits put on a musical revue.
Mammoth musical flagwaver.

w Casey Robinson, Claude Binyon *d* Michael
Curtiz *ph* Bert Glennon, Sol Polito *songs Irving
Berlin m* Ray Heindorf

George Murphy, Joan Leslie, Irving Berlin,
George Tobias, Alan Hale, Charles Butterworth,
Rosemary de Camp, Dolores Costello, Una
Merkel, Stanley Ridges, Ruth Donnelly, Kate
Smith, Frances Langford, Gertrude Niesen,
Ronald Reagan, Joe Louis

AA: Ray Heindorf

This Island Earth**
US 1955   86m   Technicolor
U-I (William Alland)

Scientists at a mysterious research station are
really visitors from a planet in outer space, to
which they kidnap brilliant minds who they hope
can help them.
Absorbing science fiction mystery with splendid
special effects and only one mutant monster to
liven the last reels.

*w Franklin Coen, Edward G. O'Callaghan,
novel* Raymond F. Jones *d Joseph Newman
ph/sp* Clifford Stine, David S. Horsley *m* Joseph
Gershenson *ad* Alexander Golitzen, Richard H.
Riedel

Jeff Morrow, Faith Domergue, Rex Reason,
Lance Fuller, Russell Johnson, Robert Nicholas,
Karl Lindt

This Land Is Mine*
US 1943   103m   bw
RKO (Jean Renoir, Dudley Nichols)

A European village fights for freedom under
occupying Nazis, and a schoolmaster becomes a
hero.
Rather superfluous flagwaver with good
performances wasted in a totally predictable and

rather uninspiring script which gives the director little scope.

w Dudley Nichols d Jean Renoir ph Frank Redman m Lothar Perl

Charles Laughton, Maureen O'Hara, George Sanders, Walter Slezak, Una O'Connor, Kent Smith, Philip Merivale, Thurston Hall, George Coulouris

'Directed with the same Zolaesque intensity, the same excited obsession with locomotives, the same exquisite pictorial sense, that informed *La Bête Humaine*.'—*Guardian*

This Love of Ours

US 1945   90m   bw
U-I (Edward Dodds)

A jealous doctor leaves his wife but years later saves her from an unhappy second marriage. Stupid romantic melodrama with characters in whose idiotic behaviour one can take no interest. Remade as *Never Say Goodbye* (qv).

w Bruce Manning, John Klorer, Leonard Lee, *play* Comè Prima Meglio di Prima by Luigi Pirandello d William Dieterle ph Lucien Ballard m Hans Salter

Merle Oberon, Charles Korvin, Claude Rains, Carl Esmond, Jess Barker, Harry Davenport, Ralph Morgan, Fritz Leiber

'About as captivating as a funeral dirge.'—*Thomas M. Pryor, New York Times*

'A juicy example of masochistic team work . . . my favourite bad film in two years.'—*Richard Winnington*

AAN: Hans Salter

This Man Is News **

GB 1938   77m   bw
(Paramount) Pinebrook (Anthony Havelock-Allan)

A reporter tracks down jewel thieves.
Thoroughly brisk and lively comedy-thriller on *Thin Man* lines. *This Man in Paris* followed two years later.

w *Allan MacKinnon, Roger Macdougall, Basil Dearden d David MacDonald*

Barry K. Barnes, Valerie Hobson, Alastair Sim, John Warwick, Garry Marsh

This Modern Age

US 1931   68m   bw
MGM

The socialite child of divorced parents goes to Paris to stay with her sophisticated mother. Mildly daring melodrama typical of its star and year.

w Sylvia Thalberg, Frank Butler, *story* Mildred Cram d Nick Grinde ph Charles Rosher

Joan Crawford, Pauline Frederick, Monroe Owsley, Neil Hamilton, Hobart Bosworth, Emma Dunn

This Property is Condemned*

US 1966   110m   Technicolor
Paramount / Seven Arts / Ray Stark (John Houseman)

Sexual adventures of a tubercular but beautiful girl in her mother's boarding house in a Mississippi town.
The Tennessee Williams mixture as before, quite well done but almost entirely resistible.

w Francis Ford Coppola, Fred Coe, Edith Sommer, *play* Tennessee Williams d Sydney Pollack ph James Wong Howe m Kenyon Hopkins

Natalie Wood, Robert Redford, Mary Badham, Kate Reid, Charles Bronson, Jon Provost, John Harding, Alan Baxter, Robert Blake

This Sporting Life **

GB 1963   134m   bw
Rank / Independent Artists (Karel Reisz)

A tough miner becomes a successful rugby player, but his inner crudeness and violence keep contentment at bay.
Skilful movie-making around an unattractive hero in dismal settings; for all the excellent detail, we do not care sufficiently for the film to become any kind of classic.

w David Storey d Lindsay Anderson ph Denys Coop m Roberto Gerhard

Richard Harris, Rachel Roberts, Alan Badel, William Hartnell, Colin Blakely, Vanda Godsell, Arthur Lowe

AAN: Richard Harris; Rachel Roberts

This Thing Called Love*

US 1941   98m   bw
Columbia (William Perlberg)
GB title: *Married But Single*

A lady executive insists on proving that marriage is best if the partners start out just good friends. Amusing comedy which at the time seemed a little saucy, and got itself banned by the Legion of Decency.

w George Seaton, Ken Englund, P. J. Wolfson d Alexander Hall ph Joseph Walker m Morris Stoloff

Rosalind Russell, Melvyn Douglas, Binnie Barnes, Allyn Joslyn, Gloria Dickson, Lee J. Cobb, Gloria Holden, Don Beddoe

This Time for Keeps
US 1947 105m Technicolor
MGM (Joe Pasternak)

The son of a famous singer falls in love with a swimming star.
Dim star musical with no outstanding sequences.

w Gladys Lehman d Richard Thorpe ph Karl Freund songs various

Esther Williams, Jimmy Durante, Lauritz Melchior, Johnnie Johnston, Xavier Cugat and his Orchestra

This Woman Is Dangerous
US 1952 97m bw
Warner (Robert Sisk)

A woman gangster goes blind and falls in love with her doctor.
Glossy hokum without much dramatic movement; strictly for star fans.

w Geoffrey Homes, George Worthing Yates d Felix Feist ph Ted McCord m David Buttolph

Joan Crawford, David Brian, Dennis Morgan, Mari Aldon, Phil Carey

The Thomas Crown Affair **
US 1968 102m De Luxe Panavision
UA / Mirisch / Simkoe / Solar (Norman Jewison)

A bored property tycoon masterminds a bank robbery and is chased by a glamorous insurance investigator.
Not so much a movie as an animated colour supplement, this glossy entertainment makes style its prime virtue, plays cute tricks with multiple images and has a famous sexy chess game, but is not above being boring for the rest of the way.

w Alan R. Trustman d Norman Jewison ph Haskell Wexler m Michel Legrand ad Robert Boyle

Steve McQueen, Faye Dunaway, Paul Burke, Jack Weston, Yaphet Kotto

'Jewison and Wexler seem to have gone slightly berserk, piling up tricks and mannerisms until the film itself sinks out of sight, forlorn and forgotten.'—Tom Milne

'A glimmering, empty film reminiscent of an haute couture model—stunning on the surface, concave and undernourished beneath.'—Stefan Kanter

AA: song 'The Windmills of Your Mind' (m Michel Legrand, ly Alan and Marilyn Bergman)
AAN: Michel Legrand

Thoroughly Modern Millie *
US 1967 138m Technicolor
Universal (Ross Hunter)

In the twenties, a young girl comes to New York, becomes thoroughly modern, falls for her boss, and has various adventures unmasking a white slave racket centring on a Chinese laundry.
Initially most agreeable but subsequently very patchy spoof of twenties fads and films, including a Harold Lloyd thrill sequence which just doesn't work and a comedy performance from Beatrice Lillie which does. Tunes and performances are alike variable.

w Richard Morris d George Roy Hill ph Russell Metty ad Alexander Golitzen, George Webb m Elmer Bernstein md André Previn, Joseph Gershenson ch Joe Layton songs various

Julie Andrews, Mary Tyler Moore, John Saxon, James Fox, Carol Channing, Beatrice Lillie, Jack Soo, Pat Morita, Anthony Dexter

'What a nice 65-minute movie is buried therein!'—Judith Crist

AA: Elmer Bernstein
AAN: André Previn, Joseph Gershenson; title song (m James Van Heusen, ly Sammy Cahn); Carol Channing

Those Calloways
US 1964 131m Technicolor
Walt Disney (Winston Hibler)

Adventures of a marsh trapper and his family who live near a Maine village and try to protect wild geese from hunters.
Predictable family saga with pleasant backgrounds.

w Louis Pelletier, novel Swift Water by Paul Annixter d Norman Tokar ph Edward Colman m Max Steiner

Brian Keith, Vera Miles, Brandon de Wilde, Walter Brennan, Ed Wynn, Linda Evans, Philip Abbott, John Larkin, John Qualen

Those Daring Young Men in Their Jaunty Jalopies
US / Italy / France 1969 125m
Technicolor Panavision
Paramount / Dino de Laurentiis / Marianne (Ken Annakin, Basil Keys)
GB title: Monte Carlo or Bust

Accidents befall various competitors in the Monte Carlo Rally.
Rough-edged imitation of The Great Race and Those Magnificent Men in Their Flying Machines, much feebler than either but with the waste of a big budget well in evidence.

w Jack Davies, Ken Annakin *d* Ken Annakin
ph Gabor Pogany *m* Ron Goodwin

Peter Cook, Dudley Moore, Tony Curtis,
Bourvil, Walter Chiari, Terry-Thomas, Gert
Frobe, Susan Hampshire, Jack Hawkins, Eric
Sykes

Those Magnificent Men in Their Flying Machines, or How I Flew from London to Paris in 25 hours and 11 Minutes**
GB 1965   133m   Technicolor   Todd-AO
TCF (Stan Marguilies, Jack Davies)

In 1910, a newspaper owner sponsors a London
to Paris air race.

Long-winded, generally agreeable knockabout
comedy with plenty to look at but far too few
jokes to sustain it.

w Jack Davies, Ken Annakin *d Ken Annakin*
ph Christopher Challis m Ron Goodwin
pd Tom Morahan

Sarah Miles, Stuart Whitman, Robert Morley,
Eric Sykes, Terry-Thomas, James Fox, Alberto
Sordi, Gert Frobe, Jean-Pierre Cassel, Karl
Michael Vogler, Irina Demich, Benny Hill, Flora
Robson, Sam Wanamaker, Red Skelton, Fred
Emney, Cicely Courtneidge, Gordon Jackson,
John Le Mesurier, Tony Hancock, William
Rushton

'There is many a likely gag, but none that
survives the second or third reprise. It could have
been a good bit funnier by being shorter: the
winning time is 25 hours 11 minutes, and by
observing some kind of neo-Aristotelian unity
the film seems to last exactly as long.'—*John
Simon*

AAN: script

Those Were the Days*
GB 1934   80m   bw
BIP (Walter C. Mycroft)

In the nineties, a magistrate seeks out his teenage
stepson in a music hall.

Lively comedy which is valuable as giving the
screen's best recreation of an old-time music hall.

w Fred Thompson, Frank Miller, Frank
Launder, Jack Jordan, *play* The Magistrate by
Arthur Wing Pinero *d Thomas Bentley ph* Otto
Kanturek *md* Idris Lewis

Will Hay, John Mills, Iris Hoey, Angela
Baddeley, Claud Allister, George Graves, Jane
Carr, H. F. Maltby

Those Were the Days
US 1940   74m   bw
Paramount (J. Theodore Reed)

During their 40th anniversary celebrations, a

married couple look back to their courtship days
at college.

Pleasant, light, nostalgic escapades.

w Don Hartman, *stories* George Fitch *d* J.
Theodore Reed *ph* Victor Milner

William Holden, Bonita Granville, Ezra Stone,
Judith Barrett, Vaughan Glazer, Lucien
Littlefield, Richard Denning

A Thousand Clowns*
US 1965   115m   bw
UA / Harell (Fred Coe)

A New Yorker who has abdicated from work
leads a cheerful, useless life with his young
nephew, but the school board have their doubts.

Imitative nonconformist comedy with frequent
reminiscences of older, better plays such as *You
Can't Take It with You*. Good lines occasionally
make themselves felt, but the overall effect is
patchy, the lead is miscast, and the location
montages only emphasize the basic one-room
set.

w Herb Gardner, from his play *d* Fred Coe
ph Arthur J. Ornitz *m* Don Walker

Jason Robards, Martin Balsam, Barry Gordon,
Barbara Harris, *William Daniels*, Gene Saks

AA: Martin Balsam
AAN: best picture; Herb Gardner; Don Walker

Thousands Cheer*
US 1943   126m   Technicolor
MGM (Joe Pasternak)

An army base stages an all-star variety show.

Ho-hum studio extravaganza with some good
numbers.

w Paul Jarrico, Richard Collins *d* George
Sidney *ph* George Folsey *md* Herbert Stothart
songs various

Kathryn Grayson, Gene Kelly, John Boles,
Mary Astor, Jose Iturbi, Kay Kyser and his
Orchestra, Lionel Barrymore, Margaret
O'Brien, June Allyson, Mickey Rooney, Judy
Garland, Red Skelton, Eleanor Powell, Bob
Crosby and his Orchestra, Lena Horne, Frank
Morgan

AAN: George Folsey; Herbert Stothart

Three Blind Mice*
US 1938   75m   bw
TCF (Raymond Griffith)

Three Kansas girls in the big city seek rich
husbands.

Mild comedy remade as *Three Little Girls in
Blue* and *How to Marry a Millionaire*, and not
all that different from any of the *Gold Diggers*
comedy musicals.

w Brown Holmes, Lynn Starling *d* William A. Seiter *ph* Ernest Palmer

Loretta Young, Joel McCrea, David Niven, Stuart Erwin, Marjorie Weaver, Pauline Moore, Binnie Barnes, Jane Darwell, Leonid Kinskey

Three Brave Men*
US 1956 88m bw Cinemascope
TCF (Herbert B. Swope Jnr)

A civilian employee in the US Navy is suspended as a security risk and it takes a lawsuit to set things straight.
Semi-factual anti-McCarthy drama proving that America is a great place to live—when you're winning. Good courtroom scenes.

wd Philip Dunne, *articles* Anthony Lewis
ph Charles G. Clarke *m* Hans Salter

Ray Milland, Ernest Borgnine, Nina Foch, Dean Jagger, Frank Lovejoy, Edward Andrews, Frank Faylen, James Westerfield, Joseph Wiseman

The Three Caballeros***
US 1945 70m Technicolor
Walt Disney (Norman Ferguson)

A programme of shorts about South America, linked by Donald Duck as a tourist.
Rapid-fire mélange of fragments supporting the good neighbour policy, following the shorter *Saludos Amigos* of 1943. The kaleidoscopic sequences and the combination of live action with cartoon remain of absorbing interest.

w various *d* various *m* Edward Plumb, Paul J. Smith, Charles Wolcott

† Stories include Pablo the Penguin, Little Gauchito, a Mexican sequence and some adventures with Joe Carioca.

AAN: Edward Plumb, Paul J. Smith, Charles Wolcott

Three Came Home**
US 1950 106m bw
TCF (Nunnally Johnson)

In 1941 writer Agnes Newton Keith tries to escape from Borneo but is interned and ill-used by the Japanese.
Well-made, harrowing war adventure.

w Nunnally Johnson, *book* Agnes Newton Keith *d* Jean Negulesco *ph* Milton Krasner *m* Hugo Friedhofer *md* Lionel Newman

Claudette Colbert, Patric Knowles, Sessue Hayakawa, Florence Desmond, Sylvia Andrew, Phyllis Morris

Three Cases of Murder*
GB 1954 99m bw
British Lion / Wessex / London Films (Ian Dalrymple, Hugh Perceval)

'In the Picture': a painting comes to life. 'You Killed Elizabeth': a man suspects himself of his faithless fiancée's murder. 'Lord Mountdrago': the foreign secretary dreams of killing an MP he hates.
Unlinked compendium, in which the first and third stories are quite interesting and well done, the second very commonplace.

w Donald Wilson, Sidney Caroll, Ian Dalrymple (original stories Roderick Wilkinson, Brett Halliday, W. Somerset Maugham) *d* Wendy Toye, David Eady, George More O'Ferrall *ph* Georges Périnal *m* Doreen Carwithen

Alan Badel, Hugh Pryse, Leueen MacGrath, Elizabeth Sellars, John Gregson, Emrys Jones, Orson Welles, André Morell

Three Cheers for the Irish
US 1940 100m bw
Warner (Sam Bischoff)

An Irishman's daughter causes family trouble when she falls for a Scot.
Pleasant, unpretentious but overlong romantic comedy.

w Richard Macaulay, Jerry Wald *d* Lloyd Bacon *ph* Charles Rosher

Thomas Mitchell, Priscilla Lane, Dennis Morgan, Alan Hale, Virginia Grey, Irene Hervey, William Lundigan

Three Coins in the Fountain**
US 1954 102m De Luxe Cinemascope
TCF (Sol C. Siegel)

Three American girls find romance in Rome.
An enormous box office hit, the pattern of which was frequently repeated against various backgrounds; it was actually remade in Madrid as *The Pleasure Seekers*. In itself a thin entertainment, but the title song carried it.

w John Patrick, *novel* John H. Secondari *d* Jean Negulesco *ph* Milton Krasner *m* Victor Young *song* Jule Styne, Sammy Cahn

Clifton Webb, Dorothy McGuire, Louis Jourdan, Jean Peters, Rossano Brazzi, Maggie McNamara, Howard St John, Kathryn Givney, Cathleen Nesbitt

AA: Milton Krasner
AAN: best picture; title song

Three Comrades ✻✻
US 1938 98m bw
MGM (Joseph L. Mankiewicz)

In twenties Germany, three friends find life hard
but derive some joy from their love for a high-
spirited girl who is dying of tuberculosis.
Despairing romance becomes a sentimental
tearjerker with all the stops out; immaculately
produced and very appealing to the masses, but
prevented by censorship from being the intended
indictment of Nazi Germany. The final scene in
which the two surviving comrades are joined in
the churchyard by their ghostly friends still
packs a wallop.

*w F. Scott Fitzgerald, Edward A. Paramore,
novel* Erich Maria Remarque *d Frank Borzage
ph* Joseph Ruttenberg *m* Franx Waxman

Margaret Sullavan, Robert Taylor, Robert
Young, Franchot Tone, Guy Kibbee, Lionel
Atwill, Henry Hull, Charley Grapewin

AAN: Margaret Sullavan

Three Cornered Moon ✻
US 1933 72m bw
Paramount

A newly-poor Depression family has trouble
finding work.
Slightly screwball romantic comedy, a
predecessor of *You Can't Take It with You*; the
humour now seems very faded, but it was a
signpost of its day.

w S. K. Lauren, Ray Harris d Elliott Nugent
ph Leon Shamroy

Claudette Colbert, Mary Boland, Richard Arlen,
Wallace Ford, Lyda Roberti, Tom Brown,
Hardie Albright

Three Daring Daughters
US 1948 115m Technicolor
MGM (Joe Pasternak)
GB title: *The Birds and the Bees*

Three girls dismayed to hear that their mother is
remarrying.
Cheerful comedy with music, but nothing to
write home about.

w Albert Mannheimer, Frederick Kohner,
Sonya Levien, John Meehan *d* Fred M. Wilcox

Jeanette MacDonald, Jose Iturbi, Jane Powell,
Anne Todd, Mary Elinor Donahue, Larry Adler,
Edward Arnold, Harry Davenport, Moyna
MacGill

Three Days of the Condor ✻✻
US 1975 118m Technicolor Panavision
Paramount / Dino de Laurentiis / Wildwood
(Stanley Schneider)

An innocent researcher for a branch of the CIA
finds himself marked for death by assassins
employed by another branch.
Entertaining New York-based thriller which
shamelessly follows most of the twists of *The 39
Steps*. It is just possible to follow its
complexities, and the dialogue is smart.

w Lorenzo Semple Jnr, David Rayfiel, novel Six
Days of the Condor by James Grady *d Sydney
Pollack ph* Owen Roizman *m* Dave Grusin

Robert Redford, Faye Dunaway, Cliff
Robertson, Max Von Sydow, John Houseman,
Walter McGinn

Three Faces East ✻
US 1930 71m bw
Warner (Darryl F. Zanuck)

The butler to the British war minister is a
German spy, and the German nurse sent to help
him is really a British agent . . .
Slow, melodramatic remake of 1926 silent, later
turned into a karloff vehicle, *British Intelligence*
(qv).

w Oliver H. P. Garrett, Arthur Caesar, *play*
Anthony Paul Kelly *d* Roy del Ruth *ph* Chick
McGill

Constance Bennett, Erich Von Stroheim,
Anthony Bushell, William Holden

The Three Faces of Eve ✻✻
US 1957 95m bw Cinemascope
TCF (Nunnally Johnson)

A psychiatrist discovers that a female patient has
three distinct personalities: a drab housewife, a
good time girl and a mature sophisticated
woman.
Alistair Cooke introduces this tall tale as if he
believed it; as presented, it is entertaining but not
very convincing. Its box office success was
sufficient to start a schizophrenia cycle.

w Nunnally Johnson, *book* Corbett H. Thigpen
MD, Hervey M. Cleckley MD *d Nunnally
Johnson ph Stanley Cortez m* Robert Emmett
Dolan

Joanne Woodward, Lee J. Cobb, David Wayne,
Nancy Kulp, Edwin Jerome

AA: Joanne Woodward

Three Faces West
US 1940 79m bw
Republic (Sol C. Siegel)

A dust bowl community is helped by an Austrian
doctor fleeing from the Nazis, but his daughter is
followed by a Nazi suitor.
Unusual modern western, blandly told.

w F. Hugh Herbert, Joseph Moncure March,

Samuel Ornitz *d* Bernard Vorhaus *ph* John Alton *m* Victor Young

John Wayne, Charles Coburn, Sigrid Gurie, Roland Varno, Spencer Charters, Sonny Bupp

Three for Bedroom C

US 1952 74m Natural Color
Brenco (Edward L. Alperson Jnr)

Confusion reigns on a train when a film star takes a compartment booked for a Harvard scientist.

Inept farce which never rises above mediocrity and coasts along well below it.

wd Milton H. Bren *ph* Ernest Laszlo *m* Heinz Roemheld

Gloria Swanson, Fred Clark, James Warren, Hans Conried, Steve Brodie, Margaret Dumont

Three for Jamie Dawn

US 1956 81m bw
AA (Hayes Goetz)

A crooked lawyer bribes three members of a murder jury.

Minor courtroom melodrama, limply developed.

w John Klempner *d* Thomas Carr *ph* Duke Green *m* Walter Scharf

Laraine Day, Ricardo Montalban, Richard Carlson, June Havoc

Three for the Show*

US 1955 93m Technicolor
Cinemascope
Columbia (Jonie Taps)

A married Broadway star finds that her first husband is still alive.

Adequate musical remake of *Too Many Husbands* (qv); not bad, not good.

w Edward Hope, Leonard Stern, *play* Too Many Husbands by W. Somerset Maugham *d* H. C. Potter *ph* Arthur E. Arling *ch* Jack Cole *songs* various

Betty Grable, Jack Lemmon, Marge Champion, Gower Champion, Myron McCormick, Paul Harvey

Three Girls about Town*

US 1942 71m bw
Columbia

Three sisters in New York find a corpse in their hotel bedroom.

A funny 'B' picture: fast paced and lively from start to finish.

w Richard Carroll *d* Leigh Jason *ph* Franz Planer

Joan Blondell, Binnie Barnes, Janet Blair, John Howard, Robert Benchley, Eric Blore, Una O'Connor

Three Godfathers*

US 1948 106m Technicolor
MGM / Argosy (John Ford)

Three outlaws escaping across the desert take charge of an orphan baby.

'Orrible sentimental parable partly redeemed by splendid scenery.

w Laurence Stallings, Frank S. Nugent, *story* Frank B. Kyne *d John Ford ph Winton Hoch m* Richard Hageman

John Wayne, Pedro Armendariz, Harry Carey Jnr, Ward Bond

† The story also appeared in 1909 as *Bronco Billy and the Baby*; in 1916 as *Three Godfathers*, with Harry Carey; in 1920 as *Marked Men*, with Harry Carey; in 1929 as *Hell's Heroes*, with Charles Bickford; in 1936 as *Three Godfathers*, with Chester Morris; and in 1975 as a TV movie, *The Godchild*, with Jack Palance.

The 300 Spartans*

US 1962 114m De Luxe Cinemascope
TCF (Rudolph Maté, George St George)

Sparta leads the ancient Greek states against Persia's attack at Thermopylae.

Quite a lively epic with some dignity.

w George St George *d* Rudolph Maté *ph* Geoffrey Unsworth *m* Manos Hadjikakis

Richard Egan, Ralph Richardson, David Farrar, Diane Baker, Barry Coe, Donald Houston, Kieron Moore, John Crawford, Robert Brown

Three Husbands

US 1950 76m bw
UA / Gloria (I. G. Goldsmith)

Three husbands receive letters from a dead friend claiming that he had affairs with each of their wives.

Silly copy of *A Letter to Three Wives*, with neither style nor sophistication.

w Vera Caspary, Edward Eliscu *d* Irving Reis *ph* Franz Planer *m* Herschel Burke Gilbert

Emlyn Williams, Eve Arden, Howard da Silva, Ruth Warrick, Shepperd Strudwick, Vanessa Brown, Billie Burke, Jonathan Hale

Three in the Attic

US 1968 90m Pathecolor
AIP / Hermes (Richard Wilson)

A college Casanova is locked in an attic by three girls who seduce him by rota until he cries for mercy.

One of the first outspoken comedies of the sexual revolution, but not a particularly funny one.

w Stephen Yafa, from his novel Paxton Quigley's Had the Course d Richard Wilson ph J. Burgi Contner m Chad Stuart

Chris Jones, Yvette Mimieux, Judy Pace, Maggie Turett, Nan Martin

Three into Two Won't Go*
GB 1969 100m Technicolor
Universal (Julian Blaustein)

An executive has an affair with a girl hitch-hiker who later moves into his house to his wife's astonishment.
Palatable sex drama with good performances, rather flabbily written and directed.

w Edna O'Brien, *novel* Andrea Newman d Peter Hall ph Walter Lassally m Francis Lai

Rod Steiger, Claire Bloom, Judy Geeson, Peggy Ashcroft, Paul Rogers

Three Little Girls in Blue
US 1946 90m Technicolor
TCF (Mack Gordon)

Musical remake of *Three Blind Mice* (qv); adequate and quite forgettable.

w Valentine Davies d Bruce Humberstone ph Ernest Palmer *songs* Mack Gordon, Joseph Myrow

June Haver, George Montgomery, Vivian Blaine, Celeste Holm, Vera-Ellen, Frank Latimore, Charles Smith, Charles Halton

Three Little Words*
US 1950 102m Technicolor
MGM (Jack Cummings)

The careers of songwriters Bert Kalmar and Harry Ruby.
Disappointingly ordinary musical in which two witty people are made to seem dull, and the plot allows Fred Astaire only one dance.

w George Wells d Richard Thorpe ph Harry Jackson md André Previn ch Hermes Pan *songs* Bert Kalmar, Harry Ruby and various collaborators

Fred Astaire, Red Skelton, Vera-Ellen, Arlene Dahl, Keenan Wynn, Gale Robbins, Gloria de Haven, Phil Regan, *Debbie Reynolds*

The Three Lives of Thomasina
GB 1963 97m Technicolor
Walt Disney

In a Scottish village in 1912, a vet finds that his methods are no match for a local girl who treats animals by giving them love.

Syrupy film for children: the animals are the main interest and one of them narrates . . .

w Robert Westerby, *novel* Thomasina by Paul Gallico d Don Chaffey ph Paul Beeson m Paul Smith

Susan Hampshire, Patrick McGoohan, Karen Dotrice, Vincent Winter, Laurence Naismith, Finlay Currie, Wilfrid Brambell

Three Loves Has Nancy
US 1938 69m bw
MGM (Norman Krasna)

A jilted bride takes her time about her next selection.
Adequate star comedy.

w Bella and Sam Spewack, George Oppenheimer, David Hertz d Richard Thorpe ph William Daniels

Janet Gaynor, Robert Montgomery, Franchot Tone, Guy Kibbee, Claire Dodd, Reginald Owen, Charley Grapewin, Emma Dunn, Cora Witherspoon

The Three Maxims
GB 1937 87m bw
GFD / Pathé Consortium (Herbert Wilcox)

Two trapezists love the girl member of the team, and the situation leads to attempted murder.
Effective Paris-set treatment of a well worn theme (see *Trapeze*).

w Herman Mankiewicz d Herbert Wilcox

Anna Neagle, Tullio Carminati, Leslie Banks, Horace Hodges

Three Men in a Boat
GB 1956 94m Eastmancolor
  Cinemascope
Romulus (Jack Clayton)

In the 1890s, misadventures befall three men holidaying on the Thames.
Flabby burlesque of a celebrated comic novel whose style is never even approached.

w Hubert Gregg, Vernon Harris, *novel* Jerome K. Jerome d Ken Annakin ph Eric Cross m John Addison

David Tomlinson, Jimmy Edwards, Laurence Harvey, Shirley Eaton, Robertson Hare, Jill Ireland, Lisa Gastoni, Martita Hunt, A. E. Matthews, Ernest Thesiger, Adrienne Corri

Three Men on a Horse*
US 1936 85m bw
Warner (Sam Bischoff)

A timid Brooklynite finds he can always pick winners, and gangsters get interested.

Smooth New Yorkish comedy which pleased at the time.

w Laird Doyle, *play* John Cecil Holm, George Abbott d Mervyn Le Roy ph Sol Polito

Frank McHugh, Sam Levene, Joan Blondell, Guy Kibbee, Carol Hughes, Allen Jenkins, Edgar Kennedy, Eddie Anderson, Harry Davenport

The Three Mesquiteers

A three-man cowboy team who operated in popular B features at the Hopalong Cassidy level. The make-up of the team varied: the actors most often found in it were John Wayne, Max Terhune, Bob Livingston, Ray Corrigan, Bob Steele, Rufe Davis, Tom Tyler, Raymond Hatton, Duncan Renaldo and Jimmy Dodd. The first film was made for RKO, all the rest for Republic: most frequent directors were George Sherman, Mack V. Wright, Joseph Kane, John English and Lester Orlebeck.

1935: POWDERSMOKE RANGE, THE THREE MESQUITEERS
1936: GHOST TOWN, GOLD, ROARIN' LEAD
1937: RIDERS OF THE WHISTLING SKULL, HIT THE SADDLE, GUNSMOKE RANCH, COME ON COWBOYS, RANGE DEFENDERS, HEART OF THE ROCKIES, THE TRIGGER TRIO, WILD HORSE RODEO
1938: THE PURPLE VIGILANTES, CALL THE MESQUITEERS, CALL OF THE MESQUITEERS, OUTLAWS OF SONORA, RIDERS OF THE BLACK HILLS, HEROES OF THE HILLS, PALS OF THE SADDLE, OVERLAND STAGE RAIDERS, SANTA FE STAMPEDE, RED RIVER RANGE
1939: THE NIGHT RIDERS, THREE TEXAS STEERS, WYOMING OUTLAW, NEW FRONTIER, THE KANSAS TERRORS, COWBOYS FROM TEXAS
1940: HEROES OF THE SADDLE, PIONEERS OF THE WEST, COVERED WAGON DAYS, ROCKY MOUNTAIN RANGERS, OKLAHOMA RENEGADES, UNDER TEXAS SKIES, THE TRAIL BLAZERS, LONE STAR RAIDERS
1941: PRAIRIE PIONEERS, PALS OF THE PECOS, SADDLEMATES, GANGS OF SONORA, OUTLAWS OF THE CHEROKEE TRAIL, GAUCHOS OF EL DORADO, WEST OF CIMARRON
1942: CODE OF THE OUTLAW, RIDERS OF THE RANGE, WESTWARD HO, THE PHANTOM PLAINSMAN, SHADOWS ON THE SAGE, VALLEY OF HUNTED MEN
1943: THUNDERING TRAILS, THE

BLOCKED TRAIL, SANTA FE SCOUTS, RIDERS OF THE RIO GRANDE

The Three Musketeers **

US 1939 73m bw
TCF
GB title: *The Singing Musketeer*

A burlesque of the familiar story with pauses for song.

A very satisfactory entertainment with all concerned in top form.

w M. M. Musselman, William A. Drake, Sam Hellman d Allan Dwan ph Peverell Marley

Don Ameche, the Ritz Brothers, Binnie Barnes, *Joseph Schildkraut*, Lionel Atwill, Miles Mander, Gloria Stuart, Pauline Moore, John Carradine

The Three Musketeers ***

US 1948 125m Technicolor
MGM (Pandro S. Berman)

High-spirited version of the famous story, with duels and fights presented like musical numbers. Its vigour and inventiveness is a pleasure to behold.

w Robert Ardrey d George Sidney ph Robert Planck m Herbert Stothart

Gene Kelly, Lana Turner, June Allyson, Frank Morgan, Van Heflin, Angela Lansbury, Vincent Price, Keenan Wynn, John Sutton, Gig Young, Robert Coote, Reginald Owen, Ian Keith, Patricia Medina

AAN: Robert Planck

The Three Musketeers (The Queen's Diamonds) **

Panama 1973 107m Technicolor
Film Trust (Alex Salkind)

Jokey version with realistic blood; despite very lively highlights it wastes most of its high production cost by not giving its plot a chance; but money was saved by issuing the second half separately as *The Four Musketeers (The Revenge of Milady)*. The latter section was less attractive.

w George MacDonald Fraser d Richard Lester ph David Watkin m Michel Legrand pd Brian Eatwell

Michael York, Oliver Reed, Richard Chamberlain, Frank Finlay, Raquel Welch, Geraldine Chaplin, Spike Milligan, Faye Dunaway, Charlton Heston, Christopher Lee, Jean-Pierre Cassel

'It's one dragged-out forced laugh. No sweep, no romance, no convincing chivalric tradition to mock.'—*Stanley Kauffmann*

Three on a Match
US 1932   63m   bw
Warner (Sam Bischoff)

Three schoolgirl friends meet again in the big
city, after which their paths cross
melodramatically.
Predictable, watchable multi-story dramatics
with an ironic twist: remade in 1938 as
Broadway Musketeers.

w Lucien Hubbard *d* Mervyn Le Roy *ph* Sol
Polito

Joan Blondell, Bette Davis, Ann Dvorak,
Warren William, Grant Mitchell, Lyle Talbot,
Humphrey Bogart, Glenda Farrell, Clara
Blandick

Three Ring Circus
US 1954   103m   Technicolor   Vistavision
Paramount / Hal B. Wallis

Ex-army veterans join a circus.
The mixture as before from Martin and Lewis:
variety acts interspersed with sentiment and
heavy mugging.

w Don McGuire, Joseph Pevney *ph* Loyal
Griggs *d* Joseph Pevney *m* Walter Scharf

Dean Martin, Jerry Lewis, Joanne Dru, Zsa Zsa
Gabor, Wallace Ford, Sig Rumann, Gene
Sheldon, Nick Cravat, Elsa Lanchester

Three Sailors and a Girl
US 1953   95m   Technicolor
Warner (Sammy Cahn)

A ship's funds are unofficially invested in a
musical show.
Undernourished comedy musical.

w Roland Kibbee, Devery Freeman, *play* The
Butter and Egg Man by George S. Kaufman
d Roy del Ruth *ph* Carl Guthrie *songs* Sammy
Fain, Sammy Cahn

Jane Powell, Gordon Macrae, Gene Nelson,
Sam Levene, George Givot, Veda Ann Borg

Three Secrets*
US 1949   98m   bw
(Warner) US Pictures (Milton Sperling)

Three women wait anxiously to find out whose
child survived a plane crash.
Well-made, formula woman's picture.

w Martin Rackin, Gina Kaus   *d* Robert Wise
ph Sid Hickox *m* Davis Buttolph

Eleanor Parker, Patricia Neal, Ruth Roman,
Frank Lovejoy, Leif Erickson, Ted de Corsia,
Edmon Ryan, Larry Keating

The Three Sisters*
GB 1970   165m   Eastmancolor
Alan Clore Films

At the turn of the century, three fatherless sisters
dream of abandoning Russian provincial life for
the big city.
Filmed Chekhov, better than most but still
lacking cinematic vigour.

translator Moura Budberg *d* Laurence Olivier
ph Geoffrey Unsworth *m* William Walton

Laurence Olivier, Joan Plowright, Jeanne Watts,
Louise Purnell, Derek Jacobi, Alan Bates,
Ronald Pickup

Three Smart Girls**
US 1936   86m   bw
Universal (Joe Pasternak)

Three sisters bring their parents back together.
Pleasant, efficient family film which made a
world star of Deanna Durbin.

w Adele Comandini, Austin Parker   *d* Henry
Koster *ph* Joseph Valentine *md* Charles Previn

Deanna Durbin, Barbara Read, Nan Grey,
Charles Winninger, Binnie Barnes, Ray Milland,
Alice Brady, Mischa Auer, Ernest Cossart,
Hobart Cavanaugh
   'The awkward age has never been so
laundered and lavendered and laid away.'—
Graham Greene
   'Idiotically tuned in to happiness, but it isn't
boring.'—*New Yorker, 1978*

AAN: best picture; script

Three Smart Girls Grow Up*
US 1939   87m   bw
Universal (Joe Pasternak)

A girl helps her sisters to find beaus.
More of the above, quite palatable but inevitably
warmed over.

w Bruce Manning, Felix Jackson *d* Henry
Koster *ph* Joe Valentine

Deanna Durbin, Helen Parrish, Nan Grey,
Charles Winninger, Robert Cummings, William
Lundigan, Ernest Cossart, Nella Walker

Three Strangers*
US 1945   92m   bw
Warner (Wolfgang Reinhardt)

A sweepstake ticket brings fortune and tragedy
to three ill-assorted people.
Humdrum pattern play: the stars work hard to
bring a little magic to it.

w John Huston, Howard Koch *d* Jean
Negulesco *ph* Arthur Edeson *m* Adolph
Deutsch

Sidney Greenstreet, Peter Lorre, Geraldine
Fitzgerald, Joan Lorring, Robert Shayne,
Marjorie Riordan, Arthur Shields

Three Stripes in the Sun
US 1955   93m   bw
Columbia (Fred Kohlmar)
GB title: *The Gentle Sergeant*

After World War II, a Japanese-hating sergeant
in the US occupation forces helps a poverty-
stricken orphanage.
Predictable sentimentality based on fact, with
good background detail.

wd Richard Murphy, *articles* E. J. Kelly
ph Burnett Guffey *m* George Duning

Aldo Ray, Phil Carey, Dick York, Chuck
Connors, Mitsuko Kimura

3.10 to Yuma**
US 1957   92m   bw
Columbia (David Heilwell)

A sheriff has to get his prisoner on to a train
despite the threatening presence of the prisoner's
outlaw friends.
Tense, well-directed but rather talky low-budget
western; excellent performances and atmosphere
flesh out an unconvincing physical situation.

w Halsted Welles *d* Delmer Daves *ph* Charles
Lawton Jnr *m* George Duning

Glenn Ford, Van Heflin, Felicia Farr, Leora
Dana, Henry Jones, Richard Jaeckel, Robert
Emhardt

Three Violent People
US 1956   100m   Eastmancolor
   Vistavision
Paramount (Hugh Brown)

Brother ranchers quarrel over the wife of one of
them, an ex-saloon hostess.
Characterless 'character' western, a long way
after *Duel in the Sun*.

w James Edward Grant *d* Rudolph Maté
ph Loyal Griggs *m* Walter Scharf

Charlton Heston, Anne Baxter, *Gilbert Roland*,
Tom Tryon, Bruce Bennett, Forrest Tucker,
Elaine Stritch, Barton MacLane

The Three Weird Sisters
GB 1948   82m   bw
British National (Louis H. Jackson)

Three old maids in a Welsh village plot to kill
their rich half-brother but are swept away by a
flood.
All-stops-out melodrama which doesn't quite
work and is generally remembered, if at all, for
the last third of its writing team.

w Louise Birt, David Evans, Dylan Thomas,
novel Charlotte Armstrong *d* Dan Birt

Nancy Price, Mary Clare, Mary Merrall, Nova
Pilbeam, Raymond Lovell, Anthony Hulme

Three Wise Fools
US 1946   90m   bw
MGM (William Wright)

Three crusty old gents adopt an orphan, who
softens them.
Antediluvian whimsy without the expected fun,
remade from a silent.

w John McDermott, James O'Hanlon, *play*
Austin Strong *d* Edward Buzzell

Margaret O'Brien, Lionel Barrymore, Thomas
Mitchell, Edward Arnold, Lewis Stone, Jane
Darwell, Harry Davenport, Cyd Charisse

Three Wise Girls
US 1932   80m approx   bw
Columbia

Three small-town girls gain wisdom in New
York.
Three millgirls' romances for the price of one.
Adequate, predictable romantic fodder of its
time.

w Robert Riskin, Agnes C. Johnson *d* William
Beaudine *ph* Ted Tetzlaff

Jean Harlow, Mae Clarke, Walter Byron, Marie
Prevost, Andy Devine, Natalie Moorhead,
Jameson Thomas

The Three Worlds of Gulliver
US / Spain 1959   100m   Technicolor
Columbia / Morningside (Charles Schneer)

Gulliver's adventures in Lilliput and
Brobdingnag.
Flat treatment of marvellous material, with all
the excitement squeezed out of it and not even
much pizazz in the trick photography.

w Arthur Ross, Jack Sher *d* Jack Sher
m Bernard Herrmann *sp* Ray Harryhausen

Kerwin Mathews, Basil Sydney, Mary Ellis, Jo
Morrow, June Thorburn, Grégoire Aslan,
Charles Lloyd Pack, Martin Benson

Thrill of a Romance
US 1945   105m   Technicolor
MGM (Joe Pasternak)

A lady swimmer falls for a returning serviceman.
Empty musical vehicle with nothing memorable
about it except the waste of time and money.

w Richard Connell, Gladys Lehmann *d* Richard
Thorpe *ph* Harry Stradling *md* George Stoll

Esther Williams, Van Johnson, Lauritz

Melchior, Frances Gifford, Henry Travers,
Spring Byington, Tommy Dorsey

The Thrill of it All*
US 1963   104m   Eastmancolor
U-I / Ross Hunter / Arwin (Ross Hunter,
  Marty Melcher)

The wife of a gynaecologist becomes an
advertising model, and work pressures disrupt
her marriage.
Glossy matrimonial farce which starts brightly
but eventually flags and becomes exhausting. Its
better jokes linger in the memory.

w Carl Reiner d Norman Jewison ph Russell
Metty m Frank de Vol

Doris Day, James Garner, Anne Francis,
Edward Andrews, Reginald Owen, Zasu Pitts,
Elliot Reid
  'Pleasantly reminiscent of some of the
screwball comedies of the thirties.'—MFB

Throne of Blood*
Japan 1957   105m   bw
Toho (Akira Kurosawa, Sojiro Motoki)
original title: Kumonosu-Jo

A samurai, spurred on by his wife and an old
witch, murders his lord at Cobweb Castle.
A Japanese version of Macbeth with a savage
and horrifying final sequence. The whole film is a
treat to look at.

w Hideo Oguni, Shinobu Hashimoto, Ryuzo
Kikushima, Akira Kurosawa, from
Shakespeare's play d Akira Kurosawa
ph Asaichi Nakai m Masaru Sato

Toshiro Mifune, Isuzu Yamada
  'Its final impression is of a man who storms
into a room with an impassioned speech to
deliver and then discovers that he has forgotten
what he came to say.'—Kenneth Cavander,
MFB

Through a Glass Darkly*
Sweden 1961   91m   bw
Svensk Filmindustri

Four unfulfilled people on a remote island fail to
communicate with each other or to understand
what God is.
It sounds like a parody Bergman film, and it
almost is. The same themes were carried through
in Winter Light and The Silence.

wd Ingmar Bergman ph Sven Nykvist m Bach

Harriet Andersson, Gunnar Bjornstrand, Max
Von Sydow, Lars Passgard

AAN: Ingmar Bergman (as writer)

Thumb Tripping*
US 1972   94m   De Luxe
Avco (Robert Chartoff, Irwin Winkler)

A boy and a girl hitch-hiker in California have a
variety of violent adventures.
Tail end of the Easy Rider fashion, with odd
moments of interesting detail.

w Don Mitchell, from his novel d Quentin
Masters ph Harry Stradling Jnr m Bob
Thompson

Michael Burns, Meg Foster, Marianna Hill,
Bruce Dern

Thunder Bay*
US 1953   102m   Technicolor
U-I (Aaron Rosenberg)

An engineer is convinced that oil can be raised
from the Louisiana sea-bed.
Well-produced outdoor actioner.

w Gil Doud, John Michael Hayes d Anthony
Mann ph William Daniels m Frank Skinner

James Stewart, Joanne Dru, Dan Duryea, Jay C.
Flippen, Anthony Moreno, Gilbert Roland,
Marcia Henderson

Thunder in the City
GB 1937   88m   bw
Atlantic (Akos Tolnay, Alexander Esway)

An American salesman in London helps a
penniless duke promote a non-existent metal.
Mild satire on British and American
idiosyncrasies, now very faded.

w Robert Sherwood, Abem Kandel, Akos
Tolnay d Marion Gering ph Al Gilks

Edward G. Robinson, Lulu Deste, Ralph
Richardson, Nigel Bruce, Constance Collier,
Arthur Wontner

Thunder in the East
US 1951   98m   bw
Paramount (Everett Riskin)

When India becomes independent in 1947, an
American wanting to sell arms clashes with the
peace-loving chief of a principality, but the arms
are needed when rebels attack.
Artificial and boring action melodrama with
platitudinous conversations.

w Jo Swerling, novel Rage of the Vulture by Alan
Moorehead d Charles Vidor ph Lee Garmes

Alan Ladd, Charles Boyer, Deborah Kerr,
Corinne Calvet, Cecil Kellaway

Thunder in the Sun
US 1958   81m   Technicolor
Seven Arts / Carollton (Clarence Greene)

In 1847 an Indian scout guides a group of Basques to California with their vines. Overwritten and melodramatic wagon train story.

wd Russel Rouse *ph* Stanley Cortez *m* Cyril Mockridge

Susan Hayward, Jeff Chandler, Jacques Bergerac, Blanche Yurka, Carl Esmond

A Thunder of Drums*

US 1961   97m   Metrocolor
  Cinemascope
MGM (Robert J. Enders)

Trouble with Apaches at a frontier post in 1870. Solid, unexciting first feature western, some way after Ford.

w James Warner Bellah *d* Joseph Newman *ph* William Spencer *m* Harry Sukman

Richard Boone, George Hamilton, Arthur O'Connell, Luana Patten, Richard Chamberlain, Charles Bronson

Thunder on the Hill

US 1951   84m   bw
U-I (Michael Kraike)
GB title: *Bonaventure*

In Norfolk, a nun solves a murder mystery during a flood.
Modest whodunnit with an unusual background but not much suspense.

w Oscar Saul, André Solt, *play* Bonaventure by Charlotte Hastings *d* Douglas Sirk *ph* William Daniels *m* Hans Salter

Claudette Colbert, Ann Blyth, Robert Douglas, Anne Crawford, Philip Friend, Gladys Cooper, John Abbott, Connie Gilchrist, Gavin Muir

Thunder Road*

US 1958   92m   bw
UA / DRM

Hillbilly bootleggers defy a Chicago gangster. Downbeat but actionful crime melodrama with an unusual background and plenty of car chases.

w James Arlee Philips, Walter Wise *d Arthur Ripley* *ph* Alan Stensvold *m* Jack Marshall

Robert Mitchum, Gene Barry, Jacques Aubuchon, Keely Smith

Thunder Rock***

GB 1942   112m   bw
Charter Films (John Boulting)

A journalist disgusted with the world of the thirties retires to a lighthouse on Lake Michigan and is haunted by the ghosts of immigrants drowned a century before.

Subtle adaptation of an impressive and topical anti-isolationist play, very well acted and presented.

w Jeffrey Dell, Bernard Miles, *play Robert Ardrey d Roy Boulting ph* Mutz Greenbaum (Max Greene) *m* Hans May

Michael Redgrave, Lilli Palmer, Barbara Mullen, James Mason, Frederick Valk, Frederick Cooper, Finlay Currie, Sybilla Binder
  'Boldly imaginative in theme and treatment.'—*Sunday Express*
  'More interesting technically than anything since *Citizen Kane.'—Manchester Guardian*

Thunderball**

GB 1965   132m   Technicolor   Panavision
UA / Eon / Kevin McClory

James Bond goes underwater.
Commercially the most successful Bond, but certainly not the best despite a plethora of action sequences.

w Richard Maibaum, John Hopkins, *novel* Ian Fleming *d* Terence Young *ph* Ted Moore *m* John Barry

Sean Connery, Adolfo Celi, Claudine Auger, Luciana Paluzzi, Rik Van Nutter, Bernard Lee, Lois Maxwell
  'The screenplay stands on tiptoe at the outermost edge of the suggestive and gazes yearningly down into the obscene.'—*John Simon*

Thunderbird Six

GB 1968   90m   Techniscope
UA / AP / Century 21 (Gerry and Sylvia Anderson)

International Rescue combats the Black Phantom.
Bright, suspenseful puppetoon based on the TV series.

w Gerry and Sylvia Anderson *d* David Lane *ph* Harry Oakes *m* Barry Gray *ad* Bob Bell
  'Holds some charm for adults, or at least for those who enjoy playing with miniature trains.'—*MFB*

Thunderbirds

US 1942   79m   Technicolor
TCF (Lamar Trotti)

Problems of Arizona flight instructors during World War II.
Very minor flagwaver.

w Lamar Trotti *d* William A. Wellman *ph* Ernest Palmer

Gene Tierney, Preston Foster, John Sutton, Jack

Holt, May Whitty, George Barbier, Richard
Haydn, Reginald Denny, Ted North

Thunderbirds
US 1952   99m   bw
Republic (John H. Auer)

An Oklahoma unit covers itself in glory during
World War II.
Scrappy, noisy war actioner with much newsreel
footage.

w Mary McCall Jnr d John H. Auer ph Reggie
Lanning m Victor Young

John Derek, John Barrymore Jnr, Mona
Freeman, Ward Bond, Gene Evans

Thunderbolt**
US 1929   94m   bw
Paramount

A gangster is caught, tried, and repents.
Gloomy melodrama with interesting style and
credits.

w Jules Furthman, Herman J. Mankiewicz
d Josef Von Sternberg ph Henry Gerrard

George Bancroft, Fay Wray, Richard Arlen,
Tully Marshall, Eugénie Besserer

AAN: George Bancroft

Thunderbolt and Lightfoot*
US 1974   115m   De Luxe   Panavision
UA / Malpaso (Robert Daley)

A bank robber escapes prison, disguises himself
as a preacher, befriends a young drifter, and
discovers that a new building stands on the spot
where the loot is hidden.
Violent melodrama reworking an ancient
comedy situation; well made on its level.

wd Michael Cimino ph Frank Stanley m Dee
Barton

Clint Eastwood, Jeff Bridges, George Kennedy,
Geoffrey Lewis, Catherine Bach

AAN: Jeff Bridges

Thunderhead, Son of Flicka*
US 1945   78m   Technicolor
TCF (Robert Bassler)

More where My Friend Flicka came from.
Unexceptionable family film with excellent
outdoor photography.

w Dwight Cummins, Dorothy Yost, novel Mary
O'Hara d Louis King ph Charles Clarke
m Cyril Mockridge

Roddy McDowall, Preston Foster, Rita
Johnson, James Bell, Carleton Young

Thunderstorm
GB 1955   88m   bw
Hemisphere / Binnie Barnes

A Spanish fisherman rescues a mysterious girl
from a derelict yacht and falls in love with her
although the villagers regard her as a witch.
Heady stuff on a low budget, quite smoothly
done for lovers of peasant drama.

w George St George, Geoffrey Holmes d John
Guillermin ph Manuel Berenguer m Paul
Misraki

Linda Christian, Carlos Thompson, Charles
Korvin

THX 1138*
US 1970   95m   Technicolor / scope
Warner / American Zoetrope (Francis Ford
Coppola,
    Lawrence Sturhahn)

In a future society, computer programmed and
emotionless, an automated human begins to
break the rules.
Orwellian science fiction; a thoughtful, rather
cold affair which is always good to look at.

w George Lucas, Walter Murch d George
Lucas ph Dave Meyers, Albert Kihn m Lalo
Schifrin

Robert Duvall, Donald Pleasence, Pedro Colley,
Maggie McOmie, Ian Wolfe

Thy Soul Shall Bear Witness*
Sweden 1920   70m approx (24 fps)   bw
    silent   Svensk Filmindustri
original title: Korkarlen; aka: The Phantom
    Carriage

A drunkard is knocked senseless, retraces his
misspent life, hears the carriage of death
approaching and returns to his family.
Old-fashioned moralistic saga which hit the right
note at the time and has scenes which still
impress.

wd Victor Sjostrom, novel Selma Lagerlöf ph J.
Julius Jaenzon

Victor Sjostrom, Hilda Borgstrom, Astrid Holm
† Remade in France in 1939 by Julien Duvivier,
as La Charette Fantome, with Pierre Fresnay
and Louis Jouvet; and again in Sweden in 1958
as Korkarlen, by Arne Mattson.

Tiara Tahiti*
GB 1962   100m   Eastmancolor
Rank / Ivan Foxwell

An up-from-the-ranks colonel and an
aristocratic smoothie captain continue their
antipathy in peacetime Tahiti, where one is

nearly murdered and the other gets his come-uppance.

Uneasy mixture of light comedy and character drama; enjoyable in parts, but flabbily assembled and muddily photographed.

w Geoffrey Cotterell, Ivan Foxwell, *novel* Geoffrey Cotterell *d* William T. Kotcheff *ph* Otto Heller *m* Philip Green

John Mills, James Mason, Herbert Lom, Claude Dauphin, Rosenda Monteros

Tick, Tick, Tick . . .*
US 1969 100m Metrocolor Panavision
MGM / Nelson-Barrett (Ralph Nelson, James Lee Barrett)

The first black sheriff in a southern community has trouble with murder and rape cases.
Socially conscious suspenser, well enough made from predictable elements and leading surprisingly to an upbeat ending.

w James Lee Barrett *d* Ralph Nelson *ph* Loyal Griggs *m* Jerry Stynes

Jim Brown, George Kennedy, Fredric March, Lynn Carlin, Don Stroud, Clifton James

A Ticket to Tomahawk*
US 1950 90m Technicolor
TCF (Robert Bassler)

A stagecoach line defies the new western railroad.
Would-be satirical western which doesn't quite have the stamina and after some pleasing touches settles for dullness.

w Mary Loos *d* Richard Sale *ph* Harry Jackson *m* Cyril Mockridge

Anne Baxter, Dan Duryea, Rory Calhoun, Walter Brennan, Charles Kemper, Connie Gilchrist, Arthur Hunnicutt, Sen Yung

Tickle Me
US 1965 90m De Luxe Panavision
AA (Ben Schwalb)

An unemployed rodeo star accepts a job at a health ranch and helps a girl escape from villains after hidden treasure.
Wispy star vehicle with an unexpected haunted ghost town climax.

w Elwood Ullman, Edward Bernds *d* Norman Taurog *ph* Loyal Griggs *m* Walter Scharf

Elvis Presley, Julia Adams, Jocelyn Lane, Jack Mullaney, Merry Anders, Connie Gilchrist

A Ticklish Affair
US 1963 95m Metrocolor Panavision
MGM / Euterpe (Joe Pasternak)

A naval commander in San Diego falls for a widow with several children.
Thin romantic comedy with too many juvenile antics.

w Ruth Brooks Flippen *d* George Sidney *ph* Milton Krasner *m* George Stoll, Robert Van Eyps

Shirley Jones, Gig Young, Red Buttons, Carolyn Jones, Edgar Buchanan

Tiger Bay*
GB 1959 105m bw
Rank / Wintle–Parkyn (John Hawkesworth)

A Polish seaman in Cardiff kills his faithless girl friend and kidnaps a child who proves more than a match for him.
Generally very proficient police chase melodrama with strong characterizations: a considerable box office success of its time.

w John Hawkesworth, Shelley Smith *d* J. Lee-Thompson *ph* Eric Cross *m* Laurie Johnson

Hayley Mills, John Mills, Horst Buchholz, Megs Jenkins, Anthony Dawson, Yvonne Mitchell

Tiger in the Smoke*
GB 1956 94m bw
Rank (Leslie Parkyn)

Ex-commando criminals comb London for hidden loot and threaten a young girl.
Odd little melodrama with a complex plot and a different, Graham Greene-like atmosphere.

w Anthony Pelissier, *novel* Marjorie Allingham *d* Roy Baker *ph* Geoffrey Unsworth *m* Malcolm Arnold

Tony Wright, Muriel Pavlow, Donald Sinden, Bernard Miles, Alec Clunes, Laurence Naismith, Christopher Rhodes, Kenneth Griffith, Beatrice Varley

The Tiger Makes Out*
US 1967 94m Technicolor
Columbia / Elan (George Justin)

A middle-aged New York postman takes revenge on society by kidnapping a young girl—who rather enjoys the experience.
Semi-surrealist comedy misguidedly extended from a two-character play; frantic pace prevents more than a few effective moments.

w Murray Shisgal, from his play *d* Arthur Hiller *ph* Arthur J. Ornitz *m* Milton Rogers

Eli Wallach, Anne Jackson, Bob Dishy, David Burns, Charles Nelson Reilly

Tiger Shark*
US 1932   80m   bw
Warner

A tuna fisherman who has lost a hand to a shark
marries the daughter of an old friend, finds she
loves someone else, and is conveniently killed by
another shark.
Vivid melodrama with a plot partly borrowed
from *Moby Dick* and itself partly borrowed by
innumerable other Warner films including *Kid
Galahad*, *The Wagons Roll at Night* and
Manpower.

w Wells Root, *story* Tuna by Houston Branch
d Howard Hawks ph Tony Gaudio

Edward G. Robinson, J. Carrol Naish, Zita
Johann

A Tiger Walks*
US 1963   91m   Technicolor
Walt Disney (Ron Miller)

In a small western town, a tiger escapes from the
circus.
A splendid animal and a happy ending help to
make this a pretty good film for children.

w Lowell S. Hawley, *novel* Ian Niall d Norman
Tokar ph William Snyder m Buddy Baker

Sabu, Brian Keith, Vera Miles, Pamela Franklin,
Kevin Corcoran, Edward Andrews, Una
Merkel, Frank McHugh
  'The Disney message runs true to form—
grown-ups should practise what they preach and
children are right about animals.'—*MFB*

Tight Spot
US 1955   97m   bw
Columbia (Lewis J. Rachmil)

A material witness in the trial of a gangster is
released from prison in the custody of an
attorney.
Fairly routine crime melodrama with unexciting
star performances.

w William Bowers, *play* Dead Pigeon by
Leonard Kantor d Phil Karlson ph Burnett
Guffey m Morris Stoloff

Edward G. Robinson, Ginger Rogers, Brian
Keith, Lorne Greene, Lucy Marlow, Katherine
Anderson

Till Death Us Do Part*
GB 1969   100m   Eastmancolor
British Lion / Associated London Films (Jon
  Pennington)

From the thirties to the sixties with loud-
mouthed, bigoted Londoner Alf Garnett.
Unremarkable and frequently misguided

opening-up of a phenomenally successful TV
series, adapted for the US as
All in the Family. The original cast wades
cheerfully enough through a bitty script; the
sequel, *The Alf Garnett Saga*, defeated them.

w Johnny Speight d Norman Cohen ph Harry
Waxman m Wilfrid Burns

Warren Mitchell, Dandy Nichols, Anthony
Booth, Una Stubbs, Liam Redmond, Bill
Maynard, Sam Kydd, Brian Blessed

Till the Clouds Roll By**
GB 1946   137m   Technicolor
MGM (Arthur Freed)

The life and times of composer Jerome Kern.
Better-than-average biopic with better-than-
average tunes and stars.

w Myles Connolly, Jean Holloway d Richard
Whorf ph Harry Stradling, George J. Folsey
md Lennie Hayton

Robert Walker, Judy Garland, Lucille Bremer,
Van Heflin, Mary Nash, Dinah Shore, Van
Johnson, *June Allyson*, Tony Martin, Kathryn
Grayson, *Lena Horne, Frank Sinatra, Virginia
O'Brien*

Till the End of Time*
US 1946   105m   bw
RKO

Three returning GIs find romance and problems
in their small town.
Downbeat variation on *The Best Years of Our
Lives* with a theme tune which puts words to a
Chopin Polonaise.

w Allen Rivkin d Edward Dmytryk ph Harry J.
Wild m Leigh Harline

Dorothy McGuire, Guy Madison, Robert
Mitchum

'Til We Meet Again
US 1939   99m   bw
Warner (David Lewis)

On a ship bound from Hong Kong to San
Francisco, a dying woman falls for a crook
about to be executed.
Stolid remake of *One Way Passage* (qv).

w Warren Duff, *story* Robert Lord d Edmund
Goulding ph Tony Gaudio

Merle Oberon, George Brent, Frank McHugh,
Pat O'Brien, Geraldine Fitzgerald, Eric Blore,
Binnie Barnes, Henry O'Neill, George Reeves

Till We Meet Again
US 1944   88m   bw
Paramount (David Lewis)

A French nun helps an American aviator escape
from the Nazis.
Very moderate, nicely photographed, romantic
war actioner.

w Lenore Coffee, *play* Alfred Maury *d* Frank
Borzage *ph Theodor Sparkuhl m* David
Buttolph

Ray Milland, Barbara Britton, Walter Slezak,
Lucile Watson, Konstantin Shayne, Vladimir
Sokoloff, Mona Freeman

Tillie and Gus*
US 1933 61m bw
Paramount (Douglas MacLean)

Two middle-aged cardsharps return home, help
their niece and nephew win an inheritance, and
come first in a paddleboat race.
Jumbled comedy with good moments and a
rousing climax.

w Walter de Leon, Francis Martin *d* Francis
Martin *ph* Benjamin Reynolds

W. C. Fields, Alison Skipworth, Baby Le Roy,
Jacqueline Wells, Clifford Jones, Clarence
Wilson, Edgar Kennedy, Barton MacLane

Tillie's Punctured Romance*
US 1914 60m approx (24 fps) bw silent
Keystone

A country maid falls for a con man who steals
her money; but she finally gets her revenge.
Museum piece comedy which no longer irritates
the funny bone but has clear historical interest.

w Hampton Del Ruth, *play* Tillie's Nightmare
by Edgar Smith *d* Mack Sennett

Marie Dressler, Charles Chaplin, Mabel
Normand, Mack Swain

Time Bomb*
GB 1952 72m bw
MGM (Richard Goldstone)
US title: *Terror on a Train*

A saboteur places a bomb on a goods train
travelling from the north of England to
Portsmouth.
Tolerable suspenser padded out with domestic
asides.

w Ken Bennett *d* Ted Tetzlaff *ph* Frederick A.
Young *m* John Addison

Glenn Ford, Anne Vernon, Maurice Denham,
Harcourt Williams, Harold Warrender, Bill
Fraser, John Horsley, Victor Maddern

Time Flies*
GB 1944 88m bw
GFD / Gainsborough (Edward Black)

A professor invents a time machine and takes his
friends back to the court of Good Queen Bess.
Very passable star farce.

w J. O. C. Orton, Ted Kavanaugh, Howard
Irving Young *d* Walter Forde *ph* Basil Emmott
md Louis Levy

Tommy Handley, Felix Aylmer, Evelyn Dall,
George Moon, Moore Marriott, Graham
Moffatt, John Salew, Olga Lindo. Stephane
Grappelly

A Time for Killing
US 1967 83m Pathecolor Panavision
Columbia / Sage Western (Harry Joe Brown)
GB title: *The Long Ride Home*

Confederate prisoners escape from a Union fort
and the commander sets off in pursuit.
Fairly savage western with Something to Say
about the corruption of war.

w Halsted Welles, *novel* Southern Blade by
Nelson and Shirley Wolford *d* Phil Karlson
ph Kenneth Peach *m* Mundell Lowe

Glenn Ford, George Hamilton, Inger Stevens,
Max Baer, Paul Petersen, Timothy Carey, Todd
Armstrong

A Time for Loving
GB 1971 104m colour
London Screen Plays / Mel Ferrer

Short romantic comedies set at different times in
the same Paris flat.
Portmanteau ooh-la-la, quite neat but pitifully
undernourished; certainly no *Plaza Suite.*

w Jean Anouilh *d* Christopher Miles
ph Andreas Winding *m* Michel Legrand
pd Theo Meurisse

Joanna Shimkus, Mel Ferrer, Britt Ekland,
Philippe Noiret, Lila Kedrova, Robert Dhery,
Michael Burns

Time Gentlemen Please
GB 1952 83m bw
Group Three (Herbert Mason)

A lazy tramp is the one blot on a prize-winning
English village.
Artificial, thinly scripted and overlit sub-Ealing
comedy with familiar characters and situations.

w Peter Blackmore, *novel* Nothing to Lose by R.
J. Minney *d* Lewis Gilbert *ph* Wilkie Cooper
m Antony Hopkins

Eddie Byrne, Hermione Baddeley, Jane Barrett,
Robert Brown, Raymond Lovell, Marjorie
Rhodes, Dora Bryan, Thora Hird, Sidney
James, Edie Martin, Ivor Barnard, Sidney Tafler
   'Quite a nice little picture.'—*Karel Reisz*

Time in the Sun***
Mexico 1933   60m   bw
Marie Seton

Unfinished fragments of Eisenstein's incomplete *Que Viva Mexico*, snippets from which were later released in various forms. This is the longest and presumably best version, with splendidly pictorial sequences of peasant and Indian life culminating with *Death Day*, all skulls and fireworks. Clearly the work of a master, though if completed the film might well have been a bore.

w Marie Seton, Paul Burnford *d* Sergei Eisenstein *ph* Edouard Tissé

Time Limit*
US 1957   95m   bw
UA / Richard Widmark, William Reynolds

During the Korean war an officer is courtmartialled for suspected collaboration. Suspenseful talk piece from a somewhat intellectualized play.

w Henry Denker, *play* Henry Denker, Ralph Berkey *d* Karl Malden *ph* Sam Leavitt *m* Fred Steiner

Richard Widmark, Richard Basehart, Dolores Michaels, June Lockhart, Carl Benton Reid, Martin Balsam, Rip Torn

'The tightly constructed story leads logically and unfalteringly to a tense climax.'—*Lindsay Anderson*

Time Lock*
GB 1957   73m   bw
Romulus (Peter Rogers)

A small boy is trapped in a bank vault just as it is being locked for the weekend.
Acceptable expansion of a Canadian TV suspenser.

w Peter Rogers, *play* Arthur Hailey *d* Gerald Thomas *ph* Peter Hennessy *m* Stanley Black

Robert Beatty, Betty McDowall, Vincent Winter, Lee Patterson, Alan Gifford, Robert Ayres

The Time Machine*
US 1960   103m   Metrocolor
MGM / Galaxy (George Pal)

A Victorian scientist builds a machine which after some trial and error transports him into the year 802701.
Surprisingly careful recreation of a period, and an undeniably charming machine, go for little when the future, including the villainous Morlocks, is so dull.

w David Duncan, *novel* H. G. Wells *d* George

Pal *ph* Paul C. Vogel *m* Russell Garcia
ad George W. Davis, William Ferrari

Rod Taylor, Yvette Mimieux, Alan Young, Sebastian Cabot, Tom Helmore, Whit Bissell, Doris Lloyd

The Time of Their Lives*
US 1946   82m   bw
Universal (Val Burton)

Revolutionary ghosts haunt a country estate. Unusual, quite effective Abbott and Costello vehicle with the comedians not playing as a team.

w Val Burton, Walter de Leon, Bradford Ropes, John Grant *d* Charles Barton *ph* Charles Van Enger *m* Milton Rosen

Bud Abbott, Lou Costello, Marjorie Reynolds, Binnie Barnes, Gale Sondergaard, John Shelton

The Time of Your Life*
US 1948   109m   bw
William Cagney

A group of lovable eccentrics spend much of their time philosophizing in a San Francisco bar. Not really a film at all, this essence of Saroyan contains much to enjoy or to annoy. The performances are pretty good.

w Nathaniel Curtis, *play William Saroyan* *d* H. C. Potter *ph* James Wong Howe *m* Carmen Dragon

James Cagney, William Bendix, Wayne Morris, Jeanne Cagney, Gale Page, Broderick Crawford, *James Barton*, Ward Bond, Paul Draper, James Lydon, Richard Erdman, Natalie Schaefer

'They have done so handsomely by Saroyan that in the long run everything depends on how much of Saroyan you can take.'—*Time*

Time out of Mind
US 1947   88m   bw
U-I

The housekeeper's daughter finances music studies for the master's ungrateful son. Silly romantic melodrama with few visible compensations.

w Abem Finkel, Arnold Phillips, *novel* Rachel Field *d* Robert Siodmak *ph* Maury Gertsman

Phyllis Calvert, Robert Hutton, Ella Raines, Eddie Albert, Leo G. Carroll

The Time, the Place and the Girl
US 1946   105m   Technicolor
Warner (Alex Gottlieb)

Two nightclub owners have problems.

Lightweight musical, indistinguishable from a dozen others.

w Francis Swann, Agnes Christine Johnson, Lynn Starling d David Butler ph William V. Skall m Arthur Schwartz

Dennis Morgan, Jack Carson, Janis Paige, Martha Vickers, S. Z. Sakall, Alan Hale, Donald Woods, Angela Greene, Florence Bates

AAN: song 'A Girl in Calico' (m Arthur Schwartz, ly Leo Robin)

A Time to Love and a Time to Die*
US 1958   132m   Eastmancolor
  Cinemascope
U-I (Robert Arthur)

During World War II, a German officer on his last leave solves problems at home but is killed on his return to the front.
Interesting but preachy and generally misguided attempt, by the studio which made All Quiet on the Western Front and The Road Back, to repeat the dose in colour and wide screen.

w Orin Jannings, novel Erich Maria Remarque d Douglas Sirk ph Russell Metty m Miklos Rozsa

John Gavin, Lilo Pulver, Keenan Wynn, Jock Mahoney, Thayer David, Agnes Windeck, Erich Maria Remarque

The Time Travelers*
US 1964   84m   Pathecolor
AIP / Dobie (William Redlin)

Scientists venture 107 years into the future, and on escaping find themselves in a time trap. Ingenious and lively low-budget science fiction with a sobering ending.

wd Ib Melchior ph William Zsigismond m Richard La Salle

Preston Foster, Phil Carey, Merry Anders, John Hoyt, Joan Woodbury

Time without Pity*
GB 1957   88m   bw
Harlequin (John Arnold, Anthony Simmons)

An alcoholic arrives in London to seek new evidence which will prevent his son from being executed for murder.
Heavy-going, introspective, hysterical, downbeat melodrama which takes itself with a seriousness which is almost deadly.

w Ben Barzman play Someone Waiting by Emlyn Williams d Joseph Losey ph Freddie Francis m Tristam Cary

Michael Redgrave, Alec McCowen, Leo McKern, Renée Houston, Ann Todd, Peter

Cushing, Paul Daneman, Lois Maxwell, George Devine, Richard Wordsworth, Joan Plowright
'It hammers home its effects with the concentration of a heavyweight out for the kill.'—Philip Oakes

Timetable*
US 1955   79m   bw
(UA) Mark Stevens

An insurance investigator is assigned to a train robbery which he actually committed himself. Concise suspenser with good script and treatment.

w Aben Kandel d Mark Stevens ph Charles Van Enger

Mark Stevens, Felicia Farr, King Calder, Wesley Addy

Tin Pan Alley***
US 1940   95m   bw
TCF (Kenneth MacGowan)

During World War I and after, two dancing girls love the same composer.
Archetypal musical, full of Broadway clichés, razzmatazz and zip. Remade 1950 as I'll Get By, not to such peppy effect.

w Robert Ellis, Helen Logan d Walter Lang ph Leon Shamroy ch Seymour Felix songs Mack Gordon, Harry Revel m Alfred Newman

Alice Faye, Betty Grable, John Payne, Jack Oakie, Allen Jenkins, Esther Ralston, The Nicholas Brothers, John Loder, Elisha Cook Jnr

AA: Alfred Newman

The Tin Star*
US 1957   93m   bw   Vistavision
Paramount / Perlberg–Seaton

An ex-sheriff turned bounty hunter helps a new young sheriff to catch bandits.
Dignified and well-characterized western with customary pleasures.

w Dudley Nichols d Anthony Mann ph Loyal Griggs m Elmer Bernstein

Henry Fonda, Anthony Perkins, Betsy Palmer, Michel Ray, Neville Brand, John McIntire

AAN: original story (Barney Slater, Joel Kane)

The Tingler
US 1959   82m   bw
Columbia / William Castle

Fear (it says here) can create on the spinal column a parasite removable only by screaming. A scientist isolates it and it runs amok in a silent cinema.

Ridiculous shocker with generally dull handling but effective moments.

w Robb White d William Castle ph Wilfrid Cline m Von Dexter

Vincent Price, Judith Evelyn, Darryl Hickman, Patricia Cutts

'The sheer effrontery of this piece of hokum is enjoyable in itself.'—*MFB*

Tip on a Dead Jockey
US 1957 99m bw
MGM (Edwin H. Knopf)
GB title: *Time for Action*

A flier loses his nerve and turns international smuggler, but reforms.
Gloomy, pedestrian star melodrama, dully cast.

w Charles Lederer, *novel* Irwin Shaw d Richard Thorpe m Miklos Rozsa

Robert Taylor, Dorothy Malone, Gia Scala, Martin Gabel, Marcel Dalio, Jack Lord

Titanic*
US 1953 98m bw
TCF (Charles Brackett)

Personal dramas aboard the *Titanic* in 1912 come to a head as the ship hits an iceberg.
An excellent example of studio production is squandered on a dim script which arouses no excitement.

w Charles Brackett, Walter Reisch, Richard Breen d Jean Negulesco ph *Joe MacDonald* m Sol Kaplan ad Lyle Wheeler, Maurice Ransford

Clifton Webb, Barbara Stanwyck, Robert Wagner, Audrey Dalton, Thelma Ritter, Brian Aherne, Richard Basehart, Allyn Joslyn

AAN: script

The Titfield Thunderbolt***
US 1952 84m Technicolor
Ealing (Michael Balcon)

When a branch railway line is threatened with closure, the villagers take it over as a private concern.
Undervalued on its release in the wake of other Ealing comedies, this now seems among the best of them as well as an immaculate colour production showing the England that is no more; the script has pace, the whole thing is brightly polished and the action works up to a fine climactic frenzy.

w T. E. B. Clarke d Charles Crichton ph Douglas Slocombe m Georges Auric

Stanley Holloway, George Relph, John Gregson,

Godfrey Tearle, *Edie Martin*, Naunton Wayne, Gabrielle Brune, Sidney James, Jack McGowran, Ewan Roberts, Reginald Beckwith

To Be or Not to Be****
US 1942 99m bw
(Alexander Korda) Ernst Lubitsch

Warsaw actors get involved in an underground plot and an impersonation of invading Nazis, including Hitler.
Marvellous free-wheeling entertainment which starts as drama and descends through romantic comedy and suspense into farce; accused of bad taste at the time, but now seen as an outstanding example of Hollywood moonshine, kept alight through sheer talent and expertise.

w Edwin Justus Mayer, story Ernst Lubitsch, Melchior Lengyel d Ernst Lubitsch ph Rudolph Maté m Werner Heymann ad Vincent Korda

Jack Benny, Carole Lombard, Robert Stack, Stanley Ridges, Felix Bressart, Lionel Atwill, Sig Rumann, Tom Dugan, Charles Halton

'As effective an example of comic propaganda as *The Great Dictator* and far better directed.'—Charles Higham, 1972
'Based on an indiscretion, but undoubtedly a work of art.'—*James Agee*

To Catch a Thief*
US 1955 97m Technicolor Vistavision
Paramount / Alfred Hitchcock

A famous cat burglar who has retired to the Riviera catches a thief who is imitating his old style.
Very slow, floppy and rather boring entertainment enlivened by the scenery and the odd Hitchcock touch.

w John Michael Hayes, *novel* David Dodge d Alfred Hitchcock ph Robert Burks m Lyn Murray

Cary Grant, Grace Kelly, *Jessie Royce Landis*, John Williams, Charles Vanel, Brigitte Auber

AAN: Robert Burks

To Each His Own**
US 1946 100m bw
Paramount (Charles Brackett)

During World War II, a middle-aged woman in London meets the soldier who is her own illegitimate and long-since-adopted son.
The woman's picture par excellence, put together with tremendous Hollywood flair and extremely enjoyable to watch.

w Charles Brackett, Jacques Théry d Mitchell Leisen ph Daniel L. Fapp m Victor Young ad Hans Dreier, Roland Anderson

Olivia de Havilland, John Lund, Roland Culver, Mary Anderson, Philip Terry, Bill Goodwin, Virginia Welles, Virginia Horne

AA: original story (Charles Brackett); Olivia de Havilland

To Find a Man*
US 1971   93m   Eastmancolor
Columbia / Rastar (Irving Pincus)

The spoiled daughter of a rich family becomes pregnant and is helped by a young chemist.
Quiet, well-made minor drama about maturity, with good small-town atmosphere.

w Arnold Schulman, novel S. J. Wilson *d* Buzz Kulik *ph* Andy Laszlo *m* David Shire

Pamela Martin, Darrell O'Connor, *Lloyd Bridges,* Phyllis Newman, Tom Ewell, Tom Bosley

To Have and Have Not**
US 1945   100m   bw
Warner (Howard Hawks)

An American charter boat captain in Martinique gets involved with Nazis.
Fairly routinely made studio adventure notable for first pairing of Bogart and Bacall, as an imitation of *Casablanca,* and for its consistent though not outstanding entertainment value. Remade later as *The Breaking Point* (qv) and *The Gun Runners* (qv), and not dissimilar from *Key Largo* (qv).

w Jules Furthman, William Faulkner, novel Ernest Hemingway *d Howard Hawks ph* Sid Hickox *m* Franz Waxman (uncredited) *md* Leo F. Forbstein

Humphrey Bogart, Lauren Bacall, Walter Brennan, Hoagy Carmichael, Dolores Moran, Sheldon Leonard, Dan Seymour, Marcel Dalio

'Remarkable for the ingenuity and industry with which the original story and the individualities of Ernest Hemingway have been rendered down into Hollywood basic.'— *Richard Winnington*

'Sunlight on the lattice, sex in the corridors, a new pianist at the café, pistol shots, the fat sureté man coming round after dark.'— *William Whitebait*

To Hell and Back
US 1955   106m   Technicolor
    Cinemascope
U-I (Aaron Rosenberg)

The war career of America's most decorated infantryman.
Routine war story which happens to be about a fellow who later became a film star.

w Gil Doud, *book* Audie Murphy *d* Jesse Hibbs *ph* Maury Gertsman *m* Joseph Gershenson

Audie Murphy, Marshall Thompson, Charles Drake, Gregg Palmer, Jack Kelly, Paul Picerni, Susan Kohner

'The emotion is congealed and there is no real personal response to the anguish of war.'—*John Gillett*

To Kill a Clown
GB 1971   104m   De Luxe
Palomar (Theodore Sills)

A painter and his wife move to a New England isle and are menaced by a crippled Vietnam veteran and his vicious dogs.
Pretentious, politically oriented rehash of *The Most Dangerous Game* (qv), carefully made but too slow for suspense.

w George Bloomfield, I. C. Rapoport, *novel* Master of the Hounds by Algis Budrys
d George Bloomfield *ph* Walter Lassally *m* Richard Hill, John Hawkins

Alan Alda, Blyth Danner, Heath Lamberts, Eric Clavering

To Kill a Mockingbird**
US 1963   129m   bw
U-I (Alan Pakula)

A lawyer in a small southern town defends a black man accused of murder.
Familiar dollops of social conscience, very well presented with a child interest and excellent atmosphere, but a mite overlong.

w Horton Foote, *novel* Harper Lee *d Robert Mulligan ph* Russell Harlan *m* Elmer Bernstein

Gregory Peck, Mary Badham, Philip Alford, John Megna, Frank Overton, Rosemary Murphy, Ruth White, Brock Peters

AA: script; Gregory Peck
AAN: best picture; Robert Mulligan; Russell Harlan; Elmer Bernstein; Mary Badham

To Paris with Love
GB 1954   78m   Technicolor
GFD / Two Cities (Anthony Darnborough)

A middle-aged widower and his son go to Paris on holiday and devise matrimonial plans for each other.
Thin, disappointing taradiddle which is short but seems long.

w Robert Buckner *d* Robert Hamer *ph* Reg Wyer *m* Edwin Astley

Alec Guinness, Vernon Gray, Odile Versois, Jacques François, Elina Labourdette, Austin Trevor

'The general impression is somehow too
aimless, too muted.'—*Gavin Lambert*

To Please a Lady*
US 1951   91m   bw
MGM (Clarence Brown)

A ruthless midget-car racer falls for the lady
journalist who is hounding him.
Good action programmer with no frills.

w Barre Lyndon, Marge Decker *d* Clarence
Brown *ph* Harold Rosson *m* Bronislau Kaper

Clark Gable, Barbara Stanwyck, Adolphe
Menjou, Will Geer, Roland Winters, Emory
Parnell, Frank Jenks

To Sir with Love
GB 1967   105m   Technicolor
Columbia (James Clavell)

A West Indian teacher comes to a tough East
End school.
Sentimental non-realism patterned after *The
Blackboard Jungle* but much softer; its influence
led to a TV situation comedy, *Please Sir*.

w James Clavell, *novel* E. R. Braithwaite
d James Clavell *ph* Paul Beeson *m* Ron Grainer

Sidney Poitier, Christian Roberts, Judy Geeson,
Suzy Kendall, Lulu, Faith Brook, Geoffrey
Bayldon, Patricia Routledge

'The sententious script sounds as if it has been
written by a zealous Sunday school teacher after
a particularly exhilarating boycott of South
African oranges.'—*MFB*

To the Devil a Daughter
GB / Germany 1975   93m   Technicolor
EMI / Hammer–Terra Filmkunst (Roy Skeggs)

An occult novelist is asked to take care of a girl
who has been 'promised' to a group of Satanists.
Confusingly told, high camp diabolic thriller.

w Chris Wicking, *novel* Dennis Wheatley
d Peter Sykes *ph* David Watkin *m* Paul Glass

Richard Widmark, Christopher Lee, Denholm
Elliott, Honor Blackman, Michael Goodliffe,
Anthony Valentine, Derek Francis, Nastassja
Kinski

To the Ends of the Earth**
US 1948   107m   bw
Columbia (Sidney Buchman)

A government agent follows a world-wide trail
after a narcotics gang.
Thoroughly riveting conventional thriller, nicely
made and photographed.

w Jay Richard Kennedy *d* Robert Stevenson
ph Burnett Guffey

Dick Powell, Signe Hasso, Ludwig Donath,
Vladimir Sokoloff, Edgar Barrier

To the Shores of Tripoli
US 1942   82m   Technicolor
TCF (Milton Sperling)

A cocky playboy becomes a tough marine.
Despite the title, this modest flagwaver with
romantic trimmings never moves out of the San
Diego training grounds.

w Lamar Trotti *d* Bruce Humberstone
ph Edward Cronjager *m* Alfred Newman

Maureen O'Hara, John Payne, Randolph Scott,
Nancy Kelly, William Tracy, Maxie
Rosenbloom, Henry Morgan, Russell Hicks,
Minor Watson

To the Victor
US 1948   100m   bw
Warner (Jerry Wald)

French collaborators stand trial for war crimes.
Glum melodrama with inadequate cast.

w Richard Brooks *d* Delmer Daves *ph* Robert
Burks *m* David Buttolph

Dennis Morgan, Viveca Lindfors, Bruce
Bennett, Victor Francen, Dorothy Malone, Tom
d'Andrea, Eduardo Ciannelli, Joseph Buloff,
Luis Van Rooten, William Conrad

The Toast of New Orleans
US 1950   97m   Technicolor
MGM (Joe Pasternak)

A Bayou villager becomes a star of the New
Orleans opera.
Very ordinary setting for a new singing star.

w Sy Gomberg, George Wells *d* Norman
Taurog *ph* William Snyder *md* George Stoll
ch Eugene Loring

Kathryn Grayson, David Niven, Mario Lanza,
J. Carrol Naish, James Mitchell, Richard
Hageman, Clinton Sundberg, Sig Arno

AAN: song 'Be My Love' (*m* Nicholas
Brodszky, *ly* Sammy Cahn)

The Toast of New York**
US 1937   109m   bw
RKO (Edward Small)

A 19th-century medicine showman becomes a
notorious Wall Street financier.
Smart biopic of Jim Fisk; good entertainment
with accomplished production.

w Dudley Nichols, John Twist, Joel Sayre
d Rowland V. Lee *ph* Peverell Marley
m Nathaniel Shilkret

Edward Arnold, Cary Grant, Frances Farmer,

Jack Oakie, Donald Meek, Clarence Kolb, Thelma Leeds

Tobacco Road***
US 1941 84m bw
TCF (Jack Kirkland, Harry H. Oshrin)

Poor whites in Georgia are turned off their land. This bowdlerized version of a sensational book and play has superbly orchestrated farcical scenes separated by delightfully pictorial quieter moments: it isn't what was intended, but in its own way it's quite marvellous.

w *Nunnally Johnson, novel* Erskine Caldwell, *play* Jack Kirkland *d John Ford ph Arthur Miller m David Buttolph*

Charley Grapewin, Elizabeth Patterson, Dana Andrews, Gene Tierney, *Marjorie Rambeau,* Ward Bond, William Tracy, Zeffie Tilbury, Slim Summerville, Grant Mitchell, Russell Simpson, Spencer Charters

Tobruk
US 1967 110m Techniscope
Universal / Corman / Gibraltar (Gene Corman)

During the North African war, a British major and some German Jews try to blow up the Nazi fuel bunkers.
Routine war adventure, quite tough and spectacular but undistinguished.

w Leo V. Gordon d Arthur Hiller ph Russell Harlan m Bronislau Kaper

Rock Hudson, George Peppard, Nigel Green, Guy Stockwell, Jack Watson, Liam Redmond, Leo Gordon, Norman Rossington, Percy Herbert

Toby Tyler*
US 1959 96m Technicolor
Walt Disney (Bill Walsh)

In 1910, a young orphan runs away to join a travelling circus in the midwest, and with the help of a chimp becomes a famous star.
Acceptable, predictable family fare.

w Bill Walsh, Lillie Hayward, *novel* James Otis Kaler d Charles Barton ph William Snyder m Buddy Baker

Kevin Corcoran, Henry Calvin, Gene Sheldon, Bob Sweeney, James Drury

Today We Live*
US 1933 113m bw
MGM (Howard Hawks)

During World War I, an aristocratic English girl and her three lovers all find themselves at the front, and two fail to return.

Stilted romantic melodrama with imposing credentials.

w Edith Fitzgerald, Dwight Taylor, William Faulkner, *story* Turnabout by William Faulkner d Howard Hawks ph Oliver T. Marsh

Joan Crawford, Gary Cooper, Robert Young, Franchot Tone, Roscoe Karns, Louise Closser Hale, Rollo Lloyd

The Todd Killings*
US 1970 93m Technicolor Panavision
National General (Barry Shear)

In a small American town, a 23-year-old boy starts out on a rampage of rape and murder.
Violent psychological melodrama, based on fact, with inventive direction.

w Dennis Murphy, Joe L. Oliansky d Barry Shear ph Harold E. Stine m Leonard Rosenman

Robert F. Lyons, Richard Thomas, Belinda Montgomery, Barbara Bel Geddes, Gloria Grahame
'The most striking of the many recent film versions of the souring of the American dream.'—*Tony Rayns*

Together Again
US 1944 93m bw
Columbia (Virginia Van Upp)

The widow of a New England mayor commissions a statue in his honour.
The title refers to the reteaming of the stars who were so popular in *Love Affair* and *When Tomorrow Comes*, which is a sign of the lack of invention elsewhere. A comedy without laughs.

w Virgina Van Upp, F. Hugh Herbert d Charles Vidor ph Joseph Walker m Werner Heymann

Charles Boyer, Irene Dunne, Charles Coburn, Mona Freeman, Jerome Courtland, Elizabeth Patterson, Charles Dingle, Walter Baldwin

Tokyo Joe
US 1949 88m bw
Columbia / Santana (Robert Lord)

A former nightclub owner returns to postwar Japan to reclaim his fortune and his ex-wife.
Dispirited star melodrama.

w Cyril Hume, Bertram Millhauser d Stuart Heisler ph Charles Lawton Jnr m George Antheil

Humphrey Bogart, Florence Marly, Alexander Knox, Sessue Hayakawa, Lora Lee Michel, Jerome Courtland

Tolable David *
US 1921   80m approx (24 fps)   bw   silent
First National / Inspiration

A quiet farming community is disrupted by three
marauding convicts, who are finally despatched
by the peace-loving youngest son.
Fresh, sympathetic David-and-Goliath story
which was a huge popular success on its release.

w Edmund Goulding, Henry King, *novel* Joseph
Hergesheimer *d Henry King ph* Henry
Cronjager

Richard Barthelmess, Gladys Hulette, Ernest
Torrence, Warner Richmond
† Columbia remade the story in 1931 with
Richard Cromwell, but its time had passed.

Tom Brown's Schooldays *
US 1940   86m   bw
(RKO) The Play's the Thing (Gene Towne,
   Graham Baker)

Tom Brown finds life at Rugby brutal, but helps
to become a civilizing influence.
Pretty lively Hollywood version of a rather
unattractive semi-classic.

w Walter Ferris, Frank Cavell, *novel* Thomas
Hughes *d* Robert Stevenson *ph* Nicholas
Musuraca *m* Anthony Collins

Jimmy Lydon, Cedric Hardwicke, Billy Halop,
Freddie Bartholemew, Gale Storm, Josephine
Hutchinson

Tom Brown's Schooldays
GB 1951   96m   bw
Renown (George Minter)

Unexciting remake featuring one surprisingly
strong performance.

w Noel Langley *d* Gordon Parry *ph* C.
Pennington-Richards *m* Richard Addinseli

Robert Newton, John Howard Davies, Diana
Wynyard, Francis de Wolff, Kathleen Byron,
Hermione Baddeley, James Hayter, Rachel
Gurney, Amy Veness, Max Bygraves, Michael
Hordern, John Charlesworth, John Forrest
'An odd mixture of the brutal and the solemnly
improving.'—*Richard Mallett, Punch*

Tom, Dick and Harry **
US 1940   86m   bw
RKO (Robert Sisk)

A girl daydreams about her three boy friends,
but can't make up her mind.
Brightly-handled comedy which became a minor
classic but does seem to have faded a little.
Remade as *The Girl Most Likely* (qv).

w Paul Jarrico *d* Garson Kanin *ph* Merrit
Gerstad *m* Roy Webb

Ginger Rogers, Burgess Meredith, Alan
Marshal, George Murphy, *Phil Silvers*, Joe
Cunningham, Jane Seymour, Lenore Lonergan
'Foot by foot the best made picture of this
year.'—*Otis Ferguson*

AAN: Paul Jarrico

Tom Jones ***
GB 1963   129m   Eastmancolor
UA / Woodfall (Tony Richardson)

In 18th-century England a foundling is brought
up by the squire and marries his daughter after
many adventures.
Fantasia on Old England, at some distance from
the original novel, with the director trying every
possible jokey approach against a meticulously
realistic physical background. Despite trade
fears, the *Hellzapoppin* style made it an
astonishing box office success (the sex helped),
though it quickly lost its freshness and was much
imitated.

w John Osborne, *novel* Henry Fielding *d Tony
Richardson ph Walter Lassally, Manny Wynn
m John Addison pd* Ralph Brinton

Albert Finney, Susannah York, Hugh Griffith,
Edith Evans, Joan Greenwood, Diane Cilento,
George Devine, Joyce Redman, David Warner,
Wilfrid Lawson, Freda Jackson, Rachel
Kempson

'Uncertainty, nervousness, muddled method
. . . desperation is writ large over it.'—*Stanley
Kauffmann*

'Much of the time it looks like a home movie,
made with sporadic talent by a group with more
enthusiasm than discipline.'—*Tom Milne*

'It is as though the camera had become a
method actor: there are times when you wish you
could buy, as on certain juke boxes, five minutes'
silence . . . Obviously a film which elicits such
lyric ejaculations from the reviewers cannot be
all good.'—*John Simon*

AA: John Osborne; Tony Richardson; Walter
Lassally; Albert Finney
AAN: Hugh Griffith; Edith Evans; Diane
Cilento; Joyce Redman

Tom Sawyer
US 1973   103m   De Luxe   Panavision
UA / Readers Digest (Arthur P. Jacobs)

Reverential, rather tediously over-produced
version for family audiences of the seventies,
with brief songs and real Mississippi locations.

w/m/ly Richard and Robert Sherman *d* Don
Taylor *ph* Frank Stanley *md* John Williams
pd Philip Jefferies

Johnnie Whitaker, Celeste Holm, Warren Oates,
Jeff East, Jodie Foster

AAN: Richard and Robert Sherman; John Williams

Tom Thumb*
GB 1958 98m Eastmancolor
MGM / Galaxy (George Pal)

A tiny forest boy outwits a couple of thieves.
Slight musical built round the legend of a two-inch boy; good trickwork and songs make it a delightful film for children.

w Ladislas Fodor d George Pal ph Georges Périnal m Douglas Gamley, Kenneth V. Jones sp Tom Howard

Russ Tamblyn, Jessie Matthews, Peter Sellers, Terry-Thomas, Alan Young, June Thorburn, Ian Wallace

The Tomb of Ligeia**
GB 1964 81m Eastmancolor
Cinemascope
American International (Roger Corman)

A brooding Victorian metamorphoses his dead wife into a cat, then into the beautiful Lady Rowena.
Complex but rather fascinating horror suspenser which rejogs familiar elements into something new; the best of the Corman Poes.

w Robert Towne, story Edgar Allan Poe d Roger Corman ph Arthur Grant m Kenneth V. Jones

Vincent Price, Elizabeth Shepherd, John Westbrook, Oliver Johnson, Richard Johnson, Derek Francis

Tommy*
GB 1975 108m colour
Hemdale / Robert Stigwood

A deaf, dumb and blind child is eventually cured and becomes a rock celebrity.
Mystical rock opera screened with the director's usual barrage of effects and an ear-splitting score. Of occasional interest.

w Ken Russell, from the opera by Pete Townshend and the Who d Ken Russell ph Dick Bush, Ronnie Taylor m Pete Townshend and the Who

Roger Daltrey, Ann-Margret, Oliver Reed, Elton John, Eric Clapton, Keith Moon

Tomorrow at Ten*
GB 1962 80m bw
Mancunian (Tom Blakeley)

A crook kidnaps a small boy and locks him up with a time bomb while he makes his demands in person. When the kidnapper is killed, the police have to hunt against time.

Tense second feature, well acted and efficiently done.

w Peter Millar, James Kelly d Lance Comfort ph Basil Emmott m Bernie Fenton

Robert Shaw, John Gregson, Alec Clunes, Alan Wheatley, Ernest Clark, Kenneth Cope

Tomorrow Is Forever*
US 1946 105m bw
RKO—International (David Lewis)

A man supposed dead in the war returns with an altered face to find his wife has remarried.
Enoch Arden rides again in a rampant woman's picture which is well enough made to be generally entertaining.

w Lenore Coffee d Irving Pichel ph Joe Valentine m Max Steiner

Orson Welles, Claudette Colbert, George Brent, Lucile Watson, Richard Long, Natalie Wood

Tomorrow Never Comes
Canada / GB 1977 109m colour
Rank / Classic / Montreal Trust / Neffbourne (Michael Klinger, Julian Melzack)

A jealous lover shoots a caller at his girl's beach cabana and a police siege begins.
Far from the class of Le Jour Se Lève, this is an exploitative and violent melodrama which need never have been made.

w David Pursall, Jack Seddon, Sydney Banks d Peter Collinson ph François Protat m Roy Budd

Oliver Reed, Susan George, Raymond Burr, Stephen McHattie, John Ireland, Donald Pleasence, John Osborne, Cec Linder

Tomorrow the World*
US 1944 86m bw
UA / Lester Cowan

A college professor adopts his orphaned German nephew, who turns out to be an ardent 12-year-old Nazi.
Adequate, predictable screen version of a once-topical play.

w Ring Lardner Jnr, Leopold Atlas, play James Gow, Armand D'Usseau d Leslie Fenton m Louis Applebaum

Fredric March, Betty Field, Skip Homeier, Agnes Moorehead, Joan Carroll

Tomorrow We Live
GB 1942 85m bw
British Aviation (George King)
US title: At Dawn We Die

French villagers help a spy escape to Britain.
Minor flagwaver marred by cheap sets.

w Anatole de Grunwald, Katherine Strueby
d George King

John Clements, Greta Gynt, Hugh Sinclair, Judy
Kelly, Godfrey Tearle, Yvonne Arnaud,
Bransby Williams

Tonight and Every Night
US 1945   92m   Technicolor
Columbia (Victor Saville)

The lives and loves of London showgirls during
the blitz.
Ludicrous concoction looking nothing like
London and certainly nothing like the Windmill,
the theatre to which it allegedly pays tribute.
There are some tolerable numbers along the way.

w Lesser Samuels, Abem Finkel, *play* Heart of a
City by Lesley Storm d Victor Saville
ph Rudolph Maté md Morris Stoloff, Marvin
Skiles

Rita Hayworth, Lee Bowman, Janet Blair, Marc
Platt, Leslie Brooks, Dusty Anderson, Florence
Bates, Ernest Cossart

AAN: Morris Stoloff, Marvin Skiles; song
'Anywhere' (m Jule Styne, ly Sammy Cahn)

Tonight or Never
US 1931   80m   bw
Samuel Goldwyn

A prima donna falls for a man she thinks is a
Venetian gigolo, but he turns out to be an
impresario from New York.
Flimsy comedy which turned out to be its star's
last vehicle of any consequence for twenty years.

w Ernest Vajda, *play* Lily Hatvany d Mervyn
Le Roy ph Gregg Toland md Alfred Newman

Gloria Swanson, Melvyn Douglas (debut),
Ferdinand Gottschalk, Robert Greig, Alison
Skipworth, Boris Karloff

Tonight We Sing*
US 1953   109m   Technicolor
TCF (George Jessel)

Sol Hurok stifles his own talent to become a
great musical impresario.
Blameless uppercrust biopic, with plenty of well-
staged guest talent.

w Harry Kurnitz, George Oppenheimer
d Mitchell Leisen ph Leon Shamroy md Alfred
Newman ch David Lichine

David Wayne, Anne Bancroft, Ezio Pinza
(Chaliapin), Roberta Peters, Tamara
Toumanova (Pavlova), Isaac Stern (Eugene
Ysaye), Jan Peerce

Tonka
US 1958   97m   Technicolor
Walt Disney

A Sioux Indian tames a magnificent white horse,
and after many adventures is reunited with him
at Little Big Horn.
Unremarkable and overlong adventure story.

w Lewis R. Foster, Lillie Hayward, *novel*
Comanche by David Appel d Lewis R. Foster
ph Loyal Griggs

Sal Mineo, Phil Carey, Jerome Courtland,
Rafael Campos, H. M. Wynant

Tony Rome*
US 1967   111m   De Luxe   Panavision
TCF / Arcola / Millfield (Aaron Rosenberg)

A seedy Miami private eye runs into murder
when he guards a millionaire's daughter.
Complex old-fashioned murder mystery
decorated with the new amorality and
fashionable violence. Tolerable for its
backgrounds and professional expertise. Sequel:
Lady in Cement (qv).

w Richard L. Breen, *novel* Miami Mayhem by
Marvin H. Albert d Gordon Douglas ph Joe
Biroc m Billy May

Frank Sinatra, Jill St John, Richard Conte,
Gena Rowlands, Simon Oakland, Jeffrey Lynn,
Lloyd Bochner, Sue Lyon

Too Hot to Handle*
US 1938   105m   bw
MGM (Lawrence Weingarten)

Adventures of a scoop-seeking newsreel
cameraman.
Boisterous comedy-melodrama with as many
sags as highlights but generally making a
cheerful star entertainment.

w Laurence Stallings, John Lee Mahin d Jack
Conway ph Harold Rosson m Franz Waxman

Clark Gable, Myrna Loy, Walter Connolly,
Walter Pidgeon, Leo Carrillo, Johnny Hines,
Virginia Weidler

'It's like an old-fashioned serial . . . no one can
call it dull.'—*Howard Barnes*

'Breathlessly paced, witty, and violent, this is
one of the more acid comedies to have been
produced by the Thirties.'—*John Baxter*

Too Hot to Handle
GB 1960   100m   Eastmancolor
ABP / Wigmore (Selim Cattan)

Two Soho strip club owners join forces to hunt
down a blackmailer.

Rotten, hilarious British gangster film set in a totally unreal underworld and very uncomfortably cast.

w Herbert Kretzmer *d* Terence Young *ph* Otto Heller *m* Eric Spear

Leo Genn, Jayne Mansfield, Karl Boehm, Danik Patisson, Christopher Lee, Patrick Holt

Too Late Blues
US 1961   100m   bw
Paramount (John Cassavetes)

A jazz musician falls for a neurotic girl and has fears of going commercial.
Uninteresting professional feature from a director whose reputation was made with the amateur *Shadows*.

w John Cassavetes, Richard Carr *d* John Cassavetes *ph* Lionel Lindon *m* David Raksin

John Cassavetes, Stella Stevens, Bobby Darin, Everett Chambers, Nick Dennis, Rupert Crosse, Vince Edwards

Too Late for Tears
US 1949   99m   bw
(UA) Hunt Stromberg

A lady bluebeard disposes of both husbands and boyfriends.
Silly melodrama, poorly cast.

w Roy Huggins *d* Byron Haskin *ph* William Mellor *m* Dale Butts

Lizabeth Scott, Don Defore, Arthur Kennedy, Dan Duryea, Kristine Miller, Barry Kelley

Too Late the Hero*
US 1969   144m   Technicolor   70mm
Associates and Aldrich / Palomar

In World War II the Japanese hold one end of a small Pacific island, British and Americans the other.
Semi-cynical, long and bloody war adventure of competence but no great merit.

w Robert Aldrich, Lukas Heller *d* Robert Aldrich *ph* Joseph Biroc *m* Gerald Fried

Michael Caine, Cliff Robertson, Ian Bannen, Henry Fonda, Harry Andrews, Denholm Elliott, Ronald Fraser, Percy Herbert

Too Many Crooks*
GB 1958   87m   bw
Rank / Mario Zampi

Incompetent crooks plot a kidnapping.
Agreeable farce with black edges and an excellent chase sequence.

w Michael Pertwee *d* Mario Zampi *ph* Stan Pavey *m* Stanley Black

Terry-Thomas, George Cole, Brenda de Banzie, Bernard Bresslaw, Sidney James, Joe Melia, Vera Day, John Le Mesurier

Too Many Girls
US 1940   85m   bw
RKO (Harry Edgington, George Abbott)

The father of a wealthy co-ed hires four football heroes to protect her.
Witless nonsense, flabbily derived from a Broadway show.

w John Twist, *play* George Marion Jnr, Richard Rodgers, Lorenz Hart *d* George Abbott *ph* Frank Redman *songs* Rodgers and Hart

Lucille Ball, Desi Arnaz, Richard Carlson, Ann Miller, Eddie Bracken, Frances Langford, Harry Shannon
† The film on which Ball and Arnaz first met.

Too Many Husbands*
US 1940   84m   bw
Columbia (Wesley Ruggles)
GB title: *My Two Husbands*

Allegedly drowned on a boat cruise, a man turns up again after his wife has remarried.
Modest variation on a familiar theme, professional but unexciting; later remade as *Three for the Show* (qv).

w Claude Binyon, *play* Home and Beauty by W. Somerset Maugham *d* Wesley Ruggles *ph* Joseph Walker

Jean Arthur, Melvyn Douglas, Fred MacMurray, Harry Davenport, Dorothy Peterson, Melville Cooper, Edgar Buchanan

Too Much Too Soon*
US 1958   121m   bw
Warner (Henry Blanke)

Young actress Diana Barrymore goes to Hollywood to look after her alcoholic father John, but mild success goes to her head and she too turns to drink.
Rather dismal and murkily photographed account of an absorbing real-life situation; one performance holds the first half together.

wd Art Napoleon, *memoirs* Diana Barrymore *ph* Nicholas Musuraca, Carl Guthrie *m* Ernest Gold *ad* George James Hopkins

Dorothy Malone, *Errol Flynn*, Efrem Zimbalist Jnr, Neva Patterson, Martin Milner, Ray Danton, Murray Hamilton

Too Young to Kiss
US 1951   89m   bw
MGM (Sam Zimbalist)

A girl pianist poses as an infant prodigy, and falls for the impresario who wants to adopt her.
Dull conveyor belt comedy.

w Frances Goodrich, Albert Hackett *d* Robert Z. Leonard *ph* Joseph Ruttenberg *m* Johnny Green

June Allyson, Van Johnson, Gig Young, Paula Corday, Larry Keating, Hans Conried

Too Young to Love
GB 1959   89m   bw
Rank / Welbeck (Herbert Smith)

A 15-year-old prostitute is brought before a Brooklyn juvenile court.
Tepid filming of a popular exploitation play of the fifties, mysteriously made in England.

w Sydney and Muriel Box, *play* Pick Up Girl by Elsa Shelley *d* Muriel Box *ph* Gerald Gibbs *m* Bruce Montgomery

Thomas Mitchell, Pauline Hahn, Joan Miller, Austin Willis, Jess Conrad, Bessie Love, Alan Gifford

Top Banana*
US 1953   100m   Color Corporation
Roadshow / Harry M. Popkin

A TV comedian invites an attractive salesgirl to join his show.
A wisp of plot is the excuse for a revue, and the interest is in the old-time burlesque acts, some of which survive the generally shoddy treatment.

w Gene Towne *d* Alfred E. Green *ph* William Bradford *m/ly* Johnny Mercer

Phil Silvers, Rose Marie, Danny Scholl, Jack Albertson

Top Hat***
US 1935   100m   bw
RKO (Pandro S. Berman)

The path of true love is roughened by mistaken identities.
Marvellous Astaire-Rogers musical, with a more or less realistic London supplanted by a totally artificial Venice, and show stopping numbers in a style which is no more separated by amusing plot complications lightly handled by a team of deft *farceurs.*

w Dwight Taylor, Allan Scott *d* Mark Sandrich *ph* David Abel, Vernon Walker *m/ly* Irving Berlin *ch* Hermes Pan *ad* Van Nest Polglase, Carroll Clark

Fred Astaire, Ginger Rogers, Edward Everett Horton, Helen Broderick, Eric Blore, Erik Rhodes

'In 25 years *Top Hat* has lost nothing of its gaiety and charm.'—*Dilys Powell, 1960*

AAN: best picture; song 'Cheek to Cheek'

Top o'the Morning
US 1949   100m   bw
Paramount (Robert L. Welch)

Investigations follow the theft of the Blarney Stone.
More Irish whimsy from the *Going My Way* stars.

w Edmund Beloin, Richard Breen *d* David Miller *ph* Lionel Lindon *m* James Van Heusen

Bing Crosby, Barry Fitzgerald, Ann Blyth, Hume Cronyn, Eileen Crowe, John McIntire

Top Secret*
GB 1952   94m   bw
ABP (Mario Zampi)
US title: *Mr Potts Goes to Moscow*

A sanitary engineer, mistaken for a spy, is kidnapped to Moscow when his blueprints are taken for atomic secrets.
Farcical satire full of chases and lavatory humour; much of it comes off nicely.

w Jack Davies, Michael Pertwee *d* Mario Zampi *ph* Stan Pavey *m* Stanley Black

George Cole, Oscar Homolka, Nadia Gray, Frederick Valk, Wilfrid Hyde White, Geoffrey Sumner, Ronald Adam

Top Secret Affair*
US 1956   100m   bw
Warner / United States (Martin Rackin)
GB title: *Their Secret Affair*

A female news publisher tries to discredit a military diplomat but falls in love with him.
Curious comedy adaptation of a rather heavy novel, moderately skilled in all departments.

w Roland Kibbee, Allan Scott, *novel* Melville Goodwin USA by John P. Marquand *d* H. C. Potter *ph* Stanley Cortez *m* Roy Webb

Kirk Douglas, Susan Hayward, Jim Backus, Paul Stewart, John Cromwell, Roland Winters

Topaz*
US 1969   124m   Technicolor
Universal / Alfred Hitchcock

In 1962 the CIA enlists a French agent to break up a Russian spy ring.
Oddly halting, desultory and unconvincing spy thriller shot mainly in flat TV style, with just a few short sequences in its director's better manner. A measure of its unsatisfactoriness is

that three different endings were shot and
actually used at various points of release.

w Samuel Taylor, *novel* Leon Uris *d* Alfred
Hitchcock *ph* Jack Hildyard *m* Maurice Jarre

Frederick Stafford, John Forsythe, John Vernon,
Roscoe Lee Browne, Dany Robin, Karin Dor,
Michel Piccoli, Philippe Noiret

'A larger, slower, duller version of the spy
thrillers he used to make in the thirties.'—*New
Yorker, 1975*

Topaze*
US 1933 78m bw
David O. Selznick

A simple schoolmaster allows himself to be
exploited.
Interesting little comedy with the star playing
against type: remade as *Mr Topaze* (qv).

w Benn W. Levy, *play* Marcel Pagnol *d* Harry
d'Abbabie d'Arrast *ph* Lucien Andriot *m* Max
Steiner

John Barrymore, Myrna Loy, Jobyna Howland,
Jackie Searl

Topkapi*
US 1964 119m Technicolor
UA / Filmways (Jules Dassin)

International thieves try to rob the Istanbul
museum.
Light-hearted caper story which gets out of
control because of the variety of styles and
accents, the director's impression that his wife
can do no wrong, and the general slowness and
lack of wit; but there are bright moments,
colourful backgrounds, and a final suspense
sequence in the *Rififi* manner.

w Monja Danischewsky, *novel* The Light of Day
by Eric Ambler *d* Jules Dassin *ph* Henri
Alekan *m* Manos Hadjidakis

Melina Mercouri, Maximilian Schell, Peter
Ustinov, Robert Morley, Akim Tamiroff, Gilles
Segal, Jess Hahn

AA: Peter Ustinov

Topper**
US 1937 96m bw
Hal Roach

A stuffy banker is haunted by the ghosts of his
sophisticated friends the Kirbys, who are visible
only to him.
Influential supernatural farce, still pretty funny
and deftly acted though a shade slow to get
going.

w Jack Jevne, Eric Hatch, Eddie Moran, *novel*
The Jovial Ghosts by Thorne Smith *d* Norman

Z. McLeod *ph* Norbert Brodine *md* Arthur
Morton

*Cary Grant, Constance Bennett, Roland Young,
Billie Burke, Alan Mowbray*, Eugene Pallette,
Arthur Lake, Hedda Hopper

AAN: Roland Young

Topper Returns***
US 1941 87m bw
Hal Roach

A girl ghost helps Topper solve her own murder.
Spirited supernatural farce which spoofs murder
mysteries, spooky houses, frightened servants,
dumb cops, etc, in a pacy, accomplished and
generally delightful manner.

w Jonathan Latimer, Gordon Douglas, with
additional dialogue by Paul Gerard Smith
d Roy del Ruth

Roland Young, Joan Blondell, Eddie Anderson,
Carole Landis, Dennis O'Keefe, *H. B. Warner*,
Billie Burke, *Donald McBride*, Rafaela Ottiano

Topper Takes a Trip*
US 1939 85m bw
Hal Roach

Ghostly Mrs Kirby helps Topper to save his wife
from a Riviera philanderer.
Mildly pleasant follow-up, with a dog replacing
Cary Grant who had become too expensive.

w Eddie Moran, Jack Jevne, Corey Ford
d Norman Z. McLeod *ph* Norbert Brodine

Constance Bennett, Roland Young, Billie Burke,
Alan Mowbray, Verree Teasdale, Franklin
Pangborn, Alexander D'Arcy

Tora! Tora! Tora!*
US 1970 144m De Luxe Panavision
TCF (Elmo Williams)

A reconstruction from both sides of the events
leading up to Pearl Harbor.
Immense, largely studio-bound, calcified war
spectacle with much fidelity to the record but no
villains and no hero, therefore no drama and no
suspense.

w Larry Forrester, Hideo Oguni, Ryuzo
Kikushima *d* Richard Fleischer, Ray Kellogg,
Toshio Masuda, Kinji Fukasaku *ph* Charles F.
Wheeler and Japanese crews
sp L. B. Abbott, Art Cruickshank

Martin Balsam, Joseph Cotten, James
Whitmore, Jason Robards, Edward Andrews,
Leon Ames, George Macready, Soh Yamamura,
Takahiro Tamura

'One of the least stirring and least photogenic

historical epics ever perpetrated on the
screen.'—*Gary Arnold*

AAN: Charles F. Wheeler

Torch Singer

US 1933   72m   bw
Paramount
aka: *Broadway Singer*

An unwed mother supports her child by singing
in night clubs.
Banal melodrama.

w Lenore Coffee, Lynn Starling, *play* Mike by
Grace Perkins *d* Alexander Hall *ph* Karl Struss

Claudette Colbert, Ricardo Cortez, David
Manners, Lyda Roberti, Baby LeRoy, Florence
Roberts, Ethel Griffies, Helen Jerome Eddy

Torch Song

US 1953   90m   Technicolor
MGM (Henry Berman, Sidney Franklin Jnr)

A temperamental musical comedy star falls for a
blind pianist.
Ossified star vehicle which looks great but is too
often unintentionally funny.

w John Michael Hayes, Jan Lustig, *story* Why
Should I Cry? by I. A. R. Wylie *d* Charles
Walters *ph* Robert Planck *m* Adolph Deutsch

Joan Crawford, Michael Wilding, Gig Young,
Marjorie Rambeau, Henry Morgan, Dorothy
Patrick

'Here is Joan Crawford all over the screen, in
command, in love and in color.'—*Otis L.
Guernsey Jnr*

AAN: Marjorie Rambeau

Torchy Blane

Glenda Farrell played the hard-boiled girl
reporter and Barton MacLane the tough police
inspector who puts up with her in seven out of the
nine second features made by Warners in the late
thirties. The characters were created in short
stories by Frederick Nebel, and the films were
mostly directed by William Beaudine or Frank
McDonald.

1936: SMART BLONDE
1937: FLY AWAY BABY, THE
ADVENTUROUS BLONDE
1938: BLONDES AT WORK, TORCHY
BLANE IN PANAMA (with Lola Lane, Paul
Kelly), TORCHY GETS HER MAN
1939: TORCHY BLANE IN CHINATOWN,
TORCHY RUNS FOR MAYOR, TORCHY
PLAYS WITH DYNAMITE (with Jane
Wyman, Allen Jenkins)

Torn Curtain**

US 1966   119m   Technicolor
Universal / Alfred Hitchcock

A defector who is really a double agent is
embarrassed when his wife follows him into East
Germany.
Patchy Hitchcock with some mechanically
effective suspense sequences, a couple of efforts
at something new, a few miscalculations, some
evidence of carelessness, and a little enjoyable
repetition of old situations.

w Brian Moore *d Alfred Hitchcock ph* John F.
Warren *m* John Addison

Paul Newman, Julie Andrews, *Wolfgang
Kieling*, Ludwig Donath, Lila Kedrova, Hans-
Joerg Felmy, Tamara Toumanova

Torpedo Run*

US 1958   98m   Metrocolor
            Cinemascope
MGM (Edmund S. Grainger)

A US submarine in World War II destroys a
Japanese aircraft carrier in Tokyo Bay.
Well-staged potboiler with excellent action
sequences marred slightly by excessive
platitudinizing.

w Richard Sale, William Wister Haines
d Joseph Pevney *ph* George J. Folsey

Glenn Ford, Ernest Borgnine, Diane Brewster,
Dean Jones

The Torrent*

US 1925   75m (24 fps)   bw   silent
MGM

Spanish sweethearts are parted by a domineering
mother, and the girl consoles herself by
becoming a Paris prima donna.
Adequate emotional vehicle of its day which
happened to be Garbo's first American film.

w Dorothy Farnum, *novel* Vicente Blasco
Ibanez *d* Monta Bell *ph* William Daniels

Ricardo Cortez, Greta Garbo, Gertrude
Olmsted, Edward Connelly, Lucien Littlefield

Torrid Zone**

US 1940   88m   bw
Warner (Mark Hellinger)

In Central America, a banana plantation
manager is tricked by his boss into staying on,
and helps a wandering showgirl as well as foiling
bandits.
Enjoyable, fast-paced hokum with a plot
borrowed from both *The Front Page* and *Red
Dust*.

w Richard Macaulay, Jerry Wald *d* William

Keighley *ph* James Wong Howe *m* Adolph
Deutsch

James Cagney, Pat O'Brien, Ann Sheridan,
Helen Vinson, Andy Devine, Jerome Cowan,
George Tobias, George Reeves

Tortilla Flat*
US 1942   106m   bw
MGM (Sam Zimbalist)

The problems of poor Mexican half-breeds in
California.
Expensive but unappealing variation on *The
Grapes of Wrath*, with none of the cast quite
getting under the skin of their parts, and no sense
of reality, rather that of a musical without music.

w John Lee Mahin, Benjamin Glazier, *novel*
John Steinbeck *d* Victor Fleming *m* Franz
Waxman

Spencer Tracy, Hedy Lamarr, John Garfield,
Frank Morgan, Akim Tamiroff, Connie
Gilchrist, John Qualen, Sheldon Leonard,
Donald Meek, Allen Jenkins, Henry O'Neill

AAN: Frank Morgan

Torture Garden*
GB 1967   93m   Technicolor
Columbia / Amicus (Milton Subotsky)

Five fairground visitors are told their future by
the mysterious Dr Diablo.
Crude but effective horror portmanteau
including one story about the resurrection of
Edgar Allan Poe.

w Robert Bloch *d* Freddie Francis

Burgess Meredith, Jack Palance, Peter Cushing,
Beverly Adams, Michael Bryant, John Standing

The Touch*
Sweden / US 1970   112m   Eastmancolor
ABC / Cinematograph AB (Lars–Owe
    Carlburg)

The wife of a provincial surgeon falls in love with
an archaeologist.
Freedom versus security: the Bergman
treatment is given to a familiar love story, but the
expected finesse is lacking.

wd Ingmar Bergman *ph* Sven Nykvist *m* Jan
Johansson

Bibi Andersson, Elliott Gould, Max Von Sydow

Touch and Go
GB 1956   85m   Technicolor
Ealing (Seth Holt)

A family has doubts about its decision to
emigrate to Australia.
Very mild comedy which fails to engage

sympathy because the characters don't seem
real.

w William Rose *d* Michael Truman *ph* Douglas
Slocombe *m* John Addison

Jack Hawkins, Margaret Johnston, June
Thorburn, John Fraser, Roland Culver, Alison
Leggatt, James Hayter

A Touch of Class**
GB 1972   106m   Technicolor   Panavision
Avco / Brut / Gordon Films (Melvin Frank)

A married American businessman in London
has a hectic affair with a dress designer.
Amiable and very physical sex farce with
hilarious highlights and a few longueurs
between; the playing keeps it above water.

w Melvin Frank, Jack Rose *d* Melvin Frank
ph Austin Dempster *m* John Cameron

Glenda Jackson, George Segal, Paul Sorvino,
Hildegarde Neil
    'Machine-tooled junk.'—*William S. Pechter*

AA: Glenda Jackson
AAN: best picture; script; John Cameron; song
'All That Love Went to Waste' (*m* George
Barrie, *ly* Sammy Cahn)

Touch of Evil**
US 1958   95m or 114m   bw
    Cinemascope
U-I (Albert Zugsmith)

A Mexican narcotics investigator
honeymooning in a border town clashes with the
local police chief over a murder.
Overpoweringly atmospheric melodrama
crammed with Wellesian touches, but very cold
and unsympathetic, with rather restrained
performances (especially his) and a plot which
takes some following. Hardly the most
auspicious return to Hollywood for a wanderer,
but now becoming a cult classic.

wd Orson Welles, novel Badge of Evil by Whit
Masterson *ph Russell Metty m* Henry Mancini

Charlton Heston, Orson Welles, Janet Leigh,
Marlene Dietrich, Akim Tamiroff, Joseph
Calleia, Ray Collins, Dennis Weaver

A Touch of Larceny*
GB 1959   92m   bw
Paramount / Ivan Foxwell

A naval commander mysteriously disappears in
the hope that he will be branded a traitor and can
sue for libel.
Fairly amusing light comedy with lively
performances.

w Roger MacDougall, Guy Hamilton, Ivan
Foxwell, *novel* The Megstone Plot by Andrew

Garve *d* Guy Hamilton *ph* John Wilcox
m Philip Green

James Mason, Vera Miles, George Sanders,
Robert Flemyng, Ernest Clark, Duncan
Lamont, Peter Barkworth

'A beguilingly polished comedy, reminiscent
in its style, urbanity and sheen of the sort of thing
Lubitsch was doing in the 30s.'—*Daily Mail*

A Touch of Love
GB 1969   107m   Eastmancolor
Amicus / Palomar (Milton Subotsky)
US title: *Thank You All Very Much*

A pregnant London student tries to get an
abortion but later decides against it.
Curious bid for serious drama by horror
producers; all very conscientious but rather
dreary.

w Margaret Drabble, from her novel The
Millstone *d* Waris Hussein *ph* Peter Suschitsky
m Michael Dress

Sandy Dennis, Ian McKellen, Michael Coles,
John Standing, Eleanor Bron

A Touch of the Sun
GB 1956   80m   bw
Eros / Raystro (Raymond Stross)

A hall porter is left a fortune but after living it up
for a while returns to his old hotel which is on the
rocks.
Limp comedy vehicle.

w Alfred Shaughnessy *d* Gordon Parry
ph Arthur Grant *m* Eric Spear

Frankie Howerd, Ruby Murray, Dorothy
Bromiley, Gordon Harker, Reginald Beckwith,
Richard Wattis, Dennis Price, Alfie Bass,
Willoughby Goddard

Touchez pas au Grisbi *
France / Italy 1953   90m approx   bw
Del Duca / Antares
aka: *Honour among Thieves; Hands Off the
Loot*

Two crooks succeed in stealing a consignment of
gold, but that's only the start of their worries.
Smooth underworld hokum, with a slightly
comic attitude implied if not stated.

w Jacques Becker, Maurice Griffe, *novel* Albert
Simonin *d* Jacques Becker *ph* Pierre Montazel
m Jean Wiener

Jean Gabin, Jeanne Moreau, Gaby Basset,
Daniel Cauchy, Marilyn Buferd, Lino Ventura,
René Dary

Toughest Man in Arizona
US 1952   90m   Trucolor
Republic (Sidney Picker)

In 1861 a US marshal falls in love with the wife
of an outlaw.
Easy-going, pleasant western aimed at the top
half of a double bill.

w John K. Butler *d* R. G. Springsteen *ph* Reggie
Lanning *m* Dale Butts

Vaughn Monroe, Joan Leslie, Edgar Buchanan,
Victor Jory, Jean Parker, Henry Morgan

Tovarich **
US 1937   98m   bw
Warner (Robert Lord)

A royal Russian husband and wife flee the
revolution to Paris and take jobs as servants in
an eccentric household.
A lively comedy of its time; though many of the
jokes now seem obvious, the playing preserves
its essential quality.

w Casey Robinson, *play adaptation Robert E.
Sherwood, original* Jacques Deval *d* Anatole
Litvak *ph* Charles Lang *m* Max Steiner

*Claudette Colbert, Charles Boyer, Basil
Rathbone*, Anita Louise, Melville Cooper, Isabel
Jeans, Maurice Murphy, Morris Carnovsky,
Gregory Gaye, Montagu Love, Fritz Feld

'The most exciting screen event of all time!'—
publicity

Toward the Unknown
US 1956   115m   Warnercolor
  Warnerscope
Warner / Toluca (Mervyn Le Roy)
GB title: *Brink of Hell*

An over-age officer takes part in the X2
experiments with rocket-firing aircraft.
Humourless flagwaver, very forgettable.

w Beirne Lay Jnr *d* Mervyn Le Roy *ph* Harold
Rosson *m* Paul Baron

William Holden, Lloyd Nolan, Virginia Leith,
Charles McGraw, Murray Hamilton, L. Q.
Jones, James Garner, Paul Fix, Karen Steele

Tower of London **
US 1939   92m   bw
Universal (Rowland V. Lee)

With the help of Mord the executioner, Richard
Crookback kills his way to the throne but is
destroyed at Bosworth.
The Shakespearean view of history played as a
horror comic: despite an overall lack of pace,
spirited scenes and good performances win the
day.

w Robert N. Lee *d* Rowland V. Lee *ph* George Robinson *m* Charles Previn

Basil Rathbone, Boris Karloff, Barbara O'Neil, Ian Hunter, Vincent Price, Nan Grey, John Sutton, Leo G. Carroll, Miles Mander

Tower of London *
US 1962 79m bw
AIP / Admiral (Gene Corman)

A variation on the same events, with Price graduating from Clarence to Crookback, and the addition of ghostly visions. All very cheap, but occasionally vivid melodrama, despite intrusive American accents.

w Leo V. Gordon, Amos Powell, James B. Gordon *d* Roger Corman *ph* Arch Dalzell *m* Michael Anderson

Vincent Price, Michael Pate, Joan Freeman, Robert Brown, Justice Eatson, Sara Salby, Richard McCauly, Bruce Gordon

The Towering Inferno ***
US 1974 165m De Luxe Panavision
TCF / Warner (Irwin Allen)

The world's tallest building is destroyed by fire on the night of its inauguration.
Showmanlike but relentlessly padded disaster spectacular, worth seeing for its cast of stars, its sheer old-fashioned expertise, and its special effects.

w Stirling Silliphant, *novels* The Tower by Richard Martin Stern, The Glass Inferno by Thomas M. Scortia, Frank M. Robinson *d* John Guillermin, Irwin Allen *ph* Fred Koenekamp *m* John Williams *sp* Bill Abbott *pd* William Creber

Paul Newman, Steve McQueen, William Holden, Faye Dunaway, Fred Astaire, Susan Blakely, Richard Chamberlain, Robert Vaughn, Jennifer Jones, O. J. Simpson, Robert Wagner

'Several generations of blue-eyed charmers act their roles as if each were under a separate bell jar.'—*Verina Glaessner*

'Each scene of someone horribly in flames is presented as a feat for the audience's delectation.'—*New Yorker*

'The combination of Grade A spectacle and B-picture characters induces a feeling of sideline detachment.'—*Michael Billington, Illustrated London News*

AA: Fred Koenekamp; song 'We May Never Sing Like That Again' (*m/ly* Al Kasha, Joel Hirschhorn)
AAN: best picture; John Williams; Fred Astaire

A Town Called Bastard
GB 1971 97m Technicolor Franscope
Benmar / Zurbano (Ben Fisz)
aka: *A Town Called Hell*

Mexican revolutionaries massacre a priest and his congregation and take over the town. Ten years later a widow arrives seeking vengeance.
Sadistic western with an opening massacre followed by twenty-two killings (count 'em). Pretty dull otherwise.

w Richard Aubrey *d* Robert Parrish *ph* Manuel Berenguer *m* Waldo de Los Rios

Robert Shaw, Stella Stevens, Telly Savalas, Martin Landau, Michael Craig, Fernando Rey, Dudley Sutton

A Town like Alice **
GB 1956 117m bw
Rank / Vic Films (Joseph Janni)
US title: *The Rape of Malaya*

Life among women prisoners of the Japanese in Malaya, especially one who is finally reunited with her Australian lover.
Genteelly harrowing war film, formlessly adapted from the first part of a popular novel; a big commercial success of its day.

w W. P. Lipscomb, Richard Mason, *novel* Nevil Shute *d* Jack Lee *ph* Geoffrey Unsworth *m* Matyas Seiber

Virginia McKenna, Peter Finch, Takagi, Marie Lohr, Maureen Swanson, Jean Anderson, Renée Houston, Nora Nicholson

Town on Trial *
GB 1956 96m bw
Columbia / Marksman (Maxwell Setton)

A police inspector solves the murder of a girl after a tennis club dance in a British country town.
Straightforward murder mystery shot in Weybridge, with a wide variety of suspects having something to hide; settings and characters are quite realistic and also a little dreary.

w Ken Hughes, Robert Westerby *d* John Guillermin *ph* Basil Emmott *m* Tristam Cary

John Mills, Charles Coburn, Derek Farr, Barbara Bates, Alec McCowen, Geoffrey Keen, Elizabeth Seal, Margaretta Scott, Fay Compton

Town without Pity *
US / Switzerland / Germany 1961 103m bw
UA / Mirisch / Osweg / Gloria (Gottfried Reinhardt)

A German girl is raped and four American

soldiers are accused; the defence counsel's wiles lead to the girl's suicide.

Dour drama with overpowering expressionist technique but not much real sympathy, interest or surprise.

w Silvia Reinhardt, George Hurdalek, *novel* The Verdict by Manfred Gregor *d* Gottfried Reinhardt *ph* Kurt Hasse *m* Dmitri Tiomkin

Kirk Douglas, E. G. Marshall, Christine Kaufmann, Barbara Rutting, Robert Blake, Richard Jaeckel

AAN: title song (*m* Dmitri Tiomkin, *ly* Ned Washington)

Toy Tiger
US 1956   88m   Technicolor
  Cinemascope
U-I (Howard Christie)

The imaginative small son of a widow 'adopts' her business friend as his father.

Flat sentimental comedy off the studio's conveyor belt, a remake of *Mad about Music*.

w Ted Sherdeman *d* Jerry Hopper *ph* George Robinson *m* Joseph Gershenson

Jeff Chandler, Laraine Day, Tim Hovey, Cecil Kellaway, Richard Haydn, David Janssen

The Toy Wife*
US 1938   95m   bw
MGM (Merian C. Cooper)
GB title: *Frou Frou*

In the early 19th century in Louisiana, a flirtatious girl causes jealousy and tragedy.

Another bid in the *Jezebel/Gone with the Wind* stakes, this handsome production proved a commercial misfire and hastened the end of its star's career.

w Zoe Akins *d* Richard Thorpe *ph* Oliver T. Marsh *m* Edward Ward

Luise Rainer, Melvyn Douglas, Robert Young, Barbara O'Neil, H. B. Warner, Alma Kruger, Walter Kingsford

Toys in the Attic*
US 1963   90m   bw   Panavision
UA / Claude / Mirisch

In a shabby New Orleans home, two ageing spinsters struggle to look after their ne'er-do-well brother.

Play into film doesn't go in this case, but the script and acting are interesting.

w James Poe, play Lillian Hellman d George Roy Hill *ph* Joseph Biroc *m* George Duning *ad* Cary Odell

Geraldine Page, Wendy Hiller, Dean Martin, Yvette Mimieux, Gene Tierney, Larry Gates

Track of the Cat*
US 1954   102m   Warnercolor
  Cinemascope
Warner / Wayne–Fellows / Batjac (Robert Fellows)

In the northern California backwoods one winter in the 1880s a farming family is menaced by a marauding mountain lion.

With the lion a symbol of evil, this is real Cold Comfort Farm country and despite good intentions all round becomes irresistibly funny before the end, largely because everyone moves and speaks so s-l-o-w-l-y. The bleached colour is interesting but would suit only snowy settings.

w A. I. Bezzerides, *novel* Walter Van Tilburg Clark *d William A. Wellman ph William H. Clothier m* Roy Webb

Robert Mitchum, Diana Lynn, Beulah Bondi, Teresa Wright, Tab Hunter, Philip Tonge, William Hopper, Carl Switzer

'Cinemascope's first genuine weirdie . . . the script is redolent of Eugene O'Neill, and to its presentation the director brings a touch of Poe . . . Despair hangs in the air like a curse . . . unfortunately ambition overreaches itself, and the film topples over into barnstorming melodrama.'—*MFB*

Trackdown
US 1976   98m   De Luxe
UA / Essaness (Bernard Schwarz)

A Montana rancher follows his sister to Los Angeles and avenges her ill-treatment there by gangsters.

Routine action thriller with fashionable realism and violence.

w Paul Edwards *d* Richard T. Heffron *ph* Gene Polito *m* Charles Bernstein

Jim Mitchum, Karen Lamm, Anne Archer, Erik Estrada, Cathy Lee Crosby, Vince Cannon

Trade Winds
US 1939   93m   bw
Walter Wanger

A girl who thinks she has committed murder flees to the Far East, and a cynical detective is sent to bring her back. Guess what happens.

Smartly written mixture of comedy, drama, mystery and travelogue which comes off only in spots; it needed a firmer hand.

w Dorothy Parker, Alan Campbell, Frank R. Adams *d* Tay Garnett *ph* Rudolph Maté

Fredric March, Joan Bennett, Ralph Bellamy, Ann Sothern, Sidney Blackmer, Thomas Mitchell, Robert Elliott

Trader Horn*
US 1931   120m   bw
MGM

An experienced African trader overcomes tribal hostility.
Primitive talkie for which second units were sent to Africa amid much publicity hoo-ha. After forty-five years, nothing of interest remains to be seen.

w Richard Schayer, Dale Van Every, Thomas Neville, *novel* Alfred Aloysius Horn, Etheldreda Lewis w W. S. Van Dyke *ph* Clyde de Vinna

Harry Carey, Edwina Booth, Duncan Renaldo, Mutia Omoolu, C. Aubrey Smith

AAN: best picture

Trader Horn
US 1973   105m   Metrocolor
MGM (Lewis J. Rachmil)

Pitiful remake patched together largely from stock footage.

w William Norton, Edward Harper *d* Reza Badiyi *ph* Ronald W. Browne *m* Shelly Manne

Rod Taylor, Anne Heywood, Jean Sorel
'Laughably inept . . . it cannot face word of mouth for long.'—*Variety*

Traffic
France / Italy 1970   96m   Eastmancolor
Corona / Gibe / Selenia (Robert Dorfman)

The designer of a camping car has various little accidents on the way from the works to a show.
Rambling comedy with understated jokes and an almost invisible star.

w Jacques Tati, Jacques Legrange *d* Jacques Tati (with Bert Haanstra) *ph* Edouard Van Den Enden, Marcel Weiss *m* Charles Dumont

Jacques Tati

The Trail of the Lonesome Pine*
US 1936   102m   Technicolor
Paramount (Walter Wanger)

A hillbilly girl goes back home when her brother is killed in a family feud.
Antediluvian Ozarkian melodrama, notable as the first outdoor film to be shot in three-colour Technicolor.

w Grover Jones, Horace McCoy, Harvey Thew, *novel* John Fox Jnr *d* Henry Hathaway *ph Howard Green m* Hugo Friedhofer, Gerrard Carbonara

Sylvia Sidney, Fred MacMurray, Henry Fonda, Fred Stone, Nigel Bruce, Beulah Bondi, Robert Barrat, Spanky McFarland, Fuzzy Knight
'Unnatural as it is, the colour does no serious

damage to the picture. This moldy bit of hokum . . . takes movies back to the days of their childhood.'—*Newsweek*

AAN: song 'A Melody from the Sky' (*m* Louis Alter, *ly* Sidney Mitchell)

The Train**
US 1965   140m   bw
UA / Ariane / Dear (Jules Bricken)

In 1944, the French resistance tries to prevent the Nazis from taking art treasures back to Germany on a special train.
Proficient but longwinded suspense actioner with spectacular sequences; a safe bet for train enthusiasts.

w Franklin Coen, Frank Davis, Walter Bernstein *d John Frankenheimer ph* Jean Tournier, Walter Wottitz *m* Maurice Jarre

Burt Lancaster, *Paul Scofield*, Jeanne Moreau, Michael Simon, Wolfgang Preiss, Suzanne Flon

AAN: script

Train of Events
GB 1949   89m   bw
Ealing (Michael Relph)

Portmanteau of stories à la Friday the 13th or Dead of Night, linked by a train disaster.
A rather mechanical entertainment, proficiently made.

w Basil Dearden, T. E. B. Clarke, Ronald Millar, Angus MacPhail *d* Basil Dearden, Charles Crichton, Sidney Cole *ph* Lionel Banes, Gordon Dines *m* Leslie Bridgewater

Valerie Hobson, John Clements, Jack Warner, Gladys Henson, Peter Finch, Irina Baronova, Susan Shaw, Patric Doonan, Joan Dowling, Laurence Payne, Mary Morris

The Train Robbers
US 1973   92m   Technicolor   Panavision
Warner / Batjac (Michael Wayne)

A widow asks three gunmen to help her clear her husband's name by retrieving gold he had stolen.
Shaggy dog western, sadly lacking in comic situation and detail.

wd Burt Kennedy *ph* William Clothier *m* Dominic Frontière

John Wayne, Ann-Margret, Rod Taylor, Ben Johnson, Bobby Vinton, Christopher George

The Traitor*
GB 1957   88m   bw
New Realm (E. J. Fancey)

At the annual reunion of a resistance group, the

host announces that one of their number was a traitor.
Heavy-handed theatrical melodrama, helped by a stout plot and some directional flair.

wd Michael McCarthy ph Bert Mason
m Jackie Brown

Donald Wolfit, Robert Bray, Jane Griffiths, Carl Jaffe, Anton Diffring, Oscar Quitak, Rupert Davies, John Van Eyssen

The Traitors*
GB 1962 69m bw
Ello (Jim O'Connelly)

A top scientist is killed and MI5 springs into action.
Commendable second feature with narrative virtues absent in most big films.

*w Jim O'Connelly d Robert Tronson
ph* Michael Reed *m* Johnny Douglas

Patrick Allen, James Maxwell, Ewan Roberts, Zena Walker

Traitor's Gate
GB 1965 80m bw
Columbia / Summit (Ted Lloyd)

A London businessman organizes a gang to steal the Crown Jewels.
Modest caper melodrama, routine but watchable.

w John Sansom, novel Edgar Wallace *d* Freddie Francis *ph* Denys Coop

Albert Lieven, Gary Raymond, Margot Trooger, Klaus Kinski, Catherina Von Schell, Edward Underdown

The Tramp*
US 1915 20m approx (24 fps) bw silent
Mutual

A tramp saves a girl from crooks, is wounded and cared for by her, deliriously happy – until her lover arrives.
Fairly funny star comedy, the first with sentimental touches and the origin of the into-the-sunset fade-out.

wd Charles Chaplin *ph* Rollie Totheroh

Charles Chaplin, Edna Purviance, Bud Jamison, Leo White, Lloyd Bacon

Tramp Tramp Tramp*
US 1926 65m approx (24 fps) bw silent
Harry Langdon

Harry enters a cross-country walking contest in order to impress his girl.
Well-staged peripatetic comedy, the star's first feature.

w Frank Capra, Tim Whelan, Hal Conklin, Gerald Duffy, Murray Roth, J. Frank Holliday
d Harry Edwards

Harry Langdon, Joan Crawford, Alec B. Francis

Trans-Europe Express*
France 1966 90m bw
Como Film (Samy Halfon)

Film-makers on a train invent a violent plot and then find life aping it.
A theme beloved of Hollywood is treated intellectually, and almost succeeds in attracting all classes.

wd Alain Robbe-Grillet *ph* Willy Kurant
m Verdi

Jean-Louis Trintignant, Marie-France Pisier, Nadine Verdier, Christian Barbier, Charles Millot, Alain Robbe-Grillet

The Trap*
US 1958 84m Technicolor
Paramount / Parkwood–Heath (Melvin Frank, Norman Panama)
GB title: *The Baited Trap*

A lawyer helps a vicious killer to escape into Mexico, but the plan backfires.
Reasonably tense action thriller with desert backgrounds.

w Richard Alan Simmons, Norman Panama
d Norman Panama *ph* Daniel L. Fapp *m* Irvin Talbot

Richard Widmark, Lee J. Cobb, Earl Holliman, Tina Louise, Carl Benton Reid, Lorne Green

Trapeze**
US 1956 105m De Luxe Cinemascope
UA / Hecht–Lancaster (James Hill)

A circus partnership almost breaks up when a voluptuous third member is engaged.
Concentrated, intense melodrama filmed almost entirely within a French winter circus and giving a very effective feel, almost a smell, of the life therein. Despite great skill in the making, however, the length is too great for a wisp of plot that goes back to *The Three Maxims* and doubtless beyond.

w James R. Webb *d* Carol Reed *ph* Robert Krasker *m* Malcolm Arnold

Burt Lancaster, Tony Curtis, Gina Lollobrigida, Thomas Gomez, Johnny Puleo, Katy Jurado, Sidney James

The Travelling Executioner*
US 1970 95m Metrocolor Panavision
MGM (Jack Smight)

In 1918 an ex-carnival showman travels the
American south with his portable electric chair
and charges a hundred dollars per execution, but
falls for one of his proposed victims.
Oddball fable without apparent moral; neither
fantastic nor funny enough.

w Garrie Bateson d Jack Smight ph Philip
Lathrop m Jerry Goldsmith

Stacy Keach, Mariana Hill, Bud Cort, Graham
Jarvis

Travels with My Aunt*
US 1972   109m   Metrocolor   Panavision
MGM (Robert Fryer, James Cresson)

A staid bank accountant is landed in a series of
continental adventures by his eccentric life-
loving aunt.
Busy but fairly disastrous adaptation of a
delightful novel, ruined by ceaseless chatter, lack
of characterization, shapeless incident and an
absurdly caricatured central performance.

w Jay Presson Allen, Hugh Wheeler, novel
Graham Greene d George Cukor ph Douglas
Slocombe m Tony Hatch pd John Box

Maggie Smith, Alec McCowen, Lou Gossett,
Robert Stephens, Cindy Williams

'It seems to run down before it gets started.'—
New Yorker, 1977

AAN: Douglas Slocombe; Maggie Smith

Tread Softly Stranger*
GB 1958   91m   bw
Alderdale (George Minter)

In a north country town, two brothers in love
with the same girl rob a safe.
Hilarious murky melodrama full of glum faces,
with a well-worn trick ending; rather well
photographed.

w George Minter, Denis O'Dell, play Jack
Popplewell d Gordon Parry ph Douglas
Slocombe m Tristam Cary

George Baker, Terence Morgan, Diana Dors,
Wilfrid Lawson, Patrick Allen, Jane Griffith,
Joseph Tomelty, Norman Macowan

Treasure Hunt
GB 1952   79m   bw
Romulus (Anatole de Grunwald)

The eccentric middle-aged members of an Irish
family find their father's fortune is missing.
Theatrical comedy with some charm and
humour, but very much a photographed play.

w Anatole de Grunwald, play M. J. Perry
d John Paddy Carstairs ph C. Pennington-
Richards m Mischa Spoliansky

Jimmy Edwards, Martita Hunt, Athene Seyler,
Naunton Wayne, June Clyde, Susan Stephen,
Brian Worth

Treasure Island**
US 1934   105m   bw
MGM

An old pirate map leads to a long sea voyage, a
mutiny, and buried treasure.
Nicely mounted Hollywood version of a classic
adventure story, a little slow in development but
meticulously produced.

w John Lee Mahin, novel Robert Louis
Stevenson d Victor Fleming ph Ray June,
Clyde de Vinna, Harold Rosson m Herbert
Stothart

Wallace Beery, Jackie Cooper, Lewis Stone,
Lionel Barrymore, Otto Kruger, Douglass
Dumbrille, Nigel Bruce, Chic Sale

Treasure Island*
GB 1950   96m   Technicolor
Walt Disney (Perce Pearce)

Cheerful Disney remake, poor on detail but
transfixed by a swaggeringly overplayed and
unforgettable leading performance.

w Lawrence Edward Watkin d Byron Haskin
ph F. A. Young m Clifton Parker pd Thomas
Morahan

Robert Newton, Bobby Driscoll, Walter
Fitzgerald, Basil Sydney, Denis O'Dea, Geoffrey
Wilkinson, Ralph Truman

'Serviceable rather than imaginative.'—
Lindsay Anderson

Treasure Island
GB / France / Germany / Spain 1971   95m
colour
Massfilms / FDL / CCC / Eguiluz (Harry Alan
Towers)

Spiritless and characterless international remake
with poor acting, production and dubbing.

w Wolf Mankowitz, O. W. Jeeves (Welles)
d John Hough ph Cicilio Paniagua m Natal
Massara

Orson Welles, Kim Burfield, Lionel Stander,
Walter Slezak, Rik Battaglia

The Treasure of Lost Canyon
US 1952   82m   Technicolor
U-I (Leonard Goldstein)

A small boy robbed of his inheritance finds it
with the help of a country doctor who turns out
to be his uncle.

Modest juvenile adventure, rather boringly narrated.

w Brainerd Duffield, Emerson Crocker, *story* by Robert Louis Stevenson *d* Ted Tetzlaff *ph* Russell Metty *m* Joseph Gershenson

William Powell, Julia Adams, Charles Drake, Rosemary de Camp, Henry Hull, Tommy Ivo

Treasure of Matecumbe
US 1976   116m   Technicolor
Walt Disney (Bill Anderson)

Two boys seek buried gold in the Florida keys. Cheerful adventure tale with a few nods to *Treasure Island*; all very competent in the Disney fashion.

w Don Tait *d* Vincent McEveety *ph* Frank Phillips *m* Buddy Baker

Robert Foxworth, Joan Hackett, Peter Ustinov, Vic Morrow, Jane Wyatt, Johnny Duran, Billy Attmore

The Treasure of Pancho Villa
US 1955   96m   Technicolor   Superscope
RKO / Edmund Grainger

Mexico 1915: an American adventurer becomes involved with the revolutionary Pancho Villa; both seek a gold consignment but it is buried in an avalanche.
Modestly well made, routine action drama.

w Niven Busch *d* George Sherman *ph* William Snyder *m* Leith Stevens

Rory Calhoun, Shelley Winters, *Gilbert Roland*, Joseph Calleia

Treasure of San Teresa
GB 1959   81m   bw
Orbit (John Nasht, Patrick Filmer-Sankey)

An American secret service agent finds Nazi loot in a Czech convent.
Roughly-made, watchable actioner.

w Jack Andrews, Jeffrey Dell *d* Alvin Rakoff *ph* Wilkie Cooper *m* Philip Martell

Eddie Constantine, Dawn Addams, Marius Goring, Christopher Lee, Walter Gotell

Treasure of the Golden Condor
US 1952   93m   Technicolor
TCF

A young Frenchman flees to the South Seas but returns to discredit his wicked uncle.
Ineffectual remake of *Son of Fury* (qv) with Guatemalan backgrounds and no punch at all.

wd Delmer Daves *ph* Edward Cronjager *m* Sol Kaplan

Cornel Wilde, Finlay Currie, Constance Smith, George Macready, Walter Hampden, Anne Bancroft, Fay Wray, Leo G. Carroll

The Treasure of the Sierra Madre **
US 1948   126m   bw
Warner (Henry Blanke)

Three gold prospectors come to grief through greed.
Well-acted but partly miscast action fable on the oldest theme in the world; rather tedious and studio-bound for a film with such a high reputation.

wd John Huston, *novel* B. Traven *ph* Ted McCord *m* Max Steiner *md* Leo F. Forbstein

Humphrey Bogart, Walter Huston, Tim Holt, Alfonso Bedoya, John Huston, Bruce Bennett, Barton MacLane
    'This bitter fable is told with cinematic integrity and considerable skill.'—*Henry Hart*
    'The faces of the men, in close-up or in a group, achieve a kind of formal pattern and always dominate the screen.'—
Peter Ericsson

AA: John Huston (as writer and director); Walter Huston
AAN: best picture

A Tree Grows in Brooklyn ****
US 1945   128m   bw
TCF (Louis D. Lighton)

Life for an Irish family with a drunken father in New York's teeming slums at the turn of the century.
A superbly-detailed studio production of the type they don't make any more: a family drama with interest for everybody.

w Tess Slesinger, Frank Davis, *novel* Betty Smith *d* Elia Kazan *ph* Leon Shamroy *m* Alfred Newman

Peggy Ann Garner, James Dunn, Dorothy McGuire, Joan Blondell, Lloyd Nolan, Ted Donaldson, James Gleason, Ruth Nelson, John Alexander, Adeline de Walt Reynolds, Charles Halton
    'He tells a maximum amount of story with a minimum of film. Little touches of humour and human understanding crop up throughout.'—
Frank Ward, NBR

AA: James Dunn
AAN: script

Trent's Last Case
GB 1952   90m   bw
Wilcox—Neagle (Herbert Wilcox)

A journalist suspects that the death of a tycoon was murder.

Desultory version of a famous novel, with none of the original style and a few naïveties of its own.

w Pamela Bower, *novel* E. C. Bentley *d* Herbert Wilcox *ph* Max Greene *m* Anthony Collins

Michael Wilding, Margaret Lockwood, Orson Welles, John McCallum, Miles Malleson

Trial*
US 1955 109m bw
MGM (Charles Schnee)

A young lawyer defends a Mexican boy accused of rape and murder.

Stereotyped but pacy and watchable racial drama with political overtones, Our Hero having to resist bigots, Commies *and* McCarthyites.

w Don M. Mankiewicz, from his novel *d* Mark Robson *ph* Robert Surtees *m* Daniele Amfitheatrof

Glenn Ford, Dorothy McGuire, Arthur Kennedy, John Hodiak, Katy Jurado, Rafael Campos, Juano Hernandez, Robert Middleton, John Hoyt

AAN: Arthur Kennedy

The Trial*
France / Italy / West Germany 1962   120m bw
Paris Europa / FICIT / Hisa
original title: *Le Procès*

Joseph K is tried and condemned for an unspecified crime.

Kafka's nightmares tend to go on too long, and this film of one of them is no exception, despite its pin-screen prologue by Alexeieff and its inventive setting in the old Gare d'Orsay. Once again Welles the magician badly needs a Hollywood studio behind him.

wd, ed Orson Welles *ph* Edmond Richard *m* Jean Ledrut *pd* Jean Mandarut

Orson Welles, Jeanne Moreau, Anthony Perkins, Madeleine Robinson, Elsa Martinelli, Suzanne Flon, Akim Tamiroff, Romy Schneider

Trial by Combat
GB 1976   90m   Technicolor
Warner / Combat (Fred Weintraub, Paul Heller)
aka: *Choice of Weapons*

An apparently harmless secret society of 'medieval knights' rededicates itself to the ritual execution of criminals who have escaped the law.

A rare specimen of comic macabre apparently

inspired by the TV series *The Avengers*. Sadly, not much of it really works.

w Julian Bond, Steven Rossen, Mitchell Smith *d* Kevin Conner *ph* Alan Hume *m* Frank Cordell *pd* Edward Marshall

John Mills, Donald Pleasence, Peter Cushing, Barbara Hershey, David Birney, Margaret Leighton, Brian Glover

The Trials of Oscar Wilde**
GB 1960   123m   Super Technirama 70
Warwick / Viceroy (Harold Huth)
US title: *The Man with the Green Carnation*

Oscar Wilde fatally sues the Marquis of Queensberry for libel, and loses; he is then prosecuted for sodomy.

Plush account of a fascinating event; narrative drive is unfortunately lacking, but one is left with interesting performances.

wd Ken Hughes *ph* Ted Moore *m* Ron Goodwin *ad* Ken Adam, Bill Constable

Peter Finch, Yvonne Mitchell, *John Fraser*, Lionel Jeffries, *Nigel Patrick*, James Mason, Emrys Jones, Maxine Audley, Paul Rogers, James Booth

Tribute to a Bad Man
US 1956   95m   Eastmancolor
Cinemascope
MGM (Sam Zimbalist)

A Wyoming horse breeder is callous in his treatment of rustlers, and wins the woman he wants when he becomes more understanding.

Somewhere behind an unsympathetic story and hesitant development lies a convincing picture of life in the old west.

w Michael Blankfort, *story* Jack Schaefer *d* Robert Wise *ph* Robert Surtees *m* Miklos Rozsa

James Cagney, Irene Papas, Don Dubbins, Stephen McNally, Vic Morrow, Royal Dano, Lee Van Cleef

Trio*
GB 1950   91m   bw
Rank / Gainsborough (Antony Darnborough)

Following *Quartet* (qv), three more stories from Somerset Maugham: 'The Verger', 'Mr Knowall', and 'Sanatorium'.

An enjoyable package, unpretentiously handled but with full weight to the content.

w W. Somerset Maugham, R. C. Sherriff, Noel Langley, *stories* W. Somerset Maugham *d* Ken Annakin, Harold French *ph* Reg Wyer, Geoffrey Unsworth *m* John Greenwood *ad* Maurice Carter

James Hayter, Kathleen Harrison, Michael Hordern, Felix Aylmer; *Nigel Patrick*, Anne Crawford, Naunton Wayne, Wilfrid Hyde White; Michael Rennie, Jean Simmons, *John Laurie, Finlay Currie*, Roland Culver, Betty Ann Davies, Raymond Huntley, André Morell

The Trip*
US 1967 85m Pathecolor
AIP (Roger Corman)

A director of TV commercials tries LSD and has hallucinations.
Much-banned plotless wallow, the ultimate opt-out movie; well done for those who can take it.

w Jack Nicholson *d* Roger Corman *ph Arch Dalzell psychedelic effects Peter Gardiner montage Dennis Jakob*

Peter Fonda, Susan Strasberg, Bruce Dern, Salli Sachse, Dennis Hopper

Triple Cross
GB 1967 140m colour
Warner / Fred Feldkamp

A small-time crook imprisoned on Jersey at the start of World War II offers to spy for the Nazis but reports to the English.
Ho-hum biopic of double agent Eddie Chapman; effective scenes merely interrupt the general incoherence.

w Renè Hardy, *book* The Eddie Chapman Story by Frank Owen *d* Terence Young *ph* Henri Alekan *m* Georges Garvarentz

Christopher Plummer, Yul Brynner, Trevor Howard, Romy Schneider, Gert Frobe, Claudine Auger

Triple Echo*
GB 1972 94m colour
Hemdale

In 1942, a soldier's wife welcomes another soldier to her farm for tea; he deserts and poses as her sister.
Foolish story which would possibly have worked as a TV play but hardly justifies a film despite the talent on hand.

w Robin Chapman, *novel* H. E. Bates *d* Michael Apted *ph* John Coquillon *m* Marc Wilkinson

Glenda Jackson, Brian Deacon, Oliver Reed

Triumph of the Will****
Germany 1936 120m bw
Leni Riefenstahl / Nazi Party

The Official record of the Nazi party congress held at Nuremberg in 1934.
A devastatingly brilliant piece of film-making—right from the opening sequence of Hitler descending from the skies, his plane shadowed against the clouds. The rally scenes are a terrifying example of the camera's power of propaganda. After World War II it was banned for many years because of general fears that it might inspire a new Nazi party.

d, ed Leni Riefenstahl ph Sepp Allgeier and 36 assistants *m* Herbert Windt

Trog
GB 1970 91m Technicolor
Warner / Herman Cohen

A man-ape is discovered in a pothole and trained by a lady scientist.
Ridiculous semi-horror film which degrades its star.

w Aben Kandel *d* Freddie Francis *ph* Desmond Dickinson *m* John Scott

Joan Crawford, Michael Gough, Bernard Kay, David Griffin

The Trojan Women*
US 1971 111m Eastmancolor
Josef Shaftel (Michael Cacoyannis, Anis Nohra)

Troy has fallen to the Greeks and its women bemoan their fate.
And oh, how they bemoan! Even with this cast, Greek tragedy does not fill the big screen.

w Michael Cacoyannis, *play* Euripides *d* Michael Cacoyannis *ph* Alfio Contini *m* Mikis Theodorakis

Katharine Hepburn, Vanessa Redgrave, Geneviève Bujold, Irene Papas, Patrick Magee, Brian Blessed, Pauline Letts

Trooper Hook
US 1957 92m bw
UA / Sol Baer Fielding

A woman prisoner of the Indians has a half-breed son and becomes an outcast when returned to her people.
Peculiar western with good moments, but generally very slow and downbeat.

w Charles Marquis Warren, David Victor, Herbert Little Jnr, *story* Jack Schaefer *d* Charles Marquis Warren *ph* Ellsworth Fredericks *m* Gerald Fried

Barbara Stanwyck, Joel McCrea, Earl Holliman, Edward Andrews, John Dehner, Susan Kohner, Royal Dano

Trottie True*
GB 1949 98m Technicolor
GFD / Two Cities (Hugh Stewart)
US title: *The Gay Lady*

Adventures of a Gaiety girl who married a lord.
Self-conscious period comedy which could have
been highly diverting but manages only to be
sporadically charming in a whimsically
amateurish way.

w C. Denis Freeman, *novel* Caryl Brahms, S. J.
Simon *d* Brian Desmond Hurst *ph* Harry
Waxman *m* Benjamin Frankel *ad* Ralph
Brinton

Jean Kent, James Donald, Hugh Sinclair, Bill
Owen, Andrew Crawford, Lana Morris

Trouble along the Way

US 1953 110m bw
Warner (Melville Shavelson)

A famous football coach is co-opted to help a
bankrupt college but some of his methods are not
quite above board.
American college comedy with dollops of
religiosity—a double threat.

w Melville Shavelson, Jack Rose *d* Michael
Curtiz *ph* Archie Stout *m* Max Steiner

John Wayne, Donna Reed, Charles Coburn,
Tom Tully, Sherry Jackson, Marie Windsor

'No opportunites for a laugh or a tear are
missed by the entire cast.'—*MFB*

Trouble for Two*

US 1936 75m bw
MGM
GB title: *The Suicide Club*

A European prince in London for an arranged
wedding gets involved with an ingenious
organization for murder.
Light-hearted, black-edged Victorian literary
spoof which starts nicely but can't quite keep up
the pace.

w Manuel Seff, Edward Paramore Jnr, *stories*
New Arabian Nights by Robert Louis
Stevenson *d* J. Walter Rubin *ph* Charles G.
Clarke *m* Franz Waxman

Robert Montgomery, Rosalind Russell, *Reginald
Owen*, Frank Morgan, *Louis Hayward*, E. E.
Clive, Walter Kingsford

Trouble in Paradise****

US 1932 86m bw
Paramount (Ernst Lubitsch)

Jewel thieves insinuate themselves into the
household of a rich Parisienne, and one falls in
love with her.
A masterpiece of light comedy, with sparkling
dialogue, innuendo, great performances and
masterly cinematic narrative. For connoisseurs,
it can't be faulted, and is the masterpiece of
American sophisticated cinema.

w *Samson Raphaelson, Grover Jones, play* The
Honest Finder by Laszlo Aladar *d Ernst
Lubitsch ph* Victor Milner

*Herbert Marshall, Miriam Hopkins, Kay
Francis, Edward Everett Horton, Charles
Ruggles*, C. Aubrey Smith, Robert Greig,
Leonid Kinskey

'One of the gossamer creations of Lubitsch's
narrative art . . . it would be impossible in this
brief notice to describe the innumerable touches
of wit and of narrative skill with which it is
unfolded.'—*Alexander Bakshy*

'A shimmering, engaging piece of work . . . in
virtually every scene a lively imagination shines
forth.'—*New York Times*

'An almost continuous musical background
pointed up and commented on the action. The
settings were the last word in modernistic
design.'—*Theodor Huff, 1948*

Trouble in Store*

GB 1953 85m bw
GFD / Two Cities (Maurice Cowan)

A stock assistant causes chaos in a department
store.
First, simplest and best of the Wisdom farces.

w John Paddy Carstairs, Maurice Cowan, Ted
Willis *d* John Paddy Carstairs *ph* Ernest
Steward *m* Mischa Spoliansky

Norman Wisdom, Jerry Desmonde, Margaret
Rutherford, Moira Lister, Derek Bond, Lana
Morris, Megs Jenkins, Joan Sims

Trouble in the Glen

GB 1954 91m Trucolor
Republic / Wilcox–Neagle (Stuart Robertson)

An Argentinian laird in a Scottish glen causes ill-
feeling.
Heavy-handed Celtic comedy whose
predictability and sentimentality could have
been forgiven were it not for the most garish
colour ever seen.

w Frank S. Nugent, *novel* Maurice Walsh
d Herbert Wilcox *ph* Max Greene *m* Victor
Young

Margaret Lockwood, Orson Welles, Forrest
Tucker, Victor McLaglen, John McCallum,
Eddie Byrne, Archie Duncan, Moultrie Kelsall

The Trouble with Angels

US 1966 112m Pathecolor
Columbia / William Frye

Two mischievous new pupils cause trouble at a
convent school.
Fun with the nuns, for addicts only.

w Blanche Hanalis, *novel* Life with Mother

Superior by Jane Trahey *d* Ida Lupino
ph Lionel Lindon *m* Jerry Goldsmith

Rosalind Russell, Hayley Mills, June Harding,
Marge Redmond, Binnie Barnes, Gypsy Rose
Lee, Camilla Sparv, Mary Wickes, Margalo
Gillmore

'A relentless series of prankish escapades.'—
MFB

The Trouble with Girls

US 1969 105m Metrocolor Panavision
MGM (Lester Welch)

In the twenties the manager of a travelling
chautauqua (educational medicine show) gets
involved in a small-town murder.
Curious vehicle for a very bored singing star,
with some interesting background detail.

w Arnold and Lois Peyser, *novel* The
Chautauqua by Day Keene, Dwight Babcock
d Peter Tewksbury *ph* Jacques Marquette
m Billy Strange

Elvis Presley, Marlyn Mason, Nicole Jaffe,
Sheree North, Edward Andrews, John
Carradine, Vincent Price, Joyce Van Patten

The Trouble with Harry**

US 1955 99m Technicolor Vistavision
(Paramount) Alfred Hitchcock

In the New England woods, various reasons
cause various people to find and bury the same
body.
Black comedy which never quite, despite bright
moments, catches the style of the book; however,
it is finely performed and the autumnal
backgrounds are splendid.

w John Michael Hayes, *novel* Jack Trevor Story
d Alfred Hitchcock *ph* Robert Burks
m Bernard Herrmann

Edmund Gwenn, Mildred Natwick, John
Forsythe, Shirley Maclaine, Mildred Dunnock

True as a Turtle

GB 1956 96m Eastmancolor
Rank (Peter de Sarigny)

Honeymooners join a variety of friends on a
yacht crossing the Channel, and get involved in
smuggling.
Artless, undemanding comedy for those who like
messing about in boats.

w Jack Davies, John Coates, Nicholas Phipps
d Wendy Toye *ph* Reg Wyer *m* Robert Farnon

John Gregson, June Thorburn, Cecil Parker,
Elvi Hale, Keith Michell, Avice Landone

True Confession**

US 1937 85m bw
Paramount (Albert Lewin)

A fantasy-prone girl confesses to a murder she
didn't commit, and her upright lawyer husband
defends her.
Archetypal crazy comedy with fine moments
despite longueurs and a lack of cinematic
inventiveness. Remade as *Cross My Heart* (qv).

w Claude Binyon, *play* Mon Crime by Louis
Verneuil, George Berr *d* Wesley Ruggles
ph Ted Tetzlaff *m* Frederick Hollander

Carole Lombard, Fred MacMurray, *John
Barrymore*, Una Merkel, Porter Hall, Edgar
Kennedy, Lynne Overman, Fritz Feld, *Irving
Bacon*

'The best comedy of the year.'—*Graham
Greene*

The True Glory****

GB/US 1945 90m bw
Ministry of Information / Office of War
   Information

The last year of the war, retold by edited
newsreels: D-Day to the Fall of Berlin.
A magnificent piece of reportage, worth a dozen
fiction films in its exhilarating Shakespearean
fervour, though the poetic commentary does
occasionally go over the top. One of the finest of
all compilations.

w Eric Maschwitz, Arthur Macrae, Jenny
Nicholson, Gerald Kersh, Guy Trosper *d* Carol
Reed, Garson Kanin *research* Peter Cusick
m William Alwyn

'Dwarfs all the fiction pictures of the year.'—
Richard Mallett, Punch

True Grit*

US 1969 128m Technicolor
Paramount / Hal B. Wallis (Paul Nathan)

In the old west, a young girl wanting to avenge
her murdered father seeks the aid of a hard-
drinking old marshal.
Disappointingly slow-moving and uninventive
semi-spoof western with a roistering
performance from a veteran star, who won a
sentimental Oscar for daring to look fat and old.

w Marguerite Roberts, *novel* Charles Portis
d Henry Hathaway *ph* Lucien Ballard *m* Elmer
Bernstein

John Wayne, Kim Darby, Glen Campbell,
Dennis Hopper, Jeremy Slate, Robert Duvall,
Strother Martin, Jeff Corey

'Readers may remember it as a book about a
girl, but it's a film about John Wayne.'—*Stanley
Kauffmann*

† *Rooster Cogburn* featured more adventures of

the Wayne character, who also showed up on
TV in 1978 in the guise of Warren Oates

AA: John Wayne

AAN: title song (*m* Elmer Bernstein, *ly* Don
Black)

True Heart Susie*
US 1919 67m approx (24 fps) bw silent
D. W. Griffith / Artcraft

A country girl sells her cow to send her boy
friend to college, but he is ungrateful.
Lavender-flavoured rustic romance, with the
director at his most sentimental. But of its kind it
is carefully done.

wd D. W. Griffith, *story* Marion Fremont
ph Billy Bitzer

Lillian Gish, Robert Harron, Clarine Seymour

The True Story of Jesse James
US 1956 92m Eastmancolor
    Cinemascope
TCF (Herbert Swope Jnr)
GB title: *The James Brothers*

After the Civil War, Jesse and Frank James
become outlaws and train robbers.
Fairly slavish remake of *Jesse James*, without
the style.

w Walter Newman *d* Nicholas Ray *ph* Joe
MacDonald *m* Leigh Harline

Robert Wagner, Jeffrey Hunter, Hope Lange,
Agnes Moorehead, John Carradine, Alan Hale
Jnr, Alan Baxter

The Truth about Women
GB 1957 107m Eastmancolor
British Lion / Beaconsfield (Sydney Box)

An old roué recounts to his son-in-law his early
amorous adventures.
Tedious charade with neither wit nor grace.

w Muriel and Sydney Box *d* Muriel Box
ph Otto Heller *m* Bruce Montgomery

Laurence Harvey, Julie Harris, Diane Cilento,
Mai Zetterling, Eva Gabor, Michael Denison,
Derek Farr, Roland Culver, Wilfrid Hyde
White, Christopher Lee, Marius Goring, Thorley
Walters, Ernest Thesiger, Griffith Jones

The Truth about Spring*
GB 1964 102m Technicolor
U-I / Quota Rentals (Alan Brown)

The bored nephew of a millionaire cruising in the
Caribbean jumps at the chance to join friends on
a scruffy yacht, but they all get involved with
pirates.
Pleasing family film with good scenery and a
friendly cast.

w James Lee Barrett, *novel* H. de Vere
Stacpoole *d* Richard Thorpe *ph* Ted Scaife
m Robert Farnon

Hayley Mills, James MacArthur, David
Tomlinson, Lionel Jeffries, John Mills, Harry
Andrews, Niall MacGinnis

Try and Get Me*
US 1951 92m bw
(UA) Robert Stillman
GB title: *The Sound of Fury*

Two men are arrested for kidnapping and
murder, and a journalist stirs the small town to
lynch fury.
Harrowing, relentless melodrama, possibly the
best on this subject.

w Jo Pagano, from his novel The Condemned
d Cyril Endfield *ph* Guy Roe *m* Hugo
Friedhofer

Frank Lovejoy, Lloyd Bridges, Kathleen Ryan,
Richard Carlson, Katherine Locke, Adele
Jergens, Art Smith

'The characterization and the handling of the
drama are remarkable, at times reaching a
complexity rare in films of this type.'—*Gavin
Lambert*

'A strange, uncomfortable, sometimes brutal
and depressing picture.'—*Richard Mallett,
Punch*

The Trygon Factor*
GB 1966 88m Technicolor
Rank / Rialto Film / Preben Phillipsen (Ian
    Warren)

Bogus nuns plan a million pound bank raid.
When you get used to its mixture of styles, this
Anglo-German production is pretty good
imitation Edgar Wallace, with bags of mystery
and melodramatic goings-on involving larger
than life characters most of whom come to sticky
ends.

w Derry Quinn, Stanley Munro, Kingsley Amis
d Cyril Frankel *ph* Harry Waxman *m* Peter
Thomas

Stewart Granger, Susan Hampshire, Cathleen
Nesbitt, Robert Morley, James Culliford,
Brigitte Horney, Sophie Hardy, James
Robertson Justice

Tudor Rose*
GB 1936 78m bw
GFD / Gainsborough (Michael Balcon)
US title: *Nine Days a Queen*

The brief life and reign of Lady Jane Grey.
Modestly well made historical textbook.

w Robert Stevenson, Miles Malleson *d* Robert
Stevenson

Cedric Hardwicke, Nova Pilbeam, John Mills, Felix Aylmer, Leslie Perrins, Frank Cellier, Desmond Tester, Gwen Frangcon Davies, Sybil Thorndike, Martita Hunt, Miles Malleson, John Laurie

Tugboat Annie**
US 1933   88m   bw
MGM

An elderly waterfront lady and her boozy friend smooth out the path of young love.
Hilarious and well-loved comedy vehicle for two great stars of the period.

w Zelda Sears, Eve Greene, *stories* Norman Reilly Raine d Mervyn Le Roy ph Gregg Toland

Marie Dressler, Wallace Beery, Robert Young, Maureen O'Sullivan, Willard Robertson, Paul Hurst

Tulsa*
US 1949   88m   Technicolor
Eagle—Lion (Walter Wanger)

The daughter of a cattle owner builds an oil empire.
Splendid Hollywood hokum of the second grade, very predictable but well-oiled.

w Frank Nugent, Curtis Kenyon d Stuart Heisler ph Winton Hoch m Frank Skinner

Susan Hayward, Robert Preston, Pedro Armendariz, Lloyd Gough, Chill Wills, Ed Begley

Tumbleweeds**
US 1925   80m (24 fps)   bw   silent
United Artists / William S. Hart

A wandering cowboy helps a family of settlers.
The same plot as *Shane* works wonders in the last film of William S. Hart, which has the apparently authentic flavour of the old west.

w C. Gardner Sullivan, *story* Hal G. Evarts d King Baggott ph Joseph August

William S. Hart, Barbara Bedford, Lucien Littlefield, Monte Collins

† Reissued in 1939 with an added eight-minute introduction by Hart, showing how the west has changed.

Tunes of Glory**
GB 1960   107m   Technicolor
UA / Knightsbridge (Albert Fennell)

The new disciplinarian CO of a highland regiment crosses swords with his lax, hard-drinking predecessor.
Wintry barracks melodrama, finely acted and well made with memorable confrontation scenes

compensating for a somewhat underdeveloped script.

w James Kennaway, from his novel d Ronald Neame ph Arthur Ibbetson

Alec Guinness, John Mills, Susannah York, Dennis Price, Kay Walsh, *Duncan Macrae,* Gordon Jackson, John Fraser, Allan Cuthbertson

The Tunnel*
GB 1935   94m   bw
Gaumont (Michael Balcon)
US title: *Transatlantic Tunnel*

Crooked finances mar the completion of an undersea tunnel to America.
A rare example of British science fiction.

w Curt Siodmak, L. DuGarde Peach, Clemence Dane, *novel* Bernard Kellerman d Maurice Elvey

Richard Dix, Leslie Banks, Madge Evans, Helen Vinson,
C. Aubrey Smith, George Arliss, Walter Huston, Basil Sydney, Jimmy Hanley

The Tunnel of Love
US 1958   98m   bw   Cinemascope
MGM / Joseph Fields

A husband applying to adopt an orphan thinks he may, while drunk, have seduced the glamorous orphan agency official.
Tasteless and not very funny comedy, somewhat miscast.

w Joseph Fields, *play* Joseph Fields, Peter de Vries, *novel* Peter de Vries d Gene Kelly ph Robert Bronner

Richard Widmark, Doris Day, Gig Young, Gia Scala, Elizabeth Fraser, Elizabeth Wilson

Turksib*
USSR 1929   60m approx (24 fps)   bw   silent
Vostok Kino

The making of the Turkestan—Siberia railway.
A highly fluent and pictorial documentary with an especially famous climax as the men struggle to lay the last rails and meet a deadline.

w Victor Turin and others d Victor Turin ph Yevgeni Slavinsky, Boris Frantzisson

Turn of the Tide*
GB 1935   80m   bw
British National (John Corfield)

A feud between two fishing families ends in marriage.
Low-key, location-set action drama with a moral. The film which brought J. Arthur Rank

into the business, which he saw had religious possibilities.

w L. DuGarde Peach, J. O. C. Orton, *novel* Three Fevers by Leo Walmsley *d* Norman Walker

Geraldine Fitzgerald, John Garrick, Niall MacGinnis, J. Fisher White, Joan Maude, Sam Livesey, Wilfrid Lawson, Moore Marriott

Turn the Key Softly

GB 1953 81m bw
GFD / Chiltern (Maurice Cowan)

The problems of three women released from prison.
Soppy formula multi-drama with contrived and uninteresting plots and characters.

w Jack Lee, Maurice Cowan, *novel* John Brophy *d* Jack Lee *ph* Geoffrey Unsworth *m* Mischa Spoliansky

Yvonne Mitchell, Terence Morgan, Joan Collins, Kathleen Harrison, Thora Hird, Dorothy Alison, Glyn Houston, Geoffrey Keen, Clive Morton

Turnabout*

US 1940 83m bw
Hal Roach

A benevolent god enables a quarrelsome couple to change bodies and see how they like it.
'The man's had a baby instead of the lady', said the ads. Well, not quite, but it did seem pretty daring at the time, and it still provides a hilarious moment or two.

w Mickell Novak, Berne Giler, John McLain, *novel* Thorne Smith *d* Hal Roach *ph* Norbert Brodine

Adolphe Menjou, John Hubbard, Carole Landis, Mary Astor, Verree Teasdale, Donald Meek, William Gargan, Joyce Compton

The Turning Point

US 1952 85m bw
Paramount (Irving Asher)

A young lawyer is appointed by the state governor to smash a crime syndicate.
Familiar exposé drama of its time, quite crisply done.

w Warren Duff *w* William Dieterle *ph* Lionel Lindon *md* Irwin Talbot

William Holden, Alexis Smith, Edmond O'Brien, Tom Tully, Ray Teal

The Turning Point*

US 1977 119m De Luxe
TCF / Hera (Nora Kaye)

The American Ballet Theatre visits Oklahoma City, and its ageing star revisits an ex-colleague, now a housewife.
Posh person's soap opera, rather boringly made and interesting only for its performances, which are certainly vivid.

w Arthur Laurents *d* Herbert Ross *ph* Robert Surtees *m* John Lanchbery *pd* Albert Brenner

Anne Bancroft, Shirley Maclaine, Mikhail Baryshnikov, Leslie Browne, Tom Skerritt, Martha Scott, Marshall Thompson

'A backstage musical dressed up with smart cultural trimmings.'—*Alan Brien*

'We get a glimpse of something great in the movie—Mikhail Baryshnikov dancing—and these two harpies out of the soaps block the view.'—*New Yorker, 1978*

Twelve Angry Men****

US 1957 95m bw
(UA) Orion–Nova (Henry Fonda, Reginald Rose)

A murder case jury about to vote guilty is convinced otherwise by one doubting member.
Though unconvincing in detail, this is a brilliantly tight character melodrama which is never less than absorbing to experience. Acting and direction are superlatively right, and the film was important in helping to establish television talents in Hollywood.

w Reginald Rose, from his play *d Sidney Lumet ph Boris Kaufman m* Kenyon Hopkins

Henry Fonda, Lee J. Cobb, E. G Marshall, Jack Warden, Ed Begley, Martin Balsam, John Fiedler, Jack Klugman, George Voskovec, Robert Webber, Edward Binns, Joseph Sweeney

AAN: best picture; Reginald Rose; Sidney Lumet

The Twelve Chairs

US 1970 93m Movielab
UMC / Crossbow (Michael Hertzberg)

A Russian bureaucrat chases twelve dining chairs, in one of which is hidden the family jewels.
Tedious Mel Brooks romp with not too many laughs, from a yarn better handled in *Keep Your Seats Please* and *It's in the Bag,* from both of which he might have learned something about comedy timing.

w Mel Brooks, *novel* Ilf and Petrov *d* Mel Brooks *ph* Dorde Nikolic *m* John Morris

Ron Moody, Frank Langella, Dom De Luise, Bridget Brice, Diana Coupland, Mel Brooks

'In the end it runs out of both steam and

jokes.'—*Michael Billington, Illustrated London News*

Twelve O'Clock High•••
US 1949   132m   bw
TCF (Darryl F. Zanuck)

During World War II, the commander of a US bomber unit in Britain begins to crack under the strain.

Absorbing character drama, justifiably a big box office success of its day, later revived as a TV series. All production values are excellent.

w Sy Bartlett, Beirne Lay Jnr   d Henry King ph Leon Shamroy   m Alfred Newman

Gregory Peck, Hugh Marlowe, Gary Merrill, Millard Mitchell, Dean Jagger, Robert Arthur, Paul Stewart, John Kellogg

AA: Dean Jagger
AAN: best picture; Gregory Peck

Twentieth Century•••
US 1934   91m   bw
Columbia

A temperamental Broadway producer trains an untutored actress, but when a star she proves a match for him.

Though slightly lacking in pace, this is a marvellously sharp and memorable theatrical burlesque, and the second half, set on the train of the title, reaches highly agreeable peaks of insanity.

w Ben Hecht, Charles MacArthur, play Napoleon of Broadway by Charles Bruce Millholland   *d Howard Hawks   ph* Joseph August

John Barrymore, Carole Lombard, Roscoe Karns, Walter Connolly, Ralph Forbes, *Etienne Girardot,* Charles Lane, Edgar Kennedy

  'Notable as the first comedy in which sexually attractive, sophisticated stars indulged in their own slapstick instead of delegating it to their inferiors.'—*Andrew Sarris, 1963*

  'In the role of Jaffe John Barrymore fits as wholly and smoothly as a banana in a skin.'— *Otis Ferguson*

Twenty-Four Hours of a Woman's Life
GB 1952   90m   Technicolor
ABPC (Ivan Foxwell)

A young widow tries to reform an inveterate gambler, but he kills himself.

Stilted, over-literary romantic melodrama with philosophical dialogue, flashback framing and Riviera settings.

w Warren Chetham Strode, *novel* Stefan Zweig

d Victor Saville   *ph* Christopher Challis *m* Robert Gill, Philip Green .

Merle Oberon, Leo Genn, Richard Todd, Stephen Murray, Peter Illing, Isabel Dean

Twenty Million Miles to Earth
US 1957   82m   bw
Columbia (Charles Schneer)

An American rocket ship returning from Venus breaks open and a scaly monster escapes into the Mediterranean and is cornered in the Roman coliseum.

Cheeseparing monster fiction which doesn't wake up till the last five minutes, and looks pretty silly even then.

w Bob Williams, Chris Knopf   *d* Nathan Juran *ph* Irving Lippmann   *m* Mischa Bakaleinikoff *sp* Ray Harryhausen

William Hopper, Joan Taylor, Frank Puglia, John Zaremba

Twenty Million Sweethearts
US 1934   89m   bw
Warner

Singing radio sweethearts are kept apart because of their images.

Thin musical with moderate numbers, remade as *My Dream Is Yours.*

w Warren Duff, Harry Sauber   *d* Ray Enright *ph* Sid Hickox *songs* Harry Warren, Al Dubin

Dick Powell, Ginger Rogers, Pat O'Brien, the Mills Brothers, Ted Fio Rito and his band, the Radio Rogues, Allen Jenkins, Grant Mitchell

Twenty Mule Team•
US 1940   84m   bw
MGM (J. Walter Ruben)

Rivalry among the borax miners in Death Valley.

Adequate semi-western with an unusual theme and setting.

w Robert C. DuSoe, Owen Atkinson   *d* Richard Thorpe *ph* Clyde De Vinna   *m* David Snell

Wallace Beery, Leo Carrillo, Marjorie Rambeau, Anne Baxter, Douglas Fowley, Berton Churchill, Noah Beery Jnr, Arthur Hohl, Clem Bevans, Charles Halton, Minor Watson

Twenty-One Days•
GB 1937   75m   bw
London Films (Alexander Korda)
aka: The First and the Last

A barrister's brother accidentally kills a man and lets an old eccentric take the blame.

Watchable but very stilted melodrama with

interesting early performances by Olivier and
Leigh and a few good moments.

w Graham Greene, *play* John Galsworthy
d Basil Dean

Laurence Olivier, Vivien Leigh, Leslie Banks,
Hay Petrie, Francis L. Sullivan, Esmé Percy,
Robert Newton, Victor Rietti

Twenty Thousand Leagues under the Sea**
US 1954 122m Technicolor
Cinemascope
Walt Disney

Victorian scientists at sea are wrecked and
captured by the mysterious captain of a
futuristic submarine.
Pretty full-blooded adaptation of a famous yarn,
with strong performances and convincing art
and trick work.

w Earl Felton, *novel Jules Verne d Richard
Fleischer ph* Franz Lehy, Ralph Hammeras,
Till Gabbani *m* Paul Smith *ad John Meehan*

Kirk Douglas, James Mason, Paul Lukas, Peter
Lorre, Robert J. Wilke, Carlton Young, Ted de
Corsia

Twenty Thousand Years in Sing Sing**
US 1932 77m bw
Warner (Robert Lord)

A tough criminal escapes from prison but his girl
kills a man during the attempt, and he takes the
blame.
Dated but fast-moving and still-powerful crime
melodrama, remade to less effect as *Castle on the
Hudson* (qv).

w Wilson Mizner, Brown Holmes, *book* Lewis
E. Lawes *d Michael Curtiz ph* Barney McGill
m Bernhard Kaun

Spencer Tracy, Bette Davis, Arthur Byron, Lyle
Talbot, Louis Calhern, Warren Hymer, Sheila
Terry, Edward McNamara

Twenty-Three Paces to Baker Street*
US 1956 103m Eastmancolor
Cinemascope
TCF (Henry Ephron)

A blind playwright in a pub overhears a murder
plot and follows the trail to the bitter end despite
attacks on his life.
Sufficiently engrossing murder mystery with a
weird idea of London's geography: the hero's
Portman Square apartment has a balcony
overlooking the Thames two miles away.
Perhaps this is part of the script's light touch.

w Nigel Balchin, *novel* Philip MacDonald

d Henry Hathaway *ph* Milton Krasner *m* Leigh
Harline

Van Johnson, Vera Miles, *Cecil Parker,* Patricia
Laffan, Maurice Denham, *Estelle Winwood,*
Liam Redmond

Twice round the Daffodils
GB 1962 89m bw
Anglo Amalgamated / GHW (Peter Rogers)

Comic and serious episodes in the lives of male
patients at a TB sanatorium.
Acceptable broadening, almost in *Carry On*
style, of a modestly successful play.

w Norman Hudis, *play* Ring for Catty by
Patrick Cargill, Jack Beale *d* Gerald Thomas
ph Alan Hume *m* Bruce Montgomery

Juliet Mills, Donald Sinden, Donald Houston,
Kenneth Williams, Ronald Lewis, Joan Sims,
Andrew Ray, Lance Percival, Jill Ireland, Sheila
Hancock, Nanette Newman

Twilight for the Gods
US 1958 120m Eastmancolor
U-I (Gordon Kay)

The captain of an old sailing ship takes her for a
last voyage from Mexico to Tahiti.
Dull and miscast adventure story lacking the
spark of the original novel; watchable only for
the travelogue elements.

w Ernest K. Gann, from his novel *d* Joseph
Pevney *ph* Irving Glassberg *m* David Raskin
md Joseph Gershenson

Rock Hudson, Cyd Charisse, Arthur Kennedy,
Leif Erickson, Charles McGraw, Ernest Truex,
Richard Haydn, Wallace Ford, Celia Lovsky,
Vladimir Sokoloff
'Rock Hudson has difficulty in suggesting a
dedicated seaman who has served under sail for
thirty years.'—*MFB*

Twilight of Honor
US 1963 115m bw Panavision
MGM / Perlsea
GB title: *The Charge Is Murder*

A young small-town lawyer defends a neurotic
no-good on a murder charge.
Modest courtroom melodrama in which the
detail is better than the main plot.

w Henry Denker, *novel* Al Dewlen *d* Boris
Sagal *ph* Philip Lathrop *m* John Green

Richard Chamberlain, *Claude Rains,* Joey
Heatherton, Nick Adams, Joan Blackman,
James Gregory, Pat Buttram, Jeanette Nolan

AAN: Nick Adams

Twilight's Last Gleaming
US/West Germany 1977   146m
  Technicolor
Lorimar / Bavaria Studios (Helmut Jedele)

An ex-general commandeers an atomic missile
plant and blackmails the president into telling
some political truths.
Suspense thriller, fairly incompetent on its level
and with ideas above its station. A distinctly
overlong and unlikeable entertainment.

w Ronald M. Cohen, Edward Huebsch,
novel Viper Three by Walter Wager d Robert
Aldrich ph Robert Hauser m Jerry Goldsmith

Burt Lancaster, Richard Widmark, Charles
Durning, Melvyn Douglas, Paul Winfield, Burt
Young, Joseph Cotten, Roscoe Lee Brown,
Gerald S. O'Loughlin, Charles Aidman

Twin Beds*
US 1942   84m   bw
Edward Small

A married couple are embarrassed by the antics
of a drunken neighbour.
Slight pretext for a pretty funny old-fashioned
farce.

w Curtis Kenyon, Kenneth Earl, E. Edwin
Moran, play Margaret Mayo, Edward Salisbury
Field d Tim Whelan ph Hal Mohr m Dmitri
Tiomkin

George Brent, Joan Bennett, Mischa Auer, Una
Merkel, Glenda Farrell, Ernest Truex, Margaret
Hamilton, Charles Coleman

The Twinkle in God's Eye
US 1955   73m   bw
Republic (Mickey Rooney)

A parson rebuilds a church in a western town
where his father was killed by Indians.
Amiable if unlikely western drama with the star
more convincing than one might expect.

w P. J. Wolfson d George Blair ph Bud
Thackery m Van Alexander

Mickey Rooney, Hugh O'Brian, Colleen Gray,
Michael Connors, Don Barry

Twinky
GB 1969   98m   Technicolor
Rank / World Film Services (Clive Sharp)
US title: Lola

A 16-year-old London schoolgirl marries a
dissolute 40-year-old American author.
Dreary sex comedy drama, the fag end of
London's swinging sixties.

w Norman Thaddeus Vane d Richard Donner
ph Walter Lassally m John Scott

Charles Bronson, Susan George, Trevor
Howard, Michael Craig, Honor Blackman,
Robert Morley, Jack Hawkins

Twins of Evil
GB 1971   87m   Eastmancolor
Rank / Hammer (Harry Fine, Michael Style)

Identical Austrian twins become devotees of a
vampire cult.
Vampire-chasing Puritans add a little flavour to
a routine Hammer horror.

w Tudor Gates d John Hough ph Dick Bush
m Harry Robinson

Madeleine and Mary Collinson, Peter Cushing,
Kathleen Byron, Dennis Price, Isobel Black

Twist around the Clock
US 1961   83m   bw
Columbia / Sam Katzman

An astute manager discovers a small-town dance
called the twist and promotes it nationally.
Rock around the Clock revisited, with an even
lower budget and fewer shreds of talent.

w James B. Gordon d Oscar Rudolph
ph Gordon Avil md Fred Karger

Chubby Checker, the Marcels, Dion, John
Cronin, Mary Mitchell

A Twist of Sand
GB 1968   91m   De Luxe
UA / Christina (Fred Engel)

An ill-matched set of criminals seek hidden
diamonds on Africa's skeleton coast.
Pattern melodrama of thieves falling out, quite
nicely put together but with performances too
high pitched.

m Marvin H. Albert, novel Geoffrey Jenkins
d Don Chaffey ph John Wilcox m Tristam Cary

Richard Johnson, Honor Blackman, Roy
Dotrice, Peter Vaughan, Jeremy Kemp

Twisted Nerve
GB 1968   118m   Eastmancolor
British Lion / Charter (John Boulting)

A rich, disturbed young man disguises himself as
a retarded teenager in order to kill his hated
stepfather.
Absurd, unpleasant, longwinded and naïvely
scripted shocker, rightly attacked because it
asserted that brothers of mongoloids are apt to
become murderers. A long way behind the worst
Hitchcock.

w Leo Marks, Roy Boulting d Roy Boulting
ph Harry Waxman m Bernard Herrmann

Hayley Mills, Hywel Bennett, Phyllis Calvert,

Billie Whitelaw, Frank Finlay, *Barry Foster*, Salmaan Peer

'Curious and in some respects disagreeable . . . never thrilling enough to reach the Hitchcock level and without sufficient medical credibility to be taken seriously as a case history.'—*Michael Billington, Illustrated London News*

Two a Penny

GB 1967 98m Eastmancolor
World Wide (Frank R. Jacobson)

An idle art student becomes involved in the drug racket but finally sees the light.
Naïve religious propaganda sponsored by the Billy Graham movement and featuring the evangelist in a cameo. A curiosity.

w Stella Linden *d* James F. Collier *ph* Michael Reed *m* Mike Leander

Cliff Richard, Dora Bryan, Ann Holloway, Avril Angers, Geoffrey Bayldon, Peter Barkworth

Two against the World

US 1936 64m bw
Warner (Bryan Foy)
GB title: *The Case of Mrs Pembroke*

A gutter newspaper unnecessarily digs up a sordid murder case and causes the suicide of two people involved.
Remake of *Five Star Final* with the interest boringly shifted to the do-gooders who *don't* want to publish the story.

w Michel Jacoby, *play* Louis Weitzenkorn *d* William McGann *ph* Sid Hickox *m* Heinz Roemheld

Humphrey Bogart, Beverly Roberts, Helen MacKellar, Henry O'Neill, Linda Perry, Virginia Brissac

Two and Two Make Six

GB 1961 89m bw
Bryanston / Prometheus (Monja Danischewsky)

Two motor cycling couples almost accidentally swap partners.
Reasonably fresh little romantic comedy.

w Monja Danischewsky *d* Freddie Francis *ph* Desmond Dickinson, Ronnie Taylor *m* Norrie Paramor

George Chakiris, Janette Scott, Alfred Lynch, Jackie Lynch, Malcolm Keen, Ambrosine Philpotts, Bernard Braden

The Two Faces of Dr Jekyll

GB 1960 88m Technicolor Megascope
Hammer (Anthony Nelson-Keys)
US title: *House of Fright*

A variation on the much-filmed story: the schizo's evil half is the more handsome.
Surprisingly flat and tedious remake.

w Wolf Mankowitz, *novel* Robert Louis Stevenson *d* Terence Fisher *ph* Jack Asher *m* David Heneker, Monty Norman

Paul Massie, Dawn Addams, Christopher Lee, David Kossoff, Francis de Wolff

Two-Faced Woman*

US 1941 90m bw
MGM (Gottfried Reinhardt)

A ski instructress who fears she may be losing her publisher husband to another woman poses as her own more vivacious twin sister.
The failure of this scatterbrained comedy is alleged to be the reason for Garbo's premature retirement. Looked at half a century later, it is no great shakes but harmless and eager to please; what sabotages it is a shoddy production and flagging pace.

w S. N. Behrman, Salka Viertel, George Oppenheimer *d* George Cukor *ph* Joseph Ruttenberg *m* Bronislau Kaper

Greta Garbo, Melvyn Douglas, *Constance Bennett*, Roland Young, Robert Sterling, Ruth Gordon, George Cleveland

'It is almost as shocking as seeing your mother drunk.'—*Time*

Two Flags West*

US 1950 92m bw
TCF (Casey Robinson)

Sixty Confederate prisoners of war are granted an amnesty and go west to fight the Indians.
Laboured but good-looking Civil War western.

w Casey Robinson *d Robert Wise* *ph Leon Shamroy* *m* Hugo Friedhofer

Joseph Cotten, Jeff Chandler, Linda Darnell, Cornel Wilde, Dale Robertson, Jay C. Flippen, Noah Beery Jnr, Harry Von Zell

'Its period reconstruction is remarkable.'— *Gavin Lambert*

Two for the Road*

GB 1967 113m De Luxe Panavision
TCF / Stanley Donen

An architect and his wife motoring through France recall the first twelve years of their relationship.
Fractured, fashionable light romantic comedy dressed up to seem of more significance than the gossamer thing it really is; and some of the gossamer has a Woolworth look.

w Frederic Raphael *d* Stanley Donen
ph *Christopher Challis* *m* Henry Mancini

Albert Finney, Audrey Hepburn, Eleanor Bron,
William Daniels, Claude Dauphin

AAN: Frederic Raphael

Two for the Seesaw
US 1962   120m   bw   Panavision
UA / Seesaw / Mirisch / Argyle / Talbot
(Robert Wise)

A New York dance instructress has a
tempestuous affair with a Wyoming doctor on
the verge of divorce.
Serious comedy or light drama, meticulously
detailed but immensely long for its content and
too revealing of its stage origins.

w Isabel Lennart, *play* William Gibson *d* Robert
Wise *ph* Ted McCord *m* André Previn
ad Boris Leven

Robert Mitchum, Shirley Maclaine

AAN: Ted McCord; song 'Second Chance'
(*m* André Previn, *ly* Dory Langdon)

Two Girls and a Sailor **
US 1944   124m   bw
MGM (Joe Pasternak)

The title says it all.
Loosely-linked wartime musical jamboree with
first-class talent; a lively entertainment of its
type.

w Richard Connell, Gladys Lehman *d* Richard
Thorpe *ph* Robert Surtees *m* George Stoll
songs various

June Allyson, Gloria de Haven, Van Johnson,
Xavier Cugat and his Orchestra, *Jimmy
Durante*, Tom Drake, Lena Horne, Carlos
Ramirez, Harry James and his Orchestra, Jose
Iturbi, *Gracie Allen*, Virginia O'Brien, Albert
Coates

AAN: script

The Two-Headed Spy *
GB 1958   93m   bw
Columbia (Hal E. Chester)

A bogus Nazi worms his way into the Gestapo
hierarchy.
Adequate, not too exciting biopic of Colonel
Alex Schottland; standard production values.

w James O'Donnell *d* André de Toth *ph* Ted
Scaife *m* Bernard Schurmann

Jack Hawkins, Gia Scala, Alexander Knox, Erik
Schumann, Felix Aylmer, Laurence Naismith,
Donald Pleasence, Kenneth Griffith

Two Lane Blacktop
US 1971   103m   Technicolor   scope
Universal / Michael S. Laughlin

In the American southwest, the aimless owners
of two souped-up cars have an interminable race.
Occasionally arresting, generally boring
eccentricity by a big studio looking for another
Easy Rider.

w Rudolph Wurlitzer, Will Corry *d* Monte
Hellman *ph* Jack Deerson *m* Billy James

James Taylor, Warren Oates, Laurie Bird,
Dennis Wilson

Two Left Feet
GB 1963   93m   bw
British Lion / Roy Baker (Leslie Gilliat)

A callow 19-year-old has girl trouble.
Ponderous sex comedy with no apparent
purpose but some well observed scenes.

w Roy Baker, John Hopkins, *novel* In My
Solitude by David Stuart Leslie *d* Roy Baker
ph Wilkie Cooper *m* Philip Green

Michael Crawford, Nyree Dawn Porter, Julia
Foster, David Hemmings, Dilys Watling, David
Lodge, Bernard Lee

Two Loves
US 1961   100m   Metrocolor
Cinemascope
MGM / Julian Blaustein
GB title: *Spinster*

An American teacher in New Zealand teaches
Maoris and whites and falls for two men.
Pretentious romantic drama with unspeakable
dialogue and eccentric characters.

w Ben Maddow, *novel* Sylva Ashton Warner
d Charles Walters *ph* Joseph Ruttenberg
m Bronislau Kaper

Shirley Maclaine, Jack Hawkins, Laurence
Harvey, Nobu McCarthy

Two Minute Warning
US 1976   115m   Technicolor   Panavision
Universal / Filmways (Edward S. Feldman)

A sniper terrifies the crowd at a championship
football game.
Smartly directed but weakly plotted and scripted
disaster movie: the mystery gunman remains a
mystery at the end.

w Edward Hume, *novel* George LaFountaine
d Larry Peerce *ph* Gerald Hirschfeld *m* Charles
Fox

Charlton Heston, John Cassavetes, Martin
Balsam, Beau Bridges, David Janssen, Marilyn
Hassett, Jack Klugman, Gena Rowlands,
Walter Pidgeon, Brock Peters, Mitch Ryan

The Two Mrs Carrolls
US 1945 (released 1947)   99m   bw
Warner (Mark Hellinger)

A psychopathic artist paints his wives as the
Angel of Death, then murders them with
poisoned milk.
Stilted film of an old warhorse of a play,
unhappily cast but working up some last-minute
tension.

w Thomas Job, *play* Martin Vale *d* Peter
Godfrey *ph* Peverell Marley *m* Franz Waxman

Barbara Stanwyck, Humphrey Bogart, Alexis
Smith, Nigel Bruce, Isobel Elsom, Pat O'Moore,
Peter Godfrey

Two Mules for Sister Sara
US 1969   116m   Technicolor   Panavision
Universal / Malpaso (Martin Rackin)

A wandering cowboy kills three men trying to
rape a nun, but she is not what she seems.
Vaguely unsatisfactory western with patches of
nasty brutality leading to an action-packed
climax.

w Albert Maltz, Budd Boetticher *d* Don Siegel
ph Gabriel Figueroa, Gabriel Torres *m* Ennio
Morricone

Clint Eastwood, Shirley Maclaine, Manolo
Fabregas, Alberto Morin

Two of a Kind
US 1951   75m   bw
Columbia (William Dozier)

A man is picked up by a glamorous girl who
involves him in an elaborate scheme to defraud
an elderly couple.
Modest suspenser.

w Lawrence Kimble, James Grunn *d* Henry
Levin *ph* Burnett Guffey *m* George Duning

Edmond O'Brien, Lizabeth Scott, Terry Moore,
Alexander Knox, Griff Barnett, Virginia Brissac

Two on a Guillotine*
US 1965   107m   bw   Panavision
Warner (William Conrad)

An illusionist arranges to be chained into his
coffin at his funeral but promises to return from
the dead.
Longwinded and unconvincing shocker with
some effectively scary sequences.

w Henry Slesar, John Kneubuhl *d* William
Conrad *ph* Sam Leavitt *m* Max Steiner

Connie Stevens, Dean Jones, Cesar Romero,
Parley Baer, Virginia Gregg, Connie Gilchrist,
John Hoyt

Two People
US 1973   100m   Technicolor
Universal (Robert Wise)

An army deserter returns home and falls for a
fashion photographer.
Solemn, inconsequential topical drama which
made no impact whatever.

w Richard de Roy *d* Robert Wise *ph* Gerald
Hirschfeld *m* David Shire

Peter Fonda, Lindsay Wagner, Estelle Parsons,
Alan Fudge

'Sluggish pacing, lifeless looping and
terminally ludicrous dialogue eventually turn the
film into a travesty of its own form.'—*Variety*

Two Rode Together
US 1961   109m   Technicolor
Columbia / John Ford / Shpetner

An army commander and a tough marshal
negotiate with Comanches for the return of
prisoners.
Substandard Ford, moderately good-looking but
uninteresting of plot and dreary of development.

w Frank Nugent, *novel* Will Cook *d* John Ford
ph Charles Lawton Jnr *m* George Duning

James Stewart, Richard Widmark, Shirley
Jones, Linda Cristal, Andy Devine, John
McIntire

Two Seconds*
US 1932   68m   bw
Warner

In the last two seconds of his life a criminal
reviews the events leading up to his execution.
Competent, pacy crime melodrama.

w Harvey Thew, *play* Elliott Lester *d* Mervyn
Le Roy *ph* Sol Polito

Edward G. Robinson, Preston Foster, Vivienne
Osborne,
J. Carrol Naish, Guy Kibbee, Adrienne Dare
'A film that compels attention.'—*Mordaunt
Hall, New York Times*

Two Sisters from Boston*
US 1946   112m   bw
MGM (Joe Pasternak)

Two girls visiting New York find work in a
Bowery saloon.
Nicely-detailed turn-of-the-century musical with
pleasant talent.

w Myles Connolly *d* Henry Koster *ph* Robert
Surtees *md* Charles Previn *songs* Sammy Fain,
Ralph Freed

June Allyson, Kathryn Grayson, Lauritz
Melchior, Jimmy Durante, Peter Lawford, Ben
Blue

Two Smart People
US 1946   93m   bw
MGM (Ralph Wheelwright)

A con man on parole in New Orleans is chased by a lady crook in search of his hidden loot.
Dog-eared comedy drama.

w Ethel Hill, Leslie Charteris d Jules Dassin
ph Karl Freund m George Bassman

Lucille Ball, John Hodiak, Lloyd Nolan, Hugo Haas, Lenore Ulric, Elisha Cook Jnr, Lloyd Corrigan, Vladimir Sokoloff

2001: A Space Odyssey***
GB 1968   141m   Metrocolor   Panavision
MGM / Stanley Kubrick (Victor Lyndon)

From ape to modern space scientist, mankind has striven to reach the unattainable.
A lengthy montage of brilliant model work and obscure symbolism, this curiosity slowly gathered commercial momentum and came to be cherished by longhairs who used it as a trip without LSD.

w Stanley Kubrick, Arthur C. Clarke, story The Sentinel by Arthur C. Clarke d Stanley Kubrick ph Geoffrey Unsworth, John Alcott m various classics pd Tony Masters, Harry Lange, Ernie Archer ad John Hoesli

'Somewhere between hypnotic and immensely boring.'—Renata Adler

'Morally pretentious, intellectually obscure and inordinately long . . . intensely exciting visually, with that peculiar artistic power which comes from obsession . . . a film out of control, an infuriating combination of exactitude on small points and incoherence on large ones.'—Arthur Schlesinger Jnr

AAN: script; Stanley Kubrick

Two Thousand Women
GB 1944   97m   bw
GFD / Gainsborough (Edward Black)

Two pilots try to rescue British women from a French concentration camp.
Routine mix of laughter and tears; hardly an outstanding film of its time, but mildly entertaining.

wd Frank Launder ph Jack Cox md Louis Levy

Phyllis Calvert, Flora Robson, Patricia Roc, Renée Houston, Anne Crawford, Jean Kent, James McKechnie, Reginald Purdell, Robert Arden, Thora Hird, Dulcie Gray, Carl Jaffe, Muriel Aked

Two Tickets to Broadway
GB 1951   106m   Technicolor
RKO

Small-town college girl finds romance and success in the big city.
Very mild musical with TV studio backdrop.

w Sid Silvers, Hal Kanter d James V. Kern
ph Edward Cronjager, Harry J. Wild m Walter Scharf

Janet Leigh, Eddie Bracken, Gloria de Haven, Tony Martin, Barbara Lawrence, Joe Smith and Charlie Dale

Two Way Stretch**
GB 1960   87m   bw
British Lion / Shepperton (M. Smedley Aston)

Three convicts break jail to rob a maharajah.
Amusing comedy with good performances and situations, unofficially borrowed in part from Convict 99.

w John Warren, Len Heath d Robert Day
ph Geoffrey Faithfull m Ken Jones

Peter Sellers, Lionel Jeffries, Wilfrid Hyde White, Bernard Cribbins, David Lodge, Maurice Denham, Beryl Reid, Liz Fraser, Irene Handl, George Woodbridge

Two Weeks in Another Town*
US 1962   107m   Metrocolor
  Cinemascope
MGM (John Houseman)

An ex-alcoholic film director gets his comeback chance in Rome but is plagued by old memories.
Self-indulgent melodrama with entertaining patches for cinéastes, especially those who saw The Bad and the Beautiful.

w Charles Schnee, novel Irwin Shaw d Vincente Minnelli ph Milton Krasner m David Raksin

Kirk Douglas, Edward G. Robinson, Cyd Charisse, Daliah Lavi, George Hamilton, Claire Trevor, Rosanna Schiaffino, James Gregory, George Macready

Two Weeks with Love*
US 1950   92m   Technicolor
MGM (Jack Cummings)

Adventures on a family summer holiday at the turn of the century.
Pleasant family musical.

w John Larkin, Dorothy Kingsley d Roy Rowland ph Al Gilks m Georgie Stoll

Jane Powell, Ricardo Montalban, Louis Calhern, Ann Harding, Phyllis Kirk, Debbie Reynolds, Carleton Carpenter, Clinton Sundberg

Two Women*
Italy / France 1960   110m   bw
Champion / Marceau / Cocinor / SGC (Carlo
  Ponti)
original title: *La Ciociara*

During the Allied bombing of Rome a woman
and her daughter travel arduously south and
have a hard time at the hands of invading
soldiers.
Rather hysterical character drama allowing for a
splendid top-note performance from its star.

w Cesare Zavattini, Vittorio de Sica,
novel Alberto Moravia *d* Vittorio de Sica
ph Gabor Pogany *m* Armando Trovaioli

Sophia Loren, Eleonora Brown, Jean-Paul
Belmondo, Raf Vallone

AA: Sophia Loren

Two Years before the Mast*
US 1946   98m   bw
Paramount

In the mid-19th century, a writer becomes a
sailor to expose bad conditions.
Well-made but unconvincing-looking
picturization of a famous book.

w Seton I. Miller, George Bruce, *book* Richard
Henry Dana *d* John Farrow *ph* Ernest Laszlo
m Victor Young

Alan Ladd, Brian Donlevy, William Bendix,
Barry Fitzgerald, Howard da Silva, Albert
Dekker, Luis Van Rooten, Darryl Hickman

Tycoon
US 1947   129m   Technicolor
RKO

An engineer is hired to drive a tunnel through the
Andes, and starts a feud with his boss when he
falls in love with his daughter.
Boring, studio-set action saga with too many
stops for romance.

w Borden Chase, John Twist *d* Richard
Wallace *ph* Harry J. Wild *m* Leigh Harline

John Wayne, Cedric Hardwicke, Laraine Day,
James Gleason, Judith Anderson, Anthony
Quinn, Grant Withers

Typhoon
US 1940   70m   Technicolor
Paramount (Anthony Veiller)

On a Dutch Guianan island, two sailors find a
girl who has been a castaway since childhood.
One of Lamour's several sarongers, quite
entertaining in its way and commendably brisk.

w Allen Rivkin *d* Louis King *ph* William
Mellor *m* Frederick Hollander

Dorothy Lamour, Robert Preston, Lynne
Overman, J. Carrol Naish, Frank Reicher

  'One of the most emphatically silly pictures I
ever saw in my life.'—*Richard Mallet, Punch*

U

Ugetsu Monogatari*
Japan 1953 94m bw
Daiei (Masaichi Nagata)

During a 16th century civil war two potters find a way of profiteering, but their ambitions bring disaster on their families.

Unique mixture of action, comedy and the supernatural, with strong, believable characters participating and a delightfully delicate touch in script and direction. On its first release it began to figure in many best ten lists, but quickly seemed to fade from public approbation.

w Matsutaro Kawaguchi, from 17th-century collection by Akinara Ueda, Tales of a Pale and Mysterious Moon after the Rain d Kenji Mizoguchi ph Kazuo Miyagawa m Fumio Hayasaka

Masayuki Mori, Machiko Kyo, Sakae Ozawa, Mitsuko Mito

The Ugly American
US 1962 120m Eastmancolor
U-I / George Englund

A publisher is made ambassador to a south-east Asian state.
Self-dating anti-communist drama which was muddled and boring when new.

w Stewart Stern, novel William J. Lederer, Eugene Burdick d George Englund

Marlon Brando, Eiji Okada, Sandra Church, Pat Hingle, Arthur Hill, Jocelyn Brando, Kukrit Pramoj

The Ugly Dachshund*
US 1965 93m Technicolor
Walt Disney (Winston Hibler)

A dachshund bitch fosters among its puppies an orphan Great Dane.
Cheerful, fast-moving animal farce.

w Albert Aley, novel G. B. Stern d Norman Tokar ph Edward Colman m George Bruns

Dean Jones, Suzanne Pleshette, Charles Ruggles, Kelly Thordsen, Parley Baer, Mako, Charles Lane

The Ultimate Warrior
US 1975 94m Technicolor
Warner (Fred Weintraub, Paul Heller)

In AD 2012 New York is ruled by a gangster, the atmosphere is poisoned, and the only hope is a new community on an island off North Carolina.
Curious pretentious fantasy without the courage of its convictions or much entertainment value.

wd Robert Clouse ph Gerald Hirschfeld m Gil Melle

Yul Brynner, Max Von Sydow, Joanna Miles, William Smith, Richard Kelton, Stephen McHattie

'Less a prophetic vision than a kind of thick-ear West Side Story.'—Richard Combs

Ulysses*
Italy 1954 103m Technicolor
Lux Film / Ponti–de Laurentiis (Fernando Cinquini)

Ulysses and his crew sail under the curse of Cassandra, and encounter Circe, the sirens and the cyclops.
Peripatetic adventure yarn not too far after Homer; narrative style uncertain but highlights good.

w Franco Brusati, Mario Camerini, Ennio de Concini, Hugh Gray, Ben Hecht, Ivo Perelli, Irwin Shaw, poem The Odyssey by Homer d Mario Camerini ph Harold Rosson m Alessandro Cicognini

Kirk Douglas, Silvana Mangano, Anthony Quinn, Rosanna Podesta

Ulysses*
GB 1967 132m bw Panavision
Walter Reade (Joseph Strick)

Twenty-four hours in Dublin with a young poet and a Jewish newspaper man.
A pleasant enough literary exercise, a decent précis of an unmanageably prolix classic novel, this specialized offering would have passed unnoticed were it not for its language, which got it banned in many places but now seems mild indeed.

w Joseph Strick, Fred Haines, novel James

Joyce *d Joseph Strick ph Wolfgang Suschitsky*
m Stanley Myers

Maurice Roeves, Milo O'Shea, Barbara Jefford,
T. P. McKenna, Anna Manahan, Maureen
Potter

'No amount of pious invoking of Joyce's name
can disguise the fact that a cheaply produced
film is being sold at exorbitant prices so that
someone can make his boodle off "culture".'—
John Simon

'An act of homage in the form of readings
from the book plus illustrated slides.'—*Pauline
Kael*

'A facile and ludicrous reduction.'—*Stanley
Kauffmann*

AAN: script

Ulzana's Raid

US 1972   103m   Technicolor
Universal / Carter de Haven / Robert Aldrich

An ageing Indian fighter and a tenderfoot officer
lead a platoon sent out to counter a murderous
Apache attack.

Bloodthirsty, reactionary western with
unpleasant shock moments.

w Alan Sharp *d* Robert Aldrich *ph* Joseph
Biroc *m* Frank de Vol

Burt Lancaster, Bruce Davison, Jorge Luke,
Richard Jaeckel, Lloyd Bochner

Umberto D**

Italy 1952   89m   bw
Dear Films

A retired civil servant can barely afford his rent
but won't part with his dog.

Downbeat, immensely moving study of old age
in a society which fails to provide for it.

w Cesare Zavattini, Vittorio de Sica *d Vittorio
de Sica ph* G. R. Aldo *m* Alessandro Cicognini

Carlo Battista

AAN: Cesare Zavattini (original story)

Uncensored

GB 1942   108m   bw
GFD / Gainsborough (Edward Black)

In Brussels during the Nazi occupation, the
leader of a toe-the-line paper secretly leads the
patriots.

Unconvincing underground melodrama with
stilted presentation and performances.

w Wolfgang Wilhelm, Terence Rattigan,
Rodney Ackland, *novel* Oscar Millard
d Anthony Asquith *ph* Arthur Crabtree
m Hans May

Eric Portman, Phyllis Calvert, Griffith Jones,

Raymond Lovell, Peter Glenville, Irene Handl,
Carl Jaffe, Felix Aylmer

Uncertain Glory

US 1944   102m   bw
Warner (Robert Buckner)

During World War II, a French playboy
sacrifices himself for his country.

Tame star vehicle needing more action and less
philosophy.

w Laszlo Vadnay, Max Brand *d* Raoul Walsh
ph Sid Hickox *m* Adolph Deutsch

Errol Flynn, Paul Lukas, Jean Sullivan, Lucile
Watson, Faye Emerson, James Flavin, Douglass
Dumbrille, Dennis Hoey

Unchained

US 1955   75m   bw
Warner / Hall Bartlett

A new governor experiments with a prison
without bars.

Decent documentary drama which reaches no
great heights.

wd Hall Bartlett, *book* Prisoners Are People by
Kenyon J. Scudder *ph* Virgil Miller *m* Alex
North

Chester Morris, Elroy Hirsch, Barbara Hale,
Todd Duncan, Johnny Johnston, Peggy
Knudsen, Jerry Paris, John Qualen

AAN: title song (*m* Alex North, *ly* Hy Zarek)

Uncle Silas*

GB 1947   103m   bw
GFD / Two Cities (Josef Somlo, Laurence
Irving)
US title: *The Inheritance*

A young Victorian heiress finds herself menaced
by her uncle and his housekeeper.

Slow-starting but superbly made period
suspenser; unfortunately the characters are all
sticks.

w Ben Travers, *novel* Sheridan Le Fanu
d Charles Frank

Jean Simmons, Derrick de Marney, Katina
Paxinou, Derek Bond, Esmond Knight, Sophie
Stewart, Manning Whiley, Reginald Tate,
Marjorie Rhodes

Unconquered

US 1947   146m   Technicolor
Paramount / Cecil B. de Mille

An 18th-century English convict girl is deported
to the American colonies and suffers various
adventures before marrying a Virginia
militiaman.

Cardboard epic, expensive and noisy but totally

unpersuasive despite cannon, arrows, fire and dynamite.

w Charles Bennett, Frederic M. Frank, Jesse Lasky Jnr, *novel* Neil H. Swanson *d* Cecil B. de Mille *ph* Ray Rennahan *m* Victor Young

Paulette Goddard, Gary Cooper, Boris Karloff, Howard da Silva, Cecil Kellaway, Ward Bond, Katherine de Mille, Henry Wilcoxon, C. Aubrey Smith, Victor Varconi, Virginia Grey, Porter Hall, Mike Mazurki

'De Mille bangs the drum as loudly as ever but his sideshow has gone cold on us.'—*Richard Winnington*

'A five-million dollar celebration of Gary Cooper's virility, Paulette Goddard's femininity, and the American frontier spirit.'—*Time*

The Undefeated
US 1969 119m De Luxe Panavision
TCF (Robert L. Jacks)

After the Civil War, two colonels from opposite sides meet on the Rio Grande.
Sprawling, lethargic star western with moments of glory.

w James Lee Barrett *d* Andrew V. McLaglen *ph* William H. Clothier *m* Hugo Montenegro

John Wayne, Rock Hudson, Lee Meriwether, Tony Aguilar, Roman Gabriel

Under Capricorn
GB 1949 117m Technicolor
Transatlantic (Sidney Bernstein, Alfred Hitchcock)

In Australia in 1830 an English immigrant stays with his cousin Henrietta, who has become a dipsomaniac because of her husband's cruelty.
Cardboard 'woman's picture' with elements of *Rebecca,* shot with vestiges of Hitch's ten-minute take. A pretty fair disaster.

w James Bridie, *novel* Helen Simpson *d* Alfred Hitchcock *ph* Jack Cardiff, Paul Beeson, Ian Craig *m* Richard Addinsell

Ingrid Bergman, Joseph Cotten, Michael Wilding, Margaret Leighton, Jack Watling, Cecil Parker, Denis O'Dea

Under Milk Wood*
GB 1971 88m Technicolor
Timon (Hugo French, Jules Buck)

Life in the Welsh village of Llareggub, as seen by the poet's eye.
Attractive but vaguely unsatisfactory screen rendering of an essentially theatrical event (originally a radio play); everything is much too literal, a real place instead of a fantasy.

wd Andrew Sinclair, *play Dylan Thomas ph* Bob Huke *m* Brian Gascoigne

Richard Burton, Elizabeth Taylor, Peter O'Toole, Glynis Johns, Vivien Merchant, Sian Phillips, Victor Spinetti, Rachel Thomas, Angharad Rees, Ann Beach

Under My Skin
US 1949 86m bw
TCF (Casey Robinson)

A crooked jockey is idolized by his son and finally reforms rather than disillusion the boy.
Hokey sentimental melodrama with racetrack backgrounds.

w Casey Robinson, *short story* My Old Man by Ernest Hemingway *d* Jean Negulesco *ph* Joseph La Shelle *m* Daniele Amfitheatrof

John Garfield, Micheline Presle, Luther Adler, Orley Lindgren, Ann Codee

Under Ten Flags
US 1960 92m bw
Paramount / Dino de Laurentiis

In World War II, a German surface raider in disguise menaces British shipping.
Muddled naval epic with too many allegiances.

w Vittorio Petrilli, Duilio Coletti, Ulrich Mohr, William Douglas Home *d* Duilio Coletti, Silvio Narizzano *ph* Aldo Tonti *m* Nino Rota

Van Heflin, Charles Laughton, John Ericson, Mylène Demongeot, Cecil Parker, Folco Lulli, Alex Nicol, Liam Redmond

Under the Red Robe*
GB 1937 82m bw
(TCF) Robert T. Kane

A hell-raising nobleman is persuaded by Cardinal Richelieu to unmask the ringleader of an anti-monarchist conspiracy.
Smart, unusual swashbuckler on the lines of *The Prisoner of Zenda,* modestly but quite effectively made.

w Lajos Biro, Philip Lindsay, J. L. Hodson, *novel* Stanley J. Weyman *d* Victor Sjostrom *ph* Georges Périnal

Conrad Veidt, Raymond Massey, Annabella, Romney Brent, Sophie Stewart, Wyndham Goldie, Lawrence Grant

Under the Yum Yum Tree
US 1963 110m Eastmancolor
Columbia / Sonnis / Swift (Frederick Brisson)

Two college students have a trial marriage in an apartment block with a lecherous landlord.
Coy, non-erotic and extremely tedious comedy which runs out of jokes after reel one.

w Lawrence Roman, David Swift *d* David Swift *ph* Joseph Biroc *m* Frank de Vol

Jack Lemmon, Carol Lynley, Dean Jones, Imogene Coca, Edie Adams, Paul Lynde, Robert Lansing

Under Two Flags*
US 1936 111m bw
TCF (Raymond Griffith)

A dashing French Foreign Legionaire is helped by a café girl.

Despite a highly predictable plot (of *Destry Rides Again)* this was a solidly-produced epic with a nice deployment of star talent.

w W. P. Lipscomb, Walter Ferris, *novel* 'Ouida' *d* Frank Lloyd *ph* Ernest Palmer *m* Louis Silvers

Ronald Colman, Claudette Colbert, Rosalind Russell, Victor McLaglen, J. Edward Bromberg, Nigel Bruce, Herbert Mundin, Gregory Ratoff, C. Henry Gordon, John Carradine, Onslow Stevens

Under Your Hat*
GB 1940 79m bw
Grand National (Jack Hulbert)

Film stars chase spies and recover a stolen carburettor.

Light-hearted adaptation of a stage musical, showing the stars in their best film form.

w Rodney Ackland, Anthony Kimmins, *play* Jack Hulbert, Archie Menzies, Geoffrey Kerr, Arthur Macrae *d* Maurice Elvey

Jack Hulbert, Cicely Courtneidge, Austin Trevor, Leonora Corbett, Cecil Parker, H. F. Maltby, Glynis Johns, Charles Oliver

Undercover Man*
US 1949 89m bw
Columbia (Robert Rossen)

US treasury agents indict a gang leader for tax evasion.

Good semi-documentary crime melodrama based on the Al Capone case.

w Sidney Boehm, Malvin Wald *d* Joseph H. Lewis *ph* Burnett Guffey *m* George Duning

Glenn Ford, Nina Foch, Barry Kelley, James Whitmore, David Wolf, Esther Minciotti

Undercurrent*
US 1946 116m bw
MGM (Pandro S. Berman)

A professor's daughter marries an industrialist and is frightened and finally endangered by the mystery surrounding his brother.

Overlong suspenser with solid performances and production values; a variation on *Gaslight.*

w Edward Chodorov, *story* Thelma Strabel *d* Vincente Minnelli *ph* Karl Freund *m* Herbert Stothart

Katharine Hepburn, Robert Taylor, Robert Mitchum, Edmund Gwenn, Marjorie Main, Jayne Meadows, Clinton Sundberg, Dan Tobin

Underground
US 1941 95m bw
Warner (William Jacobs)

Underground leaders in Germany during World War II send out radio messages under the noses of the Nazis.

Forgotten actioner, quite solidly made.

w Charles Grayson *d* Vincent Sherman *ph* Sid Hickox *m* Adolph Deutsch

Jeffrey Lynn, Philip Dorn, Karen Verne, Mona Maris, Frank Reicher, Martin Kosleck, Ilka Gruning

Underground
US 1970 100m De Luxe
UA / Levy—Gardner—Laven

An American paratrooper joins a French resistance group to kidnap a Nazi general. Routine war actioner.

w Ron Bishop, Andy Lewis *d* Arthur H. Nader *ph* Ken Talbot *m* Stanley Myers

Robert Goulet, Danièle Gaubert, Laurence Dobkin, Carl Duering

Underworld*
US 1927 82m (24 fps) bw silent
Paramount
GB title: *Paying the Penalty*

A gangster is rescued from prison by his moll and his lieutenant, and when he realizes they are in love he allows them to escape when the law closes in.

An innovative film in its time, this melodrama was the first to look at crime from the gangsters' point of view. Its main appeal now lies in its lush direction.

w Ben Hecht, Robert N. Lee, Josef Von Sternberg *d* Josef Von Sternberg *ph* Bert Glennon *ad* Hans Dreier

George Bancroft, Evelyn Brent, Clive Brook, Larry Semon

† The film was a great international success and had an influence on the pessimistic French school of the thirties.

AA: Ben Hecht

Underworld USA*
US 1960   99m   bw
Columbia / Globe (Samuel Fuller)

A young gangster takes elaborate revenge for the killing of his father.
Violent syndicate melodrama with a semi-documentary veneer and some brutal scenes. Well done but heavy going.

wd Samuel Fuller *ph* Hal Mohr *m* Harry Sukman

Cliff Robertson, Beatrice Kay, Larry Gates, Dolores Dorn, *Robert Emhardt*, Paul Dubov, Richard Rust

The Undying Monster*
US 1943   63m   bw
TCF
GB title: *The Hammond Mystery*

A curse hangs over the English ancestral home of the Hammonds.
Silly but well-photographed and directed minor horror on wolf man lines.

w Lillie Hayward, Michel Jacoby, *novel* Jessie D. Kerruish *d* John Brahm *ph* Lucien Ballard *m* Emil Newman, David Raksin

James Ellison, John Howard, Heather Angel, Bramwell Fletcher, Heather Thatcher, Eily Malyon, Halliwell Hobbes, Aubrey Mather

Unearthly Stranger*
GB 1963   75m   bw
Independent Artists (Julian Wintle, Leslie Parkyn, Albert Fennell)

Scientists working on a time-space formula find that the bride of one of them is an alien in search of their secret.
Surprisingly effective minor science fiction, in some ways all the better for its modest, TV-style production values.

w Rex Carlton *d* John Krish *ph* Reg Wyer *m* Edward Williams

John Neville, Gabriella Licudi, Philip Stone, Jean Marsh, Patrick Newell, Warren Mitchell

The Unfaithful*
US 1947   109m   bw
Warner (Jerry Wald)

A wife gets involved in a murder while her husband is out of town.
Glossy romantic melodrama, an unofficial remake of *The Letter*.

w David Goodis, James Gunn *d* Vincent Sherman *ph* Ernest Haller *m* Max Steiner

Ann Sheridan, Zachary Scott, Lew Ayres, Eve Arden, Steve Geray, Jerome Cowan, John Hoyt

Unfaithfully Yours**
US 1948   105m   bw
TCF (Preston Sturges)

An orchestral conductor believes his wife is unfaithful, and while conducting a concert thinks of three different ways of dealing with the situation.
A not entirely happy mixture of romance, farce, melodrama and wit, but in general a pretty entertaining concoction and the last major film of its talented writer-director.

wd Preston Sturges *ph* Victor Milner *m* Alfred Newman

Rex Harrison, Linda Darnell, Barbara Lawrence, Rudy Vallee, Kurt Kreuger, Lionel Stander, *Edgar Kennedy, Al Bridge*, Julius Tannen, Torben Meyer, Robert Greig

Unfinished Business
US 1941   95m   bw
Universal (Gregory La Cava)

A wife has thoughts that she should have married her husband's brother.
Smooth but disappointing romantic comedy; the detail is good enough, but it sadly lacks drive.

w Eugene Thackery *d* Gregory La Cava *ph* Joseph Valentine *m* Franz Waxman

Irene Dunne, Robert Montgomery, Eugene Pallette, Preston Foster, Walter Catlett, June Clyde, Phyllis Barry, Esther Dale, Samuel S. Hinds
    'Once sentiment gets the upper hand, reach for the exit.'—*Otis Ferguson*

The Unfinished Dance
US 1947   101m   Technicolor
MGM

The young star of a ballet school becomes jealous of a talented newcomer, and causes her injury in an accident.
The delicacies of the French original, *La Mort du Cygne*, give way to standard Hollywood hokum and produce an accomplished but totally uninteresting film.

w Myles Connolly, *story* Paul Morand *d* Henry Koster *ph* Robert Surtees *md* Herbert Stothart

Margaret O'Brien, Cyd Charisse, Karin Booth, Danny Thomas, Esther Dale
    'The same old story, with pathos, humour and ballet substituted for pathos, humour and chorus girls.'—*MFB*

The Unforgiven*
US 1960   125m   Technicolor   Panavision
UA / James Productions /
    Hecht–Hill–Lancaster (James Hill)

A rancher's daughter is suspected of being an Indian orphan, and violence results.
Good-looking, expensive but muddled racist western, hard to enjoy.

w Ben Maddow, *novel* Alan le May *d* John Huston *ph* Franz Planer *m* Dmitri Tiomkin

Burt Lancaster, Audrey Hepburn, Audie Murphy, Lillian Gish, Charles Bickford, Doug McClure, John Saxon, Joseph Wiseman, Albert Salmi

'How much strain can a director's reputation take? Of late, John Huston seems to have been trying to find out. I think he has carried the experiment too far with *The Unforgiven* . . . a work of profound phoniness, part adult western, part that *Oklahoma!* kind of folksy Americana.'—*Dwight MacDonald*

'Ludicrous . . . a hodgepodge of crudely stitched sententiousness and lame story-conference inspirations.'—*Stanley Kauffmann*

The Unguarded Moment

US 1956   85m   Technicolor
U-I (Gordon Kay)

A schoolmistress who receives anonymous love notes from a psychotic pupil is discredited by his even more unbalanced father.
Well-meaning but boring melodrama with the star attractively out of her usual element.

w Herb Meadow, Larry Marcus, *story* Rosalind Russell *d* Harry Keller *ph* William Daniels *m* Herman Stein

Esther Williams, George Nader, John Saxon, *Edward Andrews*, Jack Albertson

Unholy Partners*

US 1941   95m   bw
MGM (Samuel Marx)

The editor of a sensational newspaper has to accept finance from a gangster, but friction results when the newspaper exposes some of the gangster's activities.
Agreeable twenties melodrama with two solid stars battling it out.

w Earl Baldwin, Lesser Samuels, Bartlett Cormack *d* Mervyn Le Roy *ph* George Barnes *m* David Snell

Edward G. Robinson, Edward Arnold, Laraine Day, Marsha Hunt, William T. Orr, Don Beddoe, Charles Dingle, Walter Kingsford, Marcel Dalio

The Unholy Three*

US 1925   76m approx (24 fps)   bw   silent
MGM

A ventriloquist, a dwarf and a strong man carry out a series of crimes which end in murder.
Curious melodrama which set its star and director off on a series of seven more and even weirder eccentricities.

w Waldemar Young, *story* Clarence Robbins *d* Tod Browning *ph* David Kesson

Lon Chaney, Harry Earles, Victor McLaglen, Mae Busch, Matt Moore
† A talkie remake (Chaney's last film) appeared in 1930 (70m) with Earles, Lila Lee, Elliott Nugent and John Miljan.

The Unholy Wife

US 1957   94m   Technicolor   RKOscope
RKO (John Farrow)

A bored wife shoots a friend in mistake for her husband but is sentenced for the accidental death of her mother-in-law.
Totally uninteresting melodrama in the *Double Indemnity* style, professionally made but turgid.

w Jonathan Latimer *d* John Farrow *ph* Lucien Ballard *m* Daniele Amfitheatrof

Diana Dors, Rod Steiger, Tom Tully, Beulah Bondi, Marie Windsor, Arthur Franz, Luis Van Rooten

The Uninvited**

US 1944   98m   bw
Paramount (Charles Brackett)

A girl returns to her family house and is haunted by her mother's spirit, which seems to be evil.
One of the cinema's few genuine ghost stories, and a good one, though encased in a rather stiff production; it works up to a fine pitch of frenzy.

w Dodie Smith, *novel* Uneasy Freehold by Dorothy Macardle *d* Lewis Allen *ph* Charles Lang *m* Victor Young

Ray Milland, Ruth Hussey, *Gail Russell*, Donald Crisp, Cornelia Otis Skinner, Dorothy Stickney, Barbara Everest, Alan Napier

'Thirty-five first-class jolts, not to mention a well-calculated texture of minor frissons.'—*James Agee*
'Still manages to ice the blood with its implied horrors . . . you can almost smell the ghostly mimosa.'—*Peter John Dyer, 1966*
† British critics of the time congratulated the director on not showing the ghosts: in fact the visible manifestations had been cut by the British censor.

AAN: Charles Lang

Union Pacific**

US 1939   133m   bw
Paramount / Cecil B. de Mille

Indians and others cause problems for the railroad builders.

Standard big-scale western climaxing in a spectacular wreck; not exactly exciting, but very watchable.

w Walter de Leon, C. Gardner Sullivan, Jesse Lasky Jnr *d* Cecil B. de Mille *ph* Victor Milner, Dewey Wrigley *m* John Leipold, Sigmund Krumgold *ad* Hans Dreier, Roland Anderson

Barbara Stanwyck, Joel McCrea, Akim Tamiroff, Robert Preston, Lynne Overman, Brian Donlevy, Robert Barrat, Anthony Quinn, Stanley Ridges, Henry Kolker, Evelyn Keyes, Regis Toomey

Union Station**
US 1950   80m   bw
Paramount (Jules Schermer)

Kidnappers nominate a crowded railroad station as their ransom collection point.
Compelling little thriller modelled after *Naked City*, with real locations and plenty of excitement.

w Sidney Boehm, *novel* Thomas Walsh *d* Rudolph Maté *ph* Daniel L. Fapp *m* David Buttolph, Heinz Roemheld *md* Irvin Talbot

William Holden, *Barry Fitzgerald*, Nancy Olson, *Lyle Bettger*, Jan Sterling, Allene Roberts

Universal Soldier
GB 1971   96m   colour
Appaloosa / Ionian (Frank J. Schwarz, Donald L. Factor)

A mercenary returns to London but can't escape his past.
Solemnly meaningful melodrama on a tight budget.

wd Cy Endfield *ph* Tony Imi *m* Philip Goodhand-Tait

George Lazenby, Edward Judd, Benito Carruthers, Germaine Greer, Rudolph Walker

The Unknown Man
US 1951   86m   bw
MGM (Robert Thomsen)

A civil court lawyer of high principles successfully undertakes a criminal case, finds his client was really guilty, and sets matters straight.
Contrived but entertaining morality with standard production and performances.

w Ronald Millar, George Froeschel *d* Richard Thorpe *ph* William Mellor *m* Conrad Salinger

Walter Pidgeon, Ann Harding, Lewis Stone, Barry Sullivan, Keefe Brasselle, Eduard Franz, Richard Anderson, Dawn Addams

Unman, Wittering and Zigo
GB 1971   102m   colour
Paramount / Mediarts

A nervous schoolmaster discovers that his predecessor was murdered by the boys.
Macabre school story which overreaches itself and peters out.

w Simon Raven, *TV play* Giles Cooper *d* John Mackenzie *ph* Geoffrey Unsworth *m* Michael J. Lewis

David Hemmings, Douglas Wilmer, Hamilton Dyce, Carolyn Seymour

An Unmarried Woman*
US 1977   124m   Movielab
TCF (Paul Mazursky, Tony Ray)

A sophisticated New York woman is deserted by her husband, fights with her daughter, and takes up with two men.
Frank, well observed depiction of one woman in New York's new society; as modern as all get out but not very attractive.

wd Paul Mazursky *ph* Arthur J. Ornitz *m* Bill Conti *ph* Pato Guzman

Jill Clayburgh, Alan Bates, Michael Murphy, Cliff Gorman, Pat Quinn, Kelly Bishop

Unpublished Story
GB 1942   91m   bw
Columbia / Two Cities (Anthony Havelock-Allan)

A reporter exposes the Nazis behind a pacifist organization.
Ho-hum formula flagwaver with generally stilted production.

w Anatole de Grunwald, Patrick Kirwan *d* Harold French *ph* Bernard Knowles *m* Nicholas Brodzky

Valerie Hobson, Richard Greene, Basil Radford, Roland Culver, Brefni O'Rourke, Miles Malleson, George Carney, André Morell

The Unseen
US 1945   82m   bw
Paramount

A London governess comes to suspect that dark deeds have taken place in the empty house next door.
Period suspenser with good atmosphere but an insubstantial plot.

w Hagar Wilde, Raymond Chandler *d* Lewis Allen

Joel McCrea, Gail Russell, Herbert Marshall, Richard Lyon, Nona Griffith
† The film seems to have been a hurried attempt

to repeat and combine the previous year's success, *Gaslight* and *The Uninvited*.

The Unsinkable Molly Brown*
US 1964 128m Metrocolor Panavision
MGM / Marten (Lawrence Weingarten)

Western orphan Molly Brown grows up determined to become a member of Denver society.

Semi-western comedy-musical about a real lady who wound up surviving the *Titanic*. Bouncy and likeable but not at all memorable.

w Helen Deutsch, *musical play* Richard Morris *d* Charles Walters *ph* Daniel L. Fapp *md* Robert Armbruster *ad* George W. Davis, Preston Ames

Debbie Reynolds, Harve Presnell, *Ed Begley*, Jack Krischen, Hermione Baddeley, Martita Hunt

AAN: Daniel L. Fapp; Robert Armbruster; Debbie Reynolds

The Unsuspected*
US 1947 103m bw
Warner (Charles Hoffman)

A writer-producer of radio crime shows commits a murder and is forced to follow the clues on air. Sleek, new look mystery thriller with a disappointing plot which gives its interesting cast little to do, and allows itself to peter out in chases.

w Ranald MacDougall, *novel* Charlotte Armstrong *d Michael Curtiz ph Woody Bredell m* Franz Waxman *ad* Anton Grot

Claude Rains, Joan Caulfield, Audrey Totter, Constance Bennett, Michael North, Hurd Hatfield, Fred Clark

Untamed
US 1955 109m Technicolor
  Cinemascope
TCF (Bert E. Friedlob, William A. Bacher)

A Dutchman and an Irish girl meet again on a Boer trek to South Africa, and survive Zulu attacks.

A long and involved epic-style plot provides standard excitements and predictable romantic complications.

w Talbot Jennings, Michael Blankfort, Frank Fenton, *novel* Helga Moray *d* Henry King *ph* Leo Tover *m* Franz Waxman

Tyrone Power, Susan Hayward, Richard Egan, John Justin, Agnes Moorehead, Rita Moreno, Hope Emerson, Brad Dexter, Henry O'Neill

'A not unenjoyable essay in hokum.'—*MFB*

Untamed Frontier
US 1952 78m Technicolor
U-I (Leonard Goldstein)

The son of an unpopular Texan landowner commits murder.

Stolid minor western.

w Gerald Drayson Adams, Gwen and John Bagni *d* Hugo Fregonese *ph* Charles P. Boyle *m* Hans Salter

Joseph Cotten, Shelley Winters, Scott Brady, Suzan Ball, Minor Watson

Until They Sail
US 1957 95m bw Cinemascope
MGM (Charles Schnee)

Four New Zealand sisters have wartime romances.

Solid 'woman's picture', well enough presented.

w Robert Anderson, *novel* James A. Michener *d* Robert Wise *ph* Joseph Ruttenberg *m* David Raksin

Jean Simmons, Joan Fontaine, Paul Newman, Piper Laurie, Charles Drake, Wally Cassell, Sandra Dee

Up from the Beach*
US 1965 98m bw Cinemascope
TCF / Panoramic (Christian Ferry)

Just after D-Day, GIs have trouble in a Normandy village.

A kind of subdued sequel to *The Longest Day*, well made for war action addicts, but barely memorable.

w Stanley Mann, Claude Brule, *novel* Epitaph for an Enemy by George Barr *d Robert Parrish ph Walter Wottitz m* Edgar Cosma

Cliff Robertson, Red Buttons, Françoise Rosay, Marius Goring, Irina Demick, Broderick Crawford, James Robertson Justice, Slim Pickens

Up in Arms**
US 1944 106m Technicolor
Samuel Goldwyn

A hypochondriac joins the army.
Loose, generally pleasant introductory vehicle for Danny Kaye.

w Don Hartman, Robert Pirosh, Allen Boretz *d* Elliott Nugent *ph* Ray Rennahan *md* Ray Heindorf, Louis Forbes

Danny Kaye, Dinah Shore, Constance Dowling, Dana Andrews, Louis Calhern, Lyle Talbot

AAN: song 'Now I Know' (*m* Harold Arlen, *ly* Ted Koehler); Ray Heindorf, Louis Forbes

Up in Central Park
US 1948   88m   bw
U-I

In turn-of-the-century New York, an Irish girl becomes involved in a crooked political set up.
Stiff and unyielding star musical.

w Karl Tunberg d William A. Seiter ph Milton Krasner songs Sigmund Romberg

Deanna Durbin, Vincent Price, Dick Haymes, Albert Sharpe, Tom Powers

Up in the Cellar
US 1970   94m   Movielab
AIP (William J. Immerman)

A dejected freshman tries various schemes to revenge himself on the college president.
Youth satire aimed at a number of targets which quickly became obsolete; mildly interesting sociologically.

wd Theodore J. Flicker, novel The Late Boy Wonder by Angus Hall ph Earl Roth m Don Randi

Wes Stern, Joan Collins, Larry Hagman, Judy Pace

Up in the World
GB 1956   91m   bw
Rank (Hugh Stewart)

A window cleaner becomes friendly with a boy millionaire.
Slow and unattractive comedy star vehicle.

w Jack Davies, Henry Blyth, Peter Blackmore d John Paddy Carstairs ph Jack Cox m Philip Green

Norman Wisdom, Martin Carida, Jerry Desmonde, Maureen Swanson, Ambrosine Philpotts, Colin Gordon

Up Periscope
US 1959   111m   Technicolor
    Warnerscope
Warner / Lakeside (Aubrey Schenck)

During World War II a submarine frogman is landed on a Pacific island to steal a Japanese code book.
Stock adventure story given stock presentation.

w Richard Landau, novel Robb White d Gordon Douglas ph Carl Guthrie m Ray Heindorf

James Garner, Edmond O'Brien, Alan Hale Jnr, Carleton Carpenter

Up Pompeii
GB 1971   90m   Technicolor

A wily slave outwits Nero and escapes the eruption of Vesuvius.
Yawnmaking spinoff of a lively TV comedy series: the jokes just lie there, and die there.

w Sid Colin d Bob Kellet ph Ian Wilson m Carl Davis

Frankie Howerd, Patrick Cargill, Michael Hordern, Barbara Murray, Lance Percival, Bill Fraser, Adrienne Posta
† Sequels: Up the Front, Up the Chastity Belt (qv).

Up the Chastity Belt*
GB 1971   94m   Technicolor
EMI / Associated London Films (Ned Sherrin)

Medieval adventures of the serf Lurkalot and his master Sir Coward de Custard.
Patchy pantomime which doesn't always have the courage of its own slapdash vulgarity.

w Sid Colin, Ray Galton, Alan Simpson d Bob Kellett ph Ian Wilson m Carl Davis

Frankie Howerd, Graham Crowden, Bill Fraser, Roy Hudd, Hugh Paddick, Anna Quayle, Eartha Kitt, Dave King, Fred Emney

Up the Creek*
GB 1958   83m   bw   Hammerscope
Byron (Henry Halsted)

A none-too-bright naval lieutenant is assigned command of a broken-down shore establishment.
Cheeky remake of Oh Mr Porter. Jokes fair, atmosphere cheerful and easy-going.

wd Val Guest ph Arthur Grant

David Tomlinson, Peter Sellers, Wilfrid Hyde White, Vera Day, Tom Gill, Michael Goodliffe, Reginald Beckwith, Lionel Jeffries
† Sequel: Further Up the Creek.

Up the Down Staircase*
US 1967   124m   Technicolor
Warner / Pakula–Mulligan

Problems of a schoolteacher in one of New York's tough sections.
Earnest, well-acted, not very likeable melodrama.

w Tad Mosel, novel Bel Kaufman d Robert Mulligan ph Joseph Coffey m Fred Karlin

Sandy Dennis, Patrick Bedford, Eileen Heckart, Ruth White, Jean Stapleton, Sorrel Booke, Roy Poole

Up the Front
GB 1972   89m   Technicolor
EMI / Associated London Films (Ned Sherrin)

A footman is hypnotized into enlisting in World War I and has an enemy 'plan' tattooed on his buttocks.
Threadbare end-of-the-pier romp.

w Sid Colin, Eddie Braben *d* Bob Kellet *ph* Tony Spratling *m* Patrick Greenwell *ad* Seamus Flannery

Frankie Howerd, Bill Fraser, Zsa Zsa Gabor, Stanley Holloway, Hermione Baddeley, Robert Coote, Lance Percival, Dora Bryan

Up the Junction
GB 1967   119m   Techniscope
Paramount / Collinson–Crasto

A well-off girl crosses London's river to live among the workers of Clapham.
Socially obsolete sensationalism based on a television semi-documentary. An irritating heroine move hygienically among motorbikes, discos and mild orgies.

w Roger Smith, *book* Nell Dunn *d* Peter Collinson *ph* Arthur Lavis *m* Mike Hugg, Manfred Mann

Suzy Kendall, Dennis Waterman, Adrienne Posta, Maureen Lipman, Michael Gothard, Liz Fraser, Hylda Baker, Alfie Bass

Up the River
US 1930   80m   bw
Fox

An ex-convict is threatened with exposure, but his two pals escape to help him.
Very minor comedy with interesting credits.

w Maurine Watkins *d* John Ford *ph* Joseph August

Spencer Tracy, Warren Hymer, Claire Luce, Humphrey Bogart, William Collier Snr

Up the Sandbox
US 1972   98m   Technicolor
Barwood / First Artists (Robert Chartoff, Irwin Winkler)

A professor's wife finds she is pregnant again and fantasizes about her future life.
Muddled comedy-drama with little point and less entertainment value.

w Paul Zindel, *novel* Anne Richardson Roiphe *d* Irwin Kershner *ph* Gordon Willis, Andy Marton *m* Billy Goldenberg *ad* Harry Horner

Barbra Streisand, David Selby, Ariane Heller, Jane Hoffman

'A magical mystery tour through the picture book mind of one Manhattan housewife.'—*Richard Combs*

Up Tight
US 1968   104m   Technicolor
Paramount / Marlukin (Jules Dassin)

A black street cleaner betrays his criminal pals for money and is hunted down by them.
Ponderous black remake of *The Informer*, too schematic to make any dramatic or human impression.

w Jules Dassin, Ruby Dee, Julian Mayfield *d* Jules Dassin *ph Boris Kaufman m* Booker T. Jones *pd* Alexander Trauner

Raymond St Jacques, Ruby Dee, Julian Mayfield, Frank Silvera, Roscoe Lee Browne, Juanita Moore

Upstairs and Downstairs
GB 1959   101m   Eastmancolor
Rank (Betty E. Box)

Newlyweds have trouble with maids and au pair girls.
Glossy, cheerful, empty-headed domestic comedy.

w Frank Harvey, *novel* Ronald Scott Thorn *d* Ralph Thomas

Michael Craig, Anne Heywood, Mylène Demongeot, James Robertson Justice, Sidney James, Daniel Massey, Claudia Cardinale, Joan Hickson, Joan Sims

Uptown Saturday Night*
US 1974   104m   Technicolor
Warner / Verdon / First Artists (Melville Tucker)

Three friends pursue crooks who have inadvertently stolen a winning lottery ticket.
Witless but high-spirited star comedy for blacks, with a variety of sordid backgrounds.

w Richard Wesley *d* Sidney Poitier *ph* Fred J. Koenekamp *m* Tom Scott

Sidney Poitier, Bill Cosby, Harry Belafonte, Flip Wilson, Roscoe Lee Browne, Richard Pryor, Rosalind Cash, Paula Kelly

'If it had been filmed with a white cast this collection of atrophied comedy routines would have been indistinguishable from a Monogram farce of the forties.'—*David McGillivray*

The Upturned Glass*
GB 1947   86m   bw
GFD / Triton (Sydney Box, James Mason)

A Harley Street surgeon murders the woman responsible for the death of the girl he loved.
Rather pointless psychopathology with an ill-explained title; an interesting example of a top star not knowing what's best for him.

w Jon P. Monaghan, Pamela Kellino
d Lawrence Huntington *ph* Reg Wyer
m Bernard Stevens

James Mason, Pamela Kellino, Rosamund John, Ann Stephens, Henry Oscar, Morland Graham, Brefni O'Rourke

'The psychology is genuine; so too is the tension; the camera plays some good quiet tricks.'—*William Whitebait*

V

The Vagabond King

US 1956 88m Technicolor Vistavision
Paramount (Pat Duggan)

The life and loves of French medieval poet and
rebel François Villon.

Shiny, antiseptic studio-set remake of an old
musical warhorse. (The 1930 version is lost; a
straight version was made in 1938 as *If I Were
King*.)

w Ken Englund, Noel Langley, *operetta* Rudolf
Friml *d* Michael Curtiz *ph* Robert Burks
md Victor Young, *songs* Rudolf Friml

Oreste, Kathryn Grayson, Rita Moreno, *Walter
Hampden*, Leslie Nielsen, Cedric Hardwicke,
William Prince

The Valachi Papers

France / Italy 1972 127m Technicolor
Euro France / de Laurentiis Intermarco (Dino
de Laurentiis)

A convicted gangster talks to an FBI agent
about his life in the Mafia.

Rough, violent gangster melodrama, none the
better for being based on actual events.

w Stephen Geller, *book* Peter Maas *d* Terence
Young *ph* Aldo Tonti *m* Riz Ortolani

Charles Bronson, Fred Valleca, Gerald S.
O'Loughlin, Lino Ventura, Walter Chiari,
Amedeo Nazzari, Joseph Wiseman

Valdez Is Coming

US 1970 90m De Luxe
UA / Norlan / Ira Steiner

A Mexican confronts a rancher who has double-
crossed him.

Simply-conceived western which doesn't quite
manage to be the classic intended.

w Roland Kibbee, David Rayfiel *d* Edwin
Sherin *ph* Gabor Pogany *m* Charles Gross

Burt Lancaster, Susan Clark, Jon Cypher,
Barton Heyman, Frank Silvera

Valentino

US 1951 105m Technicolor
Columbia (Edward Small)

An Italian immigrant to the US becomes a
world-famous romantic film star but dies young.
Disastrously flat attempt to recapture the feel of
Hollywood in the twenties as a background to a
flatulent romance.

w George Bruce *d* Lewis Allen *ph* Harry
Stradling *m* Heinz Roemheld

Anthony Dexter, Eleanor Parker, Richard
Carlson, Patricia Medina, Joseph Calleia, Dona
Drake, Lloyd Gough, Otto Kruger

'One can almost see the decorated border
round the words . . . it mixes fact, speculation,
needless inaccuracy and bathos.'—*Gavin
Lambert*

'The dialogue is unbelievably ham, the
"entirely imaginary" story commonplace; the
players deserve sympathy.'—*Richard Mallett,
Punch*

Valentino*

GB 1977 127m De Luxe
UA / Aperture / Chartoff—Winkler (Harry
Benn)

Reporters quiz celebrities at a star's funeral, and
his eccentric life unfolds.

Sensationalist 'exposé' of Valentino's rise to
fame, with excellent period detail but no
sympathy for its subject.

w Ken Russell, Mardik Martin, *book* Brad
Steiger, Chaw Mank *d* Ken Russell *ph* Peter
Suschitzky *m* Ferde Grofe, Stanley Black
ad Philip Harrison

Rudolf Nureyev, Leslie Caron, Michelle Phillips,
Carol Kane, Felicity Kendal, Huntz Hall, David
de Keyser, Alfred Marks, Anton Diffring, Jennie
Linden, John Justin

Valerie

US 1957 80m bw
UA / Hal R. Makelim

A western rancher is accused of wounding his
wife and murdering her parents.
Curious little *Rashomon*-like courtroom
melodrama, quite well made and acted.

w Leonard Heidemann, Emmett Murphy
d Gerd Oswald *ph* Ernest Laszlo *m* Albert
Glasser

Anita Ekberg, Sterling Hayden, Anthony Steel, John Wengraf

The Valiant

GB/Italy 1961   89m   bw
(UA) BHP / Euro International

During World War II, a battleship in Alexandria harbour is mined, and the captain tries desperately to avert disaster.
Ill-made war fodder, of no interest at any level.

w Keith Waterhouse, Willis Hall d Roy Baker ph Wilkie Cooper, Egil Woxholt m Christopher Whelen

John Mills, Ettore Manni, Robert Shaw, Liam Redmond, Ralph Michael, Colin Douglas, Dinsdale Landen

Valiant Is the Word for Carrie

US 1936   110m   bw
RKO (Wesley Ruggles)

A childless woman devotes her life to orphan children.
Tedious soap opera.

w Claude Binyon, novel Barry Benefield d Wesley Ruggles ph Leo Tover

Gladys George, John Howard, Dudley Digges, Arline Judge, Harry Carey, Isabel Jewell

AAN: Gladys George

The Valley of Decision*

US 1945   119m   bw
MGM

In old Pittsburgh, an Irish housemaid marries the master's son.
Trouble at t' mill epic romance, American style; starrily cast but not excitingly made.

w John Meehan, Sonya Levien, novel Marcia Davenport d Tay Garnett ph Joseph Ruttenberg m Herbert Stothart

Greer Garson, Gregory Peck, Lionel Barrymore, Donald Crisp, Preston Foster, Gladys Cooper, Marsha Hunt, Reginald Owen, Dan Duryea, Jessica Tandy, Barbara Everest, Marshall Thompson

AAN: Herbert Stothart; Greer Garson

The Valley of Gwangi

US 1968   95m   Technicolor
Warner / Morningside

Cowboys and scientists discover prehistoric monsters in a 'forbidden' Mexican valley.
Tedious adventure yarn enhanced by good special effects.

w William E. Bast d James O'Connelly

ph Erwin Hillier m Jerome Moross sp Ray Harryhausen

Richard Carlson, Laurence Naismith, James Franciscus, Gila Golan, Freda Jackson

Valley of the Dolls*

US 1967   123m   De Luxe   Panavision
TCF / Red Lion (David Weisbart)

An innocent young actress is corrupted by Broadway and Hollywood, and takes to drugs.
Cliché-ridden but good-looking road-to-ruin melodrama from a bitchy bestseller; production values high, but the whole thing goes over the top at the end.

w Helen Deutsch, Dorothy Kingsley, novel Jacqueline Susann d Mark Robson ph William H. Daniels md John Williams ad Jack Martin Smith, Richard Day

Barbara Parkins, Patty Duke, Susan Hayward, Paul Burke, Sharon Tate, Martin Milner, Tony Scotti, Charles Drake, Alex Davion, Lee Grant, Robert H. Harris

AAN: John Williams

Valley of the Kings

US 1954   86m   Eastmancolor
MGM

Archaeologists fight looters in the tomb of a Pharaoh.
Thin as drama, with little action or suspense and dispirited acting, this hokum piece nevertheless benefits from splendid locations.

w Robert Pirosh, Karl Tunberg d Robert Pirosh ph Robert Surtees m Miklos Rozsa

Robert Taylor, Eleanor Parker, Carlos Thompson, Kurt Kasznar, Victor Jory

Valley of the Sun

US 1942   79m   bw
RKO (Graham Baker)

A government spy in old Arizona outwits a crooked Indian agent.
Cheapjack western with nothing to commend it.

w Horace McCoy, story Clarence Budington Kelland d George Marshall ph Harry J. Wild m Paul Sawtell

James Craig, Lucille Ball, Dean Jagger, Billy Gilbert, Cedric Hardwicke, Peter Whitney, Tom Tyler, Antonio Moreno, George Cleveland

Value for Money

GB 1955   93m   Technicolor   Vistavision
Rank / Group Films (Sergei Nolbandov)

A Yorkshire businessman determines to broaden

his outlook, and falls in love with a London showgirl.

Highly undistinguished north country romantic farce which wastes a good production and cast.

w R. F. Delderfield, William Fairchild, *novel* Derick Boothroyd *d* Ken Annakin *ph* Geoffrey Unsworth *m* Malcolm Arnold

John Gregson, Diana Dors, Susan Stephen, Derek Farr, Frank Pettingell, Jill Adams, *Ernest Thesiger*, Charles Victor, Joan Hickson

Vampira

GB 1974 88m colour
Columbia / Jack H. Wiener
US title: *Old Dracula*

A vampire count lures beauty-contest winners to his castle and uses their blood to revive his dead wife.

Would-be spoof which falls flat on its fangs.

w Jeremy Lloyd *d* Clive Donner *ph* Tony Richmond *m* David Whitaker

David Niven, Teresa Graves, Peter Bayliss, Jennie Linden, Linda Hayden, Nicky Henson, Bernard Bresslaw, Veronica Carlson

The Vampire

US 1957 74m bw
UA / Gardner—Levy

A research scientist takes bat essence and becomes a vampire.

Silly attempt to turn a legend into science fiction: more risible than sinister.

w Pat Fielder *d* Paul Landres *ph* Jack Mackenzie *m* Gerald Fried

John Beal, Coleen Gray, Kenneth Tobey, Lydia Reed

The Vampire Bat

US 1933 71m bw
Majestic

A mad doctor kills townsfolk in search of 'blood substitute'.

Primitive but vigorous low budget chiller.

w Edward Lowe *d* Frank Strayer *ph* Ira Morgan

Lionel Atwill, Fay Wray, Melvyn Douglas, Maude Eburne, George E. Stone, Dwight Frye, Lionel Belmore

Vampire Circus

GB 1971 87m colour
Hammer (Wilbur Stark)

In 1825 a plague-ridden village is visited by a circus of animal vampires.

Silly but quite inventive horror thriller.

w Judson Kinberg *d* Robert Young *ph* Moray Grant *m* Philip Martell *ad* Scott MacGregor

Adrienne Corri, Laurence Payne, Thorley Walters, John Moulder Brown, Elizabeth Seal, Lynne Frederick, Robert Tayman, Robin Hunter

The Vampire Lovers

GB 1970 91m Technicolor
Hammer / AIP (Harry Fine, Michael Style)

A lady vampire worms her way into several noble households.

Reasonably close retelling of Sheridan Le Fanu's *Carmilla*, complete with lesbian love scenes. Adequate production but not much spirit.

w Tudor Gates, Harry Fine, Michael Styles *novel* Carmilla by Sheridan Le Fanu *d* Roy Ward Baker

Ingrid Pitt, Peter Cushing, Pippa Steele, Madeleine Smith, George Cole, Dawn Addams, Douglas Wilmer, Kate O'Mara

Vampyr**

Germany / France 1931 83m bw
Tobis Klangfilm / Carl Dreyer
aka: *The Strange Adventure of David Gray*

A young man staying in a remote inn suspects that he is surrounded by vampires and has a dream of his own death.

Vague, misty, virtually plotless but occasionally frightening and always interesting to look at, this semi-professional film long since joined the list of minor classics for two scenes: the hero dreaming of his own death and the villain finally buried by flour in a mill.

w Christen Jul, Carl Dreyer, *story* 'Carmilla' by Sheridan Le Fanu *d Carl Dreyer ph Rudolph Maté, Louis Née m* Wolfgang Zeller

Julian West, Sybille Schmitz, Maurice Schutz, Jan Hieronimko

Vanessa, Her Love Story

US 1935 76m bw
MGM (David O. Selznick)

When her husband becomes insane, a Victorian lady falls for a gypsy.

Very dated romance which finished Helen Hayes's star career, for thirty years at least.

w Lenore Coffee, *novel* Hugh Walpole *d* William K. Howard *ph* Ray June

Helen Hayes, Robert Montgomery, May Robson, Otto Kruger, Lewis Stone, Henry Stephenson, Violet Kemble-Cooper, Jessie Ralph

The Vanishing Corporal*
France 1961   106m   bw
Films du Cyclope
original title: *Le Caporal Epinglé*

After several attempts, three Frenchmen succeed
in escaping from a detention camp.
Symbolic World War II drama told in mainly
comic terms. Not one of its director's great films,
but a warm and assured one.

w Jean Renoir, Guy Lefranc   *d* Jean Renoir
ph Georges Leclerc   *m* Joseph Kosma

Jean-Pierre Cassel, Claude Brasseur, Claude
Rich, O. E. Hasse

Vanishing Point*
US 1971   107m   De Luxe
TCF / Cupid (Norman Spencer)

An ex-racing driver who delivers cars for a living
becomes hepped up on benzedrine and leads
police a rare chase through the Nevada desert.
Strange, fashionable action suspenser which is
better to look at than to understand.

w Guillermo Cain   *d Richard Sarafian ph John
A. Alonzo md* Jimmy Brown

Barry Newman, Cleavon Little, Dean Jagger,
Victoria Medlin, Paul Koslo, Bob Donner
    'Uncomfortably reminiscent of *Easy Rider* as
an odyssey through an unknown America in its
discovery of strange alliances and unpredictable
hostilities.'—*Tom Milne*

The Vanishing Virginian
US 1941   97m   bw
MGM

A conservative Virginian finds that he harbours
suffragettes in his household.
Life with Father in another setting; rather yawn-
provoking.

w Jan Fortune, *novel* Rebecca Yancey Williams
d Frank Borzage

Frank Morgan, Spring Byington, Kathryn
Grayson, Elizabeth Patterson, Louise Beavers

Variety**
Germany 1925   104m (24 fps)   bw   silent
UFA
aka: *Vaudeville*

An ageing acrobat seduces a young girl and later
kills another man who is interested in her.
Crude, vivid backstage story, inventively
presented to overcome the dullness and
tawdriness of the plot.

w E. A. Dupont, Leo Birinsky, *novel* Frederick
Hollander   *d E. A. Dupont ph* Karl Freund

Emil Jannings, Lya de Putti, Maly Delschaft,
Warwick Ward

    'A continually roving lens seizes the best angle
for every detail, expression and scene.'—*Leon
Moussinac*

Variety Girl
US 1947   83m   bw
Paramount (Daniel Dare)

Of all the young hopefuls arriving in Hollywood,
one girl becomes a star.
The slightest of excuses for a tour of the
Paramount studios, with all the contract stars
doing bits. It doesn't add up to much.

w Edmund Hartmann, Frank Tashlin, Monte
Brice, Robert Welch   *d* George Marshall
ph Lionel Lindon, Stuart Thompson   *md* Joseph
J. Lilley, Troy Saunders

Mary Hatcher, Olga San Juan, De Forrest
Kelley, Glenn Tryon; and Bob Hope, Bing
Crosby, Gary Cooper, Ray Milland, Alan Ladd,
Barbara Stanwyck, Paulette Goddard, Dorothy
Lamour, Veronica Lake, Sonny Tufts, Joan
Caulfield, William Holden, Lizabeth Scott, Burt
Lancaster, Gail Russell, Diana Lynn, Sterling
Hayden, Robert Preston, William Bendix, Barry
Fitzgerald, Billy de Wolfe, George Pal
Puppetoons, Cecil B. de Mille, Mitchell Leisen,
George Marshall, Spike Jones and his City
Slickers, etc.

Varsity Show
US 1937   80m   bw
Warner (Louis F. Edelman)

Collegians stage a revue.
Mild musical.

w Warren Duff, Richard Macaulay, Jerry Wald,
Sig Herzig   *d* William Keighley   *ph* Sol Polito,
George Barnes   *ch* Busby Berkeley
songs Richard Whiting, Johnny Mercer

Dick Powell, Priscilla Lane, Rosemary Lane,
Fred Waring and his Pennsylvanians, Buck and
Bubbles, Johnny 'Scat' Davis, Ted Healy

Vault of Horror*
GB 1973   86m   Eastmancolor
Metromedia / Amicus (Milton Subotsky)

Five men trapped in the basement of a
skyscraper tell of their recurring dreams.
All-star horror omnibus, plainly but well staged.

w Milton Subotsky, *stories* William Gaines
d Roy Ward Baker   *ph* Denys Coop   *m* Douglas
Gamley

Daniel Massey, Anna Massey, Terry-Thomas,
Glynis Johns, Curt Jurgens, Dawn Addams,
Michael Craig, Edward Judd, Tom Baker,
Denholm Elliott

The Velvet Touch*
US 1948   97m   bw
(RKO) Independent Artists

A famous actress murders her producer and is
struck by conscience but allows a detective to
find his own way to the truth.
Solid murder melodrama with an excellent
theatrical atmosphere.

w Leo Rosten *d* John Gage *ph* Joseph Walker
m Leigh Harline

Rosalind Russell, Leo Genn, Sidney
Greenstreet, Claire Trevor, Leon Ames, Frank
McHugh

Vendetta
US 1950   84m   bw
RKO / Howard Hughes

The daughter of an esteemed Corsican family
takes vengeance on her father's enemies.
Outmoded ethnic melodrama with nothing to
recommend it.

w W. R. Burnett, *novel* Columba by Prosper
Mérimée *d* Mel Ferrer *ph* Franz Planer, Al
Gilks *m* Roy Webb *md* Constantin
Bakaleinikoff

Faith Domergue, George Dolenz, Donald Buka,
Hilary Brooke, Nigel Bruce, Joseph Calleia,
Hugo Haas

The Venetian Affair
US 1966   92m   Metrocolor   Panavision
MGM / Jerry Thorpe

A reporter investigates the death in Venice of an
American diplomat.
Uninteresting and complicated spy thriller with
pleasant locations.

w E. Jack Neuman, *novel* Helen MacInnes
d Jerry Thorpe *ph* Milton Krasner, Enzo
Serafin *m* Lalo Schifrin

Robert Vaughn, Karl Boehm, Elke Sommer, Ed
Asner, Boris Karloff, Felicia Farr, Roger C.
Carmel, Luciana Paluzzi, Joe de Santis

Venetian Bird*
GB 1952   95m   bw
Rank / British Film Makers (Betty E. Box)
US title: *The Assassin*

A private detective goes to Venice to reward a
wartime partisan, who turns out to have become
a notorious criminal.
Standard action fare with a nod to *The Third
Man* but not much excitement or sense of place.

w Victor Canning, from his novel *d* Ralph
Thomas *ph* Ernest Steward *m* Nino Rota
Richard Todd, Eva Bartok, John Gregson,

George Coulouris, Margot Grahame, Walter
Rilla, Sidney James

Vengeance
GB / Germany 1962   83m   bw
CCC / Raymond Stross

After a fatal accident, the brain of a tycoon is
kept alive and persuades a doctor to find his
murderer.
Twisty remake of *Donovan's Brain* (qv), not too
badly done.

w Robert Stewart, Philip Mackie *d* Freddie
Francis *ph* Bob Hulke *m* Ken Jones

Anne Heywood, Peter Van Eyck, Cecil Parker,
Bernard Lee, Maxine Audley, Jeremy Spenser,
Miles Malleson

The Vengeance of Fu Manchu
GB 1967   92m   Eastmancolor
Anglo Amalgamated / Harry Alan Towers

The Yellow Peril plans a crime syndicate to
counter Interpol, and creates a double for
Nayland Smith . . .
Limp addition to a series which started well, but
was subsequently robbed of period flavour.

w Harry Alan Towers, *novels* Sax Rohmer
d Jeremy Summers *ph* John Von Kotze
m Malcolm Lockyer

Christopher Lee, Douglas Wilmer, Tony Ferrer,
Tsai Chin, Howard Marion Crawford,
Wolfgang Kieling

The Vengeance of She
GB 1967   101m   Technicolor
Hammer (Aida Young)

A girl is possessed by the spirit of long-dead
Queen Ayesha.
Grotesquely unpersuasive reincarnation
melodrama, a long long way from its inspiration.

w Peter O'Donnell *d* Cliff Owen *ph* Wolfgang
Suschitsky *m* Mario Nascimbene

John Richardson, Olinka Berova, Edward Judd,
Colin Blakely, Derek Godfrey, Noel Willman,
André Morell, Jill Melford

Vengeance Valley
US 1951   82m   Technicolor
MGM (Nicholas Nayfack)

A western rancher keeps his foster-brother's
misdeeds from their father.
Well-made character western, a little short on
action.

w Irving Ravetch, *novel* Luke Short *d* Richard
Thorpe *ph* George Folsey *m* Rudolph G. Kopp

Burt Lancaster, Robert Walker, Ray Collins,

Joanne Dru, Sally Forrest, John Ireland, Carleton Carpenter, Ted de Corsia

Vera Cruz***
US 1953 94m Technicolor Superscope
UA / Hecht–Hill–Lancaster (James Hill)

Adventurers in 1860 Mexico become involved in a plot against Emperor Maximilian.
Terse, lively western melodrama with unusual locations and comedy and suspense touches.
Great outdoor entertainment.

w Roland Kibbee, James R. Webb, Borden Chase d Robert Aldrich ph Ernest Laszlo m Hugo Friedhofer

Gary Cooper, Burt Lancaster, Denise Darcel, Cesar Romero, George Macready, Sarita Montiel, Ernest Borgnine, Morris Ankrum, Charles Bronson

The Verdict*
US 1946 86m bw
Warner (William Jacobs)

A retired Scotland Yard inspector continues to work on a case which vexes him.
Victorian murder mystery with very unconvincing Hollywood sets and curious casting, but rather nicely detailed.

w Peter Milne, novel The Big Bow Mystery by Israel Zangwill d Don Siegel ph Ernest Haller m Frederick Hollander

Sidney Greenstreet, Peter Lorre, Joan Lorring, George Coulouris, Rosalind Ivan, Paul Cavanagh, Arthur Shields

Vertigo**
US 1958 128m Technicolor Vistavision
(Paramount) Alfred Hitchcock

A detective with a fear of heights is drawn into a complex plot in which a girl he loves apparently falls to her death. Then he meets her double . . .
Double identity thriller which doesn't really hang together but has many sequences in Hitchcock's best style despite central miscasting.

w Alec Coppel, Samuel Taylor, novel D'entre les Morts by Pierre Boileau, Thomas Narcejac d Alfred Hitchcock ph Robert Burks m Bernard Herrmann

James Stewart, Kim Novak, Barbara Bel Geddes, Tom Helmore, Henry Jones

The Very Edge
GB 1962 89m bw Cinevision
British Lion / Garrick / Raymond Stross

An obsessive young man menaces a mother-to-be.

Rather unpleasant suspenser, adequately presented.

w E. J. Howard d Cyril Frankel ph Bob Huke m David Lee

Anne Heywood, Richard Todd, Jack Hedley, Jeremy Brett, Nicole Maurey, Barbara Mullen, Maurice Denham, William Lucas

Very Important Person**
GB 1961 98m bw
Rank / Independent Artists (Julian Wintle, Leslie Parkyn)
US title: A Coming-Out Party

A senior British scientist is caught by the Nazis and has to be rescued.
Very satisfactory British comedy with a few suspense scenes; POW fare with a difference.

w Jack Davies d Ken Annakin ph Ernest Steward m Reg Owen

James Robertson Justice, Stanley Baxter, Leslie Phillips, Eric Sykes, Richard Wattis, Colin Gordon

A Very Special Favor*
US 1965 105m Technicolor
Universal / Lankershim (Robert Arthur)

A Frenchman with a spinster daughter asks an American lawyer to 'initiate' her.
Tasteless, smirking comedy with several funny scenes, glossily photographed in the lap of luxury and interesting in its early use of homosexuality as a comedy subject.

w Nate Monaster, Stanley Shapiro d Michael Gordon ph Leo Tover m Vic Mizzy

Rock Hudson, Charles Boyer, Leslie Caron, Nita Talbot, Dick Shawn, Walter Slezak, Larry Storch

The Very Thought of You
US 1944 99m bw
Warner (Jerry Wald)

Problems of a wartime marriage.
Tepid romantic potboiler.

w Alvah Bessie, Delmer Daves d Delmer Daves ph Bert Glennon m Franz Waxman

Dennis Morgan, Eleanor Parker, Dane Clark, Faye Emerson, Beulah Bondi, Henry Travers, William Prince, Andrea King

Vessel of Wrath***
GB 1938 93m bw
Mayflower (Erich Pommer)
US title: The Beachcomber

In the Dutch East Indies, the missionary's spinster sister falls for a drunken beachcomber.

First-rate character comedy, remade as *The Beachcomber* (qv).

w Bartlett Cormack, B. Van Thal, *story W. Somerset Maugham d* Erich Pommer

Charles Laughton, Elsa Lanchester, Robert Newton, Tyrone Guthrie, Dolly Mollinger, Eliot Makeham

Vice Squad

US 1953 88m bw

UA / Jules Levy, Arthur Gardner

GB title: *The Girl in Room 17*

A police captain tracks down two bank robbers who have killed a cop.

A day in the life of a police captain, quite watchable but scarcely engrossing.

w Lawrence Roman, *novel* Harness Bull by Leslie T. White *d* Arnold Laven *ph* Joseph C. Biroc *m* Herschel Burke Gilbert

Edward G. Robinson, Paulette Goddard, K. T. Stevens, Porter Hall, Adam Williams, Edward Binns, Lee Van Cleef

Vice Versa *

GB 1947 111m bw

Rank / Two Cities (Peter Ustinov, George H. Brown)

A magic stone enables an unhappy Victorian boy to change places with his pompous father. Funny moments can't disguise the fact that this overlong comedy is a bit of a fizzle, its talented creator not being a film-maker. A pity, as British films have so rarely entered the realms of fancy.

w Peter Ustinov, *novel* F. Anstey *d* Peter Ustinov

Roger Livesey, Kay Walsh, Anthony Newley, *James Robertson Justice*, David Hutcheson, Petula Clark, Joan Young

The Vicious Circle *

GB 1957 84m bw

Romulus (Peter Rogers)

An actress is found dead in Dr Latimer's flat and the weapon turns up in the boot of his car . . . Entertaining whodunnit from a TV serial.

w Francis Durbridge, from his serial The Brass Candlestick *d* Gerald Thomas *ph* Otto Heller *m* Stanley Black

John Mills, Derek Farr, Noelle Middleton, Roland Culver, Wilfrid Hyde White, Mervyn Johns, René Ray, Lionel Jeffries, Lisa Daniely

Vicki *

US 1953 85m bw

TCF (Leonard Goldstein)

A girl model is murdered, and her sister proves that her boy friend is innocent, despite the efforts of a brutal detective.

Very competent if uninspired remake of *I Wake Up Screaming* (qv).

w Dwight Taylor *d* Harry Horner *ph* Milton Krasner *m* Leigh Harline

Jeanne Crain, Jean Peters, Richard Boone, Elliott Reid, Casey Adams, Alex D'Arcy, Carl Betz, Aaron Spelling

Victim ***

GB 1962 100m bw

Rank / Allied Film Makers / Parkway (Michael Relph)

A barrister with homosexual inclinations tracks down a blackmailer despite the risk to his own reputation.

A plea for a change in the law is very smartly wrapped up as a murder mystery which allows all aspects to be aired, and the London locations are vivid.

w Janet Green, John McCormick d Basil Dearden ph Otto Heller m Philip Green

Dirk Bogarde, Sylvia Syms, John Barrie, Norman Bird, Peter McEnery, Anthony Nicholls, Dennis Price, *Charles Lloyd Pack*, Derren Nesbitt, John Cairney, Hilton Edwards, Peter Copley, Donald Churchill, Nigel Stock

Victoria the Great ***

GB 1937 112m bw (Technicolor sequence)

British Lion / Imperator / Herbert Wilcox

Episodes in the life of Queen Victoria.

A decent film with all the British virtues, and a milestone in the cinema of its time. Script and performances are excellent; production sometimes falters a little.

w Robert Vansittart, Miles Malleson, plays Victoria Regina by Laurence Housman *d* Herbert Wilcox

Anna Neagle, Anton Walbrook, H. B. Warner, Walter Rilla, Mary Morris, C. V. France, Charles Carson, Felix Aylmer, Derrick de Marney

The Victors *

GB 1963 175m bw Panavision

Columbia / Open Road (Carl Foreman)

World War II adventures of an American infantry platoon.

Patchy compendium with moral too heavily stressed but plenty of impressive scenes and performances along the way. The mixture of realism and irony, though, doesn't really mix.

w Carl Foreman, *novel* The Human Kind by Alexander Baron *d* Carl Foreman *ph* Christopher Challis *m* Sol Kaplan

George Peppard, George Hamilton, Albert Finney, Melina Mercouri, Eli Wallach, Vince Edwards, Rosanna Schiaffino, James Mitchum, *Jeanne Moreau*, Elke Sommer, Senta Berger, Peter Fonda, Michael Callan

   'Doggerel epic.'—*John Coleman*

   'War has revealed Mr Foreman as a pompous bore.'—*John Simon*

   'Having made a point through an image it continually feels the need to state it all over again by way of dialogue.'—*Penelope Houston*

Victory*
US 1940 77m bw
Paramount (Anthony Veiller)

A Dutch East Indies recluse rescues a girl and is menaced by three villains who think he is wealthy.
Curious, ineffective but occasionally compelling attempt to translate the untranslatable to the screen.

w John L. Balderston, *novel* Joseph Conrad *d* John Cromwell *ph* Leo Tover *m* Frederick Hollander

Fredric March, Betty Field, *Cedric Hardwicke*, Sig Rumann, Margaret Wycherly, Jerome Cowan, Fritz Feld, Rafaela Ottiano

   'There is achieved a combination of amateur theatricals and earnest emptiness of motive and motion that will throw a blanket of reminiscent affection around this solemn, unusual and exotic buffoonery.'—*Otis Ferguson*

Victory through Air Power***
US 1943 65m Technicolor
Walt Disney

The history of aviation and the theories of Major Alexander de Seversky.
What was thought by many to be propaganda was in fact a demonstration of Disney's own fascination with the theories of a controversial figure. The cartoon segments are put together with the studio's accustomed brilliance.

w various *d* H. C. Potter (live action), various *m* Edward J. Plumb, Paul J. Smith, Oliver J. Wallace

AAN: Edward J. Plumb, Paul J. Smith, Oliver J. Wallace

The View from Pompey's Head*
US 1955 97m Eastmancolor
  Cinemascope
TCF (Philip Dunne)
GB title: *Secret Interlude*

A New York lawyer returns on a case to the small town of his youth, and falls in love again with his old sweetheart.
Routine Marquand-type novelette, long on atmosphere and short on plot.

wd Philip Dunne, *novel* Hamilton Basso *ph* Joe MacDonald *m* Elmer Bernstein

Richard Egan, Dana Wynter, Cameron Mitchell, *Sidney Blackmer, Marjorie Rambeau*

A View from the Bridge
France 1961 117m bw
Transcontinental (Paul Graetz)
original title: *Vu du Pont*

A longshoreman on the New York waterfront has passionate feelings for his wife's niece, and these erupt when she announces her engagement.
Solemn, self-examining melodrama, poorly adapted from the stage.

w Norman Rosten, *play* Arthur Miller *d* Sidney Lumet *ph* Michel Kelber *m* Maurice Leroux

Raf Vallone, Maureen Stapleton, Carol Lawrence, Jean Sorel, Raymond Pellégrin, Morris Carnovsky, Harvey Lembeck, Vincent Gardenia

† The film was shot in several languages.

Vigil in the Night
US 1940 96m bw
RKO (George Stevens)

Two nurses are attracted to the same doctor; one dies during an epidemic.
Dull, downbeat romantic melodrama with a miscast lead.

w Fred Guiol, P. J. Wolfson, Rowland Leigh, *novel* A. J. Cronin *d* George Stevens *ph* Robert de Grasse *m* Alfred Newman

Carole Lombard, Anne Shirley, Brian Aherne, Julien Mitchell, Robert Coote, Peter Cushing, Ethel Griffies

The Viking Queen
GB 1967 91m Technicolor
Warner / Hammer (John Temple-Smith)

During the first century AD, the queen of the Iceni tries to keep peace with the occupying Romans but has trouble with hot-headed Druids.
Stuff and nonsense from the Dark Ages; light should not have been shed upon it.

w Clarke Reynolds *d* Don Chaffey *ph* Stephen Dade *m* Gary Hughes

Don Murray, Carita, Donald Houston, Andrew Keir, Patrick Troughton, Adrienne Corri, Niall MacGinnis, Wilfrid Lawson, Nicola Pagett

The Vikings***
US 1958   116m   Technirama
UA / KD Productions (Jerry Bresler)

Two Viking half-brothers quarrel over the throne of Northumbria.
Slightly unpleasant and brutal but extremely well-staged and good-looking epic in which you can almost feel the harsh climate. Fine colour, strong performances, natural settings, vivid action, and all production values as they should be.

w Calder Willingham, *novel* The Viking by Edison Marshall *d Richard Fleischer ph Jack Cardiff m Mario Nascimbene credit titles United Productions of America narrator* Orson Welles

Kirk Douglas, Tony Curtis, Ernest Borgnine, Janet Leigh, Frank Thring, James Donald, Maxine Audley, Eileen Way

Villa Rides!
US 1968   125m   Technicolor   Panavision
Paramount (Ted Richmond)

1912 Mexico: an American pilot who has been gun-running for the rebels is pressed into more active service.
Bang-bang actioner which pauses too often for reflection and local colour.

w Robert Towne, Sam Peckinpah *d* Buzz Kulik *ph* Jack Hildyard *m* Maurice Jarre *ad* Ted Howarth

Yul Brynner, Robert Mitchum, Charles Bronson, Grazia Bucetta, Herbert Lom, Alexander Knox, Fernando Rey

Village of Daughters
GB 1961   86m   bw
MGM (George H. Brown)

An unemployed commercial traveller in an Italian village finds himself choosing a bride for a successful emigré.
Voluble, gesticulating minor comedy.

w David Pursall, Jack Seddon *d* George Pollock *ph* Geoffrey Faithfull *m* Ron Goodwin

Eric Sykes, Warren Mitchell, Scilla Gabel, Carol White, Grègoire Aslan, John Le Mesurier

Village of the Damned**
GB 1960   78m   bw
MGM (Ronald Kinnoch)

Children born simultaneously in an English village prove to be super-intelligent and deadly beings from another planet.
Modestly made but absorbing and logical science fiction, cleanly presented.

w Stirling Silliphant, *Wolf Rilla, Geoffrey Barclay, novel* The Midwich Cuckoos by *John Wyndham d Wolf Rilla ph* Geoffrey Faithfull *m* Ron Goodwin

George Sanders, Barbara Shelley, Michael Gwynn, Martin Stephens, Laurence Naismith
† Sequel: *Children of the Damned* (qv).

Villain
GB 1971   98m   Technicolor   Panavision
EMI / Kastner / Ladd / Kanter

The come-uppance of a cowardly, sadistic, homosexual East End gang boss with a mother fixation.
Very unpleasant and unentertaining British low life shocker, plainly inspired by *White Heat*.

w Dick Clement, Ian La Frenais, *novel* The Burden of Proof by James Barlow *d* Michael Tuchner *ph* Christopher Challis *m* Jonathan Hodge

Richard Burton, Ian MacShane, Nigel Davenport, Joss Ackland, Cathleen Nesbitt, Donald Sinden, T. P. McKenna, Fiona Lewis

The Villain Still Pursued Her*
US 1940   66m   bw
(RKO) Harold B. Franklin

An innocent family suffers at the hands of a villainous landlord.
Clumsy burlesque of old time melodrama, interesting that it was done at all and with this cast.

w Elbert Franklin *d* Edward Cline *ph* Lucien Ballard *m* Frank Tours

Buster Keaton, Alan Mowbray, Anita Louise, Hugh Herbert, Joyce Compton, Margaret Hamilton, Billy Gilbert

The Vintage
US 1957   92m   Metrocolor   Cinemascope
MGM (Edwin H. Knopf)

Two fugitives from justice cause trouble when they become grape pickers.
Steamy drama with an unconvincing French setting; a Hollywood aberration.

w Michael Blankfort, *novel* Ursula Keir *d* Jeffrey Hayden *ph* Joseph Ruttenberg *m* David Raksin

Mel Ferrer, John Kerr, Michèle Morgan, Pier Angeli, Theodore Bikel, Leif Erickson

The Violent Enemy
GB 1968   98m   Eastmancolor
Trio / Group W. (Wilfrid Eades)

An IRA explosives expert escapes from a British
jail but quarrels with his leaders.
Dullish political melodrama needlessly rubbing
salt in old wounds.

w Edmund Ward, *novel* A Candle for the Dead
by Hugh Marlowe *d* Don Sharp *ph* Alan
Hume *m* John Scott

Tom Bell, Ed Begley, Susan Hampshire, Noel
Purcell, Michael Standing

The Violent Men*
US 1955   96m   Technicolor
Columbia (Lewis J. Rachmil)
GB title: *Rough Company*

A crippled cattle baron drives small landowners
from his valley, while his wife has an affair with
his younger brother.
So much snarling goes on that this seems like a
gangster film in fancy dress, but it does hold the
attention.

w Harry Kleiner, *novel* Donald Hamilton
d Rudolph Maté *ph* Burnett Guffey, W. Howard
Greene *m* Max Steiner

Edward G. Robinson, Barbara Stanwyck, Glenn
Ford, Brian Keith, Dianne Foster, May Wynn,
Warner Anderson, Basil Ruysdael

The Violent Ones*
US 1967   90m   Eastmancolor
Madison / Harold Goldman

In a small Mexican town, three American hobos
are interrogated after the rape and murder of a
local girl.
Rather well shot murder mystery with emphasis
on character, leading to a desert chase climax.

w Doug Wilson, Charles Davis *d Fernando
Lamas ph Fleet Southcott m* Martin Skiles

Fernando Lamas, Aldo Ray, David Carradine,
Tommy Sands

Violent Playground
GB 1958   108m   bw
Rank (Michael Relph)

A junior liaison officer in the Liverpool slums
falls in love with the sister of a fire-raiser.
'Realistic' melodrama sabotaged by an entirely
schematic and predictable plot; enervatingly dull
until the siege climax.

w James Kennaway *d* Basil Dearden *ph* Reg
Wyer *m* Phillip Green

Stanley Baker, Anne Heywood, David

McCallum, Peter Cushing, John Slater, Clifford
Evans

Violent Saturday*
US 1955   90m   De Luxe   Cinemascope
TCF (Buddy Adler)

Crooks move quietly into a small town with the
intention of robbing the bank.
Interesting little melodrama which the wide
screen robs of its proper tension. Adequate
presentation and performance.

w Sidney Boehm *d* Richard Fleischer
ph Charles G. Clarke *m* Hugo Friedhofer

Richard Egan, Victor Mature, Stephen
McNally, Sylvia Sidney, Virginia Leith, Tommy
Noonan, Lee Marvin, Margaret Hayes, J. Carrol
Naish, Ernest Borgnine

The VIPs**
GB 1963   119m   Metrocolor   Panavision
MGM (Anatole de Grunwald)

Passengers at London Airport are delayed by
fog and spend the night at a hotel.
Multi-story compendium cunningly designed to
exploit the real-life Burton–Taylor romance. In
itself, competent rather than stimulating.

w Terence Rattigan *d* Anthony Asquith
ph Jack Hildyard *m* Miklos Rozsa

Richard Burton, Elizabeth Taylor, Maggie
Smith, Rod Taylor, *Margaret Rutherford*, Louis
Jourdan, Elsa Martinelli, Orson Welles, Linda
Christian, Dennis Price, Richard Wattis, David
Frost, Robert Coote, Joan Benham, Michael
Hordern, Lance Percival, Martin Miller

'If Mr Rattigan's Aunt Edna still goes to the
pictures she should like his latest offering,
especially if she has a good lunch first.'—*Brenda
Davies*

AA: Margaret Rutherford

The Virgin and the Gypsy*
GB 1970   95m   colour
Kenwood / Dimitri de Grunwald (Kenneth
Harper)

A Midlands clergyman's daughter falls in love
with a gypsy fortune teller.
Slow, sensitive, stylish picturization of a
Lawrence novella, with generally good
performances.

w *Alan Plater, story* D. H. Lawrence
d Christopher Miles ph Robert Huke *m* Patrick
Gowers *pd* Terence Knight

Joanna Shimkus, Franco Nero, Honor
Blackman, Michael Burns, Maurice Denham,
Fay Compton, Kay Walsh, Norman Bird

Virgin Island
GB 1958   94m   Eastmancolor
British Lion / Countryman (Leon Clore,
   Graham Tharp)

A young couple set up house on a tiny Caribbean
island.
Pleasant comedy slowed down by lack of plot
and too much conversation.

w Philip Rush, Pat Jackson, *book* Our Virgin
Island by Robb White d Pat Jackson
ph Freddie Francis m Clifton Parker

Virginia Maskell, John Cassavetes, Sidney
Poitier, Isabel Dean, Colin Gordon

The Virgin Queen*
US 1955   92m   De Luxe   Cinemascope
TCF (Charles Brackett)

The relationship of Queen Elizabeth I and Sir
Walter Raleigh.
Unhistorical charade, quite pleasantly made and
worth noting for its star performance.

w Harry Brown, Mindret Lord d Henry Koster
ph Charles G. Clarke m Franz Waxman

Bette Davis, Richard Todd, Joan Collins,
Herbert Marshall, Jay Robinson, Dan
O'Herlihy, Robert Douglas,
Romney Brent

The Virgin Soldiers**
GB 1969   96m   Technicolor
Columbia / Carl Foreman (Leslie Gilliat, Ned
   Sherrin)

Serio-comic adventures of recruits in the British
army in 1960 Singapore.
Autobiographical fragments, mostly from below
the belt, sharply observed and often very funny.

w *John Hopkins, novel Leslie Thomas d John
Dexter ph Ken Higgins m* Peter Greenwell

Hywel Bennett, Nigel Patrick, *Lynn Redgrave*,
Nigel Davenport, *Rachel Kempson*, Michael
Gwynn, Tsai Chin

'A kind of monstrous mating of *Private's
Progress* and *The Family Way*, with bits of *The
Long and the Short and the Tall* thrown in for
good measure.'—*David Pirie*
† Sequel 1977: *Stand Up Virgin Soldiers*.

The Virgin Spring*
Sweden 1959   87m   bw
Svensk Filmindustri (Allan Ekelund)
original title: *Jungfrakällan*

When her murderers are killed, a spring bubbles
up from the spot where a young maiden met her
death.
Stark and rather lovely filming of a medieval

legend, with heavy symbolism and a strong
pictorial sense.

w Ulla Isaakson d Ingmar Bergman ph Sven
Nykvist m Erik Nordgren

Max Von Sydow, Brigitta Valberg, Gunnel
Lindblom, Brigitta Pettersson

Virginia City*
US 1940   121m   bw
Warner (Robert Fellows)

A dance hall girl is really a southern spy helping
a rebel colonel to steal a gold shipment from her
Yankee boy friend.
Lumpy western in Warner's best budget but
worst manner: the stars look unhappy and the
plot progresses in fits and starts.

w Robert Buckner d Michael Curtiz ph Sol
Polito m Max Steiner

Errol Flynn, Randolph Scott, Miriam Hopkins,
Humphrey Bogart, Frank McHugh, Alan Hale,
Guinn Williams, John Litel, Moroni Olsen,
Russell Hicks, Douglass Dumbrille

The Virginian*
US 1929   95m   bw
Paramount

A stalwart ranch foreman has to see his best
friend hanged for rustling, and defeats the local
bad man.
Standard western with famous clichés, e.g.
'Smile when you say that . . .'

w Edward E. Paramore Jnr, Howard
Estabrook, *novel* Owen Wister d Victor
Fleming ph J. Roy Hunt

Gary Cooper, Walter Huston, Richard Arlen,
Mary Brian, Chester Conklin, Eugene Pallette

The Virginian
US 1946   90m   Technicolor
Paramount

Forgettable remake of the above.

d Stuart Gilmore

Joel McCrea, Brian Donlevy, Sonny Tufts,
Barbara Britton, William Frawley, Henry
O'Neill, Fay Bainter

Viridiana**
Spain / Mexico 1961   91m   bw
Uninci / Films 59 / Gustavo Alatriste (Munoz
   Suay)

A novice about to take her vows is corrupted by
her wicked uncle and installs a load of beggars in
his house.
Often hilarious surrealist melodrama packed

with shades of meaning, most of them
sacrilegious. A fascinating film to watch.

w Luis Bunuel, Julio Alajandro *d Luis Bunuel*
ph Josè F. Agayo

Silvia Pinal, Francisco Rabal, Fernando Rey
  'One of the cinema's few major philosophical
works.'—*Robert Vas*

The Virtuous Bigamist see Four Steps in
the Clouds

The Virtuous Sin
US 1930   81m   bw
Paramount

A girl tries to help her student husband when war
takes him away from bacteriology.
Stilted romantic drama.

w Martin Brown, Louise Long, *novel* Lajos
Zilahy *d* George Cukor, Louis Gasnier
ph David Abel

Walter Huston, Kay Francis, Kenneth
MacKenna, Paul Cavanagh

The Visit
US 1964   100m   bw   Cinemascope
TCF / Deutschefox / Cinecittà / Dear Film /
    Films du Siècle / PECF (Julien Derode,
    Anthony Quinn)

A millionairess offers a fortune to her home
town, providing someone will kill her ex-lover.
A realistic production ill befits an essentially
theatrical play, and all the effort goes for nothing.

w Ben Barzman, *play* Friedrich Durrenmatt
d Bernhard Wicki *ph* Armando Nannuzzi
m Hans-Martin Majewski

Ingrid Bergman, Anthony Quinn, Paolo Stoppa,
Hans- Christian Vlech, Valentina Cortesa, Irina
Demick, Claude Dauphin, Eduardo Ciannelli

Visit to a Chief's Son
US 1974   92m   De Luxe   Panavision
UA / Robert Halmi

An American anthropologist and his son hope to
film the rituals of an African tribe.
Minor adventure film with a happy resolution,
based on a photomontage by the producer, a
Life photographer.

w Albert Ruben *d Lamont Johnson ph* Ernest
Day *m* Francis Lai

Robert Mulligan, Johnny Sekka, John Philip
Hodgdon

Visit to a Small Planet
US 1959   101m   bw
Paramount / Wallis–Hazen

A young man from outer space takes a look at
Earth and falls in love.
A satirical play disastrously adapted for the
moronic comedy of an unsuitable star.

w Edmund Beloin, Henry Garson, *play* Gore
Vidal *d* Norman Taurog *ph* Loyal Griggs
m Leigh Harline

Jerry Lewis, Joan Blackman, Earl Holliman,
Fred Clark, John Williams, Jerome Cowan,
Gavin Gordon, Lee Patrick

Les Visiteurs du Soir *
France 1942   110m   bw
André Paulvé
aka: *The Devil's Envoys*

The devil sends messengers to earth to corrupt
two lovers, but he fails: even though he turns
them to stone, their hearts still beat.
Made during the Occupation, this stately
medieval fable was intended to be significant: the
devil was Hitler, and the heartbeat that of
France. Perhaps because it is so conscious of
hidden meanings, it moves rather stiffly but is
often beautiful to behold.

w Jacques Prévert, Pierre Laroche *d Marcel
Carné ph* Roger Hubert *m* Joseph Kosma,
Maurice Thiriet *ad* Alexandre Trauner,
Georges Wakhevitch

Arletty, *Jules Berry*, Marie Déa, Alain Cuny,
Fernand Ledoux, Marcel Herrand

I Vitelloni
Italy / France 1953   109m   bw
Peg / Cité (Lorenzo Pegoraro)
aka: *Spivs*

In a small Italian resort, aimless young people
get into various kinds of trouble.
Interesting in its realistic detail, this sharply
observed slice of life is long enough for its basic
purposelessness to become apparent.

w Federico Fellini, Ennio Flaiano, Tullio Pinelli
d Federico Fellini *ph* Otello Martelli, Tasatti,
Carlini *m* Nino Rota

Franco Fabrizi, Franco Interlenghi, Eleonora
Ruffo, Alberto Sordi

AAN: script

Viva Las Vegas
US 1964   85m   Metrocolor
MGM (Jack Cummins, George Sidney)
GB title: *Love in Las Vegas*

A sports car racer has fun in the gambling city.
Tolerable star musical.

w Sally Benson *d* George Sidney *ph* Joseph
Biroc *md* George Stoll

Elvis Presley, Ann-Margret, Cesare Danova,
William Demarest, Nicky Blair, Jack Carter

Viva Maria!
France / Italy 1965   120m   Eastmancolor
  Panavision
Novelles Éditions / Artistes Associés / Vides
  (Oscar Dancigers, Louis Malle)

An Irish anarchist girl arrives in Central
America and joins a group of strolling players.
All show and no substance, this is a colour
supplement of a film, neither fish, flesh nor good
red herring.

w Louis Malle, Jean-Claude Carrière d Louis
Malle ph Henri Decaë m Georges Delerue
ad Bernard Evein

Jeanne Moreau, Brigitte Bardot, George
Hamilton, Paulette Dubost, Claudio Brook

Viva Max
US 1969   93m   Eastmancolor
Commonwealth United / Mark Carliner

A Mexican general marches his troops into
Texas and seizes the Alamo.
Flat comedy with mildly amusing passages but
too much noise, bluster and sentiment.

w Elliott Baker, novel James Lehrer d Jerry
Paris ph Jack Richards m Hugo Montenegro

Peter Ustinov, John Astin, Pamela Tiffin,
Jonathan Winters, Keenan Wynn, Henry
Morgan, Alice Ghostley

Viva Villa**
US 1934   110m   bw
MGM (David O. Selznick)

The career of a Mexican rebel.
Gutsy action drama with some smoothing over
of fact in the name of entertainment. A big,
highly competent production of its year.

w Ben Hecht d Jack Conway ph James Wong
Howe, Charles G. Clarke m Herbert Stothart

Wallace Beery, Fay Wray, Leo Carrillo, Donald
Cook, Stuart Erwin, George E. Stone, Joseph
Schildkraut, Henry B. Walthall, Katherine de
Mille

  'A strange poem of violence.'—John Baxter,
1968

  'A glorified horse opera . . . the spectator's
excitement is incited by the purely physical
impact of the furious riding and war sequences,
by the frequent sadism, and by the lively musical
score.'—Irving Lerner

AAN: best picture; script

Viva Zapata**
US 1952   113m   bw
TCF (Darryl F. Zanuck)

A Mexican revolutionary is finally betrayed by a
friend.
Moody, good-looking star vehicle taking a
romanticized but glum view of history.

w John Steinbeck d Elia Kazan ph Joe
MacDonald m Alex North md Alfred Newman

Marlon Brando, Jean Peters, Joseph Wiseman,
Anthony Quinn, Arnold Moss, Margo, Frank
Silvera

AAN: John Steinbeck; Alex North; Marlon
Brando

Vivacious Lady*
US 1938   90m   bw
RKO (George Stevens)

A nightclub singer marries a botany professor
and has trouble with his parents.
Pleasant romantic comedy for two popular stars.

w P. J. Wolfson, Ernest Pagano d George
Stevens ph Robert de Grasse m Roy Webb

Ginger Rogers, James Stewart, Charles Coburn,
Beulah Bondi, James Ellison, Frances Mercer,
Franklin Pangborn, Grady Sutton, Jack Carson

AAN: Robert de Grasse

Vogues of 1938*
US 1937   108m   Technicolor
Walter Wanger

Rival fashion houses compete at the Seven Arts
Ball.
A fashion show with threads of plot, interesting
for clothes and cast, all working hard.

w Bella and Samuel Spewack d Irving
Cummings ph Ray Rennahan md Boris
Morros ch Seymour Felix

Joan Bennett, Walter Baxter, Helen Vinson,
Mischa Auer, Alan Mowbray, Jerome Cowan,
Alma Kruger, Marjorie Gateson, Penny
Singleton, Hedda Hopper

AAN: song 'That Old Feeling' (m Sammy Fain,
ly Lew Brown)

The Voice of Bugle Ann*
US 1936   70m   bw
MGM (John Considine Jnr)

When a dog is killed its embittered owner seeks
revenge.
Old-fashioned country tale, rather heavy-going
but emotionally strong.

w Harvey Gates, Samuel Hoffenstein,
novel Mackinlay Kantor d Richard Thorpe

Lionel Barrymore, Maureen O'Sullivan, Eric

Linden, Dudley Digges, Spring Byington, Charley Grapewin

'A very fine movie indeed.'—*Pare Lorentz*

The Voice of Merrill
GB 1952 84m bw
Tempean (Robert Baker, Monty Berman)
US title: *Murder Will Out*

Three men are suspected of murder but one becomes a potential victim.
Complicated murder thriller which intrigues but hardly satisfies.

wd John Gilling *ph* Monty Berman *m* Frank Cordell

Valerie Hobson, James Robertson Justice, Edward Underdown, Henry Kendall, Garry Marsh, Sam Kydd

The Voice of the Turtle **
US 1948 103m bw
Warner (Charles Hoffman)
aka: *One for the Book*

A girl shares her apartment with a soldier on leave.
A three-character play is smoothly filmed, slightly broadened, and burnished till its pale wit glows nicely.

w John Van Druten, from his play *d Irving Rapper ph* Sol Polito *m* Max Steiner

Eleanor Parker, Ronald Reagan, *Eve Arden*, Wayne Morris, Kent Smith

Voices
GB 1973 91m Technicolor
(Hemdale) Warden (Robert Enders)

A young couple in an old country house are haunted by the voice of their dead son.
Twisty little ghost story which would have been more effective at one third of its length.

w George Kirgo, Robert Enders, *play* Richard Lortz *d* Kevin Billington *ph* Geoffrey Unsworth *m* Richard Rodney Bennett

Gayle Hunnicutt, David Hemmings

Voltaire *
US 1933 72m bw
Warner (Ray Griffith)

The life and times of the 18th-century French wit.
One of the better Arliss charades, because the film is as stagey as his performance.

w Paul Green, Maude T. Howell, *novel* George Gibbs. E. Laurence Dudley *d* John Adolfi *ph* Tony Gaudio

Georges Arliss, Doris Kenyon, Margaret

Lindsay, Reginald Owen, Alan Mowbray, David Torrence, Douglass Dumbrille, Theodore Newton

Von Richthofen and Brown
US 1971 97m De Luxe
UA / Roger Corman (Gene Corman)
GB title: *The Red Baron*

During World War I, a Canadian pilot takes on Germany's air ace.
The airplanes are nice, but the film is grounded by plot and dialogue.

w John and Joyce Corrington *d* Roger Corman *ph* Michael Reed *m* Hugo Friedhofer

John Phillip Law, Don Stroud, Barry Primus, Karen Huston, Corin Redgrave, Hurd Hatfield

Von Ryan's Express **
US 1965 117m De Luxe Cinemascope
TCF (Saul David)

In an Italian POW camp during World War II, an unpopular American captain leads English prisoners in a train escape.
Exhilarating action thriller with slow spots atoned for by nail-biting finale, though the downbeat curtain mars the general effect.

w Wendell Mayes, Joseph Landon, *novel* Davis Westheimer *d* Mark Robson *ph* William H. Daniels, Harold Lipstein *m* Jerry Goldsmith

Frank Sinatra, Trevor Howard, Sergio Fantoni, Edward Mulhare, Brad Dexter, John Leyton, Wolfgang Preiss, James Brolin, Adolfo Celi

Voyage of the Damned *
GB 1976 155m Eastmancolor
ITC / Associated General (Robert Fryer)

In 1939, a ship leaves Hamburg for Cuba with Jewish refugees; but Cuba won't take them.
High-minded, expensive, but poorly devised rehash of *Ship of Fools*, with too many stars in cameos and not enough central plot.

w Steve Shagan, David Butler, *book* Gordon Thomas, Max Morgan-Witts *d* Stuart Rosenberg *ph* Billy Williams *m* Lalo Schifrin

Faye Dunaway, Max Von Sydow, Oskar Werner, Malcolm McDowell, James Mason, Orson Welles, Katharine Ross, Ben Gazzara, Lee Grant, Sam Wanamaker, Julie Harris, Helmut Griem, Luther Adler, Wendy Hiller, Nehemiah Persoff, Maria Schell, Fernando Rey, Donald Houston, Jose Ferrer, Denholm Elliott, Janet Suzman

'Not a single moment carries any conviction.'—*New Yorker*

AAN: script; Lalo Schifrin; Lee Grant

Voyage to the Bottom of the Sea*
US 1961   105m   De Luxe   Cinemascope
TCF / Windsor (Irwin Allen)

USN Admiral Nelson takes scientists in his futuristic atomic submarine to explode a belt of radiation.

Childish but sometimes entertaining science fiction which spawned a long-running TV series.

w Irwin Allen, Charles Bennett *d* Irwin Allen
ph Winton Hoch, John Lamb *m* Paul Sawtell, Bert Shefter
ad J. M. Smith, Herman A. Blumenthal

Walter Pidgeon, Robert Sterling, Joan Fontaine, Peter Lorre, Barbara Eden, Michael Ansara, Henry Daniell, Regis Toomey, Frankie Avalon

W

W
US 1973 95m De Luxe
Bing Crosby Productions (Mel Ferrer)

A young wife is threatened by her psychotic first
husband.

Tedious rehash of several frightened lady
themes, all rather sick.

w Gerald di Pego, James Kelly d Richard
Quine ph Gerry Hirschfeld m Johnny Mandell

Twiggy, Michael Witney, Eugene Roche, Dirk
Benedict, John Vernon

The W Plan*
GB 1930 105m bw
BIP / Wardour (Victor Saville)

A British spy helps destroy Germany's secret
tunnels.

Slightly fantasticated spy/war action which was
a big popular success at the time.

w Victor Saville, Miles Malleson, Frank
Launder, novel Graham Seton d Victor Saville

Brian Aherne, Madeleine Carroll, Gordon
Harker, Gibb McLaughlin, George Merritt,
Mary Jerrold

'Fast, spectacular action, fine acting and
notably realistic war scenes.'—NFT, 1971

W. C. Fields and Me
US 1976 112m Technicolor
Universal (Jay Weston)

The rise to Hollywood fame of alcoholic
comedian W. C. Fields.

Untruthful and rather boring biopic, with minor
compensations.

w Bob Merrill, book Carlotta Monti d Arthur
Hiller ph David M. Walsh m Henry Mancini
pd Robert Boyle

Rod Steiger, Valerie Perrine, John Marley, Jack
Cassidy (as John Barrymore), Paul Stewart (as
Ziegfeld), Billy Barty, Bernadette Peters

'Steiger's impersonation largely keeps pace
with the overriding vulgarity of the enterprise.'—
Sight and Sound

'A stupid and pointless slander.'—Judith
Crist

WW and the Dixie Dancekings
US 1975 94m TVC
TCF (Stanley S. Canter)

In a southern state in the 1950s, a crook uses a
travelling band as an alibi and stays to promote
them.

Combination of American Graffiti and Easy
Rider, either tiresome or tolerable according to
one's mood. Very flashy, anyway.

w Thomas Rickman d John G. Avildsen ph Jim
Crabe m Dave Grusin

Burt Reynolds, Art Carney, Conny Van Dyke,
Jerry Reed, Ned Beatty

Wabash Avenue*
US 1950 92m Technicolor
TCF (William Perlberg)

During the Chicago World's Fair of 1892, a
shimmy dancer is pursued by two men.

Bright rehash of Coney Island (qv), with solid
tunes and performances.

w Harry Tugend, Charles Lederer d Henry
Koster ph Arthur E. Arling md Lionel
Newman

Betty Grable, Victor Mature, Phil Harris,
Reginald Gardiner, Margaret Hamilton, James
Barton, Barry Kelley

AAN: song 'Wilhelmina' (m Josef Myrow,
ly Mack Gordon)

The Wackiest Ship in the Army
US 1960 99m Technicolor
Cinemascope
Columbia / Fred Kohlmar

In the South Pacific during World War II a
decrepit sailing ship with an inexperienced crew
manages to confuse Japanese patrols and land a
scout behind enemy lines.

Slapstick war comedy with fragments of action;
effect rather muddled.

wd Ralph Murphy, story Herbert Carlson
ph Charles Lawton m George Duning

Jack Lemmon, Ricky Nelson, John Lund, Chips
Rafferty, Tom Tully, Joby Baker, Warren
Berlinger, Richard Anderson

The Wages of Fear ***
France / Italy 1953   140m   bw
Filmsonor / CICC / Vera
original title: *Le Salaire de la Peur*

The manager of a Central American oilfield
offers big money to drivers who will take nitro-
glycerine into the jungle to put out an oil well fire.
After too extended an introduction to the less
than admirable characters, this fascinating film
resolves itself into a suspense shocker with one
craftily managed bad moment after another.

wd Henri-Georges Clouzot, novel Georges
Arnaud *ph Armand Thirard m* Georges Auric

*Yves Montand, Folco Lulli, Peter Van Eyck,
Charles Vanel*, Vera Clouzot, William Tubbs

'As skilful as, in its preoccupation with
violence and its unrelieved pessimism, it is
unlikeable.'—*Penelope Houston, Sight and
Sound*

† See *Sorcerer*, a lamentable remake.

Wagonmaster **
US 1950   86m   bw
RKO / Argosy (John Ford, Merian C. Cooper)

Adventures of a Mormon wagon train
journeying towards Utah in 1879.
Low-key western, essentially a collection of
incidents, fondly and enjoyably presented.

w Frank Nugent, Patrick Ford   *d John Ford*
ph Bert Glennon   *m* Richard Hageman

Ben Johnson, Joanne Dru, Harry Carey Jnr,
Ward Bond, Charles Kemper, Alan Mowbray,
Jane Darwell, Russell Simpson

'The feel of the period, the poetry of space and
of endeavour, is splendidly communicated.'—
Lindsay Anderson

The Wagons Roll at Night
US 1941   83m   bw
Warner (Harlan Thompson)

The sweetheart of a circus owner makes a pass at
the new young lion-tamer.
Dull remake of *Kid Galahad* (qv), whose plot
was borrowed from *Tiger Shark* (qv). Warners
were good at this kind of retreading, but
gradually poor quality began to show.

w Fred Niblo Jnr, Barry Trivers   *d* Ray Enright
ph Sid Hickox   *m* Heinz Roemheld

Humphrey Bogart, Sylvia Sidney, Eddie Albert,
Joan Leslie, Sig Rumann, Cliff Clark, Frank
Wilcox

Waikiki Wedding *
US 1937   89m   bw
Paramount (Arthur Hornblow Jnr)

A press agent in Hawaii promotes a Pineapple
Queen contest.
Light-hearted, empty-headed musical very
typical of this studio . . . except that this one is
quite good.

w Frank Butler, Walter de Leon, Don Hartman,
Francis Martin   *d* Frank Tuttle   *ph* Karl Struss
m Leo Shukin   *md* Boris Morros

Bing Crosby, Shirley Ross, Bob Burns, Martha
Raye, George Barbier, Leif Erickson, Grady
Sutton, Granville Bates, Anthony Quinn

AA: song 'Sweet Leilani' (*m/ly* Harry Owens)

Wait til the Sun Shines, Nellie *
US 1952   108m   Technicolor
TCF (George Jessel)

The life of a small-town barber, from marriage
through tragedy to retirement.
Amiable, leisurely family drama with pleasant
settings; small beer, but oddly compulsive.

w Allan Scott, *novel* Ferdinand Reyher
d Henry King   *ph* Leon Shamroy   *m* Alfred
Newman

David Wayne, Jean Peters, Hugh Marlowe,
Albert Dekker, Alan Hale Jnr, Helene Stanley

Wait until Dark **
US 1967   108m   Technicolor
Warner Seven Arts (Mel Ferrer)

A photographer unwittingly smuggles a drug-
filled doll into New York, and his blind wife,
alone in their flat, is terrorized by murderous
crooks in search of it.
Sharp suspenser with shock moments, from a
successful play; in this case the claustrophobic
atmosphere helps, though a lack of light relief
makes itself felt.

w Robert and Jane Howard-Carrington,
play Frederick Knott   *d* Terence Young
ph Charles Lang   *m* Henry Mancini   *ad* George
Jenkins

Audrey Hepburn, Alan Arkin, Richard Crenna,
Efrem Zimbalist Jnr, Jack Weston

AAN: Audrey Hepburn

Wake Island *
US 1942   78m   bw
Paramount (Joseph Sistrom)

During World War II, marines fight to hold an
American base on a small Pacific island.
Terse, violent flagwaver, well done within its
limits.

w W. R. Burnett, Frank Butler   *d* John Farrow
ph Theodor Sparkuhl, William C. Mellor
m David Buttolph

Brian Donlevy, Macdonald Carey, Robert
Preston, William Bendix, Albert Dekker, Walter
Abel, Mikhail Rasumny, Rod Cameron,
Barbara Britton

AAN: best picture; script; John Farrow;
William Bendix

Wake Me When It's Over

US 1960   126m   De Luxe   Cinemascope
TCF / Mervyn Le Roy

Soldiers holding a Pacific island build a de luxe
hotel from surplus war material.
Aptly-titled army farce on the lines of *The
Teahouse of the August Moon* but constructed
from inferior material. Yawningly tedious.

w Richard Breen, *novel* Howard Singer
d Mervyn Le Roy ph Leon Shamroy m Cyril
Mockridge

Ernie Kovacs, Dick Shawn, Jack Warden,
Margo Moore, Nobu McCarthy, Don Knotts,
Robert Emhardt

Wake of the Red Witch**

US 1948   106m   bw
Republic (Edmund Grainger)

The owner and captain of a ship settle their
differences to seek treasure on an East Indian
island.
Rattling good action yarn told in flashback, with
adequate production and performances.

w *Harry Brown, Kenneth Gamet, novel* Garland
Roark d Edward Ludwig ph Reggie Lanning
m Nathan Scott

John Wayne, *Luther Adler*, Gail Russell, Gig
Young, Adele Mara, Eduard Franz, Grant
Withers, Henry Daniell, Paul Fix, Dennis Hoey

Wake Up and Dream

US 1946   92m   Technicolor
TCF (Walter Morosco)

A little girl is determined to find her brother who
is missing in action in World War II.
Ambitious but unappealing whimsy which
descends into sentimentality; either way it
bewildered audiences and critics.

w Elick Moll, *novel* The Enchanted Voyage by
Robert Nathan d Lloyd Bacon ph Harry
Jackson m Cyril Mockridge md Emil Newman

June Haver, John Payne, Connie Marshall,
Charlotte Greenwood, John Ireland, Clem
Bevans, Lee Patrick

Wake Up and Live*

US 1937   91m   bw
TCF (Kenneth MacGowan)

Success and failure in the radio world as a
commentator and a bandleader fight a verbal
duel in public.
Fast-moving spoof in which something is always
happening, and usually something funny.

w Harry Tugend, Jack Yellen, *book* Dorothea
Brande d Sidney Lanfield ph Edward
Cronjager m Louis Silvers

Walter Winchell, Ben Bernie and his band, Alice
Faye, Jack Haley, Patsy Kelly, Ned Sparks,
Grace Bradley, Walter Catlett, Joan Davis,
Douglas Fowley, Miles Mander, Etienne
Girardot

Walk a Crooked Mile

US 1948   91m   bw
Columbia (Edward Small)

British and American agents investigate the
leakage of atomic secrets.
Moderate semi-documentary spy thriller.

w George Bruce d Gordon Douglas ph George
Robinson m Paul Sawtell

Louis Hayward, Dennis O'Keefe, Louise
Allbritton, Carl Esmond, Raymond Burr,
Onslow Stevens

Walk a Crooked Path

GB 1969   88m   Eastmancolor
Hanover (John Brason)

A housemaster at a boys' school is accused of
homosexuality.
Po-faced melodrama in a minor key; reasonably
effective but not exciting.

w Barry Perowne d John Brason ph John
Taylor m Leslie Bridgewater

Tenniel Evans, Faith Brook, Christopher Coll,
Patricia Haines, Pat Endersby, Margery Mason,
Peter Copley

Walk, Don't Run*

US 1966   114m   Technicolor   Panavision
Columbia (Sol C. Siegel)

In Tokyo during the Olympics accommodation
is hard to find, and two men move in with a girl.
Witless reprise of *The More the Merrier*, notable
only for the Tokyo backgrounds and for Cary
Grant's farewell appearance.

w Sol Saks d Charles Walters ph Harry
Stradling m Quincy Jones

Cary Grant, Samantha Eggar, Jim Hutton, *John
Standing*, Miiko Taka

Walk East on Beacon*

US 1952   98m   bw
Columbia (Louis de Rochemont)
GB title: *The Crime of the Century*

The FBI exposes communist spies in the US.
Fast-moving semi-documentary spy thriller
modelled on the same producer's *The House on
92nd Street.*

w Leo Rosten *d* Alfred Werker *ph* Joseph Brun
m Louis Applebaum

George Murphy, Finlay Currie, Virginia
Gilmore, Karel Stepanek, Louisa Horton

A Walk in the Spring Rain
US 1969 98m Technicolor Panavision
Columbia / Pingee (Stirling Silliphant)

A college lecturer's wife, on holiday in the
mountains, falls in love with a local man.
Romance for the middle-aged, nicely done if
lacking in surprise.

w Stirling Silliphant, *novel* Rachel Maddox
d Guy Green *ph* Charles B. Lang *m* Elmer
Bernstein

Ingrid Bergman, Anthony Quinn, Fritz Weaver,
Katherine Crawford

'Not one line or scene is believably written or
acted and the direction is so lazy it appears to
have been mailed in during the postal strike.'—
Richard Roud

A Walk in the Sun***
US 1946 117m bw
Lewis Milestone Productions

The exploits of a single army patrol during the
Salerno landings of 1943, on one vital morning.
Vivid war film in a minor key, superbly
disciplined and keenly acted.

w Robert Rossen, *novel* Harry Brown *d* Lewis
Milestone *ph* Russell Harlan *m* Fredric Efrem
Rich

Dana Andrews, Richard Conte, Sterling
Holloway, John Ireland, George Tyne, Herbert
Rudley, Richard Benedict, Norman Lloyd,
Lloyd Bridges, Huntz Hall

'Concerned with the individual rather than the
battlefield, the film is finely perceptive, exciting,
and very moving.'—*Penelope Houston*

'A swiftly overpowering piece of work.'—
Bosley Crowther

'A notable war film, if not the most notable
war film to come from America.'—*Richard
Winnington*

'After nearly two hours one is sorry when it
ends.'—*Richard Mallett, Punch*

Walk like a Dragon
US 1960 95m bw
Paramount / James Clavell

In 1870 San Francisco, a cowboy sets free a

Chinese slave girl but incurs racial intolerance
when he takes her home.
Curious 'liberated' western which gets itself in a
muddle and doesn't come off at all.

w James Clavell, Dan Mainwaring *d* James
Clavell *ph* Loyal Griggs *m* Paul Dunlap

Jack Lord, James Shigeta, Nobu McCarthy, Mel
Tormé, Josephine Hutchinson, Rodolfo Acosta

Walk on the Wild Side
US 1962 114m bw
Columbia / Famous Artists (Charles K.
 Feldman)

In the thirties, a penniless farmer finds the girl he
once loved working in a New Orleans brothel.
A brilliant title sequence heralds the dreariest
and most verbose of self-conscious melodramas,
quite missing the sensational effect promised by
the advertising.

w John Fante, Edmund Morris, *novel* Nelson
Algren *d* Edward Dmytryk *ph* Joe
MacDonald *m* Elmer Bernstein *credits Saul
Bass*

Jane Fonda, Capucine, Barbara Stanwyck,
Laurence Harvey, Anne Baxter, Richard Rust

'Since the film prides itself in calling a spade a
spade, it is surprising to find all concerned
reacting to their material as though they were up
to their waists in a quagmire.'—*MFB*

AAN: title song (*m* Elmer Bernstein, *ly* Mack
David)

Walk Softly Stranger
US 1950 81m bw
RKO (Robert Sparks)

A crook on the run falls for a crippled girl, who
promises to wait for him.
Dismal love-conquers-all melodrama.

w Frank Genton *d* Robert Stevenson *ph* Harry
J. Wild *m* Frederick Hollander

Alida Valli, Joseph Cotten, Spring Byington,
Paul Stewart, Jack Paar, Jeff Donnell, John
McIntire

Walk the Proud Land
US 1956 88m Technicolor
 Cinemascope
U-I (Aaron Rosenberg)

An Indian agent persuades the army to use less
violent methods.
Fair standard western with a thoughtful and
sympathetic attitude.

w Gil Doud, Jack Sher *d* Jesse Hibbs *ph* Harold
Lipstein *m* Joseph Gershenson

Audie Murphy, Anne Bancroft, Pat Crowley,

Robert Warwick, Charles Drake, Tommy Rall, Jay Silverheels

Walkabout*
Australia 1970 100m Eastmancolor
Max L. Raab / Si Litvinoff

A man kills himself in the desert and his small children trek among the aborigines to safety.
Eerily effective contrast of city with native life, a director's and photographer's experimental success.

w Edward Bond, *novel* James Vance Marshall d/ph Nicolas Roeg m John Barry

Jenny Agutter, Lucien John, David Gimpell

The Walking Dead*
US 1936 66m bw
Warner

A man is revived after electrocution and takes revenge on his enemies.
Dour but well mounted horror thriller in a shadowy style very typical of its director.

w Ewart Adamson, Peter Milne, Robert Adams, Lillie Hayward d Michael Curtiz ph Hal Mohr

Boris Karloff, Edmund Gwenn, Marguerite Churchill, Ricardo Cortez, Barton MacLane, Warren Hull, Henry O'Neill

Walking My Baby Back Home*
US 1953 95m Technicolor
U-I (Ted Richmond)

Ex-army musicians hit on a combination of symphonic and dixieland jazz.
The lightest of light musicals, this highly polished offering remains mildly pleasing though thinly written throughout.

w Don McGuire, Oscar Brodney d Lloyd Bacon ph Irving Glassberg md Joseph Gershenson

Donald O'Connor, Janet Leigh, Buddy Hackett, Lori Nelson, Scat Man Crothers, Kathleen Lockhart, George Cleveland, John Hubbard

The Walking Stick*
GB 1970 101m Metrocolor Panavision
MGM / Winkast (Alan Ladd Jnr)

A repressed girl polio victim falls reluctantly in love with a painter who involves her in his criminal schemes.
Slow moving character romance which has its heart in the right place but too often promises suspense which never comes, and is made in a chintzy cigarette commercial style.

w George Bluestone, *novel* Winston Graham

d Eric Till ph Arthur Ibbetson m Stanley Myers

David Hemmings, Samantha Eggar, Phyllis Calvert, Ferdy Mayne, Emlyn Williams, Francesca Annis, Dudley Sutton

Walking Tall*
US 1973 125m De Luxe
Bing Crosby Productions (Mort Briskin)

A Tennessee farmer-sheriff meets violence with violence and becomes a local hero.
True story of an American vigilante, made with modest competence; its great commercial success may have been due to the support of the righteous, or of those who revel in violence.

w Mort Briskin d Phil Karlson ph Jack Marta m Walter Scharf

Joe Don Baker, Elizabeth Hartman, Gene Evans, Noah Beery Jnr

'A terrifying image of Nixon's silent majority at work.'—*Gareth Jones*
'It generates a primitive, atavistic sort of power: it awakens more apprehension and dredges up more complicated and contradictory emotions than one anticipates.'—*Gary Arnold*
† Sequel 1976: *Part Two Walking Tall*. (GB title: *Legend of the Lawman*.) 1977: *Walking Tall: Final Chapter*

Wall of Noise
US 1963 112m bw
Warner (Joseph Landon)

A racehorse trainer falls for the boss's wife.
Complex but predictable melodrama of the old school, adequately presented and performed.

w Joseph Landon, *novel* Daniel Michael Stein d Richard Wilson ph Lucien Ballard m William Lava

Suzanne Pleshette, Ty Hardin, Dorothy Provine, Ralph Meeker, Simon Oakland, Murray Matheson, Robert F. Simon

The Walls of Jericho
US 1948 106m bw
TCF (Lamar Trotti)

An influential small-town newspaperman is undermined by his vindictive wife.
Filmed novel of standard competence but minimum interest, ending in a courtroom scene.

w Lamar Trotti, *novel* Paul Wellman d John M. Stahl ph Arthur Miller m Cyril Mockridge

Cornel Wilde, Linda Darnell, Anne Baxter, Kirk Douglas, Ann Dvorak, Marjorie Rambeau, Henry Hull, Colleen Townsend

The Waltz King
US 1963   95m   Technicolor
Walt Disney (Peter V. Herald)

The life of young Johann Strauss in 1850s
Vienna.
Medium-budget international family musical,
tolerably well done.

w Maurice Tombragel d Steve Previn
ph Gunther Anders md Helmuth Froschauer

Kerwin Mathews, Brian Aherne, Senta Berger,
Peter Kraus, Fritz Eckhardt

The Waltz of the Toreadors*
GB 1962   105m   Technicolor
Rank / Wintle—Parkyn (Peter de Sarigny)

A lecherous retired general finds his past
creeping up on him and loses his young mistress
to his son.
Lukewarm adaptation of a semi-classic comedy,
disastrously translated to English settings and
characters.

w Wolf Mankowitz, play Jean Anouilh d John
Guillermin ph John Wilcox m Richard
Addinsell pd Wilfrid Shingleton

Peter Sellers, Margaret Leighton, Dany Robin,
John Fraser, Cyril Cusack, Prunella Scales

Waltzes from Vienna
GB 1933   80m   bw
GFD / Gaumont
US title: Strauss's Great Waltz

A romance of the Strausses.
There is very little music and very little
Hitchcock in this extremely mild romantic
comedy.

w Alma Reville, Guy Bolton, play Guy Bolton
d Alfred Hitchcock

Jessie Matthews, Esmond Knight, Frank
Vosper, Fay Compton, Edmund Gwenn, Robert
Hale, Hindle Edgar

The Wandering Jew*
GB 1933   111m   bw
Gaumont / Twickenham (Julius Hagen)

A Jew is condemned to live forever, but dies in
the Spanish Inquisition.
Ambitious fantasy which comes off pretty well
for those in the mood, but was a curious choice
for a British studio at the time.

w H. Fowler Mear, play E. Temple Thurston
d Maurice Elvey

Conrad Veidt, Marie Ney, Basil Gill, Anne
Grey, Dennis Hoey, John Stuart, Peggy
Ashcroft, Francis L. Sullivan, Felix Ayler,
Abraham Sofaer

Wanted for Murder*
GB 1946   103m   bw
Marcel Hellman

A man, obsessed with the fact that his father was
the public hangman, becomes a murderer
himself.
Curiously stagey melodrama with intermittent
use of London backgrounds; an interesting
curiosity.

w Emeric Pressburger, Rodney Ackland,
Maurice Cowan d Lawrence Huntington

Eric Portman, Dulcie Gray, Derek Farr, Roland
Culver, Stanley Holloway, Barbara Everest,
Bonar Colleano, Kathleen Harrison

The War against Mrs Hadley*
US 1942   86m   bw
MGM (Irving Asher)

A Washington matron tries to ignore the war
and preserve her social life.
Efficient little propaganda piece with a middle-
aged heroine.

w George Oppenheimer d Harold S. Bucquet

Fay Bainter, Edward Arnold, Richard Ney, Jean
Rogers, Sara Allgood, Spring Byington, Van
Johnson, Isobel Elsom, Halliwell Hobbes, Miles
Mander, Frances Rafferty, Connie Gilchrist

AAN: George Oppenheimer

War and Peace**
US / Italy 1956   208m   Technicolor
Vistavision
Carlo Ponti / Dino de Laurentiis

A Russian family's adventures at the time of
Napoleon's invasion.
Despite miscasting and heavy dubbing, the
pictorial parts of this précis of a gargantuan
novel are powerful and exciting enough; the
human side drags a little.

w Bridget Boland, Robert Westerby, King
Vidor, Mario Camerini, Ennio de Concini, Ivo
Perelli, novel Leo Tolstoy d King Vidor, (battle
scenes) Mario Soldati ph Jack Cardiff, (battle
scenes) Aldo Tonti m Nino Rota ad Mario
Chiari

Audrey Hepburn, Henry Fonda, Mel Ferrer,
Herbert Lom, John Mills, Oscar Homolka,
Wilfrid Lawson, Vittorio Gassman, Anita
Ekberg, Helmut Dantine, Milly Vitale, Barry
Jones

'The film has no more warmth than pictures in
an art gallery.'—Philip T. Hartung

AAN: King Vidor; Jack Cardiff

War and Peace***
USSR 1967 507m Sovcolor 'Scope
  70mm
Mosfilm

An immensely long Russian version with some
of the most magnificently spectacular battle
scenes ever filmed. A treat for the eyes
throughout, and perhaps less taxing than reading
the novel, which it follows punctiliously.

w Sergei Bondarchuk, Vasili Solovyov d Sergei
Bondarchuk ph Anatoli Petritsky
m Vyacheslav Ovchinnikov

Lyudmila Savelyeva, Sergei Bondarchuk,
Vyacheslav Tikhonov
† The film was five years in production and cost
forty million dollars.

The War between Men and Women
US 1972 105m Technicolor Panavision
National General / Jalem / Llenroc / 4D
  (Danny Arnold)

A half-blind cartoonist marries a divorcee and is
troubled by her ex-husband.
Semi-serious comedy vaguely based on Thurber,
but not so that you'd notice, apart from the blind
hero; generally neither funny nor affecting.

w Mel Shavelson, Danny Arnold, based on the
writings of James Thurber d Melville Shavelson
ph Charles F. Wheeler m Marvin Hamlisch
pd Stan Jolley

Jack Lemmon, Barbara Harris, Jason Robards
Jnr, Herb Edelman, Lisa Gerritsen

War Hunt
US 1961 83m bw
TD Enterprises (Terry Sanders)

Korea 1953: a kill-crazy private is befriended by
a war orphan but finally has to be shot.
Vaguely commendable but not very expert
indictment of the realities of war.

w Stanford Whitmore d Denis Sanders ph Ted
McCord m Bud Shank

John Saxon, Robert Redford, Sidney Pollack,
Charles Aidman, Tommy Matsuda

The War Lord**
US 1965 121m Technicolor Panavision
Universal / Court (Walter Seltzer)

An officer of the Duke of Normandy has trouble
with Druids and the law of *droit de seigneur*.
Complex medieval melodrama with an air of
fantasy about it; generally likeably strange, but
the production should have been more stylized
and fanciful.

w John Collier, Millard Kaufman, *play* The
Lovers by Leslie Stevens d Franklin Schaffner

ph Russell Metty m Jerome Moross
ad Alexander Golitzen, Henry Bumstead

Charlton Heston, Richard Boone, Rosemary
Forsyth, Maurice Evans, Guy Stockwell, Niall
MacGinnis, Henry Wilcoxon, James Farentino

The War Lover
GB 1962 105m bw
Columbia / Arthur Hornblow Jnr

In 1943, a Flying Fortress commander based in
East Anglia has the wrong ideas about women
and war.
Solemn character drama punctuated by aerial
battles.

w Howard Koch, *novel* John Hersey d Philip
Leacock ph Bob Huke m Richard Addinsell

Steve McQueen, Shirley Anne Field, Robert
Wagner, Gary Cockrell, Michael Crawford

The War of the Worlds*
US 1952 85m Technicolor
Paramount / George Pal

Terrifying aliens invade Earth via the American
midwest.
Spectacular battle scenes are the mainstay of this
violent fantasy, which goes to pieces once the
cardboard characters open their mouths.

w Barre Lyndon, *novel* H. G. Wells d Byron
Haskin ph George Barnes ad Hal Pereira,
Albert Nozaki

Gene Barry, Ann Robinson, Les Tremayne, Bob
Cornthwaite, Sandra Giglio

The War Wagon**
US 1967 99m Technicolor Panavision
Universal / Batjac (Marvin Schwartz)

Two cowboys and an Indian plan to ambush the
gold wagon of a crooked mining contractor.
Exhilarating but simply-plotted action western
with strong comedy elements and a cast of old
reliables.

w *Clair Huffaker*, from his novel Badman
d Burt Kennedy ph William H. Clothier
m Dmitri Tiomkin

John Wayne, Kirk Douglas, Howard Keel,
Robert Walker, Keenan Wynn, Bruce Cabot,
Gene Evans, Bruce Dern
  'It all works splendidly.'—MFB

The Ware Case*
GB 1938 79m bw
Ealing / Capad (S. C. Balcon)

A nobleman is suspected of murdering his wife's
rich brother.
Courtroom melodrama twice filmed as a silent;
stagey but reasonably compelling in its way.

w Robert Stevenson, Roland Pertwee, E. V. H. Emmett, *play* G. P. Bancroft *d* Robert Stevenson

Clive Brook, Jane Baxter, Barry K. Barnes, C. V. France, Francis L. Sullivan, Frank Cellier, Edward Rigby, Peter Bull, Athene Seyler, Ernest Thesiger

Warlock*
US 1959 123m De Luxe Cinemascope TCF (Edward Dmytryk)

The cowardly citizens of a small western town hire a gunman as their unofficial marshal. Overlong, talkative and somewhat pretentious star western with good sequences.

w Robert Alan Aurthur, *novel* Oakley Hall *d* Edward Dmytryk *ph* Joe MacDonald *m* Leigh Harline

Henry Fonda, Richard Widmark, Anthony Quinn, Dorothy Malone, Dolores Michaels, Wallace Ford, Tom Drake, Richard Arlen, Regis Toomey, Don Beddoe, De Forrest Kelley

Warlords of Atlantis
GB 1978 96m Technicolor EMI / John Dark, Kevin Connor

Victoria sea scientists discover a lost land under the Mediterranean. Predictable compote of monsters and unwearable costumes, without a trace of wit in the script. For infants only.

w Brian Hayles *d* Kevin Connor *ph* Alan Hume *m* Mike Vickers *pd* Elliot Scott

Doug McClure, Peter Gilmore, Shane Rimmer, Lea Brodie, Michael Gothard

A Warm December
GB / US 1972 101m Technicolor First Artists / Verdon (Melville Tucker)

A widowed American doctor in London falls for a mysterious African girl who turns out to be the dying niece of a diplomat. Weird mishmash of *Love Story, Brief Encounter* and *Dark Victory*, getting the worst of all worlds.

w Lawrence Roman *d* Sidney Poitier *ph* Paul Beeson *m* Coleridge-Taylor Parkinson

Sidney Poitier, Esther Anderson, George Baker, Johnny Sekka, Earl Cameron

Warning Shot*
US 1966 100m Technicolor Paramount / Bob Banner (Buzz Kulik)

While looking for a psychopathic killer, a cop shoots dead a man who draws a gun on him. But the dead man's gun cannot be found, and the officer is suspended...

Watchable mystery decked out with guest stars; possibly intended as a TV movie.

w Mann Rubin, *novel* 711—Officer Needs Help by Whit Masterson *d* Buzz Kulik *ph* Joseph Biroc *m* Jerry Goldsmith

David Janssen, Lillian Gish, Ed Begley, Keenan Wynn, Sam Wanamaker, Eleanor Parker, Stefanie Powers, Walter Pidgeon, George Sanders, George Grizzard, Steve Allen, Carroll O'Connor, Joan Collins

Warpath
US 1951 93m Technicolor Paramount (Nat Holt)

An ex-army captain tracks down the outlaws who murdered his girl. Goodish standard western.

w Frank Gruber *d* Byron Haskin *ph* Ray Rennahan *m* Paul Sawtell

Edmond O'Brien, Dean Jagger, Forrest Tucker, Harry Carey Jnr, Wallace Ford, Polly Bergen

Washington Story
US 1952 82m bw MGM (Dore Schary) GB title: *Target for Scandal*

A lady reporter goes to Washington to expose corruption, but falls for an honest congressman. Standard flagwaver which takes itself a shade too seriously.

wd Robert Pirosh *ph* John Alton *m* Conrad Salinger

Van Johnson, Patricia Neal, Louis Calhern, Sidney Blackmer, Philip Ober, Patricia Collinge, Elizabeth Patterson, Moroni Olsen

Watch on the Rhine**
US 1943 114m bw Warner (Hal B. Wallis)

A German refugee and his family are pursued by Nazi agents in Washington. Talky play doesn't make much of a film, though the talk is good talk and the performances outstanding; but it made a prestige point or two for Hollywood.

w Dashiell Hammett, *play* Lillian Hellman *d* Herman Shumlin *ph* Merritt Gerstad, Hal Mohr *m* Max Steiner

Paul Lukas, Bette Davis, Lucile Watson, *George Coulouris*, Donald Woods, Geraldine Fitzgerald, Beulah Bondi, Henry Daniell

AA: Paul Lukas

The Watchmaker of St Paul*
France 1973   105m   Eastmancolor
Lira (Raymond Danon)
original title: *L'Horlorgier de St Paul*

A watchmaker's tranquil life is shattered when
he learns that his son is wanted for murder.
Solid character drama with careful writing and
acting.

w Jean Aurenche, Pierre Bost, Bertrand
Tavernier, *novel* L'Horlorger D'Everton by
Georges Simenon d Bertrand Tavernier
ph Pierre William Glenn m Philippe Sarde

Philippe Noiret, Jean Rochefort, Sylvain
Rougerie, Christine Pascal

Water Birds see The Living Desert

Waterhole Three
US 1967   100m   Techniscope
Paramount

Sheriff, crooks and a gambler seek buried loot.
Rather irritatingly immoral western with a hero
who defines rape as assault with a friendly
weapon; in between it tries hard for the ballad
style.

w Joseph Steck, Robert R. Young d William
Graham ph Robert Burks m Dave Grusin

James Coburn, Carroll O'Connor, Margaret
Blye, Claude Akins, Joan Blondell, Timothy
Carey

Waterloo*
Italy / USSR 1970   132m   Technicolor
Panavision
Columbia / DDL / Mosfilm (Dino de
    Laurentiis)

Historical events leading up to the 1815 battle.
The battle forms the last hour of this historical
charade, and looks both exciting and splendid,
though confusion is not avoided. The rest is a
mixed blessing.

w H. A. L. Craig, Sergei Bondarchuk d Sergei
Bondarchuk ph Armando Nannuzzi m Nino
Rota pd Mario Garbuglia

Rod Steiger, Christopher Plummer, Orson
Welles, Jack Hawkins, Virginia McKenna, Dan
O'Herlihy, Rupert Davies, Ian Ogilvy, Michael
Wilding

Waterloo Bridge*
US 1931   72m   bw
Universal (Carl Laemmle Jnr)

An army officer marries a ballerina; when he is
reported missing his family ignore her and she
sinks into prostitution.
One for the ladies, who lapped it up.

w Tom Reed, Benn W. Levy, *play* Robert E.
Sherwood d James Whale ph Arthur Edeson

Mae Clarke, Kent Douglass, Doris Lloyd, Ethel
Griffies, Enid Bennett, Frederick Kerr, Bette
Davis

Waterloo Bridge**
US 1940   103m   bw
MGM (Sidney Franklin)

Lush, all-stops-out remake of the above; for yet
another version see *Gaby*.

w S. N. Behrman, Hans Rameau, George
Froeschel d Mervyn Le Roy ph Joseph
Ruttenberg m Herbert Stothart

Vivien Leigh, Robert Taylor, Lucile Watson,
Virginia Field, Maria Ouspenskaya, C. Aubrey
Smith, Steffi Duna

'The director uses candlelight and rain more
effectively than he does the actors.'—*New
Yorker, 1977*

AAN: Joseph Ruttenberg; Herbert Stothart

Waterloo Road
US 1944   76m   bw
GFD / Gainsborough (Edward Black)

A soldier whose wife is enamoured of a petty
crook absents himself to settle matters.
What at the time seemed cheerful realism now
seems chronically forced, but amusing moments
can still be found.

w Sidney Gilliat, *story* Val Valentine d Sidney
Gilliat ph Jack Cox md Louis Levy

John Mills, Stewart Granger, Joy Shelton,
Alastair Sim, Beatrice Varley, Alison Leggatt,
Jean Kent

'The harsh rattle of trains over a viaduct, the
clamour of the street market, the wailing of
sirens and the crash of bombs are the
accompaniment of this wartime love story.'—
Richard Winnington

'Unpretentious, credible, continuously
entertaining and just the right length.'—*Richard
Mallett, Punch*

Watermelon Man
US 1970   100m   Technicolor
Columbia / Johanna

A bigoted insurance salesman wakes up one
morning to find he has turned into a black man.
Spasmodically funny racial comedy,
compromised by the impossibility of a black
man playing white even with heavy make-up.

w Herman Raucher d Melvin Van Peebles
ph W. Wallace Kelley m Melvin Van Peebles

Godfrey Cambridge, Estelle Parsons, Howard
Caine, Mantan Moreland

Watusi
US 1959   85m   Technicolor
MGM (Al Zimbalist)

Harry Quartermain retraces his father's
footsteps to King Solomon's Mines.
Skilful re-use of *King Solomon's Mines* footage;
acceptable Boys' Own Paper stuff.

w James Clavell *d* Kurt Neumann *ph* Harold E.
Wellman

George Montgomery, Taina Elg, David Farrar,
Rex Ingram, Dan Seymour

Waxworks*
Germany 1924   62m approx (24 fps)   bw
    silent
Neptun-Film
original title: *Das Wachsfigurenkabinett*

A young poet in a fairground waxwork museum
concocts stories about Haroun al Raschid, Ivan
the Terrible and Jack the Ripper.
The form later became familiar in such horror
films as *Torture Garden* and *Tales from the
Crypt*, but here the emphasis is not on horror but
on grotesquerie, and indeed the idea is somewhat
more entertaining than the rather plodding
execution.

w Henrik Galeen *d* Paul Leni *ph* Helmar
Lerski *ad* Paul Leni, Ernst Stern, Alfred Junge

William Dieterle, Emil Jannings, Conrad Veidt,
Werner Krauss

The Way Ahead***
GB 1944   115m   bw
GFD / Two Cities (John Sutro, Norman
    Walker)
US title: *Immortal Battalion*

Adventures of a platoon of raw recruits during
World War II.
Memorable semi-documentary originally
intended as a training film; the warm humour of
the early scenes, however, never leads quite
naturally into the final action and tragedy.

w Eric Ambler, Peter Ustinov *d Carol Reed*
ph Guy Green

David Niven, Stanley Holloway, Raymond
Huntley, *William Hartnell*, James Donald, John
Laurie, Leslie Dwyer, Hugh Burden, Jimmy
Hanley, Renée Asherson, Penelope Dudley
Ward, Reginald Tate, Leo Genn, Mary Jerrold,
Peter Ustinov

Way Down East**
US 1920   110m approx (24 fps)   bw with
    colour sequence   silent
D. W. Griffith

A country girl is seduced; her baby dies; her
shame is revealed; but a kindly farmer rescues
her from drowning and marries her.
Old-fashioned tearjerker impeccably mounted
and very typical of its director in its sentimental
mood. The ice floe sequence is famous for its
excitement and realism.

w Anthony Paul Kelly, Joseph R. Grismer, D.
W. Griffith, *play* Lottie Blair Parker *d D. W.
Griffith ph* Billy Bitzer, Henrik Sortov

Lillian Gish, Richard Barthelmess, Lowell
Sherman, Creighton Hale

Way Down East
US 1935   85m   bw
TCF (Winfield Sheehan)

Tedious and unwise remake.

w Howard Estabrook, William Hurlbut
d Henry King

Rochelle Hudson, Henry Fonda, Slim
Summerville, Edward Trevor, Margaret
Hamilton, Andy Devine, Spring Byington,
Russell Simpson, Sara Haden

Way for a Sailor
US 1930   83m   bw
MGM

Adventures of a tough seafarer and a pet seal.
Thin vehicle for a declining star whose talkie
voice was at odds with his image.

w Laurence Stallings, W. L. River, *novel* Albert
Richard Wetjen *d* Sam Wood *ph* Percy Hilburn

John Gilbert, Wallace Beery, Leila Hyams, Jim
Tully, Polly Moran, Doris Lloyd

Way of a Gaucho
US 1952   91m   Technicolor
TCF (Philip Dunne)

An Argentine gaucho joins the militia and fights
Indians.
Mildly interesting western-in-disguise.

w Philip Dunne, *novel* Herbert Childs *d* Jacques
Tourneur *ph* Harry Jackson *m* Sol Kaplan

Rory Calhoun, Gene Tierney, Richard Boone,
Hugh Marlowe, Everett Sloane, Enrique Chaico

The Way of All Flesh*
US 1928   94m (24 fps)   bw   silent
Paramount

A respectable man leaves his wife, goes to the
dogs, and is too ashamed to come back.
Star character drama, most watchable now
when it goes over the top.

d Victor Fleming
Emil Jannings

† Remade 1940 with Akim Tamiroff.
AA: Emil Jannings
AAN: best picture

Way Out West****
US 1937 66m bw
Hal Roach (Stan Laurel)

Laurel and Hardy come to Brushwood Gulch to deliver the deed to a gold mine.
Seven reels of perfect joy, with the comedians at their very best in brilliantly-timed routines, plus two song numbers as a bonus.

w Jack Jevne, Charles Rogers, James Parrott, Felix Adler d James Horne ph Art Lloyd, Walter Lundin *m* Marvin Hatley

Stan Laurel, Oliver Hardy, James Finlayson, Sharon Lynne, Rosina Lawrence

'Not only one of their most perfect films, it ranks with the best screen comedy anywhere.'— *David Robinson, 1962*

AAN: Marvin Hatley

The Way to Love
US 1933 80m bw
Paramount (Benjamin Glazer)

A would-be Paris tourist guide works as a pavement hawker and helps a showgirl evade her knife-thrower partner.
Thin star vehicle with a few pleasant moments.

w Gene Fowler, Benjamin Glazer *d* Norman Taurog *ph* Charles Lang *m/ly* Ralph Rainger, Leo Robin

Maurice Chevalier, Edward Everett Horton, Ann Dvorak, Arthur Pierson, Minna Gombell, Blanche Frederici, Douglass Dumbrille, John Miljan

The Way to the Gold
US 1957 94m bw Cinemascope
TCF (David Weisbart)

An ex-convict seeks hidden loot but is pursued by competitors.
Gloomy, self-pitying melodrama.

w Wendell Mayes, *novel* Wilber Steele *d* Robert D. Webb *ph* Leo Tover *m* Lionel Newman

Jeffrey Hunter, Sheree North, Barry Sullivan, Walter Brennan, Ruth Donnelly, Neville Brand

The Way to the Stars****
GB 1945 109m bw
Two Cities (Anatole de Grunwald)
US title: *Johnny in the Clouds*

World War II as seen by the guests at a small hotel near an airfield.
Generally delightful comedy drama suffused with tragic atmosphere but with very few flying shots, one of the few films which instantly bring back the atmosphere of the war in Britain for anyone who was involved.

w Terence Rattigan, Anatole de Grunwald poem John Pudney d Anthony Asquith

John Mills, Rosamund John, Michael Redgrave, Douglass Montgomery, Basil Radford, Stanley Holloway, Joyce Carey, Renée Asherson, Felix Aylmer, Bonar Colleano, Trevor Howard, Jean Simmons

'Not for a long time have I seen a film so satisfying, so memorable, or so successful in evoking the precise mood and atmosphere of the recent past.'—*Richard Mallett, Punch*

Way Way Out
US 1966 105m De Luxe Cinemascope
TCF / Coldwater / Jerry Lewis (Malcolm Stuart)

In 1994 a weather expert on the moon has woman trouble.
Dismal sex farce with an unusual backdrop; painful to sit through.

w William Bowers, Laslo Vadnay *d* Gordon Douglas *ph* William H. Clothier *m* Lalo Schifrin

Jerry Lewis, Connie Stevens, Robert Morley, Dick Shawn, Anita Ekberg, Dennis Weaver, Howard Morris, Brian Keith

The Way We Were**
US 1973 118m Eastmancolor
Panavision
Columbia / Rastar (Ray Stark)

The romance and marriage of an upper-crust young novelist and a Jewish bluestocking girl, from college to Hollywood in the thirties, forties and fifties.
Instant nostalgia for Americans, some fun and a lot of boredom for everybody is provided by this very patchy star vehicle which makes a particular mess of the McCarthy witch hunt sequence but has undeniable moments of vitality.

w Arthur Laurents, from his novel *d* Sydney Pollack *ph* Harry Stradling Jnr *m* Marvin Hamlisch

Barbra Streisand, Robert Redford, Patrick O'Neal, Viveca Lindfors, Bradford Dillman, Lois Chiles, Allyn Ann McLerie, Herb Edelman, Murray Hamilton

'Not one moment of the picture is anything but garbage under the gravy of false honesty.'— *Stanley Kauffmann*

AA: Marvin Hamlisch; title song (*m* Marvin Hamlisch, *ly* Alan and Marilyn Bergman)

The Way West*
US 1967 122m De Luxe Panavision
UA / Harold Hecht

Hazards of a wagon train between Missouri and
Oregon in 1843.
Semi-spectacular western which looks good but
falls apart dramatically, especially in its
insistence on a sub-plot about a most unlikely
nymphet.

w Ben Maddow, Mitch Lindemann, *novel* A. B.
Guthrie Jnr *d* Andrew V. McLaglen
ph William H. Clothier m Bronislau Kaper

Kirk Douglas, Robert Mitchum, Richard
Widmark, Lola Albright, Michael Witney, Sally
Field, Stubby Kaye, Jack Elam

'A jerk's idea of an epic; big stars, big
landscapes, bad jokes, folksy-heroic music to
plug up the holes, and messy hang-ups.'—
Pauline Kael

The Wayward Bus
US 1957 89m bw Cinemascope
TCF (Charles Brackett)

A landslide strands an assortment of bus
passengers in a lonely farmhouse . . .
. . . but not the old dark house, unfortunately:
this lot does nothing but talk, and the plot never
really forms.

w Ivan Moffat, *novel* John Steinbeck *d* Victor
Vicas *ph* Charles G. Clarke *m* Leigh Harline

Dan Dailey, Jayne Mansfield, Joan Collins, Rick
Jason, Dolores Michaels, Larry Keating, Betty
Lou Keim

We Are Not Alone*
US 1939 112m bw
Warner (Henry Blanke)

A man having an innocent affair is accused of
murdering his wife.
Gloomy, well-acted drama with a rather uneasy
English setting.

w James Hilton, Milton Krims, *novel* James
Hilton *d* Edmund Goulding *ph* Tony Gaudio
m Max Steiner

Paul Muni, Jane Bryan, Flora Robson,
Raymond Severn, Una O'Connor, Henry
Daniell, Montagu Love, James Stephenson,
Cecil Kellaway

We Dive at Dawn
GB 1943 98m bw
GFD / Gainsborough (Edward Black)

World War II adventures of a British submarine
disabled in the Baltic.
Fairly routine war suspenser.

w J. P. Williams, Val Valentine, Frank Launder
d Anthony Asquith

John Mills, Eric Portman, Reginald Purdell,
Niall MacGinnis, Joan Hopkins, Josephine
Wilson, Jack Watling

We Joined the Navy
GB 1962 105m Eastmancolor
Cinemascope
Dial / Daniel M. Angel

A carefree naval commander and three cadets
get involved in the affairs of a small
Mediterranean country.
Desperate naval farce which sinks from script
malnutrition in reel two.

w Arthur Dales, *novel* John Winton *d* Wendy
Toye *ph* Otto Heller *m* Ron Grainer

Kenneth More, Lloyd Nolan, Mischa Auer, Joan
O'Brien, Jeremy Lloyd, Dinsdale Landen, Derek
Fowlds

We Live Again*
US 1934 85m bw
Samuel Goldwyn

A Russian prince is brought up in the country
and falls in love with a servant girl whose life
later takes a downward path.
Beautifully made but dramatically uninteresting
version of a Russian classic.

w Preston Sturges, Maxwell Anderson, Leonard
Praskins, *novel* Resurrection by Leo Tolstoy
d Rouben Mamoulian *ph* Gregg Toland
m Alfred Newman

Fredric March, Anna Sten, Jane Baxter, C.
Aubrey Smith, Ethel Griffies, Jessie Ralph, Sam
Jaffe

We Were Dancing
US 1942 93m bw
MGM (Robert Z. Leonard, Orville Dull)

A Polish princess elopes from her engagement
party with a gigolo.
Leaden romantic comedy produced in high style.

w Claudine West, Hans Rameau, George
Froeschel, partly based on the play Tonight at
8.30 by Noel Coward
d Robert Z. Leonard *ph* Robert Planck
m Bronislau Kaper

Norma Shearer, Melvyn Douglas, Gail Patrick,
Lee Bowman, *Marjorie Main,* Reginald Owen,
Alan Mowbray, Florence Bates, Sig Rumann,
Dennis Hoey, Heather Thatcher, Connie
Gilchrist

We Were Strangers*

US 1949 105m bw
Columbia / Horizon (Sam Spiegel)

Cuban rebels in the thirties plan to assassinate a politician and have to build a tunnel through a cemetery.

Well-made but very downbeat adventure story, too cheerless to be exciting.

w Peter Viertel, John Huston, *novel* Rough Sketch by Robert Sylvester *d John Huston* *ph* Russell Metty *m* Georges Antheil

John Garfield, Jennifer Jones, Pedro Armendariz, Gilbert Roland, Wally Cassell, Ramon Novarro, David Bond, Jose Perez

'There is so much about this film I cannot swallow – the implausibilities of detail, the convention of broken accents, the literary conversaziones, the naïve doctrines of revolution . . . [but] it continues to haunt the mind and has therefore had its say.'—*Richard Winnington*

The Weapon

GB 1956 81m bw Superscope 235
Penclean (Frank Bevis)

A boy finds a loaded revolver on a bomb site and mistakenly thinks he has killed someone with it.

Standard suspenser with a cast worthy of something more interesting.

w Fred Freiburger *d* Val Guest *ph* Reg Wyer *m* James Stevens

Lizabeth Scott, Steve Cochran, George Cole, Herbert Marshall, Nicole Maurey, Jon Whiteley, Laurence Naismith

The Web*

US 1947 87m bw
U-I

A financier hires a young lawyer as his bodyguard and lures him into committing murder.

Modestly well staged and glossy thriller.

w William Bowers, Bertram Millhauser *d* Michael Gordon *ph* Irving Glassberg *m* Hans Salter

Edmond O'Brien, Vincent Price, Ella Raines, William Bendix

The Webster Boy

GB 1961 83m bw
Emmet Dalton

A teenager suffers at the hands of a sadistic schoolmaster.

Curious, totally unbelievable melodrama.

w Ted Allen *d* Don Chaffey *ph* Gerald Gibbs *m* Wilfrid Joseph

Richard O'Sullivan, John Cassavetes, David Farrar, Elizabeth Sellars, Niall MacGinnis

A Wedding*

US 1978 125m De Luxe
TCF / Lion's Gate (Thommy Thompson, Robert Altman)

Two families converge for a fashionable wedding, but the day is beset by calamities.

Wide-ranging satirical comedy which despite excellent moments goes on far too long, is rather too black, and is sabotaged by the director's *penchant* for having fourteen people talking at the same time. An exhausting experience.

w John Considine, Patricia Resnick, Allan Nicholls, Robert Altman *d* Robert Altman *ph* Charles Rosher *md* Tom Walls

Carol Burnett, Paul Dooley, Amy Stryker, Mia Farrow, Peggy Ann Garner, Lillian Gish, Nina Van Pallandt, Vittorio Gassman, Howard Duff, Desi Arnaz Jnr, Dina Merrill, Geraldine Chaplin, Viveca Lindfors, Lauren Hutton, John Cromwell

The Wedding March**

US 1928 196m approx (24 fps) bw silent
Paramount / Celebrity

A Habsburg prince loves a poor girl but is forced to marry a crippled princess, who dies; he is then murdered by the poor girl's enraged defender.

A marathon dose of Stroheim's favourite subject, sex, with some violence and a few fetishes thrown in. Full of fascinating touches, but desperately overlong, it was originally released in two parts, but failed to draw.

w Harry Carr, Erich Von Stroheim *d Erich Von Stroheim ph* Hal Mohr, Ben Reynolds *ad* Erich Von Stroheim, Richard Day

Erich Von Stroheim, Fay Wray, Zasu Pitts, Matthew Betz, Maude George, Cesare Gravina, George Fawcett

'A pitilessly authentic portrait of decadent Imperialist Austria."—*Georges Sadoul*
† In 1975 there was published a pictorial record, *The Complete Wedding March*, by Herman G. Weinberg.

The Wedding Night*

US 1935 83m bw
Samuel Goldwyn

A Connecticut author causes tragedy when he takes an interest in the local Polish immigrant farmers and especially in the daughter of one of them.

Interesting and unusual but slightly tediously told drama.

w Edith Fitzgerald *d* King Vidor *ph* Gregg Toland *m* Alfred Newman

Gary Cooper, Anna Sten, Sig Rumann, Helen Vinson, Ralph Bellamy, Esther Dale

Wedding Present*
US 1936 81m bw
Paramount (B. P. Schulberg)

A pair of crack newspaper reporters take their jobs and themselves lightly.
Whimsical star comedy with some funny scenes.

w Joseph Anthony, *story* Paul Gallico *d* Richard Wallace *ph* Leon Shamroy

Cary Grant, Joan Bennett, George Bancroft, Conrad Nagel, Gene Lockhart, William Demarest, Edward Brophy

Wedding Rehearsal
GB 1932 84m bw
Ideal / Alexander Korda

A Guards officer foils his grandmother's plans to get him married by finding suitors for all the young ladies offered.
Frail comedy with unsure technique.

w Lajos Biro, Arthur Wimperis *d* Alexander Korda

Roland Young, George Grossmith, John Loder, Lady Tree, Wendy Barrie, Maurice Evans, Joan Gardner, Merle Oberon, Kate Cutler, Edmund Breon

Wee Willie Winkie**
US 1937 99m bw
TCF (Gene Markey)

A small girl becomes the mascot of a British regiment in India.
Vaguely based on a Kipling tale, this was the most expensive Temple vehicle and a first-rate family action picture with sentimental asides.

w Ernest Pascal, Julien Josephson, *story* Rudyard Kipling *d John Ford ph Arthur Miller*

Shirley Temple, Victor McLaglen, C. Aubrey Smith, June Lang, Michael Whalen, Cesar Romero, Constance Collier, Gavin Muir

Weekend at the Waldorf*
US 1945 130m bw
MGM (Arthur Hornblow Jnr)

Four stories about guests at New York's largest hotel.
Disguised version of *Grand Hotel,* with the same stories twisted; the talent at hand, however, is serviceable rather than inspiring.

w Sam and Bella Spewack *d* Robert Z. Leonard *ph* Robert Planck *md* Johnny Green

Ginger Rogers, Walter Pidgeon, Van Johnson, Lana Turner, Robert Benchley, Edward Arnold, Constance Collier, Leon Ames, Warner Anderson, Phyllis Thaxter, Keenan Wynn, Porter Hall, Samuel S. Hinds, George Zucco, Xavier Cugat

Weekend in Havana
US 1941 80m Technicolor
TCF (William Le Baron)

A shopgirl in Havana falls for a shipping executive.
Routine Fox musical showcasing familiar talents: adequate wartime escapist fare.

w Karl Tunberg, Darrell Ware *d* Walter Lang *ph* Ernest Palmer *md* Alfred Newman

Alice Faye, John Payne, Carmen Miranda, Cesar Romero, Cobina Wright Jnr, George Barbier, Sheldon Leonard, Leonid Kinskey /

Weekend with Father
US 1951 83m bw
U-I (Ted Richmond)

A widow and a widower fall in love when taking their respective children to a summer camp.
Mechanical comedy of upsets and embarrassments.

w Joseph Hoffman *d* Douglas Sirk *ph* Clifford Stine *m* Frank Skinner

Van Heflin, Patricia Neal, Gigi Perreau, Virginia Field, Richard Denning

Welcome Danger*
US 1929 110m bw
Harold Lloyd

The meek son of a police chief gets involved in a tong war.
Moderate early talkie comedy showing the star in some trouble with pace and dialogue.

w Clyde Bruckman, Lex Neal, Felix Adler, Paul Gerard Smith *d* Clyde Bruckman *ph* Walter Lundin, Henry Kohler

Harold Lloyd, Barbara Kent, Noah Young, Charles Middleton

Welcome Stranger
US 1947 107m bw
Paramount (Sol C. Siegel)

A genial young doctor fills in for a crusty old one on vacation in a small town.
Formula sentimental comedy, one of several reuniting the stars of *Going My Way.*

w Arthur Sheekman *d* Elliott Nugent *ph* Lionel Lindon *m* Robert Emmett Dolan

Bing Crosby, Barry Fitzgerald, Joan Caulfield,

Wanda Hendrix, Frank Faylen, Elizabeth
Patterson, Robert Shayne, Percy Kilbride

Welcome to Hard Times*
US 1967   103m   Metrocolor
MGM / Max E. Youngstein, David Carr
GB title: *Killer on a Horse*

A small western town arms itself against a
mysterious bandit.
Curiously likeable, almost symbolic suspense
western which has a good start and middle but
not much idea how to end.

wd Burt Kennedy, *novel* E. L. Doctorow
ph Harry Stradling Jnr *m* Harry Sukman

Henry Fonda, Janice Rule, Keenan Wynn, Janis
Paige, John Anderson, Warren Oates, Fay
Spain, Edgar Buchanan, Aldo Ray, Lon Chaney
Jnr, Elisha Cook Jnr

Welcome to LA*
US 1976   106m   De Luxe
Lion's Gate / Robert Altman

A young composer in Los Angeles has a varied
sex life.
Fragmentary, vaguely mystical, momentarily
interesting, frequently confusing slice of life as
seen through misty glasses.

wd Alan Rudolph *ph* Dave Myers *m* Richard
Baskin

Keith Carradine, Sally Kellerman, Geraldine
Chaplin, Harvey Keitel, Lauren Hutton, Viveca
Lindfors, Sissy Spacek, Denver Pyle

  'The supposedly free-form, improvisational
dynamics of an Altman movie have here become
a strictly choreographed ballet.'—*Richard
Combs, MFB*

Welcome to the Club
GB 1970   88m   bw
Welcome (Sam Lomberg)

Hiroshima 1945; an American Quaker sergeant
upsets military protocol.
Pale satirical comedy shot in Copenhagen.

w Clement Biddle Wood, from his novel
d Walter Shenson *ph* Mikael Salomon *m* Ken
Thomas

Brian Foley, Jack Warden, Lee Meredith, Andy
Jarrett

The Well*
US 1951   85m   bw
Cardinal / Harry M. Popkin (Clarence Greene,
Leo Popkin)

A black child falls down a well, and the town
unites to save her.

Forceful high-pitched melodrama, cut to a do-
gooder pattern which became very familiar.

w Russel Rouse, Clarence Greene *d* Leo
Popkin, Russel Rouse *ph* Ernest Laszlo
m Dmitri Tiomkin

Richard Rober, Henry Morgan, Barry Kelley,
Christine Larson

AAN: script

The Well Groomed Bride*
US 1946   75m   bw
Paramount (Fred Kohlmar)

A naval officer searches San Francisco for a
magnum of champagne with which to launch a
ship.
Thin but cheerful star comedy.

w Claude Binyon, Robert Russell *d* Sidney
Lanfield *ph* John F. Seitz *m* Roy Webb

Ray Milland, Olivia de Havilland, Sonny Tufts,
James Gleason, Constance Dowling, Percy
Kilbride, Jean Heather

Wells Fargo*
US 1937   115m   bw
Paramount (Frank Lloyd)

How the express delivery service was built up.
Large-scale, entertaining western with overmuch
emphasis on domestic issues.

w Paul Schofield, Gerald Geraghty, John
Boland, *story* Stuart N. Lake *d* Frank Lloyd
ph Theodor Sparkuhl *m* Victor Young

Joel McCrea, Bob Burns, Frances Dee, Lloyd
Nolan, Henry O'Neill, Mary Nash, Ralph
Morgan, John Mack Brown, Porter Hall,
Clarence Kolb

Went the Day Well?*
GB 1942   92m   bw
Ealing (S. C. Balcon)
US title: *Forty-eight Hours*

Villagers resist when German paratroopers
invade an English village and the squire proves to
be a quisling.
Could-it-happen melodrama which made
excellent wartime propaganda; generally well
staged.

w Angus MacPhail, John Dighton, Diana
Morgan, *story* Graham Greene *d* Alberto
Cavalcanti *m* William Walton

Leslie Banks, Elizabeth Allen, Frank Lawton,
Basil Sydney, Valerie Taylor, Mervyn Johns,
Edward Rigby, Marie Lohr, C. V. France, David
Farrar

We're No Angels*
US 1954 106m Technicolor Vistavision
Paramount (Pat Duggan)

Three escaped Devil's Island convicts help a
downtrodden storekeeper and his family to
outwit a scheming relative.
Whimsical, overstretched period comedy
suffering from miscasting but with some
pleasantries along the way.

w Ranald MacDougall, *play* La Cuisine des
Anges by Albert Husson *d* Michael Curtiz
ph Loyal Griggs *m* Frederick Hollander

Humphrey Bogart, *Peter Ustinov*, Aldo Ray,
Joan Bennett, Basil Rathbone, Leo G. Carroll,
John Smith

We're Not Dressing*
US 1934 77m bw
Paramount (Benjamin Glazer)

A spoiled heiress shipwrecked on a Pacific island
is tamed by an easy-going sailor.
Pleasant, madly dated, light-hearted variation on
a much-filmed play, resolving itself into a series
of comic turns.

w Horace Jackson, Francis Martin, George
Marion Jnr, *play* The Admirable Crichton by J.
M. Barrie *d* Norman Taurog *ph* Charles Lang
songs Harry Revel, Mack Gordon

Bing Crosby, Carole Lombard, George Burns,
Gracie Allen, Leon Errol, Ethel Merman, Jay
Henry, Ray Milland

We're Not Married*
US 1952 85m bw
TCF (Nunnally Johnson)

Six couples find that they were never legally
married.
Amiable, smartly-played compendium of
sketches on a familiar theme.

w Nunnally Johnson *d* Edmund Goulding
ph Leo Tover *m* Cyril Mockridge

Ginger Rogers, Fred Allen, Victor Moore, Paul
Douglas, Eve Arden, Marilyn Monroe, David
Wayne, Louis Calhern, Zsa Zsa Gabor, Mitzi
Gaynor, Eddie Bracken, James Gleason, Jane
Darwell

The Werewolf
US 1956 80m bw
Columbia / Clover (Sam Katzman)

In a small mountain town, a victim of radiation
exposure periodically becomes a werewolf and is
hounded down.
Absurd and tedious thriller which wastes an
interesting background.

w Robert E. Kent, James B. Gordon *d* Fred F.
Sears *ph* Edwin Linden *m* Mischa Bakaleinikoff

Steven Ritch, Don McGowan, Joyce Holden

Werewolf of London*
US 1935 75m bw
Universal

Werewolves fight for a rare Tibetan flower with
curative properties.
Patchy horror film which lurches from excellent
suspense scenes to tedious chunks of superfluous
dialogue. In many ways a milestone in the
history of its kind.

w Robert Harris *d* Stuart Walker *ph* Charles
Stumar

Henry Hull, *Warner Oland*, Valerie Hobson,
Spring Byington, Lester Matthews, Zeffie
Tilbury, Ethel Griffies

West Eleven
GB 1963 93m bw
(ABP) Daniel M. Angel (Vivian Cox)

A young London drifter is offered £10,000 to
commit murder.
Dingy but not very convincing 'realist'
melodrama with a jazzy style which induces
weariness.

w Keith Waterhouse, Willis Hall, *novel* The
Furnished Room by Laura del Rivo *ph* Otto
Heller *m* Stanley Black, Acker Bilk

Alfred Lynch, Eric Portman, Kathleen
Harrison, Diana Dors, Kathleen Breck, Freda
Jackson, Finlay Currie, Harold Lang

West Point of the Air
US 1935 90m bw
MGM (Monta Bell)

The army sergeant father of an air cadet has
great hopes for him.
Routine sentimental flagwaver.

w James J. McGuinness, John Monk Saunders,
Frank Wead, Arthur J. Beckhard *d* Richard
Rosson *ph* Clyde de Vinna, Charles A.
Marshall, Elmer Dyer

Wallace Beery, Robert Young, Maureen
O'Sullivan, Lewis Stone, James Gleason,
Rosalind Russell, Russell Hardie, Henry
Wadsworth, Robert Taylor

West Point Story*
US 1950 107m bw
Warner (Louis F. Edelman)
GB title: *Fine and Dandy*

A Broadway producer stages a show at the
military academy.

Thin and rather tedious musical saved by its irrepressible star.

w John Monks Jnr, Charles Hoffman, Irving Wallace *d* Roy del Ruth *ph* Sid Hickox *md* Ray Heindorf *songs* Sammy Cahn, Jule Styne

James Cagney, Virginia Mayo, Doris Day, Gordon Macrae, Gene Nelson, Alan Hale Jnr, Roland Winters, Jerome Cowan

AAN: Ray Heindorf

West Side Story***
US 1961   155m   Technicolor   Panavision 70
(UA) Mirisch / Seven Arts (Robert Wise)

The Romeo and Juliet story in a New York dockland setting.
The essentially theatrical conception of this entertainment is nullified by determinedly realistic settings which make much of it seem rather silly, but production values are fine and the song numbers electrifying.

w Ernest Lehman, *play* Arthur Laurents, after Shakespeare *d* Robert Wise, Jerome Robbins *ph* Daniel L. Fapp *m* Leonard Bernstein *ly* Stephen Sondheim *pd* Boris Leven

Natalie Wood (sung by Marni Nixon), Richard Beymer (sung by Jimmy Bryant), Russ Tamblyn, *Rita Moreno*, George Chakiris

AA: best picture; Robert Wise, Jerome Robbins; Daniel L. Fapp; Rita Moreno; George Chakiris
AAN: Ernest Lehman; musical direction (Saul Chaplin, Johnny Green, Sid Ramin, Irwin Kostal)

Western Union**
US 1941   94m   Technicolor
TCF (Harry Joe Brown)

Politicians and crooks hamper the laying of cross country cables.
First rate western with familiar excitements.

w Robert Carson, *novel* Zane Grey *d* Fritz Lang *ph* Edward Cronjager *m* David Buttolph

Randolph Scott, Robert Young, Dean Jagger, Virginia Gilmore, Slim Summerville, John Carradine, Chill Wills, Barton MacLane

'It is impossible to know what clichés the director may have prevented, but it is enough and too much to see those he left in.'—*Otis Ferguson*

The Westerner**
US 1940   99m   bw
Samuel Goldwyn

Judge Roy Bean comes to grief through his love for Lily Langtry.

Moody melodramatic western with comedy touches; generally entertaining, the villain more so than the hero.

w Jo Swerling, Niven Busch, *story* Stuart N. Lake *d* William Wyler *ph* Gregg Toland *m* Dmitri Tiomkin

Gary Cooper, *Walter Brennan*, Doris Davenport, Fred Stone, Paul Hurst, Chill Wills, Charles Halton, Forrest Tucker, Dana Andrews, Lilian Bond, Tom Tyler

AA: Walter Brennan
AAN: Stuart N. Lake

Westward Ho the Wagons
US 1956   85m   Technicolor Cinemascope
Walt Disney (Bill Walsh)

A wagon train defends itself against Indians.
Slow and simple-minded family western.

w Tom Blackburn *d* William Beaudine *ph* Charles Boyle *m* George Bruns

Fess Parker, Kathleen Crowley, Jeff York, David Stollery, Sebastian Cabot, George Reeves

Westward Passage
US 1932   73m   bw
RKO (David O. Selznick)

A wealthy girl weds a poor novelist but wants the rich full life for their children.
Dogged romantic drama with only the casting of interest.

w Bradley and Humphrey King, *novel* Margaret Ayer Barnes *d* Robert Milton *ph* Lucien Andriot *m* Max Steiner

Ann Harding, Laurence Olivier, Zasu Pitts, Irving Pichel, Juliette Compton, Florence Roberts

Westward the Women*
US 1951   118m   bw
MGM (Dore Schary)

In the 1850s an Indian scout leads 150 Chicago women to meet husbands in California.
Good-looking episodic western, apparently intended mainly to amuse but seldom rising to the occasion.

w Charles Schnee *d* William Wellman *ph* William Mellor *m* Jeff Alexander

Robert Taylor, Denise Darcel, John McIntire, Marilyn Erskine, Hope Emerson, Lenore Lonergan, Julie Bishop

Westworld**
US 1973   89m   Metrocolor   Panavision
MGM (Paul N. Lazarus III)

In a millionaire holiday resort which recreates the past, a western badman robot goes berserk and relentlessly attacks two visitors.
Unusual and amusing but under-produced melodrama with slipshod story development and continuity, atoned for by memorable moments and underlying excitement.

wd Michael Crichton ph Gene Polito *m* Fred Karlin *ad* Herman Blumenthal

Yul Brynner, Richard Benjamin, James Brolin, Norman Bartold, Alan Oppenheimer

The Wet Parade*
US 1932   122m   bw
MGM (Hunt Stromberg)

A politician points to the corruption caused by prohibition.
Sociologically interesting melodrama.

w John Lee Mahin, *novel* Upton Sinclair *d* Victor Fleming *ph* George Barnes

Walter Huston, Myrna Loy, Neil Hamilton, Lewis Stone, Jimmy Durante, Wallace Ford, Dorothy Jordan, John Miljan, Robert Young

What a Way to Go*
US 1963   111m   De Luxe   Cinemascope
TCF / APJAC / Orchard (Arthur P. Jacobs)

An immensely rich girl tells her psychiatrist how all her husbands proved not only successful but accident-prone.
Wild, mainly agreeable, star-and-gag-laden black comedy which starts on too high a note and fails to sustain.

w Betty Comden, Adolph Green *d* J. Lee-Thompson *ph* Leon Shamroy *md* Nelson Riddle *ly* Comden and Green *songs* Jule Styne

Shirley Maclaine, Bob Cummings, Dick Van Dyke, Robert Mitchum, Gene Kelly, Dean Martin, Paul Newman, Reginald Gardiner, Margaret Dumont

What Became of Jack and Jill?
GB 1971   90m   De Luxe
Palomar / Amicus (Milton Subotsky)

A young man tries to hasten his grandmother's death but she has the last laugh.
Feeble suspenser with a dim ending.

w Roger Marshall, *novel* The Ruthless Ones by Laurence Moody *d* Bill Bain *ph* Gerry Turpin *m* Carl Davis

Vanessa Howard, Paul Nicholas, Mona Washbourne, Peter Copley, Peter Jeffrey

What Changed Charley Farthing
GB 1975   101m   Eastmancolor
Patina—Hidalgo (Tristam Cones)

A philandering sailor has adventures in Cuba.
Weirdly ineffective comedy actioner which never gets started and should never have been thought of.

w David Pursall, Jack Seddon, *novel* Mark Hebdon *d* Sidney Hayers *ph* Graham Edgar *m* Angela Arteaga

Doug McClure, Lionel Jeffries, Warren Mitchell, Hayley Mills, Dilys Hamlett, Fernando Sancho

What Did You Do in the War, Daddy?
US 1966   115m   De Luxe   Panavision
UA / Mirisch / Geoffrey (Owen Crump, Blake Edwards)

In 1943, an Italian town surrenders readily to the Americans providing its wine festival and football match can take place.
Silly war comedy with insufficient jokes for its wearisome length. The performances are bright enough.

w William Peter Blatty *d* Blake Edwards *ph* Philip Lathrop *m* Henry Mancini

James Coburn, Dick Shawn, Sergio Fantoni, Giovanni Ralli, Aldo Ray, Harry Morgan, Carroll O'Connor, Leon Askin

What Price Glory?*
US 1952   111m   Technicolor
TCF (Sol. C. Siegel)

In 1917 France Captain Flagg and Sergeant Quirt spar for the same girl.
Stagey remake of the celebrated silent film and play; watchable if not exactly inspired.

w Phoebe and Henry Ephron, *play* Maxwell Anderson, Lawrence Stallings *d* John Ford *m* Alfred Newman

James Cagney, Dan Dailey, Corinne Calvet, William Demarest, Robert Wagner, Marisa Pavan, James Gleason

What Price Hollywood?*
US 1932   87m   bw
RKO (Pandro S. Berman)

A waitress becomes a film star with the help of a drunken director who later commits suicide.
Fairly trenchant early study of the mores of the film city, later revamped as *A Star Is Born*.

w Jane Murfin, Ben Markson, Gene Fowler, Rowland Brown, *story* Adela Rogers St John *d George Cukor ph* Charles Rosher *m* Max Steiner *montage* Slavko Vorkapitch

Constance Bennett, Lowell Sherman, Neil Hamilton, Gregory Ratoff, Brooks Bendict, Louise Beavers, Eddie Anderson
'Many of the scenes are like sketches for the later versions, but this film has its own interest,

especially because of its glimpses into the studio
life of the time.'—*New Yorker, 1977*

AAN: Adela Rogers St John

Whatever Happened to Aunt Alice?*
US 1969   101m   Metrocolor
Associates and Aldrich / Palomar

A genteel widow murders her housekeepers for
their private incomes.
Ladylike shocker with some black humour and
good performances.

w Theodore Apstein, *novel* The Forbidden
Garden by Ursula Curtiss   *d* Lee H. Katzin
ph Joseph Biroc   *m* Gerald Fried

Geraldine Page, Ruth Gordon, Rosemary
Forsyth, Robert Fuller, Mildred Dunnock

Whatever Happened to Baby Jane?*
US 1962   132m   bw
Warner Seven Arts / Associates and Aldrich
  (Robert Aldrich)

In middle age, a demented ex-child star lives in
an old Hollywood mansion with her invalid
sister, and tension leads to murder.
Famous for marking the first time Hollywood's
ageing first ladies stooped to horror, and
followed by *Hush Hush Sweet Charlotte* and the
other *Whatevers*, this dreary looking melodrama
only occasionally grabs the attention and has
enough plot for about half its length. The
performances, however, are striking.

w Lukas Heller   *d* Robert Aldrich   *ph* Ernest
Haller   *m* Frank de Vol

Bette Davis, Joan Crawford, Victor Buono,
Anna Lee

  'It goes on and on, in a light much dimmer
than necessary, and the climax, when it belatedly
arrives, is a bungled, languid mingling of
pursuers and pursued . . .'—*New Yorker*

AAN: Ernest Haller; Bette Davis; Victor Buono

What's Good for the Goose
GB 1969   104m   Eastmancolor
Tigon (Tony Tenser, Norman Wisdom)

An assistant bank manager falls for a girl hitch-
hiker and tries to recover his youth.
Embarrassing attempt to build a sexy vehicle for
a star whose sentimental mugging always
appealed mainly to children.

w Norman Wisdom   *d* Menahem Golan
ph William Brayne   *m* Reg Tilsley

Norman Wisdom, Sally Geeson, Sally Bazeley,
Derek Francis, Terence Alexander

What's New Pussycat?
US / France 1965   108m   Technicolor
UA / Famous Artists (Charles K. Feldman)

A fashion editor is distracted by beautiful girls.
Zany sex comedy with many more misses than
hits, a product of the wildly swinging sixties
when it was thought that a big budget and stars
making fools of themselves would automatically
ensure a success.

w Woody Allen   *d* Clive Donner   *ph* Jean Badal
m Burt Bacharach

Peter O'Toole, Peter Sellers, Woody Allen,
Ursula Andress, Romy Schneider, Capucine,
Paula Prentiss

  'Unfortunately for all concerned, to make
something enjoyably dirty a lot of taste is
required.'—*John Simon*

AAN: title song (*m* Burt Bacharach, *ly* Hal
David)

What's So Bad About Feeling Good?
US 1965   94m   Technicolor
Universal (George Seaton)

A 'happy virus' is carried into New York by a
toucan, and affects the lives of various people.
Flimsy pretext for a comedy, further hampered
by a less than sparkling script. The actors have
their moments.

w George Seaton, Robert Pirosh   *d* George
Seaton   *ph* Ernesto Caparros   *m* Frank de Vol

George Peppard, Mary Tyler Moore, Dom De
Luise, John McMartin, Susan St James, Don
Stroud, Charles Lane

What's the Matter with Helen?*
US 1971   101m   De Luxe
Filmways / Raymax (George Edwards, James
C. Pratt)

In 1934 Hollywood, two women run a dancing
school for child stars; one of them is a killer.
More *Baby Jane* melodramatics, quite lively and
with interesting period detail.

w Henry Farrell   *d* Curtis Harrington   *ph* Lucien
Ballard   *m* David Raksin   *pd* Eugene Lourié

Debbie Reynolds, Shelley Winters, Micheal
MacLiammoir, Dennis Weaver, Agnes
Moorehead

  'A cast of seasoned troupers cannot quite alter
the impression that they are all working to revive
a stiff.'—*Bruce Williamson*

What's Up, Doc?**
US 1972   94m   Technicolor
Warner / Saticoy (Peter Bogdanovich)

In San Francisco, an absent-minded young
musicologist is troubled by the attentions of a

dotty girl who gets him involved with crooks and a series of accidents.

Madcap comedy, a pastiche of several thirties originals. Spectacular slapstick and willing players are somewhat let down by exhausted patches and a tame final reel.

w Buck Henry, David Newman, Robert Benton d Peter Bogdanovich ph Laszlo Kovacs m Artie Butler pd Polly Pratt

Barbra Streisand, Ryan O'Neal, Kenneth Mars, Austin Pendleton, Madeleine Kahn, Mabel Albertson, Sorrell Booke

'A comedy made by a man who has seen a lot of movies, knows all the mechanics, and has absolutely no sense of humour. Seeing it is like shaking hands with a joker holding a joy buzzer: the effect is both presumptuous and unpleasant.'—Jay Cocks

'It's all rather like a 19th-century imitation of Elizabethan blank verse drama.'—Stanley Kauffmann

'It freely borrows from the best screen comedy down the ages but has no discernible style of its own.'—Michael Billington, Illustrated London News

The Wheeler Dealers
US 1963 106m Metrocolor Panavision
MGM / Filmways
GB title: Separate Beds

A Texas tycoon with a flair for the stock market sets Wall Street agog by manipulating a mysterious and non-existent new product.
Fun for financiers, but barely worth following for the rest. A slick, loud, hollow show.

w G. J. W. Goodman, Ira Wallach d Arthur Hiller ph Charles Lang Jnr m Frank de Vol

James Garner, Lee Remick, Phil Harris, Chill Wills, Jim Backus, Louis Nye, John Astin

When Dinosaurs Ruled the Earth
GB 1969 100m Technicolor
Hammer (Aida Young)

In prehistoric times, a girl is swept out to sea by a cyclone and adopted by a dinosaur.
Sequel to One Million Years BC, all very silly but tolerably well done.

wd Val Guest ph Dick Bush m Mario Nascimbene sp Jim Danforth

Victoria Vetri, Patrick Allen, Robin Hawdon, Patrick Holt, Imogen Hassall

When Eight Bells Toll*
GB 1971 94m Eastmancolor
Panavision
Winkast (Elliott Kastner)

A naval secret service agent investigates the pirating of gold bullion ships off the Scottish coast.
Acceptable kill-happy thriller: humourless James Bondery graced by splendid Scottish landscapes.

w Alistair MacLean, from his novel d Etienne Perier ph Arthur Ibbetson m Wally Stott

Anthony Hopkins, Robert Morley, Corin Redgrave, Jack Hawkins, Ferdy Mayne, Derek Bond, Nathalie Delon

When I Grow Up*
US 1951 90m bw
Horizon (S. P. Eagle)

A boy about to run away changes his mind after reading his grandfather's diaries.
Pleasant, sentimental family film with an unusual approach.

wd Michael Kanin ph Ernest Laszlo m Jerome Moross

Bobby Driscoll, Robert Preston, Charley Grapewin, Martha Scott, Ralph Dumke

When in Rome
US 1952 78m bw
MGM (Clarence Brown)

A gangster in Rome steals a priest's clothes and is accepted in his place.
Typically American religious comedy, nicely made but straying somewhat over the top when the gangster reforms and becomes a monk.

w Charles Schnee, Dorothy Kingsley, Robert Buckner d Clarence Brown ph William Daniels m Carmen Dragon

Van Johnson, Paul Douglas, Joseph Calleia, Carlo Rizzo, Tudor Owen, Aldo Silvani, Dono Nardi

When Ladies Meet*
US 1933 73m bw
RKO

A successful lady novelist falls in love with her married publisher.
Smartish comedy of manners which still has a sting.

w John Meehan, Leon Gordon, play Rachel Crothers d Harry Beaumont ph Ray June

Ann Harding, Robert Montgomery, Myrna Loy, Alice Brady, Frank Morgan, Margaret Burton, Luis Alberni

When Ladies Meet
US 1941 108m bw
MGM (Robert Z. Leonard, Orville O. Dull)

Over-produced and very talkative remake of the above.

w S. K. Lauren, Anita Loos d Robert Z. Leonard ph Robert Planck m Bronislau Kaper

Joan Crawford, Robert Taylor, Greer Garson, Spring Byington, Herbert Marshall, Rafael Strom, Olaf Hytten

When My Baby Smiles at Me
US 1948 98m Technicolor
TCF (George Jessel)

A vaudevillian goes on the skids but is saved by his wife.
Routine musical handling of a dreary drama previously filmed as *Dance of Life* (1929) and *Swing High Swing Low* (qv).

w Lamar Trotti, *play* Burlesque by George Manker Walters, Arthur Hopkins d Walter Lang ph Harry Jackson md Alfred Newman

Betty Grable, Dan Dailey, Jack Oakie, June Havoc, Richard Arlen, James Gleason, Jean Wallace

AAN: Alfred Newman; Dan Dailey

When Strangers Marry*
US 1944 67m bw
Monogram
aka: *Betrayed*

A young bride in New York discovers that she may have married a murderer.
Much-praised second feature: a bit stodgy now, but still entertaining.

w Philip Yordan, Dennis Cooper d William Castle ph Ira Morgan m Dmitri Tiomkin

Dean Jagger, Kim Hunter, Robert Mitchum, Neil Hamilton, Lou Lubin, Milt Kibbee, Dewey Robinson

'The obviousness of the low budget is completely overcome by the solid craftsmanship of the direction, script, music, editing and performances.'—*Don Miller*

When the Daltons Rode*
US 1940 80m bw
Universal

Adventures of the Dalton Gang.
Good standard western with whitewashed bad men for heroes. .

d George Marshall m Frank Skinner

Randolph Scott, Kay Francis, Brian Donlevy, Andy Devine, George Bancroft, Stuart Erwin

When the Legends Die*
US 1972 105m De Luxe
Sagoponack (Stuart Millar)

A young Indian boy, frustrated by life on the reservations, is helped by an old rodeo rider who becomes his guardian.
Dour modern western, rather stylishly done and an eloquent plea for freedom, but dramatically uncompelling.

w Robert Dozier, *novel* Hal Borland d Stuart Millar ph Richard Kline m Glenn Paxton

Richard Widmark, Frederic Forrest, Luana Anders, Vito Scotti

When Tomorrow Comes**
US 1939 82m bw
Universal (John M. Stahl)

A waitress falls for a concert pianist with a mad wife.
Fascinating star romantic drama, a successful follow-up to *Love Affair*; full of clichés, but impeccably set and acted. The stuff that Hollywood dreams were made of.

w Dwight Taylor, *story* James M. Cain d John M. Stahl ph John Mescall

Charles Boyer, Irene Dunne, Barbara O'Neil, Nydia Westman, Onslow Stevens
† The same story was remade twice in 1956, as *Serenade* and *Interlude*, and in 1968 as *Interlude* (all qv).

When We Are Married**
GB 1942 98m bw
British National (John Baxter)

In 1890s Yorkshire, three couples celebrating their silver wedding are told they were never legally married.
A very funny play smartly filmed with a superb cast of character actors.

w Austin Melford, Barbara K. Emery, *play J. B. Priestley* d Herbert Mason

Raymond Huntley, Marian Spencer, Lloyd Pearson, Olga Lindo, Ernest Butcher, Ethel Coleridge, Sydney Howard, Barry Morse, Lesley Brook, Marjorie Rhodes, Charles Victor, Cyril Smith, George Carney

When Willie Comes Marching Home*
US 1949 82m bw
TCF (Fred Kohlmar)

During World War II, events suddenly transform a small-town air training instructor into a war hero.
Awkwardly paced comedy which could have been much funnier but does amuse in fits and starts.

w Mary Loos, Richard Sale d John Ford ph Leo Tover m Alfred Newman

Dan Dailey, Colleen Townshend, Corinne

Calvet, William Demarest, Evelyn Varden, James Lydon, Mae Marsh, Lloyd Corrigan

AAN: original story (Sy Gomberg)

When Worlds Collide
US 1951   82m   Technicolor
Paramount (George Pal)

Another planet is found to be rushing inevitably towards earth, but before the collision a few people escape in a space ship.
Stolid science fiction with a spectacular but not marvellous climax following seventy minutes of inept talk.

w Sidney Boehm, *novel* Philip Wylie, Edwin Balmer d Rudolph Maté ph John Seitz, W. Howard Greene m Leith Stevens

Richard Derr, Barbara Rush, Larry Keating, Peter Hanson, John Hoyt

AAN: John Seitz, W. Howard Greene

When You're in Love *
US 1937   110m   bw
Columbia (Everett Riskin)
GB title: *For You Alone*

A European opera singer takes on a husband in order to get into the United States.
Pleasing musical star vehicle with comedy touches.

wd Robert Riskin ph Joseph Walker md Alfred Newman

Grace Moore, Cary Grant, Aline MacMahon, Henry Stephenson, Thomas Mitchell, Catherine Doucet, Luis Alberni, Emma Dunn

Where Angels Go, Trouble Follows
US 1968   95m   Eastmancolor
Columbia / William Frye

Nuns from a convent school take pupils to a California youth rally, and learn a thing or two.
Peripatetic comedy, rather frantically assembled; a sequel to *The Trouble with Angels.*

w Blanche Hanalis d James Neilson ph Sam Leavitt m Lalo Schifrin

Rosalind Russell, Stella Stevens, Binnie Barnes, Mary Wickes, Milton Berle, Arthur Godfrey, Robert Taylor, Van Johnson, Susan St James

Where Danger Lives
US 1950   84m   bw
RKO (Irving Cummings Jnr)

A doctor falls in love with a murderous patient and is drawn into her schemes.
Standard *film noir* of its time, competent enough in its depressing way.

w Charles Bennett d John Farrow ph Nicholas Musuraca m Roy Webb

Faith Domergue, Robert Mitchum, Claude Rains, Maureen O'Sullivan, Charles Kemper

Where Do We Go from Here? *
US 1945   77m   Technicolor
TCF (William Perlberg)

A writer stumbles on a genie who takes him through periods of American history, including a voyage with Christopher Columbus.
Well-staged and rather funny charade with at least one memorable song.

w Morrie Ryskind d Gregory Ratoff ph Leon Shamroy *songs* Kurt Weill, Ira Gershwin

Fred MacMurray, June Haver, Joan Leslie, Gene Sheldon, Anthony Quinn, Carlos Ramirez, Fortunio Bonanova, Alan Mowbray, Herman Bing, Otto Preminger
'Nine parts heavy facetiousness to one part very good fun.'—*James Agee*

Where Does it Hurt?
US 1971   88m   colour
Josef Shaftel (Rod Amateau, William Schwarz)

Adventures of a profiteering hospital adminstrator.
Dislikeable, plodding smut in the form of black comedy.

wd Rod Amateau, *novel* The Operator by Budd Robinson, Rod Amateau ph Brick Marquard m Keith Allison

Peter Sellers, Jo Ann Pflug, Rick Lenz, Eve Druce

Where Eagles Dare **
GB 1969   155m   Metrocolor   Panavision 70
MGM / Winkfast (Elliott Kastner)

During World War II, seven British paratroopers land in the Bavarian Alps to rescue a high-ranking officer from an impregnable castle.
Archetypal schoolboy adventure, rather unattractively photographed but containing a sufficient variety of excitements.

w Alistair MacLean, from his novel d Brian G. Hutton ph Arthur Ibbetson, H. A. R. Thompson m Ron Goodwin

Richard Burton, Clint Eastwood, Mary Ure, Patrick Wymark, Michael Hordern, Donald Houston, Peter Barkworth, Robert Beatty

Where It's At
US 1969　106m　De Luxe
UA / Frank Ross

The owner of a Las Vegas gambling hotel tries to make his son take an interest in the business. Flaccid comedy drama which belies its credits.

wd Garson Kanin *ph* Burnett Guffey *m* Benny Olsen

David Janssen, Rosemary Forsyth, Robert Drivas, Brenda Vaccaro

Where Love Has Gone*
US 1964　114m　Techniscope
Paramount / Embassy (Joseph E. Levine)

A middle-aged man is appalled to hear that his teenage daughter has killed her mother's lover. Squalid, glossy pulp fiction lightly based on the Lana Turner case, distinguished only by the game performances of its leading ladies.

w John Michael Hayes, *novel* Harold Robbins *d* Edward Dmytryk *ph* Joe MacDonald *m* Walter Scharf

Susan Hayward, Bette Davis, Mike Connors, Joey Heatherton, Jane Greer, George Macready
　'A typical Robbins pastiche of newspaper clippings liberally shellacked with sentiment and glued with sex.'——*Newsweek*

AAN: title song (*m* James Van Heusen, *ly* Sammy Cahn)

Where No Vultures Fly*
GB 1951　107m　Technicolor
Ealing (Leslie Norman)
US title: *Ivory Hunter*

Adventures of an East African game warden. Pleasantly improving family film, nicely shot on location; a sequel, *West of Zanzibar*, was less impressive.

w W. P. Lipscomb, Ralph Smart, Leslie Norman *d* Harry Watt *ph* Geoffrey Unsworth *m* Alan Rawsthorne

Anthony Steele, Dinah Sheridan, Harold Warrender, Meredith Edwards
　'These expeditionary films are really journalistic jobs. You get sent out to a country by the studio, stay as long as you can without getting fired, and a story generally crops up.'—*Harry Watt*

Where the Boys Are
US 1960　99m　Metrocolor
　Cinemascope
MGM / Euterpe (Joe Pasternak)

Four college girls spend the Easter vacation near a Florida military post in search of conquests.

Mindless, frothy youth musical, quite smoothly done.

w George Wells, *novel* Glendon Swarthout *d* Henry Levin *ph* Robert Bronner *m* George Stoll

George Hamilton, Dolores Hart, Paula Prentiss, Jim Hutton, Yvette Mimieux, Connie Francis, Frank Gorshin, Chill Wills, Barbara Nichols

Where the Sidewalk Ends
US 1950　95m　bw
TCF (Otto Preminger)

A tough policeman accidentally kills a suspect and tries to implicate a gang leader. Gloomy *policier* with curious moral values.

w Rex Connor (Ben Hecht), *novel* William L. Stuart *d* Otto Preminger *ph* Joseph La Shelle *m* Cyril Mockridge

Dana Andrews, Gene Tierney, Gary Merrill, Bert Freed, Tom Tully, Karl Malden, Ruth Donnelly, Craig Stevens, Robert Simon

Where There's a Will*
GB 1936　81m　bw
Gainsborough (Edward Black, Sidney Gilliat)

A seedy education expert sponges on his rich relations but redeems himself by rounding up gangsters at a Christmas party.
Rather slapdash star comedy with very good scenes along the way.

w Will Hay, Robert Edmunds, Ralph Spence *d* William Beaudine *ph* Charles Van Enger *md* Louis Levy

Will Hay, Hartley Power, Gibb McLaughlin, Graham Moffatt, Norma Varden, Gina Malo

Where There's Life
US 1947　75m　bw
Paramount

A timid New Yorker turns out to be heir to the throne of a Ruritanian country, and is harassed by spies of both sides.
　Mild star comedy with slow patches.

w Allen Boretz, Melville Shavelson *d* Sidney Lanfield *ph* Charles Lang Jnr

Bob Hope, Signe Hasso, William Bendix, George Coulouris

Where Were You When the Lights Went Out?*
US 1966　94m　Metrocolor　Panavision
MGM (Everett Freeman, Martin Melcher)

New York's famous electrical blackout in 1965 has its effect on the life of a musical comedy star. Cheerful sex farce with intriguing beginnings; the later confinement to one set is just a bit harmful.

w Everett Freeman, Karl Tunberg, *play* Claude Magnier *d* Hy Averback *ph* Ellsworth Fredericks *m* Dave Grusin

Doris Day, Terry-Thomas, Patrick O'Neal, Robert Morse, Lola Albright, Jim Backus, Ben Blue

Where's Charley?*
GB 1952 97m Technicolor
Warner

An Oxford undergraduate impersonates the rich aunt of his best friend.
Slow and rather stately musical version of the famous farce *Charley's Aunt*, unsatisfactorily shot on a mixture of poor sets and sunlit Oxford locations; worth cherishing for the ebullient performance of its over-age star.

w John Monks Jnr, *play* Brandon Thomas (via stage musical, *book* George Abbott *m* Frank Loesser) *d* David Butler *ph* Erwin Hillier *ch* Michael Kidd

Ray Bolger, Robert Shackleton, Mary Germaine, Allyn McLerie, Margaretta Scott, Horace Cooper

Where's Jack?*
GB 1968 119m Eastmancolor
Paramount / Oakhurst (Stanley Baker)

In 18th-century London Jack Sheppard becomes a romantic highwayman at the behest of underworld leader Jonathan Wild.
Deliberately unromantic, squalid and 'realistic' period piece which takes no hold on the fancy despite the considerable care which was obviously taken in all departments.

w Rafe and David Newhouse *d* James Clavell *ph John Wilcox m* Elmer Bernstein *pd Cedric Dawe*

Tommy Steele, Stanley Baker, Fiona Lewis, Alan Badel, Dudley Foster, Sue Lloyd, Noel Purcell

Where's Poppa?*
US 1970 82m De Luxe
Jerry Tokovsky / Martin Worth

A Jewish lawyer's aged mother constantly harms his love life, and he considers various means of getting rid of her.
Much-censored black comedy which might have been funnier in a complete form. Even so, it has its moments.

w Robert Klane, from his novel *d* Carl Reiner *ph* Jack Priestly *m* Jack Elliott

George Segal, Ruth Gordon, Trish Van Devere, Ron Leibman

Where's That Fire?*
GB 1939 73m bw
TCF (Edward Black)

An incompetent village fire brigade accidentally saves the crown jewels from thieves.
Routine but not despicable star comedy, long thought lost; flat patches are well separated by hilarious sequences.

w Marriott Edgar, Val Guest, J. O. C. Orton *d* Marcel Varnel

Will Hay, Moore Marriott, Graham Moffatt, Peter Gawthorne, Eric Clavering, Charles Hawtrey

W.H.I.F.F.S.
US 1975 92m Technicolor Panavision
Brut (C. O. Erickson)
GB title: *C.A.S.H.*

An impotent army veteran finds that a criminal career, helped by stolen army gas, helps his sex life.
Over-the-top comedy with vaguely anti-war and anti-pollution leanings.

w Malcolm Marmorstein *d* Ted Post *ph* David M. Walsh *m* John Cameron

Elliott Gould, Eddie Albert, Harry Guardino, Godfrey Cambridge, Jennifer O'Neill
† Rather typical of the film was its ambiguous catch line: 'The biggest bang in history!'

While I Live
GB 1947 85m bw
Edward Dryhurst

Reissue title: *The Dream of Olwen.*
A Cornishwoman believes an amnesiac girl to be the reincarnation of her dead sister.
Silly melodrama which achieved phenomenal popularity, despite poor production, because of its haunting theme tune *The Dream of Olwen* by Charles Williams.

w John Harlow, Doreen Montgomery, *play* This Same Garden by Robert Bell *d* John Harlow

Tom Walls, Sonia Dresdel, Carol Raye, Clifford Evans, Patricia Burke, John Warwick, Edward Lexy

While the City Sleeps
US 1956 100m bw
RKO (Bert Friedlob)

Three chief executives of a newspaper empire are pitted against each other in a search for a murder scoop.
Star-packed but leaden-paced news bureau melodrama; a major disappointment considering the talent.

w Casey Robinson, *novel* The Bloody Spur by

Charles Einstein *d* Fritz Lang *ph* Ernest
Laszlo *m* Herschel Burke Gilbert

Dana Andrews, George Sanders, Ida Lupino,
Sally Forrest, Thomas Mitchell, Rhonda
Fleming, Vincent Price, Howard Duff, James
Craig, Robert Warwick, John Barrymore Jnr

The Whip Hand
US 1951   82m   bw
RKO (Lewis J. Rachmil)

A fisherman finds himself unwelcome in a lonely
town run by ex-Nazi, now communist,
bacteriologists.
Preposterous, pretentious anti-communist low-
budgeter, mildly enjoyable for its sheer gall.

w George Bricker, Frank L. Moss *d/pd* William
Cameron Menzies *ph* Nicholas Musuraca
m Paul Sawtell

Elliott Reid, Carla Balenda, Edgar Barrier,
Raymond Burr

Whiplash
US 1948   90m   bw
Warner (William Jacobs)

A painter becomes a prizefighter.
Hokey, unpersuasive romantic melodrama.

w Maurice Geraghty, Harriet Frank Jnr
d Lewis Seiler *ph* Peverell Marley *m* Franz
Waxman

Dane Clark, Alexis Smith, Zachary Scott, Eve
Arden, Jeffrey Lynn, S. Z. Sakall, Alan Hale,
Douglas Kennedy

Whipsaw*
US 1935   88m   bw
MGM (Harry Rapf)

A G-man infiltrates a gang by wooing its girl
member.
Fairly snappy romantic drama which further
established both its stars.

w Howard Emmett Rogers *d* Sam Wood
m William Axt

Spencer Tracy, Myrna Loy, Harvey Stephens,
Clay Clements, William Harrigan

Whirlpool*
US 1950   98m   bw
TCF (Otto Preminger)

A girl is accused of a murder committed by her
hypnotist, who has willed himself out of a
hospital bed.
Silly murder melodrama; glossy production
makes it entertaining.

w Lester Barstow, Andrew Solt, *novel* Guy
Endore *d* Otto Preminger *ph* Arthur Miller
m David Raksin

Gene Tierney, *Jose Ferrer*, Richard Conte,
Charles Bickford, Barbara O'Neil, Eduard
Franz, Fortunio Bonanova

'It is sometimes difficult to discover from Miss
Tierney's playing whether she is or is not under
hypnosis.'—*MFB*

Whirlpool
GB 1959   95m   Eastmancolor
Rank (George Pitcher)

A killer escapes in Cologne; his girl friend
separates from him and gets a lift down the
Rhine in a barge; the trip reforms her and she
betrays her lover.
Modestly attractive travelogue with the burden
of a very boring melodrama.

w Lawrence P. Bachmann *d* Lewis Allen
ph Geoffrey Unsworth *m* Ron Goodwin

Juliette Greco, O. W. Fischer, William Sylvester,
Marius Goring, Muriel Pavlow

Whisky Galore****
GB 1948   82m   bw
Ealing
US title: *Tight Little Island*

During World War II, a ship full of whisky is
wrecked on a small Hebridean island, and the
local customs and excise man has his hands full.
Marvellously detailed, fast-moving, well-played
and attractively photographed comedy which
firmly established the richest Ealing vein.

*w Compton Mackenzie, Angus Macphail,
novel* Compton Mackenzie *d Alexander
Mackendrick ph* Gerald Gibbs *m Ernest Irving*

Basil Radford, Joan Greenwood, Jean Cadell,
Gordon Jackson, James Robertson Justice,
Wylie Watson, John Gregson, Morland
Graham, Duncan Macrae, Catherine Lacey,
Bruce Seton, Henry Mollinson, Compton
Mackenzie, A. E. Matthews

The Whisperers*
GB 1966   106m   bw
UA / Seven Pines (Michael S. Laughlin,
   Ronald Shedlo)

An old lady hears voices and is put upon by her
son, her wandering husband, and various others.
Interesting but cold and finally unsatisfactory
character melodrama; even the acting, though in
a sense admirable, is too genteel.

w Bryan Forbes, *novel* Robert Nicolson
d Bryan Forbes *ph* Gerry Turpin *m* John Barry

Edith Evans, Eric Portman, Avis Bunnage,
Nanette Newman, Gerald Sim, Ronald Fraser

Whispering Smith*
US 1948   88m   Technicolor
Paramount (Mel Epstein)

A government agent investigating robberies
finds his friend is implicated.
Fairly entertaining detective western.

w Frank Butler, Karl Lamb, *novel* Frank H.
Spearman *d* Leslie Fenton *ph* Ray Rennahan
m Adolph Deutsch

Alan Ladd, Robert Preston, Brenda Marshall,
Donald Crisp, William Demarest, Fay Holden,
Murvyn Vye, Frank Faylen

The Whistle at Eaton Falls*
US 1951   96m   bw
Columbia (Louis de Rochemont)
GB title: *Richer than the Earth*

The story of a strike at a small-town plastics
factory.
Reasonably absorbing semi-documentary with a
final 'solution' which rather evades the issues.

w Lemist Esler, Virginia Shaler *d* Robert
Siodmak *ph* Joseph Brun *m* Louis Applebaum

Lloyd Bridges, Dorothy Gish, Carleton
Carpenter, Murray Hamilton, James
Westerfield, Lenore Lonergan

Whistle Down the Wind*
GB 1961   99m   bw
Rank / Allied Film Makers / Beaver (Richard
   Attenborough)

Three north country children think a murderer
on the run is Jesus Christ.
Charming allegorical study of childhood
innocence, extremely well made, amusing, and
avoiding sentimentality.

w *Keith Waterhouse, Willis Hall, novel* Mary
Hayley Bell *d Bryan Forbes ph* Arthur
Ibbetson *m* Malcolm Arnold

Hayley Mills, Bernard Lee, Alan Bates, Norman
Bird, Elsie Wagstaff, Alan Barnes

The Whistler

Originally a radio series of suspense stories
introduced by someone whistling the theme tune,
this was turned into a fairly workmanlike series
of second features quite unrelated to each other
except for the leading actor, Richard Dix, who
alternated as hero and villain, and William
Castle, who directed or produced most of them.

1944: THE WHISTLER, THE MARK OF
THE WHISTLER
1945: THE POWER OF THE WHISTLER
1946: THE VOICE OF THE WHISTLER
1947: MYSTERIOUS INTRUDER, THE

SECRET OF THE WHISTLER, THE 12th
HOUR
1948: THE RETURN OF THE WHISTLER

Whistling in the Dark*
US 1941   77m   bw
MGM (George Haight)

A radio detective is kidnapped by a criminal who
wants him to devise a perfect murder which will
then be pinned on him.
Scatty comedy-thriller which, though it now
seems slow to start, was popular enough to
warrant two sequels (*Whistling in Brooklyn,
Whistling in Dixie*).

w Robert McGonigle, Harry Clark, Albert
Mannheimer, *play* Laurence Gross, Edward
Childs Carpenter *d* S. Sylvan Simon *ph* Sidney
Wagner

Red Skelton, Conrad Veidt, Ann Rutherford,
Virginia Grey, Eve Arden, Rags Ragland, Don
Douglas, Lloyd Corrigan
† The play was previously filmed in 1933 with
Ernest Truex, and this version is now shown on
TV as *Scared*.

The White Angel*
US 1935   91m   bw
Warner (Henry Blanke)

The life of Florence Nightingale.
Starchy biopic; the Victorian atmosphere is
never quite caught.

w Mordaunt Shairp, Michael Jacoby *d* William
Dieterle *ph* Tony Gaudio

Kay Francis, Ian Hunter, Donald Woods, Nigel
Bruce, Donald Crisp, Henry O'Neill, Billy
Mauch, Halliwell Hobbes

White Banners*
US 1938   88m   bw
Warner (Henry Blanke)

A social worker tries to solve the problems of a
troubled family.
Moderate middle-class drama.

w Lenore Coffee, Cameron Rogers, Abem
Finkel *d* Edmund Goulding *ph* Charles Rosher
m Max Steiner

Fay Bainter, Claude Rains, Jackie Cooper,
Bonita Granville, Henry O'Neill, James
Stephenson, Kay Johnson

AAN: Fay Bainter

The White Buffalo
US 1977   97m   Technicolor
Dino de Laurentiis (Pancho Kohner)

Wild Bill Hickok and Chief Crazy Horse join
forces to kill a marauding white buffalo.

Ridiculous symbolic western, not helped by the very artificial looking beast of the title.

w Richard Sale, from his novel d J. Lee Thompson ph Paul Lohmann m John Barry

Charles Bronson, Jack Warden, Will Sampson, Kim Novak, Clint Walker, Stuart Whitman, John Carradine, Slim Pickens, Cara Williams, Douglas Fowley

'The dried husk of a *Moby Dick* allegory seems to be rattling around here amidst all the other dead wood.'—*Jonathan Rosenbaum, MFB*

White Cargo*
US 1942 90m bw
MGM (Victor Saville)

White rubber planters are driven mad with desire for a scheming native girl.
Antediluvian melodrama previously filmed in 1930. Good for laughing at, and the star looked great as Tondelayo.

w Leon Gordon, from his play and *novel* Hell's Playground by Vera Simonton d Richard Thorpe m Bronislau Kaper

Hedy Lamarr, Walter Pidgeon, Richard Carlson, Frank Morgan, Bramwell Fletcher, Richard Ainley, Reginald Owen

White Christmas*
US 1954 120m Technicolor Vistavision
Paramount (Robert Emmett Dolan)

Two entertainers boost the popularity of a winter resort run by an old army buddy.
Humdrum musical lifted only by its stars; a revamp of *Holiday Inn*, which was much better.

w Norman Krasna, Norman Panama, Melvin Frank d Michael Curtiz ph Loyal Griggs *songs* Irving Berlin

Bing Crosby, Danny Kaye, Rosemary Clooney, Vera-Ellen, Dean Jagger, Mary Wickes, Sig Rumann, Grady Sutton

AAN: 'Count Your Blessings Instead of Sheep'

The White Cliffs of Dover*
US 1944 126m bw
MGM (Sidney Franklin)

An American girl who marries into the British aristocracy loses a husband in World War I and a son in World War II.
Tearful flagwaver with some entertaining scenes in the first half and the general sense of an all-stops-out production.

w Claudine West, Jan Lustig, George Froeschel, *poem* Alice Duer Miller d Clarence Brown ph George Folsey m Herbert Stothart

Irene Dunne, Alan Marshal, Frank Morgan,
May Whitty, Roddy McDowall, C. Aubrey Smith, Gladys Cooper, Peter Lawford, Van Johnson

'A long, earnest, well-intentioned, over-emotionalized cliché.'—*Richard Mallett, Punch*

AAN: George Folsey

White Corridors*
GB 1951 102m bw
GFD / Vic (Joseph Janni, John Croydon)

Life in a small Midlands hospital.
Competent multi-drama which found a big audience.

w Jan Read, Pat Jackson, *novel* Yeoman's Hospital by Helen Ashton d Pat Jackson ph C. Pennington-Richards

James Donald, Googie Withers, Godfrey Tearle, Petula Clark, Jack Watling, Moira Lister, Barry Jones, Megs Jenkins, Basil Radford

'This quality of professionalism is comparatively rare in British films.'—*Gavin Lambert*

The White Dawn
US 1976 110m Movielab
Paramount / American Film Properties (Martin Ransohoff)

In 1900, survivors from a whaling ship are cared 'or by Eskimos, who turn on them when nature proves unkind.
Unpleasant fable with lots of bitter weather and subtitled Eskimos. Scarcely an entertainment, and its message is mumbled.

w James Houston, Tom Rickman d Philip Kaufman ph Michael Chapman m Henry Mancini

Warren Oates, Timothy Bottoms, Lou Gossett, Eskimo cast

White Feather*
US 1955 100m Technicolor Cinemascope
TCF / Panoramic (Robert L. Jacks)

A cavalry colonel tries to hold back gold prospectors until the Cheyenne have moved on to their new reservations.
Old-fashioned cowboys and (sympathetic) Indians, very efficiently done.

w Delmer Daves, Leo Townsend d Robert Webb ph Lucien Ballard m Hugo Friedhofer

Robert Wagner, John Lund, Jeffrey Hunter, Debra Paget, Eduard Franz, Noah Beery Jnr, Hugh O'Brian, Virginia Leith, Emile Meyer

White Heat***
US 1949 114m bw
Warner (Louis F. Edelman)

A violent, mother-fixated gangster gets his comeuppance when a government agent is infiltrated into his gang.

This searing melodrama reintroduced the old Cagney and then some: spellbinding suspense sequences complemented his vivid and hypnotic portrayal.

w Ivan Goff, Ben Roberts, *story* Virginia Kellogg d Raoul Walsh ph Sid Hickox m Max Steiner

James Cagney, Edmond O'Brien, *Margaret Wycherly*, Virginia Mayo, Steve Cochran, John Archer

'The most gruesome aggregation of brutalities ever presented under the guise of entertainment.'—*Cue*

'In the hurtling tabloid traditions of the gangster movies of the thirties, but its matter-of-fact violence is a new post-war style.'—*Time*

AAN: Virginia Kellogg

White Savage
US 1943 75m Technicolor
Universal (George Waggner)
GB title: *White Captive*

The queen of beautiful South Sea island has trouble with shark hunters and crooks after her mineral deposits.

Self-admitted hokum strung loosely and colourfully around its star: big box office in the middle of the war.

w Richard Brooks d Arthur Lubin ph Lester White, William Snyder m Frank Skinner

Maria Montez, Jon Hall, Sabu, Thomas Gomez, Sidney Toler, Paul Guilfoyle, Turhan Bey, Don Terry

White Shadows in the South Seas*
US 1927 88m (sound version) bw
MGM

An alcoholic doctor in Tahiti finds happiness with a native girl until he is killed by white colonials.

Rather boring melodrama illuminated by superb photography.

w Ray Doyle, Jack Cunningham, *book* Frederick J. O'Brien d W. S. Van Dyke (and Robert Flaherty) ph Clyde de Vinna and others (including Flaherty)

Monte Blue, Raquel Torres

AA: Clyde de Vinna

The White Sister
US 1933 110m bw
MGM

When her lover is reported killed in the war, an Italian noblewoman takes the veil . . . but he comes back.

Tiresome romantic drama from another age, a big prestige production of its time.

w Donald Ogden Stewart, *novel* F. Marion Crawford, Walter Hackett d Victor Fleming ph William Daniels m Herbert Stothart

Helen Hayes, Clark Gable, Lewis Stone, Louise Closser Hale, May Robson, Edward Arnold

The White Tower
US 1950 98m Technicolor
RKO (Sid Rogell)

Various people have personal reasons for climbing an Alpine mountain.

Pretentiously symbolic melodrama with some good action sequences and curiously stilted performances.

w Paul Jarrico, *novel* James Ramsay Ullman d Ted Tetzlaff ph Ray Rennahan m Roy Webb

Glenn Ford, Claude Rains, Alida Valli, Oscar Homolka, Cedric Hardwicke, Lloyd Bridges, June Clayworth

'The main interest is a curiosity as to who will fall over which precipice when.'—*Penelope Houston*

The White Unicorn
GB 1947 97m bw
GFD / John Corfield (Harold Huth)
US title: *Bad Sister*

In a home for delinquent girls, the worst offender exchanges reminiscences with the warden.

Peg's Paper melodrama in complex flashback form.

w Robert Westerby, A. R. Rawlinson, Moie Charles, *novel* Flora Sandstrom d Bernard Knowles ph Reg Wyer m Bretton Byrd

Margaret Lockwood, Joan Greenwood, Ian Hunter, Dennis Price, Guy Middleton, Catherine Lacey, Mabel Constanduros, Paul Dupuis

White Witch Doctor
US 1953 96m Technicolor
TCF (Otto Lang)

A nurse in the Congo converts a gold-seeking adventurer.

Stale hokum in which the animals are the most interesting feature.

w Ivan Goff, Ben Roberts, *novel* Louise A. Stinetorf *d* Henry Hathaway *ph* Leon Shamroy *m* Bernard Herrmann

Susan Hayward, Robert Mitchum, Walter Slezak, Timothy Carey

White Woman
US 1933   68m   bw
Paramount

A cockney overseer in the Malaysian jungle takes back a cabaret singer as his bride.
Risible melodrama with an obvious outcome.

w Norman Reilly Raine, Frank Butler *d* Stuart Walker *ph* Harry Fischbeck

Charles Laughton, Carole Lombard, Kent Taylor, Charles Bickford, Percy Kilbride, Charles Middleton, James Bell
† Remade as *Island of Lost Men*.

White Zombie**
US 1932   74m   bw
Halperin

Haitian zombies work a sugar mill for a white schemer.
Genuinely eerie horror film with a slow, stagey, out-of-this world quality coupled with an interesting sense of composition.

w Garnett Weston *d* Victor Halperin *ph* Arthur Martinelli

Bela Lugosi, Madge Bellamy, John Harron, Joseph Cawthorn

'A Gothic fairy tale filled with dreamlike imagery, traditional symbols, echoes of Romanticism, and (probably unintentional) psychosexual overtones.'—*Carlos Clarens*

'For those absolutely dedicated to gothic silliness.'—*New Yorker, 1977*

Who Done It?
US 1942   77m   bw
Universal (Alex Gottlieb)

Soda jerks in a New York radio station catch a murderer.
So-so comedy thriller, fatally lacking atmosphere (and good jokes).

w Stanley Roberts, Edmund Joseph, John Grant *d* Erle C. Kenton *ph* Charles Van Enger *m* Frank Skinner

Bud Abbott, Lou Costello, William Gargan, Louise Allbritton, Patric Knowles, Don Porter, Jerome Cowan, William Bendix, Mary Wickes, Thomas Gomez

Who Done It?
GB 1956   85m   bw
Ealing (Michael Relph, Basil Dearden)

An ice-rink sweeper sets up as a private eye and captures a ring of spies.
Lively but disappointing film debut for a star comic whose screen personality proved too bland.

w T. E. B. Clarke *d* Basil Dearden *ph* Otto Heller *m* Philip Green

Benny Hill, Belinda Lee, David Kossoff, Garry Marsh, Ernest Thesiger, Thorley Walters

Who Goes There?
GB 1952   85m   bw
British Lion / London Films (Anthony Kimmins)
US title: *The Passionate Sentry*

In a Grace and Favour house near St James' Palace, a guardsman is involved in a trail of romantic intrigue.
Very British romantic farce, dully and quickly filmed from a West End success.

w John Dighton, from his play *d* Anthony Kimmins *ph* John Wilcox, Ted Scaife *m* Muir Mathieson

Peggy Cummins, Valerie Hobson, George Cole, Nigel Patrick, A. E. Matthews, Anthony Bushell

Who Is Harry Kellerman and Why Is He Saying These Terrible Things About Me?
US 1971   108m   De Luxe
Cinema Center (Ulu Grosbard, Herb Gardner)

A New York composer is persecuted by a mysterious figure which turns out to be himself.
Wild, shapeless, satirical psycho-comedy-melodrama. Not very good.

w Herb Gardner *d* Ulu Grosbard *ph* Victor Kemper *pd* Harry Horner

Dustin Hoffman, Barbara Harris, Jack Warden, David Burns, Gabriel Dell, Dom De Luise

AAN: Barbara Harris

Who Is Killing the Great Chefs of Europe?*
US 1978   112m   Metrocolor
Warner / Aldrich / Lorimar (Merv Adelson, Lee Rich, William Aldrich)
GB title: *Too Many Chefs*

A fast food entrepreneur in London finds himself at the centre of a series of grisly murders.
Unusual and lighthearted black comedy against the background of international gastronomy.

w Peter Stone, *novel* Nan and Ivan Lyons *d* Ted Kotcheff *ph* John Alcott *m* Henry Mancini

George Segal, Jacqueline Bisset, *Robert Morley*, Jean-Pierre Cassel, Philippe Noiret, Jean Rochefort, Madge Ryan

Who Killed Mary What's Her Name?
US 1971   90m   De Luxe
Cannon (George Manasse)

An ex-boxer determines to solve the murder of a
prostitute.
Old-fashioned whodunnit with something to say
grafted on every five minutes: an unsatisfactory
mix.

w John O'Toole d Ernest Pintoff ph Greg
Sandor m Gary McFarland

Red Buttons, Alice Playten, Sylvia Miles, Sam
Waterston

Who Slew Auntie Roo?
GB 1972   91m   Movielab
AIP / Hemdale (John Pellatt)

A madwoman menaces two orphan children.
Pointless and slenderly plotted adaptation of
Hansel and Gretel, crude in all departments.

w Robert Blees, Jimmy Sangster d Curtis
Harrington ph Desmond Dickinson m Ken
Jones

Shelley Winters, Ralph Richardson, Mark
Lester, Lionel Jeffries, Chloe Franks, Hugh
Griffith, Rosalie Crutchley, Pat Heywood

'Not content with being a delicate fantasy of
childish nightmare, it tries to add a totally
inappropriate seasoning of Grand Guignol.'—
Tom Milne

Who Was That Lady?*
US 1960   115m   bw
Columbia / Ansark / George Sidney

A professor seen kissing a student persuades a
friend to tell his wife that they are both FBI
agents on duty. Foreign spies believe them . . .
Agreeably wacky comedy with a strained and
prolonged middle section leading to a totally
zany climax.

w Norman Krasna, from his play d George
Sidney ph Harry Stradling m André Previn

Tony Curtis, Dean Martin, Janet Leigh, James
Whitmore, John McIntire, Barbara Nichols,
Larry Keating

The Whole Town's Talking*
US 1935   86m   bw
Columbia (Lester Cowan)
GB title: *Passport to Fame*

A gangster finds it convenient occasionally to
pose as his double, a meek little clerk.
Pleasingly neat comedy, well staged and acted.

w Jo Swerling, Robert Riskin, *novel* W. R.
Burnett d John Ford ph Joseph August

Edward G. Robinson, Jean Arthur, Arthur Hohl,
Wallace Ford, Arthur Byron, Donald Meek,
Edward Brophy, Etienne Girardot

'A lively and satisfactory combination of farce
and melodrama.'—*Richard Watts Jnr*

The Whole Truth*
GB 1958   84m   bw
Columbia / Romulus (Jack Clayton)

A jealous husband poses as a detective in order
to murder his wife and incriminate a film
producer.
A filmed play, but quite a solidly carpentered
murder thriller with a couple of neat twists.

w Jonathan Latimer, *play* Philip Mackie d John
Guillermin ph Wilkie Cooper m Mischa
Spoliansky

Stewart Granger, George Sanders, Donna Reed,
Gianna Maria Canale

Who'll Stop the Rain?
US 1978   125m   colour
UA / Gabriel Katzka, Herb Jaffe
GB title: *Dog Soldiers*

A Vietnam veteran takes to smuggling heroin
into the US, but gets his wife and friend involved
with gangsters.
Heavy-going, downbeat character drama with
action sequences; well enough done, but the kind
of movie that does nothing for anybody.

w Judith Roscoe, *book* Dog Soldiers by Robert
Stone d Karel Reisz ph Richard H. Kline
m Laurence Rosenthal

Nick Nolte, Tuesday Weld, Michael Moriarty,
Anthony Zerbe, Richard Masur, David
Opatoshu, Roy Sharkey, Gail Strickland

Whoopee*
US 1930   94m   Technicolor
Samuel Goldwyn, Florenz Ziegfeld

A timid young man is catapulted into various
adventures.
Early sound musical from a popular Broadway
show, later remade as *Up in Arms* (qv).

w William Conselman, *musical play* William
Anthony McGuire, *play* The Nervous Wreck by
Owen Davis d Thornton Freeland ph Lee
Garmes, Ray Rennahan, Gregg Toland
ch Busby Berkeley

Eddie Cantor, Eleanor Hunt, Paul Gregory,
Jack Rutherford, Ethel Shutta

Who's Afraid of Virginia Woolf?***
US 1966   129m   bw
Warner (Ernest Lehman)

A college professor and his wife have an all-night
shouting match and embarrass their guests.

As a film of a play, fair to middling; as a
milestone in cinematic permissiveness, very
important; as an entertainment, sensational for
those in the mood.

w Ernest Lehman, *play Edward Albee* d Mike
Nichols ph Haskell Wexler m Alex North

*Richard Burton, Elizabeth Taylor, George
Segal, Sandy Dennis*

'A magnificent triumph of determined
audacity.'—*Bosley Crowther*

'One of the most scathingly honest American
films ever made.'—*Stanley Kauffmann*

AA: Haskell Wexler; Elizabeth Taylor; Sandy
Dennis
AAN: best picture; Ernest Lehman; Mike
Nichols; Alex North; Richard Burton; George
Segal

Who's Been Sleeping in My Bed?
US 1963   103m   Technicolor   Panavision
Paramount / Amro (Jack Rose)

A TV matinee idol finds he is a sex symbol also in
his private life.
Coy bedroom farce with no real action but a
smattering of jokes.

w Jack Rose d Daniel Mann ph Joseph
Ruttenberg m George Duning

Dean Martin, Elizabeth Montgomery, Martin
Balsam, Jill St John, Richard Conte, Carol
Burnett, Louis Nye, Yoko Tani, Elizabeth
Fraser

Who's Got the Action?
US 1962   93m   Technicolor   Panavision
Paramount / Amro (Jack Rose)

A bored wife and her law partner husband have
remarkable success betting on horses.
Badly cast and rather slow comedy with flashes
of wit.

w Jack Rose, *novel* Four Horse Players Are
Missing by Alexander Rose d Daniel Mann
ph Joseph Ruttenberg m George Duning

Dean Martin, Lana Turner, Eddie Albert,
Walter Matthau, Nita Talbot, Margo, Paul
Ford, John McGiver

Who's Minding the Mint?*
US 1967   97m   Technicolor
Columbia / Norman Maurer

An employee of the US mint and his friends find
a means of printing bills at night.
Smartly-made action comedy with good
performances.

w R. S. Allen, Harvey Bullock d Howard
Morris ph Joseph Biroc m Lalo Schifrin

Jim Hutton, Dorothy Provine, Milton Berle,
Joey Bishop, Bob Denver, Walter Brennan,
Victor Buono, Jack Gilford

Who's Minding the Store?*
US 1963   90m   Technicolor
Paramount / York / Jerry Lewis (Paul Jones)

An accident-prone young man gets a job in a
department store.
Better-than-average star comedy, slapstick being
allowed precedence over sentimentality.

w Frank Tashlin, Harry Tugend d Frank
Tashlin ph W. Wallace Kelley m Joseph J.
Lilley

Jerry Lewis, Jill St John, Agnes Moorehead,
John McGiver, Ray Walston, Nancy Kulp

Why Shoot the Teacher?
Canada 1976   99m   colour
WSTT / Fraser Films (Lawrence Hertzog)

In 1935 a school teacher finds a chilly reception
when he settles in a Saskatchewan village.
Unsatisfactory but occasionally quite
entertaining comedy-drama which hovers
around the *Cold Comfort Farm* mark.

w James Defilice, *novel* Max Braithwaite
d Silvio Narizzano ph Marc Champion
m Ricky Hyslop

Bud Cort, Samantha Eggar, Chris Wiggins,
Gary Reineke

Why We Fight****
US War Office 1942–5 (*Frank Capra*)   bw

A series of feature-length compilations for
primary showing to the armed forces, these were
superbly vigorous documentaries which later
fascinated the public at large. Editing, music and
diagrams were all used to punch home the
message. Individual titles were:

'Prelude to War' (53m) w *Eric Knight, Anthony
Veiller d Frank Capra*
'The Nazis Strike' (42m) w as above d as above
'Divide and Conquer' (58m) w *Anthony Veiller,
Robert Heller d Frank Capra, Anatole Litvak*
'The Battle of Britain' (54m) wd *Anthony Veiller*
'The Battle of Russia' (80m) w *Anthony Veiller,
Robert Heller, Anatole Litvak, d Anatole Litvak*
'The Battle of China' (60m) w *Eric Knight,
Anthony Veiller d Frank Capra, Anatole Litvak*
'War Comes to America' (70m) w *Anthony
Veiller d Anatole Litvak*

All had editing by *William Hornbeck*, music by
Dmitri Tiomkin and commentary by *Walter
Huston*.

Why Worry?*
US 1923 60m approx (24 fps) bw
silent Hal Roach / Harold Lloyd

A hypochondriac is cured when he gets mixed up
in a South American revolution.
Moderate star comedy with highlights well
spaced out.

d Sam Taylor, Fred Newmeyer

Harold Lloyd, Jobyna Ralston, Leo White

Wicked as They Come
GB 1957 94m bw
Columbia / Film Locations (Maxwell Setton)
US title: *Portrait in Smoke*

A beauty contest winner from the slums makes
money and luxury her goal.
Busy melodrama which interests without
edifying.

wd Ken Hughes *co-w* Robert Westerby,
Sigmund Miller *ph* Basil Emmott *m* Malcolm
Arnold

Arlene Dahl, Herbert Marshall, Phil Carey,
Michael Goodliffe, David Kossoff, Sidney
James, Ralph Truman, Faith Brook

The Wicked Lady*
GB 1945 104m bw
GFD / Gainsborough (R. J. Minney)

In the days of Charles II, Lady Skelton befriends
a highwayman and takes to crime.
The most commercially successful of the
Gainsborough costume charades because of its
atmosphere of gloomy sin. Dramatically turgid
and surprisingly poorly acted and directed, but
with good period detail. It had to be reshot for
America because of the ladies' décolletage.

wd Leslie Arliss, *novel* The Life and Death of the
Wicked Lady Skelton by Magdalen King-Hall
ph Jack Cox *m* Hans May *md* Louis Levy

Margaret Lockwood, James Mason, Griffith
Jones, Patricia Roc, Michael Rennie, Enid
Stamp-Taylor, Felix Aylmer, Martita Hunt,
David Horne

'A mixture of hot passion and cold suet
pudding.'—*Manchester Guardian*

'Rather dull and juvenile in its determination
to be daring.'—*Richard Mallett, Punch*

A Wicked Woman
US 1934 71m bw
MGM (Harry Rapf)

A woman kills her drunken husband to protect
her children, later confesses and is exonerated.
The tail end of the mother love saga, better made
than most.

w Florence Ryerson, Zelda Sears, *novel* Anne
Austin *d* Charles Brabin *ph* Lester White

Mady Christians, Charles Bickford, Betty
Furness, William Henry, Jackie Searle, Robert
Taylor, Paul Harvey

The Wicker Man*
GB 1973 86m Eastmancolor
British Lion (Peter Snell)

A policeman flies to a remote Scottish isle to
investigate the death of a child, and finds himself
in the hands of diabolists.
Old-fashioned but remarkably well made scare
story, with effective shock moments.

w Anthony Shaffer *d* Robin Hardy *ph* Harry
Waxman *m* Paul Giovanni *ad* Seamus
Flannery

Edward Woodward, Britt Ekland, Christopher
Lee, Ingrid Pitt, Diane Cilento

'An encouraging achievement for those who
had begun to despair of the British cinema.'—
David McGillivray

Wife, Doctor and Nurse*
US 1937 84m bw
TCF (Raymond Griffith)

A romantic triangle as the title suggests.
Agreeable fluff with a mildly surprising end (for
1937) suggesting a *ménage à trois.*

w Kathryn Scola, Darrell Ware, Lamar Trotti
d Walter Lang *ph* George Cronjager *m* Arthur
Lange

Loretta Young, Warner Baxter, Virginia Bruce,
Jane Darwell, Sidney Blackmer, Maurice Cass,
Minna Gombell, Elisha Cook Jnr, Lon Chaney
Jnr

Wife, Husband and Friend*
US 1939 80m bw
TCF (Nunnally Johnson)

A man sabotages his wife's efforts to become a
professional singer.
Modestly agreeable romantic comedy later
remade as *Everybody Does It* (qv).

w Nunnally Johnson, *story* James M. Cain
d Gregory Ratoff *ph* Ernest Palmer

Loretta Young, Warner Baxter, Binnie Barnes,
Cesar Romero, George Barbier, J. Edward
Bromberg, Eugene Pallette, Helen Westley

The Wife Takes a Flyer
US 1942 86m bw
Columbia (B. P. Schulberg)
GB title: *A Yank in Dutch*

A Dutchwoman whose husband is in the asylum
takes in a fugitive USAF pilot in his place

although a Nazi officer is billeted on the household.

Downright peculiar World War II comedy which at the time seemed the height of bad taste—and no laughs.

w Gina Kaus, Jay Dratler d Richard Wallace ph Franz Planer

Joan Bennett, Franchot Tone, Allyn Joslyn, Cecil Cunningham, Lloyd Corrigan, Georgia Caine

'Kicks in the pants, belching, and exaggerated face-making are lifted from burlesque to decorate his feeble attempt.'—*New York Post*

Wife versus Secretary*
US 1936 88m bw
MGM (Hunt Stromberg)

A publisher's wife starts to believe rumours about his attention to his secretary.
Practised star comedy drama which provided thoroughly satisfactory entertainment of a kind the cinema seems to have forgotten.

w Norman Krasna, Alice Duer Miller, John Lee Mahin, *novel* Faith Baldwin d Clarence Brown ph Ray June m Herbert Stothart, Edward Ward

Clark Gable, Myrna Loy, Jean Harlow, May Robson, George Barbier, James Stewart, Hobart Cavanaugh

'See this picture if you enjoy the spectacle of three clever stars shining for all they are worth.'—*Film Weekly*

The Wilby Conspiracy*
GB 1975 105m De Luxe
UA / Optimus / Baum—Dantine (Stanley Sopel)

A British mining engineer is persuaded to help a black revolutionary in his flight from Cape Town to Johannesburg.
Reasonably exciting political chase thriller with a sufficiency of twists and action sequences; philosophy is present but secondary.

w Rod Amateau, Harold Nebenzal, *novel* Peter Driscoll d Ralph Nelson ph John Coquillon m Stanley Myers

Sidney Poitier, Michael Caine, Nicol Williamson, Prunella Gee, Saeed Jaffrey, Persis Khambatta

The Wild Affair*
GB 1965 87m bw
Seven Arts (Richard Patterson)

An office Christmas party nearly turns into an orgy.
Curious little comedy drama which plays almost

like the Road to Ruin and has an attractive but miscast leading lady. Interesting elements.

wd John Krish, *novel* The Last Hours of Sandra Lee by William Sansom ph Arthur Ibbetson m Martin Slavin

Nancy Kwan, Terry-Thomas, Jimmy Logan, Bud Flanagan, Betty Marsden, Gladys Morgan, Paul Whitsun-Jones, Donald Churchill, Victor Spinetti

The Wild and the Willing
GB 1962 112m bw
Rank / Box—Thomas (Betty E. Box)

A troublesome student at a provincial university seduces the wife of his professor.
Watchable sex melodrama with an interesting background on which no one seems to have quite enough grip; 'realism' is simply there to be exploited.

w Nicholas Phipps, Mordecai Richler, *play* The Tinker by Laurence Dobie, Robert Sloman d Ralph Thomas ph Ernest Steward m Norrie Paramor

Virginia Maskell, Paul Rogers, Ian McShane, Samantha Eggar, John Hurt, Catherine Woodville, John Standing, Jeremy Brett

Wild and Wonderful
US 1963 88m Eastmancolor
U-I / Harold Hecht

A French film star poodle makes friends with an American gambler.
Amiable zany comedy in a set-bound Gay Paree.

w Larry Markes, Michael Morris, Waldo Salt d Michael Anderson ph Joseph La Shelle m Morton Stevens

Tony Curtis, Christine Kaufmann, Larry Storch, Marty Ingels, Jacques Aubuchon, Jules Munshin

The Wild Angels*
US 1966 85m Pathecolor Panavision
AIP (Roger Corman)

A Californian motorcycle gang is run on semi-religious, ritualistic, Nazi lines.
Much-banned melodrama, cheaply made but vigorously handled and of some interest on social and historical levels.

w Charles B. Griffith d Roger Corman ph Richard Moore m Mike Curb

Peter Fonda, Nancy Sinatra, Bruce Dern, Michael J. Pollard

The Wild Blue Yonder
US 1952 98m bw
Republic (Herbert J. Yates)
GB title: *Thunder Across the Pacific*

Incidents in the lives of bomber pilots in the
Pacific during World War II.
Routine action flagwaver.

w Richard Tregaskis *d* Allan Dwan *ph* Reggie
Lanning *m* Victor Young

Wendell Corey, Vera Hruba Ralston, Forrest
Tucker, Phil Harris, Walter Brennan, Ruth
Donnelly

Wild Boys of the Road*
US 1933 88m bw
Warner (Robert Presnell)
GB title: *Dangerous Days*

Boys of poor families take to the road in gangs.
Vivid social melodrama of its day, now rather
overstated.

w Earl Baldwin *d* William Wellman *ph* Arthur
Todd

Frankie Darro, Rochelle Hudson, Edwin Philips,
Arthur Hohl

The Wild Bunch***
US 1969 145m Technicolor Panavision
70
Warner Seven Arts / Phil Feldman

In 1914, Texas bandits are ambushed by an old
enemy and die bloodily in defence of one of their
number against a ruthless Mexican
revolutionary.
Arguably the director's best film, and one which
set a fashion for blood-spurting violence in
westerns. Undeniably stylish, thoughtful, and in
places very exciting.

w Walon Green, Sam Peckinpah *d* Sam
Peckinpah *ph* Lucien Ballard *m* Jerry Fielding
ad Edward Carrere

William Holden, Ernest Borgnine, Robert Ryan,
Edmond O'Brien, Warren Oates, Jaime
Sanchez, Ben Johnson, Strother Martin, L. Q.
Jones, Albert Dekker

'A western that enlarged the form
aesthetically, thematically, demonically.'—
Stanley Kauffmann, 1972

'We watch endless violence to assure us that
violence is not good.'—*Judith Crist, 1976*

AAN: script; Jerry Fielding

The Wild Country
US 1970 100m Technicolor
Walt Disney (Ron Miller)

In the late 1880s a farmer buys a dilapidated

Wyoming ranch and falls foul of a local rancher
who controls the water supply.
Predictable family western in the familiar Disney
style.

w Calvin Clements Jnr, Paul Savage, *novel* Little
Britches by Ralph Moody *d* Robert Totten
ph Frank Phillips *m* Robert Bronner

Steve Forrest, Vera Miles, Jack Elam, Ronny
Howard, Morgan Woodward

The Wild Geese
GB 1978 134m Eastmancolor
Rank / Richmond (Euan Lloyd)

Adventures of four British mercenaries in a
central African state.
All-star blood and guts with a few breezy
touches in the script.

w Reginald Rose, *novel* Daniel Carney
d Andrew V. McLaglen *ph* Jack Hildyard
m Roy Budd

Roger Moore, Richard Burton, Richard Harris,
Hardy Kruger, Stewart Granger, Jack Watson,
Frank Finlay, Kenneth Griffith, Barry Foster,
Jeff Corey, Ronald Fraser, Percy Herbert,
Patrick Allen, Jane Hylton

Wild Geese Calling
US 1941 77m bw
TCF (Harry Joe Brown)

A young adventurer in Oregon weds the girl
friend of a conniving gambler.
Minor semi-western which never really finds a
style.

w Horace McCoy, *novel* Stewart Edward White
d John Brahm *ph* Lucien Ballard

Joan Bennett, Henry Fonda, Warren William,
Ona Munson, Barton MacLane, Russell
Simpson, Iris Adrian

Wild Harvest
US 1947 92m bw
Paramount (Robert Fellows)

A romantic triangle develops among wheat
harvesters on the western plains.
Standard star hokum.

w John Monks Jnr *d* Tay Garnett *ph* John F.
Seitz *m* Hugo Friedhofer

Alan Ladd, Dorothy Lamour, Robert Preston,
Lloyd Nolan, Dick Erdman, Allen Jenkins, Will
Wright

Wild in the Country
US 1961 114m De Luxe Cinemascope
TCF / Company of Artists (Jerry Wald)

A rebellious hillbilly is involved with three women.

Weird confection designed to show the star in all his facets.

w Clifford Odets, *novel* The Lost Country by J. R. Salamanca *d* Philip Dunne *ph* William C. Mellor *m* Kenyon Hopkins

Elvis Presley, Hope Lange, Tuesday Weld, Millie Perkins, John Ireland, Gary Lockwood

'One can't help feeling he was better off prior to this misguided bid for class.'—*MFB*

Wild in the Sky

US 1971 83m colour
AIP / Bald Eagle (William T. Naud, Dick Gautier)

Three young offenders skyjack a B52 jet bomber.

Black comedy melodrama, uncontrolled but with some engaging absurdities.

w William T. Naud, Dick Gautier *d* William T. Naud *ph* Thomas E. Spalding *m* Jerry Styner

Brandon de Wilde, Keenan Wynn, Dick Gautier, Tim O'Connor, James Daly, Robert Lansing

Wild in the Streets*

US 1968 97m Perfectcolor
AIP (Jack Cash)

In the imminent future, a pop singer becomes president and launches a campaign for teenage emancipation.

Satirical melodrama with a profusion of wild gags, some of which hit the target.

w Robert Thom *d* Barry Shear *ph* Richard Moore *m* Les Baxter

Shelley Winters, Chris Jones, Diane Varsi, Hal Holbrook, Millie Perkins

'Blatant, insensitive, crummy-looking . . . enjoyable at a pop, comic-strip level.'—*New Yorker, 1977*

Wild Is the Wind

US 1957 114m bw Vistavision
Paramount / Hal B. Wallis

A widowed Italian sheep rancher in Nevada marries his wife's sister from Italy, but she falls for his adopted son.

Intense Cold Comfort Farm melodrama with a strong similarity to *They Knew What They Wanted*; the strain shows, and the performances are tiresomely noisy.

w Arnold Schulman *d* George Cukor
ph Charles Lang Jnr *m* Dmitri Tiomkin

Anna Magnani, Anthony Quinn, Tony Franciosa, Dolores Hart, Joseph Calleia

AAN: title song (*m* Dmitri Tiomkin, *ly* Ned Washington); Anna Magnani; Anthony Quinn

The Wild North

US 1951 97m Anscocolor
MGM (Stephen Ames)

Standard adventure story with avalanche and wolf attacks.

A mountie gets his man but needs his help getting back to base.

w Frank Fenton *d* Andrew Marton *ph* Robert Surtees *m* Bronislau Kaper

Stewart Granger, Wendell Corey, Cyd Charisse

The Wild One **

US 1954 79m bw
Columbia / Stanley Kramer

Hoodlum motorcyclists terrorize a small town.

Brooding, compulsive, well-made little melodrama which was much banned because there was no retribution. As a narrative it does somewhat lack dramatic point.

w John Paxton, *story* The Cyclists' Raid by Frank Rooney *d Laslo Benedek ph* Hal Mohr *m* Leith Stevens

Marlon Brando, Lee Marvin, Mary Murphy, Robert Keith, Jay C. Flippen

The Wild Party

US 1956 81m bw
UA / Security (Sidney Harmon)

An ex-football player and some Los Angeles layabouts plot a kidnap.

Unpleasant melodrama laced with sex, violence and loud music.

w John McPartland *d* Harry Horner *ph* Sam Leavitt *m* Buddy Bregman

Anthony Quinn, Carol Ohmart, Jay Robinson, Arthur Franz, Nehemiah Persoff, Kathryn Grant, Paul Stewart

The Wild Party

US 1974 91m Movielab
AIP (Edgar Lansbury, Joseph Beruh)

In 1929, a silent film comedian on the skids throws a party to show his latest movie.

Evocative of its period but virtually confined to a single set which becomes boring, this collection of unlikely events and tedious people has only obvious points to make and its final descent into tragedy is not compelling.

w Walter Marks, *poem* Joseph Moncure March

d James Ivory *ph* Walter Lassally *m* Larry Rosenthal

James Coco, Raquel Welch, Perry King, Tiffany Bolling, Royal Dano, David Dukes, Dena Dietrich

'Seems to promise a pointillist precision about its characters and milieu which it never quite delivers.'— *Jonathan Rosenbaum*

Wild River*
US 1960 115m De Luxe Cinemascope
TCF (Elia Kazan)

In 1933 a Tennessee Valley Authority inspector incurs the wrath of a local matriarch who will not leave her valley even though it is to be flooded. Interesting liberal-minded sociological drama marred by an added love story, as the similar *Last Days of Dolwyn* was marred by melodrama. Well made but somehow unmemorable.

w Paul Osborn, *novels* Borden Deal, William Bradford Huie *d* Elia Kazan *ph* Ellsworth Fredericks *m* Kenyon Hopkins

Montgomery Clift, *Jo Van Fleet*, Lee Remick, Albert Salmi, Jay C. Flippen, James Westerfield, Bruce Dern

Wild Rovers
US 1971 132m Metrocolor Panavision 70
MGM / Geoffrey (Blake Edwards, Ken Wales)

A middle-aged cowboy, depressed with the state of his life, joins with a younger man to become a bank robber.
Fashionable, derivative, quite unsuccessful western tragi-comedy mixing in shades of every director from Ford to Peckinpah.

wd Blake Edwards *ph* Philip Lathrop *m* Jerry Goldsmith

William Holden, Ryan O'Neal, Karl Malden, Lynn Carlin, Tom Skerritt, Joe Don Baker, Rachel Roberts, Leora Dana, Moses Gunn

Wild Strawberries***
Sweden 1957 93m bw
Svensk Filmindustri (Allan Ekelund)
original title: *Smultronstället*

An elderly professor has a nightmare and thinks back over his long life.
A beautifully paced and acted, but somewhat obscure piece of probing symbolism.

wd Ingmar Bergman *ph* Gunnar Fischer *m* Erik Nordgren

Victor Sjostrom, Ingrid Thulin, Gunnar

Bjornstrand, Bibi Andersson, Naima Wifstrand, Jullan Kindahl

'The work of a man obsessed by cruelty, especially spiritual cruelty, trying to find some resolution.'—*Kenneth Cavander, MFB*

Will Penny**
US 1967 109m Technicolor
Paramount / Fred Engel /Walter Seltzer / Tom Gries

A middle-aged cowpuncher falls foul of a family of maniacal cut-throats.
Realistically spare, laconic, uncomforting western with a curiously melodramatic set of villains.

wd Tom Gries *ph* Lucien Ballard *m* David Raksin

Charlton Heston, Joan Hackett, Donald Pleasence, Lee Majors, Bruce Dern, Anthony Zerbe, Clifton James, Ben Johnson

Will Success Spoil Rock Hunter?
US 1957 95m Eastmancolor Cinemascope
TCF (Frank Tashlin)
GB title: *Oh! For a Man!*

A timid advertising executive is touted for a publicity stunt as the world's greatest lover.
A too-wild satire on TV commercials: less frenzied direction and gag-writing would have prised more humour from the situations.

w Frank Tashlin, *play* George Axelrod *d* Frank Tashlin *ph* Joe MacDonald *m* Cyril Mockridge

Jayne Mansfield, Tony Randall, Betsy Drake, Joan Blondell, John Williams, Henry Jones, Mickey Hargitay

Willard*
US 1971 95m De Luxe
Cinerama / Bing Crosby

A shy, withdrawn young man breeds and trains rats to kill his enemies.
Modest, rather unusual suspenser which builds well after a slow start; only horrifying to people who can't stand rats. A sequel, *Ben* (qv), later appeared.

w Gilbert Ralston, *novel* Ratman's Notebooks by Stephen Gilbert *d* Daniel Mann *ph* Robert B. Hauser *m* Alex North *rat trainer* Moe de Sesso

Bruce Davison, Elsa Lanchester, Ernest Borgnine, Sondra Locke, Michael Dante, J. Pat O'Malley

Willy Wonka and the Chocolate Factory*
US 1971   100m   Technicolor
David Wolper

A boy wins a tour of the local chocolate factory
and finds himself in the power of a magician.
Semi-satiric Grimms Fairy Tale pastiche which
looks good but never seems quite happy with
itself.

w Roald Dahl, from his novel d Mel Stuart
ph Arthur Ibbetson songs Leslie Bricusse,
Anthony Newley md Walter Scharf ad Harper
Goff

Gene Wilder, Jack Albertson, Peter Ostrum,
Roy Kinnear, Aubrey Woods

Wilson*
US 1944   154m   Technicolor
TCF (Darryl F. Zanuck)

The rise and fall of an American president.
Admirably careful biopic which raises no
particular excitement but entertains and
instructs on various levels.

w Lamar Trotti d Henry King ph Leon
Shamroy m Alfred Newman ad James Basevi,
Wiard Ihnen

Alexander Knox, Charles Coburn, Cedric
Hardwicke, Geraldine Fitzgerald, Thomas
Mitchell, Ruth Nelson, William Eythe, Vincent
Price, Mary Anderson, Ruth Ford, Sidney
Blackmer, Stanley Ridges, Eddie Foy Jnr,
Charles Halton, Thurston Hall, J. M. Kerrigan,
Francis X. Bushman

'Not without tedium, but worth seeing as an
enormous expensive curiosity.'—Richard
Mallett, Punch

AA: Lamar Trotti; Leon Shamroy
AAN: best picture; Henry King; Alfred
Newman; Alexander Knox

Winchester 73**
US 1950   92m   bw
U-I (Aaron Rosenberg)

Long-time enemies settle an old grudge.
Entertaining, popular, hard-riding, hard-
shooting western of the old school.

w Robert L. Richards, Borden Chase, story
Stuart N. Lake d Anthony Mann ph William
Daniels m Frank Skinner md Joseph
Gershenson

James Stewart, Shelley Winters, Dan Duryea,
Stephen McNally, Millard Mitchell, Charles
Drake, John McIntire, Will Geer, Jay C.
Flippen, Rock Hudson, Tony Curtis, John
Alexander, Steve Brodie

The Wind*
US 1927   75m (sound version 1928)   bw
MGM

A sheltered Virginia girl goes to live on the rough
and windy Texas prairie, marries a man she
doesn't love and kills a would-be rapist.
Heavy melodrama with a strong visual sense.

w Frances Marion, novel Dorothy Scarborough
d Victor Sjostrom ph John Arnold

Lillian Gish, Lars Hanson, Montagu Love,
Dorothy Cummings

'So penetrating is the atmosphere that one can
almost feel the wind itself and taste the endless
dust.'—Georges Sadoul

Wind across the Everglades
US 1958   93m   Technicolor
(Warner) Schulberg Productions (Stuart
    Schulberg)

Florida 1900: a young schoolteacher tracks
down those responsible for hunting rare birds for
their feathers, and becomes a game warden.
Dull, meandering adventure story with a
purpose, relying heavily on violence and
eccentric characters.

w Budd Schulberg d Nicholas Ray ph Joseph
Brun

Christopher Plummer, Burl Ives, Gypsy Rose
Lee, Emmett Kelly, George Voskovec, Tony
Galento, Mackinlay Kantor

The Wind and the Lion
US 1975   119m   Metrocolor   Panavision
Columbia / MGM (Herb Jaffe, Phil Rawlins)

In 1904 Tangier, an American widow and her
children are kidnapped by a Riffian chief, and the
eyes of the world are focused on the incident.
Basing itself very lightly on an actual event, this
adventure story is both confused as a narrative
and unexciting as an action piece: the camera
stops too often to look at sunsets, the plot stops
too often for philosophizing, and there are too
many underexplained characters and incidents
fitting into the international jigsaw.

wd John Milius ph Billy Williams m Jerry
Goldsmith

Sean Connery, Candice Bergen, Brian Keith,
John Huston, Geoffrey Lewis, Steve Kanaly,
Vladek Sheybal

AAN: Jerry Goldsmith

The Wind Cannot Read
GB 1958·   115m   Eastmancolor
Rank (Betty E. Box)

In India and Burma during World War II, a

flying officer falls in love with a Japanese
language instructor suffering from a brain
disease.
Or, love is a many-splendored dark victory. Old-
fashioned romance for addicts, well enough
produced.

w Richard Mason, from his novel *d* Ralph
Thomas *ph* Ernest Steward *m* Angelo
Lavagnino

Dirk Bogarde, Yoko Tani, Ronald Lewis, John
Fraser, Anthony Bushell, Michael Medwin

Windbag the Sailor
GB 1936 85m bw
Gainsborough (Edward Black)

An incompetent seaman is washed away on an
old ketch and lands on a South Sea isle.
Rather uninventive star comedy with inevitable
pleasing moments.

w Marriott Edgar, Stafford Dickens, Will Hay
d William Beaudine *ph* Jack Cox *md* Louis
Levy

Will Hay, Moore Marriott, Graham Moffatt,
Norma Varden

Windom's Way*
GB 1957 108m Technicolor
Rank (John Bryan)

A doctor on a Far Eastern island tries to quell a
native uprising.
Tolerably well intentioned action melodrama,
topical because of Malaya; dramatically rather
sober and predictable.

w Jill Craigie, *novel* James Ramsay Ullman
d Ronald Neame *ph* Christopher Challis
m James Bernard

Peter Finch, Mary Ure, Natasha Parry, Robert
Flemyng, Michael Hordern

The Window***
US 1949 73m bw
RKO

A New York slum boy is always telling tall tales,
so no one believes him when he actually
witnesses a murder . . . except the murderer.
Classic little second feature, entertaining and
suspenseful; unfortunately it had few successful
imitators.

w Mel Dinelli d Ted Tetzlaff ph William Steiner
m Roy Webb

Bobby Driscoll, Barbara Hale, Arthur Kennedy,
Paul Stewart, Ruth Roman
  'Logical, well-shaped, cohesive, admirably
acted, beautifully photographed and cut to a
nicety.'—*Richard Winnington*

Wing and a Prayer*
US 1944 97m bw
TCF

Life aboard an aircraft carrier.
Standard action flagwaver.

w Jerome Cady *d* Henry Hathaway *ph* Glen
MacWilliams

Don Ameche, Cedric Hardwicke, Dana
Andrews, Charles Bickford, Richard Jaeckel,
Henry Morgan

AAN: Jerome Cady

Winged Victory**
US 1944 130m bw
TCF (Darryl F. Zanuck)

During World War II, pilots are inducted,
trained and sent on dangerous missions.
Solid, competent, best-foot-forward flagwaver of
the highest inspirational intention.

w Moss Hart, from his play *d* George Cukor
ph Glen MacWilliams *m* David Rose

Lon McCallister, Jeanne Crain, Edmond
O'Brien, Jane Ball, Mark Daniels, Don Taylor,
Lee J. Cobb, Judy Holliday, Peter Lind Hayes,
Alan Baxter, Red Buttons, Barry Nelson, Gary
Merrill, Karl Malden, Martin Ritt, Jo-Carroll
Dennison

Wings*
US 1927 136m (24 fps) bw silent
Paramount (B. P. Schulberg)

Two young men join the Air Service during
World War I, and one eventually shoots down
the other by accident.
An epic of early aviation, still stirring in its action
sequences.

w Hope Loring, Harry D. Lighton *d William
Wellman ph Harry Perry*

Clara Bow, Charles Buddy Rogers, Richard
Arlen, Gary Cooper, Jobyna Ralston, El Brendel

AA: best picture; best engineering effects (Roy
Pomeroy)

Wings for the Eagle
US 1942 85m bw
Warner (Robert Lord)

Aircraft workers do their bit during World War
II.
Home Front propaganda, well enough
produced.

w Byron Morgan, Harrison Orkow *d* Lloyd
Bacon *ph* Tony Gaudio

Ann Sheridan, Dennis Morgan, Jack Carson,
George Tobias, Don Defore

Wings in the Dark*
US 1935   75m   bw
Paramount (Arthur Hornblow Jnr)

Embittered after being blinded in an accident, a
research flier finally leaps into action when his
stranded girl friend needs help.
Satisfactory romantic melodrama.

w Jack Kirkland, Frank Partos d James Flood
ph William C. Mellor

Cary Grant, Myrna Loy, Roscoe Karns, Hobart
Cavanaugh, Dean Jagger, Bert Hanlon, Samuel
S. Hinds

The Wings of Eagles*
US 1957   110m   Metrocolor
   Cinemascope
MGM (Charles Schnee)

A navy flier breaks his neck in an accident and
on recovery becomes a Hollywood writer.
Sentimental biopic of Frank 'Spig' Wead, a
routine, easy-going assignment for its director
(who is caricatured by Ward Bond as John
Dodge).

w Frank Fenton, William Wister Haines d John
Ford ph Paul C. Vogel m Jeff Alexander

John Wayne, Maureen O'Hara, Ward Bond,
Dan Dailey, Ken Curtis, Edmund Lowe,
Kenneth Tobey, Sig Rumann, Henry O'Neill

Wings of the Hawk
US 1953   81m   Technicolor   3-D
U-I (Aaron Rosenberg)

Mexico 1911: a gold miner falls into the hands of
revolutionaries.
Routine bang-bang, rather sloppily produced.

w James E. Moser d Budd Boetticher
ph Clifford Stine m Frank Skinner

Van Heflin, Julie Adams, George Dolenz, Pedro
Gonzales-Gonzales, Rodolfo Acosta, Antonio
Moreno, Abbe Lane

Wings of the Morning*
GB 1937   89m   Technicolor
TCF (Robert T. Kane)

In 1899, a gypsy princess marries an Irish
nobleman; in 1937, romance again blooms
between their descendants.
Britain's first Technicolor film was great to look
at and quite charming, though slight; its major
attractions being horse races, songs from John
McCormack, and a heroine dressed for plot
purposes as a boy.

w Tom Geraghty, story Donn Byrne d Harold
Schuster

Henry Fonda, Annabella, Stewart Rome, John
McCormack, Leslie Banks, Irene Vanbrugh,
Harry Tate, Edward Underdown, Helen Haye
   'A wholesome, refreshing and altogether
likeable little romance.'—Frank S. Nugent

Wings of the Navy
US 1939   89m   bw
Warner (Lou Edelman)

The loves and careers of navy pilots.
Competent animated recruiting poster.

w Michael Fessier d Lloyd Bacon ph Arthur
Edeson, Elmer Dyer

George Brent, Olivia de Havilland, John Payne,
Frank McHugh, John Litel, Victor Jory, Henry
O'Neill, John Ridgely

Winning*
US 1969   123m   Technicolor   Panavision
   70
Universal / Newman–Foreman (John
   Foreman)

A racing driver's professional problems strain
his relationship with his wife.
Cliché track melodrama with pretensions, well
but needlessly made.

w Howard Rodman d James Goldstone
ph Richard Moore m Dave Grusin

Paul Newman, Joanne Woodward, Richard
Thomas, Robert Wagner, David Sheiner, Clu
Gulager

The Winning Team
US 1952   98m   bw
Warner (Bryan Foy)

A telephone linesman becomes a great baseball
player despite trouble with his vision after an
accident.
Standard biopic of Grover Cleveland Alexander;
all very pleasant but no surprises.

w Ted Sherdeman, Seeleg Lester, Merwin
Gerard d Lewis Seiler ph Sid Hickox m David
Buttolph

Doris Day, Ronald Reagan, Frank Lovejoy, Eve
Miller, James Millican, Russ Tamblyn

The Winslow Boy***
GB 1948   117m   bw
British Lion / London Films (Anatole de
   Grunwald)

A naval cadet is expelled for stealing a postal
order; his father spends all he had on proving his
innocence.
Highly enjoyable middle-class British
entertainment based on an actual case;

performances and period settings are alike
excellent, though the film is a trifle overlong.

w Terence Rattigan, Anatole de Grunwald, play
Terence Rattigan *d Anthony Asquith*
ph Frederick Young *m* William Alwyn

Robert Donat, Cedric Hardwicke, Margaret
Leighton, Frank Lawton, Jack Watling, Basil
Radford, Kathleen Harrison, Francis L.
Sullivan, Marie Lohr, Neil North, Wilfrid Hyde
White, Ernest Thesiger

Winter Carnival
US 1939   89m   bw
UA

College romances over a holiday weekend.
Nondescript romantic comedy.

d Charles Riesner

Ann Sheridan, Richard Carlson, Helen Parrish,
Virginia Gilmore, Robert Walker

Winter Light*
Sweden 1962   80m   bw
Svensk Filmindustri (Allan Ekelund)
original title: *Nattvardsgasterna*

A widowed village pastor loses his vocation.
In a sense almost parody Bergman; in another,
one of his clearest statements of despair. The
middle section of a pessimistic trilogy which also
included *Through a Glass Darkly* and *The
Silence.*

wd Ingmar Bergman *ph* Sven Nykvist *m* none

Max Von Sydow, Ingrid Thulin, Gunnar
Bjornstrand, Gunnel Lindblom

Winter Meeting
US 1948   104m   bw
Warner (Henry Blanke)

A repressed spinster falls for a naval hero intent
on becoming a priest.
Dreary talk marathon which did its star's career
no good at all.

w Catherine Turney, *novel* Ethel Vance
d Bretaigne Windust *ph* Ernest Haller *m* Max
Steiner

Bette Davis, James Davis, Janis Paige, John
Hoyt, Florence Bates, Walter Baldwin

Winterset**
US 1936   78m   bw
RKO

On the New York waterfront, a drifter
determines to avenge his father's death.
Very dated poetic melodrama, here given a talky,
artificial production which at the time impressed
many critics but is now fairly difficult to endure.

w Anthony Veiller, *play* Maxwell Anderson
d Alfred Santell *ph* Peverell Marley
md Nathaniel Shilkret

Burgess Meredith, Eduardo Ciannelli, Margo,
Paul Guilfoyle, John Carradine, Edward Ellis,
Stanley Ridges, Maurice Moscovitch, Myron
McCormick, Mischa Auer

'Still in a grand manner that just won't do on
the screen . . . but there are fine moments in the
performances, and there's something childishly
touching in the florid dramatic effects.'—*New
Yorker, 1978*

AAN: Nathaniel Shilkret

Wintertime
US 1943   82m   bw
TCF (William Le Baron)

A Norwegian skating star comes to Canada
where her uncles's winter resort is on its uppers.
The last of the star's Fox musicals is pure
routine.

w Edward Moran, Jack Jevne, Lynn Starling
d John Brahm *ph* Glen MacWilliams
md Charles Henderson

Sonja Henie, Jack Oakie, Cesar Romero, S. Z.
Sakall, Carole Landis, Cornel Wilde, Woody
Herman and his Band

The Wistful Widow of Wagon Gap*
US 1947   78m   bw
U-I (Robert Arthur)

In old Montana, an accident-prone wayfarer
accidentally kills a man and has to look after his
family.
Tame and disappointing comedy vehicle.

w D. D. Beauchamp, William Bowers *d* Charles
T. Barton, Robert Lees, Frederic I. Rinaldo,
John Grant *ph* Charles Van Enger *m* Walter
Shumann

Bud Abbott, Lou Costello, Marjorie Main,
Audrey Young, George Cleveland

Witchcraft*
GB 1964   79m   bw
TCF / Lippert (Robert Lippert, Jack Parsons)

A family of witches take revenge on their
longtime enemies.
Spasmodically arresting horror film spoiled by
too complex a plot line and some variable acting.

w Harry Spaulding *d Don Sharp ph* Arthur
Lavis *m* Carlo Martelli

Jack Hedley, Lon Chaney Jnr, Marie Ney, Jill
Dixon, David Weston

'Unpretentious and uncommonly gripping.'—
MFB

Witchcraft through the Ages **
Sweden 1922   83m approx (24 fps)   bw
  silent
Svensk Filmindustri
original title: *Haxan*

A 'documentary' investigation of the history of
witchcraft, with acted examples.
Fascinating reconstruction of ancient rituals,
still maintaining its power to frighten.

wd Benjamin Christensen ph Johan
Ankarstjerne

Oscar Stribolt, Clara Pontoppidan, Karen
Winther

The Witches
GB 1967   90m   Technicolor
Hammer (Anthony Nelson Keys)
US title: *The Devil's Own*

A schoolmistress finds witchcraft in an English
village.
Chintzy horror with predictable development
and risible climax.

w Nigel Kneale, *novel* The Devil's Own by Peter
Curtis *d* Cyril Frankel *ph* Arthur Grant
m Richard Rodney Bennett

Joan Fontaine, Kay Walsh, Alec McCowen,
Gwen Ffrangcon Davies, Ingrid Brett, John
Collin, Michèle Dotrice, Leonard Rossiter,
Martin Stephens, Carmel McSharry

The Witches of Salem *
France / East Germany 1957   143m   bw
Borderie / CICC / DEFA / Pathé (Raymond
Borderie)
original title: *Les Sorcieres de Salem*

In 1692 Massachussetts, jealousies lead to
accusations of witchcraft and multiple trials and
executions.
An account of a horrifying historical fact which
was also intended to reflect on the McCarthy
witch hunts of the fifties; but the film, despite
splendid acting, is too literal and slow-moving.

w Jean-Paul Sartre, *play* The Crucible by Arthur
Miller *d* Raymond Rouleau *ph* Claude Renoir
m Georges Auric

Simone Signoret, Yves Montand, Mylène
Demongeot, Jean Debucourt

Witchfinder General *
GB 1968   87m   Eastmancolor
Tigon (Arnold Miller)
US title: *The Conqueror Worm*

In 1645 a villainous lawyer finds it profitable to
travel the country instigating witch hunts.
Savage, stylish minor horror melodrama with a
growing reputation as the best work of its young

director. Not for the squeamish despite its
pleasing countryside photography.

w Michael Reeves, Tom Baker, *novel* Ronald
Bassett *d Michael Reeves ph John Coquillon*
m Paul Ferris, Jim Morahan

Vincent Price, Rupert Davies, Ian Ogilvy,
Patrick Wymark, Hilary Dwyer

With a Song in My Heart *
US 1952   117m   Technicolor
TCF (Lamar Trotti)

Singer Jane Froman is crippled in a plane crash
but finally makes a comeback.
Romanticized showbiz biopic with the singer
providing voice only. Adequate production and
plenty of familiar tunes made this a successful
mass appeal sob story.

w Lamar Trotti *d* Walter Lang *ph* Leon
Shamroy *md* Alfred Newman

Susan Hayward, David Wayne, Rory Calhoun,
Thelma Ritter, Una Merkel, Robert Wagner,
Helen Westcott

AA: Alfred Newman
AAN: Susan Hayward; Thelma Ritter

With Six You Get Egg Roll
US 1968   99m   De Luxe   Panavision
Cinema Center / Arwin (Martin Melcher)

A widow with three sons marries a widower with
one daughter.
Quite a bright and inventive family comedy.

w Gwen Bagni, Paul Dubov *d* Howard Morris
ph Ellsworth Fredericks, Harry Stradling Jnr

Doris Day, Brian Keith, Pat Carroll, Barbara
Hershey

Without Love *
US 1945   111m   bw
MGM (Lawrence Weingarten)

The housing shortage in wartime Washington
causes a widow to allow a scientist to move in
with her, quite platonically.
Altered version of a popular play; rather long-
drawn-out and disappointing considering the
talent on hand.

w Donald Ogden Stewart, *play* Philip Barry
d Harold S. Bucquet *ph* Karl Freund
m Bronislau Kaper

Spencer Tracy, Katharine Hepburn, Lucille Ball,
Keenan Wynn, Carl Esmond, Patricia Morison,
Felix Bressart, Gloria Grahame
  'One of those glossy conversation pieces that
MGM does up so handsomely.'—*Rose Pelswick*

Without Reservations
US 1946 101m bw
RKO / Jesse L. Lasky

A famous woman writer heads for Hollywood
by train and meets a marine who seems ideal for
her male lead.
Would-be zany romantic comedy à la *It
Happened One Night*; doesn't quite come off.

w Andrew Solt *d* Mervyn Le Roy *ph* Milton
Krasner *m* Roy Webb

Claudette Colbert, John Wayne, Don Defore,
Phil Brown, Frank Puglia

Without Warning
US 1952 70m bw
UA / Allart

A sex maniac murders a succession of blondes.
Semi-documentary, low-budget police thriller
with all elements adequate for their purpose.

w Bill Raynor *d* Arnold Laven *ph* Joseph Biroc
m Herschel Burke Gilbert

Adam Williams, Edward Binns, Meg Randall

Witness for the Prosecution***
US 1957 114m bw
UA / Theme / Edward Small (Arthur
    Hornblow Jnr)

A convalescent QC takes on a murder defence
and finds himself in a web of trickery.
Thoroughly likeable though relentlessly over-
expanded movie version of a clever stage thriller.
Some miscasting and artificiality is condoned by
smart dialogue and handling, one celebrated
performance, and a handful of surprises.

*w Billy Wilder, Harry Kurnitz, play Agatha
Christie d Billy Wilder ph* Russell Harlan
m Matty Melneck

Charles Laughton, Tyrone Power, Marlene
Dietrich, John Williams, Henry Daniell, Elsa
Lanchester, Norma Varden, Una O'Connor, Ian
Wolfe

AAN: best picture; Billy Wilder; Charles
Laughton; Elsa Lanchester

Witness to Murder*
US 1954 81m bw
UA / Chester Erskine

A lonely woman sees a strangling in the flat
across the street; the police don't believe her but
the murderer does.
Predictable but quite effective screamer with a
nick-of-time dénouement.

w Chester Erskine *d* Roy Rowland *ph* John
Alton *m* Herschel Burke Gilbert

Barbara Stanwyck, George Sanders, Gary

Merrill, Jesse White, Harry Shannon, Claire
Carleton

Wives and Lovers
US 1963 103m bw
(Paramount) Hal B. Wallis

A successful author moves his family into
Connecticut, where sex rears its ugly head.
Would-be sophisticated comedy with insufficient
bubbles.

w Edward Anhalt, *play* The First Wife by Jay
Presson Allen *d* John Rich *ph* Lucien Ballard
m Lyn Murray

Van Johnson, Janet Leigh, Ray Walston, Shelley
Winters, Martha Hyer, Jeremy Slate

The Wiz*
US 1978
Universal 134m Technicolor

A black version of *The Wizard of Oz*, set in New
York.
Glossy version of the Broadway musical hit; it
offers some rewards, but on the whole the first is
the best.

w Joel Schumacher, from play with ly/m by
Charlie Smith, book by William Brown
d Sidney Lumet *ph* Oswald Morris *pd* Tony
Walton

Diana Ross, Michael Jackson, Nipsey Russell,
Ted Ross, Lena Horne, Richard Pyror, Mabel
King, Theresa Merritt

The Wizard of Oz***
US 1939 102m Technicolor
MGM (Mervyn Le Roy)

Unhappy Dorothy runs away from home, has
adventures in a fantasy land, but finally decides
that happiness was in her own back yard all the
time.
Classic fairy tale given vigorous straightforward
treatment, made memorable by performances,
art direction and hummable tunes.

w Noel Langley, Florence Ryerson, Edgar Allan
Wolfe, *book* Frank L. Baum *d Victor Fleming
ph* Harold Rosson *songs* E. Y. Harburg, Harold
Arlen *md* Herbert Stothart *ad Cedric Gibbons,
William A. Horning*

*Judy Garland, Frank Morgan, Ray Bolger, Jack
Haley, Bert Lahr, Margaret Hamilton*, Billie
Burke, Charley Grapewin, Clara Blandick
  'I don't see why children shouldn't like it, but
for adults there isn't very much except Bert
Lahr.'—*Richard Mallett, Punch*
  'As for the light touch of fantasy, it weighs like
a pound of fruitcake soaking wet.'—*Otis
Ferguson*

AA: song 'Over the Rainbow'
AAN: best picture; Herbert Stothart

Wolf Larsen

US 1958 83m bw
AA (Lindsley Parsons)

Serviceable remake of *The Sea Wolf* (qv)
without the Nietzschean overtones.

w Jack de Witt, Turnley Walker *d* Harlan Jones
ph Floyd Crosby *m* Paul Dunlap

Barry Sullivan, Peter Graves, Thayer David,
Gita Hall

The Wolf Man**

US 1940 70m bw
Universal

The son of an English squire comes home, is
bitten by a gypsy werewolf, and becomes one
himself.
Dazzlingly cast, moderately well staged, but
dramatically very disappointing horror piece
which established a new Universal monster who
later met Frankenstein, Abbott and Costello,
and several other eccentrics.

w Curt Siodmak *d* George Waggner *ph* Joseph
Valentine *m* Hans Salter, Frank Skinner
md Charles Previn

Lon Chaney Jnr, Claude Rains, Warren
William, Ralph Bellamy, Bela Lugosi, *Maria
Ouspenskaya*, Patric Knowles, Evelyn Ankers,
Fay Helm

Woman Accused*

US 1933 73m bw
Paramount

A woman kills her ex-lover in a struggle and goes
on the run.
Intriguing rigmarole written as a magazine serial
by ten well-known authors contributing a
chapter each. The result confirms the method.

w Bayard Veiller, *serial* Rupert Hughes, Vicki
Baum, Zane Grey, Vina Delmar, Irvin S. Cobb,
Gertrude Atherton,
J. P. McEvoy, Ursula Parrott, Polan Banks,
Sophie Kerr *d* Paul Sloane *m* Karl Struss

Nancy Carroll, Cary Grant, John Halliday,
Irving Pichel, Louis Calhern, Jack La Rue, John
Lodge

Woman Hater

GB 1948 105m bw
GFD / Two Cities

An English nobleman tries to disprove a film
star's statement that she hates men and loves
solitude.

Incredibly slight material is interminably
stretched out, well beyond an excellent cast's
ability to help.

w Robert Westerby, Nicholas Phipps *d* Terence
Young *ph* André Thomas *m* Lambert
Williamson

Stewart Granger, Edwige Feuillère, Ronald
Squire, Mary Jerrold, Jeanne de Casalis

The Woman I Love*

US 1937 85m bw
RKO (Albert Lewis)
GB title: *The Woman Between*

In World War I France, a pilot loves his superior
officer's wife.
Well-made romantic action melodrama from a
well-praised original.

w Mary Borden, French film L'Equipage and
novel of same name by Joseph Kessel *d* Anatole
Litvak *ph* Charles Rosher *m* Arthur Honegger,
Maurice Thiriet

Paul Muni, Miriam Hopkins, Louis Hayward,
Colin Clive, Minor Watson, Elizabeth Risdon,
Paul Guilfoyle, Mady Christians

Woman in a Dressing Gown*

GB 1957 94m bw
Godwin / Willis / J. Lee-Thompson

After twenty years of marriage, a wife's
slatternly ways alienate her once devoted
husband, and he asks for a divorce.
Classic British TV play adequately filmed but
now rather dated and irritating.

w Ted Willis, from his play *d* J. Lee-Thompson
ph Gilbert Taylor *m* Louis Levy

Yvonne Mitchell, Anthony Quayle, Sylvia Syms,
Andrew Ray, Carole Lesley

Woman in Hiding

US 1949 92m bw
U-I (Michael Kraike)

After escaping her husband's attempts to murder
her, a woman goes into hiding while evidence is
being accumulated against him.
Modest suspenser with too many near escapes
and not much else.

w Oscar Saul *d* Michael Gordon *ph* William
Daniels *m* Frank Skinner

Ida Lupino, Howard Duff, Stephen McNally,
John Litel, Taylor Holmes, Irving Bacon, Peggy
Dow, Joe Besser, Don Beddoe
  'The detail is full of things interesting and
amusing at the time and pleasant to remember
afterwards.'—*Richard Mallett, Punch*

The Woman in Question*
GB 1949 88m bw
GFD / Javelin (Teddy Baird)
US title: *Five Angles on Murder*

Police investigating a woman's death build up several different impressions of her.
Multi-flashback melodrama which somehow doesn't quite come off despite effort all round.

w John Cresswell *d* Anthony Asquith *ph* Desmond Dickinson *m* John Wooldridge

Jean Kent, Dirk Bogarde, Susan Shaw, John McCallum, Hermione Baddeley, Charles Victor, Duncan Macrae, Lana Morris, Vida Hope

The Woman in the Window***
US 1944 95m bw
International (Nunnally Johnson)

A grass widow professor befriends a girl who gets him involved with murder.
A refreshingly intelligent little thriller which was criticized at the time for a cop-out ending; this can now be seen as a decorative extra to a story which had already ended satisfactorily. Good middlebrow entertainment.

w Nunnally Johnson, novel Once Off Guard by J. H. Wallis *d Fritz Lang ph Milton Krasner m* Arthur Lang, Hugo Friedhofer

Edward G. Robinson, Joan Bennett, *Raymond Massey,* Dan Duryea, Edmund Breon, Thomas Jackson, Dorothy Peterson, Arthur Loft

'A perfect example of its kind, and a very good kind too.'—*James Shelley Hamilton*

'The accumulation of tiny details enlarged as though under a district attorney's magnifying glass gives reality a fantastic and anguishing appearance.'—*Jacques Bourgeois*

'In its rather artificial, club library style an effective and well made piece, absorbing, diverting and full of often painful suspense.'—*Richard Mallett, Punch*

AAN: Arthur Lang, Hugo Friedhofer

The Woman in White**
US 1948 109m bw
Warner (Henry Blanke)

The new tutor of a strange household finds himself among eccentrics, villains and ill-used ladies.
A Victorian thriller which is long on atmosphere but not so hot on suspense or plot development. The cast helps a lot.

w Stephen Morehouse Avery, *novel* Wilkie Collins *d* Peter Godfrey *ph Carl Guthrie m* Max Steiner

Gig Young, Eleanor Parker, *Sidney Greenstreet,*

Alexis Smith, Agnes Moorehead, John Emery, *John Abbott,* Curt Bois

'The Wilkie Collins novel is given the studious, stolid treatment ordinarily reserved for the ritual assassination of a great classic. This is not intended as a recommendation.'—*James Agee*

'Greenstreet and others move through the murky passages of the story like visitors in some massive Gothic museum, and they move, on the whole, with stately discretion, and do not scribble on the objects or show anything but the greatest veneration for them.'—*C. A. Lejeune*

Woman Obsessed
US 1959 102m De Luxe Cinemascope
TCF (Sidney Boehm)

In the Canadian Rockies, a pioneer woman's small son does not take to his new stepfather.
Antediluvian pulp fiction with quicksand and a forest fire for highlights. Shades of D. W. Griffith, and badly done into the bargain.

w Sidney Boehm, *novel* John Mantley *d* Henry Hathaway *ph* William C. Mellor *m* Hugo Friedhofer

Susan Hayward, Stephen Boyd, Dennis Holmes, Theodore Bikel, Barbara Nichols, Ken Scott, Arthur Franz

A Woman of Affairs
US 1928 90m (24 fps) bw silent
MGM

A wild rich girl goes from man to man and finally kills herself in a car crash.
Romantic star tosh from a fashionable novel of the time.

w Bess Meredyth, *novel* The Green Hat by Michael Arlen *d* Clarence Brown *ph* William Daniels

Greta Garbo, Lewis Stone, John Gilbert, John Mack Brown, Douglas Fairbanks Jnr, Hobart Bosworth

A Woman of Distinction
US 1950 85m bw
Columbia (Buddy Adler)

The lady dean of a New England school falls for a British astronomer.
Pratfall farce for ageing stars. No go.

w Charles Hoffman *d* Edward Buzzell *ph* Joseph Walker *m* Morris Stoloff

Rosalind Russell, Ray Milland, Edmund Gwenn, Janis Carter, Mary Jane Saunders, Francis Lederer, Jerome Courtland

A Woman of Paris**
US 1923   85m (24 fps)   bw   silent (music
   track added 1976)
Charles Chaplin

A country girl goes to the city, becomes a demi-
mondaine, and inadvertently causes the death of
the one man she loves.
Remarkably simply-handled 'road to ruin'
melodrama; its subtleties of treatment make it
still very watchable for those so inclined.

wd *Charles Chaplin m* Rollie Totheroh, Jack
Wilson

Edna Purviance, Adolphe Menjou, Carl Miller,
Lydia Knott
† Chaplin appeared unbilled as a railway porter.
The film was not a commercial success and he
withdrew it for fifty years.

Woman of Straw*
GB 1964   114m   Eastmancolor
UA / Novus (Michael Relph)

A rich old man's nurse conspires with his
nephew in a murder plot.
Rather half-hearted but good-looking star
melodrama which ventures into Hitchcock
territory.

w Robert Muller, Stanley Mann, Michael Relph,
novel Catherine Arley *d* Basil Dearden *ph* Otto
Heller *m* Muir Mathieson *pd* Ken Adam

Gina Lollobrigida, Sean Connery, *Ralph
Richardson*, Johnny Sekka, Laurence Hardy,
Alexander Knox

Woman of the Dunes*
Japan 1964   127m   bw
Teshigahara (Kiichi Ichikawa)
original title: *Suna no Onna*

An entomologist on a deserted beach finds an
attractive young widow living in a shack at the
bottom of a huge sand pit, spends the night with
her, can't escape, and finally doesn't want to.
Unique sex melodrama, all shifting sand and
picturesque angles, with a clear meaning; but far
too long.

w Kobo Abe *d Hiroshi Teshigahara
ph* Hiroshi Segawa

Eiji Okada, Kyoko Kishoda
   'Teasingly opaque, broodingly erotic.'—*MFB*

AAN: Hiroshi Teshigahara

Woman of the North Country
US 1952   90m   Trucolor
Republic (Joseph Kane)

Minnesota 1890: rivalry over an iron ore mine

erupts between a young engineer and an
ambitious woman.
Standard western.

w Norman Reilly Raine *d* Joseph Kane *ph* Jack
Marta *m* R. Dale Butts

Ruth Hussey, Rod Cameron, John Agar, Gale
Storm, Jim Davis, J. Carrol Naish

Woman of the Year***
US 1942   114m   bw
MGM (Joseph L. Mankiewicz)

A sports columnist marries a lady politician;
they have nothing in common but love.
Simple, effective, mildly sophisticated comedy
which allows two splendid stars, in harness for
the first time, to do their thing to the general
benefit.

w *Ring Lardner Jnr, Michael Kanin d George
Stevens ph* Joseph Ruttenberg *m* Franz
Waxman

Spencer Tracy, Katharine Hepburn, Fay
Bainter, Reginald Owen, William Bendix, Dan
Tobin, Minor Watson, Roscoe Karns
   'Between them they have enough charm to
keep any ball rolling.'—*William Whitebait*

AA: script
AAN: Katharine Hepburn

The Woman on Pier 13
US 1949   73m   bw
RKO (Jack J. Gross)
aka: *I Married a Communist*

A shipping executive is blackmailed by
communists, who know of a youthful crime, into
helping them spy.
Laboured witch-hunt melodrama.

w Charles Grayson, Robert Hardy Andrews
d Robert Stevenson *ph* Nicholas Musuraca
m Leigh Harline

Laraine Day, Robert Ryan, John Agar, Thomas
Gomez, Janis Carter, Richard Rober, William
Talman

Woman on the Beach
US 1947   71m   bw
RKO (Jack J. Gloss)

A mentally ailing coastguard meets a *femme
fatale* and comes between her and her sadistic
husband.
Nuthouse melodrama which neither convinces
nor compels for a moment.

w Frank Davis, Jean Renoir, *novel* None So
Blind by Mitchell Wilson *d* Jean Renoir *ph* Leo
Tover, Harry Wild *m* Hanns Eisler

Joan Bennett, Robert Ryan, Charles Bickford, Nan Leslie, Walter Sande

A Woman Rebels*
US 1936 88m bw
RKO (Pandro S. Berman)

A Victorian miss fights for women's rights and has an illegitimate baby.
Interesting, half-forgotten star drama.

w Anthony Veiller, Ernest Vajda, *novel* Portrait of a Rebel by Netta Syrett *d* Mark Sandrich *ph* Robert de Grasse *m* Roy Webb *ad* Van Nest Polglase

Katharine Hepburn, Herbert Marshall, Elizabeth Allan, Donald Crisp, Doris Dudley, David Manners, Van Heflin, Lucile Watson, Eily Malyon

Woman Times Seven
US / France 1967 99m De Luxe
TCF / Embassy (Arthur Cohn)

Seven sketches, in each of which a woman behaves typically of her sex.
Humourless after-dinner entertainment.

w Cesare Zavattini *d* Vittorio de Sica *ph* Christian Matras *m* Riz Ortolani

Shirley Maclaine, Peter Sellers, Rossano Brazzi, Vittorio Gassman, Lex Barker, Elsa Martinelli, Robert Morley, Adrienne Corri, Patrick Wymark, Alan Arkin, Michael Caine, Anita Ekberg, Philippe Noiret

A Woman under the Influence*
US 1974 146m colour
Faces International (Sam Shaw)

A white collar worker's marriage goes sour. Insanely long case history in close up, with all parties constantly on the brink of hysteria. Often sharply observed, but hard to sit through.

wd John Cassavetes *ph* Mitch Breit *m* Bo Harwood

Peter Falk, Gena Rowlands

AAN: John Cassavetes (as director); Gena Rowlands

The Woman's Angle
GB 1952 86m bw
ABP / Leslie Arliss / Bow Belles (Walter Mycroft)

In a divorce court three flashbacks tell of the life of a composer.
Damp little formula drama for matinee audiences, refashioned from a successful silent film.

wd Leslie Arliss, *novel* Three Cups of Coffee by

Ruth Feiner *ph* Erwin Hillier *m* Robert Gill; the Mansell Concerto by Kenneth Leslie Smith

Edward Underdown, Cathy O'Donnell, Lois Maxwell, Claude Farrell, Peter Reynolds, Marjorie Fielding

A Woman's Face**
US 1941 105m bw
MGM (Victor Saville)

A scarred and embittered woman turns to crime but jibs at murder.
Curious, unexpected but very entertaining melodrama with a courtroom frame, Swedish settings, an excellent cast and some bravura sequences.

w Donald Ogden Stewart, *play* Il Était une Fois by Francis de Croisset *d* George Cukor *ph* Robert Planck *m* Bronislau Kaper

Joan Crawford, Melvyn Douglas, *Conrad Veidt*, Osa Massen, Reginald Owen, Albert Basserman, Marjorie Main, Donald Meek, Connie Gilchrist

A Woman's Secret
US 1949 85m bw
RKO (Herman J. Mankiewicz)

An ex-singer grooms a girl as her successor but lives to regret it.
Downright peculiar little *film noir* by the co-author of *Citizen Kane* (though not so that you'd notice).

w Herman J. Mankiewicz, *novel* Mortgage on Life by Vicki Baum *d* Nicholas Ray *ph* George Diskant *m* Constantin Bakaleinikoff

Maureen O'Hara, Gloria Grahame, Melvyn Douglas, Bill Williams, Victor Jory, Mary Phillips

A Woman's Vengeance*
US 1948 96m bw
U-I

A man is convicted for the murder of his invalid wife, actually committed by a jealous woman in love with him but later spurned.
Interesting but very stagey melodrama from one of its author's more commercial ventures.

w Aldous Huxley, from his story and play The Gioconda Smile *d* Zoltan Korda *ph* Russell Metty

Charles Boyer, Jessica Tandy, Ann Blyth, Cedric Hardwicke, Mildred Natwick

Woman's World**
US 1954 94m Technicolor
Cinemascope
TCF (Charles Brackett)

Three top salesmen and their wives are summoned to New York by the boss, who seeks to choose a new general manager.

Amusing, superficial pattern comedy-drama for an all-star cast, backed by all-round technical competence.

w Claude Binyon, Mary Loos, Richard Sale d Jean Negulesco ph Joe MacDonald m Cyril Mockridge

Clifton Webb, Lauren Bacall, Van Heflin, June Allyson, Fred MacMurray, Arlene Dahl, Cornel Wilde, Elliott Reid, Marhalo Gillmore

The Women***

US 1939   132m   bw (Technicolor sequence)
MGM (Hunt Stromberg)

A New York socialite gets a divorce but later thinks better of it.

Bitchy comedy drama distinguished by an all-girl cast ('135 women with men on their minds'). An over-generous slice of real theatre, skilfully adapted, with rich sets, plenty of laughs, and some memorable scenes between the fighting ladies.

w *Anita Loos, Jane Murfin, play Clare Boothe d George Cukor ph Oliver T. Marsh,* Joseph Ruttenberg m Edward Ward, David Snell

Norma Shearer, Joan Crawford, *Rosalind Russell,* Mary Boland, Paulette Goddard, Joan Fontaine, Lucile Watson, Phyllis Povah, Virginia Weidler, Ruth Hussey, Margaret Dumont, Marjorie Main, Hedda Hopper

'Whether you go or not depends on whether you can stand Miss Shearer with tears flowing steadily in all directions at once, and such an endless damn back fence of cats.'—*Otis Ferguson*

Women in Love***

GB 1969   130m   De Luxe
UA / Brandywine (Larry Kramer)

Two girls have their first sexual encounters in the Midlands during the twenties.

Satisfactory rendering of a celebrated novel, with excellent period detail atoning for rather irritating characters. The nude wrestling scene was a famous first.

w Larry Kramer, *novel D. H. Lawrence d Ken Russell ph Billy Williams m* Georges Delerue

Glenda Jackson, Jennie Linden, Alan Bates, Oliver Reed, Michael Gough, Alan Webb

'They should take all the pretentious dialogue off the soundtrack and call it Women in Heat.'—*Rex Reed*

'Two-thirds success, one-third ambitious

failure.'—*Michael Billington, Illustrated London News*

AA: Glenda Jackson
AAN: Larry Kramer; Ken Russell; Billy Williams

Women of All Nations

US 1931   72m   bw
Fox

Flagg and Quirt, back in the Marines, have amorous adventures in Sweden, Nicaragua and Egypt.

Routine fun and games with the heroes of *What Price Glory.*

w Barry Connors d Raoul Walsh ph Lucien Andriot m Reginald H. Bassett

Edmund Lowe, Victor McLaglen, Greta Nissen, El Brendel, Fifi D'Orsay, Bela Lugosi, Humphrey Bogart

Women of Twilight

GB 1952   89m   bw
Romulus (Daniel M. Angel)

Unmarried mothers are victimized by a professional baby farmer.

Sordid, claustrophobic and ham-handed version of an exploitation play designed to provide another monstrous part for its star.

w Anatole de Grunwald, *novel* Sylvia Rayman d Gordon Parry ph Jack Asher m Alan Gray

Freda Jackson, René Ray, Lois Maxwell, Joan Dowling, Dora Bryan, Vida Hope, Mary Germaine, Laurence Harvey

Won Ton Ton, the Dog Who Saved Hollywood

US 1976   92m   colour
Paramount / David V. Picker, Arnold Schulman, Michael Winner

In twenties Hollywood, a lost Alsatian dog becomes a movie star but later suffers some ups and downs before being reunited with his mistress.

Scatty, unlikeable comedy with too frantic a pace, apparently in desperation at the dearth of funny lines and situations. The sixty 'guest stars' barely get a look in; the director seems to think (erroneously) that their appearance makes some kind of point even though they have nothing to do. Altogether, an embarrassment.

w Arnold Schulman, Cy Howard d Michael Winner ph Richard H. Kline m Neal Hefti

Madeleine Kahn, Art Carney, Bruce Dern, Ron Leibman; and Dennis Morgan, William Demarest, Virginia Mayo, Rory Calhoun, Henry Wilcoxon, Ricardo Montalban, Jackie

Coogan, Johnny Weissmuller, Aldo Ray, Ethel Merman, Joan Blondell, Yvonne de Carlo, Andy Devine, Broderick Crawford, Richard Arlen, Jack La Rue, Dorothy Lamour, Phil Silvers, Gloria de Haven, Stepin Fetchit, Rudy Vallee, George Jessel, Ann Miller, Janet Blair, the Ritz Brothers, Victor Mature, Fernando Lamas, Cyd Charisse, Huntz Hall, Edgar Bergen, Peter Lawford, Regis Toomey, Alice Faye, Milton Berle, John Carradine, Walter Pidgeon, etc.

Wonder Bar**
US 1934   84m   bw
Warner (Robert Lord)

Love and hate backstage at a Paris night club.
Curious musical drama with an interesting cast and fairly stunning numbers.

w Earl Baldwin, *play* Geza Herczeg, Karl Farkas, Robert Katscher d Lloyd Bacon ch Busby Berkeley songs Harry Warren, Al Dubin ad Jack Okey

Al Jolson, Kay Francis, Dolores del Rio, Ricardo Cortez, Dick Powell, Guy Kibbee, Ruth Donnelly, Hugh Herbert, Louise Fazenda, Fifi D'Orsay

Wonder Man***
US 1945   97m   Technicolor
Samuel Goldwyn

A mild-mannered student is persuaded by the ghost of his dead twin to avenge his murder.
Smooth, successful mixture of *Topper*, a nightclub musical, a gangster drama and the star's own brand of fooling; this is possibly his best vehicle.

w Don Hartman, Melville Shavelson, Philip Rapp, story Arthur Sheekman d Bruce Humberstone ph Victor Milner, William Snyder md Louis Forbes, Ray Heindorf sp John Fulton

Danny Kaye, Vera-Ellen, Virginia Mayo, Steve Cochran, S. Z. Sakall, Allen Jenkins, Ed Brophy, Donald Woods, Otto Kruger, Richard Lane, Natalie Schaefer

AAN: Louis Forbes, Ray Heindorf; song 'So in Love' (m David Rose, ly Leo Robin)

The Wonderful Country
US 1959   96m   Technicolor
UA / DRM (Chester Erskine)

A wandering gunman is offered a job by the Texas Rangers.
Complexly plotted western offering a range of familiar exploits.

w Robert Ardrey, novel Tom Lea d Robert Parrish ph Floyd Crosby, Alex Phillips

Robert Mitchum, Julie London, Pedro Armendariz, Gary Merrill, Jack Oakie, Albert Dekker, Charles McGraw, John Banner, Jay Novello

Wonderful Life*
GB 1964   113m   Techniscope
EMI / Elstree Distributors / Ivy (Kenneth Harper)

Four entertainers on a luxury liner are hired by a film crew in Africa.
Slight but zestful youth musical with highly illogical detail; the highlight is a ten-minute spoof history of the movies.

w Peter Myers, Ronald Cass d Sidney J. Furie ph Ken Higgins pd Stanley Dorfman

Cliff Richard, Walter Slezak, Susan Hampshire, Melvyn Hayes, Richard O'Sullivan, Una Stubbs, Derek Bond, Gerald Harper, the Shadows

The Wonderful World of the Brothers Grimm*
US 1962   134m   Technicolor   Cinerama
MGM / Cinerama / George Pal

An account of the lives of the German fairy tale writers is supplemented by three of their stories, *The Dancing Princess, The Cobbler and the Elves* and *The Singing Bone*.
Saccharine, heavy-handed pantomime with insufficient comedy, menace or spectacle.

w David P. Harmon, Charles Beaumont, William Roberts d Henry Levin, George Pal ph Paul C. Vogel m Leigh Harline ad George W. Davis, Edward Carfagno

Laurence Harvey, Karl Boehm, Claire Bloom, Barbara Eden, Walter Slezak, Oscar Homolka, Martita Hunt, Russ Tamblyn, Yvette Mimieux, Jim Backus, Beulah Bondi, Terry-Thomas, Buddy Hackett, Otto Kruger

AAN: Paul C. Vogel; Leigh Harline

The Wonders of Aladdin
Italy 1961   92m   Technicolor   Cinemascope
Embassy / Lux

With the help of a genie, Aladdin defeats a usurper and wins the princess's hand.
Flat and disappointing pantomime with virtually no charm.

w Luther Davis d Henry Levin, Mario Bava ph Tonino Delli Colli m Angelo Lavagnino

Donald O'Connor, Vittorio de Sica, Aldo Fabrizi, Michèle Mercier

The Wooden Horse **
GB 1950 101m bw
British Lion / Wessex / London Films (Ian Dalrymple)

During World War II, British prisoners escape from Stalag Luft III by tunnelling under a vaulting horse.
Standard, solid POW drama with predictable but exciting and occasionally moving developments.

w Eric Williams, from his novel d Jack Lee
ph C. Pennington-Richards m Clifton Parker

Leo Genn, David Tomlinson, Anthony Steele, David Greene, Michael Goodliffe, Bryan Forbes, Jacques Brunius

Words and Music **
US 1948 121m Technicolor
MGM (Arthur Freed)

The songwriting collaboration of Richard Rodgers and Lorenz Hart.
Musical biopic which packs in a lot of good numbers and manages a script which is neither too offensive nor too prominent.

w Fred Finklehoffe d Norman Taurog
ph Charles Rosher, Harry Stradling md Lennie Hayton ch Robert Alton, Gene Kelly

Tom Drake, Mickey Rooney, Perry Como, Mel Tormé, Betty Garrett, June Allyson, Lena Horne, Ann Sothern, Allyn McLerie, Gene Kelly, Vera-Ellen, Cyd Charisse, Janet Leigh, Marshall Thompson

Work Is a Four-Letter Word
GB 1968 93m Technicolor
Universal / Cavalcade (Thomas Clyde)

A power station attendant is interested only in growing mushrooms, which have a chaotic effect on his private life.
Weakly futuristic industrial fantasy which the author would probably claim to be about lack of communication. Bored audiences might have a similar view.

w Jeremy Brooks, play Eh? by Henry Livings
d Peter Hall ph Gilbert Taylor m Guy Woolfenden

David Warner, Cilla Black, Elizabeth Spriggs, Zia Mohyeddin, Joe Gladwin

The World Changes *
US 1933 91m bw
Warner (Robert Lord)

A simple farmer becomes a powerful executive, and success goes to his head.

Adequate moral drama of its time, well staged and acted.

w Edward Chodorov d Mervyn Le Roy
ph Tony Gaudio

Paul Muni, Aline MacMahon, Mary Astor, Donald Cook, Patricia Ellis, Jean Muir, Margaret Lindsay, Guy Kibbee, Alan Dinehart

The World in His Arms *
US 1952 104m Technicolor
Universal (Aaron Rosenberg)

In old San Francisco, a seal-poaching sea captain meets a Russian countess.
Romantic melodrama with plushy period backgrounds and a fair measure of action, climaxing in a boat race.

w Borden Chase d Raoul Walsh ph Russell Metty m Frank Skinner

Gregory Peck, Ann Blyth, Anthony Quinn, John McIntire, Andrea King, Carl Esmond, Eugenie Leontovitch

World in My Corner *
US 1955 85m bw
U-I (Aaron Rosenberg)

A penniless would-be prizefighter becomes the protégé of a millionaire and wins his daughter but not the crucial fight.
Well-done minor melodrama.

w Jack Sher d Jesse Hibbs ph Maury Gertsman
m Joseph Gershenson

Audie Murphy, Barbara Rush, Jeff Morrow, John McIntire, Tommy Rall, Howard St John

The World Moves On *
US 1934 90m bw
Fox (Winfield Sheehan)

The saga of a Louisiana family up to World War I.
Careful, good-looking general entertainment.

w Reginald C. Berkeley d John Ford ph George Schneiderman m Max Steiner

Madeleine Carroll, Franchot Tone, Reginald Denny, Stepin Fetchit, Lumsden Hare, Louise Dresser, Sig Rumann

The World of Henry Orient **
US 1964 106m De Luxe Panavision
UA / Pan Arts (Jerome Hellman)

Two rich 14-year-old New York girls build fantasies around a concert pianist.
Charming, immaculately mounted, refreshingly unusual but overlong comedy.

w Nora and Nunnally Johnson, novel Nora

Johnson *d George Roy Hill ph* Boris Kaufman, Arthur J. Ornitz *m* Elmer Bernstein *pd James Sullivan*

Tippy Walker, Merri Spaeth, Peter Sellers, Angela Lansbury, Paula Prentiss, Phyllis Thaxter, Tom Bosley, Bibi Osterwald

The World of Suzie Wong
GB 1960 129m Technicolor
Paramount / Ray Stark (Hugh Perceval)

A Hong Kong prostitute falls in love with the artist for whom she poses.
Dull, set-bound romantic melodrama without much gusto.

w John Patrick, *play* Paul Osborn *d* Richard Quine *ph* Geoffrey Unsworth *m* George Duning

William Holden, *Nancy Kwan*, Sylvia Syms, Michael Wilding, Laurence Naismith, Jackie Chan

'Maybe one day it will all make the grade as a musical.'—*MFB*

World Premiere*
US 1940 70m bw
Paramount

A zany film producer thinks up some wild publicity schemes for his new film and accidentally traps some Nazi spies.
Occasionally amusing farce mainly notable for its star.

w Earl Felton *d* Ted Tetzlaff

John Barrymore, Ricardo Cortez, Frances Farmer, Sig Rumann, Fritz Feld, Eugene Pallette, Luis Alberni, Virginia Dale, Don Castle

The World Ten Times Over
GB 1963 93m bw
Cyclops (Michael Luke)
US title: *Pussycat Alley*

Two semi-prostitutes try to improve their lot.
Dreary, derivative low-life drama with flashy technique.

wd Wolf Rilla *ph* Larry Pizer *m* Edwin Astley

Sylvia Syms, June Ritchie, Edward Judd, William Hartnell, Francis de Wolff

The World, the Flesh and the Devil*
US 1959 95m bw Cinemascope
MGM / Sol C. Siegel / Harbel

Trapped for five days in a mine cave-in, a man struggles to the surface to find a dead world devastated by atomic war; but still alive are the elements of an eternal triangle . . .

Enterprising but rather disappointing fantasy which tends to become merely glum and rather self-consciously carries a panic button message.

wd Ranald MacDougall *ph* Harold J. Marzorati *m* Miklos Rozsa *ad* William A. Horning, Paul Groesse

Harry Belafonte, Inger Stevens, Mel Ferrer

World without End
US 1956 80m Technicolor
Cinemascope
AA (Richard Heermance)

A space ship breaks the time barrier and returns to earth in 2508, to find that intelligent humans have been driven underground by mutants.
Reasonably lively sci-fi with horror elements, and a plot borrowed from H. G. Wells.

wd Edward Bernds *ph* Ellsworth Fredericks *m* Leith Stevens

Hugh Marlowe, Nancy Gates, Rod Taylor

The World's Greatest Athlete
US 1973 92m Technicolor
Walt Disney (Bill Walsh)

An American sports coach on an African holiday finds a young Tarzan with amazing powers.
Simple-minded comedy with lame tomfoolery and trickwork.

w Gerald Gardiner, Dee Caruso *d* Robert Scheerer *ph* Frank Phillips *m* Marvin Hamlisch

Tim Conway, John-Michael Vincent, John Amos, Roscoe Lee Browne

The World's Greatest Lover
US 1977 89m De Luxe
TCF (Gene Wilder)

In the twenties, a rival studio starts a search for a man to surpass Valentino.
Imitative slapstick extravaganza in which . anything goes but hardly anything pleases.

wd Gene Wilder *ph* Gerald Hirschfeld *m* John Morris

Gene Wilder, Carol Kane, Dom DeLuise, Fritz Feld

Worm's Eye View
GB 1951 77m bw
ABFD / Byron (Henry Halsted)

Incidents in the lives of a group of RAF billetees.
Plotless comedy from a highly successful stage romp; plainly made and empty-headed but not disagreeable.

w R. F. Delderfield, from his play *d* Jack

Raymond *ph* James Wilson *m* Tony Lowry, Tony Fones

Ronald Shiner, Garry Marsh, Diana Dors, Eric Davis, John Blythe

The Wrath of God
US 1972 111m Metrocolor Panavision
MGM / Rainbow / Cineman (William S. Gilmore Jnr)

During a twenties Central American revolution, a bootlegger joins forces with a defrocked priest. Noisy, violent adventure yarn which works up to a gory climax but does not take itself too seriously.

wd Ralph Nelson, *novel* James Graham *ph* Alex Phillips Jnr *m* Lalo Schifrin

Robert Mitchum, Frank Langella, Rita Hayworth, Victor Buono, John Colicos

The Wreck of the Mary Deare*
US 1959 108m Metrocolor Cinemascope
MGM / Blaustein–Baroda (David Blaustein)

An insurance fraud comes to light when a salvage boat is rescued from high seas. Curious, star-studded amalgam of seafaring action and courtroom melodrama, originally intended for Hitchcock.

w Eric Ambler, *novel* Hammond Innes *d* Michael Anderson *ph* Joseph Ruttenberg, F. A. Young *m* George Duning

Charlton Heston, Gary Cooper, Michael Redgrave, Emlyn Williams, Cecil Parker, Alexander Knox, Virginia McKenna, Richard Harris

The Wrecking Crew
US 1968 104m Technicolor
Columbia / Meadway / Claude (Irving Allen)

Special agent Matt Helm recovers bullion stolen from a Danish train.
Camped-up spy buffoonery with the usual nubile ladies and a production which seeks to be flashy but succeeds only in being tatty.

w William McGivern, *novel* Donald Hamilton *d* Phil Karlson *ph* Sam Leavitt *m* Hugo Montenegro

Dean Martin, Elke Sommer, Sharon Tate, Nancy Kwan, Nigel Green, Tina Louise

Written on the Wind**
US 1956 99m Technicolor
U-I (Albert Zugsmith)

A secretary marries her oil tycoon boss and finds herself the steadying force in a very rocky family.

The sheerest Hollywood moonshine: high-flying melodramatic hokum which moves fast enough to be very entertaining.

w George Zuckerman, *novel* Robert Wilder *d* Douglas Sirk *ph* Russell Metty *m* Frank Skinner

Lauren Bacall, *Robert Stack, Dorothy Malone*, Rock Hudson, Robert Keith, Grant Williams

AA: Dorothy Malone
AAN: title song (*m* Victor Young, *ly* Sammy Cahn); Robert Stack

The Wrong Arm of the Law*
GB 1962 94m bw
Romulus / Robert Verlaise (Aubrey Baring, E. M. Smedley Aston)

London gangsters plan retaliation against Australian interlopers, and offer Scotland Yard a temporary truce.
Forgettable but pretty funny crook comedy in the British vein, with pacy script and excellent comedy timing.

w John Warren, Len Heath *d* Cliff Owen *ph* Ernest Steward *m* Richard Rodney Bennett

Peter Sellers, Lionel Jeffries, Bernard Cribbins, Davy Kaye, Nanette Newman, Bill Kerr, John Le Mesurier

The Wrong Box*
GB 1966 110m Technicolor
Columbia / Salamander (Bryan Forbes)

Two elderly Victorian brothers are the last survivors of a tontine (an involved form of lottery) and try to murder each other.
Well-intentioned and star-studded black farce in which the excellent period trappings and stray jokes completely overwhelm the plot.

w Larry Gelbart, Burt Shevelove, *novel* Robert Louis Stevenson, Lloyd Osbourne *d* Bryan Forbes *ph* Gerry Turpin *m* John Barry *ad* Ray Simm

Ralph Richardson, John Mills, Michael Caine, *Wilfrid Lawson*, Nanette Newman, Peter Cook, Dudley Moore, Peter Sellers, Tony Hancock, Thorley Walters, Cicely Courtneidge, Irene Handl, John Le Mesurier, Gerald Sim, Norman Bird, Tutte Lemkow

'A slapdash affair in which anything goes, irrespective of whether or not it fits.'—*Tom Milne*

The Wrong Man*
US 1957 105m bw
Warner (Herbert Coleman)

A New York musician is mistaken by police for an armed bandit, and both witnesses and circumstances prevent the truth from emerging. True but downbeat story from the headlines, filmed with remarkably little persuasion; not its director's *métier* despite evidence of his usual thoroughness.

w Maxwell Anderson, Angus MacPhail *d* Alfred Hitchcock *ph* Robert Burks *m* Bernard Herrmann

Henry Fonda, Vera Miles, Anthony Quayle, Harold J. Stone, Esther Minciotti

WUSA*
US 1970 117m Technicolor Panavision Paramount / Mirror / Coleytown / Stuart Rosenberg (Paul Newman, John Foreman)

A penniless wanderer causes chaos when he becomes the announcer for a right-wing radio station.
A farcical melodrama for the intelligentsia, and for the most part a thoroughgoing bore. The last part offers a compensation or two.

w Robert Stone, from his novel Hall of Mirrors *d* Stuart Rosenberg *ph* Richard Moore *m* Lalo Schifrin

Paul Newman, Joanne Woodward, Laurence Harvey, Anthony Perkins, Pat Hingle, Cloris Leachman, Don Gordon, Robert Quarry, Bruce Cabot, Moses Gunn, Wayne Rogers

Wuthering Heights****
US 1939 104m bw
Samuel Goldwyn

The daughter of an unhappy middle-class Yorkshire family falls passionately in love with a gypsy who has been brought up with her.
Despite American script and settings, this wildly romantic film makes a pretty fair stab at capturing the power of at least the first half of a classic Victorian novel, and in all respects it's a superb Hollywood production of its day and a typical one, complete with ghostly finale and a first-rate cast.

w Ben Hecht, Charles MacArthur, novel Emily Brontë *d* William Wyler *ph* Gregg Toland *m* Alfred Newman

Laurence Olivier, Merle Oberon, David Niven, Hugh Williams, Flora Robson, Geraldine Fitzgerald, Donald Crisp, Leo G. Carroll, Cecil Kellaway, Miles Mander

'Unquestionably one of the most distinguished pictures of the year.'—*Frank S. Nugent, New York Times*

'A pattern of constant forward motion, with overtones maintained throughout the rise of interest and suspense.'—*Otis Ferguson*

'A strong and sombre film, poetically written as the novel not always was, sinister and wild as it was meant to be, far more compact dramatically than Miss Brontë had made it.'— *Richard Mallett, Punch*

AA: Gregg Toland
AAN: best picture; script; William Wyler; Alfred Newman; Laurence Olivier; Geraldine Fitzgerald

Wuthering Heights*
GB 1970 105m Movielab
AIP (John Pellatt)

Somewhat rewritten and overkeen to find a 1970 mood and interpretation for what can only be a period piece, this disappointing version marks a Z-film company's first determined effort to enter the big-time.

w Patrick Tilley *d* Robert Fuest *ph* John Coquillon *m* Michel Legrand

Anna Calder-Marshall, Timothy Dalton, Harry Andrews, Pamela Brown, Judy Cornwell, James Cossins, Rosalie Crutchley, Julian Glover, Hugh Griffith, Ian Ogilvy, Aubrey Woods

X

X—The Man with X-Ray Eyes

US 1963   80m   Pathecolor
'Spectarama'
AIP (Roger Corman)
GB title: *The Man with the X-Ray Eyes*

A scientist gives himself X-ray vision and goes mad.

Interesting but rather unpleasant horror story with moments of cleverness but a general air of disappointment.

w Robert Dillon, Ray Russell *d Roger Corman*
ph Floyd Crosby *m* Les Baxter

Ray Milland, Diana Van Der Vlis, Harold J. Stone, John Hoyt, Don Rickles, John Dierkes

'When the dialogue suggests that Xavier is being driven insane by strange and satanic visions, what one actually sees is rather a comedown.'—*MFB*

'Concise, confident, and not an ounce overweight.'—*NFT, 1967*

X the Unknown*

GB 1956   81m   bw
Hammer (Anthony Hinds)

A mysterious force feeds on radiation from a research station on a Scottish moor, and becomes a seeping mass.

Minor sci-fi horror with a monster like liquid lino, rushed into release to cash in on *The Quatermass Experiment*.

w Jimmy Sangster *d* Leslie Norman *ph* Gerald Gibbs *m* James Bernard

Dean Jagger, Edward Chapman, Leo McKern, William Lucas, John Harvey, Peter Hammond, Michael Ripper, Anthony Newley

Y

Yangtse Incident*
GB 1957 113m bw
British Lion / Wilcox–Neagle (Herbert Wilcox)
US title: *Battle Hell*; aka: *Escape of the Amethyst*

In 1949 a British frigate is shelled and held captive by communist shore batteries in the Yangtse.
Stalwart but not very exciting British war heroics.

w Eric Ambler, *book* Franklin Gollings
d Michael Anderson *ph* Gordon Dines
m Leighton Lucas

Richard Todd, William Hartnell, Akim Tamiroff, Donald Houston, Keye Luke, Sophie Stewart, Robert Urquhart, James Kenney, Barry Foster

The Yakuza
US 1975 112m Technicolor Panavision
Warner (Sydney Pollack, Michael Hamilburg)
Japanese gangsters kidnap the daughter of a Los Angeles shipping magnate.
Violent thriller roughly exploiting an ancient Japanese genre.

w Paul Schrader, Robert Towne *d* Sydney Pollack *ph* Okazaki Kozo, Duke Callaghan *m* Dave Grusin

Robert Mitchum, Takakura Ken, Brian Keith, Kishi Keilo, Okada Eiji
'No more than a curious footnote to the western exploitation of oriental action movies.'—*Tony Rayns*

A Yank at Eton
US 1942 88m bw
MGM (John Considine Jnr)
A rich, wild American boy is sent to Eton to cool down.
Tame, tasteless imitation of *A Yank at Oxford* with younger participants.

w George Oppenheimer, Lionel Houser, Thomas Phipps *d* Norman Taurog

Mickey Rooney, Freddie Bartholemew, Ian Hunter, Edmund Gwenn, Alan Mowbray, Tina Thayer, Marta Linden, Alan Napier, Terry Kilburn

A Yank at Oxford**
GB 1938 105m bw
MGM (Michael Balcon)

A cocky young American student comes to Oxford and meets all kinds of trouble.
A huge pre-war success which now seems naïve, this was the first big Anglo-American production from a team which went on to make *The Citadel* and *Goodbye Mr Chips* before war stymied them.

w Malcolm Stuart Boylan, Walter Ferris, George Oppenheimer, Leon Gordon, Roland Pertwee, John Monk Saunders, Sidney Gilliat, Michael Hogan *d* Jack Conway

Robert Taylor, Vivien Leigh, Maureen O'Sullivan, Lionel Barrymore, Robert Coote, Edmund Gwenn, C. V. France, Griffith Jones, Morton Selten

A Yank in the RAF*
US 1941 98m bw
TCF (Lou Edelman)
An American chorine stranded in London falls for the titular gentleman.
Silly but entertaining wartime flagwaver.

w Karl Tunberg, Darrell Ware, *story* Melville Crossman (Zanuck) *d* Henry King *ph* Leon Shamroy *m* Alfred Newman

Tyrone Power, Betty Grable, John Sutton, Reginald Gardiner, Donald Stuart, Morton Lowry, Richard Fraser, Bruce Lester

A Yank on the Burma Road
US 1942 66m bw
MGM (Samuel Marx)
GB title: *China Caravan*

A tough truck driver in the Far East abandons profit for heroism when he hears of Pearl Harbor.
Crass action flagwaver.

w George Kahn, Hugo Butler, David Lang *d* George B. Seitz

Barry Nelson, Laraine Day, Stuart Crawford, Keye Luke, Sen Yung
'Glib humbug, playing tiddleywinks with high stakes.'—*Theodore Strauss*

Yankee Doodle Dandy****
US 1942 126m bw
Warner (Hal B. Wallis, William Cagney)

The life story of dancing vaudevillian George M. Cohan.

Outstanding showbiz biopic, with unassuming but effective production, deft patriotic backdrops and a marvellous, strutting, magnetic star performance.

w Robert Buckner, Edmund Joseph d Michael Curtiz ph James Wong Howe m Heinz Roemheld md Heinz Roemheld, Ray Heindorf songs George M. Cohan

James Cagney, Joan Leslie, Walter Huston, Rosemary de Camp, Richard Whorf, George Tobias, Jeanne Cagney, Irene Manning, S. Z. Sakall, George Barbier, Frances Langford, Walter Catlett, Eddie Foy Jnr

AA: James Cagney

AAN: best picture; original story (Robert Buckner); Michael Curtiz; Heinz Roemheld, Ray Heindorf; Walter Huston

The Yearling**
US 1946 134m Technicolor
MGM (Sidney Franklin)

The son of an old-time country farmer is attached to a stray deer.
Excellent family film for four-handkerchief patrons.

w Paul Osborn, novel Marjorie Kinnan Rawlings d Clarence Brown ph Charles Rosher, Leonard Smith m Herbert Stothart

Gregory Peck, Jane Wyman, Claude Jarman Jnr, Chill Wills, Clem Bevans, Margaret Wycherly, Henry Travers, Forrest Tucker

AA: Charles Rosher, Leonard Smith (and Arthur Arling)
AAN: best picture; Clarence Brown; Gregory Peck; Jane Wyman

The Years Between
GB 1946 100m bw
GFD / Sydney Box

An MP returns after being presumed dead in the war and finds his wife has been elected in his place.
Stilted variation on the Enoch Arden theme; plot and performances alike unpersuasive.

w Muriel and Sydney Box, play Daphne du Maurier d Compton Bennett

Michael Redgrave, Valerie Hobson, Flora Robson, Felix Aylmer, James McKechnie, Dulcie Gray, Edward Rigby

The Yellow Balloon
GB 1952 80m bw
ABP (Victor Skuzetsky)

A small boy who thinks he has killed his friend is terrorized by a murderer.
Tense but not especially rewarding suspenser, clearly borrowed from The Window.

w Anne Burnaby, J. Lee-Thompson d J. Lee-Thompson ph Gilbert Taylor m Philip Green

Kenneth More, William Sylvester, Kathleen Ryan, Andrew Ray, Bernard Lee, Veronica Hurst

The Yellow Cab Man
US 1950 84m bw
MGM (Richard Goldstone)

A taxi-driving inventor is pursued by crooks after his secret formula.
Moderate star comedy.

w Devery Freeman, Albert Beich d Jack Donohue ph Harry Stradling m Scott Bradley

Red Skelton, Gloria de Haven, Walter Slezak, Edward Arnold, James Gleason, Paul Harvey, Jay C. Flippen

Yellow Canary*
GB 1943 98m bw
RKO / Imperator (Herbert Wilcox)

A socialite suspected of being a Nazi sympathizer is really a British spy.
Mild wartime melodrama chiefly notable for allotting an apparently unsympathetic part to the beloved Miss Neagle.

w De Witt Bodeen, Miles Malleson, story Pamela Bower d Herbert Wilcox ph Max Greene

Anna Neagle, Richard Greene, Nova Pilbeam, Lucie Mannheim, Cyril Fletcher, Albert Lieven, Margaret Rutherford, Marjorie Fielding

Yellow Canary
US 1963 93m bw Cinemascope
TCF / Cooga Mooga (Maury Dexter)

The baby son of a singing idol is kidnapped.
Rather dreary suspenser with too much dialogue.

w Rod Serling, novel Easy Come Easy Go by Whit Masterson d Buzz Kulik ph Floyd Crosby m Kenyon Hopkins

Pat Boone, Barbara Eden, Steve Forrest, Jack Klugman, Jesse White, John Banner, Jeff Corey

Yellow Dog

GB 1973   101m   Eastmancolor
Scotia–Barber / Akari (Terence Donovan)

A Japanese agent in London keeps watch on a
mysterious scientist.

Incoherent spy thriller with a few hybrid
oddities.

w Shinobu Hashimoto d Terence Donovan
ph David Watkin m Ron Grainer

Jiro Tamiya, Robert Hardy, Carolyn Seymour,
Joseph O'Conor

Yellow Jack*

US 1938   83m   bw
MGM (Jack Cummings)

In 1899 Cuba a marine offers himself as a guinea
pig to combat yellow fever.

Solid, unsurprising, period medical melodrama
with conventional romantic sidelights.

w Edward Chodorov, play Sidney Howard, Paul
de Kruif d George B. Seitz ph Lester White
m William Axt

Robert Montgomery, Virginia Bruce, Lewis
Stone, Andy Devine, Henry Hull, Charles
Coburn, Buddy Ebsen, Henry O'Neill, Janet
Beecher

The Yellow Rolls Royce*

GB 1964   122m   Metrocolor   Panavision
MGM (Anatole de Grunwald)

Three stories about the owners of an expensive
car; an aristocrat, a gangster, and a wandering
millionairess.

Lukewarm all-star concoction lacking either
good stories or a connecting thread.

w Terence Rattigan d Anthony Asquith
ph Jack Hildyard m Riz Ortolani pd Vincent
Korda

Rex Harrison, Jeanne Moreau, Edmund
Purdom, Moira Lister, Roland Culver, Shirley
Maclaine, George C. Scott, Alain Delon, Art
Carney, Ingrid Bergman, Omar Sharif, Joyce
Grenfell

'Tame, bloodless, smothered in elegance and
the worst kind of discreetly daring good taste.'—
Peter John Dyer

Yellow Sky**

US 1948   98m   bw
TCF (Lamar Trotti)

Outlaws on the run take over a desert ghost
town.

Gleaming, stylish western melodrama which
benefits from its unusual and confined setting.

w Lamar Trotti, story W. R. Burnett d William

Wellman ph Joe MacDonald m Alfred
Newman

Gregory Peck, Anne Baxter, Richard Widmark,
Robert Arthur, John Russell, Henry Morgan,
James Barton

Yellow Submarine*

GB 1968   87m   De Luxe
King Features / Apple (Al Brodax)

The happy kingdom of Pepperland is attacked
by the Blue Meanies.

Way-out cartoon fantasia influenced by
Beatlemania and the swinging sixties; hard to
watch for non-addicts.

w Lee Minoff, Al Brodax, Jack Mendelsohn,
Erich Segal d George Duning m John Lennon,
Paul McCartney

The Yellow Ticket*

US 1931   76m   bw
Fox
GB title: The Yellow Passport

In Russia during the pogroms, a Jewish girl
pretends to be a prostitute in order to get a travel
permit to see her dying father.

Curious anti-Russian melodrama deriving its
plot from La Tosca.

w Jules Furthman, Guy Bolton, play Michael
Morton d Raoul Walsh ph James Wong Howe

Elissa Landi, Laurence Olivier, Lionel
Barrymore, Walter Byron, Sarah Padden,
Mischa Auer, Boris Karloff

Yellowstone Kelly

US 1959   91m   Technicolor
Warner

A fur trapper prevents war between Indians and
whites.

Standard western with routine excitements and a
cast of TV faces.

w Burt Kennedy d Gordon Douglas ph Carl
Guthrie m Howard Jackson

Clint Walker, Edd Byrnes, John Russell, Ray
Danton, Claude Akins

Yes My Darling Daughter

US 1939   86m   bw
Warner (Ben Glazer)

Lovers elope and are pursued by her family.
Mildly amusing domestic comedy.

w Casey Robinson, play Mark Reed d William
Keighley ph Charles Rosher

Priscilla Lane, Jeffrey Lynn, Roland Young, Fay
Bainter, May Robson, Genevieve Tobin, Ian
Hunter

Yes Sir, That's My Baby

US 1949   82m   Technicolor
U-I (Leonard Goldstein)

Ex-service undergraduates and their wives have
trouble settling down to studies.
Witless and exhausting college comedy.

w Oscar Brodney d George Sherman ph Irving
Glassberg m Walter Scharf

Donald O'Connor, Gloria de Haven, Charles
Coburn, Barbara Brown, Joshua Shelley

Yesterday, Today and Tomorrow

Italy / France 1963   119m   Techniscope
CCC / Concordia / Joseph E. Levin (Carlo
   Ponti)

Three stories of naughty ladies.
A relentlessly boring compendium with
everybody shouting at once.

w Eduardo de Fillipp, Cesare Zavattini, others
d Vittorio de Sica ph Giuseppe Rotunno
m Armando Trovajoli

Marcello Mastroianni, Sophia Loren
  'A sad intimation of the sort of rainy day the
Italian cinema is currently having.'—*MFB*

Yesterday's Enemy

GB 1959   95m   bw   Megascope
Columbia / Hammer (T. S. Lyndon-Haynes)

In 1942 Burma, a British unit violently takes
over a village and finds an unsolved puzzle.
Would-be ironic war suspenser, economically
made but quite effective in putting its message
across.

w Peter R. Newman, from his TV play d Val
Guest ph Arthur Grant m none

Stanley Baker, Guy Rolfe, Leo McKern, Philip
Ahn, Gordon Jackson, David Oxley, Richard
Pasco, Russell Waters, Bryan Forbes, David
Lodge, Percy Herbert

Yield to the Night*

GB 1956   99m   bw
ABP (Kenneth Harper)
US title: *Blonde Sinner*

A condemned murderess relives the events which
led to her arrest.
Gloomy prison melodrama vaguely based on the
Ruth Ellis case and making an emotional plea
against capital punishment.

w John Cresswell, Joan Henry, *novel* Joan
Henry d J. Lee-Thompson ph Gilbert Taylor
m Ray Martin

Diana Dors, Yvonne Mitchell, Michael Craig,
Marie Ney, Athene Seyler, Geoffrey Keen

Yolanda and the Thief*

US 1945   108m   Technicolor
MGM (Arthur Freed)

A con man poses as the guardian angel of a naïve
heiress.
Laboured musical fantasy with arty Mexican
settings; not a success in any way, but with a few
effective moments.

w Irving Brecher, *story* Ludwig Bemelmans,
Jacques Théry d Vincente Minnelli ph Charles
Rosher .m Lennie Hayton *songs* Harry Warren,
Arthur Freed

Fred Astaire, Lucille Bremer, Frank Morgan,
Leon Ames, Mildred Natwick

You and Me

US 1938   90m   bw
Paramount (Fritz Lang)

A department store owner employs ex-convicts,
one of whom has not quite reformed.
Curious comedy drama which never has a hope
of coming off.

w Virginia Van Upp, *story* Norman Krasna
d Fritz Lang ph Charles Lang Jnr

Sylvia Sidney, George Raft, Harry Carey,
Barton MacLane, Warren Hymer, Roscoe
Karns, George E. Stone, Adrian Morris

You Belong to Me*

US 1941   94m   bw
Columbia (Wesley Ruggles)
GB title: *Good Morning, Doctor*

A playboy becomes jealous of the male patients
of his doctor wife.
Mild comedy for two stars who are well capable
of keeping it afloat.

w Claude Binyon, Dalton Trumbo d Wesley
Ruggles ph Joseph Walker m Frederick
Hollander

Barbara Stanwyck, Henry Fonda, Edgar
Buchanan, Roger Clark, Ruth Donnelly,
Melville Cooper, Maude Eburne

You Came Along

US 1945   103m   bw
Paramount (Hal B. Wallis)

A girl from the treasury department falls in love
with one of three GIs she takes on a war bond
tour, but he dies of leukemia.
Weird mishmash of farce and sentimentality;
quite watchable in its way, but an odd showcase
for a new female star.

w Robert Smith, Ayn Rand d John Farrow
ph Daniel L. Fapp m Victor Young

Lizabeth Scott, Robert Cummings, Don Defore,

Charles Drake, Julie Bishop, Kim Hunter, Rhys Williams, Franklin Pangborn, Minor Watson

You Can't Cheat an Honest Man*
US 1939   79m   bw
Universal (Lester Cowan)

Trials and tribulations of a circus owner.
Flat, desultory and generally disappointing comedy vehicle for an irresistible star combination.

w George Marion Jnr, Richard Mack, Everett Freeman, *story* Charles Bogle (W. C. Fields) d George Marshall ph Milton Krasner m Charles Previn

W. C. Fields, Edgar Bergen (with Charlie McCarthy and Mortimer Snerd), Constance Moore, Mary Forbes, Thurston Hall, Charles Coleman, Edward Brophy

You Can't Get Away with Murder
US 1939   78m   bw
Warner (Sam Bischoff)

A juvenile delinquent teams up with a gangster and takes a prison rap for him.
Standard-post-Dead End crime melodrama with no surprises.

w Robert Buckner, Don Ryan, Kenneth Gamet, *play* Chalked Out by Lewis Lawes, Jonathan Finn d Lewis Seiler ph Sol Polito

Humphrey Bogart, Billy Halop, Gale Page, John Litel, Henry Travers, Harvey Stephens, Harold Huber

You Can't Have Everything*
US 1937   99m   bw
TCF (Lawrence Schwab)

A failed play is turned into a musical.
Lively backstage comedy with good moments.

w Harry Tugend, Jack Yellen, Karl Tunberg d Norman Taurog ph Lucien Andriot md David Buttolph

Alice Faye, *the Ritz Brothers*, Don Ameche, Charles Winninger, Gypsy Rose Lee, Tony Martin, Arthur Treacher, Louis Prima, Tip Tap and Toe, Wally Vernon

You Can't Have Everything
US 1970   90m   Eastmancolor
Koala (Lou Brandt)
aka: *Cactus in the Snow*

An 18-year-old virgin GI is about to leave for Vietnam when he picks up a girl and spends a happy but platonic twenty-four hours.
An agreeably understated little love story for those absorbed by teenage sex problems.

wd Martin Zweibach ph David M. Walsh m Joe Parnello

Richard Thomas, Mary Layne, Lucille Benson, Oscar Beregi

You Can't Run Away from It
US 1956   96m   Technicolor
  Cinemascope
Columbia (Dick Powell)

An heiress runs away from a marriage arranged by her father, and falls for an amiable reporter.
Flat remake of *It Happened One Night*, with practically no comic sense or talent.

w Claude Binyon, Robert Riskin d Dick Powell ph Charles Lawton Jnr m George Duning md Morris Stoloff

June Allyson, Jack Lemmon, Charles Bickford, Jim Backus, Stubby Kaye, Paul Gilbert, Allyn Joslyn

You Can't Take It with You**
US 1938   127m   bw
Columbia (Frank Capra)

The daughter of a highly eccentric New York family falls for a rich man's son.
A hilarious, warm and witty play is largely changed into a tirade against big business, but the Capra expertise is here in good measure and the stars all pull their weight.

w Robert Riskin, *play* George S. Kaufman, Moss Hart d Frank Capra ph Joseph Walker m Dmitri Tiomkin

Jean Arthur, Lionel Barrymore, James Stewart, Edward Arnold, Spring Byington, Mischa Auer, Ann Miller, Samuel S. Hinds, Donald Meek, H. B. Warner, Halliwell Hobbes, Mary Forbes, Dub Taylor, Lillian Yarbo, Eddie Anderson, *Harry Davenport*

'Shangri-La in a frame house.'—*Otis Ferguson*

AA: best picture; Frank Capra
AAN: Robert Riskin; Joseph Walker; Spring Byington

You Can't Win 'em All
GB 1970   99m   Technicolor   Panavision
Columbia / SRO (Gene Corman)

In 1922, two rival American mercenaries have adventures in the Mediterranean.
Hectic, overplotted comedy actioner.

w Leo V. Gordon d Peter Collinson ph Ken Higgins m Bert Kaempfert

Tony Curtis, Charles Bronson, Michèle Mercier, Grégoire Aslan, Patrick Magee

You for Me

US 1952 71m bw
MGM (Henry Berman)

A millionaire patient is courted by a needy hospital and falls for a popular nurse.
Cheerful but thin little programme-filler.

w William Roberts d Don Weis ph Virgil Vogel m Alberto Columbo

Peter Lawford, Jane Greer, Gig Young, Paula Corday, Elaine Stewart

You Gotta Stay Happy

US 1948 100m bw
Universal (Karl Tunberg)

A runaway heiress joins cargo pilots on a transcontinental hop with some very queer passengers.
Ho-hum imitation of a Capra comedy; the effort shows.

w Karl Tunberg, story Robert Carson d H. C. Potter ph Russell Metty m Daniele Amfitheatrof

Joan Fontaine, James Stewart, Eddie Albert, Roland Young, Willard Parker, Percy Kilbride, Porter Hall, Paul Cavanagh, Halliwell Hobbes

You Must Be Joking*

GB 1965 100m bw
Columbia / Ameran (Charles H. Schneer)

Assorted army personnel vie in an extended initiative test.
Slam-bang location comedy with more hits than misses: cheerful entertainment.

w Alan Hackney d Michael Winner ph Geoffrey Unsworth m Laurie Johnson

Terry-Thomas, Lionel Jeffries, Michael Callan, Gabriella Licudi, *Denholm Elliott*, Lee Montague, Bernard Cribbins, Wilfrid Hyde White, James Robertson Justice, Richard Wattis, James Villiers

You Never Can Tell*

US 1951 78m bw
U-I (Leonard Goldstein)
GB title: *You Never Know*

An Alsatian dog is murdered and is sent back from heaven in the guise of a private detective to expose his killer.
Self-confidently outrageous comedy fantasy in the wake of *Here Comes Mr Jordan;* not badly done if you accept the premise.

w Lou Breslow, David Chandler d Lou Breslow ph Maury Gertsman m Hans Salter

Dick Powell, Peggy Dow, Charles Drake, Joyce Holden, Albert Sharpe, Sara Taft

You Only Live Once**

US 1937 85m bw
Walter Wanger

A petty crook framed for murder breaks out of prison and tries to escape to Canada with his wife.
Gloomy melodrama partly based on Bonnie and Clyde and incorporating a plea for justice; very well made and acted.

w Graham Baker, *story* Gene Towne d Fritz Lang ph Leon Shamroy m Alfred Newman

Sylvia Sidney, Henry Fonda, Barton MacLane, Jean Dixon, William Gargan, Jerome Cowan, Chic Sale, Margaret Hamilton, Warren Hymer

'Again and again in this film we find what can only be described as camera style, the use of the pictorial image to narrate with the maximum of emotional impact.'—*Dilys Powell*

You Only Live Twice**

GB 1967 117m Technicolor Panavision
UA / Eon (Harry Saltzman, Albert R. Broccoli)

James Bond goes to Japan.
The Bond saga at its most expensive and expansive, full of local colour and in-jokes, with an enormously impressive set for the climactic action.

w Roald Dahl, *novel* Ian Fleming d Lewis Gilbert ph Freddie Young, Bob Huke m John Barry pd Ken Adam

Sean Connery, Tetsuro Tamba, Akiko Wakabayashi, Mie Hama, Karin Dor, Bernard Lee, Lois Maxwell, Desmond Llewellyn, *Charles Gray, Donald Pleasence*

You Were Meant for Me

US 1948 92m bw
TCF (Fred Kohlmar)

A small-town girl marries a bandleader.
Mildly pleasing, muted, musical romance, with good twenties atmosphere.

w Elick Moll, Valentine Davies d Lloyd Bacon ph Victor Milner md Lionel Newman *songs* various

Jeanne Crain, Dan Dailey, Oscar Levant, Barbara Lawrence, Selena Royle, Percy Kilbride, Herbert Anderson

You Were Never Lovelier*

US 1942 97m bw
Columbia (Louis F. Edelman)

An Argentinian hotel tycoon tries to interest his daughter in marriage by creating a mysterious admirer.
Pleasing musical, a follow up for the stars of *You'll Never Get Rich.*

w Michael Fessier, Ernest Pagano, Delmer Daves *d* William A. Seiter *ph* Ted Tetzlaff *songs* Jerome Kern, Johnny Mercer *m* Leigh Harline

Fred Astaire, Rita Hayworth, Adolphe Menjou, Leslie Brooks, Adele Mara, Isobel Elsom, Gus Schilling, Xavier Cugat and his Orchestra, Larry Parks

AAN: Leigh Harline; song 'Dearly Beloved'

You'll Find Out *
US 1940 97m bw
RKO

Kay Kyser's band is hired to play for a 21st birthday party at a gloomy mansion; they help save the life of the girl concerned.
Cheerful if slow-starting spooky house send-up with a splendid trio of villains.

w James V. Kern, David Butler *d* David Butler *ph* Frank Redman *songs* James McHugh, Johnny Mercer

Kay Kyser, Boris Karloff, Peter Lorre, Bela Lugosi, Dennis O'Keefe, Ginny Simms, Helen Parrish, Alma Kruger, Ish Kabibble

AAN: song 'I'd Know You Anywhere'

You'll Like My Mother
US 1972 92m Technicolor
Universal / Bing Crosby Productions (Mort Briskin)

Pregnant widow visits neurotic mother-in-law in a snowbound mansion.
Predictable frightened lady shocker aiming somewhere between *Psycho* and *Fanatic*; of strictly routine interest.

w Jo Heims, *novel* Naomi Hintze *d* Lamont Johnson *ph* Jack Marta *m* Gil Melle

Rosemary Murphy, Patty Duke, Richard Thomas, Sian Barbara Allen

You'll Never Get Rich *
US 1941 88m bw
Columbia (Sam Bischoff)

A Broadway dance director helps his philandering producer by taking a romantically-inclined showgirl off his hands.
Smart comedy-musical which set its female lead as a top star.

w Michael Fessier, Ernest Pagano *d* Sidney Lanfield *ph* Philip Tannura *ch* Robert Alton *songs* Cole Porter *m* Morris Stoloff

Fred Astaire, Rita Hayworth, Robert Benchley, John Hubbard, Osa Massen, Frieda Inescort, Guinn Williams, Donald MacBride

AAN: Morris Stoloff; song 'Since I Kissed My Baby Goodbye'

Young America
US 1932 74m bw

Two young boys get into trouble with the law.
Dog-eared domestic flagwaver.

w William Conselman, *play* John Frederick Ballard *d* Frank Borzage *ph* George Schneiderman

Spencer Tracy, Doris Kenyon, Tommy Conlon, Ralph Bellamy, Beryl Mercer, Sarah Padden

Young and Innocent ***
GB 1937 80m bw
GFD / Gainsborough (Edward Black)
US title: *A Girl Was Young*

A girl goes on the run with her boy friend when he is suspected of murder.
Pleasant, unassuming chase melodrama with a rather weak cast but plenty of its director's touches.

w Charles Bennett, Alma Reville, *novel* A Shilling for Candles by Josephine Tey *d Alfred Hitchcock ph* Bernard Knowles *m* Louis Levy

Nova Pilbeam, Derrick de Marney, Mary Clare, Edward Rigby, Basil Radford, George Curzon, Percy Marmont, John Longden

Young and Willing
US 1942 83m bw
UA (made by Paramount) (Edward H. Griffith)

Impecunious actors in a New York boarding house hit on a great play.
Very mild, innocuous comedy which passed quickly from the public memory.

w Virginia Van Upp, *play* Francis Swann *d* Edward H. Griffith *ph* Leo Tover

William Holden, Susan Hayward, Eddie Bracken, Robert Benchley, Martha O'Driscoll, Barbara Britton, James Brown, Mabel Paige

Young at Heart **
US 1954 117m Warnercolor
(Warner) Arwin (Henry Blanke)

The daughters of a small-town music teacher have romantic problems.
Softened, musicalized remake of *Four Daughters* (qv), an old-fashioned treat with roses round the door and a high standard of proficiency in all departments.

w Julius J. Epstein, Lenore Coffee, *novel* Fannie Hurst *d* Gordon Douglas *ph* Ted McCord

Doris Day, Frank Sinatra, Ethel Barrymore,

Gig Young, Dorothy Malone, Robert Keith,
Elizabeth Fraser, Alan Hale Jnr

Young Bess*
US 1953　112m　Technicolor
MGM (Sidney Franklin)

The early years of Elizabeth I and her romance
with Tom Seymour.

Historical fiction, wildly unreliable as to fact and
dramatically not very rewarding. The character
actors have the best of it.

w Arthur Wimperis, Jan Lustig, *novel* Margaret
Irwin d George Sidney ph Charles Rosher
m Miklos Rozsa

Jean Simmons, Stewart Granger, Charles
Laughton (as Henry VIII), Kay Walsh, Deborah
Kerr, Guy Rolfe, Kathleen Byron, Cecil
Kellaway, Robert Arthur, Leo G. Carroll, Elaine
Stewart, Dawn Addams, Rex Thompson

Young Billy Young
US 1969　89m　De Luxe
UA / Talbot–Youngstein (Max Youngstein)

A young western gunman is helped out of
scrapes by a mysterious stranger bent on
revenge.

Good-looking but rather ineffective western
which throws away good production values.

wd Burt Kennedy, *novel* Who Rides with Wyatt
by Will Henry ph Harry Stradling Jnr m Shelly
Manne

Robert Mitchum, Angie Dickinson, Robert
Walker Jnr, David Carradine, John Anderson,
Paul Fix

Young Cassidy*
GB 1964　110m　Technicolor
MGM / Sextant (Robert D. Graff, Robert
Emmett Ginna)

A romantic view of the early Dublin life of writer
Sean O'Casey.

Ambling, unconvincing but generally interesting
picture of a past time.

w John Whiting, from the writings of Sean
O'Casey d Jack Cardiff, John Ford ph Ted
Scaife m Sean O'Riada

Rod Taylor, Maggie Smith, Edith Evans, Flora
Robson, Michael Redgrave, Julie Christie, Jack
MacGowran, Sian Phillips, T. P. McKenna

Young Dillinger
US 1964　102m　bw
Alfred Zimbalist

An embittered young convict becomes Public
Enemy Number One.

Fantasized, forgettable biopic with violent
moments.

w Arthur Hoerl, Don Zimbalist d Terry Morse
ph Stanley Cortez m Shorty Rogers

Nick Adams, John Ashley, Robert Conrad,
Mary Ann Mobley, Victor Buono, John Hoyt,
Reed Hadley

The Young Doctors*
US 1961　102m　bw
UA / Drexel / Stuart Millar / Laurence Turman

Old Dr Pearson resents his modern young
assistant and almost causes a tragedy.

Routine medical melo of the Kildare/Gillespie
kind, given a Grade A production and cast.

w Joseph Hayes, *novel* The Final Diagnosis by
Arthur Hailey d Phil Karlson ph Arthur J.
Ornitz m Elmer Bernstein

Fredric March, Ben Gazzara, Dick Clark, Eddie
Albert, Ina Balin, Aline MacMahon, Edward
Andrews, Arthur Hill, George Segal, Rosemary
Murphy

Young Eagles*
US 1930　71m　bw
Paramount

The adventures of American aviators in World
War I.

Spirited early sound actioner.

w William McNutt, Grover Jones d William
Wellman ph Archie Stout

Charles Rogers, Jean Arthur, Paul Lukas, Stuart
Erwin, Virginia Bruce, James Finlayson

Young Frankenstein**
US 1974　108m　bw
TCF / Gruskoff / Venture / Jouer / Crossbow
(Michael Gruskoff)

Young Frederick Frankenstein, a brain surgeon,
goes back to Transylvania and pores over his
grandfather's notebooks.

The most successful of Mel Brooks' parodies,
Mad Magazine style; the gleamingly reminiscent
photography is the best of it, the script being far
from consistently funny, but there are splendid
moments.

w Gene Wilder, Mel Brooks d Mel Brooks
ph Gerald Hirschfeld m John Morris ad Dale
Hennesy

Gene Wilder, Marty Feldman, Madeleine Kahn,
Peter Boyle, Cloris Leachman, Kenneth Mars,
Gene Hackman, Richard Haydn

AAN: script

The Young Girls of Rochefort

France 1967   126m   Eastmancolor
  Franscope
Parc Film / Madeleine / Seven Arts (Mag
  Bodard, Gilbert de Goldschmidt)
original title: *Les Demoiselles de Rochefort*

Two country girls join a travelling dancing
troupe, and find love on the day of the fair.
Flat, empty tribute to the Hollywood musical,
which never inspires despite the presence of one
of its greatest stars.

wd Jacques Demy *ph* Ghislain Cloquet
m Michel Legrand

Catherine Deneuve, Françoise Dorléac, George
Chakiris, Gene Kelly, Danielle Darrieux, Grover
Dale, Michel Piccoli

AAN: Jacques Demy; Michel Legrand

The Young in Heart***

US 1938   91m   bw
David O. Selznick

A family of charming confidence tricksters move
in on a rich old lady but she brings out the best in
them.
Delightful, roguish romantic comedy, perfectly
cast and pacily handled.

w Paul Osborn, Charles Bennett, novel The Gay
Banditti by I. A. R. Wylie *d Richard Wallace*
ph Leon Shamroy *m* Franz Waxman

*Douglas Fairbanks Jnr, Janet Gaynor, Roland
Young, Billie Burke, Minnie Dupree,* Paulette
Goddard, Richard Carlson, Henry Stephenson

AAN: Leon Shamroy; Franz Waxman

The Young Land

US 1957   89m   Technicolor
(Columbia) C. V. Whitney (Patrick Ford)

A young sheriff arrests a gunman and after the
trial has to save him from lynching.
Rather stiff attempt at a youth western.

w Norman Shannon Hall *d* Ted Tetzlaff
ph Winton C. Hoch, Henry Sharp

Dan O'Herlihy, Patrick Wayne, Yvonne Craig,
Dennis Hopper

AAN: song 'Strange Are the Ways of Love'
(*m* Dmitri Tiomkin, *ly* Ned Washington)

The Young Lions**

US 1958   167m   bw   Cinemascope
TCF (Al Lichtman)

World War II adventures of two Americans and
a German skiing instructor.
Three strands are loosely interwoven into a
would-be modern epic; the result is well mounted

and generally absorbing but uneven and
decidedly overlong.

w Edward Anhalt, *novel* Irwin Shaw *d* Edward
Dmytryk *ph* Joe MacDonald *m* Hugo
Friedhofer

Marlon Brando, Montgomery Clift, Dean
Martin, Hope Lange, Barbara Rush, May Britt,
Maximilian Schell, Lee Van Cleef

AAN: Joe MacDonald; Hugo Friedhofer

The Young Lovers*

GB 1954   96m   bw
GFD / Group Films (Anthony Havelock-Allan)
US title: *Chance Meeting*

A US Embassy man in London falls in love with
the daughter of an Iron Curtain minister.
Romeo and Juliet, cold war style, quite nicely put
together with a thriller climax.

w Robin Estridge, *story* George Tabori
d Anthony Asquith

Odile Versois, David Knight, David Kossoff,
Joseph Tomelty, Paul Carpenter, Theodore
Bikel, Jill Adams

Young Man with a Horn*

US 1950   112m   bw
Warner (Jerry Wald)
GB title: *Young Man of Music*

The professional and romantic tribulations of a
trumpet player.
Overwrought character melodrama based on the
life of Bix Beiderbecke; quite absorbing though
occasionally risible.

w Carl Foreman, Edmund H. North, *novel*
Dorothy Baker *d* Michael Curtiz *ph* Ted
McCord *m* Ray Heindorf

Kirk Douglas, Lauren Bacall, Doris Day,
Hoagy Carmichael, Juano Hernandez, Jerome
Cowan, Mary Beth Hughes, Nestor Paiva

Young Man with Ideas*

US 1952   84m   bw
MGM (Gottfried Reinhardt, William H.
  Wright)

A small-town lawyer tries to better himself in
Los Angeles.
Modestly likeable comedy which doesn't add up
to much.

w Arthur Sheekman *d* Mitchell Leisen
ph Joseph Ruttenberg *m* David Rose

Glenn Ford, Ruth Roman, Nina Foch, Denise
Darcel, Donna Corcoran, Mary Wickes,
Sheldon Leonard

Young Mr Lincoln***

US 1939   100m   bw
TCF (Kenneth MacGowan)

Abraham Lincoln as a young country lawyer
stops a lynching and proves a young man
innocent of murder.
Splendid performances and period atmosphere
are rather nipped in the bud by second-feature
courtroom twists, but this is a marvellous old-
fashioned entertainment with its heart in the right
place.

w Lamar Trotti d John Ford ph Bert Glennon
w Alfred Newman

Henry Fonda, Alice Brady, Marjorie Weaver,
Arleen Whelan, Eddie Collins, Richard
Cromwell, Donald Meek, Eddie Quillan,
Spencer Charters

'Its simple good faith and understanding are
an expression of the country's best life that says
as much as forty epics.'—*Otis Ferguson*

'Period details are lovingly sketched in—a log
splitting contest, a tug of war, a tar barrel rolling
match . . .'—*Charles Higham*

'Its source is a womb of popular and national
spirit. This could account for its unity, its
artistry, its genuine beauty.'—*Sergei Eisenstein*

AAN: Lamar Trotti

The Young Mr Pitt*

GB 1942   118m   bw
TCF (Edward Black)

Britain's youngest prime minister quells the
threat of invasion by Napoleon.
Shapeless and overlong but generally diverting
historical pastiche timed as wartime propaganda
against Hitler.

w Frank Launder, Sidney Gilliat d Carol Reed
ph Frederick A. Young m Charles Williams
ad Vetchinsky

Robert Donat, Robert Morley, Phyllis Calvert,
John Mills, Raymond Lovell, Max Adrian, Felix
Aylmer, Albert Lieven

The Young Ones*

GB 1961   108m   Technicolor
      Cinemascope
ABP (Kenneth Harper)

The son of a tycoon starts a youth club and puts
on a musical to raise funds.
A shopworn idea is the springboard for a brave
try in a field where Britain was presumed to have
failed; despite the enthusiasm with which it was
greeted at the time, it has dated badly.

w Peter Myers, Ronald Cass d Sidney J. Furie
ph Douglas Slocombe m Stanley Black

Cliff Richard, Robert Morley, Carole Grey,

Richard O'Sullivan, Melvyn Hayes, Gerald
Harper, Robertson Hare

The Young Philadelphians*

US 1959   136m   bw
Warner (producer not credited)
GB title: *The City Jungle*

A forceful young lawyer pushes his way to the
top of the snobbish Philadelphia heap despite
threats to expose his illegitimacy.
Novel on film, gleamingly done and acted with
assurance.

w James Gunn, *novel* The Philadelphian by
Richard Powell d Vincent Sherman ph Harry
Stradling m Ernest Gold

Paul Newman, Barbara Rush, Alexis Smith,
Brian Keith, Billie Burke, John Williams, Otto
Kruger, Diane Brewster, Robert Vaughn, Paul
Picerni, Robert Douglas

AAN: Harry Stradling; Robert Vaughn

The Young Savages*

US 1961   103m   bw
UA / Contemporary (Pat Duggan)

An assistant DA prosecutes three hoodlums for
murder but begins to feel that one is not guilty.
Tough, realistic melodrama of the New York
slums, with roughhouse climaxes and a political
conscience.

w Edward Anhalt, J. P. Miller, *novel* A Matter of
Conviction by Evan Hunter d John
Frankenheimer ph Lionel Lindon m David
Amram

Burt Lancaster, Shelley Winters, John David
Chandler, Dina Merrill, Edward Andrews, Telly
Savalas

The Young Stranger*

US 1957   84m   bw
RKO (Stuart Millar)

The 16-year-old son of a film executive gets into
trouble with the police.
Reasonably stimulating film of a TV play about
the kind of causeless rebel who quickly became a
cliché.

w Robert Dozier d John Frankenheimer
ph Robert Planck m Leonard Rosenman

James MacArthur, Kim Hunter, James Daly,
James Gregory, Whit Bissell

Young Tom Edison*

US 1940   82m   bw
MGM (John Considine Jnr)

First of a two-parter (see *Edison the Man*)
tracing Edison's first experiments.
Reasonably factual and absorbing junior biopic.

w Bradbury Foote, Dore Schary, Hugo Butler
d Norman Taurog *ph* Sidney Wagner
m Edward Ward

Mickey Rooney, Eugene Pallette, George Bancroft, Fay Bainter, Virginia Weidler, Victor Kilian, Lloyd Corrigan

The Young Widow
US 1946 100m bw
UA / Hunt Stromberg

The widow of a World War II flier returns to the Virginia farm where they had spent happy hours.
Glum sudser with talent all at sea.

w Richard Macaulay, Margaret Buell Wilder, *novel* Clarissa Fairchild Cushman *d* Edwin L. Marin *ph* Lee Garmes *m* Carmen Dragon *pd* Nicolai Remisoff

Jane Russell, Louis Hayward, Faith Domergue, Marie Wilson, Kent Taylor, Penny Singleton, Connie Gilchrist, Cora Witherspoon

Young Winston**
GB 1972 157m Eastmancolor Panavision
Columbia / Open Road / Hugh French (Carl Foreman)

The adventurous life of Winston Churchill up to his becoming an MP.
Generally engaging if lumpy film which switches too frequently from action to family drama to politics to character study and is not helped by irritating directorial tricks.

w Carl Foreman, *book* My Early Life by Winston Churchill *d* Richard Attenborough *ph* Gerry Turpin *m* Alfred Ralston *pd* Don Ashton, Geoffrey Drake

Simon Ward, Robert Shaw, Anne Bancroft, Jack Hawkins, Ian Holm, *Anthony Hopkins*, John Mills, Patrick Magee, Edward Woodward

AAN: Carl Foreman

Youngblood Hawke
US 1964 137m bw
Warner (Delmer Daves)

A Kentucky truck driver becomes a successful novelist and is spoiled by New York success.
Absurdly archetypal soap opera from a bestseller, spilling over with every imaginable cliché; some of its excesses are glossily entertaining.

w Delmer Daves, *novel* Herman Wouk
d Delmer Daves *ph* Charles Lawton *m* Max Steiner

James Franciscus, Genevieve Page, Suzanne Pleshette, Eva Gabor, *Mary Astor*, Lee

Bowman, Edward Andrews, John Emery, Don Porter

The Youngest Profession
US 1943 82m bw
MGM (B. F. Ziedman)

Teenage autograph hounds cause trouble at the MGM studio.
Innocuous comedy with guest stars.

w George Oppenheimer, Charles Lederer, Leonard Spiegelgass, *book* Lillian Day
d Edward Buzzell *ph* Charles Lawton *m* David Snell

Virginia Weidler, Jean Porter, Edward Arnold, John Carroll, Agnes Moorehead, Greer Garson, William Powell, Lana Turner, Walter Pidgeon, Robert Taylor

Your Witness*
GB 1950 100m bw
Warner (David E. Rose, Joan Harrison)
US title: *Eye Witness*

An American lawyer comes to an English village to defend a war buddy on a murder charge.
Interesting but ineffective blend of comedy and courtroom procedure intended to contrast English and American ways.

w Hugo Butler, Ian Hunter, William Douglas Home *d* Robert Montgomery *ph* Gerald Gibbs *m* Malcolm Arnold

Robert Montgomery, Leslie Banks, Patricia Cutts, Felix Aylmer, Andrew Cruickshank, Harcourt Williams, Jenny Laird, Michael Ripper

You're a Big Boy Now*
US 1967 96m Eastmancolor
Warner Seven Arts (William Fadiman)

A young assistant librarian discovers girls.
Freewheeling semi-surrealist comedy with exhilarating moments and the inevitable letdowns associated with this kind of campy high style.

wd Francis Ford Coppola, *novel* David Benedictus *ph* Andy Laszlo *m* Bob Prince

Peter Kastner, Elizabeth Hartman, Geraldine Page, Julie Harris, Rip Torn, Tony Bill, Karen Black, Michael Dunn

AAN: Geraldine Page

You're a Sweetheart
US 1937 96m bw
Universal (B. G. De Sylva)

A Broadway star suffers from her press agent's bright ideas.
Muffed musical with all concerned ill at ease with below par material.

w Monte Brice, Charles Grayson *d* David
Butler *ph* George Robinson *md* Charles Previn
songs various

Alice Faye, George Murphy, Ken Murray,
William Gargan, Frances Hunt, Frank Jenks,
Andy Devine, Charles Winninger, Donald Meek

You're in the Army Now**
US 1941   79m   bw
Warner (Ben Stoloff)

Two incompetent vacuum cleaner salesmen
accidentally join the army.
An excellent vehicle for two star comedians who
have often suffered from poor material, with a
silent-comedy-style climax involving a house on
wheels.

w Paul Gerard Smith, George Beatty *d* Lewis
Seiler *ph* James Van Trees

Jimmy Durante, Phil Silvers, Donald MacBride,
Jane Wyman, Regis Toomey

You're in the Navy Now*
US 1951   93m   bw
TCF (Fred Kohlmar)
aka: *USS Teakettle*

Trouble results when the navy instals steam
turbines in an experimental patrol craft.
Amusing service comedy with good script
touches and capable performances.

w Richard Murphy *d* Henry Hathaway *ph* Joe
MacDonald *m* Cyril Mockridge

Gary Cooper, Millard Mitchell, Jane Greer,
Eddie Albert, John McIntire, Ray Collins, Harry
Von Zell, Jack Webb, Richard Erdman

You're My Everything*
US 1949   94m   Technicolor
TCF (Lamar Trotti)

A Boston socialite marries a hoofer and becomes
a movie star.
Pleasant twenties comedy with good period
detail and lively performances.

w Lamar Trotti, Will Hays Jnr *d* Walter Lang
ph Arthur E. Arling *m* Alfred Newman

Anne Baxter, Dan Dailey, Anne Revere, Stanley
Ridges, Shari Robinson, Henry O'Neill, Selena
Royle, Alan Mowbray, Buster Keaton

You're Never Too Young
US 1955   103m   Technicolor   Vistavision
Paramount / Hal B. Wallis (Paul Jones)

An apprentice barber on the run from a
murderer poses as a 12-year-old child to travel
half fare.
Unattractive revamping of *The Major and the
Minor* (qv), with the star team trying too
obviously to make bricks with inferior straw.

w Sidney Sheldon *d* Norman Taurog *ph* Daniel
L. Fapp *m* Arthur Schwarz

Dean Martin, Jerry Lewis, Diana Lynn, Nina
Foch, Raymond Burr, Veda Ann Borg

You're Only Young Once see The Hardy
Family

You're Only Young Twice
GB 1952   81m   bw
Group Three (Terry Bishop)

The puritanical head of a Scottish university is
laid low by circumstance and his own folly.
Misfire eccentric comedy which deserves marks
for trying but fails to amuse.

w Reginald Beckwith, Lindsay Galloway, Terry
Bishop, *play* What Say They by James Bridie
d Terry Gilbert *ph* Jo Jago

Duncan Macrae, Charles Hawtrey, Joseph
Tomelty, Patrick Barr, Diane Hart, Robert
Urquhart

You're Telling Me*
US 1934   66m   bw
Paramount

A small-town inventor meets a princess and
makes the social grade.
Meaninglessly-titled star vehicle which is often
defiantly unamusing but does include the famous
golf routine.

w Walter de Leon, Paul M. Jones *d* Erle C.
Kenton *ph* Alfred Gilks *m* Arthur Johnston

W. C. Fields, Larry 'Buster' Crabbe, Joan
Marsh, Adrienne Ames, Louise Carter

Yours Mine and Ours*
US 1968   111m   Technicolor
UA / Desilu / Walden (Robert F. Blumofe)

A widower with nine children marries a widow
with eight, and they settle in an old San
Francisco house.
Generally appealing comedy, based on fact and
well suited to its stars.

w Mel Shavelson, Mort Lachman *d* Mel
Shavelson *ph* Charles Wheeler *m* Fred Karlin

Lucille Ball, Henry Fonda, Van Johnson

Z

Z***
France / Algeria 1968   125m
Eastmancolor
Reggane / ONCIC / Jacques Pérrin

A leading opposition MP is murdered at a rally.
The police are anxious to establish the event as
an accident, but the examining magistrate proves
otherwise.
An exciting police suspense drama which also
recalls events under the Greek colonels and was
therefore highly fashionable for a while both as
entertainment and as a political *roman à clef*.

w Costa-Gavras, Jorge Semprun, novel Vassili
Vassilikos *d Costa-Gavras ph* Raoul Coutard
m Mikis Theodorakis

Jean-Louis Trintignant, Jacques Pérrin, Yves
Montand, François Périer, Irene Papas, Charles
Denner

AAN: script

Zabriskie Point
US 1969   112m   Metrocolor   Panavision
MGM / Carlo Ponti

A rebellious Los Angeles student steals a private
airplane, meets an aimless girl, and finds a
revelation in Death Valley . . .
Highly self-indulgent and unattractive fantasy
about escape from the crudities of our over-
civilized world. An expensive failure and an
awful warning of what happens if you give an
arty director carte blanche.

wd Michelangelo Antonioni *ph* Alfio Contini
m pop songs

Mark Frechette, Daria Halprin, Rod Taylor,
Paul Fix

'Not even a good tourist's notebook . . . from
the choice of Death Valley as a symbol of
American civilization to the inclusion of gag
signs on bar-room walls to the shots of garish
billboards, this film sticks to the surface,
stranded.'—*Stanley Kauffman*

Zandy's Bride
US 1974   116m   Technicolor   Panavision
Warner (Harry Matofsky)

Life for a frontier family.
Dour semi-western.

w Marc Norman, *novel* The Stranger by Lillian
Bos Ross *d* Joan Troell *ph* Jordan Cronenweth
m Fred Karlin

Gene Hackman, Liv Ullmann, Eileen Heckart,
Harry Dean Stanton, Joe Santos, Frank Cady

Zarak*
GB 1956   99m   Technicolor
Cinemascope
Columbia / Warwick

An Afghan outlaw finally saves a British officer
at the cost of his own life.
Box-office actioner, shot in Morocco with a
weird cast and the help of old movie clips.

w Richard Maibaum *d* Terence Young *2nd
unit* Yakima Canutt *ph* John Wilcox, Ted
Moore, Cyril Knowles *ad* John Box

Victor Mature, Michael Wilding, Anita Ekberg,
Bonar Colleano, Finlay Currie, Bernard Miles,
Eunice Gayson, Peter Illing, Frederick Valk,
André Morell

Zardoz
GB 1973   105m   De Luxe   Panavision
TCF / John Boorman

Life in 2293, when the earth has become
wasteland and a mass of Brutals are ruled by a
few Exterminators who have both memory and
intelligence.
Pompous, boring fantasy for the so-called
intelligentsia.

wd John Boorman *ph* Geoffrey Unsworth
m David Munrow *pd* Anthony Pratt

Sean Connery, Charlotte Rampling, John
Alderton

Zazie dans le Metro**
France 1960   88m   Eastmancolor
Nouvelles Editions (Irène Leriche)

A naughty little girl has a day in Paris and causes
chaos.
Inventive little comedy which almost turns into a
French *Hellzapoppin*, with everybody chasing
or fighting everybody else.

wd Louis Malle, *novel* Raymond Queneau
ph Henri Raichi

Catherine Demongeot, Philippe Noiret, Vittorio Caprioli

Zebra in the Kitchen

US 1965   93m   Metrocolor
MGM / Ivan Tors

A young boy tries to improve the lot of zoo animals.
Pleasing family film.

w Art Arthur d Ivan Tors

Jay North, Martin Milner, Andy Devine, Joyce Meadows, Jim Davis

Zee and Co. *

GB 1971   109m   colour
Columbia / Zee Films (Kastner–Ladd–Kanter)
US title: *X, Y and Zee*

A successful architect battles with his termagant wife and seeks an affair.
Overwritten but entertaining sexual melodrama about an absolute bitch. The flow of bad language was new at the time.

w Edna O'Brien d Brian G. Hutton ph Billy Williams m Stanley Myers ad Peter Mullins

Elizabeth Taylor, Michael Caine, Susannah York, Margaret Leighton, John Standing
'Miss Taylor is rapidly turning into a latterday Marie Dressler.'—*Tom Milne*
'A slice-of-jet-set-life nightmare far beyond the dreams of the piggiest male chauvinist . . . the distinction of this film is that its characters are repulsive, its style vulgar, its situations beyond belief and its dialogue moronic.'—*Judith Crist*

Zeppelin *

GB 1971   97m   Technicolor   Panavision
Warner / Getty and Fromkess (Owen Crump)

In 1915, the British need to steal secrets from the zeppelin works at Friedrichshafen.
Undistinguished but entertaining period actioner with adequate spectacle but wooden performances.

w Arthur Rowe, Donald Churchill d Etienne Périer ph Alan Hume m Roy Budd sp Wally Veevers

Michael York, Elke Sommer, Peter Carsten, Marius Goring, Anton Diffring, Andrew Keir, Rupert Davies

Zéro de Conduite **

France 1933   45m approx   bw
Gaumont / Franco Film / Aubert

Boys return from the holiday to a nasty little boarding school, where the headmaster is an unpleasant dwarf and all the staff are hateful. A revolution breaks out . . .

A clear forerunner of *If . . .* and one of the most famous of surrealist films, though it pales beside Bunuel and is chiefly valuable for being funny.

w *Jean Vigo* ph Boris Kaufman m Maurice Jaubert

Jean Dasté, Louis Lefébvre, Gilbert Pruchon, le nain Delphin
'One of the most influential films ever made.'—*New Yorker, 1978*

Zero Hour !

US 1957   83m   bw
(Paramount) Bartlett / Champion (John Champion)

Half the passengers and all the crew of a jet plane are stricken with food poisoning and a shell-shocked ex-fighter pilot has to land the plane.
Adequate air melodrama with a premise which later served for *Terror in the Sky* (TV) and *Airport 75*.

w Arthur Hailey, John Champion, Hall Bartlett, *teleplay* Flight into Danger by Arthur Hailey d Hall Bartlett ph John F. Warren m Ted Dale

Dana Andrews, Linda Darnell, Sterling Hayden, Elroy Hirsch, Jerry Paris

Zero Population Growth

US 1971   96m   Eastmancolor
Sagittarius (Thomas F. Madigan)

In the 21st century there is a death penalty for having children, but a young couple defy the authorities.
Good sci-fi quickly develops into sticky sentimentality.

w Max Ehrlich, Frank de Felita d Michael Campus ph Michael Reed m Jonathan Hodge pd Tony Masters

Oliver Reed, Geraldine Chaplin, Diane Cilento, Don Gordon, Bill Nagy, Aubrey Woods

Ziegfeld Follies **

US 1944 (released 1946)   110m   Technicolor
MGM (Arthur Freed)

In heaven, Florenz Ziegfeld dreams up one last spectacular revue.
A rather airless all-star entertainment in which the comedy suffers from the lack of an audience but some of the production numbers are magnificently stylish.

w various d *Vincente Minnelli* ph George Folsey, *Charles Rosher* m various ad Cedric Gibbons, Merrill Pye, Jack Martin Smith

Fred Astaire, Lucille Ball, Bunin's Puppets, William Powell, Jimmy Durante, Edward Arnold, *Fannie Brice*, Lena Horne, Lucille

Bremer, Esther Williams, Judy Garland, *Red Skelton, Gene Kelly,* James Melton, Hume Cronyn, Victor Moore, Marion Bell

'Between opening and closing is packed a prodigious amount of material, some of which is frankly not deserving of the lavish treatment accorded it.'—*Film Daily*

Ziegfeld Girl*
US 1941   131m   bw
MGM (Pandro S. Berman)

The professional and romantic problems of Ziegfeld chorus girls.
Adequate big-budget drama with music.

w Marguerite Roberts, Sonya Levien *d* Robert Z. Leonard *ph* Ray June *m* Herbert Stothart *ch* Busby Berkeley *songs* various

James Stewart, Judy Garland, Hedy Lamarr, Lana Turner, Tony Martin, Jackie Cooper, Ian Hunter, *Charles Winninger, Al Shean,* Edward Everett Horton, Philip Dorn, Paul Kelly, Eve Arden, Dan Dailey, Fay Holden, Felix Bressart

'Heaping portions of show life in the opulent days of Flo Ziegfeld, the man who wanted bigger and better staircases.'—*C. A. Lejeune*

Zigzag*
US 1970   104m   Metrocolor   Panavision
MGM / Freeman–Enders
GB title: *False Witness*

A dying man frames himself for an unsolved murder so that the reward money, claimed under another name, will go to his wife.
Complex thriller which sustains itself pretty well most of the way, but lacks humour and character.

w John T. Kelley *d* Richard A. Colla *ph* James A. Crabe *m* Oliver Nelson

George Kennedy, Anne Jackson, Eli Wallach, Steve Ihnat, William Marshall, Joe Maross

Zoltan, Hound of Dracula
US 1977   88m   De Luxe
Vic (Albert Band, Frank Ray Perelli)

The resurrected servant of Dracula tries to use his vampire dog to create a new master.
Ingenious but unattractive addition to the saga, with dogs as chief villains; the style varies between spoof and rather nasty horror.

w Frank Ray Perelli *d* Albert Band *ph* Bruce Logan *m* Andrew Belling

Jose Ferrer, Reggie Malder, Michael Pataki, Jan Shutan

Zoo in Budapest*
US 1933   83m   bw
Fox (Jesse Lasky)

An orphan waif runs away to live with a zookeeper.
Curious little romance remembered for its luminescent photography.

w Dan Totheroh, Louise Long, Rowland V. Lee *d* Rowland V. Lee *ph* Lee Garmes

Loretta Young, Gene Raymond, O. P. Heggie, Wally Albright, Paul Fix

'Richly composed impressionistic images, assisted by highly imaginative use of sound and background music, create a poem that Murnau himself would have envied.'—*NFT, 1971*

Zorba the Greek**
GB 1964   142m   bw
TCF / Rockley / Cacoyannis

A young English writer in Crete is befriended by a huge gregarious Greek who comes to dominate his life.
A mainly enjoyable character study of a larger-than-life character, this film made famous by its music does not really hang together dramatically and has several melodramatic excrescences.

wd Michael Cacoyannis, novel Nikos Kazantzakis *ph Walter Lassally m Mikis Theodorakis*

Anthony Quinn, Alan Bates, Lila Kedrova, Irene Papas

'For all its immense length, the film never gets down to a clear statement of its theme, or comes within measuring distance of its vast pretensions.'—*Brenda Davies*

AA: Walter Lassally; Lila Kedrova
AAN: best picture; Michael Cacoyannis (as writer and director); Anthony Quinn

Zotz!
US 1962   87m   bw
Columbia / William Castle

A professor finds a rare coin with occult powers.
Footling farce patterned after *The Absent-Minded Professor*. Poor, to say the least.

w Ray Russell, *novel* Walter Karig *d* William Castle *ph* Gordon Avil *m* Bernard Green

Tom Poston, Fred Clark, Jim Backus, Cecil Kellaway, Margaret Dumont

Zulu*
GB 1964   135m   Technirama
Paramount / Diamond (Stanley Baker, Cyril Endfield)

In 1879 British soldiers stand fast against the
Zulus at Rorke's Drift.
Standard period heroics, well presented and
acted.

w John Prebble, Cy Endfield *d* Cy Endfield
ph Stephen Dade *m* John Barry

Stanley Baker, Jack Hawkins, *Michael Caine*,
Ulla Jacobsson, James Booth, Nigel Green, Ivor
Emmanuel, Paul Danceman

The Decline and Fall of the Movie

It is only fair that the author of a book which categorizes forty-five years of film should give some account of his own prejudices. I have spent more than forty years seeing, talking about and writing about films, so my affection for the medium in its 'golden age' can hardly be doubted. Even then, however, the worthwhile movies were the tip of the iceberg: probably eighty per cent of what was produced was ghastly rubbish, which is why this book deals with eight thousand movies, not all of them good, out of a total output of four times that number. The best kind of film buff loves the movie business for what it can be at its best, not for its journeyman 'B' features, its crackpot experiments, its cheapjack exploitation screamies or those relentlessly boring bottom-of-the-bill fillers.

Jonathan Swift said in 1725: 'I hate and detest that animal called man, although I heartily love John, Peter, Thomas and so forth.' This book encapsulates my Johns, my Peters and my Thomases; this essay complains bitterly that they have lately been so few in number, and attempts, admittedly by some slight use of exaggeration, to throw light on a confused and unhappy segment of cinema history.

When Sam Peckinpah made *Straw Dogs* from a novel called *The Siege of Trencher's Farm* he thought it unnecessary to explain to his audience the significance of his new title which, his publicists informed us on request, was taken from an old Chinese proverb. And when Stanley Kubrick made *A Clockwork Orange* he did not bother to retain the section of the Anthony Burgess novel which explained why it was so called. These almost identical incidents exemplify the kind of arrogance which besets film-makers in the seventies. Steeped in the history of Hollywood's golden age, they have no idea what made it work so well, and as soon as they become successful they begin to despise their audiences and are concerned only to over-spend enormous budgets while putting across some garbled self satisfying message which is usually anti-establishment, anti-law-and-order and anti-entertainment.

In this they are assisted by such long-haired publications as *Sight and Sound* and a variety of earnest critics who bend over backwards to see 'significance' where none exists and to ascribe all the film's virtues and faults to the director, or in the current jargon the *auteur*. (Would any theatrical critic dream of judging a play solely on the director's contribution, or a literary critic of reviewing a book solely on the basis of its layout on the printed page?) If cinema, which is the creation of so many people, can be an art at all, it must be a folk art which appeals to innocent and sophisticate alike, and can be easily appreciated by both. This happy state of affairs was reached thirty-five years ago by unpretentious and slick productions of the studio system such as *The Maltese Falcon* and *Stagecoach* which used every camera trick in the book without blinding the audience to the characters and the plot. Nowadays one has to fight one's way through the thick showy surface in order to get to a story which all too often is not worth following.

One problem is that modern films are largely made by people with no sense of humour, people who do not realize that they must please the mass audience if the industry in which they work is to survive. Old-time screenwriters such as Ben Hecht, Dudley Nichols and Lamar Trotti would no doubt be viewed by these young men as cynical hacks, but at least they took pains to please their audience with all the expertise at their command, and they still expressed their own views in a vein of sardonic humour which ran through most of the scripts of the thirties and forties and was there to please and satisfy the minority of film-goers who sought it out.

The absurd pretensions of some modern film-makers certainly cause amusement wherever sensible people congregate, but the advocates of sanity are in no position to have the last word. The present set-up of the film industry encourages wilder and wickeder sensations, from homicidal sharks to diabolical babies, as these are the only subjects which lure large audiences. The successes, however, are all one-offs: no one is much interested in sequels, preferring to wait for horrors of some other variety. The result is that only one film in twenty or thirty makes a profit, but the custodians of the cash have no option but to go on investing in the hope that the occasional fluke will make a fortune, which will then be quickly dissipated by a string of failures. Universal's phenomenally successful *Jaws*, for instance, was immediately followed by such commercial duds as *Gable and Lombard*, *W. C. Fields and Me*, *The Great Waldo Pepper* and *The Hindenberg*, and the studio is still looking for another hit. The sad fact is that no policy can be devised because the people in charge of the money have no idea what is likely to appeal, and they are forced to put their faith in reputedly brilliant directors who have no idea either but are quite prepared to spend large sums of other people's money in flying their own flimsy kites. The flimsiness is sometimes astonishing. The director of an abysmal 1976 comedy called *Harry and Walter go to New York* announced to the press, as a selling point, that it was 'Laurel and Hardy with real people.' Had he inquired of his mass audience, he would surely have been told that Stan and Ollie had more reality in their little fingers than was to be found in the entire crew of *Harry and Walter go to New York*, whether before or behind the camera.

One should of course add that many films these days are not supposed to make money. The adage which used to run 'you're only as good as your last picture' has been changed to 'you're only as big as your last budget', and it is no trick to get a big budget when many films are conceived by industrialists as tax losses: all you have to do is get in the news by holding outlandish views or even making pornography, and Hollywood these days opens its doors to you because at least you must have learnt how to point a camera or arrest public attention. The ones to suffer are the audiences, who have foisted upon them material which they have every right to expect to be professional, and which all too often is not, just the result of untalented exhibitionists spending someone else's money in whatever way happens to divert them most. Even if there is a profit, their habit is to take the money and run, not to invest it in better production facilities as used to happen in the good old days.

Work is thus produced for a small group of jet-setters; meanwhile that patient paying audience discovers that not only the films but the standards of physical cinema comfort are far worse than they were thirty years ago; since then the cost of admission has risen at a phenomenal rate, the average cost in Britain now being twenty times more than in 1956. What other commodity has risen in price to this extent? Television is infinitely cheaper and can be viewed in the comfort of one's own home: no wonder so many people prefer it.

So the movie industry hastens on its way to perdition and catastrophe, a fate which surely cannot be delayed more than another few years, and for which simple-minded greed, lack of foresight and a large measure of incompetence are chiefly responsible. Those of us who are old enough and who still care about the movies sigh frequently for the halcyon days when Harry Cohn and Louis B. Mayer sat in their front offices, for their intellectual limitations were far less harmful and sometimes far more stimulating to the medium than the excesses of the present incumbents, who seldom stay long enough to make their presences felt and certainly not long enough for any sense of continuity to develop. There is for instance no continuity of employment, which makes the unions tougher and tougher to deal with in an industry which was always volatile in its labour relations: every film is a fresh project for which cast and crew have to be accumulated, and the way things are there is no bank of trained talent to fall back on. As Billy Wilder said, you spend eighty per cent of your time making deals and twenty per cent making pictures. The old moguls had enough common sense and business acumen to keep the system working so that costs were comparatively low and one could afford the occasional interesting failure to please the intellectuals.

How did the movie world go so wrong? You can trace it to the restlessness after World War II, when the regular audience declined and television was a coming threat and the bosses knew that new trends had to be found but no one knew what they might be in a glum and depressed world. When actors began to want a say in production and seemed willing to risk their own money, the bosses were delighted to share the possible losses; instead they found themselves being eased out and their profits halved, their studios no longer vast employment centres with a constant production line but simply enclosed space and facilities which could be rented out to the highest bidder.

The old moguls were getting older and couldn't fight the developing situation, the new young ones were businessmen who often backed the wrong horse because they didn't understand the industry. Meanwhile the old showmen had one last irrelevant fling. If television was the enemy, they reasoned, then give the paying public what television cannot provide. Technology now allowed films to be shot on real locations, which was splendid but had two handicaps. First, the units were away from central control for a long time, and the costs were phenomenal; second, the magic was lost, for the real Paris was by no means so romantic or mysterious as Paramount's backlot which had served as Paris for so many years, nor could the lighting of it be so carefully controlled. The new realistic films were slower, because the travel costs had to be justified and travelogue largely took the place of drama. (Did anyone complain about the lack of shots of San Francisco in *The Maltese Falcon*?)

The other way to combat television was to change the shape and effect of the entertainment screen. 3-D was tried, but audiences hated wearing polaroid glasses in order to get a three-dimensional image which producers largely utilized by hurling knives, tennis balls, spiders and even grubby redskins into the audience's lap: this was fairground stuff. Cinemascope was then seized upon by Hollywood: twice as wide as the ordinary image and capable of the most spectacular effects. There is no record that the paying audience ever especially liked Cinemascope, or could even remember whether or not a film was in the process, but once the expensive equipment was installed in theatres there was no turning back. Unfortunately the technique involved a reversion in many cinematic effects to the days of D. W. Griffith. The compression of the wide image on to the film and its subsequent expansion in the projector made the photography grainy, especially in black and white, which was henceforth virtually abandoned. (At about the same time a transference to safety stock lost us the glamorous luminescent 'Feel' which had been possible with nitrate and which can still be seen in old prints.) The new shape was impossible to compose for, as Fritz Lang said, it was fine for funerals, but what painter through the ages had ever selected it unless to cut up into a triptych? Editing was cut to a minimum because on an image so large each cut made the audience jump. Instead, and cheaper, the camera stayed still while the cast roved around the empty spaces in front of it, and there was an absurd number of shots in which the leading actors reclined so as better to fit the frame. Close-ups and subtle nuances were forgotten: no longer did the camera direct you to the drama, you had to look around and find it yourself. It is rather astonishing that directors with an eye to their reputations still persist in using the scope format, for after initial release the future of any film these days is on the television, and no scope film, will satisfactorily adapt to the TV screen.

In many cinemas Cinemascope was even a fraud, for it had to be on a screen smaller in area than the old image, which was now being referred to sneeringly as 'Postage stamp'. This happened when the old screen had already occupied all the width allowed by the cinema's structure: to get the cinemascope shape, if you could not go any wider, height had to be sacrificed, and audiences wondered why suddenly they were looking at a ribbon of picture across the middle of the space which the fine old screen had occupied.

Cinemascope was patented by Fox, so the other companies all hastened to produce their own variations: Warnerscope, Metroscope, Techniscope, Superscope, Megascope, Camerascope, Panavision, each with its own cheap colour process. Projectionists all over the world were confused by these new names, and seldom knew whether they were projecting a film as they were supposed to. The results were often truly appalling, with lack of focus, too much brightness and wrong screen masking among the most common faults. Paramount's Vistavision, a non-anamorphic process, used the full frame ratio but was intended for projection at anything between 1.33:1 and 2:1, so that the essential action had to take place in a strip along the centre of the picture; consequently, to see a Vistavision print on a 1.33:1 screen was painful indeed, as all the action seemed to take place in the middle distance with great areas of unused space at the top and bottom of the image, and composition, which any painter knows to be all-important, was no longer possible. By the mid-fifties, however, 1.33:1 was no longer generally available, as 'wide screen' had become *de rigueur* even for non-anamorphic films: these cut off the top and bottom of the frame and magnified the rest. This meant that revivals were impossible unless one was prepared to suffer dancers without feet and actors without heads!

The result of all this technical uncertainty was that by the mid-fifties movies were in danger of becoming mere expensive sideshows, uninteresting to anyone of sensitivity. At the same time, an element of sophistication crept away from the popular arts: whereas in the thirties and forties smooth and educated idols had been set up for general approbation, the fifties and sixties showed an alarming tendency not merely to make heroes of 'people like us' but to rub our noses firmly in the gutter by devising stories whose leading characters had few redeeming features. Censorship had been absurdly tight and must obviously relax, but it was unwise and unexpected that the floodgates should open as they did, to admit movies which would previously have been considered anti-social rubbish. It was right, for instance, for Otto Preminger to fight the idiocies of the Production Code with his *The Moon Is Blue* and *The Man with the Golden Arm*, but it was a pity he won his battle with a leaden piece of schoolboy smut and an absurdly melodramatic updating of The Road to Ruin. Such films simply made one yearn to go back to the days of *Trouble in Paradise* and *The Palm Beach Story*, or for the true social concern expressed in the considered, powerful and moving masterpieces of Frank Capra, John Ford, or the early Chaplin.

The talents which had made Hollywood great were certainly nearing retirement by now, but it was perhaps unwise as well as churlish for the new wave to pension them off quite as hurriedly as they did, because there was no comparable talent to take their place. Great art directors like Anton Grot and Hans Dreier, great cameramen like Arthur Miller and James Wong Howe, great directors like Michael Curtiz and William Dieterle were either tossed aside or forced to work on material totally unsuited to their talents and not at all comparable to the films which had made their names. The results were big-budget disasters such as *The Egyptian* and *Omar Khayyam*; meanwhile the young directors were copying low-budget television techniques which for every *Marty* produced a dozen flatly realistic bores.

By the early sixties Hollywood had decided on a new image, but it had lost its old loyalties – the golden age audiences as well as the talents were getting older – and had to appear deliberately to the 'emancipated' young generation. This meant a virtual abolition of censorship, and from the release of *Who's Afraid of Virginia Woolf?* in 1966 to that of *The Texas Chainsaw Massacre* and *The Devil in Miss Jones* ten years later is but a short step. The film is no longer an art, or even a craft: after a brief 'swinging' period it became an exploitation industry designed to take quick money from suckers, led by maverick Ken Russells rather than conscientious Irving Thalbergs, to plaudits from irresponsible critics whenever some totally untalented new director 'does his thing'. There is no justification except box office for films like *The Exorcist* or *Mandingo*, none except self-indulgence for a $12 million coffee-table film like *Barry Lyndon*, while the popularity even in sophisticated circles of shoddy pornography like *Deep Throat* and *Death Weekend* should stand as an awful warning to the leaders of our society that a vivid young art form has overreached itself and is well and truly on the verge of disaster. It is all very well to say in defence of such films that large numbers of people flock to see them: so they did once to bear-baiting and public executions and witch hunts, but the human race long ago prided itself on having passed that stage.

The movies will be lucky if, in their search for sensationalism, they do not check themselves out altogether. Audiences have dwindled rapidly and are still dwindling; so is the number of cinemas. The lush old two-thousand seaters have turned into supermarkets, and instead each city has its ineptly-run boxes of mini-cinemas, the effect of which is rather like sitting in cheaply decorated funeral parlours and paying through the nose for the privilege. The family outing to the cinema is a thing of the past: few families can afford it or can find a suitable film, except once or twice a year when the Disney organization stirs itself; and *their* standards are by no means as high as they were, as a comparison of *Robin Hood* with *Bambi* or *Pinocchio* will immediately show. (The fact that such an uninventive computerized cartoon as *Robin Hood* can do well at the box office is an instance of how starved the public is for the older, gentler forms of entertainment.)

Another problem besetting the cinema in the sixties was its adoption by verbose and pompous critics who were determined to turn it into serious art. True art is the work of one man, or at least his personal vision: each film is the work of several hundred people. Of these, admittedly the director has the most control, but to assign to him the role of *auteur* and to ignore the contribution of producer, writer, photographer, composer and editor is arrant nonsense, except possibly in the cases of such as Hitchcock and Kubrick who do control almost every aspect of their output. The new cinema journalism simply encouraged the worst motives of the new breed of film-maker, who came to know that whatever idiocy he perpetrated would be staunchly defended, researched and psychoanalysed by one of these mercenaries in search of a cause. If a character spat on the pavement this would be taken as his final shedding of his working-class upbringing; if he went to bed with a girl it would symbolize his treachery to his own beliefs and his giving in to the snares of Mammon. Listen to a modern critic in the British Film Institute's *Monthly Film Bulletin*, once a terse and reliable guide to film trends, on *Alice Doesn't Live Here Any More*: 'What Scorsese has done, however, is to rescue an American cliché from the bland, flat but much more portentous naturalism of such as *Harry and Tonto* and restore it to an emotional and intellectual complexity through his particular brand of baroque realism.' Or on Rafelson's *Stay Hungry*: 'What distinguishes him from other film-makers of the "head" generation is both the poetic sureness of his fragmentary, allusive style, and the elliptical observation which prevents his social themes from being spiked too easily on the cultural antitheses of that bygone era.' Spare us.

Some of the elements missing from modern cinema are to be found in television, certainly in the UK with its brilliant documentaries, sharp comedies, serious art programmes and single plays; Americans are less lucky except on their public broadcasting system. But television is a private enjoyment, and one inevitably misses the sense of comradeship, of sharing a pleasure, that the cinema used to fulfil. Who having experienced them can forget the feeling of a full house being pleasurably chilled by *The Cat and the Canary*, or rolling in the aisles at Laurel and Hardy, or hoping against hope that Colman will find his *Lost Horizon*? What modern films can produce the sheer entertainment value and unforgettable, vivid scenes of such as *The Philadelphia Story*, *Stagecoach*, *Rebecca*, *Camille*, *Casablanca*, *Citizen Kane*, *Singin' in the Rain*, *A Night at the Opera*, *The Lady Vanishes*, and *The Third Man*? These were all intelligent films, all made for the despised mass audience, and they all made money because they were produced

with impeccable professionalism and star talent, and because to these qualitie
they added heart and good humour. Where is the good humour in *Jaws*? Where
the heart in *The Exorcist*? These are rides on fairground ghost trains: one pays fo
the thrill, but one comes out more depressed than uplifted.

Of course there are some genuine talents at work in films today. One respect
the likes of Jack Nicholson and Ellen Burstyn and Al Pacino and Glenda Jackso
but they are all depressingly committed to their own self-expression and to th
depiction of mankind with warts and all, not to pleasing, stimulating or improvin
the public. They need control; but where are the likes of Lubitsch to control them
Of Sturges? Of Ben Hecht? Of James Whale? Of Donald Ogden Stewart? Of S.
Perelman? Of Robert Benchley and Dorothy Parker? The films produced b
Altman and Scorsese and Ashby are doubtless stimulating in their violen
abrasive way but they are not the whole of life. David Lean and John Schlesinge
and Arthur Penn are meticulous craftsmen, but they are driven by commerce int
the excesses of *Ryan's Daughter* and *Marathon Man* and *The Missouri Break*
In the acting league, where are our up-and-coming replacements for David Niver
Cary Grant, Melvyn Douglas, Katharine Hepburn, Ronald Colman? When agai
will it be the turn of grace and elegance? When indeed will actors want to work
Steve McQueen, Elizabeth Taylor and their like prefer to demand an impossibl
high fee, and if they do not get it to sit comfortably at home on the proceeds o
their previous hits.

Hollywood at its best – and for Hollywood also read Ealing and Tobi
Klangfilm and Svenske Filmindustri – was the purveyor of an expensive an
elegant craft which at times touched art, though seldom throughout a whole film
Reality was seldom sought, but why should it be? Real life is not dramati
anyway: even *Taxi Driver* is a heightening, a selection, an emphasis. So are all th
great realist films from *The Battleship Potemkin* to *The Grapes of wrath*. And s
are the great works of Beethoven, of Rembrandt, of Michelangelo. Film stands t
life as poetry to prose, and its comments were at their most apt and stylish whe
movies were confined to the sound stage and the backlot. Freedom from tha
confinement has not made them any better: it has only made them diffuse an
patchy and overlong, and colour has made things worse because it apes realit
whereas black and white conjured up its own mood and its own comment
Today's screens are too large for the eye to take in. Sound tracks are so 'realistic
as to be incoherent. Big budgets are wasted on movies which would have been te
times as effective if a little imagination had been used or required. Kaleidoscopi
effects dazzle the eye and befuddle the brain; immensely long precredits sequence
make one think the film is nearly over before it actually starts; characterizatio
flies out the window because sex and violence must be fitted in somehow. Plo
doesn't matter; since swinging London was invented every film has become
'happening': which is another way of saying that anything goes and lack o
professionalism cannot be criticized.

All right, this essay is a deliberate hatchet job by a disappointed fan who ha
turned devil's advocate. Some of the new films clearly have virtues which the ol
ones didn't possess: one is grateful for *The Graduate* and *Charlie Bubbles* and
Cabaret and *One Flew over the Cuckoo's Nest*, which for various reasons coul
never have been made in the old Hollywood. But if my thesis were not largely true
how would one explain the enormous popularity of old movies on television, or th

recent deluge of books about them? Why, out of more than sixty films on British television over the Christmas of 1976, were *White Heat* (1948), *A Night at the Opera* (1935) and *Yankee Doodle Dandy* (1942) the most discussed and appreciated? Nostalgia is only a trendy word to describe something which people have at last learned to appreciate because it has been taken away from them. No one in his right mind would be nostalgic for PRC second features or for much of the pure assembly line product which inevitably poured out of the studios when they were working at full pitch. And one must progress. But surely not to the wasteful ineptitude which confront us at the cinema these days. Not to *Lucky Lady*, *Mother Jugs and Speed*, *At Long Last Love* or *Harry and Walter go to New York*. Must modern audiences really put up with inane or violent rubbish and appear to enjoy it simply because they are supposed not to know any better? We may not be able to get the golden age back, but we can cry for it. If 'they' fail to respond we can at least appreciate the best of it, and learn from that best. This book, I hope, may help a few people to do that.

Alphabetical Index of Alternative Titles

If the film you seek does not appear in the main section of the book and you suspect it to have more than one title, check it here. (NB: Foreign-language films are listed here only if they have more than one foreign- or English-language title. See the following lists for original titles or English-language versions.)

Breath of Scandal see His Glorious Night
The Bride Wasn't Willing see Frontier Gal
Brink of Hell see Toward the Unknown
Broadway Singer see Torch Singer
Brotherly Love see Country Dance
Build My Gallows High see Out of the Past
Burn! see Queimada!
By Hook or by Crook see I Dood It

Cactus in the Snow see You Can't Have
    Everything
Café of Seven Sinners see Seven Sinners
California Holiday see Spinout
Call Harry Crown see 99 and 44/100 Per Cent
    Dead
Call it Murder see Midnight
Call Me Genius see The Rebel
Cargo of Innocents see Stand By for Action
Caribbean Gold see Caribbean
Carnival of Thieves see The Caper of the Golden
    Bulls
Carquake see Cannonball
The Case of Mrs Pembroke see Two Against the
    World
The Case of the Missing Blonde see Lady in the
    Morgue
C.A.S.H. see W.H.I.F.F.S.
Cash and Carry see Maisie (Ringside Maisie)
Casino de Paree see Go Into Your Dance
The Cave Dwellers see One Million BC
Chained to Yesterday see Limbo
The Chairman see The Most Dangerous Man in
    the World
Chamber of Horrors see The Door with Seven
    Locks
Chance Meeting see The Young Lovers
The Charge is Murder see Twilight of Honor
Charley's American Aunt see Charley's Aunt
Chicago, Chicago see Gaily, Gaily
China Caravan see A Yank on the Burma Road
Choice of Weapons see Trial by Combat
City After Midnight see That Woman Opposite
The City Jungle see The Young Philadelphians
Clouds Over Europe see Q Planes
Code of Scotland Yard see The Shop at Sly
    Corner
Colonel Blimp see The Life and Death of Colonel
    Blimp
A Coming-Out Party see Very Important Person
Company of Cowards see Advance to the Rear
The Concrete Jungle see The Criminal
The Confession (1965) see Quick Let's Get
    Married
Confessions of a Counterspy see Man on a
    String
The Conqueror Worm see Witchfinder General
The Contact Man see Alias Nick Beal
Contest Girl see The Beauty Jungle
The Courageous Mr Penn see Penn of
    Pennsylvania
Court Martial see Carrington VC
The Courtney Affair see The Courtneys of
    Curzon Street
The Cowboy and the Girl see A Lady Takes a
    Chance
The Crash of Silence see Mandy
The Creeping Unknown see The Quatermass
    Experiment

Crest of the Wave see Seagulls over Sorrento
The Crime of the Century see Walk East on
    Beacon
The Crimson Blade see The Scarlet Blade
Crossed Swords see The Prince and the Pauper
    (1977)
Curse of the Demon see Night of the Demon
Czar of the Slot Machines see King of Gamblers
Czarina see A Royal Scandal

Damn the Defiant see HMS Defiant
Dance of the Vampires see The Fearless
    Vampire Killers
Dangerous Days see Wild Boys of the Road
Daniel and the Devil see All That Money Can
    Buy
Dark of the Sun see The Mercenaries
The Dark Page see Scandal Sheet
Daughters of Destiny see Love, Soldiers and
    Women
The Day They Gave Babies Away see All Mine
    to Give
Dead Image see Dead Ringer
Deadline see Deadline USA
Deadline Midnight see –30–
Deadly Is the Female see Gun Crazy
Decision Against Time see The Man in the Sky
Decoy see Mystery Submarine
Dédée see Dédée d'Anvers
Desert Attack see Ice Cold in Alex
Desperate Siege see Rawhide
The Destructors see The Marseilles Contract
The Detective see Father Brown
The Devil and Daniel Webster see All That
    Money Can Buy
The Devil Never Sleeps see Satan Never Sleeps
The Devil Takes the Count see The Devil is a
    Sissy
The Devil Within Her see I Don't Want to be
    Born
The Devil's Bride see The Devil Rides Out
The Devil's Brother see Fra Diavolo
The Devil's Impostor see Pope Joan
The Devil's Own see The Witches
Diabolique see Les Diaboliques
Die! Die! My Darling see Fanatic
The Dividing Line see The Lawless
Dog Soldiers see Who'll Stop the Rain?
The Domino Killings see The Domino Principle
Doomed Cargo see Seven Sinners
Doppelganger see Journey to the Far Side of the
    Sun
Down Went McGinty see The Great McGinty
Dracula Is Alive and Well and Living in London
    see The Satanic Rites of Dracula
Drake the Pirate see Drake of England
The Dream of Olwen see While I Live
Drum Crazy see The Gene Krupa Story
Drums see The Drum
Drums Along the Amazon see Angel on the
    Amazon
Du Rififi chez les Hommes see Rififi
Duck, You Sucker see A Fistful of Dynamite
Dulcimer Street see London Belongs to Me
Dynamite Man from Glory Jail see Fools Parade

East End Chant see Limehouse Blues
East of Shanghai see Rich and Strange

East of the Rising Sun see Malaya
Edge of Divorce see Background
The Electric Man see Man Made Monster
Elizabeth of England see Drake of England
Emperor of the North see Emperor of the North Pole
End as a Man see The Strange One
End of the Rainbow see Northwest Outpost
Enemies of the Public see The Public Enemy
Enemy Agent see British Intelligence
Enemy from Space see Quatermass II
Entebbe: Operation Thunderbolt see Operation Thunderbolt
Escapade see Robinson Crusoeland
Escape of the Amethyst see Yangtse Incident
Escape to Happiness see Intermezzo
Every Other Inch a Lady see Dancing Co-Ed
Every Woman's Man see The Prizefighter and the Lady
Everybody's Cheering see Take Me Out to the Ball Game
Evils of Chinatown see Confessions of an Opium Eater
Eye Witness (1950) see Your Witness

The Fall of the House of Usher see House of Usher
False Faces see Let 'Em Have It
False Witness see Zigzag
Falstaff see Chimes at Midnight
The Fantastic Disappearing Man see The Return of Dracula
Fear o' God see The Mountain Eagle
Fellini Satyricon see Satyricon
The Fifth Chair see It's in the Bag
The Fighting Pimpernel see Pimpernel Smith
The Fighting Seventh see Little Big Horn
The Fighting Sullivans see The Sullivans
Fine and Dandy see West Point Story
Finger of Guilt see The Intimate Stranger
The First and the Last see Twenty-One Days
The First Rebel see Allegheny Uprising
Fitzwilly Strikes Back see Fitzwilly
Five Angles on Murder see The Woman in Question
Five Million Years to Earth see Quatermass and the Pit
Flame over India see Northwest Frontier
The Flight of the White Stallions see The Miracle of the White Stallions
For Love of a Queen see The Dictator
For You Alone see When You're in Love
Forbidden Alliance see The Barretts of Wimpole Street
Forbidden Music see Land without Music
The Forbidden Street see Britannia Mews
Forever England see Brown on Resolution
Forever in Love see Pride of the Marines
Forever Yours see Forget Me Not
The Forsyte Saga see That Forsyte Woman
Forty Eight Hours see Went the Day Well?
Four Against Fate see Derby Day
Four Dark Hours see The Green Cockatoo
Fraternally Yours see Sons of the Desert
Free to Live see Holiday (1938)
The French They Are a Funny Race see The Diary of Major Thompson

Frenzy see Latin Quarter
The Frightened Bride see The Tall Headlines
Frightened City see The Killer That Stalked New York
Frou Frou see The Toy Wife
The Fugitive (1939) see On the Night of the Fire
Full House see O. Henry's Full House
Fuss over Feathers see Conflict of Wings

G Man's Wife see Public Enemy's Wife
Gang War see Odd Man Out
The Gay Divorce see The Gay Divorcee
The Gay Duellist see Meet Me at Dawn
The Gay Imposters see Gold Diggers in Paris
The Gay Lady see Trottie True
The Gay Mrs Trexel see Susan and God
A Genius in the Family see So Goes My Love
Gestapo see Night Train to Munich
Get Charlie Tully see Ooh, You Are Awful
Gideon of Scotland Yard see Gideon's Day
The Girl Getters see The System (GB)
Girl in Distress see Jeannie
The Girl in Overalls see Maisie (Swing Shift Maisie)
The Girl in Pawn see Little Miss Marker
The Girl in Room 17 see Vice Squad
Girl of the Year see The Petty Girl
A Girl Was Young see Young and Innocent
The Girls He Left Behind see The Gang's All Here (1943)
Girls in the Street see London Melody
Glory at Sea see The Gift Horse
The Golden Hour see Pot o' Gold
The Golden Mask see South of Algiers
The Golden Virgin see The Story of Esther Costello
Good Morning Doctor see You Belong to Me
The Grace Moore Story see So This Is Love
Grand Rue see Calle Mayor
The Great Adventure see The Adventurers
The Great Manhunt (US) see State Secret
The Great Spy Mission see Operation Crossbow
Green Eyed Woman see Take a Letter Darling
The Grip of Fear see Experiment in Terror
The Guest see The Caretaker
The Gun Runner see Santiago
Guns in the Afternoon see Ride the High Country
Guns of Wyoming see Cattle King
Gypsy Girl see Sky West and Crooked

Hallelujah I'm a Bum see Hallelujah I'm a Tramp
The Hammond Mystery see The Undying Monster
The Hands of Orlac (1935) see Mad Love
Happy Times see The Inspector General
Hara Kiri see The Battle
Hard Driver see The Last American Hero
Harmony Parade see Pigskin Parade
The Harp of Burma see The Burmese Harp
Harry Black see Harry Black and the Tiger
The Haunted and the Hunted see Dementia 13
Haunted Honeymoon see Busman's Honeymoon
The Haunted Strangler see Grip of the Strangler
Having a Wild Weekend see Catch Us If You Can

One for the Book *see* The Voice of the Turtle
One Hour with You *see* The Marriage Circle
One Hundred Per Cent Pure *see* The Girl from Missouri
One Man Mutiny *see* The Court Martial of Billy Mitchell
The One Piece Bathing Suit *see* Million Dollar Mermaid
One Woman's Story *see* The Passionate Friends
Only the Best *see* I Can Get It for You Wholesale
Operation Disaster *see* Morning Departure
Operation Snafu *see* On the Fiddle
Operation Undercover *see* Report to the Commissioner
Operation X *see* My Daughter Joy
O'Rourke of the Royal Mounted *see* Saskatchewan
Outpost in Malaya *see* The Planter's Wife
The Outsider (US 1948) *see* The Guinea Pig
Over the River *see* One More River

Panic in the Parlor *see* Sailor Beware (1956)
Panther's Moon *see* Spy Hunt
Paradise Lagoon *see* The Admirable Crichton
Paratrooper *see* The Red Beret
Paris Express *see* The Man Who Watched Trains Go By
Passing Clouds *see* Spellbound (GB)
Passion *see* Madame Dubarry
The Passionate Sentry *see* Who Goes There?
Passport to Fame *see* The Whole Town's Talking
Patterns of Power *see* Patterns
Patton—Lust for Glory *see* Patton
Pay the Devil *see* Man in the Shadow
Paying the Penalty *see* Underworld
The Persecution and Assassination of Jean-Paul Marat . . . *see* The Marat/Sade
Personal Column *see* Lured
Peter Rabbit and the Tales of Beatrix Potter *see* Tales of Beatrix Potter
The Phantom Carriage *see* Thy Soul Shall Bear Witness
The Phantom Fiend *see* The Lodger
The Phantom Strikes *see* The Gaunt Stranger
Pickup Alley *see* Interpol
Pier 13 (1932) *see* Me and My Gal
Pioneer Builders *see* The Conquerors
The Playboy *see* Kicking the Moon Around
The Playgirl and the War Minister *see* The Amorous Prawn
Pluck of the Irish *see* Great Guy
Polly Fulton *see* BF's Daughter
Pookie *see* The Sterile Cuckoo
Portrait in Smoke *see* Wicked as They Come
Power *see* Jew Suss (1934)
Pride of Kentucky *see* The Story of Seabiscuit
The Private Wore Skirts *see* Never Wave at a WAC
Profession: Reporter *see* The Passenger
Project M 7 *see* The Net
The Promoter *see* The Card
The Public Eye *see* Follow Me
Pursuit of the Graf Spee *see* The Battle of the River Plate
Pussycat Alley *see* The World Ten Times Over

Queen of Destiny *see* Sixty Glorious Years

Race Gang *see* The Green Cockatoo
The Randolph Family *see* Dear Octopus
The Rape of Malaya *see* A Town Like Alice
Rasputin the Mad Monk *see* Rasputin and the Empress
The Red Baron *see* Von Richthofen and Brown
Reign of Terror *see* The Black Book
The Remarkable Mr Kipps *see* Kipps
Remember That Face *see* The Mob
Rendezvous *see* Darling How Could You?
Reprieve *see* Convicts Four
Reputation *see* Lady with a Past
Reserved for Ladies *see* Service for Ladies
Rhodes *see* Rhodes of Africa
The Rich Full Life *see* Cynthia
Richer than the Earth *see* The Whistle at Eaton Falls
Ring of Treason *see* Ring of Spies
The Rise of Helga *see* Susan Lenox, Her Fall and Rise
The Road to Frisco *see* They Drive by Night
Romance and Riches *see* The Amazing Quest Bliss
Rommel Desert Fox *see* The Desert Fox
Rookies *see* Buck Privates
Rookies Come Home *see* Buck Privates Come Home
Rough Company *see* The Violent Men
Rudyard Kipling's Jungle Book *see* The Jungle Book
A Run on Gold *see* Midas Run
Runaway Daughter *see* Red Salute

The Sabre and the Arrow *see* Last of the Comanches
Sabrina Fair *see* Sabrina
Salt to the Devil *see* Give Us This Day
Saraband *see* Saraband for Dead Lovers
Satan's Skin *see* Blood on Satan's Claw
The Scarlet Buccaneer *see* Swashbuckler
Scotch on the Rocks *see* Laxdale Hall
Scream of Fear *see* Taste of Fear
Season of Passion *see* Summer of the Seventeenth Doll
The Second Best Secret Agent in the Whole Wide World *see* Licensed to Kill
Secret Flight *see* School for Secrets
The Secret Four *see* The Four Just Men
Secret Interlude *see* The View from Pompey's Head
See No Evil *see* Blind Terror
See You in Hell Darling *see* An American Dream
Separate Beds *see* The Wheeler Dealers
Serenade *see* Broadway Serenade
Seven Different Ways *see* Quick Let's Get Married
The Shame of a Nation *see* Scarface
She Got Her Man *see* Maisie (Maisie Gets Her Man)
She Played with Fire *see* Fortune is a Woman
Sherlock Holmes (1939) *see* The Adventures of Sherlock Holmes
Shoot First *see* Rough Shoot
The Shop on the High Street *see* The Shop on Main Street
Sidewalks of London *see* St Martin's Lane
The Silent Stranger *see* Step Down to Terror

English-Language Titles of Foreign Films

Are We All Murderers? *see* Nous Sommes Tous Les Assassins
An Artist with Ladies *see* Coiffeur pour Dames

The Baker's Wife *see* La Femme du Boulanger
The Ballad of Berlin *see* Berliner Ballade
The Battle of Austerlitz *see* Austerlitz
Bay of Angels *see* La Baie des Anges
Beyond the Gates *see* Au dela des Grilles
Bluebeard *see* Landru
Boudu Saved from Drowning *see* Boudu Sauvé des Eaux
Breathless *see* A Bout de Souffle
The Butcher *see* Le Boucher

Carnival in Flanders *see* La Kermesse Héroïque
Children of Paradise *see* Les Enfants du Paradis
Christine *see* Un Carnet de Bal
Comradeship *see* Kameradschaft
The Crazy Ray *see* Paris Qui Dort
The Cry *see* Il Grido

A Day in the Country *see* Une Partie de Campagne
Daybreak *see* Le Jour Se Lève
Days of Hope *see* Espoir
Devil in the Flesh *see* Le Diable au Corps
The Devil's Envoys *see* Les Visiteurs du Soir
Dirty Hands *see* Les Mains Sales
The Does *see* Les Biches
A Dog's Life *see* Mondo Cane
Doomed *see* Ikiru

The Earrings of Madame de *see* Madame de
Ecstasy *see* Extase
Every Second Counts *see* Les Assassins du Dimanche

Father and Master *see* Padre Padrone
The Fiends *see* Les Diaboliques
Film without Title *see* Film ohne Titel
Forbidden Games *see* Les Jeux Interdits
Frontier *see* Aerograd

Gate of Lilacs *see* Porte des Lilacs
Gates of Night *see* Les Portes de la Nuit
The Girl Friends *see* Le Amiche
Girls in Uniform *see* Maedchen in Uniform
God Needs Men *see* Dieu a Besoin des Hommes
The Goddess *see* Devi
Golden Marie *see* Casque d'Or

Hands off the Loot *see* Touchez pas au Grisbi
Hanged Man's Farm *see* La Ferme du Pendu

Heroism *see* Eroica
The Hole *see* Onibaba
Holiday for Henrietta *see* La Fête à Henriette
Honour Among Thieves *see* Touchez pas au Grisbi
The Human Beast *see* La Bête Humaine

I Have a New Master *see* L'Ecole Buissonière
In the Woods *see* Rashomon
Isle of Sinners *see* Dieu a Besoin des Hommes
It Happened at the Inn *see* Goupi Mains Rouges
It's in the Bag *see* L'Affaire est dans le Sac

Judas Was a Woman *see* La Bête Humaine

Keep an Eye on Amelia *see* Occupe-Toi d'Amélie

Living *see* Ikiru
The Long Absence *see* Une Aussi Longue Absence
Love Is My Profession *see* En Cas de Malheur
Love Story *see* Une Histoire d'Amour
The Lovers *see* Les Amants
The Lovers of Verona *see* Les Amants de Vérone
The Lower Depths *see* Les Bas-fonds

Man's Hope *see* Espoir
My Night at Maud's *see* Ma Nuit chez Maud

Nights of Cabiria *see* Cabiria

The Outsiders *see* Bande à Part

The Phantom Baron *see* Le Baron Fantôme
Port of Shadows *see* Quai des Brumes

The Road *see* La Strada
The Road to Hope *see* Il Cammino della Speranza
The Rules of the Game *see* La Règle du Jeu

The Saga of Anatahan *see* Anatahan
Savage Princess *see* Aan
Scarlet and Black *see* Le Rouge et le Noir
The Secret Game *see* Les Jeux Interdits
Spivs *see* I Vitelloni
Stormy Waters *see* Remorques
The Story of a Cheat *see* Le Roman d'un Tricheur
The Strange Adventure of David Gray *see* Vampyr

Original Titles of Foreign-Language Films Listed in English

Aimez-Vous les Femmes? *see* Do You Like Women?
Akahige *see* Redbeard
Akasen Chitai *see* Street of Shame
Alskande Par *see* Loving Couples
Les Amants du Tage *see* The Lovers of Lisbon
Les Amours de la Reine Elisabeth *see* Queen Elizabeth
El Angel Exterminador *see* The Exterminating Angel
Ansiktet *see* The Face
L'Argent de Poche *see* Small Change
Ascenseur pour l'Echafaud *see* Lift to the Scaffold
Attilo Flagello di Dio *see* Attila the Hun
Au Hasard, Balthazar *see* Balthazar
L'Auberge Rouge *see* The Red Inn
Un Autre Homme, une Autre Chance *see* Another Man, Another Chance
L'Aveu *see* The Confession

Babette S'en Va-t-en Guerre *see* Babette Goes to War
Baisers Volés *see* Stolen Kisses
Ballada o Soldate *see* Ballad of a Soldier
Banditi a Orgoloso *see* Bandits of Orgoloso
Baron Prasil *see* Baron Munchausen
La Battaglia di Algeri *see* The Battle of Algiers
Berlin, die Symphone einer Grossstadt *see* Berlin, Symphony of a Great City
Betrogen bis zum Jungsten Tag *see* Duped Till Doomsday
Bezhin Lug *see* Bezhin Meadow
Les Bijoutiers du Clair de Lune *see* Heaven Fell That Night
Biruma no Tategoto *see* The Burmese Harp
Bronenosets Potemkin *see* Battleship Potemkin
El Bruto *see* The Brute
Die Büchse der Pandora *see* Pandora's Box
Il Buono, il Bruto, il Cattivo *see* The Good, the Bad and the Ugly
Cadaveri Eccellenti *see* Illustrious Corpses
La Caida *see* The Fall
O'Cangaceiro *see* The Bandit
Le Caporal Epinglè *see* The Vanishing Corporal
Les Carnets de Major Thompson *see* The Diary of Major Thompson
Le Carrosse d'Or *see* The Golden Coach
La Casa del Angel *see* The House of the Angel
La Casse *see* The Burglars
Celui Qui Doit Mourir *see* He Who Must Die
Le Charm Discret de la Bourgeoisie *see* The Discreet Charm of the Bourgeoisie
Chelovek s Kinoapparatom *see* The Man with the Movie Camera
La Ciociara *see* Two Women

Compartiment Tueurs *see* The Sleeping Car Murders
Cybèle ou les Dimanches de Ville d'Avray *see* Sundays and Cybèle

Dama s Sobachkoi *see* The Lady with the Little Dog
Déjeuner sur l'Herbe *see* Lunch on the Grass
Les Demoiselles de Rochefort *see* The Young Girls of Rochefort
La Dentellière *see* The Lacemaker
Il Deserto Rosso *see* The Red Desert
Destinées *see* Love, Soldiers and Women
Ditte Menneskebarn *see* Ditte, Child of Man
Divorzio all'Italiana *see* Divorce Italian Style
En Djungelsaga *see* The Flute and the Arrow
Doktor Mabuse, der Spieler *see* Doctor Mabuse
Don Camillo e l'Onorevolo Peppone *see* Don Camillo's Last Round
Dorp aan de Rivier *see* Doctor in the Village

L'Eclisse *see* The Eclipse
En Compagnie de Max Linder *see* Laugh with Max Linder
Ensayo de un Crimen *see* The Criminal Life of Archibaldo de la Cruz
Ercole e la Regina di Lidia *see* Hercules Unchained
Es Geschah am 20 Juli *see* Jackboot Mutiny
L'Espion *see* The Defector
Et Dieu Crèa la Femme *see* And God Created Woman
Et Mourir de Plaisir *see* Blood and Roses
L'Eternel Retour *see* Love Eternal

Fängelse *see* The Devil's Wanton
Le Fatiche di Ercole *see* Hercules
Die Freudlose Gasse *see* Joyless Street
Le Fruit Défendu *see* Forbidden Fruit

Il Gattopardo *see* The Leopard
Giulietta degli Spiriti *see* Juliet of the Spirits
Gosta Berlings Saga *see* The Atonement of Gosta Berling
Götterdamerung *see* The Damned (1969)
La Grande Vadrouille *see* Don't Look Now... We're Being Shot At!
Gruppo di Famiglia in un Interno *see* Conversation Piece
Gycklarnas Afton *see* Sawdust and Tinsel

Hadaka no Shima *see* The Island
Haxan *see* Witchcraft through the Ages
Les Héros Sont Fatigués *see* The Heroes Are Tired

Tagebuch einer Verliebten *see* The Diary of a Married Woman
Tagebuch einer Verlorenen *see* Diary of a Lost Girl
Taiheiyo Hitoribochi *see* Alone on the Pacific
To Telefteo Psemma *see* A Matter of Dignity
Tirez sur le Pianiste *see* Shoot the Pianist
Le Trou *see* The Hole
Tystnaden *see* The Silence

Utvandrarna *see* The Emigrants

Les Vacances de Monsieur Hulot *see* Monsieur Hulot's Holiday
La Vache et le Prisonnier *see* The Cow and I
Il Vangelo Secondo Matteo *see* The Gospel According to St Matthew

Vargtimmen *see* The Hour of the Wolf
Vérités et Mensonges *see* F for Fake
Vesolye Rebyata *see* Jazz Comedy
La Vie à l'Envers *see* Life Upside Down
Viskingar och Rop *see* Cries and Whispers
Vivre pour Vivre *see* Live for Life
Vredens Dag *see* Day of Wrath
Vu du Pont *see* A View from the Bridge

Das Wachsfigurenkabinett *see* Waxworks

Les Yeux sans Visage *see* Eyes without a Face
Yukinojo Henge *see* An Actor's Revenge

Zemlya *see* Earth